THE OFFICIAL® PRICE GUIDE TO

Movie/TV Soundtracks & Original Cast Albums

SECOND EDITION

JERRY OSBORNE

Editor: Judith M. Ihnken Ebner

Associate Editors: Paul Aguirre, R. Michael Murray, Joe Lindsay

HOUSE OF COLLECTIBLES • NEW YORK

Important Notice. All of the information, including valuations, in this book has been compiled from the most reliable sources, and every effort has been made to eliminate errors and questionable data. Nevertheless, the possibility of error, in a work of such immense scope, always exists. The publisher will not be held responsible for losses which may occur in the purchase, sale, or other transaction of items because of information contained herein. Readers who feel they have discovered errors are invited to *write* and inform us, so they may be corrected in subsequent editions. Those seeking further information on the topics covered in this book are advised to refer to the complete line of *Official Price Guides* published by the House of Collectibles.

CONTENTS

ACKNOWLEDGMENTS

The single most important element in updating and revising a price and reference guide is reader input. From dealers and collectors scattered throughout the country we receive suggestions, additions and corrections. Every single piece of data we receive is carefully reviewed, with all appropriate and usable information utilized in the next edition of this guide.

As enthusiastically as we encourage your contribution, let us equally encourage that when you write, you will either type or print your name clearly on both the envelope and contents. It's as frustrating for us to receive a mailing of useful information, and not be able to credit the sender, as it probably is for the sender to not see his or her name in the Acknowledgments section.

In compiling this edition, information supplied by the people whose names appear below was of great importance. To these good folks, our deepest gratitude is extended. The amount of data and investment of time, of course, varied, but without each and every one of them this book would have been something less than it is.

Here then is an alphabetical listing of the contributors to this edition:

June Abernathy
Paul Aguirre
Bob Alaniz
Gino Albanese
Grant Aldridge
Robert C. Anderson
Louis Andrew
Nicholas Anez
Dave Antonopoulos
Alice M. Ashley
J.V. Baglio
Larry Bailey
John R. Bandoni
Charles L. Behrend
Rosanna L. Bencoach
Lynn Benton
Bob Blackburn
Blue Chip Records
Brian Bodine
Bill Boehlke
Bo Bohannan
Daryl R. Bosteels
R.E. Brouwer
James Burt
Richard F. Butler
Marco A. Camarema
Don Carroll
Donald S. Capen
Mary E. Benton Chay
Sean A. Chichure
Betty L. Chrisman

Herman M. Clark Jr.
John C. Conrad
Michael L. Cooper
Lorin Copeland
Perry Cox
Dan Crawford
S. James Culbertson
Troy Cullison
Brian Curtis
Tom Daffin
Tim Darcy
John S. David
Judy Davis
Chuck Dawson
Devon Dawson
Bill Derick
Gregory K. Donabedian
Charles D. Donley
William Drell
Judith M. Ihnken Ebner
Kevin L. Edwards
Arthur C. Ernist
David N. Ferguson
Dave Ferrier
Thomas C. Flynn
Colleen Fochi
Jim Forkenbrock
Alex Frazer-Hamilton
Cheron Frazier
Columbus G. Freiermuth
Arnie Ganem

Jack Gardner
Jean-Marc Gargiulo
Glenn Garvie
Bruce "Brucie Baby" Garthe
Rich Gesner
Jim Gibbons
Glen A. Gil
Bob Gillan
Charles T. Gray
Claire Griffin
Larry M. Griffin
Steven Grunberg
Butch Guest
David Harfeld
Michael Harrah
Ross Hartsough
John Hazard
George Held
Barry Hirschberg
Lin Holland
John Hornsby Jr.
Pauline Hubbard
David Hulsman
D. Husson
Raul A. Jackson
Robert Jackson
Ed Johnson
Robert Jordan
Roland Julean
Thomas Kaltenbach
Nicholas Kent

Dick Kissell
John Knapp
Bob Kolba
Mark Koldys
Tony Kolodziej
Tracy Kolodziej
Timothy A. Kraetsch
Milt Krantz
Randy Ladenheim-Gil
Raye E. Lang
William R. Lawson
Marianne LeButt
Howard Levine
Joe Lindsay
Wayne Long
Earl F. Loomis
Grant Lorelle
René Lucas
David Luhn
Peter C. Mallon
Chris Mancini
Rev. David E. Manly
Donald J. McDonough
C. Messner
Judge Ron Meyers
John Mlachnik
Kevin Moltner
Marjorie Moore
Charles Morgan
Eddie Morris
R. Michael Murray
Carolyn E. Myers
David Nadolski
Dennis W. Nicholson

Phil Nohl
Roger Osborne
Maryann Ost
Larry Padgett
Steve Paintner
Joanne Palmer
Tony Palumbo
Alexis E. Peavey
Marty Pekar
Rose Perkins
S.N. Perry
David M. Petersen
Naomi Plinsky
Don Pressman
Chester Prudhomme
Robert Ramsdell
George Reed
Edward R. Rose
Beverly Rosen
Shade L. Rupe
Bernie Ryder
Richard J. Salvatore
John A. Sargent
David N. Schecter
Marc R. Schwartzman
K. Selvaraja
Peter Sergides
William Shaman
Richard R. Sherwin
H. Gardner Smith Jr.
James Smith III
John Smith
Dr. Robert Smith
Loren Francis Spain

Kevin Spicer
Louis Speichler
John Stanley
Tom Stein
Robert J. Stern
Mike Stewart
Matt Stitzel
John L. Sullivan Jr.
Kevin Sweeney
Bruce Tannin
Ed Tataryn
Robert Temple
David Terralavoro
Joe Thomas
Jeff Thompson
Harley Toberman
George Trabant
Victor Valentine
Bernie Vogel
Sally Vande Voort
James von Rummelhoff
Ron Washington
Jim Weaver
Bruce C. Wemett
Danny A. White
Robert P. Wicker
John Winfrey
Jahn Wolfgang
Ronald Zabor
Phil Zafiridis
Karl Zirkel
Stanley Zyphur

INTRODUCTION

Collecting original cast and soundtrack recordings is an area quite unlike any other in music collecting — truly a world of its own.

Most of us who are cast and soundtrack collectors developed our interest in the hobby as members of the audience. From box seats at the lavish Broadway show palaces to the rickety ones at the nearly extinct downtown local theaters, we came into the fold. While watching the show, we heard this magical music that added immeasurably to the overall enjoyment of the spectacle. Our subsequent purchase of the cast or soundtrack album allowed us to relive those cherished moments of escapism over and over on our turntables, to our heart's delight.

If the music of a certain show is truly overwhelming, one might be inclined to seek out other recordings by that same composer, conductor, or performer. When that happens it is safe to say you've become a collector!

Sometimes the scenario is reversed. We hear a piece of music – perhaps even a pop hit – that steals our hearts, then can't wait to see the show from which this wonderful music came. Then, after seeing the show, we go home and play the album again.

Like a train on a spherical track, it doesn't matter where you climb on board, sooner or later you're going to come full circle, and in the process you will multiply your appreciation of this fascinating genre.

Unlike the bottomless pit that is most areas of record collecting — no one is likely to ever have a truly complete collection of R&B, Elvis, or Beatles recordings — collectors of soundtracks can, in many cases, amass a complete collection. More so if one's collection focuses on U.S. pressings — as do the listings in this guide.

By aiming first to comprehensively document records issued in the United States, or widely distributed here, we feel we can lay the best foundation. Both previous editions of this guide centered on that task.

Effective this edition, however, we have added hundreds of releases from outside the 50 states. While by no means a source for every foreign soundtrack and cast album ever made, we have begun with a collection of discs popular with collectors primarily because of content (often material not issued domestically) or cover design.

Oh yes, to eliminate any confusion about regarding two previous publications of a guide that is labeled "second edition," this is the second book for the House of Collectibles. The "first edition" for them came out in 1991, however we published an earlier soundtracks and casts guide, in 1981, for another company.

COMING TO TERMS

Many releases are original soundtracks or original cast recordings, and many others contain music actually recorded in a studio and merchandised in such a way as to appear to be *original* recordings. Such recordings, often as collectible as the original recording of the show, are designated as "Studio Casts" or "Studiotracks" in this guide. Although there is really not much difference in the two terms, the preferred format of listing casts before soundtracks (if any), created the need for having two terms meaning the same thing.

Either way, these recordings were done at a studio recording session and are from neither the film score nor from a live stage show in front of an audience.

With the more popular shows, many studio session albums were made – far more than issued with the music of the original cast. A highly successful show with great music has always been a bandwagon upon which many others couldn't wait to jump. We have included as many of these studio cast releases as possible, realizing that a fan of a particular show may want to own or at least know about other renditions of that show.

There are only two types of soundtracks in this guide: movie soundtracks and television soundtracks. TV soundtracks are identified as such, which is to say that any soundtrack not shown as a TV soundtrack is from a motion picture release.

Not to be confused with studiotrack releases is the type of LP where an artist performs an assortment of tunes, one of which is a popular show tune. We make no attempt to be comprehensive in this area since there are probably a million albums of this type, though a few are sprinkled throughout the guide for one reason or another. An exception might be records where the title is the same as that of a show. Such albums are listed in the guide more for identification purposes than actual content, as well as to inform collectors that a particular LP is not exactly what its title might indicate.

Another borderline type of cast album is one made during a live performance. If the concert was broadcast via radio, television, or film, then it clearly belongs in this guide. The gray area involves significant concerts issued only on records, such as a Madison Square Garden or Hollywood Bowl performance. Feeling such recordings are usually outside the boundaries of this book, we have included very few. Those we have listed appear not because they contain a live show, but based on other factors – such as a Broadway theater performance or to complete the section of a certain artist.

INFINITE REISSUES

One area of endless complexities is the matter of original pressings vs. reissues. Many of the successful show albums have never gone out of print – many now on CD – which may result in a considerably lower value for the original issues than other releases of the same vintage. For some of these, it may be the death of vinyl recordings in favor of compact discs and cassettes, more than just because they are old, which will ultimately increase their value.

Prices in the guide are for the first pressing, even if means the first pressing of a reissue. As often as possible, we will provide the information necessary to identify each pressing. If a reissue uses the exact same prefix, catalog number, and packaging, it may create a situation where collectors are not overly concerned about having the first pressing. After all, reissues usually contain the exact same music. Sometimes only by having an original and reissue in hand can one discover some little detail that can be documented as the key to identifying which is which. In this area, the slight premium placed on these first pressings is more token than authentic.

An $8 or $10 reissue that is easily available will likely have a noticeably different label design than its original pressing. We may then show the original pressing at $10 to $12, knowing that any collector who was particularly seeking a first pressing would gladly pay the token premium.

Looking at any of the Elvis Presley or Beatles soundtracks, for example, will reveal how prices can vary from original to reissue, to later reissue. While these are accurate prices among Presley and Beatles collectors – most of whom do not collect soundtracks per se – they may not be representative of prices paid by collectors of soundtracks for the sake of film music.

Still, if offered to the proper market, these prices can be obtained. Many similar examples exist with albums by other rock 'n' roll artists that have their own following outside the realm of soundtrack collecting. None of the prices in this guide were determined by what people who *do not* want the records would be willing to pay.

SURE IT SAYS "STEREO" – BUT IS IT?

Opinions certainly do vary with regard to rechanneled stereo. Some feel that a rechanneled (electronically simulated) stereo album is absolutely worthless – tantamount to the commission of an audio felony on the part of the record company. Their position is that the pure, original monaural sound is ruined by the fake stereo process, which, depending on the skill of the engineers, often makes the artists sound as though they were performing at the bottom of, well – a well.

Then there are those who actually prefer rechanneled stereo to monaural. They admit that while nearly everyone prefers true stereo, the rechanneled stereo tracks have an enhanced sound. They also point out – accurately – that because they didn't sell well, many of the rechanneled issues from the late '50s and early '60s are quite a bit rarer than their mono counterparts.

When the dust settles, we will likely find most rechanneled stereo releases priced about the same, if they were released simultaneously. Individual tastes can and ultimately will dictate any variances. An exception would be a rechanneled stereo release that appeared several years after the original monaural issue, in which case the mono LP would usually have the higher value.

When an album is known to be in rechanneled stereo, the designation "SE" (Stereo is Electronic) is used in parenthesis ahead of the catalog number.

"M" indicates a monaural release. "S" means either: a) definitely true stereo, b) we believe the LP to be true stereo, c) it is logical to assume it's stereo, or d) it is labeled "stereo" and we have yet to disprove that claim. Having not auditioned each and every one of the records in this guide, we know there are likely to be some that we show as "S" (stereo), that actually make use of some form of electronic stereo. It is also possible we may show an LP as "SE," when it does, in fact, contain true stereo. If you discover such errors, please bring them to our attention.

HOW THE PRICES ARE DETERMINED

Record values shown in this guide were averaged using information derived from a number of reliable sources. One of our most influential sources is our long-established price review board, with dozens of the country's top dealers and collectors pricing listings within their area of interest.

Then, assisted by some sophisticated computer software, we averaged all of the input to arrive at the most accurate price range possible.

Besides the review board (see Acknowledgments page), we regularly receive an abundance of mail from folks like yourself, suggesting corrections and changes for the next edition of the guide.

Marketplace publications are another extremely important source of pricing information. Through these, hobbyists buy, sell, and trade music collectibles. We painstakingly review those periodicals, as well as other related publications, carefully comparing prices being asked to those shown in our most recent edition. Keep in mind, however, that while *asking* prices are considered, greater weight is given actual *sales* prices.

Record prices, as with most collectibles, can vary drastically from one area of the country to another. Having reviewers and annotators in nearly every state, as well as outside our borders enables us to present a realistic average of the highest and lowest current asking prices for an identically graded copy of each record.

Other sources of consequential information include set sales and auction lists from individuals who produce and mail their own catalogs, record convention trading, personal visits with collectors and to retail locations around the country, and hundreds of hours on the telephone and e-mail with key advisors.

Although the record marketplace information in this edition was believed accurate at press time, it is ever subject to market changes. At any time, major bulk discoveries, quantity dumps, sudden price increases wrought by a singer or composer's death, overnight stardom that creates a greater demand for earlier material, and other such events and trends can easily affect scarcity and demand. Through regular research, keeping track of the day-to-day changes and discoveries taking place in the fascinating world of record collecting is a relatively simple and ongoing procedure.

To ensure the greatest possible accuracy, the prices in this guide are averaged from data culled from all of the aforementioned sources.

It is important to remember that this book is merely a guide, not a gospel of absolutes and undeniable, inflexible truths. Used properly, it can be of immense help to the record collector. Our position is to reflect existing trends and values, not to establish them. Use it with an element of flexibility.

WHEN SOME PRICES DON'T CHANGE

Some prices go unchanged book after book because their values simply do not fluctuate beyond the range given. Others, however, should be shifted and are not. This is because *no one* bothers to advise us of those market changes. With the thousands of records priced here, we cannot keep track of all of them without lots of help.

Don't keep such news a secret. And please don't wait for someone else to do it. Let us know of corrections and updates as soon as possible.

A word of caution here, however. Please *do not* submit any information to us merely because it appears in another record guide. Make certain all information can be verified in some other manner.

RECORD GRADING AND THE PRICE RANGE

The pricing shown in this edition represents the price *range* for NEAR-MINT condition copies. The value range allows for the countless variables that affect record pricing. Often, the range will widen as the dollar amount increases, making a $500 to $1,000 range as logical as a $5.00 to $10.00 range.

One standardized system of record grading, used and endorsed by Osborne's *Official Price Guide to Records* series – and buyers and sellers worldwide – is as follows:

MINT: A *mint* item must be absolutely perfect. Nothing less can be honestly described as mint. Even brand new purchases can easily be flawed in some manner and not qualify as mint. To allow for tiny blemishes, the highest grade used in our record guide series is *near-mint*. An absolutely pristine mint, or still sealed, item may carry a slight premium above the near-mint range shown in this guide.

VERY GOOD: Records in *very good* condition should have a minimum of visual or audible imperfections, which should not detract much from your enjoyment of owning them. This grade is halfway between good and near-mint.

GOOD: Practically speaking, the grade of *good* means that the item is good enough to fill a gap in your collection until a better copy becomes available. Good condition merchandise will show definite signs of wear and tear, probably evidencing that no protective care was given the item. Even so, records in good condition should play all the way through without skipping.

Most older records are going to be in something less than near-mint, or "excellent" condition. It is very important to use the near-mint price range in this guide only as a starting point in record appraising. Be honest about actual condition. Apply the same standards to the records you trade or sell as you would want one from whom you were buying to observe. Visual grading may be unreliable. Accurate grading may require playing the record (play-grading).

Use the following formula to determine values on lesser condition copies:

For **VERY GOOD** condition, figure about 40% to 60% of the near-mint price range given in this guide.

With many of the older pieces that cannot be found in near-mint, VG or VG+ may be the highest grade available. This significantly narrows the gap between VG and the near-mint range.

For **GOOD** condition, figure about 10% to 20% of the near-mint price range given in this guide.

THE 10 POINT GRADING SYSTEM

Another recommended grading system is based on the often-used 10 point scale. Many feel that grading with the 10 point system allows for a more precise description of records that are in less than mint condition. Instead of vague terms, such as VG++ (is this the same as M- -?), assigning a specific number provides a more accurate classification of condition.

Most of the records you are likely to buy or sell will no doubt be graded somewhere between 5 and 10.

After using this system ourselves for a few years, we are inclined to agree that it is more precise. Customers who have purchased records from us have, without exception, been pleased with this way of grading.

The table below shows how the 10 point system equates with the more established terms:

10: MINT
9: NEAR-MINT
8: Better than VG but below NM
7: VERY GOOD
6: Better than G but below VG
5: GOOD
4: Better than POOR but below G
3: POOR
2: Really trashed
1: It hurts to think about it

THE EVER-WIDENING GRADING GAP

It will surprise no one to learn that the gulch between GOOD and MINT is gradually becoming a canyon. The drift toward widening the grading gap that began about 10 years ago shows no signs of slowing. To keep pace with this phenomena, changes have been made in the guide to reflect the ever-increasing premiums being paid for mint condition items.

A value spread that a decade ago rated GOOD at about 20% of MINT is now closer to 10%. Look for the gap to widen further in years ahead. Most industry observers do not foresee a narrowing trend during this millennium.

THE BOTTOM LINE

All the price guides and reporting of previous sales in the world won't change the fundamental fact that true value is nothing more than what one person is willing to accept and what another is prepared to pay. Actual value is based on scarcity and demand. It's always been that way and always will.

A recording — or anything for that matter — can be 50 or 100 years old, but if no one wants it, the actual value will certainly be minimal. Just because something is old does not necessarily make it valuable. Someone has to want it!

On the other hand, a recent release, perhaps just weeks old, can have exceptionally high value if it has already become scarce and is by an artist whose following has created a demand. A record does not have to be old to be valuable.

PROMOTIONAL ISSUES

Separate documenting and pricing of everyday promotional issues is, in most cases, unnecessary. Because most of the records issued during the primary four decades covered in this guide were simultaneously pressed for promotional purposes, a separate listing of them would theoretically double the size of an already large book.

Rather, we've chosen to list promotional copies separately when we have the knowledge that an alternate price (either higher or lower) consistently is asked for them. For the most part, promos of everyday releases will fall into the same range — usually toward the high end — given for store stock copies. Some may stretch the range slightly, but not enough to warrant separate pricing. Premiums may be paid for promos that have different (longer, shorter, differently mixed, etc.) versions of tunes, even though the artist may not be particularly hot in the collecting marketplace.

When identified as a "Promotional issue," we are usually describing a record with a special promotional ("Not For Sale," "Dee Jay Copy," etc.) label or sleeve, and not a *designate* promo. Designate promos are identical to commercial releases, except they have been rubber or mechanically stamped, stickered, written on by hand, or in some way altered to accommodate their use for promotional purposes. There are very few designate promos listed in this edition, and those that are clearly identified as such.

Another type of promotional item popular among some soundtracks and casts collectors, are discs containing radio commercials, or "spots." Often single-sided pressings made in small quantities, these were made specifically for radio station use.

Since discs of commercial spots were quite common in the '50s and '60s, one or more discs may exist for nearly every successful or widely-advertised show – too many to attempt to list in this guide. Furthermore, very few have a value beyond the top end of the commercial album of the same show. Those on which collectors have placed a premium – such as for the Beatles' films – are included in this edition.

BOOTLEGS AND COUNTERFEITS

Bootleg and counterfeit records are not intentionally priced in this guide, which is not to say that a few didn't sneak past us. In fact, there are several in our pages that we strongly suspect are boots, but were unable to verify before press time. Some have been in circulation so long that even seasoned collectors are not certain of their legitimacy.

For the record, a bootleg recording is one illegally manufactured, usually containing material not previously available in a legitimate form – such as a show from which the music has never been legitimately issued. Often, with the serious collector in mind, a boot will package previously issued tracks that have achieved some degree of value or scarcity. If the material is easily available, legally, then there would be no gain for the bootlegger.

The counterfeit record is one manufactured as close as possible in sound and appearance to the source disc from which it was inspired. Not all counterfeits were created to fool an unsuspecting buyer into thinking he or she was buying an authentic issue, but some were. Many were designated in some way, such as a slight marking or variance, so as not to allow them to be confused with originals. Such a fake record primarily exists to fill a gap in the collector's file. Very few of us own an original RCA Victor copy of *The Caine Mutiny*, however many are content to have one of the boots – until the real thing comes along.

With both bootleg and with counterfeit records, the appropriate and deserving recipients of royalties are, of course, denied remuneration for their works.

Since most of the world's valuable records have been counterfeited, it is always a good idea to consult with an expert when there is any doubt. The trained eye can usually spot a fake.

This is not to say *unauthorized* releases are excluded from the book. There are many legitimate releases that are unauthorized by one entity or another; records that are neither bootleg or counterfeit. Unauthorized does not necessarily mean illegal.

HOW YOU CAN HELP

We can never get too much input or have too many reviewers. We wholeheartedly encourage you to submit anything and everything you feel would be useful in building a better record guide. The quantity of data is not a factor — no amount is too little or too much.

The extensive list of names always found in the Acknowledgments chapter indicates the development of our board of advisors. We want *you* to join the team.

When preparing additions, please try to list records in generally the same format as is used in the guide: artist's name, label, selection number, title, year of release (if known), and price range. Since our data base is stored alphabetically by artist, there's no need to note the current page number. Please submit information accurately, exactly as it appears on the label. Better yet, photocopy the covers and labels.

WAX FAX AND E-MAIL

Two frequently used methods of forwarding data to us is by fax and by e-mail. For your convenience, we have a dedicated fax line: (360) 385-6572. Use it to instantly transmit additions, corrections, price updates, and suggestions. Be sure to include (legibly) your name, address, and phone number so we can acknowledge your contribution and, if necessary, contact you.

Our e-mail address is **jpo@olympus.net.** Again, remember to provide your full name separately since Internet letters sometimes relay only the sender's e-mail address. While you're on line, visit – and bookmark – our informative web site: **http://www.olympus.net/personal/jpo**.

If you help, we want to credit you properly. Just make sure we have — and can read — the information with which to do it.

Send all additions, corrections, comments and suggestions to:

Jerry Osborne
Box 255
Port Townsend, WA 98368
Fax: (360) 385-6572

USING THIS GUIDE: ADDITIONAL POINTS

• Titles are listed in the alphabetical order of the first word. This means you'll find *Red Tent* before *Redhead*.

• Articles "A," "An" and "The" have been dropped from the beginning of alphabetized show titles in this guide even though they may appear on the records as part of the name.

• As important as composers and conductors in determining the collectibility of a record is the cast – the performers actually heard on the disc. We list as many of the performers as are known for each separate record, with special notations of interesting information occasionally included. A major source of confusion in this area is based on the way recorded music is marketed by the labels. Usually, and in large lettering, the stars of the *show* or *film* are billboarded on the front cover. However, the stars of the show are often not the same as is heard on the record. It is only the performers who appear on the record that we want listed in the cast section. When a film star is not a singer, but must appear to be singing in the film, a qualified singer will go into a studio and record the songs. The film star then simply lip synchs the lyrics. When this is done, it is the actual vocalist whose name we want to list. For this reason, many a well-known star is not listed in our cast, even though commonly associated with the show.

• For the sake of consistency, we have narrowed the many different descriptive job titles down to two: composer and conductor. Both in the listings and in the Composer/Conductor/Cast Index, you will find those names who may actually be shown on the album cover as "lyricist," "musical director," "musical arranger," etc.

• The Composer/Conductor/Cast Index has the names of all individuals known to have contributed to the records listed in *this guide only*. It is not intended to provide a complete filmography of its personnel.

• With few exceptions, all titles listed are those of the record release and not necessarily the exact title of the show – though in most cases they are identical. When a likelihood exists that one might first look elsewhere for a show, a cross-reference should be there to point you in the right direction.

• For shows recorded from both stage and screen performances, the stage (Original Cast, Original Revival Cast, etc.) listings are usually listed first. Following those are Movie and TV Soundtracks, and then Studiotracks. These groupings are irrespective of performance and release dates – casts precede soundtracks even if the cast came out after the soundtrack. Those dates are taken into consideration when sorting the listings within a grouping.

• We believe the years of shows and releases in the guide to be accurate. If we don't know the correct year, the column is left blank. Any assistance to help fill in the blanks would be appreciated. When the release date of a reissue is not known, the designation "Re" will appear in the year of release column, thus identifying the album as a reissue.

• Comments and informative notes placed on the line directly below the record listing generally apply only to the release above the note. When the note describes more than just that one record above, appropriate wording, such as "Gatefold covers" (plural) is used. With most, common sense easily dictates to which entries a note applies.

• Inexplicably, some show albums exist on discs without a label name, some without a selection number, and, in some cases, they have neither. When a label name is either not shown or is just not known to us, wording such as "No Label Shown" is used. If the selection number is either missing or is not known to us, we'll indicate "No Number Used." If a label name or number is in fact used on any of these, please contact us with the appropriate data and we will make the corrections.

• Effective this edition, we have added some 45 and 78 rpm soundtrack *singles*. Usually more important than the records themselves, however, are accompanying sleeves that picture a film scene and/or film stars. Other singles of special interest are those that make available a tune not found on the albums of the show in question. It is ones from these categories we have selected for inclusion in this printing. So, while the few you'll find here represent merely a step in yet another direction, we will not be making any claims of comprehensiveness in this area in the near future.

• There are hundreds of multi-disc LPs and EPs documented in the guide, and most are identified as such. If there are ones we've missed, please let us know. The same goes for other noteworthy details, such as boxed sets, inserts, bonus booklets, photos and posters.

• Since virtually all "soundtracks" that are merely a collection of assorted popular tunes (which may or may not be heard during the film), those composers are not indicated as being "various."

WHAT TO EXPECT WHEN SELLING RECORDS TO A DEALER

As most know, there is a noteworthy difference between the prices reported in this guide and the prices that one can expect a dealer to pay when buying records for resale. Unless a dealer is buying for a personal collection and without thoughts of resale, he or she is simply not in a position to pay full price. Dealers work on a percentage basis, largely determined by the total dollar investment, quality, and quantity of material offered as well as the general financial condition and inventory of the dealer at the time.

Another very important consideration is the length of time it will take the dealer to recover at least the amount of the original investment. The greater the demand for the stock and the better the condition, the quicker the return and therefore the greater the percentage that can be paid. Our experience has shown that, day-in and day-out, most dealers will pay from 25% to 50% of *guide* prices. And that's assuming they are planning to resell at guide prices. If they traditionally sell below guide, that will be reflected in what they can pay for stock.

If you have records to sell, it would be wise to check with several shops. In doing so you'll begin to get a good idea of the value of your collection to a dealer.

Also, consult the Directory of Buyers and Sellers in this guide for the names of many dealers who not only might be interested in buying, but from whom many collectible records are available for purchase.

Whether you wish to sell the records you have, or add out-of-print discs to your collection, check out *DISCoveries* magazine. Each issue is packed with ads, features, discographies, collecting tips and more. For more information, contact: Trader Publications, PO Box 1050, Dubuque, Iowa 52003. A sample issue is available upon request.

CONCLUDING THOUGHTS

The purpose of this guide is to report as accurately as possible the most recent prices asked and paid for records within the area of its coverage. There are two key words here that deserve emphasis: **Guide** and **Report**.

As mentioned earlier, this book is only a guide. There always have been and always will be instances of records selling well above and below the prices shown within these pages. These extremes are recognized in the final averaging process; but it's still important to understand that just because we've reported a 30-year-old record as having a $25.00 to $50.00 near-mint value, doesn't mean that a collector of that material should be hesitant to pay $75.00 for it. How badly he or she wants it and how often it's possible to purchase it *at any price* should be the prime factors considered, not the fact that we last reported it at a lower price. Of course, we'd like to know about sales of this sort so that the next edition can reflect the new pricing information.

We may report a record for $50 to $100, which may have been an accurate appraisal at press time. However, before the new edition hits the streets, the price might be $100 to $150. One or two transactions and a year later it jumps to $150 to $200. By the time we're ready to publish a new edition, this same disc may be considered a bargain at $500.

At that point, people may look at the book and wonder how we could show $50 to $100 for a $500 record. "That price is a joke," you'll hear. And at that point it is.

If we came out monthly perhaps we could keep pace, but this volatile marketplace coupled with a quinquennial publishing schedule requires the reader to allow for inflation. Check the copyright date (page ii), and consider an allowance for the passage of time.

Meanwhile, please keep in mind that any of the world's more valuable records now have the potential to be worth considerably more in the near future than when work ended on this edition.

We encourage record companies, artist management organizations, talent agencies, publicists, and performers to make certain that we are on the active mailing list for new release information, press releases, bios, publicity photos, and anything pertaining to recordings.

There is an avalanche of helpful information in this guide to aid the collector in determining what is valuable and what may not be worth fooling with, but the wise fan will also keep abreast of current trends and news through the pages of the fanzines and publications devoted to his or her favorite forms of music.

SOME DINOSAURS HAVE BEEN SHAFTED

By Paul Aguirre

A dealer gets a copy of Raintree County in. He looks it up in the price guide, sees it books for up to $125.00 and gets happy. Leaving room for doubt, he prices it at $100.00 and puts it on the wall. It sits there for one month ... two months ... six months. Then he moves it from the wall – where the high ticket items are – and into the bins. People may come in and try to negotiate on it, but he keeps seeing that $125.00 price tag dancing in front of his eyes. So he declines, and the album just sits there gathering dust. And everyone concerned is understandably confused and frustrated.

Sound familiar? If you're a dealer it does. This is precisely what's been happening in recent years – like mad on the coasts and to a lesser extent overseas and in the Midwest where vinyl album shops are fewer and farther between.

The soundtracks and original casts market has dipped considerably. The "dinosaurs" – one San Francisco dealer's affectionate term for the $100+ collectibles – just aren't selling. Meanwhile, customers keep coming in wanting a copy of *Shaft in Africa*. What's going on here?

I called Osborne Enterprises to inquire about advertising in this book. However, after a few minutes of conversation with Jerry, I inadvertently admitted I had been collecting and dealing in soundtracks and casts for over 20 years. Before I knew it, I had agreed to review the manuscript and help in updating the new edition. At the outset, I planned to give it the once-over and send it back, but I ended up venturing on a rediscovery of a topic I've always been passionate about. Aside from correcting and/or adding information to the book, the further I researched, the more I learned about a category of music I thought I knew inside-out. I didn't learn about who composed the score, who starred in the movie version or what label would have recorded the show had it lasted more than a week. No, that much I knew. It's ironic; most people who collect this kind of music must – to a certain extent – live in the past. If not live there, then be able to tap into it very easily. And what I learned was how much the world we live in *today* has effected this category of music we who read this book care so much about.

I've spent several months trying to determine why, in the last five years, there has been such a decline in interest where soundtracks and casts are concerned. My perspective came from my own experiences as both dealer and collector over the past 20 years, and also from the many others I work with, both in San Francisco and around the world. I grilled them all, and came up with virtually a unanimous account as to what has happened.

Everyone seems to agree that most albums of this type, despite their alleged values, are gathering dust on shelves across the country and beyond. And everyone seemed to agree that there are three main reasons: economics, compact discs and the plague.

The after-effects we're still feeling from Reaganomics has killed the once-mighty dollar value of soundtracks (among other things). Obviously, if a score is easily available on CD, its vinyl value is likely to drop. But I find this is only the tip of the CD iceberg. What seems to be forgotten is that every time the industry changes formats, a number of titles fall between the cracks.

For example, in 1949, when 78 sets were outmoded by the EP and LP, *Carmen Jones* and *Oklahoma!* were issued in truncated versions. *Duel in the Sun, Forever Amber, Panama Hattie, A Connecticut Yankee, Inside USA* and a score of others were not issued at all by their original labels. Likewise, when CDs outmoded LPs, there was a lot of excitement – no more skips, no more flips, easy fit, additional material, better sound.

Now, several years after the advent, the mist has cleared and things are once again pretty much as they were in 1949: certain items have disappeared from circulation. After the initial glut of Broadway cast releases by Columbia (now Sony), RCA (now BMG), MCA and Capitol (now Angel/EMI), the well dried up. As a result, it's entirely possible that shows like *Christine, Ernest in Love, Darling of the Day* and *Juno*, and film score masterworks like *The Roots of Heaven* and *Peyton Place* will never find their way to the new format, save for an occasional foreign disc. Also, there are still more titles that, while not masterworks, are still worth preserving – musicals like *Jumbo, State Fair, Athena* and dozens of others that haven't been heard from since the 10-inch LP kicked the bucket in the mid-1950s. Don't listen to those who junked their LP collections because "everything is on CD." It just isn't so. In fact, the majority of titles that emerged on LP will likely never see the light of day again.

The difference is that until lately, people were satisfied to switch formats once every 30 years. As those of us who lived through the "CD invasion" no doubt remember, any format change is traumatic and bothersome to all but the techno-fascinated. In today's world, with computers outdating themselves by the week, no format is expected to last longer than a moment in time.

A missed point by both collectors and marketers is that every time we are forced to uproot ourselves from a format, more titles will be lost. This is why collectors in particular must wake up and realize that *all* modes of music reproduction need to be kept alive. It is the only way every show and film score can be preserved.

I still pay a small fortune to have my grandfather's turntable serviced when necessary – not so much for sentimental reasons as that I can scarcely find one that operates at 78 rpm. From the pioneering Liberty Music Shop releases of the 1920s and 30s to the latest John Williams soundtrack, this is a field of music that redefines the word longevity! Very few categories of music date back as far as does the recording of shows.

Then there's the plague. Most dealers I spoke with had another, far more complex reason for the decline in this market. A vast majority feel that AIDS has depleted the ranks of soundtrack and cast collectors – meaning those in the gay community. This issue is two-fold: not only have the seriously ill or deceased stopped collecting, but the whereabouts of many of their collections is largely undetermined. In some cases, those collections have been left in caring, knowing hands. But in as many others, I fear albums were either given to thrift stores or – perish the thought – disposed of and destined for a landfill. Either way, are fewer copies of *Tender is the Night* and *Francis of Assisi* than ever before.

On the grand scale, this is a tragedy of humanity, but on a smaller one it's a tragedy for those left who covet these items.

How to find them? I have acquired a lot of my gems from the pages of marketplace publications, such as *DISCoveries,* and while these serve as an Internet of sorts, it's no secret that they hardly cater to the soundtrack collector; the majority of their subscribers having decidedly different tastes.

Many of the major mail-order dealers – ones I'm sure most readers of this guide have done business with – have expressed to me a feeling that there is as yet no venue to bring the small circle of soundtrack and cast album aficionados together. Apparently, the amount of die-hard vinyl collectors has dwindled and those left are keyed into their local record shop, content to wait there for the items they want. Soundtrack newsletters and periodicals exist – as do ones aimed at collectors of movie memorabilia -- but none have been successful thus far at closing the gap between those who have albums for sale and those who seek them.

At any rate, I believe all of the above findings are to some extent true. But regardless of the reasons, the unimaginable has happened: an entire category of music has depreciated. I still have Jerry Osborne's 1978 guide (contains the first soundtracks and casts pricing in print) as a reference. Amazingly, some albums were worth more 20 years ago than they are today. But this is the way it is, no denying it. Then again, 1978 is pre-Reganomics, pre-CD and pre-plague

Since joining the team of advisors, I have encountered many varying opinions on the guide. Some scoff at it, others swear by it. One fellow read me up and down for having anything to do with a price guide. In his estimation, "True collectors know the values. Anyone who needs to look it up is just following a trend." He contends that one item will be worth varying amounts to different collectors. This is true, of course, but I think he misses the larger point. There are different types of collectors. One type sees *The Ipcress File* on the late show, falls in love with the John Barry score and – still in disbelief that it's not on CD – is willing to pay *anything* to get their hands on that soundtrack. Another type wants *The Ipcress File* as only one of all the Barry scores. They'll want to pay less for that one album because they have more to collect. Finally, there's the avid soundtrack collector who wants them all, from *The Jazz Singer* of 1927 to *The Jazz Singer* of 1980. They will want to pay even less because there are many more to track down in a single lifetime.

So, yes, it's all relative, but that's all the more reason for a dealer to have a range to go by in pricing it. Ideally, a seller should try to peg which kind of collector he's dealing with and price things accordingly.

How to peg them? It's the difference between someone who comes in to a shop and asks specifically for *Mary Poppins* as opposed to one who asks to see the soundtrack section. Chances are you'll never see the first customer again after they find *Mary Poppins*. The second one you'll get to know very well, and they likely will always ask you to cut a deal, at least until you offer them ongoing discount.

Collectors and dealers both turn to price guides for a variety of reasons. One dealer (who shall remain nameless) published his own guide not long ago, but his infamous reputation and unsavory business practices have rendered it worthless. No one will deal with this guy twice, and I've heard that from San Francisco to Australia (with too many points between to mention).

Clearly, the Osborne book is the one to which people are referring, and it's no wonder. There are so many soundtracks and cast albums in existence that, unless you do this full-time, there's no way to even keep up with approximate values. So dealers in particular are *constantly* turning to this book for pricing help. I'd wager this is true here more than in any other music category. As a result, the editors and reviewers have thoroughly re-evaluated the price ranges, to consider the above-mentioned wide spectrum of collectors and also the overwhelmed dealers.

There has been one other important emphasis placed on this edition. Previously, the major interest for those who use this book seems to have been checking out revised prices. But readers will find quite a lot more here. A great deal of effort has gone into incorporating accurate and integral information about the albums themselves. This ranges from standard composer, conductor and cast listings, to articulate differentiations between cover issues, to the revelation of the long-withheld names of singers who "ghosted" vocals for such non-singing performers as Kim Novak, Rita Hayworth, Jeanne Crain and Audrey Hepburn. These efforts have gone beyond reporting only the information listed on album covers – information which, incidentally, is often wrong (e.g. Columbia mistakenly credits Stephen Boyd as singing his own vocals on the *Jumbo* soundtrack album). Rather, reference books have been checked, experts have been called in and the results – I think – are very satisfying. In fact, the guide now serves as a bona fide reference book on the subject – something that has been needed for a long time.

One inescapable problem with any price guide is that it begins to outdate itself the minute it hits the shelves. In the years since the 1991 edition came out, values have shifted both up and down in unheard of patterns. It's possible that some areas of the world will be unsettled by some of the price ranges following. Yes, some of the new price ranges are drastically lower and others significantly higher, but the important thing is that they are *collectively correct* – not just according to the editors' table, but to the myriad of people who have been consulted on some of these items. In some areas – Los Angeles comes to mind as one – the stakes are higher. People are more willing, and more able to spend top dollar for albums that seem to be plentiful in that region. But this is not the norm. A few hours north finds San Francisco, where the sheer volume of used record shops is unrivaled in North America. In my neck of the woods, there are literally too many soundtrack bins given the number of people collecting. But this is not the norm either.

Another essential reality to keep in mind while eyeing this guide: soundtrack collecting has become fad-oriented. Up until the late 1980s, it was the dinosaurs (*Raintree County, Alexander the Great,* etc.) that were perpetually hot. Then factory-recalled albums like *Valley Girl* became the rage, prompting not one, but three bootlegs of *The Caine Mutiny.* In the last few years, it's been '60s TV stuff, like *The Flintstones* and *Mister Ed*, that have shot from $15 to $200. Now, those are simmering down and '70s black exploitation and biker flick albums are coming up.

In an ironic twist, I can't tell you why such '50s collectibles like *Kings Go Forth, Bell, Book and Candle* and *Vertigo* won't sell, while similar items like *The Barbarian and the Geisha* and *The Night of the Hunter* are worth more than ever. In short, the normal appreciation philosophy of collecting just doesn't apply here anymore. But it's still exciting to watch a once worthless item suddenly skyrocket in value. It makes us realize no record is expendable in the soundtrack market. The cover you are using as a box filler today might soon be the most sought-after on the market.

Is there any way to keep ahead of it all? I personally think it all depends on who's growing up and looking back on their childhood at what time. It is advisable to keep an eye on each generation that turns 30 and watch values soar on items released when that generation was in its blaze of adolescence. Better think twice before you sell *Saturday Night Fever* or *Grease* at a garage sale for fifty cents.

In every Osborne guide of any kind that comes out, the author wisely reminds his readers that it is just a guide – not a bible; and that the prices are estimates – not price tags. However true this has been as a rule, it's even more so as of late. With what's hot and what's not switching places at the speed of light, it's more than likely that many of the items selling at record highs at press time will be decreasing in value between now and our next edition. By the same token, keep an eye on some of those $8 to $15 trifles that will be making the climb over the next few years.

Finally, the most agonizing part of this editing process for me was differentiating the *historical* value of a record from its current *financial* value. Often, I couldn't believe the figures I was putting down.

It's a beautiful thing when can you take an album like *The Barbarian and the Geisha*, where you can say: a) great score; b) spectacular cover art; c) next-to-impossible to find; and, d) its value is as high as $200.00. It all adds up and it all makes sense.

But there are remarkably few cases like this in today's market. Everything goes along fine until you get to the price range. Then it doesn't add up, and yet there it is in front of you. Those at the point of selling their rarities are often shocked at how little green they're making back for a lifetime of investing. But the flip side of this is that now is a good time for beginners in the collecting game. Maybe this bear market will encourage people to dig in and keep the buyer-to-seller chain going, albeit at a less-than-fair rate of exchange. Obviously, this will change in time. It always does.

Once we thought 78 albums were dead. Now that we see their original art work constantly being reproduced on microscopic CD covers, and now that we've realized how many 78 sets never made their way to commercial LP, there's a renewed interest.

Readers will notice an enormous number of 78 rpm releases are now included in the guide. It's nice to have them back.

Oh yes, one last word on compact discs: despite any drawbacks, they're coming out with some truly amazing things, from the imported Franz Waxman soundtrack of *The Story of Ruth* to MGM's stunning releases of their vintage musicals. Enjoy them all, but don't forget about what came before!

In closing, collecting and dealing in soundtracks and cast albums is very much like a game of Old Maid right now. No one wants to be left holding a spinster with no selling power. But, unlike the game, the old maid in soundtrack collecting can very easily turn into a swan with no warning whatsoever. Maybe that's where the real fun is.

© 1997 Paul Aguirre, San Francisco, California

RECORDMAN PONTIFICATES ON VINYL SOUNDTRACK COLLECTING IN THE '90s – AND BEYOND

"C'mon, Recordman," I sighed. "We promised Jerry we would prepare a short essay on collecting vinyl soundtrack recordings in the '90s – and beyond. You know, what's going on lately, why collect soundtracks at all, what's hot and what's not, how CD reissues affect the market..." I paused right there, awaiting the inevitable.

"CD's," huffed Recordman, "reissues ... don't ever mention those words in my presence again! I am a *record* collector, I am an original soundtrack record collector ... well, maybe a few good studio tracks as well. But friends never let friends listen to digital products," he smiled. "Look, people collect soundtracks, mainly because of the glorious music that has been produced for films over the last 65 years, and soundtrack collecting is one of the most esoteric, most satisfying

... and most difficult and expensive specialties in record collecting. It's the field knowledgeable record collectors finally gravitate to when they finally grow beyond pop and rock," he sneered, curling his upper lip. "The only people further out on the vinyl spiral are the classical collectors, and those people spend their time running around talking about 'shaded dogs' or something like that," he grinned.

"Actually I like to kid my classical vinyl buddies, but many soundtrack collectors are born out of their classical roots, and many soundtrack collectors develop new appreciation of the classical influences which fueled the early soundtrack composers.

"Many people become soundtrack collectors because they once sat in a darkened theater in their youth, enjoying a milestone picture with a great score, such as *Gone with the Wind, Ben-Hur, Star Wars* or ... *The Brady Bunch Movie,* then left in awe of the absolutely breathtaking music they just heard. 'Who wrote that music and is there more like it out there', they might ask themselves. Thus the search begins and a new collector is born as the quest for recordings is underway.

"The novice starts to hear and recognize the names of composers such as Korngold, Rozsa, Tiomkin, Goldsmith, Williams, Horner and many others that were unfamiliar before but which quickly become easily recognizable in style and content.

"Initially, on entering the field of collecting soundtrack vinyl recordings, one must realize that it is driven essentially by composer 'underscores' – the actual music scored for the film, not the vocals or songs being sung.

"In pop or rock, the singers and musicians are usually the reason something is collectible. With us, it is the individual composers and/or the specific film or TV score. Many soundtrack collectors are composer completists who seek out all recorded scores of any type by an individual composer. Other collectors specialize in scores of certain film genres – Disney, westerns, horror; action/adventure; wars, epics, and TV shows and scores.

"Then again, many a soundtrack album is highly collectible – not for the music that's in its grooves – but for the beautiful, unusual or sexy art found on the cover."

"Those are some good points and interesting observations. Please continue," I asked.

"Many vinyl format variations exist: 78 rpm multi-disc albums; 33 rpm long plays, on either 10- or 12-inch discs; extended play (EP) 45 and 33 rpms (usually seven-inch); 45 and 78 rpm singles; and even a few 12-inch singles, or EPs, made for disco play. All of these formats are desirable to collectors as a group, though not all collectors collect all formats."

He's right. In fact, there are now many 78 rpm soundtrack and cast releases listed in this guide, for they are sought-after by collectors as well. New interest has arisen in these 78s of the film scores of the 1940s and '50s, several of which now book for over $100.

Black plastic is the norm for the record industry; however, countless different colors have been used to make records. History has shown that those of some color or combination of colors are more desirable, and usually more valuable. Some are pictured in full color in this edition.

Promotional records are always collectible, whether made for radio station play or for some other publicity purpose. Their appeal is often bolstered by packaging and/or content not commercially available.

Then there are albums produced for varied businesses as adjunct scores for product films and documentaries, or special company events. Scored by many of the top notch composers of the day, these are known in the hobby as *industrial* soundtracks. Most exist in very limited quantities, generally just enough to satisfy the needs of a particular function.

We also have "special edition" vanity pressings from fan clubs and random entrepreneurs, bootleg issues of scores never commercially released, and some counterfeits, produced in an attempt to cash in on the high demand of some extremely rare albums.

Most of the more popular records have been reissued many times. Numerous reissues are included and noted in the guide, but as with nearly all antiques and collectibles, soundtrack collectors place a premium on first pressings.

In our field, *original* has a dual meaning. While it does refer to a first pressing, it is more commonly used to distinguish a film score made from the actual film's sound track, not a studio recording later done especially for records.

If the film score is recorded apart from the film track – even if with the same conductor, orchestra, vocalists, etc. – it is a "studiotrack," and is identified in the guide as such. Determining which is which is a matter of examining them one at a time. Many albums labeled on as "original soundtracks" by the film studios are really studiotracks, but until that claim is disproved, they are shown as soundtracks in this guide.

Studiotrack compilation LPs have started to rise in value as collectors find these albums to be the only source for many of the cues or tracks from many old films. Numerous films had no original soundtrack record released at the time, and their scores exist only on these older, compilation albums.

Television show scores have also gained in both popularity and price as collectors discover that many of them were scored by some of today's hot composers, when they were just starting in the business.

Film and TV scores to many children's films are also very hot, especially many of the original Disney records and the Hanna-Barbera releases on Colpix.

Values for film scores of "Blaxploitation" movies of the late '60s and early '70s have also increased, based on rarity as well as the great soul, funk and R&B music they contain.

The universe of collectible vinyl soundtracks is essentially a closed one in numbers now, following the emergence and dominance of the compact disc format which began in 1984. From then until around the end of the decade, most new film scores came out on both vinyl and on CD.

While there have been a few sporadic soundtracks issued after 1990 on vinyl – usually those of the rock music or oldies-compilation variety – the listings you see in the guide are very close to being complete. In addition to the value of this guide to the collector, for its pricing and useful information, it can also serve as general checklist for the general film music enthusiast to review what has been produced over the years. Many of these time-honored vinyl records will probably never be issued on CD. This for various reasons, among them: demand or lack of it, lost master tapes, legal clearances, etc.

Without rehashing the "Records vs. CD" argument of last decade, suffice it to say that, between the two formats, there really is a difference in the sound. Many term the vinyl sound as warm, and CD's as having a more brittle or cooler sound. While subjective with each listener, in playing both versions of the same recording on equivalent audio equipment, the difference in the ambiance of the two becomes apparent. The big drawback to the entire spectrum of vinyl discs is the emphasis on condition. This is why record collectors place premiums on mint and near-mint grades. Vinyl records, unless properly cared for and stored, can easily get damaged, scratched and abused, which affects their playback characteristics. A compact disc is much more forgiving.

So why collect *vinyl* soundtrack recordings in the supposedly glorious era of the CD? The reissue on CD of a film score does not make a rare vinyl album any less rare. All it does is decrease the demand somewhat for the record. Those who only want to hear the music –

regardless of format – will be content with a CD, or even a cassette tape. These folks are film and cast music aficionados, perhaps, but not *record collectors*.

Soundtrack collectors initially enter this field primarily because of their love of the music. Film scores can be exciting, contemplative, sorrowful, boisterous, bombastic and of epic proportions in their musical appeal.

Beautiful-sounding CDs exist for many of the better-known scores in this guide. However, a collector of anything from the past – whether comic books, cars, antiques or even records – the emphasis is on originality and condition. We collect not only the sound but the physical artifact which first produced that sound. This also includes original packaging – covers, sleeves, inserts, etc.

Possessiveness is certainly one characteristic of collecting. "Here it is … I own it and you don't!" is a statement of the force often driving collectors. We are amateur historians who create our own repositories of the world's musical heritage and output. Our breed has been around since the inception of the phonograph disc, at the turn of the century.

The emergence of the CD has also given rise to new appreciation for one thing taken for granted during the 40-year dominance of vinyl albums: cover artwork. Simply put, many of those 12" by 12" illustrated soundtrack gems are downright framable. Some CD enthusiasts, having seen the tiny, pitiful excuse for what passes as CD cover art, say "You can't play the cover!" But the condition and quality of the LP cover art has always been a strong selling point for records. Beautiful art or photos, with extensive liner notes, allow extra enjoyment for many of the soundtracks listed here. It's no wonder that the condition of the cover has always been as important as that of the disc itself.

Recently, "lounge" or "cocktail" music records of the 1950's have achieved recognition, primarily for their sexy, girlie covers. This then made collectors realize that, of all the record genres, it is soundtracks that offer the best examples of the seductive covers.

The 1991 edition of this guide made the general public more aware of this highly-specialized field. Good buys heretofore available in the standard collector haunts, the flea market and garage sales, have sometimes risen dramatically as the dealers sit there with a well-worn copy of the old guide in their pockets.

For those of you interested in following the collectible soundtrack field on a continuing basis, the following two publications are highly recommended: *The Soundtrack Collector* is a quarterly publication devoted to vinyl soundtrack collecting. Write: The Soundtrack Collector, 5824 West Galena, Milwaukee, WI, 53208. *Film Score Monthly* is primarily new film score and CD-oriented, featuring composer interviews, reviews, and general articles of interest for those who love film music. Plus, the continuing, sporadic, and pontificating column, *The Adventures of Recordman*, on vinyl soundtrack collecting, is graciously tolerated by the readership. Write: Film Score Monthly, 5967 Chula Vista Way, #7, Los Angeles, CA 90068.

"Not bad, in fact I think that's a wrap," Recordman said, wiping his brow and hitching up his pants. I smiled, saying "Yea, let's go with it. Hey, we're a pretty good team – this could be the beginning of a beautiful friendship."

"That'll be the day," he garbled.

Then, unable to resist, I looked him right in the eyes and said, "Recordman, you were kidding about *The Brady Bunch Movie,* weren't you?"

He laughed …and left without saying another word. Moments later, from the other room, I swear I heard the voice of Shelley Long.

©1997 R. Michael Murray

USING YOUR PC TO CLEAN THE
SOUND . . . NOT THE RECORD

By Jeff Klinedinst

For many years, collectors have cleaned records in much the same way as taking on other forms of domestic cleaning — with soap, water and some elbow grease. However, if you have a PC available, there is a dryer alternative.

Modern software science has finally connected with the world of record restoration and right *now* your IBM personal computer has the capability to be a recording studio, editing suite, and even a noise reduction laboratory.

Noise reduction, or sound cleaning, has existed almost as long as personal computers themselves, but, as with most new technologies, it took awhile for the prices to tumble to reality. Now, owning this system is possible for most of us. As you no doubt know, computers offer incredible power with a wide variety of tools for everyday use — easily justifying their modest price.

For this walk through, we'll be using:

1. Any 486 DX (or faster) computer equipped with: a) Windows 3.1 or Windows 95, b) compatible 16 bit sound card, c) mouse.

2. DART PRO software from Tracer Technologies.

3. Any normal setup for playing records, or other source.

To set up the computer for recording, simply run a line from the amplifier's outputs to the inputs of your sound card. Here your sound card functions exactly like a tape recorder, though it will use your computer's hard drive for storage rather than analog tape.

For recording, any good sound editing program will provide computerized level meters to aid you in finding the appropriate levels for recording. In DART PRO, the controls for recording work exactly like those on an analog tape recorder.

With the levels set, you then begin the recording process. It is a good idea to record several seconds of surface noise before the actual music begins. This noise at the beginning contains important information which is crucial to the noise reduction process. More about that later.

DECLICKING

Removing clicks and pops during the restoration process is critical in the restoration of worn vinyl recordings. With DART PRO, this is a fairly straightforward and uncomplicated process. An "Outlier Detector" analyzes the material and automatically searches out disturbances which do not fit within the parameters of the source material. It marks these areas and then replaces them with "good" source material, found immediately before or after the disturbance. The program automatically searches out disturbances that are 100 samples or less — so it won't haphazardly remove cymbal crashes or any other "good" source material.

For dealing with large scratches or cuts in the source material, DART PRO has a manual reparation mode that allows highlighting an area up to 1500 samples, and replacing it with "good" source material. DeClicking is usually the first stage of the noise restoration process and provides amazing results.

DENOISE

Groove noise, distortion, and any other "constant" noise associated with age and poor quality discs are the next targets. You'll recall that when we recorded the source material, it was mentioned that you should leave a bit at the beginning. Now we make use of that noise. Usually, the noise residing at the beginning of the file is the same as found in the rest of the file. DART PRO can analyze that material then remove it from the entire file. This process is called "Noise Printing."

DEHISS

For the record, DeHiss is an intelligent filtering process which provides maximum hiss removal with minimal source material degradation.

THE NOISE AUDITION

One major concern of noise reduction is the fear of damaging the source material in the quest to remove the noise. A key feature of DART PRO allows you to actually subtract your "cleaned" file from your original source and hear *only* the noise that you've removed. Then, if you hear what you determine to be too much source material amidst the noise, you can always have DART PRO attack the file less aggressively.

The final step is to use the Play function to record your cleaned material to tape, DAT tape, or even a writable CD. Now you can enjoy your music the way it was meant to be — noise free.

Noise reduction is like any other tool. It takes a bit of playing around to become familiar with all of its features. Once mastered, your PC can be a powerful ally in your pursuit to eliminate noise from your treasured recordings.

"THE CAINE MUTINY"
The Official Unofficial Story

By Gareth L. Pawlowski

The official history of the destroyer minesweeper USS DOYLE (DMC 34) briefly states, "The DOYLE returned to the Western Pacific and between February 2 to July 31, 1953, visited Midway, ports in Guam, Kwajalein, and the Philippines, as well as Hong Kong for five weeks.

One event not mentioned in the ship's history – etched in my mind forever – took place June 29 and 30, and July 3, 1953 at 1010 dock in Pearl Harbor. I was a 13 year-old navy brat at the time, and my father had been recalled to active duty at the outbreak of the Korean conflict. We spent three years on the island of Oahu, arriving at the downtown piers late January 1951 aboard the U.S.N.S. DANIEL I. SULTAN, complete with portholes blackened out.

I spent many months during those years boarding all the ships that entered Pearl Harbor, collecting match covers and watching the hula girls dance to the crews of warships returning from the Korean war zone. Once, when I was in the crew's berthing compartment of the destroyer BLUE, there was an announcement over the 21MC for personnel to leave the ship. There had been mine damage and the ship was slowly sinking from the stern and had to be towed to dry-dock for repairs. Such events were a part of my life growing up and meeting new adventures.

It was summer vacation from Pearl Harbor Intermediate School (P.H.I.S.) and my friend George Olson and I were walking along Mike Pier, towards the longer 1010 dock. As we walked I could see the DOYLE ahead of us with a slight, five degree list to port.

There was a lot of activity along the dockside. After we reached the dock area, I saw miles of electrical cables, overhead booms and camera equipment. In a flash the noise was gone and someone motioned to us with his hands to keep quiet. The cameras were rolling and the actors were plying their trade. In progress was the filming of the Stanley Kramer production of *The Caine Mutiny*, based on the Pulitzer Prize novel by Herman Wouk.

Because of all the commotion, we couldn't see what was being filmed from where we stood. I thought to myself that Humphrey Bogart was probably at CincPac (Commander in Chief, Pacific) having coffee with Admiral Arthur W. Eadford, and we would not see any of the major stars. Someone said, "Cut, that's a print" or something to that effect, followed by an announcement there would be an hour break.

George and I started to walk toward the DOYLE, not saying anything to each other, and quickly stepped onto the after starboard bow and on the ship, heading back to the fantail and down a hatch into the crew's berthing compartment.

I noticed a sailor by his bunk and open locker and asked if he had any of the ship's match covers. He reached into the locker and pulled out one and gave it to me. This match cover has always been something special in my collection because the sailor told me that the match cover had been in his locker during all of the at-sea filming, including the famous tow cutting scene.

The main reason we first went to the after crew's berthing compartment was to make sure we were not noticed by a sharp-eyed Officer of the Deck, and when we reached topside, we proceeded along the port side of the ship. There I noticed large concrete blocks positioned that gave the ship the slight list I had noticed earlier.

22

The DOYLE was a broken deck ex-destroyer of the BRISTON class, so when we got just past mid-ship, we climbed a station and a ladder up to the outer port bridge and walked into the pilot house, stopping short in our tracks in front of the wheel and engine room telegraph. With all the excitement running through me, I saw several officers standing there but my first reaction was that they were ship's company. But not George. He said, "Look there's Humphrey Bogart" and as I looked in the direction where George pointed, there he was, just two feet away from us. His eyes caught both of us. That expression of his made me think he was saying to himself, "How did these kids get on the ship?" But that thought left as quickly as it came. Then we noticed Van Johnson and Fred MacMurray. They were too busy discussing the dialogue to even notice us. George said to me, "Get Bogie's autograph." I never answered.

In those days, motion picture stars were in a world apart from us regular folks. Their presence on the giant silver screen made them seem larger than life. We just stood there, silently watching for about three minutes, then the three actors went into the chart room, and George and I looked at each other with big smiles.

We quickly left the wheel house, climbed down the ladder to the main deck and went through a center passageway under the main torpedo tube station to the after bow back onto the 1010 dockside. We took about ten paces and turned around and looked at the ship for a few minutes, then went home.

The July 10, 1953 issue of the *Pearl Harbor Shipyard Log* (Vol. VII No. 28) tells the story of the movie making at Pearl Harbor. Looking at the article years later, one part haunts me: "...amateur shooters, cameras galore, out all along the dock when the stars arrived. Humphrey Bogart, Fred MacMurray, Van Johnson ... often posed for the amateurs between scenes." Wow! Imagine a photo of me with Humphrey Bogart in 1953! Unfortunately, I did not own a camera at that age, and wouldn't have thought to ask someone to take a photo for me. Another thought: I wonder if during the filming I might have seen Meatball (Lee Marvin) or Horrible (Claude Akins) at the time.

They released the motion picture on June 24, 1954. We were back in the states by that time but I made sure that I saw the film as soon as it premiered. For many years, whenever I'd see it on television, and the typhoon scene plays, I think of the time George and I were in that same wheel house with Bogart, Johnson and MacMurray in 1953.

RCA Victor Records scheduled for release, in June 1954, "The Original Music and Dialogue" [soundtrack] album, *The Caine Mutiny* (LOC-1013). Commercial pressings of the album were made but never released for public sale. Ever since I began speaking with collectors about *The Caine Mutiny*, I have been met with flack from people telling me that "the album was on sale for two weeks and pulled off the market." They give so many explanations, one of the most widespread being that author Herman Wouk was not credited on the album cover. Now that the original Caine Mutiny cover has at long last been photographed and published, you can see Wouk is indeed credited. Below the actor credits, is: "Based upon the Pulitzer prize winning novel by HERMAN WOUK."

Regarding the purported commercial release of the album, along with any other concocted explanations, I did my own extensive research over an extended period of time and am satisfied with my findings.

Knowing the significance of this album – one of the five most valuable LPs ever – Jerry Osborne hounded me for many years to tell the complete story behind the most famous of all soundtrack records. Request granted.

Even before the record company's publicity department floods record reviewers with the standard promotional materials for an upcoming record release, there are many in-house communiqués – before, during and after actual production. Each company has its own method of inter-company correspondence, the one in use by RCA Victor at the time being the RCA Victor Record Bulletin. Each Bulletin would have a specific heading that relates to the subject matter. The "RCA Victor Record Bulletin"(RLY 66) dated May 10, 1954 announced *The Caine Mutiny* LOC-1013 album and a scheduled release date for July of that year.

A second follow-up Merchandising Tip, *RCA Victor Record Bulletin* (RLY 74), dated June 7, 1954 announced: "If any album is released on record, it will be released on RCA Victor, but at the present time, it looks very unlikely that it will be released for records," signed S.L. York, Merchandising Manager.

Also stated is that those concerned would be notified if there was any change on the album. RLY 74 was the last official in-house communication concerning *The Caine Mutiny* soundtrack album because the decision had been made and there was to be no change in status for the record album.

There are several hand-written notes on the Listing Notice of *The Caine Mutiny* album. The Notice for the 12-inch long-play album shows on April 5,1954, reference 32a changes the title to read "... soundtrack of the Technicolor film ..." Reference 32c indicates the date the withdrawal information was added to the Listing Notice.

Reference on the Listing Notice about the album not being released is not specific regarding details, but it clearly shows the ultimate fate for *The Caine Mutiny* LP. "Appeared in tips (Merchandising Tips) but not in catalog. 6m [6,000] pressed but not shipped. Withdrawn, not to be released per composer's [Max Steiner] request."

The truth is that Steiner, composer-conductor of the film score, objected. RCA Victor simply abided by his request. At any rate, there were no further Merchandising Tips or in-house communications regarding *The Caine Mutiny* soundtrack from the Technicolor film production.

The official Listing Notice for *The Caine Mutiny* 45 rpm Extended Play (RCA Victor EOD 1013), also has a hand-written notation: "Withdrawn Not to Be Released per 31d July 1, 1954." I must emphasize the use of the word "Withdrawn" used by RCA Victor in the decision not to release the album. Accompanying that notation is: "Not to Be Released." This should dispel old rumors that the album was released and then later withdrawn from record stores.

For those unfamiliar with RCA's Index and Classification of records in the '50s, there is a logical explanation why the 45 rpm equivalent is referred to as EOC 1013 in the Listing Notices instead of EOD 1013. Using the coding for popular records as an example: "E" is for Extended Play, "P" is for popular and "A" indicates a single pocket (thus EPA) 45 rpm Extended Play album. EPB is a two-disc, double-pocket set, EPC a triple-pocket EP, and EPD a four-disc EP set. *The Caine Mutiny* EP would have been four records, and since the 12-inch LP is designated LOC (long play original cast), the typist of the listing notices typed EOC thinking EOC referred to Extended Original Cast, when in reality EOC refers to Extended Play Original Cast *three-disc* album.

Normally, RCA Victor issued four-record EP albums in a different configuration than single-, double- and triple-pocket EPs. The latter three variations were packaged in single or gatefold, individual pocket, rigid cardboard jackets – like 10- and 12-inch LP covers. However, the four record EP sets came in a binder, similar to those commonly used in the '40s for 78 rpm album sets – four discs in paper sleeves with a hard cover binder and thick spine, glued or stapled together. There is no evidence whatsoever to indicate a 78 rpm album set was ever planned for *The Caine Mutiny*.

The Listing Notice for the 45 rpm Extended Play (EOD 1013) also carries the handwritten notations: "Withdrawn, not to be released per 32c, July 1, 1954. 6m pressed but not shipped (per Tom Potter) ... Composer objected."

There is no indication that the "6,000 albums pressed" refers to a combined quantity of both 12-inch LPs and 45 rpm EPs.

At the time, the record industry always referred to 45 rpm EPs as albums – both in catalogs and in their promotional advertising.

One thing is certain, whenever a record is manufactured, but not officially released, despite what those in-house directives dictate, a few copies always manage to get out. And a handful of the 12-inch *Caine Mutiny* albums did escape the factory, as most anyone reading this already knows. However, no copies of the EP have ever surfaced, indicating the extended play was surely never pressed. Of course, somewhere in a long-retired RCA employee's attic, there may rest a 45 rpm EP of *The Caine Mutiny* waiting to be discovered. Until then, I don't believe one was ever made.

The Caine Mutiny was not just another film soundtrack album. As the liner notes proclaim: "Now, Wouk's stirring book has been brought to the screen by Stanley Kramer ... and here, in an unusual record album, is the story of the Caine Mutiny, taken from the soundtrack of the film and including the voices of Humphrey Bogart, Jose Ferrer, Van Johnson, Fred MacMurray, Robert Francis, May Wynn and E.G. Marshall. Here, in this judicious blending of music and dialogue, the emotional intensity of the film is preserved as a home entertainment milestone."

To score the dramatic values of the Stanley Roberts screenplay, Max Steiner composed and conducted a special score. Outstanding portions of it are heard in this album both as bright pieces of original music and as bridges for the major scenes which are recreated here.

A final notation following the third column of liner notes states: "The material contained in these records was duly copyrighted by Columbia Pictures Corporation as part of its motion picture, *The Caine Mutiny*, in the year 1954."

Had *The Caine Mutiny* LP been released, the entire family could sit in the living room, and listen to the album as if it were a complete radio show. Alas, this home entertainment milestone was never to be.

There is a final note of irony in the way RCA Victor classified the LP as LOC 1013. The album is correct as original cast (L "OC"). But if one were to play the video of *The Caine Mutiny*, and the record on an audio cassette, they would have the exact, identical music and dialogue included on the original cast record album. This is because the original cast album is taken directly from the Columbia Film soundtrack.

It is truly a film soundtrack but with an original cast prefix and classification. Usually, original cast albums were of the Broadway show-type productions and not a motion picture adaptation.

In the mid-'70s, I met separately with Van Johnson and Fred MacMurray. Johnson spoke almost the same words as MacMurray when I mentioned *The Caine Mutiny* soundtrack album: "Oh, I didn't even know there was one." But in the end, it was the composer of the film's music score, Max Steiner who had the final word regarding whether or not RCA Victor released the album.

Humphrey Bogart himself, may well have provided an epitaph for both *The Caine Mutiny* and scores of future soundtrack collectors who seek one, when he spoke his closing lines in the 1941 film, *The Maltese Falcon*: ... the stuff that dreams are made of."

This essay originally appeared in a 1987 issue of DISCoveries *magazine. We present it now – for the first time in book format – both for both its historical content and as a tribute to the late Gareth L. Pawlowski (1939-1996).*

25

SAMPLE LISTING

Title of show →

Recording type and year of performance →

Informative notes →

Composer, conductor and cast lineup →

References to other shows somehow related →

Label, format and number ←

Price range for near-mint copy ←

Year of record release ←

Talent lineups for other shows on this release ←

OKLAHOMA!

Original Cast [Vol. 1] (1943) • Decca DA-359 10-15   43
Six 78 rpms. Makes up the 12 tracks eventually issued on EPs and LPs.
> **Composer:** Richard Rodgers, Oscar Hammerstein II. **Conductor:** Jay Blackton. **Cast:** Alfred Drake, Joan Roberts, Howard Da Silva, Celeste Holm, Lee Dixon.

Original Cast [Vol. 2] (1943) • Decca DA-383 40-45   43
Two 78 rpms. Includes *Lonely Room* – by Alfred Drake instead of Howard Da Silva – plus *The Farmer and the Cowman* and *It's a Scandal! It's a Outrage!* These tracks are omitted from the EPs and LPs.
> **Composer:** Richard Rodgers, Oscar Hammerstein II. **Conductor:** Jay Blackton. **Cast:** Alfred Drake, Betty Garde, Ralph Riggs, Joseph Buloff.

Original Cast (1943) • Decca (EP) EDM 9-6 15-25
Boxed, six-disc set.

Original Cast (1943) • Decca (M) DL-8000 20-25   49
Black and gold label. Thick plastic discs.

Original Cast (1943) • Decca (M) DL-9017 12-15   55
Red label. Original cover with new number.

Original Cast (1943) • Decca (M) DL-9017 20-25   55

Original Cast (1943) • Decca (SE) DL-79017 12-15   59
Both have red labels, with new covers picturing "The Farmer and the Cowman."

Original Cast (1943) • Decca (M) DL-9017 12-15   68

Original Cast (1943) • Decca (SE) DL-79017 15-18   68
Special 25th Anniversary Edition, with yellow drawing on cover and picture sleeve with liner notes. Red label.

Original Cast (1943) • MCA (SE) 2030e 8-10   72
> **Composer:** Richard Rodgers, Oscar Hammerstein II. **Conductor:** Jay Blackton. **Cast:** Alfred Drake, Joan Roberts, Howard Da Silva, Celeste Holm, Lee Dixon.

Original Cast • JJA (M) 19761 20-25   76
Includes the selections omitted from the Decca LP: *Lonely Room, The Farmer and the Cowman* and *It's a Scandal! It's a Outrage!*, as well as music from *Main Street to Broadway, Happy Birthday* and *State Fair*.
> **Composer:** Richard Rodgers, Oscar Hammerstein II. **Conductor:** Jay Blackton. **Cast:** Alfred Drake, Betty Garde, Ralph Riggs, Joseph Buloff. MAIN STREET TO BROADWAY: **Cast:** Mary Martin. STATE FAIR: **Conductor:** Victor Young. **Cast:** Dick Haymes.

→ Also see ANNIE GET YOUR GUN
Also see CAROUSEL

A

A-5,6,7,8
Original Cast (1976) • Spotlight (S) 22 5-10   76
    Composer: Stanloch, Scanttin. **Conductor:** Jerry Sternbach. **Cast:** Suzanna Buirgy, Fred Dawson.

A.N.T.A. ALBUM OF STARS, VOL. 1
Original Cast • Decca (M) DL 9002 15-20   51
    Subtitled *(American National Theatre and Academy) - Great Moments from Great Plays.*
    Cast: Helen Hayes, Sir John Gielgud, Eva Le Gallienne, Fredric March, Florence Eldridge.

A.N.T.A. ALBUM OF STARS, VOL. 2
Original Cast • Decca (M) DL 9009 15-20   51
    Full title: *ANTA Album of Stars Great Moments from Great Plays, Vol. 2.* Has excerpts from *The Farmer Takes a Wife, The Seagull, The Barretts of Wimpole Street* and *The Little Foxes.*
    Cast: Henry Fonda, Julie Harris, Dame Edith Evans, Tallulah Bankhead, others.

AARON SLICK FROM PUNKIN CRICK
Soundtrack (1952) • RCA Victor (EP) WP 3006 25-35   52
    Two discs.
Soundtrack (1952) • RCA Victor (EP) WP 342 25-35   52
    Boxed, three-disc set.
Soundtrack (1952) • RCA Victor (M) LPM-3006 100-150   52
    10-inch LP.
Soundtrack (1952) • Motion Picture Tracks (M) MPT-4 10-15   Re
    Contains additional material not found on the RCA release, plus music from *Satins and Spurs.*
    Composer: Jay Livingston, Ray Evans. **Conductor:** Henri Rene, Hugo Winterhalter. **Cast:** Dinah Shore, Robert Merrill, Alan Young. SATINS AND SPURS: **Composer:** Jay Livingston, Ray Evans. **Conductor:** Nelson Riddle. **Cast:** Betty Hutton, Earl Wrightson.

ABC HOLLYWOOD PALACE
TV Soundtrack (1966) • Command (S) RS-902-SD 10-15

ABC SCOPE
TV Soundtrack (1966) • ABC (M) No Number Used 10-15   67
    Highlights from ABC News weekly series on the Viet Nam War.
    Cast: Howard K. Smith (narrator), President Lyndon B. Johnson, Bob Young, Vice President Hubert Humphrey, Secretary of State Dean Rusk, Premier Ky, Peter Jennings, others.

ABE LINCOLN IN ILLINOIS
Studiotrack • RCA Victor MM-591 35-40
    78 rpm album.
    Cast: Raymond Massey.

ABOMINABLE DR. PHIBES: see DR. PHIBES

ABOUT LAST NIGHT
Soundtrack (1986) • EMI America (S) SV-17210 8-10   86
    Cast: Sheena Easton, John Oates, Jermaine Jackson, J.D. Souther, Bob Seger, Nancy Shanks, Michael Henderson, Paul Davis, Del Lords, John Waite.

ABSENT-MINDED DRAGON
Original Cast (1964) • Simon Says (M) M-25 12-18   64

ABSENT-MINDED PROFESSOR
Soundtrack (1961) • Disneyland (M) ST-1911 15-20   61
Soundtrack (1961) • Disneyland (M) DQ-1323 10-15   67
   Also contains selections from *The Shaggy Dog*.
    Composer: Richard M. Sherman, Robert B. Sherman. **Cast:** Fred MacMurray, Sterling
    Holloway, Roberta Shore, Kevin Corcoran, Paul Frees, Four Dachshunds. (With dialogue.)

ABSOLUTE BEGINNERS
Soundtrack (1986) • EMI America (S) SV-17182 8-10   86
Soundtrack (1986) • Virgin (S) V3286 8-10   80s
    Cast: David Bowie, Slim Gaillard, Style Council, Ray Davies, Gil Evans, Eighth Wonder,
    Working Week, Sade Adu, Jerry Dammers.

ABYSS
Soundtrack (1989) • Varese Sarabande (S) VS-5235 8-10   89
    Composer: Alan Silvestri. **Conductor:** Alan Silvestri.

ACADEMY AWARD HIT SONGS
Studiotrack (1969) • London (S) CHAS-1 5-10   69
   Two discs. Music from 1934-1967 award winners.
    Conductor: Frank Chacksfield. **Cast:** Frank Chacksfield and His Orchestra.

ACADEMY AWARD SONGS, VOL. 2
Studiotrack • RCA Victor (M) PRM-175 8-12   60s
Studiotrack • RCA Victor (S) PRS-175 8-12   60s
   Made for B.F. Goodrich Tires. Songs from *Swing Time, Big Broadcast of 1938, Wizard of
   Oz, Going My Way, State Fair, Here Comes the Groom, Three Coins in the Fountain, Love
   Is a Many Splendored Thing, A Hole in the Head, Never on Sunday* and *Papa's Delicate
   Condition*.
    Cast: Henry Mancini with Orchestra and Chorus.

ACADEMY AWARD THEATER
Original Radio Cast • Golden Age (M) 5032 8-10   78
   Radio broadcasts of *Watch on the Rhine* and *The Informer*.

ACADEMY AWARD WINNERS
Studiotrack (1963) • Reprise (M) R-6079 8-12   63
Studiotrack (1963) • Reprise (S) R9-6079 8-12   63
   Music from *Hatari, Taras Bulba, Days of Wine and Roses, Wonderful World of Brothers
   Grimm, Gay Puree, Two for the Seesaw, State Fair, Lawrence of Arabia, Mutiny on the
   Bounty, Walk on the Wild Side, The Boys' Night Out* and *Tender is the Night*.
    Conductor: Les Baxter. **Cast:** Les Baxter and Chorus.

ACADEMY AWARD WINNERS ON THE AIR
Original Radio Cast • Startone (M) ST-215 10-20
   Limited edition with previously unreleased performances by several artists.

ACADEMY AWARD WINNING SONGS
Studiotrack (1960s) • Columbia Special Products (M) CSM-467 10-12   60s
   Full title: *Eastman Kodak Album Academy Award Winning Songs*.
    Cast: Patti Page, Doris Day, Eydie Gorme, Robert Goulet, Steve Lawrence, others.

ACADEMY AWARDS PRESENTATION
Studiotrack • Columbia (S) LSS-1006/7 10-15
   Collection of movie songs, made for General Electric
    Cast: Anita Bryant, Jerry Vale, John Davidson, Eydie Gorme, Doris Day, Julie Andrews, others.

ACCENTUATE THE POSITIVE: see BING'S HOLLYWOOD

ACCIDENTAL TOURIST
Soundtrack (1988) • Warner Bros. (S) 1-25846 8-10   89
    Composer: John Williams.

ACROSS 110TH STREET
Soundtrack (1972) • United Artists (S) UAS-5225 12-25   72
    Composer: J.J. Johnson. Conductor: J.J. Johnson. Cast: Bobby Womack and Peace.

ACROSS THE GREAT DIVIDE
Soundtrack (1977) • Bella Linda (S) BLS-1001 10-15   77
    Composer: Gene Kauer, Douglas Lackey. Conductor: Gene Kauer, Douglas Lackey.

ACT
Original Cast (1977) • DRG (S) DRG-6101 5-8   78
    Composer: John Kander, Fred Ebb. Conductor: Stanley Lebowsky. Cast: Liza Minnelli, Roger Minami, Gayle Crofoot.

ACTION HISTORY
Studio Cast (1957) • Columbia (M) KL-5270 20-30   57
    Cast: Buddy Blattner (narrator).

ACTION JACKSON
Soundtrack (1988) • Lorimar (S) 90886-1 8-12   88
    Cast: Pointer Sisters, Madame X, Levert, Vanith, Sister Sledge, David Koz, Skyy, M.C. Jam & Pee Wee Jam.

ADDAMS FAMILY
TV Soundtrack (1964) • RCA Victor (M) LPM-3421.................................... 50-75   64
TV Soundtrack (1964) • RCA Victor (S) LSP-3421.................................... 100-150   64
    Composer: Vic Mizzy. Cast: Plas Johnson, Vic Mizzy and His Orchestra.

ADIOS AMIGO
Soundtrack (1976) • London (S) PS-666.................................... 8-10   76
    Composer: Luchi DeJesus. Cast: Infernal Blue Machine.

ADRIFT
Soundtrack (1964) • MPO (S) 1001 50-100   71
    Composer: Zdenek Liska. Conductor: Frantisek Belfin. Cast: Prague Symphony Orchestra.

ADVANCE TO THE REAR
Studiotrack (1964) • Columbia (M) CL-2159.................................... 15-35   64
Studiotrack (1964) • Columbia (S) CS-8959.................................... 20-45   64
    Composer: Randy Sparks. Cast: New Christy Minstrels.

ADVENTURERS
Soundtrack (1970) • Paramount (S) 6001 15-25   70
    Composer: Antonio Carlos Jobim.

Soundtrack (1970) • Symbolic (S) SYS-9000.................................... 20-25   70
Actual title: *Harold Robbins Presents Music from the Adventurers.*
    Composer: Antonio Carlos Jobim. Conductor: Ray Brown. Cast: Sally Kellerman, Morgan Ames, Peter Christlieb, Ray Brown and Orchestra.

ADVENTURES IN AGAPELAND
Soundtrack (1983) • MCA/Sparrow (S) SP 2054.................................... 10-15   83
Picture disc.

ADVENTURES IN PARADISE
Studiotrack (1960) • ABC Paramount (M) ABC-329 20-25   60
Studiotrack (1960) • ABC Paramount (S) ABCS-329 20-30   60
    Composer: Alfred Newman, others. Conductor: Al Apaka.

ADVENTURES OF A YOUNG MAN: see HEMINGWAY'S ADVENTURES OF A YOUNG MAN

ADVENTURES OF BARON MUNCHAUSEN
Soundtrack (1988) • Warner Bros. (S) 1-25826 8-12   88
   Composer: Michael Kamen, Eric Idle. Conductor: Michael Kamen.

ADVENTURES OF BULLWHIP GRIFFIN
Soundtrack (1967) • Disneyland (M) DQ-1291 10-15   67
   Composer: Richard M. Sherman, Robert B. Sherman.

ADVENTURES OF DON JUAN
Soundtrack (1948) • Tony Thomas (M) MS-11 20-45
   Composer: Max Steiner. Conductor: Max Steiner.

ADVENTURES OF FORD FAIRLANE
Soundtrack (1990) • Elektra (S) 60952-1 8-10   90
   Cast: Yello, Billy Idol, Motley Crew, Ton Loc, Andrew Dice Clay, Sheila E., Queensryche, Richie Samboro, Teddy Pendergrass, Lisa Fisher, Dion.

ADVENTURES OF HUCKLEBERRY FINN: see BIG RIVER

ADVENTURES OF JAMIE McPHEETERS
TV Soundtrack (1960s) • MGM (S) PM-7 15-20   62
   Side two is commercials and narrative for show sponsor, AC Spark Plug Division.)
   Cast: Osmonds, Kurt Russell. (With Dialogue.)

ADVENTURES OF MARCO POLO
TV Soundtrack (1956) • Columbia (M) ML-5111 10-15   56
TV Soundtrack (1956) • Columbia (M) OL-5111 8-12
   Composer: Clay Warnick, Mel Pahl. Conductor: Charles Sanford. Cast: Alfred Drake, Doretta Morrow.

ADVENTURES OF RIN TIN TIN
Studiotrack (1958) • Columbia (M) CL-679.............................. 30-50   58
   Composer: Various. Conductor: Nelson Riddle. Cast: Nelson Riddle Orchestra.
TV Soundtrack (1958) • Columbia (M) CL-699.............................. 50-60   58
TV Soundtrack (1959) • Harmony (M) HL-9502 30-45   59
   Composer: Ray Carter. Cast: Original TV cast. (With dialogue.)

ADVENTURES OF ROBIN HOOD
Studiotrack (1938) • Delos (M) DEL/F2540 10-12   75
   Also contains *Requiem for a Cavalier* (biography of Errol Flynn in sound, with interview by Tony Thomas).
   Composer: Erich Wolfgang Korngold. Conductor: Erich Wolfgang Korngold. Cast: Basil Rathbone (narrator).
Studiotrack • Varese Sarabande (S) 704-180 8-12   83
Studiotrack • That's Entertainment (S) TER-1066 8-12   80s
   UK release.
   Composer: Erich Wolfgang Korngold. Conductor: Varujan Kojian. Cast: Utah Symphony Orchestra.

ADVENTURES OF SHERLOCK HOLMES
Original Radio Cast • Golden Age (M) 5030............................. 8-10   78

ADVENTURES OF THE LONE RANGER: see LONE RANGER

ADVENTURES OF ZORRO: see ZORRO

ADVISE AND CONSENT
Soundtrack (1962) • RCA Victor (M) LOC-1068 20-25   62
Soundtrack (1962) • RCA Victor (S) LSO-1068...................... 35-50   62
   Composer: Jerry Fielding. Conductor: Jerry Fielding.

AFFAIR TO REMEMBER
Soundtrack (1957) • Columbia (M) CL-1013 25-30   57
   Composer: Hugo Friedhofer, Harry Warren, Harold Adamson, Leo McCarey. Conductor: Lionel
   Newman. Cast: Marni Nixon (performs vocals for Deborah Kerr in the film), Vic Damone.

AFRICA
TV Soundtrack (1967) • MGM (M) E-4462 35-40   67
TV Soundtrack (1967) • MGM (S) SE-4462.. 40-45   67
   Both LPs include booklet.
   Composer: Alex North. Conductor Alex North.

AFRICA ADDIO
Soundtrack (1966) • United Artists (M) UAL-4141............................. 10-25   66
Soundtrack (1966) • United Artists (S) UAS-6141 12-15   66
   Composer: Riz Ortolani. Conductor: Riz Ortolani.

AFRICAN QUEEN
Original Radio Cast • Mark 56 (M) 668... 10-15   75
   Cast: Humphrey Bogart, Greer Garson.

AFTER THE BALL
Original London Cast (1954) • AMR (M) 301... 50-60
   Musical version of Oscar Wilde's Lady Windermere's Fan.
   Composer: Noel Coward. Conductor: Philip Martell. Cast: Vanessa Lee,
   Peter Graves, Dennis Bowen, Tom Gill, Lois Green, Pam Marmont, Mary
   Ellis, Marion Grimaldi, Irene Browne, Graham Payn, Patricia Cree, Betty
   Felstead, Anna Halinka, Alisa Gamley.

AFTER THE FALL
Original Cast (1962) • Mercury (S) OCS-4-620 12-20   65
   Four discs. A dramatic play by Arthur Miller with the Lincoln Center Repertory Theatre
   Production Cast.
   Composer: David Amram. Cast: Jason Robards Jr., Barbara Loden, Faye Dunaway, Michael
   Strong, Ralph Meeker.
Original Cast • Caedmon (S) TRS 326.. 20-30   Re

AFTER THE FOX
Soundtrack (1966) • United Artists (M) UAL-4148................................ 10-12   66
Soundtrack (1966) • United Artists (S) UAS-5148 12-18   66
Soundtrack (1966) • United Artists (S) UA-LA-286-G........................... 6-12   74
Soundtrack (1966) • MCA (S) 25132.. 5-8   86
   Composer: Burt Bacharach. Conductor: Burt Bacharach. Cast: Peter Sellers, Hollies.

AGAINST A CROOKED SKY
Soundtrack (1975) • Embryo (Q) EM-1005-S... 25-30   75
   Composer: Lex de Azevedo. Conductor: Lex de Azevedo.

AGAINST ALL ODDS
Soundtrack (1984) • Atlantic (S) 80152-1... 8-10   84
Soundtrack (1984) • Atlantic (S) A1 80152.. 5-8   84
   Columbia House Record Club issue.
   Composer: Michel Colombier, Larry Carlton, others. Cast: Phil Collins, Stevie Nicks, Peter
   Gabriel, Big Country, Mike Rutherford, Kid Creole and the Coconuts, Larry Carlton, Michel
   Colombier.

AGATHA
Soundtrack (1975) • Casablanca (S) NBLP-7142 10-12   75
   Composer: Johnny Mandell, Paul Williams (lyrics). Cast: Pattie Brooks.

AGE OF TELEVISION
Studio Cast (1972) • RCA Victor (S) LL-8 10-20   72
Full title: *The Age of Television — A Chronicle of the First 25 Years*. From NBC, includes 32-page booklet.
Cast: Narrated by Milton Berle, Hugh Downs and Arlene Francis. Includes: *Howdy Doody Time*, President Truman, First Moon Walk, *Great Gildersleeve, Your Hit Parade*, Giants vs. Dodgers, *Kukla, Fran & Ollie*, Arlene Francis, *Strike It Rich, People Are Funny*, Fred Allen, Pat Weaver, Roy Rogers, Gene Autry, *All Star Review*, President Dwight D. Eisenhower, *Texaco Star Theatre*, President John F. Kennedy, *Today Show, Captain Kangaroo*, Assassination of Lee Harvey Oswald, *My Little Margie, Life of Riley, Dick Van Dyke Show*, President Lyndon B. Johnson, *Beverly Hillbillies, Secret Storm, Guiding Light, The Doctors, Let's Make a Deal*, Hubert H. Humphrey, *What's My Line, Sesame Street*, Moon Trek, *Superman*, Vice President Agnew, *Ding Dong School, Ben Casey, Peter Pan, Ed Sullivan Show, Tonight Show with Jack Paar, Tonight Show with Johnny Carson*, Apollo 15.

AGNES OF GOD
Soundtrack (1985) • Varese Sarabande (S) STV-81257 8-15   85
Soundtrack (1985) • That's Entertainment (S) TER-1108...................... 8-10   80s
UK release.
Composer: Georges Delerue. **Conductor:** Georges Delerue.

AGONY AND THE ECSTASY
Soundtrack (1965) • Capitol (M) MAS-2427 20-50   65
Soundtrack (1965) • Capitol (S) SMAS-2427 35-75   65
Gatefold covers and bound-in 11-page booklet.
Composer: Alex North, Franco Potenza. **Conductor:** Alex North, Franco Potenza. **Cast:** Laurindo Almeida, others.

AH, WILDERNESS!
Studio Cast • Caedmon (S) TRS 340 20-25
Author: Eugene O'Neill.

AIN'T MISBEHAVIN'
Original Cast (1978) • RCA Victor (S) CBL2-2965 5-10   78
Two discs.
Composer: Fats Waller, others. **Conductor:** Luther Henderson. **Cast:** Nell Carter, Andre DeShields, Armelia McQueen, Ken Page, Charlaine Woodard.

AIN'T SUPPOSED TO DIE A NATURAL DEATH
Original Cast (1972) • A&M (S) SP-3510 5-10   72
Two discs.
Composer: Melvin Van Peebles. **Conductor:** Harold Wheeler. **Cast:** Arthur French, Gloria Edwards, Ralph Wilcox, Marilyn Coleman, Joe Fields, Carl Gordon, Madge Wells, Barbara Alston, Toney Brealond, Bill Duke, Clebert Ford, Minnie Gentry, Albert Hall, Jimmy Hayeson, Sati Jamal, Lauren Jones, Garrett Morris, Dick Williams, Beatrice Winde.

AIR AMERICA
Soundtrack (1990) • MCA (S) 6467.. 8-10   90
Cast: Aerosmith, B.B. King, Bonnie Raitt, Charles Sexton, Steely Dan, Edgar Winter, Rick Derringer, Mamas and the Papas, Four Tops, Temptations, Fontella Bass, Seeds.

AIR FORCE PANORAMA
Original Cast (1972) • USAF (S) 2972.. 5-10   72
Live performance for 25th Anniversary of U.S. Air Force in Washington, D.C.
Conductor: Col. Arnold D. Gabriel. **Cast:** Arthur Godfrey, U.S. Air Force Band and the Singing Sergeants.

AIR POWER
TV Soundtrack (1957) • Columbia (M) ML-5214 20-30   57
TV Soundtrack (1957) • Columbia (S) MS-6029.................................. 35-55   58
Composer: Norman Dello Joio. **Conductor:** Eugene Ormandy. **Cast:** Eugene Ormandy and the Philadelphia Symphony Orchestra.

AIRBORNE SYMPHONY
Studio Cast (1946) • Columbia (S) M-34136 15-20   76
Composer: Marc Blitzstein. **Conductor:** Leonard Bernstein. **Cast:** Orson Welles, New York Philharmonic.

AIRPLANE!
Soundtrack (1980) • Regency (S) RY-9601 8-10   80
Composer: Elmer Bernstein. **Conductor:** Elmer Bernstein. **Cast:** Shadoe Stevens (narrator), Robert Hays, Julie Hagerty, Peter Graves, Lloyd Bridges, Lorna Patterson. (With dialogue.)

AIRPORT
Soundtrack (1970) • Decca (S) DL-79173 8-12   70
Composer: Alfred Newman. **Conductor:** Alfred Newman.

AIRPORT 1975
Soundtrack (1975) • MCA (S) 2082 8-10   75
Composer: John Cacavas. **Conductor:** John Cacavas.

AISLE SEAT
Studiotrack (1982) • Philips (S) 6514328 10-15   82
Composer: John Williams, Dimitri Tiomkin, Max Steiner. **Cast:** John Williams and the Boston Pops.

AL JOLSON
Soundtrack • Decca A-469 15-25   40s
Album of two 78 rpms. Music from *April Showers* and *Swanee, Sonny Boy* and *My Mammy*
Cast: Al Jolson.
Soundtrack • Decca A-575 10-15   40s
78 rpm album. Music from *Carolina in the Morning* and *Lisa*.
Cast: Al Jolson.

AL JOLSON STORY SOUNDTRACK: OUTTAKES & ALTERNATE TAKES
Soundtrack (1945) • Take Two (M) TT 103 12-18   78
Composer: Morris Stoloff. **Conductor:** Morris Stoloff. **Cast:** Al Jolson, Rudy Wissler.

ALADD
TV Soundtrack (1976) • Bag-A-Tale (S) BAT-1000 12-15   76
Composer: Jo Adler, Hannah Price. **Conductor:** Jo Adler. **Cast:** Original Stage Cast - Beverly Cohen, Debra DeLuca, Kathy DeSalvo, Michelle Kahan, Erwin Kaufman, Trish Kondra, Justin Paul, Joyce Schulman.

ALADDIN
Original London Cast (1960) • Stet (M) DS 15027 15-20   Re
Stage version based on the television production, which interpolated songs from other Cole Porter shows. First issued in the UK on EMI, not listed since we lack its selection number.
Composer: Cole Porter. **Conductor:** Bobby Howell. **Cast:** Bob Monkhouse, Doretta Morrow, Ronald Shiner (listed as Robert Shiner on front cover), Ian Wallace, Alan Wheatley, Philip Hogan, Eddie Fargent, David Fallon, Bill Shepherd Singers.
Original London Cast (1979) • President (S) PTLS 1072 8-10   80
Composer: Sandy Wilson.
TV Soundtrack (1958) • Columbia (M) CL-1117 20-45   58
Composer: Cole Porter. **Conductor:** Robert Emmett Dolan. **Cast:** Sal Mineo, Anna Maria Alberghetti, Dennis King, Cyril Ritchard, Basil Rathbone, Una Merkel, Akim Tamiroff, George Hall.

ALAKAZAM THE GREAT
Soundtrack (1961) • Vee Jay (M) LP-6000 60-65   61
Composer: Les Baxter. **Conductor:** Ian Freebairn-Smith, Albert Harris. **Cast:** Bobby Adano, Frankie Avalon, Dodie Stevens, Jonathan Winters, Arnold Stang, Sterling Holloway

ALAMO

Soundtrack (1960) • Columbia (M) CL-1558 10-20   60
Soundtrack (1960) • Columbia (S) CS-8358.................................... 15-25   60
  Both have gray label.
Soundtrack (1960) • Columbia (S) CS-8358.................................... 8-12   60
  Red label.
    Composer: Dimitri Tiomkin. **Conductor:** Dimitri Tiomkin. **Cast:** Marty Robbins, Brothers Four, John Wayne (with dialogue).
Studiotrack (1960) • Camden (M) CAL-655... 5-10   60
Studiotrack (1960) • Camden (S) CAS-655... 8-10   60
  Full title: *Music from the Film The Alamo.*
    Cast: Tex Beneke and His Orchestra.

ALAMO BAY

Soundtrack (1985) • Slash (S) 1-25311... 8-10   85
    Composer: Ry Cooder. **Cast:** Ed Harris, Amy Madigan, Ry Cooder.

ALBERT PECKINGPAW'S REVENGE

Soundtrack (1967) • Sidewalk (M) T-5907 15-20   67
Soundtrack (1967) • Sidewalk (S) ST-5907 20-25   67
    Composer: Harley Hatcher. **Conductor:** Harley Hatcher. **Cast:** Don Epperson, Jimmy August, Lydia Marcelle, Davie Allan and the Arrows, Jan Sweet.

ALBUM OF THE SOUNDTRACK OF THE TRAILER OF THE FILM OF MONTY PYTHON AND THE HOLY GRAIL: see MONTY PYTHON AND THE HOLY GRAIL

ALCHEMIST: see ZONE TROOPERS / THE ALCHEMIST

ALDRICH FAMILY

Original Radio Broadcast • Mark 56 (M) 692 10-15   70s

ALEXANDER

Soundtrack • Polydor (S) 24-7001.. 25-30   70
    Composer: Vladimir Cosma. **Conductor:** Vladimir Cosma. **Cast:** Philippe Noivet, Françoise Brion, Marlene Jobert.
  Also see SURVIVAL RUN

ALEXANDER NEVSKY

Studiotrack (1939) • Vanguard (M) VRS 451.. 10-20   60s
    Composer: Sergei Prokofiev. **Conductor:** Mario Rossi. **Cast:** Sergei Prokofiev Orchestra.
Studiotrack (1939) • Odyssey (M) Y 31014 10-20   60s
    Cast: New York Philharmonic.
Studiotrack (1960) • RCA Victor (M) LM-2395...................................... 20-30   60
Studiotrack (1960) • RCA Victor (S) LSC-2395 30-45   60
  Both includes booklet insert.
    Conductor: Fritz Reiner. **Cast:** Chicago Symphony Orchestra.
Studiotrack (1975) • RCA Victor (S) ARL1-1551 10-20   75
    Conductor: Eugene Ormandy. **Cast:** Philadelphia Orchestra.

ALEXANDER THE GREAT

Soundtrack (1956) • Mercury (M) MG-20148 200-225   56
    Composer: Mario Nascimbene. **Conductor:** Mario Nascimbene. **Cast:** Dennis Lotis. (With dialogue.)
TV Soundtrack (1964) • ABC (S) ATG1 250-300   64
    Composer: Leonard Rosenman.

ALEXANDER'S RAGTIME BAND

Soundtrack (1938) • Hollywood Soundstage (M) HS-408...................... 8-12   77
    Composer: Irving Berlin. **Conductor:** Alfred Newman. **Cast:** Alice Faye, Don Ameche, Ethel Merman.

ALFIE
Soundtrack (1966) • Impulse (M) A-9111 12-15   66
Soundtrack (1966) • Impulse (S) AS-9111 15-25   66
    Composer: Sonny Rollins. **Conductor:** Oliver Nelson.

ALFRED HITCHCOCK'S FILM MUSIC
Soundtrack • Milan (S) ACH-022 10-20   85
    Composer: Bernard Herrmann. **Conductor:** Bernard Herrmann.

ALFRED NEWMAN CONDUCTS HIS GREAT FILM MUSIC
Studiotrack • Angel (S) S-36066 8-10   73
    Composer: Alfred Newman. **Conductor:** Alfred Newman. **Cast:** Hollywood Bowl Symphony
    Orchestra.
   Also see MOTION PICTURE MUSIC

ALFRED NEWMAN CONDUCTS THEMES
Studiotrack • Capitol (S) ST-1652 10-20   62
    Conductor: Alfred Newman. **Cast:** Alfred Newman Orchestra.

ALI BABA AND THE 40 THIEVES
Studio Cast (1952) • MGM (M) E-110 20-35   52
   10-inch LP.
    Cast: Lionel Barrymore.
Studiotrack (1957) Golden Masterpiece (M) A298-20 15-25   57
    Composer: Mary Rogers, Sammy Cahn. **Cast:** Bing Crosby.

ALICE FAYE
Soundtrack • Curtain Calls (M) 100/3 8-12
   Previously unreleased music from *Now I'll Tell, George White's Scandals, Every Night
   at Eight, Poor Little Rich Girl, Sally, Irene and Mary, In Old Chicago* and others.
    Composer: Various. **Conductor:** Various. **Cast:** Alice Faye, John Payne, Frances Langford,
    Jack Oakie, Patsy Kelly, June Havoc.

ALICE FAYE IN HOLLYWOOD 1934-1937
Studiotrack • Columbia (M) CL-3068 8-12   69
   Vocals from Fox and Paramount films.
    Composer: Various. **Conductor:** Various. **Cast:** Alice Faye.

ALICE IN WONDERLAND
Studio Cast (1944) • Decca DA-376 30-35   44
   78 rpm album.
Studio Cast (1944) • Decca (M) DL-5040 30-45   49
   10-inch LP.
    Cast: Ginger Rogers.
Studio Cast (1949) • Columbia (M) ML-4148 25-35   49
   10-inch LP.
Studio Cast (1949) • Columbia (M) CL-986 20-30   57
    Composer: Carmen Dragon. **Conductor:** Carmen Dragon. **Cast:** Jane Powell.
Studio Cast (1952) • Mercury (M) MG-25096 25-50   52
   10-inch LP.
Studio Cast • Disneyland (M) ST-3909 15-20
   Includes story booklet.
Studiotrack (1952) • Disneyland (M) WDL-4015 250-350   58
   Shortly after this LPs release, Disney deleted this and the entire "WDL" series. Collectible
   for both its rarity and cover art.
Studiotrack (1952) • Disneyland (M) DQ-1208 10-12   59
    Composer: Sammy Fain, Bob Hilliard, Mack David, Al Hoffman, Jerry Livingston, Don Raye,
    Gene de Paul, Cy Cohen, Oliver Wallace. **Conductor:** Camarata. **Cast:** Darlene Gillespie (as
    "Alice"), Camarata Orchestra and Chorus.
Studiotrack (1958) • Rondo-lette (M) A12 8-15   58
   Also see PETER PAN
   Also see TREASURE ISLAND

ALICE THROUGH THE LOOKING GLASS

TV Soundtrack (1966) • RCA Victor (M) LOC-1130 15-20   66
TV Soundtrack (1966) • RCA Victor (S) LSO-1130 25-30   66
    Composer: Moose Charlap. **Conductor:** Harper MacKay. **Cast:** Roy Castle, Robert Coote,
    Jimmy Durante, Nanette Fabray, Judi Rolin, Jack Palance, Agnes Moorehead, Ricardo
    Montalban.

ALICE'S ADVENTURES IN WONDERLAND

Studio Cast (1957) • Riverside (M) SDP-22 45-65   58
    Boxed, four-disc set, with hard-bound book.
    Composer: Alec Wilder. **Conductor:** Barrett Clark. **Cast:** Cyril Ritchard (vocals and narration).
Soundtrack (1972) • Warner Bros. (S) BS-2671 15-25   72
    Composer: John Barry. **Conductor:** John Barry. **Cast:** Peter Sellers, Dudley Moore, Fiona
    Fullerton, Davy Kaye, Michael Crawford.

ALICE'S RESTAURANT

Soundtrack (1969) • United Artists (S) UAS-5195 8-12   69
    Composer: Arlo Guthrie, Garry Sherman. **Conductor:** Garry Sherman. **Cast:** Arlo Guthrie,
    Tigger Outlaw, Al Schookman.

ALIEN

Soundtrack (1979) • 20th Century-Fox (S) T-593 15-20   79
    Composer: Jerry Goldsmith. **Conductor:** Lionel Newman. **Cast:** National Philharmonic
    Orchestra.
    Also see FREUD

ALIENS

Soundtrack (1986) • Varese Sarabande (S) STV 81283 10-30   86
Soundtrack (1986) • That's Entertainment (S) TER-1115 8-10   80s
    UK release.
    Composer: James Horner. **Conductor:** James Horner. **Cast:** London Symphony Orchestra.

ALIKI, MY LOVE

Soundtrack (1963) • Fontana (M) MGS-27523 15-20   63
Soundtrack (1963) • Fontana (S) SRF-67523 20-25   63
    Composer: Manos Hadjidakis. **Conductor:** Manos Hadjidakis.

ALL ABOUT LIFE

Original Cast • Industrial OC Life XTV 89424/5 40-50
    Composer: Jerry Powell. **Conductor:** Rod Warren. **Cast:** Michael Allinson, Gloria Bleezarde,
    Bill Linton, Eliza Ross, Jay Stuart, Ronny Whyte.

ALL AMERICAN

Original Cast (1962) • Columbia (M) KOL-5760 8-12   62
Original Cast (1962) • Columbia (S) KOS-2160 12-15   62
    Both have gatefold covers.
Original Cast (1962) • Columbia (S) AKOS-5760 5-8   Re
    Conductor: John Morris. **Cast:** Ray Bolger, Eileen Herlie, Ron Husmann, Anita Gillette, Fritz
    Weaver.
Studio Cast (1962) • Challenge (M) CHL-614 10-12   62
Studio Cast (1962) • Challenge (S) CHS-2514 12-15   62
    Cast: Champs, Lionel Hampton, Les Elgart.
Studio Cast (1962) • MGM (M) E-4034 5-10   62
Studio Cast (1962) • MGM (S) SE-4034 5-10   62
    Composer: Charles Strouse, Lee Adams. **Conductor:** Leroy Holmes. **Cast:** Leroy Holmes and
    His Orchestra.
Studio Cast (1962) • Mercury (M) MG-20707 10-15   62
Studio Cast (1962) • Mercury (S) SR-60707 10-15   62
    Actual title: *All American Goes Country Style*.
    Cast: Margie Singleton, Leroy Van Dyke, others.
Studio Cast (1962) • Columbia (M) CL-1790 8-12   62

Studio Cast (1962) • Columbia (S) CS-8590 8-12   62
Cast: Duke Ellington Orchestra.

Studio Cast (1962) • Columbia (M) CL-1791 8-12   62

Studio Cast (1962) • Columbia (S) CS-8591 8-12   62
Cast: Andre Kostelanetz, Dukes of Dixieland, Banjo Barons, Les Elgart and His Orchestra, Marlowe Morris, Jerry Murad's Harmonicats, Lionel Hampton, Art Van Damme, J.J. Johnson, Banjo Barons, Bobby Hackett.

ALL AMERICAN BOY

Original Radio Cast • Golden Age (M) 5033 5-10   78

ALL AMERICAN GOES COUNTRY STYLE: see ALL AMERICAN

ALL BY MYSELF: see ANNA RUSSELL'S LITTLE SHOW

ALL DOGS GO TO HEAVEN

Soundtrack • Curb (S) CRB-10403 8-10
Composer: Ralph Burns. Cast: Irene Cara, Freddie Jackson.

ALL HANDS ON DECK

Soundtrack (1961) • Dot (EP) DEP-1098 25-35   61
Composer: Jay Livingston, Ray Evans. Cast: Pat Boone, Buddy Hackett.

ALL IN LOVE

Original Cast (1961) • Mercury (M) OCM-2204 12-15   61

Original Cast (1961) • Mercury (S) OCS-6204 20-25   61
Composer: Jacques Urbont, Bruce Geller. Conductor: Jacques Urbont. Cast: David Atkinson, Lee Cass, Gaylea Byrne, Dom DeLuise, Christina Gillespie, Mimi Randolph, Michael Davis.

ALL IN ONE: see TROUBLE IN TAHITI

ALL IN THE FAMILY

TV Soundtrack (1971) • Atlantic (M) SD-7210 10-12   71
Includes four-page booklet.
Cast: Carroll O'Connor, Jean Stapleton.

ALL IN THE FAMILY – 2ND ALBUM

TV Soundtrack (1971) • Atlantic (M) SD-7232 10-12   72
Cast: Carroll O'Connor, Jean Stapleton.

ALL IN THE YORK FAMILY

Original Cast (1972) • Borg-Warner (S) Y-72 25-35   72
Made for Bermuda sales convention, based on TV's *All in the Family*.
Cast: James Harder, Charlotte Fairchild, Charles Braswell, Gil Gerard, Dorthea Alfred.

ALL NIGHT LONG

Soundtrack (1962) • Epic (M) LA-16032 25-30   62

Soundtrack (1962) • Epic (S) BA-17032 30-35   62
Cast: Philip Green, Johnny Scott, Dave Brubeck, Johnny Dankworth.

ALL NIGHT STRUT

Original Cast (1976) • Playhouse Square (S) PHS-CLE 1S-1001 40-60   76
Composer: Various. Conductor: Tom Fitt. Cast: Robert Chidsey, Dean Hill, Elaine Psihountas, Laura Robinson.

ALL-STAR COLOR TV REVUE

TV Soundtrack • Hollywood (M) LPH-110 10-15
Conductor: Camarata. Cast: Vic Damone, Peggy Mann, Mullen Sisters, Lanny Ross.

TV Soundtrack [Vol. 2] • Hollywood (M) LPH-126 10-15
Conductor: Allen Roth. Cast: Vic Damone, Allen Roth Orchestra.

ALL-STAR PARADE, HITS FROM THE MOVIES
Studiotrack • Columbia (M) CL 1421 10-15
> Songs from *Modern Times, Say One for Me, Gigi, Anatomy of a Murder, A Summer Place, Happy Anniversary, On the Beach, Pillow Talk, The FBI Story, The Best of Everything* and *Holiday for Lovers.*
>> **Cast:** Tony Bennett, Bing Crosby, Vic Damone, Doris Day, Duke Ellington, Percy Faith, Four Lads, Norman Luboff Choir, Richard Maltby, Johnny Mathis, Mitch Miller.

ALL-STAR SALUTE, THE VERY BEST OF GERSHWIN
Studiotrack • MGM (M) E-4242 10-15
> Songs from *Show Girl, Porgy and Bess, Funny Face, The French Doll, Rosalie, A Damsel in Distress, Rhapsody in Blue, Girl Crazy, Scandals* and *The Man I Love.*
>> **Cast:** David Rose, Ray Charles Singers, Maurice Chavalier, Larry Elgart, Anna Maria Alberghetti, Bing Crosby, Judy Garland, Georges Guetary, Jaye P. Morgan, Art Tatum.

ALL THAT JAZZ
Soundtrack (1979) • Casablanca (S) NBLP-7198 5-10   79
Soundtrack (1979) • Casablanca (S) 822869-1 5-8   Re
> **Composer:** Various. **Conductor:** Ralph Burns. **Cast:** George Benson, Peter Allen, Ben Vereen.

ALL THAT MONEY CAN BUY: see GREAT FILM CLASSICS

ALL THE LOVING COUPLES
Soundtrack (1969) • GNP/Crescendo (S) 2051 25-30   69
> **Composer:** Casanova (Les Baxter).

ALL THE RIGHT MOVES
Soundtrack (1983) • Casablanca (S) 422-814494 8-10   83
> **Cast:** Jennifer Warnes, Frankie Miller, Junior, others.

ALL THE RIGHT NOISES
Soundtrack (1971) • Buddah (S) BDS-5132 20-25   71
> **Composer:** Melanie Safka.

ALL THIS AND WORLD WAR II
Soundtrack (1977) • 20th Century-Fox (S) 2T-522 10-12   76
> Boxed, two-disc set. Includes 36-page booklet and T-shirt ad flyer.
>> **Cast:** Ambrosia, Elton John, Bee Gees, David Essex, Frankie Laine, 4 Seasons, Henry Gross, Tina Turner, Leo Sayer, Rod Stewart, Keith Moon, Helen Reddy, Status Quo, Frankie Valli, Bryan Ferry, Jeff Lynne, Roy Wood, Brothers Johnson, Richard Cocciante, London Symphony Orchestra.

ALL TIME GREAT BLOOPERS
TV/Radio Soundtrack • Brookville (M) 406 15-20   73
> Two-disc set, compiled by Kermit Schafer.

ALL YOU NEED IS CASH
TV Soundtrack (1978) • Warner Bros. (S) HS-3151 10-12   78
> From an NBC-TV broadcast.
>> **Cast:** The Rutles.

ALLEGRO
Original Cast (1947) • RCA Victor CBMI-2758 20-40   47
> 78 rpm album.
Original Cast (1947) • RCA Victor (M) LOC-1099 25-30   65
Original Cast (1947) • RCA Victor (SE) LSO-1099 40-45   65
Original Cast (1947) • RCA Victor (SE) CBM1-2758 15-18   78
> **Composer:** Richard Rodgers, Oscar Hammerstein. **Conductor:** Salvatore Dell'Isola. **Cast:** John Battles, Annamary Dickey, Lisa Kirk, Patricia Bybell, William Ching, Julia Humphries, Roberta Jonay, Sylvia Karlton, Kathryn Lee, Muriel O'Malley, Robert Reeves (performing John Conte's vocals from the show), Gloria Wills.

ALLEN, STEVE: see STEVE ALLEN

ALLNIGHTER
Soundtrack (1987) • Chameleon (S) CHST-9601................................... 8-12   87
Soundtrack (1987) • Chameleon (S) CHST-9601................................ 15-25   87
  Picture disc. Some copies have Susan Hoff's autograph on picture under vinyl.
Soundtrack (1987) • Chameleon (S) D1-74792...................................... 8-10   Re

ALMOST PERFECT AFFAIR
Soundtrack (1979) • Varese Sarabande (S) STV-81132........................ 8-10   79
  Composer: Georges Delerue. **Conductor:** Georges Delerue.

ALMOST SUMMER
Soundtrack (1978) • MCA (S) MCA-3037.. 10-20   78
  Composer: Ron Altbach, Charles Lloyd, Brian Wilson, Mike Love, Al Jardine. **Cast:** Mike Love
  and Celebration, Fresh, High Inergy.

ALOHA FROM HAWAII VIA SATELLITE: see ELVIS - ALOHA FROM HAWAII VIA SATELLITE

ALTERED STATES
Soundtrack (1980) • RCA Victor (S) ABL1-3983 8-10   80
  Composer: John Corigliano. **Conductor:** Christopher Keene.

ALVIN SHOW
TV Soundtrack (1961) • Liberty (M) LRP-3209..................................... 10-15   61
TV Soundtrack (1961) • Liberty (S) LST-7209...................................... 15-20   61
  Composer: Ross Bagdasarian (David Seville). **Cast:** David Seville and the Chipmunks (Alvin,
  Theodore and Simon).

ALWAYS
Soundtrack (1990) • MCA (S) 8036.. 8-10   90
  Composer: John Williams (original music), others. **Conductor:** John Williams, others. **Cast:**
  J.D. Souther, Jimmy Buffett, Lyle Lovett, Denette Hoover, Michael Smotherman, Platters, John
  Williams and His Orchestra.

AMADEUS
Soundtrack (1984) • A&M (S) SP-91001 8-10   84
Soundtrack (1984) • Fantasy (S) WAM-1791 8-10   84
  Two-disc set with booklet.
  Composer: Wolfgang Amadeus Mozart. **Conductor:** Neville Marriner.
Soundtrack [Vol. 2] (1984) • Fantasy (S) WAM-1205 8-10   80s

AMAHL AND THE NIGHT VISITORS
TV Soundtrack (1951) • RCA Victor (EP) ERA-1701 10-20   52
TV Soundtrack (1951) • RCA Victor (M) LPM-1701.............................. 20-40   52
  10-inch LP.
TV Soundtrack (1951) • RCA Victor (M) LPM-1701.............................. 20-25   52
  12-inch LP.
TV Soundtrack (1951) • RCA Victor (M) LM-1701 20-30   52
  Hinged boxed set with libretto booklet.
TV Soundtrack (1951) • RCA Victor (M) VIC-1512............................... 15-25   57
TV Soundtrack (1951) • Victrola (M) VIC-1512...................................... 8-10   71
  Conductor: Thomas Schippers. **Cast:** Chet Allen, Rosemary Kuhlmann (NBC-TV cast).
TV Soundtrack (1963) • RCA Victor (M) LPM-2762.............................. 8-10   63
TV Soundtrack (1963) • RCA Victor (S) LSC-2762 10-12   63
  Composer: Gian-Carlo Menotti. **Conductor:** Herbert Grossman. **Cast:** Kurt Yaghijian, Martha
  King, NBC Opera Co.

AMARCORD NINO ROTA
Soundtrack (1975) • RCA Victor (S) ARL1-0907 20-30   75
    Composer: Nino Rota. **Conductor:** Carlo Savina.
Studiotrack (1975) • Hannibal (S) HNBL-9301 15-18   81
  Interpretations of Nino Rota's music from Frederico Fellini films.
    Composer: Nino Rota. **Cast:** Carla Bley, David Amram, Steve Lacy, others.

AMAZING GRACE AND CHUCK
Soundtrack (1987) • Varese Sarabande (S) STV-81312 8-10   87
    Composer: Elmer Bernstein. **Conductor:** Elmer Bernstein.

AMAZING SPIDER MAN #1
Studio Cast (1966) • Golden (S) SLP-187 150-175   66
  Includes comic book. Recording follows comic book script with sound effects and music.

AMBASSADOR
Original Cast (1972) • RCA Victor (S) SER-5618 40-50   72
  Recorded for UK release, though the show ran in both London and New York.
    Composer: Don Gohman, Hal Hackady. **Conductor:** Gareth Davies. **Cast:** Howard Keel,
    Danielle Darrieux, Margaret Courtenay, Toni-Sue Burley, Blain Fairman, Neville Jason, Judith
    Paris, Isobel Stuart, Nevil Whiting.

AMEN CORNER
Original Cast (1983) • SV (S) 001 15-25   83
  Off-Broadway show made for private use by producers.
    Composer: Garry Sherman, Peter Udell. **Cast:** Rhetta Hughes, Rober Robinson, Ruth Brown,
    Keith Amos.

AMERICA, AMERICA
Soundtrack (1963) • Warner Bros. (M) W-1527 10-12   63
Soundtrack (1963) • Warner Bros. (S) WS-1527 15-20   63
    Composer: Manos Hadjidakis, Nikos Gatsos. **Conductor:** Manos Hadjidakis. **Cast:** Athens
    Experimental Orchestra.

AMERICA THE BEAUTIFUL
Studio Cast (1962) • Columbia (M) ML-5668 10-20   61
    Cast: Vincent Price.

AMERICA, WHY I LOVE HER
Studio Cast (1973) • RCA Victor (S) LSP1-4848 10-15   73
Studio Cast (1973) • RCA Victor (S) AYL1-3959 10-15   Re
    Composer: Billy Liebert, Les Taylor, John Mitchum, Howard Barnes. **Cast:** John Wayne
    (narrator).

AMERICAN ANTHEM
Soundtrack (1986) • Atlantic (S) 81661-1 8-12   86
    Cast: John Parr, Stevie Nicks, Graham Nash, Andy Taylor, Chris Thompson, Alan Silvestri,
    INXS.

AMERICAN DREAMER
Soundtrack (1971) • Mediarts (S) 41-12 10-15   71
    Cast: Gene Clark, Hello People, John Manning, John Buck Wilkin, Abbey Road Singers.

AMERICAN FLYERS
Soundtrack (1985) • GRP (S) AP-2001 8-10   85
    Composer: Lee Ritenour, Greg Mathieson, others. **Cast:** Creedence Clearwater Revival, Glenn
    Shorrock, Danny Hutton, Chris Isaak.

AMERICAN FREEDOM TRAIN
Soundtrack (1976) • Semaphore (S) SRLP 2116 60-90   76
Boxed set. Includes both picture disc and black vinyl LPs, an EP, poster, book, and a patch.
Soundtrack (1976) • Semaphore (S) SRLP 2116 25-35   76
Price for picture disc only.

AMERICAN FRIEND
Soundtrack • Enigma (S) SJ 73286.. 5-10   87
Also has original music from *State of Things* and *River's Edge.*

AMERICAN GAME
Soundtrack (1980) • Buddah (S) BDS-5724 10-12   80
Composer: Jeffrey Kaufman. **Conductor:** Jeffrey Kaufman. **Cast:** Richie Havens, Gail Wynters.

AMERICAN GIGOLO
Soundtrack (1980) • Polydor (S) PD-1-6259 8-10   80
Soundtrack (1980) • Polydor (S) 2391 447.. 5-8   Re
Composer: Giorgio Moroder. **Conductor:** Giorgio Moroder. **Cast:** Blondie, Cheryl Barnes, Giorgio Moroder, Harold Faltermeyer (keyboards).

AMERICAN GRAFFITI
Soundtrack (1973) • MCA (S) 2-8001.. 10-12   73
Two discs in gatefold cover.
Soundtrack (1973) • MCA (S) 2-8001.. 6-10   73
Standard cover.
Cast: Bill Haley and the Comets, Buddy Holly, Crests, Beach Boys, Fats Domino, Buster Brown, Chuck Berry, Platters, Flamingos, Silhouettes, Five Satins, Bobby Freeman, Buddy Knox, Del-Vikings, Johnny Burnette, Lee Dorsey, Mark Dinning, Flash Cadillac and the Continental Kids, Monotones, Big Bopper, Sonny Til and the Orioles, Spaniels, Booker T. and the MGs, Fleetwoods, Diamonds, Clovers, Joey Dee and the Starliters, Tempos, Heartbeats, Frankie Lymon and the Teenagers, Regents, Skyliners, Del Shannon, Wolfman Jack (with dee jay chatter, some of which is over the music).

AMERICAN HOT WAX
Soundtrack (1978) • A&M (SP) SP-6500... 8-12   78
Two discs. Stereo LP has 'live' tracks, whereas the mono one is original versions.
Cast: Chuck Berry, Buddy Holly, Jerry Lee Lewis, Bobby Darin, Little Richard, Jackie Wilson, Delights, Chesterfields, Professor LaPlanto & the Planatones, Clark Otis, Tammy and the Tulips, Screamin' Jay Hawkins, Spaniels, Moonglows, Drifters, Mystics, Maurice Williams & the Zodiacs, Elegants, Turbans, Frankie Ford, Big Beat Band, Delights.

AMERICAN IDEA SOUVENIR ALBUM
TV Soundtrack • Ford (S) Number Not Known...................................... 75-85   72
Limited edition of 500, made for Ford employees.
Composer: Richard Rodgers.

AMERICAN IN PARIS
Soundtrack (1951) • MGM (EP) K-93.. 10-15   51
Four discs.
Soundtrack (1951) • MGM - MGM-93... 15-20   51
Album of four 78 rpms. Made of Metrolite vinyl.
Soundtrack (1951) • MGM (M) E-93... 20-25   51
10-inch LP.
Soundtrack (1951) • MGM (M) E-3767... 15-18   59
Gatefold cover. One side has music from *Show Boat.*
Soundtrack (1951) • Metro (M) M-552.. 8-12   66
Soundtrack (1951) • Metro (SE) MS-552.. 10-12   66
Soundtrack (1951) • MCA (SE) 1427 5-8   Re

Soundtrack (1951) • JJA (M) 19773 30-35   77
>   **Composer:** George Gershwin, Ira Gershwin, Buddy DeSylva. **Conductor:** Johnny Green, Saul
>   Chaplin. **Cast:** Gene Kelly, Georges Guetary, MGM Studio Orchestra.
>   Also see GERSHWINS IN HOLLYWOOD
>   Also see IN THE GOOD OLD SUMMERTIME

AMERICAN MUSICAL THEATER
Studiotrack (1960) • Time (S) 52003 10-15   60
>   **Composer:** Cole Porter, Meredith Willson, Rodgers and Hart, Stephen Sondheim, Alan Jay
>   Lerner, Frederick Loewe, Irving Berlin. **Conductor:** Hal Mooney. **Cast:** Gene Lowell Singers.

AMERICAN POP
Soundtrack (1981) • MCA (S) 5201 20-25   81
>   **Cast:** Pat Benatar, Big Brother and the Holding Company, Mamas and the Papas, Peter, Paul
>   and Mary, Marcy Levy, Jimi Hendrix Experience, Dave Brubeck Quartet, Sam Cooke, Fabian,
>   Doors.

AMERICAN RABBIT
Soundtrack • Rhino (S) RNEP-70614 8-10   80s
>   **Cast:** Flo and Eddie.

AMERICAN SPIRIT
Studio Cast (1975) • Decca/London (S) SP-44242 10-15   75
>   **Cast:** Lee Bowman (narrator), Henry Fonda, Burt Lancaster, Jonathan Winters, Forrest Tucker,
>   Rosalind Russell, Hugh O'Brian, Anne Baxter, Walter Pidgeon, Lorne Green, Ernest Borgnine,
>   John Forsythe, Richard Carlson, Lloyd Nolan, Cesar Romero, Roscoe Lee Browne, Virginia
>   Gregg, Susan Oliver, George Hamilton, Joan Foster, Daws Butler.

AMERICAN TAIL
Soundtrack (1986) • MCA (S) 39096 8-10   86
>   **Composer:** James Horner. **Conductor:** James Horner. **Cast:** Linda Ronstadt, James Ingram,
>   Dom Deluise, Philip Glasser, Nehemiah Persoff, John Guarnieri, Warren Hays, Christopher
>   Plummer, Betsy Cathcart.

AMERICAN WEREWOLF IN LONDON
Soundtrack (1981) • Casablanca (S) NBLP-7260 8-10   81
Soundtrack (1981) • Casablanca (S) 6480 065 8-10   81
>   Full LP title is *Meco's Impressions of An American Werewolf in London.*
>   **Composer:** Elmer Bernstein, others. **Cast:** Meco.

AMERICANIZATION OF EMILY
Soundtrack (1964) • Reprise (M) R-6151 10-12   64
Soundtrack (1964) • Reprise (S) RS-6151 12-15   64
>   **Composer:** Johnny Mandel. **Conductor:** Johnny Mandel. **Cast:** James Garner, Julie Andrews.
Studiotrack (1964) • MGM (M) E-4271 5-10   64
Also has themes from other films.
>   **Conductor:** David Rose. **Cast:** David Rose and His Orchestra.

AMERICATHON
Soundtrack (1979) • Lorimar (S) JS-36174 10-12   79
>   **Cast:** Beach Boys, Elvis Costello, Nick Lowe, Eddie Money, Tom Scott, Harvey Korman, Zane
>   Buzby.

AMITYVILLE HORROR
Soundtrack (1979) • American Int'l/Casablanca (S) AILP-3003 8-10   79
>   **Composer:** Lalo Schifrin. **Conductor:** Lalo Schifrin.

AMO NON AMO: see I LOVE YOU, I LOVE YOU, I LOVE YOU NOT

AMONG FRIENDS – WAA-MU SHOW OF 1960

Original Cast (1960) • RCA Victor Custom (M) L70P-5670 100-150   60
By the cast of Northwestern University. One of the dancers in the cast is Ann-Margret Olson, later known as Ann-Margret. Since she is neither featured nor sings, this LP is of interest primarily to Ann-Margret completists.
Composer: Lawrence Grossman. **Conductor:** John Paynter. **Cast:** Hal Warren, Show Girls, Choral Girls, Martha Stickney, Suzanne Lehman, James Rusk, Scott Smith, Gary Crabb, David Soltzer, Thomas Phillips, Robin Deck, Ann Fraser, Mimi Romann, Jill Milliken, Lawrence Gossman (orchestra), Ann-Margret (dancer).
Also see BE MY GUEST

AMORE IN 4 DIMENSIONI: see LOVE IN 4 DIMENSIONS

AMOROUS ADVENTURES OF MOLL FLANDERS

Soundtrack (1965) • RCA Victor (M) LOC-1113 30-35   65
Soundtrack (1965) • RCA Victor (S) LSO-1113 45-65   65
Composer: John Addison. **Conductor:** John Addison.

AMY

Original Cast (1975) • Custom (S) 006 5-10   75

ANASTASIA

Soundtrack (1956) • Decca (M) DL-8460 20-25   56
Black label.
Soundtrack (1956) • Decca (M) DL-8460 15-18   56
Rainbow label.
Soundtrack (1956) • Brunswick (M) LAT-8175 18-20   56
UK pressing of DL-8460, with different artwork.
Soundtrack (1956) • Varese Sarabande (S) STV 81125 12-15   82
First time issued in stereo.
Composer: Alfred Newman. **Conductor:** Alfred Newman.

ANASTASIA – THE MYSTERY OF ANNA

Soundtrack • Southern Cross (S) SCRS-1015 8-10   86
Conductor: Laurence Rosenthal. **Cast:** Munich Philharmonic Orchestra.

ANATOMY OF A MURDER

Soundtrack (1959) • Columbia (EP) B-13601 10-20   59
Soundtrack (1959) • Columbia (M) CL-1360 20-25   59
Soundtrack (1959) • Columbia (S) CS-8166 35-50   59
Soundtrack (1959) • Columbia Special Products (S) JCS-8166 8-10   82
Soundtrack (1959) • MFSL (S) 214 20-25   95
Half-speed mastered.
Composer: Duke Ellington. **Conductor:** Duke Ellington.
Studiotrack (1959) • Coronet (M) CX-99 8-12   59
Studiotrack (1959) • Coronet (S) CXS-99 8-15   59
Conductor: Bob Friedman. **Cast:** Bob Friedman Orchestra.

ANCHORS AWEIGH

Soundtrack (1945) • Columbia J-25 100-125   45
78 rpm album. Has the *King Who Couldn't Dance* sequence from the film. Gene Kelly narrates the story and sings *The Worry Song* to Jerry the Mouse (of the "Tom & Jerry" cartoon team).
Composer: Ralph Freed, Sammy Fain. **Cast:** Gene Kelly.
Soundtrack (1945) • Curtain Calls (M) 100/17 10-15
Soundtrack (1945) • Sandy Hook (M) SH-2024 8-10
Composer: Ralph Freed, Sammy Fain. **Cast:** Frank Sinatra, Gene Kelly, Kathryn Grayson, Jose Iturbi.

AND GOD CREATED WOMAN: see GOD CREATED WOMAN

AND GOD SAID: see GOD SAID

AND THEN I WROTE: see RICHARD RODGERS

ANDERSONVILLE TRIAL
Original Cast (1960) • 20th Century-Fox (M) FOX-4000 15-20   60
Original Cast (1960) • 20th Century-Fox (S) SFX-4000 18-25   60
   Dramatic play by Saul Levitt, produced by Jose Ferrer.
    Composer: Henry Nemo. **Conductor:** Hugo Montenegro. **Cast:** George C. Scott, Albert Dekker, Herbert Berghof, Russell Hardie, Robert Carroll, Robert Gerringer, James Greene.

ANDRE PREVIN: see MUSIC OF THE YOUNG HOLLYWOOD COMPOSERS

ANDRE PREVIN - COMPOSER, CONDUCTOR, ARRANGER: see INVITATION TO THE DANCE

ANDREZJ JAJDA TRILOGY
Studiotrack • That's Entertainment (S) TER-1053 10-20   80s
   UK release.

ANDROCLES AND THE LION
TV Soundtrack (1967) • RCA Victor (M) LOC-1141 12-25   67
TV Soundtrack (1967) • RCA Victor (S) LSO-1141 20-25   67
    Composer: Richard Rodgers. **Conductor:** Jay Blackton. **Cast:** Noel Coward, Ed Ames, Inga Swenson, John Cullum, Kurt Kasznar, Norman Wisdom.

ANDROMEDA STRAIN
Soundtrack (1971) • Kapp (S) KRS-5513 30-35   71
   Standard cover.
Soundtrack (1971) • Kapp (S) KRS-5513 50-75   71
   Hexagon-shaped cover.
    Composer: Gil Melle.

ANDY GRIFFITH SHOW
TV Soundtrack (1961) • Capitol (M) T-1611 50-75   61
TV Soundtrack (1961) • Capitol (S) ST-1611 100-125   61
    Composer: Earle Hagen. **Conductor:** Earle Hagen. **Cast:** Andy Griffith.

ANDY WARHOL'S DRACULA
Soundtrack • Varese Sarabande (S) STV 81156 8-12   82
    Composer: Claudio Gizzi.

ANDY WARHOL'S FRANKENSTEIN
Soundtrack (1974) • Varese Sarabande (S) STV 81157 8-12   82
    Composer: Claudio Gizzi.

ANDY WILLIAMS SHOW
TV Soundtrack (1971) • Columbia (S) KC-30105 8-12   71
   Includes illustrated booklet.
    Cast: Andy Williams.

ANGEL
Original Cast (1978) • No Label Name Used (S) GUA-001 40-45   78
   Broadway show, recorded privately by the producers.
    Composer: Gary Geld, Peter Udell. **Conductor:** William Cox. **Cast:** Don Scardino, Joel Higgins, Frances Sternhagen, Fred Gwynne.

ANGEL, ANGEL, DOWN WE GO
Soundtrack (1970) • Tower (S) ST-5161 15-25   70
   This film is also known as *Cult of the Damned.*
    Composer: Barry Mann, Cynthia Weil, Fred Karger.

ANGEL HEART
Soundtrack (1987) • Antilles New Directions (S) 91035 8-10   87
    Composer: Trevor Jones. **Conductor:** Trevor Jones. **Cast:** Bessie Smith, Brownie McGhee, Courtney Pine, LaVern Baker, Lilian Boutte, Glen Gray and the Casa Loma Orchestra.

ANGEL UNCHAINED
Soundtrack (1970) • American Int'l (S) A-1037 10-15   70
   Composer: Randy Sparks. **Conductor:** Randy Sparks. **Cast:** Randy Sparks, Don Stroud, Luke Askew, Larry Bishop, Tyne Daly.

ANGEL'S SPRINGTIME WORLD OF LIGHT OPERA
Studio Cast (1961) • Angel (M) PRO 1498 10-20   61
   White label. Promotional issue only. Selections from *Bitter Sweet, Lilac Time, The Merry Widow* and *White Horse Inn*.
   Conductor: William Reid. **Cast:** Rita Williams Singers, Michael Collins and His Orchestra, Sadler's Wells Opera Company and Orchestra, Tony Osborne and His Orchestra.

ANGELS DIE HARD
Soundtrack (1970) • UNI (S) 73091 20-25   70
   Conductor: Richard Hieronymous. **Cast:** Fever Tree, Sylvanus, Dewey Martin and Medicine Ball, East-West Pipeline, Mark Eric, Rabbit MacKay.

ANGELS FROM HELL
Soundtrack (1968) • Tower (S) ST-5128 35-50   68
   Composer: Stu Phillips. **Conductor:** Stu Phillips. **Cast:** Peanut Butter Conspiracy, Lollipop Shoppe, Ted Marckland.

ANIMAL HOUSE: see NATIONAL LAMPOON'S ANIMAL HOUSE

ANIMALS (FIVE SAVAGE MEN)
Soundtrack • Vee Jay (S) VJS-1211 10-15
   Composer: Rupert Holmes.

ANIMALYMPICS
Soundtrack (1980) • A&M (S) SP-4810 8-10   80
   Composer: Graham Gouldman.

ANKLES AWEIGH
Original Cast (1955) • Decca (M) DL-9025 25-35   55
Original Cast (1955) • AEI (M) AEI-1104 8-12   76
   Composer: Sammy Fain, Dan Shapiro. **Conductor:** Salvatore dell'Isola. **Cast:** Betty Kean, Jane Kean, Lew Parker, Mark Dawson, Gabriel Dell, Betty George, Ray Mason.

ANNA
Soundtrack (1951) • MGM (EP) X-1108 75-85   54
   Full title: *Anna/Hell Raiders of the Deep.* Also has music from *Hell Raiders of the Deep.*
   Cast: Silvana Mangano.
Soundtrack (1987) • Varese Sarabande (S) STV 81353 10-12   87
   Cast: Greg Hawkes.

ANNA RUSSELL'S LITTLE SHOW (ALL BY MYSELF)
Original Cast (1953) • Columbia (M) ML-4594 10-12   53
   Also known as *Anna Russell Sings.*
Original Cast (1953) • Columbia (M) ML-4733 10-12   53
   Actual title: *Anna Russell Sings Again.*
Original Cast (1953) • Columbia (M) ML-4928 10-12   54
   Actual title: *Anna Russell's Guide to Concert Audiences.*
Original Cast (1956) • Columbia (M) ML-5036 10-12   56
   Actual title: *Anna Russell's Square Talk on Popular Music.*
Original Cast (1957) • Columbia (M) ML-5195 10-12   57
   Actual title: *Anna Russell in Darkest Africa.*
Original Cast (1958) • Columbia (M) ML-5295 10-12   58

Original Cast (1953-1958) • Columbia (M) MG-31199.......................... 10-12   72
  Actual title: *The Anna Russell Album.* Two-disc reissue of ML-4594 and ML-4733. A 1964
  revival carried the title *All By Myself,* though no such LP exists. Each of the original six LPs
  is different, as the show was regularly changed. For example, each show has a different
  pianist.
  Composer: Anna Russell, others. **Cast:** Anna Russell, others.

ANNE OF GREEN GABLES
Original London Cast (1969) • CBS (S) 70053 35-45   69
  UK release.
  Composer: Norman Campbell, Donald Harron. **Conductor:** Martin Goldstein. **Cast:** Polly James,
  Barbara Hamilton, Hiram Sherman, Bettina Dickson, Susan Anderson, Robert Ainslie, Pat Starr, Ian
  Burford, Liz Edmiston.
Canadian Studio Cast (1971) • Dominion (S) LP-1368........................ 20-30   71
  Side two has one song from each of the following Canadian musicals: *The Navy Show, Mr.
  Scrooge, Turvey, The Pied Piper, Willie the Squouse* and *Wild Rose.*
  Composer: Norman Campbell, Donald Harron. **Conductor:** John Fenwick, Al Baculis.

ANNE OF THE THOUSAND DAYS
Soundtrack (1970) • Decca (S) DL-79174... 12-15   70
  One side has samples of Tudor Court music, by the New York Pro Musica, arranged by
  John Reeves White and Noah Greenberg.
  Composer: Georges Delerue, John Hale. **Cast:** Gary Bond.

ANNETTE (AND OTHER WALT DISNEY SERIALS)
TV Soundtrack (1958) • Mickey Mouse (M) MM-24.......................... 100-125   58
  Cast: Annette Funicello, others.

ANNIE
Original Cast (1977) • Columbia (S) QAL-34712................................. 8-10   77
  Promotional issue, white label.
Original Cast (1977) • Columbia (S) PS-34712................................... 8-10   77
Original Cast (1977) • Columbia (Q) PS-34712.................................. 8-10   77
  Label has QBL-34712, cover has PS-34712.
Original Cast (1977) • Columbia Masterworks (S) JS-34712.................. 8-10   Re
Original Cast (1977) • Columbia (S) HS-44712 10-12   79
  Half-speed mastered.
  Composer: Charles Strouse, Martin Charnin. **Conductor:** Peter Howard. **Cast:** Andrea
  McArdle, Dorothy Loudon, Reid Shelton, Laurie Beechman, Edie Cowan, Donald Craig, Barbara
  Erwin, Sandy Faison, Robert Fitch, Raymond Thorne, Penny Worth.
Soundtrack (1982) • Columbia (S) JS-38000 12-15   82
  Includes *You're Never Fully Dressed Without a Smile* within the song title list on the back
  cover.
Soundtrack (1982) • Columbia (S) JS-38000 8-10   82
  Has sticker saying "Also including the song "You're Never Fully Dressed Without a Smile"
  on the back cover. On this issue, the song title doesn't appear within the listing.
  Composer: Charles Strouse, Martin Charnin. **Conductor:** Ralph Burns. **Cast:** Aileen Quinn,
  Carol Burnett, Albert Finney, Ann Reinking, Tim Curry, Bernadette Peters.
Soundtrack (1982) • Columbia (S) CR-38168 10-20   82
  Actual title: *Annie: Original Children's Soundtrack and Story.* Dialogue and music.

ANNIE GET YOUR GUN
Original Cast (1946) • Decca (EP) ED-805 10-20   49
Original Cast (1946) • Decca A-468 12-18   49
  78 rpm album.
Original Cast (1946) • Decca (M) DL-8001... 15-20   49
  Exists with two back cover variations.
Original Cast (1946) • Decca (M) DL-9018.. 12-15   55
Original Cast (1946) • Decca (SE) DL-79018....................................... 10-12   59
Original Cast (1946) • MCA (SE) 2031e... 8-10   73

Original Cast (1946) • MCA (SE) 37092 5-8   81
Composer: Irving Berlin. Conductor: Jay Blackton. Cast: Ethel Merman, Ray Middleton, Robert Lenn, Garth, Turner and Bibb, Kathleen Carnes.
London Revival Cast (1986) • First Night (S) 4 10-12   86
UK release.
Composer: Irving Berlin. Cast: Suzi Quatro.
Revival Cast (1966) • RCA Victor (M) LOC-1124 8-10   66
Revival Cast (1966) • RCA Victor (S) LSO-1124 10-12   66
Some copies of these two have a sticker on the shrink wrap with "Includes the new Irving Berlin Hit *An Old Fashioned Wedding.*" Copies with orange, black or tan labels are worth considerably less than original, which has black label with RCA dog on top.
Conductor: Franz Allers. Cast: Ethel Merman, Bruce Yarnell, Benay Venuta, Jerry Orbach, Ronn Carrol, Rufus Smith.
Studio Cast (1963) • Columbia (M) OL-5960 8-12   63
Studio Cast (1963) • Columbia (S) OS-2360 12-15   63
Gray label.
Studio Cast (1963) • Columbia (S) CS-2360 5-8   Re
Studio Cast (1963) • Columbia (S) PC-2360 5-8   Re
Red label.
Studio Cast (1963) • Harmony (S) KH-30396 8-10   71
Studio Cast (1963) • Columbia Special Products (S) CS-2360 5-8   76
Conductor: Franz Allers. Cast: Doris Day, Robert Goulet, Kelly Brown, Renee Winters, Leonard Stokes, Jack and Jill Little People, Malcolm Dodds Quartet.
Studio Cast (1973) • London Phase 4 (S) XPS-905 8-10   73
Conductor: Stanley Black. Cast: Ethel Merman, Neilson Taylor, Neil Howlett, London Festival Orchestra and Chorus, Leslie Fyson, Benay Venuta.
Soundtrack (1950) • MGM - MGM-50 15-20   50
78 rpm album.
Soundtrack (1950) • MGM (M) E-509 25-30   50
10-inch LP.
Soundtrack (1950) • MGM (EP) X-50 15-20   50
Soundtrack (1950) • Metro (M) M-548 10-12   65
Soundtrack (1950) • Metro (SE) MS-548 10-12   65
Soundtrack (1950) • MCA (M) 1626 8-10   Re
Conductor: Adolph Deutsch. Cast: Betty Hutton, Howard Keel, Louis Calhern, Keenan Wynn, MGM Studio Orchestra.
Soundtrack (1949) • Sound Stage (M) 2302 25-45
Special edition marketed for the Judy Garland Fan Club.
Soundtrack (1949) • Sandy Hook (M) SH-2053 8-10   81
Above two contain previously unreleased soundtrack sessions featuring Judy Garland, who was to have played Annie Oakley. The rest of the cast is identical to that of the finished film listed above, except for Frank Morgan, who was replaced by Louis Calhern. Above two also include songs from the finished film that don't appear on the MGM releases.
Composer: Irving Berlin. Composer: Adolph Deutsch. Cast: Judy Garland, Howard Keel, Keenan Wynn, Benay Venuta, Frank Morgan.
TV Soundtrack (1957) • Capitol (EP) EDM-913 10-15   57
TV Soundtrack (1957) • Capitol (M) W2-913 40-45   57
Gatefold cover. Promotional issue only.
TV Soundtrack (1957) • Capitol (M) W-913 12-18   57
Composer: Irving Berlin. Conductor: Louis Adrian. Cast: Mary Martin, John Raitt.
Studiotrack (1950) • Wing (M) SRW 11005 8-12
Actual title: *Annie Get Your Gun/Oklahoma!* One side has music from *Oklahoma!*
Studiotrack (1954) • RCA Victor (EP) ERA-1798 8-10   54
Studiotrack (1954) • RCA Victor (M) LM-1798 8-12   54
Conductor: Arthur Fiedler. Cast: Boston Pops Orchestra.

Studiotrack (1955) • RCA Camden (M) CAL-411 10-12   55
Actual title: *Annie Get Your Gun and Selections from the Helen Morgan Story.*
Conductor: Al Goodman, Nat Brandywine. **Cast:** Al Goodman and His Orchestra, Maxine & Jimmy Carroll, Audrey Marsh, Earl Oxford, Mullen Sisters, Guild Choristers, Nat Brandywine Orchestra, Johnny Guarnieri and His Group, Larry Green and His Orchestra, Achille Scotti and his Group, Nat Brandwynne and His Orchestra.

Studiotrack (1955) • Camden (M) CL-154 10-12   55
Actual title: *Annie Get Your Gun Gems (and Others).*
Conductor: Harold Coates (Al Goodman). **Cast:** Harold Coates and His Orchestra.

Studiotrack (1959) • National Academy Record Club (M) ES-8 10-15   59
From the *Ed Sullivan Presents Songs and Music of...* series.
Cast: Ed Sullivan All Star Cast.

Studiotrack • RCA Victor (EP) WEPR-4 5-15   50s
Colored vinyl. Also has medley from *Kiss Me Kate.*
Conductor: Arthur Fiedler. **Cast:** Boston Pops Orchestra.

Studiotrack (1961) • Columbia (M) CL-1623.. 15-20   61

Studiotrack (1961) • Columbia (S) CS-8432.. 15-25   61
Actual title: *(Hit Songs from) Annie Get Your Gun.* One side has music from *Do Re Mi.*
Conductor: Luther Henderson. **Cast:** Polly Bergen.

Studiotrack • Design (S) DCF 1050... 8-10
Also has music from *Call Me Madam.*
Composer: Irving Berlin. **Cast:** Judy Lynn, Larry Douglas, Warren Vincent and His Orchestra.
Also see CAROUSEL
Also see DO RE MI
Also see EASTER PARADE
Also see OKLAHOMA!
Also see THOSE GLORIOUS MGM MUSICALS
Also see THREE LITTLE WORDS

ANNIE'S CHRISTMAS
Studio Cast (1982) • Columbia (S) CC-38361 8-10   82

ANONYMOUS VENETIAN
Soundtrack (1971) • United Artists (S) UAS-5218................................. 20-25   71
Composer: Stelvio Cipriani. **Conductor:** Stelvio Cipriani.

ANOTHER EVENING WITH FRED ASTAIRE
TV Soundtrack (1959) • Chrysler (M) KHOP-1087 45-65   59
Chrysler sponsored this NBC-TV production, November 4, 1959.
Composer: Various. **Conductor:** David Rose. **Cast:** Fred Astaire, Barrie Chase, Jonah Jones Quartet, Ken Nordine, Bill Thompson Singers, David Rose and His Orchestra.

ANOTHER FINE MESS
Soundtrack • Mark 56 (M) 579 20-40   78
Picture disc.
Cast: Laurel and Hardy.

ANOTHER 48 HOURS
Soundtrack (1990) • Scotti Bros. (S) 5205-1 45-55   90
Composer: James Horner. **Conductor:** James Horner. **Cast:** Curio, Michael Stanton, Jesse Johnson, James Horner.

ANOTHER TIME, ANOTHER PLACE
Soundtrack (1958) • Columbia (M) CL-1180 30-35   58
Composer: Douglas Gamley. **Conductor:** Muir Mathieson.

ANTIGONE
Studio Cast • Caedmon (M) TRS 320-M 5-10

ANY WEDNESDAY
Soundtrack (1966) • Warner Bros. (M) W-1669 10-20   66
Soundtrack (1966) • Warner Bros. (S) WS-1669 15-30   66
Composer: George Duning. **Conductor:** George Duning.

ANY WHICH WAY YOU CAN

Soundtrack (1980) • Warner Bros. (S) HS-3499 8-10   80
    Conductor: Steve Dorff. Cast: Ray Charles, Clint Eastwood, Glen Campbell, David Frizell, Shelly West, Fats Domino, Sondra Locke, Jim Stafford, Johnny Duncan, Gene Watson, Cliff Crofford, John Durrill, Texas Opera Company.

ANYA

Original Cast (1965) • United Artists (M) UAL-4133 12-18   65
Original Cast (1965) • United Artists (S) UAS-5133 40-45   65
    Composer: Robert Wright, George Forrest. Conductor: Hal Hastings. Cast: Constance Towers, Michael Karmoyan, Lillian Gish, Barbara Alexander, Boris Aplon, George S. Irving, John Michael King, Irra Petina, Michael Quinn, Karen Shepard, Ed Steffe.

ANYONE CAN WHISTLE

Original Cast (1964) • Columbia (M) KOL-6080 10-12   64
Original Cast (1964) • Columbia (S) KOS-2480 12-18   64
  Both have gatefold covers.
Original Cast (1964) • Columbia Special Products (S) AKOS-2480........ 8-10   72
Original Cast (1964) • Columbia (S) S-32608.. 5-8   73
Original Cast (1964) • Columbia Special Products (S) AS-32608............. 5-8   Re
  Above three have standard covers.
    Composer: Stephen Sondheim. Conductor: Herbert Greene. Cast: Lee Remick, Angela Lansbury, Harry Guardino, Sterling Clark, Gabriel Dell, Harvey Evans, James Frawley, Larry Roquemore, Arnold Soboloff, Tucker Smith.

ANYTHING GOES

Original Cast (1934) • Smithsonian (M) R-007 12-18   77
  Gatefold cover. With members of the original Broadway and London productions.
    Composer: Cole Porter. Cast: Ethel Merman, Jack Whiting, Jeanne Aubert, Cole Porter.
Original Revival Cast (1962) • Epic (M) FLM-13100 8-10   62
Original Revival Cast (1962) • Epic (S) FLS-13100 10-12   62
Original Revival Cast (1962) • Epic (S) JS-15100 8-10   Re
    Composer: Cole Porter. Conductor: Julian Stein. Cast: Eileen Rodgers, Hal Linden, Mickey Deems, Margery Gray, Mildred Chandler, Barbara Lang, Kenneth Mars, Warren Wade.
London Revival Cast (1969) • That's Entertainment (S) TER-1080........ 8-10   80s
  UK release.
    Composer: Cole Porter. Cast: Marion Montgomery.
Revival Cast • RCA Victor (S) 7769-1 8-10   88
    Composer: Cole Porter. Conductor: Edward Strauss. Cast: Patti LuPone, Howard McGillin, Bill McCutcheon, Rex Everhart, Linda Hart, Anne Francine, Anthony Heald.
Studio Cast (1950) • Columbia (EP) A-1732 10-12   51
Studio Cast (1950) • Columbia (M) CL-2582 15-18
  10-inch LP.
Studio Cast (1950) • Columbia (M) CL-2159 15-18   51
  10-inch LP.
Studio Cast (1950) • Columbia (M) ML-2159.. 12-15   51
Studio Cast (1950) • Columbia (M) ML-4751.. 15-20   53
  One side has music from *The Band Wagon*.
Studio Cast (1950) • Columbia (M) DL-193.. 8-12   56
Studio Cast (1950) • Columbia Special Products (M) AML-4751.............. 5-8   Re
    Composer: Cole Porter. Conductor: Lehman Engel. Cast: Mary Martin.

Studio Cast (1953) • RCA Victor (EP) EPA-489 10-20   53
Studio Cast (1953) • RCA Victor (M) LPM-3157 15-20   53
  10-inch LP. One side has music from *Kiss Me Kate*.
  Cast: Helena Bliss, George Britton, Lisa Kirk.
Soundtrack (1936) • Caliban (M) 6043 12-18
  Composer: Cole Porter, Leo Robin, Richard A. Whiting, Hogie Carmichael, Frederick Hollander, Edward Heyman. **Cast:** Bing Crosby, Ethel Merman, Charlie Ruggles, Ida Lupino, Grace Bradley, Arthur Treacher, Margaret Dumont. (With dialogue).
Soundtrack (1956) • Decca (EP) ED-845 18-20   56
Soundtrack (1956) • Decca (M) DL-8318 30-35   56
Soundtrack (1956) • Decca (M) LAT-8118 25-30   56
  UK release of Decca DL-8318. Blue cover.
Soundtrack (1956) • DRG/Stet (M) DS-15025 20-30   55
  This issue appears on many back covers in this series, but copies are not yet known to exist. Price range is estimated in the event the album surfaces.
  Composer: Cole Porter, Jimmy Van Heusen, Sammy Cahn. **Conductor:** Joseph J. Lilley. **Cast:** Bing Crosby, Donald O'Connor, Jeanmaire, Mitzi Gaynor.
TV Soundtrack (1954) • Larynx (M) 567 10-15
TV Soundtrack (1954) • Sandy Hook (M) SH-2043 8-12   81
  One side is from the CBS-TV production of *Panama Hattie*.
  Composer: Cole Porter. **Cast:** Ethel Merman, Frank Sinatra, Bert Lahr, Sheree North.
Studiotrack (1936) • Decca (M) DL-6009 45-55   50
  10-inch LP.
Studiotrack (1936) • Brunswick (M) LA 8723 30-35   50s
  10-inch LP. UK release of Decca LP.
  Both have music from *Two for Tonight* on one side.
  Composer: Cole Porter, Richard Whiting. **Conductor:** George Stoll. **Cast:** Bing Crosby, Ethel Merman.
  Also see BING'S HOLLYWOOD
  Also see EVERGREEN
  Also see PENNIES FROM HEAVEN

APARTMENT

Soundtrack (1960) • United Artists (M) UAL-3105 15-35   60
Soundtrack (1960) • United Artists (S) UAS-6105 20-45   60
Soundtrack (1960) • Ascot (M) UM-13500 12-15   64
Soundtrack (1960) • Ascot (S) US-16500 12-18   64
  Also has selections from *Some Like It Hot, Exodus* and *Odds Against Tomorrow*.
  Composer: Adolph Deutsch, Charles Williams. **Conductor:** Mitchell Powell. **Cast:** Hollywood Studio Symphony Orchestra.

APOCALYPSE NOW

Soundtrack (1979) • Elektra (S) DP-90001 20-25   79
  Two discs.
  Composer: Carmine Coppola, Francis Coppola, others. **Cast:** Marlon Brando, Robert Duvall, Martin Sheen, Doors, Frederic Forrest, Albert Hall, Sam Bottoms, Dennis Hopper, Vienna Philharmonic Orchestra, Flash Cadillac, Harrison Ford. (With dialogue.)

APOLOGY

Soundtrack (1986) • Varese Sarabande (S) STV 81284 10-12   86
  Composer: Maurice Jarre.

APPEARING NIGHTLY

Original Cast (1977) • Arista (S) AB-4142 8-10   77
  Cast: Lily Tomlin.

APPLAUSE

Original Cast (1970) • ABC (S) ABCS-OC-11 8-10   70
Original Cast (1970) • ABC SO-93210 5-10   70
  Capitol Record Club issue.
Original Cast (1970) • MCA (S) OCS-11 4-5   Re
  Composer: Charles Strouse, Lee Adams. **Conductor:** Donald Pippin. **Cast:** Lauren Bacall, Len Cariou, Robert Mandan, Bonnie Franklin, Penny Fuller, Brandon Maggart, Lee Roy Reams, Ann Williams.

APPLE

Soundtrack (1980) • Cannon (S) 1001 50-60   80
  Composer: Coby Recht, others. **Cast:** Grace Kennedy, Allan Love, Mary Hylan, George Gilmour, Joss Ackland, Vladek Sheybal, Ray Shell.

APPLE TREE

Original Cast (1966) • Columbia (M) KOL-6620 8-10   66
Original Cast (1966) • Columbia (S) KOS-3020 10-12   66
Original Cast (1966) • Columbia (S) AKOS-3020 5-8   Re
  Composer: Jerry Bock, Sheldon Harnick. **Conductor:** Elliot Lawrence. **Cast:** Barbara Harris, Larry Blyden, Alan Alda, Marc Jordan.
Original Canadian Cast (1966) • Trillium (S) TR-2000 30-35   66
  Act I only.
  Composer: Jerry Bock, Sheldon Harnick. **Conductor:** Hank Monis. **Cast:** Tom Kneebone, Dinah Christie.

APPLECART

Original Cast (1958) • Caedmon (M) 1084 8-12   58

APRIL FOOLS

Soundtrack (1969) • Columbia (S) OS-3340 10-15   69
  For covers without clipped corners.
Soundtrack (1969) • Columbia (S) OS-3340 5-10   69
  For covers with clipped corners.
  Composer: Marvin Hamlisch, Burt Bacharach. **Cast:** Chambers Brothers, Mongo Santamaria, Taj Mahal, Robert John, Percy Faith, Jack Lemmon, Catherine Deneuve, Sally Kellerman, Peter Lawford. (With dialogue.)

APRIL FOOLS DAY

Soundtrack (1986) • Varese Sarabande (S) STV 81278 8-10   86
  Composer: Charles Bernstein.

APRIL IN PARIS

Soundtrack (1952) • Titania (M) 500 8-10
  One side has music from *Young At Heart*.
  APRIL IN PARIS: **Composer:** Sammy Cahn, Vernon Duke, E.Y. Harburg. **Conductor:** Ray Heindorf. **Cast:** Doris Day, Ray Bolger, Claude Dauphin. YOUNG AT HEART: **Composer:** Cole Porter, George Gershwin, others. **Conductor:** Ray Heindorf. **Cast:** Doris Day, Frank Sinatra.
Studiotrack (1952) • Columbia (EP) B-1581 20-25   52
  Doris Day sings four songs from the film.
  Composer: Sammy Cahn, Vernon Duke, E.Y. Harburg. **Conductor:** Paul Weston. **Cast:** Doris Day, Norman Luboff Choir.

APRIL LOVE

Soundtrack (1957) • Dot (M) DLP-9000 12-18   57
Soundtrack (1957) • London (M) HA-D 2078.. 20-25   57
  UK release. Has different cover art than US issue.
Soundtrack (1957) · MCA (M) VIM-7253 12-18   Re
  Japan release, with cover printed entirely in English.
  Composer: Sammy Fain, Paul Francis Webster (musical adaptation by Alfred Newman and Cyril J. Mockridge). **Conductor:** Lionel Newman. **Cast:** Pat Boone, Shirley Jones.

ARABESQUE
Soundtrack (1966) • RCA Victor (M) LPM-3623 12-15   66
Soundtrack (1966) • RCA Victor (S) LSP-3623 15-20   66
    Composer: Henry Mancini. **Conductor:** Henry Mancini.

ARABIAN NIGHTS
Original Cast (1954) • Decca (EP) ED-816 15-20   54
Original Cast (1954) • Decca (M) DL-9013 60-65   54
    Composer: Carmen Lombardo, John Jacob Loeb. **Conductor:** Pembroke Davenport. **Cast:** Lauritz Melchior, Helena Scott, Ralph Herbert, William Chapman, James McCracken, Hope Holiday, Gloria Van Dorp.
Studio Cast (1954) • Decca (EP) ED-687 15-20   54
Studio Cast (1954) • Decca (M) DL-5542 20-25   54
    10-inch LP.
    Conductor: Guy Lombardo. **Cast:** Guy Lombardo and the Royal Canadians, Bill Flanagan, Kenny Gardner.

ARCADIANS
Original Cast (1968) • EMI (S) 233 15-18

ARCHIES
TV Soundtrack (1968) • Calendar (S) KES-101 15-25   68
    Composer: Jeff Barry. **Conductor:** Don Kirshner.

ARCHY AND MEHITABEL / ECHOES OF ARCHY
Studio Cast (1954) • Columbia (M) ML-4963 10-12   54
Studio Cast (1954) • Columbia (M) OL-4963 8-12   54
    This recording served as the basis for *Shinbone Alley* (1957).
    Composer: George Kleinsinger, Joe Darion. **Conductor:** George Kleinsinger. **Cast:** Carol Channing, Eddie Bracken, David Wayne, Percival Dove.
    Also see SHINBONE ALLEY.

ARE YOU LONESOME TONIGHT? ("THE KING STILL LIVES")
Original London Cast (1985) • First Night (S) CAST-1 8-10   85
    A stage show about the life of Elvis Presley.
    Composer: Alan Bleasdale, others. **Cast:** Martin Shaw, Simon Bowman, Michael Keating, Julian Ashton, Roger Booth, others.

ARIA
Soundtrack (1988) • RCA Victor (S) 6587-1 8-10   88

ARISTOCATS
Soundtrack (1971) • Disneyland (S) DQ-1333 8-10   71
    Composer: Various. **Cast:** Mike Sammes Singers, Robbie Lester, Susan Novack, Victor Sweier, Phil Harris, Wellingtons, Louis Prima.
Studiotrack (1971) • Disneyland (S) STER-3995 8-10   71
    Composer: Richard M. Sherman, Robert B. Sherman, Terry Gilkyson, Floyd Huddleston, Al Rinker. **Cast:** Sterling Holloway (narration), Phil Harris, Robbie Lester, Susan Novack, Gregory Novack, Victor Sweier and the Mike Sammes Singers.

ARMED AND DANGEROUS
Soundtrack (1986) • Manhattan (S) SJ-53041 8-10   86
    Cast: Atlantic Starr, Escapades, Maurice White, Cheryl Lynn, Tito Puente and His Latin Ensemble, Glenn Burtrick, Eve, Sigue Sigue Sputnik, Michael Henderson, Bill Meyers.

ARMS AND THE GIRL
Original Cast (1950) • Decca A-759 20-30   50
    78 rpm album.
Original Cast (1950) • Decca (M) DL-5200 65-85   50
    10-inch LP.

Original Cast • JJA (M) 19752 15-20   75
Also includes music from *As the Girls Go, Texas Li'l Darlin'* and *Meet the People*.

Original Cast • Columbia Special Products (M) X-14879 8-10   Re
Also has music from *Look Ma, I'm Dancin'!*
    Composer: Morton Gould, Dorothy Fields. **Conductor:** Frederick Dvonch. **Cast:** Nanette Fabray, George Guetary, Pearl Baily, Florenz Ames. LOOK MA, I'M DANCIN'!: **Composer:** Hugh Martin. **Conductor:** Pembroke Davenport. **Cast:** Nancy Walker, Harold Lang, Sandra Deel, Bill Shirley, Hugh Martin.

ARNOLD'S WRECKING CO.

Soundtrack • East Coast (S) EC-10 55S 30-60   70s
    Composer: Howie Solomon, Steve Blackstone, Ray Laurel, Richard Riggs.

AROUND THE WORLD IN 80 DAYS

Soundtrack (1956) • Decca (EP) ED-836 10-15   56
Three-disc set.

Soundtrack (1956) • Decca (M) DL-9046 10-20   56
Exists with two different covers. The earlier edition has a black band across the top which says "Music from the Sound Track" and another below which says "Music by Victor Young." The later edition has no black bands, but states the information within the picture on the cover.

Soundtrack (1956) • Decca (S) DL-79046 15-30   58

Soundtrack (1956) • Decca (S) SW-94840 10-12   Re
Capitol Record Club issue on Decca's rainbow label.

Soundtrack (1956) • MCA (S) 2062 8-10   74

Soundtrack (1956) • MCA (S) 37086 8-10   86
    Composer: Victor Young. **Conductor:** Victor Young.

Studiotrack (1956) • Tops (M) L-1591 5-10   57
    Conductor: Lew Raymond.

Studiotrack (1957) • Masterseal (M) MS-12 5-10   57
Labels do not have selection number.
    Conductor: Jack Hansen. **Cast:** Hollywood Transcription Orchestra.

Studiotrack (1957) • Musirama (M) 33-1875 5-10   57

Studiotrack (1958) • Specialty (M) SP-2101 5-10   58

Studiotrack (1958) • Specialty (M) SP-2101 5-10   87
Above reissue has a 1987 copyright date on back cover.
    Cast: Gerald Wiggins Trio: Gerald Wiggins (piano), Eugene Wright (bass), Bill Douglass (drums).

Studiotrack (1960) • Craftsmen (M) C-8022 5-10   60
    Conductor: Gordon Fleming. **Cast:** Gordon Fleming and His Orchestra.

Studiotrack • Alshiré (S) ST-5085 5-10
    Cast: 101 Strings.

Studiotrack • Bravo (M) K-102 5-10

Studiotrack • Bravo (S) KS-102 5-10
One side has music from *The King and I*.
    Conductor: John Senati. **Cast:** Bravo Pops Symphony Orchestra.

Studiotrack • Crown (M) CLP 5030 5-10
Label indicates the selection number as "101," cover shows "CLP 5030."

Studiotrack • Design (M) DLP-52 5-10
One side has music from *My Fair Lady*.
    Conductor: Warren Edward Vincent. **Cast:** Royal Farnsworth Symphony Orchestra.

Studiotrack • Everest (M) LPBR-4001 5-10

Studiotrack • Everest (S) SDBR-4001 5-10

Studiotrack • Everest (S) SDBR-1020 5-10
    Composer: Victor Young, Harold Adamson. **Conductor:** Franz Allers. **Cast:** Jack Saunders Orchestra.

Studiotrack • Golden Tone (M) C 4208 5-10
    Conductor: Carlton Miller.

Studiotrack • Grand Award (S) 214-SD 5-10
    Conductor: Enoch Light. **Cast:** Enoch Light Orchestra.
Studiotrack • International Award Series (S) ASK-102 5-10
  One side has music from *The King and I.*
    Conductor: John Senati. **Cast:** Bravo Pops Symphony Orchestra.
Studiotrack • Mayfair (S) 9591S 5-10
  Yellow vinyl.
    Conductor: Lew Raymond.
Studiotrack • Paris (M) P-129 5-10
  One side has "International Favorites."
    Cast: Hugo Devries and His Orchestra.
Studiotrack • Somerset (M) P-2800 5-10
Studiotrack • Somerset (S) SF-2800 5-10
    Cast: Cinema Sound Stage Orchestra.
Studiotrack • Valiant (S) V-4926 5-10
    Cast: Hollywood Orchestra.
Studiotrack • Unart (S) 21025 5-10
    Cast: Motion Picture Studio Orchestra.
Studiotrack • Waldorf (M) MHK33-1225 5-10
    Cast: Enoch Light and His Orchestra.

AROUND THE WORLD UNDER THE SEA
Soundtrack (1966) • Monument (M) 8050 15-30   66
Soundtrack (1966) • Monument (S) 18050 20-40   66
    Composer: Harry Sukman. **Conductor:** Harry Sukman.

ARRANGEMENT
Soundtrack (1968) • Warner Bros. (M) W-1824 10-12   68
Soundtrack (1968) • Warner Bros. (S) WS-1824 12-15   68
    Composer: David Amram. **Conductor:** David Amram.

ARRIVEDERCI, BABY!
Soundtrack (1966) • RCA Victor (M) LOC-1132 12-15   66
Soundtrack (1966) • RCA Victor (S) LSO-1132 15-30   66
    Composer: Dennis Farnon, Earl Shuman. **Conductor:** Dennis Farnon, Ernie Freeman. **Cast:** Vic Damone.

ART OF LOVE
Soundtrack (1965) • Capitol (M) T-2355 10-12   65
Soundtrack (1965) • Capitol (S) ST-2355 12-18   65
    Composer: Cy Coleman. **Conductor:** Cy Coleman.

ARTHUR (OR THE DECLINE AND FALL OF THE BRITISH EMPIRE)
TV Soundtrack (1970) • Reprise (S) RS-6366 10-15   70

ARTHUR (THE ALBUM)
Soundtrack (1981) • Warner Bros. (S) BSK-3582 8-10   81
    Composer: Christopher Cross, Nicolette Larson, others. **Cast:** Liza Minnelli, Christopher Cross, Nicolette Larson, Ambrosia, Stephen Bishop.

ARTHUR 2: ON THE ROCKS
Soundtrack (1988) • A&M (S) SP-3916 8-10   88

ARTHUR GODFREY
Studio Cast (1953) • Columbia (M) CL-521 25-35   53
  Full title: *Arthur Godfrey's TV Calendar Show.*
    Composer: Joan Edwards, Lyn Duddy. **Conductor:** Archie Bleyer. **Cast:** Arthur Godfrey, Julius LaRosa, Lu Ann Simms, Marion Marlowe, Frank Parker, Jeanette Davis, Mariners, Haleloke Kahauolopua, Chordettes.

Studio Cast • Columbia (M) CL 576 15-25   50s
  Full title: *TV Sweethearts.*
  Cast: Marion Marlowe, Frank Parker.
Studio Cast • Columbia (M) CL 6113 15-25
  Full title: *Arthur Godfrey and His Friends.*
TV Soundtrack (1954) • Columbia (M) CL-540 25-35   54
  Full title: *Christmas with Arthur Godfrey.*
  Composer: Various. **Conductor:** Archie Bleyer. **Cast:** Arthur Godfrey, Jeanette Davis,
  Mariners, Julius LaRosa, McGuire Sisters, Frank Parker, Marion Marlowe, Haleloke
  Kahauolopua, Lu Ann Simms.

ARTHUR SCHWARTZ REVISITED
Studiotrack • Crewe (S) CR 1350 8-12
  Composer: Arthur Schwartz.

ARTIE SHAW PLAYS COLE PORTER
Studiotrack • MGM (M) E-517 10-20   50s
  Film and stage music from *Gay Divorcee, Leave It to Me, Born to Dance, New Yorker,*
  Wake Up and Dream, Rosalie and *Fifty Million Frenchmen.*
  Cast: Artie Shaw and His Orchestra, Mel Torme and His Mel-Tones, Teddy Walters, Kitty
  Kallen.

ARTISTS AND MODELS
Studiotrack (1955) • Capitol (EP) EAP 1-702 50-75   55
  Composer: Jack Brooks, Harry Warren. **Conductor:** Dick Stabile. **Cast:** Dean Martin.

AS I HEAR IT
Studiotrack (1959) • Warner Bros. (M) B-1247 20-30   59
Studiotrack (1959) • Warner Bros. (S) BS-1247 25-35   59
  Music from such William Holden movies as *Sabrina, Stalag 17, The Moon Is Blue, Sunset*
  Boulevard, The Fleet's In, The Key, Love Is a Many-Splendored Thing, Picnic and *Bridge*
  on the River Kwai.
  Composer: Various. **Conductor:** Matty Malneck.

AS THE GIRLS GO: see ARMS AND THE GIRL

ASPECTS OF LOVE
Original London Cast (1989) • Polydor (S) 422 841 126-1 10-12   89
Original London Cast (1989) • Really Use (S) 126-1 5-10
  Two discs in gatefold cover. Custom inner sleeves. Includes 24-page lyrics booklet.
  Composer: Andrew Lloyd Webber (music), Don Black and Charles Hart (lyrics). **Conductor:**
  Michael Reed. **Cast:** Ann Crumb, Michael Ball, Kevin Colson, Kathleen Rowe McAllen, Paul
  Bentley, Diana Morrison, Sally Smith, Laurel Ford, David Greer, David Oakley, Patrick Clancy.

ASSAULT OF THE KILLER BIMBOS
Soundtrack (1988) • Rhino (S) R1-70311 8-10   88
  Cast: Knight and Day, Fierce, Linda Strick, Attila the Hun, Billion Dollar Babies, Lois Blaisch,
  Andy Landis and Rockslide, Third Language, Mavis Vegas Davis, Idolls.

ASTAIRE TIME
TV Soundtrack (1960) • Chrysler (M) M80P-1003 65-85   60
  Presented by Chrysler Corporation for NBC-TV on September 28, 1960. Identification
  number shown since no selection number is used.
  Composer: Various. **Conductor:** David Rose. **Cast:** Fred Astaire, Barrie Chase, David Rose
  and His Orchestra, Count Basie Band.

AT HOME ABROAD
Original Cast (1935) • Smithsonian (M) RO-24 10-20   81
  Gatefold cover. Archival album, featuring members of the original New York production.
  Composer: Arthur Schwartz, Howard Deitz. **Conductor:** Russell Wooding, Tommy Dorsey.
  Cast: Beatrice Lillie, Ethel Waters, Eleanor Powell, Reginald Gardner (all from the original cast),
  Karen Morrow, Nancy Dussault, Clifford David.
  Also see SET TO MUSIC

AT HOME WITH ETHEL WATERS
Original Cast (1951) • Monmouth Evergreen (SE) MES-6812............ 15-20
  Cast: Ethel Waters, Reginald Bean (piano).

AT HOME WITH THE MUNSTERS
TV Soundtrack (1964) • Golden Records (M) LP-139 60-85   64
  Composer: Jack Marshall, Bob Mosher. Cast: Fred Gwynne, Yvonne De Carlo, Al Lewis, Pat
  Priest, Butch Patrick.
  Also see MUNSTERS

AT LONG LAST LOVE
Soundtrack (1975) • RCA Victor (S) ABL2-0967 15-18   75
  Two discs in gatefold cover. There have been several versions of this film in circulation.
  Songs and scenes were dropped from some prints and left in others. This album contains
  only the songs used in the initial release print.
  Composer: Cole Porter. Conductor: Artie Butler. Cast: Burt Reynolds, Cybill Shepherd,
  Madeline Kahn, Duilio Del Prete, Eileen Brennan, John Hillerman, Mildred Natwick.

AT THE DROP OF A HAT
Original London Cast (1959) • Angel (M) 65042..................................... 8-10   59
Original London Cast (1959) • Angel (M) 35797..................................... 8-10   59
Original London Cast (1959) • Angel (S) S-35797................................... 10-12   59
  Composer: Michael Flanders, Donald Swann. Cast: Michael Flanders, Donald Swann (piano).

AT THE DROP OF ANOTHER HAT
Original Cast (1966) • Angel (M) 36388 8-10   66
Original Cast (1966) • Angel (S) S-36388 10-12   66
  Composer: Michael Flanders, Donald Swann. Cast: Michael Flanders, Donald Swann (piano).

AT THE MOVIES WITH THE RAY CHARLES SINGERS
Studiotrack • Command/ABC (S) RS 923 SD... 5-8
  Music from *Doctor Dolittle, The Gentle Rain, Thoroughly Modern Millie, Run for Your Wife,
  Mon Amour, Rosie, The Happiest Millionaire, Gone with the Wind, Born Free, Camelot* and
  A Countess from Hong Kong.
  Cast: Ray Charles Singers.

ATHENA
Soundtrack (1954) • Mercury (EP) EP-2-3284 35-55   54
  Two discs.
Soundtrack (1954) • Mercury (M) MG-25202 100-125   54
  10-inch LP.
  Composer: Ralph Blane, Hugh Martin. Conductor: George Stoll. Cast: Jane Powell, Debbie
  Reynolds, Vic Damone, MGM Studio Orchestra.
Soundtrack (1954) • Motion Picture Tracks (M) MPT-2 15-20
  Contains additional material not found on the Mercury issue, plus "Faster Than Sound," a
  deleted number sung by Vic Damone.
  Composer: Ralph Blane, Hugh Martin. Conductor: George Stoll. Cast: Jane Powell, Debbie
  Reynolds, Vic Damone, Louis Calhern, Virginia Gibson, MGM Studio Orchestra.

ATHENIAN TOUCH
Original Cast (1964) • Broadway East (M) OCM-101 130-140   64
Original Cast (1964) • Broadway East (S) OCS-101 150-160   64
  Composer: Willard Straight, David Eddy. Conductor: Glen Clugston. Cast: Marion Marlowe,
  Butterfly McQueen, Robert Cosden, Alice Cannon, Ken Cantril, Ron Hansen, James Harder,
  Mark Holliday, Richard Ianni, Janet McCall, Peter Sands.

ATHENS, GA. – INSIDE/OUT
Soundtrack (1987) • I.R.S. (S) RS-6185.. 8-10   87
  Cast: Squalls, Flat Duo Jets, R.E.M., Love Tractor, Kilkenny Cats, Time Toy, Pylon, Bar-B-Q
  Killers, Dreams So Real.

ATLANTIC CITY
Soundtrack (1982) • DRG (S) DRG-6104... 8-10   81
   Composer: Michel Legrand. Conductor: Michel Legrand.

ATLANTIS IN HI-FI (FORBIDDEN ISLAND)
Soundtrack (1959) • Carlton (M) 106...................................... 60-70   59
   Composer: Alexander Laszlo. Conductor: Carl Wolfgang. Cast: Bavarian State Symphony Orchestra.

AU REVOIR LES ENFANTS (GOODBYE, CHILDREN)
Soundtrack (1988) • Varese Sarabande (S) 704 430 10-12   88
   Composer: Franz Schubert. Cast: Jean-François Heisser.

AUNTIE MAME
Soundtrack (1958) • Warner Bros. (M) W-1242 20-25   58
Soundtrack (1958) • Warner Bros. (S) WS-1242 20-40   58
  Also has music from *Green Dolphin Street, Invitation* and *The Glass Slipper*.
   Composer: Bronislau Kaper. Conductor: Ray Heindorf.

AVALANCHE
Soundtrack (1978) • Delos (S) DLS-25452 8-12   78
   Composer: William Kraft. Conductor: William Kraft. Cast: National Philharmonic Orchestra.

AVENGERS
TV Soundtrack (1966) • HBR (M) 8506... 35-45   66
TV Soundtrack (1966) • HBR (S) 9506.. 60-65   66
   Conductor: Laurie Johnson. Cast: Laurie Johnson Orchestra.
Studiotrack (1982) • Varese Sarabande (S) ASV-95003 10-15   82
  Also has music from *The New Avengers* and *The Professionals*.
   Composer: Laurie Johnson. Conductor: Laurie Johnson. Cast: Laurie Johnson Orchestra.

AVENGERS #4
Studio Cast (1966) • Golden (S) SLP-187... 75-100   66
  Includes comic book. Performances follow comic script with sound effects and music.

AVIATOR
Soundtrack (1985) • Varese Sarabande (S) STV 81240 12-18   85
   Composer: Dominic Frontiere. Conductor: Dominic Frontiere.

AWAKENING
Soundtrack (1980) • Entr'acte (S) ERS-6520-ST 8-10   80
   Composer: Claude Bolling. Conductor: Claude Bolling.

AWARD WINNING ORIGINAL MOTION PICTURE SOUND TRACKS AND THEMES
Studiotrack (1966) • Mainstream (M) 56076... 8-12   66
Studiotrack (1966) • Mainstream (S) S-6076.. 8-12   66
   Conductor: Johnny Mandel, Maurice Jarre, Jerry Goldsmith. Cast: Bill Brown Singers.

AWA-A-Y WE GO
TV Soundtrack (1954) • Capitol (M) EBF-511 25-35   54
  Boxed, two-disc set.
TV Soundtrack (1954) • Capitol (M) H-511.. 75-125   54
  10-inch LP. Jackie Gleason performs as the following characters, popularized on his television show: Ralph Kramden, Joe the Bartender, Reggie Van Gleason III, The Poor Soul, The Loud Mouth, and Fenwick Babbit.
   Cast: Jackie Gleason.

B.S. I LOVE YOU
Soundtrack (1971) • Mercury (S) SRM1-610 12-15   71
  Composer: Mark Shekter, Jim Dale. **Conductor:** Jim Dale. **Cast:** Stouffville Grit.

BAAL
Soundtrack (1982) • RCA Victor (M) CPL1-4346 8-12   82
  Cast: David Bowie, others.

BABES IN ARMS
Studio Cast (1951) • Columbia (EP) A-1024 10-12   52
Studio Cast (1951) • Columbia (M) ML-4488......................... 12-18   52
  10-inch LP.
Studio Cast (1951) • Columbia (M) CL-823............................ 12-18   56
Studio Cast (1951) • Columbia (M) OL-7070........................... 10-12   65
Studio Cast (1951) • Columbia (SE) OS-2570......................... 10-12   65
Studio Cast (1951) • Columbia Special Products (SE) AOS-2570.......... 8-10   Re
  Composer: Richard Rodgers, Lorenz Hart. **Conductor:** Lehman Engel. **Cast:** Mary Martin, Mardi Bayne, Jack Cassidy.
Studio Cast (1953) • RCA Victor (EP) EPA-478 15-20   53
Studio Cast (1953) • RCA Victor (M) LPM-3152....................... 20-45   53
  10-inch LP. Also has music from *Jumbo*.
  Conductor: Jay Blackton. **Cast:** Lisa Kirk, William Tabbert, Sheila Bond. JUMBO: **Conductor:** Lehman Engel. **Cast:** Lisa Kirk, Jack Cassidy, Jordan Bentley.
Soundtrack (1939) • Curtain Calls (M) CC-100 6/7..................... 10-15
  Two discs in gatefold cover. Also has music from *Babes on Broadway*.
  Composer: Richard Rodgers, Lorenz Hart, Roger Edens, Arthur Freed, Nacio Herb Brown.
  Cast: Judy Garland, Mickey Rooney, Douglas McPhail, Betty Jaynes, Charles Winninger, June Preisser.
  Also see PANAMA HATTIE

BABES IN TOYLAND
Original Cast • Bit (S) 91550 12-18   79
  Composer: Victor Herbert, Glen MacDonough. **Conductor:** Bob Christiansen.
Studio Cast (1950) • Decca (EP) 9-165............................... 10-20   50
  Boxed, three-disc set.
Studio Cast (1950) • Decca (M) DLP-7004............................ 15-25   50
  10-inch LP. Prefix on disc is "DL."
Studio Cast (1950) • Decca (M) DL-8458 20-25   57
  One side of this LP contains music from *The Red Mill*
  Composer: Victor Herbert, Glen MacDonough. **Conductor:** Alexander Smallens. **Cast:** Kenny Baker, Karen Kemple.
Soundtrack (1961) • Buena Vista (M) BT-1/BT-2 50-100   61
  Commercial spots for film on one side, other has songs by Annette Funicello, Tommy Sands and Ray Bolger. Picture label has drawing of Annette and Sands. Not issued with cover. Made for radio station use only.
Soundtrack (1961) • Buena Vista (M) BV-4022...................... 20-25   61
Soundtrack (1961) • Buena Vista (S) STER-4022................... 20-30   61
  Composer: Victor Herbert, George Bruns, Mel Leven. **Conductor:** Tutti Camarata. **Cast:** Ray Bolger, Henry Calvin, Tommy Sands, Annette Funicello, Ed Wynn, Mary McCarty, Kevin Corcoran, Ann Jillian.

Soundtrack (1934) • Mark 56 (M) 577 8-12   78
   Black label.
Soundtrack (1934) • Mark 56 (M) 577 ..../................................... 20-50   78
   Picture disc.
     Composer: Victor Herbert, Glen MacDonough. **Cast:** Laurel & Hardy, Charlotte Henry, Felix
     Knight (with dialogue).
Studiotrack (1961) • Disneyland (M) 1219.. 8-10   62
Studiotrack (1961) • Disneyland (M) ST-3913...................................... 8-12   62
   Music tracks and chorus numbers identical to the Buena Vista issues, but with unidentified
   vocalists and the stars' voices added.
     Composer: Victor Herbert, George Bruns.

BABES ON BROADWAY: see BABES IN ARMS

BABY

Original Cast • Polydor (S) 422-821593-1 8-10   84
     Composer: David Shire, Richard Maltby. **Conductor:** B. Howard. **Cast:** Liz Callaway, James
     Longdon, Catherine Cox, Beth Fowler, Todd Graff, Martin Vidnovic, Kim Criswell, Philip
     Hoffman, Dennis Warning.

BABY DOLL

Soundtrack (1956) • Columbia (M) CL-958 40-60   57
   Back cover has ads for other Columbia albums.
Soundtrack (1956) • Columbia (M) CL-958 30-50   57
   Back cover does not have ads.
     Composer: Kenyon Hopkins. **Conductor:** Ray Heindorf.
Studiotrack • Columbia (EP) B-2114 30-45   50s
     Composer: Kenyon Hopkins. **Conductor:** Percy Faith. **Cast:** Percy Faith and His Orchestra.

BABY FACE NELSON

Soundtrack (1957) • Jubilee (M) JLP-2021... 90-100   57
     Composer: Van Alexander. **Conductor:** Van Alexander.

BABY MAKER

Soundtrack (1972) • Ode '70 (S) 77002 10-12   72
     Composer: Fred Karlin. **Cast:** Ole Blue.

BABY, THE RAIN MUST FALL

Soundtrack (1965) • Ava (M) A-53 15-30   65
Soundtrack (1965) • Ava (S) AS-53 20-40   65
     Conductor: Elmer Bernstein.
Soundtrack (1965) • Mainstream (M) 56056.. 12-25   65
Soundtrack (1965) • Mainstream (S) S-6056.. 15-30   65
   Though issued the same year as the Ava releases, the Mainstream LPs are reissues.
     Composer: Elmer Bernstein. **Conductor:** Elmer Bernstein.

BACHELOR PARTY

Soundtrack (1984) • I.R.S. (S) 70047.. 8-10   84
     Cast: Fleshtones, Oingo Boingo, R.E.M., Jools Holland, Alarm.

BACK STREET

Soundtrack (1961) • Decca (M) DL-9097 20-30   61
Soundtrack (1961) • Decca (S) DL-79097.. 45-65   61
     Composer: Frank Skinner. **Conductor:** Joseph Gershenson. **Cast:** John Gavin, Susan
     Hayward.

BACK TO SCHOOL

Soundtrack (1986) • MCA (S) 6175.. 8-10   86
     Cast: Jude Cole, Bobby Caldwell, Tyson and Schwartz, Michael Bolton, Philip Ingram, Rodney
     Dangerfield, Aretha Franklin.
     Also see PEE-WEE'S BIG ADVENTURE

BACK TO THE BEACH
Soundtrack (1987) • Columbia (S) JS-40892 10-12   87
> **Cast:** Annette Funicello, Frankie Avalon, Eddie Money, Stevie Ray Vaughan, Dick Dale, Aimee Mann, Private Domain, Pee-Wee Herman, Marti Jones, Fishbone, Herbie Hancock, Dweezil Zappa, Terry Bozzio, Dave Edmunds.
> Also see PEE-WEE'S BIG ADVENTURE

BACK TO THE FUTURE
Soundtrack (1985) • MCA (S) 6144.. 8-10   85
> **Composer:** Alan Silvestri, others. **Cast:** Huey Lewis and the News, Outatime Orchestra, Eric Clapton, Lindsay Buckingham, Etta James, Marty McFly (Michael J. Fox) and the Starlighters.

BACK TO THE FUTURE, PART 2
Soundtrack (1989) • MCA (S) 6361 8-10   89
> **Composer:** Alan Silvestri. **Conductor:** Alan Silvestri.
Soundtrack (1989) • Chameleon (S) D1-74792.................................... 8-10   Re

BACKGROUND TO VIOLENCE: see LUST FOR LIFE

BACKGROUNDS FOR BRANDO
Studiotrack (1958) • Dot (M) DLP-3107.. 20-25   58
Studiotrack (1958) • Dot (S) DLP-25107 30-35   58
> Elmer Bernstein arrangements of music from films starring Marlon Brando, including *Sayonara, On the Waterfront, Viva Zapata, The Men, Guys and Dolls, A Streetcar Named Desire, The Teahouse of the August Moon, Desiree, Julius Caesar* and *The Wild One*.
> **Composer:** Various. **Conductor:** Elmer Bernstein.

BACKSTAGE AT "TWO BY TWO": see TWO BY TWO

BAD AND THE BEAUTIFUL: see OF HUMAN BONDAGE

BAD BOYS
Soundtrack (1983) • Capitol (S) ST-12272... 8-10   83
> **Cast:** Ebonee Webb, Melba Moore, T-Connection, others.

BAD COMPANY
Soundtrack (1972) • Private Label (S) STK-1069................................. 50-60   76
> One side has music from *A Texas Romance, 1909*.
> **Composer:** Harvey Schmidt. **Cast:** Harvey Schmidt (piano).

BAD DREAMS
Soundtrack (1988) • Varese Sarabande (S) 704-560 10-15   88
> **Composer:** Jay Ferguson.

BAD GUYS
Soundtrack (1986) • Casablanca (S) 826 610-1 8-10   86
> **Composer:** William Goldstein, others. **Cast:** Spyder Turner, Precious Metal, Kane Gang, Paul Chiten, Redskins, Hand Tools, William Goldstein, Robert John, Stars on 45, Jeff Tyzik.

BAD INFLUENCE
Soundtrack (1990) • Mango (S) MLPS-9860 5-10   90
> **Composer:** Trevor Jones (original music), others. **Conductor:** Trevor Jones, others. **Cast:** Toots, Nana Vasconcelos and the Bushdancers, Lloyd Cole, Etta James, Chaba Fadela, Thomas Mapfump, Skinny Puppy, Les Negresses Vertes, Gavin Friday and the Man, Trevor Jones.

BAD SEED
Soundtrack (1956) • RCA Victor (EP) EPA-4010 90-100   56
Soundtrack (1956) • RCA Victor (M) LPM-1395 200-250   56
> **Composer:** Alex North. **Conductor:** Ray Heindorf.

BAGDAD CAFE
Soundtrack (1988) • Great Jones (S) GJ 6002..................................... 5-10   88
> **Composer:** Bob Telson.

BAJOUR

Original Cast (1964) • Columbia (M) KOL-6300 10-12   64
Original Cast (1964) • Columbia (S) KOS-2700 12-18   64
    Composer: Walter Marks. **Conductor:** Lehman Engel. **Cast:** Chita Rivera, Nancy Dussault, Herschel Bernardi, Robert Burr, Herbert Edelman, Mae Questel, Gus Trikonis.

BAKER STREET

Original Cast (1965) • MGM (M) E-7000 8-10   65
Original Cast (1965) • MGM (S) SE-7000.. 10-15   65
    Composer: Marian Grudeff, Raymond Jessel. **Conductor:** Hal Hastings. **Cast:** Fritz Weaver, Inga Swenson, Martin Gabel, Teddy Green, Patrick Horgen, Daniel Keyes, Peter Sallis, Virginia Vestoff, Martin Wolfson.
Studio Cast • MGM (M) E-4293.. 10-12   65
Studio Cast • MGM (S) SE-4293.. 10-12   65
    Full title: *Hit Songs from Baker Street…and Other Broadway Musicals.* One side has original cast selections from *She Loves Me, Carnival* and *Whoop-Up.* Selections from *Baker Street* are studio tracks.
    Composer: Marian Grudeff, Raymond Jessel, Jerry Bock, Sheldon Harnick, Bob Merrill, others. **Cast:** Richard Burton, Felicia Sanders, Richard Hayman, Fran Jeffries, Kai Winding, Danny Davis Orchestra, Jack Cassidy, Kaye Ballard, Henry Lascoe, Barbara Cook, Susan Johnson.

BAKER'S WIFE

Original Cast (1976) • Take Home Tunes (S) THT-772........................ 8-10   76
Original Cast (1976) • Take Home Tunes (S) THT-773........................ 15-20   76
    Seven-inch disc. Stephen Schwartz is heard on piano on this (#773) disc only. Also has five tracks not heard on #772.
Original London Cast (1990) • That's Entertainment (S) TER-1175 20-25   90
    Two discs. UK release.
    Composer: Stephen Schwartz, Carol Schwartz. **Cast:** Paul Sorvino, Portia Nelson, Darlene Conley, Carol Schwartz, Stephen Schwartz (piano).

BAL, LE: see LE BAL

BALCONY

Original Cast (1965) • Caedmon (M) TRS-316................................... 10-12   65
    Three discs.

BALLAD FOR BIMSHIRE

Original Cast (1963) • London (M) AM-48002 25-35   63
Original Cast (1963) • London (S) AMS-78002 45-65   63
    Composer: Irving Burgie. **Conductor:** Sammy Benskin. **Cast:** Frederick O'Neal, Christine Spencer, Jimmy Randolph, Ossie Davis, Robert Dolphin, Eugene Edwards, Clebert Ford, Alyce Webb.

BALLAD OF BABY DOE

Original Cast (1958) • MGM (S) 3GC-1... 100-125   58
    Boxed, three-disc set.
Original Cast (1958) • Heliodor (S) 250-35-3...................................... 25-35   Re
    Composer: Douglas Moore, John Latouche. **Conductor:** Emerson Buckley. **Cast:** New York City Opera Company, Beverly Sills, Walter Cassell, Frances Bible, New York City Opera Orchestra and Chorus, Jack DeLon, Joshua Heicht, Beatrice Krebs, Grant Williams.

BALLAD OF FANNY HILL

Original Cast (1963) • Fax (S) FALP 5201 15-20   63
    "An original Musical Monodrama."
    Cast: Julie Hamilton.

BALLET MUSIC FROM MGM MUSICALS
Soundtrack (1955) MGM (M) E-3148 10-12   55
 Ballet pieces from *An American in Paris, Words and Music, The Pirate, The Band Wagon,*
 Lili and *Singin' in the Rain.*
  Composer: Cole Porter, George Gershwin, Richard Rodgers, Arthur Schwartz, Arthur Freed,
  Bronislau Caper. **Conductor:** Johnny Green, Lennie Hayton, Adolph Deutsch, Hans Sommer.
  Cast: MGM Studio Orchestra.

BALLET MUSIC FROM WEST SIDE STORY: see WEST SIDE STORY

BALLET ON BROADWAY
Studiotrack • Painted Smiles (S) PS-1364 8-12

BALLROOM
Original Cast (1978) • Columbia (S) JS-35762 12-18   78
  Composer: Billy Goldenberg, Marilyn and Alan Bergman. **Conductor:** Dan Jennings. **Cast:**
  Dorothy Loudon, Vincent Gardenia, Bernie Knee, Lynn Roberts.

BALLYHOO
Original Cast (1958) • Audiosonic (M) No Number Used 20-25   58
 From performances at Adams Memorial Theatre, by Williams College student drama
 organization.
  Composer: Michael Small, Howell Price.

BALTIMORE AND OHIO MARCHING BAND PLAYS MUSIC FROM THE
COMICS
Studiotrack (1967) • Jubilee (S) JGS-8014 25-35   67
 Has cartoon cover with Batman, Popeye, others.

BAMBI
Studio Cast (1954) • RCA Victor (M) LBY-1012 15-25   54
Studio Cast (1954) • Camden (M) CAL-1012 10-15   62
  Composer: Frank Churchill, Ed Plumb, Larry Morey. **Cast:** Shirley Temple.
Soundtrack (1942) • Disneyland (EP) DEP-4010 40-60   57
Studiotrack (1957) • Disneyland (M) WDL-4009 50-75   57
 One side has music from *Cinderella.*
  Conductor: Tutti Camarata. **Cast:** Camarata and His Orchestra.
Studiotrack • Disneyland (S) 3108 10-15   82
 Picture Disc. Full title: *Story and Songs of Bambi.*

BANANA SPLITS
TV Soundtrack (1969) • HBR (EP) 34578 25-35   69
TV Soundtrack (1969) • HBR (EP) 34579 25-35   69
 Special products issues for Kellogg's, sponsor of the NBC-TV series.
TV Soundtrack (1969) • Decca (S) DL-75075 25-30   69
 Full title: *(We're the) Banana Splits.*
  Composer: Various. **Conductor:** Jack Eskew. **Cast:** Banana Splits.

BAND OF ANGELS
Soundtrack (1957) • RCA Victor (M) LPM-1557 65-85   57
Soundtrack (1957) • Entr'acte (M) ERM-6003 10-15   Re
  Composer: Max Steiner. **Conductor:** Max Steiner.

BAND OF THE HAND
Soundtrack (1986) • MCA (S) 61675 8-12   86
  Cast: Bob Dylan with the Heartbreakers, Shriekback, Reds, Andy Summers, Tiger Tiger,
  Michael Rubini.

BAND WAGON
Original Cast (1931) • "X" (M) LVA-1001 50-60   55
Original Cast (1931) • RCA Victor (M) LSA-3082 20-25   Re

Original Cast (1931) · RCA Victor (M) RD-7756 35-45   66
  UK release.
Original Cast (1931) · RCA Victor (M) 751-003 12-18   66
  French release. Very few of the 1931 records – an early experiment in marketing 33 1/3
  rpms to the public – were manufactured. Though specifics are apparently undocumented,
  their value is estimated at $200 to $250.
    Composer: Arthur Schwartz, Howard Dietz. **Conductor:** Leo Reisman. **Cast:** Fred Astaire,
    Adele Astaire, Arthur Schwartz.
Original Cast (1931) • Smithsonian (M) R-021 12-18   79
  Gatefold cover. Archival reconstruction of material from the original production.
    Composer: Arthur Schwartz, Howard Dietz. **Conductor:** Leo Reisman. **Cast:** Fred Astaire,
    Adele Astaire, Arthur Schwartz.
Studio Cast (1951) • Columbia (EP) A-1734 8-12   51
  Full title: *Hits from The Band Wagon.*
Studio Cast (1951) • Columbia (M) ML-2160 12-15   51
  10-inch LP.
    Composer: Arthur Schwartz, Howard Dietz. **Conductor:** Lehman Engel. **Cast:** Mary Martin.
Studio Cast (1953) • RCA Victor (EP) EPA-484 15-20   53
Studio Cast (1953) • RCA Victor (M) LPM-3155 30-40   53
  10-inch LP. One side has music from *The Little Shows.*
    Composer: Arthur Schwartz, Howard Dietz. **Conductor:** Jay Blackton. **Cast:** Harold Lang,
    George Britton, Edith Adams.
Studio Cast • Monmouth Evergreen (SE) MRS-6605 15-20
    Composer: Arthur Schwartz, Howard Dietz. **Conductor:** Paul Trueblood. **Cast:** Nancy Dussault,
    Clifford David, Karen Morrow.
Studio Cast (1953) • Clef (EP) CL-183 10-15   53
    Cast: Fred Astaire.
Soundtrack (1953) • MGM (EP) X-207 10-15   53
Soundtrack (1953) • MGM (M) E-3051 20-25   53
  Yellow label.
Soundtrack (1953) • MGM (M) E-3051 15-18   53
  Black label.
Soundtrack (1953) • MGM (EP) X-1013 15-25   53
  Contains only *The Girl Hunt Ballet.*
Soundtrack (1953) • MCA (M) 25015 5-8   86
    Composer: Arthur Schwartz, Howard Dietz. **Conductor:** Adolph Deutsch. **Cast:** Fred Astaire,
    Nanette Fabray, Jack Buchanan, India Adams (performs vocals for Cyd Charisse in the film),
    MGM Studio Orchestra.
Studiotrack (1951) • Decca (EP) ED-2094 8-15   51
Studiotrack (1951) • Decca (M) DL-5317 15-18   51
  10-inch LP.
    Conductor: Tommy Dorsey. **Cast:** Tommy Dorsey Orchestra.
    Also see ANYTHING GOES
    Also see THOSE GLORIOUS MGM MUSICALS

BANDIT OF SHERWOOD FOREST
Soundtrack • AEI (S) AEI-3104 10-15   80
  Also has music from *A Double Life, Force of Evil* and *Time Out of Mind.*

BANDOLERO!
Soundtrack (1968) • Project 3 (S) PR-5026-SD 12-15   68
Soundtrack (1968) • Cinema Show (S) TCS-1001-1 5-10   Re
    Composer: Jerry Goldsmith. **Conductor:** Lionel Newman.

BANG THE DRUM SLOWLY
Soundtrack (1973) • Paramount (S) PAS-1014 8-10   73
    Composer: Stephen Lawrence. **Conductor:** Stephen Lawrence.

BANJOMAN

Soundtrack (1977) • Sire (S) SA-7527 12-18   77
  Composer: Bob Dylan, Earl Scruggs, Jimmy Driftwood, others. Cast: Byrds, Joan Baez, Nitty
  Gritty Dirt Band, Earl Scruggs Revue, Doc and Merle Watson, Jack Elliot.

BARABBAS

Soundtrack (1962) • Colpix (M) CP-510 25-35   62
Soundtrack (1962) • Colpix (S) SCP-510 30-70   62
  Composer: Mario Nascimbene. Conductor: Mario Nascimbene.
Soundtrack (1962) • Citadel (S) CT 7034 8-10   81
  Composer: Mario Nascimbene, Ennio Morricone. Conductor: Mario Nascimbene. Cast: Chuck
  Bruce (narration).

BARBARA COOK AT CARNEGIE HALL

Original Cast (1975) • Columbia (S) M-33438 8-10   75
  Conductor: Wally Harper. Cast: Barbara Cook.

BARBARELLA

Soundtrack (1968) • Dyno Voice (M) DY-1908 25-30   68
Soundtrack (1968) • Dyno Voice (S) DY-31908 40-50   68
  Composer: Charles Fox, Bob Crewe. Conductor: Bob Crewe. Cast: Glitter House, Bob Crewe.

BARBARIAN AND THE GEISHA

Soundtrack (1958) • 20th Century-Fox (M) FOX-3004 175-200   58
  Composer: Hugo Friedhofer. Conductor: Kurt Graunke.

BARBRA STREISAND ... AND OTHER MUSICAL INSTRUMENTS

TV Soundtrack (1973) • Columbia (S) KC 32685 8-10   73
  Composer: Various. Conductor: Peter Matz. Cast: Barbra Streisand.

BARE KNUCKLES

Soundtrack (1977) • Gucci (S) G303 45-55   77

BAREFOOT ADVENTURE

Soundtrack (1961) • Pacific Jazz (M) PJ-35 20-30   61
Soundtrack (1961) • Pacific Jazz (S) PJS-35 40-55   61
  Composer: Bud Shank. Conductor: Bud Shank. Cast: Bob Cooper, Shelly Manne, Carmell
  Jones.

BAREFOOT IN THE PARK

Soundtrack (1967) • Dot (M) DLP-3803 15-18   67
Soundtrack (1967) • Dot (S) DLP-25803 20-25   67
  Composer: Neal Hefti. Conductor: Neal Hefti.

BARKLEYS OF BROADWAY

Soundtrack (1949) • MGM L-8 35-45   49
  Two 78 rpms. Packaged in an LP cover instead of the standard 78 rpm album binder.
Soundtrack (1949) • MGM (M) E-503 60-65   49
  10-inch record.
    Composer: Harry Warren, George and Ira Gershwin. Conductor: Lennie Hayton. Cast: Fred
    Astaire, Ginger Rogers.
    Also see THOSE GLORIOUS MGM MUSICALS

BARNUM

Original Cast (1980) • Columbia (S) JS-36576 8-10   80
  Composer: Cy Coleman, Michael Stewart. Conductor: Peter Howard. Cast: Jim Dale, Glenn
  Close, Leonard John Crofoot, Terri White, Marianne Tatum, William C. Witter, Terrence Mann.
Original London Cast (1981) • Chrysalis (S) 37627 10-12   81
  UK release.
    Composer: Cy Coleman, Michael Stewart. Cast: Michael Crawford.
Studiotrack (1980) • Gryphon (S) G 918 8-12   80
  Includes libretto. Full title: Cy Coleman Presents Barnum.
    Cast: Cy Coleman Trio.

Studiotrack (1983) • Bainbridge (S) BT 6247 8-10   83
   Cast: Cy Coleman Trio.

BARRETT PRESENTS THEY'RE THE TOP
Studiotrack (1964) • RCA Victor (M) PRM-165...................................... 10-20   64
   Promotional issue only. We have yet to learn the purpose or contents of this item.

BARRY LYNDON
Soundtrack (1975) • Warner Bros. (S) BS-2903................................. 8-10   75
   Two different cover designs exist; one with a red rose on black and white, the other
   pictures various drawings.
Soundtrack (1975) • Warner Bros. (S) K-56189.................................... 8-10   Re
   Conductor: Leonard Rosenman, Rudolf Baumgartner. **Cast:** National Philharmonic Orchestra,
   Paddy Moloney and Sean Potts, Derek Bell, Festival Strings Lucerne, Munich Bach Orchestra,
   others.

BASHVILLE
Original London Cast (1983) • That's Entertainment (S) TER-1072 8-10   83
   UK release.
   Composer: Denis King, Benny Green.

BASIL RATHBONE READS EDGAR ALLAN POE
Studio Cast • Caedmon (M) TC-1028.. 5-10

BAT MASTERSON
TV Studiotrack (1960) • Sea Horse/Chancellor (M) CSH-7002 50-75   60
   Full title: *The Official Album of NBC's Bat Masterson*.
   Cast: Eddie Bracken (narrator), Michael Avallone & the Night Riders.

BAT-21
Soundtrack (1988) • Varese Sarabande (S) VS-5202 8-15   88
   Composer: Christopher Young.

BATHROOMS ARE COMING
Original Cast • American Standard (S) AMC 2371 20-40   69
   Souvenir from a bathroom fixtures, industrial show.
   Composer: Side Siegel. **Cast:** Sandi Freeman, Steve Strong, Dick Gjonola, David Shelley,
   Suellen Estley, Patricia Smith Stanton, Barbara Lang.

BATMAN (1966)
Studio Cast (1966) • MGM/Leo (M) CH-1027 10-15   66
   Full title: *More Official Adventures of Batman*.
TV Soundtrack (1966) • Mercury (S) Batman 1 50-75   66
TV Soundtrack (1966) • 20th Century-Fox (M) TFM-3180.................... 50-60   66
TV Soundtrack (1966) • 20th Century-Fox (S) TFS-4180.................... 60-100   66
   Music and dialogue from various episodes of the TV series.
   Composer: Nelson Riddle. **Conductor:** Nelson Riddle. **Cast:** Adam West, Burt Ward, Frank
   Gorshin, Burgess Meredith, George Sanders, Anne Baxter, Jack Kruschen (with dialogue).
TV Studiotrack (1966) • RCA Victor (M) LPM-3573.............................. 15-35   66
TV Studiotrack (1966) • RCA Victor (S) LSP-3573.............................. 20-50   66
   Has the *Batman Theme*, plus studio renditions inspired by the series.
   Composer: Neal Hefti. **Conductor:** Neal Hefti. **Cast:** Neal Hefti and His Orchestra.

BATMAN (1989)
Soundtrack (1989) • Warner Bros. (S) 25936-1 8-10   89
   Composer: Prince, John L. Nelson. **Cast:** Prince, John L. Nelson, Sheena Easton.
Soundtrack (1989) • Warner Bros. (S) 1-25977 15-20   89
   Composer: Danny Elfman. **Conductor:** Shirley Walker. **Cast:** Sinfonia of London Orchestra.
Studiotrack (1966) • Design (S) SDLP-249 8-12   66
   Cast: Bat Boys.
Studiotrack (1966) • Panda (M) Pan-3035 8-12   66

BATTERIES NOT INCLUDED
Soundtrack (1987) • MCA (S) 6225.. 8-12   87
  Composer: James Horner. Conductor: James Horner. Cast: James Horner.

BATTLE BEYOND THE STARS
Soundtrack (1980) • Rhino (S) RNSP-300 8-10   80
  Composer: James Horner. Conductor: James Horner.

BATTLE FOR STALINGRAD / FALL OF BERLIN
Soundtrack • Classic Editions (S) CE-3009...................... 250-300
  Composer: Aram Khachaturian, Dimitri Shostakovich.

BATTLE OF ALGIERS
Soundtrack (1967) • United Artists (M) UAL-4171 10-12   67
Soundtrack (1967) • United Artists (S) UAS-5171 12-15   67
Soundtrack (1967) • United Artists (S) UA-LA293-G 8-10   74
  Composer: Ennio Morricone, Gillo Pontecorvo. Conductor: Bruno Nicolai.

BATTLE OF BRITAIN
Soundtrack (1969) • United Artists (S) UAS-5201 18-20   69
Soundtrack (1969) • MCA (S) 25008.. 5-10   86
  Composer: Ron Goodwin, Sir William Walton. Conductor: Ron Goodwin, Malcolm Arnold.

BATTLE OF NERETVA
Soundtrack (1971) • Entr'acte (Q) ERQ-7001-ST................................. 10-12   75
Soundtrack (1971) • Entr'acte (S) ERS-6501 10-12   76
Soundtrack • Southern Cross (S) SCAR-5005 8-10
  Composer: Bernard Herrmann. Conductor: Bernard Herrmann. Cast: London Philharmonic Orchestra.

BATTLE OF THE BULGE
Soundtrack (1965) • Warner Bros. (EP) PRO-223 20-25   65
  Promotional issue only.
Soundtrack (1965) • Warner Bros. (M) W-1617 30-40   65
  White label. Promotional issue only.
Soundtrack (1965) • Warner Bros. (M) W-1617 20-40   65
Soundtrack (1965) • Warner Bros. (S) WS-1617 30-35   65
  Composer: Benjamin Frankel. Conductor: Benjamin Frankel. Cast: New Philharmonia Orchestra of London.

BATTLEFIELD EARTH
Soundtrack (1984) • BPI (S) BPILS-01................................... 8-10   84

BATTLESTAR GALACTICA
Soundtrack (1978) • MCA (S) 3051.. 8-10   78
  Composer: Stu Phillips. Conductor: Stu Phillips.
Soundtrack (1978) • MCA (S) 3078.. 10-15   78
  Complete title: The Saga of Battlestar Galactica. Story with dialogue.
  Cast: Lorne Greene, Richard Hatch, Dirk Benedict, Ray Milland, Lew Ayres, Jane Seymour, Laurette Spang, Terry Carter.

BE MY GUEST
Original Cast (1959) • XCTV (M) 10303.. 150-200   59
  Full title: Lagniappe '59 Presents Be My Guest. From the Cast of New Trier High School in Chicago. Includes Ann-Margret Olson – later to be known as Ann-Margret – singing Heat Wave.
  Cast: Ann-Margret (Olson), others.
  Also see AMONG FRIENDS – WAA-MU SHOW OF 1960

BEACH BLANKET BINGO
Soundtrack (1965) • Capitol (M) T-2323.. 20-25   65
Soundtrack (1965) • Capitol (S) ST-2323.. 40-50   65
    Composer: Jerry Styner, others. **Conductor:** H.B. Barnum. **Cast:** Donna Loren.

BEACH GIRLS
Soundtrack (1982) • Peter Pan (S) TAS 12116..................................... 15-25   82
    Composer: Michael Lloyd, others. **Cast:** Arsenel.

BEACH PARTY
Soundtrack (1963) • Buena Vista (M) BV-3316 45-50   63
Soundtrack (1963) • Buena Vista (S) ST-3316.................................... 90-100   63
Soundtrack (1963) • Rhino (S) RNDF 204 8-12   86
    Cast: Annette Funicello.

BEACHES
Soundtrack (1988) • Atlantic (S) 81933-1... 8-10   88
    Cast: Bette Midler.

BEAR
Soundtrack (1984) • RCA Victor (S) CBL1-5328 8-10   84

BEAR
Soundtrack (1988) • Polydor (S) 841584-1 8-10   88
    Composer: Phillipe Sarde. **Conductor:** Phillipe Sarde. **Cast:** London Symphony Orchestra.

BEAR COUNTRY: see WALT DISNEY'S TRUE LIFE ADVENTURES

BEAST
Soundtrack (1988) • A&M (S) SP-3919 8-10   88
    Composer: Mark Isham.

BEASTMASTER
Soundtrack (1983) • Varese Sarabande (S) STV 81174 15-20   83
    Composer: Lee Holdridge. **Conductor:** Lee Holdridge.

BEAT GIRL
Soundtrack (1961) • Big Beat (M) WIK-31-A.. 20-30   61
    Composer: John Barry. **Cast:** John Barry, Shirley Anne Field, Adam Faith.

BEAT STREET
Soundtrack [Vol. 1] (1984) • Atlantic (S) 80154-1.................................. 8-10   84
Soundtrack [Vol. 2] (1984) • Atlantic (S) 80158-1.................................. 8-10   84
    Cast: Jazz Jay, Juicy, Tina B, Jenny Burton, others.

BEATLEMANIA
Original Cast (1977) • Arista (S) AL-8501 8-10   77
    Two discs. Some copies have large sticker on shrinkwrap with review excerpts.
    Composer: John Lennon, Paul McCartney, George Harrison. **Cast:** Joe Pecorino, Mitch
    Weissman, Leslie Fradkin, Justin McNeill.

BEATRICE LILLIE SINGS: see SET TO MUSIC

BEAU JAMES
Soundtrack (1957) • Imperial (M) 9041 20-30   57
    Composer: Richard Rodgers, Lorenz Hart, George and Ira Gershwin, others. **Conductor:**
    Joseph J. Lilley. **Cast:** Bob Hope, Imogene Lynn (performs vocals lip-synched by Vera Miles in
    the film), Jimmy Durante, Skylarks, Walter Winchell. (With dialogue.)

BEAUTY AND THE BEAST
Original Cast (1974) • Take Home Tunes (S) THT-775.......................... 8-10   74
    One side has music from *Snow White and the Seven Dwarfs*.
    Composer: Michael Valenti, Elsa Rael. **Conductor:** Michael Valenti. **Cast:** Christine Andreas,
    Steve Sterner, Howard Cutler.

TV Soundtrack (1989) • Capitol (S) C1-91583 10-20   89
  Full title: *Beauty and the Beast: of Love & Hope.* Ballet production.
    Composer: Lee Holdridge, Don Davis.

BEAVER VALLEY: see WALT DISNEY'S TRUE LIFE ADVENTURES

BEBO'S GIRL
Soundtrack (1964) • Capitol (M) T-2316.. 12-15   64
Soundtrack (1964) • Capitol (S) ST-2316... 15-18   64
    Composer: Carlo Rustichelli.

BECAUSE THEY'RE YOUNG
Studiotrack (1960) • Jamie (EP) JEP-304 20-30   60
    Composer: Aaron Schroeder, Ernest Gold, Don Costa. **Cast:** Duane Eddy.

BECAUSE YOU'RE MINE
Studiotrack (1952) • RCA Victor (EP) ERA-51 15-20   52
Studiotrack (1952) • RCA Victor (M) LM-7015.................................... 20-30   52
  10-inch LP.
    Conductor: Ray Sinatra, Constantine Callinicos. **Cast:** Mario Lanza, Jeff Alexander Choir.

BECKET
Soundtrack (1964) • Decca (M) DL-9117 15-30   64
Soundtrack (1964) • Decca (S) DL-79117 20-45   64
  Background music from the film.
    Composer: Laurence Rosenthal. **Conductor:** Muir Mathieson.
Soundtrack (1964) • RCA Victor (M) LOC-1091 15-30   64
Soundtrack (1964) • RCA Victor (S) LSO-1091................................. 15-25   64
  Dialogue from the film.
    Composer: Laurence Rosenthal. **Conductor:** Laurence Rosenthal. **Cast:** Richard Burton, Peter
    O'Toole, Sir John Gielgud.

BEDAZZLED
Soundtrack (1967) • London (S) MS-82009 50-75   67
    Composer: Dudley Moore. **Conductor:** Dudley Moore.

BEDKNOBS AND BROOMSTICKS
Soundtrack (1971) • Buena Vista (S) STER-5003................................. 8-10   71
Soundtrack (1971) • Disneyland (S) 1326 5-10   Re
    Composer: Richard M. Sherman, Robert B. Sherman. **Conductor:** Irwin Kostal. **Cast:** Angela
    Lansbury, David Tomlinson.

BEDROOM WINDOW
Soundtrack (1987) • Varese Sarabande (S) STV 81307 10-15   87
    Composer: Michael Shreive, Patrick Gleeson.

BEEHIVE
Original Cast (1988) • Rock Dream (S) RDR 003................................. 10-12   88
  Two discs.
    Conductor: Skip Drevis. **Cast:** Patti Darcy, Alison Fraser, Jasmine Guy, Adriane Lenox, Laura
    Theodore, Cookie Watkins.

BEETLEJUICE
Soundtrack (1988) • Geffen (S) GHS-24202 8-15   88
    Composer: Danny Elfman. **Conductor:** Danny Elfman.

BEG, BORROW OR STEAL
Studio Cast (1960) • Commentary (M) CNT-02.................................... 30-35   60
  Actual title: *Clara.* The album inspired the cast production.
    Composer: Leon Pober, Bud Freeman. **Conductor:** Hal Hidey. **Cast:** Betty Garrett, Jimmie
    Komack, Johnny Standley, Sid Tomack.

BEGATTING OF THE PRESIDENT
Studio Cast (1969) • Mediarts (S) 41-2 10-12   69
Written by Myron Roberts, Lincoln Haynes and Sasha Gilien.
Composer: Myron Roberts. **Conductor:** Luchi De Jesus. **Cast:** Orson Welles.

BEGGAR'S HOLIDAY
Original Cast (1946) • Blue Pear (M) BP 1013 20-30
One side has the Original London Cast of *Bet Your Life* (originally released in the UK on four 78 rpms).
Composer: Duke Ellington, John LaTouche. **Cast:** Alfred Drake, Avon Long, Libby Holman, Mildred Smith. BET YOUR LIFE: **Composer:** Kenneth Leslie-Smith, Charles Zwar, Alan Melville. **Conductor:** Bretton Byrd. **Cast:** Arthur Askey, Sally Ann Howes, Julie Wilson, Brian Reece.

BEGGAR'S OPERA
Original London Cast (1968) • CBS (S) 70046 40-45   68
UK release from the Harold Prince/Richard Pilbrow London production.
Composer: John Gay. **Conductor:** Neil Rhoden. **Cast:** Peter Gilmore, Frances Cuka, Angela Richards, Hy Hazell, Jan Waters, John Cater, James Cossins.
Studio Cast (1957) • RCA Victor (M) LPM-6048................... 40-45   57
Two discs.
Studio Cast (1957) • Everest (SE) 3127-2............................ 35-45
Two discs.
Studio Cast (1957) • Library of Recorded
   Masterpieces (SE) LRM-2523 30-35   62
Studio Cast (1957) • Argo (M) 110/111 10-15
Two discs.
Composer: John Gay. **Conductor:** Max Goberman. **Cast:** William McAlpine, Ronald Lewis, John Frost.
Studio Cast (1957) • Seraphim (SE) S-6023 10-15
Two discs.
Conductor: Sir Malcolm Sargent. **Cast:** Old Victor Company, Pro Arte Orchestra.

BEHIND THE GREAT WALL
Soundtrack (1959) • Monitor (M) MP-525............................ 30-40   59
Soundtrack (1959) • Monitor (S) MFS-525 60-75   59
Chinese documentary with traditional Chinese songs.

BEHOLD A PALE HORSE
Soundtrack (1964) • Colpix (M) CP-519 30-45   64
Soundtrack (1964) • Colpix (S) SCP-519 40-60   64
Composer: Maurice Jarre. **Conductor:** Maurice Jarre.

BEI MIR BISTU SCHOEN
Original Cast (1961) • Decca (M) DL-9115............................ 10-12   61
Original Cast (1961) • Decca (S) DL-79115 12-15   61
Composer: Sholom Secunda, Jacob Jacobs. **Conductor:** Sholom Secunda. **Cast:** Leo Fuchs, Jacob Jacobs, Miriam Kressyn, Charlotte Cooper, Leon Liebgold, Seymour Rexite, Rebecca Richman.
Studio Cast (1961) • Tikva (M) T-72................................. 40-50   61
One side has music from *Go Fight City Hall*.
Composer: Sholom Secunda, Jacob Jacobs. **Cast:** Alan Chester, Doris Colen.

BELAFONTE (THREE FOR TONIGHT): see THREE FOR TONIGHT

BELIEVERS (1968)
Original Cast (1968) • RCA Victor (M) LOC-1151 10-12   68
Original Cast (1968) • RCA Victor (S) LSO-1151 12-18   68
Off-Broadway production.
Composer: Voices, Inc. **Conductor:** Brooks Alexander. **Cast:** Benjamin Carter, Dorothy Dinroe, Jesse DeVore, Ladji Camara, Barry Hemphill, Jo Jackson, Shirley McKie, Don Oliver, Anje Ray, Veronica Redd, Ron Steward, Joseph Walker.

BELIEVERS (1987)
Soundtrack (1987) • Varese Sarabande (S) STV-81328 15-20   87
    Composer: J. Peter Robinson.

BELIZAIRE THE CAJUN
Soundtrack (1987) • Arhoolie (S) 5038 8-10   87
    Cast: Michael Doucet and Beausoleil.

BELL, BOOK AND CANDLE
Soundtrack (1959) • Colpix (M) CP-502 45-60   59
    On the back covers of several 1959 Colpix soundtrack releases, this album is listed as
    being available in stereo (SCP-502). Thus far, none have been verified.
Soundtrack (1959) • Citadel (M) CT-6006 15-20   76
Soundtrack (1959) • Citadel (M) CT-7006 12-15   79
    Remastered.
    Composer: George Duning. **Conductor:** George Duning.

BELL FOR ADANO: see FOUR TELEVISION MUSICALS

BELLE
Original London Cast (1955) • That's Entertainment (M) TER-1048 8-10   80s
    UK release.
    Composer: Monty Norman.

BELLE OF AMHERST
Original Cast (1976) • Credo (S) 5 50-60   76
    Two discs. Non-musical play by William Luce.
    Cast: Julie Harris (dialogue).

BELLE OF NEW YORK
Soundtrack (1952) • MGM (EP) K-108 15-18   52
    Boxed, four-disc set.
Soundtrack (1952) • MGM (M) E-108 30-35   52
    10-inch LP.
Soundtrack (1952) • DRG (M) DS-15004 10-12   78
    Also has eight songs composed by Fred Astaire that are not from the film.
    Composer: Harry Warren, Johnny Mercer. **Conductor:** Adolph Deutsch. **Cast:** Fred Astaire,
    Anita Ellis (performs vocals for Vera-Ellen in the film), MGM Studio Orchestra and Chorus.
    Also see TWO WEEKS WITH LOVE

BELLS ARE RINGING
Original Cast (1956) • Columbia (M) OL-5170 10-20   57
    Front cover, in black and white, pictures Judy Holliday with telephone headset. Does not
    have black stereo band across the top. Label is gray with six Columbia "eye" boxes.
Original Cast (1956) • Columbia (SE) OS-2006 10-20   58
Original Cast (1956) • Columbia Special Products (SE) AOS-2006 5-8   Re
    Front covers (in color) of above two picture Judy Holliday at left, with title and credits on
    right side. Label is gray with six Columbia "eye" boxes.
    Composer: Jule Styne, Betty Comden, Adolph Green. **Conductor:** Milton Rosenstock. **Cast:**
    Judy Holliday, Sydney Chaplin, Jean Stapleton, Eddie Lawrence, Peter Gennaro.
Soundtrack (1960) • Capitol (M) W-1435 15-20   60
Soundtrack (1960) • Capitol (S) SW-1435 18-22   60
Soundtrack (1960) • Stet (S) DS-15011 10-12   Re
    Conductor: Andre Previn. **Cast:** Judy Holliday, Dean Martin, Fred Clark, Eddie Foy Jr., Hal
    Linden.
Studiotrack (1959) • Contemporary (M) 3559 5-10   59
    Cast: Shelley Manne, Irene Kral, Jack Sheldon.
Studiotrack (1960) • Capitol (M) T-1453 8-10   60
Studiotrack (1960) • Capitol (S) ST-1453 8-10   60
    Cast: Guy Lombardo and the Royal Canadians.
Studiotrack (1960) • Richmond (M) B-20089 8-10   60

Studiotrack (1960) • Richmond (S) S-30089 8-10   60
    Cast: London Repertory Co.

Studiotrack (1961) • RCA Victor (M) LPM-2279 8-12   61

Studiotrack (1961) • RCA Victor (S) LSP-2279 8-12   61
    Cast: Melachrino Strings and Orchestra.

BELLS OF ST. MARY'S: see BING'S HOLLYWOOD

BELOVED CHRISTMAS HYMNS AND CAROLS: see ON THE TWELFTH DAY

BELOW THE BELT: see MIXED DOUBLES/BELOW THE BELT

BEN

Soundtrack (1972) • Motown (S) M755L 50-75   72
    First issue pictures a black rat and Michael Jackson on cover.

Soundtrack (1972) • Motown (S) M755L 10-15   72
    No rat shown – pictures only Michael Jackson on cover.
    Cast: Michael Jackson.

BEN BAGLEY'S ALAN JAY LERNER REVISITED

Studio Cast • Battery (M) PS 1337 8-10

BEN BAGLEY'S VINCENT YOUMANS REVISITED

Studio Cast • Battery (M) PS 1352 8-10

BEN BAGLEY'S GEORGE GERSHWIN REVISITED

Studio Cast • MGM (M) E-4375 8-10   66

Studio Cast • MGM (S) SE-4375 8-10   66

BEN BAGLEY'S NOEL COWARD REVISITED

Studio Cast • MGM (S) SE-4430 8-10   66

BEN BAGLEY'S COLE PORTER REVISITED

Studio Cast • Painted Smiles (S) PS 1340 8-10
    Cast: Kaye Ballard, David Allen, Bibi Osterwald, Bobby Short, Norman Paris, Ronny Graham.

BEN BAGLEY'S IRA GERSHWIN REVISITED

Studio Cast • Painted Smiles (S) PS 1353 8-10
    Cast: Blossom Dearie, Mary McCarty, Danny Meehan, Ethel Shutta, Margaret Whiting, Charles Rydell.

BEN BAGLEY'S OSCAR HAMMERSTEIN REVISITED

Studio Cast • Painted Smiles (S) PS 1365 8-10
    Cast: Gloria Swanson, Blossom Dearie, Cab Calloway, Patrice Munsel, Elaine Stritch, E.Y. Harburg, Dorothy Loudon, Alfred Drake, Carl Freiwald.

BEN CASEY / DR. KILDARE

Studiotrack • Strand (M) SL-1065 10-12

Studiotrack • Strand (S) SLS-1065 12-15
    Also has music from other TV shows.

BEN CASEY (AND OTHER THEMES)

Studiotrack (1961) • Carlton (M) LP-143 10-15   61

Studiotrack (1961) • Carlton (S) STLP-143 10-15   61
    Compilation of TV themes, including: *Ben Casey, Naked City, Bonanza, Perry Como Show, Peter Gunn, Bell Telephone Hour, Dr. Kildare, Checkmate, G.E. Theater, Gunsmoke, Alcoa Premiere* and *Wagon Train*.
    Composer: Various **Cast:** Valjean Johns (piano).

BEN FRANKLIN IN PARIS

Original Cast (1964) • Capitol (M) VAS-2191 10-12   64

Original Cast (1964) • Capitol (S) SVAS-2191 12-15   64
    Composer: Mark Sandrich Jr., Sidney Michaels. **Conductor:** Donald Pippin. **Cast:** Robert Preston, Ulla Sallert, Franklin Kiser, Jack Fletcher, Sam Greene, Bob Kaliban, Jerry Schaefer, Susan Watson.

Studiotrack (1964) • Wyncote (M) W-9033.. 5-8   64
Studiotrack (1964) • Wyncote (S) SW-9033... 5-8   64
Also has music from *Golden Boy*.

BEN-HUR
Soundtrack (1959) • MGM (M) 1E1 15-25   60
Soundtrack (1959) • MGM (S) S-1E1 15-30   60
Deluxe boxed edition. Includes hard-bound book.
Soundtrack (1959) • MGM (M) 1E1 10-12   60
Soundtrack (1959) • MGM (S) S-1E1 12-15   60
Gatefold cover. Black label.
Soundtrack (1959) • MGM (M) E-3900....................................... 8-10   61
Soundtrack (1959) • MGM (S) SE-3900 10-12   61
Full title: *More Music from Ben-Hur*.
Soundtrack (1959) • MGM (S) S-1E1 8-10   Re
Gatefold cover. Blue and yellow label.
Composer: Miklos Rozsa. **Conductor:** Miklos Rozsa, Erich Kloss. **Cast:** Rome Symphony
Orchestra.
Studiotrack (1959) • Lion (M) L-70123 10-15   59
Studiotrack (1959) • Lion (S) SL-70123.................................... 15-20   59
Soundtrack (1959) • Metro (M) M-503....................................... 8-10   64
Soundtrack (1959) • Metro (S) MS-503 10-12   64
Full title: *Music from Ben-Hur*.
Composer: Miklos Rozsa. **Conductor:** Miklos Rozsa, Erich Kloss. **Cast:** Frankenland State
Symphony Orchestra.
Studiotrack • London (S) SPC-21166 10-12   76
Conductor: Miklos Rozsa. **Cast:** Miklos Rozsa.

BENEATH THE PLANET OF THE APES
Soundtrack (1970) • Amos (S) AAS-8001 30-35   70
Composer: Leonard Rosenman. **Conductor:** Leonard Rosenman.

BENITO CERENO
Original Cast (1964) • Columbia (M) DOL-319 12-15   64
Original Cast (1964) • Columbia (S) DOS-719 18-20   64
Complete play with background music.
Composer: Yehudi Wyner.

BENJI
Soundtrack (1974) • Epic (S) KSE-33010 10-12   74
Composer: Euel Box. **Conductor:** Euel Box. **Cast:** Charlie Rich.
Studio Cast (1975) • Mulberry Square (S) MSR-3936 10-12   75
Full title: *The Story of Benji*. Includes color booklet.
Composer: Euel Box. **Conductor:** Euel Box. **Cast:** Jesse Davis.

BENNY GOODMAN STORY
Soundtrack [Vol. 1] (1956) • Decca (EP) ED-797 10-30   59
Two discs.
Soundtrack [Vol. 2] (1956) • Decca (EP) ED-798 10-30   59
Two discs.
Soundtrack [Vol. 1] (1956) • Decca (M) DL-8252 15-20   56
Soundtrack [Vol. 1] (1956) • Decca (SE) DL-78252 15-20   59
Soundtrack [Vol. 2] (1956) • Decca (M) DL-8253 15-20   56
Soundtrack [Vol. 2] (1956) • Decca (SE) DL-78253 15-25   59
Soundtrack (1956) • Decca (SE) DXSB7-188 25-30   65
Two discs.

Soundtrack (1956) • MCA (SE) 4055e 10-12   80
   Two discs.
    Composer: Benny Goodman, others. **Cast:** Benny Goodman (performed clarinet solos for
    Steve Allen in the film), Gene Krupa, Stan Getz, Lionel Hampton, Teddy Wilson, Martha Tilton.
Studiotrack • Capitol (M) 706 10-15
    Cast: Benny Goodman and His Orchestra.

BENNY HILL-WORDS AND MUSIC
TV Soundtrack (1972) • Capitol (S) SN-16139 8-10   81
    Composer: Benny Hill. **Conductor:** Harry Robinson. **Cast:** Benny Hill.

BEOWULF
Studio Cast (1977) • Daffodil (S) DAF-30050 50-70   77
   Two discs.
Studio Cast (1977) • Leap Frog (S) WRC 7-2293 20-30   Re
   Three discs.
    Composer: Victor Davies, Betty Jane Wylie. **Conductor:** Victor Davies. **Cast:** Chad Allen, Doug
    Mallory, Christine Chandler.

BERGEN SINGS MORGAN: see HELEN MORGAN STORY

BERLIN ALEXANDERPLATZ
Soundtrack (1983) • Varese Sarabande (S) STV-81217 10-15   84
    Composer: Peer Raben.

BERLIN TO BROADWAY WITH KURT WEILL
Original Cast (1972) • Paramount (S) PAS-4000 15-18   74
   Two discs.
    Composer: Kurt Weill. **Conductor:** Newton Wayland. **Cast:** Margery Cohen, Ken Kercheval,
    Judy Landers, Jerry Lanning, Hal Watters.

BERNARD HERRMANN
Original Radio/TV Soundtrack • Cerberus (M) Number Not Known 5-10   86
   Music from CBS Radio programs *Walt Whitman Suite* and *CBS Radio Workshop Brave
   New World* (1956), TV pilot series of *Collector's Item* and documentary theme song for
   Landmark.
    Composer: Bernard Herrmann. **Conductor:** Bernard Herrmann. **Cast:** (Brave New World)
    Aldous Huxley (reading), William Conrad (host.)
Soundtrack • London (S) SPC 21151 15-25   76
   Full title: *The Composer Conducts Music From…* Has music from *Citizen Kane, Snows of
   Kilimajaro, North By Northwest, Mysterious Island, Vertigo, 7th Voyage of Sinbad, Jason
   and the Argonauts, Three Worlds of Gulliver, Journey to the Center of the Earth, Devil and
   Daniel Webster* and *Psycho.*
    Composer: Bernard Herrmann. **Conductor:** Bernard Herrmann.
Soundtrack • London (S) SPC-21149 15-20   76
   Full title: *Bernard Herrmann Conducts Great British Film Scores.* Music from: *Anna
   Karenina, Oliver Twist, The Ideal Husband, The Invaders, Escape Me Never* and *Things to
   Come.*
    Conductor: Bernard Herrmann. **Cast:** National Philharmonic Orchestra.
Soundtrack • London (S) SPC-21177 15-20   77
   Full title: *Bernard Herrmann Conducts Great British Film Scores, Volume 2.* Music from:
   *Jane Eyre, Fahrenheit 451, The Devil and Daniel Webster, The Trouble with Harry, The 7th
   Voyage of Sinbad, Citizen Kane* and *The 3 Worlds of Gulliver.*
    Conductor: Bernard Herrmann.

BERNSTEIN CONDUCTS BERNSTEIN
Studio Cast • Varese Sarabande (M) VC-81055 10-15   78
   Music from Bernstein's *Fancy Free* and Chavez' *Daughter of Colchis.*
    Conductor: Leonard Bernstein

BEST FOOT FORWARD

Original Cast (1941) • JJA (M) 19743.. 20-25   74
Also contains music from *Look, Ma! I'm Dancin'*.
Composer: Hugh Martin, Ralph Blane. **Cast:** Nancy Walker, The Martins.
Original Revival Cast (1963) • Cadence (M) CLP-4012........................ 12-15   63
Original Revival Cast (1963) • Cadence (S) CLP-24012 20-25   63
Original Revival Cast (1963) • Piccadilly (S) PIC 3485 8-10   80
Original Revival Cast (1963) • Stet (M) DS-15003................................. 8-10   Re
Plays mono though shown as stereo (#15003).
Composer: Hugh Martin, Ralph Blane. **Conductor:** Buster Davis. **Cast:** Paula Wayne, Liza Minnelli, Glenn Walken, Karin Wolfe, Gene Castle, Paul Charles, Kay Cole, Edmund Gaynes, Jack Irwin, Don Slaton, Grant Walden, Ronald Walken, Renee Winters.

BEST LITTLE WHOREHOUSE IN TEXAS

Original Cast (1978) • MCA (S) MCA-3049 8-10   78
Original Cast (1978) • MCA (S) MCA-37218 5-8   80
Composer: Carol Hall. **Conductor:** Robert Billig. **Cast:** Clint Allmon, Pamela Blair, Lisa Brown, Gerry Burkhardt, Jay Bursky, Henderson Forsythe, Jay Garner, Carlin Glynn, Delores Hall, Susan Mansur, Michael Scott, Paul Ukena, Jr.
Soundtrack (1982) • MCA (S) MCA-6112... 8-10   82
Soundtrack (1982) • MCA (S) MCA-1499... 5-8   80s
Composer: Carol Hall, Dolly Parton. **Cast:** Dolly Parton, Burt Reynolds, Teresa Merritt, Dom De Luise, Charles Durning, Jim Nabors (narrator).

BEST OF ALLEN FUNT'S CANDID MIKE

Radio/TV Soundtrack • RCA/Bloopers (M) CM 0001.............................. 5-10
Cast: Allen Funt.

BEST OF BROADWAY / BEST OF HOLLYWOOD

Original Cast/Soundtrack • Columbia (S) 86200 30-45
Boxed, five-disc set. Made for JCPenny's.
Cast: Roy Rogers, others.

BEST OF BROADWAY MUSICALS

Original Cast (1973) • Columbia (SE) P65 5936 20-30   73
Boxed, six-disc set.

BEST OF BROADWAY 1973

Studio Cast (1973) • Century (S) 42226... 6-12   73
Two discs.
Cast: Jim Askren, Ken Kensler, Bill Madden, Jim Talmadge, Julie VanDeVort Curry, Kim McKean, Dee Ruoff, Cyndi Olson, Faye Jonason, Nicki Bettencourt, Laurel Talmadge, Kelly Brock, John Ormond, Linda Davis, David MacDonald, Lani Norskog, Gayle Pulley, Bob Bowen, Melinda Fong, Sharon Baker.

BEST OF BURLESQUE

Original Cast (1957) • MGM (M) E-3644 50-60   57
Original Cast (1957) • MGM (SE) SE-3644 75-85   58
Conductor: Herb Harris. **Cast:** Sherry Britton, Tom Poston, Vini Faye, Sugar Glaze, Emmett Rose, Nancee Ward, Lilly White, Nelle's Belles.

BEST OF DISNEY

Soundtrack [Vol. 1] • Disneyland (M) 2502.. 15-25   76
Music from *Song of the South, Alice in Wonderland, Cinderella, Aristocats, Jungle Book, Snow White, Three Little Pigs, Sleeping Beauty, Lady and the Tramp* and *It's a Small World*.
Cast: James Baskett, Camarata Chorus, Phil Harris, Louis Prima, Peggy Lee.
Soundtrack [Vol. 2] • Disneyland (M) 2503.. 15-25   78

BEST OF FRED ASTAIRE

Studiotrack (1955) • Epic (M) LN-3137... 12-15   55

BEST OF FRED ASTAIRE FROM MGM CLASSIC FILMS
Soundtrack • MCA (S) 25985 5-8   87
    Cast: Fred Astaire.

BEST OF GENE KELLY FROM MGM CLASSIC FILMS
Soundtrack • MCA (S) 25166 5-8   87
    Cast: Gene Kelly.

BEST OF JUDY GARLAND FROM MGM CLASSIC FILMS
Soundtrack • MCA (S) 25165 5-8   87
    Cast: Judy Garland.

BEST OF MANCINI
Soundtrack • RCA Victor (M) LPM-2693 10-15   64
Soundtrack • RCA Victor (S) LSP-2693 15-20   64
Soundtrack [Vol. 2] • RCA Victor (M) LPM-3557 10-15   66
Soundtrack [Vol. 2] • RCA Victor (S) LSP-3557 15-20   66
    Composer: Henry Mancini. Conductor: Henry Mancini. Cast: Henry Mancini's Orchestra and
    Chorus.

BEST OF NELSON RIDDLE
Soundtrack • Capitol (S) SY-4603 8-12
   Includes TV themes from *Route 66, The Untouchables* and *Naked City.*
    Conductor: Nelson Riddle. Cast: Nelson Riddle and His Orchestra.

BEST OF THE BEST
Soundtrack (1989) • Relativity (S) 88561-1034-1 10-20   89
    Composer: Paul Gilman. Cast: Paul Gilman, Jim Capaldi, Charlie Major, Stubblefield and Hall,
    Kirsten Nash, Golden Earring.

BEST OF THE GREAT MOTION PICTURE THEMES, VOLUME 5
Studiotrack • Capitol Creative Products (S) SL 6601 10-15
   Music from *Gone with the Wind, Exodus, Lili, Lawrence of Arabia, Love Is a Many-*
   Splendored Thing, Ben-Hur, Mondo Cane, Black Orpheus, The Robe, Umbrellas of
   Cherbourg, King of Kings and *Captain from Castille.*
    Conductor: Glen Osser, David Rose, Alfred Newman, Miklos Rozsa. Cast: Whittemore and
    Lowe, Frank Barber's Sound-In-The-Round, Jackie Gleason, Franck Pourcel.

BEST OF THE NEW FILM THEMES
Soundtrack • London (M) LL-3347 10-15   64
Soundtrack • London (S) PS-347 15-20   64
   Film themes from 1962 and '63, including *A New Kind of Love, The Cabinet of Dr. Caligari,*
   Divorce Italian Style, The V.I.P.'s, Charade, 8-1/2, Lord of the Flies, Tiara Tahiti, The
   Victors, Mondo Cane, The Cardinal and *Toys in the Attic.*
    Composer: Various. Conductor: Frank Chacksfield. Cast: Frank Chacksfield and His
    Orchestra.

BEST OF TODAY'S MOTION PICTURE THEME MUSIC, VOL. 1
Studiotrack • Unart (S) S-21015 10-15   67
   Themes from: *Dr. Doolittle, Gone with the Wind, In the Heat of the Night, You Only Live*
   Twice, The Whisperers, For a Few Dollars More, Hawaii, Triple Cross and *The Honey Pot.*

BEST OF VICTOR HERBERT
Studiotrack (1956) • Somerset (M) P-400 10-20   56
    Cast: Stockholm String Orchestra.

BEST ORIGINAL SOUNDTRACKS AND GREAT THEMES FROM MOTION PICTURES
Soundtrack • United Artists (M) UAL-3570 10-12   67
Soundtrack • United Artists (S) UAS-6570 12-15   67
    Themes from: *Hawaii, Return of the Seven, The Fortune Cookie, After the Fox, Viva Maria, Escorts Away* and *Comedy Tonight.*

BEST SHOT
Soundtrack • That's Entertainment (S) TER-1141 8-10   80s
    UK release.

BEST THINGS IN LIFE ARE FREE
Studiotrack (1956) • Capitol (EP) ECF-765 12-15   56
Studiotrack (1956) • Capitol (M) T-765 20-25   56
    Though back cover lists film credits, these selections are studio recordings, all performed by Gordon MacRae.
      Composer: Buddy DeSylva, Ray Henderson, Lew Brown. **Cast:** Gordon MacRae.
Studiotrack (1956) • Liberty (M) LRP-3017 30-35   56
    Instrumental recordings of songs from the film, arranged by Billy May.
      Composer: Buddy DeSylva, Ray Henderson, Lew Brown, Al Jolson. **Conductor:** Lionel Newman, Van Alexander.
    Also see LIFE IS JUST A BOWL OF CHERRIES

BEST YEARS OF OUR LIVES
Studiotrack (1946) • Entr'acte (S) EDP-8101 10-12   78
    Includes bonus 45 rpm single.
      Composer: Hugo Friedhofer. **Conductor:** Frank Collura. **Cast:** London Philharmonic Orchestra.

BET YOUR LIFE: see BEGGAR'S HOLIDAY

BETJEMANIA
Original London Cast (1980) • That's Entertainment (S) TER-1002 8-10   80
    UK release.
      Composer: John Gould, John Betjeman. **Conductor:** Rowland Davies, John Gould, Gay Soper, Barry Stokes.

BETRAYAL
Soundtrack (1977) • Inner City (S) IC-4001 8-10   77
      Composer: Teo Macero, Janis Ian. **Conductor:** Teo Macero. **Cast:** Janis Ian.

BETRAYED
Soundtrack (1988) • Varese Sarabande (S) 704.700 20-25   88
Soundtrack (1988) • That's Entertainment (S) TER-1163 8-10   90s
    UK release.
      Composer: Bill Conti. **Conductor:** Bill Conti.

BETTER OFF DEAD
Soundtrack (1985) • A&M (S) SP-5071 8-10   85
      Composer: Rupert Hine, others. **Cast:** Cy Curnin, Martin Ansell, Teri Nunn, Thinkman, E.G. Daily.

BETTY BLUE
Soundtrack (1988) • Virgin Movie Music (S) 90913-1 8-10   88
      Cast: Gabriel Yared.

BETTY BOOP
Studio Cast (1930) • Mark 56 (M) 639 10-15   73
      Cast: Cab Calloway, Fannie Brice, Maurice Chevalier, Louis Armstrong.

BETTY BOOP: SCANDALS OF 1974
Studio Cast • Mark 56 (M) 658 40-80   74
   Picture disc.

BETTY GRABLE
Soundtrack • Scarce Rarities (M) 5501 10-12
Soundtrack • Curtain Calls (M) 100/5 12-15
   Both LPs are of the same recording, packaged in the same cover with different labels and
   logos. Vocals from TV and movies, 1930-1970.
   Cast: Betty Grable.

BETWEEN BROADWAY AND HOLLYWOOD
Studiotrack (1963) • MGM (M) E-4156 10-15   63
Studiotrack (1963) • MGM (S) SE-4156 15-20   63
   Includes suite from *Hud*.
   Cast: Lalo Schifrin.

BEVERLY HILLBILLIES
Studio Cast • Harmony (S) HS 11269 10-15   Re
TV Soundtrack (1965) • Columbia (M) CL-2402 20-35   65
TV Soundtrack (1965) • Columbia (S) CS-9202 35-55   65
   Composer: Various. **Conductor:** Zeke Manners. **Cast:** Lester Flatt, Earl Scruggs, Buddy
   Ebsen, Irene Ryan, Max Baer, Donna Douglas, Nancy Kulp, Raymond Bailey.

BEVERLY HILLS COP
Soundtrack (1984) • MCA (S) 554747 8-10   84
   Contains *BHC (I Can't Stop)* by Rick James.
Soundtrack (1984) • MCA (S) 5553 8-10   84
   Emergency by Rockie Robbins replaces the Rick James track.
   Composer: Harold Faltermeyer, Danny Elfman, others. **Cast:** Patti LaBelle, Shalamar, Junior,
   Rockie Robbins, Pointer Sisters, Glenn Frey, Danny Elfman, System, Harold Faltermeyer, Rick
   James.

BEVERLY HILLS COP II
Soundtrack (1987) • MCA (S) 6207 8-10   87
   Composer: Harold Faltermeyer, others. **Cast:** Bob Seger, Charlie Sexton, Corey Hart, Jets,
   Pointer Sisters, Sue Ann, Jermaine Jackson, James Ingram, George Michael, Pebbles, Ready
   for the World.

BEYOND THE BLUE HORIZON
Soundtrack • Caliban (M) 6033 5-10
   Full title: *Victor Herbert - Beyond the Blue Horizon*.
   Composer: Victor Herbert. **Cast:** Mary Martin, Allan Jones, Dorothy Lamour, Jack Haley, Doris
   Day.

BEYOND THE FOREST
Soundtrack (1949) • Citadel (M) CT-MS 8 8-10   79
   Background score from the film.
Soundtrack (1949) • Citadel (M) CT-MS 8 15-20   79
   Two-disc gatefold edition, including all the film's dialogue.
   Composer: Max Steiner. **Conductor:** Max Steiner.

BEYOND THE FRINGE
Original Cast (1962) • Capitol (M) W-1792 10-12   62
Original Cast (1962) • Capitol (S) SW-1792 10-12   62
   Composer: Dudley Moore, others. **Cast:** Alan Bennett, Peter Cook, Jonathan Miller, Dudley
   Moore.

BEYOND THE FRINGE '64
Original Cast (1964) • Capitol (M) W-2072 10-12   64
Original Cast (1964) • Capitol (S) SW-2072 10-12   64

Original Cast (1964) • Capitol (S) ST-11654 8-10   77
  Composer: Dudley Moore. Cast: Alan Bennett, Peter Cook, Dudley Moore, Paxton Whitehead.

BEYOND THE GREAT WALL
Soundtrack (1965) • Capitol (M) T-10401... 35-40   65
  Chinese documentary with traditional Chinese songs.
  Cast: Tsin Ting Kiang Hung.

BEYOND THE MOON: see GULLIVER'S TRAVELS BEYOND THE MOON

BEYOND THE RAINBOW
Original Cast • MCA (S) 2874 5-10   80s

BEYOND THE SOUND BARRIER [VOL. 2]
Studio Cast • Varese Sarabande (S) RTS-2....................................... 10-12
  Music from *Tribute to a Badman* (1956), *Star Wars* (1977), *Boy with a Goldfish* (1980).
  Composer: Miklos Rozsa, John Williams, Lee Holdridge. Conductor: Morton Gould, Lee
  Holdridge. Cast: London Symphony Orchestra.

BEYOND THE VALLEY OF THE DOLLS
Soundtrack (1970) • 20th Century-Fox (S) TFS-4211 100-150   70
  Composer: Stu Phillips. Conductor: Stu Phillips. Cast: Sandpipers, Strawberry Alarm Clock,
  Carrie Nations.
  Also see VALLEY OF THE DOLLS

BIBLE
Soundtrack (1966) • 20th Century-Fox (M) TF-3184 8-10   66
Soundtrack (1966) • 20th Century-Fox (S) TFS-4184 10-12   66
  Composer: Toshiro Mayuzumi. Conductor: Franco Ferrara. Cast: John Huston (narration).
Soundtrack (1966) • 20th Century-Fox (M) TF-3187 12-15   66
Soundtrack (1966) • 20th Century-Fox (S) TFS-4187 12-15   66
  Includes four-page dialogue booklet.
  Composer: Toshiro Mayuzumi. Conductor: Franco Ferrara. Cast: Art Linkletter (narration),
  Michael Parks, Richard Harris, John Huston, Stephen Boyd, George C. Scott, Ava Gardner,
  Peter O'Toole. (With dialogue).
Studiotrack (1966) • MGM (M) E 4417 10-12   66
Studiotrack (1966) • MGM (S) SE 4417 10-12   66
  Full title: *Music from the Motion Picture, the Bible.*
Studiotrack (1966) • Metro (M) M-593 8-10   60s
Studiotrack (1966) • Metro (M) M-593 8-10   60s
  Full title: *Music from the Bible.* Also has original film music from *The Ten Commandments,
  Ben-Hur, King of Kings* and *The Greatest Story Ever Told.*
  Composer: Toshiro Mayuzumi. Conductor: Henri Rene, Carlo Savina, Miklos Rozsa. Cast:
  Metropolitan Pops Orchestra, others.

BICYCLETTES DE BELSIZE, LES: see TWISTED NERVE

BIG BAD WOLF
Soundtrack (1966) • Camden (M) CAL-1087....................................... 15-18   66
Soundtrack (1966) • Camden (S) CAS-1087....................................... 18-20   66
  Composer: Milton Delugg, Anne Delugg. Conductor: Milton Delugg. Cast: Peter Tripp
  (narration).

BIG BEAT
Soundtrack (1958) • RCA Victor (EP) EPA-4185 15-20   58
  Cast: Gogi Grant.

BIG BLUE
Soundtrack • Virgin Movie Music (S) 90963-1 8-10
  Cast: Eric Serra.

BIG BLUE MARBLE
TV Soundtrack (1974) • A&M (S) SP-3401 8-12   75

BIG BOUNCE
Soundtrack (1969) • Warner Bros. (S) WS-17818 12-18   69
Composer: Mike Curb. Conductor: Mike Curb.

BIG BROADCAST OF 1936
Soundtrack (1950) • Decca (M) DL-6008 50-60   50
10-inch LP.
Composer: Rainger-Parker. Conductor: Tommy Dorsey. Cast: Bing Crosby.
Also see BING'S HOLLYWOOD

BIG CHILL
Soundtrack (1983) • Motown (S) 6062 8-10   83
Cast: Marvin Gaye, Three Dog Night, Rascals, Smokey Robinson and the Miracles, Procol
Harum, Exciters, Aretha Franklin, Temptations.

BIG CHILL (MORE SONGS FROM THE ORIGINAL SOUNDTRACK)
Soundtrack (1984) • Motown (S) 6094 8-12   84
Cast: Creedence Clearwater Revival, Beach Boys, Four Tops, Percy Sledge, Martha Reeves &
the Vandellas, Marvin Gaye, Rascals, Steve Miller Band, Spencer Davis Group, Marvelettes,
The Band.

BIG CIRCUS
Soundtrack (1959) • Todd (M) MT-5001 50-60   59
Soundtrack (1959) • Todd (S) ST-5001 70-80   59
Composer: Paul Sawtell, Bert Shefter, Sammy Fain, Roy Webb, Sid Cutner. Conductor: Kurt
Graunke.

BIG COUNTRY
Soundtrack (1958) • United Artists (M) UAL-4004 18-20   58
Soundtrack (1958) • United Artists (SE) UAS-5004 20-50   58
Blue label. Cover has drawing of horses.
Soundtrack (1958) • United Artists (SE) UAS-5004 5-10   68
Pink and orange label. Cover has drawing with people in foreground.
Soundtrack (1958) • Ascot (M) UM-13504 8-10   64
Soundtrack (1958) • Ascot (SE) US-16504 10-12   64
Both Ascot LPs also have music from *Taras Bulba, Johnny Cool* and *Dr. No.*
Soundtrack (1958) • United Artists (SE) UA-LA270-G 8-10   74
Composer: Jerome Moross. Conductor: Jerome Moross.

BIG EASY
Soundtrack (1987) • Antilles (S) AN-7087 8-12   87
Composer: Brad Fiedel, others. Cast: Dixie Cups, Professor Longhair, Buckwheat Zydeco,
Zachary Richard, Aaron Neville & the Neville Brothers, Beausoleil, Terrance Simien & the Mallet
Playboys, The Wild Tchoupitoulas, Dennis Quaid, Swan Silvertones.

BIG GUNDOWN
Soundtrack (1967) • United Artists (S) UAS-5190 30-35   67
Soundtrack (1967) • United Artists (S) UA-LA297-G 8-10   74
Composer: Ennio Morricone. Conductor: Bruno Nicolai.

BIG HITS FROM BROADWAY
Studiotrack • Richmond (M) 20043 8-12
Music from *South Pacific, Can-Can, Carousel, Kismet, The King and I, Pajama Game, Call
Me Madam, Paint Your Wagon* and *Pal Joey.*
Cast: Cyril Stapleton and His Orchestra.

BIG HITS FROM COLUMBIA PICTURES
Studiotrack (1957) • Mayfair (S) 9632S 10-15   59
Reissue of *John Williams Orchestra Plays Sounds from Screen Spectaculars.*
Composer: Various. Conductor: John Williams. Cast: John Williams and the Hollywood Grand
Studio Orchestra.
Studiotrack • Golden Tone (S) 9632S 10-15
Composer: Various. Conductor: John Williams.

Studiotrack (1958) • Tops (M) L-1632 10-15   58
  Cover pictures Kim Novak and Rita Hayworth.
  Also see JOHN WILLIAMS ORCHESTRA PLAYS SOUNDS FROM SCREEN
  SPECTACULARS

BIG JAKE: see DIGITAL PREMIERE RECORDINGS FROM THE FILMS OF JOHN WAYNE, VOLUME 2

BIG KNIFE

Soundtrack (1955) • Columbia (EP) ZTSP-23721 25-45   55
  Two discs. Identification number – lowest of those on the four sides – shown since no
  selection number is used. Promotional issue only.
  Cast: Frank De Vol & His Orchestra

BIG OPERATOR (JAZZ FROM MOVIES)

Soundtrack • Cinema (M) LP-8001.. 60-90
  Music from *The Criminal, The Wild One* and *The Room*.

BIG RED: see STORY OF BIG RED

BIG RIVER

Original Cast (1985) • MCA (S) MCA-6147 5-10   85
  Inspired by the Mark Twain story *The Adventures of Huckleberry Finn*.
  Composer: Roger Miller. **Conductor:** Linda Twine. **Cast:** John Goodman, Daniel Jenkins, Rene
  Auberjonois, William Youmans, Peggy Harmon, Andi Henig, Bob Gunton, Ron Richardson, Patti
  Cohenour, John Short.

BIG SCREEN HITS OF JOHN BARRY

Studiotrack (1980) • CBS (S) 31862 5-15   80
  Themes from *Thunderball, Born Free, Midnight Cowboy, Goldfinger, You Only Live Twice,*
  The James Bond Theme and others.
  Composer: John Barry.

BIG SCREEN / LITTLE SCREEN

Movie/TV Soundtrack • RCA Victor (S) LSP-4630................................. 10-12   72
  Composer: Henry Mancini. **Conductor:** Henry Mancini. **Cast:** Henry Mancini and His
  Orchestra.

BIG SKY: see LOST HORIZON: THE CLASSIC FILM SCORES OF DIMITRI TIOMKIN

BIG SLEEP

Soundtrack • Cinema (M) LP-8001.. 40-55
  Includes a 12-minute suite by Max Steiner, plus other selections from soundtracks.
  Composer: Max Steiner, others.

BIG TIME

Soundtrack (1977) • Tamla (S) T6-3555-S1.. 8-10   77
  Composer: Smokey Robinson. **Cast:** Smokey Robinson.

BIG TOP PEE-WEE

Soundtrack (1988) • Arista (S) AL-8568... 8-10   88
  Has insert with five punch-out postcards.
  Composer: Danny Elfman. **Cast:** Pee-Wee Herman, Big Top Company, Chuck Rio, Vance the
  Pig.

BIG TOWN

Soundtrack (1987) • Atlantic (S) 81769-1... 8-10   87
  Cast: Little Willie John, Ray Charles, Johnny Cash, Jesse Belvin, LaVern Baker, Drifters,
  Ronnie Self, Bobby Darin.

BIG TROUBLE IN LITTLE CHINA

Soundtrack (1986) • Enigma (S) SJ-73227 8-12   86
  Composer: John Carpenter. **Cast:** John Carpenter, Coup De Villes.

BIG VALLEY
TV Soundtrack (1965) • ABC (M) ABC-527 30-35   65
TV Soundtrack (1965) • ABC (S) ABCS-527 35-45   65
   Composer: George Duning. **Conductor:** George Duning.

BIGGEST BUNDLE OF THEM ALL
Soundtrack (1967) • MGM (M) E-4446 15-20   67
Soundtrack (1967) • MGM (S) SE-4446 20-25   67
   Composer: Riz Ortolani. **Conductor:** Riz Ortolani. **Cast:** Johnny Mathis, Eric Burdon and the
   Animals.

BIKINI BEACH
Soundtrack (1964) • Buena Vista (M) BV-3324 20-40   64
Soundtrack (1964) • Buena Vista (S) STER-3324 25-50   64
   Side two has songs by Annette Funicello (written by the Sherman Brothers, Cynthia Weil
   and others).
   Composer: Jerry Styner, Guy Hemric. **Cast:** Annette Funicello.

BILKO MARCHES
Soundtrack (1956)• Promenade 2088 15-25   56
   Cover pictures Phil Silvers as Sgt. Bilko. Cast is uncredited.

BILL AND COO
Soundtrack (1947) • Mercury Miniature Playhouse MMP-20 50-75   47
   Album of two 78 rpms.
   Conductor: Lionel Newman. **Cast:** Elizabeth Walters (narration).

BILL AND TED'S EXCELLENT ADVENTURE
Soundtrack (1989) • A&M (S) SP-3915 8-10   89
   Cast: Extreme, Vital Signs, Glen Burtnick, Shark Island, Bricklin, Robbie Robb, Power Tool,
   Tora Tora.

BILLIE
Soundtrack (1965) • United Artists (M) UAL-4131 10-15   65
Soundtrack (1965) • United Artists (S) UAS-5131 18-20   65
   Composer: Dominic Frontiere, others. **Cast:** Patty Duke.

BILLION DOLLAR BRAIN
Soundtrack (1967) • United Artists (M) UAL-4174 12-15   67
Soundtrack (1967) • United Artists (S) UAS-5174 15-18   67
Soundtrack (1967) • MCA (S) 25091 5-8   86
   Composer: Richard Rodney Bennett. **Conductor:** Marcus Dods.

BILLY
Original Cast (1974) • CBS (S) 70133 40-45   74
   UK release. Gatefold cover.
   Composer: John Barry, Don Black. **Conductor:** Alfred Ralston. **Cast:** Michael Crawford, Bryan
   Pringle, Avis Bunnage, Christopher Hancock, Diana Quick, Gay Soper, Elaine Paige, Lockwood
   West, Betty Turner, Billy Boyle.

BILLY BARNES' L.A.
Original Los Angeles Cast (1962) • B.B. Records (M) 1001 25-30   62
Original Los Angeles Cast (1962) • AEI (S) AEI-1134 8-10   80s
   Composer: Billy Barnes. **Conductor:** Ray Henderson. **Cast:** Joyce Jameson, Ken Berry, Sylvia
   Lewis.

BILLY BARNES' REVUE
Original Cast (1959) • Decca (M) DL-9076 12-15   59
Original Cast (1959) • Decca (S) DL-79076 15-18   59
   Composer: Billy Barnes. **Conductor:** Billy Barnes. **Cast:** Joyce Jameson, Bert Convy, Patti
   Regan, Jackie Joseph, Ken Berry, Ann Guilbert, Bob Rodgers, Len Weinrib.

Original Cast • AEI (S) AEI-1142.. 8-10   80s
    Actual title: *Billy Barnes Sings Movie Star*.

BILLY BISHOP GOES TO WAR
Original Cast (1979) • Tapestry (S) GD-7372.................................... 8-10   79
    Composer: John Gray. **Cast:** John Gray (piano and background vocals), Eric Peterson.

BILLY BUDD
Original Radio Cast (1963) • General Electric (M) GESD-1.................. 25-35   63
    Cast: Peter Ustinov, Frank Murphy, Helen Hayes (narration).

BILLY GOLDENBERG: HIS FILM AND TELEVISION MUSIC
Studiotrack • No Label Name (S) 20 60-70
    Promotional issue only. Music from films *Up the Sandbox* and *Change of Habit* and TV
    themes, *The Harness* (TV movie) and *Columbo* (*Ransom for a Dead Man* episode).
    Composer: Billy Goldenberg. **Conductor:** Billy Goldenberg.

BILLY JACK
Soundtrack (1971) • Billy Jack (S) BJS-1001 10-15   71
    Includes bonus 45 rpm, fold-out poster and 12-page booklet.
Soundtrack (1971) • Warner Bros. (S) WS-1926 15-20   71
Soundtrack (1971) • Warner Bros. (S) BJS-1001............................... 15-20   73
    Composer: Mundell Lowe. **Conductor:** Mundell Lowe. **Cast:** Coven, Teresa Kelly, Lynn Baker,
    Gwen Smith, Katy Moffatt.

BILLY NONAME
Original Cast (1970) • Roulette (S) SROC-11 30-35   70
    Composer: Johnny Brandon. **Conductor:** Sammy Benskin. **Cast:** Donny Burks, Alan Weeks,
    Hatti Winston, Thommie Bush, Doris DeMendez, Eugene Edwards, Marilyn Johnson, Roger
    Lawson, Urylee Leonardos, Joni Palmer, Andrea Saunders, Andy Torres, Glory Van Scott.

BILLY ROSE'S JUMBO: see JUMBO

BILLY SUNDAY
Studio Cast • Word (S) W-3267 8-12
    Cast: Homer Rodeheaver, Mel Dibble (narrator).

BING CROSBY IN HOLLYWOOD (1930-1934)
Studiotrack • Columbia (M) C2L-43... 10-15   67
    Two discs. Songs from *The King of Jazz, The Big Broadcast, College Humor, Too Much*
    Harmony, Going Hollywood, We're Not Dressing and *She Loves Me Not*.
    Composer: Various. **Conductor:** Paul Whiteman, Lennie Hayton, Jimmy Grier, Nat W. Finston,
    Anson Weeks. **Cast:** Bing Crosby, Mills Brothers, Rhythm Boys, Brox Sisters.

BING CROSBY ON BROADWAY (BING CROSBY AT THE LONDON PALADIUM)
Original Cast (1976) • United Artists/K-Tel (S) NE-951 10-15   76
    Two discs.
    Cast: Bing Crosby, Rosemary Clooney, Crosby Family.

BING CROSBY RADIO SHOWS
Radio Cast • Golden Age (M) 5023 8-10
    Cast: Bing Crosby, others.

BING CROSBY RADIO YEARS
Radio Cast [Vol. 1] • GNP Crescendo (M) 9044................................... 8-10
Radio Cast [Vol. 2] • GNP Crescendo (M) 9046................................... 8-10
Radio Cast [Vol. 3] • GNP Crescendo (M) 9047................................... 8-10
Radio Cast [Vol. 4] • GNP Crescendo (M) 9048................................... 8-10

BING CROSBY SINGS THE HITS FROM ...

Studiotrack (1949) • Decca (M) DL 5000.. 20-25   49
> 10-inch LP. Songs from *Annie Get Your Gun, Song of Norway, Carousel, Bloomer Girl, Up in Central Park* and *Oklahoma!*
>> **Conductor:** Camarata. **Cast:** Bing Crosby.

BING'S HOLLYWOOD

Studiotrack • Decca (M) DL-4250.. 25-45   62
> Actual title: *Easy to Remember.* Music from *Here Is My Heart, Mississippi, Two for Tonight* and *The Big Broadcast of 1936.*
>> **Composer:** Various. **Conductor:** Various. **Cast:** Bing Crosby.
>> Also see BIG BROADCAST OF 1936

Studiotrack • Decca (M) DL-4251.. 25-40   62
> Actual title: *Pennies from Heaven.* Music from *Anything Goes, Pennies from Heaven* and *Rhythm on the Range.*
>> **Composer:** Various. **Conductor:** Georgie Stoll, Victor Young, Jimmy Dorsey. **Cast:** Bing Crosby.

Studiotrack • Decca (M) DL-4252.. 25-30   62
> Actual title: *Pocket Full of Dreams.* Music from *Waikiki Wedding, Double or Nothing* and *Sing, You Sinners.*
>> **Composer:** Various. **Conductor:** Various. **Cast:** Bing Crosby.

Studiotrack • Decca (M) DL-4253.. 25-45   62
> Actual title: *East Side of Heaven.* Music from *Doctor Rhythm, East Side of Heaven* and *Paris Honeymoon.*
>> **Composer:** Various. **Conductor:** Various. **Cast:** Bing Crosby.

Studiotrack • Decca (M) DL-4254.. 25-30   62
> Actual title: *The Road Begins.* Music from *The Road to Singapore, Star Maker* and *If I Had My Way.*
>> **Composer:** James V. Monaco, Victor Schertzinger, John Burke. **Conductor:** John Scott Trotter. **Cast:** Bing Crosby, Foursome, John Scott Trotter's Frying Pan Five.

Studiotrack • Decca (M) DL-4255.. 25-30   62
> Actual title: *Only Forever.* Music from *Birth of the Blues, Rhythm on the River* and *The Road to Zanzibar.*
>> **Composer:** James Van Heusen, John Burke, others. **Conductor:** Various. **Cast:** Bing Crosby, Mary Martin.

Studiotrack (1942) • Decca (M) DL-4256 25-30   62
> Actual title: *Holiday Inn.* Songs are from the film.
>> **Composer:** Irving Berlin. **Conductor:** John Scott Trotter, Bob Crosby. **Cast:** Bing Crosby, Fred Astaire, Margaret Lenhart, Ken Darby Singers.

Studiotrack • Decca (M) DL-4257.. 25-30   62
> Actual title: *Swinging on a Star.* Music from *The Road to Morocco, Dixie* and *Going My Way.*
>> **Composer:** James Van Heusen, John Burke. **Conductor:** Vic Schoen, John Scott Trotter. **Cast:** Bing Crosby, Bob Hope.

Studiotrack • Decca (M) DL-4258.. 30-40   62
> Actual title: *Accentuate the Positive.* Music from *Here Come the Waves, The Road to Utopia* and *The Bells of St. Mary's.*
>> **Composer:** James Van Heusen, Johnny Burke. **Conductor:** John Scott Trotter, Vic Schoen, Eddie Condon. **Cast:** Bing Crosby, Bob Hope.

Studiotrack • Decca (M) DL-4259.. 25-45   62
> Actual title: *Blue Skies.* Music from *Out of This World* and *Blue Skies.*
>> **Composer:** Irving Berlin. **Conductor:** John Scott Trotter. **Cast:** Bing Crosby, Fred Astaire, Trudy Erwin (performed vocals for Joan Caulfield in the film).

Studiotrack • Decca (M) DL-4260.. 25-40   62
> Actual title: *But Beautiful.* Music from *Welcome Stranger, The Road to Rio, The Emperor Waltz* and *Variety Girl.*
>> **Composer:** James Van Heusen, Johnny Burke. **Conductor:** Victor Young, Vic Schoen. **Cast:** Bing Crosby, Andrews Sisters, Nan Wynn, Callico Kids.

Studiotrack • Decca (M) DL-4261.. 25-35   62
  Actual title: *Sunshine Cake*. Music from: *A Connecticut Yankee in King Arthur's Court, Top o' the Morning* and *Riding High*.
    Composer: James Van Heusen, Johnny Burke, others. **Conductor:** Victor Young. **Cast:** Bing Crosby, Rhonda Fleming, William Bendix, Sir Cedric Hardwicke, Ken Darby Choir, Rhythmmakers.

Studiotrack • Decca (M) DL-4262.. 25-50   62
  Actual title: *Cool of the Evening*. Music from *Mr. Music* and *Here Comes the Groom*.
    Composer: James Van Heusen, Johnny Burke, Hoagy Carmichael, Jay Livingston, Johnny Mercer, Ray Evans. **Conductor:** Victor Young, Vic Schoen, John Scott Trotter, Jay Blackton, Matty Matlock. **Cast:** Bing Crosby, Andrews Sisters, Jane Wyman, Dorothy Kirsten.

Studiotrack • Decca (M) DL-4263.. 25-30   62
  Actual title: *Zing a Little Zong*. Music from *Road to Bali* and *Just for You*.
    Composer: James Van Heusen, Johnny Burke. **Conductor:** Sonny Burke, Joseph J. Lilley, Axel Stordahl. **Cast:** Bing Crosby, Bob Hope, Peggy Lee, Rhythmaires, Mellomen.

Soundtrack • Decca (M) DL-4264 20-30   62
  Actual title: *Anything Goes*. Music from *Anything Goes, Little Boy Lost* and *The Country Girl*.
    Composer: Cole Porter, Jimmy Van Heusen, Sammy Cahn. **Conductor:** Joseph J. Lilley. **Cast:** Bing Crosby, Donald O'Connor, Jeanmaire, Mitzi Gaynor.

BINGO LONG TRAVELING ALL-STARS AND MOTOR KINGS
Soundtrack (1976) • Motown (S) MCA 2094 8-10   76
    Composer: William Goldstein. **Conductor:** William Goldstein. **Cast:** Thelma Houston.

BIOGRAPH GIRL
Soundtrack • That's Entertainment (S) TER-1003................................. 8-10   80
  UK release.
    Composer: David Heneker. **Cast:** Sheila White, Jane Hardy, Bruce Barry, Kate Revill, Guy Siner.

BIONIC WOMAN
Studio Cast • Wonderland (S) Number Not Known 8-12   70s

BIRD
Soundtrack (1988) • Columbia (S) SC-44299... 8-10   88
  Biography of Charlie "Bird" Parker.
    Composer: Lennie Niehaus. **Cast:** Charlie Parker, Forest Whitaker, Diane Venora.

BIRD OF PARADISE
Soundtrack (1932) • Medallion (M) ML 305/306 30-35   80
  Two-disc set. Contains the entire film.
    Composer: Max Steiner. **Conductor:** Max Steiner. **Cast:** Joel McCrea, Dolores Del Rio, John Halliday, Skeets Gallegher, Lon Chaney Jr. (With dialogue.)

Soundtrack (1932) • Medallion (M) ML 309 15-30   80
  Also has music from *Sante Fe Trail* (1941), *Life with Father* (1947) and *A Star Is Born* (1937)
    Composer: Max Steiner.

BIRD WITH THE CRYSTAL PLUMAGE
Soundtrack (1970) • Capitol (S) ST-642.. 65-85   70
Soundtrack (1970) • Cerberus (S) CEMS 0108..................................... 8-15   81
    Composer: Ennio Morricone. **Conductor:** Bruno Nicolai.

BIRDS, THE BEES AND THE ITALIANS
Soundtrack (1966) • United Artists (M) UAL-4157................................ 10-12   66
Soundtrack (1966) • United Artists (S) UAS-5157 12-15   66
    Composer: Carlo Rustichelli. **Conductor:** Pier Luigi Urbini.

BIRDY
Soundtrack (1984) • Geffen (S) GHS-24070... 8-10   84
    Cast: Peter Gabriel.

BIRTH OF THE BLUES: see BING'S HOLLYWOOD

BISTRO CAR
Original Cast (1978) • Berandol (S) BER-9096 30-35   78
Off-Broadway show, based on the Canadian musical, *Jubalay.*
Composer: Patrick Rose, Richard Ouzounian, Merv Campone. **Cast:** Patrick Rose, Diane
Stapley, Ross Douglas, Nora McClellan.
Also see JUBALAY

BITE THE BULLET
Soundtrack (1975) • RFO (S) RFO-102 45-65   80
Composer: Alex North. **Conductor:** Alex North.

BITTER SWEET
Original London Cast (1929) • World (M) SH-179/80 20-25
Original London Cast (1929) • Monmouth Evergreen (SE) MES-7062 ... 8-10
London Studio Cast (1958) • RCA Victor/EMI (M) CLP-1260 20-25   58
London Studio Cast (1958) • RCA Victor/EMI (S) CSD-1260 25-35   58
Above are UK releases.
London Studio Cast (1958) • Angel (M) 35814.................................... 15-20   61
London Studio Cast (1958) • Angel (S) S-35814................................. 20-25   61
Composer: Noel Coward. **Conductor:** Michael Collins. **Cast:** Vanessa Lee, Roberto Cardinali,
Julie Dawn, John Hauxvell.

BLACK AND WHITE IN COLOR
Soundtrack (1977) • Buddah (S) BDS-5698...................................... 25-30   77
Composer: Pierre Bachelet. **Conductor:** Mat Camison.

BLACK BELLY OF THE TARANTULA
Soundtrack (1972) • Cerberus (S) CEMS 0116................................. 10-15   82
Includes music from *My Dear Assassin*, which is also by Ennio Morricone.
Composer: Ennio Morricone. **Conductor:** Ennio Morricone.

BLACK CAESAR
Soundtrack (1973) • Polydor (S) PD-6014 50-65   73
Composer: James Brown. **Cast:** James Brown.

BLACK CAULDRON
Soundtrack (1985) • Varese Sarabande (S) STV-81253...................... 10-15   85
Composer: Elmer Bernstein. **Conductor:** Elmer Bernstein. **Cast:** Utah Symphony Orchestra.

BLACK EMANUELLE
Soundtrack (1976) • West End (S) WE 100 75-85   76
Composer: Nico Fidenco.

BLACK FIST
Soundtrack (1976) • Happy Fox (S) HF-1101.................................... 50-75   76

BLACK GIRL
Soundtrack (1972) • Fantasy (S) 9420 50-65   73
Composer: Ray Shanklin, Ed Bogas, Jesse Osborne. **Cast:** Leslie Uggams, Brock Peters,
Ruby Dee, others.

BLACK HOLE
Soundtrack (1979) • Buena Vista (S) STER-5008.............................. 30-50   79
Composer: John Barry. **Conductor:** John Barry.
Soundtrack (1979) • Disneyland (S) DIS-3821 25-30   79
Has 12-page photo booklet. Full title: *The Black Hole (The Story of the Black Hole)*. Music
and dialogue from film.
Composer: John Barry. **Conductor:** John Barry. **Cast:** Maximilian Schell, Anthony Perkins,
Robert Forster, Joseph Bottoms, Yvette Mimieux, Ernest Borgnine. (With dialogue.)

BLACK NATIVITY
Original Cast (1961) • Vee Jay (M) VJ-8503 10-15   61

Original Cast (1961) • Vee Jay (S) VJS-8503 .... 20-25　61
Original Cast (1961) • Vee Jay (M) LP-5022 .... 10-15　61
Original Cast (1961) • Vee Jay (S) SR-50202 .... 15-20　61
Original Cast (1961) • Trip (S) 7022 .... 10-12　Re
   Show focuses on traditional gospel songs.
    Cast: Marion Williams, Stars of Faith, Princess Stewart.

BLACK ORCHID
Soundtrack (1959) • Dot (M) DLP-3178 .... 25-30　59
Soundtrack (1959) • Dot (S) DLP-25178 .... 30-35　59
   Composer: Alessandro Cicognini. **Conductor:** Carlo Savina.

BLACK ORPHEUS (ORFEU NEGRO)
Soundtrack (1959) • Epic (M) LN-3672 .... 25-35　59
Soundtrack (1959) • Fontana (M) MFG-27520 .... 10-15　64
Soundtrack (1959) • Fontana (SE) SRF-67520 .... 10-15　64
   Composer: Antonio Carlos Jobim, Luiz Bonfa.
Studiotrack (1965) • Fantasy (M) 3337 .... 20-30　65
   Red vinyl. Full title: *Jazz Impressions of Black Orpheus.*
Studiotrack (1965) • Fantasy (M) 3337 .... 10-15　65
   Black vinyl. Full title: *Cast Your Fate to the Wind (Jazz Impressions of Black Orpheus).*
Studiotrack (1965) • Fantasy (S) 8089 .... 15-25　65
   Black vinyl. Full title: *Jazz Impressions of Black Orpheus.* Despite title variations, all three
   Fantasy LPs have the same contents.
    Composer: Antonio Carlos Jobim, Vince Guaraldi, Henry Mancini, others. **Conductor:** Vince
   Guaraldi. **Cast:** Vince Guaraldi Trio.

BLACK RAIN
Soundtrack (1989) • Virgin (S) 91292-1 .... 8-10　89
   Composer: Hans Zimmer, others. **Conductor:** Shirley Walker. **Cast:** Gregg Allman, UB40, Iggy
   Pop, Soul II, Soul with Caron Wheeler, Les Rita Mitsouko and Sparks, Ryuichi Sakamoto.

BLACK SABBATH
Soundtrack (1964) • Tony Thomas (M) BAX LB 1000 .... 50-60　80
   Composer: Les Baxter. **Conductor:** Les Baxter.

BLACK STALLION
Soundtrack (1979) • United Artists (S) LOO-1040 .... 8-10　80
   Composer: Carmine Coppola. **Conductor:** Carmine Coppola.

BLACK STALLION RETURNS
Soundtrack (1983) • Liberty (S) LO-51144 .... 8-10　83
   Composer: Georges Delerue. **Conductor:** Georges Delerue. **Cast:** Kelly Reno, Teri Garr, Allen
   Goorwitz, Vincent Spano, Woody Strode.

BLACK TIGHTS
Soundtrack (1962) • RCA Victor (M) FOC-3 .... 15-20　62
Soundtrack (1962) • RCA Victor (S) FSO-3 .... 25-35　62
   Composer: George Bizet, others. **Cast:** Maurice Chevalier (narration).

BLACKBEARD'S GHOST
Soundtrack (1968) • Disneyland (M) DQ-1305 .... 10-12　68
Soundtrack (1968) • Disneyland (M) ST-3978 .... 8-10　Re
   Cast: Peter Ustinov (narration), Dean Jones, Suzanne Pleshette. (With dialogue.)

BLACKBIRDS OF 1928
Studio Cast (1953) • RCA Victor (EP) EPA-483 .... 10-20　53
   Composer: Jimmy McHugh, Dorothy Fields. **Cast:** Cab Calloway, Thelma Carpenter.
Studio Cast • Columbia (M) OL-6770 .... 10-12　68
   With Original Cast stars. Has 14 tracks, four of which are alternate takes.
    Composer: Jimmy McHugh, Dorothy Fields. **Conductor:** Duke Ellington, Don Redmond. **Cast:**
   Adelaide Hall, Bill Robinson, Cab Calloway, Mills Brothers, Ethel Waters, Cecil Mack Choir.

Studio Cast (1970) • Monmouth Evergreen (SE) MES-7080 8-10   76
  Composer: Jimmy McHugh, Dorothy Fields. **Cast:** Adelaide Hall.
Studio Cast • Revue (M) 1... 15-25
  Has 12 tracks.
Studio Cast • Sutton (SE) SSU-270 10-20   Re
  Has 10 tracks.
  Also see SHUFFLE ALONG

BLACULA
Soundtrack (1972) • RCA Victor (S) LSP-4806 25-75   72
  Composer: Gene Page, Wally Holmes, Karl Russell. **Conductor:** Gene Page, Don Peake.
  Cast: 21st Century, Ltd., Hues Corporation.

BLADE RUNNER
Soundtrack (1982) • Full Moon/Warner Bros. (S) 1-23748 15-20   82
  Composer: Vangelis. **Conductor:** Jack Elliott, Patrick Williams. **Cast:** John Bahler, New
  American Orchestra.

BLAME IT ON RIO
Soundtrack (1983) • Varese Sarabande (S) STV-81210 8-10   83
  Conductor: Ken Wannberg.

BLAZE
Soundtrack (1989) • A&M (S) SP-3932 8-10   89
  Composer: Bennie Wallace (original music), others. **Conductor:** Bennie Wallace, others. **Cast:**
  Bennie Wallace, Fats Domino, Hank Williams Sr., Bonnie Sheridan, Randy Newman.

BLAZING SADDLES
Soundtrack (1973) • Warner Bros. (S) BS-2781................................. 75-100   74
  Australia release. Also has music from *The Producers* and *The Twelve Chairs*.
  Composer: John Morris, Mel Brooks, Cole Porter, Vernon Duke, E.Y. Harburg. **Conductor:**
  John Morris. **Cast:** Frankie Laine, Madeline Kahn, Mel Brooks.

BLESS THE BEASTS AND CHILDREN
Soundtrack (1971) • A&M (S) SP-4322 8-12   71
Soundtrack (1971) • A&M (S) 85797 5-10   Re
  Composer: Barry DeVorzon, Perry Botkin Jr. **Cast:** Carpenters.

BLESS THE BRIDE: see WATER GYPSIES

BLIND DATE
Soundtrack (1987) • Rhino (S) RNIN-70705.. 8-10   87
  Cast: Jennifer Warnes, Billy Vera and the Beaters, Keith L'Neire, Hubert Tubbs, Henry Mancini,
  Stanley Jordan.
Soundtrack • Varese Sarabande (S) 81202 8-10   80s
  Composer: Stanley Myers. **Cast:** John Kongos.

BLISS OF MRS. BLOSSOM
Soundtrack (1968) • RCA Victor (S) LSP-4080 15-18   68
  Composer: Riz Ortolani. **Cast:** New Vaudeville Band, Shirley MacLaine, Spectrum.

BLITHE SPIRIT
Original Cast • Original Touring Cast Recording (S) NOCA 1100 10-15
  Limited edition. Reads: "Non-profit collectors disk dedicated to Sir Noel's close buddy and
  theatre goer, Dr. Roy, East Cool Inlet, Florida."
TV Soundtrack (1956) • Sandpiper (M) 1 40-60
  Ford Star Jubilee TV presentation, January 14, 1956.
  Cast: Noel Coward, Claudette Colbert, Lauren Bacall, Mildred Natwick.

BLITZ!
Original London Cast • AEI (S) AEI-1117.. 8-10   70s
Original London Cast • That's Entertainment (S) TER-1056................... 8-10   80s
  UK release.
  Composer: Lionel Bart.

BLONDE BOMBSHELL
Soundtrack • AEI (M) AEI-2120.. 10-12   80s
Songs from various Betty Hutton films.
   Composer: Various. **Conductor:** Various. **Cast:** Betty Hutton.

BLONDEL
Original London Cast (1983) • MCA (S) DBL 1/MAPS 11504............... 20-25   83
UK release.
   Composer: Tim Rice, Stephen Oliver. **Conductor:** Martin Koch.

BLONDIE
Original Radio Cast • Mark 56 (M) 624................................ 20-40   70s
Picture disc.

BLOOD AND SAND
Soundtrack (1941) • Decca A-265.................................... 15-20   52
Album of three 78 rpms.
Soundtrack (1941) • Decca (M) DL-5380 20-75   52
10-inch LP.
Soundtrack (1941) • Decca (M) DL-4629 30-60   56
Soundtrack (1941) • Decca (SE) DL-74629 10-20   59
   Composer: Vincente Gómez. **Cast:** Vincente Gómez Quintet, Graciela Parraga.
Soundtrack (1941) • Varese Sarabande (M) STV 81117................. 8-15   82
Also includes music from *Golden Earrings*.

BLOOD ON THE SUN
Soundtrack (1945) • Citadel (M) CT-6031 30-40   79
   Composer: Miklos Rozsa. **Conductor:** Miklos Rozsa.

BLOOD SIMPLE: see RAISING ARIZONA

BLOODLINE
Soundtrack (1979) • Varese Sarabande (S) STV-81131 8-12   79
   Composer: Ennio Morricone. **Conductor:** Ennio Morricone.

BLOODY MAMA
Soundtrack (1970) • American Int'l (S) STA-1031 10-12   70
   Composer: Don Randi. **Conductor:** Don Randi. **Cast:** Bigfoot.

BLOOMER GIRL
Original Cast (1944) • Decca DA-381................................ 15-20   44
Eight-disc 78 rpm set.
Original Cast (1944) • Decca (M) DL-8015.......................... 20-25   50
Black and gold label on thick wax.
Original Cast (1944) • Decca (M) DL-8015.......................... 12-18   50
Red label.
Original Cast (1944) • Decca (M) DL-9126.......................... 10-15   65
Original Cast (1944) • Decca (SE) DL-79126 15-20   65
Original Cast (1944) • MCA (SE) 2072e............................. 5-8   72
   Composer: Harold Arlen, E.Y. Harburg. **Conductor:** Leon Leonardi. **Cast:** Celeste Holm, David Brooks, Toni Hart, Harold Arlen, Hubert Dilworth, Richard Huey, Joan McCracken, Mabel Taliaferro, Dooley Wilson.

BLOOMFIELD: see HERO

BLOSSOM TIME
Studio Cast (1947) • RCA Victor (M) LK-1018...................... 18-20
   Composer: Franz Schubert, Heinrich Berte, Dorothy Donnelly (adapted by Sigmund Romberg). **Conductor:** Al Goodman. **Cast:** Earl Wrightson, Donald Dame, Mary Martha Briney, Blanka Peric, Mullen Sisters, Guild Choristers.

BLOW-UP
Soundtrack (1966) • MGM (M) E-4447 .... 25-30 67
Soundtrack (1966) • MGM (S) SE-4447 .... 30-35 67
 Composer: Herbie Hancock. **Conductor:** Herbie Hancock. **Cast:** Yardbirds, Herbie Hancock.

BLOWN AWAY
Soundtrack • Passport (S) PJ 88029 .... 5-10 87
 Cast: The Elements.

BLUE
Soundtrack (1968) • Dot (S) DLP-25855 .... 12-18 68
 Composer: Manos Hadjidakis. **Conductor:** Manos Hadjidakis.

BLUE CITY
Soundtrack (1986) • Warner Bros. (S) 1-25386 .... 8-10 86
 Cast: Ry Cooder, True Believers, Pops and Timer.

BLUE COLLAR
Soundtrack (1978) • MCA (S) 3034 .... 8-12 78
 Composer: Jack Nitzsche. **Conductor:** Jack Nitzsche. **Cast:** Captain Beefheart.

BLUE EYED BANDIT
Soundtrack • Cerberus (S) CEMS-0114 .... 8-10 82
 Composer: Ennio Morricone. **Conductor:** Ennio Morricone.

BLUE HAWAII
Soundtrack (1961) • RCA Victor (M) LPM-2426 .... 60-90 61
 Black label, reads "Long Play" at bottom.
Soundtrack (1961) • RCA Victor (S) LSP-2426 .... 75-100 61
 Black label, reads "Living Stereo" at bottom.
Soundtrack (1961) • RCA Victor (M) LPM-2426 .... 40-50 63
 Black label, reads "Mono" at bottom.
Soundtrack (1961) • RCA Victor (M) LPM-2426 .... 25-30 65
 Black label, reads "Monaural" at bottom.
Soundtrack (1961) • RCA Victor (S) LSP-2426 .... 25-30 65
 Black label, reads "Stereo" at bottom.
Soundtrack (1961) • RCA Victor (S) LSP-2426 .... 10-25 69
 Orange or tan label. (Tan label issued in 1976.)
Soundtrack (1961) • RCA Victor (S) AFL1-2426 .... 8-10 77
Soundtrack (1961) • RCA Victor (S) AYL1-3683 .... 5-8 81
 Composer: Sid Tepper, Roy C. Bennett, Fred Wise, Ben Weisman, others. **Cast:** Elvis Presley, Scotty Moore (guitar), Bob Moore (bass), D.J. Fontana (drums), Floyd Cramer (piano), Boots Randolph (sax), Hank Garland (guitar), Jordanaires (vocals), Surfers (vocals).

BLUE IGUANA
Soundtrack (1988) • Polydor (S) 835592-1 .... 8-10 88
 Cast: Kurtis Blow, Zodiac Mindwarp and the Love Reaction, Fat Boys, Del-Vikings, Chuck Brown and the Soul Searchers, James Brown, Platters, Dirge, Fela Anikulapo Kuti, Ethan James, White Boys.

BLUE LAGOON
Soundtrack (1980) • Marlin (S) 2236-X 10-12 80
 White label. Promotional issue only.
Soundtrack (1980) • Marlin (S) 2236-X 8-10 80
 Includes bonus poster.
 Composer: Basil Poledouris.

BLUE MAX
Soundtrack (1966) • Mainstream (M) 56081 .... 20-35 66
Soundtrack (1966) • Mainstream (S) S-6081 .... 25-60 66

Soundtrack (1966) • Mainstream (S) T-90799 12-15
  Capitol Record Club issue.
Soundtrack (1966) • Citadel (S) CT-6008 10-15   76
Soundtrack (1966) • Citadel (S) CT-7007 10-15   79
  Remastered edition.
    Composer: Jerry Goldsmith. **Conductor:** Jerry Goldsmith.

BLUE MONDAY
Studio Cast (1925) • Vox Turnabout (SE) TV-S 3463 15-20   76
  Side two contains Gershwin production numbers.
    Composer: George Gershwin. **Conductor:** Gregg Smith. **Cast:** Joyce Andrews, Patrick Mason.

BLUE SKIES
Studiotrack (1946) • Decca A-481 15-20   50
  Album of five 78 rpms, with booklet
Studiotrack (1946) • Decca (M) DLP-5042 40-50   50
  10-inch LP.
    Composer: Irving Berlin. **Conductor:** John Scott Trotter. **Cast:** Bing Crosby, Fred Astaire,
    Trudy Erwin (performed vocals for Joan Caulfield in the film), Olga San Juan.
  Also see BING'S HOLLYWOOD

BLUE THUNDER
Soundtrack (1983) • MCA (S) 6122 8-10   83
    Composer: Arthur Rubinstein. **Conductor:** Arthur Rubinstein. **Cast:** Beepers.

BLUE VELVET
Soundtrack (1986) • Varese Sarabande (S) STV-81292 15-20   86
Soundtrack (1986) • That's Entertaiment (S) TER-1127 8-10   80s
  UK release.
    Composer: Angelo Badalamenti, others. **Conductor:** Angelo Badalamenti. **Cast:** Julee Cruise,
    Ketty Lester, Roy Orbison.

BLUEBEARD
Soundtrack • Cerberus (S) CEM-S-0105 25-35   80
    Composer: Ennio Morricone. **Conductor:** Franco Tamponi.

BLUES
Soundtrack (1967) • Asch (M) 101 8-10
    Cast: J.D. Short, Pink Anderson, Furry Lewis, Baby Tate, Memphis Willie B., Gus Cannon,
    Sleepy John Estes.

BLUES, BALLADS AND SIN SONGS
Original Cast (1954) • Monmouth Evergreen (SE) MRS-6501 10-15
    Cast: Libby Holman, Gerald Cook (piano).

BLUES BROTHERS
Soundtrack (1980) • Atlantic (S) SD-16017 8-10   80
    Conductor: Ira Newborn. **Cast:** Blues Brothers (John Belushi and Dan Aykroyd), Ray Charles,
    James Brown, Aretha Franklin, Cab Calloway, James Cleveland Choir.

BLUES IN THE NIGHT
Original London Cast (1987) • First Night (S) SCENE 9 8-10   87

BLUES OPERA: see FREE AND EASY

BOAT, THE: see DAS BOOT

BOB AND CAROL AND TED AND ALICE
Soundtrack (1969) • Bell (S) 1200 12-18   69
  Also has two tracks from *Handel's Halleluhah Chorus* and *What the World Needs Now Is
  Love* by Merrilee Rush.
    Composer: Quincy Jones. **Conductor:** Quincy Jones. **Cast:** Quincy Jones & His Orchestra.
    Merrilee Rush.

BOB AND RAY – THE TWO AND ONLY
Original Cast (1970) • Columbia (S) S-30412...................................... 10-12   70
    Composer: Bob Elliot, Ray Goulding. **Cast:** Bob Elliot, Ray Goulding (comedy skits without music).

BOB CROSBY SHOW
TV Soundtrack • Columbia (M) CL 766 15-20
    Composer: Various. **Conductor:** Bob Crosby. **Cast:** Bob Crosby, Paula Kelly, Carole Richards.

BOB DYLAN
TV Soundtrack (1995) • Columbia (S) C2-67000 10-15   95
Two discs. Limited edition.
    Cast: Bob Dylan, others.

BOB HOPE IN HOLLYWOOD
Studiotrack • MCA (M) MCA-906.. 8-12   84
Original recordings from various films.
    Cast: Bob Hope, Bing Crosby, Peggy Lee, Shirley Ross, others.

BOBBY DEERFIELD
Soundtrack (1977) • Casablanca (S) NBLP-7071 8-10   77
    Composer: Dave Grusin. **Conductor:** Dave Grusin.

BOBO
Soundtrack (1967) • Warner Bros. (M) W-1711 12-18   67
Soundtrack (1967) • Warner Bros. (S) WS-1711 15-20   67
    Composer: Francis Lai. **Conductor:** Francis Lai. **Cast:** Peter Sellers.

BOCCACCIO '70
Soundtrack (1962) • RCA Victor (M) FOC-5... 30-35   62
Soundtrack (1962) • RCA Victor (S) FSO-5 50-100   62
    Composer: Nino Rota, Armando Trovajoli. **Conductor:** Nino Rota, Armando Trovajoli, Franco Ferrara.

BODY
Soundtrack (1973) • Harvest (S) SHSP 4008.. 20-25   73
Fulll title: *Music from the Body*.
    Cast: Ron Geesin, Roger Waters.

BODY BEAUTIFUL
Original Cast (1958) • Blue Pear (M) BP-1006 30-35
Live recording from a theater's sound system. This musical was scheduled to be recorded by Columbia until it closed shortly after opening on Broadway.
    Composer: Jerry Bock, Sheldon Harnick. **Conductor:** Milton Greene. **Cast:** Mindy Carson, Jack Warden, Steve Forrest, Jack DeLon, Mara Lynn, Barbara McNair, Brock Peters.

BODY HEAT
Soundtrack (1983) • Label X (S) LXSE 1-002 90-100   83
Demand for this LP is high since it is the only source of *Ladd Co. Fanfare*.
    Composer: John Barry. **Conductor:** John Barry.

BODY IN THE SEINE
Original Cast (1955) • Private Label-Alden-Shaw (M) VB-001.......... 200-400
Tracks from a musical that got no farther than this collection of songs. From the producers of *The Athenian Touch*.
    Composer: David Lippincott. **Conductor:** Buster Davis. **Cast:** Alice Pearce, Jim Symington, Barbara Ashley, George S. Irving, Laurel Selby, Terry Turner, Pat Wilkes, Don Liberto.

BODY ROCK
Soundtrack (1984) • EMI America (S) SO-17140 8-10   84
    Cast: Maria Vidal, David Lasley, Laura Branigan, others.

BODY SLAM
Soundtrack (1987) • MCA (S) 6197 8-10   87
    Cast: Moses Tyson Jr., Bachman-Turner Overdrive, Kick, Frankie Valli and the 4 Seasons, Debbie Lytton, Jimmy Scarlet and the Dimensions.

BODYGUARD
Soundtrack (1992) • Arista (S) 18699 8-10   92
    Cast: Whitney Houston, others.

BOEING, BOEING
Soundtrack (1965) • RCA Victor (M) LOC-1121 18-20   65
Soundtrack (1965) • RCA Victor (S) LSO-1121 25-30   65
    Composer: Neal Hefti. **Conductor:** Neal Hefti.

BOGIE: A SALUTE
Soundtrack • MGM (M) E-4359 10-12
Soundtrack • MGM (S) SE-4359 10-12

BOLD VENTURES
Studio Cast (1969) • Revell (S) 87-8162 15-20   69
  Promotional issue from Revell, makers of toy models.
    Composer: Jack Shaindlin. **Cast:** James Maguire, Mike Geller, Donald Hirsh, Fred Clements Jr., Walter Hoffman, Don Rickles.

BOLERO
Soundtrack (1981) • Polydor (S) PD-1-6353 8-10   82
    Composer: Michel Legrand, Francis Lai.
Soundtrack (1984) • Varese Sarabande (S) 81228 8-10   84
    Conductor: Peter Bernstein. **Cast:** Peter Bernstein and His Orchestra.

BOLSHOI BALLET '67
Soundtrack (1966) • Command (S) S-11035 10-12   66
    Cast: Members and dancers of the Bolshoi (translation: Big) Ballet Company.

BONANZA
TV Soundtrack (1958) • MGM (M) E-3960 25-35   61
TV Soundtrack (1958) • MGM (S) SE-3960 45-60   61
    Composer: David Rose, Jay Livingston, Ray Evans. **Conductor:** David Rose. **Cast:** David Rose and His Orchestra.

BONANZA BOUND
Original Cast (1947) • JJA (M) 19764 15-20   76
  Unreleased recordings by the original cast. Side two has *The Revuers 1938 - 1944.*
    Composer: Saul Chaplin, Betty Comden, Adolph Green (lyrics). **Conductor:** Lehman Engel. **Cast:** Carol Raye, Hal Hackett, Adolph Green, Allyn Ann McLerie, George Colouris. REVUERS: Judy Holliday, Betty Comden, Adolph Green, Leonard Bernstein (piano).

BONANZA – CHRISTMAS ON THE PONDEROSA
TV Soundtrack (1963) • RCA Victor (M) LPM-2557 20-25   63
TV Soundtrack (1963) • RCA Victor (S) LSP-2557 25-30   63
    Cast: Lorne Greene, Michael Landon, Pernell Roberts, Dan Blocker.

BONANZA – PONDEROSA PARTY TIME
TV Soundtrack (1962) • RCA Victor (M) LPM-2583 20-25   62
TV Soundtrack (1962) • RCA Victor (S) LSP-2583 25-30   62
    Conductor: Billy Liebert. **Cast:** Lorne Greene, Michael Landon, Pernell Roberts, Dan Blocker.

BONJOUR, TRISTESSE
Soundtrack (1958) • RCA Victor (M) LOC-1040 25-60   58
    Composer: Georges Auric. **Conductor:** Georges Auric.

BONNIE AND CLYDE
Soundtrack (1967) • Warner Bros. (M) W-1742 10-12   67
Soundtrack (1967) • Warner Bros. (S) WS-1742 12-15   67
Soundtrack (1967) • Warner Bros. (S) ST-91414................... 8-10
  Capitol Record Club issue.
    Composer: Charles Strouse, others. **Cast:** Warren Beatty, Faye Dunaway, Michael J. Pollard, Gene Hackman, Estelle Parsons. (With dialogue.)
Studiotrack (1967) • Mercury (S) SR 61162 10-20   67
  Cast: Flatt & Scruggs, others.
Studiotrack • Diplomat (S) DS 2449 8-12   60s
  Full title: *Themes from Bonnie and Clyde & The Graduate.*
  Cast: Limelite Singers and Orchestra.

BOOGALOO
Soundtrack (1984) • Polydor (S) 422-82369........................... 8-10   84

BOOGEY MAN
Soundtrack (1980) • Synthe-Sound-Trax (S) No Number.................... 20-40   80
  Limited edition of 1000 copies.

BOOGIE
Original London Cast • That's Entertainment (S) STGR-001.................. 8-10   80s
  UK release.

BOOK OF NUMBERS
Soundtrack (1973) • Brut (S) 6002 12-15   73
  Cast: Sonny Terry, Brownie McGhee.

BOOM!
Soundtrack (1968) • MCA (S) 3600.................................... 8-10
  Composer: John Barry. **Conductor:** John Barry. **Cast:** John Barry & Orchestra, Georgie Fame.

BORA, BORA
Soundtrack (1970) • American Int'l (S) STA-1029 20-25   70
  Composer: Les Baxter. **Conductor:** Les Baxter.

BORDER
Soundtrack (1982) • Backstreet (S) BSR-6105 8-10   82
  Composer: Ry Cooder, John Hiatt, Jim Dickinson, Sam Samudio, Dan Penn. **Conductor:** Ry Cooder. **Cast:** Ry Cooder, Willie Greene Jr., Jim Dickinson, Sam (Samudio) the Sham, John Hiatt, Brenda Patterson, Bobby King.

BORDER RADIO
Soundtrack (1987) • Enigma (S) SJ-73221 8-10   87
  Cast: Divine Horsemen, Green on Red, Dave Alvin, John Doe, Chris D., The Tonys.

BORN AGAIN
Soundtrack (1978) • Lamb & Lion (S) LL-1041....................... 8-10   78
  Composer: Les Baxter. **Conductor:** Les Baxter. **Cast:** Larnelle Harris (with dialogue).

BORN FREE
Soundtrack (1966) • MGM (M) E-4368................................ 8-10   66
Soundtrack (1966) • MGM (S) SE-4368 8-10   66
  Composer: John Barry. **Conductor:** John Barry. **Cast:** Matt Monro, John Barry.
Studiotrack (1971) • Disneyland (S) ST-3803........................... 5-8   71
  Full title: *The Story and Songs of Born Free.*

BORN LOSERS
TV Soundtrack (1967) • Tower (M) T-5082 15-20   67
TV Soundtrack (1967) • Tower (S) DT-5082 20-25   67
  Composer: Mike Curb, others. **Cast:** Terry Stafford, Sidewalk Sounds, Summer Saxophones.

BORN ON THE FOURTH OF JULY
Soundtrack (1990) • MCA (S) 6340.. 8-10   90
  Composer: John Williams. Cast: Edie Brickell and New Bohemians, Broken Homes, Van
  Morrison, Don McLean, Temptations, Shirelles, Frankie Avalon, Henry Mancini.

BORN TO DANCE
Soundtrack (1936) • Classic International Filmusicals (M) CIF-3001.... 10-12
  Composer: Cole Porter. Cast: Eleanor Powell, James Stewart, Virginia Bruce, Frances
  Langford, Buddy Ebsen, Una Merkel, Sid Silvers.

BORROWERS
TV Soundtrack (1973) • Stanyan (Q) SRQ-4014.................................... 30-40   74
  Composer: Rod McKuen. Conductor: Billy Byers. Cast: Rod McKuen, Shelby Flint.

BORSALINO
Soundtrack (1970) • Paramount (S) PAS-5019..................................... 20-25   70
  Composer: Claude Bolling, Jacques Deray. Conductor: Claude Bolling. Cast: Odette Piquet,
  Claude Bolling.

BOSTONIANS
Soundtrack (1984) • Audiotrax Ltd. (S) ATXLPO-2 8-10   84
  Composer: Richard Robbins. Conductor: Richard Robbins.

BOULEVARD NIGHTS
Soundtrack (1979) • Warner Bros. (S) BSK-3328 8-10   79
  Composer: Lalo Schifrin. Conductor: Lalo Schifrin. Cast: George Benson.

BOUND FOR GLORY
Soundtrack (1976) • United Artists (S) UA-LA695-H 10-12   76
Soundtrack (1976) • Liberty (S) LKAO-695 8-10   Re
  Composer: Woody Guthrie, Leonard Rosenman. Conductor: Leonard Rosenman. Cast: David
  Carradine.

BOURBON STREET BEAT
TV Soundtrack (1960) • Warner Bros. (M) W-1321.............................. 15-20   60
TV Soundtrack (1960) • Warner Bros. (S) WS-1321........................... 18-25   60
  Composer: Max David, Jay Livingston, others. Conductor: Don Ralke. Cast: Don Ralke and
  His Orchestra.

BOX-OFFICE BLOCKBUSTERS
Studiotrack • MGM (M) E 3894 8-12   60s
Studiotrack • MGM (S) SE 3894.. 8-12   60s
  Themes from *Exodus, Spellbound, Cimarron, Gone with the Wind, Around the World in 80
  Days, Bridge on the River Kwai, Spartacus, Gigi, Alamo, Butterfield 8* and *Ben-Hur*.
  Cast: David Rose and His Orchestra.

BOY FRIEND
Original London Cast (1953) • HMV (M) DLP-1078.............................. 45-50   50s
  UK release.
Original London Cast (1953) • Stanyan (SE) SR-10008...................... 12-18
  This musical originated in London and came to New York the following season.
  Composer: Sandy Wilson. Conductor: Stan Edwards. Cast: Anne Rogers, Anthony Hayes,
  Denise Hirst, Maria Charles, Joan Sterndale Bennett, Larry Drew, Hugh Paddick.
Original Cast (1954) • RCA Victor (EP) EOC-1018 12-15   54
  Three discs.
Original Cast (1954) • RCA Victor (M) LOC-1018 20-25   54
  Green label.
Original Cast (1954) • RCA Victor (M) LOC-1018 12-15   54
  Black label.

Original Cast (1954) • RCA Victor (M) LOC-1018 8-10   Re
  Cover indicates "RE" printed
    Composer: Sandy Wilson. **Conductor:** Anton Coppola. **Cast:** Julie Andrews, Ann Wakefield,
    John Hewer, Ruth Altman, Eric Berry, Paulette Girard, Geoffrey Hibbert, Dilys Lay, Bob
    Scheerer.
London Cast (1968) • That's Entertainment (S) TER-1054 8-10   80s
London Cast (1984) • That's Entertainment (S) TER-1095 8-10   80s
  UK releases.
Original Australian Cast (1968) • Ace of Clubs (S) SCL-1263 15-20   68
    Composer: Sandy Wilson. **Conductor:** Peter Narroway. **Cast:** Deidre Rubenstein, Laurel
    Veitch, Julia Day.
Original Revival Cast (1970) • Decca (S) DL-79177 10-12   70
Original Revival Cast (1970) • MCA (S) 2074 8-10   74
Original Revival Cast (1970) • MCA (S) 1537 5-8   80s
    Composer: Sandy Wilson. **Conductor:** Jerry Goldberg. **Cast:** Judy Carne, Sandy Duncan,
    Ronald Young, Jeanne Beauvais, Leon Shaw, Barbara Andres, Harvey Evans, Simon McQueen,
    David Vaughan, Ronald Young.
Soundtrack (1971) • MGM (S) 1SE-32 12-18   71
  Gatefold cover.
Soundtrack (1971) • MCA (S) MCA-39069 8-10   86
    Composer: Sandy Wilson, Arthur Freed, Nacio Herb Brown. **Conductor:** Peter Maxwell Davies.
    Cast: Twiggy, Christopher Gable, Tommy Tune, Max Adrian, Antonia Ellis, Bryan Pringle, Moyra
    Fraser, Georgina Hale, Sally Bryant, Barbara Windsor .
  Also see DIVORCE ME, DARLING

BOY MEETS BOY

Original Cast (1975) • JO R&P (S) JO-13 15-20   75
    Composer: Billy Solly. **Conductor:** David Friedman. **Cast:** Joe Barrett, Bobby Bower, David
    Gallegly, Jan Crean, Rita Gordon, Monica Grignon, Richard King, Paul Ratkevich, Bobby Reed,
    Dan Rounds, Raymond Wood.
Original Cast (1975) • AEI (S) AEI-1102 8-10   77
    Composer: Billy Solly. **Conductor:** David Friedman. **Cast:** Joe Barrett, Bobby Bower, David
    Gallegly.
Original Cast (1980) • Private Editions Series (S) FRC PES-1 10-15
  Gatefold cover. Based on the 1979 production by The Out & About Theatre, Minneapolis.
    Conductor: Brad Callahan, Patti Haight. **Cast:** Farrell Batley, Vic Campbell, Mick Isackson,
    Thomas Freiberg.
Studio Cast • Camay (SE) CA 3034-S 5-10
    Cast: Mel Torme, June Valli.

BOY NAMED CHARLIE BROWN

Soundtrack (1970) • Columbia (S) OS-3500 12-18   70
Soundtrack (1970) • Columbia Special Products (S) AOS-3500 8-10   Re
  Music and dialogue from a full-length animated feature.
    Composer: Rod McKuen, Vince Guaraldi, John Scott Trotter, Bill Melendez, Al Shean, Ludwig
    van Beethoven. **Conductor:** John Scott Trotter. **Cast:** Rod McKuen (vocal), voices by: Peter
    Robbins, Pamelyn Ferdin, Glenn Gilger, Andy Pforsich, Sally Dryer, Anne Alteri, Erin Sullivan.
TV Soundtrack (1964) • Fantasy (M) 5017 20-25   64
TV Soundtrack (1970) • Fantasy (S) 84-30 10-12   70
  Full title: *A Boy Named Charlie Brown, Jazz Impressions.*
    Composer: Vince Guaraldi. **Cast:** Vince Guaraldi Trio.

BOY ON A DOLPHIN

Soundtrack (1957) • Decca (M) DL-8580 25-65   57
  Black label or pink label promo.
Soundtrack (1957) • Decca (M) DL-8580 15-20   60s
  Rainbow (or multi-color) label.
Soundtrack (1957) • Varese Sarabande (M) STV-81119 8-10   81
    Composer: Hugo Friedhofer. **Conductor:** Lionel Newman. **Cast:** Marni Nixon, Mary Kaye, 20th
    Century-Fox Orchestra and Chorus.

BOY WHO COULD FLY

Soundtrack (1986) • Varese Sarabande (S) STV-81299 10-20   86
   Composer: Bruce Broughton. **Cast:** Sinfonia of London.
  Also see OLYMPUS ON MY MIND

BOYS FROM BRAZIL

Soundtrack (1978) • A&M (S) SP-4731 8-10   78
   Composer: Jerry Goldsmith. **Conductor:** Jerry Goldsmith.

BOYS FROM SYRACUSE

Original London Cast (1963) • Decca (M) LK-4564 40-45   64
Original London Cast (1963) • Decca (S) SKL-4564 45-65   64
  UK releases.
Original London Cast (1963) • Stet (S) DS-15016................................. 12-18   Re
Original London Cast (1963) • That's Entertainment (S) TER-1078 8-10   Re
  UK releases.
   Composer: Richard Rodgers, Lorenz Hart. **Conductor:** Robert Lowe. **Cast:** Bob Monkhouse,
  Denis Quilley, Pat Turner, Ronnie Corbett, Maggie Fitzgibbon, Lynn Kennington, Paula Hendrix.
Original Revival Cast (1963) • Capitol (M) TAO-1933 20-25   63
Original Revival Cast (1963) • Capitol (S) STAO-1933........................ 20-25   63
  Capitol LPs have gatefold covers.
   Composer: Richard Rodgers, Lorenz Hart. **Conductor:** Rene Weigert. **Cast:** Ellen Hanley,
  Danny Carroll, Cathryn Damon, Stuart Damon, Richard Nieves, Fred Kimbrough, Matt Tobin,
  Gary Oakes, Rudy Tronto, Clifford David, Julienne Marie, Karen Morrow.
Studio Cast (1954) • Columbia (M) ML-4837.. 12-15   54
Studio Cast (1954) • Columbia (M) CL-847 12-15   56
Studio Cast (1954) • Columbia (M) OL-7080 10-12   64
Studio Cast (1954) • Columbia (SE) OS-2580...................................... 8-10   64
Studio Cast (1954) • Columbia Special Products (SE) COS-2580............ 5-8   Re
   Composer: Richard Rodgers, Lorenz Hart. **Conductor:** Lehman Engel. **Cast:** Portia Nelson,
  Jack Cassidy, Bob Shaver.

BOYS IN THE BAND

Original Cast (1969) • A&M (S) SP-6001 12-15   69
  Two discs. Contains a complete play.
   Cast: Burt Bacharach, Martha & Vandellas, Kenneth Nelson, Frederick Combs, Cliff Gorman,
  Keith Prentice, Laurence Luckinbill, Beuben Greene, Peter White, Robert La Tourneaux,
  Leonard Frey.

BRAINCHILD

Original Cast (1974) • Demo (M) RFP-104.. 75-100   74
  Limited edition of 1,000.
   Composer: Michel Legrand, Hal David. **Cast:** Dorian Harewood.

BRAINSTORM

Soundtrack (1983) • Varese Sarabande (S) STV-81197 8-12   83
  Digital recording.
Soundtrack (1983) • That's Entertainment (S) TER-1074...................... 8-10   80s
  UK release.
   Composer: James Horner. **Conductor:** James Horner. **Cast:** London Symphony Orchestra.

BRASS ARE COMIN'

TV Soundtrack • A&M (S) SP-4228... 12-15
  Herb Alpert TV Special.
   Cast: Herb Alpert and the Tijuana Brass, others.

BRASS TARGET

Soundtrack (1978) • Varese Sarabande (S) VC-81082 8-10   78
   Composer: Laurence Rosenthal. **Conductor:** Laurence Rosenthal. **Cast:** Laurence Rosenthal.

BRAVE ONE
Soundtrack (1956) • Decca (EP) ED-847 18-25   56
Soundtrack (1956) • Decca (M) DL-8344 30-35   56
Soundtrack (1956) • AEI (M) AEI-3107 8-10   81
   Composer: Victor Young. **Conductor:** Victor Young. **Cast:** Munich Symphony Orchestra.

BRAVO, GIOVANNI
Original Cast (1962) • Columbia (M) KOL-5800 10-12   62
Original Cast (1962) • Columbia (S) KOS-2200 18-20   62
   Composer: Milton Schafer, Ronny Graham. **Conductor:** Anton Coppola. **Cast:** Cesare Siepi,
   Michele Lee, Maria Karnilova, Nino Banome, Rico Froehlich, George S. Irving, Buzz Miller,
   David Opatoshu, Gene Varrone.
Studiotrack (1961) • Columbia (M) CL-1820 8-10   62
Studiotrack (1961) • Columbia (S) CS-8620 10-12   62
   Composer: Milton Schafer, Ronny Graham. **Conductor:** Luther Henderson. **Cast:** Luther
   Henderson Orchestra.

BREAKER MORANT
Soundtrack (1980) • First American (S) FA7783 8-10   81
   Cast: Edward Woodward.

BREAKFAST AT TIFFANY'S
Original Cast (1966) • S.P.M. (M) CO-4788 125-150   78
   Live recording from the Society for the Preservation of Musicals. Full color cover and liner
notes.
   Composer: Bob Merrill. **Cast:** Mary Tyler Moore, Richard Chamberlain, Sally Kellerman, Art
   Lund.
Soundtrack (1961) • RCA Victor (M) PRS-159-2 20-25   61
   Promotional issue only.
Soundtrack (1961) • RCA Victor (M) LPM-2362 12-15   61
Soundtrack (1961) • RCA Victor (S) LSP-2362 15-20   61
   Black label.
Soundtrack (1961) • RCA Victor (S) LSP-2362 5-8   75
   Orange label.
   Composer: Henry Mancini, Johnny Mercer. **Conductor:** Henry Mancini.

BREAKFAST CLUB
Soundtrack (1985) • A&M (S) SP-5045 10-12   85
Soundtrack (1985) • A&M (S) SP-3294 8-10   Re
   Cast: Elizabeth Daily, Wang Chung, Jesse Johnson, Karla De Vito, Joyce Kennedy, Simple
   Minds.

BREAKIN'
Soundtrack (1984) • Polydor (S) 821 919-1 8-10   84
   Cast: Bar-Kays, Carol Lynn James, Rufus, Chaka Khan, Chris Taylor and David Storrs, Ollie
   and Jerry, Hotstreak, 3V, Fire Fox, Re-Flex.

BREAKIN' 2 – ELECTRIC BOOGALOO
Soundtrack (1984) • Polydor (S) 823 696-1 8-12   84
   Cast: Ollie and Jerry, Fire Fox, George Krantz, Steve Donn, Carol Lynn Townes, Mark Scott,
   Rags and Riches.

BREAKING GLASS
Soundtrack (1980) • A&M (S) SP-4820 8-10   80
   Composer: Hazel O'Connor. **Cast:** Hazel O'Connor.

BREATH OF SCANDAL
Soundtrack (1959) • Imperial (M) 9132W 20-40   59
Soundtrack (1959) • Imperial (S) 12068W 60-65   59
   Composer: Alessandro Cicognini. **Conductor:** Carlo Savina. **Cast:** Maurice Chevalier.

BRECHT ON BRECHT
Original Cast (1962) • Columbia (M) O2L-278.................................... 10-12   62
Original Cast (1962) • Columbia (S) O2S-203..................................... 12-15   62
 Both are two-disc sets.
  Composer: George Tabori. **Cast:** Dane Clark, Anne Jackson, Lotte Lenya, Viveca Lindfors.

BREEZY
Soundtrack (1973) • MCA (S) MCA-384.. 12-15   73
  Composer: Michel Legrand. **Conductor:** Michel Legrand.

BREL, JACQUES: see JACQUES BREL IS ALIVE AND WELL AND LIVING IN PARIS

BREMEN TOWN MUSICIANS
Soundtrack • Golden (M) LP-168 10-20
  Composer: Milton Delugg, Anne Delugg. **Conductor:** Lehman Engel. **Cast:** Paul Tripp (narration).

BREWSTER McCLOUD
Soundtrack (1970) • MGM (S) 1SE-28 10-12   70
  Composer: John Phillips, Gene Page. **Conductor:** Gene Page. **Cast:** Merry Clayton, John Phillips, Sally Kellerman.

BRIAN'S SONG – THEMES AND VARIATIONS
Studiotrack (1972) • Bell (S) 6071 10-15   72
 Also includes music from *Summer of '62* and *Wuthering Heights*.
  Composer: Michel Legrand. **Conductor:** Michel Legrand.

BRICE, FANNY: see FANNY BRICE

BRIDE
Soundtrack (1985) • Varese Sarabande (S) STV 81254 10-15   85
  Composer: Maurice Jarre. **Conductor:** Maurice Jarre. **Cast:** Maurice Jarre and His Orchestra.

BRIDE WORE YOLANDE: see SOPHIA LOREN IN ROME

BRIDE OF FRANKENSTEIN: see FRANZ WAXMAN

BRIDESHEAD REVISITED
TV Soundtrack (1982) • Chrysalis (S) CHR-1367................................. 10-15   82
  Composer: Geoffrey Burgon. **Conductor:** Geoffrey Burgon. **Cast:** Jeremy Irons, Anthony Andrews, Diana Quick, Sir Laurence Olivier.
TV Soundtrack (1982) • Chrysalis (S) FV-41367 8-10   82
 Produced by Granada Television.
  Composer: Geoffrey Burgon. **Conductor:** Geoffrey Burgon. **Cast:** Sir Laurence Olivier, Sir John Gielgud.

BRIDGE ON THE RIVER KWAI
Soundtrack (1957) • Columbia (M) CL-1100 12-15   57
Soundtrack (1957) • Columbia (SE) CS-9426 8-12   67
  Composer: Malcolm Arnold, Kenneth Alford. **Conductor:** Malcolm Arnold. **Cast:** Mitch Miller's Orchestra and Chorus.

BRIDGE TOO FAR
Soundtrack (1977) • United Artists (S) UA-LA762-H 10-12   77
Soundtrack (1977) • Liberty (S) LKAO-762 8-10   Re
  Composer: John Addison. **Conductor:** John Addison.

BRIGADOON
Original Cast (1947) • RCA Victor K-7... 20-30   47
 Boxed set of five blue plastic 78 rpms.
Original Cast (1947) • RCA Victor (EP) EOB-1001 10-15   51
 Two discs.
Original Cast (1947) • RCA Victor (M) LOC-1001 18-20   51
 Green label. Front cover is green.

Original Cast (1947) • RCA Victor (M) LOC-1001 10-15   50s
  Black label. Front cover has photo of dancers wearing kilts.
Original Cast (1947) • RCA Victor (M) LOC-1001 10-12   63
Original Cast (1947) • RCA Victor (SE) LSO-1001 10-12   63
  Above two have a drawing of dancers in kilts on front cover.
Original Cast (1947) • RCA Victor (SE) AYL1-3901 5-8   81
  Same cover as above, with orange trim around edges. *Brigadoon* was RCA's first original
  cast recording, made for 78s in 1947, then issued on LP in 1951.
  Composer: Alan Jay Lerner, Frederick Loewe. **Conductor:** Franz Allers. **Cast:** David Brooks,
  Marion Bell, Pamela Britton, Lee Sullivan, Delbert Anderson, Hayes Gordon, Earl Redding,
  Shirley Robbins, Jeff Warren.
London Studio Cast • Wing (M) WL-1051 10-15
  One side has music from *Kiss Me Kate*.
  Conductor: John Gregory. KISS ME KATE: **Cast:** Elizabeth Larner, Barry Kent, Mike Sammes
  Singers.
Studio Cast (1953) • RCA Victor (EP) ERA-129 5-10   53
  Conductor: Arthur Fiedler. **Cast:** Boston Pops Orchestra.
Studio Cast (1958) • Columbia (M) CL-1132 10-12   58
Studio Cast (1958) • Columbia (M) OL-7040 10-12   65
Studio Cast (1958) • Columbia (SE) OS-2540 8-10   65
Studio Cast (1958) • Columbia Special Products (SE) COS-2540e 5-8   Re
  Composer: Alan Jay Lerner, Frederick Loewe. **Conductor:** Lehman Engel. **Cast:** Shirley
  Jones, Jack Cassidy, Susan Johnson, Frank Porretta.
Studio Cast (1959) • National Academy Record Club (M) ES-12 10-15   59
  From the *Ed Sullivan Presents Songs and Music of…* series.
  Cast: Ed Sullivan All Star Cast.
Soundtrack (1954) • MGM (EP) X-263 10-25   54
Soundtrack (1954) • MGM (M) E-3135 (Yellow label) 20-25   54
Soundtrack (1954) • MGM (M) E-3135 (Black label) 15-18   Re
Soundtrack (1954) • MCA (M) 39062 5-8   Re
  Composer: Alan Jay Lerner, Frederick Loewe. **Conductor:** Johnny Green. **Cast:** Gene Kelly,
  Van Johnson, Carole Richards (performed vocals for Cyd Charisse in the film), John Gustafson
  (performed vocals for Jimmy Thompson in the film).
TV Soundtrack (1968) • Columbia Special Products (M) CSM-385 12-18   68
  Two slight back cover variations exist for this LP.
  Composer: Frederick Loewe, Alan Jay Lerner. **Conductor:** Irwin Kostal. **Cast:** Robert Goulet,
  Sally Ann Howes, Marlyn Mason, Tommy Carlisle.
  Also see EVENING WITH LERNER AND LOEWE
  Also see FINIAN'S RAINBOW AND BRIGADOON REMEMBERED
  Also see LYRICS BY LERNER
  Also see THOSE GLORIOUS MGM MUSICALS.

BRIGHT LIGHTS, BIG CITY
Soundtrack (1986) • Warner Bros. (S) 1-25688 8-10   86
  Composer: Michael Small. **Cast:** Prince, New Order, Narada Michael Walden, Bryan Ferry,
  Depeche Mode, Donald Fagen, Noise Club, Konk, Jennifer Hall, M/A/R/R/S.

BRIGHTON BEACH MEMOIRS
Soundtrack (1987) • MCA (S) 6193 8-10   87
  Composer: Various. **Cast:** Steve Clayton, George Hall Orchestra.

BRIMSTONE AND TREACLE
Soundtrack (1982) • A&M (S) SP-4915 8-12   82
  Composer: Police, Sting, Go-Go's, Squeeze. **Cast:** Police, Sting, Go-Go's, Squeeze, Finchley
  Children's Music Group, Brimstone Chorale.

BRING BACK BIRDIE
Original Cast (1981) • Original Cast (S) OC-8132 20-25   81
  Composer: Charles Strouse, Lee Adams. **Conductor:** Milton Rosenstock. **Cast:** Chita Rivera,
  Donald O'Connor, Marcel Forestieri, Betsy Friday, Maurice Hines, Maria Karnilova, Robin Morse,
  Rebecca Renfroe.

BROADWAY
Studio Cast (1958) • Columbia (EP) B-11101 5-10   58
Studio Cast (1958) • Columbia (M) CL-1110 10-15   58
Studio Cast (1958) • Columbia (S) CS-8052 15-20   58
   Composer: Various. **Cast:** Norman Luboff Orchestra and Choir.

BROADWAY BABIES
Original Cast (1972) • Columbia (S) C3-10643 20-30   72
   Boxed, three-disc set, includes previously released songs. Also has Revival Cast songs
   from Broadway shows from 1924-1971.
   Cast: Barbra Streisand, Ruby Keeler, Ethel Merman, others.

BROADWAY BALLET: see SINGIN' IN THE RAIN

BROADWAY, BROADWAY, BROADWAY
Studio Cast • Longines Symphonette (S) LWS-117 10-15
   Composer: Various. **Cast:** Judy Garland, Lena Horne, Jimmy Durante, Bing Crosby, Maurice
   Chevalier.

BROADWAY CAVALCADE
Studio Cast (1958) • Capitol (M) WBO-1079 10-20   58
   Composer: Various. **Conductor:** Fred Waring. **Cast:** Fred Waring and His Orchestra.

BROADWAY CHORUS CALL
Studio Cast (1959) • Epic (M) LN-3546 10-15   59
Studio Cast (1959) • Epic (S) BN-519 15-20   59
   Composer: Various. **Cast:** Merrill Staton Choir.

BROADWAY CLASSICS
Studio Cast (1954) • RCA Victor (EP) EPA-561 10-15   54
   Music from *Kismet, By the Beautiful Sea, The Golden Apple* and *The Girl in Pink Tights.*
   Composer: Various. **Conductor:** Hugo Winterhalter. **Cast:** Eddie Fisher, Hugo Winterhalter
   and His Orchestra.

BROADWAY COMPLEAT
Studio Cast (1959) • Warner Bros. (M) B-1253 10-15   59
Studio Cast (1959) • Warner Bros. (S) BS-1253 10-20   59
   Cast: Warren Barker Orchestra.

BROADWAY EXTRAVAGANZA
Studio Cast (1987) • MCA (S) 6219 8-10   87
   Composer: Various. **Conductor:** Paul Gemignani. **Cast:** Royal Philharmonic Orchestra.

BROADWAY '55
Studio Cast [Vol. 1] (1955) • Decca (EP) ED-2169 5-10   55
Studio Cast [Vol. 2] (1955) • Decca (EP) ED-2175 5-10   55
Studio Cast [Vol. 3] (1955) • Decca (EP) ED-2182 5-10   55
Studio Cast (1955) • Decca (M) DL-8099 10-20   55
   Composer: Various. **Conductor:** Fred Waring. **Cast:** Fred Waring and His Orchestra.

BROADWAY '58-'59
Studio Cast • Warner Bros. (M) B 1304 10-15
   Music from *Gypsy, Redhead, Flower Drum Song* and *Destry Rides Again.*
   Cast: Eddie LeMar and Orchestra.

BROADWAY GOES HOLLYWOOD
Studiotrack [Vol. 1] (1955) • Decca (EP) ED-2270 5-10   55
Studiotrack [Vol. 2] (1955) • Decca (EP) ED-2271 5-10   55
Studiotrack [Vol. 3] (1955) • Decca (EP) ED-2272 5-10   55
Studiotrack (1955) • Decca (M) DL-8167 10-20   55
   Composer: Various. **Conductor:** Jack Pleis. **Cast:** Jack Pleis and His Orchestra.

BROADWAY GOES TO COLLEGE
Studio Cast (1959) • Mercury (M) MG-20456 10-15   59
Studio Cast (1959) • Mercury (S) SR-60139 15-20   59
    Composer: Various. **Cast:** Northwestern Men's Glee Club.

BROADWAY GOLD
Studio Cast • Audio Award (S) AA 101...................................... 6-12   81
    Double LP set.

BROADWAY HIGHLIGHTS
Studio Cast [Vol. 1] (1955) • Capitol (EP) EAP 1-583............................ 5-10   55
Studio Cast [Vol. 2] (1955) • Capitol (EP) EAP 2-583............................ 5-10   55
Studio Cast [Vol. 3] (1955) • Capitol (EP) EAP 3-583............................ 5-10   55
Studio Cast (1955) • Capitol (M) T-583 15-25   55
    Composer: Various. **Cast:** John Raitt.

BROADWAY HITS IN HI-FI
Studio Cast (1954) • ABC-Paramount (M) ABC-154 10-20   54
    Composer: Various. **Conductor:** Irving Fields. **Cast:** Irving Fields' Orchestra.

BROADWAY HITS OF YESTERDAY
Studio Cast (1954) • Varsity (EP) E-20 5-10   54
Studio Cast (1954) • Varsity (EP) E-45 5-10   54
Studio Cast (1954) • Varsity (M) VLP-6011 10-20   54
    Composer: Various. **Conductor:** Russell Bennett. **Cast:** Russell Bennett and His Orchestra.

BROADWAY IN RHYTHM
Studio Cast • Columbia (M) CL 1252 8-12
    Music from *The King and I, My Fair Lady* and *South Pacific.*
    Conductor: Ray Conniff. **Cast:** Ray Conniff Orchestra and Chorus.

BROADWAY MAGIC
Original Cast [Vol. 1] (1979) • Columbia (S) JS-36282............................ 8-10   79
    Original performances from musicals recorded by Columbia Records.
    Composer: Various. **Conductor:** Various. **Cast:** Joel Grey, Priscilla Lopez, Angela Lansbury,
    Elaine Stritch, Ethel Merman, Gwen Verdon, Larry Kert, Julie Andrews, Carol Lawrence, Betty
    Wolfe, others.
Original Cast [Vol. 2] (1980) • Columbia (S) JS-36409............................ 8-10   80
    Sub-title: *The Great Performers.*
    Composer: Various. **Conductor:** Various. **Cast:** Debbie Reynolds, Danny Kaye, John Travolta,
    Barbra Streisand, Ruby Keeler, Julie Andrews, Rex Harrison, Angela Lansbury, Beatrice Arthur,
    Ethel Merman.
Original Cast [Vol. 3] (1980) • Columbia (S) JS-36409............................ 8-10   80
    Sub-title: *The Showstoppers.* Songs are from *A Chorus Line, Gypsy, My Fair Lady, Annie,
    Bye Bye Birdie, South Pacific, West Side Story, Mame, Sweet Charity* and *Li'l Abner.*
    Composer: Various. **Conductor:** Various. **Cast:** Chita Rivera, Stanley Holloway, Helen
    Gallagher, Stubby Kaye, others.
Original Cast [Vol. 4] (1981) • Columbia (S) JS-36409............................ 8-10   81
    Sub-title: *Super Hits.* Songs are from *Mame, South Pacific, George M!, Cabaret, On the
    Town, Candide, My Fair Lady, West Side Story, The Sound of Music* and *A Chorus Line.*
    Composer: Various. **Conductor:** Various. **Cast:** Angela Lansbury, Joel Grey, Stanley Holloway,
    Mary Martin, Adolph Green, Jill Haworth, others.
Original Cast [Vol. 5] (1981) • Columbia (S) JS-36409............................ 8-10   81
    Sub-title: *The Great Performances.* Songs are from *Bells Are Ringing, Camelot, Sweet
    Charity, Gypsy, Flower Drum Song, Hallelujah Baby!, A Chorus Line* and others.
    Composer: Various. **Conductor:** Various. **Cast:** Ethel Merman, Sandra Church, Larry Blyden,
    Pat Suzuki, Leslie Uggams, Donna McKechnie, Gwen Verdon, Dorothy Loudon, Judy Holliday,
    Rex Harrison, others.

BROADWAY MELODIES
Studiotrack (1956) • Kapp (M) KL-1033 15-20   56
    Composer: Various. **Cast:** Buddy Greco Quartet.

Studiotrack (1953) • London (M) LL-509 15-20   53
> **Composer:** Various. **Conductor:** Frank Chacksfield. **Cast:** Frank Chacksfield and His Orchestra.

BROADWAY MELODY OF 1938
Soundtrack (1937) • Motion Picture Tracks (M) MPT-3 12-18
> **Composer:** Cole Porter. **Cast:** Eleanor Powell, Judy Garland, Sophie Tucker, Buddy Ebsen, George Murphy.

BROADWAY MELODY OF 1940
Soundtrack (1940) • Classic International Filmusicals (M) C.I.F. 3002 ... 8-10
> **Composer:** Cole Porter. **Cast:** Fred Astaire, Eleanor Powell, George Murphy.

BROADWAY MUSICALS
Studiotrack • Columbia Special Products (S) CSS 520 8-12   60s
> Full title: *Zenith Salutes the Broadway Musicals.*
>> **Cast:** Andy Williams, Robert Goulet, Julie Andrews with Henri Rene and Orchestra, Eydie Gorme, Ray Coniff, Andre Kostelanetz, Barbra Streisand, Steve Lawrence.

BROADWAY OPENING NIGHT
Original Cast • RCA Victor (S) ARL1-4049.. 8-10   81
> Full title: *Broadway Opening Night – Vol. 1. The 60s.*
Original Cast • RCA Victor (S) ARL1-4050.. 8-10   81
> Full title: *Broadway Opening Night – Vol. 2. The 70s.*

BROADWAY PLAYBILL
Studiotrack • Columbia (M) CL 1416 10-15
> Music from *Gypsy, Sound of Music* and *Fiorello.*
>> **Conductor:** Warren Barker. **Cast:** Hi-Lo's, Warren Barker and His Orchestra.

BROADWAY SHOW STOPPERS
Studio Cast • Seeco (M) CELP-475 8-12
> **Cast:** Stubby Kaye, Lilo, Larry Kert.
Studiotrack (1959) • Forum (M) F 9021... 15-25   60
> **Cast:** Playmates (Donny, Morey, Chic.)
Studiotrack • Coronet (S) CXS-189... 8-12   60s
> Music from *My Fair Lady, South Pacific, Sound of Music,* others.
>> **Cast:** Santiago and His Silver Strings.

BROADWAY SHOWCASE
Studiotrack (1957) • Verve (M) MG-2033.. 10-20   57
> **Composer:** Various. **Conductor:** Buddy De Franco. **Cast:** Buddy De Franco and His Orchestra.

BROADWAY SONG BOOK
Studiotrack [Vol. 1] (1959) • Coral (M) CRL-57274 10-12   59
Studiotrack [Vol. 1] (1959) • Coral (S) CRL7-57274 10-15   59
Studiotrack [Vol. 2] (1959) • Coral (M) CRL-57275 10-12   59
Studiotrack [Vol. 2] (1959) • Coral (S) CRL7-57275 10-15   59
Studiotrack [Vols. 1 & 2] (1959) • Coral (M) CX-4 12-15   59
Studiotrack [Vols. 1 & 2] (1959) • Coral (S) CX-7 15-20   59
> Both "CX" issues are two-disc sets
>> **Composer:** Various. **Conductor:** Dick Jacobs. **Cast:** Dick Jacobs and His Orchestra.

BROADWAY SPECTACULAR
Studiotrack (1969) • Premier (S) PS-6003 15-20   69
> Two discs.

BROADWAY SUCCESS STORY
Studiotrack (1955) • Epic (M) LN-1122.. 15-25   55
> 10-inch LP. Also has music from *Ross.*
>> **Composer:** Various. **Cast:** Delores Hawkins and the Mellow-Larks.

BROADWAY TO HOLLYWOOD
Studiotrack • Columbia (M) CL 1607 8-12
    Cast: Ferrante and Teicher.

BROADWAY TUNESMITH CY COLEMAN SINGS CY COLEMAN
Studiotrack (1974) • Columbia (S) C-32804 10-12   74
    Previously issued as *If My Friends Could See Me Now.*
    Composer: Cy Coleman. **Cast:** Cy Coleman.
    Also see IF MY FRIENDS COULD SEE ME NOW

BROADWAY'S BEST: see THIS IS BROADWAY'S BEST

BROADWAY'S BEST SHOWS, 1963
Studiotrack (1963) • Mercury (M) MG-60757 10-15   63
Studiotrack (1963) • Mercury (S) SR-60757 10-15   63
    Themes from *Stop the World I Want to Get Off, Mr. President, Oliver* and *Little Me.*
    Cast: Harry Simeone Chorale.

BROADWAY'S BIG HITS
Studiotrack (1963) • Mercury (M) MG-20811 10-15   63
Studiotrack (1963) • Mercury (S) SR-60811 10-20   63
    Composer: Various. **Cast:** Harry Simeone Chorale, Caesar Giovannini, Clebanoff, Quincy
    Jones, Art Farmer, others.

BRONCO BILLY
Soundtrack (1980) • Elektra (S) 5E-512 8-10   80
    Composer: Steve Dorff. **Conductor:** Steve Dorff. **Cast:** Ronnie Milsap, Penny DeHaven, Merle
    Haggard, Clint Eastwood, Reinsmen.

BRONTES
Original Cast • Vanguard (S) VRS-9176/7 40-50
    Two discs.
    Cast: Margaret Webster.

BROTHER FROM ANOTHER PLANET
Soundtrack (1984) • Daring (S) DR1007 10-15   84
    Composer: Mason Daring, others. **Cast:** Joe Morton, Ren Woods, Efrain Salgado, Lee
    "Scratch" Perry, Dee Dee Bridgewater, Jeff Anderson.

BROTHER ON THE RUN
Soundtrack (1973) • Perception (S) PLP-45 25-30   73
    Composer: Johnny Pate, Adam Wade. **Conductor:** Johnny Pate. **Cast:** Adam Wade.

BROTHERHOOD
Soundtrack (1969) • Dot (S) DLP 25925 10-15   69
    Also has themes from *Artists and Models, Romeo and Juliet, Anyone Can Play, Captain
    Carey, USA* and *The Caddy.*
    Composer: Lalo Schifrin, others. **Cast:** Creative Cast.

BROTHERS
Soundtrack (1977) • Warner Bros. (S) BS-3024 10-12   77
    Composer: Taj Mahal. **Conductor:** Taj Mahal. **Cast:** Taj Mahal.

BROWN, MARY C.: see MARY C. BROWN

BRUTE FORCE
Soundtrack (1947) • Tony Thomas (S) MR-3 30-35   80
    Also contains music from *Naked City.*
    Composer: Miklos Rozsa. **Conductor:** Miklos Rozsa.
    Also see LUST FOR LIFE

BUBBLING BROWN SUGAR
Original Cast (1976) • H&L (S) HL-69011-698 8-10   76
Original Cast (1986) • Amherst (S) 3310.. 5-8   86
   Composer: Danny Holgate, others. **Conductor:** Danny Holgate. **Cast:** Avon Long, Vivian Reed, Josephine Premice, Chip Garnett, Joseph Attles, Carolyn Byrd, Ethel Beatty, Barry Preston.

BUCCANEER (1958)
Soundtrack (1958) • Columbia (M) CL-1278 15-20   58
Soundtrack (1958) • Columbia (S) CS-8096.. 25-35   58
Soundtrack (1958) • Columbia Special Products (S) ACS-8096............. 8-10   Re
   Composer: Elmer Bernstein. **Conductor:** Elmer Bernstein.

BUCCANEER
Original Cast • AEI (S) AEI-1114... 8-10   70s
  British musical.
   Composer: Sandy Wilson. **Cast:** Betty Warren, Ronald Radd.

BUCK ROGERS
Soundtrack (1979) • MCA (S) 3097... 8-10   79
   Composer: Stu Phillips, Glen A. Larson. **Conductor:** Stu Phillips.

BUD SHANK PLAYS MUSIC FROM TODAY'S MOVIES
Studiotrack • World Pacific (M) WP-1864.. 10-20   60s
Studiotrack • World Pacific (S) WPS-21864... 10-20   60s
   Cast: Bud Shank.

BUDDY
Original London Cast (1989) • First Night (S) QUE VE 1....................... 8-12   89
   Cast: Paul Hipp, Gareth Marks, David Howarth.

BUDDY HOLLY STORY
Soundtrack (1978) • Epic/American Int'l (S) SE-35412 8-12   78
  Songs made famous by Buddy Holly.
   Composer: Buddy Holly, others. **Cast:** Gary Busey, Eddie Cochran Band.

BUDGIE
Original London Cast (1988) • MCA (S) 6035 10-12   88
   Composer: Mort Shuman, Don Black. **Cast:** Adam Faith, Anita Dobson, John Turner.

BUGALOOS
TV Soundtrack (1970) • Capitol (S) SW-621 40-50   70
   Composer: Hal Yoergler. **Cast:** John McIndoe, Caroline Ellis.

BUGS BUNNY AND FRIENDS
Studiotrack • Capitol (M) J-3257 15-25   61
   Composer: Warren Foster, Ted Pierce, Michael Maltese. **Conductor:** Billy May, Van Alexander.
   Cast: Mel Blanc, Arthur Bryan.

BUGS BUNNY IN STORYLAND
Studiotrack • Capitol (M) J-3266 15-20   61
   Composer: Warren Foster, Ted Pierce, Billy May, Alan Livingston, Michael Maltese.
   Conductor: Billy May. **Cast:** Mel Blanc.

BUGS BUNNY STORIES FOR CHILDREN
Studio Cast (1947) • Capitol CC-64.. 5-10   47
  Album of three 78 rpms.
   Cast: Mel Blanc (voices), Billy May (music).

BUGSY MALONE
Soundtrack (1976) • RSO (S) RS-1-3501... 10-12   76
   Composer: Paul Williams. **Cast:** Paul Williams, others.

BULL DURHAM
Soundtrack (1988) • Capitol (S) C1-90586 8-10   88
    Cast: George Thorogood and the Destroyers, Fabulous Thunderbirds, House of Schock, Los Lobos, John Fogerty, Pat Laughlin, Dr. Bennie Wallace, Blasters.

BULLET FOR A PRETTY BOY
Soundtrack (1970) • American Int'l (S) STA-1034 10-15   70
    Composer: Harley Hatcher. **Conductor:** Harley Hatcher. **Cast:** The Source.

BULLITT
Soundtrack (1968) • Warner Bros. (S) WS-1777 40-50   68
Soundtrack (1968) • Warner Bros. (S) ST-20152 20-30   68
    Composer: Lalo Schifrin. **Conductor:** Lalo Schifrin.

BULLWHIP GRIFFIN: see ADVENTURES OF BULLWHIP GRIFFIN

BUNCH
Soundtrack (1966) • RCA Victor (M) LPM-3629 10-15   66
Soundtrack (1966) • RCA Victor (S) LSP-3629 10-15   66
    Cast: Sally Gracie, Dian Kagan, Linda Lavin, Renee Taylor, Mary Louise Wilson.

BUNDLE OF JOY
Soundtrack (1956) • RCA Victor (EP) EPA-4018 15-20   56
Soundtrack (1956) • RCA Victor (M) LPM-1399 30-35   56
    Composer: Josef Myrow, Mack Gordon. **Conductor:** Hugo Winterhalter, Walter Scharf. **Cast:** Eddie Fisher, Debbie Reynolds, Nita Talbot, RKO Studio Orchestra.

BUNNY LAKE IS MISSING
Soundtrack (1965) • RCA Victor (M) LOC-1115 25-35   65
Soundtrack (1965) • RCA Victor (S) LSO-1115 40-60   65
    Composer: Paul Glass. **Conductor:** Paul Glass. **Cast:** Zombies.

BUNNY O'HARE
Soundtrack (1971) • American Int'l (S) STA-1041 12-18   71
    Composer: Mike Curb, Billy Strange. **Conductor:** Billy Strange. **Cast:** Billy Strange, Mike Curb Congregation, Full Circle.

BUONA SERA, MRS. CAMPBELL
Soundtrack (1969) • United Artists (M) UAL-5192 15-20   69
Soundtrack (1969) • United Artists (S) UAS-5192 20-25   69
    Composer: Riz Ortolani. **Conductor:** Riz Ortolani. **Cast:** Jimmy Roselli.

BURGLAR
Soundtrack (1987) • MCA (S) 6201 8-10   87
    Cast: Sly Stone, Belinda Carlisle, Jets, Smithereens, Wax, Jacksons, Distance, Belle Stars, Bobcat Goldthwaite.

BURGLARS
Soundtrack (1971) • Bell (S) 1105 20-30   71
    Composer: Ennio Morricone. **Conductor:** Ennio Morricone.

BURKE'S LAW
TV Soundtrack (1964) • Liberty (M) LRP-3374 40-50   64
TV Soundtrack (1964) • Liberty (S) LST-7374 45-60   64
    Composer: Herschel Burke Gilbert, others. **Conductor:** Herschel Burke Gilbert.

BURLESQUE SHOW
Studio Cast (1963) • Cameo (M) C-2002 30-40   63
    Composer: Kermit Schafer.

BURN!
Soundtrack (1970) • United Artists (S) UA-LA303-G 10-15   70
    Composer: Ennio Morricone. **Conductor:** Ennio Morricone.

BURNING
Soundtrack (1981) • Charisma CLASS (S) 12........................ 8-10   81
Soundtrack (1981) • Varese Sarabande (S) 81162.............. 8-10   81
  Cast: Rick Wakeman.

BURNS AND ALLEN
Original Radio Cast • Mark 56 (M) 614............................ 15-20   73
  Sponsored by Maxwell House Coffee Time.

BUSTER
Soundtrack (1988) • Atlantic (S) 81905-1........................ 8-10   88
  Cast: Phil Collins, Gerry and the Pacemakers, Spencer Davis Group, Dusty Springfield, London Film Orchestra, Anne Dudley, Sonny and Cher, Four Tops, Searchers.

BUSTIN' LOOSE
Soundtrack (1981) • MCA (S) 5141................................. 8-10   81
  Cast: Roberta Flack, Luther Vandross.

BUT BEAUTIFUL: see BING'S HOLLYWOOD

BUTCH CASSIDY AND THE SUNDANCE KID
Soundtrack (1969) • A&M (S) SP-4227.............................. 8-12   69
Soundtrack (1969) • A&M (S) SP-3159.............................. 8-10   Re
  Composer: Burt Bacharach. **Conductor:** Burt Bacharach. **Cast:** B.J. Thomas, others.

BUTTERFIELD 8
Studiotrack (1960) • MGM (M) E-3952............................ 10-15   60
Studiotrack (1960) • MGM (S) SE-3952........................... 15-20   61
  Composer: Bronislau Kaper, others. **Conductor:** David Rose. **Cast:** David Rose and His Orchestra.

BUTTERFLY
Soundtrack (1982) • Applause (S) APLP-1017..................... 10-15   82
  Composer: Ennio Morricone. **Conductor:** Ennio Morricone.

BY JUPITER
Studio Cast (1964) • Roulette (M) R-25278....................... 30-40   64
  One side has music from *Girl Crazy*.
  Composer: Richard Rodgers, Lorenz Hart. GIRL CRAZY: George Gershwin, Ira Gershwin. **Cast:** Jackie Cain, Roy Kral.
Original Revival Cast (1967) • RCA Victor (M) LOC-1137.......... 30-35   67
Original Revival Cast (1967) • RCA Victor (M) LSO-1137.......... 45-65   67
  Composer: Richard Rodgers, Lorenz Hart. **Conductor:** Milton Setzer. **Cast:** Bob Dishy, Jackie Alloway, Irene Byatt, Emory Bass, Ronnie Cunningham, Norma Doggett, Rosemarie Heyer, Robert R. Kaye, Richard Marshall, Sheila Doggett.

BY REQUEST: THE BEST OF JOHN WILLIAMS & THE BOSTON POPS
Studiotrack (1987) • Philips (S) 420178-1......................... 10-15   87
  Music from *Close Encounters of the Third Kind, Midway, Return of the Jedi, E.T., Superman, Empire Strikes Back, 1941, Jaws* and *Star Wars*.
  Composer: John Williams. **Conductor:** John Williams. **Cast:** John Williams and the Boston Pops Orchestra.

BY THE BEAUTIFUL SEA
Original Cast (1954) • Capitol (EP) EDM-531..................... 15-20   54
Original Cast (1954) • Capitol (M) S-531........................ 45-65   54
Original Cast (1954) • Capitol (M) T-11652...................... 8-10   77
  Composer: Arthur Schwartz, Dorothy Fields. **Conductor:** Jay Blackton. **Cast:** Shirley Booth, Wilbur Evans, Cameron Prud'homme, Richard France, Mae Barnes, Libi Staiger, Thomas Gleason, Mary Harmon, Larry Howard, Cindy Robbins, Eddie Roll, Gloria Smith.
Studiotrack (1954) • Capitol (EP) EPA-535....................... 10-20   54
  Composer: Arthur Schwartz, Dorothy Fields. **Cast:** Nat "King" Cole, Betty Hutton, Helen O'Connell, Les Baxter.

BY THE LIGHT OF THE SILVERY MOON

Studiotrack (1953) • Capitol (EP) EBF-422 20-25   53
  Two discs.

Studiotrack [Vol. 1] (1953) • Capitol (EP) EAP 1-422 10-15   55

Studiotrack [Vol. 2] (1953) • Capitol (EP) EAP 2-422 10-15   55

Studiotrack [Vol. 3] (1953) • Capitol (EP) EAP 3-422 10-15   55

Studiotrack (1953) • Capitol (M) H-422 30-35   53
  10-inch LP.

Studiotrack (1953) • Capitol (M) T-422 .... 20-25·   55
  Because film stars Doris Day and Gordon MacRae were under contract to different
  recording companies, a soundtrack album from this film could not be released. Instead,
  Day recorded the score for Columbia and MacRae recorded it for Capitol.
  Composer: Various. **Conductor:** Axel Stordahl. **Cast:** Gordon MacRae, June Sutton.

Studiotrack (1953) • Columbia (EP) B-334 12-18   53

Studiotrack (1953) • Columbia (M) CL-6248 30-35   53
  10-inch LP.
  Conductor: Paul Weston. **Cast:** Doris Day, Norman Luboff Choir.

BYE BYE BIRDIE

Original Cast (1960) • Columbia (M) KOL-5510 8-12   60

Original Cast (1960) • Columbia (S) KOS-2025 10-12   60
  Above two have gatefold covers and picture a female hand against a black background.

Original Cast (1960) • Columbia (M) OL-5510 8-10   Re

Original Cast (1960) • Columbia (S) OS-2025 10-12   Re
  Above two have standard covers with "The Telephone Hour" photo on cover.

Original Cast (1960) • Columbia Special Products (S) COS-2025 8-10   Re
  Has two covers, one a reissue of "The Telephone Hour" cover, the other with the show's
  title up against a blue "Columbia Special Products" background.
  Composer: Charles Strouse, Lee Adams. **Conductor:** Elliot Lawrence. **Cast:** Chita Rivera, Dick
  Van Dyke, Paul Lynde, Michael J. Pollard, Jessica Albright, Johnny Borden, Dick Gautier,
  Sharon Lerit, Marijane Maricle, Susan Watson.

Original London Cast (1961) • Wing (M) MGW-13000 35-45   61

Original London Cast (1961) • Wing (S) SRW-17000 45-65   61
  Composer: Charles Strouse, Lee Adams. **Conductor:** Alyn Ainsworth. **Cast:** Chita Rivera,
  Peter Marshall, Angela Baddeley, Sylvia Tysick, Robert Nichols, Mary Laura Wood, Clive
  Endersby, Kenneth Nash, Marty Wilde.

Studio Cast (1961) • Columbia (M) CL-1590 10-12   61

Studio Cast (1961) • Columbia (S) CS-8390 10-15   61
  Cast: Chico Hamilton Quintet.

Studio Cast (1962) • Design (M) DLP-171 8-12   64

Studio Cast (1962) • Design (S) DLP-171 8-12   64
  One side has music from *Hello Dolly*.
  Cast: Johnny Mack Singers, Jim Vickers, Mary Hurt, Sue Singleton.

Soundtrack (1963) • RCA Victor (M) LOC-1081 12-15   63

Soundtrack (1963) • RCA Victor (S) LSO-1081 20-25   63
  On above two, Ann-Margret is not shown on cover.

Soundtrack (1963) • RCA Victor (M) LOC-1081 10-12   Re

Soundtrack (1963) • RCA Victor (S) LSO-1081 15-20   Re
  Above two picture Ann-Margret on the cover without credits below.

Soundtrack (1963) • RCA Victor (M) LOC-1081 8-10   Re

Soundtrack (1963) • RCA Victor (S) LSO-1081 12-15   Re
  Above two picture Ann-Margret on the cover with credits below.

Soundtrack (1963) • RCA Victor (S) AYL1-3947 5-10   81
  Cover pictures Ann-Margret, with credits below. No dog logo.
  Conductor: Johnny Green, Hank Levine. **Cast:** Janet Leigh, Dick Van Dyke, Ann-Margret,
  Maureen Stapleton, Bobby Rydell, Paul Lynde, Jesse Pearson, Mary LaRoche, Bryan Russell.

Studiotrack (1963) • Colpix (M) CP-451 8-10   63

Studiotrack (1963) • Colpix (S) SCP-451 10-12   63
    Conductor: Bill Potts. **Cast:** Bill Potts and His Orchestra.
Studiotrack (1963) • Cameo (M) C-1043 20-25   63
Studiotrack (1963) • Cameo (S) CS-1043 30-35   63
    Composer: Charles Strouse, Lee Adams. **Conductor:** Jack Pleis. **Cast:** Bobby Rydell.
Studiotrack (1964) • Colpix (M) CP-454 25-30   64
Studiotrack (1964) • Colpix (S) SCP-454 30-40   64
    Conductor: Stu Phillips. **Cast:** James Darren, Marcels, Shelley Fabares, Paul Peterson.

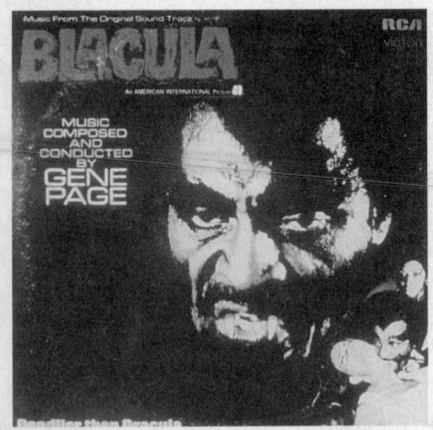

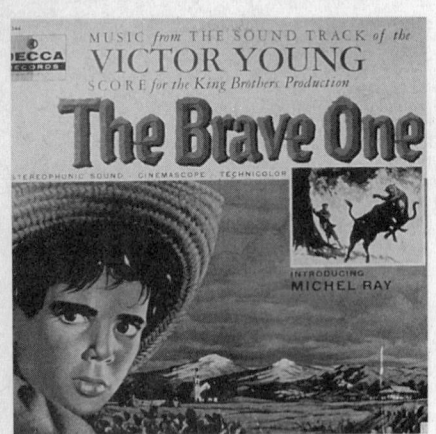

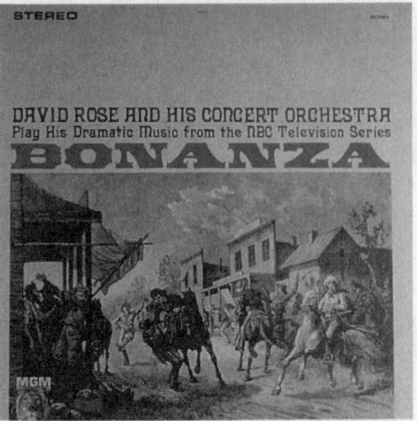

C

C'MON, LET'S LIVE A LITTLE
Soundtrack (1966) • Liberty (M) LRP-3430 15-20   66
Soundtrack (1966) • Liberty (S) LST-7430 20-25   66
   Composer: Don Crawford, others. **Conductor:** Don Ralke. **Cast:** Jackie DeShannon, Bobby Vee, Eddie Hodges.

C.C. AND COMPANY
Soundtrack (1970) • Avco Embassy (S) AVE-0-110 15-20   70
   Composer: Lenny Stack. **Conductor:** Lenny Stack.

CABARET
Original Cast (1966) • Columbia (M) KOL-6640 5-10   66
Original Cast (1966) • Columbia (S) KOS-3040 8-12   66
Some copies have a shrinkwrap sticker reading: "Winner of 8 Tony Awards…" Mono copies have artwork at top of front cover. Stereo copies have artwork between title and credits.
   Composer: John Kander, Fred Ebb. **Conductor:** Hal Hastings. **Cast:** Joel Grey, Jill Haworth, Jack Gilford, Bert Convy, Lotte Lenya, Mary Ehara, Rita O'Connor, Robert Sharp.
Original London Cast (1968) • CBS (S) 70039 60-65   68
Original London Cast (1968) • Embassy (S) 31026 20-25   Re
UK releases.
   Composer: John Kander, Fred Ebb. **Conductor:** Gareth Davies. **Cast:** Judi Dench, Kevin Colson, Barry Dennen, Lila Kedrova, Peter Sallis.
Studio Cast (1966) • Columbia (M) CL-2575 5-10   66
Studio Cast (1966) • Columbia (S) CS-9375 5-10   66
   Conductor: Joe Basile. **Cast:** Joe Basile Orchestra.
Soundtrack (1972) • ABC (S) ABCD-752 5-10   72
Back cover is white.
Soundtrack (1972) • MCA (S) MCA-752 5-8   Re
Soundtrack (1972) • MCA (S) MCA-37125 5-8   86
Above two MCA LPs have a black back cover.
   Conductor: Ralph Burns. **Cast:** Liza Minnelli, Joel Grey, Greta Keller.
Studiotrack • Custom (S) CS-1070 8-12   60s
Full title: *Theme from the Broadway Musical Cabaret & Others.*
   Cast: Glenn Rogers Orchestra.

CABIN IN THE SKY
Original Cast (1940) • AEI (M) AEI-1107 15-20   70s
Features Original Cast star, Ethel Waters along with the Martin Beck Theatre Orchestra, also from the Original Cast. These recordings first appeared on individual 78 rpm singles.
   Composer: Vernon Duke, John Latouche. **Conductor:** Max Meth. **Cast:** Ethel Waters.
Studio Cast (1940) • Columbia (M) CL-2792 10-12   68
Studio Cast (1940) • Columbia Special Products (M) CCL-2792 8-10   76
Actual title of Columbia LPs: *Ethel Waters.*
   Composer: Vernon Duke, John Latouche. **Cast:** Ethel Waters.
Original Revival Cast (1964) • Capitol (M) W-2073 20-25   64
Original Revival Cast (1964) • Capitol (S) SW-2073 40-45   64
   Composer: Vernon Duke, John Latouche. **Conductor:** Sy Oliver. **Cast:** Rosetta LeNoire, Ketty Lester, Tony Middleton, Helen Ferguson, Bernard Johnson, Sam Laws, Harold Pierson, Morton Winston.
Also see PORGY AND BESS

Soundtrack (1943) • Hollywood Soundstage (M) HS-5003 8-12
Includes a deleted number from the score.
   Composer: Vernon Duke, John Latouche, Harold Arlen, E.Y. Harburg. **Conductor:** Georgie
   Stoll. **Cast:** Ethel Waters, Eddie "Rochester" Anderson, Lena Horne, Louis Armstrong, Duke
   Ellington, Rex Ingram, Butterfly McQueen.

CACTUS FLOWER
Soundtrack (1969) • Bell (S) 1201 12-15   70
   Composer: Quincy Jones, Neil Diamond, others. **Conductor:** Eric W. Knight. **Cast:** Sarah
   Vaughan.

CADDYSHACK
Soundtrack (1980) • Columbia (S) JS-36737 5-8   80
   Composer: Johnny Mandel, Kenny Loggins, others. **Cast:** Kenny Loggins, Beat, Hilly Michaels.

CADDYSHACK II
Soundtrack (1988) • Columbia (S) SC-44317 5-8   88
   Cast: Tamara Champlin, Cheap Trick, Earth, Wind and Fire, Full Force, Lisa Lisa and Cult Jam,
   Kenny Loggins, Patty Smyth, Eric Martin, Ira Newborn, Pointer Sisters.

CAESAR AND CLEOPATRA
Studio Cast • Caedmon (M) TRS 304-M 5-10   60s

CAGE AUX FOLLES, LA: see LA CAGE AUX FOLLES

CAHILL - U.S. MARSHALL: see DIGITAL PREMIERE RECORDINGS FROM THE FILMS OF JOHN WAYNE, VOLUME 2

CAINE MUTINY
Soundtrack (1954) • RCA Victor (M) LOC-1013 5,000-10,000   54
   Recalled shortly after release, with very few copies making their way into circulation. Has
   original music and dialogue from the film, including the entire court martial scene.
Soundtrack (1954) • RCA Victor (M) LOC-1013 200-250   93
   Complete reproduction of the original issue. Non-commercial, limited edition of 100 copies,
   with full-color front cover, liner notes on back and green label disc in an original RCA paper
   sleeve.
   Composer: Max Steiner. **Conductor:** Max Steiner. **Cast:** Humphrey Bogart, Jose Ferrer, Van
   Johnson, Fred MacMurray, Robert Francis, May Wynn. (With dialogue.)

CAINE MUTINY COURT MARTIAL
TV Soundtrack (1955) • Mark 56 (S) 741 15-25   76
Two discs.
   Cast: Barry Sullivan, Lloyd Nolan, Frank Lovejoy.
TV Soundtrack (1955) • Mark 56 (S) 751 10-15   70s

CAL
Soundtrack (1984) • Mercury (S) 422-822769 8-10   84
   Composer: Mark Knopfler. **Conductor:** Mark Knopfler. **Cast:** Mark Knopfler.

CALAMITY JANE
Soundtrack (1953) • Columbia (EP) B-347 25-30   53
Two discs.
Soundtrack (1953) • Columbia (EP) B-1803 10-20   53
Soundtrack (1953) • Columbia (EP) B-1804 10-20   53
Soundtrack (1953) • Columbia (M) CL-6273 30-35   53
   10-inch LP. The Columbia releases include some music from the soundtrack along with
   some studio recordings by Doris Day.
Soundtrack (1953) • Columbia Special Products (M) P-19611 8-10   Re
Soundtrack (1953) • CBS (M) 63032 20-25   Re
   UK release. Side 1 is same as CL-6273. Side 2 is an abridged version of *The Pajama
   Game*.
   Composer: Sammy Fain, Paul Francis Webster. **Conductor:** Ray Heindorf. **Cast:** Doris Day,
   Howard Keel.

CALIFORNIA: see MANHATTAN TOWER

CALIFORNIA DREAMING
Soundtrack (1978) • Casablanca/American Int'l (S) AILP-3001.............. 8-12   78
   Composer: Fred Karlin. **Conductor:** Fred Karlin. **Cast:** Glynnis O'Connor, Seymour Cassel,
   Dorothy Tristan, Dennis Christopher, John Calvin.

CALIFORNIA SUITE
Soundtrack (1978) • Columbia (S) JS-35727 5-8   79
   Composer: Claude Bolling. **Conductor:** Claude Bolling.

CALIGULA – THE MUSIC
Soundtrack (1980) • Penthouse (S) 101... 8-12   80
  Two discs.

CALL IT LOVE
Original London Cast • That's Entertainment (S) TER-1083 8-10   80s
  UK release.
   Composer: Sandy Wilson.

CALL ME MADAM
Original Cast (1950) • RCA Victor (EP) EOA-438 20-30   50
Original Cast (1950) • RCA Victor (EP) WOC-1.................................... 25-35   50
  Boxed, five-disc set. Each record is separated by white inserts listing other RCA albums.
Original Cast (1950) • RCA Victor (M) LOC-1000 55-65   50
Original Cast (1950) • RCA Victor (M) CBM1-2032 12-15   68
  With Ethel Merman – the show's star – under exclusive contract to Decca, Dinah Shore,
  who did not appear in the show, sings Merman's vocals on these recordings.
  Accompaniment is by the rest of the Original Cast players and orchestra.
   Composer: Irving Berlin. **Conductor:** Jay Blackton. **Cast:** Dinah Shore, Paul Lukas, Russell
   Nype, Galina Talva, Pat Harrington, Ralph Chambers, Jay Velie.
Original Cast (1950) • Decca (EP) ED-806 10-12   50
Original Cast (1950) • Decca (M) DL-5304.. 15-20   50
  10-inch LP.
Original Cast (1950) • Decca (M) DL-8035.. 18-20   50
Original Cast (1950) • Decca (M) DL-9022.. 12-15   55
Original Cast (1950) • Decca (SE) DL-79022 10-12   59
Original Cast (1950) • MCA (SE) 2055e.. 8-10   72
  Ethel Merman with an otherwise assembled studio cast and orchestra.
   Composer: Irving Berlin. **Conductor:** Gordon Jenkins. **Cast:** Ethel Merman, Dick Haymes,
   Eileen Wilson, Gordon Jenkins with His Orchestra and Chorus.
Original London Cast (1952) • Monmouth Evergreen (SE) MES-7073 ... 8-12
  UK release. Also has selections from the original London cast of Cole Porter's *Can-Can*.
   Composer: Irving Berlin. **Conductor:** Cyril Ornadel. **Cast:** Billie Worth,
   Anton Walbrook, Jeff Warren, Shani Wallis.
Studio Cast (1951) • MGM (M) E-531 20-30   51
  10-inch LP.
   Composer: Irving Berlin. **Cast:** Billy Eckstine, Johnny Desmond, Art Lund.
Studio Cast (1951) • Mercury (M) 25088.. 15-30   51
  10-inch LP.
   Composer: Irving Berlin. **Cast:** Various Mercury artists.
Soundtrack (1953) • Decca (EP) ED-508.. 10-15   53
Soundtrack (1953) • Decca (M) DL-5465 30-35   53
  10-inch LP.
  Also see ANNIE GET YOUR GUN
  Also see CAN-CAN
  Also see GUYS AND DOLLS

CALL ME MISTER

Original Cast (1946) • Decca A-466 25-75   46
  78 rpm album, with booklet.
Original Cast (1946) • Decca (M) DLP-7005 65-85   50
  10-inch LP.
    Composer: Harold Rome, Mack Gordon, Sammy Fain, Frances Ash. **Conductor:** Alfred
    Newman. **Cast:** Betty Grable, Dan Dailey, Danny Thomas.
Studio Cast (1957) • Coral (M) CRL-57082 20-25   57
    Composer: Harold Rome. **Conductor:** Harold Rome. **Cast:** Harold Rome (piano).
  Also see STARLIFT
  Also see THIS IS THE ARMY

CAMELOT

Original Cast (1960) • Columbia (M) KOL-5620 8-12   60
Original Cast (1960) • Columbia (S) KOS-2031 10-15   60
  Gatefold cover. Indicates *Follow Me* is by Marjorie Smith. Disc label lists vocalist as Mary
  Sue Berry. A three-inch record of Camelot, with special paper sleeve was used as a
  Christmas gift certificate for this LP by retail stores. The value with the mini-disc is $15-20.
Original Cast (1960) • Columbia KOL-5620.. 15-25   60
  Three-inch disc promotional novelty, with special paper sleeve. Made to be used by
  retailers as Christmas gift certificates, which could be redeemed for the LP.
Original Cast (1960) • Columbia (S) OS-2031.. 8-12   Re
  Standard cover, picturing the stars of the show.
Original Cast (1960) • Columbia Masterworks (S) JS-32602.................... 5-8   73
    Composer: Alan Jay Lerner, Frederick Loewe. **Conductor:** Franz Allers. **Cast:** Julie Andrews,
    Richard Burton, Robert Goulet, Roddy McDowell, Bruce Yarnell, John Cullum, Mary Sue Berry,
    James Gannon.
Original London Cast (1963) • RCA Victor (M) CLP-1756 20-25   63
Original London Cast (1963) • RCA Victor (S) CSD-1559 20-30   63
Original London Cast (1964) • Stet (S) DS-15022................................. 12-18   Re
  UK releases.
    Composer: Alan Jay Lerner, Frederick Loewe. **Conductor:** Kenneth Alwyn. **Cast:** Laurence
    Harvey, Elizabeth Larner, Barry Kent, Miles Malleson, Moyra Fraser, Nicky Henson, Cardew
    Robinson.
London Cast (1967) • Music for Pleasure (M) MFP-1198 18-20   67
London Cast (1967) • Music for Pleasure (S) MFP-50368.................... 18-20   67
  UK releases.
    Composer: Alan Jay Lerner, Frederick Loewe. **Conductor:** Alyn Ainsworth. **Cast:** Paul
    Daneman (who replaced Laurence Harvey during original London run in 1965), Pat Michael,
    Peter Regan.
London Studio Cast • World (S) T-851 15-20
    Composer: Alan Jay Lerner, Frederick Loewe. **Conductor:** Gareth Davies. **Cast:** Patrick
    Macnee, Madge Stephens, Geoffrey Chard.
  UK release.
London Revival Cast (1982) • Varese Sarabande (S) OCV-81168......... 8-10   82
London Revival Cast (1982) • That's Entertainment (S) TER-1030........ 8-10   80s
  UK release.
    Composer: Alan Jay Lerner, Frederick Loewe. **Cast:** Richard Harris.
Studio Cast • Ambassador (S) S98070 8-10
    Conductor: Al Goodman. **Cast:** Richard Torigi, Lois Winters, Earl Rogers.
Studio Cast • Mayfair (S) 9719... 10-12
  Colored vinyl.
    Cast: Russ Williams Orchestra, Richard Saunders, Janice Sherwood, Raymond Andrews,
    Johnny Lang.
Studio Cast • Pickwick (M) PC-3103 5-8
Studio Cast • Pickwick (S) SPC-3103 5-8
    Cast: Parris Mitchell Strings - Full Cast & Orchestra.

Soundtrack (1967) • Warner Bros. (S) PRO-268.................................. 20-25   67
   Promotional issue only.
Soundtrack (1967) • Warner Bros. (M) B-1712 10-12   '67
Soundtrack (1967) • Warner Bros. (S) BS-1712................................. 10-12   67
   Gold label.
Soundtrack (1967) • Warner Bros. (S) BS-1712................................. 8-10
   Green label.
Soundtrack (1967) • Warner Bros. (S) BSK-3102 5-8   77
Soundtrack (1967) • Warner Bros. (S) SW 91347.................................... 5-8   Re
   Capitol Record Club issue.
     Composer: Alan Jay Lerner, Frederick Loewe. **Conductor:** Alfred Newman. **Cast:** Richard
     Harris, Vanessa Redgrave, Gene Merlino (performed vocals for Franco Nero in the film).
Studiotrack (1967) • Mainstream (M) 56101... 8-12   67
Studiotrack (1967) • Mainstream (S) 6101 10-12   67
     Composer: Alan Jay Lerner, Frederick Loewe. **Conductor:** Hugo Montenegro. **Cast:** Hugo
     Montenegro and His Orchestra.
Studiotrack • Alshire (S) ST-5058 8-12
     Cast: 101 Strings.
Studiotrack • Columbia (S) CS-8369 12-15
Studiotrack • Columbia Special Products (S) C-10258........................ 20-30
     Conductor: Andre Previn. **Cast:** Andre Previn.
Studiotrack • Columbia (M) CL-1570.. 8-12   60
Studiotrack • Columbia (S) CS-8370 8-12   60
   Full title: *Music from Lerner and Loewe's Camelot.*
     Conductor: Percy Faith. **Cast:** Percy Faith and His Orchestra.
Studiotrack • Design (S) SDLP-281 8-12
Studiotrack • RCA Camden (S) CAS 988.. 8-12
   Full title: *Living Strings Play Music from the Motion Picture Camelot.*
     Conductor: Hill Bowen. **Cast:** Living Strings.
Studiotrack • Somerset (S) 13400... 8-12
     Cast: 101 Strings.
Studiotrack • Sutton (M) SU 205 8-12
   Full title: *Selections from Camelot and My Fair Lady.*
     Cast: London Pops Orchestra and Chorus
Studiotrack • Time (M) T-52022 8-12
Studiotrack • Time (S) ST-2022 10-15
     Conductor: Hugo Montenegro. **Cast:** Hugo Montenegro and Orchestra.

CAN-CAN

Original Cast (1953) • Capitol (EP) EDM-452....................................... 15-20   53
Original Cast (1953) • Capitol (M) S-452... 15-18   53
   Red label.
Original Cast (1953) • Capitol (M) W-452.. 12-15   62
Original Cast (1953) • Capitol (SE) DW-452e 10-12   62
     Composer: Cole Porter. **Conductor:** Milton Rosenstock. **Cast:** Lilo, Hans Conried, Gwen
     Verdon, Erik Rhodes, Peter Cookson.
Original London Cast (1954) • Monmouth Evergreen (SE) MES-7073 ... 8-12
   UK release. Also has selections from the original London cast of *Call Me Madam.*
     Composer: Cole Porter. **Conductor:** Charles Prentice. **Cast:** Irene Hilda, Edmund Hockridge,
     Alfred Marks, Gillian Lynne, Warren Mitchell, Vincent Charles, Alan Gabriel, Eve Ashley, Joy
     Turpin, Gloria George, Aleta Morrison. CALL ME MADAM: **Composer:** Irving Berlin. **Conductor:**
     Cyril Ornadel. **Cast:** Billie Worth, Anton Walbrook, Jeff Warren, Shani Wallis.
Studio Cast • Design (M) DLP-111... 5-8
Studio Cast • Design (S) 1009 8-10
   One side has music from *Kiss Me Kate.*
     Composer: Cole Porter. **Conductor:** Warren Vincent. **Cast:** Mimi Benzell, Felix Knight.
Soundtrack (1960) • Capitol (M) W-1301 10-12   60

Soundtrack (1960) • Capitol (S) SW-1301 15-18   60
Soundtrack (1960) • Capitol (S) SM-1301 8-10   Re
   Composer: Cole Porter. **Conductor:** Nelson Riddle. **Cast:** Frank Sinatra, Shirley MacLaine, Maurice Chevalier, Louis Jourdan, Juliet Prowse.
Studiotrack • Royale (M) 18141 5-10   50s
   10-inch LP. Full title: *Hits from Can-Can by Cole Porter + Other Hits.*
   Cast: Royale Singers and Orchestra.
Studiotrack • Coronet (M) CX 119 5-10
Studiotrack • Crown (S) CST 178 5-8
   Red vinyl. Full title: *Sounds of a Thousand Strings Play Can-Can.*
   Cast: Glenn Hart, Barbara Newcomb, Lido Can-Can Singers and Dancers.
Studiotrack • Halo (M) 50217 5-8
   Cast: National Strings and Orchestra.
Studiotrack • Paris (M) P-114 5-8
   Cast: International Festival Orchestra.
   Also see KISMET
   Also see ME AND JULIET

CAN HEIRONYMUS MERKIN EVER FORGET MERCY HUMPPE AND FIND TRUE HAPPINESS?

Soundtrack (1969) • Kapp (S) KRS-5509 10-12   69
   Composer: Anthony Newley, Herbert Kretzmer. **Cast:** Anthony Newley, Joan Collins, Stubby Kaye, Bruce Forsythe, Ron Rubin.

CAN'T HELP SINGING

Soundtrack (1944) • Decca A-387 30-35   44
   78 rpm album.
   Composer: Jerome Kern, E.Y. Harburg. **Conductor:** Edgar Fairchild. **Cast:** Deanna Durbin, Robert Paige.
Soundtrack (1944) • Coral (M) CP-43 30-35   70
   UK release.
Soundtrack (1944) • Ace of Hearts (M) AH-60 15-20   Re
   UK release. Both have the songs from the Decca album plus music from other Deanna Durbin films.
Soundtrack (1944) • Titania (M) 509 8-10
   Also includes music from *Du Barry Was a Lady.*
   Composer: Jerome Kern, E.Y. Harburg. **Conductor:** Edgar Fairchild. **Cast:** Deanna Durbin, Robert Paige.
   Also see DU BARRY WAS A LADY

CAN'T STOP THE MUSIC

Soundtrack (1980) • Casablanca (S) NBLP-7220 8-10   80
   Composer: Jacques Moral, others. **Conductor:** Horace Ott. **Cast:** David London, Ritchie Family, Village People.

CANADA

Original Cast (1977) • Broadway Baby Demos (S) BBD-776 8-10   77
   Composer: Bruce Molloy, Zachary Morfogen. **Conductor:** Bruce Molloy. **Cast:** Carol Lee Gorson, Bruce Molloy Sr.

CANDIDATE

Soundtrack (1964) • Jubilee (M) JGM-5029 15-20   64
Soundtrack (1964) • Jubilee (S) 5029 20-25   64
   Composer: Steve Karmen. **Conductor:** Steve Karmen.

CANDIDE

Original Cast (1956) • Columbia (M) OL-5180 10-12   56
Original Cast (1956) • Columbia (SE) OS-2350 10-12   63
   Has alternate takes.

Original Cast (1956) • Columbia (SE) PST-2350 8-10   Re
  Composer: Leonard Bernstein, Richard Wilbur, John Latouche, Dorothy Parker. **Conductor:** Samuel Krachmalnick. **Cast:** Max Adrian, Robert Rounseville, Barbara Cook, George Blackwell, William Chapman, Robert Mesrobian, William Olvis, Irra Petina, Thomas Pyle, Norman Roland, Robert Rue.

Original Revival Cast (1973) • Columbia (Q) Q2S-32923 15-18   73
Original Revival Cast (1973) • Columbia (S) S2X-32923 10-15   73
  Both are two-disc sets.
  Composer: Leonard Bernstein, Stephen Sondheim. **Conductor:** John Mauceri. **Cast:** Lewis J. Stadlen, Mark Baker, Maureen Brennan, Sam Freed, June Gable, Jim Corti, David Horwitz, Gail Boggs, Lynne Gannaway, Chip Garnett, Robert Henderson, David Horwitz, Becky McSpadden, Carolann Page, Deborah St. Darr, Renee Semes.

Original Revival Cast (1982) • New World (S) NW-340/1 10-15   82
  Two discs.
  Composer: Leonard Bernstein, Stephen Sondheim. **Conductor:** John Mauceri. **Cast:** David Eisler, Ralph Bassett, Robert Brubaker, Joyce Castle, Ivy Austin, Erie Mills, Scott Reeve, James Billings, Rhoda Butler, Maris Clement, Jack Harrold, William Ledbetter, Don Yule, John Lankston. (With Dialogue.)

CANDY
Soundtrack (1968) • ABC (S) ABCS-OC-9 12-18   68
  Composer: Dave Grusin. **Conductor:** Dave Grusin. **Cast:** Steppenwolf, Byrds.

CANNIBALS: see SONNY AND JED

CANNONBALL RUN
Soundtrack (1981) • Warner Bros. (S) HS-3580 10-15   81
Soundtrack (1981) • RCA Victor (S) VIP-28036 8-10   81
  Has sound effects.
  Conductor: Al Capps. **Cast:** Ray Stevens, Lou Rawls, Chuck Mangione, Al Capps, California Childrens Chorus.

CANTERBURY TALES
Original London Cast (1968) • Decca (M) LK-4956 10-15   68
Original London Cast (1968) • Decca (S) SKL-4956 12-18   68
  UK releases.
  Composer: Richard Hill, John Hawkins, Nevil Coghill. **Conductor:** Richard Hill, John Hawkins, Gordon Rose. **Cast:** Wilfrid Brambell, Jessie Evans, Kenneth J. Warren, Nicky Henson, Billy Boyle, Pamela Charles, Gay Soper, Michael Logan, Kevin Brennan, Daniel Thorndike, Martin Starkie.

Original London Cast (1968) • That's Entertainment (S) TER-1076 8-10   80s
  UK release.
Original Cast (1969) • Capitol (S) SW-229 10-12   69
Original Cast (1969) • Capitol (S) SWCR-292(3) 15-18   69
  Three discs. Other two are Capitol Original Cast LPs *Celebration* and *Zorba*.
  Composer: Richard Hill, John Hawkins, Nevil Coghill. **Conductor:** Oscar Kosarin. **Cast:** George Rose, Hermione Baddeley, Martyn Green, Roy Cooper, Sandy Duncan, Ed Evanko, Ann Gardner, Bruce Hyde, Evelyn Page, Suzan Sidney, Edwin Steffe.

CANTERVILLE GHOST: see FOUR TELEVISION MUSICALS

CANTOR, EDDIE, STORY: see EDDIE CANTOR STORY

CAPER OF THE GOLDEN BULLS
Soundtrack (1967) • Tower (M) T-5086 10-12   67
Soundtrack (1967) • Tower (S) ST-5086 12-15   67
  Composer: Vic Mizzy. **Conductor:** Vic Mizzy.

CAPRICORN ONE
Soundtrack (1978) • Warner Bros. (S) BSK 3201 8-10   78
  Composer: Jerry Goldsmith. **Conductor:** Jerry Goldsmith.

CAPTAIN BLOOD: CLASSIC FILM SCORES FOR ERROL FLYNN
Studiotrack • RCA Victor (S) ARL-1-0912 8-10   75

Studiotrack • RCA Victor (Q) ARD-1-0912 10-15   75
    Music from: *They Died with Their Boots On, The Sun Also Rises, Dodge City, Adventures of Don Juan, Objective Burma, The Adventures of Robin Hood, Captain Blood* and *The Sea Hawk*.
    Composer: Max Steiner, Erich Wolfgang Korngold, Franz Waxman, Hugo Friedhofer.
    Conductor: Charles Gerhardt.

CAPTAIN FROM CASTILE

Studiotrack (1947) • Majestic MZ-6 30-50   47
    78 rpm album.
Soundtrack • Mercury MH-2 30-50   47
    78 rpm album.
Soundtrack (1947) • Mercury (EP) EP-1-3040 15-20   52
Soundtrack (1947) • Mercury (M) MG-20005 100-125   52
    Yellow cover "Special Edition." Also has selections from operettas and films
Soundtrack (1947) • Mercury (M) MG-20005 15-25   Re
    Red cover.
Soundtrack • Delos (M) F-25411 8-10   Re
    Composer: Alfred Newman. **Conductor:** Alfred Newman. **Cast:** 20th Century-Fox Studio Orchestra.
Studiotrack (1947) • Mercury (EP) EP-1-30401 15-20   52
Studiotrack (1947) • Mercury (M) MG-25072 30-50   52
    10-inch LP.
Studiotrack (1947) • Citadel (M) 7-7015 8-10   79
    Includes themes from: *All About Eve, Pinky, The Song of Bernadette, Wuthering Heights, A Royal Scandal, The Razor's Edge, How Green Was My Valley* and *A Letter to Three Wives*.
Studiotrack • Philips (M) PHM-200-098 8-10   63
    Full title: *Captain from Castile and Other Great Movie Themes*.
    Composer: Various. **Conductor:** Robert Farnon. **Cast:** Robert Farnon Orchestra.
Studiotrack • RCA Victor (S) ARL1-0184 10-12   73
    Full title: *Captain from Castile: The Classic Film Scores of Alfred Newman*. Also has music from *How to Marry a Millionaire, Wuthering Heights, Down to the Sea in Ships, The Song of Bernadette, The Bravados, Anastasia, The Best of Everything, Airport* and *The Robe*.
    Composer: Alfred Newman. **Conductor:** Charles Gerhardt.

CAPTAIN HORATIO HORNBLOWER

Studiotrack (1960) • Delyse (M) D-6057 125-150   60
Studiotrack (1960) • Delyse (SE) DS-6057 90-100   60
Studiotrack (1960) • Citadel (SE) CT-7009 15-20   79
    Includes *Rhapsody for Violin and Orchestra*.
    Composer: Robert Farnon. **Conductor:** Robert Farnon. **Cast:** London Festival Symphony Orchestra.

CAPTAIN JINKS OF THE HORSE MARINES

Original Cast (1975) • RCA Victor (S) ARL2-1727 20-25   75
    Boxed, two-disc set.
    Composer: Jack Beeson, Sheldon Harnick. **Conductor:** Russell Patterson. **Cast:** Eugene Green, George Livings, Keith Harmon, William Latimer, James Ditsch, Robert Owens Jones, Caro Wilcox, Brian Steel, Walter Hook.

CAPTAIN KANGAROO

TV Cast • Columbia (M) CL-1012 15-20   57
    Full title: *Captain Kangaroo Songs and Dances*.
    Cast: Bob Keeshan.
TV Cast • Columbia (M) CL-678 20-25   55
    Full title: *Captain Kangaroo – Treasure House*.
    Cast: Bob Keeshan.
TV Cast • Harmony (M) HL-9520 10-20   60
    Cast: Bob Keeshan with Orchestra and Chorus.

CAPTAIN MIDNIGHT

Radio Cast (1935) • Radiola (M) Release 6, Series 1 60-90   71
Limited edition of 1,000 numbered copies. Also has *Jack Armstrong* (1935), *Buck Rogers in the 25th Century* (1938) and *Dick Tracy* (1946).

Radio Cast • Golden Age (M) 5006 8-10   78
Limited edition of 1,000.

Radio Cast • Mark 56 (M) 594 40-80   70s
Picture disc.

CAPTIVE

Soundtrack (1987) • Virgin (S) 90609-1 10-12   87
Composer: The Edge, Michael Berkeley. **Cast:** The Edge.

CAR WASH

Soundtrack (1976) • MCA (EP) 1947 10-15   76
Promotional issue only. Actual title: *Mini Wash*.

Soundtrack (1976) • MCA (S) 2-6000 12-15   76
Two discs.
Composer: Norman Whitfield, others. **Conductor:** Norman Whitfield, others. **Cast:** Rose Royce, Pointer Sisters, Spinners, Hot Chocolate, Jane Rose, others.

CARAVANS

Soundtrack (1978) • Epic (S) ASE-35787 8-10   78
White label. Promotional issue only.

Soundtrack (1978) • Epic (S) ASE-35787 8-10   78
Composer: Mike Batt. **Conductor:** Mike Batt.

CARD

Original London Cast (1973) • Pye (S) NSPL-18408 25-35   73
UK release.

Original London Cast (1973) • AEI (S) AEI-1124 8-10   70s
Composer: Tony Hatch, Jackie Trent. Conductor: Ray Holder. **Cast:** Jim Dale, Millicent Martin, Joan Hickson, Marti Webb, Eleanor Bron, John Savident, Michael Malnick.

CARDINAL

Soundtrack (1963) • RCA Victor (M) LOC-1084 20-25   63
Soundtrack (1963) • RCA Victor (S) LSO-1084 30-35   63
Soundtrack (1963) • Entr'acte (S) ERS-6518 8-10   80
Composer: Jerome Moross. **Conductor:** Jerome Moross.
Also see CHARADE

CARE BEARS MOVIE

Soundtrack (1985) • Kid Stuff (S) DAR-3901-LP 10-20   85
Composer: Carole King, John Sebastian, Walt Woodward, David Bird. **Cast:** Carole King, Mickey Rooney, John Sebastian, Walt Woodward, David Bird.

CAREFREE: see FLYING DOWN TO RIO

CAREFUL, HE MIGHT HEAR YOU

Soundtrack (1983) • Varese Sarabande (S) STV-81221 8-10   83
Composer: Ray Cook.

CARETAKERS

Soundtrack (1963) • Ava (M) A-31 12-15   63
Soundtrack (1963) • Ava (S) AS-31 15-20   63
Composer: Elmer Bernstein. **Conductor:** Elmer Bernstein.

CARMELINA

Original Cast (1979) • Original Cast (S) OC-8019 12-15   79
Composer: Burton Lane, Alan Jay Lerner. **Conductor:** Don Jennings. **Cast:** Georgia Brown, Paul Sorvino, Jossie De Guzman, Grace Keagy, Bernie Knee, Gordon Ramsey, Howard Ross.

CARMEN

Studio Cast • Harmony (M) 2086.. 10-15
    Cast: Milton Cross (narrator).

CARMEN JONES

Original Cast (1944) • Decca DA-366... 20-30   44
    Album of six 78 rpms. Includes two tracks, *You Talk Jus' Like My Maw* and *Card Song*, not
    included on later LPs. Because of the vocal demands of this show, the original production
    was double cast; however, only one set of principals recorded the album.

Original Cast (1943) • Decca (EP) ED-904 15-20   50

Original Cast (1943) • Decca (M) DL-8014.. 25-30   50

Original Cast (1943) • Brunswick (M) LAT-8057 20-25   50s
    UK release of Decca DL-8014.

Original Cast (1943) • Decca (M) DL-9021.. 10-12   55

Original Cast (1943) • Decca (SE) DL-79021 10-12   59

Original Cast (1943) • MCA (SE) 2054e 5-10   72

Original Cast (1943) • MCA (SE) 1531.. 5-8   80s
    Composer: Oscar Hammerstein II, Georges Bizet. **Conductor:** Joseph Littau. **Cast:** Muriel
    Smith, Luther Saxon, Cozy Cole, Glenn Bryant, Carlotta Franzell, June Hawkins, Dick
    Montgomery, Jessica Russell, Randall Steplight, Carmen Jones Orchestra.

Soundtrack (1954) • RCA Victor (EP) ERA-233 10-15   54

Soundtrack (1954) • RCA Victor (EP) ERC-1881 12-18   54
    Both are three-disc sets.

Soundtrack (1954) • RCA Victor (M) LM-1881 12-18   54

Soundtrack (1954) • RCA (M) RD-27074 20-30   54
    UK release of RCA Victor LM-1881, but with different cover art.

Soundtrack (1954) • RCA Victor (SE) ARL1-0046............................... 10-12   73

Soundtrack (1954) • RCA Victor (SE) ARL1-0046................................. 8-10   Re
    Composer: Georges Bizet. **Conductor:** Herschel Burke Gilbert. **Cast:** Pearl Bailey, Marilyn
    Horne (performs vocals for Dorothy Dandridge in the film), LeVern Hutcherson (performs vocals
    for Harry Belafonte), Olga James, Bernice Peterson (performs vocals for Diahann Carroll), Joe
    Crawford (performs vocals for Nick Stewart), Brock Peters, Marvin Hayes (performs vocals for
    Joe Adams).

Studiotrack • Heliodor (M) H-25046.. 8-10

Studiotrack • Heliodor (S) HS-25046... 8-10
    Full title: *Grace Bumbry As Carmen Jones*.
    Cast: Grace Bumbry, George Webb, Ena Babb, Elizabeth Welch, Thomas Baptiste, Ursula
    Connors, Edward Darling.

CARMILLA: A VAMPIRE TALE

Original Cast (1972) • Vanguard (S) VSD-79322 8-10   72
    Based on a novel by J.S. Le Fanu.
    Composer: Ben Johnston, Wilford Leach. **Conductor:** Zizi Mueller. **Cast:** Margaret Benczak,
    Donald Harrington, Camille Tibaldeo, Sandra Johnson.

CARNEGIE HALL

Soundtrack (1947) • Columbia (M) ML-2113 45-50   50
    10-inch LP. Fulll title: *A Night at Carnegie Hall.*
    Composer: Wolfgang Amadeus Mozart, Guiseppe Verdi, Léo Delibes. **Conductor:** Pietro
    Cimara, George Sebastian, Fausto Cleva. **Cast:** Lily Pons, Ezio Pinza, Risë Stevens, Raoul
    Jobin.

CARNIVAL

Original Cast (1961) • MGM (M) E-3946 8-10   61

Original Cast (1961) • MGM (S) SE-3946.. 12-15   61
    Black label. Some copies have gold MGM Stereo sticker on front of mono cover, others
    have "STEREO" printed on upper right of front cover.

Original Cast (1961) • MGM (S) SE-3946.. 5-8   Re
  Blue and yellow label. Has "STEREO" printed on upper right of front cover, with letters of
  title only in red, whereas they were multi-colored on the original release.
    Composer: Bob Merrill. Conductor: Saul Schectman. Cast: Anna Maria Alberghetti, James
    Mitchell, Kaye Ballard, Jerry Orbach, Henry Lascoe, Pierre Olaf.
Studio Cast • Verve (M) V4051 10-20
  Full title: Carnival! In Percussion.
    Cast: Paul Smith Ensemble.
Studio Cast • Grand Prix (M) K-169 8-12
    Cast: Sound Stage Calliope Band.
Studio Cast • International Award Series (S) AKS-169........................... 8-12
    Cast: Sound Stage Calliope Band.
Studio Cast • World Pacific (M) WP-1410 10-20
    Cast: Ben Di Tosti.

CARNIVAL IN FLANDERS

Original Cast (1953) • Blue Pear (M) BP-1014 15-20
  Actual title: Miss Dolores Gray. Has previously unreleased vocals from stage and screen,
  including a live (stage) recording of Here's That Rainy Day.
    Composer: James Van Heusen, Johnny Burke. Cast: Dolores Gray.

CARNY

Soundtrack (1980) • Warner Bros. (S) AS-3455................................ 10-12   80
    Composer: Alex North, Robbie Robertson.

CAROL CHANNING

Original Cast • Vanguard (M) VRS-9056... 20-25
Original Cast (1961) • Vanguard (M) D-2041 10-15   61
Original Cast (1961) • Vanguard (S) VSD-2041 12-15   61
  Carol Channing's nightclub act, recorded live. Much of the material is from Channing's
  Broadway revue, Show Girl (1961).
    Composer: Charles Gaynor, others. Conductor: George Bauer, Robert Hunter. Cast: Carol
    Channing.
    Also see SHOW GIRL

CAROUSEL

Original Cast (1945) • Decca (EP) ED-804 15-20   49
  Three discs in gatefold cover.
Original Cast (1945) • Decca DA-400.. 12-15   49
  78 rpm album.
Original Cast (1945) • Decca (M) DL-8003.. 15-18   49
Original Cast (1945) • Brunswick (M) LAT-8006.................................. 18-20   49
  UK release, with different cover art.
Original Cast (1945) • Decca (M) DL-9020... 8-12   55
Original Cast (1945) • Decca (SE) DL-79020 8-10   59
Original Cast (1945) • MCA (SE) 2033... 5-8   72
Original Cast (1945) • MCA (SE) 37093... 5-8   81
Original Cast (1945) • MCA (SE) 1627.. 5-8   80s
    Composer: Richard Rodgers, Oscar Hammerstein II. Conductor: Joseph Littau. Cast: John
    Raitt, Jan Clayton, Jean Darling, Connie Baxter, Christine Johnson, Eric Mattson, Murvyn Vye.

Original London Cast (1950) • World (M) SH-393 40-45
UK release. Excerpts from London show. Single disc, also includes selections from the
London productions of *Oklahoma!!* and *Annie Get Your Gun*. This LP was reissued in part
on Stanyan 10069, which, since it omits the *Carousel* tracks, is found under *Oklahoma!*
Composer: Richard Rodgers, Oscar Hammerstein II. **Conductor:** Reginald Burston. **Cast:**
Stephen Douglass, Iva Withers, Margot Moser, Eric Mattson, Marion Ross, Morgan Davies.
OKLAHOMA!: **Composer:** Richard Rodgers, Oscar Hammerstein II. **Conductor:** Reginald
Burston. **Cast:** Howard Keel, Betty Jane Watson, Dorthea MacFarland, Walter Donahue, Henry
Clarke. ANNIE GET YOUR GUN: **Composer:** Irving Berlin. **Conductor:** Lew Stone. **Cast:**
Dolores Gray, Bill Johnson, Irving Davies, Wendy Toye.

Original Revival Cast (1965) • RCA Victor (M) LOC-1114 5-8   65
Original Revival Cast (1965) • RCA Victor (S) LSO-1114........................ 8-10   65
Conductor: Franz Allers. **Cast:** John Raitt, Eileen Christy, Susan Watson, Benay Venuta,
Edward Everett Horton, Katherine Hilgenberg, Jerry Orbach, Reid Shelton.

Studio Cast (1953) • RCA Victor (EP) EPA-475 10-20   53
Composer: Richard Rodgers, Oscar Hammerstein II. **Conductor:** Jay Blackton. **Cast:** Doretta
Morrow, John Raitt, Brenda Lewis, Orchestra and Chorus.

Studio Cast (1953) • RCA Victor (M) LPM-3150................................. 12-15   53
10-inch LP. One side has music from *Oklahoma!*

Studio Cast (1954) • RCA Victor (EP) EPC-1048.................................. 8-10   55
Three discs in triple-pocket cover.

Studio Cast (1954) • RCA Victor (M) LPM-1048................................... 10-12   54
Studio Cast (1954) • RCA Victor (SE) LSP-1048 8-10   Re
Conductor: Lehman Engel. **Cast:** Patrice Munsel, Robert Merrill, Gloria Lane, Herbert Banke,
George S. Irving.

Studio Cast (1955) • RCA Victor (EP) ERA-234.................................... 5-10   55
Full title: *Carousel Suite*.
Cast: Morton Gould and His Orchestra.

Studio Cast (1960) • Epic (M) LN-3679 8-10   60
Studio Cast (1960) • Epic (S) BN-3679 10-12   60
Cast: Lois Hunt, Harry Snow, Charmaine Harma, Kay Lande, Charles Green, Helena Seymour.

Studio Cast (1962) • Command (M) RS-33-843 5-8   62
Studio Cast (1962) • Command (S) RS-843-SD...................................... 5-8   62
With four-page bound-in booklet.
Conductor: Jay Blackton. **Cast:** Alfred Drake, Roberta Peters, Lee Venora, Claramae Turner,
Jon Crain, Command Chorus, Norman Treigle.

Studio Cast (1966) • Buena Vista (M) BV-4029.................................... 10-15   66
Studio Cast (1966) • Buena Vista (S) STER-4029 12-15   66
Above two have gatefold cover and bound-in booklet.

Studio Cast (1966) • Disneyland (M) ST 3939..................................... 8-12   66
Conductor: Tutti Camarata. **Cast:** Jan Clayton, Gloria Wood Chorus.

Soundtrack (1956) • Capitol (EP) EDM-694 12-18   56
Soundtrack (1956) • Capitol (M) W-694 12-18   56
Soundtrack (1956) • Capitol (M) LCT-6105.. 20-25   56
Unbanded disc. UK release of Capitol W-694. Both mono issues include the complete
version of *The Carousel Waltz*.

Soundtrack (1956) • Capitol (S) SW-694 8-12   62
Soundtrack (1956) • Capitol (S) SLCT-6105.. 20-25   62
Banded disc. UK release of Capitol SW-694. Both stereo issues have an edited version of
The Carousel Waltz. Though reissued many times, the difference in value between
pressings is minimal. In general, gray or black labels are in the high end of this price range,
red, green or purple labels are at the low end.

TV Soundtrack (1969) • Columbia Special Products (M) CSM-479 12-15   69
Limited edition.
Conductor: Jack Elliot. **Cast:** Robert Goulet, Mary Grover, Pernell Roberts, Marlyn Mason, Jack
DeLon, Patricia Neway.

Studiotrack (1960) • Craftsmen (M) 208.. 8-12   60
Cast: Elly Eliason.

Studiotrack (1957) • Halo (M) 50126 8-10   57
Full title: *Selections from Carousel and Other Standard Hits.* Also has music from *Porgy and Bess* and *Oklahoma!*
Cast: National Singers and Orchestra.

Studiotrack (1959) • National Academy Record Club (M) ES 11 10-12   59
From the *Ed Sullivan Presents Songs and Music of..."* series.
Cast: Ed Sullivan All Star Cast.

Studiotrack (1960) • Richmond (M) B-20064 5-8   60
Studiotrack (1960) • Richmond (S) S-30064 5-8   60
One side has music from *Oklahoma!*
Cast: Frank Chacksfield and His Orchestra.

Studiotrack • MCA (S) 6209 8-10   87
Conductor: Paul Gemignani. Cast: Barbara Cook, Royal Philharmonic Orchestra.
Also see OSCAR HAMMERSTEIN II MEMORIAL ALBUM
Also see RODGERS AND HAMMERSTEIN DELUXE SET

CARPETBAGGERS

Soundtrack (1964) • Ava (M) A-45 12-15   64
Soundtrack (1964) • Ava (S) AS-45 15-18   64
Composer: Elmer Bernstein. Conductor: Elmer Bernstein.

Studiotrack (1964) • Wyncote (M) W-9015 8-10   64
Studiotrack (1964) • Wyncote (S) SW-9015 8-10   64
Also has music from *Dr. Strangelove* and other films.
Cast: Wyncote Orchestra and Chorus.

CARRIE

Soundtrack (1976) • United Artists (S) UA-LA716-H 12-18   76
Composer: Pino Donaggio. Conductor: Pino Donaggio. Cast: Katie Irving.

CARRY IT ON

Soundtrack (1971) • Vanguard (S) VSD-79313 15-20   71
Cast: Joan Baez, David Harris.

CARRY NATION

Original Cast (1968) • Desto (S) DC-6463/64/65 20-25   68
Three discs.
Composer: Douglas Moore, William North Jayme. Conductor: Samuel Krachmalnick. Cast: Beverly Wolf, Ellen Faull, Julian Patrick, Arnold Voketaitis.

CASABLANCA

Soundtrack • Warner Bros. (EP) WB-7741 5-10   73
Has Dooley Wilson's *As Time Goes By,* with dialogue and additional music from the movie.
Cast: Dooley Wilson, others.

CASABLANCA: CLASSIC FILM SCORES FOR HUMPHREY BOGART

Studiotrack • RCA Victor (S) ARL1-0422 10-12   74
Studiotrack • RCA Victor (Q) ARD1-0422 10-20   74
Studiotrack • RCA Victor (S) AGL1-3782 8-10   81
Also has music from *Passage to Marseille, The Treasure of the Sierra Madre, The Big Sleep, The Caine Mutiny, To Have and Have Not, The Two Mrs. Carrolls, Sabrina, The Left Hand of God, Sahara, Virginia City* and *Key Largo.*
Composer: Max Steiner, Franz Waxman, Frederick Hollander, Victor Young, others.
Conductor: Charles Gerhardt. Cast: National Philharmonic Orchestra.

CASANOVA '70: see TRIPLE FEATURE

CASEY'S SHADOW

Soundtrack (1978) • Columbia (S) PS-35344 8-12   78
White label. Promotional issue only.
Soundtrack (1978) • Columbia (S) PS-35344 6-10   78
Composer: Patrick Williams. Conductor: Patrick Williams.

CASINO ROYALE
Soundtrack (1967) • Colgems (M) COMO-5005 25-35   67
Soundtrack (1967) • Colgems (S) COSO-5005 50-100   67
    Composer: Burt Bacharach. **Conductor:** Burt Bacharach. **Cast:** Herb Alpert and the Tijuana Brass, Dusty Springfield.

CASSANDRA CROSSING
Soundtrack (1977) • Citadel (S) CT-6020 20-45   77
    Composer: Jerry Goldsmith. **Conductor:** Jerry Goldsmith.

CAST A GIANT SHADOW
Soundtrack (1966) • United Artists (M) UAL-4138 10-12   66
Soundtrack (1966) • United Artists (S) UAS-5138 12-15   66
Soundtrack (1966) • MCA (S) 25093 5-8   86
    Composer: Elmer Bernstein. **Conductor:** Elmer Bernstein.

CASUALTIES OF WAR
Soundtrack • MCA (S) 6340 8-10   88
    Composer: Ennio Morricone. **Conductor:** Ennio Morricone.

CAT AND THE FIDDLE
Original London Cast (1931) • World (M) SH-171 15-20
  UK release.
    Composer: Jerome Kern, Otto Harbach. **Conductor:** Carroll Gibbons. **Cast:** Peggy Wood.
Studio Cast (1953) • RCA Victor (EP) EPA-477 10-20   53
    Conductor: Lehman Engel. **Cast:** Patricia Neway, Stephen Douglass.
Studio Cast (1959) • Epic (M) LN-3569 10-12   59
  "Excerpts" from shows. One side has music from *Hit the Deck.*
    Composer: Various. **Conductor:** Johnny Gregory. **Cast:** Doreen Hume, Denis Quilley, Michael Sammes Singers.
Soundtrack (1934) • Hollywood Soundstage (M) HS-5015 15-20
  Also has music from *The Merry Widow.* This is the rarest album in an otherwise fairly accessible series.
    Composer: Jerome Kern, Otto Harbach. **Conductor:** Herbert Stothart. **Cast:** Jeanette MacDonald, Ramon Novarro, Frank Morgan, Vivienne Segal. MERRY WIDOW: **Composer:** Jerome Kern, Otto Harbach. **Conductor:** Herbert Stothart. **Cast:** Jeanette MacDonald, Maurice Chevalier.
  Also see SHOW BOAT

CAT BALLOU
Soundtrack (1965) • Capitol (M) T-2340 10-12   65
Soundtrack (1965) • Capitol (S) ST-2340 12-15   65
  Full title: *Nat King Cole Sings His Songs from Cat Ballou and Other Motion Pictures.* Also has songs from *Blue Gardenia, St.Louis Blues, Raintree County, China Gate, Night of the Quarter Moon, Scarlet Hour* and *Adventures of Hajji Baba.*
    Cast: Nat "King" Cole, Stubby Kaye.

CAT PEOPLE
Soundtrack (1982) • Backstreet Records (S) BSR-6107 15-20   82
Soundtrack (1982) • MCA (S) 6107 8-12   82
Soundtrack (1982) • MCA (S) 37263 8-12   Re
    Composer: Giorgio Moroder. **Conductor:** Giorgio Moroder. **Cast:** David Bowie.

CAT'S EYE
Soundtrack (1985) • Varese Sarabande (S) STV-81241 8-12   85
    Composer: Alan Silvestri.

CATCH MY SOUL
Original Cast (1971) • Polydor (S) 2383 035 10-15   71
Soundtrack (1973) • Metromedia (S) BML1-0176 8-12   73
    Cast: Ritchie Havens, Tony Joe White, Lance LeGault, Delaney Bramlett, Bonnie (Bramlett) Sheridan, Season Hubley, Susan Tyrell.

CATHERINE WHEEL
Soundtrack (1981) • Sire (S) SRK-3645.. 8-12   81
  Composer: David Byrne.

CATLOW & FAMOUS THEMES
Soundtrack (1973) • Eros (S) EOP 80544.. 60-80   73
  Themes from *The Carey Treatment, Something To Hide, Soldier Blue, Zeppelin* and *Get Carter.*
  Cast: Roy Budd, others.

CATS
Original London Cast (1981) • Polydor (S) CATX-001........................... 8-10   81
Original London Cast (1981) • Geffen (S) 2GHS-2017......................... 8-10   82
Original London Cast (1981) • Geffen (S) 2GHS-2031......................... 8-10   83
  Above three are all two-disc sets.
  Composer: Andrew Lloyd Webber. Conductor: Andrew Lloyd Webber. Cast: Wayne Sleep, Paul Nicholas, Elaine Paige, Brian Blessed.
Original Cast (1981) • Geffen (S) GHS-2026 5-8   82
  Selections from the original Broadway show, on one LP. Some copies have black sticker on front cover with print "Contains the single version of the song *Memory*"
Original Cast (19821) • Geffen (S) 2GHS-2031 8-10   82
  Two discs.
  Composer: Andrew Lloyd Webber. Conductor: Rene Wiegert. Cast: Kenneth Ard, Betty Buckley, Rene Ceballos, Wendy Edmead, Steven Gelfer, Harry Groener, Stephen Hanan, Janet L. Hubert, Reed Jones, Donna King, Anna McNeely, Terrence V. Mann, Hector Jaime Mercado, Cynthia Onrubia, Ken Page, Timothy Scott, Bonnie Simmons.

CAUGHT IN THE ACT
Original Cast (1953) • Columbia (M) CL-646.. 12-15   55
Original Cast (1953) • Columbia Special Products (M) CCL-646............ 8-10   Re
  Cast: Victor Borge.
  Also see VICTOR BORGE PROGRAM

CAVALCADE
Original Radio Cast • AEI (M) AEI-1149.. 10-12   80s
  Composer: Noel Coward. Cast: Herbert Marshall, Madeleine Carroll, Una O'Conner, David Niven.

CEASE FIRE
Soundtrack • Paramount (M) SP-236... 8-12
  "Special Advance Edition."

CELEBRATION
Original Cast (1969) • Capitol (S) SW-198.. 8-12   69
  Composer: Harvey Schmidt, Tom Jones. Conductor: Ron Dereninko. Cast: Keith Charles, Michael Glenn Smith, Susan Watson, Ted Thurston.
Original Revival Cast (1978) • Pacific Arts (S) 122................................ 5-10   78
  Also see CANTERBURY TALES

CELTICS PRIDE
Radio Broadcast • Fleetwood (S) FCLP 3098 5-10
  Full title: *A&P Presents Celtics Pride.* Radio Broadcast compilation of highlights from WBZ Radio.
  Cast: Johnny Most (narrator and play-by-play announcer).

CENSORED
Studiotrack • Jubilee (M) JGM 2028.. 10-15
  Songs from Broadway shows: *Paris, Annie Get Your Gun, Pal Joey, Spring Is Here, Follow the Girls, The New Yorkers, America's Sweetheart* and *Band Wagon.*
  Cast: Martha Wright, Joe Harnell Trio.

CENSUS TAKER
Soundtrack (1985) • Episode (S) ED 21 8-12   85
    Composer: Residents. Cast: Residents, Greg Mullavey, Meredith Macrae.

CENTENNIAL SUMMER: see STATE FAIR

CERTAIN FURY
Soundtrack (1985) • Varese Sarabande (S) 81239 8-10   85
    Composer: Payne, Kunkel.

CERTAIN SMILE
Soundtrack (1958) • Columbia (M) CL-1194 30-35   58
Soundtrack (1958) • Columbia (S) CS-8068 60-65   58
    Composer: Alfred Newman. Conductor: Alfred Newman. Cast: Johnny Mathis.

CHAIRMAN
Soundtrack (1969) • Tetragrammaton (S) 5007 20-25   69
Soundtrack (1969) • AEI (S) AEI-3110 8-10   82
    Composer: Jerry Goldsmith. Conductor: Jerry Goldsmith.

CHALIAPIN AS BORIS
Original Cast • RCA Victor (M) LCT-3 20-35   49
  10-inch LP. Excerpts of *The Prologue* (1925), *The Monologue and Clock Scenes* (1931) and *The Death* (1928) – as originally recorded for Gramophone (HMV).
    Conductor: Albert Coates, Max Steimann, Vincenzo Bellezza. Cast: Feodor Chaliapin. (With dialogue.)
    Also see DON QUICHOTTE

CHALLENGE OF THE SALT (I'M GOING TO SET MYSELF ON FIRE)
Soundtrack (1973) • MVC (S) 1001 60-70   73
    Composer: Charles Bernstein.

CHAMP
Soundtrack (1979) • Planet (S) PL-9001 8-10   79
    Composer: Dave Grusin, Carole Bayer Sager, Marvin Hamlisch. Conductor: Dave Grusin. Cast: Dave Grusin, Chris Thompson.

CHANGES
Soundtrack (1970) • Nocturne (S) NRS-901 40-50   70
    Cast: Ralna English and Chapp-Lipp Voices.

CHAPLIN REVUE
Soundtrack (1960) • Decca (M) DL-4040 15-45   60
    Composer: Charlie Chaplin. Conductor: Eric Spears. Cast: Charlie Chaplin.

CHAPLIN'S ART OF COMEDY
Soundtrack (1966) • Mainstream (M) 56089 15-20   66
Soundtrack (1966) • Mainstream (S) 6089 20-25   66
  Score is based on an original Charlie Chaplin documentary.
    Composer: Elias Breeskin. Conductor: Elias Breeskin.

CHAPLIN'S BACK
Studiotrack • Paramount (S) PAS-6026 10-20
  Music from *Modern Times, City Lights, Limelight, Monsieur Verdoux, The Great Dictator, The Chaplin Review* and *A King in New York*.
    Conductor: Darius Brubeck. Cast: Darius Brubeck, Amos Garrett, others.
    Also see MUSIC FROM THE FILMS OF CHARLIE CHAPLIN

CHAPMAN REPORT
Soundtrack (1962) • Warner Bros. (M) W-1478 10-12   62
Soundtrack (1962) • Warner Bros. (S) WS-1478 12-15   62
    Composer: Leonard Rosenman. Conductor: Leonard Rosenman.

CHAPPAQUA

Soundtrack (1968) • Columbia (S) OS-3230 10-12   68
    Composer: Ravi Shankar. **Cast:** Ravi Shankar.

CHARADE

Soundtrack (1963) • RCA Victor (M) LPM-2755 10-15   63
Soundtrack (1963) • RCA Victor (S) LSP-2755 12-18   63
    Composer: Henry Mancini, Johnny Mercer. **Conductor:** Henry Mancini.
Studiotrack (1964) • Wyncote (M) W-9009 8-12   64
Studiotrack (1964) • Wyncote (S) SW-9009 8-12   64
  Also has music from *The Pink Panther* and *Tom Jones*.
Studiotrack • Capitol (M) T-2043 10-15
Studiotrack • Capitol (S) ST-2043 15-20
    Cast: Ray Anthony and Orchestra.
Studiotrack • Diplomat (S) DS-2305 8-12
  Full title: *Music from Charade, The Cardinal, & The Victors*.

CHARGE OF THE LIGHT BRIGADE

Soundtrack (1968) • United Artists (S) UAS-5177 10-12   68
    Composer: John Addison. **Conductor:** John Addison. **Cast:** Manfred Mann. (With dialogue.)
Also see DEATH OF A SCOUNDREL

CHARIOTS OF FIRE

Soundtrack (1981) • Polydor (S) PD 1-6335 8-10   81
  Some copies have an "Academy Award" sticker.
    Composer: Vangelis, Sir Hubert Parry. **Conductor:** Vangelis. **Cast:** Ambrosian Singers,
    Vangelis.

CHARIOTS OF THE GODS

Soundtrack (1974) • Polydor (S) PD-6504 12-15   74
    Composer: Peter Thomas. **Conductor:** Peter Thomas.

CHARLEY WEAVER – LETTERS FROM MAMA

TV Soundtrack • Coral (M) CRL-57458 10-15
  From the soundtrack of *The Steve Allen TV Show*.
    Cast: Cliff Arquette.

CHARLIE AND ALGERNON: see FLOWERS FOR ALGERNON

CHARLIE BROWN CHRISTMAS

TV Soundtrack (1964) • Fantasy (M) 5019 25-30   64
TV Soundtrack (1964) • Fantasy (S) 85019 30-35   64
TV Soundtrack (1964) • Fantasy (S) 8431 8-10   70
  Background score from the CBS-TV special.
TV Soundtrack (1964) • Charlie Brown Records (M) 3701 12-15
  Unipak (disc opening faces gutter rather than outer edge) fold-open cover with storybook
  and color photos. Has the entire special, including dialogue.
    Composer: Vince Guaraldi. **Conductor:** Vince Guaraldi. **Cast:** Vince Guaraldi Trio.

CHARLIE CHAN AT THE OPERA

Soundtrack (1936) • Medallion (M) MED 310 8-10   81
  Also has *Gershwin: A Portrait by Levant and Levant - Piano Concerto*.
    Composer: Oscar Levant.

CHARLIE GIRL

Original London Cast (1965) • CBS (M) 62627 25-30   65
Original London Cast (1965) • CBS (S) 62627 25-35   65
  UK release. Mono and stereo have the same selection number.
    Composer: David Heneker, John Taylor. **Conductor:** Kenneth Alwyn. **Cast:** Anna Neagle, Joe
  Brown, Hy Hazell, Christine Holmes, Stuart Damon.

Original Australian Cast (1971) • EMI (S) CSD-7687 30-35   71
   Australian release.
    Cast: Anna Neagle, Derek Nimmo.
London Revival Cast (1986) • First Night (S) CAST 3 12-18   86
   UK release.
    Composer: David Heneker, John Taylor. **Conductor:** Michael Reed. **Cast:** Cyd Charisse, Dora
   Bryan, Paul Nicholas, Lisa Hull, Nicholas Parsons, Mark Wynter.

CHARLIE SENT ME
Original Cast (1984) • Glendale (S) 603584 8-10   84

CHARLOTTE SWEET
Original Cast (1982) • John Hammond (S) W2X-38680 8-10   82
    Cast: Mara Beckerman, Lynn Eldredge, Jeffrey Keller, Timothy Landfield, Merle Louise, Michael
   McCormick, Polly Pen, Christopher Seppe.

CHARLOTTE'S WEB
Soundtrack (1973) • Paramount (S) PAS-1008 20-25   73
   Gatefold cover.
    Composer: Richard M. Sherman, Robert B. Sherman. **Conductor:** Irwin Kostal. **Cast:** Henry
   Gibson, Debbie Reynolds, Paul Lynde, Agnes Morehead, Pamelyn Ferdin.

CHARLY
Soundtrack (1968) • World Pacific (S) WPS-21454 8-10   68
   Gatefold cover.
    Composer: Ravi Shankar. **Cast:** Ravi Shankar.

CHASE
Soundtrack (1966) • Columbia (M) OL-6560 25-30   66
Soundtrack (1966) • Columbia (S) OS-2960 40-65   66
Soundtrack (1966) • CBS (M) 62668 30-40   66
   UK release.
    Composer: John Barry. **Conductor:** John Barry. **Cast:** John Barry Orchestra.
Studiotrack (1978) • Casablanca (S) 20146 10-12   78
   12-inch disco pressing.

CHASE AND SANBORN SHOW
Original Radio Cast • Mark 56 (M) 615.. 40-80   70s
   Picture disc.
    Cast: Edgar Bergan, Charlie McCarthy.

CHASTITY
Soundtrack (1969) • Atco (S) SD-33-302 15-18   69
    Composer: Sonny Bono, Elyse Weinberg. **Cast:** Cher.

CHE!
Soundtrack (1969) • Tetragrammaton (S) T-5006............................... 25-30   69
Soundtrack (1969) • AEI (S) AEI-3111 8-10   82
    Composer: Lalo Schifrin. **Conductor:** Lalo Schifrin. **Cast:** Strings of the Baja California
   Chamber Orchestra, Kaskara.

CHECKMATE
TV Soundtrack (1960) • Columbia (M) CL-1591.................................... 30-35   60
TV Soundtrack (1960) • Columbia (S) CS-8391 40-55   60
    Composer: Johnny Williams. **Conductor:** Johnny Williams.
Studiotrack (1961) • Contemporary (M) 3599...................................... 10-15   62
Studiotrack (1961) • Contemporary (S) S-7599.................................... 15-20   62
   Jazz selections, based on music from the TV show.
    Composer: Johnny Williams. **Conductor:** Shelly Manne. **Cast:** Shelly Manne.

CHEE CHEE: see REMEMBER THESE

CHEECH AND CHONG'S UP IN SMOKE: see UP IN SMOKE

CHERRY, HARRY AND RAQUEL
Soundtrack (1969) • Beverly Hills (S) BHS-23 25-50   69
Composer: Bill Loose. Conductor: Bill Loose.

CHESS
Original London Cast (1984) • RCA Victor (S) CPL2-5340 8-10   84
Two discs.
Composer: Tim Rice. Cast: Elaine Paige, Murray Head, others.

Original London Cast (1984) • RCA Victor (S) AFL1-7163 8-10
Full title: *Chess Pieces*.
Cast: Elaine Paige, Murray Head, others.

Original Cast (1988) • RCA Victor (S) 7700-1 8-12   88
From the Broadway production.
Composer: Benny Anderson, Bjorn Ulvaeus. Conductor: Paul Bogaev. Cast: Judy Kuhn, David Carroll, Philip Casnoff.

CHET HUNTLEY PRESENTS THE BEST OF WASHINGTON HUMOR
Studio Cast • Cameo (M) C-1044 8-12   63
Cast: John F. Kennedy, Barry Goldwater, others.

CHEYENNE AUTUMN
Soundtrack (1963) • Label X (S) LXSE 1-003 30-40   83
45 rpm, 12-inch disc. Audiophile pressing.
Composer: Alex North. Conductor: Alex North.

CHICAGO
Original Cast (1975) • Arista (S) AL 9005 8-10   75
Composer: John Kander, Fred Ebb. Conductor: Stanley Lebowsky. Cast: Gwen Verdon, Chita Rivera, Jerry Orbach, Barney Martin, Mary McCarty, M. O'Haughey.

CHICAGO CONSPIRACY
Original Cast • Capitol (S) SABB-1020 10-20
Cast: Odyssey Theatre Ensemble.

CHICKEN CHRONICLES
Soundtrack (1977) • United Artists (S) UA-LA-830-H 8-10   77
Composer: Ken Lauber, others. Conductor: Ken Lauber. Cast: Classics IV, Nitty Gritty Dirt Band, Canned Heat, Boffalongo, Kutee, Jackie De Shannon.

CHILD IS BORN
TV Soundtrack (1955) • MCA-TV (M) C-55 450-500
Composer: Bernard Herrmann.
Also see DAVID AND BATHSHEBA

CHILD'S INTRODUCTION TO THE MELODY AND THE INSTRUMENTS OF THE ORCHESTRA
Studiotrack (1962) • Disneyland (M) DQ-1232 8-12   62

CHILD'S PLAY
Soundtrack (1989) • Milan (S) A382 8-10   89
Composer: Joe Renzetti.

CHILDREN, CHILDREN, CHILDREN
Original Cast (1955) • Capitol (EP) EAXP-305 15-20   55
Also has music from *Lady and the Tramp*.

CHILDREN OF A LESSER GOD
Soundtrack (1986) • GNP/Crescendo (S) GNPS-8007 8-15   86
Composer: Michael Convertino. Conductor: Shirley Walker.

CHILDREN OF SANCHEZ
Soundtrack (1978) • A&M (S) SP-6700 10-15   78
   Two discs.
    Composer: Chuck Mangione. **Conductor:** Chuck Mangione.

CHILDREN OF THE CORN
Soundtrack (1984) • Varese Sarabande (S) STV 81203 8-10   84
    Composer: Jonathan Elias. **Conductor:** Jonathan Elias.

CHILDREN'S HOUR
Studio Cast (1950) • Decca (M) DL-8013 20-30   50
   One side has music from *Cinderella*.
    Cast: Donald Crisp, Edna Best, others.

CHINA BEACH: MUSIC AND MEMORIES
TV Soundtrack • SBK (S) K1-93744 10-15   90
   Dialogue and songs by various artists, including *Stand by Me*, by John Lennon.
    Cast: John Lennon, others.

CHINATOWN
Soundtrack (1974) • ABC (S) ABDP-848 25-35   74
    Composer: Jerry Goldsmith, others. **Conductor:** Jerry Goldsmith.

CHITTY CHITTY BANG BANG
Soundtrack (1968) • United Artists (S) UAS-5188 15-20   68
   Unipak cover (disc opening faces gutter rather than outer edge).
    Composer: Richard M. Sherman, Robert B. Sherman. **Conductor:** Irwin Kostal. **Cast:** Dick Van
    Dyke, Sally Ann Howes, Anna Quayle, Lionel Jeffries.
Studiotrack • Alshire (S) S-5120 8-10
   Also has music from *Funny Girl* and *Finian's Rainbow*.
    Cast: 101 Strings.

CHOCALONIA
Original Cast (1976) • Crissy (S) CR-2034 15-20   76
    Composer: Glenn Houle. **Conductor:** Glenn Houle. **Cast:** Frankie Marshall, Dennis Lybe, Jim
    Hayes, Gary Fuller, Chris Costello.

CHOCOLATE SOLDIER
Studio Cast • Columbia (M) ML-54060 15-18
   10-inch LP. One side has music from *The Student Prince*.
    STUDENT PRINCE: **Cast:** Nelson Eddy, others.
Studio Cast (1948) • Columbia (M) ML-4060 12-15
   12-inch LP.
Studio Cast (1948) • Columbia Special Products (M) P-13707 5-8   Re
   One side has music from *The Naughty Marietta*.
    Composer: Oscar Straus. **Conductor:** Robert Armbruster. **Cast:** Risë Stevens, Nelson Eddy.
Studio Cast (1951) • RCA Victor (EP) EKB-1006 12-15   51
   Two discs.
Studio Cast (1951) • RCA Victor (M) LK-1006 12-15   51
    Composer: Oscar Straus. **Conductor:** Al Goodman. **Cast:** Ann Ayars, Charles Fredericks,
    John Percival, Jimmy Carroll.
Studio Cast (1958) • RCA Victor (M) LOP-6005 12-15   58
Studio Cast (1958) • RCA Victor (S) LSO-6005 15-18   58
   Both are two-disc sets.
Studio Cast (1958) • RCA Victor (M) LOP-1506 10-12   59
Studio Cast (1958) • RCA Victor (S) LSO-1506 12-15   59
   Excerpts only.
    Composer: Oscar Straus. **Conductor:** Lehman Engel. **Cast:** Risë Stevens, Robert Merrill, Jo
    Sullivan, Peter Palmer.

CHOICE CUTS: SOUNDTRACKS FROM HOLLYWOOD'S CUTTING ROOM FLOOR

Soundtrack • Choice Cuts (M) ST-500/1 20-30
Previously unreleased outtakes from *Lady in the Dark, Song of the Islands, Athena, Barkleys of Broadway, Meet Me in Las Vegas, Bitter Sweet, Three Little Girls in Blue, Annie Get Your Gun, Hollywood Hotel, Hellazpoppin', Stormy Weather* and others.
Composer: Various. **Conductor:** Various. **Cast:** Michael Douglas, Alyson Reed, Terrence V. Mann, Audrey Landers, Yamil Borges, Nicole Fosse, Vicki Frederick, Justin Ross, Matt West, Cameron English, Pam Klinger, Charles McGowan.

CHOICE OF ARMS: see CHOIX DES ARMES

CHOIRBOYS

Soundtrack (1977) • MCA (S) 2326.. 8-10   77
Composer: Frank De Vol. **Conductor:** Frank De Vol.

CHOIX DES ARMES (CHOICE OF ARMS)

Soundtrack (1981) • DRG (S) SL-9510 8-10   81
Conductor: Philippe Sarde. **Conductor:** Peter Knight. **Cast:** London Symphony Orchestra.

CHORUS LINE

Original Cast (1975) • Columbia (S) JS-33581.. 5-8   75
Original Cast (1975) • Columbia (Q) KSQ-33581 10-15   76
Original Cast (1975) • Columbia (S) PS-33581....................................... 3-5   Re
Original Cast (1975) • Columbia (S) HS-43581 10-15   81
Half-speed mastered.
Composer: Marvin Hamlisch, Edward Kleban. **Conductor:** Donald Pippin. **Cast:** Carole Bishop, Renee Baughman, Pamela Blair, Wayne Cilento, Ronald Dennis, Kay Cole, Nancy Lane, Priscilla Lopez, Donna McKechnie, Don Percassi.
Soundtrack (1985) • Casablanca (S) 826306-1 8-10   85
Composer: Marvin Hamlisch, Edward Kleban. **Conductor:** Ralph Burns. **Cast:** Michael Douglas, Alyson Reed, Terrence V. Mann, Audrey Landers, Yamil Borges, Nicole Fosse, Vicki Frederick, Justin Ross, Matt West, Cameron English, Pam Klinger, Charles McGowan.

CHOSEN

Soundtrack (1978) • Cerberus (S) CEMS 0103..................................... 8-12   79
Original film title is *Holocaust 2000*.
Composer: Ennio Morricone. **Conductor:** Ennio Morricone.

CHRISTIANE F.

Soundtrack (1982) • RCA Victor (S) ABL1-4239 8-10   82
Cast: David Bowie.

CHRISTINE (1960)

Original Cast (1960) • Columbia (M) OL-5520...................................... 45-55   60
Original Cast (1960) • Columbia (S) OS-2026...................................... 65-85   60
Composer: Sammy Fain, Paul Webster. **Conductor:** Jay Blackton. **Cast:** Maureen O'Hara, Morley Meredith, Nancy Andrews, Janet Pavek, Phil Leeds.

CHRISTINE (1983)

Soundtrack (1983) • Motown (S) M-6086 8-10   83
Cast: George Thorogood and the Destroyers, Buddy Holly and the Crickets, Johnny Ace, Robert and Johnny, Little Richard, Dion and the Belmonts, Viscounts, Thurston Harris, Danny and the Juniors, Larry Williams.
Soundtrack (1983) • Varese Sarabande (S) VS-5240 8-12   89
Composer: John Carpenter.

CHRISTMAS CAROL

Original Irish Cast (1959) • Vanguard (M) VRS-9040 10-15   59
Original Cast (1980) • MMG (S) 3-MMG-302 20-30   80
Boxed, three-disc set. Includes 24-page booklet/libretto. From the world premiere performance.
Composer: Thea Musgrave.

Studio Cast (1949) • Columbia (M) ML-4081 40-50   49
Studio Cast (1950) • Decca (M) DL-8010 30-40   50
  Actual title: Mister Pickwick's Christmas.
  Cast: Charles Laughton.
Studio Cast (1950) • MCA (M) DL-734684 10-12   Re
  Composer: Victor Young, Hanns Eisler. **Conductor:** Victor Young, Hanns Eisler. **Cast:** Ronald
  Colman, Eric Snowden, Barbara Jean Wong, Lou Merrill, Hans Conried, Cy Kendall, Gale
  Gordon, Heather Thatcher, Fred MacKaye, Stephen Muller, Duane Thompson, Ferdinand
  Munier, Charles Laughton.
Studio Cast (1940s) • MGM (M) E-520 25-35   50s
  10-inch LP.
Studio Cast (1940s) • MGM (M) CH-112 10-15   Re
Studio Cast (1940s) • MGM (SE) PMS-32 8-10   Re
  Composer: Samuel Timberg. **Conductor:** Samuel Timberg. **Cast:** Richard Hale (narration),
  Lionel Barrymore.
Studio Cast (1961) • Caedmon (M) 1135 10-15   61
  Cast: Paul Scofield (narration), Sir Ralph Richardson, Frederick Treves, David Dodimead,
  Willoughby Goddard, Norman Mitchell, Douglas Wilmer, Colette Wilde, Edgar Wreford, James
  Culliford, Pauline Jameson, John Mitchell, Michael Lewis.
Studio Cast • Disneyland (S) ST-3811 5-10   74
Studio Cast • Disneyland (S) D-3811 5-8   74
TV Studiotrack • Pepsi (M) AAB-1367 10-20
  Side two has *Mister Micawber's Difficulties*, from *David Copperfield* (Sir Laurence Olivier).
  Produced by Towers of London.
TV Studiotrack • Spin-O-Rama (M) XMK-4014 8-12
  Reissue (side one of Pepsi AAB-1367).
  Cast: Sir Laurence Olivier.
Studiotrack (1959) • Harmony (M) HL-9523 10-15   60
  Composer: Leith Stevens. **Conductor:** Leith Stevens. **Cast:** Basil Rathbone, Francis X.
  Bushman, Lyn Murray Singers.
  Also see IT'S A WONDERFUL LIFE

CHRISTMAS IN HAWAII
TV Soundtrack (1981) • Blue Water (S) 725 8-12   81
  Full title: *Christmas in Hawaii with Jim Nabors and Guest Star Carol Burnett.*
  Cast: Jim Nabors, Carol Burnett, others.

CHRISTMAS ON THE PONDEROSA: see BONANZA

CHRISTMAS RAPPINGS
Original Cast (1979) • Judson (S) 1002 20-30   79
  Two discs.
  Composer: Al Carmines. **Conductor:** Al Carmines. **Cast:** Judson Poets' Theatre Chorus.

CHRISTMAS SING WITH BING
Radio Soundtrack (1955) • Decca (M) DL-8419 10-20   56
  From international broadcast of *CBS Radio's 1955 Christmas Show.*
  Conductor: Paul Weston, Norman Luboff, J. Spencer Cornwall. **Cast:** Bing Crosby, Paul
  Weston and His Orchestra, Norman Luboff and His Choir, St. Louis Carol Association, Little
  Singers of Granby, Quebec, Salt Lake City Tabernacle Choir, Voices of Christmas (Hollywood),
  Delores Short, Village of Neuilly Children's Choir (France), Reed Warbler's Choir (Holland),
  Vatican Choir, Dedham Choral Society (England).

CHRISTMAS STORY: see DRAGNET

CHRISTMAS THAT ALMOST WASN'T
Soundtrack (1966) • Camden (M) CAL-1086 20-35   66
Soundtrack (1966) • Camden (S) CAS-1086 20-55   66
  Composer: Ray Carter, Paul Tripp. **Cast:** Paul Tripp, Mischa Auer, Sonny Fox, Rossano Brazzi.

CHRISTMAS TIME WITH THE THREE STOOGES
Soundtrack • Rhino (M) RNEP-606 8-10   83
Six-track mini-LP.
Cast: Three Stooges.

CHRISTMAS WITH ARTHUR GODFREY: see ARTHUR GODFREY

CHRISTOPHER COLUMBUS
TV Soundtrack (1985) • Varese Sarabande (S) STV-81245 10-12   85
Composer: Riz Ortolani. Conductor: Riz Ortolani. Cast: Placido Domingo.

CHRISTY
Original Cast (1975) • Original Cast (S) OC-7913 8-10   75
Composer: Lawrence J. Blank, Bernie Spiro. Conductor: Robert Billig. Cast: Jim Elmer, Betty Forsyth, John Canary, Marie Ginnetti, Lynn Kearney, Martha T. Kearns, Bebe Sacks Landis, Gene Lefkowitz, Brian Pizer, Alexander Sokoloff, Bee Swanson.

CHRONOS
Soundtrack (1984) • Sonic Atmospheres (S) 112 15-20   85
Omnimax film produced for the Rueben H. Fleet Space Theater in San Diego.
Composer: Michael Stearns.

CHRYSANTHEMUM
London Cast • AEI (S) AEI-1108 8-10   70s
Composer: Robb Stewart.

CHU CHIN CHOW
London Studio Cast • World (S) WRS-1007 10-20
Material from an earlier performance of this show was previously issued in England.
London Studio Cast • Music for Pleasure (S) MFP-1012 10-15
Composer: Fredrick Norton, Oscar Asche. Conductor: John Hollingsworth.

CHUCK BERRY: HAIL, HAIL ROCK 'N' ROLL: see HAIL, HAIL ROCK 'N' ROLL

CIAO, RUDY: see RUDY CIAO

CIMARRON
Studiotrack (1960) • MGM (M) E-3953 10-12   61
Studiotrack (1960) • MGM (S) SE-3953 12-18   61
Composer: David Rose. Cast: David Rose and His Orchestra.

CINCINNATI KID
Soundtrack (1965) • MGM (M) E-4313 10-20   65
Soundtrack (1965) • MGM (S) SE-4313 15-25   65
Soundtrack (1965) • MCA (S) 25012 5-8   86
Composer: Lalo Schifrin. Conductor: Lalo Schifrin. Cast: Ray Charles.

CINDERELLA (1949)
Studio Cast (1959) • RCA Victor (M) LPM-2012 12-18   59
Studio Cast (1959) • RCA Victor (S) LSP-2012 15-20   59
Composer: Jerry Livingston, Norman Leyden. Conductor: Thomas Scherman. Cast: Mary Martin.
Studio Cast (1962) • Disneyland (M) ST-3908 10-12
Composer: Jerry Livingston, Norman Leyden. Conductor: Paul J. Smith. Cast: Ilene Woods, Disney cast.
Soundtrack (1949) • Disneyland (M) WDL-4007 50-150   57
Feature-length cartoon musical. First pressing
Soundtrack (1949) • Disneyland (M) DQ-1207 8-10   59
Soundtrack (1949) • Disneyland (M) 3107 10-30   81
Limited edition picture disc.
Composer: Mack David, Al Hoffman, Jerry Livingston. Conductor: Jerry Livingston.

Studiotrack (1950) • RCA Y399 35-45   49
   Two 78 rpms.
     Composer: Norman Leyden. **Conductor:** Paul Smith. **Cast:** Ilene Woods, James McDonald,
     Eleanor Audley, Helen Stanley, Lucille Bliss, Verna Felton, John Brown, Clarence Nash.
     Also see CHILDREN'S HOUR
     Also see 20,000 LEAGUES UNDER THE SEA

CINDERELLA (1957)

Original London Cast (1959) • Decca (S) SKL-4050 25-30   59
   UK release. Stage version of the Rodgers and Hammerstein television production.
     Composer: Richard Rodgers, Oscar Hammerstein II. **Conductor:** Bobby Howell. **Cast:** Tommy
     Steele, Jimmie Edwards, Yana, Bruce Trent, Kenneth Williams, Betty Marden.

Studio Cast (1965) • MGM (M) CH-1007 12-15   65
     Composer: Richard Rodgers, Oscar Hammerstein II. **Cast:** Sybil Trent.

TV Soundtrack (1957) • Columbia (M) OL-5190 10-12   57

TV Soundtrack (1957) • Columbia (SE) OS-2005 20-25   59
   Has black stereo band across top of front cover.

TV Soundtrack (1957) • Columbia Special Products (SE) AOS-2005 8-10   82
     Composer: Richard Rodgers, Oscar Hammerstein II **Conductor:** Alfredo Antonini. **Cast:** Julie
     Andrews, Howard Lindsay, Dorothy Stickney, Ilka Chase, Kaye Ballard, Alice Ghostley, Jon
     Cypher, Edith Adams, Iggie Wolfington, George Hall.

TV Soundtrack (1965) • Columbia (M) OL-6330 15-20   65

TV Soundtrack (1965) • Columbia (S) OS-2730 20-25   65
   Second television production of the Rodgers and Hammerstein version.
     Composer: Richard Rodgers, Oscar Hammerstein II. **Conductor:** John Green. **Cast:** Lesley
     Ann Warren, Ginger Rogers, Celeste Holm, Pat Carroll, Barbara Ruick, Jo Van Fleet, Don
     Heitgerd, Walter Pidgeon. (With dialogue.)
     Also see SLIPPER AND THE ROSE

CINDERELLA ITALIAN STYLE: see MORE THAN MIRACLE

CINDERELLA LIBERTY

Soundtrack (1973) • 20th Century-Fox (S) ST-100 10-12   73
     Composer: John Williams. **Conductor:** John Williams.

CINDERFELLA

Studiotrack (1960) • Dot (M) DLP-8001 35-45   60

Studiotrack (1960) • Dot (S) DLP-38001 50-75   60
   Discs are rainbow splash vinyl. Although cover lists the film cast, only Jerry Lewis appears
   on the recording. Gatefold cover. Includes: a) road race board game on inside front cover;
   b) metal arrow spinner; c) cut-out strip with game pieces; d) cardboard flip-up music stand
   on inside back cover; e) 24-page, 4" x 6" color booklet of film pictures and song lyrics; f)
   magic wand baton; g) elastic-bound crown. Price range may be much higher overseas.
     Composer: Walter Scharf, Harry Warren, Jack Brooks. **Conductor:** Walter Scharf. **Cast:** Jerry
     Lewis.

CINDY

Original Cast (1964) • ABC-Paramount (M) OC-2 15-25   64

Original Cast (1964) • ABC-Paramount (S) OCS-2 30-45   64
     Composer: Johnny Brandon. **Conductor:** Clark McClellan, Sammy Benskin. **Cast:** Sylvia
     Mann, Johnny Harmon, Lizabeth Pritchett, Thelma Oliver, Dena Dietrich, Mike Sawyer, Tommy
     Karaty, Joe Masiell, Jacqueline Mayro, Frank Nastasi, Mark Stone, Amelia Varney.

CINDY-ELLA OR I GOTTA SHOE

Soundtrack • Stet (S) DS-15023 8-10
     Composer: Ron Grainer. **Cast:** Cleo Laine.

CINEMA LEGRAND

Studiotrack • MGM (M) E-4491 10-15
   Music from *Umbrellas of Cherbourg, Young Girls of Rochefort, Plastic Dome of Norma
   Jean, Gone with the Wind, Two for the Road, Orfeu Negro, Fitzwilly, Le Vie De Chateau,
   An American Dream* and *Doctor Dolittle*.
     Composer: Michel Legrand, others. **Conductor:** Michel Legrand.

CINEMA RHAPSODIES
Studiotrack [Vol. 1] (1953) • Decca (EP) ED-2034 10-15
Studiotrack [Vol. 2] (1953) • Decca (EP) ED-2076 10-15
Studiotrack (1953) • Decca (SE) DL-8051.. 10-12   60s
   Composer: Victor Young. Conductor: Victor Young.

CINEMA SCENE TODAY
Studiotrack (1967) • Mercury (M) MG-21149... 8-15   67
Studiotrack (1967) • Mercury (S) SR-61149 10-15   67
   Composer: Various. Conductor: Marty Gold. Cast: Derek and Ray.

CINEMA '76
Studio Cast (1964) • Industrial (M) CILP 500 65-75   64
   Ggatefold cover. Includes 15-page booklet. Subtitled: *Songs of the Continental Soldier*.
   Originally presented at the New York World's Fair by Continental Insurance.
   Composer: Ray Charles. Conductor: Tony Mottola.

CINEMOOG
Studiotrack (1973) • Mercury (S) SR-61279... 8-10   73
   Composer: Various. Cast: Electronic Concept Orchestra featuring Eddie Higgins on the Moog
   Synthesizer.

CINERAMA HOLIDAY
Soundtrack (1955) • Mercury (EP) EP-1-3303 15-20   55
Soundtrack (1955) • Mercury (M) MG-20059 20-30   55
   Composer: Morton Gould, Van Cleave, Jack Shaindlin, others. Conductor: Jack Shaindlin.
Studiotrack (1955) • RCA Victor (EP) ERA-258 20-25   55
   Conductor: Morton Gould. Cast: Morton Gould and His Orchestra.

CIRCLE OF LOVE
Soundtrack (1965) • Monitor (M) MP-602.. 25-30   65
Soundtrack (1965) • Monitor (S) MPS-602.. 35-40   65
   Composer: Michel Magne. Conductor: Michel Magne.

CIRCUS OF HORRORS
Soundtrack (1960) • Imperial (M) LP-9129.. 50-125   60
   Composer: Muir Mathieson, Franz Reizenstein, Mark Anthony. Conductor: Muir Mathieson.
   Cast: Gary Mills.

CIRCUS WORLD
Soundtrack (1964) • MGM (M) E-4252 10-25   64
Soundtrack (1964) • MGM (S) SE-4252 12-30   64
   Composer: Dimitri Tiomkin. Conductor: Dimitri Tiomkin.

CITIZEN KANE
Soundtrack (1941) • Mark 56 (M) 810 10-20   80
   Two-disc set of the complete film.
   Composer: Bernard Herrmann. Conductor: Bernard Herrmann. Cast: Orson Welles, Joseph
   Cotten, Everett Sloane, Agnes Moorehead, Dorothy Comingore, Ray Collins, George Coulouris,
   Ruth Warrick.
Studiotrack (1941) • United Artists (S) UA-LA372-G 10-12   75
   Composer: Bernard Herrmann. Conductor: Leroy Holmes.
   Also see GREAT FILM CLASSICS
   Also see WELLES RAISES KANE

CITIZEN KANE / DEVIL AND DANIEL WEBSTER
Studiotrack (1940) • Virtuoso (S) TPLS-13010..................................... 15-25   68
Studiotrack (1940) • Unicorn (S) UN1-72008 8-10   73
   Actual title: *Welles Raises Kane/The Devil and Daniel Webster*.
   Composer: Bernard Herrmann. Conductor: Bernard Herrmann. Cast: London Philharmonic
   Orchestra.

CITIZEN KANE: THE CLASSIC FILM SCORES OF BERNARD HERRMANN

Studiotrack • RCA Victor (S) ARL1-0707 8-10   74

Studiotrack • RCA Victor (Q) ARD1-0707 10-15   74

Music from *On Dangerous Ground, White Witch Doctor, Hangover Square* and *Beneath the 12-Mile Reef.*

Composer: Bernard Herrmann. **Conductor:** Charles Gerhardt. **Cast:** National Philharmonic, Kiri Te Kanawa, Joaquin Achucrro (piano).

CITY BACKGROUNDS

TV Soundtrack • CBS EZ Cue (M) XTV-133194 15-20

Music cues from *The Fugitive, Perry Mason* and other TV shows.

Composer: Wilber Hatch, Fred Steiner, Nathan Van Cleave, others.

CITY HEAT

Soundtrack (1984) • Warner Bros. (S) 1-25219 8-10   84

Composer: Lennie Niehaus. **Cast:** Irene Cara, Al Jarreau, Joe Williams, Mike Lang, Pete Jolly, Clint Eastwood, Eloise Laws.

CITY OF ANGELS

Original Cast (1989) • Columbia (S) 46067 8-10   90

Composer: Cy Coleman, David Zippel. **Conductor:** Gordon Lowry Harrell. **Conductor:** Gordon Lowery Harrell. **Cast:** James Naughton, Gregg Edelman, Randy Graff, Dee Hoty, Kay McClelland, Shawn Elliot, Rene Auberjonois.

CIVILIZATION, PART II

Soundtrack (1988) • Capitol (S) C1-90205 8-10   88

CLAMBAKE

Soundtrack (1967) • RCA Victor (M) LPM-3893 150-250   67

Black label reads "Monaural" at bottom. Includes 12" x 12" bonus photo, which represents about $40 to $60 of the value.

Soundtrack (1967) • RCA Victor (S) LSP-3893 50-80   67

Black label reads "Stereo" at bottom. Includes 12" x 12" bonus photo, which represents about $40 to $60 of the value.

Soundtrack (1967) • RCA Victor (S) AFL1-2565 8-10   77

Composer: Sid Tepper, Roy C. Bennett, Jerry Reed, Ben Weisman, Sid Wayne, Randy Starr, others. **Cast:** Elvis Presley, Bob Moore (bass), Floyd Cramer (piano), Jerry Reed (guitar), Buddy Harman (drums), Harold Bradley (guitar), Grady Martin (guitar), Pete Drake (steel guitar), Jordanaires (vocals), Millie Kirkham (vocals).

CLAMS ON THE HALF SHELL

Original Cast (1975) • Atlantic (S) SD2-9000 10-15   75

Two discs.

CLAN OF THE CAVE BEAR

Soundtrack (1986) • Varese Sarabande (S) STV-81274 8-12   86

Composer: Alan Silvestri. **Conductor:** Alan Silvestri.

CLARA: see BEG, BORROW OR STEAL

CLARK GABLE ON RADIO

Radio Cast (1949) • Radiola (M) MR-1132 8-12   82

Personality Series 15, Release 132. Has *Command Decision* (March 1949) and *China Seas* (Dec. 4, 1944).

Cast: Clark Gable.

CLASH OF THE TITANS

Soundtrack (1981) • Columbia (S) JS-37386 10-15   81

Composer: Laurence Rosenthal. **Conductor:** Laurence Rosenthal. **Cast:** London Symphony Orchestra, Sir Laurence Olivier (narration).

CLASSIC FILM SCORES FOR BETTE DAVIS
Studiotrack • RCA Victor (S) ARL1-0183 10-12   73
Includes booklet.
Studiotrack • RCA Victor (S) AGL1-3706 8-10   80
Without booklet.
Music from *Now, Voyager, Dark Victory, A Stolen Life, The Private Lives of Elizabeth and Essex, Mr. Skeffington, In This Our Life, All About Eve, Jezebel, Beyond the Forest, Juarez, The Letter* and *All This and Heaven Too.*
Composer: Max Steiner, Erich Wolfgang Korngold, Franz Waxman, Alfred Newman.
Conductor: Charles Gerhardt.

CLASSIC HORROR MUSIC OF HANS J. SALTER
Soundtrack • Tony Thomas (M) HS-4 45-55   78
Includes original soundtrack music from *Creature of the Black Lagoon* and *The Incredible Shrinking Man.*
Composer: Hans J. Salter. **Conductor:** Hans J. Salter.

CLASSIC MIKLOS ROZSA FILM THEMES
Studiotrack • That's Entertainment (S) TER-1130 8-10   80s
UK release.
Composer: Miklos Rozsa. **Conductor:** Georges Delerue.

CLASSICS OF THE SILVER SCREEN
Studiotrack • RCA Victor (S) R233758 8-12
Two discs.
Cast: Arthur Fiedler and Boston Pops Orchestra.

CLAUDINE
Soundtrack (1974) • Buddah (S) BDS-5602 20-25   74
Composer: Curtis Mayfield. **Cast:** Curtis Mayfield, Gladys Knight and the Pips.

CLEAN SLATE: see COUP DE TORCHON

CLEAVAGE
Original Cast (1982) • BI (S) 36-24-36 40-80   82
Composer: Buddy Sheffield. **Cast:** Daniel David, Tom Elias, Mark Fiti, Terese Garguilo.

CLEO LAINE AT CARNEGIE HALL
Original Cast (1973) • RCA Victor (S) LPL1-5015 10-12   73
Conductor: John Dankworth. **Cast:** Cleo Laine.

CLEO LAINE RETURNS TO CARNEGIE HALL
Original Cast (1976) • RCA Victor (S) APL1-2407 8-10   76
Conductor: John Dankworth. **Cast:** Cleo Laine.

CLEOPATRA
Soundtrack (1963) • 20th Century-Fox (M) FXG-5008 12-15   63
Soundtrack (1963) • 20th Century-Fox (S) SXG-5008 12-18   63
Composer: Alex North. **Conductor:** Alex North.
Studiotrack (1963) • Design (S) DLP 161 8-12   63
Composer: Alex North. **Conductor:** Russ Case.
Studiotrack (1963) • RCA Victor (M) LPM-2766 10-12   63
Studiotrack (1963) • RCA Victor (S) LSP-2766 12-15   63
Conductor: Riz Ortolani. **Cast:** Rome Sound Stage Orchestra.
Studiotrack (1963) • Columbia (M) CL-2050 8-12   63
Studiotrack (1963) • Columbia (S) CS-8850 10-15   63
Full title: *Impressions of Cleopatra.*
Cast: Paul Horn.
Studiotrack • Coronet (M) CX-197 8-10
Studiotrack • Coronet (S) CXS-197 8-10
Full title: *Theme Music from the Film Cleopatra and Music from the Nile.*

Studiotrack • Crown (M) 5316 8-10
    Conductor: William Rodgers.
Studiotrack • Diplomat (M) 2298 8-10
    Full title: *Cleopatra Themes and Other Memorable Themes.* Also has music from *The
    Outlaw, War and Peace, Song of Norway, Cleopatra, Till the End of Time, I've Always
    Loved You* and *Red Shoes.*
    Conductor: Nicholas Andriano.
Studiotrack • Hurrah (M) H-1041 8-10
Studiotrack • Hurrah (S) HS-1041 8-10
    Conductor: Russ Case.
Studiotrack (1963) • MGM (M) E-4144 8-10
Studiotrack (1963) • MGM (S) SE-4144 8-10
    Full title: *Cleopatra (Love Themes And Music From Other Elizabeth Taylor Films).*
    Conductor: David Rose. **Cast:** David Rose & His Orchestra.
Studiotrack • Palace (M) M-749 8-10
Studiotrack • Palace (S) S-749 8-10
    One side has *Excerpts from Scheherazado Suite.*
    Cast: Bill Ewing, Viennese Symphonic Orchestra, Helen Alexandria.
Studiotrack (M) P-20200 8-10
    Cast: Cinema Sound Stage Orchestra.
Studiotrack (1963) • Time (M) T-52080 8-10   63
Studiotrack (1963) • Time (S) S-2080 8-10   63
    Conductor: Richard Hayman. **Cast:** Richard Hayman and His Orchestra.
Studiotrack (1963) • United Artists (M) UAL-3290 10-12   63
Studiotrack (1963) • United Artists (S) UAL-9290 15-20   63
    Full title: *Love Themes from Cleopatra (and Others).*
    Composer: Alex North, others. **Cast:** Ferrante and Teicher.

CLEOPATRA JONES
Soundtrack (1973) • Warner Bros. (S) BS 2719 20-30   73
    Composer: Joe Simon, others. **Cast:** Joe Simon, Millie Jackson, J.J. Johnson.

CLIVE BARKER'S NIGHT BREED: see NIGHT BREED

CLOCKERS
Soundtrack • MCA (S) 11304 8-10   95

CLOCKWORK ORANGE
Soundtrack (1971) • Warner Bros. (S) BS-2573 10-12   71
    With gatefold cover.
Soundtrack (1971) • Warner Bros. (S) BS-2573 8-10   70s
    Standard cover.
    Composer: Walter Carlos, Rachel Elkind, Gioacchino Rossini, Ludwig van Beethoven, Sir
    Edward Elgar, Terry Tucker, Erika Elgen, Arthur Freed, Nacio Herb Brown. **Cast:** Walter Carlos
    (moog synthesizer), Gene Kelly, Erika Elgen.
Soundtrack (1972) • Columbia (S) KC-31480 8-12   72
    Complete collection of Walter Carlos' music for the film.
    Composer: Walter Carlos, Rachel Elkind, Ludwig van Beethoven, Gioacchino Rossini.
    Conductor: Walter Carlos.
Studiotrack (1972) • Pickwick (S) SPC 3302 8-10   72
    Full title: *Music from the Movie Clockwork Orange.*
Studiotrack (1972) • RCA Victor (S) LSC 3268 8-10   72

CLOSE ENCOUNTERS OF THE THIRD KIND
Soundtrack (1977) • Arista (S) AL-9500 15-25   77
    Gatefold cover. Includes bonus, single-sided 7-inch, 33 single (AS-9500) of title theme.
    Deduct $10 if single is missing. Some copies have large blue sticker with review excerpts
    and mention of "Special Bonus Record."
Soundtrack (1977) • Arista (S) AL5-8078 8-10   Re

Soundtrack (1977) • Arista (S) ALB6-8365.. 8-10   Re
    Composer: John Williams. **Conductor:** John Williams.

Studiotrack (1978) • Wonderland (S) WLP-5001 10-15   78
    Full title: *The Official Dramatized Recordings of Close Encounters of the Third Kind*
    (Complete with Sound Effects and Music. Specially Created for This Record). Includes
    copy of 42-page *Close Encounters of the Third Kind* magazine,
      Composer: John Williams, Matt Kaplowitz. **Cast:** Dominick Farone, Dyan Forest, Ruth Last,
      Tom Cipolla, Herb Duncan, Jim Dukas.

Studiotrack • Pickwick (S) SPC 3616 8-10
    Composer: John Williams. **Conductor:** Pat DeVuono.
    Also see STAR WARS/CLOSE ENCOUNTERS OF THE THIRD KIND

CLOWN AND THE KIDS

Soundtrack (1968) • Golden (M) LP-215.. 20-25   68
    Composer: Tony Velona. **Conductor:** Artie Beck. **Cast:** Jazz Philharmonic of Sofia.

CLOWNAROUND

Original Cast (1972) • RCA Victor (S) LSP-4741.............................. 200-250   72
    Composer: Alvin Cooperman, Moose Charlap. **Conductor:** Harper MacKay.

CLOWNS

Soundtrack (1971) • Columbia (S) S-30772 20-30   71
    Composer: Nino Rota. **Conductor:** Carlo Savina.

CLUB 15

Original Cast (1949) • Decca (M) DL-5155.. 40-45   49
    10-inch LP.
      Conductor: Jerry Gray. **Cast:** Jerry Gray and Orchestra, Dick Haymes, Andrews Sisters, Evelyn
      Knight, Modernaires.

CLUES TO A LIFE

Original Cast • Original Cast (S) OC-8237 8-12
      Composer: Alec Wilder. **Conductor:** Elliott Weiss. **Cast:** Christine Andreas, D'Jamin Bartlett,
      Keith David, Craig Lucas.

CO-STAR

Studio Cast • Co-Star (M) CS-101.. 10-12
    Co-star with Cesar Romero. Includes script, which allows buyer to act scenes opposite the
    actor on the record.
      Cast: Cesar Romero, You.

Studio Cast • Co-Star (M) CS-102.. 10-12
    Co-star with Fernando Lamas. Includes script, which allows buyer to act scenes opposite
    the actor on the record.
      Cast: Fernando Lamas, You.

Studio Cast • Co-Star (M) CS-103.. 10-12
    Co-star with Arlene Dahl. Includes script, which allows buyer to act scenes opposite the
    actress on the record.
      Cast: Arlene Dahl, You.

Studio Cast • Co-Star (M) CS-104.. 10-12
    Co-star with George Raft. Includes script, which allows buyer to act scenes opposite the
    actor on the record.
      Cast: George Raft, You.

Studio Cast • Co-Star (M) CS-105.. 10-12
    Co-star with June Havoc. Includes script, which allows buyer to act scenes opposite the
    actress on the record.
      Composer: Jack Ragotzy. **Cast:** June Havoc, You.

Studio Cast • Co-Star (M) CS-106.. 10-12
    Co-star with Sir Cedric Hardwicke. Includes script, which allows buyer to act scenes
    opposite the actor on the record.
      Cast: Sir Cedric Hardwicke, You.

Studio Cast • Co-Star (M) CS-107.. 10-12
  Co-star with Basil Rathbone. Includes script, which allows buyer to act scenes opposite the actor on the record.
  Cast: Basil Rathbone, You.

Studio Cast • Co-Star (M) CS-108.. 10-12
  Co-star with Virginia Mayo. Includes script, which allows buyer to act scenes opposite the actress on the record.
  Cast: Virginia Mayo, You.

Studio Cast • Co-Star (M) CS-109.. 20-25
  Co-star with Tallulah Bankhead. Includes script, which allows buyer to act scenes opposite the actress on the record.
  Cast: Tallulah Bankhead, You.

Studio Cast • Co-Star (M) CS-110.. 10-12
  Co-star with Vincent Price. Includes script, which allows buyer to act scenes opposite the actor on the record.
  Cast: Vincent Price, You.

Studio Cast • Co-Star (M) CS-111.. 10-12
  Co-star with Paulette Goddard. Includes script, which allows buyer to act scenes opposite the actor on the record.
  Cast: Paulette Goddard, You.

Studio Cast • Co-Star (M) CS-112.. 10-12
  Co-star with Don Ameche. Includes script, which allows buyer to act scenes opposite the actor on the record.
  Cast: Don Ameche, You.

Studio Cast • Co-Star (M) CS-113.. 10-12
  Co-star with Jimmie Rodgers. Includes script, which allows buyer to act scenes opposite the actor on the record.
  Cast: Jimmie Rodgers, You.

Studio Cast • Co-Star (M) CS-114.. 10-12
  Co-star with Pearl Bailey. Includes script, which allows buyer to act scenes opposite the actress on the record.
  Cast: Pearl Bailey, You.

Studio Cast • Co-Star (M) CS-115.. 10-12
  Co-star with "Slapsy" Maxie Rosenbloom. Includes script, which allows buyer to act scenes opposite the actor on the record.
  Cast: "Slapsy" Maxie Rosenbloom, You.

COACH WITH THE SIX INSIDES
Original Cast (1967) • ESP Disc (M) 1019... 15-20   67
  Composer: Teiji Ito, James Joyce. **Conductor:** Teiji Ito. **Cast:** Sheila Roy, Van Dexter, Anita Dangler, Leonard Frey, Jean Erdman.

COAL MINER'S DAUGHTER
Soundtrack (1980) • MCA (S) 5107... 8-10   80
  Includes insert.
Soundtrack (1980) • MCA (S) 1699... 5-8   Re
  Composer: Loretta Lynn, Willie Nelson, others. **Cast:** Sissy Spacek, Levon Helm, Beverly D'Angelo, Jordanaires.

COAST TO COAST
Soundtrack (1980) • Full Moon (S) FM-3490... 8-10   80
  Cast: Rita Coolidge, Johnny Lee, Ambrosia.

COBRA
Soundtrack (1986) • Scotti Bros. (S) SZ-40325..................................... 8-10   86
  Cast: John Cafferty and the Beaver Brown Band, John Beauvoir, Gladys Knight, Bill Medley, Gary Wright, Georgia Satellites, Beach Boys, John Cougar Mellancamp, Ry Cooder, Preston Smith, Little Richard.

COBWEB
Soundtrack (1957) • MGM (M) E-3501 75-125   57
One side has music from *Edge of the City*.
Composer: Leonard Rosenman. **Conductor:** Johnny Green.

COCKTAIL
Soundtrack (1988) • Elektra (S) 60806-1 8-10   88
Composer: Maurice Jarre, others. **Conductor:** Maurice Jarre, others. **Cast:** Starship, Robbie Nevil, Fabulous Thunderbirds, Beach Boys, Ry Cooder, Little Richard, Bobby McFerrin, Georgia Satellites, Preston Smith, John Cougar Mellencamp.

COCKTAIL PARTY
Original Cast [Vol. 1] (1951) • Decca (M) DL-9004 15-20   51
Original Cast [Vol. 2] (1951) • Decca (M) DL-9005 15-20   51
Original Cast [Vols. 1&2] (1951) • Decca (M) DX-100 20-25   51
"Featuring members of the Original New York production."
Cast: Sir Alec Guinness, Cathleen Nesbitt, Robert Flemyng, Eileen Peel, Irene Worth, Ernest Clark, Grey Blake.

COCO
Original Cast (1969) • Paramount (S) PMS-1002 15-20   69
Unipak cover (disc opening faces gutter rather than outer edge).
Composer: Andre Previn, Alan Jay Lerner. **Conductor:** Robert Emmett Dolan. **Cast:** Katharine Hepburn, George Rose, Gale Dixon, David Holliday, Rene Auberjonois, Jean Arnold, Will B. Abel, Chad Block, Jon Cypher, Jack Dabdoub, Robert Fitch, Dan Siretta.

COCOANUTS
Soundtrack (1929) • Sandy Hook (M) 2059 8-10
Soundtrack (1929) • Soundtrack (M) STK-108 8-10   77
Composer: Irving Berlin. **Cast:** Marx Brothers, others.

COCOON
Soundtrack (1985) • Polydor (S) 827041-1 8-10   85
Composer: James Horner. **Conductor:** James Horner. **Cast:** Michael Sembello.

COCOON: THE RETURN
Soundtrack (1988) • Varese Sarabande (S) VS-5211 8-12   88
Composer: James Horner. **Conductor:** James Horner.

CODE OF SILENCE
Soundtrack (1985) • Easy Street (S) ESA-9900 8-10   85
Composer: David Frank.

COFFY
Soundtrack (1973) • Polydor (S) PD-5048 90-100   73
Composer: David Frank. **Cast:** Roy Ayers.

COLE
Original London Cast (1974) • RCA Victor (S) CRL2-5054 8-12   74
Original London Cast (1974) • RCA Victor (S) LRL2-5054 8-12   74
Composer: Cole Porter. **Cast:** Julie McKenzie, Kenneth Nelson, Bill Kerr, Angela Richards.

COLE PORTER AND ME
Studiotrack (1956) • RCA Victor (M) LPM-1340 15-25   56
Composer: Cole Porter. **Cast:** Eddie Cano (piano).

COLE PORTER IN HOLLYWOOD (1929-1956)
Soundtrack • JJA (M) 19767 25-35   76
Two discs. Songs recorded from the soundtracks of *Battle of Paris, Rosalie, Born to Dance, Broadway Melody of 1940, Anything Goes, Panama Hattie, Du Barry Was a Lady, Let's Face It, You'll Never Get Rich, Something for the Boys, Something to Shout About, Adam's Rib* and *Night and Day*.
Composer: Cole Porter. **Cast:** Gertrude Lawrence, Eleanor Powell, Nelson Eddy, Ethel Merman, Bing Crosby, Bob Hope, Betty Hutton, Fred Astaire, Vivian Blaine and others.

COLE PORTER IN LONDON: see KISS ME KATE

COLE PORTER IN PARIS

TV Soundtrack (1973) • No label Shown (M) No Number Shown......... 85-95   73
From the Bell System Family theater television special, which aired January 17, 1973. Plain white cover with green sticker affixed to front. Promotional issue only.
   Composer: Cole Porter. **Cast:** Perry Como, Diahann Carroll, Connie Stevens, Louis Jourdan, Twiggy, Charles Aznavour.

COLE PORTER REVIEW: see NIGHT AND DAY

COLE PORTER REVISITED

Studio Cast • Crewe (S) CR-3002.. 10-20
One source shows this as being on Painted Smiles, but provides no selection number.
   Composer: Cole Porter.

COLETTE

Original Cast (1970) • Mio (S) MCS-3001 12-15   70
   Composer: Harvey Schmidt, Tom Jones. **Conductor:** Harvey Schmidt. **Cast:** Zoe Caldwell, Ruth Nelson, Keith Charles, Holland Taylor.

Original London Cast (1979) • Sepia (S) RSR-100996......................... 10-12   80
   Composer: John Dankworth. **Cast:** Cleo Laine.

COLLECTOR

Soundtrack (1965) • Mainstream (M) 56053.. 12-35   65
Soundtrack (1965) • Mainstream (S) S-6053.................................... 25-55   65
   Composer: Maurice Jarre. **Conductor:** Maurice Jarre.

COLLECTOR'S COMPANION TO MUSICAL THEATRE

Studiotrack • AEI (S) AEI-1172 5-10   80s
Music from *Pink Lady* and *Prince of Pilsen*.

COLLECTOR'S SONDHEIM: see SONDHEIM

COLLEGE CONFIDENTIAL

Soundtrack (1960) • Chancellor (M) CHL-5016............................ 30-40   60
Soundtrack (1960) • Chancellor (S) CHLS-5016 40-50   60
   Composer: Dean Elliot. **Cast:** Shelly Manne, Bud Shank, Jimmy Rowles, Milt Bernhart, Bob Cooper.

COLOR ME BARBRA

TV Soundtrack (1965) • Columbia (M) CL-2478................................. 8-10   65
TV Soundtrack (1965) • Columbia (S) CS-9278 8-12   65
   Composer: Various. **Conductor:** Peter Matz. **Cast:** Barbra Streisand.

COLOR OF MONEY

Soundtrack (1986) • MCA (S) 6189....................................... 8-10   86
   Cast: Don Henley, Warren Zevon, Robert Palmer, Eric Clapton, Mark Knopfler, Willie Dixon, B.B. King, Robbie Robertson.

COLOR PURPLE

Soundtrack (1985) • Warner Bros./Qwest (M) WBMS-135-2 15-20   85
Boxed promotional issue with music and an interview with Quincy Jones.
   Cast: Quincy Jones.

Soundtrack (1985) • Qwest (S) 25356-1 10-15   85
Two colored vinyl discs. "Limited Edition."

Soundtrack (1985) • Qwest (S) 25289-1 10-20   86
Two colored vinyl discs. Includes 20-page booklet.
   Composer: Quincy Jones. **Conductor:** Quincy Jones.

COLORS

Soundtrack (1988) • Warner Bros. (S) 1-25713 8-10   88
   Cast: 44 Mag Mix, Decadent Dub Team, Salt-N-Pepa, Big Daddy Kane, Eric B., Kool G., 7A3, Roxanne Shante, M.C., Rick James.

COLUMBIA ALBUM OF COLE PORTER

Studiotrack (1956) • Columbia (M) C2L-4 10-12   56
  Two discs.
    Composer: Cole Porter. **Cast:** Michel Legrand and his Orchestra.

COLUMBO: see BILLY GOLDENBERG: HIS FILM AND TELEVISION MUSIC

COMA

Soundtrack (1978) • MGM (S) MG-1-5403 10-12   78
    Composer: Jerry Goldsmith, Don Peake. **Conductor:** Jerry Goldsmith.

COMANCHE

Soundtrack (1956) • Coral (M) CRL-57046 250-350   56
    Composer: Herschel Burke Gilbert. **Conductor:** Herschel Burke Gilbert.

COMANCHEROS: see DIGITAL PREMIERE RECORDINGS FROM THE FILMS OF JOHN WAYNE

COMDEN AND GREEN: SHOW MUSIC AT ITS BEST

Studio Cast • Heritage (M) H-0057 65-75   55
Studio Cast • DRG (M) Number Not Known 10-15   80s
  Betty Comden and Adolph Green perform their songs.
    Composer: Betty Comden, Adolph Green, Leonard Bernstein, Morton Gould, Roger Edens.
    Conductor: Herb Harris. **Cast:** Betty Comden and Adolph Green.

COME BACK CHARLESTON BLUE

Soundtrack (1972) • Atco (S) SD-7010 25-30   72
    Composer: Donny Hathaway. **Conductor:** Donny Hathaway. **Cast:** Donny Hathaway.

COME BLOW YOUR HORN

Soundtrack (1963) • Reprise (M) R-6071 20-25   63
Soundtrack (1963) • Reprise (S) R9-6071 30-45   63
    Composer: Nelson Riddle, James Van Heusen. **Conductor:** Nelson Riddle.

COME MEET U.S.

Soundtrack • No Label Shown (S) No Number Used 40-50
  Promotional album from Trans World Airlines.

COME NEXT SPRING

Soundtrack (1956) • Citadel (M) CT 7019 8-10   80
  Also has music from Steiner's *The Last Command*.
    Composer: Max Steiner. **Conductor:** Max Steiner.

COME ON, LET'S LIVE A LITTLE: see C'MON, LET'S LIVE A LITTLE

COME SPY WITH ME

Original London Cast (1966) • Decca (M) LK-4810 20-25   66
Original London Cast (1966) • Decca (S) SKL-4810 20-30   66
  UK release.
    Composer: Bryan Blackburn. **Conductor:** Sam Harding. **Cast:** Danny LaRue, Barbara Windsor,
    Richard Wattis, Dennis Lotis, Rose Hill, Barrie Gosney, Valerie Walsh.

COME TO THE MOVIES

Studiotrack (1976) • Tee Vee (S) TA-1041 8-12   76
  Two discs.

COMEDIANS

Soundtrack (1962) • MGM (M) E-4494 10-15   62
Soundtrack (1962) • MGM (S) SE-4494 12-18   62
Soundtrack (1962) • MCA (S) 25002 8-10   86
    Composer: Laurence Rosenthal. **Conductor:** Laurence Rosenthal.

COMEDY IN MUSIC
Original Cast (1953) • Columbia (M) CL 6292 20-25   53
  10-inch LP.
Original Cast (1953) • Columbia (M) CL-554 12-15   54
Original Cast (1953) • Columbia Special Products (M) CCL-554 8-10   Re
  From a 1953 performance at the John Golden Theatre in New York.
    Cast: Victor Borge.
    Also see VICTOR BORGE PROGRAM

COMIC RELIEF
Studio Cast (1986) • WEA (S) 240939 8-10   86
Studio Cast (1986) • Rhino (S) RHIN-70704 8-10   86

COMING OF CHRIST
TV Soundtrack (1960) • Decca (M) DL-9093 25-30   60
TV Soundtrack (1960) • Decca (S) DL-79093 40-45   60
  Includes booklet.
    Composer: Robert Russell Bennett. **Cast:** Alexander Scourby (narration).

COMING TO AMERICA
Soundtrack (1988) • Atco (S) 0-90958/DMD 1189 10-15   88
  Promotional issue only.
Soundtrack (1988) • Atco (S) 90958-1 8-10   88
    Composer: Nile Rodgers, others. **Cast:** System, Cover Girls, Chico DeBarge, Michael Rodgers,
    Laura Branigan, Joe Esposito, JJ Fad, Mell & Kim, Levert, Sister Sledge, Nona Hendrix.

COMMAND PERFORMANCE
London Cast (1956) • DRG (M) DARC-1-1106 15-25   79
  From performance "Night Of 100 Stars", June 28, 1956 at the London Palladium.
    Cast: Bob Hope, Sir Laurence Olivier, Tyrone Power, Gracie Field, Vivian Leigh, Noel Coward,
    Maurice Chevalier, Beatrice Lillie, Tallulah Bankhead, Paul Scofield, Peter Ustinov, Laurence
    Harvey, Jack Benny, John Mills.

COMMITTEE
Original Cast (1964) • Reprise (M) FR-2023 20-25   64
Original Cast (1964) • Reprise (S) FS-2023 25-30   64
    Composer: Ellsworth Milburn, Irene Riordan. **Cast:** Scott Beach, Hamilton Camp, Garry
    Goddrow, Larry Hankin.

COMPANY
Original Cast (1970) • Columbia (S) OS-3550 8-10   70
Original Cast (1970) • Columbia (Q) SQ-30993 15-25   70s
  Quad issue has different mix versions.
    Composer: Stephen Sondheim. **Conductor:** Hal Hastings. **Cast:** Dean Jones, Barbara Barrie,
    George Coe, John Cunningham, Teri Ralston, Beth Howland, Charles Braswell, Susan
    Browning, Steve Elmore, Charles Kimbrough, Merle Louise, Donna McKechnie, Pamela Myers,
    Elaine Stritch.
Original London Cast (1971) • CBS (S) 70108 60-65   71
  UK release. Essentially a revised Broadway cast recording made on the occasion of the
  London production's opening. Includes Larry Kert, who replaced Dean Jones in New York
  shortly after the show opened. Only seven of the cast members on this recording actually
  appeared in the London production.
    Composer: Stephen Sondheim. **Conductor:** Harold Hastings. **Cast:** Larry Kert, Barbara Barrie,
    George Coe, John Cunningham, Teri Ralston, Beth Howland, Elaine Stritch, Donna McKechnie,
    Steve Elmore.

COMPANY OF WOLVES
Soundtrack (1985) • Varese Sarabande (S) STV-81242 8-10   85
Soundtrack (1985) • That's Entertainment (S) TER-1094 8-10   80s
  UK release.
    Composer: George Fenton. **Conductor:** George Fenton.

COMPETITION

Soundtrack (1980) • MCA (S) MCA-5185.. 8-10   80
  Composer: Randy Crawford, Lalo Schifrin. **Conductor:** Lalo Schifrin.

COMPLETE SHIRLEY TEMPLE SONG BOOK

Soundtrack • 20th Century-Fox (SE) TCS-103-2.................................. 20-35
  Two discs in gatefold cover. Music from *Bright Eyes, Curly Top, Stowaway, Rebecca of
  Sunnybrook Farm* and others.
  Composer: Various. **Conductor:** Various. **Cast:** Shirley Temple.

COMPOSER'S HOLIDAY

Studiotrack (1957) • Capitol (M) T-886.. 15-25   57
  Composer: Alfred Newman, Andre Previn, Elmer Bernstein, George Duning, Dominick
  Frontiere. **Conductor:** Les Brown. **Cast:** Les Brown and His Band of Renown.

COMPULSION

Soundtrack (1959) • 20th Century-Fox (EP) FEP-101.......................... 50-75   59
  Cast: Orson Welles.

COMETOGETHER

Soundtrack (1971) • Apple (S) SW-3377 15-20   71
  Composer: Stelvio Cipriani, others. **Cast:** Joe South, Dells.

CONAN THE BARBARIAN

Soundtrack (1982) • MCA (S) 6108.. 8-10   82
Soundtrack (1982) • MCA (S) 1566.. 8-10   80s
  Composer: Basil Poledouris, Zoe Poledouris. **Conductor:** Basil Poledouris.

CONAN THE DESTROYER

Soundtrack (1984) • MCA (S) 6135.. 8-10   84
  Cast: Basil Poledouris.

CONCERT JOHN BARRY

Studiotrack (1972) • Polydor (S) 2383-156... 5-10   72
  Composer: John Barry. **Conductor:** John Barry. **Cast:** Royal Philharmonic Orchestra.

CONCERT OF FILM MUSIC

Soundtrack • RCA Victor (S) APL1-1379 6-12   76
  Music from *White Dawn* and others.
  Composer: Henry Mancini. **Conductor:** Henry Mancini.

CONFIDENTIALLY YOURS

Soundtrack (1984) • DRG (S) SL-9519 8-10   83
  Also has music from four other Truffaut/Delerue soundtracks.
  Composer: François Truffaut, Georges Delerue.

CONNECTICUT YANKEE

Broadway Revival Cast (1943) • Decca DA-367..................,................. 30-40
  Album of five 78 rpms, with booklet.
Broadway Revival Cast (1943) • JJA (M) 19733................................... 15-20   73
  Also has music from *Inside U.S.A.*
Broadway Revival Cast (1943) • AEI (M) AEI-1138 15-20   80s
  Gatefold cover.
Broadway Revival Cast (1943) • AEI (M) AEI-1138 10-12   80s
  Standard cover.
    Composer: Richard Rodgers, Lorenz Hart. **Cast:** Vivienne Segal, Robert Chisholm, Dick Foran,
    Vera-Ellen, Chester Stratton, Julie Warren.
Studio Cast (1952) • RCA Victor (EP) EKB-1026 10-12   52
Studio Cast (1952) • RCA Victor (M) LK-1026..................................... 15-20   52
  One side has music from *Rio Rita*.
    Composer: Richard Rodgers, Lorenz Hart. **Conductor:** Al Goodman. **Cast:** Earl Wrightson,
    Elaine Malbin, Guild Choristers.

CONNECTICUT YANKEE IN KING ARTHUR'S COURT: see BING'S HOLLYWOOD

CONNECTION
Original Cast (1959) • Blue Note (M) 4027 20-25   59
Original Cast (1959) • Blue Note (S) 84027 30-35   59
    Composer: Freddie Redd. **Conductor:** Freddie Redd.
Original Cast (1961) • Parker (M) PLP-806 15-20   62
Original Cast (1961) • Parker (S) PLP-8065 20-25   62
    Composer: Cecil Payne, Kenny Drew. **Conductor:** Cecil Payne.

CONQUEST OF SPACE
Studio Cast • Vox (M) DL-522 10-15
Studio Cast • Vox (S) STDL-522 15-20
    Cast: Dr. Wernher Von Braun, Willy Lea.

CONSUL
Original Cast (1950) • Decca (M) DX-101 40-50   51
  Two discs. Features members of the New York Production.
    Composer: Gian-Carlo Menotti. **Conductor:** Lehman Engel. **Cast:** Marie Powers, Patricia Neway, Gloria Lane, Cornell MacNeil, George Jone-yan, Andrew McKinley, Lydia Summers, Maria Androssi, Leon Lishner, Francis Monachino, Maria Marlo.

CONTINENTAL TWIST
Soundtrack (1961) • Capitol (M) T-1677 25-35   61
Soundtrack (1961) • Capitol (S) ST-1677 35-45   61
    Conductor: Sam Butera. **Cast:** Sam Butera and the Witnesses.

CONVERSATION PIECE
Original London Cast (1951) • World (M) SH-179-80 15-20
Original London Cast (1951) • Monmouth
  Evergreen (SE) MES-7062/3 8-10   Re
    Conductor: Reginald Burston. **Cast:** Noel Coward, Sidney Grammer, Yvonne Printemps, George Sanders.
Studio Cast • Columbia (M) SL-163 20-25
Studio Cast • Columbia Special Products (M) ASL-163 10-12   Re
  Both are boxed, two-disc sets with libretto.
    Composer: Noel Coward. **Conductor:** Lehman Engel. **Cast:** Noel Coward, Lily Pons, Richard Burton, Cathleen Nesbitt, Ethel Griffies.

CONVOY
Soundtrack (1978) • United Artists (S) UA-LA910-H 8-10   78

COOKIE
Soundtrack • UNI (S) 600 8-10
    Cast: Holly Johnson, Transvision Vamp, Bobby Helms, Nanci Griffith, Thomas Newman.

COOL BREEZE
Soundtrack (1972) • MGM (S) 1SE-35 15-20   72
    Composer: Solomon Burke. **Cast:** Solomon Burke.

COOL HAND LUKE
Soundtrack (1967) • Dot (M) DLP-3833 25-35   68
Soundtrack (1967) • Dot (S) DLP-25833 45-65   68
    Composer: Lalo Schifrin. **Conductor:** Lalo Schifrin.

COOL OF THE EVENING: see BING'S HOLLYWOOD

COOL WORLD
Soundtrack (1964) • Philips (M) 200-138 35-45   64
Soundtrack (1964) • Philips (S) 600-138 55-65   64
    Composer: Mal Waldron. **Cast:** Dizzy Gillespie Quintet.

COOLEY HIGH
Soundtrack (1975) • Motown (S) M7-840R2.. 15-20   75
  Two discs.
  Cast: Diana Ross and the Supremes, Stevie Wonder, Four Tops, Luther Allison, Martha Reeves
  and the Vandellas, Marvelettes, Smokey Robinson and the Miracles, Jr. Walker and the All-
  Stars, Barrett Strong, Mary Wells, Freddie Perren.

COP SHOW THEMES
TV Soundtrack (1976) • RCA Victor (S) APL1-1896............................ 12-15
  Themes from: *NBC Mystery Movie, The Streets of San Francisco, Bumper's Theme (The
  Blue Knight), Kojak, S.W.A.T., Baretta's Theme (Keep Your Eye on the Sparrow), The
  Rockford Files, Hawaii Five-O* and *Police Woman.*
  Composer: Henry Mancini, others. **Conductor:** Henry Mancini.

COPLAND CONDUCTS COPLAND: see QUIET CITY

CORNBREAD EARL AND ME
Soundtrack (1975) • Fantasy (S) F-9483... 20-25   75

CORRUPT ONES
Soundtrack (1967) • United Artists (M) UAL-4158............................... 15-30   67
Soundtrack (1967) • United Artists (S) UAS-5158 20-40   67
  Composer: Georges Garvarentz. **Conductor:** Georges Garvarentz. **Cast:** Dusty Springfield.

COSA NOSTRA STORY
Studio Cast (1963) • Smash (M) MGS-27045 10-20   63

COSMOS
TV Soundtrack (1981) • RCA Victor (S) ABL1-4003............................. 8-10   81
  Full title: *(Music of) Cosmos.* Score from a PBS television presentation.
  Cast: Vangelis.

COSTEAU: see COUSTEAU

COTTON CLUB
Soundtrack (1984) • Geffen (S) GHS-24062.. 8-10   84
  Composer: John Barry, others. **Conductor:** John Barry.

COTTON CLUB REVUE OF 1958
Original Cast (1958) • Gone (M) GLP-101 50-60   58
  Side two has assorted selections by Cab Calloway.
  Composer: Clay Boland, Benny Davis. **Conductor:** Eddie Barefield. **Cast:** Cab Calloway.

COTTON COMES TO HARLEM
Soundtrack (1970) • United Artists (S) UAS-5211 25-30   70
Soundtrack (1970) • MCA (S) 25133.. 8-10   86
  Composer: Galt MacDermott. **Cast:** Melba Moore, Leta Galloway, George Tipton, Sakinah.

COTTON PATCH GOSPEL
Original Cast (1981) • Chapin Productions (S) CP-101 12-15   81
  Composer: Harry Chapin, Tom Chapin. **Cast:** Scott Ainslie, Pete Corum, Tom Key, Jim
  Lauderdale, Michael Mark.

COUNT OF LUXEMBOURG
Studio Cast • London (M) 5352 10-15   60s

COUNT OF MONTE CRISTO
Studio Cast (1950) • Decca (M) DL-5147 20-70   50
  10-inch LP.
  Composer: Victor Young. **Conductor:** Victor Young. **Cast:** Herbert Marshall, Pedro De
  Cordoba, Lou Merrill, Elliott Lewis, Frederic Worlock, Fred MacKaye, Paula Winslowe.

COUNT THREE AND PRAY: see NO SAD SONGS FOR ME

COUNTESS FROM HONG KONG
Soundtrack (1967) • Decca (M) DL-1501 8-12   67
Soundtrack (1967) • Decca (S) DL-71501 10-12   67
  Some copies have "Exclusive souvenir photo album-biography of Charles Chaplin."
  Composer: Charlie Chaplin. **Conductor:** Lambert Williamson.

COUNTRY
Soundtrack (1984) • Windham Hill Records (S) WH-9-1039 8-10   84
  Composer: Charles Gross. **Conductor:** Charles Gross. **Cast:** George Winston, Darol Anger, Mark Isham, Mike Marshall.

COUNTRY BEAR JAMBOREE
Soundtrack (1972) • Disneyland (S) ST-3994 20-25   72
  From Disney's theme park attraction of the same name.

COUNTRY COUSIN
Studiotrack (1959) • Disneyland (M) ST-1903 25-30   59
Studiotrack (1959) • Disneyland (SE) DQ-1306 15-20   67
  Composer: Buddy Baker. **Cast:** Disney cast. (With dialogue.)

COUNTRY GIRL
Soundtrack (1954) • Decca (M) DL-5556 20-35   54
  10-inch LP. Also has music from *Little Boy Lost* and *Anything Goes*.
  Composer: Harold Arlen, Ira Gershwin. **Conductor:** Joseph J. Lilley. **Cast:** Bing Crosby.

COUNTRY MUSIC HOLIDAY
Soundtrack (1958) • Capitol (EP) EAP-1-921 15-25   58
  Cast: Ferlin Husky.

COUNTRY MUSIC USA OPRYLAND
Original Cast (1982) • Opryland (S) OP-1009 5-10   82

COUP DE TORCHON (CLEAN SLATE)
Soundtrack (1981) • DRG (S) SL-9511 8-10   81
  Conductor: Philippe Sarde. **Conductor:** Peter Knight. **Cast:** Philippe Sarde.

COUPE DE VILLE
Soundtrack (1990) • Cypress (S) 71334... 8-10   90
  Cast: Kingsmen, Dion, Flamingos, Temptations, Cadillacs, Joey Dee and the Starliters, Chips, Everly Brothers, Nervous Norvous, Young MC.

COURIER
Soundtrack • Virgin Movie Music (S) 90954-1 8-10
  Cast: Dangerous Games, Cry Before Dawn, Declan MacManus, Something Happens, Hothouse Flowers, Lord John White, U2.

COURT JESTER
Soundtrack (1956) • Decca (EP) ED-776 20-25   56
  Two discs.
Soundtrack (1956) • Decca (M) DL-8212 40-60   56
  Black (commercial) or pink (promotional) label.
Soundtrack (1956) • Decca (M) DL-8212 25-30   60s
  Rainbow label.
  Composer: Sylvia Fine. **Conductor:** Vic Schoen. **Cast:** Danny Kaye, Notables, Lee Gordon Singers.

COURT MARTIAL OF BILLY MITCHELL
Studio Cast (1955) • Mark 56 (SE) 633 10-15   74
  Composer: Dimitri Tiomkin. **Conductor:** Dimitri Tiomkin. **Cast:** Gary Cooper, Rod Steiger, Ralph Bellamy. (With dialogue.)

COUSINS
Soundtrack (1989) • Warner Bros. (S) 25901-1 8-10   89
  Composer: Angelo Badalamonti. **Conductor:** Angelo Badalamonti.

COUSTEAU / AMAZON

TV Soundtrack (1984) • Varese Sarabande (S) STV-81220 8-10   84
Also has music from *Amazon*.
Composer: John Scott. **Cast:** National Philharmonic Orchestra.

COVER GIRL

Soundtrack (1944) • Curtain Calls (S) CC 100/20 8-12
Also has music from *You Were Never Lovelier*.
Composer: Jerome Kern, Ira Gershwin. **Conductor:** Morris Stoloff. **Cast:** Gene Kelly, Nan Wynn (performed vocals for Rita Hayworth in the film), Phil Silvers. YOU WERE NEVER LOVELIER: **Cast:** Fred Astaire, Nan Wynn (performed vocals for Rita Hayworth in the film), Rita Hayworth (dialogue), Xavier Cugat and His Orchestra, Lina Romay.

COWARDLY CUSTARD

Original London Cast (1973) • RCA Victor (S) LSO-6010 10-15   73
Two discs.
Composer: Noel Coward. **Conductor:** John Burrows. **Cast:** Olivia Breeze, Geoffrey Burridge, Jonathan Cecil, Tudor Davies, Elaine Delmar, Peter Gale, Laura Ford, John Mohatt, Patricia Routledge, Una Stubbs, Anna Sharkey, Derek Waring.

COWBOY

Soundtrack (1958) • Decca (M) DL-8684 35-60   58
Black (commercial) or pink (promotional) label.
Soundtrack (1958) • Decca (M) DL-8684 15-20   60s
Rainbow label.
Composer: George Duning, Rafael Mendez. **Conductor:** Morris Stoloff

CRADLE WILL ROCK

Original Cast (1937) • American Legacy (M) T-1001.......................... 75-100
Composer: Marc Blitzstein. **Cast:** Howard DaSilva, Edward Fuller, Olive Stanton, Peggy Coudray, Blanche Collins, Marc Blitzstein (piano), John Adair, Howard Bird, George Fairchild, Dulce Fox, Maynard Holmes, Ralph MacBane, Frank Marvel, Charles Niemeyer, Marion Rudley, Jules Schmidt, Bert Weston.
Original Revival Cast (1964) • MGM (M) E-4289-2.............................. 20-25   64
Original Revival Cast (1964) • MGM (S) SE-4289-2............................ 20-25   64
Both are two-disc sets.
Original Revival Cast (1964) • CRI (S) S-266... 8-10   Re
Original Revival Cast (1964) • That's Entertainment (S) TER-1105........ 8-10   80s
UK releases.
Composer: Marc Blitzstein. **Conductor:** Gershon Kingsley. **Cast:** Jerry Orbach, Lauri Peters, Nancy Andrews, Hal Buckley, Gordon Clarke, Clifford David, Nichols Grimes, Joseph Bova, Karen Cleary, Dean Dittman, Rita Gardner, Micki Grant, Peter Meersman, Ted Scott, Wayne Tucker, Chris Warfield.
Original Revival Cast (1985) • Polydor (S) 827 937-1 12-15   85
Composer: Marc Blitzstein. **Conductor:** Michael Barrett. **Cast:** Dennis Bacigalupi, Brooks Baldwin, Casey Biggs, Daniel Corcoran, Leslie Geraci, Patti LuPone, Anderson Matthews, Randle Mell, Mary Lou Rosato, David Schramm, Norman Snow, Henry Stram, Michele-Denise Woods.

CRAWLSPACE

Soundtrack (1986) • Varese Sarabande (S) STV 81279 8-10   86
Composer: Pino Donaggio. **Conductor:** Natale Nassara.

CREATIVE FREAKOUT

Studio Cast (1967) • Brief (S) No Number Used 30-35   67
10-inch LP. Issued in a paper sleeve. Promotional issue only.
Composer: Hugh Heller, Jacques Wilson, Dave Williams, Dick Hamilton. **Cast:** Ben Chandler, Hellers.

CREATURE FROM THE BLACK LAGOON: see CLASSIC HORROR MUSIC OF HANS J. SALTER

CREEPERS
Soundtrack (1986) • Enigma (S) SJ-73205 8-10   86
    Cast: Claudio Simonetti, Ron Maiden, Goblin, Sex Gang Andi, Bill Wyman, Terry Taylor, Simon Boswell, Motorhead.

CREEPSHOW (FIVE JOLTING TALES OF HORROR!)
Soundtrack (1982) • Varese Sarabande (S) STV-81160 8-10   82
    Composer: John Harrison. **Conductor:** John Harrison. **Cast:** John Harrison.

CRICKET ON THE HEARTH
TV Soundtrack (1967) • RCA Victor (M) LSC-1140 10-15   67
TV Soundtrack (1967) • RCA Victor (S) LSO-1140 15-40   67
    Composer: Maury Laws, Jules Bass. **Cast:** Danny Thomas, Marlo Thomas, Ed Ames, Abbe Lane, Norman Luboff Choir.

CRIME IN THE STREETS
Soundtrack (1956) • Decca (M) DL-8376 45-50   56
  Black (commercial) or pink (promotional) label.
Soundtrack (1956) • Decca (M) DL-8376 35-45   56
  Rainbow label.
Studiotrack • Entr'acte (M) 6001 15-20   79
  Also has music from *Three Sketches* and *Theme, Variations and Fugato*, both by Waxman.
    Composer: Franz Waxman. **Conductor:** Franz Waxman.

CRIMES OF PASSION
Soundtrack (1986) • TBG/President (S) RW 3 12-15   86
    Composer: Rick Wakeman. **Cast:** Maggie Bell.

CRIMES OF THE HEART
Soundtrack (1986) • Varese Sarabande (S) STV-81298 8-12   86
Soundtrack (1986) • That's Entertainment (S) TER-1130 8-10   80s
  UK release.
    Composer: Georges Delerue.

CRIMINAL: see BIG OPERATOR

CRIMINAL LAW
Studiotrack (1989) • Varese Sarabande (S) VS-5210 8-10   89
    Composer: Jerry Goldsmith.

CRISIS
Studio Cast (1950) • Decca (M) DXSA-7194 15-20
Studio Cast (1950) • Citadel (SE) CT-7004 8-12
    Composer: Miklos Rozsa. **Conductor:** Miklos Rozsa.
  Also see FILM MUSIC OF MIKLOS ROZSA

CRITIC
Original Cast • Decca (M) DL-9154 10-15
Original Cast • Decca (S) DL-79154 12-15
    Composer: Noel Coward. **Cast:** Noel Coward, Mel Ferrer.

CRITTERS
Soundtrack (1986) • Restless (S) 72154 10-12   86
    Composer: David Newman. **Conductor:** David Newman.

CROCODILE DUNDEE
Soundtrack (1986) • Varese Sarabande (S) STV-81296 8-10   86
    Composer: Peter Best. **Conductor:** Peter Best.

CROMWELL
Soundtrack (1970) • Capitol (S) ST-640 15-18   70
Soundtrack (1970) • Capitol (S) ST-80640 8-10
    Composer: Frank Cordell. **Conductor:** Frank Cordell. **Cast:** Richard Harris, Sir Alec Guinness, Robert Morley. (With dialogue.)

CROOKED MILE
Soundtrack • AEI (S) AEI-1115 8-12   70s
   Composer: Peter Greenwell.

CROSBY'S RADIO SHOWS: see BING CROSBY'S RADIO SHOWS

CROSS AND THE SWITCHBLADE
Soundtrack (1970) • Light (S) LS-5550 20-25   70
   Composer: Ralph Carmichael. Conductor: Ralph Carmichael. Cast: Pat Boone (Biblical readings), Young People, John Bahler, Ron Hicklin, Stan Farber, Gene Morford.

CROSSED SWORDS
Soundtrack (1978) • Warner Bros. (S) BSK-3161 8-10   78
   Composer: Maurice Jarre. Conductor: Maurice Jarre. Cast: National Philharmonic Orchestra.

CROSSING DELANCEY
Soundtrack (1988) • Varese Sarabande VS 5201-1 8-12   88
   Composer: Paul Chihara.

CROSSOVER DREAMS
Soundtrack (1986) • Elektra (S) 60470-1 8-10   86
   Composer: Reuben Blades, Andy and Jerry Gonzales, Yomo Toro, Marco Rizo, Johnny Colon, Virgilio Marti, Ballistic Kisses, others. Cast: Reuben Blades, Virgilio Marti, Tito Puente, Chase, Jose Gallegos, Rooftop, Marco Rizo, Javier Vazquez.

CROSSROADS
Soundtrack (1986) • Warner Bros. (S) 1-25399 8-10   86
   Composer: Ry Cooder. Cast: Ry Cooder.

CROWNING EXPERIENCE
Soundtrack • Capitol (S) LB 2306/7 15-25   60
   Presented by Moral Re-Armament. Narration and songs.
   Composer: Paul Dunlap. Cast: Muriel Smith, Ann Buckles.

CRUISING
Soundtrack (1980) • Columbia (S) JC-36410 30-35   80
   Cast: Willy DeVille, Cripples, John Hiatt, Madelynn Von Ritz, Mutiny, Rough Trade, Germs.

CRY FOR US ALL
Original Cast (1970) • Project 3 (S) TS-1000SD 30-35   70
   Composer: Mitch Leigh, William Alfred, Phyllis Robinson. Conductor: Herbert Grossman. Cast: Joan Diener, Robert Weede, Steve Arlen, Tommy Rall, Helen Gallagher, Scott Jacoby, Steve Arlen, Darel Glaser, William Griffis, Todd Jones, Robert Weede.

CRY FREEDOM
Soundtrack (1987) • MCA (S) 6224.. 8-10   87
   Cast: George Fenton.

CRY OF THE BANSHEE
Soundtrack (1970) • Varese Sarabande (S) CT 7013 8-10   80s
   Composer: Les Baxter.
Studiotradel (1970) • Citadel (S) CTV-7013 10-15   80
   Symphonic suite based on themes from the film. Contains the *Edgar Allan Poe Suite* from the television special and *An Evening with Edgar Allan Poe*, starring Vincent Price.
   Composer: Les Baxter. Conductor: Les Baxter.

CRYER AND FORD
Original Cast (1975) • RCA Victor (S) APL1-1235................................ 10-15   75
Original Cast (1977) • RCA Victor (S) APL1-2146................................ 10-12   77
   Manhattan Theatre Club performance.
   Composer: Gretchen Cryer, Nancy Ford. Cast: Gretchen Cryer, Nancy Ford (with musical accompaniment).

CRYSTAL HEART
Original Cast (1960) • Blue Pear (M) BP-1001 10-15   83
> **Composer:** Baldwin Bergersen, William Archibald. **Conductor:** Baldwin Bergersen. **Cast:** John Baylis, Mildred Dunnock, Bob Fitch, Margot Harley, Barbara Janezic, Katherine Litz, Byron Mitchell, Joe Ross, Jeanne Shea, John Stewart, Virginia Vestoff, Vincent Warren.

CULT OF THE DAMNED: see ANGEL, ANGEL DOWN WE GO

CURIOUS EVENING WITH GYPSY ROSE LEE
Original Cast (1961) • Stereoddities (S) CG-1 20-25   61
Original Cast (1961) • AEI (S) AEI-1131 8-10   80s
> **Composer:** Bobby Kroll, Eli Basse. **Cast:** Gypsy Rose Lee.

CURTAIN GOING UP
Studiotrack (1957) • RCA Victor (M) LM 2093 8-10   57
> Music from *My Fair Lady, Carousel, Brigadoon, Can-Can, Wonderful Town* and *South Pacific.*
> **Conductor:** Arthur Fiedler. **Cast:** Boston Pops Orchestra.

CURTAIN GOING UP (MUSICAL GUIDE TO PLAY ACTING)
Original Cast • Leo (M) CH-1025 10-12
> **Composer:** Ruth Roberts, others. **Conductor:** Frank Motis. **Cast:** Richard Kiley, Julie Harris, Andrea Dolin, Glen Richards.

CUSTER OF THE WEST
Soundtrack (1968) • ABC (M) OC-5 50-60   68
Soundtrack (1968) • ABC (S) ABCS-OC-5 70-80   68
> Gatefold cover.
> **Composer:** Bernardo Segall. **Conductor:** Bernardo Segall.

CUT! OUT-TAKES FROM HOLLYWOOD'S GREATEST MUSICALS
Soundtrack [Vol. 1] • Out Take (M) OTF-1 10-20   74
> Edited out-takes from movie musicals.
> **Cast:** Judy Garland, Ann Sothern, Alice Faye, Ray Bolger, Debbie Reynolds, Jack Nicholson, Betty Garrett, Nanette Fabray, Fred Astaire, Betty Grable, June Havoc, Judy Holliday, others.

Soundtrack [Vol. 2] • Out Take (M) OTF-2 10-20   75
Soundtrack [Vol. 2] • DRG (M) SBL 12587 8-12   Re
> **Cast:** Nanette Fabray, Frank Sinatra, Bing Crosby, Frances Farmer, Gene Kelly, Lena Horne, Betty Hutton, Nancy Walker, Judy Garland, Mickey Rooney, others.

Soundtrack [Vols. 1&2] • DRG (M) OTF-1&2 20-25
> **Cast:** Judy Garland, Ann Sothern, Alice Faye, Ray Bolger, Debbie Reynolds, Jack Nicholson, Betty Garrett, Nanette Fabray, Fred Astaire, Betty Grable, June Havoc, Judy Holliday, Nanette Fabray, Frank Sinatra, Bing Crosby, Frances Farmer, Gene Kelly, Lena Horne, Betty Hutton, Nancy Walker, Judy Garland, Mickey Rooney, others.

Soundtrack [Vol. 3] • Out Take (M) OTF-3 18-20
> **Cast:** Jane Powell, Helen Traubel, Judy Garland, Lena Horne, Irene Dunne, Allan Jones, Red Skelton, Ann Sothern, Gene Kelly, Ethel Merman, Betty Grable, Howard Keel, Alice Faye, others.

CY COLEMAN PRESENTS BARNUM: see BARNUM

CYCLE SAVAGES
Soundtrack (1970) • American Int'l (S) STA-1033 20-25   70
> **Composer:** Jerry Styner, Randy Johnson, Mike Stevens, Guy Hemric, others. **Conductor:** Jerry Styner.

CYRANO
Original Cast (1973) • A&M (S) SP 8131 10-15   73
> Referred to as the "Pre-Original Cast" recording.
Original Cast (1973) • A&M (S) SP-3702 8-12   73
> Two discs.
> **Composer:** Michael Lewis. **Conductor:** Thomas Pierson. **Cast:** Christopher Plummer, Leigh Berry, Mark Lamos, James Blendick, Patrick Hines, Louis Tureen, J. Kenneth Campbell, Anita Dangler, Arnold Soboloff.

CYRANO DE BERGERAC

Studio Cast (1965) • Caedmon (S) TRS-306-S 10-20
  Three discs, with complete text booklet.
Soundtrack (1950) • Capitol (EP) EDM-283 15-20   51
Soundtrack (1950) • Capitol (M) S-283 20-25   51
  Red label. Front cover has artwork framed in a speckled gray background.
Soundtrack (1950) • Capitol (M) W-283 12-15   Re
  Black label. Front cover has artwork framed in a solid gray background.
    Composer: Paul Bowles. **Conductor:** Paul Bowles. **Cast:** Edmund Trzcinski (narration), Jose
    Ferrer, Robert Carroll, Fran Letton, Vincent Donahue, Ralph Clanton, Patricia Wheel.

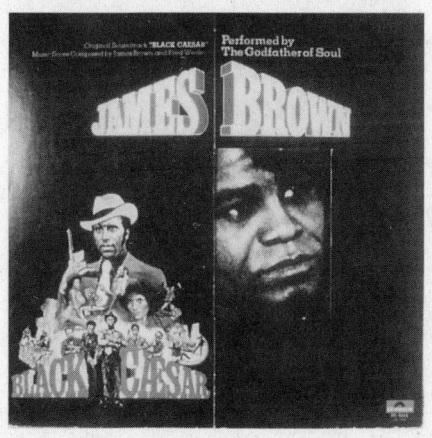

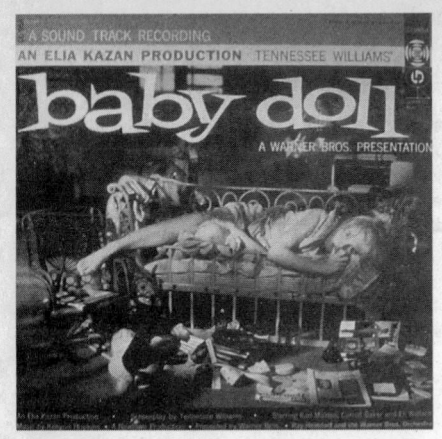

154

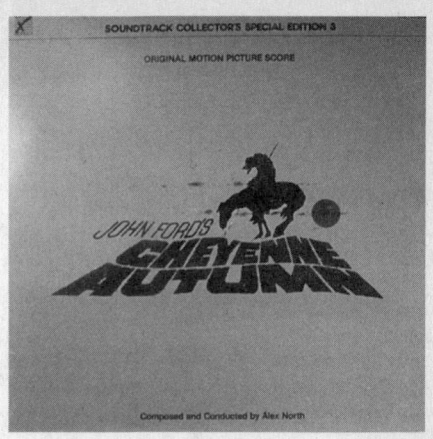

ORIGINAL SOUNDTRACK ALBUM

Cole Porter's
CAN-CAN

STARRING
FRANK SINATRA · SHIRLEY MacLAINE

MAURICE CHEVALIER

LOUIS JOURDAN

JACK CUMMINGS · WALTER LANG · SAUL CHAPLIN · DOROTHY KINGSLEY & CHARLES LEDERER

ORIGINAL CAST ALBUM

CALDWELL · NELSON

COLETTE

The Official Dramatized Recording of
CLOSE ENCOUNTERS
OF THE THIRD KIND

INCLUDED: 42 page magazine with color photos, and story about this astonishing film.

WE ARE NOT ALONE

Complete with Sound Effects and Music

COSO-5005 STEREO

CHARLES K. FELDMAN'S
CASINO ROYALE

COLGEMS

AN ORIGINAL SOUNDTRACK RECORDING

Music Composed and Conducted by
BURT BACHARACH

"Casino Royale Theme" played by
HERB ALPERT & the TIJUANA BRASS

"The Look of Love" sung by
DUSTY SPRINGFIELD

JAMES BOND 007 CASINO ROYALE

A COLUMBIA PICTURES RELEASE / PANAVISION* / TECHNICOLOR*

ORIGINAL MOTION PICTURE SOUNDTRACK

FIRST ISSUE COLLECTORS' EDITION! 10¢

CREEPSHOW
FIVE JOLTING TALES OF HORROR!

Music Composed and Performed by
JOHN HARRISON

STEREO ABCS-DC-5

The Original Motion Picture Soundtrack
CUSTER
OF THE WEST

Music Composed and Conducted by Bernardo Segall
With the Royal Philharmonic Orchestra

D-DAY

Radio Broadcast • Mark 56 (M) 728 15-20   78
Excerpts from the first 24 hours of radio broadcasts.

D-DAY PLUS 20

Radio Broadcast • Columbia Special Products (M) XTV 88815.............. 8-15   64
Two discs. Broadcasts of June 6, 1944. Made for Philco. Produced by CBS News.
Cast: Quentin Reynolds (narrator), Dwight D. Eisenhower, Winston Churchill, Adolf Hitler, others.

D.C. CAB

Soundtrack (1984) • MCA (S) MCA-5469.. 8-10   84
Promotional issue only.

Soundtrack (1984) • MCA (S) 6128.. 8-10   84
Cast: Irene Cara, Peabo Bryson, Shalamar, others.

D.O.A.

Soundtrack (1988) • Varese Sarabande (S) 704.610 25-35   88
Composer: Chaz Jankel.

DAD

Soundtrack • MCA (S) 6359... 8-10   89
Composer: James Horner.

DADDY LONG LEGS

Soundtrack (1955) • Capitol (EP) EAP-1-597....................................... 35-65   55
Composer: Johnny Mercer, Ray Anthony, George Williams. **Conductor:** Ray Anthony. **Cast:** Ray Anthony and His Orchestra, Skyliners.

DAKTARI

TV Soundtrack (1967) • MGM (M) CH 1043.. 20-25   67
TV Soundtrack (1967) • Leo the Lion (S) CH-1043 10-15   67
TV Soundtrack (1967) • Atlantic (M) 8157 15-20   68
TV Soundtrack (1967) • Atlantic (S) SD-8157 35-40   68
Composer: Shelly Manne. **Conductor:** Shelly Manne. **Cast:** Shelly Manne and His Men. (With dialogue.)

DALLAS

TV Soundtrack (1979) • First American (S) FA-780 8-10   79
Composer: John Parker. **Conductor:** John Parker.

Studiotrack (1980) • RCA Victor (S) AHL1-3613 8-10   80
Also has TV themes from: *Incredible Hulk, Taxi, All in the Family, The Waltons, Little House on the Prairie, The Restless, M*A*S*H, Laverne and Shirley* and *Knots Landing.*
Composer: Various. **Conductor:** Bill McElainey. **Cast:** Floyd Cramer.

Studiotrack (1985) • Warner Bros. (S) 1-25325.................................... 5-8   85
Full title: *Dallas - The Music Story.*
Cast: Howard Keel, Gary Morris, Johnny Lee, others.

DAMES: see GOLDEN AGE OF THE HOLLYWOOD MUSICAL

DAMES AT SEA

Original Cast (1969) • Columbia (S) OS-3330....................................... 8-12   69
Composer: Jim Wise, George Haimsohn, Robin Miller. **Conductor:** Richard J. Leonard. **Cast:** David Christmas, Steve Elmore, Tamara Long, Bernadette Peters, Sally Stark, Joseph R. Sicari.

Original London Cast (1969) • CBS (S) 70063 60-65   69
UK release.
Composer: Jim Wise, George Haimsohn, Robin Miller. **Conductor:** Ray Bishop. **Cast:** Joyce Blair, Blayne Barrington, Rita Burton, William Ellis, Sheila White, Kevin Scott.

DAMIEN – OMEN II
Soundtrack (1978) • 20th Century-Fox (S) T-563 12-15   78
Composer: Jerry Goldsmith. **Conductor:** Lionel Newman.

DAMN THE DEFIANT
Soundtrack (1962) • Colpix (M) CP-511 12-35   62
Soundtrack (1962) • Colpix (S) SCP-511 20-65   62
Composer: Clifton Parker. **Conductor:** Muir Mathieson.

DAMN YANKEES
Original Cast (1955) • RCA Victor (EP) EOC-1021 15-20   55
Original Cast (1955) • RCA Victor (M) LOC-1021 25-30   55
Green cover.
Original Cast (1955) • RCA Victor (M) LPC-1108 35-45   55
UK release. Green cover.
Original Cast (1955) • RCA Victor (M) LOC-1021 10-12   55
Orange cover.
Original Cast (1955) • RCA Victor (SE) LSO-1021(e).......................... 10-15   65
Composer: Richard Adler, Jerry Ross. **Conductor:** Hal Hastings. **Cast:** Gwen Verdon, Stephen Douglass, Ray Walston, Jean Stapleton, Rae Allen, Shannon Bolin, Russ Brown, Ronn Cummins, Cherry Davis, Nathaniel Frey, Jimmie Komack, Albert Linville, Eddie Phillips, Jackie Scholle, Robert Shafer.
Soundtrack (1958) • RCA Victor (M) LOC-1047 25-30   58
Soundtrack (1955) • RCA Victor (M) AYL1-3948................................ 8-10   Re
Composer: Richard Adler, Jerry Ross. **Conductor:** Ray Heindorf. **Cast:** Tab Hunter, Gwen Verdon, Ray Walston, Shannon Bolin, Russ Brown, Rae Allen, Nathaniel Frey, Jimmie Komack, Robert Shafer, Bob Fosse.

DAMNED
Soundtrack (1969) • Warner Bros. (S) WS-1829 20-25   69
Composer: Maurice Jarre. **Conductor:** Maurice Jarre.
Also see RAIN PEOPLE

DAMSEL IN DISTRESS
Soundtrack (1936) • Scarce Rarities (M) SR-5505............................ 12-15
One side contains music from *Follow the Fleet.*
Composer: George Gershwin, Ira Gershwin. **Cast:** Fred Astaire, Gracie Allen, George Burns. FOLLOW THE FLEET: **Composer:** Irving Berlin. **Cast:** Fred Astaire, Ginger Rogers, Harriet (Hilliard) Nelson.
Also see SKY'S THE LIMIT

DANCE A LITTLE CLOSER
Original Cast (1983) • IBR (S) 9011 100-125   87
Composer: Charles Strouse, Alan Jay Lerner. **Conductor:** Peter Howard. **Cast:** Len Cariou, Liz Robertson, George Rose, Don Chastain.

DANCE CRAZE
Soundtrack • Chrysalis (S) PV-41299 8-10
Cast: Specials, English Beat, Bad Manners, Selecter, Madness, Bodysnatchers.

DANCE TO THE MUSIC OF IRVING BERLIN
Studiotrack (1959) • Vocalion (M) VL-3664 10-20   59
Composer: Irving Berlin. **Cast:** Jimmy Smith.

DANCE WITH A STRANGER
Soundtrack (1985) • Varese Sarabande (S) STV 81251 8-10   85
Composer: Richard Hartley.

DANCERS OF BALI
Original Cast (1952) • Columbia (M) ML-4618 25-30   52
Original Cast (1952) • Columbia Special Products (M) AML-4618 8-10   Re
    Conductor: Anak Agung Gde Mandera. **Cast:** Gamelan Orchestra (from the village of Pliatan, Bali, Indonesia).

DANCES WITH WOLVES
Soundtrack (1990) • Epic (S) 467591 5-10   90
    Composer: John Barry. **Conductor:** John Barry.

DANCING YEARS
Original London Cast (1939) • RCA Victor (M) DLP-1028 100-150   50s
    UK release. 10-inch LP. Premiered in 1939 and played on and off in London throughout World War II. Recording made at the end of Drury Lane Theatre run, presumably in the early 1950s though no date of release is given on the cover or disc.
    Composer: Ivor Novello. **Conductor:** Charles Prentice. **Cast:** Ivor Novello, Mary Ellis, Olive Gilbert, Roma Beaumont, Dunstan Hart.

DANGER
TV Soundtrack (1951) • MGM (EP) X-1111 15-25   51
TV Soundtrack (1951) • MGM (M) E-111 75-100   51
10-inch LP.
    Composer: Tony Mottola. **Conductor:** Tony Mottola. **Cast:** Ray Charles Singers.

DANGEROUS CHRISTMAS OF RED RIDING HOOD
TV Soundtrack (1965) • ABC-Paramount (M) ABC-536 12-15   65
TV Soundtrack (1965) • ABC-Paramount (S) ABCS-536 15-25   65
    Composer: Jule Styne, Robert Merrill. **Conductor:** Walter Scharf. **Cast:** Liza Minnelli, Vic Damone, Cyril Ritchard, Animals.

DANGEROUS LIAISONS
Soundtrack (1988) • Virgin Movie Music (S) 791057-1 8-10   88
    Composer: George Fenton. **Conductor:** George Fenton. **Cast:** Glenn Close, Michelle Pfeiffer, John Malkovich.

DANGEROUS MINDS
Soundtrack • MCA (S) 11228 8-10   **95**

DANGEROUSLY CLOSE
Soundtrack (1986) • Enigma (S) SJ-73204 8-10   86
    Cast: Smithereens, Black Uhuru, Green on Red, T.S.O.L., Lords of the New Church, Lost Pilots, Michael McCarty.

DANNY ELFMAN: MUSIC FOR A DARKENED THEATRE
Soundtrack (1990) • MCA (S) 10065 8-10   90
    Composer: Danny Elfman. **Conductor:** Danny Elfman, Shirley Walker, John Coleman, Bill Ross, Steve Bartek. **Cast:** Sinfonia of London Orchestra, National Philharmonic Orchestra.

DANTON
Soundtrack (1983) • DRG (S) SL-9518 8-10   83
    Composer: Jean Prodromides. **Conductor:** Jan Prusak. **Cast:** Choral Music Society of Warsaw.

DARBY O'GILL AND THE LITTLE PEOPLE
Soundtrack (1959) • Disneyland (M) ST-1901 40-45   59
    Mostly dialogue, but does include the seldom-heard singing voice of Sean Connery.
    Composer: Lawrence Edward Watkin, Oliver Wallace. **Conductor:** Tutti Camarata. **Cast:** Sean Connery, Arthur Shields, J. Pat O'Malley, Janet Munro.

DARK CRYSTAL
Soundtrack (1982) • Warner Bros. (S) 1-23749 8-10   82
    Includes poster.
    Composer: Trevor Jones. **Conductor:** Marcus Dods. **Cast:** London Symphony Orchestra.

DARK EYES
Soundtrack (1987) • DRG (S) SBL-12592 8-10   87

DARK OF THE SUN
Soundtrack (1968) • MGM (M) E-4544 20-25   68
Soundtrack (1968) • MGM (S) SE-4544 30-35   68
    Composer: Jacques Loussier.

DARK SHADOWS
TV Soundtrack (1969) • Philips (S) PHS-600-314 20-25   69
Includes bonus poster.
    Composer: Robert Cobert, Charles Green. **Conductor:** Robert Cobert. **Cast:** Jonathan Frid
(narration), David Selby, Robert Cobert Orchestra.
TV Soundtrack [Vol. 2] (1966) • Media Sound (S) MS-00001 8-10   86
TV Soundtrack [Vol. 3] (1966) • Media Sound (S) MS-00002 8-10   87
    Full title: *Original Music from Dark Shadows.*
TV Soundtrack [Vol. 4] (1966-71) • Media Sound (S) MS-00003 8-10   88
TV Soundtrack • Ranwood (S) RLP-8055 12-15
    Full title: *Dark Shadows (Quentin's Theme).*

DARK STAR
Soundtrack (1974) • Citadel (S) CT-7022 25-30   80
    Composer: John Carpenter. **Cast:** John Carpenter, Miles Watkins, "Cookie" Knapp, Dan
O'Bannon, Cal Kuniholm, Brian Narelle, John Yager. (With dialogue and effects.)

DARKMAN
Soundtrack (1990) • MCA (S) MCA-10094 8-10   90
    Composer: Danny Elfman. **Conductor:** Shirley Walker. **Cast:** Liam Neeson, Frances
McDormand.

DARLING: see TRIPLE FEATURE

DARLING LILI
Soundtrack (1969) • RCA Victor (S) LSPX-1000 8-30   69
Gatefold cover.
    Composer: Henry Mancini, Johnny Mercer. **Conductor:** Henry Mancini. **Cast:** Julie Andrews,
Gloria Paul, Le Lycee Francais de Los Angeles Children's Choir.
Studiotrack (1970) • Camden (S) CAS-2421 6-8   70
    Full title: *Living Strings Play the Music from Darling Lili.*
    Conductor: Johnny Douglas. **Cast:** Living Strings.

DARLING OF THE DAY
Original Cast (1968) • RCA Victor (M) LOC-1149 30-35   68
Original Cast (1968) • RCA Victor (S) LSO-1149 45-55   68
    Composer: Jule Styne, E.Y. Harburg. **Conductor:** Buster Davis. **Cast:** Vincent Price, Patricia
Routledge, Brenda Forbes, Teddy Greene, Beth Howland, Mitchell Jason, Marc Jordan, Reid
Klein, Joy Nichols, Charles Welch, Peter Woodthorpe.

DARWIN'S THEORIES
Original Cast (1960) • Town Hall Records (M) THM-1002 100-125   60
    Composer: Darwin Venneri. **Cast:** Darwin Venneri.

DAS BOOT (THE BOAT)
Soundtrack (1981) • Atlantic (S) SD-19348 8-10   82
    Composer: Klaus Doldinger. **Conductor:** Klaus Doldinger.

DAVID AND LISA
Soundtrack (1963) • Ava (M) A-21 15-20   63
Soundtrack (1963) • Ava (S) AS-21 20-35   63
One side has *Jazz Impressions of David and Lisa.*
    Composer: Mark Lawrence. **Conductor:** Norman Paris.

DAVID COPPERFIELD
Original Cast (1978) • Argo (S) 707/708.. 12-20   78
   Two discs.
TV Soundtrack (1970) • GRT (S) GRT-10008.................................. 125-150   70
    Composer: Malcolm Arnold. **Conductor:** Malcolm Arnold.
Studiotrack • X (S) 10-1061 50-60

DAVID MERRICK PRESENTS HITS FROM HIS BROADWAY HITS
Studiotrack • RCA Victor (M) LPM 2947... 10-15
Studiotrack • RCA Victor (S) LSP 2947.. 10-20
    Has songs from *Fanny, Carnival, DoRe Mi, Gypsy, Irma la Douce, Take Me Along, Stop the World - I Want to Get Off, Oliver, Subways Are for Sleeping, Destry Rides Again, 110 in the Shade* and *Hello Dolly*.
    Composer: Various. **Conductor:** Henri Rene, Joe Lipiman. **Cast:** John Gary, Ann-Margret, Merrill Staton Voices.

DAVID RAKSIN CONDUCTS HIS GREAT FILM SCORES
Studiotrack (1976) • RCA Victor (Q) ARD1-1490 15-25   76
Studiotrack (1976) • RCA Victor (S) ARL1-1490 12-18   76
    Contains music from: *Laura, The Bad and the Beautiful* and *Forever Amber*.
    Composer: David Raksin. **Conductor:** David Raksin. **Cast:** New Philharmonia Orchestra.

DAVID RAKSIN / MUSIC FOR FILMS
Soundtrack [Vol. 1] (1978) • Library of Congress (S) 223781............... 10-20   78
    Contains music from *Force of Evil* and *Carrie*.
Soundtrack [Vol. 2] (1978) • Library of Congress (S) 223782............... 10-20   78
    Music from *Separate Tables* and *The Redeemer*.
    Both LPs were distributed only with the July 1978 issue of the *Quarterly Journal of the Library of Congress*.
    Composer: David Raksin. **Conductor:** David Raksin.

DAVID ROSE AMONG THE STARS
Studiotrack (1966) • Metro (M) M-585 8-12   66
    Has music from *Exodus, Gone With the Wind, The V.I.P.'s* and others.
    Conductor: David Rose. **Cast:** David Rose and His Orchestra.

DAVID ROSE AND HIS ORCHESTRA PLAY THE MUSIC Of GEORGE GERSHWIN
Studiotrack • MGM (M) E-85 8-12
    Songs from *An American in Paris, Oh Kay, Somebody Loves Me* and *Porgy and Bess*.
    Composer: George Gershwin. **Conductor:** David Rose. **Cast:** David Rose and His Orchestra.

DAVY CROCKETT
TV Soundtrack (1955) • Columbia (EP) B-2031 30-40   55
    Episode: *Davy Crockett, Indian Fighter*.
TV Soundtrack (1955) • Columbia C-516... 15-25   55
    Episode: *Davy Crockett, Indian Fighter*. Boxed set of two 78 rpms.
TV Soundtrack (1955) • Columbia (EP) B-2032 30-40   55
    Episode: *Davy Crockett Goes to Congress*.
TV Soundtrack (1955) • Columbia C-517... 15-25   55
    Episode: *Davy Crockett Goes to Congress*. Boxed set of two 78 rpms.
TV Soundtrack (1955) • Columbia (EP) B-2033 30-40   55
    Episode: *Davy Crockett at the Alamo*.
TV Soundtrack (1955) • Columbia C-518... 15-25   55
    Episode: *Davy Crockett at the Alamo*. Boxed set of two 78 rpms.
TV Soundtrack (1955) • Columbia (EP) B-2073 30-50   55
    Episode: *Davy Crockett and Mike Fink*.
TV Soundtrack (1955) • Columbia C-519... 15-25   55
    Episode: *Davy Crockett and Mike Fink*. Boxed set of two 78 rpms.
Soundtrack (1955) • Columbia (M) CL-666 50-75   55

Soundtrack (1955) • Disneyland (M) WDA-3602 35-45   58
Soundtrack (1955) • Disneyland (M) DQ-1315 15-25   68
   Composer: George Bruns. **Conductor:** George Bruns. **Cast:** Fess Parker, Buddy Ebsen. (With dialogue.)

DAVY CROCKETT (THE REAL STORY)
Studio Cast (1955) • Folkways (M) FP-205 15-25   55
   Cast: Bill Hayes. (With narration.)

DAWGS
Original L.A. Cast (1983) • Glendale (S) GL 6032.............................. 8-10   83
   Composer: Robert Band, Richard M. Sherman, John Henry. **Cast:** Eliana Carlough, Many Garripoli, John Michael Kelly, Marsha Kramer, Anthony Morgan.

DAWN OF THE DEAD
Soundtrack (1979) • Varese Sarabande (S) VC-81106 25-30   79
   Composer: Goblin. **Cast:** David Emge, Ken Foree, Goblin.

DAY AFTER HALLOWEEN
Soundtrack (1981) • Citadel (S) CT-7020.. 15-20   81
   Composer: Brian May. **Conductor:** Brian May.

DAY BEFORE SPRING: see LYRICS BY LERNER

DAY IN HOLLYWOOD / A NIGHT IN THE UKRAINE
Original Cast (1980) • DRG (S) SBL-12580 8-10   80
   Composer: Frank Lazarus, Jerry Herman. **Conductor:** Wally Harper. **Cast:** Frank Lazarus, Priscilla Lopez, Peggy Hewett, Kate Draper, David Garrison, Stephen James.

DAY OF ANGER
Soundtrack (1969) • RCA Victor (S) LSO-1165.................................... 15-20   69
   Composer: Riz Ortolani. **Conductor:** Riz Ortolani.

DAY OF THE DEAD
Soundtrack (1985) • Saturn (S) SR-LP-1701 8-10   85
   Composer: John Harrison. **Cast:** Modern Man, Sputzy Sparacino and Delilah, others.

DAY OF THE DOLPHIN
Soundtrack (1973) • Avco Embassy (S) AV-11014 18-20   73
   Composer: Georges Delerue. **Conductor:** Georges Delerue.

DAY OF THE LOCUST
Soundtrack (1975) • London (S) PS-912... 12-15   75
Cover has no clipped corners.
Soundtrack (1975) • London (S) PS-912... 8-10   75
Cover has one or more clipped corners.
   Composer: John Barry, others. **Conductor:** John Barry. **Cast:** Louis Armstrong, Pamela Myers, Michael Dees, Nick Lucas.

DAY THE EARTH STOOD STILL: see GREAT SCIENCE FICTION FILM MUSIC

DAY THE FISH CAME OUT
Soundtrack (1967) • 20th Century-Fox (M) 4194................................... 12-30   67
Soundtrack (1967) • 20th Century-Fox (S) S-4194.............................. 15-40   67
   Composer: Mikis Theodorakis.

DAY TIME ENDED
Soundtrack (1981) • Varese Sarabande (S) STV-81140 10-15   81
   Composer: Richard Band. **Conductor:** Richard Band.

DAYDREAMER
Soundtrack (1966) • Columbia (M) OL-6540 15-25   66
Soundtrack (1966) • Columbia (S) OS-2940 25-35   66
   Composer: Maury Laws, Jules Bass. **Conductor:** Maury Laws. **Cast:** Robert Goulet, Ray Bolger, Paul O'Keefe, Ed Wynn, Patty Duke, Hayley Mills.

DAYS OF HEAVEN
Soundtrack (1978) • Pacific Arts (S) PAC8-128 25-30   78
   Composer: Ennio Morricone, Camille Saint-Saens, Leo Kottke, Doug Kershaw. **Conductor:** Ennio Morricone.

DAYS OF THUNDER
Soundtrack (1990) • David Geffen Co. (S) DGC 24294 10-15   90
   Cast: Cher, Dhicago, David Coverdale, Guns N' Roses, Joan Jett & the Blackhearts, Elton John, Maria McKee, Terry Reid, Apollo Smile, Tina Turner, John Waite.

DAYS OF WILFRED OWEN
Soundtrack (1966) • Warner Bros. (M) B-1635 10-12   66
Soundtrack (1966) • Warner Bros. (S) BS-1635................................. 12-15   66
   Composer: Richard Lewine. **Conductor:** Richard Lewine. **Cast:** Richard Burton (recitation of poems from the film).

DE HAVEN IN HOLLYWOOD
Soundtrack • Vedette (M) 8703.. 12-15
   Gloria De Haven with songs from *Three Little Words, Summer Stock* and others.
   Composer: Various. **Conductor:** Various. **Cast:** Gloria DeHaven.

DE SADE
Soundtrack (1969) • Tower (S) ST-5170... 25-30   69
   Composer: Billy Strange. **Conductor:** Billy Strange.

DEAD
Soundtrack (1987) • Varese (S) STV 81341 8-10   87
   Also has music from *Journey into Fear* (1975.)
   Composer: Alex North. **Conductor:** Alex North. **Cast:** Angelica Huston, Donald McCann, others.

DEAD HEAT
Soundtrack (1988) • Varese Sarabande (S) 704 570 8-12   88
   Composer: Ernest Troost.

DEAD RINGER
Soundtrack (1964) • Warner Bros. (M) W-1536 12-30   64
Soundtrack (1964) • Warner Bros. (S) WS-1536 20-40   64
   Composer: Andre Previn. **Conductor:** Andre Previn.

DEADFALL
Soundtrack (1968) • 20th Century-Fox (S) S-4203.............................. 40-50   68
   Composer: John Barry. **Conductor:** John Barry. **Cast:** Shirley Bassey, Renata Tarrago.

DEADLY AFFAIR
Soundtrack (1967) • Verve (M) V-8679 20-25   67
Soundtrack (1967) • Verve (S) V6-8679... 25-30   67
   Composer: Quincy Jones. **Conductor:** Quincy Jones. **Cast:** Astrud Gilberto.

DEADLY FRIEND
Soundtrack (1986) • Varese Sarabande (S) STV-81291 8-12   86
   Composer: Charles Bernstein.

DEADLY SPAWN
Soundtrack (1985) • Deadly (S) DS 6041.. 5-10   85
   Composer: Michael Perilstein.

DEAN, JAMES, STORY: see JAMES DEAN STORY

DEAN MARTIN SINGS: see STOOGE

DEAN MARTIN TESTIMONIAL DINNER
Assembled Cast (1959) • Dean Martin Testimonial (M) No Number
  Used... 100-150   59
    Three discs in triple-pocket cover. Sold for $25 at the door as a souvenir of the Friars Club roast of Dean Martin.
    Cast: Frank Sinatra, Sammy Davis Jr., George Jessel, Jimmy Durante, Joey Bishop, Tony Martin, Dinah Shore, Danny Thomas, Bob Hope, Barry Mirkin, George Burns, Mort Sahl, Judy Garland, Sammy Cahn, Al Hart, Eugene Debs, Glenn Wallichs, Dean Martin.

DEAN MARTIN TV SHOW
Studiotrack (1966) • Reprise (M) R-6223 10-20   66
Studiotrack (1966) • Reprise (S) RS-6233 15-20   66
    Composer: Various. **Conductor:** Les Brown. **Cast:** Dean Martin, Ken Lane (piano).

DEAR HEART (AND OTHER THEMES)
Studiotrack (1965) • RCA Victor (S) LSP-2990 10-20   65
    Also has original theme from *Soldier in the Rain* and others.
    Composer: Henry Mancini. **Conductor:** Henry Mancini. **Cast:** Henry Mancini and His Orchestra.

DEAR JOHN
Soundtrack (1966) • Dunhill (M) OCD-55001 15-20   66
Soundtrack (1966) • Dunhill (S) OCDS-5500 20-25   66
    Composer: Bengt Arne Wallin. **Conductor:** Bengt Arne Wallin.

DEAR WORLD
Original Cast (1969) • Columbia (S) BOS-3260 8-12   69
Original Cast (1969) • Columbia Special Products (S) ABOS-3260.......... 5-8   Re
    Composer: Jerry Herman. **Conductor:** Donald Pippin. **Cast:** Angela Lansbury, Jane Connell, Carmen Mathews, Milo O'Shea, Pamela Hall, Kurt Peterson.

DEAREST ENEMY
Studio Cast (1981) • Beginners Prod. (S) BRP 1 12-15   81
    Composer: Richard Rodgers. **Cast:** John Dietrich, Michelle Summers, Charles West.

DEATH BEFORE DISHONOR
Soundtrack (1986) • Varese Sarabande (S) STV 81310 10-12   86
    Composer: Brian May. **Conductor:** Brian May.

DEATH IN VENICE
Soundtrack (1971) • RCA Victor (S) LSC-3224 8-12   71
    Full title: *Death In Venice (And Other Great Motion Picture Themes)*.
    Composer: Gustav Mahler. **Conductor:** Eric Leinsdorf, Van Cliburn, Eugene Ormandy. **Cast:** Boston Symphony Orchestra.

DEATH OF A SALESMAN
Original Cast (1951) • Decca DAU-774 15-25   51
    Album of eight 78 rpms.
Original Cast (1951) • Decca (M) DL-9006.. 15-20   51
Original Cast (1951) • Decca (M) DL-9007.. 15-20   51
Original Cast (1951) • Decca (M) DX-102 20-25   51
    Boxed, two-disc set. Has members of the original New York production with Thomas Mitchell playing Lee J. Cobb's role.
Original Cast (1951) • MCA (M) 204182... 10-12   84
    Boxed, two-disc set. Reissue.
    Composer: Alex North. **Conductor:** Alex North. **Cast:** Thomas Mitchell, Arthur Kennedy, Mildred Dunnock, Cameron Mitchell, Arthur Miller (narrator.)
Original Cast (M) TRS-310 10-20
    Boxed, three-disc set, with script. Has Lee J. Cobb and Mildred Dunnock, from the original cast, plus a supporting studio cast.
    Composer: Alex North. **Conductor:** Alex North. **Cast:** Lee J. Cobb, Mildred Dunnock, Michael Tolan, Dustin Hoffman.

Studiotrack (1951) • Elmer Bernstein Film Music
Collection (S) FMC-9 20-25   77
Score of the 1951 film version, plus music from *Viva Zapata.*
Composer: Alex North. **Conductor:** Elmer Bernstein. **Cast:** Royal Philharmonic Orchestra.

DEATH OF A SCOUNDREL
Soundtrack (1956) • RCA Victor (EP) EPA-919 150-175   56
Soundtrack (1956) • Entr'acte (M) ERM-6004 10-25   80
One side has music from four other Max Steiner scores: *The Charge of the Light Brigade,*
Four Wives, The Searchers and *A Stolen Life.* This side was first issued as side two of the
RCA LP *Music from Gone with the Wind and Selections from Other Motion Pictures.*
Composer: Max Steiner. **Conductor:** Max Steiner.
Also see GONE WITH THE WIND

DEATH ON THE NILE
Soundtrack (1978) • Capitol (S) SW-11866... 12-15   78
Soundtrack (1978) • EMI (S) EMC-3256 20-25   78
UK release. Has British artwork on textured cover.
Composer: Nino Rota, H. Warren and B. Green, Jacob Gade, N. Brown and A. Freed.
Conductor: Nino Rota.

DEATH RACE 2000
Soundtrack (1975) • Citadel (S) CTV-7024 5-10   75

DEATH WISH
Soundtrack (1974) • Columbia (S) PC-33199...................................... 12-15   74
White label. Promotional issue only.
Soundtrack (1974) • Columbia (S) PC-33199...................................... 12-15   74
Composer: Herbie Hancock, Jerry Peters. **Conductor:** Herbie Hancock, Jerry Peters. **Cast:**
Herbie Hancock.

DEATH WISH II
Soundtrack (1982) • Swan Song (S) SS 8511................................... 8-10   82
Composer: Jimmy Page, Gordon Edwards.

DECADE OF BROADWAY AND CINEMA
Studiotrack (1961) • Decca (S) DL-734094 15-20   61
Cast: Lawrence Welk, Wayne King, Four Aces, Peter Duchin, Carol Burnett, Liberace, Teresa
Brewer.

DECEIVERS
Soundtrack (1988) • RCA Victor (S) 7722-1 8-10   88
Composer: John Scott.

DECLINE AND FALL OF THE ENTIRE WORLD AS SEEN THROUGH THE EYES OF COLE PORTER
Original Cast (1965) • Columbia (M) OL-6410.................................... 8-10   65
Original Cast (1965) • Columbia (S) OS-2810.................................... 10-12   65
Original Cast (1965) • Columbia Special Products (S) COS-2810.......... 8-10   Re
Original Cast (1965) • Columbia Special Products (S) AOS-2810............ 5-8   Re
Composer: Cole Porter. **Conductor:** Skip Redwine. **Cast:** Kaye Ballard, Harold Lang, Carmen
Alvarez.
Studio Cast (1965) • Ric (S) ST-3002 15-20   65
This release inspired the off-Broadway revue. Columbia issued the rest of the show.
Studio Cast (1965) • Painted Smiles (S) PS-1340.................................. 8-10   Re
Composer: Cole Porter. **Conductor:** Norman Paris. **Cast:** Kaye Ballard, David Allen, Ronny
Graham.

DECLINE OF WESTERN CIVILIZATION
Soundtrack (1981) • Slash (S) 1-23934.. 8-10   81
    Cast: Black Flag, X, Circle Jerks, Fear, Catholic Discipline.
Soundtrack (1988) • Capitol (S) C1-90205..................................... 5-8   88
    Full title: *Decline Of Western Civilization Part II, The Metal Years.*
    Cast: Alice Cooper, others.

DEEP
Soundtrack (1977) • Casablanca (S) NBLP 7060................................ 12-15   77
    Colored vinyl. Promotional issue only.
Soundtrack (1977) • Casablanca (S) CAL-2018................................... 10-12   77
    Composer: John Barry. Conductor: John Barry, Frankie McIntosh. Cast: Donna Summer.

DEEP IN MY HEART
Soundtrack (1954) • MGM (EP) X-276 15-20   54
    Three discs.
Soundtrack (1954) • MGM (M) E-3153................................... 30-60   54
    Boxed, three-disc edition.
Soundtrack (1954) • MGM (M) E-3153................................... 20-40   55
    Standard LP.
    Composer: Sigmund Romberg. Conductor: Adolph Deutsch. Cast: Jose Ferrer, Rosemary
    Clooney, Helen Traubel, Gene Kelly, Fred Kelly, Jane Powell, Vic Damone, Ann Miller, Howard
    Keel, Tony Martin, William Olvis.
    Also see THOSE GLORIOUS MGM MUSICALS

DEEP THROAT
Soundtrack (1973) • DT Productions (S) No Number Used................ 50-75   73
    Souvenir promotional issue given away to select theatre-goers. White cover reads: "Now
    for the First Time, the One and Only Deep Throat."
Soundtrack (1971) • Sandy Hook (M) SH 2036..................................... 8-10   80

DEEP THROAT PART II
Soundtrack (1974) • Bryan (S) BRS-101 75-100   74
    Composer: Michael Colicchio, others. Cast: T.J. Stone, Laura Greene.

DEER HUNTER
Soundtrack (1979) • Capitol (S) SOO-11940 8-10   79
    Composer: Stanley Myers, Irving Berlin.

DELICATE BALANCE
Soundtrack (1973) Caedmon (S) TRS-360 15-18   73
    Boxed, three-disc set. Includes the entire film version of the Edward Albee play.
    Cast: Katharine Hepburn, Paul Scofield, Lee Remick, Kate Reid, Joseph Cotten, Betsy Blair.

DELIVERANCE
Soundtrack (1972) • Warner Bros. (S) BS-2683................................... 8-10   73
    Actual title: *Dueling Banjos from Deliverance.*
    Cast: Eric Weissberg, Steve Mandel.

DELTA FORCE
Soundtrack (1986) • Enigma (S) SJ 73201 8-10   86
    Composer: Alan Silverstri. Conductor: Alan Silverstri.

DEMI DOZEN
Original Cast (1957) • Offbeat (M) O-4015............................ 12-15   57
    Cast: Jean Arnold, Ceil Cabot, Jane Connell, Jack Fletcher, Stan Keen, Gordon Connell,
    George Hall, Jerry Matthews.

DEMON BARBER OF FLEET STREET: see SWEENEY TODD

DENNIS THE MENACE
TV Soundtrack (1960) • Colpix (M) CP-204..................... 100-200   60
    Cast: Jay North, Gloria Henry, Herbert Anderson, Joseph Kearns. (With dialogue.)

DEPUTY DAWG
TV Soundtrack (1960) • Camden (M) CAL-1048 15-20   60
Cast: Dayton Allen.

DERNIER AMANT ROMANTIQUE, LE: see LE DERNIER AMANT ROMANTIQUE

DES JASAGER
Studio Cast (1955) • MGM (M) E-3270.. 10-20   55
Composer: Kurt Weill.

DESERT SONG
Original London Cast • Monmouth Evergreen (SE) MES-7054 8-12
One side has music from *The Student Prince.*
Composer: Oscar Hammerstein II, Sigmund Romberg, Otto Harbach. Conductor: Herman
Finck. Cast: Sidney Pointer, Edith Day, Harry Welchman, Dennis Hoey.

Studio Cast (1945) • Decca DA-370... 10-12   45
Album of five 78 rpms.
Cast: Kitty Carlisle, Wilbur Evans, Felix Knight, Isaac Van Grove, Jeffrey Alexander.

Studio Cast (1950) • Decca (EP) 9-59... 8-12   50
Boxed, five-disc set.

Studio Cast (1950) • Decca (M) DL-7000.. 12-15   50
10-inch LP.
Conductor: Isaac Van Grove. Cast: Kitty Carlisle, Wilbur Evans, Felix Knight, Jeff Alexander
Chorus.

Studio Cast (1953) • Columbia (EP) A-1060 10-20   53
Studio Cast (1953) • Columbia (M) ML-4636.. 18-20   53
Studio Cast (1953) • Columbia (EP) A-1717 10-15   56
Studio Cast (1953) • Columbia (M) CL-831 12-15   56
Studio Cast (1953) • Columbia Special Products (M) ACL-831 8-10   Re
Conductor: Lehman Engel. Cast: Nelson Eddy, Doretta Morrow, Lee Cass, David Atkinson,
Wilton Clary.

Studio Cast (1955) • RCA Victor (EP) EKB-1013 10-12   55
Two discs.

Studio Cast (1955) • RCA Victor (M) LK-1013....................................... 10-12   55
Conductor: Al Goodman. Cast: Earl Wrightson, Francis Greer, Jimmy Carroll.

Studio Cast (1959) • RCA Victor (M) LOP-1000.................................... 10-12   59
Studio Cast (1959) • RCA Victor (S) LSO-1000 10-12   59
Conductor: Lehman Engel. Cast: Giorgio Tozzi, Kathy Barr, Peter Palmer, Warren Galjour,
Eugene Morgan.

Studio Cast (1960) • RCA Victor (M) LM-2440 10-12   60
Studio Cast (1960) • RCA Victor (S) LSC-2440...................................... 12-15   60
Conductor: Constantine Callinicos. Cast: Mario Lanza, Judith Raskin, Raymond Murcell,
Donald Arthur.

Studio Cast (1963) • Capitol (M) W-1842.. 10-12   63
Studio Cast (1963) • Capitol (S) SW-1842 12-15   63
Studio Cast (1963) • Angel (S) S-37319... 8-10   73
Conductor: Van Alexander. Cast: Gordon MacRae, Lucille Norman, Dorothy Kirsten, Gerald
Shirkey, Lloyd Bunnell, Roger Wagner Chorale.

London Studio Cast (1962) • Angel (S) S-35905 15-18   62
Conductor: Michael Collins. Cast: June Bronhill, Edmund Hockridge, Julie Dawn, Leonard
Weir, Bruce Forsyth.

Studiotrack (1953) • Capitol (EP) EBF-351 15-20   53
Studiotrack (1953) • Capitol (M) L-351 18-20   53
10-inch LP.

Studiotrack (1953) • Capitol (M) T-384... 12-15   56
One side has music from *Roberta.* Capitol issues feature Gordon MacRae, star of the 1953
film version.
Conductor: George Greeley. Cast: Gordon MacRae, Lucille Norman, Thurl Ravenscroft, Robert
Sands.

Studiotrack (1953) • RCA Victor (EP) EPB-3105.................................. 15-20   53
  Two discs.
Studiotrack (1953) • RCA Victor (M) LPM-3105 30-35   53
  10-inch LP. Above two feature Kathryn Grayson, of the 1953 film version.
    Conductor: Arthur Fiedler. **Cast:** Kathryn Grayson, Tony Martin.
Studiotrack (1957) • Halo (M) 50207 8-15   57
  Also see RIO RITA

DESIGNING WOMAN
Soundtrack (1957) • Blue Pear (M) BP-1014....................................... 15-20
  Actual title: *Miss Dolores Gray*. Has previously unreleased vocals from stage and screen,
  including *There'll Be Some Changes Made*.
    Composer: Billy Higgins, W. Benton Overstreet. **Cast:** Dolores Gray.

DESIRE UNDER THE ELMS
Soundtrack (1958) • Dot (M) DLP-3095 65-85   58
Soundtrack (1958) • MCA (M) VIM-7254.. 20-30   79
  Japanese release.
    Composer: Elmer Bernstein. **Conductor:** Elmer Bernstein.

DESPERATELY SEEKING SUSAN
Soundtrack (1985) • Varese Sarabande (S) STV-81320 8-10   85
  Full title: *Desperately Seeking Susan/Making Mr. Right*. Also has music from *Making Mr.
  Right*.
    Composer: Thomas Newman, Jenkel.

DESPERATE TEENAGE LOVEDOLLS
Soundtrack • SST (S) SST-072... 8-10

DESTINATION MOON
Soundtrack (1950) • Columbia (M) CL-6151 100-120   50
  10-inch LP.
    Composer: Leith Stevens. **Conductor:** Leith Stevens.
Studiotrack (1950) • Omega (M) OL-3 20-45   58
Studiotrack (1950) • Omega (SE) OSL-3 25-70   59
  Two cover variations exist. One reads "Omega Stereophonic Disk OSL-3" in upper right
  front with gold-leaf trim cover art. Other has "Omega Disk OSL-3 Stereo" spine print,
  without gold-leaf trim.
    Composer: Leith Stevens. **Conductor:** Henry Sandauer. **Cast:** Omega Orchestra.
Studiotrack (1950) • Varese Sarabande (SE) STV-81130.................... 12-15   80
    Conductor: Henry Sandauer.
Studiotrack • Cinema (SE) LP-8005 50-60   Re
    Conductor: Leith Stevens.

DESTRY RIDES AGAIN
Original London Cast • That's Entertainment (S) TER-1034 8-12   80s
Original Cast (1959) • Decca (M) DL-9075.. 12-15   59
Original Cast (1959) • Decca (S) DL-79075 18-25   59
    Composer: Harold Rome. **Conductor:** Lehman Engel. **Cast:** Andy Griffith, Dolores Gray, Scott
    Brady, Don Crabtree, Rosetta LeNoire, Jack Prince, Elizabeth Watts.
Studio Cast (1959) • Camden (M) CAL-540 8-10   59
Studio Cast (1959) • Camden (S) CAS-540 10-12   59
    Composer: Harold Rome. **Conductor:** Lehman Engel. **Cast:** Louise O'Brien, Jack Haskell.
Studio Cast (1959) • United Artists (M) UAL-4045............................... 10-15   59
Studio Cast (1959) • United Artists (S) UAS-5045............................... 15-20   59
    Cast: Randy Weston Trio, Four Trombones.

DE SYLVA, BROWN & HENDERSON REVISITED
Studio Cast (1967) • Painted Smiles (M) PS-1351 8-10   Re

DEVIL AND DANIEL WEBSTER
Studio Cast (1939) • Desto (SE) 6450.. 20-25
 Composer: Douglas Moore, Stephen Vincent Benet. Conductor: Armando Aliberti. Cast:
 Lawrence Winters, Joe Blankenship, Doris Young.
Studiotrack (1941) • Unicorn (M) UNS-237 20-25
 Composer: Bernard Herrmann. Conductor: Bernard Herrmann. Cast: Bernard Herrmann and
 His Orchestra.
 This film is also known as *All That Money Can Buy*.
 Also see GREAT FILM CLASSICS

DEVIL AT 4 O'CLOCK
Soundtrack (1962) • Colpix (M) CP-509 20-35   62
Soundtrack (1962) • Colpix (S) SCP-509 45-65   62
Soundtrack (1962) • Varese Sarabande (S) VC-81136 8-15   80
 Composer: George Duning. Conductor: George Duning.

DEVIL IN MISS JONES
Soundtrack (1973) • Janus (S) JLS-3059.. 10-25   73
 Composer: Roy Straigis, Peter De Angelis, Alden Shuman. Conductor: Roy Straigis, Peter De
 Angelis, Alden Shuman.

DEVIL'S ANGELS
Soundtrack (1967) • Tower (M) T-5074... 20-25   67
Soundtrack (1967) • Tower (S) DT-5074... 25-35   67
 Composer: Mike Curb. Conductor: Mike Curb. Cast: Davie Allan and the Arrows.

DEVIL'S BRIGADE
Soundtrack (1968) • United Artists (M) UAL-3654................................ 12-15   68
Soundtrack (1968) • United Artists (S) UAS-6654 15-20   68
 Composer: Alex North. Conductor: Leroy Holmes.

DEVIL'S EIGHT
Soundtrack (1969) • Tower (S) DT-5160... 15-20   69
 Composer: Mike Curb, Jerry Styner.

DEVIL'S SISTER
Radio Cast • Photon Disco (M) JOAC-X-20 8-10
 Cast: Joan Crawford.

DIAMOND HEAD
Soundtrack (1963) • Colpix (M) CP-440 20-25   63
Soundtrack (1963) • Colpix (S) SCP-440 30-60   63
 Composer: John Williams. Conductor: John Williams.
Studiotrack (1963) • Colpix (M) CP-439 10-12   63
Studiotrack (1963) • Colpix (S) SCP-439 12-15   63
 Full title: *Music Inspired by the Motion Picture Diamond Head.*
 Cast: Diamond Head Beachcombers.

DIAMOND STUDS
Original and Studio Cast (1975) • Pasquotank (S) PS-33 7-003 15-20   75
 7-inch disc.
 Composer: Jim Wann, Bland Simpson. Cast: Jim Wann, Bland Simpson, Cass Morgan.

DIAMONDS ARE FOREVER
Soundtrack (1971) • United Artists (S) UAS-5220 12-18   71
Soundtrack (1971) • United Artists (S) UA-LA301-G 8-10   74
Soundtrack (1971) • Liberty (S) LT-50301... 5-8   Re
 Composer: John Barry, Don Black. Conductor: John Barry. Cast: Shirley Bassey.

DIANA!
TV Soundtrack (1971) • Motown (S) 719.. 10-12   71
 Cast: Diana Ross.

DIARY OF ANNE FRANK
Soundtrack (1959) • 20th Century-Fox (M) FOX-3012 20-40   59
Soundtrack (1959) • 20th Century-Fox (S) SFX-3012 50-75   59
   Composer: Alfred Newman. **Conductor:** Alfred Newman.

DICK POWELL IN HOLLYWOOD
Studiotrack (1969) • Columbia (M) C2L44.................................... 15-20   69
   Two discs. Songs from Dick Powell's films.
   Composer: Various. **Conductor:** Various. **Cast:** Dick Powell.

DICK POWELL PRESENTS (THEMES FROM THE ORIGINAL SOUNDTRACK OF FOUR STAR TELEVISION PRODUCTIONS)
TV Soundtrack (1962) • Dot (M) DLP-3421 20-25   62
TV Soundtrack (1962) • Dot (S) DLP-25421 35-45   62
   Music from *Target: The Corrupters, Gertrude Berg Show, Rifleman, Robert Taylor's
   Detectives, Dick Powell Show, Law and Mr. Jones, Black Saddle, Wanted: Dead or Alive,
   Law of the Plainsman, June Allyson Show, Michael Shayne, Tom Ewell Show* and *Zane
   Grey Theater.*
   Composer: Herschel Burke Gilbert, Jerry Goldsmith, Leonard Rosenman, Leith Stevens, Jerry
   Fielding, others. **Conductor:** Herschel Burke Gilbert.

DICK TRACY IN BB
Original Radio Cast (1945) • Scarce Rarities (M) 5504 5-10
   From a February 15, 1945 broadcast.
   Cast: Judy Garland, Bing Crosby, Bob Hope, Frank Sinatra, Jimmy Durante, Dinah Shore,
   Andrews Sisters, Cass Daley.

DICKENS' CHRISTMAS CAROL: see CHRISTMAS CAROL

DIE FLEDERMAUS
Original Cast (1951) • Columbia (S) SL-108... 20-30   51
   Two discs, with booklet. Metropolitan Opera Version.
   Composer: Johann Strauss. **Cast:** Lily Pons, Ljuba Welitch, Richard Tucker, Charles Kullman,
   Martha Lipton, John Brownlee.

DIFFERENT TIMES
Original Cast (1972) • Painted Smiles (S) PS 1332................................. 8-10   87
   Composer: Michael Brown. **Conductor:** Rene Wiegert. **Cast:** James Ross, Barbara Williams,
   Ronald Young, Patti Karr, Many Bracken Phillips, Dorothy Frank, Sam Stonebauer, Mary Jo
   Catlett, Joe Masiell.

DIGITAL HOLLYWOOD – MEMORABLE FILM SCORES
Studiotrack (1988) • MCA (S) 25192... 15-25   88
   Audiophile pressing.
   Cast: Stanley Black and the London Symphony Orchestra.

DIGITAL PREMIERE RECORDINGS FROM THE FILMS OF ALFRED HITCHCOCK
Studiotrack • Varese Sarabande (S) 704-250 8-12   85
   Music from *Family Plot, Strangers on a Train, Suspicion* and *Notorious.*
   Composer: John Williams, Dimitri Tiomikin, Roy Webb, Franz Waxman. **Conductor:** Charles
   Ketchum. **Cast:** Utah Symphony Orchestra.

DIGITAL PREMIERE RECORDINGS FROM THE FILMS OF JOHN WAYNE
Studiotrack [Vol. 1] • Varese Sarabande (S) 704-280 10-20   85
   Volume one. Music from *True Grit* and *Comancheros.*
Studiotrack [Vol. 2] • Varese Sarabande (S) 704-350 10-20   86
   Volume two. Music from *The Shootist, Big Jake* and *Cahill – U.S. Marshall.*
   Composer: Elmer Bernstein. **Conductor:** Elmer Bernstein. **Cast:** Utah Symphony Orchestra.

DIGITAL SPACE
Studiotrack (1979) • Varese Sarabande (S) 100020 15-25   79
Music from *Star Wars* and *The Big Country*.
Composer: John Williams, Jerome Moross, Ralph Vaughan Williams, Sir William Walton. **Cast:** Morton Gould, London Symphony Orchestra.

DIGITAL TRIP DOWN BROADWAY
Studiotrack • MCA (S) 6220 8-10   87
Symphonic recollections.
Conductor: Paul Gemignani. **Cast:** Royal Philharmonic Orchestra.

DILLINGER
Soundtrack (1973) • MCA (S) 360 12-15   73
Composer: Barry DeVorzon, Gus Levene.

DIME A DOZEN
Original Cast (1962) • Cadence (M) CLP-3063 15-18   62
Original Cast (1962) • Cadence (S) CLP-25063 18-20   62
Both have two discs.
Cast: Gerry Matthew, Jack Fletcher, Mary Louise Wilson (pianos), Susan Browning, Fredricka Weber, Rex Robbins.

DINAH SHORE TV SHOW
TV Soundtrack (1954) • RCA Victor (EP) EPB 3214 30-35   54
Two discs.
TV Soundtrack (1954) • RCA Victor (M) LPM 3214 45-55
10-inch LP.
Cast: Dinah Shore.

DINER
Soundtrack (1982) • Elektra (S) E1-60107 10-15   82
Two discs.
Cast: Elvis Presley, Jerry Lee Lewis, Dion and the Belmonts, Heartbeats, Eddie Cochran, Carl Perkins, Fleetwoods, Lowell Fulson, Clarence Henry, Del Vikings, Bobby Darin, Jane Morgan, Dick Haymes, Tommy Edwards, Fats Domino, Jimmy Reed, Jane Morgan, Jack Scott.

DINGAKA
Soundtrack (1965) • Mercury (M) MG-21013 12-15   65
Soundtrack (1965) • Mercury (S) SR-61013 15-18   65
Composer: Eddie Domingo, Bertha Egnos.

DINO
Soundtrack (1957) • Epic (EP) EG-7187 20-35   57
Issued with paper picture sleeve. Has vocal of *Dino*, written by Pockriss and Vance, but is from neither the soundtrack nor the album (LN-3404). Promotional issue only.
Composer: Gerald Fried, Paul Vance, Lee Pockriss. **Conductor:** Gerald Fried, Mark Ellis. **Cast:** Sal Mineo.
Soundtrack (1957) • Epic (M) LN-3404 25-75   57
Composer: Gerald Fried, Paul Vance, Lee Pockriss. **Conductor:** Gerald Fried, Mark Ellis.

DINO DE LAURENTIIS PRESENTS ORIGINAL SOUNDTRACKS
Soundtrack (1974) • Project 3 (S) PR 5085-SD 25-35   74
Music from *The Valachi Papers, Crazy Joe* and *The Stone Killers*.
Composer: Riz Ortolani, Giancario Chiaramello, Roy Budd.

DINOSAURUS!
Studiotrack (1966) • Leo the Lion (S) CH-1016 8-10   66
From *The Lost World* by Arthur Conan Doyle.
Cast: Basil Rathbone.

DIRTY DANCING
Soundtrack [Vol. 1] (1987) • RCA Victor (S) 6408-1 8-10   87
Soundtrack [Vol. 1] (1987) • RCA Victor (S) R-8209 5-8   Re

Soundtrack [Vol. 2] (1987) • RCA Victor (S) 695-1 8-10   88
Soundtrack [Vol. 2] (1987) • RCA Victor (S) ST-46 5-8   Re
    Actual title: *More Dirty Dancing*. Music from the film not included on the first volume.
    Cast: Ronettes, Patrick Swayze, Maurice Williams and the Zodiacs, Merry Clayton, Blow
    Monkeys, Bruce Channel, Zappacosta, Mickey and Sylvia, Tom Johnson, Five Satins, Bill
    Medley, Jennifer Warnes.

DIRTY DINGUS MAGEE
Soundtrack (1970) • MGM (S) 1SE-24 10-12   70
Soundtrack (1970) • MCA (S) 25095 8-10   86
    Composer: Jeff Alexander. **Conductor:** Jeff Alexander. **Cast:** Mike Curb Congregation, Jeff
    Alexander.

DIRTY DOZEN
Soundtrack (1967) • MGM (M) E-4445 8-12   67
Soundtrack (1967) • MGM (S) SE-4445 10-12   67
Soundtrack (1967) • MCA (S) 39064 5-8   86
    Composer: Frank DeVol. **Conductor:** Frank DeVol. **Cast:** Trini Lopez, Sibylle Siegfried.

DIRTY FEET
Soundtrack (1965) • Fink (M) 1007 45-50   65
    Composer: M. Bartoo.

DIRTY GAME
Soundtrack (1966) • Laurie (M) 2034 15-20   66
Soundtrack (1966) • Laurie (S) SLP-2034 20-25   66
    Composer: Robert Mellin, Piero Reverberi.

DISINHAIRITED: see HAIR

DISORDERLIES
Soundtrack (1987) • Tin Pan Apple (S) 833274-1 8-10   87
    Cast: Fat Boys, Bananarama, Latin Rascals, Cashflow, Anita, Bon Jovi, Art of Noise, Tom
    Kimmel, Gwen Guthrie, Laura Hunter.

DIVA
Soundtrack (1982) • DRG (S) SL-9503 8-10   82
    Composer: Vladimir Cosma. **Conductor:** Vladimir Cosma. **Cast:** Wilhelmina Wiggins
    Fernandez.

DIVINE HAIR MASS IN F: see HAIR

DIVINE MADNESS
Soundtrack (1979) • Atlantic (S) SD-16022 8-10   79
    Conductor: Tony Berg, Randy Kerber. **Cast:** Bette Midler.

DIVINE NYMPH
Soundtrack (1980) • Cerberus (S) CEMS-0104 8-10   80
    Composer: Cesare Andrea Bixio. **Conductor:** Cesare Andrea Bixio.

DIVORCE AMERICAN STYLE
Soundtrack (1967) • United Artists (M) UAL-4163 12-15   67
Soundtrack (1967) • United Artists (S) UAS-5163 15-20   67
    Composer: Dave Grusin. **Conductor:** Dave Grusin.

DIVORCE ITALIAN STYLE
Soundtrack (1962) • United Artists (M) UAL-4106 25-30   62
Soundtrack (1962) • United Artists (S) UAS-5106 35-45   62
Studiotrack (1962) • Ascot (M) UM-13505 8-10   64
Studiotrack (1962) • Ascot (S) US-16505 10-12   64
    Composer: Carlo Rustichelli. **Conductor:** Peri Luigi Urbini.
    Also has selections from *Phaedra, West Side Story* and *Two for the Seesaw*.
    Composer: Carlo Rustichelli. **Conductor:** Peri Luigi Urbini.

DIVORCE ME, DARLING!

Original London Cast (1965) • Stet (S) DS-15009 10-15   81

Original London Cast (1965) • That's Entertainment (S) TER-1077 8-10   80s

UK release. A continuation of Sandy Wilson's *Boy Friend*.

   Composer: Sandy Wilson. **Conductor:** Ian MacPherson. **Cast:** Patricia Michael, Philip Gilbert, Anna Sharkey, Cy Young, Joan Heal, others.

  Also see BOY FRIEND

DIXIE: see BING'S HOLLYWOOD

DIXIELAND GOES BROADWAY

Studiotrack (1957) • Coral (M) CRL-57185 10-20   57

   Composer: Various. **Cast:** Stan Rubin.

DIZZY GOES HOLLYWOOD

Studiotrack • Philips (M) PHM 200-123 10-15   63

Studiotrack • Philips (S) PHS 600-123 12-18   63

Music from *Exodus, Breakfast at Tiffany's, Cleopatra, Mondo Cane, Lolita, Picnic, Never on Sunday, Lawrence of Arabia*, others.

   Cast: Dizzy Gillespie.

D.O.A.

Soundtrack • Varese Sarabande (S) STV 81358 8-10   80s

   Composer: Jankel.

DO BLACK PATENT LEATHER SHOES REALLY REFLECT UP?

Original Cast (1982) • Columbia Special Products (S) P-18852 8-10   86

   Composer: James Quinn, Alaric Jans. **Conductor:** Larry Hochman. **Cast:** Russ Thacker, Eileen Blackman, Carol Estey, Mary Buehrle, Louis DiCrescenzo, Susann Fletcher, Peter Heuchling, Patti Hoffman, Max Showalter, Don Stitt.

DO I HEAR A WALTZ?

Original Cast (1965) • Columbia (M) KOL-6370 8-10   65

Original Cast (1965) • Columbia (S) KOS-2770 12-15   65

Both have a four-page booklet insert.

Original Cast (1965) • Columbia Special Products (S) AKOS-2770 5-8   Re

   Composer: Richard Rodgers, Stephen Sondheim. **Conductor:** Frederick Dvonch. **Cast:** Elizabeth Allen, Sergio Franchi, Madeleine Sherwood, Carol Bruce, Stuart Damon, Fleury D'Antonakis, Jack Manning, Julienne Marie.

Studiotrack (1965) • Columbia (M) CL-2317 5-10   65

Studiotrack (1965) • Columbia (S) CS-9117 5-10   65

   Conductor: Percy Faith. **Cast:** Percy Faith and His Orchestra.

Studiotrack (1965) • Columbia (M) CL-2321 5-10   65

Studiotrack (1965) • Columbia (S) CS-9121 5-10   65

   Cast: Ralph Sharon Trio.

DO RE MI

Original Cast (1960) • RCA Victor (M) LOCD-2002 15-18   61

Original Cast (1960) • RCA Victor (S) LSOD-2002 25-30   61

Both have boxed black cover with inserted orange paper sleeve.

Original Cast (1960) • RCA Victor (M) LOC-1105 12-15   65

Original Cast (1960) • RCA Victor (S) LSO-1105 15-20   65

Both have red cover and no box.

   Composer: Jule Styne, Betty Comden, Adolph Green. **Conductor:** Lehman Engel. **Cast:** Phil Silvers, Nancy Walker, John Reardon, David Burns, George Matthews, Nancy Dussault, George Givot.

Original London Cast (1961) • Decca (M) LK-4413 35-45   61

Original London Cast (1961) • Decca (S) SKL-4145 45-65   61

UK release.

Original London Cast (1961) • That's Entertainment (M) TER-1075..... 12-15   Re
UK release.
    Composer: Jule Styne, Betty Comden, Adolph Green. **Cast:** Max Bygraves, Maggie Fitzgibbon, Steve Arlen, Jan Waters, Danny Green, David Lander, Harry Ross.
Studio Cast (1960) • Capitol (M) T-1586 10-12   61
Studio Cast (1960) • Capitol (S) ST-1586 10-12   61
    Composer: Jule Styne, Betty Comden, Adolph Green. **Cast:** June Christy, Bob Cooper.
Studio Cast (1960) • Time (M) T-52032 10-15   61
Studio Cast (1960) • Time (S) ST-2032.. 12-15   61
    Composer: Jule Styne, Betty Comden, Adolph Green. **Conductor:** Maury Laws. **Cast:** Jim Tyler, Maury Laws Orchestra.
Studio Cast • Tops (M) L-1720.. 8-10
Studio Cast (1961) • RCA Victor (M) LPM-2375................................... 10-12   61
Studio Cast (1961) • RCA Victor (S) LSP-2375.................................... 10-12   61
Actual title: *Do Re Mi in Dance Time.* Jazz interpretations.
    Composer: Jule Styne. **Conductor:** Jule Styne. **Cast:** Eddie Heywood (piano).
Also see ANNIE GET YOUR GUN

DO-RE-MI CHILDREN'S CHORUS: see MARY POPPINS

DO THE RIGHT THING
Soundtrack (1989) • Motown (S) MOT-6272 10-15   89
    Cast: Public Enemy, Teddy Riley, EU, Steel Pulse, Perri, Take 6, Keith John, Al Jarreau, Ruben Blades.

DOBIE!
TV Studiotrack • Capitol (M) T-1441 20-25   61
Songs by Dwayne Hickman, TV's *Dobie Gillis.*
    Cast: Dwayne Hickman.

DOCTOR DETROIT
Soundtrack (1983) • Backstreet (S) 6120.. 8-10   83
    Composer: Various. **Cast:** Dan Aykroyd, Devo, T. Carter, James Brown, Pattie Brooks, others.

DOCTOR DOLITTLE
Soundtrack (1967) • 20th Century-Fox (M) TF-5101 5-10   67
Soundtrack (1967) • 20th Century-Fox (S) DTCS-5101 10-12   67
Soundtrack (1967) • 20th Century-Fox (S) WAO-91208 5-8   Re
Both have gatefold cover with eight-page booklet.
    Composer: Leslie Bricusse. **Conductor:** Lionel Newman. **Cast:** Rex Harrison, Samantha Eggar, Anthony Newley, Richard Attenborough, William Dix.
Studiotrack (1967) • RCA Victor (S) LSP 3839.................................... 10-12   67
    Conductor: Gordon Jenkins, Ernie Freeman, Don Costa. **Cast:** Anthony Newley.
Studiotrack • Atlantic (S) SD-8151 15-25
Full title: *Bobby Darin Sings Doctor Dolittle.*
    Conductor: Roger Kellaway. **Cast:** Bobby Darin.
Studiotrack • Disneyland (S) STER-1325... 10-15
    Cast: Camarata, Mike Sammes Singers.

DOCTOR FAUSTUS
Studio Cast (1966) • Angel (S) 36378 10-15   66
    Cast: Richard Burton, Oxford University Dramatic Society.
Soundtrack (1972) • CBS (S) S63189 100-150   72
Canadian release.
    Composer: Mario Nascimbene. **Conductor:** Mario Nascimbene. **Cast:** Richard Burton. (With dialogue.)

DOCTOR GOLDFOOT AND THE GIRL BOMBS
Soundtrack (1966) • Tower (M) T-5053.. 12-15   66
Soundtrack (1966) • Tower (SE) DT-5053 15-25   66
    Composer: Jerry Styner, Guy Hemric, Les Baxter, Harley Hatcher, others. **Cast:** Terry Stafford, Sloopys, Mad Doctors, Bobby Lile, Paul and the Pack, Candles.

DOCTOR IN SPITE OF HIMSELF
Studio Cast • Magic Tone (M) CTG 4009 8-12

DR. NO
Soundtrack (1963) • United Artists (M) UAL-4108 25-30   63
Soundtrack (1963) • United Artists (S) UAS-5108 35-45   63
Soundtrack (1963) • United Artists (M) UA-LA-275-G 8-12   Re
Soundtrack (1963) • Liberty (S) LT-50275 6-10   Re
   Composer: John Barry. **Conductor:** Monty Norman.
   Also see BIG COUNTRY
   Also see INCREDIBLE WORLD OF JAMES BOND

DR. PHIBES
Soundtrack (1971) • American Int'l (S) A-1040 40-50   71
   Film title is *The Abominable Dr. Phibes.*
   Composer: Basil Kirchin, Jack Nathan, Sheldon Brooks, Johnny Mercer, others. **Conductor:**
   Paul Frees. **Cast:** Clockwork Wizzards.

DOCTOR RHYTHM: see BING'S HOLLYWOOD, STAR MAKER

DOCTOR SELAVY'S MAGIC THEATRE
Original Cast (1972) • United Artists (S) UA-LA196-G 20-25   74
   Composer: Tom Hendry, Stanley Silverman. **Conductor:** Stanley Silverman. **Cast:** Denise
   Delapenha, Mary Delson, Jessica Harper, George McGrath, Steve Menken, Jackie Paris, Barry
   Primus, Robert Schlee, Amy Taubin.

DOCTOR STRANGELOVE (AND OTHER GREAT MOVIE THEMES)
Studiotrack (1964) • Colpix (M) CP-464 10-25   64
Studiotrack (1964) • Colpix (S) SCP-464 15-45   64
   Composer: Various. **Cast:** Laurie Johnson Orchestra, Sol Kaplan Orchestra, Leith Stevens
   Orchestra, Morris Stoloff Orchestra, Norman Percival Orchestra, Muir Mathieson Orchestra.

DOCTOR WHO
Radio Cast (1979) • BBC (SE) 22001 20-25   79
   Two-disc set, includes poster, seven souvenir photos and bonus 45 rpm single. Music and
   sound effects from episode, *Genesis of the Daleks,* plus *The Dr. Who Theme.*
Radio Cast (1979) • BBC (SE) 22364 10-20   79
   Full title: *Doctor Who – Genesis of the Daleks.*
   Composer: Ron Grainer. **Cast:** Ron Grainer, Derek Goom (narrator), Tom Baker, others.
Radio Cast (1983) • BBC (SE) BBC-22462 20-25   83
   Full title: *Doctor Who – The Music.* No dialogue.
   Composer: Ron Grainer, Roger Limb, Peter Howell, Malcolm Clarke.

DOCTOR ZHIVAGO
Soundtrack (1965) • MGM (M) 1E-6 8-12   65
Soundtrack (1965) • MGM (S) S1E-6ST 8-12   65
   Both have gatefold cover and booklet. May also be shown as "1SE6ST."
Soundtrack (1965) • MGM (M) 1E-6ST 8-10   66
Soundtrack (1965) • MGM (S) S1E-6ST 8-10   66
   Both have gatefold cover. May or may not have booklet. Has alternate music for *Yuri*
   Writes a Poem for Lara. Some have "Academy Award Winner" sticker on cover. May also
   be shown as "1SE6ST."
Soundtrack (1965) • MGM (S) S1E6-STX 10-12   66
   Gatefold cover. With original music for *Yuri Writes a Poem for Lara.*
Soundtrack (1965) • MGM (S) SWAE-90620 8-10
   Capitol Record Club issue. Gatefold cover.
Soundtrack (1965) • MCA (S) 89042 5-8   86
   Composer: Maurice Jarre. **Conductor:** Maurice Jarre. **Cast:** MGM Studio Orchestra.

Studiotrack • Diplomat (M) 2382 8-12
Studiotrack • Diplomat (S) DS-2382 8-12
   Full title: *The Hits Songs from Doctor Zhivago.*
    Cast: Peter Kasanewitz Trio.
Studiotrack (1966) • Metro (M) M 570 8-12   66
Studiotrack (1966) • Metro (S) MS 570 8-12   66
    Conductor: Bruno Nicolai. **Cast:** Metropolitan Pops Orchestra
Studiotrack • Somerset (S) SF-24800 8-12
    Cast: Cinema Sound Stage Orchestra.

DOG OF FLANDERS
Soundtrack (1959) • 20th Century-Fox (M) FOX-3026 50-75   59
Soundtrack (1959) • 20th Century-Fox (S) SFX-3026 225-250   59
    Composer: Paul Sawtell, Bert Shefter. **Cast:** Santa Cecilia Academy Orchestra and Choir of
    Rome.

DOG'S LIFE
Radio Cast • Folkways (M) FW-5580 15-25
    Cast: Cast of a CBS Radio Workshop Broadcast.
Soundtrack (1953) • Decca (M) DL-4040 30-50   53

DOGS IN SPACE
Soundtrack (1987) • Atlantic (S) 81789-1 8-10   87

DOLCE VITA, LA: see LA DOLCE VITA

DOLL'S HOUSE
Studio Cast • Caedmon (S) TRS 343 5-10

DOLL'S LIFE
Original Cast (1982) • Original Cast (S) OC-8241 30-40   82
   Gatefold cover.
    Composer: Larry Grossman. **Conductor:** Paul Gemignani. **Cast:** George Hearn, Betsy Joslyn,
    Peter Gallagher, Barbara Lang, Norman A. Large, Edmund Lyndeck, David Vosburgh.
Original Cast (1982) • Columbia Special Products (S) 18846 8-12   86
    Composer: Larry Grossman, Betty Comden, Adolph Green. **Conductor:** Paul Gemignani. **Cast:**
    George Hearn, Betsy Joslyn.

$ (DOLLARS)
Soundtrack (1971) • Reprise (S) MS-2051 15-20   71
    Composer: Quincy Jones. **Cast:** Little Richard, Roberta Flack, Doug Kershaw, Don Elliott
    Voices.

DOLLY SISTERS
Soundtrack (1945) • Classic Int'l Filmusicals (M) CIF-3010 8-10
    Composer: Various. **Conductor:** Alfred Newman. **Cast:** Betty Grable, June Havoc, John
    Payne.

DOMINIC AND EUGENE
Soundtrack (1988) • Varese Sarabande (S) 704 540 8-12   88
    Composer: Trevor Jones. **Conductor:** Trevor Jones.

DON HO TV SHOW!
TV Soundtrack • Reprise (M) R-6161 8-12
TV Soundtrack • Reprise (S) RS-6367 8-12
    Cast: Don Ho, others.

DON JUAN IN HELL
Studio Cast (1952) • Columbia (M) SL-166 25-30
   A play without music, by Bernard Shaw.
    Cast: First Drama Quartette: Charles Boyer, Charles Laughton, Cedric Hardwick, Agnes
    Moorehead.

DON QUICHOTTE

Soundtrack (1933) • EJS (M) 143 10-20   59
Includes English and French versions. Actual title: *The Golden Age of Opera: "Scenes from the Film Don Quixote/Scenes from the Film Don Quichotte."* Includes dialogue and music. Also has music from *Bolero: Sierra Nevada.*
Composer: Ronsard, Jacques Ibert. **Conductor:** Jacques Ibert.

DON QUIXOTE

Soundtrack (1973) • Angel (S) S-37008 8-12   73
Composer: Minkus, John Lanchberry.

DONA FLOR AND HER TWO HUSBANDS

Soundtrack (1978) • Peters International (S) PLD 1011 10-12   77
Composer: Chico Buarque, Francis Hime.

DON'T BOTHER ME, I CAN'T COPE

Original Cast (1972) • Polydor (S) PD-6013 8-10   72
Composer: Micki Grant. **Conductor:** Danny Holgate. **Cast:** Alex Bradford, Hope Clarke, Bobby Hill, Alberta Bradford, Charles Campbell, Micki Grant, Arnold Wilkerson.

DON'T KNOCK THE TWIST

Soundtrack (1962) • Parkway (M) P-7011 20-40   62
Composer: Kal Mann, Bo Diddley, John Sheldon, others. **Cast:** Chubby Checker, Dovells, Carroll Brothers, Dee Dee Sharp.

DON'T LOOK NOW

Soundtrack (1974) • That's Entertainment (S) TER-1007 8-12   81
UK release.
Composer: Pino Donaggio. **Conductor:** Giampiero Boneschi.

DON'T MAKE WAVES

Soundtrack (1967) • MGM (M) E-4483 12-25   67
Soundtrack (1967) • MGM (S) SE-4483 15-30   67
Soundtrack (1967) • MCA (S) 25134 8-10   86
Composer: Vic Mizzy. **Conductor:** Vic Mizzy. **Cast:** Byrds.

DON'T PLAY US CHEAP

Original Cast (1972) • Stax (S) STS 2-3006 12-15   72
Two discs.
Composer: Melvin Van Peebles. **Conductor:** Harold Wheeler. **Cast:** Thomas Anderson, Joshie Jo Armstead, Nate Barnett, Frank Carey, Robert Dunn, Rhetta Hughes, Joe Keyes, Jr., Mabel King, Avon Long, George ("Ooppee") McCurn, Esther Rolle, Jay Vanleer.

DONNY & MARIE SINGING SONGS FROM THEIR TELEVISION SHOW

TV Soundtrack (1976) • Kolob (S) PD 6068 5-10   76
Cast: Donny & Marie Osmond.

DONNYBROOK!

Original Cast (1961) • Kapp (M) KDL-8500 12-15   61
Original Cast (1961) • Kapp (S) KD-8500-S 18-20   61
Composer: Johnny Burke. **Conductor:** Clay Warnick. **Cast:** Eddie Foy, Art Lund, Joan Fagan, Susan Johnson, Darrell Askey, Sibyl Bowan, Grace Carney, Alfred DeSio, Eddie Ericksen, James Gannon, Bruce MacKay, Clarence Nordstrom, Charles C. Welch, Darrell J. Askey.

DOONESBURY

Original Cast (1984) • MCA (S) 6129 8-10   84
Composer: Elizabeth Swados, Gary Trudeau. **Conductor:** Jeff Waxman. **Cast:** Barbara Andres, Laura Dean, Gary Beach, Reathel Bean, Ralph Bruneau, Kate Burton, Mark Linn-Baker, Albert Macklin, Keith Szarabajka, Lauren Tom.

DOONESBURY'S JIMMY THUDPUCKER

TV Soundtrack (1977) • RCA Victor/Windsong (S) BXL1-2589 10-12   77
From an NBC-TV special. Includes eight-page cartoon storybook.
Cast: Walden Street Rhythm Section.

DORA'S WORLD

TV Soundtrack • Cozy (S) PLS-0301 8-10
On some copies, neither cover nor label indicate a selection number.
Cast: Dora Hall, Harry Hickox, Milton Frome, Dave Barry, Peter Barbutti, Stubby Kaye, Sid Melton, Scatman Crothers, Sammy Shore.

DOROTHY LAMOUR – MOON OF MANAKOORA / THANKS FOR THE MEMORY

Soundtrack • West Coast (M) LP-14002 20-25
Lamour vocals from various films. "Fan Club Pressing," for the Dorothy Lamour Fan Club.
Cast: Dorothy Lamour.

DOUBLE DECKERS

TV Soundtrack • Capitol (S) ST-672 8-10   71
British performances: *Saturday TV Adventure Set in London.*
Cast: Peter Firth, Michael Audreson, Bruce Clark, Brinsely Forde, Douglas Simonds, Gillian Bailey, Debbie Ross.

DOUBLE DYNAMITE

Soundtrack • Motion Picture Tracks (M) MPT-7 12-18
Also includes music from *The Kissing Bandit.*
Cast: Frank Sinatra, Jane Russell, Groucho Marx. KISSING BANDIT: **Composer:** Nacio Herb Brown, Earl Brent, Edward Heyman. **Conductor:** George Stoll. **Cast:** Frank Sinatra, Kathryn Grayson, Sono Osato.

DOUBLE FEATURE: see THAT MIDNIGHT KISS

DOUBLE IMPACT

Studiotrack (1960) • RCA Victor (M) LPM-2180 25-30   60
Studiotrack (1960) • RCA Victor (S) LSP-2180 55-70   60
Sequel to *Impact.* TV themes from: *Riverboat, Bourbon Street Beat, Johnny Staccato, The Lineup, Twilight Zone, The Untouchables, Hawaiian Eye, Bonanza, International Detective, Markham, The Deputy* and *Men Into Space.*
Composer: David Rose, David Livingston, Elmer Bernstein, Mack David, Jerry Goldsmith, S.J. Wilson, Sidney Shaw, Leroy Holmes, Bernard Herrmann. **Conductor:** Buddy Morrow. **Cast:** Buddy Morrow and His Orchestra.
Also see IMPACT

DOUBLE LIFE: see BANDIT OF SHERWOOD FOREST

DOUBLE OR NOTHING: see BING'S HOLLYWOOD

DOUBLE TROUBLE

Soundtrack (1967) • RCA Victor (M) LPM-3787 40-60   67
Black label reads "Monaural" at bottom. Includes 7" x 9" bonus photo, which represents $10 to $20 of the value.
Soundtrack (1967) • RCA Victor (S) LSP-3787 40-60   67
Black label reads "Stereo" at bottom. Includes a 7" x 9" bonus photo, which represents $10 to $20 of the value.
Soundtrack (1967) • RCA Victor (S) AFL1-2564 10-25   69
Orange or tan label. (Tan label issued in 1976.)
Soundtrack (1967) • RCA Victor (S) AFL1-2564 8-10   77
Composer: Doc Pomus, Mort Schuman, Randy Starr, Sid Tepper, Roy C. Bennett, Sid Wayne, Ben Weisman, others. **Cast:** Elvis Presley, Scotty Moore (guitar), Bob Moore (bass), D.J. Fontana (drums), Charlie Hodge (vocals), Jordanaires (vocals).

DOVE

Soundtrack (1974) • ABC (S) ABDP-852 12-15   74
Composer: John Barry, Don Black. **Conductor:** John Barry. **Cast:** Lyn Paul.

DOWN AND OUT IN BEVERLY HILLS

Soundtrack (1986) • MCA (S) MCA-6160 8-10   87
Cast: Little Richard, Mariachi Vargas De Tecalitlan, David Lee Roth, Randy Newman.

DOWN BY LAW AND VARIETY

Soundtrack (1986) • Intuition (S) C1-90968 8-10   86
    Cast: John Lurie.

DOWN IN THE VALLEY

Studio Cast (1950) • Decca (M) DL 6017 15-25   50
    10-inch LP.

Studio Cast (1950) • Decca (M) DL-4239 12-15   62

Studio Cast (1950) • Decca (SE) DL-74239 15-18   62
    Composer: Kurt Weill, Arnold Sundgaard. **Conductor:** Maurice Levine. **Cast:** Alfred Drake,
    Jane Wilson, Daniel Slick, Norman Atkins.

TV Soundtrack (1950) • RCA Victor (M) LM-16 25-30   50
    10-inch LP.

TV Soundtrack (1950) • RCA Victor (EP) WDM-1367 20-25   50
    Three discs.

TV Soundtrack (1950) • RCA Victor (M) LPV-503 12-15   64
    Full title: *The Kurt Weill Classics: Lady in the Dark / Down in the Valley.* One side has
    music from *Lady in the Dark.*
    Composer: Kurt Weill, Arnold Sundgaard. **Conductor:** Peter Herman. **Cast:** Marion Bell,
    William McGraw, Kenneth Smith, Ray Jacquemot, Richard Barrows, Robert Holland. LADY IN
    THE DARK: **Composer:** Kurt Weill, Ira Gershwin. **Conductor:** Leonard Joy. **Cast:** Gertrude
    Lawrence.

DOWN TO THE SEA IN SHIPS

Studiotrack (1949) • Entra'cte (SE) ERS-6506 25-35   77
    Also has music from: *The Kentuckian* (1955, Bernard Herrmann), *In Love and War* (1958,
    Hugo Friedhofer) and *Sunrise at Campobello* (1960, Franz Waxman).
    Composer: Alfred Newman, Bernard Herrmann, Hugo Friedhofer, Franz Waxman. **Conductor:**
    Fred Steiner.

DOWN TWISTED

Soundtrack (1987) • Varese Sarabande (S) STV 81305 10-12   87
    Composer: Berlingame.

DOWNRIVER

Original Cast (1975) • Take Home Tunes (S) THT-7811 8-10   75
    Composer: Johnny Braden. **Conductor:** Jeff Waxman. **Cast:** Richard Donne, Marcia McLain,
    Donald Arrington, Michael Corbett, Alvin Fields, Robert Price.

DRACULA

Original Radio Cast • Mark 56 (M) 760 50-100   70s
    Picture disc.
    Cast: Orson Wells.

Studiotrack (1964) • Stamford (M) CO-1553 10-20
    Two discs.
    Cast: Christopher Lee.

Studiotrack (1974) • Capitol (S) ST-11340 10-12   74
    Side two, titled *Four Faces of Evil*, has music from: *Fear in the Night, She, The Vampire
    Lovers* and *Dr. Jekyll and Sister Hyde.*
    Composer: James Bernard, John McCabe, Harry Robinson, David Whitaker. **Conductor:** Philip
    Martell. **Cast:** Christopher Lee, Bill Mitchell, Hammer City Orchestra.

Soundtrack (1979) • MCA (S) 3166 8-10   79
    Composer: John Williams. **Conductor:** John Williams.

DRAGNET

Original Radio Cast (1950) • Radiola (M) MR-1059 10-15   75
    From a December 7, 1950 broadcast.
    Cast: Jack Webb, others.

Original Radio Cast • Golden Age (M) 5003 8-10   78

TV Soundtrack (1953) • RCA Victor (EP) EPB-3199 25-35   53
    Two discs.

TV Soundtrack (1953) • RCA Victor (M) LPM-3199............................. 75-90   53
Contains the episode "The Christmas Story." 10-inch LP
Composer: Walter Schumann. Conductor: Walter Schumann. Cast: Jack Webb, Ben
Alexander. (With dialogue.)

DRAGNET (1987)
Soundtrack (1987) • MCA (S) MCA-6210............................. 10-15   87
Composer: Ira Newborn, others. Conductor: Ira Newborn, others. Cast: Dan Aykroyd, Tom
Hanks, Art of Noise, New Edition, Peter Aykroyd, Pat Thrall, Ira Newborn.
Soundtrack (1987) • China (EP) 4V9 43135............................. 4-8   87
12-inch 45 rpm.
Cast: Art of Noise.

DRAGONSLAYER
Soundtrack (1981) • Label X (S) LXSE 2-001 100-125   83
Boxed, limited edition, half-speed mastered, audiophile recording. Plays at 45 rpm. 2,500
made.
Composer: Alex North. Conductor: Alex North.

DRANGO
Soundtrack (1957) • Liberty (M) LRP-3036 100-125   57
Composer: Elmer Bernstein. Conductor: Elmer Bernstein.

DRAT! THE CAT!
Original Cast (1965) • Blue Pear (M) BP 1005 30-35
Live recording made from the sound system of the Martin Beck Theater. Columbia planned
to record the show, but it closed shortly after opening.
Composer: Milton Schafer, Ira Levin. Conductor: Herbert Grossman. Cast: Lesley Ann
Warren, Elliott Gould, Jane Connell, Jack Fletcher, Charles Durning, Sandy Ellen, David Gold,
Lu Leonard, Gene Varrone.

DRAUGHTSMAN'S CONTRACT
Soundtrack (1982) • DRG (S) SL-9513 8-10   82
Composer: Michael Nyman.

DREAM A LITTLE DREAM
Soundtrack (1989) • Cypress (S) YL9-0125 8-10   89
Cast: Mike Reno, R.E.M., Michael Damian, Fee Waybill, Chris Thompson, Otis Redding.

DREAM GIRLS
Original Cast (1982) • Geffen (S) GHSP-2007 8-10   82
Composer: Henry Krieger. Conductor: Yolanda Segovia. Cast: Obba Babatunde, Cleavant
Derricks, Loretta Devine, Ben Harney, Jennifer Holliday, Sheryl Lee Ralph, Deborah Burrell,
Tony Franklin.

DREAM OF KINGS
Soundtrack (1969) • National General (S) NG-1000 15-25   69
Composer: Alex North. Conductor: Alex North. Cast: Frankie Valli, others.

DREAMLIFE
Soundtrack • Earwax (S) 001 15-20
Promotional only picture disc. 800 made.
Soundtrack • Earwax (S) 001 20-30
Picture disc with movie program insert. 200 made. Promotional issue only.

DREAMS
TV Soundtrack (1984) • Columbia (S) BFC-39886............................. 8-10   84

DREAMSCAPE
Soundtrack (1984) • Sonic Atmospheres (S) 102................................. 30-35   84
Composer: Maurice Jarre.

DRESSED TO KILL
Soundtrack (1980) • Varese Sarabande (S) STV-81148 8-12   80
   Composer: Pino Donaggio. **Conductor:** Natale Massara.

DRESSED TO THE NINES
Original Cast (1960) • MGM (M) E-3914 15-20   60
Original Cast (1960) • MGM (S) SE-3914............................... 25-35   60
   Composer: Various. **Conductor:** William Roy. **Cast:** Ceil Cabot, Gordon Connell, Bill Hinnant,
   Gerry Matthews, William Roy and Carl Norman (pianos), Pat Ruhl, Mary Louise Wilson.

DRIVE-IN
Radio Cast (1946) • Command Performance (M) 8.............................. 35-40
   From Suspence Series. Broadcast November 21, 1946.
   Cast: Judy Garland, others.

DRIVING MISS DAISY
Soundtrack (1989) • Varese Sarabande (S) VS-5246 8-12   89
   Composer: Hans Zimmer. **Conductor:** Hans Zimmer. **Cast:** Louis Armstrong, Eartha Kitt.

DROP DEAD! (AN EXERCISE IN HORROR)
Radio Cast • Capitol (M) T-1763 30-40   62
Radio Cast • Capitol (S) ST-1763 40-50   62
   Radio dramas.
   Cast: Bea Benederet, Jack Kruschen, Junius Matthews, Mercedes McCambridge, Arch Oboler
   (narration).

DROWNING OF LUCY HAMILTON
Soundtrack (1985) • Window Speak (S) SSP-2 10-20   85
   12-inch 45 rpm.
   Composer: Lucy Hamilton, L. Lunch.

DRUGSTORE COWBOY
Soundtrack • Novus (S) 3077-1-N9 8-10
   Cast: Bobby Goldsboro, Abbey Lincoln, Jackie De Shannon, John Fred and His Playboy Band,
   Desmond Dekker and Aces, others.

DU BARRY WAS A LADY
Soundtrack (1943) • Titania (M) 509 8-10
   Also includes music from *Can't Help Singing.*
   Composer: Cole Porter, others. **Conductor:** George Stoll. **Cast:** Lucille Ball, Martha Mears
   (performs some vocals for Lucille Ball in the film), Red Skelton, Gene Kelly, Virginia O'Brien, Zero
   Mostel, Tommy Dorsey and His Orchestra. CAN'T HELP SINGING: **Composer:** Jerome Kern, E.Y.
   Harburg. **Conductor:** Edgar Fairchild. **Cast:** Deanna Durbin, Robert Paige.
      Also see MUSIC AND LYRICS BY COLE PORTER

DUCHIN, EDDY: see EDDY DUCHIN STORY

DUCK, YOU SUCKER
Soundtrack (1972) • United Artists (S) UAS-5221 25-35   72
Soundtrack (1972) • United Artists (S) UALA 302 10-15
   Composer: Ennio Morricone. **Conductor:** Ennio Morricone.

DUDE (THE HIGHWAY LIFE)
Original Cast (1972) • Kilmarnock (S) KIL-72007 20-25   72
Original Cast (1972) • Kilmarnock (Q) KIL-72007............................ 20-25   72
   Composer: Galt MacDermot, Gerome Ragni. **Conductor:** Galt MacDermot. **Cast:** Nell Carter,
   Salome Bey, Nat Morris, Jim Farrell, Leta Galloway.
Studio Cast (1972) • Kilmarnock (S) KIL-72003 20-25   72
   Actual title: *Salome Bey Sings Dude.*
   Composer: Galt MacDermot, Gerome Ragni. **Cast:** Salome Bey, Alan Braunstein, Nell Carter,
   Jim Farrell, Leta Galloway, David Lasley, Nat Morris.

DUDES

Soundtrack (1987) • MCA (S) 6212 8-10   87
  Composer: Charles Bernstein.

DUEL

Original Cast (1979) • Original Cast (S) OC-7917 8-10   79
  Composer: Randal Wilson. Cast: Thomas Young, Randal Wilson, Kurt Yahjian, Karen Kraft,
  Kate DeZina, Bertilla Baker.

DUEL AT DIABLO

Soundtrack (1966) • United Artists (M) UAL-4139 10-25   66
Soundtrack (1966) • United Artists (S) UAS-5139 12-35   66
  Composer: Neal Hefti. Conductor: Neal Hefti. Cast: Neal Hefti and His Orchestra.
Soundtrack (1966) • MCA (S) 1436 8-10   80s
  Conductor: Ernie Sheldon. Cast: Ernie Sheldon.

DUEL IN THE SUN

Studiotrack (1946) • RCA Victor DM-1083 75-100   48
  Album of four 78 rpms, with bound-in booklet.
  Composer: Dimitri Tiomkin. Conductor: Arthur Fiedler. Cast: Boston Pops.
  Also see FOREVER AMBER

DUELING BANJOS FROM DELIVERANCE: see DELIVERANCE

DUKES OF HAZZARD

TV Soundtrack (1981) • Scotti Bros. (S) FZ-37712 15-25   82
  Cast: Catherine Bach, James Best (narrator), Johnny Cash, Sorrell Booke (narrator), Doug
  Kershaw, Hazzard County Boys, Tom Wopat, John Schneider.

DUMBO

Studio Cast (1960) • RCA Camden (M) CAS-1026 20-25   59
Studio Cast (1960) • RCA Camden (SE) CAS-1026 (e) 10-12   59
  One side has *The Tootlepipers' Circus*.
  Cast: Shirley Temple (narrator); others.
Soundtrack (1941) • Disneyland (M) WDL-4013 175-200   57
Soundtrack (1941) • Disneyland (M) DQ-1204 20-25   59
Soundtrack (1941) • Disneyland (M) ST-4904 125-150   63
  Special edition (ST-4904) has six-piece accordian gatefold cover with pop-up figures.
  Composer: Frank Churchill; Oliver Wallace. Cast: Cliff Edwards.

DUNE

Soundtrack (1984) • Polydor (S) 422-823 770 20-25   84
  Cast: Toto.

DUNWICH HORROR

Studio Cast • Caedmon (S) TC-1467 10-12   76
  Cast: David McCallum.
Soundtrack (1970) • American Int'l (S) STA-1028 25-30   70
Soundtrack (1970) • Varese Sarabande (S) VC-81103 10-15   79
  Composer: Les Baxter. Conductor: Les Baxter. Cast: Les Baxter Orchestra.

DUSTY AND SWEETS McGEE

Soundtrack (1971) • Warner Bros. (S) SW-1936 15-20   71
  Cast: Van Morrison, Monotones, Marcels, Gene Chandler, Del Shannon, Little Eva, Blues
  Image, Bruce Channel, Jake Holmes, Jimmy Forest.

DYLAN

Original Cast (1964) • Columbia (M) DOL-301 15-20   64
Original Cast (1964) • Columbia (S) DOS-701 18-25   64
  Three discs. Has the complete dramatic play plus special booklet.
  Composer: Laurence Rosenthal, Teo Macero. Cast: Sir Alec Guinness, Kate Reid, James Ray,
  Barbara Berger, Martin Garner, Jenny O'Hara, Gordon B. Clarke, Paul Larson, Jonathan Moore,
  Carol Gustafson, Louisa Cabot, Margaret Braidwood, Ernest Graves, Grant Code, Janet Sarno.

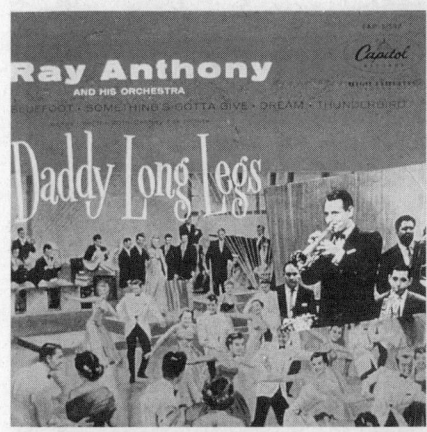

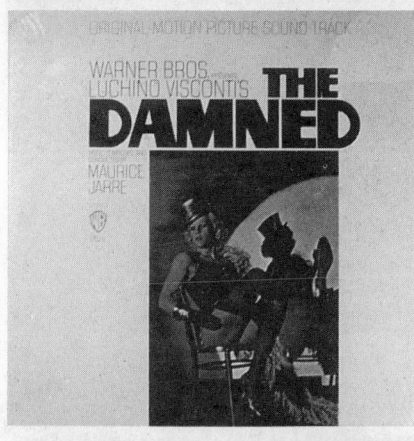

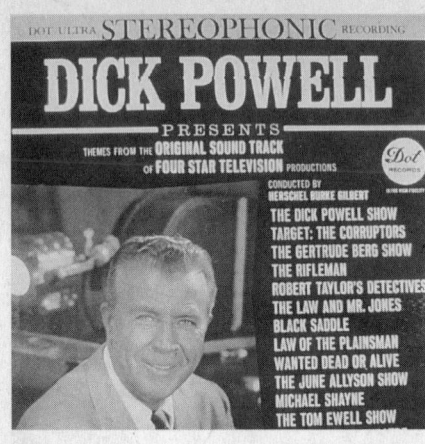

DOT ULTRA STEREOPHONIC RECORDING

DICK POWELL

PRESENTS

THEMES FROM THE ORIGINAL SOUND TRACK
OF FOUR STAR TELEVISION PRODUCTIONS

CONDUCTED BY
HERSCHEL BURKE GILBERT

THE DICK POWELL SHOW
TARGET: THE CORRUPTORS
THE GERTRUDE BERG SHOW
THE RIFLEMAN
ROBERT TAYLOR'S DETECTIVES
THE LAW AND MR. JONES
BLACK SADDLE
LAW OF THE PLAINSMAN
WANTED DEAD OR ALIVE
THE JUNE ALLYSON SHOW
MICHAEL SHAYNE
THE TOM EWELL SHOW

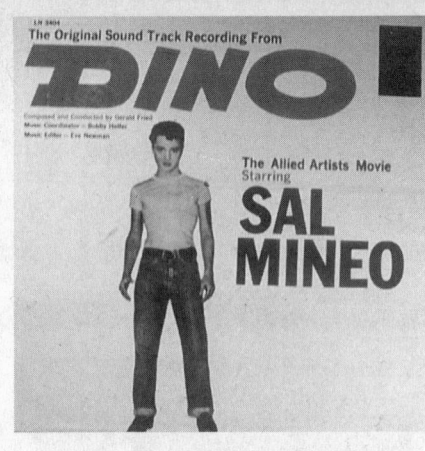

The Original Sound Track Recording From

DINO

The Allied Artists Movie
Starring

SAL
MINEO

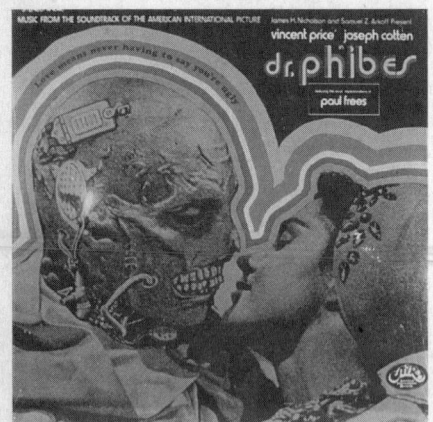

MUSIC FROM THE SOUNDTRACK OF THE AMERICAN INTERNATIONAL PICTURE

vincent price   joseph cotten

dr. phibes

paul frees

DOCTOR WHO

THE MUSIC

THE BBC RADIOPHONIC WORKSHOP

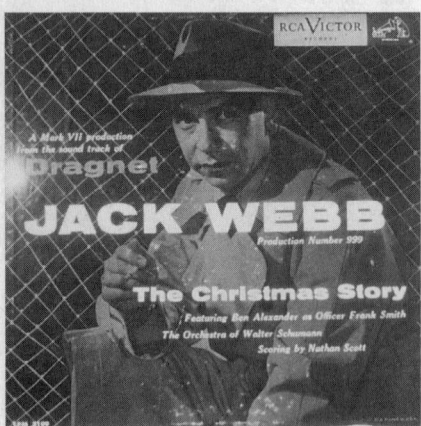

RCA VICTOR

A Mark VII production
from the sound track of
Dragnet

JACK WEBB

Production Number 999

The Christmas Story

Featuring Ben Alexander as Officer Frank Smith
The Orchestra of Walter Schumann
Scoring by Nathan Scott

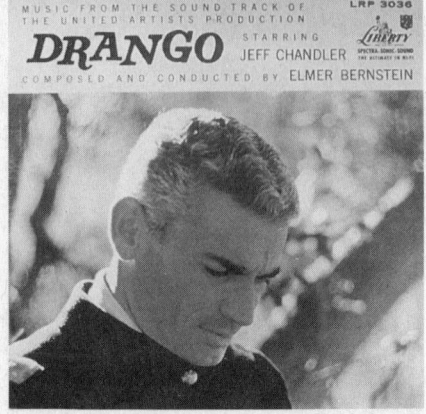

MUSIC FROM THE SOUND TRACK OF
THE UNITED ARTISTS PRODUCTION

DRANGO   STARRING   JEFF CHANDLER

COMPOSED AND CONDUCTED BY ELMER BERNSTEIN

E

E.T.: THE EXTRA-TERRESTRIAL
Soundtrack (1982) • MCA (S) 70000 25-60   82
  Boxed, storybook edition. Includes 20-page program/photo booklet and a poster. Some copies have "MCA 71000 suggested list price $12.98" printed on a sticker on cover spine with 70000 on back cover and label.
Soundtrack (1982) • MCA (S) MCA-6145 20-40   85
  Same as above except has Grammy Awards sticker on shrinkwrap and 24-page booklet. Some copies have "MCA-6145" sticker on cover spine over "70000" number.
  Cast: Michael Jackson (narration and vocal).
Soundtrack (1982) • MCA (S) 6113 10-20   82
  Picture disc. Packaged in clear plastic cover.
Soundtrack (1982) • MCA (S) 6109 8-10   82
  Digital edition (recorded, mixed and edited digitally).
Soundtrack (1982) • MCA (S) 16014 30-40   82
  Audiophile edition.
Soundtrack (1982) • MCA (S) 3160 8-10   82
Soundtrack (1982) • MCA (S) 37264 8-10   88
  Composer: John Williams. **Conductor:** John Williams. **Cast:** John Williams and His Orchestra.

EAGLE HAS LANDED (1969)
TV Soundtrack (1969) • Capitol (SP) SLAO-6660 5-10   69
  From TV broadcast of Lunar expedition.
TV Soundtrack (1969) • Intrepid (SP) IT-2-7401 6-12   69
  Two discs.

EAGLE HAS LANDED (1978)
Soundtrack (1978) • Entr'acte (S) ERS-6510 8-12
  Also has music from *The Four Musketeers.*
  Composer: Lalo Schifrin. **Conductor:** Lalo Schifrin.

EARL OF RUSTON
Original Cast (1971) • Capitol (S) ST-465 30-40   71
  Composer: Peter Link, Ragan Courtney, C.C. Courtney. **Cast:** Peter Link, C.C. Courtney, Leecy R. Woods, Yolande Bavan, Boni Enten, Marta Heflin, Salvation Company.

EARTH GIRLS ARE EASY
Soundtrack (1989) • Sire/Reprise (S) 25835 8-10   89
  Cast: Darryl Hall, John Oates, Royalty, Information Society, Jill Jones, The "N," B-52s, Depeche Mode, Jesus and Mary Chain, Stewart Copeland, Julie Brown.

EARTHA KITT SINGS SONGS FROM NEW FACES: see NEW FACES OF 1952

EARTHQUAKE (1973)
Original Cast (1973) • Inner City (S) LRS RT-60 20-25   73
  Composer: C. Bernard Jackson. **Conductor:** Larry Nash. **Cast:** Bernie Cowens, Karmello Brooks, Lupe Zuniga, Rod Perry, Nikki Sanz, Peter Salas, Lee Hampton.

EARTHQUAKE (1974)
Soundtrack (1974) • MCA (S) 2081 8-12   74
  Includes *Something for Remy.*
Soundtrack (1974) • MCA (S) 2081 30-35   74
  Limited edition, with "Sensurround" band at the end of side two. *Something for Remy* does not appear on this issue. Back cover has white sticker with revised theme titles placed over original theme listing.
  Composer: John Williams. **Conductor:** John Williams.

EAST OF EDEN
TV Soundtrack (1981) • Elektra (S) 5E-520 8-10   81
    Composer: Lee Holdridge. **Conductor:** Lee Holdridge.
    Also see JAMES DEAN STORY
    Also see TRIBUTE TO JAMES DEAN

EAST SIDE OF HEAVEN: see BING'S HOLLYWOOD

EAST SIDE, WEST SIDE
TV Soundtrack (1963) • Columbia (M) CL-2123 20-25   63
TV Soundtrack (1963) • Columbia (S) CS-8923 25-35   63
    Composer: Kenyon Hopkins. **Conductor:** Kenyon Hopkins.

EASTER PARADE
Soundtrack (1948) • MGM - MGM-40 20-30   48
    78 rpm album.
Soundtrack (1948) • MGM (EP) X-40 30-35   50
Soundtrack (1948) • MGM (M) E-502 45-75   50
    10-inch LP.
Soundtrack (1948) • MGM (M) E-3227 12-18   55
    One side has music from *Annie Get Your Gun*.
Soundtrack (1948) • MCA (M) MCA-1459 8-10   86
    Composer: Irving Berlin. **Conductor:** Johnny Green. **Cast:** Judy Garland, Fred Astaire, Peter
    Lawford, Ann Miller.
    Also see THOSE GLORIOUS MGM MUSICALS

EASTMAN KODAK ALBUM ACADEMY AWARD WINNING SONGS: see ACADEMY AWARD WINNING SONGS

EASY COME, EASY GO
Soundtrack (1967) • RCA Victor (EP) EPA-4387 50-75   67
    Black label.
Soundtrack (1967) • RCA Victor (EP) EPA-4387 75-100   67
    White label. Promotional issue only. Reads "EASY COME, EASY GO - Elvis Presley" at top
    of the label.
Soundtrack (1967) • RCA Victor (EP) EPA-4387 75-100   67
    White label. Promotional issue only. Reads "RCA Victor Presents Elvis in the Original
    Soundtrack Recording from the Paramount Picture EASY COME, EASY GO, a Hal Wallis
    Production" at top of the label.
    Composer: Bill Giant, Bernie Baum, Florence Kaye, Gerald Nelson, Fred Burch, Ben Weisman,
    others. **Cast:** Elvis Presley, Scotty Moore (guitar), Bob Moore (bass), Jerry Scheff (bass), D.J.
    Fontana (drums), Hal Blaine (drums), Jordanaires (vocals).

EASY MONEY
Soundtrack (1983) • Columbia (S) JS-38968 8-10   83
    Cast: Billy Joel, Scandal, Heaven, Nick Lowe, Weather Girls.

EASY RIDER
Soundtrack (1969) • Dunhill (S) DSX-50063 15-20   69
    Composer: Hoyt Axton, Jimi Hendrix, Bob Dylan, Roger McGuinn, others. **Cast:** Byrds,
    Steppenwolf, Jimi Hendrix Experience, Roger McGuinn, Fraternity of Man, Electric Prunes, Holy
    Modal Rounders.

EASY TO REMEMBER: see BING'S HOLLYWOOD

EATING RAOUL
Soundtrack (1982) • Varese Sarabande (S) STV-81164 8-12   82
    Composer: Arlon Ober.

ECCO

Soundtrack (1965) • Warner Bros. (M) W-1600 10-20   65
Soundtrack (1965) • Warner Bros. (S) WS-1600 15-30   65
    Composer: Riz Ortolani. **Conductor:** Riz Ortolani.

ECHO PARK

Soundtrack (1986) • A&M (S) SP-5119 8-10   86
    Cast: Jimmie Wood and the Immortals, Shandi, Dean Chamberlain, David Baerwald, Sights,
    Johnette Napolitano, David Ricketts, Patti Black, Mike Sherwood, Julie Christensen.

ECHOES OF HOLLYWOOD

Studiotrack (1956) • Vox (M) VX 800 10-15   56
    10-inch LP.
Studiotrack (1956) • Vox (M) VX 25-400 10-15   56
    Music from *Love Is a Many Splendored Thing, Flying Down to Rio, Love Me Tonight, The*
    Gay Divorcee, Limelight, Murder at the Vanities, Firefly, Lili, Easter Parade, Top Hat and
    An American in Paris.
    Cast: George Feyer, Alexander's Ragtime Band.

EDDIE ALBERT ALBUM

TV Studiotrack (1967) • Columbia (M) CL-2599 10-12   67
TV Studiotrack (1967) • Columbia (S) CS-9399 12-15   67
    Includes the *Green Acres* theme.
    Composer: Various. **Cast:** Eddie Albert.

EDDIE AND THE CRUISERS

Soundtrack (1983) • Scotti Bros. (S) FZ-38929 8-10   83
    Composer: John Cafferty. **Cast:** John Cafferty and the Beaver Brown Band, Ben E. King.

EDDIE CANTOR AT CARNEGIE HALL

Original Cast (1950) • Audio Fidelity (M) AFLP-702 20-25
    Cast: Eddie Cantor.

EDDIE CANTOR STORY

Soundtrack (1953) • Capitol (EP) FBF-467 20-25   53
    Boxed, two-disc set.
Soundtrack (1953) • Capitol (M) L-467 40-45   53
    10-inch LP.
    Composer: Walter Donaldson, James J. Monaco, others. **Conductor:** Ray Heindorf. **Cast:**
    Eddie Cantor. (Cantor performs vocals lip-synched by Keefe Braselle in the film.)
Studiotrack (1953) • Decca (EP) ED-592 15-20   53
Studiotrack (1953) • Decca (M) DL-5504 20-25   53
    10-inch LP. Actual title: *Eddie Cantor Sings.*

EDDY DUCHIN STORY

Soundtrack (1956) • Decca (EP) ED-844 12-15   56
    Three discs in triple-pocket cover.
Soundtrack (1956) • Decca (M) DL-8289 30-35   56
    Cover pictures Tyrone Power and Kim Novak sitting at a piano.
Soundtrack (1956) • Decca (M) DL-8289 10-12   56
Soundtrack (1956) • Decca (S) DL-78289 12-15   59
    Cover of above two has a drawing of Tyrone Power kissing Kim Novak.
Soundtrack (1956) • Decca (M) DL-9121 8-12   65
Soundtrack (1956) • Decca (S) DL-79121 10-15   65

Soundtrack • MCA (S) 2041 5-10   73
Soundtrack • MCA (S) 37088 5-8   86
  Cover pictures Tyrone Power holding Kim Novak against a blue background. All issues
  have Carmen Cavallaro's piano selections, but no background score.
  Composer: Various. **Conductor:** Morris Stoloff. **Cast:** Carmen Cavallaro, Columbia Pictures
  Studio Orchestra.
Soundtrack (1956) • Decca (M) DL-8396 45-50   56
  Music from George Duning's background score, plus soundtrack music from *On the
  Waterfront, From Here to Eternity* and *You Can't Run Away from It.*
  Composer: George Duning. **Conductor:** Morris Stoloff.
Studiotrack (1956) • Capitol (EP) EAP-1-716 8-12   56
Studiotrack (1956) • Capitol (EP) EAP-2-716 8-12   56
Studiotrack (1956) • Capitol (EP) EAP-3-716 8-12   56
Studiotrack (1956) • Capitol (M) T-716 15-20   56
  Capitol releases have additional music not found on the Decca recordings.
  Composer: Various. **Conductor:** Harry Geller. **Cast:** Harry Sukman, George Greeley.
Studiotrack (1956) • Columbia (M) CL-790 12-15   56
Studiotrack (1956) • Columbia (S) CS 9420 10-12   80
  Composer: Various. **Cast:** Eddy Duchin (original recordings), Tony Leonard (vocal).
Studiotrack • Mercury (M) MG 20134 8-12
  Composer: Various. **Conductor:** David Le Winter. **Cast:** David Le Winter.
Studiotrack • Tops (M) L 1510 8-10
  Full title: *A Tribute to Eddy Duchin.*
  Cast: Al Lerner.

EDGE OF THE CITY: see COBWEB

EDITH AND MARCEL
Soundtrack (1984) • Atlantic (S) 80153-1 8-10   84
  Two discs.

EDITH'S DIARY
Soundtrack • Varese Sarabande (S) STV-81255 8-10   80s
  Composer: Knieper.

EDUCATION OF SONNY CARSON
Soundtrack (1974) • Paramount (S) PAS-1045 10-25   74
  Composer: Taylor Perkinson. **Conductor:** Taylor Perkinson.

EDWARD AND MRS. SIMPSON
TV Soundtrack (1978) • Stet/DRG (S) DS-15019 10-12   79
  Mobil Showcase Network mini-series.
  Composer: Ron Grainer, others. **Conductor:** Ron Grainer. **Cast:** Ron Grainer Orchestra, Jenny
  Wren.

EDWARD THE KING
TV Soundtrack (1980) • DRG (S) DARC 21104 10-12   80
  Two discs.
  Composer: Cyril Ornadel. **Conductor:** Cyril Ornadel.

EDWARD THE SEVENTH
TV Soundtrack (1975) • Polydor (S) 2659 041 8-12   75
  Two discs.

EDWIN DROOD: see MYSTERY OF EDWIN DROOD

EGYPTIAN
Soundtrack (1954) • Decca (M) DL-9014 20-60   54
Soundtrack (1954) • Decca (SE) DL-79014 12-25   59
Soundtrack (1954) • MCA (SE) 2029e 8-10   72
  Composer: Alfred Newman, Bernard Herrmann. **Conductor:** Alfred Newman. **Cast:** Doreen
  Tryden, Hollywood Symphony Orchestra and Chorus.

EIGER SANCTION
Soundtrack (1975) • MCA (S) 2088.. 10-12   75
   Composer: John Williams. Conductor: John Williams.

8½
Soundtrack (1963) • RCA Victor (M) FOC-6........................... 30-35   63
Soundtrack (1963) • RCA Victor (S) FSO-6 35-45   63
   Composer: Nino Rota. Conductor: Nino Rota.

EIGHT MEN OUT
Soundtrack (1988) • Varese Sarabande (S) 704.600 20-25   88
   Composer: Mason Daring.

EIGHT ON THE LAM
Soundtrack (1967) • United Artists (M) UAL-4156................................ 10-12   67
Soundtrack (1967) • United Artists (S) UAS-5156 12-15   67
Soundtrack (1967) • MCA (S) 25096.. 8-12   86
   Composer: George Romanis. Conductor: Al Caiola.

18 INTERESTING SONGS FROM UNFORTUNATE MUSICALS
Studio Cast • Take Home Tunes (S) THT-777 10-12

84 CHARING CROSS ROAD
Soundtrack (1986) • Varese Sarabande (S) STV-81306........................ 8-10   86
Soundtrack (1986) • That's Entertainment (S) TER-1129...................... 8-10   80s
   UK release.
   Composer: George Fenton.

81 PROOF
Original Cast (1981) • Cym (S) 8236.. 8-10   81
   Composer: John Everest. Cast: Suzanne Alseaw, Paul Wong, Jean Elderkin, Judy Berkowitz.

EILEEN
Studio Cast (1917) • Camden (M) CAL-210 80-100   54
   One side has music from *Polonaise*.
   Composer: Victor Herbert, Henry Blossom. POLONAISE: Composer: Bronislau Kaper, John
   Latouche. Conductor: Harold Coates.

EL CID
Soundtrack (1961) • MGM (M) E-3977 20-30   62
Soundtrack (1961) • MGM (S) SE-3977 25-35   62
   Composer: Miklos Rozsa. Conductor: Miklos Rozsa. Cast: Symphony Orchestra Graunke of
   Munich.

EL DORADO
Soundtrack (1967) • Epic (M) FLM-13114 35-45   67
Soundtrack (1967) • Epic (S) FLS-15114 60-65   67
   Composer: Nelson Riddle. Conductor: Nelson Riddle.

EL GRANDE DE COCA COLA
Original Cast (1973) • Bottle Cap (S) BC-1001 50-55   73
   7-inch LP.
   Composer: The Cast. Cast: Ron House, Allan Sherman, John Neville-Andrews, Sally Willis.

EL TOPO
Soundtrack (1972) • Apple (S) SWAO-3388 25-35   72
   Includes insert.
   Composer: Alexandro Jodorowsky.

ELECTRA GLIDE IN BLUE
Soundtrack (1973) • United Artists (S) UA-LA062-H 35-45   73
   Gatefold cover. Includes 24-page booklet and two posters.
   Composer: James William Guercio, others.

ELECTRIC COMPANY TV SHOW (SONGS FROM)
TV Soundtrack (1973) • Disneyland (S) 1350............................. 8-15   73
   Cast: Tom Bahlor, Diana Lee, Idasue McCune, Jerry Whitman.

TV Soundtrack (1974) • Sesame Street (S) 22052............................. 6-12   74
   Composer: Joe Raposo, others. **Cast:** Luis Avalos, Jim Boyd, Morgan Freeman, Judy Graubart, Skip Hinnant, Rita Moreno, Hattie Winston, June Angela, Gregory Burge, Stephen Gustafson, Melanie Henderson, Bayn Johnson, Victor Borge, Mel Brooks, Tom Lehrer.

ELECTRIC DREAMS
Soundtrack (1984) • Virgin (S) SE-39600............................. 8-10   84
   Cast: Giorgio Moroder, Philip Oakey, Jeff Lynne, Culture Club, Helen Terry, Heaven 17, P.P. Arnold.

ELECTRIC HORSEMAN
Soundtrack (1980) • Columbia (S) JS-36327 8-10   80
   Composer: Dave Grusin. **Cast:** Willie Nelson.

ELEPHANT CALF
Original Cast (1967) • Asch (M) FL-9831 15-20   67
   Composer: Arnold Black, Bertolt Brecht, Eric Bently. **Cast:** James Antonio, Hilda Brauner, Beeson Carroll, Logan Ramsey (piano).

ELEPHANT CALLED SLOWLY
Soundtrack (1970) • Bell (S) B-1202 10-12   70
   Composer: Howard Blake. **Conductor:** Howard Blake.

ELEPHANT MAN
Soundtrack (1980) • 20th Century Fox (S) T-1000 10-12   80
Soundtrack (1981) • Pacific Arts (S) 143............................. 10-12   81
Soundtrack (1981) • 20th Century-Fox (S) 632 8-12   Re
   Composer: John Morris. **Conductor:** John Morris.

ELEPHANT STEPS
Original Cast (1970) • Columbia (S) M2X-33044............................. 15-20   70
Original Cast (1970) • Columbia (S) 2MG-33044 8-10   Re
Both are two-disc sets.
   Composer: Stanley Silverman, Richard Foreman. **Conductor:** Michael Tilson Thomas. **Cast:** Karen Altman, Susan Belling, Luther Enstad.

ELEPHANT'S CHILD
Soundtrack • Windham Hill (S) WH-0701............................. 5-10

ELEVEN AGAINST THE ICE
TV Soundtrack (1958) • RCA Victor (M) LPM-1618............................. 45-55   58
   Composer: Kenyon Hopkins. **Conductor:** Kenyon Hopkins. **Cast:** Jimmy Simmons.

ELIZABETH AND ESSEX: THE CLASSIC FILM SCORES OF ERICH WOLFGANG KORNGOLD
Studiotrack • RCA Victor (S) ARL 1-0185 10-12   73
   Music from *The Private Lives of Elizabeth and Essex, The Prince and the Pauper, The Sea Wolf, Another Dawn, Of Human Bondage, Anthony Adverse* and *Deception*.
   Composer: Erich Wolfgang Korngold. **Conductor:** Charles Gerhardt.

ELIZABETH TAYLOR IN LONDON
TV Soundtrack (1963) • Colpix (M) CP-459............................. 20-30   63
TV Soundtrack (1963) • Colpix (S) SCP-459............................. 40-45   63
   Composer: John Barry. **Conductor:** Johnnie Spence. **Cast:** Elizabeth Taylor (narration).

ELMER BERNSTEIN: A MAN AND HIS MOVIES
Studiotrack (1967) • Mainstream (M) 56094 10-15   67
Studiotrack (1967) • Mainstream (S) S-6094 15-20   67
> Movie themes from *To Kill a Mockingbird, Walk on the Wild Side, The Man with the Golden Arm, Mutiny on the Bounty, The Carpetbaggers, Rat Race, Sweet Smell of Success, Anna Lucasta* and *Sudden Fear.*
> **Composer:** Elmer Bernstein.

ELMER BERNSTEIN CONDUCTS
Soundtrack • Dot (S) DLP-3364 15-20
Soundtrack • Dot (S) DLP-25364 20-25
> Full title: *Elmer Bernstein Conducts Gone with the Wind and Other Great Movie Themes.*
> **Conductor:** Elmer Bernstein.

ELMER GANTRY
Soundtrack (1960) • United Artists (M) UAL-4069 20-45   60
Soundtrack (1960) • United Artists (S) UAS-5069 30-40   60
Soundtrack (1960) • MCA (S) 39070 8-10   86
> Above three have music only from *Elmer Gantry.*
Soundtrack (1960) • United Artists (M) DF-6 12-15   63
Soundtrack (1960) • United Artists (S) DFS-56 15-20   63
> Above two have music from *The Vikings* on one side.
Studiotrack (1960) • Mercury (S) SR 60260 10-12   60
> **Conductor:** Malcolm Dodds. **Cast:** Patti Page.

ELSA LANCHESTER HERSELF
Original Cast (1961) • Verve (M) MGV-15024 12-15   61
Original Cast (1961) • Verve (S) V6-15024 18-20   61
> **Cast:** Elsa Lanchester.
Studio Cast (1961) • Hi-Fi (M) R-405 15-20   61
> Contains only three show tunes.
Studio Cast (1961) • Tradition (S) 2065 10-12   Re
Studio Cast (1961) • Tradition (SE) 2091 10-12
> **Cast:** Elsa Lanchester.

ELVIS
TV Soundtrack (1979) • Dick Clark (S) TVLP-79DC................................ 10-15   79
> **Cast:** Ronnie McDowell (performs the vocals lip synced by Kurt Russell, who portrayed Elvis in the film), Chip Young (guitar), Dale Sellers (guitar), David Briggs (keyboards), Bobby Ogden (keyboards), Buddy Harmon (drums), Mike Leech (bass), Charlie McCoy (harmonica), Jordanaires (vocals), Kathy Westmoreland (vocals).

ELVIS (NBC-TV SPECIAL)
TV Soundtrack (1968) • RCA Victor (M) LPM-4088.............................. 20-30   68
> Orange label. Rigid disc.
TV Soundtrack (1968) • RCA Victor (M) LPM-4088.............................. 15-20   72
> Orange label. Flexible disc.
TV Soundtrack (1968) • RCA Victor (M) LPM-4088.............................. 10-20   76
> Tan label.
TV Soundtrack (1968) • RCA Victor (M) AFM1-4088 10-15   77
TV Soundtrack (1968) • RCA Victor (M) AYM1-3894 5-10   81
TV Soundtrack (1968) • RCA Victor (M) DVM1-0704 25-35   85
> Special Products issue. Exclusive offer from HBO (Home Box Office) for cable TV subscribers. Actual title of HBO broadcast of the 1968 Burbank sessions: *Elvis – One Night With You.* Includes poster.
> **Composer:** Elvis Presley, Jerry Leiber, Mike Stoller, W. Earl Brown, others. **Cast:** Elvis Presley, Scotty Moore (guitar), D.J. Fontana (drums), Charlie Hodge (guitar, vocals), Tom Tedesco (guitar), Hal Blaine (drums), Mike Deasy (guitar), Alan Fortas (tambourine), NBC Studio Orchestra. (With dialogue.)

ELVIS: ALOHA FROM HAWAII VIA SATELLITE

TV Soundtrack (1973) • RCA Victor (EP) DTFO-200 75-100   73
Six-song, stereo EP for jukebox play. Includes 10 jukebox title strips.

TV Soundtrack (1973) • RCA Victor (Q) VPSX-6089 2,000-2,500   73
With "Chicken of the Sea" sticker applied to front cover. Includes programming insert sheet Promotional issue for the Van Camps Company only.

TV Soundtrack (1973) • RCA Victor (Q) VPSX-6089 75-100   73
Song titles not printed on cover itself, but on a gold sticker applied to cover.

TV Soundtrack (1973) • RCA Victor (Q) VPSX-6089 500-750   73
Promotional issue only. Titles and programming information are printed on a white sticker, applied to front cover.

TV Soundtrack (1973) • RCA Victor (Q) VPSX-6089 25-30   73
Song titles are printed on back cover.

TV Soundtrack (1973) • RCA Victor (Q) CPD2-2642 10-15   74
All are two-disc sets.
    Conductor: Joe Guercio. **Cast:** Elvis Presley, James Burton (guitar), John Wilkinson (guitar), Ronnie Tutt (drums), Jerry Scheff (bass), Glen D. Hardin (piano), Charlie Hodge (guitar, vocals), Kathy Westmoreland (vocals), Sweet Inspirations (vocals), J.D. Sumner and the Stamps (vocals), Joe Guercio and His Orchestra. (With dialogue.)

ELVIS IN CONCERT

TV Soundtrack (1977) • RCA Victor (S) APL2-2587............................ 15-25   77
TV Soundtrack (1977) • RCA Victor (S) CPL2-2587 12-18   82
Both are two-disc sets.
    Conductor: Joe Guercio. **Cast:** Elvis Presley, James Burton (guitar), John Wilkinson (guitar), Jerry Scheff (bass), Ronnie Tutt (drums), Glen D. Hardin (piano), Sherrill Nielsen (vocals), Vernon Presley (dialogue), J.D. Sumner and the Stamps (vocals), Sweet Inspirations (vocals), Joe Guercio and His Orchestra. (With dialogue.)

ELVIS LIVE AT THE LOUISIANA HAYRIDE

Radio Cast (1954-1956) • Louisiana Hayride (M) LH-3061 15-20   83
Full title: *Elvis . . . the Beginning Years 1954 to '56 Live At the Louisiana Hayride, Where It All Began.* From KWKH radio broadcasts, Shreveport, Louisiana.

Radio Cast (1955-1956) • Music Works (M) PB-3601 10-15   82
Actual title: *Elvis: The First Live Recordings.* A partial reissue of LH-3061.

Radio Cast (1954-1955) • Music Works (M) PB-3602 10-15   82
Actual title: *Elvis: The Hillbilly Cat.* A partial reissue of LH-3061.

Radio Cast (1954-56) • Premore (M) PL-589 8-12   90
Full title: *Early Elvis 1954-1956 Live At the Louisiana Hayride.* A mail-order only offer from the Solo Cup Co. Reissue of Louisiana Hayride LH-3061.
    Cast: Elvis Presley, Scotty Moore (guitar), Bill Black (bass), D.J. Fontana (drums), Frank Page (emcee), David Kent (narration).

EMERALD FOREST

Soundtrack (1985) • Varese Sarabande (S) STV-81244........................ 8-15   85
    Composer: Junior Homrich, Brian Gascoigne.

EMIL AND THE DETECTIVES

Soundtrack (1964) • Disneyland (M) DQ-1262 30-35   64
    Cast: Walter Slezak (narration).

EMILY

Soundtrack (1976) • Stanyan (Q) SRQ-4025 20-30   76
    Composer: Rod McKuen. **Conductor:** Alyn Ainsworth.

EMMANUELLE

Soundtrack (1975) • Arista (S) AL-4036... 12-15   75
    Composer: Pierre Bachelet, Herve Roy, Howard Blaikley. **Conductor:** Pierre Bachelet, Herve Roy.

EMPEROR AND THE NIGHTINGALE

Soundtrack • Windham Hill (S) WH-0706... 5-10

EMPEROR WALTZ

Studiotrack (1949) • Decca (M) DL-5272 40-45   49
10-inch LP. One side has music from *Top o' the Morning*.
Composer: James VanHeusen, Johnny Burke, others. **Conductor:** Victor Young, Simon Rady.
Cast: Bing Crosby, Ann Blyth, Jeff Alexander Chorus.
Also see BING'S HOLLYWOOD

EMPIRE OF THE SUN

Soundtrack (1987) • Warner Bros. (S) 25668-1 8-10   87
Composer: John Williams. **Conductor:** John Williams. **Cast:** Ambrosian Junior Choir, James Rainbird (soloist).

EMPIRE STRIKES BACK

Soundtrack (1980) • RSO (S) RS-1-3081... 10-12   80
Soundtrack (1980) • RSO (S) 827580-1... 8-10   Re
Soundtrack (1980) • RSO (S) RS-2-4201... 15-20   80
All are two-disc sets and each includes a 12-page booklet.
Composer: John Williams. **Cast:** Malachi Throne (narration), Mark Hamill, Harrison Ford, Carrie Fisher, Billy Dee Williams, Anthony Daniels, James Earl Jones, Frank Oz, London Symphony Orchestra.

Soundtrack (1980) • Buena Vista (S) BV-62102................................... 15-20   83
Has 16-page booklet. Music and dialogue.
Cast: Various.

Studiotrack (1980) • Chalfont (S) SDG-313... 12-20   80
Digital recording.
Conductor: Charles Gerhardt. **Cast:** National Philharmonic Orchestra.

Studiotrack (1980) • RSO (S) RS-1-3079... 8-12   80
Disco version.
Conductor: Boris Midney. **Cast:** London Symphony Orchestra.

Studiotrack (1980) • RSO (S) RO-1-3086 8-12   80
10-inch LP. Full title: *Meco Plays Music from The Empire Strikes Back*.
Conductor: Meco. **Cast:** Meco.
Also see STAR WARS

ENCHANTED COTTAGE: see JUNGLE BOOK

ENCORE OF BROADWAY GOLDEN HITS

Studiotrack • Mercury (M) MG-20613... 25-30   61
Studiotrack • Mercury (S) SR-60613 30-40   61
Songs from *Porgy and Bess, Great Day, Hit the Deck, Girl Crazy, Cotton Club Revue, Madame Sherry, Senior Prom, Big Show, Leave It to Me, Knickerbocker Holiday* and *Oklahoma!*
Conductor: David Carroll. **Cast:** Platters.

ENCORE! MORE OF THE MUSIC OF HENRY MANCINI

Studiotrack (1967) • RCA Victor (M) LPM-3887 10-15   67
Studiotrack (1967) • RCA Victor (S) LSP-3887 10-20   67
Music from *Exodus, The Man with the Golden Arm, Lili, Doctor Zhivago, Captain from Castile, Laura, Days of Wine and Roses, Charade, Moon River, A Hard Day's Night, Born Free, Moulin Rouge, Mondo Cane, Black Orpheus, Zorba the Greek* and *The Umbrellas of Cherbourg*.
Composer: Henry Mancini, others. **Conductor:** Henry Mancini.

ENCORES OF HOLLYWOOD

Studiotrack (1956) • Allegro (M) 1694 30-40   56
Cast: Kurt Maier.

ENDLESS LOVE

Soundtrack (1981) • Mercury/Polygram (S) SRM 1-2001 10-12   81
Soundtrack (1981) • Mercury (S) 826277-1.. 8-10   81
Composer: Jonathan Tunick, Lionel Richie. **Cast:** Diana Ross, Lionel Richie, Kiss, Cliff Richard.

ENDLESS SUMMER
Soundtrack (1966) • World Pacific (M) WP-1832 15-20   66
Soundtrack (1966) • World Pacific (S) ST-1832 20-25   66
    Composer: John Blakeley, Walter Georis, John Gibson, Hank Marvin, Jet Harris. **Cast:** Sandals.

ENEMY MINE
Soundtrack (1985) • Varese Sarabande (S) STV-81271 10-15   85
Soundtrack (1985) • That's Entertainment (S) TER-1112 8-10   80s
    UK release.
    Composer: Maurice Jarre. **Conductor:** Maurice Jarre. **Cast:** Munich Studio Orchestra.

ENFORCER
Soundtrack (1951) • Mark 56 (M) 707 40-80   79
    Picture disc.

ENGLAND MADE ME
Soundtrack (1973) • East Coast (S) 1062 8-12
    Composer: John Scott. **Conductor:** John Scott. **Cast:** Peter Finch, Michael York, London Philharmonic Orchestra, Lana Cantrell.

ENIGMA
Studiotrack • That's Entertainment (S) TER-1027 8-10   80s
    UK release.
    Composer: Marc Wilkinson.

ENNIO MORRICONE FILM MUSIC
Studiotrack [Vol. 1] • Virgin (S) 7 90674-1 5-10
Studiotrack [Vol. 2] • Virgin (S) 7 90901-1 5-10
Studiotrack [Vol. 3] • Virgin (S) 7 25769-1 5-10

ENOLA GAY
TV Soundtrack (1980) • Varese Sarabande (S) STV-81149 8-12   81
    Digital mix.
    Composer: Maurice Jarre. **Conductor:** Maurice Jarre.

ENTER LAUGHING
Soundtrack (1967) • Liberty (M) LOM-17004 10-25   67
Soundtrack (1967) • Liberty (S) LOS-17004 15-30   67
    Composer: Quincy Jones. **Conductor:** Quincy Jones.

ENTER THE DRAGON
Soundtrack (1973) • Warner Bros. (S) BS-2727 35-50   73
    Composer: Lalo Schifrin. **Conductor:** Lalo Schifrin.

ENTERTAINERS
Original Cast (1964) • London (S) SW-99436 20-25   64

EQUALIZER AND OTHER CLIFF HANGERS
Soundtrack (1988) • I.R.S. (S) IRS-42099 8-10   88
    Composer: Stewart Copeland. **Cast:** Stewart Copeland.

EQUUS
Soundtrack (1977) • United Artists (S) UA-LA839-H 10-12   77
Soundtrack (1977) • Liberty (S) LT-839 8-10   Re
    Composer: Richard Rodney Bennett. **Conductor:** Angela Morley. **Cast:** Richard Burton, Peter Firth. (With dialogue.)

ERASERHEAD
Soundtrack (1977) • I.R.S. (S) SP-70027 8-10   82
    Composer: Thomas "Fats" Waller, Peter Ivers, David Lynch. **Cast:** John Nance, Charlotte Stewart, Allen Joseph, Jeanne Bates, Laurel Near. (With dialogue.)

ERIC SOYA'S 17
Soundtrack (1967) • Mercury (M) MG-21115 10-12   67
Soundtrack (1967) • Mercury (S) SR-61115... 12-30   67
    Composer: Ole Hoyer.

ERNEST IN LOVE
Original Cast (1960) • Columbia (M) OL-5530.............................. 35-50   60
Original Cast (1960) • Columbia (S) OS-2027..................................... 65-85   60
    Composer: Lee Pockriss, Anne Croswell. Conductor: Liza Redfield. Cast: Leila Martin, John
    Irving, Gerrianne Raphael, Louis Edmonds, Sara Seeger, Christina Gillespie, George Hall,
    Margot Harley, Lucy Landau, Alan Shayne.

ESCAPE FROM NEW YORK
Soundtrack (1981) • Varese Sarabande (S) STV-81134 8-10   81
Studiotrack • That's Entertainment (S) TER-1027 8-10   80s
  UK release.
    Composer: John Carpenter. Conductor: John Carpenter. Cast: John Carpenter, Alan Howarth.

ESCAPE ME NEVER: see BERNARD HERRMANN CONDUCTS GREAT BRITISH
    FILM SCORES

ESCAPE TO WITCH MOUNTAIN
Soundtrack (1975) • Disneyland (S) ST-3809 8-10   75
Soundtrack (1975) • Disneyland (S) DS-3809 8-10   75
    Composer: Johnny Mandel.

ESTABLISHMENT
Original Cast (1963) • Riverside (M) RM-850 35-50   63
    Composer: Peter Cook, The Cast. Cast: Eleanor Bron, John Bird, Original London Company.

ETERNAL SEA
Soundtrack (1955) • Citadel (M) CT 7021 8-10   82
  Also has the Elmer Bernstein soundtrack from *Make Haste to Live*.
    Composer: Elmer Bernstein. Conductor: Elmer Bernstein.

ETHEL MERMAN
Original Cast • Decca (M) DL-5053... 25-45   49
  10-inch LP. Full title: *Ethel Merman Sings Songs She Has Made Famous*. Selections from
  Take a Chance, Anything Goes, Girl Crazy, Red Hot and Blue and *George White's*
  Scandals of 1931.
    Composer: George Gershwin, Ira Gershwin, Cole Porter, others. Conductor: Jay Blackton. Cast:
    Ethel Merman.
Original Cast (1956) • Vik (M) LVA-1004.. 25-40   56
  Full title: *Ethel Merman on Stage (with Gertrude Niesen.)*
    Cast: Ethel Merman, Gertrude Niesen.
Original Cast (1963) • Reprise (M) R-6062.. 12-15   63
Original Cast (1963) • Reprise (M) R9-6062.. 15-20   63
  Actual title: *Merman in Vegas.*
Studio Cast • Decca (M) DX-153... 40-60   60s
  Boxed, two-disc set.
Studio Cast • Decca (M) DX-153... 25-35   Re
  Two discs in gatefold cover. Full title for both: *Ethel Merman - A Musical Autobiography*.
  Narrated by Ethel Merman, with 34 songs from various shows, some drawn from Decca
  original cast recordings.
    Composer: George Gershwin, Ira Gershwin, Cole Porter, Irving Berlin, others. Conductor:
    Buddy Cole, Jay Blackton, Gordon Jenkins, Sy Oliver. Cast: Ethel Merman, Buddy Cole Quartet,
    Joan Carroll, Harry Sosnik, John Garth, Turner and Bibb, Ray Middleton, Ray Bolger.
Soundtrack • Encore (M) ST 101 15-25
  Actual title: *Merman in the Movies, 1930-38*. Includes rare material from nine films.
    Cast: Ethel Merman, Bing Crosby.

Studiotrack (1950-1951) • MCA (M) MCL 1839 10-12   87
    Actual title: *Ethel Merman – The Moon Is Your Balloon*. Contains original show tunes for
    Decca.
      Cast: Ethel Merman, Ray Bolger, Jimmy Durante.
Studiotrack • Reprise (M) R-6032 12-18
Studiotrack • Reprise (S) R9-6032 15-20
    Actual title: *Merman – Her Greatest!*
      Cast: Ethel Merman.
Studiotrack • Stanyan (S) SR 10070 10-20   73
    Actual title: *Ethel Merman – Her Greatest Hits*. Reissue of *Merman – Her Greatest!*
      Cast: Ethel Merman.

ETHEL WATERS: see CABIN IN THE SKY

EUBIE!
Original Cast (1978) • Warner Bros. (S) HS-3267 8-10   78
    Composer: Eubie Blake, others. **Conductor:** Vicki Carter. **Cast:** Ethel Beatty, Gregory Hines,
    Lonnie McNeil, Terry Burrell, Lynnie Godfrey, Maurice Hines, Mel Johnson, Jr., Janet Powell,
    Marion Ramsey, Alaina Reed, Jeffrey V. Thompson.

EUROPEAN HOLIDAY
Studio Cast • SAS Airlines (M) TV-22216/7 50-60   50s
    10-inch LP. Gatefold cover. A Mitch Miller Musical, produced for Scandinavian Airlines.
    Side two has three native Scandinavian tunes. Promotional issue only.
Studio Cast • Columbia (M) CL-2586 25-30   50s
    Also includes Mitch Miller arrangements of popular songs.
    Composer: Lee Thornsby, Douglas Lance, Johan Halvorsen, Lars Erik Larsson, H.C. Lumbye.
    Conductor: Jimmy Carroll, Tippe Lumbye, Stig Westerberg, Olvin Fjedlstad. **Cast:** Michael
    Stewart, Jill Corey, Jerry Vale, Jonathan Winters, George Perrin, Mitch Miller and His Orchestra,
    Oslo Philharmonic Orchestra, Stockholm Radio Orchestra, Tivoli Concert Orchestra.

EUROPEANS
Soundtrack (1980) • Gramavision (S) 1010 10-12   81
    Composer: Stephen Foster, Clara Schumann, Franz Schubert.

EVE OF THE WAR
Soundtrack (1980) • Columbia (S) 43-11148 8-10   80
    12-inch disco pressing. One side has *Horsell Common and the Heat Ray*.

EVENING WITH ALAN JAY LERNER
Original Cast (1971) • Laureate Records (S) LL-602 10-12   77
    Part of the *Lyrics and Lyricists Series*.
      Cast: Alan Jay Lerner, Bobbi Baird, J.T. Cromwell, Barbara Williams.
Original London Cast • Relativity/First Night (S) 88561 8261-1 15-20   87
    Two discs. Recorded live at London's Theatre Royale.

EVENING WITH BEATRICE LILLIE
Original Cast (1952) • London (M) LL-1373 25-35   56
Original Cast (1952) • London (M) LL-5212 15-20   Re
    Opened on Broadway in 1952 and moved to London in 1954. Recording made in London
    after the run ended.
    Composer: Richard Rodgers, Lorenz Hart, Noel Coward, Bert Kalmar, Harry Ruby, George
    Gershwin, Irving Berlin, Arthur Schwartz, Howard Dietz, others. **Cast:** Beatrice Lillie, Eadie and
    Rack (pianos).

EVENING WITH BORIS KARLOFF AND HIS FRIENDS
Soundtrack (1967) • Decca (M) DL-4833 30-45   67
Soundtrack (1967) • Decca (SE) DL-74833 65-75   67
    Boris Karloff narrates music sequences from *Dracula* (1931), *Frankenstein* (1932), *Bride of
    Frankenstein* (1935), *Son of Frankenstein* (1939), *The Wolfman* (1941) and *House of
    Frankenstein* (1944).
    Composer: William Loose, Frank Skinner, Hans J. Salter, Charles Previn, Franz Waxman.
    Cast: Boris Karloff (narrator).

EVENING WITH DIANA ROSS
Original Cast (1976) • Motown (S) M7-877R2 10-12   76
Two discs.
Conductor: Gil Askey. Cast: Diana Ross, Brenda Jones, Shirley Jones, Valorie Jones.

EVENING WITH FRED ASTAIRE
TV Soundtrack (1958) • Chrysler (M) No Number Used 45-65   58
Presented by Chrysler Corporation for NBC-TV, October 17, 1958.
Composer: Various. Conductor: David Rose. Cast: Fred Astaire, Barrie Chase, David Rose
Orchestra, Jonah Jones Quartet.

EVENING WITH FRED EBB AND JOHN KANDER
Original Cast (1973) • Laureate Records (S) LL-605 10-12   78
Part of the *Lyrics and Lyricists Series*.
Cast: Fred Ebb, John Kander.

EVENING WITH GROUCHO
Soundtrack • A&M (M) SP-3515 10-15   72
Two discs. Excerpts from Marx Brothers films and Groucho Marx performances.
Cast: Groucho Marx, Marx Brothers.

EVENING WITH GYPSY ROSE LEE: see CURIOUS EVENING

EVENING WITH JEROME KERN
Original Cast (1959) • United Artists (M) UAL 3039 20-25   59
Composer: Jerome Kern, Oscar Hammerstein II, Otto Harbach, E.Y. Harburg, Ira Gershwin,
others. Conductor: Joseph Ricardel. Cast: Wilbur Evans, Dolores Perry, Bill Tabbert.

EVENING WITH JERRY HERMAN
Original Cast (1974) • Laureate Records (S) LL-606 10-12   78
Part of the *Lyrics and Lyricists Series*.
Cast: Jerry Herman, Lisa Kirk, Joe Masiell, Carol Dorian.

EVENING WITH JOHNNY MERCER
Original Cast Live (1971) • Laureate Records (S) LL-601 10-12   77
Part of the *Lyrics and Lyricists Series*.
Cast: Johnny Mercer, Margaret Whiting, Robert Sands.

EVENING WITH LERNER AND LOEWE
Studio Cast (1959) • RCA Victor (M) LPM-6005 10-15   59
Studio Cast (1959) • RCA Victor (S) LSP-6005 15-20   59
Two discs. Selections from *My Fair Lady* and *Paint Your Wagon, Brigadoon* and *Gigi*.
Composer: Alan Jay Lerner, Frederick Loewe. Conductor: Johnny Green. Cast: Jane Powell,
Phil Harris, Jan Peerce, Robert Merrill, RCA Victor Symphony Orchestra and Chorale.
Studio Cast (1959) • RCA Victor (S) LPM-2274 10-15   60
Studio Cast (1959) • RCA Victor (S) LSP-2274 15-20   60
Full title: *My Fair Lady/Paint Your Wagon*. Partial reissue of *An Evening with Lerner and
Loewe*.
Composer: Alan Jay Lerner, Frederick Loewe. Conductor: Johnny Green. Cast: Johnny Green
and RCA Victor Symphony and Chorale, Jan Peerce, Robert Merrill, Jane Powell, Phil Harris.

EVENING WITH MIKE NICHOLS AND ELAINE MAY
Original Cast (1960) • Mercury (M) OCM-2200 12-15   60
Original Cast (1960) • Mercury (S) OCS-6200 15-25   60
Both have a gatefold cover.
Original Cast (1960) • Mercury (M) MG-20865 12-15   64
Original Cast (1960) • Mercury (S) SR-60865 15-25   64
Original Cast (1960) • Mercury (S) 2-628 10-15   Re
Includes Nichols and May material previously unissued on LP.
Cast: Mike Nichols, Elaine May.

EVENING WITH PETERS SELLERS
TV Soundtrack (1974) • BBC (S) 22402............................... 15-25   80s
From the BBC Parkinson program.
Cast: Peter Sellers, Harry Stoneham Trio.

EVENING WITH QUENTIN CRISP
Original Cast (1978) • DRG (S) S26-5188............................ 10-12   78
Two discs.
Cast: Quentin Crisp (dialogue).

EVENING WITH RICHARD NIXON
Original Cast (1972) • Ode (S) SP-77015 20-30   72
From an original play by Gore Vidal.
Cast: Saliva Sisters, Gene Rupert, Humbert Allen Astredo, Phillip Sterling, George S. Irving,
Robert King.

EVENING WITH SAMMY CAHN
Original Cast (1972) • Laureate Records (S) LL-604.............. 10-12   78
Part of the *Lyrics and Lyricists Series.*
Composer: Sammy Cahn. Cast: Sammy Cahn, Bobbi Baird, Shirley Lemmon, Jon Peck.

EVENING WITH SHELDON HARNICK
Original Cast (1971) • Laureate Records (S) LL-603.............. 10-12   77
Part of the *Lyrics and Lyricists Series.*
Cast: Sheldon Harnick, Margery Gray, Mary Louise.

EVENING WITH W.S. GILBERT
Original Cast • Original Cast (S) OC-8026 8-12
Composer: Arthur Sullivan, Osmond Carr, Edward German, W.S. Gilbert. Cast: Lloyd Harris,
Alfred Heller (piano).

EVENING WITH WILLIAM SHAKESPEARE
Original Cast (1952) • Theatre Masterpieces (M) No Number Used. 100-125   52
Two red vinyl discs. Gatefold cover. Includes program insert. Recording from Hartford
Shakespeare Festival performance, December 5, 1952.
Cast: Wesley Addy, Staats Cotsworth, Richard Dyer-Bennet, Faye Emerson, Nina Foch, Eva Le
Gallienne, Leueen MacGrath, Arnold Moss, Claude Rains.

EVERGREEN
Original London Cast (1930) • Monmouth Evergreen (M) MES 7049 ... 15-18
One side has music from *Anything Goes.*
Composer: Richard Rodgers, Lorenz Hart. Cast: Jessie Matthews.

EVERY GOOD BOY DESERVES FAVOUR
Original London Cast (1979) • RCA Victor (S) ABL1-2855.................... 8-12   79
Gatefold cover.
Original London Cast (1979) • RCA Victor (S) ABL1-2855.................... 8-10   Re
Standard cover.
Composer: Andre Previn, Tom Stoppard. Conductor: Andre Previn. Cast: Ian McKellen, Ian
Richardson, Patrick Stewart, Elizabeth Spriggs, Philip Locke, Andrew Sheldon.

EVERY WHICH WAY BUT LOOSE
Soundtrack (1979) • Elektra (S) 5E-503............................... 8-10   79
Conductor: Steve Dorff. Cast: Eddie Rabbitt, Charlie Rich, Mel Tillis, Sondra Locke, Cliff
Crofford, Larry Collins, Phil Everly, Hank Thompson.

EVERYBODY SING
Soundtrack (1938) • Pilgrim (M) 4000 8-10
Also has songs from *Pigskin Parade* (1936.)
Cast: Judy Garland, Betty Grable, Allan Jones, Fanny Brice: PIGSKIN PARADE: Cast: Judy
Garland, Betty Grable, Stuart Erwin, Dixie Dunbar.

EVERYBODY'S ALL-AMERICAN

Soundtrack (1988) • Capitol (S) C1-91184 8-10   88
> **Cast:** Nat "King" Cole, Shirley and Lee, Lloyd Price, Jesse Hill, Hank Ballard and the Midnighters, Jaguars, Barbara Lynn, Smiley Lewis, Dietra Hicks and Evan Rogers, Don Gardner and Dee Dee Ford.

EVERYTHING I HAVE IS YOURS

Soundtrack (1952) • MGM (M) E-187 20-25   53
> 10-inch LP.

Soundtrack (1952) • MCA (M) MCA-39081 8-10   86
> Both also have music from *Lili*.
> **Composer:** Johnny Green, Johnny Mercer, Harold Adamson, Burton Lane, Saul Chaplin, others. **Conductor:** Johnny Green, David Rose. **Cast:** Marge and Gower Champion, Monica Lewis, MGM Studio Orchestra. LILI: **Composer:** Bronislau Kaper. **Conductor:** Hans Sommer. **Cast:** Leslie Caron, Mel Ferrer, MGM Studio Orchestra.
> Also see THOSE GLORIOUS MGM MUSICALS.

EVIL DEAD

Soundtrack (1982) • Varese Sarabande (S) STV-81199 15-20   84

Soundtrack [Vol. 2] (1987) • Varese Sarabande (S) STV-81313 12-15   87
> Actual title: *Evil Dead 2*.

Soundtrack (1982) • That's Entertainment (S) TER-1142 8-10   80s
> **Composer:** Joseph LoDuca

EVIL UNDER THE SUN

Studiotrack (1982) • RCA Victor (SE) AYL1-4309 10-12   82
> Although this release displays cover art from the film, the recording contains original big band renditions of Cole Porter songs used as underscoring in the film.
> **Composer:** Cole Porter. **Cast:** Various.

EVITA

Original London Cast (1976) • MCA (S) 1951 10-12   76
> White label. Promotional issue only. Full title: *Excerpts from Evita*.

Original London Cast (1976) • MCA (S) 2-11003 10-20   76
> Original concept album. Two-disc set with booklet.
> **Composer:** Andrew Lloyd Webber, Tim Rice. **Conductor:** Anthony Bowles. **Cast:** Paul Jones, Julie Covington, C.T. Wilkinson, London Philharmonic Orchestra, Tony Christie, Barbara Dickson, Mike Smith, Mike d'Abo, Christopher Neil.

Original London Cast (1978) • MCA (S) 3527 8-10   78

Original London Cast (1978) • MCA (S) 3069 20-30   78
> UK releases.
> **Composer:** Andrew Lloyd Webber, Tim Rice. **Conductor:** Anthony Bowles. **Cast:** Elaine Page, David Essex, Joss Ackland, Siobhan McCarthy, Mark Ryan.

Original New York Cast (1979) • MCA (S) 2-11007 8-10   79
> Two discs. White label. Includes libretto booklet. Promotional issue only.

Original New York Cast (1979) • MCA (S) 2-11007 8-10   79
> Two discs. This opera is based on the life of Eva Peron.
> **Composer:** Andrew Lloyd Webber, Tim Rice. **Conductor:** Rene Weigert. **Cast:** Patti Lupone, Mandy Patinkin, Bob Gunton, Jane Ohringer, Mark Syers.

Studio Cast (1979) • RSO (S) RS-1-3061 10-12   79
> Disco version.
> **Composer:** Andrew Lloyd Webber, Tim Rice. **Cast:** Festival.

EWOK ADVENTURE

Soundtrack • Varese Sarabande (S) STV-81281 40-50   80s
> **Composer:** Peter Bernstein.

EXCALIBUR

Soundtrack (1981) • Island (S) ILPS 19682 8-10   81
> **Composer:** Richard Wagner, Carl Orff. **Conductor:** Sir Adrian Boult, Rafael De Burgos. **Cast:** Nicol Williamson, Nigel Berry, Helen Mirren, Nicholas Clay.

EXCHANGE: see TAMALPIAS EXCHANGE

EXCITING HONG KONG: see HONG KONG

EXODUS

Soundtrack (1960) • RCA Victor (EP) LPC-129...................................... 8-10　　60

Soundtrack (1960) • RCA Victor (M) LOC-1058 .... 8-10　　60

Soundtrack (1960) • RCA Victor (S) LSO-1058................................... 10-12　　60
　Above three have black label with dog on top.

Soundtrack (1960) • RCA Victor (S) LSO-1058...................................... 5-8　　Re

Soundtrack (1960) • RCA Victor (S) AYL1-3872 .... 5-8　　81
　Price for labels *other than* black with dog on top. Includes orange, tan, or black labels with
　dog on side.
　Composer: Ernest Gold. **Conductor:** Ernest Gold.

Studiotrack (1960) • United Artists (M) UAL-3123 .... 8-10　　60

Studiotrack (1960) • United Artists (S) UAS-6123 .... 10-12　　60

Studiotrack (1960) • United Artists (M) UAL-3125 .... 8-10　　61

Studiotrack (1960) • United Artists (S) UAS-6125 .... 10-12　　61

Studiotrack • MCA (S) 39065 .... 8-10　　86
　Composer: Ernest Gold. **Conductor:** Mitchell Powell. **Cast:** Hollywood Studio Orchestra.

Studiotrack • Palace (S) PST-654 5-8
　Cast: Hollywood Transcription Orchestra, Don Raleigh Orchestra.

Studiotrack • Spin-O-Rama (M) MK-3112 5-8
　Full title: *Theme from Exodus and Other Great Themes.*
　Cast: Stradivari Strings.

Studiotrack • Venise (S) 10012 5-8
　Colored vinyl. Full title: *Theme from Exodus and Other Great Films.*
　Cast: Greig McRitchie Orchestra.

Studiotrack (1961) • Vee Jay (M) VJLP-3016................................... 10-12　　61

Studiotrack (1961) • Vee Jay (S) SR-3016 .... 10-15　　61
　Actual title: *Exodus to Jazz.*
　Cast: Eddie Harris.
　Also see APARTMENT

EXORCIST

Soundtrack (1974) • Warner Bros. (S) W-2774.................................... 15-30　　74
　Composer: Krzysztof Penderecki, Mike Oldfield, George Crumb, others. **Conductor:** Leonard
　Slatkin.

EXORCIST II – THE HERETIC

Soundtrack (1977) • Warner Bros. (S) BS-3068.................................. 10-15　　77
　Composer: Ennio Morricone. **Conductor:** Ennio Morricone.

EXPERIMENT IN TERROR

Soundtrack (1962) • RCA Victor (M) LPM-2442 .... 20-25　　62

Soundtrack (1962) • RCA Victor (S) LSP-2442 .... 35-70　　62
　Both picture Lee Remick being attacked from behind.

Soundtrack (1962) • RCA Victor (M) LPM-2442 .... 15-20　　63

Soundtrack (1962) • RCA Victor (S) LSP-2442 .... 20-25　　63
　Both picture two mannequins, but not Lee Remick.
　Composer: Henry Mancini. **Conductor:** Henry Mancini.

EXPLORERS

Soundtrack (1985) • MCA (S) 6148... 8-10　　85
　Composer: Jerry Goldsmith. **Conductor:** Jerry Goldsmith. **Cast:** Robert Palmer, Red 7, Night
　Ranger.

EXPLORING THE UNKNOWN

Studiotrack (1955) • RCA Victor (EP) EPC-1025 .... 20-25　　55
　Three discs.

Studiotrack (1955) • RCA Victor (M) LPC-1025.................................... 30-35　55
　　Composer: Leith Stevens. Conductor: Leith Stevens. Cast: Walter Schurmann Chorus, Paul
　　Frees (narration).

EXPRESSO BONGO
London Cast (1958) • AEI (S) AEI-1110... 8-10　70s

EXTREME PREJUDICE
Soundtrack (1987) • Intermedia/Intrada (S) MAF-7001 .... 8-10　87
　　Composer: Jerry Goldsmith. Conductor: Jerry Goldsmith. Cast: Hungarian State Opera
　　Orchestra.

EYDIE GORME SINGS: see STEVE & EYDIE

EYE OF THE NEEDLE
Soundtrack (1981) • Varese Sarabande (S) STV-81138 .... 8-10　81
Soundtrack (1981) • That's Entertainment (S) TER-1010...................... 8-10　80s
　　UK release.
　　Composer: Miklos Rozsa. Conductor: Miklos Rozsa. Cast: Nürnberg Symphony Orchestra.

EYES OF LAURA MARS
Soundtrack (1978) • Columbia (S) JS-35487 .... 10-12　78
　　Gatefold cover.
　　Composer: Artie Kane. Conductor: Artie Kane. Cast: Barbra Streisand, Odyssey, K.C. and the
　　Sunshine Band, Michalski and Oosterveen, Michael Zager Band.

STEREO

ORIGINAL MUSIC FROM THE MOTION PICTURE SOUND TRACK

BURT LANCASTER
JEAN SIMMONS
IN
ELMER GANTRY

MUSIC COMPOSED AND CONDUCTED BY
ANDRÉ PREVIN

CHRYSLER CORPORATION

presents musical excerpts from

An Evening with Fred Astaire

OCTOBER 17, 1958 · NBC-TV

FREBERG
UNDERGROUND!
SHOW #1

Introducing a ZOWIE! new medium: PAY RADIO!

MUSIC FROM THE SOUND TRACK

FIRE DOWN BELOW

Footloose

Footloose

F

F.I.S.T.
Soundtrack (1978) • United Artists (S) UA-LA-897-H 8-10   79
Composer: Bill Conti. **Conductor:** Bill Conti.

FM
Soundtrack (1978) • MCA (S) MCA2-12000 10-12   78
Soundtrack (1978) • MCA (S) 2-6900 5-10   78
Both are two-disc sets.
Cast: Boston, Jimmy Buffett, Doobie Brothers, Eagles, Dan Fogelberg, Foreigner, Billy Joel, Randy Meisner, Steve Miller, Tom Petty and Heartbreakers, Queen, Boz Scaggs, Bob Seger and Silver Bullet Band, Steely Dan, James Taylor, Joe Walsh, Linda Ronstadt.

Studiotrack (1978) • Springboard (S) SPB-4108 8-10   78
Cast: Studio 78.
Studiotrack (1978) • Pickwick (S) SPC-3647 8-10   78
Full title: *Music from FM.*

F/X
Soundtrack (1986) • Varese Sarabande (S) STV-81276 8-12   86
Composer: Bill Conti.

FABULOUS BAKER BOYS
Soundtrack • GRP (S) GR-2002 8-10
Composer: Dave Grusin. **Cast:** Dave Grusin, Michelle Pfeiffer, Duke Ellington Orchestra, Benny Goodman Orchestra, Earl Palmer Trio.

FABULOUS GENERATION OF MOTION PICTURE THEMES
Studiotrack (1966) • Time (S) TDS 3000 8-12   66
Two discs. Themes from *Tom Jones, Pink Panther, Never on Sunday, Charade, Exodus, Lawrence of Arabia, Days of Wine and Roses, La Dolce Vita, Bye Bye Birdie, Cardinal, Fall of the Roman Empire, America America, Mondo Cane, How the West Was Won, Victors, Longest Day, Breakfast at Tiffany's, West Side Story, Gigi* and *Lolita.*
Composer: Various. **Conductor:** Richard Hayman.

FACADE
Original Cast (1955) • London (M) A-4104 20-30   55
Boxed set with lyrics booklet.
Conductor: Anthony Collins. **Cast:** Dame Edith Sitwell, Peter Pears, English Opera Group Ensemble.

FACE IN THE CROWD
Soundtrack (1957) • Capitol (EP) EAP-1-863 20-40   57
Soundtrack (1957) • Capitol (M) W-872 20-40   57
Composer: Tom Glazer, Budd Schulberg. **Cast:** Andy Griffith, Lee Remick, Walter Matthau, Girls' Trio. (With dialogue.)

FACES
Soundtrack (1968) • Columbia (S) OS-3290 12-15   68
Composer: Jack Ackerman. **Cast:** Jack Ackerman.

FADE OUT, FADE IN
Original Cast (1964) • ABC (M) ABC-OC-3 12-18   64
Original Cast (1964) • ABC (S) ABCS-OCS-3 20-25   64
Gatefold cover.
Composer: Jule Styne, Betty Comden, Adolph Green. **Conductor:** Colin Romoff. **Cast:** Carol Burnett, Jack Cassidy, Dick Patterson, Tina Louise, Tiger Haynes, Lou Jacobi, Mitchell Jason.

FAGGOT

Original Cast (1973) • Blue Pear (M) BP-1008 12-15   73
  Composer: Al Carmines. **Cast:** Peggy Atkinson, Essie Borden, Lou Bullock, Al Carmines, Marilyn Child, Tony Clark, Frank Coppola, Lee Guilliatt, Bruce Hopkins, Julie Kurnitz, Philip Owens, David Pursley, Bill Reynolds, Ira Siff, David Summers.

FAHRENHEIT 451: see FANTASY FILM WORLD OF BERNARD HERRMANN

FALCON AND THE SNOWMAN

Soundtrack (1985) • EMI America (S) SV-17150 8-10   85
  Composer: Pat Metheny, Lyle Mays. **Cast:** Pat Metheny Group, David Bowie.

FALL OF THE HOUSE OF USHER

Soundtrack • American Int. (M) No Number Used 25-30
  Composer: Les Baxter.

FALL OF THE ROMAN EMPIRE

Soundtrack (1964) • Columbia (M) OL-6060 20-25   64
Soundtrack (1964) • Columbia (S) OS-2460 30-35   64
  Composer: Dimitri Tiomkin. **Conductor:** Dimitri Tiomkin.

FAME

Soundtrack (1980) • RSO (S) RPO-1023 10-15   80
  Three-track sampler. Limited edition.
Soundtrack (1980) • RSO (S) RX-1-3080 5-8   80
  Silver label. Gatefold cover.
Soundtrack (1980) • RSO (S) RX-1-3080 5-8   80
  Tan label.
Soundtrack (1980) • RSO (S) 825388-1 5-8   80
  Composer: Michael Gore, Dean Pitchford, others. **Cast:** Irene Cara, Paul McCrane, Linda Clifford, Wade Lassiter, Michael Gore and Steven Margoshes (pianos).

TV Soundtrack (1982) • RCA Victor (S) AFL1-4525 5-8   82
TV Soundtrack (1982) • RCA Victor (S) AFL1-4259 5-8   82
TV Soundtrack (1982) • MGM (S) AFL1-4259 5-8   82
  Full title for above three: *The Kids from Fame.*
  Cast: Debbie Allen, Erica Gimpel, Carlo Imperato, Valerie Landsburg, Gene Anthony Ray, Lori Singer, Lee Curreri.
TV Soundtrack (1983) • RCA Victor (S) APL1-4852 5-8   83
  Full title: *Fame: Rock and Roll World.*
  Cast: Carlo Imperato, others.

FAMILY AFFAIR

Original Cast (1962) • United Artists (M) UAL-4099 20-25   62
Original Cast (1962) • United Artists (S) UAS-5099 35-45   62
  Composer: John Kander, James Goldman, William Goldman. **Conductor:** Stanley Lebowsky. **Cast:** Shelley Berman, Eileen Heckart, Morris Carnovsky, Larry Kert, Bibi Osterwald, Gino Conforti, Jack DeLon, Rita Gardner, Linda Lavin, Alice Nunn, Bill McDonald, Bibi Osterwald, Beryl Towbin.

FAMILY PLOT: see MUSIC FROM HITCHCOCK FILMS

FAMILY WAY

Soundtrack (1967) • Warner Bros. (M) A/B 150-250   66
  10-inch disc. Commercial spots. Made for radio station use only.
Soundtrack (1967) • London (M) M-76007 30-50   67
Soundtrack (1967) • London (S) MS-82007 40-75   67
  Price is for London copies either with or without "For Radio Station Use" sticker on cover. Counterfeit copies can be identified by the poor quality reproduction of the back cover.
  Composer: Paul McCartney.

FAMOUS BROADWAY
Studiotrack • Polydor (S) 24-5003 10-15
Music from *Hair, Fiddler on the Roof, Man of La Mancha* and *Company*.
Conductor: Arthur Fiedler. **Cast:** Boston Pops Orchestra.

FANCY FREE
Original Cast • Capitol (M) P 8136 12-15
Also contains music from *Rodeo*.
Studiotrack • Decca (M) DL-6023 55-60
Composer: Leonard Bernstein. **Conductor:** Joseph Levine. RODEO: **Composer:** Aaron
Copland. **Conductor:** Joseph Levine.

FANNY
Original Cast (1954) • RCA Victor (EP) EOC-1015 10-15   54
Three discs.
Original Cast (1954) • RCA Victor (M) LOC-1015 10-15   54
Front cover has "An Original Cast Recording" written in a yellow triangle on top left corner.
Black label, with "Long Play" at bottom.
Original Cast (1954) • RCA Victor (M) LOC-1015 8-10   59
Original Cast (1954) • RCA Victor (SE) LSO-1015 10-15   59
Front cover on both have "An Original Cast Recording" at top left. Black label, with either
"Mono" or "Stereo," depending on issue.
Original Cast (1954) • RCA Victor (M) LOC-1015 5-8   Re
Original Cast (1954) • RCA Victor (SE) LSO-1015 5-8   Re
For either orange or tan labels.
Composer: Harold Rome. **Conductor:** Lehman Engel. **Cast:** Ezio Pinza, Walter Slezak,
Florence Henderson, Nejla Ates, Mohammed El Bakkar, Edna Preston, Gerald Price, Lloyd
Reese, William Tabbert.
Studio Cast (1955) • Heritage (M) H-0055 45-55   55
10-inch LP. Dialogue and vocals by Harold Rome.
Composer: Harold Rome. **Cast:** Harold Rome.
Soundtrack (1961) • Warner Bros. (M) W-1416 10-15   61
Soundtrack (1961) • Warner Bros. (S) WS-1416 15-20   61
Composer: Harold Rome. **Conductor:** Morris Stoloff. **Cast:** Leslie Caron, Maurice Chevalier,
Charles Boyer, Horst Buchholz.

FANNY BRICE: STORY IN SONG
Studio Cast (1958) • MGM (M) E-3704 12-15   58
Studio Cast (1958) • MGM (S) SE-3704 15-18   58
Cast: Kaye Ballard.

FANNY HILL
Soundtrack (1971) • Canyon (S) S-7700 12-15   71
Composer: Clay Pitts. **Conductor:** Clay Pitts. **Cast:** Oven, Frank Thomas.

FANTASIA
Soundtrack (1940) • Disneyland/Buena Vista (M) WDS-101 15-18   57
Soundtrack (1940) • Disneyland/Buena Vista (S) WDX-101e 25-30   57
Soundtrack (1940) • Buena Vista (S) STER-101 15-20   Re
Above three are three-disc sets with gatefold covers and color booklets.
Conductor: Leopold Stokowski.
Soundtrack (1940) • Disneyland (M) WDL-4101 15-20   61
Also has music from *Night on Bald Mountain*.
Conductor: Leopold Stokiwski. **Cast:** Philadelphia Orchestra.
Studiotrack (1982) • Buena Vista (S) V-104 15-20   82
Digital recording.
Conductor: Irwin Kostal.
Studiotrack • RCA Victor (S) VCS-7079 8-12
Conductor: Eugene Ormandy, Robert Shaw, Arthur Fiedler.
Also see PETER AND THE WOLF

FANTASTIC FILM MUSIC OF ALBERT GLASSER, VOL.1
Soundtrack • Starlog (S) SR-1001 8-10   79
    Music from *The Amazing Colossal Man, The Buckskin Lady, Beginning of the End, The Cyclops, Top of the World, The Cisco Kid, Big Town* and *The Boy and the Pirates.*
    Composer: Albert Glasser. **Conductor:** Albert Glasser.

FANTASTIC FOUR #1
Studio Cast (1966) • Golden (S) SLP-185 100-175   66
    Includes *Fantastic Four* comic book, Marvel's first-ever comic to go into second printing and Marvel's first comic book/record. Performance follows comic script with sound effects and music

FANTASTIC PLASTIC MACHINE
Soundtrack (1969) • Epic (S) BN-26469 20-25   69
    Composer: Harry Betts. **Conductor:** Harry Betts.

FANTASTICKS
Original Cast (1960) • MGM (M) E-3872 10-15   60
Original Cast (1960) • MGM (S) SE-3872 15-20   60
    Standard cover.
Original Cast (1960) • MGM (M) E-3872 5-8   61
Original Cast (1960) • MGM (S) SE-3872 8-10   61
    White gatefold cover.
Original Cast (1960) • MGM (S) SE-3872 8-10   Re
    Black gatefold cover.
Original Cast (1960) • That's Entertainment (S) TER-1099 8-10   80s
    UK release.
    Composer: Harvey Schmidt, Tom Jones. **Conductor:** Julian Stein. **Cast:** Kenneth Nelson, Jerry Orbach, Rita Gardner, William Larsen, Hugh Thomas.

FANTASY FILM WORLD OF BERNARD HERRMANN
Studiotrack • London (S) SPC-44207 15-20
    Music from *Journey to the Center of the Earth, The 7th Voyage of Sinbad, The Day the Earth Stood Still* and *Fahrenheit 451*.
    Composer: Bernard Herrmann. **Conductor:** Bernard Herrmann. **Cast:** National Philharmonic Orchestra.
Soundtrack • MFSL (S) 240 15-25   95

FANTASY FILM WORLD OF HANS J. SALTER
Soundtrack • Medallion (M) ML-312 30-40   82
    Original music from *The Golden Horde, The Black Shield of Falworth* and *The Prince Who Was a Thief*.
    Composer: Hans J. Salter. **Conductor:** Hans J. Salter.

FANTASY – SPACE
TV Soundtrack • CBS EX Cue (M) XTV 133214 10-15
    Music cues from various TV shows and Fred Steiner's original music for the *Twilight Zone* episode *A Hundred Yards over the Rim*.
    Composer: Fred Steiner, William Josephs, Jerry Goldsmith.

FAR FROM THE MADDING CROWD
Soundtrack (1967) • MGM (M) 1E-11 8-10   67
Soundtrack (1967) • MGM (S) S1E-11 10-30   67
    Composer: Richard Rodney Bennett. **Conductor:** Marcus Dods. **Cast:** Isla Cameron, Trevor Lucas.

FAR HORIZONS – THE WESTERN FILM SCORES OF HANS J. SALTER
Soundtrack • Medallion (M) ML-313 8-10   82
    Music from *Battle of Apache Pass, Walk the Proud Land, Man Without a Star, Bend of the River, The Spoilers, Day of the Badman, The Tall Stranger, Untamed Frontier, The Oklahoman, Four Guns to the Border* and *The Horizons*.
    Composer: Hans J. Salter. **Conductor:** Hans J. Salter.

FAR NORTH

Soundtrack (1988) • Sugar Hill (S) SH-8502 8-10   88
   Cast: Red Clay Ramblers.

FAR OUT MAN

Soundtrack (1990) • Chameleon (S) D1-74829............................ 10-15   90
   Cast: DV8, Kool Moe Dee, Bobby Dee, Bobby Taylor & Carolyn Majors, Bonedaddys, Samantha Fox, Tommy Chong, Don Dokken.

FAR PAVILIONS

Soundtrack (1983) • Chrysalis (S) FV-41464 8-15   83
   Composer: Carl Davis. Conductor: Carl Davis.

FAREWELL, MY LOVELY

Soundtrack (1975) • United Artists (S) LT-556 10-12   75
Soundtrack (1975) • United Artists (S) UA-LA556-G 8-10   75
   Composer: David Shire. Conductor: David Shire. Cast: Artie Kane (piano), Dick Nash (trombone), Justin Gordon (clarinet, saxophone), others.

FAREWELL TO ARMS

Soundtrack (1957) • Capitol (EP) EDM-918 15-25   57
Soundtrack (1957) • Capitol (M) W-918 35-45   57
   Composer: Mario Nascimbene. Conductor: Franco Ferrara.

FAREWELL TO THE KING

Soundtrack (1989) • Varese Sarabande (S) VS-5216 10-15   89
   Composer: Basil Poledouris. Conductor: Basil Poledouris.

FARMER

Soundtrack • HM (S) 1001 40-60   76
  Promotion issue only.
Soundtrack • Red Earth (S) 44039.................................. 40-50   77
  Also has three Gene Clark tracks from 1971 film *The American Dreamer.*
   Composer: Hugo Montenegro. Cast: Hugo Montenegro, Gene Clark.

FASHIONS OF 1934: see HOORAY FOR HOLLYWOOD

FAST BREAK

Soundtrack (1979) • Motown (S) M7-915-R1 8-10   79
   Composer: David Shire, James DiPasquale, Carol Connors. Conductor: David Shire, James DiPasquale. Cast: Billy Preston, Syreeta.

FAST TIMES AT RIDGEMONT HIGH

Soundtrack (1982) • Full Moon/Island (S) 982...................... 15-25   82
  Six-track picture disc sampler. Promotional issue only.
Soundtrack (1982) • Full Moon/Asylum (S) 4-60158 10-12   82
  Two discs.
Soundtrack (1982) • Full Moon/Island (S) 99246.................... 5-10   82
  Single disc.
   Cast: Jackson Browne, Jimmy Buffett, Don Felder, Go-Go's, Louise Goffin, Sammy Hagar, Don Henley, Gerard McMahon, Graham Nash, Oingo Boingo, Palmer-Jost, Poco, Quarterflash, Ravyns, Timothy B. Schmit, Stevie Nicks, Billy Squier, Donna Summer, Joe Walsh.

FASTEST GUITAR ALIVE

Soundtrack (1968) • MGM (M) E-4475.............................. 10-20   68
Soundtrack (1968) • MGM (S) SE-4475 15-30   68
Soundtrack (1968) • MCA (S) 1437.................................. 8-10   86
   Composer: Roy Orbison, Bill Dees. Conductor: Fred Karger. Cast: Roy Orbison.

FATAL ATTRACTION (1980)

Soundtrack (1980) • Fast Fire (S) FST-7500....................... 20-30   85
  Original film title was *Head On.*
   Composer: Max Hitchcock, Barry Coates, Rich Eames. Cast: Max Hitchcock, Barry Coates, Rich Eames.

FATAL ATTRACTION (1987)
Soundtrack (1987) • GNP/Crescendo (S) GNPS-8011............................ 8-10   87
> **Composer:** Maurice Jarre. **Conductor:** Maurice Jarre.

FATAL BEAUTY
Soundtrack (1987) • Atlantic (S) 81809-1................................ 8-10   87
> **Composer:** Harold Faltermeyer, others. **Cast:** Donna Allen, Le Vert, Madam X, Miki Howard, Shannon, Debbie Gibson, War, System.

FATHOM
Soundtrack (1967) • 20th Century-Fox (M) TFM-4195 20-30   67
Soundtrack (1967) • 20th Century-Fox (S) TFS-4195 30-50   67
> **Composer:** John Dankworth. **Conductor:** John Dankworth.

FAVORITE THEMES FROM MASTERPIECE THEATRE (1971-1981)
TV Soundtrack (1971-81) • Gloucester (S) GPM T10 5-8   81

FAWLTY TOWERS – SECOND SITTING
TV Soundtrack (1981) • BBC (SE) 22405 10-20   81
> From the episodes *The Rat* and *The Builders*.
> **Cast:** John Cleese, Prunella Scales, Connie Booth, Andrew Sachs.

FEAR NO EVIL
Soundtrack (1981) • Web (S) LP-106.. 8-12   81
> **Composer:** Frank Laloggia, David Spear. **Conductor:** Frank Laloggia.

FEATHERTOP
TV Soundtrack (1961) • No Label Used (M) No Number Used......... 100-125   61
> Promotional issue, made by Mars Candy Co. for ABC, October 19, 1961.
TV Soundtrack (1961) • No Label Used (M) LB 2931/32 20-25   Re
> **Composer:** Mary Rodgers, Martin Charnin. **Conductor:** Richard Priborsky. **Cast:** Jane Powell, Hugh O'Brian, Hans Conried, Cathleen Nesbitt.

FEDORA
Soundtrack (1978) • Varese Sarabande (S) STV-81108 8-10   79
> **Composer:** Miklos Rozsa. **Conductor:** Miklos Rozsa.

FEDS
Soundtrack (1988) • GNP/Crescendo (S) GNPS-8014........................... 8-10   88
> **Composer:** Randy Edelman. **Cast:** Albert Collins, Roy Gaines, Barry Goldberg, Electric Boys, Joe Louis Walker.

FEELING GOOD WITH ANNIE
Studio Cast • Columbia (S) CC-38362 10-12
> **Conductor:** Brian Mann. **Cast:** William Woodson (narration), Robin Ignico, Brenda Baker, Bill Martin, Al Chalk.

FELIX THE CAT
TV Soundtrack (1959) • Cricket (M) CR-28 20-25   59
> **Composer:** Win Sharples. **Cast:** Jack Mercer.

FELLINI SATYRICON
Soundtrack (1969) • United Artists (S) UAS-5208 15-35   70
> **Composer:** Nino Rota. **Conductor:** Nino Rota.

FELLINI'S GINGER AND FRED
Soundtrack (1986) • Varese Sarabande (S) STV-81277 8-10   86
> **Composer:** Nicola Plovani.

FELLINI'S ROMA
Soundtrack (1972) • United Artists (S) UA-LA052-F............................. 20-30   72
> **Composer:** Nino Rota. **Conductor:** Carlo Savina.

FEMALE ANIMAL
Soundtrack (1970s) • Canyon (S) LP-7702 50-75   70s
     Composer: Clay Pitts, Don Payne, Rick Hitchcock. **Conductor:** Clay Pitts, Don Payne, Rick Hitchcock.

FEMALE PRISONER
Soundtrack (1969) • Columbia (S) OS-3320 15-35   69
     Composer: Anton Webern, Gustav Mahler, Luciano Berio. **Conductor:** Pierre Boulez, Leonard Bernstein.

FEMININE FORUM
Original Radio Cast • Mark 56 (M) 578.. 15-20   70s
   Picture disc.
     Cast: Bill Ballance.

FERRY CROSS THE MERSEY
Soundtrack (1965) • United Artists (M) UAL-3387 15-20   65
Soundtrack (1965) • United Artists (S) UAS-6387 25-35   65
     Composer: Gerry Marsden. **Conductor:** George Martin. **Cast:** Gerry and the Pacemakers.

FESTIVAL
Original Cast (1974) • Original Cast (S) OC-7916 8-10   74
     Composer: Stephen Downs, Randal Martin. **Conductor:** David Spear. **Cast:** Bill Hutton, Maureen McNamara, Tina Johnson, Michael Magnusen, Lindy Nisbet, Roxann Parker, Michael Rupert, Leon Stewart, Robin Taylor, John Windsor.

FEUDIN' RHYTHM / HOEDOWN
Soundtrack • RCA Victor (EP) Number Not Known 20-25   50s
   Both are Columbia movies starring Eddy Arnold. Verification is pending.
     Cast: Eddy Arnold.

FIBBER McGEE AND MOLLY
Original Radio Cast • Golden Age (M) 5011 8-10   78
     Cast: Jim and Marion Jordan.

FIDDLER ON THE ROOF
Original Cast (1964) • RCA Victor (M) LOC-1093 5-8   64
Original Cast (1964) • RCA Victor (S) LSO-1093 6-12   64
   Credits are on front cover.
Original Cast (1964) • RCA Victor (S) LSO-1093 8-10   Re
   Credits are on back cover.
     Composer: Jerry Bock, Sheldon Harnick. **Conductor:** Milton Greene. **Cast:** Zero Mostel, Maria Karnilova, Beatrice Arthur, Bert Convy, Leonard Frey, Sue Babel, Tanya Everett, Michael Granger, Paul Lipson, Joanna Merlin, Julia Migenes, Austin Pendleton, Carol Sawyer.
London Studio Cast • Pickwick (S) SPC-3291 10-12   64
     Composer: Jerry Bock, Sheldon Harnick. **Cast:** Gerry Grant, Rita Williams.
Original Israeli Cast (1965) • Columbia (M) OL-6650 10-12   65
Original Israeli Cast (1965) • Columbia (S) OS-3050 10-12   65
   Sung in Hebrew. All text and credits appear in both English and Hebrew.
     Composer: Jerry Bock, Sheldon Harnick. **Conductor:** Izhak Graziani. **Cast:** Shmuel Rudenski, Lya Dulitzkaya, Alina Stranitska, Albert Cohen, Etty Grottes.
Original London Cast (1967) • CBS (M) 70030 20-25   67
Original London Cast (1967) • CBS (S) 70030 25-35   67
   UK release. Same number used for both mono and stereo.
Original London Cast (1967) • Columbia (S) SX-30742 8-12   67
   US release.
     Composer: Jerry Bock, Sheldon Harnick. **Conductor:** Gareth Davies. **Cast:** Topol, Miriam Karlin, Paul Whitsun-Jones, Cynthia Grenville, Linda Gardner.
Original German Cast • London (S) SW-99470 10-12   64
   UK release.
     Composer: Jerry Bock, Sheldon Harnick. **Conductor:** Dailbor Brazda. **Cast:** Shmuel Rudenski, Lilly Towska, Eva Berthold.

German Cast • Preiser (S) SPR-3200 10-12   64
  Austrian release.
    Composer: Jerry Bock, Sheldon Harnick. **Conductor:** Johannes Fehring. **Cast:** Yossi Yadin, Lya
    Dulizkaya, Gretl Elb, Peter Frohlich, Eva Pilz, Sylvia Anders.
Studio Cast • MGM (M) LAT 10,013 5-10   65
  Full title: *Fiddler on the Roof Goes Latin.*
    Cast: Joe Quijano.
Studio Cast (1968) • London (S) SP-44121 8-10   68
  Phase 4 stereo.
Studio Cast (1968) • London (S) SMAS 93020 8-10   68
  Phase 4 stereo. Capitol Record Club issue.
    Composer: Sheldon Harnick, Jerry Bock. **Conductor:** Stanley Black. **Cast:** Robert Merrill, Molly
    Picon, Jacob Kalich, Robert Bowman, Andy Cole, Margaret Eaves, Barbara Moore, Sylvia King,
    Eddie Lester, Margaret Savage, Mary Thomas, James Tullett, Patricia Whitmore, London
    Festival Orchestra and Chorus.
Studio Cast • Diplomat (M) D 2349 8-12
Studio Cast • Diplomat (S) DS 2349 8-12
    Conductor: Al Goodman. **Cast:** Phillip Golden, Martha Garry, Al Goodman and His Orchestra.
Soundtrack (1971) • United Artists (S) UAS-10900 10-12   71
  Two-disc set. Includes six-page booklet..
    Composer: Jerry Bock, Sheldon Harnick. **Conductor:** John Williams. **Cast:** Topol, Norma
    Crane, Leonard Frey, Molly Picon, Paul Mann.
Studiotrack (1964) • Capitol (M) T-2216 10-15   64
Studiotrack (1964) • Capitol (S) ST-2216 15-20   64
    Cast: Cannonball Adderley.
Studiotrack (1965) • RCA Victor (M) LPM 2964 8-12   65
Studiotrack (1965) • RCA Victor (S) LSP 2964 8-12   65
  Full title: *Music from the Broadway Hit Fiddler on the Roof.*
    Cast: Claus Ogerman and His Orchestra.
Studiotrack (1965) • RCA Victor (M) LPM 3363 8-12   65
Studiotrack (1965) • RCA Victor (S) LSP 3363 8-12   65
  Full title: *Gypsy Violin of Emery Deutsch Playing Selections from Fiddler on the Roof.*
    Cast: Emery Deutsch.
Studiotrack • Columbia (M) OL-6610 8-10   60s
Studiotrack • Columbia (S) OS-3010 8-12   60s
Studiotrack • Columbia (S) PST-3010 8-10   Re
  Full title: *Herschel Bernardi Sings Fiddler on the Roof.*
    Conductor: Peter Matz. **Cast:** Herschel Bernardi.
Studiotrack • Capitol Special Products (Q) QL-6765 5-10   70s
    Conductor: Arthur Greenslade. **Cast:** Hollywood Pops Orchestra.
Studiotrack • Disneyland (S) STER-1339 5-10
    Conductor: Camarata. **Cast:** Camarata, Mike Sammes Orchestra.
Studiotrack • MMO (S) 1037 5-10
    Conductor: William Harrison. **Cast:** Music Minus One Orchestra.

FIELD OF DREAMS
Soundtrack (1989) RCA/Novus (S) 3060-1 8-10   89
    Composer: James Horner. **Conductor:** James Horner.

50th ANNIVERSARY OF GEORGE JESSEL IN SHOW BUSINESS
Original Cast • Cabot (M) 1001 20-40
  Carnegie Hall show.
    Composer: George Jessel. **Cast:** Gus Edwards, Eddie Foy, Eddie Leonard, Anna Held, Sam
    Bernard, George M. Cohan, Eddie Cantor, Al Jolson.

50th ANNIVERSARY SHOW: see GENERAL MOTORS' 50th ANNIVERSARY

50 GREAT SHOWTUNES
Studio Cast • Brigade (S) P-1311S 10-20
  Two discs. Cast is not credited.

50 HAPPY YEARS OF DISNEY FAVORITES
Soundtrack • Disneyland (S) STER 3513 8-10
Two discs. With gatefold cover and booklet.

50 YEARS OF BROADWAY MUSIC
Studiotrack • Musicor/Springboard (S) MU3-3801 8-15
Boxed, three-disc set.

50 YEARS OF FILM
Soundtrack • Warner Bros. (S) PRO-573 20-25   73
Two discs. With gatefold cover and booklet. Full title: *50 Years of Film, All Talking-All Singing-All Rocking*. Includes excerpts from both Warner Bros. album sets that follow (#2736 & #2737).
Promotional issue only.
Cast: Elizabeth Taylor, Richard Burton, Humphrey Bogart, Alfonso Bedoya, James Dean, Bugs Bunny (Mel Blanc), Barbra Streisand, James Cagney, Ingrid Bergman, Dooley Wilson.

Soundtrack • Warner Bros. (S) 3XX-2736 15-20   73
Full title: *50 Years of Film Music (1923 - 1973)*. Boxed, three-disc set with slip-case. Includes 28-page booklet. (With dialogue.)

Soundtrack • Warner Bros. (M) 3XX-2737 15-20   73
Boxed, three-disc set with slip-case. Includes 60-page booklet. Completely different than 3XX-2736. (With dialogue.)
Conductor: Erich Wolfgang Korngold, Max Steiner, Franz Waxman, Dimitri Tiomkin, Alex North, others. **Cast:** Ginger Rogers, Louis Armstrong, Mary Martin, Frank Sinatra, Al Jolson, Ruby Keeler, Dick Powell, James Melton, Doris Day, Harry James, Joan Blondell, Judy Garland, James Cagney, Frances Langford, Johnny "Scat" Davis, others.

50 YEARS OF FILM MUSIC: see 50 YEARS OF FILM

50 YEARS OF MOVIE MUSIC: FROM FLICKERS TO WIDE SCREEN
Studiotrack (1959) • Decca (S) DL-79079 8-10   59
Conductor: Jack Shaindlain. **Cast:** Jack Shaindlain & Orchestra.

55 DAYS AT PEKING
Soundtrack (1963) • Columbia (M) CL-2028 20-35   63
Soundtrack (1963) • Columbia (S) OS-8828 25-60   63
Composer: Dimitri Tiomkin. **Conductor:** Dimitri Tiomkin. **Cast:** Andy Williams.

51 GREATEST MOTION PICTURE FAVORITES
Studiotrack (1964) • Music Voice (M) MM-2009 10-20   64
Studiotrack (1964) • Music Voice (S) MS-3009 15-25   64
Composer: Various. **Cast:** Vinnie Bell, his guitar and orchestra.

52 PICK UP
Soundtrack (1986) • Varese Sarabande (S) STV 81300 8-10   86
Composer: Chang.

FIGHTER
Soundtrack (1952) • Decca (M) DL-5415 60-75   52
10-inch LP.
Composer: Vicente Gómez. **Cast:** Vicente Gómez (guitar solos).

FILM CLASSICS
Studiotrack • RCA Victor (S) ARL 1-4020 8-10   81
Classical music as used in films.

FILM CLASSICS: TAKE 2
Studiotrack • RCA Victor (S) XRL 1-4316 8-10   82
Classical music from *Four Seasons*, *Victor Victoria*, *Cannery Row*, *Excalibur*, *Gallipoli* and *Caligula*.

FILM FAME
Studiotrack (1967) Project 3 (S) PR-5013SD 10-15   67
> Music from *To Sir With Love, For a Few Dollars More, When the World Is Ready, In the Heat of the Night* and others.
> **Cast:** Enoch Light and the Light Brigade.

FILM FAME MARVELOUS MOVIE THEMES
Studiotrack • Project 3 (S) CST 178... 8-12
> Music from *Camelot, To Sir with Love, Gone with the Wind, More Than a Miracle, The Long Duel, In the Heat of the Night, Wait Until Dark, Live for Life* and *The Bobo.*

FILM FESTIVAL AT CANNES (EUROPE'S FAMOUS MOTION PICTURE THEMES)
Studiotrack (1956) • Mercury (M) MG-20188.. 12-15   56
> **Cast:** Eddie Barclay and Orchestra.

FILM FESTIVAL – 16 GREATEST MOVIE THEMES.
Soundtrack (1969) • Colgems (S) 116 15-20   69
> Music from *The Night of the Generals, Lord Jim, Behold a Pale Horse, The Victors, Murderer's Row* and others.

FILM MUSIC
Soundtrack [Vol. 2] • WA (S) WA-15.. 30-40   Re
> Original soundtrack recordings from *Mister Roberts, Travels with My Aunt, Two Minute Warning, Frenzy, Yakuza, Bananas, Master Gunfighter, Conversation, Hunting Party, War Wagon, Last Safari, Full of Life, Seven Faces of Dr. Lao, John Goldfarb Please Come Home, World's Greatest Athlete, the 3:10 to Yuma, Right Cross, Wrong Man, Islands in the Stream* and *The Comancheros.*
> **Composer:** Franz Waxman, Tony Hatch, Charles Fox, Ron Goodwin, Dave Grusin, Marvin Hamlisch, Lalo Schifirin, David Shire, Riz Ortolani, Dimitri Tiomkin, John Dankworth, George Duning, Leigh Harline, John Williams, Marvin Hamlisch, David Raksin, Bernard Herrmann, Jerry Goldsmith, Elmer Bernstein. **Cast:** Franz Waxman Orchestra, Tony Hatch Orchestra, Ron Goodwin Orchestra, Dave Grusin Orchestra, Marvin Hamlisch Orchestra & Chorus, Lalo Schifrin Orchestra, Riz Ortolani Orchestra, Mike Callahan, John Dankworth Orchestra, Judy Holliday, Shirley MacLaine, Frankie Laine, David Raksin Orchestra, Bernard Herrmann Orchestra, Jerry Goldsmith Orchestra, Elmer Bernstein Orchestra.

Studiotrack [Vol. 1] (1987) • Virgin Movie Music (S) 90674-1 8-10   87
Studiotrack [Vol. 2] (1988) • Virgin Movie Music (S) 90901-1 8-10   88
> **Composer:** Ennio Morricone. **Conductor:** Ennio Morricone. **Cast:** Ennio Morricone and His Orchestra.
> Also see MRS. SOFFEL

FILM MUSIC BY ALEX NORTH
Studiotrack • Citadel (S) CT 6023 20-25
> **Conposer:** Alex North.

FILM MUSIC BY MANCINI
Soundtrack (1973) • RCA Camden (S) ADL2-0293............................... 10-15   73
> Two discs.
> **Composer:** Henry Mancini. **Conductor:** Henry Mancini.

FILM MUSIC FROM FRANCE
Soundtrack (1962) • Philips (M) PHM-200-071...................................... 15-20   62
Soundtrack (1962) • Philips (S) PHS 600-071....................................... 20-30   62
> Music from 12 French films.
> **Composer:** Georges Delerue, Mikis Theodorakis, Michel Legrand, T. Albinoni. **Conductor:** Georges Delerue, Mikis Theodorakis, Michel Legrand, T. Albinoni.

FILM MUSIC ITALIAN STYLE
Studiotrack (1968) • Sunset (M) 1188 6-12   68
Soundtrack (1968) • Sunset (S) 5188 5-10   68
> Music from *La Dolce Vita, 8½, Ecco, Malamondo, La Strada, Mondo Cane* and others.
> **Cast:** Sunset Strings.

FILM MUSIC OF BRONISLAU KAPER
Soundtrack • Delos (S) F-25421 15-20   75
Music from *San Francisco, Mutiny on the Bounty, Lili, The Glass Slipper, Butterfield 8, Auntie Mame, The Chocolate Soldier, Invitation, The Brothers Karamazov, Green Door, The Swan* and *Lord Jim.*
Composer: Bronislau Kaper.

FILM MUSIC OF DIMITRI TIOMKIN
Soundtrack • Cinema (M) LP-8012...................... 50-60
Also has music from *Town Without Pity, Night Passage* and *Hotel De Paree.*
Composer: Dimitri Tiomkin.

FILM MUSIC OF HANS J. SALTER
Soundtrack • Tony Thomas Productions (M) TT-HS-1/2 30-40
Two discs. Limited edition, with soundtracks of *The Ghost of Frankenstein, The Magnificent Doll, Bend of the River* and *Against All Flags.*
Composer: Hans J. Salter.

FILM MUSIC OF HERBERT STOTHART
Soundtrack • Tony Thomas Productions (M) TT-ST 1/2....................... 30-45   80
Two discs. Music from *Mutiny on the Bounty, David Copperfield, Anna Karenina* and *Viva Villa!*

FILM MUSIC OF HUGO FRIEDHOFER
Soundtrack (1972) • Delos (S) DEL-25420 10-15   79
Music from *Von Richtofen and Brown* and *Private Parts.*
Composer: Hugo Friedhofer. **Conductor:** Hugo Friedhofer, Kurt Graunke.

FILM MUSIC OF MAX STEINER: see BIRD OF PARADISE

FILM MUSIC OF MIKLOS ROZSA
Soundtrack (1966) • Citadel (M) CT-MR-1 25-30   78
Actual title: *The Power/Sodom and Gomorrah.* Outtakes and previously unreleased tracks from both films.
Studiotrack • Capitol (S) ST-2837 15-25   67
Actual title: *Miklos Rozsa Conducts His Great Film Music.*
Studiotrack • Angel (S) 36063............................ 10-20   Re
Studiotrack • Cloud Nine (S) 7013 5-10   Re
Music from *Quo Vadis, King of Kings* and *Ben-Hur.*
Composer: Miklos Rozsa. **Conductor:** Miklos Rozsa.

FILM ON FILM
Studiotrack (1966) • Project 3 (S) PR-5005SD.................... 10-15   66
Composer: Enoch Light and the Light Brigade.

FILM SPECTACULAR
Studiotrack [Vol. 1] (1964) • London (S) Number Not Known 15-25   64
Studiotrack [Vol. 1] (1964) • London (S) SP-44025 15-25   64
Studiotrack [Vol. 2] (1964) • London (M) LL-3327 15-25   64
Studiotrack [Vol. 3] (1964) • London (S) SP-44078 15-25
Studiotrack [Vol. 4] (1972) • London (S) SP-44173 15-25   72
Full title: *Film Spectacular – The Epic.*
Themes from *Stagecoach, For Whom the Bell Tolls, Doctor Zhivago, Ben-Hur, 2001: A Space Odyssey, The Sea Hawk, The Alamo* and *Patton.*

Studiotrack [Vol. 5] (1964) • London (S) SP-44225 15-25   75
Full title: *Film Spectacular – The Love Story*. Music from *Casablanca, A Man and a Woman, Intermezzo, Blood & Sand, La Strada, Love Story* and *Gone with the Wind*.
Studiotrack [Vol. 6] (1976) • London (S) SP-44248 15-25   76
Full title: *Film Spectacular – World War II*. Music from *The Longest Day, Suite from Mrs. Miniver, Spitfire Prelude and Fugue (The First of the Few), Western Approaches, Bridge on the River Kwai, Guns of Navarone, Great Escape* and *Victory at Sea*.
Composer: Various. **Conductor:** Stanley Black. **Cast:** London Festival Orchestra and Chorus.
Studiotrack • Diplomat (M) 2305 8-12
Music from *Charade, The Cardinal* and *The Victors*.
Conductor: Miklos Andriano. **Cast:** Soundtrack Orchestra.

FILM THEMES OF ALFRED NEWMAN
Soundtrack • Capricorn (M) CP-1286... 25-35   74
Music from *12 O'Clock High, Mark of Zorro, President's Lady, A Man Called Peter, Razor's Edge* and nine other films.
Composer: Alfred Newman.

FILM THEMES OF ERNEST GOLD
Studiotrack (1962) • London (M) LL-3320 25-30   62
Studiotrack (1962) • London (S) PS-320 40-50   62
Music from *Pressure Point, Saddle Pals, Young Philadelphians, A Child Is Waiting, The Last Sunset* and others.
Composer: Ernest Gold. **Conductor:** Ernest Gold. **Cast:** Ernest Gold and His Orchestra.

FILMUSIC SCENE
Studiotrack (1960s) • Columbia Special Products (S) CSS 521 8-10   60s
Full title: *Zenith Salutes the Filmusic Scene*.
Cast: Andy Williams, Andre Kostelanetz, Jerry Vale, Eydie Gorme, Tony Bennett, Jane Morgan, Robert Goulet, Barbra Streisand.

FILMS OF ALFRED HITCHCOCK
Studiotrack • Varese Sarabande (S) 704 250.. 8-12   80s
Cast: Utah Symphony Orchestra.

FILMS OF RUSS COLUMBO
Soundtrack • Golden Legends (S) 2000/2.. 8-10
Soundtracks from *Broadway Thru a Keyhole* (1933), *Moulin Rouge* (1933) and *Wake Up and Dream* (1934).
Composer: Russ Columbo.

FINAL COMEDOWN
Soundtrack (1972) • Blue Note (S) BST-84415...................................... 25-30   72
Composer: Wade Marcus. **Conductor:** Wade Marcus. **Cast:** Grant Green.

FINAL CONFLICT
Soundtrack (1981) • Varese Sarabande (S) STV-81272......................... 8-10   84
Composer: Jerry Goldsmith. **Conductor:** Jerry Goldsmith. **Cast:** National Philharmonic Orchestra.

FINAL COUNTDOWN
Soundtrack (1980) • Casablanca (S) NBLP-7232 25-30   80
Composer: John Scott. **Conductor:** John Scott.

FINAL EXAM
Soundtrack (1981) • AEI (S) AEI-3105... 8-10   81
Composer: Gary Scott. **Conductor:** Gary Scott.

FINAL OPTION
Soundtrack (1983) • Varese Sarabande (S) STV 81188 8-10   83
Composer: Roy Budd. **Conductor:** Roy Budd.

FINE MESS
Soundtrack (1986) • Motown (S) 6180 8-10   86
   Cast: Temptations, Mary Jane Girls, Chico De Barge, Henry Mancini, Smokey Robinson, Nick Jameson, Keith and Darryl, Los Lobos, Christine McVie.

FINEST HOURS
Soundtrack (1964) • Mercury (M) MGP2-104 25-30   64
   Two discs.
Soundtrack (1964) • Mercury (S) SRP2-604 30-35   64
   Composer: Ron Grainer. **Cast:** Orson Welles, Pat Wymark. Narration by Welles and Wymark, with voices of Sir Winston Churchill, Neville Chamberlain and Franklin D. Roosevelt.

FINGS AIN'T WOT THEY USED T' BE
Original London Cast • That's Entertainment (S) TER-1047 8-12   80s
   UK release.
   Composer: Lionel Bart.

FINIAN'S RAINBOW
Original Cast (1947) • Columbia (EP) A-1520 15-20   48
Original Cast (1947) • Columbia (M) ML-4062 12-18   48
   Green label. Yellow cover, with no photo.
Original Cast (1947) • Columbia (M) OL-4062 8-12   Re
   Grey label. Two covers exist; pink one pictures Ella Logan, white one pictures Ella Logan and David Wayne.
Original Cast (1947) • Columbia (SE) OS-2080 8-12   63
Original Cast (1947) • Columbia (SE) CS-2080 8-10   Re
   Composer: Burton Lane, E.Y. Harburg. **Conductor:** Ray Charles. **Cast:** Ella Logan, Donald Richards, David Wayne, Delores Martin, Sonny Terry, Alan Gilbert, Jerry Laws, Lorenzo Fuller, Maude Simmons, Lewis Sharp, Lyn Murray Singers.
Original Revival Cast (1960) • RCA Victor (M) LOC-1057 10-12   60
Original Revival Cast (1960) • RCA Victor (S) LSO-1057 12-15   60
   Cover shows rainbow leading to a pot of gold.
Original Revival Cast (1960) • RCA Victor (M) LOC-1057 8-10   60
Original Revival Cast (1960) • RCA Victor (S) LSO-1057 8-10   60
   Green cover. Pictures Jeannie Carson and Howard Morris hiding in trees.
   Composer: Burton Lane, E.Y. Harburg. **Conductor:** Max Meth. **Cast:** Jeannie Carson, Howard Morris, Biff McGuire, Jerry Laws, Carol Brice, Bill Glover, Sorrell Booke, Colonel Tiger Haynes, Bobby Howes.
Studio Cast (1951) • RCA Victor (M) LKT-1000 30-40   51
   Composer: Burton Lane, E.Y. Harburg. **Conductor:** Russ Case. **Cast:** Audrey Marsh, Jimmy Carroll, Jimmy Blair, Deep River Boys.
Studio Cast (1954) • Capitol (EP) EBF-561 10-20   54
   Boxed, two-disc set.
Studio Cast (1954) • Capitol (M) H-561 25-30   54
   10-inch LP. Made after plans fell through for an animated film version of the show, starring Ella Logan and Frank Sinatra.
   Composer: Burton Lane, E.Y. Harburg. **Cast:** Ella Logan, George Greeley (pianos).
Studio Cast (1963) • Reprise (M) F-2015 10-15   63
Studio Cast (1963) • Reprise (S) FS-2015 15-20   63
Studio Cast • Harmony (S) HS-11286 8-12   Re
   Composer: Burton Lane, E.Y. Harburg. **Conductor:** Morris Stoloff, Ken Lane. **Cast:** Dean Martin, Frank Sinatra, Debbie Reynolds, Sammy Davis Jr., Bing Crosby, Rosemary Clooney, McGuire Sisters, Hi-Lo's, Clark Dennis, Lou Monte, Mary Kaye Singers.
Studio Cast (1959) • National Academy Record Club (M) ES 13 10-15   59
   From *Ed Sullivan Presents Songs and Music of...* series.
   Cast: Ed Sullivan All Star Cast.
Studio Cast • Pickwick (S) SPC 3132 8-12
   Cast: Bugs Bower and Orchestra.
Soundtrack (1968) • Warner Bros. (M) B-2550 8-10   68

Soundtrack (1968) • Warner Bros. (S) BS-2550 8-10   68
Includes music deleted from the released print of the film.
Composer: Burton Lane, E.Y. Harburg. **Conductor:** Ray Heindorf. **Cast:** Fred Astaire, Petula Clark, Tommy Steele, Keenan Wynn, Ken Darby Singers, Don Francks, Brenda Arnau, Avon Long, Jester Hairston, Barbara Hancock.
Studiotrack • Somerset (S) SF-32900 8-12
Cast: Cinema Sound Stage Orchestra.
Also see REPRISE REPERTORY THEATRE

FINIAN'S RAINBOW AND BRIGADOON REMEMBERED
Studiotrack (1959) • United Artists (M) UAL-3135 15-20   59
Studiotrack (1959) • United Artists (S) UAS-6035 20-30   59
Jazz interpretations.
Cast: Lee and Hal Schaefer.

FINNEGAN'S WAKE
Soundtrack (1968) • RCA Victor (M) VDM-118 12-15   68
Soundtrack (1968) • RCA Victor (S) VDS-118 12-30   68
Composer: Elliot Kaplan. **Conductor:** Elliot Kaplan. **Cast:** Martin J. Kelly, Jane Reilly.
(Passages from the James Joyce work.)

FIORELLO!
Original Cast (1959) • Capitol (M) WAO-1321 8-10   59
Original Cast (1959) • Capitol (S) SWAO-1321 12-15   59
Gatefold cover. Black label.
Original Cast (1959) • Capitol (S) SWAO-1321 10-15   59
Standard cover. Red label.
Composer: Jerry Bock, Sheldon Harnick. **Conductor:** Hal Hastings. **Cast:** Tom Bosley, Patricia Wilson, Ellen Hanley, Howard DaSilva, Pat Stanley, Nathaniel Frey, Eileen Rodgers, Bob Holiday.
Studio Cast (1959) • Capitol (M) T1343 8-10   59
Also has music from *The Sound of Music*.
Conductor: Alfred Newman.
Studio Cast • Camden (M) CAL-599 10-12   59
Studio Cast • Camden (S) CAS-599 12-15   59
One side has music from *The Sound of Music*
Composer: Jerry Bock, Sheldon Harnick. **Cast:** Florence Henderson, Sid Bass with His Orchestra and Chorus.

FIRE AND ICE
Soundtrack (1987) • MCA (S) 6206 8-10   87
Composer: Various. **Cast:** Marietta, Gary Wright, Panarama, John Denver, Laurie Alda.

FIRE DOWN BELOW
Soundtrack (1957) • Decca (M) DL-8597 35-75   57
Composer: Ken Jones. **Conductor:** Muir Mathieson. **Cast:** Jeri Southern, Ned Washington, Lester Lee, Jack Lemmon, Vivian Comma.

FIREFLY
Studio Cast (1951) • RCA Victor (M) LM-121 15-20   51
Composer: Rudolf Friml, Otto Harbach. **Conductor:** Al Goodman. **Cast:** Allan Jones, Martha Wright, Elaine Malbin, Hayes Gordon.
Studio Cast (1959) • Lion (M) L-70090 10-15
Composer: Rudolf Friml, Otto Harbach. **Conductor:** Paul Britton. **Cast:** Paul Britton Orchestra.

FIRESTARTER
Soundtrack (1984) • MCA (S) 6131 8-10   84
Composer: Tangerine Dream. **Cast:** Tangerine Dream.

FIREWALKER
Soundtrack (1986) • Varese Sarabande (S) STV-81303 8-10   86
Composer: Chang.

FIREWIND
Soundtrack • Sparrow (S) SPR-1004 8-10

FIRST BLOOD
Soundtrack (1982) • Regency (S) 9505... 8-10   82
Soundtrack (1982) • That's Entertainment (S) TER-1038....................... 8-10   80s
UK release.
Composer: Jerry Goldsmith. Conductor: Jerry Goldsmith. Cast: Dan Hill.

FIRST BORN
Soundtrack (1984) • EMI (S) ST-17144.. 8-10   84

FIRST GREAT TRAIN ROBBERY: see GREAT TRAIN ROBBERY

FIRST IMPRESSIONS
Original Cast (1959) • Columbia (M) OL-5400.. 15-20   59
Original Cast (1959) • Columbia (S) OS-2014....................................... 35-50   59
Original Cast (1959) • Columbia Special Products (S) AOS-2014.......... 8-10   Re
Composer: Glenn Paxon, Robert Goldman, George Weiss. Conductor: Frederick Dvonch.
Cast: Polly Bergen, Farley Granger, Hermione Gingold, Donald Madden, Phyllis Newman,
Christopher Hewett, Lynn Ross, Ellen Hanley, Lois Bewley, Lauri Peters.

FIRST LIVE RECORDINGS: see ELVIS LIVE AT THE LOUISIANA HAYRIDE

FIRST MEN IN THE MOON
Studiotrack • Starlog/Varese Sarabande (S) SV-95002 15-20   80
Digital recording. Also includes *Dr. Strangelove, Captain Kronos, Vampire Hunter* and
Hedda.
Composer: Laurie Johnson. Conductor: Laurie Johnson.

FIRST NUDIE MUSICAL
Soundtrack (1976) • Northal (S) 1001 12-15   76
Soundtrack (1976) • Varese Sarabande (S) VC-81028 10-15   78
Composer: Bruce Kimmel. Conductor: Rene Hall. Cast: Stephen Nathan, Cindy Williams,
Bruce Kimmel, Annette O'Toole, Debbie Shapiro, Valerie Gillett, Diana Canova.

FISH THAT SAVED PITTSBURGH
Soundtrack (1979) • Lorimar (S) SZ-36303... 8-12   80
Cast: Four Tops, Phyllis Hyman, Bell and James.

FISTFUL OF DOLLARS
Soundtrack (1966) • RCA Victor (M) LOC-1135 12-18   67
Soundtrack (1966) • RCA Victor (S) LSO-1135..................................... 20-30   67
Black label with dog on top.
Soundtrack (1966) • RCA Victor (S) LSO-1135..................................... 10-15   75
Orange, tan, or new black label.
Composer: Ennio Morricone. Conductor: Ennio Morricone.
Also see MUSIC FROM A FISTFUL OF DOLLARS, FOR A FEW DOLLARS MORE AND
THE GOOD, THE BAD AND THE UGLY

FITZCARRALDO
Soundtrack (1982) • Polydor (S) H-6363.. 8-10   82

FITZWILLY
Soundtrack (1967) • United Artists (M) UAL-4173................................. 10-15   68
Soundtrack (1967) • United Artists (S) UAS-5173 15-20   68
Soundtrack (1967) • MCA (S) 25098... 8-10   86
Composer: John Williams. Conductor: John Williams.

FIVE AFTER EIGHT
Original Cast (1979) • Original Cast (S) OC-8027 8-12   79
Composer: Michael Bitterman. Conductor: Ron Williams. Cast: Sally Funk, James Handakas,
Dena Olstad, Arthur Sorenson, Barbara Walker.

FIVE CORNERS
Soundtrack (1988) • Varese Sarabande (S) STV 81354 8-10   88
    Composer: James Newton Howard. **Conductor:** James Newton Howard.

FIVE DAYS FROM HOME
Soundtrack (1978) • MCA (S) 2362 10-12   78
    Composer: Bill Conti. **Conductor:** Bill Conti.

FIVE EASY PIECES
Soundtrack (1970) • Epic (S) KE-30456 15-20   71
  Includes classical selections by Mozart and Chopin.
    Cast: Tammy Wynette, Pearl Kaufman, Jack Nicholson, Karen Black. (With dialogue.)

FIVE PENNIES
Soundtrack (1959) • Dot (EP) DEP-102 20-25   59
Soundtrack (1959) • Dot (M) DLP-9500 15-20   59
Soundtrack (1959) • Dot (S) DLP-29500 25-40   59
Soundtrack (1959) • London (S) SAHU-6044 35-45   59
  UK release. Full-color foldout cover.
    Composer: Sylvia Fine, Leith Stevens, others. **Conductor:** Leith Stevens. **Cast:** Red Nichols,
    Danny Kaye, Eileen Wilson (performs vocals for Barbara Bel Geddes in the film), Louis
    Armstrong, Bob Crosby, Ray Anthony.
Studiotrack • Coronet (M) CX-100 8-12
    Cast: Bob Freeman Orchestra.

FIVE PORTRAITS: see LOUISIANA STORY

FIVE SAVAGE MEN
Soundtrack (1977) • Vee Jay (S) VJS 1211 40-60   77
    Cast: Rupert Holmes.

FIVE SUMMER STORIES
Soundtrack (1972) • Granite (S) GR 7720 25-30   72
    Cast: Honk.

5,000 FINGERS OF DR. T
Soundtrack (1953) • GSF (M) GSF-1007 20-25
  Side one is the movie soundtrack; side two has outtakes and alternate versions.
    Composer: Frederick Hollander, Dr. Seuss. **Cast:** Peter Lind Hayes, Mary Healy, Hans
    Conried, Tommy Rettig.

FLAHOOLEY
Original Cast (1951) • Capitol (EP) EDM-284 25-50   51
Original Cast (1951) • Capitol (M) S-284 100-125   51
Original Cast (1951) • Capitol (M) T-11649 10-15   77
    Composer: Sammy Fain, E.Y. Harburg, Moises Vivanco. **Conductor:** Maurice Levine. **Cast:**
    Yma Sumac, Barbara Cook, Jerome Courtland, Irwin Corey, Fay DeWitt, Marilyn Ross.

FLAME AND THE FLESH
Soundtrack (1954) • MGM (EP) X-1080 35-50   54
    Composer: Nicholas Brodsky, Jack Lawrence. **Cast:** Carlos Thompson.

FLAME IN THE WIND
Soundtrack (1970) • Unusual (S) 1004 45-60   70
    Composer: Dwight Gustafson. **Conductor:** Dwight Gustafson.

FLAMINGO KID
Soundtrack (1984) • Varese Sarabande (S) 81232 25-30   84
Soundtrack (1984) • Motown (S) 613ML 10-15   84
    Cast: Chiffons, Jesse Frederick, Acker Bilk, Dion, Crystals, Barrett Strong, Impressions, Hank
    Ballard and Midnighters, Martha and the Vandellas.

FLANAGAN AND ALLEN STORY

Original Cast • Encore (M) ENC 151 10-15
British stage, radio and film performances from 1935-51.
Cast: Bud Flanagan, Chesney Allen.

FLASH GORDON

Original Radio Cast (1930s) • Mark 56 (M) 609 15-20   73
Two radio episodes.

Original Radio Cast • Golden Age (M) 5007 8-10   78

Soundtrack (1938) • Pelican (M) LP-2006 8-12   76
Full title: *Flash Gordon's Trip to Mars*.
Composer: Franz Waxman. **Conductor:** Franz Waxman. **Cast:** Buster Crabbe, Jean Rogers, Frank Shannon, Charles Middleton, Beatrice Roberts, Richard Alexander, Donald Kerr, Wheeler Oakman, G. Montague Shaw.

Soundtrack (1980) • Elektra (S) 5E-518 8-12   80
Includes photo insert. May have a "Queen" sticker on shrinkwrap.
Composer: Queen. **Cast:** Queen.

FLASHDANCE

Soundtrack (1983) • Casablanca (S) NBLP-7278 8-10   83
Composer: Giorgio Moroder, others. **Conductor:** Sylvestor Levay. **Cast:** Irene Cara, Shandi, Helen St. John, Karen Kamon, Joe Esposito, Laura Branigan, Donna Summer, Cycle V, Kim Carnes, Michael Sembello.

Soundtrack (1983) • Casablanca (S) 422-811 492-1 8-10   83
May have a sticker on shrinkwrap with credits.
Composer: Giorgio Moroder, others. **Conductor:** Phil Ramone. **Cast:** Irene Cara, Shandi, Helen St. John, Karen Kamon, Joe Esposito, Laura Branigan, Donna Summer, Cycle V, Kim Carnes, Michael Sembello.

FLASHER

Soundtrack (1972) • Green (S) GBS-1008 20-25   72
Composer: Pool-Pah. **Conductor:** Rupert Holmes.

FLASHPOINT

Soundtrack (1984) • EMI America (S) ST-17141 8-10   84
Cast: Tangerine Dream, Gems.

FLEA IN HER EAR

Soundtrack (1968) • 20th Century-Fox (S) TFS-4200 10-35   68
Composer: Bronislau Kaper. **Conductor:** Lionel Newman.

FLEET'S IN

Soundtrack (1942) • Hollywood Soundstage (M) HS-405 8-10
Composer: Johnny Mercer, Victor Schertzinger. **Cast:** Betty Hutton, William Holden, Eddie Bracken, Dorothy Lamour, Jimmy Dorsey, Bob Eberly, Helen O'Connell.

FLESH AND BLOOD

Soundtrack (1985) • Varese Sarabande (S) STV-81256 8-10   85
Composer: Basil Poledouris. **Conductor:** Basil Poledouris.

FLETCH

Soundtrack (1985) • MCA (S) 6142 8-10   85
Composer: Harold Faltermeyer, others. **Cast:** Stephanie Mills, Dan Hartman, John Farnum, Fixx, Kim Wilde, Harold Faltermeyer.

FLIGHT OF THE CONDOR

TV Soundtrack (1982) • ABC (S) REB 440 30-40   82

FLIGHT OF THE DOVES

Soundtrack (1971) • London (S) XPS-591 15-20   71
Composer: Roy Budd. **Cast:** Roy Budd (piano).

FLINTSTONES
TV Soundtrack (1961) • Colpix (M) CP-302... 75-150   61
Two half-hour TV episodes.
Cast: Alan Reed, Jean Vander Pyl, Mel Blanc, Bea Benadaret. (With dialogue.)
TV Soundtrack (1961) • Golden (M) 66.. 125-175   61
Cast characters singing songs from the TV show.
Cast: Mel Blanc, Alan Reed, Jean Vander Pyl, Bea Benadaret.
Studiotrack (1966) HBR (M) HLP-2052 40-50   66
Full title: *Flintstones & Jose Jiminez in the Time Machine.*
Cast: Bill Dana, others.

FLIP WILSON SHOW
TV Soundtrack • Little David (S) LD-2000 10-15   70s
Cast: Flip Wilson.

FLOOD
TV Soundtrack (1962) • Columbia (M) ML-5757 15-20   62
TV Soundtrack (1962) • Columbia (S) MS-6357................................... 20-25   62
Full title: *The Flood – A Biblical Allegory Based on Noah and the Ark.* Premiere CBS TV
telecast from June 14, 1962. One side has original Stravinsky music from *The Mass.*
Composer: Igor Stravinsky. **Conductor:** Igor Stravinsky, Robert Craft. **Cast:** Laurence Harvey
(narrator), Sebastian Cabot, John Reardon, Robert Oliver, Elsa Lanchester, Paul Tripp, Richard
Robinson, Columbia Symphony Orchestra and Chorus.

FLORA, THE RED MENACE
Original Cast (1965) • RCA Victor (M) LOC-1111 10-12   65
Original Cast (1965) • RCA Victor (S) LSO-1111 15-18   65
Original Cast (1965) • RCA Victor (S) CBL1-2760 10-12   Re
Composer: John Kander, Fred Ebb. **Conductor:** Hal Hastings. **Cast:** Liza Minnelli, Mary Louise
Wilson, Cathryn Damon, Robert Kaye, Stephanie Hill, Bob Dishy, Danny Carroll, Joe E. Marks,
Dortha Duckworth, James Cresson.
Original Revival Cast (1987) • That's Entertainment (S) TER-1159...... 10-12   89
UK release.
Composer: John Kander, Fred Ebb. **Conductor:** Hal Hastings. **Cast:** Veanne Cox, Peter
Frechette, Lyn Greene, John Kander (piano).

FLOWER DRUM SONG
Original Cast (1958) • Columbia (EP) A-5350 10-15   58
Original Cast (1958) • Columbia (M) OL-5350...................................... 8-10   58
Original Cast (1958) • Columbia (S) OS-2009.. 8-12   58
First issues have artwork in gold base. Reissues, valued at roughly the same as originals,
have a yellow base.
Composer: Richard Rodgers, Oscar Hammerstein II. **Conductor:** Salvatore Dell'Isola. **Cast:**
Pat Suzuki, Miyoshi Umeki, Larry Blyden, Juanita Hall, Ed Kenney, Keye Luke, Jack Soo,
Conrad Yama, Rose Quong, Pat Adiarte, Anita Ellis, Susan Lynn, Baayork Lee, Arabella Hong,
Cely Carrillo, Luis Robert Hernandez, Linda Ribuca, Yvonne Ribuca.
Original London Cast (1960) • RCA Victor (M) CLP-1359 30-35   60
Original London Cast (1960) • RCA Victor (S) CSD-1359 40-45   60
UK release.
Original London Cast (1960) • Angel (M) 35886................................. 12-15   60
Original London Cast (1960) • Angel (S) S-35886.............................. 15-18   60
Original London Cast (1960) • That's Entertainment (S) TER 1060 8-10   Re
UK release.
Composer: Richard Rodgers, Oscar Hammerstein II. **Conductor:** Robert Lowe. **Cast:** Kevin Scott,
Ida Shepley, Yau Shang Tung, George Pastell, Yama Saki, Zed Zakari.
Studio Cast (1958) • Rondo-lette (M) 843 10-15   58
Also has music from *Porgy and Bess.*
Studio Cast (1959) • ABC-Paramount (M) ABC-272 8-12   59
Studio Cast (1959) • ABC-Paramount (S) ABCS-272........................... 10-20   59
Cast: Harold Lanin.

Studio Cast (1959) • Bell (M) BLP-13 8-12   59
Studio Cast (1959) • Bell (S) BLP-13 10-20   59
    Same prefix and selection number used for both mono and stereo.
    Conductor: Jimmy Carroll. **Cast:** Wayne Sherwood, Cely Carillo and Chorus, Edna McGriff.
Studio Cast (1959) • Columbia (EP) B-2151 15-20   59
    Composer: Richard Rodgers, Oscar Hammerstein II. **Cast:** Tony Bennett, Doris Day, Four
    Lads, Johnny Mathis.
Studio Cast (1959) • Design (M) DL-98 10-12   59
Studio Cast (1959) • Design (S) SS-41 10-12   59
Studio Cast • Design (M) DCF-1011 10-12   60
    Reissue with "Design Uni-Groove System."
    Conductor: Dean Franconi. **Cast:** Bill Hyer, Patricia Wong, Marchicko Lee, Rose Katagiri,
    Jonathon Hallee, Berea Lum, Gene Sands Chorus, Sound Stage Orchestra.
Studio Cast (1959) • Dot (M) DLP-3173 15-20   59
    Jazz interpretations.
    Cast: Muriel Roberts.
Studio Cast (1959) • Rondo (S) SA-79 10-12   59
    Cast: Ira Wright.
Studio Cast (1959) • Roost (M) LP 2231 10-15   59
Studio Cast (1959) • Roost (S) SLP 2231 15-20   59
    Cast: Johnny Smith Quartet.
Studio Cast (1959) • Waldorf (S) 1412SD 10-20   59
    Cast: Waldorf Music Hall Show Orchestra.
Studio Cast (1959) • Warner Bros. (M) B-1256 15-20   59
Studio Cast (1959) • Warner Bros. (S) BS-1256 15-25   59
    Actual title: *Flower Drum Song Original Jazz Performance.*
    Cast: Morris Nanton Trio.
Studio Cast (1960) • Richmond (M) B-20081 10-15   60
Studio Cast (1960) • Richmond (S) S-30081 15-20   60
    Also has music from *West Side Story.*
    Cast: London Theatre Orchestra.
Studio Cast • Bravo (S) K 120 8-12
    Conductor: John Senati. **Cast:** Bravo Pops Symphony Orchestra.
Studio Cast • Crown (M) CLP-5105 8-12
Studio Cast • Treasure (S) 809 8-12
Studio Cast • Ultraphonic (M) 50325 8-12
    Cast: Halo Orchestra and Singers.
Soundtrack (1961) • Decca (M) DL-9098 10-15   61
Soundtrack (1961) • Decca (S) DL-79098 8-10   61
    Both have a red label.
Soundtrack (1961) • MCA (S) 2069 5-8   74
    Composer: Richard Rodgers, Oscar Hammerstein II. **Conductor:** Alfred Newman. **Cast:** B.J.
    Baker (performs vocals for Nancy Kwan in the film), James Shigeta, Juanita Hall, Miyoshi
    Umeki, Jack Soo, Marilyn Horne (performs vocals for Reiko Sato), Benson Fong.

FLOWERING PEACH

Original Cast (1954) • MGM (M) E-3164 75-90   54
    Incidental music.
    Composer: Alan Hovhaness.

FLOWERS FOR ALGERNON

Original London Cast (1980) • Original Cast (S) OC-8021 8-10   80
    Composer: Charles Strouse, David Rogers. **Conductor:** Alexander Farris. **Cast:** Michael
    Crawford, Cheryl Kennedy, Aubrey Woods, Ralph Nossek.

FLOWERS IN THE ATTIC

Soundtrack • Varese Sarabande (S) STV 81358 8-10   87
    Composer: Christopher Young. **Conductor:** Paul Francis Witt. **Cast:** Evalon Witt.

FLUSH LEFT, STAGGER RIGHT
Original Cast • Insights IV (S) Number Not Known................................ 10-20
  Composer: Jerry Powell, Michael McWhinney. **Cast:** Robert Ryan, Hal Linden, Arte Johnson, Marilyn Cooper, others.

FLY
Soundtrack (1986) • Varese Sarabande (S) STV-81289 10-15   86
Soundtrack (1986) • That's Entertainment (S) TER-1120....................... 8-10   80s
  UK release.
  Composer: Howard Shore. **Conductor:** Howard Shore. **Cast:** London Philharmonic Orchestra.

FLY II
Soundtrack (1989) • Varese Sarabande (S) VS-5220 8-12   89
  Composer: Christopher Young. **Conductor:** Allan Wilson. **Cast:** Munich Studio Orchestra.

FLY BLACKBIRD
Original West Coast Cast (1962) • Imaginate (M) LK-1-V13786 40-50   62
  Preceded original Broadway cast recording.
  Composer: C. Jackson, James Hatch. **Cast:** Ellen Gordon, Jack Crowder, Vera Oliver, George Takei.
Original Cast (1962) • Mercury (M) OCM-2206 20-25   62
Original Cast (1962) • Mercury (S) OCS-6206 30-50   62
  Composer: C. Jackson, James Hatch. **Conductor:** Gershon Kingsley. **Cast:** Avon Long, Leonard Parker, Paul Reid Roman, Jack Crowder, Jim Bailey, Robert Guillaume, Mary Louise, John Anania, Helen Blount, Thelma Oliver, William Sugihara, Glory Van Scott.

FLY BY NIGHT
Soundtrack (1979) • Parachute (S) 20525 8-10   79
  Disco pressing.

FLY WITH ME
Original Cast (1980) • Original Cast (S) OC-8023................................. 12-15   80
  Columbia University production of a 1920 show, presented when the composers were students at the University.
  Composer: Richard Rodgers, Lorenz Hart, Oscar Hammerstein II. **Conductor:** Howard Shanet. **Cast:** Daniel Frank, Rod Melucas, Cheryl S. Horowitz, Francis Larson, Annie Laurita, Marci Pliskin, Avi Simon (Columbia University students).

FLYING DOWN TO RIO
Soundtrack (1933) • Sandy Hook (M) SH-2010.. 5-8   78
  Also has music from *Carefree*.
  Composer: Vincent Youmans, others. **Cast:** Fred Astaire, Ginger Rogers. CAREFREE:
  Composer: Irving Berlin. **Cast:** Fred Astaire, Ginger Rogers.

FLYING NUN
TV Studiotrack (1967) • Colgems (M) COM-106 20-35   67
TV Studiotrack (1967) • Colgems (S) COS-106 30-55   67
  Full title of both: *Sally Field - Star of the Flying Nun*. Contains *Who Needs Wings to Fly*, original theme from the TV series.
  Composer: Various. **Conductor:** Bob Mitchell, Ernie Freeman, Don McGinnis. **Cast:** Sally Field, Bob Mitchell Choir.

FOG
Soundtrack (1980) • Varese Sarabande (S) STV-81191 10-35   84
  Composer: John Carpenter.

FOLIES BERGERE (1958)
Soundtrack (1958) • Decca (M) DL-8571 15-20   58
  Composer: P.Gerard, Henri Betti, others. **Conductor:** Roger Roger. **Cast:** Roger Roger and His Orchestra.

FOLIES BERGERE (1964)

Original Cast (1964) • Audio Fidelity (M) 2135 10-15   64
Original Cast (1964) • Audio Fidelity (S) AFSD-6135 12-18   64
    Composer: P. Gerard, Henri Betti, others. **Conductor:** Joe Basile. **Cast:** Patachou, Georges
    Ulmer.

FOLLIES

Original Cast (1971) • Capitol (S) SO-761 10-12   71
    Red label with circular Capitol logo at top. Includes insert with photos, synopsis and song
    titles.
Original Cast (1971) • Capitol (S) SO-761 5-8   71
    Purple or red label. Without insert.
    Composer: Stephen Sondheim. **Conductor:** Hal Hastings. **Cast:** Alexis Smith, Gene Nelson,
    Dorothy Collins, John McMartin, Arnold Moss, Yvonne DeCarlo, Fifi D'Orsay, Mary McCarty,
    Ethel Shutta, Michael Bartlett, Harvey Evans, Justine Johnston, Victoria Mallory, Rita O'Connor,
    Kurt Peterson, Suzanne Rogers.
Original Lincoln Center Cast (1985) • RCA Victor (S) HBC2-7128 10-12   85
    Two discs. Recorded live during a concert. Includes a 16-page booklet..
    Composer: Stephen Sondheim. **Conductor:** Paul Gemignani. **Cast:** Mandy Patinkin, Barbara
    Cook, George Hearn, Lee Remick, Elaine Stritch, Carol Burnett, Andre Gregory, Arthur Rubin,
    Jim Walton, Howard McGillin, Liz Callaway, Daisy Prince, Betty Comden, Adolph Green, Liliane
    Montevecchi, Phyllis Newman, Licia Albanese, Erie Mills, New York Philharmonic.
Original London Cast (1987) • First Night (S) Encore 3 18-20   87
    UK release. Two discs. Gatefold cover. Includies libretto and color poster. Has new songs
    in place of several dropped from the original production.
    Composer: Stephen Sondheim. **Conductor:** Chris Walker. **Cast:** Diana Rigg, Daniel Massey,
    Julia McKenzie, David Healy, Dolores Gray.

FOLLOW ME

Soundtrack (1969) • Uni (S) 73056 20-25   69
    Composer: Stu Phillips. **Conductor:** Stu Phillips. **Cast:** Dino, Desi and Billy.

FOLLOW THAT BIRD

Soundtrack (1985) • RCA Victor (S) CBL1-5475 8-10   85
    Composer: Van Dyke Parks, Lennie Niehaus. **Cast:** Waylon Jennings, Alabama, Ronnie
    Milsap, Sesame Street Cast, Frank Oz, Muppets.

FOLLOW THAT DREAM

Soundtrack (1962) • RCA Victor (EP) EPA-4368 100-150   62
    Paper sleeve. Red printing on one side, back side is blank. Made especially for coin
    (jukebox) operators and radio stations. Well-duplicated counterfeits exist.
Soundtrack (1962) • RCA Victor (EP) EPA-4368 175-250   62
    Black label, dog on top. Marked "Not For Sale." Promotional issue only. With paper sleeve.
Soundtrack (1962) • RCA Victor (EP) EPA-4368 75-100   62
    Black label, dog on top. Marked "Not For Sale." Promotional issue only. Disc only.
Soundtrack (1962) • RCA Victor (EP) EPA-4368 45-60   62
    Black label, dog on top.
Soundtrack (1962) • RCA Victor (EP) EPA-4368 30-40   65
    Black label, dog on side.
Soundtrack (1962) • RCA Victor (EP) EPA-4368 30-40   69
    Orange label.
    Composer: Sid Tepper, Roy C. Bennett, Ben Weisman, Sid Wayne, Jerry Livingston, others.
    Cast: Elvis Presley, Scotty Moore (guitar), Boots Randolph (sax), Dudley Brooks (piano), D.J.
    Fontana (drums), Hal Blaine (drums), Jordanaires (vocals).

FOLLOW THAT GIRL
Original London Cast (1960) • RCA (M) CLP-1366 20-25   60
Original London Cast (1960) • RCA (S) CSD-1366 25-35   60
  UK release.
London Cast (1960) • AEI (S) AEI-1121 8-10   70s
    Composer: Julian Slade, Dorothy Reynolds. **Conductor:** Philip Martell. **Cast:** Susan
    Hampshire, Peter Gilmore, Patricia Routledge, James Cairncross, Marion Grimaldi.

FOLLOW THE BOYS (1944)
Soundtrack (1944)• Hollywood Soundstage (S) HS 5012 8-10
    Composer: Roy Turk, Fred Ahlert, Jule Styne, Sammy Cahn, others. **Cast:** Jeanette
    MacDonald, George Raft, Vera Zorina, Dinah Shore, Sophie Tucker, The Andrews Sisters,
    Donald O'Connor.

FOLLOW THE BOYS (1962)
Soundtrack (1962) • MGM (M) E-4123 10-12   62
Soundtrack (1962) • MGM (S) SE-4123 12-15   62
    Composer: Benny Davis, Ted Murry. **Conductor:** Leroy Holmes. **Cast:** Connie Francis.

FOOL BRITANNIA!
Studio Cast • Acappella (M) AC-1 15-18
    Composer: Leslie Bricusse, Anthony Newley. **Conductor:** Marvin Holtzman. **Cast:** Peter
    Sellers, Joan Collins, Anthony Newley, Leslie Bricusse, Daniel Massey, Michael Lipton.

FOOL FOR LOVE
Soundtrack (1985) • MCA (S) 6156 8-10   85

FOOLS
Soundtrack (1970) • Reprise (S) RS-6429 12-15   71
    Composer: Shorty Rogers, Paul Parrish, Alex Harvey, Mimi Farina. **Conductor:** Shorty Rogers.
    Cast: Kenny Rogers and the First Edition, Mimi Farina, Shorty Rogers, Katherine Ross.

FOOTLIGHT PARADE: see GOLDEN AGE OF THE HOLLYWOOD MUSICAL

FOOTLOOSE
Soundtrack (1984) • Columbia (S) 9C9-39404 10-15   84
  Picture Disc.
Soundtrack (1984) • Columbia (S) JS-39242 8-10   84
    Composer: Michael Gore, Dean Pitchford, Jim Steinman, others. **Cast:** Kenny Loggins,
    Shalamar, Deniece Williams, Mike Reno and Ann Wilson, Bonnie Tyler, Sammy Hagar, Karla
    Bonoff, Moving Pictures.

FOOTSTEPS ON THE MOON
TV Soundtrack (1969) • CBS News (M) XSV 144899 8-12   69
TV Soundtrack (1969) • Command (S) 948-S 8-12   69
  ABC TV and radio news programs for Apollo 11 space flight, July 1969. Includes booklet.
    Cast: Charles Kuralt (narrator).

FOR A FEW DOLLARS MORE
Studiotrack (1967) • United Artists (M) UAL-3608 12-15   67
Studiotrack (1967) • United Artists (S) UAS-6608 15-20   67
  One side has music from *A Fistful of Dollars, Zorba the Greek, Topkapi, Viva Maria, The*
  Train and *Tom Jones*.
    Composer: Ennio Morricone. **Conductor:** Leroy Holmes.
  Also see MUSIC FROM A FISTFUL OF DOLLARS

FOR COLORED GIRLS WHO HAVE CONSIDERED SUICIDE WHEN THE
RAINBOW IS ENUF
Original Cast (1976) • Buddah (S) BDS-95007 8-10   76
    Cast: Diana Wharton (vocal), Ntozake Shange (poetry).

FOR HEAVEN'S SAKE
Original Cast (1961) • NAEYA (M) EYA-100 8-12   61
Limited subcription edition. "A Cast Recording of the musical revuew," at University of Michigan.
Composer: Frederick Silver, Helen Kromer.

FOR LOVE OF IVY
Soundtrack (1968) • ABC (S) SOC-7 12-15   68
Composer: Quincy Jones, Maya Angelou. **Conductor:** Quincy Jones. **Cast:** B.B. King, Cashman, Pistilli & West, Shirley Horn.

FOR PETE'S SAKE
Soundtrack (1974) • Grason (EP) BG-6618 6-12   74
Composer: Ralph Carmichael. **Conductor:** Ralph Carmichael. **Cast:** Al Freeman, Jr., George Beverly Shea, Young People.

FOR THE FIRST TIME
Soundtrack (1959) • RCA Victor (EP) EPA-4344 15-20   59
Soundtrack (1959) • RCA Victor (M) LM-2338 10-25   59
Soundtrack (1959) • RCA Victor (S) LSC-2338 12-50   59
Composer: George Stoll, others. **Conductor:** George Stoll, Carlo Savina, Johannes Rediske, C. Callinicos. **Cast:** Mario Lanza.

FOR THE LOVE OF BENJI
Soundtrack (1977) • Epic (S) KSE-34867 8-12   77
Composer: Euel Box. **Conductor:** Euel Box.

FOR WHOM THE BELL TOLLS
Studiotrack (1943) • Decca A-360 30-45   50
Album of three 78 rpms.
Studiotrack (1957) • Jubilee (M) JCM-1034 20-30   57
Tribute to Victor Young with 12 selections from various films.
Composer: Victor Young. **Cast:** Harry Sukman (piano).
Studiotrack (1958) • Warner Bros. (M) B-1201 20-25   58
Silver label.
Studiotrack (1968) • Warner Bros. (S) BS-1201 25-30   58
Gold label.
Studiotrack (1968) • Warner Bros. (S) WS-1201 10-12   Re
Green label.
Studiotrack (1968) • Stanyan (Q) SRQ-4013 25-30   73
Composer: Victor Young. **Conductor:** Ray Heindorf.
Also see GOLDEN EARRINGS

FOR YOUR EYES ONLY
Soundtrack (1981) • Liberty (S) LOO-1109 20-25   81
Composer: Bill Conti, Michael Leeson. **Conductor:** Bill Conti. **Cast:** Sheena Easton, Rage, Bill Conti.

FORBIDDEN BROADWAY
Original Cast (1982) • DRG (S) SBL-12585 10-15   84
Off-Broadway parody of Broadway shows and stars.
Composer: Gerald Alessandrini (parody lyrics). **Conductor:** Fred Barton. **Cast:** Gerard Alessandrini, Fred Barton, Bill Carmichael, Nora Mae Lyng, Chloe Webb.

FORBIDDEN ISLAND: see ATLANTIS IN HI-FI

FORBIDDEN PLANET
Studiotrack (1956) • MGM 12243 4-6   56
78 rpm. Backed with *The Swan*.
Studiotrack (1956) • MGM 12243 15-25   56
Picture sleeve for 78 rpm. Sleeve pictures scene from each film on each side.

Studiotrack (1956) • MGM K12243... 5-8   56
45 rpm. Backed with *The Swan*.
Studiotrack (1956) • MGM K12243... 15-25   56
Picture sleeve for 45 rpm. Sleeve pictures scene from each film on each side.
Composer: Bronislau Kaper, David Rose. **Conductor:** David Rose. **Cast:** David Rose and His Orchestra.
Studiotrack (1956) • Planet (S) PR-001.................................... 30-40   78
Composer: Louis Barron, Bebe Barron. **Cast:** Walter Pidgeon, Anne Francis.

FORBIDDEN WORLD
Soundtrack (1982) • Web (S) LP 107.. 8-10   82
Composer: Susan Justin. **Conductor:** Susan Justin.

FORBIDDEN ZONE
Soundtrack (1980) • Varese Sarabande (S) STV-81170..................... 8-10   80s
Composer: Danny Elfman. **Cast:** Mystic Knights of the Oingo Boingo.

FORCE OF EVIL: see BANDIT OF SHERWOOD FOREST

FORD 50TH ANNIVERSARY TELEVISION SHOW
TV Soundtrack (1953) • Decca DU-999 20-25   53
12-inch 78 rpm album.
TV Soundtrack (1953) • Decca (EP) ED-593 15-20   53
TV Soundtrack (1953) • Decca (M) DL-7027............................... 20-25   53
10-inch LP.
Composer: Irving Berlin, others. **Conductor:** Jay Blackton. **Cast:** Ethel Merman, Mary Martin.

FOREIGN FILM FESTIVAL
Studiotrack • London Phase 4 (S) SP 44112.............................. 8-12
Conductor: Frank Chacksfield. **Cast:** Frank Chacksfield Orchestra.

FOREIGN INTRIGUE
Soundtrack (1956) • MGM (EP) X-1323.................................... 15-20   56
Composer: Robert Durand.

FOREST OF THE AMAZON
Soundtrack (1971) • United Artists (S) UAS-5506 5-10   71
Composer: Heitor Villo-Lobos.

FOREVER AMBER
Soundtrack (1947) • RCA Victor P-197 60-65   47
Album of three 78 rpms.
Soundtrack • Cinema (M) LP-8007.. 12-50   74
One side has music from *Duel In The Sun*.
Composer: David Raksin. **Conductor:** David Raksin. DUEL IN THE SUN: **Composer:** Dimitri Tiomkin. **Conductor:** Dimitri Tiomkin.
Also see DAVID RAKSIN CONDUCTS HIS GREAT FILM SCORES.

FOREVER JUDY: see JUDY

FOREVER YOUNG, FOREVER FREE
Soundtrack (1976) • MCA (S) 2093...................................... 8-10   76
Composer: Lee Holdridge. **Conductor:** Lee Holdridge.

FORGOTTEN BROADWAY
Original Cast • No Label Shown (M) T-101 20-25

White label disc in plain white cover without liner notes. Includes additional songs from *New Faces of 1956* which don't appear on the RCA Victor cast album, plus previously unreleased or cut songs from *I Do! I Do!, A Mother's Kisses, Carnival in Flanders, Molly, Chicago* and *High Button Shoes.*

Composer: Various. Conductor: Various. Cast: Inga Swenson, Jane Connell, T.C. Jones, Billie Hayes, Tiger Haynes, John Reardon, Beatrice Arthur, Kaye Ballard, Mary Martin, Robert Preston, Dolores Gray, Johnny Burke, Chita Rivera, Gwen Verdon, Nanette Fabray.
Also see NEW FACES OF 1956

FORMULA
Soundtrack (1980) • Varese Sarabande (S) STV-81153 8-10   80

Composer: Bill Conti. Conductor: Bill Conti.

FORMULA FOR LOVE
Soundtrack • Atco (M) 33-128 15-25   61

Single-sided disc.
Cast: Louis Armstrong, Nina & Frederick.

FORTUNA
Studio Cast (1962) • Owl (M) ORLP-4.. 30-35   62

Composer: Francis Thorne, Arnold Weinstein. Cast: Francis Thorne (piano).

FORTUNATE PILGRIM
Soundtrack (1988) • RCA Victor (S) 7788-1 8-10   88

FORTUNE AND MEN'S EYES
Soundtrack (1971) • MGM (S) 1SE-29 10-12   71

Cast: Ronnie Dyson, Galt McDermot, Leata Galloway.

FORTUNE COOKIE
Soundtrack (1966) • United Artists (M) UAL-4145 10-12   66
Soundtrack (1966) • United Artists (S) UAS-5145 12-15   66

Composer: Andre Previn. Conductor: Andre Previn.

FORTY FIVE MINUTES FROM BROADWAY
Studio Cast • AEI (S) AEI-1159... 5-10   80s

Composer: George M. Cohan. Cast: Tammy Grimes, Larry Blyden, Russell Nype.

40 POUNDS OF TROUBLE
Soundtrack (1963) • Mercury (M) MG-20784 20-25   63
Soundtrack (1963) • Mercury (S) SR-60784... 25-35   63

Composer: Mort Lindsey. Conductor: Mort Lindsey.

42nd STREET
Original Cast (1980) • RCA Victor (S) CBL1-3891 8-10   80

Composer: Harry Warren, Al Dubin. Conductor: John Lesko. Cast: Tammy Grimes, Jerry Orbach, Carole Cook, Lee Roy Reams, Joseph Bova, Danny Carroll, James Congdon, Jeri Kansas, Ginny King, Karen Prunczik, Wanda Richert.

FOSTER BROOKS' ROASTS
TV Soundtrack • Roast (S) RR-1002.. 10-15   76

From Friar's Roasts of those named in the cast.
Cast: Foster Brooks roasts: Dean Martin, Hubert Humphrey, Joe Namath, Carroll O'Connor, Johnny Carson, Ralph Nader, Don Rickles.

FOUL PLAY
Soundtrack (1978) • Arista (S) AL-9501 8-10   78

Composer: Charles Fox. Conductor: Charles Fox. Cast: Barry Manilow.

FOUR ALFRED HITCHCOCK FILMS: see MUSIC FROM HITCHCOCK FILMS

FOUR BELOW STRIKES BACK
Original Cast (1960) • Offbeat (M) O-4017 35-45   60
> **Composer:** William Roy, others. **Cast:** Jenny Lou Law, Nancy Dussault, George Furth, Cy Young, Robert Colston, Paul Trueblood (pianos).

FOUR GIRLS IN TOWN
Soundtrack (1956) • Decca (EP) ED-2487 20-25   56
> **Composer:** Alex North. **Conductor:** Joseph Gershenson. **Cast:** Universal-International Orchestra.
> Also see WRITTEN ON THE WIND

FOUR HIT SHOWS
Studiotrack • Rondo-lette (M) 841 8-12
> Suites from *South Pacific, The King and I, Carousel* and *Oklahoma!*
> **Cast:** Suzanne Auber and Broadway Orchestra.

FOUR HORSEMEN OF THE APOCALYPSE
Soundtrack (1962) • MGM (M) E-3993 15-20   62
Soundtrack (1962) • MGM (S) SE-3993 20-25   62
> **Composer:** Andre Previn. **Conductor:** Andre Previn.

FOUR IN THE MORNING
Soundtrack (1966) • Roulette (M) OS-805 25-30   66
Soundtrack (1966) • Roulette (S) OSS-805 35-40   66
> Includes dialogue.
> **Composer:** John Barry. **Conductor:** John Barry.

FOUR JILLS IN A JEEP
Soundtrack (1944) • Hollywood Soundstage (M) HS-407 10-25
> **Composer:** Harold Adamson, Jimmy McHugh, Sonny Burke. **Cast:** Kay Francis, Carole Landis, Martha Raye, Mitzi Mayfair, Jimmy Dorsey Orchestra, Betty Grable, Dick Haymes, Alice Faye, Carmen Miranda, George Jessel.

FOUR MUSKETEERS
Original London Cast (1967) • Philips (S) SAL-3655 12-18   67
UK release.
> **Composer:** Laurie Johnson, Herbert Kretzmer. **Conductor:** Derek New. **Cast:** Harry Secombe, Elizabeth Larner, Stephanie Voss, Aubrey Woods, Glyn Owen, John Junkin, Jeremy Lloyd, Sheena Marshe, Kenneth Connor.

FOUR MUSKETEERS: see EAGLE HAS LANDED

FOUR ORIGINAL SOUNDTRACK RECORDINGS BY PHILIPPE SARDE
Soundtrack (1982) • DRG Concord Series (S) SL 9512 8-12   82
> Music from French films: *L'Etoile Du Nord, La Veuve Couderc, Le Chat* and *Le Train.*
> **Composer:** Philippe Sarde.

FOUR SAINTS IN THREE ACTS
Original Cast (1947) • RCA Victor (M) LCT-1139 75-100   54
Original Cast (1947) • RCA Victor (M) LM-2756 25-30   64
> **Composer:** Virgil Thomson, Gertrude Stein. **Conductor:** Virgil Thomson. **Cast:** Beatrice Robinson-Wayne, Ruby Greene, Inez Matthews, Edward Matthews, Charles Holland.

FOUR SEASONS
Soundtrack (1981) Private Stock (S) PS-7000 20-60   81
> Two discs.

FOUR TELEVISION MUSICALS

TV Soundtrack • Blue Pear (M) BP-1019 30-35

Selections from *A Bell for Adano, Junior Miss, No Man Can Tame Me* and *The Canterville Ghost.*

A BELL FOR ADANO: **Composer:** Howard Dietz, Arthur Schwartz. **Cast:** Anna Maria Alberghetti, Frank Yaconelli, Edwin Steffe. JUNIOR MISS: **Composer:** Burton Lane, Dorothy Fields. **Cast:** Carol Lynley, Don Ameche, Joan Bennett, Jill St. John, Paul Ford, David Wayne, Diana Lynn. NO MAN CAN TAME ME: **Composer:** Jay Livingston, Ray Evans. **Cast:** John Raitt, Gisele Mackenzie, Eddie Foy, Jr. CANTERVILLE GHOST: **Composer:** Jerry Bock, Sheldon Harnick. **Cast:** Sir Michael Redgrave, Douglas Fairbanks, Jr., Natalie Schafer, Tippy Walker.

FOUR WIVES: see DEATH OF A SCOUNDREL

FOURPOSTER: see LOST HORIZON: THE CLASSIC FILM SCORES OF DIMITRI TIOMKIN

FOURTH MAN

Soundtrack (1979) • Varese Sarabande (S) STV-81222 8-10   84

Composer: Loek Dikker. **Cast:** Willem Frederik Bon.

FOURTH PROTOCOL

Soundtrack (1987) • DRG (S) SBL-12591 10-15   87

Composer: Lalo Schifrin. **Conductor:** Lalo Schifrin.

FOX

Soundtrack (1968) • Warner Bros. (M) W-1738 20-30   68

Soundtrack (1968) • Warner Bros. (S) WS-1738 20-25   68

Composer: Lalo Schifrin. **Conductor:** Lalo Schifrin. **Cast:** Anne Heywood, Sally Stevens.

FOX AND THE HOUND

Soundtrack • Disneyland (S) 3106 25-30   81

Picture disc.

Soundtrack • Disneyland (S) JT-3823 15-20   81

Cast: Mickey Rooney, Kurt Russell, Pearl Bailey, Sandy Denny.

FOXES

Soundtrack (1980) • Casablanca (S) 7206 10-12   80

Two discs.

Composer: Giorgio Moroder.

FOXY

Original Cast (1964) • S.P.M. (M) CO-4636 100-125   64

Live recording by the Society for the Preservation of Musicals. This show closed before reaching New York.

Composer: Robert Emmett Dolan, Johnny Mercer. **Conductor:** Donald Pippin. **Cast:** Larry Blyden, Cathryn Damon, John Davidson, Robert H. Harris, Gerald Hiken, Bert Lahr, Julienne Marie.

FOXY BROWN

Soundtrack (1974) • Motown (S) MS-811 10-15   74

Composer: Willie Hutch.

FRANCES

Soundtrack (1983) • Southern Cross (S) SCRS-1001 10-12   83

Composer: John Barry. **Conductor:** John Barry.

FRANCES LANGFORD PRESENTS

TV Soundtrack (1959) • NBC-TV/Splendex (M) 59................................ 25-35   59

From an NBC TV Special, aired March 15, 1959, plus an open-end interview with Frances Langford. Includes script. Promotional issue only.

Composer: Various. **Conductor:** David Rose. **Cast:** Frances Langford, Hugh O'Brian, Julie London, Edgar Bergen and Charlie McCarthy, George Sanders, Jerry Colonna, Bobby Troup, Tony Romano, Four Freshmen, Murray McEachern, Bob Hope, David Rose and His Orchestra.

TV Soundtrack (1960) • Chanford (M) 2176 50-60   60
  Full title: *Frances Langford Show: NBC-TV, Sunday May 1, 1960, 8-9 PM, N.Y. Time.*
  Designated a "Complimentary LP."
    Conductor: Ray Heindorf. **Cast:** Frances Langford, Johnny Mathis, Don Ameche, Hermoine
    Gingold, Robert Cummings, Mary Costa.

FRANCIS LAI PERFORMS HIS GREAT FILM MUSIC
Soundtrack • DRG (S) MRS-508 5-10
  Music from *Love Story, A Man and a Woman, Live for Life, Mayerling* and *International
  Velvet.*
    Composer: Francis Lai. **Conductor:** Francis Lai. **Cast:** Royal Philharmonic Orchestra.

FRANCIS OF ASSISI
Soundtrack (1961) • 20th Century-Fox (M) FOX-3053 125-150   61
Soundtrack (1961) • 20th Century-Fox (S) SFX-3053 175-200   61
    Composer: Mario Nascimbene. **Conductor:** Franco Ferrara. **Cast:** Choir of the Porziuncola,
    Children of Assisi Chorus, Poor Sisters of Clare.

FRANCIS X. BUSHMAN TALKS ABOUT HIS LIFE & TIMES
Soundtrack (1975) • Mark 56 (M) 708 5-8   75
    Cast: Francis X. Bushman.

FRANK SINATRA CONDUCTS TONE POEMS OF COLOR: see TONE POEMS OF COLOR

FRANK SINATRA SINGS GEORGE GERSHWIN
Studiotrack (1950s) • Columbia (EP) B-1673 10-15   50s
  Songs from *Girl Crazy, Strike Up the Band* and *Porgy and Bess.*
    Composer: George Gershwin. **Conductor:** Axel Stordahl. **Cast:** Frank Sinatra.

FRANK'S WILD YEAR
Original Cast (1986) • Island (S) 7-90572-1 10-15   86
    Composer: Tom Waits, Greg Cohen. **Cast:** Tom Waits.

FRANKENSTEIN: see WEIRD CIRCLE

FRANKIE AND JOHNNY
Soundtrack (1966) • RCA Victor (M) LPM-3553 150-250   66
  Black label reads "Monaural" at bottom. Includes bonus 12" x 12" color photo.
Soundtrack (1966) • RCA Victor (M) LPM-3553 75-125   66
  Black label reads "Monaural" at bottom. Without bonus photo.
Soundtrack (1966) • RCA Victor (S) LSP-3553 150-250   6€
  Black label reads "Stereo" at bottom. Includes bonus 12" x 12" color photo.
Soundtrack (1966) • RCA Victor (S) LSP-3553 80-120   66
  Black label reads "Stereo" at bottom. Without bonus photo.
Soundtrack (1966) • RCA Victor (S) APL1-2559 10-15   77
Soundtrack (1966) • Pickwick/Camden (S) ACL-7007 10-12   76
  Excludes three tracks that were on the 1966 RCA Victor issues.
    Composer: Fred Karger, Ben Weisman, Sid Tepper, Roy C. Bennett, Sid Wayne, Fred Wise,
    Randy Starr, Doc Pomus, Mort Schuman, Bill Giant, Bernie Baum, Florence Kaye, others. **Cast:**
    Elvis Presley, Scotty Moore (guitar), Barney Kessel (guitar), D.J. Fontana (drums), Hal Blaine
    (drums), Jordanaires (vocals).

FRANTIC (1958)
Soundtrack (1958) • Columbia (M) CL-1268 50-60   58
Soundtrack (1958) • Columbia Special Products (M) ACL-1268 8-12   Re
Soundtrack (1958) • Fontana (M) MGF-27532 15-20   64
Soundtrack (1958) • Fontana (S) SRF-67532 20-25   64
    Composer: Miles Davis. **Cast:** Miles Davis Quintet.

FRANTIC (1988)
Soundtrack (1988) • Elektra (S) 60782-1 8-10   88
    Composer: Ennio Morricone.

FRANZ LEHAR MEMORIAL ALBUM
Studio Cast • RCA Victor (M) LK-1004 10-15   54
> **Composer:** Franz Lehar. **Conductor:** Al Goodman. **Cast:** Eileen Farrell, Charles Fredericks, Al Goodman and His Orchestra.

FRANZ LISZT STORY: see SONG WITHOUT END

FRANZ WAXMAN
Studiotrack • Varese Sarabande (S) 704,320..................... 8-12   80s
> Music from *Bride of Frankenstein, Paradine Case, Horn Blows at Midnight* and others. **Conductor:** Richard Mills. **Cast:** Queensland Symphony.

FRAULEIN
Studiotrack (1958) • Audition (M) Aud-33-5926 20-30   58
> Although cover pictures film stars Mel Ferrer and Dana Wynter, the album inexplicably contains no music from *Fraulein*. Music is from *Gigi, The Seven Hills of Rome, Sayonara, Raintree County, The Joker is Wild, Sitting Pretty, Times Square Lady, Rose of Washington Square, Vogues of 1938* and *A Song is Born*.
> **Composer:** Various. **Conductor:** Richard Mills. **Cast:** The Ink Spots, The Monarchs, Bob Eberly.

FRED ASTAIRE AND GINGER ROGERS
Soundtrack • EMI (SE) 184-95807/8 12-18
> Two discs. UK release with liner notes in French. Obvious electronic stereo. Scores of *Top Hat, The Gay Divorcee, Shall We Dance?* and *Swing Time*.
> **Cast:** Fred Astaire, Ginger Rogers. TOP HAT: **Composer:** Irving Berlin. SWING TIME: **Composer:** Jerome Kern, Dorothy Fields. GAY DIVORCEE: **Composer:** Cole Porter. SHALL WE DANCE?: **Composer:** George Gershwin, Ira Gershwin.
> Also see GAY DIVORCEE
> Also see TOP HAT

FRED ASTAIRE SINGS AND SWINGS IRVING BERLIN
TV Soundtrack • MGM (M) PR-1 10-20
> Excerpts. Released in conjunction with Alcoa Premiere.
> **Cast:** Fred Astaire, Oscar Peterson, Ray Brown, Flip Phillips.
> Also see BEST OF FRED ASTAIRE

FREE AND EASY
Studio Cast (1957) • Columbia (M) CL-1099......................... 20-25   57
> Based on the musical *St. Louis Woman*, rewritten as *Blues-Opera*, then titled *Free and Easy*.
> **Composer:** Harold Arlen, Johnny Mercer. **Conductor:** Andre Kostelanetz.

FREE TO BE ... YOU & ME
Soundtrack (1972) • Arista (S) 4003 8-10   72

FREEDOM'S FINEST HOUR
Soundtrack (1968) • Decca (S) DL-74943............................. 10-15   68
> Documentary of the American Revolution.
> **Cast:** Ronald Reagan (narrator).

FRENCH LIEUTENANT'S WOMAN
Soundtrack (1981) • DRG (S) DRG 6106................................ 8-10   81
> **Composer:** Carl Davis. **Conductor:** Carl Davis.

FRENCH LINE
Soundtrack (1954) • Mercury (EP) EP-2-3183 20-30   54
> Two discs.
Soundtrack (1954) • Mercury (M) MG-25182 60-75   54
> 10-inch LP.
> **Composer:** Josef Myrow, Walter Scharf. **Conductor:** Constantin Bakaleinkoff. **Cast:** Jane Russell, Mary McCarty, Gilbert Roland.

FRESH HAIR: see HAIR

FRESHMAN: see HAROLD LLOYD'S WORLD OF LAUGHTER

FREUD

Soundtrack (1962) • Citadel (S) CT-6019... 15-20   77
> Some music originally composed in 1962 for *Freud* was discarded and used in 1979 for *Alien*.

Soundtrack (1962) • Citadel (M) CT 7011 10-12   79
> **Composer:** Jerry Goldsmith. **Conductor:** Joseph Gershenson.
> Also see ALIEN

FRIDAY THE 13TH

Soundtrack (1983) • Gramavision (S) 1030.. 8-10   83
> Has theme from *Friday the 13th, Part 3*, plus background score from *Friday the 13th*, parts 1, 2 and 3.
> **Composer:** Harry Manfredini. **Conductor:** Harry Manfredini. **Cast:** Harry Manfredini and His Orchestra.

TV Soundtrack (1989) • GNP/Crescendo (S) GNPS-8018 8-10   89
> Full title: *Friday the 13th – The Series*.
> **Composer:** Fred Mollin.

FRIENDLY PERSUASION

Soundtrack (1956) • Dot (EP) DEP-1054 15-20   56
> **Composer:** Dimitri Tiomkin, Paul Francis Webster. **Cast:** Pat Boone (includes main title theme, *Friendly Persuasion [Thee I Love]*).

Soundtrack (1956) • RKO/Unique (M) LP-110...................................... 50-60   56

Soundtrack (1956) • Venise (M) V-7026.. 45-55   60
> Actual title: *Dimitri Tiomkin Conducts Sound Tracks*.

Soundtrack (1956) • Varese Sarabande (M) STV-81165 8-12   82
> **Composer:** Dimitri Tiomkin. **Conductor:** Dimitri Tiomkin.

Studiotrack (1956) • Coral (EP) EC-81144... 15-30
> **Composer:** Dimitri Tiomkin. **Conductor:** Dimitri Tiomkin. **Cast:** Dimitri Tiomkin.

Studiotrack (1956) • Coral (EP) CXP45-1280....................................... 10-20   56
> **Composer:** Dimitri Tiomkin, Paul Francis Webster. **Conductor:** Dimitri Tiomkin.
> Above three do not include Pat Boone's title theme, *Friendly Persuasion [Thee I Love]*.
> Also see LOST HORIZON: THE CLASSIC FILM SCORES OF DIMITRI TIOMKIN

FRIENDS

Soundtrack (1973) • Paramount (S) DJS-1 20-30   73
> Full title: *Paramount Records Presents an Open-end Interview with Elton John about Friends Soundtrack*. Includes song introductions by Elton. Promotional issue only.

Soundtrack (1973) • Paramount (S) PAS-6004 12-15   73

Soundtrack (1973) • Pickwick (S) SPC 3598.. 8-12   78
> **Composer:** Elton John, Bernie Taupin, Paul Buckmaster. **Cast:** Elton John, Liza Strike, Lesley Duncan, Madeline Bell.

FRIENDS: see SIGMUND AND THE SEA MONSTERS

FRIGHT NIGHT

Soundtrack (1985) • Private I (S) SZ-40087 8-10   85
> **Composer:** Brad Fiedel, others. **Cast:** J. Geils Band, Ian Hunter, Autograph, April Wine, Devo, Sparks, White Sister, Fabulous Fontaines, Evelyn "Champagne" King.

FRITZ THE CAT

Soundtrack (1972) • Fantasy (S) F-9406.. 20-25   72

Soundtrack (1972) • Fantasy (S) MPF-4532 10-12   Re
> **Cast:** Bo Diddley, Alice Stuart, Innocent, Bystanders, Cal Tjader, Watson Sisters, others.

FROM BROADWAY TO HOLLYWOOD
Studiotrack • Columbia Special Products (M) CSP-213........................ 15-20
Studiotrack • Columbia Special Products (S) CSP-213 15-20
> Songs from *Wives and Lovers, Breakfast at Tiffany's, Papa's Delicate Condition, West Side Story, My Fair Lady, Fiddler on the Roof, Kismet* and *Mary Poppins*. Made for Zenith.
> **Cast:** Percy Faith, Don Costa, Johnny Mathis, Andre Kostelanetz, Julie Andrews, Ray Conniff.

FROM HELL TO TEXAS
Studiotrack (1958) • Colortone (S) C33-4937.. 8-12   58
> Full title: *Themes from Hollywood As Inspired By the 20th Century-Fox Cinemascope Production – From Hell to Texas*. Also has music from *Raintree County, Wild is the Wind* and others.
> **Conductor:** Mark Warren. **Cast:** Mark Warren.

FROM HERE TO ETERNITY
Soundtrack (1953) • Coral (M) CRL-56105 50-100   53
> 10-inch LP. Hawaiian music from the soundtrack. Issued with four different covers.
> **Cast:** Danny Stewart and His Islanders.
> Also see EDDY DUCHIN STORY

FROM ISRAEL WITH LOVE
Original Cast (1972) • Hed Arzi (S) BAN-14278 20-30   72
> **Conductor:** Rafi Ben Moshe. **Cast:** Micha Adir, Dani Amihud, Chaya Arad.

FROM RUSSIA WITH LOVE
Soundtrack (1964) • United Artists (M) UAL-4114................................ 10-15   64
Soundtrack (1964) • United Artists (S) UAS-5114 15-20   64
> **Composer:** John Barry, Lionel Bart. **Conductor:** John Barry. **Cast:** Matt Monro, John Barry and His Orchestra.

Soundtrack (1964) • Liberty (M) LRP-3356 10-15   64
Soundtrack (1964) • Liberty (S) LST-7356 15-20   64
> Soundtrack recording of the title song, plus 11 other film songs.
> **Composer:** Various. **Cast:** Matt Monro.

Studiotrack (1964) • Liberty (M) LRP-3353.. 10-15   64
Studiotrack (1964) • Liberty (S) LST-7353 10-15   64
> Full title: *From Russia with Love (and Other Themes)*. 12 title tracks from films including *Dragnet* and *The Fugitive*.
> **Composer:** Various. **Conductor:** Si Zentner. **Cast:** Si Zentner and His Orchestra.

Studiotrack (1964) • Capitol (M) T-2075.. 10-15   64
Studiotrack (1964) • Capitol (S) ST-2075 10-15   64
> 12 assorted film title tunes.
> **Composer:** Various. **Conductor:** Jimmie Haskell. **Cast:** Jimmie Haskell and His Orchestra.
> Also see INCREDIBLE WORLD OF JAMES BOND
> Also see THUNDERBALL/FROM RUSSIA WITH LOVE

FROM THE HIP
Soundtrack (1987) • Varese Sarabande (S) STV 81309 8-10   87
> **Composer:** Zaza.

FROM THE SECOND CITY
Original Cast [Vol. 1] (1961) • Mercury (M) OCM-2201 20-25   61
Original Cast [Vol. 1] (1961) • Mercury (S) OCS-6201 25-30   61
Original Cast [Vol. 2] (1961) • Mercury (M) OCM-2202 20-25   61
Original Cast [Vol. 2] (1961) • Mercury (S) OCS-6202 25-30   61
Original Cast [Vol. 3] (1961) • Mercury (M) OCM-2203 20-25   62
Original Cast [Vol. 3] (1961) • Mercury (S) OCS-6203 25-30   62
> **Composer:** William Mathieu. **Conductor:** William Mathieu. **Cast:** Howard Alk, Alan Arkin, Roger Bowen, Severn Darden, Andrew Duncan, Barbara Harris, Mina Kolb, Paul Sand, Eugene Troobnick, William Mathieu (piano). (Skits.)

Original Cast • Mercury (S) SR-61224 20-30   69
  Actual title: *The Second City Writhes Again!*
    Cast: Howard Alk, Alan Arkin, Roger Bowen, Severn Darden, Andrew Duncan, Barbara Harris, Mina Kolb, Paul Sand, Eugene Troobnick, Jack Burns, Avery Schrieber, Del Close, Omar Shapli, Ann Elder (skits).

FROM THE TERRACE
Studiotrack (1974) • Cinema (S) LP-8009 25-35   74
  Also has music from *The Liberation of L.B. Jones*.
    Composer: Elmer Bernstein. Conductor: Elmer Bernstein.

FRONT ROW CENTER
Studiotrack • Columbia (EP) B-2030 5-15
  Songs from *Can-Can, Knickerbocker Holiday, Girl Crazy* and *Pal Joey*.
    Cast: Paul Weston, Michel Legrand, Morton Gould.

FRONT STREET GAIETIES
Original Cast • AEI (S) AEI-1133 8-10   80s
    Composer: Walter Willison, Jeffrey Silverman.

FROSTY THE SNOWMAN
Soundtrack (1970) • MGM (S) SE-4733 45-50   70
    Composer: Steve Nelson, Jack Rollins. Conductor: Maury Laws. Cast: Jimmy Durante, Billy DeWolfe, Jackie Vernon, Paul Frees, June Foray.

FUGITIVE KIND
Soundtrack (1959) • United Artists (M) UAL-4065 30-40   60
Soundtrack (1959) • United Artists (S) UAS-5065 45-65   60
    Composer: Kenyon Hopkins. Conductor: Kenyon Hopkins.

FULL METAL JACKET
Soundtrack (1987) • Warner Bros. (S) 9-25613-1 10-15   87
    Cast: Abigail Mead, Nigel Goulding, Johnny Wright, Dixie Cups, Sam the Sham and the Pharoahs, Chris Kenner, Nancy Sinatra, Trashmen, Goldman Band.

FULL OF LIFE: see NO SAD SONGS FOR ME

FUN AND FANCY FREE
Soundtrack (1947) • Disneyland (M) DQ-1248 15-20   64

FUN IN ACAPULCO
Soundtrack (1963) • RCA Victor (M) LPM-2756 40-50   63
  Black label, reads "Mono" at bottom.
Soundtrack (1963) • RCA Victor (S) LSP-2756 40-50   63
  Black label with RCA silver top logo, reads "Stereo" at bottom.
Soundtrack (1963) • RCA Victor (M) LPM-2756 20-30   65
  Black label, reads "Monaural" at bottom.
Soundtrack (1963) • RCA Victor (S) LSP-2756 20-30   65
  Black label with RCA white top logo, reads "Stereo" at bottom.
Soundtrack (1963) • RCA Victor (S) LSP-2756 10-25   69
  Orange label.
Soundtrack (1963) • RCA Victor (S) AFL1-2756 8-10   77
    Composer: Ben Weisman, Sid Wayne, Sid Tepper, Roy C. Bennett, Bill Giant, Bernie Baum, Florence Kaye, Fred Wise, Don Robertson, Hal Blair, Jerry Leiber, Mike Stoller, Pepe Guizar, others. Cast: Elvis Presley, Scotty Moore (guitar), Barney Kessel (guitar), D.J. Fontana (drums), Hal Blaine (drums), Dudley Brooks (piano), Jordanaires (vocals), Amigos (vocals).

FUNERAL IN BERLIN
Soundtrack (1966) • RCA Victor (M) LOC-1136 20-25   67
Soundtrack (1966) • RCA Victor (S) LSO-1136 30-40   67
    Composer: Konrad Elfers. Conductor: Konrad Elfers.

FUNNY FACE

Original Cast (1927) • World (M) SH-14420-25 20-25

Original Cast (1927) • Monmouth Evergreen (SE) MES-7037 8-12
UK releases.

Original Cast (1927) • Smithsonian (M) R-019 12-18
Gatefold cover with bound-in booklet.
Composer: George Gershwin, Ira Geshwin. **Conductor:** Julian Jones. **Cast:** Fred Astaire,
Adele Astaire, Bernard Clifton, Leslie Henson, Sydney Howard, George Gershwin.

Soundtrack (1957) • Verve (M) MGV-15001 30-35   57
Pink gatefold cover, without insert.

Studiotrack (1957) • Verve (M) MGV-2064 25-35   57
Standard cover, pictures Audrey Hepburn and Fred Astaire in a scene from the film.
Composer: George Gershwin, Ira Gershwin. **Conductor:** Buddy Bregman. **Cast:** Buddy
Bregman Orchestra.

Soundtrack (1957) • Stet (M) DS-15001 18-20   77
Red gatefold cover, with insert.

Soundtrack (1957) • Stet (M) DS-15001 8-10   77
Pink, standard cover, without insert.
Composer: George Gershwin, Ira Gershwin, Roger Edens, Leonard Gershe. **Conductor:**
Adolph Deutsch. **Cast:** Fred Astaire, Audrey Hepburn, Kay Thompson.

Studiotrack • Verve (M) MGV-2064 10-12
Composer: George Gershwin, Ira Gershwin. **Cast:** Buddy Bregman and Orchestra.

FUNNY GIRL

Original Cast (1964) • Capitol (M) VAS-2059 8-12   64

Original Cast (1964) • Capitol (S) SVAS-2059 8-12   64
Back cover pictures both Barbra Streisand and Sydney Chaplin. Has song titles on bottom.

Original Cast (1964) • Capitol (S) STAO-2059 8-10   Re
Back cover pictures only Barbra Streisand. Has song titles on the right.

Original Cast (1964) • Capitol (M) W-2059 20-25   64

Original Cast (1964) • Capitol (S) SW-2059 20-30   64
UK release.
Composer: Jule Styne, Bob Merrill. **Conductor:** Milton Rosenstock. **Cast:** Barbra Streisand,
Sydney Chaplin, Danny Meehan, Kay Medford, Jean Stapleton, John Lankston.

Studio Cast (1968) • Motown (S) MS-672 15-20   68
Composer: Jule Styne, Bob Merrill. **Cast:** Diana Ross and the Supremes.

Soundtrack (1968) • Columbia (S) BOS-3220 8-12   68
Gray label. Unipak cover (disc opening faces gutter rather than outer edge). Inside cover
has liner notes on a black background.

Soundtrack (1968) • Columbia (S) BOS-3220 8-10   68
Brownish label. Unipak cover (disc opening faces gutter rather than outer edge). Inside
cover has liner notes on a tan background.

Soundtrack (1968) • CBS (S) S-70044 15-20   68
UK release. Unipak cover (disc opening faces gutter rather than outer edge).

Soundtrack (1968) • Columbia (Q) SQ-30992 25-30   71

Soundtrack (1968) • Columbia (S) JS-3220 8-10   Re
Standard cover. Features an extended overture.
Composer: Jule Styne, Bob Merrill. **Conductor:** Walter Scharf. **Cast:** Barbra Streisand, Omar
Sharif, Kay Medford, Mae Questel.

Studiotrack • Diplomat (S) DS 2462 8-12
Also has music from *Finian's Rainbow.*
Cast: Al Goodman's Show Orchestra.

Studiotrack • Pickwick (S) SPC-3131 8-12
Cast: Pete King Chorale and Orchestra.

Studiotrack (1964) • Wyncote (M) W-9019... 8-12   64
Studiotrack (1964) • Wyncote (S) SW-9019... 8-15   64
   Also has music from *Hello, Dolly*.
    Conductor: Rudolph Statler. **Cast:** Rudolph Statler Orchestra & Chorus.
   Also see HELLO, DOLLY!

FUNNY LADY
Soundtrack (1975) • Arista (S) AL-9004.. 8-12   75
    Composer: John Kander, Fred Ebb, Billy Rose, others. **Conductor:** Peter Matz. **Cast:** Barbra
    Streisand, James Caan, Ben Vereen.

FUNNY THING HAPPENED ON THE WAY TO THE FORUM
Original Cast (1962) • Capitol (M) WAO-1717...................................... 8-12   62
Original Cast (1962) • Capitol (S) SWAO-1717................................... 10-12   62
   Both have gatefold cover.
Original Cast (1962) • Capitol (M) WAO-1717...................................... 5-10   62
Original Cast (1962) • Capitol (S) SW-1717.. 5-10   66
   Both have standard cover.
    Composer: Stephen Sondheim. **Conductor:** Hal Hastings. **Cast:** Zero Mostel, Jack Gilford,
    David Burns, Ruth Kobart, John Carradine, Brian Davies, Ronald Holgate, Preshy Marker.
Original London Cast (1963) • RCA Victor (M) CLP-1685 45-60   63
   UK release. A stereo issue is presumed to exist – likely with a "CSD" prefix – but we have
   yet to confirm one.
Original London Cast (1963) • Stet (S) DS-15028.............................. 12-18   Re
   UK release.
    Composer: Stephen Sondheim. **Cast:** Frankie Howard, Kenneth Connor, Jon Pertwee,
    Robertson Hare, Eddie Gray, Leon Greene, Linda Gray, John Rye, Isla Blair.
Soundtrack (1966) • United Artists (M) UAL-4144............................... 8-10   66
Soundtrack (1966) • United Artists (S) UAS-5144.............................. 10-12   66
Soundtrack (1966) • United Artists (S) UA-LA284-G........................... 8-10   74
    Composer: Stephen Sondheim, Ken Thorne. **Conductor:** Ken Thorne. **Cast:** Zero Mostel, Phil
    Silvers, Jack Gilford, Buster Keaton, Michael Crawford, Annette Andre, Michael Hordern, Leon
    Greene.

FURY
Soundtrack (1978) • Arista (S) AB-4175... 10-15   78
    Composer: John Williams. **Conductor:** John Williams.

FUZZY PINK NIGHTGOWN
Soundtrack (1957) • Imperial (M) LP-9042-W...................................... 40-50   57
Soundtrack (1957) • Imperial (SE) LPS-9042-W................................. 100-150   59
    Composer: Billy May. **Conductor:** Billy May.

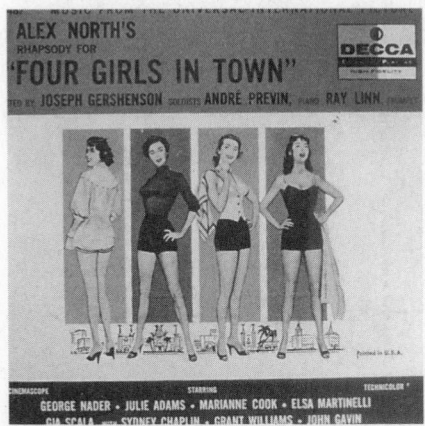

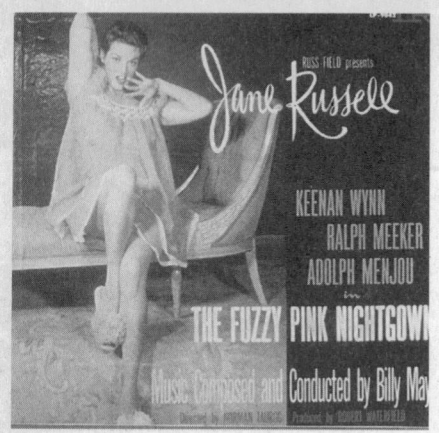

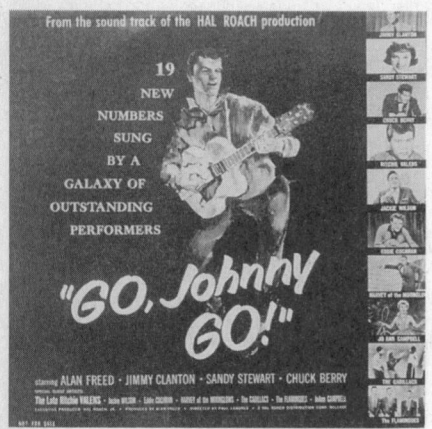

G

G.I. BLUES
Soundtrack (1960) • RCA Victor (M) LPM-2256............................... 200-300   60
  Black label, reads "Long Play" at bottom. Cover has heart-shaped "Featuring Wooden Heart" sticker.
Soundtrack (1960) • RCA Victor (M) LPM-2256................................... 90-110   60
  Black label, reads "Long Play" at bottom. Without heart-shaped "Featuring Wooden Heart" sticker.
Soundtrack (1960) • RCA Victor (S) LSP-2256................................. 200-300   60
  Black label, reads "Long Play" at bottom. Cover has heart-shaped "Featuring Wooden Heart" sticker.
Soundtrack (1960) • RCA Victor (S) LSP-2256 100-125   60
  Black label, reads "Living Stereo" at bottom. Without heart-shaped "Featuring Wooden Heart" sticker.
Soundtrack (1960) • RCA Victor (M) LPM-2256 40-50   63
  Black label, reads "Mono" at bottom.
Soundtrack (1960) • RCA Victor (S) LSP-2256 25-30   65
  Black label, reads "Stereo" at bottom.
Soundtrack (1960) • RCA Victor (M) LPM-2256 25-30   65
  Black label, reads "Monaural" at bottom.
Soundtrack (1960) • RCA Victor (S) LSP-2256 10-25   69
  Orange or tan label. (Tan label issued in 1976).
Soundtrack (1960) • RCA Victor (S) AFL1-2256 8-10   78
Soundtrack (1960) • RCA Victor (S) AYL1-3735 5-8   81
  Composer: Sid Wayne, Sid Tepper, Roy C. Bennett, Fred Wise, Ben Weisman, Doc Pomus, Mort Schuman, Carl Perkins, others. **Cast:** Elvis Presley, Scotty Moore (guitar), Tiny Timbrell (guitar), D.J. Fontana (drums), Dudley Brooks (piano), Ray Siegel (bass), Jimmie Haskell (accordion), Jordanaires (vocals).

GABLE AND LOMBARD
Soundtrack (1976) • MCA (S) 2091.. 8-10   76
  Composer: Michel Legrand. **Conductor:** Michel Legrand.

GABRIELLA
Soundtrack (1984) • RCA Victor (S) ABL1-5186 8-10   84
  Composer: Antonio Carlos Jobim. **Conductor:** Oscar Castro Neeves.

GAILY, GAILY
Soundtrack (1969) • United Artists (S) UAS-5202................................. 8-10   69
Soundtrack (1969) • United Artists (S) ST-93038.................................... 5-8   69
  Capitol Record Club issue.
  Composer: Henry Mancini, Marilyn Bergman, Alan Bergman. **Conductor:** Henry Mancini. **Cast:** Jimmie Rodgers, Henry Mancini, Anita Nye, Melina Mercouri.

GALLANT MEN
Studio Cast (1967) • Capitol (M) T-2643 10-12   67
Studio Cast (1967) • Captiol (S) ST-2643 12-15   67
  Composer: John Cacavas. **Conductor:** John Cacavas. **Cast:** U.S. Senator Everett McKinley Dirksen.

GAME IS OVER
Soundtrack (1967) • Atco (M) 205... 15-20   67
Soundtrack (1967) • Atco (S) SD-33-205 20-25   67
   Composer: Jean-Peirre Bourtayre, Jean Bouchety.

GAME OF LIFE
Soundtrack • Word (S) W-2006 6-12

GAMES
Soundtrack (1970) • Viking (S) LPS-105.......................... 150-175   70
   Limited Edition.
   Composer: Francis Lai. Conductor: Francis Lai. Cast: Barbara Moore Singers, Elton John.

GAMES OF XXI OLYMPIAD, MONTREAL
Assembled Cast (1976) • Polydor (S) 2424124................................... 10-12   76
   Canadian release.
   Composer: Andre Mathieu.

GANDHI
Soundtrack (1982) • RCA Victor (S) ABL1-4557 8-10   82
   Composer: Ravi Shankar, George Fenton. Conductor: George Fenton. Cast: Ravi Shankar,
   Lakshmi Shankar, Sultan Khan, Ashish Khan, Sharad Kumar, Ashit Desai, T.K. Ramakrishnan,
   Parasher Desai, Alla Rakha, Wren Orchestra, Ben Kingsley (narrator).

GANG'S ALL HERE
Soundtrack (1943) • Classic International Filmusicals (M) CIF-3003...... 8-12   78
Soundtrack (1943) • Sandy Hook (M) SH-2009.................................... 8-12   78
   Composer: Harry Warren, Leo Robin. Cast: Alice Faye, Carmen Miranda, James Ellison, Phil
   Baker, Edward Everett Horton, Charlotte Greenwood, Tony De Marco, Benny Goodman and His
   Orchestra.

GANGBUSTERS
Original Radio Cast • Golden Age (M) 5018.. 8-10   78

GARBAGE PAIL KIDS
Soundtrack (1987) • MCA (S) 6221... 8-10   87
   Cast: David Lawrence, Beat Farmers, Ed Keupper, Hakim and Lady Dianna, Jimmy Scarlett and
   Dimensions, Debbie Lytton, Garbage Pail Kids.

GARBO
Soundtrack • MGM (M) E-4201 10-12   64
   Music from *Anna Christie, Susan Lennox, Mata Hari, Grand Hotel, Queen Christina, Anna
   Karenina, Camille, Conquest* and *Ninotchka.*
   Composer: Various. Cast: Greta Garbo, John Barrymore, Robert Taylor, Charles Boyer, others.

GARDEN OF THE FINZI-CONTINIS
Soundtrack (1971) • RCA Victor (S) LSP-4712 10-12   72
   Composer: Manuel DeSica. Conductor: Carlo Savina.

GARRETT, PAT: see PAT GARRETT AND BILLY THE KID

GAS-S-S-S
Soundtrack (1970) • American Int'l (S) A-1038.................................... 12-15   71
   Cast: Robert Corff, Gourmet's Delight, Johnny and the Tornados.

GATOR
Soundtrack (1976) • United Artists (S) UA-LA646-G 8-10   76
Soundtrack (1976) • United Artists (S) LT-646 5-8   76
   Composer: Charles Bernstein, Jerry Reed, Bobby Goldsboro. Conductor: Charles Bernstein.
   Cast: Jerry Reed, Bobby Goldsboro.

GAUNTLET
Soundtrack (1978) • Warner Bros. (S) BSK-3144 8-12   78
    Cover art is by Frank Frazetta.
    Composer: Jerry Fielding. **Conductor:** Jerry Fielding.

GAY DIVORCEE
Soundtrack • EMI (SE) EMTC-101 15-20   74
    UK release. Gatefold cover with photo insert. Also has music from *Swing Time*.
    Composer: Cole Porter. **Conductor:** Max Steiner. **Cast:** Fred Astaire, Ginger Rogers, Betty
    Grable, Edward Everett Horton, Erik Rhodes. SWING TIME: **Composer:** Jerome Kern, Dorothy
    Fields.
    Also see FRED ASTAIRE AND GINGER ROGERS

GAY LIFE
Original Cast (1961) • Capitol (M) WAO-1560 15-20   61
Original Cast (1961) • Capitol (S) SWAO-1560 25-45   61
    Composer: Arthur Schwartz, Howard Dietz. **Conductor:** Herbert Greene. **Cast:** Walter Chiari,
    Barbara Cook, Jules Munshin, Loring Smith, Elizabeth Allen, Jeanne Bal, Lu Leonard.

GAY PURR-EE
Soundtrack (1963) • Warner Bros. (M) B-1479 12-18   62
Soundtrack (1963) • Warner Bros. (S) BS-1479 20-25   62
    Composer: Harold Arlen. **Conductor:** Mort Lindsey. **Cast:** Judy Garland, Red Buttons, Robert
    Goulet, Paul Frees, Hermione Gingold.

GEISHA BOY
Soundtrack (1958) • Jubilee (M) JLP-1096 35-45   58
Soundtrack (1958) • Jubilee (S) JGS-1096 65-75   58
    Some stereo copies came in a mono jacket with a gold stereo sticker added to the mono
    label. Others have a stereo band across the top of the front cover. Both the cover and side
    one of disc show the selection number as JGS-1096, but side two of disc shows it as
    SDJLP-1096.
    Composer: Walter Scharf. **Conductor:** Muir Mathieson.

GEMS FROM GERSHWIN
Studiotrack (1954) • RCA Victor (EP) EPBT-3055 10-15   54
    Two discs.
Studiotrack (1954) • RCA Victor (M) LPT-3055 25-35   54
    10-inch LP.
    Composer: George Gershwin. **Conductor:** Nathaniel Shilkret. **Cast:** Jane Froman, Felix Knight,
    Sunny Skylar, RCA Victor Salon Group.

GENE KRUPA STORY
Soundtrack (1959) • Verve (M) MGV-15010 30-45   59
Soundtrack (1959) • Verve (S) MGVS-6105 65-85   59
Soundtrack (1959) • Verve (S) V6-15010 60-70   63
    This reissue is as scarce as the original. Front cover shows the mono number (MGV-
    15010). Back cover and disc have the proper stereo number. Back cover is slightly different
    from original.
    Composer: Leith Stevens. **Conductor:** Leith Stevens. **Cast:** Gene Krupa, Red Nichols, Anita
    O'Day, Shelly Manne, Ruby Lane.

GENERAL ELECTRIC THEATER
TV Soundtrack (1959) • Columbia (M) CL-1395 30-35   59
TV Soundtrack (1959) • Columbia (S) CS-8190 40-45   59
TV Soundtrack (1959) • Columbia Special Products (S) ACS-8190 12-25   81
    Cover pictures Ronald Reagan, then the General Electric spokesman.
    Composer: Elmer Bernstein. **Conductor:** Elmer Bernstein.

GENERAL MOTORS' 50th ANNIVERSARY SHOW
TV Soundtrack (1958) • RCA Victor (M) LOC-1037 50-75   58
From an NBC-TV color special, aired November 17, 1957.
> **Composer:** Various. **Conductor:** Hugo Winterhalter. **Cast:** Pat Boone, Carol Burnett, Dan Dailey, Dinah Shore, Doretta Morrow, Steve Lawrence, Howard Keel, Cyril Ritchard, Claudia Crawford, Hugo Winterhalter and His Orchestra.

GENGHIS KHAN
Soundtrack (1965) • Liberty (M) LPR-3412 15-45   65
Soundtrack (1965) • Liberty (S) LST-7412 25-65   65
> **Composer:** Dusan Radic. **Conductor:** Muir Mathieson.

GENIE
Studiotrack (1983) • Columbia (S) AL-38678 8-10   83
Themes and variations from the TV Series *Taxi*.
> **Cast:** Bob James.

GENTLE RAIN
Soundtrack (1966) • Mercury (M) MG-21016 12-15   66
Soundtrack (1966) • Mercury (S) SR-61016.. 15-18   66
> **Composer:** Luis Bonfa. **Conductor:** Eumir Deodata.

GENTLEMEN MARRY BRUNETTES
Soundtrack (1955) • Coral (M) CRL-57013 45-65   55
> **Composer:** Richard Rodgers, Lorenz Hart, Bert Kalmar, Harry Ruby, others. **Conductor:** Robert Farnon. **Cast:** Jane Russell, Jeanne Crain, Rudy Vallee, Johnny Desmond, Anita Ellis (performed some vocals for Jeanne Crain in the film), Robert Farnon (performed vocals for Scott Brady).

GENTLEMEN PREFER BLONDES
Original Cast (1949) • Columbia (EP) A-895 15-20   50
Three discs.
Original Cast (1949) • Columbia (EP) A-1736 12-15   50
Boxed, three-disc set.
Original Cast (1949) • Columbia (M) ML-4290 15-18   50
Original Cast (1949) • Columbia (M) OL-4290.. 10-12
Original Cast (1949) • Columbia (SE) OS-2310 8-10   63
Original Cast (1949) • Columbia (SE) S-32610 5-8   73
Original Cast (1949) • Columbia (SE) CSO-AOS-2 5-8   Re
> **Composer:** Jule Styne, Leo Robin. **Conductor:** Milton Rosenstock. **Cast:** Carol Channing, Yvonne Adair, Jack McCauley, Eric Brotherson, George S. Irving, Rex Evans, Alice Pearce, Cholly Atkins, Honi Coles.

Original London Cast (1962) • RCA Victor (M) CLP-1602 60-65   62
Original London Cast (1962) • RCA Victor (S) CSD-1464 65-85   62
London production includes several songs not in the original Broadway production. Later issues have Odeon sticker placed over RCA logo on both disc and cover.
> **Composer:** Jule Styne, Leo Robin. **Conductor:** Alyn Ainsworth. **Cast:** Dora Bryan, Guy Middleton, Donald Stewart, Anne Hart, Bessie Love, Valerie Walsh.

Studio Cast (1962) • Caedmon (M) TC-1148 10-15   62
Has dialogue from the original story, but original score is replaced with hit tunes from the 1920s.
> **Composer:** Jule Styne, Leo Robin. **Conductor:** Charlie Katz. **Cast:** Carol Channing.

Soundtrack (1953) • MGM (EP) X-208... 30-75   53
Two discs.
Soundtrack (1953) • MGM (M) E-208... 75-100   53
10-inch LP.
Soundtrack (1953) • MGM (M) E-3231... 25-35   55
One side has music from *Till the Clouds Roll By*.

Soundtrack (1953) • Stet (M) DS-15005.. 15-20   Re
  Actual title: *Never Before and Never Again*. Also has music from other Marilyn Monroe
  films: *There's No Business Like Show Business*, *Niagara* and *River of No Return*.
    Composer: Jule Styne, Leo Robin, Hoagy Carmichael, Harold Adamson. **Cast:** Marilyn Monroe,
    Jane Russell.
    Also see MARILYN
    Also see MARILYN MONROE
    Also see REMEMBER MARILYN

GEORGE GERSHWIN REVISITED
Studiotrack • Painted Smiles (S) 1357 10-12

GEORGE K. ARTHUR'S PRIZE PACKAGE
Soundtrack • MGM (M) E-3151 40-45   54
  Music from *The Stranger Left No Card*, *Martin and Gaston* and *A Prince for Cynthia*.
    Composer: Hugo Alfven, Temple Abady. **Conductor:** Muir Mathieson.

GEORGE M!
Original Cast (1968) • Columbia (M) KOL-6800 8-10   68
Original Cast (1968) • Columbia (S) KOS-3200 10-12   68
Original Cast (1968) • Columbia (S) PS-3200 5-8   Re
    Composer: George M. Cohan. **Conductor:** Jay Blackton. **Cast:** Joel Grey, Betty Ann Grove, Jill
    O'Hara, Bernadette Peters, Loni Ackerman, Jerry Dodge, Danny Carroll, Jonelle Allen,
    Jacqueline Alloway, Susan Batson, Jamie Donnelly, Harvey Evans, Angela Martin.
Studiotrack • Columbia (S) CS-9643 8-10
  Full title: *Songs from the Hit Musical George M!*
    Conductor: Teo Macero, Howard Roberts. **Cast:** Banjo Barons, Chorus and Orchestra.
Studiotrack • Design (SE) SDLP 288 8-12
  Full title: *Yankee Doodle Dandy Songs of Broadway's George M. Cohan*.
Studiotrack • RCA Camden (S) CAS-2275... 8-12
    Cast: Living Voices.

GERSHWIN HOLIDAY
Studiotrack (1963) • RCA Victor (M) VPM-6011 10-20   63
  Two discs.
    Cast: Frankie Carle, Morton Gould, Al Hirt, Norman Luboff, Peter Nero, Three Suns, Hugo
    Winterhalter.

GERSHWIN RARITIES
Studiotrack • Painted Smiles (M) 7017 10-20   80
    Cast: Kaye Ballard, David Craig, Nancy Walker, Louis Carlyle, Betty Gillett.

GERSHWINS IN HOLLYWOOD (1931-1964)
Soundtrack • JJA (M) 19773 30-35   77
  Two discs. Contains previously unreleased music from *An American in Paris* (including
  outtakes) and songs from *Delicious, Girl Crazy, Shall We Dance?, Lady Be Good, The
  Goldwyn Follies, The Man I Love, Starlift, Rhapsody in Blue, Kiss Me Stupid, Somebody
  Loves Me* and *Three for the Show*.
    Composer: George Gershwin, Ira Gershwin. **Conductor:** Various. **Cast:** Dean Martin, Betty
    Hutton, Gene Kelly, Oscar Levant, Betty Grable, Jack Lemmon, Doris Day, others.

GERTRUDE STEIN'S FIRST READER
Original Cast (1970) • Polydor (S) 24-7002... 15-25   70
    Composer: Ann Sternberg, Gertrude Stein. **Cast:** Michael Anthony, Joy Garrett, Frank
    Giordano, Sandra Thornton, Ann Sternberg (piano).

GET CRAZY
Soundtrack (1983) • Morocco (S) 6065CL 8-10   83
    Cast: Sparks, Ramones, Lou Reed, Lori Eastside & Nada, Marshall Crenshaw, Malcolm
    McDowell, Bill Henderson, Michael Boddicker, Howard Kaylan, Fear with Lee Ving.

GET SMART

TV Soundtrack (1965) • United Artists (M) UAL-3533 25-35   65
TV Soundtrack (1965) • United Artists (S) UAS-6533 35-55   65
    Cast: Don Adams. (With dialogue.)

GET YOURSELF A COLLEGE GIRL

Soundtrack (1964) • MGM (M) E-4273 12-18   65
Soundtrack (1964) • MGM (S) SE-4273 20-30   65
    Conductor: Fred Karger, others. Cast: Dave Clark Five, Animals, Stan Getz, Astrude Gilberto, Jimmy Smith Trio, Mary Ann Mobley, Standells, Freddie Bell and the Bell Boys, Roberta Linn.

GETTING STRAIGHT

Soundtrack (1970) • Colgems (S) COSO-5010 20-25   70
    Composer: Ron Stein, others. Conductor: Ron Stein, others. Cast: P.K. Limited, New Establishment, Elliott Gould, Candice Bergen. (With dialogue.)

GHOST AND MRS. MUIR

Studiotrack (1947) • Elmer Bernstein's Film Music
   Collection (M) FMC-4 25-35   75
Soundtrack (1947) • Varese Sarabande (M) 704 340 8-12   80s
    Composer: Bernard Herrmann. Conductor: Elmer Bernstein.

GHOST OF FRANKENSTEIN

Soundtrack (1942) • Tony Thomas (M) TT-HS-3 8-10   79
    Composer: Hans J. Salter. Conductor: Hans J. Salter.
   Also see FILM MUSIC OF HANS J. SALTER

GHOST STORY

Soundtrack (1981) • MCA (S) 5287 8-10   81
Soundtrack (1981) • MCA (S) MCA-27118 8-10   86
    Composer: Philippe Sarde. Conductor: Philippe Sarde.

GHOSTBUSTERS

Soundtrack (1984) • Arista (S) AL 8-8246 8-10   84
   Includes ad flyer.
    Composer: Elmer Bernstein, others. Conductor: Elmer Bernstein. Cast: Ray Parker Jr., Busboys, Alessi, Thompson Twins, Air Supply, Laura Branigan, Mick Smiley.

GHOSTBUSTERS II

Soundtrack (1989) • MCA (S) MCA-6306 8-10   89
    Composer: Randy Edelman, Bobby Brown. Cast: Bobby Brown, New Edition, James Taylor, Doug E. Fresh & the Get Fresh Crew, Run DMC, Oingo Boingo, Elton John, Glen Frey, Howard Huntsberry.

GHOSTS OF THE CIVIL DEAD

Soundtrack • Mute (S) 71433-1 8-10
    Cast: Blixa Bargeld, Nick Cave, Mick Harvey.

GIANT

Soundtrack (1956) • Capitol (EP) EDM-773 15-25   56
Soundtrack (1956) • Capitol (M) W-773 15-20   56
Soundtrack (1956) • Capitol (SE) DW-773 12-15   63
    Composer: Dimitri Tiomkin. Conductor: Dimitri Tiomkin, Ray Heindorf.
   Also see TRIBUTE TO JAMES DEAN

GIDGET GOES HAWAIIAN

Soundtrack (1961) • Colpix (M) CP 418 35-45   61
    Cast: James Darren, others.

GIFT OF LOVE

TV Soundtrack (1958) • Columbia (M) CL-1113.................................. 20-25   58
  Composer: Cyril Mockridge, Alfred Newman, Sammy Fain. **Conductor:** Lionel Newman. **Cast:** Vic Damone.

GIFT OF THE MAGI

TV Soundtrack (1959) • United Artists (M) UAL-4013 25-30   59
TV Soundtrack (1959) • United Artists (S) UAS-5013 35-45   59
  Composer: Richard Adler. **Conductor:** Hal Hastings. **Cast:** Eli Wallach (narration), Sally Ann Howes, Allen Case, Bibi Osterwald, Howard St. John, Jersey Quartet.

GIGI

Original Cast (1973) • RCA Victor (S) ABL1-0404.................................. 8-10   73
  Composer: Frederick Loewe, Alan Jay Lerner. **Conductor:** Ross Reimueller. **Cast:** Alfred Drake, Agnes Moorehead, Karin Wolfe, Daniel Massey, Maria Karnilova, Howard Chitjian, George Gaynes.
Original London Cast (1985) • Safari (S) Gigi-1 18-20   85
  UK release.
  Composer: Frederick Loewe, Alan Jay Lerner. **Conductor:** Ray Cook. **Cast:** Jean Pierre Aumont, Sian Phillips, Beryl Reid, Geoffrey Burridge, Amanda Waring.
Soundtrack (1958) • MGM (M) MG-1 20-40   58
  Three-disc, special promotional package.
  Composer: Frederick Loewe, Alan Jay Lerner. **Cast:** Leslie Caron, Maurice Chevalier, Louis Jourdan, Hermione Gingold, Dick Hyman Trio, David Rose.
Soundtrack (1958) • MGM (M) E-3641... 10-12   58
Soundtrack (1958) • MGM (S) SE-3641 12-15   58
  Yellow and black label.
Soundtrack (1958) • MGM (M) E-3641... 8-10   Re
Soundtrack (1958) • MGM (S) SE-3641 8-10   Re
  Black label, standard cover.
Soundtrack (1958) • MGM (M) E-3641... 8-10   68
Soundtrack (1958) • MGM (S) SE-3641 8-10   68
  Gatefold cover with new artwork. Blue and gold label.
Soundtrack (1958) • MGM (S) SW-90523.. 5-10   Re
  Capitol Record Club issue.
Soundtrack (1958) • MCA (S) 39045... 5-8   86
  Conductor: Andre Previn. **Cast:** Leslie Caron, Betty Wand (performed some vocals for Leslie Caron in the film), Louis Jourdan, Maurice Chevalier, Hermione Gingold.
Studiotrack (1958) • Columbia (M) CL-1122.. 10-15   58
  Actual title: *Dancing With Gigi*
  Conductor: Ray Ellis.
Studiotrack (1958) • Camden (M) CAL 436... 8-10   58
Studiotrack (1958) • Camden (S) CAS 436... 8-10   58
  Full title: *Instrumental Hits from Gigi.*
  Cast: Hill Bowen & His Orchestra.
Studiotrack (1958) • Golden Crest (M) CR-3042 8-12   58
  Cast: Hank Jones.
Studiotrack (1958) • Grand Award (S) GA-215....................................... 8-10   58
  Conductor: Enoch Light. **Cast:** Enoch Light and His Orchestra.
Studiotrack (1958) • Masterseal (M) MS-71 8-10   58
  Conductor: Fontanna. **Cast:** Fontanna and His Orchestra and Chorus.
Studiotrack [Vol. 1] (1958) • MGM (EP) X-1601 5-10   58
Studiotrack [Vol. 2] (1958) • MGM (EP) X-1602 5-10   58
Studiotrack (1958) • MGM (M) E-3640 8-12   58
  Conductor: David Rose. **Cast:** David Rose Orchestra.
Studiotrack (1958) • Rondolette (M) A32... 8-15   58
  Also has music from *Oklahoma!*

Studiotrack (1958) • Columbia (M) WL-158.. 12-15   58
French language version.
Conductor: Paul Baron. **Cast:** Maurice Chevalier, Sacha Distel, Marie-France, Jean Marker.
Studiotrack (1958) • Crown (S) CST-103 8-12   58
Studiotrack (1958) • Crown (M) 5064 8-10   Re
Conductor: Bernie Anders. **Cast:** Richard Hill, Billy Mason, Madeline Carey, Rena Ritchie, Sonny Patrick.
Studiotrack (1958) • Mercury (M) MG-20367 10-12   58
Conductor: Pete Rugolo. **Cast:** Robert Clary, Faith Winthrop.
Studiotrack (1958) • RCA Victor (EP) EPA-4258............................. 15-20   58
Studiotrack (1958) • RCA Victor (M) LPM-1716 8-10   58
Studiotrack (1958) • RCA Victor (S) LSP-1716 10-30   58
Conductor: Dennis Farnon. **Cast:** Gogi Grant, Tony Martin, Dennis Farnon's Orchestra.
Studiotrack (1958) • Waldorf (M) MHK 33-1249.................................. 5-8   58
Cast: Michael Stewart, Jack Brown, Dottie Evans, Lois Winter, Jerry Duane, Enoch Light Orchestra and Chorus, Gay Blades, Three Gossips.
Studiotrack (1958) • Design (M) DLP-56 5-8   58
Conductor: Warren Edward Vincent. **Cast:** Helen Halpin, Jack Searle.
Studiotrack • Golden Tone (M) C4035 5-8
Conductor: Gordon Fleming. **Cast:** Rene Beaumont, Susan Ellen, Babette George, Jack Andrews, John Bennett, Ted Sheldon.
Studiotrack (1959) • Mercury (S) SR-60042 5-8   59
Cast: Robert Clary.
Studiotrack • Tops (M) L1652.. 5-8
Conductor: Norman Leslie. **Cast:** Jack Forrest, Sheila Foray, Pierre Collette, Jean De Vol, Richard Phillips.
Studiotrack (1960) • Craftsmen (M) C-8028 5-8   60
Conductor: Leslie Carlton. **Cast:** Jacques Darieux and His Orchestra.
Studiotrack (1960) • Richmond (M) B-20074....................................... 5-8   60
Studiotrack (1960) • Richmond (S) S-30074 5-10   60
One side has music from *South Pacific*.
Conductor: Cyril Stapleton. **Cast:** Bryan Johnson, Joy Worth, Ray Merril, Janet Waters, Andy Cole, Pat Whitworth.
Studiotrack (1960) • Rondolette (M) 864 5-8   60
Cast: Muriel Rahn, Tom O'Leary, others.
Studiotrack (1963) • Bellflower (M) BFR-8009.................................... 5-8   63
Cast: Helen Halpin, Jack Searle.
Studiotrack • Coronet (M) CX 68... 5-8
Studiotrack • Coronet (S) CXS 68... 5-8
Studiotrack • Halo (M) 50300 5-8
Studiotrack • Koko (M) LM 2215 5-8
Studiotrack • Palace (S) PST-609 5-8
Full title: *Gigi and The Music Man*. Also has music from *The Music Man*.
Studiotrack • Saga (S) XID-5017... 5-8
Also has music from *Porgy and Bess*.
Studiotrack • Sutton (S) SSU-201 5-8
Also has music from *French Can-Can*.
Also see BRIGADOON
Also see EVENING WITH LERNER AND LOEWE

GIGOT
Soundtrack (1962) • Capitol (M) W-1754 15-25   62
Soundtrack (1962) • Capitol (S) SW-1754 20-35   62
Composer: Jackie Gleason. **Conductor:** Jackie Gleason.

GILBERT & SULLIVAN
Studio Cast (1950) • Decca (M) DL-5094 10-15   50
  Cast: Danny Kaye.
Studiotrack (1956) • Concertone (M) 2061 8-10   56
  Cast: Savoy Players & Orchestra.

GILDA RADNER LIVE
Original Cast (1979) • Warner Bros. (S) HS-3320 10-12   79
  Conductor: Howard Shore. **Cast:** Gilda Radner.

GINGER AND FRED: see FELLINI'S GINGER AND FRED

GINGER ROGERS
Soundtrack • Curtain Calls (M) CC 100/21 10-12
  Previously unreleased vocals from *Flying Down to Rio, Lady in the Dark,*
  Carefree, Vivacious Lady, The Barkleys of Broadway, In Person, Dreamboat
  plus stage versions of *Mame* and *Hello, Dolly!*
  Cast: Ginger Rogers, Fred Astaire, Oscar Levant, Jack Oakie, Ray Milland, Warner Baxter, Dick
  Powell.

GINGERBREAD BOY
Studio Cast (1960) • Harmony (M) HL-9528 10-15   60
  One side is music and story from *Goldilocks and the Three Bears.*
  Composer: Curtis Biever. **Conductor:** Curtis Biever. **Cast:** David Allen (narration).

GIRL CAN'T HELP IT
Soundtrack (1956) • Capitol (M) EAP-1-823 100-150   56
  Cast: Little Richard, Fats Domino, Platters, Gene Vincent and His Blue Caps.

GIRL CRAZY
Studio Cast (1952) • Columbia (M) ML-4475 12-18   52
Studio Cast (1952) • Columbia (M) CL-822 10-12   56
Studio Cast (1952) • Columbia (M) OL-7060 10-12   59
Studio Cast (1952) • Columbia (SE) OS-2560 10-12   59
Studio Cast (1952) • Columbia Special Products (SE) COS-2560 5-8   Re
  Composer: George Gershwin, Ira Gershwin. **Cast:** Mary Martin, Louise Carlyle, Eddie Chappell.
Studio Cast (1953) • RCA Victor (EP) EPA-486 15-20   53
Studio Cast (1953) • RCA Victor (M) LPM-3156 25-30   53
  10-inch LP. One side has music from *Porgy and Bess.*
  Composer: George Gershwin, Ira Gershwin, Dubose Heyward. **Conductor:** Lehman Engel, Jay
  Blackton, Milton Rosenstock. **Cast:** Lisa Kirk, Helen Gallagher, Edith Adams, Cab Calloway,
  Helen Thigpen.
Studio Cast (1962) • Reprise (M) R-6032 10-15   62
Studio Cast (1962) • Reprise (S) RS-6032 15-20   62
  Composer: George Gershwin, Ira Gershwin. **Conductor:** Morris Stoloff.
Soundtrack (1943) • Hollywood Soundstage (M) HS-5008 10-12   70s
Soundtrack (1943) • Curtain Calls (M) CC-100 9/10 15-20   70s
  Two discs. Silver Screen Soundtrack Series. Also has music from *Strike Up the Band.*
  Composer: George Gershwin. **Cast:** Judy Garland, Mickey Rooney, June Allyson,
  Nancy Walker.
Studiotrack (1943) • Decca DA-362 35-45   52
  Album of three 78 rpms.
Studiotrack (1943) • Decca (M) DL-5412 60-65   52
  10-inch LP.
  Composer: George Gershwin, Ira Gershwin. **Conductor:** George Stoll. **Cast:** Judy Garland,
  Mickey Rooney.

Studiotrack (1943) • Decca (EP) ED-2022 75-100   52
  Four Judy Garland songs from the original release.
    Composer: George Gershwin, Ira Gershwin. **Conductor:** George Stoll. **Cast:** Judy Garland.
    Also see BY JUPITER
    Also see WHEN THE BOYS MEET THE GIRLS

GIRL FRIEND
Studio Cast (1960) • Epic (M) BN 566 15-18
Studio Cast (1960) • Epic (M) LN-3685 20-25   60
  Also has music from *White Horse Inn* and *The New Moon*.
    Composer: Richard Rodgers, Lorenz Hart. **Conductor:** Johnny Gregory. **Cast:** Doreen Hume,
    Bruce Trent.
London Revival Cast (1987) • That's Entertainment (S) TER-1148 10-12   87
  UK release.
    Composer: Richard Rodgers, Lorenz Hart. **Cast:** Barbara King, Mark Hutchinson, Amanda Daintz,
    Catherine Francone, Mark Barrett.

GIRL FROM JONES BEACH
Soundtrack • Co-Star (S) CS 108 5-10   77
  Cast: Ed Stokes (narrator).

GIRL FROM U.N.C.L.E.
TV Soundtrack (1966) • MGM (M) E-4410 25-35   66
TV Soundtrack (1966) • MGM (S) SE-4410 35-50   66
    Composer: Dave Grusin, Jerry Goldsmith, others. **Conductor:** Teddy Randazzo.

GIRL GROUPS: THE STORY OF A SOUND
Soundtrack (1983) • Motown (S) 5322ML 8-12   83
    Cast: Supremes, Shangri-Las, Martha and the Vandellas, Dixie Cups, Mary Wells, Angels,
    Marvelettes, Shirelles, Velvelettes.

GIRL HAPPY
Soundtrack (1965) • RCA Victor (M) LPM-3338 40-60   65
  Black label, reads "Monaural" at bottom.
Soundtrack (1965) • RCA Victor (S) LSP-3338 40-60   65
  Black label, reads "Stereo" at bottom.
Soundtrack (1965) • RCA Victor (S) LSP-3338 15-25   Re
  Black label, reads "Stereo" at bottom. Has "RE" in lower left front cover and "LSP 3338
  (SPRS 2041)" on label.
Soundtrack (1965) • RCA Victor (S) LSP-3338 10-25   69
  Orange or tan label. (Tan label issued in 1976.)
Soundtrack (1965) • RCA Victor (S) AFL1-3338 8-10   78
    Composer: Doc Pomus, Bill Giant, Bernie Baum, Florence Kaye, Sid Tepper, Roy C. Bennett,
    Sid Wayne, Ben Weisman, others. **Cast:** Elvis Presley, Scotty Moore (guitar), D.J. Fontana
    (drums), Ray Siegel (bass), Jordanaires (vocals), Carole Lombard Trio (vocals), Jubilee Four
    (vocals).

GIRL HUNT BALLET: see BAND WAGON

GIRL IN PINK TIGHTS
Original Cast (1954) • Columbia (EP) A-1105 15-20   58
Original Cast (1954) • Columbia (M) ML-4890 40-45   58
Original Cast (1954) • Columbia Special Products (M) AOL-4890 8-10   81
    Composer: Sigmund Romberg, Leo Robin. **Conductor:** Sylvan Levin. **Cast:** Jeanmarie,
    Charles Goldner, David Atkinson, Brenda Lewis, Lydia Fredericks, Kalem Kermoyan, John
    Stamford.

GIRL IN THE BIKINI
Soundtrack (1952) • Poplar (M) PLP 33-1002 300-350   52
    Composer: Jean Yatove. **Cast:** Brigitte Bardot.

GIRL MOST LIKELY
Soundtrack (1957) • Capitol (M) W-930 40-60   58
Composer: Hugh Martin, Ralph Blane, Nelson Riddle. Conductor: Nelson Riddle. Cast: Jane
Powell, Cliff Robertson, Keith Andes, Kaye Ballard, Tommy Noonan, Jud Conlon Singers.

GIRL ON A MOTORCYCLE
Soundtrack (1969) • Tetragrammaton (S) T-5000 20-25   69
Composer: Les Reed. Cast: Douglas Gamley.

GIRL WHO CAME TO SUPPER
Original Cast (1963) • Columbia (M) KOL-6020 12-15   63
Original Cast (1963) • Columbia (S) KOS-2420 15-18   63
Composer: Noel Coward. Conductor: Jay Blackton. Cast: Jose Ferrer, Florence Henderson,
Roderick Cook, Sean Scully, Tessie O'Shea, Carey Nairnes.
Studio Cast • DRG (M) SL-5178 8-10
Noel Coward narrates and sings songs from the score.
Composer: Noel Coward. Conductor: Jay Blackton. Cast: Noel Coward.

GIRLS...AND MORE GIRLS
Soundtrack • Lion (M) L 70118.. 20-30
Songs from *Pandora and the Flying Dutchman, I'll Cry Tomorrow, Annie Get Your Gun,
Gentlemen Prefer Blondes, Lovely to Look At, The King and I, Tender Trap, Pirate, Student
Prince, Good News, Words and Music* and *Pagan Love Song*.
Conductor: Johnny Green, Charles Henderson, Adolph Deutsch, Lionel Newman, Carmen
Dragon, David Rose, Lennie Hayton. Cast: Debbie Reynolds, Susan Hayward, Lena Horne,
Judy Garland, Ava Gardner, Jane Powell, Jane Russell, Betty Hutton, Ann Blyth, Kathryn
Grayson, June Allyson, Esther Williams, MGM Studio Orchestra, Johnny Green and His
Orchestra, David Rose and His Orchestra.

GIRLS, LES: see LES GIRLS

GIRLS! GIRLS! GIRLS!
Soundtrack (1962) • RCA Victor (M) LPM-2621 60-90   62
Black label, reads "Long Play" at bottom.
Soundtrack (1962) • RCA Victor (S) LSP-2621 75-100   62
Black label, reads "Living Stereo" at bottom.
Soundtrack (1962) • RCA Victor (M) LPM-2621 40-50   63
Black label, reads "Mono" at bottom.
Soundtrack (1962) • RCA Victor (M) LPM-2621 25-30   65
Black label, reads "Monaural" at bottom.
Soundtrack (1962) • RCA Victor (S) LSP-2621 25-30   65
Black label, reads "Stereo" at bottom.
Soundtrack (1962) • RCA Victor (S) LSP-2621 10-25   69
Orange or tan label. (Tan label issued in 1976.)
Soundtrack (1962) • RCA Victor (S) AFL1-2621 8-10   77
Composer: Jerry Leiber, Mike Stoller, Bill Giant, Bernie Baum, Florence Kaye, Ruth Batchelor,
Dudley Brooks, Sid Tepper, Roy C. Bennett, Otis Blackwell, others. Cast: Elvis Presley, Scotty
Moore (guitar), Tiny Timbrell (guitar), Barney Kessel (guitar), Ray Siegel (bass), D.J. Fontana
(drums), Dudley Brooks (piano), Boots Randolph (sax), Jordanaires (vocals), Amigos (vocals).

GIRLS JUST WANT TO HAVE FUN
Soundtrack (1985) • Mercury (S) 422-824.. 10-12   85
Soundtrack (1985) • Mercury (S) 824510-1... 8-10   Re
Cast: Alex Brown, Chris Farren, Rainey, Q-Feel, Deborah Galli, Tami Holbrook, Meredith
Marshall, Animotion, Amy Hart, Holland.

GIRLS OF THE '30s
Soundtrack • Pelican (M) LP 122 5-10

GIVE 'EM HELL, HARRY!
Original Broadway Cast (1975) • United Artists (S) UA-LA540-H2 12-18   75
Two discs. Dialogue only.
Cast: James Whitmore (as U.S. President Harry Truman).

GIVE MY REGARDS TO BROAD STREET
Soundtrack (1984) • Columbia (S) SC-39613... 10-12   84
"Re-recorded Beatles and Wings classics." Some copies have black sticker with track information.
Composer: Paul McCartney, John Lennon. **Cast:** Paul McCartney, Linda McCartney, Ringo Starr.

GLASS MENAGERIE
Studio Cast (1964) • Caedmon (M) TRS-M-301 20-35   64
Boxed, two-disc set, with portfolio insert. A complete play by Tennessee Williams.
Composer: Paul Bowles. **Cast:** Jessica Tandy, David Wayne, Julie Harris, Montgomery Clift.
Soundtrack (1987) • MCA (S) 6222.. 8-10   87
Composer: Henry Mancini, Paul Bowles. **Conductor:** Henry Mancini. **Cast:** Henry Mancini and His Orchestra.
Studiotrack • Major (M) SR4M-3085.. 8-12
Composer: Max Marlin. **Conductor:** Max Marlin.

GLASS SLIPPER: see AUNTIE MAME

GLENN MILLER: GOLDEN HITS FROM HIS ORIGINAL SOUNDTRACKS
Soundtrack • 20th Century-Fox (M) FOX 1001...................................... 15-20
Music from *Orchestra Wives* and *Sun Valley Serenade*.
Composer: Mack Gordon, Harry Warren. **Conductor:** Glenn Miller. **Cast:** Glenn Miller and His Orchestra, Tex Beneke, Ray Eberle, Pat Friday, Marion Hutton and the Modernaires.
Also see ORCHESTRA WIVES
Also see SUN VALLEY SERENADE

GLENN MILLER STORY
Soundtrack [Vol. 1] (1954) • Decca (EP) ED-2124 20-25   56
Soundtrack [Vol. 2] (1954) • Decca (EP) ED-2125 20-25   56
Soundtrack [Vol. 2] (1954) • Decca (EP) ED-2126 20-25   56
Soundtrack (1954) • Decca (M) DL-5519 20-25   54
10-inch LP.
Soundtrack (1954) • Decca (M) DL-8226 20-25   56
Soundtrack (1954) • Decca (SE) DL-78226 15-20   59
Soundtrack (1954) • Decca (M) DL-9123 12-18   65
Soundtrack (1954) • Decca (SE) DL-79123 12-18   65
Soundtrack (1954) • MCA (SE) 2036e 8-10   72
Additional music not found on the 10-inch LP.
Soundtrack (1954) • MCA (S) 1624.. 10-15   80s
Reissued in true stereo in conjunction with the stereophonic theatrical re-release.
Conductor: Joseph Gershenson. **Cast:** Universal-International Studio Orchestra, Glenn Miller Orchestra, Louis Armstrong and All Stars.
Studiotrack • RCA Victor (EP) EPB-3057 20-25   54
Two discs.
Studiotrack • RCA Victor (M) LPT-3057 20-25   54
10-inch LP.
Conductor: Glenn Miller. **Cast:** Glenn Miller Orchestra.
Studiotrack • RCA Victor (EP) EPA-733... 10-15   56
Studiotrack • RCA Victor (EP) EPB-1192... 15-20   56
Two discs.

Studiotrack • RCA Victor (M) LPM-1192.. 10-15   56
Studiotrack • RCA Victor (SE) LPM-1192e.. 12-18
    Conductor: Glenn Miller. **Cast:** Glenn Miller Orchestra, Tex Beneke, Marion Hutton, Modernaires.
Studiotrack (1956) • Decca (M) DL-5532 15-20   56
    Cast: Louis Armstrong and the All Stars.
  Also see ORCHESTRA WIVES
  Also see GOLDEN HITS FROM HIS ORIGINAL SOUND TRACKS

GLORY
Soundtrack (1989) • Virgin Movie Music (S) 91329-4 15-25   89
    Composer: James Horner. **Conductor:** James Horner. **Cast:** Boys Choir of Harlem.

GLORY GUYS
Soundtrack (1965) • United Artists (M) UAL-4126 10-12   65
Soundtrack (1965) • United Artists (S) UAS-5126 12-15   65
    Composer: Riz Ortolani. **Conductor:** Riz Ortolani.

GLORY STOMPERS
Soundtrack (1968) • Sidewalk (S) DT-5910 35-45   68
    Composer: Mike Curb, Harley Hatcher, Davie Allan. **Cast:** Davie Allan and the Arrows, Max Frost and the Troopers, Casey Kasem, Eddie and the Stompers, Sidewalk Sounds.

GNOME MOBILE
Soundtrack (1967) • Disneyland (M) CR-282 10-20   67
  Commercial spots. Made for radio station use only.
    Cast: Walter Brennan, Ed Wynn, Matthew Garber, Karen Dotrice.

GO FIGHT CITY HALL: see BEI MIR BISTU SCHOEN

GO FLY A KITE
Original Cast (1966) • General Electric (S) No Number Used 75-100   66
  Two discs. General Electric presented this show at the Fifth Electric Utility Conference, in Williamsburg, Virginia, September 19 - 21, 1966. Distributed there as a souvenir.
    Composer: John Kander, Walter Marks, Fred Ebb. **Conductor:** Ted Simons. **Cast:** Valerie Harper, Henry Hamilton, Nancy Haywood, Joel Warfield.

GO, GO, GO WORLD
Soundtrack (1965) • Musicor (M) MM-2059... 30-35   65
Soundtrack (1965) • Musicor (S) MS-3059... 45-50   65
    Composer: Bruno Nicolai, Nino Oliviero.

GO INTO YOUR DANCE: see WONDER BAR

GO, JOHNNY, GO!
Soundtrack (1959) • No Label Shown (EP) No Number Used.......... 200-300   60
    Composer: Various. **Conductor:** Hal Roach. **Cast:** Jimmy Clanton.
Soundtrack (1959) • No Label Shown (M) No Number Used............ 500-750   59
  Promotional issue only.
    Cast: Jimmy Clanton, Sandy Stewart, Jackie Wilson, Chuck Berry, Cadillacs, Flamingos, Eddie Cochran, Ritchie Valens, Harvey Fuqua, Jo Ann Campbell.

GOBLIN MARKET
Original Cast (1985) • That's Entertainment (S) TER-1144 10-12   85
  UK release.
    Composer: Polly Penn. **Cast:** Terri Klausner, Ann Morrison, Polly Penn, Sharon Scruggs.

GOD CREATED WOMAN
Soundtrack (1957) • Decca (M) DL-8685 50-100   57
  Full title: *And God Created Woman.*
    Composer: Paul Misraki. **Cast:** Brigitte Bardot (French dialogue).

GOD SAID
Studio Cast (1959) • Epic (M) 5LN-3534 10-15   59
Studio Cast (1959) • Epic (S) 6BN-511 10-15   59
   Full title: *And God Said*. Biblical stories.
    Composer: God. **Cast:** Dana Andrews (narrator).

GOD'S HOUSE
Soundtrack (1965) • No Label Used (M) No Number Used 60-80   65
   Private pressing made by TV composer, Ingram Walters. Each is autographed as a
   Christmas gift for friends. Also has music from other TV and film scores.
    Composer: Ingram Walters.

GOD'S LITTLE ACRE
Soundtrack (1958) • United Artists (M) UAL-40002 125-150   58
    Composer: Elmer Bernstein, Erskine Caldwell. **Conductor:** Elmer Bernstein.

GODFATHER
Soundtrack (1972) • Paramount (S) PAS-1003 15-20   72
   First issue has tri-fold cover with 17 color photos on inside cover.
Soundtrack (1972) • Paramount (S) PAS-1003 10-15   72
   Gatefold cover. Has fewer black and white photos.
    Composer: Nino Rota, Carmine Coppola, others. **Conductor:** Carmine Coppola, Carlo Savina.
    Cast: Al Martino.
Soundtrack (1972) • Paramount (S) PAS-6034 10-15   72
   Full title: *The Godfather's Family Wedding Album*.

GODFATHER, PART II
Soundtrack (1975) • ABC (S) DP-856 15-18   75
    Composer: Nino Rota, Carmine Coppola. **Conductor:** Carmine Coppola. **Cast:** Livio Giorgi,
    Nino Palermo, Marcia Religioso.

GODFATHER, PARTS I & II
TV Soundtrack (1972-74) • Sunnyvale (S) SSP2000 10-20   77
   Music from TV's *The Godfather* Saga.
    Composer: Carmine Coppola, Nino Rota, Francesco Pennino. **Conductor:** Carmine Coppola.
    Cast: Milan Philarmonia Orchestra.

GODS MUST BE CRAZY
Soundtrack (1981) • Varese Sarabande (S) STV 81243 8-10   80s
    Composer: Johnny Boshoff.

GODS MUST BE CRAZY II
Soundtrack (1990) • Novus (S) 3091-1-N... 8-10   90
    Composer: Charles Fox. **Conductor:** Charles Fox.

GODSPELL
Original Cast (1971) • Bell (S) 1102 8-10   71
Original Cast (1971) • Arista (S) AL 4001.. 5-8   75
Original Cast (1971) • Arista (Q) AQ-4001 10-12   75
Original Cast (1971) • Arista (S) ALB6-8304 5-8   Re
    Composer: Stephen Schwartz. **Conductor:** Stephen Schwartz. **Cast:** Lamar Alford, Jesse
    Cutler, Peggy Gordon, David Haskell, Joanne Jonas, Richard LaBonte, Robin Lamont, Gilmer
    McCormick, Sonia Manzano, Jeffrey Mylett, Stephen Nathan, Steve Reinhardt, Herb Simon.
Original Australian Cast (1971) • Lewis Young Prod. (S) SFL-934486 . 12-18   71
    Composer: Stephen Schwartz. **Conductor:** Rory Thomas. **Cast:** Domenic Luca, Chris Sheil,
    Karen Corbett, Christopher Pate, Paul Reid Roman, Colette Mann, Julian Archer, Rob Ellis.

Soundtrack (1973) • Bell (S) 1118.. 8-12   73
Soundtrack (1973) • Arista (S) 4005 8-10   75
Soundtrack (1973) • Arista (S) ALB6-8337.. 5-8   Re
    Composer: Stephen Schwartz, Jay Hamburger, Peggy Gordon. **Cast:** Victor Garber, Robin
    Lamont, Lynne Thigpen, David Haskell, Merrell Jackson, Jerry Stroka, Gilmer McCormick,
    Jeffrey Mylett, Katie Hanley, Stephen Reinhardt, Richard LaBonte.
Soundtrack (1973) • Pickwick (S) SPC 3304.. 5-10   73
    Opera excerpts.
    Composer: Stephen Schwartz. **Conductor:** Stephen Reinhardt. **Cast:** David Haskell, Victor
    Garber, Robin Lamont, Joanne Jonas.

GOIN' BACK TO INDIANA
TV Soundtrack (1971) • Motown (S) M-742... 10-12   71
    Composer: Various. **Cast:** Jackson Five, Bill Cosby, Tom Smothers.

GOING HOLLYWOOD
Soundtrack • Crosbyana (SE) Volume 17 10-12
    Soundtracks from Bing Crosby films, 1928 - 1964.
    Cast: Bing Crosby.
    Also see TEN NORTH FREDERICK

GOING MY WAY
Studiotrack (1944) • Decca A-405... 15-25   44
    78 rpm album.
Studiotrack (1944) • Decca (EP) ED-2036 15-25   49
    Composer: James Van Heusen, others. **Conductor:** John Scott Trotter, Victor Young. **Cast:**
    Bing Crosby, Williams Brothers Quartet, Ken Darby Singers, John Scott Trotter and His
    Orchestra, Victor Young and His Orchestra.
Studiotrack (1944) • Decca (M) DL-5052 40-45   49
    10-inch LP. One side has music from *The Bell's of St. Mary's.*
    Also see BING'S HOLLYWOOD

GOING SURFIN'
Soundtrack (1975) • Cowabunga (S) 1001... 15-20   75

GOLD
Soundtrack (1975) • ABC (S) ABCD-855 10-35   75
    Composer: Elmer Bernstein, Don Black. **Conductor:** Elmer Bernstein. **Cast:** Maureen
    McGovern, Jimmy Helms, Trevor Chance.

GOLD DIGGERS (OF 1933 AND 1935): see GOLDEN AGE OF THE
HOLLYWOOD MUSICAL

GOLD TURKEY
Radio Cast (1975) • Epic (S) PE-33410 10-12   75
    National Lampoon Radio Hour program.

GOLDBERG, WHOOPI: see WHOOPI GOLDBERG

GOLDEN AGE OF BRITISH FILM MUSIC
Soundtrack • Citadel (S) CT-OFI-1... 15-20   82
    Composer: Sir Arthur Bliss, Hopkins, Alwyn, Greenwood, Irving, others.

GOLDEN AGE OF MOVIE MUSICALS
Soundtrack (1972) • MGM (S) SQBO-93890... 10-15   72
    Two discs. Includes a 12-page guidebook and full-color posters from *Annie Get Your Gun,
    Singin' in the Rain* and *Kismet.*
    Cast: Judy Garland, Fred Astaire, Jane Powell, Ava Gardner, Gene Kelly, Georges Guetary,
    Bert Lahr, Kathryn Grayson, Debbie Reynolds, Ann Miller, Howard Keel, Esther Williams,
    Ricardo Montalban, others.

GOLDEN AGE OF THE HOLLYWOOD MUSICAL
Soundtrack • United Artists (S) UA-LA215-H..10-12   72
Soundtrack • Liberty (S) LKAO-215 8-10   Re
  Music from *Gold Diggers of 1933*, *Dames*, *42nd Street*, *Footlight Parade* and *Gold Diggers of 1935*.
    Composer: Harry Warren, others. **Conductor:** Ray Heindorf, Leo F. Forbstein. **Cast:** George Raft (narration), Joan Blondell, Ruby Keeler, Dick Powell.

GOLDEN APPLE
Original Cast (1954) • RCA Victor (EP) EOD-1014 20-30   54
Original Cast (1954) • RCA Victor (M) LOC-1014 75-90   54
Original Cast (1954) • Elektra (M) EKL-5000......................................45-65   60
    Composer: Jerome Moross, John Latouche. **Conductor:** Hugh Ross. **Cast:** Priscilla Gillette, Stephen Douglass, Kaye Ballard, Bibi Osterwald, Portia Nelson, Martha Larrimore, Dean Michener, Geraldine Viti, Jack Whiting.

GOLDEN BOY
Original Cast (1964) • Capitol (M) VAS-2124 10-12   64
Original Cast (1964) • Capitol (S) SVAS-2124 12-15   64
  Both have gatefold covers.
Original Cast (1964) • Capitol (S) STAO-11165 10-12   77
  Features an alternate finale.
    Composer: Charles Strouse, Lee Adams. **Conductor:** Elliot Lawrence. **Cast:** Sammy Davis Jr., Billy Daniels, Paula Wayne, Kenneth Tobey, Louis Gossett, Lola Falana, John Brown, Terrin Miles.
Studiotrack (1964) • Capitol (M) T-2278..8-10   64
Studiotrack (1964) • Capitol (S) ST-2278..8-12   64
    Conductor: H.B. Barnum.
Studiotrack • Colpix (M) CP-478...8-12   64
Studiotrack • Colpix (S) SCP-478...8-12   64
  Full title: *Selections from Golden Boy.*
    Cast: Art Blakey and the Jazz Messengers.

GOLDEN BREED
Soundtrack (1967) • Capitol (S) ST-2886...20-25   67
    Composer: Mike Curb, Jerry Styner, Harley Hatcher. **Cast:** Mike Clifford, Davie Allen.

GOLDEN CHILD
Soundtrack (1986) • Capitol (S) SJ-12544 8-10   867
    Composer: John Barry, others. **Cast:** Ann Wilson, Melissa Morgan, Ashford and Simpson, Martha Davis, Ratt, Marlon Jackson, Robbie Buchanen, John Barry.

GOLDEN COACH
Soundtrack (1952) • MGM (M) E-3111 65-125   54
    Composer: Antonio Vivaldi, others. **Conductor:** Gino Marinuzzi Jr. **Cast:** Rome Symphony Orchestra, Anna Magnani.

GOLDEN EARRINGS
Studiotrack (1947) • Decca (M) DL-8008 20-25   50
Studiotrack (1947) • Decca (M) DL-8481 15-18   57
  Both also have music from *For Whom the Bell Tolls.*
    Composer: Victor Young. **Conductor:** Victor Young. **Cast:** Victor Young's Concert Orchestra.
    Also see BLOOD AND SAND

GOLDEN HOLLYWOOD THEMES
Soundtrack (1963) • Decca (M) DL-4362 10-15   63
Soundtrack (1963) • Decca (S) DL-74362...15-20   63

GOLDEN HORSESHOE REVIEW
Original Cast • Disneyland (M) WDL-3013 10-12

GOLDEN LAND
Original Cast (1986) • Continuity Products (S) GL-001 10-20   86
Composer: Zalmen Miloten, Moiske Rosenfeld. Cast: Bruce Adler, Marc Krause, Neva Small, Phyllis Berk, Stuart Zagnit.

GOLDEN MOTION PICTURE THEMES AND ORIGINAL SOUND TRACKS
Soundtrack • United Artists (M) UAL-3376 8-10   64
Soundtrack • United Artists (S) UAS-6376 8-10   64
Composer: Various. Conductor: Various. Cast: Al Caiola, Leroy Holmes, Ferrante and Teicher, Riz Ortolani, Hollywood Studio Orchestra, Ken Lauber, Billy May, John Barry, John Addison, Frank DeVol, Ernest Gold.

GOLDEN RAINBOW
Original Cast (1968) • Calendar (M) KOM-1001 20-30   68
Original Cast (1968) • Calendar (S) KOS-1001 35-45   68
Composer: Walter Marks. Conductor: Elliot Lawrence. Cast: Steve Lawrence, Eydie Gorme, Scott Jacoby, Joseph Sirola.

GOLDEN SCREW
Original Cast (1967) • Atco (M) 33-208 25-30   67
Original Cast (1967) • Atco (S) SD-33-208.. 30-40   67
Composer: Tom Sankey. Cast: Tom Sankey, Jack Hopper, Inner Sanctum.

GOLDEN SEAL
Soundtrack (1983) • Compleat (S) CSTR-6001.................................... 10-15   83
Composer: John Barry, Dana Kaproff. Cast: Glen Campbell.

GOLDEN THEMES FROM MOTION PICTURES
Studiotrack (1962) • United Artists (M) UAL-3210 8-10   62
Studiotrack (1962) • United Artists (S) UAS-6210 8-10   62
Music from *Picnic, Spellbound, Mona Lisa, As Time Goes By, Moulin Rouge, My Foolish Heart, Be My Love, All the Way, Tammy, Secret Love, True Love* and *The High and the Mighty*.
Composer: Various. Cast: Ferrante and Teicher.

GOLDEN TURKEY ALBUM
Soundtrack • Rhino (S) RNSP 307... 10-12   85
Concept collection of the 12 worst movie scores of all time.

GOLDEN VOYAGE OF SINBAD
Soundtrack (1974) • United Artists (S) UA-LA308-G 12-15   74
Soundtrack (1974) • United Artists (S) UAS-29576 8-10   Re
Composer: Miklos Rozsa. Conductor: Miklos Rozsa.

GOLDFINGER
Soundtrack (1964) • United Artists (M) UAL-4117 10-15   64
Soundtrack (1964) • United Artists (S) UAS-5117 15-20   64
Composer: John Barry, Leslie Bricusse, Anthony Newley. Conductor: John Barry. Cast: Shirley Bassey, John Barry.
Studiotrack (1964) • Camden (M) CAL-913.. 8-12   64
Studiotrack (1965) • Camden (S) CAS-913.. 10-12   65
Full title: *Goldfinger (and Other Music from James Bond Thrillers)*.
Composer: John Barry, others. Cast: Ray Martin and His Orchestra.
Studiotrack (1965) • United Artists (S) UAS-6424 10-12   65
Full title: *John Barry Plays Goldfinger*. Also has other Barry film themes.
Conductor: John Barry. Cast: John Barry.
Studiotrack (1965) • Wyncote (M) W-9086... 8-12   65
Full title: *Songs from Goldfinger and Other James Bond Favorites*.
Cast: Cheltenham Orchestra and Chorus.

Studiotrack • Regina (M) R 319.. 8-12   60s
   Full title: *Goldfinger and Other Great Movie Themes*.
    Cast: Jack La Forge and Orchestra.
    Also see INCREDIBLE WORLD OF JAMES BOND
    Also see JAMES BOND

GOLDILOCKS (1958)
Original Cast (1958) • Columbia (M) OL-5340 15-20   58
Original Cast (1958) • Columbia (S) OS-2007 40-50   58
Original Cast (1958) • Columbia Special Products (S) COS-2007 8-10   Re
    Composer: Leroy Anderson, Joan Ford, Walter Kerr, Jean Kerr. **Conductor:** Lehman Engel.
    Cast: Don Ameche, Elaine Stritch, Russell Nype, Pat Stanley, Nathaniel Frey, Margaret
    Hamilton, Gene Varrone, Richard Armbruster.

GOLDILOCKS (1970)
TV Soundtrack (1970) • Evans-Black Carpets/Armstrong (S) DL-3511 10-12   70
    Composer: Richard M. Sherman, Robert B. Sherman. **Cast:** Bing Crosby, Mary Frances
    Crosby, Kathryn Crosby, Nathaniel Crosby, Paul Winchell (narrator), Avery Schrieber.

GOLDILOCKS AND THE THREE BEARS: see GINGERBREAD BOY

GOLIATH AND THE BARBARIANS
Soundtrack (1960) • American International (M) 1001-M 30-35   60
Soundtrack (1960) • American International (S) 1001-S...................... 45-65   60
Soundtrack (1960) • Varese Sarabande (S) VC-81078 8-10   78
    Composer: Les Baxter. **Conductor:** Muir Mathieson.

GOMER PYLE U.S.M.C.
Studiotrack • Columbia (M) CL-2368.. 15-20
    Cast: Jim Nabors.

GONE WITH THE WAVE
Soundtrack (1965) • Colpix (M) CP-492 25-30   65
Soundtrack (1965) • Colpix (S) SCP-492 50-55   65
    Composer: Lalo Schifrin. **Conductor:** Lalo Schifrin. **Cast:** Shelly Manne, Laurindo Almeida.

GONE WITH THE WIND
Original London Cast (1972) • Columbia EMI (S) SCXA 9252 ....:. 25-45   72
   UK release.
Original London Cast (1972) • AEI (S) AEI-1113................................... 12-18   70s
   Both from the musical version which opened at the Theatre Royale, Drury Lane, London,
   May 3, 1972.
    Composer: Harold Rome. **Conductor:** Ray Cook. **Cast:** Harve Presnell, June Ritchie, Patricia
    Michael, Robert Swann, Brian Davies.
Studio Cast (1973) • Chappell (S) CHP-101... 25-30   73
    Composer: Harold Rome. **Cast:** Harold Rome (singing the complete score, including songs cut
    from the show), Et Tu Brutus Ensemble.
Soundtrack (1939) • MGM (M) 1E-10.. 10-12   67
Soundtrack (1939) • MGM (SE) S1E-10.. 12-15   67
   Gatefold cover "Limited Editions." Both include a 32-page color booklet.
Soundtrack (1939) • MGM (M) 1E-10.. 8-10   67
Soundtrack (1939) • MGM (SE) S1E-10.. 8-10   67
   Gatefold covers, but without the booklet.
Studiotrack (1954) • RCA Victor (EP) EPB-3227................................... 10-20   54
   Two discs. Gatefold cover.
    Composer: Max Steiner. **Conductor:** Max Steiner.
Studiotrack (1954) • RCA Victor (M) LPM-3227 20-25   54
   10-inch LP.
Studiotrack (1954) • Camden (M) CAL-625.. 12-18   61
Studiotrack (1954) • RCA Victor (M) LSM-3859 12-15   67

Studiotrack (1954) • RCA Victor (SE) LSP-3859 12-15   67

Studiotrack (1956) • RCA Victor (M) LPM-1287 20-25   56
   Full title: *Music from Gone with the Wind and Selections from Other Motion Pictures.* One side has music from *The Searchers, The Stolen Life, The Charge of the Light Brigade* and *Four Wives.*

Studiotrack (1959) • Warner Bros. (M) W-1322 15-45   59

Studiotrack (1959) • Warner Bros. (S) WS-1322.................................. 30-80   59
   Gatefold covers (cover has hand-painted carriage scene), with booklet. Both labeled "20th Anniversary Edition."

Studiotrack (1959) • Warner Bros. (M) W-1322 12-15   61

Studiotrack (1959) • Warner Bros. (S) WS-1322.................................. 12-15   61
   Gatefold covers. Both labeled "Official Centennial Edition – Deluxe Souvenir Edition."

Studiotrack (1959) • Warner Bros. (M) W-1322 10-12   67

Studiotrack (1959) • Warner Bros. (S) WS-1322.................................. 10-12   67
   Either standard or gatefold covers. Both labeled "Spectacular Wide Screen Sound" with black border covers.

Studiotrack (1959) • Warner Bros. (S) WS-1322.................................... 8-12   72

Studiotrack (1959) • Stanyan (S) SR-10090... 8-10   73
   Composer: Max Steiner. **Conductor:** Muir Mathieson. **Cast:** London Symphony Orchestra.

Studiotrack (1961) • Columbia (S) L3-10004.. 10-12   61
   Full title: *Tara's Theme from Gone with the Wind.* Also has themes from other films.
   Composer: Max Steiner. **Conductor:** Percy Faith. **Cast:** Percy Faith Orchestra.

Studiotrack (1961) • MGM (M) E-3954 35-40   61

Studiotrack (1961) • MGM (SE) SE-3954 35-45   61
   Gatefold covers. Both are "Commemorative editions."

Studiotrack (1961) • Metro (M) M-613 10-15   66

Studiotrack (1961) • Metro (SE) MS-613 15-20   66
   Metros are abridged versions of MGM 3954.

Studiotrack (1961) • MCA (SE) 39063 8-10   86
   Reissue of MGM SE-3954.
   Composer: Max Steiner. **Conductor:** Cyril Ornadel. **Cast:** Starlight Symphony Orchestra.

Studiotrack (1967) • RCA Camden (S) CAS-2161 8-10   67
   Full title: *Living Strings Play Music from Gone with the Wind and Other Motion Pictures.*
   Cast: Living Strings.

Studiotrack • RCA Victor (S) ARL1-0452 10-12   74
   Full title: *Max Steiner's Classic Film Score, Gone with the Wind.*
   Composer: Max Steiner. **Conductor:** Charles Gerhardt. **Cast:** National Philharmonic Orchestra.

Studiotrack • Design (S) DLP-274... 8-12
   Also has themes from other films.
   Cast: Dean Franconi and the Hollywood Strings.

Studiotrack • Pickwick (M) PC-3087... 8-10

Studiotrack • Pickwick (S) SPC-3087 8-10
   Composer: Max Steiner. **Conductor:** Walter Stott.

Studiotrack (1939) • Polydor (M) PDM-1-7001 10-12   83
   Previously unreleased soundtrack music. Includes reprint of original movie poster.
   Composer: Max Steiner. **Conductor:** Max Steiner.
   Also see PARRISH

GOOD COMPANIONS

Original London Cast (1974) • EMI (S) EMC 3042 20-25   74
   UK release.

Original London Cast (1974) • Stet (S) DS-15020.................................. 8-12   Re
   Composer: Andre Previn, Johnny Mercer. **Conductor:** Marcus Dods. **Cast:** John Mills, Judi Dench, Marti Webb, Malcolm Rennie.

GOOD EVENING
Original Cast (1973) • Island (S) ILPS-9298... 10-15   73
    Composer: Peter Cook, Dudley Moore. **Cast:** Peter Cook, Dudley Moore.

GOOD MORNING, BABYLON
Soundtrack (1987) • Varese Sarabande (S) STV-81317 10-15   87
    Composer: Nicola Piovani.

GOOD MORNING, VIETNAM
Soundtrack (1987) • A&M (S) SP-3913 8-10   87
    Cast: Martha Reeves and Vandellas, Beach Boys, Wayne Fontana and the Mindbenders, Searchers, Castaways, James Brown, Them, Marvelettes, Vogues, Rivieras, Louis Armstrong, Robin Williams.

GOOD NEWS
Original Cast (1974) • No Label Used (S) SA-101-4.......................... 200-250   74
    Two discs in gatefold cover. Live recording of the show's score on one record, outtakes and alternate versions on the other. Limited editon of 1,000 numbered copies. Shown as stereo on cover, but recording appears to be mono.
    Composer: Ray Henderson, Lew Brown, Buddy DeSylva. **Conductor:** Liza Redfield. **Cast:** Alice Faye, John Payne, Stubby Kaye, Scott Stevenson, Marti Rolph, Barbara Lail, Wayne Bryan, Jana Robbins, Joseph Burke, Tommy Breslin.
Studio Cast (1974) • Signature (S) BSL1-0577 10-12   74
    Composer: Ray Henderson, Lew Brown, Buddy DeSylva. **Cast:** Teresa Brewer.
Studio Cast • World (M) WRC-7065.. 20-25
    One side has music from *Sally*.
Soundtrack (1947) • MGM - MGM-17... 18-20   47
    78 rpm album.
Soundtrack (1947) • MGM (EP) X-17 12-15   50
Soundtrack (1947) • MGM (M) E-504... 35-45   50
    10-inch LP.
Soundtrack (1947) • MGM (M) E-3229 15-18   55
    One side has music from *Three Little Words*.
Soundtrack (1947) • MGM (M) E-3771 18-20   59
    Gatefold cover. One side has music from *Words and Music*. Because he was contracted to another label, Mel Torme is not heard on the MGM releases.
    Composer: Ray Henderson, Lew Brown, Buddy DeSylva, Betty Comden, Adolph Green, Roger Edens. **Conductor:** Lennie Hayton. **Cast:** June Allyson, Peter Lawford, Patricia Marshall, Joan McCracken.
Studiotrack (1957) • Halo (M) 50257 10-15   57
    Also see IN THE GOOD OLD SUMMERTIME
    Also see THOSE GLORIOUS MGM MUSICALS

GOOD NEWS ABOUT OLDS
TV Soundtrack (1959) • WDR (M) 112272... 10-20   59
    Full title: *Good News About Olds (Oldsmobile's 1959 Announcement Show)*. Label and number are shown only in trail-off area of disc.
    Conductor: Glen Osser. **Cast:** Florence Henderson, Bill Hayes.
    Also see OLD FOR '60 MUSICAL
    Also see THIS IS OLDSMOBILITY

GOOD OLD BAD OLD DAYS!
Original London Cast • EMI (S) EMA-751 12-15   73
    Gatefold cover.
Original London Cast • AEI (S) AEI-1116... 8-12   70s
    Composer: Anthony Newley, Leslie Bricusse.

GOOD, THE BAD AND THE UGLY
Soundtrack (1968) • United Artists (M) UAL-4172 8-12   68
Soundtrack (1968) • United Artists (S) UAS-5172 10-15   68
Soundtrack (1968) • United Artists (S) ST-91464 8-12   Re
    Composer: Ennio Morricone. **Cast:** Hugo Montenegro.

GOOD TIMES
Soundtrack (1967) • Atco (M) 33-214 10-25   67
Soundtrack (1967) • Atco (S) SD-33-214 12-35   67
    Composer: Sonny Bono. **Conductor:** Sonny Bono. **Cast:** Sonny and Cher. (With dialogue.)

GOOD TO GO
Soundtrack (1986) • Island (S) 90509-1 8-10   86
    Cast: Trouble Funk, Ini Kamoze, Hot Cold Sweat, Sly and Robbie, Wally Badarou, Chuck
    Brown, Donald Banks, Redds and the Boys.
    Also see MUSIC FROM A FISTFUL OF DOLLARS

GOODBYE AGAIN
Soundtrack (1961) • United Artists (M) UAL-4091 20-25   61
Soundtrack (1961) • United Artists (S) UAS-5091 20-30   61
    Composer: Georges Auric, Dory Langdon. **Cast:** Anthony Perkins (dialogue), Ferrante and
    Teicher, Diahann Carroll.

GOODBYE, CHARLIE
Soundtrack (1964) • 20th Century-Fox (M) TFM-3165 12-25   64
Soundtrack (1964) • 20th Century-Fox (S) TFS-4165 20-25   64
    Composer: Andre Previn. **Conductor:** Andre Previn.

GOODBYE COLUMBUS
Soundtrack (1969) • Warner Bros. (S) WS-1786 12-15   69
    Composer: Charles Fox, Association, others. **Cast:** Association.

GOODBYE DEAR, I'LL BE BACK IN A YEAR
Original L.A. Cast (1983) • No Label Used (S) No Number Used 8-10   83
    Cast: Martin Bratter, Lisa Kae Matso, Bruce Steele, Lori Moore.

GOODBYE GEMINI
Soundtrack (1971) • DJM (S) DJLPS-408 25-30   71
    Composer: Christopher Gunning, others. **Conductor:** Marcus Dods. **Cast:** Jackie Lee,
    Peddlers, Peter Lee Stirling.

GOODBYE MR. CHIPS
Original London Cast (1982) • That's Entertainment (S) TER-1025 10-12   82
    UK release. London stage production based on the 1969 film.
    Composer: Leslie Bricusse. Conductor: John Owen Edwards. Cast: John Mills, Colette Gleeson,
    Nigel Stock.
Soundtrack (1969) • MGM (S) 1SE-19 10-15   69
    White label. Standard cover. Promotional issue only.
Soundtrack (1969) • MGM (S) 1SE-19 8-10   69
Soundtrack (1969) • MCA (S) MCA-39006 5-8   86
    Composer: Leslie Bricusse. **Conductor:** John Williams. **Cast:** Petula Clark, Peter O'Toole.

GOODTIME CHARLEY
Original Cast (1975) • RCA Victor (S) ARL1-1011 20-25   75
    Composer: Hal Hackady, Larry Grossman. **Conductor:** Arthur B. Rubinstein. **Cast:** Joel Grey,
    Ann Reinking, Louis Zorich, Ed Becker, Susan Browning, Rhoda Butler, Peggy Cooper, Jay
    Garner, Grace Keagy, Nancy Killmer, Hal Norman, Charles Rule, Richard B. Shull, Brad Tyrrell.

GOODY TWO SHOES
Studio Cast • MGM/Young Directional (S) YDS 301 8-12
    Cast: Efrem Zimbalist Jr. (narrator).

GOOFY'S TV SPECTACULAR
TV Soundtrack • Disneyland (S) 1252.................................. 20-25

GOONIES
Soundtrack (1985) • Epic (S) SE-40067................................ 8-10   85
    Composer: Dave Grusin, others. **Cast:** Cyndi Lauper, REO Speedwagon, Luther Vanderdross, Joseph Williams, 14K, Philip Bailey, Bangles, Dave Grusin.

GORDON JENKINS CONDUCTS 26 YEARS OF ACADEMY AWARD WINNERS
Studiotrack (1959) • CG Records (M) CGM 1002 10-15   59
    Conductor: Gordon Jenkins.

GORDON'S WAR
Soundtrack (1973) • Buddah (S) BDS-5137 25-30   73
    Cast: Barbara Mason, New Birth, Badder Than Evil.

GORILLAS IN THE MIST
Soundtrack (1988) • MCA (S) 6255....................................... 8-10   88
    Composer: Maurice Jarre. **Conductor:** Maurice Jarre.

GORKY PARK
Soundtrack (1983) • Varese Sarabande (S) STV-81206 8-12   83
Soundtrack (1983) • That's Entertainment (S) TER-1086.................... 8-10   80s
UK release.
    Composer: James Horner. **Conductor:** James Horner.

GOSPEL
Soundtrack (1983) • Savoy (S) 14753................................... 8-10   83

GOSPEL ACCORDING TO ST. MATTHEW
Soundtrack (1966) • Mainstream (M) 54000.. 15-20   66
Soundtrack (1966) • Mainstream (S) S-54000...................................... 30-90   66
    Traditional African-American spirituals.
    Composer: Johann Sebastian Bach, Wolfgang Amadeus Mozart, Sergei Prokofiev, others.

GOSPEL AT COLONUS
Original Cast (1985) • Warner Bros. (S) 1-25182.................................. 8-10
    Composer: Bob Tilson, Lee Breuer. **Cast:** Jeuetta Steele, Wille Rogers, Five Blind Boys of Alabama.
Original Cast (1985) • Elektra/Nonesuch (S) 97919-1 20-25   85

GOSPEL ROAD
Soundtrack (1982) • Priority (S) CG-32253 10-15   82
Soundtrack (1982) • Columbia (S) CG-32253 10-15   82
    Two discs. The story of Jesus Christ, told and sung by Johnny Cash. Issued by Columbia on both labels at approximately the same time.
    Cast: Johnny Cash.

GOT TO INVESTIGATE SILICONES
Original Cast • GE (S) QP-1001.. 40-55
    Souvenir cast album from General Electric about the making of silicones.

GOTCHA
Soundtrack (1985) • MCA (S) 5596....................................... 8-10   85
    Composer: Bill Conti, others. **Cast:** Thereza Bazar, Giuffria, Camelflage, Hubert Kah, Joan Jett and the Blackhearts, Bill Conti, Bronski Beat, Nik Kershaw.

GOTHIC
Soundtrack (1987) • Virgin (S) 90607-1 15-20   87
    Composer: Thomas Dolby. **Conductor:** Thomas Dolby. **Cast:** Thomas Dolby, Timothy Spall, Screamin' Lord Byron.

GOYA

Soundtrack (1959) • Decca (M) DL-8236 90-110   59
Film biography of painter Francisco Goya.
Composer: Vincente Gomez. Cast: Vincente Gomez (guitar).

GRAB ME A GONDOLA

Original London Cast • RCA (M) MCLP-1103..................................... 25-35
UK release. Year of show not given.
Original London Cast • AEI (S) AEI-1119.. 8-12   70s
Composer: James Gilbert, Julian More. Conductor: Frank Cordell. Cast: Joan Heal, Denis
Quilley, Joyce Blair, Jane Wenham, Guido Lorraine, Donald Hewlett, Johnny Ladd, Trevor Jones.

GRADUATE

Soundtrack (1968) • Columbia (S) OS-3180 8-12   68
Soundtrack (1968) • Columbia (S) JS-3180 5-8   Re
Soundtrack (1968) • Columbia (S) PS-3180.. 5-8   Re
Composer: Paul Simon, Additional music by David Grusin. Cast: Paul Simon, Art Garfunkel.

GRAND CANYON SUITE

Soundtrack (1959) • Disneyland (M) WDL-4019 15-20   59
Soundtrack (1959) • Disneyland (S) STER-4019 45-50   59
Composer: Ferde Grofe. Conductor: Frederick Stark. Cast: Frederick Stark and the
Symphonie Orchester Graunke.
Studiotrack (1955) • Columbia (EP) A-1088.. 10-15   55
Studiotrack (1955) • Columbia (M) CL-716.. 25-35   55
Composer: Ferde Grofe. Conductor: Andre Kostelanetz. Cast: New York Philharmonic
Orchestra.
Studiotrack (1950s) • Capitol (EP) ED 804.. 10-20   50s
Boxed, three-disc set. Actual title: *Ferde Grofe Conducts His Grand Canyon Suite.*
Composer: Ferde Grofe. Conductor: Ferde Grofe.
Also see LURE OF THE GRAND CANYON

GRAND MOTEL

Soundtrack (1932) • Caliban (M) 6040 10-15
Cast: Marlene Dietrich, Warren William, Alan Mowbray.

GRAND MUSIC HALL OF ISRAEL

Original Cast (1967) • London (S) SW-99463 15-20   67
Recorded live at L'Olympia, Paris.

GRAND PRIX

Soundtrack (1966) • MGM (M) 1E-8.. 10-12   66
Soundtrack (1966) • MGM (S) 1SE-8.. 12-15   66
Gatefold cover with three-page booklet.
Soundtrack (1966) • MCA (S) 25101.. 5-10   86
Composer: Maurice Jarre. Conductor: Maurice Jarre. Cast: MGM Studio Orchestra.

GRAND TOUR

Original Cast (1979) • Columbia (S) JS-35761..................................... 8-12   79
Composer: Jerry Herman. Conductor: Wally Harper. Cast: Joel Grey, Florence Lacey, Ronald
Holgate, Chevi Colton, Travis Hudson, Gene Varrone, Stephen Vinovich.

GRANDE BOURGEOISE, LA: see LA GRANDE BOURGEOISE

GRANDMA MOSES SUITE

Soundtrack (1950) • Columbia (M) ML-2185 85-100   50
10-inch LP.
Composer: Hugh Martin. Conductor: Daniel Saidenberg. Cast: Grandma Moses.

GRAPES OF WRATH

Studio Cast • Caedmon (S) TC-1570 10-20   77
Cast: Henry Fonda (narrator.)

GRASS HARP
Original Cast (1971) • Painted Smiles (S) PS-1354.............................. 5-10   71
   Composer: Claude Richardson, Kenward Elmslie. **Conductor:** Theodore Saidenberg. **Cast:**
   Barbara Cook, Carol Brice, Karen Morrow, Ruth Ford, Max Showalter, Russ Thacker.

GRASSHOPPER
Soundtrack (1970) • National General (S) NG-1001 10-12   70
   Composer: Billy Goldenberg. **Conductor:** Billy Goldenberg. **Cast:** Brooklyn Bridge, Vicki
   Lawrence, Bobby Russell, Shawn and David.

GREASE
Original Cast (1972) • MGM (S) 1SE-34 8-12   72
Original Cast (1972) • Polydor (S) 827548-1 5-8   Re
   Composer: Jim Jacobs, Warren Casey. **Conductor:** Louis St. Louis. **Cast:** Adrienne Barbeau,
   Walter Bobbie, Barry Bostwick, James Canning, Carole Demas, Katie Hanley, Tom Harris, Ilene
   Kristen, Dorothy Leon, Timothy Meyers, Kathi Moss, Alan Paul, Marya Small, Garn Stephens.
Soundtrack (1978) • RSO (S) RS 2-4002... 8-12   78
   Two discs.
   Composer: Jim Jacobs, Warren Casey. **Conductor:** James Getzoff, Bill Oakes. **Cast:** Frankie
   Valli, John Travolta, Olivia Newton-John, Frankie Avalon, Stockard Channing, Jeff Conaway,
   Cindy Bullens, Sha-Na-Na, Louis St. Louis.

GREASE 2
Soundtrack (1982) • RSO (S) RS-1-3803.. 8-12   82
   Composer: Various. **Cast:** Four Tops, others.

GREAT ACADEMY AWARD SONGS
Studiotrack • RCA Victor (M) PRM-151 8-12   64
Studiotrack • RCA Victor (S) PRS-151 10-15   64
   Music from *Gigi, Days of Wine and Roses, Breakfast at Tiffany's, Gay Divorcee, Pinocchio,
   Hello Frisco Hello,, Song of the South, Captain Carey USA, Calamity Jane, The Man Who
   Knew too Much* and *The Joker Is Wild*.
   Composer: Henry Mancini, others. **Conductor:** Henry Mancini. **Cast:** Henry Mancini Orchestra
   and Chorus.

GREAT AMERICAN BACKSTAGE MUSICAL
Original Cast (1976) • AEI (S) AEI-1101 8-10   76
   Composer: Billy Solly. **Conductor:** Billy Solly. **Cast:** Gaye Kruger, Jerry Clark, Tamara Long.

GREAT AMERICAN FILM SCORES: see DOWN TO THE SEA IN SHIPS

GREAT AMERICAN FOURTH OF JULY PARADE
Soundtrack (1976) • Columbia (S) P-13246 5-10   76
   Cast: John Houseman, Melvyn Douglas, George Grizzard, Baker Salsbury.

GREAT AMERICAN MUSICAL
Original Cast (1979) • Fleetwood (S) FMS-1017 10-15   79
   Two discs.

GREAT AMERICAN SHOW TUNES
Studiotrack • Epic (M) LG 3085... 10-15
   Composer: Irving Berlin, George Gershwin, Ira Gershwin. **Conductor:** Wally Stott. **Cast:** Wally
   Stott and His Orchestra.

GREAT BANK ROBBERY: see RAIN PEOPLE

GREAT BOOKS, GREAT MOVIES, GREAT SONGS
Studiotrack (1962) • MGM (M) E-4132 10-15
Studiotrack (1962) • MGM (S) SE-4132 10-20
   Conductor: David Rose, Leroy Holmes. **Cast:** David Rose and His Orchestra, Leroy Holmes
   and His Orchestra, Russ Conway.

GREAT BRITISH FILM SCORES
Soundtrack • London Phase 4 (S) 21149 10-12
    Composer: Bernard Herrmann. Conductor: Bernard Herrmann.

GREAT CARUSO
Studiotrack (1951) • RCA Victor DM-1506 18-22   51
    78 rpm album.
Studiotrack (1951) • RCA Victor (M) LM-1127 15-20   51
    Exists with two similar front cover designs.
Studiotrack (1951) • RCA Victor (M) LM-1127 12-15   59
Studiotrack (1951) • RCA Victor (SE) LSC-1127 10-12   59
    Conductor: Constantine Callinicos. Cast: Mario Lanza.

GREAT DEBATES
Studio Cast (1979) • Caedmon (S) TC-2087 10-12
    Two discs.
    Conductor: Don Heckman. Cast: Fritz Weaver, Jose Ferrer.

GREAT EPIC FILM THEMES
Studiotrack (1967) • Sunset (S) SLS 50243 8-12   67

GREAT ESCAPE
Soundtrack (1963) • United Artists (M) UAL-4107 8-10   63
Soundtrack (1963) • United Artists (S) UAS-5107 10-12   63
    Composer: Elmer Bernstein. Conductor: Elmer Bernstein.

GREAT EXPECTATIONS
Soundtrack (1974) • Pye (S) NSPL-18452 35-45   75
    UK release. Film made for television but released theatrically in England.
    Composer: Maurice Jarre. Conductor: Maurice Jarre.

GREAT FILM CLASSICS (MUSIC FROM)
Soundtrack • London (S) SP-44144 10-12
    Music from *Jane Eyre, The Snows of Kilimanjaro, Citizen Kane* and *The Devil and Daniel
    Webster* (also known as *All That Money Can Buy*).
    Composer: Bernard Herrmann. Conductor: Bernard Herrmann. Cast: National Philharmonic
    Orchestra.

GREAT GATSBY
Soundtrack (1974) • Paramount (S) PAS-2-3001 10-12   74
    Two discs.
    Composer: Nelson Riddle. Conductor: Nelson Riddle. Cast: Nick Lucas, Bill Atherton (vocals),
    Jess Stacy (piano solo).

GREAT GILDERSLEEVE
Original Radio Cast • Golden Age (M) 5024 8-10   78
Original Radio Cast • Mark 56 (M) 620 8-10   73
    Cast: Hal Peary.

GREAT HITS FROM STAGE & SCREEN
Soundtrack • Capitol Creative Products (S) SL-6562 5-10
    Full title: *Zenith Presents the Best of the Great Hits from Stage & Screen.* Music from
    *Gypsy, Sand Pebbles, Sweet Charity, On a Clear Day You Can See Forever, Dr. Zhivago,
    Dr. No, Mame, Fiddler on the Roof, Sandpiper, Man and a Woman, West Side Story* and
    Born Free.
    Cast: Jackie Gleason, Matt Monro, Peggy Lee, Laurindo Almeida, Al Martino, Jimmie Haskell,
    Vic Damone, Lettermen.

GREAT IMPOSTOR: see HIGH TIME

GREAT LOVE THEMES FROM MOTION PICTURES: see MAX STEINER - GREAT LOVE THEMES FROM MOTION PICTURES

GREAT MOMENTS FROM HALLMARK HALL OF FAME
TV Soundtrack (1966) • Hallmark Cards (M) PRM-202 8-12   66
Two discs.Tracks from 1951-52 and 1965-66.

GREAT MOMENTS FROM THE SILVER SCREEN
Soundtrack • Harmony (SE) H-30549 5-8   70s
Cast: Fred Astaire, Bing Crosby, Marlene Dietrich, Judy Garland, etc.

GREAT MOMENTS FROM THE WORLD OF SPORTS
TV Soundtrack (1972) • Columbia (S) C-11056 20-25   72
Documentary sponsored by International Rec. Vehicles.
Cast: Jim McKay (narrator), others.

GREAT MOMENTS IN SHOW BUSINESS
Soundtrack • Epic (M) LN-3234... 10-20   57

GREAT MOMENTS WITH MR. LINCOLN
Studio Cast (1964) • Buena Vista (M) BV-3981................................... 15-20   64
Studio Cast (1964) • Buena Vista (S) STER-3981 20-25   64
Composer: Buddy Baker. Conductor: Buddy Baker. Cast: Royal Dano (narrator, as Abraham Lincoln).

GREAT MOTION PICTURE CONCERTOS
Studiotrack (1960s) • Warner Bros. (M) W 1319.................................. 8-10   60s
Studiotrack (1960s) • Warner Bros. (S) WS 1319 10-12   60s
Conductor: George Greeley. Cast: George Greeley and Orchestra.

GREAT MOTION PICTURE THEMES
Studiotrack (1961) • United Artists (M) UAL-3122 10-15   60
Studiotrack (1961) • United Artists (S) UAS-6122 10-20   60
Music from *Exodus, Never on Sunday, The Apartment, Magnificent Seven, The Alamo, Big Country, Vikings, Unforgiven, On the Beach, Some Like It Hot, Solomon & Sheba, Horse Soldiers, Wonderful Country* and *Smile*.
Cast: Ferrante and Teicher, Don Costa, Al Caiola, Nick Perito, Gerry Mulligan, Shelly Manne.
Soundtrack [Vol. 2] (1967) • United Artists (M) UAL-3625.................... 10-15   67
Soundtrack [Vol. 2] (1967) • United Artists (S) UAS-6625 10-20   67
Music from *A Man and a Woman, For a Few Dollars More, Corrupt Ones, The Birds the Bees and the Italians, Gone with the Wind, Honey Pot, In the Heat of the Night, You Only Live Twice, Alfie, Whisperers, Divorce American Style, Triple Cross* and *The Way West*.
Composer: Various. Conductor: Francis Lai, Leroy Holmes, Georges Garvarentz, Pier Luigi Urbini, John Addison, Quincy Jones, John Barry, Henry Jerome, Dave Grusin. Cast: Leroy Holmes Orchestra, Ferrante and Teicher, Henry Jerome Orchestra, Serendipity Singers, others.

GREAT MOTION PICTURE THEMES FROM JEAN HARLOW FILMS
Studiotrack • World Artists (M) WAM-2007 10-15   60s

GREAT MOVIE HITS OF THE FORTIES
Studiotrack (1963) • Kapp (M) ML-7531.. 8-10   63
Studiotrack (1963) • Kapp (S) ML-7531-S.. 10-12   63
Composer: Various. Cast: Jack Elliott Orchestra.

GREAT MOVIE HITS OF THE THIRTIES
Studiotrack (1963) • Kapp (M) ML-7530.. 8-10   63
Studiotrack (1963) • Kapp (S) ML-7530-S.. 10-12   63
Composer: Various. Cast: Vardi Orchestra.

GREAT MOVIE THEMES

Studiotrack (1964) • RCA Victor (M) LPM-2895 10-15   64

Studiotrack (1964) • RCA Victor (S) LSP-2895 10-15   64

   Music from *Moulin Rouge, Days of Wine and Roses, Uninvited, Lili, A Streetcar Named Desire, David and Lisa, Unchained, Ruby Gentry, Green Street Dolphin* and others.
   Cast: Norman Luboff Choir.

Studiotrack (1974) • London (S) STCO 95534 10-20   74

   Boxed, three-disc set.

GREAT MOVIE THEMES COMPOSED BY MIKLOS ROZSA

Studiotrack • MGM (M) E-4112 10-12   63

Studiotrack • MGM (S) SE-4112 15-20   63

GREAT MOVIE THEMES OF OUR TIMES

Studiotrack • Daffodil (S) SBA 16010 8-12

   Conductor: Waldo de Los Rios.

GREAT MOVIE THRILLERS

Soundtrack • London Phase 4 (S) SP-44126 8-10   60s

   Music from Bernard Herrmann scores for the Alfred Hitchcock films, *North By Northwest, Psycho, Vertigo, Marnie* and *The Trouble with Harry*.
   Composer: Bernard Herrmann. **Conductor:** Bernard Herrmann. **Cast:** London Philharmonic Orchestra.

GREAT MUPPET CAPER

Soundtrack (1981) • Atlantic (S) SD-16047 8-10   81

   Has fan club insert.
   Composer: Joe Raposo. **Conductor:** Joe Raposo. **Cast:** The Muppets.

GREAT MUSIC FROM THE MOVIES

Studiotrack • Reader's Digest (S) RD3-39 12-18   66

   Boxed, four-disc set, with 12-page booklet. Actual title: *The Fascinating Story of Film Music*. Music from *Love Is a Many-Splendored Thing, Laura, Three Coins in the Fountain, Zorba the Greek, The Third Man, Now Voyager, Saratoga Trunk, King's Row, The Glenn Miller Story, Sandpiper, A Woman Commands, Cleopatra, Jezebel, East of Eden, Shane, The Way of the Gold, Lili, Moulin Rouge, Around the World in 80 Days, Charade, Lawrence of Arabia, El Cid, Exodus* and *Gone with the Wind*.
   Composer: Max Steiner, various. **Conductor:** Charles Gerhardt. **Cast:** RCA Symphony Orchestra.
   Also see MOOD MUSIC FROM THE MOVIES

GREAT MUSIC THEMES OF TELEVISION

Studiotrack (1954) • RCA Victor (EP) EPB-1020 ....:.......... 10-20   54

   Two discs.

Studiotrack (1954) • RCA Victor (M) LPM-1020 15-20   54

   Composer: Various. **Conductor:** Hugo Winterhalter. **Cast:** Hugo Winterhalter Orchestra.

GREAT NEW MOTION PICTURE THEMES

Studiotrack (1967) • Musicor (M) 2133 8-12   67

   Cast: Harmonicats.

Studiotrack (1967) • Musicor (S) 3133 10-12   67

   Cast: Sounds Spectacular.

GREAT ORIGINAL SOUNDTRACKS AND MOVIE THEMES

Soundtrack (1965) • Mainstream (M) 56063 12-15   65

Soundtrack (1965) • Mainstream (S) S-6063 15-20   65

   Music from *King Rat, Zorba the Greek, The Sandpiper, Ship of Fools, Mary Poppins, Sound of Music, Moment of Truth, Juliet of the Spirits* and *The Collector*.
   Composer: John Barry, Nino Rota, Maurice Jarre, Piero Piccioni. **Conductor:** Maurice Jarre, Carlo Savina, John Barry, Piero Piccioni. **Cast:** John Barry, Nino Rota, Maurice Jarre, Piero Piccioni, New Manhattan Philharmonic.

GREAT OUTDOORS
Soundtrack (1988) • Atlantic (S) 81859-1 8-10   88
  Composer: Various. Cast: Joe Walsh, David Wilcox, Thomas Newman and Lazy.

GREAT PERSONALITIES OF BROADWAY
Studio Cast (1963) • Camden (M) CAL-745 10-15   63
Studio Cast (1963) • Camden (S) CAS-745 15-20   63
  Cast: George M. Cohan, Fanny Brice, Al Jolson, Rudy Vallee, Ethel Merman, Ezio Pinza, Helen
  Morgan, Harry Lauder, Bea Lillie.

GREAT RACE
Soundtrack (1965) • RCA Victor (M) LPM-3402 10-12   65
Soundtrack (1965) • RCA Victor (S) LSP-3402 12-15   65
  Composer: Henry Mancini. Conductor: Henry Mancini. Cast: Dorothy Provine.
Studiotrack • Coronet (M) CX-266 8-12
Studiotrack • Coronet (S) CXS-266 8-12
  Also has other Mancini themes.

GREAT RADIO COMEDIANS
Radio Cast • Murray Hill (M) 931699 20-25
  Five-disc set.

GREAT SCIENCE FICTION FILM MUSIC
Studiotrack • London (S) CSL-1001 30-40
  Made for the Science Fiction Book Club. Music from *The Day the Earth Stood Still*, *Psycho*,
  Journey to the Center of the Earth and *Fahrenheit 451*.
  Composer: Barnard Herrmann. Conductor: Bernard Herrmann. Cast: National Philharmonic
  Orchestra.
  Also see FANTASY FILM WORLD OF BERNARD HERRMANN

GREAT SONGS FROM ITALIAN FILMS
Studiotrack • Epic (M) LN-3593 10-20   59
  Music from *Anna*, *Le Ragazze Di San Frediano*, *Gli Uomini Che Mascalzoni*, *Le Notti Di
  Cabriria*, *Le Notti Bianche*, *Addio Giovinezza*, *Roma Citta Aperta*, *Una Famiglia Impossible*,
  La Strada, *Anna Di Borrklyn*, *Seven Hills of Rome* and *Souvenir D'Italie*.
  Conductor: Gian Stellari. Cast: Gian Stellari Orchestra.

GREAT SONGS FROM MOTION PICTURES, VOLUME I (1927 - 1937)
Studiotrack (1961) • Time (M) T-2044 10-15   61
Studiotrack (1961) • Time (S) S-2044 10-20   61
  Composer: Various. Conductor: Hugo Montenegro. Cast: Hugo Montenegro.

GREAT SONGS FROM MOTION PICTURES, VOLUME II (1938 - 1944)
Studiotrack (1961) • Time (M) T-2045 10-15   61
Studiotrack (1961) • Time (S) S-2045 10-20
  Composer: Various. Conductor: Hugo Montenegro. Cast: Hugo Montenegro.

GREAT SONGS FROM MOTION PICTURES, VOLUME III (1945 - 1960)
Studiotrack (1961) • Time (M) T-2046 10-15   61
Studiotrack (1961) • Time (S) S-2046 10-20   61
  Composer: Various. Conductor: Hugo Montenegro. Cast: Hugo Montenegro.

GREAT THEMES FROM FOREIGN MOVIES
Studiotrack (1950s) • MGM (M) E-3731 15-20   57
  Cast: Metropolitan Jazz Quartet.

GREAT THEMES FROM GREAT AMERICAN MOVIES
Studiotrack (1950s) • MGM (M) E-3727 15-20   57
  Cast: Metropolitan Jazz Quartet.

GREAT THEMES FROM GREAT BROADWAY SHOWS
Studiotrack (1950s) • MGM (M) E-3728 15-20   57
    Cast: Metropolitan Jazz Quartet.

GREAT THEMES FROM HIT FILMS
Studiotrack (1962) • Command (S) RS-835-SD 15-20   62
    Music from *West Side Story, Never on Sunday, El Cid, La Dolce Vita, The Light in the
    Piazza, Four Horsemen of the Apocalypse, Breakfast at Tiffany's, Exodus, King of Kings,
    Tender is the Night, The Hustler* and *Satan Never Sleeps.*
    Conductor: Enoch Light. **Cast:** Enoch Light Orchestra.

GREAT THEMES FROM MOTION PICTURES: see TWELVE GREAT THEMES
    OF THE SOARING 60s

GREAT THEMES FROM TV AND MOTION PICTURES
Studiotrack (1967) • Harmony (M) 7423.. 5-10   67
Studiotrack (1967) • Harmony (S) 11223 6-12   67
    Cast: Harmonicats.

GREAT THEMES FROM TV SHOWS
Studiotrack (1959) • MGM (M) E-3729.. 20-30   59
    Jazz interpretations from TV's *Medic, Mickey Mouse Show, Loretta Young Show, Jack
    Paar Show, Dave Garroway Show, Jan Murray Show, Bob Cummings Show, Playhouse
    90, Our Town, Patti Page Show, Red Buttons* and *Perry Como Show.*
    Cast: Metropolitan Jazz Quartet.

GREAT TRAIN ROBBERY
Soundtrack (1978) • United Artists (S) UA-LA962-I 8-12   79
    Also known as *The First Great Train Robbery.*
Soundtrack (1978) • MCA (S) 25102.. 8-12   86
    Composer: Jerry Goldsmith. **Conductor:** Jerry Goldsmith. **Cast:** National Symphony Orchestra.
    Also see RAIN PEOPLE

GREAT WALDO PEPPER
Soundtrack (1975) • MCA (S) 2085.. 8-12   75
    Composer: Henry Mancini. **Conductor:** Henry Mancini.

GREAT WALTZ
Original Cast (1965) • Capitol (M) VAS-2426 12-15   65
Original Cast (1965) • Capitol (S) SVAS-2426 15-18   65
    From the Los Angeles Civic Light Opera revival.
    Composer: Johann Strauss Sr., Johann Strauss Jr., Erich Wolfgang Korngold. **Conductor:** Karl
    Kritz (musical adaptation by Erich Wolfgang Korngold, Robert Wright and George Forrest).
    Cast: Giorgio Tozzi, Jean Fenn, Frank Porretta, Anita Gillette, Leo Fuchs, Wilbur Evans, Eric
    Brotherson, Fred Essler, Lucy Andonian.
Original London Cast (1970) • Columbia (S) SCX-6429........................ 35-45   70
    UK release. London version of the Los Angeles Civic Light Opera revival.
    Composer: Robert Wright, George Forrest, Erich Wolfgang Korngold, Julius Bittner. **Conductor:**
    Alexander Faris. **Cast:** Sari Barabas, Walter Cassel, Diane Todd, David Watson, Eric Brotherson,
    Robert Dorning, Robert Howe.
London Studio Cast • World (S) S-7056.. 12-15
    UK release.
    One side has music from *Rio Rita.*
Studio Cast (1936) • AEI (S) AEI-1153.. 15-18   80s
    The only American recording of the original New York production. Recorded in 1936.
    Composer: Johann Strauss, Desmond Carter. **Conductor:** Al Goodman. **Cast:** Jessica
    Dragonette, James Melton.
Soundtrack (1972) • MGM (S) 1SE-39.. 8-10   72
    Composer: Robert Wright, George Forrest. **Conductor:** Roland Shaw. **Cast:** Kenneth McKellar,
    Mary Costa, Ken Barrie, Joan Baxter, Carlos Villa (violin), Mike Sammes Singers.

GREAT WAR
TV Soundtrack • Project XX (S) G8-OP-8961 60-75
Produced by NBC-TV.
Cast: Robert Russell Bennett.

GREAT WESTERN THEMES
Studiotrack • United Artists (S) UA-LA-082 8-15   70s
Two discs. Music from *The Magnificent Seven, Fistful of Dollars, Hour of the Gun* and others.

GREAT WHITE HOPE
Original Cast • Tetragrammaton (S) TDL-5200 15-25
Boxed, three-disc set, with script.
Composer: Charles Gross. **Conductor:** Charles Gross. **Cast:** James Earl Jones, Jane Alexander.

GREAT ZIEGFELD
Soundtrack (1936) • Classic International Filmusicals (M) CIF-3005.... 12-15
Also includes outtakes from the film.
Composer: Irving Berlin, George Gershwin and others. **Conductor:** Herbert Stothart. **Cast:** Luise Rainer, Fanny Brice, Allan Jones (performed vocals for Dennis Morgan in the film).

GREATEST
Soundtrack (1977) • Arista (S) AL-7000 8-12   77
Composer: Michael Masser, Linda Creed, Gerry Goffin. **Conductor:** Michael Masser. **Cast:** George Benson, Mandrill, Michael Masser.

GREATEST HIT SONGS FROM SPECIAL TV OFFERS
Studiotrack [Vol. 1] • RCA Victor (S) ARL1-0510 10-15
Studiotrack [Vol. 2] • RCA Victor (S) ARL1-0551 10-15   74
Studiotrack [Vol. 3] • RCA Victor (S) ARL1-0614 10-15
Conductor: Arthur Fiedler. **Cast:** Boston Pops.

GREATEST HITS OF WALT DISNEY: see WALT DISNEY

GREATEST SCIENCE FICTION HITS
Studiotrack (1980) • GNP/Crescendo (S) GNPS-2128........................... 8-10   80
Music from *Alien, Star Wars, The Day the Earth Stood Still* and Dominic Frontiere's *Outer Limits*.
Composer: Various. **Conductor:** Neil Norman. **Cast:** Neil Norman.
Studiotrack [Vol.2] • GNP/Crescendo (S) GNPS-2133 8-10   81
Music from *The Twilight Zone* and *The Adventures of Superman*.
Composer: Various. **Conductor:** Neil Norman. **Cast:** Neil Norman.
Studiotrack [Vol. 3] (1984) • GNP/Crescendo (S) GNPS 2163 8-10   84
Music from *Return of the Jedi, E.T.: The Extraterrestrial, War of the Worlds, Lost in Space 1 & 2, Flash Gordon, Into the Alternate Universe, Raiders of the Lost Ark, The Thing, Blade Runner, The Prisoner, Land of the Giants, Capricorn 1, Space: 1999, The Invaders, Angry Red Planet, Voyage to the Prehistoric Planet* and *U.F.O.*
Conductor: Hall Daniels, Neil Norman. **Cast:** Neil Norman, others.

GREATEST SHOW ON EARTH
Soundtrack (1952) • RCA Victor (EP) EPB-3018 30-60   52
Two discs.
Soundtrack (1952) • RCA Victor (M) LPM-3018 100-150   52
10-inch LP. Circus music from the motion picture played by the Paramount Studio Band.
Composer: Victor Young, John Ringling North, E. Ray Goetz, others. **Conductor:** Irvin Talbot.

GREATEST STORY EVER TOLD
Soundtrack (1965) • United Artists (M) UAX-5120 225-275   65
White label. Has alternate tracks not heard on commercial issues. Promotional issue only.
Soundtrack (1965) • United Artists (M) UAL-4120................................. 8-15   65
Soundtrack (1965) • United Artists (S) UAS-5120................................. 8-15   65

Soundtrack (1965) • United Artists (M) UA-LA277-G.................................. 5-8   74
Soundtrack (1965) • MCA (S) 39057.. 5-8   86
    Composer: Alfred Newman. **Conductor:** Alfred Newman.

GREEK PEARLS
Soundtrack (1968) • Lyra (M) LY-1008.. 20-25   68
Soundtrack (1968) • Lyra (SE) LYS-1008 25-30   68
    Composer: Mimis Plessas. **Conductor:** Mimis Plessas. **Cast:** Nelly Manou, Yannis
    Poulopoulos.

GREEN ACRES: see EDDIE ALBERT ALBUM

GREEN DOLPHIN STREET: see AUNTIE MAME

GREEN FIRE: see FILM MUSIC OF MIKLOS ROZSA

GREEN HORNET
Original Radio Cast • Mark 56 (M) 509.. 10-15   73
    Two episodes.
Original Radio Cast • Golden Age (M) 5010.. 8-10   78
TV Soundtrack (1966) • 20th Century-Fox (M) TF-3186.................. 150-200   66
TV Soundtrack (1966) • 20th Century-Fox (S) S-3186 200-250   66
    Composer: Billy May. **Conductor:** Billy May.
Studiotrack (1966) • Coronet (M) CX-282 10-15   66

GREEN ICE
Soundtrack (1981) • Polydor (S) POLS-1031 8-10   81
    Composer: Bill Wyman. **Cast:** Maria Muldaur.

GREENWICH VILLAGE, U.S.A.
Original Cast (1960) • 20th Century-Fox (M) TCFP-105-12.................. 50-55   60
Original Cast (1960) • 20th Century-Fox (S) TCF-105-2S 75-100   60
    Both are two-disc sets. Contains the complete show.
Original Cast (1960) • 20th Century-Fox (M) FOX-4005........................ 30-35   60
Original Cast (1960) • 20th Century-Fox (S) SFX-4005........................ 35-50   60
    Both have only excerpts from the show.
Original Cast (1960) • AEI (M) AEI-1129... 12-15   80
    Two discs. Reissued in monaural only.
    Composer: Jeanne Bargy, Frank Gehrecke, Herb Corey. **Conductor:** Bill Costa. **Cast:** Jack
    Betts, Saralou Cooper, Pat Finley, Judy Guyll, Dawn Hampton, James Harwood, Jane A.
    Johnston, Burke McHugh, James Pompeii, Ken Urmston.

GREENWILLOW
Original Cast (1960) • RCA Victor (M) No Number Used 15-25   60
    White label. Promotional issue only.
Original Cast (1960) • RCA Victor (M) LOC-2001 12-15   60
Original Cast (1960) • RCA Victor (S) LSO-2001 45-55   60
    May also be found in a limited edition replica candy box with a leaf insert. This package is
    known as "Mrs. Loesser's pressing."
Original Cast (1960) • Columbia Special Products (S) P-13974 8-10   77
    Composer: Frank Loesser. **Conductor:** Abba Bogin. **Cast:** Anthony Perkins, Cecil Kellaway,
    Pert Kelton, Ellen McCown, William Chapman, Lee Cass, Saralou Cooper, Bruce MacKay, Jan
    Tucker, Brenda Harris, Lynn Brinker, John Megna.
Studio Cast (1960) • RCA Victor (M) LPM-2229.. 5-8   60
Studio Cast (1960) • RCA Victor (S) LSP-2229...................................... 5-10   60
    Composer: Frank Loesser. **Conductor:** George Melachrino. **Cast:** Melachrino Strings
    (instrumental renditions of the score).

GREETINGS FROM BROADWAY
Studiotrack • AEI (S) AEI-1176 5-10   80s

GREMLINS
Soundtrack (1984) • Geffen (S) GHSP-24044.. 8-10   84
Seven-track mini-album.
Composer: Jerry Goldsmith. **Conductor:** Jerry Goldsmith. **Cast:** Michael Sembello, Quarter Flash, Peter Gabriel.

GREMLINS 2: THE NEW BATCH
Soundtrack (1990) • Varese Sarabande (S) VS-5269 5-8   90
Composer: Jerry Goldsmith. **Conductor:** Jerry Goldsmith.

GREY FOX
Soundtrack (1982) • DRG (S) SL-9515 8-10   83
Composer: Michael Conway Baker. **Cast:** Chieftains.

GREYFRIARS BOBBY
Soundtrack (1961) • Disneyland (M) ST-1914 20-25   61
Composer: Richard M. Sherman, Robert B. Sherman, others. **Cast:** Ginny Tyler, others.

GREYSTOKE – THE LEGEND OF TARZAN, LORD OF THE APES
Soundtrack (1984) • Warner Bros. (S) 1-25120-1 8-10   84
Composer: John Scott. **Conductor:** John Scott. **Cast:** Royal Philharmonic Orchestra.

GRIND
Original Cast (1985) • Polydor (S) 827072-1 8-12   85
Standard cover.
Original Cast • That's Entertainment (S) TER-1103 12-15   80s
UK release. Gatefold cover.
Composer: Larry Grossman, Ellen Fitshugh. **Conductor:** Paul Gemignani. **Cast:** Ben Vereen, Stubby Kaye, Leilani Jones, Timothy Nolen, Sharon Murray, Carol Woods.

GRIZZLY
Soundtrack (1976) • Truluv (S) HWR 301 40-50   76
Composer: Jerry Goldsmith, Robert Ragland. **Conductor:** Harry Rabinowitz, Robert O. Ragland.

GROUNDS FOR MARRIAGE
Soundtrack (1950) • MGM (M) E-536.. 60-70   50
10-inch LP.
Composer: Various. **Conductor:** Johnny Green. **Cast:** Kathryn Grayson.

GROWING PAINS
TV Soundtrack (1988) • Reprise (S) 1-25735... 8-12   88
Composer: Steve Dorff and Friends. **Cast:** B.J. Thomas, Dusty Springfield, Jill Colucci, Take 6, Bill Medley, Eddie Rabbitt, Anne Murray, Kenny Rogers.

GUERRE EST FINIE, LA: see LA GUERRE EST FINIE

GUESS WHO'S COMING TO DINNER?
Soundtrack (1967) • Colgems (M) COM-108...................................... 20-25   68
Soundtrack (1967) • Colgems (S) COS-108....................................... 20-30   68
Composer: Frank DeVol. **Conductor:** Frank DeVol. **Cast:** Billy Hill.

GUIDING LIGHT
Original Radio Cast • Golden Age (M) 5020.. 8-10   78

GULLIVER
Soundtrack • Soundwings (S) SW-2101 8-10   86
Conductor: Patrick Williams. **Cast:** Royal Philharmonic Orchestra, Sir John Gielgud (narrator).

GULLIVER IN LILLIPUT
Studio Cast • United Artists (M) UAC-11024 15-20
Cast: Denise Bryer & the Famous Theatre Company, Hollywood St. Orchestra.

GULLIVER'S TRAVELS
Soundtrack • Decca (M) 100 80-100
  Composer: Victor Young

GULLIVER'S TRAVELS BEYOND THE MOON
Soundtrack (1966) • Mainstream (M) 54001.. 20-25   65
Soundtrack (1966) • Mainstream (S) 4001 20-40   65
  Composer: Milton Delugg, Anne Delugg. **Conductor:** George Brackman.

GULLIVER'S TRAVELS: JOURNEY TO BROBDINGNAG
Original Radio Cast • Tot (M) 1811 25-30   73
  Adventure Hour Series, Volume 5.
  Cast: Professor Margaret C. Tyler.

GUNFIGHT AT THE O.K. CORRAL: see LAND OF THE PHARAOHS

GUNN ... NUMBER ONE
Soundtrack (1967) • RCA Victor (M) LPM-3840 10-20   67
Soundtrack (1967) • RCA Victor (S) LSP-3840 10-30   67
  Composer: Henry Mancini, Jay Livingston, Ray Evans, Leslie Bricusse. **Conductor:** Henry
  Mancini. **Cast:** Henry Mancini Orchestra, others.

GUNS FOR SAN SEBASTIAN
Soundtrack (1968) • MGM (M) E-4565.. 35-40   68
Soundtrack (1968) • MGM (S) SE-4565.. 50-55   68
Soundtrack (1968) • MCA (S) 25103.. 8-10   86
  Composer: Ennio Morricone.

GUNS OF NAVARONE
Soundtrack (1961) • Columbia (M) CL-1655 15-18   61
Soundtrack (1961) • Columbia (S) CS-8455... 25-50   61
  Composer: Dimitri Tiomkin. **Conductor:** Dimitri Tiomkin. **Cast:** Mitch Miller and His Gang.
  Also see LOST HORIZON: THE CLASSIC FILM SCORES OF DIMITRI TIOMKIN

GUNSMOKE
Original Radio Cast • Golden Age (M) 5004... 8-10   78
  Cast: William Conrad (as Sheriff Matt Dillon).

GURU
Soundtrack (1969) • RCA Victor (S) LSO-1158.................................... 15-20   69
  Composer: Ustad Khan. **Conductor:** V. Balsara.

GUYS AND DOLLS
Original Cast (1950) • Decca (EP) ED-803 15-20   50
Original Cast (1950) • Decca (M) DL-8036... 18-22   50
Original Cast (1950) • Decca (M) DL-9023... 15-20   55
Original Cast (1950) • Decca (SE) DL-79023 12-15   59
Original Cast (1950) • MCA (SE) 2034e 8-10   72
Original Cast (1950) • MCA (SE) 37094 5-8   81
Original Cast (1950) • MCA (SE) 1628 5-8   80s
Original Cast (1950) • Brunswick (M) LAT-8022.................................. 20-25   50
  UK release. Different cover art than on US issues.
  Composer: Frank Loesser. **Conductor:** Irving Actman. **Cast:** Robert Alda, Vivian Blaine, Sam
  Levene, Stubby Kaye, Johnny Silver, Isabel Bigley, Pat Rooney, Douglas Deane.
Studio Cast (1955) • Decca (EP) ED-2308... 10-15   55
  Cast: Sammy Davis Jr.
Studio Cast (1956) • Columbia (EP) B-2077 10-15   56
  Cast: Frankie Laine, Jo Stafford, Jerry Vale, Rosemary Clooney.

Studio Cast (1956) • Columbia (M) CL-2567 20-40   56
  10-inch LP.
    Conductor: Percy Faith, Harry James. **Cast:** Rosemary Clooney, Frankie Laine, Jerry Vale, Jo
    Stafford, Harry James.

Studio Cast [Vol. 1] • Camden (EP) CAE 172 10-15   50s
Studio Cast [Vol. 2] • Camden (EP) CAE 173 10-15   50s
    Cast: Harold Coates Orchestra with Chorus and Soloists.

Studio Cast • RCA Victor (M) LK-1000 10-15   50s
    Composer: Frank Loesser. **Conductor:** Al Goodman. **Cast:** Ray Charles, Audrey Marsh, Morey
    Amsterdam, Guild Choristers, Donald Richards, Al Goodman and His Orchestra.

Studio Cast (1960) • Richmond (S) S-30072 10-15   60
  Also contains music from *The Music Man*.
    Composer: Jule Styne, Stephen Sondheim. **Cast:** London Theatre Company.

Studio Cast (1963) • Reprise (M) F-2016 12-18   64
Studio Cast (1963) • Reprise (S) FS-2016 18-25   64
  Gatefold covers.

Studio Cast (1963) • Reprise (M) F-2016 10-12   64
Studio Cast (1963) • Reprise (S) FS-2016 12-15   64
  Standard covers.

Studio Cast (1963) • Harmony (S) HS-11374 10-12   Re
    Composer: Frank Loesser. **Conductor:** Morris Stoloff. **Cast:** Frank Sinatra, Dean Martin,
    Sammy Davis Jr., Bing Crosby, Dinah Shore, Alan Sherman, Debbie Reynolds, McGuire Sisters.

Studio Cast (1976) • 20th Century-Fox (S) ST-514 10-12   76
  Disco version.
    Composer: Frank Loesser. **Conductor:** Al Capps. **Cast:** Broadway Brass.

Soundtrack (1955) • Decca (EP) ED-2332 40-45   56
Soundtrack (1955) • Brunswick (EP) ED-2332 25-35   56
  UK release.
  Both EPs contain four soundtrack songs.
    Composer: Frank Loesser. **Conductor:** Jay Blackton. **Cast:** Marlon Brando, Jean Simmons.

Soundtrack (1955) • Ace of Hearts (M) AH-137 15-20   67
  UK release. Four songs from the EP plus music from the film *Call Me Madam*.

Soundtrack • Stet (M) DS-25001 12-15   Re
  Also has music from *I'll Cry Tomorrow* (including the title song which did not appear on the
  original release) and *Call Me Madam*.

Soundtrack (1955) • Motion Picture Tracks (M) MPT-1 20-25
  First LP release of the film soundtrack in its entirety. Yellow cover. Normal weight cover
  stock.

Soundtrack (1955) • Motion Picture Tracks (M) MPT-1 8-10   Re
  Yellow cover, but much brighter than on the original. Lighter weight cover stock.
    Composer: Frank Loesser. **Conductor:** Jay Blackton. **Cast:** Marlon Brando, Jean Simmons,
    Frank Sinatra, Vivian Blaine, Stubby Kaye, Johnny Silver.

Soundtrack (1955) • JJA (M) 19762 30-35   76
  Actual title: *Frank Loesser in Hollywood*. Two-disc set with most of the soundtrack score,
  plus songs from other Frank Loesser films.
    Composer: Frank Loesser. **Conductor:** Jay Blackton. **Cast:** Marlon Brando, Jean
    Simmons. CALL ME MADAM: **Composer:** Irving Berlin. **Conductor:** Alfred Newman.
    Cast: Ethel Merman, George Sanders, Donald O'Connor, Carole Richards (performed
    vocals for Vera-Ellen in the film). I'LL CRY TOMORROW: **Composer:** Various.
    Conductor: Charles Henderson. **Cast:** Susan Hayward.

Studiotrack (1956) • Decca (M) DL-8290 10-12   56
    Cast: Carmen Cavallaro.

Studiotrack • Columbia (M) CL-1426 8-10
    Cast: Manhattan Jazz All Stars.

Original Revival Cast (1976) • Motown (S) M6-876S1 10-12   76
Original Revival Cast (1976) • Motown (S) 5277ML 8-10   Re
   Composer: Frank Loesser. **Conductor:** Howard Roberts. **Cast:** Norma Donaldson, Robert Guillaume, Ernestine Jackson, James Randolph, Ken Page, Christopher Pierre, Bardell Connor, Irene Datcher, Sterling McQueen, Marion Moore, Emmet "Babe" Wallace.
   Also see REPRISE REPERTORY THEATRE

GYPSY

Original Cast (1959) • Columbia (EP) EPA-5420 10-12   59
Original Cast (1959) • Columbia (M) OL-5420.. 8-10   59
Original Cast (1959) • Columbia (S) OS-2017..................................... 15-18   59
   Above LPs have white cover with drawings.
Original Cast (1959) • Columbia (M) OL-5420.. 8-10   62
Original Cast (1959) • Columbia (S) OS-2017..................................... 12-15   62
   Above two have brown covers with photos from the show.
Original Cast (1959) • Columbia (S) S-32607.. 8-10   73
   Composer: Jule Styne, Stephen Sondheim. **Conductor:** Milton Rosenstock. **Cast:** Ethel Merman, Jack Klugman, Sandra Church, Maria Karnilova, Paul Wallace, Lane Bradbury, Faith Dane, Chotzi Foley, Jacqueline Mayro, Karen Moore.
Original London Cast (1974) • RCA Victor (S) SER-5686 15-18   74
   UK release. Gatefold cover.
Original London Cast (1974) • RCA Victor (S) LBL1-5004 8-12   74
   US release. Gatefold cover.
Studio Cast (1959) • Columbia (M) CL-1352.. 8-12   59
Studio Cast (1959) • Columbia (S) CS-8160 10-12   59
   Actual title: *Teddy Wilson and His Trio Play Gypsy in Jazz.*
   Cast: Teddy Wilson and His Trio.
Soundtrack (1962) • Warner Bros. (M) B-1480 15-20   62
Soundtrack (1962) • Warner Bros. (S) BS-1480.................................. 20-25   62
Soundtrack (1962) • Capitol (M) RW 90000 30-35   62
Soundtrack (1962) • Capitol (S) SRW 90000 45-50   62
   Capitol releases don't appear to be reissues. Same cover art, except the Warner Bros. logo has been replaced by a Capitol one on front and back.
   Composer: Jule Styne, Stephen Sondheim. **Conductor:** Frank Perkins, Jule Styne. **Cast:** Rosalind Russell, Lisa Kirk (partially dubbed the vocals of Rosalind Russell in the film), Natalie Wood, Karl Malden, Paul Wallace, Roxanne Arlen, Faith Dane, Betty Bruce, Ann Jillian.
London Studio Cast • Music for Pleasure (S) MFP-1308...................... 15-18
   Composer: Jule Styne, Stephen Sondheim. **Cast:** Jimmy Blackburn, Kay Medford, Sonya Petrie, Lorraine Smith.
Original London Cast (1974) • RCA Victor (S) LBL1-5004 20-25   74
   US pressing. Gatefold cover.
   Composer: Jule Styne, Stephen Sondheim. **Conductor:** Richard Leonard. **Cast:** Angela Lansbury, Barrie Ingham, Zan Charisse, **Bonnie Langford, Debbie Bowen, Andrew Norman, Laurie Webb, Kelly Wilson, Valerie Walsh, Judy Cannon.**
Original Revival Cast (1990) • Elektra/Nonesuch (S) 79239-1 8-10   90
   Composer: Jule Styne, Stephen Sondheim. **Cast:** Tyne Daly, Christa Moore, Jonathan Hadary, Robert Lambert.

GYPSY GIRL

Soundtrack (1966) • Mainstream (M) 56090.. 20-25   66
Soundtrack (1966) • Mainstream (S) 6090 35-40   66
   Original film title was *Sky West and Crooked.*
   Composer: Milton Delugg, Anne Delugg. **Cast:** Hayley Mills.

GYPSY MOTHS

Soundtrack (1969) • Cinema (M) LP-8011 25-65
   Composer: Elmer Bernstein. **Conductor:** Hans Rossbach.

GYPSY ROSE LEE REMEMBERS BURLESQUE

Original Cast (1962) • Stereoddities (S) CG-1 .... 20-25　　62

Composer: Eli Basse, Bobby Kroll. **Cast:** Gypsy Rose Lee, others.

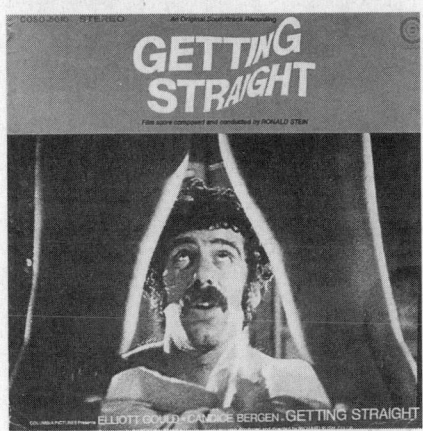

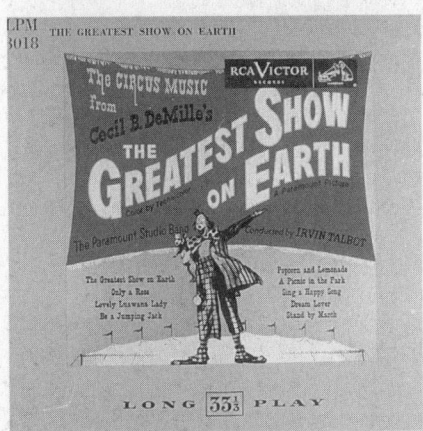

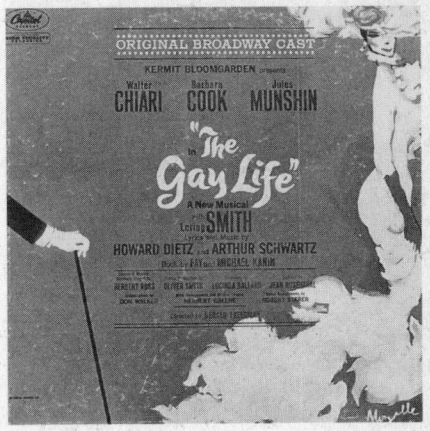

H.M.S. PINAFORE
Studio Cast • RCA Victor (M) LK-1002 12-15
    Conductor: Al Goodman. **Cast:** Al Goodman Orchestra, Earl Wrightson, Audrey Marsh, Jimmy
    Carroll, Martha Wright, Leonard Stokes, John Percival, Guild Choristers.
Studiotrack (1960) • Hudson (M) 274 5-10   60
    Vocals.
Studiotrack (1960) • Hudson (M) 223 5-10   60
    Instrumentals.

HAIL, HAIL, ROCK 'N' ROLL
Soundtrack (1987) • MCA (S) 6217 8-10   87
    Film title: *Chuck Berry: Hail, Hail Rock 'n' Roll*. Film highlights Chuck Berry's life and career,
    much of which is told by Berry himself.
    Cast: Chuck Berry, Linda Ronstadt, Robert Cray, Eric Clapton, Julian Lennon.

HAIR
Original Off-Broadway Cast (1967) • RCA Victor (M) LOC-1143 8-12   67
Original Off-Broadway Cast (1967) • RCA Victor (S) LSO-1143 10-12   67
Original Off-Broadway Cast (1967) • RCA Victor (S) ANL1-0986 8-10   75
    Composer: Galt MacDermot, Gerome Ragni, James Rado. **Conductor:** John Morris. **Cast:**
    Walker Daniels, Gerome Ragni, Steve Dean, Sally Eaton, Marijane Maricle, Jonelle Allen,
    Susan Batson, Linda Compton, Suzannah Evans, Paul Jabara, Jill O'Hara, Shelley Plimpton,
    Alma Robinson, Arnold Wilkerson, Jonathan Kramer, Suzannah Norstrand, Natalie Mosco, Mary
    Davis, Emmaretta Marks, Lynn Kellogg, Donnie Burks, Walter Harris.
Off-Broadway Cast (1967) • RCA Special Products (S) PRS-319 5-8   Re
    Cast: N.Y. Shakespeare Festival Public Theatre.
Original Cast (1967) • RCA Victor (M) LOC-1150 8-10   68
Original Cast (1967) • RCA Victor (S) LSO-1150 10-12   68
    Black label.
Original Cast (1967) • RCA Victor (S) LSO-1150 5-8   Re
    Orange label.
Original Cast (1967) • RCA Victor (Q) ABD1-0245 15-20   70s
    Composer: Galt MacDermot, Gerome Ragni, James Rado. **Conductor:** Galt MacDermot. **Cast:**
    Ronnie Dyson, Gerome Ragni, Steve Curry, Lamont Washington, Diane Keaton, Melba Moore,
    James Rado.
Original London Cast [Vol. 1] (1967) • Atco (S) SD-7002 12-15   69
Original London Cast [Vol. 2] (1967) • Polydor (S) 24-5501 10-12   71
    Full title of Vol. 2: *Fresh Hair*.
    Composer: Galt MacDermot, Gerome Ragni, James Rado. **Conductor:** Derek Wadsworth.
    Cast: Vince Edwards, Oliver Tobias, Michael Feast, Paul Nicholas.
Broadway Cast (1969) • RCA Victor (S) LSP-4174 12-15   69
    Full title: *Divine Hair Mass in F*. Recorded at Cathedral of St. John the Divine.
Original French Cast (1969) • Philips (S) PHS-600-329 10-15   69
    Composer: Galt MacDermot, Gerome Ragni. **Cast:** Gloria Carter, Herve Wattine, Julien Clerc,
    Bill Combs, Gerard Palaprat, Charles Austin, Gregory Ken, Serge Godinho, Ann Ballester,
    Clement Marshall, Henry Hay, Jeaniene Bennett.

Studio Cast (1969) • RCA Victor (M) LOC-1163.................................. 10-15   69
Studio Cast (1969) • RCA Victor (S) LSO-1163 15-20   69
  Full title: *DisinHAIRited*. Has original cast members and composers plus future cast
  members doing songs written for – but not included in – the show.
    Composer: Galt MacDermot, Gerome Ragni, James Rado. **Conductor:** Galt MacDermot. **Cast:**
    Robin McNamara, Galt MacDermot (piano), Jim Rado, Jerry Ragni, Melba Moore, Leata
    Galloway.
Studiotrack (1969) • RCA Victor (S) LSP-4632 12-15   69
  Full title: *Don Kirschner Cuts Hair*.
    Composer: Galt MacDermot, Gerome Ragni, James Rado. **Conductor:** Don Kirschner. **Cast:**
    Don Kirschner (instrumental renditions).
Studiotrack (1970) • Capitol (S) ST-305 10-15   70
  Jazz interpretations.
    Cast: Stan Kenton.
Original Japanese Cast (1971) • RCA Victor (S) LSO-1170 20-25   71
    Conductor: Danny Hurd.
Studio Cast (1979) • Pickwick (S) SPC-3655 8-10   79
  Full title: *Music from Hair*.
    Cast: Sunshine Generation.
Studio Cast • Kilmarnock (S) KIL-69001 10-15
  Jazz instrumentals. From a Carleton University concert.
    Composer: Galt MacDermot, Jerry Ragni, James Rado. **Conductor:** Galt MacDermot. **Cast:**
    Galt MacDermot, Charlie Brown, Jimmy Lewis, Idris Mohammed.
Studio Cast • Pickwick (S) SPC-3169 5-10
    Conductor: Geoff Love. **Cast:** Dave Wintour, Pat Whitmore.
Studiotrack • Ambassador (S) S 98084... 5-10
    Cast: Ray Bloch Singers.
Studiotrack • Polydor (S) 24-6005.. 5-10
    Cast: James Last.
Soundtrack (1979) • RCA Victor (S) CBL2-3274 10-12   79
  Two discs.
    Conductor: Galt MacDermot. **Cast:** John Savage, Treat Williams, Beverly D'Angelo, Annie
    Golden, Melba Moore, Cheryl Barnes, Dorsey Wright, Don Dacus.

HAIRSPRAY
Soundtrack (1988) • MCA (S) 6228.. 8-10   88
    Cast: Rachel Sweet, Ray Bryant Combo, Jan Bradley, Gene and Wendell, Flares, Jerry Dallman
    and Knightcaps, Little Peggy March, Barbara Lynn, Gene Pitney, Ikettes, Toussaint McCall, Five
    Du-Tones.

HALF A SIXPENCE
Original London Cast (1960s) • Decca (S) LK-4521 15-20   60s
Original London Cast (1960s) • Decca (S) SKL-4521.......................... 15-20   60s
Original London Cast (1960s) • That's Entertainment (S) TER-1041...... 8-12   Re
  UK releases.
    Composer: David Heneker. **Cast:** Tommy Steele, Marti Webb, Anna Barry, James Grout.
London Studio Cast • World (S) T-852... 12-15
  UK release.
    Composer: David Heneker. **Conductor:** Gareth Davies. **Cast:** Barbara Windsor, Marty Wilde,
    Mike Sammes Singers.
Original Cast (1965) • RCA Victor (M) LOC-1110 8-12   65
Original Cast (1965) • RCA Victor (S) LSO-1110 10-12   65
    Composer: David Heneker. **Conductor:** Stanley Lebowsky. **Cast:** Tommy Steele, Grover Dale,
    James Grout, Polly James, Will MacKenzie, Norman Allen, Eleanor Treiber.
Soundtrack (1967) • RCA Victor (M) LOC-1146 8-10   68
Soundtrack (1967) • RCA Victor (S) LSO-1146.................................... 10-12   68
    Composer: David Heneker. **Conductor:** Irwin Kostal. **Cast:** Tommy Steele, Julia Foster, Cyril
    Ritchard.

HALF MAN – HALF ALLIGATOR
Original Cast (1966) • RCA Victor (M) VDM 113 15-20   66
Cast: William Mooney.

HALF PAST WEDNESDAY
Original Cast (1962) • Columbia (M) CL-1917...................................... 25-30   62
Original Cast (1962) • Columbia (S) CS-8717 30-35   62
Original Cast (1962) • Harmony (M) HL-9560 5-10   Re
Original Cast (1962) • Harmony (S) HS-14560....................................... 10-15   Re
Composer: Robert Colby, Nita Jones. Conductor: Julian Stein. Cast: Dom DeLuise, Sean Garrison, Audre Johnston, Robert Fitch, David Winters.

HALL OF PRESIDENTS
Soundtrack (1972) • Disneyland (S) STER-3806 15-20   72
Includes booklet.
Composer: Buddy Baker. Conductor: Buddy Baker. Cast: Lawrence Dobkin (narration), Royal Dano (as Abraham Lincoln).

HALLELUJAH, BABY!
Original Cast (1967) • Columbia (M) KOL-6690 8-10   67
Original Cast (1967) • Columbia (S) KOS-3090 12-18   67
Composer: Jule Styne, Betty Comden, Adolph Green. Conductor: Buster Davis. Cast: Leslie Uggams, Robert Hooks, Allen Case, Clifford Allen, Lillian Hayman, Barbara Sharma, Winston Dewitt Hemsley.

HALLELUJAH THE HILLS
Soundtrack (1964) • Fontana (M) F-27524.. 18-20   64
Soundtrack (1964) • Fontana (S) SRF-67524 20-25   64
Composer: Meyer Kupferman. Conductor: Meyer Kupferman.

HALLELUJAH TRAIL
Soundtrack (1965) • United Artists (M) UAL-4127 12-15   65
Soundtrack (1965) • United Artists (S) UAS-5127 20-25   65
Composer: Elmer Bernstein. Conductor: Elmer Bernstein.

HALLOWEEN
Soundtrack (1978) • Varese Sarabande (S) STV-81176 10-15   83
Composer: John Carpenter. Conductor: John Carpenter. Cast: John Carpenter.

HALLOWEEN II
Soundtrack (1981) • Varese Sarabande (S) STV-81152 12-15   81
Composer: John Carpenter. Conductor: John Carpenter. Cast: John Carpenter, Alan Howarth, Chordettes.

HALLOWEEN III – SEASON OF THE WITCH
Soundtrack (1982) • MCA (S) 6115.. 12-15   82
Composer: John Carpenter, Alan Howarth. Conductor: John Carpenter. Cast: John Carpenter, Alan Howarth.

HALLOWEEN IV – RETURN OF MICHAEL MEYERS
Soundtrack (1988) • Varese Sarabande (S) VS-5205 10-12   88
Composer: John Carpenter, Alan Howarth. Conductor: Alan Howarth.

HALLOWEEN V – REVENGE OF MICHAEL MEYERS
Soundtrack (1989) • Varese Sarabande (S) VS-5239 10-12   89
Composer: John Carpenter, Alan Howarth. Conductor: Alan Howarth.

HAMLET
Original Cast (1964) • Columbia (M) DOL-302 20-25   64
Original Cast (1964) • Columbia (S) DOS-702 20-25   64
Boxed, four-disc sets, with booklets. Complete recording from Sir John Gielgud's Broadway revival. Covers show credits on white background.
Original Cast (1964) • Columbia (M) OL-8020..................................... 12-15   64

Original Cast (1964) • Columbia (S) OS-2620...................................... 12-18   64
Highlights from the boxed set. Cover pictures Richard Burton against a dark background.
Cast: Richard Burton, Hume Cronyn, Alfred Drake, Eileen Herlie, William Redfield, George Rose, Sir John Gielgud, Linda Marsh, Robert Milli, John Cullum, George Voskovec.

Studio Cast • Caedmon (S) SRS 232.. 5-10
Soundtrack (1948) • RCA Victor DM-1273 20-75
78 rpm album.

Soundtrack (1948) • RCA Victor (M) LCT-5 25-30   51
10-inch LP.

Soundtrack (1948) • RCA Victor (M) LM-1924 20-25   55
One side has music from *Henry V.*
Composer: Sir William Walton. **Conductor:** Muir Mathieson. **Cast:** Sir Laurence Olivier, Jean Simmons, Eileen Herlie, Stanley Holloway, Harcourt Williams, Basil Sydney, Philharmonic Orchestra. (With dialogue.)

TV Soundtrack (1970) • RCA Victor (M) VDM-119 10-12   70
Two discs. A Hallmark production.
Composer: John Addison. **Conductor:** John Addison. **Cast:** Richard Chamberlain, Sir Michael Redgrave, Margaret Leighton, Sir John Gielgud.

Soundtrack (1990) • Virgin (S) VMM3 8-10   90
Composer: Ennio Morricone. **Cast:** Mel Gibson, Glenn Close.
Also see MUSIC FROM SHAKESPEAREAN FILMS
Also see WALTON CONDUCTS HIS GREAT FILM MUSIC

HAMMERHEAD
Soundtrack (1968) • Colgems (S) COS-110.. 25-30   68
Composer: David Whitaker. **Conductor:** David Whitaker. **Cast:** Madeline Bell.

HAMMERSMITH IS OUT
Soundtrack (1972) • Capitol (S) SW-861 20-25   72
Composer: Dominic Frontiere. **Conductor:** Dominic Frontiere. **Cast:** Sally Stevens.

HAND IS ON THE GATE
Original Cast (1966) • Verve (M) FV-9040-2 12-15   66
Original Cast (1966) • Verve (S) FVS-9040-2...................................... 15-20   66
Both have two discs.
Cast: Leon Bibb, Roscoe Lee Browne, Gloria Foster, Moses Gunn, James Earl Jones, Cicely Tyson, Ellen Holly, Josephine Premice.

HANDFUL OF DUST
Soundtrack (1988) • DRG (S) 6110.. 12-15   88

HANDMAID'S TALE
Soundtrack (1990) • GNP/Crescendo (S) GNPD-8020 8-10   90
Composer: Ryuchi Sakamoto. **Cast:** Natasha Richardson, Faye Dunaway, Aiden Quinn, Robert Duvall.

HANG 'EM HIGH
Soundtrack (1968) • United Artists (S) UAS-5179 12-18   68
Soundtrack (1968) • MCA (S) 1435.. 8-10   Re
Composer: Dominic Frontiere. **Conductor:** Dominic Frontiere.

Studiotrack (1968) • RCA Victor (S) 4022 8-10   68
Also has themes from *In the Heat of the Night, Valley of the Dolls, The Fox, For Love of Ivy* and others.
Composer: Various. **Conductor:** Hugo Montenegro. **Cast:** Hugo Montenegro and His Orchestra.

HANG YOUR HAT ON THE WIND
Soundtrack (1969) • Disneyland (M) DQ-1332 15-20   69
With dialogue.
Composer: Randy Sparks. **Conductor:** Jim Helms.

HANK

TV Soundtrack (1965) • RCA Victor (M) LPM-3489............................ 20-30   65
TV Soundtrack (1965) • RCA Victor (S) LSP-3489.............................. 30-40   65
   Full title: *Dick Kallman Drops in As Hank*, from the NBC TV series.
   Cast: Dick Kallman.
TV Soundtrack (1965) • Capitol (S) 6150 30-40   65
   Full title: *Hank Sings.*
   Cast: Dick Kallman.

HANNAH AND HER SISTERS

Soundtrack (1987) • MCA (S) 6190.. 5-8   87
   Composer: Various. **Cast:** Count Basie and His Orchestra, Bobby Short, Derek Smith, Harry
   James, Dick Hyman, Roy Eldridge, George Malcolm, Simon Preston, Lloyd Nolan, Maureen
   O'Sullivan.

HANNIBAL BROOKS

Soundtrack (1969) • United Artists (S) UAS-5196................................ 8-10   69
Soundtrack (1969) • MCA (S) 25104.. 5-8   86
   Composer: Francis Lai. **Conductor:** Francis Lai.

HANS ANDERSEN

Original London Cast • PYE (S) 18551 30-35
   UK release. British stage version of the film *Hans Christian Andersen*, utilizing the same
   Frank Loesser score.
   Composer: Frank Loesser. **Cast:** Tommy Steele, Sally Anne Howes.

HANS BRINKER

TV Soundtrack (1958) • Dot (M) DLP-9001 30-35   58
   Composer: Hugh Martin. **Conductor:** Irwin Kostal. **Cast:** Tab Hunter, Peggy King, Sheila
   Smith, Jarmila Novotna, Vinny Corrod.

HANS BRINKER AND THE SILVER SKATES

Soundtrack (1969) • Disneyland (S) DQ-1282..................................... 15-20   69
Soundtrack (1972) • Disneyland (S) DDF-5.. 15-20   72
   Reissue has two discs. Also has music from *Toby Tyler in the Circus*.
   Cast: Henry Calvin (narrator), others.

HANS CHRISTIAN ANDERSEN

Studiotrack (1952) • Decca (EP) ED 556 15-18   52
   Two discs. Gatefold cover.
Studiotrack (1952) • Decca (EP) 9-364 15-20   52
   Boxed, four-disc set.
Studiotrack (1952) • Decca (M) DL-5433 25-35   52
   10-inch LP.
Studiotrack (1952) • Decca (M) DL-8479 10-15   57
Studiotrack (1952) • Decca (SE) DL-78479... 8-15   59
Studiotrack (1952) • MCA (SE) 148... 8-10   Re
   Above three also have music from *Tubby the Tuba*.
   Composer: Frank Loesser, Paul Tripp, George Kleinsinger. **Conductor:** Gordon Jenkins, Victor
   Young. **Cast:** Danny Kaye, Jane Wyman, Gordon Jenkins and His Chorus and Orchestra, Victor
   Young and His Orchestra.

HANS CHRISTIAN ANDERSEN STORIES

Studiotrack (1963) • Disneyland (M) ST-3964 10-20   63
   Gatefold cover, with booklet.
   Composer: Tutti Camarata. **Conductor:** Tutti Camarata.

HANSEL AND GRETEL

Studio Cast (1949) • Columbia (M) ML 2055 40-45   49
10-inch LP.
Composer: Engelbert Humperdinck, Adelheid Wette. **Conductor:** Carmen Dragon. **Cast:** Basil Rathbone, Jane Powell, Ted Donaldson, Lurene Tuttle, Frank Graham, Rece Saxon.

TV Soundtrack (1955) • Bluebird (M) LXA-1013 30-35   55
TV Soundtrack (1955) • RCA Victor (M) LBY-1024 25-30   59
TV Soundtrack (1955) • Camden (M) CAL-1024 8-10   61
TV Soundtrack (1955) • Camden (SE) CAS-1024 8-12   61
Composer: Engelbert Humperdinck. **Conductor:** Franz Allers. **Cast:** Mildred Dunnock.

TV Soundtrack (1958) • MGM (M) E-3690 50-60   58
Composer: Alec Wilder. **Conductor:** Glenn Osser. **Cast:** Red Buttons, Barbara Cook, Rudy Vallee, Stubby Kaye, Paula Laurence.

Studiotrack (1964) • Disneyland (M) DQ-1253 10-20   64
Studiotrack (1964) • Disneyland (S) ST-3955 15-20   67
Soundtrack (1965) • Golden (M) LP-167 20-45   65
Dialogue from soundtrack with studiotrack music added.
Composer: Anne & Milton Delugg.

HAPPENING

Soundtrack (1967) • Colgems (M) COMO-5006 20-25   67
Soundtrack (1967) • Colgems (S) COSO-5006 30-40   67
Composer: Frank DeVol. **Conductor:** Frank DeVol. **Cast:** Stephen Doyle Smith.

HAPPENING IN CENTRAL PARK

TV Soundtrack • Columbia (S) CS-9710 8-12   68
Composer: Various. **Conductor:** Peter Matz. **Cast:** Barbra Streisand.

HAPPIEST GIRL IN THE WORLD

Original Cast (1961) • Columbia (M) KOL-5650 30-35   61
Original Cast (1961) • Columbia (S) KOS-2050 35-55   61
Yellow covers with drawings and credits.
Original Cast (1961) • Columbia (M) KOL-5650 30-35   61
Original Cast (1961) • Columbia (S) KOS-2050 45-60   61
White photo covers with credits.
Composer: Jacques Offenbach, E.Y. Harburg. **Conductor:** Robert DeCormier. **Cast:** Cyril Ritchard, Janice Rule, Dran Seitz, Bruce Yarnell, Lu Leonard, Nancy Windsor.

HAPPIEST MILLIONAIRE

Soundtrack (1967) • Buena Vista (M) BV-5001 8-12   67
Soundtrack (1967) • Buena Vista (S) STER-5001 8-12   67
Gatefold covers. Both have a 12-page bound-in booklet.
Composer: Richard M. Sherman, Robert B. Sherman. **Conductor:** Jack Elliot. **Cast:** Tommy Steele, Lesley Ann Warren, John Davidson, Paul Petersen, Fred MacMurray, Eddie Hodges, Geraldine Page, Gladys Cooper, Joyce Bulifant.

HAPPY AS A SANDBAG

Original London Cast (1975) • Decca (S) SKL 5217 25-35   75
UK release.
Composer: Various. **Conductor:** Nigel Hess. **Cast:** Lesley Duff, Trevor Jones, David Ashton, Martin Duncan, Julian Hough, Robert McIntosh, Yvonne Edgell, Darlene Johnson, Roy Macready, Geraldine Wright.

HAPPY BIRTHDAY: see OKLAHOMA!

HAPPY END

Studio Cast • Columbia (M) OL-5630 8-12   77
Studio Cast • Columbia (S) OS-2032 10-12   77
Performed in the German language.

Studio Cast (1977) • Columbia Special Products (S) COS-2032 5-8   Re
  Composer: Kurt Weill, Bertolt Brecht. **Conductor:** Wilhelm Bruckner-Ruggeberg. **Cast:** Lotte Lenya.

HAPPY ENDING
Soundtrack (1969) • United Artists (S) UAS-5203 10-12   69
Soundtrack (1969) • MCA (S) 25105 5-8   86
  Composer: Michel Legrand. **Conductor:** Michel Legrand. **Cast:** Michael Dees, Bill Eaton, Michel Legrand.

HAPPY GO LUCKY: see THANKS A MILLION

HAPPY HUNTING
Original Cast (1956) • RCA Victor (EP) EOC-1026 15-20   56
  Three discs.
Original Cast (1956) • RCA Victor (M) LOC-1026 20-30   56
  Composer: Harold Karr, Matt Dubey. **Conductor:** Jay Blackton. **Cast:** Ethel Merman, Fernando Lamas, Virginia Gibson, Gordon Polk, Mary Finney, Leon Belasco.

HAPPY MOTHER GOOSE (BY KUKLA, FRAN AND OLLIE)
Studio TV Cast • RCA Victor Y-423 15-25   53
  Two 78 rpm EPs.
Studio TV Cast • RCA Victor (EP) WY-423 15-25   53
  Two 45 rpm EPs.
  Composer: Jack Fascinato. **Conductor:** Jack Fascinato. **Cast:** Fran Allison, Burr Tillstrom, Jack Fascinato (piano).
  Also see MERRY CHRISTMAS FROM KUKLA, FRAN AND OLLIE
  Also see SONGS BY KUKLA, FRAN AND OLLIE

HAPPY PRINCE
Studio Cast (1950) • Decca (M) DLP-6000 30-40   50
  10-inch LP. One side has music from *The Small One.*
  Composer: Bernard Herrmann, Victor Young. **Conductor:** Victor Young. **Cast:** Bing Crosby, Orson Welles.
Studio Cast (1965) • Decca (S) RNF-5 10-20   65
  We have yet to verify the format and purpose of this disc.
Soundtrack (1980) • Disneyland (S) ST-3820 10-15   80
  Songs and dialogue. One side has music from *The Small One.*
  Cast: Sean Marshall, Olan Soule, Joe Higgins, William Woodson, Hal Smith, Gordon Jump.

HAPPY TIME
Original Cast (1968) • RCA Victor (M) LOC-1144 8-12   68
Original Cast (1968) • RCA Victor (S) LSO-1144 10-15   68
  Composer: John Kander, Fred Ebb. **Conductor:** Oscar Kosarin. **Cast:** Robert Goulet, David Wayne, Mike Rupert, Julie Gregg.

HARD COUNTRY
Soundtrack (1981) • Epic (S) SE-37367 8-10   81
  Composer: Michael Murphey, others. **Cast:** Kim Basinger, Tanya Tucker.

HARD DAY'S NIGHT
Soundtrack (1964) • United Artists (M) SP-2359/60 600-1,000   64
  Open-end interview. Includes 12-page script. Made for radio station use only.
Soundtrack (1964) • United Artists (M) SP-2362/3 500-700   64
  Commercial spots. Made for radio station use only.
Soundtrack (1964) • United Artists (M) UAL-3366 1,000-2,000   64
  White label. Promotional issue only.
Soundtrack (1964) • United Artists (M) UAL-3366 100-150   64
  Black label.
Soundtrack (1964) • United Artists (S) UAS-6366 150-200   64
  Black label.

Soundtrack (1964) • United Artists (S) UAS-6366 30-50   68
   Pink label.
Soundtrack (1964) • United Artists (S) UAS-6366 30-50   70
   Black and orange label.
Soundtrack (1964) • United Artists (S) UAS-6366 10-20   71
   Tan label.
Soundtrack (1964) • Capitol (S) SW-11921 10-15   77
   Yellow and orange sunrise label.
Soundtrack (1964) • Capitol (S) SW-11921 10-20   80s
   Purple label or black label.
Soundtrack (1964) • MFSL (S) 1-103 20-40   87
   Half-speed mastered.
Soundtrack (1964) • Capitol/Parlophone (M) CLJ-46437 10-20   80s
   Purple label or black label.
   Composer: John Lennon, Paul McCartney. **Conductor:** George Martin. **Cast:** Beatles, George
   Martin Orchestra.
Soundtrack Interview (1964) • Cicadelic/BIOdisc 001 10-15   90
   Seven-inch disc. Open-end interview. 700 numbered copies made. Promotional issue only.
Soundtrack Interview (1964) • Cicadelic/BIOdisc 001 20-30   90
   Seven-inch disc. Open-end interview. 55 numbered copies made with "Specially prepared
   for Records, Etc. of Payson, Arizona" printed on disc. A promotional bonus to book buyers.
   Includes script.

HARD JOB BEING GOD
Studio Cast (1972) • GWP (S) ST-2036 20-25   72
   Composer: Tom Martel. **Conductor:** John O'Reilly. **Cast:** Dorothy Lerner, Tom Martel, John
   O'Reilly, Tom Troxell, Joe Valentine, Susie Walcher.

HARD PART BEGINS
Soundtrack (1974) • A&M (S) SP-9016 8-12   74
   Cast: Donnelly Rhodes, Paul Bradley, Nancy Bellefuller, Cliff Carol.

HARD RIDE
Soundtrack (1971) • Paramount (S) PAS-6005 20-25   71
   Composer: Harley Hatcher. **Cast:** Bill Medley, Thelma Camacho, Junction, Sounds of Harley,
   Bob Moline, Bluewater.

HARD TO HOLD
Soundtrack (1984) • RCA Victor (S) ABL1-4935 8-10   84
   Cast: Rick Springfield, Randy Crawford, Graham Parker, Nona Hendryx, Peter Gabriel.

HARDER THEY COME
Soundtrack (1973) • Mango (S) SMAS-7400 10-12   73
Soundtrack (1973) • Mango (S) SMAS-9202 8-12   Re
   Composer: Jimmy Cliff, others. **Cast:** Jimmy Cliff, Desmond Dekker, Slickers, Maytals.

HARK!
Original Cast (1972) • Private Label (S) STK-1016 50-75   72
   Two discs.
   Conductor: Sande Campbell.
Original Touring Cast (1972) • Theatre Archives (S) JGR-300 25-30   72
   Composer: Dan Goggin, Marvin Solley, Robert Lorick. **Cast:** Dan Goggin, Marvin Solley,
   Sharon Miller, Elaine Petricoff, Jack Blackton, Danny Guerreo.

HARLOW
Soundtrack (1965) • Columbia (M) OL-6390 10-12   65
Soundtrack (1965) • Columbia (S) OS-2790 12-15   65
   From the film starring Carroll Baker.
   Composer: Neal Hefti. **Conductor:** Neal Hefti.
Soundtrack (1965) • Warner Bros. (M) W-1599 10-12   65

Soundtrack (1965) • Warner Bros. (S) WS-1599 12-15   65
From the film starring Carol Lynley.
Composer: Nelson Riddle, Al Ham. Conductor: Nelson Riddle.

HAROLD ARLEN REVISITED
Studio Cast • Crewe (S) CR 1345 10-15
Composer: Harold Arlen.

HAROLD J. MIRISCH – MOVIE PIONEER OF THE YEAR 1964
Studiotrack (1964) • United Artists (M) UAL-9004 10-15   64

HAROLD LLOYD'S WORLD OF LAUGHTER
Soundtrack • Citadel (S) CT-6018... 10-20   77
Music made for reissue of *The Freshman*.
Composer: Walter Scharf.

HAROLD ROBBINS PRESENTS MUSIC FROM THE ADVENTURERS: see ADVENTURERS

HAROLD SINGS ARLEN
Studiotrack (1966) • Columbia (M) OL-6520 8-10   66
Studiotrack (1966) • Columbia (S) OS-2920 8-12   66
Studiotrack • Columbia Special Products (S) AOS-2920 5-8
Conductor: Peter Matz. Cast: Harold Arlen, Barbra Streisand.

HARPER
Soundtrack (1966) • Mainstream (M) 56078....................................... 15-18   66
Soundtrack (1966) • Mainstream (S) 6078 20-25   66
Composer: Johnny Mandel, Andre Previn, Dory Previn. Conductor: Johnny Mandel. Cast: Ruth Price.

HARPER VALLEY P.T.A.
Soundtrack (1978) • Plantation (S) PLP-700.............................. 8-10   78
Green vinyl.
Composer: Tom T. Hall, others. Conductor: Nelson Riddle. Cast: Jeannie C. Riley, Nelson Riddle, Jerry Lee Lewis, Johnny Cash, Carol Channing, Rita Remington.

HARRAD EXPERIMENT
Soundtrack (1973) • Capitol (S) ST-11182........................... 15-20   73
Composer: Artie Butler. Cast: Ace Trucking Company, Lori Lieberman, Don Johnson.

HARRAD SUMMER
Soundtrack (1974) • Capitol (S) ST-11338........................... 15-20   74
Film sequel to *The Harrad Experiment*.
Composer: Artie Butler. Cast: Pat Williams, Gene Redding.

HARRY AND LENA
TV Soundtrack (1970) • RCA Victor (S) PRS-295 8-10   70
Conductor: Alfred Brown. Cast: Harry Belafonte, Lena Horne.

HARRY AND THE HENDERSONS
Soundtrack (1987) • MCA (S) 6208.. 10-15   87
Composer: Bruce Broughton. Conductor: Bruce Broughton. Cast: Joe Cocker, others.

HARRY AND TONTO
Soundtrack (1974) • Casablanca (S) NBLP-7010 12-15   75
Composer: Bill Conti. Cast: Art Carney, Geraldine Fitzgerald, Chief Dan George, Barbara Rhoades. (With dialogue.)

HARUM SCARUM
Soundtrack (1965) • RCA Victor (M) LPM-3468 150-250   65
Black label, dog on top, reads "Monaural" at bottom. Includes bonus 12" x 12" color photo.
Soundtrack (1965) • RCA Victor (M) LPM-3468 75-125   65
Black label, dog on top, reads "Monaural" at bottom. Without bonus photo.

Soundtrack (1965) • RCA Victor (S) LSP-3468 150-250   65
   Black label, dog on top, reads "Stereo" at bottom. Includes bonus 12" x 12" color photo.
Soundtrack (1965) • RCA Victor (S) LSP-3468 80-120   65
   Black label, dog on top, reads "Stereo" at bottom. Without bonus photo.
Soundtrack (1965) • RCA Victor (S) APL1-2558 10-15   78
Soundtrack (1965) • RCA Victor (S) AYL1-3734 8-10   81
   Composer: Bill Giant, Bernie Baum, Florence Kaye, Sid Tepper, Roy C. Bennett, others. **Cast:**
   Elvis Presley, Scotty Moore (guitar), D.J. Fontana (drums), Bob Moore (bass), Jordanaires
   (vocals).

HARVEY GIRLS

Studiotrack (1946) • Decca A-388 20-30   46
   78 rpm album, with booklet.
Soundtrack (1946) • Hollywood Soundstage (M) HS-5002 8-15
   Soundtrack score plus outtakes from the film.
   Composer: Johnny Mercer, Harry Warren. **Conductor:** Lennie Hayton. **Cast:** Judy Garland,
   Ray Bolger, Kenny Baker, Virginia O'Brien, Betty Russell (performed vocals for Cyd Charisse in
   the film), Marion Doenges (performed vocals for Angela Lansbury).
   Also see MEET ME IN ST. LOUIS.

HATARI

Soundtrack (1962) • RCA Victor (M) LPM-2559 20-30   62
   Cover has "Newest Album by 1962's Double Oscar Winner Mancini," without cover
   graphics. Promotional issue only.
Soundtrack (1962) • RCA Victor (M) LPM-2559 15-20   62
Soundtrack (1962) • RCA Victor (S) LSP-2559 20-30   62
   Black labels with dog on top.
Soundtrack (1962) • RCA Victor (S) LSP-2559 10-12   Re
   Orange or tan labels.
   Composer: Henry Mancini, Johnny Mercer, Hoagy Carmichael. **Conductor:** Henry Mancini.
   Cast: Henry Mancini and His Orchestra.

HAUNTED

Soundtrack (1977) • Midland Int'l (S) BKL1-2131 10-12   77
   Composer: Lor Crane, Freya Crane, Ronald Romano. **Conductor:** Lor Crane. **Cast:** Billy Vera,
   Carol Douglas, Herb Oscar Anderson, Freya Crane, Ronald Romano.

HAVE GUN WILL TRAVEL

TV Soundtrack (1957) • Columbia (M) CL-1788 20-25   62
TV Soundtrack • Columbia (S) CS-8588 30-35   62
   Composer: Bernard Herrmann. **Cast:** Johnny Western.
TV Soundtrack (1957) • Cerberus (M) CST-0209 15-20   84
   Also has music from *Ethan Allen* and *The Western Suite*.

HAVING A WILD WEEKEND

Soundtrack (1965) • Epic (M) LN-24162 15-18   65
Soundtrack (1965) • Epic (S) BN-26162 15-30   65
   Has the hit, *Catch Us If You Can*, originally intended as the film title.
   Composer: Dave Clark, Mike Smith, Denis Payton, Lenny Davidson. **Cast:** Dave Clark Five.

HAWAII

Soundtrack (1966) • United Artists (M) UAL-4143 5-10   66
Soundtrack (1966) • United Artists (S) UAS-5143 8-10   66
Soundtrack (1966) • United Artists (S) SW-90935 8-10   Re
   Capitol Record Club issue.
   Composer: Elmer Bernstein. **Conductor:** Elmer Bernstein.
Studiotrack (1966) • Liberty (M) LRP-3488 8-10   66
Studiotrack (1966) • Liberty (S) LST-7488 10-12   66
   Full title: *Hawaii, Music from the Film . . . and Other Selections*.
   Composer: Elmer Bernstein, others. **Conductor:** Martin Denny. **Cast:** Martin Denny.

Studiotrack • Somerset (S) SF-26900 5-10   60s
   Side 2 is songs from *Pacific Paradise*.
     Composer: Elmer Bernstein, J. Kuhn, others. **Cast:** Cinema Sound Stage Orchestra.
Studiotrack • Wyncote (M) W 9172 5-10   60s
Studiotrack • Wyncote (S) WS 9172 10-12   60s
   Both also have music from *Alfie* and *The Wrong Box*.
     Cast: Hollywood Studio Orchestra.

HAWAII FIVE-0

TV Soundtrack (1969) • Capitol (S) ST-410 25-30   69
TV Soundtrack (1969) • Capitol (S) SM-410 15-20   Re
     Composer: Morton Stevens. **Conductor:** Morton Stevens.

HAWAIIAN EYE

TV Soundtrack (1959) • Warner Bros. (M) W-1355 20-25   59
TV Soundtrack (1959) • Warner Bros. (S) WS-1355 25-30   59
     Composer: Jerry Livingston, Mack David, others. **Conductor:** Warren Barker. **Cast:** Connie
   Stevens, Robert Conrad, Poncie Ponce.

HAWAIIANS

Soundtrack (1970) • United Artists (S) UAS-5210 10-12   70
Soundtrack (1970) • United Artists (S) SW-93297 15-20   70
   Capitol Record Club issue.
     Composer: Henry Mancini. **Conductor:** Henry Mancini.

HAZEL FLAGG

Original Cast (1953) • RCA Victor (EP) WOC-1010 25-35   53
Original Cast (1953) • RCA Victor (M) LOC-1010 100-125   53
Original Cast (1953) • RCA Victor (M) CBM1-2207 20-30   Re
   Film rendering is titled *Living It Up*.
     Composer: Jule Styne, Bob Hilliard. **Conductor:** Pembroke Davenport. **Cast:** Helen Gallagher,
   Thomas Mitchell, Benay Venuta, John Howard, Jack Whiting, Dean Campbell.
   Also see LIVING IT UP

HE'S MY GIRL

Soundtrack (1987) • Scotti Bros. (S) SZ-40906 8-10   87
     Cast: David Hallyday, Sylvie Vartan, Paul Revere and the Raiders, Mountain, Chambers
   Brothers, Mickey Barrera, Kim Bullard.

HEAD

Soundtrack (1968) • Colgems (S) COSO-5008 40-50   68
Soundtrack (1968) • Rhino (S) RNLP-145 8-10   Re
     Composer: Ken Thorne. **Conductor:** Ken Thorne. **Cast:** Monkees (Mike Nesmith, Peter Tork,
   Davy Jones, Micky Dolenz). (With dialogue.)

HEAR! HEAR!

Original Cast (1955) • Decca (EP) ED 841 20-25   55
   Three discs.
Original Cast (1955) • Decca (M) DL-9031 35-45   55
     Composer: Fred Waring, others. **Conductor:** Fred Culley. **Cast:** Norma Douglas, Fred Waring
   and His Pennsylvanians, Glee Club, Leonard Kranendonk, Bob Sands, Gordon Goodman.

HEART BEAT

Soundtrack (1980) • Capitol (S) SOO-12029 10-12   80

HEART IS A LONELY HUNTER

Soundtrack (1968) • Warner Bros. (S) WBS-1759 20-25   68
     Composer: Dave Grusin. **Cast:** Scott Davis.

HEART IS A REBEL

Soundtrack • Chancel (EP) CR-2005 10-15
     Composer: Ralph Carmichael. **Conductor:** Ralph Carmichael. **Cast:** Ethel Waters, Georgia
   Lee, Ralph Carmichael's Orchestra.

HEART OF DIXIE
Soundtrack (1989) • A&M (S) SP-3930 10-20   89
    Composer: Kenny Vance, Philip Namanworth, others. **Cast:** Elvis Presley, Kenny Vance,
    Delbert McClinton, Charlie Jacobs, Rebecca Russell, Ivory Joe Hunter, Snakes.

HEARTBREAK HOTEL
Soundtrack (1988) • RCA Victor (S) 8533 1-R 5-8   88
    Composer: Georges Delerue (original music), Mae Axton, Tom Durden, Elvis Presley, others.
    Cast: Elvis Presley, David Keith and the T. Graham Brown Band, Dobie Gray, Alice Cooper.

HEARTBREAK KID
Soundtrack (1972) • Columbia (S) S-32155 8-12   73
    Composer: Garry Sherman, Cy Coleman, others. **Conductor:** Garry Sherman. **Cast:** Bill Dean,
    Eddie Albert, Charles Grodin, Cybill Shepherd, Audra Lindley, Jeannie Berlin. (With dialogue.)

HEARTS OF FIRE
Soundtrack (1987) • Columbia (S) SC-40870 8-12   87
    Cast: Bob Dylan, Fiona, Rupert Everett.

HEAT AND DUST
Soundtrack (1983) • Varese Sarabande (S) STV-81194 8-10   83
Soundtrack (1983) • That's Entertainment (S) TER-1032 8-10   80s
    UK release.
    Composer: Richard Robbins. **Conductor:** Harry Rabinowitz.

HEATHERS
Soundtrack (1989) • Varese Sarabande (S) VS-5223 8-12   89
    Composer: David Newman. **Conductor:** David Newman.

HEAVEN'S GATE
Soundtrack (1980) • Liberty (S) LOO-1073 10-15   80
    Composer: David Mansfield, Ennio Morricone. **Conductor:** David Mansfield. **Cast:** Doug
    Kershaw.

HEAVENLY BODIES
Soundtrack (1985) • Private Bodies (S) SZ 39930 8-12   85
    Cast: Bonnie Pointer, Tubes, Cheryl Lynn, others.

HEAVENLY KID
Soundtrack (1985) • Elektra (S) 60425-1 8-10   85
    Cast: Joe Lynn Turner, Jon Fiore, Jamie Bond, Debra Laws, George Duke, Lynn Turner,
    Howard Hewett, Mickey Thomas, Niko-Meka.

HEAVY METAL – THE SCORE
Soundtrack (1981) • Asylum (S) 5E 547 35-40   81
    Composer: Elmer Bernstein. **Conductor:** Elmer Bernstein.
Soundtrack (1981) • Asylum (S) DP-9004 12-15   81
    Two discs.
    Composer: Elmer Bernstein. **Cast:** Black Sabbath, Blue Oyster Cult, Cheap Trick, Devo,
    Donald Fagen, Don Felder, Grand Funk Railroad, Sammy Hagar, Journey, Nazareth, Stevie
    Nicks, Riggs, Trust.

HEAVY TRAFFIC
Soundtrack (1973) • Fantasy (S) 9436 10-25   73
    Cast: Sergio Mendes & Brazil '66, Chuck Berry, Isley Brothers, Dave Brubeck Quartet, Merl
    Saunders, Ed Bogas, Ray Shanklin.

HECTOR, THE STOWAWAY PUP
TV Soundtrack (1964) • Disneyland (M) ST-1921 30-35   64
    Composer: Richard M. Sherman, Robert B. Sherman.

HEIDI
TV Soundtrack (1968) • Capitol (S) SKAO-2995 10-40   68
    Composer: John Williams. **Conductor:** John Williams. **Cast:** Sir Michael Redgrave, Jennifer
    Edwards (dialogue), Carri Chase (vocal on *Heidi's Theme*).

HEIDI'S SONG
Soundtrack (1982) • K-Tel (S) NU 5310 15-20   82
   Composer: Sammy Cahn, Burton Lane.

HEIFETZ ON TELEVISION
TV Soundtrack • RCA LSC 3205 15-20
"A Presentation of the Bell System Family Theater on NBC-TV."
   Conductor: Jascha Heifetz, Sir Malcolm Sargent. **Cast:** New Symphony Orchestra of London, Jascha Heifetz.

HELD OVER! TODAY'S GREAT MOVIE THEMES
Studiotrack • Columbia (S) CS-1019 10-15
   Composer: Various. **Conductor:** Percy Faith. **Cast:** Percy Faith Orchestra.

HELEN MORGAN STORY
Soundtrack (1957) • RCA Victor (EP) EPA-4112 15-20   57
Soundtrack (1957) • RCA Victor (M) LOC-1030 35-45   57
   Conductor: Ray Heindorf. **Cast:** Gogi Grant (performs vocals for Ann Blyth in the film.)
TV Soundtrack (1957) • Columbia (M) CL-994 15-20   57
   Actual title: *Bergen Sings Morgan*. Songs from the television production of *The Helen Morgan Story*.
   Conductor: Luther Henderson. **Cast:** Polly Bergen.

HELEN OF TROY
Studiotrack (1974) • Elmer Bernstein Film Music Collection (S) FMC-1 35-40   74
   Also has music from *A Summer Place* (1959).
   Composer: Max Steiner. **Conductor:** Elmer Bernstein

HELL CAN BE HEAVEN
Original London Cast • That's Entertainment (S) TER-1068 8-10   80s
   UK release.
   Composer: Hereward K.

HELL RAIDERS OF THE DEEP: see ANNA

HELL TO ETERNITY
Soundtrack (1960) • Warwick (M) W-2030 75-100   60
Soundtrack (1960) • Warwick (S) WST-2030 150-200   60
   Composer: Leith Stevens. **Conductor:** Leith Stevens.

HELL UP IN HARLEM
Soundtrack (1974) • Motown (S) M-802V1 20-25   74
   Composer: Fonce Mizell, Freddie Perren. **Cast:** Edwin Starr.

HELL'S ANGELS ON WHEELS
Soundtrack (1967) • Smash (M) 27094 20-25   67
Soundtrack (1967) • Smash (S) 67094 20-30   67
   Composer: Stu Phillips. **Conductor:** Stu Phillips.

HELL'S ANGELS '69
Soundtrack (1969) • Capitol (S) SKAO-303 20-25   69
   Cast: Tony Bruno, Sonny Valdez, Wendy Cole.

HELL'S BELLS
Soundtrack (1969) • Sidewalk (S) 5919 20-30   69
   Composer: Les Baxter. **Conductor:** Les Baxter.

HELLBOUND: HELLRAISER II – TIME TO PLAY
Soundtrack (1988) • GNP/Crescendo (S) GNPS-8015 8-10   88
   Film sequel to *Hellraiser*.
   Composer: Christopher Young. **Conductor:** Allan Wilson. **Cast:** Graunke Symphony Orchestra.
   Also see HELLRAISER

HELLCATS

Soundtrack (1968) • Tower (M) T-5124 15-20   68
Soundtrack (1968) • Tower (S) ST-5124 20-25   68
    Cast: Davie Allen and the Arrows, Davy Jones.

HELLO AGAIN

Soundtrack (1987) • Pro-Arte (S) CDC-1004 8-10   87
    Conductor: William Goldstein. **Cast:** William Goldstein.

HELLO, CAROL!: see HELLO, DOLLY!

HELLO, DOLLY!

Original Cast (1964) • RCA Victor (M) LOCD-1087 10-12   64
Original Cast (1964) • RCA Victor (S) LSOD-1087 12-15   64
    Black-and-white back covers have *Come and Be My Butterfly* spotlighted. As that number
    was deleted from the show soon after opening, cover was recalled.
Original Cast (1964) • RCA Victor (S) LOCD-1087 8-10   64
Original Cast (1964) • RCA Victor (S) LSOD-1087 8-10   64
    Color back covers picture Carol Channing. Black label.
Original Cast (1964) • RCA Victor (S) LOCD-1087 5-8   Re
Original Cast (1964) • RCA Victor (S) LSOD-1087 5-8   Re
    Color back covers picture Carol Channing. Covers have "RE." Label may be either orange
    or tan.
Original Cast (1964) • RCA Victor (S) AYL1-3814 8-10   81
    Composer: Jerry Herman. **Conductor:** Shepard Coleman. **Cast:** Carol Channing, David Burns,
    Eileen Brennan, Sondra Lee, Charles Nelson Reilly, Jerry Dodge, Igors Gavon.
Original Cast Interview (1964) • RCA Victor (M) SP-33-282 15-25   64
    Has an interview titled *Hello, Carol!*
    Cast: Carol Channing.
Original Cast • Bar-Mike (EP) No Number Used 20-25   70
    Full title: *Ethel Merman Sings The New Songs from Hello Dolly*. Two selections added to
    the show when Merman joined the cast in 1970.
    Composer: Jerry Herman. **Cast:** Ethel Merman, Goldie Hawkins, Wayne Sanders, Bill Halfacre.
Original London Cast (1965) • RCA Victor (M) RD-7768 20-25   65
Original London Cast (1965) • RCA Victor (S) SF-7768 25-35   65
Original London Cast (1966) • RCA Victor (M) LOCD-2007 25-35   66
Original London Cast (1966) • RCA Victor (S) LSOD-2007 25-30   66
    UK releases.
    Composer: Jerry Herman. **Conductor:** Alyn Ainsworth. **Cast:** Mary Martin, Loring Smith,
    Marilynn Lovell, Coco Ramirez.
Original All-Black Cast (1967) • RCA Victor (M) LOC-1147 8-10   67
Original All-Black Cast (1967) • RCA Victor (S) LSO-1147 8-12   67
Original All-Black Cast (1967) • RCA Victor (S) ANL1-2849 5-8   Re
    Composer: Jerry Herman. **Conductor:** Saul Schectman. **Cast:** Pearl Bailey, Cab Calloway,
    Jack Crowder, Winston DeWitt Hemsley, Chris Calloway, Roger Lawson, Emily Yancy.
Original German Cast (1967) • Columbia (M) OL-6710 12-15   67
Original German Cast (1967) • Columbia (S) OS-3110 15-18   67
    Composer: Jerry Herman. **Conductor:** Klaus Doldinger. **Cast:** Tatjana Iwanow, Wolfgang Arps,
    Ingrid Ernest, Evelyn Balser.
Soundtrack (1969) • 20th Century-Fox (S) DTCS-5103 10-12   69
    Gatefold cover.
Soundtrack (1969) • 20th Century-Fox (S) 102 8-10   74
    Standard cover.
      Composer: Jerry Herman. **Conductor:** Lionel Newman, Lennie Hayton. **Cast:** Barbra
      Streisand, Walter Matthau, Michael Crawford, Louis Armstrong.
Studiotrack (1964) • RCA Victor (M) LPM-2916 8-10   64
Studiotrack (1964) • RCA Victor (S) LSP-2916 10-12   64
    Cast: Tommy Dorsey Orchestra, Sam Donahue Orchestra.

Studiotrack • Diplomat (M) 2323 5-10
  One side has music from *Funny Girl*.
    Conductor: Al Goodman.
    Also see FUNNY GIRL

HELLO FRISCO, HELLO
Soundtrack (1943) • Caliban (M) 6005 8-10
  One side has music from Spring Parade.
    Cast: Alice Faye, June Havoc, John Payne. SPRING PARADE: Deanna Durbin, Robert
    Cummings.

HELLO OUT THERE
Studio Cast (1953) • Desto (SE) DST-6451 15-20
    Composer: Jack Beeson, William Saroyan. **Conductor:** Frederick Waldman. **Cast:** John
    Reardon, Lenya Gabriele, Marvin Worden.

HELLO, SOLLY!
Original Cast (1967) • Capitol (M) W-2731 8-12   67
Original Cast (1967) • Capitol (S) SW-2731 10-12   67
    Conductor: Al Hausman. **Cast:** Mickey Katz, Larry Best, Stan Porter, Vivian Lloyd.

HELLO-GOODBYE
Soundtrack (1970) • 20th Century-Fox (S) S-4210............................... 25-30   70
    Composer: Francis Lai. **Conductor:** Francis Lai.

HELLRAISER
Soundtrack (1987) • Pro-Arte (S) CDC-1001 8-10   87
    Cast: Christopher Young.
    Also see HELLBOUND: HELLRAISER II – TIME TO PLAY

HELP!
Soundtrack (1964) • United Artists (M) UA-Help-A/B......................... 500-800   65
  Commercial spots. Made for radio station use only.
Soundtrack (1964) • United Artists (M) UA-Help-INT.......................750-1000   65
  Open-end interview. Includes script. Promotional issue only.
Soundtrack (1964) • Cicadelic/BIOdisc (M) 002 8-10   90
  Seven-inch disc. Open-end interview. Includes script. A promotional bonus to book buyers.
  Includes paper sleeve and script insert.
Soundtrack (1965) • Capitol (M) MAS-2386 75-100   65
  Black label.
Soundtrack (1965) • Capitol (S) SMAS-2386 50-75   65
  Black label.
Soundtrack (1965) • Apple (S) SMAS-2386 20-30   68
  With Capitol logo on Apple label.
Soundtrack (1965) • Capitol (S) SMAS-2386 20-40   69
  Green label.
Soundtrack (1965) • Apple (S) SMAS-2386 15-25   70s
  Apple label without Capitol logo.
Soundtrack (1965) • Capitol (S) SMAS-2386 10-12   70s
  Orange label or purple label.
Soundtrack (1965) • Capitol (S) SMAS-2386 10-12   83
  Black label with print in colorband.
Soundtrack (19654) • MFSL (S) 1-105... 20-40   85
  Half-speed mastered.
Soundtrack (1965) • Capitol (S) C1-90454... 10-20   88
  Purple label.
Soundtrack (1965) • Capitol/Parlophone (S) CLJ-46439 10-20   88
  Purple label, or black label with colorband.
    Composer: John Lennon, Paul McCartney, George Harrison. **Cast:** Beatles.

HEMINGWAY'S ADVENTURES OF A YOUNG MAN
Soundtrack (1962) • RCA Victor (M) LOC-1074 30-35   62
Soundtrack (1962) • RCA Victor (S) LSO-1074 60-65   62
Soundtrack (1962) • Entr'acte (S) ERS-6516 15-20   79
Soundtrack (1962) • Label X (S) LXRS-201 8-10   Re
   Composer: Franz Waxman. Conductor: Franz Waxman.

HENNESEY
TV Soundtrack (1959) • Signature (M) 1049 40-50   59
TV Soundtrack (1959) • Signature (S) SS-1049 60-70   59
   Composer: Sonny Burke. Conductor: Jackie Cooper.

HENRY VIII AND HIS SIX WIVES
Soundtrack (1972) • Angel (S) SFO-36895 8-20   72
   Gatefold cover. Authentic Tudor Court music and original pieces composed in a sixteenth-
   century style for the film.
   Composer: David Munrow, others. Conductor: David Munrow. Cast: Early Music Consort of
   London.

HENRY V
Studiotrack (1945) • RCA DM-1128 150-250   45
   Album of four 12-inch, 78 rpms. Includes nine-page booklet. Music and dialogue.
   Composer: Sir William Walton. Cast: Sir Laurence Olivier, Sir William Walton and the
   Philadelphia Orchestra and Chorus.
   Also see HAMLET

HENRY MANCINI PRESENTS THE ACADEMY AWARD SONGS
Studiotrack (1966) • RCA Victor (M) LPM-6013 10-12   66
Studiotrack (1966) • RCA Victor (S) LSP-6013 12-15   66
   Two discs. 31 Oscar winning songs from 1934 - 1964.
   Composer: Various. Conductor: Henry Mancini. Cast: Henry Mancini's Orchestra and Chorus.

HENRY, SWEET HENRY
Original Cast (1967) • Ampco Music (S) No Number Used 20-30   67
   Single-sided demonstration disc, with 7 tracks. Promotional issue only.
Original Cast (1967) • ABC (M) OC-4 20-25   67
Original Cast (1967) • ABC (S) SOC-4 25-45   67
   Composer: Robert Merrill. Conductor: Shepard Coleman. Cast: Don Ameche, Carol Bruce,
   Neva Small, Louise Lasser, Robin Wilson, Alice Playten, Laried Montgomery.

HER FIRST ROMAN
Original Cast (1968) • S.P.M. (M) CO-7751 100-125
   Live recording by the Society for the Preservation of Musicals.
   Composer: Ervin Drake. Conductor: Peter Howard. Cast: Cal Bellini, Richard Kiley, Bruce
   MacKay, Claudia McNeil, Brooks Morton, Leslie Uggams.

HERCULES (1959)
Soundtrack (1959) • RCA/Bluebird (M) LBY-1036 100-125   59
   Composer: Enzo Masetti. Cast: Conrad Nagel (narration), Steve Reeves (dialogue).

HERCULES (1983)
Studiotrack (1983) • Varese Sarabande (S) STV-81187 15-20   83
   Includes poster. Background score from the film.
   Composer: Pino Donaggio. Conductor: Natale Massara.

HERCULES (THE MUSIC)
Soundtrack • Phoenix (S) PHC AM-01 50-65   84
   Composer: Enzo Masetti. Conductor: Enzo Masetti.

HERE COME THE GIRLS
Studiotrack • Epic (M) LN 3188 8-12
Studiotrack • Epic (M) LN 25145 8-15
   Cast: Mary Martin, Martha Raye, Grace Moore, Ella Logan, Alice Faye, Connie Boswell, Helen Morgan, Ethel Merman, Jane Froman, Gertrude Niesen, Bebe Daniels, Irene Dunne.

HERE COME THE WAVES: see BING'S HOLLYWOOD

HERE COMES GARFIELD
TV Soundtrack (1982) • Epic (S) FE 38136 8-10   82
   Composer: Desiree Goyette, Ed Bogas. **Cast:** Lou Rawls, Desiree Goyette.

HERE COMES THE GROOM: see BING'S HOLLYWOOD

HERE IS MY HEART: see BING'S HOLLYWOOD, MISSISSIPPI

HERE WE GO ROUND THE MULBERRY BUSH
Soundtrack (1968) • United Artists (M) UAL-5175 10-12   68
Soundtrack (1968) • United Artists (S) UAS-5175 10-15   68
   Composer: Traffic, Spencer Davis Group. **Cast:** Traffic, Steve Winwood, Spencer Davis Group.

HERE'S JOHNNY: see MAGIC MOMENTS FROM THE TONIGHT SHOW

HERE'S LOVE
Original Cast (1963) • Columbia (M) KOL-6000 8-20   63
Original Cast (1963) • Columbia (S) KOS-2400 12-30   63
   Composer: Meredith Willson. **Conductor:** Elliot Lawrence. **Cast:** Janis Paige, Craig Stevens, Laurence Naismith, Fred Gwynne, Paul Reed, Cliff Hall, Arthur Rubin, Valerie Lee, Kathy Cody.
Studiotrack (1963) • Columbia (M) CL-2099 10-15   63
Studiotrack (1963) • Columbia (S) CS-8899 15-20   63
   Full title: *Hit Songs from the New Broadway Musical Meredith Willson's Here's Love.*
   Composer: Meredith Willson. **Conductor:** Frank Hunter. **Cast:** Merrill Staton Voices.

HERO
Soundtrack (1972) • Capitol (S) SW-11098 15-20   72
   Composer: Johnny Harris, others. **Conductor:** Johnny Harris. **Cast:** Bloomfield's Heads Hands and Feet.

HERO AIN'T NOTHIN' BUT A SANDWICH
Soundtrack (1978) • Columbia (S) PS-35046 8-10   78

HEROES
Soundtrack (1977) • MCA (S) 2320 12-15   77
   Composer: Jack Nitzche, Richard Hazard. **Conductor:** Richard Hazard. **Cast:** Kim Carnes, Sounds of Sunshine.

HEROES OF TELEMARK
Soundtrack (1965) • Mainstream (M) 56064 12-18   65
Soundtrack (1965) • Mainstream (S) S-6064 20-25   65
   Composer: Malcolm Henry Arnold. **Conductor:** Malcolm Henry Arnold.
Soundtrack (1965) • No Label Shown (M) No Number Used 30-40   65
   Open-end interview with script. Promotional issue only.

HEY BOY, HEY GIRL
Soundtrack (1959) • Capitol (M) T-1160 20-30   59
   Conductor: Nelson Riddle. **Cast:** Louis Prima, Keely Smith, Sam Butera and the Witnesses.

HEY, LET'S TWIST
Soundtrack (1961) • Roulette (M) R-25168 20-25   62
Soundtrack (1961) • Roulette (S) SR-25168 25-30   62
   Composer: Henry Glover. **Cast:** Joey Dee and the Starlighters, Jo Ann Campbell, Teddy Randazzo.

HEY THERE, IT'S YOGI BEAR

Soundtrack (1964) • Kellogg (M) CR-6010 10-15   64
  Seven-inch 33 rpm.
   Composer: Warren Foster, David Gates. **Conductor:** Marty Maich. **Cast:** Daws Butler, Don
   Messick

Soundtrack (1964) • Colpix (M) CP-472 25-35   64

Soundtrack (1964) • Colpix (S) SCP-472 40-50   64
   Composer: Ray Gilbert, Doug Goodwin, David Gates, Marty Paich. **Conductor:** Marty Paich.
   Cast: Mel Blanc, Daws Butler, Pat O'Malley, Jackie Ward, Jonah & Wailers, Billy Lee & Ernest
   Newton, James Darren, Don Messick. (With dialogue.)

HIDDEN

Soundtrack (1987) • Varese Sarabande (S) STV 81349 10-12   87
   Composer: Michael Convertino.

HIDING OUT

Soundtrack (1987) • Virgin (S) 90661-1 8-10   87
   Cast: Boy George, Lolita Pop, Pretty Poison, Scarlett and Black, Felix Cavaliere, All That Jazz,
   Hue and Cry, Roy Orbison, K.D. Lang, Lee Anthony Brisdon, David L. Brisdon, Black Britain,
   Public Image Limited.

HIDING PLACE

Soundtrack (1975) • Word (S) WST-8697.. 10-15   75
   Composer: Tedd Smith.

HIGH AND THE MIGHTY

Studiotrack (1954) • E. Bernstein Film Music Coll. (S) FMC-14............ 20-25   79
  Also contains music from *Search for Paradise* (1957).
   Composer: Dimitri Tiomkin. **Conductor:** Elmer Bernstein.

HIGH ANXIETY

Soundtrack (1977) • Asylum (S) 5E-501 15-20   77
  Side two has music from five other Mel Brooks films, composed by John Morris: *The
  Producers, Young Frankenstein, Silent Movie, Blazing Saddles* and *Twelve Chairs.* Some
  covers have yellow shrinkwrap sticker listing tracks.
   Composer: John Morris. **Conductor:** John Morris. **Cast:** Mel Brooks, Madeline Kahn, others.

HIGH BUTTON SHOES

Original Cast (1947) • RCA Victor K-10.. 25-40   47
  78 rpm album. Has original artwork from the show not seen on any of the LPs.

Original Cast (1947) • Camden (M) CAL-457 20-30   58

Original Cast (1947) • RCA Victor (M) LOC-1107 20-35   64

Original Cast (1947) • RCA Victor (SE) LSO-1107 25-30   64
   Composer: Jule Styne, Sammy Cahn. **Conductor:** Milton Rosenstock. **Cast:** Phil Silvers,
   Nanette Fabray, Lois Lee, Mark Dawson, Jack McCauley, Johnny Stewart.

HIGH ROAD TO CHINA

Soundtrack (1983) • Scar (S) 5003 30-40   83
   Composer: John Barry. **Conductor:** John Barry.

HIGH SOCIETY

Original London Cast (1987) • CBS (S) SCX-6707 40-45   87
  UK release. London stage version has film score plus other Cole Porter show tunes.
   Composer: Cole Porter. **Conductor:** David Mellor. **Cast:** Trevor Eve, Natasha Richardson,
   Stephen Rea, Angela Richards, Ronald Fraser, Ann Firbank, Robert Swales, Alan Barry.

Soundtrack (1956) • Capitol PRO-306 10-20   56
  Has *True Love* on one side, interviews with Bing Crosby and Grace Kelly on the flip.
   Composer: Cole Porter. **Conductor:** Johnny Green. **Cast:** Bing Crosby, Grace Kelly.

Soundtrack (1956) • Capitol (EP) PRO 281 20-25   56
  Single-sided "Disc Jockey Interview Record." White label. Promotional issue only.
   Cast: Bing Crosby, Grace Kelly, Frank Sinatra, Celeste Holm.

Soundtrack (1956) • Capitol (EP) EDM-750 12-18   56

Soundtrack (1956) • Capitol (M) W-750 10-15   56
Soundtrack (1956) • Capitol (S) SW-750 20-30   61
Soundtrack (1956) • Capitol (S) SW-750 8-10   Re
  Red label.
    Composer: Cole Porter. **Conductor:** Johnny Green. **Cast:** Bing Crosby, Grace Kelly, Frank Sinatra, Louis Armstrong, Celeste Holm.

HIGH SPIRITS (1964)
Original Cast (1964) • ABC (M) ABC-OC-1 10-12   64
Original Cast (1964) • ABC-Paramount (S) ABCS-OC-1 15-20   64
    Composer: Hugh Martin, Timothy Gray. **Conductor:** Fred Werner. **Cast:** Beatrice Lillie, Tammy Grimes, Edward Woodward, Timothy Gray, Louise Troy.
Original London Cast (1965) • Pye (M) NPL-18100 45-55   65
Original London Cast (1965) • Pye (S) NSPL-83022 50-65   65
    Composer: Hugh Martin, Timothy Gray. **Conductor:** Michael Moores. **Cast:** Cicely Courtneidge, Marti Stevens, Denis Quilley, Jan Waters.

HIGH SPIRITS (1988)
Soundtrack (1988) • SRG (S) SL-5180 8-10   88
Soundtrack • GNP/Crescendo (S) GNPS-8016 8-10   88
    Composer: George Fenton. **Conductor:** George Fenton. **Cast:** Graunke Symphony Orchestra.

HIGH TIME
Studiotrack (1960) • RCA Victor (M) LPM-2314 12-15   60
Studiotrack (1960) • RCA Victor (S) LSP-2314 20-25   60
    Composer: Henry Mancini, James Van Heusen. **Conductor:** Henry Mancini.
Studiotrack • Camden (M) CAL-928 10-12   66
Studiotrack • Camden (S) CAS-928 12-15   66
  Also has music from *The Great Impostor*.
    Composer: Henry Mancini. **Conductor:** Henry Mancini.

HIGH TOR
TV Soundtrack (1956) • Decca (M) DL-8272 100-150   56
    Composer: Arthur Schwartz, Maxwell Anderson. **Conductor:** Joseph J. Lilley. **Cast:** Bing Crosby, Julie Andrews, Everett Sloane. (With dialogue).

HIGH, WIDE AND HANDSOME: see SWEET ADELINE

HIGHER AND HIGHER
Soundtrack (1943) • Hollywood Soundstage (M) HS-411 12-15
    Composer: Richard Rodgers, Lorenz Hart, Jimmy McHugh, Harold Adamson. **Conductor:** Constantin Bakaleinikoff. **Cast:** Michele Morgan, Frank Sinatra, Jack Haley, Mel Torme, Leon Errol, Marcy McGuire, Paul and Grace Hartman, Barbara Hale, Dooley Wilson, Ivy Scott.

HIGHLANDER: see KIND OF MAGIC

HIGHLIGHTS FROM THE PHANTOM OF THE OPERA: see PHANTOM OF THE OPERA

HI-HO: see MARY MARTIN SINGS AND SWINGS

HILLBILLY CAT: see ELVIS LIVE AT THE LOUISIANA HAYRIDE

HIMSELF (BILL COSBY)
Soundtrack (1982) • Motown (S) 6026ML 8-10   82
  Cast: Bill Cosby.

HINDENBERG
Soundtrack (1975) • MCA (S) 2090 8-18   75
    Composer: David Shire. **Conductor:** David Shire. **Cast:** Hugh Douglas (narrator of newsreel prologue), Peter Donat, Robert Clary, Herb Morrison (newsman from original radio broadcast).

HIS LAND
Soundtrack • Light (S) LS-5532.. 10-15   70s
    Composer: Ralph Carmichael. **Conductor:** Ralph Carmichael. **Cast:** Cliff Richard, Cliff
    Barrows, Ralph Carmichael Orchestra and Chorus.

HIS WIFE'S HABIT
Soundtrack (1970) • Capitol (S) SW-641 12-15   70
    Composer: Jim Helms, Norma Green, Gary Lemel. **Conductor:** Jim Helms. **Cast:** Gary Lemel,
    Sonny Geraci.

HISTORY OF MGM MOVIE MUSIC – VOL. 1
Soundtrack (1973) • MGM (SE) 2-SES-15 10-12   73
    Two discs. Instrumental excerpts from *Gone with the Wind, Till the Clouds Roll By, The
    Pirate, Words and Music, An American in Paris, Singin' in the Rain, Lili, The Band Wagon,
    Brigadoon, Raintree County, Gigi, Ben-Hur, How the West Was Won, Mutiny on the Bounty*
    and *The Unsinkable Molly Brown.* There is no "Vol. 2."
    Composer: Various. **Conductor:** Various.

HISTORY OF THE WORLD, PART I
Soundtrack (1981) • Warner Bros. (S) BSK 3579 8-10   81
    Composer: John Morris, Mel Brooks, Ronny Graham. **Conductor:** John Morris. **Cast:** Mel
    Brooks, Orson Welles. (With dialogue.)

HIT INSTRUMENTALS FROM TV WESTERN THEMES
Studiotrack (1959) • United Artists (M) UAL-3161 10-12   59
Studiotrack (1959) • United Artists (S) UAS-6161 12-15   59
    Music from *Wagons Ho!, Bonanza, The Rebel, Law Man, Maverick, Bat Masterson, Ballad
    of Paladin, Tall Man, Laramie, Gunslinger, The Deputy* and *Rawhide.*
    Cast: Al Caiola Guitars Orchestra.

HIT MOTION PICTURE THEMES
Studiotrack • Mercury (M) MG 20810................................... 12-15   62
Studiotrack • Mercury (S) SR 60810 12-20   62
    Themes from *Walk on the Wild Side, 40 Pounds of Trouble, Mutiny on the Bounty,
    Wonderful World of Brothers Grimm, Rome Adventure, Breakfast at Tiffany's, Exodus, La
    Dolce Vita, High Time, Hatari, Tender Is the Night, Guns of Navarone* and *Diamond Head.*
    Composer: Various. **Cast:** Brook Benton, Dick Contino, Caesar Giovannini, Xavier Cugat, Billy
    Eckstine, Shirley Horn, Carl Stevens, Clebanoff.

HIT MOVIE SONGS FROM THE EXOTIC ISLANDS
Studiotrack (1963) • Warner Bros. (S) WS-1493.................... 20-30   63
    Composer: Various. **Cast:** Surfers.

HIT SONGS FROM BAKER STREET: see BAKER STREET

HIT THE DECK
Original London Cast • World (M) SH-176 12-15
    One side has music from *No No Nanette.*
    Composer: Vincent Youmans, Clifford Grey, Leo Robin, Irving Caesar. **Cast:** Stanley Holloway,
    Barry Twins, Ivy Tresmand.
Soundtrack (1955) • MGM (EP) X-287 10-15   55
Soundtrack (1955) • MGM (M) E-3163................................. 20-25   55
Soundtrack (1955) • MCA (M) 25033 8-10   86
    Composer: Vincent Youmans, Clifford Grey, Leo Robin, Irving Caesar. **Conductor:** George
    Stoll. **Cast:** Jane Powell, Tony Martin, Debbie Reynolds, Vic Damone, Ann Miller, Kay Armen,
    Clark Burroughs (performed vocals for Russ Tamblyn in the film).
    Also see CAT AND THE FIDDLE
    Also see THOSE GLORIOUS MGM MUSICALS.

HIT THEMES FROM MOTION PICTURES
Studiotrack • United Artists (S) S-21001 8-10   67

HITCHHIKER: see OUTER SPACE SUITE

HITCH-HIKERS GUIDE TO THE GALAXY – PART ONE
BBC Radio Series (1979) • Hannibal (S) HNBL 2301 15-20   82
> Composer: Tim Souster. Cast: Simon Jones, Geoffrey McGivern, Mark Wing-Davey, Stephen Moore, Cindy Oswin, Richard Vernon, Valentine Dyall, David Tate, Jim Broadbent, Bill Wallis, Peter Jones.

HITLER
Soundtrack (1962) • Medallion (S) MED-302 25-30   80
> Composer: Hans J. Salter. Conductor: Hans J. Salter.

HITLER'S INFERNO
Assembled Cast • Audio Rarities (M) 2445 15-25
> Cast: Adolph Hitler (speeches and music).

HITLER IS ON THE AIR
Radio Cast • Radiola (M) Series 3 & 4 20-30   89
> Two discs. Radiola Actuality Series program on "Nazi WW2 Propaganda Broadcasts."

HITS FROM BAKER STREET AND OTHER BROADWAY MUSICALS
Studio Cast • MGM (M) E-4293... 8-15
> Cast: Richard Burton, Felicia Sanders, Richard Hayman, Fran Jeffries, Kai Winding, Danny Davis Orchestra, Jack Cassidy, Kaye Ballard, Henry Lascoe, Barbara Cook, Susan Johnson.

HITS FROM BROADWAY SHOWS
Studiotrack (1955) • RCA Victor (EP) EPA-728....................................... 8-15   55
Studiotrack (1955) • RCA Victor (EP) EPB-728.................................... 10-20   55
Studiotrack (1955) • RCA Victor (M) LPM-3124 15-30   55
> 10-inch LP.

Studiotrack (1955) • RCA Victor (M) LPM-1191 10-15   55
> Full title: *Perry Como Sings the Hits from Broadway Shows.* Music from *Guys and Dolls, Call Me Madam, South Pacific* and *The King and I.*
> Composer: Various. Cast: Perry Como, Betty Hutton, Fontane Sisters, Mitchell Ayres Orchestra.

HITS FROM HOLLYWOOD
Studiotrack (1957) • RCA Custom (M) RAL-1003 15-20   57
> Volume three in the *For HI-Fi Living* Series.
> Cast: Ronnie Ogden and Orchestra.

HITTER
Soundtrack (1978) • Capitol (S) SW-11920... 8-10   78
> Composer: Garfeel Ruff, others. Cast: Raul de Souza, Gloria Jones, Taste of Honey, Maze, Garfeel Ruff.

HOBBIT
Original Cast (1974) • Argo (S) 1196/9 15-25   74
> Three discs.

TV Soundtrack (1977) • Disneyland (S) ST-3819................................... 12-30   77
TV Soundtrack (1977) • Buena Vista (S) 103....................................... 10-30   77
> Boxed, two-disc set, with booklet. Music and dialogue.

TV Soundtrack (1977) • Buena Vista (S) 103A...................................... 40-45   77
> Boxed set with decals and poster. Sears and Roebuck premium offer.
> Composer: Maury Laws, Jules Bass, Glenn Yarbrough, others.

HOGAN'S HEROES
Studiotrack (1969) • Sunset (M) SUM-1137 20-25   69
Studiotrack (1969) • Sunset (S) SUS-5137 20-35   69
> Full title: *Hogan's Heroes Sing the Best of WWII.*
> Composer: Various. Conductor: Jerry Fielding. Cast: Robert Clary, Richard Dawson, Ivan Dixon, Larry Hovis.

HOLD ON!
Soundtrack (1966) • MGM (M) E-4342 10-15   66
Soundtrack (1966) • MGM (S) SE-4342 15-20   66
    Cast: Herman's Hermits (featuring Peter Noone), Shelley Fabares.

HOLD ON TO YOUR HATS
Studio Cast (1940) • Painted Smiles (S) PS 1372 8-10   80
    Composer: Burton Lane, H.Y. Hamburg. **Cast:** Helen Gallagher, Carleton Carpenter, Arthur
    Siegel.

HOLIDAY IN MANHATTAN
Studiotrack • Design (S) SS-47 10-15
    Cast: Cole Porter, Addison Bailey Orchestra.

HOLIDAY IN MEXICO
Studiotrack (1946) • Columbia X-271 20-25   46
  Album of two 78 rpms.
    Composer: Victor Herbert, others. **Conductor:** Carmen Dragon. **Cast:** Jane Powell.

HOLIDAY INN
Studiotrack (1942) • Decca A-306 20-25   50
  Album of six 78 rpms.
Studiotrack (1942) • Decca (M) DL-5092 40-50   50
  10-inch LP.
Studiotrack (1942) • MCA (SE) 25205 8-10   87
    Composer: Irving Berlin. **Conductor:** John Scott Trotter, Bob Crosby. **Cast:** Bing Crosby, Fred
    Astaire, Margaret Lenhart, Ken Darby Singers.
  Also see BING'S HOLLYWOOD

HOLLY, BUDDY, STORY: see BUDDY HOLLY STORY

HOLLYWOOD
TV Soundtrack (1979) • Stet (S) DS-15006 15-20   79
  Music used to accompany silent film classics.
    Composer: Carl Davis, Charles Chaplin, others. **Conductor:** Carl Davis.

HOLLYWOOD CANTEEN
Soundtrack • Curtain Calls (M) 100/11-12 8-12
  Two discs. Also has music from *Stage Door Canteen*.
    Composer: Various. **Conductor:** Benny Goodman, Xavier Cugat, Count Basie, Kay Kyser, Guy
    Lombardo. **Cast:** Andrews Sisters, Jack Benny, Joe E. Brown, Eddie Cantor, Kitty Carlisle, Jack
    Carson, Joan Crawford, Bette Davis, John Garfield, Joan Leslie, Ida Lupino, Irene Manning,
    Dennis Morgan, Eleanor Parker, Alexis Smith, Barbara Stanwyck, Jane Wyman. STAGE DOOR
    CANTEEN: **Cast:** Ethel Merman, Gracie Fields, Ethel Waters, Ray Bolger, Gypsy Rose Lee,
    Peggy Lee.

HOLLYWOOD GOLD, VOL. I
Studiotrack (1973) • Ovation (S) QVQD-1601 10-12   73
  Gatefold cover.
    Composer: Various. **Cast:** Quadrastrings.

HOLLYWOOD HITS BY NACIO HERB BROWN
Studiotrack (1957) • MGM (M) E-3566 15-25   57
    Composer: Nacio Herb Brown. **Cast:** Richard Ellsasser and Theatre Organ.

HOLLYWOOD HOTEL
Soundtrack (1937) • EOH (M) 99601 12-15   75
Soundtrack (1937) • Hollywood Soundstage (M) HS-5004 8-10   81
    Composer: Johnny Mercer, Richard Whiting. **Cast:** Dick Powell, Frances Langford, Benny
    Goodman Orchestra, Rosemary Lane, Johnny "Scat" Davis, Ted Healy, Jerry Cooper.
  Also see HOORAY FOR HOLLYWOOD

HOLLYWOOD IS ON THE AIR
Radio Soundtrack (1930s-1940s) • Radiola (M) 2MR-1718................. 15-25
Pomotional radio spots for films.

HOLLYWOOD KNIGHTS
Soundtrack (1980) • Casablanca (S) 7218.. 8-10   80
Cast: Frankie Valli and the 4 Seasons, Martha and the Vandellas, Brooklyn Dreams.

HOLLYWOOD MAESTRO – ALFRED NEWMAN
Soundtrack • Citadel (M) CT 6003 25-30   76
Side 1 has music from *Pinky*, *A Royal Scandal*, *All About Eve* and others. Side 2 is a pops concert.
Composer: Alfred Newman. Conductor: Alfred Newman.

HOLLYWOOD OR BUST
Soundtrack (1957) • Capitol (EP) EAP 1-806 50-75   57
Composer: Sammy Fain, Paul Francis Webster. Cast: Dean Martin.

HOLLYWOOD PARTY
Studio Cast • Beginner's Productions (S) BRP-2 12-18   80
Complete score as intended for the 1934 MGM musical, of which only a few songs remained in the finished film.
Composer: Richard Rodgers, Lorenz Hart. Conductor: Tom Gilhooly. Cast: Pat Whitmore, Barbara Rosenblatt, Robert Daws, Richard Quin.

HOLLYWOOD POPS
Studiotrack • Capitol (M) P-8639 15-25
Composer: Alfred Newman, others. Conductor: Alfred Newman. Cast: Hollywood Bowl Symphony Orchestra.

HOLLYWOOD SONG BOOK – ACADEMY AWARD WINNERS
Studiotrack [Vol. 1] (1958) • Coral (M) CRL-57241 8-10   58
Studiotrack [Vol. 1] (1958) • Coral (S) CRL7-57241 10-12   58
Studiotrack [Vol. 2] (1958) • Coral (M) CRL-57242 8-10   58
Studiotrack [Vol. 2] (1958) • Coral (S) CRL7-57242 10-12   58
Studiotrack [Vol. 1&2] (1958) • Coral (M) CX-2 15-18   58
Studiotrack [Vol. 1&2] (1958) • Coral (S) 7CX-2 15-18   58
Composer: Various. Conductor: Neal Hefti. Cast: Neal Hefti and His Orchestra.

HOLLYWOOD SQUARES
TV Soundtrack • Event (M) EV 6903 10-12   74
Full title: *Zingers from the Hollywood Squares*.
Cast: Rose Marie, Charlie Weaver, Lily Tomlin, Paul Lynde.

HOLLYWOOD: THE POST WAR YEARS (1946 - 1949)
Soundtrack • AEI (M) AEI-3104 15-20   80
Music from *The Bandit of Sherwood Forest* (Hugo Friedhofer), *Time Out of Mind* (Miklos Rozsa), *A Double Life* (Miklos Rozsa), *Force of Evil* (David Raksin).
Composer: Hugo Friedhofer, Miklos Rozsa, David Raksin. Conductor: Hugo Friedhofer, Miklos Rozsa, David Raksin.

HOLLYWOOD THEMES
Studiotrack • Forum (M) F-9008 10-20
Monaural version is titled *Hollywood U.S.A.*
Studiotrack • Forum (S) SF-16010 20-40
Composer: Various. Cast: Jack Shaindlain Orchestra.

HOLLYWOOD'S BAD BUT BEAUTIFUL GIRLS
Studiotrack (1960) • Warner Bros. (M) W-1502 40-60   60
Cast: Stan Applebaum Orchestra.

HOLLYWOOD'S GREAT THEMES

Studiocast (1962) • Columbia (M) CL-1783..........................8-12   62
Studiocast (1962) • Columbia (S) CS-8583..........................8-12   62
    Conductor: Percy Faith. **Cast:** Percy Faith Orchestra.

HOLLYWOOD'S HEROES ON THE AIR

Radio Cast • Murray Hill (M) 937239..........................20-25
   Boxed, four-disc set. Includes eight original radio broadcast programs.
    Cast: Clark Gable, Errol Flynn, Tyrone Power, Humphrey Bogart, others.

HOLOCAUST

TV Soundtrack (1978) • RCA Victor (S) ARL1-2785 10-25   78
   Includes synopsis insert.
    Composer: Morton Gould. **Conductor:** Morton Gould. **Cast:** National Philharmonic Orchestra.

HOLOCAUST 2000: see CHOSEN

HOME MOVIES

Soundtrack (1979) • Varese Sarabande (S) STV-81139..........................10-15   80
    Composer: Pino Donaggio. **Conductor:** Pino Donaggio.

HOME OF THE BRAVE

Soundtrack (1986) • Warner Bros. (S) 134-2 15-20   86
   Two discs. Interview. Promotional issue only.
    Cast: Laurie Anderson.
Soundtrack (1986) • Warner Bros. (S) 1-25400 8-10   86
    Cast: Laurie Anderson.

HOMER

Soundtrack (1970) • Cotillion (S) SD-9037..........................10-12   70
    Cast: Byrds, Buffalo Springfield, Cream, Led Zeppelin, Don Scardino.

HOMER AND EDDIE

Soundtrack (1989) • Apache (S) D1-71654..........................20-25   89
    Composer: Eduard Artemyev.

HOMETOWN U.S.A.

Soundtrack (1979) • K-TEL (S) NU-94460 8-10   79
    Cast: Betty Everett, Ritchie Valens, Little Richard, Five Satins, Chiffons, Skyliners, Del Vikings, Teen Queens, Dion & the Belmonts, Penguins, Jerry Lee Lewis, Rosie & the Originals, Dion, Paris Sisters, Willows, Marvin & Johnny.

HONEY POT

Soundtrack (1967) • United Artists (M) UAL-4159..........................8-12   67
Soundtrack (1967) • United Artists (S) UAS-5159..........................10-12   67
Soundtrack (1967) • MCA (S) 25106..........................5-8   Re
    Composer: John Addison. **Conductor:** John Addison.

HONEY WEST

TV Soundtrack (1965) • ABC-Paramount (M) 532..........................20-30   65
TV Soundtrack (1965) • ABC-Paramount (S) S-532..........................30-40   65
    Composer: Joseph Mullendore. **Conductor:** Alfred Perry.

HONEYBABY

Soundtrack (1974) • RCA Victor (S) APL1-0994 8-10   74
    Cast: Diana Sands, Calvin Lockhart.

HONEYSUCKLE ROSE

Soundtrack (1980) • Columbia (S) S2-36752..........................8-10   80
   Two discs.
    Composer: Willie Nelson, others. **Cast:** Willie Nelson, Dyan Cannon, Amy Irving, Johnny Gimble, Jody Payne, Hank Cochran, Emmylou Harris, Jeannie Seely, Kenneth Threadgill.

HOTEL PARADISO
Soundtrack (1966) • MGM (M) E-4419............................... 10-20   66
Soundtrack (1966) • MGM (S) SE-4419.............................. 12-25   66
Both have cover art by Frank Frazetta.
Composer: Laurence Rosenthal. **Conductor:** Laurence Rosenthal.

HOUDINI, MAN OF MAGIC
Original London Cast (1966) • CBS (S) 70027.................... 25-30   66
UK release.
Composer: Wilfred Wylam, John Morley, Aubrey Cash. **Conductor:** Jan Cervenka. **Cast:** Stuart Damon, Judith Bruce, Stubby Kaye, Doris Hare, Colin Welland, Gaye Brown.

HOUR OF THE GUN
Soundtrack (1967) • United Artists (M) UAL-4166................. 25-35   67
Soundtrack (1967) • United Artists (S) UAS-5166................ 50-60   67
Composer: Jerry Goldsmith. **Conductor:** Jerry Goldsmith.

HOUR WITH IRVING BERLIN
Studio Cast • Royale (M) 1343.. 10-15   50s
Composer: Irving Berlin. **Cast:** Morton Downey, Jack Smith, Georgia Gibbs, Thelma Carpenter, Danny O'Neill.

HOUSE / HOUSE II: THE SECOND STORY
Soundtrack (1987) • Varese Sarabande (S) STV-81324......... 8-10   87
Composer: Harry Manfredini.

HOUSE IS NOT A HOME
Soundtrack (1964) • Ava (M) A-50 10-20   64
Soundtrack (1964) • Ava (S) AS-50 12-25   64
Composer: Joseph Weiss, Burt Bacharach. **Conductor:** Joseph Weiss.

HOUSE OF FEAR
TV Soundtrack (1980) • Murray Hill (M) M55439.................. 12-15   80
Cast: Basil Rathbone, Nigel Bruce.

HOUSE OF FLOWERS
Original Cast • Columbia (M) LP-12508 8-10
Promotional issue only.
Original Cast (1954) • Columbia (EP) A-1113 12-18   54
Three discs.
Original Cast (1954) • Columbia (M) ML-4969 20-35   54
Blue label. Has cardboard photo sleeve listing other cast albums in the Columbia Records library.
Original Cast (1954) • Columbia (M) OL-4969...................... 10-20
Gray label.
Original Cast (1954) • Columbia (SE) OS-2320 12-18   63
Original Cast (1954) • Columbia Special Products (SE) COS-2320 5-10   Re
Composer: Harold Arlen, Truman Capote. **Conductor:** Jerry Arlen. **Cast:** Pearl Bailey, Diahann Carroll, Juanita Hall, Rawn Spearman, Ada Moore, Miriam Burton, Dolores Harper, Enid Mosier.
Original Revival Cast (1968) • United Artists (M) UAL-4180................ 15-25   68
Original Revival Cast (1968) • United Artists (S) UAS-5180................ 20-35   68
Composer: Harold Arlen, Truman Capote. **Conductor:** Joseph Raposo. **Cast:** Yolande Bavan, Thelma Oliver, Hope Clarke, Josephine Premice, Tom Helmore, Robert Jackson, Charles Moore, Novella Nelson, Carla Pinza.
Studio Cast • Columbia (M) CL-640 8-12
Conductor: Percy Faith.

HOUSE OF LEATHER
Studio Cast (1970) • Fontana (S) SRF-67591 20-25   70
Composer: Dale Menten, Frederick Gaines. **Cast:** Dale Menten, Dennis Craswell, Tom Hustin, Dennis Libby, Blackwood Apology.

HOUSE OF USHER: see FALL OF THE HOUSE OF USHER

HOUSE PARTY
Soundtrack (1990) • Motown (S) MOT-6296 8-10   90
    Cast: Arts and Crafts, Today, Force MDs, Full Force Family, Flavor Flav, Kid 'N' Play, Kenny
    Vaughan and Art of Love.

HOUSE PARTY KID INTERVIEWS
TV Soundtrack (1956) • Columbia (M) CL-703 5-10   56
    Cast: Art Linkletter.

HOUSEBOAT
Soundtrack (1958) • Columbia (M) CL-1222 40-45   58
    Composer: George Duning, Jay Livingston, Ray Evans. **Conductor:** George Duning, Frank
    DeVol. **Cast:** Sophia Loren, George Duning and His Orchestra.

HOUSEFUL OF LOVE: MUSIC FROM THE BILL COSBY SHOW
TV Soundtrack (1986) • Columbia (S) FC-40270 10-15   86
Music from the TV series.
    Composer: Stu Gardiner, Arthur Hill. **Cast:** Lori Fulton, Bill Cosby, Patti Austin, Michael Bolton,
    James Ingram, others.

HOUSEKEEPING
Soundtrack (1987) • Varese Sarabande (S) STV 81338 10-12   87
    Composer: Michael Gibbs.

HOUSEWIFE SUPERSTAR
Original Cast (1977) • Charisma (S) CAS-1123 15-20   77
    Composer: Barry Humphries. **Cast:** Barry Humphries (piano).

HOUSEWIVES' CANTATA
Original Cast (1980) • Original Cast (S) OC-8133 10-12   80
    Composer: Mira Spektor, June Siegel. **Conductor:** Bob Goldstone. **Cast:** Lawrence Chelsi,
    Maida Meyers, Mira J. Spektor, Sharon Talbot.

HOW FUNNY CAN SEX BE?
Soundtrack (1976) • West End (S) WE 101 20-25   76
    Composer: Armando Trovaioli.

HOW NOW, DOW JONES
Original Cast (1967) • RCA Victor (M) LOC-1142 15-20   67
Original Cast (1967) • RCA Victor (S) LSO-1142 25-30   67
    Composer: Elmer Bernstein, Carolyn Leigh. **Conductor:** Peter Howard. **Cast:** Anthony Roberts,
    Marlyn Mason, Brenda Vaccaro, Sammy Smith, Hiram Sherman, Mara Worth, Charlotte Jones,
    Fran Stevens.

HOW SWEET IT IS
Soundtrack (1968) • RCA Victor (M) LPM-4037 10-12   68
Soundtrack (1968) • RCA Victor (S) LSP-4037 12-18   68
    Composer: Pat Williams, Jim Webb. **Conductor:** Pat Williams, Jim Webb. **Cast:** Picardy
    Singers.

HOW THE GRINCH STOLE CHRISTMAS
TV Soundtrack (1966) • Leo (M) LE-901 20-45   66
TV Soundtrack (1966) • Leo (S) LES-901 45-65   66
From MGM-TV Christmas special. Gatefold cover.
TV Soundtrack • Polydor (S) 528439 8-15   90s
Picture disc.
    Composer: Albert Hague, Dr. Seuss (Ted Geisel), Eugene Poddany. **Conductor:** Eugene
    Poddany. **Cast:** Boris Karloff (narration).

HOW THE WEST WAS WON
Soundtrack (1963) • MGM (M) 1E-5 8-10   63
Soundtrack (1963) • MGM (S) S1E-5 8-12   63
Black label.

Soundtrack (1963) • MGM (S) S1E-5 5-15   Re
  Blue and gold label.
Soundtrack (1963) • MCA (S) 39043 5-8   86
    Composer: Alfred Newman, Ken Darby, Dave Guard, Faeyar, Henske, Sammy Cahn.
    Conductor: Alfred Newman, Robert Armbruster. **Cast:** Debbie Reynolds, Ken Darby Singers,
    Dave Guard, Whiskeyhill Singers, MGM Studio Orchestra.
Studiotrack (1960) • RCA Victor (M) LOP-6070 25-35   60
Studiotrack (1960) • RCA Victor (S) LSO-6070 45-55   60
  Both have gatefold covers and booklets. Based on a Life Magazine series that inspired the
  film.
    Composer: Alan Lomax, Sam Hinton, others. **Conductor:** Bob Thompson, Richard P. Condie.
    Cast: Bing Crosby, Rosemary Clooney, Sam Hinton, Jack Halloran Singers, Jimmie Driftwood,
    Tarry Town Trio, Mormon Tabernacle Choir.
Studiotrack (1963) • Epic (M) LN-24058 8-10   63
Studiotrack (1963) • Epic (S) BN-26058 10-12   63
    Cast: Voices Eleven.
Studiotrack (1963) • Colpix (M) CP-452 15-20   63
Studiotrack (1963) • Colpix (S) SCP-452 15-20   63
    Cast: Burgess Meredith.
  Also see UNDEFEATED

HOW TO BEAT THE HIGH COST OF LIVING
Soundtrack (1980) • Columbia (S) JS-36741 10-12   80
    Composer: Patrick Williams. **Cast:** Hubert Laws, Earl Klugh.

HOW TO GET THE MOST OUT OF YOUR STEREO
Studiotrack • Warner Bros. (S) XS-1400 100-125   60
  Gold vinyl, audiophile issue. Themes from *Singin' in the Rain, Mickey Mouse Club Theme,*
  Over the Rainbow and others.
    Composer: Various.

HOW TO MURDER YOUR WIFE
Soundtrack (1965) • United Artists (M) UAL-4119 10-15   65
Soundtrack (1965) • United Artists (S) UAS-5119 15-20   65
    Composer: Neal Hefti. **Conductor:** Neal Hefti.

HOW TO SAVE A MARRIAGE AND RUIN YOUR LIFE
Soundtrack (1968) • Columbia (S) OS-3140 15-18   68
    Composer: Michel Legrand. **Conductor:** Michel Legrand.

HOW TO STEAL A MILLION
Soundtrack (1966) • 20th Century-Fox (M) TFM-3183 20-30   66
Soundtrack (1966) • 20th Century-Fox (S) TFS-4183 40-50   66
    Composer: John Williams. **Conductor:** John Williams.

HOW TO STEAL AN ELECTION (A DIRTY POLITICS MUSICAL)
Original Cast (1968) • RCA Victor (S) LSO-1153 10-12   68
    Composer: Oscar Brand. **Conductor:** Bhen Lanzaroni. **Cast:** Bill McCutcheon, Del Hinkley,
    Dennis Allen, Barbara Anson, Beverly Ballard, Ed Crowley, Thom Koutsoukos, Carole Demas,
    Clifton Davis.

HOW TO STUFF A WILD BIKINI
Soundtrack (1965) • Wand (M) 671 20-25   65
Soundtrack (1965) • Wand (S) S-671 30-40   65
    Composer: Jerry Styner, Guy Hemric, others. **Cast:** Annette Funicello, Kingsmen, Mickey
    Rooney, Lu Ann Simms, Brian Donlevy, Harvey Lembeck.

HOW TO SUCCEED IN BUSINESS WITHOUT REALLY TRYING
Original Cast (1961) • RCA Victor (M) LOC-1066 8-10   61
Original Cast (1961) • RCA Victor (S) LSO-1066 8-12   61
  Black labels. Both include inserts.

Original Cast (1961) • RCA Victor (S) LSO-1066 5-8   Re
Tan or orange label.
   Composer: Frank Loesser. **Conductor:** Elliot Lawrence. **Cast:** Robert Morse, Rudy Vallee,
   Bonnie Scott, Charles Nelson Reilly, Claudette Sutherland, Sammy Smith, Paul Reed, Virginia
   Martin, Ruth Kobart, Mara Landi.
Original London Cast (1960s) • RCA Victor (M) RD-7564 40-50   60s
Original London Cast (1960s) • RCA Victor (S) SF-7564 65-85   60s
UK release.
   Composer: Frank Loesser. **Cast:** Warren Berlinger, Billy DeWolfe, David Knight.
Studiotrack (1961) • RCA Victor (M) LPM-2493 8-10   61
Studiotrack (1961) • RCA Victor (S) LSP-2493 8-10   61
   Composer: Frank Loesser. **Conductor:** Ray Ellis. **Cast:** Ray Ellis Orchestra.
Soundtrack (1967) • United Artists (M) UAL-4151 8-12   67
Soundtrack (1967) • United Artists (S) UAS-5151 12-18   67
Soundtrack (1967) • United Artists (M) W-92240 8-10   Re
Capitol Record Club issue.
   Composer: Frank Loesser. **Conductor:** Nelson Riddle. **Cast:** Robert Morse, Rudy Vallee,
   Michele Lee, Sammy Smith, Anthony Teague, Maureen Arthur, Kay Reynolds, John Myhers,
   Ruth Kobart.

HOWARD THE DUCK
Soundtrack (1986) • MCA (S) 6173.. 15-20   86
Includes poster insert.
   Composer: John Barry. **Conductor:** John Barry. **Cast:** Dolby's Cube, Cheery Bomb, Tata Vega.

HOWDY DOODY
Original Cast • Leslie (M) PIP-6808.. 15-20
Also see IT'S HOWDY DOODY TIME

HOWLING
Soundtrack (1981) • Varese Sarabande (S) STV-81150 8-10   81
   Composer: Pino Donaggio. **Conductor:** Natale Massara, Pino Donaggio.

HOWLS, BONERS AND SHOCKERS FROM ART LINKLETTER'S

HUCKLEBERRY FINN
Soundtrack (1974) • United Artists (S) UA-LA229-F.............................. 8-12   74
   Composer: Richard M. Sherman, Robert B. Sherman. **Conductor:** Fred Werner. **Cast:** Roberta
   Flack, Paul Winfield, Jeff East, Harvey Korman, Gary Merrill, David Wayne.
Studiotrack (1983) • Troubador (S) 1ER-23-5009 8-12   83

HUCKLEBERRY HOUND
TV Soundtrack (1959) • Colpix (M) CP-202..................................... 100-200   59
   Cast: Daws Butler, Don Messick.
Studio Cast • Columbia (SE) P-13829.. 10-12   77

HUCKLEBERRY HOUND: HERE COMES HUCKLEBERRY HOUND
TV Soundtrack • Colpix (M) CP-207... 50-100   61
   Cast: Daws Butler, Don Messick, Chris Allen (narrator).

HUGH O'BRIEN, TV'S WYATT EARP SINGS: see WYATT EARP

HUGHIE
Original Cast (1965) • Columbia (M) OL-6260.................................... 18-20   65
Original Cast (1965) • Columbia (S) OS-2760.................................... 20-25   65
Complete Broadway play.
   Cast: Jason Robards, Jack Dodson.

HUGO MONTENEGRO – GOOD VIBRATIONS
Studiotrack (1969) • RCA Victor (S) LSP-4104 8-12   69
Music from *The Lady in Cement, Promises, Promises, Rosemary's Baby, The Outcasts* (TV) and *The Big Valley* (TV).
Composer: Hugo Montenegro. **Conductor:** Hugo Montenegro. **Cast:** Hugo Montenegro Orchestra.

HUGO THE HIPPO
Soundtrack (1976) • United Artists (S) UA-LA637-G 15-20   76
Cartoon soundtrack.
Composer: Burt Keys. **Conductor:** Burt Keys. **Cast:** Marie Osmond, Jimmy Osmond, Burl Ives, Robert Morley, Paul Lynde.

HUK
Soundtrack • Screen Archives (M) SAAG 10.001................................. 10-15
Gatefold cover. Includes eight-page booklet and "Academy Award Nomination" insert sheet. Private pressing.
Composer: Albert Glasser.

HUMANOIDS FROM THE DEEP
Soundtrack (1980) • Cerberus (S) CST-0203....................................... 20-25   81
Composer: James Horner. **Conductor:** James Horner.

HUMORESQUE
Soundtrack (1947) • Columbia (M) ML 2103 100-150
10-inch LP.
Composer: Franz Waxman.

HUNDRA
Soundtrack (1984) • Macola (S) MRC-0903... 15-20   84
Composer: Ennio Morricone. **Conductor:** Ennio Morricone.

HUNGER
Soundtrack (1983) • Varese Sarabande (S) STV-81184 15-20   83
Composer: Michael Rubini, Denny Jaeger, others.

HUNT FOR RED OCTOBER
Soundtrack (1990) • MCA (S) MCA-6428... 20-25   90
Composer: Basil Poledouris. **Conductor:** Basil Poledouris.

HURRICANE
Soundtrack (1979) • Elektra (S) EKL 5E-5014 15-20   79
Composer: Nino Rota. **Conductor:** Nino Rota.

HURRY SUNDOWN
Soundtrack (1967) • RCA Victor (M) LOC-1133................................... 15-20   67
Soundtrack (1967) • RCA Victor (S) LSO-1133................................... 20-25   67
Composer: Hugo Montenegro. **Conductor:** Hugo Montenegro.

HUSTLER
Soundtrack (1961) • Kapp (M) KL-1264 45-55   61
Soundtrack (1961) • Kapp (S) KS-3264 75-100   61
Composer: Kenyon Hopkins. **Cast:** Doc Severinsen, others.

HUTTON IN HOLLYWOOD
Soundtrack • Vedette (M) 8702.. 10-15
Previously unreleased songs from *Happy Go Lucky, And the Angels Sing, Incendiary Blonde, Duffy's Tavern, The Perils of Pauline* and *Red, Hot and Blue*.
Composer: Various. **Conductor:** Various. **Cast:** Betty Hutton.

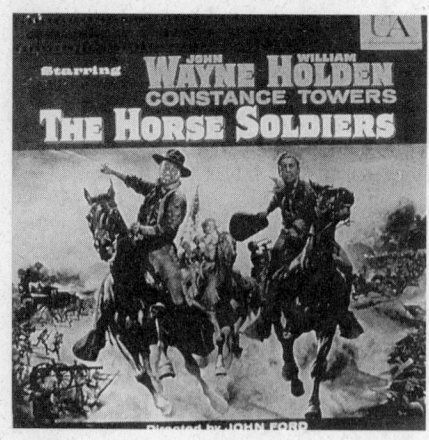

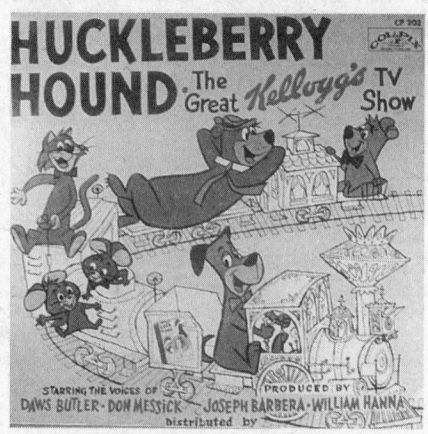

I, A WOMAN, PART 2
Soundtrack (1969) • MGM (S) S1E-18 ST 10-20   69
   Also known as *2*
    Composer: Sven Gyldmark. **Conductor:** Sven Gyldmark.

I AND ALBERT
Original London Cast (1972) • That's Entertainment (S) TERS-1004 ... 20-25   81
   UK release. Limited edition.
    Composer: Charles Strouse, Lee Adams. **Cast:** Polly James, Sven-Bertil Taube, Lewis Fiander, Aubrey Woods, Gay Soper.

I CAN GET IT FOR YOU WHOLESALE
Original Cast (1962) • Columbia (M) KOL-5780 8-12   62
Original Cast (1962) • Columbia (S) KOS-2180 12-18   62
Original Cast (1962) • Columbia Special Products (S) AKOS-2180........ 8-10   Re
    Composer: Harold Rome. **Conductor:** Lehman Engel. **Cast:** Lillian Roth, Jack Kruschen, Harold Lang, Barbra Streisand, Elliott Gould, Sheree North, Luba Lisa, Ken LeRoy, Marilyn Cooper, Bambi Linn, Steve Curry, Francine Bond, Kelly Brown, Wilma Curley, James Hickman, Barbara Monte, William Reilly, Pat Turner, Edward Verson.
Studio Cast (1962) • Columbia (M) CL-1815 8-10   62
Studio Cast (1962) • Columbia (S) CS-8615 8-12   62
    Composer: Harold Rome. **Conductor:** Sy Oliver. **Cast:** Sy Oliver Orchestra.

I CAN HEAR IT NOW
TV Soundtrack (1956) • Columbia (M) No Number Used 15-20   56
    Cast: David Ben-Gurion. (Dialogue.)
TV Soundtrack (1956) • Columbia (M) ML-5110 15-20   56
   Interview from the CBS-TV special *See It Now*, broadcast March 13, 1956.
    Cast: Gamal Abdel Nasser. (Dialogue.)
TV Soundtrack • Columbia (M) ML-4095... 15-20
   Volume 1 (1933-1945).
    Cast: Edward R. Murrow, Fred W. Friendly.
TV Soundtrack (1970) • Columbia (M) F3M 38858............................. 10-15   87
   Boxed, three-disc set. Of interest to Beatles collectors is the inclusion of excerpts of two of their songs. Reissued as *The Way It Was - The Sixties*.
TV Soundtrack (1970) • Columbia (M) M3X-30353 10-15   70
   Reissue, titled: *The Way It Was - The Sixties*
    Cast: Walter Cronkite (narrator).
TV Soundtrack (1955) • Columbia (EP) A-5066 10-15   55
TV Soundtrack (1955) • Columbia (M) ML-5066 15-20   55
TV Soundtrack (1955) • Columbia (M) KOL-7000 10-15   Re
    Cast: Winston Churchill. (Dialogue).

I CAN'T KEEP RUNNING IN PLACE
Original Cast (1981) • Painted Smiles (S) PS-1346................................ 8-10   81
    Composer: Barbara Schottenfeld. **Conductor:** Robert Hirschhorn. **Cast:** Evalyn Baron, Joy Franz, Helen Gallagher, Bev Larson, Phyllis Newman, Marcia Rodd.

I COULD GO ON SINGING
Soundtrack (1963) • Capitol (M) W-1861 12-15   63
Soundtrack (1963) • Capitol (S) SW-1861 15-20   63
   Composer: Mort Lindsey, Harold Arlen, Kurt Weill, others. **Conductor:** Mort Lindsey.
   Cast: Judy Garland.

I DO! I DO!
Original Cast (1966) • RCA Victor (M) LOC-1128 8-10   66
Original Cast (1966) • RCA Victor (S) LSO-1128 8-12   66
   Black label, dog on top.
Original Cast (1966) • RCA Victor (S) LSO-1128 5-8   Re
   Orange or tan labels.
   Composer: Harvey Schmidt, Tom Jones. **Conductor:** John Lesko. **Cast:** Mary Martin,
   Robert Preston.

I HAD A BALL
Original Cast (1964) • Mercury (M) OCM-2210 8-12   64
Original Cast (1964) • Mercury (S) OCS-6210 10-15   64
Original Cast (1964) • Mercury (M) OCM-2210/MGD-2-24 20-25   64
   Two discs. Open-end interviews with cast members, plus songs by Sarah
   Vaughan and Louis Armstrong not heard in the show. Since original cover of the
   cast LP is used, mono number is also used. Interview disc is numbered MGD-2-
   24. Promotional issue only.
   Composer: Jack Lawrence, Stan Freeman. **Conductor:** Pembroke Davenport. **Cast:**
   Buddy Hackett, Richard Kiley, Karen Morrow, Luba Lisa, Steve Roland, Rosetta
   LeNoire.
Studio Cast (1965) • Philips (S) PHS-600-165 10-12   65
   Promotional issue only.
Studio Cast (1965) • Philips (M) PHM-200-165 8-12   65
Studio Cast (1965) • Philips (S) PHS-600-165 10-12   65
   Cast: Lester Lanin.

I LOVE LUCY
TV Soundtrack (1951) • Star Merchants (SE) SM-1951 8-10
   Songs and music from the television series.
   Composer: Various. **Conductor:** Wilbur Hatch. **Cast:** Desi Arnaz, Lucille Ball.

I LOVE MELVIN
Soundtrack (1953) • MGM (EP) K-190 15-30   53
   Boxed, four-disc set.
Soundtrack (1953) • MGM (M) E-190 40-45   53
   10-inch LP.
Soundtrack (1953) • MCA (M) 39081 8-10   86
   Also has music from *Everything I Have Is Yours*.
   Composer: Josef Myrow, Mack Gordon. **Conductor:** Georgie Stoll. **Cast:** Debbie
   Reynolds, Donald O'Connor, Noreen Corcoran.
   Also see THOSE GLORIOUS MGM MUSICALS.

I LOVE MOVIES
Studiotrack (1958) • Columbia (M) CL-1178 12-15   58
   Composer: Various. **Conductor:** Michel Legrand. **Cast:** Michel Legrand and his
   Orchestra.

I LOVE MY WIFE
Original Cast (1977) • Atlantic (S) SD-19107 8-10   77
   Composer: Cy Coleman, Michael Stewart. **Conductor:** John Miller. **Cast:** Lenny
   Baker, Joanna Gleason, Ilene Graff, James Naughton, Ken Bichel, Michael Mark, John
   Miller, Joe Saulter.

I LOVE YOU, ALICE B. TOKLAS
Soundtrack (1967) • Cinema (M) LP-8010 25-35   75
   Composer: Elmer Bernstein. **Conductor:** Hans Rossbach, Elmer Bernstein.

I MARRIED AN ANGEL

Original Cast • AEI (M) AEI-1150 15-18   80s
  Archival album of songs from the show including members of the original New York
  production culled from 78 rpm singles and excerpts from a radio broadcast.
  Composer: Richard Rodgers, Lorenz Hart. **Cast:** Wynn Murray, Audrey Christie, Eve
  Symington, Gordon MacRae, Lucille Norman.
  Also see NEW MOON

I NEVER SANG FOR MY FATHER

Soundtrack (1970) • Bell (S) 1204 20-35   71
  Composer: Barry Mann, Al Gorgoni, Cynthia Weil. **Cast:** Roy Clark.

I REMEMBER MAMA

Studio Cast (1979) • Polydor (S) 827336-1 12-18   79
  Recorded after the Broadway production closed but still includes several members of the
  original cast.
  Composer: Richard Rodgers, Martin Charnin, Raymond Jessel. **Conductor:** Bruce
  Pomahac. **Cast:** Charlotte Edwards, Joanna Borman, George Hearn, Sally Ann
  Howes, Ann Morrison, George S. Irving, Tom Woodman.

I SHALL RETURN

Original Cast (1977) • CMI (S) DMA 1945 25-30   77
  Two discs.
  Cast: Carl Betz, others.

I SPY

TV Soundtrack [Vol. 1] (1965) • Warner Bros. (M) W-1637 20-25   65
TV Soundtrack [Vol. 1] (1965) • Warner Bros. (S) WS-1637 25-30   65
TV Soundtrack [Vol. 2] (1965) • Capitol (M) T-2839 15-20   68
TV Soundtrack [Vol. 2] (1965) • Capitol (S) ST-2839 20-30   68
  Composer: Earle Hagen, Hugo Friedhofer. **Conductor:** Earle Hagen.

I WALK THE LINE

Soundtrack (1970) • Columbia (S) S-30397 12-15   70
  Composer: Johnny Cash. **Cast:** Johnny Cash and the Tennessee Three.

I WANT TO BE AN ACTOR LADY

Original Cast • New World (S) 221 10-15

I WANT TO LIVE

Soundtrack (1958) • United Artists (EP) UAE-1000 15-20   58
Soundtrack (1958) • United Artists (M) UAL-4005 18-20   58
Soundtrack (1958) • United Artists (S) UAS-5005 20-30   58
  Blue label.
  Composer: Johnny Mandel. **Conductor:** Johnny Mandel.
Soundtrack [Jazz] (1958) • United Artists (M) UAL-4006 20-25   58
Soundtrack [Jazz] (1958) • United Artists (S) UAS-5006 20-30   58
  Jazz themes from the film.
  Composer: Johnny Mandel. **Cast:** Gerry Mulligan, Shelly Manne, Art Farmer (jazz
  combo).
Soundtrack (1958) • United Artists (M) UXL-1 40-50   58
  Two discs. Combines UAL-4005 and UAL-4006.
Soundtrack (1958) • United Artists (S) UXS-51 50-70   59
  Two discs. Combines UAS-5005 and UAS-5006.
Soundtrack (1958) • United Artists (M) DF-3 12-15   63
Soundtrack (1958) • United Artists (S) DFS-53 12-18   63
  One side has music from *Odds Against Tomorrow*. Part of United Artists'
  "Double Feature" series.

Soundtrack (1958) • United Artists (S) UA-LA271-G 8-10   74
Soundtrack (1958) • Ascot (M) UM-13501... 15-20   64
Soundtrack (1958) • Ascot (S) US-16501.. 25-30   64
    Also has music from *The Vikings, Never on Sunday* and *Wonderful Country*.
    Also see JOHNNY COOL
    Also see ODDS AGAINST TOMORROW

I WAS A TEENAGE ZOMBIE
Soundtrack (1987) • Enigma (S) SJ-73296 8-10   87
    Cast: Smithereens, Los Lobos, Alex Chilton, Ben Vaughn Group, Bob Pfeifer,
    Fleshtones, Del Fuegos, DB's, Dream Syndicate, Violent Femmes, Waitresses.

I WILL
Original L.A. Cast (1984) • KM (S) 10966 20-30   84
    Composer: Marty Gaetz, Rand Hopkins. **Cast:** Darin Barber, Dexter Hamlett,
    Elizabeth Oakes.

I'LL CRY TOMORROW
Soundtrack (1955) • MGM (EP) X-1180 15-25   55
    Does not include the title song.
    Composer: Various. **Conductor:** Charles Henderson. **Cast:** Susan Hayward.
Studio Cast • Epic (M) LN 3206 15-20
    Conductor: Don Costa. **Cast:** Lillian Roth.
    Also see GUYS AND DOLLS
    Also see SUSAN HAYWARD
    Also see TEN NORTH FREDERICK

I'LL NEVER FORGET WHAT'S 'IS NAME
Soundtrack (1967) • Decca (M) DL-9163 15-20   68
Soundtrack (1967) • Decca (S) DL-79163... 20-25   68
    Composer: Francis Lai. **Conductor:** Francis Lai.

I'LL SEE YOU IN MY DREAMS
Studiotrack (1951) • Columbia (EP) B-289 12-18   51
Studiotrack (1951) • Columbia (M) CL-6198.. 35-45   51
    10-inch LP.
    Composer: Gus Kahn, others. **Conductor:** Paul Weston. **Cast:** Doris Day, Danny
    Thomas, Norman Luboff Choir, Lee Brothers.
Soundtrack (1951) • Caliban (M) 6008 8-10
    Also has music from *Lullaby of Broadway*.
    Composer: Gus Kahn, others. **Conductor:** Ray Heindorf. **Cast:** Doris Day, Danny
    Thomas.

I'LL TAKE SWEDEN
Soundtrack (1965) • United Artists (M) UAL-4121................................. 10-12   65
Soundtrack (1965) • United Artists (S) UAS-5121 ..../.................... 12-15   65
    Composer: Jimmie Haskell, By Dunham, others. **Cast:** Frankie Avalon, Bob Hope,
    Tuesday Weld.

I'M GETTING MY ACT TOGETHER AND TAKING IT ON THE ROAD
Original London Cast (1978) • Columbia Special Prod. (S) X-14885...... 8-10   78
Original London Cast (1978) • That's Entertainment (S) TER-1006 8-10   80s
    UK release.
    Composer: Nancy Ford, Gretchen Cryer. **Cast:** Joel Fabiani, Gretchen Cryer, Margot
    Rose, Betty Aberlin, Don Scardino.

I'M GONNA GIT YOU SUCKA
Soundtrack (1988) • Arista (S) AL8-8574 8-10   88
    Some covers have an oval sticker with credits.
      Cast: Gap Band, Jennifer Holliday, Jermaine Jackson, Boogie Down Productions,
      Four Tops, Aretha Franklin, K-9 Posse, Too Nice, Friends of Distinction, Curtis
      Mayfield.

IBM PRESENTS SCROOGE: see SCROOGE

ICE CASTLES
Soundtrack (1979) • Arista (S) AL-9502 8-10   79
Soundtrack (1979) • Arista (S) AL 58064 5-8   Re
      Composer: Marvin Hamlisch. **Conductor:** Marvin Hamlisch. **Cast:** Melissa
      Manchester, Alan Parsons Project.

ICE FOLLIES
Original Cast (1967) • Dot (M) DLP-3757 18-20   67
Original Cast (1967) • Dot (S) DLP-25757 20-25   67
      Conductor: Pete King. **Cast:** Mike Minor, Debbie Williams, Sally Sweetland.

ICE STATION ZEBRA
Soundtrack (1968) • MGM (S) S1E-14 ST 20-30   68
Soundtrack (1968) • MCA (S) 25017 8-15   86
      Composer: Michel Legrand. **Conductor:** Michel Legrand.

ICEMAN
Soundtrack (1983) • Southern Cross (S) SCRS-1006 15-20   83
      Composer: Bruce Smeaton. **Conductor:** Bruce Smeaton.

ICHABOD (THE LEGEND OF SLEEPY HOLLOW)
Studio Cast (1949) • Decca (M) DL-6001 50-70   49
    10-inch LP. One side has story of *Rip Van Winkle*.
Studio Cast (1949) • Decca (M) DL-9106 20-25   61
Studio Cast • Mr. Pickwick (M) SPC-5156 10-15   77
    One side has music from *Rip Van Winkle*.
      Cast: Boris Karloff (narrator.)
Soundtrack (1949) • Disneyland (M) ST-1920 20-25   63
    One side has music from Rip Van Winkle.
      Composer: Victor Young. **Conductor:** Victor Young. **Cast:** Bing Crosby. RIP VAN
      WINKLE: Walter Huston.
TV Soundtrack (1988) • Windham Hill (S) WH 0700 15-25   88
    From a Showtime cable TV movie.
      Composer: Tim Story. **Cast:** Glenn Close, others.

IDEAL HUSBAND: see BERNARD HERRMANN CONDUCTS GREAT BRITISH
    FILM SCORES

IDOL
Soundtrack (1966) • Fontana (M) MGF-27559 20-25   66
Soundtrack (1966) • Fontana (SE) SRF-67559 25-35   66
    Stereo release lists the catalog number as SRS-67559 on the front cover and spine and as
    SRF-67559 on the back cover and disc label.
      Composer: John Dankworth. **Conductor:** John Dankworth. **Cast:** Cleo Laine.

IDOLMAKER
Soundtrack (1980) • A&M (S) SP-4840 10-15   80
      Composer: Jeff Barry. **Cast:** Darlene Love, Jess Frederick, Nino Tempo, Colleen
      Fitzpatrick, Peter Gallagher, Sweet Inspirations & London Fog, Ray Sharkey.

IF EVER I SEE YOU AGAIN

Soundtrack (1978) • Warner Bros. (S) 2WB-3199 8-12   78
  Two discs.
    Composer: Joe Brooks. **Conductor:** Joe Brooks. **Cast:** Kenny Karen, Debby Boone,
    Jamie Carr.

IF HE HOLLERS, LET HIM GO

Soundtrack (1968) • Tower (S) ST-5152 25-30   68
    Composer: Harry Sukman, Sammy Fain, Coleridge Perkinson.

IF I HAD MY WAY: see BING'S HOLLYWOOD

IF IT'S TUESDAY, THIS MUST BE BELGIUM

Soundtrack (1969) • United Artists (S) UAS-5197 10-12   69
Soundtrack (1969) • MCA (S) 967.. 5-8   86
    Composer: Walter Scharf, Donovan Leitch. **Conductor:** Walter Scharf. **Cast:** J.P.
    Rags, Hopscotch.

IF MY FRIENDS COULD SEE ME NOW

Studiotrack • Columbia (S) CS-9378.. 15-18   74
  Reissue is titled *Broadway Tunesmith Cy Coleman Sings Cy Coleman*.
    Composer: Cy Coleman. **Cast:** Cy Coleman.
  Also see BROADWAY TUNESMITH CY COLEMAN SINGS CY COLEMAN

IF THEY COULD SEE ME NOW

Studio Cast • That's Entertainment (S) TERX-1087 8-10   80s
  UK release.

ILLUSTRATED MAN

Soundtrack (1969) • Warner Bros.-Seven Arts (M) No Number
Used.. 25-30   69
  Commercial spots. Made for radio station use only.

ILLYA DARLING

Original Cast (1967) • United Artists (M) UAL-8901 8-10   67
  Musical based on the film *Never on Sunday*.
Original Cast (1967) • United Artists (S) UAS-9901 10-15   67
    Composer: Joe Darion, Manos Hadjidakis. **Conductor:** Karen Gustafson. **Cast:**
    Melina Mercouri, Titos Vandis, Nikos Kourkoulos, Orson Bean, Hal Linden, Rudy
    Bond.

IMAGINE – THE MOTION PICTURE

Soundtrack (1988) • Capitol (S) C1-90803.. 8-10   88
    Composer: John Lennon, Paul McCartney. **Cast:** John Lennon, Beatles, Plastic Ono
    Band.

IMAGINE THAT – SONGS FROM THE TV SPECIAL

TV Soundtrack • Premore (S) PL-280 8-10
    Cast: Dora Hall.

IMITATION OF LIFE

Soundtrack (1959) • Decca (M) DL-8879 35-45   59
Soundtrack (1959) • Decca (S) DL-78879... 60-70   59
    Composer: Frank Skinner, Sammy Fain. **Conductor:** Joseph Gershenson.

IMPACT
Studiotrack (1959) • RCA Victor (M) LPM-2042 25-30   59
Studiotrack (1959) • RCA Victor (S) LSP-2042 45-60   59
  TV themes from *Waterfront, Rawhide, Peter Gunn, Black Saddle, Highway
  Patrol, Richard Diamond, Racket Squad, Sea Hunt, Mike Hammer, Perry
  Mason, M-Squad* and *The Naked City*. Sequel is titled *Double Impact*.
    Composer: George Duning, Ned Washington, Dimitri Tiomkin, Dave Kahn, Melvin
    Lenard, Pete Rugolo, Fred Steiner, Joe Mullendore, Count Basie, Ray Llewellyn, J.
    Michael Hennagin, Alexander Laszio, Henry Mancini. **Conductor:** Buddy Morrow.
    Cast: Buddy Morrow and His Orchestra.
    Also see DOUBLE IMPACT

IMPORTANCE OF BEING EARNEST
Original Cast • Angel (M) B 3504 15-20
  Two discs.
    Cast: Sir John Gielgud, Dame Edith Evans, Pamela Brown, Cecilia Johnson, Roland
    Culver.

IMPOSSIBLE DREAM – THE STORY OF THE 1967 BOSTON RED SOX
Studio Cast • Fleetwood (S) FCLP 3024 15-20
    Conductor: Bill Green. **Cast:** Ken Coleman (narrator), Ned Martin, Mel Parnell, Jess
    Cain.

IMPRESSIONS OF - A PATCH OF BLUE: see PATCH OF BLUE

IN A SHALLOW GRAVE
Soundtrack (1988) • Varese Sarabande (S) STV 81359 35-40   88
    Composer: Jonathan Sheffer.

IN A SILLY SYMPHONY: see WHO'S AFRAID OF THE BIG BAD WOLF?

IN CALIENTE: see HOORAY FOR HOLLYWOOD

IN CIRCLES
Original Cast (1967) • Avant Garde (M) M-108 20-25   67
Original Cast (1967) • Avant Garde (S) AV-108 30-40   67
    Composer: Al Carmines, Gertrude Stein. **Cast:** Theo Barnes, Al Carmines, Jacque
    Lynn Colton, David Vaughan, Lee Crespi, Lee Guilliatt, James Hilbrandt, Julie Kurnitz,
    George McGrath, Arlene Rothlein, Elaine Summers, David Tice, Arthur Williams,
    Nancy Zala.

IN COLD BLOOD
Soundtrack (1967) • Colgems (M) COM-107 20-25   67
Soundtrack (1967) • Colgems (S) COS-107 25-30   67
    Composer: Quincy Jones. **Conductor:** Quincy Jones.

IN GAY COMPANY
Revival Cast (1984) • WEB (S) OC-111 10-15   84
  Includes program booklet.
    Cast: Los Angeles Cast.

IN HARM'S WAY
Soundtrack (1965) • RCA Victor (M) LOC-1100 20-30   65
Soundtrack (1965) • RCA Victor (S) LSO-1100 45-85   65
    Composer: Jerry Goldsmith. **Conductor:** Jerry Goldsmith.

IN HOLLYWOOD
Studiotrack (1963) • Columbia (M) CL-2034 10-15   63
Studiotrack (1963) • Columbia (S) CS-8834 15-20   63
    Composer: Various. **Conductor:** John Williams. **Cast:** Andre Previn (piano).

IN LIKE FLINT
Soundtrack (1967) • 20th Century-Fox (M) 4193 30-35   67
Soundtrack (1967) • 20th Century-Fox (S) S-4193 40-95   67
Film sequel to *Our Man Flint*.
Composer: Jerry Goldsmith. **Conductor:** Jerry Goldsmith.
Also see OUR MAN FLINT

IN PARIS: see SOMEBODY BAD STOLE DE WEDDING BELL

IN SEARCH OF
TV Soundtrack (1977) • AVI (S) AVL-6008 12-15   77
Composer: Laurin Rinder, W. Michael Lewis, Steve Stewart. **Conductor:** W. Michael
Lewis.

IN SEARCH OF THE CASTAWAYS
Soundtrack (1962) • Disneyland (M) ST-3916 55-65   62
Composer: Richard M. Sherman, Robert B. Sherman. **Conductor:** Muir Mathieson.
Cast: John Mills (narration), Hayley Mills, Maurice Chevalier, Wilfrid Hyde White,
George Sanders. (With dialogue.)
Soundtrack (1962) • Disneyland (S) DQ-1318 20-25   68
Also has music from *The Parent Trap* and *Summer Magic*.
Composer: Richard M. Sherman, Robert B. Sherman. **Conductor:** Tutti Camarata.
Cast: Hayley Mills, Maureen O'Hara, Tommy Sands, Annette Funicello, Maurice
Chevalier, Burl Ives.

IN THE GOOD OLD SUMMERTIME
Soundtrack (1949) • MGM - Number Not Known 25-35   49
78 rpm album.
Soundtrack (1949) • MGM (M) E-169 65-85   49
10-inch LP.
Soundtrack • MGM (M) E-3232 15-18   55
One side has music from *An American In Paris*.
Composer: Harold Arlen, E.Y. Harburg, others. **Conductor:** Georgie Stoll. **Cast:** Judy Garland,
The King's Men. AMERICAN IN PARIS: **Composer:** George Gershwin (music), Ira Gershwin
(lyrics), Buddy DeSylva. **Conductor:** Johnny Green, Saul Chaplin. **Cast:** Gene Kelly, Georges
Guetary, MGM Studio Orchestra.
Soundtrack (1949) • MCA (M) MCA-39083 8-10   86
Also has music from *Good News* (1947).
Composer: Harold Arlen, E.Y. Harburg, others. **Conductor:** Georgie Stoll. **Cast:** Judy Garland,
The King's Men. GOOD NEWS: **Composer:** Ray Henderson, Lew Brown, Buddy DeSylva, Betty
Comden, Adolph Green, Roger Edens. **Conductor:** Lennie Hayton. **Cast:** June Allyson, Peter
Lawford, Patricia Marshall, Joan McCracken.
Also see THOSE GLORIOUS MGM MUSICALS.

IN THE HEAT OF THE NIGHT
Soundtrack (1967) • United Artists (M) UAL-4160 10-12   67
Soundtrack (1967) • United Artists (S) UAS-5160 12-18   67
Soundtrack (1967) • United Artists (S) UA-LA290-G 8-10   74
Soundtrack (1967) • Liberty (S) LT-51133 8-10   Re
Composer: Quincy Jones, Alan and Marilyn Bergman. **Conductor:** Quincy Jones.
Cast: Ray Charles, Glen Campbell, Gil Bernal, Boomer and Travis.

IN THE MATTER OF J. ROBERT OPPENHEIMER
Studio Cast • Caedmon (S) SRS 336 15-20

IN THE MOOD
Soundtrack (1987) • Atlantic (S) 81788-1 8-10   87
Composer: Various. **Conductor:** Ralph Burns. **Cast:** Ralph Burns' Big Band featuring
Beverly D'Angelo and Jennifer Holliday.

IN THE NAVY

Soundtrack • Universal Studios - No Number Used 15-25
78 rpm album. Made for motion picture theatre use.
Cast: Bud Abbott, Lou Costello, Dick Powell, Andrews Sisters.

IN THE PINK

Studiotrack (1984) • RCA Victor (S) CRC1-5315 10-15   84
Columbia House Record Club issue.
Composer: Henry Mancini. **Conductor:** Henry Mancini, James Galway. **Cast:** James
Galway and the National Philharmonic Orchestra.

IN TROUBLE AGAIN

Soundtrack • Mark 56 (M) 600 15-25   75
Cast: Laurel and Hardy.

IN TROUSERS

Original Cast (1979) • Original Cast (S) OC-7915 8-10   79
Composer: William Finn. **Conductor:** Michael Starobin. **Cast:** Alison Fraser, Joanna
Green, Mary Testa, Chip Zien.

IN WHITE AMERICA

Original Cast (1964) • Columbia (M) KOL-6030 10-12   64
Original Cast (1964) • Columbia (S) KOS-2430 12-18   64
Conductor: Oscar Brand. **Cast:** Gloria Foster, James Greene, Moses Gunn,
Claudette Nevins, Michael O'Sullivan, Fred Pinkard.

IN WITH THE OLD

Original Cast • That's Entertainment (S) TER-1122 10-15   80s
UK release.

INCHON

Soundtrack (1982) • Regency International (S) RI-8502 20-25   82
Composer: Jerry Goldsmith.

INCREDIBLE JOURNEY

Soundtrack (1963) • Disneyland (M) ST-1927 25-30   63

INCREDIBLE SHRINKING MAN: see CLASSIC HORROR MUSIC OF HANS J. SALTER

INCREDIBLE WORLD OF JAMES BOND

Soundtrack (1965) • United Artists (S) SP-3 15-20   65
Special Products issue. Music from *Dr. No, From Russia with Love* and
Goldfinger.
Soundtrack (1965) • Unart (M) M-20010 10-15   67
Soundtrack (1965) • Unart (S) S-20010 10-15   67
Composer: John Barry, Monty Norman. Conductor: John Barry, Leroy Holmes, Monty
Norman. **Cast:** Leroy Holmes Orchestra, others.
Also see JAMES BOND

INDIAN SUMMER

Soundtrack (1960) • Folkways (M) FS 3851 15-25   60
Also has music from *Horizontal Lines, Country Fiddle* and *The Many Colored
Paper.*
Cast: Pete Seeger, Michael Seeger.

INDIANA JONES AND THE LAST CRUSADE

Soundtrack (1989) • Warner Bros. (S) 25883-1 10-15   89
Composer: John Williams. **Conductor:** John Williams.

INDIANA JONES AND THE TEMPLE OF DOOM
Soundtrack (1984) • Polydor (S) 422-821592-1 Y-1 15-20   84
  Composer: John Williams. Conductor: John Williams. Cast: John Williams
  Orchestra.
Soundtrack (1984) • Buena Vista (S) 62107 15-20   84
  Full title: *The Story of Indiana Jones and the Temple of Doom.* Gatefold cover.
  Includes 16-page booklet. Dialogue and music.
  Composer: John Williams. Conductor: John Williams. Cast: John Williams
  Orchestra.

INDISCRETION OF AN AMERICAN WIFE
Soundtrack (1954) • Columbia (EP) B-366... 25-60   54
  Two discs.
Soundtrack (1954) • Columbia (M) CL-6277 50-75   54
  10-inch LP.
  Composer: Alessandro Cicognini. Conductor: Franco Ferrara.
  Also see SONG OF BERNADETTE

INFORMER: see MUSIC BY MAX STEINER

INHERITANCE
Soundtrack (1964) • AFL-CIO (M) ACWA MS1 30-45   64
  Made by Amalgamated Clothing Workers of America, AFL-CIO for 50th
  anniversary film.
  Composer: George Kleinsinger, Millard Lampall. Conductor: George Kleinsinger.
  Cast: Robert Ryan (narrator), Joan Baez (uncredited).

INN OF THE SIXTH HAPPINESS
Soundtrack (1958) • 20th Century-Fox (M) FOX-3011 25-50   58
Soundtrack (1958) • 20th Century-Fox (S) SFX-3011 60-65   58
  Composer: Malcolm Arnold. Conductor: Malcolm Arnold. Cast: Ingrid Bergman, Curt
  Jurgens, Robert Donat, London Royal Philharmonic, Athene Seyler (with dialogue).

INNER CITY
Original Cast (1971) • RCA Victor (S) LSO-1171 8-12   71
  Composer: Helen Miller, Eve Merriman. Conductor: Gordon Harrell. Cast: Joy
  Garrett, Linda Hopkins, Carl Hall, Fluffer Hirsch, Delores Hall, Paulette Ellen Jones,
  Larry Marshall, Allan Nicolls, Florence Tarlow.

INNERSPACE
Soundtrack (1987) • Geffen (S) GHS-24161 10-15   87
  Composer: Jerry Goldsmith, others. Conductor: Jerry Goldsmith. Cast: Rod Stewart,
  Wang Chung, Narada Michael Walden, Berlin, Sam Cooke, Jerry Goldsmith.

INNOCENT YEARS
TV Soundtrack • Project XX (S) HO-8P-0935 25-35
  Produced by NBC-TV.
  Cast: Robert Russell Bennett.

INSEMINOID
Soundtrack • Citadel (S) CT 7023 15-20   81
Soundtrack • Varese Sarabande (S) CT 7023.. 8-10   80s
  Composer: John Scott.

INSIDE DAISY CLOVER
Soundtrack (1965) • Warner Bros. (M) W-1616 18-20   65
Soundtrack (1965) • Warner Bros. (S) WS-1616 25-30   65
  Composer: Andre Previn. Conductor: Andre Previn.

INSIDE MOVES
Soundtrack (1980) • Full Moon (S) FMH-3506 8-10   80
  Composer: John Barry, others. Cast: Spinners, Boz Scaggs, Ambrosia, Lady Sylvia,
  Leo Sayers, Eagles, Pablo Cruise.

318

INSIDE SINA
Studio Cast • Charm (M) CM-110.. 10-20
From the Society for Indecency to Naked Animals.

INSIDE STAR TREK: see STAR TREK

INSIDE U.S.A.
Original Cast (1948) • RCA Victor K-14................................. 65-85   48
78 rpm album. Never issued commercially by RCA as a long-playing record.
Features members of the original New York production, with Perry Como, who
was not in the show.
  Composer: Howard Dietz, Arthur Schwartz. **Conductor:** Russ Case. **Cast:** Beatrice
  Lillie, Jack Haley, Billy Williams, Perry Como.

Original Cast (1948) • JJA (M) 19733.................................... 15-20   73
Includes material from the RCA album of 78s, plus selections from the show
performed by Pearl Bailey. Perry Como's recordings are not included. Also has
music from *A Connecticut Yankee.*
  Composer: Howard Dietz, Arthur Schwartz. **Conductor:** Russ Case. **Cast:** Beatrice
  Lillie, Jack Haley, Billy Williams, Pearl Bailey.

INSIGNIFICANCE
Soundtrack (1985) • Zenith (S) ZIT-1Q4 10-20   85
Produced as "a souvenir of music and dialogue to remind us of Nicolas Roeg's
Insignificance."
  Composer: Stanley Myers, Hans Zimmer. **Cast:** Stanley Myers, Hans Zimmer,
  Theresa Russell, Roy Orbison, Gil Evans, Will Jennings, Glenn Gregory, Claudia
  Bruken, Lew Soloff, Tony Curtis, Michael Emil, Gary Busey.

INSPECTOR CLOUSEAU
Soundtrack (1968) • United Artists (S) UAS-5186..................... 20-25   68
Soundtrack (1968) • MCA (S) 25107....................................... 8-10   86
  Composer: Ken Thorne. **Conductor:** Ken Thorne.

INSPIRED THEMES FROM THE INSPIRED FILMS
Studiotrack (1963) • Liberty Premiere Series (M) LMM-13019 15-20   63
Studiotrack (1963) • Liberty Premiere Series (S) LSS-14019............... 25-30   63
Die-cut cover. Includes music from *Sampson and Delilah, El Cid, Man Called Peter,
Francis of Assisi, Prodigal, King Of Kings, Ten Commandments, Song of Bernadette, Ben-
Hur, David and Bathsheba, Quo Vadis* and *The Robe.*

INTERLUDE (1957)
Soundtrack (1957) • Coral (M) CRL-57159 45-75   57
One side has music from *Tammy and the Bachelor.*
  Composer: Frank Skinner (both). TAMMY AND THE BACHELOR: Jay Livingston, Ray
  Evans. **Conductor:** Joseph Gershenson (both). **Cast:** TAMMY AND THE BACHELOR:
  Debbie Reynolds.

INTERLUDE (1968)
Soundtrack (1968) • Colgems (S) COSO-5007 18-25   68
Excerpts of compositions by Ludwig van Beethoven, Johannes Brahms, Pyotr
Ilyich Tchaikovsky, Antonin Dvorak and Sergei Rachmaninoff.
  Composer: Georges Delerue, Hal Shaper. **Conductor:** Georges Delerue, Ernest
  Fleischmann. **Cast:** Timi Yuro, Royal Philharmonic Orchestra conducted by Ernest
  Fleischmann.

INTERNATIONAL FILM FESTIVAL
Studiotrack (1963) • Warner Bros. (S) WS 1548................................... 10-15   63
  Conductor: Werner Muller.

INTERNATIONAL SOIRÉE
Original Cast (1958) • Audio Fidelity (M) AF-1881................................ 15-20   58
  Standard cover.
Original Cast (1958) • Audio Fidelity (S) AFSD-5881 20-40   58
  Gatefold cover, devoted to explaining new stereo process.
    Composer: Jo Basile, others. **Conductor:** Jo Basile. **Cast:** Patachou and Co., Jo
    Basile (accordion, orchestra).

INTERNATIONAL VELVET
Soundtrack (1978) • MGM (S) 1-5405.. 10-15   78
    Composer: Francis Lai. **Conductor:** Francis Lai.

INTERNS
Soundtrack (1962) • Colpix (M) CP-427 20-30   62
Soundtrack (1962) • Colpix (S) SCP-427 30-35   62
    Composer: Leith Stevens. **Conductor:** Leith Stevens, Stu Phillips.

INTERRUPTED MELODY
Soundtrack (1955) • MGM (EP) X-304 10-25   55
Soundtrack (1955) • MGM (M) E-3185 20-25   55
Soundtrack (1955) • MGM (M) E-3984 15-20   62
  Actual title: *The Voice of Eileen Farrell.*
    Conductor: Walter Ducloux. **Cast:** Eileen Farrell (performed vocals for Eleanor Parker
    in the film), Heinz Blankenburg, Rudolf Petrak, William Olvis, Marcella Reale, Charles
    Gonzales.

INTO THE NIGHT
Soundtrack (1985) • MCA (S) 5561.. 8-10   85
    Composer: Ira Newborn, others. **Cast:** B.B. King, Patti LaBelle, Thelma Houston,
    Marvin Gaye, Four Tops.

INTO THE WOODS
London Cast (1987) • RCA Victor (S) 6796-1-RC 15-20   88
  Two discs.
    Composer: Stephen Sondheim. **Conductor:** Paul Gemignani. **Cast:** Bernadette
    Peters, Joanna Gleason, Chip Zien, Tom Aldredge, Robert Westenberg, Barbara
    Bryne, Kim Crosby, Merle Louise, Ben Wright, Edmund Lyndeck, Kay McClelland,
    Chuck Wagner.

INVADERS FROM MARS
Soundtrack (1986) • Enigma (S) SJ-73226 10-15   86
    Composer: David Storrs. **Conductor:** David Storrs.

INVADERS: see BERNARD HERRMANN CONDUCTS GREAT BRITISH FILM SCORES

INVASION OF THE BODY SNATCHERS
Soundtrack (1979) • United Artists (S) UA-LA940-H 10-15   79
    Composer: Denny Zeitlin. **Conductor:** Denny Zeitlin. **Cast:** Royal Scots Dragoon
    Guards.

INVASION U.S.A.
Soundtrack (1985) • Varese Sarabande (S) 81263 10-15   85
    Composer: Jay Chattaway. **Conductor:** Jay Chattaway.

INVESTIGATION OF A CITIZEN ABOVE SUSPICION
Soundtrack (1970) • Cerberus (S) GEMS-0110 15-20   81
    Composer: Ennio Morricone. **Conductor:** Ennio Morricone.

INVITATION: see AUNTIE MAME

INVITATION AU VOYAGE
Soundtrack (1982) • Varese Sarabande (S) STV-81189 10-15   82
    Composer: Gabriel Yared. **Cast:** Nina Scott and Lawlessness.

INVITATION TO THE DANCE
Soundtrack (1956) • MGM (M) E-3207 30-40   56
Soundtrack (1956) • MCA (SE) 25037 8-15   86
 Has the scores for the *Circus* and *Ring Around the Rosy* sections of the film. The *Sinbad* section is not included.
  Composer: Andre Previn, Jacques Ibert. **Conductor:** Andre Previn, John Hollingsworth.
Soundtrack (1956) • MGM (M) E-4186.. 15-20   63
Soundtrack (1956) • MGM (SE) SE-4186.. 10-15   63
 Actual titles: *Andre Previn: Composer, Conductor, Arranger, Pianist.*
  Composer: Andre Previn, Jacques Ibert. **Conductor:** Andre Previn, John Hollingsworth.

IPCRESS FILE
Soundtrack (1965) • Decca (M) DL-9124 20-30   65
Soundtrack (1965) • Decca (S) DL-79124... 35-45   65
  Composer: John Barry. **Conductor:** John Barry.

IPI-TOMBI
Original Cast (1977) • Ashtree (S) ASH-26000 10-25   77
 Two discs.
  Composer: Bertha Egnos, Gail Lakier. **Cast:** Count Wellington Judge, Dan Pule, Jabu Mbalo, Matthew Bodibe, Ruby Morare, Petunia Seakatsi, Joe Seakatsi, Gasta Mnguni, Andy Chabeli, Patrick Moletsane.

IRENE
Original London Cast (1919) • Monmouth
 Evergreen (SE) MES-7057 10-15
  Composer: Harry Tierney, Joseph McCarthy. **Conductor:** G.W. Byng, Frank Tours.
  Cast: Edith Day, Daisy Hancox, Winnie Collins, Robert Hale.
Original London Cast • EMI (M) EMC-3139................................... 20-30
  Composer: Harry Tierney, Joseph McCarthy. **Cast:** John Pertwee, Jessie Evans, Eric Flynn, Julie Anthony.
Original Revival Cast (1973) • Columbia (S) KS-32266......................... 8-12   73
  Composer: Harry Tierney, Joseph McCarthy, Charles Gaynor, Otis Clements.
  Conductor: Jack Lee. **Cast:** Debbie Reynolds, Monte Markham, George S. Irving, Patsy Kelly, Ruth Warrick, Ted Pugh, Carmen Alvarez, Jeanne Lehman, Monte Markham, Meg Scanlon, Janie Sell, Penny Worth.
  Also see RIO RITA

IRMA LA DOUCE
Original London Cast (1958) • Philips (M) BBL-7274 25-35   60
 UK release.
  Composer: Marguerite Monnot, Julian More, David Heneker, Monty Norman. **Conductor:** Alexander Faris. **Cast:** Elizabeth Seal, Keith Michell, Clive Revill, Ronald Barker, John East, David Evans, Frank Olegario, Gary Raymond.
Original Cast (1960) • Columbia (M) OL-5560..................................... 8-10   60
Original Cast (1960) • Columbia (S) OS-2029..................................... 10-12   60
Original Cast (1960) • Columbia Special Products (SE) AOS-2029.......... 5-8   Re
  Composer: Marguerite Monnot. **Conductor:** Stanley Lebowsky. **Cast:** Elizabeth Seal, Keith Michell, Clive Revill, George S. Irving, Osborne Smith, Fred Gwynne, Stuart Damon, George Del Monte, Aric Lavie, Zack Matalon, Rudy Tronto.
London Studio Cast (1960) • London (M) LL-3197 15-20   61
London Studio Cast (1960) • London (S) PS-221................................. 20-25   61
  Composer: Julian Moore, Marguerite Monnot, David Heneker, Monty Norman.
  Conductor: Bob Sharples. **Cast:** Joyce Blair, Ian Paterson, Cliff Adams Chorus.
Original French Revival Cast (1960) • Columbia (M) WL-177 15-20   60
  Composer: Marguerite Monnot, Alexandre Breffort. **Conductor:** Andre Popp. **Cast:** Zizi Jeanmaire, Roland Petit, Les Quatre Barbus, Luc Davis.

Soundtrack (1963) • United Artists (M) UAL-4109................................ 10-12   63
Soundtrack (1963) • United Artists (M) UAS-5109 12-18   63
  Both have the complete score from the film.
Studiotrack (1961) • Columbia (M) CL-1590.. 8-10   61
Studiotrack (1961) • Columbia (S) CS-8390.. 8-10   61
  Cast: Chico Hamilton Quintet.
Studiotrack (1961) • Richmond (M) B-20089... 8-12   61
Studiotrack (1961) • Richmond (S) S-30089 8-12   61
  Cast: London Repertory Theatre.
Studiotrack (1963) • Capitol (M) T-1943.. 12-18   63
Studiotrack (1963) • Capitol (S) ST-1943 15-20   63
  Full title: *Jack Lemmon Plays Piano Selections from Irma La Douce.*
  Conductor: Jack Marshall. **Cast:** Jack Lemmon (piano).
  Also see TOM JONES (1963)

IRON EAGLE

Soundtrack (1986) • Capitol (S) SV-12499.. 8-10   86
  Cast: Queen, Katrina and the Waves, Dio, Helix, King Kobra, Eric Martin, Adrenelin,
  Urgent, The Jon Butcher Axis, George Clinton.

IRON EAGLE II

Soundtrack (1986) • Epic (S) SE-45006... 8-10   86
  Cast: Insiders, Alice Cooper, Mike Reno, Sweet Obsession, Doug and Slugs, Britny
  Fox, FM/UK, Henry Lee Summer, Ruth Pointer, Billy Vera, Rick Springfield.

IRVING BERLIN: 100TH ANNIVERSARY COLLECTION

Studio Cast (1988) • MCA (S) 39324 10-15   88
  Composer: Irving Berlin. **Cast:** Bing Crosby, Fred Astaire, Linda Ronstadt, others.
  Also see IRVING BERLIN TRIBUTE
  Also see ON THE AVENUE

IRVING BERLIN REVISITED

Studio Cast (1967) • MGM (M) E-4435... 20-25   67
Studio Cast (1967) • MGM (M) SE-4435 15-20   67
Studio Cast (1967) • Painted Smiles (M) PS 1356 8-10   Re
  Issued as part of The *New American Theatre Series.*
  Composer: Irving Berlin. **Conductor:** Norman Paris.

IRVING BERLIN TRIBUTE

Radio Cast • Famous Personalities (M) 1001.. 15-25
  Cast: Ethel Merman, Walter Winchell, Al Jolson, Sophie Tucker, Eddie Cantor, Lew
  Lahr, Connie Boswell, Rudy Vallee, Tommy Dorsey, Alice Faye, others.

IS PARIS BURNING?

Soundtrack (1966) • Columbia (M) OL-6630 15-30   66
Soundtrack (1966) • Columbia (M) OS-3030.. 20-40   66
  Composer: Maurice Jarre. **Conductor:** Maurice Jarre.
Soundtrack (1966) • No Label Shown (M) No Number Used................ 30-40   66
  Open-end interview, with script. Promotional issue only.

IS THERE LIFE AFTER HIGH SCHOOL?

Original Cast (1982) • Original Cast (S) OC-8240 20-25   82
  Composer: Craig Carnilia. **Conductor:** Bruce Coughlin. **Cast:** Raymond Baker,
  Cynthia Carle, Alma Cuervo, Sandy Faison, Harry Groener, Philip Hoffman, David
  Patrick Kelly, Maureen Shilliman, James Widdoes.

ISABEL'S A JEZEBEL

Original London Cast (1974) • United Artists (S) UAG-29148 25-45   74
  Composer: Galt McDermott. **Conductor:** Galt McDermott.

ISADORA: see LOVES OF ISADORA

ISLAND
Soundtrack (1979) • Varese Sarabande (S) VC-81147 15-20   79
  Composer: Ennio Morricone. **Conductor:** Ennio Morricone.

ISLAND AT THE TOP OF THE WORLD
Soundtrack (1974) • Disneyland (S) ST 3814..................................... 20-25   74
  Gatefold cover. Includes 12-page booklet.
  Composer: Maurice Jarre. **Conductor:** Maurice Jarre. **Cast:** David Hartman, Donald
  Sinden, Thurl Ravenscroft (narrator.)

ISLAND IN THE SKY
Soundtrack (1953) • Decca (M) DL-7029 250-275   53
  10-inch LP.
  Composer: Emil Newman, Hugo Friedhofer, Herb Spencer. **Conductor:** Emil
  Newman. **Cast:** John Wayne.
  Also see SONG OF BERNADETTE

ISLAND OF DR. MOREAU
Soundtrack (1981)• No Label Shown (S) HG-4000 20-30   81
  Promotional issue only. Although cover uses the film title, disc title is *Island of Horror*.
  Composer: Laurence Rosenthal. **Conductor:** Laurence Rosenthal.

ISLAND OF HORROR: see ISLAND OF DR. MOREAU

ISLANDS IN THE STREAM
Soundtrack (1977) • Intrada (S) RVF-6003 15-20   77
  Composer: Jerry Goldsmith. **Conductor:** Jerry Goldsmith.

ISRAEL NOW
Soundtrack • United Artists (M) UAL-3609... 10-12   68
  Music from *Exodus* and *Cast a Giant Shadow*, plus incidental selections.
Soundtrack • United Artists (S) UAS-6609 12-15   68
  Composer: Ernest Gold, Elmer Bernstein, Henry Sandaver. **Cast:** Elmer Bernstein,
  Ferrante and Teicher, Zemel Choir, Hollywood Studio Orchestra.

ISRAEL SPEAKS
Assembled Cast (1963) • United Artists (M) UAL-9002 8-12   63
  Cast: Abba Eban (speech).

IT HAPPENED AT THE WORLD'S FAIR
Soundtrack (1963) • RCA Victor (M) LPM-2697 150-200   63
  Black label, reads "Long Play" at bottom. Includes bonus 8" x 10" color photo.
Soundtrack (1963) • RCA Victor (M) LPM-2697 70-100   63
  Black label, reads "Long Play" at bottom. Without bonus photo.
Soundtrack (1963) • RCA Victor (S) LSP-2697 150-200   63
  Black label, reads "Living Stereo" at bottom. Includes bonus 8" x 10" color
  photo.
Soundtrack (1963) • RCA Victor (S) LSP-2697 75-100   63
  Black label, reads "Living Stereo" at bottom. Without bonus photo
Soundtrack (1963) • RCA Victor (M) LPM-2697 40-50   63
  Black label, reads "Mono" at bottom.
Soundtrack (1963) • RCA Victor (M) LPM-2697 25-30   65
  Black label, reads "Monaural" at bottom.
Soundtrack (1963) • RCA Victor (S) LSP-2697 25-30   65
  Black label, reads "Stereo" at bottom.
Soundtrack (1963) • RCA Victor (S) APL1-2568 8-10   78
  Composer: Bill Giant, Bernie Baum, Florence Kaye, Sid Wayne, Ben Weisman, Ruth
  Batchelor, Fred Wise, Sid Tepper, Roy C. Bennett, Don Robertson, Otis Blackwell,
  others. **Cast:** Elvis Presley, Scotty Moore (guitar), D.J. Fontana (drums), Dudley
  Brooks (piano), Jordanaires (vocals), Mellow Men (vocals).

IT HAPPENED IN BROOKLYN
Soundtrack (1947) • Hollywood Soundstage (M) HS-5006 8-10
Composer: Jule Styne, Sammy Cahn. **Conductor:** Johnny Green. **Cast:** Frank Sinatra, Jimmy Durante, Kathryn Grayson, Peter Lawford.
Also see ON MOONLIGHT BAY

IT HAPPENED ONE BITE
Soundtrack (1978) • Warner Bros. (S) K-3158 8-10-15   78
Cast: Dan Hicks.

IT STARTED IN NAPLES
Soundtrack (1960) • Dot (M) DLP-3324 35-60   60
Soundtrack (1960) • Dot (S) DLP-25324 65-100   60
Soundtrack (1960) • Varese Sarabande (S) STV-81122 10-15   82
Composer: Alessandro Cicognini, Carlo Savina. **Conductor:** Carlo Savina. **Cast:** Sophia Loren.

IT'S A BIRD IT'S A PLANE IT'S SUPERMAN
Original Cast (1966) • Columbia (M) KOL-6570 8-10   66
Original Cast (1966) • Columbia (S) KOS-2970 8-12   66
Original Cast (1966) • Columbia Special Products (M) AKOS-2970 5-8   Re
Composer: Charles Strouse, Lee Adams. **Conductor:** Hal Hastings. **Cast:** Jack Cassidy, Bob Holliday, Eric Mason, Patricia Marand, Linda Lavin, Michael O'Sullivan, Don Chastain, Flying Lings.

IT'S A MAD, MAD, MAD, MAD WORLD
Soundtrack (1963) • United Artists (M) UAL-4110 12-15   63
Soundtrack (1963) • United Artists (S) UAS-5110 12-18   63
Soundtrack (1963) • United Artists (S) UA-LA276-G 8-10   74
Soundtrack (1963) • MCA (S) 39076 5-10   86
Composer: Ernest Gold, Mack David. **Conductor:** Ernest Gold.

IT'S A REVOLUTION MOTHER
Soundtrack (1971) • Entertainment Systems. (S) No Number Used 60-80   71
Documentary about demonstrations and riots of late 1960s and early '70s. A "Royce Adams Enterprises Production."
Composer: Chris Martell. **Cast:** Mandarin Gate.

IT'S A SMALL WORLD
Original Cast (1964) • Disneyland (S) ST 3925 30-35   63
Full title: *Walt Disney Presents at the New York World's Fair, It's a Small World.* Abstract white cover.
Original Cast (1964) • Disneyland (S) ST 3925 15-20   Re
Yellow cover, with photo.
Cast: Richard M. Sherman, Robert B. Sherman, Winston Hibler (narrator).

IT'S A WONDERFUL LIFE
Studiotrack (1988) • Telarc (S) Number Unknown 15-20   88
Also has original scores from *A Christmas Carol* and *Miracle on 34th Street.*
Composer: Dimitri Tiomkin, Richard Addinsell, Cyril Mockridge. **Conductor:** David Newman.

IT'S ALIVE II (IT LIVES AGAIN)
Soundtrack (1978) • Starlog (S) SR-1002 12-18   78
Same score as *It's Alive.* It was reworked by Laurie Johnson for the sequel, after Bernard Herrmann's death.
Composer: Bernard Herrmann, Laurie Johnson. **Conductor:** Laurie Johnson.

IT'S ALWAYS FAIR WEATHER
Soundtrack (1955) • MGM (EP) X-331 15-20   55
Soundtrack (1955) • MGM (M) E-3241 35-45   55
Soundtrack (1955) • DRG/Stet (M) DS-15020 20-25   Re
    This issue is listed on back covers of many others in this series, but no copies
    are known to exist. Price range is estimated in the event the album surfaces.
Soundtrack (1955) • MCA (M) 25018 8-10   86
    Composer: Andre Previn, Adolph Green, Betty Comden. **Conductor:** Andre Previn.
    Cast: Gene Kelly, Dan Dailey, Carole Richards (performed vocals for Cyd Charisse in
    the film), Dolores Gray, Jud Conlon (performed vocals for Michael Kidd).
Studiotrack (1955) • Heritage (M) H-0058 45-65   55
    10-inch LP. Betty Comden & Adolph Green perform songs written for the film.
    Composer: Andre Previn, Adolph Green, Betty Comden. **Cast:** Betty Comden, Adolph
    Green.

IT'S HONEYMOONERS TIME
TV Soundtrack (1985) • Murray Hill (SE) 000237 10-15   85
    Cast: Jackie Gleason, Art Carney, others.

IT'S HOWDY DOODY TIME
Studio Cast • RCA Victor (S) LSP-4546 15-20   71
    Cast: Buffalo Bob Smith, Howdy Doody Cast.

IT'S MY TURN
Soundtrack (1980) • Motown (S) M8-947M1 8-10   80
    Composer: Patrick Williams, Michael Masser, Carole Bayer Sager, Teddy Randazzo,
    Tony Travalini, Ozone. **Conductor:** Richard Berres. **Cast:** Diana Ross, Tony Travalini,
    Ozone, other.

IT'S TIME TO PRAY, AMERICA!
TV Soundtrack (1976) • House Top (M) HTR-702 8-10   76
    Cast: Former President Gerald R. Ford, The Honorable Jimmy Carter, Pat Boone,
    Johnny Cash, Yitzak Rabin, Dr. Zvi Almog, Cr. Bill Bright, Charles Colson, Terence
    Cardinal Cooke, Billy Graham, James Hampton, Jack Hayford, Rex Humbard, Tom
    Landry, Janet Lynn, Samuel Piccolo, Jim Ryun, Lefty Scumaci, Demos Shakarian,
    Tom Skinner, David Wilkerson, Pat Robertson (host).

ITALIAN JOB
Soundtrack (1969) • Paramount (S) PAS-5007 25-35   69
    Composer: Quincy Jones. **Conductor:** Quincy Jones. **Cast:** Matt Monro, Quincy
    Jones.

IVAN THE TERRIBLE
Studiotrack (1945) • Angel (SE) SB-3851 15-20   78
    Boxed, two-disc set.
    Composer: Sergei Prokofiev.

IVANHOE
Soundtrack (1952) • MGM K-179 25-35   52
    Boxed set of four singles, four sides of which have music from *Ivanhoe*. The
    other four contain music from *Plymouth Adventure*.
Soundtrack (1952) • MGM (M) E-179 45-85   52
    10-inch LP. Also has music from *Plymouth Adventure*.
Soundtrack (1952) • MGM (M) E-3507 30-35   57
    Also has music from *Madame Bovary* and *Plymouth Adventure*.
    Composer: Miklos Rozsa. **Conductor:** Miklos Rozsa. **Cast:** MGM Studio Orchestra.

IVANOV
Original Cast (1966) • RCA Victor (M) VDM-109 15-20   66
Original Cast (1966) • RCA Victor (S) VDS-109 25-35   66
    A dramatic play by Anton Chekov.
    Cast: Vivien Leigh, Sir John Gielgud, Roland Culver, Jennifer Hilary, John Merivale.

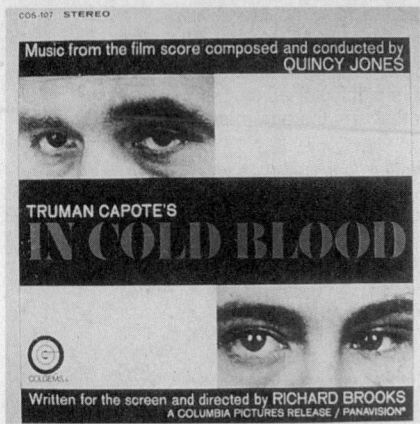

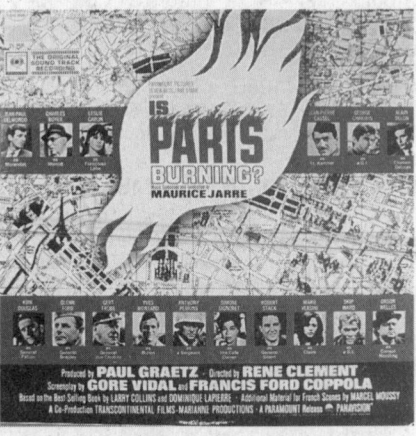

J

J.B.
Original Cast (1959) • RCA Victor (M) LD-6075 40-50   59
Original Cast (1959) • RCA Victor (S) LDS-6075 .... 50-60 .   59
   Two discs. Dramatic play in verse by Archibald MacLeish.
   Composer: David Amram. **Conductor:** David Amram. **Cast:** Raymond Massey, Christopher
   Plummer, James Daly, James Olson, Ford Rainey.

JACK AND THE BEANSTALK
TV Soundtrack (1956) • RKO/Unique (M) LP-111 25-35   56
   Composer: Jerry Livingston, Helen Deutsch. **Conductor:** Joe Lehay. **Cast:** Bob Graybo, Lynn
   Roberts, Dale Collyer, Petticoats.
TV Soundtrack (1966) • HBR (M) HLP-8511 50-100   67
TV Soundtrack (1966) • HBR (S) HST-9511 125-175   67
   Black label or white-label promo.
TV Soundtrack (1967) • HBR (M) HLP-8511 40-50   67
   Blue "Cartoon Series" label.
   Composer: James Van Heusen, Sammy Cahn. **Conductor:** Lennie Hayton. **Cast:** Gene Kelly,
   Ted Cassidy, Bobby Rina, Marion McNight, Marni Nixon.

JACK BENNY STORY
Soundtrack • Radiola 45/46 10-15
   Two discs.

JACK JOHNSON
Soundtrack (1971) • Columbia (S) KC-30455 20-30   71
   Composer: Miles Davis. **Cast:** Jack Johnson, Miles Davis, Brock Peters. (With dialogue.)

JACK PAAR: THE BEST OF 'WHAT'S HIS NAME'
TV Soundtrack • Ramrod/Columbia Special Products (M) R-8001 10-15
   Special products issue, made for Jiffy Sew Instant Mending.

JACK THE RIPPER
Soundtrack (1960) • RCA Victor (M) LPM-2199 25-30   60
Soundtrack (1960) • RCA Victor (S) LSP-2199 45-50   60
   Background score from the film.
   Composer: Pete Rugolo, Jimmy McHugh. **Conductor:** Pete Rugolo.
Soundtrack (1960) • Camden (M) CAL-590 25-75   60
   Music and dialogue from the film.
   Composer: Stanley Black. **Cast:** Sir Cedric Hardwicke (narration).

JACQUES BREL IS ALIVE AND WELL AND LIVING IN PARIS
Original Cast (1968) • Columbia (S) D2S-779 8-10   68
   Two discs. Includes four-page booklet.
Original Cast (1968) • Columbia (S) CGK-40817 8-10   Re
   Composer: Jacques Brel, Eric Blau, Mort Shuman. **Conductor:** Mort Shuman. **Cast:** Elly Stone,
   Mort Shuman, Shawn Elliott, Alice Whitfield.
Original Detroit Cast (1968) • Synchronicity (S) 1306 20-25   68
   Composer: Jacques Brel, Eric Blau, Mort Shuman. **Conductor:** Marc Chover.
Soundtrack (1973) • Atlantic (S) SD-2-1000 10-12   73
   Composer: Jacques Brel, Eric Blau, Mort Shuman. **Conductor:** François Rauber. **Cast:**
   Jacques Brel, Mort Shuman, Elly Stone, Shawn Elliott, Judy Landers, Joseph Neal, Annette
   Perrone, Joe Masiell.

JAGGED EDGE

Soundtrack (1985) • Varese Sarabande (S) 81252 10-15   85
Soundtrack (1985) • That's Entertainment (S) TER-1107 8-10   80s
  UK release.
    Composer: John Barry. **Conductor:** John Barry.

JAILHOUSE ROCK

Soundtrack (1957) • RCA Victor (EP) EPA-4114 50-75   57
  Black label, dog on top.
Soundtrack (1957) • RCA Victor (EP) EPA-4114 30-40   65
  Black label, dog on side.
Soundtrack (1957) • RCA Victor (EP) EPA-4114 50-100   69
  Orange label.
    Composer: Jerry Leiber, Mike Stoller, Ben Weisman, Aaron Schroeder, others. **Cast:** Elvis
    Presley, Scotty Moore (guitar), D.J. Fontana (drums), Bill Black (bass), Dudley Brooks, Mike
    Stoller (piano), Jordanaires (vocals).

JAKE SPEED

Soundtrack (1986) • Varese Sarabande (S) STV 81285 8-10   86
    Composer: Mark Snow.

JAMAICA

Original Cast (1957) • RCA Victor (M) LOC-1036 10-15   57
  Each issue of this album contains different material, making it necessary to have all three in
  order to obtain the entire score. This one has abridged versions of some numbers to allow
  for the inclusion of four songs not included on LSO-1036 but heard on LSO-1103.
Original Cast (1957) • RCA Victor (S) LSO-1036 40-45   57
  Has an overture not included on other releases.
Original Cast (1957) • RCA Victor (M) LOC-1103 12-18   65
Original Cast (1957) • RCA Victor (S) LSO-1103 35-40   65
  Has extended versions of some songs, thereby eliminating others found on LOC-1036.
    Composer: Harold Arlen, E.Y. Harburg, Peter Matz. **Conductor:** Lehman Engel. **Cast:** Lena
    Horne, Ricardo Montalban, Josephine Premice, Adelaide Hall, Ossie Davis, Augustine Rios, Joe
    Adams, Hugo Dilworth.
Studio Cast • MGM (M) E-3612 10-20   57
    Composer: Harold Arlen. **Conductor:** David Rose. **Cast:** Lena Horne, Ricardo Montalban,
    David Rose and His Orchestra.
Studiotrack (1956) • RCA Victor (EP) EPA-4038 10-15   56
    Cast: Lena Horne.
Studiotrack (1958) • Jubilee (EP) EP-5062 10-15   58
Studiotrack (1958) • Jubilee (M) JLP-1062 15-25   59
    Cast: Cy Coleman and His Orchestra.

JAMBOREE!

Soundtrack (1957) • Warner Bros. (M) No Number Used 2,000-3,000   57
  Promotional issue only. Front cover is a slick pasted on generic, unprinted cardboard
  cover. Notes on back are printed right on the cardboard (no slick used on back). Original
  covers have a smooth surface. Front cover photos have gray-green background hue. Trail-
  off area on disc has "Jam 1," & "Jam 2" stamped (not etched) in vinyl. Label is light yellow.
  Warner "shield" logo has parallel lines as background, all with sharp, distinct lettering.
  Counterfeit identification: Front cover graphics are printed on posterboard. Back cover
  notes are pasted on. Cover has textured feel. Front cover photos have pinkish hue.
  background. Trail-off area has "Jam 1" & "Jam 2" hand-etched. Label is dark yellow.
  Warner "shield" logo has black background with broken lettering.
    Composer: Aaron Schroeder, Claude DeMetruis, Ernie Wilkins, Bernie Lowe, Kal Mann, Roy C.
    Bennett, Sid Tepper, Otis Blackwell, Teddy Randazzo, Leone M. Richards, Count Basie, Buddy
    Knox, Fats Domino, Dave Bartholomew. **Cast:** Fats Domino, Buddy Knox, Jimmy Bowen,
    Charlie Gracie, Slim Whitman, Jerry Lee Lewis, Connie Francis, Four Coins, Carl Perkins,
    Frankie Avalon, Jodie Sands, Count Basie, Joe Williams (Joseph Goreed), Andy Martin, Martha
    Lou Harp, Paul Carr, Lewis Lymon and the Teenchords, Ron Coby.

JAMES BLONDE (SECRET AGENT 006.95, MARKED DOWN FROM 007.00)

Studio Cast (1965) • Colpix (M) CP-495 10-15   65
Comedy skits based on James Bond characters.
Cast: Marty Brill, Larry Foster.

JAMES BOND

Studiotrack (1966) • Metro (M) M-520 10-12   66
Studiotrack (1966) • Metro (S) MS-520 15-18   66
Full title: *Music From James Bond Motion Pictures (Plus Other Music of Mystery, Mayhem and Murder).* Themes from *Goldfinger, Peter Gunn, From Russia With Love* and others.
Composer: Henry Mancini, John Barry, others. **Cast:** Danny Davis and Orchestra, Kenyon Hopkins and Orchestra, Ray Ellis and Orchestra.

Studiotrack (1971) • London Phase 4 (S) 2 BSP-24 15-25   71
Two discs. Full title: *Return of James Bond in Diamonds Are Forever and Others.* Also has music from *The Avengers* and *The Saint.*
Composer: John Barry, Jerry Goldsmith, Laurie Johnson, Henry Mancini, Lalo Schifrin, others. **Conductor:** Roland Shaw. **Cast:** Roland Shaw and His Orchestra.

Studiotrack (1983) • Discovery (S) 8513 10-15   83
Full title: *16 James Bond Film Themes.*
Composer: John Barry, H. Dussein, others. **Conductor:** Nicky North. **Cast:** Studio London Orchestra.

Studiotrack (1985) • Bulldog (S) BDL-1036 10-15   85
Full title: *Bond by Barry.*
Composer: John Barry. **Conductor:** John Barry.

Studiotrack • London (S) PS 514 10-15
Full title: *Themes from James Bond Thrillers – Vol. 3.*

Studiotrack/Soundtrack • United Artists (S) 6415 15-20
Full title: *Music to Read James Bond By.*
Composer: John Barry, Monty Norman. **Cast:** (soundtrack artists), Leroy Holmes and Orchestra.
Also see GOLDFINGER
Also see INCREDIBLE WORLD OF JAMES BOND

JAMES BOND – 13 ORIGINAL THEMES

Soundtrack • Liberty (S) LO-51138 10-15   83
Soundtrack • Liberty/Columbia House (S) LO-51138 10-15   80s
Record club issue.
Soundtrack • Liberty/RCA Victor (S) R-151594 10-15   80s
Record club issue.
Soundtrack • Liberty (S) LJ-51138 15-20   80s
Themes from *Live and Let Die, From Russia with Love, Goldfinger, Thunderball, You Only Live Twice, We Have All the Time in the World, Diamonds Are Forever* and *The James Bond Theme.*
Composer: John Barry, others. **Conductor:** John Barry, others. **Cast:** Matt Monro, Shirley Bassey, Tom Jones, Nancy Sinatra, Louis Armstrong, Paul McCartney, Lulu, Carly Simon, Sheena Easton, Rita Coolidge.
Cast: Sounds of Screen Orchestra.

Studiotrack • Somerset (S) SF 232 8-12
Music from *Goldfinger, James Bond Theme, From Russia with Love* and others.
Composer: John Barry, others. **Cast:** Zero Zero Seven Band.

JAMES BOND – 10th ANNIVERSARY
Soundtrack • United Artists (S) UXS-91 20-25   72
Two discs. Music from: *Goldfinger, Dr. No, From Russia with Love, Thunderball, You Only Live Twice, On Her Majesty's Secret Service* and *Diamonds Are Forever.*
Composer: John Barry, Monty Norman, Lionel Bart, Leslie Bricusse, Anthony Newley, Don Black, Hal David. **Conductor:** John Barry, Eric Rodgers. **Cast:** Matt Monro, Shirley Bassey, Louis Armstrong.

JAMES BOND – 25 YEARS OF 007
Studiotrack • Bainbridge (S) BT-6274 8-10   87

JAMES DEAN STORY
Soundtrack (1957) • Capitol (EP) EDM 1-881 25-30
Soundtrack (1957) • Capitol (M) W-881 35-45   57
Composer: Leith Stevens, Jay Livingston, Ray Evans. **Conductor:** Leith Stevens.
Studiotrack (1956) • Unique (M) LP-109 150-160   56
Actual title: *Music James Dean Lived By.*
Studiotrack (1956) • Coral (M) CRL-57099........................... 30-50   56
Cast: Steve Allen and Bill Randle and Gigi Perreau (narrators), George Cates and His Orchestra & Chorus, Dick Jacobs and His Orchestra & Chorus, Jimmy Wakely, Eddie Stuart.
Studiotrack (1957) • World Pacific (M) 2005 50-75   57
Jazz interpretation.
Studiotrack (1960) • Kimberly (M) 2016 20-25   60
Reissue of World Pacific 2005.
Cast: Chet Baker.
Soundtrack (1955) • Warner Bros. (M) BS-2843 10-12   75
Actual title: *James Dean.* Has dialogue excerpts from *Giant, East of Eden* and *Rebel Without a Cause.*
Composer: Leonard Rosenman, Dimitri Tiomkin. **Conductor:** Ray Heindorf, Dimitri Tiomkin. **Cast:** James Dean, Jo Van Fleet, Raymond Massey, Julie Harris, Barbara Baxley, Jim Backus, Ann Doran, Rock Hudson, Elizabeth Taylor, Mercedes McCambridge, Charles Watts, Monte Hale, Chill Wills, Carroll Baker.
Also see TRIBUTE TO JAMES DEAN

JANE, MARY: see MARY JANE

JANE EYRE
TV Soundtrack (1971) • Capitol (S) SW-749......................... 20-25   71
TV Soundtrack (1971) • That's Entertainment (S) TER-1022 12-15   80s
UK release.
Composer: John Williams. **Conductor:** John Williams.

JANE POWELL
Soundtrack • Scarce Rarities (M) 5503 12-20
Selections from Jane Powell's films and radio shows.
Composer: Various. **Cast:** Jane Powell, Four Freshmen, Vic Damone.
Soundtrack • Curtain Calls (M) CC 100/4 10-12
Silver Screen Star Series. Previously unreleased selections from *Holiday in Mexico, Three Daring Daughters, Rich, Young and Pretty, A Date With Judy, Small Town Girl, Delightfully Dangerous, Song of the Open Road* and the 1959 TV version of *Meet Me in St. Louis.*
Composer: Various. **Conductor:** Various. **Cast:** Jane Powell, Frank Sinatra, Vic Damone, Jeanette MacDonald, Jose Iturbi, Gordon MacRae.

JANIS
Soundtrack (1975) • Columbia (S) CGT-33345..................... 10-12   75
Cast: Janis Joplin (vocals, monologues and interviews).

JARRE BY JARRE
Composer: Maurice Jarre. **Conductor:** Maurice Jarre. **Cast:** Royal Philharmonic Orchestra.

JAWS
Soundtrack (1975) • MCA (S) 2087 15-20   75
Soundtrack (1975) • MCA (S) 1660 8-10   Re
  Composer: John Williams. **Conductor:** John Williams. **Cast:** John Williams and His Orchestra.

JAWS 2
Soundtrack (1978) • MCA (S) 3045 8-15   78
  Composer: John Williams. **Conductor:** John Williams. **Cast:** John Williams and His Orchestra.

JAWS 3-D
Soundtrack (1983) • MCA (S) 6124 8-15   83
  Composer: Alan Parker. **Conductor:** Alan Parker.

JAZZ AGE
TV Soundtrack • Project XX (S) F8-MP-0935 20-25
  Produced by NBC-TV.
  Cast: Robert Russell Bennett.

JAZZ DANCE
Soundtrack • Jaguar (EP) EP-801 50-60
Soundtrack • Jaguar (S) JP-801 100-125
  10-inch LP.
  Cast: Pee Wee Russell, Jimmy McPartland, Jimmy Archey, Pops Foster, George Wettling, Willie "The Lion" Smith.

JAZZ SINGER (1953)
Studiotrack (1953) • Decca (EP) EPB-3118 15-20   53
  Two discs.
Studiotrack (1953) • Decca (EP) ED-2003 15-20   53
  Composer: Various. **Conductor:** Gordon Jenkins. **Cast:** Peggy Lee, Gordon Jenkins with His Chorus and Orchestra.
Studiotrack (1953) • RCA Victor (EP) EPB-3118 10-20   53
  Two discs.
Studiotrack (1953) • RCA Victor (M) LPM-3118 25-35   53
  10-inch LP.
  Composer: Sammy Fain, Peggy Lee, Jerry Seelen, others. **Conductor:** Frank DeVol. **Cast:** Danny Thomas.

JAZZ SINGER (1980)
Soundtrack (1980) • Capitol (S) SWAV-12120 8-10   80
Soundtrack (1980) • Capitol (S) R-132877 8-10   Re
  Composer: Neil Diamond. **Conductor:** Neil Diamond. **Cast:** Neil Diamond, Sir Laurence Olivier, Lucie Arnaz, Catlin Adams.

JAZZ THEMES FOR COPS AND ROBBERS: see PRIVATE HELL 36

JAZZ TRACK
Soundtrack • Columbia (M) CL-1268 15-20
Soundtrack • Columbia (S) KCL-1268 20-25
  One side has music from French film *Elevator to the Scaffold*.
  Composer: Miles Davis. **Cast:** Miles Davis, John Coltrane.

JEAN DE FLORETTE
Soundtrack (1986) • TVT (S) 3004 15-20   86
  Composer: Jean-Claude Petit. **Conductor:** Jean-Claude Petit.

JEANETTE MACDONALD AND NELSON EDDY
Studiotrack • RCA Victor (M) LPV-526 20-25   66
  Full title: *Nostalgic Recordings of Music From Their Golden Years In Hollywood*. Vocals from *Rose Marie, Maytime, Naughty Marietta, Girl of the Golden West, Sweethearts, New Moon, Bitter Sweet, I Married an Angel, Song of Love*.
  Cast: Jeanette MacDonald, Nelson Eddy.

Soundtrack • Sandy Hook (M) 3SH1 15-20
   Boxed, three-disc set. Full title: *Original Soundtrack Recordings*. Music from six films.
   Cast: Jeanette MacDonald, Nelson Eddy.

JEANNE EAGLES
Soundtrack (1957) • Decca (M) DL-8574 30-70   57
   Full title: *This Is Kim as Jeanne Eagles*. Music from the film and other traditional pop
   themes associated with Kim Novak.
   Composer: George Duning. **Conductor:** Morris Stoloff.

JEEVES
Original London Cast (1975) • MCA (S) 2726 150-250   75
   UK release.
   Composer: Andrew Lloyd Webber, Alan Ayckbourn.

JEKYLL AND HYDE
Original Cast (1990) • London (S) 21137 10-15   90

JENNIE
Original Cast (1963) • RCA Victor (M) LOC-1083 15-20   63
Original Cast (1963) • RCA Victor (S) LSO-1083 35-45   63
   Composer: Arthur Schwartz, Howard Dietz. **Conductor:** John Lesko. **Cast:** Mary Martin,
   George Wallace, Ethel Shutta, Jack DeLon, Robin Bailey.

JEREMIAH JOHNSON
Soundtrack (1972) • Warner Bros. (S) BS-2902................................... 12-18   72
   Composer: John Rubenstein, Tim McIntire.

JEREMY
Soundtrack (1973) • United Artists (S) UA-LA145-G 10-15   73
   Composer: Lee Holdridge, Joseph Brooks, Dorothea Joyce. **Conductor:** Lee Holdridge. **Cast:**
   Robby Benson, Glynnis O'Connor.

JEREMY O'BRIAN
Original Cast (1972) • Sentry Custom (S) USR-5711 10-15   72
   Full title: *Academy D Presents Jeremy O'Brian*.

JERICO-JIM CROW
Original Cast (1964) • Folkways (M) FL-9671 15-20   64
   Two discs.
   Composer: Langston Hughes, Paul Campbell. **Conductor:** Hugh Porter. **Cast:** Gilbert Price,
   Micki Grant, Rosalie King, Joseph Attles, Dorothy Drake, William Cain, Hugh Porter Gospel
   Singers, Metrogene Myles.

JEROME KERN GOES TO HOLLYWOOD
London Cast (1986) • Safari (S) 86 8-10
   Composer: Jerome Kern, Bernard Dougall, Dorothy Fields, Ira Gershwin, Oscar Hammerstein
   II, Otto Harbach, Jimmy McHugh, Johnny Mercer, M.E. Rourke, P.G. Wodehouse. **Conductor:**
   Clive Chaplin. **Cast:** Elaine Delmar, David Kernan, Liz Robertson, Elisabeth Welch.

JEROME KERN IN LONDON
Original Cast • Manmouth (S) MES 7064 10-15
   Composer: Jerome Kern.

JEROME KERN REVISITED
Studio Cast • Columbia (M) OL-6440 10-15
   Composer: Jerome Kern.

JEROME MOROSS: see WELLES RAISES KANE

JEROME ROBBINS' BROADWAY
Original Cast (1988) • RCA Victor (S) 60150-1-RC 12-15   88
   Boxed, two-disc set. Includes 63-page booklet. Music from various Robbins musicals.
   Conductor: Paul Gemignani. **Cast:** Jason Alexander, Robert La Fosse, Susann Fletcher, Nancy
   Hess, Susan Kikuchi, Michael Kubala, Jane Lanier, Joey McKneely, Luis Perez, Faith Prince,
   Debbie Shapiro, Scott Wise, Charlotte d'Amboise.

JERRY'S GIRLS

Original Cast (1984) • Polydor (S) 820207-1 8-10   84
Original Cast (1984) • That's Entertainment (S) TER2-1093 8-10   80s
  UK release.
    Composer: Jerry Herman. **Conductor:** Janet Glazenar. **Cast:** Carol Channing, Leslie Uggams,
    Andrea McArdle, Ellyn Arons, Deborah Graham, Jerry Herman, Suzanne Ishee, Diane Myron,
    Laura Soltis, Helena-Joyce Wright.

JESSICA

Soundtrack (1962) • United Artists (M) UAL-4096 12-18   62
Soundtrack (1962) • United Artists (S) UAS-5096 15-20   62
    Composer: Mario Nascimbene, Marguerite Monnot, others. **Cast:** Maurice Chevalier.

JESUS CHRIST SUPERSTAR

Original Cast (1971) • Decca (S) DXSA-7206 25-30   71
  Boxed, two-disc set. Made before production of the stage show. Includes 28-page program
  booklet. Some covers have "DXA" prefix.
Original Recording (1971) • Decca (S) DXSA-7206 20-25   71
  Two discs in gatefold cover (no box). Made before production of the stage show. Includes a
  28-page program booklet.
Original Recording (1971) • MCA (S) MCA2-10000 10-12   73
  Two discs in gatefold cover. Includes insert.
    Composer: Andrew Lloyd Webber, Tim Rice. **Conductor:** Alan Doggett, Andrew Lloyd Webber.
    Cast: Murray Head, Ian Gillan, Yvonne Elliman, Brian Keith, Mike D'Abo, Paul Raven, Barry
    Dennen, Victor Brox, John Gustafson, Paul Davis, City of London Ensemble, others.
Original Cast (1971) • Decca (S) DL-71503 15-20   71
Original Cast (1971) • MCA (S) 5000 10-12   72
    Composer: Andrew Lloyd Webber, Tim Rice. **Conductor:** Marc Pressel. **Cast:** Ben Vereen, Jeff
    Fenholt, Yvonne Elliman, Barry Dennen, Paul Ainsley, Bob Bingham, Phil Jethro, Steven Bell,
    Alan Braunstein, Michael Meadows.
Original London Cast (1971) • Decca (EP) No Number Used 20-30   71
  Boxed set of four stereo discs. Promotional issue only.
Original London Cast (1971) • MCA (S) 2503 25-30   71
    Composer: Andrew Lloyd Webber, Tim Rice. **Conductor:** Anthony Bowles. **Cast:** Paul Nichols,
    Stephen Tate, Dana Gillespie, John Parker.
London Studio Cast (1971) • Pickwick (S) SPC-3262 10-12   71
    Composer: Andrew Lloyd Webber, Tim Rice. **Cast:** Mike Trounce, Martin Jay, Michael Allen,
    Jenny Mason.
Studio Cast • Springboard (S) SP-4000 8-10
    Composer: Andrew Lloyd Webber, Tim Rice. **Conductor:** Nick Ingram.
Soundtrack (1973) • MCA (S) MCA2-11000 10-12   73
  Two discs. Includes two-page lyric sheet.
    Composer: Andrew Lloyd Webber, Tim Rice. **Conductor:** Andre Previn. **Cast:** Ted Neeley, Carl
    Anderson, Yvonne Elliman, Barry Dennen, Bob Bingham, Larry Marshall, Joshua Mostel, Kurt
    Yaghjian.
Studiotrack • Ambassador (S) S-98103... 8-10
  Also has music from *Tommy* and *Godspell.*
    Cast: Sweet Peace.
Studiotrack • Columbia (S) C-31042 8-12
    Cast: Percy Faith and His Orchestra and Chorus.

JESUS OF NAZARETH

TV Soundtrack (1977) • RCA Victor (S) CBL3-3929 20-25   81
  Three discs. Though the film premiered in April 1977, the album didn't come out until 1981.
    Composer: Maurice Jarre. **Conductor:** Maurice Jarre. **Cast:** National Philharmonic Orchestra.
    (With dialogue.)
TV Soundtrack (1982) • RCA Victor (S) ABL1-4284.............................. 8-12   82
    Composer: Maurice Jarre. **Conductor:** Maurice Jarre.

JETSONS: THE MOVIE

Soundtrack (1990) • MCA (S) MCA-6431 12-15   90
    Cast: XXL, Shane Sutton, Tiffany, Steve McClintock, Gayle Rose, John Duarte, Stunners.

TV Soundtrack • Columbia Special Products (S) P-13903 8-10   77

JEWEL IN THE CROWN

TV Soundtrack (1985) • Chrysalis (S) CDL-1465 10-15   85
  Gatefold cover.

TV Soundtrack (1985) • Chrysalis (S) FV-41465.............................. 10-15   85
  14-part series, produced by Granada Television.
    Composer: George Fenton. **Conductor:** Anthony Randall, Booker Isobel Griffiths.

JEWEL OF THE NILE

Soundtrack (1985) • Jive/Arista (S) JL9-8406 10-15   85
    Composer: Jack Nitzsche, others. **Cast:** Billy Ocean, Ruby Turner, Hugh Masekela and
    Jonathan Butler, Willesden Dodgers, Whodini, Precious Wilson, Mark Shreeve, Nubians, Jack
    Nitzsche.

JIMI HENDRIX

Soundtrack (1973) • Reprise (S) 2RS-6481 15-25   73
  Two discs.
    Composer: Jimi Hendrix, others. **Cast:** Jimi Hendrix. (Includes music and interviews.)

JIMI PLAYS MONTEREY

Soundtrack • Reprise (S) 1-25358 8-10
    Cast: Jimi Hendrix.

JIMMY

Original Cast (1969) • RCA Victor (S) LSO-1162 12-18   69
    Composer: Bill Jacob, Patti Jacob. **Conductor:** Milton Rosenstock. **Cast:** Frank Gorshin, Anita
    Gillette, Julie Wilson, Jack Collins, William Griffis, Dorothy Claire, Paul Forrest, Edward Becker,
    Carol Conte, Clifford Fearl, Henry Lawrence, Stanley Simmonds, Evan Thompson.

JIMMY DURANTE TV SHOW

TV Soundtrack (1955) • Royale (M) 1812 60-80   55
  10-inch LP.
    Conductor: Louis Prima. **Cast:** Jimmy Durante, Eddie Jackson, Paul Douglas, Lilyann Carne.

JINGLE JANGLE

Original London Cast • That's Entertainment (S) JJ-1093 8-10   80s
  UK release.
    Composer: Geoff Morrow, Hal Shaper. **Cast:** Norman Wisdom.

JO JO DANCER, YOUR LIFE IS CALLING

Soundtrack (1986) • Warner Bros. (SP) 11-25444 8-10   86
    Composer: Various. **Cast:** Herbie Hancock, O'Jays, Gladys Knight and the Pips, Mahalia
    Jackson, Muddy Waters, Spinners, Chaka Khan, Junior Walker and the All Stars, Marvin Gaye.

JOAN

Original Cast (1971) • Judson (S) JU-1001 120-130   71
  Two discs.
    Composer: Al Carmines. **Conductor:** Al Carmines. **Cast:** Joe Cecil, Julie Kurnitz, Phyllis
    MacBryde, Tracy Moore, Sandy Padilla, Ira Siff, Margaret Wright, Lee Guilliant, Emily Adams,
    Jeffrey Apter, David Vaughan, Al Carmines (piano), Essie Borden, Tony Clark, Teresa King.

JOAN CRAWFORD

Soundtrack • Curtain Calls (M) CC 100/23.. 20-25
  Previously unreleased songs from *Untamed, Hollywood Revue of 1929, Montana Moon,*
  Dancing Lady, Mannequin, Ice Follies of 1939, Flamingo Road, Torch Song and others.
  Part of the *Silver Screen Star Series,* and the scarcest entry in that series.
    Composer: Various. **Conductor:** Various. **Cast:** Joan Crawford, Robert Montgomery, Conrad
    Nagel, Art Jarrett, Fred Astaire, Greer Garson, Fred MacMurray, India Adams (performs vocals for
    Joan Crawford in *Torch Song*), Marjorie Rambeau.

JOANNA

Soundtrack (1968) • 20th Century-Fox (S) S-4202................................. 8-12   68
  Composer: Rod McKuen. **Conductor:** Arthur Greenslade. **Cast:** Rod McKuen, Michael Sarne, Barbara Kay.

JOE

Soundtrack (1970) • Mercury (S) SRM1-605.. 10-12   70
Soundtrack (1970) • Mercury (S) SRM1-607.. 12-15   70
  Full title: *Joe Speaks*. Dialogue and music from the soundtrack.
  Composer: Bobby Scott. **Conductor:** Bobby Scott. **Cast:** Jerry Butler, Dean Michaels, Exuma, Peter Boyle, Dennis Patrick. (With dialogue.)

JOE COCKER: MAD DOGS AND ENGLISHMEN

Soundtrack (1970) • A&M (S) SP-6002 10-15   70
  The *Mad Dogs and Englishmen* tour film came out in 1971.
  Cast: Joe Cocker, Leon Russell, Rita Coolidge, Chris Stainton, others.

JOE LOUIS STORY

Soundtrack (1953) • MGM (EP) X-221 20-50   53
  Two discs.
Soundtrack (1953) • MGM (M) E-221 50-70   53
  10-inch LP.
  Composer: George Bassman, others. **Conductor:** George Bassman.

JOE PALOOKA

Original Radio Cast • Mark 56 (M) 663... 20-40   70s
  Picture disc.

JOE SPEAKS: see JOE

JOHN AND MARY

Soundtrack (1970) • A&M (S) SP-4230 12-18   70
  Adaptations of compositions by Johann Sebastian Bach, Wolfgang Amadeus Mozart, Felix Mendelssohn and George Frideric Handel.
  Composer: Quincy Jones, Alan and Marilyn Bergman, others. **Conductor:** Quincy Jones. **Cast:** Evie Sands, Strange Things, Jeff Bridges, Morgan Ames Singers.

JOHN BARRY

Studiotrack (1966) • Capitol (M) T-2527 15-20   66
Studiotrack (1966) • Capitol (S) ST-2527 15-25   66
  Full title: *John Barry Plays Film and TV Themes.*
  Composer: John Barry. **Conductor:** John Barry.
Studiotrack (1966) • Columbia (M) CL-2493.. 10-15   66
Studiotrack (1966) • Columbia (S) CS-9293.. 15-20   66
  Full title: *John Barry Plays His Great Movie Themes.* Includes: *Thunderball, 007 (From Russia with Love), The James Bond Theme (Dr. No), The Chase, Theme from King Rat, The Knack, Seance on a Wet Afternoon, The Ipcress File* and *Born Free.*
Studiotrack (1968) • Columbia (M) CL-2708.. 15-20   68
Studiotrack (1968) • Columbia (S) CS-9508.. 20-25   68
  Full title: *John Barry Conducts His Greatest Movie Hits.*
  Conductor: John Barry, Monty Norman.
Studiotrack (1970) • Columbia (S) CS-1003.. 10-15   70
  Full title: *Ready When You Are, J.B.*
  Composer: John Barry. **Conductor:** John Barry.
  Also see CONCERT JOHN BARRY

JOHN BROWN'S BODY

Original Cast (1953) • Columbia (M) OSL-181 20-25   53
  Boxed, two-disc set.
  Composer: Walter Schumann. **Conductor:** Walter Schumann. **Cast:** Tyrone Power, Judith Anderson, Raymond Massey, Betty Benson, Roger Miller.

TV Soundtrack (1962) • A.D.L. (M) XTV 87288/87289 50-75   62
  Composer: George Kleinsinger. **Cast:** Richard Boone, Douglas Campbell.

JOHN F. KENNEDY

TV & Radio Cast (1963) • Colpix (M) CP-2500 50-60   64
  Actual title: *Four Days That Shocked the World (Nov. 22-25, 1963 – The Complete Story.*
  Cast: John F. Kennedy (dialogue).

TV Studiotrack (1963) • Columbia (M) L2L-1017 15-20   63
  Full title: *John Fitzgerald Kennedy As We Remember Him.*
  Cast: John F. Kennedy (dialogue).

TV Studiotrack (1963) • Continental (M) 770 10-15   63
  Actual title: *Memorial Tribute: Ask Not What Your Country Can Do for Your, Ask What You
  Can Do for Your Country.* Speeches and excerpts from "Oath of Office," "Inaugural
  Address," "Speech on Berlin," "Speech on the Cuban Crisis," "Fort Worth Speech," and
  "Last Speech, Dallas, Texas." Issued with two different back cover pictures. Same album
  as Universal MS-197.

TV Studiotrack (1963) • Decca (M) DL-2500 10-20   63

TV Studiotrack (1963) • Decca (M) DL-9116 10-20   63

TV Studiotrack (1963) • Decca (S) DL-79116 15-20   63
  Actual title: *That Was the Week That Was.* From a British Broadcasting telecast, November
  23, 1963.
  Composer: Herbert Kretzmer, Dave Lee, Caryl Brahms. **Conductor:** Dave Lee. **Cast:** David
  Frost, David Kernan, Kenneth Cope, Lance Percival, Millicent Martin, Roy Kinnear, Al Mancini,
  William Rushton, Robert Lang, Dame Sybil Thorndike, Bernard Levin.

TV Studiotrack (1963) • Decca (S) DL-72500 10-20   63
  Cast: John F. Kennedy (dialogue).

TV Studiotrack (1963) • Diplomat (M) 1000 10-15   63
  Label may be either burgandy or white.
  Cast: John F. Kennedy (dialogue).

TV Studiotrack (1963) • Documentaries Unlimited (M) Vol. 1 10-20   63
  Full title: *J.F.K., the Man, the President.*
  Cast: John F. Kennedy (dialogue), Barry Gray (narrator).

TV Studiotrack (1963) • Harmonica (M) HLP-3005 10-20   63
  Actual title: *Kennedy Speaks.*
  Cast: John F. Kennedy (dialogue).

TV Studiotrack (1963) • Pickwick (M) DLP-169 8-12   63
  Actual title: *The Presidential Years (1960 - 1963).* Reissue of 20th Century-Fox release.

Radio Studiotrack (1963) • Premier (M) 2099 10-20   63
  White label. Actual title: *Highlights of (Kennedy) Speeches.* Memorial tribute broadcast by
  WMCA, New York, November 22, 1963.
  Cast: John F. Kennedy (dialogue), Ed Brown (narrator).

TV Studiotrack (1963) • Premier (M) 2099 10-15   63
  Same as above except black label.

TV Studiotrack (1963) • Somerset (M) P-16100 10-20   63
  Labeled *United States' Presidents' Speeches*, has speeches by John F. Kennedy and
  Franklin D. Roosevelt.
  Cast: John F. Kennedy, Franklin D. Roosevelt. (With dialogue.)

TV Studiotrack (1963) • 20th Century-Fox (M) TMF 3127 10-20   63
  Actual title: *The Presidential Years (1960 - 1963).*
  Cast: John F. Kennedy (dialogue), David Teig (narrator).

TV Studiotrack (1963) • Universal (M) MS 197 10-15   63
  Actual title *Memorial Tribute: Ask Not What Your Country Can Do for Your, Ask What You
  Can Do for Your Country.* Speeches and excerpts from "Oath of Office," "Inaugural
  Address," "Speech on Berlin," "Speech on the Cuban Crisis," "Fort Worth Speech," and
  "Last Speech, Dallas, Texas." Same album as Continental 770.
  Cast: John F. Kennedy (dialogue).

TV Studiotrack (1964) • RCA Victor (M) VDM-101 10-20   64
  Actual title: *The Kennedy Wit.*
  Cast: John F. Kennedy (dialogue).
Studiotrack • Ebony (M) No Number Used 10-15
  Full title: *John F. Kennedy and the Negro.* Produced by Ebony Magazine. Civil rights-
  related speeche excerpts.
  Cast: John F. Kennedy (dialogue).
Assembled Cast (1963) • RCA Victor (M) LMM-7030 10-20   63
  Labeled *Pontifical Requiem* (Mozart Requiem).
  Cast: Cardinal Cushing, Boston Symphony and Choir.
Studiotrack (1963) • Reprise (M) R-6199 10-15   65
  Cast: Tom Lehrer.
  Also see YEARS OF LIGHTNING, DAY OF DRUMS

JOHN PAUL JONES
Soundtrack (1959) • Warner Bros. (M) W-1293 50-60   59
Soundtrack (1959) • Warner Bros. (S) WS-1293 90-110   59
Soundtrack (1959) • Varese Sarabande (S) STV-81146 12-18   81
  Composer: Max Steiner. **Conductor:** Muir Mathieson.

JOHN WAYNE: see DIGITAL PREMIERE RECORDINGS FROM THE FILMS OF JOHN WAYNE

JOHN WILLIAMS ORCHESTRA PLAYS SOUNDS FROM SCREEN SPECTACULARS
Studiotrack (1957) • Craftsmen (M) C-8043 15-25   57
  Reissued as *Big Hits from Columbia Pictures*
  Composer: Various. **Cast:** John T. Williams and the Hollywood Grand Studio Orchestra.
  Also see BIG HITS FROM COLUMBIA PICTURES

JOHN WILLIAMS' SYMPHONIC SUITES
Studiotrack (1982) • EMI-Angel (S) RL-32109 10-20   82
  Full title: *John Williams' Symphonic Suites of Music from E.T. The Extraterrestrial, Close
  Encounters of the Third Kind, Star Wars.*
  Composer: John Williams. **Cast:** Frank Barber and the London Symphony Orchestra, National
  Philharmonic Orchestra.

JOHNNY APPLESEED
Studiotrack (1948) • RCA Victor Y-390 35-40   49
  Album of three 78 rpms.
Studiotrack (1948) • Camden (M) CAL-1054 15-20   64
Studiotrack (1948) • Camden (SE) CAS-1054 5-10   64
  One side has music from *Pecos Bill.*
  Composer: Walter Kent. **Conductor:** Ken Darby. **Cast:** Dennis Day (narration, vocals). PECOS
  BILL: **Cast:** Roy Rogers, Sons of the Pioneers.
Studio Cast (1964) • Disneyland (M) DQ-1260 15-20
  Composer: Kim Gannon, Walter Kent. **Cast:** Dennis Day.

JOHNNY B. GOODE
Soundtrack (1986) • Capitol (S) MLP-15022 10-12   86

JOHNNY BE GOOD
Soundtrack (1988) • Atlantic (S) 81837-1 8-10   88
  Composer: Jay Ferguson. **Cast:** Frozen Ghost and Friends, Bernie Shanahan, Dirty Looks,
  Judas Priest, Myles Goodwyn, Kix, Fiona, John Astley, Saga, Ted Nugent.

JOHNNY CONCHO

Soundtrack (1956) • Capitol (EP) EAP 1-754 30-60   56
    Composer: Nelson Riddle, Doc Stanford. **Conductor:** Nelson Riddle. **Cast:** Nelson Riddle and
    His Orchestra.

JOHNNY COOL

Soundtrack (1963) • United Artists (M) UAL-4111 15-20   63
Soundtrack (1963) • United Artists (S) UAS-5111 20-25   63
Soundtrack (1963) • Ascot (M) ALM-13012 15-20   64
Soundtrack (1963) • Ascot (S) ALS-16012 20-25   64
    Also has jazz selections from *Odds Against Tomorrow, I Want to Live, The Misfits* and
    Paris Blues.
Soundtrack (1961) • United Artists (S) UA-LA273-G 10-12   74
    Reissue of Ascot ALS-16012.
    Composer: Alex North. **Conductor:** Alex North. **Cast:** Sammy Davis Jr.
    Also see BIG COUNTRY

JOHNNY GREEN ON THE HOLLYWOOD SOUNDSTAGE

Studiotrack • MGM (M) E-3694 20-25
    Composer: Various. **Conductor:** Johnny Green. **Cast:** MGM Symphony Orchestra.

JOHNNY GUITAR

Soundtrack (1954) • Citadel (M) CIT-7026 15-20   81
    Composer: Victor Young. **Conductor:** Victor Young.

JOHNNY HANDSOME

Soundtrack (1989) • Warner Bros. (S) 1-25996 8-10   89
    Composer: Ry Cooder.

JOHNNY JOHNSON

Studio Cast (1936) • MGM (M) E-3447 40-50   55
Studio Cast (1936) • Heliodor (M) H-25024 10-12   66
Studio Cast (1936) • Heliodor (SE) HS-25024 10-15   66
Studio Cast (1936) • Polydor (SE) 831384 8-10   86
    Composer: Kurt Weill, Paul Green. **Conductor:** Samuel Matlowsky. **Cast:** Burgess Meredith,
    Hiram Sherman, Evelyn Lear, Lotte Lenya, Thomas Stewart, Jane Connell, Scott Merrill, Jean
    Sanders, Bob Shaver, William Malten.

JOHNNY THE PRIEST

Original London Cast • That's Entertainment (S) TERS-1044 8-10   80s
    UK release.
    Composer: Peter Powell.

JOHNNY TREMAIN

Soundtrack (1957) • Disneyland (M) WDL-4014 45-50   57
    One side, titled *Songs of Our Soldiers,* has assorted soldier-related selections.
    Composer: George Bruns. **Conductor:** George Bruns.

JOLLY THEATRICAL SEASON

Studio Cast (1963) • Capitol (M) T-1862 10-15   63
Studio Cast (1963) • Capitol (S) ST-1862 15-20   63
    Composer: Various. **Cast:** Robert Morse, Charles Nelson Reilly.

JOLSON REVUE

Original Cast (1975) • Sunset (S) 50426 10-15   75

JOLSON SINGS AGAIN

Studiotrack • Decca (M) DLP-5006 15-20   49
    10-inch LP.
    Composer: Various. **Conductor:** Morris Stoloff, Matty Matlock. **Cast:** Al Jolson, Morris Stoloff
    and His Orchestra, Matty Matlock and His Orchestra, Four Hits and a Miss, Lee Gordon Singers.

JONATHAN LIVINGSTON SEAGULL

Studio Cast (1973) • Dunhill (S) DSD-50160 10-12   73
  From a book by Richard Bach, told by Richard Harris.
    Composer: Terry James. **Conductor:** Terry James. **Cast:** Richard Harris (narration).

Soundtrack (1973) • Columbia (S) KS-32550 10-12   73

Soundtrack (1973) • Columbia (S) HS-42550 20-25   81
  Half-speed mastered. Includes 12-page booklet.

Soundtrack (1973) • Columbia (S) JS-32550 8-10   Re
    Composer: Neil Diamond. **Cast:** Neil Diamond.

Soundtrack (1973) • Varese Sarabande (S) VC-81081 10-15   78
    Cast: Lee Holdridge.

Studiotrack (1974) • Pickwick (S) SPC 3369 5-10   74

JONNY QUEST

TV Soundtrack (1965) • Hanna Barbera (M) HLP-2030 40-50   65
    Composer: Hoyt Curtian.

JOPLIN, SCOTT: see SCOTT JOPLIN

JOSE MELIS ON BROADWAY

Studiotrack • Mercury (M) MG 20610 5-10

Studiotrack • Mercury (S) SR 60610 10-15
  Has songs from *My Fair Lady, West Side Story, Kiss Me Kate, Most Happy Fella, Gypsy, Bells Are Ringing, Out of This World, Brigadoon, The King and I, Sound of Music, Music Man* and *Kismet.*
    Cast: Jose Melis.

JOSE MELIS PLAYS JACK PAAR'S FAVORITES

Studiotrack • Seeco (S) CELP-4620 10-12
    Cast: Jose Melis.

JOSEPH AND THE AMAZING TECHNICOLOR DREAMCOAT

Original Recording (1968) • Scepter (S) SPS-588X 12-18   68
  Gatefold cover with libretto insert.

Original Recording (1968) • Scepter/Capitol (S) SMAS 93738 8-12   Re
  Recorded before the London show. First performed in 1968 at the Colet Court School in England.
    Composer: Andrew Lloyd Webber. **Conductor:** Alan Doggett. **Cast:** Terry Saunders, David Daltrey, Malcolm Parry, Tim Rice, John Cook, Bryan Watson, Colet Court Choir, Joseph Consortium, Dr. W.S. Lloyd Webber (organ), Martin Wilcox (harpsichord).

Original Cast (1982) • Chrysalis (S) CHR-1387 8-10   82

Original Cast (1982) • Chrysalis (S) PV41387 8-10   Re
    Composer: Andrew Lloyd Webber, Tim Rice. **Conductor:** David Friedman. **Cast:** David Ardao, Laurie Beechman, Kenneth Bryan, Tom Carder, Bill Hutton, Robert Hyman, Randon Lo, Steve McNaughton, Charlie Serrano, Gordon Stanley, Barry Tarallo.

Studio Cast (1973) • MCA (S) 399 8-10   73
  First recording of the revised complete work. (Has original London cast stars.)
    Composer: Andrew Lloyd Webber, Tim Rice. **Conductor:** Chris Hamelcooke. **Cast:** Gary Bond, Peter Reeves, Maynard Williams, Gordon Waller, Roger Watson.

JOSEPH ANDREWS

Soundtrack (1977) • Tony Thomas (S) TT-JA-2 25-35   77
  Private recording.
    Composer: John Addison. **Conductor:** John Addison.

JOSEPH McCARTHY IS ALIVE AND WELL AND LIVING IN DADE COUNTY

Original Cast (1977) • AEI (S) AEI-1103 8-10   77
    Composer: Ray Scantlin. **Cast:** Paul Baccus, Kim Brassner, Mary Jo Gillis, Amanda McBroom, Hal James Pederson, Jay Pevney, Daniel Trent, Gerrard Wagner, Alfred Wilson, Dennis Wood.

JOSEPHINE BAKER SHOW
Original Cast (1961) • RCA Victor (M) LPM-2427 20-25   61
Original Cast (1961) • RCA Victor (S) LSP-2427 30-40   61
   Conductor: Joe Bouillon. **Cast:** Josephine Baker.

JOSIE AND THE PUSSYCATS
TV Soundtrack (1970) • Capitol (S) ST-665 100-150   70
   Composer: Danny Janssen, Bobby Hart, Austin Roberts. **Cast:** Cathy Dougher, Patrice
   Holloway, Cherie Moor (a.k.a. Cheryl Ladd).

JOURNEY BACK TO OZ
TV Soundtrack (1974) • Filmation (S) No Number Used 30-50   80
   From the TV special presented by Texize.

TV Soundtrack (1974) • RFO (S) RFO-101 65-70   80
   Actual title of LP is *The Return to Oz,* which is an error. From the TV special *Journey Back
   to Oz.*
   Composer: Sammy Cahn, James Van Heusen. **Conductor:** Walter Scharf. **Cast:** Liza Minnelli,
   Jack E. Leonard, Herschel Bernardi, Mickey Rooney, Ethel Merman, Danny Thomas, Milton
   Berle, Paul Lynde, Risë Stevens.

JOURNEY INTO FEAR: see DEAD

JOURNEY THROUGH THE PAST
Soundtrack (1972) • Warner Bros. (S) 2XS-6480 12-15   72
   Two discs.
   Composer: Neil Young, others. **Cast:** Neil Young.

JOURNEY TO THE CENTER OF THE EARTH (1959)
Soundtrack (1959) • Dot (EP) DEP-1091 25-30   59
   Cast: Pat Boone.
   Also see FANTASY FILM WORLD OF BERNARD HERRMANN

JOURNEY TO THE CENTER OF THE EARTH (1974)
Original Cast (1974) • A&M (S) SP-3621 10-15   74
   Includes poster.

Original Cast (1974) • A&M (Q) QU-53621 20-25   74
   Includes booklet.
   Composer: Rick Wakeman. **Conductor:** David Measham. **Cast:** David Hemmings (narration),
   Rick Wakeman, Garry Pickford-Hopkins, Ashley Holt, Mike Egan, Roger Newell, Barney James,
   John Cleary, English Chamber Choir, others.

JOURNEY TO THE MOON
TV Broadcast • Buddah (S) BDS-5045 15-20   69
   From broadcasts made by moon landing expedition.

JOURNEY WITHIN
Soundtrack (1969) • Atlantic (S) SD 1519 10-15   69
   Composer: Charles Lloyd. **Cast:** Charles Lloyd, Keith Jarrett.

JOY
Original Cast (1970) • RCA Victor (S) LSO-1166 5-10   70
   Composer: Oscar Brown Jr., Luiz Henrique, others. **Conductor:** Sivuca. **Cast:** Oscar Brown Jr.,
   Jean Pace, Sivuca, Norman Shobey.

JOYCE GRENFELL REQUESTS THE PLEASURE
Original Cast (1955) • Philips (M) BBL-7004 30-40
   UK release.

Original Cast (1955) • DRG (M) SL-5186 8-10   Re
   Composer: Joyce Grenfell, Richard Addinsell. **Conductor:** William Blizard. **Cast:** Joyce
   Grenfell, Beryl Kaye, Paddy Stone, Irving Davies.

JOYFUL NOISE

Original Cast (1966) • Blue Pear (M) BP-1018 20-50

Composer: Oscar Brand, Paul Nausseau. **Cast:** John Raitt, Karen Morrow, Susan Watson, Swen Swenson.

JOYRIDE

Soundtrack (1977) • United Artists (S) UA-LA-784-H 8-15   77

Composer: Barry Mann, Jimmie Haskell, others. **Cast:** Electric Light Orchestra, Barry Mann.

JUBALAY

Original Cast (1974) • Jubalay Productions (S) JP-9001 55-65   74

Canadian musical which later emerged off-Broadway as *Bistro Car*.

Composer: Patrick Rose, Merv Campone. **Cast:** Patrick Rose, Diane Stapley, Ruth Nichol, Brent Carver.

Also see BISTRO CAR

JUD

Soundtrack (1971) • Ampex (S) A-50101 15-20   71

Composer: Stu Phillips, Bob Dylan, others. **Cast:** John Hartford, American Breed, Mason Proffit, Crow, Barbara Robison.

JUDGMENT AT NUREMBERG

Soundtrack (1961) • United Artists (M) UAL-4095 15-18   61

Soundtrack (1961) • United Artists (S) UAS-5095 35-45   61

Soundtrack (1961) • MCA (S) 39055 8-10   86

Composer: Ernest Gold. **Conductor:** Ernest Gold. **Cast:** Spencer Tracy, Burt Lancaster, Maximilian Schell. (With dialogue.)

Also see HORSE SOLDIERS

JUDITH

Soundtrack (1966) • RCA Victor (M) LOC-1119 12-15   66

Soundtrack (1966) • RCA Victor (S) LSO-1119 20-30   66

Composer: Sol Kaplan. **Conductor:** Sol Kaplan.

JUDY AT CARNEGIE HALL

Original Cast (1961) • Capitol (EP) EAP 1-1569 10-15   61

Original Cast (1961) • Capitol (M) WBO-1569 12-15   61

Original Cast (1961) • Capitol (S) SWBO-1569 12-18   61

Above two LPs are two-disc sets. "Recorded live and complete, Sunday, April 23, 1961 at 8:30 pm."

Conductor: Mort Lindsey. **Cast:** Judy Garland.

JUDY AT THE PALACE

Studio Cast (1951) • Decca (EP) ED-6020 20-25   51

Two discs.

Studio Cast (1951) • Decca (M) DL-6020 50-60   51

10-inch LP. Though seeming to be a concert album, this is a collection of studio recordings of songs performed during Garland's Palace engagement.

Composer: Harold Arlen, E.Y. Harburg, Roger Edens, James V. Monaco, Joe McCarthy. **Conductor:** Harry Sosnik, Victor Young, George Stoll, David Rose, others. **Cast:** Judy Garland, Gene Kelly.

JUDY GARLAND

Original Cast (1969) • Juno (SE) S-1000 15-20

Actual title: *Judy, London 1969*. Recordings of her last concert performances.

Cast: Judy Garland.

Original Radio Cast • Accessor Pro (Starcast) (M) STCT-1001 15-25

Full title: *Judy Garland, Rare Early Broadcast Performances*. From radio broadcasts 1935-1952.

Cast: Judy Garland.

Original Broadway Cast (1967) • ABC (M) ABC-620 .... 10-15 67
Original Broadway Cast (1967) • ABC (S) ABCS-620 .... 15-25 67
  Actual title: *At Home at the Palace.*
  Conductor: Bobby Cole. **Cast:** Judy Garland, Joe Luft, Lorna Luft.
Soundtrack • MGM (M) E-82 .... 40-60 50s
Soundtrack • MGM (M) E-3149 .... 15-40 55
  Full title of both: *Judy Garland.* Music from *Summer Stock, Till the Clouds Roll By, Words and Music, The Pirate, In the Good Old Summertime.*
  Cast: Judy Garland.
Soundtrack • MGM (SE) F3989P 15-25 62
  Full title: *Judy Garland – The Star Years.* From MGM films (1947-1950).
  Cast: Judy Garland.
Soundtrack • MGM (M) E-4202 .... 10-15 62
Soundtrack • MGM (SE) SE-4202 .... 15-20 62
  Full title: *Very Best of Judy Garland.*
  Cast: Judy Garland.
Soundtrack • MGM (SE) PX-102 40-60
  Includes poster. Actual title: *Forever Judy.* Music from *Wizard of Oz, Little Nellie Kelly, Meet Me in St. Louis* and other films from 1939-1949. Promotional issue only.
  Cast: Judy Garland.
Soundtrack • MGM (SE) DCLA 1405 20-30
  Actual title: *Forever Judy.* Music from *Wizard of Oz, Little Nellie Kelly, Meet Me in St. Louis* and other films from 1939-1949. Promotional issue only.
  Cast: Judy Garland.
Soundtrack • MGM (M) SDP1-2 20-25
  Two discs. Full title: *Judy Garland: The Golden Years at MGM.* Also has previously unreleased songs.
  Cast: Judy Garland.
TV Soundtrack (1955) • Capitol (M) 676 .... 20-30 55
  Actual title: *Miss Show Business.* From CBS special *Ford Star Jubilee.*
  Cast: Judy Garland.
TV Soundtrack (1963) • Capitol (M) W-2062 .... 20-30 63
  From *The Judy Garland Show.*
  Cast: Judy Garland.
TV Soundtrack • Broadcast Tributes (M) BTRIB 0002 15-25
  Full title: *Greatest Duets – Judy Garland.*
  Cast: Judy Garland, Bobby Darin, Steve Allen, June Allyson, Peggy Lee, Mickey Rooney, Van Johnson, Jane Powell, Ray Bolger, Ethel Merman, Martha Raye.
TV Soundtrack • Paragon (M) 1001 15-25
  Actual title: *Great Garland Duets.*
  Cast: Judy Garland, Count Basie Orchestra, Ethel Merman, Diahann Carroll, Liza Minnelli, Frank Sinatra, Dean Martin, Jack Jones, Barbra Streisand.
TV Soundtrack • Radiant (S) 711-0105 10-15
  Actual title: *The Unforgettable Judy Garland.*
  Cast: Judy Garland, others.

(JUDY) GARLAND AT THE GROVE

Original Cast (195859) • Capitol (M) T-1118 .... 15-25 59
Original Cast (19589) • Capitol (S) ST-1118 .... 20-30 59
  Composer: Various. **Conductor:** Freddy Martin. **Cast:** Judy Garland.

JUDY GARLAND & LIZA MINNELLI LIVE AT THE LONDON PALLADIUM

Original Cast • Capitol (S) SWBO-2295 .... 20-25 65
  Two discs. Unabridged version.
  Cast: Judy Garland, Liza Minnelli.
Original Cast • Capitol (S) ST-11191 .... 10-12 73
  Two discs. Abridged version.
  Cast: Judy Garland, Liza Minnelli.

Original Cast • Mobile Fidelity (S) MFSL-1-048 35-45   81
Audiophile reissue.

JULIA AND JULIA
Soundtrack (1988) • Varese Sarabande (S) STV-81327 8-10   88
Composer: Maurice Jarre. Conductor: Maurice Jarre.

JULIE AND CAROL AT CARNEGIE HALL
Original Cast (1962) • Columbia (S) OL-5840 8-10   62
Original Cast (1962) • Columbia (S) OS-2240 8-12   62
Composer: Robert Allen, Al Stillman, Mike Nichols, Ken Welch. Conductor: Irwin Kostal. Cast: Julie Andrews, Carol Burnett.

JULIE AND CAROL AT LINCOLN CENTER
Original Cast (1971) • Columbia (S) S-31153 12-15   71
Composer: Various. Conductor: Peter Matz. Cast: Julie Andrews, Carol Burnett.

JULIET OF THE SPIRITS
Soundtrack (1965) • Mainstream (M) 56062 18-20   65
Soundtrack (1965) • Mainstream (S) S-6062 40-50   65
Composer: Nino Rota. Conductor: Carlo Savina.

JULIUS CAESAR
Soundtrack (1953) • MGM (EP) X-204 35-40   53
Soundtrack (1953) • MGM (M) E-3033 25-35   53
Soundtrack (1953) • MCA (M) 39055 5-10   86
Composer: Miklos Rozsa. Conductor: Miklos Rozsa. Cast: John Houseman, Marlon Brando, James Mason, Sir John Gielgud, Louis Calhern, Edmond O'Brien, Greer Garson, Deborah Kerr. (With dialogue)

JULIUS CAESAR JONES
Original Cast (1966) • Argo (S) 2RG 529 20-25   66

JUMBO
Studio Cast (1953) • RCA Victor (EP) EPA-479 15-20   53
Composer: Richard Rodgers, Lorenz Hart. Conductor: Lehman Engel. Cast: Lisa Kirk, Jack Cassidy, Jordan Bentley.
Soundtrack (1962) • Columbia (M) OL-5860 10-15   62
Soundtrack (1962) • Columbia (S) OS-2260 15-20   62
Both have gatefold covers. Film version's full title is *Billy Rose's Jumbo.*
Soundtrack (1962) • Columbia Special Products (S) AOS-2260 10-12   Re
Standard cover, which is a blue Columbia Special Products cover.
Soundtrack (1962) • Columbia Special Products (S) AOS-2260 8-10   Re
Standard cover that reproduces original front cover (1962) artwork.
Composer: Richard Rodgers, Lorenz Hart. Conductor: George Stoll. Cast: Doris Day, Stephen Boyd, James Joyce (performed some vocals for Stephen Boyd, although album gives Boyd credit), Jimmy Durante, Martha Raye.
Also see BABES IN ARMS

JUMPIN' JACK FLASH
Soundtrack (1986) • Mercury (S) 830545-1 8-10   86
Cast: Rene and Angela, Bananarama, Kool and the Gang, Gwen Guthrie, Billy Branigan, Rolling Stones, Face to Face, Supremes, Thomas Newman.

JUNGLE BOOK
Studiotrack (1940) • RCA Victor DM 905 50-75   40
Album of four 78 rpms. Adapted from the Alexander Korda Production.
Composer: Miklos Rozsa. Conductor: Miklos Rozsa. Cast: Sabu (narrator), Victor Symphony Orchestra.
Studiotrack (1942) • RCA Victor (M) LM-2118 50-60   57
Actual title: *Rozsa-Kipling's Jungle Book/Thief of Bagdad.*

Studiotrack (1942) • United Artists (M) UAS-29725.............................. 10-15   Re
  Also has music from *Thief of Bagdad*.
    Composer: Miklos Rozsa. **Conductor:** Miklos Rozsa. **Cast:** Leo Genn (narrator).
Studiotrack (1945) • Entr'acte (M) ERM-6002 15-20   79
  Side two has *Enchanted Cottage* and *The Paradine Case*, by Franz Waxman, music
  originally issued on 78 rpm singles.
    Composer: Miklos Rozsa. **Conductor:** Miklos Rozsa. **Cast:** Sabu (narrator). PARADINE CASE:
    Composer: Franz Waxman. **Conductor:** Constantin Bakaleinikoff, Franz Waxman.
    ENCHANTED COTTAGE: **Composer:** Roy Webb.
  Also see FILM MUSIC OF MIKLOS ROZSA

JUNGLE BOOK (1967)
Soundtrack (1967) • Disneyland (M) ST-3948... 12-15   67
Soundtrack (1967) • Disneyland (S) STER-3948 15-20   67
Soundtrack (1967) • Buena Vista (M) BV-4041 10-15   67
Soundtrack (1967) • Buena Vista (S) STER-4041.................................. 15-20   67
Soundtrack (1967) • Disneyland (S) 3105 25-30   81
  Picture disc. Limited edition.
    Composer: Richard M. Sherman, Robert B. Sherman. **Cast:** Louis Prima, Phil Harris, Sterling
    Holloway.

JUNGLE FEVER
Soundtrack (1991) • Motown (S) MOT-6291 10-15   91
    Composer: Stevie Wonder.

JUNGLE JIM
Original Radio Cast • Golden Age (M) 5014.. 8-10   78

JUNIOR MISS: see FOUR TELEVISION MUSICALS

JUNO
Original Cast (1959) • Columbia (M) OL-5380................................. 30-35   59
Original Cast (1959) • Columbia (S) OS-2013................................. 45-65   59
    Composer: Marc Blitzstein. **Conductor:** Robert Emmett Dolan. **Cast:** Shirley Booth, Melvyn
    Douglas, Jack MacGowran, Jean Stapleton, Monte Amundsen, Nancy Andrews, Loren Driscoll,
    Rico Froehlich, Beulah Garrick, Robert Hoyem, Julian Patrick, Arthur Rubin, Robert Rue, Sada
    Thompson.

JUPITER MENACE
Soundtrack (1982) • Passport (S) PB 6014.. 8-10   82
    Composer: Larry Fast. **Cast:** Synergy.

JURASSIC PARK
Soundtrack (1993) • MCA/BMG (S) No Number Shown.................800-1,200   93
  Picture disc. Made in very small quantity for in-house use.

JUST A GIGOLO: see SCHÖNER GIGOLO – ARMER GIGOLO

JUST BETWEEN FRIENDS
Soundtrack (1986) • Warner Bros. (S) 1-25391 8-10   86
    Composer: Pat Williams. **Cast:** Pat Williams, Earl Klugh.

JUST FOR OPENERS
Original Cast (1965) • Upstairs (S) UD-37W56 70-75   65
    Conductor: Michael Cohen. **Cast:** Betty Aberlin, Richard Blair, Madeline Kahn, Fannie Flagg,
    Stockton Brigel, R.G. Brown, Michael Cohen and Edward Morris (twin pianos).

JUST FOR YOU
Studiotrack (1952) • Decca (EP) 9-350 20-35   52
Studiotrack (1952) • Decca (M) DL-5417 50-100   52
  10-inch LP.
    Composer: Harry Warren, Leo Robin. **Conductor:** Van Cleave, Camarata, Dave Barbour, John
    Scott Trotter. **Cast:** Bing Crosby, Jane Wyman, Ben Lessey, Andrews Sisters, Jud Conlon's
    Rhythmaires.

JUST ONE OF THE GUYS
Soundtrack (1985) • Elektra (S) 60426-1 8-10   85
   Composer: Various. **Cast:** Shalamar, Ronnie Spector, Berlin, others.

JUST TELL ME YOU LOVE ME
Soundtrack (1980) • MCA (S) 3255.. 8-10   80
   Cast: England Dan and John Ford Coley.

JUSTINE
Soundtrack (1969) • Monument (S) SLP 18123 20-30   69
   Composer: Jerry Goldsmith, others. **Conductor:** Jerry Goldsmith.

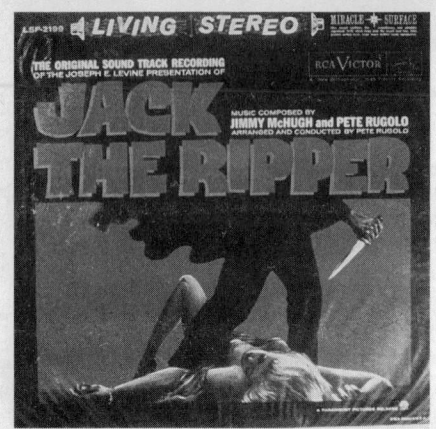

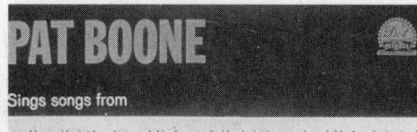

KA-BOOM!
Original Cast (1980) • CYM (S) 8130 8-10   80
   Composer: Joe Ercole, Bruce Kluger. **Conductor:** John Lehman. **Cast:** Ben Agresti, Judith Bro, John Hall, Ken Ward, Valerie Williams, Andrea Wright.

KALEIDOSCOPE
Soundtrack (1966) • Warner Bros. (M) W-1663 12-18   66
Soundtrack (1966) • Warner Bros. (S) WS-1663 15-20   66
   Composer: Stanley Myers. **Conductor:** Stanley Myers.

KAMIKAZE 1989
Soundtrack (1982) • Virgin (S) V 12255 15-20   82
   Composer: Edgar Froese. **Cast:** Edgar Froese.

KARATE KID
Soundtrack (1984) • Casablanca (EP) PRO-293-1 8-15   84
12-inch EP. Promotional issue only.
   Cast: Commuter, St. Regis, Baxter Robertson, Broken Edge.
Soundtrack (1984) • Casablanca (S) NBLP-7282 8-10   84
Soundtrack (1984) • Casablanca (S) 822 213-1 8-10   Re
   Cast: Survivor, Gang of Four, Broken Edge, Commuter, Paul Davis, Shandi, St. Regis, Baxter Robertson, Flirts, Jan and Dean, Joe "Bean" Esposito.

KARATE KID II
Soundtrack (1986) • Urania/United Artists (S) SW-40414 8-10   86
   Cast: Peter Cetera, Moody Blues, Mancrab, Paul Rodgers, Southside Johnny, Dennis DeYoung, New Edition, Carly Simon, Bill Conti.

KARATE KID III
Soundtrack (1989) • MCA (S) 6308 8-10   89
   Cast: Little River Band, Glenn Medeiros, Boys Club, Jude Cole, Pointer Sisters, Winger, PBF, Money Talks.

KARL MARX PLAY
Original Cast (1973) • Kilmarnock (S) KIL-72010 30-40   73
   Composer: Galt MacDermott, Rochelle Owens. **Conductor:** Galt MacDermott. **Cast:** Phyllis Newman, Ralph Carter, Harold Gould, Jamie Sanchez, Norman Matlock, Linda Mulrean, Louie Piday, Linda Swenson.

KAZABLAN
Soundtrack (1973) • CBS (S) 70128 20-25   73
UK release. Gatefold cover.
   Composer: Dov Seltzer. **Conductor:** Dov Seltzer. **Cast:** Arie Elias, Etty Grotes, Efrat Lavie, Yehuda Efroni.
Soundtrack (1973) • MGM (S) 1SE-48 12-15   73
   Composer: Dov Seltzer, Laim Hefer, Sam Almagor, Amos Ettinger. **Conductor:** Dov Seltzer. **Cast:** Yehoram Gaon, Aliza Azikri.

KEAN
Original Cast (1961) • Columbia (M) CL-1732 25-30   61
White label. Promotional issue only.
Original Cast (1961) • Columbia (M) KOL-5720 10-20   61

Original Cast (1961) • Columbia (S) KOS-2120 15-30   61
  Gatefold cover.
  Composer: George Forrest, Robert Wright. **Conductor:** Pembroke Davenport. **Cast:** Alfred
  Drake, Lee Venora, Oliver Gray, Joan Weldon, Patricia Cutts, Truman Smith, Alfred Desio,
  Christopher Hewett, Robert Penn, Arthur Rubin, Elie Siegmeister, Patrick Waddington.

KEEP UP THE GRASS
Soundtrack • East Coast (S) EC-10-55-S 8-10
  Cast: Arnold Wrecking Co.

KELLY
Original Cast (1966) • Original Cast (S) OC-8025 10-12   80

KELLY'S HEROES
Soundtrack (1970) • MGM (S) 1SE-23 20-25   70
  Composer: Lalo Schifrin. **Conductor:** Lalo Schifrin. **Cast:** Hank Williams Jr, Mike Curb
  Congregation.

KELLY, PETE: see PETE KELLY'S BLUES

KEN MURRAY'S BLACKOUTS
Original Cast (1975) • Mark 56 (S) 701 8-12
  Cast: Ken Murray, Marie Wilson.

KENNEDY, JOHN F.: see JOHN F. KENNEDY

KENNEDY WIT: see JOHN F. KENNEDY

KENNY ROGERS AND THE FIRST EDITION 'ROLLIN'
TV Soundtrack (1973) • Jolly Rogers/MGM (S) JR-5003 15-20   73
  Cast: Kenny Rogers and the First Edition.

KENT STATE
TV Soundtrack (1981) • RCA Victor (S) ABL1-3928 15-20   81
  Composer: Ken Lauber. **Conductor:** Ken Lauber. **Cast:** Grace Slick, Richie Havens, John
  Sebastian.

KENTUCKIAN: see DOWN TO THE SEA IN SHIPS

KEY
Soundtrack (1958) • Columbia (M) CL-1185 40-75   58
  Composer: Malcolm Henry Arnold. **Conductor:** Muir Mathieson.

KHARTOUM
Soundtrack (1966) • United Artists (M) UAL-4140 10-12   66
Soundtrack (1966) • United Artists (S) UAS-5140 12-15   66
  Composer: Frank Cordell. **Conductor:** Frank Cordell.

KID GALAHAD
Soundtrack (1962) • RCA Victor (EP) EPA-4371 40-80   62
  Black label, dog on top.
Soundtrack (1962) • RCA Victor (EP) EPA-4371 30-40   65
  Black label, dog on side.
Soundtrack (1962) • RCA Victor (EP) EPA-4371 50-100   69
  Orange label.
  Composer: Ben Weisman, Fred Wise, Ruth Batchelor, Hal David, others. **Cast:** Elvis Presley,
  Scotty Moore (guitar), D.J. Fontana (drums), Bob Moore (bass), Boots Randolph (sax), Dudley
  Brooks (piano), Jordanaires (vocals).

KID MILLIONS
Soundtrack • Classic International (M) CIF-3007 8-10
  Also has music from *Roman Scandals*.
  Composer: Various. **Cast:** Eddie Cantor, others.

KID POWER
TV Soundtrack (1972) • Pride (S) PRD-0010 8-12   72
Cartoon soundtrack from Rankin-Bass.
Composer: Perry Botkin Jr., Jules Bass. **Conductor:** Perry Botkin Jr., Jules Bass. **Cast:** Jeff and Greg Thomas, Jay Silverheels Jr., Curbstones.

KIDNAPPED
Soundtrack (1971) • American Int'l (S) A-1042.................................... 12-15   72
Composer: Roy Budd. **Conductor:** Roy Budd. **Cast:** Mary Hopkin.

KIDS ARE ALRIGHT
Soundtrack (1979) • MCA (S) 2-11005... 12-15   79
Soundtrack (1979) • MCA (S) 2-6899.. 10-12   Re
Two discs.
Composer: Peter Townshend, John Entwistle, Mose Allison, E. McDaniels. **Cast:** The Who.

KIDS FROM FAME: see FAME

KIDS SAY THE DARNDEST THINGS
TV Soundtrack • Columbia Harmony (EP) ZTV 29206/7 10-15
Promotional item made for Royal Gelatin.
Cast: Art Linkletter, others.

KILLER FORCE
Soundtrack (1976) • Audio Fidelity (S) AFSD-6277 25-30   76
Composer: Georges Garvarentz. **Conductor:** Georges Garvarentz.

KILLERS: see LUST FOR LIFE

KILLERS THREE
Soundtrack (1968) • Tower (EP) SPRO-4647/8 10-15   68
Promotional issue only.
Soundtrack (1968) • Tower (S) ST-5141 15-20   68
Composer: Harley Hatcher, Jerry Styner, others. **Cast:** Merle Haggard, Bonnie Owens, Dick Curless, Kaye Adams.

KILLING FIELDS
Soundtrack (1984) • Virgin (S) V-2328... 10-15   84
Soundtrack (1984) • Virgin (S) 90591-1 8-10   Re
Composer: Mike Oldfield, David Bedford. **Conductor:** Mike Oldfield. **Cast:** Orchestra of the Bavarian State Opera and Tolzer Boys Choir (conducted by Eberhard Schoener).

KIMBERLEY JIM
Soundtrack (1965) • RCA Victor (M) LPM-2780 20-25   65
Soundtrack (1965) • RCA Victor (S) LSP-2780 25-30   65
Composer: Various. **Conductor:** Bill Walker. **Cast:** Jim Reeves, Madeleine Usher.

KIND OF MAGIC
Soundtrack • Capitol/EMI (S) SMAS-12476 10-15   86
A partial reissue of what would have been a *Highlander* soundtrack, if one were issued.
Cast: Queen, others.

KINDRED
Soundtrack (1987) • Varese Sarabande (S) STV 81308 10-12   86
Composer: David Newman. **Conductor:** David Newman.

KING, A MUSICAL TESTIMONY
Original London Cast (1990) • London (S) 425212-4 8-12   90
Composer: Richard Blackford, Maya Angelou, Alistair Beaton. **Cast:** Simon Estes, Cynthia Hayman, Shezwae, Ray Shell.

KING AND I
Original Cast (1951) • Decca DA-876... 20-25   51
78 rpm album.
Original Cast (1951) • Decca (EP) ED-800 10-15   51

Original Cast (1951) • Decca (EP) 9-260 12-15   51
  Boxed, six-disc set.
Original Cast (1951) • Decca (M) DL-9008... 12-18   51
  Cover has original poster graphics with credits. Black and gold label on thick wax.
Original Cast (1951) • Decca (M) DL-9008... 8-12   59
  Cover has original poster graphics with credits. Red label.
Original Cast (1951) • Decca (M) DL-9008... 35-45   59
  Cover has a drawing of Gertrude Lawrence and Yul Brynner, with the title on three lines. In order to make room for the electronic stereo band across the top of the stereo edition of this release, a new cover was created with the title on two lines.
Original Cast (1951) • Decca (M) DL-9008... 8-10   59
Original Cast (1951) • Decca (SE) DL-79008 8-12   59
Original Cast (1951) • MCA (SE) 2028 8-10   72
Original Cast (1951) • MCA (SE) 37095 5-8   81
Original Cast (1951) • MCA (SE) 1629 5-8   Re
  Covers on above five have the drawing of Gertrude Lawrence and Yul Brynner, with the title on two lines.
    Composer: Richard Rodgers, Oscar Hammerstein II. **Conductor:** Frederick Dvonch. **Cast:** Gertrude Lawrence, Yul Brynner, Dorothy Sarnoff, Doretta Morrow, Larry Douglas.
Original London Cast (1953) • Philips (M) BBL-7002 65-85   53
Original London Cast (1953) • Stet (M) DS-15014 12-18   Re
  UK releases.
    Composer: Richard Rodgers, Oscar Hammerstein II. **Conductor:** Reginald Burston. **Cast:** Valerie Hobson, Herbert Lom, Muriel Smith, Doreen Duke, Jan Mazarus, Martin Benson.
Original Revival Cast (1964) • RCA Victor (M) LOC-1092 8-10   64
Original Revival Cast (1964) • RCA Victor (S) LSO-1092....................... 8-12   64
  Black label with dog on top.
Original Revival Cast (1964) • RCA Victor (S) LSO-1092......................... 5-8   Re
  Tan, black or orange label. These are the only records that include *The Small House of Uncle Thomas* ballet (albeit abridged).
    Composer: Richard Rodgers, Oscar Hammerstein II. **Conductor:** Franz Allers. **Cast:** Risë Stevens, Darren McGavin, Lee Venora, James Harvey, Patricia Neway, Frank Porretta.
Original Revival Cast (1977) • RCA Victor (S) ABL1-2610 10-12   77
    Composer: Richard Rodgers, Oscar Hammerstein II. **Conductor:** Milton Rosenstock. **Cast:** Yul Brynner, Constance Towers, Hye-Young Choi, Martin Vidnovic, June Angela, Gene Profanato, Alin Amick.
Studio Cast (1952) • Remington (M) R-199-144................................... 10-15   52
Studio Cast (1952) • Remington (M) R-149-55.................................... 10-15   52
  Cast: Frank Chacksfield, Elizabeth Humphries, Lucille Graham.
Studio Cast (1953) • RCA Victor (EP) EPA-411 10-15   53
  Cast: Dinah Shore.
Studio Cast (1954) • Decca (EP) ED-2057.. 10-15   54
  Cast: Bing Crosby.
Studio Cast (1955) • RCA Victor (EP) EKB-1022 10-20   55
  Two discs.
Studio Cast (1955) • RCA Victor (M) LK-1022...................................... 18-20   55
  Cast: Dinah Shore, Patricia Munsel, Tony Martin, Robert Merrill.
Studio Cast (1960) • Columbia (M) OL-8040 8-12   60
Studio Cast (1960) • Columbia (S) OS-2640 10-12   60
    Composer: Richard Rodgers, Oscar Hammerstein II. **Conductor:** Lehman Engel. **Cast:** Barbara Cook, Theodore Bikel, Anita Darian, Jeanette Scovotti, Daniel Ferro.
Studio Cast (1977) • Rediffusion (S) RIM-1000................................... 15-20   77
Studio Cast • Diplomat (S) DS 2211.. 8-15
  Cast: Al Goodman and His Orchestra and Chorus, Susan Shaute, Richard Torigi, Gretchen Rhoads, Edgar Powell.
Studio Cast • Rondo-lette (S) SA143 8-15
  Cast: Eddie Ruhl, Barbara Altman, Alberta Hopkins, Tom O'Leary, others.

Studio Cast • Spin-O-Rama (S) MK-3045 8-15
    Conductor: Al Goodman. **Cast:** Richard Torigi, Edgar Powell, Susan Shaute, Gretchen Rhoads.

Soundtrack (1956) • Capitol (EP) EDM-740 10-15   56
    Actual title: *Shall We Dance?*

Soundtrack (1956) • Capitol (M) W-740 5-10   56
    Mono pressings include the complete fan dance music for *Getting to Know You.*

Soundtrack (1956) • Capitol (S) SW-740 5-12   59
    Stereo pressings omit the fan dance music for *Getting to Know You.* This album has been
    reissued many times, though the difference in value between editions is minimal. In
    general, gray or black labels are in the high end of this price range, red, green or purple
    labels are at the low end.
      Composer: Richard Rodgers, Oscar Hammerstein II. **Conductor:** Alfred Newman. **Cast:**
      Deborah Kerr, Yul Brynner, Rita Moreno, Marni Nixon (performed some vocals for Deborah Kerr
      in the film), Terry Saunders, Gene Merlino (performed vocals for Carlos Rivas).

Studiotrack (1957) • Halo (M) 50197 8-10   57

Studiotrack (1957) • Paris (M) MS-33-1823/4 8-10   57
    Cast: Frank Chacksfield, Elizabeth Humphries, Lucille Graham.

Studiotrack (1958) • Warner Bros. (M) W-1205 8-12   58

Studiotrack (1958) • Warner Bros. (S) WS-1205 10-12   58
    Cast: Warren Barker Orchestra.

Studiotrack (1959) • Columbia (EP) B-12522 5-10   59

Studiotrack (1959) • Columbia (M) CL-1252 8-10   59

Studiotrack (1959) • Columbia (S) CS-8064 8-10   59
    Conductor: Ray Conniff. **Cast:** Ray Conniff and His Orchestra.

Studiotrack (1959) • Decca (M) DL-8305 10-12   59
    Cast: Carmen Cavallaro.

Studiotrack (1959) • Richmond (M) B-20071 8-10   59

Studiotrack (1959) • Richmond (S) S-30071 8-10   59
    Cast: Frank Chacksfield.

Studiotrack (1959) • Savoy (M) MG-12134 8-10   59

Studiotrack (1959) • Savoy (S) SST-13002 8-10   59
    Cast: Wilbur Harden.

Studiotrack (1959) • World Pacific (M) 1272 8-10   59

Studiotrack (1959) • World Pacific (S) S-1272 8-10   59
    Cast: Mastersounds.

Studiotrack (1959) • National Academy Record Club (M) ES 4 10-15   60
    From *Ed Sullivan Presents Songs and Music of....* series. May also be shown as "NA-8."
    Cast: Ed Sullivan All Star Cast.

Studiotrack (1960) • Craftsmen (M) 211 8-12   60

Studiotrack (1960) • Epic (M) BN-564 10-12   60

Studiotrack (1960) • Epic (M) LN-3680 10-15   60
    Cast: Lois Hunt, Charmaine Harma, Samuel Jones, Harry Snow, Irene Carroll.

Studiotrack (1960) • Richmond (M) B-20065 8-15   60

Studiotrack (1960) • Richmond (S) S-30065 8-15   60
    One side has music from *My Fair Lady.*
    Cast: Cyril Stapleton and His Orchestra.

Studiotrack • Harmony (M) 7194 8-12

Studiotrack • Harmony (S) HS-11007 8-12
    Also has music from *Flower Drum Song.*
    Cast: Dino Martinelli and His Orchestra.

Studiotrack • Masterseal (M) MS-8 8-12
    Cast: Frank Chacksfield and His Orchestra, Elizabeth Humphries, Lucille Graham.

Studiotrack • Mercury (S) SR 60640 8-12
    Conductor: Clebanoff.

Studiotrack • Plymouth (M) P-12-39 8-12
   One side has various classical tracks.
     Cast: Plymouth Players.
Studiotrack • Rondo-lette (S) SA83 8-12
   Also has other film themes.
     Conductor: Ira Wright. **Cast:** Ira Wright Orchestra.
Studiotrack • Somerset (M) P-2700 8-12
Studiotrack • Somerset (S) SF-2700 8-12
   Also has music from *My Fair Lady.*
     Conductor: Robert Russell Bennett. **Cast:** New World Theatre Orchestra.
Studiotrack • Vox (M) PL 21300 8-12
   Full title: *The King and I and Carousel.* One side has music from *Carousel.*
     Cast: George Feyer.
Studiotrack • Design (S) DLP-236 8-12
    Also see AROUND THE WORLD IN 80 DAYS
    Also see MY FAIR LADY
    Also see RODGERS AND HAMMERSTEIN DELUXE SET

KING CREOLE

Soundtrack [Vol. 1] (1958) • RCA Victor (EP) EPA-4319 50-75   58
   Volume one. Black label, dog on top.
Soundtrack [Vol. 1] (1958) • RCA Victor (EP) EPA-4319 30-40   65
   Volume one. Black label, dog on side.
Soundtrack [Vol. 1] (1958) • RCA Victor (EP) EPA-4319 50-100   69
   Volume one. Orange label.
Soundtrack [Vol. 2] (1958) • RCA Victor (EP) EPA-4321 50-75   58
   Volume two. Black label, dog on top.
Soundtrack [Vol. 2] (1958) • RCA Victor (EP) EPA-4321 30-40   65
   Volume two. Black label, dog on side.
Soundtrack [Vol. 2] (1958) • RCA Victor (EP) EPA-4321 50-100   69
   Orange label.
Soundtrack (1958) • RCA Victor (M) LPM-1884 250-350   58
   Black label, reads "Long Play" at bottom. Includes bonus 8" x 10" black-and-white photo of
   Elvis in uniform.
Soundtrack (1958) • RCA Victor (M) LPM-1884 100-125   58
   Black label, reads "Long Play" at bottom. Without bonus photo.
Soundtrack (1958) • RCA Victor (SE) LSP-1884e 50-100   59
   Black label, RCA silver-top logo. Reads "Stereo Electronically Reprocessed" at bottom.
Soundtrack (1958) • RCA Victor (M) LPM-1884 40-60   63
   Black label, reads "Mono" at bottom.
Soundtrack (1958) • RCA Victor (M) LPM-1884 25-30   65
   Black label, reads "Monaural" at bottom.
Soundtrack (1958) • RCA Victor (SE) LSP-1884e 25-30   60
   Black label, RCA white-top logo.
Soundtrack (1958) • RCA Victor (SE) LSP-1884e 10-25   69
   Orange or tan label. (Tan label issued in 1976.)
Soundtrack (1958) • RCA Victor (SE) AFL1-1884 8-10   77
Soundtrack (1958) • RCA Victor (SE) AYL1-3733 5-8   80
     Composer: Fred Wise, Ben Weisman, Sid Wayne, Jerry Leiber, Mike Stoller, Sid Tepper, Roy
   C. Bennett, others. **Cast:** Elvis Presley, Scotty Moore (guitar), D.J. Fontana (drums), Bill Black
   (bass), Jordanaires (vocals).

KING FAMILY CHRISTMAS

TV Soundtrack • Mobile (S) FCLP 3031 10-15   60s
     Cast: King Family.

KING KONG

Studiotrack (1933) • United Artists (S) UA-LA373-G 12-15   76
   Composer: Max Steiner. **Conductor:** Leroy Holmes.
Studiotrack (1933) • Entr'acte (S) ERS-6504 10-12   76
Studiotrack (1933) • Southern Cross (S) SCAR-5006 8-10   Re
   Composer: Max Steiner. **Conductor:** Fred Steiner. **Cast:** National Philharmonic Orchestra.
Soundtrack (1976) • Reprise (S) MS-2260 12-15   76
   From the 1976 film. Includes bonus poster.
   Composer: John Barry. **Conductor:** John Barry.
   Also see ORIGINAL TV ADVENTURES OF KING KONG.

KING KONG

Original South African Cast (1960) • Gallotone (M) GALP-1040 35-45   60
   South African release. All-African jazz opera..
   Composer: Pat Williams, Todd Matshikiza. **Conductor:** Mackay Devashe. **Cast:** Nathan
   Mdledle, Miriam Makeba, Joseph Mogotsi, Helen Gama, Stephen Moloi, Dan Poho.
Original London Cast (1961) • London (M) 5762 35-55   61
   UK release.
   Composer: Pat Williams, Todd Matshikiza. **Conductor:** Stanley Glasser. **Cast:** Nathan Mdledle,
   Peggy Phango, Joseph Mogotsi, Ben Masinga, Stephen Moloi, Sophie Mgcina, Patience Gowabe.

KING KONG LIVES

Soundtrack (1987) • MCA (S) 6203 20-25   87
   Digital audiophile LP.
   Composer: John Scott. **Conductor:** John Scott. **Cast:** Graunke Symphony Orchestra.

KING OF COMEDY

Soundtrack (1983) • Warner Bros. (S) 1-9 23765- 1 8-10   83
   Cast: Pretenders, B.B. King, Talking Heads, Bob James, Rickie Lee Jones, Robbie Robertson,
   Ric Ocasek, Ray Charles, David Sanborn, Van Morrison.

KING OF HEARTS (1967)

Soundtrack (1967) • United Artists (M) UAL-4150 10-12   67
Soundtrack (1967) • United Artists (S) UAS-5150 12-15   67
Soundtrack (1967) • United Artists (M) UA-LA287-G 8-10   74
   Composer: Georges Delerue. **Conductor:** Georges Delerue.

KING OF HEARTS (1980)

Original Cast (1980) • Original Cast (S) OC-8028 10-12   81
   Composer: Peter Link, Jacob Brackman. **Conductor:** Peter Link. **Cast:** Don Scardino, Millicent
   Martin, Pamela Blair, Bob Gunton, Michael McCarty, Gordon Weiss, Rex Hays, Marilyn
   D'Honau, A. Lacoonis.

KING OF KINGS

Soundtrack (1961) • MGM (M) 1E2 12-15   61
Soundtrack (1961) • MGM (S) S1E2 15-20   61
   Boxed sets, each with a hard-bound book and four 8" x 10" photos. At least seven different
   photos exist for this.
Soundtrack (1961) • MGM (M) 1E2-ST 12-15   61
Soundtrack (1961) • MGM (S) S1E2-ST 12-18   61
Soundtrack (1961) • MCA (S) 39056 5-8   86
   Composer: Miklos Rozsa. **Conductor:** Miklos Rozsa.
Studiotrack (1962) • Varese Sarabande (S) VC 81104 8-12   79
   Also has music from *El Cid* and *Ben Hur.* First released as *Wide-Screen Spectaculars*
   (Somerset 16400).
   Composer: Miklos Rozsa. **Conductor:** Miklos Rozsa.
Soundtrack (1961) • MGM (M) E-3971 10-12   61
Soundtrack (1961) • MGM (S) SE-3971 10-12   61
   Full title: *King of Kings – The Story of Jesus for Children.* Has story narration with original
   soundtrack music.
   Composer: Miklos Rozsa. **Conductor:** Miklos Rozsa. **Cast:** Richard Boone.

Studiotrack (1961) • MGM (M) E-3970 15-20   61
Studiotrack (1961) • MGM (S) SE-3970 20-25   61
   Cast: Robert Ryan (narrator).
   ALSO SEE WIDE-SCREEN SPECTACULARS

KING OF THE ENTIRE WORLD
Original Cast (1978) • 4th Wall Repertory Co. (S) WRC-4 20-25   78
   Composer: Daniel Pisello. **Conductor:** Kit McClure. **Cast:** 4th Wall Repertory Co.

KING OF THE MOUNTAIN
Soundtrack (1981) • Polygram (S) 4445 25-35   81
   Promotional picture disc with two soundtrack songs. 1,500 made.
   Cast: Deborah Van Valkenburgh.

KING OF THE WHOLE DAMN WORLD
Original Cast (1962) • Blue Pear (S) 1017 10-20
   Composer: Robert Larimer. **Conductor:** Dobbs Franks. **Cast:** Sheldon Patts, Boris Aplin, Tom
   Pedi, Francine Beens, Floria Mari, Alan Howard.

KING RAT
Soundtrack (1965) • Mainstream (M) 56061 20-25   65
Soundtrack (1965) • Mainstream (S) S-6061 35-45   65
   Composer: John Barry. **Conductor:** John Barry.

KING SOLOMON'S MINES
Soundtrack (1985) • Restless (S) 72106-1 15-20   85
   Composer: Jerry Goldsmith. **Conductor:** Jerry Goldsmith. **Cast:** Hungarian State Opera
   Orchestra.

KINGS ROW
Studiotrack (1942) • Chalfont (SE) SDG-305 15-30   79
   Digital recording.
   Composer: Erich Wolfgang Korngold. **Conductor:** Charles Gerhardt. **Cast:** National
   Philharmonic Orchestra.

KING'S STORY
Soundtrack (1967) • DRG (S) SL-5185 8-10   80
   Composer: Ivor Slaney. **Conductor:** Ivor Slaney. **Cast:** Orson Welles, Flora Robson, Patrick
   Wymark, David Warner. (With dialogue.)

KINGDOM OF FREE
Soundtrack • Custom Fidelity (S) CFS-1816 8-12

KINGS GO FORTH
Soundtrack (1958) • Capitol (M) W-1063 75-125   58
   Composer: Elmer Bernstein, Red Norvo. **Conductor:** Elmer Bernstein.

KINGSMILL SUITE
Soundtrack (1974) • Friendly Eagle (S) FER-BG-101 5-10   74
   One side has *Themes from the Old Country.*
   Composer: Donald Spect. **Conductor:** Donald Spect.

KIPLING'S JUNGLE BOOK: see JUNGLE BOOK

KIRI SINGS GERSHWIN
Studiotrack (1987) • EMI/Angel (S) 47454 10-12   87
   Gershwin songs written for stage shows and films.
   Composer: George Gershwin, Ira Gershwin, others. **Conductor:** John McGlinn. **Cast:** Kiri Te
   Kanawa, New Princess Theater Orchestra.

KISMET
Original Cast (1953) • Columbia MM-1100 15-20   54
   78 rpm album.
Original Cast (1953) • Columbia (EP) A-1100 10-15   54
   Boxed, four disc set.

Original Cast (1953) • Columbia (M) ML-4850 8-12   54
  Brown cover with drawing and credits.
Original Cast (1953) • Columbia (M) OL-4850.................................... 8-10   Re
  Some copies have same cover as ML-4850, others have credits superimposed over photo
  of Alfred Drake.
Original Cast (1953) • Columbia (SE) OS-2060 8-15   59
Original Cast (1953) • Columbia (SE) S-32605 5-8   73
  Composer: Alexander Borodin, Robert Wright, George Forrest. **Conductor:** Louis Adrian. **Cast:**
  Alfred Drake, Doretta Morrow, Joan Diener, Richard Kiley, Henry Calvin, Richard Oneto, Hal
  Hackett, Lucy Andonian.
Studio Cast (1954) • Columbia (EP) B-1800 10-15   54
  Cast: Tony Bennett.
Studio Cast (1954) • Mercury (EP) EP 1-3160 10-15   54
  Cast: Vic Damone, Ross Bagdasarian, Terry Gibbs.
Studio Cast (1954) • Decca (EP) ED-2117.. 10-15   54
  Composer: Alexander Borodin, Robert Wright, George Forrest. **Cast:** Four Aces, Peggy Lee,
  Danny Kaye.
Soundtrack (1955) • MGM (EP) X-3281 10-15   55
Soundtrack (1955) • MGM (M) E-3281 15-20   55
  Yellow label.
Soundtrack (1955) • MGM (M) E-3281 10-12
  Black label. Above three include the song *Rahadlakum*
Soundtrack (1955) • Metro (M) 526 8-12   65
Soundtrack (1955) • Metro (SE) MS-526.. 8-12   65
  Metro reissues omit *Rahadlakum*.
Soundtrack (1955) • MCA (M) 1424 5-8   Re
  Composer: Alexander Borodin, Robert Wright, George Forrest. **Conductor:** Andre Previn.
  Cast: Howard Keel, Ann Blyth, Dolores Gray, Vic Damone, Sebastian Cabot.
  Also see TEN NORTH FREDERICK

KISS ME KATE
Original Cast (1948) • Columbia C-200 10-25   49
  78 rpm album.
Original Cast (1948) • Columbia (M) ML-4140 10-20   49
  Kiss Me Kate was the first original cast performance recorded especially for a long-play
  album. Yellow and red cover with black-and-white photos of Alfred Drake (without beard)
  and Patricia Morison. Green or blue disc label.
Original Cast (1948) • Columbia (M) OL-4140.................................... 10-12   58
  Some copies have the same cover as above with new number on it. Others have white
  cover with color photo of Drake (with beard) and Morison. Gray label.
Original Cast (1948) • Columbia (SE) OS-2300 8-10   63
Original Cast (1948) • Columbia (M) OL-4140.................................... 12-15
  Variation of white cover, with credits for the TV production. However, this is the same
  recording as the other issues.
Original Cast (1948) • Columbia (M) S-32609 5-10   73
  Composer: Cole Porter. **Conductor:** Pembroke Davenport. **Cast:** Alfred Drake, Patricia
  Morison, Lisa Kirk, Harold Lang, Jack Diamond, Lorenzo Fuller, Annabelle Hill, Edwin Clay,
  Charles Wood, Eddie Sledge, Fred Davis, Harry Clark.
Original London Cast (1951) • World (M) SHB-26................................. 25-35
  UK release. Two discs. Actual title: *Cole Porter in London.* Complete score from London
  production, plus music from *Wake Up and Dream, The Gay Divorcee, Nymph Errant,
  Anything Goes, The Sun Never Sets, O Mistress Mine, The Fleet's Lit Up, The Eclipse, A
  Night Out* and *Black Velvet* (retitled London production of *Leave it to Me*).
  Composer: Cole Porter. **Conductor:** Freddie Bretherton. **Cast:** Patricia
  Morison, Bill Johnson, Julie Wilson, Walter Long, Adelaide Hall, Archie
  Savage, Danny Green, Sidney James.
Original Revival Cast (1965) • RCA Victor (M) LOC-1112 8-12   65

Original Revival Cast (1965) • RCA Victor (S) LSO-1112..................... 10-12   65
Composer: Alexander Borodin, Robert Wright, George Forrest. **Conductor:** Franz Allers. **Cast:** Alfred Drake, Anne Jeffreys, Henry Calvin, Don Baddoe, Lee Venora, Richard Banke, Rudy Vejar, Albert Toigo, Anita Alpert.

Studio Cast (1953) • Columbia (M) CL-6275 20-30   53
10-inch LP.

Studio Cast (1953) • Columbia (EP) B-399 10-15   55
Two discs.

Studio Cast (1953) • Columbia (M) CL-550 15-20   55
Conductor: Percy Faith. **Cast:** Percy Faith and His Orchestra.

Studio Cast • London (M) PM-55001.. 10-15
Studio Cast • London (S) SP-44043.. 15-20
Composer: Alexander Borodin, Robert Wright, George Forrest. **Conductor:** Mantovani. **Cast:** Robert Merrill, Regina Resnik, Kenneth McKellar, Adele Leigh, Ian Wallace, Mike Sammes Singers.

Studio Cast • London (S) S 30077 10-15
Also has music from *Can-Can*.
Cast: London Theatre Company.

Studio Cast • Capitol (S) SW-2022 10-15   64
Studio Cast • Angel (S) S-37321.. 8-10   73
Composer: Alexander Borodin, Robert Wright, George Forrest. **Conductor:** Van Alexander. **Cast:** Gordon MacRae, Dorothy Kirsten, Bunny Bishop, Salli Terri, Richard Levitt.

Studio Cast (1948) • Capitol (EP) CDF-157 15-20   49
Boxed, four-disc set.

Studio Cast (1948) • Capitol CD-144.. 20-25   49
Album of four 78 rpms.

Studio Cast (1948) • Capitol (M) LP H-157... 20-25   49
10-inch LP.
Conductor: Paul Weston. **Cast:** Gordon MacRae, Jo Stafford, Paul Weston and Orchestra.

Studio Cast (1959) • Capitol (M) TAO-1267 8-10   59
Studio Cast (1959) • Capitol (S) STAO-1267 8-12   59
Includes principal members of the original cast, reassembled for a high fidelity stereo recording, which was also released in mono.
Composer: Cole Porter. **Conductor:** Pembroke Davenport. **Cast:** Alfred Drake, Patricia Morison, Lisa Kirk, Harold Lang, Bob Sands, Ray Drakely, Lorenzo Fuller, Aloysius Donovan, Alex Dubroff.

Studio Cast (1959) • RCA Victor (M) LPM-1984.................................. 10-15   59
Studio Cast (1959) • RCA Victor (S) LSP-1984................................... 12-18   59
Composer: Porter. **Conductor:** Henri Rene. **Cast:** Howard Keel, Gogi Grant, Anne Jeffreys.

Studio Cast (1962) • Columbia (M) CL-1768 8-10   62
Studio Cast (1962) • Columbia (S) CS-8568 8-10   62
Studio Cast (1962) • Harmony (M) HL-7155.. 5-8
Studio Cast (1962) • Harmony (S) HS 11001 5-8
Conductor: Glenn Osser. **Cast:** Earl Wrightson, Lois Hunt, Mary Mayo.

Studio Cast (1964) • Reprise (M) F-2017 10-15   64
Studio Cast (1964) • Reprise (S) FS-2017 20-25   64
Both have gatefold covers.

Studio Cast (1964) • Reprise (M) F-2017 10-12   64
Studio Cast (1964) • Reprise (S) FS-2017 12-18   64
Both have standard covers.
Composer: Cole Porter. **Conductor:** Morris Stoloff, Ken Lane. **Cast:** Frank Sinatra, Dean Martin, Sammy Davis Jr., Jo Stafford, Phyllis McGuire, Hi-Lo's, Lou Monte, Keely Smith, Johnny Prophet, Dinah Shore.

German Studio Cast • Ariola (S) S-74343 25-30
Composer: Cole Porter. **Conductor:** Johannes Fehring. **Cast:** Olive Moorefield, Peter Alexander.

Soundtrack (1953) • MGM (EP) X-223 12-15   53
  Boxed, three-disc set.
Soundtrack (1953) • MGM (M) E-3077 15-18   53
  Above MGM issues contain the entire score.
Soundtrack (1953) • Metro (M) M-525 8-10   65
Soundtrack (1953) • Metro (SE) MS-525 8-12   65
  Metro reissues have only ten selections from the score.
Soundtrack (1953) • MCA (M) 25003 8-10   86
  Composer: Cole Porter. **Conductor:** Andre Previn. **Cast:** Kathryn Grayson, Howard Keel, Ann Miller, Keenan Wynn, James Whitmore, Bobby Van, Tommy Rall, Bob Fosse.
TV Soundtrack (1968) • Columbia Special Products (S) CSS-645 12-25   68
  Full title: *Armstrong Presents Cole Porter's Kiss Me Kate.*
  Composer: Cole Porter. **Conductor:** Jack Elliott. **Cast:** Robert Goulet, Carol Lawrence, Jessica Walter, Marty Ingels, Michael Callan, Jules Munshin, Hendra and Ullett.
Studiotrack (1953) • RCA Victor (EP) ERA-187 10-15   53
  Conductor: Harry Geller. **Cast:** Kathryn Grayson, Johnnie Johnston.
Studiotrack (1959) • Somerset (M) P-9800 8-10   59
Studiotrack (1959) • Somerset (S) SF-9800 8-10   59
  Full title: *Kiss Me Kate and Oklahoma!*
  Composer: Cole Porter. **Conductor:** Robert Russell Bennett. **Cast:** New World Theatre Orchestra.
Studiotrack (1960) • National Academy Record Club (M) ES 2 10-15   60
  From the *Ed Sullivan Presents Songs and Music of...* series.
  Cast: Ed Sullivan All Star Cast.
Studiotrack (1958) • World Pacific (M) WP-1243 10-15   58
  Cast: Four Aces, Peggy Lee, Danny Kaye.
  Also see ANNIE GET YOUR GUN
  Also see ANYTHING GOES
  Also see BRIGADOON
  Also see CAN-CAN
  Also see REPRISE REPERTORY THEATRE
  Also see THOSE GLORIOUS MGM MUSICALS

KISS OF THE SPIDER WOMAN

Soundtrack (1985) • Island (S) 90475-1 8-10   85
  Cast: Sonia Braga, others.

KISS THEM FOR ME

Soundtrack (1957) • Coral (M) CRL-57160 65-75   57
  Big band music of the early '40s.
  Composer: Lionel Newman, others. **Conductor:** Lionel Newman.

KISSIN' COUSINS

Soundtrack (1964) • RCA Victor (M) LPM-2894 40-60   64
  Black label, reads "Mono" at bottom.
Soundtrack (1964) • RCA Victor (S) LSP-2894 40-60   64
  Black label, RCA silver-top logo.
Soundtrack (1964) • RCA Victor (M) LPM-2894 20-30   65
  Black label, reads "Monaural" at bottom.
Soundtrack (1964) • RCA Victor (S) LSP-2894 20-30   65
  Black label, RCA white-top logo.
Soundtrack (1964) • RCA Victor (S) LSP-2894 10-25   69
  Orange label.
Soundtrack (1964) • RCA Victor (S) AFL1-2894 10-12   77
Soundtrack (1964) • RCA Victor (S) AYL1-4115 8-10   81
  Composer: Bill Giant, Bernie Baum, Florence Kaye, Sid Tepper, Roy C. Bennett, Fred Wise, others. **Conductor:** Fred Karger. **Cast:** Elvis Presley, Scotty Moore (guitar), Harold Bradley (guitar), D.J. Fontana (drums), Floyd Cramer (piano), Bob Moore (bass), Boots Randolph (sax), Jordanaires (vocals).

KISSING BANDIT
Soundtrack (1948) • MGM (EP) X-1037 12-18   53
Four songs by Kathryn Grayson from her MGM musicals, including *Love is Where You Find It.*
  Composer: Nacio Herb Brown, Earl Brent, Edward Heyman. **Conductor:** George Stoll. **Cast:** Kathryn Grayson.
Soundtrack (1948) • MGM (M) E-3257 20-25   55
Actual title: *Kathryn Grayson Sings.* Songs from her MGM musicals, including *All of a Sudden My Heart Sings* and *Jalousie.*
  Composer: Harold Rome, Jacob Gabe, Vera Bloom, others. **Conductor:** George Stoll. **Cast:** Kathryn Grayson.
   Also see DOUBLE DYNAMITE

KITTIWAKE ISLAND
Original Cast (1960) • Blue Pear (M) BP-1003 20-30
  Composer: Alec Wilder, Arnold Sundgaard. **Cast:** Joe Lautner, Kathleen Murray, G. Wood, Lainie Kazan.

KITTY FOYLE
Original Radio Cast • Mark 56 (M) 675... 15-20   75
  Cast: Ginger Rogers.

KNACK (AND HOW TO GET IT), THE
Soundtrack (1965) • United Artists (M) UAL-4129............................... 12-15   65
Soundtrack (1965) • United Artists (S) UAS-54129 15-18   65
Soundtrack (1965) • United Artists (S) UA-LA270-G 10-12   70s
Soundtrack (1965) • MCA (S) 25109.. 8-10   86
  Composer: John Barry. **Conductor:** John Barry. **Cast:** Johnny Delittle.

KNICKERBOCKER HOLIDAY
Original Radio Cast • Mark 56 (M) 613... 8-12   70s
  Composer: Kurt Weill, Maxwell Anderson. **Cast:** Walter Huston, Jeanne Madden.
Original Cast (1938) • Joey (M) 7243 10-12
Original Cast (1938) • AEI (M) AEI-1148... 15-18   84
Archival recording featuring members of the original New York production and excerpts from a 1945 radio broadcast.
  Composer: Kurt Weill, Maxwell Anderson. **Conductor:** Maurice de Abravanel, Harold Levy. **Cast:** Walter Huston, Jeanne Madden, Jean Darling, David Brooks, Robert Shackleton.
  Also see MISTER IMPERIUM
  Also see KURT WEILL IN HOLLYWOOD

KNIGHTS OF THE CITY
Soundtrack (1986) • Private I (S) SZ-40317 8-10   86

KNIGHTS OF THE ROUND TABLE
Soundtrack (1953) • Varese Sarabande (S) STV-81128 10-15   80
  Composer: Miklos Rozsa. **Conductor:** Muir Mathieson.

KNOCK ON WOOD
Studiotrack (1954) • Decca (EP) ED 2141 20-35   54
Studiotrack (1954) • Decca (M) DL-5527 75-85   54
10-inch LP. Music from the film, plus other selections sung by Danny Kaye that are not on the EP.
  Composer: Sylvia Fine. **Conductor:** Vic Schoen. **Cast:** Danny Kaye, Lee Gordon Singers, Victor Young and His Singing Strings.

KOSHER WIDOW
Original Cast (1959) • Golden Crest (M) 4018.................................... 25-30   59
Original Cast (1959) • Golden Crest (S) 4018 30-35   59
  Composer: Sholom Secunda, Molly Picon. **Conductor:** Sholom Secunda. **Cast:** Molly Picon, Irving Jacobson, Mae Schoenfeld.

KOYAANISQATSI (LIFE OUT OF BALANCE)
Soundtrack (1983) • Antilles (S) 90626-1 15-20   83
   Film sequel is *Powaqqatsi*
     Composer: Philip Glass. **Conductor:** Philip Glass. **Cast:** Philip Glass.

KRAFT TELEVISION THEATER
TV Soundtrack (1957) • RKO/Unique (M) ULP-127 30-35   57
TV Soundtrack (1957) • RKO/Unique (SE) SLP-D1270 20-30   58
TV Soundtrack (1957) • Golden Tone (M) C-4065 20-25   Re
   Actual title: *Profile in Music*. Though LP states "conductor Wladimir Selinsky conducts his
   own scores from TV productions," it is simply a reissue of the RKO/Unique release.
     Composer: Wladimir Selinsky. **Conductor:** Wladimir Selinsky.

KRAKATOA, EAST OF JAVA
Soundtrack (1969) • ABC (S) ABCS-OC-8.................................... 12-15   69
     Composer: Frank DeVol, Mack David. **Conductor:** Frank DeVol. **Cast:** Barbara Werle.

KRAMER VS. KRAMER
Soundtrack (1979) • Columbia (S) 35727................................ 8-10   79
Soundtrack (1979) • Columbia (S) 35873................................ 10-15   79
   Full title: *Kramer vs. Kramer (Baroque Suite)*
     Composer: Antonio Vivaldi, Henry Purcell.

KRONOS
Soundtrack (1957) • Cacophonic (M) CLP-1001 10-20
   Gatefold cover. Includes eight-page booklet and portrait print of the composers.
     Composer: Paul Sawtell, Bert Shefter.

KRULL
Soundtrack (1983) • Southern Cross (S) SCRS-1004......................... 15-20   83
     Composer: James Horner. **Conductor:** James Horner. **Cast:** London Symphony Orchestra.

KRUPA, GENE, STORY: see GENE KRUPA STORY

KRUSH GROOVE
Soundtrack (1985) • Warner Bros. (S) 1-25295 8-10   85
     Cast: Sheila E., Chaka Khan, L.L., Blow Kurtis, Fat Boys, Debbie Harry, Beastie Boys, Gap
     Band, Force M.D.'s, Run D.M.C.

KUNG-FU
TV Soundtrack (1971) • Warner Bros. (S) BS-2726 10-15   73
     Composer: Jim Helms. **Conductor:** Jim Helms. **Cast:** David Carradine, Keye Luke, Philip Ahn,
     Radames Pera. (With dialogue.)

KUKLA, FRAN AND OLLIE: see SONGS BY KUKLA, FRAN AND OLLIE

KURT WEILL CABARET
Original Cast (1963) • MGM (M) E-4180 15-20   63
Original Cast (1963) • MGM (S) SE-4180... 20-25   63
     Composer: Kurt Weill. **Conductor:** Abraham Stokman. **Cast:** Martha Schlamme, Will Holt.

KURT WEILL CLASSICS: see DOWN IN THE VALLEY

KURT WEILL IN HOLLYWOOD
Soundtrack • Ariel (M) KWH-10 25-35   82
   Music from the film versions of *One Touch of Venus, Where Do We Go from Here?,*
   Knickerbocker Holiday and *You and Me.*
     ONE TOUCH OF VENUS: **Composer:** Kurt Weill, Ogden Nash, Ann Ronnell. **Conductor:** Leon
     Arnaud. **Cast:** Robert Walker, Eileen Wilson (performed Ava Gardner's vocals in the film), Dick
     Haymes, Eve Arden, Olga San Juan. YOU AND ME: **Composer:** Kurt Weill, Sam Coslow.
     Conductor: Victor Young. **Cast:** Carol Paige. KNICKERBOCKER HOLIDAY: **Composer:** Kurt
     Weill, Maxwell Anderson. **Conductor:** Jacques Samossud. **Cast:** Nelson Eddy, Charles Coburn,
     Ernest Cossert. WHERE DO WE GO FROM HERE: **Composer:** Kurt Weill, Ira Gershwin.
     Conductor: Emil Newman. **Cast:** Fred MacMurray, Joan Leslie, June Haver, Herman Bing,
     Carlos Ramirez, Fortunio Bonanova, Gene Sheldon.

KURT WEILL REVISITED

Studio Cast [Vol. 1] • Painted Smiles (S) PS 1375 8-15
  Composer: Kurt Weill.
Studio Cast [Vol. 2] • Painted Smiles (S) PS 1376 8-15
  Composer: Kurt Weill.

KWAMINA

Original Cast (1961) • Capitol (M) W-1645 20-25   61
Original Cast (1961) • Capitol (S) SW-1645 35-45   61
  Composer: Richard Adler. **Conductor:** Colin Romoff. **Cast:** Sally Ann Howes, Terry Carter,
  Brock Peters, Robert Guillaume.
Studio Cast (1961) • Mercury (M) MG-20654 10-20
Studio Cast (1961) • Mercury (S) SR-60654 15-25
  Composer: Richard Adler. **Conductor:** Billy Taylor. **Cast:** Billy Taylor Orchestra.

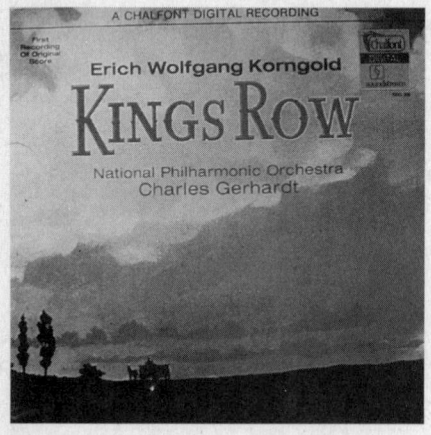

L

LA BAMBA
Soundtrack (1987) • Slash (S) 1-25605.. 8-15   87
Soundtrack (1987) • Slash (S) R-120062 8-10   Re
Composer: Ritchie Valens, Carlos Santana, Miles Goodman, others. **Cast:** Los Lobos, Marshall Crenshaw, Howard Huntsberry, Brian Setzer, Bo Diddley.

LA CAGE AUX FOLLES (1980)
Soundtrack (1980) • Cerberus (S) 0102 10-12   80
Soundtrack (1980) • Cerberus (S) CEM-0102 25-50   80
Pink vinyl. Limited edition.
Composer: Ennio Morricone. **Conductor:** Ennio Morricone.

LA CAGE AUX FOLLES (1983)
Original Cast (1983) • RCA Victor (S) HBC1-4824 8-10   83
Composer: Jerry Herman. **Conductor:** Donald Pippin. **Cast:** George Hearn, Gene Barry, Jay Garner, John Weiner, Elizabeth Parrish, Leslie Stevens, William Thomas Jr., Merle Louise, Walter Charles.

LA CAGE AUX FOLLES II
Soundtrack (1981) • Cerberus (S) CEMS-0107................................... 10-12   81
Composer: Ennio Morricone. **Conductor:** Ennio Morricone.

LA DOLCE VITA
Soundtrack (1961) • RCA Victor (EP) LPC-136.................................... 15-20   61
Soundtrack (1961) • RCA Victor (M) FOC-1 20-30   61
Soundtrack (1961) • RCA Victor (S) FSO-1 35-60   61
Composer: Nino Rota, others. **Conductor:** Nino Rota.
Studiotrack (1961) • RCA Victor (M) LPM-2410 10-12   61
Studiotrack (1961) • RCA Victor (S) LSP-2410 10-12   61
Full title: *La Dolce Vita and Other Great Motion Picture Themes.* Also has music from *The High and the Mighty, The Misfits, Spellbound, The Joker Is Wild, Love Is a Many-Splendored Thing. Gone with the Wind, A Summer Place, The Man Who Knew Too Much, April Love* and *Exodus.*
Composer: Nino Rota. **Conductor:** Ray Ellis. **Cast:** Ray Ellis and Orchestra.

LA GRANDE BOURGEOISE
Soundtrack (1974) • Cerberus (S) CEMS-0109................................... 10-15   81
Composer: Ennio Morricone. **Conductor:** Ennio Morricone.

LA GUERRE EST FINIE
Soundtrack (1967) • Bell (M) 6012 10-20   67
Soundtrack (1967) • Bell (S) 6012-S 15-25   67
Composer: Giovanni Fusco. **Conductor:** Jean Gitton.

LA MELODIA PROHIBIDA
Studiotrack (1930s) • RCA VICTOR 17-5002.................................... 200-250   30s
78 rpm picture disc. Actual title: *Siempre.*
Cast: Jose Mojica.

LA PERICHOLE
Original Cast (1957) • RCA Victor (M) LOC-1029 35-45   57
Boxed set with libretto. Has original cast of the Metropolitan Opera production.

Original Cast (1957) • Met Opera Club (M) MO-713............................. 12-15   57
   Composer: Jacques Offenbach, Maurice Valency. **Conductor:** Jean Morel. **Cast:** Patrice Munsel, Theodor Uppman, Cyril Ritchard, Ralph Herbert, Paul Franke, Keidi Krall, Madelaine Chambers, Rosalind Elias, Charles Anthony, Calvin Marsh, Alessio de Paolis.

LA STRADA
Studio Cast (1969) • United Artists (S) UAS-6688................................ 25-30   69
   Cast: Sir Julian (piano).

LA TRAVIATA
Soundtrack (1983) • Elektra/Asylum (S) 60267-1................................ 10-15   83
   Two discs.

LA VIE PARISIENNE
Original London Cast (1961) • RCA Victor/EMI (M) CLP-1468 20-30   61
Original London Cast (1961) • RCA Victor/EMI (S) CSD-1468 25-35   61
   UK release.
   Composer: Jacques Offenbach, Geoffrey Dunn. **Conductor:** Alexander Faris. **Cast:** June Bronhill, Eric Shilling, Anna Pollak, Kevin Miller, Suzanne Steele, Jon Weaving, Cynthia Morey, John Fryatt.

LA VIOLETERA
Soundtrack (1959) • Columbia (M) EX-5056 30-40   60
   Composer: Martinez Abades. **Cast:** Sarita Montiel.

LA VOIX HUMAINE (THE HUMAN VOICE)
Original Cast • RCA Victor (S) LSS-2385... 15-20

LABYRINTH
Soundtrack (1986) • EMI America (S) SV-17206 10-15   86
   Composer: Trevor Jones, David Bowie. **Conductor:** Trevor Jones. **Cast:** Trevor Jones, David Bowie.

LADIES DON'T SPIT AND HOLLER
Original Cast (1981) • Perfection Sound (S) 31982.............................. 10-20   81
   Composer: Lynn Lavner. **Cast:** Lynn Lavner, Phyllis Young.

LADIES OF BURLESQUE
Soundtrack • Legends (M) 1000/2... 25-35
   Previously unreleased vocals from *Panama Hattie, DuBarry Was a Lady, She Loves Me Not, Kiss the Boys Goodbye, Eadie Was a Lady, Wabash Avenue, Nora Prentiss, Let's Do It Again, So This Is Love, Pal Joey, Girl Happy, The Stripper* and *Meet Me in Las Vegas.* Figure on front cover combines features from each singer to create a "composite burlesque beauty."
   Cast: Alice Faye, Mary Martin, Ann Sothern, Ann Miller, Lucille Ball, Shelley Winters, Jane Wyman, Virginia O'Brien, Barbara Stanwyck, Grace Bradley, Glenda Farrell, Miriam Hopkins, Betty Grable, Adele Jergens, Ann Sheridan, Kathryn Grayson, Jo Ann Greer (performed vocals for Rita Hayworth in *Pal Joey*), Joanne Woodward, Cara Williams, Nita Talbot.

LADIES WHO WROTE THE LYRICS
Original Cast (1985) • Battery (S) PS-1334... 8-10   85
   Cast: Michael's Pub Show.

LADY AND THE TRAMP
Soundtrack (1955) • Capitol DBX-3056.. 40-50   54
   78 rpm album. Gatefold cover with full-color picture book, "Featuring members of the original cast."
Soundtrack (1955) • Capitol (EP) EAXP-3056...................................... 20-30   55
   Composer: Peggy Lee, Sonny Burke, Dave Cavanaugh. **Conductor:** Dave Cavanaugh. **Cast:** Daws Butler, June Foray, Art Gilmore, Barbara Luddy, Larry Roberts, Bill Thompson.
Studiotrack (1955) • Decca (M) DL-5557 40-60   55
   10-inch LP.

Studiotrack (1955) • Decca (M) DL-8462 30-75   57
   Composer: Peggy Lee, Sonny Burke, Oliver Wallace. Conductor: Victor Young. Cast: Peggy
   Lee, Sonny Burke.
Soundtrack (1955) • Disneyland (M) ST-3917 15-20   62
Soundtrack (1955) • Disneyland (M) DQ-1231 20-25   63
Soundtrack (1955) • Disneyland (M) 3103 25-30   80
   Picture disc. Limited edition.
   Composer: Peggy Lee, Sonny Burke, Oliver Wallace. Conductor: Sonny Burke, Oliver
   Wallace. Cast: Peggy Lee, Sonny Burke, Oliver Wallace
Studiotrack (1955) • MGM (EP) X-1145 20-25   55
   Cast: Kay Armen, Marion Sisters.
   Also see CHILDREN, CHILDREN, CHILDREN

LADY BE GOOD

Original Cast (1924) • Smithsonian (M) R-008 12-18
   Gatefold cover. Smithsonian archival recreation of the original production.
   Composer: George Gershwin, Ira Gershwin. Conductor: J. Heuvel, Carl Fenton. Cast: Fred
   Astaire, Adele Astaire, George Gershwin (piano), William Kent, George Vollaire, Irving Berlin,
   Victor Arden and Phil Ohman (pianos), Cliff Edwards.
Soundtrack (1941) • Hollywood Soundstage (M) HS-5010 10-15
   Composer: George Gershwin, Ira Gershwin, Jerome Kern, Oscar Hammerstein II, others.
   Conductor: George Stoll. Cast: Ann Sothern, Eleanor Powell, Robert Young, Red Skelton,
   Virginia O'Brien, John Carroll.

LADY BEWARE

Soundtrack (1987) • Scotti Bros. (S) AL-40971 8-10   87
   White label. Promotional issue only.
Soundtrack (1987) • Scotti Bros. (S) SZ-40971 8-10   87
   Composer: Craig Safan. Cast: David Hallyday, LaMarca, Craig Safan.

LADY CAROLINE LAMB

Soundtrack (1972) • Angel (S) S-36946 12-18   73
   Composer: Richard Rodney Bennett. Conductor: Marcus Dods. Cast: New Philharmonic
   Orchestra, Peter Mark (viola).

LADY FROM PHILADELPHIA

TV Soundtrack (1957) • RCA Victor (M) LM-2212 12-15   57
   From the TV series See It Now.
   Cast: Edward R. Murrow (narration), Marian Anderson, Franz Rupp (piano).

LADY IN CEMENT

Soundtrack (1968) • 20th Century-Fox (S) S-4204 15-20   68
   Composer: Hugo Montenegro, Sammy Fain, others. Conductor: Hugo Montenegro.

LADY IN THE DARK

Original Cast (1941) • RCA P-60 25-35   41
   78 rpm album.
Original Radio Cast (1941) • AEI (M) AEI-1145 18-20   80s
   Featuring both Gertrude Lawrence and Macdonald Carey from the Broadway production.
   Composer: Kurt Weill, Ira Gershwin. Cast: Gertrude Lawrence, Hume Cronyn, Macdonald
   Carey.
Original Radio Cast • Command Performance (M) LP-10 20-50
   Dialogue from the play, with music primarily used only as underscoring for this radio
   production.
   Composer: Kurt Weill, Ira Gershwin. Cast: Judy Garland, John Lund.
Studio Cast (1953) • Columbia (M) CL-6249 25-35   53
Studio Cast (1953) • Harmony (M) HL-7012 15-18   56
   Composer: Kurt Weill, Ira Gershwin. Conductor: Maurice Abravanel. Cast: Danny Kaye.
Studio Cast (1963) • Columbia (M) OL-5990 20-30   63
Studio Cast (1963) • Columbia (S) OS-2390 25-30   63

Studio Cast (1963) • Columbia (S) COS-2390 8-10   Re
    Composer: Kurt Weill, Ira Gershwin. **Conductor:** Lehman Engel. **Cast:** Risë Stevens, Adolph
    Green, John Reardon, Stephanie Augustine, Kenneth Bridges, Roger White.
TV Soundtrack (1954) • RCA Victor (M) LM-1882 175-225   54
    Composer: Kurt Weill, Ira Gershwin. **Conductor:** Charles Sanford. **Cast:** Ann Sothern, Carleton
    Carpenter, Clay-Warnick Choir.
    Also see DOWN IN THE VALLEY
    Also see NYMPH ERRANT

LADY IN WHITE
Soundtrack (1988) • Varese Sarabande (S) 704 530 8-12   88
    Composer: Frank Laloggia. **Conductor:** John Massari. **Cast:** Lukas Haas.

LADY SINGS THE BLUES
Soundtrack (1972) • Paramount/Dick Strout (S) 181/182 30-40   72
    Labeled "MRA (Multiple Record Album, serving the requirements of both radio and TV
    stations)." Has complete as well as open-end interviews, including a 15-minute interview
    with Diana Ross. Includes scripts.
Soundtrack (1972) • Motown (S) M-78558D 10-12   72
    Two discs. Includes eight-page booklet.
    Composer: Michel Legrand, others. **Conductor:** Michel Legrand. **Cast:** Diana Ross (sings
    songs of Billie Holliday).

LADY'S NOT FOR BURNING
Original Cast (1951) • Decca (M) DL-9508/9 35-45   51
    Two discs.
    Cast: Sir John Gielgud, Pamela Brown, Richard Burton.

LADYHAWKE
Soundtrack (1985) • Atlantic (S) 81248-1 15-20   85
    Composer: Andrew Powell. **Conductor:** Andrew Powell. **Cast:** Philharmonic Orchestra.

LAGNIAPPE '59 PRESENTS BE MY GUEST: see BE MY GUEST

LAMBERT'S HOROSCOPE: see RED SHOES

LAND BEFORE TIME
Soundtrack (1988) • MCA (S) 6266 10-15   88
    Conductor: James Horner. **Cast:** James Horner, London Symphony Orchestra, King's College
    Choir, Diana Ross.

LAND OF THE PHARAOHS
Studiotrack (1978) • Elmer Bernstein Film Music
    Collection (S) FMC-13 15-18   78
    Also has music from *Gunfight at the O.K. Corral.*
    Composer: Dimitri Tiomkin. **Conductor:** Elmer Bernstein.

LAND RAIDERS
Soundtrack (1970) • Beverly Hills (S) BHS-21 20-25   70
    Composer: Bruno Nicolai. **Conductor:** Bruno Nicolai.

LANDLORD
Soundtrack (1970) • United Artists (S) UAS-5209 15-20   70
    Composer: Al Kooper. **Conductor:** Al Kooper. **Cast:** Martha Stewart Singers, Lorraine Ellison,
    Manny Green, Joe Farrell, Staple Singers, Al Kooper.

LANGFORD, FRANCES: see FRANCES LANGFORD PRESENTS

LAS VEGAS NIGHTS: see SHIP AHOY

LASERIUM ZODIAC
Soundtrack (1978) • Polydor (S) 1-6122 8-10   78

LASSIE: see MAGIC OF LASSIE

LASSITER

Soundtrack (1984) • Varese Sarabande (S) STV-81208 12-15   84
Soundtrack (1984) • That's Entertainment (S) TER-1092 8-10   80s
   UK release.
    Composer: Ken Thorne. **Conductor:** Ken Thorne. **Cast:** Danny Street.

L'ASSOLUTO NATURALE

Soundtrack (1980) • Cerberus (S) CEMS 0112 8-10   81
    Composer: Ennio Morricone. **Conductor:** Ennio Morricone.

LAST AMERICAN VIRGIN

Soundtrack (1982) • Columbia (S) JS-38279 8-10   82
    Cast: Oingo Boingo, Phil Seymour, Tommy Tutone, others.

LAST ANGRY MAN: see NO SAD SONGS FOR ME

LAST COMMAND: see COME NEXT SPRING

LAST DRAGON

Soundtrack (1985) • Motown (S) 6128ML 8-10   85
    Cast: DeBarge, Stevie Wonder, Smokey Robinson, Rockwell, Willie Hutch, Temptations, Dwight
    David, Vanity, Alfie, Charlene.

LAST EMBRACE

Soundtrack (1979) • Varese Sarabande (S) STV-81166 15-20   83
    Composer: Miklos Rozsa. **Conductor:** Miklos Rozsa. **Cast:** Nürnberg Symphony Orchestra,
    Albert Dominguez (piano).

LAST EMPEROR

Soundtrack (1987) • Virgin Movie Music (S) 90690-1 10-15   87
    Composer: Ryuichi Sakamoto, David Byrne, others. **Cast:** David Byrne, Cong Su, Red Guard
    Accordion Band, Girls Red Guard Dancers, Ryuichi Sakamoto, Ball Orchestra of Vienna.

LAST EXIT TO BROOKLYN

Soundtrack (1989) • Warner Bros. (S) 25986-1 10-12   89
    Composer: Mark Knopfler. **Cast:** Mark Knopfler.

LAST METRO

Soundtrack (1980) • DRG (S) SL-9504 10-14   80
    Composer: Georges Delerue. **Conductor:** Georges Delerue. **Cast:** Lucienne Delyle, Rina
    Ketty, Leo Marjane.

LAST OF THE AMERICAN HOBOES

Soundtrack (1978) • Beegee (S) BGS-1041 15-20   70
    Composer: Gary Revel, Eddie Downs, others. **Conductor:** Judd Phillips. **Cast:** Gary Revel,
    Chapparral Brothers, Brian Mark, Wayne Storm, Noble "Kid" Chissel, Mike DeTemple.

LAST OF THE SECRET AGENTS

Soundtrack (1966) • Dot (M) DLP-3714 15-20   66
Soundtrack (1966) • Dot (S) DLP-25714 20-25   66
    Composer: Pete King, Neal Hefti. **Conductor:** Frank Comstock. **Cast:** Steve Rossi.

Studiotrack • Musicor (M) MM 2086 10-15
   Full title: *Steve Rossi Sings You Are, from The Last of the Secret Agents*. Also has songs
   from other films.
    Cast: Steve Rossi.

LAST OF THE SKI BUMS

Soundtrack (1969) • World Pacific (S) WPS-21884 15-25   69
   Orange cover.
Soundtrack (1969) • World Pacific (S) WPS-21884 10-20   69
   Blue cover.
    Composer: John Blakeley, Jud Strunk, John Gibson, Gaston Georis. **Cast:** Sandals.

LAST PICTURE SHOW

Soundtrack (1971) • Columbia (SE) S-31143 10-12   72
    Cast: Tony Bennett, Eddie Fisher, Pee Wee King, Hank Snow, Frankie Laine, Lefty Frizzell, Johnny Ray, Jo Stafford.

Studiotrack (1971) • MGM (SE) 1SE-33 8-10   71
    Cast: Hank Williams (collection of his early '50s recordings).

LAST PORNO FLICK

Soundtrack (1974) • BRS (S) 103 10-12   75
    Composer: Tony Bruno. **Conductor:** Tony Bruno.

LAST REBEL

Soundtrack (1971) • Capitol (S) SW-827 12-15   71
    Composer: Jon Lord, Tony Ashton. **Cast:** Ashton, Gardner and Dyke, Royal Liverpool Symphony Orchestra.

LAST RUN

Soundtrack (1971) • MGM (S) 1SE-30 15-25   71
Soundtrack (1971) • MCA (S) 25116 8-10   86
    Composer: Jerry Goldsmith. **Conductor:** Jerry Goldsmith. **Cast:** Steve Lawrence.

LAST STARFIGHTER

Soundtrack (1984) • Southern Cross (S) SCRS-1007 20-25   84
    Conductor: Craig Safan. **Cast:** Craig Safan.

LAST SUMMER

Soundtrack (1969) • Warner Bros. (S) WS-1791 15-20   69
    Composer: John Simon. **Conductor:** John Simon.

LAST SWEET DAYS OF ISAAC

Original Cast (1970) • RCA Victor (S) LSO-1169 8-10   70
    Composer: Nancy Ford, Gretchen Cryer. **Conductor:** Clay Fullum. **Cast:** Austin Pendleton, Fredicka Weber, Charles Collins, C. David Colson, Louise Heath, John Long, Zeitgeist.

LAST TANGO IN PARIS

Soundtrack (1972) • United Artists (S) UA-LA045-F 12-15   72
Soundtrack (1972) • Pickwick (S) SPC-3314 8-10   72
    Composer: Gato Barbieri. **Conductor:** Gato Barbieri.

LAST TEMPTATION OF CHRIST

Soundtrack (1988) • Real World (S) GHS-24206 10-15   88
    Two discs. Full title: *Passion: Music for The Last Temptation of Christ.*
    Cast: Peter Gabriel.

LAST TIME I SAW PARIS

Studiotrack (1954) • MGM (EP) X1124 20-25   54
    Cast: Odetta.

LAST VALLEY

Soundtrack (1971) • Dunhill (S) X-50102 25-35   71
Soundtrack (1971) • Dunhill (S) SW-50102 12-15   Re
    Composer: John Barry. **Conductor:** John Barry.

LAST WALTZ

Soundtrack (1978) • Warner Bros. (S) 3WS-3146 25-30   78
    Three discs.
    Cast: The Band, Paul Butterfield, Eric Clapton, Neil Diamond, Bob Dylan, Emmylou Harris, Ronnie Hawkins, Mac "Dr. John" Rebennac, Joni Mitchell, Van Morrison, Staples, Ringo Starr, Muddy Waters, Ron Wood, Neil Young.

LATE GREAT PLANET EARTH

Soundtrack • RCR Productions (S) ACAB-10022 12-15   76
    Cast: Hal Lindsey, Orson Welles.

LATE NITE COMIC (A NEW AMERICAN MUSICAL)

Original Cast • Original Cast (S) OC-8843 8-10   87
    Cast: Lee Shapiro, Brian Gari, Michael McAssey, Julie Budd, Robin Kaiser.

LAUGH-IN: see ROWEN AND MARTIN'S LAUGH-IN

LAURA: see DAVID RAKSIN CONDUCTS HIS GREAT FILM SCORES

LAUREL & HARDY

Soundtrack • Mark 56 (M) 575 10-15   78

Soundtrack • Music Box (M) TMH 4305 25-35   82
   Numbered (1,000 made), autographed edition of original scores from *Saps at Sea*, *Way Out West* (music and dialogue*)*, *Bonnie Scotland*, *Blockheads*, *Them Thar Hills*, *Sons of the Desert*, *Topper Takes a Trip* (Cosmo Topper), plus demo recordings and newly recorded Hatley selections (1982).
    Composer: T. Marvin Hatley. **Conductor:** T. Marvin Hatley. **Cast:** T. Marvin Hatley, others.
   Also see ANOTHER FINE MESS
   Also see BABES IN TOYLAND.

LAWRENCE OF ARABIA

Soundtrack (1962) • Colpix (M) LE-1000............................. 35-40   62

Soundtrack (1962) • Colpix (S) LES-1000............................ 40-45   62
   Boxed sets, with booklets.

Soundtrack (1962) • Colpix (M) CP-514 8-10   62

Soundtrack (1962) • Colpix (S) SCP-514 12-18   62
   Cover pictures Arab band in lower right corner. Side 2 is *Whose Name Do You Ride*. First issues do not have "Academy Award Winner" on cover.

Soundtrack (1962) • Colpix (S) SCP-514 10-12   62
   Cover shows a sword being brandished in lower right corner. Side 2 is *Continuation of the Miracle*. First issues do not have "Academy Award Winner" on cover.

Soundtrack (1962) • Colgems (M) COMO-5004................... 12-15   67

Soundtrack (1962) • Colgems (S) COSO-5004 15-18   67
   Reissue of Colpix release.

Soundtrack (1962) • Bell (S) B-1205 10-12   71

Soundtrack (1962) • Arista (S) ABM-4009........................... 8-12   Re
    Composer: Maurice Jarre, Kenneth Alford. **Conductor:** Maurice Jarre. **Cast:** London Philharmonic Orchestra.

Studiotrack (1962) • Colpix (M) CP-458 10-12   62

Studiotrack (1962) • Colpix (S) SCP-458 10-15   62
   Full title for both is *Lawrence of Arabia and Other Wonderful Movie Themes*. Includes soundtrack and studiotrack music.
    Composer: Various. **Cast:** Various.

Studiotrack • Palace (M) M-747 8-10

Studiotrack • Palace (S) PST-747 8-10
   Also has *Music of the Orient*, by the Alexander Maloof Orchestra.
    Composer: Maurice Jarre, Kenneth J. Alford. **Cast:** Bill Ewing (organ), Alexander Maloof Orchestra.

Studiotrack • United Artists (M) UAL-3278 8-12

LAWRENCE WELK SHOW: 10TH ANNIVERSARY SPECIAL

TV Soundtrack (1965) • Dot (M) DLP-3591........................... 8-12   65

TV Soundtrack (1965) • Dot (S) DLP-25591 10-15   65
    Conductor: Lawrence Welk. **Cast:** Lawrence Welk and featured guests.

LE MANS

Soundtrack (1971) • Columbia (S) S-30891 12-15   71
    Composer: Michel Legrand. **Conductor:** Michel Legrand. **Cast:** Peggy Taylor Woodward. Gene Morford.

LE RETOUR DE MARTIN GUERRE: see RETURN OF MARTIN GUERRE

LEADBELLY
Soundtrack (1976) • ABC (S) ABDP-939 12-15   76
  Composer: Huddie Ledbetter (a.k.a. "Leadbelly"). Conductor: Fred Karlin.

LEADER OF THE PACK
Original Cast (1985) • Elektra (S) 9 60420-1 8-10   85
  Full title: *Greatest Hits from Leaders of the Pack.* Promotional issue only.
Original Cast (1985) • Elektra (S) 60409-1 10-25   85
  Two discs.
  Composer: Ellie Greenwich, Jeff Barry. Cast: Dinah Manoff, Patrick Cassidy, Dennis Bailey,
  Annie Golden, Darlene Love, Ellie Greenwich.

LEAN ON ME
Soundtrack (1989) • Warner Bros. (S) 1-25843 10-15   89
  Cast: Thelma Houston, Winans, Stetsasonic, Roxanne Shante, TKA, Siedah Garrett, Force
  M.D.'s, Riff, Teen Dream, Taja Sevelle, Big Daddy Kane, Guns 'N' Roses.

LEARNING TREE
Soundtrack (1969) • Warner Bros. (S) WS-1812 12-15   69
  Composer: Gordon Parks. Conductor: Tom McIntosh.
  Also see RAIN PEOPLE

LEAVE IT TO JANE
Original Revival Cast (1959) • Strand (M) SL-1002 10-12   59
Original Revival Cast (1959) • Strand (S) SLS-1002 12-18   59
Original Revival Cast (1959) • Stet (S) DS-15002 8-10   Re
Original Revival Cast (1959) • AEI (S) AEI-1143 8-10   80s
  Composer: Jerome Kern, Guy Bolton, P.G. Wodehouse. Conductor: Joseph Stecko. Cast:
  Kathleen Murray, Dorothy Greener, George Segal, Angelo Mango, Jeanne Allen, Art Matthews,
  Ray Tudor, Jan Speers.

LEAVE IT TO ME: see LET'S FACE IT

LEGAL EAGLES
Soundtrack (1986) • MCA (S) 6172 8-10   86
  Digital recording.
  Composer: Elmer Bernstein. Conductor: Elmer Bernstein. Cast: Rascals, Darryl Hannah,
  Steppenwolf, United Kingdom Symphony.

LEGEND (1976)
Original Cast (1976) • Theatre Archives (M) TA-7801 8-10   76
  Background music heard during the play.
  Composer: Dan Goggin. Cast: Tangerine Dream, Bryan Ferry, Jon Anderson.

LEGEND (1986)
Soundtrack (1986) • Moment (S) 100 25-35   86
  Composer: Jerry Goldsmith. Conductor: Jerry Goldsmith.
Soundtrack (1986) • MCA (S) 6165 10-15   86
  Composer: Tangerine Dream members. Cast: Jon Anderson, Bryan Ferry, Tangerine Dream.

LEGEND OF JESSE JAMES
Soundtrack (1980) • A&M SP-3718 10-15   80

LEGEND OF SLEEPY HOLLOW: see ICHABOD (THE LEGEND OF SLEEPY
  HOLLOW)

LEGEND OF THE LONE RANGER
Soundtrack (1981) • MCA (S) 5212 10-15   81
  Includes Rossini's *William Tell Overture.*
  Composer: John Barry, Gioacchino Rossini. Conductor: John Barry. Cast: Merle Haggard.
  Also see LONE RANGER

LEGEND OF THE SEVEN GOLDEN VAMPIRES
Soundtrack (1974) • Warner Bros. (S) K-56085 12-15   74
    Composer: James Bernard. **Composer:** Philip Martell. **Cast:** Peter Cushing (narration).

LEGENDS OF THE MUSICAL STAGE
Soundtrack (1980) • Take Two (S) TT-104 12-18   80
   Warner Brothers early film soundtracks, with vocals.
    Composer: Various. **Cast:** Nick Lucas, Harry Richman, Marilyn Miller, Eddie Cantor, Fanny
    Brice, Sophie Tucker, Ethel Merman, Al Jolson.

LEGS DIAMOND
Original Cast (1988) • RCA Victor (S) 7983-1-RC 20-25   89
   One of the last original cast recordings released primarily on vinyl.
    Composer: Peter Allen. **Conductor:** Eric Stern. **Cast:** Peter Allen, Julie Wilson, Randall Edwards,
    Joe Silver, Raymond Serra, Christian Kauffmann, Pat McNamara, Jim Fyfe, Brenda Baxton.

LEINENGEN VS. THE ANTS: see SORRY, WRONG NUMBER

LEMMINGS: see NATIONAL LAMPOON LEMMINGS

LENA HORNE: THE LADY AND HER MUSIC
Original Cast (1981) • Qwest (S) 2QW-3597 8-20   81
   Two discs.
    Conductor: Linda Twine, Bob Freedman. **Cast:** Lena Horne, Clare Bathe, Tyra Ferrell, Vondie
    Curtis-Hall.

LENNY
Original Cast (1971) • Blue Thumb (S) BTS-9001 12-15   71
   Two discs.
    Composer: Tom O'Horgan. **Cast:** Cliff Gorman, Joe Silver, Erica Yohn, Jane House, Robert
    Weil.
Soundtrack (1974) • United Artists (S) UA-LA-359-H 15-20   74
    Composer: Ralph Burns, others. **Conductor:** Ralph Burns. **Cast:** Dustin Hoffman (monologues
    from his portrayal of Lenny Bruce).

LEONARD BERNSTEIN & THE NEW YORK PHILHARMONIC ON CHRISTMAS DAY
TV Soundtrack (1960) • Kenyon/Eckhardt (M) no number used 25-30   60
   Sponsored by Ford Motor Company.
    Conductor: Leonard Bernstein. **Cast:** New York Philharmonic Orchestra, Marian Anderson,
    Schola Cantorum Chorus, St. Paul's London Boy's Choir.

LEONARD NIMOY PRESENTS MR. SPOCK'S MUSIC FROM OUTER SPACE
Studiotrack • Dot (M) DLP 3794 35-50
Studiotrack • Dot (S) DLP 25794 55-80
    Cast: Leonard Nimoy (music and dialogue.)

LEOPARD
Soundtrack (1963) • 20th Century-Fox (M) FXG-5015 20-25   63
Soundtrack (1963) • 20th Century-Fox (S) SXG-5015 20-40   63
Soundtrack (1963) • Varese Sarabande (S) STV 81190 8-12
    Composer: Nino Rota. **Conductor:** Franco Ferrara.

LES BICYCLETTES DE BELSIZE: see TWISTED NERVE

LES GIRLS
Soundtrack (1957) • MGM (M) E-3590.. 20-30   57
Soundtrack (1957) • MCA (M) MCA-1426 8-10   Re
  Also has music from *Lili*.
  Composer: Cole Porter. **Conductor:** Adolph Deutsch. **Cast:** Gene Kelly, Mitzi Gaynor, Kay
  Kendall, Taina Elg. LILI: **Composer:** Bronislau Kaper. **Conductor:** Hans Sommer. **Cast:** Leslie
  Caron, Mel Ferrer, MGM Studio Orchestra.
  Also see TEN NORTH FREDERICK
  Also see THOSE GLORIOUS MGM MUSICALS.

LES LIAISONS DANGEREUSES
Soundtrack (1961) • Epic (M) LA-16022.. 25-30   61
Soundtrack (1961) • Fontana (M) MGF-27539 12-18   65
Soundtrack (1961) • Fontana (SE) SRF-67539 12-18   65
  Composer: J. Marray. **Cast:** Art Blakey and the Jazz Messengers with Barney Wilen.
Studiotrack (1962) • Parker (M) PLP-813... 12-18   62
Studiotrack (1962) • Parker (S) PLPS-813-S 15-20   62
  Composer: Duke Jordan. **Conductor:** Duke Jordan.

LES MISERABLES
Original French Cast (1985) • First Night (S) No Number Used 15-20   85
Original London Cast (1985) • Relativity (S) 88561 8140-1 15-20   85
  Two discs.
  Composer: Claude-Michel Schonberg, Herbert Kretzmer. **Cast:** Colm Wilkinson, Roger Allam.
Original London Cast (1985) • First Night (S) Encore 1....................... 10-15   86
  Cast: Patti LuPone, others.
Original Cast (1987) • Geffen (S) GHS-24151 10-12   87
Original Cast (1987) • Geffen (S) M5G-24151 10-12   87
  Two discs. From the Broadway production.
  Composer: Claude-Michel Schonberg, Herbert Kretzmer. **Conductor:** Robert Billig. **Cast:** Colm
  Wilkinson, Terrence Mann, Randy Graff, Donna Vivino, Jennifer Butt, Leo Burmester, Frances
  Ruffelle, David Bryant, Judy Kuhn, Michael Maguire.

LES POUPEES DE PARIS
Original Cast (1964) • RCA Victor (M) LOC-1090 15-18   64
Original Cast (1964) • RCA Victor (S) LSO-1090 20-25   64
  A show created for the 1964 New York World's Fair, featuring the puppets of Sid and Marty
  Krofft.
  Composer: Jimmy Van Heusen, Sammy Cahn. **Conductor:** Joe Reisman. **Cast:** Pearl Bailey,
  Milton Berle, Cyd Charisse, Annie Farge, Gene Kelly, Liberace, Jayne Mansfield, Tony Martin,
  Phil Silvers, Loretta Young, Edith Adams.

LESLIE UGGAMS ON TV
TV Soundtrack • Columbia (M) CL-1706 10-12
TV Soundtrack • Columbia (S) CS-8506 12-15
  Cast: Leslie Uggams, Mitch Miller's Sing Along Chorus.

LESS THAN ZERO
Soundtrack (1987) • Def Jam/Columbia (S) SC-44042 5-8   87
  Cast: Aerosmith, Roy Orbison, Poison, L., Glen Danzig and Power and Fury Orchestra, Slayer,
  Public Enemy, Black Flames, Joan Jett and Blackhearts, Oran "Juice" Jones, Alyson Williams,
  Bangles.

LET 'EM EAT CAKE: see OF THEE I SING

LET IT BE
Soundtrack (1970) • Apple (S) AR-34001 15-25   70
Soundtrack (1970) • Capitol (S) SW-11922... 8-12   79
  Purple or black label.

Soundtrack (1970) • MFSL (S) 1-109 25-35   79
Half-speed mastered. Has gatefold cover.
Composer: John Lennon, Paul McCartney, George Harrison. **Cast:** Beatles.

LET IT RIDE
Original Cast (1961) • RCA Victor (M) LOC-1064 10-15   61
Original Cast (1961) • RCA Victor (S) LSO-1064 30-35   61
Composer: Jay Livingston, Ray Evans. **Conductor:** Jay Blackton. **Cast:** George Gobel, Sam Levene, Barbara Nichols.

LET MY PEOPLE COME
Original Cast (1974) • Libra (S) LR-1069 15-20   74
Composer: Earl Wilson Jr. **Conductor:** Billy Cunningham. **Cast:** Christine Rubens, Tobie Columbus, Lorraine Davidson, Marty Duffy, Joe Jones, Larry Paulette, Shezwae Powell.

LET NO MAN WRITE MY EPITAPH
Soundtrack (1960) • Verve (M) MG-V-4043 20-25   60
Soundtrack (1960) • Verve (S) V6-4043 30-35   60
Cast: Ella Fitzgerald, Paul Smith (piano).

LET THE GOOD TIMES ROLL
Soundtrack (1973) • Bell (S) 9002 20-25   73
Two discs. Includes introductions and documentary tracks
Cast: Chuck Berry, Chubby Checker, Shirelles, Little Richard, Bo Diddley, Coasters, Five Satins, Fats Domino, Danny and the Juniors, Bill Haley & His Comets.
Soundtrack (1974) • Kory (S) KK-1003 8-12

L'ETOILE DU NORD
Soundtrack • DRG (S) SL 9512 10-15   83
Also has music from *La Vueve Couderc, Le Chat* and *Le Train.*
Composer: Philippe Sarde. **Conductor:** Philippe Sarde, Carlo Savina, Jean-Michel Defaye. **Cast:** Philippe Sarde, Jean Sablon, Santa Cecilia Orchestra.

LET'S BE HAPPY
Soundtrack (1957) • RCA Victor (EP) EPA-4060 35-45   57
Four tracks taken directly from the sound track, performed by Tony Martin.
Composer: Nicholas Brodszky, Paul Francis Webster. **Conductor:** Louis Levy. **Cast:** Tony Martin.

LET'S DANCE TO THE MOVIE THEMES
Studiotrack (1961) • Mercury (M) MG 20688 10-12   61
Studiotrack (1961) • Mercury (S) SR 60688 10-15   61
Music from *Exodus, Never on Sunday, The Sundowners, Moon River, Tunes of Glory* and *Dark at the Top of the Stairs.*
Cast: David Carroll and His Orchestra.

LET'S DO IT AGAIN
Soundtrack (1975) • Curstom (S) CU-5005 10-12   75
Composer: Curtis Mayfield, Quinton Joseph, Phillip Upchurch, Gary Thompson, Floyd Morris, Joseph Scott. **Cast:** Staple Singers.

LET'S FACE IT
Original Cast • Smithsonian (M) RO-16 15-18   79
With members of the original New York production, plus Hildegarde's Decca recordings (from 78 rpms). Also has music from *Leave it to Me* and *Red, Hot and Blue.*
Composer: Cole Porter. **Conductor:** Max Meth, Harry Sosnik, Johnny Green. **Cast:** Danny Kaye, Mary Jane Walsh, Hildegarde. LEAVE IT TO ME: **Composer:** Cole Porter. **Conductor:** Eddy Duchin. **Cast:** Mary Martin. RED HOT AND BLUE: **Composer:** Cole Porter. **Conductor:** Fairchild and Carroll. **Cast:** Ethel Merman, Yvonne Printemps.
Studio Cast (1941) • Decca A-291 15-18   41
78 rpm album. Six songs performed by Hildegarde, who was not actually in the show.
Composer: Cole Porter. **Conductor:** Harry Sosnik. **Cast:** Hildegarde.

LET'S GET HARRY
Soundtrack (1986) • Varese Sarabande (S) STV-81301 10-12   86
    Composer: Brad Fiedel.

LET'S GET LOST
Soundtrack (1989) • Novus (S) 35054-1-N9.................................... 8-10   89

LET'S MAKE LOVE
Soundtrack (1960) • Columbia (M) CL-1527 20-25   60
Soundtrack (1960) • Columbia (S) CS-8327......................... 35-50   60
Soundtrack (1960) • Columbia Special Products (S) ACS-8327............. 8-10   Re
    Composer: James Van Heusen, Sammy Cahn, Cole Porter. **Conductor:** Lionel Newman. **Cast:** Marilyn Monroe, Yves Montand, Frankie Vaughan.

LETHAL WEAPON
Soundtrack (1987) • Warner Bros. (S) 1-25561 8-10   87
    Composer: Michael Kamen, Eric Clapton. **Cast:** Eric Clapton, David Sanborn, Michael Kamen, Honeymoon Suite.

LETHAL WEAPON 2
Soundtrack (1989) • Warner Bros. (S) 1-25985 8-10   89
    Composer: Michael Kamen, Eric Clapton, Bob Dylan, George Harrison, Terry Melcher, Mike Love, David Sanborn. **Conductor:** Michael Kamen. **Cast:** George Harrison, Eric Clapton, Beach Boys, David Sanborn, Randy Crawford, Michael Kamen.

LETTER TO BREZHNEV
Soundtrack (1985) • MCA (S) 6162.. 8-10   85
    Cast: Redskins, Fine Young Cannibals, Carmel, Sandie Shaw, Alan Gill, Bronski Beat, Flesh, Certain Ratio, Paul Quinn, Margi Clarke.

LEVIATHAN
Soundtrack (1989) • Varese Sarabande (S) VS-5226 15-20   89
    Composer: Jerry Goldsmith. **Conductor:** Jerry Goldsmith. **Cast:** Orchestra di Santa Cecilia di Roma.

LIAISONS DANGEREUSES, LES: see LES LIAISONS DANGEREUSES

LIBERACE PLAYS GOLDEN THEMES FROM HOLLYWOOD
Studiotrack (1963) • Coral (S) 757452 10-15   63
    Cast: Liberace.

LIBERACE SHOW: A PROGRAM OF TV FAVORITES
TV Soundtrack (1958) • Harmony (M) HL-7154 10-20
    Cast: Liberace.

LIBERATION OF L.B. JONES: see FROM THE TERRACE

LIBERTY
TV Soundtrack (1986) • Citadel (S) CTD-8100.................................... 15-20   86
    Composer: William Goldstein. **Cast:** Chris Sarandon, Frank Langella, Carrie Fisher, Dana Delaney, George Kennedy, Claire Bloom, LeVar Burton.

LICENSE TO DRIVE
Soundtrack (1988) • MCA (S) 6241.. 8-10   88
    Cast: Breakfast Club, Belinda Carlisle, Boys Club, Billy Ocean, New Edition, D.J., Jonathan Butler, Femme Fatale, Slave Raider, Brenda K. Starr.

LICENSE TO KILL
Soundtrack (1989) • MCA (S) 6307.. 8-10   89
    Conductor: Michael Kamen. **Cast:** Gladys Knight, Ivory, Tim Feehan, Michael Kamen and National Philharmonic Orchestra, Patti La Belle.

LIE OF THE MIND
Soundtrack • Sugar Hill (S) SH-8501 8-10
    Cast: Red Clay Ramblers.

LIFE AND TIMES OF A SHE-DEVIL
TV Soundtrack (1986) • BBC (S) REB-615 15-20   86
    Composer: Peter Filleul, Richard Rodgers, Wolfgang Amadeus Mozart, etc. **Conductor:** Del Newman. **Cast:** Peter Filleul, Christine Collister, Claire Moore.

LIFE AND TIMES OF JUDGE ROY BEAN
Soundtrack (1972) • Columbia (S) S-31948 20-25   72
    Composer: Maurice Jarre. **Conductor:** Maurice Jarre. **Cast:** Andy Williams, Paul Newman (dialogue.)

LIFE IN THE THIRTIES
TV Soundtrack • NBC-TV (M) K08P.. 30-50
    Full title: *Project 20, NBC Television Network Presents: Life in the Thirties.*
    Conductor: Robert Russell Bennett.

LIFE IS JUST A BOWL OF CHERRIES
Studiotrack • Bethlehem (M) BCP-61 10-15   56
    Has music from *Best Things in Life Are Free.*

LIFE OF BRIAN
Soundtrack (1979) • Warner Bros. (S) BSK-3396 8-10   79
    Composer: Geoffrey Burgon, Michael Palin, Andre Jacquemin, David Howman, Eric Idle. **Conductor:** Marcus Dods. **Cast:** Terry Jones, Graham Chapman, Michael Palin, John Cleese, Eric Idle, Terry Gilliam.

LIFEFORCE
Soundtrack (1985) • Varese Sarabande (S) STV-81249 20-25   85
    Composer: Henry Mancini. **Conductor:** Henry Mancini. **Cast:** London Symphony Orchestra.

LIGHT FANTASTIC
Soundtrack (1963) • 20th Century-Fox (M) FXG-5016 15-20   63
Soundtrack (1963) • 20th Century-Fox (S) SXG-5016.......................... 20-25   63
    Composer: Joseph Leibman. **Conductor:** Judd Woldin.

LIGHT OF DAY
Soundtrack (1987) • CBS/Blackheart (S) ZK-40654 8-10   87
    Cast: Barbusters, Fabulous Thunderbirds, Ian Hunter, Dave Edmunds, Bon Jovi, Joan Jett and Blackhearts, Michael J. Fox, Rick Cox, Chas Smith, Jon C.

LIGHTER SIDE OF LAURITZ MELCHIOR: see THRILL OF A ROMANCE

LIGHTHORSEMEN: see SHAME

LI'L ABNER
Original Cast (1956) • Columbia (EP) A-5150 10-15   56
Original Cast (1956) • Columbia (M) OL-5150...................................... 10-15   56
Original Cast (1956) • Columbia Special Products (M) AOL-5150.......... 5-12   Re
    Composer: Gene de Paul, Johnny Mercer. **Conductor:** Lehman Engel. **Cast:** Edith Adams, Peter Palmer, Howard St. John, Stubby Kaye, Stanley Simmonds, Marc Breaux, Ralph Linn, Jack Matthew, Carmen Alvarez, Pat Creighton, Hope Holiday, Deedee Wood, Robert McClure, George Reeder, Lillian D'Honau, Bonnie Evans.
Soundtrack (1959) • Columbia (M) OL-5460 20-25   59
Soundtrack (1959) • Columbia (S) OS-2021 30-35   59
    Credits are printed within bottom of the photo.
Soundtrack (1959) • Columbia (M) OL-5460 12-18   Re
Soundtrack (1959) • Columbia (S) OS-2021 15-20   Re
    Credits are printed on red strip across bottom of the photo.
    Composer: Gene de Paul, Johnny Mercer. **Conductor:** Nelson Riddle, Joseph J. Lilley. **Cast:** Peter Palmer, Stubby Kaye, Carmen Alvarez, Billie Hayes, Joe E. Marks, Bern Hoffman.
Soundtrack (1959) • Philips (S) SBBL-565.. 15-20   59
    UK release.
    Composer: Gene de Paul, Johnny Mercer. **Conductor:** Nelson Riddle, Joseph J. Lilley. **Cast:** Peter Palmer, Stubby Kaye, Carmen Alvarez, Billie Hayes, Joe E. Marks, Bern Hoffman.

Studiotrack • Columbia (EP) B-2119 20-25   59
  Composer: Gene de Paul, Johnny Mercer. **Cast:** Doris Day.
Studiotrack (1957) • Contemporary (M) C-3533 15-20   57
  Actual title: *Modern Jazz Performance of Li'l Abner.*
  Cast: Shelley Mann, Andre Previn, L. Vinnegar.
Studiotrack [Vol. 1] (1959) • Columbia (EP) B-9551 8-12   59
Studiotrack [Vol. 2] (1959) • Columbia (EP) B-9552 8-12   59
Studiotrack [Vol. 3] (1959) • Columbia (EP) B-9553 8-12   59
Studiotrack (1959) • Columbia (M) CL-955 10-15   59
  Conductor: Percy Faith. **Cast:** Percy Faith and His Orchestra.

LILAC TIME (BLOSSOM TIME)
London Studio (1961) • Angel (M) 35817 25-30   61
London Studio Cast (1961) • Angel (S) 35817 35-40   61
  Composer: Franz Schubert, Adrian Ross. **Conductor:** Michael Collins. **Cast:** June Bronhill,
  Thomas Round, John Cameron, Rita Williams Singers.

LILI
Soundtrack (1953) • MGM (EP) X-1025 20-25   53
  Composer: Bronislau Kaper. **Conductor:** Hans Sommer. **Cast:** Leslie Caron, Mel Ferrer, MGM
  Studio Orchestra.
  Also see EVERYTHING I HAVE IS YOURS
  Also see LES GIRLS

LILI MARLENE
Soundtrack (1981) • DRG (S) SL 9506 10-15   81
  Composer: Peer Raben. **Conductor:** Peer Raben.

LILIES OF THE FIELD
Soundtrack (1963) • Epic (M) LN-26094 12-15   64
Soundtrack (1963) • Epic (S) BN-26094 15-18   64
  Composer: Jerry Goldsmith. **Conductor:** Jerry Goldsmith. **Cast:** Jester Hairston.

LILITH
Soundtrack (1964) • Colpix (M) CP-520 10-15   64
Soundtrack (1964) • Colpix (S) SCP-520 12-18   64
  Composer: Kenyon Hopkins. **Conductor:** Kenyon Hopkins.

LINK
Soundtrack (1986) • Varese Sarabande (S) STV-81294 10-15   86
  Composer: Jerry Goldsmith. **Conductor:** Jerry Goldsmith.

LINUS THE LIONHEARTED
TV Soundtrack (1964) • Post Cereals (M) No Number Used 10-20   64
  A Post Cereal mail-order item, to promote the cartoon show.
  Cast: Sheldon Leonard, Carl Reiner, Gerry Matthews, Bob McFadden, Ruth Buzzi, Jesse White.

LION
Soundtrack (1962) • London (M) M-76001 275-325   62
  Cover printed in U.S, disc made in England.
  Composer: Malcolm Arnold. **Conductor:** Malcolm Arnold.

LION IN WINTER
Soundtrack (1968) • Columbia (S) OS-3250 10-12   68
  Composer: John Barry. **Conductor:** John Barry. **Cast:** Jane Merrow, Voices of the Accademia
  Monteverdiana.

LION KING
Soundtrack (1994) • Walt Disney (S) 60858-7 8-12   94
  Composer: Hans Zimmer. **Conductor:** Nick Glenie-Smith. **Cast:** Elton John, Whoopi Goldberg,
  Carmen Twillie, Lebo M., Jason Weaver, Jim Cummings, Joe Williams, Laura Williams, Rowen
  Atkinson, Cheech Marin, Nathan Lane, Jeremy Irons, Ernie Sabella, Sally Dworski.

LION OF THE DESERT

Soundtrack (1981) • Quality (S) SV-2082... 15-20   81
Soundtrack (1981) • Project 3 (S) PR-5107 20-25   81
    Composer: Maurice Jarre. **Conductor:** Maurice Jarre. **Cast:** London Symphony Orchestra.

LIONHEART

Soundtrack [Vol. 1] (1987) • Varese Sarabande (S) STV-81304 10-15   87
    Composer: Jerry Goldsmith. **Conductor:** Jerry Goldsmith.
Soundtrack [Vol. 2] (1987) • Varese Sarabande (S) STV-81311 50-60   87
  Has additional music from film.

LIPSTICK

Soundtrack (1976) • Atlantic (S) SD-18178... 10-15   76
    Composer: Michel Polnareff. **Conductor:** Michel Polnareff, Jimmie Haskell.

LIQUID SKY

Soundtrack (1982) • Varese Sarabande (S) STV-81181 10-15   83
    Composer: Slava Tsukerman, Brenda Hutchinson, Clive Smith.

LIQUIDATOR

Soundtrack (1966) • MGM (M) E-4413.. 12-18   66
Soundtrack (1966) • MGM (S) SE-4413.. 15-20   66
Soundtrack (1966) • MCA (S) 25137.. 8-10   86
    Composer: Lalo Schifrin. **Conductor:** Lalo Schifrin. **Cast:** Shirley Bassey.

LISTEN, LET'S MAKE LOVE

Soundtrack (1984) • GSF (S) 1003 10-15   84
    Composer: Ennio Morricone. **Conductor:** Ennio Morricone.

LISZTOMANIA

Soundtrack (1975) • A&M (S) SP-4546 10-12   75
    Composer: Rick Wakeman, Franz Liszt, Richard Wagner. **Cast:** Roger Daltrey, English Rock
    Ensemble, John Forsythe, Linda Lewis, George Michie, National Philharmonic Orchestra, Paul
    Nicholas, Rick Wakeman, David Wilde.

LITTLE ABNER: see LI'L ABNER

LITTLE BIG MAN

Soundtrack (1970) • Columbia (S) S-30545 18-20   70
    Composer: John Hammond. **Cast:** John Hammond, Dustin Hoffman (narrator), Richard
    Mulligan, Faye Dunaway, Chief Dan George (with dialogue).

LITTLE BOY LOST

Soundtrack (1953) • Decca (EP) ED-2085 25-30   53
    Cast: Bing Crosby.
  Also see BING'S HOLLYWOOD
  Also see COUNTRY GIRL.

LITTLE DRUMMER BOY: see MOUSE ON THE MAYFLOWER

LITTLE FAUSS AND BIG HALSY

Soundtrack (1970) • Columbia (S) S-30385 15-18   70
    Composer: Bob Dylan, Johnny Cash, others. **Cast:** Johnny Cash and the Tennessee Three,
    Carl Perkins.

LITTLE FUGITIVE

Soundtrack (1953) • Folkways (M) 2070 100-200   53
  10-inch.
    Composer: Eddy Manson.

LITTLE MARY SUNSHINE

Original Cast (1959) • Capitol (M) WAO-1240.. 8-10   60
Original Cast (1959) • Capitol (S) SWAO-1240.................................... 10-12   60
  Black label.

Original Cast (1959) • Capitol (S) SWAO-1240 5-8   60
   Red label.
    Composer: Rick Besoyan. **Conductor:** Glenn Osser, Arnold Goland. **Cast:** Eileen Brennan,
    William Graham, Elmarie Wendel, John Aniston, John McMartin, Elizabeth Parrish, Mario Siletti.
Original London Cast • PYE (M) NLP-18071 40-45
   UK release.
Original London Cast • AEI (S) AEI-1105 12-15   70s
    Composer: Rick Besoyan. **Cast:** Bernard Cribbins, Patricia Routledge, Joyce Blair, Terence
    Cooper, Gita Denise, Erik Chitty.

LITTLE ME

Original Cast (1962) • RCA Victor (M) LOC-1078 8-10   62
Original Cast (1962) • RCA Victor (S) LSO-1078 12-15   62
   Black label.
Original Cast (1962) • RCA Victor (S) LSO-1078 5-10   Re
   Orange or tan labels, often with clipped covers.
Original Cast (1962) • RCA Victor (S) AYL1-4237 5-8   81
    Composer: Cy Coleman, Carolyn Leigh. **Conductor:** Charles Sanford. **Cast:** Sid Caesar,
    Virginia Martin, Nancy Andrews, Swen Swenson, Mort Marshall, Joey Faye, Mickey Deems.
Original London Cast (1964) • Pye (M) NPL-18107 45-55   64
Original London Cast (1964) • Pye (S) NSPL-83029 55-65   64
   UK release.
Original London Cast (1964) • World (M) T-789 30-35   Re
Original London Cast (1964) • World (S) ST-789 35-45   Re
   UK release.
    Composer: Cy Coleman, Carolyn Leigh. **Conductor:** Ed Coleman. **Cast:** Bruce Forsyth, Eileen
    Gourlay, Swen Swenson, Avril Angers, Bernard Spear.

LITTLE MISS SHIRLEY TEMPLE

Soundtrack • Pickwick (SE) PTP-2034 20-35
   Two discs, with songs from various films.
    Cast: Shirley Temple.

LITTLE NELLY KELLY

Soundtrack (1940) • Cheerio (M) 5000 8-10
   Also has music from *Thousands Cheer* (1943)
    Cast: Judy Garland.

LITTLE NIGHT MUSIC

Original Cast (1973) • Columbia (S) KS-32265 10-15   73
   Dark blue gatefold cover. Include libretto.
Original Cast (1973) • Columbia (Q) JS-32265 20-25   73
Original Cast (1973) • Columbia (Q) SQ-32265 8-10   Re
   Light blue gatefold cover. Includes libretto.
    Composer: Stephen Sondheim. **Conductor:** Hal Hastings. **Cast:** Glynis Johns, Len Cariou,
    Hermione Gingold, Victoria Mallory, Patricia Elliott, Teri Ralston, Mark Lambert, Gene Varrone.
Original London Cast (1973) • RCA Victor (S) LRL1-5090 8-15   73
    Composer: Stephen Sondheim. **Conductor:** Ray Cook. **Cast:** Jean Simmons, Hermione
    Gingold, Joss Ackland, Maria Aitken, Veronica Page.
Soundtrack (1978) • Columbia (S) JS-35333 12-18   78
    Composer: Stephen Sondheim. **Conductor:** Jonathan Tunick. **Cast:** Elizabeth Taylor, Len
    Cariou, Diana Rigg, Lesley-Anne Down, Hermione Gingold, Laurence Guittard, Christopher
    Guard, Chloe Franks.

LITTLE ORPHAN ANNIE

Original Radio Cast • Mark 56 (M) 593 20-40   79
   Picture disc.

LITTLE PRINCE

Soundtrack (1974) • ABC (S) ABDP-854 12-18   74
    Composer: Frederick Loewe, Alan Jay Lerner. **Conductor:** Angela Morley. **Cast:** Richard Kiley, Bob Fosse, Gene Wilder, Donna McKechnie, Steven Warner, Joss Ackland.

Studio Cast (1974) • Pip (S) 6813 10-12   75
    Composer: Mort Garson. **Cast:** Richard Burton (narration), John Carradine, Billy Simpson, Jim Backus, Jonathan Winters, Claudine Longet, Mark Conrad (dialogue, performing the novel by Antoine De Saint-Exupery).

LITTLE RASCALS

Soundtrack • Mark 56 (M) 653 10-15   74
    Various tracks from *Our Gang* and *Little Rascals*.

LITTLE ROMANCE

Soundtrack (1979) • Varese Sarabande (S) STV-81109 10-15   79
    Composer: Georges Delerue. **Conductor:** Georges Delerue.

LITTLE SHOP OF HORRORS (1960)

Soundtrack (1960) • Rhino (S) RNSP-304 10-15   84

LITTLE SHOP OF HORRORS (1982)

Original Cast (1982) • Geffen (S) GHSP-2020 20-25   82
    Composer: Alan Menken, Howard Ashman. **Conductor:** Robert Billig. **Cast:** Ellen Greene, Lee Wilkof, Hy Anzell, Frane Luz, Sheila Kay Davis, Leilani Jones, Jennifer Leigh Warren, Martin P. Robinson, Ron Taylor.

Soundtrack (1986) • Geffen (S) GHS-24125 15-20   86
    Composer: Alan Menken. **Cast:** Rick Moranis, Ellen Greene, Vincent Gardenia, Steve Martin, Jim Belushi, John Candy, Levi Stubbs, Christopher Guest, Bill Murray.

LITTLE SHOWS: see BAND WAGON

LITTLE WILLIE JR.'S RESURRECTION

Original Cast (1977) • Glori (S) JC-1044 20-25   77
    Composer: Johnny Thompson, Oscar L. Johnson. **Conductor:** Johnny Thompson. **Cast:** Darrah Gustafson, Tom O'Neill, Belle Weil.

LITTLE WOMEN

TV Soundtrack (1958) • Kapp (M) KL-1104 40-50   58
    One side is *Music for Little Women by the Golden Strings*.
    Composer: Richard Adler. **Conductor:** Hal Hastings. **Cast:** Jeannie Carson, Risë Stevens, Florence Henderson, Bill Hayes, Roland Winters, Zina Bethune.

LITTLEST ANGEL

Studio Cast (1950) • Decca (EP) ED-549 12-20   50
    Two discs. Gatefold cover.

Studio Cast (1950) • Decca (M) DLP-8009 15-20   50
    Cover has a drawing of an angel and stable scene. One side has *Lullaby of Christmas*.

Studio Cast (1950) • Decca (M) DL-8009 12-15   Re
    Cover pictures a little girl. One side has *Lullaby of Christmas*.
    Composer: Charles Paul. **Conductor:** Victor Young, **Cast:** Loretta Young, Ken Darby Choir.
    LULLABY OF CHRISTMAS: **Composer:** Carmen Dragon. **Conductor:** Carmen Dragon. **Cast:** Gregory Peck.

TV Soundtrack (1969) • Mercury (S) SRM-1603 12-15   69
    Composer: Lan O'Kun. **Cast:** Fred Gwynne (narration), Cab Calloway, Tony Randall, Connie Stevens, Johnnie Whitaker, Corinna Manetto.

LITTLEST OUTLAW

Studiotrack (1955) • Disneyland (M) DQ-1246 15-20   64
    Cast: Cliff Edwards (narration, as Jiminy Cricket).

LITTLEST REBEL

Radio Cast (1940) • Radiola (M) MR-1097 8-15   80
    Complete Lux Radio Theatre show, October 14, 1940.
    Cast: Shirley Temple, others.

LITTLEST REVUE
Original Cast (1956) • Epic (M) LN-3275 30-40   56
Original Cast (1956) • Painted Smiles (M) PS-1361 8-10   79
    Composer: Vernon Duke, others. **Conductor:** Will Irwin. **Cast:** Beverly Bozeman, Joel Grey,
    Tammy Grimes, Charlotte Rae, Larry Storch, George Marcy, Tommy Morton.

LIVE A LITTLE, STEAL A LOT: see MURPH THE SURF

LIVE AND LET DIE
Soundtrack (1973) • United Artists (S) UA-LA100-G 10-12   73
    With corners intact (not clipped). Tan label.
Soundtrack (1973) • United Artists (S) UA-LA100-G 8-10   73
    Cover has clipped corner. Tan label.
Soundtrack (1973) • United Artists (S) UA-LA100-G 5-8   Re
    Orange and yellow label.
Soundtrack (1973) • Liberty (S) LMAS-100 5-8   Re
    Issued on orange/yellow label, and on gray label.
Soundtrack (1973) • Liberty (S) LT-50100 5-8   Re
    Gray label.
    Composer: Paul McCartney, Linda McCartney, George Martin, Monty Norman, others. **Cast:**
    Paul McCartney and Wings, George Martin and His Orchestra, B.J. Arnau, Harold A. "Duke"
    Degan and the Olympia Brass Band.

LIVE FOR LIFE
Soundtrack (1967) • United Artists (M) UAL-4165 5-8   67
Soundtrack (1967) • United Artists (S) UAS-5165 5-10   67
Soundtrack (1967) • United Artists (S) UA-LA291-G 5-8   74
    Composer: Francis Lai, Raymond Le Senechal, Sonny Miller, Pierre Barouh, Jerry Keller.
    Conductor: Francis Lai. **Cast:** Nicole Croisille, Annie Girardot, Louis Aldebert.
Studiotrack (1967) • Unart (S) S-21026 10-15   68
    Composer: Francis Lai. **Cast:** Motion Picture Studio Orchestra.

LIVELY SET
Soundtrack (1964) • Decca (M) DL-9119 20-25   64
Soundtrack (1964) • Decca (S) DL-79119 25-35   64
    Composer: Bobby Darin. **Conductor:** Joseph Gershenson. **Cast:** James Darren, Wink
    Martindale, Joanie Sommers, Ron Wilson and the Surfaris.

LIVING DAYLIGHTS
Soundtrack (1987) • Warner Bros. (S) 1-25616 12-15   87
    Composer: John Barry. **Conductor:** John Barry. **Cast:** John Barry, A-Ha, Pretenders.

LIVING DESERT
Soundtrack • RCA Victor (EP) ERAS-1 60-75   53
    Includes 24-page illustrated booklet.
Soundtrack (1953) • Buena Vista (M) BV-3326 30-40   65
    One side has *The Vanishing Prairie*.
    Composer: Paul J. Smith. **Conductor:** Paul J. Smith. **Cast:** Winston Hubler (narration).

LIVING FREE
Soundtrack (1972) • RCA Victor (S) LSO-1172 8-15   72
    Film sequel to *Born Free*.
    Composer: Sol Kaplan. **Conductor:** Sol Kaplan.
Studiotrack (1972) • Camden (S) CAS-2564 5-10   72
    Full title: *Living Strings Play Music from Living Free*.
    Conductor: Johnny Douglas. **Cast:** Living Strings.

LIVING IT UP
Soundtrack (1954) • Capitol (EP) EAP 1-533 50-75   54
Film inspired by *Hazel Flagg*.
Composer: Jule Styne, Bob Hilliard. **Conductor:** Walter Scharf. **Cast:** Dean Martin, Jerry Lewis.
Also see HAZEL FLAGG

LIVING LEGEND
Soundtrack (1980) • No Label Used (S) 005013 15-20   80
Cast: Roy Orbison.

LIVING WORD
Soundtrack • AEI (S) AEI-3112 8-10   82
Composer: Edward David Zeliff. **Conductor:** Edward David Zeliff.

LIZA MINNELLI AT THE WINTER GARDEN
Original Cast (1974) • Columbia (S) PC-32854 10-12   74
Composer: John Kander, Fred Ebb, others. **Conductor:** Jack French. **Cast:** Liza Minnelli.

LIZA WITH A "Z"
TV Soundtrack (1972) • Columbia (S) KC-31762 10-12   72
Composer: Fred Ebb, John Kander, others. **Cast:** Liza Minnelli.

LOCAL HERO
Soundtrack (1983) • Warner Bros. (S) 1-23827 10-15   83
Soundtrack (1983) • Vertigo (S) VOG-1-3321 10-15   83
Composer: Mark Knopfler. **Cast:** Mark Knopfler, Gerry Rafferty.

LOCK UP YOUR DAUGHTERS
Original London Cast (1960) • London (M) 5766............................... 30-35   63
Original London Cast (1960) • That's Entertainment (M) TER-1049 8-10   Re
UK releases.
Composer: Laurie Johnson, Lionel Bart. **Conductor:** Laurie Johnson. **Cast:** Richard Wordsworth, John Sharp, Terence Cooper, Robin Wentworth, Stephanie Voss, Madeleine Newbury, Hy Hazell, Keith Marsh, Brendan Barry.

LOGAN'S RUN
Soundtrack (1976) • MGM (S) MG-1-5302 20-30   76
Composer: Jerry Goldsmith. **Conductor:** Jerry Goldsmith.

LOLA
Studio Cast (1982) • Painted Smiles (S) PS 1335 8-10   82
Composer: Claude Richardson, Kenward Elmslie. **Cast:** Christine Andrews, Judy Kaye, David Carroll.
Also see VERONIKA VOSS AND LOLA

LOLA MONTEZ
Original Cast (1955) • Columbia (M) CX-7514 85-100   55
Australian release. This show was produced in Sydney, Australia.
Composer: Peter Benjamin, Peter Stannard. **Conductor:** Leo Packer. **Cast:** Mary Preston, Frank Wilson, Jane Martin, Michael Cole, Alan Hopgood, Bernard Shine.

LOLITA
Soundtrack (1962) • MGM (M) E-4050 10-25   62
Soundtrack (1962) • MGM (S) SE-4050 30-40   62
Soundtrack (1962) • MCA (S) 39067 8-10   86
Composer: Nelson Riddle, Bob Harris. **Conductor:** Nelson Riddle, Bob Harris. **Cast:** Nelson Riddle and His Orchestra.
Studiotrack • Sonodor (S) SON-105 10-12

LOLLIPOP COVER
Soundtrack (1966) • Mainstream (M) 56067..................................... 10-20   66
Soundtrack (1966) • Mainstream (S) S-6067..................................... 12-30   66
Composer: Ruby Raksin. **Conductor:** Ruby Raksin. **Cast:** Carol Selfinger.

LONE RANGER

Original Radio Cast • Decca (M) K-29/30/31/32 .... 60-80　　51
　Four 78 rpms: *He Becomes the Lone Ranger* (K-29), *He Finds Silver* (K-30), *He Finds Dan Reid* (K-31), *He Helps the Colonel's Son* (K-32). Each disc has a color picture sleeve.

Original Radio Cast • Decca (SE) DL-75125 .... 15-20　　50s
　Six 78 rpms, the four above plus: *He Meets the War Horse* and *He Saves the Booneville Gold*. Full title: *Adventures of the Lone Ranger*.
　Cast: Narrator. (With sound effects and orchestral accompaniment.)

Original Radio Cast • Unedited Radio Programs (M) RR4M................... 8-10

Original Radio Cast • Golden Age (M) 5002.. 8-10　　78
　Also see LEGEND OF THE LONE RANGER

LONE WOLF MCQUADE

Soundtrack (1983) • Citadel (S) CT 7024.. 10-20　　83

Soundtrack (1983) • That's Entertainment (S) TER-1071....................... 8-10　　80s
　UK release.
　Composer: Francesco DeMasi.

LONELY GUY

Soundtrack (1984) • MCA (S) 36010... 8-10　　83
　Composer: Jerry Goldsmith, others. **Cast:** America, Max Carl, Winston Ford, Gerard McMahon.

LONELY LADY

Soundtrack (1984) • Allegiance (S) 441 .... 8-10　　84
　Cast: Ellis Hall Jr., Pia Zadora, others.

LONESOME TRAIN

Studio Cast (1944) • Decca (M) DL-5054... 25-40　　49
　10-inch LP.
　Composer: Earl Robinson, Millard Campell. **Conductor:** Lyn Murray. **Cast:** Burl Ives, Earl Robinson, Richard Huey, Lon Clark.

LONG DUEL

Soundtrack (1967) • Atco (M) 33-228... 10-12　　67

Soundtrack (1967) • Atco (S) SD 33-228 .... 12-15　　67
　Composer: Patrick John Scott, Don Black. **Conductor:** Patrick John Scott. **Cast:** Vince Hill.

LONG HOT SUMMER

Soundtrack (1958) • Roulette (M) R-25026 .... 45-65　　58
　Composer: Alex North. **Conductor:** Lionel Newman. **Cast:** Jimmie Rodgers.

LONG JOHN SILVER

Soundtrack (1954) • RCA Victor (EP) EPB-3279 .... 50-125　　55

Soundtrack (1954) • RCA Victor (M) LPM-3279 .... 200-350　　55
　10-inch LP.
　Composer: David Buttolph. **Conductor:** David Buttolph.

LONG RIDERS

Soundtrack (1980) • Warner Bros. (S) HS-3448 ......:............................ 8-10　　80
　Composer: Ry Cooder, David Lindley. **Cast:** Ry Cooder, Jim Keach, Mitch Greenhill, Pico Payne.

LONG SHIPS

Soundtrack (1964) • Colpix (M) CP-517 .... 30-40　　64

Soundtrack (1964) • Colpix (S) SCP-517 .... 50-60　　64
　Composer: Dusan Radic. **Conductor:** Borislav Pascan.

LONGEST DAY
Soundtrack (1962) • 20th Century-Fox (M) FXG-5007 12-15   62
Soundtrack (1962) • 20th Century-Fox (S) SXG-5007 18-20   62
   Two different covers exist. First issued with white background on red and black foreground.
     Composer: Paul Anka, others. **Cast:** Lowell Thomas (narration), John Wayne, Rod Steiger,
     Red Buttons, Peter Lawford. (With dialogue presenting a condensed version of the film).
Studiotrack • Diplomat (S) DS-2284 8-12
     Composer: Al Goodman.

LOOK AT MONACO
TV Soundtrack (1963) • Columbia (M) CL-2019 30-40   63
   From a CBS-TV special that aired February 17, 1963.
TV Soundtrack (1963) • Columbia (SE) CS-8819 45-65   63
     Composer: Percy Faith. **Conductor:** Percy Faith. **Cast:** Princess Grace [Kelly] (narrator), Percy
     Faith and the Orchestre National De L'Opera De Monte Carlo.

LOOK MA, I'M DANCIN'!
Original Cast (1948) • Decca DA-637 20-25   48
   78 rpm album. Includes booklet.
     Composer: Hugh Martin. **Conductor:** Pembroke Davenport. **Cast:** Nancy Walker, Harold
     Lang, Sandra Deel, Bill Shirley, Hugh Martin.
Original Cast (1948) • Decca (M) DL-5231 75-85   50
   10-inch LP. Since this show was recorded during a strike at Decca, some songs are
   performed by Hugh Martin (composer), Sandra Deel and Bill Shirley, none of whom were
   actually in the show.
Original Cast (1948) • JJA (M) 19743 20-25   74
   Actual title: *Three by Hugh Martin.* Also contains music from *Best Foot Forward* and *Love
   from Judy.*
   Also see ARMS AND THE GIRL

LOOK TO THE LILIES
Studio Cast (1970) • Blue Pear (M) BP 1010 15-18
   One side has *Pleasures and Palaces* (1965). Both are "demo" productions.
     Composer: Jule Styne, Sammy Cahn, Frank Loesser.

LOOKING FOR LOVE
Soundtrack (1964) • MGM (M) E-4229 10-12   64
Soundtrack (1964) • MGM (S) SE-4229 12-15   64
     Composer: Hank Hunter, Stan Vincent, Gary Geld, Richard Udele, Claus Ogerman, others.
     Conductor: Claus Ogerman, Joe Mazzu. **Cast:** Connie Francis.

LOOKING FOR MR. GOODBAR
Soundtrack (1977) • Columbia (S) JS-35029 8-10   77
     Composer: Artie Kane, others. **Cast:** Donna Summer, Commodores with Lionel Richie, Thelma
     Houston, Diana Ross, Bill Withers, O'Jays, Boz Scaggs, Marlena Shaw.

LOOT
Soundtrack (1970) • CBS (S) 70073 100-150   70
   UK release.
     Composer: Keith Mansfield, Richard Willing Denton. **Conductor:** Keith Mansfield. **Cast:** Richard
     Attenborough, Lee Remick, Hywel Bennett, Milo O'Shea, Steve Ellis.

LORCA AND THE OUTLAWS
Soundtrack (1986) • Atlantic (S) 8160-1 10-15   86
     Composer: Tony Banks. **Cast:** Tony Banks.

LORD JIM
Soundtrack (1965) • Colpix (M) CP-521 12-15   65
Soundtrack (1965) • Colpix (S) SCP-521 15-18   65
     Composer: Bronislau Kaper. **Conductor:** Muir Mathieson.

LORD LOVE A DUCK
Soundtrack (1966) • United Artists (M) UAL-4137 10-15   66
Soundtrack (1966) • United Artists (S) UAS-5137 20-25   66
  Composer: Neal Hefti. **Conductor:** Neal Hefti.

LORD OF THE FLIES
Studiotrack (1963) • Ava (M) A-30 10-12   63
Studiotrack (1963) • Ava (S) AS-30 12-15   63
  Composer: Raymond Leppard.

LORD OF THE RINGS
Soundtrack (1978) • Fantasy (S) LOR-1 15-20   78
  Two discs. Includes fan club insert.
Soundtrack (1978) • Fantasy (S) LOR-PD2 20-30   78
  Two picture discs. Includes booklet.
  Composer: Leonard Rosenman. **Conductor:** Leonard Rosenman.

LORDS OF FLATBUSH
Soundtrack (1974) • ABC (S) ABCD-828 20-25   74
  Composer: Joe Brooks.

LORELEI
Original Cast (1974) • MGM/Verve (S) MV-5097-OC 20-25   74
  Recorded pre-Broadway.
  Composer: Jule Styne, Leo Robin. **Conductor:** Milton Rosenstock. **Cast:** Carol Channing,
  Dody Goodman, Peter Palmer, John Mineo, Lee Roy Reams, Brandon Maggart, Jean Bruno,
  Bob Fitch, Tamara Long.
Original Cast (1974) • MGM (S) M3G-55 20-30   74
  Recorded after Broadway opening, with several changes in cast and score since (#5097
  pre-Broadway recording.
  Composer: Jule Styne, Leo Robin. **Conductor:** Milton Rosenstock. **Cast:** Carol Channing,
  Peter Palmer, Jack Fletcher, Lee Roy Reams, Bob Fitch, Tamara Long, John Mineo.

LOREN, SOPHIA: see SOPHIA LOREN IN ROME

LORETTA YOUNG SHOW see MUSIC FOR LORETTA

LOSIN' IT
Soundtrack (1982) • Regency (S) RI-8507 10-15   82
  Composer: K. Wannberg. **Conductor:** K. Wannberg.

LOSS OF INNOCENCE
Soundtrack (1961) • Colpix (M) CP-508 20-30   62
  Composer: Richard Addinsell. **Conductor:** Richard Addinsell.

LOST ANGELS
Soundtrack (1989) • A&M (S) SP-3926 8-10   89
  Cast: Apollo Smile, Happy Mondays, Cure, Soundgarden, Poghes, Toni Childs, Soul Asylum,
  Raheem, Royal Court of China, John Williams, Wayne Shorter.

LOST BOYS
Soundtrack (1987) • Atlantic (S) 81767-1 8-10   87
  Cast: Eddie and Tide, Thomas Newman, INXS and Jimmy Barnes, Roger Daltrey, Lou Gramm,
  Echo and the Bunnymen, Gerard McMann, Tim Cappello, Mummy Calls.

LOST CONTINENT
Soundtrack (1957) • MGM (M) E-3635 175-200   57
  Composer: Francesco Lavagnino. **Conductor:** Francesco Lavagnino.
Studiotrack (1957) • Columbia (EP) B-2128 15-20   57
  Full title: *Lost Continent, Music from the Film.*
  Composer: Francesco Lavagnino. **Cast:** Michel Legrand Orchestra.

LOST EMPIRES
TV Soundtrack • That's Entertainment (S) TER-1119 8-10   80s
UK release.
Composer: Derek Milton.

LOST FILMS (TRAILERS FROM THE FIRST YEARS OF SOUND)
Soundtrack • Take Two (M) TT-110 12-18   84
Trailer film music from: *Gold Diggers of Broadway, My Man, Under a Texas Moon, No No Nanette, Queen of the Nightclubs, Honky Tonk* and *Little Johnny Jones.*
Cast: Nick Lucas, Fanny Brice, Texas Guinan, Sophie Tucker, Eddie Buzzell.

LOST HORIZON
Studio Cast (1937) • Decca (M) DL-5154 50-60   50
10-inch LP.
Composer: Dimitri Tiomkin. **Cast:** Ronald Colman, others.

Original Radio Cast (1941) • Pelican (M) LP 140 10-15   75
Cast: Cecil B. DeMille (narrator), others.

Soundtrack (1973) • Bell (S) LH-1 20-25   73
Promotion only. Colored vinyl.

Soundtrack (1973) • Bell (S) B-1300 12-15   73
Composer: Burt Bacharach, Hal David. **Conductor:** Burt Bacharach. **Cast:** Jerry Hutman (performs vocals for Peter Finch), Diana Lee (performs vocals for Liv Ullmann), Sally Kellerman, James Shigeta, Bobby Van, Andrea Willis (performs vocals for Olivia Hussey), Shawn Phillips. Also see TALE OF TWO CITIES.

LOST HORIZON: THE CLASSIC FILM SCORES OF DIMITRI TIOMKIN
Studiotrack • RCA Victor (S) ARL1-1669 10-15   76
Studiotrack • RCA Victor (Q) ARD1-1669 20-25   76
Also has music from *The Big Sky, Friendly Persuasion, Search for Paradise, The Fourposter* and *The Guns of Navarone.*
Composer: Dimitri Tiomkin. **Conductor:** Charles Gerhardt.

LOST IN THE STARS
Original Cast (1949) • Decca (M) DL-8028 30-40   49
Unbanded (continuous play) disc. Includes six-page booklet.

Original Cast (1949) • Decca (M) DL-9120 10-12   65
Original Cast (1949) • Decca (SE) DL-79120 10-12   65
Original Cast (1949) • MCA (SE) 2071e 8-10   72
Original Cast (1949) • MCA (SE) 1535 5-8   Re
Composer: Kurt Weill, Maxwell Anderson. **Conductor:** Maurice Levine. **Cast:** Todd Duncan, Inez Matthews, Sheila Guyse, Herbert Coleman, Frank Roane, Julian Mayfield, Guy Spaull.

LOST MAN
Soundtrack (1969) • Uni (S) 73060 12-15   69
Composer: Quincy Jones, Dick Cooper, Ernie Shelby, Diane Hilderbrand, Cora Martin. **Conductor:** Stanley Wilson. **Cast:** Nate Turner, Mirettes, Benetta Fields, Ernestine Anderson & Pree Sisters, Church Choir, Geraldine Jones.

LOST WEEKEND
Soundtrack (1945) • TT (Tony Thomas) (M) MR-2 20-45   80
Composer: Miklos Rozsa. **Conductor:** Miklos Rozsa.

LOUIS, JOE, STORY: see JOE LOUIS STORY

LOUISIANA HAYRIDE
Radio Cast (1976) • Louisiana Hayride (M) NR-8454 300-700   19
Yellow label. Issued only to subscribing radio stations. Features various artists, including guest Bobby G. Rice. Has the first ever issue of Elvis Presley's version of *Tweedle Dee,* from a 1954 Louisiana Hayride performance.

Radio Cast (1976) • Louisiana Hayride (M) NR-8454 200-300   Re
   Gold label.
     Cast: David Kent (host), Frank Page (emcee), Elvis Presley, Bill Black (bass), Scotty Moore
     (guitar), Bobby G. Rice (vocals).
     Also see ELVIS LIVE AT THE LOUISIANA HAYRIDE

LOUISIANA PURCHASE
Original Cast / TV Soundtrack • JJA (M) 19746 20-25   74
   With members of the original New York production, plus excerpts from the 1951 TV
   production.
     Composer: Irving Berlin. **Cast:** Victor Moore, Irene Bordoni, Vera Zorina, William Gaxton,
     Sandra Deel, Carol Bruce.

LOUISIANA STORY
Soundtrack • Columbia (M) ML-2087 150-200
   10-inch LP. Also has Thomson's *Five Portraits.*
     Composer: Virgil Thomson. **Conductor:** Virgil Thomson, Eugene Ormandy.

LOUISIANE
Soundtrack (1984) • Columbia (S) FM-39353 10-15   84
     Composer: Claude Bolling. **Cast:** Dee Dee Bridgewater, Baton Rouge Community Choir,
     Claude Bolling.

LOVE AMERICAN STYLE
Soundtrack (1973) • Capitol (S) ST-11250... 35-40   73
Soundtrack (1973) • Capitol (S) SM-11250.. 12-15   Re
     Composer: Charles Fox. **Conductor:** Charles Fox.

LOVE AMONG THE RUINS
TV Soundtrack (1975) • No Label Used (S) 15-20   75
     Cast: Kathrine Hepburn, Sir Laurence Olivier, others.

LOVE AND LET LOVE
Original Cast (1968) • Sam Fox (S) X4RS-0371 100-120   68
   Covers have art and printing. Promotional issue only.
Original Cast (1968) • Sam Fox (S) X4RS-0371 50-70   68
   Has plain white cover (no printing).
     Composer: Stanley Gelber, Don Christopher, John Lollos. **Cast:** Marcia Rodd, Tom Lacy, John
     Cunningham, Virginia Vestoff.

LOVE AT FIRST BITE
Soundtrack (1979) • Parachute (S) RRLP-9016.................................... 10-15   79
     Composer: Charles Bernstein, others. **Conductor:** Charles Bernstein. **Cast:** Pat Hodges,
     Sidney Barnes.

LOVE AT LARGE
Soundtrack (1990) • Virgin Movie Music (S) 91359-1........................... 10-15   90
     Composer: Mark Isham. **Conductor:** Mark Isham. **Cast:** Leonard Cohen, Warren Zevon, Mark
     Isham.

LOVE BUG
Soundtrack (1969) • Disneyland (M) ST-3986...................................... 25-30   69
   Story, music and songs. Includes 12-page booklet.
     Cast: Buddy Hackett (narration).

LOVE FOR LOVE
Original London Cast (1966) • RCA Victor (M) VDM-112 25-30   66
Original London Cast (1966) • RCA Victor (S) VDS-112 35-40   66
   Both are three-disc sets with the complete dramatic play by William Congreve.
     Composer: Marc Wilkinson. **Cast:** Sir Laurence Olivier, Lynn Redgrave, Joyce Redman,
     Anthony Hopkins, Len Whiting, Colin Blakely (dialogue).

LOVE FROM JUDY

Original London Cast (1952) • JJA (M) 19743...................................... 20-25   74
Music from the 1952 London production. Actual title: *Three by Hugh Martin*. Also contains music from *Best Foot Forward* and *Look, Ma! I'm Dancin'*.
Composer: Hugh Martin, Timothy Gray. **Conductor:** Philip Martell. **Cast:** Jeannie Carson, Adelaide Hall, Bill O'Connor, Audrey Freeman, Johnny Brandon, June Whitfield, Rita Williams Singers.

LOVE GODDESSES

Soundtrack (1965) • Columbia (M) CL-2209 20-25   65
Soundtrack (1965) • Columbia (S) CS-9009... 25-30   65
Composer: Percy Faith. **Conductor:** Percy Faith. **Cast:** Percy Faith Orchestra.

LOVE IN 4 DIMENSIONS

Soundtrack (1966) • Request (M) RLP-8090....................................... 15-20   66
Soundtrack (1966) • Request (S) SRLP-8090 20-25   66
Composer: Franco Mannio.

LOVE IN GERMANY

Soundtrack (1984) • AVI (S) Number Not Known................................. 5-10   84
Composer: Michel Legrand.

LOVE IN THE AFTERNOON

Soundtrack (1957) • Verve (EP) EPV-5055... 65-85   57
Composer: Johnny Mercer, Matty Malneck. **Conductor:** Matty Malneck.

LOVE IS A BALL

Soundtrack (1963) • Philips (M) PHM-200-082.................................... 8-12   63
Soundtrack (1963) • Philips (S) PHS-600-082..................................... 12-15   63
Composer: Michel Legrand. **Conductor:** Michel Legrand. **Cast:** Charles Boyer (narration).

LOVE IS A FUNNY THING

Soundtrack (1970) • United Artists (S) UAS-5207 8-20   70
Soundtrack (1970) • MCA (S) 25111... 5-10   86
Composer: Francis Lai. **Conductor:** Francis Lai.

LOVE IS A MANY-SPLENDORED THING

Studiotrack (1956) • Mercury (M) MG-20123....................................... 10-15   56
Actual title: *Love is a Many-Splendored Thing and All Time Motion Picture Theme Favorites*.
Composer: Sammy Fain, others. **Conductor:** Richard Hayman. **Cast:** Richard Hayman Orchestra.

LOVE IS MY PROFESSION

Soundtrack (1959) • Everest (M) LPBR-5076....................................... 30-40   60
Soundtrack (1959) • Everest (S) SDBR-1076....................................... 45-65   60
One side has music from *Where the Hot Wind Blows*.
Composer: Rene Cloerec. **Conductor:** Ray Ventura.

LOVE LIFE: see LYRICS BY LERNER

LOVE MACHINE

Soundtrack (1971) • Scepter (S) SPS-595 10-15   71
Composer: Artie Butler. **Conductor:** Artie Butler. **Cast:** Dionne Warwick.

LOVE ME OR LEAVE ME

Soundtrack (1955) • Columbia (EP) B-540... 15-25   55
Three discs.
Soundtrack (1955) • Columbia (EP) B-2090... 10-15   55
Soundtrack (1955) • Columbia (M) CL-710 15-18   55
Soundtrack (1955) • Columbia (SE) CS-8773 10-12   63

Soundtrack (1955) • Columbia Special Products (SE) ACS-8773 8-10   63
   Composer: Richard Rodgers, Lorenz Hart, Irving Berlin, Walter Donaldson, others. **Conductor:** Percy Faith. **Cast:** Doris Day.

LOVE ME TENDER
Soundtrack (1956) • RCA Victor (EP) EPA-4006 150-200   56
   Black label, no dog on label.
Soundtrack (1956) • RCA Victor (EP) EPA-4006 75-85   56
   Black label, dog on top. With horizontal silver line across label.
Soundtrack (1956) • RCA Victor (EP) EPA-4006 50-75   56
   Black label, dog on top. Without horizontal silver line across label.
Soundtrack (1956) • RCA Victor (EP) EPA-4006 30-40   65
   Black label, dog on side.
Soundtrack (1956) • RCA Victor (EP) EPA-4006 50-100   69
   Orange label.
      Composer: Elvis Presley, Vera Matson, Ken Darby. **Cast:** Elvis Presley, Ken Darby Trio (vocals).

LOVE ME TONIGHT
Soundtrack (1932) • Ariel (M) CMF-23 30-35
   Also has music from *The Love Parade* and *One Hour with You*.
   Composer: Richard Rodgers, Lorenz Hart. **Conductor:** Nat W. Finston. **Cast:** Maurice Chevalier, Jeanette MacDonald, Marion Byron, Gabby Hayes, Bert Roach, Rolf Sedan, Tyler Brooke, Joseph Cawthorn. ONE HOUR WITH YOU: **Composer:** Oscar Straus, Richard Whiting, Leo Robin. **Conductor:** Nat W. Finston. **Cast:** Maurice Chevalier, Jeanette MacDonald, Genevieve Tobin, Donald Novis, Charles Ruggles. LOVE PARADE: **Composer:** Victor Schertzinger, Clifford Grey. **Conductor:** Victor Schertzinger. **Cast:** Maurice Chevalier, Jeanette MacDonald.

LOVE MUSIC FROM HOLLYWOOD
Studiocast • Columbia (EP) B-7941 5-10   50s
Studiocast • Columbia (EP) B-7942 5-10   50s
Studiocast • Columbia (EP) B-7943 5-10   50s
Studiocast • Columbia (M) CL-794 20-25   50s
   Conductor: Paul Weston. **Cast:** Paul Weston Orchestra.

LOVE PARADE: see LOVE ME TONIGHT

LOVE SCENE
Studiotrack (1959) • Dot (M) DLP-3097... 20-25   59
Studiotrack (1959) • Dot (S) DLP-25097 20-40   59
   Music from *Raintree County, Laura, A Place in the Sun* and others.
   Composer: Various. **Conductor:** Elmer Bernstein.

LOVE SONG
Original Cast (1976) • Original Cast (S) OC-8022 8-10   76
   Composer: Michael Valenti. **Conductor:** Michael Valenti. **Cast:** Melanie Chartoff, Sigrid Heath, Jess Richards, Robert Manzari.

LOVE SONGS
Soundtrack (1985) • Varese Sarabande (S) STV 81258 10-15   85
   Composer: Michel Legrand. **Cast:** Christopher Lambert, Catherine Deneuve.

LOVE STORY (1946): see SUICIDE SQUADRON

LOVE STORY (1970)
Soundtrack (1970) • Paramount (S) PAS-6002.................................... 10-15   70
Soundtrack (1970) • Paramount (S) SW 93442 10-15   70
   Capitol Record Club issue.
Soundtrack (1970) • Paramount (S) PAS-7000.................................... 12-15   71
   Two discs, with music and dialogue.
      Composer: Francis Lai. **Conductor:** Francis Lai. **Cast:** Ryan O'Neal, Ali McGraw, Georges Pludermacher.

Studiotrack (1970) • RCA Victor (S) LSC-3210 10-12   71
  Classical music heard in the film, plus *The Heart Is a Lonely Hunter, Romeo and Juliet, The Thomas Crown Affair* and others.
  Conductor: Eugene Ormandy. **Cast:** Eugene Ormandy, Philadelphia Orchestra.

LOVE THEME FROM CLEOPATRA: see CLEOPATRA

LOVE THEMES FROM MOTION PICTURES

Studiotrack (1952) • Decca (M) DL-5413 15-20   52
  10-inch LP.

Studiotrack (1952) • Decca (M) DL-8364 12-18
  Music from *Wuthering Heights, Best Years of Our Lives, Invitation, My Foolish Heart,* others
  Composer: Miklos Rozsa, Franz Waxman, Jay Livingston, Ray Evans, Max Steiner, Erich Wolfgang Korngold, Hugo Friedhofer, Bronislau Kaper, Victor Young, Alfred Newman, Ned Washington. **Conductor:** Victor Young. **Cast:** Victor Young and His Orchestra.

LOVEDOLLS SUPERSTAR

Soundtrack • SST (S) 062 8-10
  Cast: Lovedolls, Redo Kross, Black Flag, Sonic Youth, Painted Willie, Lawndale, Gone, Anarchy 6, Meat Puppets, Dead Kennedys.

LOVELESS

Soundtrack (1983) • Roadshow (SP) RS-102 8-12   83
  Composer: Robert Gordon, others. **Cast:** Bill Justis, Sandy Nelson, Diamonds, Little Richard, Robert Gordon, Eddy Dixon.

LOVELY TO LOOK AT

Soundtrack (1952) • MGM (M) K-150 15-20   52
  Boxed, four-disc set.

Soundtrack (1952) • MGM (M) E-150 20-30   52
  10-inch LP.

Soundtrack (1952) • MGM (M) E-3230 15-18   55
  Also has music from *Show Boat.*
  Composer: Jerome Kern, Oscar Hammerstein II, Otto Harbach, others. **Conductor:** Carmen Dragon. **Cast:** Howard Keel, Kathryn Grayson, Red Skelton, Ann Miller, Marge and Gower Champion.
  Also see SUMMER STOCK
  Also see THOSE GLORIOUS MGM MUSICALS.

LOVER COME BACK

Soundtrack (1961) • Columbia Special Products (M) XTV-82021 20-25   61
  Actual title: *Wonderful Day.* Record envelope has promo credits and photos for *Lover Come Back* on one side and a discography of Doris Day's Columbia releases on the other. Also has songs from *The Man Who Knew Too Much, Pillow Talk, Teacher's Pet, Young at Heart, Julie, It Happened to Jane, Love Me Or Leave Me* and *Romance on the High Seas.*
  Cast: Doris Day.

LOVERS

Original Cast (1974) • Golden Gloves (M) PG-723 30-35   74
  Labeled stereo but is monaural.
  Composer: Steve Sterner, Peter DelValle. **Conductor:** Steve Sterner. **Cast:** Reathel Bean, Mike Coscone, John Ingle, Martin Rivera, Robert Sevra, Gary Sneed.

LOVERS AND OTHER STRANGERS

Soundtrack (1970) • ABC (S) ABCS OC-15 8-15   70

Soundtrack (1970) • Capitol (S) SW 93479 8-25   70
  Capitol Record Club issue.
  Composer: Fred Karlin. **Conductor:** Fred Karlin. **Cast:** Larry Meredith, Country Coalition.

LOVES OF ISADORA

Soundtrack (1968) • Kapp (S) KRS-5511 15-18   69
This film is also known as *Isadora.*
    Composer: Maurice Jarre, Ludwig van Beethoven, Johann Sebastian Bach, Johannes Brahms, Alexander Borodin, Pyotr Ilyich Tchaikovsky. **Conductor:** Maurice Jarre.

LOVING COUPLES

Soundtrack (1980) • Motown (S) M8-949 8-10   80
    Composer: Fred Karlin, Greg Wright. **Cast:** Temptations, Billy Preston, Jermaine Jackson, Syreeta.

LOVING YOU

Soundtrack [Vol. 1] (1957) • RCA Victor (EP) EPA-1-1515 60-90   57
    Black label, dog on top. With horizontal silver line across label.
Soundtrack [Vol. 1] (1957) • RCA Victor (EP) EPA-1-1515 50-75   57
    Black label, dog on top. Without horizontal silver line across label.
Soundtrack [Vol. 1] (1957) • RCA Victor (EP) EPA-1-1515 30-40   65
    Black label, dog on side.
Soundtrack [Vol. 1] (1957) • RCA Victor (EP) EPA-1-1515 50-100   69
    Orange label.
Soundtrack [Vol. 2] (1957) • RCA Victor (EP) EPA-2-1515 60-90   57
    Black label, dog on top. With horizontal silver line across label.
Soundtrack [Vol. 2] (1957) • RCA Victor (EP) EPA-2-1515 50-75   57
    Black label, dog on top. Without horizontal silver line across label.
Soundtrack [Vol. 2] (1957) • RCA Victor (EP) EPA-2-1515 30-40   65
    Black label, dog on side.
Soundtrack [Vol. 2] (1957) • RCA Victor (EP) EPA-2-1515 50-100   69
    Orange label.
Soundtrack (1957) • RCA Victor (M) LPM-1515 100-125   57
    Black label, reads "Long Play" at bottom.
Soundtrack (1957) • RCA Victor (SE) LSP-1515e 50-100   59
    RCA silver-top logo, reads "Stereo Electronically Reprocessed" at bottom.
Soundtrack (1957) • RCA Victor (M) LPM-1515 40-60   63
    Black label, reads "Mono" at bottom.
Soundtrack (1957) • RCA Victor (M) LPM-1515 25-30   57
    Black label, reads "Monaural" at bottom.
Soundtrack (1957) • RCA Victor (SE) LSP-1515e 25-30   59
    Black label, RCA white-top logo.
Soundtrack (1957) • RCA Victor (SE) LSP-1515e 10-25   69
    Orange or tan label. (Tan label issued in 1976.)
Soundtrack (1957) • RCA Victor (SE) AFL1-1515e 8-10   77
    Composer: Kal Mann, Bernie Lowe, Jerry Leiber, Mike Stoller, Sid Tepper, Roy C. Bennett, Ben Weisman, Aaron Schroeder, others. **Cast:** Elvis Presley, Scotty Moore (guitar), Bill Black (bass), D.J. Fontana (drums), Dudley Brooks (piano), Jordanaires (vocals).

LOVING YOU / G.I. BLUES

Soundtrack (1957) • RCA Victor (M) LPM-1515 4,000-6,000   60s
    Picture disc. Photo imbedded in vinyl (side 1) is the front cover art of a European *G.I. Blues* LP. Side 2 has no photo. Plays five songs from the standard *Loving You* album (*Loving You, Got a Lot o' Livin' to Do, Lonesome Cowboy, Blueberry Hill* and *True Love*). The remaining five tracks are random instrumentals by unidentified artists that have nothing whatsoever to do with Elvis.

LUCKY LADY

Soundtrack (1976) • Arista (S) AL-4069 8-15   76
    Composer: Ralph Burns, John Kander, Fred Ebb, Cecil Masklin, Bessie Smith, others. **Conductor:** Ralph Burns. **Cast:** Liza Minnelli, Bessie Smith, Burt Reynolds.

LUDWIG

Soundtrack (1973) • Philips (S) PHS 1-5401.. 15-25   73
  Composer: Richard Wagner, Jacques Offenbach, Walter Schumann. **Conductor:** Franco
  Mannino. **Cast:** Franco Mannino.

LULLABY LAND OF NOWHERE: see WHO'S AFRAID OF THE BIG BAD WOLF

LULLABY OF BROADWAY

Studiotrack (1951) • Columbia (EP) B-235.. 15-18   50s
  Two discs.
Studiotrack (1951) • Columbia (M) CL-6168.. 30-35   51
  10-inch LP.
  Conductor: Frank Comstock. **Cast:** Doris Day, Norman Luboff Choir, Buddy Cole Quartet.
Studiotrack (1956) • Coral (M) CRL-57029... 15-20   56
  Cast: George Auld Orchestra.
Studiotrack (1953) • London (M) LL-1426 15-20   53
  Cast: Woolf Phillips and His Orchestra.
  Also see I'LL SEE YOU IN MY DREAMS

LULLABY OF CHRISTMAS: see LITTLEST ANGEL

LUM 'N ABNER

Original Radio Cast • Golden Age (M) 5022... 8-10   78

LURE OF THE GRAND CANYON

Studio Cast (1961) • Columbia (M) CL-1622 12-15   61
Studio Cast (1961) • Columbia (S) CS-8422 12-18   61
  Conductor: Andre Kostelanetz. **Cast:** Johnny Cash (narration), Andre Kostelanetz Orchestra.
  Also see GRAND CANYON SUITE

LUSH THEMES FROM MOTION PICTURES

Studiotrack • MGM (M) E-3172 15-20   58
  Music from *The High and the Mighty, A Bullet Is Waiting, Land of the Pharaohs, Strategic
  Air Command, Rear Window, Tight Spot, Gone with the Wind, The Bridges at Toko-Ri, The
  Prodigal, Unchained, President's Lady* and *Spellbound.*
  Conductor: Leroy Holmes. **Cast:** Leroy Holmes Orchestra.

LUST FOR LIFE

Soundtrack (1956) • Decca (M) DL-10015 25-35   59
Soundtrack (1956) • Decca (S) DL-710015.. 40-45   59
Soundtrack (1956) • Varese Sarabande (S) VC-81053......................... 12-18   78
  Full title: *Rozsa: Lust for Life Suite – Background to Violence.* Also has music from *Brute
  Force, The Killers* and *The Naked City.*
Soundtrack • High Street Station (M) 3301 20-30   74
  Also has music from *Spellbound, Naked City* and *The Killers.*
  Composer: Miklos Rozsa. **Conductor:** Miklos Rozsa. **Cast:** The Frankenland State Symphony
  Orchestra.

LUTE SONG

Original Cast (1946) • Decca A-445 25-35   46
  78 rpm album. Includes booklet.
Original Cast • Decca (M) DL-8030.. 60-65   50
  Black and gold label on thick wax. One side has music from *On The Town.*
Original Cast • Decca (M) DL-8030.. 30-35   50
  Black label.
Original Cast • Decca (M) DL-8030.. 20-25   50
  Rainbow label. Above three also have music from *On the Town.*
  Composer: Raymond Scott, Bernard Hanighen. **Conductor:** Raymond Scott. **Cast:** Mary
  Martin. ON THE TOWN: **Composer:** Leonard Bernstein, Adolph Green, Betty Comden.
  Conductor: Lyn Murray, Leonard Jay, Tutti Camarata. **Cast:** Nancy Walker, Betty Comden,
  Adolph Green, Mary Martin (not in the show).

LUTHER
Soundtrack (1973) • Caedmon (S) TRS-363 25-50   73
   Two discs.

LUV
Original Cast (1965) • Columbia (M) DOL-318 10-12   65
Original Cast (1965) • Columbia (S) DOS-318 10-12   65
   Boxed, two-disc set with eight-page booklet.
     Composer: Irving Joseph, Murray Schisgal. **Cast:** Eli Wallach, Anne Jackson, Alan Arkin.

LYDIA
Studiotrack (1979) • Citadel (S) CT-7010 20-30   79
   Actual title: *Film Music for Piano*. Also has music from *Between Two Worlds, A Bill of
   Divorcement* and *City for Conquest*.
     Composer: Erich Wolfgang Korngold, Miklos Rozsa, Stein.

LYRICS BY LERNER
Studio Cast (1955) • Heritage (M) 0600 60-70   55
Studio Cast (1955) • DRG (M) MRS-903 10-12   Re
   Music from *Brigadoon, The Day Before Spring, Love Life* and *Paint Your Wagon*.
     Composer: Alan Jay Lerner, Kurt Weill, Frederick Loewe. **Conductor:** Billy Taylor. **Cast:** Alan
   Jay Lerner, Kaye Ballard, Billy Taylor Quartet.

LYSISTRATA
Studio Cast • Caedmon (M) TRS 313-M 5-10

M - SQUAD
TV Soundtrack (1958) • RCA Victor (M) LPM-2062............................ 20-25   59
TV Soundtrack (1958) • RCA Victor (S) LSP-2062............................. 30-35   59
   Full title: *The Music from M Squad.*
    Composer: John Williams, Stanley Wilson, Count Basie, Benny Carter. **Conductor:** Stanley
    Wilson.

MGM YEARS
Soundtrack • MGM (S) PG-5878.. 18-20
   Boxed set. Previously released soundtrack recordings from MGM musicals.
    Composer: Various. **Conductor:** Various. **Cast:** Judy Garland, Betty Hutton, Howard Keel, Fred
    Astaire, Gene Kelly, Esther Williams, Ricardo Montalban, William Warfield, Leslie Caron, others.

MGM'S 30th ANNIVERSARY ALBUM
Soundtrack • MGM (M) E-3118 20-25   54
   Music from *Easter Parade, An American in Paris, Neptune's Daughter, Lili, Good News,
   Singin' in the Rain, Show Boat, Annie Get Your Gun* and others.
    Composer: Various. **Conductor:** Various. **Cast:** Judy Garland, Betty Hutton, Howard Keel, Fred
    Astaire, Gene Kelly, Esther Williams, Ricardo Montalban, William Warfield, Leslie Caron, others.

MA PERKINS
Original Radio Cast • Golden Age (M) 5015........................... 8-10   78

MA RAINEY'S BLACK BOTTOM
Original Cast (1984) • Manhattan (S) SVBO-53001 8-15   85

MAC AND ME
Soundtrack (1988) • Curb (S) CRB-10401 8-10   88
    Composer: Alan Silvestri. **Conductor:** Alan Silvestri.

MacARTHUR
Soundtrack (1977) • MCA (S) 2287...................................... 10-25   77
    Composer: Jerry Goldsmith. **Conductor:** Jerry Goldsmith.

MACBETH
Studio Cast (1953) • RCA Victor (M) LM-6010 40-50   53
   Boxed, two-disc set with booklet. Dialogue and minimal sound effects.
    Cast: Sir Alec Guinness, Pamela Brown, Anthony Service, Andrew Cruickshank, Robin Bailey,
    Rachel Gurney, John Bushelle, Gabrielle Blunt, Mary O'Farrell, Margaret Vines, Philip Guard,
    Stanley Van Beers, Mark Dignan, Jill Nyasa, Pat Doonan, others.

MACBIRD
Original Cast (1967) • Evergreen (S) EVR-004 20-30   67
   Boxed, two-disc set with 109-page paperback text of the show. Dramatic play by Barbara
   Garson, with music and songs by John Duffy.
    Composer: John Duffy. **Conductor:** John Duffy. **Cast:** Dalton Dearborn, Jennifer Darling,
    Cleavon Little, Paul Hecht, William Devane, Stacy Keach, Rue McClanahan, John Pleshette.

MACK, THE
Soundtrack (1973) • Motown (S) M766L 10-12   73
    Composer: Willie Hutch. **Cast:** Willie Hutch.
Soundtrack (1973) • Ala (S) 1995 30-40   83
    Composer: Alan Silvestri.

MACK AND MABEL
Original Cast (1974) • ABC (S) ABCH-830... 10-12   74
  Has complete credits on front cover.
Original Cast (1974) • ABC (S) ABCH-830... 10-12   74
  Partial credits only on front cover.
    Composer: Jerry Herman. **Conductor:** Donald Pippin. **Cast:** Robert Preston, Bernadette
    Peters, Lisa Kirk, Stanley Simmonds.

MACK THE KNIFE
Soundtrack (1989) • CBS (S) 45630 10-15   89
  Film version of the 1976 Broadway revival of *The Threepenny Opera*.
    Composer: Kurt Weill. **Cast:** Raul Julia, Julia Migenes, Richard Harris, Roger Daltrey.

MACKENNA'S GOLD
Soundtrack (1969) • RCA Victor (S) LSP-4096 10-15   69
    Composer: Quincy Jones, Freddie Douglas. **Conductor:** Quincy Jones. **Cast:** Jose Feliciano.

MACKINTOSH AND T.J.
Soundtrack (1975) • RCA Victor (S) APL1-1520 8-12   76
    Composer: Waylon Jennings. **Cast:** Waylon Jennings, Roy Rogers.

MAD ADVENTURES OF RABBI JACOB
Soundtrack (1974) • London (S) PS-652... 10-20   74
  Cover is intact (no clipped corners or punched holes).
Soundtrack (1974) • London (S) PS-652... 5-8   74
  Cover has clipped corners or punched holes.
    Composer: Vladimir Cosma. **Conductor:** Vladimir Cosma.

MAD DOGS AND ENGLISHMEN: see JOE COCKER: MAD DOGS AND
ENGLISHMEN

MAD MAX
Soundtrack (1980) • Varese Sarabande (S) STV-81144 10-15   80
Soundtrack • That's Entertainment (S) TER-1016................................. 8-10   80s
  UK release.
    Composer: Brian May. **Conductor:** Brian May.

MAD MAX – BEYOND THUNDERDOME
Soundtrack (1985) • Capitol (S) SWAV-12429 10-15   85
    Composer: Maurice Jarre. **Conductor:** Maurice Jarre. **Cast:** Tina Turner, Royal Philharmonic
    Orchestra.

MAD MONSTER PARTY
Soundtrack (1967) • Rankin Bass (S) RB-1001............................... 100-125   67
  Originally intended for commercial release on RCA Victor. Promotional issue only.
    Composer: Maury Laws, Jules Bass. **Cast:** Boris Karloff, Phyllis Diller, Ethel Ennis, Gale
    Garnett.

MAD SHOW
Original Cast (1965) • Columbia (M) OL-6530.. 35-45   65
Original Cast (1965) • Columbia (S) OS-2930... 65-85   65
    Composer: Mary Rodgers, Stephen Sondheim, Marshall Barer. **Conductor:** Sam Pottle. **Cast:**
    Jo Anne Worley, Linda Lavin, MacIntyre Dixon, Paul Sand, Richard Libertini.

MADAME BOVARY
Soundtrack (1949) • MGM 43.. 100-150
  78 rpm album.
Soundtrack (1949) • MGM (M) E-3507 100-150
  The first score to be transferred directly from the film soundtrack to LP.
Studiotrack • Elmer Bernstein Film Music Collection (S) FMC-12......... 25-30
    Composer: Miklos Rozsa. **Conductor:** Elmer Bernstein.
  Also see IVANHOE

MADAME CLAUDE
Soundtrack (1977) • Philips (S) 9101-144 10-12   77
   Composer: Serge Gainsbourg. Conductor: Jean Pierre Sabar. Cast: Jane Birkin.

MADAME SOUSATZKA
Soundtrack (1988) • Varese Sarabande (S) VS 5204 8-10   88

MADAME X
Soundtrack (1966) • Decca (M) DL-9152 10-12   66
Soundtrack (1966) • Decca (S) DL-79152 12-15   66
   Composer: Frank Skinner, others. Conductor: Joseph Gershenson.

MADE FOR EACH OTHER
Soundtrack (1971) • Buddah (S) BDS-5111 10-15   72
   Composer: Trade Martin. Conductor: Trade Martin.

MADE IN HEAVEN
Soundtrack (1987) • Elektra (S) 60729-1 8-10   87
   Cast: Martha Davis, R.E.M., Ric Ocasek, Luther Vandross, Nylons, Buffalo Springfield, Mark Isham.

MADEMOISELLE MODISTE
Studio Cast (1953) • RCA Victor (EP) EPA-480 15-20   53
Studio Cast (1953) • RCA Victor (M) LPM-3153.................................. 20-30   53
   10-inch LP. One side has music from *Naughty Marietta*.
   Composer: Victor Herbert, Henry Blossom, Rida Johnson Young. Conductor: Jay Blackton. Cast: Doretta Morrow, Felix Knight, Edward Roecker.

MADRON
Soundtrack (1970) • Quad (S) QUS-5001 10-12   70
   Composer: Riz Ortolani. Conductor: Riz Ortolani.

MADWOMAN OF CHAILLOT
Soundtrack (1969) • Warner Bros. (S) WS-1805 10-15   69
   Composer: Michael Lewis. Conductor: Michael Lewis.
   Also see RAIN PEOPLE

MAE WEST – THE ORIGINAL VOICE TRACKS FROM HER GREATEST MOVIES
Soundtrack • Decca (M) DL-9176 10-12   70
Soundtrack • Decca (SE) DL-79176.. 10-15   70
   Cast: Mae West.

MAGGIE
London Cast (1977) • Overtures (S) 1002.. 10-15   80

MAGGIE FLYNN
Original Cast (1968) • RCA Victor (S) LSOD-2009.............................. 12-18   68
   Gatefold cover.
    Composer: Hugo Peretti, Luigi Creatore, George David Weiss. Conductor: John Lesko. Cast: Shirley Jones, Jack Cassidy, Robert Kaye, Jennifer Darling, Sybil Bowan, Austin Colyer, Stanley Simmonds, William James.
Studio Cast • RCA Victor (S) LSP-4083 8-10
   Cast: Hugo & Luigi Chorus.

MAGGIE MAY
Original London Cast (1964) • Decca (EP) STO/DFE-8602 40-45   64
   Has four additional cast songs not available on LP.
Original London Cast • Decca (M) LK-4643 20-25   64
Original London Cast • Decca (S) SKL-4643.. 25-35   64
   UK releases.
Original London Cast • That's Entertainment (S) TER-1046 8-12   80s
   UK release.

MAGIC CHRISTIAN
Soundtrack (1970) • Commonwealth United (S) CU-6004.................... 15-20   70
At least three sleeve and label variations exist.
    Composer: Ken Thorne, Paul McCartney, others. **Cast:** Badfinger, Thunderclap Newman, Ringo Starr, Peter Sellers, Ken Thorne. (With dialogue.)

MAGIC FIRE
Soundtrack (1956) • Varese Sarabande (SE) STV-81179.................... 15-20   80s
Film biography of composer Richard Wagner.
    Composer: Richard Wagner. **Conductor:** Erich Wolfgang Korngold.

MAGIC FLUTE
Soundtrack (1976) • A&M (S) SP-4577 10-12   76
Swedish performances of Mozart compositions.
    Composer: Wolfgang Amadeus Mozart.

MAGIC GARDEN OF STANLEY SWEETHEART
Soundtrack (1970) • MGM (S) 1SE-20 10-15   70
    Composer: Michel Legrand, Bee Gees, War, others. **Conductor:** Jerry Styner. **Cast:** Bill Medley, Eric Burdon and War, Mike Curb Congregation, Crow, David Lucas, Wheel, Angeline Butler, Stilroc, Michael Greer, Angeline Butler.

MAGIC MOMENTS FROM THE TONIGHT SHOW
TV Soundtrack • Casablanca (S) SPNB-1296................................ 10-20   76
Two discs. Includes show's 25th anniversary poster.
    Cast: Johnny Carson, Ed McMahon, Doc Severinsen and His Band, Jay Silverheels, Bette Midler, Groucho Marx, George Carlin, Dean Martin, Pearl Bailey, Lenny Bruce, Billie Holiday, Judy Garland, Aretha Franklin, Smothers Brothers, Richard M. Nixon, Peter Falk, Ike and Tina Turner, Lucille Ball, Desi Arnaz Jr., Buddy Hackett, Jack Benny, Glen Campbell, Don Rickles, Sammy Davis Jr., George Burns, Joey Bishop, Jerry Lewis, others.

MAGIC OF LASSIE
Soundtrack (1978) • Peter Pan (M) 155 8-20   78
Issued with two similar – though slightly different – covers.
    Composer: Richard M. Sherman, Robert B. Sherman. **Conductor:** Irwin Kostal. **Cast:** Pat Boone, Mickey Rooney, Alice Faye, James Stewart, Debbie Boone.

MAGIC OF MUSICAL COMEDY
Original Cast (1965) • Columbia (M) DJ-10 20-25   65
Interviews conducted by Broadway critic Lee Jordan, interspersed with selections from musicals recorded by Columbia. Script printed on back cover.
    Composer: Various. **Conductor:** Various. **Cast:** Richard Rodgers, Dick Van Dyke, Robert Goulet, Julie Andrews, Rex Harrison, Barbra Streisand, Mary Martin, Stephen Douglass.

MAGIC SHOW
Original Cast (1974) • Bell (S) 9003 12-20   74
Some covers have a sticker on the front reading: "Inside! Hexaflexagon."
Original Cast (1974) • Arista (S) 9003.. 8-10   76
    Composer: Stephen Schwartz. **Conductor:** Stephen Reinhardt. **Cast:** Doug Henning, Dale Soules, David Ogden Stiers, Cheryl Barnes, Anita Morris, Annie McGreevey, Robert LuPone, Loyd Sannes, Ronald Stafford.

MAGICAL MYSTERY TOUR
Soundtrack (1967) • Capitol (M) MAL-2835.................................... 100-150   67
Black label. Gatefold cover. Includes 24-page booklet.
Soundtrack (1967) • Capitol (S) SMAL-2835.. 50-75   67
Black label. Gatefold cover. Includes 24-page booklet.
Soundtrack (1967) • Apple (S) SMAL-2835.. 20-40   68
With Capitol logo on Apple label. Includes booklet.
Soundtrack (1967) • Capitol (S) SMAL-2835.. 20-40   69
Green label. Includes booklet.
Soundtrack (1967) • Capitol (S) SMAL-2835.. 10-12   76
Orange label. Includes booklet.

Soundtrack (1967) • Capitol (S) SMAL-2835.. 10-12   83
     Black label. Includes booklet.
Soundtrack (1967) • Capitol (S) C1-48062.. 8-10   88
     Purple label. Includes booklet.
Soundtrack (1967) • MFSL (S) 1-047 40-60   80
     Half-speed mastered.
       Composer: John Lennon, Paul McCartney, George Harrison. **Cast:** Beatles.

MAGNAVOX PRESENTS FRANK SINATRA
TV Soundtrack (1973) • Reprise (S) PRO-578 10-15   73
     Conductor: Nelson Riddle. **Cast:** Frank Sinatra, Association, Count Basie, Harpers Bizarre, Barbara NcNair, Don Ho.

MAGNIFICENT MOMENTS FROM MGM MOVIES
Soundtrack • MGM (M) E-4017 20-25
     Has music from *Words and Music, Gigi, Annie Get Your Gun, An American In Paris, Singin' in the Rain, Band Wagon, Lili, Kiss Me Kate, Wizard of Oz, Kismet* and *Show Boat.*
       Cast: Judy Garland, Louis Jourdan, Howard Keel, Georges Guetary, Gene Kelly, Adolph Deutsch, Leslie Caron & Mel Ferrer, Kathryn Grayson, Ann Blyth & Vic Damone, William Warfield, Lennie Hayton.

MAGNIFICENT MOTION PICTURE MUSIC
Studiotrack (1961) • United Artists (M) UAL-3134 10-12   61
Studiotrack (1961) • United Artists (S) UAS-6134 10-12   61
     Conductor: Don Costa. **Cast:** Don Costa Voices & Orchestra.

MAGNIFICENT MOVIE MUSIC
Soundtrack • United Artists (M) UAL-3476 8-12
Soundtrack • United Artists (S) UAS-6476 8-12
     Music from *The Knack – and How to Get It, Greatest Story Ever Told, Zorba the Greek, Thunderball, Hallelujah Trail, How to Murder Your Wife, The Train, Rage to Live, Help!, Sound of Music, What's New Pussycat?, I'll Take Sweden, The Glory Guys* and *Return from the Ashes.*
       Cast: Ferrante and Teicher, Leroy Holmes, John Barry, Elmer Bernstein, Neal Hefti, George Martin, Burt Bacharach, Riz Ortolani, Arnold Goland.

MAGNIFICENT MOVIE THEMES
Studiotrack (1965) • Command (M) R-887 8-12   65
Studiotrack (1965) • Command (S) RS-887SD 8-12   65
Studiotrack (1965) • Command (S) SMAS-90485 8-12   Re
     Capitol Record Club issue. Music from *Ship of Fools, The Amorous Adventures of Moll Flanders, Von Ryan's Express* and others.
       Composer: Various. **Cast:** Enoch Light and the Light Brigade.

MAGNIFICENT OBSESSION
Soundtrack (1954) • Decca (EP) ED-815 20-25   54
     Three discs.
Soundtrack (1954) • Decca (M) DL-8078 45-55   54
     Black label with gold print.
Soundtrack (1954) • Decca (M) DL-8078 30-35
     Rainbow label.
Soundtrack (1954) • Varese Sarabande (M) STV-81118 8-10   81
       Composer: Frank Skinner (based on themes by Chopin, Beethoven and Bach). **Conductor:** Joseph Gershenson.

MAGNIFICENT ROGUE
Original Radio Cast (1956) • Radiola (M) MR-1049............................... 10-12   75
     Cast: W.C. Fields, Fred Allen (narration), Ed Wynn, Errol Flynn, Mack Sennett, Baby Leroy, Edgar Bergen.

MAGNIFICENT SEVEN
Soundtrack (1960) • United Artists (M) UAL-3133 15-20   60
Soundtrack (1960) • United Artists (S) UAS-6133 20-25   60
  Above two both have the main title plus 11 other selections which are not from the film.
  Composer: Elmer Bernstein. **Conductor:** Al Caiola. **Cast:** Al Caiola (guitar).
  Also see RETURN OF THE SEVEN

MAGNIFICENT XII
Studiotrack (1963) • Liberty Premiere Series (S) LSS-14004 15-20   63
  Die-cut cover. Music from *The Magnificent Seven, Theme From The Sundowners, Laura,*
  Unchained Melody, Theme From Moulin Rouge, Never on Sunday, Exodus and others.
  Cast: Fantastic Strings of Felix Slatkin.

MAGOO IN HI-FI
Studio Cast (1957) • RCA Victor (M) LPM-1362 50-70   57
  Full title: *Magoo in Hi-Fi / Mother Magoo Suite.*
  Composer: Dennis Farnon. **Conductor:** Dennis Farnon. **Cast:** Jim Backus.

MAHABHARATA
Soundtrack (1990) • Virgin/Real World (S) 1-91363 10-12   90

MAHOGANY
Soundtrack (1975) • Motown (S) M6-858S1 5-10   75
  Composer: Michael Masser, others. **Conductor:** Lee Holdridge. **Cast:** Diana Ross.

MAHONEY'S LAST STAND
Soundtrack (1976) • Atlantic (S) SD-36-126 8-12   76
  Composer: Ron Wood, Ronnie Lane. **Cast:** Ron Wood, Ronnie Lane, Ian McLagan, Bruce
  Rowlands, Rick Grech, Ian Stewart, Kenney Jones, Pete Townshend, Bubby Keys, Jim Price,
  Benny Gallagher, Glynis Johns, Billy Nicholls.

MAID OF THE MOUNTAINS
Original London Cast (1918) • World (M) SH-169 18-20   81
  UK release.
  Composer: Harold Fraser-Simson, Harry Graham, Brian Hooker. **Conductor:** Merlin Morgan.
  Cast: Jose Collins, Thorpe Bates, Lauri DeFrece, Mable Sealby.
Original London Cast (1972) • Columbia/EMI (S) SCX-6504 20-25   72
  UK release. From London revival. Includes songs not found in previous productions.
  Composer: Harold Fraser-Simson, Harry Graham, Brian Hooker, Rudolf Friml, others. **Conductor:**
  Derek Taverner. **Cast:** Jimmy Edwards, Lyn Kennington, Gordon Clyde, Jimmy Thompson, Janet
  Mahoney.

MAIGRET
TV Soundtrack • London (M) LL-3281 10-15   63
  Themes and music from the BBC-TV show.
  Composer: Ron Grainer.

MAIN EVENT
Soundtrack (1979) • Columbia (S) JS-36115 8-10   79
  Composer: Paul Jabara, Bob Esty, Bruce Roberts, others. **Conductor:** Bob Esty. **Cast:** Barbra
  Streisand, Frankie Valli and the 4 Seasons, Loggins and Messina.

MAIN STREET TO BROADWAY: see OKLAHOMA!

MAJOR DUNDEE
Soundtrack (1965) • Columbia (M) OL-6380 12-18   65
Soundtrack (1965) • Columbia (S) OS-2780 15-25   65
  Composer: Daniele Amfitheatrof, Michael Melvoin. **Conductor:** Daniele Amfitheatrof. **Cast:**
  Mitch Miller's Gang.

MAJOR LEAGUE
Soundtrack (1989) • Curb (S) CRB 10402 10-12   89
  Composer: Randy Newman, James Newton Howard.

MAKE A WISH
Original Cast (1951) • RCA Victor (M) LOC-1002 100-125   51
Original Cast (1951) • RCA Victor (M) CBM1-2033 8-10   77
> **Composer:** Hugh Martin. **Conductor:** Milton Rosenstock. **Cast:** Nanette Fabray, Stephen Douglass, Helen Gallagher, Harold Lang, Dean Campbell.

MAKE HASTE TO LIVE: see ETERNAL SEA

MAKE ME AN OFFER
Original London Cast (1959) • RCA Victor (M) CLP-1333 35-45   59
UK release.
Original Cast (1959) • AEI (M) AEI-1112 10-15   70s
> **Composer:** David Heneker. **Cast:** Daniel Massey.

MAKE MINE MANHATTAN
Studio Cast (1948) • Painted Smiles (SE) PS-1369 8-10   79
One side has music from other revues.
> **Composer:** Richard Lewine, Arnold Horwitt. **Conductor:** Dennis Deal. **Cast:** Nancy Andrews, Carleton Carpenter, Helen Gallagher, Dolores Gray, Estelle Parsons, Lynn Redgrave, Arthur Siegel, Elaine Stritch.

MAKING MR. RIGHT: see DESPERATELY SEEKING SUSAN

MAKING OF THE PRESIDENT, 1960
TV Soundtrack (1963) • United Artists (M) UXL-9 20-25   63
TV Soundtrack (1963) • United Artists (S) UXS-59 20-25   63
Both are two-disc sets. Aired on ABC TV, December 29, 1963.
> **Composer:** Elmer Bernstein, others. **Cast:** Martin Gabel (narration), John F. Kennedy, Richard M. Nixon (voices used in TV documentary).

MAKING THE GRADE
Soundtrack (1984) • Varese Sarabande (S) STV-81204 10-15   84
> **Composer:** Basil Poledouris. **Conductor:** Francesco DeMasi. **Cast:** Shandi.

MALAMONDO
Soundtrack (1964) • Epic (M) LN-24126 25-30   64
Soundtrack (1964) • Epic (S) BN-26126 35-40   64
> **Composer:** Ennio Morricone. **Conductor:** Ennio Morricone. **Cast:** Ken Coleman.

MALCOLM X
Soundtrack (1972) • Warner Bros. (S) BS-2619 10-12   72
> **Cast:** Malcolm X.

MAMA I WANT TO SING
Original London Cast (1983) • Reach (S) WS-50000 15-25   83
> **Composer:** Rudolph Hawkins, Vy Higginson, others. **Cast:** Deitra Icks, Doris Tracy, Randy Higginson.

MAME
Original Cast (1966) • Columbia (M) KOL-6600 8-10   66
Original Cast (1966) • Columbia (S) KOS-3000 8-15   66
Original Cast (1966) • Columbia (S) PS-3000 8-10   Re
> **Composer:** Jerry Herman. **Conductor:** Donald Pippin. **Cast:** Angela Lansbury, Beatrice Arthur, Jane Connell, Charles Braswell, Jerry Lanning, Frankie Michaels, Sab Shimono.

Original Cast (1966) • Columbia (M) DJ-23 20-25   66
Full title: *Opening Night at the Winter Garden: Mame.* Cast interviews and songs from the show. Promotional issue only.
> **Composer:** Jerry Herman. **Conductor:** Donald Pippin. **Cast:** Angela Lansbury, Neil Simon, Jerry Herman, Jack L. Warner, Fred Robbins (interviewer).

London Studio Cast • Musico (S) MOS-1024 15-18
> **Composer:** Jerry Herman. **Cast:** Beryl Reid, Joan Turner, Keith Knight, Charlie Young.

Studio Cast (1966) • Epic (S) 15107 8-18   66
Also has music from *Sweet Charity.*
> **Composer:** Jerry Herman. **Conductor:** Frank Hunter. **Cast:** Bobby Hackett, Ronnie David.

Studio Cast • Gladwynne (S) GL 2022 8-12
    Cast: Jerry Choder, Gini Dee, Richard Rome and Orchestra.
Studio Cast • Diplomat (S) DS-2385 8-12
    Cast: Monterey Brass, Mary Louise, Michaels Brothers.
Soundtrack (1973) • Warner Bros. (S) PRO-580.................................. 35-45   73
    Gatefold cover. Front has close-up of Lucille Ball in a Christmas hat, back has credits and "Happy holidays! See you at Easter with Mame. Love, Lucy." Inside has photos from the film and liner notes. Has some alternate takes not on the commercial release (W-2773). Promotional issue only.
Soundtrack (1974) • Warner Bros. (S) W-2773...................................... 10-12   74
    Composer: Jerry Herman. **Conductor:** Fred Werner. **Cast:** Lucille Ball, Beatrice Arthur, Robert Preston, Jane Connell, Bruce Davison, Kirby Furlong.

MAMMY: see 20 MILLION SWEETHEARTS

MAN AND A WOMAN (UN HOMME ET UNE FEMME)

Soundtrack (1966) • United Artists (EP) UA-5147 10-12   66
    Stereo. White label. Promotional issue only.
Soundtrack (1966) • United Artists (M) UAL-4147 12-15   66
Soundtrack (1966) • United Artists (S) UAS-5147 15-20   66
    Composer: Francis Lai, Pier Barouh. **Conductor:** Francis Lai. **Cast:** Pierre Barouh, Nicole Croisille, Braden Powell and His Orchestra.
Soundtrack (1966) • United Artists (S) UAS-5184 15-20   66
    English language version.
Studiotrack (1966) • Liberty (S) LST-7490 8-12   66
    Composer: Francis Lai. **Cast:** Johnny Mann Singers.
Studiotrack (1967) • Unart (M) M-20019 10-15   67
Studiotrack (1967) • Unart (S) S-21019.. 10-15   67
    Full title: *Music from the Score of A Man and a Woman.*
    Composer: Francis Lai. **Cast:** Motion Picture Studio Orchestra.

MAN AND A WOMAN: 20 YEARS LATER

Soundtrack (1986) • Finnadar (S) 90562-1 8-10   86
    Composer: Francis Lai.

MAN AND BOY

Soundtrack (1971) • Sussex (S) SXBS-7011 10-15   71
    Composer: Johnny Johnson. **Conductor:** Quincy Jones. **Cast:** Bill Withers, Douglas Turner-Ward (monologue).

MAN CALLED ADAM

Soundtrack (1966) • Reprise (M) R-6180 12-15   66
Soundtrack (1966) • Reprise (S) RS-6180 15-18   66
    Composer: Benny Carter, others. **Conductor:** Benny Carter. **Cast:** Sammy Davis Jr., Mel Torme, Louis Armstrong, Nat Adderley.

MAN CALLED DAGGER

Soundtrack (1967) • MGM (M) E-4516... 12-15   68
Soundtrack (1967) • MGM (S) SE-4516 15-18   68
    Composer: Steve Allen, Buddy Kaye. **Conductor:** Ronald Stein. **Cast:** Maureen Arthur.

MAN CALLED FLINTSTONE

Soundtrack (1966) • HBR (M) HLP-2055 60-65   67
    Composer: John McCarthy, Ted Nichols, Doug Goodwin. **Cast:** Mel Blanc, Henry Corden (voices heard in feature-length cartoon).

MAN CALLED HORSE

Soundtrack (1970) • Columbia (S) OS-3530 12-15   70
    Composer: Leonard Rosenman. **Conductor:** Leonard Rosenman.

MAN COULD GET KILLED
Soundtrack (1966) • Decca (M) DL-4750 12-15   66
Soundtrack (1966) • Decca (S) DL-74750 15-18   66
    Composer: Bert Kaempfert. **Conductor:** Bert Kaempfert.

MAN FOR ALL SEASONS
Soundtrack (1966) • RCA Victor (M) VDM-116 20-25   66
    Two discs. Contains the entire film.
    Composer: Georges Delerue. **Conductor:** Georges Delerue. **Cast:** Paul Scofield, Robert Shaw,
    Orson Welles, Wendy Hiller, Leo McKern, Susannah York. (With dialogue.)

MAN FROM BROADWAY
Original Cast • No Label Used (S) S1J-003 10-15
    Composer: Lou Fortunate. **Cast:** Lou Fortunate, Imogene Wiel.

MAN FROM INTERPOL
TV Soundtrack (1962) • Top Rank (M) RM-327 30-40   62
TV Soundtrack (1962) • Top Rank (S) RS-627 50-60   62
    Composer: Tony Crombie. **Conductor:** Tony Crombie.

MAN FROM SHAFT
Studiotrack (1972) • MGM (S) SE-4836 15-25   72
    Cast: Richard Roundtree.
    Also see SHAFT

MAN FROM SNOWY RIVER
Soundtrack (1982) • Varese Sarabande (S) STV 81167 10-15   82
    Composer: Bruce Rowland. **Conductor:** Bruce Rowland.

MAN FROM THE EAST
Original Cast (1973) • Island (S) SMAS-9334 10-15   73
    Original music from the play.
    Composer: Stomu Yamashita. **Conductor:** Stomu Yamashita.

MAN FROM U.N.C.L.E.
TV Soundtrack [Vol. 1] (1965) • RCA Victor (M) LPM-3475 30-50   65
TV Soundtrack [Vol. 1] (1965) • RCA Victor (S) LSP-3475 55-70   65
    Composer: Jerry Goldsmith, Morton Stevens, Walter Scharf, Lalo Schifrin. **Conductor:** Hugo
    Montenegro.
TV Soundtrack [Vol. 2] (1965) • RCA Victor (M) LPM-3574 30-35   66
TV Soundtrack [Vol. 2] (1965) • RCA Victor (S) LSP-3574 40-45   66
    Composer: Gerald Fried, Robert Drasnin. **Conductor:** Hugo Montenegro.
Studiotrack (1965) • Metro (M) M-544 10-15   65
Studiotrack (1965) • Metro (S) MS-544 10-15   65
    Full title: *The Man from U.N.C.L.E. and Other TV Themes.* Also has music from: *Mr. Novak,*
    Daniel Boone, Flipper, Bonanza, Return to Peyton Place, Dr. Kildare and *12 O'Clock High.*
    Composer: Milton DeLugg, others. **Conductor:** Milton DeLugg, David Rose, Leroy Holmes.
    Cast: Milton DeLugg, Richard Chamberlain.

MAN IN THE MIDDLE
Soundtrack (1965) • 20th Century-Fox (M) TFM-3128 20-30   65
Soundtrack (1965) • 20th Century-Fox (S) TFS-4128 40-50   65
    Composer: John Barry, Lionel Bart, others. **Conductor:** John Barry.

MAN IN THE MOON
Original Cast (1963) • Golden (M) LP-104 35-40   63
    A completely different show than the 1961 space race satire film of the same name.
    Composer: Jerry Bock, Sheldon Harnick. **Cast:** Marionettes of Bil Baird and Cora Baird, Frank
    Sullivan, Franz Fazakas, Cari Harms, George Baird.

MAN NAMED BROWN

Original Cast • Brown-Forman Distillers Corp. (M) No Number Used... 10-20
Produced by Brown-Forman in conjunction with their 100th anniversary.
  Composer: Raymond Scott, Dick Stern.

MAN OF A THOUSAND FACES

Soundtrack (1957) • Decca (M) DL-8623 40-45   57
For either commercial (black label) or promotional issues.

Soundtrack (1957) • Decca (M) DL-8623 25-35   57
Rainbow (or multi-color) label.

Soundtrack (1957) • Varese Sarabande (M) STV-81121 8-10   Re
  Composer: Frank Skinner. **Conductor:** Joseph Gershenson.

MAN OF LA MANCHA

Original Cast (1965) • Kapp (M) KRL-4505 8-10   65

Original Cast (1965) • Kapp (S) KRS-54505 8-12   65
Covers may be found with either black or blue star and with "Best Musical 1966" shown.

Original Cast (1965) • MCA (S) 2018 8-10   Re

Original Cast (1965) • MCA (S) 1672 5-8   Re
  Composer: Mitch Leigh, Joe Darion. **Conductor:** Neil Warner. **Cast:** Richard Kiley, Irving
  Jacobson, Ray Middleton, Robert Rounseville, Joan Diener, Eleanore Knapp, Mimi Turque, Gino
  Conforti, Harry Theyard.

Studio Cast (1965) • Buena Vista (M) BV-4027 8-20   65

Studio Cast (1965) • Buena Vista (S) STER-4027 10-30   65
Gatefold covers and bound-in booklets.

Studio Cast (1965) • Disneyland (M) 1322 10-15
Songs and music from the stage play.
  Composer: Mitch Leigh, Joe Darion. **Conductor:** Tutti Camarata. **Cast:** Mike Sammes Singers.

Original London Cast (1968) • Decca (S) DXSA-7203 15-18   68
UK release.

Original London Cast (1968) • MCA (S) 10010 10-12   Re
Two disc sets. Contains the entire show.
  Composer: Mitch Leigh, Joe Darion. **Conductor:** Denys Rawson. **Cast:** Keith Michell, Joan
  Diener, Bernard Spear, David King, Edward Atienza, Peter Gordeno, Patricia Bredin, Alan
  Crofoot, Olive Gilbert.

Original Mexican Cast • Decca (M) DL-9171 12-18   63

Original Mexican Cast • Decca (S) DL-79171 15-20   63
  Conductor: Mario Ruiz Armengol.

Studio Cast (1972) • Columbia (S) S-31237 8-10   72
  Conductor: Paul Weston. **Cast:** Jim Nabors, Madeline Kahn, Marilyn Horne, Jack Gilford,
  Richard Tucker, Ron Husman, Irene Clark, David Bender.

Studio Cast (1972) • Golden (S) 265 8-10   72
Children's version.
  Cast: Richard Kiley.

Soundtrack (1972) • United Artists (S) UAS-9906 15-20   72
Cover is intact (no clipped corners or punched holes).

Soundtrack (1972) • United Artists (S) UAS-9906 5-8   72
Cover has clipped corners or punch-out holes.
  Composer: Mitch Leigh, Joe Darion. **Conductor:** Laurence Rosenthal. **Cast:** Peter O'Toole,
  Sophia Loren, James Coco.

MAN ON FIRE

Soundtrack (1987) • Varese Sarabande (S) STV 81343 10-15   87
  Composer: John Scott. **Conductor:** John Cast. **Cast:** Graunke Symphony Orchestra.

MAN ON THE MOON
Radio Broadcast (1969) • CBS (S) No Number Used........................... 15-20   69
    CBS News production, sponsored by Rolex. Includes letter insert from Rolex.
      Cast: Walter Cronkite (narrator.)
Radio Broadcast (1969) • Evolution (S) 3004... 8-10   69
      Cast: Roy Neal (narrator).

MAN WHO SHOT LIBERTY VALENCE
Soundtrack (1962) • Paramount (M) SP-1890....................................... 20-30   62
    Commercial spots for film. Dialogue and music. Made for radio station use only.
      Cast: James Stewart, John Wayne.

MAN WHO WOULD BE KING
Soundtrack (1975) • Capitol (S) SW-11474.. 15-20   75
      Composer: Maurice Jarre. **Conductor:** Maurice Jarre.

MAN WITH A LOAD OF MISCHIEF
Original Cast (1966) • Kapp (M) KRL-4508 8-12   66
Original Cast (1966) • Kapp (S) KRS-5508 10-12   66
      Composer: John Clifton, Ben Tarver. **Conductor:** Sande Campbell. **Cast:** Alice Cannon,
      Lesslie Nicol, Tom Noel, Reid Shelton, Raymond Thorne, Virginia Vestoff.

MAN WITH BOGART'S FACE
Soundtrack (1980) • Web (S) LP 104.. 12-15   81
      Composer: George Duning. **Conductor:** George Duning.

MAN WITH THE GOLDEN ARM
Soundtrack [Vol. 1] (1955) • Decca (EP) ED-2335 10-15   55
Soundtrack [Vol. 2] (1955) • Decca (EP) ED-2336 10-15   55
Soundtrack [Vol. 3] (1955) • Decca (EP) ED-2337 10-15   55
Soundtrack (1955) • Decca (M) DL-8257 12-18   55
Soundtrack (1955) • Decca (SE) DL-78257 12-15   59
Soundtrack (1955) • MCA (SE) 2043e 8-10   72
Soundtrack (1955) • MCA (SE) 1528 5-8   Re
      Composer: Elmer Bernstein. **Conductor:** Elmer Bernstein. **Cast:** Shorty Rogers and His
      Giants, Shelly Manne, Bud Shank (jazz renditions).

MAN WITH THE GOLDEN GUN
Soundtrack (1974) • United Artists (S) UA-LA358-G 10-20   74
Soundtrack (1974) • Liberty (S) LT-5358.. 8-12   Re
      Composer: John Barry, Monty Norman, Don Black. **Conductor:** John Barry. **Cast:** Lulu (title
      song).

MAN WITHOUT A COUNTRY
Studio Cast (1950) • Decca (M) DL-8020 20-30   50
    One side has music from *What So Proudly We Hail.*
      Cast: Bing Crosby, Frank Lovejoy, others.

MAN'S A MAN
Original Cast (1964) • Spoken Arts (M) 870 10-12   64
    Musical adaptation of the Brecht play.
      Conductor: Joe Raposo. **Cast:** Joe Raposo (piano).

MANCINI GENERATION
TV Soundtrack (1972) • RCA Victor (S) LSP-4689................................ 12-15   72
      Composer: Henry Mancini. **Conductor:** Henry Mancini. **Cast:** Henry Mancini and His
      Orchestra.

MANCINI'S ANGELS
Studiotrack (1977) • RCA Victor (S) APL1-2290 10-15   77
Music from *Charlie's Angels*, *A Star Is Born*, *Car Wash*, *Silver Streak*, *What's Happening!!*,
The Moneychangers, *Rocky* and *Roots*.
Conductor: Henry Mancini. **Cast:** Henry Mancini.

MANHATTAN
Soundtrack (1979) • Columbia (S) JS-36020 10-15   79
Composer: George Gershwin. **Conductor:** Zubin Mehta. **Cast:** Gary Graffman (piano), New
York Philharmonic.

MANHATTAN PROJECT
Soundtrack (1986) • Varese Sarabande (S) STV-81282 10-15   86
Composer: Philippe Sarde. **Conductor:** Harry Rabinowitz.

MANHATTAN TOWER
Studio Cast (1946) • Decca DAU-723 15-20
78 rpm album.
Studio Cast (1950) • Decca (EP) ED-562.. 10-20   50
Two discs.
Studio Cast (1950) • Decca (M) DLP-8011... 20-25   50
Also has music from *California*.
Composer: Gordon Jenkins **Conductor:** Gordon Jenkins **Cast:** Gordon Jenkins' Orchestra and
Chorus, Elliot Lewis (narrator), Beverly Mahr. CALIFORNIA: **Composer:** Gordon Jenkins, Tom
Adair. **Conductor:** Gordon Jenkins, Tom Adair. **Cast:** Beverly Mahr, Lee Sweetland, Betty
Brewer, Art Gentry, Gordon Jenkins' Orchestra and Chorus.
Studio Cast [Vol. 1] (1956) • Capitol (EP) EDM 1-766......................... 8-12   56
Studio Cast [Vol. 2] (1956) • Capitol (EP) EDM 2-766.......................... 8-12   56
Studio Cast [Vol. 3] (1956) • Capitol (EP) EDM 3-766.......................... 8-12   56
Studio Cast (1956) • Capitol (M) T-766.. 15-25   56
Studio Cast (1956) • Capitol (SE) DT-766 12-20   60s
Composer: Gordon Jenkins. **Cast:** Gordon Jenkins' Orchestra, Ralph Brewster Singers, Elliot
Lewis, Beverly Mahr, Bill Lee, Shirley Mitchell.
Studio Cast (1957) • Mercury (M) MG-20226 15-25   57
Conductor: Vic Schoen. **Cast:** Patti Page.
Studiotrack • Columbia (M) OL-6050... 10-15   64
Studiotrack • Columbia (S) OS-2450... 15-20   64
One side is the "First recording" of *The Man Who Loves Manhattan*
Composer: Gordon Jenkins. **Conductor:** Gordon Jenkins. **Cast:** Robert Goulet.

MANHUNTER
Soundtrack (1986) • MCA (S) 6182.. 8-10   86
Cast: Iron Butterfly, Prime Movers, Reds, Red 7, Michael Rubini, Shriekback.

MANIAC
Soundtrack (1980) • Varese Sarabande (S) STV-81143 15-20   80
Composer: Jay Chattaway.

MANNIX
TV Soundtrack (1969) • Paramount (S) PAS-5004 20-35   69
Composer: Lalo Schifrin. **Conductor:** Lalo Schifrin.

MANON OF THE SPRING
Soundtrack (1986) • TVT (S) 3005.. 10-15   86
Composer: Jean-Claude Petit.

MANS, LE: see LE MANS

MANTOVANI

Studiotrack • London (M) LL-1700 8-12
Titled *Film Encores*, has themes from *High Noon, Unchained, Intermezzo, My Foolish
Heart, Wizard of Oz, Summertime, Three Coins in the Fountain, Love Is a Many-
Splendored Thing, Laura, High Noon, Lili, Knickerbocker Holiday* and *Limelight*.
Cast: Mantovani and Orchestra.

Studiotrack • London (S) PS-516 8-12
Title: *Hollywood*.

Studiotrack • London (S) PS 270 8-12
Titled *Mantovani Plays Music from Two New David Merrick Broadway Musical Productions*,
has music from *Stop the World I Want to Get Off* and *Oliver*.

Studiotrack • London (S) PS 419 8-12
Titled *The Mantovani Sound*, has music from *Dear Heart, Funny Girl, Charade, Fiddler on
the Roof, Roar of the Greasepaint, Hello Dolly, Stop the World I Want to Get Off, Oliver,
The King and I, No Strings, My Fair Lady* and *The Sound of Music*.
Cast: Mantovani and His Orchestra.

MANY MOONS: see MERRY CHRISTMAS FROM KUKLA, FRAN AND OLLIE

MARACAIBO

Soundtrack (1958) • Decca (M) DL-8756 30-45   58
For either commercial (black label) or promotional issues.

Soundtrack (1958) • Decca (M) DL-8756 20-25   60s
Rainbow (or multi-color) label.
Composer: Laurindo Almeida, others. **Conductor:** Laurindo Almeida. **Cast:** Laurindo Almeida,
Jean Wallace.

MARAT (DE) SADE

Original Cast (1966) • Caedmon (M) 312M 15-20   66

Original Cast (1966) • Caedmon (S) TRS 312S 20-25   66
Boxed, three-disc set, with book.
Composer: Richard Peaslee, Geoffrey Skelton, Adrian Mitchell. **Conductor:** Patrick Gowers.
Cast: Clifford Rose, Brenda Kempner, Ruth Baker, Patrick Magee.

Soundtrack (1966) • United Artists (M) UAL-4153 10-15   66

Soundtrack (1966) • United Artists (S) UAS-5153 12-18   66
Composer: Richard Peaslee, Geoffrey Skelton, Adrian Mitchell. **Conductor:** Patrick Gowers.
Cast: Glenda Jackson, John Steiner, Jeanette Landis.

MARCH OF THE FALSETTOS

Original Cast (1981) • DRG (S) SBL-12581 10-15   81
Composer: William Finn. **Cast:** M. Rupert, A. Fraser.

MARCHES FROM THE MOVIES

Studiotrack (1965) • London (S) PS 434 15-25   65
Music from *Dr. Strangelove, The Longest Day, Ben Hur, The Inn of the Sixth Happiness,
The Music Man, Babes in Toyland, Captain from Castile, The Victors, Guns of Navarone,
How the West Was Won, Bridge on the River Kwai, The King and I* and *Guns at Batasi*.
Conductor: Captain Rodney Bashford. **Cast:** Band of the Grenadier Guards.

MARCO POLO

TV Soundtrack (1982) • Arista (S) AL-8304 10-15   82
Composer: Ennio Morricone. **Conductor:** Ennio Morricone. **Cast:** Dino Asciolla, Unione
Musicisti di Roma.

MARCO THE MAGNIFICENT

Soundtrack (1966) • Columbia (M) OL-6470 15-20   66

Soundtrack (1966) • Columbia (S) OS-2870 25-35   66
Composer: Georges Garvarentz, Charles Aznavour. **Conductor:** Georges Garvarentz. **Cast:**
Jerry Vale.

MARDI GRAS (1958)

Studiotrack (1958) • Dot (EP) DEP-1075 20-25   58
    Four film songs: *Loyalty, Bourbon Street Blues, Bigger Than Texas* and *A Fiddle, a Rifle, an Axe and a Bible.*
      Composer: Sammy Fain, Paul Francis Webster. **Conductor:** Billy Vaughn. **Cast:** Pat Boone, Steve Allen.

Studiotrack (1958) • Bell (M) LP-11 10-12   58
      Composer: Sammy Fain, Paul Francis Webster. **Conductor:** Enoch Light. **Cast:** Barry Frank, Janet Eden, Ralph Nyland, Lois Winter, Michael Stewart Quartet.

Studiotrack (1958) • Waldorf (S) MHK-SD-1405 10-12   58
      Composer: Sammy Fain, Paul Francis Webster. **Conductor:** Jimmy Carroll. **Cast:** Lou McGarity, Milt Hinton, Kenny Davern, Panama Francis, Loren Becker, Dottie Evans, Jack Brown.

MARDI GRAS (1965)

Original Cast (1965) • Decca (M) DL-4696 20-30   65
Original Cast (1965) • Decca (S) DL-74696 30-35   65
    Music from the Jones Beach Marine Theatre Guy Lombardo musical.
      Composer: Carmen Lombardo, John Jacob Loeb. **Conductor:** Mitchell Ayers. **Cast:** Jones Beach Marine Theatre Orchestra.

MARIA GOLOVIN

Original Cast (1958) • RCA Victor (M) LM-6142 200-225   58
    Boxed, three-disc set.
      Composer: Gian-Carlo Menotti.

MARIE: A TRUE STORY

Soundtrack (1985) • Varese Sarabande (S) STV-81265 10-15   85
      Composer: Francis Lai. **Conductor:** Francis Lai.

MARIE WARD

Soundtrack • Varese Sarabande (S) STV 81268 35-45   85
      Composer: Elmer Bernstein.

MARIGOLD

London Cast • AEI (S) AEI-1120 8-12   70s

MARILYN

Soundtrack • 20th Century-Fox (M) FXG-5000 50-75   59
Soundtrack • 20th Century-Fox (SE) SXG-5000 75-100   59
    Music from *There's No Business Like Show Business, River of No Return* and *Gentlemen Prefer Blondes.* Yellow cover. Includes an 8" x 10" black-and-white glossy – same as used on front cover – in a plastic frame.

Soundtrack • 20th Century-Fox (M) FXG-5000 45-55   59
Soundtrack • 20th Century-Fox (SE) SXG-5000 50-75   59
    Yellow cover. Without the bonus photo.

Soundtrack • 20th Century-Fox (M) FXG-5000 35-45   63
Soundtrack • 20th Century-Fox (SE) SXG-5000 40-60   63
    Black cover. Without the bonus photo.
      Composer: Irving Berlin, Jule Styne, Leo Robin, others. **Conductor:** Lionel Newman. **Cast:** Marilyn Monroe, Eileen Wilson (originally set to dub Jane Russell's vocals in *Gentlemen Prefer Blondes).*
      Also see MARILYN

MARILYN MONROE

Soundtrack • Audio Fidelity (M) PD 50,005 15-20   84
   Picture disc. Actual title: *The Ten*.

Soundtrack • Legends (S) 1000/1 25-30
   Gatefold cover. Previously unreleased recordings, including a Royal Triton TV commercial, an award acceptance for 1952 *Photoplay* Award, a press interview, a rendition of *Happy Birthday* at JFK's 1962 birthday party at Madison Square Garden, plus songs and dialogue excerpts from *Love Happy, Ladies of the Chorus, River of No Return, Gentlemen Prefer Blondes, The Jack Benny Show, How to Marry a Millionaire, Bus Stop, The Prince and the Show Girl, Some Like It Hot, Something's Gotta Give, Niagara, Seven Year Itch* and *There's No Business Like Show Business*.
   Cast: Marilyn Monroe.

Soundtrack • Rave (S) SH-2013 15-20   72
   Cast: Marilyn Monroe.

Soundtrack • Sandy Hook (M) SH-2013 15-20   84
   Picture disc. Actual title: *Rare Recordings 1948-1962*.
   Also see MARILYN
   Also see REMEMBER MARILYN
   Also see GENTLEMEN PREFER BLONDES.

MARIO LANZA SINGS BECAUSE

Studiotrack (1954) RCA Victor (EP) ERA-222 12-15   54
   Re-recordings from *The Great Caruso* and *That Midnight Kiss*.
   Conductor: Constantine Callinicos, Ray Sinatra. **Cast:** Mario Lanza, RCA Victor Orchestra.

MARJOE

Soundtrack (1972) • Warner Bros. (S) BS-2667 10-12   72
   Cast: Marjoe Gortner, Rev. Jerry Short, Mattie Clark, Andrae Crouch. (With dialogue.)

MARJORIE MORNINGSTAR

Soundtrack (1958) • RCA Victor (M) LOC-1044 50-60   58
   Has "An Original Soundtrack Recording" on spine.

Soundtrack (1958) • RCA Victor (M) LOC-1044 25-35   Re
   Does not have "An Original Soundtrack Recording" on spine. Has "Especially recorded in Hollywood for this album" on back at bottom and "RE" next to label number.
   Composer: Max Steiner, Sammy Fain, others. **Conductor:** Ray Heindorf. **Cast:** Gene Kelly.

MARK TWAIN TONIGHT

Original Cast [Vol. 1] (1959) • Columbia (M) OL-5440 8-12   59
Original Cast [Vol. 1] (1959) • Columbia (S) OS-2019 10-12   59
Original Cast [Vol. 2] (1959) • Columbia (M) OL-5610 8-12   61
Original Cast [Vol. 2] (1959) • Columbia (S) OS-2030 10-12   61
   Cast: Hal Holbrook (as Mark Twain).

TV Soundtrack (1967) • Columbia (M) OL-6680 12-15   67
TV Soundtrack (1967) • Columbia (S) OS-3080 12-18   67
   TV version of Holbrook's performance.
   Cast: Hal Holbrook (as Mark Twain).

MARKED FOR DEATH

Soundtrack (1990) • Delicious (S) 443-002-1 10-12   90

MARNIE: see GREAT MOVIE THRILLERS

MARRIAGE ITALIAN-STYLE: see TRIPLE FEATURE

MARRIED TO THE MOB

Soundtrack (1988) • Reprise (S) 1-25763 8-10   88
   Cast: Ziggy Marley and Melody Makers, New Order, Chris Isaak, Debbie Harry, Q. Lazzarus, Voodooist Corporation, Brian Eno, Feelies, Sinead O'Connor, Tom Tom Club.

MARRY ME A LITTLE
Original Cast (1981) • RCA Victor (S) ABL1-4159................................ 10-15   81
Original Cast (1981) • RCA Victor (S) AGL1-7142 5-8   Re
   Composer: Stephen Sondheim. **Conductor:** E. Martin Perry. **Cast:** Suzanne Henry, Craig Lucas.

MARRY ME, MARRY ME
Soundtrack (1969) • RCA Victor (S) LSO-1160.............................. 8-20   69
   Composer: Emil Stern, others. **Conductor:** Johnny Spence, Marty Manning, others. **Cast:** Jane Morgan.

MARTIN
Soundtrack (1977) • Varese Sarabande (S) VC-81127 8-10   79
   Composer: Donald Rubinstein. **Conductor:** Donald Rubinstein.

MARTIN CHARNIN: FIVE GREAT SONGS FROM NOT-SO-GREAT SHOWS
Studio Cast • Take Home Tunes (S) THT-771 5-10
   Also see UPSTAIRS AT O'NEALS

MARTIN, DEAN: see DEAN MARTIN

MARVELOUS PARTY WITH BEA LILLIE
Soundtrack • AEI (M) AEI-2103... 10-15   79
   Material from shows starring Beatrice Lillie.
   Cast: Bea Lillie.
   Also see QUEEN BEA

MARVIN AND TIGE
Soundtrack (1983) • Capitol (S) ST-12307... 8-10   83
   Composer: Patrick Williams.

MARX BROTHERS – ORIGINAL VOICE TRACKS FROM THEIR GREATEST MOVIES
Soundtrack • Decca (M) DL-9168 10-12   69
Soundtrack • Decca (SE) DL-79168... 10-15   69
   Material from various Marx Brothers' movies.
   Conductor: Charles Bud Dant. **Cast:** Marx Brothers.

MARY C. BROWN AND THE HOLLYWOOD SIGN
Studio Cast (1972) • United Artists (S) UAS-5657.............................. 12-15   72
   Composer: Dory Previn. **Cast:** Dory Previn, Joe Osborn, Peter Jameson, David Cohen, Laurindo Almeida, Bryan Garofolo.

MARY JANE
Soundtrack (1968) • Sidewalk (S) DT-5911 20-25   68
   Composer: Mike Curb, Lawrence Brown, Valjean Johns, Guy Hemric.

MARY POPPINS
Soundtrack (1964) • Buena Vista (M) BV-4026 10-15   64
Soundtrack (1964) • Buena Vista (S) STER-4026............................... 20-25   64
   Gatefold covers and bound-in booklets.
Soundtrack (1964) • Buena Vista (M) BV-4026 8-12   64
Soundtrack (1964) • Buena Vista (S) STER-4026............................... 10-15   64
   Gatefold covers without booklet.
Soundtrack (1964) • Buena Vista (S) STER-5005.............................. 8-15   73
Soundtrack (1964) • Disneyland (S) 3104 25-30   81
   Picture disc.

Soundtrack (1964) • RCA Victor (M) CPO-111.................................... 12-18

Soundtrack (1964) • RCA Victor (S) CSO-111 15-18
RCA's reissue of Buena Vista issues.
Composer: Richard M. Sherman, Robert B. Sherman. **Conductor:** Irwin Kostal. **Cast:** Julie Andrews, Dick Van Dyke, David Tomlinson, Glynis Johns, Ed Wynn, Karen Dotrice, Matthew Garber.

Soundtrack (1965) • Buena Vista (M) BV-3335 15-20   65

Soundtrack (1965) • Buena Vista (S) STER-3335................................ 20-25   65
Full title: *Mary Poppins En Francais*. Film score performed in French.
Composer: Richard M. Sherman, Robert B. Sherman. **Conductor:** Irwin Kostal. **Cast:** Christiane Legrand, Bob Martin.

Studiotrack (1964) • Reprise (M) R-6141 10-15   64

Studiotrack (1964) • Reprise (S) RS-6141 20-25   64
Full title: *Duke Ellington Plays Mary Poppins*.
Cast: Duke Ellington and His Orchestra.

Studiotrack (1964) • Disneyland (M) DQ-1256 8-20   64
Full title: *10 Songs from Mary Poppins*.
Cast: Marni Nixon, Bill Lee, Richard M. Sherman.

Studiotrack (1964) • Vee Jay (M) VJLP-1110...................................... 12-15   64

Studiotrack (1964) • Vee Jay (S) SR-1110.. 12-25   64
Full title: *Songs from Mary Poppins (and Other Songs)*.
Conductor: Ray Walston. **Cast:** Ray Walston's Children's Chorus.

Studiotrack (1965) • Hamilton (M) 152 8-12   65

Studiotrack (1965) • Hamilton (S) 12152.. 10-20   65
Full title: *Songs from Mary Poppins*.
Cast: Lawrence Welk and His Orchestra.

Studiotrack (1965) • Monument (M) M-8034 8-15   65

Studiotrack (1965) • Monument (S) SM-18034..................................... 15-20   65
Full title: *A Swinger's Guide to Mary Poppins*.
Cast: Tupper Saussy Quartet, Charlie McCoy.

Studiotrack (1965) • Buena Vista (M) BV-3333 12-20   65

Studiotrack (1965) • Buena Vista (S) STER-3333 15-30   65
Full title: *Let's Fly with Mary Poppins*.
Cast: Louis Prima, Gia Malone.

Studiotrack (1965) • Disneyland (M) DQ-1288 10-12   65
Actual title: Marching Along with Mary Poppins.
Cast: University of California Bruin Band.

Studiotrack • Wyncote (M) W-9049... 8-10   60s

Studiotrack • Wyncote (S) SW-9049.. 8-15   60s
Cast: Cheltenham Orchestra and Chorus.

Studiotrack (1965) • Columbia (M) CL-2366.. 8-10   65

Studiotrack (1965) • Columbia (S) CS-9166 10-12   65
Full title: *Music from Mary Poppins and Other Movie Hits*.
Conductor: Ray Conniff. **Cast:** Ray Conniff Orchestra.

Studiotrack (1973) • Camden (S) ACLI-0379 8-10   Re
Composer: Richard M. Sherman, Robert B. Sherman. **Cast:** Living Voices.

Studiotrack • Happy Time (S) HT-1034 10-15

Studiotrack • Kapp (M) KL-1419... 10-15

Studiotrack • Kapp (S) KS-3419 15-20
Full title: *Do-Re-Mi Children's Chorus Songs from Mary Poppins with Special Guest Mary Martin*. Also has songs from *Peter Pan, Pinocchio, Unsinkable Molly Brown, Cinderella* and *So Dear to My Heart*.
Cast: Do-Re-Mi Children's Chorus, Mary Martin.

MARY, QUEEN OF SCOTS
Soundtrack (1971) • Decca (S) DL-79186 20-30   72
    Composer: John Barry. Conductor: John Barry. Cast: Vanessa Redgrave.
Original Cast (1978) • MMG (S) 3 MMG-301 25-30   78
  Boxed, three-disc set. Includes 40-page booklet/libretto. Has the U.S. premiere
  performance.
    Composer: Thea Musgrave. Conductor: Peter Mark.

MASADA
TV Soundtrack (1981) • MCA (S) 5168 15-20   81
TV Soundtrack (1981) • MCA (S) 1564 5-8   Re
    Composer: Jerry Goldsmith. Conductor: Jerry Goldsmith.

M*A*S*H
Soundtrack (1970) • Columbia (S) OS-3520 10-15   70
  Does not have Ahmad Jamal's M*A*S*H Theme.
Soundtrack (1970) • Columbia (S) S-32753 8-12   73
  Includes Ahmad Jamal's M*A*S*H Theme.
    Composer: Johnny Mandel, Mike Altman, others. Cast: Ahmad Jamal (on '73 issue only),
    Johnny Mandel, Donald Sutherland, Elliott Gould, Sally Kellerman, Robert Duvall, Tom Skerritt,
    Gary Burghoff, Jo Ann Pflug, Fred Williamson, Rene Auberjonois, Roger Bowen, David Arkin,
    Kim Atwood, Tim Brown, Indus Arthur, John Schuck, Ken Prymus, Dawn Damon, G. Wood,
    Bobby Troup, Danny Goldman, Corey Fisher, Cathleen Cordell, Jerry Jones, Ted Knight, Marvin
    Miller, Rick Neilan. (With dialogue.)

MASK
Soundtrack (1985) • MCA (S) 6140 8-10   85
    Cast: Steppenwolf, Gary "U.S." Bonds, Steely Dan, Little Richard, Lynyrd Skynyrd, Grateful
  Dead.

MASK
Soundtrack (1994) • Chaos (S) OAS-6455 20-30   94
  White label. Plain cover. Promotional issue only.

MASK AND GOWN
Original Cast (1957) • GNP/Crescendo (M) 602 10-25   57
Original Cast (1957) • GNP/Crescendo (S) 602ST 15-35   57
Original Cast (1957) • AEI (M) AEI-1178 10-12   80s
    Composer: T.C. Jones. Cast: T.C. Jones.

MASS
Original Cast (1971) • Columbia (S) M2-31008 10-20   71
  Boxed, two-disc set with booklet.
Original Cast (1971) • Columbia (Q) M2Q-31008 12-20   71
  Single disc. Has excerpts from show.
    Composer: Leonard Bernstein, Stephen Schwartz. Conductor: Leonard Bernstein. Cast: Alan
    Titus, Norman Scribner Choir, Berkshire Boys Choir.

MASTER OF THE WORLD
Soundtrack (1961) • Vee Jay (M) VJLP-4000 15-20   61
Soundtrack (1961) • Vee Jay (S) SR-4000 25-35   61
Soundtrack (1961) • Varese Sarabande (S) VC-81070 12-18   78
    Composer: Les Baxter. Conductor: Calvin Carter.

MASTERS OF THE MUSICAL
Studiotrack • AEI (S) AEI-1160 8-10   80s
  Subtitle: Songs by Ira Gershwin.
Studiotrack • AEI (S) AEI-1161 8-10   80s
  Subtitle: Songs by Cole Porter.
Studiotrack • AEI (S) AEI-1164 8-10   80s
  Subtitle: Songs by Rodgers & Hart.

Studiotrack • AEI (S) AEI-1165 8-10   80s
  Subtitle: *Songs by Arthur Schwartz.*
Studiotrack • AEI (S) AEI-1168 8-10   80s
  Subtitle: *Songs by Jerome Kern.*

MASTERS OF THE UNIVERSE
Soundtrack (1987) • Varese Sarabande (S) STV 81333 15-20   87
  Composer: Bill Conti. **Conductor:** Harry Rabinowitz.

MATEWAN
Soundtrack (1987) • Daring (S) DR-1011.. 8-10   87
  Cast: Mason Daring.

MATING URGE
Soundtrack (1958) • International (M) LP-7777 30-40   58
Soundtrack (1958) • International (S) LP-7777-S................................ 35-45   58
  Also known as *Primitive.*
Soundtrack (1958) • Capitol (M) T-1552... 25-35   61
Soundtrack (1958) • Capitol (S) ST-1552.. 25-35   61
  Reissue title: *Pagan Love.*
  Composer: Stanley Wilson. **Conductor:** Stanley Wilson.

MATTER OF INNOCENCE
Soundtrack (1968) • Decca (M) DL-9160 10-12   68
Soundtrack (1968) • Decca (S) DL-79160... 12-15   68
  Composer: Michel Legrand. **Conductor:** Michel Legrand. **Cast:** Matt Monro.

MAURICE
Soundtrack (1987) • RCA Victor (S) 6618-1 8-12   87
  Composer: Richard Robbins. **Conductor:** Richard Robbins. **Cast:** Richard Robbins.

MAX MORATH AT THE TURN OF THE CENTURY
Original Cast (1969) • RCA Victor (S) LSO-1159 20-25   69
  Conductor: Fred Karlin. **Cast:** Max Morath (piano).

MAX STEINER – FOUR CLASSIC FILM SCORES
Soundtrack • Tony Thomas (M) TT-MS-13/14...................................... 45-75   81
  Two discs. Music from *Treasure of the Sierra Madre, Tomorrow Is Forever, Johnny Belinda*
  and *The Fountainhead.*
  Composer: Max Steiner.

MAX STEINER – GREAT LOVE THEMES FROM MOTION PICTURES
Studiotrack (1955) • RCA Victor (EP) EPA-704..................................... 25-30   55
  Music from *Johnny Belinda, The McConnell Story, The Last Command* and *Helen of Troy.*
Studiotrack (1955) • RCA Victor (M) LPM-1170 35-40   55
  Composer: Max Steiner. **Conductor:** Max Steiner.

MAX STEINER: MEMORIES
Soundtrack • Tony Thomas (M) TT-MS 17... 40-60   81
  Suites from *Escapade in Japan, Dr. Ehrlich's Magic Bullet, A Dispatch from Reuters,*
  Arsenic and Old Lace and *Fighter Squadron.*
  Composer: Max Steiner. **Conductor:** Max Steiner.

MAX STEINER: MUSIC FOR WESTERNS
Studiotrack • Tony Thomas (M) TT-MS 9/10.. 50-75   79
  Two discs. Music from *Dallas, San Antonio, Charge at Feather River, Raton Pass, Violent*
  Men, Silver River, Jim Thorpe – All American, A Distant Trumpet, Lion and the Horse, The
  Oklahoma Kid and *Virginia City.*
  Composer: Max Steiner. **Conductor:** Max Steiner.

MAX STEINER REVISITED

Soundtrack (1964) • Citadel (M) CT-MS-7... 50-55   78
  Music from *Spencer's Mountain, Lady Takes a Sailor, So Big, Ice Palace, City for Conquest, Operation Pacific* and *The Life of Emile Zola*.
  Composer: Max Steiner. **Conductor:** Max Steiner.

MAX STEINER: THE MAGIC OF

Soundtrack • Citadel (M) CT-MS-6.. 15-20   78
  Suites from *Tovarich, Gold Is Mine, Find It, Young Man with a Horn, They Died With Their Boots On, The Garden of Allah, Rocky Mountain, Saratoga Trunk, Deep Valley* and *The Woman in White*.
  Composer: Max Steiner. **Conductor:** Max Steiner.

MAX STEINER: THE RKO YEARS (1932-1935)

Soundtrack (1975) • Del/F (M) 25410.. 40-50   75
  Suites from *Symphony For Six Million, Bird of Paradise, King Kong, Morning Glory, Lost Patrol, Of Human Bondage, Little Minister* and *The Three Musketeers*.
  Composer: Max Steiner. **Conductor:** Max Steiner.

MAX STEINER: THE WARNER YEARS

Soundtrack • Citadel (M) CT-MS-2.. 50-70   75
  Suites from *Dive Bomber, Santa Fe Trail, One Foot in Heaven, The Adventures of Mark Twain, Glass Menagerie* and *The Flame and the Arrow*.
  Composer: Max Steiner. **Conductor:** Max Steiner.

MAXIMUM OVERDRIVE: see WHO MADE WHO

MAYA

Soundtrack (1966) • MGM (M) E-4376... 8-12   66
Soundtrack (1966) • MGM (S) SE-4376.. 8-12   66
  Composer: Riz Ortolani. **Conductor:** Riz Ortolani.
TV Soundtrack (1967) • MGM (M) CH-1044... 15-20   67
  With dialogue.
  Composer: Hans J. Salter. **Cast:** Jay North, Sajid Khan.
TV Soundtrack • Citadel (S) CT-6017 20-25
  Without dialogue.
  Composer: Hans J. Salter.

MAYERLING

Soundtrack (1969) • Philips (S) SBL-7876 100-125   69
  UK release.
  Composer: Francis Lai. **Conductor:** Francis Lai.

MAYOR

Original Cast (1985) • New York Music Co. (S) NYM-21 8-10   85
  Composer: Charles Strouse. **Cast:** Lenny Wolpe, Douglas Bernstein, Marion Caffey, Keith Curran, Nancy Giles, Ken Jennings, Ilene Kristen, Kathryn McAteor.

MAYTIME

Original Radio Cast (1944) • Pelican (M) LP-121 8-10
  With the stars of the 1937 film version.
  Composer: Sigmund Romberg, Rida Johnson Young, Cyrus Wood. **Cast:** Jeanette MacDonald, Nelson Eddy, Edgar Barrier.

McLINTOCK!

Soundtrack (1963) • United Artists (M) UAL-4112................................ 30-50   63
Soundtrack (1963) • United Artists (S) UAS-5112................................ 65-75   63
  Composer: Frank DeVol. **Conductor:** Frank DeVol.

McVICAR

Soundtrack (1980) • Polydor (S) PD-1-6284 8-12   80
  Cast: Roger Daltrey, John Entwistle, Kenney Jones, Pete Townshend, others.

1.

2.

3.

4.

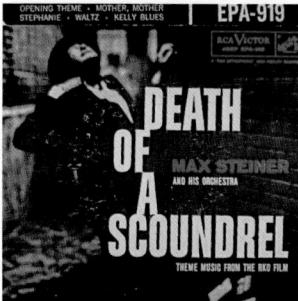

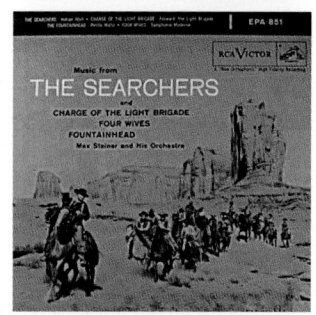

5.

6.

7.

8.

1. *Flame and the Flesh* ($40–$60). 2. *Guys and Dolls* ($35–$45). 3. *Compulsion* ($50–$75). 4. *I'll Cry Tomorrow* ($15–$25). 5. *Death of a Scoundrel* ($150–$175). 6. *The Searchers* ($100–$200). 7. *Samson and Delilah* ($25–$35). 8. *Johnny Concho* ($30–$60).

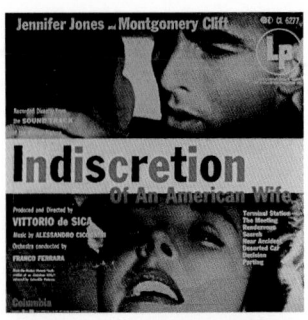

1.

2.

3.

4.

5.

6.

7.

8.

1. *Indiscretion of an American Wife* ($45–$65). 2. *Snow White and the Seven Dwarfs* ($60–$70). 3. *Danger* ($75–$100). 4. *European Holiday* ($50–$60). 5. *White Christmas* ($40–$50). 6. *Lady and the Tramp* ($40–$60). 7. *The Vanishing Prairie* ($60–$75). 8. *Gentlemen Prefer Blondes* ($75–$100).

1.

2.

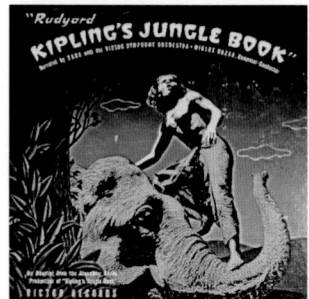

3.

4.

5.

6.

7.

8.

1. *Henry V* ($150–$250). 2. *Duel in the Sun* ($35–$45). 3. *The Red House* ($75–$100). 4. *Forever Amber* ($40–$50). 5. *Kipling's Jungle Book* ($50–$75). 6. *Rachel and the Stranger* ($100–$125). 7. *Madame Bovary* ($100–$150). 8. *Gulliver's Travels* ($80–$100).

1.

2.

3.

4.

5.

6.

1. *The Girl Most Likely* ($40–$60). 2. *Panic Button* ($100–$125). 3. *Love Is My Profession* ($45–$65). 4. *Fatal Attraction* ($20–$30). 5. *Boccaccio '70* ($50–$100). 6. *She Loves the Movies* ($60–$90).

1.

2.

3.

4.

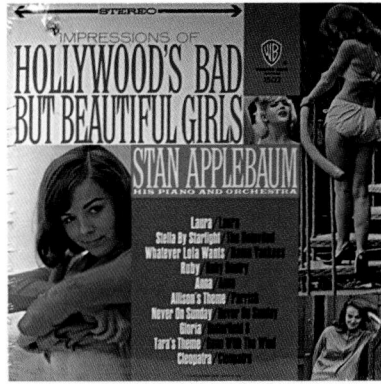

5.

6.

1. *Amarcord Nino Rota* ($20–$30). 2. *Barbarella* ($40–$50). 3. *Music from the Modern Screen* ($20–$30). 4. *The Minx* ($75–$100). 5. *Hollywood's Bad But Beautiful Girls* ($40–$60). 6. *Themes from Italian Films* ($30–$40).

1.

2.

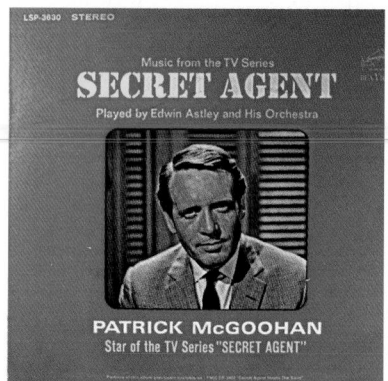
3.

4.

5.

6.

1. *Adventures of Rin Tin Tin* ($50–$60). 2. *How the Grinch Stole Christmas* ($45–$65). 3. *Secret Agent* ($225–$250). 4. *Davy Crockett* ($50–$75). 5. *Mister Ed* ($100–$200). 6. *Ozzie and Harriet* ($175–$200).

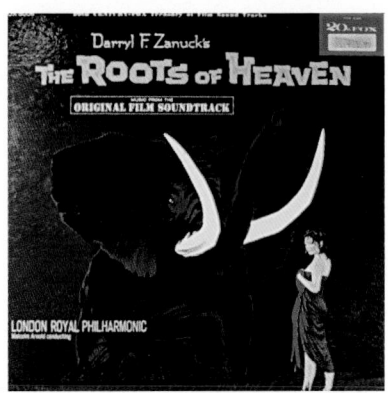

1.   2.

3.   4.

5.   6.

1. *The 7th Voyage of Sinbad* ($175–$200). 2. *The Roots of Heaven* ($250–$300).
3. *Jamboree* ($2,000–$3,000). 4. *The Barbarian and the Geisha* ($175–$225).
5. *A Dog of Flanders* ($225–$250). 6. *Comanche* ($250–$350).

1.

2.

3.

4.

5.

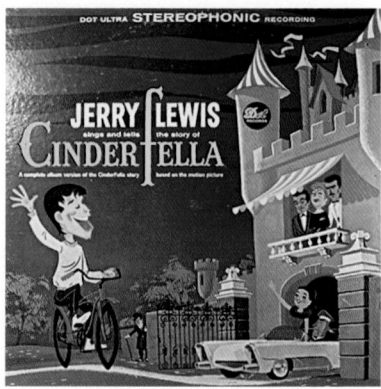

6.

1. *Trapeze* ($20–$25). 2. *The Bad Seed* ($200–$250). 3. *La Cage Aux Folles* ($25–$50). 4. *Marnie* ($50–$60). 5. *How to Get the Most Out of Your Stereo* ($100–$125). 6. *Cinderfella* ($50–$75).

ME AND BESSIE

Original Cast (1975) • Columbia (S) PC-34032 8-12   76
    Conductor: Howlett Smith. **Cast:** Linda Hopkins.

ME AND JULIET

Original Cast (1953) • RCA Victor (EP) EOA-458 15-20   53
Original Cast (1953) • RCA Victor (EP) EOC-1012 15-30   53
    Three discs.
Original Cast (1953) • RCA Victor (M) LOC-1012 45-65   53
Original Cast (1953) • RCA Victor (M) LOC-1098 20-25   65
Original Cast (1953) • RCA Victor (SE) LSO-1098............................... 25-30   65
    Composer: Richard Rodgers, Oscar Hammerstein. **Conductor:** Salvatore Dell'isola. **Cast:** Isabel Bigley, Bill Hayes, Joan McCracken, Mark Dawson, Arthur Maxwell, Bob Fortier, Barbara Carroll Trio.
Studio Cast (1953) • Decca (M) DL 5469 10-20   53
    10-inch LP. Also has music from *Can-Can*.
    Composer: ME AND JULIET: Richard Rodgers, Oscar Hammerstein, CAN-CAN: Cole Porter. **Conductor:** Gordon Jenkins. **Cast:** Gordon Jenkins and His Orchestra.
Studio Cast • Columbia (M) CL-6264 10-15   50s
    10-inch LP. Also has music from *Can-Can*.
    Cast: Art Ferrante, Lou Teicher.
Studio Cast • Royale (EP) EP-276 10-15   50s
    Colored vinyl.
    Cast: Royale Singers and Orchestra.
Studio Cast • Royale (M) 1423... 10-15   50s
    Also has music from *Can-Can*.
    Cast: Royale Singers and Orchestra, Freddy Gardner, Cello Quartet with Orchestra.

ME AND MY GIRL

Original London Cast (1985) • EMI (S) 46932.. 8-10   85
Original London Cast (1985) • That's Entertainment (S) TER-1145 8-10   80s
    UK releases.
    Composer: Noel Gay, Arthur Rose, Douglas Furber. **Cast:** Robert Lindsay.
Original Cast (1986) • MCA (S) 6196 12-15   81
Original Cast (1986) • EMI (S) PV-53030... 8-10   Re
    From the Broadway production.
    Composer: Noel Gay, Arthur Rose, Douglas Furber. **Cast:** Robert Lindsay, Maryann Plunkett, George S. Irving.

ME AND THE COLONEL

Soundtrack (1958) • RCA Victor (M) LOC-1046 30-45   58
    Composer: George Duning. **Conductor:** George Duning.

ME, NATALIE

Soundtrack (1969) • Columbia (S) OS-3350 12-15   69
    Composer: Henry Mancini. **Conductor:** Henry Mancini. **Cast:** Rod McKuen, Patty Duke. (With dialogue.)

ME NOBODY KNOWS

Original Cast (1970) • Atlantic (S) SD-1566 5-10   70
    Composer: Gary Friedman, Will Holt. **Conductor:** Edward Strauss. **Cast:** Melanie Henderson, Jose Fernandez, Northern J. Calloway, Beverly Ann Bremers, Irene Cara, Gerri Dean, Douglas Grant, Kevin Lindsay, Hattie Winston, Carla Thomas.

MEANING OF LIFE

Soundtrack (1983) • A&M (S) SP-4931 8-10   83
Soundtrack (1983) • MCA (S) 6121.. 8-10   83
    Cast: Monty Python.

MEATBALLS
Soundtrack (1979) • RSO (S) 1-3056.................................... 8-10   79
    Composer: Elmer Bernstein, Norman Gimbel. **Conductor:** Elmer Bernstein. **Cast:** Bill Murray,
    Rick Dees, Terry Black, Mary MacGregor, David Naughton.

MECO'S IMPRESSIONS OF AN AMERICAN WEREWOLF IN LONDON: see AMERICAN WEREWOLF IN LONDON

MEDEA
Original Cast (1950) • Decca (M) DLP-9000 20-25   50
    Black and gold label.
Original Cast (1950) • Decca (M) DLP-9000 15-18
    Rainbow (or multi-color) label.
    Cast: Judith Anderson, Vera Allen, Doris Rich, Raymond Edward Johnson, Arnold Moss, Everett
    Sloane.
Studio Cast • Caedmon (M) TRS-M-302 5-10

MEDICAL CENTER
TV Soundtrack (1971) • MGM (S) SE-4742............................... 18-20   71
    Also has other Lalo Schifrin scores.
    Composer: Lalo Schifrin. **Conductor:** Lalo Schifrin.

MEDICINE BALL CARAVAN
Soundtrack (1971) • Warner Bros. (S) BS-2565................................ 10-12   71
    Cast: Alice Cooper, B.B. King, Youngbloods, Delaney and Bonnie, Sal Valentino and
    Stoneground, Doug Kershaw.

MEDITERRANEAN HOLIDAY
Soundtrack (1964) • London (M) M-76003 30-45   64
Soundtrack (1964) • London (S) MS-82003 60-75   64
    Composer: Riz Ortolani. **Conductor:** Riz Ortolani.

MEDIUM
Original Cast (1947) • Columbia (M) OSL-154 20-25   49
    Two discs, one of which is *The Telephone*.
    Composer: Gian-Carlo Menotti. **Conductor:** Emanuel Balaban. **Cast:** Marie Powers, Evelyn
    Keller, Beverly Dame, Frank Rogier, Catherine Mastice.
Studio Cast • Columbia (S) MS-7387 8-12
    Composer: Gian-Carlo Menotti. **Conductor:** Jorge Mester. **Cast:** Opera Society of Washington,
    Regina Resnik, Judith Blegen, Emily Derr, Julian Patrick, Claudine Carlson.
Soundtrack (1951) • Mercury (M) MGL-7 100-150   51
    Boxed, two-disc set. Complete recording from the film.
    Composer: Gian-Carlo Menotti. **Conductor:** Thomas Schippers. **Cast:** Anna Maria Alberghetti,
    Marie Powers, Beverly Dame, Belva Kibler, Donald Morgan. (With dialogue.)

MEET ME AFTER THE SHOW: see PAINTING THE CLOUDS WITH SUNSHINE

MEET ME IN ST. LOUIS
Studiotrack (1944) • Decca A-380............................... 25-35   44
    Three-78 rpm album. Includes booklet.
Studiotrack (1944) • Decca (M) DL-8498 25-30   57
Studiotrack (1944) • AEI (M) AEI-3101................................... 8-12   78
    On both, one side is *The Harvey Girls*. Decca issues include *Boys and Girls Like You and
    Me* – deleted from the film.
    Composer: Hugh Martin, Ralph Blane, Johnny Mercer, Harry Warren, others. **Conductor:**
    George Stoll. **Cast:** Judy Garland, Kenny Baker, Virginia O'Brien, Betty Russell.
Soundtrack (1944) • Hollywood Soundstage (M) HS-5007 8-10
    Composer: Hugh Martin, Ralph Blane. **Conductor:** George Stoll. **Cast:** Judy Garland, Margaret
    O'Brien, Arthur Freed (performed vocals for Leon Ames in the film), D. Markas (performed
    vocals for Mary Astor) (with dialogue).

Radio Cast (1946) • Pelican (M) 118.. 8-12
Recording of a complete dress rehearsal on Dec. 1, 1946, one day before the actual
broadcast on the air.
Cast: Judy Garland, Margaret O'Brien, Tom Drake.

MEET THE PEOPLE: see ARMS AND THE GIRL

MEETINGS WITH REMARKABLE MEN
Soundtrack (1979) • Varese Sarabande (S) VC-81129 10-15   79
Composer: Laurence Rosenthal. **Conductor:** Laurence Rosenthal.

MEGILLA OF ITZIG MANGER
Original Cast (1968) • Columbia (S) OS-3270...................................... 35-40   68
Composer: Dov Seltzer, Joe Darion. **Conductor:** Dov Seltzer, Max Meth. **Cast:** Pesach
Burstein, Lillian Lux, Mike Burstein.

MELACHRINO ON BROADWAY
Studiotrack (1956) • RCA Victor (EP) EPA-874................................ 10-15   56
Act 1. Music from *My Fair Lady*. Each of three Acts are packaged separately.
Studiotrack (1956) • RCA Victor (EP) EPA-875................................ 10-15   56
Act 2. Music from *My Fair Lady, Guys and Dolls* and *Damn Yankees*.
Studiotrack (1956) • RCA Victor (EP) EPA-876................................ 10-15   56
Act 3. Music from *The King and I, Can-Can, South Pacific* and *The Pajama Game*.
Conductor: George Melachrino. **Cast:** Melachrino Orchestra.

MELACHRINO ORCHESTRA PLAYS MEDLEYS FROM CALL ME MADAM AND IRVING BERLIN SHOW TUNES
Studiotrack (1954) • RCA Victor (EP) EPA-507.................................... 10-15   54
Composer: Irving Berlin. **Conductor:** Melachrino. **Cast:** Melachrino Orchestra.

MELACHRINO ORCHESTRA PLAYS MEDLEYS FROM SHOW BOAT AND KISS ME KATE
Studiotrack (1954) • RCA Victor (EP) EPA-508.................................... 10-15   54
Composer: Oscar Hammerstein II, Jerome Kern, Cole Porter. **Conductor:** Melachrino. **Cast:**
Melachrino Orchestra.

MELACHRINO ORCHESTRA PLAYS MEDLEYS FROM SHOWS
Studiotrack (1954) • RCA Victor (LP) LPM-1008.................................. 15-25   54
Composer: Oscar Hammerstein II, Richard Rodgers, Irving Berlin, Jerome Kern, Cole Porter.
Conductor: Melachrino. **Cast:** Melachrino Orchestra.

MELACHRINO ORCHESTRA PLAYS MEDLEYS FROM SOUTH PACIFIC AND CAROUSEL
Studiotrack (1954) • RCA Victor (EP) EPA-509.................................... 10-15   54
Composer: Oscar Hammerstein II, Richard Rodgers. **Conductor:** Melachrino. **Cast:** Melachrino
Orchestra.

MELBA
Soundtrack (1953) • RCA Victor (M) LM-7012 30-60   53
10-inch LP.
Composer: Wolfgang Amadeus Mozart, Gaetano Donizetti, Felix Mendelssohn, Johann
Sebastian Bach, Charles François Gounod, Giacomo Puccini, Gioacchino Rossini. **Conductor:**
Muir Mathieson, Warwick Braithwaite. **Cast:** Patrice Munsel.

MELINDA
Soundtrack (1972) • Pride (S) 0006 8-12   72
Composer: Jerry Butler.

MELODY
Soundtrack (1971) • Atco (S) SD-33-363 10-12   71
Composer: Barry Gibb, Robin Gibb, Maurice Gibb. **Cast:** Bee Gees, Crosby, Stills, Nash and
Young, Richard Hewson Orchestra.

MELODY OF BROADWAY
Studiotrack • AEI (S) AEI-1154 10-15   80s

MEMED MY HAWK
Soundtrack (1984) • That's Entertainment (S) TER-1099...................... 8-10   80s
   UK release.
   Composer: Manos Hadjidakis.

MEMORABLE MOMENTS IN MUSICAL COMEDY
Original Cast • Decca A-865 20-30   51
   78 rpm album.
Original Cast • Decca (M) DL-6019....................................... 30-45   51
   10-inch LP. Music from *Knickerbocker's Holiday, The Girl from Utah, Leave It to Me, Pins and Needles, Foursome, Girl Crazy, Panama Hattie* and *Follow the Girls*. Some of these tracks appeared later on *They Stopped the Show!*
   Cast: Walter Huston with Victor Young and His Orchestra, Julie Sanderson with Harry Sosnik Orchestra, Millie Weitz with Harold J. Rome and Baldwin Bergersen, Mary Martin with Ray Sinatra Orchestra, Ethel Merman with Jay Blackton Orchestra, Gertrude Niesen with Harry Sosnik Orchestra, Foursome.

MEMORABLE MUSIC FROM THE MOVIES
Studiotrack (1954) • RCA Camden (M) CAL-233 15-20   54
   Music from *Moulin Rouge, Laura, Story of Three Loves, Limelight, Under Paris Skies, Lydia, Blithe Spirit, Love Story, Spellbound* and *Flesh and Fantasy.*
   Conductor: Werner Janssen, Harlan Ramsey. **Cast:** Harold Coates and Orchestra, Mitchell Ayres Orchestra, Henri Rene Orchestra, Al Goodman Orchestra, Janssen Symphony of Los Angeles.

MEMORIES AUX BRUXELLES
Soundtrack (1959) • Carlton (M) LP 12/112 15-25   59
Soundtrack (1959) • Carlton (S) STLP 12/112 20-35   59
   Cast: Alexander Laszlo.

MEMORIES OF A MIDDLE-AGED MOVIE FAN
Studiotrack (1968) • Atco (S) SD-33-263 20-30   68
   Music from films of 1936: *Suzy, Born to Dance, Rhythm on the Range, Rose of the Rancho, The Great Ziegfeld, Pennies from Heaven, Sing Me a Love Song, Trail of the Lonesome Pine, Swingtime, Sing Baby Sing, Stowaway* and *Poor Little Rich Girl.*
   Cast: Ray Charles (not *the* Ray Charles, but a different artist/conductor.)

MEN IN WAR
Soundtrack (1957) • Imperial (M) LP-9032-W 125-150   57
   Monaural even though labeled as "Recorded in Stereophonic Sound."
   Composer: Elmer Bernstein. **Conductor:** Elmer Bernstein.

MERCHANT IVORY PRODUCTIONS 25th ANNIVERSARY
Soundtrack • RCA Victor (S) 6658-1-RC16.. 10-12   88
   Two discs.

MERMAN IN VEGAS: see ETHEL MERMAN

MERRIEST SONGS
Soundtrack (1968) • Disneyland (S) DL-3510 10-15   68
   Made for Gulf Oil. Soundtracks studiotracks from *Mary Poppins, Snow White, Cinderella, Pinocchio, Lady and the Tramp, Three Little Pigs, So Dear to My Heart, Family Band, Babes in Toyland, Winnie the Pooh, Jungle Book* and *Alice in Wonderland.*
   Cast: Julie Andrews, Louis Armstrong, Phil Harris, Burl Ives, Mary Martin, Louis Prima, Dick Van Dyke, Ed Wynn.

MERRILY WE ROLL ALONG
Original Cast (1982) • RCA Victor (S) CBL1-4197 25-30   81
   Half-speed master audiophile recording. Includes booklet.
   Composer: Stephen Sondheim. **Cast:** Jim Walton, Ann Morrison, Lonny Price.

MERRY ANDREW
Soundtrack (1958) • Capitol (M) T-1016... 30-45   58
   Composer: Saul Chaplin, Johnny Mercer. **Conductor:** Nelson Riddle. **Cast:** Danny Kaye, Pier Angeli, Salvatore Baccaloni, Robert Coote, Rex Evans.

MERRY CHRISTMAS
TV Soundtrack (1975) • Sesame Street (S) CTW-25516 10-15   75

MERRY CHRISTMAS FROM KUKLA, FRAN AND OLLIE
TV Soundtrack (1955) • Decca (M) DL-8192... 60-75   55
One side has James Thurber's *Many Moons*.
Composer: Jack Fascinato. **Cast:** Fran Allison, Burr Tillstrom.
Also see HAPPY MOTHER GOOSE (BY KUKLA, FRAN AND OLLIE)
Also see SONGS BY KUKLA, FRAN AND OLLIE

MERRY CHRISTMAS, MR. LAWRENCE
Soundtrack (1983) • MCA (S) 6125.. 10-15   83
Composer: Ryuichi Sakamoto. **Cast:** Ryuichi Sakamoto, David Sylvian.

MERRY WIDOW
Original Revival Cast (1964) • RCA Victor (M) LOC-1094 8-10   64
Original Revival Cast (1964) • RCA Victor (S) LSO-1094...................... 8-12   64
Composer: Franz Lehar, Paul Francis Webster. **Conductor:** Franz Allers. **Cast:** Patrice
Munsel, Robert Wright, Sig Arno, Frank Porretta, Mischa Aver, Joan Weldon, Joseph Leon,
Robert Goss.

Original London Revival Cast • Angel (S) 35816 20-25
Composer: Franz Lehar, Paul Francis Webster. **Conductor:** William Reid. **Cast:** Thomas
Round, June Bronhill, Howell Glynne, Marion Lowe.

Studio Cast (1948) • Decca DA-364.. 12-18   48
78 rpm album.

Studio Cast (1950) • Decca (M) DL-8004.. 20-30   50
Pink cover.

Studio Cast (1950) • Decca (M) DL-8819.. 20-25   58
Alternate cover. Decca issues featur cast members from various 1940s New York revivals.
Composer: Franz Lehar, Paul Francis Webster. **Conductor:** Isaac Van Grove. **Cast:** Kitty
Carlisle, Wilbur Evans, Felix Knight, Lisette Verea, Merry Widow Orchestra and Chorus.

Studio Cast (1951) • London (M) 5354.. 15-20   50s
Conductor: Victor Reinshagen.

Studio Cast (1951) • RCA Victor (EP) WK 28 15-20   51
Boxed, four-disc set.

Studio Cast (1951) • RCA Victor (M) LK-1020...................................... 15-20   51

Studio Cast (1951) • Camden (M) CAL-397 12-15   57
Composer: Franz Lehar, Paul Francis Webster. **Conductor:** Al Goodman. **Cast:** Donald
Richards, Elaine Malbin, Nino Ventura, Guild Choirsters.

Studio Cast (1952) • Capitol (EP) EBF-335.. 15-25   52
Two discs.

Studio Cast (1952) • Capitol (M) L-335 15-18   52
10-inch LP.

Studio Cast (1952) • Capitol (M) T-437 10-12   55
One side has music from *The Student Prince*.
Composer: Franz Lehar, Adrian Ross, Forman Brown, Paul Francis Webster, Sigmund
Romberg, Dorothy Donnelly. **Conductor:** George Greeley. **Cast:** Gordon MacRae, Lucille
Norman, Dorothy Warenskjold.

Studio Cast (1953) • Columbia (M) ML-4666.. 12-15   53
Studio Cast (1953) • Columbia (M) CL-838 10-12   56
Conductor: Lehman Engel. **Cast:** Dorothy Kirsten, Robert Rounseville.

Studio Cast (1964) • Columbia (M) OL-5880... 8-10   64
Studio Cast (1964) • Columbia (S) OS-2280 10-12   64
Conductor: Franz Allers. **Cast:** Lisa Della Casa, John Reardon, Laurel Hurley, American Opera
Society Orchestra and Chorus, Paul Franke, Charles K. L. Davis, Howard Kahl, Paul Richards.

Studio Cast • London (M) A 4233... 15-18
Boxed, two-disc set. Includes booklet.
Conductor: Robert Stolz. **Cast:** Hilde Gueden, Per Gruden, Waldemar Kmentt, Emmy Loose,
Karl Donch, Peter Klein, Kurt Equiluz, Marjan Rus, Hans Duhan, Peter Preses, Ljubomir
Pantscheff, Edith Winkler, others.

Studio Cast • Kapp (M) KL-1152 8-10
Studio Cast • Kapp (S) KS-3035 10-15
An "Operetta without words."
  Composer: Franz Lehar. Conductor: Conrad Lieder. Cast: Vienna Theater-Konzert Orchestra.
Studio Cast (1957) • Halo (M) 5073 8-15   57
Studio Cast (1960) • Craftsmen (M) 205 8-12   60
Studio Cast • Celebrity (M) UT 602 8-12
  Cast: New World Strings.
Studio Cast • Classics International (S) CIS-1813.................................. 8-12
Studio Cast • Spin-O-Rama (S) S-80 8-12
  Cast: Stradivari Strings.
Soundtrack (1952) • MGM (EP) X-157 12-15   52
Soundtrack (1952) • MGM E-157 20-30   52
  78 rpm album.
Soundtrack (1952) • MGM (M) E-3228... 15-18   55
  One side has music from *Rose Marie*.
  Composer: Franz Lehar, Paul Francis Webster. Conductor: Jay Blackton. Cast: Fernando
  Lamas, Trudy Erwin (performed Lana Turner's vocals in the film), Richard Haydn, MGM Studio
  Orchestra and Chorus.
  Also see CAT AND THE FIDDLE

MERTON OF THE MOVIES
Radio Cast (1941) • Pelican (M) LP-139 12-18
  Broadcast November 17, 1941.
  Cast: Judy Garland, Mickey Rooney.

MESSAGE
Soundtrack • Namara (S) SLOW 1033.. 5-10

MET STARS ON BROADWAY
Studio Cast • Met/RCA Special Products (M) 204 10-15
  Cast: Ezio Pinza, Leontyne Price, Robert Weede, Risë Stevens, Cesare Siepi, Renata Tebaldi,
  Roberta Peters, Eileen Farrell, Giulietta Simionato, Dorothy Kirsten, Birgit Nilsson, Renata
  Scotto.

METROPOLIS
Soundtrack (1984) • Columbia (S) JS-39526 8-12   84
Soundtrack (1984) • Columbia (S) CK-39526.. 5-10   Re
  Score composed for 1984 theatrical rerelease of a 1927 silent film.
  Composer: Giorgio Moroder, others. Cast: Freddie Mercury, Pat Benatar, Jon Anderson, Cycle
  V, Giorgio Moroder, Bonnie Tyler, Loverboy, Billy Squier, Adam Ant.
Original London Cast • That's Entertainment (S) TER 2-1168 12-18   80s
  Two discs. UK release.
  Composer: Joe Brooks. Cast: Brian Blessed, Judy Kuhn, Graham Bickley, Jonathan Adams, Paul
  Keown, Stifyn Parri.

MEXICAN HAYRIDE
Original Cast (1944) • Decca A-372 20-30   44
  Album of four 78 rpms. Includes booklet.
Original Cast (1944) • Decca (M) DL-5232... 75-100   50
  10-inch LP.
Original Cast (1944) • Columbia (M) X-14878...................................... 8-10   Re
  Music from *Texas, Li'l Darlin'*.
  Composer: Cole Porter. Conductor: Harry Sosnik. Cast: June Havoc, Wilbur Evans, Corinna
  Mura.

MIAMI VICE
TV Soundtrack (1985) • MCA (S) 6150 8-10   85
  Composer: Jan Hammer, others. Conductor: Jan Hammer, others. Cast: Jan Hammer, Glenn
  Frey, Chaka Khan, Phil Collins, Grandmaster Melle Mel, Tina Turner.

MIAMI VICE II

TV Soundtrack (1986) • MCA (S) 6192 8-10   86
  Composer: Jan Hammer, others. Conductor: Jan Hammer, others. Cast: Jan Hammer, Phil Collins, Roxy Music, Jackson Browne, Damned, Patti LaBelle and Bill Champlin, Steve Jones, Andy Taylor.

MICKEY AND THE BEANSTALK

Studio Cast (1968) • Disneyland (M) ST-3974 20-25   68
  Gatefold cover. Includes bound-in 10-page color booklet. Side two is Disney-related songs.
  Composer: Jimmie Dodd, Oliver Wallace, others. Cast: Robbie Lester (narrator), Jim Macdonald (Mickey Mouse, Giant), Clarence Nash (Donald Duck), Pinto Colvig (Goofy), Marilyn Hooven (singing harp), Jimmie Dodd and the Mouseketeers Chorus and Orchestra.

MICKEY MOUSE CLUB: see WALT DISNEY'S MICKEY MOUSE CLUB

MICKEY'S CHRISTMAS CAROL

Soundtrack • Disneyland (S) 3109 20-30   82
  Picture disc.

MICKEY ONE

Soundtrack (1965) • MGM (M) E-4312 10-15   65
Soundtrack (1965) • MGM (S) SE-4312 15-18   65
  Both have four-page booklet.
  Composer: Eddie Sauter. Conductor: Eddie Sauter. Cast: Stan Getz.

MIDAS RUN

Soundtrack (1968) • Citadel (S) CT-6016 35-65   68
  Composer: Elmer Bernstein.

MIDNIGHT COWBOY

Soundtrack (1969) • United Artists (S) UAS-5198 15-20   69
Soundtrack (1969) • EMI America (S) E1-48409 8-10   Re
  Composer: John Barry. Conductor: John Barry. Cast: Harry Nilsson, Groop, Leslie Miller, Elephant's Memory, John Barry.

MIDNIGHT EXPRESS

Soundtrack (1978) • Casablanca (S) NBLP-7114 15-20   78
Soundtrack (1978) • Casablanca (S) 822561-1 8-10   Re
  Composer: Giorgio Moroder, David Castle, William Hayes, Oliver Stone, Chris Bennett.
  Conductor: Giorgio Moroder, H. Faltermeier. Cast: David Castle, Chris Bennett.

MIDNIGHT RUN

Soundtrack (1988) • MCA (S) 6250 10-15   88
  Composer: Danny Elfman. Conductor: Danny Elfman. Cast: Danny Elfman.

MIDSUMMER NIGHT'S DREAM

Original Cast (1954) • RCA Victor (EP) ERB-46 15-18   55
  Two discs. Excerpts from the LP set.
Original Cast (1954) • RCA Victor (M) LM-6115 40-45   55
  Boxed, three-disc set with booklet. Based on the Old Vic 1954 production of Shakespeare's play.
Original Cast (1954) • RCA Victor (M) LM-1863 20-25   54
  Highlights from boxed set. Based on Old Vic 1954 production of Shakespeare's play.
  Composer: Felix Mendelssohn. Conductor: Sir Malcolm Sargent. Cast: Moira Shearer, Robert Helpmann, Stanley Holloway, B.B.C. Orchestra.
Original Cast (1978) • Doda (S) LPM-78D1 15-20   78
  Composer: Randolph Tallman. Conductor: Jim Abbott.

MIDSUMMER NIGHT'S SEX COMEDY

Soundtrack (1982) • CBS (S) 37789 8-10   82
  Composer: Felix Mendelssohn. Conductor: George Szell, Leonard Bernstein, Eugene Ormandy, Seiji Ozawa. Cast: Cleveland Orchestra, New York Philharmonic, Philadelphia Orchestra, Isaac Stern and Boston Symphony Orchestra.

MIGHTY QUINN

Soundtrack (1989) • A&M (S) SP-3924 8-10   89
    Cast: UB40, Arrow, Michael Rose, Sheryl Lee Ralph, Cedella Marley, Sharon Marley
    Pendergast, Half Pint, Yello, Neville Brothers, Little Twitch, Seventeen Plus.

MIKADO

Studio Cast (1954) • RCA Victor (EP) EKL-1001 10-20   54
    Two discs.

Studio Cast (1954) • RCA Victor (M) LK-1001 20-30   54
    Composer: William S. Gilbert, Arthur Sullivan. **Conductor:** Al Goodman. **Cast:** Al Goodman
    and His Orchestra, Jimmy Carroll, Audrey Marsh, John Percival, Sally Sweetland, Martha
    Wright, Earl Wrightson.

Studio Cast (1957) • Halo (M) 5061 10-15   57

Studio Cast • Royale (M) 1882 10-15   50s
    10-inch LP. Full title: *Mikado – Excerpts.*
    Cast: Savoyards.

Studio Cast (1958) • Angel (M) 3573 15-25   58

Studio Cast (1958) • Angel (S) S-3573 25-35   58
    Composer: William S. Gilbert, Arthur Sullivan. **Conductor:** Sir Malcolm Sargent. **Cast:** Pro Arte
    Orchestra.

Studio Cast • Everest (S) 3412 20-30
    Conductor: Richard Korn. **Cast:** North German Radio Orchestra, Martyn Green, Barbara
    Troxell, James Pease.

Studio Cast • London (M) LLP 189/90 10-15
    Two discs.
    Conductor: Isidore Godfrey. **Cast:** Darrell Fancourt, Leonard Osborne, Martyn Green, Richard
    Watson, Alan Styler.

TV Soundtrack (1960) • Columbia (M) OL-5480 20-25   60

TV Soundtrack (1960) • Columbia (S) OS-2022 65-85   60

TV Soundtrack (1960) • Columbia Special Products (M) AOL-5480 8-10   Re
    From the NBC-TV Bell Telephone Hour presentation.
    Composer: William S. Gilbert, Arthur Sullivan. **Conductor:** Donald Voorhees. **Cast:** Groucho
    Marx, Stanley Holloway, Robert Rounseville, Barbara Meister, Dennis King, Helen Traubel,
    Norman Luboff Choir, Bell Telephone Orchestra.

Studiotrack (1960) • Hudson (M) 221 5-10   60

Studiotrack • Bell (M) BLP 31 5-10
    Cast: Martyn Green.

Studiotrack • Classics International (SE) CIS-1812 15-20
    Cast: Savoyards.

Studiotrack • World Pacific (M) WP 1262 15-20
    Cast: Freddie Gambrel, Paul Horn.

MIKE HAMMER

TV Soundtrack (1959) • RCA Victor (M) LPM-2140 15-20   59

TV Soundtrack (1959) • RCA Victor (S) LSP-2140 20-40   59
    Composer: Dave Kahn, Melvyn Lenard. **Conductor:** Skip Martin. **Cast:** Skip Martin's Orchestra.

MIKE POST

Soundtrack (1984) • RCA Victor (S) AFL1-5183 8-10   84
    Collection of television and movie themes.
    Composer: Mike Post, others. **Conductor:** Mike Post. **Cast:** Mike Post.
    Also see MUSIC FROM L.A. LAW (AND OTHERWISE)
    Also see TELEVISION THEME SONGS

MIKE TODD'S BROADWAY
Studio Cast (1958) • Everest (M) LPBR-5011 8-12   58
Studio Cast (1958) • Everest (S) SPBR-5011 10-15   58
     Boxed set containing an LP in a gatefold cover. Music from *The Hot Mikado, Gay New Orleans, Streets of Paris, Star & Garter, Mexican Hayride, A Night in Venice, As the Girls Go, Up in Central Park, Peep Show, Something for the Boys* and *Around the World in 80 Days.*

MIKE'S MURDER
Soundtrack (1983) • A&M (S) SP-4931 8-10   83
     Composer: Joe Jackson. **Cast:** Joe Jackson.

MIKLOS ROZSA
Studiotrack (1985) • Varese Sarabande (S) 704,260 8-10   85
     Music from *Spellbound, Time Out of Mind, World the Flesh and the Devil, Lydia* and *Because of Him.*
     Composer: Miklos Rozsa. **Conductor:** Elmer Bernstein. **Cast:** Cynthia Millar; Utah Symphony Orchestra with Joshua Pierce and Dorothy Jonas.

MIKLOS ROZSA CONDUCTS HIS GREAT FILM MUSIC
Studiotrack • Polydor (S) 2383-327 15-25   75
     Music from *The Thief of Bagdad, A Double Life, The Lost Weekend, A Time to Love – A Time to Die, The Naked City, Knights of the Round Table, Diane – Story of Three Loves* and *Young Bess.*
     Composer: Miklos Rozsa. **Conductor:** Miklos Rozsa. **Cast:** Royal Philharmonic Orchestra.

MIKLOS ROZSA CONDUCTS HIS GREAT THEMES
Studiotrack • Capitol (S) ST-2837 15-25   67
     Music from *Ben-Hur, El Cid, Quo Vadis* and *King of Kings.*
Studiotrack • Angel (S) S-36063 15-20   73
     Actual title: *Miklos Rozsa Conducts His Great Film Music.* Reissue of Capitol LP.
     Composer: Miklos Rozsa. **Conductor:** Miklos Rozsa.

MIKLOS ROZSA – MUSIC FOR FILMS
Soundtrack • Tony Thomas (M) TT-MR-4 30-40   81
     Music from *The Killers, Dark Waters* and *Time Out of Mind.*
     Composer: Miklos Rozsa. **Conductor:** Miklos Rozsa.

MILANESE STORY
Soundtrack (1962) • Atlantic (M) 1388 10-15   62
Soundtrack (1962) • Atlantic (S) SD-1388 15-20   62
     Composer: John Lewis. **Conductor:** John Lewis.

MILDRED PIERCE (AND OTHER MELODRAMATIC LADIES)
Soundtrack • Tony Thomas (M) TT-MS-15 50-70   81
     Music from *Without Honor, Caged, The Breaking Point* and *Four Daughters.*
     Composer: Max Steiner, others.

MILK AND HONEY
Original Cast (1961) • RCA Victor (M) LOC-1065 8-10   61
Original Cast (1961) • RCA Victor (S) LSO-1065 12-15   61
     Front covers have only credits.
Original Cast (1961) • RCA Victor (M) LOC-1065 8-10   61
Original Cast (1961) • RCA Victor (S) LSO-1065 10-12   61
     Covers picture Tommy Rall and two dancers.
     Composer: Jerry Herman. **Conductor:** Max Goberman. **Cast:** Robert Weede, Mimi Benzell, Molly Picon, Tommy Rall, Juki Arkin.

MILLION DOLLAR MOVIES
Studiotrack (1960) • RCA Victor (M) LM-2380.................................... 10-20   60
Studiotrack (1960) • RCA Victor (S) LSC-2380 15-25   60
   Full title: *Music from Million Dollar Movies*.
    Conductor: Arthur Fiedler. **Cast:** Arthur Fiedler and Boston Pops.
Studiotrack [Vol. 2] (1965) • RCA Victor (M) LM-2782.......................... 10-15   65
Studiotrack [Vol. 2] (1965) • RCA Victor (S) LSC-2782 15-20   65
   Full title: *More Music from Million Dollar Music*. Music from *Mondo Cane*, *Tom Jones*, *Days of Wine and Roses*, *The Longest Day*, *The Cardinal*, *Charade*, *My Fair Lady*, *Breakfast at Tiffany's*, *Mary Poppins*, *Cleopatra*, *Snow White*, *Lawrence of Arabia* and others.
    Conductor: Arthur Fiedler. **Cast:** Arthur Fiedler and Boston Pops.

MILLION DOLLAR MYSTERY
Soundtrack (1987) • MRC (S) 1024.. 8-12   87
    Conductor: Al Gorgoni.

MILLION SELLERS FROM THE MOVIES
Studiotrack (1971) • Alshire (S) S-5254 8-10   71
    Cast: 101 Strings.

MILTON BERLE SINGS RODGERS AND HART SONGS
Studiotrack • RCA Victor P-170.. 25-30
   78 rpm album.
    Cast: Milton Berle, Vic Damone, others.

MINI-WASH: see CAR WASH

MINNIE'S BOYS
Original Cast (1970) • Project 3 (S) TS-6002-SD 12-15   70
   Off-white cover.
Original Cast (1970) • Project 3 (S) TS-6002-SD 8-12   Re
   White cover.
    Composer: Larry Grossman, Hal Hackady. **Conductor:** John Berkman. **Cast:** Shelley Winters, Arny Freeman, Mort Marshall, Julie Kurnitz, Lewis J. Stadlen, Daniel Fortus, Irwin Pearl, Alvin Kupperman and Gary Raucher (as the Marx Brothers).

MINOR MIRACLE
Soundtrack (1984) • Varese Sarabande (S) STV-81193 8-10   84
    Composer: Rick Patterson. **Conductor:** Rich Patterson.

MINX
Soundtrack (1970) • Amsterdam (S) 12007 75-100   70
    Composer: Tom Dawes, Don Danneman. **Cast:** Cyrkle.

MIRACLE
Studiotrack • Elmer Bernstein Film Music Collection (S) FMC-2........... 20-25
   Also has music from *Toccata for Toy Trains*.
    Composer: Elmer Bernstein.

MIRACLE GOES ON
Soundtrack (1977) • Paragon (S) 33035 8-12   77
    Cast: John Peterson. **Conductor:** Ronn Huff. **Cast:** Doug Oldham and His Orchestra, Peterson Trio, Dave Boyer, Lillie Knauls, Truth, John Peterson, Ken Peterson, Festival Choir, others.

MIRACLE ON 34TH STREET: see IT'S A WONDERFUL LIFE

MIRAGE
Soundtrack (1965) • Mercury (M) MG-21025 10-12   65
Soundtrack (1965) • Mercury (S) SR-61025....................................... 12-15   65
    Composer: Quincy Jones. **Conductor:** Quincy Jones.

MISANTHROPE
Studio Cast • Caedmon (S) TRS 337 8-12   66

MISER
Studio Cast • Caedmon (S) TRS 338 8-12   66
MISERABLES, LES: see LES MISERABLES
MISFITS
Soundtrack (1961) • United Artists (M) UAL-4087 40-45   61
Soundtrack (1961) • United Artists (S) UAS-5087 75-100   61
Soundtrack (1961) • United Artists (M) UALA-273 10-12   Re
    Composer: Alex North. **Conductor:** Alex North.
    Also see JOHNNY COOL
MISHIMA
Soundtrack (1985) • Nonesuch/Elektra (S) 79113-1 10-15   85
    Composer: Philip Glass.
MISS AMERICA (AND OTHER ABERATIONS)
Original Cast (1961) • Brave New World (M) CO-638 15-20
    Pageant satire from Minneapolis. Limited edition, 1,000 copies made.
MISS GINGER ROGERS
Studiotrack (1978) • EMI (S) ODN 1002.. 10-20   78
    Rerecordings of songs from her films.
    Conductor: John Mealing, Harry South, John Hawkins. **Cast:** Ginger Rogers.
MISS GULCH RETURNS
Original Cast (1986) • Gulch Mania (S) MGR-5757 10-15   86
MISS JULIE
Original Revival Cast (1979) • Painted Smiles (S) PS-1338 8-10   79
    Composer: Ned Rorem, Kenward Elmslie. **Conductor:** Peter Leonard. **Cast:** Judith James,
    Ronald Madden, Veronica August.
MISS LIBERTY
Original Cast (1949) • Columbia MM-860.. 12-15   49
    Album of six 78 rpms.
Original Cast (1949) • Columbia (M) ML-4220 20-25   49
    Green label.
Original Cast (1949) • Columbia (M) OL-4220...................................... 12-15   Re
    Gray label.
Original Cast (1949) • Columbia Special Products (M) AOL-4220.......... 8-10   Re
    Composer: Irving Berlin. **Cast:** Eddie Albert, Allyn McLerie, Mary McCarty, Ethel Griffles,
    Johnny Thompson.
Studio Cast (1949) • Decca (M) DL-5009 20-25   49
    10-inch LP.
    Composer: Irving Berlin. **Conductor:** Fred Waring. **Cast:** Joe Marine, Daisy Bernier, Gordon
    Goodman, Jane Wilson, Joanne Wheatley and Chorus, Fred Waring and His Pennsylvanians.
MISS SADIE THOMPSON
Soundtrack (1953) • Mercury (EP) EP-2-3147 25-35   54
Soundtrack (1953) • Mercury (M) MG-25181 45-65   54
    10-inch LP.
Soundtrack (1953) • Mercury (M) MG-20123 100-150   56
    12-inch LP.
    Composer: George Duning, Lester Lee, Ned Washington. **Conductor:** Morris Stoloff. **Cast:**
    Rita Hayworth, Jo Ann Greer (performs vocals lip-synched by Rita Hayworth in the film), Jose
    Ferrer, Aldo Ray. (With dialogue.)
MISS SAIGON
Original London Cast • Geffen (S) GHS-24271 12-18   80s
    Two discs.
    Composer: Claude-Michel Schonberg. **Cast:** Jonathan Pryce, Lea Salonga.

MISS SHOW BUSINESS: see JUDY GARLAND

MISSION
Soundtrack (1986) • Virgin (S) 90567-1 12-15   86
    Composer: Ennio Morricone. **Conductor:** Ennio Morricone. **Cast:** London Philharmonic
    Orchestra, Incantation (Indian instrumentation), London Voices (choir).
    Also see VIRGIN

MISSION: IMPOSSIBLE
TV Soundtrack (1967) • Dot (M) DLP-3831 20-30   67
TV Soundtrack (1967) • Dot (S) DLP-25831 25-35   67
    Composer: Lalo Schifrin, Jack Urbont, Bruce Geller, Bud Shank, Stu Williamson. **Conductor:**
    Lalo Schifrin.
TV Soundtrack [Vol. 2] (1967) • Paramount (S) PAS-5002 20-40   69
    Composer: Lalo Schifrin. **Conductor:** Lalo Schifrin.
Studiotrack • Custom (S) CS-1102 8-12
    Cast: Larry Schaffer Orchestra.

MISSISSIPPI
Studiotrack (1935) • Decca (M) DL-6008 50-60   51
    10-inch LP. One side has music from *Here Is My Heart*.
    Composer: Richard Rodgers, Lorenz Hart, Stephen Foster. **Conductor:** George Stoll. **Cast:**
    Bing Crosby.

MISSISSIPPI BURNING
Soundtrack (1988) • Antilles (S) 91236-1 10-15   88
    Composer: Trevor Jones.

MISSOURI BREAKS
Soundtrack (1976) • United Artists (S) UA LA623-G 15-40   76
Soundtrack (1976) • MCA (S) 25113 8-10   86
    Composer: John Williams. **Conductor:** John Williams.

MISTRAL'S DAUGHTER
TV Soundtrack (1984) • Carrere (S) SZ-39902 8-10   84
    Composer: Vladimir Cosma. **Conductor:** Vladimir Cosma.

MISTY: see TO CATCH A THIEF

MISUNDERSTOOD
Soundtrack (1984) • Polydor (S) 821 238 8-10   84
    Composer: Michael Hoppe, Carlos Franzetti. **Conductor:** Carlos Franzetti.

MIXED DOUBLES / BELOW THE BELT
Original Cast (1966) • Upstairs (S) UD-37W56 80-100   66
    Two discs.
    Cast: Judy Graubart, Madeline Kahn, Larry Moss, Lily Tomlin, Richard Blair, Genna Carter,
    Robert Rovin, Janie Sell, Gary Sneed.

MOAT FARM MURDERS: see OUTER SPACE SUITE

MOBY DICK
Studio Cast (1950) • Decca (M) DL-5146 50-75   50
    10-inch LP.
    Cast: Charles Laughton and Supporting Cast.
Studio Cast (1950) • Decca (M) DL-9071 20-35   59
    One side has music and dialogue from *Treasure Island*.
    Composer: Victor Young. **Conductor:** Victor Young. **Cast:** Charles Laughton (*Moby Dick*),
    Thomas Mitchell (*Treasure Island*).
Soundtrack (1956) • RCA Victor (EP) EPB-1247 20-40   56
    Two discs. Omits closing segment heard on the LP (LPM-1247) below.
Soundtrack (1956) • RCA Victor (M) LPM-1247 100-125   56
    Composer: Philip Sainton. **Conductor:** Louis Levy.

MODERN GIRLS

Soundtrack (1986) • Warner Bros. (S) 1-25526 8-10   86
    Cast: Depeche Mode, Anthony & the Camp, Fly Joy, Toni Basil, Female Body Inspectors, George Black, Club Nouveau, Ice House, TKA, Jesus & Mary Chain.

MODERN TIMES

Soundtrack (1936) • United Artists (M) UAL-4049 15-20   59
Soundtrack (1936) • United Artists (SE) UAS-5049 30-35   59
  Gatefold covers.
Soundtrack (1936) • United Artists (SE) UAS-5222 8-10   71
  Standard cover.
    Composer: Charlie Chaplin. **Conductor:** Alfred Newman.

MODERNS

Soundtrack (1988) • Virgin Movie Music (S) 90922-1 8-10   88
    Composer: Mark Isham, Charlelie Couture. **Conductor:** Mark Isham, Charlelie Couture. **Cast:** L'Orchestre Moderne, Charlelie Couture.

MODESTY BLAISE

Soundtrack (1966) • 20th Century-Fox (M) 3182 25-30   66
Soundtrack (1966) • 20th Century-Fox (S) 4182 40-50   66
    Composer: John Dankworth. **Conductor:** John Dankworth. **Cast:** David and Jonathan.

MOHAMMAD, MESSENGER OF GOD

Soundtrack (1977) • Namara (S) 79001-798 20-25   77
    Composer: Maurice Jarre. **Conductor:** Maurice Jarre.

MOLLY MAGUIRES

Soundtrack (1970) • Paramount (S) PAS-6000 12-18   70
    Composer: Henry Mancini. **Conductor:** Henry Mancini.

MOLLY'S PILGRIM

Soundtrack • Musicmasters (S) 20138K 8-10

MOMENT BY MOMENT

Soundtrack (1978) • RSO (S) RS-1-3040 8-12   78
  White label. Promotional issue only.
Soundtrack (1978) • RSO (S) RS-1-3040 8-10   78
    Composer: Lee Holdridge, Molly-Ann Leikin. **Cast:** Yvonne Elliman, Michael Franks, Stephen Bishop, Charles Lloyd, Dan Hill, 10CC.

MOMENT OF TRUTH

Soundtrack (1965) • Mainstream (M) 56057 10-12   65
Soundtrack (1965) • Mainstream (S) S-6057 12-18   65
  This Italian movie should not be confused with a 1952 French film of the same title.
    Composer: Piero Piccioni. **Conductor:** Piero Piccioni.

MON ONCLE D'AMERIQUE

Soundtrack (1979) • DRG (S) SL-9505 8-10   79
    Composer: Arie Dzierlatka. **Conductor:** Arie Dzierlatka.

MONDO CANE

Soundtrack (1963) • United Artists (M) UAL-4105 12-18   63
Soundtrack (1963) • United Artists (S) UAS-5105 15-20   63
  Cover may show Riz Ortolani as "Ritz" Ortolani.
    Composer: Riz Ortolani, Nino Oliviero. **Conductor:** Riz Ortolani.
Studiotrack (1965) • Liberty (S) LST-7307 8-10   65
  Full title: *Theme from Mondo Cane.* Also has other film music.
    Conductor: Martin Denny. **Cast:** Martin Denny and Orchestra.

MONDO CANE NO. 2
Soundtrack (1964) • 20th Century-Fox (M) TFM-3147 25-30   64
Soundtrack (1964) • 20th Century-Fox (S) TFS-4147 35-40   64
    Composer: Nino Oliviero.

MONDO HOLLYWOOD
Soundtrack (1967) • Tower (M) T-5083.. 15-20   67
Soundtrack (1967) • Tower (S) DT-5083.. 20-25   67
    Composer: Mike Curb, others. **Conductor:** Mike Curb. **Cast:** Davie Allan and the Arrows, Mugwump Establishment, Mike Clifford, Riptides, Bobby Jameson, God Pan, Darrell Dee, 18th Century Concepts, Teddy and Darrell.

MONOLOGUES AND SONGS
Original Cast (1958) • Elektra (M) EKL-184 25-30   58
    Composer: Joyce Grenfell, Richard Addinsell. **Cast:** Joyce Grenfell, George Bauer (piano).

MONSIEUR DE POURCEAUGNAC
Original Cast (1978) • Broadway Baby Demos (S) BBD-789.................. 8-10   78
    Composer: Howard Harris, Tony Schuman. **Cast:** Lisa Loomer, Tony Calabro, Homer Foil.

MONSIGNOR
Soundtrack (1982) • Casablanca (S) 7277... 10-15   82
    Composer: John Williams. **Conductor:** John Williams. **Cast:** London Symphony Orchestra.

MONSTERS, MUNSTERS, MUMMIES, AND OTHER TV FIENDS
TV Soundtrack • Epic BN-26125 75-80

MONTEREY POP
Soundtrack • Reprise (S) SW-93371.. 15-20
    Full title: *Music from Monterey Pop Soundtrack.* Capitol Record Club issue.
    Cast: Jimi Hendrix Experience, Otis Redding.

MONTEZ, LOLA: see LOLA MONTEZ

MONTY PYTHON AND THE HOLY GRAIL
Soundtrack (1975) • Arista (S) AB-4050.. 10-12   75
    Full title: *The Album of the Soundtrack of the Trailer of the Film of Monty Python and the Holy Grail.*
Soundtrack (1975) • Arista (S) ALB-68355... 8-10   Re
    Composer: Neil Innes. **Cast:** Terry Jones, Eric Idle, Graham Chapman, Terry Gilliam, John Cleese, Michael Palin, Douglas Adams, John Young, Bee Duffell, Connie Booth.

MOOD MUSIC FROM STAGE & SCREEN
Studiotrack (1965) • Columbia (SP) XSV-88912 10-15   65
    Made for Zenith.
    Cast: Andre Previn, Percy Faith, others.

MOOD MUSIC FROM THE MOVIES
Studiotrack (1971) • Reader's Digest (S) RD4-141 20-30   71
    Boxed, six-disc set. Music from *Adventures of Robin Hood, Spellbound, Jane Eyre, The Private Lives of Elizabeth & Essex, 2001: A Space Odyssey, Rashomon, Of Human Bondage, The Spector of the Rose, Julie* and others. Mail order offer.
    Composer: Various. **Conductor:** Charles Gerhardt. **Cast:** London Symphony Orchestra.
    Also see GREAT MUSIC FROM THE MOVIES

MOOD MUSIC OF THE SILENT MOVIES
Studio Cast • Barbary (M) BC 33020... 5-10
    Cast: Maurice Ellenhorn (piano), Alan Lurie (narrator).

MOON IN THE GUTTER
Soundtrack (1983) • DRG (S) SL-9516 8-10   83
    Composer: Gabriel Yared.

MOON IS BLUE

Soundtrack (1953) • Crown (M) CLP-5095... 15-20   56
  Black vinyl.
Soundtrack (1953) • Crown (SE) CST-130... 30-35   56
  Colored vinyl.
  Composer: Hershel Burke Gilbert, Sylvia Fine. **Conductor:** Hershel Burke Gilbert.

MOON OF MANAKOORA: see DOROTHY LAMOUR – THE MOON OF MANAKOORA

MOON OVER PARADOR

Soundtrack (1988) • MCA (S) 6249.. 20-25   88
  Composer: Maurice Jarre. **Conductor:** Maurice Jarre.

MOON SPINNERS

Soundtrack (1964) • Buena Vista (M) BV-3323 25-35   64
  Composer: Ron Grainer, Terry Gilkyson. **Conductor:** Ron Grainer.

MOONLIGHT IS SILVER: see WE WERE DANCING

MOONLIGHTING

TV Soundtrack (1987) • MCA (S) 6214 8-10   87

MOONRAKER

Soundtrack (1979) • United Artists (S) UA-LA971-I............................... 8-10   79
  Composer: John Barry, Hal David. **Conductor:** John Barry. **Cast:** Shirley Bassey.

MOONSTRUCK

Soundtrack (1988) • Capitol (S) C1-90231 8-10   88
  Composer: Various. **Cast:** Dean Martin, Dick Hyman, Vikki Carr.

MORE

Soundtrack (1968) • Tower (S) ST-5169 25-40   68
Soundtrack (1968) • Harvest (S) SW-11198 10-20   73
  Composer: Pink Floyd. **Cast:** Pink Floyd.

MORE AMERICAN GRAFFITI

Soundtrack (1979) • MCA (S) No Number Used 25-35   79
  Picture disc. Promotional issue only.
Soundtrack (1979) • MCA (S) 2-11006.. 8-12   79
  Two discs.
  Cast: Martha and the Vandellas, Andy Williams, Byrds, Angels, Simon and Garfunkel, Donovan, Supremes, Cream, Bob Dylan, Aretha Franklin, Zombies, ? and the Mysterians, Chantays, Lenny Welch, Marvelettes, Bobby Vinton, Capitols, Country Joe and the Fish, Barry Sadler, Mary Wells, Doug Sahm, McCoys, Percy Sledge, Wolfman Jack. (With dialogue.)

MORE FUNNY FONE CALLS: see STEVE ALLEN'S FUNNY FONE CALLS

MORE GREAT MOTION PICTURE THEMES

Studiotrack (1961) • United Artists (M) UAL-3158 8-10   61
Studiotrack (1961) • United Artists (S) UAS-6158 8-12   61
  Music from *Bonanza, Goodbye Again, Gone with the Wind, Elmer Gantry, Paris Blues, Misfits, One-Eyed Jacks, Never on Sunday, Odds Against Tomorrow, Porgy and Bess, Houseboat, God's Little Acre, Naked Maja, Some Like It Hot* and *Moulin Rouge.*
  Cast: Leroy Holmes Orchestra, Ferrante & Teicher, Henry Jerome Orchestra, Melina Mercouri, Al Caiola, Louis Armstrong, Andre Previn, Don Costa, Bill Potts, Marilyn Monroe, Mitchell Powell, Elmer Bernstein, Modern Jazz Quartet.

MORE HIT TV THEMES

Studiotrack (1963) • Capitol (M) T-1869 10-20   63
Studiotrack (1963) • Capitol (S) ST-1869 20-40   63

Music from *The Beverly Hillbillies, Bonanza, Andy Williams Show, Stoney Burke, McHale's Navy, Have Gun Will Travel, I Love Lucy, Lawrence Welk Show, Dick Van Dyke Show* and others.
Conductor: Nelson Riddle. **Cast:** Nelson Riddle Orchestra.

MORE LUSH THEME FROM MOTION PICTURES

Studiotrack • MGM (M) E-3480 20-25
Conductor: Leroy Holmes.

MORE MUSIC FROM MILLION DOLLAR MOVIES: see MILLION DOLLAR MOVIES

MORE OFFICIAL ADVENTURES OF BATMAN: see BATMAN

MORE STATELY MANSIONS

Studio Cast • Caedmon (S) TRS 331 8-12   67

MORE THAN A MIRACLE

Soundtrack (1967) • MGM (M) E-4515 12-15   67
Soundtrack (1967) • MGM (S) SE-4515 15-20   67

Also known as *Cinderella, Italian Style*.
Composer: Piero Piccioni. **Conductor:** Piero Piccioni. **Cast:** Roger Williams' Orchestra and Chorus.

MORE THEMES FROM THE JAMES BOND THRILLERS

Studiotrack (1966) • London (M) LL 3445 8-12   66
Cast: Roland Shaw Orchestra.

MOSCOW ON THE HUDSON

Soundtrack (1984) • RCA Victor (S) ABL1-5036 8-10   84
Composer: David McHugh.

MOSES THE LAWGIVER

Soundtrack (1976) • RCA Victor (S) TBL1-1106 15-20   76
Composer: Ennio Morricone. **Conductor:** Bruno Nicolai. **Cast:** Gianna Spagnolo.

MOSQUITO COAST

Soundtrack (1986) • Fantasy (S) FSP-21005 8-10   87
Composer: Maurice Jarre. **Conductor:** Maurice Jarre.

MOST HAPPY FELLA

Original Cast (1956) • Columbia (EP) A-5118 10-20   56
Original Cast (1956) • Columbia (M) OL-5118 12-15   56
Original Cast (1956) • Columbia (SE) OS-2330 8-12   63

Both LPs are one disc with show highlights.

Original Cast (1956) • Columbia (M) O3L-240 20-25   56

Boxed, three-disc set with booklet. Entire show, including dialogue.

Original Cast (1956) • Columbia Special Products (M) CO3L-240 10-15   76

Boxed, three-disc set without booklet.
Composer: Frank Loesser. **Conductor:** Herbert Greene. **Cast:** Robert Weede, Jo Sullivan, Art Lund, Susan Johnson, Lee Cass, Shorty Long, Mona Paulee, John Henson, Alan Gilbert, Roy Lazarus, Arthur Rubin, Keith Kaldenberg, Rico Froehlich. (With dialogue.)

Original London Cast (1960) • RCA (M) CLP-1365 30-35   60
Original London Cast (1960) • RCA (S) CSD-1365 45-65   60

UK release.

Original London Cast (1960) • Angel (M) 35887 20-25   60
Original London Cast (1960) • Angel (S) S-35887 35-40   60

Composer: Frank Loesser. **Conductor:** Kenneth Alwyn. **Cast:** Helena Scott, Art Lund, Inia Wiata, Libi Staiger, Jack DeLon, John Clifford, Ralph Farnsworth, William Dickie.

London Studio Cast • World (M) LMP-17 20-25
UK release.
  Composer: Frank Loesser. Conductor: Jan Cervenka. Cast: Edwin Steffe, Stella Moray, Peter Hudson.
Studio Cast • Camden (EP) CAE-375 5-15
  Cast: Jack Say and His Orchestra.
Studio Cast • Camden (M) CAL 319 8-12
  Full title: *12 Instrumental Hits from The Most Happy Fella, My Fair Lady and Pipe Dream.*
  Cast: Domenico Savino and His Orchestra, Jack Say and His Orchestra, Guy Lupar and His Orchestra.
Studio Cast • Columbia (M) 904 10-15
  Cast: Les Elgart and His Orchestra.
Studio Cast • Columbia (M) 905 10-15
  Cast: Percy Faith and His Orchestra.
Studio Cast • Golden Music (S) LPG 3004 8-12
  Conductor: Maury Laws. Cast: Broadway Stars and the G.M.S. Orchestra.

MOTHER EARTH
Original Cast (1972) • Environmental (S) SP-1001 50-75   72
From a pre-Broadway show.
  Composer: Toni Shearer, Ron Thronson. Conductor: Bill Hollman. Cast: Patti Austin, Dee Ervin, Carol Christy, Bill Hathaway, Indira Danks, Hap Palmer.

MOTHER, JUGS AND SPEED
Soundtrack (1976) • A&M (S) SP-4590 8-12   76
  Cast: Paul Jabara, Steve Marriott, Peter Frampton, Billy Preston, Michelle Phillips, Brothers Johnson, Pete Jolly, Crusaders.

MOTHER OF ALL OF US
Original Revival Cast (1976) • New World (S) NW-288/28 12-18   76
Two discs.
  Composer: Virgil Thomson, Gertrude Stein. Conductor: Raymond Leppard. Cast: Mignon Dunn, Philip Booth, James Atherton.

MOTHER WORE TIGHTS: see SHOCKING MISS PILGRIM

MOTION PICTURE MUSIC
Studiotrack (1953) • Mercury (EP) EP-1-3045 12-18   53
  Music from *Wuthering Heights, All About Eve, A Letter to Three Wives* and *The Razor's Edge.*
Studiotrack (1953) • Mercury (M) MG-20037 20-25   53
  10-inch LP. One side has *Wuthering Heights*, other has *An American in Paris.*
  Composer: Alfred Newman. Conductor: Alfred Newman. Cast: Hollywood Symphony.

MOTION PICTURE SOUNDSTAGE
Studiotrack • (1957) Capitol (M) T-875 10-15   57
  Full title: *Motion Picture Soundstage (Great Songs from the Hollywood Screen).*
  Conductor: Van Alexander. Cast: Gordon MacRae.

MOTION PICTURE THEME SUPERPAK
Soundtrack (1972) • United Artists (S) UXS-89 15-18   72
Two discs. Also has studiotrack themes.

MOTION PICTURE THEMES
Studiotrack (1952) • MGM (EP) X-1016 5-8   52
  Conductor: David Rose. Cast: David Rose Orchestra.

MOUNTAIN: see OMAR KHAYYAM

MOUNTBATTEN: THE LAST VICEROY
Soundtrack • Varese Sarabande (S) STV 81273 10-15   85
Soundtrack • That's Entertainment (S) TER-1113 8-10   80s
UK release.
  Composer: John Scott. Conductor: John Scott. Cast: Royal Philharmonic Orchestra.

MOUSE ON THE MAYFLOWER

TV Soundtrack (1968) • No Label Shown (M) GRC-11398................ 75-100   68
Side two has *The Little Drummer Boy*. Promotional issue for an NBC-TV special titled "Presented By Your Gas Company."
Composer: Maury Laws, Jules Bass. **Cast:** Tennessee Ernie Ford (narration and vocals), John Gary, Eddie Albert, Joanie Sommers, Greer Garson (narration), Jose Ferrer, Teddy Eccles, Vienna Boys Choir.

MOVIE AND TV THEMES

Studiotrack (1962) • Ava (M) A-11 10-15   62
Studiotrack (1962) • Ava (S) AS-31..................................... 20-25   62
Studiotrack (1962) • Choreo (M) A-11 10-15   62
Studiotrack (1962) • Choreo (S) AS-11 20-25   62
Music from *Anna Lucasta, Rat Race, Sweet Smell of Success, Sudden Fear, Take Five, Walk on the Wild Side, Man with the Golden Arm, Anna Lucasta* and *Saints and Sinners*.
Composer: Elmer Bernstein. **Conductor:** Elmer Bernstein.

MOVIE HITS BY BRONISLAU KAPER

Studiotrack • MGM (M) E-3511 15-25
Composer: Bronislau Kaper. **Cast:** Richard Ellsasser and Theatre Organ.

MOVIE MOODS

Studiotrack (1957) • Coral (M) 57125.................................. 15-20   57
Cast: George Cates and Orchestra.

MOVIE MOVIE

Studiotrack (1979) • Filmscore Records (S) FS-7914............... 8-10   79
Composer: Ralph Burns, Buster Davis, Larry Gelbart, Sheldon Keller. **Conductor:** Buster Davis. **Cast:** Patricia Marshall, Gene Merlino, Jerry Whitman.

MOVIE PARADE POP, VOL. 1

Soundtrack • MGM (M) E-3220 30-50
Features music from *Blackboard Jungle* along with various studiotrack themes.

MOVIE SONG ALBUM – TONY BENNETT

Studiotrack • Columbia (M) CL-2472................................... 10-15   66
Studiotrack • Columbia (S) CS-9272................................... 10-15   66
Conductor: Johnny Mandel. **Cast:** Tony Bennett.

MOVIE STAR

Studio Cast (1981) • AEI (S) AEI-1142................................. 10-15   81
Composer: Billy Barnes. **Cast:** Billy Barnes.

MOVIE STAR, AMERICAN STYLE

Soundtrack (1966) • Mira (M) 3007.................................... 12-15   66
Soundtrack (1966) • Mira (S) 3007.................................... 15-20   66
Composer: Joseph Greene. **Conductor:** Joseph Greene.

MOVIE THEMES

Studiotrack • Magic Violins (M) 2506.................................. 10-15
Music from *Moulin Rouge, Gigi, True Love* and *If I Loved You*.
Cast: Eric Drucker and His Magic Violins.

Studiotrack • Richmond (M) B 20095 10-15
Music from *The Apartment, The Alamo, Never On Sunday, A Summer Place, Bells Are Ringing, Pepe, The Unforgiven, The Sundowners* and *The Bridge on the River Kwai*.
Cast: Frank Chacksfield and His Orchestra.

MOVIE THEMES FOR LOVERS ONLY

Studiotrack (1963) • Capitol (M) W-1877 10-12   63
Studiotrack (1963) • Capitol (S) SW-1877........................... 10-15   63
Cast: Jackie Gleason Orchestra.

MOVIE THEMES FROM HOLLYWOOD

Studiotrack (1955) • Coral (M) CRL-57006... 20-30   55

Music from *The High and the Mighty, The Champion, A Bullet Is Waiting, Strange Lady in Town, Dial "M" for Murder, Return to Paradise, High Noon, Land of The Pharaohs, Hajji-Baba, Duel in the Sun, I Confess,* and *Lost Horizon.*
Composer: Dimitri Tiomkin. **Conductor:** Dimitri Tiomkin.

MOVIES 'N' ME

Studiotrack (1974) • RCA Victor (M) LPL1-5092 5-10   74

Music *from Modesty Blaise, The Servant, Look Stranger* and others.
Conductor: John Dankworth. **Cast:** John Dankworth and His Orchestra.

MOVIN' ON

TV Soundtrack (1969) • Harold Mayer Prod. (M) HMP 69 10-15   69

Documentary about United Transportation Union, AFL-CIO.
Cast: Arthur Kennedy (narrator), Hank Snow, New Lost City Ramblers, Bonnie Dobson.

MOVIN' WITH NANCY

TV Soundtrack (1967) • Reprise (M) R-6277.. 10-15   67

TV Soundtrack (1967) • Reprise (S) RS-6277...................................... 15-20   67

Pink, gold and green label.

TV Soundtrack (1967) • Reprise (S) RS-6277...................................... 12-15   Re

Brown and gold label.

TV Soundtrack (1967) • Reprise (S) ST-91349 12-15   Re

Capitol Record Club issue.
Conductor: Billy Strange. **Cast:** Nancy Sinatra, Frank Sinatra, Lee Hazelwood, Dean Martin.

MR. BLACKWELL SHOW

Original Show Recording (1967) • Rob Rich (S) 7-11........................... 10-15   67

Composer: Harper MacKay. **Conductor:** Harper MacKay.

MR. BROADWAY

TV Soundtrack (1957) • RCA Victor (M) LPM-1520............................... 25-30   57

Composer: George M. Cohan. **Cast:** Mickey Rooney.

MR. BUDDWING

Soundtrack (1966) • Verve (M) V-8638 10-15   66

Soundtrack (1966) • Verve (S) V6-8638 10-30   66

Composer: Kenyon Hopkins. **Conductor:** Kenyon Hopkins. **Cast:** Kenyon Hopkins.

MR. CINDERS

Original London Cast • That's Entertainment (S) TER-1037 8-10   80s

UK release.
Composer: Vivian Ellis, R. Myers, Clifford Grey, G. Newman, Leo Robin.

London Revival Cast • That's Entertainment (S) TER-1069 8-10   80s

UK release.

MR. ED

TV Soundtrack (1962) • Colpix (M) CP-209...................................... 150-250   62

Dialogue and skits from the television show.
Cast: Alan Young, Connie Hines, Larry Keating, Edna Skinner.

MR. ED – STRAIGHT FROM THE HEART

Soundtrack (1962) • Golden (M) OL 5210... 20-25   62

Cast: Mike Stewart and the Stable Hands.

MR. IMPERIUM

Studiotrack (1951) • RCA Victor (M) LM-61... 65-80   51

10-inch LP. One side has music from *Knickerbocker Holiday, Roberta, One Night of Love* and *Spring Is Here.*
Conductor: Johnny Green. **Cast:** Ezio Pinza, Fran Warren, Guadalajara Trio.

MR. JINKS, PIXIE & DIXIE

TV Soundtrack • Colpix (S) CP 208.................................. 25-30
  Cast: Daws Butler, others.

MR. LUCKY

TV Soundtrack (1959) • RCA Victor (EP) EPA 4363 12-15   60
TV Soundtrack (1959) • RCA Victor (M) LPM-2198.............................. 12-15   60
  Full title: *Music from Mr. Lucky.*
TV Soundtrack (1959) • RCA Victor (S) LSP-2198.............................. 12-18   60
  Black label.
TV Soundtrack (1959) • RCA Victor (S) LSP-2198................................ 8-10   72
  Orange label.
    Composer: Henry Mancini. **Conductor:** Henry Mancini. **Cast:** Henry Mancini and His
    Orchestra.
Studiotrack (1960) • Camden (M) CAL-600... 10-15   60
Studiotrack (1960) • Camden (S) CAS-600... 15-20   60
    Composer: Henry Mancini. **Conductor:** Richard Maltby. **Cast:** Richard Maltby and His
    Orchestra.
Studiotrack • RCA Victor (M) LPM 2360.................................. 10-15
  Full title: *Mr. Lucky Goes Latin.*
    Composer: Henry Mancini, others. **Cast:** Henry Mancini and His Orchestra.

MR. MEAN

Soundtrack • Mercury (S) SRM-3707 8-10

MR. MICAWBER'S DIFFICULTIES: see CHRISTMAS CAROL

MR. MUSIC

Studiotrack (1950) • Decca (M) DL-5284 45-55   50
  10-inch LP.
    Conductor: Victor Young, Vic Schoen, Jay Blackton. **Cast:** Bing Crosby, Dorothy Kirsten,
    Andrews Sisters, Ken Lane Singers.
    Also see BING'S HOLLYWOOD

MR. NOVAK

TV Soundtrack (1963) • MGM (M) E-4222 15-20   63
TV Soundtrack (1963) • MGM (S) SE-4222... 20-25   63
  Both have title track plus nine other high school-related themes.
    Conductor: Lyn Murray.

MR. PICKWICK'S CHRISTMAS: see CHRISTMAS CAROL

MR. PRESIDENT

Original Cast (1962) • Columbia (M) KOL-5870 8-12   62
Original Cast (1962) • Columbia (S) KOS-2270 12-18   62
  Both have glossy, silver gatefold covers.
Original Cast (1962) • Columbia (M) KOL-5870 8-10   63
Original Cast (1962) • Columbia (S) KOS-2270 10-15   63
Original Cast (1962) • Columbia Special Products (S) AKOS-2270........ 5-10   Re
  Above three have white, standard covers.
    Composer: Irving Berlin. **Conductor:** Jay Blackton. **Cast:** Robert Ryan, Nanette Fabray, Anita
    Gillette, Jack Haskell, Jack Washburn, Stanley Grover, Jerry Strickler, Wisa D'Orso.
Studio Cast (1962) • RCA Victor (M) LPM-2630.................................. 10-12   62
Studio Cast (1962) • RCA Victor (S) LSP-2630................................... 12-15   62
    Composer: Irving Berlin. **Conductor:** Mitchell Ayers. **Cast:** Perry Como, Kaye Ballard, Sandy
    Stewart, Ray Charles Singers.
Studio Cast • Diplomat (M) 2287 8-12
Studio Cast • Diplomat (S) DS-2287 8-12
    Cast: Douglas Gamley Orchestra.

MR. ROCK & ROLL (SCENE 2)
Soundtrack • Vik (M) EXA-301 25-30
Composer: Clyde Otis. Cast: Teddy Randazzo, Brook Benton, others.

MR. WONDERFUL
Original Cast (1956) • Decca (M) DL-9032............................ 35-45   56
Composer: Jerry Bock, George Weiss, Larry Holofcener. Conductor: Morton Stevens. Cast: Sammy Davis Jr., Will Mastin Trio, Jack Carter, Chita Rivera, Pat Marshall, Olga James, Hal Loman.

MRS. BROWN, YOU'VE GOT A LOVELY DAUGHTER
Soundtrack (1968) • MGM (S) SE-4548 15-18   68
Composer: Graham Gouldman, G. Stephens, K. Young, others. Cast: Herman's Hermits.

MRS. PATTERSON
Original Cast (1954) • RCA Victor (EP) EOC-1017 30-50   54
Original Cast (1954) • RCA Victor (M) LOC-1017 130-150   54
Composer: Charles Sebree, Greer Johnson, James Shelton. Conductor: Abba Bogin. Cast: Eartha Kitt, Enid Markey, Ruth Attaway, Terry Carter, Alonzo Basan, Helen Dowdy, Jay Riley, Mary Harmon, Mary Ann Hoxworth, Joan Morgan.

MRS. SOFFEL
Soundtrack (1984) • Windham Hill Records (S) WH-91041 10-15   85
Actual title: *Film Music*. Also has music from *The Times of Harvey Milk* and *Never Cry Wolf*.
Composer: Mark Isham.

MUCH ADO ABOUT NOTHING
Original London Cast (1965) • RCA Victor (M) VDM-104 30-40   65
Original London Cast (1965) • RCA Victor (S) VDS-104 45-55   65
Two discs. Franco Zeffirelli's production of William Shakespeare's play.
Composer: Nino Rota. Cast: Maggie Smith, Robert Stephens, Albert Finney, Frank Finlay, Lynn Redgrave, Michael York, Derek Jacobi, Gerald James. (With dialogue.)

MUNSTERS
TV Soundtrack (1964) • Decca (M) DL-4588....................................... 30-60   64
TV Soundtrack (1964) • Decca (S) DL-74588 50-100   64
Composer: J. Marshall.
Also see AT HOME WITH THE MUNSTERS

MUPPET MOVIE
Soundtrack (1979) • Atlantic (S) SD-16001 8-10   79
Composer: Paul Williams, Kenny Ascher. Conductor: Ian Freebairn-Smith. Cast: Jim Henson, Frank Oz, Jerry Nelson, Richard Hunt, Dave Goelz.

MUPPET SHOW
TV Soundtrack (1977) • Arista (S) AB-41952 8-12   77
Cast: Jim Henson, Muppets.

MUPPETS TAKE MANHATTAN
Soundtrack (1984) • Warner Bros. (S) 1-25114 8-10   84
Cast: Muppets.

MURDER INC.
Soundtrack (1960) • Canadian-American (M) CALP-1003 75-80   60
Composer: Frank DeVol, George Weiss. Conductor: Jeff Alexander. Cast: Sarah Vaughan.

MURDER ON THE ORIENT EXPRESS

Soundtrack (1974) • Capitol (S) ST-11361 12-15   74
Soundtrack (1974) • EMI (S) EMC-3054 20-25   74
    UK release. Has British artwork on textured cover. Later reissued in abridged form, backed
    with *Lady Caroline Lamb*. Covers are similar, but this the more valuable edition.
    Composer: Richard Rodney Bennett. **Conductor:** Marcus Dods. **Cast:** Royal Opera House
    Orchestra.
Studiotrack (1975) • Columbia (S) PC 33437 5-10   75
    Conductor: Andre Kostelanetz.

MURDER WAS THE CASE

Soundtrack • Warner Bros. (S) 92484 10-15   90s
    Two discs.

MURDERER'S ROW

Soundtrack (1966) • Colgems (M) COMO-5003 45-50   67
Soundtrack (1966) • Colgems (S) COSO-5003 75-100   67
    Composer: Lalo Schifrin. **Conductor:** Lalo Schifrin.

MURMUR OF THE HEART

Soundtrack (1972) • Roulette (S) SR-3006 15-20   72
    Composer: Sidney Bechet, Dizzy Gillespie, Henri Renaud, Charlie Parker.

MURPH THE SURF

Soundtrack (1975) • Motown (S) M6-839-S1 12-18   75
    Film later titled *Live a Little, Steal a Lot*, then retitled *You Can't Steal Love*.
    Composer: Philip Lambro. **Conductor:** Philip Lambro.

MUSCLE BEACH PARTY

Soundtrack (1964) • Buena Vista (M) BV-3314 20-50   64
Soundtrack (1964) • Buena Vista (S) STER-3314 50-110   64
Soundtrack (1964) • Rhino (S) RNDF 205 15-20   86
    Cast: Frankie Avalon, Annette Funicello.
Studiotrack (1964) • United Artists (M) UAL-3371 15-20   64
Studiotrack (1964) • United Artists (S) UAS-6371 20-25   64
    Full title: *Frankie Avalon Sings Songs from Muscle Beach Party*.
    Cast: Frankie Avalon.

MUSIC AND LYRICS BY COLE PORTER

Original Cast • JJA (M) 19745 15-20   74
    Music from *Mexican Hayride, Panama Hattie, The Seven Lively Arts, Du Barry Was A Lady*
    and *Around the World in 80 Days* (1946). Live recordings.
    Composer: Cole Porter. **Cast:** Ethel Merman, Enzo Stuarti, Bert Lahr.

MUSIC AND SONGS FROM ITALIAN FILMS

Soundtrack (1962) • RCA Victor (M) FOC-4 15-20   62
Soundtrack • RCA Victor (S) FSO-4 25-30   62
    12 Italian film tracks by various artists, including *La Dolce Vita, Rocco and His Brothers,*
    Che Gioia Vivere, La Grande Olimpiade and others.

MUSIC BY MAX STEINER

Studiotrack • Capitol (M) L-250 45-55
    10-inch LP. Music from *The Informer, Now Voyager* and *Since You Went Away*.
Studiotrack • Capitol (M) T-387 60-65   53
    Music from *The Informer, Now Voyager* and *Since You Went Away*, plus Alex North's
    music from *A Streetcar Named Desire*.
Studiotrack • Angel (M) S-36068 10-12   73
    Reissue of Capitol T-387, but with booklet and extra tracks by Steiner.
    Composer: Alex North, Max Steiner. **Conductor:** Ray Heindorf, Max Steiner.

Studiotrack • Citadel (M) CT-MS-5 30-40
  Music from *The Searchers* and *Pursued*.
  Composer: Max Steiner. **Conductor:** Max Steiner.

MUSIC FOR A DARKENED THEATRE: see DANNY ELFMAN: MUSIC FOR A DARKENED THEATRE

MUSIC FOR A PRIVATE EYE
Studiotrack • Mercury (S) SR 60109 15-30
  Full title: *Music for a Private Eye (Swinging Themes of Famous TV Whodunits.)* Music from *Richard Diamond, Thin Man, Perry Mason, Alfred Hitchcock Presents* and others.
  Conductor: Pete Rugolo, Skippy Martin, Ralph Marterie. **Cast:** Ralph Marterie and His Marlboro Men.

MUSIC FOR EPIC MOTION PICTURES
Studiotrack (1984) • AEI (S) AEI-3114 10-12   84
  Suites from *Cimarron, King of Kings, El Cid, Cleopatra* and *War and Peace*.
  Conductor: Vladimir Shustakewicz.

MUSIC FOR FILMS
Studiotrack • Columbia (M) RL-3029 50-75
  Music of British films from the 1940s and early '50s.
  Composer: Allan Gray, Miklos Rozsa, Vaughan Williams, Mischa Spoliansky, Lord Berners.
  Conductor: Charles Williams, Sidney Torch, Ernest Irving. **Cast:** Queen's Hall Light Orchestra, Philharmonic Orchestra.

MUSIC FOR JENNIFER
Studiotrack (1953) • Columbia (EP) B-369 15-25   53
  Two discs.
Studiotrack (1953) • Columbia (M) CL-6281 40-50   53
  10-inch LP. Also has music from *Ruby Gentry, Portrait of Jennie, Duel in the Sun, Song of Bernadette, Love Letters, Since You Went Away* and *Indiscretion of an American Wife*.
  Composer: Various. **Conductor:** Paul Weston. **Cast:** Paul Weston and His Orchestra.

MUSIC FOR LORETTA
TV Soundtrack (1960) • Decca (M) DL-4124 15-18   60
TV Soundtrack (1960) • Decca (S) DL-74124 25-30   60
  Black or red label.
TV Soundtrack (1960) • Decca (M) DL-4124 12-15
TV Soundtrack (1960) • Decca (S) DL-74124 15-20
  Rainbow label. Also known as *Music from The Loretta Young Show*.
  Composer: Harry Lubin. **Conductor:** Harry Lubin.

MUSIC FOR RADIO AND TELEVISION
Soundtrack • Cerberus (S) CST- 0210 8-10   85
  Music from *The Walt Whitman Suite, Brave New World, Collector's Item* and *Landmark*.
  Composer: Bernard Herrmann. **Conductor:** Bernard Herrmann.

MUSIC FROM A FISTFUL OF DOLLARS, FOR A FEW DOLLARS MORE, AND THE GOOD, THE BAD AND THE UGLY
Soundtrack (1968) • RCA Victor (M) LPM-3927 10-15   68
Soundtrack (1968) • RCA Victor (S) LSP-3927 15-20   68
Soundtrack (1968) • RCA Victor (S) ANL1-1094 8-10   Re
  Composer: Ennio Morricone. **Conductor:** Hugo Montenegro. **Cast:** Hugo Montenegro and His Orchestra and Chorus.
Studiotrack (1968) • Sunset (S) SUS-5286 8-12   68
Studiotrack (1968) • United Artists (S) S-21032 10-15   68
  Full title: *Great Music from A Fistful of Dollars, For a Few Dollars More* and *The Good, the Bad And the Ugly*
  Composer: Ennio Morricone. **Conductor:** Ennio Morricone. **Cast:** Hollywood Soundmakers.

MUSIC FROM DISNEY MOTION PICTURES
Soundtrack • Disneyland (S) DQ-1318.. 20-25   68
Cast: Hayley Mills, Burl Ives, Annette Funicello, Maurice Chevalier, others.

MUSIC FROM GREAT AUSTRALIAN FILMS
Soundtrack • DRG (S) SBL 12582 10-15   83
Music from *Picnic at Hanging Rock, Gallipoli, My Brilliant Career, The Chant of Jimmy Blacksmith, The Mango Tree* and eight other films.

MUSIC FROM GREAT FILMS
Studiotrack (1957) • Design (M) DLP 90 8-12   57
Music from *Around the World in 80 Days, Spellbound, Slaughter on Tenth Avenue, Moulin Rouge, The Way You Look Tonight, Gigi, From Here to Eternity, I've Got You Under My Skin* and *Warsaw Concerto.*
Cast: Dean Franconi and Soundstage Orchestra.

MUSIC FROM GREAT FRENCH MOTION PICTURES
Studiotrack • Capitol (S) SP 8603 10-15
Conductor: Franck Pourcel. Cast: Franck Pourcel and His Orchestra.

MUSIC FROM GREAT ITALIAN MOTION PICTURES
Studiotrack • Capitol (S) SP 8608 20-25
Music from *Four Days of Naples, La Strada, Il Gattopardo (The Leopard), Mondo Cane, I Basilischi (The Basilisks), Il Camino Della Speranza (The Street of Dreams), Divorzio All'Italiana (Divorce - Italian Style), Anna, 8 1/2* and *Crimen.*
Conductor: Pino Calvi and His Orchestra.

MUSIC FROM GREAT MOTION PICTURES
Studiotrack • Time (S) S/2187.. 10-15
Music from *Never on Sunday, Three Coins in the Fountain, Third Man, Limelight, Picnic, Anna, Spellbound, A Summer Place, Gone with the Wind* and *Hi-Lili Hi-Lo.*
Conductor: Richard Hayman. Cast: Manhattan Pops Orchestra.

MUSIC FROM GREAT SHAKESPEAREAN FILMS
Studiotrack • London (S) SPC-21132.................................... 20-25   76
Has music from Hamlet, Richard III and Julius Caesar.
Composer: Dimitri Shostakovich, Sir William Walton, Miklos Rozsa. Conductor: Bernard Herrmann. Cast: National Philharmonic Orchestra.

MUSIC FROM HITCHCOCK FILMS
Studiotrack • Varese Sarabande (S) 704 250...................................... 15-20   85
Music from *Family Plot, Strangers on a Train, Suspicion* and *Notorious.*
Studiotrack • That's Entertainment (S) TER-1109 8-10   80s
Actual title: *Four Alfred Hitchcock Films.*
Composer: John Williams, Dimitri Tiomkin, Franz Waxman, Roy Webb. Conductor: Charles Ketcham. Cast: Utah Symphony Orchestra.

MUSIC FROM HOLLYWOOD
Studiotrack (1953) • RCA Victor (M) LPM-1007 15-20   53
Music from *The Snows of Kilimanjaro, High Noon, Ivanhoe, David and Bathsheba, The Fourposter, Moulin Rouge, The Happy Time, A Place in the Sun, Shane* and *Quo Vadis.*
Composer: Various. Conductor: Al Goodman. Cast: Al Goodman and His Orchestra.
Studiotrack (1953) • Columbia (M) CL-6255.. 15-20   53
10-inch LP.
Studiotrack (1955) • Columbia (EP) B-1692... 8-12   55
Studiotrack (1955) • Columbia (EP) B-1693... 8-12   55
Studiotrack (1955) • Columbia (EP) B-376... 10-20   55
Two discs. Combines B-1692 and B-1693.
Studiotrack (1955) • Columbia (M) CL-577... 15-18   55
Composer: Various. Conductor: Percy Faith. Cast: Percy Faith and His Orchestra.

Studiotrack (1963) • Columbia (M) CL-2113... 30-40　　63
Studiotrack (1963) • Columbia (S) CS-8913... 50-60　　63
　　Composer: Lionel Newman, Alex North, Miklos Rozsa, Max Steiner, Dimitri Tiomkin, Franz
　　Waxman, Bernard Herrmann, others. **Conductor:** Lionel Newman, Alex North, Miklos Rosza,
　　Max Steiner, Dimitri Tiomkin, Franz Waxman, Bernard Herrmann, others.

MUSIC FROM L.A. LAW (AND OTHERWISE)
Soundtrack • Polydor (S) 833985-1... 8-10　　80s
　　Composer: Mike Post, others. **Conductor:** Mike Post. **Cast:** Mike Post.
　　Also see MIKE POST

MUSIC FROM MARLBORO COUNTRY
TV Soundtrack (1967) • United Artists (S) SP-107 .... 30-40　　67
　　Music from Marlboro commercials. Special Products issue.
　　Composer: Elmer Bernstein. **Conductor:** Elmer Bernstein.

MUSIC FROM MILLION DOLLAR MOVIES: see MILLION DOLLAR MOVIES

MUSIC FROM MOTION PICTURES
Studiotrack (1964) • Capitol (S) SP-8598.. 20-25　　64
　　Music from *David and Bathsheba, The Robe, Captain from Castile, Dangerous Moonlight*
　　and others.
　　Composer: Alfred Newman, Richard Addinsell, others. **Cast:** Hollywood Bowl Symphony
　　Orchestra.
Studiotrack (1956) • MGM (M) E-3397 .... 40-50　　56
　　Music from *Love is a Many Splendored Thing, Giant, Summertime, Julie, Catered Affair, La
　　Strada, The Glass Slipper, Friendly Persuasion, The Swan, Public Pigeon No. 1, Serenade*
　　and *Forbidden Planet.*
　　Conductor: David Rose. **Cast:** David Rose and His Orchestra.

MUSIC FROM MOVIELAND
Soundtrack • Mercury (M) MG25203.. 60-65　　54
　　10-inch LP.
　　Composer: Various. **Conductor:** Morris Stoloff. **Cast:** Columbia Pictures Studio Orchestra.

MUSIC FROM NATIONAL FOOTBALL LEAGUE FILMS
TV Soundtrack (1972) NFL .... 15-20　　72
　　Composer: Sam Spence.

MUSIC FROM PETER GUNN: see PETER GUNN

MUSIC FROM SHAKESPEAREAN FILMS
Soundtrack • Angel (M) 36198 .... 12-18　　64
Soundtrack • Angel (S) S-36198 .... 15-20　　64
　　Music from *Hamlet, Henry V* and *Richard III.*
　　Composer: Sir William Walton. **Conductor:** Sir William Walton.
　　Also see WALTON CONDUCTS HIS GREAT FILM MUSIC

MUSIC FROM SHUBERT ALLEY
TV Soundtrack (1959) • Sinclair (S) OSS-2250.................................... 25-35　　59
　　White label. From a November 13, 1959, NBC TV show hosted by Andy Williams.
　　Promotional issue only.
　　Composer: Various. **Conductor:** Vic Shoen. **Cast:** Andy Williams, Alfred Drake, Lisa Kirk, Ray
　　Walston, Doretta Morrow, Betty Comden, Adolph Green.

MUSIC FROM SIESTA
Soundtrack (1987) • Warner Bros. (S) 1-25655 .... 8-10　　87
　　Composer: Miles Davis, Marcus Miller.

MUSIC FROM SPLASH, BEASTMASTER, ETC.: see SPLASH

MUSIC FROM THE BODY: see BODY

MUSIC FROM THE FILM THE ALAMO: see ALAMO

MUSIC FROM THE FILMS

Studiotrack • Epic (S) BC 1147 10-15
Music from *Louisiana Story, Henry V* and others.
Composer: Virgil Thomson, Sir William Walton. **Conductor:** Louis Lane. **Cast:** Cleveland Pops.

Studiotrack • London (S) PS-112 10-15
Cast: Mantovani and Orchestra.

Studiotrack • Spin-O-Rama (M) S-43 8-12
Music from *Story of Three Lives, Moulin Rouge, Love Story, Gigi, The Third Man,
Spellbound, High Society, Undercurrent, Show Boat* and *Carousel.*
Conductor: Eddie Maynard. **Cast:** Stradivari Strings, Eddie Maynard.

MUSIC FROM THE FILMS OF CHARLIE CHAPLIN

Studiotrack (1972) • GNP Crescendo (S) GNPS 2064 15-25   72
Studiotrack (1972) • GNP Crescendo (S) GNPS 2064 8-10   90s
Conductor: Michel Villard. **Cast:** Michel Villard and His Orchestra.

MUSIC FROM THE FILMS OF FEDERICO FELLINI

Studiotrack • Silver Screen (S) FILM 004 10-15   87
Cast: Nino Rota, Carlo Savina.

MUSIC FROM THE FILMS OF RAINER WERNER FASSBINDER

Studiotrack • That's Entertainment (S) TER-1085 8-10   80s
UK release.
Composer: Peer Raben.

MUSIC FROM THE GALAXIES

Studiotrack (1980) • CBS (S) DAL-5876 12-20   80
Music from *Superman, Star Wars, Star Trek, Moonraker, Battlestar Galactica* and *Meteor.*
Composer: John Williams, Jerry Goldsmith, Andrew Courage, John Barry, G. Larson, Laurence
Rosenthal. **Cast:** Ettore Stratta and London Symphony Orchestra.

MUSIC FROM THE GREAT MOVIE THRILLERS

Studiotrack • London (S) SP-44126 20-25
Composer: Bernard Herrmann. **Conductor:** Bernard Herrmann. **Cast:** London Philharmonic
Orchestra.

MUSIC FROM THE MODERN SCREEN

Studiotrack (1959) • MGM (M) E-3753 12-18   59
Studiotrack (1959) • MGM (S) SE-3753 20-30   59
Composer: Various. **Cast:** Leroy Holmes and Orchestra.

MUSIC FROM THE MOVIES

Studiotrack (1957) • Goldentone (M) C-4002 10-15   57
Music from *Around the World in 80 Days, Long Ago and Far Away, Manhattan* and
Anniversary Waltz.
Cast: Mayfair All-Star Orchestra.

Studiotrack (1982) • Seagull (S) LG-8207 10-15   82
Cast: Enoch Light and the Light Brigade.

MUSIC IN THE AIR

Original Cast (1951) • RCA Victor (M) LK-1025 125-150   51
Scheduled as an original cast recording of the 1951 revival; however, due to the show's
unsuccessful run, the only cast member whose songs appear on the LP is Jane Pickens.
Composer: Jerome Kern, Oscar Hammerstein II. **Conductor:** Al Goodman. **Cast:** Jane Pickens
(with chorus).

Studio Cast (1932) • RCA Victor (M) 39001 300-400   32
12-inch, full-color 33 rpm picture disc. One side has a caricature of Paul Whiteman, the
other a scene from the stage production with studio cast and song listings. Issued in a plain
white sleeve.
Composer: Jerome Kern, Oscar Hammerstein II. **Conductor:** Nathaniel Shilkret. **Cast:** Marjorie
Horton, Robert Simmons, Jack Parker, Conrad Thibault.

London Studio Cast (1932) • World (M) T-121 20-25
UK release.
Cast: Marion Grimaldi, Andy Cole, Maggie Fitzgibbon.

MUSIC LOVERS
Soundtrack (1971) • United Artists (S) UAS-5217 12-15   71
Soundtrack (1971) • Sunset (S) SLS 50410 8-10   Re
Includes music of Tchaikovsky.
Conductor: Andre Previn. **Cast:** Andre Previn, London Symphony Orchestra.

MUSIC MAN
Original Cast (1957) • Capitol (EP) EDM-990 15-20   57
Boxed, four-disc set.
Original Cast (1957) • Capitol (M) WAO-990 8-10   57
Original Cast (1957) • Capitol (S) SWAO-990 10-12   57
Gatefold covers with drawings and credits on front.
Original Cast (1957) • Capitol (M) W-990 8-10   Re
Original Cast (1957) • Capitol (S) SW-990 8-10   Re
Standard covers with photo of Robert Preston.
Composer: Meredith Willson. **Conductor:** Herbert Greene. **Cast:** Robert Preston, Barbara Cook, David Burns, Buffalo Bills, Eddie Hodges, Pert Kelton, Paul Reed, Helen Raymond, Iggie Wolfington.
Original London Cast (1961) • RCA Victor (M) CLP-1444 30-35   61
Original London Cast (1961) • RCA Victor (S) CSD-1444 35-45   61
Original London Cast (1961) • Odeon (S) PCSD-1361 20-25
UK releases.
Original London Cast (1961) • Stanyan (S) SR-10039 10-15   72
Composer: Meredith Willson. **Conductor:** Gareth Davies. **Cast:** Van Johnson, Patricia Lambert, Bernard Spear, Iowa Four, Michael Malnick, Denis Waterman, Ruth Kettlewell.
Studio Cast (1957) • Capitol (EP) 1-991/4-991 10-15   57
Boxed, four-disc set. Full title: *The Music From Meredith Willson's The Music Man.*
Conductor: Sidney Fine, Larry Rosenthal.
Studio Cast (1957) • Capitol (M) T-966 10-15   57
Full title: *Dance to the Music Man.*
Cast: Glen Gray and the Casa Loma Orchestra, Pee Wee Hunt and His Orchestra, Guy Lombardo and His Royal Canadians, Don Radney, Kenny Gardner, Freddy Martin and His Orchestra.
Studio Cast (1957) • Capitol (M) T-989 10-15   57
Cast: Fred Waring and the Pennsylvanians.
Studio Cast (1957) • Capitol (M) T-991 10-20   57
Made by Capitol Custom Services Dept. as a "Music Man Contest Prize."
Conductor: Meredith Willson.
Studio Cast (1958) • Atlantic (M) 1276 20-30   58
Studio Cast (1958) • Atlantic (S) SD-1276 30-40   58
Cast: Jimmy Giuffre.
Studio Cast (1958) • Columbia/Epic (M) LN-3463 20-25   58
Cast: Jimmy McPartland's All-Stars.
Studio Cast (1958) • Crown (M) 5062 10-20   58
Conductor: Thomas M. Davis, Hans Hagan. **Cast:** Ken Harp, Donna Cook, Connie Conway, Don Garley, Patti Steele, Jackie Allen, others.
Studio Cast (1958) • Camden (M) CAL 428 8-15   58
Studio Cast (1958) • Camden (S) CAS 428 8-15   58
Full title: *Instrumental Hits from The Music Man.*
Cast: Hill Bowen and His Orchestra.
Studio Cast (1958) • Rondo-lette (M) A27 8-15   58
Also has music from *South Pacific.*
Studio Cast (1959) • Lion (M) L-70091 8-15   59

Studio Cast (1960) • Capitol (M) T-1320 25-30   60
Actual title: *...And Then I Wrote The Music Man*. By Mr. and Mrs. Meredith Willson.
Cast: Rini Willson, Meredith Willson.

Studio Cast • Crown (M) 5062.. 8-15
Conductor: Thomas M. Davis, Hans Hagen. **Cast:** Ken Harp, Donna Cook, Connie Conway,
Don Grilley, Cornhuskers, Patti Steele, Jackie Allen, Barbara Ford, Lucille Smith, Ken Remo,
Ray Vasquez, Paul Ely.

Studio Cast • Promenade (M) 2097.. 8-15
Conductor: Frank Meyers. **Cast:** Geri Gray, Marty Kaye, Bobby Thompson, others.

Studio Cast • Waldorf (M) 33-1248 8-15
Cast: Enoch Light Orchestra and Chorus, Lois Winter, Artie Malvin, Buckin' Broncos, Jerry
Duane, Willie Winkle.

Soundtrack (1962) • Warner Bros. (EP) S-1459................................. 10-15   62
Stereo 33 rpm. Promotional issue only.

Soundtrack (1962) • Warner Bros. (M) B-1459 10-15   62
Gray label.

Soundtrack (1962) • Warner Bros. (S) BS-1459................................. 12-18   62
Gold label.

Soundtrack (1962) • Warner Bros. (S) BS-1459................................. 5-10   66
Composer: Meredith Willson. **Conductor:** Ray Heindorf. **Cast:** Robert Preston, Shirley Jones,
Buddy Hackett, Hermione Gingold, Pert Kelton, Ronnie Howard, Buffalo Bills.

Studiotrack (1962) • MGM (M) E-4065 8-10   62
Studiotrack (1962) • MGM (S) SE-4065 8-10   62
Full title: *Paul Smith Quartet Plays The Music Man & Other Motion Picture Favorites*. One
side has themes from *Breakfast at Tiffany's, Walk on the Wild Side, West Side Story, Lolita*
and *Lisa*.
Cast: Paul Smith Quartet.

Studiotrack (1962) • United Artists (M) UAL-3235 8-10   62
Studiotrack (1962) • United Artists (S) UAS-6235 8-10   62
Full title: *Dance to the Music Man*.
Conductor: Ralph Marterie. **Cast:** Ralph Marterie and His Marlboro Orchestra.

Studiotrack • Masterseal (M) 70 8-12
Conductor: Fontana. **Cast:** Fontana and His Orchestra and Chorus.
Also see GIGI
Also see GYPSY
Also see SOUTH PACIFIC

MUSIC OF ERICH WOLFGANG KORNGOLD
Studiotrack (1962) • Warner Bros. (M) W-1438 20-45   62
Studiotrack (1962) • Warner Bros. (S) WS-1438................................ 30-75   62
Full title is *Anthony Adverse – Music of Erich Wolfgang Korngold*. Also has music from
*King's Row, Elizabeth and Essex, The Sea Hawk, The Prince and the Pauper, The
Constant Nymph* and *Robin Hood*.
Composer: Erich Wolfgang Korngold. **Conductor:** Lionel Newman.

MUSIC OF GEORGE GERSHWIN
Studiotrack • Columbia (M) ML-2026 10-20   50s
10-inch LP. Music from *Girl Crazy, Lady Be Good, Funny Face, Oh Kay* and *Strike Up the
Band*.
Cast: Andre Kostelanetz and His Orchestra.

MUSIC OF JEROME KERN
Studiotrack (1955) • Columbia (EP) A-1531 5-10   55
Studiotrack (1955) • Columbia (M) CL-776... 10-20   55
Composer: Jerome Kern. **Conductor:** Andre Kostelanetz. **Cast:** Andre Kostelanetz and His
Orchestra.

MUSIC OF REPUBLIC
Studiotrack • Cinema Sound (S) 1001... 20-25   85
Numbered edition of 1,000 made. Full title: *The Music of Republic (1937-1941)*.
Studiotrack • Varese Sarabande (S) VS 81250.................................... 15-20   85
Music from Republic Pictures western films and serials.
   Composer: Cy Feuer, William Lava, Mort Glickman, Alberto Colombo, Paul Sawtell.
   Conductor: James King.

MUSIC OF RICHARD RODGERS: see RICHARD RODGERS

MUSIC Of RODGERS AND HAMMERSTEIN
Studiotrack • RCA Victor (M) LPM 2513... 8-12
Studiotrack • RCA Victor (S) LSP 2513.. 8-12
Music from *Me and Juliet, South Pacific, The King and I, State Fair, Sound of Music, Carousel, Flower Drum Song, South Pacific* and *Oklahoma!*
   Cast: Melachrino Strings and Orchestra.

MUSIC OF RODGERS AND HART
Studiotrack (1962) • RCA Victor (M) LPM-2535 10-15   62
Studiotrack (1962) • RCA Victor (S) LSP-2535 10-20   62
   Cast: Marty Gould and His Orchestra.

MUSIC OF THE MOVIES
Studiotrack (1977) • Time-Life (S) STLF-0007 25-30   77
Boxed, three-disc set.
   Conductor: Arthur Fiedler. **Cast:** Boston Pops.

MUSIC OF THE YOUNG HOLLYWOOD COMPOSERS (ANDRE PREVIN PLAYS)
Studiotrack • RCA Victor (M) LPM-3491... 10-12   63
Studiotrack • RCA Victor (S) LSP-3491.. 12-15   63
   Composer: Various. **Cast:** Andre Previn.

MUSIC OF VICTOR HERBERT
Studiotrack (1975) • Angel (S) SFO-37160 8-12   75
Studiotrack (1975) • Angel (Q) SFO-37160... 10-15   75
Gatefold cover. Includes lyrics sheet.
   Conductor: Andre Kostelanetz. **Cast:** Andre Kostelanetz and the London Symphony Orchestra, Beverly Sills.

MUSIC OF VICTOR YOUNG
Studiotrack (1957) • International (M) LP-5051 15-25   57
   Composer: Victor Young. **Cast:** Bud Herrmann (piano).

MUSIC OF WALT DISNEY
Soundtrack • Buena Vista (M) BV-2000 25-30   67

MUSIC TO BE MURDERED BY
Studiotrack (1959) • Imperial (M) LP-9052 30-60   59
Studiotrack (1959) • Imperial (S) LP-12005.. 40-80   59
Studiotrack (1959) • DRG (S) SL-5183 10-15   80
Instrumental versions of pop standards. Narrated by Alfred Hitchcock.
   Conductor: Jeff Alexander. **Cast:** Jeff Alexander Orchestra, Alfred Hitchcock (narration).

MUSIC TO READ LIFE'S YEAR END ISSUE BY
Studiotrack (1963) • Decca (M) DL-34155 15-20   63
Companion LP for a *Life Magazine* year-end issue on "The Movies."

MUSIC TO READ "THE PRETENDERS" BY: see PRETENDERS

MUSIC TO REMEMBER
Studiotrack • Mercury (EP) EP-1-3030.. 15-20

Music from *Intermezzo, How Green Was My Valley, None But the Lonely Heart* and *Drink to Me Only with Thine Eyes.*

Composer: Alfred Newman, others. **Conductor:** Alfred Newman.

MUSICAL CHAIRS
Original Cast (1980) • Original Cast (S) OC-8024 8-12   80

Composer: Tom Savage. **Conductor:** Barry Gordon. **Cast:** Brandon Maggart, Lee Meredith, Tom Urich, Patti Karr, Jess Richards, Joy Franz, Helen Blount, Leslie-Anne Wolfe, Rick Emery, Scott Ellis.

MUSICAL COMEDY AND OPERETTA FAVORITES, VOL. 2
Studio Cast • Hollywood (M) LPH-115... 8-10

Conductor: Sylvan Levin. **Cast:** Felix Knight, Mac Morgan, Vivian della Chiesa, Virginia Haskens, Martha Wright.

MUSICAL COMEDY FAVORITES
Studiotrack (1955) • Columbia (M) CL-775... 10-15   55

Music from *Jubilee, Roberta, The Boys from Syracuse, No No Nanette, Ziegfeld Follies, Between the Devil, Very Warm for May, Girl Crazy, The Gay Divorcee, Smiles, Scandals, Spring Is Here, As Thousands Cheer, Bitter Sweet* and *The Band Wagon.*

Composer: Cole Porter, Jerome Kern, Richard Rodgers, Vincent Youmans, Irving Berlin, Arthur Schwartz, George Gershwin, Noel Coward. **Cast:** Andre Kostelanetz and His Orchestra.

MUSICAL TOUCH OF FAR AWAY PLACES
Studiotrack (1959) • Warner Bros. (M) B 1308.................................... 10-20   59

Full title: *William Holden Presents a Musical Touch of Far Away Places.*

Conductor: Warren Barker. **Cast:** Warren Barker & Orchestra.

MUSICAL WORLD Of LERNER AND LOEWE
Studiotrack • MGM (M) E 3781 12-18

Music from *My Fair Lady, Paint Your Wagon, Gigi* and *Brigadoon.*

Conductor: Cyril Ornadel. **Cast:** Starlight Symphony Orchestra.

MUTANT
Soundtrack (1982) • Varese Sarabande (S) STV-81209 10-15   82

Film is also known as *Forbidden World.*

Conductor: Richard Band. **Cast:** National Philharmonic Orchestra.

MUTINY ON THE BOUNTY
Soundtrack (1962) • MGM (M) 1E4 10-15   62

Soundtrack (1962) • MGM (S) S1E4 10-15   62

Boxed sets. Both include a book and painting. Includes *The Bounty Theme.*

Soundtrack (1962) • MGM (M) 1E4 10-15   62

Soundtrack (1962) • MGM (S) S1E4 10-15   62

Boxed sets. Both include a book and painting. Includes *The Bounty Love Theme Tahitian Chant.*

Soundtrack (1962) • MGM (M) 1E4-ST 8-10   62

Soundtrack (1962) • MGM (S) S1E4-ST 10-12   62

Soundtrack (1962) • MCA (S) 25007 8-10   86

Standard covers.

Composer: Bronislau Kaper. **Conductor:** Robert Armbruster.

Studiotrack (1962) • Golden (S) 289 8-10   73

Cast: Nordhoff and Hall.

Studiotrack • Diplomat (M) D-2276.. 8-12

Studiotrack • Diplomat (S) DS-2276.. 8-12

Also has themes from *El Cid, Cimarron, King of Kings* and *Four Horsemen of the Apocalypse.*

Conductor: Nicholas Andriano. **Cast:** Film Spectacular Sound Track Orchestra.

Studiotrack • United Artists (M) UAL-3249 8-10

Studiotrack • United Artists (S) UAS-6249 10-12

Full title: *Music to Remember from Mutiny on the Bounty and Others.* Also has other film themes.

Conductor: Andre Previn, Ferrante and Teicher, Franz Waxman. Cast: Andre Previn, Ferrante & Teicher, others.

MY COUSIN JOSEFA

Original Cast (1969) • Harlequin (S) H-3270 30-35   69

Original Cast (1969) • AEI (S) AEI-1139 8-12   80s

Composer: Robert Austin. Conductor: Richard Braun. Cast: Carla Alberghetti, Jack Ritschel, Leslie Cozzens, Michael Hall, Walt Ritter, Graciela Franks, Nola Roeper, Ellard Davis, Asaad Kelada.

MY DEAR ASSASSIN: see BLACK BELLY OF THE TARANTULA

MY DEMON LOVER

Soundtrack (1987) • Varese Sarabande (S) STV-81322 10-15   87

Composer: David Newman, Ed Alton.

MY FAIR LADY

Original Cast (1956) • Columbia (EP) A-5090 10-25   56

Boxed, four-disc set.

Original Cast (1956) • Columbia (M) OL-5090 8-40   56

White label. Promotional issue only.

Original Cast (1956) • Columbia (M) OL-5090 8-10   56

Gray label.

Original Cast (1956) • Columbia Special Products (M) XOL-5090 5-8

Composer: Alan Jay Lerner, Frederick Loewe. Conductor: Franz Allers. Cast: Rex Harrison, Julie Andrews, Stanley Holloway, Robert Coote, Rod McLennan, John Michael King, Gordon Dilworth, Philippa Bevans.

Original London Cast (1959) • Columbia (S) OS-2015 8-12   59

Original London Cast (1959) • Columbia (S) PS-2015 5-8   Re

Gatefold covers.

Original London Cast (1959) • CBS (S) 68001 20-25   59

UK release. Unipak fold-open cover (disc opening faces gutter rather than outer edge).

Composer: Alan Jay Lerner, Frederick Loewe. Conductor: Cyril Ornadel. Cast: Rex Harrison, Julie Andrews, Stanley Holloway, Robert Coote, Leonard Weir, Robert Chisholm, Alan Dudley, Betty Woolfe.

Original Italian Cast (1959) • Columbia (M) OL-8060 8-12

Original Italian Cast (1959) • Columbia (S) OS-2660 12-15

Composer: Alan Jay Lerner, Frederick Loewe. Conductor: Mario Migliardi. Cast: Delia Scala, Gianrico Tedeschi, Mario Carotenuto.

Original Spanish Cast • Columbia (S) OS-2980 12-15

Composer: Alan Jay Lerner, Frederick Loewe. Conductor: Mario Ruiz Armengol. Cast: Manolo Fabregas, Cristina Rojas, Placido Domingo, Mario Alberto Rodriquez, Miguel Suarez, Salvador Quiroz, Natalia Gentil Arcos, Tomas Saro, others.

Original Radio Cast (1959) • Radiola (M) MR-1122 10-15   81

Full title: *My Fair Lady, Guys and Dolls.* Two 15-minute radio shows aired February 1959 for the American Heart Association.

Cast: Rex Harrison, Julie Andrews, Cathleen Nesbitt, Stanley Holloway, Vivian Blaine, Sam Levene, Stubby Kaye, Robert Alda, Isabel Bigley.

London Cast (1959) • Classic Club (M) 505 10-20   59

10-inch LP.

Composer: Alan Jay Lerner, Frederick Loewe. Conductor: John Gregory. Cast: Hubert Gregg, John Slater, John Harvey, others.

London Cast (1959) • Avon (M) 3001 12-15   59

London Cast (1959) • Avon (S) S-3001 12-18   59

London Cast (1959) • Forum Circle (M) FC 9105 5-10

London Cast (1959) • Forum Circle (S) FCS 9105 5-10

Composer: Alan Jay Lerner, Frederick Loewe. Conductor: John Gregory. Cast: Hubert Gregg, Elizabeth Larner, John Slater, John Harvey.

Studio Cast (1957) • Masterseal (M) MSLP-5001................................. 20-30   57
   Composer: Alan Jay Lerner, Frederick Loewe. **Conductor:** Jack Hansen. **Cast:** Lanny Ross, Marcia Neil.

Studio Cast (1957) • Halo (M) 50202 8-15   57

Studio Cast (1957) • Vox (M) VX 25 340.. 8-15   57
   Cast: George Feyer.

Studio Cast (1958) • Rondo-lette (M) A6.. 8-15   58
  Also has music from *Pal Joey*.

Studio Cast (1958) • Ultraphonic (M) 50202.. 8-15   58

Studio Cast (1959) • Lion (M) L-70092.. 8-15   59
   Cast: Ann Maria Pallys, John Rvark.

Studio Cast • Mercury (M) MG-20192 8-15   50s
   Cast: Richard Hayman and His Orchestra.

Studio Cast • Waldorf (M) MHK 33-1205.. 10-15   50s
  Full title: *Songs from My Fair Lady.*
   Cast: Enoch Light Orchestra and Chorus, Bob Eberly, Lois Winter, Artie Malvin, Dottie Evans, Mike Stewart, Loren Becker.

Studio Cast (1959) • Camden (M) CAL-520 15-20   60

Studio Cast (1959) • Camden (S) CAS-520 20-30   60

Studio Cast (1959) • Camden (M) CAL 819 8-10   Re

Studio Cast (1959) • Camden (S) CAS 819... 8-12   Re
  Full title of Camden issues: *Music from My Fair Lady.*
   Composer: Alan Jay Lerner, Frederick Loewe. **Conductor:** Hill Bowen. **Cast:** Hill Bowen and His Orchestra and Chorus, Kathy Lane, Mike Sammes.

Studio Cast (1960) • National Academy Record Club (M) ES-1 10-15   60
  From the *Ed Sullivan Presents Songs and Music of...* series.
   Cast: Ed Sullivan All Star Cast.

Studio Cast (1960) • Craftsmen (M) C-8020 8-12   60

Studio Cast • Waldorf (M) MH 33-156.. 10-20   50s
  10-inch LP.

Studio Cast • Waldorf (M) MHK 33-1227.. 10-20   50s
   Composer: Alan Jay Lerner, Frederick Loewe. **Cast:** Enoch Light Orchestra and Chorus, Bob Eberly, Lois Winter, Artie Malvin, Dottie Evans, Mike Stewart, Loren Becker.

Studio Cast (1964) • Capitol (M) T-2173 12-15   64

Studio Cast (1964) • Capitol (S) ST-2173 15-20   64
   Conductor: John Williams. **Cast:** Shelly Manne and His Men, Jack Sheldon, Irene Kral.

Studio Cast (1964) • Century Custom (M) 18381 10-15   64
  "A Production of Whitehaven High School," Tennessee.
   Conductor: Kenneth Canestrari. **Cast:** Tom McDaniel, Barbara Woods, Jim Pentecost, others.

Studio Cast • Celebrity (S) UTS 104 10-12
   Conductor: Lawrence Nash. **Cast:** Julie Jones, Tex Howard, Margaret Young.

Studio Cast • Coronet (S) CXS-243 10-12
   Cast: Lola Fisher, Richard Torigi, William Reynolds, Edgar Powell, Roxy Theatre Orchestra.

Studio Cast • Coronet (M) CX 28 10-12

Studio Cast • Coronet (S) CXS 28 10-12
   Cast: Coronet Studio Orchestra and Chorus, Margaret Young, Andrew Harris, Conrad Josephs, Sam Whatson.

Studio Cast • Design (M) DLP-212... 10-12

Studio Cast • Design (S) SDLP-212 10-12
   Conductor: Dean Franconi. **Cast:** Lola Fisher, Edgar Powell, William Reynolds, Richard Torigi.

Studio Cast • Diplomat (M) ND-2214.. 10-12

Studio Cast • Diplomat (S) DS-2214 10-12

Studio Cast • Diplomat (S) FM-78 10-12
   Composer: Alan Jay Lerner, Frederick Loewe. **Conductor:** Al Goodman. **Cast:** Lola Fisher, Richard Torigi, Edgar Powell, William Reynolds, Al Goodman and His Orchestra.

Studio Cast • Grand Prix (S) K-409 10-12

Conductor: Dean Franconi. Cast: Lola Fisher, Richard Torigi, Edgar Powell, William Reynolds, Mal Hasset and His Orchestra.

Studio Cast • Hurrah (M) H-1036 10-12

Studio Cast • Hurrah (S) HS-1036 10-12

Conductor: Dean Franconi. Cast: Lola Fisher, Richard Torigi, Edgar Powell, William Reynolds, Dean Franconi and His Orchestra.

Studio Cast • Mayfair (S) 9537-S 10-20

Colored vinyl.

Conductor: Lew Raymond. Cast: Evelyn Sharpe, Charles Peck, Robert Back.

Studio Cast • Parade (M) SP-357... 10-12

Conductor: Al Goodman. Cast: Lola Fisher, Richard Torigi, Edgar Powell, William Reynolds, Al Goodman and His Orchestra ahd Chorus.

Studio Cast • Rondo-lette (S) SA 144 10-12

Conductor: Richard Muller-Lampertz. Cast: Lawrence Chelsi, Alberta Hopkins, Tom O'Leary, Eddie Ruhl.

Studio Cast • Pirouette (S) FM 78 10-12

One side has music from *The King and I.*

Studio Cast • Spin-O-Rama (M) MK-3057... 10-12

Studio Cast • Spin-O-Rama (S) S-82 10-12

Conductor: Al Goodman. Cast: Lola Fisher, Richard Torigi, William Reynolds, Edgar Powell, Al Goodman and His Orchestra.

Studio Cast • Tops (M) L1537 10-12

Conductor: Lew Raymond. Cast: Evelyn Sharpe, Charles Peck, Robert Back.

Studio Cast (1987) • London (S) 421200-1 8-12   87

Conductor: John Mauceri. Cast: Kiri Te Kanawa, Jeremy Irons, Sir John Gielgud, Warren Mitchell, Jerry Hadley, Meriel Dickenson, David Beavan, Joseph Cornwell, Lindsey Benson, Judith Rees, Susan Bickley, London Voices, Terry Edwards, London Symphony Orchestra.

Soundtrack (1964) • Columbia (M) KOL-8000.......................... 50-75   64

Soundtrack (1964) • Columbia (S) KOS-2600.......................... 50-75   64

Limited Edition. Colored vinyl, white label. Gatefold cover. According to insert letter from Columbia Vice President, "This specially prepared and pressed album is a mint edition copy. This number appearing below is one of 8,475. Guard it well. It is already a rare piece of property." Promotional issue only.

Soundtrack (1964) • Columbia (M) KOL-8000............................ 8-10   64

Soundtrack (1964) • Columbia (S) KOS-2600............................ 8-12   64

Gatefold cover. Front and back cover have title in white letters.

Soundtrack (1964) • Columbia (S) KOS-2600............................ 8-12   60s

Gatefold cover. Front and back cover have title in black letters. Credits on back cover are different from above issue.

Soundtrack (1964) • Columbia (S) JS-2600 10-15   Re

Reworked gatefold cover. Title in white script with more complete credits in black ink. Back cover has titles on top over new photo of Rex Harrison and Audrey Hepburn. Inside cover is same as original release.

Soundtrack (1964) · CBS (S) 70000 20-25

UK release.

Composer: Alan Jay Lerner, Frederick Loewe. Conductor: Andre Previn. Cast: Audrey Hepburn, Rex Harrison, Marni Nixon (performed some of Audrey Hepburn's vocals in the film), Stanley Holloway, Wilfrid Hyde-White, Bill Shirley (performed Jeremy Brett's vocals), Theodore Bikel.

Studiotrack • United Artists (M) UAL 3361 8-12   64

Studiotrack • United Artists (S) UAS 6361.............................. 8-12   64

Conductor: Nick Perito. Cast: Ferrante and Teicher.

Studiotrack (1964) • Capitol (M) W 2117.............................. 10-12   64

Studiotrack (1964) • Capitol (S) SW 2117............................. 10-15   64

Conductor: Ralph Carmichael. Cast: Nat "King" Cole.

Studiotrack (1964) • Wyncote (M) W-9044.. 8-12   64
Studiotrack (1964) • Wyncote (S) W-9044 8-12   64
   Conductor: Dave Stephens. **Cast:** Hollywood Studio Orchestra and Chorus.
Studiotrack (1964) • Wyncote (S) W-9073 8-12   64
   Also has music from *Mary Poppins* and *Sound of Music*.
   Cast: Rudolf Statler.
Studiotrack • Allegro (M) 1686 8-12
   Full title: *The Songs from My Fair Lady*. First issue has themes from "Other Broadway
   Hits," on one side.
   Cast: Allegro Singers and Orchestra, Royal Singers and Orchestra.
Studiotrack • Allegro (M) 1686 8-12
   Full title: *The Songs from the Broadway Success, My Fair Lady*. Reissue has themes from
   Pal Joey on one side with different cover.
   Cast: Allegro Singers and Orchestra.
Studiotrack • Bravo (M) K-104.. 8-12
   One side has music from *Gigi*.
   Conductor: John Senati. **Cast:** Bravo Pops Symphony Orchestra.
Studiotrack • Camden (EP) CAE 357 5-10
   First issue has art sketch cover.
Studiotrack • Camden (EP) CAE 357 5-10
   Reissue has photo cover.
   Cast: Domenico Savino and His Orchestra.
Studiotrack • Columbia (M) CL-895... 8-12
Studiotrack • Columbia (S) CS-9004.. 8-12   64
   Cast: Percy Faith and His Orchestra.
Studiotrack • Columbia (M) CL-2195... 8-15   64
Studiotrack • Columbia (S) CS-8995... 8-15   64
   Cast: Andre Previn and His Quartet.
Studiotrack • Columbia (M) CL-2205... 8-12   64
Studiotrack • Columbia (S) CS-9005.. 10-15   64
   Full title: *Great Songs from My Fair Lady and Other Musicals*. Also has songs from *Hello
   Dolly, Babes in Toyland, Jubilee, All American, Funny Girl* and *No Strings*.
   Cast: Andy Williams.
Studiotrack • Command (S) CC 11041.. 8-15
   One side has music from *The Sound of Music*.
   Conductor: William Steinberg. **Cast:** Pittsburgh Symphony Orchestra.
Studiotrack • Concert-Disc (S) CS-23 5-10
   One side has music from *Gigi*.
   Conductor: Caesar Giovanninni. **Cast:** Radiant Velvet Orchestra.
Studiotrack (1956) • Contemporary (M) 3527...................................... 20-30   56
   Actual title: *Modern Jazz Performances of Songs from My Fair Lady*.
   Cast: Shelly Manne and His Friends, Andre Previn, Leroy Vinnegar.
Studiotrack • Crown (S) CST-107 8-12
   Conductor: Tom Davis, Hans Hagen.
Studiotrack • Crown (M) CLP-5042 8-12
   Conductor: Thomas M. Davis, Hans Hagen, Lloyd Hanna, Irene Cummings.
Studiotrack • Custom (S) CS-1001... 8-12
Studiotrack • Forum Circle (S) FCS 9105.. 8-12
Studiotrack • Four Corners (S) FCS-4203... 8-12
   Cast: All Stars.
Studiotrack • Goldentone (M) C-4034 8-12
Studiotrack • Gramophone (M) 20202... 8-12
   Cast: Varsity Singers and Orchestra.
Studiotrack • Grand Award (S) 216 8-12
   Cast: Enoch Light Orchestra and Chorus.
Studiotrack • Harmony (M) HL 7032... 8-12
   Cast: Harwyn Quartet.

Studiotrack • Harmony (M) HL 7195...8-12
Studiotrack • Harmony (S) HS 11008...8-12
One side has music from *Brigadoon*.
Conductor: Dino Martinelli. **Cast:** Dino Martinelli and His Orchestra.
Studiotrack • La Brea (M) L-8007 8-12
Credits not shown on either cover or label.
Studiotrack • MGM (M) E 4280 8-12
Studiotrack • MGM (S) SE 4280..8-12
Cast: Mel Torme, Fran Jeffries, Maurice Chevalier, Robert Sebastian Orchestra, Melanchrino Strings, Cyril Ornadel and the Starlight Symphony, Oscar Peterson.
Studiotrack • Palace (M) M-637 8-12
Studiotrack • Palace (S) PST-637 8-12
One side has classical "Mood Music."
Cast: James Campbell, Margo Mason, Fontana & His Orchestra.
Studiotrack • Parade (M) SP 321 8-12
Cast: Dick Richards Orchestra, Jennie Feathers, Don Lawrence.
Studiotrack • Promenade (M) 2061 8-12
Thirteen tracks. One side has music from *The King and I*.
Conductor: Al Goodman. **Cast:** Al Goodman and His Orchestra, Lola Fisher, Richard Torigi, Edgar Powell, Susan Shaute, Gretchen Rhoads, William Reynolds.
Studiotrack • Promenade (M) R 2061..8-12
Eleven tracks. One side has music from *The King and I*.
Conductor: Al Goodman. **Cast:** Al Goodman and His Orchestra, Lola Fisher, Richard Torigi, Edgar Powell, Susan Shaute, Gretchen Rhoads, William Reynolds.
Studiotrack • Somerset (M) P-22100..8-12
Studiotrack • Somerset (S) SF-22100 8-12
Cast: 101 Strings.
Studiotrack • Valiant (S) V-4916..8-12
One side has music from Broadway and Manhattan shows.
Conductor: Robert Russel Bennett. **Cast:** Broadway Theatre Orchestra.
Original Revival Cast (1976) • Columbia (S) PS-34197.........................8-10   76
Original Revival Cast (1976) • Columbia (Q) PS-34197 20-25   76
Above two are from the 20th anniversary production. Quad issue reads QBL-34197 on label.
Composer: Alan Jay Lerner, Frederick Loewe. **Conductor:** Theodore Saindenberg. **Cast:** Robert Coote, Ian Richardson, Christine Andreas, George Rose, Jerry Lanning, Sylvia O'Brien.
Studiotrack (1978) • Music Minus One (S) MMO 1030 10-15   78
Conductor: William Harrison. **Cast:** Music Minus One Theatre Orchestra.
Also see AROUND THE WORLD IN 80 DAYS
Also see CAMELOT
Also see KING AND I
Also see EVENING WITH LERNER AND LOEWE

MY FAIRFAX LADY
Original Cast (1957) • Jubilee (M) JGM-2030......................................40-50   57
Satire of *My Fair Lady* by the Los Angeles Cast.
Composer: Sid Kuller. **Conductor:** Jerry Fielding. **Cast:** Billy Gray, Bert Gordon, Carol Shannon, Kirby Stone Four.

MY FAVORITE BRUNETTE
Soundtrack • Capitol 381 25-35
78 rpm.
Cast: Bob Hope, Dorothy Lamour.

MY FUR LADY
Original Cast (1957) • McGill (M) MRS LPM-3 25-35   57
Original Cast (1957) • McGill (M) MRS LPM-5 40-50   57
  Recorded June 12, 1957 by a Canadian College.
    Composer: James Domville, Galt MacDermot, Timothy Porteous, Harry Garber, Roy Wolvin.
    Conductor: Edmund Assaly. **Cast:** Ann Golden, Jim Hugessen, Nancy Bacal, John MacLeod,
    Sheila McCormick, Douglas Robertson, Graham Wright.

MY GEISHA
Soundtrack (1962) • RCA Victor (M) LOC-1070 30-50   62
Soundtrack (1962) • RCA Victor (S) LSO-1070 75-80   62
    Composer: Franz Waxman, others. **Conductor:** Franz Waxman.

MY LEFT FOOT
Soundtrack (1989) • Varese Sarabande (S) 8-12   89
    Composer: Elmer Bernstein.

MY NAME IS BARBRA
TV Soundtrack (1965) • Columbia (M) CL-2336 8-10   65
TV Soundtrack (1965) • Columbia (S) CS-9136 8-12   65
  Contains some material from the 1965 CBS-TV special, with additional songs not from the
  show.
    Composer: Various. **Conductor:** Peter Matz. **Cast:** Barbra Streisand.
TV Soundtrack • Columbia (M) CL-2409 8-10
TV Soundtrack • Columbia (S) CS-9209 8-12
  Full title: *My Name Is Barbra, Two.* Has Bergdorf-Goodman medley not found on the first
  album.
    Composer: Various. **Conductor:** Peter Matz. **Cast:** Barbra Streisand.

MY NAME IS NOBODY
Soundtrack (1974) • Cereberus (S) CEM-S 0101 10-15   80
    Composer: Ennio Morricone. **Conductor:** Ennio Morricone.

MY ONE AND ONLY
Original Cast (1983) • Atlantic (S) 80110-1 8-10   83
    Composer: George Gershwin, Ira Gershwin. **Cast:** Tommy Tune, Twiggy.

MY PEOPLE
Original Chicago Cast (1963) • Contact (M) C-1 15-20   66
Original Chicago Cast (1963) • Contact (S) CS-1 20-25   66
Original Chicago Cast (1963) • Flying Dutchman (S) FDS-112 10-15   Re
    Composer: Duke Ellington. **Conductor:** Jimmy Jones. **Cast:** Joya Sherrill, Lil Greenwood,
    Jimmy McPhail, Irving Bunton Singers, Bunny Briggs, Jimmy Grissom.

MY PLEASURE IS MY BUSINESS
Soundtrack (1975) • Daffodil (S) DAF-10051 10-15   75
  Canadian release.
    Composer: Thomas W. Cochrane. **Cast:** Xaviera Hollander.

MY SIDE OF THE MOUNTAIN
Soundtrack (1969) • Capitol (S) ST-245 20-25   69
    Composer: William Josephs. **Conductor:** Muir Mathieson. **Cast:** Teddy Eccles, Theodore Bikel,
    Tudi Wiggins. (With dialogue.)

MY SONG GOES ROUND THE WORLD
Soundtrack (1950) • Continental (M) CON-1 30-40   50
  10-inch LP. "A Joseph Schmidt Memorial Album."
    Cast: Joseph Schmidt.

MY SQUARE LADDIE
Studio Cast • Foremost (M) FMLS-1 20-25
Studio Cast • AEI (M) AEI-1132 8-10   80s
Lampoon of *My Fair Lady*.
Composer: Max Showalter, William Howe. **Conductor:** Eddie Dunstedter. **Cast:** Reginald Gardner, Zasu Pitts, Nancy Walker.

MY STEPMOTHER IS AN ALIEN
Soundtrack (1988) • Polydor (S) 837798-1 8-10   88
Cast: Animotion, M/A/R/R/S, Ivan Neville, Kim Basinger, Dan Aykroyd, Cameo, Jackie Jackson, Siren.

MY TURN ON EARTH
Original Cast (1977) • Embryo (S) ER-2003A 12-15   77
Two discs.
Composer: Lex de Azevedo, Carol Lynn Pearson. **Conductor:** Lex de Azevedo. **Cast:** Candy Brand, Laurette Conkling, Shawn Engemann, Brad Murdoch, Paul Engemann.

MY TUTOR
Soundtrack (1983) • Regency International (S) RI 8406....................... 10-15   83
Composer: Webster Lewis.

MY UNCLE
Soundtrack (1958) • Fontana (EP) TFE-17175 10-15   58
Cast: Jacques Tati.

MY WILD IRISH ROSE
Soundtrack (1947) • RCA Victor (EP) EPB-3036 10-15   52
Two discs.
Soundtrack (1947) • RCA Victor (M) LPM-3036 20-25   52
10-inch LP.
Composer: Chauncy Olcott, others. **Conductor:** Russ Case, Mark Warnow, Charles Dant. **Cast:** Dennis Day.

MYRA BRECKINRIDGE
Studiotrack • 20th Century-Fox (M) DS-1924/1925 50-100   70
Has "Special Radio Programming Material" printed on label. A cast radio show, interview and open-end interview album with scripts. No music. Promotional issue only.
Cast: Mae West, Rex Reed, Calvin Lockhart, Raquel Welch, John Huston.

MYSTERIOUS FILM WORLD OF BERNARD HERRMANN
Studiotrack • London (S) SPC-21137.. 25-30   76
Selections from *The Three Worlds of Gulliver* with more music from that film than the Colpix issue, which is mostly dialogue. Also has music from *Mysterious Island* and *Jason and the Argonauts*.
Composer: Bernard Herrmann. **Conductor:** Bernard Herrmann. **Cast:** National Philharmonic Orchestra.
Also see THREE WORLDS OF GULLIVER

MYSTERY OF EDWIN DROOD
Original Cast (1985) • Polydor (S) 422 827 969-1 5-8   86
Composer: Rupert Holmes. **Conductor:** Michael Starobin. **Cast:** Betty Buckley, Cleo Laine, George Rose, Patti Cochenour, Howard McGillian, others.

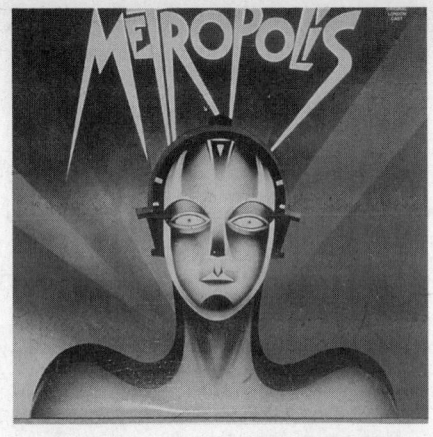

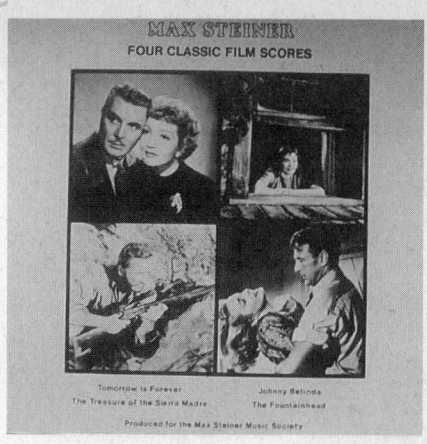

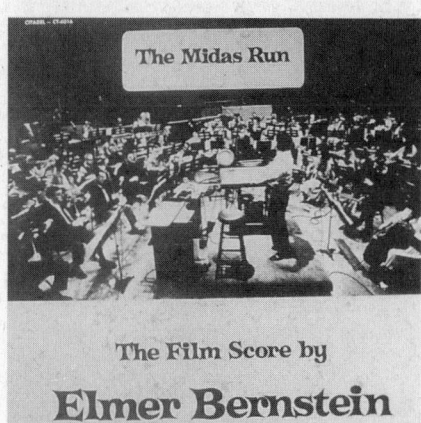

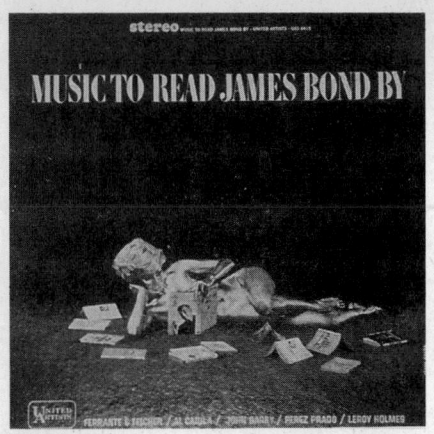

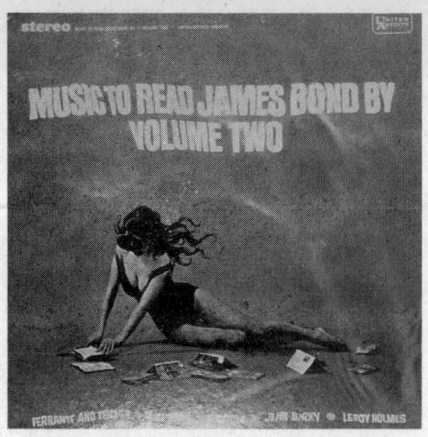

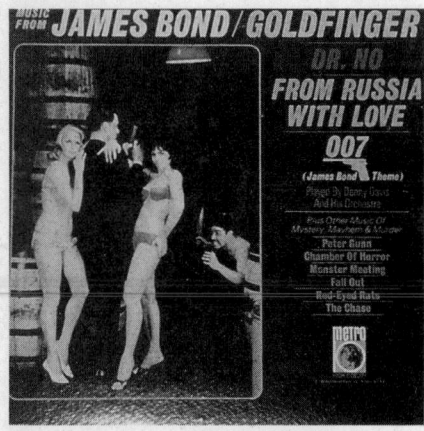

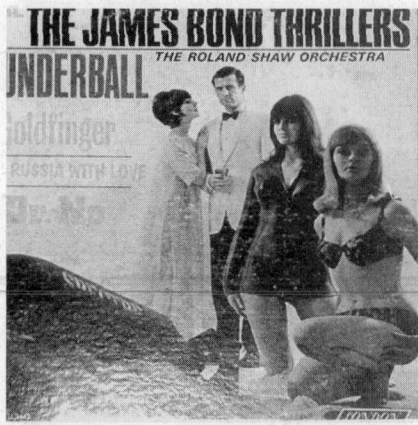

NARM'S GOLDEN DECADE
Studiotrack • RCA Victor (S) PRS-264 20-40   69
> Promotional souvenir disc, distributed at NARM's tenth anniversary meeting and awards banquet. Tracks were recorded in the studio but were "suggestive of the spirit of the artists' performances at the RCA parties or the NARM [National Association of Record Merchandisers] banquets."
> **Cast:** Limeliters, Ann-Margret, Al Hirt, Paul Anka, Homer and Jethro, Peter Nero, Eddy Arnold, John Gary, Chet Atkins, Floyd Cramer, Anita Kerr Singers, Boots Randolph, Myron Cohen, SSGT. Barry Sadler, Henry Mancini, Jack Jones, Harry Belafonte.

NBC'S SATURDAY NIGHT LIVE: see SATURDAY NIGHT LIVE

NAGSHEAD
Original Cast (1974) • O. Barton (S) OBS-1114-45 15-20   70s
> From a Broadway demo recording, since this show did not open as planned.
> **Composer:** Ovid Lewis. **Conductor:** Lou Toby. **Cast:** Phyllis Craig, Donald Lombardi, Lou Toby, Dick Gardner.

NAKED ANGELS
Soundtrack (1969) • Straight (S) STS-1056 15-20   69
> **Composer:** Jeffrey Simmons, Randy Steirling.

NAKED APE
Soundtrack (1973) • Playboy (S) PB-125 12-15   73
> **Composer:** Jimmy Webb, Johann Sebastian Bach. **Conductor:** Jimmy Webb. **Cast:** Donald Driver, Jimmy Webb, Clydie King, others.

NAKED CARMEN
Studiotrack (1970) • Mercury (S) SRM 1-604 10-15   70
> **Composer:** John Corigliano, Paul Paray. **Cast:** Detroit Symphony Orchestra.

NAKED CITY (1948): see LUST FOR LIFE

NAKED CITY
TV Soundtrack (1958) • Colpix (S) CP-505 30-35   58
TV Soundtrack (1958) • Colpix (S) SCP-505 40-50   58
> Full title: *Naked City – A Musical Portrait.*
> **Composer:** George Duning, Ned Washington. **Conductor:** Morris Stoloff. **Cast:** John McIntire (narration), JoAnn Greer, James Darren.
> Also see BRUTE FORCE

NAKED MAJA
Soundtrack (1959) • United Artists (M) UAL-4031 20-25   59
Soundtrack (1959) • United Artists (S) UAS-5031 25-30   59
> **Composer:** Francesco Angelo Lavagnino. **Conductor:** Francesco Angelo Lavagnino.

NAKED PREY
Soundtrack (1966) • Folkways (S) 3854 8-10   66

NAKED SEA
Soundtrack • Capitol (EP) EAP 1-675 50-60   55
> **Cast:** Laurindo Almeida, George Fields.

NAMU THE KILLER WHALE
Soundtrack (1965) • United Artists (S) UAL 3540 15-25   65
Soundtrack (1965) • United Artists (S) UAS 6540 35-45   65
 Full title: *Namu the Killer Whale (and Other Ballads of Adventure)*. Original film title theme
 plus other whale-related songs.
 Composer: Tom Glaser. **Cast:** Tom Glaser.

NANCY GOES TO RIO
Soundtrack (1950) • MGM (M) E-508 25-60   50
 10-inch LP.
Soundtrack (1950) • MCA (M) 39079 5-10   86
 Also has music from *Rich, Young and Pretty*.
 Composer: Ray Gilbert, others. **Conductor:** George Stoll. **Cast:** Jane Powell, Ann Sothern,
 Carmen Miranda, Danny Scholl, MGM Studio Orchestra and Chorus.
 Also see THOSE GLORIOUS MGM MUSICALS.

NANCY WALKER: THE BROADWAY BOMBSHELL SINGS SHOW
STOPPERS
Studio Cast • Stet (M) SOT-2002 8-10   76
 Cast: Nancy Walker.

NAPOLEON
Studiotrack (1927) • CBS (SE) FMT-37230 10-15   81
 Composer: Carmine Coppola. **Conductor:** Carmine Coppola.

NASHVILLE
Soundtrack (1975) • ABC (S) ABCD-893 8-20   75
 Conductor: Richard Baskin. **Cast:** Keith Carradine.

NASHVILLE / NEW YORK
London Cast • That's Entertainment (S) TER-1001 10-12   80s
 UK release.
 Composer: Ogden Nash, others.

NASHVILLE REBEL
Soundtrack (1966) • RCA Victor (M) LPM-3736 15-20   66
Soundtrack (1966) • RCA Victor (SE) LSP-3736e 10-15   66
 Composer: Waylon Jennings, Paul McCartney, others. **Cast:** Waylon Jennings.

NATIONAL LAMPOON LEMMINGS
Original Cast (1971) • Blue Thumb (S) 9001 10-20   71
 Two discs. Includes insert.
Original Cast (1973) • Banana (S) BTS-6006 10-12   73
 Conductor: Paul Jacobs. **Cast:** Chevy Chase, Alice Playten, John Belushi, Gary Goodrow, Paul
 Jacobs, Christopher Guest, Mary Jennifer Mitchell.

NATIONAL LAMPOON'S ANIMAL HOUSE
Soundtrack (1978) • MCA (S) L33-1981 25-35   78
 Full title: *Animal House - An interview with John Belushi*. Four songs from film.
 Promotional issue only.
 Cast: John Belushi, others.
Soundtrack (1978) • MCA (S) 3046 8-10   78
 Composer: Elmer Bernstein, others. **Conductor:** Elmer Bernstein. **Cast:** John Belushi, Sam
 Cooke, Bobby Lewis, Lloyd Williams, Paul and Paula, Stephen Bishop, Chris Montez, Elmer
 Bernstein, National Lampoon. (With dialogue.)

NATIONAL LAMPOON'S VACATION
Soundtrack (1983) • Warner Bros. (S) 1-23909 8-10   83
 Cast: Lindsey Buckingham, Fleetwoods, Ramones, Ralph Burns, Nicolette Larson, June
 Pointer, Vanity.

NATIVE SON
Soundtrack (1986) • MCA (S) 6198 15-20   86
 Composer: James Mtume.

NATIVES ARE RESTLESS
Original Cast (1968) • RCA Victor (S) 865N-4022.................................. 5-10   68
For a Northwestern University Waa-Mu Show.
Cast: Choral Group, Shelley Long.

NATURAL
Soundtrack (1984) • Warner Bros. (S) 1-25116 10-15   84
Composer: Randy Newman. **Conductor:** Randy Newman.

NATURAL HIGH
Original Cast • Light (S) L5-5558-L 10-12
Composer: Ralph Carmichael, Kurt Kaiser.

NATURE'S HALF ACRE: see WALT DISNEY'S TRUE LIFE ADVENTURES

NAUGHTY MARIETTA
Original Cast (1910) • Smithsonian (M) N-026 10-15   81
Two discs.
Composer: Victor Herbert, Rida Johnson Young. **Conductor:** James R. Morris. **Cast:** Judith Blazer, Leslie Harrington, Elvira Green.
Studio Cast (1950) • Columbia (M) ML-2094 12-18   50
Composer: Victor Herbert, Rida Johnson Young. **Conductor:** Robert Armbruster. **Cast:** Nelson Eddy, Nadine Conner.
Studio Cast (1951) • RCA Victor (M) LK-1005 12-18   51
Composer: Victor Herbert, Rida Johnson Young. **Conductor:** Al Goodman. **Cast:** Earl Wrightson, Elaine Malbin, Jimmy Carroll.
Studio Cast (1953) • RCA Victor (EP) EPA-481................................... 15-20   53
Studio Cast (1954) • Capitol (M) L-468 12-18   54
10-inch LP.
Studio Cast (1954) • Capitol (M) P-551 12-15   54
Studio Cast (1954) • Capitol (M) T-551 12-15   54
Above two also have music from *The Red Mill.*
Composer: Victor Herbert, Rida Johnson Young. **Conductor:** George Greeley. **Cast:** Gordon MacRae, Marguerite Piazza, Katherine Hilgenberg.
Studio Cast (1959) • Lion (M) L-70090.. 10-15   59
Composer: Victor Herbert, Rida Johnson Young. **Conductor:** Paul Britton.
Studiotrack (1952) • RCA Victor (M) LCT-16 35-45   52
10-inch LP.
Studiotrack (1952) • RCA Victor (M) LPV-526..................................... 15-20   66
Also contains songs from seven other films starring Nelson Eddy and Jeanette MacDonald.
Composer: Victor Herbert, Rida Johnson Young. **Conductor:** Nathaniel Shilkret, Herbert Stothart. **Cast:** Nelson Eddy, Jeanette MacDonald.
Also see CHOCOLATE SOLDIER
Also see MADEMOISELLE MODISTE

NAVAJO JOE
Soundtrack (1966) • United Artists (S) UA-LA292-G............................. 20-25   74
Composer: Leo Nichols (Ennio Morricone). **Conductor:** Leo Nichols (Ennio Morricone).

NAVY SEALS
Soundtrack (1990) • Atlantic (S) 82125-1... 8-10   90
Cast: Mr. Big, Bon Jovi, Richie Havens, Planet 3, Gowan, Vicki Thomas, Lisa Hartman, Blue Rodeo.

NEAR DARK
Soundtrack (1987) • Varese Sarabande (S) STV 81345......................... 8-10   87
Composer: Tangerine Dream. **Cast:** Tangerine Dream.

NED KELLY
Soundtrack (1970) • United Artists (S) UAS-5213................................. 15-20   70
Soundtrack (1970) • United Artists (S) UA-LA300-G............................. 10-12   74
Composer: Shel Silverstein. **Cast:** Waylon Jennings, Mick Jagger, Kris Kristofferson, Tom Ghent.

NEFERTITI
Original Cast (1977) • Take Home Tunes (S) THT-7810 8-10   77
Composer: David Spangler, Christopher Gore. Conductor: John Demain. Cast: Robert
Lupone, Andrea Marcovicci, Michael Nouri, Michael Smartt, Jane White.

NERVOUS SET
Original Cast (1959) • Columbia (M) OL-5430 20-30   59
Original Cast (1959) • Columbia (S) OS-2018 45-55   59
Composer: Tommy Wolf, Fran Landesman. Cast: Richard Hayes, Tani Seitz, Larry Hagman,
Del Close, Tommy Wolf (piano), William Schneider (drum), Kenny Burrell (guitar), Joe Benjamin
(bass).

NEVADA SMITH
Soundtrack (1966) • Dot (M) DLP-3718 18-20   66
Soundtrack (1966) • Dot (S) DLP-25718 25-35   66
Composer: Alfred Newman. Conductor: Alfred Newman.

NEVER A DULL MOMENT
Soundtrack (1968) • Custom Recorders (M) CR 2872 25-30   68
Single-sided. Commercial spots. Made for radio station use only.

NEVER CRY WOLF: see MRS. SOFFEL

NEVER ENDING STORY
Soundtrack (1984) • EMI America (S) ST-17139 15-20   84
Cast: Limahl, others.

NEVER ON SUNDAY
Soundtrack (1960) • United Artists (M) UAL-4070................................ 8-10   60
Soundtrack (1960) • United Artists (S) UAS-5070................................ 8-25   6
Soundtrack (1960) • United Artists/Capitol (S) SW-90834 8-10   60.
Capitol Record Club issue.
Soundtrack (1960) • Liberty (S) 4N-10280 5-8   Re
Composer: Manos Hadjidakis. Conductor: Manos Hadjidakis. Cast: Melina Mercouri.
Also see I WANT TO LIVE
Also see ILLYA DARLING

NEVER SAY DIE: see $1000 A TOUCHDOWN

NEVER SAY NEVER AGAIN
Soundtrack (1983) • Seven Seas (S) K28P-4122 12-15   83
Composer: Michel Legrand. Cast: Sean Connery, Barbara Carrera.

NEW FACES OF 1952
Original Cast (1952) • RCA Victor OC-1008 15-20   52
78 rpm album.
Original Cast (1952) • RCA Victor (EP) EOA-433 12-18   52
Original Cast (1952) • RCA Victor (M) LOC-1008 15-20   52
Original Cast (1952) • RCA Victor (M) CBM1-2206................................ 8-15   77
Includes Time for Tea, not found on 1952 issues.
Composer: Ronny Graham, June Carroll, Arthur Siegel, Sheldon M. Harnick, Michael Brown,
others. Conductor: Anton Coppola. Cast: Virginia Bosler, June Carroll, Robert Clary, Allen
Conroy, Virginia DeLuce, Alice Ghostley, Ronny Graham, Patricia Hammerlee, Eartha Kitt,
Joseph Lautner, Paul Lynde, Bill Mullikin, Rosemary O'Reilly.
Soundtrack (1954) • RCA Victor (EP) EPA-557 20-25   54
Composer: Ronny Graham, June Carroll, Arthur Siegel, others. Conductor: Henri Rene, Anton
Coppola. Cast: Eartha Kitt.

NEW FACES OF 1956

Original Cast (1956) • RCA Victor (EP) EOC-1025 15-20   56
Original Cast (1956) • RCA Victor (M) LOC-1025 35-45   56
> The album titled *Forgotten Broadway* offers additional songs from *New Faces of 1956* that do not appear on the RCA Victor albums.
>> **Composer:** June Carroll, others. **Conductor:** Jay Blackton. **Cast:** T.C. Jones (host), Suzanne Bernard, Jane Connell, Billie Hayes, Johnny Haymer, Tiger Haynes, Ann Henry, Virginia Martin, John Reardon, Amru Sani, Bob Shaver, Maggie Smith, Inga Swenson.
> Also see FORGOTTEN BROADWAY

NEW FACES OF 1968

Original Cast (1968) • Warner Bros. (S) BS-2551 20-25   68
> **Composer:** Ronny Graham, others. **Conductor:** Ted Simons. **Cast:** Michael Allen, Suzanne Astor, Gloria Bleezarde, Trudy Carson, Marilyn Child, Elaine Giftos, Madeline Kahn, Robert Klein, Brandon Maggart, George Ormiston, Rod Perry, Nancie Phillips, Leonard Sillman.

NEW GIRL IN TOWN

Original Cast (1957) • RCA Victor (EP) EOC-1027 10-20   57
> Three discs. Gatefold cover.
Original Cast (1957) • RCA Victor (M) LOC-1027 12-18   57
Original Cast (1957) • RCA Victor (S) LSO-1027 35-45   58
Original Cast (1957) • RCA Victor (M) LOC-1106 15-18   65
Original Cast (1957) • RCA Victor (S) LSO-1106 20-25   65
> **Composer:** Bob Merrill. **Conductor:** Hal Hastings. **Cast:** Mark Dawson, Lulu Bates, Eddie Phillips, Delbert Anderson, H.F. Green, Mara Landi, Gwen Verdon, Thelma Ritter, Cameron Prud'Homme, George Wallace.

NEW INTERNS

Soundtrack (1964) • Colpix (M) CP-473 20-25   64
Soundtrack (1964) • Colpix (S) SCP-473 30-35   64
> Film sequel to *The Interns.*
> **Composer:** Earle Hagen. **Conductor:** Earle Hagen.

NEW KIND OF LOVE

Soundtrack (1963) • Mercury (M) MG-20859 10-12   63
Soundtrack (1963) • Mercury (S) SR-60859 12-18   63
> **Composer:** Sammy Fain, Erroll Garner, others. **Conductor:** Leith Stevens. **Cast:** Erroll Garner.

NEW MESSIAH

Soundtrack (1972) • Columbia KC-31713 15-20   72

NEW MOON

Original London Cast (1928) • Monmouth Evergreen (SE) MES-7051 8-10
> **Composer:** Sigmund Romberg, Oscar Hammerstein II. **Conductor:** Sigmund Romberg (instrumentals), Herman Finck (vocals). **Cast:** Evelyn Laye, Ben Williams, Howett Worster, Gene Gerrard.
Studio Cast (1950) • Decca (EP) EP-522 15-20   50
Studio Cast (1950) • Decca (M) DL-5378 10-25   50
> 10-inch LP.
> **Cast:** Florence George, Frank Forest, Paul Gregory.
Studio Cast (1950) • Capitol (M) P-219 12-18   50
> Green label.
Studio Cast (1950) • Capitol (M) T-219 10-20   Re
> One side has music from *The Vagabond King.*
> **Composer:** NEW MOON: Sigmund Romberg, Oscar Hammerstein II, VAGABOND KING: Rudolf Friml, Brian Hooker. **Conductor:** Paul Weston. **Cast:** Gordon MacRae, Lucille Norman, Chorus and Orchestra.
Studio Cast (1950) • Columbia (M) ML-2164 10-15   50
> 10-inch LP.
Studio Cast (1950) • Columbia Special Products (M) P-13878 5-8   77
> One side has music from *Rose Marie.*
> **Composer:** Sigmund Romberg, Oscar Hammerstein II. **Conductor:** Leon Arnaud. **Cast:** Nelson Eddy, Eleanor Steber.

Studio Cast (1951) • RCA Victor (EP) EKB-1011 8-12   51
 Two discs.
Studio Cast (1951) • RCA Victor (M) LK-1011 10-15   51
  Composer: Sigmund Romberg, Oscar Hammerstein II. **Conductor:** Al Goodman. **Cast:** Earl
  Wrightson, Al Goodman Orchestra, Frances Greer, Donald Dame, Earl Oxford, Guild Chorister.
Studio Cast (1953) • Decca (M) DL-5472 12-18   53
 10-inch LP.
  Composer: Sigmund Romberg, Oscar Hammerstein. **Conductor:** Victor Young. **Cast:** Thomas
  Hayward, Jane Wilson, Lee Sweetland.
Studio Cast (1957) • Halo (M) 50262 8-15   57
Studio Cast (1963) • Capitol (M) W-1966 8-12   63
Studio Cast (1963) • Capitol (S) SW-1966 10-12   63
Studio Cast (1963) • Angel (S) S-37320 8-10   73
  Composer: Sigmund Romberg, Oscar Hammerstein II. **Conductor:** Van Alexander. **Cast:**
  Gordon MacRae, Dorothy Kirsten, Richard Robinson, Roger Wagner Chorale, Earle Wilkie,
  Jeanine Wagner, James Tippey.
Soundtrack (1930) • Raviola (M) BMPB1929/Flicker 8/69 8-10   80
 Also has music from *Broadway Melody*.
Soundtrack (1930) • Pelican (M) LP-2020 12-15   80
 Above two contain the score from the lost 1930 film version.
  Composer: Sigmund Romberg, Oscar Hammerstein II. **Conductor:** Herbert Stothart. **Cast:**
  Grace Moore, Lawrence Tibbett, Roland Young, Emily Fitzroy, Gus Shy, Adolph Menjou.
Soundtrack (1940) • Pelican (M) LP-103 8-12   80
 Score of the 1940 film version. Also has a 1942 radio broadcast of *I Married an Angel*.
  Composer: Sigmund Romberg, Oscar Hammerstein II. **Cast:** Jeanette MacDonald, Nelson
  Eddy.
 Also see GIRL FRIEND

NEW ORLEANS
Soundtrack (1947) • Giants Of Jazz GOJ-1025 40-50   47
 78 rpm demos from studio recordings for the film.
  Cast: Louis Armstrong, Billie Holiday, Woody Herman, Arturo De Cordova, Dorothy Patrick,
  Marjorie Patrick, Marjorie Lord, Irene Rich, John Alexander, Richard Hagemen.

NEW THEMES FROM MOTION PICTURES
Studiotrack • Time (S) S/2065 10-20
 Music from *Lolita, Advise and Consent, State Fair, Road to Hong Kong, Music Man, Gypsy,
 West Side Story, La Dolce Vita, Young Savages, Naked Island* and others.

NEW WORLD OF STAINLESS STEEL
Soundtrack • Republic Steel L8-OP-5735/36 100-125

NEW YEAR'S RADIO DANCING PARTY 1945-46
Radio Cast (1945/46) • Radiola (M) MR-1031 20-25   74

NEW YORK, NEW YORK
Soundtrack (1977) • United Artists (S) UAMG-113 25-35   77
 Boxed set with sheet music and accessories. Promotional issue only.
Soundtrack (1977) • United Artists (S) UA-LA750-L2 8-12   77
Soundtrack (1977) • Liberty (S) LKBL-750 8-10   Re
 Both are two-disc sets.
  Composer: John Kander, Fred Ebb. **Conductor:** Ralph Burns, Gary Miller. **Cast:** Liza Minnelli,
  Larry Kert, Mary Kay Place, Dianne Abbott, Georgie Auld.

NEW YORK STORIES
Soundtrack (1989) • Elektra (S) 60857-1 10-15   89
  Cast: Kid Creole and Coconuts, Pianosaurus, Frankie Carle, Wilbur De Paris, Bernie Leighton,
  Procol Harum, Transvision Vamp, Hot Club of France, Bob Dylan, The Band.

NEXT MAN
Soundtrack (1976) • Buddah (S) BDS-5685............................ 10-15   76
Composer: Michael Kamen, Rosko Mercer. **Conductor:** Michael Kamen. **Cast:** Tasha Thomas, Robert Fitoussi, Michael Kamen.

NIAGARA: see MARILYN; REMEMBER MARILYN

NICHOLAS AND ALEXANDRA
Soundtrack (1971) • Bell (S) 1103 20-25   71
Composer: Richard Rodney Bennett. **Conductor:** Marcus Dods. **Cast:** New Philharmonia Orchestra of London.

NICHOLAS NICKLEBY
TV Soundtrack (1982) • DRG (S) SBL-12583 10-15   82
TV Soundtrack (1982) • That's Entertainment (S) TER-1029 8-10   80s
UK release.
Composer: Stephen Oliver. **Conductor:** Harry Rabinowitz. **Cast:** Roger Rees, Jane Downs, Emily Richards, John Woodvine, David Threlfall, Edward Petherbridge, Susanne Bertish, Lila Kaye, Alun Armstrong, others.

NIGHT AND DAY
Studiotrack (1946) • RCA Victor P-158 15-20   46
Four 78 rpms in gatefold cover.
Studiotrack (1946) • RCA Victor (EP) EPA-421 10-15   51
Studiotrack (1946) • RCA Victor (EP) EPA-158 10-15   51
Studiotrack (1946) • RCA Victor (EP) WP-158.................................... 15-20   51
Boxed set of four discs.
Studiotrack (1946) • RCA Victor (M) LPM-32.. 20-25   51
10-inch LP. Actual title: *A Cole Porter Review*. Based on the life of Cole Porter, as presented by Warner Brothers in the film *Night and Day*.
Composer: Cole Porter. **Conductor:** David Rose. **Cast:** David Rose Orchestra.
Soundtrack (1946) • Motion Picture Tracks (M) MPT-6......................... 35-45
Based on the life of Cole Porter, as presented by Warner Brothers in the film *Night and Day*.
Composer: Cole Porter. **Conductor:** Ray Heindorf. **Cast:** Cary Grant, Jane Wyman, Ginny Simms, Mary Martin, Monty Woolley, Eve Arden, Carlos Ramirez.

NIGHT AT CARNEGIE HALL: see CARNEGIE HALL

NIGHT BREED
Soundtrack (1990) • MCA (S) 8037 10-15   90
Shown on cover as *Clive Barker's Night Breed*.
Composer: Danny Elfman. **Conductor:** Shirley Walker.

NIGHT CLUB CONFIDENTIAL
Original Cast (1984) • Confidential (S) No Number Used..................... 10-12   84
Composer: Dennis Deal, Albert Evans. **Conductor:** Albert Evans. **Cast:** Fay DeWitt, Stephen Berger, Denise Nolan, Steve Gideon.

NIGHT CROSSING
Soundtrack (1981) • Intrada (S) RVF-6004 15-20   81
Composer: Jerry Goldsmith. **Conductor:** Jerry Goldsmith.

NIGHT IN HEAVEN
Soundtrack (1983) • A&M (S) SP-4966.. 8-10   83
Cast: Mike Des Barres & Holly Knight, Europeans, English Beat, Tom Teeley, Kiddo, Bryan Adams, Jan Hammer & the Next, Rita Coolidge, Gary U.S. Bonds.

NIGHT IN VENICE

Original Cast (1952) • Everest (M) LPBR-6028 20-25   59
Original Cast (1952) • Everest (S) SDBR-3028 30-35   59
    Features cast of the 1952 Jones Beach Marine Theatre production. Gray foil back cover.
Original Cast (1952) • Everest (M) LPBR-6028 15-20   59
Original Cast (1952) • Everest (S) SDBR-3028 20-25   59
    Standard, white back cover.
      Composer: Johann Strauss Jr., Ruth Martin, Thomas Martin. **Conductor:** Thomas Martin. **Cast:**
      Enzo Stuarti, Thomas Tibbett Hayward, Norwood Smith, Jack Russell, Nola Fairbanks, Laurel
      Hurley, David Kurlan, Guen Omeron, Kenneth Schon.

NIGHT OF THE COMET

Soundtrack (1984) • Macola (S) MRCO 900 10-15   84
    Cast: Revolver, Diana DeWitt, Thom Pace, Skip Adams, Chris Farren, John Townsend, Stallion,
    Amy Holland.

NIGHT OF THE GENERALS

Soundtrack (1967) • Colgems (M) COMO-5002 30-35   67
Soundtrack (1967) • Colgems (S) COSO-5002 45-65   67
    Composer: Maurice Jarre. **Conductor:** Maurice Jarre.

NIGHT OF THE HUNTER

Soundtrack (1955) • RCA Victor (EP) EPC-1136 65-75   55
    Three discs.
Soundtrack (1955) • RCA Victor (M) LPM-1136 150-225   55
    Composer: Walter Schumann. **Conductor:** Walter Schumann. **Cast:** Charles Laughton
    (narration).

NIGHT OF THE IGUANA

Soundtrack (1964) • MGM (M) PR-4 30-35   64
    Limited "Collector's Edition" in black gatefold cover. Dialogue and music from the film.
    Composer: Benjamin Frankel. **Conductor:** Benjamin Frankel. **Cast:** John Huston
    (commentary), Richard Burton, Ava Gardner, Deborah Kerr, Sue Lyon, others.
Soundtrack (1964) • MGM (M) E-4247 8-12   64
Soundtrack (1964) • MGM (S) SE-4247 12-15   64
    Composer: Benjamin Frankel. **Conductor:** Benjamin Frankel.
Studiotrack (1964) • Wyncote (M) W-9038 8-10   64
Studiotrack (1964) • Wyncote (S) SW-9038 8-10   64
    Also has themes from *Robin and the 7 Hoods, Unsinkable Molly Brown* and *My Fair Lady.*

NIGHT OF THE LIVING DEAD

Soundtrack (1968) • Varese Sarabande (M) STV-81151 10-15   82
    Assortment of '50s recordings heard in the film.
    Composer: Spencer Moore, William Loose, George Hormel, Ib Glindemann, others.

NIGHT OF THE SHOOTING STARS

Soundtrack (1983) • Varese Sarabande (S) STV-81175 12-15   83
    Composer: Nicola Piovani.

NIGHT PASSAGE: see FILM MUSIC OF DIMITRI TIOMKIN

NIGHT SHIFT

Soundtrack (1982) • Warner Bros. (S) 1-23702 8-10   821
    Composer: Burt Bacharach, Carole Bayer Sager (some additional music and lyrics by Marv
    Ross and David Foster). **Cast:** Quarterflash, Burt Bacharach, Al Jarreau, Pointer Sisters, Rod
    Stewart, Marshall Crenshaw, Heaven 17, Talk Talk, Rufus with Chaka Khan.

NIGHT THE LIGHTS WENT OUT IN GEORGIA

Soundtrack (1981) • Mirage (S) WTG-16051 10-15   81
    Composer: David Shire. **Conductor:** Gene Armond (music coordinator). **Cast:** Tanya Tucker,
    Glen Campbell, George Jones, Tammy Wynette, Dennis Quaid, Kristy McNichol, Billy Preston,
    Syreeta.

NIGHT THEY RAIDED MINSKY'S
Soundtrack (1968) • United Artists (S) UAS-5191 12-15   69
> **Composer:** Charles Strouse, Lee Adams. **Conductor:** Philip J. Lang, Leroy Holmes. **Cast:** Rudy Vallee, Dexter Maitland, Lillian Hayman, Jason Robards, Norman Wisdom.

NIGHT TRAIN GOES TO HOLLYWOOD
Studio Cast (1962) • Mercury (M) MG-20702 10-15   62
Studio Cast (1962) • Mercury (S) SR-60702 15-20   62
> Songs from: *Porgy and Bess, Never on Sunday, Man with a Golden Arm, High Noon, Jailhouse Rock, Exodus, The Rat Race, Dragnet, Sunset Strip* and *West Side Story*. **Composer:** Various. **Conductor:** Buddy Morrow. **Cast:** Buddy Morrow.

NIGHT VISITOR: see TOUCH OF EVIL

NIGHT WITH JEROME KERN
Studio Cast (1959) • Columbia (M) CL-1386 8-12   59
Studio Cast (1959) • Columbia (S) CS-8181 10-15   59
> **Composer:** Jerome Kern. **Conductor:** Percy Faith. **Cast:** Earl Wrightson, Lois Hunt, Percy Faith Orchestra.

NIGHT WITH RUDOLF FRIML
Studio Cast (1961) • Columbia (M) CL-1630 10-15   61
Studio Cast (1961) • Columbia (S) CS-8430 12-18   61
> **Composer:** Rudolf Friml. **Conductor:** Frank DeVol. **Cast:** Earl Wrightson, Lois Hunt.

NIGHTCOMERS
Soundtrack (1976) • Citadel (S) CTJF-1 75-125
> **Composer:** Jerry Fielding. **Conductor:** Jerry Fielding.

NIGHTFLYERS
Soundtrack (1987) • Varese Sarabande (S) STV 81344 12-15   87
> **Composer:** Timm.

NIGHTHAWKS
Soundtrack (1981) • Backstreet (S) 5196 12-15   81
Soundtrack (1981) • MCA (S) 1521 8-10   80s
> MCA reissue merely has "MCA 1521" stamped on cover of Backstreet album. **Cast:** Keith Emerson.

NIGHTINGALE
Original London Cast (1982) • That's Entertainment (S) TER-1031 10-12   83
> UK release.
> **Composer:** Charles Strouse. **Cast:** Sarah Brightman, Andrew Shore, Gordon Sandison.

NIGHTMARE IN RED
TV Soundtrack • NBC-TV (S) F8-OP-3406 40-50
> **Cast:** Robert Russell Bennett.

NIGHTMARE ON ELM STREET
Soundtrack (1984) • Varese Sarabande (S) STV-81236 8-12   84
> **Composer:** Charles Bernstein.

NIGHTMARE ON ELM STREET 2 – FREDDY'S REVENGE
Soundtrack (1986) • Varese Sarabande (S) STV-81275 10-15   86
> **Composer:** Christopher Young. **Conductor:** Paul Francis Witt.

NIGHTMARE ON ELM STREET 3 – DREAM WARRIORS
Soundtrack (1987) • Varese Sarabande (S) STV-81314 12-15   87
Soundtrack (1987) • That's Entertainment (S) TER-1143 8-10   80s
> UK release.
> **Composer:** Angelo Badelamenti.

NIGHTMARE ON ELM STREET 4 – THE DREAM MASTER
Soundtrack (1988) • Varese Sarabande (S) VS-5203 12-15   88
  Composer: Craig Safan.
Soundtrack (1988) • Chrysalis (S) OV-41673 8-10   88
  Cast: Sea Hags, Angels from Angel City, Go West, Divinyls, Jimmy Davis and Junction, Vinnie
  Vincent Invasion, Vigil, Blondie, Love/Hate, Craig Safan.

NIGHTMARE ON ELM STREET 5 – THE DREAM CHILD
Soundtrack (1989) • Varese Sarabande (S) VS-5238 8-12   89
  Composer: Jay Ferguson.
Soundtrack (1989) • Jive (S) 1258-1J 8-10   89
  Composer: Various. Cast: Bruce Dickinson, Romeo's Daughter, Samantha Fox.

NIKKI, WILD DOG OF THE NORTH
Soundtrack (1961) • Disneyland (M) DQ-1913 25-30   61
Soundtrack (1961) • Disneyland (M) DQ-1281 15-20   65
  Composer: Paul J. Smith. Conductor: Paul J. Smith. Cast: Don Haldane, Jean Coutu, Emile
  Geneste. (With dialogue.)

NINA, THE PINTA, AND THE SANTA MARIA
Studiotrack (1960) • Dot (M) DLP-9009 20-30   60
Studiotrack (1960) • Dot (S) DLP-29009 35-45   60
  Original musical created especially for records.
  Composer: Ray Gilbert, Ray Rasch. Conductor: Neely Plumb. Cast: Eddie Albert, Joanne Gilbert,
  Lee Miller, Thurl Ravenscroft. (With dialogue.)

NINA SIMONE SINGS PORGY
Studiotrack • Palace (M) 771 15-20
  Cast: Nina Simone, Village Allstars.

NINE
Original Cast (1982) • Columbia (S) JS-38325 10-15   82
Original Cast (1982) • Columbia (S) PC-38325 8-12   Re
  LP version is abridged. Additional material is included on both cassettes and compact
  discs.
  Composer: Maury Yeston. Conductor: Wally Harper. Cast: Raul Julia, Karen Akers, Shelly
  Burch, Taina Elg, Liliane Montevecchi, Anita Morris.

9½ WEEKS
Soundtrack (1986) • Capitol (S) SV-12470 8-10   86
  Cast: Corey Hart, John Taylor, Eurythmics, Joe Cocker, Luba, Bryan Ferry, Dalbello, Devo,
  Stewart Copeland.

NINE HOURS TO RAMA
Soundtrack (1963) • London (M) M-76002 250-300   63
  Covers printed in US., discs made in England.
  Composer: Malcolm Arnold. Conductor: Malcolm Arnold.

9-30-55
Soundtrack (1977) • MCA (S) 2313 15-20   77
  Includes background music from *Rebel Without a Cause* and *East of Eden*, both scored
  by Rosenman.
  Composer: Leonard Rosenman, others. Conductor: Leonard Rosenman. Cast: Richard
  Thomas (narration), Webb Pierce, Kitty Wells (with dialogue relating to James Dean).

NINE TO FIVE
Soundtrack (1980) • 20th Century-Fox (S) T-627 8-10   80
  Composer: Dolly Parton, Charles Fox. Conductor: Charles Fox. Cast: Dolly Parton.

1900
Soundtrack (1976) • RCA Victor (S) TBL1-1221 12-15   76
  Composer: Ennio Morricone. Cast: Ennio Morricone.

1984 (FOR THE LOVE OF BIG BROTHER)
Soundtrack (1984) • RCA Victor (S) ABL1-5349 12-15   84
> **Composer:** Annie Lennox, David A. Stewart. **Cast:** Eurythmics.

1941
Soundtrack (1979) • Arista (S) AL-9510 12-15   79
> **Composer:** John Williams, Harold R. Atteridge, Harry Carroll. **Conductor:** John Williams, others. **Cast:** Louis Bellson, Abe Most.

1984 (FOR THE LOVE OF BIG BROTHER)
Soundtrack (1984) • RCA Victor (S) ABL1-5349 12-15   84
> **Composer:** Annie Lennox, David A. Stewart. **Cast:** Eurythmics.

1963: THE YEAR'S MOST POPULAR THEMES
Studiotrack (1963) • Command (S) RS-854-SD 10-12   63
> **Cast:** Enoch Light Orchestra.

1963's MAJOR MOTION PICTURE AND TV THEMES
Studiotrack (1963) • 20th Century-Fox (M) TFM-3105 10-12   63
Studiotrack (1963) • 20th Century-Fox (S) TFS-4105 10-12   63
> Full title: *Silver Screen '63, Magic Screen '63: 1963's Major Motion Picture and TV Themes.* Includes: *Irma La Douce, Cleopatra, The V.I.P.'s, Papa's Delicate Condition, It's a Mad, Mad, Mad, Mad World, Phil Silvers' Show, The Lieutenant, Breaking Point, Mr. Novak, Dick Van Dyke Show, Bill Dana Show* and others. **Composer:** Various. **Conductor:** Lionel Newman. **Cast:** Lionel Newman and His Orchestra & Chorus.

1969
Soundtrack (1988) • Polydor (S) 837362-1 8-10   88
> **Cast:** Jimi Hendrix, Cream, Animals, Creedence Clearwater Revival, Canned Heat, Zombies, Jesse Colin Young, Blind Faith, Moody Blues, Crosby, Nash and Young, Pretenders.

NO EXIT
Studio Cast • Caedmon (S) TRS 337 10-15   67

NO FOR AN ANSWER
Original Cast (1941) • Theme (M) TALP-103 500-525   51
> Reissue of Musicraft 78 rpm recordings.

Original Cast (1941) • JJA (M) 19772 15-20   77
> Includes demo version of *Juno*, sung and played by Marc Blitzstein.

Original Cast (1941) • AEI (M) AEI-1140 8-10   82
> **Composer:** Marc Blitzstein. **Cast:** Carol Channing, Olive Deering, Lloyd Gough, Marc Blitzstein (piano).

NO GO
Soundtrack (1976) • Island (S) SMAS-9333 10-15   76

NO HARD FEELINGS
Original Cast • Hasty Pudding Theatricals of Harvard (M) HPT-117 10-15
> **Composer:** Tod Cobey, Mike Tschudin, Timothy Mayer.

NO MAN CAN TAME ME
TV Soundtrack (1959) • Empire (M) EBC-59748 100-125   59
> Single-sided disc.
> **Composer:** Jay Livingston, Ray Evans. **Cast:** Gisele MacKenzie, John Raitt.
> Also see FOUR TELEVISION MUSICALS

NO MAN'S LAND
Soundtrack (1987) • Varese Sarabande (S) STV 81352 10-15   87
> **Composer:** Basil Poledouris.

NO MERCY
Soundtrack (1987) • TVT (S) 3002 10-15   87
> **Composer:** Alan Silvestri.

NO NO NANETTE

Original Revival Cast (1971) • Columbia (S) S-30563 8-10   71
From the 1971 Broadway revival. Gatefold cover with insert. Purple covers are worth more than pink covers.

Original Revival Cast (1971) • Columbia (Q) SQ-30563 10-15   71

Original Revival Cast (1971) • Columbia (S) AS-2-1023 30-35   71
Full title: *Backstage at No No Nanette.* Lee Jordan interviews members of the cast. Also has excerpts from the Columbia cast recording.
Composer: Vincent Youmans, Otto Harbach, Irving Caesar. **Conductor:** Buster Davis. **Cast:** Ruby Keeler, Jack Gilford, Bobby Van, Helen Gallagher, Susan Watson, Patsy Kelly, Roger Rathburn.

Original London Cast • Stanyan (M) SR-10035 12-15   72
One side has music from *Sunny.*
Composer: Vincent Youmans, Otto Harbach, Irving Caesar. **Conductor:** Percival Mackey. **Cast:** Binnie Hale, Seymour Beard, Joseph Coyne, George Grossmith, Irene Brown, Zoe Ackerman, K.C. Townsend, Pat Lysinger.

Original London Revival Cast (1973) • CBS (S) 70126 65-85   73
UK release. Gatefold cover.
Composer: Vincent Youmans, Otto Harbach, Irving Caesar. **Conductor:** Buster Davis. **Cast:** Anna Neagle, Anne Rogers, Thora Hird, Teddy Green, Tony Britton, Barbara Brown, Peter Gale, Jenny Wren, Elaine Howard, Anita Graham.

Studio Cast (1958) • Epic (M) LM-3512 25-30   58

Studio Cast (1958) • Epic (M) LN-3512 10-15   Re
One side has music from *Show Boat.*
Conductor: Johnny Gregory. **Cast:** Bruce Trent, Doreen Hume.

Studio Cast (1971) • RCA Victor (S) LSP-4504 10-12   71

Studio Cast (1971) • United Artists (S) UAS-6806 10-12   71
Composer: Vincent Youmans, Otto Harbach, Irving Caesar. **Conductor:** Leroy Holmes. **Cast:** Leroy Holmes Singers and Orchestra.

Studio Cast • Ranwood (S) R 8087 8-10
Cast: Lawrence Welk, Lawrence Welk Singers.

London Studio Cast • Saga (S) 811 15-20
Composer: Vincent Youmans, Otto Harbach, Irving Caesar. **Conductor:** Ray Cook. **Cast:** Mary Preston, John Parker, John Dane, Barry Monroe.

Studiotrack (1950) • Columbia (EP) B-215 15-20   50

Studiotrack (1950) • Columbia (M) CL-6149 35-45   50
10-inch LP. Actual title: *Tea for Two,* a 1950 film version of *No, No, Nanette.*

Studiotrack (1950) • Columbia Collectors Series (S) 17660 8-10
Also has music from *On Moonlight Bay.*
Composer: Vincent Youmans, Otto Harbach, Irving Caesar, others. **Conductor:** Axel Stordahl. **Cast:** Doris Day, Gene Nelson, Ken Lane Singers, Page Cavanaugh Trio.

NO SAD SONGS FOR ME

Soundtrack (1950) • Web (M) ST-108 15-20   82
Also has music from *The Last Angry Man, Full of Life* and *Count Three and Pray,* all composed and conducted by George Duning.
Composer: George Duning. **Conductor:** George Duning.

NO SMALL AFFAIR

Soundtrack (1984) • Atlantic (S) 78-01891 8-10   84
Composer: Rupert Holmes. **Cast:** Fiona, Chrissy Faith, Rupert Holmes, Twisted Sister, Zebra, Paul Delph, Malcolm McLaren and the McLarenettes.

NO STRINGS

Original Cast (1962) • Capitol (M) OC-1695 8-15   62

Original Cast (1962) • Capitol (S) SO-1695 10-25   62
Black label.

Original Cast (1962) • Capitol (S) SO-1695 5-8   62
Red label.
Composer: Richard Rodgers. **Conductor:** Peter Matz. **Cast:** Richard Kiley, Diahann Carroll, Noelle Adam, Bernice Massi, Don Chastain, Mitchell Gregg, Alvin Epstein, Ann Hodges, Polly Rowles.

Original London Cast (1963)• Decca (M) LK-4576 30-35   63
Original London Cast (1963) • Decca (S) SKL-4576 35-45   63
  UK release.
Original London Cast (1963) • Stet (S) DS-15013.................................. 12-18
  Composer: Richard Rodgers. **Conductor:** Johnnie Spence. **Cast:** Art Lund, Beverly Todd, Hy
  Hazell, Ferdy Mayne, David Holliday, Erica Rogers, Geoffrey Hatchings, Marti Stevens.
Studio Cast • Atlantic (M) 1383.. 15-25   62
  Composer: Richard Rodgers. **Cast:** Bobby Short, Chris Connor, Lavern Baker.
Studio Cast • Epic/Columbia Special Products (S) EPSP-630 8-10
  Composer: Richard Rodgers. **Conductor:** Ralph Burns. **Cast:** Ralph Burns and His Orchestra.

NO SUN IN VENICE
Soundtrack (1958) • Atlantic (M) 1284 15-20   58
Soundtrack (1958) • Atlantic (S) SD-1284... 20-25   61
Soundtrack (1958) • London (S) LTZ-K-15140 10-15   61
  Composer: John Lewis. **Conductor:** John Lewis. **Cast:** Modern Jazz Quartet.

NO WAY OUT
Soundtrack (1987) • Varese Sarabande (S) STV 81334....................... 10-15   87
Soundtrack (1987) • That's Entertainment (S) TER-1149...................... 8-10   80s
  UK release.
  Full title: *No Way Out / Year of Living Dangerously.*
  Composer: Maurice Jarre.

NO WAY TO TREAT A LADY
Soundtrack (1968) • Dot (M) DLP-3846 10-12   68
Soundtrack (1968) • Dot (S) DLP-25846.. 12-25   68
  Composer: Stanley Myers. **Conductor:** Stanley Myers. **Cast:** American Breed.

NOBLE HOUSE
Soundtrack • Varese Sarabande (S) STV 81360 10-15   80s
  Composer: Paul Chihara.

NOBODY'S PERFECT
Soundtrack (1989) • Sisapa (S) 75782-1 8-10   89
  Cast: K.C. and the Sunshine Band, Terry Wood, Fee Waybill, Neurotica, Michael Logan, D.B
  Night, Lorraine Devon, Crybabys, Robert Randeles.

NOCTURNA
Soundtrack (1979) • MCA (S) 2-4121 10-15   79
  Two discs.
  Composer: Reid Whitelaw, Norman Bergen. **Cast:** Gloria Gaynor, Vicki Sue Robinson, Jay
  Siegel, Heaven and Hell Orchestra and Chorus, Moment of Truth.

NOEL & GERTIE
Original Cast • RCA Victor (M) LCT-1156 25-45
Original Cast• RCA/EMI (M) CLP-1050 25-35
  UK release. Has different artwork. Noel Coward and Gertrude Lawrence with songs and
  scenes from *Private Lives, Shadow Play, Red Peppers, Conversation Piece* and *Bitter*
  Sweet.
  Composer: Noel Coward. **Cast:** Noel Coward, Gertrude Lawrence, Yvonne Printemps.

NOEL COWARD ALBUM
Original Cast • Columbia MG (M) 30088... 10-15
  Two discs. Repackage of two albums: *The Las Vegas Album* and *The New York Album.*
  Composer: Noel Coward. **Cast:** Noel Coward.

NOEL COWARD: THE LAS VEGAS ALBUM
Original Cast • Columbia (M) ML-5063 10-15
  Composer: Noel Coward. **Cast:** Noel Coward.

NOEL COWARD: THE NEW YORK ALBUM
Original Cast • Columbia (M) ML-5163 10-15
  Composer: Noel Coward. **Cast:** Noel Coward.

NORTH AND SOUTH
Soundtrack (1985) • Varese Sarabande (S) 704 310............................ 12-18   86
> One side has music from *The Right Stuff*. Full title: *North and South – The Right Stuff*.
> **Composer:** Bill Conti. **Conductor:** Bill Conti. **Cast:** London Symphony Orchestra.

NORTH BY NORTHWEST
Studiotrack (1980) • Varese Sarabande (S) SV-95001 12-18   80
> **Composer:** Bernard Herrmann. **Conductor:** Laurie Johnson.

NORTH OF HOLLYWOOD
Studiotrack (1958) • RCA Victor (M) LPM-1445 20-35   58
Studiotrack (1958) • RCA Victor (S) LSP-1445 50-75   58
> Alex North themes from *American Road, Streetcar Named Desire* and others.
> **Composer:** Alex North. **Conductor:** Alex North.

NORTHWEST OUTPOST
Soundtrack (1947) • Columbia (M) MM-690.. 20-25
> Three discs.
> **Composer:** Rudolf Friml. **Conductor:** Robert Armbruster. **Cast:** Nelson Eddy.

NORWOOD
Soundtrack (1970) • Capitol (S) SW-475 10-15   70
> **Composer:** Al Delory, Mac Davis, Mitchell Torok, Ramona Reed. **Cast:** Glen Campbell.

NOSTALGIA TRIP TO THE STARS 1920-1950
Studiotrack [Vol. 1] • Monmouth-Evergreen (SE) MES/7030................. 10-15
Studiotrack [Vol. 2] • Monmouth-Evergreen (SE) MES/7031................. 10-15

NOSTALGIC RECORDINGS OF MUSIC: see JEANETTE MACDONALD AND NELSON EDDY

NOT SO LONG AGO
TV Soundtrack (1960) • RCA Victor (M) LOC-1055 12-15   60
TV Soundtrack (1960) • RCA Victor (S) LSO-1055 20-25   60
> From the NBC-TV documentary *Project Twenty*.
> **Composer:** Robert Russell Bennett. **Conductor:** Robert Russell Bennett. **Cast:** Bob Hope
> (narrator), Harry S Truman, Dwight D. Eisenhower, Winston Churchill, Babe Ruth, others.

NOT WITH *MY* WIFE, YOU DON'T
Soundtrack (1966) • Warner Bros. (M) W-1668.................................... 12-15   66
Soundtrack (1966) • Warner Bros. (S) WS-1668 18-20   66
> **Composer:** Johnny Williams. **Conductor:** Johnny Williams.

NOTHING BUT A MAN
Soundtrack (1964) • Motown (M) MT-630 12-15   65
Soundtrack (1964) • Motown (S) S-630 15-20   65
> **Cast:** Smokey Robinson and the Miracles, Little Stevie Wonder, Mary Wells, Martha Reeves
> and the Vandellas.

NOTHING BUT THE BEST
Soundtrack (1964) • Colpix (M) CP-477... 12-15   64
Soundtrack (1964) • Colpix (S) SCP-477 18-20   64
> **Composer:** Ron Grainer. **Conductor:** Ron Grainer. **Cast:** Millicent Martin, Eagles.

NOTHING IN COMMON
Soundtrack (1986) • Arista (S) AL9-8438.. 8-10   86
> **Composer:** Patrick Leonard. **Conductor:** Pat Leonard. **Cast:** Thompson Twins, Carly Simon,
> Christopher Cross, Richard Marx, Aretha Franklin, Cruzados, Real to Reel, Pat Leonard.

NOTORIOUS: see MUSIC FROM HITCHCOCK FILMS

NOW IS THE TIME FOR ALL GOOD MEN
Original Cast (1967) • Columbia (M) OL-6730 10-12   67
Original Cast (1967) • Columbia (S) OS-3130 12-18   67
    Composer: Nancy Ford, Gretchen Cryer. **Conductor:** Stephen Lawrence. **Cast:** Sally Niven, Judy Frank, David Cryer, Donna Curtis, David Sabin, Art Wallace, Anne Kaye, Murray Olson, Steve Skiles, John Bennett Perry.

NOW VOYAGER: THE CLASSIC FILM SCORES OF MAX STEINER
Studiotrack • RCA Victor (S) ARL-1-0136 15-20   73
    Music from *Now Voyager, King Kong, The Big Sleep, The Charge of the Light Brigade, The Fountainhead, Four Wives, Since You Went Away, Saratoga Trunk, The Informer* and *Johnny Belinda*.
    Composer: Max Steiner. **Conductor:** Charles Gerhardt.
    Also see MUSIC BY MAX STEINER

NOW YOU SEE HIM, NOW YOU DON'T
Soundtrack (1972) • Disneyland DIS 72-1 20-25   72
    "Complete Radio Campaign" LP with radio spots, interviews, excerpt quotes and open-end interview. Issued in custom cover. Promotional issue only.
    Cast: Kurt Russell, Dick Strout, Joe Flynn, Jim Backus, others.

NOWHERE TO HIDE
Soundtrack (1987) • Varese Sarabande (S) STV-81336 12-15   87
    Composer: Brad Fiedel.

NUN'S STORY
Soundtrack (1959) • Warner Bros. (M) B-1306 50-60   59
Soundtrack (1959) • Warner Bros. (S) WS-1306 100-110   59
Soundtrack (1959) • Stanyan (Q) SRQ-4022 10-15   Re
    Composer: Franz Waxman. **Conductor:** Franz Waxman. **Cast:** Dame Edith Evans, Dame Peggy Ashcroft (dialogue).

NUNSENSE
Original Cast (1986) • DRG (S) SBL-12589 10-15   86
    Composer: Dan Goggin. **Cast:** Christine Anderson, Semina DeLaurentis, Marilyn Farina, Edwina Lewis, Suzi Winson.
Original London Cast (1987) •That's Entertainment (S) TER-1132 10-12   87
    UK release.
    Composer: Dan Goggin. **Cast:** Honor Blackman, Anna Sharkey, Pip Hinton, Louise Gold, Bronwen Stanway.

NUNZIO
Soundtrack (1978) • MCA (S) 2374 10-12   78
    Composer: Lalo Schifrin. **Conductor:** Lalo Schifrin.

NUTCRACKER
Soundtrack (1966) • Vanguard (S) 168SD 10-15   66
    Two discs.
Soundtrack (1986) • Telarc (S) DG-10137 15-20   86
    Two discs.
    Composer: Pyotr Ilyich Tchaikovsky. **Conductor:** Charles Mackerras.

NUTS
Soundtrack (1987) • Columbia (S) AC-40876 8-10   87
    Composer: Barbra Streisand. **Conductor:** Jeremy Lubbock. **Cast:** Barbra Streisand.

NYMPH ERRANT
Original Cast (1933) • RCA Victor (M) LRT-7001 30-35   54
    10-inch LP. One side has music from *Lady in the Dark*.
    Composer: Cole Porter. **Cast:** Gertrude Lawrence.

O

O BABYLON
Studio Cast (1976) • Kilmarnock (S) KIL 72030 15-20   84
Composer: Galt MacDermot, Derek Wolcott. **Cast:** Carl Hall, David Johnson, Sheila Gibbs, Mel Novik.

O LUCKY MAN
Soundtrack (1973) • Warner Bros. (S) BDS-2710 8-15   73
Composer: Alan Price. **Conductor:** Alan Price. **Cast:** Alan Price, Colin Green, Dave Markee, Clive Thacker.

O MARRY ME
Original Cast (1961) • Blue Pear (M) 1016 10-20
Composer: Robert Kessler, Lola Pergament. **Cast:** Joe Silver, Elly Stone, Chevi Colton, Murial Greenspan.

O SAY CAN YOU SEE!
Original Cast (1962) • No Label Used (M) XTV 87195/-6 75-100   62
Red cover. Original production ran from October 8 to November 4, 1962, at New York's Provincetown Playhouse. The cast recorded the show at Columbia Studios on November 8, 1962. About 75 private nameless label copies made. Published by Sunbeam.
Composer: Jack Holmes, Bill Conklin, Bob Miller. **Conductor:** Jack Holmes. **Cast:** Elmarie Wendel, Paul B. Price, Jan Chaney, Nicolas Coster, Joel Warfield, Joyce Kerry, Thomas Gaines, Richard Nelson.

O'BRIEN, PAT: see PAT O'BRIEN

OBA KOSA (THE KING DID NOT HANG)
Original Cast (1975) • Kaleidophone (S) KS-2201 15-20   75
Composer: Duro Ladipo. **Cast:** Duro Ladipo National Theatre.

OBSCURED BY CLOUDS
Soundtrack (1972) • Harvest (S) ST-11078 10-15   72
From the film *The Valley*.
Composer: Roger Waters, Pink Floyd. **Cast:** Pink Floyd.

OBSESSION
Soundtrack (1976) • London/Phase 4 (S) SPC-21160 10-30   76
Composer: Bernard Herrmann. **Conductor:** Bernard Herrmann. **Cast:** National Philharmonic Orchestra.

OCTOPUSSY
Soundtrack (1983) • A&M (S) SP-4967 15-20   83
Composer: John Barry. **Conductor:** John Barry. **Cast:** Rita Coolidge.

ODD COUPLE
Soundtrack (1968) • Dot (S) DLP-25862 10-12   68
Composer: Neal Hefti. **Conductor:** Neal Hefti. **Cast:** Jack Lemmon, Walter Matthau. (With dialogue.)

TV Soundtrack (1973) • London Phase 4 (S) XPS-903 25-50   73
Music and dialogue.
Composer: Richard Rodgers, Cole Porter, Irving Berlin, Frank Loesser, Burton Lane, Carly Simon, others. **Conductor:** Roland Shaw. **Cast:** Jack Klugman, Tony Randall, London Festival Orchestra & Chorus.

ODDS AGAINST TOMORROW
Soundtrack (1959) • United Artists (M) UAL-4061 20-30   59
Soundtrack (1959) • United Artists (S) UAS-5061 40-50   59
Composer: John Lewis. **Conductor:** John Lewis.

Studiotrack (1959) • United Artists (M) UAL-4063 10-12   59
Studiotrack (1959) • United Artists (S) UAS-5063 12-15   59
  Jazz interpretations of film music.
    Composer: John Lewis. **Conductor:** John Lewis. **Cast:** Modern Jazz Quartet.
    Also see I WANT TO LIVE
    Also see JOHNNY COOL

ODE TO BILLY JOE
Soundtrack (1976) • Warner Bros. (S) BS-2947 12-15   76
Soundtrack (1976) • Warner Bros. (S) No Number Used 20-30   76
  Single-sided. Full title: *Special Radio Salute to Bobbie Gentry and Ode to Billy Joe.*
  Promotional issue only.
    Composer: Bobbie Gentry, Michel Legrand, others. **Conductor:** Michel Legrand. **Cast:** Bobbie
    Gentry.

ODESSA FILE
Soundtrack (1974) • MCA (S) 2084 8-10   74
    Composer: Andrew Lloyd Webber, others. **Conductor:** Anthony Bowles, Alan Doggett, Adolf
    Stahuber. **Cast:** Perry Como.

OF HUMAN BONDAGE
Soundtrack (1964) • MGM (M) E-4261 15-20   64
Soundtrack (1964) • MGM (S) SE-4261 20-30   64
Also has music from *The Bad and the Beautiful, Ziegfeld Girl, Valentino, Cat on a Hot Tin
Roof and Love is a Many-Splendored Thing.*
    Composer: David Raksin, Ron Goodwin, others. **Conductor:** Ron Goodwin, David Rose.
    Also see DAVID RAKSIN CONDUCTS HIS GREAT FILM SCORES

OF LOVE AND DESIRE
Soundtrack (1963) • 20th Century-Fox (M) FXG-5014 18-20   63
Soundtrack (1963) • 20th Century-Fox (S) SXG-5014 20-25   63
    Composer: Ronald Stein. **Conductor:** Ronald Stein. **Cast:** Sammy Davis Jr.

OF MICE AND MEN
Soundtrack (1939) • Mark 56 (M) 606 8-30   75
  Two discs. Contains entire film.
    Composer: Aaron Copland.

OF THEE I SING
Original Revival Cast (1952) • Capitol FDR-350 35-45   52
  Boxed, 78 rpm set.
Original Revival Cast (1952) • Capitol (EP) EDM-350 20-25   52
Original Revival Cast (1952) • Capitol (M) S-350 100-125   52
Original Revival Cast (1952) • Capitol (M) T-11651 8-10   77
    Composer: George Gershwin, Ira Gershwin. **Conductor:** Maurice Levine. **Cast:** Jack Carson,
    Paul Hartman, Jack Whiting, Lenore Lonegran, Betty Oakes, Florenz Ames, J. Pat O'Malley.
TV Soundtrack (1972) • Columbia (S) S-31763 12-18   72
TV Soundtrack (1972) • Columbia (S) S-31763 20-25   72
  Special promotional edition issued by AMF, the show's sponsor.
    Composer: George Gershwin, Ira Gershwin. **Conductor:** Peter Matz. **Cast:** Carroll O'Connor,
    Jack Gilford, Cloris Leachman, Michele Lee, Garrett Lewis.
Concert Cast (1987) • CBS (S) S2M 42522 8-12   87
  Two discs. Includes insert. Second LP is *Let 'Em Eat Cake.*
    Conductor: George Gershwin, Ira Gershwin. Michael Tilson Thomas. **Cast:** Maureen
    McGovern, Larry Kert, Jack Gilford, Paige O'Hara, David Garrison, Orchestra of St. Lukes.

OFF LIMITS
Soundtrack (1988) • Varese Sarabande (S) 704.450 12-15   88
    Composer: James Newton Howard.

OFFICER AND A GENTLEMAN
Soundtrack (1982) • Island (S) PR-491 10-12   82
  12-inch EP.

Soundtrack (1982) • Island (S) 90017-1.. 10-12   82
  Composer: Jack Nitzche, Buffy-Sainte Marie, Will Jennings, Lee Ritenour, others. **Cast:** Joe
  Cocker, Jennifer Warnes, Van Morrison, ZZ Top, Pat Benatar, Sir Douglas Quintet, Dire Straits,
  Lee Ritenour.

OFFICIAL ADVENTURES OF FLASH GORDON
Studiotrack (1966) • Leo the Lion (S) CH-1028...................................... 8-12
  Cast: Buster Crabbe, Ronald Liss, Rita Lloyd, Corinne Orr, George Petrie, Jackson Beck
  (narrator).

OFFICIAL ALBUM OF NBC'S BAT MASTERSON: see BAT MASTERSON

OFFICIAL GRAMMY AWARDS ARCHIVE COLLECTION (STAGE AND ORIGINAL CAST RECORDINGS)
Original Cast • Franklin Mint (S) GRAM-11 75-100   85
  Boxed set of four red vinyl discs. Includes 20-page booklet. Available by mail-order only,
  from the Franklin Mint. Mmusic from *Gypsy, Camelot, Flower Drum Song, The Sound of
  Music, Redhead, Bye Bye Birdie, What Makes Sammy Run, Do I Hear a Waltz, Fiddler on
  the Roof, Half a Sixpence, Apple Tree, Mame, Man of La Mancha, Cabaret, Hallelujah
  Baby, Sweet Charity, Hair, Godspell, Raisin, 1776, Annie, Company, Chorus Line, Ain't
  Misbehavin', Ballroom, Sweeny Todd, I Love My Wife, One Mo' Time,* and more.
  Cast: Ethel Merman, Robert Goulet, Pat Suzuki, Mary Martin, Dick Van Dyke, Steve Lawrence,
  Tommy Steele, Angela Lansbury, Joel Grey, Jack Gilford, Lotte Lenya, Leslie Uggams, Dean
  Jones, Hal Linden, Theodore Bikel, Sally Ann Howes, Paul Lynde, Zero Mostel, Ronnie Dyson,
  Andrea McArdle, Glynis Johns, Ken Page, Nell Carter, Robin Lamont, Clifton Davis, Lynn
  Kellogg, Irving Jacobson, Barbara Harris, Gwen Verdon, Elizabeth Allen, Allen Case, Robert
  Hooks, Charles Braswell, John Miller, others.

OFFICIAL MUSIC OF THE XXIIIRD OLYMPIAD, LOS ANGELES 1984
Soundtrack (1984) • Columbia (S) AS-99 1871 12-15   84
  Promotional only picture disc.
  Cast: Loverboy, Giorgio Moroder, John Williams, Quincy Jones, Bill Conti, Foreigner, Herbie
  Hancock, Philip Glass.
Studiotrack (1984) • Columbia (S) BJS-39322 8-12   84

OH BOY!
Original London Cast (1917) • World (M) SHB-32................................. 20-25
  UK release.
  Composer: Jerome Kern, P.G. Wodehouse. **Cast:** Dot Temple, Tom Powers, Beatrice Lillie,
  Billy Leonard.

OH, BROTHER
Original Cast (1981) • Original Cast (S) OC-8342.............................. 10-15   81
  Composer: Michael Valenti, Donald Driver. **Conductor:** Marvin Laird. **Cast:** Judy Kaye, David-
  James Carroll, Larry Marshall, Harry Groener, Mary Mastrantonio, Joe Morton, Alan Weeks.

OH! CALCUTTA!
Original Cast (1969) • Aidart (S) AID-9903 10-12   69
  Composer: The "Open Window." **Cast:** Peter Schickele, Stanley Walden, Robert Dennis, Boni
  Enten, Katie Drew-Wilkinson, Mark Dempsey, Leon Russom, George Welbes, Alan Rachins,
  Raina Barrett, Nancy Tribush, Margo Sappington.

OH CAPTAIN!
Original Cast (1958) • Columbia (M) OL-5280 8-12   58
Original Cast (1958) • Columbia Special Products (S) AOS-2002........... 8-10   77
  Not issued in stereo until 1977. Abbe Lane, who appeared in the show, did not participate
  in making the cast album, and her songs are by Eileen Rodgers.
  Composer: Jay Livingston, Ray Evans. **Conductor:** Jay Blackton. **Cast:** Jacquelyn McKeever,
  Edward Platt, Susan Johnson, Tony Randall, Eileen Rodgers (performing Abbe Lane's songs
  from the show), Paul Valentine, George Ritner, Bruce MacKay, Louis Polacek, Nolan Van Way.
Studio Cast (1958) • Columbia (M) CL-1167 20-30   58
  Full title: *Hits from "Oh, Captain!"*
  Composer: Jay Livingston, Ray Evans. **Conductor:** Jose Ferrer. **Cast:** Johnny Mathis,
  Rosemary Clooney, Vic Damone, Guy Mitchell, Tony Bennett, Jo Stafford, Stan Freeman,
  Norman Luboff, Jill Corey, Don Cherry.

Studio Cast (1958) • MGM (M) E-3687 12-15   58
   Composer: Jay Livingston, Ray Evans. **Conductor:** Phil Moore. **Cast:** Jose Ferrer (original cast
   producer), Rosemary Clooney, Jud Conlon Singers.
Studio Cast • Columbia (M) CL-1126 10-12
   Cast: Stan Freeman and His Quartet.
Studio Cast • Harmony (M) HL-7097 10-12
   Full title: *Dancing with Oh, Captain!*
   Cast: Bob Prince Quintet.

OH COWARD!
Original Cast (1972) • Bell (S) 9001 12-20   72
   Two discs.
   Composer: Noel Coward. **Conductor:** Rene Weigert. **Cast:** Barbara Carson, Roderick Cook,
   Jamie Ross.

OH DAD, POOR DAD, MAMMA'S HUNG YOU IN THE CLOSET AND I'M FEELIN' SO SAD
Soundtrack (1967) • RCA Victor (M) LPM-3750 15-20   67
Soundtrack (1967) • RCA Victor (S) LSP-3750 20-25   67
   Composer: Neal Hefti. **Conductor:** Neal Hefti.

OH, GOOD GRIEF!
TV Soundtrack • Warner Bros. (S) WS-1747 15-20   68
   Music from various *Peanuts* TV specials.
   Composer: Vince Guaraldi. **Conductor:** Vince Guaraldi.

OH, KAY!
Original London Cast • Monmouth Evergreen (SE) MES-7043 10-15
Original London Cast • Smithsonian (M) R-011 15-18   Re
   Composer: George Gershwin, Ira Gershwin. **Cast:** Gertrude Lawrence, Harold French, Claude
   Hulbert.
Studio Cast (1957) • Columbia (M) OL-1050 15-20   57
Studio Cast (1957) • Columbia (SE) OS-2550 20-25
Studio Cast (1957) • Columbia Special Products (M) ACL-1050 8-10   Re
   Composer: George Gershwin, Ira Gershwin. **Conductor:** Lehman Engel. **Cast:** Barbara Ruick,
   Jack Cassidy, Allen Case, Roger White, Cy Walter (piano), Bernard Leighton (piano).
Original Revival Cast (1960) • 20th Century-Fox (M) FOX-4003 15-25   60
Original Revival Cast (1960) • 20th Century-Fox (S) SFX-4003 35-45   60
Original Revival Cast (1960) • Stet (S) DS-15017 8-12
   Composer: George Gershwin, Ira Gershwin. **Conductor:** Dorothea Freitag. **Cast:** David
   Daniels, Marti Stevens, Bernie West, Dorothea Freitag (piano), Reginald Beane (piano).

OH, ROSALINDA!
Soundtrack (1957) • Mercury (M) MG-20145 40-45   57
   From the English film adaptation of the 1942 Broadway show, based on *Die Fledermaus.*
   Composer: Johann Strauss, Jr. **Cast:** Sir Michael Redgrave, Mel Ferrer, Alexander Young
   (performs vocals for Mel Ferrer in the film), Anthony Quayle, Ludmilla Tcherina, Sari Barabas
   (performs vocals for Ludmilla Tcherina), Anneliese Rothenberger, Dennis Price, Dennis Dowling
   (performs vocals for Dennis Price), Anton Walbrook, Walter Berry (performs vocals for Anton
   Walbrook), Oska Sima. (With dialogue).

OH, WHAT A LOVELY WAR!
Original Cast (1964) • London (M) 5906 10-15   64
Original Cast (1964) • London (S) OS-25906 15-20   64
   Recorded when David Merrick brought the show to New York.
   Composer: Various. **Conductor:** Alfred Ralston. **Cast:** Charles Chilton, Avis Bunnage, Barry
   Bethell, Griffith Davies, Brian Murphy.
Studio Cast • World (M) SH-130 15-20
   UK release.
   Assorted World War I period songs heard in the stage play.
Soundtrack (1969) • Paramount (S) PAS-5008 10-12   69

Soundtrack (1969) • EMI (S) SPFL-251 15-18   69
UK release. Gatefold booklet.
    Composer: Various. **Conductor:** Alfred Ralston. **Cast:** Jean Pierre Cassell, Maggie Smith, Maurice Arthur, Richard Howard, Joanne Brown, Joe Melia, Colin Redgrave, Pia Colombo, Penny Allen.

OH, YOU BEAUTIFUL DOLL
Studiotrack (1950) • RCA Victor (EP) EPA-252 10-15   50
    Cast: Tony Martin, Pied Pipers.

OIL CITY SYMPHONY
Original Cast (1987) • DRG (S) SBL 12524 8-10   86
    Composer: Mike Craven, Mark Hardwich, others. **Cast:** Mike Craven, Mark Hardwich, others.

OIL TOWN, U.S.A.
Soundtrack (1953) • RCA Victor (M) LFM-3000 50-60   53
10-inch LP.
Soundtrack (1953) • ISR (M) 10043 35-40   53
    Composer: Ralph Carmichael. **Conductor:** Ralph Carmichael. **Cast:** Billy Graham, Cindy Walker, Redd Harper.

OKLAHOMA!
Original Cast [Vol. 1] (1943) • Decca DA-359 10-15   43
Six 78 rpms. Makes up the twelve tracks eventually issued on EPs and LPs
    Composer: Richard Rodgers, Oscar Hammerstein II. **Conductor:** Jay Blackton. **Cast:** Alfred Drake, Joan Roberts, Howard Da Silva, Celeste Holm, Lee Dixon.
Original Cast [Vol. 2] (1943) • Decca DA-383 40-45   43
Two 78 rpms. Includes *Lonely Room* – by Alfred Drake, not Howard Da Silva – plus *The Farmer and the Cowman* and *It's a Scandal! It's a Outrage!* These tracks were omitted from the EPs and LPs.
    Composer: Richard Rodgers, Oscar Hammerstein II. **Conductor:** Jay Blackton. **Cast:** Alfred Drake, Betty Garde, Ralph Riggs, Joseph Buloff.
Original Cast (1943) • Decca (EP) EDM 9-6 15-25
Boxed, six-disc set.
Original Cast (1943) • Decca (EP) ED-801 20-25   49
Three discs.
Original Cast (1943) • Decca (M) DL-8000 20-25   49
Black and gold label. Thick plastic discs.
Original Cast (1943) • Decca (M) DL-9017 12-15   55
Red label. Original cover with new number.
Original Cast (1943) • Decca (M) DL-9017 20-25   55
Original Cast (1943) • Decca (SE) DL-79017 12-15   59
Both have red label with new cover art picturing "The Farmer and the Cowman" sequence.
Original Cast (1943) • Decca (M) DL-9017 12-15   68
Original Cast (1943) • Decca (SE) DL-79017 15-18   68
Special 25th anniversary edition, with yellow drawing on cover and picture sleeve with liner notes. Red label.
Original Cast (1943) • MCA (SE) 2030e 8-10   72
    Composer: Richard Rodgers, Oscar Hammerstein II. **Conductor:** Jay Blackton. **Cast:** Alfred Drake, Joan Roberts, Howard Da Silva, Celeste Holm, Lee Dixon.
Original Cast • JJA (M) 19761 20-25   76
Includes the selections omitted from the Decca LP: *Lonley Room, The Farmer and the Cowman* and *It's a Scandal! It's a Outrage!* Also has music from *Main Street to Broadway, Happy Birthday* and *State Fair.*
    Composer: Richard Rodgers, Oscar Hammerstein II. **Conductor:** Jay Blackton. **Cast:** Alfred Drake, Betty Garde, Ralph Riggs, Joseph Buloff. MAIN STREET TO BROADWAY: **Cast:** Mary Martin. STATE FAIR: **Conductor:** Victor Young. **Cast:** Dick Haymes.
Original London Cast (1947) • Stanyan (M) 10069 8-12
Does not include music from *Carousel.*
    Composer: Richard Rodgers, Oscar Hammerstein II. **Conductor:** Reginald Burston. **Cast:** Howard Keel, Betty Jane Watson, Dorthea MacFarland, Walter Donahue, Henry Clarke.

Original Revival Cast (1979) • RCA Victor (S) CBL1-3572 8-10   79
  Conductor: Jay Blackton. **Cast:** Laurence Guittard, Christine Andreas.

Studio Cast (1943) • Decca DA-378 10-12
  Two disc 78 rpm album set.

Studio Cast (1943) • Decca (M) DL-7002 10-12   50
  10-inch LP. Also has music from *Porgy and Bess*.
  Composer: Richard Rodgers, Oscar Hammerstein II. **Conductor:** Alfred Wallenstein. **Cast:** Philharmonic Orchestra of Los Angeles.

Studio Cast (1950) • Decca (M) DL-7002 30-40   50
  10-inch LP. Also has music from *Porgy and Bess*.
  Composer: Richard Rodgers, Oscar Hammerstein II. **Conductor:** Alfred Wallenstein. **Cast:** Philharmonic Orchestra of Los Angeles.

Studio Cast (1951) • Columbia (M) AL-4 10-15   51
  10-inch LP. One side has *Roumanian Fantasy*.
  Conductor: Andre Kostelanetz. **Cast:** Andre Kostelanetz Orchestra.

Studio Cast (1953) • RCA Victor (EP) EPA-474 10-20   53
  Conductor: Al Goodman.

Studio Cast (1956) • Columbia (M) ML-4598 15-18   59
Studio Cast (1956) • Columbia (SE) CS-8739 8-12   59
Studio Cast (1956) • Harmony (M) HL-7364 10-15   66
Studio Cast (1956) • Harmony (SE) HS-11164 10-15   66
  Composer: Richard Rodgers, Oscar Hammerstein II. **Conductor:** Lehman Engel. **Cast:** Nelson Eddy, Virginia Haskins, Kaye Ballard, Portia Nelson, Lee Cass, Wilton Clary.

Studio Cast (1960) • Epic (M) LN-3678 20-25   60
  Composer: Richard Rodgers, Oscar Hammerstein II. **Cast:** Stuart Foster, Lois Hunt, Fay DeWitt.

Studio Cast • Coronet (M) CX-46 10-12
Studio Cast • Coronet (S) CXS-46 10-12
  Cast: Coronet Studio Orchestra, Lee Carol, John Drake, Henry Cassidy, Earnscliffe Chorus.

Studio Cast • Crown (S) CLP 5036 10-12
  Composer: Richard Rodgers, Oscar Hammerstein II. **Cast:** Lloyd Hanna, Irene Cummings, Deeda Patrick, Jack Cassidy, Don Ralke Chorus.

Studio Cast • Fidelio (M) TLA 9083 10-12
  Conductor: Jimmy Warren. **Cast:** Carole Martin, Steve Jackson, New York Revue Orchestra.

Studio Cast • Grand Prix (S) KS-410 10-12
  Cast: Mal Hasset and His Orchestra, Richard Torigi, Edgar Powell, Susan Shaute, Gretchen Rhoads, Paula Wayne.

Studio Cast • International Award (S) AKS-207 10-12
  Cast: Richard Torigi, Edgar Powell, Gretchen Rhoads, Susan Shaute, William Reynolds, Dolores Martin, Dean Franconi and Sound Stage Orchestra.

Studio Cast (1964) • Columbia (M) OL-8010 8-12   64
Studio Cast (1964) • Columbia (S) OS-2610 10-12   64
  Features cast members of the national touring company.
  Composer: Richard Rodgers, Oscar Hammerstein II. **Conductor:** Franz Allers. **Cast:** John Raitt, Florence Henderson, Phyllis Newman, Jack Elliott, Irene Carroll, Leonard Stokes, Ara Berberian.

Studio Cast • Pirouette (S) FM 80 10-12
  Conductor: Al Goodman. **Cast:** Richard Torigi, Edgar Powell, Gretchen Rhoads, Susan Shaute, William Reynolds, Dolores Martin, Al Goodman and His Orchestra.

Studio Cast • Promenade (M) 2062 10-12
  One side has music from *South Pacific*.
  Conductor: Al Goodman. **Cast:** Richard Torigi, Edgar Powell, Gretchen Rhoads, Susan Shaute, William Reynolds, Dolores Martin, Al Goodman and His Orchestra.

Studio Cast • Spin-O-Rama (M) MK-3056 10-12
Studio Cast • Spin-O-Rama (S) S-81 10-12
  Conductor: Al Goodman. **Cast:** Al Goodman & Orchestra, Susan Shaute, Richard Torigi, William Reynolds, Dolores Martin, Paula Wayne.

Soundtrack (1955) • Capitol (EP) FDM 595 15-20   55
  Boxed, four-disc set. Includes four-page booklet.

Soundtrack (1955) • Capitol (EP) FDM-1-595 8-12   55
Soundtrack (1955) • Capitol (EP) FDM-2-595 8-12   55
Soundtrack (1955) • Capitol (EP) FDM-3-595 8-12   55
Soundtrack (1955) • Capitol (EP) FDM-595 8-12   55
Soundtrack (1955) • Capitol (M) WAO-595 20-25   55
   Blue label.
Soundtrack (1955) • Capitol (M) WAO-595 12-15   55
   Dark red label.
Soundtrack (1955) • Capitol (S) SWAO-595 10-15   59
Soundtrack (1955) • Capitol (S) SWAO-595 8-10   59
   Light red, purple or green labels.
Soundtrack (1955) · Capitol (M) LCT-6100 20-25   55
Soundtrack (1955) · Capitol (S) SLCT-6100 20-25   55
   UK releases.
Soundtrack (1955) • Capitol (M) TCL-1790 12-15   62
   Composer: Richard Rodgers, Oscar Hammerstein II. **Conductor:** Jay Blackton. **Cast:** Gordon
   MacRae, Shirley Jones, Gloria Grahame, Gene Nelson, Charlotte Greenwood, James Whitmore,
   Rod Steiger; Jay C. Flippen.
Studiotrack • RCA (M) LM-1884 8-15   55
   One side has suite from *Carousel.*
   Conductor: Morton Gould. **Cast:** Morton Gould and His Orchestra.
Studiotrack (1957) • Halo (M) 50114 8-15   57
   Cast: National Singers & Orchestra.
Studiotrack (1959) • Lion (S) L-70094 8-15   59
Studiotrack (1959) • National Academy Record Club (M) ES 6 10-15   59
   From *Ed Sullivan Presents Songs and Music of...* series.
   Cast: Ed Sullivan All Star Cast.
Studiotrack • Capitol (M) T-596 10-15   50s
   Cast: Nelson Riddle and His Orchestra.
Studiotrack • Royale (M) LP 66 8-15   50s
   10-inch LP.
Studiotrack • Royale (M) VLP 6045 8-15   50s
   Cast: Russell Bennett and His Orchestra.
Studiotrack • Royale (M) 18159 8-15   50s
   10-inch LP. Full title: *Songs from Oklahoma.*
   Cast: Royale Operetta Singers and Orchestra, Royale Salon Orchestra.
Studiotrack • Varsity (M) 69119 8-15   50s
   10-inch LP. Full title: *Songs from Oklahoma.*
   Cast: Varsity Operetta Singers and Orchestra, Varsity Concert Orchestra.
Studiotrack • Waldorf Music Hall (M) MH-33-171 8-15   50s
   10-inch LP. Also has music from *South Pacific.*
   Cast: Enoch Light Orchestra and Chorus, Lois Winter, Loren Becker, Arthur Malvin, Michael
   Stewart, Anita Lawrence.
Studiotrack (1960) • Craftsmen (M) C-8053 8-12   60
   Full title: *Oklahoma / Carousel.* Also has music from *Carousel.*
Studiotrack (1960) • Craftsmen (M) 210 8-12   60
Studiotrack (1973) • RCA APL1-0271 8-10   73
Studiotrack • Broadway (M) P 1014 8-12
   Cast: Warren Dubin Orchestra & Full Stage Chorus.
Studiotrack • Celebrity (S) UTS 118 8-12
   Conductor: Lawrence Nash. **Cast:** Julie Jonas, Tex Howard, Margaret Young.
Studiotrack • Colortone (M) C33-4930 8-12
   Full title: *Oklahoma, The King and I, and Other Great Shows.* Also has music from *Babes
   In Arms, On Your Toes, Roberta* and *Very Warm For May.*
   Cast: Colortone Studio Orchestra and Chorus.
Studiotrack • Crown (S) CST-106 8-12
   Conductor: Hans Hagen.

Studiotrack • Diplomat (M) D-2213.. 8-12
Studiotrack • Diplomat (S) DS-2213.. 8-12
  Cast: Al Goodman's Orchestra.
Studiotrack • Goldentone (M) C-4023 8-12
  One side has music from *South Pacific.*
  Cast: Mayfair Symphonette Orchestra & Singers.
Studiotrack • Harmony (M) HL-7193 8-12
  One side has music from *Carousel.*
  Cast: Dino Martinelli and His Orchestra.
Studiotrack • Wing (M) SRW 12507... 8-12
  Full title: *Oklahoma and Carousel.* Also has music from *Carousel.*
  Conductor: Cecil Wheatridge. **Cast:** Cecil Wheatridge and Orchestra.
Studiotrack • Micro (M) 51... 8-12
  Cast: Cameo All Star Orchestra, Eddie Krawll, Olga Karma, Toontimers, Larry Clinton
  Orchestra.
Studiotrack • Original Cast (S) OC-8129....................................... 8-12
  Celeste Holm gives a personal tribute.
  Cast: Celeste Holm.
Studiotrack • RCA (M) LM 1884 8-12
  Conductor: Morton Gould.
Studiotrack • Somerset (M) P-1700... 8-12
Studiotrack • Somerset (S) 1700... 8-12
  One side has music from *South Pacific.*
  Conductor: D.L. Miller. **Cast:** New World Theatre Orchestra.
  Also see ANNIE GET YOUR GUN
  Also see CAROUSEL
  Also see OSCAR HAMMERSTEIN II MEMORIAL ALBUM
  Also see RODGERS AND HAMMERSTEIN DELUXE SET

OKLAHOMA CRUDE
Soundtrack (1973) • RCA Victor (S) APL1-0271 10-20   73
  Composer: Henry Mancini. **Conductor:** Henry Mancini.

OLD BOYFRIENDS
Soundtrack (1979) • Columbia (S) JS-36072 35-45   79
  Promotional issue given to opening night patrons at a Hollywood theater.
  Conductor: David Shire. **Cast:** John Belushi.

OLD GRINGO
Soundtrack (1989) • GNP Crescendo (S) GNPS-8017........................... 8-10   89
  Composer: Lee Holdridge. **Conductor:** Lee Holdridge.

OLD MAID AND THE THIEF
Studio Cast (1941) • Turnabout (SE) TV-34745................................... 12-15
  Composer: Gian-Carlo Menotti. **Conductor:** Jorge Mester. **Cast:** Judith Blegen, Anna
  Reynolds, John Reardon, Margaret Baker.

OLD MAN AND THE SEA
Soundtrack (1958) • Columbia (M) CL-1183 20-30   58
Soundtrack (1958) • Columbia (S) CS-8013 30-50   58
Soundtrack (1958) • Columbia Special Products (S) ACS-8013................ 5-8   Re
  Composer: Dimitri Tiomkin. **Conductor:** Dimitri Tiomkin.

OLD YELLER
Soundtrack (1957) • Disneyland (M) WDL-3024 30-35   57
Soundtrack (1957) • Disneyland (M) WDL-1024 20-25   60
Soundtrack (1957) • Disneyland (M) DQ-1258..................................... 20-25   64
  One side has *The Legend Of Lobo*
  Composer: Oliver G. Wallace. **Cast:** Fess Parker (narration), Dorothy McGuire, Tommy Kirk,
  Kevin Corcoran. (With dialogue.)

OLDS FOR '60 MUSICAL

TV Soundtrack (1960) • No Label Used (M) 1190/1191 10-20   60
Identification numbers (found in trail-off area) shown since no selection number is used.
Conductor: Sherman Frank. **Cast:** Florence Henderson, Bill Hayes.
Also see GOOD NEWS ABOUT OLDS
Also see THIS IS OLDSMOBILITY

OLIVER!

Original London Cast (1960) • Decca (M) LK-4359 18-20   60
Original London Cast (1960) • Decca (S) SKL-4105 20-25   60
UK release. Opened in London before coming to New York.
Composer: Lionel Bart. **Conductor:** Marcus Dods. **Cast:** Ron Moody, Georgia Brown, Paul
Whitsun-Jones, Danny Sewell, Martin Horsey, Keith Hamshere.
Original Cast (1962) • RCA Victor (M) LOCD-2004 5-8   63
Original Cast (1962) • RCA Victor (S) LSOD-2004 8-10   63
Black labels. Some copies have only David Merrick's bio on the back cover. Others have
bios for both Merrick and Lionel Bart.
Original Cast (1962) • RCA Victor (S) LSOD-2004 5-8   Re
Orange label.
Original Cast (1962) • RCA Victor (S) AYL1-4113 5-8   Re
Composer: Lionel Bart. **Conductor:** Donald Pippin. **Cast:** Clive Revill, Georgia Brown, Bruce
Prochnik, Willoughby Goddard, Hope Jackman, Michael Goodman, Alice Playten, Danny
Sewell.
London Studio Cast (1962) • Capitol (M) T-1784 8-12   62
London Studio Cast (1962) • Capitol (S) ST-1784 12-15   62
Composer: Lionel Bart. **Conductor:** Tony Osborne. **Cast:** Stanley Holloway, Alma Cogan,
Violet Carson, Denis Waterman, Tony Tanner, Leslie Fyson, Charles Granville, Williams
Singers, Tony Osborne and His Orchestra.
Studio Cast (1962) • Golden (M) LP 105 10-15   62
Composer: Lionel Bart. **Conductor:** Jim Timmens. **Cast:** James Kenney, Myra de Groot, Janet
Eden, Gene Lowell, Gene Steck.
Soundtrack (1968) • Colgems (M) COMD-5501 8-12   68
Soundtrack (1968) • Colgems (S) COSD-5501 8-10   68
Front cover says "Best Picture of the Year!" in upper right corner and has a RE print. Both
have Unipak (disc opening faces gutter rather than outer edge) fold-open covers.
Soundtrack (1968) • RCA Victor (S) COSD-5501 8-10   Re
Gatefold cover.
Soundtrack (1968) • RCA Victor (M) RB-6777 12-15   68
UK pressing. Brown stapled gatefold booklet-cover.
Composer: Lionel Bart. **Conductor:** John Green. **Cast:** Ron Moody, Oliver Reed, Mark Lester,
Harry Secombe, Shani Wallis, Peggy Mount, Jack Wild, Sheila White.
Studiotrack • Pickwick (S) SPC-3155 8-10
Composer: Lionel Bart. **Conductor:** Laurie Ringham. **Cast:** Pickwick Children's Chorus and
Orchestra, Ron Marshall.

OLIVER & COMPANY

Soundtrack (1988) • Disneyland (S) 64101 20-25   88
Cast: Huey Lewis, Billy Joel, Ruth Pointer, Bette Midler, Myhann Tran, Ruben Blades.

OLIVER TWIST

Studio Cast • Decca (M) DL-9107 15-20   50s
Soundtrack (1948) • Columbia (M) ML-2092 100-150   50
10-inch LP. Though untitled, has music from film plus *Suicide Squadron* and *Love Story*.
Composer: Arnold Bax. **Conductor:** Muir Mathieson.
Studiotrack (1963) • Harmony (M) HL-9558 10-12   63
Also has *The Three Musketeers.*
Studiotrack • Columbia Special Products (S) P-13902 8-10   Re
Conductor: Ralph Rose. THREE MUSKETEERS: Carmen Dragon. **Cast:** Basil Rathbone
(narrator). THREE MUSKETEERS: Errol Flynn (narrator).
Also see BERNARD HERRMANN CONDUCTS GREAT BRITISH FILM SCORES
Also see SUICIDE SQUADRON

OLIVER'S STORY
Soundtrack (1978) • ABC (S) AA-1117 10-15   78
Includes Francis Lai's *Love Story* theme.
   Conductor: Lee Holdridge.

OLYMPIC ELK: see WALT DISNEY'S TRUE LIFE ADVENTURE

OLYMPUS ON MY MIND
Original Cast (1986) • That's Entertainment (S) TER-1131 10-15   87
Also known as *The Boy Who Could Fly.*
   Cast: Joyce DeWitt, Martin Vidnovic, Susan Powell, Nancy Johnson, others.
Also see BOY WHO COULD FLY

OLYMPUS 7-0000
TV Soundtrack (1966) • Command (M) CS-33-07 8-12   66
TV Soundtrack (1966) • Command (S) CS-07-SD 10-12   66
   Composer: Richard Adler. **Conductor:** Philip Della Penna. **Cast:** Donald O'Conner, Phyllis
   Newman, Eddie Foy Jr., Larry Blyden.

OMAR KHAYYAM
Soundtrack (1957) • Decca (M) DL-8449 40-45   57
Black label or pink label promo. Also has music from *The Mountain.*
Soundtrack (1957) • Decca (M) DL-8449 20-25
Rainbow (or multi-color) label. Also has music from *The Mountain.*
   THE MOUNTAIN: **Composer:** Daniele Amfitheatrof. **Conductor:** Daniele Amfitheatrof.

OMEN (AND OTHER THEMES)
Soundtrack (1976) • Tattoo (S) BJL1-1888 10-15   76
Subtitle: *50 Years of Classic Horror Film Music.*
   Composer: Jerry Goldsmith. **Conductor:** Lionel Newman.

ON A CLEAR DAY YOU CAN SEE FOREVER
Original Cast (1965) • RCA Victor (M) LOCD-2006 8-10   65
Original Cast (1965) • RCA Victor (S) LSOD-2006 8-12   65
Both include a souvenir theater program.
   Composer: Burton Lane, Alan Jay Lerner. **Conductor:** Theodore Saidenberg. **Cast:** Barbara
   Harris, John Cullum, Titos Vandis, Byron Webster, William Reilly, William Daniels, Clifford
   David, Barbara Monte, Gerald M. Teijelo.
Soundtrack (1970) • Columbia (S) S-30086 8-12   70
Unipak (disc opening faces gutter rather than outer edge) fold-open cover.
Soundtrack (1970) • Columbia Special Products (S) AS-30086 8-10   Re
Gatefold cover. Earlier copies have blue spine, later ones have white.
   Composer: Burton Lane, Alan Jay Lerner. **Conductor:** Nelson Riddle. **Cast:** Barbra Streisand,
   Yves Montand, Bob Newhart, Larry Blyden, Jack Nicholson.

ON A NOTE OF TRIUMPH
Original Radio Cast (1945) • Columbia MM-575 60-75   40s
12-inch 78 rpms. Broadcast as "V.E. Day"commemorative.
Original Radio Cast (1945) • Mark '56 (M) 704 20-25   75
   Composer: Bernard Herrmann. **Conductor:** Lud Gluskin. **Cast:** Martin Gabel (narration).

ON ANY SUNDAY
Soundtrack (1971) • Bell (S) 1206 12-18   71
   Composer: Dominic Frontiere. **Conductor:** Dominic Frontiere.

ON BROADWAY
TV Soundtrack (1969) • Motown (S) MS-699 8-10   69
TV Soundtrack (1969) • Motown (S) S-699 8-10   69
Full title: *On Broadway with the Supremes and the Temptations.*
   Conductor: H.B. Barnum. **Cast:** Diana Ross and the Supremes, Temptations.

ON GOLDEN POND
Soundtrack (1981) • MCA (S) 6106 10-15   82

Soundtrack (1981) • MCA (S) 1497.. 8-10   80s
    Composer: Dave Grusin. **Conductor:** Dave Grusin. **Cast:** Henry Fonda, Katharine Hepburn, Dabney Coleman, Jane Fonda, Doug McKeon. (With dialogue).

ON HER BED OF ROSES
Soundtrack (1966) • Mira (M) LP-3006 12-15   66
Soundtrack (1966) • Mira (S) LPS-3006................................. 15-18   66
    Composer: Joseph Green. **Conductor:** Joseph Green.

ON HER MAJESTY'S SECRET SERVICE
Soundtrack (1969) • United Artists (S) UAS-5204 12-18   69
Soundtrack (1969) • United Artists (S) UA-LA299-G 8-10   Re
Includes Monty Norman's *James Bond Theme.*
    Composer: John Barry. **Conductor:** John Barry. **Cast:** Louis Armstrong, Nina.

ON MOONLIGHT BAY
Soundtrack (1951) • Caliban (M) 6006 8-10
Also has music from *Three Smart Girls* and *It Happened in Brooklyn.*
    Composer: Various. **Conductor:** Ray Heindorf. **Cast:** ON MOONLIGHT BAY: Doris Day, Gordon MacRae. THREE SMART GIRLS: Deanna Durbin. IT HAPPENED IN BROOKLYN: Frank Sinatra, Jimmy Durante.
Studiotrack (1951) • Columbia (EP) B-267............................. 10-25   51
    Two discs.
Studiotrack (1951) • Columbia (M) CL-6186 35-45   51
    10-inch LP.
    Conductor: Paul Weston, Norman Luboff. **Cast:** Doris Day, Paul Weston and His Orchestra, Norman Luboff Choir, Jack Smith.
Studiotrack (1951) • Coral (M) CRL-56043 15-20   52
    10-inch LP.
    Cast: Lawrence Welk Orchestra, Roberta Linn, Dick Dale, Garth Andrews, Sparklers, Gene Pursell.
    Also see TEA FOR TWO

ON THE AVENUE
Soundtrack (1937) • Hollywood Soundstage (M) HS-401 8-10
    Composer: Irving Berlin. **Cast:** Dick Powell, Alice Faye, Ritz Brothers.

ON THE BEACH
Soundtrack (1959) • Roulette (M) R-25098 50-75   59
Soundtrack (1959) • Roulette (S) SR-25098 100-150   59
    Composer: Ernest Gold. **Conductor:** Ernest Gold.
Studiotrack (1959) • United Artists (M) UAL-3061 20-25   59
Studiotrack (1959) • United Artists (S) UAS-6061 30-35   59
    Also has music from *The Vikings, The Horse Soldiers, I Want to Live, The Wonderful Country, The Naked Maja* and *The Big Country.*
    Composer: Ernest Gold, others. **Conductor:** Mitchell Powell. **Cast:** Hollywood Studio Symphony Orchestra.
Studiotrack • London (M) LL 3138....................................... 15-20
Studiotrack • London (S) PS-203 15-20
    Cast: Frank Chacksfield and Orchestra.

ON THE BRIGHTER SIDE
Original London Cast (1963) • London (M) 5767.................... 50-60   63
    Conductor: Colin Beaton. **Cast:** Pip Hinton, Stanley Baxter, Betty Marsden, Ronnie Barker, David Kernan, Bob Stevenson, Judy Carne, Alan Barnes, Victor Duret.

ON THE FLIP SIDE
TV Soundtrack (1966) • Decca (M) DL-4836......................... 15-20   66
TV Soundtrack (1966) • Decca (S) DL-74836 20-25   66
    Composer: Hal David, Burt Bacharach. **Conductor:** Peter Matz. **Cast:** Rick Nelson, Joanie Sommers, Dona Jean Young.

ON THE RECORD - EVENTS OF 1977
Studio Cast (1978) • Caedmon (M) TC-1572 15-20   78
  News highlights of 1977 as compiled by United Press International. Includes segments on
  the deaths of Elvis Presley, Bing Crosby, Groucho Marx, Charlie Chaplin, and Guy
  Lombardo.

ON THE TOWN
Original Cast (1944) • Decca A-416 25-35   46
  78 rpm album. Includes booklet.
Original Cast (1944) • RCA Victor DM-995 35-45   44
  78 rpm album. No bookler.
Original Cast (1944) • Camden (M) CAL-196 20-25   54
  LP issue of DM-995. Above two have the ballet music from the show, performed by the
  original Adelphi Theater orchestra.
  Conductor: Leonard Bernstein.
Studio Cast (1961) • Columbia (M) OL-5540 20-25   61
Studio Cast (1961) • Columbia (S) OS-2028 30-35   61
  Four members of the original cast were re-assembled for this complete recording of the
  score. Above two have insert.
Studio Cast (1961) • Columbia (S) S-31005 12-18   70
Studio Cast (1961) • Columbia Special Products (S) AS-31005 8-10   Re
  Both have new covers and one song, *Carnegie Hall*, not heard on original releases.
  Composer: Leonard Bernstein, Betty Comden, Adolph Green. **Conductor:** Leonard Bernstein.
  Cast: Nancy Walker, Betty Comden, Adolph Green, Cris Alexander, John Reardon.
Original London Cast (1963) • CBS (S) 60005 65-85   63
  UK release.
  Composer: Leonard Bernstein, Betty Comden, Adolph Green. **Conductor:** Lawrence Leonard.
  Cast: Elliott Gould, Carol Arthur, Don McKay, Franklin Kiser, Andrea Jaffe, Gillian Lewis,
  Elspeth March, Rosamund Greenwood, John Humphry, Tommy Merrifield, Sylvia Ellis.
London Studio Cast • Stet (S) DS-15029 8-12
  Composer: Leonard Bernstein, Betty Comden, Adolph Green. **Conductor:** Leonard Bernstein.
  Cast: Fred Lucas, Noele Gordon, Dennis Lotis, Stella Tanner, Lionel Blair, Williams Singers,
  Shane Rimmer.
Soundtrack (1949) • Show Biz (M) 5603 20-25
  Composer: Leonard Bernstein, Betty Comden, Adolph Green, Roger Edens. **Conductor:**
  Lennie Hayton. **Cast:** Gene Kelly, Frank Sinatra, Ann Miller, Betty Garrett, Jules Munshin.
  Also see COMDEN AND GREEN: SHOW MUSIC AT ITS BEST
  Also see LUTE SONG

ON THE TWELFTH DAY
Soundtrack (1955) • MGM (M) E-3223 35-45   55
  One side has *Beloved Christmas Hymns and Carols*, conducted by Macklin Marrow.
  Composer: Doreen Carwithen. **Conductor:** Muir Mathieson.

ON THE TWENTIETH CENTURY
Original Cast (1978) • Columbia (S) JS-35330 8-12   78
  Composer: Cy Coleman, Betty Comden, Adolph Green. **Cast:** Madeline Kahn, Imogene Coca,
  John Cullum.

ON THE WATERFRONT: see EDDY DUCHIN STORY

ON YOUR TOES
Original London Cast (1936) • Monmouth Evergreen (SE) MES-7049 8-10
  Cast: Jack Whiting.
Studio Cast (1953) • Columbia (M) ML-4645 18-20   53
Studio Cast (1953) • Columbia (M) CL-837 12-18   56
Studio Cast (1953) • Columbia (M) OL-7090 10-12   Re
Studio Cast (1953) • Columbia (SE) OS-2590 8-12   Re
Studio Cast (1953) • Columbia Special Products (SE) AOS-2590 8-10   Re
  Composer: Richard Rodgers, Lorenz Hart. **Conductor:** Lehman Engel. **Cast:** Portia Nelson,
  Jack Cassidy, Laurel Shelby, Ray Hyson, Robert Eckles, Zamah Cunningham.
Original Revival Cast (1954) • Decca (EP) ED-903 15-20

Original Revival Cast (1954) • Decca (M) DL-9015 60-65   54
Original Revival Cast (1954) • Stet (M) DS-15024 12-18   Re
  Composer: Richard Rodgers, Lorenz Hart. **Conductor:** Salvatore Dell'Isola. **Cast:** Bobby Van, Elaine Stritch, Ben Astar, Kay Coulter, Joshua Shelley, Jack Williams, Eleanor Williams.
Original Revival Cast (1983) • Polydor (S) 813-667-1 Y-1 8-10   83
  Gatefold cover.
Original Revival Cast (1983) • That's Entertainment (S) TER 1063...... 10-12   80s
  UK release. Two discs. Gatefold cover.
  Composer: Richard Rodgers, Lorenz Hart. **Conductor:** John Mauceri. **Cast:** Natalia Makarova, Dina Merrill, Christine Andreas, Lara Teeter, George S. Irving, George de la Pena.
  Also see SLAUGHTER ON 10TH AVENUE

ONCE A THIEF
Soundtrack (1965) • Verve (M) V-8624 20-25   65
Soundtrack (1965) • Verve (S) V6-8624.. 30-40   65
  Above two have other Lalo Schifrin themes, such as *Joy House* and *The Man from U.N.C.L.E.*
  Composer: Lalo Schifrin. **Conductor:** Lalo Schifrin. **Cast:** Irene Reid.

ONCE BITTEN
Soundtrack (1985) • MCA/Curb (S) 6154 8-10   85
  Some copies have round yellow sticker on cover with artist credits.
  Composer: John Du Prez, others. **Cast:** 3 Speed, Hubert Kah, Real Life, Private Domain, Two of Us, Gifthorse, Maria Vidal, Moses Tyson Jr., Kevin McKnelly.

ONCE UPON A MATTRESS
Original Cast (1959) • Kapp (M) KDL-7004 15-20   59
Original Cast (1959) • Kapp (S) KDL-7004-S 20-25   59
  Both have black covers.
Original Cast (1959) • Kapp (M) KL-4507... 8-10   66
Original Cast (1959) • Kapp (S) KRS-5507 10-12   66
Original Cast (1959) • MCA (S) 2079 5-8   75
Original Cast (1959) • MCA (S) 37097 5-8   81
  All four have red covers.
  Composer: Mary Rodgers, Marshall Barer. **Conductor:** Hal Hastings. **Cast:** Carol Burnett, Joseph Bova, Allen Case, Jack Gilford, Anne Jones, Harry Snow, Robert Weil, Jane White.
Original London Cast (1960) • RCA (M) CLP-1410 35-45
Original London Cast (1960) • Stet (M) DS-15026 12-18
  Composer: Mary Rodgers, Marshall Barer. **Conductor:** Robert Lowe. **Cast:** Jane Connell, Peter Grant, Robin Hunter, Bill Kerr, Patricia Lambert, Bill Newman, Milo O'Shea, Thelma Ruby, Max Wall.

ONCE UPON A TIME IN AMERICA
Soundtrack (1984) • Mercury (S) 818697.. 10-12   84
  Composer: Ennio Morricone. **Conductor:** Ennio Morricone. **Cast:** Gheorghe Zamfir, Edda Dell Orso.

ONCE UPON A TIME IN THE WEST
Soundtrack (1969) • RCA Victor (S) LSP-4736 20-25   72
  Composer: Ennio Morricone. **Conductor:** Ennio Morricone.
Studiotrack • United Artists (S) UAS-6710 10-25
  Also has music from *100 Rifles* and others.
  Composer: Ennio Morricone, Jerry Goldsmith, others. **Cast:** Leroy Holmes and Orchestra.

ONCE UPON A TOUR
TV Soundtrack (1968) • Cozy (S) TV-2000 12-18   68
TV Soundtrack (1968) • Premore (S) PL-2000...................................... 8-12   Re
  Cast: Dora Hall, Phil Harris, Frank Sinatra Jr., Oliver, Rich Little, Roosevelt Grier.

ONE AND ONLY
Soundtrack (1978) • ABC (S) AA-1059 10-12   78
  Composer: Patrick Williams, Alan Bergman, Marilyn Bergman. **Conductor:** Bill Byers, Patrick Williams. **Cast:** Kacey Cisyk.

ONE AND ONLY, GENUINE, ORIGINAL FAMILY BAND

Soundtrack (1968) • Buena Vista (M) BV-5002 8-10   68
Soundtrack (1968) • Buena Vista (S) STER-5002 8-12   68
Soundtrack (1968) • Buena Vista (M) ST-3961 10-15   68
Soundtrack (1968) • Buena Vista (S) STER- 3961 15-20   68
> **Composer:** Richard M. Sherman, Robert B. Sherman. **Conductor:** Jack Elliot. **Cast:** Walter Brennan, Buddy Ebsen, Lesley Ann Warren, John Davidson, Janet Blair, Steve Harmon, Wally Cox, Richard Deacon, John Craig.

ONE-EYED JACKS

Soundtrack (1961) • Liberty (M) LOM-16001 20-25   61
Soundtrack (1961) • Liberty (S) LOS-17001 40-45   61
> **Composer:** Hugo Friedhofer. **Conductor:** Irving Talbot.

ONE FLEW OVER THE CUCKOO'S NEST

Soundtrack (1975) • Fantasy (S) F-9500 15-20   75
Soundtrack (1975) • Fantasy (S) MPF-4531 8-10   Re
> **Composer:** Jack Nitzsche. **Conductor:** Jack Nitzsche.

ONE FROM THE HEART

Soundtrack (1982) • Columbia (S) FC-37703 8-10   82
> **Composer:** Tom Waits. **Cast:** Tom Waits, Crystal Gayle.

ONE HOUR WITH YOU

Soundtrack (1932) • Ariel (M) CMF-23 30-35
Also has music from *Love Me Tonight* and *The Love Parade*.
> **Composer:** Oscar Straus, Richard A. Whiting, Leo Robin. **Conductor:** Nat W. Finston. **Cast:** Maurice Chevalier, Jeanette MacDonald, Genevieve Tobin, Donald Novis, Charles Ruggles.

101 DALMATIANS

Soundtrack (1961) • Disneyland (M) ST-4903 150-175   63
Pop-up edition.
Soundtrack (1961) • Disneyland (M) DQ-1308 15-20   66
> **Composer:** Mel Leven, George Bruns, others.

110 IN THE SHADE

Original Cast (1963) • RCA Victor (M) LOC-1085 15-25   63
Original Cast (1963) • RCA Victor (S) LSO-1085 20-30   63
> **Composer:** Harvey Schmidt, Tom Jones. **Conductor:** Donald Pippin. **Cast:** Robert Horton, Inga Swenson, Stephen Douglass, Will Geer, Steve Roland, Scooter Teague, Lesley Warren, George Church.

ONE MAN In HIS TIME: see AGES OF MAN

ONE MO' TIME

Original Cast (1980) • Warner Bros. (S) HS-3454 8-10   80
> **Composer:** Various. **Conductor:** Orange Kellin. **Cast:** Vernel Bagneris, Topsy Chapman, Thais Clark, Sylvia "Kuumba" Williams, John Stell, Jabbo Smith.

ONE NAKED NIGHT

Soundtrack (1965) • Vega (M) VLP-2002 15-20   65
Soundtrack (1965) • Vega (S) VS-2002 25-30   65
> **Composer:** Chet McIntyre. **Cast:** Chet McIntyre & the Combo.

ONE NIGHT OF LOVE: see MR. IMPERIUM

ONE NIGHT STAND

Original Cast (1980) • Original Cast (S) OC-8134 10-12   80
> **Composer:** Jule Styne, Herb Gardner. **Conductor:** Milton Rosenstock. **Cast:** Jack Weston, Catherine Cox, Jeff Keller, Charles Kimbrough, William Morrison, Paul Binotto.

ONE ON ONE (THE STORY OF A WINNER)

Soundtrack (1977) • Warner Bros. (S) BS-3076 8-10   77
> **Composer:** Charles Fox, Paul Williams. **Conductor:** Charles Fox. **Cast:** Seals and Crofts.

ONE OVER THE EIGHT
Original London Cast (1961) • London (M) 5760................................... 20-30   63
Composer: Lance Mulchay, others. Cast: Kenneth Williams, Sheila Hancock, Toni Eden, Lance Percival, Sheila O'Neill, Lynda Baron, John Howard, Robin Hawdon, Frank Horrox Sextet.

ONE STEP BEYOND
TV Soundtrack (1960) • Decca (M) DL-8970...................... 20-25   60
TV Soundtrack (1960) • Decca (S) DL-78970 30-40   60
TV Soundtrack (1960) • Varese Sarabande (S) STV-81120 8-10   81
Composer: Harry Lubin. Conductor: Harry Lubin.

1001 ARABIAN NIGHTS
Soundtrack (1959) • Colpix (M) CP-410 20-50   59
Soundtrack (1959) • Colpix (S) SCP-410 70-75   59
Soundtrack (1959) • Varese Sarabande (S) STV-81138........................ 8-10   81
Composer: George Duning. Conductor: George Duning. Cast: Jim Backus (as Mr. Magoo), Clark Sisters, Jud Conlon Singers.

$1000 A TOUCHDOWN
Soundtrack (1939) • Paramount Pictures PHS 100.......................... 10-15   39
Single-sided 78 rpm. Released on film as *Never Say Die.*
Cast: Martha Raye, Bob Hope.

ONE TOO MANY (HIT SONGS FROM)
Soundtrack (1951) • Kaybee/Hallmark - No Number Used................... 40-55   51
Album of five 78 rpms.
Composer: Various. Cast: Ruth Warwick, Harmonaires, Nelly Goletti, Ginger Prince.

ONE TOUCH OF VENUS
Original Cast (1943) • Decca A-361 25-35   43
Album of five 78 rpms.
Original Cast (1943) • Decca (M) DL-9122............................. 18-22   65
Original Cast (1943) • Decca (SE) DL-79122............................. 25-30   65
Original Cast (1943) • AEI (SE) AEI-1136............................. 10-12   84
Composer: Kurt Weill, Ogden Nash. Conductor: Maurice Abravanal. Cast: Mary Martin, Kenny Baker.
Studio Cast (1955) • Heritage (M) 0051 100-125   55
Composer: Kurt Weill, Ogden Nash.
Also see KURT WEILL IN HOLLYWOOD

ONE TRICK PONY
Soundtrack (1980) • Warner Bros. (S) XHS-3472...................... 8-10   80
Soundtrack (1980) • Warner Bros. (S) K 56846 8-10   80s
Composer: Paul Simon. Cast: Paul Simon.

ONE, TWO, THREE
Studiotrack (1961) • Musicor/United Artists (M) M-2002........................ 25-30   62
Studiotrack (1961) • Musicor (S) MS-3002............................. 40-45   62
Actual title: *One, Two, Three Waltz.*
Composer: Andre Previn. Conductor: Roger Wayne. Cast: Roger Wayne and His Orchestra.

ONE WAY TICKET TO BROADWAY
Original Cast (1979) • Theatre Archives (S) TA-8001 8-10   79
Composer: Dan Goggin, Robert Lorick. Cast: Katie Ander, Beth Fowler, Dan Goggin, Ann Hodapp, Elaine Petricoff, Marvin Solley.

ONLY FOREVER: see BING'S HOLLYWOOD

ONWARD VICTORIA
Original Cast (1980) • Original Cast (S) OC 8235 12-18   81
Composer: Keith Hermann, Irene Rosenberg, Charlotte Anker. Conductor: Larry Blake. Cast: Laura Waterbury, Jill Eikenberry, Beth Austin, Michael Zaslov, Lenny Wolpe.

OPENING DAY CEREMONIES
TV Soundtrack (1960) • Century (S) No Label Shown 15-20
From the 1960 Olympic Winter Games, held in Squaw Valley, Calif.

OPENING NIGHT
Studiotrack • MGM (M) E-3816 8-12   60
Studiotrack • MGM (S) SE-3816 10-15   60
Music from *The Music Man, Guys and Dolls, Damn Yankees, Kismet, The Pajama Game* and *Greenwillow.*
Conductor: Cyril Ornadel. Cast: Starlight Symphony.

OPENING NIGHT AT THE PALACE - SWEET CHARITY: see SWEET CHARITY

OPENING NIGHT AT THE WINTERGARDEN - MAME: see MAME

OPERA SAUVAGE
Soundtrack • Polydor (S) 2490-161 10-15

OPTIMISTS
Soundtrack (1973) • Paramount (S) PAS-1015 20-25   73
Composer: Lionel Bart, George Martin. Conductor: Lionel Bart. Cast: Peter Sellers, Lionel Bart.

ORANGE BIRD
Studio Cast (1971) • Disneyland (S) STER-3991 15-20   71
Includes illustrated booklet.
Composer: Richard M. Sherman, Robert B. Sherman. Conductor: Tutti Camarata. Cast: Anita Bryant.

ORCHESTRA WIVES
Soundtrack (1942) • RCA Victor (EP) EPBT-3065 10-20   54
Two discs.
Soundtrack (1942) • RCA Victor (M) LPT-3065 25-30   54
10-inch LP.
Soundtrack [Vol. 1] (1942) • 20th Century-Fox (M) 3020 15-20   59
Soundtrack [Vol. 1] (1942) • 20th Century-Fox (SE) S-3020e 15-20   59
Soundtrack [Vol. 2] (1942) • 20th Century-Fox (M) 3021 15-20   59
Soundtrack [Vol. 2] (1942) • 20th Century-Fox (SE) S-3021e 15-20   59
Soundtrack [Vols. 1 & 2] (1942) • 20th Century-Fox (M) TCF-100-2 20-30   60
Soundtrack [Vols. 1 & 2] (1942) • 20th Century-Fox (SE) TCS-100-2 .. 20-30   60
Two discs. Actual title: *Glenn Miller – Complete Soundtracks.* Also has music from *Sun Valley Serenade* (1941).
Soundtrack • Movietone (SE) MTM-1003 10-12   69
Soundtrack • 20th Century-Fox (SE) S-72018 8-10   73
Both include music from *Sun Valley Serenade.*
Composer: Mack Gordon, Harry Warren. Conductor: Glenn Miller. Cast: Glenn Miller and His Orchestra.
Also see GLENN MILLER: GOLDEN HITS FROM HIS ORIGINAL SOUNDTRACKS

ORDER IS LOVE
Original Cast (1961) • Trilogy (S) TA-1001 15-20   61
Composer: Lex de Azevedo, Carol Lynn Pearson. Conductor: Dee Winterton. Cast: Gordon Harkness, Bob Nuismer, Janey Luke, Dianne Lynne Harris, Lawrence Gardner, Doug Voet, Paul Miller, Bryce Chamberlain.

ORIGINAL AMATEUR HOUR - 25TH ANNIVERSARY
TV Soundtrack • United Artists (M) UXL-2 30-40   73
Two discs.

ORIGINAL MOTION PICTURE HIT THEMES
Studio Cast (1963) • United Artists (M) UAL-3197 10-15   63
Studio Cast (1963) • United Artists (S) UAS-6197 15-20   63
Composer: Various. Conductor: Various. Cast: Ferrante and Teicher, Ralph Marterie, Gene Pitney, Al Caiola, Roger Wayne, Nick Perito, Louis Armstrong.

ORIGINAL MOTION PICTURE THEMES

Soundtrack (1962) • United Artists (M) UAL-3122.................................. 8-12   62
Soundtrack (1962) • United Artists (S) UAS-6122................................. 10-15   62
  Music from *Exodus, Never on Sunday, The Apartment, Magnificent 7* and others.

ORIGINAL MOVIE THEMES OF DIMITRI TIOMKIN

Soundtrack (1955) • Coral (EP) EC-81069.. 40-50   55
  Composer: Dimitri Tiomkin. **Conductor:** Dimitri Tiomkin.

ORIGINAL SOUND TRACKS

Soundtrack • MGM (M) 2E-10 20-25   60s
Soundtrack • MGM (S) 2SE-10 35-40   60s
  Two discs. Full title: *Original Sound Tracks and Recordings of Original Music from Great Movies.* Has music from *Ben Hur, King of Kings, Quo Vadis, Cleopatra, Farewell to Arms, Mutiny on the Bounty, Butterfield 8, The V.I.P.s, The Robe, El Cid, Madam Bovary, Lili, How the West Was Won, Cimarron, Love Is a Many-Splendored Thing.*
  Conductor: Alfred Newman, David Rose, Robert Armbruster, Carlo Savina, Miklos Rozsa, Cyril Ornadel, Hans Sommer.

ORIGINAL SOUNDTRACK HITS

Soundtrack • Lion (M) L70122... 15-20
  Full title: *Original Soundtrack Hits Recorded Directly from the Soundtracks of MGM Musicals.*

ORIGINAL SOUNDTRACK MUSIC FROM THE FILMS OF JACQUES TATI: see PLAYTIME

ORIGINAL SOUNDTRACKS AND MUSIC

Soundtrack/Studiotrack (1962) • United Artists (M) UAL 3303 15-20   62
Soundtrack/Studiotrack (1962) • United Artists (S) UAS 6303 15-20   62
  Full title: *Original Soundtracks and Music from the Great Motion Pictures.* Has music from *The V.I.P.s, Mondo Cane, Lawrence of Arabia, How the West Was Won, Taras Bulba, Never on Sunday, The Wishing Star, Dr. No, The Apartment, Irma La Douce, Phaedra, The Great Escape, Cleopatra, Divorce Italian Style, Mutiny on the Bounty* and *Exodus.*
  Cast: Leroy Holmes Orchestra, Riz Ortolani Orchestra, Ferrante and Teicher Orchestra, Hollywood Sound Stage Orchestra, Manos Hadjidakis Orchestra, Franz Waxman Orchestra, Andre Previn Orchestra, Mikis Theodorakis Orchestra, Elmer Bernstein Orchestra, Carlo Rustichelli Orchestra.

ORIGINAL SOUNDTRACKS AND OTHER MUSIC FROM GREAT MOVIES

Soundtrack/Studiotrack • MGM (M) 2E-10 20-30   64
Soundtrack/Studiotrack • MGM (S) 2SE-10... 20-30   64
  Two discs. Music from *The Robe, Madame Bovary, Quo Vadis, Butterfield 8, King of Kings,* and others.

ORIGINAL SOUNDTRACKS RECORDED IN ITALY

Soundtrack • RCA Victor (S) FSO-4... 60-80   62
  Music from *Nude Odyssey* and 11 other films.

ORIGINAL THEMES FROM THE GREAT SOAP OPERAS

TV Soundtrack • Realm (S) 2V8056.. 10-15   75
  Two discs.
  Composer: Charles Paul.

ORIGINAL TV ADVENTURES OF KING KONG

TV Soundtrack (1966) • Epic (M) LN-24231 15-25   66
TV Soundtrack (1966) • Epic (S) BN-26231 25-30   66
  Composer: Maury Laws. **Cast:** Bob McFadden (narration).

OSCAR

Soundtrack (1966) • Columbia (M) OL-6550 15-18   66
Soundtrack (1966) • Columbia (S) OS-2950 20-25   66
Soundtrack (1966) • CBS (M) 62684.. 12-15   66

Soundtrack (1966) • CBS (S) 62684 15-20   66
CBS UK releases have the same label number for both mono and stereo.
Composer: Percy Faith, Jay Livingston, Ray Evans. **Conductor:** Percy Faith, Johnny Mandel.
Cast: Tony Bennett.

OSCAR HAMMERSTEIN II MEMORIAL ALBUM
Soundtrack • Capitol (S) CLS-1.. 45-55   65
UK release. Hammerstein commemorative of his death (1965). Two-discs. Has the UK
releases of the soundtracks, *Carousel* (SLCT-6105) and *Oklahoma!* (SLCT-6100). Black
gatefold cover with memorial text on back and reproductions of original covers inside.
Composer: Richard Rodgers, Oscar Hammerstein II. **Conductor:** Alfred Newman, Jay Blackton.
Cast: Shirley Jones, Gordon MacRae, Gene Nelson, Barbara Ruick, Gloria Grahame, Charlotte
Greenwood.

OSTERMAN WEEKEND
Soundtrack (1983) • Varese Sarabande (S) STV-81198........................ 8-10   83
Soundtrack (1983) • That's Entertainment (S) TER 1084........................ 8-10   80s
Composer: Lalo Schifrin. **Conductor:** Lalo Schifrin.

OTHELLO
Studio Cast • Columbia M-554 10-20
Seventeen 78 rpm discs.
Studio Cast • Columbia (M) SL-153 10-15
Studio Cast • Columbia (M) CSL-153.. 10-15
Three discs.
Cast: Paul Robeson, Uta Hagen, Jose Ferrer, Alexander Scourby, others.

OTHER SIDE OF MIDNIGHT
Soundtrack (1977) • 20th Century-Fox (S) T-542................................. 10-12   77
Soundtrack (1977) • 20th Century-Fox (S) T-542................................. 8-10   77
UK release.
Composer: Michel Legrand. **Conductor:** Michel Legrand.

OTHER SIDE OF THE MOUNTAIN
Soundtrack (1975) • MCA (S) 2086.. 8-12   75
Soundtrack (1975) • MCA (S) 1539.. 5-10   80s
Composer: Charles Fox. **Conductor:** Charles Fox.

OTHER SIDE OF THE MOUNTAIN, PART II
Soundtrack (1978) • MCA (S) 2335.. 8-10   78
Composer: Lee Holdridge. **Conductor:** Lee Holdridge. **Cast:** Merrily Webber.

OTHER WORLD OF WINSTON CHURCHILL
TV Soundtrack (1965) • Mercury (M) MG-21033................................... 20-25   65
TV Soundtrack (1965) • Mercury (S) SR-61033 30-35   65
From NBC-TV's *Hallmark Hall of Fame.*
Composer: Carl Davis. **Conductor:** Carl Davis. **Cast:** Paul Scofield (narration).

OTLEY
Soundtrack (1969) • Colgems (S) COS-112 20-25   69
Composer: Stanley Myers. **Conductor:** Stanley Myers. **Cast:** Don Partridge, Alex Keenan,
Pete Murray.

OUR GAL SUNDAY
Original Radio Cast • Golden Age (M) 5017... 8-10   78

OUR GANG – ORIGINAL MOTION PICTURE SOUNDTRACKS
Soundtrack (1938) • Mark 56 (M) 653 10-15   70s
Music from *The Our Gang Follies* and *Mush and Milk.*

OUR MAN FLINT
Soundtrack (1966) • 20th Century-Fox (M) TFM-3179 30-40   66
Soundtrack (1966) • 20th Century-Fox (S) TFS-4179 60-80   66
Composer: Jerry Goldsmith. **Conductor:** Jerry Goldsmith.

Studiotrack (1966) • Diplomat (M) 2380 10-12   66
  Also has music from *The Silencers* and *The Oscar*.
    Cast: Wilson Lewes Trio.
    Also see IN LIKE FLINT

OUR MAN IN HOLLYWOOD
Studiotrack (1963) • RCA Victor (M) LPM-2604 10-12   63
Studiotrack (1963) • RCA Victor (S) LSP-2604 10-15   63
  Black label.
Studiotrack (1963) • RCA Victor (S) LSP-2604 8-10   72
  Orange label.
    Composer: Henry Mancini. **Conductor:** Henry Mancini. **Cast:** Henry Mancini and His
    Orchestra.

OUR MOTHER'S HOUSE
Soundtrack (1967) • MGM (S) SE-4495 60-70   67
  Canadian release only. Monaural issue is a U.S. counterfeit.
    Composer: Georges Delerue. **Conductor:** Georges Delerue.

OUR TOWN
TV Soundtrack (1956) • Capitol (EP) EAP -1-673 50-75   56
TV Soundtrack (1956) • Capitol (M) N-16148... 10-12   Re
  Actual title: *Look to Your Heart*. Has three of the four songs from the original release.
    Composer: James Van Heusen, Sammy Cahn. **Cast:** Frank Sinatra, Eva Marie Saint.
Studiotrack • Decca (M) DL 7527 25-35   50s
  10-inch LP. Also has music from *The Plow That Broke the Plains*.
    Composer: Aaron Copland. **Conductor:** Thomas Scherman. **Cast:** Little Orchestra Society.
    THE PLOW THAT BROKE THE PLAINS: **Composer:** Virgil Thomson. **Conductor:** Neville
    Marriner. **Cast:** L.A. Chamber Orchestra.
    Also see QUIET CITY

OUT OF AFRICA
Soundtrack (1985) • MCA (S) 6158... 15-20   85
  With an extra track, *The Music of Goodbye (Love Theme from Out of Africa)* by Melissa
  Manchester and Al Jarreau.
    Composer: John Barry. **Conductor:** John Barry. **Cast:** Academy of St. Martin in the Fields,
    Melissa Manchester & Al Jarreau.
Soundtrack (1985) • MCA (S) 39303.. 8-10   88
    Composer: John Barry. **Conductor:** John Barry. **Cast:** Academy of St. Martin in the Fields.

OUT OF BOUNDS
Soundtrack (1986) • I.R.S. (S) 6180 8-10   86
    Cast: Stewart Copeland, Adam Ant, Siouxsie and the Banshees, Cult, Belinda Carlisle, Night
    Ranger, Tommy Keene, American Girls, Lords of the New Church.

OUT OF SIGHT
Soundtrack (1966) • Decca (M) DL-4751 12-18   66
Soundtrack (1966) • Decca (S) DL-74751 15-20   66
    Composer: Al DeLory, others. **Conductor:** Nick Venet. **Cast:** Gary Lewis and the Playboys,
    Astronauts, Turtles, Freddie and the Dreamers, Dobie Gray, Knickerbockers.

OUT OF THIS WORLD
Original Cast (1950) • Columbia (M) ML-54390 20-25   50
  Disc label reads "ML-4390."
Original Cast (1950) • Columbia (M) OL-4390 15-18   Re
Original Cast (1950) • Columbia Special Products (M) COL-4390 8-10   Re
    Composer: Cole Porter. **Conductor:** Pembroke Davenport. **Cast:** Charlotte Greenwood,
    Priscilla Gillette, William Redfield, David Burns, Barbara Ashley.

**OUT TAKES: see CUT! OUTTAKES FROM HOLLYWOOD'S GREATEST
  MUSICALS**

OUTER SPACE SUITE
Soundtrack (1957) • Cerberus (M) 0208 15-20   83
Also includes *The Moat Farm Murders* and *The Hitchhiker.*
Composer: Bernard Herrmann.

OUTLAND
Soundtrack (1981) • Warner Bros. (S) HS-3551 20-25   81
Composer: Jerry Goldsmith. **Conductor:** Jerry Goldsmith. **Cast:** National Philharmonic Orchestra.

OUTLAW BLUES
Soundtrack (1977) • Capitol (S) ST-11691.. 10-12   77
Composer: Charles Bernstein, Hoyt Axton. **Conductor:** Charles Bernstein. **Cast:** Hoyt Axton, Peter Fonda, Susan Saint James, John Crawford, James Callahan, Michael Lerner.

OUTLAW JOSEY WALES
Soundtrack (1976) • Warner Bros. (S) BS-2956 10-30   76
Composer: Jerry Fielding. **Conductor:** Jerry Fielding.

OUTLAW RIDERS
Soundtrack (1970) • MGM (S) 1SE-26.. 15-20   70
Composer: Michael Lloyd, Simon Stokes, others. **Cast:** Lenny McDaniel, Horsemen, Simon Stokes and the Night Hawks, Bob Correll.

OUTRAGEOUS
Soundtrack (1977) • Polydor (S) 1-8902 8-10   77
Cast: Brenda Hoffert, Cecile Frenette, Craig Russell.

OUTRE LA PORTA
Soundtrack (1984) • Varese Sarabande (S) STV-81213 10-15   84
Composer: Pino Donaggio. **Conductor:** Natale Massara.

OUTSIDE IN
Soundtrack (1972) • MGM (S) 1SE-37.. 10-12   72
Composer: Randy Edelman, others. **Conductor:** Randy Edelman. **Cast:** Randy Edelman (vocal, piano), Five Man Electrical Band.

OUTSIDERS
Soundtrack (1983) • Silva Screen (S) SIL-5051 10-12   83
French release.
Cast: Bill Hughes.

OVER HERE!
Original Cast (1974) • Columbia (S) KS-32961 12-20   74
Original Cast (1974) • Columbia (Q) KQS-32961 15-30   74
Composer: Richard M. Sherman, Robert B. Sherman. **Conductor:** Joseph Klein. **Cast:** Patty Andrews, Maxene Andrews, Douglass Watson, MacIntyre Dixon, John Travolta, April Shawhan, Janie Sell, William Griffis, Jim Weston, Phyllis Somerville, Samuel E. Wright, John Drive.

OVER THE EDGE
Soundtrack (1979) • Warner Bros. (S) BSK-3335 8-10   79
Cast: Cheap Trick, Cars, Van Halen, Jimi Hendrix, Ramones, Little Feat, Valerie Carter.

OVER THE TOP
Soundtrack (1987) • Columbia (S) SC-40655 8-10   87
Cast: Sammy Hagar, Robin Zander, Larry Greene, Big Trouble, Frank Stallone, Kenny Loggins, Asia, Giorgio Moroder, Eddie Money.

OWL AND THE PUSSYCAT
Soundtrack (1970) • Columbia (S) S-30401 10-12   70
Composer: Richard Halligan. **Cast:** Barbra Streisand, George Segal, Blood, Sweat and Tears.

OZZIE AND HARRIET
TV Soundtrack (1957) • Imperial (M) LP-9049 175-200   57
Composer: Various. **Cast:** Ozzie and Harriet Nelson (vocals).

P

PACIFIC 1860
Original London Cast (1946) • That's Entertainment (M) TER-1040..... 15-18   83
UK release.
   Composer: Noel Coward. **Conductor:** Mantovani. **Cast:** Mary Martin.

PACIFIC OVERTURES
Original Cast (1976) • RCA Victor (S) ARL1-1367 10-12   76
Original Cast (1976) • RCA Victor (S) ARL1-4007 8-10   Re
Includes libretto.
   Composer: Stephen Sondheim. **Conductor:** Paul Gemignani. **Cast:** Mako, Soon-Teck Oh, Yuki
Shimoda, Sab Shimono, Isao Sato, Alvin Ing, Ernest Harada, James Dybas, Patrick Kinser-Lau,
Jae Woo Lee, Timm Fujii, Conrad Yama, Ricardo Tobia, Gedde Watanabe, Hsu Syers, Freda
Foh Shen, Leslie Watanabe, Fusako Yoshida, Genji Ito.
Original London Cast • That's Entertainment (S) TER-21151................ 10-12   80s
UK release.
Full title: *Pacific Overtures (Highlights).*
   Composer: Stephen Sondheim.

PAGAN LOVE: see MATING URGE

PAGAN LOVE SONG
Soundtrack (1950) • MGM - MGM-64.. 15-20   50
78 rpm album.
Soundtrack (1950) • MGM (EP) K-64.. 20-25   50
Boxed, three-disc set. Includes flyer insert.
Soundtrack (1950) • MGM (M) E-534.. 25-35   50
10-inch LP.
Soundtrack (1950) • MCA (M) 39080 5-8   86
One side has music from *The Pirate.*
   Composer: Harry Warren, Nacio Herb Brown, Arthur Freed. **Conductor:** Adolph Deutsch. **Cast:**
Howard Keel, Esther Williams, MGM Studio Orchestra and Chorus.
   Also see THOSE GLORIOUS MGM MUSICALS

PAINT YOUR WAGON
Original Cast (1951) • RCA Victor OC-6... 15-20   51
78 rpm album.
Original Cast (1951) • RCA Victor (EP) WOC-1006 15-20   51
Original Cast (1951) • RCA Victor (EP) EOA-434 10-15   51
Original Cast (1951) • RCA Victor (M) LOC-1006 15-18   51
Green label.
Original Cast (1951) • RCA Victor (M) LOC-1006 10-12   51
Black label, dog on top. Has "Long Play" at bottom. Cover is brown.
Original Cast (1951) • RCA Victor (M) LOC-1006 8-15   65
Original Cast (1951) • RCA Victor (SE) LSO-1006e............................ 10-12   65
Covers picture Olga San Juan running across a mountain, with dog logo on top right of
front cover. Label is black with "Mono" or "Stereo" at bottom.
Original Cast (1951) • RCA Victor (SE) LSO-1006e 5-8   65
Cover does not have dog logo. Label may be tan, black, or orange.
   Composer: Alan Jay Lerner, Frederick Loewe. **Conductor:** Franz Allers. **Cast:** James Barton,
Olga San Juan, Tony Bavaar, Rufus Smith, Robert Penn, Dave Thomas.

Soundtrack (1969) • Paramount (S) 1609/10 15-20   69
Promotional issue made for radio stations.
  Composer: Alan Jay Lerner, Frederick Loewe, Andre Previn. **Conductor:** Andre Previn. **Cast:**
  Lee Marvin, Clint Eastwood, Jean Seberg, Harve Presnell. (With dialogue.)
Soundtrack (1969) • Paramount (S) PMS-1001 10-12   69
Gatefold, double pocket cover, with leaflet poster fold. One pocket contains disc, other has
a full-color booklet.
Soundtrack (1969) • ABC/Paramount (S) PMS-1001 8-10   Re
Gatefold cover. No poster, no booklet. Cover replaces all mention of Paramount Records
with "ABC Records" band, but label is blue with Paramount logo.
Soundtrack (1969) • MCA (S) 37099 5-8   86
  Composer: Alan Jay Lerner, Frederick Loewe, Andre Previn. **Conductor:** Nelson Riddle. **Cast:**
  Lee Marvin, Clint Eastwood, Anita Gordon (performs vocals for Jean Seberg in the film), Harve
  Presnell, Ray Walston, The Nitty Gritty Dirt Band.
Studiotrack (1970) • Forward (S) ST-F-1016 10-12   70
Instrumentals from the film, played by Nelson Riddle and his orchestra.
  Composer: Alan Jay Lerner, Frederick Loewe, Andre Previn. **Conductor:** Nelson Riddle.
Studiotrack (1970) • Flying Dutchman (S) FDS-114 10-15   70
Jazz interpretations.
  Composer: Alan Jay Lerner, Frederick Loewe, Andre Previn. **Cast:** Tom Scott Quartet (Tom
  Scott, Roger Kellaway, Chuck Domanico, John Guerin).
Studiotrack • Ambassador (S) S 98037 8-12
  Cast: Ray Bloch Singers.
Studiotrack • Diplomat (S) DS-2419 8-12
Also see EVENING WITH LERNER AND LOEWE
Also see LYRICS BY LERNER.

PAINTED SMILES OF COLE PORTER
Studio Cast (1972) • Painted Smiles (S) PS-1358 10-12   72
Unproduced revue, intended to be a Broadway musical.
Studio Cast (1972) • Painted Smiles (S) PS-1358 8-10   72
Reissue. Different cover and seven additional songs.
  Composer: Cole Porter. **Conductor:** Judd Woldin. **Cast:** Blossom Dearie, Carmen Alvarez,
  Karen Morrow, Edward Earle, Laura Kenyon, Alice Playten, Charles Rydell.

PAINTING THE CLOUDS WITH SUNSHINE
Studiotrack (1951) • Capitol (EP) KDF-291 15-20   51
Studiotrack (1951) • Capitol (M) L-291 30-35   51
10-inch LP.
  Composer: Various. **Conductor:** George Greeley. **Cast:** Dennis Morgan, Lucille Norman.
Soundtrack (1951) • Caliban (M) 6012 8-10
Also has music from *Meet Me After the Show*.
  Composer: Various. **Conductor:** Ray Heindorf. **Cast:** Virginia Mayo, Gene Nelson, Dennis
  Morgan, Lucille Norman, Virginia Gibson. MEET ME AFTER THE SHOW: **Composer:** Jule
  Styne, Leo Robin. **Cast:** Betty Grable, MacDonald Carey, Eddie Albert.

PAJAMA GAME
Original Cast (1954) • Columbia (EP) A-1098 15-20   54
Original Cast (1954) • Columbia (M) ML-4840 12-15   54
Original Cast (1954) • Columbia (M) OL-4840 8-20
Original Cast (1954) • Columbia (M) S-32606 5-8   73
  Composer: Richard Adler, Jerry Ross. **Conductor:** Hal Hastings. **Cast:** John Raitt, Janis Paige,
  Eddie Foy Jr., Carol Haney, Reta Shaw, Stanley Prager, Buzz Miller, Peter Gennaro.
Original London Cast (1955) • RCA Victor (M) CLP-1062 175-200   55
UK release. From 1955 London Coliseum production.
  Composer: Richard Adler, Jerry Ross. **Conductor:** Robert Lowe. **Cast:** Max Wall, Joy Nichols,
  Edmund Hockridge, Elizabeth Seal, Frank Lawless, Joan Emney.
Soundtrack (1957) • Columbia (EP) A-5210 15-20   57
Boxed, four-disc set.
Soundtrack (1957) • Columbia (M) OL-5210 12-18   57

Soundtrack (1957) • Columbia Special Products (M) AOL-5210 10-12   Re
Plain blue Columbia Special Products cover.
Soundtrack (1957) • Columbia Special Products (M) AOL-5210 5-8   Re
Reproduction of original cover.
Composer: Richard Adler, Jerry Ross. Conductor: Ray Heindorf. Cast: Doris Day, John Raitt,
Carol Haney, Eddie Foy Jr., Reta Shaw, Barbara Nichols, Kenneth LeRoy, Buzz Miller, Jack
Straw.
Soundtrack (1957) • Philips (M) B-07263-L 20-25   58
Dutch release. Has slightly different cover art.
Soundtrack (1957) • CBS (M) 63032 20-25
UK release. Abridged, containing primarily Doris Day vocals. Also has music
from Calamity Jane.
Composer: Richard Adler, Jerry Ross. Conductor: Ray Heindorf. Cast: Doris Day,
John Raitt, Carol Haney, Eddie Foy Jr., Reta Shaw, Barbara Nichols, Kenneth
LeRoy, Buzz Miller, Jack Straw.
Studiotrack (1957) • Masterseal (M) MS-52 8-15   57
Studiotrack (1957) • Masterseal (SE) 33-1895 8-12   Re
Composer: Richard Adler. Conductor: Jack Hansen. Cast: Hollywood Transcription Orchestra.
Studiotrack • Columbia (EP) B-1863 15-20   50s
Composer: Richard Adler, Jerry Ross. Cast: Rosemary Clooney, Johnnie Ray, Guy Mitchell,
Mariners.
Studiotrack • Somerset (M) P-3300 8-10
Studiotrack • Somerset (S) SF-3300 8-12
Also has music from Silk Stockings.
Composer: PAJAMA GAME: Richard Adler, Jerry Ross, Cole Porter. Conductor: Joseph Kuhn.
Cast: New World Theatre Orchestra. SILK STOCKINGS: Composer: Cole Porter, Joe=seph
Kuhn. Conductor: Joseph Kuhn. Cast: New World Theatre Orchestra.

PAJAMA PARTY
Soundtrack (1964) • Buena Vista (M) BV-3325 30-35   64
Soundtrack (1964) • Buena Vista (S) STER-332 70-80   64
Composer: Jerry Styner, Guy Hemric. Cast: Annette Funicello, Tommy Kirk.

PAL JOEY
Original Revival Cast (1952) • Capitol (EP) EDM-310 20-25   52
Original Revival Cast (1952) • Capitol (M) S-310 60-70   52
Original Revival Cast (1952) • World (M) T-774 20-25   Re
UK release. Although Vivienne Segal and Harold Lang played the leads in this show, they
were replaced in this recording by Jane Froman and Dick Beavers, making it necessary to
have both the Columbia and Capitol (or World) issues to have the complete show.
Composer: Richard Rodgers, Lorenz Hart. Conductor: Max Meth. Cast: Jane Froman, Dick
Beavers, Helen Gallagher, Patricia Northrop, Elaine Stritch, Lewis Bolyard.
London Revival Cast (1980) • That's Entertainment (S) TERX-1005 12-18   80
UK release. Shown as "First True Stereo Original Cast Recording."
Composer: Richard Rodgers, Lorenz Hart. Conductor: Grant Hossack. Cast: Sian Phillips, Denis
Lawson, Danielle Carson, Buster Skeggs, Darlene Johnson.
Studio Cast (1952) • Columbia (EP) A-974 10-25
Boxed, four-disc set.
Studio Cast (1952) • Columbia (EP) A-1735 10-15   52
Studio Cast (1952) • Columbia (M) ML-4364 15-20   52
Studio Cast (1952) • Columbia (M) OL-4364 12-20   Re
Covers have a drawing.
Studio Cast (1952) • Columbia (M) ML-4364 12-15
Studio Cast (1952) • Columbia (M) OL-4364 10-20
Covers have photos.

Studio Cast (1952) • Columbia Special Products (M) AOL-4364 8-10   Re
Some copies have the drawing cover, others have plain blue Columbia Special Products
cover. The success of this recording sparked the Broadway revival listed below, with
Vivienne Segal and Harold Lang also starring in the show. For that reason, this LP is often
mistakenly referred to as the revival cast album.
Composer: Richard Rodgers, Lorenz Hart. **Conductor:** Lehman Engel. **Cast:** Vivienne Segal,
Harold Lang, Barbara Ashley, Beverly Fite, Kenneth Remo, Jo Hurt.

Studio Cast • Tops (M) L-1607 10-15
Composer: Richard Rodgers, Lorenz Hart. **Conductor:** Lew Raymond. **Cast:** Martha Tilton,
June Hutton, Curt Massey, Clark Dennis, Marilyn Maxwell, Betty Baker, Clark Dennis, Bob
McKendrick.

Soundtrack (1957) • Capitol (EP) EDM-912 10-15   57
Soundtrack (1957) • Capitol (M) W-912 15-20   57
Gray label.
Soundtrack (1957) • Capitol (M) W-912 12-18   Re
Black label with colorband. On above two, front covers of some copies read "Rodgers and
Hart's *Pal Joey*," while others have only the title.
Soundtrack (1957) • Capitol (SE) DW-912 15-20   61
Soundtrack (1957) • Capitol (SE) SM-912 8-10   Re
Some selections are in electronic stereo, others are in monaural.
Composer: Richard Rodgers, Lorenz Hart. **Conductor:** Morris Stoloff. **Cast:** Frank Sinatra, Rita
Hayworth, Jo Ann Greer (performed some of Rita Hayworth's vocals in the film), Trudy Erwin
(performed vocals for Kim Novak), Barbara Nichols.

Studiotrack (1957) • Jubilee (M) JLP-1061 45-65   57
Instrumentals by Bobby Sherwood, who portrayed Ned Galvin and his Galvinizers in the
film.
Composer: Richard Rodgers, Lorenz Hart. **Conductor:** Bobby Sherwood.

Studiotrack (1957) • Contemporary (M) C 3543 30-35   57
Cast: Andre Previn & His Pals, Shelly Manne & Red Mitchell.

Studiotrack (1957) • Halo (M) 50264 10-12   57
Studiotrack (1957) • Masterseal (M) MS-56 10-15   57
Conductor: Don Raleigh. **Cast:** Don Raleigh & His Orchestra, Sandra Lee, Les Young.

Studiotrack • Design (S) DLP-60 10-12   57
Conductor: Stanley Applewaite. **Cast:** Stanley Applewaite and Orchestra.

Studiotrack • Atlantic (M) ALS 1211 10-15   50s
Cast: Charles Sherrill.

Studiotrack (1959) • National Academy Record Club (M) ES 9 10-15   60
From the *Ed Sullivan Presents Songs and Music of…* series.
Cast: Ed Sullivan All Star Cast.

Studiotrack • Crown (S) CST-110 8-12
Conductor: Duke Hazlett.

Studiotrack • Jubilee (S) JLP 1061 10-12
Studiotrack • Promenade (M) 2089 8-12
Cast: Eddie Maynard Orchestra, Bill Sinclair, Jennie Feathers.

Studiotrack • Riverside (M) RLP-12-249 15-20
Cast: Kenny Drew Trio.

Studiotrack • Spectrum (S) SS 40 8-12
Conductor: Stanley Applewaite. **Cast:** Stanley Applewaite and His Orchestra.

PALM SPRINGS WEEKEND

Soundtrack (1963) • Warner Bros. (M) W-1519 20-25   63
Soundtrack (1963) • Warner Bros. (S) WS-1519 30-35   63
Composer: Frank Perkins, others. **Conductor:** Frank Perkins. **Cast:** Connie Stevens, Troy
Donahue, Ty Hardin, Robert Conrad, Jerry Van Dyke, Modern Folk Quartet.

PANAMA HATTIE

Original Cast (1940) • Decca DA-203.. 45-65　　40
  78 rpm album. Never released by Decca in LP format. Two gatefold cover variations exist:
  one with disc envelopes in a standard page-style format, other with envelope folders
  attached to the cover.
    Composer: Cole Porter. **Conductor:** Harry Sosnik. **Cast:** Ethel Merman, June Carroll.
    Also see ANYTHING GOES

PANIC BUTTON

Soundtrack (1964) • Musicor (M) MM-2026.................................... 50-75　　64
Soundtrack (1964) • Musicor (S) MS-3026..................................... 100-125　　64
  Coveted for cover photo of Jayne Mansfield.
    Composer: Georges Garvarentz. **Conductor:** Georges Garvarentz.

PAPA WAS A PREACHER

Soundtrack (1985) • Word (S) 7-01-900210-2........................... 8-10　　84
    Composer: Ken Sutherland. **Cast:** Mac Frampton, Sandi Patti, Porter Kids, Robert Pine with
    Brandon Sokolosky and Choir.

PAPER MOON

Soundtrack (1973) • Paramount (S) PAS-1012 .... 8-10　　73
  Various songs from the mid-'30s.
    Cast: Bing Crosby, Hoagy Carmichael, Paul Whitman, Larry Stewart, Dick Powell, Jimmie Grier
    and His Orchestra, Boswell Sisters, Ozzie Nelson and His Orchestra, Donald Novis, Victor
    Young and His Orchestra, Pinky Tomlin, Leo Reisman and His Orchestra, Jimmy Davis, Tommy
    Dorsey and His Orchestra, Ken Darby and Ramona, Blue Sky Boys, Frank Luther.
Studiotrack • Harmony (SE) KH-32748 .... 8-10　　73
  Songs of the '30s, but not ones heard in the film.
    Cast: Cliff Edwards, Sophie Tucker, Dick Powell, Buddy Clark.

PAPER TIGER

Soundtrack (1975) • Capitol (S) SW-11475.. 15-20　　75
    Composer: Roy Budd. **Conductor:** Roy Budd. **Cast:** National Philharmonic Orchestra, Ray
    Conniff Singers, Mike Sammes Singers, Roy Budd (piano).

PAPILLON

Soundtrack (1973) • Capitol (S) ST-11260.. 10-25　　73
    Composer: Jerry Goldsmith. **Conductor:** Jerry Goldsmith.

PARADE

Original Cast (1960) • Kapp (M) KDL-7005 .... 175-200　　60
Original Cast (1960) • Kapp (S) KDS-7005 .... 200-225　　60
    Composer: Jerry Herman. **Cast:** Dody Goodman, Richard Tone, Fia Karin, Charles Nelson
    Reilly, Jerry Herman (piano).

PARADE: MUSIC FROM UNDER THE CHERRY MOON: see UNDER THE CHERRY MOON

PARADE OF HITS

Studiotrack • MGM (M) E 4078 15-25
  Music from *Lolita, Walk on the Wildside, King of Kings, Dr. Kildare, El Cid* and *Four
  Horsemen of the Apocalypse.*
    Cast: Andre Previn and MGM Studio Orchestra, Benton Ames and His Orchestra, Cyril Ornadel
    and Starlight Symphony, Elmer Bernstein, Leroy Holmes, Richard Chamberlain, Sue Lyon.

PARADE OF SHOW STOPPERS

Soundtrack • Columbia Special Products (S) CSP-237 10-15
  Music from *Funny Girl, Mary Poppins, Stop the World I Want to Get Off, Fiddler on the
  Roof, Kismet, My Fair Lady, Gypsy, Bye Bye Birdie, Camelot, Sound of Music, West Side
  Story* and *Hello Dolly.*
    Cast: Barbra Streisand, Ray Conniff Singers, Robert Goulet, Julie Andrews, Vic Damone, Kirby
    Stone Four, Tony Bennett, Jerry Vale, Percy Faith, Johnny Mathis, Andre Kostelanetz.

PARADINE CASE
Studiotrack (1948) • AEI (M) AEI-3103.. 8-10   79
Also has music from *Spellbound*.
Composer: Franz Waxman. SPELLBOUND: Miklos Rozsa. **Conductor:** Franz Waxman.
Also see JUNGLE BOOK

PARADISE ALLEY
Soundtrack (1978) • MCA (S) 5100.. 8-10   79
Composer: Bill Conte, others. **Conductor:** Bob Alcivar. **Cast:** Sylvester Stallone, Tom Waits,
Frank Stallone Jr.

PARADISE HAWAIIAN STYLE
Soundtrack (1966) • RCA Victor (M) LPM-3643 40-60   66
Soundtrack (1966) • RCA Victor (S) LSP-3643 40-60   66
Black label.
Soundtrack (1966) • RCA Victor (S) LSP-3643 10-25   69
Orange or tan label. (Tan label issued in 1976.)
Soundtrack (1966) • RCA Victor (S) AFL1-3643 8-10   77
Composer: Bill Giant, Bernie Baum, Florence Kaye, Fred Wise, Randy Starr, Sid Tepper, Roy
C. Bennett, others. **Cast:** Elvis Presley, Scotty Moore (guitar), Charlie McCoy (guitar), Barney
Kessel (guitar), Barnal Lewis (steel), D.J. Fontana (drums), Hal Blaine (drums), Larry
Muhoberac (keyboard), Ray Siegel (bass), Jordanaires (vocals), Mello Men (vocals).

PARAMOUNT PRESENTS FAMOUS MOVIE THEMES
Studiotrack • Paramount (S) PAS-1007 8-12
Two discs.

PARAPLUIES DE CHERBOURG: see UMBRELLAS OF CHERBOURG
PARDNERS
Soundtrack (1956) • Capitol (EP) EAP 1-752 50-75   56
Composer: Sammy Cahn, Jimmy Van Heusen. **Conductor:** Dick Stabile. **Cast:** Dean Martin,
Jerry Lewis.

PARDON MY BLOOPER!
Soundtrack • Jubilee (M) LP-2 10-15
10-inch LP. Kermit Schafer's "bloopers" from radio, film and TV productions.
Soundtrack [Vol. 4] • Jubilee (M) LP-2011 10-15
10-inch LP.
Soundtrack • K-Tel International (S) NU-431 15-25   74
Two-disc, limited edition. Kermit Schafer's "bloopers" from radio, film and TV productions.
Composer: Sam Coslow (theme song).

PARENT TRAP
Soundtrack (1961) • Buena Vista (M) BV-3309 20-40   61
Soundtrack (1961) • Buena Vista (S) STER-3309.............................. 55-60   61
One side has music from *Intermezzo, Swiss Family Robinson, Sleeping Beauty* and *Alice in
Wonderland*.
Composer: Richard M. Sherman, Robert B. Sherman. **Conductor:** Tutti Camarata. **Cast:**
Hayley Mills, Tommy Sands, Annette Funicello, Maureen O'Hara.
Also see IN SEARCH OF THE CASTAWAYS

PARENTHOOD
Soundtrack (1989) • Reprise (S) 1-26001 8-10   89
Composer: Randy Newman. **Cast:** Randy Newman.

PARIS BLUES
Soundtrack (1961) • United Artists (M) UAL-4092............................... 15-20   61
Soundtrack (1961) • United Artists (S) UAS-5092 20-30   61

Soundtrack (1961) • United Artists (S) UA-LA274-G 10-12   74
    Composer: Duke Ellington, others. **Cast:** Louis Armstrong.
    Also see HORSE SOLDIERS
    Also see JOHNNY COOL

PARIS BY NIGHT
Original Cast • AEI (S) AEI-1158 5-10   80s

PARIS HOLIDAY
Soundtrack (1958) • United Artists (M) UAL-40001 30-45   58
    In addition to film score, has solos by Bob Hope and two duets by Hope and Bing Crosby.
    Crosby does not appear in the film.
    Composer: Joseph J. Lilley, James Van Heusen, Jerome Kern, Vernon Duke. **Conductor:**
    Joseph J. Lilley. **Cast:** Bob Hope, Bing Crosby.

PARIS HONEYMOON
Studiotrack (1939) • Decca (M) DL-6012 50-60   50
    10-inch LP.
    Composer: Ralph Rainger, Leo Robin. **Conductor:** John Scott Trotter. **Cast:** Bing Crosby.
    Also see BING'S HOLLYWOOD

PARIS '90
Original Cast (1952) • Columbia (M) ML-4619 100-150   52
    Composer: Kay Swift. **Conductor:** Nathaniel Shilkret. **Cast:** Cornelia Otis Skinner.

PARIS, TEXAS
Soundtrack (1984) • Warner Bros. (S) 1-25270 8-10   84
    Cast: Ry Cooder.

PARIS WAS MADE FOR LOVERS
Soundtrack • Ala (S) 1981 15-20   78
    Composer: Michel Legrand, Hal Shaper. **Conductor:** Michel Legrand. **Cast:** Michel Legrand,
    Matt Monro, Dusty Springfield.

PARIS WHEN IT SIZZLES
Soundtrack (1964) • Reprise (M) R-6113 15-20   64
Soundtrack (1964) • Reprise (S) RS-6113 25-35   64
    Composer: Nelson Riddle, others. **Conductor:** Nelson Riddle.

PARRISH
Soundtrack (1961) • Warner Bros. (M) W-1413 20-25   61
Soundtrack (1961) • Warner Bros. (S) WS-1413 40-70   61
    Also has music from *Gone with the Wind* and *A Summer Place.*
    Composer: Max Steiner. **Conductor:** Max Steiner. **Cast:** Warner Brothers Orchestra, George
    Greeley (piano).

PARTY
Soundtrack (1968) • RCA Victor (M) LPM-3997 12-18   68
Soundtrack (1968) • RCA Victor (S) LSP-3997 15-20   68
    Composer: Henry Mancini. **Conductor:** Henry Mancini. **Cast:** Party Poops, Henry Mancini and
    His Orchestra.

PARTY PARTY
Soundtrack (1982) • A&M (S) SP-3212 8-12   82
    Cast: Elvis Costello & the Attractions, Dave Edmunds, Altered Images, Bad Manners, Sting,
    Bananarama, Madness, Modern Romance, Pauline Black, Midge Ure, Chas & Dave.

PARTY WITH BETTY COMDEN AND ADOLPH GREEN
Original Cast (1958) • Capitol (M) WAO-1197 10-25   58
Original Cast (1958) • Capitol (S) SWAO-1197 15-20   58
    Composer: Betty Comden, Adolph Green, others. **Conductor:** Peter Howard. **Cast:** Betty
    Comden, Adolph Green.

Original Revival Cast (1977) • Stet (S) S2L-5177 10-12   77
  Two discs.
    Composer: Betty Comden, Adolph Green, others. **Cast:** Betty Comden, Adolph Green.

PASCALI'S ISLAND
Soundtrack (1988) • Virgin Movie Music (S) 90976-1 8-10   88
    Composer: Loek Dikker. **Conductor:** Huub Kerstens. **Cast:** Philharmonic Orchestra of
    Flanders.

PASSAGE TO INDIA
Soundtrack (1985) • Capitol (S) SV-12389 8-12   85
    Composer: Maurice Jarre. **Conductor:** Maurice Jarre.

PASSING FAIR
Original Cast (1965) • Proscenium (M) PR-25 30-35   65
  Intended for Broadway, but this show never opened.
    Composer: James Forbes Chapin. **Cast:** James Forbes Chapin, Valentine Pringle, Mary
    Louise, Bill Dillard, Dolores Perry, Mark Donald (piano).

PASSION: see LAST TEMPTATION OF CHRIST

PAT GARRETT AND BILLY THE KID
Soundtrack (1973) • Columbia (S) KC-32460 12-15   73
Soundtrack (1973) • Columbia (S) PC-32460 8-10   Re
    Composer: Bob Dylan. **Cast:** Bob Dylan, Brenda Patterson, Donna Weiss, Priscilla Jones,
    Byron Berline, Carol Hunter.

PAT O'BRIEN
TV Soundtrack (1964) • RIK (S) M-1003 10-15   64
    Cast: Pat O'Brien.

PATCH OF BLUE
Soundtrack (1965) • Mainstream (M) 56068 12-15   65
Soundtrack (1965) • Mainstream (S) S-6068 20-30   65
Soundtrack (1965) • Mainstream (S) ST 90805 12-18
  Capitol Record Club issue.
Soundtrack (1965) • Citadel (S) CT-6028 10-12   78
Soundtrack (1965) • Citadel (S) CT-7008 8-12   80
    Composer: Jerry Goldsmith. **Conductor:** Jerry Goldsmith.
Studiotrack (1963) • MGM (M) E-4358 10-15   63
Studiotrack (1963) • MGM (S) SE-4358 10-15   63
  Full title: *Impressions of a Patch of Blue.*
    Cast: Walt Dickerson Quartet (featuring Sun Ra).

PATRICK
Soundtrack (1978) • Varese Sarabande (S) VC-81107 10-15   79
    Composer: Brian May. **Conductor:** Brian May. **Cast:** Susan Penhaligon, Robert Helpmann.

PATTON
Soundtrack (1970) • 20th Century-Fox (S) S-4208 8-20   70
Soundtrack (1970) • 20th Century-Fox (S) T-902 5-15   Re
    Composer: Jerry Goldsmith. **Conductor:** Jerry Goldsmith. **Cast:** George C. Scott. (With
    dialogue.)

PATTY
Soundtrack (1976) • Stang (S) 1027 15-20   76
    Composer: Al Goodman, Sammy Lowe, others. **Conductor:** Sammy Lowe. **Cast:** Moments,
    Rimshots, Chuck Jackson, Retta Young.

PATTY HEARST
Soundtrack (1988) • Nonesuch (S) 79186-1 8-10   88
    Composer: Scott Johnson.

PAUL SILLS' STORY THEATRE
Original Cast (1970) • Columbia (S) SG-30415...................................... 8-12   70
Full title: *Paul Sills' Story Theatre.*
Composer: Bob Dylan, Country Joe McDonald, George Harrison, Hamid Hamilton Camp. Cast: Melinda Dillon, Mary Frann, Paul Sand, Richard Libertini, Peter Bonerz, Hamid Hamilton Camp, Valerie Harper, Richard Schaal, True Brethren. (With dialogue.)

PAWNBROKER
Soundtrack (1965) • Mercury (M) MG-21011 15-20   65
Soundtrack (1965) • Mercury (S) SR-61011.. 25-30   65
Composer: Quincy Jones. Conductor: Quincy Jones. Cast: Rod Steiger, Marc Allen (With dialogue.)

PEACE
Original Cast (1969) • Metromedia (S) MP-33001 20-30   69
Composer: Al Carmines, Tim Reynolds. Conductor: Al Carmines. Cast: Julie Kurnitz, George McGarth, Essie Borden, Ann Dunbar, David Vaughan, David Pursley, David Tice, Margaret Wright, Arlene Rothlein, Marie Santell.

PEACH THIEF
Soundtrack (1966) • Roulette (M) OS-804 20-25   66
Soundtrack (1966) • Roulette (S) OSS-804.. 25-30   66
Also has music from six TV soundtracks: *The Cheaters, International Detective, The Liars, The World Tomorrow, Supposin'* and *The Man from Interpol.*
Composer: Simeon Pirankov. Conductor: Simeon Pirankov.

PECOS BILL, KING OF THE COWBOYS
Soundtrack (1986) • Windham Hill (S) WH-0709 10-12   86
Also see JOHNNY APPLESEED

PEE-WEE'S BIG ADVENTURE
Soundtrack (1985) • Varese Sarabande (S) 704 370 12-15   86
Full title: *Pee-Wee's Big Adventure / Back to the Beach.* Also has music from *Back to School* (1986).
Composer: Danny Elfman. Conductor: John Coleman. Cast: National Philharmonic Orchestra.

PEG
Original London Cast (1984) • That's Entertainment (S) TER-1024 8-10   84
UK release.
Composer: David Heneker.

PEG O' MY HEART
Original Cast • Decca (M) DL-7012.. 20-65   50
10-inch LP. Part of Decca's "Cherished Moments of the Theater" series that recreates plays from the 1920s.
Cast: Laurette Taylor, Lew White, others.

PEGGY SUE GOT MARRIED
Soundtrack (1986) • Varese Sarabande (S) STV 81295 10-15   86
Composer: John Barry, Buddy Holly, others. Conductor: John Barry. Cast: John Barry, Buddy Holly, Dion and the Belmonts, Marshall Crenshaw Band, Nicholas Cage with Pride and Joy.
Soundtrack (1986) • That's Entertainment (S) TER-1126....................... 8-10   80s
UK release.

PEKING MEDALLION
Soundtrack (1967) • Philips (S) SBL-7782 45-65   67
UK release.
Composer: Georges Garvarentz, Buddy Kaye. Cast: Dusty Springfield.

PELÉ
Soundtrack (1977) • Atlantic (S) SD-18231 10-12   77
Composer: Sergio Mendes, Pelé. Conductor: Sergio Mendes. Cast: Pelé.

PENELOPE
Soundtrack (1966) • MGM (M) E-4426... 8-20   66
Soundtrack (1966) • MGM (S) SE-4426... 12-30   66
   Composer: Johnny Williams, Leslie Bricusse, Gale Garnett. **Conductor:** Johnny Williams.
   Cast: Pennypipers, Natalie Wood, Johnny Williams.

PENITENTIARY III
Soundtrack (1987) • RCA Victor (S) 6663-1...................................... 8-10   87
   Cast: New Choice, Gap Band, Midnight Star, Yarbrough and Peoples, James Reese, Lotti Dotti,
   Diabolical, La Rue, Rodney Franklin, Shawnie G., Freda Payne, Lenny Williams.

PENNEY PROUD
Original Cast (1962) • Industrial (S) A&R-2195 15-20   62
   Composer: Michael Brown. **Conductor:** Norman Paris. **Cast:** Kenneth Nelson, Ellen Martin,
   Walter Farrell, Cynthia Wayne, Betty Ann Busch, Michael Brown, Tom Mixon.

PENNIES FROM HEAVEN: see BING'S HOLLYWOOD

PENNIES FROM HEAVEN (1981)
Soundtrack (1981) • Warner Bros. (SE) 2-HW-3639............................. 8-10   81
   Two discs.
   Conductor: Marvin Hamlisch, Billy May. **Cast:** Elsie Carlisle, Sam Browne, Connie Boswell,
   Fred Latham, Bing Crosby, Arthur Tracy, Boswell Sisters, Ida Sue McCune, Rudy Vallee, Dolly
   Dawn, George Hall, Helen Kane, Walt Harrah, Gene Merlino, Vern Rowe, Robert Tebow, Irving
   Aaronson, Ronnie Hill.

PENTHOUSE
Soundtrack (1967) • United Artists (M) UAL-4170................................ 12-18   67
Soundtrack (1967) • United Artists (S) UAS-5170 15-20   67
   Composer: John Hawksworth, others. **Conductor:** John Hawksworth. **Cast:** Lisa Shane. (With
   dialogue.)

PEOPLE NEXT DOOR
Soundtrack (1970) • Avco Embassy (S) AVE-0-11002.......................... 20-25   72
   Composer: Don Sebesky. **Conductor:** Don Sebesky.

PEOPLE'S CHOICE
Studio Cast (1968) • RCA Victor (M) PRM-263 10-15   68
   Cast: Edwin Newman (narration).

PEPE
Soundtrack (1960) • Colpix (M) CP-507 10-20   60
Soundtrack (1960) • Colpix (S) SCP-507 15-20   60
   Composer: Johnny Green, others. **Conductor:** Andre Previn, Johnny Green. **Cast:** Shirley
   Jones, Maurice Chevalier, Bobby Darin, Judy Garland, Bing Crosby, Sammy Davis, Jr.

PERCY FAITH PLAYS THE ACADEMY AWARD WINNER AND OTHER
GREAT MOVIE THEMES
Studiotrack (1967) • Columbia (M) CL-2650.. 8-12   67
Studiotrack (1967) • Columbia (S) CS-9450.. 10-12   67
   Composer: Various. **Conductor:** Percy Faith. **Cast:** Percy Faith and His Orchestra.

PERFECT
Soundtrack (1985) • Arista (S) AL-8278 8-10   85
   Composer: Ralph Burns, others. **Cast:** Jermaine Jackson, Pointer Sisters, Thompson Twins,
   Wham, Berlin, Jermaine Stewart, Dan Hartman, Nona Hendryx, Lou Reed, Whitney Houston.

PERFECT COUPLE
Soundtrack (1979) • Lion Gate (S) AQR-524 20-25   79
   Composer: Tony Berg, Ted Neeley, Allan Nichols, others. **Conductor:** Tony Berg. **Cast:**
   Keepin' 'Em Off the Streets (Ted Neeley, Heather MacRae, Tomi-Lee Bradley, Steven Sharp,
   Marta Heflin).

PERFORMANCE

Soundtrack (1970) • Warner Bros. (S) BS-1846.................................. 25-30   70
Soundtrack (1970) • Warner Bros. (S) BS-2554.................................. 12-18   70
   Reissued (BS-2554) just months after first release (BS-1846).
     Composer: Jack Nitzsche, others. **Conductor:** Randy Newman. **Cast:** Randy Newman, Mick
     Jagger, Buffy Sainte-Marie, Merry Clayton, Merry Clayton Singers, Last Poets.

PERICHOLE, LA: see LA PERICHOLE

PERMANENT RECORD

Soundtrack (1988) • Epic (S) SE-40879.............................. 8-10   88
     Composer: Joe Strummer, others. **Cast:** Joe Strummer and the Latino Rockabilly War,
     Godfathers, Bodeans, J.D. Souther, Lou Reed, Stranglers.

PERRI

Soundtrack (1957) • Disneyland (M) ST-3902.. 40-50   57
Soundtrack (1957) • Disneyland (M) ST-1909.. 20-25   61
Soundtrack (1957) • Disneyland (M) DQ-1309 15-20   67
     Composer: Winston Hibler, George Bruns, Paul Smith, Gil George, Ralph Wright, Tutti
     Camarata. **Cast:** Jimmy Dodd, Darlene Gillespie. (With dialogue.)

PET SEMATARY

Soundtrack (1989) • Varese Sarabande (S) VS-5227 8-12   89
     Composer: Elliott Goldenthal. **Conductor:** Steven Mercurio. **Cast:** Zarathustra Boys Choir,
     Orchestra of St. Luke's.

PETE KELLY'S BLUES

Soundtrack (1955) • Columbia (M) CL-690 20-25   55
   Background score and jazz tunes from the film.
     Composer: Various. **Conductor:** Ray Heindorf, Matty Matlock. **Cast:** Matty Matlock and His
     Jazz Band.
Soundtrack (1955) • Decca (M) DL-8166 20-25   55
   Has vocals by Peggy Lee and Ella Fitzgerald not found on the Columbia issue.
     Composer: Various. **Conductor:** Harold Mooney. **Cast:** Peggy Lee, Ella Fitzgerald.
TV Soundtrack (1959) • Warner Bros. (M) W-1303............................. 10-15   59
TV Soundtrack (1959) • Warner Bros. (S) WS-1303............................ 12-18   59
     Composer: Various. **Conductor:** Dick Cathcart.
Studiotrack (1955) • RCA Victor (EP) EPB-1126................................ 15-20   55
   Two discs.
Studiotrack (1955) • RCA Victor (EP) EPA-649................................... 10-25   55
Studiotrack (1955) • RCA Victor (EP) EPM-2053A-649........................ 20-25   55
Studiotrack (1955) • RCA Victor (M) LPM-1126 20-25   55
Studiotrack (1955) • RCA Victor (M) LPM-2040 15-20   59
Studiotrack (1955) • RCA Victor (SE) LSP-2040e 15-20   59
   RCA Victor issues are background music from film, plus narration.
     Cast: Jack Webb (narration), Matty Matlock, Dick Cathcart, Nick Fatool, Elmer "Moe" Schneider,
     George Van Eps, Ray Sherman, Jud DeNaut (jazz combo).
Studiotrack (1957) • RCA Victor (M) LPM-1413 20-25   57
   Actual title: *Pete Kelly At Home.*
     Cast: Jack Webb.
Studiotrack (1959) • RCA Victor (M) LPM-2053 10-12   59
     Conductor: Matty Matlock. **Cast:** Matty Matlock, Dick Cathcart, Eddie Miller, Elmer Schneider,
     Nick Fatool, George Van Eps, Ray Sherman, Jud DeNaut.

PETE'S DRAGON

Soundtrack (1977) • Capitol (S) SW-11704... 15-20   77
     Composer: Al Kasha, Joel Hirschhorn. **Conductor:** Irwin Kostal. **Cast:** Helen Reddy, Mickey
     Rooney, Red Buttons, Shelley Winters, Sean Marshall, Jim Dale, Charlie Callas, Charles Tyner,
     Gary Morgan, Jeff Conaway, others.
Studiotrack (1977) • Disneyland (S) Storyteller 3 8-12   77
   Story of *Pete's Dragon* with music and dialogue from the film, plus 11-page color booklet.

Studiotrack (1977) • Disneyland (S) ST-3818..................................... 20-25   77
  Composer: Al Kasha, Joel Hirschhorn. **Cast:** Helen Reddy, Jim Dale, Mickey Rooney, Red Buttons, Shelley Winters, Sean Marshall, Bob Holt (narrator).

PETER AND THE WOLF

Studio Cast (1979) • Caedmon (S) TC 1623 5-8   79
  Full title: *Peter and the Wolf / Tubby the Tuba.*
  Cast: Carol Channing.

Soundtrack (1946) • Disneyland (M) WDL-3016 35-40   58
Soundtrack (1946) • Disneyland (M) WDL-1016 15-20   60
Soundtrack (1946) • Disneyland (M) DQ-1242 10-15   64
  One side has *The Sorcerer's Apprentice* from *Fantasia.*
  Composer: Sergei Prokofiev. **Cast:** Sterling Holloway (narrator).

Studiotrack • RCA Victor (S) AYLI-4450.. 8-10   82
  Also includes *Pinocchio.*
  Cast: Sterling Holloway (narrator). PINOCCHIO: Cliff Edwards (narrator).
  Also see SNOW WHITE AND THE SEVEN DWARFS

PETER GUNN

TV Soundtrack (1958) • RCA Victor (EP) EPA-4333........................... 10-12   59
  Monaural.
TV Soundtrack (1958) • RCA Victor (EP) ESP-4333........................... 20-25   59
  Stereo.
TV Soundtrack (1958) • RCA Victor (M) LPM-1956........................... 10-12   59
TV Soundtrack (1958) • RCA Victor (S) LSP-1956............................ 12-15   59
  Full title: *The Music from Peter Gunn.*
  Composer: Henry Mancini. **Conductor:** Henry Mancini. **Cast:** Henry Mancini and His Orchestra.

TV Soundtrack [Vol. 2] (1958) • RCA Victor (EP) EPA-4339................ 10-15   59
  Monaural.
TV Soundtrack [Vol. 2] (1958) • RCA Victor (EP) ESP-4339................ 20-25   59
  Stereo.
TV Soundtrack (1958) • RCA Victor (M) LPM-2040........................... 12-15   59
TV Soundtrack (1958) • RCA Victor (S) LSP-2040............................. 12-18   59
  Above two, titled *More Music from Peter Gunn*, may be found with either a red or blue front cover.
  Composer: Henry Mancini. **Conductor:** Henry Mancini. **Cast:** Henry Mancini and His Orchestra.

TV Studiotrack (1959) • Comtemporary (M) C-3560 15-25   59
  Actual title *Shelly Manne and His Men Play Peter Gunn.*
  Composer: Henry Mancini. **Conductor:** Shelly Manne. **Cast:** Shelly Manne and His Combo.

TV Studiotrack (1959) • Crown (M) CLP-5101 10-15   59
TV Studiotrack (1959) • Crown (S) 138... 15-20   59
TV Studiotrack (1959) • Crown (S) 138... 20-25   59
  Red vinyl.
  Composer: Henry Mancini. **Cast:** Ted Nash and His Orchestra.

TV Studiotrack • Lion (M) L-70112 10-12
TV Studiotrack • Lion (S) L-70112.. 10-12
  Full title: *Music from Peter Gunn.*
  Composer: Henry Mancini. **Cast:** Aaron Bell & Orchestra.

TV Studiotrack • MGM (M) CE-3813 10-12
  Full title: *The Best Of Peter Gunn.* May also be shown as E-3813.
  Composer: Henry Mancini. **Conductor:** Ray Ellis. **Cast:** Ray Ellis Orchestra.

PETER PAN (1950)

Original Cast (1950) • Columbia (EP) J-1526..................................... 15-20   50
Original Cast (1950) • Columbia (M) ML-4312 15-20   50
Original Cast (1950) • Columbia (M) OL-4312................................... 12-20   50

Original Cast (1950) • Columbia Special Products (M) AOL-4312.......... 5-10   Re
   Composer: Leonard Bernstein, Alec Wilder. **Conductor:** Ben Steinberg. **Cast:** Jean Arthur,
   Boris Karloff, Marcia Henderson, Deg Hillias, Joe E. Marks.

PETER PAN (1953)

Soundtrack (1953) • Disneyland (M) DQ-1206 20-25   63
   Composer: Sammy Fain, Sammy Cahn, Oliver Wallace, Ed Penner, Ted Sears, Winston Hibler.
   Cast: Bobby Driscoll, Kathryn Beaumont, Hans Conried, Bill Thompson, Candy Candido,
   Jimmie Dodd, Henry Calvin.

Soundtrack (1953) • Disneyland (M) ST 3910 25-30   62
   Die-cut cover and bound-in 11-page booklet.

Soundtrack (1953) • Disneyland (S) 3110 25-30   82
   Picture disc.

Studiotrack (1953) • RCA Victor (EP) EPA-407..................................... 10-15   53

Studiotrack (1953) • RCA Victor (M) LPM-3101 15-25   53
   Conductor: Hugo Winterhalter. **Cast:** Hugo Winterhalter and His Orchestra.

Studiotrack (1954) • Columbia (EP) B-1590.............................. 10-15   54
   Composer: Sammy Fain, Sammy Cahn, Oliver Wallace, Ed Penner, Ted Sears, Winston Hibler.
   Cast: Doris Day.

Studiotrack (1960) • Camden (M) CAL-1009....................................... 10-15   60
   Also has *Alice in Wonderland*.
   Cast: Bobby Driscoll, Kathryn Beaumont, Norman Leyden, Henri Rene and His Orchestra.

Studiotrack • RCA Victor (S) AYLI-4448.................................. 8-10   82
   Cast: Disney artists.

PETER PAN (1954)

Original Cast (1954) • RCA Victor (EP) EYA-48................................. 15-20   54

Original Cast (1954) • RCA Victor (EP) EOC-1019 40-50   54
   Does not have "6 Enchanting Tunes " at top left of front cover.

Original Cast (1954) • RCA Victor (EP) EOC-1019 15-20   54
   Has "6 Enchanting Tunes " on front cover.

Original Cast (1954) • RCA Victor (EP) PR-136 8-15   62
   Six track, stereo 33 EP. Promotional issue only.

Original Cast (1954) • RCA Victor (M) LOC-1019 20-30   54

Original Cast (1954) • RCA Victor (M) LOC-1019 8-12   59

Original Cast (1954) • RCA Victor (SE) LSO-1019e.......................... 10-15   59

Original Cast (1954) • RCA Victor (SE) AYL1-3762 5-10   Re
   Composer: Mark Charlap, Carolyn Leigh, Jule Styne, Betty Comden, Jaye Ribanoff, Trude
   Rittman, Elmer Bernstein, Adolph Green. **Conductor:** Louis Adrian. **Cast:** Mary Martin, Cyril
   Ritchard, Kathy Nolan, Sondra Lee, Robert Harrington, Joseph Stafford, Margalo Gillmore.

PETER RABBIT AND TALES OF BEATRIX POTTER

Soundtrack • Angel (S) S-36789 10-15
   From the Royal Ballet Film.
   Composer: John Lanchberry. **Conductor:** John Lanchberry. **Cast:** Royal Opera House
   Orchestra.

PETEY WHEATSTRAW (THE DEVIL'S SON-IN-LAW)

Soundtrack (1977) • Magic Disc (S) MD-112.. 10-12   77
   Composer: Nat Dove, Mary Love. **Cast:** Nat Dove and the Devils.

PETTICOATS AND PETTIFOGGERS

Original Cast (1969) • Creative Sound (S) CSS-1525 25-30   69
   Composer: James Prigmore, Buddy Youngreen. **Cast:** Neldon Maxfield, Lynne Youngreen,
   Michael Edwards.

PETULIA

Soundtrack (1968) • Warner Bros. (S) WS-1755 20-25   68
   Composer: John Barry. **Conductor:** John Barry.

PEYTON PLACE

Soundtrack (1957) • RCA Victor (M) LOC-1042 20-25   58
Black label. Reads "Long Play" at bottom.
Soundtrack (1957) • RCA Victor (S) LSO-1042................................. 85-100   58
Black label. Reads "Living Stereo" at bottom.
Soundtrack (1957) • RCA Victor (M) LOC-1042 20-25   65
Black label. Reads "Monaural" at bottom.
Soundtrack (1957) • RCA Victor (S) LSO-1042................................. 50-55   65
Black label. Reads "Stereo" at bottom.
Soundtrack (1957) • Entr'acte (S) ERS-6515 10-12   Re
Composer: Franz Waxman. Conductor: Franz Waxman.
TV Soundtrack (1965) • Epic (M) LN-24147 20-25   65
TV Soundtrack (1965) • Epic (S) BN-26147 25-30   65
Composer: Randy Newman, Franz Waxman. Conductor: Randy Newman.

PHAEDRA

Soundtrack (1962) • United Artists (M) UAL-4102................................. 8-10   62
Soundtrack (1962) • United Artists (S) UAS-5102 10-12   62
Soundtrack (1962) • United Artists (S) UA-LA280-G 8-10   74
Composer: Mikis Theodorakis. Conductor: Mikis Theodorakis. Cast: Melina Mercouri.
Also see DIVORCE ITALIAN STYLE

PHANTASM

Soundtrack (1979) • Varese Sarabande (S) VC-81105 8-10   79
Composer: Fred Myrow, Malcolm Seagrave. Conductor: Fred Myrow, Malcolm Seagrave.
Cast: Michael Baldwin, Bill Thornberry.

PHANTOM OF THE OPERA (1987)

Original London Cast (1987) • Polydor (S) 831273-1 15-20   87
Two discs. Includes libretto.
Composer: Andrew Lloyd Webber. Cast: Michael Crawford, Sarah Brightman.
Original Cast (1987) • Polydor (S) 831563-1 10-15   88
"Highlights" from *Phantom of the Opera*.
Composer: Andrew Lloyd Webber. Cast: Michael Crawford.

PHANTOM OF THE OPERA (1989)

Soundtrack (1989) • Restless (S) 72386-1 8-10   89
Composer: Mischa Segal. Conductor: Mischa Segal.

PHANTOM OF THE PARADISE

Soundtrack (1974) • A&M (S) SP-3653 12-15   74
Soundtrack (1974) • A&M (S) SP-3176 8-10   82
Composer: Paul Williams. Cast: Paul Williams, William Finlay, Jessica Harper, Juicy Fruits,
Beach Bums, Undead, Ray Kennedy.

PHAR LAP

Soundtrack (1983) • Varese Sarabande (S) STV 81230 10-15   84
Composer: Bruce Roland.

PHIL THE FLUTER

Original London Cast (1969) • Philips (S) SBL-7916 45-55   69
UK release.
Composer: David Heneker, Percy French. Conductor: Ray Cook. Cast: Evelyn Laye, Mark
Wynter, Stanley Baxter, Basil Lord, John Gower, Sarah Atkinson, Caryl Little, Fred Evans.

PHILADELPHIA EXPERIMENT

Soundtrack (1984) • Rhino (S) RNSP-306 20-25   84
Composer: Ken Wannberg. Conductor: Ken Wannberg.

PHILEMON
Original Cast (1975) • Gallery (S) OC-1 30-40   75
> **Composer:** Harvey Schmidt, Tom Jones. **Conductor:** Ken Collins. **Cast:** Michael Glenn-Smith, Virginia Gregory, Dick Latessa, Leila Martin, Howard Ross, Kathryn King Segal.

PHOTOPLAY PICKS THE GREAT LOVE THEMES OF HOLLYWOOD
Studiotrack (1960) • Warner Bros. (S) WS-1368.................. 15-25   60

PIANO BAR
Original Cast (1978) • Original Cast (S) OC-7812 8-10   78
> **Composer:** Rob Fremont, Doris Willens. **Conductor:** Joel Silberman. **Cast:** Kelly Bishop, Karen DeVito, Steve Elmore, Jim McMahon, Richard Ryder, Joel Silberman.

PICASSO
Soundtrack (1956) • Folkways (M) FS-3860.......................... 50-60   57
> **Composer:** Roman Vlad. **Conductor:** Franco Ferrara. **Cast:** Gangi (flamenco guitar).

PICASSO SUMMER: see SUMMER OF '42

PICKWICK
Original London Cast (1965) • Philips (M) AL-3431 20-25   65
Original London Cast (1965) • Philips (S) SAL-3431 25-30   65
  UK releases. Gatefold – rigid cardboard – covers.
Original London Cast (1965) • World (S) T-487 20-25   Re
  UK release. Gatefold – flexible cardboard – cover.
> **Composer:** Cyril Ornadel, Leslie Bricusse. **Conductor:** Marcus Dods. **Cast:** Harry Secombe, Jessie Evans, Anton Rodgers, Teddy Green, Gerald James, Oscar Quitak, Julian Orchard, Hilda Braid, Norman Warwick, Ian Burford, Robin Wentworth, Tony Simpson.

PICNIC
Soundtrack (1955) • Decca (EP) ED-846 10-15   55
Soundtrack (1955) • Decca (EP) ED-346 15-25   55
  Three discs.
Soundtrack (1955) • Decca (M) DL-8320 20-25   55
  Pink lettering on front covers. Black label.
Soundtrack (1955) • Decca (S) DL-78320......................... 25-35   59
  Pink lettering on front covers. Has gold stereo box affixed over mono number. Black label.
Soundtrack (1955) • Decca (S) DL-78320......................... 15-20   59
  Yellow lettering on front cover, with a stereo band across the top. Rainbow (or multi-color) label.
> **Composer:** George Duning. **Conductor:** Morris Stoloff.

Soundtrack (1955) • MCA (S) 2049........................... 8-10   72
Soundtrack (1955) • MCA (S) 1527........................... 5-8   80s
Studiotrack (1955) • Coral (EP) EC 81132 10-15   55
> **Cast:** Steve Allen and Orchestra, George Cates and Orchestra.

PIECE OF THE ACTION
Soundtrack (1977) • Curtom (S) CU 5019........................... 10-25   77
> **Composer:** Curtis Mayfield. **Cast:** Mavis Staples.

PIECES OF EIGHT
Original Cast (1959) • Offbeat (M) O-4016........................... 60-65   59
  Julius Monk's *Upstairs At the Downstairs* revue.
> **Composer:** William Roy, others. **Cast:** Ceil Cabot, Del Close, Jane Connell, Estelle Parsons, Gerry Matthews, William Roy and Carl Norman (pianos).

Original London Cast (1959) • London (M) 5761 35-45   63
  UK release.
> **Composer:** Laurie Johnson. **Conductor:** Frank Horrox. **Cast:** Kenneth Williams, Fenella Fielding, Myra deGroot, Peter Reeves, Josephine Blake, Terence Theobald, Valerie Walsh, Peter Brett, Frank Horrox Quintet.

PIED PIPER OF HAMELIN (1957)

TV Soundtrack (1957) • RCA Victor (M) LPM-1563............................. 30-50   57
   Composer: Edvard Grieg, Hal Stanley, Irving Taylor. **Conductor:** Peter Dudley King. **Cast:**
   Joseph Sargent (narration), Van Johnson.

PIED PIPER OF HAMELIN (1968)

Studio Cast (1968) • Columbia (S) CS-9572 10-12   68
   Cast: Gene Kelly (narrator).

PIGSKIN PARADE: see EVERYBODY SING

PILLOW TALK

Soundtrack (1959) • Columbia (EP) B-2156... 40-45   59
Soundtrack (1959) • Universal International (M) 1318.......................... 50-60   59
   Red vinyl single. Has interview with Doris Day.
Soundtrack (1959) • Universal International (M) DCLA 1316 250-325   59
   Single-sided. Narrated by Doris Day. Die-cut cover is shaped like a round pillow. Reads:
   "Selections from the soundtrack of *Pillow Talk*. This special recording is personally for you."
   Conductor: Joseph Gershenson. **Cast:** Doris Day, Rock Hudson, Perry Blackwell.
Studiotrack (1959) • Decca (EP) 9-30966 45-65   59
   Rock Hudson sings four songs from the film.
   Conductor: Joseph Gershenson. **Cast:** Rock Hudson.

PINK CADILLAC

Soundtrack (1989) • Warner Bros. (S) 1-25922 8-10   89
   Cast: Michael Martin Murphey, Hank Williams, Jr., Hank Williams, Sr., Jill Hollier, Randy Travis,
   Southern Pacific, J.C. Crowley, Billy Hill, Dion, Robben Ford.

PINK PANTHER

Soundtrack (1964) • RCA Victor (M) LPM-2795 8-12   64
Soundtrack (1964) • RCA Victor (S) LSP-2795 10-25   64
Soundtrack (1964) • RCA Victor (S) ANL1-1389 8-10   Re
   Composer: Henry Mancini. **Conductor:** Henry Mancini. **Cast:** Meglio Stasera.
   Also see CHARADE

PINK PANTHER STRIKES AGAIN

Soundtrack (1976) • United Artists (S) UA-LA-694-G 12-15   76
Soundtrack (1976) • Liberty (S) LT-51135... 8-10
   Composer: Henry Mancini. **Conductor:** Henry Mancini. **Cast:** Tom Jones.

PINOCCHIO

Soundtrack (1940) • Disneyland (M) WDL-4002 200-250   56
   Yellow label.
Soundtrack (1940) • Disneyland (M) ST-4905.................................... 75-150   63
   Six-page, accordian-style, gatefold cover with pop-up figures.
Soundtrack (1940) • Disneyland (M) DQ-1202 20-25   59
Soundtrack (1940) • Disneyland (M) 3102... 25-30   81
   Picture disc.
   Composer: Leigh Harline, Ned Washington, Paul J. Smith, Ed Plumb. **Conductor:** Leigh
   Harline, Paul J. Smith. **Cast:** Cliff Edwards (as Jiminy Cricket), Walter Catlett.
Studiotrack (1940) • RCA Victor Y385 45-5253.................................... 10-20   49
   "Little Nipper" storybook, 78 rpm album set.
   Composer: Norman Leyden. **Conductor:** Henri Rene. **Cast:** Cliff Edwards, Sandy Fussell,
   Jackson Beck, Patsy Camperc, Frank Milano, Cliff Edwards (narrator).
Studiotrack (1950) • Decca (EP) ED-719 10-15   50
Studiotrack (1940) • Decca (M) DL-5151 55-65   50
   10-inch LP. Full title: *Song Hits from Pinocchio*
   Conductor: Victor Young. **Cast:** Cliff Edwards, Victor Young and His Orchestra.
Studiotrack (1940) • Decca (M) DL-8387 20-30   56
Studiotrack (1940) • Decca (SE) DL-78387... 10-15   Re
   One side has music from *The Wizard of Oz*.

Composer: Leigh Harline, Ned Washington. **Composer:** Harold Arlen, E.Y. Harburg.
Conductor: Victor Young. **Cast:** Cliff Edwards, Julietta Novis, Ken Darby Singers, King's Men,
Judy Garland, Ken Darby Singers. WIZARD OF OZ: **Composer:** Harold Arlen, E.Y. Harburg.
Conductor: Victor Young. **Cast:** Cliff Edwards, Julietta Novis, Ken Darby Singers, King's Men,
Judy Garland, Ken Darby Singers.

Studiotrack (1940) • Disneyland (S) 3905 45-50   57
   Cast: Cliff Edwards (as Jiminy Cricket), others.

TV Soundtrack (1957) • Columbia (M) CL-1055 30-35   57
   Composer: Alec Wilder. **Conductor:** Glenn Osser. **Cast:** Mickey Rooney, Fran Allison, Jerry
   Colonna, Stubby Kaye, Martyn Green, Gordon B. Clarke.

Studiotrack • MCA (S) 13301 15-25   83
Picture disc. One side has music from *The Wizard of Oz.*
   Cast: Judy Garland, others
Also see PETER AND THE WOLF

PINS AND NEEDLES

Original Cast (1937) / TV Soundtrack (1966) • JJA (M) 19783 20-25   78
Originally presented in 1937 by the International Ladies Garment Workers Union. Side one
is original cast members in songs remastered from 78 rpm singles. Side two is selections
from the 1966 television production.
   Composer: Harold Rome. **Cast:** Millie Weitz, Kay Weber, Sonny Schuyler, Ruth Rubinstein,
   Clarence Palmer, Harold Rome (from the original New York production), Elaine Stritch, Bobby
   Short, Phil Leeds, Josephine Premice, Bob Dishy (from the television production).

Studio Cast (1962) • Columbia (M) OL-5810 8-10   62
Studio Cast (1962) • Columbia (S) OS-2210 8-12   62
Labeled "25th Anniversary Edition."
Studio Cast (1962) • Columbia Special Products (S) AOS-2210 8-10   Re
   Composer: Harold J. Rome, others. **Conductor:** Stan Freeman. **Cast:** Harold Rome, Barbra
   Streisand, Jack Carroll, Rose Marie Jun, Alan Sokoloff.

PIPE DREAM

Original Cast (1955) • RCA Victor (EP) EOC-1023 30-40   55
Three discs. Has "Special Advance Edition" on cover.

Original Cast (1955) • RCA Victor (M) LOC-1023 45-65   55
Front cover originally listed the names of William Johnson and Helen Traubel in the wrong
order. A white "Special Advance Edition" banner was added to cover the error. Price here is
for those copies.

Original Cast (1955) • RCA Victor (M) LOC-1023 35-45   55
Text errors corrected. Reworked cover has drawings on pink background with credits in a
white box.

Original Cast (1955) • RCA Victor (M) LOC-1097 18-20   65
Original Cast (1955) • RCA Victor (SE) LSO-1097e 30-35   65
White cover with credits on top, picture on bottom.
   Composer: Richard Rodgers, Oscar Hammerstein II. **Conductor:** Salvatore Dell'isola. **Cast:**
   Helen Traubel, William Johnson, Judy Tyler, George D. Wallace, Mike Kellin.

PIPE DREAMS

Soundtrack (1976) • Buddah (S) BDS-5676 15-20   76
   Composer: Dominic Frontiere, others. **Conductor:** Dominic Frontiere. **Cast:** Gladys Knight and
   the Pips.

PIPPI IN THE SOUTH SEAS

Soundtrack (1974) • GG (S) 6305 10-15   74
   Cast: Henry Jerome.

PIPPIN
Original Cast (1972) • Motown (S) M-760L.. 10-15   72
Gatefold cover.
Original Cast (1972) • Motown (S) 5342-ML.. 5-8   Re
Standard cover.
    Composer: Stephen Schwartz. **Conductor:** Stanley Lebowsky. **Cast:** Eric Berry, Jill Clayburgh, Leland Palmer, Ben Vereen, Irene Ryan, John Rubinstein.

PIRANHA
Soundtrack (1978) • Varese Sarabande (S) STV-81126 12-18   79
    Composer: Pino Donaggio. **Conductor:** Pino Donaggio.

PIRATE
Soundtrack (1948) • MGM MGM-21 20-25   51
78 rpm album.
Soundtrack (1948) • MGM (M) E-21 45-80   51
10-inch LP.
Soundtrack (1948) • MGM (M) E-3234 15-18   55
One side of this LP is music from *Summer Stock.*
    Composer: Cole Porter. **Conductor:** Lennie Hayton. **Cast:** Judy Garland, Gene Kelly.
Also see THOSE GLORIOUS MGM MUSICALS.

PIRATE MOVIE
Soundtrack (1982) • Polydor (S) PD-2-9503 8-10   82
Two discs.
    Composer: Terry Britten, Sue Shifrin, others. **Conductor:** Peter Sullivan. **Cast:** Christopher Atkins, Brain Robertson, Pirates & Mike Brady, Kristy McNichol, Ian Mason, Kool & the Gang, Peter Cupples Band, Peter Sullivan & Orchestra, Ted Hamilton, Bill Kerr, Gary McDonald & Policemen, The Sisters.

PIRATES
Soundtrack (1986) • Varese Sarabande (S) STV-81287 12-15   86
Actual title: *Roman Polanski's Pirates.*
    Composer: Philippe Sarde. **Cast:** Philippe Sarde Orchestra De Paris, Bill Byers.

PIRATES OF PENZANCE
Studio Cast (1960) • Hudson (M) 222 8-10   60
Studio Cast • Acorn (S) 637 8-10
Original Cast (1981) • Elektra (S) VE-601 12-15   81
Two discs. Complete performance of the 1981 Broadway revival.
    Composer: William S. Gilbert, Arthur Sullivan. **Cast:** Linda Ronstadt, Kevin Kline, Estelle Parsons, George Rose, Rex Smith.

PIZZA HUT '73 (ANNUAL MEETING)
Assembled Cast (1973) • Pizza Hut (M) No Number Used.................. 15-20   73
Recorded at the Town & Country Hotel, San Diego, California, January 7 - 10, 1973.
    Cast: Rich Little (doing impressions of Elvis Presley, Dean Martin, Johnny Cash, Bing Crosby and others).

PLACES IN THE HEART
Soundtrack (1984) • Varese Sarabande (S) 81229 10-15   84
    Cast: Doc and Merle Watson, Texas Playboys.

PLAIN AND FANCY
Original Cast (1955) • Capitol (EP) EDM-603....................................... 15-20   55
Original Cast (1955) • Capitol (M) S-603.. 15-20   55
Red label. Blue cover.
Original Cast (1955) • Capitol (M) W-603... 12-15   55
Black label. Cover is a much lighter blue than original.

Original Cast (1955) • Capitol (SE) DW-603 10-12   59
Cover has staged (studio) photo, not one made druing the original production.
Composer: Albert Hague, Arnold Horwitt. **Conductor:** Franz Allers. **Cast:** Richard Derr,
Barbara Cook, David Daniels, Gloria Marlowe, Nancy Andrews, Elaine Lynn, Shirl Conway,
Douglas Fletcher Rodgers.

London Studio Cast (1957) • Dot (M) DLP-3048 25-30   57
One side has music from *The Water Gypsies.*
Composer: Albert Hague, Arnold Horwitt. **Conductor:** Cyril Ornadel. **Cast:** Virginia Somers,
Jack Drummond, Grace O'Connor, Joan Hovis, Malcolm Keen.

PLAN 9 FROM OUTER SPACE
Soundtrack (1958) • Pendulum (S) EROS-009 15-20   78
Soundtrack (1958) • Performance (M) 391... 10-15   89
Cast: Bela Lugosi, Vampira, others.

PLANES, TRAINS, AND AUTOMOBILES
Soundtrack (1988) • Hughes/MCA (S) MCA-6223................................. 8-10   88
Composer: Ira Newborn **Cast:** Dream Academy, Steve Earle and Dukes, Dave Edmunds,
Emmylou Harris, Silicon Teens, Stars of Heaven, E.T.A. featuring Steve Martin & John Candy,
Westworld, Balaam & the Angel.

PLANET OF THE APES
Soundtrack (1968) • 20th Century-Fox (M) No Number Used 10-25   68
"College – General Spot Announcements." Label shows "45 RPM" but disc plays at 33 rpm.
Seven-inch single. Promotional issue only.
Cast: Charlton Heston (narrator.)

Soundtrack (1968) • Project 3 (S) PR-5023SD.................................... 10-35   68
Standard cover.

Soundtrack (1968) • Project 3 PR 5023 20-25   68
Gatefold cover.
Composer: Jerry Goldsmith. **Conductor:** Jerry Goldsmith.
Also see BENEATH THE PLANET OF THE APES

PLATINUM
Original Cast (1978) • No Label Name Used (S) No Number Used.. 125-150   78
Live recording.
Composer: Gary William Friedman, Will Holt. **Cast:** Alexis Smith, Richard Cox, Lisa Mordente.

PLATOON (AND SONGS FROM THE ERA)
Soundtrack (1986) • Atlantic (S) 81742-1... 8-10   87
Composer: Georges Delerue. **Conductor:** George Delerue. **Cast:** Vancouver Symphony
Orchestra, Smokey Robinson, Merle Haggard, Doors, Jefferson Airplane, Aretha Franklin, Otis
Redding, Percy Sledge, Rascals.

PLATOON LEADER
Soundtrack (1988) • GNP/Crescendo (S) GNPS-8013........................... 8-10   88
Cast: George S. Clinton.

PLAY IT AGAIN, SAM
Soundtrack (1972) • Paramount (S) 1004 10-15   72
Composer: Billy Goldenberg, others. **Conductor:** Billy Goldenberg. **Cast:** Woody Allen, Diane
Keaton, Tony Roberts, Oscar Peterson Trio.

PLAYGIRLS
Original Cast (1964) • Warner Bros. (M) W-1530................................. 20-25   64
Original Cast (1964) • Warner Bros. (S) WS-1530.............................. 30-35   64
Composer: Jackie Barnett. **Conductor:** Dean Elliott. **Cast:** Cara Williams, Kay Stevens, Julie
Wilson, Connie Russell.

PLAYING FOR KEEPS
Soundtrack (1986) • Atlantic (S) 81678-1.. 8-10   86
Cast: Peter Frampton, Sister Sledge, Eugene Wilde, Chris Thompson, Pete Townshend, Joe
Cruz, Arcadia, Julian Lennon, Phil Collins.

PLAYTIME (ORIGINAL SOUNDTRACK MUSIC FROM THE FILMS OF JACQUES TATI)

Soundtrack • UA International (S) UNS 15554 20-30   68
Also has music from *Mon Oncle, Mr. Hulot's Holiday, Jour De Fete* and *Cours Du Soir.*
Composer: Jacques Tati, Jan Yatove, Leo Petit. **Conductor:** François Lemarque, François Rauber, Jan Yatove, Leo Petit.

PLEASURE SEEKERS

Soundtrack (1964) • RCA Victor (M) LOC-1101 35-45   65
Soundtrack (1964) • RCA Victor (S) LSO-1101 70-80   65
Though some covers have an "RE", this album came out only once.
Composer: James Van Heusen, Lionel Newman, others. **Conductor:** Lionel Newman. **Cast:** Ann-Margret.

PLEASURES AND PALACES: see LOOK TO THE LILIES

PLOW THAT BROKE THE PLAINS

Studiotrack (1936) • RCA DM-1116 165-175   47
Two 12-inch, 78 rpms in an album with pictures. 1936 documentary for the U.S. Farm Security Administration.
Composer: Virgil Thomson. **Conductor:** Leopold Stokowski. **Cast:** Hollywood Bowl Orchestra. Also see OUR TOWN, RIVER

Studiotrack • AEI (M) AEI-3501 5-10   80s
Composer: Virgil Thomson. **Conductor:** Neville Marriner. **Cast:** L.A. Chamber Orchestra.

PLYMOUTH ADVENTURE: see IVANHOE

POCKET FULL OF DREAMS: see BING'S HOLLYWOOD

POINT

Original London Cast (1977) • MCA (S) 2331 8-10   77
TV Soundtrack (1971) • RCA Victor (S) LSPX-1003 12-15   71
Includes eight-page storybook.
TV Soundtrack (1971) • RCA Victor (S) LSP-4417 8-10   71
Without booklet.
Composer: Harry Nilsson. **Conductor:** Harry Nilsson. **Cast:** Harry Nilsson, Micky Dolenz, Davy Jones.

POINT OF ORDER

TV Soundtrack (1964) • Columbia (S) KOL-6070 10-12   64
TV Soundtrack (1964) • Columbia (S) KOS-2470 12-15   64
Documentary of the U.S. Army/Joseph McCarthy Senate Hearings.
Cast: Eric Sevareid (narration), Joseph McCarthy, Joseph L. Welch, Robert T. Stevens, James Jullana, Roy M. Cohn, Senators: Karl E. Mundt, John G. McClellan, Henry Jackson, Stuart Symington. (Dialogue).

POITIER MEETS PLATO

Studio Cast (1964) • Warner Bros. (M) W-1561 12-15   64
Cast: Sidney Poitier (narrator), Fred Katz (music.)

POLICE ACADEMY IV – CITIZENS ON PATROL

Soundtrack (1987) • Motown (S) 6235ML 8-10   87
Cast: Darryl Duncan, S., Stacy Lattisaw, Brian Wilson, Michael Winslow and L., Family Dream, Chico De Barge, Garry Glenn, Southern Pacific.

POLICE ACADEMY VI

Soundtrack (1989) • Posse (S) POS-1234 12-15   89
Promotional issue only.

POLLYANNA

Soundtrack (1960) • Disneyland (M) ST-1906 45-50   60
Soundtrack (1960) • Disneyland (M) DQ-1307 20-25   67
Composer: Paul J. Smith, others. **Cast:** Kevin Corcoran, Hayley Mills, Karl Malden, Jane Wyman, Adolphe Menjou, Agnes Moorehead. (With dialogue.).

POLONAISE: see EILEEN

POLTERGEIST
Soundtrack (1982) • MGM (S) 1-5408.. 35-40   82
    Composer: Jerry Goldsmith. Conductor: Jerry Goldsmith.

POLTERGEIST II – THE OTHER SIDE
Soundtrack (1986) • Intrada (S) RVF-6002 10-12   86
    Composer: Jerry Goldsmith. Conductor: Jerry Goldsmith.
Soundtrack (1986) • That's Entertainment (S) TER-1116...................... 8-10   80s
  UK release.

POLTERGEIST III
Soundtrack (1988) • Varese Sarabande (S) 704.620 50-75   88
    Composer: Joe Renzetti.

POMEGRANADA
Original Cast (1966) • Patsan (M) PS-1101.. 80-100   66
    Composer: Alvin Carmines, H.M. Koutoukas. Cast: Alvin Carmines (piano), Michael Elias,
    Burton Supree, Margaret Wright, David Vaughan, Julie Kurnitz, Meredith Monk, Sandy Padilla.

PONTIFICAL REQUIEM: see JOHN F. KENNEDY

POP GOES THE MOVIES
Studiotrack (1982) • Arista (S) SP 129 8-12   82
Studiotrack (1982) • Arista (S) AL-9598 10-15   82
  Has specially banded excerpts of selections from *Casablanca*, *The Harvey Girls*, *Zorba the
  Greek*, *Strike Up the Band*, *Love Story*, *Laura*, *M*A*S*H*, *Three Coins in the Fountain*,
  Secret Love, *The Godfather*, *Never on Sunday*, *Goldfinger* and 15 others.
    Conductor: Meco. Cast: Meco.

POPE JOHN PAUL II – LIVE IN AMERICA
TV Soundtrack (1979) • Bethleham (S) BA 5555 8-12   79
  Includes photo insert.

POPEYE
Original Radio Cast • Mark 56 (M) 715.. 40-80   79
  Picture disc. Die-cut cover.
Original Radio Cast • Mark 56 (M) 715.. 30-50   79
  Picture disc. Generic cover.
Original Radio Cast • Golden Age (M) 5008.. 8-10
  Full title: *Popeye The Sailor.*
Soundtrack (1980) • Boardwalk (S) SW-36880 10-15   80
    Composer: Harry Nilsson, Sam Lerner. Conductor: Van Dyke Parks. Cast: Robin Williams,
    Shelley Duvall, Ray Walston, Paul L. Smith, Falcons, Ray Cooper, Doug Dillard, Harry Nilsson,
    Van Dyke Parks, Klaus Voorman, Mysterious Karsten.

POPI
Soundtrack (1969) • United Artists (S) UAS-5194 8-12   69
Soundtrack (1969) • MCA (S) 25044... 5-8   86
    Composer: Dominic Frontiere. Conductor: Dominic Frontiere.

POPPY
Soundtrack (1936) • Columbia (M) KC-33253 8-10   75
    Cast: W.C. Fields.

POPS IN SPACE
Studiotrack (1980) • Philips (S) 9500 921 10-15   80
  Music from *Superman*, *The Empire Strikes Back*, *Star Wars*, *Close* and *Encounters of the
  Third Kind.*
    Conductor: John Williams. Cast: John Williams & the Boston Pops Orchestra.

POPULAR PIANO CONCERTOS FROM THE GREAT BROADWAY MUSICALS

Studiotrack • Warner Bros. (M) W-1415....................................... 10-15   60s
Studiotrack • Warner Bros. (S) WS-1415..................................... 15-20   60s
    Conductor: George Greeley. **Cast:** George Greeley and Orchestra.

PORGY AND BESS

Original Cast (1940) • Decca (EP) ED-808 15-20   50
Original Cast [Vol. 1] (1940) • Decca A-145.............................. 15-20   50
Original Cast [Vol. 2] (1940) • Decca A-283.............................. 15-20   50
Original Cast [Vol. 3] (1940) • Decca A-351.............................. 15-20   50
  78 rpm albums.
Original Cast (1940) • Decca (M) DL-7006................................. 15-20   50
  10-inch LP.
Original Cast (1940) • Decca (M) DL-8042................................. 20-25   52
Original Cast (1940) • Decca (M) DL-9024................................. 15-20   55
  Cover art is a drawing of Catfish Row.
Original Cast (1940) • Decca (M) DL-9024................................. 12-15   59
Original Cast (1940) • Decca (SE) DL-79024.............................. 10-12   59
Original Cast (1940) • MCA (SE) 2035e..................................... 8-10   73
Original Cast (1940) • MCA (SE) 1631....................................... 5-8   80s
  Above four covers picture cast members. Decca recordings include members of several different companies (1935 to 1940) of the show.
    Composer: George Gershwin, Ira Gershwin, DuBose Heyward. **Conductor:** Alexander Smallens. **Cast:** Todd Duncan, Anne Brown, Eva Jessye Choir, Edward Matthews, Georgette Harvey, Helen Dowdy, Harriett Jackson, William Woolfolk, Avon Long, Gladys Goode, Decca Symphony Orchestra.

Original Revival Cast (1953) • RCA Victor (EP) EPA-487 10-15   53
Original Revival Cast (1953) • RCA Victor (M) LM-2679 10-15   63
Original Revival Cast (1953) • RCA Victor (SE) LSC-2679.................... 12-18   63
  Gatefold covers.
    Composer: George Gershwin, Ira Gershwin, DuBose Heyward. **Conductor:** Skitch Henderson. **Cast:** Leontyne Price, William Warfield, John W. Bubbles, McHenry Boatwright.

Original Revival Cast (1977) • RCA Victor (S) ARL3-2109 20-25   77
  Boxed, three-disc set. Includes booklet.
Original Revival Cast (1977) • RCA Victor (S) ARL1-2109 8-10   77
  One disc.
    Composer: George Gershwin, Ira Gershwin, DuBose Heyward. **Conductor:** John Demain. **Cast:** Donnie Ray Albert, Clamma Dale, Houston Grand Opera Company, Andrew Smith, Betty Lane, Carol Brice, Larry Marshall, Bernard Thacker, Glover Parhan, Melvin Wallace, Shirley Bains.

Studio Cast (1976) • RCA Victor (S) CPL2-1831................................. 12-18   76
  Two discs.
    Conductor: Frank DeVol. **Cast:** Ray Charles, Cleo Laine.

Studio Cast (1975) • London (S) OSA-13116.................................... 12-15   76
  Two discs. Includes booklet.
    Conductor: Lorin Maazel. **Cast:** Willard White, Leona Mitchell, McHenry Boatwright, Florence Quivar, Lorin Maazel with the Cleveland Orchestra and Chorus.

Studio Cast • AEI (S) AEI-1107 15-20   70s
  Also has music from *Cabin in the Sky*.
    Composer: George Gershwin, Ira Gershwin, DuBose Heyward. **Conductor:** Cy Walter. **Cast:** Todd Duncan, Cy Walter (piano), Mabel Mercer.

Studio Cast (1951) • RCA Victor (M) LM-1124 12-18   51
    Composer: George Gershwin, Ira Gershwin, DuBose Heyward. **Conductor:** Robert Russell Bennett. **Cast:** Risë Stevens, Robert Merrill, Robert Shaw Chorale.

Studio Cast (1953) • Decca (M) DL-4051 15-20   53
    Conductor: Johnny Green. **Cast:** Hollywood Bowl Pops Orchestra.

Studio Cast(1954) • MGM (M) E-3131.. 10-12   54
   Composer: George Gershwin, Ira Gershwin, DuBose Heyward. **Cast:** MGM Studio Orchestra.
Studio Cast (1954) • RCA Victor (EP) ERA-179.................................... 5-10   54
   Conductor: Arthur Fiedler. **Cast:** Arthur Fiedler and the Boston Pops Orchestra.
Studio Cast (1957) • Halo (M) 50115 8-15   57
Studio Cast • Columbia (M) AAL-31 20-25   50s
   10-inch LP.
   Conductor: Lehman Engel. **Cast:** Lawrence Winters, Camilla Williams, Inez Matthews, Avon
   Long, Eddie Matthews, June McMechen, J. Rosamond Chorus.
Studio Cast (1959) • Columbia (M) OSL-162 20-25   59
   Three discs.
Studio Cast (1959) • Columbia (M) CL-922... 8-10   59
Studio Cast (1959) • Columbia (M) OSL-162 15-20   59
   Single LPs with "Highlights" from three-disc set.
Studio Cast (1959) • Columbia/Odyssey (SE) 32-36-001 12-15   Re
   Conductor: Lehman Engel. **Cast:** Lawrence Winters, Camilla Williams, Inez Matthews, Avon
   Long, Helen Dowdy, Eddie Matthews, June McMechen, J. Rosamond Chorus.
Studio Cast (1959) • RCA Victor (M) CAL 500 10-15   59
   Conductor: Alexander Smallens. **Cast:** Lawrence Tibbett, Helen Jepson, Nathaniel Shilkret.
Studio Cast (1960) • Verve (M) MG VS-6040-2.................................... 15-20   60
Studio Cast (1960) • Verve (S) VE-2-2507.. 20-25   60
Studio Cast (1960) • Verve (M) 32472 10-15   Re
   Above three two-disc sets.
   Conductor: Russell Garcia. **Cast:** Ella Fitzgerald, Louis Armstrong.
Studio Cast (1962) • RCA Victor (M) LOP-1507.................................... 10-15   62
Studio Cast (1962) • RCA Victor (S) LSO-1507 15-20   62
   Conductor: Robert Corman, Lennie Hayton. **Cast:** Lena Horne, Harry Belafonte.
Studio Cast • Bethlehem (S) BCP 6009 5-10   76
   Conductor: Russ Garcia. **Cast:** Francis Faye, Mel Torme, Duke Ellington, Pat Moran Quartet,
   Australian Jazz Quintet.
Studiocast • Golten Tone (M) 9641 10-12
   Conductor: John T. Williams. **Cast:** Hollywood Grand Studio Orchestra, Bill Lee, Norma
   Zimmer, Marni Nixon, Earl Wilkie.
Studio Cast • Musical Masterpiece Society (M) M2035 10-12
   Includes four-page libretto.
   Conductor: Paul Belanger. **Cast:** Opera Society Orchestra and Chorus.
Studio Cast • Pirouette (S) FM-21 10-12
   Conductor: Al Goodman. **Cast:** Al Goodman and His Orchestra and Chorus, Lee Carrel, Bill St.
   Clair, Bob Storm, Gene Jones.
Soundtrack (1959) • Columbia (M) OL-5410 10-12   59
Soundtrack (1959) • Columbia (S) OS-2016 12-30   59
   White labels. Banded LP with playing times next to song titles. Promotional issue only.
Soundtrack (1959) • Columbia (M) OL-5410 8-10   59
Soundtrack (1959) • Columbia (S) OS-2016 8-12   59
Soundtrack (1959) • Columbia (S) PS-2016... 5-8   Re
   Unbanded. Playing times not shown next to song titles.
Soundtrack (1959) • Philips (S) SABL-119... 20-25   59
   UK release. Gatefold cover with booklet.
   Composer: George Gershwin, Ira Gershwin, DuBose Heyward. **Conductor:** Andre Previn.
   Cast: Robert McFerrin (performs vocals for Sidney Poitier in the film), Adele Addison (performs
   vocals for Dorothy Dandridge), Pearl Bailey, Cab Calloway (performs songs sung in the film by
   Sammy Davis Jr.), Brock Peters, Loulie Jean Norman (performs vocals for Diahann Carroll),
   Inez Matthews (performs vocals for Ruth Attaway), Clarence Muse.
Studiotrack (1959) • Decca (M) DL-8854 12-15   59

Studiotrack (1959) • Decca (S) DL-78854 15-20   59
> Because of conflicting recording contracts, Decca issued Sammy Davis Jr's *Porgy and Bess*. He does not appear on the Columbia soundtrack.
> **Conductor:** Jack Pleis, Buddy Bregman, Morty Stevens. **Cast:** Sammy Davis Jr., Carmen McRae, Bill Thompson Singers.

Studiotrack • Roulette (M) R 25063.. 15-25
> Full title: *Pearl Bailey Sings Porgy and Bess and other Gershwin Melodies.*
> **Composer:** George Gershwin. **Conductor:** Buddy Baker. **Cast:** Pearl Bailey.

Studiotrack (1959) • Interlude (M) MO-505 8-15   59
> **Cast:** Buddy Collette.

Studiotrack (1959) • National Academy Record Club (M) ES 7 10-15   60
> From *Ed Sullivan Presents Songs and Music of...* series.
> **Cast:** Ed Sullivan All Star Cast.

Studiotrack (1959) • Richmond (M) B-20059.. 10-15   59
Studiotrack (1959) • Richmond (S) S-30059 10-15   59
> Also has music from *Show Boat.*
> **Conductor:** Frank Chacksfield. **Cast:** Frank Chacksfield and His Orchestra.

Studiotrack (1959) • United Artists (M) UAL-4021 15-20   59
Studiotrack (1959) • United Artists (S) UAS-5021 15-25   59
> **Cast:** Diahann Carroll, Andre Previn Trio.

Studiotrack (1960) • Craftsmen (M) 209.. 8-12   60
Studiotrack (1959) • Columbia (M) CL-1274.. 8-10   59
Studiotrack (1959) • Columbia (S) CS-8085.. 8-12   59
> **Cast:** Miles Davis, Gil Evans Orchestra.

Studiotrack (1959) • Dot (M) DLP-3193... 8-10   59
Studiotrack (1959) • Dot (S) DLP-25193 8-12   59
> **Cast:** Bob Crosby and His Bobcats.

Studiotrack • Bethlehem (M) EXLP-1 40-45
> Jazz renditions.

Studiotrack • Bethlehem (M) 3 BP-1.. 8-12   Re
> **Cast:** Francis Faye, Mel Torme.

Studiotrack • Acorn (S) 642... 8-12
> One side has theme track *Music of the South.*
> **Cast:** Albert Cohen and Orchestra.

Studiotrack • Bravo (M) K-119... 8-12
> One side has *Rhapsody in Blue.*
> **Conductor:** John Denati. **Cast:** Bravo Pops Symphony Orchestra.

Studiotrack • Carlton (M) LP 12/111.. 8-12
Studiotrack • Carlton (S) STLP 12/111... 8-12
> **Cast:** Monty Kelly and Orchestra.

Studiotrack • Celebrity (S) UTS 111 8-12
> **Cast:** Clara Ford, Jack Engels, William Enright, Martha Hill.

Studiotrack • Clarity (M) 807 8-12
> One side has music from *Carousel.*
> **Cast:** Hollywood Symphonette Orchestra and Singers.

Studiotrack • Goldentone (M) C 4017.. 8-12
> One side has music from *Carousel.*
> **Cast:** Hollywood Orchestra and Singers.

Studiotrack • Harmony (M) 7169 8-12
> **Cast:** Dino Martinelli and His Orchestra.

Studiotrack • Heliodor (S) HS-25052... 10-15
> **Conductor:** Kenneth Alwyn. **Cast:** Lawrence Winters, Isabelle Lucas, Ray Ellington, Barbara Elsy, Pauline Stevens.

Studiotrack • Hudson (M) 209 8-12
> One side has various Gospel songs.
> **Cast:** Elly Ellason and His Orchestra, Grace Gospel Singers.

Studiotrack • Mercury (S) 60050 8-12
   Cast: Eric Steele and His Orchestra.

Studiotrack • Someret (S) SF-8600 8-12
   Cast: 101 Strings.

Studiotrack • Warner Bros. (M) W 1260 8-12
   Cast: Stewart-Williams and Company.
   Also see CAROUSEL
   Also see FLOWER DRUM SONG
   Also see GIGI
   Also see GIRL CRAZY
   Also see OKLAHOMA!

PORKY'S REVENGE!
Soundtrack (1985) • Columbia (S) JS-39983 10-15   85
   Cast: Dave Edmunds, Jeff Beck, Fabulous Thunderbirds, George Harrison, Willie Nelson, Carl Perkins, Clarence Clemons, Crawling King Snakes.

PORTRAIT OF A SPLENDID AMERICAN
Radio Cast (1961) • Columbia (M) ML-5709 60-75   61
   Documentary broadcast by KMOX, St. Louis, January 1961. Tribute to Dr. Tom Dooley with speech excerpts, interviews and narration. Promotional issue only.
   Cast: Tom Dooley, others.

PORTRAITS IN BRONZE
Studio Cast (1961) • Liberty (M) LSM-13002 15-25   61
Studio Cast (1961) • Liberty (S) LSS-14002 20-30   61
   Excerpts from Robert "Bumps" Blackwell's *Portraits in Bronze.*
   Conductor: Robert Blackwell. **Cast:** Bessie Griffin, Gospel Pearls (Eddie Lee Kendrix, Joe Clayton, Marlene Gwynn, Tony Harris, Delores Addison).

PORTS OF PARADISE
Studiotrack (1960) • Capitol (M) TAO-1447 20-25   60
Studiotrack (1960) • Capitol (S) STAO-1447 40-45   60
   Includes 16-page color booklet.
   Composer: Alfred Newman. **Conductor:** Alfred Newman, Ken Darby.

POSTCARD FROM MOROCCO
Original Cast (1975) • Desto (S) DC-7137-8 15-20   75
   Two discs.
   Composer: Dominick Argento, John Donahue. **Conductor:** Philip Brunelle. **Cast:** Barbara Brandt, Barry Busse, Edward Foreman, Janis Hardy, Yale Marshall, Sarita Roche, Vern Sutton (original cast of the Center Opera of Minnesota).

POUPEES DE PARIS, LES: see LES POUPEES DE PARIS

POWAQQATSI
Soundtrack (1988) • Nonesuch/Elektra (S) FM-37230 10-12   88
   Promotional issue only.
Soundtrack (1988) • Nonesuch (S) 79192-1 10-15   88
   Film sequel to *Koyaanisqatsi.*
   Composer: Philip Glass. **Cast:** Philip Glass.

POWER: see FILM MUSIC OF MIKLOS ROZSA

POWER
Soundtrack (1984) • Cerberus (S) CST-0211 15-20   84
   Composer: Chris Young. **Conductor:** Paul Francis Witt.

POWER IS YOU
Studio Cast (1979) • Clarus (S) CL-1233 10-15   79
   Composer: Rosemary Caggiano, Bernie Fass. **Conductor:** Marty Gold. **Cast:** Tony Randall, Lynn Redgrave, Bob Brown, Steve Clayton, Rose Marie Jun.

PRANKS
Soundtrack (1982) • Citadel (S) CT-7031.. 10-15   82
   Composer: Chris Young. **Conductor:** Chris Young.

PREACHERMAN MEETS WIDDERWOMAN
Soundtrack • PRO (S) 1001 8-12

PREMIER RADIO PERFORMANCES
Studiotrack • Premier (M) PR-1201 20-25
  Music from *A Double Life* and *Time Out of Mind* (Miklos Rozsa), *The Bandit of Sherwood Forest* (Hugo Friedhofer) and *Force of Evil* (David Raksin).
   Composer: Miklos Rozsa, Hugo Friedhofer, David Raksin. **Conductor:** Miklos Rozsa, Hugo Friedhofer, David Raksin.

PREMIERE
Studio Cast (1950s) • Zephyr (M) ZP 12010 35-50   50s
   Conductor: Bob Thompson. **Cast:** Ricardo Montalban, Debra Paget, Howard Duff, Eve Arden, Pat O'Brien, Rita Moreno, Marge & Gower Champion, Ida Lupino, Preston Foster, Corinne Calvet.

PREMISE
Original Cast (1960) • Vanguard (M) VRS-9092.................................. 35-40   60
   Cast: Theodore J. Flicker, Joan Darling, George Segal, Thomas Aldredge. (With dialogue.)

PREPPIES
Original Cast (1984) • Alchemy Records (S) AL-1001-D 10-12   84
   Composer: Gary Portnoy, Judy Hart Angelo. **Cast:** Dennis Bailey, Kathleen Rowe McAllen, Bob Walton, Beth Fowler, Michael Ingram, David Sabin.

PRESSURE IS ON
Soundtrack • Curb (S) 5E-535... 10-15
   Cast: Hank Williams Jr.

PRETENDERS
Studiotrack (1970) • Philips (S) PHS- 600-327 10-15   70
  Full title: *Music to Read* [Gwen Davis'] "The Pretenders" by.
   Composer: Jackie Reinach. **Conductor:** Joe Reinach. **Cast:** Joe Reinach Complex.

PRETTY BABY
Soundtrack (1978) • ABC (S) AA-1076 12-15   78
   Composer: Scott Joplin, Jelly Roll Morton, others. **Conductor:** Jerry Wexler.

PRETTY BOY FLOYD
Soundtrack (1960) • Audio Fidelity (M) AFLP-1936.............................. 40-50   60
Soundtrack (1960) • Audio Fidelity (M) AFSD-5936 70-80   60
   Composer: William Sandord, Del Serino. **Conductor:** William Sandord.

PRETTY IN PINK
Soundtrack (1986) • Virgin (S) SP-17376.. 5-8   86
  12-inch single. Has *If You Leave* on side two.
   Cast: Psychedelic Furs.
Soundtrack (1986) • A&M (S) SP-3293 8-12   86
Soundtrack (1986) • A&M (S) SP-51133293 8-10   86
   Cast: Psychedelic Furs, Jesse Johnson, Suzanne Vega, Orchestral Manoeuvres in the Dark, Smiths, Echo and Bunnymen, New Order, INXS, Belouis Some, Danny Hutton, Hitters, Smiths.

PRETTY WOMAN
Soundtrack (1990) • EMI (S) E1-93492.. 8-10   90
   Composer: Roy Orbison, William Dees, others. **Cast:** Roy Orbison, Natalie Cole, David Bowie, Go West, Jane Wiedlin, Roxette, Robert Palmer, Peter Cetera, Lauren Wood, Red Hot Chili Peppers, Christopher Ocasek.

PRETTYBELLE

Original Cast • Original Cast (S) OC-8238 35-50   82
Show closed out of town in 1971. Members of the original cast were regrouped in 1982 to
make this recording.
> **Composer:** Jule Styne, Bob Merrill. **Conductor:** Milton Rosenstock. **Cast:** Angela Lansbury, Mark
> Dawson, Peter Lombard, Bert Michaels, Maggie Task, Bobby Lee, Michael Jason, Igors Gavon.

PRICK UP YOUR EARS

Soundtrack (1987) • Silver Screen (S) FILM 014 10-15   87
> **Cast:** Stanley Myers, John Harle, Berliner Band.

PRIDE AND THE PASSION

Soundtrack (1957) • Capitol (M) W-873 25-65   57
> **Composer:** George Antheil. **Conductor:** Ernest Gold.

PRIEST OF LOVE

Soundtrack (1981) • That's Entertainment (S) TER-1014....................... 8-10   80s
UK release.
> **Composer:** Joseph James.

PRIME OF MISS JEAN BRODIE

Soundtrack (1969) • 20th Century-Fox (S) S-4207................................. 8-10   69
> **Composer:** Rod McKuen. **Conductor:** Arthur Greenslade. **Cast:** Rod McKuen, Mike Redway,
> Andrew Downey.

Soundtrack (1969) • Warner Bros. (S) WS-1787 10-15   69
Gatefold cover.

Soundtrack (1969) • Stanyan/Warner Bros. (S) WS-1853 10-15   69
Has special overture that was played for Queen Elizabeth and her mother.
> **Composer:** Rod McKuen. **Conductor:** Arthur Greenslade. **Cast:** Rod McKuen.

PRIMITIVE: see MATING URGE

PRIMROSE

Original London Cast (1924) • World (M) SH-214 45-55   74
UK release. Remastered from original 78 rpms, recorded in 1924 when the show opened.
Also has piano selections played by George Gershwin.
> **Composer:** George Gershwin, Ira Gershwin, Desmond Carter. **Conductor:** J. Ansell. **Cast:**
> Margery Hicklin, Percy Heming, Leslie Henson, Heather Thatcher, Thomas Weguelen, Claude
> Hulbert, George Gershwin.

PRINCE AND THE PAUPER

Original Cast (1963) • London (M) AM-28001 20-25   63

Original Cast (1963) • London (S) AMS-98001 20-30   63
> **Composer:** George Fischoff, Verna Tomasson. **Conductor:** Burt Farber. **Cast:** Budd Mann, Joe
> Bousard, Joan Shepard, Robert McHaffey, John Davidson, Carol Blodgett, Flora Elkins.

Studio Cast (1963) • Disneyland (M) ST-1912 20-25   61

Studio Cast (1963) • Disneyland (M) DQ-1311...................................... 10-15   67
First cover is purple, second is red.

Studio Cast (1963) • Pickwick (S) SPC 3204 8-10   Re
Based on Mark Twain's *Prince and the Pauper*.
> **Composer:** Mark Twain.

PRINCE OF DARKNESS

Soundtrack (1987) • Varese Sarabande (S) STV 81340 10-15   87

Soundtrack (1987) • That's Entertainment (S) TER-1157....................... 8-10   80s
UK release.
> **Composer:** John Carpenter.

PRINCE OF THE CITY
Soundtrack (1981) • Varese Sarabande (S) STV-81137 8-10   81
Soundtrack (1981) • That's Entertainment (S) TER-1012 8-10   80s
   UK release.
   Composer: Paul Chihara. **Conductor:** Paul Chihara.

PRINCESS BRIDE
Soundtrack (1987) • Warner Bros. (S) 1-25610 15-20   87
   Composer: Mark Knopfler. **Cast:** Mark Knopfler, Willy Deville.

PRISON
Studio Cast (1974) • Pacific Arts (S) PAC-101 15-20   74
   Boxed set. Includes booklet.
   Composer: Michael Nesmith. **Cast:** Michael Nesmith, David Kempton, Red Rhodes, Michael Cohen, Chura, Don Whaley, Aanami Choir.
Soundtrack (1988) • Varese Sarabande (S) STV 81361 8-10   88
   Composer: Richard Band, Christopher L. Stone.

PRISONER OF ZENDA
Studiotrack • United Artists (S) UA-LA-374-G 10-20   75
   Composer: Alfred Newman. **Conductor:** Leroy Holmes.

PRISONERS OF LOVE: see PRODUCERS

PRIVATE HELL 36
Soundtrack (1954) • Coral (M) CRL-56122 75-100   54
   10-inch LP.
Soundtrack (1954) • Coral (M) CRL-57283 35-45   58
   Actual title: *Jazz Themes for Cops and Robbers*. Also has music from *The Thin Man, Perry Mason, Peter Gunn* and *M Squad*.
   Composer: Leith Stevens. **Conductor:** Leith Stevens.

PRIVATE LESSONS
Soundtrack (1981) • MCA (S) 5275 8-10   81

PRIVATE LIVES: see NOEL AND GERTIE

PRIVATE PARTS: see FILM MUSIC OF HUGO FRIEDHOFER

PRIVATE SCHOOL
Soundtrack (1983) • MCA (S) 36005 8-10   83
   Six-track, "Mini-LP."
   Cast: Phoebe Cates, Men's Room, Bill Wray, Rick Springfield.

PRIVILEGE
Soundtrack (1967) • Uni (M) 3005 15-20   67
Soundtrack (1967) • Uni (S) 73005 20-25   67
   Composer: Mike Leander, Mark London, others. **Conductor:** Mike Leander. **Cast:** Paul Jones, George Bean and the Runner Beans.

PRIZE
Soundtrack (1963) • MGM (M) E-4192 10-12   63
Soundtrack (1963) • MGM (S) SE-4192 12-18   63
   Above two also have eight tracks from eight films, none of which are by Jerry Goldsmith.
   Composer: Jerry Goldsmith. **Conductor:** Jerry Goldsmith.

PRODUCERS
Soundtrack (1968) • RCA Victor (M) LPM-4008 15-20   68
Soundtrack (1968) • RCA Victor (S) LSP-4008 25-30   68

Soundtrack (1968) • RCA Victor (S) ANL1-1132 8-10   75
  Composer: John Morris, Mel Brooks, Norman Blagman, Herb Hartig, Morton Goode.
  Conductor: John Morris. **Cast:** Gene Wilder, Zero Mostel, Dick Shawn, Kenneth Mars, Madlyn
  Cates, Lee Meredith, Christopher Hewett, Mary Love, Amelie Barleon, Nell Harrison, Elsie Kirk,
  Andreas Voutsinas, Arthur Rubin, Zale Kessler, Bernie Allen, Rusty Blitz, Anthony Gardell, John
  Zoller, Renee Taylor. (With dialogue.)
  Also see BLAZING SADDLES

PROFESSIONALS
Soundtrack (1966) • Colgems (M) COMO-5001 55-60   66
Soundtrack (1966) • Colgems (S) COSO-5001 100-150   66
  Composer: Maurice Jarre. **Conductor:** Maurice Jarre.

PROFILE IN MUSIC: see KRAFT TELEVISION THEATRE

PROFILES IN COURAGE
Studio Cast • RCA Victor (M) VDM-103 15-20   65
  Composer: Nelson Riddle. **Cast:** Edward M. Kennedy (narration).

PROGRESS IN SOUND
Studio Cast • Sonic Arts Form (M) 99T645770 K8 20-30
  10-inch LP. Die-cut cover. Promotional issue from Motorola.
  Cast: Norman Ross (narration), Jonathan Winters (dialogue).

PROMENADE
Original Cast (1969) • RCA Victor (S) LSO-1161 12-18   69
  Composer: Al Carmines, Marie Irene Fornes. **Conductor:** Susan Romann, Al Carmines. **Cast:**
  Margot Albert, Shannon Bolin, Michael Davis, Glenn Kezer, Ty McConnell, Alice Playten, Gilbert
  Price, Sandra Schaeffer, Carrie Wilson, Florence Tarlow.

PROMISE
Soundtrack (1979) • MCA (S) 3082 8-20   79
  Composer: David Shire. **Conductor:** David Shire. **Cast:** Melissa Manchester.

PROMISE AT DAWN
Soundtrack (1970) • Polydor (S) 24-5502 25-30   70
  Composer: Georges Delerue, others. **Conductor:** Georges Delerue. **Cast:** Melina Mercouri.

PROMISE HER ANYTHING
Soundtrack (1966) • Kapp (M) KL-1476 10-12   66
Soundtrack (1966) • Kapp (S) KS-3476 10-15   66
  Composer: Lynn Murray, Burt Bacharach, Hal David, Ron Grainer. **Conductor:** John Keating.
  Cast: Tom Jones, others.

PROMISED LAND
Original Cast (1947) • Varese Sarabande (SE) 704 230 10-15   83
  Composer: Crawford Gates, Arnold Sundgaard. **Cast:** Joann Attley, Robert Peterson, Noel
  Twitchell.
Soundtrack (1988) • Private Music (S) 2035-1 10-15   88
  Cast: James Newton Howard.

PROMISES, PROMISES
Original Cast (1968) • United Artists (S) UAS-9902 10-15   68
Original Cast (1968) • United Artists (M) SPOC-1 20-25   68
  Cast interviews and songs. Promotional issue only.
Original Cast (1968) • EMI (S) LO-9902 8-10   Re
  Composer: Burt Bacharach, Hal David. **Conductor:** Harold Wheeler. **Cast:** Jerry Orbach, Jill
  O'Hara, Edward Winter, Donna McKechnie, A. Larry Haines, Marian Mercer, Paul Reed, Dick
  O'Neill, Norman Shelly, Vince O'Brien, Millie Slavin, Adrienne Angel, Margo Sappington,
  Baayork Lee, Kay Oslin, Rita O'Connor, Julane Stites, Neil Jones.
Original London Cast • United Artists (S) 2907 150-175   60s
  UK release.
  Composer: Burt Bacharach, Hal David. **Cast:** Betty Buckley, Tony Roberts, James Congdon,
  Donna McKechnie.

Original Italian Cast • CGD (S) FGS-5063 40-50   60s
  Composer: Burt Bacharach, Hal David. **Cast:** Catherine Spaak, Johnny Dorelli, Bice Valori.
Studio Cast • Fontana (S) SFL-13192.. 10-15   60s
  Composer: Burt Bacharach, Hal David. **Conductor:** Keith Roberts. **Cast:** Aimi MacDonald,
  Ronnie Carroll.

PROPER TIME
Soundtrack (1960) • Contemporary (M) 3587....................................... 15-20   60
Soundtrack (1960) • Contemporary (S) S-7587..................................... 25-30   60
  Cast: Shelly Manne and His Men.

PROPHET
Original Cast (1974) • Atlantic (Q) QD-18120 10-15   74
  Composer: Arif Mardin. **Conductor:** Arif Mardin. **Cast:** Richard Harris.

PROTECTOR
Soundtrack (1985) • Seven Seas (S) K28P-4152................................... 8-10   85
  Composer: Ken Thorne.

PROUDLY THEY CAME
Studio Cast (1970) • Landmark (S) PR-LP-101..................................... 15-20   70
  Two discs.
  Composer: Various. **Cast:** Kate Smith, Bob Hope, Teresa Graves, Young Americans, Jack
  Benny, Centurymen, Dinah Shore, Glen Campbell, Dorothy Lamour, Red Skelton, Jeannie C.
  Riley, New Christy Minstrels, Pat Boone, Esther Phillips, Fred Waring, Les Brown and His Band,
  James Stewart (narration).

PROVIDENCE
Soundtrack (1977) • DRG (S) SL-9502 15-20   80
  Composer: Miklos Rosza. **Conductor:** Miklos Rosza.

**PROWLERS OF THE EVERGLADES: see WALT DISNEY'S TRUE LIFE
  ADVENTURES**

PRUDENCE AND THE PILL
Soundtrack (1968) • 20th Century-Fox (S) S-4199............................... 12-25   68
  Composer: Bernard Ebbinghouse. **Conductor:** Bernard Ebbinghouse. **Cast:** Mike Sammes
  Singers.

PSYCH-OUT
Soundtrack (1968) • Sidewalk (S) ST-5913.. 12-15   68
  Composer: Ron Stein, others. **Cast:** Strawberry Alarm Clock, Seeds, Storybook, Boenzee
  Cryque.

PSYCHO
Studiotrack (1974) • Unicorn (S) RHS-336... 20-25   74
  Composer: Bernard Herrmann. **Conductor:** Bernard Herrmann. **Cast:** National Philharmonic
  Orchestra.
Studiotrack (1974) • Unicorn (S) UNI-75001 20-25   78
  Remastered.
Studiotrack • London (SE) SPC 21151... 20-25   76
  Also has music from 10 other Herrmann film scores.
  Composer: Bernard Herrmann. **Conductor:** Bernard Herrmann.
  Also see GREAT MOVIE THRILLERS

PSYCHO II
Soundtrack (1983) • MCA (S) 6119.. 15-20   83
  Composer: Jerry Goldsmith. **Conductor:** Jerry Goldsmith. **Cast:** Jerry Goldsmith and His
  Orchestra.

PSYCHO III
Soundtrack (1986) • MCA (S) 6174.. 10-15   86
  Composer: Carter Burwell.

PUFNSTUF
Soundtrack (1970) • Capitol (S) SW-542 25-50   70
    Composer: Charles Fox. Conductor: Charles Fox. Cast: "Mama" Cass Elliot, Martha Raye,
    Billie Hayes, Jack Wild.

PULL BOTH ENDS
Original London Cast • That's Entertainment (S) TER-1028.................. 8-10   80s
    UK release.
    Composer: John Schroeder, Anthony King.

PULP FICTION
Soundtrack (1994) • MCA (S) 11103.. 10-15   94

PUMP BOYS AND DINETTES
Original Cast (1982) • Columbia (S) FM-37790...................................... 5-15   82
    Composer: Jim Wann, others. Cast: Jim Wann, Cass Morgan, John Schimmel, Debra Monk,
    John Foley, Mark Hardwick.

PUMP UP THE VOLUME
Soundtrack (1990) • MCA (S) 8039.. 8-10   90
    Cast: Concrete Blonde, Ivan Neville, Liquid Jesus, Pixies, Peter Murphy, Bad Brains with Henry
    Rollins, Above the Law, Soundgarden, Sonic Youth, Cowboy Junkies.

PUMPING IRON 2 – THE WOMEN
Soundtrack (1985) • Island (S) 90273 8-10   85
    Cast: Art of Noise, Skipworth and Turner, Grace Jones, Will Powers, New York City Peech
    Boys, Black Uhuru, Roach, Fast Forward.

PUNCH LINE
Soundtrack (1988) • A&M (S) SP 3922 12-15   88
    Composer: Charles Gross. Conductor: Charles Gross.

PURE GOLD – HENRY MANCINI
Soundtrack • RCA Victor (S) AYL1-3667 10-15   75
    Composer: Henry Mancini. Conductor: Henry Mancini.

PURE GOLD MOVIES
Studiotrack (1976) • RCA Victor (SE) ANL1-1978.................................... 5-10   76
    Music from *Innocents of Paris, A Woman Commands, Lady Be Good, Lilac Time, Gone
    with the Wind, San Francisco, A Night at the Opera, Cabin in the Sky, Sadie MacKee* and
    The Funniest Man in the World.
    Cast: Maurice Chevalier, Russ Columbo, Lanny Ross, Wayne King and His Orchestra with
    Chorus, Living Strings with Johnny Douglas, Jeanette MacDonald, RCA Victor Orchestra with
    Robert Russell Bennett, Allan Jones Orchestra with Robert Armbruster, Rosemary Clooney with
    Nelson Riddle, Gene Austin.

PURLIE
Original Cast (1970) • Ampex (S) A-40101 8-12   70
    Includes *The Harder They Fall.*
Original Cast (1970) • Ampex (Q) A-40101-S....................................... 20-25   70
    Omits *The Harder They Fall.*
    Composer: Gary Geld, Peter Udell. Conductor: Joyce Brown. Cast: Cleavon Little, Melba
    Moore, John Heffernan, Linda Hopkins, Sherman Hemsley, Novella Nelson, C. David Colson.

PURPLE PEOPLE EATER
Soundtrack (1988) • AJK (S) A227-1 10-15   88
    Conductor: Bob Summers, others. Cast: Little Richard, Jan and Dean, D.K., Chubby Checker,
    Sha Na Na, Bobby Day, Mike Harris, Penny and Sondra, Longfellow, Happenings, Bob
    Summers Orchestra.

PURPLE RAIN
Soundtrack (1984) • Warner Bros. (S) 1-25110 8-10   84
    Composer: Prince. Cast: Prince and the Revolution.

PURPLE ROSE OF CAIRO
Soundtrack (1985) • MCA (S) 6139.. 12-15   85
    Composer: Dick Hyman. **Conductor:** Dick Hyman.

PURSUED: see MUSIC BY MAX STEINER

PURSUIT OF D.B. COOPER
Soundtrack (1981) • Polydor (S) PD-1-6344 10-15   81
    Composer: James Horner. **Cast:** Waylon Jennings, Rita Coolidge, Jessi Coulter, Marshall
    Tucker Band.

PUTTIN' ON THE RITZ
Soundtrack (1930) • Meet-Patti Discs (M) PRW-1930............................ 8-10
  Also has music from *Whoopee*.
    Cast: Harry Richman.

Q

Q THE WINGED SERPENT
Soundtrack (1983) • Cerberus (S) CST-0206..................................... 15-20   83
    Composer: Robert O. Ragland. **Conductor:** Robert O. Ragland.

QB VII
TV Soundtrack (1974) • ABC (S) ABCD-822...................................... 15-18   74
    Composer: Jerry Goldsmith. **Conductor:** Jerry Goldsmith.

QUADROPHENIA
Soundtrack (1979) • Polydor (S) PD-2-6235 10-15   80
  Two discs.
    Composer: Peter Townshend, others. **Conductor:** John Entwhistle. **Cast:** The Who (Pete
    Townshend, Keith Moon, Roger Daltrey, John Entwhistle), High Numbers, Cross Section, James
    Brown, Kingsmen, Booker T. & the MGs, Cascades, Chiffons, Ronettes, Crystals, others.

QUANDO L'AMORE E'SENSUALITA
Soundtrack (1981) • Cerberus (S) CEMS-0113................................... 10-15   82
    Composer: Ennio Morricone. **Conductor:** Ennio Morricone.

QUARTET
Soundtrack (1981) • Gramavision (S) GR 1020 10-15   81
    Composer: Richard Robbins. **Conductor:** Richard Robbins.

QUEEN BEA
Studiotrack (1961) • DRG (M) DARC-2-1101 15-18   79
  Two discs. Full title: *Queen Bea, Bea Lillie – A Musical Autobiography*. Bea discusses her
  career and sings songs.
    Cast: Bea Lillie.
  Also see MARVELOUS PARTY WITH BEA LILLIE

QUERELLE
Soundtrack (1982) • DRG (S) 9509.. 10-15   82
    Composer: Peer Raben. **Conductor:** Peer Raben.

QUEST FOR FIRE
Soundtrack (1982) • RCA Victor (S) ABL1-4274 15-20   82
Soundtrack (1982) • RCA Victor (S) 6034/BL-14274........................... 8-10   82
    Composer: Philippe Sarde. **Conductor:** Philippe Sarde.

QUICK AND THE DEAD – THE STORY OF THE ATOM BOMB
Original Radio Cast [Vol. 1] (1950) • RCA Victor (EP) WDM-1507....... 20-25   50

Original Radio Cast [Vol. 1] (1950) • RCA Victor (M) LM-1129............. 40-60   50
Original Radio Cast [Vol. 2] (1950) • RCA Victor (EP) WDM-1508....... 20-25   50
Original Radio Cast [Vol. 2] (1950) • RCA Victor (M) LM-1130............. 40-60   50
    From an NBC public service broadcast.
     Composer: Fred Friendly (writer). **Cast:** Bob Hope, William L. Laurence, President Harry S Truman, Franklin D. Roosevelt, Winston Churchill, General Dwight D. Eisenhower, General Leslie R. Groves, Admiral William S. Parsons, Captain Robert Lewis, Helen Hays, Paul Lukas, Robert Trout.

QUICK BEFORE IT MELTS
Soundtrack (1964) • MGM (M) E-4285................................ 12-15   64
Soundtrack (1964) • MGM (S) SE-4285.............................. 15-18   64
    Both have eight David Rose selections not from this soundtrack.
     Composer: David Rose. **Conductor:** David Rose.

QUICK DRAW MCGRAW
TV Soundtrack (1962) • Colpix (M) CP-203............................ 30-40   62
     Cast: Daws Butler, Don Messick, Doug Young.

QUICKSILVER
Soundtrack (1986) • Atlantic (S) 81631 8-10   86
     Composer: Tony Banks, others. **Cast:** Roger Daltrey, Fiona, Peter Frampton, Ray Parker Jr., Helen Terry, Larry John McNally, Thomas Newman, Tony Banks, Fish, John Parr & Marilyn Martin.

QUIET CITY
Original Cast • Columbia (S) MS-7375................................. 15-25
    Actual title: *Copland Conducts Copland.* Also has music from *Our Town* and other classical selections.
     Composer: Aaron Copland. **Conductor:** Aaron Copland.

QUIET DAYS IN CLICHY
Soundtrack (1970) • Vanguard (S) VSD-79303..................... 10-12   70
     Composer: Country Joe McDonald, Ben Webster, Andy Sundstrom. **Cast:** Country Joe McDonald, Ben Webster, Andy Sundstrom, Young Flowers, Papa Blue's Viking Jazz Band.

QUIET MAN
Soundtrack (1952) • Decca (M) DL-5411 100-120   52
    10-inch LP.
Soundtrack (1952) • Decca (M) DL-8566 75-150   57
Soundtrack (1952) • Varese Sarabande (M) STV-81073 10-15   78
    Both have music from *Samson and Delilah* on one side.
     Composer: Victor Young, others. **Conductor:** Victor Young. **Cast:** Bing Crosby, Victor Young and His Orchestra.
Studiotrack (1952) • RCA Victor (M) LPM-3089 50-65   52
    10-inch LP.
     Composer: Victor Young. **Conductor:** Sydney Green. **Cast:** Merv Griffin.

QUILLER MEMORANDUM
Soundtrack (1966) • Columbia (M) OL-6660 25-30   66
Soundtrack (1966) • Columbia (S) OS-3060 45-60   66
     Composer: John Barry, Tony Hatch, others. **Conductor:** John Barry. **Cast:** Matt Monro.

QUILP
Soundtrack • Chap (S) 12574 50-60
     Composer: Elmer Bernstein.

QUO VADIS
Soundtrack (1951) • MGM (EP) K-134 35-50   51
    Boxed, seven-disc set.
Soundtrack (1951) • MGM (EP) K-103 30-40   57
    Boxed, four-disc set.

Soundtrack (1951) • MGM (M) E-103.. 30-45   51
  10-inch LP. Above have background music from the film, but no dialogue.
Soundtrack (1951) • MGM (M) E-134.. 45-55   51
  Boxed set of two 10-inch discs.
Soundtrack (1951) • MGM (M) E-3524... 18-25   57
Soundtrack (1951) • MCA (SE) 39075 8-10   86
  Full title of above three: *(Dramatic Highlights from) Quo Vadis*. These have dialogue from the film.
  Conductor: Miklos Rozsa. **Cast:** Walter Pidgeon (introduction), Robert Taylor, Deborah Kerr, Leo Genn, Peter Ustinov, Patricia Laffan, Felix Aylmer, Peter Miles, Finlay Currie, Abraham Sofaer, Nora Swinburne. (With dialogue.)
Studiotrack (1953) • Capitol (EP) FAP-454 15-20   53
Studiotrack (1953) • Capitol (EP) EBF-454 20-25   53
  Two discs.
Studiotrack (1951) • Capitol (M) L-454... 30-35   53
  10-inch LP. Combines *Quo Vadis Suite* with *Spellbound Concerto*.
Studiotrack (1953) • Capitol (M) T-456... 35-45   53
  Includes the *Quo Vadis Suite*. Also has *Spellbound Concerto* and *The Red House*.
  Conductor: Erich Kloss. **Cast:** Orchestra of Nurnberg.
Studiotrack (1978) • London (S) SPC-21180...................................... 8-10   78
  Standard cover.
Studiotrack (1978) • London (S) SPC-21180...................................... 20-25   78
  Gatefold cover.
  Composer: Miklos Rozsa. **Conductor:** Miklos Rozsa. **Cast:** Royal Philharmonic Orchestra.
Studiotrack • Decca/Phase 4 (S) PFS 4430 10-15
  Also see FILM MUSIC OF MIKLOS ROZSA

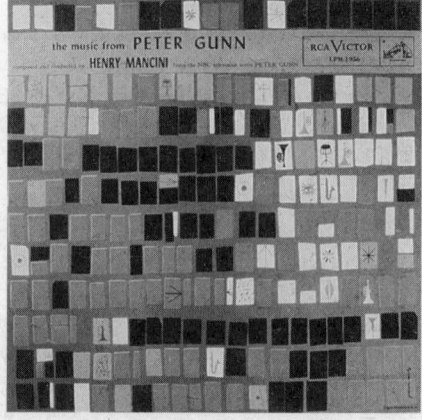

R

R.P.M.
Soundtrack (1970) • Bell (S) 1203.. 10-12   70
    Composer: Barry DeVorzon, Perry Botkin Jr, Melanie. **Cast:** Melanie, Chris Morgan.

R.S.V.P. THE COLE PORTERS
Original Cast (1974) • Respond (S) PMS-299 30-40   74
    Composer: Cole Porter. **Conductor:** Mac Frampton. **Cast:** Mary Margaret McBride (prologue), Jack Jenkins, Sally Jenkins.

RACE FOR THE WIRE
Soundtrack • Anaconda Industrial (M) XB-491 50-75
   Wire-related industrial film by Anaconda Wire & Cable Company.
    Composer: Marion Evans

RACHEL AND THE STRANGER
Soundtrack (1948) • Decca (M) 695................................. 100-125

RAD
Soundtrack (1986) • MCA (S) 6166.. 8-10   86
    Cast: John Farnham, Beat Farmers, 3-Speed, Hubert Kah, Real Life, Sparks, Jimmy Haddox.

RADIO DAYS
Soundtrack (1987) • Novus/RCA Victor (S) 3917-1-N9 8-10   87
    Cast: Tommy Dorsey, Artie Shaw, Allan Jones, Sammy Kaye, Guy Lombardo, Duke Ellington, Xavier Cugat.

RADIO'S GREATEST BROADCASTS
Radio Cast • Longines Symphonette (M) SYS-5387 20-25
    Cast: Jack Armstrong, Ted Kennedy, others.

RAGA
Soundtrack (1971) • Apple (S) SWAO-3384 15-20   71
    Composer: Ravi Shankar, Colin Walcott. **Cast:** Ravi Shankar.

RAGE TO LIVE
Soundtrack (1965) • United Artists (M) UAL-4130................................. 8-10   65
Soundtrack (1965) • United Artists (S) UAS-5130................................. 8-12   65
    Composer: Nelson Riddle, Arthur Ferrante, Louis Teicher. **Conductor:** Nelson Riddle. **Cast:** Ferrante and Teicher.

RAGGEDY ANN AND ANDY
Soundtrack (1977) • Columbia (S) S-34686 12-15   77
    Composer: Joe Raposo. **Conductor:** Joe Raposo.

RAGTIME
Soundtrack (1981) • Electra (S) 5E-565................................. 15-20   81
    Composer: Randy Newman. **Conductor:** Randy Newman. **Cast:** Randy Newman, Jennifer Warnes.

RAGTIME YEARS
Original Cast (1978) • Vanguard (S) VSD-79391 8-10   78
    Cast: Max Morath (piano).

RAIDERS OF THE LOST ARK
Soundtrack (1981) • Columbia (S) JS-37373 8-10   81
> Gatefold cover. Includes 16-page booklet.

Soundtrack (1981) • Polydor (S) 821-583 8-10   84

Soundtrack (1981) • DCC Compact Classics (S) LPZ 2-2009 25-35   95
> Two discs. Audiophile, virgin vinyl. Limited edition, 2,000 made. Over 80 minutes of music.
> **Composer:** John Williams. **Conductor:** John Williams.

Soundtrack (1981) • Columbia (S) JS-37696 10-12   81
> Actual title: *Raiders of the Lost Ark: The Movie on Record.* Includes dialogue.
> **Composer:** John Williams. **Conductor:** John Williams. **Cast:** Harrison Ford, Karen Allen, Paul
> Freeman, Ronald Lacey, John Rhys-Davies, Denholm Elliott. (With dialogue.)

RAILWAY CHILDREN
Soundtrack (1972) • Capitol (S) SW-871 18-20   72
> **Composer:** Johnny Douglas, Vince Hill. **Conductor:** Johnny Douglas, Vince Hill.

RAIN MAN
Soundtrack (1989) • Capitol (S) C1-91866.. 8-10   89
> **Cast:** Delta Rhythm Boys, Etta James, Johnny Clegg and Savuka, Ian Gillan, Roger Glover,
> Bananarama, Hans Zimmer, Lou Christie, Belle Stars, Rob Wasserman, Aaron Neville.

RAIN PEOPLE
Soundtrack (1968) • Warner Bros. (S) PRO-329............................. 100-150   68
> Full title: *The Rain People, The Great Train Robbery, The Damned, The Learning Tree,
> The Wild Bunch, The Madwoman of Chaillot.* Some songs were not commercially available.
> Cover has art by Al Hirshfeld. Promotional issue only.

RAINBOW BRIDGE
Soundtrack (1971) • Reprise (S) MS-2040... 12-15   71
> **Cast:** Jimi Hendrix.

RAINBOW 'ROUND MY SHOULDER
Soundtrack (1952) • Columbia (EP) B-1512... 15-20   52
> **Cast:** Frankie Laine.

RAINMAKER
Soundtrack (1956) • RCA Victor (EP) EPA-1434 25-30   56
Soundtrack (1956) • RCA Victor (M) LPM-1434 50-125   57
> **Composer:** Alex North. **Conductor:** Alex North.

RAINTREE COUNTY
Soundtrack (1957) • RCA Victor (M) LOC-6000 100-125   57
> Two discs. Gatefold cover. Has entire score. Issued only in mono.

Soundtrack (1957) • RCA Victor (M) LOC-1038................................. 25-30   58
Soundtrack (1957) • RCA Victor (S) LSO-1038................................. 40-45   58
> Single discs in standard covers. Highlights from LOC-6000.

Soundtrack (1957) • Entr'acte (S) ERS-6503-ST 15-20   Re
> Two discs. Gatefold cover. First stereo issue of the entire score.
> **Composer:** Johnny Green. **Conductor:** Johnny Green.

RAISIN
Original Cast (1973) • Columbia (S) KS-32754 8-12   73
> **Composer:** Judd Woldin, Robert Brittan. **Conductor:** Howard A. Roberts. **Cast:** Virginia
> Capers, Joe Morton, Ernestine Jackson, Robert Jackson, Deborah Allen, Helen Martin, Ralph
> Carter, Herb Downer, Marenda Perry.

RAISIN IN THE SUN
Original Revival Cast (1972) • Caedmon (S) TRS 355 15-25   72
> Boxed, three-disc set.
> **Cast:** Ruby Dee, Ossie Davis, Claude McNeil, Diana Sands.

RAISINETS MOVIE GREATS

Soundtrack (1982) • Ward-Johnson (S) BU-5400 5-10   82
   Music from *Car Wash, Midnight Cowboy, Star Wars, Rocky, Summer of '42, Romeo & Juliet, Pink Panther, The Godfather* and others.

RAISING ARIZONA

Soundtrack (1987) • Varese Sarabande (S) STV 81318 10-15   87
   Full title: *Raising Arizona / Blood Simple.* Also has music from *Blood Simple* (1984).

Soundtrack (1987) • That's Entertainment (S) TER-1141........................ 8-10   80s
   UK release.
   Composer: Carter Burwell.

RAISINS WITH ALMONDS

Radio Cast • Living Arc (M) LAL1977 10-15   79
   Two discs.

RAMBO: FIRST BLOOD – PART II

Soundtrack (1985) • Jackal/Varese Sarabande (S) WOW-728 15-20   85
   Digital recording.

Soundtrack (1985) • Varese Sarabande (S) STV-81246 10-15   85

Soundtrack (1985) • That's Entertainment (S) TER-1104........................ 8-10   80s
   UK release.
   Composer: Jerry Goldsmith. **Conductor:** Jerry Goldsmith. **Cast:** Jerry Goldsmith and the National Philharmonic Orchestra, Frank Stallone.

RAMBO III

Soundtrack (1988) • Scotti Bros. (S) SZ-44319............................... 10-15   88
   Composer: Jerry Goldsmith. **Cast:** Bill Medley, Jerry Goldsmith, Giorgio Moroder, Joe Pizullo.

RAMPAGE

Soundtrack (1988) • Virgin Movie Music (S) 90644-1 10-15   88
   Composer: Ennio Morricone.

RAN

Soundtrack (1985) • Fantasy (S) FSP-21004.................................. 15-20   85
   Composer: Toru Takemitsu. **Conductor:** Hiroyuki Iwaki.

RANCHO DELUXE

Soundtrack (1975) • United Artists (S) UA-LA466-G 10-12   75
   Composer: Jimmy Buffet. **Cast:** Jimmy Buffet.

RAP MASTER RONNIE

Original Cast (1986) • AEI (S) AEI-1177 5-10   86
   San Francisco production of *'84 Top of the Gate.*
   Composer: Elizabeth Swados, Gary Trudeau.

RAP TO ROCK

TV Soundtrack (1990) • Rap to Rock (S) 3101 10-15   90

RAPPIN'

Soundtrack (1985) • Atlantic (S) 81252-1.................................. 8-10   85
   Cast: Mario Van Peebles, Kadeem Hardison, Eriq La Salle, Tuff Inc., Warren Mills.

RASHOMON

Original Cast (1959) • Carlton (M) LPX-5000 20-25   59

Original Cast (1959) • Carlton (S) STLPX-5000 25-30   59
   Incidental music from the Broadway play.
   Composer: Laurence Rosenthal. **Conductor:** Laurence Rosenthal.

RAT RACE

Soundtrack (1960) • Dot (M) DLP-3306 20-25   60
Soundtrack (1960) • Dot (S) DLP-25306 30-35   60
     Jazz renditions of pop standards, some of which were performed by Sam Butera and the Witnesses in the film. Does not have background score.
       Composer: Elmer Bernstein, others. **Cast:** Sam Butera and the Witnesses.

RATTLE AND HUM

Soundtrack (1988) • Island (S) 91003-1 8-10   88
     Two discs.
       Cast: U2, Jimi Hendrix, B.B. King.

RAW DEAL

Soundtrack (1986) • Varese Sarabande (S) STV-81286 10-12   86
       Cast: Cinemascore.

RAZOR'S EDGE

Soundtrack (1984) • Southern Cross (S) SCRS-1009 10-15   84
       Composer: Jack Nitzsche. **Conductor:** Stanley Black. **Cast:** Stanley Black and His Orchestra.

RE-ANIMATOR

Soundtrack (1985) • Varese Sarabande (S) STV-81261 10-15   85
       Composer: Richard Band. **Conductor:** Richard Band. **Cast:** Rome Philharmonic Orchestra.

REAL AMBASSADORS

Studio Cast (1963) • Columbia (M) OL-5850 15-20   63
Studio Cast (1963) • Columbia (S) OS-2250 20-25   63
       Composer: Dave Brubeck, Iola Brubeck. **Cast:** Louis Armstrong, Dave Brubeck, Dave Lambert, Jon Hendricks, Annie Ross, Carmen McRae.

REAL THING

Original Cast • Nonesuch (S) 78027-1 10-15   84
     Two discs. Contains the entire play.
       Cast: Glenn Close, Jeremy Irons.

REALLY ROSIE

Original Cast (1980) • Caedmon (S) TRS-368 10-20   80
       Composer: Carole King, Maurice Sendak. **Conductor:** Joel Silberman. **Cast:** Jermaine Campbell, Trisha Campbell, April Herman.
TV Soundtrack (1975) • Ode (S) SP-77027 10-12   75
TV Soundtrack (1975) • Ode (S) PE-34955 8-10   80
       Composer: Carole King. **Conductor:** Carole King, Maurice Sendak. **Cast:** Carole King.

REBECCA: see OBJECTIVE, BURMA!

REBEL WITHOUT A CAUSE: see TRIBUTE TO JAMES DEAN

RED BALLOON

Soundtrack • Nonesuch (S) H-2001 8-12
     Adapted from a classic French film by Albert Lamorisse.
       Composer: Al Barr. **Conductor:** Al Barr. **Cast:** Jean Vallin (story narrator).

RED DAWN

Soundtrack (1985) • Intrada (S) RVF-6001 30-35   85
       Composer: Basil Poledouris. **Conductor:** Basil Poledouris.

RED DETACHMENT OF WOMEN

Original Cast (1972) • Everest (SE) 3338 5-15   72
     Performed for President Nixon during his visit to China.
       Cast: China Ballet Troupe.

RED GARTERS

Soundtrack (1954) • Columbia (EP) B-377 15-20   54
     Two discs.

Soundtrack (1954) • Columbia (M) CL-6282 35-45   54
  10-inch LP.
  Composer: Jerry Livingston, Ray Evans. **Conductor:** Joseph J. Lilley, Percy Faith, Mitch Miller.
  Cast: Rosemary Clooney, Guy Mitchell, Joanne Gilbert.

RED HEAT
Soundtrack (1988) • Virgin Movie Music (S) 90891-1 15-25   88
  Composer: James Horner. **Conductor:** James Horner.

RED HOT AND BLUE
Original Cast (1936) • AEI (M) AEI-1147 10-18   70s
  Also includes music from *Stars in Your Eyes.*
  Composer: Cole Porter. **Conductor:** Fairchild and Carroll. **Cast:** Ethel Merman. STARS IN
  YOUR EYES: **Composer:** Arthur Schwartz, Dorothy Fields. **Conductor:** Al Goodman. **Cast:** Ethel
  Merman.
  Also see LET'S FACE IT

RED HOUSE
Studiotrack (1947) • Capitol (EP) FAP-2-453 15-20   51
Studiotrack (1947) • Capitol CB-48 75-100   51
  78 rpm album.
Studiotrack (1947) • Capitol (M) L-453 50-60   51
  10-inch LP. One side has *Spellbound.*
  Composer: Miklos Rozsa. **Conductor:** Miklos Rozsa, Erich Kloss.
  Also see QUO VADIS

RED MANTLE
Soundtrack (1972) • RCA Victor (S) LSP-4815 12-18   72
  Composer: Marc Fredericks. **Cast:** Judy Scott.

RED MILL
Studio Cast (1945) • Decca (M) A-411 20-25   45
  78 rpm album. Includes booklet.
Studio Cast (1945) • Decca (EP) 9-165 20-25   50
  Boxed, three-disc set.
  Composer: Victor Herbert, Henry Blossom. **Conductor:** Jay Blackton. **Cast:** Eileen Farrell,
  Wilbur Evans, Felix Knight.
Studio Cast (1945) • RCA Victor (M) K-1 20-30   45
  78 rpm album. Includes bound-in booklet.
Studio Cast (1945) • RCA Victor (M) LK-1016 30-40   52
Studio Cast (1945) • Camden (M) CAL-437 15-25   58
  Although covers of above RCA Victor issues state "From the Paula Stone and Hunt
  Stromberg, Jr. Production," these have a studio cast. Since liner notes speak of the show in
  terms of this production; it appears the producers intended these releases to serve in lieu
  of an original cast album for the 1945 Broadway revival.
  Composer: Victor Herbert, Henry Blossom. **Conductor:** Al Goodman. **Cast:** Earl Wrightson,
  Mary Martha Briney, Donald Dame, Mullen Sisters, Guild Choristers.
Studio Cast (1952) • Camden (M) CAL-408 15-25   58
  Composer: Victor Herbert, Harry Blossom. **Cast:** Charles Fredericks, Marion Bell, Christina
  Lind.
Studio Cast • Turnabout (S) TV 34766 15-25
  Composer: Victor Herbert, Harry Blossom. **Cast:** Rosalind Rees, Leonard Van Camp, Michael
  Wilson, Kimball Wheeler, Samantha Genton.
  Also see BABES IN TOYLAND
  Also see NAUGHTY MARIETTA
  Also see UP IN CENTRAL PARK

RED PONY
Soundtrack (1949) • Columbia (M) ML-5983 20-25
Soundtrack (1949) • Columbia (SE) MS-6583 25-30

Soundtrack (1949) • Varese Sarabande (SE) STV 81259 20-25   86
Above issue was processed from original film acetate masters.
Composer: Aaron Copland. Conductor: Andre Previn.

RED SCORPION
Soundtrack (1988) • Varese Sarabande (S) VS-5230 10-15   88
Composer: Jay Chattaway.

RED SHOES
Soundtrack (1949) • Columbia (M) ML-2083 20-30
10-inch LP. Also has music from *Lambert's Horoscope*.
Composer: Brian Easdale. Conductor: Muir Mathieson.

RED SKY AT MORNING
Soundtrack (1970) • Decca (S) DL-79180 12-18   71
Composer: Billy Goldberg, others. Conductor: Billy Goldberg, Leonard Slatkin, Vic Schoen,
Benny Carter. Cast: Mills Brothers, Andrews Sisters, Louis Jordan, Miriam Gulager.

RED SONJA
Soundtrack (1985) • Varese Sarabande (S) STV-81248 10-15   85
Composer: Ennio Morricone. Conductor: Ennio Morricone.

RED TENT
Soundtrack (1971) • Paramount (S) PAS-6019 15-25   71
Soundtrack (1971) • Paramount (S) 5019 20-30   71
Promotional issue only.
Composer: Ennio Morricone. Conductor: Ennio Morricone.

REDHEAD
Original Cast (1959) • RCA Victor (M) LOC-1048 10-15   59
Original Cast (1959) • RCA Victor (S) LSO-1048 40-45   59
Instrumental track *Essie's Vision* was omitted from above stereo issue and added to later
reissues.
Original Cast (1959) • RCA Victor (M) LOC-1104 12-15   65
Original Cast (1959) • RCA Victor (S) LSO-1104 20-30   65
Composer: Albert Hague, Dorothy Fields. Conductor: Jay Blackton. Cast: Gwen Verdon,
Richard Kiley, Leonard Stone, Doris Rich, Cynthia Latham, Joy Nichols, Bob Dixon, Pat Ferrier.
Studio Cast (1959) • RCA Camden (M) CAL-521 10-12   59
Studio Cast (1959) • RCA Camden (S) CAS-521 10-12   59
Conductor: Mike Sammes. Cast: Rita Williams, Bryan Johnson, Fred Lucas, Hill Bowen and
His Orchestra.
Studio Cast (1959) • RCA Victor (M) LPM-2039 8-12   59
Full title: *Meyer Davis Plays "Redhead" for Dancing*.
Composer: Albert Hague, Dorothy Fields. Conductor: Meyer Davis. Cast: Meyer Davis.
Studio Cast • Design (S) DCF-1047 10-15
Composer: Albert Hague, Dorothy Fields. Cast: Rex Stewart Quintet.

REDS
Soundtrack (1981) • Columbia (S) BJS-37690 15-20   81
Includes pieces by P. Wingate, H.W. Petrie, E. Pottier, P. Degeyter & E.J. Mellinger.
Composer: Stephen Sondheim, Dave Grusin, others. Conductor: Dave Grusin. Cast: Jean-
Pierre Rampal, Claude Bolling, Moscow Radio Chorus, Heaton Vorse.

REFORM SCHOOL GIRLS
Soundtrack (1984) • Rhino (S) RNLP-70310 10-15   84
Cast: Wendy O. Williams, others.

REGINA
Original Revival Cast (1959) • Columbia (M) O3L-260 25-30   59
Original Revival Cast (1959) • Columbia (S) O3S-202 30-35   59
Three-disc sets.

Original Revival Cast (1959) • Columbia/Odyssey (S) YS-35236 15-20   Re
  Composer: Marc Blitzstein. **Conductor:** Samuel Krachmalnick. **Cast:** Brenda Lewis, Elisabeth
  Carron, Carol Brice, Joshua Hecht, Helen Strine, George S. Irving, Emil Renan.

REIVERS
Soundtrack (1969) • Columbia (S) OS-3510 12-15   70
  Composer: John Williams. **Conductor:** John Williams.

RELAX WITH VICTOR HERBERT
Studiotrack (1954) • RCA Victor (EP) EPB-1023................................. 10-15   54
Studiotrack (1954) • RCA Victor (M) LPM-1023 15-25   54
  Composer: Victor Herbert. **Conductor:** Al Goodman. **Cast:** Al Goodman and His Orchestra.

RELUCTANT DRAGON
TV Soundtrack • HBR (M) HBR-2029... 15-40
  Cast: Touche and Dum Dum (original TV stars).

REMEMBER MARILYN
Soundtrack • 20th Century-Fox (SE) T-901... 20-25   72
  Gatefold cover. Includes 12-page booklet, originally available through a television offer.
  Booklet has two different covers. One has a small, boxed, color photo of Monroe against a
  white background. Other has an abstract, speckled, color digital image of Monroe. Disc is a
  reissue of *Marilyn* (SXG-5000), with music from *There's No Business Like Show Business,*
  River of No Return and *Gentlemen Prefer Blondes.*
  Composer: Irving Berlin, Jule Styne, Leo Robin, others. **Conductor:** Lionel Newman. **Cast:**
  Marilyn Monroe, Eileen Wilson (originally set to dub Jane Russell's vocals in *Gentlemen Prefer*
  Blondes).
  Also see MARILYN
  Also see MARILYN MONROE.

REMEMBER MY NAME
Soundtrack (1978) • Columbia (S) JS-35553 8-10   78
  Composer: Alberta Hunter. **Cast:** Alberta Hunter.

REMEMBER THE ALAMO
Studiotrack • Kapp (M) KL-1216.. 45-55
  Composer: Dimitri Kiomkin, others. **Cast:** Terry Gilkyson and the Easy Riders.

REMEMBER THE GOLDEN DAYS OF RADIO, VOL. 2
Radio Cast • Longines Symphonette (M) SY 5184................................ 20-25
  Material from *Jack Armstrong - All American Boy, Lone Ranger, Terry and the Pirates,*
  Famous Jury Trials, Dangerous Assignment, Mr. Keene - Tracer of Lost Persons, Gang
  Busters, Shadow. Also has radio news broadcasts of *First Presidential Election Broadcast*
  Returns, President Coolidge and Charles Lindberg Before Congress, Billy Sunday opposes
  repeal of prohibition, F.D.R. inaugurated, Adoft Hitler, Edwin C. Hill, Greatest 'Eye Witness'
  Report in History and *The Von Hindenburg crashes in flames.*

REMEMBER THESE
Studio Cast (1963) • Ava (M) A-26.. 20-25   63
Studio Cast (1963) • Ava (S) AS-26 20-30   63
Studio Cast (1963) • DRG (M) MRS-905.. 8-10   85
  Music from *Treasure Girl* and *Chee-Chee.*
Studio Cast (1963) • That's Entertainment (S) TER-1039 8-10   80s
  UK release.
  Composer: TREASURE GIRL: George Gershwin, Ira Gershwin. CHEE-CHEE: Richard
  Rodgers, Lorenz Hart. **Conductor:** Richard Lewine. **Cast:** Betty Comden.

RENALDO AND CLARA
Soundtrack (1978) • Columbia (S) AO-422 25-35   78
  Four tracks from the film. Promotional issue only.
  Composer: Bob Dylan. **Cast:** Bob Dylan.

RENT-A-COP
Soundtrack (1988) • Intrada (S) MAF-7002... 15-20   88
    Composer: Jerry Goldsmith. **Conductor:** Jerry Goldsmith. **Cast:** Hungarian State Opera Orchestra.

REPO MAN
Soundtrack (1984) • San Andreas/MCA (S) 39019 8-10   84
    Cast: Iggy Pop, Black Flag, Suicidal Tendencies, Plugz, Juicy Bananas, Circle Jerks, Burning Sensations, Fear.

REPORTER
TV Soundtrack (1964) • Columbia (M) CL-2269.................................... 25-30   64
TV Soundtrack (1964) • Columbia (S) CS-9069 35-40   64
    Composer: Kenyon Hopkins. **Conductor:** Kenyon Hopkins.

REPRISE REPERTORY THEATRE
Studio Cast (1964) • Reprise (S) 4FS-2019 45-60   64
    Four LPs (each of which was also issued individually) in special slip cover: *Finian's Rainbow* (FS-2015), *Guys and Dolls* (FS-2016), *Kiss Me Kate* (FS-2017) and *South Pacific* (FS-2018). Except for *Finian's Rainbow*, the gatefold edition is used in this set.
    Composer: See individual show listings. **Conductor:** Morris Stoloff, Ken Lane. **Cast:** See individual show listings.

REPUBLIC YEARS (ROY ROGERS)
Soundtrack • Varese Sarabande (S) STV-81212 10-15   84

REQUIEM FOR A CAVALIER: see ADVENTURES OF ROBIN HOOD

RESCUERS
Soundtrack (1977) • Disneyland (M) ST-3816.. 8-25   77
Soundtrack (1977) • Disneyland (M) DQ-1369...................................... 8-12   77
    Story, songs and dialogue.
    Composer: Artie Butler. **Conductor:** Artie Butler. **Cast:** Shelby Flint (vocals), Bob Newhart, Eva Gabor, Joe Flynn, Geraldine Page. (With dialogue.)

RESTLESS ONES
Soundtrack (1965) • Grason (EP) BG-6515 10-15   60s
    Labeled a "Souvenir EP."
Soundtrack (1965) • Supreme (M) M-110 15-20   65
Soundtrack (1965) • Supreme (S) MS-210.. 25-30   65
    Composer: Ralph Carmichael. **Conductor:** Ralph Carmichael. **Cast:** Johnny Crawford.

RETURN OF A MAN CALLED HORSE
Soundtrack (1976) • United Artists (S) UA-LA692-G 12-15   76
Soundtrack (1976) • Liberty (S) LT-692... 8-10   Re
    Composer: Laurence Rosenthal. **Conductor:** Laurence Rosenthal.

RETURN OF MARTIN GUERRE
Soundtrack (1983) • DRG (S) SL-9514 10-15   83
    Audiophile pressing. Also has music for *Julia*.
    Composer: M. Portal.

RETURN OF THE JEDI
Soundtrack (1983) • Buena Vista/Lucas Film (S) 63155 25-30   83
    Picture disc.
Soundtrack (1983) • Buena Vista (S) 62103 15-20   83
    Full title: *The Story of Return of the Jedi*. Music and dialogue. Includes booklet.
    Composer: John Williams. **Conductor:** John Williams. **Cast:** London Symphony Orchestra.
    Also see RETURN OF THE JEDI
    Also see STAR WARS

RETURN OF THE LIVING DEAD
Soundtrack (1984) • Enigma (S) 72004-1 8-10   85
Soundtrack (1984) • Enigma (S) 72085-1 15-20   85
Picture disc.
Cast: Cramps, 45 Grave, TSOL, Flesheaters, Roky Erickson, Damned, Tall Boys, Jet Black Berries, SSQ.

RETURN OF THE LIVING DEAD, PART II
Soundtrack (1988) • Island (S) 90854-1 8-10   88
Soundtrack (1988) • Island (S) ISTA-17 8-10   88
Cast: Julian Cope, Anthrax, Mantronic, Leatherwolf, Lamont, Big O, J. Peter Robinson, Zodiac Mindward and the Love Reaction.

RETURN OF THE PINK PANTHER
Soundtrack (1975) • RCA Victor (S) ABL1-0968 .... 10-12 . 75
Includes poster.
Soundtrack (1975) • RCA Victor (Q) ABDL1-0968 15-18   75
Composer: Henry Mancini. **Conductor:** Henry Mancini. **Cast:** Henry Mancini and His Orchestra.

RETURN OF THE SEVEN
Soundtrack (1966) • United Artists (M) UAL-4146 10-12   66
Soundtrack (1966) • United Artists (S) UAS-5146 12-18   66
Cover incorrectly states the "previously issued as *The Magnificent Seven.*" This soundtrack album has re-recordings of *The Magnificent Seven* plus new music
Composer: Elmer Bernstein. **Conductor:** Elmer Bernstein.
Also see MAGNIFICENT SEVEN

RETURN OF THE SOLDIER
Soundtrack (1985) • That's Entertainment (S) TER-1036 8-10   80s
UK release.
Composer: Richard Rodney Bennett.

RETURN TO EDEN
TV Soundtrack (1983) • Varese Sarabande (S) STV 81260 10-15   85
From an Australian TV mini-series.
Composer: Brian May. **Conductor:** Brian May.

RETURN TO MACON COUNTY
Soundtrack (1985) • United Artists (S) UALA-491 8-10   85
Cast: Various.

RETURN TO OZ
Soundtrack (1985) • Sonic Atmospheres (S) 113 25-35   85
Audiophile disc.
Composer: David Shire. **Conductor:** David Shire. **Cast:** London Symphony Orchestra.
Also see JOURNEY BACK TO OZ

RETURN TO PARADISE
Soundtrack (1953) • Decca (EP) ED-542 20-35   53
Soundtrack (1953) • Decca (M) DL-5489 150-175   53
10-inch LP.
Composer: Dimitri Tiomkin, Charles Daufman. **Conductor:** Dimitri Tiomkin. **Cast:** Gary Cooper (narration).

RETURN TO SNOWY RIVER
Soundtrack (1988) • Varese Sarabande (S) 704.510 10-15   88
Composer: Bruce Rowland.

RETURN TO WATERLOO
Soundtrack (1985) • Arista (S) AL6-8386 8-10   85
Composer: Ray Davies. **Cast:** Ray Davies, Mick Avery, Jim Rodford, Ian Gibbons.

REVENGE
Soundtrack (1986) • United Entertainment Pictures (S) UEP-6212 8-12   86
Composer: Rod Slane, Jon Slazer. Cast: Michael Brewer.
Soundtrack (1990) • Silva Screen (S) FILM 065 10-12   90
Composer: Jack Nitzche.

REVENGE OF THE NERDS
Soundtrack (1984) • Scotti Bros. (S) AL-39599 10-12   84
Promotional issue only.
Soundtrack (1984) • Scotti Bros. (S) BFZ-39599 8-12   84
Cast: Andrea and Hot Mink, Ya Ya, Rubinoos, others.

REVENGE OF THE NINJA
Soundtrack (1983) • Varese Sarabande (S) STV-81195 10-15   83
Composer: Rob Walsh.

REVENGE OF THE PINK PANTHER
Soundtrack (1978) • United Artists (S) UA-LA913-H 10-15   78
Composer: Henry Mancini, others. Conductor: Henry Mancini. Cast: Peter Sellers (as
Inspector Clouseau), Lon Satton.

REVOLUTION
Soundtrack (1968) • United Artists (S) UAS-5185 20-25   68
Soundtrack (1968) • United Artists (S) UA-LA296-G 12-15   74
Composer: Buffy St. Marie, others. Cast: Quicksilver Messenger Service, Steve Miller Band,
Mother Earth.

REVUERS 1938-1944: see BONANZA BOUND

REX
Original Cast (1976) • RCA Victor (S) ABL1-1683 12-15   76
Composer: Richard Rodgers, Sheldon Harnick. Conductor: Jay Blackton. Cast: Nicol
Williamson, Penny Fuller, Tom Aldredge, Barbara Andres, Glenn Close, Ed Evanko, Michael
John, Merwin Goldsmith.
Studio Cast (1977) • Discovery (S) DS 783 10-12   77
Cast: Shelly Manne.

RHAPSODY IN BLUE
Studiotrack (1954) · RCA Victor (EP) EPA-565 10-15   54
Composer: George Gershwin. Conductor: Hugo Winterhalter. Cast: Byron Janis (piano); Hugo
Winterhalter and His Orchestra.
Studiotrack (1966) • Columbia (S) P2S-5092 10-20   66
Two discs. Also has music from An American in Paris, Concerto in F, Slaughter on Tenth
Avenue, Warsaw Concerto plus the Spellbound Concerto.
Conductor: Kenneth Alwyn; Morgan Lewis. Cast: Sinfonia of London Orchestra; Malcolm Binns;
William Davies.

RHAPSODY OF STEEL
Soundtrack (1958) • US Steel (M) JB-502/3 65-85   58
Soundtrack (1958) • Aduco (M) 804-RM5 20-40   59
Industrial film Side two has music by the Pittsburgh Symphony Orchestra.
Composer: Dimitri Tiomkin. Conductor: Dimitri Tiomkin. Cast: Gary Merrill (narration).

RHAPSODY UNDER THE STARS
Studiotrack (1957) • Capitol (M) P-8494 15-25   57
Music from Spellbound and others.
Composer: Miklos Rozsa. Conductor: Miklos Rozsa. Cast: Hollywood Bowl Symphony.

RHINESTONE
Soundtrack (1984) • RCA Victor (S) 1-5032 8-10   84
Includes flyer insert.
Composer: Dolly Parton, others. Cast: Dolly Parton, Sylvester Stallone, Randy Parton, Kim
Vassy.

RHYTHM ON THE RANGE

Studiotrack (1950) • Decca (M) DL-6010 50-60   50
   10-inch LP. One side has music from *Pennies from Heaven.*
     Composer: Johnny Mercer, others. **Conductor:** Jimmy Dorsey. **Cast:** Bing Crosby, Martha
     Raye.
   Also see BING'S HOLLYWOOD.

RHYTHM ON THE RIVER: see BING'S HOLLYWOOD

RICH MAN, POOR MAN

TV Soundtrack (1976) • MCA (S) 2095 15-25   76
     Composer: Alex North. **Conductor:** Alex North, Harold Mooney.

RICH, YOUNG AND PRETTY

Soundtrack (1951) • MGM - MGM-86... 15-20   51
   78 rpm album.
Soundtrack (1951) • MGM (EP) K-86 18-20   51
   Boxed, four-disc set.
Soundtrack (1951) • MGM (EP) X-86 12-15   51
Soundtrack (1951) • MGM (M) E-86... 30-35   51
   10-inch LP.
Soundtrack • MGM (M) E-3236 15-18   55
   One side has music from *Singin' in the Rain.*
     Composer: Nicholas Brodszky, Sammy Cahn. **Conductor:** David Rose. **Cast:** Jane Powell,
     Danielle Darrieux, Fernando Lamas.
Soundtrack • Curtain Calls (M) CC 100/4 10-12
   Actual title: *Jane Powell.* Previously unreleased selections by Powell and Vic Damone.
   Damone's Mercury contract prevented him from appearing on the MGM soundtrack album.
     Composer: Nicholas Brodszky, Sammy Cahn. **Conductor:** David Rose. **Cast:** Jane Powell, Vic
     Damone.
   Also see NANCY GOES TO RIO
   Also see THOSE GLORIOUS MGM MUSICALS

RICHARD BOONE READS THE STORY OF JESUS FOR CHILDREN

Soundtrack • MGM E-3971 25-35
   Background score is from Rozsa's *King of Kings.*
     Composer: Miklos Rozsa. **Cast:** Richard Boone, others.

RICHARD DIAMOND

TV Soundtrack (1959) • Mercury (M) MG-36162................................... 35-45   59
TV Soundtrack (1959) • Mercury (S) SR-80045 65-75   59
     Composer: Pete Rugulo. **Conductor:** Pete Rugulo.

RICHARD RODGERS

Studiotrack (1955) • Columbia (M) CL-810... 15-25   55
   Full title: *Richard Rodgers Conducting The Philharmonic Symphony Orchestra of New
   York.* Music from *Victory at Sea, Slaughter on 10th Avenue, Carousel Waltz* and others.
     Composer: Richard Rodgers. **Conductor:** Richard Rodgers. **Cast:** Philharmonic Symphony
     Orchestra of New York.
Studiotrack (1956) • Columbia (M) CL-1140.. 10-15   56
   Full title: *The Columbia Album of Richard Rodgers, Vol.1.*
     Conductor: Andre Kostelanetz. **Cast:** Andre Kostelanetz and His Orchestra.
Studiotrack (1971) • RCA/Camden (S) CAS-2458 8-10   71
   Reissue of *The Golden Era of Richard Rodgers.*
     Cast: Marty Gold, Living Strings, Norman Luboff Choir, others.
Studiotrack • Columbia (M) CL-784.. 8-15
   Full title: *Music of Richard Rodgers.*
     Cast: Andre Kostelanetz and His Orchestra.

Studiotrack [Vol. 1] • Decca A-798 8-15
Studiotrack [Vol. 2] • Decca A-799 8-15
  78 prm albums.
Studiotrack [Vol. 1] • Decca (M) DL 5292 8-15
  10-inch LP. Full title: *Richard Rodgers and Oscar Hammerstein II Songs, Vol. 1.*
  Cast: Fred Waring and His Pennsylvanians.
Studiotrack [Vol. 2] • Decca (M) DL 5293 8-15
  10-inch LP. Full title: *Richard Rodgers and Oscar Hammerstein II Songs, Vol. 2.*
  Cast: Fred Waring and His Pennsylvanians.
Studiotrack • RCA Victor (M) PRM 201 8-15
  Full title: *Sound of Richard Rodgers' Music.* Made for B.F. Goodrich.
  Cast: Richard Kiley, Florence Henderson, John Raitt, Peter Nero, Mary Martin, Norman Luboff
  Choir, Andre Previn, Lena Horne, Arthur Fiedler, Sergio Franchi, Alfred Drake.
Studiotrack • Time (S) S-2115 8-12
  Actual title: *And Then I Wrote.*
  Conductor: George Siravo.

RICHARD III
Soundtrack (1955) • RCA Victor (M) LM-6126 50-100   55
  Boxed, three-disc set. Music and dialogue.
  Composer: Sir William Walton. **Cast:** Sir Laurence Olivier.
Soundtrack (1955) • RCA Victor (M) LM-1940 50-65   55
  "Highlights" from the three-disc set.
  Also see MUSIC FROM SHAKESPEAREAN FILMS

RIDE THE WILD SURF
Soundtrack (1964) • Liberty (M) LPR-3368 20-25   64
Soundtrack (1964) • Liberty (S) LST-7368 25-30   64
  Composer: Roger Christian, Jan Berry, others. **Cast:** Jan and Dean, Fantastic Baggys.

RIDER ON THE RAIN
Soundtrack (1970) • Capitol (S) ST-584 20-25   70
  Composer: Francis Lai, Severine. **Conductor:** Francis Lai.

RIDES, RAPES, AND RESCUES (THEMES FROM GREAT SILENT FILMS)
Studiotrack (1961) • Liberty (M) LRP-3185 10-15   61
Studiotrack (1961) • Liberty (S) LST-7185 15-20   61
  Composer: L. Jones, Carl Brandt. **Cast:** Hangnails Hennessey and Wingy Brubeck.

RIDING HIGH
Soundtrack (1979) • Jambo (S) JAM-2 10-15   79

RIGHT STUFF: see NORTH AND SOUTH

RIGHT TO HAPPINESS
Original Radio Cast • Golden Age (M) 5016 8-10   78

RIKKY AND PETE
Soundtrack (1988) • DRG (S) SBL-12593 8-10   88

RIN TIN TIN: see ADVENTURES OF RIN TIN TIN

RINK
Original Cast (1984) • Polydor (S) 422-823125-1 8-10   84
Original Cast (1984) • That's Entertainment (S) TER-1091 8-12   80s
Original London Cast • That's Entertainment (S) TER-1156 12-15   89
  UK releases.
  Composer: John Kander, Fred Ebb. **Cast:** Chita Rivera, Liza Minnelli.

RIO BRAVO

Soundtrack (1959) • Capitol (EP) PRO-1063 250-350   59
Has *Rio Bravo* and *My Rifle, My Pony and Me*, by Dean Martin, backed with *De Guello*, from the film soundtrack, by Nelson Riddle. Also has studiotrack music. Promotional issue only. Issued with a paper picture sleeve.
Composer: Dimitri Tiomkin, Paul Francis Webster. **Conductor:** Gus Levene, Nelson Riddle.
Cast: Dean Martin, Nelson Riddle, Manny Klein (trumpet).

Soundtrack (1959) • Warner Bros. (M) JB-2262 400-500   59
Full title: *John Wayne Introduces Dean Martin and Ricky Nelson Singing "My Rifle, My Pony and Me" from the sound track of Warner Bros. "Rio Bravo."* 45 rpm. Not issued with sleeve. Film version of this song has never been issued commercially. Promotional issue only.
Composer: Dimitri Tiomkin, Francis Webster. **Cast:** John Wayne (narration), Dean Martin, Ricky Nelson.

RIO GRANDE

Soundtrack (1950) • Varese Sarabande (SE) STV-81124 10-15   79
Composer: Victor Young. **Conductor:** Victor Young. **Cast:** Sons of the Pioneers, Ken Curtis, Ben Johnson, Harry Carey Jr., Claude Jarman Jr.

RIO RITA

Original London Cast (1927) • World (M) SH-138 20-25
Original London Cast (1927) • Monmouth Evergreen (SE) MES-7058 . 12-15   78
UK releases. Also have music from *Rose Marie* and *Show Boat*.
Actual title: *Edith Day: The Queen of Drury Lane.* Also has music from *Rose Marie, Irene, Desert Song* and *Show Boat*.
Composer: Harry Tierney, Joseph McCarthy. **Conductor:** Jack Hilton. **Cast:** Edith Day, Geoffrey Gwyther.
Also see CONNECTICUT YANKEE
Also see GREAT WALTZ

RIOT ON SUNSET STRIP

Soundtrack (1967) • Tower (M) T-5065 15-20   67
Soundtrack (1967) • Tower (S) DT-5065 20-25   67
Cast: Standells, Mugwumps, Chocolate Watch Band, Sidewalk Sounds, Debra Travis, Mom's Boys, Drew.

RIP VAN WINKLE: see ICHABOD (THE LEGEND OF SLEEPY HOLLOW)

RISE AND FALL OF THE CITY OF MAHAGONNY

Studio Cast (1970) • Columbia (M) K3L-243 15-20   70
Boxed, three-disc set. Includes booklet. Performed in German.
Composer: Kurt Weill, Bertolt Brecht. **Conductor:** Wilhelm Bruckner-Ruggeberg. **Cast:** Lotte Lenya, Gisela Litz, Sigmund Roth, Richard Munch and the North German Radio Chorus (conducted by Max Thurn), Peter Markwort, Heinz Sauerbaum.
Also see THREEPENNY OPERA

RISE AND FALL OF THE THIRD REICH

TV Soundtrack (1968) • MGM (M) 1SE-12 20-25   68
TV Soundtrack (1968) • MGM (S) 1E-12-ST 20-30   68
Composer: Lalo Schifrin, Lili Chookasian, Alfred Perry. **Conductor:** Lawrence Foster. **Cast:** Laurence Harvey (narration), Gregg Smith Singers.

RISKY BUSINESS

Soundtrack (1984) • Virgin (S) V-2302 1012   84
Composer: Tangerine Dream, others. **Cast:** Tangerine Dream, Bob Seger, Prince, Jeff Beck, Muddy Waters, Journey, Phil Collins.

RITA HAYWORTH

Soundtrack • Curtain Calls (M) CC 100/22 15-20
"Silver Screen Star Series." Previously unreleased songs and dialogue from *Pal Joey*, *Gilda, Miss Sadie Thompson, Tonight and Every Night, My Gal Sal* and others. Cover acknowledges that Hayworth never sang her own vocals – and credits those who did – but Hayworth's singing is heard in excerpts from two television appearances.
Conductor: Morris Stoloff, others. Cast: Rita Hayworth, Nan Wynn, Jo Ann Greer, Martha Mears, Anita Ellis, Jose Ferrer, others. (With dialogue).

RIVER (1937)

Soundtrack (1937) • Desto (M) D-405 10-12
Soundtrack (1937) • Desto (SE) DST-6405 10-12
Conductor: Walter Hendl. Cast: Vienna Symphony Orchestra.
Soundtrack (1937) • Vanguard (M) VRS-1071 10-12
Soundtrack (1937) • Vanguard (S) VSD-2095 10-12
One side has music from *The Plow That Broke The Plains*.
Composer: Virgil Thomson. Conductor: Leopold Stokowski. Cast: Symphony of the Air.
Soundtrack (1937) • Angel (S) S-37300 10-20
Actual title: *Music from the Films*. Includes *The Plow That Broke the Plains* and *Autumn*, a nine-minute concertino. *The River* and *The Plow That Broke the Plains* were U. S. Government documentary films.
Composer: Virgil Thomson. Conductor: Neville Marriner. Cast: L.A. Chamber Orchestra.

RIVER (1951)

Soundtrack (1951) • Polymusic (M) PR-5003 50-75   51

RIVER (1984)

Soundtrack (1984) • MCA (S) MCA-6138 10-15   84
Composer: John Williams. Conductor: John Williams.

RIVER OF NO RETURN: see MARILYN; MARILYN MONROE

RIVER RAT

Soundtrack (1984) • RCA Victor (S) CBL1-5310 8-10   84
Composer: Mike Post. Conductor: Mike Post. Cast: Alabama, Earl Thomas Conley, Deborah Allen, Bill Medley, Autograph, Joey Scarbury.

RIVER'S EDGE

Soundtrack (1986) • Enigma (S) SJ-73242 8-10   87
Cast: Slayer, Agent Orange, Wipers, Burning Spear, Hallows Eve, Fates Warning.

RIVERWIND

Original Cast (1962) • London (M) AM-48001 30-35   62
Original Cast (1962) • London (S) AMS-78001 60-80   62
Composer: John Jennings. Conductor: Abba Bogin. Cast: Elizabeth Parrish, Helen Blount, Dawn Nickerson, Brooks Morton, Lovelady Powell, Martin J. Cassidy.

ROAD BEGINS: see BING'S HOLLYWOOD

ROAD HOUSE

Soundtrack (1989) • Arista (S) AL9-8576 8-10   89
Composer: Various. Cast: Jeff Healey Band.

ROAD TO BALI

Soundtrack (1952) • Decca (M) DL-5444 60-65   52
10-inch LP. All of Bing Crosby and Bob Hope's songs are from the movie soundtrack, but Dorothy Lamour's film songs are performed here by Peggy Lee.
Composer: James Van Heusen, Johnny Burke. Conductor: Sonny Burke, Joseph J. Lilley, Axel Stordahl. Cast: Bing Crosby, Bob Hope, Peggy Lee, Rhythmaires, Mellowmen.
Also see BING'S HOLLYWOOD

ROAD TO HONG KONG

Soundtrack (1962) • Liberty (M) LOM-16002.. 15-20   62
Soundtrack (1962) • Liberty (S) LOS-17002.. 30-35   62
    Composer: James Van Heusen, Robert Farnon, Sammy Cahn. **Conductor:** Robert Farnon.
    Cast: Bing Crosby, Bob Hope, Dorothy Lamour, Joan Collins.

ROAD TO MOROCCO: see BING'S HOLLYWOOD

ROAD TO RIO: see BING'S HOLLYWOOD

ROAD TO SINGAPORE

Studiotrack (1940) • Decca (M) DL-6015 50-60   50
    10-inch LP. Also has music from *If I Had My Way*.
    Conductor: John Scott Trotter. **Cast:** Bing Crosby.
    Also see BING'S HOLLYWOOD

ROAD TO UTOPIA: see BING'S HOLLYWOOD

ROAD TO ZANZIBAR: see BING'S HOLLYWOOD

ROAD WARRIOR

Soundtrack (1982) • Varese Sarabande (S) STV-81155 10-15   82
    Composer: Brian May. **Conductor:** Brian May.

ROADIE

Soundtrack (1980) • Warner Bros. (S) PRO-A-861 15-20   80
    Promotional issue only.
    Cast: Alice Cooper, Pat Benatar, Blondie, Stephen Bishop, Yvonne Elliman, Jay Ferguson, Styx,
    Sue Sadd & the Next, Double Yellow Line, Teddy Pendergrass, Roy Orbison & Emmylou Harris,
    Cheap Trick.
Soundtrack (1980) • Warner Bros. (S) PRO-A-885 15-20   80
    Promotional issue only.
    Cast: Jerry Lee Lewis, Hank Williams, Jr., Blondie, Roy Orbison, Emmylou Harris, Eddie
    Rabbitt, Asleep at the Wheel.
Soundtrack (1980) • Warner Bros. (S) 2HS-3441 10-12   80
    Two discs.
    Cast: Cheap Trick, Pat Benatar, Teddy Pendergrass, Jay Ferguson, Blondie, Styx, Joe Ely
    Band, Alice Cooper, Eddie Rabbitt, Stephen Bishop, Yvonne Elliman, Sue Sadd & the Next,
    Asleep at the Wheel, Jerry Lee Lewis, Roy Orbison, Emmy Lou Harris, Hank Williams, Jr.

ROAR OF THE GREASEPAINT – THE SMELL OF THE CROWD

Original Cast (1965) • RCA Victor (M) LOC-1109 8-10   65
Original Cast (1965) • RCA Victor (S) LSO-1109 8-12   65
    Composer: Anthony Newley, Leslie Bricusse. **Conductor:** Herbert Grossman. **Cast:** Anthony
    Newley, Cyril Ritchard, Sally Smith, Joyce Jillson, Gilbert Price.
Studio Cast • RCA Victor (S) LSP-3394 8-12
    Cast: Dick Schory Orchestra.

ROARING '20s

TV Soundtrack (1960) • Warner Bros. (M) W-1394............................... 10-12   60
TV Soundtrack (1960) • Warner Bros. (S) WS-1394.............................. 15-18   60
    Conductor: Alexander "Sandy" Courage. **Cast:** Dorothy Provine.
Studiotrack (1960) • Forum (M) F-16002... 10-15   60
Studiotrack (1960) • Forum (S) SF-16002.. 15-20   60
    Cast: Bonnie Alden.

ROBBER BRIDEGROOM

Original Cast (1976) • Columbia Special Products (S) P-14589 8-10   78
    Some copies have the cover image reversed.
    Composer: Robert Waldman, Alfred Uhry. **Conductor:** Robert Waldman. **Cast:** Barry Bostwick,
    Rhonda Coullet, Barbara Lang, Larry Moss, Carolyn McCurry.

Studio Cast (1976) • Take Home Tunes (S) THT-761 12-15   76
Seven-inch disc.
Composer: Robert Waldman, Alfred Uhry. **Cast:** Virginia Vestoff, Jerry Orbach.

ROBBERY
Soundtrack (1967) • London (M) M-76008 10-12   67
Soundtrack (1967) • London (S) MS-82008 15-18   67
Composer: John Keating. **Conductor:** John Keating. **Cast:** Jackie Lee, John Keating and His
Orchestra.

ROBE
Soundtrack (1953) • Decca (EP) ED-901 12-30   53
Boxed, four-disc set.
Soundtrack (1953) • Decca (M) DL-9012 20-25   53
Dark maroon label with gold print and "Microgroove" at bottom.
Soundtrack (1953) • Decca (M) DL-9012 12-15   53
Soundtrack (1953) • Decca (SE) DL-79012 10-15   59
Red or black label.
Soundtrack (1953) • MCA (SE) 2052e 8-10   72
Soundtrack (1953) • MCA (SE) 1529 5-8   80s
Composer: Alfred Newman. **Conductor:** Alfred Newman. **Cast:** Hollywood Symphony
Orchestra, Carole Richards.

ROBERT AND ELIZABETH
Original London Cast (1964) • RCA Victor (M) CLP-1820 12-15   64
Original London Cast (1964) • RCA Victor (S) CSD-1575 15-18   64
UK release.
Original London Cast (1964) • Stet (S) DS-15021 10-15
Composer: Ron Grainer, Ronald Millar. **Conductor:** Alexander Faris. **Cast:** June Bronhill, John
Clements, Keith Michell, Angela Richards, Jeremy Lloyd, Stella Moray, Robert Vahey.

ROBERTA
Soundtrack (1935) • Classic Int'l Filmusicals (M) C.I.F.-3011 8-12
Includes two songs written especially for the film version, *Lovely to Look At* and *I Won't
Dance*.
Composer: Jerome Kern, Oscar Hammerstein II, Otto Harbach, Dorothy Fields. **Cast:** Irene
Dunne, Fred Astaire, Ginger Rogers.
Studio Cast (1946) • Decca DA-374 20-25   46
78 rpm album. Includes booklet.
Studio Cast (1946) • Decca (M) DL-8007 30-35   50
Composer: Jerome Kern, Oscar Hammerstein II, Otto Harbach. **Conductor:** Harry Sosnik, Jeff
Alexander. **Cast:** Alfred Drake, Kitty Carlisle, Paula Laurence, Kathryn Meisle.
Studio Cast (1952) • Columbia (EP) B-311 12-15   53
Studio Cast (1952) • Columbia (M) CL-6220 30-35   52
10-inch LP.
Studio Cast (1952) • Columbia (M) ML-4765.. 18-20   53
Studio Cast (1952) • Columbia (M) CL-841 12-18   56
Studio Cast (1952) • Columbia (M) OL-7030 10-12   Re
Studio Cast (1952) • Columbia (SE) OS-2530e.................................... 8-10   Re
Studio Cast (1952) • Columbia Special Products (SE) COS-2530e.......... 5-8   Re
Above issues have a variety of covers.
Composer: Jerome Kern, Oscar Hammerstein II, Otto Harbach. **Conductor:** Lehman Engel.
Cast: Joan Roberts, Jack Cassidy, Kaye Ballard, Portia Nelson, Stephen Douglass, Frank
Rogier.
Studio Cast (1952) • Capitol (EP) FBF-334 10-15   52
Studio Cast (1952) • Capitol (M) L-334 15-18   52
10-inch LP.

Studio Cast (1952) • Capitol (M) T-384 .... 12-15 50s
Composer: Jerome Kern, Oscar Hammerstein II, Otto Harbach. **Conductor:** George Greeley.
Cast: Gordon MacRae, Lucille Norman, Anne Triola.

Soundtrack (1952) • MGM (M) K-150 .... 15-20 52
Boxed, four-disc.

Soundtrack (1952) • MGM (M) E-150 .... 20-30 52
10-inch LP.

Soundtrack (1952) • MGM (M) E-3230 .... 15-18 55
Also has music from *Show Boat*. These MGM releases are from the 1952 film version of
Roberta, retitled *Lovely to Look At.*
Composer: Jerome Kern, Oscar Hammerstein II, Otto Harbach. **Conductor:** Carmen Dragon.
Cast: Howard Keel, Kathryn Grayson, Red Skelton, Ann Miller, Marge and Gower Champion.

Studio Cast (1952) • RCA Victor (EP) EKB-1007 .... 10-15 52
Studio Cast (1952) • RCA Victor (M) LK-1007 .... 18-20 52
Studio Cast (1952) • Camden (M) CAL-464 .... 10-12 58
Composer: Jerome Kern, Oscar Hammerstein II, Otto Harbach. **Conductor:** Al Goodman.
Cast: Ray Charles, Eve Young, Jimmy Carroll, Marion Bell, Guild Choristers.

Studio Cast • Rondo-lette (M) 872 8-12
Studio Cast • Rondo-lette (S) SA 158 8-12
Conductor: Richard Muller-Lampertz. **Cast:** Larry Chelsi Orchestra with Boys Chorus, Frances
Martin, Hester Hasheian, Fred Weidner.

London Studio Cast • World (M) T-121 20-25
Composer: Jerome Kern, Oscar Hammerstein II, Otto Harbach. **Cast:** Marion Grimaldi, Andy
Cole, Maggie Fitzgibbon.

Studiotrack (1957) • Halo (M) 50119 .... 8-15 57
Studiotrack (1959) • National Academy Record Club (M) ES 10 .... 10-15 60
From *Ed Sullivan Presents Songs and Music of...* series.
Cast: Ed Sullivan All Star Cast.

Studiotrack • Warner Bros. (M) W 1279 8-15
Cast: Morris Nanton Trio.
Also see DESERT SONG
Also see MISTER IMPERIUM
Also see THOSE GLORIOUS MGM MUSICALS

ROBIN AND MARIAN
Soundtrack (1976) • Sherwood (S) PRO-4345 .... 100-125 76
Promotional issue only. Not issued commercially, although boots do exist.
Composer: John Barry. **Conductor:** John Barry.

ROBIN AND THE SEVEN HOODS
Soundtrack (1964) • Reprise (M) R-2021 .... 25-35 64
Soundtrack (1964) • Reprise (S) FS-2021 .... 40-45 64
Composer: Sammy Cahn, James Van Heusen, Nelson Riddle. **Conductor:** Nelson Riddle.
Cast: Frank Sinatra, Dean Martin, Bing Crosby, Sammy Davis Jr., Peter Falk.

ROBIN HOOD
Studio Cast • AEI (M) AEI-1179 .... 5-10 80s
Composer: de Koven-Smith.

Soundtrack (1964) • Disneyland (M) DQ-1249 .... 10-15 64
Full title: *The Story of Robin Hood.*
Composer: Lawrence E. Watkin, Elton Hayes, Eddie Polo, George Wyle. **Cast:** Dal McKennon
(narrator), Peter Finch, Richard Todd, Elton Hayes, James Hayter, James Robertson Justice,
Hubert Gregg, Joan Rice, Patrick Barr. (With dialogue.)

Soundtrack (1973) • Disneyland (S) ST-3810 .... 20-25 73
Gatefold cover. Includes booklet. From an animated cartoon.
Composer: Roger Miller, Floyd Huddleston, George Bruns, Johnny Mercer. **Cast:** Roger Miller,
Peter Ustinov, Phil Harris, Brian Bedford, Pat Buttram, Andy Devine, Terry-Thomas, George
Lindsay. (With dialogue.)

ROBOCOP
Soundtrack (1987) • Varese Sarabande (S) STV-81330 10-15   87
Soundtrack (1987) • That's Entertainment (S) TER-1146........................ 8-10   80s
UK release.
  Composer: Basil Poledouris. **Conductor:** Howard Blake, Tony Britton. **Cast:** Sinfonia of London Orchestra.

ROCCO AND HIS BROTHERS
Soundtrack (1960) • RCA Victor (M) FOC-2.. 20-30   61
Soundtrack (1960) • RCA Victor (S) FSO-2 30-45   61
  Composer: Nino Rota. **Conductor:** Nino Rota.

ROCK ALL NIGHT
Soundtrack (1957) • Mercury (M) MG-20293 70-80   57
  Cast: Platters, Blockbusters, Eddie Beal Combo, Nora Hayes.

ROCK BABY, ROCK IT
Soundtrack (1957) • Rhino (M) RNSP-309.. 8-10
  Cast: Johnny Carroll and the Hot Rocks, Cell Block Seven, Don Coats and Bon-Aires, Five Stars, Preacher Smith and Deacons, Rosco Gordon and the Red Tops, Belew Twins.

ROCK JUSTICE
Original Cast (1980) • EMI America (S) SWAK-17036 8-10   80

ROCK 'N' ROLL HIGH SCHOOL
Soundtrack (1979) • Sire (S) SRK-6070... 8-10   79
  Cast: Ramones, Chuck Berry, Alice Cooper, Todd Rundgren, Paley Brothers, Nick Lowe, Eddie and the Hot Rods, Brownsville Station, Devo, R.J. Soles, Brian Eno.

ROCK PRETTY BABY
Soundtrack [Vol. 1] (1956) • Decca (EP) ED 2480 50-75   56
Soundtrack [Vol. 2] (1956) • Decca (EP) ED 2481 50-75   56
Soundtrack [Vol. 3] (1956) • Decca (EP) ED 2482 50-75   56
Soundtrack (1956) • Decca (M) DL-8429 50-100   56
Black label or pink label promo.
Soundtrack (1956) • Decca (M) DL-8429 30-35   60s
Rainbow (or multi-color) label.
  Composer: Henry Mancini, others. **Conductor:** Joseph Gershenson. **Cast:** Jimmy Daley & the Ding-A-Lings, Rod McKuen, Alan Copeland, Hal Dickinson.

ROCK, ROCK, ROCK
Soundtrack (1958) • No Label Name Used (M) No Number Used.... 500-750   58
20 tracks credited to seven different lables: Atlantic, Chess, Coral, Gee, MGM, Roost and Vik. Promotional issue only.
Soundtrack (1958) • Chess (M) LP-1425 75-125   58
Soundtrack (1958) • Chess/MCA (M) CH-9254 8-12   Re
Studio recordings heard in the film.
  Cast: Lavern Baker, Bowties, Jimmy Cavallo, Moonglows, Alan Freed Orchestra, 3 Chuckles, Frankie Lymon and the Teenagers, Johnny Burnette, Connie Francis, Chuck Berry, Flamingos.

ROCKABYE HAMLET
Studio Cast (1976) • Rising (S) RILP-103 70-80   76
Pre-Broadway, demonstration record.
  Composer: Cliff Jones. **Conductor:** Gordon Lowry Harrell. **Cast:** Cal Dodd, Rory Dodd, Cliff Jones, Lisa Hartt, Irish Rovers. Lisa Hartt and The Irish Rovers were not in the actual Broadway show.

ROCKERS
Soundtrack (1979) • Mango (S) 9587... 8-10   80
  Cast: Inner Circle, Maytones, Junior Murvin, Heptones, Peter Tosh, Jacob Miller, Junior Byles, Bunny Wailer, Gregory Isaacs, Rockers All-Stars, Kiddus I, Burning Spear, Third World, Justin Hines and the Dominoes.

ROCKETSHIP X-M
Soundtrack (1950) • Starlog (M) SR-1000................................ 12-15   78
Composer: Ferde Grofe Jr. Conductor: Albert Glasser.

ROCKY
Soundtrack (1976) • United Artists (S) UA-LA693-G 10-15   76
Tan label.
Soundtrack (1976) • United Artists (S) UA-LA693-G 8-10   Re
Sunburst label.
Soundtrack (1976) • Liberty (S) LO-00693................................ 8-10   Re
Composer: Bill Conti, others. Conductor: Bill Conti. Cast: Valentine, DeEtta Little, Nelson
Pigford.

ROCKY II
Soundtrack (1979) • United Artists (S) UA-LA972-I............................ 10-15   79
Composer: Bill Conti, others. Conductor: Bill Conti. Cast: DeEtta Little, Nelson Pigford.

ROCKY III
Soundtrack (1982) • Liberty (S) LO-51130.. 10-15   82
Duotone – black and gray – front cover.
Soundtrack (1982) • Liberty (S) LO-51130.............................. 8-10   82
Full color front cover.
Composer: Bill Conti. Conductor: Bill Conti. Cast: Survivor, Frank Stallone, DeEtta Little,
Nelson Pigford.

ROCKY IV
Soundtrack (1985) • Scotti Bros. (S) SZ-40203..................................... 10-15   85
Composer: Vince diCola, others. Cast: Survivor, John Cafferty, Kenny Loggins, Gladys Knight,
James Brown, Robert Tepper, Go West, Touch.

ROCKY HORROR PICTURE SHOW
Soundtrack (1974) • Ode (S) 9009.................................... 12-18   748
Soundtrack (1974) • Ode (S) 78332.................................... 10-15   78
Ode label may be shown as "Ode Sound and Visions."
Soundtrack (1974) • Ode (S) 21653.................................... 10-12   78
Soundtrack (1975) • Ode (S) OPD-91653 20-30   78
Picture disc. Numbered edition.
Soundtrack (1975) • Ode (S) 91653..................................... 15-20   78
Picture disc. Reissue numbered edition, has "Limited edition II" sticker on cover.
Soundtrack (1975) • Rhino (S) R11H-70712 8-10   Re
Composer: Richard O'Brien. Conductor: Richard Hartley. Cast: Tim Curry, Susan Sarandon,
Barry Bostwick, Richard O'Brien, Meat Loaf.
Soundtrack • Ode (S) 1032 15-20   83
Two discs. Full title: *Rocky Horror Picture Show Audience Par-tic-ci-pation Album.*
Complete film soundtrack with live midnight audience participation. Inner sleeves have
dialogue and audience responses.

ROCKY HORROR SHOW
Original Cast (1975) • Ode (S) SP-77026 10-12   75
Original Cast (1975) • Rhino (S) R11H-70090.. 8-10   Re
Composer: Richard O'Brien. Conductor: D'Vaughn Pershing. Cast: Tim Curry, Jamie Donnelly,
Boni Enten.
Original Australian Cast (1975) • Elephant (S) ELA-7000 10-15

ROCKY THE FLYING SQUIRREL AND HIS FRIENDS
TV Soundtrack (1961) • Golden Tone (M) LP 64-A.............................. 25-35   61
Conductor: Dennis Farnon. Cast: June Foray, Paul Frees, Walter Tetley, Bill Scott.

RODEO: see FANCY FREE

RODGERS AND HAMMERSTEIN DELUXE SET

Soundtrack (1956) • Capitol (M) TCL-1790 12-15   62
Soundtrack (1956) • Capitol (S) STCL-1790 12-15   62
  Black label.
Soundtrack (1956) • Capitol (M) TCL-1790 12-15   62
Soundtrack (1956) • Capitol (S) STCL-1790 12-15   62
  Red label. All Capitol issues are boxed, three-disc sets, with booklets and the songs
  from *Oklahoma!, Carousel* and *The King and I.*
  Composer: Richard Rodgers, Oscar Hammerstein II. OKLAHOMA!: **Conductor:** Jay Blackton.
  Cast: Gordon MacRae, Shirley Jones, Gloria Grahame, Gene Nelson, Charlotte Greenwood,
  James Whitmore, Rod Steiger, Jay C. Flippen. CAROUSEL: **Conductor:** Alfred Newman. **Cast:**
  Gordon MacRae, Shirley Jones, Cameron Mitchell, Robert Rounseville, Barbara Ruick,
  Claramae Turner. THE KING AND I: **Conductor:** Alfred Newman. **Cast:** Yul Brynner, Rita
  Moreno, Marni Nixon (performs songs for Deborah Kerr in the film), Terry Saunders.

RODGERS AND HART 1927-1942

Original Cast • Show Biz (M) 5604 20-25
  Original cast performances from *Babes in Arms, Jumbo, I Married an Angel, Higher and
  Higher* and others.
  Composer: Richard Rodgers, Lorenz Hart. **Cast:** Wynn Murray, Ray Heatherton, Gloria Grafton,
  Donald Novis, Audrey Christie, Shirley Ross.

RODGERS AND HART IN HOLLYWOOD

Soundtrack [Vol. 1] • JJA (M) 19820 30-35   82
  Gatefold cover with typewritten song listing taped inside. Music from films by Rodgers and
  Hart.
  Composer: Richard Rodgers, Lorenz Hart. **Conductor:** Various. **Cast:** Various.
Soundtrack [Vol. 2] • JJA (M) 19821 30-35   82
  Gatefold cover with typewritten song listing taped inside. Music from *Too Many Girls,
  Higher and Higher, I Married an Angel, The Boys from Syracuse* and *Evergreen.*
  Composer: Richard Rodgers, Lorenz Hart. **Conductor:** Various. **Cast:** Desi Arnaz, Ann Miller,
  Trudy Erwin, Jack Haley, Jeanette MacDonald, Nelson Eddy, Allan Jones, Joe Penner, Martha
  Raye, Jessie Matthews, others.
Soundtrack [Vol. 3] • JJA (M) 19822 25-30   82
  Original MGM pre-recordings for the sound track of *Words and Music,* including outtakes.
  Has Perry Como and Mel Torme's recordings not found on the MGM issues, plus the
  seldom-heard singing voice of Vera-Ellen.
  Composer: Richard Rodgers, Lorenz Hart. **Conductor:** Lennie Hayton. **Cast:** June Allyson,
  Perry Como, Tom Drake, Judy Garland, Betty Garrett, Lena Horne, Gene Kelly, Mickey Rooney,
  Ann Sothern, Mel Torme, Vera-Ellen, Eileen Wilson (performed Cyd Charisse's vocals in the
  film), Dee Turnell.

RODGERS AND HART 1935-1939: see TOO MANY GIRLS

RODGERS AND HART REVISITED

Studio Cast • Recording Industries Corporation (S) ST-3001 10-12
  The album that started the Painted Smiles series. Although produced on R.I.C., reissues
  and all other volumes are on Painted Smiles.
Studio Cast • Spruce (M) S-101 8-12   Re
Studio Cast [Vol. 1] • Painted Smiles (S) PS-1341 8-10   Re
  Composer: Richard Rodgers, Lorenz Hart. **Conductor:** Norman Paris. **Cast:** Dorothy Loudon,
  Danny Meehan, Cy Young, Charlotte Rae.
Studio Cast [Vol. 2] • Painted Smiles (S) PS-1343 8-10
  Composer: Richard Rodgers, Lorenz Hart. **Conductor:** Norman Paris. **Cast:** Blossom Dearie,
  Gloria De Haven, Dorothy Loudon, B.B. Osterwald, Charles Rydell, Bobby Short

Studio Cast [Vol. 3] • Painted Smiles (S) PS-1366 8-10
    Composer: Richard Rodgers, Lorenz Hart. **Conductor:** Dennis Deal. **Cast:** Nancy Andrews,
    Blossom Dearie, Arthur Siegel, Johnny Desmond, Estelle Parsons, Anthony Perkins, Lynn
    Redgrave.

Studio Cast [Vol. 4] • Painted Smiles (S) PS-1367 8-10
    Composer: Richard Rodgers, Lorenz Hart. **Conductor:** Dennis Deal. **Cast:** Nancy Andrews,
    Blossom Dearie, Johnny Desmond, Anthony Perkins, Lynn Redgrave, Elaine Stritch.

ROGUE SON

Soundtrack (1930) • Pelican (M) LP-2019 12-20   80
    One of the fist "talkies," we know of no remaining prints of this film.
    Composer: Clifford Grey, Franz Lehar, Dimitri Tiomikin. **Conductor:** Herbert Stothart. **Cast:**
    Lawrence Tibbett, Cahterine Dale Owen, Judith Vasselli, Ullrich Haupt, Laurel and Hardy.

ROGUES

TV Soundtrack (1964) • RCA Victor (M) LPM-2976 15-20   64

TV Soundtrack (1964) • RCA Victor (S) LSP-2976 20-30   64
    Composer: Nelson Riddle. **Conductor:** Nelson Riddle.

ROLLER BOOGIE

Soundtrack (1979) • Casablanca (S) NBLP-2-7194 10-12   80
    Two discs. Includes insert.
    Conductor: Bob Esty. **Cast:** Earth, Wind and Fire, Cher, Ron Green, Johnny Coolrock, Mavis
    Vegas Davis, Bob Esty and Cheeks, Michelle Aller, Emotions.

ROLLERBALL

Soundtrack (1975) • United Artists (S) UA-LA470-G 10-15   75
    Music of Shostakovich, Albinoni/Giazotto, J.S. Bach and Tchaikovsky.
    Composer: Andre Previn. **Conductor:** Andre Previn. **Cast:** London Symphony Orchestra,
    Simon Preston (organ), John Brown (violin).

ROLLERCOASTER

Soundtrack (1977) • MCA (S) 2284 10-15   77
    Composer: Lalo Schifrin. **Conductor:** Lalo Schifrin.

ROMAN SCANDALS: see KID MILLIONS

ROMANCE OF A HORSETHIEF

Soundtrack (1971) • Allied Artists (S) AAS-110-100 40-50   71
    Promotional issue only.
    Composer: Mort Shuman. **Conductor:** Mort Shuman. **Cast:** Yul Brynner, Lainie Kazan.

ROMANCE / ROMANCE

Original Cast (1988) • MCA (S) 6252 8-12   88

Original Cast (1988) • That's Entertainment (S) TER-1161 8-10   89
    UK release.
    Composer: Keith Herrmann, Barry Harman. **Conductor:** Kathy Sommer. **Cast:** Scott Bakula,
    Alison Fraser, Deborah Graham, Robert Hoshour.

ROMANTIC FAVORITES FROM STAGE AND SCREEN

Studiotrack • Capitol Creative Products (S) SL-6513 8-12
    Music from *My Fair Lady, Fantasticks, Pajama Game, Roar of the Greasepaint, On a Clear
    Day You Can See Forever, South Pacific, Iceland, Days of Wine and Roses, Inside Daisy
    Clover* and *Breakfast at Tiffany's.*
    Cast: Nat "King" Cole, Lettermen, Nancy Wilson, George Shearing, Matt Monro, Les Baxter.

ROMANTIC MOMENTS

Studiotrack • Columbia (M) GB-3 10-20   50s
    Full title: *Romantic Moments from Rose Marie, New Moon, Naughty Marietta.*
    Conductor: Leon Arnaud, Robert Armbruster. **Cast:** Nelson Eddy, Nadine Conner, Dorothy
    Kirsten, Eleanor Steber, Howard Chandler Chorus.

ROMANTIC MUSICAL

Original Cast (1983) • Franklin Mint (S) Number Not Known................ 30-50   83
     Boxed set of four red vinyl discs. Includes booklet. Music from *Sound of Music, The Fantasticks, Do I Hear a Waltz?, She Loves Me, Carousel, A Little Night Music, Camelot* and *Kismet.*

ROME ADVENTURE

Soundtrack (1962) • Warner Bros. (M) W-1458 10-12   62
Soundtrack (1962) • Warner Bros. (S) WS-1458 10-25   62
     Composer: Max Steiner, others. **Conductor:** Max Steiner. **Cast:** Emilio Pericoli, Cafe Milano Orchestra.

ROMEO AND JULIET

Soundtrack (1954) • Epic (M) LC-3126 40-50   54
Soundtrack (1954) • Epic (M) FLM-13104 30-35   66
Soundtrack (1954) • Epic (SE) FLS-15104 30-35   66
     Composer: Roman Vlad. **Conductor:** Lambert Williamson. **Cast:** Sir John Gielgud (prologue), Laurence Harvey, Flora Robson, Sebastian Cabot, Susan Shentall. (With dialogue.)

Studiotrack (1950) • RCA Victor (M) LM-1019 25-30   50
     10-inch LP.
     Composer: Peter Ilyich Tchaikovsky. **Cast:** Arturo Toscanini.

Soundtrack (1968) • Capitol (S) SWDR-289 20-25   69
     Boxed, four-disc set. Includes booklet. Includes music, dialogue, special effects, etc.
     Composer: Nino Rota, Eugene Walter. **Cast:** Leonard Whiting, Olivia Hussey, Michael York, Milo O'Shea, John McEnry, Pat Heywood, Natasha Parry, Robert Stephens, Glen Weston, Keith Skinner, Bruce Robinson, Paul Hardwick, Antonio Pierfederici. (With dialogue.)

Soundtrack (1968) • Capitol (S) ST-400 8-10   69
     Excerpts of Capitol SWDR-289.
     Composer: Nino Rota. **Conductor:** Nino Rota. **Cast:** Leonard Whiting, Olivia Hussey, Michael York, Milo O'Shea, John McEnry, Pat Heywood, Natasha Parry, Robert Stephens.

Soundtrack (1968) • Capitol (S) ST-2993 10-12   68
     Black label.

RONALD REAGAN RECOMMENDS

Studiotrack • Raleigh (M) No Number Used 20-40   58
     Full title: *Ronald Reagan Recommends Award Winning Music From Hollywood.* As TV spokesmen for General Electric, Ronald Reagan presents eight Oscar-winning tracks.

ROOFTOPS

Soundtrack (1989) • Capitol (S) C1-91736 8-10   89

ROOM 43: see BIG OPERATOR

ROOM WITH A VIEW

Soundtrack (1985) • DRG (S) SBL 12588 10-15   86
     Composer: Richard Robbins. **Cast:** Kiri Te Kanawa.

ROOTS

TV Soundtrack (1978) • Warner Bros. (S) 3WS-3048 12-25   78
     Three discs.
TV Soundtrack (1977) • A&M (S) SP-4626 10-15   76
     Includes poster.
     Composer: Quincy Jones, Gerald Fried. **Conductor:** Quincy Jones, Gerald Fried. **Cast:** Quincy Jones, Letta Mbulu.

ROOTS OF HEAVEN

Soundtrack (1958) • 20th Century-Fox (M) FOX-3005 250-300   58
     Composer: Malcolm Arnold, Henri Patterson. **Conductor:** Malcolm Arnold. **Cast:** London Royal Philharmonic

ROSE

Soundtrack (1979) • Atlantic (S) SD-16010 10-15   79
   Cast: Bette Midler.

ROSE MARIE

Original London Cast • Monmouth Evergreen (SE) MES-7050 15-20
   Also has music from *The Three Musketeers*.
   Composer: Rudolf Friml, Otto Harbach. **Cast:** Edith Day, Derek Oldham, Billy Merson.

Studio Cast (1950) • Columbia (M) ML-2178....................................... 12-18   50
   10-inch LP.
   Composer: Rudolf Friml, Herbert Stothart, Otto Harbach. **Conductor:** Leon Arnaud. **Cast:**
   Nelson Eddy, Dorothy Kirsten.

Studio Cast (1952) • RCA Victor (M) LK-1012....................................... 15-18   52

Studio Cast (1952) • Camden (M) CAL-408 12-15   58
   Composer: Rudolf Friml, Herbert Stothart, Otto Harbach. **Conductor:** Al Goodman. **Cast:**
   Charles Fredericks, Marion Bell, Christina Lind, Guild Trio and Choristers, Al Goodman and His
   Orchestra.

Studio Cast (1958) • RCA Victor (M) LOP-1001 15-20   58

Studio Cast (1958) • RCA Victor (S) LSO-1001 25-35   58
   Composer: Rudolf Friml, Herbert Stothart, Otto Harbach. **Conductor:** Lehman Engel. **Cast:**
   Julie Andrews, Giorgio Tozzi, Meier Tzelniker, Frances Day, Marion Keene, Frederick Harvey,
   Tudor Evans.

Soundtrack (1936) • Hollywood Soundstage (M) HS-414..................... 10-12
   Composer: Rudolf Friml, Herbert Stothart, Otto Harbach. **Conductor:** Herbert Stothart. **Cast:**
   Jeanette MacDonald, Nelson Eddy, Allan Jones.

Soundtrack (1954) • MGM (EP) X-229... 12-15   54

Soundtrack (1954) • MGM (M) E-229.. 20-30   54
   10-inch LP.

Soundtrack (1954) • Metro (M) M-616... 10-12   67

Soundtrack (1954) • Metro (SE) MS-616... 10-12   67

Soundtrack (1954) • MCA (M) MCA-25009 5-8   86

Soundtrack (1954) • MGM (M) E-3769... 15-18   60
   MGM Original Cast Double Feature series. Gatefold cover. Also has music from *Seven
   Brides for Seven Brothers*. All of the above MGM releases include songs deleted from the
   released print of the film.
   Composer: Rudolf Friml, Herbert Stothart, Otto Harbach, Oscar Hammerstein II. **Conductor:**
   George Stoll. **Cast:** Ann Blyth, Fernando Lamas, Howard Keel, Bert Lahr, Marjorie Main.

Studiotrack (1952) • RCA Victor (EP) ERA-220 10-15   52

Studiotrack (1952) • RCA Victor (M) LCT-16....................................... 35-45   52
   10-inch LP. Actual title: *Operetta Favorites by Jeanette MacDonald and Nelson Eddy*. Also
   has music from *Naughty Marietta* and *Maytime*.
   Composer: Rudolf Friml, Herbert Stothart, Otto Harbach. **Conductor:** Nathaniel Shilkret. **Cast:**
   Nelson Eddy, Jeanette MacDonald.

Studiotrack (1957) • Halo (M) 50241 8-15   57
   Also see MERRY WIDOW
   Also see RIO RITA
   Also see THOSE GLORIOUS MGM MUSICALS

ROSE ON BROADWAY

TV Soundtrack • Cozy (S) PL-9206... 10-12
   Conductor: H.B. Barnum.

ROSE TATTOO

Soundtrack (1955) • Columbia (EP) B-727.. 20-25   55

Soundtrack (1955) • Columbia (M) CL-727 35-45   55
   Composer: Alex North. **Conductor:** Alex North.

Studio Cast (1967) • Caedmon (S) TRS-324....................................... 20-25   67
   Three discs. A dramatic play.
   Cast: Maureen Stapleton, Harry Guardino.

ROSEMARY'S BABY
Soundtrack (1968) • Dot (S) DLP-25875 15-18   68
    Composer: Christopher Komeda. **Conductor:** Dick Hazard.

ROSENCRANTZ AND GUILDENSTERN ARE DEAD
Original London Cast (1967) • London (S) AMS-88003 15-18   68
    Incidental music. Also has music from *The Royal Hunt of the Sun* and *As You Like It*.
    Composer: Marc Wilkinson. **Conductor:** Marc Wilkinson.

ROTHSCHILDS
Original Cast (1970) • Columbia (S) S-30337 20-25   70
    Composer: Jerry Bock, Sheldon Harnick. **Conductor:** Milton Greene. **Cast:** Paul Hecht, Leila
    Martin, Jill Clayburgh, Hal Linden, Keene Curtis, Leo Leyden, Timothy Jerome, David Garfield,
    Allan Gruet.

ROUGH RIDERS – MUSIC FOR ON AND OFF THE ROAD
Soundtrack (1986) • Epic (S) FE-40248 8-10   86

ROUND MIDNIGHT
Soundtrack (1986) • Columbia (S) SC-40464 10-15   86
    Conductor: Herbie Hancock. **Cast:** Dexter Gordon.

ROUSTABOUT
Soundtrack (1964) • RCA Victor (M) LPM-2999 40-60   64
    Black label, reads "Mono" at bottom.
Soundtrack (1964) • RCA Victor (S) LSP-2999 300-600   64
    Black label, with RCA Victor logo in silver print.
Soundtrack (1964) • RCA Victor (M) LPM-2999 20-30   65
    Black label, reads "Monaural" at bottom.
Soundtrack (1964) • RCA Victor (S) LSP-2999 20-30   65
    Black label, with RCA Victor logo in white print.
Soundtrack (1964) • RCA Victor (S) LSP-2999 10-25   69
    Orange or tan label.
Soundtrack (1964) • RCA Victor (S) AFL1-2999 8-10   77
    Composer: Bill Giant, Bernie Baum, Florence Kaye, Jerry Leiber, Mike Stoller, Ben Weisman,
    Sid Wayne, Fred Wise, Randy Starr, Sid Tepper, Roy C. Bennett. **Cast:** Elvis Presley, Scotty
    Moore (guitar), Tiny Timbrell (guitar), Bob Moore (bass), Floyd Cramer (piano), D.J. Fontana
    (drums), Hal Blaine (drums), Boots Randolph (saxophone), Dudley Brooks (piano), Jordanaires
    (vocals).

ROUTE 66 THEME AND OTHER GREAT TV THEMES
Studiotrack (1960) • Capitol (M) T-1771 15-25   60
Studiotrack (1960) • Capitol (S) ST-1771 20-30   60
    Also has music from *Ben Casey, The Defenders, Dr. Kildare, Naked City, The Andy Griffith
    Show, The Alvin Show, The Steve Allen Show, My Three Sons, Sing Along with Mitch, Sam
    Benedict* and *The Untouchables.*
    Conductor: Nelson Riddle. **Cast:** Nelson Riddle and His Orchestra.

ROWAN AND MARTIN'S LAUGH-IN
TV Soundtrack (1968) • Epic (S) 15118 12-18   68
TV Soundtrack (1969) • Reprise (S) RS 6335 12-18   69
    Actual title: *Laugh-In '69.*
TV Soundtrack • Harmony (S) KH-30976 10-12
    Cast: Dan Rowan, Dick Martin, Judy Carne, Arte Johnson, Ruth Buzzi, Henry Gibson, Goldie
    Hawn, Dave Madden, Gary Owens, Alan Sues, Chelsea Brown, Dick Whittington, Jo Anne
    Worley, Connie Stevens.

ROY ROGERS – THE REPUBLIC YEARS: see REPUBLIC YEARS

ROYAL AFFAIR
Soundtrack (1950) • Decca DU-758 85-100   50
    Two 78 rpms in gatefold album. From a 1950 French film.
    Conductor: Raymond Legrand. **Cast:** Maurice Chevalier.

ROYAL HUNT OF THE SUN: see ROSENCRANTZ AND GUILDENSTERN ARE DEAD

ROYAL WEDDING
Soundtrack (1951) • MGM - MGM-70... 25-30   51
   78 rpm album.
Soundtrack (1951) • MGM (EP) K-70 12-18   51
   Boxed, four-disc set.
Soundtrack (1951) • MGM (M) E-543 35-45   51
   10-inch LP.
     Composer: Burton Lane, Alan Jay Lerner. **Conductor:** Johnny Green. **Cast:** Fred Astaire, Jane Powell.
     Also see SEVEN BRIDES FOR SEVEN BROTHERS
     Also see THOSE GLORIOUS MGM MUSICALS

ROZSA CONDUCTS ROZSA
Studiotrack (1978) • Varese Sarabande (S) VC-81053 15-20   78
   Contains the suite from *Lust for Life* plus *Brute Force, The Killers* and *The Naked City*, performed as the *Background to Violence Suite*.
     Composer: Miklos Rozsa. **Conductor:** Miklos Rozsa. **Cast:** Frankenland State Symphony Orchestra.

ROZSA: LUST FOR LIFE SUITE see LUST FOR LIFE

ROZSA: SUITES FOR THE FILMS
Studiotrack (1979) • Varese Sarabande (S) VC-81104 10-12   79
   Music from *Ben-Hur, El Cid* and *King of Kings*.
     Composer: Miklos Rozsa. **Conductor:** Richard Muller-Lampertz. **Cast:** Hamburg Concert Orchestra and Chorus.

RUDE AWAKENING
Soundtrack • Elektra (S) 60873-1... 8-10
     Cast: Mike + Mechanics, Sigue Sigue Sputnik, Bill Medley, Frankie and Knockouts, Kim Carnes, Georgia Satellites, Miami Sound Machine, Jefferson Airplane, Grateful Dead, Phoebe Snow, Bob Dylan.

RUDOLPH THE RED-NOSED REINDEER
TV Soundtrack (1964) • Decca (M) DL-34327 25-35   64
TV Soundtrack (1964) • Decca (S) DL-74815 45-65   64
TV Soundtrack (1964) • MCA (S) MCA-15003 12-15   Re
   One side has complete TV soundtrack. Side two is songs from the show performed by the Decca Concert Orchestra. May or may not have lyrics printed on back cover.
     Composer: Johnny Marks. **Conductor:** Maury Laws, Herbert Rehbein. **Cast:** Burl Ives, Stan Francis, Billie Richards, Paul Soles, Janet Orenstein.

RUDY CIAO
Original Cast • RCA Italiana (M) APML-10411 65-85
   Italian release. Italian musical based on the life of Rudolph Valentino. Gatefold cover.
     Composer: Trovaioli. **Conductor:** Bruno Nicolai. **Cast:** Marcello Mastroianni, Olga Villi, Ilaria Occhini, Giuliana Lojodice, Giusi Raspani Dandolo, Raffaella Carra', Paola Pitagora, Tina Lattanzi.

RUFF & READY – ADVENTURES IN SPACE
TV Soundtrack (1958) • Colpix (M) CP 201 50-100   58

RUGANTINO
Original Cast (1964) • Warner Bros. (M) H-1528................................... 25-30   64
Original Cast (1964) • Warner Bros. (S) HS-1528................................ 35-45   64
   Includes booklet. Italian show that became the first Broadway musical presented in a foreign language. English translation by Alfred Drake.
     Composer: Armando Trovajoli, Pietro Garinei, Sandro Giovannini. **Conductor:** Anton Coppola. **Cast:** Nino Manfredi, Ornella Vanoni, Aldo Fabrizi, Bice Valor, Lando Fiorini.

RUGGLES OF RED GAP
TV Soundtrack (1957) • Verve (M) MGV-15000 35-45   57

TV Soundtrack (1957) • Stet (M) DS-15007 8-12   Re
    Composer: Jule Styne, Leo Robin. **Conductor:** Buddy Bregman. **Cast:** Sir Michael Redgrave,
    Peter Lawford, Imogene Coca, Jane Powell, David Wayne.

RULING CLASS
Soundtrack (1972) • Avco Embassy (S) AV-11003 20-25   72
    Composer: John Cameron, others. **Conductor:** John Cameron. **Cast:** Peter O'Toole, Alastair
    Sim, Arthur Lowe, Harry Andrews, Coral Browne. (With dialogue.)

RUMBLE FISH
Soundtrack (1983) • A&M (S) SP6-4983 10-15   83
    Composer: Stewart Copeland.

RUN, ANGEL, RUN
Soundtrack (1969) • Epic (S) BN-26474.. 15-20   69
    Composer: Stu Phillips, others. **Conductor:** Stu Phillips. **Cast:** Tammy Wynette, Windows.

RUN FOR YOUR WIFE
Soundtrack (1966) • RCA Victor (M) LOC-1129 10-12   66
Soundtrack (1966) • RCA Victor (S) LSO-1129.................................... 12-18   66
    Composer: Nino Oliviero. **Conductor:** Pier Luigi Urbini, Marty Manning. **Cast:** Frankie Randall.

RUN OF THE ARROW
Soundtrack (1957) • Decca (M) DL-8620 50-60   57
  Black label or pink label promo.
Soundtrack (1957) • Decca (M) DL-8620 30-35   60s
  Rainbow (or multi-color) label.
Soundtrack (1957) • AEI (M) AEI-3102 10-12   78
    Composer: Victor Young, others. **Conductor:** Constantin Bakaleinkoff.

RUN WILD, RUN FREE
Soundtrack (1969) • SGC (S) SD-5003.. 15-20   69
    Composer: David Whitaker. **Conductor:** David Whitaker. **Cast:** New Christy Minstrels.

RUNAWAY
Soundtrack (1985) • Varese Sarabande (S) STV-81234 12-15   85
    Composer: Jerry Goldsmith.

RUNAWAY TRAIN
Soundtrack (1985) • Enigma (S) 73200-1 12-15   86
    Composer: Trevor Jones.

RUNAWAYS
Original Cast (1978) • Columbia (S) JS-35410..................................... 8-12   78
  A New York Shakespeare Festival musical.
    Composer: Elizabeth Swados. **Cast:** Bernie Allison, Trini Alvarado, Mark Anthony Butler,
    Leonard Brown, Bruce Hilbok, Diane Lane, Jossie De Guzman, Nan-Lynn Nelson, Randy Ruiz,
    Venustrak Robinson, Karen Evans, Ray Contreras.

RUNNING MAN
Soundtrack (1987) • Varese Sarabande (S) STV-81356 10-15   87
Soundtrack (1987) • That's Entertainment (S) TER-1158...................... 8-10   80s
  UK release.
    Composer: Harold Faltermeyer.

RUNNING SCARED
Soundtrack (1986) • MCA (S) 6169.. 10-12   86
Soundtrack (1986) • MCA (S) 39321... 8-10   88
    Composer: Rod Temperton, others. **Cast:** Michael McDonald, Fee Waybill, Rod Temperton and
    Beat Wagon, Larry Williams, Ready for the World, Klymaxx, New Edition, Patti Labelle, Kim
    Wilde.

RUSH TO JUDGMENT
Soundtrack (1967) • Happening (M) 3210.. 15-20   67
    Cast: Mark Lane (narration).

Soundtrack (1967) • Vanguard (M) 9242.. 15-20   67
Deliberation of the Warren Commission's findings regarding Lee Harvey Oswald.
Cast: Emile De Antonio (narration).

RUSSIAN ADVENTURE
Soundtrack (1966) • Roulette (M) OS-802 15-18   66
Soundtrack (1966) • Roulette (S) OSS-802.. 20-25   66
Also known as *Cinerama's Russian Adventure*.
Conductor: Aleksandr Lokshin. Cast: Moscow State Symphony, Orchestra of the Moscow State Circus, Orchestra of the Bolshoi Ballet, Moiseyev Song and Dance Ensemble, Piantnitsky Song and Dance Ensemble.

RUSSIANS ARE COMING! THE RUSSIANS ARE COMING!
Soundtrack (1966) • United Artists (M) UAL-4142 8-10   66
Soundtrack (1966) • United Artists (S) UAS-5142 8-12   66
Soundtrack (1966) • United Artists (S) SW-90843 8-10   Re
Capitol Record Club issue.
Soundtrack (1966) • MCA (S) 1428... 8-10   80s
Composer: Johnny Mandel, others. Conductor: Johnny Mandel. Cast: Irene Kral.

RUSSKIES
Soundtrack (1987) • Varese Sarabande (S) STV 81335 10-15   87
Composer: James Newton Howard.

RUSTLER'S RHAPSODY
Soundtrack (1985) • Warner Bros. (S) 1-25284 8-10   85
Composer: Steve Dorff, others. Cast: Gary Morris, Nitty Gritty Dirt Band, John Anderson, Pinkard and Bowden, Charlie McCoy, Pam Tillis, Randy Travis, Karen Brooks, Rex Allen Jr., Rex Allen Sr., Roy Rogers.

RUTHLESS PEOPLE
Soundtrack (1986) • Epic (S) SE-40398.. 8-10   86
Cast: Mick Jagger, Billy Joel, Machinations, Luther Vandross, Dan Hartman, Kool and the Gang, Michel Colombier, Bruce Springsteen, Nicole, Paul Young.

RUTLES
TV Soundtrack (1978) • Warner Bros. (S) HS-3151 15-20   78
Composer: Neil Innes. Cast: Neil Innes, Ollie Halsall, Rikki Fataar, John Halsey.

RYAN'S DAUGHTER
Soundtrack (1970) • MGM (S) 1SE-27 10-15   70
Gatefold cover.
Composer: Maurice Jarre. Conductor: Maurice Jarre.

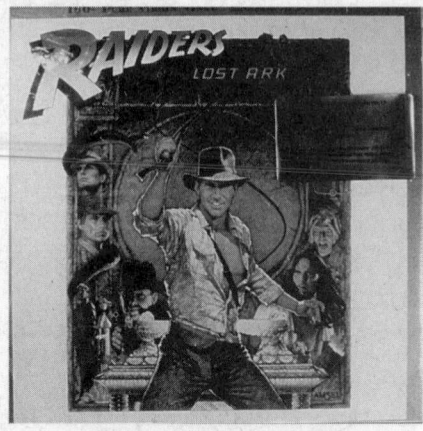

ORIGINAL MOTION PICTURE SOUNDTRACK

RAMBO
FIRST BLOOD PART II

Music composed and conducted by
JERRY GOLDSMITH

Featured song "PEACE IN OUR LIFE"
sung by
FRANK STALLONE

STALLONE

No man, no law, no war can stop him.

"RASHOMON"
THE ORIGINAL MUSIC FROM THE BROADWAY TRIUMPH

COMPOSED AND CONDUCTED BY LAURENCE ROSENTHAL

STEREO

CLAIRE BLOOM/ROD STEIGER
OSCAR HOMOLKA/AKIM TAMIROFF

in PETER GLENVILLE'S production

"RASHOMON"

A new play by FAY and MICHAEL KANIN

ORIGINAL MOTION PICTURE SOUNDTRACK

STEREO

THE ROAD
WARRIOR

ORIGINAL MOTION PICTURE SOUNDTRACK

Return To
OZ

Music Composed and
Conducted by DAVID SHIRE

THE LONDON SYMPHONY ORCHESTRA

Dimitri Tiomkin | The Pittsburgh Symphony | Gary Merrill

Rhapsody of
STEEL

Music from the Motion Picture

Music of India

from JEAN RENOIR'S
THE RIVER

The Original Musical Score
from the Motion Picture Sound Track
Recorded in India

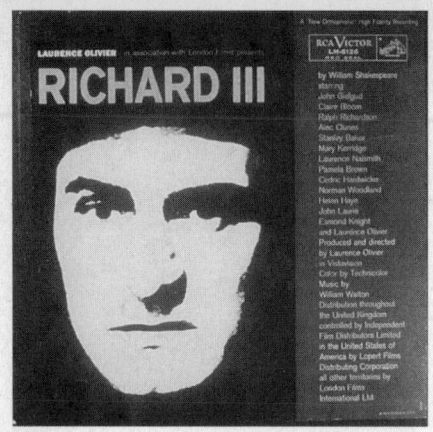

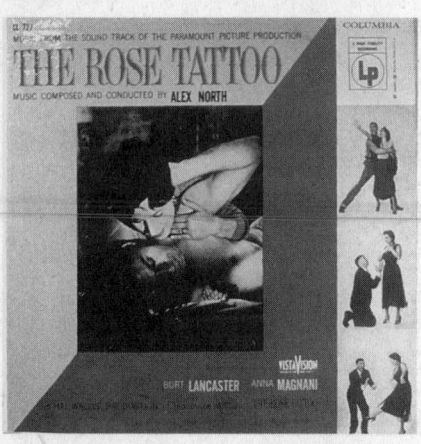

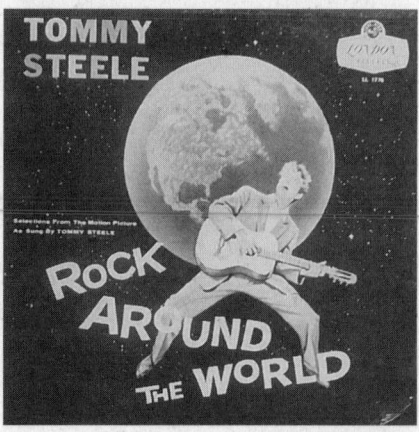

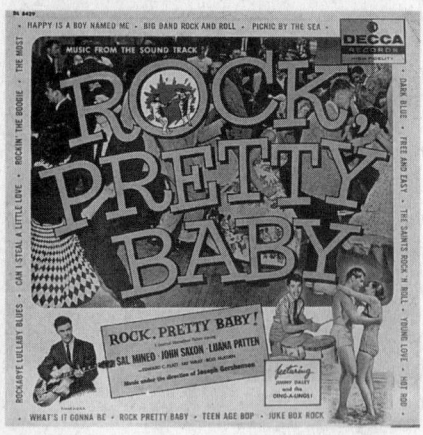

S

S'WONDERFUL, S'MARVELOUS, S'GERSHWIN
TV Soundtrack (1972) • Daybreak (M) DR-2009 10-12   72
Composer: George Gershwin, Ira Gershwin, B.G. DeSylva, DuBose Heyward. Conductor: Elliot Lawrence. Cast: Fred Astaire, Jack Lemmon, Leslie Uggams, Peter Nero, Robert Guillaume, Larry Kert, Alan Johnson, Linda Bennett.

SABRINA: see AS I HEAR IT

SACCO AND VANZETTI
Soundtrack (1971) • RCA Victor (S) LSP-4612 15-20   71
Composer: Ennio Morricone. Conductor: Ennio Morricone. Cast: Joan Baez.

SACRED IDOL
Soundtrack (1960) • Capitol (M) T-1293.. 20-25   60
Soundtrack (1960) • Capitol (S) ST-1293.. 30-35   60
Composer: Les Baxter. Conductor: Les Baxter.

SAGA OF BATTLESTAR GALACTICA: see BATTLESTAR GALACTICA

SAGA OF THE DINGBAT
Original Cast • N.Y. Herald Tribune (S) XCSV-105844/5 60-70
Industrial show.
Composer: Julian Stein, Edward Naylor. Conductor: Rolf Barnes. Cast: Ann Vivian, Hal Linden, Stan Page, Carole Woodruff, Mimi Vondra, Arline Woods, Gino Conforti, Don Grilley.

SAHARA
Soundtrack (1984) • Varese Sarabande (S) STV-81211 10-15   84
Composer: Ennio Morricone. Conductor: Ennio Morricone. Cast: Cathy Cole.

SAIL AWAY
Original Cast (1961) • Capitol (M) WAO-1643.. 8-12   61
Original Cast (1961) • Capitol (S) SWAO-1643..................................... 12-18   61
Composer: Noel Coward. Conductor: Peter Matz. Cast: Elaine Stritch, James Hurst, Alice Pearce, Patricia Harty, Grover Dale, Charles Braswell, Paul O'Keefe.
Original London Cast (1962) • Stanyan (S) SR-10027 10-15   72
Reissue. We lack details on an original release of this show, if there is such a U.S. issue.
Composer: Noel Coward. Conductor: Gareth Davies. Cast: Elaine Stritch, David Holliday, Grover Dale, Sheila Forbes, John Hewer, Edith Day, Sydney Arnold.
Studio Cast (1961) • Capitol (M) W-1667 10-15   61
Full title: *Noel Coward Sings His New Broadway Hit – Sail Away.*
Composer: Noel Coward. Conductor: Peter Matz. Cast: Noel Coward.

SAINT
TV Soundtrack (1962) • RCA Victor (M) LPM-3631........................... 50-125   66
TV Soundtrack (1962) • RCA Victor (S) LSP-3631........................... 100-200   66
Composer: Edwin Astley, Ken Jones. Conductor: Edwin Astley.

ST. ELMO'S FIRE
Soundtrack (1985) • Atlantic (S) 81261-1.. 8-10   85
Composer: David Foster. Conductor: David Foster. Cast: John Parr, Billy Squier, Elefante, Jon Anderson, Fee Waybill, David Foster, Vikki Moss, Airplay, Donny Gerrard, Amy Holland.

SAINT JOAN
Soundtrack (1957) • Capitol (M) W-865 25-30   57
Composer: Mischa Spoliansky. Conductor: Mischa Spoliansky.
Studio Cast • Caedmon (M) TRS 311-M 20-25

ST. LOUIS BLUES

Studiotrack (1958) • Capitol (M) W-993 35-45   58
Composer: William C. Handy, Nelson Riddle. **Conductor:** Nelson Riddle. **Cast:** Nat "King" Cole.
Studiotrack (1958) • Roulette (M) R-25037 12-18   58
Studiotrack (1958) • Roulette (S) SR-25037 20-25   58
Composer: William C. Handy. **Conductor:** Don Redman. **Cast:** Pearl Bailey.
Studiotrack (1958) • RCA Victor (M) LPM-1661 20-25   58
Studiotrack (1958) • RCA Victor (S) LSP-1661 25-45   58
Full title: *Selections from the Paramount Motion Picture St. Louis Blues.* Film stars Nat
"King" Cole, Pearl Bailey and Eartha Kitt were each under recording contracts to different
labels, resulting in three studio versions of a never-realized soundtrack ablum.
Composer: William C. Handy. **Conductor:** Matty Matlock, Jester Hairston. **Cast:** Eartha Kitt,
Shorty Rogers and His Giants.

ST. LOUIS WOMAN

Original Cast (1946) • Capitol CE-28 30-35   46
78 rpm album. Includes lyrics booklet and a leaflet. Capitol's first original cast album.
Original Cast (1946) • Capitol (M) L-355 60-75   52
10-inch LP.
Original Cast (1946) • Capitol (SE) DW-2742 30-35   67
Cover has drawing on white background.
Composer: Harold Arlen, Johnny Mercer. **Conductor:** Leon Leonardi. **Cast:** Pearl Bailey, Harold
Nicholas, Ruby Hill, June Hawkins, Robert Pope.
Also see FREE AND EASY.

SAINT OF BLEECKER STREET

Original Cast (1954) • RCA Victor (M) LM-6032 70-80   54
Boxed, two-disc. Includes booklet.
Original Cast (1954) • RCA Victor (M) CBM2-2714 15-20   78
Composer: Gian-Carlo Menotti. **Conductor:** Thomas Schippers. **Cast:** Maria DiGerlando, David
Aiken, Gabrielle Ruggiero, David Poleri, John Reardon, Catherine Akos, Elizabeth Carron, Russell
Goodwin.

SALAAM BOMBAY!

Soundtrack (1988) • DRG (S) SBL 12595 8-12   88
Composer: L. Subramaniam. **Conductor:** L. Subramaniam. **Cast:** L. Subramaniam.

SALAD DAYS

Original London Cast (1958) • London (M) 5474 35-40   58
Original London Cast (1958) • London (M) 5765 20-25   63
Original London Cast (1958) • Embassy (M) EMB-31046 12-15   Re
Composer: Julian Slade, Dorothy Reynolds. **Cast:** Eleanor Drew, John Warner, James
Cairncross, Cairn Cross, Michael Aldridge, Edward Rubach & Robert Docker (pianos).
Original Revival Cast • That's Entertainment (S) TER-1018 8-10   80s
UK release.
Composer: Julian Slade, Dorothy Reynolds.

SALLAH

Soundtrack (1965) • Philips (M) PHM-200-177 15-20   65
Soundtrack (1965) • Philips (S) PHS-600-177 20-25   65
Composer: Yohanan Zarai. **Conductor:** Luchi DeJesus.

SALLY

Original London Cast (1921) • Monmouth Evergreen (SE) MES-7053 ... 8-12
Composer: Jerome Kern, others. **Cast:** Dorothy Dickson, Gregory Stroud, Leslie Henson, George
Grossmith, Heather Thatcher, Seymour Beard.
Also see GOOD NEWS

SALLY FIELD: see FLYING NUN

SALOME

Soundtrack (1953) • Decca (EP) ED-515 25-35   53
Soundtrack (1953) • Decca (M) DL-6026 100-125   53
   10-inch LP.
Soundtrack (1953) • MCA (M) VIM-7267E 35-45   84
   Japanese release. One side has music from *Samson and Delilah*. Cover
   shows original 10-inch Decca front covers of each show, enlarged to 12-inch
   size.
   Composer: George Duning, Daniele Amfitheatrof. **Conductor:** Morris Stoloff. **Cast:** Rita
   Hayworth, Stewart Granger, Alan Badel. (With dialogue.)

SALSA

Soundtrack (1988) • MCA (S) 6232.. 8-10   88
   Cast: Bobby Caldwell, Ben E. King, Marisela with Edwin Hawkins Singers, Tito Puente, Robby
   Rosa, Wilkins, Mavis Vegas Davis, Grupo Niche, Laura Branagan, Kenny Ortega.

SALT AND PEPPER

Soundtrack (1968) • United Artists (S) UAS-5187 12-15   68
Soundtrack (1968) • MCA (S) 25035.. 8-10   86
   Composer: John Dankworth, Leslie Bricusse. **Cast:** Sammy Davis Jr., George Rhodes.

SALUDOS AMIGOS (MUSIC FROM SOUTH OF THE BORDER)

Soundtrack (1943) • Disneyland (M) WDL-3039 35-40   59
Soundtrack (1943) • Disneyland (M) WDL-1039 20-25   60
   Composer: Ray Barroso, Augustine Lara, Charles Wolcott, others. **Conductor:** Leo Perachi.

SALUTE TO BOGIE: HUMPHREY BOGART

Studiotrack • MGM (M) E-4359 20-25
   Cast: Singing Strings.

SALUTE TO VINCENT YOUMANS: FOUR GREAT HITS FROM HIT
SHOWS

Studiotrack (1954) • RCA Victor (EP) EPA-543.................................... 15-20   54
   Includes: *Great Day* (from *Great Day*), *Sometimes I'm Happy* and *Hallelujah* (from *Hit the
   Deck*) and *Tea for Two* (from *No No Nanette*).
   Composer: Vincent Youmans. **Conductor:** Case. **Cast:** Russ Case and His Orchestra.

SALVADOR: see WALL STREET

SALVATION

Original Cast (1969) • Capitol (S) SO-337.. 10-15   69
   Composer: Peter Link, C.C. Courtney. **Conductor:** Kirk Nurock. **Cast:** Yolande Bavan, Peter
   Link, C.C. Courtney, Joe Morton, Martha Heflin, Boni Enten, Chapman Roberts, Annie Rachel.
Studio Cast (1969) • Mio International (S) MUS-5009 15-20   69
   Promotional issue only.
   Composer: Peter Link, C.C. Courtney. **Cast:** Gallery Repertory Theatre.
Soundtrack (1988) • Giant (S) GRI-6002-1 10-12   88

SAMMY

TV Soundtrack (1973) • MGM (S) SE-4914.. 10-15   73
   Composer: Various. **Conductor:** George Rhodes, Jack Parnell. **Cast:** Sammy Davis Jr., Sammy
   Davis Sr.

SAMOA

Soundtrack (1956) • Disneyland (M) WDL-4003 40-50   56
   One side has music from *Switzerland*.
   Composer: Oliver G. Wallace. **Conductor:** Oliver G. Wallace.

SAMSON AND DELILAH (1949)
Soundtrack (1949) • Decca (EP) DA-747 25-35   52
Soundtrack (1949) • Decca (M) DL-6007 30-50   52
   10-inch LP.
   Also see QUIET MAN
   Also see SALOME

SAND CASTLE
Soundtrack (1960) • Columbia (M) CL-1455 12-15   61
Soundtrack (1960) • Columbia (S) CS-8249... 15-20   61
   Composer: Alec Wilder. **Conductor:** Samuel Baron.

SAND PEBBLES
Soundtrack (1966) • 20th Century-Fox (M) 3189................................ 20-25   66
Soundtrack (1966) • 20th Century-Fox (S) S-4189............................... 40-45   66
   Composer: Jerry Goldsmith. **Conductor:** Lionel Newman.
Soundtrack (1966) • No Label Used (M) No Number Used 35-40   66
   Single-sided. Documentary titled *The Making of Sand Pebbles*. Narrated by Richard
   Attenborough with comments by the director and cast. An Argyle-Solar Production.
   Promotional issue only.

SANDHOG
Original Cast (1954) • Vanguard (M) VRS-9001.............................. 275-325   54
   Composer: Earl Robinson, Waldo Salt. **Cast:** Earl Robinson (piano).

SANDPIPER
Soundtrack (1965) • Mercury (M) MG-21032 10-12   65
Soundtrack (1965) • Mercury (S) SR-61032... 12-18   65
   Composer: Johnny Mandel. **Conductor:** Robert Armbruster.

SANDS OF IWO JIMA
Soundtrack (1949) • Citadel (M) CT-7027 10-15   81
   Also has music from Victor Young's *The Sun Shines Bright*.
   Composer: Victor Young. **Conductor:** Victor Young.

SANFORD AND SON
TV Soundtrack (1972) • RCA Victor (M) LPM-4739.............................. 12-15   72
   Composer: Quincy Jones. **Conductor:** Quincy Jones. **Cast:** Redd Foxx, Demond Wilson, Lynn
   Hamilton, Noam Pitlik, Hal Williams, Dick Van Patten, Harold Fong. (With dialogue.)

SANTA CLAUS CONQUERS THE MARTIANS
Studio Cast (1966) • Golden (S) SLP-170... 150-200   66
   Includes comic book. Record follows script, with sound effects and music.

SANTA CLAUS IS COMIN' TO TOWN
TV Soundtrack (1970) • MGM (S) SE-4732... 45-60   70
   Composer: Maury Laws, Jules Bass, J. Fred Coots, Haven Gillespie. **Cast:** Fred Astaire
   (narration), Mickey Rooney, Keenan Wynn, Paul Frees, Joan Gardner, Robbie Lester, Gary
   White, Dina Lynn, Greg Thomas, Westminster Children's Choir. (With dialogue.)

SANTA CLAUS – THE MOVIE
Soundtrack (1985) • EMI America (S) SJ-17177 8-12   85
   Composer: Henry Mancini. **Conductor:** Henry Mancini. **Cast:** Sheena Easton, others.

SAP OF LIFE
Original Cast • Blue Pear (M) BP-1002 18-20
   Composer: David Shire, Richard Maltby, Jr. **Cast:** Kenneth Nelson, Jerry Dodge, Patricia Bruder.

SARAFINA
Original Cast • Shanachie (S) 43052.. 8-10
Original Cast • RCA Victor (S) 9307-1 RC9... 8-10

SARATOGA

Original Cast (1959) • RCA Victor (M) LOC-1051 20-25   59
Original Cast (1959) • RCA Victor (S) LSO-1051 30-50   59
    Composer: Harold Arlen, Johnny Mercer. **Conductor:** Jerry Arlen. **Cast:** Howard Keel, Carol Lawrence, Odette Myrtil, Carol Brice.

SARAVA

Original Cast (1979) • Roadshow (S) 4D-11455 5-10   79
    12-inch, disco pressing.
    Composer: Mitch Leigh.

SATAN IN HIGH HEELS

Soundtrack (1962) • Parker (M) PLP-406 15-20   62
Soundtrack (1962) • Parker (S) PLP-406S 25-30   62
    Gatefold covers.
Soundtrack (1962) • Parker (M) PLP-406 12-15   62
Soundtrack (1962) • Parker (S) PLP-406S 15-20   62
    Standard covers.
    Composer: Mundell Lowe. **Conductor:** Mundell Lowe.

SATAN'S SADISTS

Soundtrack (1969) • Smash (S) SRS-67127 25-30   69
    Composer: Harley Hatcher. **Conductor:** Harley Hatcher.

SATCHMO THE GREAT

TV Soundtrack (1958) • Columbia (M) CL-1077 35-40   58
TV Soundtrack (1958) • Columbia Special Products (M) JCL-1077 8-10   Re
    Music and excerpts from the film and from the CBS-TV series *See It Now.*
    Conductor: Leonard Bernstein. **Cast:** Louis Armstrong, Edward R. Murrow, Lewisohn Stadium Symphony Orchestra. (With dialogue.)

SATINS AND SPURS

TV Soundtrack (1954) • Capitol (EP) FBF-547 20-25   54
TV Soundtrack (1954) • Capitol (M) L-547 60-65   54
    10-inch LP.
    Composer: Jay Livingston, Ray Evans. **Conductor:** Nelson Riddle. **Cast:** Betty Hutton, Earl Wrightson.
    Also see AARON SLICK FROM PUNKIN CRICK

SATISFACTION

Soundtrack (1988) • AJK (S) A710-1 8-10   88
    Cast: Justine Bateman and Mystery, Michel Colombier, John Kay and Steppenwolf.

SATURDAY NIGHT FEVER

Soundtrack (1977) • RSO (S) RS-2-4001 10-12   77
Soundtrack (1977) • RSO (S) 825389-1 8-10   Re
    Two discs.
    Composer: Barry Gibb, Robin Gibb, Maurice Gibb, others. **Conductor:** Barry Gibb, Robin Gibb, Maurice Gibb, David Shire, others. **Cast:** Bee Gees, Yvonne Elliman, Walter Murphy, Tavares, Kool and the Gang, K.C. and the Sunshine Band, Trammps, Ralph McDonald, David Shire, M.F.S.B.

SATURDAY NIGHT LIVE

Original Cast (1976) • Arista (S) AL-4107 10-12   76
TV Soundtrack (1976) • Arista (S) ALB6-8435 8-10   Re
    Composer: Paul Shaffer, others. **Conductor:** Howard Shore. **Cast:** John Belushi, Dan Aykroyd, Chevy Chase, Jane Curtin, Garrett Morris, Laraine Newman, Gilda Radner, Peter Boyle, Buck Henry, Richard Pryor, Paul Simon, Lily Tomlin, Don Pardo, Anne Beatts, Robert King, Bill Wendell. (With dialogue.)

SATURDAY'S WARRIOR

Original Cast (1974) • Embryo (S) EM-1001 10-15   74
    Composer: Lex de Azevedo, Doug Stewart. **Conductor:** Lex de Azevedo. **Cast:** Donna Conkling, Cam Clarke, Shawn Engemann.

SAVAGE

Soundtrack (1974) • Money (S) MS-1109.. 12-15   74
    Composer: Don Julian, others.

SAVAGE SAM

Soundtrack (1963) • Disneyland (M) ST-1925....................................... 25-30   63
    Sequel to *Old Yeller.*
    Cast: Thurl Ravenscroft (narration), Wellingtons, Brian Keith, Tommy Kirk, Marta Kristen, Jeff York, Dewey Martin, Kevin Corcoran. (With dialogue.)

SAVAGE SEVEN

Soundtrack (1968) • Atco (M) 33-245... 20-25   68
Soundtrack (1968) • Atco (S) SD-33-245 20-30   68
    Composer: Guy Hemric, Jerry Styner. **Cast:** Cream, Iron Butterfly, Barbara Kelly, Morning Good.

SAVAGE STREETS

Soundtrack (1984) • MCA (S) L33-1206.. 10-15   84
    Side 1: *Justice for One.* Side 2: *Innocent Hearts.* Promotional issue only.
    Composer: John Farnham, Sue Shifrin, Randy Bishop. **Cast:** John Farnham.
Soundtrack (1984) • MCA (S) 6134... 8-10   84
    Composer: Michael Lloyd, John d'Andrea. **Cast:** John Farnham, Real Life, 3 Speed, Michael Bradley.

SAVAGE WILD

Soundtrack (1970) • American Int'l (S) STA-1032 15-20   70
    Composer: Jamie Mendoza-Nava. **Conductor:** Jamie Mendoza-Nava. **Cast:** Chris Quesada.

SAVE THE CHILDREN

Soundtrack (1973) • Motown (S) M-800-R2 8-12   73
    Two discs. Includes poster.
    Cast: Matt Robinson (narration), Jackson Five, Nancy Wilson, Roberta Flack, Brenda Lee Eager, Rev. James Cleveland, Marvin Gaye, Sammy Davis Jr., Temptations, Bill Withers, O'Jays, Gladys Knight and the Pips, Main Ingredient, Curtis Mayfield, Jerry Butler, Ramsey Lewis Trio, Quincy Jones, Rev. Jesse Jackson. (With dialogue.)

SAVING THE WILDLIFE

TV Soundtrack (1986) • American Gramaphone (S) AG 2086 10-15   86
    A PBS Television Special.
    Composer: Mannheim Steamroller. **Cast:** Mannheim Steamroller.

SAY AMEN, SOMEBODY

Soundtrack (1983) • DRG (S) SB2L-1258... 8-10   83
    Two discs. Soundtrack plus concert recordings.
    Cast: "Mother" Willie Mae Ford Smith, "Professor" Thomas Dorsey.

SAY, DARLING

Original Cast (1958) • RCA Victor (M) LOC-1045 30-35   58
Original Cast (1958) • RCA Victor (S) LSO-1045 45-55   58
    Musical based on the actual rehearsal process of *The Pajama Game.* Whereas the original show featured just piano accompaniment, this recording is augmented to include a full theater orchestra.
    Composer: Jule Styne, Betty Comden, Adolph Green. **Conductor:** Sid Ramin. **Cast:** David Wayne, Vivian Blaine, Johnny Desmond, Jerome Cowan, Mitchell Gregg, Steve Condos.

SAY ONE FOR ME
Soundtrack (1959) • Columbia (M) CL-1337 15-20   59
Soundtrack (1959) • Columbia (S) CS-8147................................ 60-65   59
   Composer: James Van Heusen, Sammy Cahn. **Conductor:** Lionel Newman. **Cast:** Debbie
   Reynolds, Bing Crosby, Robert Wagner, Buddy Cole, Judy Harriett.
Studiotrack (1959) • Buena Vista (M) BV-1302 10-20   59
   Cast: Rex Allen, Roberta Shore, Tony Paris.

SAYONARA
Soundtrack (1957) • RCA Victor (M) LOC-1041 20-50   57
Soundtrack (1957) • RCA Victor (S) LSO-1041............................ 45-65   57
Soundtrack (1957) • Entr'acte (S) ERS-6513-ST 8-10   Re
   Composer: Franz Waxman, Irving Berlin, Shiro Matsumoto, Suifo Kishimoto. **Conductor:** Franz
   Waxman. **Cast:** Miiko Taka.

SCALPHUNTERS
Soundtrack (1968) • United Artists (M) UAL-4176............................. 20-30   68
Soundtrack (1968) • United Artists (S) UAS-5176 25-40   68
Soundtrack (1968) • MCA (S) 25042 8-12   86
   Composer: Elmer Bernstein. **Conductor:** Elmer Bernstein.

SCANDAL
Soundtrack (1989) • Enigma (S) 773531-1 8-12   89
   Composer: Carl Davis, others.

SCANDALOUS JOHN
Soundtrack (1971) • Buena Vista (S) STER-5004 10-15   71
   Composer: Rod McKuen. **Cast:** Rod McKuen.

SCANDALOUS LIFE OF FRANKIE AND JOHNNY
Studio Cast (1938) • Desto (M) D-408................................ 8-10
Studio Cast • Desto (S) DST-6408 10-12   Re
   One side is *Indian Suite, Suite No. 2, Opus 48*, the classical work of Edward MacDowell.
   Composer: Jerome Moross. **Conductor:** Walter Hendl. **Cast:** Vienna Symphony Orchestra and
   Chorus.

SCARFACE
Soundtrack (1984) • MCA (S) 6126.. 15-20   83
   Composer: Giorgio Moroder. **Cast:** Paul Engemann, Deborah Harry, Amy Holland, Maria
   Conchita, Giorgio Moroder, Elizabeth Daily, Beth Andersen.

SCARLET AND THE BLACK
Soundtrack (1983) • Cerberus (S) CEM-S-0120 15-25   83
   Composer: Ennio Morricone.

SCARLET STREET
Soundtrack (1945) • Medallion (M) ML 303 20-25   79
   Composer: Hans J. Salter. **Conductor:** Hans J. Salter.

SCENES AND THEMES
Studiotrack (1972) • RCA Victor (Q) APD1-0025 10-20   72
   Music from *Lost Horizon, A Man and a Woman, Love Story, Dr. Zhivago, The Sandpipers,
   Gone with the Wind, Alfie, Casino Royale, Romeo and Juliet* and *Say Goodbye Maggie
   Cole.*
   Cast: Hugo Montenegro and Orchestra.

SCENT OF MYSTERY
Soundtrack (1960) • Ramrod (M) T-6001 40-50   60
Soundtrack (1960) • Ramrod (S) ST-6001 75-85   60
   Composer: Mario Nascimbene, Jordan Ramin, Harold Adamson. **Conductor:** Jack Saunders.
   Cast: Eddie Fisher.

SCHNAPSIE

Studio Cast • Sea Horse/Chancellor (M) CSH-7001............................ 20-30
Includes bonus photo.
Composer: Eddy Manson. **Cast:** Marla Ray and Cast (narrators).

SCHONER GIGOLO – ARMER GIGOLO (JUST A GIGOLO)

Soundtrack (1979) • Ariola (S) 200 462 320.. 25-30   79
Conductor: Jack Fishman, Frank Barber, John Altman. **Cast:** Marlene Dietrich, Manhattan
Transfer, Ragtimers, Pasadena Roof Orchestra, Gunther Fischer Orchestra, Sydne Rome,
Rebels, Barnabas Orchestra, Village People.

SCHOOL DAZE

Soundtrack (1988) • EMI (S) E1-48680.. 8-10   88
Cast: E., Tech and Effx, Rays, Jigaboo and Wannabee Ensemble, Kenny Barron and Terence
Blanchard, Morehouse College Glee Club, Keith John, Phyllis Hyman, Pieces of a Dream, Portia
Griffin.

SCHOOL FOR SCANDAL

Original Cast (1962) • Command (S) RS 13002.................................... 20-25   62
Boxed, three-disc set. Majectic Theatre, N.Y. presentation.
Studio Cast • Caedmon (M) TRS 305-M 15-20

SCORPIO

Soundtrack • Elmer Bernstein Film Music Collection (S) FMC 11......... 25-30   78
Composer: Jerry Fielding. **Conductor:** Jerry Fielding.

SCOTT JOPLIN

Soundtrack (1977) • MCA (S) 2098... 8-10   77
Soundtrack (1977) • MCA (S) 1541... 8-10   80s
Composer: Scott Joplin. **Cast:** Dick Hyman.

SCRAMBLED FEET

Original Cast (1979) • DRG (S) 6105 8-10   79
Composer: John Driver, Jeffrey Haddow. **Conductor:** Jimmy Wisner. **Cast:** Evalyn Baron, John
Driver, Jeffrey Haddow, Roger Neil.

SCREAMERS

Soundtrack (1980) • Web (S) ST-101 12-15   81
Composer: Luciano Michelini. **Conductor:** Luciano Michelini.

SCREEN THEMES

Studiotrack (1988) • Varese Sarabande (S) VS-5208 10-15   88
Music from *Masquerade, Da, Beetlejuice, The Milagro Beanfield War, Cocoon, The Return,
Die Hard* and five other films.
Composer: John Barry, Elmer Bernstein, Danny Elfman, Dave Grusin, James Horner, Michael
Kamen, others. **Conductor:** John Scott. **Cast:** Royal Philharmonic Orchestra.

SCROOGE

Soundtrack • Cinema Center Films (S) SS 273.................................... 15-25
Promotional issue only.
Soundtrack (1970) • Columbia (S) S-30258 12-18   70
Unipak fold-open cover (disc opening faces gutter rather than outer edge). Musical version
of Charles Dickens' *A Christmas Carol*.
Soundtrack (1970) • Columbia Special Products (S) P-14077................ 8-10   Re
Soundtrack (1970) • TelEd (S) S-1001.. 10-20   75
Full title: *IBM Presents Scrooge*. Highlights from *Scrooge*. An educational package for
classroom use. Includes original sleeve, insert, and a cover that serves as a classroom
poster.
Composer: Leslie Bricusse. **Conductor:** Ian Fraser. **Cast:** Albert Finney, David Collins, Laurence
Naismith, Sir Alec Guinness, Richard Beaumont, Anton Rodgers.
Original Cast (1978) • Theatre Under The Stars (S) TUTS-78 10-15   78
Seven-inch disc..
Composer: James Bernard, Mark Holden. **Conductor:** Mark Holden.

SCROOGED

Soundtrack (1988) • A&M (S) SP 3921 8-10   89
Cast: Annie Lennox, Al Green, Mark Lennon, New Voices of Freedom, Dan Hartman, Denise Lopez, Kool Moe Dee, Miles Davis, Larry Carlton, Paul Shaffer, Robbie Robertson, Buster Poindexter.

SEA HAWK

Studiotrack (1940) • Varese Sarabande (SE) 704 -380........................ 10-15   87
Studiotrack (1940) • That's Entertainment (SE) TER-1164 8-10   89
UK release.
Composer: Erich Wolfgang Korngold. Conductor: Varujan Kojian. Cast: Utah Symphony Orchestra and Chorus.

SEA HAWK: THE CLASSIC FILM SCORES OF ERICH WOLFGANG KORNGOLD

Studiotrack • RCA Victor (S) LSC-3330 12-15   72
Includes liner notes insert.
Studiotrack • RCA Victor (S) AGL-1-3707 8-10   72
Without liner notes insert. Music from *The Sea Hawk, Kings Row, Captain Blood, The Adventures of Robin Hood, Of Human Bondage, Juaurez, The Constant Nymph, Anthony Adverse, Between Two Worlds, Deception, Devotion* and *Escape Me Never.*
Composer: Erich Wolfgang Korngold. Conductor: Charles Gerhardt. Cast: National Philharmonic Orchestra of London.

SEA OF LOVE

Soundtrack (1989) • Mercury (S) 422-842-170-1 8-10   89
Composer: Trevor Jones (original music), Phil Baptiste, George Khoury. Conductor: Trevor Jones. Cast: Phil Phillips and the Twilights, Tom Waits.

SEARCH FOR PARADISE

Soundtrack (1957) • RCA Victor (M) LOC-1034 25-35   57
Composer: Dimitri Tiomkin. Conductor: Dimitri Tiomkin. Cast: Robert Merrill.
Also see HIGH AND THE MIGHTY
Also see LOST HORIZON: THE CLASSIC FILM SCORES OF DIMITRI TIOMKIN

SEARCHERS

Soundtrack • RCA Victor (EP) EPA-851... 100-200   56
Full title: *Music from the Searchers, Charge of the Light Brigade, Four Wives & Fountainhead.* Cover pictures John Wayne in The Searchers.
Composer: Max Steiner. Conductor: Max Steiner. Cast: Max Steiner and His Orchestra.
Also see DEATH OF A SCOUNDREL
Also see MUSIC BY MAX STEINER

SEASIDE SWINGERS

Soundtrack (1965) • Mercury (M) MG-21031 15-20   65
Soundtrack (1965) • Mercury (S) SR-61031... 20-25   65
Cast: Freddie and the Dreamers, John Leyton, Mike Sarne, Grazina Frame.

SEBASTIAN

Soundtrack (1968) • Dot (M) DLP-3845 15-18   68
Soundtrack (1968) • Dot (S) DLP-25845 15-20   68
Composer: Jerry Goldsmith. Conductor: Jerry Goldsmith, others. Cast: Jimmy A. Hassell.

SECOND CITY WRITHES AGAIN: see FROM THE SECOND CITY

SECOND SHEPHERD'S PLAY

Original Cast (1976) • Broadway Baby Demos (S) BBD-774.................. 8-10   76
Composer: Steve Kitsakos. Cast: Myra Quigley, Greg Cesario, Joel Stevens, Doug Holsclaw, Richard Woods, Karen Haas, Deborah Tilton, Natalia Chuma.

SECRET ADMIRER
Soundtrack (1985) • MCA (S) 5611... 8-10   85
    Composer: Jan Hammer. **Cast:** Van Stephenson, Tony Carey, Kim Wilde, Don Felder, Klymaxx, Nik Kershaw, Rosemary Butler, Arnold McCuller, Timothy B. Schmit, Jan Hammer.

SECRET AGENT
TV Soundtrack • RCA Victor (M) LPM-3630.................................... 125-225   66
TV Soundtrack • RCA Victor (S) LSP-3630..................................... 225-250   66
  Label has correct title.
TV Soundtrack • RCA Victor (S) LSP-3630..................................... 100-200   66
  Label incorrectly shows title as "Danger Man."
    Composer: Edwin Astley, others. **Conductor:** Edwin Astley.

SECRET AGENT MEETS THE SAINT
TV Soundtrack • RCA Victor (M) LPM-3467....................................... 90-175   65
TV Soundtrack • RCA Victor (S) LSP-3467...................................... 125-200   65
  Music from *Secret Agent Man* and *The Saint*.
    Composer: Edwin Astley, others. **Conductor:** Edwin Astley.

SECRET GARDEN
Studio Cast (1988) • Columbia Special Products (S) 19920................... 8-10   88
    Composer: Sharon Burgett. **Cast:** Barbara Cook, John Cullum, others.

SECRET LIFE OF WALTER MITTY
Original Cast (1964) • Columbia (M) OL-6320.. 8-12   64
Original Cast (1964) • Columbia (S) OS-2720...................................... 10-15   64
Original Cast (1964) • Columbia Special Products (S) AOS-2720............ 5-8   Re
    Composer: Leon Carr, Earl Shuman. **Conductor:** Joseph Stecko. **Cast:** Mark London, Cathryn Damon, Eugene Roche, Christopher Norris, Charles Rydell, Rudy Tronto, Lorraine Serabian, Rue McClanahan, Lette Rehnolds.

SECRET OF MY SUCCESS
Soundtrack (1987) • MCA (S) 6205.. 8-10   87
    Cast: Night Ranger, Pat Benatar, Danny Peck, Nancy Shanks, Bananarama, David Foster, Roger Daltrey, Restless Heart, Taxxi.

SECRET OF N.I.M.H.
Soundtrack (1982) • Varese Sarabande (S) STV 81169 10-15   82
    Composer: Jerry Goldsmith, Paul Williams. **Conductor:** Jerry Goldsmith. **Cast:** National Philharmonic Orchestra, Ambrosian Singers, Paul Williams, Sally Stevens.

SECRET OF SANTA VITTORIA
Soundtrack (1969) • United Artists (S) UAS-5200 20-30   69
Soundtrack (1969) • MCA (S) 25034.. 8-10   86
    Composer: Ernest Gold, others. **Conductor:** Ernest Gold. **Cast:** Sergio Franchi.

SECRETS OF LIFE
Soundtrack (1956) • Disneyland (M) WDL-4006 50-60   56
    Composer: Paul J. Smith. **Conductor:** Paul J. Smith.

SECRETS OF THE SWORD
TV Soundtrack (1985) • Kid Stuff (S) DAR-3900.................................. 10-15   85
  Gatefold cover. Includes booklet. Part of the *Masters of the Universe* TV series.
    Composer: Erika Scheimer, others. **Cast:** Erika Scheimer, Haim Saban, Shuki Levy, others.

SEDUCED AND ABANDONED
Soundtrack (1964) • CAM (M) 10001 35-40   64
    Composer: Carlo Rustichelli. **Conductor:** Pier Luigi Urbini.

SEE IT NOW: see LADY FROM BALTIMORE

SEESAW

Original Cast (1973) • Buddah (S) BDS-95006 10-12   73
Original Cast (1973) • Columbia Special Products (S) X-15563 8-10   Re
>Composer: Cy Coleman, Dorothy Fields. Conductor: Donald Pippin. Cast: Michele Lee, Ken Howard, Tommy Tune, Cecelia Norfleet, Giancarlo Esposito, LaMonte Des Fontaines.

SELMA

Original Cast (1976) • Cotillion (S) SD2-110 15-20   76
>Two discs.
>Composer: Tommy Butler. Conductor: Peggy Young. Cast: Tommy Butler, Denise Erwin, Janice Barnett, Ernie Banks, Jackie Lowe, Rubert Williams, Fred Tucks, Alzena Powell, Carlton Williams, Sandra Pitre, Eddie Turner, Mary Anderson, Chris Williams, Smokye Terrell, Susan Beaubian.

SENATOR JOSEPH R. McCARTHY

Original Broadcast • Broadside (M) 450 20-25
>Includes insert. Original Congressional testimony.

SERENADE

Soundtrack (1956) • RCA Victor (EP) ERB-70 10-20   56
>Two discs.
Soundtrack (1956) • RCA Victor (M) LM-1996 15-20   56
>Composer: Sammy Cahn, Nicholas Bordszky, various operatic composers. Conductor: Ray Heindorf. Cast: Mario Lanza, Jean Fenn, Licia Albanese.
Soundtrack (1956) Columbia B-2110 10-20   56
>Composer: Sammy Cahn, Nicholas Bordszky, various operatic composers. Conductor: Ray Heindorf. Cast: Ray Heindorf & His Orchestra.

SERENADE TO A PRINCESS

Studiotrack (1956) • Mercury (M) MG-20156 45-65   56
>Music – not recorded elsewhere – from Grace Kelly films: *The Bridges at Toko-Ri, Dial M for Murder, Rear Window, Green Fire, To Catch a Thief, Mogambo, The Country Girl, High Noon* and *The Swan*. Also has two themes commemorating Kelly's royal wedding in Monaco, written especially for this LP.
>Composer: Various. Conductor: David Carroll. Cast: Grace Kelly.
Studiotrack (1976) • Mercury (M) MG-20301 20-25   Re
>Actual reissue title: *Dreams*.
>Also see WEDDING IN MONACO

SERENADE TO THE STARS OF HOLLYWOOD

Studiotrack • Decca (M) DL-8123 15-20
>Composer: Alfred Newman. Conductor: Alfred Newman. Cast: Alfred Newman and Orchestra.

SGT. PEPPER'S LONELY HEARTS CLUB BAND

Soundtrack (1978) • RSO (S) RS-2-4-4100 10-12   78
>Two discs. Includes poster.
>Composer: John Lennon, Paul McCartney, George Harrison. Conductor: George Martin. Cast: Bee Gees, Peter Frampton, Billy Preston, Steve Martin, Earth, Wind and Fire, Paul Nicholas, George Burns, Aerosmith, Alice Cooper, Sandy Farina, Dianne Steinberg, Stargard, Frankie Howerd, Jay MacIntosh, John Wheeler.
Studiotrack • Springboard (S) SPB-4111 5-8   78
>Full title: *Music from the Movie Sgt. Pepper's Lonely Hearts Club Band*.
>Cast: Abbey Road '78.

SGT. PRESTON OF THE YUKON

Original Radio Cast • Mark 56 (M) 592 10-15   70s
Original Radio Cast • Golden Age (M) 5028 8-10   78

SERGEANTS 3

Soundtrack (1962) • Reprise (M) R-2013 25-30   62
Soundtrack (1962) • Reprise (S) R9-2013 40-45   62
>Composer: Billy May. Conductor: Billy May.

SERPENT AND THE RAINBOW
Soundtrack (1988) • Varese Sarabande (S) STV-81362 35-40   88
  Composer: Brad Fiedel.

SERPICO
Soundtrack (1973) • Paramount (S) PAS-1016 12-30   73
  Composer: Mikis Theodorakis. Conductor: Mikis Theodorakis.

SESAME STREET
TV Soundtrack (1970) • Columbia (S) CS-1069 10-15   70
  Includes book and poster.
TV Soundtrack (1970) • Sesame Street (S) CTW-79005 8-12   77
  Two discs.
  Composer: Joe Raposo, Jeffrey Moss, Jon Stone. Cast: Jim Henson.

SET TO MUSIC
Original Cast (1939) • JJC (M) M-3003 20-25
Original Cast (1939) • JJC (SE) ST-3003 20-30
Original Cast (1939) • AEI (SE) AEI-2103 8-10   80s
  Actual title: *Beatrice Lillie Sings*. Also has music from *At Home Abroad*.
  Composer: Noel Coward. Cast: Beatrice Lillie.

SEVEN ALONE
Soundtrack • Seval (S) 101 60-80   76
  Composer: Robert O. Ragland.

SEVEN BRIDES FOR SEVEN BROTHERS
Original London Cast (1982) • First Night (S) Cast-2 30-35   82
  UK release. This London stage production inspired the short-lived 1982 Broadway version,
  which apparently did not get recorded.
  Composer: Johnny Mercer, Gene De Paul, Al Kasha, Joel Hirschhorn. Conductor: Martin Yates.
  Cast: Roni Page, Steve Devereaux, Geoff Steer, Simon Howe, Mark Davis, Martyn Knight, Peter
  Bishop, Julie E. Horner, Debra Robinson, Victoria Lynson, Michaela Strachan.
London Studio Cast • DRG (S) DS-15025 8-12   80s
  Though cover has photos from the film, this is by a studio cast.
Soundtrack (1954) • MGM - MGM-244 15-20   54
  78 rpm album.
Soundtrack (1954) • MGM (EP) X-244 12-15   54
  Two discs.
Soundtrack (1954) • MGM (M) E-244 20-25   54
  10-inch LP.
Soundtrack (1951) • MGM (M) E-3235 12-18   55
  One side has music from *Royal Wedding*.
  ROYAL WEDDING: Composer: Burton Lane, Alan Jay Lerner. Conductor: Johnny Green.
  Cast: Fred Astaire, Jane Powell.
Soundtrack (1954) • MCA (M) 25021 8-10   86
  Composer: Johnny Mercer, Gene De Paul. Conductor: Adolph Deutsch. Cast: Howard Keel,
  Jane Powell, Bill Lee (performs vocals for Matt Mattox in the film), Virginia Gibson, Tommy Rall,
  Russ Tamblyn, Betty Noyes (performs vocals for Ruta Lee), Norma Zimmer (performs vocals for
  Julie Newmar), Howard Hudson (performs vocals for Jacques d'Amboise), Gene Lanham
  (performs vocals for Marc Platt), Robert Wacker (performs vocals for Jeff Richards).
  Also see ROSE MARIE
  Also see THOSE GLORIOUS MGM MUSICALS

SEVEN COME ELEVEN (A GAMING GAMBOL)
Original Cast (1961) • Columbia (M) XLP-55477 150-175   61
  Special edition – sold only at the theatre during the show's run.
Original Cast (1961) • Columbia (M) OL-5740 40-50   61
  Cast: William Roy and Carl Norman at the plural pianos.

SEVEN DEADLY SINS

Studio Cast (1971) • Columbia (M) KL-5175 15-20   71
Performed in German.
  Composer: Kurt Weill, Bertolt Brecht. **Conductor:** Wilhelm Bruckner-Ruggeberg. **Cast:** Lotte
  Lenya, Julius Katona, Fritz Gollnitz, Ernest Poettgen.

SEVEN DREAMS

Studio Cast (1953) • Decca (M) DL-9011 18-20   53
  Composer: Gordon Jenkins. **Conductor:** Gordon Jenkins. **Cast:** Bill Lee, Laurie Carroll, Jeanette
  Nolan, John McIntire, Beverly Mahr, Ernie Newton, Virginia Rees, Dick Beals, Thurl Ravenscroft,
  Keith Carver, Dave Knight, Ralph Brewster, Cornelia Davis, Ray Linn, Chuck Schrouder, Ralph
  Brewster Singers.

SEVEN GOLDEN MEN

Soundtrack (1969) • United Artists (SE) UAS-5193.............................. 20-25   69
  Composer: Armando Trovajoli. **Conductor:** Armando Trovajoli.

SEVEN HILLS OF ROME

Soundtrack (1958) • RCA Victor (EP) EPA-4222 10-15   58
Soundtrack (1958) • RCA Victor (M) LM-2211 20-25   58
  Composer: Victor Young, Harold Adamson, others. **Conductor:** Ray Heindorf. **Cast:** Mario
  Lanza.

SEVEN LITTLE FOYS

Soundtrack (1955) • RCA Victor (EP) EPB-3275 25-35   55
Two discs.
Soundtrack (1955) • RCA Victor (M) LPM-3275 50-70   55
10-inch LP.
  Composer: Joseph J. Lilley. **Conductor:** Joseph J. Lilley. **Cast:** Bob Hope, James Cagney, Milly
  Vitale.

SEVEN LIVELY ARTS: see SOMETHING FOR THE BOYS

SEVEN PERCENT SOLUTION

Soundtrack (1976) • Citadel (S) CT-JA-1 15-20   76
  Composer: John Addison. **Conductor:** John Addison.

SEVEN SAMURAI

Soundtrack (1984) • Varese Sarabande (S) STV 81142 12-15   84
  Composer: Fumio Hayazaka.

SEVEN WONDERS OF THE WORLD (IN CINERAMA)

Soundtrack • GO (M) AX-1.. 100-200   50s
10-inch LP. Reads: "Admiral High Fidelity Record - Not for Sale."Music from *Seven
Wonders of the World*, plus other songs." Promotional issue only.

SEVENTEEN

Original Cast (1951) • RCA Victor (M) LOC-1003 100-125   51
Original Cast (1951) • RCA Victor (M) CBM1-2034 20-25   77
  Composer: Walter Kent, Kim Gannon. **Conductor:** Vincent Travers. **Cast:** Ann Crowley, Kenneth
  Nelson, Doris Dalton, Frank Albertson, Dick Kallman, Helen Wood, Harrison Muller, Maurice Ellis,
  Alonzo Bonsan, Joan Bowman, Bonnie Brae, Carol Cole, Sherron McCutcheon.

1776

Original Cast (1969) • Columbia (S) BOS-3310 20-25   69
Shows Howard DaSilva as Benjamin Franklin, both in the credits and the synopsis.
Although he created the role on stage, DaSilva is not on this recording. His part is sung by
Rex Everhart. Disc label properly credits Everhart.
Original Cast (1969) • Columbia (S) BOS-3310 8-12   69
Back cover credits corrected to show Rex Everhart as Benjamin Franklin.
  Composer: Sherman Edwards. **Conductor:** Peter Howard. **Cast:** William Daniels, Paul Hecht,
  Clifford David, David Ford, Virginia Vestoff, Rex Everhart, Ken Howard, Ronald Holgate, Betty
  Buckley, Scott Jarvis, B.J. Slater, William Duell, David Vosburgh, Henry LeClair, Stephen Nathan.

Original London Cast • CBS (S) SCX-6424...35-45
UK release.
Composer: Sherman Edwards. Cast: Lewis Fiander, Bernard Lloyd, David Kernan.
Soundtrack (1972) • Columbia (S) S-31741 10-12   72
Gatefold cover.
Composer: Sherman Edwards. Conductor: Ray Heindorf. Cast: William Daniels, Howard DaSilva, Ken Howard, David Ford, Virginia Vestoff, Ronald Holgate, Rex Robbins, Blythe Danner, William Duell, Mark Montgomery, Ralston Hill, John Cullum.

SEVENTH DAWN
Soundtrack (1964) • United Artists (M) UAL-4115..............................12-40   64
Soundtrack (1964) • United Artists (S) UAS-5115 15-50   64
Composer: Riz Ortolani. Conductor: Riz Ortolani.

SEVENTH HEAVEN
Original Cast (1955) • Decca (M) DL-9001.......................................125-150   55
Composer: Victor Young, Stella Unger. Conductor: Max Meth. Cast: Gloria De Haven, Ricardo Montalban, Robert Clary, Chita Rivera, Patricia Hammerlee, Gerianne Raphael.

7th VOYAGE OF SINBAD
Soundtrack (1958) • Colpix (M) CP-504 175-200   59
Back covers of several Colpix albums, circa-'59, show this as being available in stereo (SCP-504). We have yet to confirm that any exist.
Soundtrack (1958) • Varese Sarabande (S) STV-81135......................12-18   83
First stereo issue of the score.
Composer: Bernard Herrmann.

70 GIRLS, 70
Original Cast (1971) • Columbia (S) S-30589.......................................35-45   71
Composer: John Kander, Fred Ebb. Conductor: Oscar Kosarin. Cast: Mildred Natwick, Hans Conried, Lillian Roth, Gil Lamb, Lillian Hayman, Joey Faye, Lucie Lancaster, Coley Worth, Ruth Gillette, Steve Mills, Abby Lewis, Lloyd Harris, Beau Tilden, Jay Velie.

77 SUNSET STRIP
TV Soundtrack (1958) • Warner Bros. (M) W-1289.............................20-25   59
TV Soundtrack (1958) • Warner Bros. (S) WS-1289...........................30-35   59
Composer: Jerry Livingston, Alex North, Mack David, others. Conductor: Warren Barker.
Studiotrack (1958) • Jubilee (M) J-1106 12-15   59
Studiotrack (1958) • Jubilee (S) SDJ-1106...15-20   59
Jazz selections.
Cast: Frankie Ortega Trio.
Studiotrack (1959) • Lion (M) L-70116 10-15   59
Full title: *Music from 77 Sunset Strip.*
Conductor: Aaron Bell. Cast: Aaron Bell and His Orchestra.

SEX AND THE SINGLE GIRL
Soundtrack (1964) • Warner Bros. (M) W-1572 12-15   64
Soundtrack (1964) • Warner Bros. (S) WS-1572 .:..............................18-20   64
Composer: Neal Hefti, others. Conductor: Neal Hefti. Cast: Fran Jeffries.

SEX, LIES AND VIDEOTAPE
Soundtrack (1988) • Virgin Movie Music (S) 91298-1 10-15   89
Composer: Cliff Martinez. Conductor: Cliff Martinez. Cast: Cliff Martinez.

SEX LIFE OF PRIMATE (AND OTHER BITS OF GOSSIP)
Studio Cast (1963) • Verve (M) 15043 20-25   63
Cast: Shelly Berman, Jerry Stiller, Anne Meara, Lovelady Powell. (Comedy, dialogue.)

SHADOW

Original Radio Cast • Mark 56 (M) 591 8-10   73
  Adventure No. 1.
Original Radio Cast [Vol. 2] • Mark 56 (M) 608 50-100   79
  Picture disc.
Original Radio Cast [Vol. 4] • Mark 56 (M) 771 30-60   79
  Picture disc.
Original Radio Cast • Golden Age (M) 5029 8-10   78
  Promotional item for Coca-Cola.

SHAFT

Soundtrack (1971) • Enterprise (S) ENS-2-5002 15-25   71
Soundtrack (1971) • Stax (S) 88002 8-12   Re
  Both have two discs.
  Composer: Isaac Hayes. **Conductor:** Isaac Hayes. **Cast:** Isaac Hayes.
  Also see MAN FROM SHAFT

SHAFT IN AFRICA

Soundtrack (1973) • ABC (S) ABCX-793 20-30   73
  Composer: Johnny Pate, Dennis Lambert, Brian Potter. **Conductor:** Johnny Pate. **Cast:** Four Tops.

SHAFT'S BIG SCORE

Soundtrack (1972) • MGM (S) 1SE-36 20-30   72
  Composer: Gordon Parks. **Conductor:** Richard Hazard. **Cast:** O.C. Smith.

SHAG

Soundtrack (1989) • Sire (S) 1-25800 8-10   89
  Cast: LaVern Baker, K.D. Lang and the Reclines, Randy Newman, Ben E. King, Louise Goffin, Charmettes, Hank Ballard, Chris Isaak, Tommy Page, Take 6, Moonliters.

SHAGGY DOG

Soundtrack (1959) • Disneyland (M) WDL-3044 25-30   59
Soundtrack (1959) • Disneyland (M) WDL-1044 15-20   62
  Cast: Paul Frees, Roberta Shore, Kevin Corcoran.
  Also see ABSENT-MINDED PROFESSOR
  Also see UGLY DACHSHUND

SHAKE HANDS WITH THE DEVIL

Soundtrack (1959) • United Artists (M) UAL-4043 25-30   59
Soundtrack (1959) • United Artists (SE) UAS-5043 40-45   59
  Composer: William Alwyn. **Conductor:** Muir Mathieson.

SHAKESPEARE IN HOLLYWOOD

Radio Cast (1937) • Ariel (M) SHO 1/4 20-25   82
  Boxed, four-disc set. Full title: *Shakespeare in Hollywood, Vol. 1, The Tragedies.*
  Cast: Humphrey Bogart, Burgess Meredith, Claude Rains, etc.
Radio Cast (1937) • Ariel (M) SHO 5/8 20-25   82
  Boxed, four-disc set. Full title: *Shakespeare in Hollywood, Vol. 2, The Comedies.*
  Cast: Edward G. Robinson, Rosalind Russell, Orson Welles, etc.

SHAKESPEARE WALLAH

Soundtrack (1966) • Epic (M) FLM-13110 12-15   66
Soundtrack (1966) • Epic (SE) FLS-15110 15-18   66
  Composer: Satyajit Ray, others. **Conductor:** Alok Dey. **Cast:** Mubarak Begum.

SHALAKO

Soundtrack (1968) • Philips (S) PHS-600-286 25-30   68
  Composer: Robert Farnon, Muir Mathieson, Jim Dale. **Conductor:** Muir Mathieson.

SHALL WE DANCE?: see FRED ASTAIRE AND GINGER ROGERS

SHAME
Soundtrack • DRG (S) SL 9521.. 8-10   88
  One side has music from *The Lighthorsemen*.
    Composer: Mario Millo. **Cast:** Mario Millo, Cos Russo.

SHANE
Soundtrack • Paramount (M) SP 162 40-50
  Also has music from *The Call of the Far Away Hills*. Promotional issue only.

SHANGHAI GESTURE
Original Cast (1926) • Decca (M) DL 7010............................... 40-45   50
  10-inch LP. Part of Decca's *Cherished Moments of the Theater* series of recreated plays
  from the 1920s.
    Composer: John Colton (playwright), Fritz Blocki. **Cast:** Florence Reed.

SHANGRI-LA: see SHINBONE ALLEY

SHAPE OF THE LAND
Soundtrack (1986) • Windham Hill (S) WH-1055 10-15   86
  Also known as *The Story of Naomi Uemura*.
    Composer: Philip Aaberg, Michael Hedges, William Ackerman. **Cast:** Philip Aaberg.

SHAPE OF THE UNIVERSE: see INSIGNIFICANCE

SHARE MY LETTUCE
Original Cast • Nexa (S) NPL-18011 8-12
    Composer: Keith Stratham, Patrick Gowers. **Conductor:** Anthony Bowles. **Cast:** Kenneth
  Williams, Maggie Smith, Philip Gilbert, others.

SHARKY'S MACHINE
Soundtrack (1981) • Warner Bros. (S) BSK-3653 10-15   81
    Composer: Waylon Jennings, Joe Sample, Lorenz Hart, Richard Rodgers, Snuff Garrett, others.
  Conductor: Al Capps. **Cast:** Randy Crawford, Flora Purim, Buddy De Franco, Manhattan
  Transfer, Chet Baker, Doc Severinsen, Sarah Vaughan, Joe Williams, Julie London, Peggy Lee,
  Eddie Harris.

SHAZAM: see GOMER PYLE

SHE
Soundtrack (1935) • Varese Sarabande (M) 80004............................. 12-15
    Composer: Max Steiner. **Conductor:** Max Steiner.

SHE-DEVIL
Soundtrack (1989) • Polydor (S) 841-583-1 25-35   89
    Cast: Safire, Carmel, D-Mob, Chubby Checker, Tom Kimmel, Elvis Presley, Jermaine Stewart,
  Kate Ceberano, Yello, Fatboys.

SHE LOVES ME
Original Cast (1963) • MGM (M) E-41180C-2..................................... 10-20   63
Original Cast (1963) • MGM (S) SE-41180C-2.................................... 12-30   63
  Two discs.
Original Cast (1963) • Stet (S) DS-15008... 8-15   Re
  Two discs.
    Composer: Jerry Bock, Sheldon Harnick. **Conductor:** Hal Hastings. **Cast:** Barbara Cook, Daniel
  Massey, Barbara Baxley, Jack Cassidy, Nathaniel Frey, Ralph Vaughan Williams, Jo Wilder,
  Wood Romoff, Gino Conforti, Joe Ross, Marion Brash, Trude Adams, Peg Murray, Ludwig
  Donath.

SHE LOVES THE MOVIES
Soundtrack (1955) • Decca (M) DL-8312 60-90   55
  Also has studiotrack recordings. Cover art by *Esquire* magazine's George Petty.
    Composer: Alfred Newman, Victor Young, others.

SHE'S CALLED VIRGINIA
Soundtrack (1971) • L.O.V. (S) LV 20037 10-15   71
Presentation about the State of Virginia.
  Cast: Brick Rider, Joseph Cotten (narrator).

SHE'S GOTTA HAVE IT
Soundtrack (1986) • Island (S) 90528-1 8-10   86

SHE'S HAVING A BABY
Soundtrack (1988) • I.R.S. (S) 6211 8-10   88
  Cast: Everything But the Girl, Bryan Ferry, Gene Loves Jezebel, Dr., XTC, Love and Rockets, Carmel, Dave Wakeling, Kate Bush, Kirsty MacColl.

SHE'S OUT OF CONTROL
Soundtrack (1989) • MCA (S) 6281 8-10   89
  Cast: Troy Hinton, Brenda K. Starr, Phil Thornalley, Boys Club, Harold Faltermeyer, Jim Ladd, Oingo Boingo, Brian Wilson, Frankie Avalon, Kinks, Jetboy.

SHEBA BABY
Soundtrack (1975) • Buddah (S) BDS-5634 25-30   75
  Composer: Higgins, Brown. **Conductor:** Higgins, Brown.

SHEENA
Soundtrack (1984) • Varesa Sarabande (S) STV 81225 10-15   84
  Composer: Richard Hartley. **Conductor:** Richard Hartley.

SHEIK
Original Radio Cast • Mark 56 (M) 760 40-80   70s
Picture disc.
  Cast: Rudolph Valentino.

SHENANDOAH (1965)
Soundtrack (1965) • Decca (M) DL-9125 12-15   65
Soundtrack (1965) • Decca (S) DL-79125 12-18   65
  Composer: Frank Skinner, others. **Conductor:** Joseph Gershenson. **Cast:** James Stewart (narration).

SHENANDOAH (1974)
Original Cast (1974) • RCA Victor (S) ARL1-1019 8-12   74
Original Cast (1974) • RCA Victor (S) AGL1-3763 8-10   81
  Composer: Gary Geld, Peter Udell. **Cast:** John Cullum, Donna Theodore, Penelope Milford, Joel Higgins, Chip Ford, Ted Agress, Gordon Halliday, Gary Harger, Charles Welch, David Russell, Jordan Suffin, Joseph Shapiro, Robert Rosen.

SHERLOCK HOLMES
Original Radio Cast (1938) • Radiola (M) MR 1036 12-15   74
Full title: *The Immortal Sherlock Holmes.* Crime Series 4, Release 36. Aired September 25, 1938.
  Cast: Orson Wells.
Original Radio Cast (1940) • Radiola (M) MR 1143 12-15   83
Full title: *The Adventures of Sherlock Holmes.* Crime Series 17, Release 143.
  Cast: Basil Rathbone, Nigel Bruce.
Soundtrack • Murray Hill (M) M-55358 10-20
Three discs.

SHINBONE ALLEY

Original Cast (1957) / TV Soundtrack (1960) • Sound of
  Broadway (M) 300/1 65-85
Has Eartha Kitt and Eddie Bracken from the original New York production, as well as
Tammy Grimes, who starred with Bracken in the 1960 television production. Also has
music from *Shangri-La*.
  Composer: George Kleinsinger, Joe Darion. **Cast:** Eartha Kitt, Tammy Grimes, Eddie Bracken.
  SHANGRI-LA: **Composer:** Harry Warren, Jerome Lawrence, Robert E. Lee. **Cast:** Marisa Pavan,
  Richard Basehart, Helen Gallagher, Alice Ghostley, Gene Nelson.

SHINING

Soundtrack (1980) • Warner Bros. (S) HS-3449 15-20   80
  Composer: Wendy Carlos, Rachel Elkind, Gyorgy Ligeti, Bela Bartok, others. **Conductor:** Ernest
  Bour, Herbert von Karajan, others.

SHIP AHOY

Soundtrack (1942) • Hollywood Soundstage (M) HS-5011 10-15   83
  Also has music from *Las Vegas Nights*.
  Composer: Burton Lane, E.Y. Harburg. **Cast:** Eleanor Powell, Red Skelton, Frank Sinatra, Bert
  Lahr, Virginia O'Brien, Pied Pipers, Tommy Dorsey Orchestra. LAS VEGAS NIGHTS: **Composer:**
  Frank Loesser, Burton Lane, Louis Alter. **Conductor:** Tommy Dorsey. **Cast:** Frank Sinatra, Pied
  Pipers, Lillian Cornell, Constance Moore, Buddy Rich, Phil Regan, Bert Wheeler, Virginia Dale,
  Tommy Dorsey & His Orchestra.

SHIP OF FOOLS

Soundtrack (1965) • RCA Victor (M) LM-2817 20-40   65
Soundtrack (1965) • RCA Victor (S) LSC-2817 35-50   65
  Composer: Ernest Gold. **Conductor:** Arthur Fiedler. **Cast:** Boston Pops Orchestra.

SHIRLEY MacLAINE LIVE AT THE PALACE

Original Cast (1976) • Columbia (S) PC-34223 8-12   76
  An August 19, 1976, performance.
  Composer: Various. **Conductor:** Donn Trenner. **Cast:** Shirley MacLaine, Adam Grammis, Candy
  Brown, Gary Flannery, JoAnn Lehman, Larry Vickers.

SHIRLEY TEMPLE'S HITS

Soundtrack • 20th Century-Fox (M) FOX-3006 15-25   58
  Music from *Bright Eyes, Curly Top, Stowaway, Rebecca of Sunnybrook Farm* and others.
  Composer: Various. **Conductor:** Various. **Cast:** Shirley Temple.

SHOCK TREATMENT

Soundtrack (1981) • Warner Bros. (S) PRO-A-976 10-15   81
  Promotional issue only.
Soundtrack (1981) • Warner Bros. (S) LLA-361 10-15   81
  Composer: Richard O'Brien, Richard Hartley. **Conductor:** Richard Hartley.

SHOCKER

Soundtrack (1989) • Varese Sarabande (S) VS-5247 10-15   89
  Composer: William Goldstein.
Soundtrack (1989) • SBK (S) K1-93233 5-10   89
  Cast: Megadeath, Alice Cooper, Saraya, Iggy Pop, Dangerous Toys, Born Fire, Dead On, Dudes
  of Wrath.

SHOCKING MISS PILGRIM

Soundtrack (1947) • Classic International Filmusicals (M) CIF-3008 8-10
  Also has music from *Mother Wore Tights*.
  Composer: George Gershwin, Ira Gershwin. **Cast:** Betty Grable, Dick Haymes. MOTHER WORE
  TIGHTS: **Composer:** Mack Gordon, Josef Myrow, others. **Conductor:** Alfred Newman. **Cast:**
  Betty Grable, Dan Dailey, Mona Freeman.

SHOES OF THE FISHERMAN
Soundtrack (1968) • MGM (S) S1E-15 10-15   68
   Number may also be shown as "1SE15."
Soundtrack (1968) • MCA (S) 25130 5-8   86
   Composer: Alex North. **Conductor:** Alex North.

SHOESTRING REVUE
Original Cast (1955) • Offbeat (M) O-4011 20-25   59
Original Cast (1955) • Painted Smiles (M) PS-1360 8-10   73
   Composer: Charles Strouse, David Barker, Sheldon Harnick, others. **Conductor:** Dorothea
   Freitag. **Cast:** Beatrice Arthur, Fay DeWitt, Dody Goodman, Dorothy Greener, John Bartis, Eddie
   Hilton.

SHOESTRING REVUE '57
Original Cast (1957) • Offbeat (M) O-4012 20-25   60
Original Cast (1957) • Painted Smiles (M) PS-1362 8-10   73
   Composer: Shelley Mowell, Charles Strouse, Harvey Schmidt, Lee Adams, Tom Jones.
   Conductor: Dorothea Freitag. **Cast:** Beatrice Arthur, Fay DeWitt, Dody Goodman, Dorothy
   Greener, John Bartis, Danny Carroll, Bill McCutcheon, Bud McCreery.

SHOGUN
TV Soundtrack (1981) • RSO (S) RX-1-3088 15-20   80
   Composer: Maurice Jarre. **Conductor:** Maurice Jarre.

SHOGUN ASSASSIN
Soundtrack (1980) • Baby Cart (S) 4148-49 10-15   80
   Promotional Issue only.
   Composer: W. Michael Lewis, Mark Lindsay, Robert Houston. **Conductor:** W. Michael Lewis,
   Mark Lindsay, Robert Houston.

SHOOT THE PIANO PLAYER
Soundtrack (1962) • Philips (EP) PLP-4005 25-30   62
   Composer: Georges Delerue. **Conductor:** Georges Delerue.

SHOOTING PARTY
Soundtrack (1985) • Varese Sarabande (S) STV 81235 10-15   85
   Conductor: John Scott. **Cast:** Royal Philharmonic Orchestra.

SHOOTIST: see DIGITAL PREMIERE RECORDINGS FROM THE FILMS OF JOHN WAYNE, VOLUME 2

SHOP ON MAIN STREET
Soundtrack (1966) • Mainstream (M) 56082 15-25   67
Soundtrack (1966) • Mainstream (S) S-6082 25-35   67
   Composer: Zdenek Liska.

SHORT EYES
Soundtrack (1977) • Curtom (S) CU-5017 20-25   77
   Composer: Curtis Mayfield. **Conductor:** Curtis Mayfield.

SHORTY ROGERS MEETS TARZAN: see TARZAN THE APEMAN

SHOTGUN SLADE
TV Soundtrack (1959) • Mercury (M) MG-20575 30-35   60
TV Soundtrack (1959) • Mercury (S) SR-60235 50-60   60
   Composer: Gerald Fried. **Conductor:** Stanley Wilson.

SHOW
Soundtrack • Polydor (S) 529021 8-10   90s

SHOW BIZ (FROM VAUDE TO VIDEO)
Original Cast • RCA Victor (EP) ED-1011 20-25   54
Four discs.
Original Cast • RCA Victor (M) LOC-1011.. 25-35   54
Composer: Various. **Conductor:** Norman Layden. **Cast:** Georgie Jessel (narrator), Gene Austin, Ben Bernie, Bing Crosby, Fanny Brice, Eddie Cantor, George M. Cohan, Tommy Dorsey, Jimmy Durante, Sophie Tucker, George Gershwin, Will Rogers, Kate Smith, others.

SHOW BOAT
Original Cast • RCA Victor (M) LPM-3151.. 15-25   50s
10-inch LP. Full title: *Show Boat / The Cat and the Fiddle.* Side 1 has *Show Boat,* (opened December 27,1927, Ziegfeld Threatre, New York). Side 2 is *The Cat and the Fiddle* (opened October 15, 1931, Globe Theatre, New York.).
Composer: Jerome Kern, Otto Harbach. **Conductor:** Lehman Engel. **Cast:** Bettina Hall, George Meador, Odette Myrtil, Flora LeBreton, Fred Walton. SHOW BOAT: **Composer:** Jerome Kern, Oscar Hammerstein II. **Conductor:** Lehman Engel. **Cast:** Charles Winninger, Aunt Jemima, Edna May Oliver, Eva Puck, Sammy White, Helen Morgan, Howard Marsh, Norma Terris, Eleanor Shaw, Jules Bludsoe.

Original Cast • Columbia Special Products (M) AC-55 8-10   Re
Members of the original cast, the 1932 revival cast, 1936 film cast, original London cast, and a studio cast.
Composer: Jerome Kern, Oscar Hammerstein II. **Conductor:** Victor Young. **Cast:** Helen Morgan, James Melton, Paul Robeson, Frank Munn, Countess Albani.

Original Cast • Columbia Special Products (M) XTV-82003/4 5-10   60s
Full title: *Songs from Show Boat.* Also has "Second Cast" and studiotrack recordings.
Cast: Original Cast members, Second Cast members, Polly Bergen, Percy Faith, Earl Wrightson, Louis Hunt, Roy Hamilton, Shirley Jones.

Soundtrack (1936) • Xeno (M) XLP-251... 20-25
Complete sound track from the 1936 film version.
Composer: Jerome Kern, Oscar Hammerstein II. **Cast:** Irene Dunne, Allan Jones, Helen Morgan, Paul Robeson, Charles Winninger, Helen Westley, Donald Cook.

Studio Cast (1942) • RCA Victor (M) LM-9002 10-15
One side is various show tunes by Robert Merrill.
Composer: Jerome Kern, Oscar Hammerstein II. **Conductor:** John Scott Trotter. **Cast:** Robert Merrill, Dorothy Kirsten.

Original Revival Cast (1946) • Columbia C-55..................................... 15-20   46
78 rpm album. May be found with either a red or a black folder.
Original Revival Cast (1946) • Columbia MM-611 20-25   46
78 rpm album. Gatefold cover with liner notes and photos.
Original Revival Cast (1946) • Columbia (EP) A-611............................. 20-25   46
Original Revival Cast (1946) • Columbia (M) ML-4058 12-18   48
Paper envelope-type jacket, with opening at top.
Original Revival Cast (1946) • Columbia (M) OL-4058 10-15
Standard cover.
Composer: Jerome Kern, Oscar Hammerstein II. **Conductor:** Edwin McArthur. **Cast:** Jan Clayton, Carol Bruce, Charles Fredericks, Kenneth Spencer, Helen Dowdy, Colette Lyons.

Studio Cast • Decca (M) DL 5060 20-25   50s
10-inch LP.
Cast: Bing Crosby, Kenny Baker, Frances Langford, Tony Martin, Lee Wiley.

Soundtrack (1951) • MGM - MGM-84.. 12-18   51
78 rpm album.
Soundtrack (1951) • MGM (EP) X-84 10-15   51
Soundtrack (1951) • MGM (EP) K-84 12-15   51
Boxed, four-disc set.
Soundtrack (1951) • MGM (M) E-559... 15-20   51
10-inch LP.
Soundtrack (1951) • Metro (M) M-527 8-12   65
Soundtrack (1951) • Metro (SE) MS-527.. 10-12   65

Soundtrack (1951) • MGM (M) E-3230 12-18   Re
Also has music from *Lovely to Look At.*

Soundtrack (1951) • MCA (M) 1429 5-8   Re
On above soundtracks, Ava Gardner portrays Julie, although her vocals in the film are by
Annette Warren.
Composer: Jerome Kern, Oscar Hammerstein II. **Conductor:** Adolph Deutsch. **Cast:** Kathryn
Grayson, Ava Gardner, Howard Keel, Marge and Gower Champion, William Warfield.

Studiotrack • Mercury (M) MG 25104 10-15
10-inch LP. Full title*: Show Boat: Hit Selections from the MGM Production.*
Cast: Tony Fontane, Virginia Haskins & Felix Knight, Patti Page, Sophie Tucker, Tony Martin.

Studio Cast (1956) • RCA Victor (M) LM-2008 10-15   56
Conductor: Lehman Engel. **Cast:** Robert Merrill, Patrice Stevens, Risë Stevens, Katherine
Graves, Janet Pavek, Kevin Scott, Lehman Engel and His Orchestra and Chorus.

Studio Cast (1956) • RCA Victor (EP) ERA-280 10-15   57
Cast: Robert Merrill, Patrice Munsel, Risë Stevens, Lehman Engel and His Orchestra and Chorus.

Studiotrack (1957) • Halo (M) 50127 8-10   57

Studiotrack • Columbia (M) CL-806 8-10   50s
One side has music from *South Pacific* and *Slaughter on Tenth Avenue.*
Conductor: Andre Kostelanetz. **Cast:** Philadelphia Orchestra Pops.

Studiotrack • Royale (M) 1242 8-10
Cast: Thelma Carpenter, Russell Bennett, Royale Operetta Singers & Orchestra.

Studiotrack • Royale (M) 1822 8-10
10-inch LP. Full title: *Show Boat and Other Hits of the South.*

Studiotrack (1959) • National Academy Record Club (M) ES 3 10-15   60
From *Ed Sullivan Presents Songs and Music of...* series.
Cast: Ed Sullivan All Star Cast.

Studio Cast (1959) • RCA Victor (M) LOC-1505 8-12   59

Studio Cast (1959) • RCA Victor (S) LSO-1505 10-15   59

Studio Cast (1959) • RCA Victor (M) LOP-1505 8-10   Re
"Spotlight Series" (LOP-1505).
Conductor: Henri Rene. **Cast:** Howard Keel, Anne Jeffreys, Gogi Grant, Henri Rene and His
Orchestra.

Studio Cast (1959) • Camden (S) CAS-488 8-10   59
Composer: Jerome Kern, Oscar Hammerstein II. **Conductor:** Hill Bowen. **Cast:** Barbara Leigh,
Andy Cole, Bryan Johnson, Patricia Clark, Maxine Daniels, Denis Quilley, Ivor Emmanuel.

Studiotrack (1960) • Columbia (M) CL-1419 8-10   60

Studiotrack (1960) • Columbia (S) CS-8216 8-12   60
Jazz interpretations.
Composer: Jerome Kern, Oscar Hammerstein II. **Conductor:** John Carisi. **Cast:** Guitar Choir,
Bob Brookmeyer (trombone), Phil Woods (alto sax), John Carisi (trumpet).

Studio Cast (1962) • Columbia (M) OL-5820 8-10   62

Studio Cast (1962) • Columbia (S) OS-2220 8-12   62
Composer: Jerome Kern, Oscar Hammerstein II, P.G. Wodehouse. **Conductor:** Franz Allers.
Cast: John Raitt, Barbara Cook, William Warfield, Anita Darian, Fay DeWitt, Louise Parker,
Merrill Staton Choir.

Original Revival Cast (1966) • RCA Victor (M) LOC-1126 8-10   66

Original Revival Cast (1966) • RCA Victor (S) LSO-1126 10-15   66
Black label with dog on top

Original Revival Cast (1966) • RCA Victor (S) LSO-1126 5-10   Re
Black label with dog on side, orange, or tan labels.
Composer: Jerome Kern, Oscar Hammerstein II. **Conductor:** Franz Allers. **Cast:** Barbara Cook,
Constance Towers, Stephen Douglass, David Wayne, William Warfield, Rosetta LeNoire, Allyn
Ann McLerie, Eddie Phillips.

Original London Revival Cast (1972) • Stanyan (S) 2SR-10048 10-15   72
Two discs.
Composer: Jerome Kern, Oscar Hammerstein II. **Conductor:** Ray Cook. **Cast:** Andre Jobim,
Cleo Laine, Thomas Carey, Kenneth Nelson, Lorna Dallas, Jan Hunt, Ena Cabayo.

London Studio Cast • Stanyan (S) SR-10036... 8-10   72
    Composer: Jerome Kern, Oscar Hammerstein II. **Conductor:** Michael Collins. **Cast:** Shirley
    Bassey, Marlys Watters, Don McKay, Dora Bryan, Geoffrey Webb, Isabelle Lucas, Williams
    Singers.

Studio Cast (1976) • RCA Victor (M) AVM1-1741 8-10   76

Studio Cast (1988) • Angel (M) AL-49108 10-15   88
    Boxed, three-disc set. Includes booklet. One of the most complete recordings of the show,
    with alternate versions and songs that were cut from the original production.
    Composer: Jerome Kern, Oscar Hammerstein II. **Conductor:** John McGlinn. **Cast:** Frederica
    Von Stade, Jerry Hadley, Teresa Stratas, others.

Studio Cast • Spin-O-Rama (M) MK-3044 10-12

Studio Cast • Spin-O-Rama (S) S-40 10-12
    Conductor: Al Goodman. **Cast:** Stradivari Strings, Richard Torigi, Lee Venora, Audrey Marsh.
    Also see AMERICAN IN PARIS
    Also see CAT AND THE FIDDLE
    Also see LOVELY TO LOOK AT
    Also see NO NO NANETTE
    Also see PORGY AND BESS
    Also see RIO RITA
    Also see THOSE GLORIOUS MGM MUSICALS

SHOW GIRL

Original Cast (1961) • Roulette (M) R-80001.. 10-15   61
Original Cast (1961) • Roulette (S) SR-80001 20-25   61
Original Cast (1961) • Forum (M) F-9054 8-10   63
Original Cast (1961) • Forum (S) SF-9054 10-12   63
    Composer: Charles Gaynor, others. **Conductor:** Robert Hunter. **Cast:** Carol Channing, Jules
    Munshin, Les Quat' Jeudis.
    Also see CAROL CHANNING

SHOW TIME

Studiotrack • Coral (EP) EC 81151/53 8-20
    Three discs.

Studiotrack • Coral (M) CRL 57111 8-25
    Music from Broadway shows *Happy Hunting, Lil' Abner* and *Bells Are Ringing*.
    Cast: Lawrence Welk and His Champagne Music, Lennon Sisters, Muddy Merrill, others.

SHOWCASE ALBUM, 1967

TV Soundtrack (1966) • WNDT (M) 101... 50-60   67
    Recordings excerpted from the 1966-1967 season of *Sunday Showcase* TV specials, from
    WNDT radio, New York.
    Conductor: Various. **Conductor:** Allan Miller, Abba Bogin. **Cast:** Brock Peters (narration), Rod
    Steiger, Linda Lavin, Richard Morse, James Daley, Michael Tolan, Marion Williams, Claire Bloom,
    Robert White, Joseph Ladone, Standwells, Suzanne Grossmann, Colleen Dewhurst, Lee
    Goodman, George Tipton, Jay Berliner, Kathleen Widdoes, Howard Da Silva, Nancy Dussault,
    Kenneth Haigh. (With dialogue.)

SHOWDOWN

Soundtrack (1973) • National Features (EP) 2785 20-30   73
    Interviews with film stars Dean Martin and Rock Hudson. Includes script. Promotional issue
    only.
    Cast: Dean Martin, Rock Hudson. (Dialogue.)

SHOWSTOPPERS

Studio Cast • Capitol Creative Products (S) SL 6254 15-20
    Music from *Kismet, Can-Can, Carousel, West Side Story, Funny Girl, Inside Daisy Clover,
    Broadway Melody of 1940, Thumbs Up, Three Coins in the Fountain* and *I'll Take
    Romance*.
    Cast: Nancy Wilson, Gordon MacRae, Judy Garland, Al Martino, Matt Monro.

Studio Cast • Columbia (M) ML-6129 8-10   60s
Studio Cast • Columbia (S) MS-6729 10-12   60s
　　Music from *Kiss Me Kate, South Pacific, My Fair Lady, Music Man, Show Boat, Promenade*
　　and *West Side Story.*
　　Conductor: Andre Kostelantez. **Cast:** New York Philharmonic.

SHOWTIME, THE BEST OF BROADWAY
Studiotrack • Harmony (S) KH 30132 10-15
　　Cast: Angela Lansbury, Dick Van Dyke, Mary Martin, Carol Lawrence & Larry Kert, Julie Andrews,
　　Ethel Merman, Carol Channing, Joel Grey, Barbara Streisand, Judy Holliday.

SHUFFLE ALONG
Original Cast (1921-28) • RCA Victor (M) LPM 3154 20-35   53
　　10-inch LP. Full title: *Shuffle Along / Blackbirds of 1928.* Side 1 is *Shuffle Along* (opened
　　May 23, 1921, Sixty-third St. Music Hall, New York). Side 2 is *Blackbirds of 1928* (opened
　　May 9, 1928, Liberty Theatre, New York).
　　Composer: BLACKBIRDS: Jimmy McHugh, Dorothy Fields. SHUFFLE ALONG: Eubie Blake,
　　Noble Sissle. **Conductor:** BLACKBIRDS: Lehman Engel. SHUFFLE ALONG: Eubie Blake. **Cast:**
　　BLACKBIRDS: Cab Calloway, Thelma Carpenter. SHUFFLE ALONG: Avon Long, Thelma
　　Carpenter, Louise Woods, Laurence Watson.
Original Cast (1921) • New World (M) NW-260 8-10
　　Composer: Eubie Blake, Noble Sissle. **Conductor:** Eubie Blake. **Cast:** Eubie Blake, Noble
　　Sissle, Gertrude Saunders.
Studio Cast • Columbia (S) C2S-847 15-20
　　Two discs.
　　Composer: Eubie Blake, Noble Sissle. **Cast:** Eubie Blake, Noble Sissle.
　　Also see BLACKBIRDS OF 1928

SHY PEOPLE
Soundtrack (1987) • Varese Sarabande (S) STV 81357 8-10   87
　　Composer: Tangerine Dream. **Cast:** Tangerine Dream.

SICILIAN
Soundtrack (1987) • Virgin Movie Music (S) 90682-1 10-15   87
　　Conductor: David Mansfield. **Cast:** Hungarian State Symphony.

SICILIAN CLAN
Soundtrack (1970) • 20th Century-Fox (S) TFS-4209 35-45   70
　　Composer: Ennio Morricone. **Conductor:** Ennio Morricone.

SID AND NANCY
Soundtrack (1986) • MCA (S) 6181 8-10   86

SIDE BY SIDE BY SONDHEIM
Original London Cast (1976) • RCA Victor (S) CBL2-1851 8-25   76
　　Two discs. Reissue of RCA Victor UK album – same recording but with slightly different
　　artwork.
　　Composer: Stephen Sondheim. **Conductor:** Tim Higgs, Stuart Pedlar. **Cast:** Millicent Martin,
　　Julia McKenzie, David Kernan, Tim Higgs, Stuart Pedler, Ned Sherrin.

SIDE BY SIDE 75
Original Cast (1975) • No Label Shown (S) No Number Used 10-20   75
　　Composer: Stanford Agency. **Cast:** Larry Muhoberac.

SIDEHACKERS
Soundtrack (1969) • Amaret (S) ST-5004 15-20   70
　　Composer: Jerry Styner, Guy Hemric, others. **Cast:** New Life.

SIESTA
Soundtrack (1987) • Warner Bros. (S) 1-25655 8-10   87
　　Full title: *(Music from) Siesta.*
　　Composer: Miles Davis. **Cast:** Miles Davis.

SIGMUND AND THE SEA MONSTERS
TV Soundtrack (1973) • Chelsea (S) BCL1-0332 15-20   73
  Full title: *Friends / Music from the TV series Sigmund and the Sea Monsters*. Also has
  material from *Friends*.
   Composer: Jansen and Hart. **Conductor:** Jimmie Haskell. **Cast:** Johnnie Whitaker.

SIGN OF AQUARIUS
Soundtrack (1969) • Adell (S) ASLP-216 25-30   69
   Composer: Al Zbacinc, Tom Baker, Ed Golya, Allen Baker. **Conductor:** Tom Baker.

SIGN OF FOUR
Soundtrack • That's Entertainment (S) TER-1136 8-10   80s
  UK release.
   Composer: Patrick Gowers.

SILENCERS
Soundtrack (1966) • RCA Victor (M) LOC-1120 20-30   66
Soundtrack (1966) • RCA Victor (S) LSO-1120 40-50   66
   Composer: Elmer Bernstein. **Conductor:** Elmer Bernstein. **Cast:** Vikki Carr.
Studiotrack (1966) • Reprise (EP) SR-6211 10-15   66
  Stereo, six-track juke box issue. Includes title strips and LP mini-cover, for juke box display.
Studiotrack (1966) • Reprise (M) R-6211 10-15   66
Studiotrack (1966) • Reprise (S) RS-6211 20-25   66
  Full title: *Dean Martin as Matt Helm Sings Songs from The Silencers*.
   Composer: Elmer Bernstein, Hal David, Billy Hill, Howard Greenfield, Jerry Keller, Al Jolson,
   Charlie Chaplin, others. **Conductor:** Ernie Freeman, Gene Page. **Cast:** Dean Martin.

SILENT MOVIE
Soundtrack (1976) • United Artists (S) UA-LA672-G 10-12   76
  Includes full-color poster.
   Composer: John Morris, Jacob Gade, Margarita Lecuona, Vera Bloom. **Conductor:** Lionel
   Newman.

SILENT MOVIE HITS FROM THE PIT PIANO
Studiotrack • Alshire (S) S-5108 10-15

SILENT MOVIE MUSIC
Studiotrack • Coral (M) 57024 15-25
   Composer: Jack Shaindlain. **Cast:** Jack Shaindlain.

SILENT PARTNER
Soundtrack (1979) • Pablo Today (S) 2312-103 8-10   78
   Composer: Oscar Peterson. **Cast:** Oscar Peterson, Benny Carter, Clark Terry, Zoot Sims, Milt
   Jackson, John Heard, Grady Tate.

SILENT RUNNING
Soundtrack (1972) • Decca (S) DL-79188 40-45   72
Soundtrack (1972) • Varese Sarabande (S) STV-81072 15-20
  Green vinyl.
   Composer: Peter Schickele. **Cast:** Joan Baez, Peter Schickele.

SILENT YEARS
Studiotrack (1971) • Eastbrook (S) 502 15-20   71
  Music from *The General, The Beloved Rogue, The Gold Rush, Orphans of the Storm,
  Blood and Sand* and *The Mark of Zorro*.
   Composer: William Perry. **Cast:** William Perry.

SILK STOCKINGS
Original Cast (1955) • RCA Victor (EP) EOC-1016 12-18   55
Original Cast (1955) • RCA Victor (M) LOC-1016 25-35   55
  Gatefold covers.
Original Cast (1955) • RCA Victor (M) LOC-1102 15-20   65
Original Cast (1955) • RCA Victor (SE) LSO-1102 20-25   65
Original Cast (1955) • RCA Victor (M) CBM1-2208 12-18   77
  Composer: Cole Porter. **Conductor:** Herbert Greene. **Cast:** Hildegarde Neff, Don Ameche, Gretchen Wyler, Leon Belasco, Henry Lascoe, David Opatoshu.
Soundtrack (1957) • MGM (M) E-3542 20-25   57
Soundtrack (1957) • MCA (M) 39074 8-10   86
  Composer: Cole Porter. **Conductor:** Andre Previn, Johnny Green. **Cast:** Fred Astaire, Cyd Charisse, Janis Paige, Carole Richards (performs some vocals for Cyd Charisse in the film), Peter Lorre, Joseph Buloff, Jules Munshin.
  Also see PAJAMA GAME
  Also see THOSE GLORIOUS MGM MUSICALS

SILKWOOD
Soundtrack (1984) • DRG (S) 6107 10-15   84
  Composer: Georges Delerue. **Cast:** Meryl Streep (vocal).

SILMARILLION
Studio Cast • Caedmon (S) TC-1564 20-30   77
  Cast: Christopher Tolkien.

SILVER BULLET
Soundtrack (1985) • Varese Sarabande (S) STV 81264 10-15   85
  Composer: Jay Chattaway.

SILVER CHALICE
Studiotrack • Elmer Bernstein Film Music Collection (S) FMC 3 30-45   75
  Composer: Elmer Bernstein, Franz Waxman. **Conductor:** Elmer Bernstein.

SILVER SCREEN
Studiotrack • Alshire (S) S-5041 5-10
  Music from *Around the World In 80 Days, Love Is a Many-Splendored Thing, Moulin Rouge, Ruby, High & The Mighty, Spellbound, Three Coins in the Fountain, Picnic* and *Gone with the Wind.*
  Cast: 101 Strings.

SILVER SCREEN SYMPHONY
Soundtrack • Columbia Special Products (M) C3-10710 15-25   72
  Three-disc set. Made for The Literary Guild. Original recordings from movies.
  Cast: Fred Astaire, Al Jolson, Betty Grable, Nelson Eddy, others.

SILVER THEATRE RADIO BROADCAST
Radio Cast • Mark 56 (M) 777 10-15   77
  Full title: *Silver Theatre Radio Broadcast of a George Garabedian Production Starring Clark Gable.*
  Cast: Clark Gable.

SILVERADO
Soundtrack (1985) • Geffen (S) GHS-24080 15-20   85
  Composer: Bruce Broughton. **Conductor:** Bruce Broughton.

SILVERLAKE
Original Cast (1980) • Nonesuch (S) DB-79003 10-12   80
  Two discs.
  Composer: Kurt Weill. **Conductor:** Julius Rudel. **Cast:** Joel Grey, William Neill, Elizabeth Hynes, Elaine Bonazzi, Jack Harrold.

SIMPLY HEAVENLY
Original Cast (1957) • Columbia (M) OL-5240..................... 15-20   57
> **Composer:** David Martin, Langston Hughes. **Conductor:** David Martin. **Cast:** Claudia McNeil, Melvin Stewart, Anna English, Brownie McGhee, Marilyn Berry, Duke Williams, John Boule.

SINCE YOU WENT AWAY
Soundtrack (1944) • Citadel (M) MS-3/4 45-65   76
> Two discs. Private recording – not issued commercially.
> **Composer:** Max Steiner. **Conductor:** Max Steiner.
> Also see MUSIC BY MAX STEINER

SINCERELY YOURS
Soundtrack (1955) • Columbia (EP) B-800........................ 15-25   56
> Three discs.
Soundtrack (1955) • Columbia (M) CL-800 30-40   56
> **Composer:** Various. **Conductor:** Gordon Robinson. **Cast:** Liberace (piano), Warner Bros. Symphony Orchestra.

SINFONIETTA
Soundtrack • Varese Sarabande (S) 704 200 10-15   80s
> **Composer:** Erich Wolfgang Korngold.

SING
Soundtrack (1989) • Columbia (S) 44-68207..................... 5-8   89
> Seven versions of *Birthday Suite*.
> **Cast:** Johnny Kemp.
Soundtrack (1989) • Columbia (S) SC-45086..................... 8-10   89
> **Cast:** Mickey Thomas, Art Garfunkel, Patti La Belle, Laurnea Wilkerson, Joe Williams, Bill Champlin, Paul Carrack, Terri Nunn, Michael Bolton, Cast of *Sarafina*, Nia Peeples, Johnny Kemp.

SING BOY SING
Soundtrack (1958) • Capitol (EP) EPA-1-929..................... 10-15   58
Soundtrack (1958) • Capitol (EP) EPA-2-929..................... 10-15   58
Soundtrack (1958) • Capitol (EP) EPA-3-929..................... 10-15   58
Soundtrack (1958) • Capitol (M) T-929.............................. 20-25   57
> Blue label.
> **Composer:** Tommy Sands, Lionel Newman, others. **Conductor:** Lionel Newman. **Cast:** Tommy Sands.

SING FOR YOUR SUPPER
Studio Cast (1960) • Vanguard (M) VRS-9066.................. 20-25   60
> **Composer:** Earl Robinson, John Latouche. **Conductor:** Robert DeCormier. **Cast:** Odetta, DeCormier Chorale.
Studio Cast (1974) • United Artists (S) UA-LA604-G........... 10-12   74
> **Composer:** Earl Robinson, John Latouche. **Conductor:** Leonard DePaur. **Cast:** Brock Peters.
Studio Cast (1976) • RCA Victor (M) AVM1-1739 8-10   76
> **Composer:** Earl Robinson, John Latouche. **Conductor:** Nathaniel Shilkret. **Cast:** Paul Robeson.

SING MUSE!
Original Cast (1961) • Blue Pear (S) BP-1004..................... 15-25
> **Composer:** Joseph Raposo, Erich Segal. **Conductor:** Jerry Goldberg. **Cast:** Karen Morrow, Brandon Maggart, Paul Michael, Ralph Stanley, William Reinson, Bob Spencer.

SING OUT, SWEET LAND!
Original Cast (1944) • Decca A-404 20-25   50
> 78 rpm album. Includes booklet.
Original Cast (1944) • Decca (M) DL-8023......................... 40-45   50
> Cover has drawings.

Original Cast (1944) • Decca (M) DL-4304.. 15-18   63
Original Cast (1944) • Decca (SE) DL-74304................................... 18-20   63
  Cover has photos.
Original Cast (1944) • AEI (M) AEI-1137.. 10-12   80s
  Cover has drawings.
  Conductor: Elie Siegmeister. **Cast:** Burl Ives, Alma Kaye, Alfred Drake, Bibi Osterwald, Juanita
  Hall, Ted Tiller, Jack McCauley, Herk Armstrong.

SING, YOU SINNERS: see PARIS HONEYMOON

SINGIN' IN THE RAIN
Soundtrack (1952) • MGM (EP) X-113... 12-18   52
  Boxed, four-disc set.
Soundtrack (1952) • MGM (M) E-113.. 20-25   52
  10-inch LP.
Soundtrack (1952) • MGM (M) E-3770.. 15-18   60
  Gatefold cover. One side has music from *Till the Clouds Roll By*.
Soundtrack (1952) • Metro (M) M-599.. 10-15   67
Soundtrack (1952) • Metro (SE) MS-599... 12-18   67
Soundtrack (1952) • MCA (SE) 39044 8-10   86
  Above soundtracks do not have the *Broadway Ballet* sequence, released separately.
  Composer: Nacio Herb Brown, Arthur Freed, Betty Comden, Adolph Green, Roger Edens.
  Conductor: Lennie Hayton. **Cast:** Gene Kelly, Donald O'Connor, Debbie Reynolds, MGM Studio
  Orchestra.
Soundtrack (1952) • MGM (EP) X-1026 10-15   54
  With *Broadway Ballet* sequence.
  Composer: Nacio Herb Brown, Arthur Freed. **Conductor:** Lennie Hayton. **Cast:** Gene Kelly.
Original London Cast (1983) • Rain (S) 1 12-18   84
  Gatefold cover. Also has other, unrelated, music.
  Composer: Nacio Herb Brown, Arthur Freed, Betty Comden, Adolphf Green, Roger Edens,
  Dorothy Fields, Jimmy McHugh, George Gershwin, Ira Gershwin. **Cast:** Tommy Steele, Roy
  Castle, Sarah Payne, Danielle Carson.
  Also see RICH, YOUNG AND PRETTY
  Also see THOSE GLORIOUS MGM MUSICALS

SINGING FOOL
Soundtrack (1929) • Take Two (M) TT-106.. 12-18   78
  Gatefold cover. Has *The Spaniard That Blighted My Life*, which no longer exists in film
  prints.
  Composer: Buddy De Sylva, Lew Brown, Ray Henderson, others. **Cast:** Al Jolson.

SINGING NUN
Soundtrack (1966) • MGM (M) 1E-7.. 8-12   66
Soundtrack (1966) • MGM (S) S1E-7... 12-15   66
Soundtrack (1966) • MCA (S) 25090.. 8-10   86
  Inspired by the life of Sister Luc-Gabrielle, and her hit album *The Singing Nun*. Sister Luc-
  Gabrielle (nee Jeanine Deckers) was known professionally as Soeur Sourire ("Sister
  Smile").
  Composer: Randy Sparks, Soeur Sourire, others. **Conductor:** Harry Sukman. **Cast:** Debbie
  Reynolds.
Studiotrack (1966) • Metro (M) M-569... 10-12   66
Studiotrack (1966) • Metro (S) MS-569 10-15   66
  Full title: *The Singing Nun – Music from the MGM Motion Picture*. Orchestral versions of the
  soundtrack songs.
  Composer: Randy Sparks, Soeur Sourire. **Conductor:** Joe Cain. **Cast:** Joe Cain Orchestra.

SINGLE ROOM FURNISHED
Soundtrack (1968) • Sidewalk (S) ST-5917.. 25-35   68
  Composer: James Sheldon. **Conductor:** James Sheldon. **Cast:** Paris Sisters, Jack Irwin.

SISTER, SISTER
Soundtrack (1988) • Varese Sarabande (S) STV 81355 8-10   88
    Composer: Einhorn.

SISTERS
Soundtrack (1973) • Entr'acte (Q) ERQ-7001 18-20   73
Soundtrack (1973) • Southern Cross (S) SCAR-5004 8-10   Re
    Composer: Bernard Herrmann. Conductor: Bernard Herrmann. Cast: Bernard Herrmann and
    His Orchestra.

SIX PACK
Soundtrack (1982) • Allegiance (S) AV-430 8-10   82
    Composer: Charles Fox.

633 SQUADRON
Soundtrack (1964) • United Artists (S) UA-LA305-G 20-25   74
Soundtrack (1964) • MCA (S) 25043 10-12   86
    Composer: Ron Goodwin. Conductor: Ron Goodwin.

SIXTEEN CANDLES
Soundtrack • MCA (S) 36012 8-10   84
    Cast: Stray Cats, Annie Golden, Ira Newborn & the Geeks, Patti Smith, Thompson Twins.

SIXTEEN DAYS OF GLORY (1984 SUMMER OLYMPICS)
Soundtrack (1986) • DRG (S) 419386-1 10-15   86
    Cast: Placido Domingo.

16 GREAT MOTION PICTURE THEMES
Soundtrack • ABC (S) DP-4007 10-15   74
    Music from *The Godfather, Sterile Cuckoo, Odd Couple, Rosemary's Baby, Italian Job,
    Paint Your Wagon, Ten Commandments, The Dove, Love Story, Cool Hand Luke, Will
    Penny, T.R. Baskin, Barefoot in the Park, Great Gatsby, Molly Maguires* and *Nevada
    Smith.*

67 MELODY LANE
TV Soundtrack (1955) • Columbia (M) CL-724 20-30   55
    Composer: Ken Griffin, Stephen Foster, others. Cast: Ken Griffin.

SKATEBOARD
Soundtrack (1977) • RCA Victor (S) ABL1-2769 8-10   77
    Composer: Mark Snow, others. Conductor: Mark Snow. Cast: Dr. John, Jefferson Starship,
    Mickey Thomas, Taro Meyer, Mona Lisa and Terry Young, Roger Jaep.

SKATEDATER
Soundtrack (1966) • Mira (M) LP-3004 12-15   66
Soundtrack (1966) • Mira (S) LPS-3004 15-20   66
    Composer: Mike Curb. Conductor: Nick Venet.

SKATETOWN U.S.A.
Soundtrack (1980) • Columbia (S) JC-36292 8-10   80
    Cast: Dave Mason, Earth, Wind and Fire, Emotions, Marilyn McCoo and Billy Davis Jr., Jacksons,
    Hounds, John Sebastian, Heatwave, Patrick Hernandez.

SKI CRAZY
Soundtrack (1956) • Electro-Vox (M) EV-2081 60-80   56
    Composer: Henry Vars. Conductor: Kurt Graunke. Cast: Symphonie Orchester Graunke.

SKI ON THE WILD SIDE
Soundtrack (1967) • MGM (M) E-4439 20-35   67
Soundtrack (1967) • MGM (S) SE-4439 25-50   67
    Composer: Billy Allen.

SKIDOO

Soundtrack (1968) • RCA Victor (S) LSO-1152.................................... 10-12   68
Composer: Harry Nilsson. Conductor: George Tipton. Cast: Carol Channing, Harry Nilsson.

SKY BANDITS

Soundtrack (1986) • Varese Sarabande (S) STV-81297 10-12   86
Composer: Alfi Kabilijo. Conductor: Alfi Kabilijo. Cast: National Philharmonic Orchestra.

SKY'S THE LIMIT

Soundtrack (1943) • Curtain Calls (M) CC 100/19............................... 10-12
Also has music from *A Damsel in Distress.*
Composer: Harold Arlen, Johnny Mercer. Cast: Fred Astaire, Sally Sweetland (performs vocals
for Joan Leslie in the film), Robert Benchley (dialogue). DAMSEL IN DISTRESS: Composer:
George Gershwin, Ira Gershwin. Cast: Fred Astaire, Gracie Allen, George Burns.

SKYSCRAPER

Original Cast (1965) • Capitol (M) VAS-2422 8-12   65
Original Cast (1965) • Capitol (S) SVAS-2422 12-15   65
Composer: James Van Heusen, Sammy Cahn. Conductor: John Lesko. Cast: Julie Harris,
Peter L. Marshall, Charles Nelson Reilly, Dick O'Neill, Rex Everhart, Nancy Chushman, Lesley
Stewart.
Studio Cast (1965) • Capitol (M) T-2411 8-10   65
Studio Cast (1965) • Capitol (S) ST-2411 8-10   65
Composer: James Van Heusen, Sammy Cahn. Conductor: Stu Phillips. Cast: Hollyridge
Singers.

SLAM DANCE

Soundtrack (1987) • Island (S) 90662-1 8-10   87
Cast: Stan Ridgway, Mitchell Froom, Tim Scott, Eddy Howard.

SLAPSTICK OF ANOTHER KIND

Soundtrack (1984) • Varese Sarabande (S) STV-81163 10-15   84
Composer: Morton Stevens, Michel Legrand. Cast: Morton Stevens.

SLAUGHTERHOUSE-FIVE

Studio Cast • Angel (S) S-36876... 10-15
Conductor: Yehudi Menuhin. Cast: Douglas Leedy, George Malcolm and Helmut Walcha,
Edouard Comette, Menuhin Festival Orchestra.
Soundtrack (1972) • Columbia (S) S-31333 20-25   72
Has original Glenn Gould performances, as heard in the film.
Composer: Johann Sebastian Bach. Conductor: Vladimir Golschmann, Pablo Casals. Cast:
Glenn Gould (piano), Columbia Symphony Orchestra.

SLAUGHTER ON 10TH AVENUE

Soundtrack (1957) • Decca (M) DL-8657 15-20   57
Soundtrack (1957) • Decca (S) DL-78657 25-30   58
Black labels. Stereo cover has gold stereo box affixed over original mono number.
Soundtrack (1957) • Decca (M) DL-8657 10-12
Soundtrack (1957) • Decca (S) DL-78657 15-18
Rainbow label. Film has Richard Rodgers' original ballet music from *On Your Toes* as
background music, arranged and adapted by Herschel Burke Gilbert.
Composer: Richard Rodgers. Conductor: Joseph Gershenson.
Also see WORDS AND MUSIC

SLAUGHTER'S BIG RIP-OFF

Soundtrack (1973) • Polydor (S) PD-6015 25-35   73
Composer: James Brown, Fred Wesley. Cast: James Brown, Fred Wesley and the J.B's.

SLAVE TRADE IN THE WORLD TODAY

Soundtrack (1964) • London (M) M-76006 175-200   64
Composer: Teo Usuelli.

SLAVES
Soundtrack (1969) • Skye (S) SK-11 20-25   69
   Composer: Bobby Scott, Bob Kessler. **Conductor:** Gary McFarland. **Cast:** Dionne Warwick.

SLAVES OF NEW YORK
Soundtrack (1989) • Virgin (S) 7-91229-1 8-10   89
   Composer: Richard Robbins. **Cast:** Boy George, others.

SLEEP WARM
Soundtrack • Stanyan (S) 5081 10-12
   Composer: Rod McKuen. **Cast:** Rod McKuen.

SLEEPING BEAUTY
Soundtrack (1959) • Disneyland (M) WDL-4018 20-25   59
Soundtrack (1959) • Disneyland (S) STER-4018 25-35   59
Soundtrack (1959) • Buena Vista (S) STER-4036 15-20   70
   Composer: Peter Ilyich Tchaikovsky. **Conductor:** George Bruns. **Cast:** Mary Costa, Bill Shirley.
Studiotrack • Disneyland (S) ST 3911MO 10-30
   Conductor: Camarata. **Cast:** Mary Martin.
Studiotrack (1959) • Disneyland (M) MM-32 35-40   59
   Cast: Darlene Gillespie.
Studiotrack (1964) • Disneyland (M) DQ-1228 15-20   62
Soundtrack (1966) • Roulette (M) OS-803 10-12   66
Soundtrack (1966) • Roulette (S) OSS-803 12-18   66
   Composer: Peter Ilyich Tchaikovsky. **Conductor:** Boris Khaikin. **Cast:** Leningrad Kirov Ballet Group.
Studiotrack (1966) • Golden (M) 166 8-10   66
   Cast: Paul Tripp (narration).

SLENDER THREAD
Soundtrack (1965) • Mercury (M) MG-21070 12-15   65
Soundtrack (1965) • Mercury (S) SR-61070 15-18   65
   Composer: Quincy Jones. **Conductor:** Quincy Jones.

SLEUTH
Soundtrack (1973) • Columbia (S) S-32154 12-25   73
   Composer: John Addison. **Conductor:** John Addison. **Cast:** Michael Caine, Sir Laurence Olivier. (With dialogue.)

SLIPPER AND THE ROSE
Soundtrack (1976) • MCA (S) 2097 10-15   76
   Composer: Richard M. Sherman, Robert B. Sherman. **Conductor:** Angela Morley. **Cast:** Richard Chamberlain, Gemma Craven, John Christopher Gable, Annette Crosbie, Julian Orchard, Michael Hordern, Kenneth More, Peter Graves, John Turner.
   Also see CINDERELLA

SLIPPERY WHEN WET
Soundtrack (1959) • World Pacific (M) W-1265 20-25   59
Soundtrack (1959) • World Pacific (S) WS-1265 30-35   59
   Composer: Bud Shank. **Cast:** Bud Shank.

SLOW DANCING IN THE BIG CITY
Soundtrack (1978) • United Artists (S) UA-LA939-H 8-10   78
   Composer: Bill Conti. **Conductor:** Bill Conti.

SLUGGER'S WIFE
Soundtrack (1985) • MCA (S) 5578 10-15   85
   Includes insert.
   Composer: Quincy Jones. **Cast:** Quincy Jones.

SLUMBER PARTY '57
Soundtrack (1976) • Mercury (S) SRM-1-1097 20-25   76
    Cast: Jerry Lee Lewis, Crew Cuts, Johnny Preston, Paul and Paula, Platters, Angels, Bruce Channel, Danleers, Big Bopper, Phil Phillips, Jivin' Gene and the Jokers, David Carroll and His Orchestra.

SLUMBER PARTY MASSACRE
Soundtrack (1984) • Web (S) ST 109 10-20   84
    Composer: Ralph Jones. **Conductor:** Ralph Jones.

SMALL ONE: see HAPPY PRINCE

SMASHING TIME
Soundtrack (1967) • ABC (M) OC-6 12-15   68
Soundtrack (1967) • ABC (S) ABCS OC-6 20-25   68
Soundtrack (1967) • ABC (S) 91399 8-12   Re
    Composer: John Addison. **Conductor:** John Addison. **Cast:** Lynn Redgrave, Rita Tushingham.

SMASH-UP, THE STORY OF A WOMAN: see SUSAN HAYWARD

SMILIN' THROUGH
Original Cast • Decca (M) DL-7011 25-65   50
  10-inch LP. Part of Decca's *Cherished Moments of the Theater* series of recreated plays from the 1920s.
    Cast: Jane Cowl, others.

SMILING, THE BOY FELL DEAD
Original Cast (1961) • Sunbeam (M) LB-549 30-40
    Composer: David Baker, Sheldon Harnick. **Cast:** Danny Meehan, Joseph Macauly, Claiborne Cary.

SMOKEY AND THE BANDIT
Soundtrack (1977) • MCA (EP) S33-1961 10-15   77
  Includes Jerry Reed's *West Bound and Down* and *March of the Rednecks.*
    Composer: Bill Justis, Jerry Reed, Dick Feller, Jerry R. Hubbard, Ervin T. Rouse. **Cast:** Jerry Reed, Bill Justis.
Soundtrack (1977) • MCA (S) 2099 8-10   77
    Composer: Bill Justis, Jerry Reed, Dick Feller, others. **Cast:** Jerry Reed, Burt Reynolds, Jackie Gleason. (With dialogue.)

SMOKEY AND THE BANDIT II
Soundtrack (1980) • MCA (S) 6101 8-10   80
    Conductor: Al Capps. **Cast:** Jerry Reed, Statler Brothers, Don Williams, Roy Rogers and the Sons of the Pioneers, Bandit Band, Tanya Tucker, Mel Tillis, Brenda Lee, Tommy Tedesco (guitar), Herb Pedersen (banjo), Jerry Kennedy (dobro, guitar), Bobby Thompson (banjo), Burt Reynolds. (With dialogue.)

SMOKEY AND THE BANDIT III
Soundtrack (1983) • MCA (S) 36006 8-10   83
    Cast: John Stewart, Lee Greenwood, Ed Bruce, others.

SMOTHERS BROTHERS HOUR
TV Soundtrack (1966) • Mercury (S) SR 61193 15-20   66
  Includes 8" x 10" photo.
    Cast: Smothers Brothers.

SMOTHERS BROTHERS SHOW – TOUR DE FARCE OF AMERICAN HISTORY
TV Soundtrack (1965) • Mercury (M) MG-20948 10-15   65
TV Soundtrack (1965) • Mercury (S) SR-60948 15-20   65
    Cast: Smothers Brothers (Tom Smothers, Dick Smothers).

SNOOPY
Original Cast (1975) • DRG (S) 6103 10-15   75
  Composer: Larry Grossman, Hal Hackady. **Conductor:** Jon Olson.
Original London Cast • Polydor (S) 422-820 247-1 8-10
Original London Cast • That's Entertainment (S) TER-1073.................. 8-10   80s
  UK release.

SNOOPY COME HOME
Soundtrack (1972) • Columbia (S) S-31541 15-20   72
  Composer: Richard M. Sherman, Robert B. Sherman. **Conductor:** Don Ralke. **Cast:** Shelby
  Flint, Don Ralke, Ray Pohlman, Thurl Ravenscroft, Guy Pohlman, Linda Ercoli.

SNOOPY'S CHRISTMAS
Studio Cast • Diplomat (S) S-1718.. 8-12

SNOW GOOSE
Studio Cast (1949) • Decca (M) DL-5055.. 50-55
  10-inch LP.
  Composer: Victor Young. **Conductor:** Victor Young. **Cast:** Herbert Marshall, Joan Loring, others.

SNOW QUEEN
Soundtrack (1959) • Decca (M) DL-8977 25-35   59
Soundtrack (1959) • Decca (S) DL-78977 45-65   59
  Composer: Frank Skinner, Diane Lampert, Richard Loring. **Conductor:** Joseph Gershenson.
  Cast: Paul Freed (narration), Sandra Dee, Tommy Kirk, Patty McCormick. (With dialogue.)

SNOW WHITE AND ROSE RED
Soundtrack (1966) • Camden (M) CAL-1084....................................... 10-12   66
Soundtrack (1966) • Camden (S) CAS-1084.. 12-15   66
  Composer: Milton DeLugg, Anne DeLugg. **Conductor:** Milton DeLugg. **Cast:** Paul Tripp
  (narration).

SNOW WHITE AND THE SEVEN DWARFS
Original Cast (1979) • Buena Vista (S) 5009 25-30   79
  Sold only at Radio City Music Hall.
  Composer: Frank Churchill, Joe Cook, Larry Morey, Jay Blackton. **Conductor:** Donald Pippin.
  Cast: Mary Jo Salerno, Richard Bowne, Anne Francine.
Studio Cast • Golden (M) 5-30-A.. 8-10
  Also has *Sleeping Beauty* and *Peter and the Wolf*.
Studiotrack (1937) • Decca (M) DL-5015 60-70   49
  10-inch LP.
  Composer: Frank Churchill, Larry Morey, others. **Conductor:** Paul J. Smith, Leigh Harline.
Soundtrack (1937) • Disneyland (M) WDL-4005 175-200   57
  Score, the first to be recorded directly from the soundtrack, came out originally on 78 rpms.
Soundtrack (1937) • Disneyland (M) DQ-1201 45-50   62
  Cast: Adriana Caselotti (as "Snow White"), Harry Stockwell.
Soundtrack (1937) • Disneyland (M) 3101... 25-30   80
  Limited edition picture disc.
Soundtrack (1937) • Buena Vista (M) 102 45-50   75
  Three discs. Complete soundtrack of the film.
Studiotrack (1965) • Golden (M) LP-165 10-15   65
  Music and dialogue.
  Cast: Anne and Milton Delugg.
Studiotrack (1962) • Buena Vista (M) BV-4023 25-30   62
Studiotrack (1962) • Buena Vista (S) STER-4023 35-40   62
  Conductor: Tutti Camarata.
  Also see BEAUTY AND THE BEAST

SNOW WHITE AND THE THREE STOOGES
Soundtrack (1961) • Columbia (M) CL-1650 40-60   61

Soundtrack (1961) • Columbia (S) CS-8450..65-85   61
Soundtrack (1961) • Columbia Special Products (S) ACS-8450.............8-10   Re
  Composer: Harry Harris, others. **Cast:** Carol Heiss, Three Stooges.

SNOWMAN
Soundtrack (1984) • Columbia (S) FM-39126 10-15   84
  Composer: Howard Blake. **Conductor:** Howard Blake. **Cast:** Sinfonia of London, Bernard Cribbins (narration).

SNOWS OF KILIMANJARO: see GREAT FILM CLASSICS

SO DEAR TO MY HEART, STORY OF
Studiotrack (1948) • Disneyland (M) DQ-1255 25-30   64
  Cast: Bryan Russell (narration).

SO LONG, 174TH STREET
Original Cast (1976) • Original Cast (S) OC-8131 8-12   81
  Based on the Joseph Stein comedy *Enter Laughing*.
  Composer: Stan Daniels. **Conductor:** Milton Rosenstock. **Cast:** Robert Morse, Kaye Ballard, Loni Ackerman, George S. Irving, Patti Karr.

SO THIS IS LOVE
Soundtrack (1953) • RCA Victor (M) LOC-3000 60-70   53
  10-inch LP.
  Composer: Various. **Conductor:** Ray Heindorf. **Cast:** Kathryn Grayson.

SO THIS IS PARIS
Soundtrack (1955) • Decca (EP) ED-700 20-25   55
Soundtrack (1955) • Decca (M) DL-5553 35-45   55
  10-inch LP.
  Composer: Phil Moody, Pony Sherell. **Conductor:** Joseph Gershenson. **Cast:** Gene Nelson, Tony Curtis, Gloria De Haven, Paul Gilbert.

SODOM AND GOMORRAH
Soundtrack (1963) • RCA Victor (M) LOC-1076.............................35-100   63
Soundtrack (1963) • RCA Victor (S) LSO-1076.............................65-100   63
  Composer: Miklos Rozsa. **Conductor:** Miklos Rozsa.
  Also see FILM MUSIC OF MIKLOS ROZSA

SOL MADRID
Soundtrack (1968) • MGM (M) E-4541 20-25   68
Soundtrack (1968) • MGM (S) SE-4541-ST 25-30   68
  Composer: Lalo Schifrin. **Conductor:** Lalo Schifrin, Robert Armbruster.

SOLOMON AND SHEBA
Soundtrack (1959) • United Artists (M) UAL-4051...............................20-25   59
Soundtrack (1959) • United Artists (S) UAS-5051 60-120   59
  Maroon, silk-like cover.
Soundtrack (1959) • United Artists (M) UAL-4051 50-60   59
Soundtrack (1959) • United Artists (S) UAS-5051 50-60   59
  Standard cover.
Soundtrack (1959) • MCA (S) 1425..8-10   80
  Composer: Mario Nascimbene. **Conductor:** Mario Nascimbene.

SOLOMON KING
Soundtrack • Sal-Wa (S) P-SAS 1001 8-10
  Composer: J. Steiger. **Cast:** Sal Watts, Claudia Russo.

SOME BEAUTIFUL DAY
Original Cast • Avant Garde (S) 127 8-12

SOME CAME RUNNING
Soundtrack (1958) • Capitol (M) W-1109 25-30   58
Soundtrack (1958) • Capitol (S) SW-1109 65-75   58
    Composer: Elmer Bernstein, James Van Heusen, Sammy Cahn. **Conductor:** Elmer Bernstein.

SOME KIND OF WONDERFUL
Soundtrack (1987) • MCA (S) 6200 8-10   87
    Cast: Furniture, Lick the Tins, Blue Room, Pete Shelley, Jesus and Mary Chain, Flesh for Lulu, March Violets, Stephen Duffy, Apartments, March Violets.

SOME LIKE IT HOT
Soundtrack (1959) • United Artists (EP) UAE-1005 45-50   59
Soundtrack (1959) • United Artists (M) UAL-4030 40-50   59
Soundtrack (1959) • United Artists (S) UAS-5030 60-70   59
Soundtrack (1959) • United Artists (S) UA-LA272-G 8-15   74
    Composer: Adolph Deutsch, others. **Conductor:** Adolph Deutsch, Matty Malneck. **Cast:** Marilyn Monroe, Society Syncopaters.
Studiotrack (1960) • United Artists (M) UAL-3029 40-50   60
Studiotrack (1960) • United Artists (S) UAS-6029 65-85   60
    Full title: *Some Like it Hot Cha-Cha-Cha.* Selections from the film played for dancing. Cover pictures Marilyn Monroe on front and has photos from the film on back.
    Composer: Various. **Cast:** Sweet Sue and Her Society Syncopaters, Rene Hernandez and His Orchestra.
Studiotrack • Epic (M) LN 3559 20-25
    Full title: *Jack Lemmon Sings Some Like It Hot.*
    Cast: Jack Lemmon.
    Also see APARTMENT

SOMEBODY BAD STOLE DE WEDDING BELL
Studiotrack (1954) • RCA Victor (EP) EPA-570 10-20   54
    Music from *Who's Got De Ding Dong* (from The New Copacabana Show of 1954) and In Paris.
    Composer: Cole Porter. **Conductor:** Henri Rene. **Cast:** Eartha Kitt, Henri Rene and His Orchestra.

SOMEBODY LOVES ME
Soundtrack (1952) • RCA Victor (EP) EPB-3097 15-20   52
    Two discs.
Soundtrack (1952) • RCA Victor (M) LPM-3097 40-50   52
    10-inch LP.
    Composer: Various. **Conductor:** Emil Newman. **Cast:** Betty Hutton, Pat Morgan (performs vocals for Ralph Meeker in the film).
Soundtrack (1952) • Motion Picture Tracks (M) MPT-5 25-35
    Includes previously unreleased material.
    Composer: Various. **Conductor:** Emil Newman. **Cast:** Betty Hutton, Pat Morgan (performs vocals for Ralph Meeker in the film), Adele Jurgens.
Studiotrack (1952) • Decca (M) DL-5424 20-25   52
    10-inch LP.
    Conductor: Victor Young. **Cast:** Blossom Seeley, Benny Fields.

SOMEBODY UP THERE LIKES ME
Soundtrack (1956) • RCA Victor (EP) EPA-903 20-25   56
    Title theme is the only track from the film. Also has *Dream Along with Me*, Perry Como's NBC-TV show theme.
    Composer: Various. **Cast:** Perry Como, Mitchell Ayres' Orchestra, Ray Charles Singers.

SOMETHING FOR THE BOYS
Original Cast (1948) • AEI (S) AEI-1157 10-20   80s
Original Radio Cast (1944) • Sound Stage (M) 2305 15-20   80
    Black vinyl.
Original Radio Cast (1944) • Sound Stage (M) 2305 20-25   80
    Colored vinyl. Top spine of cover reads "Original Broadway Cast Recording," but this is a
    condensed version of a 1944 radio show with members of the original New York
    production. Also has music from *Seven Lively Arts*.
    Composer: Cole Porter **Cast:** SOMETHING FOR THE BOYS: Ethel Merman, Bill Johnson, Paula
    Laurence, Betty Garrett, Allen Jenkins. SEVEN LIVELY ARTS: Benny Goodman Quintet, Gene
    Walsh, Jane Harvey, Peggy Mann, Charlotte Rae.

SOMETHING UNIQUE
Original Cast (1956) • RCA Victor (M) G8OP-6206 25-30
    Special Products issue for Singer Sewing Machine Company.
    Composer: Ken Hopkins. **Cast:** Bill Heyer, Bob Sheerer, Edith Adams.

SOMETHING WILD
Soundtrack (1986) • MCA (S) 6194 8-10   86
    Cast: Oingo Boingo, UB40, Fine Young Cannibals, Sonny Okkossun, Celia Cruz, Jerry Harrison,
    New Order, Sister Carol, Steve Jones, Jimmy Cliff.

SOMETIMES A GREAT NOTION
Soundtrack (1971) • Decca (S) DL-79185 12-18   71
    This film was retitled *Never Give an Inch*.
    Composer: Henry Mancini. **Conductor:** Henry Mancini. **Cast:** Charley Pride.

SOMEWHERE IN TIME
Soundtrack (1980) • MCA (S) 5154 15-20   80
Soundtrack (1980) • MCA (S) 39306 8-10   80s
    Composer: John Barry, others. **Conductor:** John Barry. **Cast:** Roger Williams and Chet
    Swiatkowsky (pianos).

SON OF DRACULA
Soundtrack (1972) • Rapple/RCA Victor (S) ABL1-0220 10-15   72
    Includes iron-on insert.
    Composer: Harry Nilsson, others. **Cast:** Harry Nilsson.

SONDHEIM
Studio Cast (1985) • Book of the Month Club (S) 85-7515 10-20   85
    Three discs. New recordings supervised by Sondheim.
    Composer: Stephen Sondheim. **Cast:** Mary D'Arcy, others.
Original Cast • RCA Victor (S) CRL4-5359 20-30   85
    Boxed, four-disc set. Includes 40-page booklet with lyrics. Full title: *A Collector's Sondheim
    – Anthology of earlier Original Cast recordings from 1954-1984*. Includes many previously
    unreleased tracks. Also includes music from *A Stephen Sondheim Evening*.
    Composer: Stephen Sondheim. **Conductor:** Ray Cook, Mitch Farber, Thomas Fay, Paul
    Gemignani, Herbert Green, Hal Hastings, Tim Higgs, Stuart Pedlar, E. Martin Perry, Carlo Savina,
    Stephen Sondheim. **Cast:** Liz Callaway, Cris Groenendaal, Bob Gunton, George Hearn, Steven
    Jacob, Judy Kaye, Victoria Mallory, Angela Lansbury, Jason Alexander, Ann Morrison, Stephen
    Sondheim, others.

SONDHEIM: A MUSICAL TRIBUTE
Original Cast (1973) • Warner Bros. (S) 2WS-2705 15-20   73
    Two discs. Gatefold cover. Recorded live March 11, 1973, at New York's Shubert Theatre.
    Composer: Stephen Sondheim, others. **Conductor:** Paul Gemignani. **Cast:** Jack Cassidy,
    Dorothy Collins, Pamela Hall, Larry Kert, Angela Lansbury, Mary McCarty, Donna McKechnie,
    Chita Rivera, Alexis Smith, Nancy Walker, George Lee Andrews, Mark Lambert, John McMartin,
    Tony Steven, Larry Blyden, Pamela Myers, Stephen Sondheim.

SONG AND DANCE

Original Cast (1980) • Polydor (S) POLD 5031 8-10   80
Original Cast (1980) • Polydor (S) PD-1-6260................................. 8-10   80
    Actual title: *Tell Me on a Sunday*.
    Composer: Andrew Lloyd Webber, Don Black. **Conductor:** Harry Rabinowitz, David Caddick, Paul Maguire. **Cast:** Marti Webb, Elaine Stritch, others.

SONG IS BORN

Soundtrack (1948) • Capitol - Number Not Known 30-50   48
    78 rpm album. Actual title: *Giants of Jazz*. Benefit album for the Damon Runyon Memorial Fund for Cancer Research.
    Composer: Various. **Conductor:** Various. **Cast:** Tommy Dorsey, Louis Armstrong, Benny Goodman, Charlie Barnet, Golden Gate Quartet, Mel Powell, others.

SONG OF BERNADETTE

Studiotrack (1943) • Decca DA-365 45-70   43
    78 rpm album. Includes booklet.
Studiotrack (1943) • Decca (M) DL-5358 100-125   52
    10-inch LP. Both have cover art by Norman Rockwell
    Composer: Alfred Newman. **Conductor:** Alfred Newman. **Cast:** Alfred Newman's Concert Orchestra.
Studiotrack • Varese Sarabande (M) STV-81116................................ 10-15   83
    One side has music from *Island in the Sky*.
    Composer: Emil Newman, Alfred Newman, Hugo Friedhofer. **Conductor:** Alfred Newman. **Cast:** Alfred Newman's Concert Orchestra.

SONG O' MY HEART: JOHN MCCORMACK SINGS

Soundtrack (1929) • John McCormack Assoc. (M) No Number Used .. 10-15   71
    Cast: John McCormack, others.

SONG OF NORWAY

Original Cast • Decca DA-382.. 12-18
    78 rpm album. Includes booklet.
Original Cast (1944) • Decca (EP) ED-842 10-12   49
Original Cast (1944) • Decca (M) DL-8002... 18-20   49
    Black and gold label. Cover has drawing on orange background.
Original Cast (1944) • Decca (M) DL-9019 12-15   55
    May have either original cover (above) or a photo of two bicyclists against a gray mountain background.
Original Cast (1944) • Decca (SE) DL-79019 8-12   59
Original Cast (1944) • MCA (SE) 2032e 8-10   72
    Composer: Edvard Grieg, Robert Wright, George Forrest. **Conductor:** Arthur Kay. **Cast:** Robert Shafer, Lawrence Brooks, Helena Bliss, Kitty Carlisle (sings Irra Petina's role on the LP), Sig Arno, Ivy Scott, Walter Kingsford, Gwen Jones, Kent Edwards.
Original Cast (1944) • Columbia M-562.. 20-25   44
    78 rpm album. Recorded by the show's star, Irra Petina, who does not appear on the Decca original cast album.
Original Cast • JJA (M) 19782.. 15-20   78
    First LP release of Irra Petina's recordings. Also has music from *Winged Victory* and *Up In Central Park*.
    Composer: Edvard Grieg, Robert Wright, George Forrest. **Conductor:** Sylvan Shulman. **Cast:** Irra Petina, Robert Weede. UP IN CENTRAL PARK: **Composer:** Sigmund Romberg, Dorothy Fields. **Conductor:** Max Meth. **Cast:** Eileen Farrell, Wilbur Evans, Celeste Holm, Betty Bruce. WINGED VICTORY: **Composer:** David Rose. **Conductor:** Leonard de Paur. **Cast:** Julie Warren, Red Buttons, Barry Nelson, Edmond O'Brien, Danny Scholl, John Forsythe, Peter Lind Hays, Karl Malden, Kevin McCarthy, Edward McMahon, Gary Merrill, Ray McDonald, George Reeves.

Original Revival Cast (1958) • Columbia (M) CL-1328 12-18   59
Original Revival Cast (1958) • Columbia (S) CS-8135........................... 40-45   59
From a 1958 Jones Beach Marine Theater summer production.
Composer: Edvard Grieg, Robert Wright, George Forrest. **Conductor:** Lehman Engel. **Cast:** Brenda Lewis, John Reardon, Helena Scott, Sig Arno, William Olvis, Muriel O'Malley, Stan Freeman, William Linton, Perryne Anker.

Studio Cast • Angel (S) S-35904 10-15
Composer: Robert Wright, George Forrest. **Conductor:** Michael Collins. **Cast:** Victoria Elliot, Thomas Round, Norma Hughes, John Lawrenson, Williams Singers, Michael Collins and His Orchestra.

Soundtrack (1970) • ABC (S) ABCS OC-14 8-12   70
Comes with two different covers, each with a variation in listings of musical numbers and running times. Recording is the same despite cover information.
Composer: Edvard Grieg, Robert Wright, George Forrest. **Conductor:** Roland Shaw. **Cast:** Toralv Maurstad, Florence Henderson, Frank Porretta, Harry Secombe, Elizabeth Larner, Christina Schollin.

Studiotrack • RCA Victor (S) LSC-3198 8-10
Cast: Van Cliburn, Boston Pops.

SONG OF SCHEHERAZADE
Soundtrack • Columbia X-272.. 15-20
78 rpm album. Film biography of Nikolai Rimsky-Korsakov. There may have been a Columbia LP reissue, but at press time we lack the necessary details.
Composer: Nikolai Rimsky-Korsakov, Miklos Rozsa, Jack Brooks. **Conductor:** Julius Burger. **Cast:** Charles Kullman.

SONG OF SONGS AND THE LETTERS OF HELOISE AND ABELARD
Studio Cast • Caedmon (M) TC 1085... 8-12

SONG OF THE SOUTH
Soundtrack (1946) • Disneyland (EP) DBR-28 30-40   56
Soundtrack (1946) • Disneyland (M) WDL-4001 100-250   56
Soundtrack (1946) • Disneyland (M) DQ-1205 15-25   63
Also known as *Uncle Remus.*
Composer: Allie Wrubel, Charles Wolcott, others. **Conductor:** Paul J. Smith, Daniele Amfitheatrof. **Cast:** James Baskett (as Uncle Remus), Hattie McDaniel, Horace "Nick O'demus" Stewart.

SONG REMAINS THE SAME
Soundtrack (1976) • Swan Song (S) SS2-201...................................... 15-20   76
Two discs.
Composer: Led Zeppelin (Robert Plant, Jimmy Page, John Paul Jones, John Bonham). **Cast:** Led Zeppelin.

SONG WITHOUT END
Soundtrack (1960) • Colpix (M) CP-506 15-20   60
Soundtrack (1960) • Colpix (S) SCP-506 20-25   60
Blue vinyl. Gatefold covers.
Soundtrack (1960) • Colpix (M) CP-506 10-12   60
Soundtrack (1960) • Colpix (S) SCP-506 12-15   60
Black vinyl. Gatefold covers.
Studiotrack (1960) • Colpix (M) CP-415 12-18   60
Additional music from the film.
Composer: Franz Liszt, others. **Conductor:** Morris Stoloff. **Cast:** Jorge Bolet (piano), Los Angeles Philharmonic Orchestra.

Studiotrack (1960) • Liberty (M) LRP-3151... 8-12   60
Studiotrack (1960) • Liberty (S) LST-7151 8-12   60
Actual title: *The Franz Liszt Story.*
Cast: Harry Sukman.
Studiotrack (1960) • Decca (M) DL-8999 8-12   60

Studiotrack (1960) • Decca (S) DL-78999 8-12   60
  Actual title: *The Franz Liszt Story.*
   Cast: Carmen Cavallaro.

SONGS BY KUKLA, FRAN AND OLLIE
Studio TV Cast • RCA Victor (EP) Y-425 15-25   53
  Two 78 rpm EPs.
Studio TV Cast • RCA Victor (EP) WY-425 20-35   53
  Two 45 rpm EPs.
   Composer: Jack Fascinato. **Conductor:** Jack Fascinato. **Cast:** Fran Allison, Burr Tillstrom,
   Jack Fascinato (piano).
Studio Cast • RCA Camden (S) CAS 2582 10-15   72
   Composer: Jack Fascinato. **Conductor:** Jack Fascinato. **Cast:** Fran Allison, Burr Tillstrom.
  Also see HAPPY MOTHER GOOSE (BY KUKLA, FRAN AND OLLIE)
  Also see MERRY CHRISTMAS FROM KUKLA, FRAN AND OLLIE

SONGS BY KORNGOLD & STEINER
Soundtrack • Citadel (S) CT-7005 12-18   79
   Composer: Erich Wolfgang Korngold, Max Steiner.

SONGS FROM GREAT FILMS
Studiotrack (1959) • Mercury (M) MG 20371 10-20   59
Studiotrack (1959) • Mercury (S) SR 60017 15-25   59
  Music from *Wild Is the Wind, Three Coins in the Fountain, Moonglow, Picnic, Tammy, Gigi,*
  Raintree Country, A Farewell to Arms, Sayonara, Marjorie Morningstar and *Limelite.*
   Conductor: Herman Clebanoff. **Cast:** Herman Clebanoff and Clebanoff Strings.

SONGS FROM THE GOLDEN CIRCLE
TV Soundtrack • ABC-Paramount (M) No Number Used 10-20   60s
   Composer: Don Costa. **Conductor:** Don Costa. **Cast:** Eydie Gorme, Steve Lawrence, Don Costa
   Orchestra.

SONGS FROM THE WESTERN SCREEN
Studiotrack • Capitol (M) T-971 15-20
  Music from *Wichita, The Big Land, The Searchers, The Last Frontier, Down Liberty Road,*
  High Noon, The Marshall's Daughter, Vanishing Prairie and Trooper Hook.
   Cast: Tex Ritter.

SONGS OF OUR SOLDIERS: see JOHNNY TREMAIN

SONGWRITER
Soundtrack (1984) • Columbia (S) FC-39531 8-10   84
Soundtrack (1984) • Columbia (S) PC-39531 8-10   80s
   Cast: Willie Nelson, Kris Kristofferson, others.

SONNY AND JED
Soundtrack (1973) • Cerberus (S) CEMS 0111 10-15   81
  Also has music from *The Cannibals.*
   Composer: Ennio Morricone (both). **Conductor:** Ennio Morricone (both).

SONS OF KATIE ELDER
Soundtrack (1965) • Columbia (M) OL-6420 30-50   65
Soundtrack (1965) • Columbia (S) OS-2820 60-85   65
   Composer: Elmer Bernstein. **Conductor:** Elmer Bernstein. **Cast:** John Wayne, Johnny Cash.
   (With dialogue.)

SOPHIA LOREN IN ROME
TV Soundtrack (1964) • Columbia (M) OL-6310 20-25   64
TV Soundtrack (1964) • Columbia (S) OS-2710 45-65   64
TV Soundtrack (1964) • Columbia Special Products (S) CSP-172 12-15
  Also has music from *The Bride Wore Yolande.*
   Composer: John Barry. **Conductor:** John Barry. **Cast:** Sophia Loren.

SOPHIE

Original Cast (1963) • AEI (M) AEI-1130.. 20-25   80
  Has *You'd Know It,* by Jenny Smith, not found on commercial issue. Promotional issue only.
Original Cast (1963) • AEI (M) AEI-1130.. 10-15   80
  Based on the life of Sophie Tucker.
    Composer: Steve Allen. **Cast:** Steve Allen, Linda Lavin, Kathy Keegan, Jerry Vale, Jenny Smith, Libi Staiger.

SOPHIE'S CHOICE

Soundtrack (1983) • Jackal Records/Southern Cross (S) WOW-726... 12-15   83
Soundtrack (1983) • Southern Cross (S) SCRS-1002........................... 8-10   83
    Composer: Marvin Hamlisch. **Conductor:** Marvin Hamlisch. **Cast:** Marvin Hamlisch.

SOPHISTICATED LADIES

Original Cast (1981) • RCA Victor (S) CBL2-4053 10-12   81
  Two discs. Film based on the music of Duke Ellington.
Original Cast (1983) • RCA Victor (S) DJL1-4061 8-12   83
  Single disc with highlights from CBL2-4053. Promotional issue only.
Original Cast (1983) • RCA Victor (S) ABL1-4693................................ 8-12   83
  Single disc with highlights from CBL2-4053.
    Composer: Duke Ellington, others. **Conductor:** Mercer Ellington. **Cast:** Gregory Hines, Judith Jamison, Phyllis Hyman, P.J. Benjamin, Hinton Battle, Gegg Burge, Mercedes Ellington, Priscilla Baskerville, Terri Klausner, Michael Scott Gregory, Michael Lichtefeld, Gremlinn T. Creole.

SORCERER

Soundtrack (1977) • MCA (S) 2277.. 10-15   77
Soundtrack (1977) • MCA (S) MCL 1646 10-15   80s
    Composer: Edgar Froese, Christopher Baunke, Peter Baumann. **Cast:** Tangerine Dream.

SORCERER'S APPRENTICE: see PETER AND THE WOLF

SORRY, WRONG NUMBER

Original Radio Cast (1943) • Radiola (M) 70-80
  Numbered edition of 1,000. Release #3, Horror Series #1. One side has *Leinengen Vs. the Ants* (1949).
Studio Cast (1952) • Decca (M) DL-6092.. 60-70   52
  10-inch LP. Radio thriller with supporting cast and sound effects. Directed by William Spier.
    Composer: Lucille Fletcher (writer). **Conductor:** William Spier. **Cast:** Agnes Moorehead.

SOUL HUSTLER

Soundtrack (1973) • MGM (S) SE-4943... 10-15   73
    Composer: Harley Hatcher, others. **Conductor:** Harley Hatcher. **Cast:** Marcene Harris, Mathew Crowe and His Travelin' Band.

SOUL MAN

Soundtrack (1986) • A&M (S) SP-3903 8-10   86
    Cast: Ricky, Rae Dawn Chong, Sly Stone, Models, Nu Shooz, Lou Reed, Vesta Williams, Tom Scott, Brenda Russell.

SOUL OF HOLLYWOOD

Studiotrack • Jazzland (M) JLP 63 15-20
  Music from *Never on Sunday, Gone with the Wind, Fanny, Exodus, The Apartment, Spellbound* and others.
    Conductor: Melba Liston. **Cast:** Junior Mance and Orchestra.

SOUL OF NIGGER CHARLEY

Soundtrack (1973) • MGM (S) 1SE-46... 18-20   73
  Film sequel to *Legend of Nigger Charley.*
    Composer: Don Costa. **Conductor:** Don Costa. **Cast:** Lou Rawls.

SOUL TO SOUL

Soundtrack (1971) • Atlantic (S) 7207 10-12   71

Soundtrack (1971) • Atlantic (S) 81674-1 .... 10-12　Re
Recording of an Independence Day celebration in Ghana, West Africa.
Composer: Richie Havens, Ike Cargill, others. Cast: Wilson Pickett, Ike and Tina Turner, Staple Singers, Eddie Harris, Les McCann, Amoa, Roberta Flack, Voices of East Harlem.

SOUND AND THE FURY
Soundtrack (1959) • Decca (M) DL-8885 .... 20-30　59
Soundtrack (1959) • Decca (S) DL-78885 .... 45-65　59
Composer: Alex North. Conductor: Lionel Newman.

SOUND OF BROADWAY
Studiotrack (1964) • RCA Victor (M) PRM-162 .... 15-20　64
Music from *Hello Dolly, Kismit, Bye Bye Birdie, How to Succeed in Business Without Really Trying, Kiss Me Kate, South Pacific, Sound of Music, Camelot, Pajama Game* and *Stop the World – I Want to Get Off*. Made for Helene Curtis Co.
Cast: John Gary, Ann-Margret, Ed Ames, Alfred Drake & Jane Pickens, Florence Henderson, Richard Kiley, Sergio Franchi, Hugo & Luigi Chorus, Dick Schory, Pete King Chorale.

SOUND OF HOLLYWOOD THEMES
Studiotrack (1962) • Kapp/Medallion (M) ML-7513 .... 10-15　62
Studiotrack (1962) • Kapp/Medallion (S) ML-7513-S .... 15-20　62
Music from *The Sundowners, Never on Sunday, Spellbound, A Summer Place, Black Orpheus, Midnight Lace, Green Leaves of Summer, Sons and Lovers, Suzie Wong, The Unforgiven, Moonglow* and *The Apartment*.
Composer: Various. Cast: Vardi and the Medallion Strings.

SOUND OF JAZZ
TV Soundtrack (1957) • Columbia (M) CL-1098 .... 15-25　58
TV Soundtrack (1957) • Columbia (S) CS-8040 .... 25-35　58
Cast: Billie Holiday, Lester Young, Count Basie, Gerry Mulligan.

SOUND OF MUSIC
Original Cast (1959) • Columbia (M) KOL-5450 .... 8-10　59
Original Cast (1959) • Columbia (S) KOS-2020 .... 8-12　59
Gatefold covers. Has credits on front cover.
Original Cast (1959) • Columbia (M) KOL-5450 .... 8-10　59
Original Cast (1959) • Columbia (S) KOS-2020 .... 8-12　59
Standard covers. Photo of Mary Martin and children on cover.
Original Cast (1959) • Columbia (S) S-32601 .... 8-10　73
Composer: Richard Rodgers, Oscar Hammerstein II. Conductor: Frederick Dvonch. Cast: Mary Martin, Theodore Bikel, Patricia Neway, Kurt Kasznar, Marion Marlowe, Lauri Peters, Muriel O'Malley, Karen Shepard, Brian Davies, Elizabeth Howell.
Original London Cast (1959) • Stanyan (S) SRS-5003 .... 12-15　Re
Reissue of RCA Victor UK release.
Composer: Richard Rodgers, Oscar Hammerstein II. Conductor: Robert Lowe. Cast: Jean Bayless, Sylvia Beamish, Olive Gilbert, Constance Shacklock, Roger Dann, Barbara Brown, Eunice Gayson, Harold Kasket, Nicholas Bennett, Lynn Kennington.
London Studio Cast • Music for Pleasure (S) MFP-1007 12-15
London Studio Cast • Capitol (S) DT-90134 10-12
Capitol Record Club issue.
Conductor: Sam Fonteyn. Cast: Maureen Hartley, Charles West, Shirley Chapman, Richard Loaring, Heather Bishop, Sharon Sefton, Denise Powell, Susan Challner, Helen Mathieson, Stephen Ayres, Neville Martin, Mike Sammes Singers.
Studio Cast (1959) • Richmond (M) B-20079 .... 10-12　59
Studio Cast (1959) • Richmond (S) S-30079 .... 12-15　59
Composer: Richard Rodgers, Oscar Hammerstein II. Cast: London Theatre Company.

Studio Cast (1960) • Warner Bros. (M) W-1377 12-15   60
Studio Cast (1960) • Warner Bros. (S) WS-1377 15-20   60
    Conductor: Father Frank Wasner. **Cast:** Trapp Family Singers (who inspired the story).
Studio Cast (1966) • Disneyland (S) DQ 1292 10-15   66
    Recorded in London. Full title: *Mary Martin Sings the Sound of Music.*
    Conductor: Tuttu Camarata. **Cast:** Mary Martin.
Studio Cast (1966) • Disneyland (S) ST 3936 10-15   66
    Gatefold cover. Recorded in London. Full title: *Mary Martin Tells the Story and Sings the Songs of Rodgers and Hammerstein's Sound of Music.*
    Conductor: Tuttu Camarata. **Cast:** Mary Martin.
Studio Cast • Crown (M) 5135 8-12
    Cast: Sounds of a Thousand Strings, Janice Bryant, John Page, Robert Kent Chorus.
Studio Cast • Premier (M) PM 9017 10-12
Studio Cast • Premier (S) PS 9017 10-12
    Conductor: Mitch Hacker.
Studio Cast • Rondo-lette (S) SA 156 10-12
    Conductor: Russ Cast. **Cast:** Gigi Durston, others.
Studio Cast • Spin-O-Rama (M) MK-3078 10-12
    Cast: Patrice Roselle, Rose Block, Ana Green, Babs Colon, Leonard Rogers, Rosemary Hayes, Walter Stiller, Child Chorus.
Studio Cast • Tops (M) L1626 10-12
    Conductor: William Carlisle. **Cast:** Alice Knight, Karen Leslie, Gerald Mann, Babette George, Children's Chorus, Steve Morton.
Studio Cast (1961) • Kapp (M) KL-1175 10-12   61
Studio Cast (1961) • Kapp (S) KS-3059 12-15   61
Soundtrack (1965) • RCA Victor (M) LOCD-2005 12-15   65
Soundtrack (1965) • RCA Victor (S) LSOD-2005 12-18   65
    Includes booklets. Back covers incorrectly show *I Have Confidence* as "I Have Confidence in Me." Black label with dog on top.
Soundtrack (1965) • RCA Victor (M) LOCD-2005 8-12   65
Soundtrack (1965) • RCA Victor (S) LSOD-2005 10-12   65
    Includes booklets. Back covers correctly show *I Have Confidence.* Black label with dog on top.
Soundtrack (1965) • RCA Victor (S) LSOD-2005 8-12   Re
    Orange label. Unipak fold-open cover (disc opening faces gutter rather than outer edge). Without booklet.
Soundtrack (1965) • RCA Victor (S) LSOD-2005 8-10   Re
    Gatefold cover. No booklet. Black label with dog near top.
    Composer: Richard Rodgers, Oscar Hammerstein II. **Conductor:** Irwin Kostal. **Cast:** Julie Andrews, Bill Lee (performs vocals for Christopher Plummer in the film), Charmian Carr.
Studiotrack • Imperial (M) 2038 10-12   59
Studiotrack • Imperial (S) LP 12038 10-15   59
    Cast: Mannie Klein and His Sextet.
Studiotrack (1965) • RCA Camden (M) CAL-869 8-12   65
Studiotrack (1965) • RCA Camden (S) CAS-869 8-12   65
    Cast: Living Strings.
Studiotrack • Celebrity (S) UTS-150 8-12
    Conductor: Mitch Hacker.
Studiotrack (1959) • Columbia (M) CL-1418 8-12   59
Studiotrack (1959) • Columbia (S) CS-8215 8-12   59
Studiotrack • Columbia (S) OS-2040 8-12
    Full title: *Music from Rodgers and Hammerstein's The Sound of Music.*
    Conductor: Percy Faith. **Cast:** Percy Faith and His Orchestra.
Studiotrack • Coronet (S) CXS-102 8-12
    Conductor: Lewis Merritt.

Studiotrack • Custom (M) 2033 8-12
    Cast: California Pops Orchestra.
Studiotrack • Decca (M) DL-8975.. 8-12
    Cast: Stratford Strings.
Studiotrack • Design (M) DLP-135 8-12
    Conductor: Dean Franconi. **Cast:** Dean Franconi.
Studiotrack • Diplomat (S) DS-2344 8-12
    Cast: Dale Davis and His Orchestra and Chorus, Janet Anderson, Marion Garvey.
Studiotrack (1959) • Harmony (M) HL-7235 8-10   59
Studiotrack (1959) • Harmony (S) HS-11031 8-12   59
    Cast: Norman Paris Quartet.
Studiotrack • International Award (S) ASK-139 8-12
Studiotrack • International Award (S) AKS-139 8-12   Re
  "AKS" is correct prefix for reissue.
    Cast: John Senati and His Orchestra, Bill Jacob.
Studiotrack (1959) • MGM (M) E-3810 8-10   60
Studiotrack (1959) • MGM (S) SE-3810 8-12   60
    Cast: Benny Goodman Orchestra.
Studiotrack • RCA Victor (S) LSP-2277..................................... 8-12
    Conductor: Frank Wasner.
Studiotrack • Reprise (M) R-6145 8-12
  Full title: *The Sound of Music and the Sound of Cano.*
    Cast: Eddie Cano, Tony Reyes, Fred Aguirre.
Studiotrack • Wing (S) SRW-16228 8-12
    Cast: Richard Hayman and His Orchestra.
Studiotrack • Wyncote (M) W 9076... 8-12
Studiotrack • Wyncote (S) W 9076... 8-12
    Cast: International Pop Orchestra, 110 Musicians, Cheltenham Chorus.
Original London Revival Cast (1981) • Epic (S) EPC-70212 20-25   81
  UK release.
  Gatefold cover. Songs from the film version are added to the stage score.
    Composer: Richard Rodgers, Oscar Hammerstein II. **Conductor:** Cyril Ornadel. **Cast:** Petula Clark, Honor Blackman, John Bennett, Michael Jayston, June Bronhill, Claire Parker, Paul Shearstone.
Studio Cast (1988) • Telarc Digital (S) DG-10162 10-12   88
    Cast: Frederika Von Stade, Hakan Hagegard, others.
  Also see FIORELLO!
  Also see TRAPP FAMILY

SOUND OF RICHARD RODGERS' MUSIC

Studiotrack (1966) • RCA Victor (S) PRS-201 8-12   66
  Music from *Sound of Music, Carousel, Garrick Gaieties, State Fair, South Pacific, Boys from Syracuse, The King and I, Pal Joey, Evergreen* and *Oklahoma!*
    Composer: Richard Rodgers.

SOUND STAGE – HI-FI MUSIC FROM HOLLYWOOD

Studiotrack • Columbia (M) CL-612... 10-15
  Music from *Gone with the Wind, Indiscretion of an American Wife, Quo Vadis, Ruby Gentry, A Streetcar Named Desire, Portrait of Jennie, For Whom the Bell Tolls* and others.
    Conductor: Paul Weston. **Cast:** Paul Weston and His Orchestra.

SOUNDER

Soundtrack (1972) • Columbia (S) S-31944 12-18   72
    Cast: Sam "Lightnin" Hopkins, Taj Mahal.

SOUNDS BROADWAY! SOUNDS HOLLYWOOD! SOUNDS GREAT!

Studiotrack (1961) • Epic (M) LN-3797.. 10-12   61
Studiotrack (1961) • Epic (S) BN-604... 12-15   61
    Conductor: Norman Leyden, Frank Hunter (arrangers). **Cast:** Merrill Staton Voices.

SOUNDS FROM THE SILENT SCREEN
Soundtrack (1925-26) • Pelican (SE) 2011 15-20   78
   Music from *Ben-Hur, The Temptress* and *Thief of Baghdad.*

SOUNDS FROM TRUE STORIES
Soundtrack (1986) • Sire (S) 1-25515 8-10   86
   Cast: David Byrne, Carl Finch, Panhandle Mystery Band, Kronos Quartet, Banda Eclipse, Steve
   Jordan.

SOUNDS OF REDESIGN
Soundtrack (1965) • IRI (S) No Number Used 20-25   65
   From the *The Story of Redesign*, an industrial film about the making of *Plastics World*
   magazine. Single-sided LP.
   Cast: Don Zimmers.

SOUNDSTAGE
Studiotrack (1955) • Columbia (M) CL-612... 15-25   55
   Music from *Indiscretion of an American Wife, Duel in the Sun, Song of Bernadette, Since*
   You Went Away, Portrait of Jennie and others.
   Cast: Paul Weston and Orchestra.

SOUNDSTAGE SPECTACULAR
Studiotrack (1968) • Columbia (S) P2S-5214 10-15   68
   Two discs.
   Cast: Columbia Musical Treasuries Orchestra.

SOUNDTRACKS
Soundtrack • Decca (M) DL-4362 12-15   63
Soundtrack • Decca (S) DL-74362 15-18   63

SOUNDTRACKS AND FILMSCORES – SUPERALBUM
Soundtrack • Ascot (M) UM-13500.. 10-12   63
Soundtrack • Ascot (S) US-13500... 10-15   63
   Music from *The Apartment, Some Like It Hot, Exodus* and *Odds Against Tomorrow.*
Soundtrack • Ascot (M) UM-13501.. 10-12   63
Soundtrack • Ascot (S) US-13501... 10-15   63
   Music from *The Vikings, Never on Sunday, The Wonderful Country* and *I Want to Live.*
Soundtrack • Ascot (M) UM-13502.. 10-12   63
Soundtrack • Ascot (S) US-13502... 10-15   63
   Music from *The Horse Soldiers, Paris Blues, Judgment at Nuremberg* and *The Unforgiven.*
Soundtrack • Ascot (M) UM-13504.. 10-12   64
Soundtrack • Ascot (S) US-13504... 10-15   64
   Music from *Phaedra, Two for the Seesaw, West Side Story* and *Divorce Italian Style.*

SOUNDTRACKS (MUSIC FROM GREAT MOTION PICTURES)
Soundtrack • United Artists (M) UAL-3303 12-15   63
Soundtrack • United Artists (S) UAS-6303 15-18   63
   Composer: Various. **Cast:** Leroy Holmes, Elmer Bernstein, others.

SOUNDTRACKS, VOICES AND THEMES FROM GREAT MOVIES
Soundtrack (1959) • Colpix (M) CP-503 60-65   59
Soundtrack (1959) • DRG (M) MRS-509 10-12   83
   Previously unreleased soundtrack music from Columbia's *Pal Joey, Gilda, Three for the*
   Show, From Here to Eternity, You Were Never Lovelier, Cover Girl, The Eddy Duchin
   Story, Sunny Side of the Street, Picnic, The Bridge on the River Kwai and *You Can't Run*
   Away From It.
   Composer: Richard Rodgers, Lorenz Hart, George Gershwin, Ira Gershwin, George Duning,
   Jerome Kern, others. **Conductor:** Morris Stoloff. **Cast:** June Allyson, Jo Ann Greer (performs
   vocals for Rita Hayworth in *Pal Joey* and *Gilda),* Gene Kelly, Betty Grable, Jack Lemmon, Fred
   Astaire, others.

SOUP FOR ONE
Soundtrack (1982) • Atlantic/Mirage (S) WTG 19353............................ 8-12   82
    Composer: Nile Rodgers, Bernard Edwards, Johnny Mandel. **Cast:** Chic, Carly Simon, Teddy Pendergrass, Fonzi Thornton, Sister Sledge, Deborah Harry.

SOUPY SALES SHOW
TV Soundtrack (1961) • Reprise (M) R-6010.....................................:..... 12-15   61
TV Soundtrack (1961) • Reprise (S) R9-6010 15-20   61
    Cast: Soupy Sales.

SOUTH AMERICAN WAY
Soundtrack • MCA (M) 1703 8-15   80s
   Music from Carmen Miranda's films.
    Cast: Carmen Miranda, Andrews Sisters.

SOUTH PACIFIC
Original Cast (1949) • Columbia MM-850.. 10-15   49
   Boxed 78 rpm set.
Original Cast (1949) • Columbia (EP) A-850 15-20   49
   Boxed, four-disc set.
Original Cast (1949) • Columbia (EP) A-852 10-20   49
   Three discs.
Original Cast [Vol. 1] (1949) • Columbia (EP) A-1723 10-20   49
Original Cast [Vol. 1] (1949) • Columbia (EP) B-2579 10-15   Re
   Columbia "Hall of Fame Series."
Original Cast [Vol. 2] (1949) • Columbia (EP) A-1724 8-15   49
Original Cast (1949) • Columbia (M) ML-4180 12-15   49
   Green or blue label.
Original Cast (1949) • Columbia (M) OL-4180.................................... 8-12   Re
   Gray label. Both have a large anchor pictured on green cover.
Original Cast (1949) • Columbia (M) OL-4180.................................... 8-10   Re
   Shiny gatefold cover. Pictures film stars Ezio Pinza and Mary Martin.
Original Cast (1949) • Columbia (M) OL-4180.................................... 10-12   Re
   Flat (not shiny) gatefold cover.
Original Cast (1949) • Columbia (M) OL-4180.................................... 8-12   Re
Original Cast (1949) • Columbia (SE) OS-2040 10-12   Re
   Standard covers. Picture Ezio Pinza and Mary Martin.
Original Cast (1949) • Columbia (SE) S-326014 8-10   73
    Composer: Richard Rodgers, Oscar Hammerstein II. **Conductor:** Salvatore Dell'Isola. **Cast:** Mary Martin, Ezio Pinza, Juanita Hall, William Tabbert, Barbara Luna.
Original London Cast • Columbia (EP) 50-55
   Selection number not yet known.
    Composer: Richard Rodgers, Oscar Hammerstein II. **Cast:** Mary Martin, Wilbur Evans, Muriel Smith, Peter Grant.
Studio Cast (1950) • Decca A-714 10-20   50
   78 rpm album.
Studio Cast (1950) • Decca (M) DL-5207 20-25   50
   10-inch LP.
    Cast: Bing Crosby, Danny Kaye, E. Knight, Ella Fitzgerald.
Studio Cast (1952) • Remington (M) R-149-54................................... 10-15   52
   10-inch LP. Full title: *South Pacific (Highlights)*.
    Cast: Ivor Stanley Orchestra, Walter Soul Singers.
Studiotrack (1952) • Remington (M) R-199-115 10-15   52
   Also has music from *Twilight Concert No. 2*.
    Cast: Austrian Symphony Orchestra.
Studio Cast (1954) • RCA Victor (M) LK-1008...................................... 8-12   54
    Conductor: Al Goodman. **Cast:** Sandra Deel, Jimmy Carroll, Dickenson Eastham, Thelma Carpenter, Al Goodman and His Orchestra with the Guild Choristers.

Studio Cast (1957) • Design (S) DLP 209 8-12   57
Cast: Mal Hasset and His Farnsworth Orchestra, Richard Torigi, Dolores Martin, Susan Shauto, William Reynolds, Paula Wayne.

Studio Cast (1958) • RCA Camden (M) CAL-421 8-12   58

Studio Cast (1958) • RCA Camden (S) CAS-494 10-12   59
Conductor: Hill Bowen. **Cast:** Hill Bowen and His Orchestra and Chorus, Marie Benson, Bryan Johnson, Fred Lucas, Laurie Cornell, Denis Martin.

Studio Cast • Diplomat (M) 2212 8-10

Studio Cast • Diplomat (S) FM-77 10-12
Cast: Al Goodman and His Orchestra, Richard Torigi, Dolores Martin, Susan Shauto, William Reynolds, Paula Wayne.

Studio Cast • Grand Prix (M) K-408 8-10
Cast: Mal Hasset and His Orchestra, Richard Torigi, Dolores Martin, Susan Shauto, William Reynolds, Paula Wayne.

Studio Cast • Mayfair (S) 96345 8-10
Conductor: Lew Raymond. **Cast:** Lew Raymond Orchestra and Chorus, Norma Zimmer, Bonnie Lou Williams, Charles Peck, Marni Nixon.

Studio Cast • Promenade (M) 2092 8-10
Cast: Al Goodman and His Orchestra, Richard Torigi, Dolores Martin, Susan Shauto, William Reynolds, Paula Wayne.

Studio Cast • Silver Seal (M) UT 115 8-10
Conductor: Lawrence Nash. **Cast:** Julie Jones, Tex Howard, Margaret Young.

Studio Cast • Spin-O-Rama (M) MK-3047 8-10

Studio Cast • Spin-O-Rama (S) S-3047 8-10
Cast: Al Goodman Orchestra. Richard Torigi, Dolores Martin, Susan Shauto, William Reynolds, Paula Wayne.

Studio Cast • Tops (M) L1634 10-12
Conductor: Lew Raymond. **Cast:** Lew Raymond Orchestra & Chorus, Marni Mixon, Norma Zimmer, Bonnie Lou Williams, Charles Peck.

Studiotrack (1957) • Design (M) DLP 59 8-10   57
Also has music from *The Music Man*.
Cast: Cyril Holloway and the Royal Farnsworth Orchestra.

Studiotrack (1957) • Harmony (M) HL-7092 8-10   57
Cast: Dino Martinelli Orchestra.

Soundtrack (1958) • RCA Victor (EP) EPA-4211 10-15   58

Soundtrack (1958) • RCA Victor (EP) EOC-1032 10-15   58
Three discs.

Soundtrack (1958) • RCA Victor (M) LOCD-2000 20-25   58
Gatefold cover. "Deluxe Edition," includes color photos.

Soundtrack (1958) • RCA Victor (M) LOC-1032 8-12   58

Soundtrack (1958) • RCA Victor (S) LSO-1032 10-12   58
Front covers do not have "Academy Award Winner for Achievement in Sound" on right side. Black label.

Soundtrack (1958) • RCA Victor (M) LOC-1032 8-10   Re

Soundtrack (1958) • RCA Victor (S) LSO-1032 8-12   Re
Covers have blue top with "Academy Award Winner for Achievement in Sound" on right side. Orange label.

Soundtrack (1958) • RCA Victor (S) AYL1-3681 5-8   81
Composer: Richard Rodgers, Oscar Hammerstein II. **Conductor:** Alfred Newman. **Cast:** Giorgio Tozzi (performs vocals for Rossano Brazzi in the film), Mitzi Gaynor, Bill Lee (performs vocals for John Kerr), Ray Walston, Muriel Smith (performs vocals for Juanita Hall), Ken Darby Singers.

Studiotrack (1958) • Halo (M) 50123 8-10   58
Cast: National Concert Dance Orchestra, Broadway Symphonic Jazz Orchestra.

Studiotrack (1958) • RCA Victor (M) LPM-1731 8-10   58

Studiotrack (1958) • RCA Victor (S) LSP-1731 8-12   58
Full title: *George Feyer Takes You to Rodgers and Hammerstein's South Pacific and Oklahoma!*
Cast: George Feyer.

Studiotrack (1959) • Perfect (M) PL-12028 8-10   59
Studiotrack (1959) • Perfect (S) PS-14028.. 8-12   59
Cast: Boris Mersson, Somerset Orchestra.

Studiotrack (1959) • Somerset (M) SSP-77.. 8-10   59
Studiotrack (1959) • Somerset/Stereo Fidelity (S) SF-77 8-10   59
Also has music from *The Music Man*.
Cast: Hollywood Soundstage Chorus with Theatre Orchestra.

Studiotrack (1959) • National Academy Record Club (M) ES-5............ 10-15   59
From *Ed Sullivan Presents Songs and Music of...* series.
Cast: Ed Sullivan All Star Cast.

Studiotrack • Royale (M) LP 15 8-10   50s
10-inch LP.
Cast: Paul Paine and His Society Orchestra, The Twins.

Studiotrack • Royale (M) 1238 8-10   50s
Also has music from *Carousel*.
Cast: Royale Operetta Singers and Orchestra,

Studiotrack (1960) • Craftsmen (M) C-8021 8-10   60
Cast: Gordon Fleming Orchestra.

Studiotrack (1960) • Hudson (M) 212.. 8-10   60
Complete musical score.
Cast: Elly Ellason and His Orchestra.

Studiotrack • Bravo (M) K-103.. 8-10
Studiotrack • Bravo (S) KS-103.. 8-10
One side has music from *Oklahoma!*
Conductor: John Senati. **Cast:** Bravo Pops Symphony Orchestra.

Studiotrack • Capitol (M) T-992... 8-10
Studiotrack • Capitol (S) ST-992 8-10
Cast: Fred Waring and His Orchestra.

Studiotrack • Coronet (M) CX-41... 8-10
Studiotrack • Coronet (S) CXS-41.. 8-10
Cast: Coronet Studio Orchestra and Chorus, Margaret Young, William Carson, Jeanie Gray, Cy Milano, Maureen Kennedy, Playboys.

Studiotrack • Crown (S) CST-111 8-10
Red vinyl.
Conductor: Hans Hagen.

Studiotrack • Hollywood (M) LPH-152 8-10
Cast: Maury Laws and His Orchestra.

Studiotrack • Library In Sound (M) 9907 8-10
One side has music from *Red Mill*.

Studiotrack • Masterseal (M) MS-53.. 8-10
Studiotrack • Masterseal (M) 33-1906/7 8-10
Full title: *South Pacific Highlights*. One side has *1001 Nights* by Johann Strauss.
Conductor: Gerhard Becker. **Cast:** Jean Campbell, Bob Dale, Ivor Slaney and His Orchestra, Gerhard Becker and His Orchestra, Walter Saul Singers.

Studiotrack • Music Minus One (S) MMO 1035 8-10
Conductor: William Harrison. **Cast:** Music Minus One TheatreOrchestra.

Studiotrack • Palace (M) M-607 8-10
Studiotrack • Parade (M) SP 308 8-10
One side has *Songs of the Sea*.
Cast: Al Garry and His Orchestra and Chorus.

Studiotrack • Plymouth (M) P12-40 8-10
  Full title: *South Pacific (Highlights) + Dinner Music.*
    Composer: Richard Rodgers, Johann Strauss, Mendelsohn, others. **Cast:** Vienna Tonkunstler
    Symphony Orchestra, Plymouth Players.
Studiotrack • Richmond (M) B-20046 8-10
Studiotrack • Richmond (S) S-30046 8-10
    Conductor: Frank Chacksfield. **Cast:** Frank Chacksfield and His Orchestra.
Studiotrack • Stage Door (M) NA11 8-10
  National Academy Record Club issue.
Studiotrack • Wing (S) SRW-12502 10-15   59
    Conductor: Marc La Salle. **Cast:** Marc La Salle and his Orchestra.
Studio Cast (1964) • Reprise (M) F-2018 10-12   64
Studio Cast (1964) • Reprise (S) FS-2018 15-20   64
  Gatefold cover.
Studio Cast (1964) • Reprise (S) FS-2018 12-15   64
  Standard cover.
    Composer: Richard Rodgers, Oscar Hammerstein II. **Conductor:** Morris Stoloff, Ken Lane. **Cast:**
    Frank Sinatra, Jo Stafford, McGuire Sisters, Bing Crosby, Keely Smith, Dinah Shore, Debbie
    Reynolds, Rosemary Clooney, Sammy Davis Jr., Hi-Los.
Original Revival Cast (1967) • Columbia (M) OL-6700 10-12   67
Original Revival Cast (1967) • Columbia (S) OS-3100 15-20   67
    Composer: Richard Rodgers, Oscar Hammerstein II. **Conductor:** Jonathon Anderson. **Cast:**
    Florence Henderson, Giorgio Tozzi, Justin McDonough, Eleanor Calbes, Irene Byatt, David Doyle.
Studio Cast (1986) • CBS (S) SM-42205 8-10   86
  Gatefold cover. Includes booklet.
    Conductor: Jonathon Anderson. **Cast:** Kiri Te Kanawa, Jose Carreras, Sarah Vaughan, Mandy
    Patinkin, Ambrosia Singers, London Symphony Orchestra.
    Also see GIGI
    Also see MUSIC MAN
    Also see OKLAHOMA!
    Also see REPRISE REPERTORY THEATRE

SOUTH SEAS ADVENTURE
Soundtrack (1958) • Audio Fidelity (M) 1899 20-25   59
Soundtrack (1958) • Audio Fidelity (S) AFSD-5899 35-45   59
  Gatefold cover.
Soundtrack (1958) • Audio Fidelity (M) AFLP 1899 15-18   Re
Soundtrack (1958) • Audio Fidelity (S) AFSD-5899 18-20   Re
  Standard cover.
Soundtrack (1958) • Citadel (S) CT-7014 15-20   81
  Also has music from *Journey into Fear.*
    Composer: Alex North. **Conductor:** Alex North. **Cast:** Cinerama Symphony Orchestra.

SOUTHERN STAR
Soundtrack (1969) • Colgems (S) COSO-5009 50-60   69
    Composer: Georges Garvarentz. **Conductor:** Georges Garvarentz. **Cast:** Matt Monro.

SPACE AGE: AGE OF RELIABILITY
TV Cast • Raybestos-Manhattan (M) No Number Used 15-20
  Gatefold cover. Includes program/booklet with historic broadcasts from space flights.
    Cast: Charles Daly (narrator.)

SPACE: 1999
TV Soundtrack (1975) • RCA Victor (S) ABL-1-1422 15-20   75
    Composer: Barry Gray. **Conductor:** Barry Gray. **Cast:** Martin Landau, Barbarn Bain.

SPACE ORGAN
Studiotrack • Crystal Clear (S) CCS 6003 8-10
  Music from *Star Wars, Superman, CE3K* and *Battlestar Galactica.*
    Composer: John Williams, Stu Philips. **Cast:** Jonas Nordwall.

SPACEBALLS
Soundtrack (1987) • Atlantic (S) 81770-1 10-15   87
    Composer: John Morris. **Conductor:** John Morris. **Cast:** Van Halen, Pointer Sisters, Spinners, Ladyfire, Berlin, Kim Charles, Jeffrey Osborne.

SPACECAMP
Soundtrack (1986) • RCA Victor (S) ABL1-5856 30-35   86
    Composer: John Williams.

SPANISH AFFAIR
Soundtrack (1958) • Dot (M) DLP-3078 65-85   58
    Composer: Daniele Amfitheatrof. **Conductor:** Daniele Amfitheatrof.

SPARKLE
Soundtrack (1976) • Atlantic (S) 18176 15-20   76
    Cast: Irene Cara, Curtis Mayfield, Lonette McKee.

SPARKLES
Original L.A. Cast (1976) • WEB Records (S) OC-105 10-15   81
    Composer: Jim Murdock, Michael Lewis. **Cast:** Aretha Franklin, Robert Kimbrough, Benjamin Lamb, Janell Kergner.

SPARTACUS
Soundtrack (1960) • Decca (M) DL-9092 25-30   60
   Pink label. Promotional issue only.
Soundtrack (1960) • Decca (M) DL-9092 10-15   60
Soundtrack (1960) • Decca (S) DL-79092 15-20   60
   Gatefold covers. Includes six-page booklet and poster. Maroon or black labels.
Soundtrack (1960) • Decca (M) DL-9092 8-12   60
Soundtrack (1960) • Decca (S) DL-79092 12-15   60
   Rainbow (or multi-color) labels.
Soundtrack (1960) • MCA (S) 2068 8-10   72
Soundtrack (1960) • MCA (S) 1534 5-8   80s
    Composer: Alex North. **Conductor:** Alex North.

SPECTACULAR WORLD OF CLASSIC FILM SCORES
Studiotrack • RCA Victor (S) ARL 1-2792 30-40   78
   Has "20 Highlights of the Best-Selling RCA Classic Film Score Series." Includes: *Captain Blood, Now Voyager, Gone with the Wind, Elizabeth & Essex, The Caine Mutiny, Citizen Kane, Knights of the Round Table, The Guns of Navarone* and *Objective Burma!* Also has five previously unreleased Gerhardt selections: *Julius Caesar, Peyton Place, The Thing (From Another World), King of the Khyber Rifles* and *Salome.*
    Composer: Jimmy McHugh, Franz Waxman, Alfred Newman, Max Steiner, John Williams, Erich W. Korngold, Bernard Herrmann, Miklos Rozsa, Dimitri Tiomkin, Daniele Amfitheatrof. **Conductor:** Charles Gerhardt.

SPEED ZONE
Soundtrack (1989) • Grudge (S) 4506-1-F9 8-10   89
    Cast: Stevie Wonder, Richie Havens, Billy Burnette, David Wheatley, Splash, Ross Vanelli, Felix Cavaliere, Charlie Karp, Omar and Howlers, Will to Power.

SPEEDWAY
Soundtrack (1968) • RCA Victor (M) LPM-3989 1,000-1,500   68
   Includes an 8" x 10" color photo, which represents about $10 to $20 of the value. Note: this price is *only* for monaural pressings.
Soundtrack (1968) • RCA Victor (S) LSP-3989 35-50   68
   Includes an 8" x 10" color photo, which represents about $10 to $20 of the value.
Soundtrack (1968) • RCA Victor (S) LSP-3989 10-25   69
   Orange or tan label. (Tan label issued in 1976.)
Soundtrack (1968) • RCA Victor (S) AFL1-3989 8-10   77
    Composer: Ben Weisman, Sid Wayne, Sid Tepper, Roy C. Bennett, others. **Cast:** Elvis Presley, Nancy Sinatra (vocals), Jordanaires (vocals).

SPELLBOUND

Studiotrack (1945) • Ara ARA-2 50-75   45
   Album of four 78 rpms. May have track information on leaflets in between each envelope.
    Composer: Miklos Rozsa. **Conductor:** Miklos Rozsa.
Studiotrack (1945) • REM (M) LP-1 125-150   50
   10-inch LP. Photo cover.
Studiotrack (1945) • REM (M) LP-1 75-100   50
   10-inch LP. Plain green cover.
    Composer: Miklos Rozsa. **Conductor:** Miklos Rozsa.
Studiotrack (1958) • Warner Bros. (M) W-1213 20-25   58
Studiotrack (1958) • Warner Bros. (S) WS-1213................................ 20-30   58
Studiotrack (1958) • Stanyan (Q) SRQ-4021 8-10   Re
    Composer: Miklos Rozsa. **Conductor:** Ray Heindorf.
Studiotrack • Columbia (EP) B-1718 10-15   50s
   Also has "theme and incidental music from Limelight."
    Composer: Miklos Rozsa, Charlie Chaplin. **Cast:** Wally Stott and His Orchestra.
Studiotrack • RCA Victor (S) ARL1-0911 10-12   75
Studiotrack • RCA Victor (Q) ARD1-0911 10-12   75
   Full title: *Spellbound: The Classic Film Scores of Miklos Rozsa.* Music from *Double
   Indemnity, Spellbound, The Lost Weekend, Knights of the Round Table, The Four
   Feathers, The Jungle Book, Ivanhoe, The Thief of Bagdad* and *The Red House.*
    Composer: Miklos Rosza. **Conductor:** Charles Gerhardt.
Studiotrack • Varese Sarabande (M) 704 260 8-12
   Also has overtures from *Because of Him* and *The World, The Flesh & The Devil.*
    Composer: Miklos Rozsa. **Conductor:** Miklos Rozsa, Elmer Bernstein. **Cast:** Utah Symphony
    Orchestra.
    Also see LUST FOR LIFE
    Also see PARADINE CASE
    Also see QUO VADIS
    Also see RED HOUSE
    Also see SUN ALSO RISES

SPINOUT

Studiotrack (1966) • RCA Victor (M) LPM-3702 150-250   66
   Includes a 12" x 12" color photo, which represents about $75 to $100 of the value.
Studiotrack (1966) • RCA Victor (S) LSP-3702 150-250   66
   Includes a 12" x 12" color photo, which represents about $75 to $100 of the value.
Studiotrack (1966) • RCA Victor (S) AFL1-2560................................ 8-10   78
    Composer: Fred Wise, Randy Starr, Sid Tepper, Roy C. Bennett, Bill Giant, Bernie Baum,
    Florence Kaye, Ben Weisman, Doc Pomus, Mort Shuman, Sid Wayne, others. **Cast:** Elvis
    Presley, Scotty Moore (guitar), D.J. Fontana (drums), Jordanaires and Imperials Quartet (vocals).

SPIRIT OF ST. LOUIS

Soundtrack (1957) • RCA Victor (M) LPM-1472 35-45   57
Soundtrack (1957) • Entr'acte (SE) ERS-6507................................ 8-12   77
    Composer: Franz Waxman. **Conductor:** Franz Waxman.

SPLASH

Soundtrack (1984) • Cherry Lane (S) 00301 15-25   84
   Includes 17" x 22" poster of film's star Daryl Hannah.
    Composer: Lee Holdridge. **Conductor:** Lee Holdridge. **Cast:** Royal Philharmonic Orchestra.
Soundtrack (1980s) • Varese Sarabande (S) 704 290 8-12   80s
   Full title: *Music from Splash, Beastmaster, etc.*

SPOOK WHO SAT BY THE DOOR

Soundtrack (1973) • Columbia (S) KC-32944...................................... 15-25   74
    Cast: Herbie Hancock.

SPOON RIVER ANTHOLOGY
Original Cast (1963) • Columbia (M) OL-6010... 8-10   63
Original Cast (1963) • Columbia (S) OS-2410.. 8-12   Re
  Theatrical presentation of Edgar Lee Masters' work, originally produced by the U.C.L.A.
  University Extension Theatre Group.
  Composer: Naomi C.Hirshhorn, Charles Aidman. **Cast:** Betty Garrett, Robert Elston, Joyce Van
  Patten, Naomi C. Hirshhorn, Hal Lynch. (With dialogue.)
Studio Cast (1970) • Ranwood (S) R-5000.. 5-10   70
  Conductor: Bill Justis. **Cast:** Linda Wood, Dick Whittinghill.

SPORTING CLUB
Soundtrack (1971) • Buddah (SP) BDS-95002...................................... 15-20   71
  White label. Promotional issue only.
Soundtrack (1971) • Buddah (SP) BDS-75002...................................... 15-20   71
  Composer: Michael Small. **Conductor:** Michael Small. **Cast:** Michael Small, Jerry Lee Lewis,
  Gene Pistilli.

SPOTLIGHT ON BROADWAY
Studiotrack (1977) • Time-Life (S) STLF-0003 15-20   77
  Boxed, three-disc set.
  Conductor: Arthur Fiedler. **Cast:** Boston Pops.

SPOTLIGHT ON WILD BILL HICKOCK
Radio Cast • Tiara (M) TMT-7516 8-10
Radio Cast • Tiara (SE) TST-7516.. 8-10
  Cast: Guy Madison, Andy Devine.

SPRING BREAK
Soundtrack (1983) • Warner Bros. (S) 1-23826 8-10   83
  Cast: Cheap Trick, Gerald McMahon, Jack Mack and the Heart Attack, Dreamers, Hot Date,
  NRBQ, Big Spender.

SPRING IS HERE: see MISTER IMPERIUM

SPRING PARADE: see HELLO FRISCO, HELLO

SPRINGTIME FOR HITLER: see PRODUCERS

SPRINGTIME IN THE ROCKIES
Radio Cast (1944) • Pelican (M) 128... 8-15
  Broadcast May 22, 1944.
  Cast: Betty Grable, Carmen Miranda, Dick Powell.

SPIES LIKE US
Soundtrack (1985) • Varese Sarabande (S) STV 81270 10-12   85
  Composer: Elmer Bernstein. **Conductor:** Elmer Bernstein. **Cast:** Chevy Chase, Dan Aykroyd.

SPY WHO CAME IN FROM THE COLD
Soundtrack (1965) • RCA Victor (M) LOC-1118 15-20   65
Soundtrack (1965) • RCA Victor (S) LSO-1118.................................... 30-35   65
  Composer: Sol Kaplan. **Conductor:** Sol Kaplan.

SPY WHO LOVED ME
Soundtrack (1977) • United Artists (S) UA-LA774-H 8-10   77
Soundtrack (1977) • Liberty (S) LO-50774 8-10   Re
  Composer: Marvin Hamlisch. **Conductor:** Marvin Hamlisch. **Cast:** Carly Simon, Marvin Hamlisch,
  Gibson Brothers.
Studiotrack (1977) • Springboard (S) SPB-4079 8-10   77
  Full title: *Music from the Spy Who Loved Me & Other Great James Bond Thrillers.*
  Cast: Film Festival Orchestra.

SPY WITH A COLD NOSE
Soundtrack (1966) • Columbia (M) OL-6670 12-15   66
Soundtrack (1966) • Columbia (S) OS-3070 25-30   66
    Composer: Riz Ortolani. **Conductor:** Riz Ortolani.

SQUARE ROOT OF ZERO
Soundtrack (1966) • Mainstream (M) 56070.. 10-12   66
Soundtrack (1966) • Mainstream (S) S-6070.. 12-15   66
    Composer: Elliot Kaplan. **Conductor:** Elliot Kaplan.

STACCATO
TV Soundtrack (1959) • Capitol (EP) EAP 3-1287 15-20   59
TV Soundtrack (1959) • Capitol (M) T-1287 25-30   59
TV Soundtrack (1959) • Capitol (S) ST-1287 40-45   59
  Music from the TV series *Johnny Staccato*.
    Composer: Elmer Bernstein. **Conductor:** Elmer Bernstein.

STAGE DOOR CANTEEN: see HOLLYWOOD CANTEEN

STAGECOACH (1939)
Soundtrack (1939) • Mark 56 (M) 783 10-20   77
  Two discs. Dialogue and music.
    Composer: Richard Hageman. **Cast:** John Wayne, Claire Trevor, Donald Meek, Thomas Mitchell.
    (With dialogue).

STAGECOACH (1966)
Soundtrack (1966) • Mainstream (M) 56077.. 18-20   66
Soundtrack (1966) • Mainstream (S) S-6077.. 25-30   66
Soundtrack (1966) • Mainstream (S) T-90802..................................... 15-18   60s
  Capitol Record Club issue.
    Composer: Jerry Goldsmith, Pickriss and Vance, Ruth Batchelor. **Conductor:** Alexander
    Courage. **Cast:** Bill Brown Singers, others.

STAGES
Original Cast (1978) • Varese Sarabande (S) VC-81083 10-15   78
    Composer: Bruce Kimmell. **Conductor:** Michael Goodrow. **Cast:** Bruce Kimmell, Sammy
    Williams, Randi Kallan, Linden Waddell.

STAKEOUT
Soundtrack (1958) • RCA Victor (EP) EPA-4199 90-110   58
    Composer: Irwin Schwartz, Irvin Kershner, Andrew J. Fenady. **Cast:** Hollywood Chamber Jazz
    Group.

STAN FREBERG SHOWS
Original Radio Cast • Capitol (M) WBO-1035...................................... 40-60   58
  Two discs. Full title: *The Best of the Stan Freberg Shows*.
Original Radio Cast • Capitol (M) SM-11824 8-12   Re
  Single disc. Abridged version of WBO-1035. Full title: *The Best of the Stan Freberg Shows,
  Volume 1*.
    Composer: Stan Freberg, Ken Sullet. **Conductor:** Billy May. **Cast:** Stan Freberg, Paul Freeds
    (narration), Jesse White, Jud Conlon Singers, Peter Leeds, Byron Kane, Colleen Collins, Helen
    Kleeb.
Original Radio Cast • Capitol (M) T-1694 30-50   62
  Actual title: *Face the Funnies*.
    Composer: Stan Freberg, Ken Sullet. **Conductor:** Billy May. **Cast:** Stan Freberg, Paul Frees
    (narration), Jesse White, The Jud Conlon Singers, Peter Leeds, Byron Kane, Colleen Collins,
    Helen Kleeb.
Original Radio Cast • Capitol (M) T-1242 30-50   59
  Full title: *Stan Freberg with the Original Cast*.
    Composer: Stan Freberg, Ken Sullet. **Conductor:** Billy May. **Cast:** Stan Freberg, Paul Frees
    (narration), Jesse White, Jud Conlon Singers, Peter Leeds, Byron Kane, Colleen Collins, Helen
    Kleeb.

Studio Cast (1961) • Capitol (M) W-1573 25-35   61
Studio Cast (1961) • Capitol (S) SW-1573 35-45   61
Full title: *Stan Freberg Presents the United States of America Vol. 1: The Early Years.* A
musical satire revue made especially for records.
Composer: Stan Freberg, Ken Sullet. **Conductor:** Billy May. **Cast:** Stan Freberg, Paul Frees
(narration), Jesse White, Jud Conlon Singers, Peter Leeds, Byron Kane, Colleen Collins, Helen
Kleeb.

STAND AND DELIVER
Soundtrack (1988) • Varese Sarabande (S) 704 590 10-15   88
Conductor: Craig Safan.

STAND BY ME
Soundtrack (1986) • Atlantic (S) 81677-1 8-10   86
Cast: Del Vikings, Buddy Holly, Silhouettes, Jerry Lee Lewis, Shirley and Lee, Chordettes,
Coasters, Bobbettes.

STAR!
Soundtrack (1968) • 20th Century-Fox (S) DTCS-5102 8-25   68
Gatefold cover. Includes eight-page booklet. Film biography of Gertrude Lawrence.
Conductor: Lennie Hayton. **Cast:** Julie Andrews, Daniel Massey, Bruce Forsyth, Beryl Reid,
Garrett Lewis, Daffodils.

STAR IS BORN (1937)
Studiotrack (1937) • United Artists (S) UA-LA375-G 12-15   75
Composer: Max Steiner. **Conductor:** LeRoy Holmes.
Original Radio Cast (1942) • Radiola (M) 1155 10-15
Broadcast December 28, 1942.
Cast: Judy Garland, Walter Pidgeon.

STAR IS BORN (1954)
Soundtrack (1954) • Columbia (EP) BA-1201 15-20   54
Soundtrack (1954) • Columbia (M) CL 6299 20-40   54
10-inch LP. Does not have the *Born in a Trunk* sequence, found on 12-inch LPs.
Soundtrack (1954) • Columbia (M) BL-1201 20-25   54
Boxed edition. Includes booklet.
Soundtrack (1954) • Columbia (M) CL-1101 12-18   58
Soundtrack (1954) • Columbia (SE) CS-8740 10-15   63
Soundtrack (1954) • Harmony (SE) HS-11366 10-12   69
Soundtrack (1954) • Columbia Special Products (SE) ACS-8740e 8-10   Re
Soundtrack (1954) • Columbia (SE) LE-10011 5-8   80
Composer: Harold Arlen, Leonard Gershe, Ira Gershwin. **Conductor:** Ray Heindorf. **Cast:** Judy
Garland.

STAR IS BORN (1976)
Soundtrack (1976) • Columbia (S) JS-34403 8-10   76
Gatefold cover.
Composer: Paul Williams, Rupert Holmes. **Cast:** Barbra Streisand, Kris Kristofferson.

STAR MAKER
Studiotrack (1951) • Decca (M) DL-6013 50-60   51
10-inch LP. Also has music from *Doctor Rhythm.*
Composer: Gus Edwards, James V. Monaco, Johnny Burke, others. **Conductor:** John Scott Trotter.
Cast: Bing Crosby, Connee Boswell, Music Maids.
Also see BING'S HOLLYWOOD

STAR SPANGLED RHYTHM
Soundtrack (1943) • Curtain Calls (S) CC 100/20 8-12   80s

Soundtrack (1943) • Sandy Hook (S) SH-2045 8-10
  Composer: Johnny Mercer, Harold Arlen. **Cast:** Bing Crosby, Betty Hutton, Victor Moore, Bob
  Hope, Eddie Bracken, Johnny Johnston, Dick Powell, Vera Zorina, Eddie "Rochester" Anderson,
  Mary Martin, Paulette Goddard, Martha Mears (performs vocals for Veronica Lake in the film),
  Dorothy Lamour, Fred MacMurray.

STAR STRUCK
Soundtrack (1983) • A&M (S) SP-4938 8-10   83
  Cast: Jo Kennedy, Turnaround, Swinger, Ross O'Donovan, John O'May, Mental As Regular.

STAR TREK
TV Soundtrack (1985) • GNP/Crescendo (S) 8006 8-10   85
  Two episodes: *The Cage* and *Where No Man Has Gone Before*.

TV Soundtrack • GNP/Crescendo (S) GNPS-8010 8-10   88
  Sound effects from the original TV soundtrack.

TV Soundtrack (1965) • Polygram (S) PDS 1-6423 8-10   85
  Two episodes: *The Cage* and *Where No Man Has Gone Before*.
  Composer: Alex Courage. **Conductor:** Alex Courage. **Cast:** Alexander Courage Orchestra.

TV Soundtrack [Vol. 1] • Varese Sarabande (S) 704 270 8-12   80s
  Composer: Fred Steiner.

TV Soundtrack [Vol. 2] • Varese Sarabande (S) 704 300 8-12   80s
  Music from *The Empath* episode.
  Composer: George Duning.

Studiotrack (1976) • Columbia (S) PC-34279 30-60   76
  Fulll title: *Inside Star Trek*. Gene Roddenberry interviews Isaac Asimov, William Shatner,
  DeForest Kelley and Mark Lenard. Includes *Star Trek Theme*.

Studiotrack • Synthetic Plastics (S) 6001 8-10
  Also has themes from other films.
  Cast: New Sound Orchestra.

STAR TREK – THE MOTION PICTURE
Soundtrack (1979) • Columbia (S) JS-36334 15-20   79
  Includes bonus photo.
  Composer: Jerry Goldsmith. **Conductor:** Jerry Goldsmith.

STAR TREK II: THE WRATH OF KHAN
Soundtrack (1982) • Atlantic (S) SD-19363 10-15   82
  Composer: James Horner. **Conductor:** James Horner.

STAR TREK III: THE SEARCH FOR SPOCK
Soundtrack (1984) • Capitol (S) ST-12360 10-15   84
  Gatefold cover. Includes single-sided bonus EP, with theme song.
  Composer: James Horner. **Conductor:** James Horner.

STAR TREK IV: THE VOYAGE HOME
Soundtrack (1986) • MCA (S) L-33-17251 15-20   87
  12-inch single. Has *Market Street* and *Ballad of the Whale*, by the Yellowjackets.
  Promotional issue only.

Soundtrack (1986) • MCA (S) 5972 8-12   87

Soundtrack (1986) • MCA (S) 6195 8-10   87
  Composer: Leonard Rosenman, Russell Ferrante, Jimmy Haslip. **Conductor:** Leonard
  Rosenman. **Cast:** Yellowjackets.

STAR TREK V: THE FINAL FRONTIER
Soundtrack (1989) • Epic (S) E-45267 10-15   89
  Composer: Jerry Goldsmith. **Conductor:** Jerry Goldsmith. **Cast:** Hiroshima.

STAR TREK: THE NEXT GENERATION, VOL. 1
TV Soundtrack (1988) • GNP/Crescendo (S) 8012 8-10   88
  From *Encounter at Farpoint* episode.
  Composer: Dennis McCarthy, Alexander Courage, Jerry Goldsmith. **Conductor:** Dennis
  McCarthy.

STAR TREK THEMES
Studiotrack • Wonderland (S) WLP-301 10-12

STAR WARS
Soundtrack (1977) • 20th Century-Fox (S) 2T-541 8-12   77
  Two discs. Gatefold cover. Includes poster and flyer.
Soundtrack (1977) • 20th Century-Fox (S) 813588 5-8   Re
  Composer: John Williams. **Conductor:** John Williams. **Cast:** London Symphony Orchestra.
Soundtrack (1977) • 20th Century-Fox (S) T-550 10-12   77
  Gatefold cover with attached 16-page booklet. Full title: The Story of Star Wars.
  Conductor: John Williams. **Cast:** London Symphony Orchestra, Roscoe Lee Browne (narrator).
Soundtrack (1977) • 20th Century-Fox (S) PR-103 10-15   79
  Fulll title: The Story of Star Wars. Picture disc. Has "actual dialogue, sound effects & music
  from the film."
Soundtrack (1977) • RSO (S) 1-3093.. 8-12   80
  Conductor: John Williams. **Cast:** Roscoe Lee Browne (narration), Mark Hamill, Sir Alec
  Guinness, Carrie Fisher. (With dialogue.)
Soundtrack (1977) • Buena Vista (S) 62101 10-20   83
  Includes 16-page booklet. Music and dialogue.
  Conductor: John Williams. **Cast:** London Symphony Orchestra.
Studiotrack (1977) • Musicor (S) MUS-8801 8-10   77
  Composer: John Williams. **Cast:** Electric Moog Orchestra.
Studiotrack (1977) • Gold Award/Damil (S) SGA-1000.......................... 8-10   77
  One side has music from *A Stereo Space Odyssey.*
  Composer: John Williams. **Conductor:** Colin Frechter. **Cast:** London Philharmonic Orchestra.
  STEREO SPACE ODYSSEY: **Composer:** W. Holcombe. **Conductor:** Douglas Gamley. **Cast:**
  London Philharmonic Orchestra.
Studiotrack • Millennium (S) 8001 8-10
  Composer: Meco. **Cast:** Meco.
  Also see EMPIRE STRIKES BACK

STAR WARS / CLOSE ENCOUNTERS OF THE THIRD KIND
Soundtrack • RCA Victor (S) ARL1-2698 15-20   78
  Full title: *John Williams' Classic Film Scores: Close Encounters of the Third Kind / Star*
  Wars.
Studiotrack (1977) • London (S) ZM 1001 8-10   78
  One suite devoted to each score.
  Composer: John Williams. **Conductor:** John Williams, Zubin Mehta (arranger).
Studiotrack (1978) • RCA Victor (S) AGL-3650 8-10   78
Studiotrack (1979) • MFSL (S) 008 25-50   79
  Cast: Los Angeles Philharmonic Orchestra.

STAR WARS / RETURN OF THE JEDI
Soundtrack (1983) • RSO (S) 422-811767-1... 8-10   83
  Composer: John Williams. **Conductor:** John Williams. **Cast:** London Symphony Orchestra.
Studiotrack (1983) • RCA Victor (S) CRC1-4748 8-12   83
  Full title: *John Williams' Classic Film Scores: Star Wars / Return of the Jedi.*
  Conductor: Charles Gerhardt. **Cast:** National Philharmonic Orchestra.

STAR WARS TRILOGY
Soundtrack (1983) • Varese Sarabande (S) 704.210 12-18   83
Soundtrack (1983) • That's Entertainment (S) TER-1067....................... 8-10   80s
  UK release.
  Composer: John Williams. **Conductor:** Varujan Kojian. **Cast:** Utah Symphony Orchestra.

STARDUST

Soundtrack (1975) • Arista (S) AL-5000 10-12   75
Two discs. Film sequel to *That'll Be the Day*, featuring "40 Original Hit Records."
Cast: Neil Sedaka, Maxine Brown, Bobby Vee, Zombies, Bobby Darin, Billy J. Kramer and the Dakotas, Crystals, Beach Boys, Drifters, Chiffons, Little Eva, Fortunes, Carole King, Gerry and the Pacemakers, Jan & Dean, Cat Stevens, Barbara Lewis, Shirelles, Box Tops, Mamas and the Papas, Lovin' Spoonful, Monkees, Animals, Hollies, Bee Gees, Righteous Brothers, Barry McGuire, Jefferson Airplane, Aretha Franklin.

STARLIFT

Soundtrack (1951) • Titania (M) 510 8-10
Also has music from *Call Me Mister*.
Composer: George Gershwin, Ira Gershwin, Jule Styne, Sammy Cahn, Cole Porter, others. **Conductor:** Ray Heindorf. **Cast:** Doris Day, Gordon MacRae, Gene Nelson, Virginia Mayo, James Cagney, Patrice Wymore, Janis Paige. CALL ME MISTER: **Composer:** Harold Rome, Mack Gordon, Sammy Fain, Frances Ash. **Conductor:** Alfred Newman. **Cast:** Betty Grable, Dan Dailey, Danny Thomas.

STARLIGHT EXPRESS

Studio Cast (1987) • MCA (S) 5972 10-15   87
Full title: *Songs and Music from Starlight Express*.
Composer: Andrew Lloyd Webber. **Cast:** Josie Aiello, Peter Hewlett, Earl Jordan, Richie Havens, Marc Cohn, Harold Faltermeyer, El Debarge.

STARMAN

Soundtrack (1984) • Varese Sarabande (S) STV 81233 10-15   84
Soundtrack (1984) • That's Entertainment (S) TER-1097...................... 8-10   80s
UK release.
Composer: Jack Nitzsche.

STARRING FRED ASTAIRE

Soundtrack • Columbia (S) SG-32472... 10-15   73
Two discs. Music from *Flying Down to Rio, Top Hat, Follow the Fleet* and others.
Composer: George Gershwin, Irving Berlin. **Cast:** Fred Astaire.

STARS AND STRIPES FOREVER

Soundtrack (1952) • MGM 176 (30694/95/96/97)............................... 12-15   52
Boxed set of four 78 rpms.
Soundtrack (1952) • MGM (EP) X-176 10-15   52
Two discs.
Soundtrack (1952) • MGM (M) E-176.. 20-25   52
10-inch LP.
Soundtrack (1952) • MGM (M) E-3508.. 15-20   57
Also has four selections by the *American Military Band*.
Composer: John Philip Sousa, others. **Conductor:** Alfred Newman. **Cast:** American Military Band.

STARS IN YOUR EYES

Studio Cast • JJC (M) ST-3004 8-12
Composer: Arthur Schwartz, Dorothy Fields. **Cast:** Ethel Merman.
Also see RED HOT AND BLUE

STARS OF THE SILVER SCREEN, 1929-1930

Soundtrack • RCA Victor (M) LPV 538 10-15   67
Original recordings from Hollywood Talkies.
Conductor: Ted Shapiro, Roy Shields, Nathaniel Shilkret, Leonard Joy, Victor Baravalli. **Cast:** John Boles, Fanny Brice, Maurice Chevalier, Bebe Daniels, Dolores Del Rio, Duncan Sisters, George Jessel, Helen Kane, Charles King, Dennis King, Jeanette MacDonald, Everett Marshall, Helen Morgan, Gloria Swanson, Sophie Tucker, Lupe Velez.

STARTING HERE, STARTING NOW
Original Cast (1977) • RCA Victor (S) ABL1-2360................................. 8-12   77
  Composer: David Shire, Richard Maltby Jr. **Conductor:** Robert W. Preston. **Cast:** Margery Cohen, George Lee Andrews, Loni Ackerman.

STATE FAIR
Studiotrack (1945) • Decca (M) DA-412................................ 15-20   45
  78 rpm album.
  Composer: Richard Rodgers, Oscar Hammerstein II. **Conductor:** Victor Young. **Cast:** Dick Haymes.
Soundtrack • Classic International Filmusicals (M) CIF-3009................. 8-12
  Recorded from the film itself, including dialogue and effects. Also has music from *Centennial Summer.*
  Composer: Richard Rodgers, Oscar Hammerstein II. CENTENNIAL SUMMER: **Composer:** Jerome Kern, Leo Robin, E.Y. Harburg. **Conductor:** Charles Henderson. **Cast:** Jeanne Crain (dialogue), Louanne Hogan (performs Jeanne Crain's vocals in the film), Cornel Wilde, Linda Darnell, William Eythe, Walter Brennan, Kathleen Howard, Larry Stevens, Avon Long.
Soundtrack (1962) • Dot (M) DLP-9011 12-15   62
Soundtrack (1962) • Dot (S) DLP-29011 15-18   62
  Composer: Richard Rodgers, Oscar Hammerstein II. **Conductor:** Alfred Newman. **Cast:** Pat Boone, Ann-Margret, Bobby Darin, Alice Faye, Anita Gordon (performed Pamela Tiffin's vocals in the film), Bob Smart, Tom Ewell, David Street.
Studiotrack (1962) • 20th Fox (S) FOX-3057 8-12   62
Studiotrack (1962) • 20th Fox (S) SFX-3057 10-12   62
  Composer: Richard Rodgers, Oscar Hammerstein II. **Conductor:** Sonny Lester.
  Also see OKLAHOMA!
  Also see TEN NORTH FREDERICK

STATE OF SEIGE
Soundtrack (1973) • Columbia (S) S-32352 8-12   73
  Composer: Mikos Theodorakis. **Cast:** Los Calchakis.

STAVISKY
Soundtrack (1974) • RCA Victor (S) ARL1-0952 12-15   75
  Composer: Stephen Sondheim. **Conductor:** Carlo Savina.

STAYING ALIVE
Soundtrack (1983) • RSO (S) 422-813-269-1 8-10   83
  Gatefold cover. May have black shrinkwrap sticker with credits.
  Composer: Bee Gees (Robin Gibb, Barry Gibb, Maurice Gibb), others. **Cast:** Bee Gees, Tommy Faragher, Cynthia Rhodes, Frank Stallone.

STEADFAST TIN SOLDIER
Soundtrack (1987) • Windham Hill (S) WH-0702 10-15   87
  Original score with dialogue studiotrack added.
  Composer: Mark Isham. **Cast:** Mark Isham, others.

STEALING HOME
Soundtrack (1988) • Atlantic (S) 81885-1 8-10   88
  Cast: Jerry Lee Lewis, Bo Diddley, Everly Brothers, David Foster, Shirelles, Nylons, Marilyn Martin, Four Seasons.

STEEL MAGNOLIAS
Soundtrack (1989) • Polydor (S) 841582-1 12-15   89
  Composer: Georges Delerue, others. **Conductor:** Georges Delerue. **Cast:** Ry Cooder, Wayne Toups, Tommy Funkerburk.

STEEL TOWN
Original Cast • Flying Fish (S) FF 347 8-12
  Cast: San Francisco Mime Troupe.

STEELYARD BLUES
Soundtrack (1972) • Warner Bros. (S) BS-2662.................................. 12-15   72
    Composer: Nick Gravenites, Mike Bloomfield.
Soundtrack (1972) • Sound On Film #20.. 12-15   72
    Profile of Peter Boyle. Nat Hentoff interviews Boyle and co-producer, Julia Phillips. Actual
    title: *Peter Boyle into View.*
    Cast: Peter Boyle, Julia Phillips, Nat Hentoff.

STEINER TOUCH
Soundtrack • Tony Thomas (M) TT-MS 16... 50-70   81
    Music from *Jezebel, Dark Victory, My Reputation* and *Marjorie Morningstar.*
    Composer: Max Steiner. **Conductor:** Max Steiner.

STEPHEN FOSTER STORY
Original Cast (1966) • XSBV (S) 111386.. 10-20   66
    Show runs every summer in Kentucky, during which time the album is available at the
    theatre. Though its run began in 1959, it is the 1966 cast on the LP.
    Composer: Stephen Foster. **Conductor:** Willis Beckett. **Cast:** Richard Silwell, Jeanette Sallee,
    William Lathon.

STEPHEN SONDHEIM EVENING
Original Cast • RCA Victor (S) CBL2-4745.. 8-12   83
    Composer: Stephen Sondheim. **Cast:** Liz Callaway, Cris Groenendaal, Bob Gunton, George
    Hearn, Steven Jacob, Judy Kaye, Victoria Mallory, Angela Lansbury.
    Also see SONDHEIM

STEREO ACTION GOES BROADWAY
Studiotrack • RCA Victor (S) LSA-2382... 8-12
    Cast: Dick Schory.

STEREO MAGIC OF BROADWAY
Studio Cast • Columbia (S) XSV-68544/53 15-20
    Boxed, five-disc set.

STERILE CUCKOO
Soundtrack (1969) • Paramount (S) PAS-5009 8-12   69
    Composer: Fred Karlin, Dory Previn. **Conductor:** Fred Karlin. **Cast:** Sandpipers.

STEVE & EYDIE
TV Soundtrack • Stage Two (S) 711 15-20
    Two discs. Full title: *Steve & Eydie, Our Love Is Here to Stay – The Gershwin Years.* Mail
    order offer only.
    Cast: Steve Lawrence, Eydie Gorme.

STEVE ALLEN TV SHOW
TV Soundtrack (1959) • Dot (M) DLP 3587 12-25   59
    Cast: Steve Allen.

STEVE ALLEN'S FUNNY FONE CALLS
TV Soundtrack (1963) • Dot (M) DLP-3472 10-15   63
    Cast: Steve Allen, Louis Nye.
TV Soundtrack [Vol. 2] (1963) • Dot (M) DLP-3517 10-15   63
    Full title: *More Funny Fone Calls.*
    Cast: Steve Allen, Louis Nye.

STEVIE
Soundtrack (1978) • Epic (S) SE-37726... 8-10   78
    Composer: Patrick Gowers. **Conductor:** Marcus Dodds. **Cast:** John Williams (guitarist), Glenda
    Jackson (reading poems of Stevie Smith).

STILETTO
Soundtrack (1969) • Columbia (S) OS-3360 8-25   69
    Composer: Sid Ramin. **Conductor:** Sid Ramin.

STING

Soundtrack (1974) • MCA (S) 390... 8-12   74
Soundtrack (1974) • MCA (S) 2040.. 8-10   70s
Soundtrack (1974) • MCA (S) 37091... 5-8   81
Soundtrack (1974) • MCA (S) 1625... 5-8   80s
    Composer: Marvin Hamlisch, Scott Joplin. **Conductor:** Marvin Hamlisch. **Cast:** Marvin Hamlisch (piano).

STING II

Soundtrack (1983) • MCA (S) 6116.. 10-12   83
    Composer: Lalo Schifrin. **Conductor:** Lalo Schifrin. **Cast:** Linda Hopkins.

STINGIEST MAN IN TOWN

TV Soundtrack (1956) • Columbia (M) CL-950.................................. 12-18   56
TV Soundtrack (1956) • Columbia (M) P-12637 5-10   Re
    Composer: Fred Spielman. **Conductor:** Tutti Camarata. **Cast:** Vic Damone, Johnny Desmond, The Four Lads, Patrice Munsel, Basil Rathbone, Robert Weede, Betty Madigan, Martyn Green, Robert Wright.

STIR CRAZY

Soundtrack (1981) • Posse (S) 10001.. 10-12   81
    Composer: Tom Scott, Michael Masser, others. **Cast:** Kiki Dee, Gene Wilder, Randy Goodrum, Leroy Gomez, Leata Galloway, Dorian Holley. (With dialogue.)

STOLEN LIFE: see DEATH OF A SCOUNDREL

STOMPIN' FOR MILI

Soundtrack • Columbia (EP) B-1947 20-25
    Conductor: Dave Brubeck.

STONE KILLER

Soundtrack • Project 3 (S) PR 5085.. 20-25   74
    Full title: *Stone Killer / Crazy Joe / The Valachi Papers*.
    Composer: Roy Budd, Giancarlo Chiaramello, Riz Ortolani.

STONEY ISLAND

Original Cast (1978) • Glades (S) 7516.. 8-12   78
    Conductor: Gene Barge. **Cast:** Stoney Island.

STOOGE

Studiotrack (1952) • Capitol (M) H-401 60-65   53
    10-inch LP.
Studiotrack (1952) • Capitol (EP) EBF-401 50-75   53
    Boxed, two-disc set. Full title of both: *Dean Martin Sings (Songs from the Stooge)*.
Studiotrack (1952) • Capitol (EP) EAP 1-401 25-50   53
    Actual title: *Dean Martin Sings, Vol. 1*.
Studiotrack (1952) • Capitol (EP) EAP 2-401 25-50   53
    Actual title: *Dean Martin Sings, Vol. 2*. These two single-disc EPs have the same eight tracks as on both EPF-401 and H-401.
Studiotrack (1952) • Capitol (M) T-401.. 20-30   55
    Actual title: *Dean Martin Sings*. 12-inch reissue of H-401, with four studio tracks added. No mention anywhere about "Songs from the Stooge."
Studiotrack (1952) • Capitol (SE) DT-2941 10-12   68
    Actual title: *Dean Martin Favorites*. Reissue of *Dean Martin Sings*, but with one *Stooge* song (*A Girl Named Mary and a Boy Named Bill*) missing.
    Composer: Goering-Bernie-Hirsch, Johnny Green, E.Y. Harburg, McHugh-Fields-Oppenheimer, Mack Gordon, Harry Revel, Arthur Johnson, Sam Coslow, Richard Whiting, Leo Robin, Jerry Livingston, Mack David. **Conductor:** Dick Stabile (with special arrangements by Nelson Riddle and Gus Levene). **Cast:** Dean Martin.

STOP MAKING SENSE
Soundtrack (1984) • Sire (S) 1-25121 8-10   84
  Cast: Talking Heads.

STOP THE WORLD – I WANT TO GET OFF!
Original Cast (1962) • London (M) AM-58001 8-10   62
Original Cast (1962) • London (S) AMS-88001 8-10   62
Original Cast (1962) • RCA Victor (M) CPO-106 10-12   62
Original Cast (1962) • RCA Victor (S) CSO-106 12-15   62
  Reissue of London release, with fewer copies in circulation.
  Composer: Anthony Newley, Leslie Bricusse. **Conductor:** Milton Rosenstock. **Cast:** Anthony
  Newley, Anna Quayle, Jennifer Baker, Susan Baker.
Original Cast (1962) • Polydor (S) 820261-1 5-8   Re
Original London Cast (1961) • Decca (M) LK-4408 12-18   61
  UK release.
Original London Cast (1961) • That's Entertainment (S) TER-1082 8-12   80s
  UK release.
Soundtrack (1966) • Warner Bros. (M) B-1643 10-12   66
Soundtrack (1966) • Warner Bros. (S) BS-1643.................................. 12-18   66
  Composer: Anthony Newley, Leslie Bricusse, Al Ham. **Conductor:** Al Ham. **Cast:** Tony Tanner,
  Millicent Martin.
Original Revival Cast (1978) • Warner Bros. (S) HS-3214 8-10   78
  Composer: Anthony Newley, Leslie Bricusse. **Conductor:** George Rhodes. **Cast:** Sammy Davis
  Jr., Marian Mercer, Shelly Burch.

STORMY MONDAY
Soundtrack (1988) • Virgin (S) 90962-1 8-10   88
  Cast: B.B. King, Mike Figgis, Krakow Jazz Ensemble, Linda Taylor, Stephanie De Sykes, Linda
  Allen.

STORMY WEATHER
Soundtrack (1943) • Sandy Hook (M) SH-2037..................................... 8-12   80
  Cast: Lena Horne, Cab Calloway and His Band, Bill Robinson, Fats Waller, Zutty Singleton.

STORY AND SONGS OF BAMBI: see BAMBI

STORY OF BENJI: see BENJI

STORY OF BIG RED
Soundtrack (1962) • Disneyland (S) ST-1916 25-30   62
  Composer: Richard M. Sherman, Robert B. Sherman. **Cast:** Walter Pidgeon (dialogue).

STORY OF CHRISTMAS
TV Soundtrack (1963) • Capitol (M) T-1964 10-15   63
TV Soundtrack (1963) • Capitol (S) ST-1964 10-15   63
  Includes program insert.
  Conductor: Roger Wagner. **Cast:** Tennessee Ernie Ford, Roger Wagner Chorale.

STORY OF MOBY DICK
Soundtrack (1957) • Dot (M) DLP-3043 35-40   57
  Composer: Richard Mohautt. **Conductor:** Jack Shaindlin. **Cast:** Thomas Mitchell (narration).

STORY OF NAOMI UEMURA: see SHAPE OF THE LAND

STORY OF POLLYANNA: see POLLYANNA

STORY OF STAR WARS: see STAR WARS

STORY OF THE BLACK HOLE: see BLACK HOLE

STORY OF THE GNOME-MOBILE
Soundtrack (1967) • Disneyland (S) ST-3946 25-30   67
  Composer: Buddy Baker, Robert B. Sherman, Richard M. Sherman. **Conductor:** Wayne
  Robinson. **Cast:** Tom Lowell (narration).

STORY OF THE LOVE BUG: see LOVE BUG

STORY OF TRON
Soundtrack (1982) • Disneyland (S) 2517 15-20   82
   Composer: Wendy Carlos. Cast: Chuck Riley (narration).

STORY OF TUTANKHAMEN
Studio Cast (1978) • Argo/Decca (S) ZNF-16 8-12   87
 Includes booklet.
   Composer: Gamal Salama, Kamal El Malakh, Dr. Ibrahim Ahmed.

STRADA, LA: see LA STRADA

STRAIGHT TO HELL
Soundtrack (1987) • Enigma (S) SJE-73308 8-10   87
   Composer: Various. Cast: Joe Strummer, Cait O'Riordan, Pogues, Pray for Rain, Zander Schloss.

STRANGE BREW
Soundtrack (1983) • Mercury (S) 814104 8-10   83
 Full title: *The Adventures of Bob & Doug McKenzie in Strange Brew.*
   Composer: Charles Fox. Cast: Doug & Bob McKenzie.

STRANGE INTERLUDE
Original Cast • Columbia (M) DOL-288 20-25
Original Cast • Columbia (S) DOS-688 25-30
 Boxed, five-disc set. Includes booklet. A play by Eugene O'Neill.
   Cast: Betty Field, Jane Fonda, Ben Gazzara, Pat Hingle, Geoffrey Horne, Geraldine Page, William Prince, Franchot Tone, Richard Thomas.

STRANGE LOVE OF MARTHA IVERS
Studiotrack (1946) • Medallion (M) ML-314 20-25   82
   Composer: Miklos Rozsa.
   Also see FILM MUSIC OF MIKLOS ROZSA

STRANGE ONE
Soundtrack (1957) • Coral (M) CRL-57132 45-65   57
   Composer: Kenyon Hopkins. Conductor: Kenyon Hopkins.

STRANGER THAN PARADISE – THE RESURRECTION OF ALBERT AYLER
Soundtrack (1984) • Enigma (S) SJ-73213 8-10   84
   Composer: John Lurie. Cast: John Lurie.

STRANGERS ON A TRAIN: see MUSIC FROM HITCHCOCK FILMS

STRAW DOGS
Soundtrack (1978) • Citadel (S) CTJF-2/3 50-75   78
 Has four original scores arranged into suites. Includes *The Mechanic*, *Lawman* and *Chato's Land*. Gatefold cover.
   Composer: Jerry Fielding. Conductor: Jerry Fielding.

STRAWBERRY BLONDE
Soundtrack (1941) • Radiola (M) MR-1103 10-12
   Cast: James Cagney, Olivia de Havilland.

STRAWBERRY STATEMENT
Soundtrack (1970) • MGM (S) 2SE-14 12-15   70
 Two discs.
   Composer: Ian Freebairn-Smith, Karl Bohm. Cast: Buffy Sainte-Marie, Neil Young, Crosby, Stills and Nash, Thunderclap Newman, Karl Bohm, Red Mountain Jug Band, MGM Studio Orchestra.

STREET MUSIC
Soundtrack (1982) • Regency (S) RI-8503 8-10   82
   Composer: Ed Bogas, Judy Munsen.

STREET SCENE

Original Cast (1947) • Columbia MM-683.. 15-40   49
  78 rpm album.
Original Cast (1947) • Columbia (M) ML-4139 18-20   49
  Paper envelope-type jacket, with opening at top.
Original Cast (1947) • Columbia (M) OL-4139................................... 10-12   Re
Original Cast (1947) • Columbia Special Products (M) COL-4139.......... 8-10   77
    Composer: Kurt Weill, Langston Hughes. **Conductor:** Maurice Abravanel. **Cast:** Anne Jeffreys,
    Polyna Stoska, Brian Sullivan, Hope Emerson, Don Saxon, Remo Lota, Beverly Janis, Creighton
    Thompson, Peggy Turnley, Ellen Carleen.

STREETCAR NAMED DESIRE (1951)

Soundtrack (1951) • Capitol (EP) FBF-289 25-30   51
  Two discs.
Soundtrack (1951) • Capitol (M) L-289.. 30-40   51
  10-inch LP.
    Composer: Alex North. **Conductor:** Ray Heindorf.
  Also see MUSIC BY MAX STEINER

STREETCAR NAMED DESIRE (1984)

TV Soundtrack (1984) • Allegiance (M) AV-439 8-12   84
    Composer: Alex North. **Conductor:** Ray Heindorf. **Cast:** Debra Dobkin.

STREETS OF FIRE

Soundtrack (1984) • MCA (S) 5492... 8-10   84
    Cast: Fire Inc., Fix, Blasters, Marilyn Martin, Greg Phillingames, Maria McKee, Dan Hartman, Ry
    Cooder.

STROKER ACE

Soundtrack (1983) • MCA (S) 36003.. 8-10   83
    Cast: Marshall Tucker Band, Larry Gatlin, Terri Gibbs.

STRONG TOGETHER

Soundtrack • Big Tree (S) 76016 10-12   70s
    Cast: Hot.

STUDENT PRINCE

Studio Cast (1950) • Decca (M) DL-7008 15-20   50
  10-inch LP.
Studio Cast (1950) • Decca (M) DL-8362.. 12-18   52
  10-inch LP. One side has music from *The Vagabond King*.
    Composer: Sigmund Romberg, Dorothy Donnelly. **Conductor:** Victor Young. **Cast:** Jane Wilson,
    Lee Sweetland, Gloria Lane.
Studio Cast (1951) • RCA Victor (EP) EKB 1014 12-15
  Two discs.
Studio Cast (1951) • RCA Victor (M) LK 1014 18-25
Studio Cast (1951) • Camden (M) CAL-382 12-15   Re
    Conductor: Al Goodman. **Cast:** Earl Wrightson, Frances Greer, Donald Dame, Mary Martha
    Briney, Guild Choristers, Al Goodman and His Orchestra.
Studio Cast (1953) • Columbia (M) ML-4592.. 12-15   53
Studio Cast (1953) • Columbia (M) CL-826 10-12   56
Studio Cast (1953) • Columbia/Odyssey (M) Y-32367........................... 8-10   Re
    Conductor: Lehman Engel. **Cast:** Dorothy Kirsten, Robert Rounseville, Genevieve Warner,
    Warner Dalton, Clifford Harvout, Brenda Miller.
Studiotrack (1954) • RCA Victor (EP) ERB-1837 10-15   54
Studiotrack (1954) • RCA Victor (EP) LPC-117.................................... 10-12   61
  Compact 33 Double.
Studiotrack (1954) • RCA Victor (M) LM-1837...................................... 15-20   54
    Conductor: Constantine Callinicos. **Cast:** Mario Lanza, Elizabeth Doubleday.
Studiotrack (1954) • RCA Victor (M) LM-2339...................................... 8-12   60

Studiotrack (1954) • RCA Victor (S) LSC-2339 10-15   60
    Conductor: Paul Baron. **Cast:** Mario Lanza, Norma Giusti.

Studiotrack (1954) • RCA Victor (S) LSC-3216 8-10   Re
    Cast: Mario Lanza, Elizabeth Doubleday.

Studio Cast • Capitol (M) L407 10-15   50s
  10-inch LP.
    Cast: Gordon MacRae.

Studio Cast (1962) • Capitol (W) W-1841 12-15   62

Studio Cast (1962) • Capitol (S) SW-1841 12-18   62

Studio Cast (1962) • Angel (S) S-37318 8-10   73
    Conductor: Van Alexander. **Cast:** Gordon MacRae, Dorothy Kirsten, Earle Wilkie, Richard
    Robinson, William Felber, Charles Scharbach, Howard Chitjian, Robert Johnson, Roger Wagner
    Chorale.

Studio Cast (1965) • Columbia (M) OL-5980 8-12   65

Studio Cast (1965) • Columbia (S) OS-2380 10-12   65
    Conductor: Franz Allers. **Cast:** Roberta Peters, Jan Peerce, Giorgio Tozzi, Anita Darian,
    Lawrence Avery, Merrill Staton Choir.

Studiotrack (1957) • Halo (M) 50272 8-15   57

Studiotrack • Columbia (M) CL-6051 10-15   50s
  10-inch LP. Full title: *Selections from The Student Prince.*
    Cast: Marek Weber and His Orchestra and Chorus.

Studiotrack • Mercury (EP) EP-1-3040 5-15   50s
    Conductor: Paul Baron. **Cast:** Glenn Burris, Genevieve Rowe, Paul Baron Orchestra and
    Chorus.

Studiotrack • Royale (M) 1892 8-15   50s
  10-inch LP.
    Cast: Royale Operetta Singers and Orchestra.

Studiotrack • Allegro (M) 1644 8-12
  One side has music from *The Desert Song.*
    Cast: Glenn Burris, Genevieve Rowe, Paul Baron Orchestra and Chorus.

Studiotrack • Rondo-lette (S) SA159 8-12
    Conductor: Russ Cage. **Cast:** Stephen Karayan Choir, Russ Case and Orchestra.
  Also see CHOCOLATE SOLDIER
  Also see DESERT SONG
  Also see MERRY WIDOW

STUDY IN TERROR

Soundtrack (1965) • Roulette (M) OS-801 25-35   66

Soundtrack (1965) • Roulette (S) OSS-801 60-75   66
    Composer: John Scott. **Conductor:** John Scott.

STUNT MAN

Soundtrack (1980) • 20th Century-Fox (S) T-626 12-25   80
    Composer: Dominic Frontiere. **Conductor:** Dominic Frontiere. **Cast:** Dusty Springfield.

STUNTS

Soundtrack (1977) • Amerama (S) ST-251 10-15   77
    Composer: Michael Kamen. **Conductor:** Michael Kamen.

SUBJECT WAS ROSES

Original Cast (1964) • Columbia (M) DOL-308 15-18   64

Original Cast (1964) • Columbia (S) DOS-708 20-25   64

Original Cast (1964) • Columbia (S) ADOS-708 10-15   Re
  Boxed, three-disc sets.
    Composer: Frank D. Gilroy (his dramatic play). **Cast:** Jack Albertson, Irene Dailey, Martin Sheen.
    (Dialogue.)

SUBTERRANEANS
Soundtrack (1960) • MGM (M) E-3812-ST 35-40   60
Soundtrack (1960) • MGM (S) SE-3812 60-70   60
  Composer: Andre Previn, others. **Conductor:** Andre Previn. **Cast:** Gerry Mulligan, Carmen McRae.

SUBURBIA
Soundtrack (1983) • Enigma (S) 71093-1 8-10   83
  Cast: Alex Gibson, Vandals, T.S.O.L.

SUBWAY
Soundtrack (1985) • Varese Sarabande (S) STV-81269 10-15   85
  Composer: Eric Serra. **Cast:** Eric Serra.

SUBWAYS ARE FOR SLEEPING
Original Cast (1961) • Columbia (M) KOL-5730 8-25   61
Original Cast (1961) • Columbia (S) KOS-2130 12-18   61
  Gatefold covers.
Original Cast (1961) • Columbia Special Products (S) AOS-2130 8-10   Re
  Composer: Jule Styne, Betty Comden, Adolph Green. **Conductor:** Milton Rosenstock. **Cast:** Sydney Chaplin, Carol Lawrence, Orson Bean, Phyllis Newman, Cy Young, John Sharpe, Bob Gorman, Gene Varrone.
Studio Cast (1961) • Coral (M) CRL-57398 8-12   61
Studio Cast (1961) • Coral (S) CRL7-57398 8-12   61
  Composer: Jule Styne, Betty Comden, Adolph Green. **Conductor:** Burt Farber. **Cast:** McGuire Sisters.
Studio Cast (1961) • Epic (M) LN-3829 12-15   62
Studio Cast (1961) • Epic (S) BN-622 12-15   62
  Jazz renditions.
  Cast: Dave Grusin.
Studio Cast (1962) • Columbia (M) CL-1733 8-12   62
Studio Cast (1962) • Columbia (S) CS-8533 8-12   62
  Cast: Percy Faith and His Orchestra.

SUDDEN IMPACT
Soundtrack (1983) • Viva (S) 1-23990 20-25   83
  Also has music from other "Dirty Harry" films: *Magnum Force* and *The Enforcer*.
  Composer: Lalo Schifrin. **Cast:** Roberta Flack, Enforcers.

SUGAR
Original Cast (1972) • United Artists (S) UAS-9905 12-18   72
  Cover intact (no clipped corners).
Original Cast (1972) • United Artists (S) UAS-9905 8-10   72
  Cover has clipped corners.
  Composer: Jule Styne, Robert Merrill. **Conductor:** Elliot Lawrence. **Cast:** Robert Morse, Tony Roberts, Cyril Ritchard, Elaine Joyce, Sheila Smith.

SUGAR BABIES
Original Cast (1979) • Broadway Ent. (S) BE 8302-R 10-15   83
  Additional material "deemed extraneous by the show's producers" is available on the cassette version of this album.
  Composer: Jimmy McHugh, Dorothy Fields, Harold Adamson, Al Dublin, Arthur Malvin.
  Conductor: Milton Rosenstock, Larry Blank. **Cast:** Mickey Rooney, Ann Miller, Sid Stone, Scott Stewart, Ronn Lucas, Jack Fletcher, Jane Summerhays.

SUICIDE SQUADRON

Studiotrack • Columbia (M) ML-2902 75-100   50
  10-inch LP. Album is actually untitled, but it does contain *Warsaw Concerto*; as featured in
  the film *Suicide Squadron* (original British title *Dangerous Moonlight*). Also has music from
  Oliver Twist (1948) and *Love Story* (1946).
  Composer: Richard Addinsell. **Conductor:** Muir Mathieson. OLIVER TWIST: **Composer:**
  Arnold Bax. **Conductor:** Muir Mathieson. LOVE STORY: **Composer:** Hubert Bath. **Conductor:**
  Hubert Bath.

SUMMER AND SMOKE

Soundtrack (1961) • RCA Victor (M) LOC-1067 25-50   62
Soundtrack (1961) • RCA Victor (S) LSO-1067 60-65   62
Soundtrack (1961) • Entr'acte (S) ERS-6519 8-10   Re
  Composer: Elmer Bernstein. **Conductor:** Elmer Bernstein.

SUMMER DOG

Original Soundtrack (1977) • JM (S) 1177 8-12   77
  Composer: Robin Lamont, Barry Tarallo.

SUMMER HOLIDAY (1948)

Soundtrack (1948) • Four Jays (M) HW-602 20-25
  Complete score for the 1948 musical, including numbers deleted before the film was
  released.
  Composer: Harry Warren, Ralph Blane. **Conductor:** Lennie Hayton. **Cast:** Mickey Rooney,
  Gloria De Haven, Walter Huston, Frank Morgan, Agnes Moorehead, Marilyn Maxwell, Denny
  Wilson (performs vocals for Selena Royle in the film).

SUMMER HOLIDAY (1963)

Soundtrack (1963) • Epic (M) LN-24063 20-25   63
Soundtrack (1963) • Epic (S) BN-26063 25-30   63
  Cast: Cliff Richard and the Shadows.

SUMMER LOVE

Soundtrack (1958) • Decca (M) DL-8714 50-60   58
  Black label or pink label promo.
Soundtrack (1958) • Decca (M) DL-8714 25-35   60s
  Rainbow (or multi-color) label.
  Composer: Henry Mancini, Rod McKuen, others. **Conductor:** Joseph Gershenson. **Cast:** Molly
  Bee, Rod McKuen, Kip Tyler, Jimmy Daley and the Ding-A-Lings.

SUMMER LOVERS

Soundtrack (1982) • Warner Bros. (S) 1-23695 5-8   82
  Composer: Basil Poledouris. **Conductor:** Basil Poledouris. **Cast:** Chicago, Michael Sembello,
  Depeche Mode, Stephen Bishop, Tina Turner, Nona Hendryx, Heaven 17, Elton John.

SUMMER MAGIC

Soundtrack (1963) • Buena Vista/Alcoa Wrap (EP) AL-701 20-25   63
Soundtrack (1963) • Buena Vista (M) BV-4025 12-40   63
Soundtrack (1963) • Buena Vista (S) STER-4025 15-60   63
  Composer: Richard M. Sherman, Robert B. Sherman. **Conductor:** Tutti Camarata. **Cast:** Hayley
  Mills, Burl Ives, Eddie Hodges, Deborah Walley, Wendy Turner, Marilyn Hoover.
  Also see IN SEARCH OF THE CASTAWAYS

SUMMER OF '42

Soundtrack (1971) • Warner Bros. (S) WS-1925 12-15   71
Soundtrack (1971) • Warner Bros. (S) WS-1925/ST 93822 8-10   Re
  Regarded as the *Summer of '42* soundtrack, this LP has but two tracks from that film. The
  remainder is music from *The Picasso Summer*. "ST 93822" indicates Capitol Record Club
  issue.
  Composer: Michel Legrand. **Conductor:** Michel Legrand.

SUMMER PLACE (AND OTHER GREAT HITS FROM THE MOVIES)

Studiotrack (1959) • Columbia (M) CL-1421 15-20   59

Studiotrack (1959) • Columbia (S) CS-8218.. 20-40   59
  Also has music from *Modern Times, Pillow Talk, On the Beach, Gigi* and *The F.B.I. Story.*
  Cast: Percy Faith, Tony Bennett, Doris Day, Four Lads, Johnny Mathis, Bing Crosby, Duke
  Ellington, Norman Luboff Choir, Mitch Miller, Vic Damone, Richard Maltby.
  Also see HELEN OF TROY
  Also see PARRISH

SUMMER SCHOOL
Soundtrack (1987) • Chrysalis (S) OV-41607.. 8-10   87
  Cast: Tami Show, Paul Engemann, Billy Burnette, Danny Elfman, Elisa Fiorillo, E.G. Daily,
  Fabulous Thunderbirds, Tone Norum, Tonio K.

SUMMER STOCK
Soundtrack (1950) • MGM (EP) K-56 18-30   50s
  Boxed, four-disc set.
Soundtrack (1950) • MGM - MGM-56... 12-18   50
  78 rpm album.
Soundtrack (1950) • MGM (M) E-519.. 35-40   50
  10-inch LP.
Soundtrack (1948) • MGM (M) E-3234.. 15-18   55
  One side is music from *The Pirate.*
Soundtrack (1950) • MCA (M) 39084 8-10   86
  Also has music from *Lovely To Look At.*
  Composer: Harry Warren, Harold Arlen, Saul Chaplin. **Conductor:** Johnny Green. **Cast:** Judy
  Garland, Gene Kelly, Gloria De Haven, Phil Silvers, Pete Roberts (performs vocals for Hans
  Conried in the film).
  Also see THOSE GLORIOUS MGM MUSICALS

SUMMER STORY
Soundtrack (1988) • Virgin Movie Music (S) 90961-1 10-15   88
  Composer: Georges Delerue.

SUN ALSO RISES
Soundtrack (1957) • Kapp (M) KDL-7001.. 45-55   57
Soundtrack (1957) • AEI (M) AEI-3190 12-15   81
  Also has music from *Spellbound.*
  Composer: Hugo Friedhofer, Vincente Gomez, others. **Conductor:** Lionel Newman.

SUN SHINES BRIGHT: see SANDS OF IWO JIMA

SUN VALLEY SERENADE
Soundtrack (1941) • RCA Victor (EP) EPBT-3064 15-25   54
  Two discs.
Soundtrack (1941) • RCA Victor (M) LPT-3064.................................... 40-50   54
  10-inch LP.
  Composer: Mack Gordon, Harry Warren. **Conductor:** Glenn Miller. **Cast:** Glenn Miller Orchestra.
Soundtrack [Vol. 1] (1941) • 20th Century-Fox (M) 3159..................... 10-15   65
Soundtrack [Vol. 1] (1941) • 20th Century-Fox (SE) S-4159e 10-15   65
Soundtrack [Vol. 2] (1941) • 20th Century-Fox (M) 3160..................... 10-15   65
Soundtrack [Vol. 2] (1941) • 20th Century-Fox (SE) S-4160e 10-15   65
  Also see GLENN MILLER
  Also see GOLDEN HITS FROM HIS ORIGINAL SOUNDTRACKS
  Also see ORCHESTRA WIVES

SUNBURN
Soundtrack (1979) • Arrival (S) NU-9540 20-25   77
  Composer: John Cameron, others. **Conductor:** John Cameron. **Cast:** Graham Gouldman, 10CC,
  Heatwave, Kandidate, John Ferrara.

SUNDAY IN NEW YORK
Soundtrack (1963) • RCA Victor (M) LPM-2827 15-20   64
Soundtrack (1963) • RCA Victor (S) LSP-2827 20-30   64
  Composer: Peter Nero, Roland Everett, Carroll Coates. **Conductor:** Peter Nero. **Cast:** Peter Nero.

SUNDAY IN THE COUNTRY
Soundtrack (1984) • Varese Sarabande (S) 81227 10-15   84
  One side has original score for *The Pirate*.
  Composer: Philippe Sarde.

SUNDAY IN THE PARK WITH GEORGE
Original Cast (1984) • RCA Red Seal Digital (S) HBC1-5042................. 8-15   84
  Includes 18-page booklet.
  Composer: Stephen Sondheim. **Conductor:** Paul Gemignani. **Cast:** Mandy Patinkin, Bernadette Peters.

SUNDOWNERS
Soundtrack (1960) • Cinema (MS) LP-8014 40-45   75
  Composer: Dimitri Tiomkin. **Conductor:** Hans Rossback.

SUNFLOWER
Soundtrack (1970) • Avco Embassy (S) AVE-0-110............................. 12-15   70
  Composer: Henry Mancini. **Conductor:** Henry Mancini. **Cast:** Henry Mancini and His Orchestra.

SUNNY
Original London Cast • World (M) SH-240 15-18
  Also has music from the original London production of *Show Boat*.
  Composer: Jerome Kern, Oscar Hammerstein II, Otto Harbach. **Conductor:** Philip Braham.
  Cast: Binnie Hale, Jack Hobbs, Jack Buchanan, Elsie Randolph, Claude Hulbert.
  Also see NO NO NANETTE

SUNNY SIDE OF THE STREET
Soundtrack (1951) • Mercury (M) MG 25100....................................... 40-50   51
  10-inch LP.
  Composer: Morris Stoloff. **Cast:** Frankie Laine, Terry Moore, Billy Daniels, Vic Damone.

SUNNYSIDE
Soundtrack (1979) • American Int'l (S) AILP-3002 8-10   79
  Composer: Steven Stahns, Stephen Longfellow, others. **Cast:** Harold Wheeler and the New York City Band. (With incidental music by Alan Douglas and Harold Wheeler.)

SUNSET BOULEVARD: THE CLASSIC FILM SCORES OF FRANZ WAXMAN
Studiotrack • RCA Victor (S) ARL1-0708 10-12   74
Studiotrack • RCA Victor (Q) ARD1-0708 10-20   74
  Includes insert with liner notes.
Studiotrack • RCA Victor (S) AGL 1-378 8-10   80
  Without liner notes insert. Music from *Prince Valiant, A Place in the Sun, The Bride of Frankenstein, Sunset Boulevard, Old Acquaintance, Rebecca, The Philadelphia Story* and *Taras Bulba*.
  Composer: Franz Waxman. **Conductor:** Charles Gerhardt.

SUNSHINE
TV Soundtrack (1973) • MCA (S) 387 12-15   73
  Composer: John Denver, Taffy Nivert, Bill Danoff, Dick Kniss, Mike Taylor. **Cast:** Cliff DeYoung, Christina Raines. (With dialogue.)

SUNSHINE CAKE: see BING'S HOLLYWOOD

SUPERFLY
Soundtrack (1972) • Curtom (S) CRS-8014-ST..................................... 30-35   72
  Composer: Curtis Mayfield. **Cast:** Curtis Mayfield.

SUPERFLY T.N.T.
Soundtrack (1973) • Buddah (S) 5136 25-30   73
  Cast: Osibisa

SUPERGIRL
Soundtrack (1984) • Varese Sarabande (S) STV-81231 10-15   84
  Composer: Jerry Goldsmith. **Conductor:** Jerry Goldsmith. **Cast:** National Philharmonic Orchestra.

SUPERMAN
Original Radio Cast • Radiola (M) MR 1150 8-10   84
  Cast: Bud Collyer, Joan Alexander, Julian Noa, others.
Original Radio Cast (1947) • Musette Records (M) #1 50-75   47
  Two discs. From *The Flying Train* episode. Includes 12-page storybook.
Original Radio Cast • Mark 56 (M) 588 10-12   72
Original Radio Cast • Mark 56 (M) 677 10-12   74
  Full title: *Kellogg's Presents Superman*. Four episodes from 1940s, plus Kellogg's radio commercials.
Original Radio Cast • Mark 56 (M) 812 15-25   78
  Picture disc. Four episodes from 1940s.
Original Radio Cast • Mark 56 (M) 812 20-40   78
  Promotional picture disc for Pepsi with different picture on back side.
Original Radio Cast • Nostalgia Lane (M) 2NLR-1016 8-10   77
  Full title: *Superman: Original Radio Broadcasts*.
  Also see IT'S A BIRD, IT'S A PLANE, IT'S SUPERMAN

SUPERMAN – THE MOVIE
Soundtrack (1979) • Warner Bros. (S) 2BSK-3257 8-15   79
  Two discs. Includes advertising flyer.
  Composer: John Williams. **Conductor:** John Williams. **Cast:** London Symphony Orchestra.

SUPERMAN II
Soundtrack (1980) • Warner Bros. (S) HS-3505 12-15   81
  Disc is laser-etched with five Superman logos circling each side.
  Composer: Ken Thorne (from original material composed by John Williams). **Conductor:** Ken Thorne.

SUPERMAN III
Soundtrack (1983) • Warner Bros. (S) 1-23879 10-15   83
  Composer: Ken Thorne, Giorgio Moroder, John Williams (original *Superman* theme). **Cast:** Marshall Crenshaw, Chaka Khan, Roger Miller, Helen St. John.

SUPERMAN – THE RADIO SPECIAL
Radio Cast/Soundtrack • Warner Bros. (S) PRO-A-964 15-20   81
  Full title: *The History of Superman - The Radio Special*. One-hour radio show tracing the story of Superman, from the comics, to radio and television, to films. Features soundtrack excerpts from various films. Promotional issue only.

SURF PARTY
Soundtrack (1964) • 20th Century-Fox (M) TFM-3131 15-20   64
Soundtrack (1964) • 20th Century-Fox (S) TFS-4131 25-30   64
  Composer: Jimmie Haskell, By Dunham. **Conductor:** Jimmie Haskell. **Cast:** Jackie De Shannon, Astronauts, Routers, Kenny Miller, Patricia Morrow, Lory Patrick.

SURFER GIRLS
Soundtrack (1978) • Oakwood (S) SUS-1001 85-95   78
  Composer: Michael Gabbert, Kendall Keyes. **Cast:** Michael Gabbert, Denny Gause, Shanna Greene, Terry Kiser, Abbey Roberta.

SURRENDER
Soundtrack (1987) • Varese Sarabande (S) STV 81348 10-15   87
  Composer: Michael Colombier.

SURVIVAL OF ST. JOAN
Original Cast (1971) • Paramount (S) PAS-9000 20-25   71
Two discs.
Composer: Hank Ruffin, Gary Ruffin, James Lineberger. **Conductor:** Stephen Schwartz. **Cast:** F. Murray Abraham, Willie Rook, Lenny Baker, Ronald Bishop, Richard Bright, Elizabeth Elis, Peter Lazer, Janet Samo.

SURVIVAL RUN
Soundtrack (1981) • Original Cast (S) O.C. 8020................................. 10-15   81
Also has music from Alexander. Promotional issue only.
Composer: Gary Williams Friedman. **Cast:** Peter Graves, Ray Milland, Vincent Van Patten.

SUSAN HAYWARD
Soundtrack (1952) • Legends (M) 1000/3 20-25
Previously unreleased material from *I'll Cry Tomorrow, With a Song in My Heart* and *Smash-Up*.
Composer: Various. **Conductor:** Various. **Cast:** Susan Hayward, Peg La Centra (performs vocals for Susan Hayward in *Smash-Up*), Jane Froman (performs vocals for Susan Hayward in *With a Song in My Heart*).

SUSPECT
Soundtrack (1988) • Varese Sarabande (S) 704 390 12-15   88
Composer: Michael Kamen.

SUSPICION: see MUSIC FROM HITCHCOCK FILMS

SUSPIRA
Soundtrack (1977) • Attic (S) AT LAT 1042... 10-12   77
Canadian release.
Composer: Dario Argento, Goblin. **Cast:** Dario Argento, Goblin.

SWAMP THING
Soundtrack (1982) • Varese Sarabande (S) STV-81154 10-15   82
Composer: Harry Manfredini. **Conductor:** Harry Manfredini.

SWAN
Soundtrack (1956) • MGM (M) E-3399.. 60-65   56
Soundtrack (1956) • MCA (M) 25086 8-10   86
Composer: Bronislau Kaper. **Conductor:** Johnny Green. **Cast:** MGM Studio Orchestra.
Also see FORBIDDEN PLANET

SWAN DOWN GLOVES
Original Cast • That's Entertainment (S) TER-1017 8-10   80s
UK release.
Composer: Nigel Kess, B. Brown.

SWANEE RIVER
Radio Cast (1977) • Totem (S) 1028.. 8-10   77
Composer: Stephen Foster. **Cast:** Dennis Morgan, Al Jolson, Frances Gifford, Walter Huston (host).

SWANN IN LOVE / KATHARINA BLUM
Soundtrack (1984) • Varese Sarabande (S) 81224 10-15   84
Composer: Hans Werner Henze. **Conductor:** Hans Werner Henze. **Cast:** Basel Radio Symphony Orchestra.

SWARM
Soundtrack (1978) • Warner Bros. (S) BSK-3208 25-30   78
Composer: Jerry Goldsmith. **Conductor:** Jerry Goldsmith.

SWASHBUCKLER
Soundtrack (1976) • MCA (S) 2096... 10-12   76
Composer: John Addison. **Conductor:** John Addison.

SWEDEN, HEAVEN AND HELL
Soundtrack (1969) • Ariel (S) ARS-15000 20-25   69
  Composer: Peter Umiliani. Conductor: Peter Umiliani.

SWEDISH FLY GIRLS
Soundtrack (1975) • Juno (S) S-1003 120-130   75
  Music produced by Manfred Mann.
  Composer: Mose Henry, Melanie Safka.

SWEENEY TODD (THE DEMON BARBER OF FLEET STREET)
Studio Cast (1979) • RCA Victor (S) PD-11687 12-15   79
  12-inch single of *The Ballad of Sweeney Todd*. Shows RCA's Red Seal label as "Red Seals
  Disco."
  Cast: His Master's Fish, featuring Gordon Grody.
Original Cast (1979) • RCA Victor (S) CBL2-3379 10-12   79
  Two discs. Gatefold cover. Includes 25-page booklet.
Original Cast (1979) • RCA Victor (S) CBL2-3379 8-10   79
  Two discs. Standard cover.
  Composer: Stephen Sondheim. Conductor: Paul Gemignani. Cast: Angela Lansbury, Len
  Cariou, Victor Garber, Ken Jennings, Merle Louise, Sarah Rice, Edmund Lyndeck, Joaquin
  Romanguera, Jack Eric Williams.

SWEET ADELINE
Soundtrack • Titania (M) 506 8-10
  Also has music from *High, Wide and Handsome*.
  Composer: Jerome Kern, Oscar Hammerstein II. Cast: Irene Dunne.

SWEET BYE AND BYE
Original Cast (1974) • Desto (S) DC-7179/8 15-20   74
  Composer: Jack Beeson, Kenward Elmslie. Conductor: Russell Patterson. Cast: Noel Rogers,
  Judith Anthony, Carolyn James, Paula Seibel, Robert Owen Jones, Walter Hook, Elizabeth
  Green, Dennis Howell, William Latimer.

SWEET CHARITY
Original Cast (1966) • Columbia (M) KOL-6500 8-10   66
Original Cast (1966) • Columbia (S) KOS-2900 8-12   66
  Composer: Cy Coleman, Dorothy Fields. Conductor: Fred Warner. Cast: Gwen Verdon, John
  McMartin, Thelma Oliver, James Luisi, Helen Gallagher, Arnold Soboloff, John Wheeler, Harold
  Pierson, Michael Davis, Eddie Gasper.
Original Cast (1966) • Columbia (S) DJ-17 15-20   66
  Full title: *Backstage at the Palace: Sweet Charity*. Cast interviews, songs from the play and
  interviews with celebrities after they attended opening night. Promotional issue only.
  Composer: Cy Coleman, Dorothy Fields. Cast: Gwen Verdon, Helen Gallagher, Neil Simon,
  Lena Horne.
Soundtrack (1969) • Decca (S) DL-71502 8-12   69
  Composer: Cy Coleman, Dorothy Fields. Conductor: Joseph Gershenson. Cast: Shirley
  MacLaine, John McMartin, Chita Rivera, Paula Kelly, Stubby Kaye, Sammy Davis Jr.
Studiotrack • Vocalion (S) VL 73867 8-10
  Cast: Sound Stage Orchestra.
Original Revival Cast (1986) • EMI (S) R-164190 8-12   86
Original Revival Cast (1986) • EMI (S) SV-17196 8-10
  Composer: Cy Coleman, Dorothy Fields. Cast: Deborah Allen, Michael Rupert, Bebe Neuwirth,
  others.
  Also see MAME

SWEET DREAMS
Soundtrack (1985) • MCA (S) 6149 8-10   85
Soundtrack (1985) • MCA (S) 39301 8-10   88
  Film inspired by the life and career of Patsy Cline.
  Cast: Patsy Cline.

SWEET LIES
Soundtrack (1988) • Island (S) 90855-1 8-10   88
    Cast: Compagnie Creole, Robert Palmer, Trevor Jones, Paul McGovern, Gold, Salif Keita, George Decimus.

SWEET LOVE, BITTER
Soundtrack (1967) • Impulse (M) A-9142 10-12   67
    Story inspired by jazz musician Charlie "Bird" Parker.
Soundtrack (1967) • Impulse (S) AS-9142 12-15   67
    Composer: Mal Waldron. **Cast:** Mal Waldron.

SWEET RIDE
Soundtrack (1968) • 20th Century-Fox (S) TFS-S-4198 15-20   68
    Composer: Pete Rugolo, Lee Hazlewood. **Conductor:** Pete Rugolo. **Cast:** Dusty Springfield.

SWEET SIXTEEN
Soundtrack (1983) • Regency (S) R1 8505 10-15   83
    Composer: Ray Ellis.

SWEET SMELL OF SUCCESS
Soundtrack (1957) • Decca (EP) ED 2541 20-25   57
Soundtrack (1957) • Decca (M) DL-8610 45-50   57
    Composer: Elmer Bernstein, Chico Hamilton, Fred Katz. **Conductor:** Elmer Bernstein.
Studiotrack (1957) • Decca (M) DL-8614 20-25   57
    Jazz renditions.
    Composer: Chico Hamilton, Fred Katz. **Cast:** Chico Hamilton Quintet.

SWEET SWEETBACK'S BAADASSSSS SONG
Soundtrack (1971) • Stax (S) STS-3001 25-30   71
    Conductor: Melvin Van Peebles. **Cast:** Melvin Van Peebles, Earth, Wind and Fire, Brer Soul.

SWEETHEARTS
Studio Cast (1951) • RCA Victor (EP) WK-6 10-15   51
    Boxed, four-disc set.
Studio Cast (1951) • RCA Victor (EP) EKB-1015 15-20   51
    Two discs.
Studio Cast (1951) • RCA Victor (M) LK-1015 20-25   51
Studio Cast (1951) • Camden (M) CAL-369 15-20   57
    Composer: Victor Herbert, Robert B. Smith. **Conductor:** Al Goodman. **Cast:** Earl Wrightson, Frances Greer, Jimmy Carroll, Christina Lind, Guild Choristers.

SWEPT AWAY
Soundtrack (1975) • Peters International (S) PLD 1005 30-40   75
    Composer: Piero Piccioni.

SWIMMER
Soundtrack (1968) • Columbia (S) OS-3210 20-25   68
    Composer: Marvin Hamlisch. **Conductor:** Jack Hayes.

SWING TIME: see FRED ASTAIRE AND GINGER ROGERS

SWINGER
Soundtrack (1966) • RCA Victor (M) LPM-3710 30-35   66
Soundtrack (1966) • RCA Victor (S) LSP-3710 45-65   66
    Five songs from the film, plus other vocals by Ann-Margret.
    Composer: Andre Previn, Marty Paich, Harold Arlen, Johnny Mercer. **Conductor:** Marty Paich. **Cast:** Ann-Margret.

SWINGER'S PARADISE
Soundtrack (1965) • Epic (M) LN-24145 15-20   65
Soundtrack (1965) • Epic (S) BN-26145 20-25   65
    Conductor: Stanley Black. **Cast:** Cliff Richard and the Shadows, Michael Sammes Singers, Norrie Paramor Strings.

SWINGIN' SOUNDS FOR SECRET AGENTS
Studiotrack • Columbia (M) CSM-444 10-15   60s
Record club only. Includes an alternate version of John Barry's *James Bond Theme*.

SWINGIN' SUMMER
Soundtrack (1966) • HBR (M) HLP-8500 20-25   66
Soundtrack (1966) • HBR (M) HST-98500 25-30   66
Cast: Donnie Brooks, Righteous Brothers, Rip Chords, Raquel Welch, Carol Conners, Swingers.

SWINGIN' WEST
Studiotrack (1960) • RCA Victor (M) LPM-2163 20-25   60
Studiotrack (1960) • RCA Victor (S) LSP-2163 35-45   60
TV themes from *Have Gun Will Travel*, *Bat Masterson*, *Maverick*, *Bonanza*, *Bucksin*, *The Texan*, *Black Saddle*, *The Deputy*, *Gunsmoke*, *Wyatt Earp*, *Wagon Train* and *Cheyenne*.
Cast: Marty Gold and His Orchestra.

SWINGING ON A STAR: see BING'S HOLLYWOOD

SWITZERLAND: see SAMOA

SWORD AND THE SORCERER
Soundtrack (1982) • Varese Sarabande (S) STV-81158 10-15   82
Soundtrack (1982) • That's Entertainment (S) TER-1023 8-10   80s
UK release.
Composer: David Whitaker. Conductor: David Whitaker.

SWORD IN THE STONE
Soundtrack (1963) • Disneyland (M) ST-4901 125-175   63
Gatefold, six-page accordian-style, cover with pop-up figures.
Soundtrack (1963) • Disneyland (M) DQ-1236 12-15   64
Composer: Richard M. Sherman, Robert B. Sherman.

SYLVESTER
Soundtrack (1985) • MCA/Curb (S) 39026 8-10   85
Cast: Los Lobos, Gail Davies, Cruzados, Sylvester, Rank and File.

SYLVIA
Soundtrack (1965) • Mercury (M) MG-21004 12-18   65
Soundtrack (1965) • Mercury (S) SR-61004 25-30   65
Composer: David Raksin. Conductor: David Raksin.

SYNANON
Soundtrack (1965) • Liberty (M) LRP-3413 12-15   65
Soundtrack (1965) • Liberty (S) LST-7413 15-18   65
Composer: Neal Hefti, others. Conductor: Neal Hefti. Cast: Neal Hefti and His Orchestra.

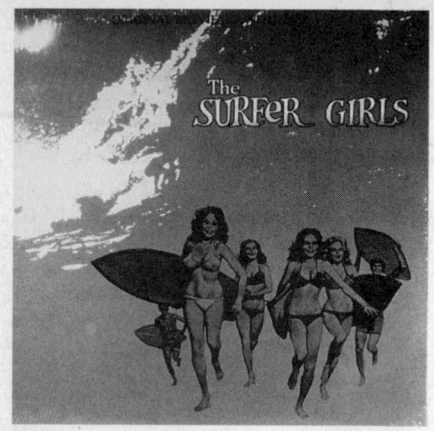

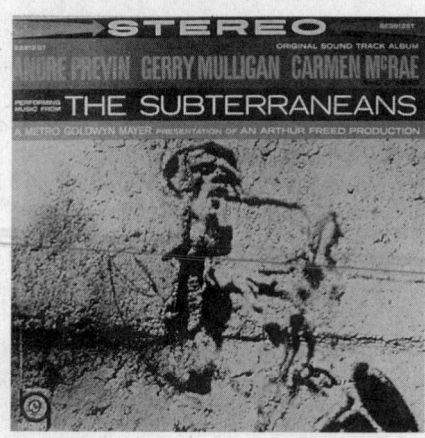

T

T.C.B. (TAKIN' CARE OF BUSINESS)
TV Soundtrack (1968) • Tamla/Motown (S) MS-682 15-20   68
TV Soundtrack (1968) • Motown (S) S-682 10-12   68
TV Soundtrack (1968) • Natural Resources (S) NR-4020T1 8-10   Re
   Composer: William Robinson, Holland-Dozier-Holland. **Cast:** Diana Ross and the Supremes, Temptations.

T.R. BASKIN
Soundtrack (1971) • Paramount (S) PAS-6018 12-18   71
   Composer: Jack Elliott, June Jackson. **Conductor:** Jack Elliott.

TV FRIENDS: see ARTHUR GODFREY

TV GUIDE TOP TELEVISION THEMES
TV Soundtracks (1959) • Warner Bros. (M) W-1290 30-40   59
   Themes from: *D.A.'s Man, Perry Mason, 77 Sunset Strip, Pete Kelly's Blues, Mickey Mouse Club, Maverick, Peter Gunn, Have Gun Will Travel, M-Squad, Richard Diamond, Playhouse 90* and *The Real McCoys.*
   Cast: Warren Barker, Frank Comstock, others.

TV HITS
Studio Cast (1977) • Pickwick (S) SPC-3566 8-12
   Composer: Various. **Cast:** Birchwood Pops Orchestra.

TV JAZZ THEMES
Studiotrack • Somerset (M) P-8800 10-15
   One side has music from *Peter Gunn,* other has music from *Richard Diamond, 77 Sunset Strip* and *The Thin Man.*
   Composer: Henry Mancini, Livingston and David, Pete Rugolo. **Conductor:** Skip Martin. **Cast:** Video All-Stars with Shelly Manne, Paul Horn.

TV SINGALONG WITH MITCH MILLER AND THE GANG
TV Soundtrack (1961) • Columbia (M) CL-1698 10-12   61
TV Soundtrack (1961) • Columbia (S) CS-8428 12-15   61
   Composer: Various. **Conductor:** Mitch Miller. **Cast:** Mitch Miller and the Gang.

TV THEME SONG SINGALONG ALBUM
TV Soundtrack (1985) • Rhino/CBS (S) RNLP-703 8-10   85

TV THRILLER THEMES
Studiotrack • Philips (S) PHS-600-027 12-15
   Themes from *Route 66, Tightrope, M Squad, Avengers, Top Secret, Perry Mason, 77 Sunset Strip, Johnny Staccato* and others.
   Cast: Johnny Gregory.

TV WESTERN THEME SONGS
Studiotrack • Coral (S) CRL-57267 35-45   59
   Themes from *Have Gun Will Travel, Restless Gun, Wagon Train, Broken Arrow, Sugarfoot, Tales of Wells Fargo, Wyatt Earp, Maverick, Cheyenne, Gunsmoke, Death Valley Days* and *Buckskin.*
   Cast: Lawrence Welk and His Orchestra.
Studiotrack • Coronet (M) CX-175 8-12   60s
Studiotrack • Coronet (S) CXS-175 8-12   60s
   Music from *Wyatt Earp, Davy Crockett, Cheyenne* and others.
   Cast: Slim Boyd & His Range Riders.

TV'S GREATEST HITS

Studiotrack (1986) • Compleat (S) 671020-1 8-10   86
Music from *Bonanza, Rawhide, Alfred Hitchcock Presents, Dr. Kildare, Peyton Place, Peter Gunn, Dragnet, The Man from U.N.C.L.E., Jackie Gleason Show* and *Dick Van Dyke Show*.
Cast: Frank Chacksfield and His Orchestra.

TV'S TOP THEMES

Studiotrack (1954) • Capitol (EP) EAP 1-9118 15-20   54
Conductor: Ray Anthony. **Cast:** Ray Anthony & His Orchestra.

Studiotrack (1962) • Mercury (M) MG-60706.............................. 8-12   62

Studiotrack (1962) • Mercury (S) SR-60706.............................. 10-15   62
Music from *Dobie Gillis, My Three Suns, Nervous Jazz* and others.
Conductor: Pete Rugolo. **Cast:** Pete Rugolo and His Orchestra.

TAI-PAN

Soundtrack (1986) • Varese Sarabande (S) STV-81293 10-15   86
Composer: Maurice Jarre. **Conductor:** Maurice Jarre.

TAKE FIVE

Original Cast (1958) • Offbeat (M) O-4013... 30-35   58
With "curtain" cover.

Original Cast (1958) • Offbeat (M) O-4013... 12-18   58
With standard (no curtain) cover.
Conductor: Stan Keen. **Cast:** Jean Arnold, Ceil Cabot, Ellen Hanley, Ronny Graham, Gerry Matthews, Stan Keen and Gordon Connell (plural pianos).

TAKE IT FROM HERE

Original Cast (1963) • Columbia (M) No Number Given 45-55   63
10-inch LP. Industrial film made for Xerox from a show performed at a September 16, 1963 company meeting.
Composer: Wilson Stone. **Conductor:** Maurice Levine.

TAKE ME ALONG

Original Cast (1959) • RCA Victor (EP) SP-45-78 15-20   59
Promotional issue only. Has paper picture sleeve.

Original Cast (1959) • RCA Victor (M) LOC-1050 8-12   59

Original Cast (1959) • RCA Victor (S) LSO-1050 15-20   59
Black label.

Original Cast (1959) • RCA Victor (M) LOC-1050 8-10   Re

Original Cast (1959) • RCA Victor (S) LSO-1050 8-10   Re
Reissues. Have "RE" on cover. Orange label.
Composer: Robert Merrill. **Conductor:** Lehman Engel. **Cast:** Jackie Gleason, Walter Pidgeon, Eileen Herlie, Robert Morse, Una Merkel, Susan Luckey, Peter Conlow.

Studio Cast (1959) • RCA Victor (M) LPM 2142 10-12   59
Conductor: Frankie Carle.

TAKE ME OUT TO THE BALL GAME

Soundtrack (1949) • Curtain Calls (M) CC-100/18.............................. 10-15
Film soundtrack plus two outtakes.
Composer: Roger Edens, Betty Comden, Adolph Green. **Conductor:** Lennie Hayton. **Cast:** Gene Kelly, Frank Sinatra, Esther Williams, Betty Garrett, Jules Munshin.

TAKE THIS JOB AND SHOVE IT

Soundtrack (1981) • Epic (S) SE-37177... 8-10   81
Cast: Johnny Paycheck.

TAKING MY TURN

Original Cast (1984) • Broadway Ltd. (S) BLR-10001-R...................... 10-12   84
Despite label name, this was an off-Broadway show.
Composer: Gary William Friedman, Will Holt. **Conductor:** Barry Levitt. **Cast:** Tiger Haynes, Marni Nixon, Margaret Whiting, Ted Thurston, Shelia Smith, Cissy Houston.

TAKING OFF

Soundtrack (1971) • Decca (S) DL-79181 10-12   71
    Cast: Nina Hart, Susan Chafitz, 48 Girls, Carly Simon, Mary Mitchell, Ike and Tina Turner, Susan Cohen, Incredible String Band, Buck Henry.

TALE OF TWO CITIES

Studio Cast (1949) • Decca (M) DL-5153 40-50   50
    10-inch LP.

Studio Cast (1949) • Decca (M) DL-9059 30-45   50s
    One side has *Lost Horizon* (1937).
    Composer: Victor Young. **Conductor:** Claude Sweeten. **Cast:** Ronald Colman.

TALES FROM THE DARK SIDE (THE MOVIE)

Soundtrack (1990) • GNP Crescendo (S) GNPS-8021 8-10   90
    Composer: Chaz Jankel, Jim Manzie, Erica Lindsay, others. **Conductor:** Donald A. Rubinstein, Pat Regan. **Cast:** Donald A. Rubinstein, Chaz Jankel

TALES OF HOFFMANN

Soundtrack (1951) • London (M) XLLPA-4 40-50   51

Soundtrack (1951) • London (M) A-4302 20-25   Re
    Boxed, three-disc sets. Include booklets.
    Composer: Jacques Offenbach. **Conductor:** Sir Thomas Beecham. **Cast:** Robert Rounseville, Dorothy Bond (performs vocals for Moira Shearer in the film), Monica Sinclair (performs vocals for Pamela Brown), Bruce Darrgavel (performs vocals for Robert Helpmann), Owen Brannigan and Grahame Clifford (both perform vocals for Leonide Massine), Ann Ayars.

Studiotrack (1957) • Halo (M) 5084 8-15   57

TALES OF THE UNEXPECTED

TV Soundtrack (1979) • Stet (S) DS-15018 10-15   80
    Also has music from: *Edward and Mrs. Simpson, Malice Aforethought, Born and Bred, Rebecca, Paul Temple* and *Dr. Who*.
    Composer: Ron Grainer. **Conductor:** Robert Kingston.

TALK RADIO

Soundtrack (1988) • Varese Sarabande (S) VS-5215 12-15   88
    One side has music from *Wall Street*.
    Composer: Stewart Copeland.

TALL TOM JEFFERSON

Studio Cast (1974) • Wonderland (M) LP-270 12-15   74
    Musical history of Thomas Jefferson.
    Cast: Richard Kiley (narrator.)

TALLULAH

Original Cast (1983) • Painted Smiles (S) PS 1348 8-10   83
    Composer: Arthur Siegel, Mae Richard. **Conductor:** Bruce W. Coyle. **Cast:** Helen Gallagher, Joel Craig, Russell Nype, Tom Hofner.

TAMALPAIS EXCHANGE

Original Cast (1970) • Atlantic (S) SD-8263 25-30   70
    From the show titled *Exchange*.
    Cast: Penelope Ann Bodry, Mike Brandt, Susan Kay, Michael Knight.

TAMBOURINES TO GLORY

Studio Cast (1958) • Folkways (M) FG-3538 15-20   58
    Composer: Jobe Huntley, Langston Hughes. **Cast:** Ernest Cook, Porter Singers.

TAMING OF THE SHREW

Soundtrack (1967) · RCA Victor (M) VDM-117 20-25   67
    Composer: Nino Rota. **Conductor:** Nino Rota. **Cast:** Elizabeth Taylor, Richard Burton, Michael York, Cyril Cusack, Michael Hordern, Alfred Lynch, Alan Webb, Victor Spinetti, Natasha Pyne. (With dialogue.)

TAMMY AND THE BACHELOR: see INTERLUDE (1957)

TANGO ARGENTINA
Original Cast (1986) • Atlantic (S) 81636 8-10   86
  Cast: Elba Beron, Rave Lavie, others.

TAP
Soundtrack (1989) • Epic (S) SE 45084 10-15   89
  Composer: James Newton Howard, Stanley Clarke.

TAP DANCE KID
Original Cast (1984) • Polydor (S) 820210-1 8-10   84
Original Cast • That's Entertainment (S) TER-1096 8-10   80s
UK release.
  Composer: Henry Krieger, Robert Lorick. Conductor: Don Jones.

TAPEHEADS
Soundtrack (1988) • Island (S) 91030-1 8-10   88
  Cast: Swanky Modes, Devo, Bo Diddley, King Cotton, Fishbone.

TARANTULA: see THEMES FROM HORROR FILMS

TARAS BULBA
Soundtrack (1962) • United Artists (M) UAL-4100 20-30   62
Soundtrack (1962) • United Artists (S) UAS-5100 35-45   62
Gatefold covers.
  Composer: Franz Waxman, Mack David. Conductor: Franz Waxman.
Also see BIG COUNTRY

TAROT
Original Cast (1970) • United Artists (S) UAS-5563 15-20   70
  Composer: Touchstone. Cast: Touchstone (Tom Constanten, Paul Dresher, Gary Hirsh, Wes
  Steele, Art Fayer, Jim Byers). Touchstone was previously known as the Original Rubber Duck
  Band.

TARZAN
Original Radio Cast • Nostalgia (M) 1017 10-12
Congo Murder and *Long Journey* episodes.
Original Radio Cast • Mark 56 (M) 644 40-80   70s
Picture disc.
  Cast: Edgar Rice Burroughs.

TARZAN AND THE EYES OF THE LION
TV Soundtrack (1966) • MGM (M) LE-902 12-15   66
TV Soundtrack (1966) • MGM (S) LES-902 15-20   66
  Cast: Ron Ely.

TARZAN THE APE MAN
Soundtrack (1960) • MGM (M) E-3798 15-20   60
Soundtrack (1960) • MGM (S) SE-3798 20-25   60
Actual title: *Shorty Rogers Meets Tarzan.*
  Composer: Shorty Rogers. Conductor: Shorty Rogers.

TASTE OF HONEY
Studio Cast (1960) • Atlantic (M) 1355 10-15   61
Studio Cast (1960) • Atlantic (S) SD-1355 15-20   61
Bobby Scott plays his original music for the original Broadway production.
  Composer: Bobby Scott. Cast: Bobby Scott.

TAWNY

TV Soundtrack (1954) • Capitol (EP) EBF-471.................................... 20-30   54
Boxed, two-discs set. Same eight tracks as on H-471.
TV Soundtrack (1954) • Capitol (M) H-471.. 50-60   54
10-inch LP.
   Composer: Jackie Gleason. **Conductor:** Jackie Gleason. **Cast:** Jackie Gleason Orchestra,
   Bobby Hackett.

TAXI: see GENIE

TAXI DRIVER

Soundtrack (1976) • Arista (S) AL-4079... 15-20   76
Soundtrack (1976) • Arista (S) AL-58179.. 10-15   Re
   Composer: Bernard Herrmann. **Conductor:** Bernard Herrmann, Dave Blume. **Cast:** Bill Phillips,
   Robert DeNiro. (With dialogue.)

TEA DANCE

Original Cast (1976) • Pyramid (S) PY-9006 10-12   76
   Composer: D.C. LaRue. **Conductor:** Adam Schefrin, Steve Tubin. **Cast:** D.C. LaRue, Lou
   Christie.

TEA FOR TWO

Studiotrack (1950) • Columbia (EP) B-215... 15-20   50
Studiotrack (1950) • Columbia (M) CL-6149... 35-45   50
10-inch LP. Film inspired by *No, No, Nanette.*
Studiotrack • Columbia Collectors Series (M) 17660............................. 8-10   Re
Also has music from *On Moonlight Bay.*
   Composer: Vincent Youmans, Richard Rodgers, Lorenz Hart, George Gershwin, Ira Gershwin,
   Harry Warren, others. **Conductor:** Axel Stordahl. **Cast:** Doris Day, Gene Nelson, Ken Lane
   Singers, Page Cavanaugh Trio. ON MOONLIGHT BAY: **Conductor:** Paul Weston, Norman
   Luboff. **Cast:** Doris Day, Paul Weston and His Orchestra, Norman Luboff Choir, Jack Smith.

TEACHERS

Soundtrack (1984) • Capitol (S) SV-1-12371.. 8-10   84
   Cast: ZZ Top, .38 Special, Roman Holliday, Joe Cocker, Night Ranger, Freddie Mercury, Bob
   Seger and Silver Bullet Band, Eric Martin and Friends, Motels, Ian Hunter.

TEEN WOLF

Soundtrack (1985) • Southern Cross (S) SCRS-1010 8-10   85
   Cast: Miles Goodman, Douglas Brayfield.

TEEN WOLF TOO

Soundtrack (1987) • Curb (S) CRB-10400 8-10   87
Sequel to *Teen Wolf.* Cover may have credits sticker.
   Composer: Mark Goldenberg, Danny Elfman, others. **Cast:** Oingo Boingo, Ragtime, B.G. Vox,
   Ed Keupper, Mark Goldenberg, Real Life, Beat Farmers, Desert Rose Band.

TEEN-AGE CRUISERS

Soundtrack (1980) • Rhino (S) 016 10-12   80
   Cast: Johnny Legend, Billy Zoom, Blasters, Ray Campi, "Wildman" Tony Conn, Jerry Sikorski,
   Alvis Wayne, Jackie Lee "Waukeen" Chochran, Charlie Feathers.

TEENAGE MILLIONAIRE

Soundtrack (1961) • Ace (M) LP-1014 50-75   61
   Cast: Jimmy Clanton.

TEENAGE MUTANT NINJA TURTLES

Soundtrack (1990) • SBK (S) K1-91066 8-10   90
   Cast: Hi Tek 3, Partners in Kryme, M.C., Riff, Spunkadelic, Johnny Kemp, Investiture and Crime
   Wave, John Du Prez, Turtles Mutate, Orchestra on the Half Shell.

TEENAGE REBELLION

Soundtrack (1967) • Sidewalk (M) T-5903 .... 12-15 67
Soundtrack (1967) • Sidewalk (S) ST-5903............................ 20-25 67
  Composer: Mike Curb, Bob Summers, others. **Cast:** Burt Topper (narrator).

TELEPHONE: see MEDIUM

TELEVISION THEME SONGS

TV Soundtrack • Elektra (S) EL-60028................................ 10-15 82
  Music from *Hill Street Blues, The Greatest American Hero, The White Shadow, Richie
  Brockelman, Private Eye, The Rockford Files* and *Magnum P.I.*
  Composer: Mike Post. **Conductor:** Mike Post. **Cast:** Mike Post.
  Also see MIKE POST

TELEVISION'S GREATEST HITS

TV Soundtrack [Vol. 1] • TeeVee Toons (M) TVT-1100 .... 10-15 85
TV Soundtrack [Vol. 2] • TeeVee Toons (M) TVT-1200 .... 10-15 86
  Two disc sets. Each volume has 65 themes from 1950s and 1960s.

TELL ME LIES

Soundtrack (1967) • Gre-Gar (M) GG-5000 .... 12-15 67
Soundtrack (1967) • Gre-Gar (S) GGS-5000 .... 15-20 67
  Composer: Richard Peaslee, Adrian Mitchell. **Conductor:** Tony Russell. **Cast:** Glenda
  Jackson, Stokely Carmichael. (Wth dialogue.)

TELL ME ON A SUNDAY: see SONG AND DANCE

TELL ME THAT YOU LOVE ME, JUNIE MOON

Soundtrack (1970) • Columbia (S) OS-3540 .... 10-25 70
  Composer: Philip Springer, Pete Seeger, PG&E, Estelle Levitt. **Conductor:** Philip Springer.
  Cast: Pete Seeger, PG&E.

TELL TALE HEART: see WEIRD CIRCLE

TEMPEST

Soundtrack (1982) • Casablanca (S) NBLPH 7269 .... 8-10 82
  Composer: Stomu Yamashita. **Conductor:** Stomu Yamashita. **Cast:** Dinah Washington.

10

Soundtrack (1979) • Warner Bros. (S) BSK-3399 .... 10-15 79
  Composer: Henry Mancini, Maurice Ravel, others. **Conductor:** Henry Mancini. **Cast:** Henry
  Mancini and His Orchestra.

TEN: see MARILYN MONROE

TEN COMMANDMENTS

Soundtrack (1956) • Dot (M) DLP-3054-D............................ 20-30 56
Soundtrack (1960) • Dot (S) DLP-25054-D 15-20 60
  Two disc sets. Re-recorded in 1960 especially for stereo release.
  Composer: Elmer Bernstein. **Conductor:** Elmer Bernstein.
Soundtrack (1956) • Paramount (S) PAS 1006 .... 10-25 73
Soundtrack (1956) • MCA (S) MCA 2-4159............................ 8-15 Re
  Two disc sets. Paramount Records (later MCA) acquired the rights to the score from Dot.
  Composer: Elmer Bernstein. **Conductor:** Elmer Bernstein.
Studiotrack (1966) • United Artists (M) UAL 3495 .... 10-12 66
Studiotrack (1966) • United Artists (S) UAS-6495 .... 10-25 66
Studiotrack (1966) • United Artists (S) UA-LA304-G 8-10 74
  Composer: Elmer Bernstein. **Conductor:** Elmer Bernstein.

TEN GOLDEN YEARS: see 36 GREAT MOTION PICTURE THEMES AND
  ORIGINAL SOUNDTRACKS

TEN NORTH FREDERICK
Studiotrack (1958) • Audition (M) AUD-33-5928.................................. 40-50   58
Has *Sweet and Lovely* (film's main theme) plus music from *State Fair, Les Girls, Going Hollywood, Hollywood Revue of 1929, Touch and Go, The Jolson Story, I'll Cry Tomorrow* and *Kismet*.
Composer: Various. **Cast:** Four Themes, Dottie Evans, Monarchs, Loren Becker.

TEN THOUSAND BEDROOMS
Studiotrack (1957) • Capitol (EP) EAP 1-840 50-75   57
Composer: Nicholas Brodszky, Sammy Cahn. **Conductor:** Gus Levene. **Cast:** Dean Martin.

TEN TO MIDNIGHT
Soundtrack (1983) • Varese Sarabande (S) STV-81172 10-15   83
Cast: Robert O. Ragland.

TENDER IS THE NIGHT
Soundtrack (1962) • 20th Century-Fox (M) FOX-3054 125-150   62
Soundtrack (1962) • 20th Century-Fox (S) SFX-3054 175-200   62
Composer: Various. **Conductor:** Bernard Herrmann.

TENDER MERCIES
Soundtrack (1983) • Liberty (S) LO-51147 10-15   83
Composer: Various. **Cast:** Robert Duvall, Charlie Craig, Sherry Grooms, Lane Brody, Craig Bickhardt, Gail Youngs.

TENDERLOIN
Original Cast (1960) • Capitol (M) WAO-1492...................................... 12-18   60
Original Cast (1960) • Capitol (S) SWAO-1492................................... 20-25   60
Includes theater program in pocket of back cover.
Composer: Jerry Bock, Sheldon Harnick. **Conductor:** Hal Hastings. **Cast:** Ron Husmann, Wynne Miller, Eileen Rodgers, Rex Everhard, Maurice Evans, Eddie Phillips, Lee Becker, Raymond Bramley, Irene Kane, Nancy Emes, Carvel Caster, Margery Gray, Lanier Davis, Jack Leigh.
Studio Cast • Capitol (M) T 1536.. 8-12
Full title: *Dance to the Music from Tenderloin.*
Cast: Nelson Riddle.

TENE BRAE
Soundtrack • That's Entertainment (S) TER-1064................................ 8-10   80s
UK release.
Cast: Goblin.

10TH ANNIVERSARY JAMES BOND ALBUM: see JAMES BOND – 10TH ANNIVERSARY

TENTH VICTIM
Soundtrack (1965) • Mainstream (M) 56071.. 30-35   65
Soundtrack (1965) • Mainstream (S) S-6071....................................... 20-55   65
Composer: Piero Piccioni. **Conductor:** Piero Piccioni. **Cast:** Mina.

TEPEPA
Soundtrack • Cerberus (S) CERS-0106 10-15   82
Composer: Ennio Morricone. **Conductor:** Ennio Morricone.

TEQUILA SUNRISE
Soundtrack (1988) • Capitol (S) C1-91185.. 8-10   88
Cast: Ann Wilson, Robin Zander, Crowded House, Everly Brothers, Beach Boys, Andy Taylor, Church, Bobby Darin, Dave Grusin, Lee Ritenour, David Sanborn, Duran Duran, Ziggy Marley and Melody Makers.

TERMINATOR
Soundtrack (1984) • Enigma (S) 72000-1 10-15   84
Composer: Brad Fiedel, others. **Cast:** Tahnee Cain & Tryanglz, Jay Ferguson and 16mm, Lin Van Hek.

TERMS OF ENDEARMENT
Soundtrack (1984) • Capitol (S) SV-12329... 10-15   84
> **Composer:** Michael Gore. **Cast:** Ethel Merman, Eddie Roll, Grover Dale and the Jets, Judy Garland.

TERROR VISION
Soundtrack (1986) • Restless (S) 72120-1... 8-10   86
> **Cast:** Fibonaccis, Richard Band.

TESS
Soundtrack (1981) • MCA (S) 5193... 10-15   81
> **Composer:** Philippe Sarde. **Conductor:** Carlo Savina. **Cast:** London Symphony Orchestra, Larry Butler.

TEVYA AND HIS DAUGHTERS
Original Cast (1957) • Columbia (M) OL-5225.................................... 20-25   57
> **Composer:** Serge Hovey. **Conductor:** Serge Hovey. **Cast:** Mike Kellin, Anna Vita Berger, Paul E. Richards, Carroll Conroy, Howard DaSilva, Joan Harvey.

TEXAS CHAINSAW MASSACRE PART 2
Soundtrack (1986) • I.R.S. (S) IRS-6184.. 8-10   86
> **Cast:** Torch Song, Lords of the New Church, Timbuk 3, Cramps, Concrete Blonde, Oingo Boingo, Stewart Copeland.

TEXAS, LI'L DARLIN'
Original Cast (1949) • Decca DA-748... 20-25   50
> 78 rpm album.

Original Cast (1949) • Decca (M) DL-5188... 65-75   50
> 10-inch LP.
> **Composer:** Robert Emmett Dolan, Johnny Mercer. **Conductor:** Will Irwin. **Cast:** Kenny Delmar, Danny Scholl, Mary Hatcher, Fredd Wayne, Loring Smith.
> Also see ARMS AND THE GIRL

TEXAS ROMANCE, 1909: see BAD COMPANY

THANK GOD IT'S FRIDAY
Studio Cast (1978) • Springboard (S) SPB-4109................................. 10-15   78
> **Cast:** Studio 78.

Soundtrack (1978) • Casablanca (S) NBLP-7099-3 15-20   78
> Two discs. Includes bonus 12-inch single by Donna Summer.
> **Cast:** Donna Summer, Commodores, Diana Ross, Thelma Houston, Santa Esmeralda, Pattie Brooks, Paul Jabara, Wright Brothers, Flying Machine, D.C. LaRue.

Soundtrack (1978) • Springboard (S) 0298 5-10   78
> **Cast:** Lionel Richie and the Commodores.

THANK YOUR LUCKY STARS
Soundtrack (1943) • Curtain Calls (M) CC-100/8 12-20
Soundtrack (1943) • Sandy Hook (M) SH-2012..................................... 8-20   Re

THANKS A MILLION
Soundtrack • Caliban (M) 6021 8-10
> Also has music from *Happy Go Lucky*.
> **Cast:** Paul Whiteman, Dick Powell, Mary Martin.

THAT DARN CAT
Soundtrack (1965) • Buena Vista (M) BV-3334 15-20   65
Soundtrack (1965) • Buena Vista (S) STER-3334................................ 25-30   65
> **Composer:** Bob Brunner, Richard M. Sherman, Robert B. Sherman. **Conductor:** Bob Brunner. **Cast:** Louis Prima, Bobby Troup.

THAT MAN IN ISTANBUL
Soundtrack (1966) • Mainstream (M) 56072....................................... 12-18   66
Soundtrack (1966) • Mainstream (S) S-6072...................................... 20-25   66
> **Composer:** Georges Garvarentz, Buddy Kaye. **Cast:** Richard Anthony.

THAT MIDNIGHT KISS
Studiotrack (1949) • RCA Victor (M) LM-86.. 30-35   51
  10-inch LP.
Studiotrack (1949) • RCA Victor (M) LM-86.. 25-30   51
Studiotrack (1949) • RCA Victor (M) LM-2422...................................... 18-20
  Also has music from *Toast of New Orleans*.
    Composer: Various. **Conductor:** Constantine Callinicos, Ray Sinatra. **Cast:** Mario Lanza,
    Elaine Malbin.

THAT NIGHT IN RIO
Soundtrack (1941) • Curtain Calls (M) CC 100/14.............................. 10-12
  Silver Screen Soundtrack Series. Also includes *Weekend in Havana*, with outtakes from
  both films.
    Composer: Harry Warren, Mack Gordon. **Cast:** Alice Faye, Carmen Miranda, Don Ameche,
    John Payne, Cesar Romero.

THAT OTHER WOMAN'S CHILD
Original L.A. Cast (1982) • Web OC 110... 10-20   82
    Composer: Sherry Landrum, George Clinton. **Cast:** Matt Boyd, Mary Angela Young, Jay
    Huguely, others.

THAT WAS THE WEEK THAT WAS: see JOHN F. KENNEDY

THAT WAS THEN, THIS IS NOW
Soundtrack (1985) • Easy Street (S) ESA-9903.................................. 10-12   85
    Composer: Keith Olsen, Bill Cuomo, others. **Cast:** Pattie Brooks, Kipp Lennon, Roach, Kevin
    Moore.

THAT'S DANCING!
Soundtrack (1985) • EMI America (SE) SJ-17149................................. 8-10   85
    Composer: Henry Mancini, others. **Conductor:** Henry Mancini, others. **Cast:** Ruby Keeler, Wini
    Shaw, Dick Powell, Fred Astaire, Ginger Rogers, Ray Bolger, Judy Garland, Gene Kelly, Donald
    O'Connor, Ann Miller, Bobby Van, Tommy Rall, Bob Fosse, Bee Gees, Irene Cara, Kim Carnes.

THAT'S ENTERTAINMENT!
Soundtrack (1974) • MCA (S) MCA2-11002.. 15-20   74
  Two discs. Gatefold cover. Some tracks are stereo, but the majority of the album is mono.
  Back cover lists film credits in small print
Soundtrack (1974) • MCA (S) MCA2-11002.. 10-15   76
  Same as above except: a) back cover lists film credits in larger print, with title printed in an
  arc at top; b) song listings provide more information on *Honeysuckle Rose* and *The Song's
  Gotta Come from the Heart*; c) includes the final song, *That's Entertainment*, which the
  original release did not.
    Conductor: Henry Mancini, others. **Cast:** Fred Astaire, Bing Crosby, Gene Kelly, Frank Sinatra,
    James Stewart, Donald O'Connor, Peter Lawford, Debbie Reynolds, Mickey Rooney, Judy
    Garland, Lena Horne, June Allyson, Jimmy Durante, Eleanor Powell, Jane Powell, Joan
    Crawford, Jean Harlow, Cary Grant, Mario Lanza, Kathryn Grayson, Howard Keel, Ann Miller,
    Maurice Chevalier, Leslie Caron, others.
Studiotrack (1974) • Columbia (S) KG-33065.................................... 10-12   74
  Two discs. Full title: *Songs Featured in That's Entertainment*.
    Conductor: Andre Kostelanetz. **Cast:** Andre Kostelanetz.

THAT'S ENTERTAINMENT, PART 2
Soundtrack (1976) • MGM (SE) MG-1-5301.. 10-15   76
  Cover intact (no clipped corners).
Soundtrack (1976) • MGM (SE) MG-1-5301.. 5-10   76
  Cover has clipped corners or punch-out holes.

Soundtrack (1976) • MCA (SE) MCA-6155 5-8   Re
On all of these, some tracks are true stereo but the majority of the album is electronically processed stereo.
Conductor: Nelson Riddle. **Cast:** Fred Astaire, Gene Kelly, Judy Garland, Lena Horne, Leslie Caron, Mel Ferrer, Kathryn Grayson, Bing Crosby, Ethel Waters, Jimmy Durante, Debbie Reynolds, Donald O'Connor, Nanette Fabray, Jack Buchanan, Betty Hutton, Howard Keel, Maurice Chevalier, others.

THAT'S THE WAY IT IS
Soundtrack (1970) • RCA Victor (S) LSP-4445 20-30   70
Orange label.
Soundtrack (1970) • RCA Victor (S) AFL1-4445 10-15   78
Conductor: Joe Guercio. **Cast:** Elvis Presley, James Burton (guitar), John Wilkinson (guitar), Jerry Scheff (bass), Ronnie Tutt (drums), Joe Guercio and His Orchestra, Glen D. Hardin (piano), David Briggs (keyboards), Charlie Hodge (guitar, vocals), Kathy Westmoreland (vocals), Imperials (vocals), Sweet Inspirations (vocals).

THEME FROM EXODUS (AND OTHER GREAT THEMES)
Studiotrack (1961) • MGM (M) E-3950 15-20   61
Studiotrack (1961) • MGM (S) SE-3950 25-30   61
Composer: Various. **Conductor:** David Rose. **Cast:** David Rose Orchestra.

THEME MUSIC FROM GREAT MOTION PICTURE SCORES
Studiotrack (1951) • RCA Victor (M) LPT 1008 15-18   51
Music from *Spellbound, Traumerei, Fantasia Mexicana, Undercurrent, Duel in the Sun, Lost Weekend, Gone with the Wind* and *Love Story.*
Composer: Max Steiner, Aaron Copland, Miklos Rozsa, Johannes Brahms, Robert Schumann, Dimitri Tiomkin. **Conductor:** Al Goodman. **Cast:** Al Goodman and His Orchestra.

THEME SCENE
Soundtrack • RCA Victor (S) ABL1-3052 10-15   78
Soundtrack • RCA Victor (Q) AQL1-3052 15-20   78
Music from *Once Is Not Enough* and eight other films.
Composer: Henry Mancini.

THEMES!
Studiotrack (1962) • Capitol (M) T-1652 15-20   62
Studiotrack (1962) • Capitol (S) ST-1652 20-25   62
Music from *Captain from Castile, Road House, Love Is a Many-Splendored Thing, The Hurricane, Anastasia* and *The Pleasure of His Company.*
Conductor: Alfred Newman. **Cast:** Alfred Newman and His Orchestra.

THEMES FROM
Studiotrack (1960) • Carlton (M) LP 12-126 15-25   60
Studiotrack (1960) • Carlton (S) ST LP 12-126 55-65   60
Audiophile stereo.
Composer: Various. **Conductor:** Lew Douglas. **Cast:** Lew Douglas and His Orchestra.

THEMES FROM BEN CASEY AND DR. KILDARE
Studiotrack (1960s) • Diplomat (M) 2269 8-12   60s

THEMES FROM BOX-OFFICE BLOCK BUSTERS
Studiotrack • MGM (M) E 3894 12-15
Conductor: David Rose.

THEMES FROM CLASSIC SCIENCE FICTION, FANTASY & HORROR FILMS
Studiotrack • Varese Sarabande (S) STV-81077 12-15   78
Same as *Themes from Horror Movies* (Coral) except for the editing of narration and sound effects, which detracted from the original. Remastered.
Composer: Hans J. Salter, Herman Stein, Fred Carling, Ed Lawrence, Henry Mancini, Paul Dressau, James Bernard, William Lava. **Conductor:** Dick Jacobs.
Also see THEMES FROM HORROR MOVIES

THEMES FROM GREAT FILMS

Studiotrack • Waldorf (M) MH 33-195 10-15   50s
    10-inch LP. Music from *An Affair to Remember, Second Chorus, April Love, Fascination, Les Girls* and *Tammy*.
      Cast: Bob Eberly, Sylvia Textor, Hi-Fi's, Dottie Evans, Monarchs, Loren Becker, Enoch Light Orchestra.

Studiotrack (1957) • Waldorf (M) MHK-22-1224 10-15   57
      Cast: Enoch Light Orchestra.

Studiotrack (1962) • Time (M) 52078 8-12   62

Studiotrack (1962) • Time (S) S/2078 10-15   62
    Music from *How the West Was Won, To Kill a Mockingbird, Days of Wine and Roses, Mutiny on the Bounty, A Girl Named Tamiko, Gigot, Lawrence of Arabia, The Longest Day, Prologue from West Side Story, Bye Bye Birdie, Jumbo* and *Gypsy*.

THEMES FROM HIT TV SHOWS

Studiotrack • Peter Pan (S) 8185 10-15
      Cast: Pop Singers & Orchestra.

THEMES FROM HOLLYWOOD

Studiotrack (1957) • Colortone (M) C33-4904 10-20   57
    Music from *April Love, Tammy, An Affair to Remember* and *The Tender Trap*.
      Cast: Bob Eberly, Sylvia Textor, Mike Stewart, Ray Bloch and His Orchestra.

Studiotrack (1957) • Colortone (M) C33-4927 10-20   57
      Cast: Colortone Studio Orchestra.

THEMES FROM HORROR MOVIES

Studiotrack • Coral (M) CRL-57240 40-45   59

Studiotrack • Coral (S) CRL-757240 40-60   59
    Music from *The Mole People, The Creature from the Black Lagoon, This Island Earth, The Incredible Shrinking Man, It Came from Outer Space, The Creature Walks Among Us, The House of Frankenstein, The Horror of Dracula, Tarantula, Son of Dracula, Revenge of the Creature* and *Deadly Mantis*.
      Composer: Hans J. Salter, Herman Stein, Fred Carling, Ed Lawrence, Henry Mancini, Paul Dressau, James Bernard, William Lava. **Conductor:** Dick Jacobs. **Cast:** Bob McFadden (narrator).
    Also see THEMES FROM CLASSIC SCIENCE FICTION, FANTASY & HORROR FILMS

THEMES FROM ITALIAN FILMS

Studiotrack (1957) • MGM (M) E-3485 30-40   57
    Cover pictures Sophia Loren, Gina Lollobrigida and Sylvana Mangano. Music from *Bitter Rice, Anna, Bread, Love and Dreams, Hell Raiders of the Deep, Indiscretion of an American Wife, Woman of the River* and *Saluti e Baci*.
      Cast: Robert Ashley Orchestra.

THEMES FROM MASTERPIECE THEATRE

TV Soundtrack [Vol. 1] (1981) • Sine Qua Non (S) GPMT 10 15-25   81

TV Soundtrack [Vol. 2] (1986) • Sine Qua Non (S) SQN-5052-1 15-25   85

TV Soundtrack (1985) • Sine Qua Non (S) SQN-5057 20-25   85
    Two discs. Gatefold cover.

THEMES FROM MUTINY ON THE BOUNTY (AND OTHER GREAT FILMS)

Studiotrack (1962) • Warner Bros. (M) W-1476 8-20   62

Studiotrack (1962) • Warner Bros. (S) WS-1476 10-25   62
    Also has music from *El Cid, The Music Man, Exodus, The Apartment, Gypsy, Gay Purr-ee, Ride the High Country, Mutiny on the Bounty* and *West Side Story*.
      Composer: Various. **Conductor:** George Greeley. **Cast:** George Greeley (piano) and His Orchestra.

THEMES FROM NEW PROVOCATIVE FILMS
Studiotrack (1970) • Liberty/United Artists (S) UAS-6742.................... 25-35   70
Music from *What Do You Say to a Naked Lady, Sweden Heaven and Hell, Lover, Women in Love, De Sade, The Libertine, Medium Cool, Fanny Hill, Bob and Carol and Ted and Alice, John and Mary, All the Loving Couples* and *The Arrangement.*
Cast: Leroy Holmes and Orchestra.

THEMES FROM PEYTON PLACE WITH OTHER TV & FILM GREATS
Studiotrack (1965) • Spinorama (S) S-161 10-20   65

THEMES FROM THE GREAT MOTION PICTURES
Soundtrack (1966) • Metro (M) M-608... 10-15   66
Soundtrack (1966) • Metro (S) MS 608 15-20   66
Music from *Grand Prix, Doctor Zhivago* and *Born Free.*
Composer: Maurice Jarre, John Barry. **Cast:** John Barry, MGM Orchestra, Metropolitan Pops Orchestra.
Soundtrack • United Artists (M) UAL 6303 15-20   60s
Music from *The V.I.P.'s, Mondo Cane, Lawrence of Arabia, How the West Was Won, Never on Sunday, Taras Bulba, Dr. No, The Apartment, Irma La Douce, Phaedra, The Great Escape, Cleopatra, Divorce Italian Style, Mutiny on the Bounty* and *Exodus.*
Cast: Leroy Holmes, Riz Ortolani, Ferrante & Teicher, Hollywood Sound Stage Orchestra, Manos Hadjidakis, Andre Previn, Mikis Theodorakis, Elmer Bernstein, Carlo Rustichelli.

THEMES FROM THE JAMES BOND THRILLERS
Studiotrack (1965) • London (M) LL-3412 10-12   65
Studiotrack (1965) • London (S) PS-412... 15-20   65
Music from *Goldfinger, From Russia with Love* and *Dr. No.*
Composer: Norman Barry, others. **Conductor:** Roland Shaw. **Cast:** Roland Shaw and His Orchestra.

THEMES FROM THE MOVIES
Studiotrack (1956) • Tops (M) L-1519.. 15-25   56
Composer: Various. **Conductor:** Lew Raymond. **Cast:** Lew Raymond and His Orchestra, Toppers, Bud Roman, Ronnie Deauville, Gayle Larson, Mimi Martel, Rhythmaires.

THEMES FROM TV
Studiotrack • Diplomat (M) 2269 8-12
Studiotrack • Diplomat (S) DS-2269.. 8-12
Music from *Ben Casey, Cheyenne, Late Show, Arthur Murray's TV Party, Dr. Kildare, Victory at Sea, Danny Thomas TV Show, Alfred Hitchcock TV Show* and *Hawaiian Spectacular.*

THEMES FROM TV'S TOP 12
Studiotrack (1962) • Reprise (M) R-6018 10-15   62
Studiotrack (1962) • Reprise (S) R9-6018.. 15-20   62
Composer: Various. **Conductor:** Neal Hefti. **Cast:** Neal Hefti and His Orchestra.

THEMES OF TV'S GREATEST WESTERNS
Studiotrack (1959) • RCA Victor (M) LBY-1027 35-45   59
Cast: Sons of the Pioneers, Prairie Chiefs, Johnny O'Neill.

THEMES TO REMEMBER (TOP TV THEMES & BACKGROUND MUSIC)
Studiotrack • Decca (S) DL-74481 30-40
Music from *The Virginian, 87th Precinct* and others.
Cast: Stanley Black Orchestra.

THEN CAME BRONSON
Soundtrack • Capitol (S) 2672.. 15-20

THERE'S NO BUSINESS LIKE SHOW BUSINESS
Soundtrack (1954) • Decca (EP) ED-828 15-20   54
Soundtrack (1954) • Decca (M) DL-8091 20-25   54
  Black label.
Soundtrack (1954) • Decca (M) DL-8091 15-18   54
  Rainbow label.
    Composer: Irving Berlin. **Conductor:** Alfred Newman, Lionel Newman. **Cast:** Ethel Merman,
    Donald O'Connor, Mitzi Gaynor, Johnnie Ray, Dan Dailey, Dolores Gray (performing vocals
    sung by Marilyn Monroe in the film).
Soundtrack (1954) • RCA Victor (EP) EPA-593 100-125   54
  Marilyn Monroe's selections from the soundtrack, that are not on the Decca issues. These
  tracks also appear on a variety of other Marilyn Monroe albums.
    Composer: Irving Berlin. **Conductor:** Alfred Newman, Lionel Newman. **Cast:** Marilyn Monroe.
    Also see GENTLEMEN PREFER BLONDES
    Also see MARILYN
    Also see MARILYN MONROE
    Also see REMEMBER MARILYN

THEY CALL IT AN ACCIDENT
Soundtrack (1982) • Island (S) WB-1457 10-12
Soundtrack (1982) • Island (S) XILP-9757 8-10   82
Soundtrack (1982) • Island (S) ILPS-9757 8-10   82
    Composer: W. DeLeon, P. Norbert. **Cast:** Steve Winwood, U2, Marianne Faithfull, Jess Roden,
    Peter Wood, Compass Point All Stars, Wallyu Badarou.

THEY CALL ME MISTER TIBBS
Soundtrack (1970) • United Artists (S) UAS-5214 20-25   70
    Composer: Quincy Jones. **Conductor:** Quincy Jones.

THEY LIVE
Soundtrack (1988) • Enigma (S) D1-73367 8-10   88
    Cast: John Carpenter, Alan Howarth.

THEY SHOOT HORSES, DON'T THEY?
Soundtrack (1969) • ABC (S) ABCS-OC-10 10-20   69
  Gatefold cover.
    Composer: Johnny Green, others. **Conductor:** Johnny Green. **Cast:** Bonnie Bedelia (vocal).

THEY STOPPED THE SHOW!
Original Cast (1954) • Decca (M) DL-9111 20-25   54
Original Cast (1954) • Decca (SE) DL-79111 20-30   59
Original Cast • MCA (SE) MCA-2070 8-12   Re
  Original performances from Broadway shows, some previously unreleased on LP: *Leave It
  to Me, Bloomer Girl, Call Me Mister, Where's Charley?, The King and I, Knickerbocker
  Holiday, Carousel, Wonderful Town, Texas Li'l Darlin', Follow the Girls, Two on the Aisle*
  and *Oklahoma!*
    Composer: Various. **Conductor:** Various. **Cast:** Mary Martin, Alfred Drake, Joan Roberts, Betty
    Garrett, Ray Bolger, Gertrude Lawrence, Walter Huston, Dooley Wilson, Danny Scholl, Rosalind
    Russell, John Raitt, Gertrude Niesen, Dolores Gray.
Original Cast • Audio Rarities (M) LPA-2290 20-25   69
  Vaudeville tracks from 1900-1918, taken from cylinders.
    Cast: George M. Cohan, Harry Lauder, Marie Dressler, Lillian Russell, others.

THEY'RE PLAYING OUR SONG
Original Cast (1979) • Casablanca (S) NBLP-7141 8-15   79
  Gatefold cover.
Original Cast (1979) • Casablanca (S) NBLP-7141 5-20   Re
  Standard cover.
    Composer: Marvin Hamlisch, Carol Bayer Sager. **Conductor:** Larry Blank. **Cast:** Robert Klein,
    Lucie Arnaz, Chorus.

Original Australian Cast (1979) • Festival (S) 37356 8-10   79
  Composer: Marvin Hamlisch, Carole Bayer Sager. **Conductor:** Dale Ringland. **Cast:** John
  Waters, Jacki Weaver.
Original London Cast (1980) • Chopper (S) CHOP-E-6 10-12   80
Original London Cast (1979) • That's Entertainment (S) TER-1035 10-12   83
  UK release.
  Composer: Marvin Hamlisch, Carole Bayer Sager. **Conductor:** Grant Hossack.

THIEF
Soundtrack (1981) • Virgin (S) VL-2213 8-12   81
  Composer: Tangerine Dream. **Cast:** Tangerine Dream.
Soundtrack (1981) • Elektra (S) 5E-521 8-10   81
  Composer: Tangerine Dream (Edgar Froese, Chris Franke, Johannes Schmoelling), Craig
  Safan. **Cast:** Tangerine Dream.

THIEF OF BAGDAD
Studiotrack (1977) • Elmer Bernstein Film Music
  Collection (S) FMC-8 30-35   77
Studiotrack (1978) • Warner Bros. (S) BSK-3183 15-20   78
  Composer: Miklos Rozsa. **Conductor:** Elmer Bernstein. **Cast:** Royal Philharmonic Orchestra,
  Saltarello Choir, Bruce Ogston (baritone), Phyllis Cannan (mezzo-soprano), Powell Jones (as
  "Abu").
  Also see JUNGLE BOOK

THIEF OF HEARTS
Soundtrack (1984) • Casablanca (S) 422-822 942 15-20   84

THIEF WHO CAME TO DINNER
Soundtrack (1973) • Warner Bros. (S) BS-2700 12-15   73
  Composer: Henry Mancini. **Conductor:** Henry Mancini.

THIN BLUE LINE
Soundtrack (1988) • Elektra/Nonesuch (S) 97 92091 15-20   88
  Composer: Philip Glass. **Conductor:** Michael Riesman.

THIN MAN
Original Radio Cast (1936) • Radiola (M) MR-1077 25-30   77
  Crime Series 11, Release 77. Broadcast from CBS Lux Radio Theatre, June 8, 1936. Also
  has interview with Theda Bara.

THING
Soundtrack (1982) • MCA (S) 6111 10-15   82
  Composer: Ennio Morricone. **Conductor:** Ennio Morricone.

THING WITH TWO HEADS
Soundtrack (1972) • Pride (S) PRD-0005 15-25   72
Studiotrack (1972) • Pride (S) LST 7353 15-20   73
  Full title: *Music Inspired By the Thing with Two Heads.*
  Cast: Perry Botkin, Jr., Jerry Butler, Ollie Nightingale, others.

THING-FISH
Original Cast (1984) • EMI (S) 24-0294-3 35-40   84
  Boxed, three-disc set. With libretto.
  Composer: Frank Zappa. **Conductor:** Frank Zappa. **Cast:** Ike Willis, Terry Bozzio, Dale Bozzio,
  Napoleon Murphy Brock, Bob Harris, Johnny "Guitar" Watson, Ray White.

THINGS TO COME
Soundtrack (1937) • London (M) STS-15112 10-12
  Excerpts from original score of *The Shape of Things to Come.*.
  Composer: Sir Arthur Bliss. **Conductor:** Sir Arthur Bliss. **Cast:** London Symphony Orchestra.

Studiotrack (1977) • EMI (Q) ASD-3416.. 15-25   77
One side has music from *A Color Symphony*.
Composer: Sir Arthur Bliss.
Also see BERNARD HERRMANN CONDUCTS GREAT BRITISH FILM SCORES

THIRD MAN

Soundtrack (1949) • London (M) LL-1560 30-40   56
Soundtrack (1949) • London (M) LL-1560 20-35   59
Full title: *Third Man Theme*. Reissue (1959) has a different front cover, picturing TV series
star Michael Rennie – though music is from the film and not the TV series. One side is
zither duets by Fritz & Jacky.
Cast: Anton Karas, Fritz & Jacky (zither).

13 DAUGHTERS

Original Cast (1961) • Mahalo (S) M-3003 20-30   61
Although this show came to Broadway the following year (starring Don Ameche), this
recording is of the original Hawaiian production.
Composer: Eaton Magoon Jr. **Conductor:** Alvina Kaulili. **Cast:** Napua Stevens, Kam Fong
Chun, Richard Kuga, Augustina Santiago, Tamara Long, Lordie Kaulili, Jack Annon.

30 IS A DANGEROUS AGE, CYNTHIA

Soundtrack (1968) • London (S) MS-82010 15-18   68
Composer: Dudley Moore. **Conductor:** Dudley Moore.

THIRTY MINUTES WITH BEATRICE LILLIE

Studio Cast • Liberty Music Shops (M) LMS-1002................................. 50-75
Beatrice Lillie performs songs from her Broadway shows. Some covers have a plain white
back cover, others have ads.
Composer: Noel Coward, Arthur Schwartz, Howard Dietz, others. **Cast:** Beatrice Lillie.

36 GREAT MOTION PICTURE THEMES & ORIGINAL SOUNDTRACKS

Soundtrack/Studiotrack [Vol. 1] (1968) • United Artists (S) UXS-68 20-30   68
Two discs. Also known as *Ten Golden Years*.
Soundtrack/Studiotrack [Vol. 2] (1969) • United Artists (S) UXS-69 20-30   69
Two discs.
Soundtrack/Studiotrack [Vol. 3] (1972) • United Artists (S) UXS-72 20-30   72
Two discs.

36 HOURS

Soundtrack (1964) • Vee Jay (M) VJLP-1131....................................... 12-15   64
Soundtrack (1964) • Vee Jay (S) VJLPS-113....................................... 12-18   64
Soundtrack (1964) • Varese Sarabande (S) VC-81071 8-10   79
Composer: Dimitri Tiomkin. **Conductor:** Dimitri Tiomkin.

33 GREAT WALT DISNEY MOTION PICTURE MELODIES

Studiotrack (1962) • Buena Vista (M) BV-3319 15-20   62
Studiotrack (1962) • Buena Vista (S) STER-3319 25-30   62
Conductor: Tutti Camarata.

THIS COULD BE THE NIGHT

Soundtrack (1957) • MGM (M) E-3530... 40-50   57
Soundtrack (1957) • MCA (M) 39085 8-10   86
Composer: Richard Rodgers, Lorenz Hart, Cole Porter, others. **Conductor:** Ray Anthony. **Cast:**
Julie Wilson, Ray Anthony Orchestra, Neile Adams.

THIS EARTH IS MINE

Soundtrack (1959) • Decca (M) DL-8915 40-80   59
Soundtrack (1959) • Decca (S) DL-78915... 90-110   59
Soundtrack (1959) • Varese Sarabande (S) VC-81076 8-12   79
Composer: Hugo Friedhofer, James Van Heusen, Sammy Cahn. **Conductor:** Joseph
Gershenson. **Cast:** Bob Grabeau, Universal-International Orchestra.

THIS IS BROADWAY'S BEST

Original Cast • Columbia (M) B2W-1 12-15
Original Cast • Columbia (S) B2WS-1 15-20
  Two discs. Gatefold cover with bound-in booklet. Music from earlier Columbia original cast albums, including some tracks that are rechanneled stereo.
    Composer: Various. **Cast:** Jan Clayton, Charles Fredericks, Ella Logan, Annabelle Hill, Ezio Pinza, Carol Channing, Harold Lang, Beverly Fite, Carol Haney, Alfred Drake, Doretta Morrow, Richard Kiley, Henry Calvin, Enid Mosier, Ada Moore, Shorty Long, John Henson, Alan Gilbert, Roy Lazarus, Irra Petina, George Blackwell, Thomas Pyle, Barbara Cook, Judy Holliday, Carol Lawrence, Larry Kert, Pat Suzuki, Rex Harrison, Julie Andrews, Ethel Merman, Mary Martin, Robert Coote, Paul Lynde, Marijane Maricle, Clive Revill, Eliza Seal, Adolph Green, John Reardon, Cris Alexander.

THIS IS CINERAMA

Soundtrack (1952) • Peter Pan (SE) 152 30-35   73
    Composer: Max Steiner, others. **Cast:** Lowell Thomas (narration).

THIS IS ELVIS

Soundtrack (1981) • RCA Victor (S) CPL2-4031 15-18   81
  Two discs. Has custom inner sleeves.
    Conductor: Joe Guercio. **Cast:** Elvis Presley, Scotty Moore (guitar), James Burton (guitar), John Wilkinson (guitar), Jerry Scheff (bass), Bill Black (bass), Bob Moore (bass), Dudley Brooks (piano), Floyd Cramer (piano), Boots Randolph (sax), D.J. Fontana (drums), Ronnie Tutt (drums), Jordanaires (vocals), Kathy Westmoreland (vocals), J.D. Summer and the Stamps (vocals), Sweet Inspirations (vocals), Joe Guercio Orchestra.

THIS IS OLDSMOBILITY

TV Soundtrack (1958) • Hudson Recording (M) HR-119 20-30   58
  Indicates "not for public performance broadcast on radio or television or commercial use." Full title: *This Is Oldsmobility (Oldsmobile's 1958 Dealer Announcement Show)*. Colored vinyl. Label and number are shown only in vinyl trail-off area.
    Conductor: Sherman Frank. **Cast:** Florence Henderson, Bill Hayes.
  Also see GOOD NEWS ABOUT OLDS
  Also see OLDS FOR '60 MUSICAL

THIS IS SPINAL TAP

Soundtrack (1984) • Polydor (S) 817846-1 10-15   84

THIS IS THE ARMY

Original Cast (1942) • Decca A-340 20-30   42
  78 rpm album.
Original Cast (1942) • Decca (M) DL-5108 75-100   50
  10-inch LP.
Original Cast • JJA (M) 19742 15-20   74
Original Cast (1946) • Columbia Special Products (M) X-14877 8-10   Re
  Also have music from *Call Me Mister*.
    Composer: Irving Berlin. **Conductor:** Corporal Milton Rosenstock. **Cast:** Earl Oxford, Ezra Stone, Philip Truex, Julie Oshins, Robert Stanley, Stuart Churchill, James "Stump" Cross, Irving Berlin and an all-soldier cast. CALL ME MISTER: **Composer:** Harold Rome. **Conductor:** Lehman Engel. **Cast:** Betty Garrett, Lawrence Winters, Paula Bane, Danny Scholl, Bill Callahan, Harry Clark, Chandler Cowles, Jules Munshin.
Soundtrack (1942) • Sandy Hook (M) SH-2035 12-15   80
    Composer: Irving Berlin. **Conductor:** Ray Heindorf. **Cast:** Ronald Reagan, Joan Leslie, George Murphy, Irving Berlin, Alan Hale, Rosemary de Camp.

THIS IS YOUR LIFE

TV Studiotrack (1958) • Imperial (M) LP-9051 75-125   58
    Conductor: Van Dexter. **Cast:** Van Dexter and Orchestra.

THIS PROPERTY IS CONDEMNED

Soundtrack (1966) • Verve (M) V-8664 18-20   66
Soundtrack (1966) • Verve (S) V6-8664 25-30   66
    Composer: Kenyon Hopkins, Jay Livingston, Ray Evans. **Conductor:** Kenyon Hopkins. **Cast:** Mary Badham.

THIS WAS BURLESQUE

Original Cast (1962) • Roulette (M) R-25185 20-25   62
Original Cast (1962) • Roulette (S) SR-25185 20-30   62
    Composer: Sonny Lester, Bill Grundy, others. **Conductor:** Sonny Lester. **Cast:** Ann Corio, Buddy Bryant, Steve Mills, Lisa Carroll, Sandy Fuller, Jackie Henkins, "Fabulous Fannie," "Taj Mahal," "Mercedie Bends," Casino Cuties.

THIS WORLD TOMORROW

Studio Cast • Guild Publications (S) GP-6258 8-12
    Composer: Alexander Laszlo. **Cast:** Vincent Price (narration).

THIS YEAR'S TOP MOVIE SONGS

Studiotrack (1963) • United Artists (S) UAS-6356 10-15   63
    Music from *Tom Jones, Lilies of the Field, Love in the Country, Toys in the Attic, Stolen Hours, It's a Mad Mad Mad World, Charade, Mondo Cane, 55 Days at Peking* and *Pappa's Delicate Condition.*
    Cast: Four Lads.

THOMAS AND THE KING

Original Cast • Varese Sarabande (S) 1009 8-10   80s
    Composer: John Williams, James Marbert.

THOMAS CROWN AFFAIR

Soundtrack (1968) • United Artists (S) UAS-5182 15-20   68
Soundtrack (1968) • United Artists (S) UA-LA295-G 8-10   74
    Composer: Michel Legrand, Marilyn Bergman, Alan Bergman. **Conductor:** Michel Legrand. **Cast:** Noel Harrison, Michel Legrand.

THOROUGHLY MODERN MILLIE

Soundtrack (1967) • Decca (M) DL-1500 8-20   67
Soundtrack (1967) • Decca (S) DL-71500 8-25   67
    Gatefold cover with eight-page bound-in booklet.
    Composer: Elmer Bernstein, James Van Heusen, Sammy Cahn. **Conductor:** Andre Previn. **Cast:** Julie Andrews, Carol Channing, John Gavin, James Fox. (With dialogue.)
Studiotrack (1967) • Alshire (S) ST-3002A 8-12   67
    Composer: Elmer Bernstein, James Van Heusen, others. **Cast:** Hollywood Sound Stage Orchestra and Chorus.
Studiotrack (1967) • Camden (S) CAS-2165 8-12   67
Studiotrack • Decca (S) DL-74864 8-15
    Cast: Dukes of Dixieland.
Studiotrack • Design (M) DLP-266 8-12
    Cast: Skidoos.
Studiotrack • MGM (S) 44 ST 8-12
Studiotrack • Somerset (S) SF-27700 8-12
    Cast: Cinema Sound Stage Orchestra and Chorus.
Studiotrack • Tifton (S) S-78008 8-12
    Cast: Sunset Singers.

THOSE CALLOWAYS

Soundtrack (1965) • Universal Cut (M) S4RG-0278 35-40   65
    Commercial spots. Made for radio station use only.

THOSE DARING YOUNG MEN IN THEIR JAUNTY JALOPIES

Soundtrack (1969) • Paramount (S) PAS-5006 12-15   69
    Composer: Ron Goodwin, others. **Conductor:** Ron Goodwin. **Cast:** Jimmy Durante.

THOSE FABULOUS STRINGS PLAY THUNDERBALL AND OTHER MOVIE HITS

Studiotrack (1965) • Metro (M) M 551 10-12   65
Studiotrack (1965) • Metro (S) MS 551 12-15   65
    Also has music from *Goldfinger, Pink Panther, Sandpiper, Yellow Rolls Royce, What's New Pussycat* and *Help!*

THOSE GLORIOUS MGM MUSICALS

Soundtrack • MGM (M) 2-SES-40-ST 10-15   73
    Two discs. Has *Easter Parade* and *Singin' in the Rain*. Contains *Broadway Ballet* sequence, omitted from original MGM releases.
Soundtrack • MGM (M) 2-SES-41-ST 10-15   73
    Two discs. Has *Seven Brides for Seven Brothers* and *Rose Marie*.
Soundtrack • MGM (M) 2-SES-42-ST 10-15   73
    Two discs. Has *Show Boat* and *Annie Get Your Gun*.
Soundtrack • MGM (M/SE) 2-SES-43-ST 30-35   73
    Two discs. Has *The Pirate, Pagan Love Song* (both electronically processed stereo) and *Hit the Deck* (mono). MGM reissued a portion of its soundtrack albums in electronic stereo in the mid-1960s, but *The Pirate* and *Pagan Love Song* were not among them. Since this album is the only release of these recordings in rechanneled stereo, it is worth more than others in the series.
Soundtrack • MGM (M) 2-SES-44-ST 10-15   73
    Two discs. Has *The Band Wagon* and *Kiss Me Kate*.
Soundtrack • MGM (M) 2-SES-45-ST 10-15   73
    Two discs. Has *Till the Clouds Roll By* and *Three Little Words*.
Soundtrack • MGM (M) 2-SES-49ST 10-15   73
    Two discs. Has *Good News, In the Good Old Summertime* and *Two Weeks with Love*. No releases were assigned to the three selection numbers skipped (46, 47 and 48).
Soundtrack • MGM (M) 2-SES-50ST 10-15   73
    Two discs. Has *Lovely to Look At* and *Brigadoon*.
Soundtrack • MGM (M) 2-SES-51ST 10-15   73
    Two discs. Has *Silk Stockings, The Barkleys of Broadway* and *Les Girls*.
Soundtrack • MGM (M) 2-SES-52ST 10-15   73
    Two discs. Has *Everything I Have Is Yours, Summer Stock* and *I Love Melvin*.
Soundtrack • MGM (M) 2-SES-53ST 10-15   73
    Two discs. Has *Nancy Goes to Rio, Rich, Young and Pretty* (previously unreleased music) and *Royal Wedding*.
Soundtrack • MGM (M) 2-SES-54ST 10-15   73
    Two discs. Has *Deep in My Heart* and *Words and Music*. Contains *Slaughter on Tenth Avenue* sequence, originally issued separate from the soundtrack album. Some discs in this series are listed as being in stereo, but with the exception of *The Pirate* and *Pagan Love Song*, they are original mono recordings. Composers, conductors and casts are found separately under each title.

THOSE MAGNIFICENT MEN IN THEIR FLYING MACHINES

Soundtrack (1965) • 20th Century-Fox (M) TFM-3174 12-15   65
Soundtrack (1965) • 20th Century-Fox (S) TFS-4174 15-18   65
    Composer: Ron Goodwin. **Conductor:** Ron Goodwin.
Soundtrack (1965) • 20th Century-Fox (M) FM-2 40-50   65
    Script and open-end interviews with Sarah Miles, Stuart Whitman, Terry-Thomas, Irina Demick, James Fox and Alberto Sordi. Made for radio station use only.

THOUSAND MILES OF MOUNTAINS

Studio Cast (1964) • Northern Pacific (M) KB-4368.............................. 20-30   64
From Northern Pacific's centennial celebration, "A Musical Adventure in Railroading,"
Composer: Norman Richards. **Conductor:** Norman Richards. **Cast:** Raymond Massey
(narration), Ken Carson, Larry Douglas, Stuart Foster, Hal Linden, Lynn Roberts, Allen Swift,
Iggie Wolfington, Mason Adams, Paul Ballantyne, Patricia Bright, John Connell, Leslie Hunter,
Leon Janney, Bart Larsen, others.

THOUSANDS CHEER

Soundtrack (1943) • Hollywood Soundstage (M) HS-409..................... 12-15
Composer: Various. **Conductor:** Georgie Stoll. **Cast:** Kathryn Grayson, Gene Kelly, Eleanor
Powell, Mickey Rooney, Virginia O'Brien, June Allyson, Gloria De Haven, Bob Crosby Orchestra,
Kay Kyser Orchestra, Lena Horne, Benny Carter Band, Red Skelton, Donna Reed, Margaret
O'Brien, Judy Garland.

THREADS OF GLORY

Original Cast (1976) • Desert Dramatics (S) 4741................................ 10-12   76
Two discs.
Composer: Lex de Azevedo, Doug Stewart. **Conductor:** Lex de Azevedo. **Cast:** Ric de
Azevedo, Kent Larson, Helen McVey, Roger McKay, Candy Wilson.

THREE AMIGOS

Soundtrack (1987) • Warner Bros. (S) 1-25558 8-10   87
Composer: Randy Newman. **Cast:** Chevy Chase, Steve Martin, Martin Short, Fred Asparagus,
Randy Newman.

THREE BILLION MILLIONAIRES

Studio Cast (1963) • United Artists (M) UXL-4 15-25   63
Studio Cast (1963) • United Artists (S) UAS-54.................................... 20-30   63
Two discs. Produced for the United Nations.
Conductor: Ray Ellis. **Cast:** Judy Garland, Bing Crosby, Sammy Davis Jr., Carol Burnett, Wally
Cox, Jack Benny, Danny Kaye, George Maharis, Terry Thomas, Adlai E. Stevenson, Robert
Allen.

THREE BITES OF THE APPLE

Soundtrack (1967) • MGM (M) E-4444... 8-15   67
Soundtrack (1967) • MGM (S) SE-4444 8-20   67
Soundtrack (1967) • MCA (S) 25010... 5-8   86
Composer: Eddy Manson, others. **Conductor:** Robert Armbruster. **Cast:** David McCallum.

THREE COINS IN THE FOUNTAIN

Soundtrack (1954) • 20th Century-Fox CT 22532/6235 30-35   54
Single-sided 78 rpm, with movie theme song and promotional radio announcements.
Soundtrack (1954) • Capitol (EP) EAP-1-542....................................... 20-25   54
Composer: Sammy Cahn, Jule Styne. **Cast:** Frank Sinatra.

THREE DAYS OF THE CONDOR

Soundtrack (1975) • Capitol (S) SW-11469.. 10-15   75
Composer: Dave Grusin. **Conductor:** Dave Grusin. **Cast:** Jim Gilstrap, Marti McCall.

THREE EVENINGS WITH FRED ASTAIRE

TV Soundtrack • Choreo (M) A-1 20-25   60
Gatefold cover. Excerpts from *An Evening With Fred Astaire* (1958), *Another Evening With
Fred Astaire* (1959) and *Astaire Time* (1960). Each of these scores was previously issued
in its entirety by Chrysler.
TV Soundtrack • DRG (M) S3L-5181 20-30   82
Boxed, three-disc set. Complete reissues of the Chrysler *An Evening With Fred Astaire*,
Another Evening With Fred Astaire and *Astaire Time*.
Composer: Various. **Conductor:** David Rose, others. **Cast:** Fred Astaire, Barrie Chase, others.
Also see ANOTHER EVENING WITH FRED ASTAIRE
Also see EVENING WITH FRED ASTAIRE
Also see ASTAIRE TIME

THREE FOR THE ROAD
Soundtrack (1987) • Varese Sarabande (S) STV 81319 12-15   87
    Composer: Jerry Goldberg.

THREE FOR THE SHOW
Soundtrack (1955) • Mercury (EP) EP-2-3283 20-25   55
    Does not contain the overture.
Soundtrack (1955) • Mercury (M) MG-25204 50-60   55
    10-inch LP. Includes the overture.
    Composer: George Duning, George Gershwin, Ira Gershwin, others. **Conductor:** Morris Stoloff.
    Cast: Betty Grable, Marge Champion, Jack Lemmon, Jud Conlon Singers.

THREE FOR TONIGHT
Studio Cast (1955) • RCA Victor (M) LPM-1150 10-15   55
Studio Cast (1955) • RCA Victor (SE) LSP-1150 8-12   59
    Actual title of above two: *Belafonte*. Has seven tracks from *Three for Tonight* plus other
    selections.
    Conductor: Tony Scott, others. **Cast:** Harry Belafonte, Millard J. Thomas (guitar), Norman
    Luboff Choir.

THREE FUGITIVES
Soundtrack (1989) • Varese Sarabande (S) VS-5219 12-15   89
    Composer: David McHugh.

THREE GUYS NAKED FROM THE WAIST DOWN
Original Cast (1985) • Polydor (S) 820244-1 8-10   85
Original Cast (1985) • That's Entertainment (S) TER-1100 8-10   80s
    UK release.
    Composer: Michael Rupert, Jerry Colker. **Conductor:** Henry Aronson. **Cast:** Scott Bakula,
    Jerry Colker, John Kassir.

THREE IN THE ATTIC
Soundtrack (1968) • Sidewalk (S) ST-5918 25-30   69
    Composer: Chad Stuart, Jeremy Clyde, Wayne Irwin, others. **Cast:** Chad Stuart, Jeremy Clyde.

THREE IN THE CELLAR
Soundtrack (1970) • American Int'l (S) A-1036 20-25   71
    From the film *Up in the Cellar*. Another album – using that title – is nearly identical, but has
    a different cover.
    Composer: Don Randi, Dory Previn. **Conductor:** Don Randi. **Cast:** Hamilton Camp.
    Also see UP IN THE CELLAR

THREE LITTLE GIRLS IN BLUE
Soundtrack (1946) • Hollywood Soundstage (M) HS-410 8-12
    Composer: Mack Gordon, Josef Myrow, Harry Warren. **Cast:** June Haver, Vivian Blaine,
    Celeste Holm, Carol Stewart (performs vocals for Vera-Ellen in the film), Del Porter (performs
    vocals for Charlie Smith), Ben Gage (performs vocals for George Montgomery).

THREE LITTLE PIGS
Studiotrack (1934) • Disneyland (M) ST-1910 12-15   61
Studiotrack (1934) • Disneyland (M) DQ-1310 10-15   66
    Composer: Frank Churchill. **Conductor:** Frank Churchill. (With dialogue.)

THREE LITTLE WORDS
Soundtrack (1950) • MGM - MGM-53 15-20   50
    78 rpm album.
Soundtrack (1950) • MGM (EP) X-53 15-20   50
Soundtrack (1950) • MGM (M) E-516 30-60   50
    10-inch LP.
Soundtrack (1950) • MGM (M) E-3768 15-18   60
    Gatefold cover. One side is music from *Annie Get Your Gun*.

Soundtrack (1950) • Metro (M) M-615... 10-12   67
Soundtrack (1950) • Metro (SE) MS-615.. 10-12   67
  Composer: Harry Ruby, Bert Kalmar. **Conductor:** Andre Previn. **Cast:** Fred Astaire, Red
  Skelton, Gloria De Haven, Arlene Dahl, Anita Ellis (performs vocals for Vera-Ellen in the film),
  Gale Robbins, Helen Kane (performs vocals for Debbie Reynolds).
Studiotrack (1950) • Decca A-567 12-20   50
  78 rpm album.
Studiotrack (1950) • Decca (M) DL-5160 15-25   50
  10-inch LP.
  Cast: Leo Reisman and His Orchestra, Bob Hannon, Sunny Skylar, Diane Courtney, Honey
  Dean, Double Daters.
  Also see GOOD NEWS
  Also see THOSE GLORIOUS MGM MUSICALS

THREE MESQUITEERS

Studiotrack (1980s) • Varese Sarabande (S) STV 81319..................... 10-15   85
  Full title: *The Three Mesquiteers – Music from Republic Westerns and Serials.*
  Composer: William Lava, others.

THREE MUSKETEERS (1928)

Original London Cast (1928) • Monmouth Evergreen (SE) MES-7050 . 15-20   72
  Also has music from *Rose Marie.*
  Composer: Rudolf Friml, Clifford Grey, P.G. Wodehouse. **Cast:** Dennis King, Adrienne Brune,
  Raymond Newell, Robert Woollard.
Studio Cast • Command Performance (S) LP-9 8-12
  Music and dialogue.

THREE MUSKETEERS (1974)

Soundtrack (1974) • Bell (S) 1310... 8-12   74
  Composer: Michel Legrand. **Conductor:** Michel Legrand.

THREE O'CLOCK HIGH

Soundtrack (1987) • Varese Sarabande (S) STV 81339 8-10   87
  Composer: Tangerine Dream. **Cast:** Tangerine Dream.

THREE PENNY OPERA: see THREEPENNY OPERA

3 SAILORS AND A GIRL

Studiotrack (1953) • Capitol (EP) FBF-485 20-25   53
  Two discs.
Studiotrack (1953) • Capitol (M) L-485 50-60   54
  10-inch LP.
  Composer: Sammy Fain. **Conductor:** George Greeley. **Cast:** Gordon MacRae, Jane Powell,
  Gene Nelson.

THREE SMART GIRLS: see ON MOONLIGHT BAY

THREE STAR STUDDED HOURS WITH HOLLYWOOD'S LEADING LADIES

Radio Cast (1946) • Nostalgia (M) 3NLR133....................................... 15-20   79
  Three discs.
  Cast: Lana Turner, Irene Dunne, others.

3:10 TO YUMA

Soundtrack • Citadel (M) GD-2... 35-45   79
  Composer: George Duning. **Conductor:** George Duning. **Cast:** Frankie Laine.

THREE THE HARD WAY

Soundtrack (1974) • Curstom (S) CRS-8602-ST.................................. 12-15   74
  Composer: Richard Tufo, Lowrell Simon, Phil Upchurch, Tom Green. **Cast:** Impressions.

THREE TO MAKE MUSIC
Original Cast (1958) • RCA Victor (M) LPM-2012.............................. 20-25   58
Original Cast (1958) • RCA Victor (S) LSP-2012.............................. 25-30   58
    Composer: Mary Rodgers, Linda R. Melnick. **Conductor:** Thomas Scherman. **Cast:** Mary Martin.

THREE TOUGH GUYS: see TOUGH GUYS

THREE WISHES FOR JAMIE
Original Cast (1952) • Capitol (EP) EDM-317...................................... 25-35   52
Original Cast (1952) • Capitol (M) S-317....................................... 100-125   52
Original Cast (1952) • Stet (M) DS-15012.. 15-18   Re
    Composer: Ralph Blane, Bert Wheeler. **Conductor:** Joseph Littau. **Cast:** Bert Wheeler, Anne Jeffreys, John Raitt, Charlotte Rae, Robert Halliday, Peter Conlow.

THREE WORLDS OF GULLIVER
Soundtrack (1960) • Colpix (M) CP-414 45-55   61
    Back covers of several Colpix albums, circa-'60 and '61, show this as being available in stereo (SCP-414). We have yet to confirm that any exist.
Soundtrack (1960) • Citadel (M) CT-7018 10-15   81
    Includes dialogue and sound effects.
    Composer: Bernard Herrmann. **Conductor:** Bernard Herrmann. **Cast:** Kerwin Mathews, Jo Morrow, June Thorburn, Lee Patterson, Gregoire Aslan, Basil Sydney.
    Also see MYSTERIOUS FILM WORLD OF BERNARD HERRMANN

THREEPENNY OPERA
Original Berlin Cast (1933) • Capitol/Telefunken (M) P-8117 20-25
    Actual title: *Kurt Weill's Die Dreigroschenoper (The Three-Penny Opera)*.
    Composer: Kurt Weill, Bert Brecht. **Conductor:** Theo Mackeben. **Cast:** Lewis Ruth Band, Willy Trenk, Lotte Lenya, Kurt Gerron (narrator), Erika Helmke, Erich Ponto
Original German Cast • Telefunken (M) 97012 25-30
    Also has music from *The Rise And Fall of the City of Mahagonny*.
Original German Cast • Telefunken (M) 641991 8-10   Re
    Composer: Kurt Weill, Marc Blitzstein.
Original Revival Cast (1954) • MGM (M) E-3121.................................. 15-18   54
Original Revival Cast (1954) • MGM (M) E-3121.................................... 8-12   Re
    Black label. There are two front cover variations for above issues.
Original Revival Cast (1954) • MGM (M) E-3121 OC............................... 8-10   59
Original Revival Cast (1954) • MGM (SE) SE-3121................................ 8-12   59
    Black label. Gatefold covers.
Original Revival Cast (1954) • Polydor (SE) 820260-1 5-8   Re
    Composer: Kurt Weill, Marc Blitzstein. **Conductor:** Samuel Matlowsky. **Cast:** Lotte Lenya, Scott Merrill, Charlotte Rae, Beatrice Arthur, Martin Wolfson, John Astin, Jo Sullivan, Paul Dooley, George Tyne, Gerald Price, Threepenny Opera Orchestra, Joseph Beruh, Bernard Bogin, William Duell.
Studio Cast • Columbia (M) O2L-257 30-35   58
Studio Cast • Columbia (SE) O2S-201 30-35   58
    Two discs. Includes booklet and poster. German language edition.
Studio Cast • Columbia/Odyssey (SE) 42-32977 8-10   Re
    Composer: Kurt Weill, Marc Blitzstein. **Conductor:** Wilhelm Bruckner-Riggeberg. **Cast:** Lotte Lenya, Wolfgang Neuss, Willy Trenk-Trebitsch.
Studio Cast • Vanguard (M) RSV-9002 20-25
Studio Cast • Vanguard (SE) S-273e 8-10
    German language.
    Composer: Kurt Weill, Bertolt Brecht (German lyrics). **Conductor:** F. Charles Adler. **Cast:** Helge Roswaenge, Alfred Jerger, Rosette Anday.

Soundtrack (1964) • RCA Victor (M) LOC-1086 125-150   64
Soundtrack (1964) • RCA Victor (S) LSO-1086 175-200   64
Above two have original cover design, quickly discarded in favor of the one that follows. Only one copy has thus far been verified of this edition. Cover has white background with pink and black drawing of Macheath's back, scarf and cane dangling, and a parade of characters dancing underneath. RCA's "An Original Soundtrack Recording" box is pink and white and not on an angle.
Soundtrack (1964) • RCA Victor (M) LOC-1086 12-15   64
Soundtrack (1964) • RCA Victor (S) LSO-1086 15-20   64
Reworked covers also have white background, but have an orange-like drawing of Macheath and Jenny, with Sammy Davis Jr. in the foreground. RCA's "An Original Soundtrack Recording" box is orange and white and on an angle. Front covers have "RE" at bottom.
Composer: Kurt Weill, Marc Blitzstein. Conductor: Samuel Matlowsky. Cast: Curt Jurgens, Hildegarde Neff, June Ritchie, Sammy Davis Jr., George S. Irving (performs vocals for Curt Jurgens in the film), Martha Schlamme (performs vocals for Hildegarde Neff), Jo Wilder (performs vocals for June Ritchie), Gert Frobe. (With dialogue.)
Soundtrack (1964) • London (M) M-76004 15-20   64
German language.
Composer: Kurt Weill, Bertolt Brecht (German lyrics). Conductor: Peter Sandloff. Cast: Hildegarde Neff, June Ritchie, Gert Frobe.
Original Revival Cast (1976) • Columbia (S) PS-34326 15-20   76
Original Revival Cast (1976) • Columbia (Q) PS-34326 15-20   76
Gatefold cover. With lyrics insert.
Composer: Kurt Weill, Marc Blitzstein. Conductor: Stanley Silverman. Cast: C.K. Alexander, Blair Brown, Ellen Greene, Raul Julia, Caroline Kava, David Sabin, Tony Azito, Elizabeth Wilson, Roy Brocksmith, Pendleton Brown, Glenn Kezer, Robert Schlee.
Soundtrack (1989) • CBS (S) 45630 10-15   89
Actual title: *Mack the Knife.* Film version of the 1976 Broadway revival.
Composer: Kurt Weill, Marc Blitzstein. Conductor: Dov Seltzer. Cast: Raul Julia, Julia Migenes, Richard Harris, Roger Daltrey, Julie Walters, Clive Revill, Elizabeth Seal.

THRILL OF A ROMANCE
Studiotrack (1945) • Camden (M) CAL-424 25-35   58
Actual title: *The Lighter Side of Lauritz Melchoir.* Also has three selections from *Two Sisters from Boston.*
Composer: Various. Cast: Lauritz Melchoir.

THRILLER
TV Soundtrack (1960) • Time (M) T-52034 20-30   60
TV Soundtrack (1960) • Time (S) S-2034 35-45   60
Composer: Pete Rugolo. Conductor: Pete Rugolo.

THUNDER ALLEY
Soundtrack (1967) • Sidewalk (M) T-5902 15-20   67
Soundtrack (1967) • Sidewalk (S) ST-5902 20-25   67
Composer: Mike Curb, Jerry Styner, Guy Hemric, others. Conductor: Mike Curb. Cast: Annette Funicello, Eddie Beram, Sidewalk Sounds, Band Without a Name, Lorraine Singers.

THUNDERBALL
Soundtrack (1965) • United Artists (M) UAL-4132 12-20   65
Soundtrack (1965) • United Artists (S) UAS-5132 20-25   65
Soundtrack (1965) • United Artists (S) SW 90820 10-20   60s
Capitol Record Club issue.
Soundtrack (1965) • Sunset (S) SLS-50396 15-20   65
Composer: John Barry, Leslie Bricusse, Don Black. Conductor: John Barry. Cast: Tom Jones.
Studiotrack (1965) • Capitol (S) ST-2455 8-12   65
Full title: *Bang! Bang! Bang! Thunderball and Other Secret-Agent Themes.*
Composer: John Barry, Jerry Goldsmith, Lionel Bart, others. Cast: Elliott Fisher and His Orchestra.

Studiotrack (1965) • Somerset (S) SF 24700 8-12   65
  Full title: *Music from Thunderball.*
Studiotrack • RCA Camden (M) CAL 927.. 8-12
Studiotrack • RCA Camden (S) CAS 927.. 8-12
  Also has music from *Thunderball, The Knack, The FBI, Man from U.N.C.L.E., Honey West,
  I Spy, Trial's of O'Brian, The Young Set* and others.
  Conductor: Ray Martin. **Cast:** Ray Martin & Orchestra.

THURBER CARNIVAL
Original Cast (1960) • Columbia (M) KOL-5500 10-20   60
Original Cast (1960) • Columbia (S) KOS-2024 12-15   60
  Gatefold covers.
Original Cast (1960) • Columbia (M) KOL-5500 8-10   60
Original Cast (1960) • Columbia (S) KOS-2024 8-12   60
Original Cast (1960) • Columbia Special Products (S) CKOS-2024 5-10   Re
  Standard covers.
  Composer: James Thurber, Don Elliott. **Cast:** Tom Ewell, Peggy Cass, Paul Ford, John
  McGiver, Alice Ghostley, Peter Turgeon, Wynne Miller.

TICK . . . TICK . . . TICK
Soundtrack (1970) • MGM (S) SE-4667 12-30   70
  Conductor: Mike Curb. **Cast:** Tompall and the Glaser Brothers.

TICKLE ME
Soundtrack (1965) • RCA Victor (EP) EPA-4383 40-60   65
  Black label, dog on side.
Soundtrack (1965) • RCA Victor (EP) EPA-4383 50-100   69
  Orange label.
  Composer: Doc Pomus, Mort Schuman, Jerry Leiber, Mike Stoller, Fred Wise, Sid Wayne, Ben
  Weisman, others. **Cast:** Elvis Presley, Scotty Moore (guitar), D.J. Fontana (drums), Bob Moore
  (bass), Floyd Cramer (piano), Boots Randolph (sax), Millie Kirkham (vocals), Jordanaires
  (vocals).

TILL THE CLOUDS ROLL BY
Soundtrack (1946) • MGM - MGM-1... 15-20   46
  78 rpm album.
Soundtrack (1946) • MGM (EP) X-1 15-20   50
Soundtrack (1946) • MGM (EP) K-1 25-30   50
  Boxed, two-disc set.
Soundtrack (1946) • MGM (M) E-501 35-45   50
  10-inch LP. MGM's first soundtrack LP and EP release. Though not the first of its kind, this
  score is credited with starting the practice of producing albums recorded directly from the
  sound track of a motion picture.
Soundtrack (1946) • Metro (M) M-578.. 8-12   66
Soundtrack (1946) • Metro (SE) MS-578... 10-12   66
Soundtrack (1946) • MCA (M) 25000 5-8   86
  All of the above contain only excerpts from the score.
  Composer: Jerome Kern, others. **Conductor:** Lennie Hayton. **Cast:** Judy Garland, Tony Martin,
  Lena Horne, June Allyson, Kathryn Grayson, Virginia O'Brien, Caleb Peterson.
  Also see GENTLEMEN PREFER BLONDES
  Also see SINGIN' IN THE RAIN
  Also see THOSE GLORIOUS MGM MUSICALS

TILT
Soundtrack (1979) • ABC (S) AA-1114 8-10   79
  Composer: Lee Holdridge. **Conductor:** Lee Holdridge. **Cast:** Brooke Shields, Ken Marshall.

TIME AFTER TIME
Soundtrack (1979) • Entr'acte (S) ERS-6517 15-20   79
  Composer: Miklos Rozsa. **Conductor:** Miklos Rozsa. **Cast:** Royal Philharmonic Orchestra.

TIME CHANGES
Original Cast (1969) ● ABC (S) ABCS-681 25-30   69
A Ford Theatre presentation.
Composer: Harry Palmer, others. **Conductor:** Bert DeCopteaux, Johnny Pate. **Cast:** John Mazzarelli, Harry Palmer, Joey Scott, Arthur "Butch" Webster, Robert Tamagni.

TIME FOR SINGING
Original Cast (1966) ● Warner Bros. (M) W-1639 30-35   66
Original Cast (1966) ● Warner Bros. (S) HS-1639 45-65   66
Based on the novel *How Green Was My Valley*.
Composer: John Morris, Gerald Freedman. **Conductor:** Jay Blackton. **Cast:** Ivor Emmanuel, Tessie O'Shea, Shani Wallis, Laurence Naismith, Frank Griso, Brian Avery, Gene Rupert.

TIME IS THEN AS WELL AS NOW
Soundtrack ● Columbia (S) P-13246 8-12

TIME MACHINE
Soundtrack (1960) ● GNP/Crescendo (S) GNPS-8008 10-15   87
Also has overture from *Atlantis, the Lost Continent*.
Composer: Russell Garcia. **Cast:** Russell Garcia.

TIME OF DESTINY
Soundtrack (1988) ● Virgin Movie Music (S) 90938-1 10-15   88
Composer: Ennio Morricone.

TIME OUT OF MIND: see BANDIT OF SHERWOOD FOREST

TIME REMEMBERED
Original Cast (1957) ● Mercury (M) MG-20380 20-25   57
Original Cast (1957) ● Mercury (S) SR-60023 30-35   58
Incidental music from the dramatic Broadway play.
Composer: Vernon Duke. **Conductor:** Pete Rugolo. **Cast:** Tony Travis, Vernon Duke (piano).

TIME TO KEEP
TV Soundtrack (1964) ● RCA Victor (M) LOC-1088 10-15   64
From NBC News.
Cast: Chet Huntley, David Brinkley (newscasters).

TIME TO LOVE AND A TIME TO DIE
Soundtrack (1958) ● Decca (M) DL-8778 65-100   58
Soundtrack (1958) ● Varese Sarabande (M) VC-81075 10-15   79
Composer: Miklos Rozsa. **Conductor:** Miklos Rozsa. **Cast:** Universal-International Orchestra.

TIME TO RUN
Soundtrack (1973) ● World Wide Recordings (S) WWR-1001 15-20   73
Limited edition private pressing. Not commercially available.
Soundtrack (1973) ● World Wide (S) CSS-1575 10-15   73
Show "Premier Edition."
Composer: Ted Smith, Randy Stonehill. **Conductor:** Ted Smith. **Cast:** Jerry Whitman, Randy Stonehill, Barbara Sigel.

TIME TO SING
Soundtrack (1968) ● MGM (S) SE-4540 12-15   68
Soundtrack (1968) ● MCA (S) 1458 8-10   86
Composer: Hank Williams Jr., William Scoggins, L. Kusik, E. Snyder, S. Karliski. **Cast:** Hank Williams Jr., Shelley Fabares, Clara Ward Singers.

TIMES OF HARVEY MILK: see MRS. SOFFEL

TIMES SQUARE
Soundtrack (1980) • RSO (S) RPD-1026 8-10   80
  Promotional issue only.
Soundtrack (1980) • RSO (S) RS-2-4203.. 8-15   80
  Two discs.
    Cast: Suzi Quatro, Pretenders, Roxy Music, Gary Numan, Marcy Levy, Robin Gibb, Talking
    Heads, Joe Jackson, XTC, Ramones, Robin Johnson, Trini Alvarado, Ruts, D.L. Byron, Lou
    Reed, Desmond Child and Rouge, Garland Jeffreys, Cure, Patti Smith Group, David Johansen.

TINSELTOWN
Original L.A. Cast (1981) • Web (S) OC 102...................................... 10-20   81
    Cast: Composer: Mark Milner. **Cast:** Diane Benedict, Linda Lyons, David Pavlosky, Mindy Dow,
    Eddie D'Angelo.

TINTYPES
Original Cast (1981) • DRG (S) S2L-5196.. 10-15   81
  Two discs.

TIP TOES
Original London Cast (1925) • Monmouth Evergreen (SE) MES-7052 ... 8-12
  One side has music from *Wildflower*.
    Composer: George Gershwin, Ira Gershwin. **Conductor:** I.A. DeOrellana. **Cast:** Allen Kearns,
    Dorothy Dickson, Laddie Cliff, John Kirby, Peggy Beatty, Evan Thomas, Vera Bryer.

TO BE OR NOT TO BE
Soundtrack (1983) • Antilles (S) ASTA-2.. 8-12   83

TO BED . . . OR NOT TO BED
Soundtrack (1963) • London (M) M-76005 35-40   63
    Composer: Piero Picciono. **Conductor:** Piero Picciono.

TO BROADWAY WITH LOVE
Original Cast (1964) • Columbia (M) OL-8030...................................... 20-25   64
Original Cast (1964) • Columbia (S) OS-2630...................................... 35-45   64
  Original 1964 New York World's Fair cast, saluting the music of Broadway.
    Composer: Jerry Bock, Sheldon Harnick, others. **Cast:** Bob Carroll, Rod Perry, Don Liberto,
    Millie Slavin, Patti Karr, Guy Rotondo, Miriam Burton, Nancy Leighton.

TO CATCH A THIEF
Soundtrack (1955) • Coral (EP) EC-81083.. 50-75   54
  Has background music later heard in the film. (EP came out a year before the film.)
Soundtrack (1955) • Coral (M) CRL-57032 30-50
  Actual title: *Misty*. Has the EP tracks, plus additional studio jazz tracks.
    Conductor: Lyn Murray. **Cast:** Georgie Auld, Lyn Murray (tenor sax solos).

TO KILL A MOCKINGBIRD
Soundtrack (1962) • Ava (M) A-20 20-25   63
Soundtrack (1962) • Ava (S) AS-20 20-30   63
Soundtrack (1962) • Citadel (S) CT-7029... 10-15   81
    Composer: Elmer Bernstein. **Conductor:** Elmer Bernstein. **Cast:** Royal Philharmonic
    Orchestra.
Studiotrack (1962) • Elmer Bernstein Film Music
  Collection (S) FMC-7 20-25   76
Studiotrack (1962) • Warner Bros. (S) BSK-3184 10-12   78
    Composer: Elmer Bernstein. **Conductor:** Elmer Bernstein.

TO LIVE AND DIE IN L.A.
Soundtrack (1985) • Geffen (S) GHS-24081 8-10   85
    Cast: Wang Chung.

TO LIVE ANOTHER SUMMER, TO PASS ANOTHER WINTER
Original Cast (1971) • Buddah (S) BDS-95004 12-18   71
  Boxed, two-disc set.

Original Cast (1971) • Buddah (S) BDS-95004 10-12   Re
  Two discs.
    Composer: David Paulsen, Dov Seltzer. **Conductor:** David Kirvoshel. **Cast:** Rivka Raz, Aric Lavie, Yona Atari, Ili Gorlizki, Hanan Goldblatt.

TO SIR WITH LOVE
Soundtrack (1967) • Fontana (MS) MGF-27569................................... 10-20   67
Soundtrack (1967) • Fontana (S) SRF-67569 12-25   67
    Composer: Ron Grainer, others. **Conductor:** Ron Grainer. **Cast:** Lulu, Mindbenders.

TO WONG FOO, THANKS FOR EVERYTHING... JULIE NEWMAR
Soundtrack (1995) • MCA (S) 11231... 8-10   95

TOAST OF NEW ORLEANS
Studiotrack (1950) • RCA Victor DM-1417 35-45   50
  Two 78 rpms. Gatefold folder. Inside cover has full liner notes and film photos of Kathryn Grayson and Mario Lanza. Includes four "popular songs" from the film not included on any later releases.
    Composer: Sammy Cahn, Nicholas Brodszky. **Conductor:** Ray Sinatra. **Cast:** Mario Lanza.
Studiotrack (1950) • RCA Victor DM 1395.. 15-20   50
  78 rpm album. Gatefold folder. Has the classical arias from the film heard in all subsequent issues.
Studiotrack (1950) • RCA Victor (EP) DWM 1395................................. 15-20   51
  Boxed, three-disc set.
Studiotrack (1950) • RCA Victor (M) LM-75.. 25-35   51
  10-inch LP.
    Conductor: Constantine Callinicos. **Cast:** Mario Lanza, Elaine Malbin.
    Also see THAT MIDNIGHT KISS

TOBY TYLER
Soundtrack (1960) • Disneyland (M) ST-1904....................................... 12-18   60
  Film also known as *Ten Weeks with the Circus.*
    Composer: Richard Loring, Diane Lampert. **Cast:** Brian Corcoran, Henry Calvin, Gene Sheldon, Dal McKennon (narration).

TOCCATA FOR TOY TRAINS: see MIRACLE

TODAY'S GREATEST MOVIE HITS
Studiotrack • Columbia (S) CS-9556... 8-12
    Cast: Andre Kostelanetz.

TOGETHER
Soundtrack (1980) • RCA Victor (S) ABL1-3541 8-10   80
    Composer: Burt Bacharach, Paul Anka. **Conductor:** Burt Bacharach. **Cast:** Jackie DeShannon, Libby Titus, Michael McDonald.

TOGETHER AGAIN
Original Cast (1983) • Cerberus (S) COC 0301..................................... 10-15   85
    Composer: Bruce Kimmel. **Cast:** Bruce Kimmel, Penny Peyser, Marsha Kramer, Jeff Maxwell, Deborah Moradzadeh, Alan Abelew, Rich Wain.

TOGETHER BROTHERS
Soundtrack (1974) • 20th Century-Fox (S) ST-101 10-12   74
Soundtrack (1974) • 20th Century-Fox (S) 95809 8-10   Re
    Composer: Barry White, Love Unlimited. **Cast:** Love Unlimited Orchestra.

TOGETHER WITH MUSIC
TV Soundtrack (1955) • Ford Star Jubilee (M) No Number Used 50-60   55
  Promotional issue only.
TV Soundtrack (1955) • DRG (M) DARC2-1103 12-18   78
  Two discs.
    Composer: Noel Coward, Richard Rodgers, Oscar Hammerstein II, Cole Porter, others. **Cast:** Noel Coward, Mary Martin.

TOKYO FILE 212

Soundtrack • Screen Archives (M) SAAG 10.002.................................. 25-30

Includes four-page booklet and information insert sheet. Private pressing, "Not for commercial distribution."

Composer: Albert Glasser.

TOKYO OLYMPIAD

Soundtrack (1966) • Monument (M) MLP-8046.................................. 12-15　66

Soundtrack (1966) • Monument (S) SLP-18046.................................. 15-20　66

Composer: Toshiro Mayuzumi. **Conductor:** Toshiro Mayuzumi. **Cast:** Yomiuri Nihon Kokyo Gakudan Orchestra.

TOKYO POP

Soundtrack (1988) • Ric (S) RCR-850.. 8-10　88

Cast: Carrie Hamilton, Red Warriors, Michael Cerveris, Yutaka Todokkor, Papaya Paranoia.

TOLLER CRANSTON'S THE ICE SHOW … ON BROADWAY

Original Cast (1977) • Robden (S) RDR-1001....................................... 10-75　77

From the Palace Theater in New York City.

Composer: Al Kasha, Joel Hirschhorn.

TOM BROWN'S SCHOOL DAYS

Original London Cast (1972) • Decca (S) SKL-5137 .... 30-35　72

UK release.

Composer: Chris Andrews, Joan Maitland, Jack Maitland. **Conductor:** Alan Braden. **Cast:** Roy Dotrice, Judith Bruce, Leon Greene, David Gwillim, Adam Walton, Jill Martin, Christopher Guard, Ray Davis, Trudi Van Doorn.

TOM JONES (1963)

Soundtrack (1963) • United Artists (M) UAL-4113.................................. 8-10　63

Soundtrack (1963) • United Artists (S) UAS-5113.................................. 8-12　63

Soundtrack (1963) • United Artists (M) UAL-4134.................................. 8-10　66

Soundtrack (1963) • United Artists (S) UAS-5134 .... 10-12　66

Reissues (4134/5134) also have music from *Irma La Douce.*

Soundtrack (1963) • MCA (S) 39068.. 5-8　86

Composer: John Addison. **Conductor:** John Addison. IRMA LA DOUCE: **Composer:** Marguerite Monnot, Andre Previn. **Conductor:** Andre Previn. **Cast:** Andre Previn.

Also see CHARADE

TOM JONES (1964)

Studio Cast (1964) • Theatre Productions (M) 59000............................ 8-12　64

Studio Cast (1964) • Theatre Productions (S) S-9000.......................... 10-15　64

Planned for stage production, but not produced as such.

Composer: Ruth Batchelor, Bob Roberts. **Conductor:** Peter Matz. **Cast:** Clive Revill (narration), Bob Roman, Karen Morrow, Carole Shaw, Iggie Wolfington, Darlene Zito, Chuck Cassey Chorus, C. Magruder.

TOM JONES (1968)

Studio Cast (1968) • No Label Used (M) PRP-4343............................. 15-25　68

Full Title: *Excerpts from Tom Jones.* Selection number only shown in vinyl trail-off area.

Composer: Paul Holden. **Cast:** Pat MacPherson, Don MacPherson, Joel Higgins, Elizabeth French, Michael McElroy, Jim Farg, Paul Holden.

TOM SAWYER (1957)

TV Soundtrack (1957) • Decca (M) DL-8432...................................... 20-30　57

Theatre Guild production, aired on the United States Steel Hour.

Composer: Frank Luther. **Conductor:** Ralph Norman. **Cast:** Jimmy Boyd, John Sharpe (as Tom Sawyer), Bennye Gatteys, Rose Bampton, Clarence Cooper, Song Spinners.

TOM SAWYER (1972)

Studio Cast (1972) • Reader's Digest/United Artists (S) UAMPG-105 .. 10-15   72
"A Musical Adaptation." Boxed set. Includes lyrics booklet.
> **Composer:** Richard M. Sherman, Robert B. Sherman. **Cast:** Johnnie Whitaker, Jeff East, Jodie Foster, Celeste Holm.

Soundtrack (1973) • United Artists (S) UA-LA057-F 15-20   73
> **Composer:** Richard M. Sherman, Robert B. Sherman. **Conductor:** John Williams. **Cast:** Johnnie Whitaker, Jeff East, Jodie Foster, Charley Pride, Celeste Holm and Chorus.

Studiotrack (1973) • Alshire (S) S-5295 5-10   73
> **Cast:** 101 Strings.

Studiotrack (1973) • Golden (S) 280 10-12   73
> **Cast:** Early Williams (narration).

TOM THUMB

Soundtrack (1958) • Lion (M) L-70084 25-30   58
Soundtrack (1958) • MGM (M) CA-104-ST 12-15   68
Soundtrack (1958) • MCA (M) 25006 8-10   86
> **Composer:** Fred Spielman, others. **Conductor:** Muir Mathieson. **Cast:** Russ Tamblyn, Peter Sellers, Terry-Thomas, Stan Freberg, Dean Jones (narration), Ian Wallace, Bernard Miles, Alan Young, Jessie Matthews, June Thorburn, Norma Zimmer. (With dialogue.)

TOMFOOLERY

Original London Cast (1980) • Multi Media Tapes (ST) MMT LP-001 ... 30-40   80
Original London Cast (1980) • That's Entertainment (S) TER-1137 8-10   80s
UK release.
> **Composer:** Tom Lehrer. **Conductor:** Chris Walker. **Cast:** Robin Ray, Jonathan Adams.

TOMMY

Original Cast (1969) • Decca (S) DXSW-7205 15-20   69
Two discs. Includes booklet.
Original Cast (1969) • MCA (S) 2-10005 12-15   72
Two discs.
> **Composer:** The Who. **Conductor:** Pete Townshend. **Cast:** The Who.

Studio Cast (1969) • Ode (S) SP-99001 20-25   69
Two discs.
> **Composer:** The Who. **Conductor:** David Measham. **Cast:** The Who, Ringo Starr, Rod Stewart, Richard Harris, Sandy Denny, Steve Winwood, Richie Havens, Merry Clayton, Graham Bell, Maggie Bell, London Symphony Orchestra.

Soundtrack (1975) • Polydor (S) PD-29502 12-15   75
Two discs.
> **Composer:** The Who (Pete Townshend, John Entwistle, Keith Moon, Roger Daltrey). **Conductor:** Pete Townshend. **Cast:** Ann-Margret, Oliver Reed, Elton John, Eric Clapton, Jack Nicholson, Tina Turner, Paul Nicholas, Simon Townshend, The Who.

Soundtrack (1975) • Polydor (S) SA-010 10-15   75
One-hour radio program. Actual title: *The Making of Tommy.* Promotional issue only.

Studiotrack • Pickwick (S) 3339 5-10   73
Full title: *Excerpts from Tommy.*
> **Conductor:** Bruce Baxter. **Cast:** Tony Rivers, Mick Trounce, Martha Smith, John Perry.

TONE POEMS OF COLOR, FRANK SINATRA CONDUCTS

Studiotrack (1956) • Capitol (M) W-735 30-50   56
> **Composer:** Victor Young, Alec Wilder, Elmer Bernstein, Andre Previn, Nelson Riddle, Jeff Alexander, Billy May, Gordon Jenkins. **Conductor:** Frank Sinatra.

TONIGHT AT 8:30: see WE WERE DANCING

TONIGHT WE SING

Soundtrack (1953) • RCA Victor (EP) WDM-7016.............................. 15-25   53
Boxed, three-disc set. Colored vinyl.
Soundtrack (1953) • RCA Victor (M) LM-7016 25-45   53
Composer: Various. **Conductor:** Alfred Newman. **Cast:** Ezio Pinza, Roberta Peters, Jan Peerce, Edwin Dunning.

TONY FONTANE STORY

Soundtrack (1962) • RCA Victor (S) LSP 2526 20-25   62
Conductor: Lyle Murphy. **Cast:** Tony Fontane.

TOO MANY GIRLS

Original Cast (1939) • Show Biz (M) 5605... 20-25
Original cast performances from *Too Many Girls* on one side; other has performances from *Tune-Up Time,* a 1939 CBS radio show.
Studio Cast (1977) • Painted Smiles (S) PS-1368................................ 8-10   77
Composer: Richard Rodgers, Lorenz Hart. **Conductor:** Dennis Deal. **Cast:** Nancy Andrews, Johnny Desmond, Estelle Parsons, Anthony Perkins, Nancy Grennan, Jerry Wyatt, Arthur Siegel, Ken Parks.

TOO MUCH, TOO SOON

Soundtrack (1958) • Mercury (M) MG-20381 20-30   58
Soundtrack (1958) • Mercury (S) SR-60019.. 65-80   58
Composer: Ernest Gold. **Conductor:** Ray Heindorf.

TOOTSIE

Soundtrack (1983) • Warner Bros. (S) 23781- 1 10-15   83
Composer: Dave Grusin, Alan Bergman, Marilyn Bergman. **Cast:** Stephen Bishop, Dave Grusin.

TOP BANANA

Original Cast (1951) • Capitol (EP) EDM-308..................................... 20-25   52
Original Cast (1951) • Capitol (M) S-308... 100-125   52
Limited edition. Rainbow, color band label.
Original Cast (1951) • Capitol (M) S-308... 65-85   52
Red label.
Original Cast (1951) • Capitol (M) T-11650 8-12   77
Composer: Johnny Mercer. **Conductor:** Hal Hastings. **Cast:** Phil Silvers, Judy Lynn, Jack Albertson, Rose Marie, Joey Faye, Herbie Faye, Lindy Doherty, Eddie Hanley, Ted "Sport" Morgan, Judy Lynn, Bob Scheerer, Zachary Charles, Joan Fields, Hal Loman, Bradford Hatton, Johnny Trama.

TOP CAT

TV Soundtrack (1962) • Colpix (M) CP-212.. 30-45   62
Has *The Unscratchables* and *Top Cat Falls in Love.*
Cast: Arnold Stang, Allen Jenkins, Leo DeLyon, Maurice Gosfield, Marvin Kaplan.

TOP GUN

Soundtrack (1986) • Columbia (S) CAS-2349 8-10   86
12-inch single of *Danger Zone,* by Kenny Loggins.
Composer: Giorgio Moroder, Tom Whitlock. **Cast:** Kenny Loggins.
Soundtrack (1986) • Columbia (S) SC-40323.. 8-10   86
Composer: Harold Faltermeyer. **Cast:** Kenny Loggins, Loverboy, Cheap Trick, Berlin, Harold Faltermeyer and Steve Stevens, Miami Sound Machine, Teena Marie, Marietta, Larry Greene.

TOP HAT

Soundtrack (1937) • EMI (SE) EMTC-102...................................... 15-20   74
UK release. Gatefold cover with photo insert. Also has music from *Shall We Dance?*
Composer: Irving Berlin. **Cast:** Fred Astaire, Ginger Rogers. SHALL WE DANCE?: **Composer:** George Gershwin, Ira Gershwin.
Also see FRED ASTAIRE AND GINGER ROGERS

TOP O' THE MORNING: see BING'S HOLLYWOOD

TOP SECRET
Soundtrack (1984) • Passport (S) 3603.............................. 10-15   84
  Cast: Val Kilmer.
Soundtrack (1984) • Varese Sarabande (S) STV-81219 10-15   84
Soundtrack (1984) • That's Entertainment (S) TER-1090..................... 8-10   80s
  UK release.
  Composer: Maurice Jarre. Conductor: Maurice Jarre. Cast: Royal Philharmonic Orchestra.

TOP TV THEMES '64
Studiotrack (1964) • Warner Bros. (S) WS 1529................................. 10-15   64
  Music from *Petticoat Junction, Burke's Law, Patty Duke, Arrest and Trial, 77 Sunset Strip*
  and *My Favorite Martian.*
  Conductor: Carl Brandt. Cast: Warner Brothers Orchestra.

TOPKAPI
Soundtrack (1964) • United Artists (M) UAL-4118............................... 10-12   64
Soundtrack (1964) • United Artists (S) UAS-5118............................... 12-30   64
Soundtrack (1964) • MCA (S) 25118... 8-10   86
  Composer: Manos Hadjidakis. Conductor: Manos Hadjidakis. Cast: Melina Mercouri.

TORCH SONG
Soundtrack (1953) • MGM (M) E-214...................................... 40-60   53
  10-inch LP. Has select film selections, but omits some in favor of non-film vocals.
  Conductor: Adolph Deutsch. Cast: India Adams (performs vocals for Joan Crawford in the film),
  Walter Gross (piano).

TORCH SONG TRILOGY
Soundtrack (1988) • Polydor (S) 837785-1 10-15   88
  Composer: Various. Cast: Harvey Fierstein, Charlie Haden and Quartet West, Charles Pierce,
  Axel Vera, Marilyn Scott, Joe Williams with Count Basie and His Orchestra, Billie Holiday, Bill
  Evans, Anita O'Day.

TORN CURTAIN
Soundtrack (1966) • Decca (M) DL-9155 12-15   66
Soundtrack (1966) • Decca (S) DL-79155............................... 15-20   66
  Composer: John Addison, Jay Livingston, Ray Evans. Conductor: John Addison.
Soundtrack (1966) • Universal (M) 666 25-30   66
  Colored vinyl. Open-end (and complete) interviews by Dick Strout (interviewer) with Alfred
  Hitchcock, Paul Newman, Julie Andrews. Promotional issue only.
Studiotrack (1966) • Elmer Bernstein's Film Music
  Collection (S) FMC-10 30-35   77
Studiotrack (1966) • Warner Bros. (S) BSK-3185 12-15   78
  Both have Bernard Herrmann's unused score for the film.
  Composer: Bernard Herrmann. Conductor: Elmer Bernstein. Cast: Royal Philharmonic
  Orchestra.

TOTAL RECALL
Soundtrack (1990) • Varese Sarabande (S) VS-5267 8-15   90
  Composer: Jerry Goldsmith. Conductor: Jerry Goldsmith.

TOUCH
Original Cast (1971) • Ampex (S) A-50102 10-12   71
  Composer: Kenn Long, Jim Crozier. Conductor: Jim Crozier, David Rodman. Cast: Norman
  Jacob, Barbara Ellis, Ken Long, Phyllis Gibbs, Gary Graham, Plowright Players.

TOUCH OF CLASS
Soundtrack (1973) • Brut (S) 6004....................................... 10-12   73
  Composer: John Cameron, George Barrie, Sammy Cahn, Mel Frank, Marvin Frank.
  Conductor: John Cameron. Cast: John Cameron, Madeline Bell.

TOUCH OF EVIL

Soundtrack (1958) • Challenge (M) CHL-602 75-90   58

Soundtrack (1958) • Warner/Challenge (M) CH-615 100-125   62
    Actual title: *The Wild Side of Henry Mancini*. Omits some tracks from the original Challenge release in favor of others.

Soundtrack (1958) • Citadel (M) CT-6015 20-30   77
    Selected tracks from above Challenge titles. Also has a suite from *The Night Visitor* by Henry Mancini.

Soundtrack (1958) • Citadel (M) CT-7016 15-20   80
    Complete soundtrack from Challenge and Warner/Challenge albums.
    Composer: Henry Mancini. **Conductor:** Joseph Gershenson.

TOUCHABLES

Soundtrack (1968) • 20th Century-Fox (S) S-4206 15-20   69
    Composer: Ken Thorne, others. **Conductor:** Ken Thorne. **Cast:** Nirvana, Ferris Wheel, Wynder K. Frog, Roy Redman.

TOUGH ENOUGH

Soundtrack (1983) • Liberty (S) LT-51147 8-10   83
    Cast: Mickey Gilley, T.G. Sheppard, Dennis Quaid, Blue Skies Band, Johnny Tillotson, Lane Brody.

TOUGH GUYS

Soundtrack (1974) • Enterprise (S) ENS-7504 15-25   74
    Film title: *Three Tough Guys*.
    Composer: Isaac Hayes. **Conductor:** Isaac Hayes.

TOUGH GUYS DON'T DANCE

Soundtrack (1987) • Varese Sarabande (S) STV-81346 10-15   87
    Composer: Angelo Badelamenti.

TOURIST TRAP

Soundtrack (1979) • Varese Sarabande (S) VC-81102 12-18   79
    Composer: Pino Donaggio. **Conductor:** Pino Donaggio.

TOVARICH

Original Cast (1963) • Capitol (M) TAO-1940 12-18   63

Original Cast (1963) • Capitol (S) STAO-1940 20-25   63

Original Cast (1963) • Capitol (S) STAO-11653 10-15   77
    Gatefold covers.
    Composer: Lee Pockriss, Anne Croswell. **Conductor:** Stanley Lebowsky. **Cast:** Vivien Leigh, Jean Pierre Aumont, George S. Irving, Louise Troy, Louise Kirtland, Byron Mitchell, Margery Gray, Paul Michael, Rita Metzger.

TOWERING INFERNO

Soundtrack (1975) • Warner Bros. (S) BS-2840 10-15   75
    Composer: John Williams, Al Kasha, Joel Hirschhorn. **Conductor:** John Williams. **Cast:** Maureen McGovern.

TOWN WITHOUT PITY: see FILM MUSIC OF DIMITRI TIOMKIN

TOYS IN THE ATTIC

Soundtrack (1963) • Citadel (S) GD-1 30-40
    Promotional issue only.
    Composer: George Duning. **Conductor:** George Duning.

TRAIL OF THE PINK PANTHER

Soundtrack (1982) • Liberty (S) LT-51139 10-15   82
    Music from *Pink Panther* films.
    Composer: Henry Mancini. **Conductor:** Henry Mancini.

TRAIN
Soundtrack (1965) • United Artists (M) UAL-4122.............................. 12-15   65
Soundtrack (1965) • United Artists (S) UAS-5122 20-40   65
    Composer: Maurice Jarre. **Conductor:** Maurice Jarre.

TRAIN RIDE TO HOLLYWOOD
Soundtrack (1975) • London (S) PS-665... 10-12   75
    Cast: Bloodstone. (With dialogue.)

TRAMP
Soundtrack • United/Superior (S) No Number Used............................. 15-20
    Cast: Lowell Fulsom.

TRANSFORMED MAN
Studiotrack • Decca (M) DL-75043... 15-20

TRANSFORMERS – THE MOVIE
Soundtrack (1986) • Scotti Bros. (S) SZ-40430.................................... 8-10   86
    Composer: Various. **Cast:** Stan Bush, Vince Di Cola, Spectre General, Weird Al Yankovic, Lion.

TRANSYLVANIA 6-5000
Soundtrack (1985) • Varese Sarabande (S) 81267 10-15   85
    Conductor: Lee Holdridge. **Cast:** Zagreb Symphony Orchestra.

TRAP
Soundtrack (1966) • Atco (M) 33-204.. 30-40   66
Soundtrack (1966) • Atco (S) SD-33-204 60-70   66
    Composer: Ron Goodwin. **Conductor:** Ron Goodwin.

TRAPEZE
Soundtrack (1956) • Columbia (M) CL-870 20-25   56
    Composer: Malcolm Arnold, others. **Conductor:** Muir Mathieson.

TRAPP FAMILY
Soundtrack (1961) • 20th Century-Fox (M) FOX-3044 20-25   61
Soundtrack (1961) • 20th Century-Fox (S) TFS-3044 30-35   61
    Composer: Frank Grothe, others. **Conductor:** Kurt Graunke.

TRAVIATA, LA: see LA TRAVIATA

TREASURE GIRL: see REMEMBER THESE

TREASURE ISLAND
Original London Cast • That's Entertainment (S) TER-1008.................... 8-12   81
    UK release.
    Composer: Corandel, N. Newell.
Studio Cast (1950) • Decca (M) DL-5125... 50-75   50
    10-inch LP.
    Composer: Victor Young. **Conductor:** Victor Young. **Cast:** Thomas Mitchell, others.
Soundtrack (1950) • RCA Victor (EP) EYA-17 20-25   50
Soundtrack (1950) • RCA Victor (M) LY-1... 50-60   51
    10-inch LP. One side is music from *Alice in Wonderland.*
    Composer: Various. **Cast:** Dal McKennon (narration), Bobby Driscoll, Robert Newton, Finlay Currie, Basil Sydney, Walter Fitzgerald, Denis O'Dea, Geoffrey Wilkinson. (With dialogue.)
Soundtrack (1950) • Disneyland (M) DQ-1251 15-20   64
    Cast: Dal McKennon (narration), Bobby Driscoll, Robert Newton, Finlay Currie, Basil Sydney, Walter Fitzgerald, Denis O'Dea, Geoffrey Wilkinson. (With dialogue.)
    Also see MOBY DICK

TREASURE OF SAN GENNARO
Soundtrack (1966) • Buddah (S) BDS-5011 30-35   68
    Composer: Armando Trovaioli. **Conductor:** Armando Trovaioli.

TREASURE OF THE SIERRA MADRE

Radio Cast (1949) • Mark 56 (M) 610.................................. 10-15   70s
> Full title: *Humphrey Bogart Starring in Treasure of the Sierra Madre.* Broadcast April 18, 1949.
>> **Cast:** Humphrey Bogart, others.

TREASURY OF EARLY MUSICAL COMEDY

Studiotrack [Vol. 1] • AEI (S) 1170 8-10   80s
Studiotrack [Vol. 1] • AEI (S) 1171 8-10   80s

TREE GROWS IN BROOKLYN

Original Cast (1951) • Columbia (EP) A-1000 10-12   51
Original Cast (1951) • Columbia (EP) A-1712 10-12   51
Original Cast (1951) • Columbia (M) ML-4405 20-25   51
Original Cast (1951) • Columbia (M) OL-4405.................................... 10-25
Original Cast (1951) • Columbia Special Products (M) AML-4405.......... 8-10   Re
> **Composer:** Arthur Schwartz, Dorothy Fields. **Conductor:** Max Goberman. **Cast:** Shirley Booth, Marcia Van Dyke, Nathaniel Frey, Johnny Johnston, Delbert Anderson, Nomi Mitty, Claudia Campbell, Beverly Purvin.

TRIAL OF BILLY JACK

Soundtrack (1974) • ABC (S) ABCD-853 12-15   74
> **Composer:** Elmer Bernstein, John Lennon, Paul McCartney, Delores Taylor, Teresa Laughlin, Lynn Baker. **Conductor:** Elmer Bernstein. **Cast:** Michelle Wilson, Teresa Laughlin, Michael Bolland, Lynn Baker.

TRIAL OF THE CANTONSVILLE NINE

Original Cast (1968) • Caedmon (S) TRS 353.................................... 15-20   68
> Two discs.
>> **Cast:** Ed Flanders, Douglass Watson, Leon Russom, Anthony Costello, Peter Strauss, Gwen Arner, Donald Moffat, Richard Jordan, Nancy Malone, David Spielberg, William Schallert, Mary Jackson, Jason Bernard, John S. Battersby, Lou Fant, Harv Selsby, Kevin Tighe.

TRIBUTE TO JAMES DEAN

Soundtrack (1955) • Columbia (M) CL-940 25-30   57
> Music from *Rebel Without a Cause, East of Eden* and *Giant.*

Soundtrack (1955) • Columbia Special Products (M) ACL-940 8-10   Re
> **Composer:** Leonard Rosenman. **Conductor:** Ray Heindorf. **Cast:** Ray Heindorf and Orchestra.

Studiotrack (1957) • Imperial (M) LP-9021 20-25   57
> Music from *East of Eden, Rebel Without a Cause* and *Giant.*
>> **Composer:** Leonard Rosenman, Dimitri Tiomkin. **Conductor:** Leonard Rosenman.
> Also see JAMES DEAN STORY

TRICK OR TREAT

Soundtrack (1986) • Columbia (S) PC-40549.. 8-10   86
> **Composer:** Fastway. **Cast:** Fastway.

TRINI LOPEZ SHOW

TV Soundtrack (1968) • Reprise (S) RS-6361................................. 10-15   68
> **Cast:** Trini Lopez, Ventures, Nancy Ames.

TRIP

Soundtrack (1967) • Tower/Sidewalk (M) T-5908................................. 20-30   67
Soundtrack (1967) • Tower/Sidewalk (S) ST-5908................................. 30-40   67
> **Composer:** Mike Bloomfield, Nick Gravenites. **Cast:** Mike Bloomfield and the Electric Flag ("An American Music Band").

TRIP TO ITALY

Soundtrack (1953) • Mercury (EP) EP-1-3273 20-25   53
> **Composer:** Renzo Rossellini. **Conductor:** Renzo Rossellini. **Cast:** Rome Symphony Orchestra.

TRIPLE CROSS

Soundtrack (1967) • United Artists (M) UAL-4162................................ 15-20   67
Soundtrack (1967) • United Artists (S) UAS-5162............................... 25-30   67
    Composer: Georges Garvarentz. **Conductor:** Georges Garvarentz. **Cast:** Tony Allen.

TRIPLE FEATURE

Soundtrack (1966) • Epic (M) LN-24195 35-40   66
Soundtrack (1966) • Epic (S) BN-26195.. 45-50   66
    Music from *Casanova '70, Marriage Italian-Style* and *Darling.*

TRIUMPH OF MAN

Studiotrack (1964) • RCA Victor (EP) R4LM-4348/4349 15-20   64
    Colored vinyl discs in triple gatefold cover. Made for Travelers Insurance for New York's World Fair Exhibit.
    Composer: Frank Ledlie Moore. **Conductor:** Fritz Mahler. **Cast:** Hartford Symphony Orchestra, Peter Thomas (narrator).

TRIUMPH OF THE SPIRIT

Soundtrack (1989) • Varese Sarabande (S) VS-5254 12-15   89
    Composer: Cliff Eidelman. **Conductor:** Cliff Eidelman.

TRIUMPH OF THE WILL

Radio Cast • Communication Archives (M) CAM-271477..................... 30-40   79
    Two discs. Has language translation notes. 1934 Nuremberg Rally.

TROCADERO LEMON BLUE

Soundtrack (1979) • Casablanca (S) NBLP-7117 10-15   79
    Composer: Alec R. Constandinos. **Conductor:** Raymond Knehnetsky.

TROLL

Soundtrack (1986) • Restless (S) 72119-1.. 10-15   86
    Composer: Richard Band. **Conductor:** Richard Band.

TRON

Soundtrack (1982) • CBS (S) SM-37782.. 10-15   82
    Composer: Wendy Carlos. **Conductor:** Wendy Carlos. **Cast:** London Philharmonic Orchestra, Journey.
Soundtrack • Disneyland (S) 2157 10-15
    Full title: *The Story of Tron.* Music, sound effects and dialogue.

TROUBADOR

London Cast • Lyntone (S) LYN-699 10-15

TROUBLE IN MIND

Soundtrack (1985) • Island/Visual Arts (S) 90501-1-E........................... 8-12   86
    Composer: Mark Isham. **Cast:** Marianne Faithfull, Mark Isham.

TROUBLE IN TAHITI

TV Soundtrack (1958) • MGM (M) E-3646 20-30   58
    Recorded in stereo though not issued until 1966.
TV Soundtrack (1958) • Heliodor (M) H25020 10-12   66
TV Soundtrack (1958) • Heliodor (S) H25020 15-20   66
    First stereo release of the 1958 recording. Originally presented as *All in One*, a three-part program with a play, dance program, and the show *Trouble in Tahiti.* LP has only *Trouble in Tahiti.*
TV Soundtrack (1958) • Polydor (S) 827845-1 8-10   Re
    Composer: Leonard Bernstein. **Conductor:** Arthur Winograd. **Cast:** Beverly Wolff, David Atkinson, Miriam Workman, Earl Rogers, Robert Bollinger. (This was also the original 1952 cast.)
Studio Cast (1974) • Columbia (Q) KMQ-32597.................................. 10-15   74

TROUBLE MAN
Soundtrack (1972) • Tamla (S) T-322L 10-12   72
  Composer: Marvin Gaye. **Cast:** Marvin Gaye.

TROUBLE WITH ANGELS
Soundtrack (1966) • Mainstream (M) 56073.......................... 25-35   66
Soundtrack (1966) • Mainstream (S) S-6073........................ 65-75   66
  Composer: Jerry Goldsmith, Ernie Sheldon. **Conductor:** Jerry Goldsmith, Harry Betts. **Cast:** Devils.

TROUBLE WITH HARRY: see GREAT MOVIE THRILLERS

TROUBLEMAKER
Studiotrack (1964) • Ava (M) A-49 12-15   64
Studiotrack (1964) • Ava (S) AS-49.. 15-20   64
  Music from *Walk on the Wild Side, The Carpetbaggers, Man with the Golden Arm* and *My Fair Lady.*
  Composer: Cy Coleman. **Conductor:** Cy Coleman.

TRUCK TURNER
Soundtrack (1974) • Enterprise (S) ENS-2-7507................................... 25-30   74
  Two discs.
  Composer: Isaac Hayes. **Cast:** Isaac Hayes.

TRUE CONFESSIONS
Soundtrack (1981) • Varese Sarabande (S) STV-81141 8-10   81
Soundtrack (1981) • That's Entertainment (S) TER-1013...................... 8-10   82
  UK release.
  Composer: Georges Delerue. **Conductor:** Georges Delerue.

TRUE GRIT
Soundtrack (1969) • Capitol (S) ST-263.. 10-20   69
Soundtrack (1969) • Capitol (S) ST-8-0263.. 10-25   69
  Capitol Record Club issue.
  Composer: Elmer Bernstein, Don Black. **Conductor:** Elmer Bernstein, Al DeLory. **Cast:** Glen Campbell.
  Also see DIGITAL PREMIERE RECORDINGS FROM THE FILMS OF JOHN WAYNE

TRUE LOVE
Soundtrack • RCA Victor (S) 9819-1-R9 8-10
  Cast: Graham Parker, Grayson Hugh, Betty Wright, Jim Capaldi, Eurythmics.

TRUE SPACE ADVENTURE: SPACE SHUTTLE
TV Soundtrack • Kids Stuff (S) KPD-6005................................. 10-15   82
  Picture Disc.

TRUE STORIES: see SOUNDS OF TRUE STORIES

TRUE STORY OF THE CIVIL WAR
Soundtrack (1958) • Coral (M) CRL-59100 65-100   58
  Includes booklet. From a documentary film short.
  Composer: Ernest Gold, others. **Conductor:** Ernest Gold. **Cast:** Raymond Massey (narrator).

TRUTH OF TRUTHS
Original Cast • Oak (S) OR 1001 8-12
  Two discs.
  Cast: Jim Backus, Lloyd Schoonmaker, Donnie Brooks, Dick & Sandy St. John, others.

TUBBY THE TUBA
Studio Cast (1950) • Columbia (M) JL-8013.. 15-20   50
  10-inch LP.
  Composer: George Kleinsinger. **Conductor:** Leon Barzin. **Cast:** Victor Jory (narrator).

Soundtrack • Disneyland (M) DQ-1287 15-25   65
Soundtrack • Disneyland (M) ST-1928 25-30   63
    Cast: Annette Funicello (narrator), others.
    Also see HANS CHRISTIAN ANDERSEN
    Also see PETER AND THE WOLF.

TUCKER (THE MAN AND HIS DREAM)
Soundtrack (1988) • A&M (S) SP-3917 10-15   88
    Composer: Joe Jackson, others. **Cast:** Joe Jackson, others.

TUFF TURF
Soundtrack (1985) • Rhino (S) RNSP-308 8-10   85
    Composer: Jonathon Elias, others. **Cast:** Southside Johnny, Jim Carroll Band, Jack Mack and
    the Heart Attack, Lene Lovich, Marianne Faithfull, Dale Gnyea with J.R. and the 2-Men.

TUNES OF GLORY
Soundtrack (1960) • United Artists (M) UAL-4086 20-25   61
Soundtrack (1960) • United Artists (S) UAS-5086 35-45   61
    Composer: Malcolm Arnold (uncredited on this release). **Conductor:** Malcolm Arnold
    (uncredited).

TURN ON, TUNE IN, DROP OUT
Soundtrack (1967) • Mercury (M) MG-21131 15-20   67
Soundtrack (1967) • Mercury (S) SR-61131 20-25   67
    Composer: Maryvonne Giercarz. **Conductor:** Lars Eric, Richard Bond. **Cast:** Timothy Leary,
    Ph.D. (With dialogue.)

TURNABOUT
Original Cast (1975) • Pelican (S) LP-142 10-15   75
    Original 1956 cast regrouped for "A Satirical Revue."
    Composer: Forman Brown. **Cast:** Elsa Lanchester, Forman Brown (piano), Bill Buck, Harry
    Burnett, Dorothy Neumann, Frances Osborne, Ray Henderson (piano).

TURNED ON BROADWAY
Studiotrack (1982) • RCA Victor (S) AFL1-4327 8-12   82
    Excerpts from over 90 Broadway songs, done in disco style.
    Conductor: Luther Henderson. **Cast:** Broadway Symphony.

TURNING POINT
Soundtrack (1977) • 20th Century-Fox (S) T-549 10-15   78
    Gatefold cover.
    Composer: John Lanchberry. **Conductor:** Lawrence Foster. **Cast:** Lawrence Foster, Los
    Angeles Philharmonic Orchestra.

TUSCALOOSA'S CALLING ME (BUT I'M NOT GOING)
Original Cast (1975) • Vanguard (S) VSD-79376 10-12   75
    Composer: Hank Beebe, Bill Heyer. **Conductor:** Jeremy Harris. **Cast:** Len Gochman, Patti
    Perkins, Renny Temple.

TWANG
Original London Cast • That's Entertainment (S) TER-1055 8-10   80s
    UK release.
    Composer: Lionel Bart.

TWELVE CHAIRS
Soundtrack (1970) • Asylum (S) 5E-501 8-10   77
    Actual title: *High Anxiety.* Also has music from *The Producers, Young Frankenstein, Silent
    Movie, Blazing Saddles* and *High Anxiety.*
Soundtrack (1970) • Varese Sarabande (S) STV-81159 8-10   83
Soundtrack (1970) • That's Entertainment (S) TER-1033 8-10   80s
    UK release.
    Composer: John Morris. **Conductor:** John Morris.
    Also see BLAZING SADDLES

TWELVE GREAT THEMES OF THE SOARING '60s

Studiotrack • 20th Fox (M) 3043.. 10-15   60

Studiotrack • 20th Fox (S) SFX 3043 15-20   60
> Music from *Sons and Lovers, Never on Sunday, Adventures in Paradise, Diary of Anne Frank, A Summer Place, Can-Can, The Apartment, The Alamo, From the Terrace, Klondike, Mr. Lucky* and *Hong Kong.*
> **Cast:** 20th Century Strings.

Studiotrack • 20th Fox (M) 1006.. 8-10   60
> Reissue of 3043. Actual title: *Great Themes from Motion Pictures.*

TWENTIETH CENTURY OZ

Soundtrack (1978) • Celestial (S) 4001 10-12   78
> **Composer:** Ross Wilson, Joy Dunstan, Graham Matters.

25th HOUR

Soundtrack (1967) • MGM (M) E-4464................................... 12-15   67
> Promotional issue only.

Soundtrack (1967) • MGM (M) E-4464................................... 12-15   67

Soundtrack (1967) • MGM (S) SE-4464 12-18   67
> **Composer:** Georges Delerue. **Conductor:** Georges Delerue.

TWENTY-FIVE YEARS OF LIFE

TV Soundtrack (1961) • No Label Shown (M) No number Used........... 40-50   61
> 10-inch LP. Deluxe, soft-stock cover.
> **Cast:** Bob Hope, Mary Martin, Sid Caesar, Peggy Cass, Ray Charles Singers, others.

25 YEARS OF RECORDED SOUND

Studiotrack • DRG (M) DARC-2-2100 12-25   79
> Two discs. Gatefold cover. Full title: *25 Years of Recorded Sound (1945-1970) from the Vaults of MGM, Vol. 1* (no second volume exists). Music from *Texas Carnival, The Kissing Bandit, The Strip, Jubilee, One Touch of Venus, Escapade* and others. Includes previously unreleased songs and some previously released on singles.
> **Composer:** Various. **Conductor:** Various. **Cast:** Fred Astaire, Bing Crosby, Lena Horne, Debbie Reynolds, Rosemary Clooney, Danny Thomas, Ava Gardner, Desi Arnaz, Esther Williams, Kay Thompson, Dan Dailey, Betty Garrett, Jimmy Durante, others.

TWENTY-FOUR KARAT GOLD (FROM THE SOUND STAGE)

Soundtrack (1968) • MGM (S) SE-242-2.............................. 15-20   68
> Original soundtrack music from 16 films.

TWENTY GREAT MOVIE THEMES

Studiotrack (1973) • Command (S) RSSD-963-1 15-20   73
> Two discs.
> **Conductor:** Enoch Light. **Cast:** Enoch Light, Bobby Byrne.

Studiotrack (1973) • Command (S) RSSD-963-2 15-20   73
> Two discs.
> **Conductor:** Enoch Light. **Cast:** Enoch Light.

TWENTY MILLION SWEETHEARTS

Soundtrack (1934) • Milloball (M) TMSM-3403....................... 8-10
> Also has music from *Mammy.*
> **Cast:** Ray Enright, Dick Powell, Ginger Rogers, Pat O'Brien, Allen Jenkins, Grant Mitchell, Mills Brothers. MAMMY: Al Jolson.

21 JUMP STREET

TV Soundtrack (1988) • I.R.S. (S) IRS-6270 10-15   89
> **Cast:** Alarm, Reckless Sleepers, One Nation, Holly Robinson, Peter Bernstein, Hunters & Collectors, dBs, Ranking Rogers, Timbuk 3.

20,000 LEAGUES UNDER THE SEA

Studio Cast • Camden (M) CAL-1057 20-25   65
Studio Cast • Camden (S) CAS-1057e... 10-15   65
    One side has music from *Cinderella*
    Cast: Studio cast.
Studiotrack (1954) • RCA Y4004.. 50-60   54
    Album of two 78 rpms.

TWILIGHT OF HONOR

Soundtrack (1963) • MGM (M) E-4185.............................. 10-20   63
Soundtrack (1963) • MGM (S) SE-4185 15-25   63
    One side has music from *Murder at Gallop, Ride the High Country, Black Orpheus* and *Hud*
    Composer: John Green, others. **Conductor:** John Green. **Cast:** Richard Chamberlain, Ron Goodwin and Orchestra, Ronny Lang, Bill Evans, Lalo Schifrin, Robert Holliday Orchestra, Harry James and His Orchestra, MGM Studio Orchestra.

TWILIGHT ZONE

TV Soundtrack [Vol. 1] • Varese Sarabande (M) STV-81171 10-15   83
    Music from episodes: *The Invaders, Perchance to Dream, Walking Distance* and *The Sixteen Millimeter Shrine.*
    Composer: Dimitri Tiomkin, Jerry Goldsmith, Bernard Hermann, Franz Waxman.
TV Soundtrack [Vol. 2] • Varese Sarabande (M) STV-81178 10-15   83
    Music from episodes: *Where Is Everybody?, One Hundred Yards over the Rim, The Big Tall Wish* and *A Stop at Willoughby.*
    Composer: Fred Steiner, Jerry Goldsmith, Bernard Herrmann, Fred Steiner, Nathan Scott.
TV Soundtrack [Vol. 3] • Varese Sarabande (M) STV-81185 10-15   83
    Music from episodes: *Back There, And When the Sky Was Opened, A World of Difference* and *The Lonely.*
    Composer: Jerry Goldsmith, Bernard Herrmann, Leonard Rosenman, Nathan Van Cleave, Marius Constant.
TV Soundtrack [Vol. 4] • Varese Sarabande (M) STV-81192 10-15   84
    Music from episodes: *King Nine Will Not Return, Two, Elegy* and *Nervous Man in a Four Dollar Room.*
    Composer: Jerry Goldsmith, Nathan Van Cleave, Fred Steiner, Bernard Herrmann, Rene Garriguenc.
TV Soundtrack [Vol. 5] • Varese Sarabande (M) STV-81205 10-15   85
    Music from episodes: *I Sing the Body Electric, The Passerby, The Trouble with Templeton* and *Dust.*
    Composer: Jerry Goldsmith, Nathan Van Cleave, Fred Steiner, Bernard Herrmann, Jeff Alexander.

TWILIGHT ZONE – THE MOVIE

Soundtrack (1983) • Warner Bros. (S) 1-23887 10-15   83
    Composer: Jerry Goldsmith. **Conductor:** Jerry Goldsmith. **Cast:** Jennifer Warnes.

TWINS

Soundtrack (1988) • WTG (S) SP-45036 8-10   88
    Cast: Bobby McFerrin, Herbie Hancock, 2 Live Crew, Nicolette Larson, Jeff Beck, Terry Bozzio, Tony Hymas, Philip Bailey, Little Richard, Nayobe, Henry Lee Summer, Marilyn Scott, Spinners, Andrew Roachford, Peter Richardson.

TWISTED NERVE

Soundtrack • Polydor (S) 583-728... 200-275   68
    One side has music from *Les Bicyclettes De Belsize.*
    Composer: Bernard Herrmann. **Conductor:** Bernard Herrmann.

TWO

Original Cast (1978) • Take Home Tunes (S) THT-788.......................... 8-10   78
    Composer: Julie Mandel. **Conductor:** Donald Oliver. **Cast:** Ann Hodapp, Hal Watters.

TWO A PENNY

Soundtrack (1971) • Light (S) LS-5530 10-12   71
> **Composer:** Mike Leander, Cliff Richard, Paul Simon, others. **Conductor:** Mike Leander. **Cast:** Cliff Richard.

TWO BY TWO

Original Cast (1970) • Columbia (S) S-30338.................................... 15-20   70
> **Composer:** Richard Rodgers, Martin Charnin. **Conductor:** Jay Blackton. **Cast:** Danny Kaye, Harry Goz, Madeline Kahn, Michael Karm, Joan Copeland, Walter Willison, Tricia O'Neil, Marilyn Cooper.

Original Cast (1970) • Columbia (S) AS-15 15-20   70
> Full title: *Backstage at Two By Two*. Richard Rodgers and Danny Kaye discussing the show as well as Rodgers' 50 years as a Broadway composer. Also has Rodgers' songs from other Columbia original cast recordings. Promotional issue only.
> **Composer:** Richard Rodgers. **Conductor:** Jay Blackton, others. **Cast:** Lee Jordan (interviewer).

Studio Cast • Camden (S) CAS-2458...................................... 8-12
> Tribute to Richard Rodgers.

TWO FILM SCORES FOR SOLO PIANO

Soundtrack • Private Label (S) STK-1069 30-35   76
> Music from *A Texas Romance, 1909* and *Bad Company*.
> **Composer:** Harvey Schmidt. **Cast:** Harvey Schmidt (piano).

TWO FOR THE ROAD

Soundtrack (1967) • RCA Victor (M) LPM-3802 12-15   67

Soundtrack (1967) • RCA Victor (S) LSP-3802 15-20   67
> Black label.

Soundtrack (1967) • RCA Victor (S) LSP-3802 8-12   Re
> Orange label.
> **Composer:** Henry Mancini. **Conductor:** Henry Mancini. **Cast:** Henry Mancini and His Orchestra.

TWO FOR THE SEESAW

Soundtrack (1962) • United Artists (M) UAL-4103............................... 10-12   62

Soundtrack (1962) • United Artists (S) UAS-5103 15-20   62

Soundtrack (1962) • MCA (S) 25016... 5-8   86
> **Composer:** Andre Previn, Dory Langdon. **Conductor:** Andre Previn. **Cast:** Jackie Cain.
> Also see DIVORCE ITALIAN STYLE

TWO FOR TONIGHT: see ANYTHING GOES, BING'S HOLLYWOOD

TWO GENTLEMEN OF VERONA

Original Cast (1971) • ABC (S) No Number Used 10-15   71
> Full title: *Excerpts from the Original Broadway Cast LP, Two Gentlemen of Verona*. Promotional issue only.

Original Cast (1971) • ABC (S) BCSY-1001 12-18   71
> Two discs.
> **Composer:** Galt McDermot, John Guare. **Conductor:** Harold Wheeler. **Cast:** Jonelle Allen, Diana Davila, Clifton Davis, Raul Julia, Norman Matlock.

Studio Cast (1971) • Kilmarnock (S) KIL-72004 20-25   71
> **Composer:** Galt MacDermot, John Guare. **Conductor:** Galt MacDermot. **Cast:** Galt MacDermot, Sheila Gibbs, Ken Lowry, P.T. Mavins.

200 MOTELS

Soundtrack (1971) • United Artists (S) UAS-9956 25-30   71

Soundtrack (1971) • MCA (S) MCA2-4183.. 15-20   Re
> Two discs.
> **Composer:** Frank Zappa. **Conductor:** Frank Zappa, Elgar Howarth. **Cast:** Theodore Bikel (narrator), Royal Philharmonic Orchestra.

TWO MOON JUNCTION

Soundtrack (1988) • Varese Sarabande (S) 704 520 8-12   88
   Composer: Elias.

TWO MULES FOR SISTER SARA

Soundtrack (1970) • Kapp (S) KRS-5512 20-25   70
   Composer: Ennio Morricone. **Cast:** Shirley MacLaine.

TWO OF A KIND

Soundtrack (1983) • MCA (S) 6127 8-10   83
   Cast: Olivia Newton-John, John Travolta, Chicago, David Foster, Magness-Ballard, Steve Kipner, Boz Scaggs, Journey.

TWO ON THE AISLE

Original Cast (1951) • Decca DA-886 25-30   51
   Boxed 78 rpm set.

Original Cast (1951) • Decca (EP) 9-275 25-30   51

Original Cast (1951) • Decca (M) DL-8040 75-85   51
   Black label with gold print.

Original Cast (1951) • Decca (M) DL-8040 45-65   51
   Black label with white print.

Original Cast (1951) • Decca (M) DL-8040 40-60   60s
   Rainbow (or multi-color) label. Though a reissue, this is quite scarce and as much in demand as originals.
   Composer: Jule Styne, Betty Comden, Adolph Green. **Conductor:** Herbert Greene. **Cast:** Bert Lahr, Dolores Gray, Kathryn Mylroie, Ellen Hanley, Fred Bryan.

TWO RODE TOGETHER

Soundtrack (1961) • Columbia Pictures (M) SP-1691 25-30   61
   Commercial spots. Made for radio station use only.
   Cast: James Stewart (dialogue).

TWO SISTERS FROM BOSTON: see THRILL OF ROMANCE

2001: A SPACE ODYSSEY

Soundtrack (1968) • MGM (S) S1E-13 8-15   68
   May also be shown as "1SE13."

Soundtrack (1968) • MGM (S) SWAK-91517 8-10

Soundtrack • MGM (S) ST 93378 8-10
   Capitol Record Club issues.

Soundtrack (1968) • MGM (S) S1E-13-STX 15-25   68
   Contains the concert version of Ligeti's *Atmospheres.*
   Composer: Richard Strauss, Gyorgy Ligeti, Johann Strauss, Aram Khachaturian, others. **Conductor:** Karl Bohm, Francis Travis, Clytus Gottwald, Herbert Von Karajan, Gennadl Rozhdestvensky, Ernest Bour. **Cast:** Berlin Philharmonic Orchestra, Bavarian Radio Orchestra, Stuttgart Schola Cantorum, Leningrad Philharmonic Orchestra, Sudwestfunk Orchestra, Radio Symphony Orchestra.

Studiotrack • Columbia (S) MS-7176 10-12
   Conductor: Eugene Ormandy, Leonard Bernstein **Cast:** Eugene Ormandy, Leonard Bernstein, Swedish Radio (effects.)

Soundtrack (1968) • MGM (S) SE-4722-ST 15-20   70

Soundtrack (1968) • MCA (S) 39049 8-10   86
   Full title of above two: *2001: A Space Odyssey, Volume 2.*
   Composer: Richard Strauss, Gyorgy Ligeti, Johann Strauss, Aram Khachaturin.

2010

Soundtrack (1984) • A&M (S) SP-5038 12-15   84
   Composer: David Shire. **Cast:** Andy Summers.

TWO TICKETS TO BROADWAY

Studiotrack (1951) • RCA Victor (M) LPM-39 30-35   51
   10-inch LP.
    Conductor: Hugo Winterhalter, Henri Rene. **Cast:** Tony Martin, Dinah Shore.

TWO TICKETS TO PARIS

Soundtrack (1962) • Roulette (M) R-25182 8-12   62
Soundtrack (1962) • Roulette (S) SR-25182 10-30   62
    Composer: Henry Glover, others. **Conductor:** Henry Glover. **Cast:** Joey Dee and the Starliters,
    Gary Crosby, Kay Medford, Jeri Lynne Fraser.

TWO WEEKS WITH LOVE

Soundtrack (1950) • MGM (M) E-530 30-35   50
   10-inch LP.
Soundtrack (1950) • MCA (M) 39082 8-10   86
    One side has soundtrack music from *The Belle of New York*.
    Conductor: Georgie Stoll. **Cast:** Jane Powell, Debbie Reynolds, Carleton Carpenter. BELLE OF
    NEW YORK: **Composer:** Harry Warren, Johnny Mercer. **Conductor:** Adolph Deutsch. **Cast:**
    Fred Astaire, Anita Ellis (performs vocals for Vera-Ellen in the film), MGM Studio Orchestra and
    Chorus.
    Also see THOSE GLORIOUS MGM MUSICALS
    Also see WORDS AND MUSIC

TWO'S COMPANY

Original Cast (1952) • RCA Victor (EP) WOC-1009 20-25   62
Original Cast (1952) • RCA Victor (M) LOC-1009 75-100   52
Original Cast (1952) • RCA Victor (M) CBM1-2757 15-18   78
    Composer: Vernon Duke, Ogden Nash, Sammy Cahn. **Conductor:** Milton Rosenstock. **Cast:**
    Bette Davis, Hiram Sherman, David Burns, George S. Irving, Bill Callahan, Ellen Hanley, Peter
    Kelley, Deborah Remson, Sue Hight.
    Composer: Lalo Schifrin. **Conductor:** Lalo Schifrin.

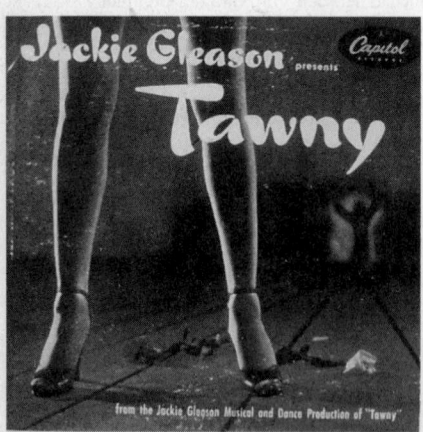

UHF AND OTHER STUFF
Soundtrack (1989) • Rock 'N Roll (S) SZ-45265 8-10   89
    Cast: "Weird Al" Yankovic.

UGLY DACHSHUND
Studiotrack (1966) • Disneyland (M) DQ-1290 20-25   66
    With narration. One side has music from *The Shaggy Dog.*
    Composer: Richard M. Sherman, Robert B. Sherman, Camarata, Dunham. **Cast:** Fred
    MacMurray, P. Harcourt Frees, Roberta Shore, Kevin Corcoran.

ULYSSES
Soundtrack (1967) • RCA Victor (M) LOC-1138 10-25   67
Soundtrack (1967) • RCA Victor (S) LSO-1138 12-30   67
    Composer: Stanley Myers. **Conductor:** Stanley Myers.
Soundtrack (1967) • Caedmon (S) TMS-300 10-15
    Boxed set. Soundtrack of the Walter Reade Jr - Joseph Strick Production.
    Cast: Milo O'Shea, Barbara Jefford, Maurice Roeves.

ULYSSES – THE GREEK SUITE
Studio Cast (1978) • 20th Century-Fox (S) 2T-1101 12-18   78
    Two discs. Includes booklet.
    Composer: Michael Rapp. **Conductor:** Michael Rapp. **Cast:** David Arias (narrator), Ted
    Neeley, Yvonne Iversen, Channen Junge, Grant Goracy, Cindy Snyder, others.

UMBRELLAS OF CHERBOURG (LES PARAPLUIES DE CHERBOURG)
Soundtrack (1964) • Philips (M) PCC-216 15-20   65
Soundtrack (1964) • Philips (S) PCC-616 25-30   65
    Gatefold cover. Includes booklet. Performed in French.
    Composer: Michel Legrand. **Conductor:** Michel Legrand. **Cast:** Jacques Demy. (With
    dialogue.)
Studiotrack (1964) CDP International (S) DCS-6806 15-20   64
    Full title: *Don Costa Plays Music from Umbrellas of Cherbourg.* Also has music from *Emily*
    Sylvia, Dear Heart, Greatest Story Ever Told, Goldfinger and *How to Murder Your Wife.*
    Composer: Michel Legrand, others. **Cast:** Don Costa Orchestra.

UNBEARABLE LIGHTNESS OF BEING
Soundtrack (1988) • Fantasy (S) FSP-21006 15-20   88
    Cast: Leo Janacek.

UNCLE JOE SHANNON
Soundtrack (1978) • United Artists (S) UA-LA935-H 12-15   79
Soundtrack (1978) • Liberty (S) D1-73234 8-10   79
    Composer: Bill Conti. **Conductor:** Bill Conti. **Cast:** Maynard Ferguson (trumpet).

UNCLE MEAT
Soundtrack (1968) • Reprise (S) RS-2024 15-20   68
    Two discs. From an unreleased film.

UNCLE REMUS: see SONG OF THE SOUTH

UNCLE TOM'S CABIN
Soundtrack (1968) • Philips (S) PHS-600-272 25-35   68
    Composer: Peter Thomas, Aldo Von Pinelli. **Conductor:** Peter Thomas. **Cast:** Juliette Greco,
    Eartha Kitt, George Goodman.

UNCLE VANYA
Studio Cast • Caedmon (M) TRS 303-M 20-25   60s
TV Soundtrack • Philips (M) PHM 2-301 20-25   64
  Two discs. Gatefold cover with booklet.
    Composer: Anton Chekhov (author), others. **Cast:** Sir Laurence Olivier, Joan Plowright, Sir Michael Redgrave, others.

UNDER COVER
Soundtrack (1987) • Enigma (S) SJ-73276 10-15   87
    Cast: Todd Rundgren, Wednesday Week, T.S.O.L., Agent Orange, Passionnel.

UNDER FIRE
Soundtrack (1983) • Warner Bros. (S) 1-23965 15-20   83
    Composer: Jerry Goldsmith. **Cast:** Pat Metheny.

UNDER MILK WOOD
Original Radio Cast (1954) • Argo (M) SW 501-2.............................. 15-20
  Boxed, two-disc set. Includes insert.
    Composer: Daniel Jones. **Cast:** Richard Burton, Richard Bebb, Hugh Griffith, Rachel Thomas, Diana Maddox, Dafydd Havard, Sybil Williams, Dilys Davies, David Close-Thomas, Ben Williams, Meredith Edwards, Gwenllian Owen, Philip Burton, Gwenyth Petty, others.
Studio Cast • Caedmon (M) TC-2005.. 40-50   53
  Two discs. Dramatic narrative by Dylan Thomas.
    Cast: Dylan Thomas, Dion Allen, Nancy Wickwire, Roy Poole, Sada Thompson, Allen F. Collins.

UNDER THE BOARDWALK
Soundtrack (1988) • Enigma (S) D1-73234....................................... 8-10   88
    Cast: Untouchables, Surf Punks, Surf MC's, Del-Lords, Ike Willis, Smithereens, Broadcasters, Wednesday Week, Drifters.

UNDER THE CHERRY MOON
Soundtrack (1986) • Warner Bros. (S) 1-25395 5-10   86
  Full title: *Parade: Music from Under the Cherry Moon.*
    Cast: Prince and the Revolution.

UNFINISHED DANCE
Soundtrack (1947) • MGM - MGM-4... 50-60   47
  Album of four 78 rpms. One of the few soundtrack albums MGM never transferred in its entirety to long playing records.
Soundtrack (1947) • MGM (M) E-540 12-18   55
  10-inch LP. Actual title: *Slaughter on Tenth Avenue and Other Ballet Music from Motion Pictures.* Music from the 78 set, plus ballet music from *Words and Music* and *The Pirate.*
    Composer: Various. **Conductor:** Herbert Stothart. **Cast:** MGM Studio Orchestra, Danny Thomas.

UNFORGIVEN
Soundtrack (1960) • United Artists (M) UAL-4068................................ 30-35   60
Soundtrack (1960) • United Artists (S) UAS-5068 60-65   60
Soundtrack (1960) • United Artists (M) DF-7 12-15   Re
Soundtrack (1960) • United Artists (S) DFS-57 12-18   Re
  Above two also have music from *Wonderful Country.*
    Composer: Dimitri Tiomkin. **Conductor:** Dimitri Tiomkin. **Cast:** Santa Cecilia Symphony Orchestra of Rome.
Studiotrack (1960) • United Artists (M) UAL-3119 15-20   60
    Cast: Don Costa and Orchestra.
  Also see HORSE SOLDIERS

UNKNOWN THEATRE SONGS OF JULE STYNE
Studiotrack • Blue Pear (M) BP 1011 10-15
  Obscure songs from *Do-Re-Mi, Hazel Flagg, Hellzapoppin, Gypsy, Two on the Aisle, Hallelujah Baby, Funny Girl, Darling of the Day, Sugar, Subways Are for Sleeping* and *Peep Show.* Cast not credited.

UNMARRIED WOMAN
Soundtrack (1978) • 20th Century-Fox (S) T-557 8-10   78
    Composer: Bill Conti. **Conductor:** Bill Conti. **Cast:** Michelle Wiley.

UNPUBLISHED COLE PORTER
Studio Cast (1972) • Painted Smiles (S) PS 1358 5-10
    Composer: Cole Porter. **Cast:** Carmen Alvarez, Karen Morrow, Edward Earle, Alice Playten,
    Laura Kenyon, Charles Rydell, Blossom Dearie.

UNSINKABLE MOLLY BROWN
Original Cast (1960) • Capitol (M) WAO-1509 10-12   60
Original Cast (1960) • Capitol (S) SWAO-1509 12-15   60
    Above two contain a program insert in pocket of back cover.
Original Cast (1960) • Capitol (M) W-2152 8-10   64
Original Cast (1960) • Capitol (S) SW-2152 8-12   64
    Composer: Meredith Willson. **Conductor:** Herbert Greene. **Cast:** Tammy Grimes, Harve
    Presnell, Cameron Prud'Homme, Edith Meiser, Mony Dalmes, Jack Harrold, Mitchell Gregg.
Studio Cast (1961) • Camden (M) CAL-667 10-15   61
    Composer: Meredith Willson. **Conductor:** Elliot Lawrence. **Cast:** Sandy Stewart, Bernie Knee,
    Elliot Lawrence's Orchestra and Chorus.
Soundtrack (1964) • MGM (M) E-4232 20-25   64
    "Special Advance Copy!" Promotional issue only.
Soundtrack (1964) • MGM (M) E-4232 8-10   64
Soundtrack (1964) • MGM (S) SE-4232 10-12   64
Soundtrack (1964) • MGM (M) W-90048 8-10
Soundtrack (1964) • MGM (S) SW-90048 8-10
    Above two are Capitol Record Club issues.
Soundtrack (1964) • MCA (S) 25011 5-8   86
    Composer: Meredith Willson. **Conductor:** Robert Armbruster. **Cast:** Debbie Reynolds, Harve
    Presnell, MGM Studio Orchestra.
Studiotrack (1961) • Columbia (M) CL-1576 8-10   61
Studiotrack (1961) • Columbia (S) CS-8376 8-12   61
    Conductor: Andre Kostelanetz. **Cast:** Andre Kostelanetz and His Orchestra.

UNTAMED YOUTH
Soundtrack • Prep (EP) MI-1 100-125
    Cover pictures Mamie Van Doren.
    Composer: Les Baxter. **Conductor:** Les Baxter.

UNTIL SEPTEMBER
Soundtrack (1984) • Varese Sarabande (S) STV-81226 8-10   84
    Composer: John Barry. **Conductor:** John Barry.

UNTOUCHABLES (1960)
TV Soundtrack (1960) • Capitol (M) T-1430 25-35   60
TV Soundtrack (1960) • Capitol (S) ST-1430 35-45   60
    Composer: Nelson Riddle. **Conductor:** Nelson Riddle.

UNTOUCHABLES (1987)
Soundtrack (1987) • A&M (S) SP-3809 8-10   87
    Composer: Ennio Morricone. **Conductor:** Ennio Morricone.

UP IN CENTRAL PARK
Original Cast (1945) • Decca DA-395 15-20   45
    78 rpm album. Includes booklet.
Original Cast (1945) • Decca (M) DL-8016 30-35   50
    Black and gold label on thick wax.
Original Cast (1945) • Decca (M) DL-8016 20-30
    Black label.

Original Cast (1945) • Decca (M) DL-8016... 15-18   50
> Rainbow (or multi-color) label. Above Decca LPs also have music from *The Red Mill*. All Decca releases feature Wilbur Evans and Betty Bruce from the original New York production and an otherwise assembled studio cast.
> > **Composer:** Sigmund Romberg, Dorothy Fields. **Conductor:** Max Meth. **Cast:** Eileen Farrell, Wilbur Evans, Celeste Holm, Betty Bruce. RED MILL: **Composer:** Victor Herbert, Henry Blossom. **Conductor:** Jay Blackton. **Cast:** Eileen Farrell, Wilbur Evans, Felix Knight.

Studio Cast • Angel (S) S-37323... 10-15
> **Cast:** Beverly Sills, Sherill Milnes.
> Also see SONG OF NORWAY

UP IN SMOKE
Soundtrack (1978) • Warner Bros. (S) BSK-3249 8-10   78
> **Composer:** Tommy Chong, Cheech Marin. **Cast:** Cheech and Chong. (With dialogue).

UP IN THE CELLAR
Soundtrack (1970) • American Int'l (S) A-1036..................................... 15-20   71
> **Composer:** Don Randi, Dory Previn. **Conductor:** Don Randi. **Cast:** Hamilton Camp.
> Also see 3 IN THE CELLAR

UP THE ACADEMY
Soundtrack (1980) • Capitol (S) SOO-12091 10-15   80
> **Composer:** Various. **Cast:** Blondie, Ian Hunter, Babys, Blow-Up, Jonathan Richman and the Modern Lovers, Cheeks, Pat Benatar, Sammy Hagar.

UP THE CREEK
Soundtrack (1984) • Pasha (S) SZ 39333.. 8-10   84
> **Composer:** William Goldstein.

UP THE DOWN STAIRCASE
Soundtrack (1967) • United Artists (M) UAL-4169.............................. 15-20   67
Soundtrack (1967) • United Artists (S) UAS-5169 25-35   67
> **Composer:** Fred Karlin. **Conductor:** Fred Karlin.

UP THE JUNCTION
Soundtrack (1968) • Mercury (S) SRP-61159 20-25   68
> **Composer:** M. Hugg, B. Hugg, Manfred Mann. **Cast:** Manfred Mann.

UP WITH PEOPLE!
TV Soundtrack [Vol. 1] (1965) • Pace (S) 1101 10-15   65
> **Composer:** Paul Colwell, Ralph Colwell, Steve Colwell, Herbert Allen, David Bliss Allen, others. **Cast:** Colwell Brothers, Green Glenn Singers (with Glenn Close), Linda Blackmore, Charles Woodward, others, Effie Galletly.

TV Soundtrack [Vol. 2] (1967) • Pace (S) S-1102 10-15   67
TV Soundtrack (1981) • Up With People (S) 1133 8-12   81
> Actual title: *Encore!*
> **Cast:** Colwell Brothers, others.

UPSTAIRS AT O'NEALS
Original Cast (1982) • Painted Smiles (S) PS-1344................................ 8-15   83
> Full title: *Martin Charnin's Upstairs at O'Neals.*
> **Conductor:** David Krane.

UPTIGHT
Soundtrack (1968) • Stax (S) STS-2006 25-30   68
> **Composer:** Booker T. Jones. **Cast:** Booker T. and the MGs.

URBAN COWBOY
Soundtrack (1980) • Asylum (S) DP-90002.. 8-15   80
> Two discs. Includes 18" x 22" poster.
> **Cast:** Jimmy Buffett, Joe Walsh, Dan Fogelberg, Bob Seger and the Silver Bullet Band, Mickey Gilley, Johnny Lee, Anne Murray, Eagles, Bonnie Raitt, Charlie Daniels Band, Gilley's Urban Cowboy Band, Kenny Rogers, Boz Scaggs, Linda Ronstadt, John David Souther.

Soundtrack (1980) • Full Moon/Epic (S) SE-36921 8-10   80
Full title: *Urban Cowboy II.* "More Music from the Original Soundtrack."
Composer: Various. **Cast:** Bayou City Beats, Charlie Daniels Band, Mickey Gilley & Johnny Lee, J.D. Souther, Mickey Gilley.

URGH – A MUSIC WAR

Soundtrack (1981) • A&M (S) SP-6019 10-15   81
Two discs.
Cast: Police, Wall of Voodoo, Toyah Wilcox, Orchestral Manoeuvres in the Dark, Oingo Boingo, XTC, Members, Go-Go's, Klaus Nomi, Athletico Spizz '80, Alley Cats, Jools Holland, Devo, Echo and Bunnymen, Au Pairs, Cramps, Joan Jett and Blackhearts, Pere Ubu, Gary Numan, Fleshtones, Gang of Four, John Otway, 999, X, Magazine, Skafish, Steel Pulse.

UTTER GLORY OF MORRISSEY HALL

Original Cast (1979) • Original Cast (S) OC-7918 8-12   79
Composer: Clark Gesner. **Conductor:** John Gordon. **Cast:** Celeste Holm, Karen Gibson, Laurie Franks, Marilyn Franks, Marilyn Caskey, Taina Elg.

UTU

Soundtrack (1983) • Southern Cross (S) SRCS-1008 8-10   83
Conductor: William Southgate. **Cast:** New Zealand Symphony Orchestra.
Composer: Lalo Schifrin. **Conductor:** Lalo Schifrin.

V

V.I.P.s
Soundtrack (1963) • MGM (M) E-4152... 8-10   63
Soundtrack (1963) • MGM (S) SE-4152... 8-12   63
Soundtrack (1963) • MCA (S) 25001.. 5-8   86
    Composer: Miklos Rozsa. **Conductor:** Miklos Rozsa. **Cast:** Rome Symphony Orchestra.

VA VA VOOM! SCREEN SIRENS SING!
Soundtrack • Rhino (M) RNTA-1999 20-30   85
    Two discs. Colored vinyl limited edition. Includes eight-page booklet.
    Cast: Marilyn Monroe, Ann-Margret, Diana Dors, Jayne Mansfield, others.

VAGABOND KING
Studio Cast (1951) • RCA Victor (M) LK-1010...................................... 12-18   51
    Composer: Rudolf Friml, Brian Hooker. **Conductor:** Al Goodman. **Cast:** Earl Wrightson,
    Frances Greer, Guild Choristers.
Studio Cast (1951) • Decca (M) DL-7014.. 20-30   56
    10-inch LP.
    Composer: Rudolf Friml, Brian Hooker. **Conductor:** Jay Blackton. **Cast:** Alfred Drake, Mimi
    Benzell, Frances Bible.
Studiotrack (1956) • RCA Victor (M) LM-2004...................................... 20-25   56
    Composer: Rudolf Friml, Brian Hooker. **Conductor:** Henri Rene. **Cast:** Oreste, Jean Fenn.
Studio Cast (1956) • RCA Victor (M) LM-2509 10-12   61
Studio Cast (1956) • RCA Victor (S) LSC-2509.................................... 12-18   61
    Composer: Rudolf Friml, Brian Hooker. **Conductor:** Constantine Callinicos. **Cast:** Mario Lanza,
    Judith Raskin.
Studiotrack (1957) • Halo (M) 50248 15-20   57
    Also see NEW MOON
    Also see STUDENT PRINCE

VALACHI PAPERS
Studiotrack • Project 3 (S) PR-5085.. 25-30
    Also has music from two other Dino DiLaurentiis films: *Crazy Joe* and *Stone Killer.*

VALENTINO (1951)
Studiotrack (1951) • Decca (M) DL-5347 30-35   51
    10-inch LP. "A collection of tangos inspired by the motion picture *Valentino: the Loves and*
    Times of Rudolph Valentino.
    Conductor: Victor Young. **Cast:** Castillians.

VALENTINO (1977)
Soundtrack (1977) • United Artists (S) UA-LA810-H 15-25   77
    Composer: Stanley Black, Ferde Grofe. **Conductor:** Stanley Black. **Cast:** Chris Ellis.

VALIANT YEARS
TV Soundtrack (1962) • ABC-Paramount (M) ABC-387 25-30   62
TV Soundtrack (1962) • ABC-Paramount (S) ABCS-387 30-35   62
    Based on the career of Winston Churchill.
    Composer: Richard Rodgers. **Conductor:** Robert Emmett Dolan.

VALLEY: see OBSCURED BY CLOUDS

VALLEY GIRL

Soundtrack (1983) • Epic (M) FE 38623.. 50-75   83
    Five tracks from the film. Promotional issue only.

Soundtrack (1983) • Roadshow (S) RS-101....................................... 50-150   83
    Six track mini-album. Recalled shortly after production, with very few copies making it into
    circulation.
    Composer: Various. **Cast:** Bonnie Hayes with the Wild Combo, Sparks, Josie Cotton,
    Plimsouls.

VALLEY OF THE DOLLS

Soundtrack (1967) • 20th Century-Fox (M) TF-4196 10-15   67

Soundtrack (1967) • 20th Century-Fox (S) TFS-4196 20-25   67

Soundtrack (1967) • 20th Century-Fox (S) SW-91374 10-12   67
    Capitol Record Club issue. May have "S-4196" on cover and "SW-91374" on label.
    Composer: Andre Previn, Dory Previn, others. **Conductor:** John Williams. **Cast:** Tony Scotti.

Studiotrack (1967) • United Artists (S) UAS-6623 25-35   67
    Full title: *Patty Duke Sings Songs from Valley of the Dolls and Other Selections.*
    Cast: Patty Duke.

Studiotrack • Spector (S) SPS-568 8-10
    Cast: Dionne Warwick.
    Also see BEYOND THE VALLEY OF THE DOLLS

VALMOUTH

Original Cast (1960) • PYE (S) NSPL-83004...................................... 20-30   60

Original Cast (1960) • AEI (S) AEI-1123 8-12   70s
    Cast of the Chichester Festival, England.

Original Cast (1960) • That's Entertainment (S) TER-1019 10-12   82
    UK releases.
    Composer: Sandy Wilson. **Cast:** Bertice Reading, Fenella Fielding, Doris Hare, Robert
    Helpmann.

VAMP

Soundtrack (1986) • Varese Sarabande (S) STV-81288 10-15   86
    Composer: Jonathan Elias.

VAN

Soundtrack (1976) • Warner Bros. (S) BS 3063................................... 10-15   77

VAN NUYS BLVD.

Soundtrack (1979) • Mercury (S) SRM-1-3794...................................... 8-12   79
    Composer: Ron Wright, Ken Mansfield. **Cast:** Ron Wright, Tere Mansfield, Jump Start.

VANESSA

Original Cast (1958) • RCA Victor (S) ARL2-2094 20-25   77
    Two discs.
    Composer: Samuel Barber, Gian-Carlo Menotti. **Conductor:** Dimitri Mitropoulos. **Cast:** Eleanor
    Steber, Rosalind Elias, Regina Resnik, Nicolai Gedda, Georgio Tozzi.

VANISHING POINT

Soundtrack (1971) • Amos (S) AAS-8002 15-20   71
    Conductor: Jimmy Bowen. **Cast:** Jerry Reed, Mountain, Delaney and Bonnie and Friends, J.B.
    Pickers, Jimmy Walker, Bobby Doyle, "Big Mama" Thornton, Doug Dillard Expedition, Segarini &
    Bishop, Eve, Kim & Dave, Jimmy Bowen Orchestra and Chorus.

VANISHING PRAIRIE

Soundtrack (1954) • Columbia (M) CL-6332 60-75   54
    10-inch LP.
    Composer: Paul J. Smith. **Conductor:** Paul J. Smith.
    Also see LIVING DESERT

VARIETY GIRL: see BING'S HOLLYWOOD

VELVETEEN RABBIT
Studio Cast (1985) • Dancing Cat (S) DC-3007 8-12   85
   Composer: George Winston. Conductor: George Winston. Cast: Meryl Streep (narration),
   George Winston.

VERNON DUKE REVISITED
Studio Cast • Crewe (S) CR-1342 8-12
   Composer: Vernon Duke.

VERONIKA VOSS / LOLA
Soundtrack (1982) • DRG (S) SL-9508 15-20
   Background score for the films *Veronika Voss* and *Lola*.
   Composer: Peer Raben.

VERTIGO
Soundtrack (1958) • Mercury (M) MG-20384 100-150   58
Soundtrack (1958) • Mercury (S) SRI 75117 25-35   77
   Composer: Bernard Herrmann. Conductor: Muir Mathieson. Cast: Sinfonia of London.

VERY BEST OF GERSHWIN: see ALL-STAR SALUTE, THE VERY BEST OF GERSHWIN

VERY BEST OF MOTION PICTURE MUSICALS
Soundtrack • MGM (M) E 4171 10-15   63
Soundtrack • MGM (SE) SE 4171 15-20   63
   Music from *Words and Music, Gigi, Annie Get Your Gun, An American in Paris, The Band
   Wagon, Lili, The Wizard of Oz, Kismet* and *Show Boat*.
   Cast: Judy Garland, Louis Armstrong, Howard Keel, George Guetary, Adolf Deutsch, Leslie
   Caron, Mel Ferrer, Louis Jourdan, Gene Kelly, Kathryn Grayson, Ann Blyth, Vic Damone,
   William Warfield.

VERY BEST OF RICHARD RODGERS
Studiotrack • Summit (S) 1054 8-10
   Music from *Carousel, South Pacific, The King and I* and *Oklahoma!*
   Composer: Richard Rogers. Conductor: Hans Jurgens-Walther. Cast: Hamburg Symphony.

VERY GOOD EDDIE
Original Revival Cast (1975) • DRG (S) DRG-6100 8-12   75
   Composer: Jerome Kern. Conductor: Lynn Crigler. Cast: David Christmas, Spring Fairbank,
   Travis Hudson, Hal Shane.

VERY WARM FOR MAY
Studio Cast • Monmouth Evergreen (SE) MES-6808 8-10
   Composer: Jerome Kern, Oscar Hammerstein II. Cast: Reid Shelton, Susan Watson, D.
   Carroll.
Original Cast (1939) • AEI (M) AEI-1156 20-25   80s
   As with most AEI albums, liner notes don't reveal the source of the material. However, front
   cover clearly states "The Original Broadway Cast Recording" and several well-known voices
   from the original cast are heard on the record.
   Composer: Jerome Kern, Oscar Hammerstein II. Conductor: Matty Melneck. Cast: Eve Arden,
   Frances Mercer, Jack Whiting, Grace McDonald, Richard Quine, Hiram Sherman, Hollace
   Shaw, Tony Martin (who didn't appear in the original production).

VIA GALACTICA
Studio Cast (1972) • Chappell (M) C-103 40-50   72
   Special demonstration disc.
Studio Cast (1972) • Kilmarnock (S) KIL-72009 25-30   72
   Composer: Galt MacDermot, Christopher Gore. Conductor: Galt MacDermot. Cast: Bill Butler
   (guitar).

VIC AND SADE
Original Radio Cast • Golden Age (M) 5027 8-10   78

VICTOR BORGE PROGRAM

Original Cast (1948) • Columbia (M) CL-6013 20-25   48
  10-inch LP
    Conductor: Paul Baron. **Cast:** Victor Borge, Paul Baron and His Orchestra.

Studio Cast (1953) • MGM (EP) X-1707 10-15   62

Studio Cast (1953) • MGM (M) E-3995 15-20   62
    Cast: Victor Borge.
    Also see CAUGHT IN THE ACT
    Also see COMEDY IN MUSIC.

VICTOR / VICTORIA

Soundtrack (1982) • MGM (S) MG-1-5407 25-35   82

Soundtrack (1982) • Polydor (S) MG-1-5407 5-10   Re
    Gatefold covers. Has same cover and selection number as MGM original.
    Composer: Henry Mancini, Leslie Bricusse. **Conductor:** Henry Mancini. **Cast:** Julie Andrews, Robert Preston, Lesley Ann Warren.

VICTOR YOUNG

Studiotrack • AEI (S) AEI-2107 10-15   80s
    Full title: *Victor Young Conducts Victor Young.*
    Composer: Victor Young. **Conductor:** Victor Young.

Studiotrack • Citadel (S) CT-6024 12-18   69
    Composer: Victor Young. **Conductor:** Victor Young.

Studiotrack • Wing (M) MGW-12247 12-15
    Full title: *Great Motion Picture Themes of Victor Young.*
    Composer: Victor Young. **Conductor:** Richard Hayman.

VICTORS

Soundtrack (1963) • Colpix (M) CP-516 12-15   63

Soundtrack (1963) • Colpix (S) SCP-516 12-18   63
    Composer: Sol Kaplan, Hugh Martin, Ralph Blane. **Conductor:** Sol Kaplan.

Studiotrack (1963) • Colpix (M) CP-460 10-12   63

Studiotrack (1963) • Colpix (S) SCP-460 12-15   63
    Cast: Jane Morgan.
    Also see CHARADE

VICTORY AT SEA

TV Soundtrack (1952) • RCA Victor (EP) ERA-150 15-20   54
    Conductor: Robert Russell Bennett. **Cast:** NBC Symphony Orchestra.

TV Soundtrack (1952) • RCA Victor (EP) EPC-1779 15-18   54
  Three discs.

TV Soundtrack [Vol. 1] (1952) • RCA Victor (M) LM-1779 15-20   54

TV Soundtrack [Vol. 1] (1952) • RCA Victor (M) LM-2335 15-20   59

TV Soundtrack [Vol. 1] (1952) • RCA Victor (S) LSC-2335 15-20   59

TV Soundtrack [Vol. 1] (1952) • RCA Victor (EP) LPC-121 10-15   61
  Compact 33.

TV Soundtrack [Vol. 1] (1952) • RCA Victor (S) ANL1-0970 8-10   75
    Composer: Richard Rodgers. **Conductor:** Robert Russell Bennett. **Cast:** RCA Symphony Orchestra.

TV Soundtrack [Vol. 2] (1952) • RCA Victor (M) LM-2226 15-20   58

TV Soundtrack [Vol. 2] (1952) • RCA Victor (S) LSC-2226 15-25   58
  Above two have gatefold covers and include booklets.

TV Soundtrack [Vol. 2] (1952) • RCA Victor (S) ANL1-1432 8-10   76

TV Soundtrack [Vol. 3] (1952) • RCA Victor (M) LM-2523 15-20   61

TV Soundtrack [Vol. 3] (1952) • RCA Victor (S) LSC-2523 12-15   61
  Above two have gatefold covers and include booklets.

TV Soundtrack (1952) • RCA Victor (EP) LPC-142 10-15   61
  Compact 33.

TV Soundtrack (1952) • RCA Victor (S) VCS-7064 15-20
  Two discs. Highlights of the 13-hour score.
TV Soundtrack (1952) • Mobile Fidelity Sound
  Lab (S) MFSL 3-150 75-100   85
  Limited edition audiophile boxed reissue of all three volumes.
    Composer: Richard Rodgers. **Conductor:** Robert Russell Bennett. **Cast:** RCA Symphony
    Orchestra.
TV Studiotrack • Lion (M) L70113 10-15
    Composer: Richard Rodgers. **Conductor:** Aaron Bell. **Cast:** Aaron Bell Orchestra.
TV Studiotrack • Promenade (M) 2220 8-12
    Cast: Los Angeles Pops Orchestra.
TV Studiotrack • Reader's Digest (S) Number Not Known 20-25
  Boxed, four-disc set.
    Conductor: Charles Gerhardt.
TV Studiotrack • Somerset/Stereo Fidelity (S) SF-10900 8-12
  One side has *Symphonic Suite of Service Anthems*.
    Conductor: Rheinhard Linz. **Cast:** London Philharmonic Orchestra, Armed Forces Symphony.
TV Studiotrack • Spin-O-Rama (S) S-44 8-12

VIDEODROME
Soundtrack (1983) • Varese Sarabande (S) 81173 10-15   83
    Composer: Howard Shore.

VIEW FROM THE BRIDGE
Original Cast (1966) • Mercury (M) OCM-2-221 20-25   66
Original Cast (1966) • Mercury (S) OCS-2-621 30-40   66
  Two discs. The complete Arthur Miller play.
Original Cast (1966) • Caedmon (S) TRS 317 20-25   67
  Boxed, two disc set. Includes booklet.

VIEW TO A KILL
Soundtrack (1985) • Capitol (S) J 818740 10-15   85
  Promotional issue only.
Soundtrack (1985) • Capitol (S) SJ -12413 15-20   85
Soundtrack (1985) • Capitol (S) SV 12413 8-10   Re
    Composer: John Barry. **Conductor:** John Barry. **Cast:** Duran Duran.

VIKINGS
Soundtrack (1958) • United Artists (M) UAL-4003 20-30   59
  "Special preview." Cover has only title, no artwork.
Soundtrack (1958) • United Artists (M) UAL-4003 20-25   59
Soundtrack (1958) • United Artists (S) UAS-5003 30-40   59
  Gatefold covers.
Soundtrack (1958) • United Artists (S) UAS-5003 8-12   72
  Yellow label.
    Composer: Mario Nascimbene. **Conductor:** Mario Nascimbene.
    Also see ELMER GANTRY
    Also see I WANT TO LIVE

VILLA RIDES!
Soundtrack (1968) • Dot (M) DLP-3870 20-25   68
Soundtrack (1968) • Dot (S) DLP-25870 25-35   68
    Composer: Maurice Jarre. **Conductor:** Maurice Jarre.

VILLAGE OF EIGHT GRAVESTONES
Soundtrack (1976) • Varese Sarabande (S) VC-81084 10-15   78
    Composer: Yasushi Akutagawa. **Conductor:** Yasushi Akutagawa.

VINCENT YOUMANS REVISITED
Studio Cast • Painted Smiles (S) PS 1352 8-15

VIRGIN

Original Cast (1972) • Paramount (S) PAA-0288 15-20   72
Also has music from *Fear No Evil, The Mission* and *Ordination Theme.* Promotional issue
only.

Original Cast (1972) • Paramount (S) PAS-8000 30-40   72
Boxed, two-disc set.

Original Cast • Pilgrim America (S) R 3822.. 5-10   81
Includes insert.
    Composer: John O'Reilly. **Cast:** Joe DeVito, Dorothy Lerner, Jim Rast, Jay Pielecki, Mission.

VIRGIN AND THE GYPSY

Soundtrack (1970) • Steady (S) S-122 25-30   70
    Composer: Patrick Gowers, others. **Conductor:** Patrick Gowers.

VIRTUE IN DANGER

Original London Cast • That's Entertainment (S) TER-1079.................. 8-10   80s
UK release.
    Composer: Paul Oeha, James Bernard.

VISION QUEST

Soundtrack (1985) • Geffen (S) GHS-24063.. 8-10   85
    Composer: Various. **Cast:** Journey, Style Council, Madonna, Don Henley, Dio, John Waite,
    Red Rider, Sammy Hagar, Foreigner.

VISIONS OF EIGHT

Soundtrack (1973) • RCA Victor (S) ABL1-0231 8-12   73
    Composer: Henry Mancini. **Conductor:** Henry Mancini.

VIVA LAS VEGAS

Soundtrack (1964) • RCA Victor (EP) EPA-4382 40-60   64
Black label, dog on top.

Soundtrack (1964) • RCA Victor (EP) EPA-4382 30-40   65
Black label, dog on side.

Soundtrack (1964) • RCA Victor (EP) EPA-4382 50-100   69
Orange label.
    Composer: Doc Pomus, Mort Schuman, Bill Giant, Bernie Baum, Florence Kaye, others. **Cast:**
    Elvis Presley, Scotty Moore (guitar), Barney Kessel (guitar), D.J. Fontana (drums), Jordanaires
    (vocals).

VIVA MARIA!

Soundtrack (1965) • United Artists (M) UAL-4135................................. 15-20   66
Soundtrack (1965) • United Artists (S) UAS-5135................................. 15-30   66
    Composer: Georges Delerue, Louis Malle, Jean Claude Carriere. **Conductor:** Georges
    Delerue. **Cast:** Brigitte Bardot, Jeanne Moreau.

VIVA MAX!

Soundtrack (1969) • RCA Victor (S) LSP-4275 15-20-25   70
    Composer: Ralph Dino, John Sembello, Hugo Montenegro. **Conductor:** Hugo Montenegro.
    Cast: Al Hirt, Hugo Montenegro, Ron Hicklin Chorus.

VIVA ZAPATA: see DEATH OF A SALESMAN

VIXEN

Soundtrack (1968) • Beverly Hills (S) BHS-22...................................... 40-50   68
    Composer: Bill Loose. **Conductor:** Bill Loose.

VOICE OF EILEEN FARRELL: see INTERRUPTED MELODY

VOICE OF F.D.R.

Studio Cast (1952) • Decca (M) DL-9628... 30-40   52
    Composer: Victor Young. **Conductor:** Victor Young. **Cast:** Quentin Reynolds (narration).

VOICES

Soundtrack (1979) • Planet (S) P-9002 8-10   79
Composer: Jimmy Webb, others. Cast: Burton Cummings, Willie Nelson, Tom Petty and the Heartbreakers.

VOICES OF LIBERTY

Original Cast (1984) • Disneyland (M) 2524 15-20   84
Daily show at Disney World's Epcot Center.
Cast: Derrick Johnson, etc.

VOIX HUMAINE, LA: see LA VOIX HUMAINE

VON RICHTHOFEN AND BROWN: see PRIVATE PARTS

VOYAGE EN BALLON

Soundtrack (1960) • Philips (M) PHM-200-029 25-30   60
Soundtrack (1960) • Philips (S) PHS-600-029 35-40   60
Soundtrack (1960) • Philips (S) FDX-290 8-10   77
Composer: Jean Prodromides. Conductor: Andre Girard.

VOYAGE OF THE DAMNED

Soundtrack (1976) • No Label Name or Number Used 25-35   77
White label. Promotional issue only.
Soundtrack (1976) • Entr'Acte (S) ERS-6508 20-25   77
Composer: Lalo Schifrin. Conductor: Lalo Schifrin.

W.C. FIELDS
Original Radio Broadcast • Mark 56 (M) 571 40-80   78
   Picture disc. Actual title: *Nostalgia*. Two variations were made. One has photo of Fields
   standing, other shows only his upper body.
   Cast: W.C. Fields.
Studio Cast • Jay (M) 2001 15-20   52
   Full title: *W.C. Fields Temperance Lecture*
   10-inch LP.
Studio Cast • Proscenium (M) PR-22 15-20   60
   Full title: *W.C. Fields ... His Only Recording.* Has *Temperance Lecture* plus eight songs by
   Mae West.
   Cast: W.C. Fields, Mae West.
Soundtrack • Decca (M) DL-9164 15-25   69
Soundtrack • Decca (SE) DL-79164 15-25   69
   Full title: *W.C. Fields – The Original Voice Tracks from His Greatest Movies.* Gatefold cover
   with poster. Includes excerpts from his Paramount and Universal films.
   Cast: W.C. Fields, Gary Owens (narrator), others.

W.C. FIELDS AND ME
Soundtrack (1976) • MCA (S) 2092 8-15   76
   Cover intact (no clipped corners).
Soundtrack (1976) • MCA (S) 2092 5-8   76
   Cover has one or more clipped corners.
   Composer: Henry Mancini. **Conductor:** Henry Mancini. **Cast:** Valerie Perrine, Rod Steiger.
   (With dialogue).

W.W. AND THE DIXIE DANCEKINGS
Soundtrack (1975) • 20th Century-Fox (S) ST-103 20-25   75
   Composer: Dave Grusin, others. **Conductor:** Lionel Newman.

WACKIEST SHIP IN THE ARMY
Soundtrack (1960) • No Label Shown (M) KB-760 40-50   60
   "Theatre Promotion Record." 45 rpm single with *Do You Know What It Means to Miss New
   Orleans.*
   Cast: Ricky Nelson, Jack Lemmon (piano).

WACKY WORLD OF MOTHER GOOSE
Soundtrack (1967) • Epic (M) LN-24230 25-30   67
Soundtrack (1967) • Epic (S) BN-26230 35-45   67
   Composer: George Wilkins, Jules Bass. **Cast:** Margaret Rutherford (as "Mother Goose").

WAGON TRAIN
TV Soundtrack (1959) • Mercury (M) MG-20502 20-55   59
TV Soundtrack (1959) • Mercury (S) SR-60179 30-75   59
   Composer: Jerome Moross, others. **Conductor:** Stanley Wilson.

WAIKIKI WEDDING
Studiotrack (1937) • Decca (M) DL-6011 50-60   51
   10-inch LP.
   Composer: Leo Robin, Ralph Rainger, Harry Owens. **Conductor:** Lani McIntire, Jimmy Dorsey,
   Victor Young. **Cast:** Bing Crosby.
   Also see BING'S HOLLYWOOD

WAIT A MINIM!

Original Cast (1966) • London (M) AM-58002 10-15   66
Original Cast (1966) • London (S) AMS-88002 12-18   66
    Composer: Andrew Tracey. **Cast:** Andrew Tracey, Paul Tracey, Kendrew Lascelles, Michel
    Martel, Nigel Pegram, Dana Valery, Sarah Atkinson.

WAITING FOR GODOT

Original Cast (1956) • Columbia (M) O2L-238..................................... 20-30   56
    Two discs. A "Tragicomedy."
    Cast: Bert Lahr, E.G. Marshall, Kurt Kasznar.

WAKE UP AND LIVE

Soundtrack (1937) • Hollywood Soundstage (M) HS-403 8-10
    Cast: Alice Faye, Jack Haley.
    Also see ALICE FAYE IN HOLLYWOOD 1934-1937.

WALK DON'T RUN

Soundtrack (1966) • Mainstream (M) 56080.. 18-20   66
Soundtrack (1966) • Mainstream (S) S-6080.. 25-35   66
    Composer: Quincy Jones, Peggy Lee. **Conductor:** Quincy Jones. **Cast:** Don Elliot Voices,
    Tony Clementi.

WALK IN THE SPRING RAIN: see LOVE IS A MANY-SPLENDORED THING

WALK ON THE WILD SIDE

Soundtrack (1962) • Columbia (M) Number Not Known 40-50   62
    Includes script and letter to clergy condemning censorship. Reportedly, included two
    theater tickets. Promotional issue only.
Soundtrack (1962) • Choreo (M) A-4-ST 20-25   62
Soundtrack (1962) • Choreo (S) AS-4-ST 30-40   62
Soundtrack (1962) • Ava (M) A-4-ST... 12-18   62
Soundtrack (1962) • Ava (S) AS-4-ST.. 20-30   62
    Some Ava label discs were packaged in a Choreo cover.
Soundtrack (1962) • Mainstream (M) 56083... 12-15   67
Soundtrack (1962) • Mainstream (S) S-6083.. 20-25   67
Soundtrack (1962) • Mainstream (S) DT-91062 12-18   60s
    Capitol Record Club issue with same cover as Ava/Choreo album.
Soundtrack (1962) • Citadel (S) CT-7028.. 8-10   82
    Composer: Elmer Bernstein. **Conductor:** Elmer Bernstein.

WALK WITH LOVE AND DEATH

Soundtrack (1969) • Citadel (M) CT-6025 55-75   69
    Composer: Georges Delerue. **Conductor:** Georges Delerue.

WALKABOUT

Soundtrack (1971) • GSF (S) GSF-1005... 10-12   78
    Composer: John Barry. **Conductor:** John Barry.

WALKER

Soundtrack (1987) • Virgin Movie Music (S) 90686-1 10-15   87
    Cast: Joe Strummer.

WALKING HAPPY

Original Cast (1966) • Capitol (M) VAS-2631 10-12   66
Original Cast (1966) • Capitol (S) SVAS-2631 12-18   66
    Composer: James Van Heusen, Sammy Cahn. **Conductor:** Herbert Grossman. **Cast:** Norman
    Wisdom, Louise Troy, George Rose, Ed Bakey, Gordon Dilworth, Emma Trekman, Gretchen
    Van Akmen, Sharon Dierking, Ian Garry, Burt Bier, Chad Black.

WALL

Original Cast (1960) • Folkways (M) FG-3558....................................... 10-20   60
    Cast: Rita Karin, Norbert Horowitz, Rochelle Horowitz.

WALL STREET
Soundtrack (1987) • Varese Sarabande (S) 704 400 12-15   88
One side has music from *Salvador* (1986).
Soundtrack (1987) • That's Entertainment (S) TER-1154 8-10   80s
UK release.
    Composer: Stewart Copeland. **Cast:** Stewart Copeland. SALVADOR: **Composer:** Georges
    Delerue. **Cast:** Georges Delerue.
    Also see TALK RADIO

WALT DISNEY'S GREATEST HITS
Soundtrack • Ronco (S) R 2100 25-30   76
Includes eight cut-outs and lyrics (price is for *uncut* figures). Full title: *Greatest Hits of Walt
Disney*. Original songs from *Jungle Book, Robin Hood, Snow White and the Seven Dwarfs,
Bedknobs & Broomsticks, Dumbo, Peter Pan, Pinocchio, Aristocats, Mary Poppins, Song of
the South, Winnie the Pooh, Davy Crockett* and *Cinderella*.

WALT DISNEY'S MICKEY MOUSE CLUB
TV Soundtrack • Disneyland (M) DQ-1229 35-40   62
Full title: *Songs from the Mickey Mouse Club Serials*.
    Cast: Jimmy Dodd, Mouseketeers Chorus and Orchestra,
TV Soundtrack • Disneyland (M) MM-24 100-125   58
Full title: *Songs from Annette and Other Walt Disney Serials*.
TV Soundtrack • Disneyland (S) STER-1362 20-25   74
Full title: *Mickey Mouse Club Mousekedances and Other Mouseketeer Favorites*.
    Cast: Annette Funicello, others.
TV Soundtrack • Disneyland (S) ST-3815 30-35   75
Full title: *Mickey Mouse Club Song Hits*. Includes 16-page photo booklet.
Studio Cast • Official Mickey Mouse Club (M) MM-28 65-75   58
Actual title: *Songs About Zorro and Other TV Heroes*.

WALT DISNEY'S TRUE LIFE ADVENTURES
Soundtrack • Disneyland (M) WDL-4011 40-50   57
Music from five Disney "True Life Adventure" film shorts: *Beaver Valley* (1950), *Bear
Country* (1953), *Prowlers of the Everglades* (1953), *Nature's Half Acre* (1951) and *Olympic
Elk* (1952).
    Composer: Paul J. Smith. **Conductor:** Paul J. Smith.

WALT DISNEY'S WONDERFUL WORLD OF COLOR
TV Soundtrack • Disneyland (M) DQ-1245 30-35   63

WALT WHITMAN SUITE: see BERNARD HERRMANN

WALTON CONDUCTS HIS GREAT FILM MUSIC
Studiotrack (1945) • Seraphin (M) 60205 20-25   73
Reissue of *Music from Shakespearean Films*.
    Composer: Sir William Walton. **Conductor:** Sir William Walton.
    Also see MUSIC FROM SHAKESPEAREAN FILMS

WALTONS CHRISTMAS ALBUM
TV Soundtrack (S) KC-33193 8-20   74
    Composer: Jerry Goldsmith, R. Kellaway, others. **Cast:** Earl Hamner, Will Geer.

WALTZING DOWN BROADWAY
Studiotrack (1958) • Warner Bros. (M) B-1218 8-15   58
Studiotrack (1958) • Warner Bros. (S) BS-1218 8-20   58
    Composer: Various. **Conductor:** Warren Barker. **Cast:** Warren Barker and Orchestra.

WANDERERS
Soundtrack (1979) • Warner Bros. (S) BSK-3359 25-30   79
    Cast: 4 Seasons, Lee Dorsey, Angels, Shirelles, Ben E. King, Contours, Isley Brothers, Dion.

WAR AND PEACE (1956)
Soundtrack (1956) • Columbia (M) CL-930 18-20   56
Soundtrack (1956) • Columbia Special Products (M) ACL-930 8-10   76
    Composer: Nino Rota. **Conductor:** Franco Ferrara.

WAR AND PEACE (1968)
Soundtrack (1968) • Capitol (S) SWAO-2918 20-25   68
Soundtrack (1968) • That's Entertainment (S) TER-1020.................... 10-12   80s
   UK release...
    Composer: Vyacheslav Ovchinnikov. **Conductor:** Vyacheslav Ovchinnikov. **Cast:** Moscow
    Symphony Orchestra and All Union Radio and TV Chorus.

WAR AND REMEMBRANCE
TV Soundtrack (1989) • Mediatrax (S) MT-R0001................................ 12-15   89
    Composer: Robert Cobert. **Cast:** Robert Cobert, Jane Seymour.
   Also see WINDS OF WAR

WAR GAMES
Soundtrack (1983) • Polydor (S) 815005-1 8-10   83
    Composer: Arthur B. Rubinstein. **Conductor:** Arthur B. Rubinstein. **Cast:** Yvonne Elliman,
    Beepers. (With dialogue.)

WAR LORD
Soundtrack (1965) • Decca (M) DL-9149 20-25   65
Soundtrack (1965) • Decca (S) DL-79149... 35-45   65
    Composer: Jerome Moross, Hans J. Salter. **Conductor:** Joseph Gershenson.

WAR LOVER
Studiotrack (1962) • Colpix (M) CP-512 15-20   62
Studiotrack (1962) • Colpix (S) SCP-512 25-50   62
    Composer: Richard Addinsell. **Conductor:** Shiro Hirosaki.

WAR OF THE WORLDS
Original Radio Cast (1938) • Evolution (SE) 4001 12-15   69
   Two discs. "Actual broadcast by the Mercury Theatre on the Air, October 30, 1938."
    Composer: Howard Koch (radio play). **Conductor:** Bernard Herrmann (musical director). **Cast:**
    Orson Welles, others. (With dialogue.)
Original Radio Cast (1938) • Audio Rarities (M) LPA-2355 10-15
Original Radio Cast (1938) • M.F. (M) 201/2 10-15
   Complete radio broadcast.
Soundtrack (1938) • Quasi (M) PAL-1953....................................... 30-35
   A "Limited Collectors Edition." One side has music from *When Worlds Collide*, also by Leith
   Stevens.
    Composer: Leith Stevens. **Conductor:** Leith Stevens.
Original Radio Cast (1938) • Longines (M) No Number Used 8-10   72
    Composer: Howard Koch. **Cast:** Orson Welles, Mercury Theatre Cast.
Studio Cast (1978) • Columbia (S) PC2-35290 15-20   78
   Two discs. Includes booklet. A musical production.
    Composer: Jeff Wayne. **Cast:** Justin Hayward, Richard Burton, David Essex, Julie Covington.

WARLOCK
Soundtrack (1989) • Intrada (S) MAF-7003.. 15-20   90
    Composer: Jerry Goldsmith. **Conductor:** Jerry Goldsmith. **Cast:** Melbourne Symphony
    Orchestra.

WARNING SHOT
Soundtrack (1967) • Liberty (M) LRP-3498 20-30   67
Soundtrack (1967) • Liberty (S) LST-7498 30-40   67
    Composer: Jerry Goldsmith, Jay Livingston, Ray Evans. **Conductor:** Si Zentner.

WARNING SIGN
Soundtrack (1985) • Southern Cross (S) SCRS 1012 10-15   85
  Composer: Craig Safan.

WARRIORS
Soundtrack (1979) • A&M (S) SP-4761 12-15   79
Soundtrack (1979) • A&M (S) SP-3151 8-10   Re
  Composer: Barry DeVorzon, others. Cast: Barry DeVorzon, Kenny Vance, Joe Walsh, Eric
  Mercury, Desmond Child.

WARSAW CONCERTO: see SUICIDE SQUADRON

WASHINGTON BEHIND CLOSED DOORS
TV Soundtrack (1977) • ABC (S) AB-1044 15-25   77
  Composer: Dominic Frontiere, Norman Gimble. Conductor: Dominic Frontiere. Cast: Sally
  Stevens, Jackie Ward, Missy Mackay, Diana Lee, Ron Hicklin, Loren S. Farber, Gene Merlino,
  Mitch Gordon.

WATER GIPSIES
Original London Cast (19545) • World (M) SH-228 20-25
  UK release. Also has music from Bless the Bride.
  Composer: Vivian Ellis, A.P. Herbert. Conductor: Jack Coles. Cast: Dora Bryan, Laurie Payne,
  Peter Graves, Pamela Charles, Doris Hare, Jerry Verno. (With dialogue.)
  Also see PLAIN AND FANCY

WATERHOLE #3
Soundtrack (1967) • Smash (M) MGS-27096 12-15   67
Soundtrack (1967) • Smash (S) SRS-67096 20-25   67
  Composer: Dave Grusin, Bob Wells. Conductor: Dave Grusin. Cast: Roger Miller (narration
  and vocals).

WATERLOO
Soundtrack (1971) • Paramount (S) PAS-6003 25-30   71
Soundtrack (1971) • Paramount (S) SW-93729 20-25   71
  Capitol Record Club issue.
  Composer: Nino Rota. Conductor: Bruno Nicolai.

WATERMELON MAN
Soundtrack (1970) • Beverly Hills (S) BHS-26 25-30   70
  Composer: Melvin Van Peebles. Conductor: Melvin Van Peebles. Cast: Melvin Van Peebles,
  Estelle Parsons.

WATERSHIP DOWN
Soundtrack (1978) • Columbia (S) JS-35707 20-25   78
  Composer: Angela Morley, Malcolm Williamson, Mike Batt. Conductor: Marcus Dods. Cast:
  Michael Hordern (prologue narration), Art Garfunkel.

WATTSTAX (THE LIVING WORD)
Soundtrack [Vol. 1] (1973) • Stax (S) STS-2-3010 15-20   73
  Two discs.
  Cast: Isaac Hayes, Staple Singers, Rufus & Carla Thomas, Eddie Floyd, Bar-Kays, Albert King,
  Soul Children.
Soundtrack [Vol. 2] (1973) • Stax (S) STS-2-3018 15-20   73
  Two discs.
  Conductor: Dale Warrenn. Cast: Isaac Hayes, Staple Singers, Luther Ingram, Richard Pryor,
  Rev. Jesse Jackson, Rufus Thomas, Carla Thomas, Bar-Kays, Johnnie Taylor, Emotions, Kim
  Weston, Eddie Floyd, Albert King, Soul Children.

WAVELENGTH
Soundtrack (1983) • Varese Sarabande (S) STV-81207 10-12   83
  Composer: Tangerine Dream. Cast: Tangerine Dream.

WAY IT WAS – THE SIXTIES: see I CAN HEAR IT NOW

WAY OF THE WORLD
Original London Cast (1968) • Caedmon (M) TR-339 15-20   68
Original London Cast (1968) • Caedmon (S) TRS-339........................ 20-25   68
  Three discs.

WAY...WAY OUT
Soundtrack (1966) • 20th Century Fox (S) 3192 15-35   66
  Composer: Lalo Schifrin. **Conductor:** Lalo Schifrin.

WAY WE WERE
Soundtrack (1974) • Columbia (S) KS-32830...................................... 12-15   74
  Composer: Marvin Hamlisch, Marilyn and Alan Bergman. **Conductor:** Marvin Hamlisch. **Cast:** Barbra Streisand.

WAY WEST
Soundtrack (1967) • United Artists (M) UAL-4149............................... 10-12   67
Soundtrack (1967) • United Artists (S) UAS-5149 12-15   67
Soundtrack (1967) • MCA (S) 25045.. 8-10   86
  Composer: Bronislau Kaper, Mack David. **Conductor:** Andre Previn. **Cast:** Serendipity Singers.

WE STILL KILL THE OLD WAY
Soundtrack (1967) • United Artists (M) UAL-4183............................... 12-15   68
Soundtrack (1967) • United Artists (S) UAS-5183 15-18   68
Soundtrack (1967) • MCA (S) 25039.. 8-10   86
  Composer: Luis Enriquez Bacalov. **Conductor:** Bruno Nicolai.

WE WERE DANCING
Original Cast • Monmouth Evergreen (SE) MES-7042 8-12
  Music from *Tonight at 8:30, Private Lives* and *Moonlight Is Silver.*
  Composer: Noel Coward. **Cast:** Noel Coward, Gertrude Lawrence, Douglas Fairbanks Jr.

WE'D RATHER SWITCH
Original Cast (1969) • Varieties (M) WRS-100 60-75   69
  Composer: Larry Crane. **Conductor:** Lorenzo Fuller. **Cast:** Tricia Sandberg, Yancy Gerber, Martha Wilcox, Howard Lemay, Ron Collins.

WEDDING IN MONACO
Soundtrack (1956) • Mercury (M) MG-20149 200-250   56
  MGM short subject, featuring the entire marriage ceremony of Grace Kelly and Prince Rainier III. Includes the ballet *Homage to the Princess*, performed at the Monte Carlo Opera House as part of the festivities. Front cover is black and white, back cover has color photographs and a black-and-white MGM publicity still with liner notes.
  Composer: Stan Kenton. **Cast:** Grace Kelly, Prince Rainier III of Monaco.
  Also see SERENADE TO A PRINCESS

WEDDING IN PARIS
Original London Cast (1953) • Parlophone (M) PMD-1011............... 100-150   53
  UK release. 10-inch LP.
Composer: Hans May, Sonny Miller. **Conductor:** Philip Green. **Cast:** Anton Walbrook, Evelyn Laye, Jeff Warren, Susan Swinford.

WEEDS
Soundtrack (1987) • Varese Sarabande (S) STV 81350 12-15   87
  Composer: Angelo Badelamenti.

WEEKEND IN HAVANA: see THAT NIGHT IN RIO

WEILL, KURT: see KURT WEILL CABARET

WEIRD CIRCLE
Original Radio Cast • Golden Age (M) 5025.. 8-10   78
  The Tell-Tale Heart and *Frankenstein.*

WEIRD SCIENCE

Soundtrack (1985) • MCA (S) 6146.. 8-10   85
Soundtrack (1985) • MCA (S) 6152.. 8-10   85
    Composer: Ira Newborn, others. **Cast:** Oingo Boingo, Max Carl, Taxxi, Cheyne, Kim Wilde, Wall of Voodoo, Broken Homes, Wild Men of Wonga, Lords of the New Church, Killing Joke.

WELCOME!

Soundtrack (1977) • Private Stock (S) PS 7004 10-15   77
    Composer: Guido & Maurizio DeAngelis.

WELCOME STRANGER: see BING'S HOLLYWOOD

WELCOME TO L.A.

Soundtrack (1977) • United Artists (S) UA-LA703-H 12-15   77
Soundtrack (1977) • MCA (S) 25040.. 8-10   86
    Composer: Richard Baskin. **Cast:** Richard Baskin, Keith Carradine.

WELLES RAISES KANE

Radio Cast • Virtuoso (M) TPCS-13010 40-45
    Also includes radio broadcast of *Jerome Moross*. Both are complete shows.
    Composer: Bernard Herrmann, Jerome Moross. **Conductor:** Bernard Herrmann.

WE'RE THE BANANA SPLITS: see BANANA SPLITS

WEST SIDE STORY

Original Cast (1957) • Columbia (EP) A-5230 10-20   58
    Boxed, four-disc set.
Original Cast (1957) • Columbia (M) OL-5230.. 10-12   58
Original Cast (1957) • Columbia (S) OS-2001.. 12-18   58
    Columbia's first true stereo Broadway cast LP.
Original Cast (1957) • Columbia (S) S-32603.. 8-10   73
Original Cast (1957) • Columbia (S) JS-32603.. 5-8   Re
    Composer: Leonard Bernstein, Stephen Sondheim. **Conductor:** Max Goberman. **Cast:** Marni Nixon (performs vocals for Natalie Wood in the film), Jim Bryant (performs vocals for Richard Beymer), Rita Moreno, Betty Wand (performs some vocals for Rita Moreno), Russ Tamblyn, Tucker Smith.
London Cast • Rondo-lette (S) 856 5-10
    Complete show.
    Cast: London Company.
London Studio Cast (1959) • Forum (M) F-9045 10-12   59
London Studio Cast (1959) • Forum (S) SF-9045 12-18   59
    Although cover says "Original English Cast," this does not have the original cast of the London production.
    Composer: Leonard Bernstein, Stephen Sondheim. **Conductor:** Lawrence Leonard. **Cast:** George Chakiris, Bruce Trent, Lucille Graham.
Studio Cast (1961) • Columbia (M) ML-5651.. 8-10   61
Studio Cast (1961) • Columbia (S) MS-6251.. 8-10   61
    One side has a suite from *On the Waterfront*.
    Composer: Leonard Bernstein, Stephen Sondheim. **Conductor:** Leonard Bernstein. **Cast:** Leonard Bernstein and His Orchestra.
Studio Cast • Vox (S) STPL 513 160.. 10-15
    Cast: C. Clark, L. Surrey, American Radio Symphony, others.
Soundtrack (1961) • Columbia (M) OL-5670 8-12   61
Soundtrack (1961) • Columbia (S) OS-2070 10-15   61
    Gatefold covers.
Soundtrack (1961) • Columbia (M) OL-5670 8-10
Soundtrack (1961) • Columbia (S) OS-2070 10-12
    Standard covers. Inner sleeve has photos and liner notes.

Soundtrack (1961) • CBS (S) SBP-153 012 15-20   60s
French release. Fold-open cover, with text in English on front and back. Liner notes on inside are in French.

Soundtrack (1961) • Columbia (S) JS-2070 8-10   Re
   Composer: Leonard Bernstein, Stephen Sondheim. **Conductor:** Johnny Green. **Cast:** Marni Nixon (performs vocals for Natalie Wood in the film), Jim Bryant (performs vocals for Richard Beymer), Rita Moreno, Betty Wand (performs some vocals for Rita Moreno in the film), Russ Tamblyn.

Studiotrack (1958) • RCA Victor (EP) EPA-4148 5-15   58
   Cast: Ramin-Kostal Orchestra.

Studiotrack (1959) • Warner Bros. (M) B-1240 10-12   59

Studiotrack (1959) • Warner Bros. (S) BS-1240 10-15   59
Full title: *Ballets U.S.A.* Includes *Ballet from West Side Story.*
   Cast: Robert Prince.

Studiotrack (1961) • Capitol (S) ST-1609 10-15   61
Full title: *West Side Story: Kenton's West Side Story.*
   Conductor: Stan Kenton. **Cast:** Stan Kenton & His Orchestra.

Studiotrack (1961) • United Artists (M) UAL-3166 10-12   61

Studiotrack (1961) • United Artists (S) UAS-6166 10-15   61
Side 2 is music from six other films.
   Conductor: Johnny Green. **Cast:** Ferrante and Teicher.

Studiotrack (1962) • Verve (M) V-8485 10-12   62

Studiotrack (1962) • Verve (S) V6-8485 10-15   62
   Cast: Oscar Peterson Trio.

Studiotrack (1962) • Atco (S) 33-141 10-20   62
Full title: *Bobby Darin Presents the Richard Behrke Trio Like West Side Story.*
   Cast: Richard Behrke Trio.

Studiotrack • Diplomat (M) 2259 8-12   60s
Studiotrack • Diplomat (S) DS 2259 8-12   60s
Studiotrack • Diplomat (S) FM-96 8-12   60s
Music from *Flower Drum Song, High Society, Spellbound, The Third Man, Gigi, Love Story* and *Undercurrent.*
   Cast: Metropolitan Strings.

Studiotrack • Ed Sullivan's Stereo (S) ESS 1000 8-15
   Cast: Ira Wright and His Orchestra.

Studiotrack • Fantasy (M) 3310 10-20   60s
   Cast: Cal Tjader, others.

Studiotrack • International Awards (M) AK-225 8-12   60s
   Conductor: Abbot Mason.

Studiotrack • Mobile Fidelity Sound Lab (S) MFSL-1-005 45-50
Half-speed mastered from original masters. Audiophile issue.
   Cast: Andre Previn, Shelly Manne, Red Mitchell.
Also see DIVORCE ITALIAN STYLE
Also see FLOWER DRUM SONG

WESTERN FILM WORLD OF DIMITRI TIOMKIN

Studiotrack (1981) • Musical Heritage (S) 48221 15-20   81

Studiotrack (1981) • Unicorn/Kanchana Digital (S) DKP 9002 15-20   81
Music from *Red River, Duel in the Sun, Night Passage, Giant, High Noon* and *Rio Bravo.*
   Composer: Dimitri Tiomkin. **Conductor:** Laurie Johnson. **Cast:** Laurie Johnson & the London Studio Symphony Orchestra, John McCarthy Singers.

WESTERN SAGA AND THE DESERT AND THE INDIAN

TV Soundtrack (1956-1957) • Cerberus (M) CST-0207 20-25   83
Music from *Gunsmoke, Rawhide* and *Have Gun Will Travel.*
   Composer: Bernard Herrmann. **Conductor:** Bernard Herrmann.

WESTWARD HO THE WAGONS
Soundtrack (1956) • Disneyland (M) WDL-4008 35-45   56
Soundtrack (1956) • Disneyland (M) WDL-3041 20-25   59
    Composer: George Bruns, Fess Parker, Tom Blackburn, Stan Jones, Gil George, Paul Smith.
    Conductor: George Bruns, Tutti Camarata. **Cast:** Fess Parker, Bill Reeve, Kathleen Crowley.
Studiotrack • Three On One (EP) 378.. 5-10
    Cast: Sandpipers.

WESTWORLD
Soundtrack (1973) • MGM (S) 1SE-47 12-15   73
Soundtrack (1973) • MCA (S) 25004.. 8-10   86
    Composer: Fred Karlin. **Conductor:** Fred Karlin.

WETHERBY
Soundtrack (1985) • Varese Sarabande (S) STV-81247 8-10   85
Soundtrack (1985) • That's Entertainment (S) TER-1010...................... 8-10   80s
UK release.
    Composer: Nick Bicat.

WHALER OUT OF NEW BEDFORD (AND OTHER SONGS OF THE WHALING ERA)
Soundtrack • Folkways (S) FS-3850 30-35
    Cast: Peggy Seeger, Ewan MacColl, A.L. Lloyd.

WHALES OF AUGUST
Soundtrack (1987) • Varese Sarabande (S) STV 81347 10-15   87
    Composer: Alan Price.

WHAT A WAY TO DYE
Soundtrack (1966) • Caprolan/Allied Chemical (S) DWC666/667 30-35   66
"A film on the history of colored dye." Selection number is found only in vinyl trail-off off area. Industrial film.
    Composer: Gershon Kingsley. **Conductor:** Gershon Kingsley. **Cast:** Gershon Kingsley, Burgess Meredith (narrator).

WHAT A WAY TO GO!
Soundtrack (1964) • 20th Century-Fox (M) TFM-3143 15-20   64
Soundtrack (1964) • 20th Century-Fox (S) TFS-4143 30-35   64
Background music from the soundtrack, but none of the musical numbers.
    Composer: Nelson Riddle, Jule Styne, Betty Comden, Adolph Green. **Conductor:** Nelson Riddle.

WHAT AM I BID?
Soundtrack (1967) • MGM (M) E-4506... 12-15   67
Soundtrack (1967) • MGM (S) SE-4506... 12-18   67
    Composer: Gene Nash, Leroy Van Dyke, Buddy Black. **Conductor:** Ernie Freeman. **Cast:** Leroy Van Dyke, Faron Young, Tex Ritter, Johnny Sea.

WHAT COMES AROUND
Soundtrack (1985) • EMI/Capitol (S) ST-12444.................................. 10-15   85
    Composer: Jerry Reed, others.

WHAT DID YOU DO IN THE WAR, DADDY?
Soundtrack (1966) • RCA Victor (M) LPM-3648 12-15   66
Soundtrack (1966) • RCA Victor (S) LSP-3648 20-25   66
    Composer: Henry Mancini, Jay Livingston, Ray Evans. **Conductor:** Henry Mancini.

WHAT DO YOU SAY TO A NAKED LADY?
Soundtrack (1970) • United Artists (S) UAS-5206 15-18   70
Soundtrack (1970) • MCA (S) 25030... 8-10   86
    Composer: Steve Karmen. **Conductor:** Steve Karmen. **Cast:** Allen Funt (narrator), others.

WHAT DO YOU WANT TO BE WHEN YOU GROW UP?

Studio Cast (1967) • Camden (M) CAL-1083 10-15   67

Studio Cast (1967) • Camden (S) CAS-1083 15-20   67

Composer: Various. **Conductor:** Billy Mure. **Cast:** Ed McMahon (narrator), Jeff McMahon, Jackson Beck, Evelyn Juster, Dick Van Patten, Rita Lloyd, Corrine Orr, Peter Fernandez, Jack Grimes, Sybil Trent, Kathy Grimes.

WHAT IT WAS, WAS LOVE

Studio Cast (1969) • RCA Victor (S) LSP-4115 12-15   69

An "Original Albumusical."

Composer: Gordon Jenkins. **Conductor:** Gordon Jenkins. **Cast:** Steve Lawrence and Eydie Gorme.

WHAT MAKES SAMMY RUN?

Original Cast (1964) • Columbia (M) KOL-6040 12-15   64

Original Cast (1964) • Columbia (S) KOS-2440 20-25   64

Composer: Ervin Drake. **Conductor:** Lehman Engel. **Cast:** Steve Lawrence, Sally Ann Howes, Robert Alda, Barry Newman, Bernice Massi.

WHAT'S A NICE COUNTRY LIKE U.S. DOING IN A STATE LIKE THIS?

Original Cast (1973) • RMSC (EP) 747003 40-45   73

Composer: Cary Hoffman, Ira Gasman. **Cast:** Trudy Desmond, Andrea Martin, Martin Short.

Original London Cast (1973) • Galaxy (S) GAL-6004 30-35   73

Composer: Cary Hoffman, Ira Gasman. **Cast:** Peter Blake, Billy Boyle, Neil McCaul, Jacque Toye, Leveen Willoughby.

WHAT'S NEW PUSSYCAT?

Soundtrack (1965) • United Artists (M) UAL-4128 12-15   65

Soundtrack (1965) • United Artists (S) UAS-5128 15-20   65

Soundtrack (1965) • United Artists (S) UA-LA278-G 10-12   74

Composer: Burt Bacharach (music), Hal David (lyrics). **Cast:** Tom Jones, Manfred Mann, Dionne Warwick.

WHAT'S THE MATTER WITH HELEN?

Soundtrack (1971) • Dynamation (S) DY-1200 40-45   71

Promotional issue only.

Composer: David Raksin. **Conductor:** David Raksin.

WHAT'S THE MEANING OF THIS?

Original Cast (1967) • Lutheran (S) S7 7956 20-25   67

Presented by the Youth Activity Division of the American Lutheran Church. Musical made especially for an August 1967 convention.

Composer: Richard Wilson. **Conductor:** Herbert Pilhofer. **Cast:** Castle Singers, John Prigge, Ken Bland, Pat Maxon, Robert Lee, Tim Schumacher.

WHAT'S UP, TIGER LILY?

Soundtrack (1966) • Kama Sutra (M) KLP-8053 12-15   66

Soundtrack (1966) • Kama Sutra (S) KLPS-8053 12-18   66

Composer: John Sebastian, others. **Cast:** Woody Allen and Lenny Maxwell (narration), Lovin' Spoonful.

WHEN HARRY MET SALLY

Soundtrack (1989) • Columbia (S) SC-45319 8-10   89

Cast: Harry Connick Jr.

WHEN THE BOYS MEET THE GIRLS

Soundtrack (1965) • MGM (M) E-4334 12-15   65

Soundtrack (1965) • MGM (S) SE-4334 25-30   65

Soundtrack (1965) • MCA (S) 25013..................................... 8-10   86
    Film version of *Girl Crazy,* including much of the original score.
      Composer: George Gershwin, Ira Gershwin, Liberace, others. **Conductor:** Ernie Freeman,
      Fred Karger. **Cast:** Connie Francis, Harve Presnell, Liberace, Louis Armstrong, Sam the Sham
      and the Pharaohs, Herman's Hermits.
    Also see GIRL CRAZY

WHEN THE WIND BLOWS
Soundtrack (1987) • Virgin (S) 790599..................................... 8-10   87
      Composer: Roger Waters, others. **Cast:** Roger Waters & Bleeding Hearts, David Bowie, Hugh
      Cornwell, Genesis, Squeeze, Paul Hardcastle.

WHEN WORLDS COLLIDE: see WAR OF THE WORLDS

WHERE DO WE GO FROM HERE? : see KURT WEILL IN HOLLYWOOD

WHERE EAGLES DARE
Soundtrack (1969) • MGM (S) S1E-16 ST 20-30   69
Soundtrack (1969) • MCA (S) 25082..................................... 8-10   86
      Composer: Ron Goodwin. **Conductor:** Ron Goodwin.

WHERE THE ACTION IS
TV Soundtrack (1965) • ABC-Paramount (M) ABC-531 20-25   65
TV Soundtrack (1965) • ABC-Paramount (S) ABCS-531 25-30   65
      Cast: Steve Alaimo.

WHERE THE BOYS ARE '84
Soundtrack (1984) • RCA Victor (S) ABL1-5039 8-10   84
      Cast: Judy Cole, Shandi, Rockats, Peter Beckett, Lisa Hartman, Toronto, Phil Seymour, Rick
      Derringer.

WHERE THE BLUE OF THE NIGHT MEETS THE GOLD OF THE DAY
Soundtrack • Biograph (M) BLP-17-1 10-20   77
    Music from the early films of Bing Crosby (1930 - 1933).
      Cast: Bing Crosby.

WHERE THE BUFFALO ROAM
Soundtrack (1980) • Backstreet/MCA (S) 5126 10-15   80
      Cast: Jimi Hendrix, Wild Bill Band of Strings, Bob Dylan, Neil Young, Four Tops, Creedence
      Clearwater Revival, Temptations.

WHERE THE HOT WIND BLOWS: see LOVE IS MY PROFESSION

WHERE THE LILIES BLOOM
Soundtrack (1974) • Columbia (S) KC-32806........................ 10-12   74
      Composer: Earl Scruggs Revue. **Conductor:** Earl Scruggs Revue. **Cast:** Earl Scruggs Revue.

WHERE THE RIVER RUNS BLACK
Soundtrack (1986) • Varese Sarabande (S) STV-81290 15-20   86
      Composer: James Horner. **Conductor:** James Horner.

WHERE'S CHARLEY?
Original Cast (1948) • Decca (M) DL-9111........................... 15-18   54
Original Cast (1948) • Decca (SE) DL-79111 20-25   54
Original Cast (1948) • MCA (SE) MCA-2070........................... 8-12   Re
    Actual title: *They Stopped the Show!* Has original performances from Broadway shows,
    some of which had not, at that time, been released on LP, including Ray Bolger's *Once in
    Love With Amy.*
      Composer: Frank Loesser. **Cast:** Ray Bolger.
Soundtrack (1952) • Decca (M) DU-9-40065........................ 35-45
    Once in Love with Amy and *Make a Miracle* on 45 rpm. Sleeve pictures scenes from the
    film and says "A DECCA Original Cast Album."
      Composer: Frank Loesser. **Conductor:** Sy Oliver. **Cast:** Ray Bolger, Allyn Ann McLerie.

Soundtrack (1952) • Ecnad (M) 216 20-25
Front cover says "Charley's Aunt," but artwork is of Ray Bolger and recording is from the
sound track of *Where's Charley?* Cover also says "mono and stereo," but recording is
mono.
    Composer: Frank Loesser. Conductor: Ray Heindorf. Cast: Ray Bolger, Allyn Ann McLerie,
    Robert Shackleton, Mary Germaine, Horace Cooper, Howard Marion Crawford, Margaretta
    Scott. (With dialogue).
Original London Cast (1957) • Columbia (M) SX-1085 45-65   58
UK release.
Original London Cast (1957) • Monmouth Evergreen (SE) MES-7029 . 15-20   Re
Composer: Frank Loesser. Conductor: Michael Collins. Cast: Norman Wisdom, Pip Hinton, Marion
Grimaldi, Terence Cooper, Pamela Gale, Felix Felton, Jerry Desmonde, Barry Kent.

WHERE'S JACK?
Soundtrack (1969) • Paramount (S) PAS-5005 20-25   69
    Composer: Elmer Bernstein. Conductor: Elmer Bernstein. Cast: Mary Hopkin, Danny Doyle.

WHERE'S POPPA?
Soundtrack (1970) • United Artists (S) UAS-5216 12-25   70
    Composer: Jack Z. Elliott. Cast: Carol Carmichael, June Jackson, Bright Cheerstrap.

WHISPERERS
Soundtrack (1967) • United Artists (M) UAL-4161 15-20   67
Soundtrack (1967) • United Artists (S) UAS-5161 20-30   67
Soundtrack (1967) • MCA (S) 25041 8-10   86
    Composer: John Barry. Conductor: John Barry.

WHISTLE BLOWER
Soundtrack (1987) • Varese Sarabande (S) STV 81315 12-15   87
Soundtrack (1987) • That's Entertainment (S) TER-1139 8-10   80s
UK release.
    Composer: John Scott. Conductor: John Scott.

WHITE CHRISTMAS
Soundtrack (1954) • Decca (EP) ED 819 18-25   54
Boxed, three-disc set.
Soundtrack (1954) • Decca (M) DL-8083 25-45   54
Because of conflicting contracts, Rosemary Clooney's vocals don't appear on the Decca
issues. This LP has some tunes directly from the sound track as well as studio recordings.
    Composer: Irving Berlin. Conductor: Joseph J. Lilley. Cast: Bing Crosby, Danny Kaye, Trudy
    Stevens (performs vocals for Vera-Ellen in the film), Peggy Lee (performing Rosemary
    Clooney's vocals), Skylarks.
Studiotrack (1954) • Columbia (M) CL-6338 40-50   54
10-inch LP.
    Composer: Irving Berlin. Conductor: Percy Faith, Paul Weston, Buddy Cole. Cast: Rosemary
    Clooney, Betty Clooney, Mellomen.

WHITE HORSE INN
Studio Cast (1961) • Angel (M) 35815 15-20   61
Studio Cast (1961) • Angel (S) S-35815 25-30   61
    Composer: Ralph Benatzky, Robert Stolz, Robert Gilbert, Harry Graham. Conductor: Tony
    Osborne. Cast: Andy Cole, Mary Thomas, Rita Williams, Charles Young, Peter Regan, Rita
    Williams Singers, Barney Gilbraith.
Studio Cast (1960) • Angel (S) SZX-3897 10-15   60
Performed in German.
    Conductor: Willy Mattes.
Studio Cast • Monmouth Evergreen (SE) MES-7055 8-10
Excerpts.
    Composer: Ralph Benatzky, Robert Stolz, Robert Gilbert, Harry Graham. Conductor: Jack
    Hylton. Cast: Jack Hylton and His Orchestra.
    Also see GIRL FRIEND

WHITE MANSIONS

Studio Cast (1978) • A&M (S) SP-6004.. 8-12   78
    Cast: Waylon Jennings, Jessi Colter, others.

WHITE MISCHIEF

Soundtrack (1987) • Varese Sarabande (S) 704.470 12-18   87
Soundtrack (1987) • That's Entertainment (S) TER-1153...................... 8-10   80s
   UK release.
    Composer: George Fenton.

WHITE NIGHTS

Soundtrack (1985) • Atlantic (S) 81273-1.. 10-15   85
   Back cover has 10 photos of Hines and Baryshnikov.
Soundtrack (1985) • Atlantic (S) 81273-1E 8-10   85
   Back cover has five photos, with clouds scene and two dancers on front cover.
Soundtrack (1985) • Atlantic (S) A1-81273 8-10   80s
   Columbia House Record Club issue.
    Composer: Michel Colombier. Conductor: Phil Ramone. Cast: Phil Collins, Marilyn Martin,
    David Pack, Robert Plant, Roberta Flack, Sandy Stewart, Nile Rodgers, John Hiatt, Chaka
    Khan, Lou Reed, David Foster, Jenny Burton.

WHITE ROCK – INNSBRUCK WINTER GAMES

TV Soundtrack (1978) • A&M (S) SP-4614 8-12   78
    Composer: Rick Wakeman. Conductor: Rick Wakeman.

WHO FRAMED ROGER RABBIT?

Soundtrack (1988) • Touchstone (S) 64100 15-20   88
    Composer: Alan Silvestri.
Soundtrack (1988) • Disneyland/Buena Vista (S) 62112 15-20   88
   Includes souvenir photo booklet. Has music and dialogue from soundtrack.
    Composer: Alan Silvestri. Cast: William Woodson (narrator), others.

WHO IS KILLING THE GREAT CHEFS OF EUROPE?

Soundtrack (1978) • Epic (S) SE-35692.. 8-10   78
    Composer: Henry Mancini. Conductor: Henry Mancini. Cast: National Philharmonic Orchestra.

WHO MADE WHO?

Soundtrack (1986) • Atlantic (S) 81650-1.. 8-10   86
   Soundtrack of the film Maximum Overdrive.
    Composer: AC/DC (Malcom Young, Angus Young, Brian Johnson). Cast: AC/DC.

WHO'S AFRAID OF THE BIG BAD WOLF

Studio Cast (1930s) • RCA Victor 224... 150-200   34
   Six-inch 78 rpm picture disc. Part one.
    Cast: Frank Luther, Frank Luther Orchestra, others.
Studio Cast (1930s) • RCA Victor 224/5/6.. 600-750   34
   Three disc. Six-inch, 78 rpm black and white picture discs. Other two Disney related picture
   discs are In A Silly Symphony (Who's Afraid of the Big Bad Wolf)/Mickey Mouse & Minnie's
   in Town, (RCA 225, $200-$300) and Lullaby Land of Nowhere/Dance of the Bogey Men
   (RCA 226, $150-$200) from Disney's Lullaby Land.
    Cast: Frank Luther Orchestra, others.

WHO'S AFRAID OF VIRGINIA WOOLF?

Studio Cast (1963) • Columbia (M) DOL-287 20-25   63
Studio Cast (1963) • Columbia (S) DOS-687 20-30   63
   Boxed, four-disc sets. Complete dramatic play.
    Cast: Arthur Hill, Uta Hagen, George Grizzard, Melinda Dillon. (Dialogue.)
Soundtrack (1966) • Warner Bros. (M) B-1656 10-15   66
Soundtrack (1966) • Warner Bros. (S) BS-1656.................................... 12-18   66
   Film background music, with some dialogue. Cover may or may not show "Directed by
   Mike Nichols."

Soundtrack (1966) • Warner Bros. (M) 2B-1657 20-25   66
Two discs. Gatefold cover. Issued only in mono. Complete film.
Composer: Alex North, Sonny Burke. **Conductor:** Alex North. **Cast:** Elizabeth Taylor, Richard Burton, George Segal, Sandy Dennis.

WHO'S GOT DE DING DONG?: see SOMEBODY BAD STOLE DE WEDDING BELL

WHO'S HARRY KELLERMAN AND WHY IS HE SAYING THOSE TERRIBLE THINGS ABOUT ME?
Soundtrack (1971) • Columbia (S) S-30791 12-15   71
Composer: Shel Silverstein, others. **Conductor:** Ron Haffkine. **Cast:** Ray Charles, Dr. Hook and the Medicine Show, Dustin Hoffman, Barbara Harris, Jack Warden, Dom DeLuise, Betty Walker. (With dialogue.)

WHO'S THAT GIRL?
Soundtrack (1987) • Sire (S) 1-25611 8-10   87
Cast: Duncan Faure, Scritti Politti, Madonna, Coati Mundi, Club Nouveau, Michael Davidson.

WHOOPEE!
Original Cast • Smithsonian (M) R-012 20-25
Composer: Gus Kahn, others. **Cast:** Eddie Cantor, Ruth Etting, George Olson.
Also see PUTTIN' ON THE RITZ

WHOOPI GOLDBERG
Original Cast (1985) • Geffen (S) GHS-24065 8-10   85
Cast: Whoopi Goldberg.

WHOOP-UP!
Original Cast (1958) • MGM (M) E-3745 25-30   58
Has the overture, not found on the stereo issue.
Original Cast (1958) • MGM (S) SE-3745............................... 45-55   58
Does not have overture, making it necessary to have both the mono and stereo to have a truly complete show.
Composer: Moose Charlap, Norman Gimble. **Conductor:** Stanley Lebowsky. **Cast:** Susan Johnson, Ralph Young, Sylvia Syms, Romo Vincent, Danny Meehan, Tony Gardell, Asia, Tom Raskin.
Original Cast (1958) • Polydor (S) 837196-1 8-10   Re
Studio Cast (1958) • MGM (M) E-3746............................... 12-15   58
Studio Cast (1958) • MGM (S) SE-3746............................... 12-18   58
Composer: Moose Charlap, Norman Gimbel. **Conductor:** David Rose. **Cast:** David Rose and His Orchestra.
Studio Cast (1958) • MGM (M) E-3747............................... 10-12   58
Studio Cast (1958) • MGM (S) SE-3747............................... 12-15   58
Composer: Moose Charlap, Norman Gimble. **Cast:** Dick Hyman.

WHY NOT?
TV Soundtrack (1960) • Grand Award (M) GA33-424 10-15
Skits from the *Steve Allen Show*.
Cast: Dayton Allen, Steve Allen.

WICHITA TOWN
TV Soundtrack (1959) • Citadel (S) CT 6022 35-50   78
Composer: Hans J. Salter. **Conductor:** Hans J. Salter.

WICKED LADY
Soundtrack (1984) • Atlantic (S) 80073-1............................... 8-12   84
Composer: Tony Banks. **Conductor:** Stanley Black. **Cast:** National Philharmonic Orchestra of London.

WIDE-SCREEN SPECTACULARS
Studiotrack • Somerset (M) P-16400.. 8-10
Studiotrack • Somerset (S) SF-16400 8-12
  Also has music from *El Cid, Ben-Hur* and *King of Kings.*
  Composer: Miklos Rozsa. **Cast:** Cinema Sound Stage Orchestra.

WIDE, WIDE WORLD
TV Soundtrack (1956) • RCA Victor (M) LPM-1280.............................. 35-40   56
  Composer: David Broekman. **Conductor:** David Broekman.

WIDE WIDE WORLD OF WAR
Original Cast (1973) • Little David (S) Number Not Known................... 15-20   73
  Cast: The Committee, San Francisco Improvisational Group.

WILD ANGELS
Soundtrack (1966) • Tower (M) T-5043.................................. 12-15   66
Soundtrack (1966) • Tower (S) DT-5043................................. 15-20   66
  Composer: Mike Curb, Harley Hatcher, Davie Allan. **Cast:** Davie Allan and the Arrows, Hands of Time, Visitors Featuring Barbara.
Soundtrack [Vol. 2] (1966) • Tower (M) T-5056.................................. 12-15   67
Soundtrack [Vol. 2] (1966) • Tower (S) DT-5056................................... 15-20   67
  Composer: Mike Curb, Harley Hatcher, Davie Allan. **Cast:** Davie Allan and the Arrows, Hands of Time, Joe Leahy.

WILD BUNCH
Soundtrack (1969) • Warner Bros. (S) WS-1814 60-75   69
Soundtrack (1969) • Varese Sarabande (S) STV-81145 10-15   80
  Composer: Jerry Fielding. **Conductor:** Jerry Fielding.
  Also see RAIN PEOPLE

WILD EYE
Soundtrack (1968) • RCA Victor (M) LPM-4003 15-18   68
Soundtrack (1968) • RCA Victor (S) LSP-4003 20-25   68
  Composer: Gianni Marchetti. **Conductor:** Gianni Marchetti, Marty Manning. **Cast:** Rufus Lumley.

WILD GEESE
Soundtrack (1978) • A&M (S) SP-4730 8-25   78
  Composer: Roy Budd, others. **Conductor:** Roy Budd. **Cast:** Joan Armatrading, Irish Guards with Jack Watson, Jerry and Marc Donahue. (With dialogue.)

WILD GUITAR
Soundtrack • Rhino (S) 307 10-12

WILD IN THE STREETS
Soundtrack (1968) • Tower (S) SKAO-5099...................................... 20-25   68
Soundtrack (1968) • Tower (S) ST-5139... 15-20   68
Soundtrack (1968) • Capitol (S) SKAO-6284...................................... 12-15   68
  Composer: Les Baxter, Barry Mann, Cynthia Weil, G. Hemric, P. Wibler. **Conductor:** Mike Curb. **Cast:** Davie Allan & the Arrows, 13th Power, Senators, Jerry Howard, Second Time, Gurus.

WILD IS THE WIND
Soundtrack (1957) • Columbia (M) CL-1090 20-25   57
  Composer: Dimitri Tiomkin. **Conductor:** Dimitri Tiomkin. **Cast:** Johnny Mathis.

WILD LIFE
Soundtrack (1984) • MCA (S) 5523.. 8-10   84
  Includes insert flyer.
  Cast: Edward Van Halen, Andy Summers, Three O'Clock, Louise Goffin, Charlotte Caffey, Peter Case, Bananarama, Charlie Sexton, Ron Wood, Van Stephenson, Hanover Fist.

WILD ON THE BEACH

Soundtrack (1965) • RCA Victor (M) LPM-3441 20-25   65
Soundtrack (1965) • RCA Victor (S) LSP-3441 25-35   65
    Composer: Jimmy Haskell, Sonny Bono, By Dunham, others. **Conductor:** Jimmie Haskell.
    Cast: Astronauts, Frankie Randall, Sonny and Cher, Sandy Nelson, Jackie and Gayle, Cindy
    Malone.

WILD ONE

Soundtrack (1954) • RCA Victor (EP) EPA-535 60-80   54
    Actual EP title: *Hot Blood*, the film's original title.
Soundtrack (1954) • RCA Victor (EP) EPA-535 40-50   54
    With film title changed, EPs were reissued reflecting new title, *The Wild One.*
    Composer: Leith Stevens. **Conductor:** Shorty Rogers. **Cast:** Shorty Rogers and His Orchestra,
    featuring Bill Perkins (tenor saxophone).
Soundtrack (1954) • Decca (M) DL-5515 40-50   54
    10-inch LP.
Soundtrack (1954) • Decca (M) DL-8349 35-45   56
    Composer: Leith Stevens. **Conductor:** Leith Stevens. **Cast:** Leith Stevens' All Stars.
Studiotrack (1954) • Decca (EP) ED-633 35-40   54
    Two discs. Full title: *Jazz Themes from The Wild One.*
    Composer: Leith Stevens. **Conductor:** Leith Stevens. **Cast:** Leith Stevens' All Stars.
    Also see BIG OPERATOR

WILD ORCHID

Soundtrack • Sire (S) 1-26127 8-10

WILD RACERS

Soundtrack (1968) • Sidewalk (S) ST-5914 20-25   68
    Cast: Arrows, Sidewalk Sounds.

WILD ROVERS

Soundtrack (1971) • MGM (S) 1SE-31 12-15   71
Soundtrack (1971) • MCA (S) 25141 8-10   86
    Composer: Jerry Goldsmith. **Conductor:** Sydney Sax. **Cast:** Ellen Smith.

WILD WHEELS

Soundtrack (1969) • RCA Victor (S) LSO-1156 15-20   69
    Composer: Harley Hatcher, others. **Cast:** Terry Stafford, Don Epperson, Thirteenth Committee,
    Billie and Blue, Saturday Revue, Three of August.

WILD, WILD WINTER

Soundtrack (1966) • Decca (M) DL-4699 12-15   66
Soundtrack (1966) • Decca (S) DL-74699 25-30   66
    Composer: Jerry Long, others. **Conductor:** Frank Wilson. **Cast:** Astronauts, Jay and the
    Americans, Beau Brummels, Dick and Deedee, Jackie and Gayle.

WILDCAT

Original Cast (1960) • RCA Victor (M) LOC-1060 10-20   61
Original Cast (1960) • RCA Victor (S) LSO-1060 20-35   61
    Composer: Cy Coleman, Carolyn Leigh. **Conductor:** John Morris. **Cast:** Lucille Ball, Keith
    Andes, Edith King, Paula Stewart, Clifford David, Swen Swenson, Charles Braswell, Bill Walker,
    Ray Mason, Al Lanti, Don Tomkins.
Studio Cast (1961) • Kapp (M) KL-1223 8-15   61
Studio Cast (1961) • Kapp (S) KS-3223 10-20   61
    Composer: Cy Coleman, Carolyn Leigh. **Conductor:** Pete King. **Cast:** Jack Jones, Beth Adlam,
    Pete King Chorale and Orchestra, Norma Zimmer, Ernie Newton.
Studio Cast (1961) • RCA Victor (M) LPM-2357 8-12   61
Studio Cast (1961) • RCA Victor (S) LSP-2357 10-12   61
    Composer: Cy Coleman, Carolyn Leigh. **Conductor:** Bob Thompson. **Cast:** Bob Thompson
    Orchestra and Chorus.

WILDCATS
Soundtrack (1986) • Warner Bros. (S) 1-25388 8-10   86
    Cast: Isley Brothers, Mavis Staples, Michael Jeffries, Randy Crawford, Sidney Justin, James Ingram, Tata Vega, James Newton Howard, Joe Cocker.

WILDERNESS TRAIL
TV Soundtrack • National Geographic Society (M) 07708 15-20
    Composer: Walter Scharf. **Conductor:** Walter Scharf.

WILDEST DREAMS
Original London Cast • AEI (S) AEI-1122 8-12   70s
    Composer: J. Slade. **Conductor:** D. Reynolds.

WILDFLOWER: see TIP TOES

WILL PENNY
Soundtrack (1968) • Dot (M) DLP-3844 15-25   68
Soundtrack (1968) • Dot (S) DLP-25844 18-20   68
    One side has *The Film Music of David Raksin* and includes selections from *Sylvia* and *Too Late Blues.*
    Composer: David Raksin. **Conductor:** David Raksin. **Cast:** Donald Pleasance (narration), Don Cherry.

WILL ROGERS' U.S.A.
Original Cast (1971) • Columbia (S) SG-30546 10-12   71
    Two discs.
    Cast: James Whitmore as Will Rogers. (Dialogue.)

WILLIAM HOLDEN PRESENTS: see MUSICAL TOUCH OF FAR AWAY PLACES

WILLIE DYNAMITE
Soundtrack (1974) • MCA (S) 393 18-20   74
    Composer: J.J. Johnson, Gilbert Moses III. **Cast:** Martha Reeves and the Sweet Things.

WILLOW
Soundtrack (1988) • Virgin Movie Music (S) 90939-1 20-25   88
    Composer: James Horner. **Conductor:** James Horner. **Cast:** London Symphony Orchestra, King's College Choir of Wimbledon.
Soundtrack (1988) • Buena Vista (S) 62113 8-12   88
    Includes 16-page booklet. Story, dialogue and music.

WILLY WONKA AND THE CHOCOLATE FACTORY
Soundtrack (1971) • Paramount (S) Number Not Known 30-35   71
    Promotional issue only. Has custom cover.
Soundtrack (1971) • Paramount (S) PAS-6012 35-40   71
Soundtrack (1971) • MCA (S) 37124 8-10   86
    Composer: Anthony Newley, Leslie Bricusse. **Conductor:** Walter Scharf. **Cast:** Gene Wilder, Diana Lee, Jack Albertson (with dialogue).

WIND AND THE LION
Soundtrack (1975) • Arista (S) AL-4048 12-15   75
Soundtrack (1975) • Arista (S) AR-4048 8-10   Re
    Composer: Jerry Goldsmith. **Conductor:** Jerry Goldsmith.

WINDJAMMER
Soundtrack (1958) • Columbia (M) CL-1158 8-12   58
    Gatefold cover.
Soundtrack (1958) • Columbia (SE) CS-8651 8-12   59
    Composer: Morton Gould, Easy Riders. **Conductor:** Jack Shaindlin. **Cast:** Cinemiracle Symphony Orchestra, S/S Christian Radrich.
Studiotrack • Harmony (M) HL 7131 8-12
    Cast: Art Lowry and His Latin-American Sounds.

WINDS OF CHANGE
Soundtrack (1979) • Casablanca (S) NBLP-7167 12-15   79
    Composer: Alec R. Costandinos, Enoch Anderson. **Conductor:** Raymond Knehnetsky.

WINDS OF WAR
Soundtrack (1983) • Varese Sarabande (S) STV 81180 10-20   83
Soundtrack (1983) • That's Entertainment (S) TER-1070...................... 8-10   80s
    UK release.
    Composer: Bob Cobert. **Conductor:** Bob Cobert. **Cast:** Robert Mitchum, Ali McGraw, Jan-Michael Vincent, John Houseman, Polly Bergen, Lisa Eilbacher, David Dukes, Topol, Ben Murphy, Peter Graves, Jeremy Kemp, Ralph Bellamy, Victoria Tennant.
    Also see WAR AND REMEMBRANCE

WINDWALKER
Soundtrack (1980) • Cerberus (S) CST-0202..................................... 10-20   81
    Composer: Merrill Jenson. **Conductor:** Merrill Jenson.

WINGED VICTORY
Original Cast • Decca A-363 30-40
    Two 12-inch 78 rpms in folder with booklet. Never released on LP by Decca.
    Composer: David Rose. **Conductor:** Leonard de Paur. **Cast:** Julie Warren, Red Buttons, Barry Nelson, Edmond O'Brien, Danny Scholl, John Forsythe, Peter Lind Hayes, Karl Malden, Kevin McCarthy, Edward McMahon, Gary Merrill, Ray McDonald, George Reeves.
    Also see SONG OF NORWAY

BOTH - NOT SOUNDTRACKs
WINNING
Soundtrack (1969) • Decca (S) DL-79169.. 12-18   69
    Maroon label.
Soundtrack (1969) • Decca (S) DL-79169.. 10-15   69
    Black label.
    Composer: Dave Grusin. **Conductor:** Dave Grusin.

WINSTON CHURCHILL: see VALIANT YEARS
WIRED
Soundtrack (1988) • Varese Sarabande (S) VSD-5237...................... 12-15   88
    Composer: Basil Poledouris. **Conductor:** Basil Poledouris. **Cast:** Michael Chicklis and the Wired Band, Brian Francis Neary, Joe Strummer, Gary Groomes, Richie Havens, Ventures, Basil Poledouris.

WISDOM
Soundtrack (1988) • Varese Sarabande (S) VS-5209 12-15   88
    Composer: Danny Elfman. **Conductor:** Danny Elfman.

WISH YOU WERE HERE
Original Cast (1952) • RCA Victor OC-1007....................................... 20-25   52
    78 rpm album.
Original Cast (1952) • RCA Victor (EP) EOA-437 10-15   52
Original Cast (1952) • RCA Victor (EP) WOC-1007 15-18   52
    Boxed, five-disc set.
Original Cast (1952) • RCA Victor (M) LOC-1007 35-50   52
Original Cast (1952) • Camden (M) CAL-621 15-18   61
Original Cast (1952) • RCA Victor (M) LOC-1108 12-15   65
Original Cast (1952) • RCA Victor (SE) LSO-1108............................. 12-18   65
    Composer: Harold Rome. **Conductor:** Jay Blackton. **Cast:** Sheila Bond, Jack Cassidy, Patricia Marand, Sammy Smith, Sidney Armus, Paul Valentine.

WITCHES OF EASTWICK
Soundtrack (1987) • Warner Bros. (S) 1-25607 25-30   87
    Composer: John Williams.

WITH A SONG IN MY HEART
Soundtrack (1952) • Capitol DNN-309 20-30   52
    Boxex set of four 78 rpms.
Soundtrack (1952) • Capitol (EP) KDF-309 15-18   52
    Boxed, four-disc set.
Soundtrack (1952) • Capitol (M) L-309 20-30   52
    10-inch LP.
Soundtrack (1952) • Capitol (M) T-309 18-25   52
Soundtrack (1952) • Capitol (M) 11891 8-10   78
    Abridged version of original release.
     Composer: Richard Rodgers, Lorenz Hart, others. **Conductor:** George Greeley. **Cast:** Jane
     Froman (performed vocals for Susan Hayward in the film).
     Also see SUSAN HAYWARD

WITHNAIL AND I
Soundtrack (1987) • DRG (S) SBL-12590 8-10   87
     Cast: Beatles, others.

WITHOUT YOU, I'M NOTHING
Original Cast • Enigma (S) 73369 8-10
     Cast: Sandra Bernhard.

WITNESS
Original Cast (1978) • Light (S) LSX-5739 10-15   78
    Two discs.
     Composer: Jimmy and Carol Owens. **Cast:** Barry McGuire.
Soundtrack (1985) • Jackal/Varese Sarabande (S) WOW-727 10-12   85
    Digital Recording.
Soundtrack (1985) • Varese Sarabande (S) STV-81237 8-10   85
Soundtrack (1985) • That's Entertainment (S) TER-1098 8-10   80s
    UK release.
     Composer: Maurice Jarre.

WIZ
Original Cast (1975) • Atlantic (Q) QD-18137 10-20   75
Original Cast (1975) • Atlantic (S) SD-18137 8-10   75
    African-American adaptation of *The Wizard of Oz.*
     Composer: Charlie Smalls, others. **Conductor:** Charles H. Coleman. **Cast:** Stephanie Mills,
     Tiger Haynes, Ted Ross, Hinton Battle, Clarice Taylor, Mabel King, Andre DeShields, Tasha
     Thomas, Dee Dee Bridgewater.
Soundtrack (1978) • MCA (S) 2-14000 10-12   78
    Two discs. Includes three inserts.
     Composer: Charlie Smalls, others. **Conductor:** Quincy Jones, Bobby Tucker, Robert
     Freedman. **Cast:** Diana Ross, Michael Jackson, Lena Horne, Richard Pryor, Nipsey Russell,
     Thelma Carpenter, Mabel King, Theresa Merritt, Ted Ross.

WIZARD OF OZ
Original Radio Cast (1939) • Jass Seventeen (M) 12017-1 15-25   88
    Complete NBC "Maxwell House Good News" radio broadcast, June 29, 1939. Has original
    movie cast performance with music, plus "behind the scenes" talk.
     Composer: Harold Arlen, E.Y. Harburg. **Cast:** Judy Garland, Ray Bolger, Jack Haley, Bert Lahr,
     Frank Morgan, Billie Burke, Margaret Hamilton.
Original London Cast • That's Entertainment (S) TER-1165 12-18   89
    UK release. From a London stage production.
     Composer: Harold Arlen, E.Y. Harburg.

Studio Cast (1976) • Caedmon (S) TC 1512 8-12   76
"An accurate abridgement of the original book" as read by Ray Bolger.
Composer: Don Heckman. **Conductor:** Don Heckman. **Cast:** Ray Bolger.
Radio Cast (1950) • Radiola (M) 1109 5-8
Broadcast December 25, 1950.
Composer: Harold Arlen, E.Y. Harburg. **Cast:** Judy Garland, others.
Soundtrack (1939) • MGM (EP) X-3464 15-25   56
Boxed, three-disc set.
Soundtrack (1939) • MGM (M) E-3464 40-50   56
Yellow cover.
Soundtrack (1939) • MGM (M) E-3996 10-12   62
Soundtrack (1939) • MGM (SE) SE-3996 10-15   62
Gatefold covers with drawing on front.
Soundtrack (1939) • MGM (M) SPX-104 20-25   66
"Merchandising Edition," originally a TV mail order offer. Cover is green with drawing of
Dorothy, Tin Man and Scarecrow on yellow brick road.
Soundtrack (1939) • MCA (M) 39046 8-10   86
Composer: Harold Arlen, E.Y. Harburg. **Conductor:** George Stoll, Herbert Stothart. **Cast:** Judy
Garland, Ray Bolger, Jack Haley, Bert Lahr, Frank Morgan, Billie Burke, Margaret Hamilton,
MGM Studio Orchestra and Chorus.
Studiotrack • Decca (M) DL-5152.. 25-35   52
10-inch LP.
Conductor: Victor Young. **Cast:** Judy Garland, Ken Darby Singers, Victor Young and His
Orchestra.
Also see PINOCCHIO

WOMAN CALLED MOSES
Soundtrack (1978) • MCA (S) 3054.. 8-12   78
Composer: Van McCoy. **Cast:** Tommie Young.

WOMAN IN RED
Soundtrack (1984) • Motown (S) 6108 8-10   84
Composer: John Morris, Stevie Wonder, Ben Bridges. **Cast:** Stevie Wonder, Dionne Warwick.

WOMAN NEXT DOOR
Soundtrack (1981) • DRG (S) SL-9507 10-15   81
Composer: Georges Delerue. **Conductor:** Georges Delerue.

WOMAN OF THE YEAR
Original Cast (1981) • Arista (S) AL-8303 10-15   81
Composer: John Kander, Fred Ebb. **Conductor:** Donald Pippin. **Cast:** Lauren Bacall, Harry
Guardino, Eivind Harum, Grace Keagy, Daren Kelly, Tom Avera, Rex Hays, Lawrence Raiken,
Gerry Vichi, Marilyn Cooper, Rex Everhart, Jamie Ross, Roderick Cook.

WOMAN TIMES SEVEN
Soundtrack (1967) • Capitol (M) T-2800.. 10-12   67
Soundtrack (1967) • Capitol (S) ST-2800... 12-18   67
Seven-episode film, wherein Shirley MacLaine portrays seven different characters.
Composer: Riz Ortolani. **Conductor:** Riz Ortolani. **Cast:** Shirley MacLaine.

WOMEN OF THE WORLD
Soundtrack (1963) • Decca (M) DL-9112 15-20   63
Soundtrack (1963) • Decca (S) DL-79112... 15-30   63
Composer: Riz Ortolani, Nino Oliviero. **Conductor:** Riz Ortolani.

WONDER BAR
Soundtrack (1934) • Hollywood Soundstage (M) HS-402...................... 8-12
Also has music from *Go Into Your Dance*.
Composer: Various. **Cast:** Al Jolson, Delores Del Rio, Dick Powell. GO INTO YOUR DANCE:
Composer: Various. **Cast:** Helen Morgan, Al Jolson, Ruby Keeler.
Also see: HOORAY FOR HOLLYWOOD.

WONDER YEARS

TV Soundtrack (1989) • Atlantic (S) 82032-1 8-15   89
    Full title: *The Wonder Years: Music from the Emmy Award Winning Show and Its Era.*
    Cast: Joe Cocker, Was (Not Was), Judson Spence, Buffalo Springfield, Indigo Girls, Debbie Gibson, Escape Club, Julian Lennon, Van Morrison, Carole King, Crosby, Stills, Nash & Young.

WONDERFUL COUNTRY

Soundtrack (1959) • United Artists (M) UAL-4050 20-60   59
Soundtrack (1959) • United Artists (SE) UAS-5050e 30-100   59
    Composer: Alex North. **Conductor:** Alex North.
    Also see I WANT TO LIVE
    Also see UNFORGIVEN

WONDERFUL DAY: see LOVER COME BACK

WONDERFUL O

Studio Cast (1963) • Colpix (M) CP-6000 20-25   63
Studio Cast (1963) • Colpix (S) SCP-6000 25-30   63
    Composer: J. Raymond Henderson. **Conductor:** J. Raymond Henderson. **Cast:** Burgess Meredith, Gordon Ewing, Ken Remo, Richard Erdman, Salli Terri, Stephen Franken, Ken Berry, Sharon Randall.

WONDERFUL TO BE YOUNG

Soundtrack (1962) • Dot (M) DLP-3474 20-25   62
Soundtrack (1962) • Dot (S) DLP-25474 30-40   62
    Composer: Peter Myers, Burt Bacharach, Hal David. **Cast:** Cliff Richard and the Shadows, Michael Sammes Singers.

WONDERFUL TOWN

Original Cast (1953) • Decca (EP) ED-802 25-30   53
    Boxed, three-disc set.
Original Cast (1953) • Decca (M) DL-9010 25-30   53
    Black label with gold lettering on thick wax.
Original Cast (1953) • Decca (M) DL-9010 10-15   53
Original Cast (1953) • Decca (SE) DL-79010 8-12   63
Original Cast (1953) • MCA (SE) 2050e 5-8   72
    Composer: Leonard Bernstein, Betty Comden, Adolph Green. **Conductor:** Lehman Engel.
    Cast: Rosalind Russell, George Gaynes, Edith Adams, Delbert Anderson, Dort Clark, Jordan Bentley, Cris Alexander.
Original West Coast Cast • Location (M) 1261-368 35-40
    Composer: Leonard Bernstein, Betty Comden, Adolph Green. **Cast:** Veronica Lehner, Jerry Lanning, Phyllis Newman.
TV Soundtrack (1958) • Columbia (M) OL-5360 10-15   58
TV Soundtrack (1958) • Columbia (S) OS-2008 20-25   58
    Composer: Leonard Bernstein, Betty Comden, Adolph Green. **Conductor:** Lehman Engel.
    Cast: Rosalind Russell, Sydney Chaplin, Jacquelyn McKeever, Cris Alexander, Jordan Bentley, Sam Kirkham.
Original London Revival Cast (1986) • Reality/First Night (S) 88561 8-12   86
    Composer: Leonard Bernstein, Betty Comden, Adolph Green. **Cast:** Maureen Lipman.

WONDERFUL WORLD OF MOTION PICTURES

Soundtrack/Studiotrack • United Artists (S) UAS-6392 10-12   65
Soundtrack/Studiotrack • United Artists (S) ST-91181 10-12   60s
    Capitol Record Club issue. Original music from *A Hard Day's Night, Dear Heart, Woman of Straw, Diary of a Bachelor* and others.

WONDERFUL WORLD OF THE BROTHERS GRIMM

Soundtrack (1962) • MGM (M) 1E-3 10-25   62
Soundtrack (1962) • MGM (M) S1E-3 12-35   62
    Boxed set. Includes hard-bound book.
Soundtrack (1962) • MGM (M) E-4077 12-15   63
Soundtrack (1962) • MGM (S) SE-4077 12-18   63

Soundtrack (1962) • MCA (S) MCA-39091 5-8   86
One side of above two has instrumentals from six other films.
Composer: Bob Merrill. **Conductor:** Gus Levene. **Cast:** Laurence Harvey, Yvette Mimieux, Russ Tamblyn, Buddy Hackett, Jim Backus, Terry-Thomas, Beulah Bondi, Karl Boehm, Otto Kruger, Arnold Stang. (With dialogue.)

WONDERWALL
Soundtrack (1968) • Apple (S) ST-3350 25-30   68
This film was not officially released, though some copies have surfaced.
Composer: George Harrison. **Cast:** George Harrison, John Barhami, Tommy Reilly, Colin Manley, Edward Anthony Ashton, Roy Duke. (With musicians of Bombay, India.)

WOODSTOCK
Soundtrack (1970) • Cotillion (S) CT3-500 15-20   70
Soundtrack (1970) • Cotillion (S) SD3-500 15-20   Re
Three discs.
Cast: Jimi Hendrix, Crosby, Stills, Nash & Young, Santana, the Who, Ten Years After, Joe Cocker, Sha-Na-Na, John Sebastian, Canned Heat, Richie Havens, Country Joe McDonald, Joan Baez, Jeffrey Shurtleff, Jefferson Airplane, Sly and the Family Stone, Butterfield Blues Band.
Soundtrack (1970) • Cotillion (S) CT2-400 15-20   71
Soundtrack (1970) • Cotillion (S) SD2-400 10-15   Re
Two discs. Actual title: *Woodstock Two*.
Cast: Jimi Hendrix, Jefferson Airplane, Butterfield Blues Band, Joan Baez, Crosby, Stills, Nash & Young, Melanie, Mountain, Canned Heat.
Soundtrack (1970) • Mobile Fidelity Sound Lab (S) MFSL-5-200 80-100   87
Five-disc set. Includes booklet.

WOOLWORTH HAD A NOTION
Original Cast (1965) • No Label Name Used (S) No Number Used...... 25-35   65
From a June 16, 1965, Woolworth's presentation at the Biltmore Hotel Ballroom.
Composer: Michael Brown.

WORDS AND MUSIC (1948)
Soundtrack (1948) • MGM MGM-37 15-20   49
78 rpm album.
Soundtrack (1948) • MGM (EP) X-37 15-20   50
Soundtrack (1948) • MGM (M) E-505 40-45   50
10-inch LP.
Soundtrack (1948) • Metro (M) M-580 10-12   66
Soundtrack (1948) • Metro (SE) MS-580 10-15   66
All above issues have only excerpts from the score and do not include *Slaughter on Tenth Avenue*, issued separately. Because of conflicting recording contracts, the vocals of Perry Como and Mel Torme do not appear on these albums.
Soundtrack (1948) • MGM (M) E-3233 12-18   55
One side has music from *Two Weeks With Love*.
TWO WEEKS WITH LOVE: **Conductor:** George Stoll. **Cast:** Jane Powell, Debbie Reynolds, Carleton Carpenter.
Soundtrack (1948) • MCA (M) 25029 8-10   86
Reissue of MGM release, but with *Slaughter on Tenth Avenue*.
Composer: Richard Rodgers, Lorenz Hart. **Conductor:** Lennie Hayton. **Cast:** June Allyson, Mickey Rooney, Judy Garland, Betty Garrett, Lena Horne, Ann Sothern.
Soundtrack (1948) • MGM (M) E-540 12-18   55
10-inch LP. Actual title: *Slaughter on Tenth Avenue and Other Ballet Music from Motion Pictures*. Also has ballet music from *The Unfinished Dance* and *The Pirate*.
Composer: Richard Rodgers. **Conductor:** Lennie Hayton.
Soundtrack (1957) • MGM (EP) X-1026 10-12   57
Contains *Slaughter on Tenth Avenue*. Also has music from *Singin' in the Rain*.
Composer: Richard Rodgers. **Conductor:** Lennie Hayton.

Soundtrack • JJA (M) 19822 25-30   82
MGM pre-recordings for the sound track of *Words and Music,* including outtakes. Has
Perry Como and Mel Torme's recordings – not on MGM issues – plus the seldom-heard
singing voice of Vera-Ellen.
Composer: Richard Rodgers, Lorenz Hart. **Conductor:** Lennie Hayton. **Cast:** June Allyson,
Perry Como, Tom Drake, Judy Garland, Betty Garrett, Lena Horne, Gene Kelly, Mickey Rooney,
Ann Sothern, Mel Torme, Vera-Ellen, Eileen Wilson (performed Cyd Charisse's vocals in the
film), Dee Turnell.
Also see GOOD NEWS
Also see THOSE GLORIOUS MGM MUSICALS.

WORDS AND MUSIC (1974)
Original Cast (1974) • RCA Victor (S) LRL1-5079 15-20   74
Conductor: Richard Leonard. **Cast:** Lorna Dallas, Terry Mitchell, Laurel Ford.
Studio Cast (1974) • World (S) WRS-1002 12-15   74
Composer: Sammy Cahn, James Van Heusen, Jule Styne, others. **Cast:** Sammy Cahn, Mike
Sammes Singers.

WORKING
Original Cast (1978) • Columbia (S) JS-35411 10-12   78
Original Cast (1978) • Columbia Special Products (S) PS-35411 5-8   Re
Composer: Stephen Schwartz, Mary Rodgers. **Conductor:** Stephen Reinhardt. **Cast:** Susan
Bigelow, Arny Freeman, Bob Gunton, Robin Lamont, Matt Landers, Bobo Lewis, David Patrick
Kelly, Matthew McGrath, David Langston Smyrl, Joe Mantegna.

WORKING GIRL
Soundtrack (1988) • Arista (S) AL6-8593 8-10   88
Composer: Various. **Cast:** Carly Simon, others.

WORLD, The (ORIGINAL CAST STARRING HOWDY DOODY)
Studio Cast • Leslee (S) PIP-6808 10-12   72
Montage of world events, from 1948 to 1960, including dialogue by political personalities.
Includes the original "Howdy Doody" TV cast.
Cast: Bob Smith (as "Buffalo Bob").

WORLD APART
Soundtrack (1988) • RCA Victor (S) 7974-1 10-15   88
Composer: Hans Zimmer.

WORLDS APART
Soundtrack • Youth Films (S) U3RS 10-15
"Promotional Premier Souvenir Album."
Composer: John W. Peterson.

WORLD IN SOUND
Radio Cast (1975) • Associated Press (M) 1975 5-8   75
News highlights of 1975 by AP Radio.
Composer: Jim Wessel (editor). **Cast:** Tom Martin (narrator).
Radio Cast (1976) • Associated Press (M) 1976 5-8   76
News highlights of 1976 by AP Radio.
Composer: Jim Wessel (editor). **Cast:** Tom Martin (narrator).
Radio Cast (1978) • Associated Press (M) 1977 50-100   78
News highlights of 1977, as compiled by the Associated Press. Includes segments on the
deaths of both Elvis Presley and Bing Crosby, accounting for higher price range.
Composer: Jim Wessel (editor). **Cast:** Tom Martin (narrator).

WORLD OF CENTURY TWENTY FIRST
Soundtrack (1962) • Capitol (M) GP-6256/6257 25-35   62
Film short shown at 1962 World Fair at Seattle.
Composer: Alexander Laszlo. **Cast:** Vincent Price (narrator), Alexander Laszlo.

WORLD OF CHARLES AZNAVOUR

Original Cast (1965) • Reprise (M) 6193 12-15   65
Original Cast (1965) • Reprise (S) S-6193 15-18   65
   Recorded at the Huntington Hartford Theatre, Hollywood, Nov. 19, 1965.
   Cast: Charles Aznavour.

WORLD OF SUZIE WONG

Soundtrack (1960) • RCA Victor (M) LOC-1059 15-20   60
Soundtrack (1960) • RCA Victor (S) LSO-1059 40-50   60
   Composer: George Duning, James Van Heusen, Sammy Cahn, others. **Conductor:** Muir
   Mathieson.

WORLD ON STAGE, VOLUME 1

Original Cast (1983) • Franklin Mint (S) Number Not Known 30-50   83
   Boxed set of four colored vinyl discs. Includes booklet. Original cast recordings from *Man of
   La Mancha, Candide, Fiddler on the Roof, The Rothschilds, Milk And Honey, Three Penny
   Opera, Cabaret, Fanny* and *Carnival.*

WORLD WAR I

TV Soundtrack (1964) • RCA Victor (M) LM-2791 20-25   64
TV Soundtrack (1964) • RCA Victor (S) LSC-2791 35-40   64
TV Soundtrack (1964) • RCA Victor (S) ANL1-2334 25-30   64
   Composer: Morton Gould. **Conductor:** Morton Gould.

WORLD'S GREATEST LOVER

Soundtrack (1978) • RCA Victor (S) ABL1-2709 8-10   78
   Composer: John Morris, Harry Nilsson. **Conductor:** John Morris. **Cast:** Gene Wilder, Carol
   Kane, Dom DeLuise, Fritz Feld, Carl Ballantine, Michael Huddleston, Matt Collins.

WRAITH

Soundtrack (1986) • Scotti Bros. (S) SZ-40429 8-10   86
   Composer: Michael Hoenig, others. **Cast:** Tim Feehan, Honeymoon Suite, Stan Bush,
   LaMarca, Jill Michaels, Ozzy Osbourne, Lion, James House, Ian Hunter, Bonnie Tyler.

WRITTEN ON THE WIND

Soundtrack (1956) • Decca (M) DL-8424 30-35   56
   Black label or pink label promo.
Soundtrack (1956) • Decca (M) DL-8424 15-20   60s
   Rainbow (or multi-color) label.
Soundtrack (1956) • Varese Sarabande (M) VC-81074 8-10   80s
   Above three also have music from *Four Girls in Town.*
   Composer: Victor Young, Sammy Cahn, Frank Skinner, others. **Conductor:** Joseph
   Gershenson. **Cast:** Four Aces. FOUR GIRLS IN TOWN: **Composer:** Alex North. **Conductor:**
   Joseph Gershenson (with orchestration by Henry Mancini). **Cast:** Andre Previn, Ray Linn.

WRONG BOX

Soundtrack (1966) • Mainstream (M) 56088 50-100   66
Soundtrack (1966) • Mainstream (S) S-6088 100-150   66
   Composer: John Barry, others. **Conductor:** John Barry.

WUTHERING HEIGHTS

Soundtrack (1971) • American Int'l (S) A-1039 25-30   71
   Composer: Marilyn Bergman, Alan Bergman. **Conductor:** Michel Legrand. **Cast:** Mike Curb
   Congregation.
Soundtrack • Elmer Bernstein's Film Music Collection (S) FMC-6 35-40   76
   Composer: Alfred Newman. **Conductor:** Elmer Bernstein.

WYATT EARP

TV Soundtrack • ABC-Paramount (EP) ABC A-203 15-20   57
TV Soundtrack • ABC-Paramount (M) ABC-203 40-60   57
   Composer: Ken Darby, others. **Cast:** Hugh O'Brien and Ken Darby Chorus.

WYATT EARP, CHEYENNE AND OTHER TV FAVORITES
Studiotrack (1958) • RCA Victor (M) LBY-1004 30-50   58
  Cast: Roy Rogers and Dale Evans, Sons of the Pioneers, Prairie Chiefs, Johnny O'Neill.

XANADU
Soundtrack (1980) • MCA (S) 6100 10-15   80
  Composer: John Farrar, Jeff Lynne. **Cast:** Olivia Newton-John, Electric Light Orchestra, Cliff Richard, Gene Kelly, Tubes.

XTRO
Soundtrack (1984) • That's Entertainment (S) TER-1052 8-10   80s
  UK release.
  Composer: Harry Bromley Davenport.

YANKEE DOODLE DANDY
Studiotrack • RCA Victor P-125 10-15
  78 rpm album.
  Cast: RCA Victor Orchestra, others.
Soundtrack (1942) • Curtain Calls (M) CC-100/13 10-15
Soundtrack (1942) • Radiola (M) MR-1103 8-10
  Composer: George M. Cohan, Richard Rodgers, Lorenz Hart. **Cast:** James Cagney, Walter Huston, Joan Leslie, Frances Langford, Jeanne Cagney, Irene Manning, Rosemary DeCamp. Also see GEORGE M!

YANKS
Soundtrack (1979) • MCA (S) 3181 10-15   79
  Composer: Richard Rodney Bennett, others. **Conductor:** Marcus Dods.

YANKS ARE COMING
TV Soundtrack (1974) • ABC (S) Number Not Known 8-12   74
  Has insert.

YEAR OF LIVING DANGEROUSLY
Soundtrack (1983) • Varese Sarabande (S) STV-81182 10-15   83
Soundtrack (1983) • That's Entertainment (S) TER-1065 8-10   80s
  UK release.
  Composer: Maurice Jarre. **Cast:** Electronic realization by Spencer Lee and Maurice Jarre. Also see NO WAY OUT

YEAR OF THE DRAGON
Soundtrack (1985) • Varese Sarabande (S) STV-81266 10-15   85
  Composer: David Mansfield, others. **Conductor:** David Mansfield.

YEARS OF LIGHTNING, DAY OF DRUMS
Soundtrack (1966) • Capitol (M) T-2486.. 12-20   66
Soundtrack (1966) • Capitol (S) ST-2486... 15-30   66
    Produced by the U.S. Information Agency.
     Composer: Bruce Herschenson. **Conductor:** Bruce Herschenson. **Cast:** John F. Kennedy
     (dialogue), Gregory Peck (narration).

YEARS TO REMEMBER
Original Radio Broadcast • Longines Symphonette (M) SY-5185......... 15-20
    Broadcasts and news from the 1930s and '40s, including war coverage.
     Cast: Frank Knight, Jack Benny, Prime Minister Neville Chamberlain, Franklin D. Roosevelt,
     Winston Churchill, President Harry S Truman, General Douglas MacArthur, Babe Ruth, Lou
     Gehrig.

YELLOW CANARY
Soundtrack (1963) • Verve (M) MG-8548... 12-18   63
Soundtrack (1963) • Verve (S) V6-8548.. 20-25   63
     Composer: Kenyon Hopkins. **Conductor:** Kenyon Hopkins.

YELLOW ROLLS-ROYCE
Soundtrack (1965) • MGM (M) E-4292 8-12   65
Soundtrack (1965) • MGM (S) SE-4292 10-12   65
     Composer: Riz Ortolani. **Conductor:** Riz Ortolani. **Cast:** Katyna Ranieri.

YELLOW SUBMARINE
Soundtrack (1969) • Apple Films Presents (M) KAL-1004................ 300-700   69
    Commercial spots. Made for radio station use only.
Soundtrack (1969) • Apple (S) SW-153 20-25   69
    Side one has film songs by the Beatles, side two is original film music by George Martin.
Soundtrack (1969) • Capitol (S) SW-153 10-12   Re
    Orange, or purple, or black label with color band.
Soundtrack (1969) • MFSL (S) 1-108 30-50   87
    Half-speed mastered.
Soundtrack (1969) • Capitol (S) C1-46445 10-15   88
     Composer: John Lennon, Paul McCartney, George Harrison, George Martin. **Conductor:**
     George Martin. **Cast:** Beatles, George Martin and His Orchestra.

YENTL
Soundtrack (1983) • Columbia (S) 1791.. 12-15   83
    Picture disc. Studio and movie versions of *The Way He Makes Me Feel* and *No Matter
    What Happens.* Promotional issue only.
     Composer: Michel Legrand. **Cast:** Barbra Streisand.
Soundtrack (1983) • Columbia (S) JS-39152 8-10   83
     Composer: Michel Legrand, Alan Bergman, Marilyn Bergman. **Conductor:** Michel Legrand.
     Cast: Barbra Streisand.

YES, GIORGIO
Soundtrack (1982) • London (S) PDV-9001 8-12   82
     Cast: Luciano Pavarotti.

YESTERDAY, TODAY AND TOMORROW
Soundtrack (1964) • Warner Bros. (M) W-1552 25-35   64
Soundtrack (1964) • Warner Bros. (S) WS-1552 40-50   64
    Cover pictures Sophia Loren.
     Composer: Armando Trovaioli, others. **Conductor:** Armando Trovaioli. **Cast:** Michele Mattera.

YESTERDAY'S HERO
Soundtrack (1979) • Warwick (S) SWW 5075...................................... 10-15   79

YIDDISH ARE COMING! THE YIDDISH ARE COMING!
Original Cast • Verve (S) V-15058 10-15

YOGI BEAR & BOO BOO
TV Soundtrack • Colpix (S) CP-205 50-100   61
    Cast: Daws Butler, others.

YOJIMBO
Soundtrack (1961) • MGM (M) E-4096... 90-100   62
Soundtrack (1961) • MGM (S) SE-4096 120-130   62
    Composer: Masaru Sato. **Conductor:** Masaru Sato.

YOL
Soundtrack (1982) • Warner Bros. (S) 23816-1 10-15   82
    Composer: Sebastian Argol.

YOLANDA AND THE THIEF
Soundtrack • Hollywood Soundstage (M) HS-5001 12-20   79
    Also has music from *You'll Never Get Rich*.
    Composer: Arthur Freed, Harry Warren. **Cast:** Fred Astaire, Trudy Erwin (performs vocals for Lucille Bremer in the film). YOU'LL NEVER GET RICH: **Composer:** Cole Porter. **Cast:** Fred Astaire, Delta Rhythm Boys, Chico Hamilton, Buddy Collette, A. Grant, Joe Comfort, Red Mack, Martha Tilton.

YOR – THE HUNTER FROM THE FUTURE
Soundtrack (1983) • Southern Cross (S) SCRS-1005 10-15   83
    Cast: John Scott.

YOU AND ME: see KURT WEILL IN HOLLYWOOD

YOU ARE WHAT YOU EAT
Soundtrack (1968) • Columbia (S) OS-3240 12-18   68
    Composer: Peter Yarrow, John Simon, Sonny Bono, others. **Cast:** Peter Yarrow, Tiny Tim, Paul Butterfield, Electric Flag, Rosko, John Herold, Hamsa El Din, John Simon, Eleanor Baruchian.

YOU BET YOUR LIFE
Original Radio Cast • Golden Age (M) 5021 8-10   78
    Cast: Groucho Marx.

YOU CAN'T RUN AWAY FROM IT: see EDDY DUCHIN STORY

YOU LIGHT UP MY LIFE
Soundtrack (1977) • Arista (S) AB-4159.. 10-12   77
    Composer: Joe Brooks. **Conductor:** Joe Brooks. **Cast:** Kasey Cisyk, Joe Brooks.

YOU NEVER KNOW
Original Revival Cast (1973) • Blue Pear (M) BP 1015.......................... 20-25   73
    Composer: Cole Porter. **Cast:** Esteban Chalbaud, Lynn Fitzpatrick, Dan Held, Rod Loomis, Grace Theveny, Jamie Thomas Barbara Norrio.

YOU ONLY LIVE ONCE
Soundtrack (1969) • London (S) PS-561 12-15   69
    Composer: Jacques Loussier. **Conductor:** Jacques Loussier. **Cast:** Jacques Loussier Orchestra.

YOU ONLY LIVE TWICE
Soundtrack (1967) • United Artists (M) UAL-4155................................. 10-15   67
Soundtrack (1967) • United Artists (S) UAS-5155 15-20   67
Soundtrack (1967) • United Artists (S) UA-LA289-G 8-10   74
    Composer: John Barry, Leslie Bricusse. **Conductor:** John Barry. **Cast:** Nancy Sinatra.

YOU WERE NEVER LOVELIER: see COVER GIRL

YOU'LL NEVER GET RICH: see YOLANDA AND THE THIEF

YOU'RE A BIG BOY NOW

Soundtrack (1966) • Kama Sutra (M) KLP-8058 .... 10-15　67
Soundtrack (1966) • Kama Sutra (S) KLPS-8058................................. 12-18　67
  Cover may have sticker promoting *Darling Be Home Soon.*
  Composer: John Sebastian. **Conductor:** Jack Lewis. **Cast:** Lovin' Spoonful.

YOU'RE A GOOD MAN, CHARLIE BROWN

Studio Cast (1967) • MGM (M) LE-900.. 12-15　67
Studio Cast (1967) • MGM (S) LES-900.. 12-15　67
  Original musical for records, which inspired the Broadway show.
  Composer: Clark Gesner. **Conductor:** Jay Blackton. **Cast:** Orson Bean, Barbara Minkus, Bill
  Hinnant, Clark Gesner.
Original Cast (1967) • MGM (M) 1E- .... 8-10　67
Original Cast (1967) • MGM (S) S1E-9 .... 8-10　67
Original Cast (1967) • Polydor (S) 820262-1 .... 5-8　Re
  Composer: Clark Gesner. **Conductor:** Joseph Raposo. **Cast:** Gary Burghoff, Bill Hinnant, Reva
  Rose, Karen Johnson, Skip Hinnant, Bob Balaban.
Studio Cast • Pickwick (M) PC-3069 8-10
Studio Cast • Pickwick (S) SPC-3069 8-10
  Composer: Clark Gesner. **Conductor:** Bugs Bower. **Cast:** Ron Marshall, Connie Zimet.
TV Soundtrack (1972) • Atlantic (S) SD-7252 .... 10-15　72
  Composer: Clark Gesner. **Conductor:** Elliot Lawrence. **Cast:** Wendell Burton, Ruby Persson,
  Barry Livingston, Mark Montgomery, Bill Hinnant, Noelle Matlovsky.

YOUNG ABE LINCOLN

Original Cast (1961) • Golden (M) LP-76 .... 15-20　61
  Children's musical with story and songs.
  Composer: Victor Ziskin.
Original Cast (1961) • Wonderland (M) WLP-76 .... 10-12　Re
  Composer: Victor Ziskin, Joan Javits, Arnold Sundgaard. **Cast:** Darrell Sandeen, Judy Foster,
  Lou Cutell, Tom Noel, Travis Hudson, Jack Blackton, Ray Hyson, Robert Darnell, Jack Kauflinn.

YOUNG AMERICA DANCES TO TV'S GREATEST THEMES

Studiotrack (1963) • 20th Century Fox (M) TFM-3109......................... 15-25　63
  Cast: Bill Ramal & Orchestra.

YOUNG AND THE RESTLESS

TV Soundtrack (1974) • P.I.P. (S) PIP-6812 .... 10-20　74
  Composer: Don McGinnis, Jerry Winn, Bob Todd, Barry DeVorzon, Perry Botkin Jr. **Cast:**
  Touch Ltd.
Studiotrack (1976) • A&M (S) SP-3412 .... 10-12　76
  Also has other TV themes.

YOUNG AT HEART

Studiotrack (1954) • Capitol (EP) EAP-1-571 .... 15-20　54
  Cast: Frank Sinatra.
Studiotrack (1954) • Columbia (EP) B-455.. 20-25　54
Studiotrack (1954) • Columbia (M) CL-6339.. 40-50　54
  Solos by Doris Day and Frank Sinatra, but not their duets from the film. Title song not
  included.
  Composer: Cole Porter, George Gershwin, others. **Conductor:** Percy Faith, Buddy Cole, Axel
  Stordahl, Frank Comstock. **Cast:** Frank Sinatra, Doris Day.
  Also see APRIL IN PARIS

YOUNG BESS

Soundtrack (1953) • Elmer Bernstein Film Music
  Collection (S) FMC-5 .... 20-40　76
  Composer: Miklos Rozsa.

YOUNG BILLY YOUNG

Soundtrack (1969) • United Artists (S) UAS-5199 20-25   69
Soundtrack (1969) • MCA (S) 25031.. 8-10   86
    Composer: Shelly Manne. **Conductor:** Shelly Manne. **Cast:** Billy Edd Wheeler.

YOUNG DOCTORS IN LOVE

Soundtrack (1982) • Regency (S) R1-8501 15-20   82
   Comedy skits with original score.
    Composer: Maurice Jarre. **Conductor:** Maurice Jarre. **Cast:** Maurice Jarre, others.

YOUNG FRANKENSTEIN

Soundtrack (1975) • ABC (S) ABCD-870 10-20   75
   Gatefold cover. Cover may or may not have "Story and Screenplay by Mel Brooks and
   Gene Wilder" on bottom.
    Composer: John Morris, others. **Conductor:** John Morris. **Cast:** Gene Wilder, Peter Boyle,
    Marty Feldman, Cloris Leachman, Teri Garr, Madeline Kahn. (With dialogue.)
    Also see HIGH ANXIETY.

YOUNG GIRLS OF ROCHEFORT

Soundtrack (1968) • Philips (M) PCC-2-226... 12-18   68
Soundtrack (1968) • Philips (S) PCC-2-626 15-40   68
   Two discs. Gatefold cover. Contains entire film.
Soundtrack (1968) • Philips (M) PCC-227 10-12   68
Soundtrack (1968) • Philips (S) PCC-627 12-15   68
   Two discs. Excerpts from film.
    Composer: Michel Legrand. **Conductor:** Michel Legrand. **Cast:** Donald Burke, Danielle
    Darrieux, Anne Germain, Claude Parent, Jean Stout, Jacques Revaux, Alice Herald, Christine
    Legrand, Claudine Meunier.
Studiotrack (1968) • United Artists (M) UAL-3662 8-12   68
Studiotrack (1968) • United Artists (S) UAS-6662 10-12   68
    Composer: Michel Legrand. **Conductor:** Michel Legrand.

YOUNG GUNS II

Soundtrack (1990) • Mercury (S) 846473-1.. 8-10   90
    Composer: Alan Silvestri, Jon Bon Jovi. **Cast,** Alan Silvestri, Jon Bon Jovi.

YOUNG LIONS

Soundtrack (1958) • Decca (M) DL-8719 20-25   58
Soundtrack (1958) • Decca (S) DL-78719... 50-75   58
Soundtrack (1958) • Varese Sarabande (S) STV-81115 10-15   81
    Composer: Hugo Friedhofer. **Conductor:** Lionel Newman. **Cast:** 20th Century-Fox Orchestra.

YOUNG LOVERS

Soundtrack (1964) • Columbia (M) OL-7010 12-18   64
Soundtrack (1964) • Columbia (S) OS-2510 15-20   64
    Composer: Sol Kaplan. **Conductor:** Sol Kaplan.

YOUNG MAN WITH A HORN

Soundtrack (1950) • Columbia (EP) B-198.. 15-20   50
Soundtrack (1950) • Columbia (M) CL-6106 40-45   50
   10-inch LP.
Soundtrack (1950) • Columbia (M) CL-582 20-30   54
Soundtrack (1950) • Columbia Special Products (M) ACL-582 8-10   81
    Compser: Richard Rodgers, Lorenz Hart, others. **Conductor:** Harry James. **Cast:** Doris Day,
    Harry James and His Orchestra.
Soundtrack (1950) • CBS (M) SOPJ-100 20-25
   Japanese release. Cover of original 10-inch LP is used. All three reissues (12-inch) have
   additional music not on the EP or the 10-inch LP.
Composer: Richard Rodgers, Lorenz Hart, others. **Conductor:** Harry James. **Cast:** Doris Day, Harry
James and His Orchestra.

YOUNG SAVAGES
Soundtrack (1961) • Columbia (M) CL-1672 20-30   61
Soundtrack (1961) • Columbia (S) CS-8472.. 65-85   61
    Composer: David Amram. **Conductor:** David Amram.

YOUNG SHERLOCK HOLMES
Soundtrack (1985) • MCA (S) 6159.. 10-15   85
    Composer: Bruce Broughton. **Conductor:** Bruce Broughton. **Cast:** Sinfonia Orchestra of London.

YOUNG WARRIORS
Soundtrack (1983) • Varese Sarabande (S) STV-81186 10-15   83
    Cast: Bob Walsh.

YOUNG WINSTON
Soundtrack (1972) • Angel (S) SFO-36901 20-25   72
    Composer: Alfred Ralston. **Conductor:** Alfred Ralston.

YOUNGBLOOD
Soundtrack (1978) • United Artists (S) UA-LA904-H 10-12   78
  May or may not have sticker on shrinkwrap listing credits and featured tracks.
Soundtrack (1978) • RCA Victor (S) ABL1-7172 8-10   86
Soundtrack (1978) • Far Out (S) 904 5-8   Re
    Composer: Lonnie Jordan. **Cast:** War, William Orbit, Mickey Thomas, Glenn Jones, John Hiatt, Starship, Jack Gilder, Marc Jordan, Autograph.

YOUR ARMS TOO SHORT TO BOX WITH GOD
Original Cast (1976) • ABC (S) AB-1004.. 10-12   76
Original Cast (1976) • MCA (S) MCA-37126 8-10   86
    Composer: Alex Bradford, Micki Grant, H.B. Barnum. **Conductor:** Eddie Brown, Chapman Roberts. **Cast:** Salome Bey, Clinton Derricks Carroll, Sheila Ellis, Delores Hall, Bobby Hill, Alex Bradford, William Hardy Jr., Michael Gray, Vinette Carroll.

YOUR CHEATIN' HEART
Soundtrack (1964) • MGM (M) E-4260.. 10-12   64
Soundtrack (1964) • MGM (S) SE-4260... 12-18   64
Soundtrack (1964) • MCA (S) 1438... 8-10   87
  Film inspired by the life and career of Hank Williams Sr.
    Composer: Hank Williams Sr. **Conductor:** Fred Karger. **Cast:** Hank Williams Jr.

YOUR OWN THING
Original Cast (1968) • RCA Victor (M) LOC-1148 10-15   68
Original Cast (1968) • RCA Victor (S) LSO-1148 15-20   68
    Composer: Hal Hester, Danny Apolinar. **Conductor:** Charles Schneider, Peter Matz. **Cast:** Rusty Thacker, Leland Palmer, Igors Gavon, Danny Apolinar, Tom Ligon, John Kuhner, Michael Valenti, Marcia Rodd.

YOURS, ANNE
Original Cast (1985) • That's Entertainment (S) TER-1118 10-12   87
  UK release.
    Composer: Michael Cohen, Enid Futterman. **Cast:** Trini Alvarado, Dana Zeller-Alexis, George Guidall.

YOURS, MINE AND OURS
Soundtrack (1968) • United Artists (S) UAS-5181 10-25   69
Soundtrack (1968) • MCA (S) 1434... 5-8   80s
    Composer: Fred Karlin. **Conductor:** Fred Karlin.

Z

Z
Soundtrack (1969) • Columbia (S) OS-3370 10-12   69
Soundtrack (1969) • Columbia Special Products (S) AOS-3370 5-10
  Composer: Mikis Theodorakis. **Conductor:** Bernard Gerard.
Studiotrack • RCA Victor (S) LSP-4350 8-10
  Full title: *Theme from Z and Other Films.*
  Conductor: Henry Mancini. **Cast:** Henry Mancini and His Orchestra.
  Also see HOSTAGE

ZABRISKIE POINT
Soundtrack (1970) • MGM (S) SE-4468 12-18   70
Soundtrack (1970) • MCA (S) 25032 8-10   86
  Cast: Pink Floyd, Jerry Garcia and the Grateful Dead, Youngbloods, Patti Page, John Fahey,
  Kaleidoscope, Roscoe Holcolmb.

ZACHARIAH
Soundtrack (1970) • ABC (S) ABC5 OC-13 15-25   70
  Composer: Jimmie Haskell, Joe McDonald, others. **Conductor:** Jimmie Haskell. **Cast:** Country
  Joe and the Fish, James Gang, Doug Kershaw, White Lightnin', New York Rock Ensemble.

ZAPPED
Soundtrack (1982) • Regency (S) 38-152 8-10   82
  Composer: Various. **Cast:** David Pomeranz, Plain Jane, Rick Derringer, others.

ZEBRA
Soundtrack (1989) • MCA (S) 42160 8-12   89
  Music from the video production *Tadayuki Naito/Zebra.*
  Composer: Jack DeJohnette. **Cast:** Jack DeJohnette, Lester Bowie.

ZEBRAHEAD
Soundtrack (1992) • Ruffhouse (S) C 53147 5-10   92
  Cast: Cool Moe Dee.

ZELLY AND ME
Soundtrack (1988) • Varese Sarabande (S) 704.420 12-15   88
  Composer: Pino Donaggio, George Duning.

ZENDA
Original Cast (1963) • Blue Pear (M) BP-1007 30-35
  Slated for a New York run, but show closed while playing elsewhere. Had it opened, it
  would have been recorded by Capitol. This is a live recording from a theater's sound
  system.
  Composer: Vernon Duke, Leonard Adelson, Sid Kuller, Martin Charnin. **Composer:** Pembroke
  Davenport. **Cast:** Alfred Drake, Anne Rogers, Chita Rivera, Carmen Mathews, Frederic
  Worlock, Peter Brandon, Marc Wilder, Jock Livingston, Karl Redcoff, Truman Gaige, Susan
  Luckey.

ZIEGFELD FOLLIES OF 1919
Original Cast (1919) • Smithsonian (M) R-009 18-20
  An archival recreation of the original production
  Composer: Irving Berlin, Joseph McCarthy, Harry Tierney, Harry Ruby, Lew Brown, others.
  Cast: Eddie Cantor, Bert Williams, Van and Schenck, John Steel.

ZIEGFELD FOLLIES OF 1946

Soundtrack (1946) • Curtain Calls (M) CC-100-15/16 12-15
Two discs. Gatefold cover.
Composer: Arthur Freed, Harry Warren, others. **Conductor:** Lennie Hayton. **Cast:** Fred Astaire, William Powell, James Melton, Marion Bell, Lena Horne, Judy Garland, Red Skelton, Gene Kelly, Harriet Lee, Kathryn Grayson.

ZIEGFELD GIRL

Soundtrack (1941) • Classic International
Filmusicals (M) CIF-3006.. 10-20
Composer: Various. **Conductor:** Herbert Stothart. **Cast:** Judy Garland, Tony Martin, Charles Winninger.
Also see OF HUMAN BONDAGE

ZIGGY STARDUST – THE MOTION PICTURE

Soundtrack (1983) • RCA Victor (S) CPL2-4862 10-15   83
Two discs.
Cast: David Bowie.

ZIGZAG

Soundtrack (1970) • MGM (S) 1SE-21 10-12   70
Composer: Oliver Nelson, others. **Conductor:** Oliver Nelson, Don Peake. **Cast:** Roy Orbison, Bobby Hatfield.

ZING A LITTLE ZONG: see BING'S HOLLYWOOD

ZINGERS FROM THE HOLLYWOOD SQUARES

TV Soundtrack (1974) • Event (M) EV 6903................................ 5-10   74
Cast: Peter Marshall, Rose Marie, Freddie Prinze, Don Rickles, Paul Lynde, Rich Little, George Gobel, others.

ZITA

Soundtrack (1968) • Philips (SE) PHS-600-287 15-20   69
Composer: François DeRoubaix, others. **Conductor:** François DeRoubaix.

ZIZI

Original Cast (1964) • Philips (S) PHS-600-287 20-25   64
Some tracks are rechanneled stereo.
Cast: Zizi Jeanmair.

ZONE TROOPERS / THE ALCHEMIST

Soundtrack (1985) • Varese Sarabande (S) STV-81262 8-12   85
One side has music from *The Alchemist.*
Composer: Richard Band.

ZOOT SUIT

Soundtrack (1981) • MCA (S) 5267 15-20   81
Soundtrack (1981) • MCA (S) 1522 8-10   80s
Composer: Daniel Valdez. **Conductor:** Shorty Rogers. **Cast:** Daniel Valdez, Edward James Olmos, American Zoot Band.

ZORBA

Original Cast (1968) • Capitol (S) SO-118.. 8-10   68
Maroon cover.
Original Cast (1968) • Capitol (S) ST-12291 5-8   Re
Green cover.
Composer: John Kander, Fred Ebb. **Conductor:** Hal Hastings. **Cast:** Herschel Bernardi, Maria Karnilova, John-Cunningham, Carmen Alvarez, Lorraine Serabian, Jerry Sappir, Ali Hafid, Angelo Saridis, Lee Hooper.

Original Revival Cast (1983) • RCA Victor (S) ABL1-4732 10-12   83
Composer: John Kander, Fred Ebb. **Conductor:** Randolph Mauldin. **Cast:** Anthony Quinn, Lila Kedrova, Frank De Sal, John Mineo, Suzanne Costallos, Robert Westenberg, Panchali Null, Debbie Shapiro, Rob Marshall, Angelina Fiordellisi, Peter Marinos, Peter Kevoian, Richard Warren Pugh, Theresa Rakov, Paul Straney, Taro Meyer.
Also see CANTERBURY TALES

ZORBA THE GREEK
Soundtrack (1964) • 20th Century-Fox (M) TFM-3167 8-12   65
Soundtrack (1964) • 20th Century-Fox (S) TFS-4167 10-12   65
Soundtrack (1964) • 20th Century-Fox (S) T-903 8-10   Re
Soundtrack (1964) • 20th Century-Fox (S) 826245-1 5-8   73
Composer: Mikis Theodorakis. **Conductor:** Mikis Theodorakis.

ZORRO
TV Soundtrack (1956) • Disneyland (EP) DEP-3601 15-25   56
Composer: William Lava, George Bruns and Norman Foster (theme). **Conductor:** William Lava. **Cast:** Guy Williams, Henry Calvin.
Soundtrack (1964) • Disneyland (M) WDA 3601 45-50   58
Includes booklet. Also known as *Four Adventures of Zorro*.
Composer: William Lava. **Conductor:** William Lava. **Cast:** Guy Williams, Henry Calvin, Phil Ross, Jan Arvan, Jimmie Dodd.
Also see WALT DISNEY'S MICKEY MOUSE CLUB

ZULU
Soundtrack (1964) • United Artists (M) UAL-4116 25-35   64
Soundtrack (1964) • United Artists (S) UAS-5116 55-65   64
Composer: John Barry. **Conductor:** John Barry. **Cast:** Richard Burton (narrator).

ZULU AND THE ZAYDA
Original Cast (1965) • Columbia (M) KOL-6480 10-12   65
Original Cast (1965) • Columbia (S) KOS-2880 12-15   65
Composer: Harold Rome, Howard DaSilva, Felix Leon. **Conductor:** Meyer Kupferman. **Cast:** Menasha Skulnik, Ossie Davis, Louis Gossett, Peter DeAnda, Christine Spencer.

ZULU DAWN
Soundtrack (1979) • Cereberus (S) CEM-201 10-12   79
Soundtrack (1979) • Cereberus (S) CST-0201 8-10   81
Composer: Elmer Bernstein. **Conductor:** Elmer Bernstein.

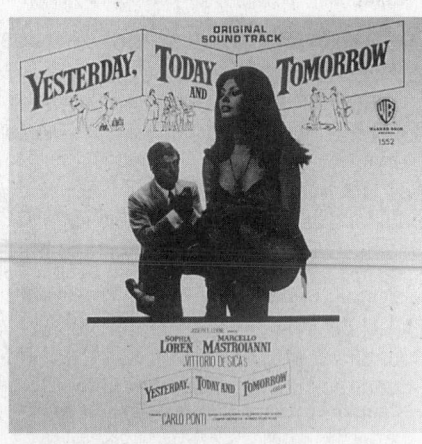

SOUNDTRACKS AND ORIGINAL CASTS – THE MONEY RECORDS

Several of the world's most valuable albums and extended play discs are from the field of soundtrack and cast releases. Especially noteworthy in this regard is the number one entry on the list, *The Caine Mutiny,* one of music collecting's two or three most priceless records of any type.

There are now hundreds of recordings in the guide with a top-end price of $100 or more. Remember, though, these titles are limited to only those recordings contained in this edition.

The prices here represent the high end of the actual dollar range. See the individual listings in the body of the book for complete pricing information.

Rather than duplicate separate monos, stereos, 78s, EPs and other variations, we will identify only the most valuable disc here. An asterisk following the selection number indicates there are others of the same title that would qualify for this list. Consult the listings for specific identification of each record.

When two or more records have the same price, the sequence here is alphabetical by title.

1. CAINE MUTINY• RCA Victor (M) LOC-1013 ....$10,000
2. LOVING YOU / G.I. BLUES (Picture Disc) • RCA Victor (M) LPM-1515 6,000
3. JAMBOREE! • Warner Bros. (M) No Number Used 3,000
4. ELVIS: ALOHA FROM HAWAII VIA SATELLITE • RCA (Q) VPSX-6089* 2,500
5. HARD DAY'S NIGHT • United Artists (M) UAL-3366* 2,000
6. SPEEDWAY • RCA Victor (M) LPM-3989 1,500
7. JURASSIC PARK • MCA/BMG (S) No Number Shown 1,200
8. HELP! • United Artists (M) No Number Used 1,000
9. GO JOHNNY GO! • No Label Shown (M) No Number Used* 750
10. ROCK, ROCK, ROCK · No Label Name Used (M) No Number Used...................750
11. WHO'S AFRAID OF THE BIG BAD WOLF • RCA Victor 224/5/6* 750
12. LOUISIANA HAYRIDE • Louisiana Hayride (M) NR-8454* 700
13. YELLOW SUBMARINE • Apple Films Presents (M) KAL-1004 700
14. ROUSTABOUT • RCA Victor (S) LSP-2999 600
15. NO FOR AN ANSWER • Theme (M) TALP-103 525
16. BILL AND COO • Mercury Miniature Playhouse (M) MMP-20...........................500
17. CHILD IS BORN • MCA-TV (M) C-55...500
18. RIO BRAVO • Warner Bros. (M) JB-2262*...500
19. BODY IN THE SEINE • Private Label-Alden-Shaw (M) VB-001...........................400
20. MUSIC IN THE AIR • RCA Victor (M) 39001* 400
21. COMANCHE • Coral (M) CRL-57046 350
22. GIRL IN THE BIKINI • Poplar (M) 33-1002 350
23. KING CREOLE • RCA Victor (M) LPM-1884* 350
24. LONG JOHN SILVER • RCA Victor (M) LPM-3279* 350
25. LION • London (M) M-76001...325
26. PILLOW TALK • Universal International (M) DCLA 1316 325
27. SANDHOG • Vanguard (M) VRS-9001 325
28. BATTLE FOR STALINGRAD / FALL OF BERLIN • Classic Editions (S) 3009 300
29. FRANCIS OF ASSISI • 20th Century-Fox (S) SFX-3053*...................................300
30. BLUES • RCA Victor (S) LSP-2256*...300
31. NINE HOURS TO RAMA • London (M) M-76002...300
32. ROOTS OF HEAVEN • 20th Century-Fox (M) FOX-3005....................................300
33. GREATEST STORY EVER TOLD • United Artists (M) UAX-5120.......................275
34. ISLAND IN THE SKY • Decca (M) DL-7029..275
35. TWISTED NERVE • Polydor (S) 583-728..275

713

191. GOYA • Decca (M) DL-8236 110
192. JOHN PAUL JONES • Warner Bros. (S) WS-1293...................110
193. MUSCLE BEACH PARTY • Buena Vista (S) STER-3314...........110
194. NUN'S STORY • Warner Bros. (S) WS-1306 110
195. STAKEOUT • RCA Victor (EP) EPA-4199................................110
196. THIS EARTH IS MINE • Decca (S) DL-78915 110
197. BABES IN TOYLAND • Buena Vista (M) BT-1/BT-2................100
198. BABY FACE NELSON • Jubilee (M) 2021................................100
199. BATMAN • 20th Century-Fox (S) TFS-4180............................100
200. BEACH PARTY • Buena Vista (S) ST-3316.............................100
201. BLAZING SADDLES • Warner Bros. (S) BS-2781....................100
202. BLUE HAWAII • RCA Victor (S) LSP-2426*.............................100
203. BOCCACCIO '70 • RCA Victor (S) FSO-5................................100
204. BODY HEAT • Label X (S) LXSE 1-002..................................100
205. BRAINCHILD • Demo (M) RFP-104.......................................100
206. CAPTAIN HORATIO HORNBLOWER • Delyse (SE) D-6057........100
207. CASINO ROYALE • Colgems (S) COSO 5005..........................100
208. COFFY • Polydor (S) PD-5048..100
209. CRADLE WILL ROCK • American Legacy (M) T-1001................100
210. DANGER • MGM (M) E-111..100
211. DEEP THROAT PART II • Bryan (S) BRS-101.........................100
212. DRACULA • Mark 56 (M) 760..100
213. EASY COME, EASY GO • RCA Victor (EP) EPA-4387 100
214. EILEEN • Camden (M) CAL-210..100
215. ENFORCER • Mark 56 (M) 707...100
216. FOUR SAINTS IN THREE ACTS • RCA Victor (M) LCT-1139 100
217. FOXY • S.P.M. (M) CO-4636 100
218. FROM HERE TO ETERNITY • Coral (M) CRL-56105................100
219. GENTLEMEN PREFER BLONDES • MGM (M) E-208 100
220. GIRL CRAZY • Decca (EP) ED-2022.....................................100
221. GIRLS! GIRLS! GIRLS! • RCA Victor (S) LSP-2621.................100
222. GO FLY A KITE • General Electric (S) No Number Used............100
223. GRANDMA MOSES SUITE • Columbia (M) ML-2185 100
224. GREENWICH VILLAGE, U.S.A. • 20th Century-Fox (S) TCF-105-2S.........100
225. GULLIVER'S TRAVELS • Decca (M) 100.................................100
226. HUCKLEBERRY HOUND (HERE COMES) • Colpix (M) CP-207 100
227. HUSTLER • Kapp (S) KS-3264 100
228. IT STARTED IN NAPLES • Dot (S) DLP-25324 100
229. JAILHOUSE ROCK • RCA Victor (EP) EPA-4114.....................100
230. JUST FOR YOU • Decca (M) DL-5417 100
231. KID GALAHAD • RCA Victor (EP) EPA-4371 100
232. LOLA MONTEZ • Columbia (M) CX-7514 100
233. MARILYN • 20th Century-Fox (SE) SXG-5000........................100
234. MEXICAN HAYRIDE • Decca (M) DL-5232 100
235. MINX • Amsterdam (S) 12007..100
236. MISFITS • United Artists (S) UAS-5087 100
237. MIXED DOUBLES / BELOW THE BELT • Upstairs (S) UD-37W56 100
238. MOUSE ON THE MAYFLOWER • No Label Shown (M) GRC-11398 100
239. MUNSTERS • Decca (S) DL-74588 100
240. MURDERER'S ROW • Colgems (S) COSO-5003......................100
241. MYRA BRECKINRIDGE • 20th Century-Fox (S) S-4210 100

COMPOSER/CONDUCTOR/CAST INDEX

AABERG, PHILIP
Shape of the Land
AANAMI CHOIR
Prison
AARONSON, IRVING
Pennies from Heaven
ABADES, MARTINEZ
La Violetera
ABADY, TEMPLE
George K. Arthur's Prize
Package
ABBEY ROAD SINGERS
American Dreamer
ABBOTT, BUD
In the Navy
ABBOTT, DIANNE
New York, New York
ABEL, WILL B.
Coco
ABELEW, ALAN
Together Again
ABERLIN, BETTY
I'm Getting My Act Together
and Taking It on the Road
Just for Openers
ABOVE THE LAW
Pump Up the Volume
ABRAHAM, F. MURRAY
Survival of St. Joan
ABRAVANAL, MAURICE
Lady In the Dark
One Touch of Venus
Street Scene
AC/DC
Who Made Who
ACADEMY OF ST. MARTIN
Out of Africa
ACE TRUCKING COMPANY
Harrad Experiment
ACE, JOHNNY
Christine
ACHUCRRO, JOAQUIN
Citizen Kane: The Classic Film
Scores of Bernard Herrmann
ACKERMAN, JACK
Faces
ACKERMAN, LONI
George M!
So Long 174th Street
Starting Here, Starting Now
ACKERMAN, WILLIAM
Shape of the Land
ACKERMAN, ZOE
No No Nanette
ACKLAND, JOSS
Apple
Evita
Little Night Music
Little Prince
ACTMAN, IRVING
Guys and Dolls
ADAIR, JOHN
Cradle Will Rock
ADAIR, TOM
California
ADAIR, YVONNE
Gentlemen Prefer Blondes
ADAM, NOELLE
No Strings
ADAMS, BRYAN
Night In Heaven
ADAMS, CATLIN
Jazz Singer
ADAMS, CLIFF
Irma La Douce
ADAMS, DON
Get Smart
ADAMS, DOUGLAS
Monty Python and the Holy
Grail
ADAMS, EDITH
Band Wagon
Cinderella
Girl Crazy
Les Poupees De Paris

Li'l Abner
Something Unique
Wonderful Town
ADAMS, EMILY
Joan
ADAMS, INDIA
Band Wagon
Joan Crawford
Torch Song
ADAMS, JOE
Jamaica
ADAMS, JONATHAN
Metropolis
Tomfoolery
ADAMS, KAYE
Killers Three
ADAMS, LEE
All American
Applause
Bring Back Birdie
Bye Bye Birdie
Golden Boy
I and Albert
It's a Bird, It's a Plane, It's
Superman
Night They Raided Minsky's
Shoestring Revue '57
ADAMS, MASON
Thousand Miles of Mountains
ADAMS, NEILE
This Could Be the Night
ADAMS, SKIP
Night of the Comet
ADAMS, TRUDE
She Loves Me
ADAMSON, HAROLD
Affair to Remember
Around the World In 80 Days
Everything I Have Is Yours
Four Jills In a Jeep
Gentlemen Prefer Blondes
Higher and Higher
Scent of Mystery
Seven Hills of Rome
Sugar Babies
ADANO, BOBBY
Alakazam the Great
ADDERLEY, CANNONBALL
Fiddler on the Roof
ADDERLEY, NAT
Man Called Adam
ADDINSELL, RICHARD
It's a Wonderful Life
Joyce Grenfell Requests the
Pleasure
Loss of Innocence
Monologues and Songs
Music from Motion Pictures
Suicide Squadron
War Lover
ADDISON, ADELE
Porgy and Bess
ADDISON, DELORES
Portraits In Bronze
ADDISON, JOHN
Amorous Adventures of Moll
Flanders
Bridge Too Far
Charge of the Light Brigade
Golden Motion Picture Themes
and Original Soundtracks
Great Motion Picture Themes
Hamlet
Honey Pot
Joseph Andrews
Seven Percent Solution
Sleuth
Smashing Time
Swashbuckler
Tom Jones
Torn Curtain
ADDY, WESLEY
Evening with William
Shakespeare
ADELSON, LEONARD
Zenda

ADIARTE, PATRICK
Flower Drum Song
ADIR, MICHA
From Israel with Love
ADLAM, BETH
Wildcat
ADLER, BRUCE
Golden Land
ADLER, F. CHARLES
Threepenny Opera
ADLER, JO
Aladd
ADLER, RICHARD
Damn Yankees
Gift of the Magi
Kwamina
Little Women
Olympus 7-0000
Pajama Game
ADRENALIN
Iron Eagle
ADRIAN, LOUIS
Annie Get Your Gun
Kismet
Peter Pan
ADRIAN, MAX
Boy Friend
Candide
ADU, SADE
Absolute Beginners
AEROSMITH
Air America
Less Than Zero
Sgt. Pepper's Lonely Hearts
Club Band
AGENT ORANGE
River's Edge
Undercover
AGNEW, SPIRO T.
Age of Television
AGRESS, TED
Shenandoah
AGRESTI, BEN
Ka-Boom!
AGUIRRE, FRED
Sound of Music
A-HA
Living Daylights
AHMED, DR. IBRAHIM
Story of Tutankhamen
AHN, PHILIP
Kung-Fu
AIDMAN, CHARLES
Spoon River Anthology
AIELLO, JOSIE
Starlight Express
AIKEN, DAVID
Saint of Bleecker Street
AINSLEY, PAUL
Jesus Christ Superstar
AINSLIE, ROBERT
Anne of Green Gables
AINSLIE, SCOTT
Cotton Patch Gospel
AINSWORTH, ALYN
Bye Bye Birdie
Camelot
Emily
Gentlemen Prefer Blondes
Hello Dolly!
Sweet Charity
AIR SUPPLY
Ghostbusters
AIRPLAY
St. Elmo's Fire
AITKEN, MARIA
Little Night Music
AKERS, KAREN
Nine
AKOS, CATHERINE
Saint of Bleecker Street
AKUTAGAWA, YASUSHI
Village of Eight Gravestones
ALABAMA
Follow That Bird

River Rat
ALAIMO, STEVE
Where the Action Is
ALAN
This Is Broadway's Best
ALARM
Bachelor Party
Music Man
ALBANESE, LICIA
Follies
Serenade
ALBANI, COUNTESS
Show Boat
ALBERGHETTI, ANNA
MARIA
Aladdin
All-Star Salute, the Very Best of
Gershwin
Carnival
Four Television Musicals
Medium
ALBERGHETTI, CARLA
My Cousin Josefa
ALBERT, DONNIE
Porgy and Bess
ALBERT, EDDIE
Eddie Albert Album
Heartbreak Kid
Miss Liberty
Mouse on the Mayflower
Nina, the Pinta, and the Santa
Maria
ALBERT, MARGOT
Promenade
Seventeen
ALBERTSON, FRANK
ALBERTSON, JACK
Subject Was Roses
Top Banana
Willy Wonka and the Chocolate
Factory
ALBINONI, T.
Film Music from France
ALBRIGHT, JESSICA
Bye Bye Birdie
ALCIVAR, BOB
Paradise Alley
ALDA, ALAN
Apple Tree
ALDA, LAURIE
Fire and Ice
ALDA, ROBERT
Guys and Dolls
What Makes Sammy Run?
ALDEBERT, LOUIS
Live for Life
ALDEN, BONNIE
Roaring '20s
ALDREDGE, THOMAS
Into the Woods
Premise
Rex
ALDRIDGE, MICHAEL
Salad Days
ALESSANDRINI, GERALD
Forbidden Broadway
ALESSI
Ghostbusters
ALEXANDER, BARBARA
Anya
ALEXANDER, BEN
Dragnet
ALEXANDER, BROOKS
Believers
ALEXANDER, C.K.
Threepenny Opera
ALEXANDER, CHRIS
On the Town
Wonderful Town
ALEXANDER, JANE
Great White Hope
ALEXANDER, JASON
Jerome Robbins' Broadway
Sondheim

ALEXANDER, JEFF
Because You're Mine
Dirty Dingus Magee
Emperor Waltz
Murder Inc.
Music to Be Murdered By
Roberta
Tone Poems of Color, Frank
Sinatra Conducts
Twilight Zone
ALEXANDER, JOAN
Superman
ALEXANDER, JOHN
New Orleans
ALEXANDER, RICHARD
Flash Gordon
ALEXANDER, VAN
Baby Face Nelson
Best Things In Life Are Free
Desert Song
Kismet
Motion Picture Soundstage
New Moon
Student Prince
**ALEXANDER'S RAGTIME
BAND**
Echoes of Hollywood
ALEXANDRIA, HELEN
Cleopatra
ALFIE
Last Dragon
ALFORD, KENNETH
Bridge on the River Kwai
Lawrence of Arabia
ALFORD, LAMAR
Godspell
ALFRED, DOROTHEA
All In the York Family
ALFRED, WILLIAM
Cry for Us All
ALFVEN, HUGO
George K. Arthur's Prize
Package
ALIBERTI, ARMANDO
Devil and Daniel Webster
ALK, HOWARD
From the Second City
ALL THAT JAZZ
Hiding Out
ALL-STARS
Cooley High
TV Jazz Themes
ALLAM, ROGER
Les Miserables
ALLAN, DAVIE, & ARROWS
Albert Peckingpaw's Revenge
Devil's Angels
Glory Stompers
Golden Breed
Hellcats
Mondo Hollywood
Wild Angels
Wild In the Streets
ALLEGRO SINGERS
My Fair Lady
ALLEN, BERNIE
Producers
ALLEN, BILLY
Ski on the Wild Side
ALLEN, CHAD
Beowulf
ALLEN, CHESNEY
Flanagan and Allen Story
ALLEN, CHET
Amahl and the Night Visitors
ALLEN, CHRIS
Huckleberry Hound
ALLEN, CLIFFORD
Hallelujah, Baby!
ALLEN, DAVID BLISS
Up with People!
ALLEN, DAVID
Ben Bagley's Cole Porter
Revisited
Decline and Fall of the Entire
World As Seen Through the
Eyes of Cole Porter
Gingerbread Boy
ALLEN, DAYTON
Deputy Dawg

Why Not?
ALLEN, DEBORAH
Fame
Raisin
River Rat
Sweet Charity
ALLEN, DENNIS
How to Steal an Election (A
Dirty Politics Musical)
ALLEN, DION
Under Milk Wood
ALLEN, DONNA
Fatal Beauty
ALLEN, ELIZABETH
Do I Hear a Waltz?
Gay Life
Official Grammy Awards
Archive Collection
ALLEN, FRED
Age of Television
Magnificent Rogue
ALLEN, GRACIE
Damsel In Distress
ALLEN, HERBERT
Up with People!
ALLEN, JACKIE
Music Man
ALLEN, JEANNE
Leave It to Jane
ALLEN, JONELLE
George M!
Hair
Two Gentlemen of Verona
ALLEN, KAREN
Raiders of the Lost Ark
ALLEN, LINDA
Stormy Monday
ALLEN, MARC
Pawnbroker
ALLEN, MICHAEL
Jesus Christ Superstar
New Faces of 1968
ALLEN, NORMAN
Half a Sixpence
ALLEN, PENNY
Oh What a Lovely War
ALLEN, PETER
All That Jazz
Legs Diamond
ALLEN, RAE
Damn Yankees
ALLEN, REX
Say One for Me
ALLEN, REX, JR.
Rustler's Rhapsody
ALLEN, ROBERT
Julie and Carol at Carnegie Hall
Three Billion Millionaires
ALLEN, STEVE
Judy Garland
Man Called Dagger
Picnic
Sophie
Steve Allen TV Show
Steve Allen's Funny Fone Calls
Why Not?
ALLEN, TONY
Triple Cross
ALLEN, VERA
Medea
ALLEN, WOODY
Play It Again, Sam
ALLER, MICHELLE
Roller Boogie
ALLERS, FRANZ
Annie Get Your Gun
Around the World In 80 Days
Brigadoon
Camelot
Carousel
Hansel and Gretel
King and I
Kismet
Merry Widow
My Fair Lady
Oklahoma
Paint Your Wagon
Plain and Fancy
Show Boat
Student Prince

ALLEY CATS
Urgh - A Music War
ALLINSON, MICHAEL
All About Life
ALLISON, BERNIE
Runaways
ALLISON, FRAN
Age of Television
Happy Mother Goose (As Told
By Kukla, Fran and Ollie)
Merry Christmas from Kukla,
Fran and Ollie
Pinocchio
Songs By Kukla, Fran and Ollie
ALLISON, LUTHER
Cooley High
ALLISON, MOSE
Kids Are Alright
ALLMAN, GREGG
Black Rain
ALLMON, CLINT
Best Little Whorehouse In
Texas
ALLOWAY, JACQUELINE
By Jupiter
George M!
ALLYSON, JUNE
Eddy Duchin Story
Girl Crazy
Girls...And More Girls
Good News
Judy Garland
Rodgers and Hart In Hollywood
Soundtracks, Voices and
Themes from Great Movies
That's Entertainment!
Thousands Cheer
Till the Clouds Roll By
Words and Music
ALMEIDA, LAURINDO
Agony and the Ecstasy
Gone with the Wave
Maracaibo
Mary C. Brown and the
Hollywood Sign
Naked Sea
ALMOG, DR. ZVI
It's Time to Pray, America!
ALMAGOR, SAM
Kazablan
ALPERT, ANITA
Kismet
ALPERT, HERB
Brass Are Comin'
Casino Royale
ALSEAW, SUZANNE
81 Proof
ALSTON, BARBARA
Ain't Supposed to Die a Natural
Death
ALTBACH, RON
Almost Summer
ALTER, LOUIS
Ship Ahoy
ALTERED IMAGES
Party Party
ALTERI, ANNE
Boy Named Charlie Brown
ALTMAN, BARBARA
King and I
ALTMAN, JOHN
Schoner Gigolo - Armer Gigolo
(Just a Gigolo)
ALTMAN, KAREN
Elephant Steps
ALTMAN, RUTH
Boy Friend
ALTON, ED
My Demon Lover
ALVARADO, TRINI
Runaways
Times Square
Yours, Anne
ALVAREZ, CARMEN
Decline and Fall of the Entire
World As Seen Through the
Eyes of Cole Porter
Irene
Li'l Abner
Painted Smiles of Cole Porter

Zorba
ALVIN, DAVE
Border Radio
ALWYN, KENNETH
Camelot
Charlie Girl
Most Happy Fella
Porgy and Bess
ALWYN, WILLIAM
Golden Age of British Film
Music
Shake Hands with the Devil
AMBROSIA
All This and World War II
Arthur (the Album)
Coast to Coast
Inside Moves
AMBROSIAN JUNIOR CHOIR
Empire of the Sun
AMBROSIAN SINGERS
Chariots of Fire
Secret of N.I.M.H.
South Pacific
AMECHE, DON
Alexander's Ragtime Band
Co-Star
Four Television Musicals
Frances Langford Presents
Goldilocks
Henry, Sweet Henry
Silk Stockings
That Night In Rio
AMERICA
Lonely Guy
AMERICAN BREED
Jud
No Way to Treat a Lady
AMERICAN GIRLS
Out of Bounds
AMERICAN MILITARY BAND
Stars and Stripes Forever
**AMERICAN OPERA SOCIETY
ORCHESTRA**
Merry Widow
AMERICAN ZOOT BAND
Zoot Suit
AMES, BENTON
Parade of Hits
AMES, ED
Androcles and the Lion
Cricket on the Hearth
Sound of Broadway
AMES, FLORENZ
Arms and the Girl
Look Ma I'm Dancin'!
Of Thee I Sing
AMES, MORGAN
Adventurers
John and Mary
AMES, NANCY
Tenderloin
Trini Lopez Show
AMFITHEATROF, DANIELE
Major Dundee
Omar Khayyam
Salome
Spanish Affair
Spectacular World of Classic
Film Scores
Uncle Remus
AMICK, ALIN
King and I
AMIGOS
Fun In Acapulco
Girls! Girls! Girls!
AMIHUD, DANI
From Israel with Love
AMOA
Soul to Soul
AMOS, KEITH
Amen Corner
AMRAM, DAVID
After the Fall
Amarcord Nino Rota
Arrangement
J.B.
Young Savages
AMSTERDAM, MOREY
Guys and Dolls

AMUNDSEN, MONTE
Juno
ANAK AGUNG GDE
MANDERA
Dancers of Bali
ANANIA, JOHN
Fly Blackbird
ANARCHY 6
Lovedolls Superstar
ANDAY, ROSETTE
Threepenny Opera
ANDERS, BERNIE
Gigi
ANDERS, KATIE
One Way Ticket to Broadway
ANDERS, SYLVIA
Fiddler on the Roof
ANDERSEN, BETH
Scarface
ANDERSON, BENNY
Chess
ANDERSON, CARL
Jesus Christ Superstar
ANDERSON, CHRISTINE
Nunsense
ANDERSON, DELBERT
Brigadoon
New Girl In Town
Tree Grows In Brooklyn
Wonderful Town
ANDERSON, EDDIE
"ROCHESTER"
Cabin In the Sky
ANDERSON, ENOCH
Winds of Change
ANDERSON, ERNESTINE
Lost Man
ANDERSON, HERB OSCAR
Haunted
ANDERSON, HERBERT
Dennis the Menace
ANDERSON, JEFF
Brother from Another Planet
ANDERSON, JOHN
Honkytonk Man
Rustler's Rhapsody
ANDERSON, JONATHAN
South Pacific
ANDERSON, JON
Legend
Metropolis
St. Elmo's Fire
ANDERSON, JUDITH
John Brown's Body
Medea
ANDERSON, LAURIE
Home of the Brave
ANDERSON, LEROY
Goldilocks
ANDERSON, MARIAN
Lady from Philadelphia
Leonard Bernstein and the New
York Philharmonic on
Christmas Day
ANDERSON, MARY
Selma
ANDERSON, MAXWELL
High Tor
Knickerbocker Holiday
Kurt Weill In Hollywood
Lost In the Stars
ANDERSON, PINK
Blues
ANDERSON, SUSAN
Anne of Green Gables
ANDERSON, THOMAS
Don't Play Us Cheap
ANDES, KEITH
Girl Most Likely
Wildcat
ANDI AND THE SEX GANG
Creepers
ANDONIAN, LUCY
Great Waltz
Kismet
ANDRE, ANNETTE
Funny Thing Happened on the
Way to the Forum

ANDREA AND HOT MINK
Revenge of the Nerds
ANDREAS, CHRISTINE
Beauty and the Beast
Clues to a Life
My Fair Lady
Oklahoma
On Your Toes
ANDRES, BARBARA
Boy Friend
Doonesbury
Rex
ANDREWS, ANTHONY
Brideshead Revisited
ANDREWS, CHRIS
Tom Brown's School Days
ANDREWS, CHRISTINE
Lola
ANDREWS, DANA
God Said
ANDREWS, GARTH
On Moonlight Bay
ANDREWS, GEORGE LEE
Sondheim: A Musical Tribute
Starting Here, Starting Now
ANDREWS, HARRY
Ruling Class
ANDREWS, JACK
Gigi
ANDREWS, JOYCE
Blue Monday
ANDREWS, JULIE
Academy Awards Presentation
Americanization of Emily
Boy Friend
Broadway Magic
Broadway Musicals
Camelot
Cinderella
Darling Lili
From Broadway to Hollywood
High Tor
Julie and Carol at Carnegie Hall
Julie and Carol at Lincoln
Center
Magic of Musical Comedy
Mary Poppins
Merriest Songs
My Fair Lady
Parade of Show Stoppers
Rose Marie
Sound of Music
Star
Thoroughly Modern Millie
Victor / Victoria
ANDREWS, MAXENE
Over Here!
ANDREWS, NANCY
Christine
Cradle Will Rock
Juno
Little Me
Make Mine Manhattan
Plain and Fancy
Rodgers and Hart Revisited
Too Many Girls
ANDREWS, PATTY
Over Here!
ANDREWS, RAYMOND
Camelot
ANDREWS SISTERS
Bing's Hollywood
Club 15
Dick Tracy In BB
Hollywood Canteen
In the Navy
Just for You
Mr. Music
Red Sky at Morning
South American Way
ANDRIANO, MIKLOS
Film Spectacular
ANDRIANO, NICHOLAS
Cleopatra
Mutiny on the Bounty
ANDROSSI, MARIA
Consul
ANGEL, ADRIENNE
Promises, Promises
ANGELA, JUNE
Electric Company TV Show

King and I
ANGELO, JUDY HART
Preppies
ANGELOU, MAYA
For Love of Ivy
King, a Musical Testimony
ANGELS FROM ANGEL CITY
Nightmare on Elm Street 4 -
The Dream Master
ANGELS
Girl Groups: The Story of a
Sound
More American Graffiti
Slumber Party '57
Wanderers
ANGER, DAROL
Country
ANGERS, AVRIL
Little Me
ANIMALS
Dangerous Christmas of Red
Riding Hood
Get Yourself a College Girl
1969
Stardust
ANIMOTION
Girls Just Want to Have Fun
My Stepmother Is an Alien
ANISTON, JOHN
Little Mary Sunshine
ANITA
Disorderlies
ANKA, PAUL
Longest Day
NARM's Golden Decade
Together
ANKER, CHARLOTTE
Onward Victoria
ANKER, PERRYNE
Song of Norway
ANN-MARGRET
Among Friends - Waa-Mu Show
of 1960
Be My Guest
Bye Bye Birdie
David Merrick Presents Hits
from His Broadway Hits
NARM's Golden Decade
Pleasure Seekers
Sound of Broadway
State Fair
Swinger
Tommy
Va Va Voom! Screen Sirens
Sing!
ANNON, JACK
13 Daughters
ANSELL, J.
Primrose
ANSELL, MARTIN
Better Off Dead
ANSON, BARBARA
How to Steal an Election (A
Dirty Politics Musical)
ANT, ADAM
Metropolis
Out of Bounds
ANTHEIL, GEORGE
Pride and the Passion
ANTHONY, JUDITH
Sweet Bye and Bye
ANTHONY, MARK
Circus of Horrors
ANTHONY, MICHAEL
Gertrude Stein's First Reader
ANTHONY, RAY
Charade
Daddy Long Legs
Five Pennies
This Could Be the Night
TV's Top Themes
ANTHONY, RICHARD
That Man In Istanbul
ANTHONY AND THE CAMP
Modern Girls
ANTHRAX
Return of the Living Dead, Part
II
ANTONINI, ALFREDO
Cinderella

ANTONIO, JAMES
Elephant Calf
APAKA, AL
Adventures In Paradise
APARTMENTS
Some Kind of Wonderful
APLON, BORIS
Anya
King of the Whole Damn World
APOLINAR, DANNY
Your Own Thing
APOLLO SMILE
Days of Thunder
Lost Angels
APPLEBAUM, STAN
Hollywood's Bad But Beautiful
Girls
APPLEWAITE, STANLEY
Pal Joey
APRIL WINE
Fright Night
APTER, JEFFREY
Joan
ARAD, CHAYA
From Israel with Love
ARCADIA
Playing for Keeps
ARCHER, JULIAN
Godspell
ARCHEY, JIMMY
Jazz Dance
ARCHIBALD, WILLIAM
Crystal Heart
ARCOS, NATALIA GENTIL
My Fair Lady
ARD, KENNETH
Cats
ARDAO, DAVID
Joseph and the Amazing
Technicolor Dreamcoat
ARDEN, EVE
Kurt Weill In Hollywood
Premiere
ARGENTO, DARIO
Suspira
ARGENTO, DOMINICK
Postcard from Morocco
ARGOL, SEBASTIAN
Yol
ARIAS, DAVID
Ulysses - The Greek Suite
ARKIN, ALAN
From the Second City
Luv
ARKIN, JUKI
Milk and Honey
ARLEN, HAROLD
Bloomer Girl
Cabin In the Sky
Country Girl
Free and Easy
Gay Purr-ee
Harold Arlen Revisited
Harold Sings Arlen
House of Flowers
I Could Go on Singing
Jamaica
Judy at the Palace
Pinocchio
St. Louis Woman
Saratoga
Sky's the Limit
Star Is Born
Summer Stock
Swinger
Wizard of Oz
ARLEN, JERRY
House of Flowers
Saratoga
ARLEN, ROXANNE
Gypsy
ARLEN, STEVE
Cry for Us All
Do Re Mi
ARMATRADING, JOAN
Wild Geese
ARMBRUSTER, RICHARD
Goldilocks
ARMBRUSTER, ROBERT
Chocolate Soldier

721

How the West Was Won
  Mutiny on the Bounty
  Naughty Marietta
  Northwest Outpost
  Pure Gold Movies
  Sandpiper
  Sol Madrid
  Three Bites of the Apple
  Unsinkable Molly Brown
ARMED FORCES SYMPHONY
  Victory at Sea
ARMEN, KAY
  Hit the Deck
  Lady and the Tramp
ARMENGOL, MARIO RUIZ
  Man of La Mancha
  My Fair Lady
ARMOND, GENE
  Night the Lights Went Out In
    Georgia
ARMSTEAD, JOSHIE JO
  Don't Play Us Cheap
ARMSTRONG, AL
  Nicholas Nickleby
ARMSTRONG, HERK
  Sing Out Sweet Land
ARMSTRONG, JACK
  Radio's Greatest Broadcasts
ARMSTRONG, LOUIS
  Betty Boop
  Cabin In the Sky
  Day of the Locust
  Driving Miss Daisy
  50 Years of Film
  Five Pennies
  Formula for Love
  Glenn Miller Story
  Good Morning, Vietnam
  Hello Dolly!
  High Society
  James Bond - Tenth
    Anniversary
  James Bond 13 Original
    Themes
  Man Called Adam
  Merriest Songs
  More Great Motion Picture
    Themes
  New Orleans
  On Her Majesty's Secret
    Service
  Original Motion Picture Hit
    Themes
  Paris Blues
  Porgy and Bess
  Real Ambassadors
  Satchmo the Great
  Song Is Born
  Very Best of Motion Picture
    Musicals
  When the Boys Meet the Girls
ARMUS, SIDNEY
  Wish You Were Here
ARNAU, B.J.
  Live and Let Die
ARNAU, BRENDA
  Finian's Rainbow
ARNAUD, LEON
  Kurt Weill In Hollywood
  New Moon
  Rose Marie
ARNAZ, DESI
  I Love Lucy
  Rodgers and Hart In Hollywood
  25 Years of Recorded Sound
ARNAZ, DESI, JR.
  Magic Moments from the
    Tonight Show
ARNAZ, LUCIE
  Jazz Singer
  They're Playing Our Song
ARNO, SIG
  Merry Widow
  Song of Norway
ARNOLD, EDDY
  Feudin' Rhythm / Hoedown
  NARM's Golden Decade
ARNOLD, JEAN
  Demi Dozen
  Coco
  Flower Drum Song
  Take Five

ARNOLD, MALCOLM HENRY
  Battle of Britain
  Bridge on the River Kwai
  David Copperfield
  Heroes of Telemark
  Inn of the Sixth Happiness
  Key
  Lion
  Nine Hours to Rama
  Roots of Heaven
  Trapeze
  Tunes of Glory
ARNOLD, P. P.
  Electric Dreams
ARNOLD, SYDNEY
  Sail Away
ARNOLD WRECKING CO.
  Keep Up the Grass
ARONS, ELLYN
  Jerry's Girls
ARONSON, HENRY
  Three Guys Naked from the
    Waist Down
ARPS, WOLFGANG
  Hello Dolly!
**ARQUETTE, CLIFF
  (CHARLEY WEAVER)**
  Charley Weaver Letters from
    Mama
  Hollywood Squares
ARRINGTON, DONALD
  Downriver
ARROW
  Mighty Quinn
ARROWS
  Wild Racers
ARSENEL
  Beach Girls
ART OF NOISE
  Disorderlies
  Dragnet
  Pumping Iron 2 - The Women
ARTEMYEV, EDUARD
  Homer and Eddie
ARTHUR, BEATRICE
  Broadway Magic
  Fiddler on the Roof
  Mame
  Shoestring Revue '57
  Shoestring Revues
  Threepenny Opera
ARTHUR, DONALD
  Desert Song
ARTHUR, JEAN
  Peter Pan
ARTHUR, MAUREEN
  How to Succeed In Business
    Without Really Trying
  Man Called Dagger
ARTHUR, MAURICE
  Oh What a Lovely War
ARTS AND CRAFTS
  House Party
ARVAN, JAN
  Zorro
ASCHE, OSCAR
  Chu Chin Chow
ASCHER, KENNY
  Muppet Movie
ASCIOLLA, DINO
  Marco Polo
ASHCROFT, DAME PEGGY
  Nun's Story
ASHFORD AND SIMPSON
  Golden Child
ASHLEY, BARBARA
  Body In the Seine
  Out of This World
  Pal Joey
ASHLEY, EVE
  Can-Can
ASHLEY, ROBERT
  Themes from Italian Films
ASHMAN, HOWARD
  Little Shop of Horrors
ASHTON, DAVID
  Happy As a Sandbag

**ASHTON, EDWARD
  ANTHONY**
  Wonderwall
**ASHTON, GARDNER AND
  DYKE**
  Last Rebel
ASHTON, JULIAN
  Are You Lonesome Tonight
ASIA
  Over the Top
  Whoop-Up!
ASKEY, ARTHUR
  Beggar's Holiday
ASKEY, DARRELL J.
  Donnybrook!
ASKEY, GIL
  Evening with Diana Ross
ASKREN, JIM
  Best of Broadway 1973
ASLAN, GREGOIRE
  Three Worlds of Gulliver
ASLEEP AT THE WHEEL
  Roadie
ASPARAGUS, FRED
  Three Amigos
ASSALY, EDMUND
  My Fur Lady
ASSOCIATION
  Goodbye Columbus
  Magnavox Presents Frank
    Sinatra
ASTAIRE, ADELE
  Band Wagon
  Funny Face
  Lady Be Good
ASTAIRE, FRED
  Another Evening with Fred
    Astaire
  Astaire Time
  Band Wagon
  Barkleys OF Broadway
  Belle of New York
  Best of Fred Astaire from MGM
    Classic Films
  Bing's Hollywood
  Blue Skies
  Broadway Melody of 1940
  Cole Porter In Hollywood
    (1929-1956)
  Cut! Out-Takes from
    Hollywood's Greatest
    Musicals
  Damsel In Distress
  Easter Parade
  Evening with Fred Astaire
  Finian's Rainbow
  Flying Down to Rio
  Fred Astaire and Ginger Rogers
  Fred Astaire Sings and Swings
    Irving Berlin
  Funny Face
  Gay Divorcee
  Ginger Rogers
  Golden Age of Movie Musicals
  Holiday Inn
  Irving Berlin: 100th
    Anniversary Collection
  Joan Crawford
  Lady Be Good
  Royal Wedding
  S'wonderful, S'marvelous,
    S'Gershwin
  Santa Claus Is Comin' to Town
  Silk Stockings
  Silver Screen Symphony
  Sky's the Limit
  Soundtracks, Voices and
    Themes from Great Movies
  Starring Fred Astaire
  That's Dancing!
  That's Entertainment!
  That's Entertainment, Part 2
  Three Evenings with Fred
    Astaire
  Three Little Words
  25 Years of Recorded Sound
  Yolanda and the Thief / You'll
    Never Get Rich
  Ziegfeld Follies of 1946
ASTAR, BEN
  On Your Toes

ASTIN, JOHN
  Threepenny Opera
ASTLEY, EDWIN
  Saint
  Secret Agent
  Secret Agent Meets the Saint
ASTLEY, JOHN
  Johnny Be Good
ASTOR, SUZANNE
  New Faces of 1968
ASTREDO, HUMBERT ALLEN
  Evening with Richard Nixon
ASTRONAUTS
  Out of Sight
  Surf Party
  Wild on the Beach
  Wild, Wild Winter
ATARI, YONA
  To Live Another Summer, to
    Pass Another Winter
ATES, NEJLA
  Fanny
**ATHENS EXPERIMENTAL
  ORCHESTRA**
  America, America
ATHERTON, BILL
  Great Gatsby
ATHERTON, JAMES
  Mother of All of Us
ATHLETICO SPIZZ '80
  Urgh - A Music War
ATIENZA, EDWARD
  Man of La Mancha
ATKINS, CHET
  NARM's Golden Decade
ATKINS, CHOLLY
  Gentlemen Prefer Blondes
ATKINS, CHRISTOPHER
  Pirate Movie
ATKINS, NORMAN
  Down In the Valley
ATKINSON, DAVID
  All In Love
  Desert Song
  Girl In Pink Tights
  Trouble In Tahiti
ATKINSON, PEGGY
  Faggot
ATKINSON, ROWEN
  Lion King
ATKINSON, SARAH
  Phil the Fluter
  Wait a Minim!
ATLANTIC STARR
  Armed and Dangerous
ATTAWAY, RUTH
  Mrs. Patterson
ATTENBOROUGH, RICHARD
  Doctor Dolittle
  Loot
ATTERIDGE, HAROLD R.
  1941
ATTILA THE HUN
  Assault of the Killer Bimbos
ATTLES, JOSEPH
  Bubbling Brown Sugar
  Jerico-Jim Crow
ATTLEY, JOANN
  Promised Land
AU PAIRS
  Urgh - A Music War
AUBER, SUZANNE
  Four Hit Shows
AUBERJONOIS, RENE
  Big River (the Adventures of
    Huckleberry Finn)
  City of Angels
  Coco
AUBERT, JEANNE
  Anything Goes
AUDLEY, ELEANOR
  Cinderella
AUDRESON, MICHAEL
  Double Deckers
AUER, MISCHA
  Christmas That Almost Wasn't
  Merry Widow
AUGER, CLAUDINE
  Thunderball

723

BAKULA, SCOTT
Romance / Romance
Three Guys Naked from the
Waist Down

BAL, JEANNE
Gay Life

BALABAN, BOB
You're a Good Man, Charlie
Brown

BALABAN, EMANUEL
Medium

BALAAM AND THE ANGEL
Planes, Trains, and
Automobiles

BALDWIN, BROOKS
Cradle Will Rock

BALDWIN, MICHAEL
Phantasm

BALL, LUCILLE
Du Barry Was a Lady
I Love Lucy
Ladies of Burlesque
Magic Moments from the
Tonight Show
Mame
Wildcat

BALL, MICHAEL
Aspects of Love

**BALL ORCHESTRA OF
VIENNA**
Last Emperor

BALLANCE, BILL
Feminine Form

BALLANTINE, CARL
World's Greatest Lover

BALLANTYNE, PAUL
Thousand Miles of Mountains

BALLARD, BEVERLY
How to Steal an Election (A
Dirty Politics Musical)

BALLARD, HANK
Everybody's All-American
Flamingo Kid

BALLARD, KAYE
Baker Street
Ben Bagley's Cole Porter
Revisited
Carnival
Cinderella
Decline and Fall of the Entire
World As Seen Through the
Eyes of Cole Porter
Fanny Brice: Story In Song
Gershwin Rarities
Girl Most Likely
Golden Apple
Lyrics By Lerner
Mr. President
Oklahoma
Roberta
So Long 174th Street

BALLESTER, ANN
Hair

BALLISTIC KISSES
Crossover Dreams

BALSARA, V.
Guru

BALSER, EVELYN
Hello Dolly!

BAMPTON, ROSE
Tom Sawyer

BANANA SPLITS
Banana Splits

BANANARAMA
Disorderlies
Jumpin' Jack Flash
Party Party
Rain Man
Secret of My Success
Wild Life

BAND
Big Chill (More Songs from the
Original Soundtrack)
Last Waltz
New York Stories

BAND, RICHARD
Day Time Ended
Mutant
Prison
Re-Animator
Terror Vision

Troll
Zone Troopers / the Alchemist

BAND, ROBERT
Dawgs

**BAND OF THE GRENADIER
GUARDS**
Marches from the Movies

BAND WITHOUT A NAME
Thunder Alley

BANDA ECLIPSE
Sounds from True Stories

BANDIT BAND
Smokey and the Bandit II

BANE, PAULA
Call Me Mister

BANGLES
Goonies
Less Than Zero

BANJO BARONS
All American
George M!

BANKE, HERBERT
Carousel

BANKE, RICHARD
Kismet

BANKHEAD, TALLULAH
ANTA Album of Stars, Vol. 2
Co-Star
Command Performance

BANKS, DONALD
Good to Go

BANKS, ERNIE
Selma

BANKS, TONY
Lorca and the Outlaws
Quicksilver
Wicked Lady

BANOME, NINO
Bravo Giovanni!

BAPTISTE, PHIL
Sea of Love

BAPTISTE, THOMAS
Carmen Jones

BAR-B-Q KILLERS
Athens, Ga. - Inside / Out

BAR-KAYS
Breakin'
Wattstax (the Living Word)

BARABAS, SARI
Great Waltz
Oh, Rosalinda!

BARAVALLI, VICTOR
Stars of the Silver Screen,
1929-1930

BARBEAU, ADRIENNE
Grease

BARBER, DARIN
I Will

BARBER, FRANK
Best of the Great Motion
Picture Themes, Volume 5
John Williams' Symphonic
Suites
Schoner Gigolo - Armer Gigolo
(Just a Gigolo)

BARBER, SAMUEL
Vanessa

BARBIERI, GATO
Last Tango In Paris

BARBOUR, DAVE
Just for You

BARBUSTERS
Light of Day

BARBUTTI, PETER
Dora's World

BARCLAY, EDDY
Film Festival at Cannes
(Europe's Famous Motion
Picture Themes)

BARDOT, BRIGITTE
Girl In the Bikini
God Created Woman
Viva Maria!

BAREFIELD, EDDIE
Cotton Club Revue of 1958

BARER, MARSHALL
Mad Show
Once Upon a Mattress

BARGE, GENE
Stony Island

BARGELD, BLIXA
Ghosts of the Civil Dead

BARGY, JEANNE
Greenwich Village U.S.A.

BARHAMI, JOHN
Wonderwall

BARKER, DAVID
Shoestring Revues

BARKER, RONALD
Irma La Douce
On the Brighter Side

BARKER, WARREN
Broadway Compleat
Broadway Playbill
Hawaiian Eye
King and I
Musical Touch of Faraway
Places
77 Sunset Strip
TV Guide Top Television
Themes
Waltzing Down Broadway

BARLEON, AMELIE
Producers

BARNABAS ORCHESTRA
Schoner Gigolo - Armer Gigolo
(Just a Gigolo)

BARNES, ALAN
On the Brighter Side

BARNES, BILLY
Billy Barnes Revue
Billy Barnes' L.A.
Movie Star

BARNES, CHERYL
American Gigolo
Hair
Magic Show

BARNES, HOWARD
America, Why I Love Her

BARNES, MAE
By the Beautiful Sea

BARNES, ROLF
Saga of the Dingbat

BARNES, SIDNEY
Love at First Bite

BARNES, THEO
In Circles

BARNET, CHARLIE
Song Is Born

BARNETT, JACKIE
Playgirls

BARNETT, JANICE
Selma

BARNETT, NATE
Don't Play Us Cheap

BARNUM, H.B.
Beach Blanket Bingo
Golden Boy
On Broadway
Rose on Broadway
Your Arm's Too Short to Box
with God

BARON, EVALYN
I Can't Keep Running In Place
Scrambled Feet

BARON, LYNDA
One Over the Eight

BARON, PAUL
Gigi
Student Prince
Victor Borge Program

BARON, SAMUEL
Sand Castle

BAROUH, PIERRE
Live for Life
Man and a Woman

BARR, AL
Red Balloon

BARR, KATHY
Desert Song

BARR, PATRICK
Robin Hood

BARRERA, MICKEY
He's My Girl

BARRETT, JOE
Boy Meets Boy

BARRETT, MARK
Girl Friend

BARRETT, MICHAEL
Cradle Will Rock

BARRETT, RAINA
Oh! Calcutta!

BARRIE, BARBARA
Company

BARRIE, GEORGE
Touch of Class

BARRIE, KEN
Great Waltz

BARRIER, EDGAR
Maytime

BARRINGTON, BLAYNE
Dames at Sea

BARRON, BEBE
Forbidden Planet

BARROSO, RAY
Saludos Amigos (Music from
South of the Border)

BARROWS, RICHARD
Down In the Valley

BARRY, ALAN
High Society

BARRY, ANNA
Half a Sixpence

BARRY, BRENDAN
Lock Up Your Daughters

BARRY, BRUCE
Biograph Girl

BARRY, DAVE
Dora's World

BARRY, GENE
La Cage Aux Folles

BARRY, JEFF
Archies
Idolmaker
Leader of the Pack

BARRY, JOHN
Alice's Adventures In
Wonderland
Beat Girl
Big Screen Hits of John Barry
Billy
Black Hole
Black Hole (the Story of the
Black Hole)
Body Heat
Boom
Born Free
Chase
Concert John Barry
Cotton Club
Dances with Wolves
Day of the Locust
Deadfall
Deep
Diamonds Are Forever
Dove
Dr. No
Elizabeth Taylor In London
Four In the Morning
Frances
From Russia with Love
Golden Child
Golden Motion Picture Themes
and Original Soundtracks
Golden Seal
Goldfinger
Great Motion Picture Themes
Great Original Soundtracks and
Movie Themes
High Road to China
Howard the Duck
Incredible World of James
Bond
Inside Moves
Ipcress File
Jagged Edge
James Bond
James Bond - 10th Anniversary
James Bond 13 Original
Themes
John Barry
King Kong
King Rat
Knack (And How to Get It)
Last Valley
Legend of the Lone Ranger
Lion In Winter
Living Daylights
Magnificent Movie Music
Man In the Middle

725

BLITZSTEIN, MARC
Airborne Symphony
Cradle Will Rock
Juno
No for an Answer
Regina
Threepenny Opera
BLIZARD, WILLIAM
Joyce Grenfell Requests the
Pleasure
BLOCH, RAY
Hair
Themes from Hollywood
BLOCKBUSTERS
Rock All Night
BLOCKER, DAN
Bonanza - Christmas on the
Ponderosa
Bonanza - Ponderosa Party
Time
BLOCKI, FRITZ
Shanghai Gesture
BLODGETT, CAROL
Prince and the Pauper
BLONDELL, JOAN
50 Years of Film
Golden Age of the Hollywood
Musical
BLONDIE
American Gigolo
Nightmare on Elm Street 4 -
The Dream Master
Roadie
Up the Academy
BLOOD, SWEAT AND TEARS
Owl and the Pussycat
BLOODSTONE
Train Ride to Hollywood
BLOOM, CLAIRE
Liberty
Showcase Album, 1967
BLOOM, VERA
Kissing Bandit
Silent Movie
BLOOMFIELD'S HEADS,
HANDS AND FEET
Hero
BLOOMFIELD, MIKE
Steelyard Blues
Trip
BLOSSOM, HENRY
Eileen
Mademoiselle Modiste
Red Mill
BLOUNT, HELEN
Fly Blackbird
Musical Chairs
Riverwind
BLOW MONKEYS
Dirty Dancing
BLOW, KURTIS
Blue Iguana
BLOW-UP
Up the Academy
BLUDSOE, JULES
Show Boat
BLUE OYSTER CULT
Heavy Metal
BLUE RODEO
Navy SEALS
BLUE ROOM
Some Kind of Wonderful
BLUE SKIES BAND
Tough Enough
BLUE SKY BOYS
Paper Moon
BLUES BROTHERS
Blues Brothers
BLUES IMAGE
Dusty and Sweets McGee
BLUEWATER
Hard Ride
BLUME, DAVE
Taxi Driver
BLUNT, GABRIELLE
Macbeth
BLYDEN, LARRY
Apple Tree
Broadway Magic
Flower Drum Song

Forty-Five Minutes from
Broadway
Foxy
Olympus 7-0000
On a Clear Day You Can See
Forever
Sondheim: A Musical Tribute
BLYTH, ANN
Emperor Waltz
Girls...And More Girls
Kismet
Magnificent Moments from
MGM Movies
Rose Marie
BOATWRIGHT, McHENRY
Porgy and Bess
BOBBETTES
Stand By Me
BOBBIE, WALTER
Grease
BOCK, JERRY
Apple Tree
Baker Street
Body Beautiful
Fiddler on the Roof
Fiorello!
Four Television Musicals
Man In the Moon
Mister Wonderful
Rothschilds
She Loves Me
Tenderloin
To Broadway with Love
BODDICKER, MICHAEL
Get Crazy
BODEANS
Permanent Record
BODIBE, MATTHEW
Ipi-Tombi
BODRY, PENELOPE ANN
Tamalpais Exchange
BODYSNATCHERS
Dance Craze
BOEHM, KARL
Strawberry Statement
2001: A Space Odyssey
Wonderful World of the
Brothers Grimm
BOENZEE CRYQUE
Psych-Out
BOFFALONGO
Chicken Chronicles
BOGAEV, PAUL
Chess
BOGART, HUMPHREY
African Queen
Caine Mutiny
50 Years of Film
Hollywood's Heroes on the Air
Shakespeare In Hollywood
Treasure of the Sierra Madre
BOGAS, ED
Black Girl
Heavy Traffic
Here Comes Garfield
Street Music
BOGGS, GAIL
Candide
BOGIN, ABBA
Greenwillow
Mrs. Patterson
Riverwind
Showcase Album, 1967
BOGIN, BERNARD
Threepenny Opera
BOLAND, CLAY
Cotton Club Revue of 1958
BOLES, JOHN
Stars of the Silver Screen,
1929-1930
BOLET, JORGE
Song Without End
BOLGER, RAY
All American
Babes In Toyland
Cut! Out-Takes from
Hollywood's Greatest
Musicals
Daydreamer
Ethel Merman
Harvey Girls

Hollywood Canteen
Judy Garland
That's Dancing!
They Stopped the Show!
Wizard of Oz
BOLIN, SHANNON
Damn Yankees
Promenade
BOLLAND, MICHAEL
Trial of Billy Jack
BOLLING, CLAUDE
Awakening
Borsalino
California Suite
Louisiane
Reds
BOLLINGER, ROBERT
Trouble In Tahiti
BOLSHOI BALLET AND
ORCHESTRA
Bolshoi Ballet '67
Russian Adventure
BOLTON, GUY
Leave It to Jane
BOLTON, MICHAEL
Back to School
Houseful of Love: Music from
the Bill Cosby Show
Sing
BOLYARD, LEWIS
Pal Joey
BON JOVI
Disorderlies
Light of Day
Navy SEALS
BON JOVI, JON
Young Guns II
BON, WILLEM FREDERIK
Fourth Man
BONANOVA, FORTUNIO
Kurt Weill In Hollywood
BONAZZI, ELAINE
Silverlake
BOND, DOROTHY
Tales of Hoffmann
BOND, FRANCINE
I Can Get It for You Wholesale
BOND, GARY
Anne of the Thousand Days
Joseph and the Amazing
Technicolor Dreamcoat
BOND, JAMIE
Heavenly Kid
BOND, RICHARD
Turn On, Tune In, Drop Out
BOND, RUDY
Illya Darling
BOND, SHEILA
Babes In Arms / Jumbo
Wish You Were Here
BONDI, BEULAH
Wonderful World of the
Brothers Grimm
BONDS, GARY "U.S."
Night In Heaven
BONEDADDYS
Far Out Man
BONERZ, PETER
Paul Sills' Story Theater (of
Magical Folk-Rock Fables)
BONESCHI, GIAMPIERO
Don't Look Now
BONFA, LUIZ
Black Orpheus (Orfeo Negro)
Gentle Rain
BONHAM, JOHN
Song Remains the Same
BONO, SONNY
Chastity
Good Times
Wild on the Beach
You Are What You Eat
BONOFF, KARLA
Footloose
BONSAN, ALONZO
Mrs. Patterson
Seventeen
BOOGIE DOWN
I'm Gonna Git You Sucka

BOOKE, SORRELL
Dukes of Hazzard
Finian's Rainbow
BOOKER T. AND THE MGs
Quadrophenia
Uptight
BOOMER AND TRAVIS
In the Heat of the Night
BOONE, DEBBY
If Ever I See You Again
BOONE, PAT
All Hands on Deck
April Love
Cross and the Switchblade
Friendly Persuasion
General Motors' 50th
Anniversary Show
It's Time to Pray, America!
Journey to the Center of the
Earth
Magic of Lassie
Mardi Gras
Proudly They Came
State Fair
BOONE, RICHARD
John Brown's Body
King of Kings
Richard Boone Reads the Story
of Jesus for Children
BOOTH, CONNIE
Fawlty Towers - Second Sitting
Monty Python and the Holy
Grail
BOOTH, PHILIP
Mother of All of Us
BOOTH, ROGER
Are You Lonesome Tonight
BOOTH, SHIRLEY
By the Beautiful Sea
Juno
Tree Grows In Brooklyn
BORDEN, ESSIE
Faggot
Joan
Peace
BORDEN, JOHNNY
Bye Bye Birdie
BORDONI, IRENE
Louisiana Purchase
BORGE, VICTOR
Caught In the Act
Comedy In Music
Electric Company TV Show
Victor Borge Program
BORGES, YAMIL
Chorus Line
BORGNINE, ERNEST
American Spirit
Black Hole (the Story of the
Black Hole)
BORMAN, JOANNA
I Remember Mama
BORN FIRE
Shocker
BORODIN, ALEXANDER
Kismet
Loves of Isadora
BORUM, MEMPHIS WILLIE
Blues
BOSHOFF, JOHNNY
Gods Must Be Crazy
BOSLER, VIRGINIA
New Faces of 1952
BOSLEY, TOM
Fiorello!
BOSTON
FM
BOSTON POPS ORCHESTRA
Song of Norway
Spotlight on Broadway
BOSTON SYMPHONY
ORCHESTRA
Death In Venice
John F. Kennedy
Midsummer Night's Sex
Comedy
BOSTWICK, BARRY
Grease
Robber Bridegroom
Rocky Horror Picture Show

BOSWELL, CONNEE
  Here Come the Girls
  Irving Berlin Tribute
  Pennies from Heaven
  Star Maker
BOSWELL, SIMON
  Creepers
BOSWELL SISTERS
  Paper Moon
  Pennies from Heaven
BOTKIN, PERRY, JR.
  Bless the Beasts and Children
  Kid Power
  R.P.M.
  Thing with Two Heads
  Young and the Restless
BOTTOMS, JOSEPH
  Black Hole (the Story of the
    Black Hole)
BOTTOMS, SAM
  Apocalypse Now
BOUCHETY, JEAN
  Game Is Over
BOUILLON, JOE
  Josephine Baker Show
BOULE, JOHN
  Simply Heavenly
BOULEZ, PIERRE
  Female Prisoner
BOULT, SIR ADRIAN
  Excalibur
BOUR, ERNEST
  2001: A Space Odyssey
BOURTAYRE, JEAN-PIERRE
  Game Is Over
BOUSARD, JOE
  Prince and the Pauper
BOUTTE, LILIAN
  Angel Heart
BOVA, JOSEPH
  Cradle Will Rock
  42nd Street
  Once Upon a Mattress
BOWAN, SYBIL
  Donnybrook!
  Maggie Flynn
BOWEN, BOB
  Best of Broadway 1973
BOWEN, DEBBIE
  Gypsy
BOWEN, DENNIS
  After the Ball
BOWEN, HILL
  Camelot
  Gigi
  Music Man
  My Fair Lady
  Redhead
  Show Boat
  South Pacific
BOWEN, JIMMY
  Jamboree!
  Vanishing Point
BOWEN, ROGER
  From the Second City
BOWER, BOBBY
  Boy Meets Boy
BOWER, BUGS
  Finian's Rainbow
  You're a Good Man, Charlie
    Brown
BOWIE, DAVID
  Absolute Beginners
  Baal
  Cat People
  Christiane F.
  Falcon and the Snowman
  Labyrinth
  Pretty Woman
  Ziggy Stardust - The Motion
    Picture
BOWIE, LESTER
  Zebra
BOWLES, ANTHONY
  Evita
  Jesus Christ Superstar
  Odessa File
  Share My Lettuce
BOWLES, PAUL
  Cyrano De Bergerac

  Glass Menagerie
BOWMAN, JOAN
  Seventeen
BOWMAN, LEE
  American Spirit
BOWMAN, ROBERT
  Fiddler on the Roof
BOWMAN, SIMON
  Are You Lonesome Tonight
BOWNE, RICHARD
  Snow White and the Seven
    Dwarfs
BOWTIES
  Rock, Rock, Rock
BOX, EUEL
  Benji
  Benji (the Story of Benji)
  For the Love of Benji
BOX TOPS
  Stardust
BOY GEORGE
  Hiding Out
  Slaves of New York
BOYD, JIM
  Electric Company TV Show
BOYD, JIMMY
  Tom Sawyer
BOYD, MATT
  That Other Woman's Child
BOYD, STEPHEN
  Bible
  Jumbo
BOYER, CHARLES
  Love Is a Ball
BOYER, DAVE
  Miracle Goes On
BOYLE, BILLY
  Billy
  Canterbury Tales
  What's a Nice Country Like the
    U.S. Doing In a State Like
    This?
BOYLE, PETER
  Joe
  Saturday Night Live
  Young Frankenstein
BOYS CHOIR OF HARLEM
  Glory
BOYS CLUB
  Karate Kid III
  License to Drive
  She's Out of Control
BOZEMAN, BEVERLY
  Littlest Revue
BOZZIO, DALE
  Thing-Fish
BOZZIO, TERRY
  Back to the Beach
  Thing-Fish
  Twins
BRACKEN, EDDIE
  Archy and Mehitabel / Echoes
    of Archy
  Bat Masterson
  Fleet's In
  Hot September
BRACKMAN, GEORGE
  Gulliver's Travels Beyond the
    Moon
BRACKMAN, JACOB
  King of Hearts
BRADBURY, LANE
  Gypsy
BRADEN, ALAN
  Tom Brown's School Days
BRADEN, JOHNNY
  Downriver
BRADFORD, ALBERTA
  Don't Bother Me, I Can't Cope
BRADFORD, ALEX
  Your Arm's Too Short to Box
    with God
BRADLEY, GRACE
  Anything Goes
  Ladies of Burlesque
BRADLEY, HAROLD
  Clambake
  Kissin' Cousins
BRADLEY, JAN
  Hairspray

BRADLEY, MICHAEL
  Savage Streets
BRADLEY, PAUL
  Hard Part Begins
BRADLEY, TOMI-LEE
  Perfect Couple
BRADY, ALICE
  Hooray for Hollywood
BRADY, MIKE
  Pirate Movie
BRADY, SCOTT
  Destry Rides Again
BRAE, BONNIE
  Seventeen
BRAGA, SONIA
  Kiss of the Spider Woman
BRAHAM, PHILIP
  Sunny
BRAHMS, CARYL
  John F. Kennedy
BRAHMS, JOHANNES
  Loves of Isadora
  Theme Music from Great
    Motion Picture Scores
BRAID, HILDA
  Pickwick
BRAIDWOOD, MARGARET
  Dylan
BRAITHWAITE, WARWICK
  Melba
BRAMBELL, WILFRID
  Canterbury Tales
BRAMLETT, DELANEY
  Catch My Soul
BRAMLEY, RAYMOND
  Tenderloin
BRAND, CANDY
  My Turn on Earth
BRAND, OSCAR
  How to Steal an Election (A
    Dirty Politics Musical)
  In White America
  Joyful Noise
BRANDO, MARLON
  Apocalypse Now
  Guys and Dolls
  Julius Caesar
BRANDON, JOHNNY
  Billy Noname
  Cindy
  Love from Judy
BRANDON, PETER
  Zenda
BRANDT, BARBARA
  Postcard from Morocco
BRANDT, CARL
  Rides, Rapes and Rescues
    (Themes from Great Silent
    Films)
  Top TV Themes '64
BRANDT, MIKE
  Tamalpais Exchange
BRANDYWINE, NAT
  Annie Get Your Gun
BRANIGAN, BILLY
  Jumpin' Jack Flash
BRANIGAN, LAURA
  Body Rock
  Coming to America
  Flashdance
  Ghostbusters
  Salsa
BRANNIGAN, OWEN
  Tales of Hoffmann
BRASH, MARION
  She Loves Me
BRASSNER, KIM
  Joseph McCarthy Is Alive and
    Well and Living In Dade
    County
BRASWELL, CHARLES
  All In the York Family
  Company
  Mame
  Official Grammy Awards
    Archive Collection
  Sail Away
  Wildcat
BRAUN, RICHARD
  My Cousin Josefa

BRAUNER, HILDA
  Elephant Calf
BRAUNSTEIN, ALAN
  Dude (the Highway Life)
  Jesus Christ Superstar
BRAVO POPS SYMPHONY
  ORCHESTRA
  Around the World In 80 Days
  Flower Drum Song
  Gigi
  My Fair Lady
BRAYFIELD, DOUGLAS
  Teen Wolf
BRAZDA, DAILBOR
  Fiddler on the Roof
BRAZZI, ROSSANO
  Christmas That Almost Wasn't
BREAKFAST CLUB
  License to Drive
BREALOND, TONEY
  Ain't Supposed to Die a Natural
    Death
BREAUX, MARC
  Li'l Abner
BRECHT, BERTOLT
  Elephant Calf
  Happy End
  Rise and Fall of the City of
    Mahogany
  Seven Deadly Sins
  Threepenny Opera
BREDIN, PATRICIA
  Man of La Mancha
BREESKIN, ELIAS
  Chaplin's Art of Comedy
BREEZE, OLIVIA
  Cowardly Custard
BREFFORT, ALEXANDRE
  Irma La Douce
BREGMAN, BUDDY
  Funny Face
  Porgy and Bess
  Ruggles of Red Gap
BREL, JACQUES
  Jacques Brel Is Alive and Well
    and Living In Paris
BREMERS, BEVERLY ANN
  Me Nobody Knows
BRENNAN, EILEEN
  At Long Last Love
  Hello Dolly!
  Little Mary Sunshine
BRENNAN, KEVIN
  Canterbury Tales
BRENNAN, MAUREEN
  Candide
BRENNAN, WALTER
  One and Only, Genuine,
    Original Family Band
BRENT, EARL
  Kissing Bandit
BRER SOUL
  Sweet Sweetback's Baadasssss
    Song
BRESLIN, TOMMY
  Good News
BRETHERTON, FREDDIE
  Kiss Me Kate
BRETT, PETER
  Pieces of Eight
BREUER, LEE
  Gospel at Colonus
BREWER, BETTY
  California
BREWER, MICHAEL
  Revenge
BREWER, TERESA
  Decade of Broadway and
    Cinema
  Good News
BREWSTER, RALPH
  Manhattan Tower
  Seven Dreams
BRICE, CAROL
  Finian's Rainbow
  Grass Harp
  Louisiana Purchase
  Porgy and Bess
  Regina
  Saratoga

730

BRICE, FANNY
Betty Boop
Everybody Sing
Great Personalities of
 Broadway
Great Ziegfeld
Legends of the Musical Stage
Lost Films: Trailers from the
 First Years of Sound
Show Biz (From Vaude to Video)
Stars of the Silver Screen,
 1929-1930
BRICKELL, EDIE
Born on the Fourth of July
BRICKLIN
Bill and Ted's Excellent
 Adventure
BRICUSSE, LESLIE
Doctor Dolittle
Fool Britannia
Goldfinger
Good Old Bad Old Days!
Goodbye Mr. Chips
Gunn...Number One
James Bond - 10th Anniversary
Penelope
Pickwick
Roar of the Greasepaint - The
 Smell of the Crowd
Salt and Pepper
Scrooge
Stop the World - I Want to Get
 Off!!
Thunderball
Victor / Victoria
Willy Wonka and the Chocolate
 Factory
You Only Live Twice
BRIDGES, BEN
Woman In Red
BRIDGES, JEFF
John and Mary
BRIDGES, KENNETH
Lady In the Dark
BRIDGES, LLOYD
Airplane!
BRIDGEWATER, DEE DEE
Brother from Another Planet
Louisiane
Wiz
BRIGEL, STOCKTON
Just for Openers
BRIGGS, BUNNY
My People
BRIGGS, DAVID
Elvis
That's the Way It Is
BRIGHT, BILL
It's Time to Pray, America!
BRIGHT CHEERSTRAP
Where's Poppa?
BRIGHT, PATRICIA
Thousand Miles of Mountains
BRIGHT, RICHARD
Survival of St. Joan
BRIGHT, ZOE
Snoopy
BRIGHTMAN, SARAH
Nightingale
Phantom of the Opera
BRILL, MARTY
James Blonde (Secret Agent
 006.95, Marked Down from
 007.00)
BRIMSTONE CHORALE
Brimstone and Treacle
BRINEY, MARY MARTHA
Blossom Time
Red Mill
Student Prince
BRINKER, LYNN
Greenwillow
BRINKLEY, DAVID
Time to Keep
BRION, FRANÇOISE
Alexander
BRISDON, DAVID L.
Hiding Out
BRITTAN, ROBERT
Raisin

BRITTEN, TERRY
Pirate Movie
BRITTON, GEORGE
Anything Goes
Band Wagon
BRITTON, PAMELA
Brigadoon
BRITTON, PAUL
Firefly
Naughty Marietta
BRITTON, SHERRY
Best of Burlesque
BRITTON, TONY
Robocop
BRO, JUDITH
Ka-Boom!
BROADBENT, JIM
Hitch-Hikers Guide to the
 Galaxy
BROADCASTERS
Under the Boardwalk
BROADWAY BRASS
Guys and Dolls
BROADWAY ORCHESTRA
Four Hit Shows
BROADWAY SYMPHONY
Turned on Broadway
**BROADWAY THEATER
 ORCHESTRA**
My Fair Lady
BROCK, KELLY
Best of Broadway 1973
**BROCK, NAPOLEON
 MURPHY**
Thing-Fish
BROCKSMITH, ROY
Threepenny Opera
BRODSZKY, NICHOLAS
Flame and the Flesh
Let's Be Happy
Rich, Young and Pretty
Serenade
Ten Thousand Bedrooms
Toast of New Orleans
BRODY, LANE
Tender Mercies
Tough Enough
BROEKMAN, DAVID
Wide, Wide World
BROKEN EDGE
Karate Kid
BROKEN HOMES
Born on the Fourth of July
Weird Science
BRON, ELEANOR
Card
Establishment
BRONHILL, JUNE
Desert Song
La Vie Parisienne
Lilac Time (Blossom Time)
Merry Widow
Robert and Elizabeth
Sound of Music
BRONSKI BEAT
Gotcha
Letter to Brezhnev
BROOKE, TYLER
Love Me Tonight
BROOKLYN BRIDGE
Grasshopper
BROOKLYN DREAMS
Hollywood Knights
BROOKMEYER, BOB
Show Boat
BROOKS, DAVID
Bloomer Girl
Brigadoon
BROOKS, DONNIE
Swingin' Summer
Truth of Truths
BROOKS, DUDLEY
Follow That Dream
Fun In Acapulco
G.I. Blues
Girls! Girls! Girls!
It Happened at the World's Fair
Jailhouse Rock
Kid Galahad
Loving You

Roustabout
This Is Elvis
BROOKS, FOSTER
Foster Brooks' Roasts
BROOKS, JACK
Artists and Models
Cinderfella
Song of Scheherazade
BROOKS, JOE
If Ever I See You Again
Jeremy
Lords of Flatbush
Metropolis
You Light Up My Life
BROOKS, KAREN
Rustler's Rhapsody
BROOKS, KARMELLO
Earthquake
BROOKS, LAWRENCE
Song of Norway
BROOKS, MEL
Blazing Saddles
Electric Company TV Show
High Anxiety
History of the World, Part I
Producers
BROOKS, PATTIE
Agatha
Doctor Detroit
Thank God It's Friday
That Was Then, This Is Now
BROOKS, SHELDON
Dr. Phibes
BROTHERS FOUR
Alamo
BROTHERS JOHNSON
All This and World War II
Mother, Jugs, and Speed
BROTHERSON, ERIC
Gentlemen Prefer Blondes
Great Waltz
BROUGHTON, BRUCE
Boy Who Could Fly
Harry and the Hendersons
Silverado
Young Sherlock Holmes
BROWN
Sheba Baby
BROWN, ALEX
Girls Just Want to Have Fun
BROWN, ALFRED
Harry and Lena
BROWN, ANNE
Porgy and Bess
BROWN, B.
Swan Down Gloves
BROWN, BARBARA
Sound of Music
BROWN, BILL, SINGERS
Award Winning Original Motion
 Picture Sound Tracks and
 Themes
Stagecoach
BROWN, BLAIR
Threepenny Opera
BROWN, BOB
Power Is You
BROWN, BOBBY
Ghostbusters II
BROWN, BUSTER
American Graffiti
BROWN, CANDY
Shirley MacLaine, Live at the
 Palace
BROWN, CHARLIE
Hair
BROWN, CHELSEA
Rowan and Martin's Laugh-In
BROWN, CHUCK
Blue Iguana
Good to Go
BROWN, EDDIE
Your Arm's Too Short to Box
 with God
BROWN, FORMAN
Merry Widow
Turnabout
BROWN, GAYE
Houdini, Man of Magic

BROWN, GEORGIA
Carmelina
Oliver!
BROWN, IRENE
No, No, Nanette
BROWN, JACK
Gigi
Mardi Gras
BROWN, JAMES
Black Caesar
Blue Iguana
Blues Brothers
Doctor Detroit
Good Morning, Vietnam
Quadrophenia
Rocky IV
Slaughter's Big Rip-Off
BROWN, JOANNE
Oh What a Lovely War
BROWN, JOE
Charlie Girl
BROWN, JOE E.
Hollywood Canteen
BROWN, JOHN
Cinderella
Golden Boy
Rollerball
BROWN, JOYCE
Purlie
BROWN, JULIE
Earth Girls Are Easy
BROWN, KELLY
Annie Get Your Gun
I Can Get It for You Wholesale
BROWN, LAWRENCE
Mary Jane
BROWN, LEONARD
Runaways
BROWN, LES
Composer's Holiday
Dean Martin TV Show
Proudly They Came
BROWN, LEW
Singing Fool
Ziegfeld Follies of 1919
BROWN, LISA
Best Little Whorehouse In
 Texas
BROWN, LOUIS
Best Things In Life Are Free
Good News
BROWN, MAXINE
Stardust
BROWN, MICHAEL
Different Times
Hot Parts
New Faces of 1952
Penney Proud
Woolworth Had a Notion
BROWN, N.
Death on the Nile
BROWN, NACIO HERB
Boy Friend
Clockwork Orange
Hollywood Hits By Nacio Herb
 Brown
Kissing Bandit
Pagan Love Song
Singin' In the Rain
BROWN, OSCAR, JR.
Joy
BROWN, PAMELA
Importance of Being Earnest
Lady's Not for Burning
Macbeth
Tales of Hoffmann
BROWN, PENDLETON
Threepenny Opera
BROWN, R.G.
Just for Openers
BROWN, RAY
Adventurers
Fred Astaire Sings and Swings
Irving Berlin
BROWN, RUSS
Damn Yankees
BROWN, RUTH
Amen Corner
BROWN, W. EARL
Elvis (NBC-TV Special)

BROWNE, CORAL
  Ruling Class
BROWNE, IRENE
  After the Ball
BROWNE, JACKSON
  Fast Times at Ridgemont High
  Miami Vice II
BROWNE, ROSCOE LEE
  American Spirit
  Hand Is on the Gate
  Star Wars
BROWNE, SAM
  Pennies from Heaven
BROWNING, SUSAN
  Company
  Dime a Dozen
  Goodtime Charley
BROWNLEE, JOHN
  Die Fledermaus
BROWNSVILLE STATION
  Rock 'N' Roll High School
BROX, VICTOR
  Jesus Christ Superstar
BROX SISTERS
  *Bing Crosby In Hollywood
    (1930-1934)*
BRUBAKER, ROBERT
  Candide
BRUBECK, DARIUS
  Chaplin's Back
BRUBECK, DAVE
  All Night Long
  American Pop
  Heavy Traffic
  Real Ambassadors
  Stompin' for Mili
BRUCE, BETTY
  Gypsy
BRUCE, CAROL
  Do I Hear a Waltz?
  Henry, Sweet Henry
  Show Boat
BRUCE, CHUCK
  Barabbas
BRUCE, ED
  Smokey and the Bandit III
BRUCE, JUDITH
  Houdini, Man of Magic
  Tom Brown's School Days
BRUCE, LENNY
  *Magic Moments from the
    Tonight Show*
BRUCE, NIGEL
  House of Fear
  Sherlock Holmes
BRUCE, VIRGINIA
  Born to Dance
BRUCKNER-RIGGEBERG,
  WILHELM
  Happy End
  *Rise and Fall of the City of
    Mahogany*
  Seven Deadly Sins
  Threepenny Opera
BRUDER, PATRICIA
  Sap of Life
BRUKEN, CLAUDIA
  Insignificance
BRUNE, ADRIENNE
  Three Musketeers
BRUNEAU, RALPH
  Doonesbury
BRUNELLE, PHILIP
  Postcard from Morocco
BRUNNER, BOB
  That Darn Cat
BRUNO, JEAN
  Lorelei
BRUNO, TONY
  Hell's Angels '69
  Last Porno Flick
BRUNS, GEORGE
  Babes In Toyland
  Davy Crockett
  Johnny Tremaine
  101 Dalmatians
  Perri
  Robin Hood
  Sleeping Beauty
  Westward Ho, the Wagons

Zorro
BRYAN, DORA
  Charlie Girl
  Gentlemen Prefer Blondes
  Show Boat
  Water Gipsies
BRYAN, FRED
  Two on the Aisle
BRYAN, KENNETH
  *Joseph and the Amazing
    Technicolor Dreamcoat*
BRYAN, WAYNE
  Good News
BRYANT, ANITA
  Academy Awards Presentation
  America Sings
  Orange Bird
BRYANT, BUDDY
  This Was Burlesque
BRYANT, DAVID
  Les Miserables
BRYANT, GLENN
  Carmen Jones
BRYANT, JIM
  West Side Story
BRYANT, RAY
  Hairspray
BRYANT, SALLY
  Boy Friend
BRYER, DENISE
  Gulliver In Lilliput
BRYER, VERA
  Tip Toes
BRYNNER, YUL
  King and I
  Romance of a Horsethief
BRYSON, PEABO
  D.C. Cab
BUARQUE, CHICO
  *Dona Flor and Her Two
    Husbands*
BUBBLES, JOHN W.
  Porgy and Bess
BUCHANAN, JACK
  Band Wagon
  Sunny
  That's Entertainment, Part 2
BUCHANAN, ROBBIE
  Golden Child
BUCK, BILL
  Turnabout
BUCKIN' BRONCOS
  Music Man
BUCKINGHAM, LINDSEY
  Back to the Future
  National Lampoon's Vacation
BUCKLES, ANN
  Crowning Experience
BUCKLEY, BETTY
  Cats
  Mystery of Edwin Drood
  Promises, Promises
  1776
BUCKLEY, EMERSON
  Ballad of Baby Doe
BUCKLEY, HAL
  Cradle Will Rock
BUCKMASTER, PAUL
  Friends
BUCKWHEAT ZYDECO
  Big Easy
BUDD, JULIE
  *Late Nite Comic (A New
    American Musical)*
BUDD, ROY
  Catlow and Famous Themes
  *Dino DeLaurentis Presents
    Original Soundtracks*
  Final Option
  Flight of the Doves
  Kidnapped
  Paper Tiger
  Stone Killer
  Wild Geese
BUEHRLE, MARY
  *Do Black Patent Leather Shoes
    Really Reflect Up?*
BUFFALO BILLS
  Music Man

BUFFALO SPRINGFIELD
  Homer
  Made In Heaven
  Wonder Years
BUFFETT, JIMMY
  Always
  Fast Times at Ridgemont High
  FM
  Rancho Deluxe
  Urban Cowboy
BUIRGY, SUZANNA
  A-5,6,7,8
BULIFANT, JOYCE
  Happiest Millionaire
BULLARD, KIM
  He's My Girl
BULLENS, CINDY
  Grease
BULLOCK, LOU
  Faggot
BULOFF, JOSEPH
  Silk Stockings
BUMBRY, GRACE
  Carmen Jones
BUNNAGE, AVIS
  Billy
BUNNELL, LLOYD
  Desert Song
BUNTON, IRVING
  My People
BURCH, FRED
  Easy Come, Easy Go
BURCH, SHELLY
  Nine
  *Stop the World - I Want to Get
    Off!!*
BURDON, ERIC
  Biggest Bundle of Them All
  *Magic Garden of Stanley
    Sweetheart*
BURFORD, IAN
  Anne of Green Gables
  Pickwick
BURGE, GREGORY
  Electric Company TV Show
  Sophisticated Ladies
BURGER, JULIUS
  Song of Scheherazade
BURGETT, SHARON
  Secret Garden
BURGHOFF, GARY
  *M*A*S*H*
  *You're a Good Man, Charlie
    Brown*
BURGIE, IRVING
  Ballad for Bimshire
BURGON, GEOFFREY
  Brideshead Revisited
  Life of Brian
BURKE, BILLIE
  Wizard of Oz
BURKE, DONALD
  Young Girls of Rochefort
BURKE, JOHNNY
  Bing's Hollywood
  Carnival In Flanders
  Donnybrook!
  Emperor Waltz
  Road to Bali
  Star Maker
BURKE, JOSEPH
  Good News
BURKE, SOLOMON
  Cool Breeze
BURKE, SONNY
  Bing's Hollywood
  Four Jills In a Jeep
  Hennesey
  Lady and the Tramp
  Road to Bali
  Who's Afraid of Virginia Woolf?
BURKHARDT, GERRY
  *Best Little Whorehouse In
    Texas*
BURKS, DONNY
  Billy Noname
  Hair
BURLEY, TONI-SUE
  Ambassador

BURMEISTER, LEO
  Les Miserables
BURNETT, CAROL
  Annie
  Christmas In Hawaii
  *Decade of Broadway and
    Cinema*
  Fade Out Fade In
  Follies
  *General Motors' 50th
    Anniversary Show*
  Julie and Carol at Carnegie Hall
  *Julie and Carol at Lincoln
    Center*
  Once Upon a Mattress
  Three Billion Millionaires
BURNETT, HARRY
  Turnabout
BURNETTE, BILLY
  Speed Zone
  Summer School
BURNETTE, JOHNNY
  American Graffiti
  Rock, Rock, Rock
BURNING SENSATIONS
  Repo Man
BURNING SPEAR
  River's Edge
  Rockers
BURNS, DAVID
  Do Re Mi
  *Funny Thing Happened on the
    Way to the Forum*
  Hello Dolly!
  Music Man
  Out of This World
  Two's Company
BURNS, GEORGE
  Damsel In Distress
  Dean Martin Testimonial Dinner
  *Magic Moments from the
    Tonight Show*
  *Sgt. Pepper's Lonely Hearts
    Club Band*
BURNS, JACK
  From the Second City
BURNS, RALPH
  All Dogs Go to Heaven
  All That Jazz
  Annie
  Cabaret
  Chorus Line
  In the Mood
  Lenny
  Lucky Lady
  Movie Movie
  National Lampoon's Vacation
  New York, New York
  No Strings
  Perfect
  Say Amen, Somebody
BURR, ROBERT
  Bajour
BURRELL, DEBORAH
  Dream Girls
BURRELL, KENNY
  Nervous Set
BURRELL, TERRY
  Eubie
BURRIDGE, GEOFFREY
  Cowardly Custard
BURROUGHS, EDGAR RICE
  Tarzan
BURROUGHS, CLARK
  Hit the Deck
BURROWS, CLIFF
  His Land
BURROWS, JOHN
  Cowardly Custard
BURSKY, JAY
  *Best Little Whorehouse In
    Texas*
BURSTEIN, MIKE
  Megilla of Itzig Manger
BURSTON, REGINALD
  Carousel
  Conversation Piece
  Oklahoma
BURTNICK, GLEN
  Armed and Dangerous

732

Bill and Ted's Excellent
Adventure
BURTON, JAMES
Elvis In Concert
Elvis: Aloha from Hawaii Via
Satellite
That's the Way It Is
This Is Elvis
BURTON, JENNY
Beat Street
White Nights
BURTON, KATE
Doonesbury
BURTON, LEVAR
Liberty
BURTON, MIRIAM
House of Flowers
To Broadway with Love
BURTON, PHILIP
Under Milk Wood
BURTON, RICHARD
Baker Street
Becket
Camelot
Conversation Piece
Days of Wilfred Owen
Doctor Dolittle
Doctor Faustus
Equus
50 Years of Film
Hamlet
Lady's Not for Burning
Little Prince
Night of the Iguana
Taming of the Shrew
Under Milk Wood
War of the Worlds
Who's Afraid of Virginia Woolf?
Zulu
BURTON, RITA
Dames at Sea
BURTON, WENDELL
You're a Good Man, Charlie
Brown
BURWELL, CARTER
Psycho III
Raising Arizona
BUSBOYS
Ghostbusters
BUSCH, BETTY ANN
Penney Proud
BUSEY, GARY
Buddy Holly Story
Insignificance
BUSH, KATE
She's Having a Baby
BUSH, STAN
Transformers - The Movie
Wraith
BUSH, THOMMIE
Billy Noname
BUSHELLE, JOHN
Macbeth
BUSHMAN, FRANCIS X.
Christmas Carol
Francis X. Bushman Talks
About His Life and Times
BUSSE, BARRY
Postcard from Morocco
BUTERA, SAM
Continental Twist
Hey Boy, Hey Girl
Rat Race
BUTLER, ANGELINE
Magic Garden of Stanley
Sweetheart
BUTLER, ARTIE
At Long Last Love
Harrad Experiment
Harrad Summer
Love Machine
Rescuers
BUTLER, BILL
Via Galactica
BUTLER, DAWS
American Spirit
Hey There, It's Yogi Bear
Huckleberry Hound
Mr. Jinks, Pixie and Dixie
Quick Draw McGraw
Yogi Bear and Boo Boo

BUTLER, JERRY
Joe
Melinda
Save the Children
Thing with Two Heads
BUTLER, JONATHAN
License to Drive
BUTLER, LARRY
Tess
BUTLER, MARK ANTHONY
Runaways
BUTLER, RHODA
Candide
Goodtime Charley
BUTLER, ROSEMARY
Secret Admirer
BUTLER, TOMMY
Selma
BUTT, JENNIFER
Les Miserables
BUTTERFIELD, PAUL
Last Waltz
You Are What You Eat
BUTTERFIELD BLUES BAND
Woodstock
BUTTOLPH, DAVID
Horse Soldiers
Long John Silver
BUTTONS, RED
Gay Pur-ee
Hansel and Gretel
Longest Day
Pete's Dragon
BUTTRAM, PAT
Robin Hood
Winged Victory
BUZBY, ZANE
Americathon
BUZZELL, EDDIE
Lost Films: Trailers from the
First Years of Sound
BUZZI, RUTH
Linus the Lionhearted
Rowan and Martin's Laugh-In
BYATT, IRENE
By Jupiter
South Pacific
BYBELL, PATRICIA
Allegro
BYERS, BILLY
Borrowers
One and Only
Pirates
BYERS, JIM
Tarot
BYGRAVES, MAX
Do Re Mi
BYLES, JUNIOR
Rockers
BYNG, G.W.
Irene
BYRD, BRETTON
Beggar's Holiday
BYRD, CAROLYN
Bubbling Brown Sugar
BYRDS
Banjoman
Candy
Don't Make Waves
Easy Rider
Homer
More American Graffiti
BYRNE, BARBARA
Into the Woods
BYRNE, BOBBY
Twenty Great Movie Themes
BYRNE, DAVID
Catherine Wheel
Last Emperor
Sounds from True Stories
BYRNE, GAYLEA
All In Love
BYRON, D.L.
Times Square
BYRON, MARION
Love Me Tonight
BYRON, SCREAMIN' LORD
Gothic

CBS RADIO WORKSHOP
CAST
Dog's Life
CAAN, JAMES
Funny Lady
CABAYO, ENA
Show Boat
CABOT, CEIL
Demi Dozen
Dressed to the Nines
Pieces of Eight
Take Five
CABOT, LOUISA
Dylan
CABOT, SEBASTIAN
Flood
Romeo and Juliet
CACAVAS, JOHN
Airport 1975
Gallant Men
Horror Express
CADDICK, DAVID
Song and Dance
CADILLACS
Coupe De Ville
Go Johnny Go!
CAESAR, IRVING
Hit the Deck
No, No, Nanette
CAESAR, SID
Little Me
CAFE MILANO ORCHESTRA
Rome Adventure
CAFFERTY, JOHN
Cobra
Eddie and the Cruisers
Rocky IV
CAFFEY, CHARLOTTE
Wild Life
CAFFEY, MARION
Mayor
CAGE, NICHOLAS
Peggy Sue Got Married
CAGGIANO, ROSEMARY
Power Is You
CAGNEY, JAMES
50 Years of Film
Seven Little Foys
Starlift
Strawberry Blond
Yankee Doodle Dandy
CAHN, SAMMY
Ali Baba and the 40 Thieves
Anything Goes
Bing's Hollywood
Dean Martin Testimonial Dinner
Evening with Sammy Cahn
Heidi's Song
High Button Shoes
How the West Was Won
It Happened In Brooklyn
Jack and the Beanstalk
Journey Back to Oz
Les Poupees De Paris
Let's Make Love
Look to the Lilies
Our Town
Pardners
Peter Pan
Rich, Young and Pretty
Road to Hong Kong
Robin and the Seven Hoods
Say One for Me
Serenade
Skyscraper
Some Came Running
Starlift
Ten Thousand Bedrooms
This Earth Is Mine
Toast of New Orleans
Touch of Class
Two's Company
Walking Happy
Words and Music
World of Suzie Wong
Written on the Wind
CAIN, JACKIE
By Jupiter
Two for the Seesaw

CAIN, JESS
Impossible Dream - The Story
of the 1967 Boston Red Sox
CAIN, JOE
Singing Nun
CAIN, TAHNEE, AND THE
TRYANGLZ
Terminator
CAIN, WILLIAM
Jerico-Jim Crow
CAINE, MICHAEL
Sleuth
CAIOLA, AL
Eight on the Lam
Golden Motion Picture Themes
and Original Soundtracks
Great Motion Picture Themes
Hit Instrumentals from TV
Western Themes
Magnificent Seven
More Great Motion Picture
Themes
Original Motion Picture Hit
Themes
CAIRNCROSS, JAMES
Hooray for Daisy!
Salad Days
CALABRO, TONY
Monsieur De Pourceaugnac
CALBES, ELANOR
South Pacific
CALDWELL, BOBBY
Back to School
Salsa
CALDWELL, ERSKINE
God's Little Acre
CALDWELL, ZOE
Colette
CALHERN, LOUIS
Annie Get Your Gun
Athena
Julius Caesar
CALIFORNIA CHILDRENS
CHORUS
Cannonball Run
CALIN, MICKEY
West Side Story
CALLAHAN, BILL
Call Me Mister
Two's Company
CALLAHAN, BRAD
Boy Meets Boy
CALLAHAN, JAMES
Outlaw Blues
CALLAN, MICHAEL
Film Music
Kiss Me Kate
CALLAS, CHARLIE
Pete's Dragon
CALLAWAY, LIZ
Baby
Follies
Sondheim
Stephen Sondheim Evening
CALLICO KIDS
Bing's Hollywood
CALLINICOS, CONSTANTINE
Because You're Mine
Desert Song
For the First Time
Great Caruso
Mario Lanza Sings Because
Student Prince
That Midnight Kiss
Toast of New Orleans
Vagabond King
CALLOWAY, CAB
Ben Bagley's Oscar
Hammerstein Revisited
Betty Boop
Blackbirds of 1928
Blues Brothers
Choice Cuts
Cotton Club Revue of 1958
Girl Crazy
Hello Dolly!
Littlest Angel
Porgy and Bess
Stormy Weather
CALLOWAY, CHRIS
Hello Dolly!

CALLOWAY, NORTHERN
  Me Nobody Knows
CALVET, CORINNE
  Premiere
CALVI, PINO
  Music from Great Italian Motion
    Pictures
CALVIN, HENRY
  Babes In Toyland
  Hans Brinker and the Silver
    Skates
  Kismet
  Peter Pan
  This Is Broadway's Best
  Toby Tyler
  Zorro
CALVIN, JOHN
  California Dreaming
CAMACHO, THELMA
  Hard Ride
CAMARA, LADJI
  Believers
CAMARATA, TUTTI
  Alice In Wonderland
  All Star Color TV Revue
  Babes In Toyland
  Bambi
  Best of Disney
  Bing Crosby Sings Hits From...
  Carousel
  Doctor Dolittle
  Darby O'Gill and the Little
    People
  Fiddler on the Roof
  Hans Christian Andersen
    Stories
  In Search of the Castaways
  Just for You
  Lute Song
  Man of La Mancha
  Orange Bird
  Parent Trap
  Perri
  Sleeping Beauty
  Snow White and the Seven
    Dwarfs
  Sound of Music
  Stingiest Man In Town
  Summer Magic
  33 Great Walt Disney Motion
    Picture Melodies
  Ugly Dachshund
  Westward Ho, the Wagons
CAMELFLAGE
  Gotcha
CAMEO
  My Stepmother Is an Alien
CAMERON, ISLA
  Far from the Madding Crowd
CAMERON, JOHN
  Lilac Time (Blossom Time)
  Ruling Class
  Sunburn
  Touch of Class
CAMISON, MAT
  Black and White In Color
CAMP, HAMILTON
  Committee
  Paul Sills' Story Theater (of
    Magical Folk-Rock Fables)
  Three In the Cellar
  Up In the Cellar
CAMPBELL, CHARLES
  Don't Bother Me, I Can't Cope
CAMPBELL, CLAUDIA
  Tree Grows In Brooklyn
CAMPBELL, DEAN
  Hazel Flagg
  Make a Wish
CAMPBELL, DOUGLAS
  John Brown's Body
CAMPBELL, GLEN
  Any Which Way You Can
  Golden Seal
  In the Heat of the Night
  Magic Moments from the
    Tonight Show
  Night the Lights Went Out In
    Georgia
  Norwood
  Proudly They Came
  True Grit

CAMPBELL, J. KENNETH
  Cyrano
CAMPBELL, JAMES
  My Fair Lady
CAMPBELL, JO ANN
  Go Johnny Go!
  Hey Let's Twist
CAMPBELL, MILLARD
  Lonesome Train
CAMPBELL, NORMAN
  Anne of Green Gables
CAMPBELL, PAUL
  Jerico-Jim Crow
CAMPBELL, SANDE
  Hark!
  Man with a Load of Mischief
CAMPBELL, TRISHA
  Really Rosie
CAMPBELL, VIC
  Boy Meets Boy
CAMPBERC, PATSY
  Pinocchio
CAMPI, RAY
  Teen-Age Cruisers
CAMPONE, MERV
  Bistro Car
  Jubalay
CANARY, JOHN
  Christy
CANDIDO, CANDY
  Peter Pan
CANDLES
  Doctor Goldfoot and the Girl
    Bombs
CANDY, JOHN
  Little Shop of Horrors
  Planes, Trains, and
    Automobiles
CANESTRARI, KENNETH
  My Fair Lady
CANNAN, PHYLLIS
  Thief of Bagdad
CANNED HEAT
  Chicken Chronicles
  1969
  Woodstock
CANNING, JAMES
  Grease
CANNON, ALICE
  Athenian Touch
  Man with a Load of Mischief
CANNON, DYAN
  Honeysuckle Rose
CANNON, GUS
  Blues
CANNON, JUDY
  Gypsy
CANO, EDDIE
  Cole Porter and Me
  Sound of Music
CANOVA, DIANA
  First Nudie Musical
CANOVA, JUDY
  Hooray for Hollywood
CANTOR, EDDIE
  Eddie Cantor at Carnegie Hall
  Eddie Cantor Story
  50th Anniversary of George
    Jessel In Show Business
  Hollywood Canteen
  Irving Berlin Tribute
  Legends of the Musical Stage
  Show Biz
  Whoopee!
  Ziegfeld Follies of 1919
CANTRELL, LANA
  England Made Me
CANTRIL, KEN
  Athenian Touch
CAPALDI, JIM
  Best of the Best
  True Love
CAPER, BRONISLAW
  Ballet Music from MGM
    Musicals
CAPERS, VIRGINIA
  Raisin
CAPITOLS
  More American Graffiti

CAPOTE, TRUMAN
  House of Flowers
CAPPELLO, TIM
  Lost Boys
CAPPS, AL
  Cannonball Run
  Guys and Dolls
  Sharky's Machine
  Smokey and the Bandit II
CAPTAIN BEEFHEART
  Blue Collar
CAPTAIN KANGAROO (Bob
    Keeshan)
  Age of Television
  Captain Kangaroo
CARA, IRENE
  All Dogs Go to Heaven
  City Heat
  D.C. Cab
  Fame
  Flashdance
  Me Nobody Knows
  Sparkle
  That's Dancing!
CARDER, TOM
  Joseph and the Amazing
    Technicolor Dreamcoat
CARDINALI, ROBERTO
  Bittersweet
CAREY, FRANK
  Don't Play Us Cheap
CAREY, HARRY, JR.
  Rio Grande
CAREY, MACDONALD
  Lady In the Dark
CAREY, MADELINE
  Gigi
CAREY, THOMAS
  Show Boat
CAREY, TONY
  Secret Admirer
CARGILL, IKE
  Soul to Soul
CARIOU, LEN
  Applause
  Dance a Little Closer
  Little Night Music
  Sweeney Todd (The Demon
    Barber of Fleet Street)
CARISI, JOHN
  Show Boat
CARL, MAX
  Lonely Guy
  Weird Science
CARLE, CYNTHIA
  Is There Life After High School?
CARLE, FRANKIE
  Gershwin Holiday
  New York Stories
  Take Me Along
CARLEEN, ELLEN
  Street Scene
CARLIN, GEORGE
  Magic Moments from the
    Tonight Show
CARLING, FRED
  Themes from Classic Science
    Fiction, Fantasy and Horror
    Films
  Themes from Horror Movies
CARLISLE, BELINDA
  Burglar
  License to Drive
  Out of Bounds
CARLISLE, ELSIE
  Pennies from Heaven
CARLISLE, KITTY
  Desert Song
  Hollywood Canteen
  Merry Widow
  Roberta
  Song of Norway
CARLISLE, THOMAS
  Brigadoon
CARLOS, WALTER
  Clockwork Orange
CARLOS, WENDY
  Shining
  Story of Tron
  Tron

CARLOUGH, ELIANA
  Dawgs
CARLSON, CLAUDINE
  Medium
CARLSON, RICHARD
  American Spirit
CARLTON, LARRY
  Against All Odds
  Scrooged
CARLTON, LESLIE
  Gigi
CARLYLE, LOUISE
  Gershwin Rarities
  Girl Crazy
CARMEL
  Letter to Brezhnev
  She-Devil
  She's Having a Baby
CARMICHAEL, BILL
  Forbidden Broadway
CARMICHAEL, CAROL
  Where's Poppa?
CARMICHAEL, HOAGY
  Anything Goes
  Bing's Hollywood
  Gentlemen Prefer Blondes
  Hatari
  Paper Moon
CARMICHAEL, RALPH
  Cross and the Switchblade
  For Pete's Sake
  Heart Is a Rebel
  His Land
  My Fair Lady
  Natural High
  Oil Town, U.S.A.
  Restless Ones
CARMICHAEL, STOKELY
  Tell Me Lies
CARMINES, AL
  Christmas Rappings
  Faggot
  In Circles
  Joan
  Peace
  Pomegranada
  Promenade
CARNE, JUDY
  Boy Friend
  On the Brighter Side
  Rowan and Martin's Laugh-In
CARNE, LILYAN
  Jimmy Durante TV Show
CARNES, KATHLEEN
  Annie Get Your Gun
CARNES, KIM
  Flashdance
  Heroes
  Rude Awakening
  That's Dancing!
CARNEY, ART
  Harry and Tonto
  It's Honeymooners Time
  Panama Hattie
CARNEY, GRACE
  Donnybrook!
CARNILIA, CRAIG
  Is There Life After High School?
CARNOVSKY, MORRIS
  Family Affair
CAROL, CLIFF
  Hard Part Begins
CAROL, LEE
  Oklahoma
CARON, LESLIE
  American In Paris
  Everything I Have Is Yours
  Gigi
  Lili
  Magnificent Moments from
    MGM Movies
  That's Entertainment!
  That's Entertainment, Part 2
  Very Best of Motion Picture
    Musicals
CAROTENUTO, MARIO
  My Fair Lady
CARPENTER, CARLETON
  Hold on to Your Hats
  Lady In the Dark
  Make Mine Manhattan

734

735

CAVALLARO, CARMEN
Eddy Duchin Story
King and I
Song Without End
CAVALLO, JIMMY
Rock, Rock, Rock
CAVANAUGH, PAGE
Tea for Two
CAVE, NICK
Ghosts of the Civil Dead
CAWTHORN, JOSEPH
Love Me Tonight
CAESAR, SID
Twenty-Five Years of Life
CEBALLOS, RENE
Cats
CEBERANO, KATE
She-Devil
CECIL, JOE
Joan
CECIL, JONATHAN
Cowardly Custard
CELI, ADOLFO
Thunderball
CELL BLOCK SEVEN
Rock Baby Rock It
CENTURYMEN
Proudly They Came
CERTAIN RATIO
Letter to Brezhnev
CERVENKA, JAN
Houdini, Man of Magic
Most Happy Fella
CERVERIS, MICHAEL
Tokyo Pop
CESARIO, GREG
Second Shepherd's Play
CETERA, PETER
Karate Kid II
Pretty Woman
CHABELI, ANDY
Ipi-Tombi
CHACKSFIELD, FRANK
Academy Award Hit Songs
Best of the New Film Themes
Broadway Melodies
Carousel
Foreign Film Festival
King and I
Movie Themes
On the Beach
Porgy and Bess
South Pacific
TV's Greatest Hits
CHAFITZ, SUSAN
Taking Off
CHAKIRIS, GEORGE
Choice Cuts
West Side Story
CHALBAUD, ESTEBAN
You Never Know
CHALIAPIN, FEODOR
Chaliapin As Boris
CHALK, AL
Feeling Good with Annie
CHAMBERLAIN, BRYCE
Order Is Love
CHAMBERLAIN, DEAN
Echo Park
CHAMBERLAIN, NEVILLE
Years to Remember
CHAMBERLAIN, RICHARD
Breakfast at Tiffany's
Hamlet
Man from U.N.C.L.E.
Parade of Hits
Slipper and the Rose
Twilight of Honor
CHAMBERS, RALPH
Call Me Madam
CHAMBERS BROTHERS
April Fools
He's My Girl
CHAMPION, GOWER
Lovely to Look At
Premiere
Show Boat
CHAMPION, MARGE
Lovely to Look At
Premiere

Show Boat
Three for the Show
CHAMPLIN, BILL
Miami Vice II
Sing
CHAMPLIN, TAMARA
Caddyshack II
CHAMPS
All American
CHAN, SAMMY
Thoroughly Modern Millie
CHANCE, TREVOR
Gold
CHANDLER, BEN
Creative Freakout
CHANDLER, CHRISTINE
Beowulf
CHANDLER, GENE
Dusty and Sweets McGee
CHANDLER, MILDRED
Anything Goes
CHANEY, JAN
O Say Can You See!
CHANEY, LON, JR.
Bird of Paradise
CHANG
52 Pick Up
Firewalker
CHANNEL, BRUCE
Dirty Dancing
Dusty and Sweets McGee
Slumber Party '57
CHANNING, CAROL
Archy and Mehitabel / Echoes
of Archy
Carol Channing
Gentlemen Prefer Blondes
Harper Valley P.T.A.
Hello Dolly!
Jerry's Girls
Lorelei
No for an Answer
Peter and the Wolf
Show Girl
Skidoo
This Is Broadway's Best
Thoroughly Modern Millie
Tubby the Tuba
CHANNING, STOCKARD
Grease
CHANTAYS
More American Graffiti
CHAPIN, JAMES FORBES
Passing Fair
CHAPLIN, CHARLIE
Chaplin Revue
Chaplin's Art of Comedy
Countess from Hong Kong
Hollywood
Modern Times
Silencers
CHAPLIN, CLIVE
Jerome Kern Goes to
Hollywood
CHAPLIN, SAUL
American In Paris
Bonanza Bound
Everything I Have Is Yours
Merry Andrew
Summer Stock
CHAPLIN, SYDNEY
Bells Are Ringing
Funny Girl
Subways Are for Sleeping
Wonderful Town
CHAPMAN, GRAHAM
Life of Brian
Monty Python and the Holy
Grail
CHAPMAN, SHIRLEY
Sound of Music
CHAPMAN, TOPSY
One Mo' Time
CHAPMAN, WILLIAM
Arabian Nights
Candide
Greenwillow
CHAPP-LIPP VOICES
Changes
CHAPARRAL BROTHERS
Last of the American Hoboes

CHAPPELL, EDDIE
Girl Crazy
CHARD, GEOFFREY
Camelot
CHARISSE, CYD
Charlie Girl
It's Always Fair Weather
Les Poupees De Paris
CHARISSE, ZAN
Gypsy
CHARLAP, MARK
Peter Pan
CHARLAP, MOOSE
Alice Through the Looking
Glass
Clownaround
Whoop-Up!
CHARLENE
Last Dragon
CHARLES, KEITH
Celebration
Colette
CHARLES, KIM
Spaceballs
CHARLES, MARIA
Boy Friend
CHARLES, PAMELA
Canterbury Tales
Water Gipsies
CHARLES, PAUL
Best Foot Forward
**CHARLES, RAY (not the
singer)**
Memories of a Middle-Aged
Movie Fan
CHARLES, RAY
Any Which Way You Can
Big Town
Blues Brothers
Cincinnati Kid
Cinema '76
Danger
Finian's Rainbow
Guys and Dolls
In the Heat of the Night
King of Comedy
Porgy and Bess
Roberta
Somebody Up There Likes Me
Twenty-Five Years of Life
Who's Harry Kellerman and
Why Is He Saying Those
Terrible Things About Me?
CHARLES, RAY, SINGERS
All-Star Salute, the Very Best of
Gershwin
At the Movies with the Ray
Charles Singers
Mr. President
CHARLES, VINCENT
Can-Can
CHARLES, WALTER
La Cage Aux Folles
CHARLES, ZACHARY
Top Banana
CHARLOTTE
Bei Mir Bistu Schoen
CHARMETTES
Shag
CHARNIN, MARTIN
Annie
Feathertop
I Remember Mama
Two By Two
Zenda
CHARTOFF, MELANIE
Love Song
CHAS AND DAVE
Party Party
CHASE
Crossover Dreams
CHASE, BARRIE
Another Evening with Fred
Astaire
Astaire Time
Evening with Fred Astaire
Three Evenings with Fred
Astaire
CHASE, CARRI
Heidi

CHASE, CHEVY
National Lampoon Lemmings
Saturday Night Live
Spies Like Us
Three Amigos
CHASE, ILKA
Cinderella
CHASTAIN, DON
Dance a Little Closer
It's a Bird, It's a Plane, It's
Superman
No Strings
CHATTAWAY, JAY
Invasion U.S.A.
Maniac
Red Scorpion
Silver Bullet
CHEAP TRICK
Caddyshack II
Heavy Metal
Over the Edge
Roadie
Spring Break
Top Gun
CHECKER, CHUBBY
Don't Knock the Twist
Let the Good Times Roll
Purple People Eater
She-Devil
CHEECH AND CHONG
Up In Smoke
CHEEKS
Up the Academy
CHEERY BOMB
Howard the Duck
CHEKHOV, ANTON
Uncle Vanya
CHELSI, LAWRENCE
Housewives' Cantata
CHELTENHAM ORCHESTRA
Goldfinger
Mary Poppins
CHER
Chastity
Days of Thunder
Roller Boogie
CHERRY, DON
Oh Captain!
Will Penny
CHERYL LYNN
Armed and Dangerous
Heavenly Bodies
CHESTER, ALAN
Bei Mir Bistu Schoen
CHESTERFIELDS
American Hot Wax
CHEVALIER, MAURICE
All-Star Salute, the Very Best of
Gershwin
Betty Boop
Black Tights
Breath of Scandal
Broadway, Broadway, Broadway
Can-Can
Command Performance
Gigi
In Search of the Castaways
Jessica
Love Me Tonight
Music from Disney Motion
Pictures
Pepe
Pure Gold Movies
Royal Affair
Stars of the Silver Screen,
1929-1930
Summer Magic
That's Entertainment!
That's Entertainment, Part 2
CHEYNE
Weird Science
CHIARAMELLO, GIANCARLO
Dino DeLaurentis Presents
Original Soundtracks
Stone Killer
CHIARI, WALTER
Gay Life
CHIC
Soup for One
CHICAGO
Days of Thunder

737

738

CUNNINGHAM, RONNIE
By Jupiter
CUNNINGHAM, ZAMAH
On Your Toes
CUOMO, BILL
That Was Then, This Is Now
CUPPLES, PETER, BAND
Pirate Movie
CURB, MIKE
Big Bounce
Born Losers
Bunny O'Hare
Devil's Angels
Devil's Eight
Dirty Dingus Magee
Glory Stompers
Golden Breed
Kelly's Heroes
Magic Garden of Stanley
Sweetheart
Mary Jane
Mondo Hollywood
Skatedater
Teenage Rebellion
Thunder Alley
Tick . . . Tick . . . Tick
Wild Angels
Wild In the Streets
Wuthering Heights
CURBSTONES
Kid Power
CURE
Lost Angels
Times Square
CURIO
Another 48 Hours
CURLESS, DICK
Killers Three
CURLEY, WILMA
I Can Get It for You Wholesale
CURNIN, CY
Better Off Dead
CURRAN, KEITH
Mayor
CURRERI, LEE
Fame
CURRIE, FINLAY
Quo Vadis?
Treasure Island
CURRY, JULIE VAN DE VORT
Best of Broadway 1973
CURRY, STEVE
Hair
I Can Get It for You Wholesale
CURRY, TIM
Annie
Rocky Horror Picture Show
Rocky Horror Show
CURTIAN, HOYT
Jonny Quest
CURTIN, JANE
Saturday Night Live
CURTIS, DONNA
Now Is the Time for All Good
Men
CURTIS, KEN
Rio Grande
Rothschilds
CURTIS, TONY
Insignificance
So This Is Paris
CURTIS-HALL, VONDIE
Lena Horne: The Lady and Her
Music
CUSACK, CYRIL
Taming of the Shrew
CUSHING, CARDINAL
John F. Kennedy
CUSHING, PETER
Legend of the Seven Golden
Vampires
CUTELL, LOU
Young Abe Lincoln
CUTLER, HOWARD
Beauty and the Beast
CUTLER, JESSE
Godspell
CUTNER, SID
Big Circus

CUTTS, PATRICIA
Kean
CYCLE V
Flashdance
Metropolis
CYPHER, JON
Cinderella
Coco
CYRKLE
Minx
D MOB
She-Devil
DB'S
I Was a Teenage Zombie
D.J.
License to Drive
D.K.
Purple People Eater
DRs
She's Having a Baby
DABDOUB, JACK
Coco
D'ABO, MIKE
Evita
Jesus Christ Superstar
DACUS, DON
Hair
DAFFODILS
Star
DAHL, ARLENE
Co-Star
Three Little Words
DAILEY, DAN
Choice Cuts
General Motors' 50th
Anniversary Show
It's Always Fair Weather
Shocking Miss Pilgrim
There's No Business Like Show
Business
25 Years of Recorded Sound
DAILEY, IRENE
Subject Was Roses
DAILY, E.G.
Better Off Dead
Summer School
DAILY, ELIZABETH
Breakfast Club
Scarface
DAINTZ, AMANDA
Girl Friend
DALBELLO
9½ Weeks
DALE, CLAMMA
Porgy and Bess
DALE, DICK
Back to the Beach
On Moonlight Bay
DALE, GROVER
Half a Sixpence
Sail Away
West Side Story
DALE, JIM
B.S. I Love You
Barnum
Card
Pete's Dragon
Shalako
DALE, VIRGINIA
Ship Ahoy
DALEY, CASS
Dick Tracy In BB
DALEY, JIMMY, AND THE
DING-A-LINGS
Rock Pretty Baby
Summer Love
DALLAS, LORNA
Show Boat
Words and Music
DALLMAN, JERRY
Hairspray
DALMES, MONY
Unsinkable Molly Brown
DALTON, DORIS
Seventeen
DALTON, WARNER
Student Prince

DALTREY, DAVID
Joseph and the Amazing
Technicolor Dreamcoat
DALTREY, ROGER
Lisztomania
Lost Boys
Mack the Knife
McVicar
Quadrophenia
Quicksilver
Secret of My Success
Tommy
DALY, CHARLES
Space Age: Age of Reliability
DALY, JAMES
J.B.
Showcase Album, 1967
DALY, TYNE
Gypsy
D'AMBOISE, CHARLOTTE
Jerome Robbins' Broadway
DAME, BEVERLY
Medium
DAME, DONALD
Blossom Time
New Moon
Red Mill
Student Prince
DAMIAN, MICHAEL
Dream a Little Dream
DAMNED
Miami Vice II
Return of the Living Dead
DAMON, CATHRYN
Boys from Syracuse
Flora the Red Menace
Foxy
Secret Life of Walter Mitty
DAMON, STUART
Boys from Syracuse
Charlie Girl
Do I Hear a Waltz?
Houdini, Man of Magic
Irma La Douce
DAMONE, VIC
Affair to Remember
All Star Color TV Revue
All-Star Parade, Hits from the
Movies
Arrivederci, Baby!
Athena
Choice Cuts
Dangerous Christmas of Red
Riding Hood
Deep In My Heart
Gift of Love
Hit the Deck
Jane Powell
Kismet
Magnificent Moments from
MGM Movies
Milton Berle Sings Rodgers and
Hart Songs
Oh Captain!
Parade of Show Stoppers
Rich, Young and Pretty
Stingiest Man In Town
Summer Place (And Other
Great Hits from the Movies)
Sunny Side of the Street
DANA, BILL
Flintstones
DANDOLO, GIUSI RASPANI
Ciao, Rudy
D'ANDREA, JOHN
Savage Streets
DANE, FAITH
Gypsy
DANE, JOHN
No, No, Nanette
DANEMAN, PAUL
Camelot
D'ANGELO, BEVERLY
Coal Miner's Daughter
Hair
Honky-Tonk Freeway
In the Mood
Say Amen, Somebody
D'ANGELO, EDDIE
Tinseltown

DANGERFIELD, RODNEY
Back to School
DANGEROUS GAMES
Courier
DANGEROUS TOYS
Shocker
DANGLER, ANITA
Coach with the Six Insides
Cyrano
DANIELS, ANTHONY
Empire Strikes Back
DANIELS, BEBE
Here Come the Girls
Stars of the Silver Screen,
1929-1930
DANIELS, BILLY
Golden Boy
Sunny Side of the Street
DANIELS, CHARLIE
Urban Cowboy
DANIELS, DAVID
Oh Kay!
Plain and Fancy
DANIELS, HALL
Greatest Science Fiction Hits
DANIELS, MAXINE
Show Boat
DANIELS, STAN
So Long 174th Street
DANIELS, WALKER
Hair
DANIELS, WILLIAM
On a Clear Day You Can See
Forever
1776
DANKS, INDIRA
Mother Earth
DANKWORTH, JOHN
All Night Long
Cleo Laine at Carnegie Hall
Cleo Laine Returns to Carnegie
Hall
Colette
Fathom
Film Music
Idol
Modesty Blaise
Movies 'N' Me
Salt and Pepper
DANLEERS
Slumber Party '57
DANN, ROGER
Sound of Music
DANNEMAN, DON
Minx
DANNER, BLYTHE
1776
DANNY AND THE JUNIORS
Christine
Let the Good Times Roll
DANO, ROYAL
Great Moments with Mr.
Lincoln
DANOFF, BILL
Sunshine
DANT, CHARLES "BUD"
Marx Brothers - Original Voice
Tracks from Their Greatest
Movies
D'ANTONAKIS, FLEURY
Do I Hear a Waltz?
DANZIG, GLEN
Less Than Zero
DARBY, KEN
Bing's Hollywood
Finian's Rainbow
Going My Way
Holiday Inn
How the West Was Won
Johnny Appleseed
Littlest Angel
Love Me Tender
Paper Moon
Pinocchio
River of No Return
South Pacific
Wyatt Earp
D'ARCY, MARY
Sondheim

DARCY, PATTI
Beehive
DARDEN, SEVERN
From the Second City
DARIAN, ANITA
King and I
Show Boat
Student Prince
DARIEUX, JACQUES
Gigi
DARIN, BOBBY
American Hot Wax
Big Town
Diner
Doctor Dolittle
Judy Garland
Lively Set
Pepe
Stardust
State Fair
Tequila Sunrise
DARING, MASON
Brother from Another Planet
Matewan
DARION, JOE
Archy and Mehitabel / Echoes
of Archy
Illya Darling
Man of La Mancha
Megilla of Itzig Manger
DARLING, EDWARD
Carmen Jones
DARLING, JEAN
Carousel
DARLING, JENNIFER
Mac Bird
Maggie Flynn
DARLING, JOAN
Premise
DARNELL, ROBERT
Young Abe Lincoln
DARREN, JAMES
Bye Bye Birdie
Gidget Goes Hawaiian
Hey There, It's Yogi Bear
Lively Set
Naked City
DARRGAVEL, BRUCE
Tales of Hoffmann
DARRIEUX, DANIELLE
Ambassador
Rich, Young and Pretty
Young Girls of Rochefort
DASILVA, HOWARD
Cradle Will Rock
Fiorello!
Oklahoma
1776
Showcase Album, 1967
Tevya and His Daughters
Zulu and the Zayda
DATCHER, IRENE
Guys and Dolls
DAUFMAN, CHARLES
Return to Paradise
DAVENPORT, HARRY
BROMLEY
Xtro
DAVENPORT, PEMBROKE
Arabian Nights
Hazel Flagg
I Had a Ball
Kean
Kiss Me Kate
Out of This World
Zenda
DAVERN, KENNY
Mardi Gras
DAVID AND JONATHAN
Modesty Blaise
DAVID, CLIFFORD
At Home Abroad
Band Wagon
Boys from Syracuse
Cradle Will Rock
On a Clear Day You Can See
Forever
1776
Wildcat
DAVID, DWIGHT
Last Dragon

DAVID, HAL
Brainchild
James Bond - 10th Anniversary
Kid Galahad
Lost Horizon
Moonraker
On the Flip Side
Promise Her Anything
Promises, Promises
Silencers
What's New Pussycat?
Wonderful to Be Young
DAVID, KEITH
Clues to a Life
DAVID, MACK
Alice In Wonderland
Cinderella
Double Impact
Hawaiian Eye
It's a Mad, Mad, Mad, Mad
World
Krakatoa, East of Java
77 Sunset Strip
Stooge
Taras Bulba
Way West
DAVID, MAX
Bourbon Street Beat
DAVID, RONNIE
Mame
DAVIDSON, JOHN
Academy Awards Presentation
Foxy
Happiest Millionaire
One and Only, Genuine,
Original Family Band
Prince and the Pauper
DAVIDSON, LENNY
Having a Wild Weekend
DAVIDSON, LORRAINE
Let My People Come
DAVIDSON, MICHAEL
Who's That Girl?
DAVIES, BRIAN
Funny Thing Happened on the
Way to the Forum
Gone with the Wind
Sound of Music
DAVIES, DILYS
Under Milk Wood
DAVIES, GAIL
Sylvester
DAVIES, GARETH
Ambassador
Cabaret
Camelot
Fiddler on the Roof
Half a Sixpence
Music Man
Sail Away
DAVIES, IRVING
Joyce Grenfell Requests the
Pleasure
Oklahoma
DAVIES, MORGAN
Carousel
DAVIES, PETER MAXWELL
Boy Friend
DAVIES, RAY
Absolute Beginners
Return to Waterloo
DAVIES, ROWLAND
Betjemania
DAVIES, TUDOR
Cowardly Custard
DAVIES, VICTOR
Beowulf
DAVILA, DIANA
Two Gentlemen of Verona
DAVIS, BENNY
Cotton Club Revue of 1958
Follow the Boys
DAVIS, BETTE
Hollywood Canteen
Two's Company
DAVIS, BUSTER
Best Foot Forward
Body In the Seine
Darling of the Day
Hallelujah, Baby!
Movie Movie

No, No, Nanette
DAVIS, CARL
Far Pavilions
French Lieutenant's Woman
Hollywood
Other World of Winston
Churchill
Scandal
DAVIS, CHARLES K.L.
Merry Widow
DAVIS, CHERRY
Damn Yankees
DAVIS, CLIFTON
How to Steal an Election (A
Dirty Politics Musical)
Official Grammy Awards
Archive Collection
Two Gentlemen of Verona
DAVIS, CORNELIA
Seven Dreams
DAVIS, DANIEL
Cleavage
DAVIS, DANNY, ORCHESTRA
Baker Street
James Bond
DAVIS, DON
Beauty and the Beast
DAVIS, ELLARD
My Cousin Josefa
DAVIS, FRED
Kiss Me Kate
DAVIS, JEANETTE
Arthur Godfrey
DAVIS, JESSE
Benji (the Story of Benji)
DAVIS, JIMMY
Nightmare on Elm Street 4 -
The Dream Master
Paper Moon
DAVIS, JOHNNY "Scat"
Hollywood Hotel
Hooray for Hollywood
DAVIS, LANIER
Tenderloin
DAVIS, LINDA
Best of Broadway 1973
DAVIS, LUC
Irma La Douce
DAVIS, MAC
Norwood
DAVIS, MARK
Seven Brides for Seven
Brothers
DAVIS, MARTHA
Golden Child
Made In Heaven
DAVIS, MARY
Hair
DAVIS, MAVIS VEGAS
Assault of the Killer Bimbos
Roller Boogie
Salsa
DAVIS, MEYER
Redhead
DAVIS, MICHAEL
All In Love
Promenade
Sweet Charity
DAVIS, MILES
Frantic
Jack Johnson
Jazz Track
Music from Siesta
Porgy and Bess
Scrooged
Siesta (Music From)
DAVIS, OSSIE
Ballad for Bimshire
Jamaica
Raisin In the Sun
Zulu and the Zayda
DAVIS, PAUL
About Last Night
Jesus Christ Superstar
Karate Kid
DAVIS, RAY
Tom Brown's School Days
DAVIS, SAMMY, JR.
Dean Martin Testimonial Dinner
Finian's Rainbow

Golden Boy
Guys and Dolls
Johnny Cool
Kiss Me Kate
Magic Moments from the
Tonight Show
Man Called Adam
Mister Wonderful
Of Love and Desire
Pepe
Porgy and Bess
Robin and the Seven Hoods
Salt and Pepper
Sammy
Save the Children
South Pacific
Stop the World - I Want to Get
Off!!
Sweet Charity
Three Billion Millionaires
Threepenny Opera
DAVIS, SAMMY, SR.
Sammy
DAVIS, SCOTT
Heart Is a Lonely Hunter
DAVIS, SHEILA KAY
Little Shop of Horrors
DAVIS, SPENCER, GROUP
Big Chill (More Songs from the
Original Soundtrack)
Buster
Here We Go Round the
Mulberry Bush
DAVIS, THOMAS M.
Music Man
My Fair Lady
DAVISON, BRUCE
Mame
DAWES, TOM
Minx
DAWN, DOLLY
Pennies from Heaven
DAWN, JULIE
Bittersweet
Desert Song
DAWS, ROBERT
Hollywood Party
DAWSON, FREDDY
A-5,6,7,8
DAWSON, MARK
Ankles Aweigh
High Button Shoes
Me and Juliet
New Girl In Town
Prettybelle
DAWSON, RICHARD
Hogan's Heroes
DAY, BOBBY
Purple People Eater
DAY, DENNIS
Johnny Appleseed
My Wild Irish Rose
DAY, DORIS
Academy Awards Presentation
Academy Award Winning Songs
All-Star Parade, Hits from the
Movies
Annie Get Your Gun
Beyond the Blue Horizon
By the Light of the Silvery Moon
Calamity Jane
50 Years of Film
Gershwins In Hollywood (1931-
1964)
I'll See You In My Dreams
Jumbo
Love Me Or Leave Me
Lover Come Back
Lullaby of Broadway
On Moonlight Bay
Pajama Game
Peter Pan
Pillow Talk
Starlift
Summer Place (And Other
Great Hits from the Movies)
Tea for Two
Young at Heart
Young Man with a Horn
DAY, EDITH
Desert Song
Irene

743

Rio Rita
Rose Marie
Sail Away
DAY, FRANCES
Rose Marie
DAY, JULIA
Boy Friend
DAYE, IRENE
Too Many Girls
DEACON, RICHARD
One and Only, Genuine,
Original Family Band
DEAD KENNEDYS
Lovedolls Superstar
DEAD ON
Shocker
DEAL, DENNIS
Make Mine Manhattan
Night Club Confidential
Rodgers and Hart Revisited
Too Many Girls
DEAN, BILL
Heartbreak Kid
DEAN, GERRI
Me Nobody Knows
DEAN, JAMES
50 Years of Film
James Dean Story
DEAN, LAURA
Doonesbury
DEAN, STEVE
Hair
DEANDA, PETER
Zulu and the Zayda
DEANE, DOUGLAS
Guys and Dolls
**DEANGELIS, GUIDO AND
MAURIZIO**
Welcome!
DEANGELIS, PETER
Devil In Miss Jones
DEARBORN, DALTON
Mac Bird
DEARIE, BLOSSOM
Ben Bagley's Ira Gershwin
Revisited
Ben Bagley's Oscar
Hammerstein Revisited
Painted Smiles of Cole Porter
Rodgers and Hart Revisited
DEASY, MIKE
Elvis (NBC-TV Special)
DEAUVILLE, RONNIE
Themes from the Movies
DE AZEVEDO, LEX
Against a Crooked Sky
My Turn on Earth
Order Is Love
Saturday's Warrior
Threads of Glory
DE AZEVEDO, RIC
Threads of Glory
DE BARGE
Last Dragon
DE BARGE, CHICO
Coming to America
Fine Mess
Police Academy IV - Citizens on
Patrol
DE BARGE, EL
Starlight Express
DEBS, EUGENE
Dean Martin Testimonial Dinner
DE BURGOS, RAFAEL
Excalibur
DECADENT DUB TEAM
Colors
DECAMP, ROSEMARY
Yankee Doodle Dandy
DECARLO, YVONNE
At Home with the Munsters
Follies
DECIMUS, GEORGE
Sweet Lies
DECK, ROBIN
Among Friends - Waa-Mu Show
of 1960
DECOPTEAUX, BERT
Time Changes

DE CORDOBA, PEDRO
Count of Monte Cristo
DE CORDOVA, ARTURO
New Orleans
DECORMIER, ROBERT
Happiest Girl In the World
Sing for Your Supper
DEDHAM CHORAL SOCIETY
Christmas Sing with Bing
DEE, BOBBY
Far Out Man
DEE, DARRELL
Mondo Hollywood
DEE, GINI
Mame
DEE, JOEY
Coupe De Ville
Hey Let's Twist
Two Tickets to Paris
DEE, KIKI
Stir Crazy
DEE, RUBY
Black Girl
Raisin In the Sun
DEE, SANDRA
Snow Queen
South Pacific
DEEL, SANDRA
Look Ma I'm Dancin'!
Louisiana Purchase
DE EMILE, ANTONIO
Rush to Judgment
DEEMS, MICKEY
Anything Goes
Little Me
DEEP RIVER BOYS
Finian's Rainbow
DEERING, OLIVE
No for an Answer
DEES, BILL
Fastest Guitar Alive
DEES, MICHAEL
Day of the Locust
Happy Ending
DEES, RICK
Meatballs
DEES, WILLIAM
Pretty Woman
DEFAYE, JEAN-MICHEL
L'Etoile Du Nord
DE FRANCO, BUDDY
Broadway Showcase
Sharky's Machine
DE FRECE, LAURI
Maid of the Mountains
DEGAN, HAROLD A.
Live and Let Die
DE GROOT, MYRA
Oliver!
Pieces of Eight
DEGUZMAN, JOSSIE
Carmelina
Runaways
DE HAVEN, GLORIA
De Haven In Hollywood
Rodgers and Hart Revisited
Seventh Heaven
So This Is Paris
Summer Stock
Thousands Cheer
Three Little Words
DEHAVEN, PENNY
Bronco Billy
DE HAVILLAND, OLIVIA
Strawberry Blond
DEITZ, HOWARD
Band Wagon
DEJESUS, LUCHI
Adios Amigo
Begatting of the President
Sallah
DEJOHNETTE, JACK
Zebra
DEKKER, DESMOND
Drugstore Cowboy
Harder They Come
DE KOVEN-SMITH
Robin Hood

DELANEY, DANA
Liberty
DELANEY AND BONNIE
Catch My Soul
Medicine Ball Caravan
Vanishing Point
DELAPENHA, DENISE
Doctor Selavy's Magic Theater
DELAURENTIS, SEMINA
Nunsense
DELEON, W.
They Called It an Accident
DELERUE, GEORGES
Agnes of God
Almost Perfect Affair
Anne of the Thousand Days
Black Stallion Returns
Classic Miklos Rozsa Film
Themes
Confidentially Yours
Crimes of the Heart
Day of the Dolphin
Film Music from France
Heartbreak Hotel
Horsemen
Interlude
King of Hearts
Last Metro
Little Romance
Man for All Seasons
Our Mother's House
Platoon (And Songs from the
Era)
Promise at Dawn
Salvador
Shoot the Piano Player
Silkwood
Steel Magnolias
Summer Story
True Confessions
25th Hour
Viva Maria!
Walk with Love and Death
Woman Next Door
DEL FUEGOS
I Was a Teenage Zombie
DELIBES, LÉO
Carnegie Hall
DELIGHTS
American Hot Wax
DELITTLE, JOHNNY
Knack (And How to Get It)
DELL, GABRIEL
Ankles Aweigh
Anyone Can Whistle
DELL ORSO, EDDA
Once Upon a Time In America
DELLA CASA, LISA
Merry Widow
DELLA CHIESA, VIVIENNE
Musical Comedy and Operetta
Favorites, Vol 2
DELL'ISOLA, SALVATORE
Allegro
Ankles Aweigh
Flower Drum Song
Me and Juliet
On Your Toes
Pipe Dream
South Pacific
DELLO JOIO, NORMAN
Air Power
DEL-LORDS
About Last Night
Under the Boardwalk
DELLS
Cometogether
DELMAR, ELAINE
Cowardly Custard
Jerome Kern Goes to
Hollywood
DELMAR, KENNY
Texas Li'l Darlin'
DEL MONTE, GEORGE
Irma La Douce
DELON, JACK
Ballad of Baby Doe
Body Beautiful
Carousel
Family Affair
Jennie

Most Happy Fella
DELORY, AL
Norwood
Out of Sight
True Grit
DE LOS RIOS, WALDO
Great Movie Themes of Our
Times
DELPH, PAUL
No Small Affair
DEL PRETE, DUILIO
At Long Last Love
DEL RIO, DOLORES
Bird of Paradise
Stars of the Silver Screen,
1929-1930
Wonder Bar
DELSON, MARY
Doctor Selavy's Magic Theater
DELTA RHYTHM BOYS
Rain Man
Yolanda and the Thief / You'll
Never Get Rich
DELUCA, DEBRA
Aladd
DELUCE, VIRGINIA
New Faces of 1952
**DELUGG, ANNE AND
MILTON**
Big Bad Wolf
Bremen Town Musicians
Gulliver's Travels Beyond the
Moon
Gypsy Girl
Hansel and Gretel
Snow White and Rose Red
Snow White and the Seven
Dwarfs
DELUGG, MILTON
Man from U.N.C.L.E.
DELUISE, DOM
All In Love
American Tail
Best Little Whorehouse In
Texas
Half Past Wednesday
Who's Harry Kellerman and
Why Is He Saying Those
Terrible Things About Me?
World's Greatest Lover
DELVALLE, PETER
Lovers
DEL-VIKINGS
American Graffiti
Blue Iguana
Diner
Hometown U.S.A.
Stand By Me
DELYLE, LUCIENNE
Last Metro
DELYON, LEO
Top Cat
DEMAIN, JOHN
Nefertiti
Porgy and Bess
DE MARCO, TONY
Gang's All Here
DEMAS, CAROLE
Grease
How to Steal an Election (A
Dirty Politics Musical)
DEMASI, FRANCESCO
Lone Wolf McQuade
Making the Grade
DEMENDEZ, DORIS
Billy Noname
DEMETRIUS, CLAUDE
Jamboree!
DEMILLE, CECIL B.
Lost Horizon
DEMPSEY, MARK
Oh! Calcutta!
DEMY, JACQUES
Umbrellas of Cherbourg
(Parapluies De Cherbourg)
DENAUT, JUD
Pete Kelly's Blues
DENCH, JUDI
Cabaret

DENEUVE, CATHERINE
April Fools
Love Songs
DE NIRO, ROBERT
New York, New York
Taxi Driver
DENISE, GITA
Little Mary Sunshine
DENNEN, BARRY
Cabaret
Jesus Christ Superstar
DENNIS, CLARK
Finian's Rainbow
Pal Joey
DENNIS, ROBERT
Oh! Calcutta!
DENNIS, RONALD
Chorus Line
DENNIS, SANDY
Who's Afraid of Virginia Woolf?
DENNY, MARTIN
Hawaii
Mondo Cane
DENNY, SANDY
Fox and the Hound
Tommy
DENTON, RICHARD WILLING
Loot
DENVER, JOHN
Fire and Ice
Sunshine
DEODATO, EUMIR
Gentle Rain
DEORELLANA, I.A.
Tip Toes
DEPARIS, WILBUR
New York Stories
DE PAUL, GENE
Alice In Wonderland
Eddy Duchin Story
Li'l Abner
Seven Brides for Seven Brothers
DEPAUR, LEONARD
Sing for Your Supper
DEPECHE MODE
Bright Lights, Big City
Earth Girls Are Easy
Modern Girls
Summer Lovers
DERAY, JACQUES
Borsalino
DEREK AND RAY
Cinema Scene Today
DERENINKO, RON
Celebration
DEROUBAIX, FRANÇOIS
Zita
DERR, EMILY
Medium
DERR, RICHARD
Plain and Fancy
DERRICKS, CLEAVANT
Dream Girls
DERRINGER, RICK
Air America
Where the Boys Are '84
Zapped
DES BARRES, MICHAEL
Night In Heaven
DES FONTAINES, LAMONTE
Seesaw
DESAI, ASHIT
Gandhi
DESAI, PARASHER
Gandhi
DE SAL, FRANK
Zorba
DESALVO, KATHY
Aladd
DESERT ROSE BAND
Teen Wolf Too
DESHANNON, JACKIE
C'mon, Let's Live a Little
Chicken Chronicles
Drugstore Cowboy
Surf Party
Together

DESHIELDS, ANDRE
Ain't Misbehavin'
Wiz
DESICA, MANUEL
Garden of the Finzi-Continis
DESIO, ALFRED
Donnybrook!
Kean
DESMOND, JOHNNY
Call Me Madam
Gentlemen Marry Brunettes
Rodgers and Hart Revisited
Say Darling
Stingiest Man In Town
Too Many Girls
DESMOND, TRUDY
What's a Nice Country Like the U.S. Doing In a State Like This?
DESMONDE, JERRY
Where's Charley?
DESOUZA, RAUL
Hitter
DESPO
Illya Darling
DESYKES, STEPHANIE
Stormy Monday
DESYLVA, BUDDY
American In Paris
Best Things In Life Are Free
Good News
S'wonderful, S'marvelous, S'Gershwin
Singing Fool
DETEMPLE, MIKE
Last of the American Hoboes
DETROIT SYMPHONY ORCHESTRA
Naked Carmen
DEUTSCH, ADOLPH
Annie Get Your Gun
Apartment
Ballet Music from MGM Musicals
Band Wagon
Belle of New York
Deep In My Heart
Funny Face
Girls...And More Girls
Les Girls
Magnificent Moments from MGM Movies
Pagan Love Song
Seven Brides for Seven Brothers
Show Boat
Some Like It Hot
Torch Song
Very Best of Motion Picture Musicals
DEUTSCH, EMERY
Fiddler on the Roof
DEUTSCH, HELEN
Jack and the Beanstalk
DEVANE, WILLIAM
Mac Bird
DEVEREAUX, STEVE
Seven Brides for Seven Brothers
DEVILLE, WILLY
Cruising
Princess Bride
DEVILS
Trouble with Angels
DEVINE, ANDY
Robin Hood
Spotlight on Wild Bill Hickock
DEVINE, LORETTA
Dream Girls
DEVITO, JOE
Virgin
DEVITO, KAREN
Piano Bar
DEVITO, KARLA
Breakfast Club
DEVO
Doctor Detroit
Fright Night
Heavy Metal
9½ Weeks
Rock 'N' Roll High School

Tapeheads
Urgh - A Music War
DE VOL, FRANK
Choirboys
Dirty Dozen
Golden Motion Picture Themes and Original Soundtracks
Guess Who's Coming to Dinner?
Happening
Houseboat
Jazz Singer
Krakatoa, East of Java
McLintock!
Murder Inc.
Night with Rudolf Friml
Porgy and Bess
DE VOL, JEAN
Gigi
DEVON, LORRAINE
Nobody's Perfect
DEVORE, JESSE
Believers
DEVORZON, BARRY
Bless the Beasts and Children
Dillinger
R.P.M.
Warriors
Young and the Restless
DEVRIES, HUGO
Around the World In 80 Days
DEVUONO, PAT
Close Encounters of the Third Kind
DEWHURST, COLLEEN
Showcase Album, 1967
DEWITT, DIANA
Night of the Comet
DEWITT, FAYE
Flahooley
Night Club Confidential
Oklahoma
Shoestring Revue '57
Shoestring Revues
Show Boat
DEWITT, JOYCE
Olympus on My Mind
DEWOLFE, BILLY
Frosty the Snowman
How to Succeed In Business Without Really Trying
DEXTER, VAN
Coach with the Six Insides
This Is Your Life
DEY, ALOK
Shakespeare Wallah
DEYOUNG, CLIFF
Sunshine
DE YOUNG, DENNIS
Karate Kid II
DEZINA, KATE
Duel
D'HONAU, LILLIAN
Li'l Abner
D'HONAU, MARILYN
King of Hearts
DIABOLICAL
Penitentiary III
DIAMOND, JACK
Kiss Me Kate
DIAMOND, NEIL
Cactus Flower
Jazz Singer
Jonathan Livingston Seagull
Last Waltz
DIAMOND HEAD BEACHCOMBERS
Diamond Head
DIAMONDS
Loveless
DIBBLE, MEL
Billy Sunday
DICK AND DEE DEE
Wild, Wild Winter
DICKENSON, MERIEL
My Fair Lady
DICKERSON, WALT
Impressions of - A Patch of Blue
DICKEY, ANNAMARY
Allegro

DICKIE, WILLIAM
Most Happy Fella
DICKINSON, BRUCE
Nightmare on Elm Street 5 - The Dream Child
DICKINSON, HAL
Rock Pretty Baby
DICKINSON, JIM
Border
DICKSON, BARBARA
Blood Brothers
Evita
DICKSON, BETTINA
Anne of Green Gables
DICKSON, DOROTHY
Sally
Tip Toes
DICOLA, VINCE
Rocky IV
Transformers - The Movie
DICRESCENZO, LOUIS
Do Black Patent Leather Shoes Really Reflect Up?
DIDDLEY, BO
Don't Knock the Twist
Fritz the Cat
La Bamba
Let the Good Times Roll
Stealing Home
Tapeheads
DIENER, JOAN
Cry for Us All
Kismet
Man of La Mancha
DIERKING, SHARON
Walking Happy
DIETRICH, DENA
Cindy
DIETRICH, JOHN
Dearest Enemy
DIETRICH, MARLENE
Schoner Gigolo - Armer Gigolo (Just a Gigolo)
DIETZ, HOWARD
At Home Abroad
Band Wagon
Evening with Beatrice Lillie
Four Television Musicals
Gay Life
Inside U.S.A.
Jennie
Thirty Minutes with Beatrice Lillie
DIGERLANDO, MARIA
Saint of Bleecker Street
DIGNAN, MARK
Macbeth
DIKKER, LOEK
Fourth Man
Pascali's Island
DILLARD, BILL
Passing Fair
DILLARD, DOUG
Popeye
Vanishing Point
DILLER, PHYLLIS
Mad Monster Party
DILLON, MELINDA
Paul Sills' Story Theater (of Magical Folk-Rock Fables)
Who's Afraid of Virginia Woolf?
DILWORTH, GORDON
My Fair Lady
Walking Happy
DILWORTH, HUBERT
Bloomer Girl
DILWORTH, HUGO
Jamaica
DI NAPOLI, MIKE
Flying Down to Rio
DINNING, MARK
American Graffiti
Hootenanny Hoot
DINO, RALPH
Viva Max!
DINO, DESI, AND BILLY
Follow Me
DINROE, DOROTHY
Believers

745

DIO
Iron Eagle
Vision Quest
DION
Adventures of Ford Fairlane
Coupe De Ville
Flamingo Kid
Pink Cadillac
Wanderers
DION AND THE BELMONTS
Christine
Diner
Hometown U.S.A.
Peggy Sue Got Married
DIPASQUALE, JAMES
Fast Break
DIRE STRAITS
Officer and a Gentleman
DIRGE
Blue Iguana
**DIRKSEN, SENATOR
EVERETT McKINLEY**
Gallant Men
DIRTY LOOKS
Johnny Be Good
DISHY, BOB
By Jupiter
Flora the Red Menace
DISNEY CAST
Cinderella
Country Cousin
Peter Pan
DISTANCE
Burglar
DISTEL, SACHA
Gigi
DI TOSTI, BEN
Carnival
DITSCH, JAMES
Captain Jinks of the Horse
Marines
DITTMAN, DEAN
Cradle Will Rock
DIVINE HORSEMEN
Border Radio
DIVINYLS
Nightmare on Elm Street 4 -
The Dream Master
DIX, WILLIAM
Doctor Dolittle
DIXIE CUPS
Big Easy
Full Metal Jacket
Girl Groups: The Story of a
Sound
DIXON, BOB
Redhead
DIXON, EDDY
Loveless
DIXON, GALE
Coco
DIXON, IVAN
Hogan's Heroes
DIXON, LEE
Oklahoma
DIXON, MACINTYRE
Mad Show
Over Here!
DIXON, MORT
Hooray for Hollywood
DIXON, WILLIE
Color of Money
DOBKIN, DEBRA
Streetcar Named Desire
DOBKIN, LAWRENCE
Hall of Presidents
DOBSON, ANITA
Budgie
DOBSON, BONNIE
Movin' On
DOCKER, ROBERT
Salad Days
DODD, CAL
Rockabye Hamlet
DODD, JIMMIE
Mickey and the Beanstalk
Perri
Peter Pan

Walt Disney's Mickey Mouse
Club
Zorro
DODD, RORY
Rockabye Hamlet
DODDS, MALCOLM
Annie Get Your Gun
Elmer Gantry
DODDS, MARCUS
Billion Dollar Brain
Dark Crystal
Far from the Madding Crowd
Goodbye Gemini
Lady Caroline Lamb
Life of Brian
Murder on the Orient Express
Nicholas and Alexandra
Stevie
Watership Down
Yanks
DODGE, JERRY
George M!
Hello Dolly!
Sap of Life
DODGERS, WILLESDEN
Jewel of the Nile
DODIMEAD, DAVID
Christmas Carol
DODS, MARCUS
Good Companions
Oliver!
Pickwick
DODSON, JACK
Hughie
DOE, JOHN
Border Radio
DOENGES, MARION
Harvey Girls
DOGGETT, ALAN
Jesus Christ Superstar
Joseph and the Amazing
Technicolor Dreamcoat
Odessa File
DOGGETT, NORMA
By Jupiter
DOHERTY, LINDY
Top Banana
DOKKEN, DON
Far Out Man
DOLAN, ROBERT EMMETT
Aladdin
Coco
Foxy
Juno
Texas Li'l Darlin'
Valiant Years
DOLBY, THOMAS
Gothic
DOLBY'S CUBE
Howard the Duck
DOLDINGER, KLAUS
Das Boot (the Boat)
Hello Dolly!
DOLENZ, MICKY
Head
Point
Stardust
DOLIN, ANDREA
Curtain Going Up (Musical
Guide to Play Acting)
DOLPHIN, ROBERT
Ballad for Bimshire
DOMINGO, EDDIE
Dingaka
DOMINGO, PLACIDO
Christopher Columbus
My Fair Lady
Sixteen Days of Glory (1984
Summer Olympics)
DOMINGUEZ, ALBERT
Last Embrace
DOMINO, FATS
American Graffiti
Any Which Way You Can
Blaze
Diner
Girl Can't Help It!
Jamboree!
Let the Good Times Roll
DOMVILLE, JAMES
My Fur Lady

DONAGGIO, PINO
Carrie
Crawlspace
Don't Look Now
Dressed to Kill
Hercules
Home Movies
Howling
Outre La Porta
Piranha
Tourist Trap
DONAHUE, JOHN
Postcard from Morocco
DONAHUE, MARC
Wild Geese
DONAHUE, SAM
Hello, Dolly!
DONAHUE, TROY
Palm Springs Weekend
DONAHUE, VINCENT
Cyrano De Bergerac
DONAHUE, WALTER
Oklahoma
DONALD, MARK
Passing Fair
DONALDSON, NORMA
Guys and Dolls
DONALDSON, TED
Hansel and Gretel
DONALDSON, WALTER
Eddie Cantor Story
Love Me Or Leave Me
DONAT, PETER
Hindenberg
DONAT, ROBERT
Inn of the Sixth Happiness
DONATH, LUDWIG
She Loves Me
DONCH, KARL
Merry Widow
DONIZETTI, GAETANO
Melba
DONLEVY, BRIAN
How to Stuff a Wild Bikini
DONN, STEVE
Breakin' 2 - Electric Boogaloo
DONNE, RICHARD
Downriver
DONNELLY, DOROTHY
Blossom Time
Merry Widow
Student Prince
DONNELLY, JAMIE
George M!
Rocky Horror Show
DONOVAN
More American Graffiti
DONOVAN, ALOYSIUS
Kiss Me Kate
DOOBIE BROTHERS
FM
DOOLEY, PAUL
Threepenny Opera
DOOLEY, TOM
Portrait of a Splendid American
DOONAN, PAT
Macbeth
DOORS
American Pop
Apocalypse Now
Platoon (And Songs from the
Era)
DORAN, ANN
James Dean Story
**DO-RE-MI CHILDREN'S
CHORUS**
Mary Poppins
DORFF, STEVE
Any Which Way You Can
Bronco Billy
Every Which Way But Loose
Growing Pains
Honkytonk Man
Rustler's Rhapsody
DORIAN, CAROL
Evening with Jerry Herman
DORNING, ROBERT
Great Waltz

DORS, DIANA
Va Va Voom! Screen Sirens
Sing!
D'ORSAY, FIFI
Follies
DORSEY, JIMMY
Bing's Hollywood
Fleet's In
Four Jills In a Jeep
Rhythm on the Range
Waikiki Wedding
DORSEY, LEE
American Graffiti
Wanderers
DORSEY, TOMMY
Band Wagon
Big Broadcast of 1936
Irving Berlin Tribute
Paper Moon
Radio Days
Ship Ahoy
Show Biz (From Vaude to Video)
Song Is Born
DORSEY ORCHESTRA
Hello Dolly!
D'ORSO, WISA
Mr. President
DOTRICE, KAREN
Mary Poppins
DOTRICE, ROY
Tom Brown's School Days
DOUBLE YELLOW LINE
Roadie
DOUBLEDAY, ELIZABETH
Student Prince
DOUCET, MICHAEL
Belizaire the Cajun
DOUG AND SLUGS
Iron Eagle II
DOUG E. FRESH
Ghostbusters II
DOUGALL, BERNARD
Jerome Kern Goes to
Hollywood
DOUGHER, CATHY
Josie and the Pussycats
DOUGLAS, CAROL
Haunted
DOUGLAS, DONNA
Beverly Hillbillies
DOUGLAS, FREDDIE
MacKenna's Gold
DOUGLAS, HUGH
Hindenberg
DOUGLAS, JOHNNY
Darling Lili
Living Free
Pure Gold Movies
Railway Children
DOUGLAS, LARRY
Annie Get Your Gun
King and I
Thousand Miles of Mountains
DOUGLAS, LEW
Themes from Motion Pictures
and TV
DOUGLAS, MELVYN
Great American Fourth of July
Parade
Juno
DOUGLAS, MICHAEL
Chorus Line
DOUGLAS, NORMA
Hear! Hear!
DOUGLAS, PAUL
Jimmy Durante TV Show
DOUGLAS, ROSS
Bistro Car
DOUGLASS, BILL
Around the World In 80 Days
DOUGLASS, STEPHEN
Carousel
Cat and the Fiddle
Damn Yankees
Golden Apple
Make a Wish
110 In the Shade
Roberta
Show Boat

748

ELECTRIC MOOG ORCHESTRA
Star Wars
ELECTRIC PRUNES
Easy Rider
ELECTRONIC CONCEPT ORCHESTRA
Cinemoog
ELEFANTE
St. Elmo's Fire
ELEGANTS
American Hot Wax
ELEMENTS
Blown Away
ELEPHANT'S MEMORY
Midnight Cowboy
ELFERS, KONRAD
Funeral in Berlin
ELFMAN, DANNY
Batman
Beetlejuice
Beverly Hills Cop
Big Top Pee-Wee
Clive Barker's Night Breed
Danny Elfman: Music for a Darkened Theatre
Darkman
Forbidden Zone
Midnight Run
New Breed
Pee Wee's Big Adventure
Screen Themes
Summer School
Teen Wolf Too
Wisdom
ELG, TAINA
Les Girls
Nine
Utter Glory of Morrissey Hall
ELGAR, SIR EDWARD
Clockwork Orange
ELGART, LARRY
All-Star Salute, the Very Best of Gershwin
ELGART, LES
All American
Most Happy Fella
ELGEN, ERIKA
Clockwork Orange
ELIAS, ARIE
Kazablan
ELIAS, JONATHAN
Children of the Corn
Tuff Turf
Vamp
ELIAS, MICHAEL
Pomegranada
ELIAS, ROSALIND
Vanessa
ELIAS, TOM
Cleavage
ELIASON, ELLY
Carousel
ELIS, ELIZABETH
Survival of St. Joan
ELKIND, RACHEL
Clockwork Orange
Shining
ELKINS, FLORA
Prince and the Pauper
ELLEN, SANDY
Drat! the Cat!
ELLEN, SUSAN
Gigi
ELLENHORN, MAURICE
Mood Music of the Silent Movies
ELLIMAN, YVONNE
Jesus Christ Superstar
Moment By Moment
Roadie
Saturday Night Fever
War Games
ELLINGTON, DUKE
All American
All-Star Parade, Hits from the Movies
Anatomy of a Murder
Beggar's Holiday
Blackbirds of 1928

Cabin In the Sky
Fabulous Baker Boys
Mary Poppins
My People
Paris Blues
Porgy and Bess
Radio Days
Sophisticated Ladies
Summer Place (And Other Great Hits from the Movies)
ELLINGTON, MERCEDES
Sophisticated Ladies
ELLINGTON, RAY
Porgy and Bess
ELLIOT, BOB
Bob and Ray - The Two and Only
ELLIOT, DON, VOICES
Dollars ($)
Walk Don't Run
ELLIOT, VICTORIA
Song of Norway
ELLIOTT, DEAN
College Confidential
Playgirls
ELLIOTT, DENHOLM
Raiders of the Lost Ark
ELLIOTT, DON
Thurber Carnival
ELLIOTT, JACK
Banjoman
Blade Runner
Carousel
Great Movie Hits of the Forties
Happiest Millionaire
Kiss Me Kate
Oklahoma
One and Only, Genuine, Original Family Band
T.R. Baskin
Where's Poppa?
ELLIOTT, PATRICIA
Little Night Music
ELLIOTT, SHAWN
City of Angels
Jacques Brel Is Alive and Well and Living In Paris
ELLIS, ANITA
Belle of New York
Flower Drum Song
Gentlemen Marry Brunettes
Rita Hayworth
Three Little Words
ELLIS, ANTONIA
Boy Friend
ELLIS, BARBARA
Touch
ELLIS, CAROLINE
Bugaloos
ELLIS, CHRIS
Valentino
ELLIS, MARK
Dino
ELLIS, MARY
After the Ball
Dancing Years
ELLIS, MAURICE
Seventeen
ELLIS, RAY
Gigi
How to Succeed In Business Without Really Trying
James Bond
La Dolce Vita
Peter Gunn
Sweet Sixteen
Three Billion Millionaires
ELLIS, ROB
Godspell
ELLIS, SCOTT
Musical Chairs
ELLIS, SHEILA
Your Arm's Too Short to Box with God
ELLIS, STEVE
Loot
ELLIS, VIVIAN
Mr. Cinders
Water Gipsies
ELLIS, WILLIAM
Dames at Sea

ELLISON, JAMES
Gang's All Here
ELLISON, LORRAINE
Landlord
ELLSASSER, RICHARD
Hollywood Hits By Nacio Herb Brown
Movie Hits By Bronislau Kaper
EL MALAKH, KAMAL
Story of Tutankhamen
ELMER, JIM
Christy
ELMORE, STEVE
Company
Dames at Sea
Piano Bar
ELMSLIE, KENWARD
Grass Harp
Lola
Miss Julie
Sweet Bye and Bye
ELSTON, ROBERT
Spoon River Anthology
ELSY, BARBARA
Porgy and Bess
ELY, JOE, BAND
Roadie
ELY, PAUL
Music Man
ELY, RON
Tarzan and the Eyes of the Lion
EMERSON, FAITH
Evening with William Shakespeare
EMERSON, HOPE
Street Scene
EMERSON, KEITH
Nighthawks
EMERY, RICK
Musical Chairs
EMGE, DAVID
Dawn of the Dead
EMIL, MICHAEL
Insignificance
EMMANUEL, IVOR
Show Boat
Time for Singing
EMNEY, JOAN
Pajama Game
EMOTIONS
Roller Boogie
Skatetown U.S.A.
Wattstax (the Living Word)
ENFORCERS
Sudden Impact
ENDERSBY, CLIVE
Bye Bye Birdie
ENGEL, LEHMAN
Anything Goes
Babes In Arms
Bajour
Band Wagon
Blackbirds of 1928
Bonanza Bound
Boys from Syracuse
Bremen Town Musicians
Brigadoon
Call Me Mister
Carousel
Cat and the Fiddle
Chocolate Soldier
Consul
Conversation Piece
Desert Song
Destry Rides Again
Do Re Mi
Fanny
Girl Crazy
Goldilocks
I Can Get It for You Wholesale
Jamaica
Jumbo
King and I
Lady In the Dark
Li'l Abner
Merry Widow
Oh Kay!
Oklahoma
On Your Toes
Pal Joey
Porgy and Bess

Roberta
Rose Marie
Show Boat
Song of Norway
Student Prince
Take Me Along
What Makes Sammy Run?
Wonderful Town
ENGEMANN, PAUL
My Turn on Earth
Scarface
Summer School
ENGEMANN, SHAWN
My Turn on Earth
Saturday's Warrior
ENGLISH, ANNA
Simply Heavenly
ENGLISH, CAMERON
Chorus Line
ENGLISH, RALNA
Changes
ENGLISH BEAT
Dance Craze
Night In Heaven
ENGLISH CHAMBER CHOIR
Journey to the Center of the Earth
ENGLISH OPERA GROUP ENSEMBLE
Facade
ENGLISH ROCK ENSEMBLE
Lisztomania
ENNIS, ETHEL
Mad Monster Party
ENO, BRIAN
Married to the Mob
Rock 'N' Roll High School
ENRIGHT, RAY
Twenty Million Sweethearts
ENSTAD, LUTHER
Elephant Steps
ENTEN, BONI
Earl of Ruston
Oh! Calcutta!
Rocky Horror Show
Salvation
ENTWHISTLE, JOHN
Kids Are Alright
McVicar
Quadrophenia
Tommy
EPPERSON, DON
Albert Peckingpaw's Revenge
Wild Wheels
EPSTEIN, ALVIN
No Strings
EQUILUZ, KURT
Merry Widow
ERCOLE, JOE
Ka-Boom!
ERCOLI, LINDA
Snoopy Come Home
ERDMAN, JEAN
Coach with the Six Insides
ERDMANN, RICHARD
Wonderful O
ERIC B.
Colors
ERIC, LARS
Turn On, Tune In, Drop Out
ERIC, MARK
Angels Die Hard
ERICKSEN, EDDIE
Donnybrook!
ERICKSON, ROKY
Return of the Living Dead
ERICSON, JUNE
Flower Drum Song
ERNEST, INGRID
Hello Dolly!
ERROL, LEON
Higher and Higher
ERVIN, DEE
Mother Earth
ERWIN, BARBARA
Annie
ERWIN, DENISE
Selma

ERWIN, STUART
Everybody Sing
ERWIN, TRUDY
Bing's Hollywood
Blue Skies
Merry Widow
Rodgers and Hart In Hollywood
Yolanda and the Thief / You'll Never Get Rich
ESCAPADES
Armed and Dangerous
ESCAPE CLUB
Wonder Years
ESKEW, JACK
Banana Splits
ESPOSITO, GIANCARLO
Seesaw
ESPOSITO, JOE
Coming to America
Flashdance
Karate Kid
ESSEX, DAVID
All This and World War II
Evita
Stardust
War of the Worlds
ESSLER, FRED
Great Waltz
ESTES, SIMON
King, a Musical Testimony
ESTES, SLEEPY JOHN
Blues
ESTEY, CAROL
Do Black Patent Leather Shoes Really Reflect Up?
ESTLEY, SUELLEN
Bathrooms Are Coming
ESTY, BOB
Main Event
Roller Boogie
ET TU BRUTUS ENSEMBLE
Gone with the Wind
ETTING, RUTH
Whoopee!
ETTINGER, AMOS
Kazablan
EUROPEANS
Night In Heaven
EURYTHMICS
9½ Weeks
True Love
EVANKO, ED
Canterbury Tales
Rex
EVANS, ALBERT
Night Club Confidential
EVANS, BILL
Torch Song Trilogy
Twilight of Honor
EVANS, BONNIE
Li'l Abner
EVANS, DALE
Wyatt Earp, Cheyenne and Other TV Favorites
EVANS, DAME EDITH
ANTA Album of Stars, Vol. 2
Importance of Being Earnest
Nun's Story
EVANS, DAVID
Irma La Douce
EVANS, DOTTIE
Gigi
Mardi Gras
Ten North Frederick
Themes from Great Films
EVANS, FRED
Phil the Fluter
Sweet Charity
EVANS, GIL
Absolute Beginners
Insignificance
Porgy and Bess
EVANS, HARVEY
Anyone Can Whistle
Boy Friend
Follies
George M!
EVANS, JESSIE
Canterbury Tales
Pickwick

EVANS, KAREN
Runaways
EVANS, MARION
Steve and Eydie
EVANS, MAURICE
Race for the Wire
Tenderloin
EVANS, RAY
Aaron Slick from Punkin Crick
All Hands on Deck
Bing's Hollywood
Bonanza
Four Television Musicals
Gunn...Number One
Houseboat
Interlude
James Dean Story
Let It Ride
Love Themes from Motion Pictures
No Man Can Tame Me
Oh Captain!
Oscar
Red Garters
Satins and Spurs
This Property Is Condemned
Torn Curtain
Warning Shot
What Did You Do In the War, Daddy?
EVANS, REX
Gentlemen Prefer Blondes
Merry Andrew
EVANS, SUZANNAH
Hair
EVANS, TUDOR
Rose Marie
EVANS, WILBUR
By the Beautiful Sea
Desert Song
Evening with Jerome Kern
Great Waltz
Merry Widow
Mexican Hayride
Red Mill
EVE
Armed and Dangerous
Vanishing Point
EVE, TREVOR
High Society
EVERETT, BETTY
Hometown U.S.A.
EVERETT, ROLAND
Sunday In New York
EVERETT, RUPERT
Hearts of Fire
EVERETT, TANYA
Fiddler on the Roof
EVEREST, JOHN
81 Proof
EVERHART, REX
Anything Goes
1776
Skyscraper
Tenderloin
Woman of the Year
EVERLY, PHIL
Every Which Way But Loose
EVERLY BROTHERS
Coupe De Ville
Stealing Home
Tequila Sunrise
EVERYTHING BUT THE GIRL
She's Having a Baby
EWELL, TOM
State Fair
Thurber Carnival
EWING, BILL
Cleopatra
Lawrence of Arabia
EWING, GORDON
Wonderful O
EXCITERS
Big Chill
EXTREME
Bill and Ted's Excellent Adventure
EXUMA
Joe
FABARES, SHELLEY
Bye Bye Birdie

Hold On!
Time to Sing
FABIAN
American Pop
High Time
FABIANI, JOEL
I'm Getting My Act Together and Taking It on the Road
FABRAY, NANETTE
Alice Through the Looking Glass
Arms and the Girl
Band Wagon
Cut! Out-Takes from Hollywood's Greatest Musicals
High Button Shoes
Make a Wish
Mr. President
That's Entertainment, Part 2
FABREGAS, MANOLO
My Fair Lady
FABRIZI, ALDO
Rugantino
FABULOUS FONTAINES
Fright Night
FABULOUS THUNDERBIRDS
Bull Durham
Cocktail
Light of Day
Porky's Revenge!
Summer School
FACE TO FACE
Jumpin' Jack Flash
FADELA, CHABA
Bad Influence
FAGAN, JOAN
Donnybrook!
FAGEN, DONALD
Bright Lights, Big City
Heavy Metal
FAHEY, JOHN
Zabriskie Point
FAIN, SAMMY
Alice In Wonderland
Ankles Aweigh
April Love
Big Circus
Calamity Jane
Christine
Flahooley
Gift of Love
Hollywood Or Bust
Hooray for Hollywood
If He Hollers, Let Him Go
Imitation of Life
Jazz Singer
Lady In Cement
Love Is a Many Splendored Thing
Mardi Gras
Marjorie Morningstar
New Kind of Love
Peter Pan
Tender Is the Night
3 Sailors and a Girl
FAIRBANK, SPRING
Very Good Eddie
FAIRBANKS, DOUGLAS, JR.
Four Television Musicals
Tonight at 8:30
FAIRBANKS, NOLA
Night In Venice
FAIRCHILD, CHARLOTTE
All In the York Family
FAIRCHILD, EDGAR
Can't Help Singing
FAIRCHILD, GEORGE
Cradle Will Rock
FAIRCHILD AND CARROLL
Red Hot and Blue
FAIRMAN, BLAIN
Ambassador
FAISON, SANDY
Annie
Is There Life After High School?
FAITH, ADAM
Beat Girl
Budgie
Stardust

FAITH, CHRISSY
No Small Affair
FAITH, PERCY
All-Star Parade, Hits from the Movies
April Fools
Baby Doll
Camelot
Do I Hear a Waltz?
From Broadway to Hollywood
Guys and Dolls
Held Over! Today's Great Movie Themes
Hollywood's Great Themes
House of Flowers
Jesus Christ Superstar
Kismet
Look at Monaco
Love Goddesses
Love Me Or Leave Me
Mood Music from Stage and Screen
Most Happy Fella
Music from Hollywood
My Fair Lady
Night with Jerome Kern
Oscar
Parade of Show Stoppers
Percy Faith Plays the Academy Award Winner and Other Great Movie Themes
Red Garters
Sound of Music
Summer Place (And Other Great Hits from the Movies)
White Christmas
Young at Heart
FAITHFULL, MARIANNE
They Call It an Accident
Trouble In Mind
Tuff Turf
FALANA, LOLA
Golden Boy
FALCONS
Popeye
FALK, PETER
Magic Moments from the Tonight Show
Robin and the Seven Hoods
FALLON, DAVID
Aladdin
FALTERMEYER, HAROLD
American Gigolo
Beverly Hills Cop
Beverly Hills Cop II
Fatal Beauty
Fletch
Midnight Express
Running Man
She's Out of Control
Starlight Express
Top Gun
FAME, GEORGIE
Boom
FAMILY DREAM
Police Academy IV - Citizens on Patrol
FANCOURT, DARRELL
Mikado
FANTASTIC BAGGYS
Ride the Wild Surf
FANTASTIC STRINGS OF FELIX SLATKIN
Inspired Themes from the Inspired Films
Magnificent XII
FARAGHER, TOMMY
Staying Alive
FARBER, BURT
Prince and the Pauper
Subways Are for Sleeping
FARBER, LOREN S.
Washington Behind Closed Doors
FARBER, MITCH
Sondheim
FARBER, STAN
Cross and the Switchblade
FARG, JIM
Tom Jones

FARGE, ANNIE
  Les Poupees De Paris
FARGENT, EDDIE
  Aladdin
FARINA, MARILYN
  Nunsense
FARINA, MIMI
  Fools
FARINA, SANDY
  Sgt. Pepper's Lonely Hearts
    Club Band
FARIS, ALEXANDER
  Great Waltz
  Irma La Douce
  La Vie Parisienne
  Robert and Elizabeth
FARMER, ART
  Broadway's Big Hits
  I Want to Live
FARMER, FRANCES
  Cut! Out-Takes from
    Hollywood's Greatest
    Musicals
FARNHAM, JOHN
  Rad
  Savage Streets
FARNON, DENNIS
  Arrivederci, Baby!
  Gigi
  Magoo In Hi-Fi
  Rocky the Flying Squirrel and
    His Friends
FARNON, ROBERT
  Captain from Castile
  Captain Horatio Hornblower
  Gentlemen Marry Brunettes
  Road to Hong Kong
  Shalako
FARNUM, JOHN
  Fletch
FARNSWORTH, RALPH
  Most Happy Fella
FARONE, DOMINICK
  Close Encounters of the Third
    Kind
FARRAR, JOHN
  Xanadu
FARRELL, EILEEN
  Franz Lehar Memorial Album
  Interrupted Melody
  Met Stars on Broadway
  Red Mill
FARRELL, GLENDA
  Ladies of Burlesque
FARRELL, JIM
  Dude (the Highway Life)
FARRELL, JOE
  Landlord
FARRELL, WALTER
  Penney Proud
FARREN, CHRIS
  Girls Just Want to Have Fun
  Night of the Comet
FARRIS, ALEXANDER
  Flowers for Algernon
FASCINATO, JACK
  Happy Mother Goose (As Told
    By Kukla, Fran and Ollie)
  Merry Christmas from Kukla,
    Fran and Ollie
  Songs By Kukla, Fran and Ollie
FASS, BERNIE
  Power Is You
FAST FORWARD
  Pumping Iron 2 - The Women
FAST, LARRY
  Jupiter Menace
FASTWAY
  Trick Or Treat
FAT BOYS
  Blue Iguana
  Disorderlies
  Krush Groove
  She-Devil
FATAAR, RIKKI
  Rutles
FATES WARNING
  River's Edge
FATOOL, NICK
  Pete Kelly's Blues

FAULL, ELLEN
  Carry Nation
FAURE, DUNCAN
  Who's That Girl?
FAY, THOMAS
  Sondheim
FAYE, ALICE
  Alexander's Ragtime Band
  Alice Faye
  Alice Faye In Hollywood 1934-
    1937
  Cut! Out-Takes from
    Hollywood's Greatest
    Musicals
  Four Jills In a Jeep
  Gang's All Here
  Good News
  Hello Frisco, Hello
  Here Come the Girls
  Irving Berlin Tribute
  Ladies of Burlesque
  Magic of Lassie
  On the Avenue
  State Fair
  That Night In Rio
  Wake Up and Live
FAYE, FRANCIS
  Porgy and Bess
FAYE, HERBIE
  Top Banana
FAYE, JOEY
  Little Me
  70 Girls, 70
  Top Banana
FAYE, VINI
  Best of Burlesque
FAYER, ART
  Tarot
FAZAKAS, FRANZ
  Man In the Moon
FEAR
  Decline of Western Civilization
  Get Crazy
  Repo Man
FEARL, CLIFFORD
  Jimmy
FEAST, MICHAEL
  Hair
FEATHERS, CHARLIE
  Teen-Age Cruisers
FEEHAN, TIM
  License to Kill
  Wraith
FEELIES
  Married to the Mob
FEHRING, JOHANNES
  Fiddler on the Roof
FELBER, WILLIAM
  Student Prince
FELD, FRITZ
  World's Greatest Lover
FELDER, DON
  Fast Times at Ridgemont High
  Heavy Metal
  Secret Admirer
FELDMAN, MARTY
  Young Frankenstein
FELICIANO, JOSE
  Mackenna's Gold
FELLER, DICK
  Smokey and the Bandit
FELSTEAD, BETTY
  After the Ball
FELTON, FELIX
  Where's Charley?
FELTON, VERNA
  Cinderella
FEMALE BODY INSPECTORS
  Modern Girls
FEMME FATALE
  License to Drive
FENADY, ANDREW J.
  Stakeout
FENHOLT, JEFF
  Jesus Christ Superstar
FENN, JEAN
  Great Waltz
  Serenade
  Vagabond King

FENTON, CARL
  Lady Be Good
FENTON, GEORGE
  Company of Wolves
  Cry Freedom
  Dangerous Liaisons
  84 Charing Cross Road
  Gandhi
  High Spirits
  Jewel In the Crown
  White Mischief
FENWICK, JOHN
  Anne of Green Gables
FERDIN, PAMELYN
  Boy Named Charlie Brown
  Charlotte's Web
FERGUSON, HELEN
  Cabin In the Sky
FERGUSON, JAY
  Bad Dreams
  Johnny Be Good
  Nightmare on Elm Street 5 -
    The Dream Child
  Roadie
  Terminator
FERGUSON, MAYNARD
  Uncle Joe Shannon
FERNANDEZ, JOSE
  Me Nobody Knows
FERNANDEZ, PETER
  What Do You Want to Be When
    You Grow Up?
FERNANDEZ, WILHELMINA
  WIGGINS
  Diva
FERRANTE, (Arthur) AND
  (Louis) TEICHER
  Broadway to Hollywood
  Can-Can
  Cleopatra
  Golden Motion Picture Themes
    and Original Soundtracks
  Golden Themes from Motion
    Pictures
  Goodbye Again
  Great Motion Picture Themes
  Israel Now
  Magnificent Movie Music
  Me and Juliet
  More Great Motion Picture
    Themes
  Mutiny on the Bounty
  Original Motion Picture Hit
    Themes
  Original Soundtracks and Music
  Rage to Live
  West Side Story
FERRANTE, RUSSELL
  Star Trek IV: The Voyage Home
FERRARA, FRANCO
  Bible
  Boccaccio '70
  Farewell to Arms
  Francis of Assisi
  Indiscretion of an American
    Wife
  Leopard
  Picasso
  War and Peace
FERRARA, JOHN
  Sunburn
FERRELL, TYRA
  Lena Horne: The Lady and Her
    Music
FERRER, JOSE
  Caine Mutiny
  Cyrano De Bergerac
  Deep In My Heart
  Girl Who Came to Supper
  Great Debates
  Miss Sadie Thompson
  Mouse on the Mayflower
  Oh Captain!
  Othello
  Rita Hayworth
FERRER, MEL
  Everything I Have Is Yours
  Lili
  Magnificent Moments from
    MGM Movies
  Oh, Rosalinda!
  That's Entertainment, Part 2

Very Best of Motion Picture
  Musicals
FERRIER, PAT
  Redhead
FERRIS WHEEL
  Touchables
FERRO, DANIEL
  King and I
FERRY, BRYAN
  All This and World War II
  Bright Lights, Big City
  Legend
  9½ Weeks
  She's Having a Baby
FESTIVAL
  Evita
FESTIVAL CHOIR
  Miracle Goes On
FESTIVAL STRINGS
  LUCERNE
  Barry Lyndon
FEUER, CY
  Music of Republic
FEVER TREE
  Angels Die Hard
FEYER, GEORGE
  Echoes of Hollywood
  King and I
  South Pacific
FIANDER, LEWIS
  I and Albert
FIBONACCIS
  Terror Vision
FIDENCO, NICO
  Black Emanuelle
FIEDEL, BRAD
  Big Easy
  Fright Night
  Let's Get Harry
  Nowhere to Hide
  Serpent and the Rainbow
  Terminator
FIEDLER, ARTHUR
  Annie Get Your Gun
  Brigadoon
  Classics of the Silver Screen
  Curtain Going Up
  Desert Song
  Duel In the Sun
  Famous Broadway
  Fantasia
  Greatest Hits Songs from
    Special TV Offers
  Million Dollar Movies
  Music of the Movies
  Porgy and Bess
  Richard Rodgers
  Ship of Fools
  Spotlight on Broadway
FIELD, BETTY
  Strange Interlude
FIELD, SALLY
  Flying Nun
FIELD, SHIRLEY ANN
  Beat Girl
FIELDING, FENELLA
  Pieces of Eight
  Valmouth
FIELDING, JERRY
  Advise and Consent
  Dick Powell Presents (Music
    from the Original Soundtrack
    of Four Star Productions)
  Gauntlet
  Hogan's Heroes
  My Fairfax Lady
  Nightcomers
  Outlaw Josey Wales
  Scorpio
  Straw Dogs
  Wild Bunch
FIELDS, ALVIN
  Downriver
FIELDS, BENETTA
  Lost Man
FIELDS, BENNY
  Somebody Loves Me
FIELDS, DOROTHY
  Arms and the Girl
  Blackbirds of 1928
  By the Beautiful Sea

Tickle Me
Viva Las Vegas

FONTANA, WAYNE
Good Morning, Vietnam

FONTANE, TONY
Show Boat

FONTANE SISTERS
Hits from Broadway Shows

FONTANNA
Gigi

FORAN, DICK
Connecticut Yankee

FORAY, JUNE
Frosty the Snowman
Rocky the Flying Squirrel and
His Friends

FORAY, SHEILA
Gigi

FORBES, BRENDA
Darling of the Day

FORBES, SHEILA
Sail Away

FORBSTEIN, LEO F.
Golden Age of the Hollywood
Musical

FORCE M.D.'S
House Party
Krush Groove
Lean on Me

FORD, BARBARA
Music Man

FORD, CHIP
Shenandoah

FORD, CLEBERT
Ain't Supposed to Die a Natural
Death
Ballad for Bimshire

FORD, DAVID
1776

FORD, FRANKIE
American Hot Wax

FORD, HARRISON
Apocalypse Now
Empire Strikes Back
Raiders of the Lost Ark

FORD, JOAN
Goldilocks

FORD, LAURA
Cowardly Custard

FORD, LAUREL
Aspects of Love
Words and Music

FORD, NANCY
Cryer and Ford
I'm Getting My Act Together
and Taking It on the Road
Last Sweet Days of Isaac
Now Is the Time for All Good
Men

FORD, PAUL
Four Television Musicals
Thurber Carnival

FORD, GERALD R.
It's Time to Pray, America!

FORD, ROBBEN
Pink Cadillac

FORD, RUTH
Grass Harp

FORD, TENNESSEE ERNIE
Mouse on the Mayflower
Story of Christmas

FORD, WINSTON
Lonely Guy

FORDE, BRINSELY
Double Deckers

FOREE, KEN
Dawn of the Dead

FOREIGNER
FM
Official Music of the XXIIIrd
Olympiad, Los Angeles 1984
Vision Quest

FOREMAN, EDWARD
Postcard from Morocco

FOREMAN, RICHARD
Elephant Steps

FOREST, DYAN
Close Encounters of the Third
Kind

FOREST, FRANK
New Moon

FOREST, JIMMY
Dusty and Sweets McGee

FORESTIERI, MARCEL
Bring Back Birdie

FORNES, MARIE IRENE
Promenade

FORREST, FREDERIC
Apocalypse Now

FORREST, GEORGE
Anya
Great Waltz
Kean
Kismet
Song of Norway

FORREST, JACK
Gigi

FORREST, PAUL
Jimmy

FORREST, STEVE
Body Beautiful

FORSTER, ROBERT
Black Hole (the Story of the
Black Hole)

FORSYTH, BETTY
Christy

FORSYTH, BRUCE
Can Hieronymus Merkin Ever
Forget Mercy Humppe (And
Find True Happiness)
Desert Song
Little Me
Star

FORSYTHE, HENDERSON
Best Little Whorehouse In
Texas

FORSYTHE, JOHN
American Spirit
Lisztomania

FORTAS, ALAN
Elvis (NBC-TV Special)

FORTIER, BOB
Me and Juliet

FORTUNATE, LOU
Man from Broadway

FORTUS, DANIEL
Minnie's Boys

FORTY-EIGHT GIRLS
Taking Off

FORTY-FIVE GRAVE
Return of the Living Dead

FORTY-FOUR MAG MIX
Colors

FOSSE, BOB
Kiss Me Kate
Little Prince
That's Dancing!

FOSSE, NICOLE
Chorus Line

FOSTER, DAVID
St. Elmo's Fire
Secret of My Success
Stealing Home
Two of a Kind
White Nights

FOSTER, GLORIA
Hand Is on the Gate
In White America

FOSTER, JOAN
American Spirit

FOSTER, JODIE
Tom Sawyer

FOSTER, JUDY
Young Abe Lincoln

FOSTER, JULIA
Half a Sixpence

FOSTER, LARRY
James Blonde (Secret Agent
006.95, Marked Down from
007.00)

FOSTER, LAWRENCE
Rise and Fall of the Third Reich
Turning Point

FOSTER, NORMAN
Zorro

FOSTER, POPS
Jazz Dance

FOSTER, PRESTON
Premiere

FOSTER, STEPHEN
Europeans
67 Melody Lane
Mississippi
Stephen Foster Story
Swanee River

FOSTER, STUART
Oklahoma
Thousand Miles of Mountains

FOSTER, WARREN
Hey There, It's Yogi Bear

FOUR ACES
Decade of Broadway and
Cinema
Eddy Duchin Story
Kismet
Written on the Wind

FOUR COINS
Jamboree!

FOUR DACHSHUNDS
Absent-Minded Professor

FOUR FRESHMEN
Frances Langford Presents
Jane Powell

FOUR HITS AND A MISS
Jolson Sings Again

FOUR LADS
All-Star Parade, Hits from the
Movies
Flower Drum Song
Stingiest Man In Town
Summer Place (And Other
Great Hits from the Movies)
This Year's Top Movie Songs

FOUR SEASONS
All This and World War II
Body Slam
Hollywood Knights
Main Event
Stealing Home
Wanderers

FOUR THEMES
Ten North Frederick

FOUR TOPS
Air America
Big Chill (More Songs from the
Original Soundtrack)
Buster
Cooley High
Fish That Saved Pittsburgh
Grease 2
I'm Gonna Git You Sucka
Into the Night
Shaft In Africa
Where the Buffalo Roam

FOUR TROMBONES
Destry Rides Again

FOURSOME
Bing's Hollywood

FOURTEEN K
Goonies

FOURTH WALL REPERTORY
CO.
King of the Entire World

FOWLER, BETH
Baby
One Way Ticket to Broadway
Preppies

FOX, BRITNY
Iron Eagle II

FOX, CHARLES
Barbarella
Film Music
Foul Play
Gods Must Be Crazy II
Goodbye Columbus
Love American Style
Nine to Five
One on One (the Story of a
Winner)
Other Side of the Mountain
Pufnstuf
Six Pack
Strange Brew

FOX, DULCE
Cradle Will Rock

FOX, JAMES
Thoroughly Modern Millie

FOX, MICHAEL J.
Light of Day

FOX, SAMANTHA
Far Out Man
Nightmare on Elm Street 5 -
The Dream Child

FOX, SONNY
Christmas That Almost Wasn't

FOXX, REDD
Sanford and Son

FOY, EDDIE, JR.
Bells Are Ringing
Donnybrook!
50th Anniversary of George
Jessel In Show Business
Four Television Musicals
Olympus 7-0000
Pajama Game

FRADKIN, LESLIE
Beatlemania

FRAME, GRAZINA
Seaside Swingers

FRAMPTON, MAC
Papa Was a Preacher
R.S.V.P. the Cole Porters

FRAMPTON, PETER
Mother, Jugs and Speed
Playing for Keeps
Quicksilver
Sgt. Pepper's Lonely Hearts
Club Band

FRANCE, RICHARD
By the Beautiful Sea

FRANCHI, SERGIO
Do I Hear a Waltz?
Richard Rodgers
Secret of Santa Vittoria
Sound of Broadway

FRANCINE, ANNE
Anything Goes
Snow White and the Seven
Dwarfs

FRANCIS, ANNE
Forbidden Planet

FRANCIS, ARLENE
Age of Television

FRANCIS, CONNIE
Follow the Boys
Jamboree!
Looking for Love
Rock, Rock, Rock
When the Boys Meet the Girls

FRANCIS, KAYE
Four Jills In a Jeep

FRANCIS, PANAMA
Mardi Gras

FRANCIS, ROBERT
Caine Mutiny

FRANCIS, STAN
Rudolph the Red-Nosed
Reindeer

FRANCKS, DON
Finian's Rainbow

FRANCONE, CATHERINE
Girl Friend

FRANCONI, DEAN
Flower Drum Song
Music from Great Films
My Fair Lady
Sound of Music

FRANK, BARRY
Mardi Gras

FRANK, DANIEL
Fly with Me

FRANK, DAVID
Code of Silence
Coffy

FRANK, DOROTHY
Different Times

FRANK, JUDY
Now Is the Time for All Good
Men

FRANK, MARVIN
Touch of Class

FRANK, MEL
Touch of Class

FRANK, SHERMAN
Olds for '60 Musical
This Is Oldsmobility

FRANKE AND KNOCKOUTS
Rude Awakening
FRANKE, PAUL
Merry Widow
FRANKEL, BENJAMIN
Battle of the Bulge
Night of the Iguana
FRANKEN, STEPHEN
Wonderful O
FRANKENLAND STATE
SYMPHONY ORCHESTRA
Ben-Hur
Rozsa Conducts Rozsa
FRANKLIN, ARETHA
Back to School
Big Chill
Blues Brothers
I'm Gonna Git You Sucka
*Magic Moments from the
Tonight Show*
More American Graffiti
Nothing In Common
*Platoon (And Songs from the
Era)*
Sparkle
Stardust
FRANKLIN, BONNIE
Applause
FRANKLIN, RODNEY
Penitentiary III
FRANKLIN, TONY
Dream Girls
FRANKS, CHLOE
Little Night Music
FRANKS, DOBBS
King of the Whole Damn World
FRANKS, GRACIELA
My Cousin Josefa
FRANKS, LAURIE
Utter Glory of Morrissey Hall
FRANKS, MICHAEL
Moment By Moment
FRANN, MARY
*Paul Sills' Story Theater (of
Magical Folk-Rock Fables)*
FRANZ, JOY
I Can't Keep Running In Place
Musical Chairs
FRANZELL, CARLOTTA
Carmen Jones
FRANZETTI, CARLOS
Misunderstood
FRASER, A.
March of the Falsettos
FRASER, ALISON
Beehive
In Trousers
Romance / Romance
FRASER, ANN
*Among Friends - Waa-Mu Show
of 1960*
FRASER, IAN
Scrooge
FRASER, JERI LYNNE
Two Tickets to Paris
FRASER, MOYRA
Boy Friend
Camelot
FRASER, RONALD
High Society
FRASER-SIMSON, HAROLD
Maid of the Mountains
FRATERNITY OF MAN
Easy Rider
FRAWLEY, JAMES
Anyone Can Whistle
FREBERG, STAN
Stan Freberg Shows
Tom Thumb
FRECHETTE, PETER
Flora the Red Menace
FRECHTER, COLIN
Star Wars
FRED, JOHN
Drugstore Cowboy
FREDDIE & DREAMERS
Out of Sight
Seaside Swingers

FREDERICK, JESSE
Flamingo Kid
Idolmaker
FREDERICK, VICKI
Chorus Line
FREDERICKS, CHARLES
Chocolate Soldier
Franz Lehar Memorial Album
Red Mill
Rose Marie
Show Boat
This Is Broadway's Best
FREDERICKS, LYDIA
Girl In Pink Tights
FREDERICKS, MARC
Red Mantle
FREEBAIRN-SMITH, IAN
Alakazam the Great
Muppet Movie
Strawberry Statement
FREED, ALAN
Rock, Rock, Rock
FREED, ARTHUR
*Ballet Music from MGM
Musicals*
Boy Friend
Clockwork Orange
Pagan Love Song
Singin' In the Rain
*Yolanda and the Thief / You'll
Never Get Rich*
Ziegfeld Follies of 1946
FREED, SAM
Candide
FREEDMAN, GERALD
Time for Singing
FREEDMAN, ROBERT
Wiz
FREEMAN, AL, JR.
For Pete's Sake
FREEMAN, ARNY
Minnie's Boys
Working
FREEMAN, AUDREY
Love from Judy
FREEMAN, BOB,
ORCHESTRA
Five Pennies
FREEMAN, BOBBY
American Graffiti
FREEMAN, BUD
Beg, Borrow Or Steal
FREEMAN, ERNIE
Arrivederci, Baby!
Doctor Dolittle
Flying Nun
Silencers
What Am I Bid?
When the Boys Meet the Girls
FREEMAN, MONA
Shocking Miss Pilgrim
FREEMAN, MORGAN
Electric Company TV Show
FREEMAN, PAUL
Raiders of the Lost Ark
FREEMAN, SANDI
Bathrooms Are Coming
FREEMAN, STAN
I Had a Ball
Oh Captain!
Pins and Needles
Song of Norway
FREES, P. HARCOURT
Ugly Dachshund
FREES, PAUL
Absent-Minded Professor
Dr. Phibes
Exploring the Unknown
Frosty the Snowman
Gay Purr-ee
*Rocky the Flying Squirrel and
His Friends*
Santa Claus Is Comin' to Town
Shaggy Dog
Snow Queen
Stan Freberg Shows
FREIBERG, THOMAS
Boy Meets Boy
FREITAG, DOROTHEA
Oh Kay!

Shoestring Revue '57
Shoestring Revues
FREIWALD, CARL
*Ben Bagley's Oscar
Hammerstein Revisited*
FREMONT, ROB
Piano Bar
FRENCH, ARTHUR
*Ain't Supposed to Die a Natural
Death*
FRENCH, ELIZABETH
Tom Jones
FRENCH, HAROLD
Oh Kay!
FRENCH, JACK
*Liza Minnelli at the Winter
Garden*
FRENCH, PERCY
Phil the Fluter
FRENETTE, CECILE
Outrageous
FRESH
Almost Summer
FREY, GLENN
Beverly Hills Cop
Ghostbusters II
Miami Vice
FREY, LEONARD
Boys In the Band
Coach with the Six Insides
Fiddler on the Roof
FREY, NATHANIEL
Damn Yankees
Fiorello!
Frankie and Johnny
Goldilocks
She Loves Me
Tree Grows In Brooklyn
FRID, JONATHAN
Dark Shadows
FRIDAY, BETSY
Bring Back Birdie
FRIDAY, GAVIN
Bad Influence
FRIDAY, PAT
*Glenn Miller: Golden Hits from
His Original Soundtracks*
FRIED, GERALD
Dino
Man from U.N.C.L.E.
Roots
Shotgun Slade
FRIEDHOFER, HUGO
Affair to Remember
Barbarian and the Geisha
Best Years of Our Lives
Boy on a Dolphin
*Captain Blood: Classic Film
Scores for Errol Flynn*
Down to the Sea In Ships
Film Music of Hugo Friedhofer
*Hollywood: The Post War Years
(1946 - 1949)*
I Spy
Island In the Sky
*Love Themes from Motion
Pictures*
One-Eyed Jacks
Premier Radio Performances
Song of Bernadette
Sun Also Rises
This Earth Is Mine
Young Lions
FRIEDMAN, BOB
Anatomy of a Murder
*Lena Horne: The Lady and Her
Music*
FRIEDMAN, DAVID
Boy Meets Boy
*Joseph and the Amazing
Technicolor Dreamcoat*
FRIEDMAN, GARY WILLIAM
Me Nobody Knows
Platinum
Survival Run
Taking My Turn
FRIENDLY, FRED
*I Can Hear It Now, Volume 1:
1933-1945*
*Quick and the Dead - The Story
of the Atom Bomb*

FRIENDS OF DISTINCTION
I'm Gonna Git You Sucka
FRIML, RUDOLF
Firefly
Maid of the Mountains
Night with Rudolf Friml
Northwest Outpost
Rose Marie
Three Musketeers
Vagabond King
FRIZELL, DAVID
Any Which Way You Can
Honkytonk Man
FRIZZELL, LEFTY
Last Picture Show
FROBE, GERT
Threepenny Opera
FROEHLICH, RICO
Bravo Giovanni!
Juno
Most Happy Fella
FROESE, EDGAR
Kamikaze 1989
Sorcerer
FROG, WYNDER K.
Touchables
FROHLICH, PETER
Fiddler on the Roof
FROMAN, JANE
Gems from Gershwin
Here Come the Girls
I'll Cry Tomorrow
Pal Joey
Susan Hayward
FROME, MILTON
Dora's World
FRONTIERE, DOMINIC
Aviator
Billie
Composer's Holiday
Hammersmith Is Out
Hang 'Em High
On Any Sunday
Pipe Dreams
Popi
Stunt Man
*Washington Behind Closed
Doors*
FROOM, MITCHELL
Slam Dance
FROST, DAVID
John F. Kennedy
FROST, JOHN
Beggar's Opera
FROST, MAX
Glory Stompers
FROZEN GHOST AND
FRIENDS
Johnny Be Good
FRYATT, JOHN
La Vie Parisienne
FUCHS, LEO
Bei Mir Bistu Schoen
Great Waltz
FUJII, TIMM
Pacific Overtures
FULL CIRCLE
Bunny O'Hare
FULL FORCE
Caddyshack II
House Party
FULLER, EDWARD
Cradle Will Rock
FULLER, GARY
Chocalonia
FULLER, LORENZO
Finian's Rainbow
Kiss Me Kate
We'd Rather Switch
FULLER, PENNY
Applause
Rex
FULLER, SANDY
This Was Burlesque
FULLERTON, FIONA
*Alice's Adventures In
Wonderland*
FULLUM, CLAY
Last Sweet Days of Isaac

GARRETT, SIEDAH
Lean on Me
GARRETT, SNUFF
Sharky's Machine
GARRICK, BEULAH
Juno
GARRIGUENC, RENE
Twilight Zone
GARRIPOLI, MARY
Dawgs
GARRISON, DAVID
Day in Hollywood / Night in the
Ukraine
Of Thee I Sing
GARRISON, SEAN
Half Past Wednesday
Hot September
GARRY, IAN
Walking Happy
GARRY, MARTHA
Fiddler on the Roof
GARSON, GREER
African Queen
Joan Crawford
Julius Caesar
Mouse on the Mayflower
GARSON, MORT
Little Prince
GARTH, JOHN
Annie Get Your Gun
Ethel Merman
GARVARENTZ, GEORGES
Corrupt Ones
Great Motion Picture Themes
Killer Force
Marco the Magnificent
Panic Button
Peking Medallion
Southern Star
That Man In Istanbul
Triple Cross
GARY
Mask
GARY, JOHN
David Merrick Presents Hits
from His Broadway Hits
Mouse on the Mayflower
NARM's Golden Decade
Sound of Broadway
GASCOIGNE, BRIAN
Emerald Forest
GASMAN, IRA
What's a Nice Country Like the
U.S. Doing In a State Like
This?
GASPER, EDDIE
Sweet Charity
GATES, CRAWFORD
Promised Land
GATES, DAVID
Hey There, It's Yogi Bear
GATLIN, LARRY
Stroker Ace
GATSOS, NIKOS
America, America
GATTEYS, BENNYE
Tom Sawyer
GAUSE, DENNY
Surfer Girls
GAUTIER, DICK
Bye Bye Birdie
GAVIN, JOHN
Thoroughly Modern Millie
GAVON, IGORS
Hello Dolly!
Prettybelle
Your Own Thing
GAXTON, WILLIAM
Louisiana Purchase
GAY, JOHN
Beggar's Opera
GAY, NOEL
Me and My Girl
GAY BLADES
Gigi
GAYE, MARVIN
Big Chill
Big Chill (More Songs from the
Original Soundtrack)
Into the Night

Jo Jo Dancer, Your Life is
Calling
Save the Children
Trouble Man
GAYLE, CRYSTAL
One from the Heart
GAYNES, EDMUND
Best Foot Forward
GAYNES, GEORGE
Gigi
Wonderful Town
GAYNOR, CHARLES
Carol Channing
Irene
Show Girl
GAYNOR, GLORIA
Nocturna
GAYNOR, MITZI
Anything Goes
Bing's Hollywood
Les Girls
South Pacific
There's No Business Like Show
Business
GAYSON, EUNICE
Sound of Music
GAZZARA, BEN
Strange Interlude
GEDDA, NICOLAI
Vanessa
GEER, WILL
110 In the Shade
Walton's Christmas Album
GEESIN, RON
Body
GEHRECKE, FRANK
Greenwich Village U.S.A.
GEHRIG, LOU
Years to Remember
GEILS, J., BAND
Fright Night
GELBART, LARRY
Movie Movie
GELBER, STANLEY
Love and Let Love
GELD, GARY
Angel
Looking for Love
Purlie
Shenandoah
GELFER, STEVEN
Cats
GELLER, BRUCE
All In Love
Mission: Impossible
GELLER, HARRY
Eddy Duchin Story
Kiss Me Kate
GELLER, MIKE
Bold Ventures
GEMIGNANI, GEORGE
Pacific Overtures
GEMIGNANI, PAUL
Broadway Extravaganza
Carousel
Digital Trip Down Broadway
Doll's Life
Follies
Grind
Into the Woods
Jerome Robbins' Broadway
Sondheim
Sondheim: A Musical Tribute
Sunday In the Park with George
Sweeney Todd (The Demon
Barber of Fleet Street)
GEMS
Flashpoint
GENE AND WENDELL
Hairspray
GENE LOVES JEZEBEL
She's Having a Baby
GENESTE, EMILE
Nikki, Wild Dog of the North
GENN, LEO
Quo Vadis?
GENNARO, PETER
Bells Are Ringing
Pajama Game

GENTON, SAMANTHA
Red Mill
GENTRY, ART
California
GENTRY, BOBBIE
Ode to Billy Joe
GENTRY, MINNIE
Ain't Supposed to Die a Natural
Death
GEORGE, BABETTE
Gigi
GEORGE, BETTY
Ankles Aweigh
GEORGE, CHIEF DAN
Harry and Tonto
Little Big Man
GEORGE, FLORENCE
New Moon
GEORGE, GIL
Perri
Westward Ho, the Wagons
GEORGE, GLORIA
Can-Can
GEORGIA SATELLITES
Cobra
Cocktail
Rude Awakening
GEORIS, WALTER
Endless Summer
Last of the Ski Bums
GERACI, LESLIE
Cradle Will Rock
GERACI, SONNY
His Wife's Habit
GERARD, BERNARD
Folies Bergere
Z
GERARD, GIL
All In the York Family
GERARD, P.
Folies Bergere
GERBER, YANCY
We'd Rather Switch
GERHARDT, CHARLES
Captain Blood: Classic Film
Scores from Errol Flynn
Captain from Castile
Casablanca: Classic Film
Scores for Humphrey Bogart
Citizen Kane: The Classic Film
Scores of Bernard Herrmann
Classic Film Scores for Bette
Davis
Elizabeth and Essex: The
Classic Film Scores of Erich
Wolfgang Korngold
Empire Strikes Back
Gone with the Wind
Great Music from the Movies
Kings Row
Lost Horizon: The Classic Film
Scores of Dimitri Tiomkin
Mood Music from the Movies
Now, Voyager: The Classic Film
Scores of Max Steiner
Sea Hawk: The Classic Film
Scores of Erich Wolfgang
Korngold
Spectacular World of Classic
Film Scores
Spellbound
Star Wars - Return of the Jedi
Star Wars / Close Encounters
of the Third Kind
Sunset Boulevard: The Classic
Film Scores of Franz Waxman
Victory at Sea
GERMAIN, ANNE
Young Girls of Rochefort
GERMAN, EDWARD
Evening with W.S. Gilbert
GERMS
Cruising
GERRARD, DONNY
St. Elmo's Fire
GERRARD, GENE
New Moon
GERRINGER, ROBERT
Andersonville Trial
GERRON, KURT
Threepenny Opera

GERRY & PACEMAKERS
Buster
Ferry Cross the Mersey
Stardust
GERSHE, LEONARD
Star Is Born
GERSHENSON, JOSEPH
Back Street
Four Girls in Town
Freud
Glenn Miller Story
Imitation of Life
Interlude
Lively Set
Madame X
Magnificent Obsession
Man of a Thousand Faces
Rock Pretty Baby
Shenandoah
Slaughter on 10th Avenue
Snow Queen
So This Is Paris
Summer Love
Sweet Charity
This Earth Is Mine
Touch of Evil
War Lord
Written on the Wind
GERSHWIN, GEORGE
American In Paris
Ballet Music from MGM
Musicals
Blue Monday
Damsel In Distress
David Rose and His Orchestra
Play the Music of George
Gershwin
Ethel Merman
Evening with Beatrice Lillie
Frank Sinatra Sings George
Gershwin
Fred Astaire and Ginger Rogers
Funny Face
Gems from Gershwin
Gershwins In Hollywood (1931-
1964)
Girl Crazy
Great American Show Tunes
Great Ziegfeld
Kiri Sings Gershwin
Lady Be Good
Manhattan
Musical Comedy Favorites
My One and Only
Of Thee I Sing
Oh Kay!
Porgy and Bess
Primrose
Remember These
S'wonderful, S'marvelous,
S'Gershwin
Shocking Miss Pilgrim
Show Biz (From Vaude to Video)
Soundtracks, Voices and
Themes from Great Movies
Starlift
Starring Fred Astaire
Tea for Two
Three for the Show
Tip Toes
Top Hat
When the Boys Meet the Girls
Young at Heart
GERSHWIN, IRA
American In Paris
By Jupiter
Country Girl
Damsel In Distress
Ethel Merman
Evening with Jerome Kern
Fred Astaire and Ginger Rogers
Funny Face
Gershwins In Hollywood (1931-
1964)
Girl Crazy
Great American Show Tunes
Jerome Kern Goes to
Hollywood
Kiri Sings Gershwin
Kurt Weill In Hollywood
Lady Be Good
Lady In the Dark
My One and Only
Of Thee I Sing

GOODMAN, MILES
La Bamba
Teen Wolf
GOODROW, GARY
National Lampoon Lemmings
GOODROW, MICHAEL
Stages
GOODRUM, RANDY
Stir Crazy
GOODWIN, DOUG
Hey There, It's Yogi Bear
Man Called Flintstone
GOODWIN, RON
Battle of Britain
Film Music
of Human Bondage (And Other
Great Themes)
633 Squadron
Those Daring Young Men In
Their Jaunty Jalopies
Those Magnificent Men In Their
Flying Machines
Trap
Twilight of Honor
Where Eagles Dare
GOODWIN, RUSSELL
Saint of Bleecker Street
GOODWYN, MYLES
Johnny Be Good
GOOM, DEREK
Doctor Who
GOORWITZ, ALLEN
Black Stallion Returns
GORACY, GRANT
Ulysses - The Greek Suite
GORDENO, PETER
Man of La Mancha
GORDON, ANITA
State Fair
GORDON, BARRY
Musical Chairs
GORDON, BERT
My Fairfax Lady
GORDON, CARL
Ain't Supposed to Die a Natural
Death
GORDON, DEXTER
'Round Midnight
GORDON, ELLEN
Fly Blackbird
GORDON, GALE
Christmas Carol
GORDON, HAYES
Brigadoon
Firefly
GORDON, JOHN
Utter Glory of Morrissey Hall
GORDON, JUSTIN
Farewell, My Lovely
GORDON, LEE
Court Jester
Jolson Sings Again
Knock on Wood
GORDON, MACK
Bundle of Joy
I Love Melvin
Orchestra Wives
Shocking Miss Pilgrim
Stooge
Sun Valley Serenade
That Night In Rio
Three Little Girls In Blue
GORDON, MITCH
Washington Behind Closed
Doors
GORDON, NOELE
On the Town
GORDON, PEGGY
Godspell
GORDON, RITA
Boy Meets Boy
GORDON, ROBERT
Loveless
GORDON, ROSCO
Rock Baby Rock It
GORE, CHRISTOPHER
Nefertiti
Via Galactica
GORE, MICHAEL
Fame

Footloose
Terms of Endearment
GORGONI, AL
I Never Sang for My Father
Million Dollar Mystery
GORLIZKI, ILI
To Live Another Summer, to
Pass Another Winter
GORMAN, BOB
Subways Are for Sleeping
GORMAN, CLIFF
Boys in the Band
Lenny
GORME, EYDIE
Academy Awards Presentation
Academy Award Winning Songs
Broadway Musicals
Filmusic Scene
Golden Rainbow
Songs from the Golden Circle
Steve and Eydie
GORSHIN, FRANK
Batman
Jimmy
GORSON, CAROL LEE
Canada
GORTNER, MARJOE
Marjoe
GOSFIELD, MAURICE
Top Cat
GOSNEY, BARRIE
Come Spy with Me
GOSPEL PEARLS
Portraits in Bronze
GOSS, ROBERT
Merry Widow
GOSSETT, LOUIS
Golden Boy
Zulu and the Zayda
GOTTWALD, CLYTUS
2001: A Space Odyssey
GOUGH, LLOYD
No for an Answer
GOULD, ELLIOTT
Drat! the Cat!
Getting Straight
I Can Get It for You Wholesale
M*A*S*H
GOULD, GLENN
Slaughterhouse-Five
GOULD, HAROLD
Karl Marx
GOULD, JOHN
Betjemania
GOULD, MORTON
Arms and the Girl
Beyond the Sound Barrier, Vol.
2
Carousel
Cinerama Holiday
Comden and Green: Show
Music at Its Best
Digital Space
Front Row Center
Gershwin Holiday
Holocaust
Oklahoma
Windjammer
World War I
GOULDING, NIGEL
Full Metal Jacket
GOULDING, RAY
Bob and Ray - The Two and
Only
GOULDMAN, GRAHAM
Animalympics
Mrs. Brown, You've Got a
Lovely Daughter
Sunburn
GOULET, ROBERT
Academy Award Winning Songs
America Sings
Annie Get Your Gun
Brigadoon
Broadway Musicals
Camelot
Carousel
Daydreamer
Filmusic Scene
Gay Purr-ee
Happy Time

Kiss Me Kate
Magic of Musical Comedy
Manhattan Tower
Official Grammy Awards
Archive Collection
Parade of Show Stoppers
GOUNOD, CHARLES
FRANÇOIS
Melba
GOURLAY, EILEEN
Little Me
GOURMET'S DELIGHT
Gas-S-S-S
GOWABE, PATIENCE
King Kong
GOWAN
Navy SEALS
GOWER, JOHN
Phil the Fluter
GOWERS, PATRICK
Marat (De) Sade
Share My Lettuce
Sign of Four
Stevie
Virgin and the Gypsy
GOYETTE, DESIREE
Here Comes Garfield
GOZ, HARRY
Two By Two
GRABEAU, BOB
This Earth Is Mine
GRABLE, BETTY
Betty Grable
Cut! Out-Takes from
Hollywood's Greatest
Musicals
Dolly Sisters
Everybody Sing
Four Jills In a Jeep
Gay Divorcee
Gershwins In Hollywood (1931-
1964)
Ladies of Burlesque
Shocking Miss Pilgrim
Silver Screen Symphony
Soundtracks, Voices and
Themes from Great Movies
Springtime In the Rockies
Three for the Show
GRACIE, CHARLIE
Jamboree!
GRACIE, SALLY
Bunch
GRAFF, ILENE
I Love My Wife
GRAFF, RANDY
City of Angels
Les Miserables
GRAFF, TODD
Baby
GRAFFMAN, GARY
Manhattan
GRAFTON, GLORIA
Rodgers and Hart 1927-1942
GRAHAM, BILLY
It's Time to Pray, America!
Oil Town, U.S.A.
GRAHAM, DEBORAH
Jerry's Girls
Romance / Romance
GRAHAM, FRANK
Hansel and Gretel
GRAHAM, GARY
Touch
GRAHAM, HARRY
Maid of the Mountains
White Horse Inn
GRAHAM, LUCILLE
King and I
West Side Story
GRAHAM, RONNY
Ben Bagley's Cole Porter
Revisited
Bravo Giovanni!
Decline and Fall of the Entire
World As Seen Through the
Eyes of Cole Porter
History of the World, Part I
New Faces of 1952
New Faces of 1968
Take Five

GRAHAM, WILLIAM
Little Mary Sunshine
GRAHAME, GLORIA
Oklahoma
Oscar Hammerstein II
Memorial Album
GRAINER, RON
Cindy-Ella Or I Gotta Shoe
Doctor Who
Edward and Mrs. Simpson
Finest Hours
Maigret
Moon Spinners
Nothing But the Best
Promise Her Anything
Robert and Elizabeth
Tales of the Unexpected
To Sir with Love
GRAMM, LOU
Lost Boys
GRAMMER, SIDNEY
Conversation Piece
GRAMMIS, ADAM
Shirley MacLaine Live at the
Palace
GRAND FUNK RAILROAD
Heavy Metal
GRANDMA MOSES
Grandma Moses Suite
GRANDMASTER FLASH AND
MELLE MEL
Miami Vice
GRANGER, FARLEY
First Impressions
GRANGER, MICHAEL
Fiddler on the Roof
GRANGER, STEWART
Salome
GRANT, A.
Yolanda and the Thief / You'll
Never Get Rich
GRANT, CARY
That's Entertainment!
GRANT, DOUGLAS
Me Nobody Knows
GRANT, GERRY
Fiddler on the Roof
GRANT, GOGI
Big Beat
Gigi
Kiss Me Kate
Show Boat
GRANT, MICKI
Cradle Will Rock
Don't Bother Me, I Can't Cope
Jerico-Jim Crow
Your Arm's Too Short to Box
with God
GRANVILLE, CHARLES
Oliver!
GRATEFUL DEAD
Mask
Rude Awakening
Zabriskie Point
GRAUBART, JUDY
Electric Company TV Show
Mixed Doubles / Below the Belt
GRAUNKE SYMPHONY
Hellbound: Hellraiser II - Time
to Play
High Spirits
King Kong Lives
Man on Fire
Ski Crazy
GRAUNKE, KURT
Barbarian and the Geisha
Big Circus
Film Music of Hugo Friedhofer
El Cid
Ski Crazy
Trapp Family
GRAVENITES, NICK
Steelyard Blues
Trip
GRAVES, ERNEST
Dylan
GRAVES, KATHERINE
Show Boat
GRAVES, PETER
After the Ball

Airplane!
Slipper and the Rose
Survival Run
Water Gipsies
Winds of War

GRAVES, TERESA
Proudly They Came

GRAY, ALLAN
Music for Films

GRAY, BARRY
Space: 1999

GRAY, BILLY
My Fairfax Lady

GRAY, DOBIE
Heartbreak Hotel
Out of Sight

GRAY, DOLORES
Carnival In Flanders
Designing Woman
Destry Rides Again
Follies
It's Always Fair Weather
Kismet
Make Mine Manhattan
Oklahoma
There's No Business Like Show
Business
They Stopped the Show!
Two on the Aisle

GRAY, EDDIE
Funny Thing Happened on the
Way to the Forum

GRAY, GERI
Music Man

GRAY, GLEN
Angel Heart
Music Man

GRAY, JERRY
Club 15

GRAY, JOHN
Billy Bishop Goes to War

GRAY, LINDA
Funny Thing Happened on the
Way to the Forum

GRAY, MARGERY
Anything Goes
Evening with Sheldon Harnick
Tenderloin
Tovarich

GRAY, MICHAEL
Your Arm's Too Short to Box
with God

GRAY, OLIVER
Kean

GRAY, TIMOTHY
High Spirits
Love from Judy

GRAYBO, BOB
Jack and the Beanstalk

GRAYSON, KATHRYN
Anchors Aweigh
Desert Song
Girls...And More Girls
Golden Age of Movie Musicals
Grounds for Marriage
It Happened In Brooklyn
Kiss Me Kate
Kissing Bandit
Ladies of Burlesque
Lovely to Look At
Magnificent Moments from
MGM Movies
Show Boat
So This Is Love
That's Entertainment!
That's Entertainment, Part 2
Thousands Cheer
Till the Clouds Roll By
Ziegfeld Follies of 1946

GRAZIANI, IZHAK
Fiddler on the Roof

GREAN, CHARLES
Dark Shadows

GRECH, RICK
Mahoney's Last Stand

GRECO, BUDDY
Broadway Melodies

GRECO, JULIETTE
Uncle Tom's Cabin

GREELEY, GEORGE
Desert Song

Eddy Duchin Story
Finian's Rainbow
Great Motion Picture Concertos
Merry Widow
Naughty Marietta
Parrish
Popular Piano Concertos from
the Great Broadway Musicals
Roberta
Themes from Mutiny on the
Bounty (And Other Great
Films)
3 Sailors and a Girl
With a Song In My Heart

GREEN GLENN SINGERS
Up with People!

GREEN ON RED
Border Radio
Dangerously Close

GREEN, ADOLPH
Bells Are Ringing
Bonanza Bound
Broadway Magic
Comden and Green: Show
Music at Its Best
Do Re Mi
Doll's Life
Fade Out Fade In
Follies
Hallelujah, Baby!
It's Always Fair Weather
Lady In the Dark
Lute Song
Music from Shubert Alley
On the Town
On the Twentieth Century
Party with Betty Comden and
Adolph Green
Peter Pan
Say Darling
Singin' In the Rain
Subways Are for Sleeping
Take Me Out to the Ball Game
Two on the Aisle
What a Way to Go!
Wonderful Town

GREEN, AL
Scrooged

GREEN, BILL
Impossible Dream - The Story
of the 1967 Boston Red Sox

GREEN, CHARLES
Carousel

GREEN, COLIN
O Lucky Man

GREEN, DANNY
Do Re Mi
Kiss Me Kate

GREEN, ELIZABETH
Sweet Bye and Bye

GREEN, ELVIRA
Naughty Marietta

GREEN, EUGENE
Captain Jinks of the Horse
Marines

GREEN, GRANT
Final Comedown

GREEN, H.F.
New Girl In Town

GREEN, JOANNA
In Trousers

GREEN, JOHN
Twilight of Honor

GREEN, JOHNNY
American In Paris
Ballet Music from MGM
Musicals
Brigadoon
Bye Bye Birdie
Cinderella
Cobweb
Easter Parade
Evening with Lerner and Loewe
Everything I Have Is Yours
Girls...And More Girls
High Society
It Happened In Brooklyn
Johnny Green on the Hollywood
Soundstage
Let's Face It
Mister Imperium
Oliver!

Pepe
Porgy and Bess
Raintree County
Royal Wedding
Silk Stockings
Stooge
Summer Stock
Swan
They Shoot Horses Don't They
West Side Story

GREEN, LOIS
After the Ball

GREEN, MANNY
Landlord

GREEN, MARTYN
Canterbury Tales
Mikado
Pinocchio
Stingiest Man In Town

GREEN, NORMA
His Wife's Habit

GREEN, PAUL
Johnny Johnson

GREEN, PHILIP
All Night Long
Wedding In Paris

GREEN, RON
Roller Boogie

GREEN, SYDNEY
Quiet Man

GREEN, TEDDY
Pickwick

GREEN, TOM
Three the Hard Way

GREENE, ELLEN
Little Shop of Horrors
Threepenny Opera

GREENE, HERBERT
Anyone Can Whistle
Gay Life
Most Happy Fella
Music Man
Silk Stockings
Sondheim
Two on the Aisle
Unsinkable Molly Brown

GREENE, JAMES
Andersonville Trial
In White America

GREENE, JOSEPH
Movie Star, American Style
On Her Bed of Roses

GREENE, LARRY
Annie Get Your Gun
Over the Top
Top Gun

GREENE, LAURA
Deep Throat Part II

GREENE, LEON
Funny Thing Happened on the
Way to the Forum
Tom Brown's School Days

GREENE, LORNE
American Spirit
Battlestar Galactica
Bonanza - Christmas on the
Ponderosa
Bonanza - Ponderosa Party
Time

GREENE, LYN
Flora the Red Menace

GREENE, MILTON
Body Beautiful
Fiddler on the Roof
Rothschilds

GREENE, REUBEN
Boys In the Band

GREENE, RUBY
Four Saints In Three Acts

GREENE, SAM
Ben Franklin In Paris

GREENE, SHANNA
Surfer Girls

GREENE, TEDDY
Baker Street
Darling of the Day

GREENE, WILLIE, JR.
Border

GREENER, DOROTHY
Leave It to Jane
Shoestring Revue '57

Shoestring Revues

GREENFIELD, HOWARD
Silencers

GREENHALGH, EDWARD
Foxy

GREENHILL, MITCH
Long Riders

GREENSLADE, ARTHUR
Fiddler on the Roof
Joanna
Prime of Miss Jean Brodie

GREENSPAN, MURIAL
O Marry Me

GREENWELL, PETER
Crooked Mile

GREENWICH, ELLIE
Leader of the Pack

GREENWOOD, CHARLOTTE
Gang's All Here
Oklahoma
Oscar Hammerstein II
Memorial Album
Out of This World

GREENWOOD, LEE
Smokey and the Bandit III

GREENWOOD, LIL
My People

GREER, DAVID
Aspects of Love

GREER, FRANCES
Desert Song
New Moon
Student Prince
Sweethearts
Vagabond King

GREER, JOANN
Ladies of Burlesque
Naked City
Rita Hayworth
Soundtracks, Voices and
Themes from Great Movies

GREER, MICHAEL
Magic Garden of Stanley
Sweetheart

GREGG, HUBERT
My Fair Lady
Robin Hood

GREGG, JULIE
Happy Time

GREGG, MITCHELL
No Strings
Say Darling
Unsinkable Molly Brown

GREGG, VIRGINIA
American Spirit

GREGORY, ANDRE
Follies

GREGORY, GLENN
Insignificance

GREGORY, JOHN
Brigadoon
Cat and the Fiddle
Girl Friend
My Fair Lady
No, No, Nanette

GREGORY, KEN
Hair

GREGORY, MICHAEL SCOTT
Sophisticated Ladies

GREGORY, PAUL
New Moon

GREGORY, VIRGINIA
Philemon

GRENFELL, JOYCE
Joyce Grenfell Requests the
Pleasure
Monologues and Songs

GRENNAN, NANCY
Too Many Girls

GRENVILLE, CYNTHIA
Fiddler on the Roof

GREY, CLIFFORD
Hit the Deck
Love Me Tonight
Mr. Cinders
Rogue Song
Three Musketeers

GREY, JOEL
Broadway Magic
Cabaret

761

HADDOW, JEFFREY
Scrambled Feet
HADDOX, JIMMY
Rad
HADEN, CHARLIE
Torch Song Trilogy
HADFELD, MARK
Snoopy
HADJIDAKIS, MANOS
Aliki My Love
America, America
Blue
Illya Darling
Memed My Hawk
Never on Sunday
Original Soundtracks and Music
Themes from the Great Motion
Pictures
Topkapi
HADLEY, JERRY
My Fair Lady
HAFFKINE, RON
Who's Harry Kellerman and
Why Is He Saying Those
Terrible Things About Me?
HAFID, ALI
Zorba
HAGAR, SAMMY
Fast Times at Ridgemont High
Footloose
Heavy Metal
Over the Top
Up the Academy
Vision Quest
HAGEGARD, HAKAN
Sound of Music
HAGEMAN, RICHARD
New Orleans
Stagecoach
HAGEN, EARLE
Andy Griffith Show
I Spy
New Interns
HAGEN, HANS
Music Man
My Fair Lady
Oklahoma
South Pacific
HAGEN, UTA
Othello
Who's Afraid of Virginia Woolf?
HAGERTY, JULIE
Airplane!
HAGGARD, MERLE
Bronco Billy
Killers Three
Legend of the Lone Ranger
Platoon (And Songs from the
Era)
HAGMAN, LARRY
Nervous Set
HAGUE, ALBERT
How the Grinch Stole
Christmas
Plain and Fancy
Redhead
HAIGH, KENNETH
Showcase Album, 1967
HAIGHT, PATTI
Boy Meets Boy
HAIMSOHN, GEORGE
Dames at Sea
HAIRSTON, JESTER
Finian's Rainbow
Lilies of the Field
St. Louis Blues
HAKIM AND LADY DIANNA
Garbage Pail Kids
HALDANE, DON
Nikki, Wild Dog of the North
HALE, BARBARA
Higher and Higher
HALE, BINNIE
No, No, Nanette
Sunny
HALE, GEORGINA
Boy Friend
HALE, JOHN
Anne of the Thousand Days

HALE, MONTE
James Dean Story
HALE, RICHARD
Christmas Carol
HALE, ROBERT
Irene
HALEY, BILL, & COMETS
Let the Good Times Roll
HALEY, JACK
Beyond the Blue Horizon
Higher and Higher
Inside U.S.A.
Rodgers and Hart in Hollywood
Wake Up and Live
Wizard of Oz
HALF PINT
Mighty Quinn
HALFACRE, BILL
Hello Dolly!
HALINKA, ANNA
After the Ball
HALL, ADELAIDE
Blackbirds of 1928
Jamaica
Kiss Me Kate
Love from Judy
HALL, ALBERT
Ain't Supposed to Die a Natural
Death
Apocalypse Now
HALL, BETTINA
Cat and the Fiddle
HALL, CARL
Inner City
O Babylon
HALL, CAROL
Best Little Whorehouse in
Texas
HALL, CLIFF
Here's Love
HALL, DARRYL
Earth Girls Are Easy
HALL, DELORES
Best Little Whorehouse in
Texas
Inner City
Your Arm's Too Short to Box
with God
HALL, DORA
Dora's World
Imagine That - Songs from the
TV Special
Once Upon a Tour
HALL, ELLIS, JR.
Lonely Lady
HALL, GEORGE
Brighton Beach Memoirs
Cinderella
Demi Dozen
Ernest in Love
Pennies from Heaven
HALL, JENNIFER
Bright Lights, Big City
HALL, JOHN
Ka-Boom!
HALL, JUANITA
Flower Drum Song
House of Flowers
Sing Out Sweet Land
South Pacific
HALL, MICHAEL
My Cousin Josefa
HALL, PAMELA
Dear World
Sondheim: A Musical Tribute
HALL, RENE
First Nudie Musical
HALL, TOM T.
Harper Valley P.T.A.
HALLEE, JONATHON
Flower Drum Song
HALLIDAY, GORDON
Shenandoah
HALLIDAY, JOHN
Bird of Paradise
HALLIDAY, ROBERT
Three Wishes for Jamie
HALLIGAN, RICHARD
Owl and the Pussycat

HALLORAN, JACK
How the West Was Won
HALLOWS EVE
River's Edge
HALLYDAY, DAVID
He's My Girl
Lady Beware
HALO ORCHESTRA
Flower Drum Song
HALPIN, HELEN
Gigi
HALSALL, OLLIE
Rutles
HALVORSEN, JOHAN
European Holiday
HAM, AL
Harlow
Stop the World - I Want to Get
Off!!
HAMBURG CONCERT
ORCHESTRA
Rozsa: Suites for the Films
HAMBURG SYMPHONY
Very Best of Richard Rodgers
HAMBURG, H.Y.
Hold on to Your Hats
HAMBURGER, LAY
Godspell
HAMELCOOKE, CHRIS
Joseph and the Amazing
Technicolor Dreamcoat
HAMILL, MARK
Empire Strikes Back
Star Wars
HAMILTON, BARBARA
Anne of Green Gables
HAMILTON, CARRIE
Tokyo Pop
HAMILTON, CHICO
Bye Bye Birdie
Irma La Douce
Sweet Smell of Success
Yolanda and the Thief / You'll
Never Get Rich
HAMILTON, DICK
Creative Freakout
HAMILTON, GEORGE
American Spirit
HAMILTON, HENRY
Go Fly a Kite
HAMILTON, JULIE
Ballad of Fanny Hill
HAMILTON, LUCY
Drowning of Lucy Hamilton
HAMILTON, LYNN
Sanford and Son
HAMILTON, MARGARET
Goldilocks
Wizard of Oz
HAMILTON, TED
Pirate Movie
HAMLETT, DEXTER
I Will
HAMLISCH, MARVIN
April Fools
Champ
Chorus Line
Film Music
Ice Castles
Pennies from Heaven
Sophie's Choice
Spy Who Loved Me
Sting
Swimmer
They're Playing Our Song
Way We Were
HAMMER, JAN
Miami Vice
Miami Vice II
Night in Heaven
Secret Admirer
HAMMER, M.C.
Colors
Teenage Mutant Ninja Turtles
HAMMER CITY ORCHESTRA
Dracula
HAMMERLEE, PATRICIA
New Faces of 1952
Seventh Heaven

HAMMERSTEIN, OSCAR, II
Allegro
Carmen Jones
Carousel
Cinderella
Desert Song
Evening with Jerome Kern
Flower Drum Song
Fly with Me
Helen Morgan Story
High, Wide and Handsome
Jerome Kern Goes to
Hollywood
King and I
Lovely to Look At
Me and Juliet
Melachrino Orchestra Plays
Medleys
Music in the Air
New Moon
Oklahoma
Oscar Hammerstein II
Memorial Album
Pipe Dream
Roberta
Rodgers and Hammerstein
Deluxe Set
Rose Marie
Show Boat
Sound of Music
South Pacific
State Fair
Sunny
Sweet Adeline
Together with Music
Very Warm for May
HAMMOND, JOHN
Little Big Man
HAMNER, EARL
Walton's Christmas Album
HAMPTON, DAWN
Greenwich Village U.S.A.
HAMPTON, JAMES
It's Time to Pray, America!
HAMPTON, LEE
Earthquake
HAMPTON, LIONEL
All American
Benny Goodman Story
Clams on the Half Shell
HAMSHERE, KEITH
Oliver!
HANAN, STEPHEN
Cats
HANCOCK, BARBARA
Finian's Rainbow
HANCOCK, CHRISTOPHER
Billy
HANCOCK, HERBIE
Back to the Beach
Blow-Up
Death Wish
Jo Jo Dancer, Your Life Is
Calling
Official Music of the XXIIIrd
Olympiad, Los Angeles 1984
'Round Midnight
Spook Who Sat By the Door
Twins
HANCOCK, SHEILA
One Over the Eight
HANCOX, DAISY
Irene
HAND TOOLS
Bad Guys
HANDAKAS, JAMES
Five After Eight
HANDS OF TIME
Wild Angels
HANDY, WILLIAM C.
St. Louis Blues
HANEY, CAROL
Pajama Game
This Is Broadway's Best
HANIGHEN, BERNARD
Lute Song
HANKIN, LARRY
Committee
HANKS, TOM
Dragnet

762

HANLEY, EDDIE
Top Banana
HANLEY, ELLEN
Boys from Syracuse
Fiorello!
First Impressions
Take Five
Two's Company
HANLEY, KATIE
Godspell
Grease
HANNA, LLOYD
Oklahoma
HANNAH, DARRYL
Legal Eagles
HANOVER FIST
Wild Life
HANSEN, JACK
Around the World In 80 Days
My Fair Lady
HANSEN, RON
Athenian Touch
HAPPENINGS
Purple People Eater
HAPPY MONDAYS
Lost Angels
HARADA, ERNEST
Pacific Overtures
HARBACH, OTTO
Cat and the Fiddle
Desert Song
Evening with Jerome Kern
Firefly
Jerome Kern Goes to
  Hollywood
Lovely to Look At
No, No, Nanette
Roberta
Rose Marie
Sunny
HARBURG, E.Y.
Ben Bagley's Oscar
  Hammerstein Revisited
Blazing Saddles
Bloomer Girl
Cabin In the Sky
Can't Help Singing
Darling of the Day
Evening with Jerome Kern
Finian's Rainbow
Flahooley
Happiest Girl In the World
Jamaica
Judy at the Palace
Pinocchio
Ship Ahoy
State Fair
Stooge
Wizard of Oz
HARDEN, WILBUR
King and I
HARDER, JAMES
All In the York Family
Athenian Touch
HARDIE, RUSSELL
Andersonville Trial
HARDIN, GLEN D.
Elvis In Concert
Elvis: Aloha from Hawaii Via
  Satellite
That's the Way It Is
HARDIN, TY
Palm Springs Weekend
HARDING, SAM
Come Spy with Me
HARDISON, KADEEM
Rappin'
HARDWICK, MARK
Oil City Symphony
Pump Boys and Dinettes
HARDWICK, PAUL
Romeo and Juliet
HARDWICKE, SIR CEDRIC
Bing's Hollywood
Co-Star
Jack the Ripper
HARDY, JANE
Biograph Girl
HARDY, JANIS
Postcard from Morocco

HARDY, WILLIAM, JR.
Your Arm's Too Short to Box
  with God
HARE, DORIS
Houdini, Man of Magic
Valmouth
Waier Gipsies
HARE, ROBERTSON
Funny Thing Happened on the
  Way to the Forum
HAREWOOD, DORIAN
Brainchild
HARGER, GARY
Shenandoah
HARKNESS, GORDON
Order Is Love
HARLE, JOHN
Prick Up Your Ears
HARLEY, MARGOT
Crystal Heart
Ernest In Love
HARLINE, LEIGH
Film Music
Pinocchio
Snow White and the Seven
  Dwarfs
HARLOW, JEAN
That's Entertainment!
HARMA, CHARMAINE
Carousel
King and I
HARMAN, BARRY
Romance / Romance
HARMAN, BUDDY
Clambake
Elvis
HARMON, JOHNNY
Cindy
HARMON, KEITH
Captain Jinks of the Horse
  Marines
HARMON, MARY
By the Beautiful Sea
Mrs. Patterson
HARMON, PEGGY
Big River (the Adventures of
  Huckleberry Finn)
HARMON, STEVE
One and Only, Genuine,
  Original Family Band
HARMONAIRES
One Too Many (Hit Songs From)
HARMONICATS
All American
Great New Motion Picture
  Themes
Great Themes from TV and
  Motion Pictures
HARMS, CARI
Man In the Moon
HARNELL, JOE
Censored
HARNEY, BEN
Dream Girls
HARNICK, SHELDON M.
Apple Tree
Baker Street
Body Beautiful
Captain Jinks of the Horse
  Marines
Evening with Sheldon Harnick
Fiddler on the Roof
Fiorello!
Four Television Musicals
Man in the Moon
New Faces of 1952
Rex
Rothschilds
She Loves Me
Shoestring Revues
Smiling, the Boy Fell Dead
Tenderloin
To Broadway with Love
HARP, KEN
Music Man
HARP, MARTHA LOU
Jamboree!
HARPER, DOLORES
House of Flowers

HARPER, JESSICA
Doctor Selavy's Magic Theater
Phantom of the Paradise
HARPER, REDD
Oil Town, U.S.A.
HARPER, VALERIE
Go Fly a Kite
Paul Sills' Story Theater (of
  Magical Folk-Rock Fables)
HARPER, WALLY
Barbara Cook at Carnegie Hall
Day in Hollywood / Night in the
  Ukraine
Grand Tour
Nine
HARPERS BIZARRE
Magnavox Presents Frank
  Sinatra
HARRAH, WALT
Pennies from Heaven
HARRELL, GORDON LOWRY
City of Angels
Inner City
Rockabye Hamlet
HARRIETT, JUDY
Say One for Me
HARRINGTON, DONALD
Carmilla
HARRINGTON, LESLIE
Naughty Marietta
HARRINGTON, PAT
Call Me Madam
HARRINGTON, ROBERT
Peter Pan
HARRIS, ALBERT
Alakazam the Great
HARRIS, BARBARA
Apple Tree
From the Second City
Official Grammy Awards
  Archive Collection
On a Clear Day You Can See
  Forever
Who's Harry Kellerman and
  Why Is He Saying Those
  Terrible Things About Me?
HARRIS, BOB
Lolita
Thing-Fish
HARRIS, BRENDA
Greenwillow
HARRIS, DAVID
Carry It On
HARRIS, DIANNE LYNNE
Order Is Love
HARRIS, ED
Alamo Bay
HARRIS, EDDIE
Exodus to Jazz
Sharky's Machine
Soul to Soul
HARRIS, EMMYLOU
Honeysuckle Rose
Last Waltz
Planes, Trains, and
  Automobiles
Roadie
HARRIS, HARRY
Snow White and the Three
  Stooges
HARRIS, HERB
Best of Burlesque
Comden and Green: Show
  Music at Its Best
Frankie and Johnny
HARRIS, HOWARD
Monsieur De Pourceaugnac
HARRIS, JET
Endless Summer
HARRIS, JEREMY
Tuscaloosa's Calling Me (But
  I'm Not Going)
HARRIS, JOHNNY
Hero
HARRIS, JULIE
ANTA Album of Stars, Vol. 2
Belle of Amherst
Curtain Going Up (Musical
  Guide to Play Acting)
Glass Menagerie

James Dean Story
Skyscraper
HARRIS, LARNELLE
Born Again
HARRIS, LLOYD
Evening with W.S. Gilbert
70 Girls, 70
HARRIS, MARCENE
Soul Hustler
HARRIS, MIKE
Purple People Eater
HARRIS, PHIL
Aristocats
Best of Disney
Brigadoon
Evening with Lerner and Loewe
Jungle Book
Merriest Songs
Once Upon a Tour
Robin Hood
HARRIS, RICHARD
Bible
Camelot
Cromwell
Jonathan Livingston Seagull
Mack the Knife
Prophet
Tommy
HARRIS, ROBERT H.
Foxy
HARRIS, THURSTON
Christine
HARRIS, TOM
Grease
HARRIS, TONY
Portraits In Bronze
HARRIS, WALTER
Hair
HARRISON, GEORGE
Beatlemania
Help!
Lethal Weapon 2
Let It Be
Magical Mystery Tour
Paul Sills' Story Theater (of
  Magical Folk-Rock Fables)
Porky's Revenge!
Sgt. Pepper's Lonely Hearts
  Club Band
Wonderwall
Yellow Submarine
HARRISON, JERRY
Something Wild
HARRISON, JOHN
Creepshow
Day of the Dead
HARRISON, NELL
Producers
HARRISON, NOEL
Thomas Crown Affair
HARRISON, REX
Broadway Magic
Doctor Dolittle
Magic of Musical Comedy
My Fair Lady
HARRISON, WILLIAM
Fiddler on the Roof
HARROLD, JACK
Candide
Silverlake
Unsinkable Molly Brown
HARRON, DONALD
Anne of Green Gables
HARRY, DEBORAH
Krush Groove
Married to the Mob
Scarface
Soup for One
HART, AL
Dean Martin Testimonial Dinner
HART, AMY
Girls Just Want to Have Fun
HART, ANN
Gentlemen Prefer Blondes
HART, BOBBY
Josie and the Pussycats
HART, COREY
Beverly Hills Cop II
9½ Weeks
HART, DUNSTAN
Dancing Years

Singin' In the Rain
Slaughter on 10th Avenue
Star
Take Me Out to the Ball Game
Till the Clouds Roll By
Words and Music
Ziegfeld Follies of 1946

HAYWARD, JUSTIN
War of the Worlds

HAYWARD, SUSAN
Back Street
Girls...And More Girls
I'll Cry Tomorrow

HAYWARD, THOMAS
New Moon
Night In Venice

HAYWOOD, NANCY
Go Fly a Kite

HAYWORTH, RITA
Miss Sadie Thompson
Pal Joey
Rita Hayworth
Salome

HAZARD, RICHARD
Heroes
Rosemary's Baby
Shaft's Big Score

HAZARD COUNTY BOYS
Dukes of Hazzard

HAZELL, HY
Charlie Girl
Little Shop of Horrors
Lock Up Your Daughters
No Strings

HAZELWOOD, LEE
Movin' with Nancy
Sweet Ride

HAZLETT, DUKE
Pal Joey

HEAD, MURRAY
Chess
Jesus Christ Superstar

HEAL, JOAN
Divorce Me, Darling!
Grab Me a Gondola

HEALEY, JEFF
Road House

HEALY, DAVID
Follies

HEALY, MARY
5,000 Fingers of Dr. T

HEALY, TED
Hollywood Hotel

HEARD, JOHN
Silent Partner

HEALD, ANTHONY
Anything Goes

HEARN, GEORGE
Doll's Life
Follies
I Remember Mama
La Cage Aux Folles
Sondheim
Stephen Sondheim Evening

HEARTBEATS
Diner

HEATH, LOUISE
Last Sweet Days of Isaac

HEATH, SIGRID
Love Song

HEATHERTON, RAY
Rodgers and Hart 1927-1942
Too Many Girls

HEATWAVE
Skatetown U.S.A.
Sunburn

HEAVEN
Easy Money

HEAVEN 17
Electric Dreams
Night Shift
Summer Lovers

**HEAVEN AND HELL
ORCHESTRA**
Nocturna

HECHT, JOSHUA
Ballad of Baby Doe
Regina

HECHT, PAUL
Mac Bird

Rothschilds
1776

HECKART, EILEEN
Family Affair

HECKMAN, DON
Great Debates
Wizard of Oz

HEDGES, MICHAEL
Shape of the Land

HEFER, LAIM
Kazablan

HEFFERNAN, JOHN
Purlie

HEFLIN, MARTA
Earl of Ruston
Perfect Couple
Salvation

HEFLIN, VAN
Airport

HEFTI, NEAL
Barefoot In the Park
Batman
Boeing, Boeing
Duel at Diablo
Harlow
Hollywood Song Book -
    Academy Award Winners
How to Murder Your Wife
Last of the Secret Agents
Lord Love a Duck
Magnificent Movie Music
Odd Couple
Oh Dad, Poor Dad, Mamma's
    Hung You In the Closet and
    I'm Feelin' So Sad
Sex and the Single Girl
Synanon
Themes from TV's Top 12

HEIFETZ, JASCHA
Heifetz on Television

HEINDORF, RAY
Auntie Mame
Baby Doll
Bad Seed
Calamity Jane
Damn Yankees
Eddie Cantor Story
Finian's Rainbow
For Whom the Bell Tolls
Frances Langford Presents
Giant
Golden Age of the Hollywood
    Musical
Helen Morgan Story
I'll See You In My Dreams
James Dean Story
Lullaby of Broadway
Marjorie Morningstar
Music Man
Pajama Game
Pete Kelly's Blues
Serenade
1776
Spellbound
Star Is Born
Starlift
Streetcar Named Desire
Too Much, Too Soon
Tribute to James Dean

HEISS, CAROL
Snow White and the Three
    Stooges

HEISSER, JEAN-FRANÇOIS
Au Revoir Les Enfants

HEITGERD, DON
Cinderella

HELD, ANNA
50th Anniversary of George
    Jessel In Show Business

HELD, DAN
You Never Know

HELIX
Iron Eagle

HELLER, ALFRED
Evening with W.S. Gilbert

HELLER, HUGH
Creative Freakout

HELLO PEOPLE
American Dreamer

HELM, LEVON
Coal Miner's Daughter

HELMKE, ERIKA
Threepenny Opera

HELMORE, TOM
House of Flowers

HELMS, BOBBY
Cookie

HELMS, JIM
Gold
Hang Your Hat on the Wind
His Wife's Habit
Kung-Fu

HELPMANN, ROBERT
Midsummer Night's Dream
Patrick
Tales of Hoffmann
Valmouth

HEMING, PERCY
Primrose

HEMMINGS, DAVID
Journey to the Center of the
    Earth

HEMPHILL, BARRY
Believers

HEMRIC, GUY
Bikini Beach
Cycle Savages
Doctor Goldfoot and the Girl
    Bombs
How to Stuff a Wild Bikini
Mary Jane
Pajama Party
Savage Seven
Sidehackers
Thunder Alley
Wild In the Streets

HEMSLEY, SHERMAN
Purlie

**HEMSLEY, WINSTON
DEWITT**
Hallelujah, Baby!
Hello Dolly!

HENDERSON, BILL
Get Crazy

HENDERSON, CHARLES
Girls...And More Girls
I'll Cry Tomorrow

HENDERSON, FLORENCE
Fanny
Fiorello!
Girl Who Came to Supper
Little Women
Oklahoma
Olds for '60 Musical
Richard Rodgers
Song of Norway
Sound of Broadway
South Pacific
This Is Oldsmobility

HENDERSON, LUTHER
Ain't Misbehavin'
Annie Get Your Gun
Bravo Giovanni!
Helen Morgan Story
Turned on Broadway

HENDERSON, MARCIA
Peter Pan

HENDERSON, MELANIE
Electric Company TV Show
Me Nobody Knows

HENDERSON, MICHAEL
About Last Night
Armed and Dangerous

HENDERSON, RAY
Best Things In Life Are Free
Billy Barnes' L.A.
Good News
Singing Fool
Turnabout
Wonderful O

HENDERSON, ROBERT
Candide

HENDERSON, SKITCH
Porgy and Bess

HENDL, WALTER
River
Scandalous Life of Frankie and
    Johnny

HENDRA AND ULLETT
Kiss Me Kate

HENDRICKS, JON
Real Ambassadors

HENDRIX, JIMI
American Pop
Easy Rider
Jimi Hendrix
Jimi Plays Monterey
Monterey Pop
1969
Over the Edge
Rainbow Bridge
Rattle and Hum
Where the Buffalo Roam
Woodstock

HENDRIX, NONA
Coming to America
Hard to Hold
Perfect
Summer Lovers

HENDRIX, PAULA
Boys from Syracuse

HENDRY, TOM
Doctor Selavy's Magic Theater

HENEKER, DAVID
Biograph Girl
Charlie Girl
Half a Sixpence
Irma La Douce
Make Me an Offer
Peg
Phil the Fluter

HENIG, ANDI
Big River (the Adventures of
    Huckleberry Finn)

HENKINS, JACKIE
This Was Burlesque

HENLEY, DON
Color of Money
Fast Times at Ridgemont High
Vision Quest

HENNAGIN, J. MICHAEL
Impact

HENNESSEY, HANGNAILS
Rides, Rapes and Rescues
    (Themes from Great Silent
    Films)

HENNING, DOUG
Magic Show

HENRIQUE, LUIZ
Joy

HENRY, ANN
New Faces of 1956

HENRY, BUCK
Saturday Night Live
Taking Off

HENRY, CLARENCE
Diner

HENRY, GLORIA
Dennis the Menace

HENRY, JOHN
Dawgs

HENRY, MOSE
Swedish Fly Girls

HENRY, SUZANNE
Marry Me a Little

HENSLEY, TOMMY
Christmas to Elvis

HENSON, JIM
Muppet Movie
Sesame Street

HENSON, JOHN
Most Happy Fella
This Is Broadway's Best

HENSON, LESLIE
Funny Face
Primrose
Sally

HENSON, NICKY
Camelot
Canterbury Tales

HENZE, HANS WERNER
Swann In Love / Katharina
    Blum

HEPBURN, AUDREY
Funny Face
My Fair Lady

HEPBURN, KATHARINE
Coco
Delicate Balance
Love Among the Ruins
On Golden Pond

766

HIRSCHHORN, JOEL
Pete's Dragon
Seven Brides for Seven
  Brothers
Toller Cranston's the Ice
  Show...On Broadway
Towering Inferno

HIRSCHHORN, ROBERT
I Can't Keep Running In Place

HIRSH, DONALD
Bold Ventures

HIRSH, GARY
Tarot

HIRSHHORN, NAOMI C.
Spoon River Anthology

HIRST, DENISE
Boy Friend

HIRT, AL
Gershwin Holiday
NARM's Golden Decade
Viva Max!

HIS MASTER'S FISH
Sweeney Todd (The Demon
  Barber of Fleet Street)

HITCHCOCK, ALFRED
Films Of Alfred Hitchcock
Music to Be Murdered By

HITCHCOCK, MAX
Fatal Attraction

HITCHCOCK, RICK
Female Animal

HITLER, ADOLPH
D-Day Plus 20
Hitler's Inferno

HITTERS
Pretty In Pink

HO, DON
Don Ho Show!
Magnavox Presents Frank
  Sinatra

HOBBS, JACK
Sunny

HOBSON, VALERIE
King and I

HOCKRIDGE, EDMUND
Can-Can
Desert Song
Pajama Game

HODAPP, ANN
One Way Ticket to Broadway
  Two

HODGE, CHARLIE
Double Trouble
Elvis (NBC-TV Special)
Elvis: Aloha from Hawaii Via
  Satellite
That's the Way It Is

HODGES, ANN
No Strings

HODGES, EDDIE
C'mon, Let's Live a Little
Happiest Millionaire
Music Man
Summer Magic

HODGES, PAT
Love at First Bite

HOENIG, MICHAEL
Wraith

HOEY, DENNIS
Desert Song

HOFFERT, BRENDA
Outrageous

HOFFMAN, AL
Alice In Wonderland
Cinderella

HOFFMAN, BERN
Li'l Abner

HOFFMAN, CARY
What's a Nice Country Like the
  U.S. Doing In a State Like
  This?

HOFFMAN, DUSTIN
Death of a Salesman
Lenny
Little Big Man
Who's Harry Kellerman and
  Why Is He Saying Those
  Terrible Things About Me?

HOFFMAN, PATTI
Do Black Patent Leather Shoes
  Really Reflect Up?

HOFFMAN, PHILIP
Baby
Is There Life After High School?

HOFFMAN, WALTER
Bold Ventures

HOFNER, TOM
Tallulah

HOGAN, PHILIP
Aladdin

HOLBROOK, HAL
Mark Twain Tonight

HOLBROOK, TAMI
Girls Just Want to Have Fun

HOLCOLMB, ROSCOE
Zabriskie Point

HOLCOMBE, W.
Stereo Space Odyssey

HOLDEN, MARK
Scrooge

HOLDEN, PAUL
Tom Jones

HOLDEN, WILLIAM
Fleet's In

HOLDER, RAY
Card

HOLDRIDGE, LEE
Beastmaster
Beauty and the Beast
Beyond the Sound Barrier, Vol.
  2
East of Eden
Forever Young, Forever Free
Jeremy
Mahogany
Moment By Moment
Old Gringo
Oliver's Story
Other Side of the Mountain,
  Part II
Splash
Tilt
Transylvania 6-5000

HOLGATE, DANNY
Bubbling Brown Sugar
Don't Bother Me, I Can't Cope

HOLGATE, RONALD
Funny Thing Happened on the
  Way to the Forum
Grand Tour
1776

HOLIDAY, BILLIE
Magic Moments from the
  Tonight Show
New Orleans
Sound of Jazz
Torch Song Trilogy

HOLIDAY, BOB
Fiorello!
It's a Bird, It's a Plane, It's
  Superman

HOLIDAY, HOPE
Arabian Nights
Li'l Abner

HOLLAND
Girls Just Want to Have Fun

HOLLAND, AMY
Night of the Comet
St. Elmo's Fire
Scarface

HOLLAND, CHARLES
Four Saints In Three Acts

HOLLAND, JOOLS
Bachelor Party
Urgh - A Music War

HOLLAND, ROBERT
Down In the Valley

**HOLLAND - DOZIER -
  HOLLAND**
T.C.B. (Takin' Care of Business)

HOLLANDER, FREDERICK
Anything Goes
Casablanca: Classic Film
  Scores for Humphrey Bogart
5,000 Fingers of Dr. T

HOLLANDER, XAVIERA
My Pleasure Is My Business

HOLLEY, DORIAN
Stir Crazy

HOLLIDAY, DAVID
Coco
Sail Away

HOLLIDAY, JENNIFER
Dream Girls
I'm Gonna Git You Sucka

HOLLIDAY, JUDY
Bells Are Ringing
Broadway Magic
Cut! Out-Takes from
  Hollywood's Greatest
  Musicals
Film Music
Revuers

HOLLIDAY, MARK
Athenian Touch

HOLLIDAY, ROBERT
Twilight of Honor

HOLLIER, JILL
Pink Cadillac

HOLLIES
After the Fox
Stardust

HOLLINGSWORTH, JOHN
Chu Chin Chow
Invitation to the Dance

HOLLMAN, BILL
Mother Earth

HOLLOWAY, PATRICE
Josie and the Pussycats

HOLLOWAY, STANLEY
Broadway Magic
Hamlet
Hit the Deck
Midsummer Night's Dream
Mikado
My Fair Lady
Oliver!

HOLLOWAY, STERLING
Absent-Minded Professor
Alakazam the Great
Aristocats
Jungle Book
Peter and the Wolf

HOLLY, BUDDY
American Graffiti
American Hot Wax
Buddy Holly Story
Christine
Peggy Sue Got Married
Stand By Me

HOLLY, ELLEN
Hand Is on the Gate

HOLLYRIDGE SINGERS
Skyscraper

**HOLLYWOOD BOWL
  ORCHESTRA**
Alfred Newman Conducts His
  Great Film Music
Hollywood Pops
Music from Motion Pictures
Plow That Broke the Plains
Porgy and Bess
Rhapsody Under the Stars

**HOLLYWOOD CHAMBER
  JAZZ GROUP**
Stakeout

**HOLLYWOOD CINEMA
  ORCHESTRA**
Duel In the Sun

**HOLLYWOOD GRAND
  STUDIO ORCHESTRA**
Big Hits from Columbia
  Pictures

HOLLYWOOD ORCHESTRA
Around the World In 80 Days

**HOLLYWOOD POPS
  ORCHESTRA**
Fiddler on the Roof

**HOLLYWOOD SOUNDSTAGE
  ORCHESTRA**
Music Man
Original Soundtracks and Music
Thoroughly Modern Millie

**HOLLYWOOD
  SOUNDMAKERS**
Music from a Fistful of Dollars
  / For a Few Dollars More /

The Good, the Bad and the
  Ugly

**HOLLYWOOD STUDIO
  ORCHESTRA**
Exodus
Gulliver In Lilliput
Hawaii

**HOLLYWOOD SYMPHONY
  ORCHESTRA**
Apartment
Egyptian
Israel Now
Motion Picture Music
On the Beach
Robe

**HOLLYWOOD
  TRANSCRIPTION
  ORCHESTRA**
Around the World In 80 Days
Exodus

HOLM, CELESTE
Bloomer Girl
Cinderella
High Society
Oklahoma
Three Little Girls In Blue
Tom Sawyer
Utter Glory of Morrissey Hall

HOLMAN, LIBBY
Beggar's Holiday
Blues, Ballads and Sin Songs

HOLMES, CHRISTINE
Charlie Girl

HOLMES, JACK
O Say Can You See!

HOLMES, JAKE
Dusty and Sweets McGee

HOLMES, LEROY
All American
Citizen Kane
Devil's Brigade
Double Impact
Follow the Boys
For a Few Dollars More
Golden Motion Picture Themes
  and Original Soundtracks
Great Motion Picture Themes
Incredible World of James
  Bond
James Bond
King Kong
Lush Themes from Motion
  Pictures
Magnificent Movie Music
Man from U.N.C.L.E.
More Great Motion Picture
  Themes
More Lush Themes from Motion
  Pictures
Music from the Modern Screen
Night They Raided Minsky's
No, No, Nanette
Once Upon a Time In the West
Original Soundtracks and Music
Parade of Hits
Prisoner of Zenda
Soundtracks (Music from Great
  Motion Pictures)
Star Is Born
Themes from New Provocative
  Films

HOLMES, MAYNARD
Cradle Will Rock

HOLMES, RUPERT
Animals (Five Savage Men)
Edwin Drood
Five Savage Men
Flasher
Mystery of Edwin Drood
No Small Affair
Star Is Born

HOLMES, WALLY
Blacula

HOLOFCENER, LARRY
Mister Wonderful

HOLSCLAW, DOUG
Second Shepherd's Play

HOLT, ASHLEY
Journey to the Center of the
  Earth

HOLT, BOB
Pete's Dragon

HOLT, WILL
Kurt Weill Cabaret
Me Nobody Knows
Platinum
Taking My Turn

HOLTZMAN, MARVIN
Fool Britannia

HOLY MODAL ROUNDERS
Easy Rider

HOMER AND JETHRO
NARM's Golden Decade

HOMRICH, JUNIOR
Emerald Forest

HONEYMOON SUITE
Lethal Weapon
Wraith

HONG, ARABELLA
Flower Drum Song

HONK
Five Summer Stories

HOOK, WALTER
Captain Jinks of the Horse
  Marines
Sweet Bye and Bye

HOOKER, BRIAN
Maid of the Mountains
Vagabond King

HOOKS, ROBERT
Hallelujah, Baby!
Official Grammy Awards
  Archive Collection

HOOPER, EWAN
Hooray for Daisy!

HOOPER, LEE
Zorba

HOOVER, DENETTE
Always

HOOVER, MARILYN
Mickey and the Beanstalk
Summer Magic

HOPE, BOB
Beau James
Bing's Hollywood
Bob Hope In Hollywood
Cole Porter In Hollywood
  (1929-1956)
Command Performance
Dean Martin Testimonial Dinner
Dick Tracy In BB
Frances Langford Presents
I'll Take Sweden
My Favorite Brunette
Not So Long Ago
$1000 a Touchdown
Paris Holiday
Proudly They Came
Quick and the Dead - The Story
  of the Atom Bomb
Road to Bali
Road to Hong Kong
Road to Singapore
Seven Little Foys
Twenty-Five Years of Life

HOPGOOD, ALAN
Lola Montez

HOPKIN, MARY
Kidnapped
Where's Jack?

HOPKINS, ALBERTA
King and I

HOPKINS, ANTHONY
Love for Love

HOPKINS, BRUCE
Faggot

HOPKINS, KENYON
Baby Doll
East Side, West Side
Eleven Against the Ice
Fugitive Kind
Hustler
James Bond
Lilith
Mister Buddwing
Reporter
Something Unique
Strange One
This Property Is Condemned
Yellow Canary

HOPKINS, LIGHTNIN'
Sounder

HOPKINS, LINDA
Honkytonk Man
Inner City
Me and Bessie
Purlie
Sting II

HOPKINS, MIRIAM
Ladies of Burlesque

HOPKINS, RAND
I Will

HOPPE, MICHAEL
Misunderstood

HOPPER, DENNIS
Apocalypse Now
Easy Rider

HOPPER, JACK
Golden Screw

HOPSCOTCH
If It's Tuesday, This Must Be
  Belgium

HORDERN, MICHAEL
Funny Thing Happened on the
  Way to the Forum
Slipper and the Rose
Taming of the Shrew
Watership Down

HORGEN, PATRICK
Baker Street

HORMEL, GEORGE
Night of the Living Dead

HORN, PAUL
Cleopatra
Mikado

HORN, SHIRLEY
For Love of Ivy
Hit Motion Picture Themes

HORNE, GEOFFREY
Strange Interlude

HORNE, LENA
Broadway, Broadway, Broadway
Cabin In the Sky
Cut! Out-Takes from
  Hollywood's Greatest
  Musicals
Girls...And More Girls
Harry and Lena
Jamaica
Lena Horne: The Lady and Her
  Music
Opening Night at the Palace -
  Sweet Charity
Porgy and Bess
Richard Rodgers
Rodgers and Hart In Hollywood
Stormy Weather
That's Entertainment!
That's Entertainment, Part 2
Thousands Cheer
Till the Clouds Roll By
25 Years of Recorded Sound
Wiz
Words and Music
Ziegfeld Follies of 1946

HORNE, MARILYN
Carmen Jones
Flower Drum Song
Man of La Mancha

HORNER, JAMES
Aliens
American Tail
Another 48 Hours
Batteries Not Included
Battle Beyond the Stars
Brainstrom
Cocoon
Cocoon: The Return
Dad
Field of Dreams
Glory
Gorky Park
Humanoids from the Deep
Krull
Land Before Time
Pursuit of D.B. Cooper
Red Heat
Screen Themes
Star Trek II: The Wrath of Khan
Star Trek III: The Search for
  Spock
Where the River Runs Black
Willow

HORNER, JULIE E.
Seven Brides for Seven
  Brothers

HOROWITZ, CHERYL S.
Fly with Me

HOROWITZ, NORBERT
Wall

HORROX, FRANK
One Over the Eight
Pieces of Eight

HORSEMEN
Outlaw Riders

HORSEY, MARTIN
Oliver!

**HORTON, EDWARD
  EVERETT**
Carousel
Gang's All Here
Gay Divorcee

HORTON, ROBERT
110 In the Shade

HORWITT, ARNOLD
Make Mine Manhattan
Plain and Fancy

HORWITZ, DAVID
Candide

HOSHOUR, ROBERT
Romance / Romance

HOSSACK, GRANT
Pal Joey
They're Playing Our Song

HOT
Strong Together

HOT CHOCOLATE
Car Wash

HOT CLUB OF FRANCE
New York Stories

HOT COLD SWEAT
Good to Go

HOT DATE
Spring Break

HOTHOUSE FLOWERS
Courier

HOTSTREAK
Breakin'

HOTY, DEE
City of Angels

HOUGH, JULIAN
Happy As a Sandbag

HOULE, GLENN
Chocalonia

HOUNDS
Skatetown U.S.A.

HOUSE, JAMES
Wraith

HOUSE, JANE
Lenny

HOUSE, RON
El Grande De Coca Cola

HOUSE OF SCHOCK
Bull Durham

HOUSEMAN, JOHN
Great American Fourth of July
  Parade
Julius Caesar
Winds of War

HOUSTON, CISSY
Taking My Turn

HOUSTON, ROBERT
Shogun Assassin

HOUSTON, THELMA
Bingo Long Traveling All-Stars
  and Motor Kings
Into the Night
Lean on Me
Looking for Mr. Goodbar
Thank God It's Friday

HOUSTON, WALTER
Knickerbocker Holiday

HOUSTON, WHITNEY
Bodyguard
Perfect

**HOUSTON GRAND OPERA
  COMPANY**
Porgy and Bess

HOVEY, SERGE
Tevya and His Daughters

HOVHANESS, ALAN
Flowering Peach

HOVIS, JOAN
Plain and Fancy

HOVIS, LARRY
Hogan's Heroes

HOWARD, ALAN
King of the Whole Damn World

HOWARD, B.
Baby

HOWARD, EDDY
Slam Dance

HOWARD, FRANKIE
Funny Thing Happened on the
  Way to the Forum

HOWARD, JAMES NEWTON
Five Corners
Major League
Promised Land
Russkies
Tap
Wildcats

HOWARD, JERRY
Wild In the Streets

HOWARD, JOHN
Hazel Flagg
One Over the Eight

HOWARD, KEN
Seesaw
1776

HOWARD, LARRY
By the Beautiful Sea

HOWARD, MIKI
Fatal Beauty

HOWARD, PETER
Annie
Barnum
Dance a Little Closer
Her First Roman
How Now, Dow Jones
Party with Betty Comden and
  Adolph Green
1776

HOWARD, RICHARD
Oh What a Lovely War

HOWARD, RON
Music Man

HOWARD, SYDNEY
Funny Face

HOWARD, TEX
My Fair Lady
Oklahoma

HOWARTH, ALAN
Escape from New York
Halloween II
Halloween III - Season of the
  Witch
Halloween IV - Return of
  Michael Meyers
Halloween V - Revenge of
  Michael Meyers They Live

HOWARTH, DAVID
Buddy

HOWARTH, ELGAR
200 Motels

HOWE, ROBERT
Great Waltz

HOWE, SIMON
Seven Brides for Seven
  Brothers

HOWE, WILLIAM
My Square Laddie

HOWELL, BOBBY
Aladdin
Cinderella

HOWELL, DENNIS
Sweet Bye and Bye

HOWELL, ELIZABETH
Sound of Music

HOWERD, FRANKIE
Funny Thing Happened on the
  Way to the Forum
Sgt. Pepper's Lonely Hearts
  Club Band

HOWES, BOBBY
Finian's Rainbow

HOWES, SALLY ANN
Beggar's Holiday
Brigadoon
Chitty, Chitty, Bang, Bang
Gift of the Magi
Hans Andersen

I Remember Mama
Kwamina
Official Grammy Awards
Archive Collection
What Makes Sammy Run?
HOWLAND, BETH
Company
Darling of the Day
HOWLETT, NEIL
Annie Get Your Gun
HOWMAN, DAVID
Life of Brian
HOXWORTH, MARY ANN
Mrs. Patterson
HOYEM, ROBERT
Juno
HOYER, OLE
Eric Soya's 17
HUBBARD, JERRY R.
Smokey and the Bandit
HUBERT, JANET L.
Cats
HUBLEY, SEASON
Catch My Soul
HUDDLESTON, FLOYD
Aristocats
Robin Hood
HUDDLESTON, MICHAEL
World's Greatest Lover
HUDSON, HOWARD
Seven Brides for Seven
Brothers
HUDSON, PETER
Most Happy Fella
HUDSON, ROCK
James Dean Story
Pillow Talk
Showdown
HUDSON, TRAVIS
Grand Tour
Very Good Eddie
Young Abe Lincoln
HUE AND CRY
Hiding Out
HUES CORPORATION
Blacula
HUEY, RICHARD
Bloomer Girl
Lonesome Train
HUFF, RONN
Miracle Goes On
HUGESSEN, JIM
My Fur Lady
HUGG, B.
Up the Junction
HUGH, GRAYSON
True Love
HUGHES, BILL
Outsiders
HUGHES, LANGSTON
Jerico-Jim Crow
Simply Heavenly
Street Scene
Tambourines to Glory
HUGHES, NORMA
Song of Norway
HUGHES, RHETTA
Amen Corner
Don't Play Us Cheap
HUGO AND LUIGI CHORUS
Sound of Broadway
HUGUELY, JAY
That Other Woman's Child
HULBERT, CLAUDE
Oh Kay!
Primrose
HULL, LISA
Charlie Girl
HUMBARD, REX
It's Time to Pray, America!
HUME, DOREEN
Cat and the Fiddle
Girl Friend
No, No, Nanette
HUMPERDINCK,
ENGELBERT
Hansel and Gretel
HUMPHREY, HUBERT H.
ABC Scope

Age of Television
Foster Brooks' Roasts
HUMPHRIES, BARRY
Housewife Superstar
HUMPHRIES, ELIZABETH
King and I
HUMPHRIES, JULIA
Allegro
HUNG, TSIN TING KIANG
Beyond the Great Wall
HUNGARIAN STATE OPERA
ORCHESTRA
Extreme Prejudice
King Solomon's Mines
Rent-A-Cop
HUNGARIAN STATE
SYMPHONY
Sicilian
HUNT, JAN
Show Boat
HUNT, LOIS
Carousel
King and I
Kiss Me Kate
Night with Jerome Kern
Night with Rudolf Friml
Oklahoma
HUNT, PEE WEE
Music Man
HUNT, RICHARD
Muppet Movie
HUNTER, ALBERTA
Remember My Name
HUNTER, CAROL
Pat Garrett and Billy the Kid
HUNTER, FRANK
Here's Love
Mame
Sounds Broadway! Sounds
Hollywood! Sounds Great!
HUNTER, HANK
Looking for Love
HUNTER, IAN
Fright Night
Light of Day
Teachers
Up the Academy
Wraith
HUNTER, IVORY JOE
Heart of Dixie
HUNTER, LAURA
Disorderlies
HUNTER, LESLIE
Thousand Miles of Mountains
HUNTER, ROBERT
Carol Channing
Show Girl
HUNTER, TAB
Damn Yankees
Hans Brinker
HUNTLEY, CHET
Time to Keep
HUNTLEY, JOBE
Tambourines to Glory
HUNTSBERRY, HOWARD
Ghostbusters II
La Bamba
HURD, DANNY
Hair
HURLEY, LAUREL
Merry Widow
Night In Venice
HURST, JAMES
Sail Away
HURT, JO
Pal Joey
HURT, MARY
Bye Bye Birdie
HUSKY, FERLIN
Country Music Holiday
HUSMANN, RON
All American
Man of La Mancha
Tenderloin
HUSSEY, OLIVIA
Lost Horizon
Romeo and Juliet
HUSTIN, TOM
House of Leather

HUSTON, ANGELICA
Dead
HUSTON, JOHN
Bible
Night of the Iguana
HUSTON, WALTER
Ichabod and Mr. Toad
Memorable Moments In
Musical Comedy
Myra Breckinridge
Swanee River
They Stopped the Show!
Yankee Doodle Dandy
HUTCH, WILLIE
Foxy Brown
Mack
HUTCHERSON, LEVERN
Carmen Jones
HUTCHINSON, BRENDA
Liquid Sky
HUTCHINSON, MARK
Girl Friend
HUTMAN, JERRY
Lost Horizon
HUTTON, BETTY
Annie Get Your Gun
Blonde Bombshell
By the Beautiful Sea
Cut! Out-Takes from
Hollywood's Greatest
Musicals
Fleet's In
Gershwins In Hollywood (1931-
1964)
Girls...And More Girls
Hits from Broadway Shows
Hutton In Hollywood
Satins and Spurs
Somebody Loves Me
That's Entertainment, Part 2
HUTTON, BILL
Festival
Joseph and the Amazing
Technicolor Dreamcoat
HUTTON, DANNY
American Flyers
Pretty In Pink
HUTTON, JUNE
Pal Joey
HUTTON, MARION
Glenn Miller: Golden Hits from
His Original Soundtracks
HUXLEY, ALDOUS
Bernard Herrmann
HYDE, BRUCE
Canterbury Tales
HYDE-WHITE, WILFRID
In Search of the Castaways
My Fair Lady
HYER, BILL
Flower Drum Song
HYLAN, MARY
Apple
HYLTON, JACK
White Horse Inn
HYMAN, DICK
Gigi
Hannah and Her Sisters
Moonstruck
Purple Rose of Cairo
Scott Joplin
Whoop-Up!
HYMAN, PHYLLIS
Fish That Saved Pittsburgh
School Daze
Sophisticated Ladies
HYMAN, ROBERT
Joseph and the Amazing
Technicolor Dreamcoat
HYMAS, TONY
Twins
HYNES, ELIZABETH
Silverlake
HYSON, RAY
On Your Toes
Young Abe Lincoln
IAN, JANIS
Betrayal
IANNI, RICHARD
Athenian Touch

IBERT, JACQUES
Don Quichotte
Invitation to the Dance
ICE HOUSE
Modern Girls
ICKS, DEITRA
Mama I Want to Sing
IDLE, ERIC
Adventures of Baron
Munchausen
Life of Brian
Monty Python and the Holy
Grail
IDOL, BILLY
Adventures of Ford Fairlane
IDOLLS
Assault of the Killer Bimbos
IGNICO, ROBIN
Feeling Good with Annie
IKETTES
Hairspray
IMPERATO, CARLO
Fame
IMPERIALS
That's the Way It Is
IMPRESSIONS
Flamingo Kid
Three the Hard Way
INCANTATION
Mission
INCREDIBLE STRING BAND
Taking Off
INDIGO GIRLS
Wonder Years
INFERNAL BLUE MACHINE
Adios Amigo
INFORMATION SOCIETY
Earth Girls Are Easy
ING, ALVIN
Pacific Overtures
INGELS, MARTY
Kiss Me Kate
INGHAM, BARRIE
Gypsy
INGLE, JOHN
Lovers
INGRAM, JAMES
American Tail
Beverly Hills Cop II
Houseful of Love: Music from
the Bill Cosby Show
Wildcats
INGRAM, LUTHER
Wattstax (the Living Word)
INGRAM, MICHAEL
Preppies
INGRAM, NICK
Jesus Christ Superstar
INGRAM, PHILIP
Back to School
INGRAM, REX
Cabin In the Sky
INK SPOTS
Fraulein
INNER CIRCLE
Rockers
INNER SANCTUM
Golden Screw
INNES, NEIL
Monty Python and the Holy
Grail
Rutles
INNOCENT BYSTANDERS
Fritz the Cat
INSIDERS
Iron Eagle II
INTERNATIONAL FESTIVAL
ORCHESTRA
Can-Can
INVESTITURE AND CRIME
WAVE
Teenage Mutant Ninja Turtles
INXS
American Anthem
Lost Boys
Pretty In Pink
IOWA FOUR
Music Man

IRISH GUARDS
 Wild Geese
IRISH ROVERS
 Rockabye Hamlet
IRON BUTTERFLY
 Manhunter
 Savage Seven
IRONS, JEREMY
 Brideshead Revisited
 Lion King
 My Fair Lady
 Real Thing
IRVING, AMY
 Honeysuckle Rose
IRVING, ERNEST
 *Golden Age of British Film
  Music*
 Music for Films
IRVING, GEORGE
 Anya
 Body In the Seine
 Bravo Giovanni!
 Carousel
 Evening with Richard Nixon
 Gentlemen Prefer Blondes
 I Remember Mama
 Irene
 Irma La Douce
 Me and My Girl
 On Your Toes
 Regina
 So Long 174th Street
 Threepenny Opera
 Tovarich
 Two's Company
IRVING, JOHN
 Ernest In Love
IRVING, KATIE
 Carrie
IRWIN, JACK
 Best Foot Forward
 Single Room Furnished
IRWIN, WAYNE
 Three In the Attic
IRWIN, WILL
 Littlest Revue
 Texas Li'l Darlin'
ISAACS, GREGORY
 Rockers
ISAAK, CHRIS
 American Flyers
 Married to the Mob
 Shag
ISACKSON, MICK
 Boy Meets Boy
ISHAM, MARK
 Beast
 Country
 Love at Large
 Made In Heaven
 Moderns
 Mrs. Soffel
 Steadfast Tin Soldier
 Trouble In Mind
ISHEE, SUZANNE
 Jerry's Girls
ISLEY BROTHERS
 Heavy Traffic
 Wanderers
 Wildcats
ITO, GENJI
 Pacific Overtures
ITO, TEIJI
 Coach with the Six Insides
ITURBI, JOSE
 Anchors Aweigh
IVERS, PETER
 Eraserhead
IVERSEN, YVONNE
 Ulysses - The Greek Suite
IVES, BURL
 Hugo the Hippo
 In Search of the Castaways
 Lonesome Train
 Merriest Songs
 *Music from Disney Motion
  Pictures*
 *Rudolph the Red-Nosed
  Reindeer*
 Sing Out Sweet Land
 Summer Magic

IVORY
 License to Kill
IWAKI, HIROYUKI
 Ran
IWANOW, TATJANA
 Hello Dolly!
J.J. FAD
 Coming to America
JABARA, PAUL
 Hair
 Honky-Tonk Freeway
 Main Event
 Mother, Jugs and Speed
 Thank God It's Friday
**JACK AND JILL LITTLE
 PEOPLE**
 Annie Get Your Gun
JACKIE AND GAYLE
 Wild on the Beach
 Wild, Wild Winter
JACKMAN, HOPE
 Oliver!
JACKSON, ANNE
 Brecht on Brecht
 Luv
JACKSON, C. BERNARD
 Earthquake
 Fly Blackbird
JACKSON, CHUCK
 Patty
JACKSON, EDDIE
 Jimmy Durante TV Show
JACKSON, ERNESTINE
 Guys and Dolls
 Raisin
JACKSON, FREDDIE
 All Dogs Go to Heaven
JACKSON, GLENDA
 Marat (De) Sade
 Stevie
 Tell Me Lies
JACKSON, HARRIETT
 Porgy and Bess
JACKSON, JACKIE
 My Stepmother Is an Alien
JACKSON, JERMAINE
 About Last Night
 Beverly Hills Cop II
 I'm Gonna Git You Sucka
 Loving Couples
 Perfect
JACKSON, JO
 Believers
JACKSON, JOE
 Mike's Murder
 Times Square
 *Tucker (the Man and His
  Dream)*
JACKSON, JUNE
 T.R. Baskin
 Where's Poppa?
JACKSON, MAHALIA
 America Sings
 *Jo Jo Dancer, Your Life Is
  Calling*
JACKSON, MARLON
 Golden Child
JACKSON, MERRELL
 Godspell
JACKSON, MICHAEL
 Ben
 E.T. - The Extra-Terrestrial
 Wiz
JACKSON, MILLIE
 Cleopatra Jones
JACKSON, MILT
 Silent Partner
JACKSON, REV. JESSE
 Save the Children
 Wattstax (the Living Word)
JACKSON, ROBERT
 House of Flowers
 Raisin
JACKSON, STEVE
 Oklahoma
JACKSON FIVE (JACKSONS)
 Burglar
 Goin' Back to Indiana
 Save the Children
 Skatetown U.S.A.

JACOB, BILL
 Jimmy
JACOB, PATTI
 Jimmy
JACOB, STEVEN
 Sondheim
 Stephen Sondheim Evening
JACOBI, DEREK
 Much Ado About Nothing
JACOBI, LOU
 Fade Out Fade In
JACOBI, NORMAN
 Touch
JACOBS, CHARLIE
 Heart of Dixie
JACOBS, DICK
 *Broadway Song Book (Volumes
  1 and 2)*
 James Dean Story
 *Themes from Classic Science
  Fiction, Fantasy and Horror
  Films*
 Themes from Horror Movies
JACOBS, JACOB
 Bei Mir Bistu Schoen
JACOBS, JIM
 Grease
JACOBS, PAUL
 National Lampoon Lemmings
JACOBSON, IRVING
 Kosher Widow
 Man of La Mancha
 *Official Grammy Awards
  Archive Collection*
JACOBSON, KENNETH
 Hot September
JACOBY, SCOTT
 Cry for Us All
 Golden Rainbow
JACQUEMIN, ANDRE
 Life of Brian
JACQUEMOT, RAY
 Down In the Valley
JAEGER, DENNY
 Hunger
JAEP, ROGER
 Skateboard
JAGGER, MICK
 Ned Kelly
 Performance
 Ruthless People
JAGUARS
 Everybody's All-American
JAMAL, SATI
 *Ain't Supposed to Die a Natural
  Death*
JAMES, BARNEY
 *Journey to the Center of the
  Earth*
JAMES, BOB
 Genie
 King of Comedy
JAMES, CAROLYN
 Sweet Bye and Bye
JAMES, ETHAN
 Blue Iguana
JAMES, ETTA
 Back to the Future
 Bad Influence
 Rain Man
JAMES, GERALD
 Much Ado About Nothing
 Pickwick
JAMES, HARRY
 50 Years of Film
 Guys and Dolls
 Hannah and Her Sisters
 Twilight of Honor
 Young Man with a Horn
JAMES, JOSEPH
 Priest of Love
JAMES, JUDITH
 Miss Julie
JAMES, OLGA
 Carmen Jones
 Mister Wonderful
JAMES, POLLY
 Anne of Green Gables
 Half a Sixpence
 I and Albert

JAMES, RICK
 Beverly Hills Cop
 Colors
JAMES, SIDNEY
 Kiss Me Kate
JAMES, STEPHEN
 *Day in Hollywood / Night in the
  Ukraine*
JAMES, TERRY
 Jonathan Livingston Seagull
JAMES, WILLIAM
 Maggie Flynn
JAMES GANG
 Zachariah
JAMESON, BOBBY
 Mondo Hollywood
JAMESON, JOYCE
 Billy Barnes Revue
 Billy Barnes' L.A.
JAMESON, NICK
 Fine Mess
JAMESON, PAULINE
 Christmas Carol
JAMESON, PETER
 *Mary C. Brown and the
  Hollywood Sign*
JAMISON, JUDITH
 Sophisticated Ladies
JAN AND DEAN
 Karate Kid
 Purple People Eater
 Ride the Wild Surf
 Stardust
JANACEK, LEO
 Unbearable Lightness of Being
JANEZIC, BARBARA
 Crystal Heart
JANIS, BEVERLY
 Street Scene
JANKEL, ANNABEL
 Desperately Seeking Susan
 DOA
JANKEL, CHAZ
 *Tales from the Dark Side (the
  Movie)*
JANNEY, LEON
 Thousand Miles of Mountains
JANS, ALARIC
 *Do Black Patent Leather Shoes
  Really Reflect Up?*
JANSEN AND HART
 Sigmund and the Sea Monsters
JANSSEN, DANNY
 Josie and the Pussycats
JANSSEN, WERNER
 *Memorable Music from the
  Movies*
JARDINE, AL
 Almost Summer
JARMAN, CLAUDE, JR.
 Rio Grande
JARRE, MAURICE
 Apology
 *Award Winning Original Motion
  Picture Sound Tracks and
  Themes*
 Behold a Pale Horse
 Bride
 Cocktail
 Collector
 Crossed Swords
 Damned
 Doctor Zhivago
 Dreamscape
 Enemy Mine
 Enola Gay
 Fatal Attraction
 Gorillas In the Mist
 Grand Prix
 Great Expectations
 *Great Original Soundtracks and
  Movie Themes*
 Is Paris Burning?
 Island at the Top of the World
 Jarre By Jarre
 Jesus of Nazareth
 Julia and Julia
 Lawrence of Arabia
 *Life and Times of Judge Roy
  Bean*
 Lion of the Desert

JOHNSTON, AUDRE
  Half Past Wednesday
JOHNSTON, JANE A.
  Greenwich Village U.S.A.
JOHNSTON, JOHNNY
  Kiss Me Kate
  Tree Grows In Brooklyn
JOHNSTON, JUSTINE
  Follies
JOLLY, PETE
  City Heat
  Mother, Jugs and Speed
JOLSON, AL
  Al Jolson
  Al Jolson Story Soundtrack:
    Outtakes and Alternate
    Takes
  Best Things In Life Are Free
  50 Years of Film
  50th Anniversary of George
    Jessel In Show Business
  Go Into Your Dance
  Great Personalities of
    Broadway
  Irving Berlin Tribute
  Jolson Sings Again
  Legends of the Musical Stage
  Silencers
  Silver Screen Symphony
  Singing Fool
  Swanee River
  Wonder Bar
JON C.
  Light of Day
JONAH AND THE WAILERS
  Hey There, It's Yogi Bear
JONAS, DOROTHY
  Miklos Rozsa
JONAS, JOANNE
  Godspell
JONASON, FAYE
  Best of Broadway 1973
JONAY, ROBERTA
  Allegro
JONES, ALLAN
  Beyond the Blue Horizon
  Cut! Out-Takes from
    Hollywood's Greatest
    Musicals
  Everybody Sing
  Firefly
  Great Ziegfeld
  Pure Gold Movies
  Radio Days
  Rose Marie
  Rodgers and Hart In Hollywood
JONES, ANNE
  Once Upon a Mattress
JONES, BRENDA
  Evening with Diana Ross
JONES, CARMELL
  Barefoot Adventure
JONES, CHARLOTTE
  How Now, Dow Jones
JONES, CLIFF
  Rockabye Hamlet
JONES, DANIEL
  Under Milk Wood
JONES, DAVY
  Head
  Hellcats
  Point
  Stardust
JONES, DEAN
  Blackbeard's Ghost
  Company
  Official Grammy Awards
    Archive Collection
  Tom Thumb
JONES, DON
  Tap Dance Kid
JONES, GEORGE
  Night the Lights Went Out In
    Georgia
JONES, GERALDINE
  Lost Man
JONES, GLENN
  Youngblood
JONES, GLORIA
  Hitter

JONES, GRACE
  Pumping Iron 2 - The Women
JONES, GWEN
  Song of Norway
JONES, HANK
  Gigi
JONES, JACK
  Judy Garland
  NARM's Golden Decade
  Wildcat
JONES, JAMES EARL
  Empire Strikes Back
  Great White Hope
  Hand Is on the Gate
JONES, JILL
  Earth Girls Are Easy
JONES, JIMMY
  My People
JONES, JOE
  Let My People Come
JONES, JOHN PAUL
  Song Remains the Same
JONES, JONAH, QUARTET
  Another Evening with Fred
    Astaire
  Evening with Fred Astaire
JONES, JULIAN
  Funny Face
JONES, JULIE
  My Fair Lady
  Oklahoma
JONES, KEN
  Fire Down Below
  Mahoney's Last Stand
  Saint
JONES, KENNEY
  McVicar
JONES, L.
  Rides, Rapes and Rescues
    (Themes from Great Silent
    Films)
JONES, LAUREN
  Ain't Supposed to Die a Natural
    Death
JONES, LEILANI
  Grind
  Little Shop of Horrors
JONES, MARTI
  Back to the Beach
JONES, NEIL
  Promises, Promises
JONES, NITA
  Half Past Wednesday
JONES, ORAN
  Less Than Zero
JONES, PAULETTE ELLEN
  Inner City
JONES, PAUL
  Evita
  Privilege
JONES, PETER
  Hitch-Hikers Guide to the
    Galaxy
JONES, POWELL
  Thief of Bagdad
JONES, PRISCILLA
  Pat Garrett and Billy the Kid
JONES, QUINCY
  Bob and Carol and Ted and
    Alice
  Broadway's Big Hits
  Cactus Flower
  Color Purple
  Deadly Affair
  Dollars ($)
  Enter Laughing
  For Love of Ivy
  Great Motion Picture Themes
  Hot Rock
  In Cold Blood
  In the Heat of the Night
  Italian Job
  John and Mary
  Lost Man
  Mackenna's Gold
  Man and Boy
  Mirage
  Official Music of the XXIIIrd
    Olympiad, Los Angeles 1984
  Pawnbroker
  Roots

Sanford and Son
Save the Children
Slender Thread
Slugger's Wife
They Call Me Mister Tibbs
Walk Don't Run
Wiz
JONES, RALPH
  Slumber Party Massacre
JONES, REED
  Cats
JONES, RICKIE LEE
  King of Comedy
JONES, ROBERT OWEN
  Captain Jinks of the Horse
    Marines
  Sweet Bye and Bye
JONES, SAMUEL
  King and I
JONES, SHIRLEY
  April Love
  Brigadoon
  Carousel
  Evening with Diana Ross
  Maggie Flynn
  Music Man
  Oklahoma
  Oscar Hammerstein II
    Memorial Album
  Pepe
JONES, SIMON
  Hitch-Hikers Guide to the
    Galaxy
JONES, STAN
  Westward Ho, the Wagons
JONES, STEVE
  Miami Vice II
  Something Wild
JONES, T.C.
  Mask and Gown
  New Faces of 1956
JONES, TERRY
  Life of Brian
  Monty Python and the Holy
    Grail
JONES, TODD
  Cry for Us All
JONES, TOM (Composer)
  Celebration
  Colette
  Fantasticks
  I Do! I Do!
  Irma La Douce
  110 In the Shade
  Philemon
  Shoestring Revue '57
JONES, TOM
  James Bond 13 Original
    Themes
  Pink Panther Strikes Again
  Promise Her Anything
  Thunderball
  What's New Pussycat?
JONES, TREVOR
  Angel Heart
  Bad Influence
  Dark Crystal
  Dominic and Eugene
  Grab Me a Gondola
  Happy As a Sandbag
  Labyrinth
  Mississippi Burning
  Runaway Train
  Sea of Love
  Sweet Lies
JONES, VALORIE
  Evening with Diana Ross
JONES BEACH MARINE
  THEATER ORCHESTRA
  Mardi Gras
JOPLIN, JANIS
  Janis
JOPLIN, SCOTT
  Pretty Baby
  Scott Joplin
  Sting
JORDAN, DUKE
  Les Liaisons Dangereuses
JORDAN, EARL
  Starlight Express

JORDAN, JIM AND MARION
  Fibber McGee and Mollie
JORDAN, LEE
  Two By Two
JORDAN, LONNIE
  Youngblood
JORDAN, MARC
  Apple Tree
  Darling of the Day
  Youngblood
JORDAN, STANLEY
  Blind Date
JORDAN, STEVE
  Sounds from True Stories
JORDANAIRES
  Christmas to Elvis
  Clambake
  Co-Star
  Double Trouble
  Easy Come, Easy Go
  Follow That Dream
  Frankie and Johnny
  G.I. Blues
  Girl Happy
  Girls! Girls! Girls!
  Harum Scarum
  Jailhouse Rock
  Kid Galahad
  King Creole
  Kissin' Cousins
  Loving You
  Paradise, Hawaiian Style
  Roustabout
  Speedway
  Spinout
  This Is Elvis
  Tickle Me
  Viva Las Vegas
JORY, VICTOR
  Tubby the Tuba
JOSEPH, ALLEN
  Eraserhead
JOSEPH, IRVING
  Luv
JOSEPH, JACKIE
  Billy Barnes Revue
JOSEPH, QUINTON
  Let's Do It Again
JOSEPHS, WILLIAM
  Fantasy - Space
  My Side of the Mountain
JOSLYN, BETSY
  Doll's Life
JOURDAN, LOUIS
  Can-Can
  Cole Porter In Paris
  Gigi
  Magnificent Moments from
    MGM Movies
  Red Sky at Morning
JOURNEY
  Heavy Metal
  Risky Business
  Tron
  Two of a Kind
  Vision Quest
JOY, LEONARD
  Down In the Valley
  Stars of the Silver Screen,
    1929-1930
JOYCE, DOROTHEA
  Jeremy
JOYCE, ELAINE
  Sugar
JOYCE, JAMES
  Coach with the Six Insides
  Ulysses
JUDAS PRIEST
  Johnny Be Good
JUDGE, COUNT
  WELLINGTON
  Ipi-Tombi
JUDSON POETS
  Christmas Rappings
JUICY
  Beat Street
JUICY BANANAS
  Repo Man
JUICY FRUITS
  Phantom of the Paradise

JULIA, RAUL
  Mack the Knife
  Nine
  Threepenny Opera
  Two Gentlemen of Verona
JULIAN, DON
  Savage
JULLANA, JAMES
  Point of Order
JUMP, GORDON
  Happy Prince
JUMP START
  Van Nuys Blvd.
JUN, ROSE MARIE
  Pins and Needles
  Power Is You
JUNCTION
  Hard Ride
JUNGE, CHANNEN
  Ulysses - The Greek Suite
JUNIOR
  All the Right Moves
  Beverly Hills Cop
JUNKIN, JOHN
  Four Musketeers
JURGENS, CURT
  Inn of the Sixth Happiness
  Threepenny Opera
  Very Best of Richard Rodgers
JUSTER, EVELYN
  What Do You Want to Be When
    You Grow Up?
JUSTICE, JAMES
  ROBERTSON
  Robin Hood
JUSTIN, SIDNEY
  Wildcats
JUSTIN, SUSAN
  Forbidden World
JUSTIS, BILL
  Hooper
  Loveless
  Smokey and the Bandit
  Spoon River Anthology
K.C. & SUNSHINE BAND
  Eyes of Laura Mars
  Nobody's Perfect
  Saturday Night Fever
K-9 POSSE
  I'm Gonna Git You Sucka
KABILIJO, ALFI
  Sky Bandits
KAEMPFERT, BERT
  Man Could Get Killed
KAGAN, DIAN
  Bunch
KAH, HUBERT
  Gotcha
  Once Bitten
  Rad
KAHAN, MICHELLE
  Aladd
KAHAUOLOPUA, HALELOKE
  Arthur Godfrey
KAHN, DAVE
  Impact
  Mike Hammer
KAHN, GUS
  Whoopee!
KAHN, HOWARD
  Merry Widow
KAHN, MADELINE
  At Long Last Love
  Blazing Saddles
  Just for Openers
  Man of La Mancha
  Mixed Doubles / Below the Belt
  New Faces of 1968
  On the Twentieth Century
  Two By Two
  Young Frankenstein
KAISER, KURT
  Natural High
KAISER, ROBIN
  Late Nite Comic (A New
    American Musical)
KALDENBERG, KEITH
  Most Happy Fella
KALEIDOSCOPE
  Zabriskie Point

KALIBAN, BOB
  Ben Franklin In Paris
KALICH, JACOB
  Fiddler on the Roof
KALLAN, RANDI
  Stages
KALLEN, KITTY
  Artie Shaw Plays Cole Porter
KALLMAN, DICK
  Hank
  Seventeen
KALMAR, BERT
  Evening with Beatrice Lillie
  Gentlemen Marry Brunettes
  Three Little Words
KAMEN, MICHAEL
  Adventures of Baron
    Munchausen
  Lethal Weapon
  Lethal Weapon 2
  License to Kill
  Next Man
  Screen Themes
  Stunts
  Suspect
KAMON, KAREN
  Flashdance
KAMOZE, INI
  Good to Go
KANDER, JOHN
  Act
  Cabaret
  Chicago
  Evening with Fred Ebb and
    John Kander
  Family Affair
  Flora the Red Menace
  Funny Lady
  Go Fly a Kite
  Happy Time
  Liza Minnelli at the Winter
    Garden
  Liza with a "Z"
  Lucky Lady
  New York, New York
  Rink
  70 Girls, 70
  Woman of the Year
  Zorba
KANDIDATE
  Sunburn
KANE, ARTIE
  Eyes of Laura Mars
  Farewell, My Lovely
  Looking for Mr. Goodbar
KANE, BIG DADDY
  Colors
  Lean on Me
KANE, BYRON
  Stan Freberg Shows
KANE, CAROL
  World's Greatest Lover
KANE, HELEN
  Pennies from Heaven
  Stars of the Silver Screen,
    1929-1930
  Three Little Words
KANE, IRENE
  Tenderloin
KANE GANG
  Bad Guys
KANSAS, JERI
  42nd Street
KAPER, BRONISLAU
  Auntie Mame
  Butterfield 8
  Eileen
  Film Music of Bronislau Kaper
  Flea In Her Ear
  Forbidden Planet
  Get Crazy
  Lili
  Lord Jim
  Love Themes from Motion
    Pictures
  Movie Hits By Bronislau Kaper
  Mutiny on the Bounty
  Swan
  That's Entertainment
  Way West

KAPLAN, ELLIOT
  Finnegan's Wake
  Square Root of Zero
KAPLAN, MARVIN
  Top Cat
KAPLAN, SOL
  Doctor Strangelove (And Other
    Great Movie Themes)
  Judith
  Living Free
  Spy Who Came In from the Cold
  Victors
  Young Lovers
KAPLOWITZ, MARK
  Close Encounters of the Third
    Kind
KAPROFF, DANA
  Golden Seal
KARAS, ANTON
  Third Man Theme
KARATY, TOMMY
  Cindy
KARAYAN, STEPHEN,
  CHOIR
  Student Prince
KAREN, KENNY
  If Ever I See You Again
KARGER, FRED
  Angel, Angel, Down We Go
  Eddy Duchin Story
  Fastest Guitar Alive
  Frankie and Johnny
  Get Yourself a College Girl
  Kissin' Cousins
  When the Boys Meet the Girls
  Your Cheatin' Heart
KARIN, FIA
  Parade
KARIN, RITA
  Wall
KARLIN, FRED
  Baby Maker
  California Dreaming
  Leadbelly
  Lovers and Other Strangers
  Loving Couples
  Max Morath at the Turn of the
    Century
  Sterile Cuckoo
  Up the Down Staircase
  Westworld
  Yours, Mine and Ours
KARLIN, MIRIAM
  Fiddler on the Roof
KARLISKI, S.
  Time to Sing
KARLOFF, BORIS
  Evening with Boris Karloff and
    His Friends
  How the Grinch Stole
    Christmas
  Ichabod (the Legend of Sleepy
    Hollow)
  Mad Monster Party
  Peter Pan
  Ugly Duckling
KARLTON, SYLVIA
  Allegro
KARM, MICHAEL
  Two By Two
KARMEN, STEVE
  Candidate
  What Do You Say to a Naked
    Lady?
KARMOYAN, MICHAEL
  Anya
  Bravo Giovanni!
  Bring Back Birdie
  Fiddler on the Roof
  Gigi
  Gypsy
  Zorba
KARP, CHARLIE
  Speed Zone
KARR, HAROLD
  Happy Hunting
KARR, PATTI
  Different Times
  Musical Chairs
  So Long 174th Street

To Broadway with Love
KASANEWITZ, PETER, TRIO
  Doctor Zhivago
KASEM, CASEY
  Glory Stompers
KASHA, AL
  Pete's Dragon
  Seven Brides for Seven
    Brothers
  Toller Cranston's the Ice
    Show...On Broadway
  Towering Inferno
KASKARA
  Che!
KASKET, HAROLD
  Sound of Music
KASSIR, JOHN
  Three Guys Naked from the
    Waist Down
KASZNAR, KURT
  Androcles and the Lion
  Sound of Music
  Waiting for Godot
KATAGIRI, ROSE
  Flower Drum Song
KATONA, JULIUS
  Seven Deadly Sins
KATRINA AND THE WAVES
  Iron Eagle
KATZ, CHARLIE
  Gentlemen Prefer Blondes
KATZ, FRED
  Poitier Meets Plato
  Sweet Smell of Success
KATZ, MICKEY
  Hello Solly!
KAUER, GENE
  Across the Great Divide
KAUFFMANN, CHRISTIAN
  Legs Diamond
KAUFLINN, JACK
  Young Abe Lincoln
KAUFMAN, ERWIN
  Aladd
KAUFMAN, JEFFREY
  American Game
KAUFMAN, PEARL
  Five Easy Pieces
KAULILI, ALVINA
  13 Daughters
KAVA, CAROLINE
  Threepenny Opera
KAY, ARTHUR
  Song of Norway
KAY, BARBARA
  Joanna
KAY, SUSAN
  Tamalpais Exchange
KAYE, ALMA
  Sing Out Sweet Land
KAYE, ANNE
  Now Is the Time for All Good
    Men
KAYE, BERYL
  Joyce Grenfell Requests the
    Pleasure
KAYE, BUDDY
  Man Called Dagger
  Peking Medallion
  That Man In Istanbul
KAYE, DANNY
  Broadway Magic
  Court Jester
  Five Pennies
  Gilbert and Sullivan
  Hans Christian Andersen
  Kismet
  Knock on Wood
  Lady In the Dark
  Let's Face It
  Merry Andrew
  South Pacific
  Three Billion Millionaires
  Two By Two
  White Christmas
KAYE, DAVY
  Alice's Adventures In
    Wonderland
KAYE, FLORENCE
  Easy Come, Easy Go

773

KISHIMOTO, SUIFO
Sayonara
KISS
Endless Love
KITSAKOS, STEVE
Second Shepherd's Play
KITT, EARTHA
Driving Miss Daisy
Mrs. Patterson
New Faces of 1952
Somebody Bad Stole De
Wedding Bell
St. Louis Blues
Uncle Tom's Cabin
KIX
Johnny Be Good
KLAUSNER, TERRI
Goblin Market
Sophisticated Ladies
KLEBAN, EDWARD
Chorus Line
KLEEB, HELEN
Stan Freberg Shows
KLEIN, JOSEPH
Over Here!
KLEIN, MANNY
Rio Bravo
KLEIN, PETER
Merry Widow
KLEIN, REID
Darling of the Day
KLEIN, ROBERT
New Faces of 1968
They're Playing Our Song
KLEINSINGER, GEORGE
Archy and Mehitabel / Echoes
of Archy
Hans Christian Andersen
Inheritance
John Brown's Body
Shinbone Alley
Tubby the Tuba
KLINE, KEVIN
Pirates of Penzance
KLINGER, PAM
Chorus Line
KLOSS, ERICH
Ben-Hur
Ben-Hur, Vol. II
Quo Vadis?
Red House
KLUGER, BRUCE
Ka-Boom!
KLUGH, EARL
How to Beat the High Cost of
Living
Just Between Friends
KLUGMAN, JACK
Gypsy
Odd Couple
KLYMAXX
Running Scared
Secret Admirer
KMENTT, WALDEMAR
Merry Widow
KNAPP, COOKIE
Dark Star
KNAPP, ELEANORE
Man of La Mancha
KNAULS, LILLIE
Miracle Goes On
KNEE, BERNIE
Ballroom
Carmelina
Unsinkable Molly Brown
KNEEBONE, TOM
Apple Tree
KNEHNETSKY, RAYMOND
Trocadero Lemon Blue
Winds of Change
KNICKERBOCKERS
Out of Sight
KNIEPER
Edith's Diary
KNIGHT, DAVE
How to Succeed In Business
Without Really Trying
Seven Dreams
KNIGHT, ERIC
Cactus Flower

KNIGHT, EVELYN
Club 15
South Pacific
KNIGHT, FELIX
Can-Can
Desert Song
Gems from Gershwin
Mademoiselle Modiste
Merry Widow
Musical Comedy and Operetta
Favorites, Vol 2
Show Boat
KNIGHT, FRANK
Years to Remember
KNIGHT, GLADYS
Claudine
Cobra
Jo Jo Dancer, Your Life Is
Calling
License to Kill
Pipe Dreams
Rocky IV
Save the Children
KNIGHT, HOLLY
Night In Heaven
KNIGHT, KEITH
Mame
KNIGHT, MARTYN
Seven Brides for Seven
Brothers
KNIGHT, MICHAEL
Tamalpais Exchange
KNIGHT, P.
Choix Des Armes
Coup De Torchon
KNIGHT AND DAY
Assault of the Killer Bimbos
KNISS, DICK
Sunshine
KNOPFLER, MARK
Cal
Color of Money
Last Exit to Brooklyn
Local Hero
Princess Bride
KNOX, BUDDY
American Graffiti
Jamboree!
KOBART, RUTH
Funny Thing Happened on the
Way to the Forum
How to Succeed In Business
Without Really Trying
KOCH, HOWARD
War of the Worlds
KOCH, MARTIN
Blondel
KOJIAN, VARUJAN
Adventures of Robin Hood
Sea Hawk
Star Wars Trilogy
KOLB, MINA
From the Second City
KOMACK, JIMMIE
Beg, Borrow Or Steal
Damn Yankees
KOMEDA, CHRISTOPHER
Rosemary's Baby
KONDRA, TRISH
Aladd
KONGOS, JOHN
Blind Date
KONK
Bright Lights, Big City
KOOL AND THE GANG
Jumpin' Jack Flash
Pirate Movie
Ruthless People
Saturday Night Fever
KOOL G.
Colors
KOOL MOE DEE
Far Out Man
Scrooged
Zebrahead
KOOPER, AL
Landlord
KORMAN, HARVEY
Americathon
Huckleberry Finn

KORN, RICHARD
Mikado
KORNGOLD, ERICH
WOLFGANG
Adventures of Robin Hood
Anthony Adverse
Captain Blood: Classic Film
Scores for Errol Flynn
Classic Film Scores for Bette
Davis
Elizabeth and Essex: Classic
Film Scores of Erich
Wolfgang Korngold
50 Years of Film
Great Waltz
Kings Row
Love Themes from Motion
Pictures
Magic Fire
Sea Hawk
Sea Hawk: The Classic Film
Scores of Erich Wolfgang
Korngold
Sinfonietta
Spectacular World of Classic
Film Scores
KOSARIN, OSCAR
Canterbury Tales
Happy Time
70 Girls, 70
KOSTAL, IRWIN
Bedknobs and Broomsticks
Brigadoon
Charlotte's Web
Chitty, Chitty, Bang, Bang
Fantasia
Half a Sixpence
Hans Brinker
Julie and Carol at Carnegie Hall
Magic of Lassie
Mary Poppins
Pete's Dragon
KOSTELANETZ, ANDRE
All American
America Sings
Broadway Musicals
Filmusic Scene
Free and Easy
From Broadway to Hollywood
Grand Canyon Suite
Lure of the Grand Canyon
Music of George Gershwin
Murder on the Orient Express
Music of Jerome Kern
Music of Victor Herbert
Musical Comedy Favorites
Oklahoma
Parade of Show Stoppers
Richard Rodgers
Showstoppers
That's Entertainment
Today's Greatest Movie Hits
KOTTKE, LEO
Days of Heaven
KOURKOULOS, NIKOS
Illya Darling
KOUTOUKAS, H.M.
Pomegranada
KOUTSOUKOS, THOM
How to Steal an Election (A
Dirty Politics Musical)
KOZ, DAVE
Action Jackson
KRACHMALNICK, SAMUEL
Candide
Carry Nation
Regina
KRAFT, KAREN
Duel
KRAFT, WILLIAM
Avalanche
KRAKOW JAZZ ENSEMBLE
Stormy Monday
KRAL, IRENE
Bells Are Ringing
My Fair Lady
Russians Are Coming! the
Russians Are Coming!
KRAL, ROY
By Jupiter

KRAMER, BILLY J., AND THE
DAKOTAS
Stardust
KRAMER, JONATHAN
Hair
KRAMER, MARSHA
Dawgs
Together Again
KRANE, DAVID
Upstairs at O'Neals
KRANENDONK, LEONARD
Hear! Hear!
KRANTZ, GEORGE
Breakin' 2 - Electric Boogaloo
KRAUSE, MARC
Golden Land
KREBS, BEATRICE
Ballad of Baby Doe
KRESSYN, MIRIAM
Bei Mir Bistu Schoen
KRETZMER, HERBERT
Can Heironymus Merkin Ever
Forget Mercy Humppe (And
Find True Happiness)
Four Musketeers
John F. Kennedy
Les Miserables
KRIEGER, HENRY
Dream Girls
Tap Dance Kid
KRISTEN, ILENE
Grease
Mayor
KRISTEN, MARTA
Savage Sam
KRISTOFFERSON, KRIS
Ned Kelly
Songwriter
Star Is Born
KRITZ, KARL
Great Waltz
KROLL, BOBBY
Curious Evening with Gypsy
Rose Lee
Gypsy Rose Lee Remembers
Burlesque
KROMER, HELEN
For Heaven's Sake
KRONOS QUARTET
Sounds from True Stories
KRUGER, GAYE
Great American Backstage
Musical
KRUGER, OTTO
Wonderful World of the
Brothers Grimm
KRUPA, GENE
Benny Goodman Story
Gene Krupa Story
KRUSCHEN, JACK
Batman
Drop Dead! (An Exercise In
Horror)
I Can Get It for You Wholesale
KUBALA, MICHAEL
Jerome Robbins' Broadway
KUGA, RICHARD
13 Daughters
KUHLMANN, ROSEMARY
Amahl and the Night Visitors
KUHN, JOSEPH
Hawaii
Pajama Game
KUHN, JUDY
Chess
Les Miserables
Metropolis
KUHNER, JOHN
Your Own Thing
KUKLA, FRAN AND OLLIE
Age of Television
Happy Mother Goose (As Told
By Kukla, Fran and Ollie)
Merry Christmas from Kukla,
Fran and Ollie
Songs By Kukla, Fran and Ollie
KULLER, SID
My Fairfax Lady
Zenda

Funny Girl

LANNING, JERRY
Berlin to Broadway with Kurt
Weill
Mame
My Fair Lady
Wonderful Town

LANSBURY, ANGELA
Anyone Can Whistle
Bedknobs and Broomsticks
Broadway Magic
Dear World
Gypsy
Harvey Girls
Mame
Official Grammy Awards
Archive Collection
Opening Night at the Winter
Garden - Mame
Prettybelle
Sondheim
Sondheim: A Musical Tribute
Stephen Sondheim Evening
Sweeney Todd (The Demon
Barber of Fleet Street)

LANTI, AL
Wildcat

LANZA, MARIO
Because You're Mine
Desert Song
For the First Time
Great Caruso
Mario Lanza Sings Because
Serenade
Seven Hills of Rome
Student Prince
That Midnight Kiss
That's Entertainment!
Toast of New Orleans
Vagabond King

LANZARONI, BHEN
How to Steal an Election (A
Dirty Politics Musical)

LARA, AUGUSTINE
Saludos Amigos (Music from
South of the Border)

LARGE, NORMAN
Doll's Life

LARIMER, ROBERT
King of the Whole Damn World

LARNER, ELIZABETH
Camelot
Four Musketeers
Kiss Me Kate
My Fair Lady
Vanishing Point

LAROCHE, MARY
Bye Bye Birdie

LAROSA, JULIUS
Arthur Godfrey

LARRIMORE, MARTHA
Golden Apple

LARSEN, BART
Thousand Miles of Mountains

LARSEN, WILLIAM
Fantasticks

LARSON, BEV
I Can't Keep Running In Place

LARSON, FRANCIS
Fly with Me

LARSON, GAYLE
Themes from the Movies

LARSON, GLEN A.
Buck Rogers
Music from the Galaxies

LARSON, KENT
Threads of Glory

LARSON, NICOLETTE
Arthur (the Album)
National Lampoon's Vacation
Twins

LARSON, PAUL
Dylan

LARSSON, LARS ERIK
European Holiday

LA RUE
Penitentiary III

LARUE, D.C.
Tea Dance
Thank God It's Friday

LA RUE, DANNY
Come Spy with Me

LA SALLE, ERIQ
Rappin'

LA SALLE, MARC
South Pacific

LASCELLES, KENDREW
Wait a Minim!

LASCOE, HENRY
Baker Street
Carnival
Silk Stockings

LASLEY, DAVID
Body Rock
Dude (the Highway Life)

LASSER, LOUISE
Henry, Sweet Henry

LASSISTER, WADE
Fame

LAST, JAMES
Hair

LAST, RUTH
Close Encounters of the Third
Kind

LAST POETS
Performance

LASZLO, ALEXANDER
Atlantis In Hi-Fi (Forbidden
Island)
Impact
Memories Aux Bruxelles
This World Tomorrow
World of Century Twenty First

LATESSA, DICK
Philemon

LATHAM, CYNTHIA
Redhead

LATHAM, FRED
Pennies from Heaven

LATHON, WILLIAM
Stephen Foster Story

LATIMER, WILLIAM
Captain Jinks of the Horse
Marines
Sweet Bye and Bye

LATIN RASCALS
Disorderlies

LATOUCHE, JOHN
Ballad of Baby Doe
Beggar's Holiday
Cabin In the Sky
Candide
Eileen
Golden Apple
Sing for Your Supper

LATTANZI, TINA
Ciao, Rudy

LA TOURNEAUX, ROBERT
Boys In the Band

LATTISAW, STACY
Police Academy IV - Citizens on
Patrol

LAUBER, KEN
Chicken Chronicles
Golden Motion Picture Themes
and Original Soundtracks
Kent State

LAUDER, HARRY
Great Personalities of
Broadway
They Stopped the Show!

LAUDERDALE, JIM
Cotton Patch Gospel

LAUGHLIN, PAT
Bull Durham

LAUGHLIN, TERESA
Trial of Billy Jack

LAUGHTON, CHARLES
Christmas Carol
Don Juan In Hell
Moby Dick
Night of the Hunter

LAUPER, CYNDI
Goonies

LAUREL, RAY
Arnold's Wrecking Co.

LAUREL AND HARDY
Another Fine Mess
Babes In Toyland
In Trouble Again

Rogue Song

LAURENCE, PAULA
Hansel and Gretel

LAURENCE, WILLIAM L.
Quick and the Dead - The Story
of the Atom Bomb

LAURITA, ANNIE
Fly with Me

LAUTNER, JOSEPH
Kittiwake Island
New Faces of 1952
Uhl and Other Stuff

LAVA, WILLIAM
Music of Republic
Themes from Classic Science
Fiction, Fantasy and Horror
Films
Themes from Horror Movies
Three Mesquiteers
Zorro

**LAVAGNINO, FRANCESCO
ANGELO**
Lost Continent
Naked Maja

LAVIE, ARIC
Irma La Douce
To Live Another Summer, to
Pass Another Winter

LAVIE, EFRAT
Kazablan

LAVIE, RAVE
Tango Argentina

LAVIN, LINDA
Bunch
Family Affair
It's a Bird, It's a Plane, It's
Superman
Mad Show
Showcase Album, 1967
Sophie

LAVNER, LYNN
Ladies Don't Spit and Holler

LAW, JENNY LOU
Four Below Strikes Back

LAWFORD, PETER
April Fools
Easter Parade
Good News
It Happened In Brooklyn
Longest Day
Ruggles of Red Gap
That's Entertainment

LAWLESS, FRANK
Pajama Game

LAWNDALE
Lovedolls Superstar

LAWRENCE, ANITA
Oklahoma

LAWRENCE, CAROL
Broadway Magic
Kiss Me Kate
Saratoga
Subways Are for Sleeping
West Side Story

LAWRENCE, DAVID
Garbage Pail Kids

LAWRENCE, EDDIE
Bells Are Ringing

LAWRENCE, ED
Themes from Classic Science
Fiction, Fantasy and Horror
Films
Themes from Horror Movies

LAWRENCE, ELLIOT
Apple Tree
Bye Bye Birdie
Golden Boy
Golden Rainbow
Here's Love
How to Succeed In Business
Without Really Trying
S'wonderful, S'marvelous,
S'Gershwin
Sugar
Unsinkable Molly Brown
You're a Good Man, Charlie
Brown

LAWRENCE, GERTRUDE
Cole Porter In Hollywood
(1929-1956)
King and I

Lady In the Dark
Nymph Errant
Oh Kay!
They Stopped the Show!
Tonight at 8:30

LAWRENCE, HENRY
Jimmy

LAWRENCE, JACK
Flame and the Flesh
I Had a Ball

LAWRENCE, MARK
David and Lisa

LAWRENCE, PAULA
Roberta
Something for the Boys

LAWRENCE, STEPHEN
Bang the Drum Slowly
Now Is the Time for All Good
Men

LAWRENCE, STEVE
Academy Award Winning Songs
Broadway Musicals
General Motors' 50th
Anniversary Show
Golden Rainbow
Last Run
Official Grammy Awards
Archive Collection
Songs from the Golden Circle
Steve and Eydie
What It Was, Was Love
What Makes Sammy Run?

LAWRENCE, VICKI
Grasshopper

LAWRENSON, JOHN
Song of Norway

LAWS, DEBRA
Heavenly Kid

LAWS, ELOISE
City Heat

LAWS, HUBERT
How to Beat the High Cost of
Living

LAWS, JERRY
Finian's Rainbow

LAWS, MAURY
Cricket on the Hearth
Daydreamer
Do-Re-Mi
Frosty the Snowman
Hobbit
Mad Monster Party
Most Happy Fella
Mouse on the Mayflower
Original TV Adventures of King
Kong
Rudolph the Red-Nosed
Reindeer
Santa Claus Is Comin' to Town

LAWS, SAM
Cabin In the Sky

LAWSON, DENIS
Pal Joey

LAWSON, ROGER
Billy Noname
Hello Dolly!

LAY, DILYS
Boy Friend

LAYE, EVELYN
New Moon
Phil the Fluter
Wedding In Paris

LAZARUS, FRANK
Day in Hollywood / Night in the
Ukraine

LAZARUS, ROY
Most Happy Fella

LAZER, PETER
Survival of St. Joan

LEA, WILLY
Conquest of Space

LEACH, WILFORD
Carmilla

LEACHMAN, CLORIS
Of Thee I Sing
Young Frankenstein

LEAHY, JOE
Jack and the Beanstalk
Wild Angels

LEANDER, MIKE
Privilege

Two a Penny

LEAR, EVELYN
Johnny Johnson

LEARY, TIMOTHY
Turn On, Tune In, Drop Out

LEATHERWOLF
Return of the Living Dead, Part II

LEBO M.
Lion King

LEBOWSKY, STANLEY
Act
Chicago
Family Affair
Half a Sixpence
Irma La Douce
Pippin
Tovarich
Whoop-Up!

LE BRETON, FLORA
Cat and the Fiddle

LECLAIR, HENRY
1776

LECUONA, MARGARITA
Silent Movie

LED ZEPPELIN
Homer
Song Remains the Same

LEDBETTER, HUDDIE
Leadbelly

LEDBETTER, WILLIAM
Candide

LEE, BAAYORK
Promises, Promises

LEE, BILL
Hey There, It's Yogi Bear
Manhattan Tower
Mary Poppins
Seven Brides for Seven Brothers
Seven Dreams
South Pacific

LEE, BOBBY
Prettybelle

LEE, BRENDA
Smokey and the Bandit II

LEE, CHRISTOPHER
Dracula
John F. Kennedy

LEE, DAVE
John F. Kennedy

LEE, DIANA
Electric Company TV Show (Songs From)
Lost Horizon
Washington Behind Closed Doors
Willy Wonka and the Chocolate Factory

LEE, GEORGIA
Heart Is a Rebel

LEE, GYPSY ROSE
Curious Evening with Gypsy Rose Lee
Gypsy Rose Lee Remembers Burlesque
Hollywood Canteen

LEE, HARRIET
Ziegfeld Follies of 1946

LEE, JACKIE
Goodbye Gemini
Robbery
Teen-Age Cruisers

LEE, JACK
Irene

LEE, JAE WOO
Pacific Overtures

LEE, JOHNNY
Coast to Coast
Dallas
Urban Cowboy

LEE, KATHRYN
Allegro

LEE, LESTER
Fire Down Below
Miss Sadie Thompson

LEE, LOIS
High Button Shoes

LEE, MARCHICKO
Flower Drum Song

LEE, MICHELE
Bravo Giovanni!
How to Succeed In Business Without Really Trying
Of Thee I Sing
Seesaw

LEE, PEGGY
Best of Disney
Bing's Hollywood
Bob Hope In Hollywood
Hollywood Canteen
Jazz Singer
Judy Garland
Kismet
Lady and the Tramp
Pete Kelly's Blues
Road to Bali
Sharky's Machine
Walk Don't Run
White Christmas

LEE, ROBERT
What's the Meaning of This?

LEE, SONDRA
Hello Dolly!
Pal Joey
Peter Pan

LEE, VALERIE
Here's Love

LEE, VANESSA
After the Ball
Bittersweet

LEE BROTHERS
I'll See You In My Dreams

LEECH, MIKE
Elvis

LEEDS, PETER
Stan Freberg Shows

LEEDS, PHIL
Christine

LEEDY, DOUGLAS
Slaughterhouse-Five

LEESON, MICHAEL
For Your Eyes Only

LEFKOWITZ, GENE
Christy

LEGALLIENNE, EVA
ANTA Album of Stars, Vol. 1
Evening with William Shakespeare

LEGAULT, LANCE
Catch My Soul

LEGEND, JOHNNY
Teen-Age Cruisers

LEGRAND, CHRISTINE
Mary Poppins
Young Girls of Rochefort

LEGRAND, MICHEL
Atlantic City
Bolero
Brainchild
Breezy
Cinema Legrand
Columbia Album of Cole Porter
Film Music from France
Front Row Center
Gable and Lombard
Happy Ending
How to Save a Marriage and Ruin Your Life
I Love Movies
Ice Station Zebra
Lady Sings the Blues
Le Jazz Grand Michel Legrand and Co.
Le Mans
Lost Continent
Love In Germany
Love Is a Ball
Love Songs
Magic Garden of Stanley Sweetheart
Matter of Innocence
Never Say Never Again
Ode to Billy Joe
Other Side of Midnight
Paris Was Made for Lovers
Slapstick of Another Kind
Summer of '42
Thomas Crown Affair
Umbrellas of Cherbourg (Parapluies De Cherbourg)
Wuthering Heights

Yentl
Young Girls of Rochefort

LEGRAND, RAYMOND
Royal Affair

LEHAR, FRANZ
Franz Lehar Memorial Album
Merry Widow
Rogue Song

LEHMAN, JEANNE
Irene

LEHMAN, JOANN
Shirley MacLaine Live at the Palace

LEHMAN, JOHN
Ka-Boom!

LEHMAN, SUZANNE
Among Friends - Waa-Mu Show of 1960

LEHNER, VERONICA
Wonderful Town

LEHRER, TOM
Electric Company TV Show
John F. Kennedy
Tomfoolery

LEIBER, JERRY
Elvis (NBC-TV Special)
Fun In Acapulco
Girls! Girls! Girls!
Jailhouse Rock
King Creole
Loving You
Roustabout
Tickle Me

LEIBMAN, JOSEPH
Dark Star
Light Fantastic

LEIGH, ADELE
Kismet

LEIGH, BARBARA
Show Boat

LEIGH, CAROLYN
How Now, Dow Jones
Little Me
Peter Pan
Wildcat

LEIGH, JACK
Tenderloin

LEIGH, JANET
Bye Bye Birdie

LEIGH, MITCH
Cry for Us All
Man of La Mancha
Sarava

LEIGH, VIVIEN
Command Performance
Ivanov
Tovarich

LEIGHTON, BERNIE
New York Stories
Oh Kay!

LEIGHTON, MARGARET
Hamlet

LEIGHTON, NANCY
To Broadway with Love

LEIKIN, MOLLY-ANN
Moment By Moment

LEIN, SANDRA
Hallelujah, Baby!

LEINSDORF, ERIC
Death In Venice

LEITCH, DONOVAN
If It's Tuesday, This Must Be Belgium

LE LYCEE FRANCAIS CHOIR
Darling Lili

LEMAR, EDDIE
Broadway '58-'59

LEMARQUE, FRANÇOIS
Playtime

LEMAY, HOWARD
We'd Rather Switch

LEMBECK, HARVEY
How to Stuff a Wild Bikini

LEMEL, GARY
His Wife's Habit

LEMMON, JACK
April Fools
Fire Down Below
Gershwins In Hollywood (1931-1964)

Irma La Douce
Odd Couple
S'wonderful, S'marvelous, S'Gershwin
Some Like It Hot
Soundtracks, Voices and Themes from Great Movies
Three for the Show
You Can't Run Away from It
Wackiest Ship In the Army

LEMMON, SHIRLEY
Evening with Sammy Cahn

LENARD, MELVYN
Impact
Mike Hammer

LENHART, MARGARET
Bing's Hollywood
Holiday Inn

LENINGRAD KIROV BALLET GROUP
Sleeping Beauty

LENINGRAD PHILHARMONIC
2001: A Space Odyssey

LENN, ROBERT
Annie Get Your Gun

LENNON, JOHN
Beatlemania
Give My Regards to Broad Street
Hard Day's Night
Help!
Imagine - The Motion Picture
Let It Be
Magical Mystery Tour
Sgt. Pepper's Lonely Hearts Club Band
Trial of Billy Jack
Yellow Submarine

LENNON, JULIAN
Hail Hail Rock 'N' Roll
Playing for Keeps
Wonder Years

LENNON, KIPP
That Was Then, This Is Now

LENNON, MARK
Scrooged

LENNON SISTERS
Show Time

LENNOX, ANNIE
1984 (For the Love of Big Brother)
Scrooged

LENOIRE, ROSETTA
Cabin In the Sky
Destry Rides Again
I Had a Ball
Show Boat

LENOX, ADRIANE
Beehive

LENYA, LOTTE
Brecht on Brecht
Cabaret
Happy End
Johnny Johnson
Official Grammy Awards Archive Collection
Rise and Fall of the City of Mahogany
Seven Deadly Sins
Threepenny Opera

LEON, DOROTHY
Grease

LEON, FELIX
Zulu and the Zayda

LEON, JOSEPH
Merry Widow
Rhinestone

LEONARD, BILLY
Oh Boy!

LEONARD, EDDIE
50th Anniversary of George Jessel In Show Business

LEONARD, JACK
Panama Hattie

LEONARD, JACK E.
Journey Back to Oz

LEONARD, LAWRENCE
West Side Story

LEONARD, LU
Drat! the Cat!

Gay Life
  Happiest Girl In the World
LEONARD, PATRICK
  Nothing In Common
LEONARD, PETER
  Miss Julie
LEONARD, RICHARD
  Dames at Sea
  Gypsy
  Words and Music
LEONARD, SHELDON
  Linus the Lionhearted
LEONARD, TONY
  Eddy Duchin Story
LEONARDI, LEON
  Bloomer Girl
  St. Louis Woman
LEONARDOS, URYLEE
  Billy Noname
LEPPARD, RAYMOND
  Lord of the Flies
  Mother of All of Us
LERIT, SHARON
  Bye Bye Birdie
LERNER, AL
  Eddy Duchin Story
LERNER, ALAN JAY
  American Musical Theater
  Brigadoon
  Camelot
  Carmelina
  Coco
  Dance a Little Closer
  Evening with Alan Jay Lerner
  Evening with Lerner and Loewe
  Gigi
  Little Prince
  Lyrics By Lerner
  My Fair Lady
  On a Clear Day You Can See
    Forever
  Paint Your Wagon
  Royal Wedding
LERNER, DOROTHY
  Hard Job Being God
  Virgin
LERNER, FREDERICK
  My Fair Lady
LERNER, MICHAEL
  Outlaw Blues
LERNER, SAM
  Popeye
LEROY, KEN
  I Can Get It for You Wholesale
  Pajama Game
LE SENECHAL, RAYMOND
  Live for Life
LESKO, JOHN
  42nd Street
  I Do! I Do!
  Jennie
  Maggie Flynn
  Skyscraper
LESLIE, JOAN
  Hollywood Canteen
  Kurt Weill In Hollywood
  Yankee Doodle Dandy
LESLIE, NORMAN
  Gigi
LESLIE-SMITH, KENNETH
  Beggar's Holiday
LES NEGRESSES VERTES
  Bad Influence
LES QUAT' JEUDIS
  Show Girl
LES QUATRE BARBUS
  Irma La Douce
LESSEY, BEN
  Just for You
LESTER, EDDIE
  Fiddler on the Roof
LESTER, KETTY
  Blue Velvet
  Cabin In the Sky
LESTER, MARK
  Oliver!
LESTER, ROBBIE
  Aristocats
  Mickey and the Beanstalk
  Santa Claus Is Comin' to Town

LESTER, SONNY
  State Fair
  This Was Burlesque
LETTERMEN
  Romantic Favorites from Stage
    and Screen
LETTON, FRAN
  Cyrano De Bergerac
LEVANT, OSCAR
  Charlie Chan at the Opera
  Gershwins In Hollywood (1931-
    1964)
  Ginger Rogers
LEVAY, SYLVESTOR
  Flashdance
LEVEN, MEL
  Babes In Toyland
  101 Dalmatians
LEVENE, GUS
  Dillinger
  Rio Bravo
  Ten Thousand Bedrooms
  Wonderful World of the
    Brothers Grimm
LEVENE, SAM
  Guys and Dolls
  Let It Ride
LEVERT
  Action Jackson
  Coming to America
  Fatal Beauty
LEVIN, BERNARD
  John F. Kennedy
LEVIN, IRA
  Drat! the Cat!
LEVIN, SYLVAN
  Girl In Pink Tights
  Musical Comedy and Operetta
    Favorites, Vol 2
LEVINE, HANK
  Bye Bye Birdie
LEVINE, JOSEPH
  Fancy Free
LEVINE, MAURICE
  Down In the Valley
  Flahooley
  Lost In the Stars
  Of Thee I Sing
  Take It from Here
LEVITT, BARRY
  Taking My Turn
LEVITT, ESTELLE
  Tell Me That You Love Me,
    Junie Moon
LEVITT, RICHARD
  Kismet
LEVY, LOUIS
  Let's Be Happy
  Moby Dick
LEVY, MARCY
  American Pop
  Times Square
LEVY, SHUKI
  Secrets of the Sword
LEWES, WILSON, TRIO
  Our Man Flint
LEWINE, RICHARD
  Chee Chee
  Days of Wilfred Owen
  Make Mine Manhattan
  Remember These
LE WINTER, DAVID
  Eddy Duchin Story
LEWIS, ABBY
  70 Girls, 70
LEWIS, AL
  At Home with the Munsters
LEWIS, BARBARA
  Stardust
LEWIS, BARNAL
  Paradise, Hawaiian Style
LEWIS, BOBBY
  National Lampoon's Animal
    House
LEWIS, BOBO
  Working
LEWIS, BRENDA
  Carousel
  Girl In Pink Tights
  Regina

LEWIS, CAPTAIN ROBERT
  Quick and the Dead - The Story
    of the Atom Bomb
LEWIS, EDWINA
  Nunsense
LEWIS, ELLIOTT
  California
  Count of Monte Cristo
  Manhattan Tower
LEWIS, FURRY
  Blues
LEWIS, GARRETT
  Of Thee I Sing
  Star
LEWIS, GARY, & PLAYBOYS
  Out of Sight
LEWIS, HUEY, & NEWS
  Back to the Future
  Oliver and Company
LEWIS, JACK
  You're a Big Boy Now
LEWIS, JERRY LEE
  American Hot Wax
  Diner
  Harper Valley P.T.A.
  Hometown U.S.A.
  Jamboree!
  Roadie
  Slumber Party '57
  Sporting Club
  Stand By Me
  Stealing Home
LEWIS, JERRY
  Cinderfella
  Living It Up
  Magic Moments from the
    Tonight Show
  Pardners
LEWIS, JIMMY
  Hair
LEWIS, JOHN
  Milanese Story
  No Sun In Venice
  Odds Against Tomorrow
LEWIS, LINDA
  Lisztamania
LEWIS, MICHAEL
  Christmas Carol
  Cyrano
  Madwoman of Chaillot
  Sparkles
LEWIS, OVID
  Nagshead
LEWIS, RAMSEY
  Save the Children
LEWIS, RONALD
  Beggar's Opera
LEWIS, SMILEY
  Everybody's All-American
LEWIS, SYLVIA
  Billy Barnes' L.A.
LEWIS, W. MICHAEL
  In Search of
  Shogun Assassin
LEWIS, WEBSTER
  My Tutor
LEWISOHN STADIUM
SYMPHONY
  Satchmo the Great
LEYDEN, LEO
  Rothschilds
LEYDEN, NORMAN
  Cinderella
  Peter Pan
  Pinocchio
  Show Biz (From Vaude to Video)
  Sounds Broadway! Sounds
    Hollywood! Sounds Great!
LEYTON, JOHN
  Seaside Swingers
LIBBY, DENNIS
  House of Leather
LIBERACE
  Decade of Broadway and
    Cinema
  Les Poupees De Paris
  Liberace Plays Golden Themes
    from Hollywood

  Liberace Show: A Program of
    TV Favorites
  Sincerely Yours
  When the Boys Meet the Girls
LIBERTINI, RICHARD
  Mad Show
  Paul Sills' Story Theater (of
    Magical Folk-Rock Fables)
LIBERTO, DON
  Body In the Seine
  To Broadway with Love
LICHTEFELD, MICHAEL
  Sophisticated Ladies
LICK THE TINS
  Some Kind of Wonderful
LIDO CAN-CAN SINGERS
AND DANCERS
  Can-Can
LIEBERMAN, LORI
  Harrad Experiment
LIEBERT, BILLY
  America, Why I Love Her
  Bonanza - Ponderosa Party
    Time
LIEBGOLD, LEON
  Bei Mir Bistu Schoen
LIEDER, CONRAD
  Merry Widow
LIGETI, GYORGY
  Shining
  2001: A Space Odyssey
LIGHT, ENOCH
  Around the World In 80 Days
  Bells Are Ringing
  Film Fame
  Film on Film
  Gigi
  Great Themes from Hit Films
  Magnificent Movie Themes
  Mardi Gras
  Music from the Movies
  Music Man
  1963: The Year's Most Popular
    Themes
  Oklahoma
  Themes from Great Films
  Twenty Great Movie Themes
LIGON, TOM
  Your Own Thing
LILE, BOBBY
  Doctor Goldfoot and the Girl
    Bombs
LILLEY, JOSEPH J.
  Anything Goes
  Beau James
  Bing's Hollywood
  Country Girl
  High Tor
  Li'l Abner
  Paris Holiday
  Red Garters
  Road to Bali
  Seven Little Foys
  White Christmas
LILLIE, BEATRICE
  At Home Abroad
  Command Performance
  Evening with Beatrice Lillie
  Great Personalities of
    Broadway
  High Spirits
  Inside U.S.A.
  Marvelous Party with Bea Lillie
  Oh Boy!
  Queen Bea
  Set to Music
  Thirty Minutes with Beatrice
    Lillie
LILO
  Broadway Show Stoppers
LIMAHL
  Never Ending Story
LIMELITE SINGERS
  Bonnie and Clyde
LIMELITERS
  NARM's Golden Decade
LINCOLN, ABBEY
  Drugstore Cowboy
LIND, CHRISTINA
  Red Mill
  Rose Marie

Sweethearts

LINDEN, HAL
Anything Goes
Bells Are Ringing
Flush Left, Stagger Right
Illya Darling
Official Grammy Awards
  Archive Collection
Rothschilds
Saga of the Dingbat
Thousand Miles of Mountains

LINDFORS, VIVECA
Brecht on Brecht

LINDLEY, AUDRA
Heartbreak Kid

LINDLEY, DAVID
Long Riders

LINDSAY, GEORGE
Robin Hood

LINDSAY, ERICA
Tales from the Dark Side (the Movie)

LINDSAY, HOWARD
Cinderella

LINDSAY, KEVIN
Me Nobody Knows

LINDSAY, MARK
Shogun Assassin

LINDSAY, ROBERT
Me and My Girl

LINDSEY, HAL
Late Great Planet Earth

LINDSEY, MORT
40 Pounds of Trouble
Gay Purr-ee
I Could Go on Singing
Judy at Carnegie Hall

LINEBERGER, JAMES
Survival of St. Joan

LINK, PETER
Earl of Ruston
King of Hearts
Salvation

LINKLETTER, ART
Bible
Howls, Boners and Shockers from Art Linkletter's House
Party Kid Interviews
Kids Say the Darndest Things

LINN, BAMBI
I Can Get It for You Wholesale

LINN, RALPH
Li'l Abner

LINN, RAY
Four Girls In Town
Seven Dreams

LINN, ROBERTA
Get Yourself a College Girl
On Moonlight Bay

LINN-BAKER, MARK
Doonesbury

LINTON, BILL
All About Life
Song of Norway

LINVILLE, ALBERT
Damn Yankees

LINZ, RHEINHARD
Victory at Sea

LION
Transformers - The Movie
Wraith

LIPIMAN, JOE
David Merrick Presents Hits from His Broadway Hits

LIPMAN, MAUREEN
Wonderful Town

LIPPINCOTT, DAVID
Body In the Seine

LIPSON, PAUL
Fiddler on the Roof

LIPTON, MARTHA
Die Fledermaus

LIPTON, MICHAEL
Fool Britannia

LIQUID JESUS
Pump Up the Volume

LISA LISA AND CULT JAM
Caddyshack II

LISA, LUBA
I Can Get It for You Wholesale

I Had a Ball

LISHNER, LEON
Consul

LISKA, ZDENEK
Adrift
Shop on Main Street

LISS, RONALD
Flash Gordon

LISTON, MELBA
Soul of Hollywood

LISZT, FRANZ
Lisztomania
Song Without End

LITTAU, JOSEPH
Carmen Jones
Carousel
Cotton Patch Gospel
Imagine - The Motion Picture
Three Wishes for Jamie

LITTLE, CARYL
Phil the Fluter

LITTLE, CLEAVON
Mac Bird
Purlie

LITTLE, DEETTA
Rocky
Rocky II
Rocky III

LITTLE, RICH
Hollywood Squares
Once Upon a Tour
Pizza Hut '73 (Annual Meeting)

LITTLE EVA
Dusty and Sweets McGee
Stardust

LITTLE FEAT
Over the Edge

LITTLE ORCHESTRA SOCIETY
Our Town

LITTLE RICHARD
American Hot Wax
Christine
Cobra
Cocktail
Dollars ($)
Down and Out In Beverly Hills
Girl Can't Help It!
Hometown U.S.A.
Let the Good Times Roll
Loveless
Mask
Purple People Eater
Twins

LITTLE RIVER BAND
Karate Kid III

LITTLE SINGERS OF GRANBY, QUEBEC
Christmas Sing with Bing

LITTLE TWITCH
Mighty Quinn

LITTLE WILLIE JOHN
Big Town

LITZ, GISELA
Rise and Fall of the City of Mahogany

LITZ, KATHERINE
Crystal Heart

LIVING STRINGS
Camelot
Darling Lili
Living Free
Pure Gold Movies
Richard Rodgers
Sound of Music

LIVING VOICES
George M!
Mary Poppins

LIVINGS, GEORGE
Captain Jinks of the Horse Marines

LIVINGSTON, BARRY
You're a Good Man, Charlie Brown

LIVINGSTON, DAVID
Double Impact

LIVINGSTON, JAY
Aaron Slick from Punkin Crick
Alice In Wonderland
All Hands on Deck

Bing's Hollywood
Bonanza
Bourbon Street Beat
Four Television Musicals
Gunn...Number One
Houseboat
James Dean Story
Let It Ride
Love Themes from Motion Pictures
No Man Can Tame Me
Oh Captain!
Oscar
Satins and Spurs
This Property Is Condemned
Torn Curtain
Warning Shot
What Did You Do In the War, Daddy?

LIVINGSTON, JERRY
Cinderella
Follow That Dream
Hawaiian Eye
Jack and the Beanstalk
Red Garters
77 Sunset Strip
Stooge

LIVINGSTON, JOCK
Zenda

LLEWELLYN, RAY
Impact

LLOYD, A.L.
Whaler Out of New Bedford (And Other Songs of the Whaling Era)

LLOYD, CHARLES
Almost Summer
Journey Within
Moment By Moment

LLOYD, JEREMY
Four Musketeers
Robert and Elizabeth

LLOYD, MICHAEL
Beach Girls
Outlaw Riders
Savage Streets

LLOYD, RITA
Flash Gordon
What Do You Want to Be When You Grow Up?

LLOYD, VIVIAN
Hello Solly!

L'NEIRE, KEITH
Blind Date

LO, RANDON
Joseph and the Amazing Technicolor Dreamcoat

LOCKE, PHILIP
Every Good Boy Deserves Favor

LOCKE, ROBERT
Snoopy

LOCKE, SONDRA
Any Which Way You Can
Every Which Way But Loose

LOCKHART, CALVIN
Honeybaby
Myra Breckinridge

LODEN, BARBARA
After the Fall

LODUCA, JOSEPH
Evil Dead

LOEB, JOHN JACOB
Arabian Nights
Mardi Gras

LOESSER, FRANK
Greenwillow
Guys and Dolls
Hans Andersen
Hans Christian Andersen
How to Succeed In Business Without Really Trying
Look to the Lilies
Most Happy Fella
Odd Couple
Ship Ahoy
Where's Charley?

LOEWE, FREDERICK
American Musical Theater
Brigadoon
Camelot
Evening with Lerner and Loewe
Gigi

Little Prince
Lyrics By Lerner
My Fair Lady
Paint Your Wagon

LOGAN, ELLA
Finian's Rainbow
Here Come the Girls
This Is Broadway's Best

LOGAN, MICHAEL
Canterbury Tales
Nobody's Perfect

LOGGINS, KENNY
Caddyshack
Caddyshack II
Footloose
Over the Top
Rocky IV
Top Gun

LOGGINS AND MESSINA
Main Event

LOJODICE, GIULIANA
Ciao, Rudy

LOKSHIN, ALEKSANDR
Russian Adventure

LOLLIPOP SHOPPE
Angels from Hell

LOLLOS, JOHN
Love and Let Love

LOM, HERBERT
King and I

LOMAN, HAL
Mister Wonderful
Top Banana

LOMAX, ALAN
How the West Was Won

LOMBARD, PETER
Prettybelle

LOMBARDI, DONALD
Nagshead

LOMBARDO, CARMEN
Arabian Nights
Mardi Gras

LOMBARDO, GUY
Arabian Nights
Bells Are Ringing
Hollywood Canteen
Music Man
Radio Days

LONDON, DAVID
Can't Stop the Music

LONDON, JULIE
Frances Langford Presents
Sharky's Machine

LONDON, MARK
Privilege
Secret Life of Walter Mitty

LONDON FESTIVAL ORCHESTRA
Annie Get Your Gun
Captain Horatio Hornblower
Fiddler on the Roof
Film Spectacular
Odd Couple

LONDON FILM ORCHESTRA
Buster

LONDON FOG
Idolmaker

LONDON PHILHARMONIC
Battle of Newetva
Best Years of Our Lives
Citizen Kane / Devil and Daniel Webster
England Made Me
Evita
Fly
Great Movie Thrillers
Lawrence of Arabia
Mission
Music from Great Movie Thrillers
Star Wars
Stereo Space Odyssey
Tron
Victory at Sea

LONDON POPS ORCHESTRA
Camelot

LONDON REPERTORY
Bells Are Ringing
Irma La Douce

LONDON ROYAL
PHILHARMONIC
Roots of Heaven
LONDON SYMPHONY
ORCHESTRA
Aliens
All This and World War II
Bear
Beyond the Sound Barrier, Vol.
2
Brainstrom
Choix Des Armes (Choice of
Arms)
Clash of the Titans
Dark Crystal
Digital Hollywood - Memorable
Film Scores
Digital Space
Empire Strikes Back
Gone with the Wind
John Williams' Symphonic
Suites
Krull
Land Before Time
Lifeforce
Lion of the Desert
Monsignor
Mood Music from the Movies
Music from the Galaxies
Music Lovers
My Fair Lady
North and South
Return of the Jedi
Return to Oz
Rollerball
South Pacific
Star Wars
Star Wars - Return of the Jedi
Superman - The Movie
Tess
Things to Come
Tommy
Western Film World of Dimitri
Tiomkin
Willow
LONDON THEATRE
COMPANY
Flower Drum Song
Gypsy
Kismet
Sound of Music
LONDON VOICES
Mission
My Fair Lady
LONEGRAN, LENORE
Of Thee I Sing
LONG, AVON
Beggar's Holiday
Bubbling Brown Sugar
Don't Play Us Cheap
Finian's Rainbow
Fly Blackbird
Porgy and Bess
Shuffle Along
LONG, JERRY
Wild, Wild Winter
LONG, JOHN
Last Sweet Days of Isaac
LONG, KENN
Touch
LONG, SHELLEY
Natives Are Restless
LONG, SHORTY
Most Happy Fella
This Is Broadway's Best
LONG, TAMARA
Dames at Sea
Great American Backstage
Musical
Lorelei
13 Daughters
LONG, WALTER
Kiss Me Kate
LONGDON, JAMES
Baby
LONGET, CLAUDINE
Little Prince
LONGFELLOW
Purple People Eater
LONGFELLOW, STEPHEN
Sunnyside

LONGHAIR, PROFESSOR
Big Easy
LOOMER, LISA
Monsieur De Pourceaugnac
LOOMIS, ROD
You Never Know
LOOSE, BILL
Cherry, Harry and Raquel
Vixen
LOOSE, EMMY
Merry Widow
LOOSE, WILLIAM
Evening with Boris Karloff and
His Friends
Night of the Living Dead
LOPEZ, DENISE
Scrooged
LOPEZ, PRISCILLA
Broadway Magic
Chorus Line
Day in Hollywood / Night in the
Ukraine
LOPEZ, TRINI
Dirty Dozen
Trini Lopez Show
L'ORCHESTRE MODERNE
Moderns
LORD, BASIL
Phil the Fluter
LORD, JON
Last Rebel
LORD, MARJORIE
New Orleans
LORD BERNERS
Music for Films
LORDS OF THE NEW
CHURCH
Dangerously Close
Out of Bounds
Texas Chainsaw Massacre Part
2
Weird Science
LOREN, DONNA
Beach Blanket Bingo
LOREN, SOPHIA
Houseboat
Man of La Mancha
Sophia Loren In Rome
LORICK, ROBERT
Hark!
One Way Ticket to Broadway
Tap Dance Kid
LORING, JOAN
Snow Goose
LORING, RICHARD
Snow Queen
Toby Tyler
LORRAINE, GUIDO
Grab Me a Gondola
LORRAINE SINGERS
Thunder Alley
LORRE, PETER
Silk Stockings
LOS ANGELES CHAMBER
ORCHESTRA
Plow That Broke the Plains
River
LOS ANGELES
PHILHARMONIC
Song Without End
Turning Point
LOS CALCHAKIS
State of Seige
LOS LOBOS
Bull Durham
Fine Mess
I Was a Teenage Zombie
La Bamba
Sylvester
LOST PILOTS
Dangerously Close
LOTA, REMO
Street Scene
LOTIS, DENNIS
Alexander the Great
Come Spy with Me
On the Town
LOTTI DOTTI
Penitentiary III

LOUDON, DOROTHY
Annie
Ballroom
Ben Bagley's Oscar
Hammerstein Revisited
Broadway Magic
Rodgers and Hart Revisited
LOUISE, MARY
Evening with Sheldon Harnick
Fly Blackbird
Mame
Passing Fair
LOUISE, MERLE
Charlotte Sweet
Company
Into the Woods
La Cage Aux Folles
Sweeney Todd (The Demon
Barber of Fleet Street)
LOUISE, TINA
Fade Out Fade In
LOUSSIER, JACQUES
Dark of the Sun
You Only Live Once
LOVE, ALLAN
Apple
LOVE, BESSIE
Gentlemen Prefer Blondes
LOVE, DARLENE
Idolmaker
Leader of the Pack
LOVE, GEOFF
Hair
LOVE, MARY
Petey Wheatstraw (the Devil's
Son-In-Law)
Producers
LOVE, MIKE
Almost Summer
Lethal Weapon 2
LOVE AND ROCKETS
She's Having a Baby
LOVE / HATE
Nightmare on Elm Street 4 -
The Dream Master
LOVE TRACTOR
Athens, Ga. - Inside / Out
LOVE UNLIMITED
Together Brothers
LOVEDOLLS
Lovedolls Superstar
LOVEJOY, FRANK
Caine Mutiny Court Martial
Man Without a Country
LOVELL, MARILYNN
Hello Dolly!
LOVERBOY
Metropolis
Official Music of the XXIIIrd
Olympiad, Los Angeles 1984
Top Gun
LOVETT, LYLE
Always
LOVICH, LENE
Tuff Turf
LOVIN' SPOONFUL
Stardust
What's Up, Tiger Lily?
You're a Big Boy Now
LOWE, ARTHUR
Ruling Class
LOWE, BERNIE
Jamboree!
Loving You
LOWE, JACKIE
Selma
LOWE, MARION
Merry Widow
LOWE, MUNDELL
Billy Jack
Satan In High Heels
LOWE, NICK
Americathon
Easy Money
Rock 'N' Roll High School
LOWE, ROBERT
Boys from Syracuse
Flower Drum Song
Pajama Game
Sound of Music

LOWE, SAMMY
Patty
LOWELL, GENE
American Musical Theater
Oliver!
LOWELL, TOM
Story of the Gnome-Mobile
LOWRY, KEN
Two Gentlemen of Verona
LUBBOCK, JEREMY
Nuts
LUBIN, HARRY
Music for Loretta
One Step Beyond
LUBOFF, NORMAN
All-Star Parade, Hits from the
Movies
Broadway
By the Light of the Silvery Moon
Christmas Sing with Bing
Cricket on the Hearth
Gershwin Holiday
Great Movie Themes
I'll See You In My Dreams
Lullaby of Broadway
Mikado
Oh Captain!
On Moonlight Bay
Richard Rodgers
Summer Place (And Other
Great Hits from the Movies)
Three for Tonight
LUCA, DOMENIC
Godspell
LUCAS, CRAIG
Clues to a Life
Marry Me a Little
LUCAS, DAVID
Magic Garden of Stanley
Sweetheart
LUCAS, FRED
On the Town
Redhead
South Pacific
LUCAS, ISABELLE
Porgy and Bess
Show Boat
LUCAS, NICK
Day of the Locust
Great Gatsby
Legends of the Musical Stage
Lost Films: Trailers from the
First Years of Sound
LUCAS, RONN
Sugar Babies
LUCAS, TREVOR
Far from the Madding Crowd
LUCKEY, SUSAN
Zenda
LUCKINBILL, LAURENCE
Boys in the Band
LUCKY, SUSAN
Take Me Along
LUFT, JOE
Judy Garland
LUFT, LORNA
Judy Garland
LUGOSI, BELA
Plan 9 from Outer Space
LUISI, JAMES
Sweet Charity
LUKAS, PAUL
Call Me Madam
Quick and the Dead - The Story
of the Atom Bomb
LUKE, JANEY
Order Is Love
LUKE, KEYE
Flower Drum Song
Kung-Fu
LULU
James Bond 13 Original
Themes
Man with the Golden Gun
To Sir with Love
LUM, BEREA
Flower Drum Song
LUMAN, BOB
Carnival Rock

LUMBYE, H.C.
European Holiday
LUMBYE, TIPPE
European Holiday
LUMLEY, RUFUS
Wild Eye
LUNA, BARBARA
South Pacific
LUND, ART
Breakfast at Tiffany's
Call Me Madam
Donnybrook!
Most Happy Fella
No Strings
LUPAR, GUY
Most Happy Fella
LUPINO, IDA
Anything Goes
Hollywood Canteen
Premiere
LUPONE, PATTI
Anything Goes
Cradle Will Rock
Evita
Les Miserables
LUPONE, ROBERT
Magic Show
Nefertiti
LURIE, ALAN
Mood Music of the Silent
Movies
LURIE, JOHN
Down By Law and Variety
Stranger Than Paradise - The
Resurrection of Albert Ayler
LUTHER, FRANK
Paper Moon
Tom Sawyer
Who's Afraid of the Big Bad
Wolf, Part 1 and 2
LUX, LILLIAN
Megilla of Itzig Manger
LUZ, FRANE
Little Shop of Horrors
LYBE, DENNIS
Chocalonia
LYMON, FRANKIE, AND THE
TEENAGERS
Rock, Rock, Rock
LYMON, LEWIS, AND THE
TEENCHORDS
Jamboree!
LYNCH, ALFRED
Taming of the Shrew
LYNCH, DAVID
Eraserhead
LYNCH, HAL
Spoon River Anthology
LYNDE, PAUL
Bye Bye Birdie
Charlotte's Web
Hollywood Squares
Journey Back to Oz
New Faces of 1952
Official Grammy Awards
Archive Collection
LYNDECK, EDMUND
Doll's Life
Into the Woods
Sweeney Todd (The Demon
Barber of Fleet Street)
LYNG, NORA MAE
Forbidden Broadway
LYNLEY, CAROL
Four Television Musicals
LYNN, BARBARA
Everybody's All-American
Hairspray
LYNN, BETTY
Choice Cuts
LYNN, DIANA
Four Television Musicals
LYNN, DINA
Santa Claus Is Comin' to Town
LYNN, ELAINE
Plain and Fancy
LYNN, IMOGENE
Beau James
LYNN, JANET
It's Time to Pray, America!

LYNN, JUDY
Annie Get Your Gun
Top Banana
LYNN, LORETTA
Coal Miner's Daughter
LYNN, MARA
Body Beautiful
LYNN, SUSAN
Flower Drum Song
LYNNE, GILLIAN
Can-Can
LYNNE, JEFF
All This and World War II
Electric Dreams
Xanadu
LYNSON, VICTORIA
Seven Brides for Seven
Brothers
LYNYRD SKYNYRD
Mask
LYON, SUE
Night of the Iguana
Parade of Hits
LYONS, COLETTE
Show Boat
LYONS, LINDA
Tinseltown
LYSINGER, PAT
No No Nanette
LYTTON, DEBBIE
Body Slam
Garbage Pail Kids
M/A/R/R/S
Bright Lights, Big City
My Stepmother Is an Alien
M.C. JAM AND PEE WEE
JAM
Action Jackson
MFSB
Saturday Night Fever
MGM STUDIO ORCHESTRA
American In Paris
Athena
Ballet Music from MGM
Musicals
Band Wagon
Belle of New York
Everything I Have Is Yours
Doctor Zhivago
Gigi
Girls...And More Girls
High Society
How the West Was Won
Ivanhoe
Johnny Green on the Hollywood
Soundstage
Kismet
Lili
Lovely to Look At
Merry Widow
Nancy Goes to Rio
Pagan Love Song
Parade of Hits
Porgy and Bess
Rose Marie
Seven Brides for Seven
Brothers
Silk Stockings
Singin' In the Rain
Slaughter on 10th Avenue
Strawberry Statement
Swan
Themes from the Great Motion
Pictures
Twilight of Honor
Unfinished Dance
Unsinkable Molly Brown
Wizard of Oz
Words and Music
MAAZEL, LORIN
Porgy and Bess
MacARTHUR, DOUGLAS
Years to Remember
MacAULY, JOSEPH
Smiling, the Boy Fell Dead
MacBANE, RALPH
Cradle Will Rock
MacBRYDE, PHYLLIS
Joan

MacCOLL, EWAN
Whaler Out of New Bedford
(And Other Songs of the
Whaling Era)
MacCOLL, KIRSTY
She's Having a Baby
MacDERMOT, GALT
Cotton Comes to Harlem
Dude (the Highway Life)
Fortune and Men's Eyes
Hair
Isabel's a Jezebel
Karl Marx
My Fur Lady
O Babylon
Two Gentlemen of Verona
Via Galactica
MacDONALD, AIMI
Promises, Promises
MacDONALD, DAVID
Best of Broadway 1973
MacDONALD, JEANETTE
Jeanette MacDonald and
Nelson Eddy
Love Me Tonight
Maytime
Naughty Marietta
New Moon
Pure Gold Movies
Rodgers and Hart In Hollywood
Rose Marie
Stars of the Silver Screen,
1929-1930
MacDONALD, JAMES
Cinderella
Mickey and the Beanstalk
MacDONOUGH, GLEN
Babes In Toyland
MACERO, TEO
Betrayal
George M!
MacFARLAND, DORTHEA
Oklahoma
MacGOWRAN, JACK
Juno
MacGRATH, LEUEEN
Evening with William
Shakespeare
MacGREGOR, MARY
Meatballs
MACHINATIONS
Ruthless People
MacINTOSH, JAY
Sgt. Pepper's Lonely Hearts
Club Band
MACK, CECIL
Blackbirds of 1928
MACK, JACK
Spring Break
Tuff Turf
MACK, JOHNNY, SINGERS
Bye Bye Birdie
MACK, RED
Yolanda and the Thief / You'll
Never Get Rich
MACKAY, ANGUS
Hooray for Daisy!
MacKAY, BRUCE
Donnybrook!
Greenwillow
Her First Roman
Oh Captain!
MacKAY, HARPER
Alice Through the Looking
Glass
Clownaround
Mr. Blackwell Show
MacKAY, MISSY
Washington Behind Closed
Doors
MacKAY, RABBIT
Angels Die Hard
MacKAYE, FRED
Christmas Carol
Count of Monte Cristo
MACKEBEN, THEO
Threepenny Opera
MacKENZIE, GISELE
Four Television Musicals
No Man Can Tame Me

MacKENZIE, WILL
Half a Sixpence
MacKERRAS, CHARLES
Nutcracker
MACKEY, PERCIVAL
No, No, Nanette
MACKLIN, ALBERT
Doonesbury
MacLAINE, SHIRLEY
Bliss of Mrs. Blossom
Can-Can
Film Music
Shirley MacLaine Live at the
Palace
Sweet Charity
Two Mules for Sister Sara
Woman Times Seven
MacLEOD, JOHN
My Fur Lady
MacMANUS, DECLAN
Courier
MacMURRAY, FRED
Absent-Minded Professor
Caine Mutiny
Happiest Millionaire
Joan Crawford
Kurt Weill In Hollywood
Shaggy Dog
MacNEE, PATRICK
Camelot
MacNEIL, CORNELL
Consul
MacPHERSON, DON
Tom Jones
MacPHERSON, PAT
Tom Jones
MacPHERSON, ROSS
Sweet Charity
MacRAE, GORDON
Best Things In Life Are Free
By the Light of the Silvery Moon
Carousel
Desert Song
Kismet
Kiss Me Kate
Merry Widow
Motion Picture Soundstage
Naughty Marietta
New Moon
Oklahoma
On Moonlight Bay
Oscar Hammerstein II
Memorial Album
Roberta
Showstoppers
Starlift
Student Prince
3 Sailors and a Girl
MacRAE, HEATHER
Perfect Couple
MacRAE, MEREDITH
Census Taker
MACREADY, ROY
Happy As a Sandbag
MAD DOCTORS
Doctor Goldfoot and the Girl
Bombs
MADAM X
Action Jackson
Fatal Beauty
MADDEN, BILL
Best of Broadway 1973
MADDEN, DAVE
Rowan and Martin's Laugh-In
MADDEN, DONALD
First Impressions
MADDEN, JEANNE
Knickerbocker Holiday
MADDEN, RONALD
Miss Julie
MADDOX, DIANA
Under Milk Wood
MADIGAN, AMY
Alamo Bay
MADIGAN, BETTY
Stingiest Man In Town
MADISON, GUY
Spotlight on Wild Bill Hickock
MADNESS
Dance Craze

Party Party
MADONNA
Vision Quest
Who's That Girl?
MAGAZINE
Urgh - A Music War
MAGEE, PATRICK
Marat (De) Sade
MAGGART, BRANDON
Applause
Lorelei
Musical Chairs
New Faces of 1968
Sing Muse!
MAGNANI, ANNA
Golden Coach
MAGNE, MICHEL
Circle of Love
MAGNESS-BALLARD
Two of a Kind
MAGNUSEN, MICHAEL
Festival
MAGOON, EATON, JR.
13 Daughters
MAGRUDER, C.
Tom Jones
MAGUIRE, JAMES
Bold Ventures
MAGUIRE, MICHAEL
Les Miserables
MAGUIRE, PAUL
Song and Dance
MAHARIS, GEORGE
Three Billion Millionaires
MAHLER, FRITZ
Triumph of Man
MAHLER, GUSTAV
Death In Venice
Female Prisoner
MAHONEY, JANET
Maid of the Mountains
MAHR, BEVERLY
California
Manhattan Tower
Seven Dreams
MAIDEN, RON
Creepers
MAIER, KURT
Encores of Hollywood
MAIN INGREDIENT
Save the Children
MAIN, MARJORIE
Rose Marie
MAIONE, GIA
Mary Poppins
MAITLAND, DEXTER
Night They Raided Minsky's
MAITLAND, JACK
Tom Brown's School Days
MAITLAND, JOAN
Tom Brown's School Days
MAJOR, CHARLIE
Best of the Best
MAJORS, CAROLYN
Far Out Man
MAKO
Pacific Overtures
MAKOROVA
On Your Toes
MALBIN, ELAINE
Connecticut Yankee
Firefly
Merry Widow
Naughty Marietta
That Midnight Kiss
Toast of New Orleans
MALCOLM, GEORGE
Hannah and Her Sisters
Slaughterhouse-Five
MALDEN, KARL
Gypsy
Pollyanna
Winged Victory
MALKOVICH, JOHN
Dangerous Liaisons
MALLE, LOUIS
Viva Maria!
MALLESON, MILES
Camelot

MALLORY, DOUG
Beowulf
MALLORY, VICTORIA
Follies
Little Night Music
Sondheim
Stephen Sondheim Evening
MALNECK, MATTY
As I Hear It
Love In the Afternoon
MALNICK, MICHAEL
Card
Music Man
MALONE, CINDY
Wild on the Beach
MALOOF, ALEXANDER
Lawrence of Arabia
MALTBY, RICHARD
*All-Star Parade, Hits from the
    Movies*
Baby
Mister Lucky
*Summer Place (And Other
    Great Hits from the Movies)*
MALTBY, RICHARD, JR.
Sap of Life
Starting Here, Starting Now
MALTEN, WILLIAM
Johnny Johnson
MALVIN, ARTHUR
Flower Drum Song
Music Man
Oklahoma
Sugar Babies
MAMAS AND THE PAPAS
Air America
American Pop
Stardust
MANCE, JUNIOR
Soul of Hollywood
MANCHESTER, MELISSA
Ice Castles
Promise
MANCINI, AL
John F. Kennedy
MANCINI, HENRY
Academy Award Songs, Vol. 2
Arabesque
Best of Mancini
Best of Mancini (Vol. 2)
Big Screen / Little Screen
Black Orpheus (Orfeu Negro)
Blind Date
Born on the Fourth of July
Breakfast at Tiffany's
Charade
Concert of Film Music
Cop Show Themes
Darling Lili
Dear Heart (And Other Themes)
*Encore! More of the Music of
    Henry Mancini*
Experiment In Terror
Film Music By Mancini
Fine Mess
Gaily, Gaily
Glass Menagerie
Great Race
Great Waldo Pepper
Gunn
Hatari
Hawaiians
*Henry Mancini Presents the
    Academy Award Songs*
High Time
Impact
In the Pink
James Bond
Lifeforce
Mancini Generation
Mancini's Angels
Me Natalie
Mister Lucky
Molly Maguires
NARM's Golden Decade
Oklahoma Crude
Our Man In Hollywood
Party
Peter Gunn
Pink Panther
Pink Panther Strikes Again
Pure Gold - Henry Mancini

Return of the Pink Panther
Revenge of the Pink Panther
Rock Pretty Baby
Santa Claus - The Movie
Sometimes a Great Notion
Summer Love
Sunflower
10
That's Dancing!
That's Entertainment!
Theme Scene
*Themes from Classic Science
    Fiction, Fantasy and Horror
    Films*
Themes from Horror Movies
Thief Who Came to Dinner
Touch of Evil
Trail of the Pink Panther
Two for the Road
Victor / Victoria
Visions of Eight
W.C. Fields and Me
*What Did You Do In the War,
    Daddy?*
*Who Is Killing the Great Chefs
    of Europe?*
Z
MANCRAB
Karate Kid II
MANDARIN GATE
It's a Revolution, Mother
MANDEL, FRANK
New Moon
MANDEL, JOHNNY
Agatha
Americanization of Emily
*Award Winning Original Motion
    Picture Sound Tracks and
    Themes*
Caddyshack
Escape to Witch Mountain
Harper
I Want to Live
*M*A*S*H*
*Movie Song Album - Tony
    Bennett*
Oscar
*Russians Are Coming! the
    Russians Are Coming!*
Sandpiper
Soup for One
MANDEL, JULIE
Two
MANDEL, STEVE
Deliverance
MANDAN, ROBERT
Applause
MANETTO, CORINNA
Littlest Angel
MANFREDI, NINO
Rugantino
MANFREDINI, HARRY
Friday the 13th
*House / House II: The Second
    Story*
Swamp Thing
MANGANO, SILVANA
*Anna / Hell Raiders of the
    Deep*
MANGIONE, CHUCK
Cannonball Run
Children of Sanchez
Leave It to Jane
MANGO, ANGELO
Heaven's Gate
**MANHATTAN POPS
ORCHESTRA**
*Music from Great Motion
    Pictures*
MANHATTAN TRANSFER
*Schoner Gigolo - Armer Gigolo
    (Just a Gigolo)*
Sharky's Machine
MANILOW, BARRY
Clams on the Half Shell
Copacabana
Foul Play
MANLEY, COLIN
Wonderwall
MANN, AIMEE
Back to the Beach
MANN, BARRY
Angel, Angel, Down We Go

I Never Sang for My Father
Joyride
Wild In the Streets
MANN, BRIAN
Feeling Good with Annie
MANN, BUDD
Prince and the Pauper
MANN, COLETTE
Godspell
MANN, JOHNNY, SINGERS
Man and a Woman
MANN, KAL
Don't Knock the Twist
Jamboree!
Loving You
MANN, MANFRED
Charge of the Light Brigade
Up the Junction
What's New Pussycat?
MANN, PAUL
Fiddler on the Roof
MANN, PEGGY
All Star Color TV Revue
Something for the Boys
MANN, SYLVIA
Cindy
MANN, V. TERRENCE
Barnum
Cats
Chorus Line
Les Miserables
MANNE, SHELLY
Barefoot Adventure
Bells Are Ringing
Checkmate
College Confidential
Daktari
Gene Krupa Story
Gone with the Wave
Great Motion Picture Themes
I Want to Live
Li'l Abner
Man with the Golden Arm
My Fair Lady
Peter Gunn
Proper Time
West Side Story
Young Billy Young
MANNERS, ZEKE
Beverly Hillbillies
MANNHEIM STEAMROLLER
Saving the Wildlife
MANNING, IRENE
Hollywood Canteen
Yankee Doodle Dandy
MANNING, JACK
Do I Hear a Waltz?
MANNING, JOHN
American Dreamer
MANNING, MARTY
Marry Me, Marry Me
Run for Your Wife
Wild Eye
MANNINO, FRANCO
*Love In 4 Dimensions (Amore
    In 4 Dimension)*
Ludwig
MANOFF, DINAH
Leader of the Pack
MANOU, NELLY
Greek Pearls
MANSFIELD, DAVID
Heaven's Gate
Sicilian
Year of the Dragon
MANSFIELD, JAYNE
Les Poupees De Paris
*Va Va Voom! Screen Sirens
    Sing!*
MANSFIELD, KEITH
Loot
MANSFIELD, KEN
Van Nuys Blvd.
MANSON, EDDY
Little Fugitive
Schnapsie
Three Bites of the Apple
MANSUR, SUSAN
*Best Little Whorehouse In
    Texas*

MANTEGNA, JOE
Working
MANTOVANI
Kismet
Mantovani
Music from the Films
Pacific 1860
MANTRONIC
Return of the Living Dead, Part II
MANZANO, SONIA
Godspell
MANZARI, ROBERT
Love Song
MANZIE, JIM
Tales from the Dark Side (the Movie)
MAPFUMP, THOMAS
Bad Influence
MARAND, PATRICIA
It's a Bird, It's a Plane, It's Superman
Wish You Were Here
MARBERT, JAMES
Thomas and the King
MARCELLE, LYDIA
Albert Peckingpaw's Revenge
MARCELS
Bye Bye Birdie
Dusty and Sweets McGee
MARCH, FREDRIC
ANTA Album of Stars, Vol. 1
MARCH, LITTLE PEGGY
Hairspray
MARCH VIOLETS
Some Kind of Wonderful
MARCHETTI, GIANNI
Wild Eye
MARCKLAND, TED
Angels from Hell
MARCOVICCI, ANDREA
Nefertiti
MARCUS, WADE
Final Comedown
MARCY, GEORGE
Littlest Revue
MARDIN, ARIF
Prophet
MARI, FLORIA
King of the Whole Damn World
MARIACHI VARGAS DE TECALITLAN
Down and Out In Beverly Hills
MARICLE, MARIJANE
Bye Bye Birdie
Hair
MARIE, JULIENNE
Boys from Syracuse
Do I Hear a Waltz?
Foxy
MARIE, TEENA
Top Gun
MARIE-FRANCE
Gigi
MARIETTA
Fire and Ice
Top Gun
MARIN, CHEECH
Lion King
Up In Smoke
MARINE, JOE
Miss Liberty
MARINERS
Arthur Godfrey
MARINOS, PETER
Zorba
MARINUZZI, GINO, JR.
Golden Coach
MARION SISTERS
Lady and the Tramp
MARISELA
Salsa
MARJANE, LEO
Last Metro
MARK, BRIAN
Last of the American Hoboes
MARK, MICHAEL
Cotton Patch Gospel
I Love My Wife

MARK, PETER
Lady Caroline Lamb
Mary, Queen of Scots
MARKEE, DAVE
O Lucky Man
MARKER, JEAN
Gigi
MARKER, PRESHY
Funny Thing Happened on the Way to the Forum
MARKEY, ENID
Mrs. Patterson
MARKHAM, MONTE
Irene
MARKS, ALFRED
Can-Can
MARKS, EMMARETTA
Hair
MARKS, GARETH
Buddy
MARKS, JOE E.
Flora the Red Menace
Li'l Abner
Peter Pan
MARKS, JOHNNY
Rudolph the Red-Nosed Reindeer
MARKS, WALTER
Bajour
Go Fly a Kite
Golden Rainbow
MARKWORT, PETER
Rise and Fall of the City of Mahogany
MARLEY, CEDELLA
Mighty Quinn
MARLEY, ZIGGY
Married to the Mob
Tequila Sunrise
MARLIN, MAX
Glass Menagerie
MARLO, MARIA
Consul
MARLOWE, GLORIA
Plain and Fancy
MARLOWE, MARION
Arthur Godfrey
Athenian Touch
Sound of Music
MARMONT, PAM
After the Ball
MARRAY, J.
Les Liaisons Dangereuses
MARRINER, NEVILLE
Amadeus
Plow That Broke the Plains
River
MARRIOTT, STEVE
Mother, Jugs and Speed
MARS, KENNETH
Anything Goes
Producers
MARSDEN, BETTY
Cinderella
On the Brighter Side
MARSDEN, GERRY
Ferry Cross the Mersey
MARSH, AUDREY
Annie Get Your Gun
Finian's Rainbow
Guys and Dolls
H.M.S. Pinafore
Mikado
Show Boat
MARSH, HOWARD
Show Boat
MARSH, KEITH
Lock Up Your Daughters
MARSH, LINDA
Hamlet
MARSHALL TUCKER BAND
Pursuit of D.B. Cooper
Stroker Ace
MARSHALL, CLEMENT
Hair
MARSHALL, E.G.
Waiting for Godot

MARSHALL, EVERETT
Stars of the Silver Screen, 1929-1930
MARSHALL, FRANKIE
Chocalonia
MARSHALL, HERBERT
Cavalcade
Count of Monte Cristo
Snow Goose
MARSHALL, JACK
At Home with the Munsters
Irma La Douce
Munsters
MARSHALL, KEN
Tilt
MARSHALL, LARRY
Inner City
Jesus Christ Superstar
Oh, Brother
Porgy and Bess
MARSHALL, MEREDITH
Girls Just Want to Have Fun
MARSHALL, MIKE
Country
MARSHALL, MORT
Little Me
Minnie's Boys
MARSHALL, PAT
Good News
Mister Wonderful
MARSHALL, PATRICIA
Movie Movie
MARSHALL, PETER
Bye Bye Birdie
Hollywood Squares
Skyscraper
MARSHALL, RICHARD
By Jupiter
MARSHALL, RON
Oliver!
You're a Good Man, Charlie Brown
Zorba
MARSHALL, SEAN
Happy Prince
Pete's Dragon
MARSHALL, YALE
Postcard from Morocco
MARSHE, SHEENA
Four Musketeers
MARTEL, MICHEL
Wait a Minim!
MARTEL, MIMI
Themes from the Movies
MARTEL, TOM
Hard Job Being God
MARTELL, CHRIS
It's a Revolution, Mother
MARTELL, PHILIP
After the Ball
Dracula
Legend of the Seven Golden Vampires
Love from Judy
MARTERIE, RALPH
Music for a Private Eye
Music Man
Original Motion Picture Hit Themes
MARTI, VIRGILIO
Crossover Dreams
MARTIN, ANDREA
What's a Nice Country Like the U.S. Doing In a State Like This?
MARTIN, ANDY
Jamboree!
MARTIN, ANGELA
George M!
MARTIN, BARNEY
Chicago
MARTIN, BILL
Feeling Good with Annie
MARTIN, BOB
Mary Poppins
MARTIN, CAROLE
Oklahoma
MARTIN, CORA
Lost Man

MARTIN, DAVID
Simply Heavenly
MARTIN, DEAN
Airport
Artists and Models
Bells Are Ringing
Dean Martin Testimonial Dinner
Dean Martin TV Show
Finian's Rainbow
Foster Brooks' Roasts
Gershwins In Hollywood (1931-1964)
Guys and Dolls
Hollywood Or Bust
Judy Garland
Kiss Me Kate
Living It Up
Magic Moments from the Tonight Show
Moonstruck
Movin' with Nancy
Pardners
Rio Bravo
Robin and the Seven Hoods
Showdown
Silencers
Stooge
Ten Thousand Bedrooms
MARTIN, DELORES
Finian's Rainbow
Oklahoma
MARTIN, DENIS
South Pacific
MARTIN, DEWEY
Angels Die Hard
Savage Sam
MARTIN, DICK
Rowan and Martin's Laugh-In
MARTIN, ELLEN
Penney Proud
MARTIN, ERIC
Caddyshack II
Iron Eagle
Teachers
MARTIN, FREDDY
Music Man
MARTIN, GEORGE
Ferry Cross the Mersey
Hard Day's Night
Honky-Tonk Freeway
Live and Let Die
Magnificent Movie Music
Sgt. Pepper's Lonely Hearts Club Band
Yellow Submarine
MARTIN, GRADY
Clambake
MARTIN, HELEN
Raisin
MARTIN, HUGH
Athena
Best Foot Forward
Girl Most Likely
Grandma Moses Suite
Hans Brinker
High Spirits
Look Ma I'm Dancin'!
Love from Judy
Make a Wish
Meet Me In St. Louis
Victors
MARTIN, JANE
Lola Montez
MARTIN, JILL
Tom Brown's School Days
MARTIN, LEILA
Ernest In Love
Philemon
Rothschilds
MARTIN, MARILYN
Quicksilver
Stealing Home
Streets of Fire
White Nights
MARTIN, MARY
Annie Get Your Gun
Anything Goes
Babes In Arms
Band Wagon
Beyond the Blue Horizon
Bing's Hollywood
Broadway Magic

787

McGRAW, ALI
Love Story
Winds of War
McGRAW, WILLIAM
Down In the Valley
McGREEVEY, ANNIE
Magic Show
McGREGOR, DION
Frankie and Johnny
McGRIFF, EDNA
Flower Drum Song
McGUINN, ROGER
Easy Rider
McGUIRE, BARRY
Stardust
Witness
McGUIRE, BIFF
Finian's Rainbow
McGUIRE, DOROTHY
Old Yeller
McGUIRE, MARCY
Higher and Higher
McGUIRE, PHYLLIS
Kiss Me Kate
McGUIRE SISTERS
Arthur Godfrey
Finian's Rainbow
Guys and Dolls
South Pacific
Subways Are for Sleeping
McHAFFEY, ROBERT
Prince and the Pauper
McHUGH, BURKE
Greenwich Village U.S.A.
McHUGH, DAVID
Moscow on the Hudson
Three Fugitives
McHUGH, JIMMY
Blackbirds of 1928
Four Jills In a Jeep
Higher and Higher
Jack the Ripper
*Jerome Kern Goes to
 Hollywood*
Singin' In the Rain
*Spectacular World of Classic
 Film Scores*
Sugar Babies
McHUGH - FIELDS -
 OPPENHEIMER
Stooge
McINDOE, JOHN
Bugaloos
McINTIRE, JOHN
Naked City
Seven Dreams
McINTIRE, LANI
Waikiki Wedding
McINTIRE, TIM
Jeremiah Johnson
McINTOSH, FRANKIE
Deep
McINTOSH, TOM
Learning Tree
McINTOSH, ROBERT
Happy As a Sandbag
McINTYRE, CHET
One Naked Night
McKAY, DON
Show Boat
McKAY, ROGER
Threads of Glory
McKEAN, KIM
Best of Broadway 1973
McKECHNIE, DONNA
Broadway Magic
Chorus Line
Company
Little Prince
Promises, Promises
Sondheim: A Musical Tribute
McKEE, LONETTE
Sparkle
McKEE, MARIA
Days of Thunder
Streets of Fire
McKEEVER, JACQUELYN
Oh Captain!
Wonderful Town

McKELLAR, KENNETH
Great Waltz
Kismet
McKELLEN, IAN
Every Good Boy Deserves Favor
McKENDRICK, BOB
Pal Joey
McKENNA, VIRGINIA
King and I
McKENNON, DAL
Robin Hood
Toby Tyler
Treasure Island
McKENZIE, JULIA
Cole
Follies
Side By Side By Sondheim
McKEON, DOUG
On Golden Pond
McKERN, LEO
Man for All Seasons
McKIE, SHIRLEY
Believers
McKINLEY, ANDREW
Consul
McKNEELY, JOEY
Jerome Robbins' Broadway
McKNELLY, KEVIN
Once Bitten
McKUEN, ROD
Borrowers
Boy Named Charlie Brown
Emily
Joanna
Me Natalie
Prime of Miss Jean Brodie
Rock Pretty Baby
Scandalous John
Sleep Warm
Summer Love
McLAGAN, IAN
Mahoney's Last Stand
McLAIN, MARCIA
Downriver
McLAREN, MALCOLM
No Small Affair
McLEAN, DON
Born on the Fourth of July
McLENNAN, ROD
My Fair Lady
Sweet Charity
McLERIE, ALLYN ANN
Bonanza Bound
Miss Liberty
Show Boat
McMAHON, ED
*Magic Moments from the
 Tonight Show*
*What Do You Want to Be When
 You Grow Up?*
McMAHON, EDWARD
Winged Victory
McMAHON, GERARD
Fast Times at Ridgemont High
Lonely Guy
Lost Boys
Spring Break
McMAHON, JEFF
*What Do You Want to Be When
 You Grow Up?*
McMAHON, JIM
Piano Bar
McMARTIN, JOHN
Follies
Little Mary Sunshine
Sondheim: A Musical Tribute
Sweet Charity
McMECHEN, JUNE
Porgy and Bess
McNAIR, BARBARA
Body Beautiful
*Magnavox Presents Frank
 Sinatra*
McNALLY, LARRY JOHN
Quicksilver
McNAMARA, MAUREEN
Festival
McNAMARA, ROBIN
Hair

McNAMARA, PAT
Legs Diamond
McNAUGHTON, STEVE
*Joseph and the Amazing
 Technicolor Dreamcoat*
McNEELY, ANNA
Cats
McNEIL, CLAUDIA
Her First Roman
Raisin In the Sun
Simply Heavenly
McNEIL, LONNIE
Eubie
McNEILL, JUSTIN
Beatlemania
McNICHOL, KRISTY
*Night the Lights Went Out In
 Georgia*
Pirate Movie
McNIGHT, MARION
Jack and the Beanstalk
McPARTLAND, JIMMY
Jazz Dance
Music Man
McPHAIL, JIMMY
My People
McPHERSON, IAN
Divorce Me, Darling!
McPHERSON, SAUNDRA
Hallelujah, Baby!
McQUEEN, ARMELIA
Ain't Misbehavin'
McQUEEN, BUTTERFLY
Athenian Touch
Cabin In the Sky
McQUEEN, SIMON
Boy Friend
McQUEEN, STERLING
Guys and Dolls
McRAE, CARMEN
Hotel
Porgy and Bess
Real Ambassadors
Subterraneans
McRITCHIE, GREIG
Exodus
McSPADDEN, BECKY
Candide
McVEY, HELEN
Threads of Glory
McVIE, CHRISTINE
Fine Mess
McWHINNEY, MICHAEL
Flush Left, Stagger Right
MDLEDLE, NATHAN
King Kong
MEAD, ABIGAIL
Full Metal Jacket
MEADOR, GEORGE
Cat and the Fiddle
MEADOWS, MICHAEL
Jesus Christ Superstar
MEALING, JOHN
Miss Ginger Rogers
MEARA, ANNE
*Sex Life of Primate (And Other
 Bits of Gossip)*
MEARS, MARTHA
Rita Hayworth
MEASHAM, DAVID
*Journey to the Center of the
 Earth*
Tommy
MEAT LOAF
Rocky Horror Picture Show
MEAT PUPPETS
Lovedolls Superstar
MECO
American Werewolf In London
Empire Strikes Back
Pop Goes the Movies
Star Wars
MEDALLION STRINGS
Sound of Hollywood Strings
MEDEIROS, GLENN
Karate Kid III
MEDFORD, KAY
Funny Girl
Gypsy

Two Tickets to Paris
MEDLEY, BILL
Cobra
Dirty Dancing
Growing Pains
Hard Ride
*Magic Garden of Stanley
 Sweetheart*
Rambo III
River Rat
Rude Awakening
MEEHAN, DANNY
*Ben Bagley's Ira Gershwin
 Revisited*
Funny Girl
Rodgers and Hart Revisited
Smiling, the Boy Fell Dead
Whoop-Up!
MEEKER, RALPH
After the Fall
Somebody Loves Me
MEERSMAN, PETER
Cradle Will Rock
MEGADEATH
Shocker
MEGNA, JOHN
Greenwillow
MEHTA, ZUBIN
Manhattan
*Star Wars / Close Encounters
 of the Third Kind*
MEISER, EDITH
Unsinkable Molly Brown
MEISLE, KATHRYN
Roberta
MEISNER, RANDY
FM
MEISTER, BARBARA
Mikado
MELACHRINO, GEORGE
Bells Are Ringing
Greenwillow
Melachrino on Broadway
*Melachrino Orchestra Plays
 Medleys*
*Music of Rodgers and
 Hammerstein*
MELANIE
R.P.M.
MELBOURNE SYMPHONY
 ORCHESTRA
Warlock
MELCHER, TERRY
Lethal Weapon 2
MELCHIOR, LAURITZ
Arabian Nights
Thrill of a Romance
MELENDEZ, BILL
Boy Named Charlie Brown
MELIA, JOE
Oh What a Lovely War
MELIS, JOSE
Jose Melis on Broadway
*Jose Melis Plays Jack Paar's
 Favorites*
MELL, RANDLE
Cradle Will Rock
MELL AND KIM
Coming to America
MELLE, GIL
Andromeda Strain
MELLENCAMP, JOHN
 COUGAR
Cobra
Cocktail
MELLIN, ROBERT
Dirty Game
MELLO MEN
It Happened at the World's Fair
Paradise, Hawaiian Style
MELLOMEN
Bing's Hollywood
Road to Bali
White Christmas
MELLOR, DAVID
High Society
MELNICK, LINDA R.
Three to Make Music
MELTON, JAMES
50 Years of Film

Show Boat
Ziegfeld Follies of 1946
MELTON, SID
Dora's World
MELUCAS, ROD
Fly with Me
MELVILLE, ALAN
Beggar's Holiday
MELVOIN, MICHAEL
Major Dundee
MEMBERS
Urgh - A Music War
MEN'S ROOM
Private School
MENDELSSOHN, FELIX
Melba
Midsummer Night's Dream
Midsummer Night's Sex
Comedy
MENDES, SERGIO
Heavy Traffic
Pelé
MENDEZ, RAFAEL
Cowboy
MENDOZA-NAVA, JAMIE
Savage Wild
MENJOU, ADOLPHE
New Moon
Pollyanna
MENKEN, ALAN
Little Shop of Horrors
MENKEN, STEVE
Doctor Selavy's Magic Theater
MENOTTI, GIAN-CARLO
Amahl and the Night Visitors
Consul
Maria Golovin
Medium
Old Maid and the Thief
Saint of Bleecker Street
Vanessa
MENTAL AS REGULAR
Star Struck
MENTEN, DALE
House of Leather
MENUHIN, YEHUDI
Slaughterhouse-Five
MERCADO, HECTOR JAIME
Cats
MERCER, JACK
Felix the Cat
MERCER, JOHNNY
Belle of New York
Bing's Hollywood
Breakfast at Tiffany's
Charade
Daddy Long Legs
Darling Lili
Dr. Phibes
Evening with Johnny Mercer
Everything I Have Is Yours
Fleet's In
Foxy
Free and Easy
Good Companions
Harvey Girls
Hatari
Hollywood Hotel
Hooray for Hollywood
Jerome Kern Goes to
Hollywood
Li'l Abner
Love in the Afternoon
Merry Andrew
Rhythm on the Range
Robin Hood
St. Louis Woman
Saratoga
Seven Brides for Seven
Brothers
Swinger
Texas Li'l Darlin'
Top Banana
You Can't Run Away from It
MERCER, MABEL
Porgy and Bess
MERCER, MARIAN
Promises, Promises
Stop the World - I Want to Get
Off!!

MERCER, ROSKO
Next Man
MERCOURI, MELINA
Gaily, Gaily
Illya Darling
More Great Motion Picture
Themes
Never on Sunday
Phaedra
Promise at Dawn
Topkapi
MERCURIO, STEVEN
Pet Sematary
MERCURY, ERIC
Warriors
MERCURY, FREDDIE
Metropolis
Teachers
MERCURY THEATER CAST
War of the Worlds
MEREDITH, BURGESS
Batman
How the West Was Won
Johnny Johnson
Shakespeare In Hollywood
What a Way to Dye
Wonderful O
MEREDITH, LARRY
Lovers and Other Strangers
MEREDITH, LEE
Musical Chairs
Producers
MEREDITH, MORLEY
Christine
MERIVALE, JOHN
Ivanov
MERKEL, UNA
Born to Dance
Take Me Along
MERLIN, JOANNA
Fiddler on the Roof
MERLINO, GENE
Camelot
King and I
Movie Movie
Pennies from Heaven
Washington Behind Closed
Doors
MERMAN, ETHEL
Alexander's Ragtime Band
Annie Get Your Gun
Anything Goes
Broadway Babies
Broadway Magic
Call Me Madam
Cole Porter In Hollywood
(1929-1956)
Cut! Out-Takes from
Hollywood's Greatest
Musicals
Ethel Merman
Ford 50th Anniversary TV Show
Great Personalities of
Broadway
Gypsy
Happy Hunting
Hello Dolly!
Here Come the Girls
Hollywood Canteen
Irving Berlin Tribute
Journey Back to Oz
Judy Garland
Legends of the Musical Stage
Memorable Moments in
Musical Comedy
Music and Lyrics By Cole
Porter
Official Grammy Awards
Archive Collection
Panama Hattie
Red Hot and Blue
Something for the Boys
Stars In Your Eyes
Terms of Endearment
There's No Business Like Show
Business
MERRIL, RAY
Gigi
MERRILL, BOB
Baker Street
Carnival
Funny Girl

New Girl In Town
Prettybelle
Wonderful World of the
Brothers Grimm
MERRILL, BUDDY
Show Time
MERRILL, DINA
On Your Toes
MERRILL, GARY
Huckleberry Finn
Rhapsody of Steel
Winged Victory
MERRILL, LOU
Christmas Carol
Count of Monte Cristo
MERRILL, ROBERT
Aaron Slick from Punkin Crick
Brigadoon
Carousel
Chocolate Soldier
Dangerous Christmas of Red
Riding Hood
Evening with Lerner and Loewe
Fiddler on the Roof
Henry, Sweet Henry
King and I
Kismet
Porgy and Bess
Search for Paradise
Show Boat
Sugar
Take Me Along
MERRILL, SCOTT
Johnny Johnson
Threepenny Opera
MERRIMAN, EVE
Inner City
MERRITT, TERESA
Best Little Whorehouse In
Texas
Wiz
MERSON, BILLY
Rose Marie
MERSSON, BORIS
South Pacific
MESROBIAN, ROBERT
Candide
MESSICK, DON
Hey There, It's Yogi Bear
Huckleberry Hound
Quick Draw McGraw
MESTER, JORGE
Medium
Old Maid and the Thief
METH, MAX
Cabin In the Sky
Finian's Rainbow
Let's Face It
Megilla of Itzig Manger
Seventh Heaven
METHENY, PAT
Falcon and the Snowman
Under Fire
**METROPOLITAN JAZZ
QUARTET**
Great Themes from Foreign
Movies
Great Themes from Great
American Movies
Great Themes from Great
Broadway Shows
Great Themes from TV Shows
**METROPOLITAN POPS
ORCHESTRA**
Bible
Doctor Zhivago
Themes from the Great Motion
Pictures
METZGER, RITA
Tovarich
MEUNIER, CLAUDINE
Young Girls of Rochefort
MEYER, TARO
Skateboard
Zorba
MEYERS, BILL
Armed and Dangerous
MEYERS, FRANK
Music Man
MEYERS, MAIDA
Housewives' Cantata

MEYERS, TIMOTHY
Grease
MGCINA, SOPHIE
King Kong
MIAMI SOUND MACHINE
Rude Awakening
Top Gun
MICHAEL, GEORGE
Beverly Hills Cop II
MICHAEL, PAT
Camelot
MICHAEL, PATRICIA
Divorce Me, Darling!
Gone with the Wind
MICHAEL, PAUL
Sing Muse!
Tovarich
MICHAEL'S PUB SHOW
Ladies Who Wrote the Lyrics
MICHAELS, BERT
Prettybelle
MICHAELS, DEAN
Joe
MICHAELS, FRANKIE
Mame
MICHAELS, HILLY
Caddyshack
MICHAELS, JILL
Wraith
MICHAELS, SIDNEY
Ben Franklin In Paris
MICHAELS BROTHERS
Mame
**MICHALSKI AND
OOSTERVEEN**
Eyes of Laura Mars
MICHELINI, LUCIANO
Screamers
MICHELL, KEITH
Irma La Douce
Man of La Mancha
Robert and Elizabeth
MICHENER, DEAN
Golden Apple
MICHIE, GEORGE
Lisztomania
MICKEY AND SYLVIA
Dirty Dancing
MIDDLETON, CHARLES
Flash Gordon
MIDDLETON, GUY
Gentlemen Prefer Blondes
MIDDLETON, RAY
Annie Get Your Gun
Ethel Merman
Man of La Mancha
MIDDLETON, TONY
Cabin In the Sky
MIDLER, BETTE
Beaches
Clams on the Half Shell
Divine Maddness
Magic Moments from the
Tonight Show
Oliver and Company
Rose, The
MIDNEY, BORIS
Empire Strikes Back
MIDNIGHT STAR
Penitentiary III
MIGENES, JULIA
Fiddler on the Roof
MIGLIARDI, MARIO
My Fair Lady
MIKE + MECHANICS
Rude Awakening
**MILAN PHILHARMONIA
ORCHESTRA**
Godfather, Parts I and II
MILANO, FRANK
Pinocchio
MILBURN, ELLSWORTH
Committee
MILES, BERNARD
Tom Thumb
MILES, PETER
Quo Vadis?
MILES, TERRIN
Golden Boy

MILES, VERA
Beau James
MILFORD, PENELOPE
Shenandoah
MILLAND, RAY
Battlestar Galactica
Ginger Rogers
Survival Run
MILLAR, CYNTHIA
Miklos Rozsa
MILLAR, RONALD
Robert and Elizabeth
MILLER, ALLAN
Showcase Album, 1967
MILLER, ANN
Deep In My Heart
Easter Parade
Golden Age of Movie Musicals
Hit the Deck
Kiss Me Kate
Ladies of Burlesque
Lovely to Look At
On the Town
Rodgers and Hart In Hollywood
Sugar Babies
That's Dancing!
That's Entertainment!
MILLER, ARTHUR
Death of a Salesman
MILLER, BOB
O Say Can You See!
MILLER, BRENDA
Student Prince
MILLER, BUZZ
Bravo Giovanni!
Pajama Game
MILLER, CARLTON
Around the World In 80 Days
MILLER, D.L.
Oklahoma
MILLER, EDDIE
Pete Kelly's Blues
MILLER, FRANKIE
All the Right Moves
MILLER, GARY
New York, New York
She Loves Me
MILLER, GLENN
Glenn Miller: Golden Hits from
His Original Soundtracks
Glenn Miller Story
Orchestra Wives
Sun Valley Serenade
MILLER, HELEN
Inner City
MILLER, JACOB
Rockers
MILLER, JOHN
I Love My Wife
Official Grammy Awards
Archive Collection
MILLER, JONATHAN
Beyond the Fringe
MILLER, KENNY
Surf Party
MILLER, KEVIN
La Vie Parisienne
MILLER, LEE
Nina, the Pinta, and the Santa
Maria
MILLER, LESLIE
Midnight Cowboy
MILLER, MARCUS
Music from Siesta
MILLER, MARILYN
Legends of the Musical Stage
MILLER, MITCH
All-Star Parade, Hits from the
Movies
America Sings
Bridge on the River Kwai
European Holiday
Guns of Navarone
Leslie Uggams on TV
Major Dundee
Red Garters
Summer Place (And Other
Great Hits from the Movies)
TV Singalong with Mitch Miller
and the Gang

MILLER, PAUL
Order Is Love
MILLER, ROBIN
Dames at Sea
MILLER, ROGER
Big River (the Adventures of
Huckleberry Finn)
John Brown's Body
Robin Hood
Superman III
Waterhole #3
MILLER, SHARON
Hark!
MILLER, SONNY
Live for Life
Wedding In Paris
MILLER, STEVE, BAND
Big Chill (More Songs from the
Original Soundtrack)
FM
Revolution
MILLER, WYNNE
Tenderloin
Thurber Carnival
MILLI, ROBERT
Hamlet
MILLIKEN, JILL
Among Friends - Waa-Mu Show
of 1960
MILLO, MARIO
Shame / Lighthorsemen
MILLS, ERIE
Candide
Follies
MILLS, GARY
Circus of Horrors
MILLS, HAYLEY
Daydreamer
Gypsy Girl
In Search of the Castaways
Music from Disney Motion
Pictures
Parent Trap
Pollyanna
Summer Magic
MILLS, JOHN
Command Performance
Good Companions
Goodbye Mr. Chips
In Search of the Castaways
MILLS, RICHARD
Franz Waxman
Fraulein
MILLS, STEPHANIE
Fletch
Wiz
MILLS, STEVE
70 Girls, 70
This Was Burlesque
MILLS, WARREN
Rappin'
MILLS BROTHERS
Bing Crosby In Hollywood
(1930-1934)
Blackbirds of 1928
Red Sky at Morning
Twenty Million Sweethearts
MILNER, MARK
Tinseltown
MILNES, SHERRILL
Up In Central Park
MILOTEN, ZALMEN
Golden Land
MILSAP, RONNIE
Bronco Billy
Follow That Bird
MILTON, DEREK
Lost Empires
MIMIEUX, YVETTE
Black Hole (the Story of the
Black Hole)
Wonderful World of the
Brothers Grimm
MINA
Tenth Victim
MINAMI, ROGER
Act
MINDBENDERS
Good Morning, Vietnam
To Sir with Love

MINEO, JOHN
Lorelei
Zorba
MINEO, SAL
Aladdin
MINKUS
Don Quixote
MINKUS, BARBARA
You're a Good Man, Charlie
Brown
MINNELLI, LIZA
Act
Arthur (the Album)
Best Foot Forward
Cabaret
Dangerous Christmas of Red
Riding Hood
Flora the Red Menace
Journey Back to Oz
Judy Garland
Judy Garland - Liza Minnelli
Live at the London Palladium
Liza Minnelli at the Winter
Garden
Liza with a "Z"
Lucky Lady
New York, New York
Rink
MINOR, MIKE
Ice Follies
MIRANDA, CARMEN
Four Jills In a Jeep
Gang's All Here
Nancy Goes to Rio
South American Way
Springtime In the Rockies
That Night In Rio
MIRETTES
Lost Man
MIRKIN, BARRY
Dean Martin Testimonial Dinner
MIRREN, HELEN
Excalibur
MISRAKI, PAUL
God Created Woman
MISSION
Virgin
MITCHELL, ADRIAN
Marat (De) Sade
Tell Me Lies
MITCHELL, BILL
Dracula
MITCHELL, BOB
Flying Nun
MITCHELL, BYRON
Crystal Heart
Tovarich
MITCHELL, CAMERON
Carousel
Death of a Salesman
MITCHELL, GRANT
Twenty Million Sweethearts
MITCHELL, GUY
Oh Captain!
Red Garters
MITCHELL, JAMES
Carnival
MITCHELL, JOHN
Christmas Carol
MITCHELL, JONI
Last Waltz
MITCHELL, LEONA
Porgy and Bess
MITCHELL, MARY
Taking Off
MITCHELL, MARY JENNIFER
National Lampoon Lemmings
MITCHELL, NORMAN
Christmas Carol
**MITCHELL, PARRIS,
STRINGS**
Camelot
MITCHELL, RED
West Side Story
MITCHELL, SHIRLEY
Manhattan Tower
MITCHELL, TERRY
Words and Music
MITCHELL, THOMAS
Death of a Salesman

Hazel Flagg
Moby Dick
Story of Moby Dick
Treasure Island
MITCHELL, WARREN
Can-Can
My Fair Lady
MITCHUM, JOHN
America, Why I Love Her
MITCHUM, ROBERT
Winds of War
MITROPOULOS, DIMITRI
Vanessa
MITSOUKO, LES RITA
Black Rain
MITTY, NOMI
Tree Grows In Brooklyn
MIXON, TOM
Penney Proud
MIZELL, FONCE
Hell Up In Harlem
MIZZY, VIC
Addams Family
Caper of the Golden Bulls
Don't Make Waves
MNGUNI, GASTA
Ipi-Tombi
MOBLEY, MARY ANN
Get Yourself a College Girl
MOCKRIDGE, CYRIL
Gift of Love
It's a Wonderful Life
MODELS
Soul Man
MODERN FOLK QUARTET
Palm Springs Weekend
MODERN JAZZ QUARTET
More Great Motion Picture
Themes
No Sun In Venice
Odds Against Tomorrow
MODERN MAN
Day of the Dead
MODERN ROMANCE
Party Party
MODERNAIRES
Club 15
Glenn Miller: Golden Hits from
His Original Soundtracks
MOFFATT, KATY
Billy Jack
MOGOTSI, JOSEPH
King Kong
MOHAMMED, IDRIS
Hair
MOHATT, JOHN
Cowardly Custard
MOHAUTT, RICHARD
Story of Moby Dick
**MOISEYEV SONG AND
DANCE ENSEMBLE**
Russian Adventure
MOLETSANE, PATRICK
Ipi-Tombi
MOLINE, BOB
Hard Ride
MOLLIN, FRED
Friday the 13th
MOLLOY, BRUCE
Canada
MOLOI, STEPHEN
King Kong
MOLONEY, PADDY
Barry Lyndon
MOM'S BOYS
Riot on Sunset Strip
MOMENT OF TRUTH
Nocturna
MOMENTS
Patty
MONA LISA
Skateboard
MONACHINO, FRANCIS
Consul
MONACO, JAMES V.
Bing's Hollywood
Eddie Cantor Story
Judy at the Palace
Star Maker

MONARCHS
Fraulein
Ten North Frederick
Themes from Great Films

MONEY, EDDIE
Americathon
Back to the Beach
Over the Top

MONEY TALKS
Karate Kid III

MONIS, HANK
Apple Tree

MONK, DEBRA
Pump Boys and Dinettes

MONK, MEREDITH
Pomegranada

MONKEES
Head
Stardust

MONKHOUSE, BOB
Boys from Syracuse

MONNOT, MARGUERITE
Irma La Douce
Jessica

MONOTONES
American Graffiti
Dusty and Sweets McGee

MONRO, MATT
Born Free
From Russia with Love
Italian Job
James Bond - 10th Anniversary
James Bond 13 Original
Themes
Matter of Innocence
Paris Was Made for Lovers
Quiller Memorandum
Romantic Favorites from Stage
and Screen
Showstoppers
Southern Star

MONROE, BARRY
No, No, Nanette

MONROE, MARILYN
Gentlemen Prefer Blondes
Let's Make Love
Marilyn Monroe
More Great Motion Picture
Themes
Remember Marilyn
River of No Return
Some Like It Hot
There's No Business Like Show
Business
Va Va Voom! Screen Sirens
Sing!

MONTAGE
Hot Parts

MONTALBAN, RICARDO
Alice Through the Looking
Glass
Golden Age of Movie Musicals
Jamaica
Premiere
Seventh Heaven

MONTAND, YVES
Let's Make Love
On a Clear Day You Can See
Forever

MONTE, BARBARA
I Can Get It for You Wholesale
On a Clear Day You Can See
Forever

MONTE, LOU
Finian's Rainbow
Kiss Me Kate

MONTENEGRO, HUGO
Andersonville Trial
Camelot
Farmer
Great Songs from Motion
Pictures, Volume I (1927 -
1937)
Great Songs from Motion
Pictures, Volume II (1938 -
1944)
Great Songs from Motion
Pictures, Volume III (1945 -
1960)
Hang 'Em High
Hugo Montenegro - Good
Vibrations

Hurry Sundown
Lady In Cement
Man from U.N.C.L.E.
Music from a Fistful of Dollars
/ For a Few Dollars More /
The Good, the Bad and the
Ugly
Scenes and Themes
Viva Max!

MONTEREY BRASS
Mame

MONTEVECCHI, LILIANE
Follies
Nine

MONTEZ, CHRIS
National Lampoon's Animal
House

MONTGOMERY, DICK
Carmen Jones

MONTGOMERY, GEORGE
Three Little Girls In Blue

MONTGOMERY, LARIED
Henry, Sweet Henry

MONTGOMERY, MARION
Anything Goes

MONTGOMERY, MARK
1776
You're a Good Man, Charlie
Brown

MONTGOMERY, ROBERT
Joan Crawford

MONTIEL, SARITA
La Violetera

MONTY PYTHON
Meaning of Life

MOODY, PHIL
So This Is Paris

MOODY, RON
Oliver!

MOODY BLUES
Karate Kid II
1969

MOON, KEITH
All This and World War II
Quadrophenia
Tommy

MOONEY, HAROLD
American Musical Theater
Pete Kelly's Blues
Rich Man, Poor Man

MOONEY, WILLIAM
Half Man - Half Alligator

MOONGLOWS
American Hot Wax
Rock, Rock, Rock

MOONLITERS
Shag

MOOR, CHERIE (Cheryl
Ladd)
Josie and the Pussycats

MOORE, ADA
House of Flowers
This Is Broadway's Best

MOORE, BARBARA
Fiddler on the Roof
Games

MOORE, BOB
Blue Hawaii
Clambake
Double Trouble
Easy Come, Easy Go
Harum Scarum
Kid Galahad
Kissin' Cousins
Roustabout
This Is Elvis
Tickle Me

MOORE, CHARLES
House of Flowers

MOORE, CHRISTA
Gypsy

MOORE, CLAIRE
Life and Times of a She-Devil

MOORE, CONSTANCE
Ship Ahoy

MOORE, DOUGLAS
Ballad of Baby Doe
Carry Nation
Devil and Daniel Webster

MOORE, DUDLEY
Alice's Adventures In
Wonderland
Bedazzled
Beyond the Fringe
Beyond the Fringe '64
Good Evening
30 Is a Dangerous Age, Cynthia

MOORE, FRANK LEDLIE
Triumph of Man

MOORE, GRACE
Here Come the Girls
New Moon

MOORE, JONATHAN
Dylan

MOORE, JULIAN
Irma La Douce

MOORE, KAREN
Gypsy

MOORE, KEVIN
That Was Then, This Is Now

MOORE, MARION
Guys and Dolls

MOORE, MARY TYLER
Breakfast at Tiffany's

MOORE, MELBA
Bad Boys
Cotton Comes to Harlem
Hair
Purlie

MOORE, PHIL
Oh Captain!

MOORE, SCOTTY
Blue Hawaii
Christmas to Elvis
Double Trouble
Easy Come, Easy Go
Elvis (NBC-TV Special)
Elvis Live at the Louisiana
Hayride
Follow That Dream
Frankie and Johnny
Fun In Acapulco
G.I. Blues
Girl Happy
Girls! Girls! Girls!
Harum Scarum
It Happened at the World's Fair
Jailhouse Rock
Kid Galahad
King Creole
Kissin' Cousins
Louisiana Hayride
Loving You
Paradise, Hawaiian Style
Roustabout
Spinout
This Is Elvis
Tickle Me
Viva Las Vegas

MOORE, SPENCER
Night of the Living Dead

MOORE, STEPHEN
Hitch-Hikers Guide to the
Galaxy

MOORE, TERRY
Sunny Side of the Street

MOORE, TRACY
Joan

MOORE, VICTOR
Louisiana Purchase

MOOREHEAD, AGNES
Alice Through the Looking
Glass
Charlotte's Web
Citizen Kane
Gigi
Pollyanna
Sorry, Wrong Number

MOORES, MICHAEL
High Spirits

MORADZADEH, DEBORAH
Together Again

MORAL, JACQUES
Can't Stop the Music

MORAN, PAT
Porgy and Bess

MORANIS, RICK
Little Shop of Horrors

MORARE, RUBY
Ipi-Tombi

MORATH, MAX
Max Morath at the Turn of the
Century
Ragtime Years

MORAY, STELLA
Most Happy Fella
Robert and Elizabeth

MORDENTE, LISA
Platinum

MORE, JULIAN
Grab Me a Gondola
Irma La Douce

MORE, KENNETH
Slipper and the Rose

MOREAU, JEANNE
Viva Maria!

MOREHOUSE COLLEGE
GLEE CLUB
School Daze

MORENO, RITA
Electric Company TV Show
King and I
Premiere
She Loves Me
West Side Story

MOREY, CYNTHIA
La Vie Parisienne

MOREY, LARRY
Bambi
Snow White and the Seven
Dwarfs

MORFOGEN, ZACHARY
Canada

MORFORD, GENE
Cross and the Switchblade
Le Mans

MORGAN, ANTHONY
Dawgs

MORGAN, CASS
Diamond Studs
Pump Boys and Dinettes

MORGAN, CHRIS
R.P.M.

MORGAN, DENNIS
Great Ziegfeld
Hollywood Canteen
Painting the Clouds with
Sunshine
Swanee River

MORGAN, DONALD
Medium

MORGAN, EUGENE
Desert Song

MORGAN, FRANK
Annie Get Your Gun
Wizard of Oz

MORGAN, GARY
Pete's Dragon

MORGAN, HELEN
Go Into Your Dance
Great Personalities of
Broadway
Here Come the Girls
Show Boat
Stars of the Silver Screen,
1929-1930

MORGAN, JANE
Diner
Filmusic Scene
Marry Me, Marry Me
Victors

MORGAN, JAYE P.
All-Star Salute, the Very Best of
Gershwin

MORGAN, JOAN
Mrs. Patterson

MORGAN, MAC
Musical Comedy and Operetta
Favorites, Vol 2

MORGAN, MELISSA
Golden Child

MORGAN, MERLIN
Maid of the Mountains

MORGAN, MICHELE
Higher and Higher

MORGAN, PAT
Somebody Loves Me

MORISON, PATRICIA
Kiss Me Kate

MORLEY, ANGELA
Equus
Little Prince
Slipper and the Rose
Watership Down
MORLEY, JOHN
Houdini, Man of Magic
MORLEY, ROBERT
Cromwell
MORMON TABERNACLE CHOIR
America Sings
How the West Was Won
MORNING GOOD
Savage Seven
MORODER, GIORGIO
American Gigolo
Cat People
Electric Dreams
Flashdance
Foxes
Metropolis
Midnight Express
Official Music of the XXIIIrd Olympiad, Los Angeles 1984
Over the Top
Rambo III
Scarface
Superman III
Top Gun
MOROSS, JEROME
Big Country
Cardinal
Digital Space
Golden Apple
Jerome Moross
Scandalous Life of Frankie and Johnny
Wagon Train
War Lord
MORRICONE, ENNIO
Barabbas
Battle of Algiers
Big Gundown
Bird with the Crystal Plumage
Black Belly of the Tarantula
Bloodline
Blue Eyed Bandit
Bluebeard
Burglars
Burn
Butterfly
Casualties of War
Chosen
Days of Heaven
Duck, You Sucker
Exorcist II - The Heretic
Film Music, Vol. 1
Film Music, Vol. 2
Fistful of Dollars
For a Few Dollars More
Frantic
Good, the Bad and the Ugly
Guns for San Sebastian
Hamlet
Heaven's Gate
Hundra
Investigation of a Citizen Above Suspicion
Island
L'assoluto Naturale
La Cage Aux Folles
La Cage Aux Folles II
La Grande Bourgeoise
Listen, Let's Make Love
Malamondo
Marco Polo
Mission
Moses the Lawgiver
Music from a Fistful of Dollars / For a Few Dollars More / The Good, the Bad and the Ugly
My Name Is Nobody
1900
Once Upon a Time In America
Once Upon a Time In the West
Quando L'amore E'sensualita'
Rampage
Red Sonja
Red Tent
Sacco and Vanzetti
Sahara

Scarlet and the Black
Sicilian Clan
Sonny and Jed
Tepepa
Thing
Time of Destiny
Two Mules for Sister Sara
Untouchables
MORRIS, ANITA
Magic Show
Nine
MORRIS, FLOYD
Let's Do It Again
MORRIS, GARRETT
Ain't Supposed to Die a Natural Death
Hallelujah, Baby!
Saturday Night Live
MORRIS, GARY
Dallas
Rustler's Rhapsody
MORRIS, HOWARD
Finian's Rainbow
MORRIS, JAMES R.
Naughty Marietta
MORRIS, JOHN
All American
Blazing Saddles
Elephant Man
Hair
High Anxiety
History of the World, Part I
Producers
Silent Movie
Spaceballs
Time for Singing
Twelve Chairs
Wildcat
Woman In Red
World's Greatest Lover
Young Frankenstein
MORRIS, MARLOWE
All American
MORRIS, NAT
Dude (the Highway Life)
MORRISON, ALETA
Can-Can
MORRISON, ANN
Goblin Market
I Remember Mama
Merrily We Roll Along
Sondheim
MORRISON, DIANA
Aspects of Love
MORRISON, HERB
Hindenberg
MORRISON, VAN
Born on the Fourth of July
Dusty and Sweets McGee
King of Comedy
Last Waltz
Officer and a Gentleman
Wonder Years
MORRISON, WILLIAM
One Night Stand
MORROW, BUDDY
Double Impact
Impact
MORROW, DORETTA
Adventures of Marco Polo
Carousel
Desert Song
General Motors' 50th Anniversary Show
King and I
Kismet
Mademoiselle Modiste
Music from Shubert Alley
This Is Broadway's Best
MORROW, GEOFF
Jingle Jangle
MORROW, JO
Three Worlds of Gulliver
MORROW, KAREN
At Home Abroad
Band Wagon
Boys from Syracuse
Grass Harp
I Had a Ball
Joyful Noise
Painted Smiles of Cole Porter
Sing Muse!

Tom Jones
MORROW, PATRICIA
Surf Party
MORSE, RICHARD
Showcase Album, 1967
MORSE, ROBERT
How to Succeed In Business Without Really Trying
Jolly Theatrical Season
So Long 174th Street
Sugar
Take Me Along
MORSE, ROBIN
Bring Back Birdie
MORTON, BROOKS
Her First Roman
Riverwind
MORTON, JELLY ROLL
Pretty Baby
MORTON, JOE
Brother from Another Planet
Oh, Brother
Raisin
Salvation
MORTON, TOMMY
Littlest Revue
MOSCO, NATALIE
Hair
MOSCOW RADIO CHORUS
Reds
MOSCOW STATE SYMPHONY
Russian Adventure
MOSCOW SYMPHONY ORCHESTRA
War and Peace
MOSER, MARGOT
Carousel
MOSES, GILBERT, III
Willie Dynamite
MOSHE, RAFI BEN
From Israel with Love
MOSHER, BOB
At Home with the Munsters
MOSIER, ENID
House of Flowers
This Is Broadway's Best
MOSS, ARNOLD
Evening with William Shakespeare
Follies
Medea
MOSS, JEFFREY
Sesame Street
MOSS, KATHI
Grease
MOSS, LARRY
Mixed Doubles / Below the Belt
Robber Bridegroom
MOSS, VIKKI
St. Elmo's Fire
MOST, ABE
1941
MOST, JOHNNY
Celtics Pride
MOSTEL, JOSHUA
Jesus Christ Superstar
MOSTEL, ZERO
Fiddler on the Roof
Funny Thing Happened on the Way to the Forum
Official Grammy Awards Archive Collection
Producers
MOTELS
Teachers
MOTHER EARTH
Revolution
MOTION PICTURE STUDIO ORCHESTRA
Around the World In 80 Days
Live for Life
Man and a Woman
MOTIS, FRANK
Curtain Going Up (Musical Guide to Play Acting)
MOTLEY CRUE
Adventures of Ford Fairlane

MOTORHEAD
Creepers
MOTTOLA, TONY
Cinema '76
Danger
MOUNT, PEGGY
Oliver!
MOUNTAIN
He's My Girl
Omar Khayyam
Vanishing Point
MOUSEKETEERS CHORUS
Walt Disney's Mickey Mouse Club
MOVING PICTURES
Footloose
MOWELL, SHELLEY
Shoestring Revue '57
MOZART, WOLFGANG AMADEUS
Amadeus
Carnegie Hall
Gospel According to St. Matthew
Life and Times of a She-Devil
Magic Flute
Melba
MR. BIG
Navy SEALS
MTUME, JAMES
Native Son
MUELLER, ZIZI
Carmilla
MUGWUMP ESTABLISHMENT
Mondo Hollywood
MUGWUMPS
Riot on Sunset Strip
MUHOBERAC, LARRY
Paradise, Hawaiian Style
Side By Side 75
MULCHAY, LANCE
One Over the Eight
MULDAUR, MARIA
Green Ice
MULLAVEY, GREG
Census Taker
MULLEN SISTERS
All Star Color TV Revue
Annie Get Your Gun
Blossom Time
Red Mill
MULLENDORE, JOSEPH
Honey West
Impact
MULLER, HARRISON
Seventeen
MULLER, STEPHEN
Christmas Carol
MULLER, WERNER
International Film Festival
MULLER-LAMPERTZ, RICHARD
Roberta
Rozsa: Suites for the Films
MULLIGAN, GERRY
Great Motion Picture Themes
Hot Rock
I Want to Live
Sound of Jazz
Subterraneans
MULLIGAN, RICHARD
Little Big Man
MULLIKIN, BILL
New Faces of 1952
MULREAN, LINDA
Karl Marx
MUMMY CALLS
Lost Boys
MUNCH, RICHARD
Rise and Fall of the City of Mahogany
MUNDT, KARL E.
Point of Order
MUNICH BACH ORCHESTRA
Barry Lyndon
MUNICH PHILHARMONIC
Anastasia - The Mystery of Anna

MUNICH STUDIO
  ORCHESTRA
  Enemy Mine
  Fly II
MUNICH SYMPHONY
  ORCHESTRA
  Brave One
MUNIER, FERDINAND
  Christmas Carol
MUNN, FRANK
  Show Boat
MUNRO, JANET
  *Darby O'Gill and the Little
  People*
MUNROW, DAVID
  Henry VIII and His Six Wives
MUNSEL, PATRICE
  *Ben Bagley's Oscar
  Hammerstein Revisited*
  Carousel
  King and I
  La Perichole
  Melba
  Merry Widow
  Show Boat
  Stingiest Man In Town
MUNSEN, JUDY
  Street Music
MUNSHIN, JULES
  Call Me Mister
  Gay Life
  Kiss Me Kate
  Show Girl
  Silk Stockings
  Take Me Out to the Ball Game
MUPPETS
  Follow That Bird
  Great Muppet Caper
  Muppet Show
  Muppets Take Manhattan
MURA, CORINNA
  Mexican Hayride
MURCELL, RAYMOND
  Desert Song
MURDOCH, BRAD
  My Turn on Earth
MURDOCK, JIM
  Sparkles
MURE, BILLY
  *What Do You Want to Be When
  You Grow Up?*
MURPHEY, MICHAEL
  MARTIN
  Hard Country
  Pink Cadillac
MURPHY, BEN
  Winds of War
MURPHY, FRANK
  Billy Budd
MURPHY, GEORGE
  Broadway Melody of 1940
MURPHY, LYLE
  Tony Fontane Story
MURPHY, PETER
  Pump Up the Volume
MURPHY, WALTER
  Saturday Night Fever
MURRAY, ANNE
  Growing Pains
  Urban Cowboy
MURRAY, BILL
  Little Shop of Horrors
  Meatballs
MURRAY, KATHLEEN
  Kittiwake Island
  Leave It to Jane
MURRAY, KEN
  Ken Murray's Blackouts
MURRAY, LYN
  Christmas Carol
  Finian's Rainbow
  Lonesome Train
  Mister Novak
  On the Town
  Promise Her Anything
  To Catch a Thief
MURRAY, PEG
  She Loves Me
MURRAY, PETE
  Otley

MURRAY, SHARON
  Grind
MURRAY, WYNN
  I Married an Angel
  Rodgers and Hart 1927-1942
MURROW, EDWARD R.
  *I Can Hear It Now, Volume 1:
  1933-1945*
  Lady from Philadelphia
  Satchmo the Great
MURRY, TED
  Follow the Boys
MURVIN, JUNIOR
  Rockers
MUSE, CLARENCE
  Porgy and Bess
MUSGRAVE, THEA
  Christmas Carol
  Mary, Queen of Scots
MUSIC MAIDS
  Star Maker
MUSIC MINUS ONE
  ORCHESTRA
  Fiddler on the Roof
MUTINY
  Cruising
MYERS, PAMELA
  Company
  Day of the Locust
  Sondheim: A Musical Tribute
MYERS, PETER
  Wonderful to Be Young
MYERS, R.
  Mr. Cinders
MYERS, STANLEY
  Blind Date
  Deer Hunter
  Insignificance
  Kaleidoscope
  No Way to Treat a Lady
  Otley
  Prick Up Your Ears
  Ulysses
MYGGEN, BENT
  Hooper
MYHERS, JOHN
  *How to Succeed In Business
  Without Really Trying*
MYLES, METROGENE
  Jerico-Jim Crow
MYLETT, JEFFREY
  Godspell
MYLROIE, KATHRYN
  Two on the Aisle
MYRON, DIANE
  Jerry's Girls
MYROW, FRED
  Phantasm
MYROW, JOSEF
  Bundle of Joy
  French Line
  I Love Melvin
  Shocking Miss Pilgrim
  Three Little Girls In Blue
MYRTIL, ODETTE
  Cat and the Fiddle
  Saratoga
MYSTERIOUS KARSTEN
  Popeye
MYSTICS
  American Hot Wax
NBC OPERA COMPANY
  Amahl and the Night Visitors
NBC STUDIO ORCHESTRA
  Elvis (NBC-TV Special)
NRBQ
  Spring Break
NABORS, JIM
  *Best Little Whorehouse In
  Texas*
  Christmas In Hawaii
  Gomer Pyle U.S.M.C.
  Man of La Mancha
NADER, RALPH
  Foster Brooks' Roasts
NAGEL, CONRAD
  Hercules
  Joan Crawford
NAIRNES, CAREY
  Girl Who Came to Supper

NAISMITH, LAURENCE
  Here's Love
  Scrooge
  Time for Singing
NAMANWORTH, PHILIP
  Heart of Dixie
NAMATH, JOE
  Foster Brooks' Roasts
NANCE, JOHN
  Eraserhead
NANTON, MORRIS
  Flower Drum Song
  Roberta
NAPOLITANO, JOHNETTE
  Echo Park
NARELLE, BRIAN
  Dark Star
NARROWAY, PETER
  Boy Friend
NASCIMBENE, MARIO
  Alexander the Great
  Barabbas
  Doctor Faustus
  Farewell to Arms
  Francis of Assisi
  Jessica
  Scent of Mystery
  Solomon and Sheba
  *Twelve Great Themes of the
  Soaring '60s*
  Vikings
NASH, CLARENCE
  Cinderella
  Mickey and the Beanstalk
NASH, DICK
  Farewell, My Lovely
NASH, GENE
  What Am I Bid?
NASH, GRAHAM
  American Anthem
  Fast Times at Ridgemont High
NASH, KENNETH
  Bye Bye Birdie
NASH, KIRSTEN
  Best of the Best
NASH, LARRY
  Earthquake
  My Fair Lady
  Oklahoma
NASH, OGDEN
  Nashville / New York
  One Touch of Venus
  Two's Company
NASH, TED
  Peter Gunn
NASSARA, NATALE
  Crawlspace
NASSER, GAMAL ABDEL
  *I Can Hear It Now - Gamal
  Abdel Nasser*
NASTASI, FRANK
  Cindy
NATHAN, JACK
  Dr. Phibes
NATHAN, STEPHEN
  First Nudie Musical
  Godspell
  1776
NATIONAL LAMPOON
  *National Lampoon's Animal
  House*
NATIONAL PHILHARMONIC
  OF LONDON
  *Sea Hawk: The Classic Film
  Scores of Erich Wolfgang
  Korngold*
  Wicked Lady
NATIONAL PHILHARMONIC
  ORCHESTRA
  Alien
  Avalanche
  Barry Lyndon
  *Bernard Herrmann Conducts
  Great British Film Scores*
  *Casablanca: Classic Film
  Scores for Humphrey Bogart*
  *Citizen Kane: The Classic Film
  Scores of Bernard Herrmann*
  Cousteau / Amazon
  Crossed Swords

*Danny Elfman: Music for a
  Darkened Theatre*
Empire Strikes Back
*Fantasy Film World of Bernard
  Herrmann*
Final Conflict
*Great Film Classics (Music
  From)*
*Great Science Fiction Film
  Music*
Holocaust
In the Pink
Jesus of Nazareth
*John Williams' Symphonic
  Suites*
King Kong
Kings Row
Lisztomania
*Music from Great
  Shakespearean Films*
Mutant
*Mysterious Film World of
  Bernard Herrmann*
Obsession
Outland
Paper Tiger
Pee Wee's Big Adventure
Psycho
Secret of N.I.M.H.
Sky Bandits
Star Wars - Return of the Jedi
*Star Wars / Close Encounters
  of the Third Kind*
Supergirl
*Who Is Killing the Great Chefs
  of Europe?*
NATIONAL SINGERS AND
  ORCHESTRA
  Can-Can
  Carousel
NATIONS, CARRIE
  Beyond the Valley of the Dolls
NATWICK, MILDRED
  At Long Last Love
  Blithe Spirit
  70 Girls, 70
NAUGHTON, DAVID
  Meatballs
NAUGHTON, JAMES
  City of Angels
  I Love My Wife
NAUSSEAU, PAUL
  Joyful Noise
NAYLOR, EDWARD
  Saga of the Dingbat
NAYOBE
  Twins
NAZARETH
  Heavy Metal
NEAGLE, ANNA
  Charlie Girl
NEAL, JOSEPH
  *Jacques Brel Is Alive and Well
  and Living In Paris*
NEAL, ROY
  Man on the Moon
NEAR, LAUREL
  Eraserhead
NEARY, BRIAN FRANCIS
  Wired
NEELEY, TED
  Jesus Christ Superstar
  Perfect Couple
  Ulysses - The Greek Suite
NEESON, LIAM
  Darkman
NEEVES, OSCAR CASTRO
  Gabriela
NEFF, HILDEGARDE
  Silk Stockings
  Threepenny Opera
NEIL, MARCIA
  My Fair Lady
NEIL, ROGER
  Scrambled Feet
NEILL, WILLIAM
  Silverlake
NELLE'S BELLES
  Best of Burlesque
NELSON, HARRIET (Hilliard)
  Ozzie and Harriet

NELSON, GENE
Follies
Lullaby of Broadway
Oklahoma
Oscar Hammerstein II
    Memorial Album
Painting the Clouds with
    Sunshine
Shinbone Alley
So This Is Paris
Starlift
Tea for Two
3 Sailors and a Girl
NELSON, GERALD
Easy Come, Easy Go
NELSON, JERRY
Muppet Movie
NELSON, JOHN L.
Batman
NELSON, KENNETH
Boys In the Band
Cole
Fantasticks
Penney Proud
Sap of Life
Seventeen
Show Boat
NELSON, NAN-LYNN
Runaways
NELSON, NOVELLA
House of Flowers
Purlie
NELSON, OLIVER
Alfie
Zigzag
NELSON, OZZIE
Ozzie and Harriet
Paper Moon
NELSON, PORTIA
Baker's Wife
Boys from Syracuse
Golden Apple
Oklahoma
On Your Toes
Roberta
NELSON, RICHARD
O Say Can You See!
NELSON, RICK
On the Flip Side
Rio Bravo
Wackiest Ship In the Army
NELSON, RUTH
Colette
NELSON, SANDY
Loveless
Wild on the Beach
NELSON, STEVE
Frosty the Snowman
NELSON, WILLIE
Coal Miner's Daughter
Electric Horseman
Honeysuckle Rose
Porky's Revenge!
Songwriter
Voices
NEMO, HENRY
Andersonville Trial
NERO, FRANCO
Camelot
NERO, PETER
Gershwin Holiday
NARM's Golden Decade
Richard Rodgers
S'wonderful, S'marvelous,
    S'Gershwin
Sunday In New York
NERVOUS NORVOUS
Coupe De Ville
NESBITT, CATHLEEN
Cocktail Party
Conversation Piece
Feathertop
My Fair Lady
NESMITH, MICHAEL
Head
Prison
Stardust
NEUMANN, DOROTHY
Turnabout
NEUROTICA
Nobody's Perfect

NEUSS, WOLFGANG
Threepenny Opera
NEUWIRTH, BEBE
Sweet Charity
NEVIL, ROBBIE
Cocktail
NEVILLE, AARON
Big Easy
Rain Man
NEVILLE, IVAN
My Stepmother Is an Alien
Pump Up the Volume
NEVILLE BROTHERS
Mighty Quinn
NEVILLE-ANDREWS, JOHN
El Grande De Coca Cola
NEVINS, CLAUDETTE
In White America
NEW, DEREK
Four Musketeers
**NEW AMERICAN
    ORCHESTRA**
Blade Runner
NEW BIRTH
Gordon's War
NEW CHOICE
Penitentiary III
NEW CHRISTY MINSTRELS
Advance to the Rear
America Sings
Proudly They Came
Run Wild, Run Free
NEW EDITION
Dragnet
Ghostbusters II
Karate Kid II
License to Drive
Running Scared
NEW ESTABLISHMENT
Getting Straight
NEW LIFE
Sidehackers
NEW LOST CITY RAMBLERS
Movin' On
**NEW MANHATTAN
    PHILHARMONIC**
Great Original Soundtracks and
    Movie Themes
NEW ORDER
Bright Lights, Big City
Married to the Mob
Pretty In Pink
Something Wild
**NEW PHILHARMONIA
    ORCHESTRA**
David Raksin Conducts His
    Great Film Scores
**NEW PHILHARMONIC
    ORCHESTRA OF LONDON**
Lady Caroline Lamb
Nicholas and Alexandra
NEW PRINCESS THEATER
Kiri Sings Gershwin
NEW SOUND ORCHESTRA
Star Trek
**NEW SYMPHONY
    ORCHESTRA OF LONDON**
Heifetz on Television
NEW VAUDEVILLE BAND
Bliss of Mrs. Blossom
NEW VOICES OF FREEDOM
Scrooged
NEW WORLD STRINGS
Merry Widow
NEW WORLD THEATRE
Kiss Me Kate
Oklahoma
Pajama Game
NEW YORK CITY OPERA
Ballad of Baby Doe
**NEW YORK CITY PEECH
    BOYS**
Pumping Iron 2 - The Women
NEW YORK PHILHARMONIC
Airborne Symphony
Follies
Grand Canyon Suite

Leonard Bernstein and the New
    York Philharmonic on
    Christmas Day
Manhattan
Midsummer Night's Sex
    Comedy
Showstoppers
**NEW YORK REVUE
    ORCHESTRA**
Oklahoma
**NEW YORK ROCK
    ENSEMBLE**
Zachariah
**NEW YORK SHAKESPEARE
    FESTIVAL PUBLIC
    THEATER**
Hair
NEW ZEALAND SYMPHONY
Utu
NEWAY, PATRICIA
Carousel
Cat and the Fiddle
Consul
King and I
Sound of Music
NEWBORN, IRA
Blues Brothers
Caddyshack II
Dragnet
Into the Night
Planes, Trains, and
    Automobiles
Sixteen Candles
Weird Science
NEWBURY, MADELEINE
Lock Up Your Daughters
NEWCOMB, BARBARA
Can-Can
NEWELL, N.
Treasure Island
NEWELL, RAYMOND
Three Musketeers
NEWELL, ROGER
Journey to the Center of the
    Earth
NEWHART, BOB
On a Clear Day You Can See
    Forever
NEWLEY, ANTHONY
Can Heironymus Merkin Ever
    Forget Mercy Humppe (And
    Find True Happiness)
Doctor Dolittle
Fool Britannia
Goldfinger
Good Old Bad Old Days!
James Bond - 10th Anniversary
Roar of the Greasepaint - The
    Smell of the Crowd
Stop the World - I Want to Get
    Off!!
Willy Wonka and the Chocolate
    Factory
NEWMAN, ALFRED
Adventures In Paradise
Airport
Alfred Newman Conducts His
    Great Film Music
Alfred Newman Conducts
    Themes
Alexander's Ragtime Band
Anastasia
Best of the Great Motion
    Picture Themes, Volume 5
Call Me Madam
Camelot
Captain from Castile
Carousel
Certain Smile
Classic Film Scores for Bette
    Davis
Composer's Holiday
Diary of Anne Frank
Dolly Sisters
Down to the Sea In Ships
Egyptian
Film Themes of Alfred Newman
Fiorello!
Flower Drum Song
Gift of Love
Greatest Story Ever Told

Hollywood Maestro - Alfred
    Newman
Hollywood Pops
How the West Was Won
King and I
Love Themes from Motion
    Pictures
Modern Times
Motion Picture Music
Music from Motion Pictures
Music to Remember
Nevada Smith
Oscar Hammerstein II
    Memorial Album
Prisoner of Zenda
Robe
Serenade to the Stars of
    Hollywood
She Loves the Movies
Shocking Miss Pilgrim
Song of Bernadette
South Pacific
Spectacular World of Classic
    Film Scores
Stars and Stripes Forever
State Fair
Themes
There's No Business Like Show
    Business
Tonight We Sing
Wuthering Heights
NEWMAN, BARRY
What Makes Sammy Run?
NEWMAN, DAVID
Critters
Heathers
It's a Wonderful Life
Kindred
My Demon Lover
NEWMAN, DEL
Life and Times of a She-Devil
NEWMAN, EDWIN
People's Choice
NEWMAN, EMIL
Island In the Sky
Kurt Weill In Hollywood
Somebody Loves Me
Song of Bernadette
NEWMAN, G.
Mr. Cinders
NEWMAN, LARAINE
Saturday Night Live
NEWMAN, LIONEL
Affair to Remember
Alien
Anthony Adverse
April Love
Bandolero!
Best Things In Life Are Free
Bill and Coo
Boy on a Dolphin
Damien - Omen II
Doctor Dolittle
Flea In Her Ear
Gift of Love
Girls...And More Girls
Hello Dolly!
Hong Kong
Kiss Them for Me
Let's Make Love
Long Hot Summer
Music from Hollywood
1963's Major Motion Picture
    and TV Themes
Omen
Pleasure Seekers
River of No Return
Sand Pebbles
Say One for Me
Silent Movie
Sing Boy Sing
Sound and the Fury
Sun Also Rises
There's No Business Like Show
    Business
W.W. and the Dixie Dancekings
Young Lions
NEWMAN, PAUL
Life and Times of Judge Roy
    Bean
NEWMAN, PHYLLIS
First Impressions
Follies

O'NEILL, TOM
Little Willie Jr.'s Resurrection
ONETO, RICHARD
Kismet
ONRUBIA, CYNTHIA
Cats
OPATOSHU, DAVID
Bravo Giovanni!
Silk Stockings
OPERA SOCIETY OF WASHINGTON
Medium
ORBACH, JERRY
Annie Get Your Gun
Carnival
Carousel
Chicago
Cradle Will Rock
Fantasticks
42nd Street
Promises, Promises
Robber Bridgegroom
ORBISON, ROY
Blue Velvet
Fastest Guitar Alive
Hiding Out
Insignificance
Less Than Zero
Living Legend
Pretty Woman
Roadie
Zigzag
ORBIT, WILLIAM
Youngblood
ORCHARD, JULIAN
Pickwick
Slipper and the Rose
ORCHESTRA OF NÜRNBERG
Quo Vadis?
ORCHESTRA OF ST. LUKES
Of Thee I Sing
Pet Sematary
ORCHESTRA OF THE BAVARIAN STATE
Killing Fields
ORCHESTRA OF THE MOSCOW STATE CIRCUS
Russian Adventure
ORCHESTRA ON THE HALF SHELL
Teenage Mutant Ninja Turtles
ORCHESTRAL MANOEUVRES IN THE DARK
Pretty In Pink
Urgh - A Music War
O'REILLY, JOHN
Hard Job Being God
Virgin
O'REILLY, ROSEMARY
New Faces of 1952
ORESTE
Vagabond King
ORFF, CARL
Excalibur
ORIGINAL LONDON COMPANY
Establishment
O'RIORDAN, CAIT
Straight to Hell
ORMANDY, EUGENE
Air Power
Alexander Nevsky
Death In Venice
Fantasia
Love Story
Midsummer Night's Sex Comedy
Louisiana Story
2001: A Space Odyssey
ORMISTON, GEORGE
New Faces of 1968
ORMOND, JOHN
Best of Broadway 1973
ORNADEL, CYRIL
Call Me Madam
Edward the King
Gone with the Wind
Musical World of Lerner and Loewe

My Fair Lady
Opening Night
Parade of Hits
Pickwick
Plain and Fancy
Sound of Music
ORR, CORRINE
Flash Gordon
What Do You Want to Be When You Grow Up?
ORTEGA, FRANKIE
77 Sunset Strip
ORTEGA, KENNY
Salsa
ORTOLANI, RIZ
Africa Addio
Biggest Bundle of Them All
Bliss of Mrs. Blossom
Buona Sera, Mrs. Campbell
Christopher Columbus
Cleopatra
Day of Anger
Dino DeLaurentis Presents Original Soundtracks
Ecco
Film Music
Glory Guys
Golden Motion Picture Themes and Original Soundtracks
Madron
Magnificent Movie Music
Maya
Mediterranean Holiday
Mondo Cane
Original Soundtracks and Music
Seventh Dawn
Spy with a Cold Nose
Stone Killer
Woman Times Seven
Women of the World
Yellow Rolls-Royce
OSATO, SONO
Kissing Bandit
OSBORN, JOE
Mary C. Brown and the Hollywood Sign
OSBORNE, FRANCES
Turnabout
OSBORNE, JEFFREY
Spaceballs
OSBORNE, JESSE
Black Girl
OSBORNE, LEONARD
Mikado
OSBORNE, TONY
Angel's Springtime World of Light Opera
Oliver!
White Horse Inn
OSBOURNE, OZZY
Wraith
O'SHEA, MILO
Dear World
Loot
Romeo and Juliet
Ulysses
O'SHEA, TESSIE
Girl Who Came to Supper
Time for Singing
OSHINS, JULIE
This Is the Army
OSIBISA
Superfly T.N.T.
OSLIN, K.T.
Promises, Promises
OSLO PHILHARMONIC ORCHESTRA
European Holiday
OSMOND, DONNY
Donny and Marie Singing Songs from Their TV Show
OSMOND, JIMMY
Hugo the Hippo
OSMOND, MARIE
Donny and Marie Singing Songs from Their TV Show
OSMONDS
Adventures of Jamie McPheeters

OSSER, GLENN
Best of the Great Motion Picture Themes, Volume 5
Hansel and Gretel
Kiss Me Kate
Little Mary Sunshine
Pinocchio
OSTERWALD, BIBI
Ben Bagley's Cole Porter Revisited
Family Affair
Gift of the Magi
Golden Apple
Rodgers and Hart Revisited
Sing Out Sweet Land
O'SULLIVAN, MAUREEN
Hannah and Her Sisters
O'SULLIVAN, MICHAEL
In White America
It's a Bird, It's a Plane, It's Superman
OSWIN, CINDY
Hitch-Hikers Guide to the Galaxy
OTIS, CLARK
American Hot Wax
OTIS, CLYDE
Mister Rock and Roll (Scene 2)
O'TOOLE, ANNETTE
First Nudie Musical
O'TOOLE, PETER
Becket
Bible
Goodbye Mr. Chips
Man of La Mancha
Ruling Class
OTT, HORACE
Can't Stop the Music
OTWAY, JOHN
Urgh - A Music War
OUTATIME ORCHESTRA
Back to the Future
OUZOUNIAN, RICHARD
Bistro Car
OVCHINNIKOV, VYACHESLAV
War and Peace
OVEN
Fanny Hill
OVERSTREET, W. BENTON
Designing Woman
OWEN, CATHERINE DALE
Rogue Song
OWEN, GLYN
Four Musketeers
OWEN, GWENLLIAN
Under Milk Wood
OWENS, BONNIE
Killers Three
OWENS, GARY
Rowan and Martin's Laugh-In
W.C. Fields
OWENS, HARRY
Waikiki Wedding
OWENS, JIMMY AND CAROL
Witness
OWENS, PHILIP
Faggot
OWENS, ROCHELLE
Karl Marx
OXFORD UNIVERSITY DRAMATIC SOCIETY
Doctor Faustus
OXFORD, EARL
Annie Get Your Gun
New Moon
This Is the Army
OZ, FRANK
Empire Strikes Back
Follow That Bird
Muppet Movie
OZAWA, SEIJI
Midsummer Night's Sex Comedy
OZONE
It's My Turn
PBF
Karate Kid III

P.K. LIMITED
Getting Straight
PAAR, JACK
Age of Television
PABLO CRUISE
Inside Moves
PACE, JEAN
Joy
PACE, THOM
Night of the Comet
PACIFIC GAS AND ELECTRIC
Tell Me That You Love Me, Junie Moon
PACK, DAVID
White Nights
PACKER, LEO
Lola Montez
PADDICK, HUGH
Boy Friend
PADILLA, SANDY
Joan
Pomegranada
PAGE, CAROLANN
Candide
PAGE, EVELYN
Canterbury Tales
PAGE, FRANK
Elvis Live at the Louisiana Hayride
Louisiana Hayride
PAGE, GENE
Blacula
Brewster McCloud
Silencers
PAGE, GERALDINE
Happiest Millionaire
Rescuers
Strange Interlude
PAGE, JIMMY
Death Wish II
Song Remains the Same
PAGE, KEN
Ain't Misbehavin'
Cats
Guys and Dolls
Official Grammy Awards Archive Collection
PAGE, PATTI
Academy Award Winning Songs
Elmer Gantry
Manhattan Tower
Show Boat
Zabriskie Point
PAGE, RONI
Seven Brides for Seven Brothers
PAGE, STAN
Saga of the Dingbat
PAGE, TOMMY
Shag
PAGE, VERONICA
Little Night Music
PAGET, DEBRA
Premiere
PAHL, MEL
Adventures of Marco Polo
PAICH, MARTY
Hey There, It's Yogi Bear
Hong Kong
Swinger
PAIGE, CAROL
Kurt Weill In Hollywood
PAIGE, ELAINE
Billy
Cats
Chess
Evita
PAIGE, JANIS
Here's Love
Pajama Game
Silk Stockings
Starlift
PAIGE, ROBERT
Can't Help Singing
PAINTED WILLIE
Lovedolls Superstar
PALAPRAT, GERARD
Hair

PALANCE, JACK
Alice Through the Looking
Glass
PALEY BROTHERS
Rock 'N' Roll High School
PALIN, MICHAEL
Life of Brian
Monty Python and the Holy
Grail
PALLYS, ANNA MARIA
My Fair Lady
PALMER, EARL
Fabulous Baker Boys
PALMER, HAP
Mother Earth
PALMER, HARRY
Time Changes
PALMER, JONI
Billy Noname
PALMER, LELAND
Pippin
Your Own Thing
PALMER, PETER
Chocolate Soldier
Desert Song
Li'l Abner
Lorelei
PALMER, ROBERT
Color of Money
Explorers
Pretty Woman
Sweet Lies
PALMER-JOST
Fast Times at Ridgemont High
PALMERMO, NINO
Godfather Part II
PALUZZI, LUCIANA
Thunderball
PANARAMA
Fire and Ice
**PANHANDLE MYSTERY
BAND**
Sounds from True Stories
PANTSCHEFF, LJUBOMIR
Merry Widow
**PAPA BLUE'S VIKING JAZZ
BAND**
Quiet Days In Clichy
PAPAYA PARANOIA
Tokyo Pop
PARAMOR, NORRIE
Judy Garland
Swinger's Paradise
PARAY, PAUL
Naked Carmen
PARDO, DON
Saturday Night Live
PARENT, CLAUDE
Young Girls of Rochefort
PARHAN, GLOVER
Porgy and Bess
PARIS, JACKIE
Doctor Selavy's Magic Theater
PARIS, JUDITH
Ambassador
PARIS, NORMAN
Ben Bagley's Cole Porter
Revisited
David and Lisa
Decline and Fall of the Entire
World As Seen Through the
Eyes of Cole Porter
Irving Berlin Revisited
Penney Proud
Rodgers and Hart Revisited
PARIS, TONY
Say One for Me
PARIS SISTERS
Hometown U.S.A.
Single Room Furnished
PARKER, ALAN
Jaws 3-D
PARKER, CHARLIE
Bird
Murmur of the Heart
PARKER, CLAIRE
Sound of Music
PARKER, CLIFTON
Damn the Defiant

PARKER, DOROTHY
Candide
PARKER, ELEANOR
Hollywood Canteen
Interrupted Melody
Sound of Music
PARKER, FESS
Davy Crockett
Old Yeller
Westward Ho, the Wagons
PARKER, FRANK
Arthur Godfrey
PARKER, GRAHAM
Hard to Hold
True Love
PARKER, JOHN
Dallas
Jesus Christ Superstar
No, No, Nanette
PARKER, LEONARD
Fly Blackbird
PARKER, LEW
Ankles Aweigh
PARKER, LOUISE
Show Boat
PARKER, RAY, JR.
Ghostbusters
Quicksilver
PARKER, ROXANN
Festival
PARKS, GORDON
Learning Tree
Shaft's Big Score
PARKS, KEN
Too Many Girls
PARKS, MICHAEL
Bible
PARKS, VAN DYKE
Follow That Bird
Popeye
PARNELL, JACK
Sammy
PARNELL, MEL
Impossible Dream - The Story
of the 1967 Boston Red Sox
PARR, JOHN
American Anthem
Quicksilver
St. Elmo's Fire
PARRAGA, GRACIELA
Blood and Sand
PARRI, STIFYN
Metropolis
PARRISH, ELIZABETH
La Cage Aux Folles
Little Mary Sunshine
Riverwind
PARRISH, LESLIE
Li'l Abner
PARRISH, PAUL
Fools
PARRY, MALCOLM
Joseph and the Amazing
Technicolor Dreamcoat
PARRY, NATASHA
Romeo and Juliet
PARRY, SIR HUBERT
Chariots of Fire
PARSON, WILLIAM
Something for the Boys
PARSONS, ALAN
Ice Castles
PARSONS, ESTELLE
Bonnie and Clyde
Make Mine Manhattan
Pieces of Eight
Pirates of Penzance
Rodgers and Hart Revisited
Too Many Girls
Watermelon Man
PARSONS, NICHOLAS
Charlie Girl
**PARSONS, (ADMIRAL)
WILLIAM S.**
Quick and the Dead - The Story
of the Atom Bomb
PARTNERS IN KRYME
Teenage Mutant Ninja Turtles

PARTON, DOLLY
Best Little Whorehouse In
Texas
Nine to Five
Rhinestone
PARTRIDGE, DON
Otley
PARTY POOPS
Party
**PASADENA ROOF
ORCHESTRA**
Schoner Gigolo - Armer Gigolo
(Just a Gigolo)
PASCAN, BORISLAV
Long Ships
PASSIONNEL
Undercover
PASTELL, GEORGE
Flower Drum Song
PATACHOU
Folies Bergere
International Soiree
PATE, CHRISTOPHER
Godspell
PATE, JOHNNY
Brother on the Run
Shaft In Africa
Time Changes
PATERSON, IAN
Irma La Douce
PATINKIN, MANDY
Evita
Follies
South Pacific
Sunday In the Park with George
PATRICK, BUTCH
At Home with the Munsters
PATRICK, DEEDA
Oklahoma
PATRICK, DENNIS
Joe
PATRICK, DOROTHY
New Orleans
PATRICK, JULIAN
Carry Nation
Juno
Medium
PATRICK, LORY
Surf Party
PATRICK, MARJORIE
New Orleans
PATRICK, SONNY
Gigi
PATTERSON, BRENDA
Border
Pat Garrett and Billy the Kid
PATTERSON, DICK
Fade Out Fade In
PATTERSON, HENRI
Roots of Heaven
PATTERSON, LEE
Three Worlds of Gulliver
PATTERSON, LORNA
Airplane!
Minor Miracle
PATTERSON, RICK
Captain Jinks of the Horse
Marines
Sweet Bye and Bye
PATTI, SANDI
Papa Was a Preacher
PATTS, SHELDON
King of the Whole Damn World
PAUL, ALAN
Grease
PAUL, CHARLES
Littlest Angel
Original Themes from the Great
Soap Operas
PAUL, GLORIA
Darling Lili
PAUL, JUSTIN
Aladd
PAUL, LYN
Dove
PAUL AND PAULA
National Lampoon's Animal
House

Slumber Party '57
PAUL AND THE PACK
Doctor Goldfoot and the Girl
Bombs
PAULEE, MONA
Most Happy Fella
PAULETTE, LARRY
Let My People Come
PAULSEN, DAVID
To Live Another Summer, to
Pass Another Winter
PAVAN, MARISA
Shinbone Alley
PAVAROTTI, LUCIANO
Yes, Giorgio
PAVEK, JANET
Christine
Show Boat
PAVLOSKY, DAVID
Tinseltown
PAXON, GLENN
First Impressions
PAYCHECK, JOHNNY
Take This Job and Shove It
PAYN, GRAHAM
After the Ball
PAYNE, CECIL
Connection
PAYNE, DON
Female Animal
PAYNE, FREDA
Penitentiary III
PAYNE, JODY
Honeysuckle Rose
PAYNE, JOHN
Alice Faye
Dolly Sisters
Good News
Hello Frisco, Hello
That Night In Rio
PAYNE, LAURIE
Water Gipsies
PAYNE, PICO
Long Riders
PAYNE, SARAH
Singin' In the Rain
PAYNTER, JOHN
Among Friends - Waa-Mu Show
of 1960
PAYTON, DENIS
Having a Wild Weekend
PEAKE, DON
Blacula
Coma
Zigzag
**PEANUT BUTTER
CONSPIRACY**
Angels from Hell
PEARCE, ALICE
Body In the Seine
Gentlemen Prefer Blondes
Sail Away
PEARS, PETER
Facade
PEARSON, CAROL LYNN
My Turn on Earth
Order Is Love
PEARSON, JESSE
Bye Bye Birdie
PEARY, HAL
Great Gildersleeve
PEASE, JAMES
Mikado
PEASLEE, RICHARD
Marat (De) Sade
Tell Me Lies
PEBBLES
Beverly Hills Cop II
PECK, CHARLES
My Fair Lady
PECK, DANNY
Secret of My Success
PECK, GREGORY
John F. Kennedy
Littlest Angel
Years of Lightning, Day of
Drums
PECK, JON
Evening with Sammy Cahn

PECORINO, JOE
Beatlemania
PEDDLERS
Goodbye Gemini
PEDERSEN, HERB
Smokey and the Bandit II
PEDERSON, HAL JAMES
*Joseph McCarthy Is Alive and
Well and Living In Dade
County*
PEDI, TOM
King of the Whole Damn World
PEDLAR, STUART
Side By Side By Sondheim
Snoopy
Sondheim
PEEL, EILEEN
Cocktail Party
PEEPLES, NIA
Sing
PEERCE, JAN
Brigadoon
Evening with Lerner and Loewe
Student Prince
Tonight We Sing
PEGRAM, NIGEL
Wait a Minim!
PELE
Pelé
PENDERECKI, KRZYSZTOF
Exorcist
PENDERGAST, SHARON
MARLEY
Mighty Quinn
PENDERGRASS, TEDDY
Adventures of Ford Fairlane
Roadie
Soup for One
PENDLETON, AUSTIN
Fiddler on the Roof
Last Sweet Days of Isaac
PENGUINS
Hometown U.S.A.
PENHALIGON, SUSAN
Patrick
PENN, DAN
Border
PENN, POLLY
Charlotte Sweet
Goblin Market
PENN, ROBERT
Kean
Paint Your Wagon
PENNA, PHILIP DELLA
Olympus 7-0000
PENNER, ED
Peter Pan
PENNER, JOE
Rodgers and Hart In Hollywood
PENNINO, FRANCESCO
Godfather, Parts I and II
PENNY AND SONDRA
Purple People Eater
PENNYPIPERS
Penelope
PENTECOST, JIM
My Fair Lady
PERA, RADAMES
Kung-Fu
PERACHI, LEO
*Saludos Amigos (Music from
South of the Border)*
PERCASSI, DON
Chorus Line
PERCIVAL, JOHN
Chocolate Soldier
H.M.S. Pinafore
Mikado
PERCIVAL, LANCE
John F. Kennedy
One Over the Eight
PERCIVAL, NORMAN
*Doctor Strangelove (And Other
Great Movie Themes)*
PERETTI, HUGO
Maggie Flynn
PEREZ, LUIS
Jerome Robbins' Broadway

PERGAMENT, LOLA
O Marry Me
PERIC, BLANKA
Blossom Time
PERICOLI, EMILIO
Rome Adventure
PERILSTEIN, MICHAEL
Deadly Spawn
PERITO, NICK
Great Motion Picture Themes
*Original Motion Picture Hit
Themes*
PERKINS, ANTHONY
*Black Hole (The Story of the
Black Hole)*
Goodbye Again
Greenwillow
Rodgers and Hart Revisited
Too Many Girls
PERKINS, BILL
Wild One
PERKINS, CARL
Diner
G.I. Blues
Jamboree!
Little Fauss and Big Halsy
Porky's Revenge!
PERKINS, FRANK
Gypsy
Palm Springs Weekend
PERKINS, PATTI
*Tuscaloosa's Calling Me (But
I'm Not Going)*
PERKINSON, COLERIDGE
If He Hollers, Let Him Go
PERKINSON, TAYLOR
Education of Sonny Carson
PERREAU, GIGI
James Dean Story
PERREN, FREDDIE
Cooley High
Hell Up In Harlem
PERRI
Do the Right Thing
PERRIN, GEORGE
European Holiday
PERRINE, VALERIE
W.C. Fields and Me
PERRONE, ANNETTE
*Jacques Brel Is Alive and Well
and Living In Paris*
PERRY, ALFRED
Honey West
Rise and Fall of the Third Reich
PERRY, DOLORES
Evening with Jerome Kern
Passing Fair
PERRY, E. MARTIN
Marry Me a Little
Sondheim
PERRY, JOHN BENNETT
*Now Is the Time for All Good
Men*
PERRY, MARENDA
Raisin
PERRY, ROD
Earthquake
New Faces of 1968
To Broadway with Love
PERRY, WILLIAM
Silent Years
PERSHING, D'VAUGHN
Rocky Horror Show
PERSOFF, NEHEMIAH
American Tail
PERSSON, RUBY
*You're a Good Man, Charlie
Brown*
PERTWEE, JON
*Funny Thing Happened on the
Way to the Forum*
PETER, PAUL AND MARY
American Pop
PETERS, BERNADETTE
Annie
Dames at Sea
George M!
Into the Woods
Mack and Mabel
Sunday In the Park with George

PETERS, BROCK
Black Girl
Body Beautiful
Carmen Jones
Jack Johnson
Kwamina
Porgy and Bess
Showcase Album, 1967
Sing for Your Supper
PETERS, JERRY
Death Wish
PETERS, LAURI
Cradle Will Rock
First Impressions
Sound of Music
PETERS, ROBERTA
Carousel
Met Stars on Broadway
Student Prince
Tonight We Sing
PETERSEN, PAUL
Happiest Millionaire
PETERSON TRIO
Miracle Goes On
PETERSON, BERNICE
Carmen Jones
PETERSON, CALEB
Till the Clouds Roll By
PETERSON, ERIC
Billy Bishop Goes to War
PETERSON, JOHN
Miracle Goes On
Worlds Apart
PETERSON, KEN
Miracle Goes On
PETERSON, KURT
Dear World
Follies
PETERSON, OSCAR
*Fred Astaire Sings and Swings
Irving Berlin*
Play It Again, Sam
Silent Partner
PETERSON, PAUL
Bye Bye Birdie
PETERSON, ROBERT
Promised Land
PETHERBRIDGE, EDWARD
Nicholas Nickleby
PETINA, IRRA
Anya
Candide
Song of Norway
PETIT, JEAN-CLAUDE
Jean De Florette
Manon of Spring
PETIT, LEO
Playtime
PETIT, ROLAND
Irma La Douce
PETRAK, RUDOLF
Interrupted Melody
PETRICOFF, ELAINE
Hark!
One Way Ticket to Broadway
PETRIE, GEORGE
Flash Gordon
PETRIE, SONYA
Gypsy
PETTICOATS
Jack and the Beanstalk
PETTY, GWENYTH
Under Milk Wood
PETTY, TOM
FM
Voices
PEVNEY, JAY
*Joseph McCarthy Is Alive and
Well and Living In Dade
County*
PEYSER, PENNY
Together Again
PFEIFER, BOB
I Was a Teenage Zombie
PFEIFFER, MICHELLE
Dangerous Liaisons
Fabulous Baker Boys
PFLUG, JO ANN
*M*A*S*H*

PFORSICH, ANDY
Boy Named Charlie Brown
PHANGO, PEGGY
King Kong
PHILHARMONIC
ORCHESTRA
Hamlet
Ladyhawke
Music for Films
Oklahoma
PHILHARMONIC
ORCHESTRA OF
FLANDERS
Pascall's Island
PHILHARMONIC SYMPHONY
ORCHESTRA OF NEW
YORK
Richard Rodgers
PHILLINGAMES, GREG
Streets of Fire
PHILLIPS, BILL
Taxi Driver
PHILLIPS, EDDIE
Damn Yankees
New Girl In Town
Show Boat
Tenderloin
PHILLIPS, ESTHER
Proudly They Came
PHILLIPS, FLIP
*Fred Astaire Sings and Swings
Irving Berlin*
PHILLIPS, JOHN
Brewster McCloud
PHILLIPS, JUDD
Last of the American Hoboes
PHILLIPS, MARY BRACKEN
Different Times
PHILLIPS, MICHELLE
Mother, Jugs and Speed
PHILLIPS, NANCIE
New Faces of 1968
PHILLIPS, PHIL
Sea of Love
Slumber Party '57
PHILLIPS, RICHARD
Gigi
PHILLIPS, SHAWN
Lost Horizon
PHILLIPS, SIAN
Pal Joey
PHILLIPS, STU
Angels from Hell
Battlestar Galactica
Beyond the Valley of the Dolls
Buck Rogers
Bye Bye Birdie
Follow Me
Hell's Angels on Wheels
Interns
Jud
Run, Angel, Run
Skyscraper
Space Organ
PHILLIPS, THOMAS
*Among Friends - Waa-Mu Show
of 1960*
PHILLIPS, WOOLF
Lullaby of Broadway
PIANOSAURUS
New York Stories
PIANTNITSKY SONG AND
DANCE ENSEMBLE
Russian Adventure
PIAZZA, MARGUERITE
Naughty Marietta
PICARDY SINGERS
How Sweet It Is
PICCIONI, PIERO
*Great Original Soundtracks and
Movie Themes*
Moment of Truth
More Than a Miracle
Swept Away
Tenth Victim
To Bed . . . Or Not to Bed
PICCOLO, SAMUEL
It's Time to Pray, America!

PICKENS, JANE
  Music In the Air
  Sound of Broadway
PICKERS, J.B.
  Vanishing Point
PICKETT, WILSON
  Soul to Soul
PICKFORD-HOPKINS,
  GARRY
  Journey to the Center of the
    Earth
PICKRISS AND VANCE
  Stagecoach
PICKWICK CHILDREN'S
  CHORUS
  Oliver!
PICON, MOLLY
  Fiddler on the Roof
  Kosher Widow
  Milk and Honey
PIDAY, LOUIE
  Karl Marx
PIDGEON, WALTER
  American Spirit
  Cinderella
  Forbidden Planet
  Quo Vadis?
  Star Is Born
  Story of Big Red
  Take Me Along
PIECES OF A DREAM
  School Daze
PIED PIPERS
  Oh You Beautiful Doll
  Ship Ahoy
PIELECKI, JAY
  Virgin
PIER ANGEL
  Merry Andrew
PIERCE, CHARLES
  Torch Song Trilogy
PIERCE, JOSHUA
  Miklos Rozsa
PIERCE, WEBB
  9-30-55
PIERFEDERICI, ANTONIO
  Romeo and Juliet
PIERRE, CHRISTOPHER
  Guys and Dolls
PIERROTS
  Oh What a Lovely War
PIERSON, HAROLD
  Cabin In the Sky
  Sweet Charity
PIERSON, THOMAS
  Cyrano
  Dude (the Highway Life)
PIGFORD, NELSON
  Rocky
  Rocky II
  Rocky III
PILHOFER, HERBERT
  What's the Meaning of This?
PILZ, EVA
  Fiddler on the Roof
PINE, COURTNEY
  Angel Heart
PINK FLOYD
  More
  Obscured By Clouds
  Zabriskie Point
PINKARD AND BOWDEN
  Rustler's Rhapsody
PINKARD, FRED
  In White America
PINZA, CARLA
  House of Flowers
PINZA, EZIO
  Carnegie Hall
  Fanny
  Great Personalities of
    Broadway
  Met Stars on Broadway
  Mister Imperium
  South Pacific
  This Is Broadway's Best
  Tonight We Sing
PIPPIN, DONALD
  Applause
  Ben Franklin In Paris

Chorus Line
Dear World
Foxy
La Cage Aux Folles
Mack and Mabel
Mame
Oliver!
110 In the Shade
Seesaw
Snow White and the Seven
  Dwarfs
Woman of the Year
PIQUET, ODETTE
  Borsalino
PIRANKOV, SIMEON
  Peach Thief
PIRATES
  Pirate Movie
PISELLO, DANIEL
  King of the Entire World
PISTILLI, GENE
  Sporting Club
PITAGORA, PAOLA
  Ciao, Rudy
PITCHFORD, DEAN
  Fame
  Footloose
PITLIK, NOAM
  Sanford and Son
PITNEY, GENE
  Hairspray
  Original Motion Picture Hit
    Themes
PITRE, SANDRA
  Selma
PITTS, CLAY
  Fanny Hill
  Female Animal
PITTS, ZASU
  My Square Laddie
PITTSBURGH SYMPHONY
  ORCHESTRA
  My Fair Lady
PIXIES
  Pump Up the Volume
PIZER, BRIAN
  Christy
PIZULLO, JOE
  Rambo III
PLACE, MARY KAY
  New York, New York
PLAIN JANE
  Zapped
PLANATONES
  American Hot Wax
PLANET 3
  Navy SEALS
PLANT, ROBERT
  White Nights
PLASTIC ONO BAND
  Imagine - The Motion Picture
PLATT, EDWARD
  Oh Captain!
PLATTERS
  Always
  American Graffiti
  Blue Iguana
  Encore of Broadway Golden
    Hits
  Girl Can't Help It!
  Rock All Night
  Slumber Party '57
PLAYMATES
  Broadway Show Stoppers
PLAYTEN, ALICE
  Henry, Sweet Henry
  National Lampoon Lemmings
  Oliver!
  Painted Smiles of Cole Porter
  Promenade
PLEASANCE, DONALD
  Will Penny
PLEIS, JACK
  Broadway Goes Hollywood
  Bye Bye Birdie
  Porgy and Bess
PLESHETTE, JOHN
  Mac Bird
PLESHETTE, SUZANNE
  Blackbeard's Ghost

PLESSAS, MIMIS
  Greek Pearls
PLIMPTON, SHELLEY
  Hair
PLISKIN, MARCI
  Fly with Me
PLOVANI, NICOLA
  Fellini's Ginger and Fred
  Night of the Shooting Stars
PLOWRIGHT PLAYERS
  Touch
PLOWRIGHT, JOAN
  Uncle Vanya
PLUDEMACHER, GEORGES
  Love Story
PLUGZ
  Repo Man
PLUMB, ED
  Bambi
  Pinocchio
PLUMB, NEELY
  Nina, the Pinta, and the Santa
    Maria
PLUMMER, CHRISTOPHER
  American Tail
  Cyrano
  J.B.
  Sound of Music
PLUNKETT, MARYANN
  Me and My Girl
PLYMOUTH PLAYERS
  King and I
  South Pacific
POBER, LEON
  Beg, Borrow or Steal
POCKRISS, LEE
  Dino
  Ernest In Love
  Tovarich
POCO
  Fast Times at Ridgemont High
PODDANY, EUGENE
  How the Grinch Stole
    Christmas
POETTGEN, ERNEST
  Seven Deadly Sins
POGUES
  Lost Angels
  Straight to Hell
POHLMAN, GUY
  Snoopy Come Home
POINDEXTER, BUSTER
  Scrooged
POINTER, BONNIE
  Heavenly Bodies
POINTER, JUNE
  National Lampoon's Vacation
POINTER, RUTH
  Iron Eagle II
  Oliver and Company
POINTER, SIDNEY
  Desert Song
POINTER SISTERS
  Action Jackson
  Beverly Hills Cop
  Beverly Hills Cop II
  Caddyshack II
  Car Wash
  Karate Kid III
  Night Shift
  Perfect
  Spaceballs
POISON
  Less Than Zero
POITIER, SIDNEY
  Desert Song
  Poitier Meets Plato
POLACEK, LOUIS
  Oh Captain!
POLEDOURIS, BASIL
  Blue Lagoon
  Conan the Barbarian
  Conan the Destroyer
  Farewell to the King
  Flesh and Blood
  Hunt for Red October
  Making the Grade
  No Man's Land
  Red Dawn
  Robocop

Summer Lovers
Wired
POLEDOURIS, ZOE
  Conan the Barbarian
POLERI, DAVID
  Saint of Bleecker Street
POLICE
  Brimstone and Treacle
  Urgh - A Music War
POLK, GORDON
  Happy Hunting
POLLAK, ANNA
  La Vie Parisienne
POLLARD, MICHAEL J.
  Bonnie and Clyde
  Bye Bye Birdie
POLNAREFF, MICHEL
  Lipstick
POLO, EDDIE
  Robin Hood
POMAHAC, BRUCE
  I Remember Mama
POMERANZ, DAVID
  Zapped
POMPEII, JAMES
  Greenwich Village U.S.A.
POMUS, DOC
  Double Trouble
  Frankie and Johnny
  G.I. Blues
  Girl Happy
  Spinout
  Tickle Me
  Viva Las Vegas
PONCE, PONCIE
  Hawaiian Eye
PONS, LILY
  Carnegie Hall
  Conversation Piece
  Die Fledermaus
PONTECORVO, GILLO
  Battle of Algiers
PONTO, ERICH
  Threepenny Opera
POOL-PAH
  Flasher
POOLE, ROY
  Under Milk Wood
POOR SISTERS OF CLARE
  Francis of Assisi
POP, IGGY
  Black Rain
  Repo Man
  Shocker
POP, LOLITA
  Hiding Out
POPE, ROBERT
  St. Louis Woman
POPP, ANDRE
  Irma La Douce
POPS AND TIMER
  Blue City
PORRETTA, FRANK
  Brigadoon
  Great Waltz
  King and I
  Merry Widow
  Song of Norway
PORTEOUS, TIMOTHY
  My Fur Lady
PORTAL, M.
  Return of Martin Guerre
PORTER, COLE
  Aladdin
  American Musical Theater
  Anything Goes
  At Long Last Love
  Ballet Music from MGM
    Musicals
  Bing's Hollywood
  Blazing Saddles
  Born to Dance
  Broadway Melody of 1940
  Can-Can
  Cole
  Cole Porter and Me
  Cole Porter In Hollywood
    (1929-1956)
  Cole Porter In Paris
  Cole Porter Revisited

800

801

Roar of the Greasepaint - The
　　Smell of the Crowd
PRICE, HANNAH
　Aladd
PRICE, HOWELL
　Ballyhoo
PRICE, JIM
　Mahoney's Last Stand
PRICE, LEONTYNE
　Met Stars on Broadway
　Porgy and Bess
PRICE, LLOYD
　Everybody's All-American
PRICE, LONNY
　Merrily We Roll Along
PRICE, PAUL B.
　O Say Can You See!
PRICE, RAY
　Honkytonk Man
PRICE, ROBERT
　Downriver
PRICE, RUTH
　Harper
PRICE, VINCENT
　America the Beautiful
　Co-Star
　Darling of the Day
　This World Tomorrow
　World of Century Twenty First
PRIDE, CHARLEY
　Sometimes a Great Notion
　Tom Sawyer
PRIEST, PAT
　At Home with the Munsters
PRIGGE, JOHN
　What's the Meaning of This?
PRIGMORE, JAMES
　Petticoats and Pettifoggers
PRIMA, LOUIS
　Aristocats
　Best of Disney
　Hey Boy, Hey Girl
　Jimmy Durante TV Show
　Jungle Book
　Mary Poppins
　Merriest Songs
　That Darn Cat
PRIME MOVERS
　Manhunter
PRIMUS, BARRY
　Doctor Selavy's Magic Theater
PRINCE
　Batman
　Bright Lights, Big City
　Purple Rain
　Risky Business
　Under the Cherry Moon
PRINCE, DAISY
　Follies
PRINCE, FAITH
　Jerome Robbins' Broadway
PRINCE, GINGER
　One Too Many (Hit Songs From)
PRINCE, JACK
　Destry Rides Again
PRINCE RAINIER III
　Wedding In Monaco
PRINCE, ROBERT
　West Side Story
PRINCE, WILLIAM
　Strange Interlude
PRINGLE, BRYAN
　Billy
　Boy Friend
PRINGLE, VALENTINE
　Passing Fair
PRINTEMPS, YVONNE
　Conversation Piece
　Red Hot and Blue
PRINZE, FREDDIE
　Hollywood Squares
PRITCHETT, LIZABETH
　Cindy
PRIVATE DOMAIN
　Back to the Beach
　Once Bitten
PRO ARTE ORCHESTRA
　Beggar's Opera
　Mikado

PROCHNIK, BRUCE
　Oliver!
PROCOL HARUM
　Big Chill
　New York Stories
PRODROMIDES, JEAN
　Danton
　Voyage En Ballon
PROFANATO, GENE
　King and I
PROKOFIEV, SERGEI
　Alexander Nevsky
　Gospel According to St.
　　Matthew
　Ivan the Terrible
　Peter and the Wolf
PROPHET, JOHNNY
　Kiss Me Kate
PROVINE, DOROTHY
　Great Race
　Roaring '20s
PROWSE, JULIET
　Can-Can
　Sweet Charity
PRUD'HOMME, CAMERON
　By the Beautiful Sea
　New Girl In Town
　Unsinkable Molly Brown
PRUNCZIK, KAREN
　42nd Street
PRUSAK, JAN
　Danton
PRYCE, JONATHAN
　Miss Saigon
PRYOR, RICHARD
　Saturday Night Live
　Wattstax (the Living Word)
　Wiz
PSIHOUNTAS, ELAINE
　All Night Strut
PSYCHEDELIC FURS
　Pretty In Pink
PUBLIC ENEMY
　Do the Right Thing
　Less Than Zero
PUBLIC IMAGE LIMITED
　Hiding Out
PUCCINI, GIACOMO
　Melba
PUCK, EVA
　Show Boat
PUENTE, TITO
　Armed and Dangerous
　Crossover Dreams
　Salsa
PUGH, RICHARD WARREN
　Zorba
PUGH, TED
　Irene
PULE, DAN
　Ipi-Tombi
PULLEY, GAYLE
　Best of Broadway 1973
PURCELL, HENRY
　Kramer Vs. Kramer
PURIM, FLORA
　Sharky's Machine
PURSELL, GENE
　On Moonlight Bay
PURSLEY, DAVID
　Faggot
　Peace
PURVIN, BEVERLY
　Tree Grows In Brooklyn
PYLE, THOMAS
　Candide
PYLON
　Athens, Ga. - Inside / Out
PYNE, NATASHA
　Taming of the Shrew
Q FEEL
　Girls Just Want to Have Fun
Q. LAZZARUS
　Married to the Mob
QUADRASTRINGS
　Hollywood Gold, Vol. I
QUAID, DENNIS
　Big Easy

Night the Lights Went Out In
　Georgia
　Tough Enough
QUARTERFLASH
　Fast Times at Ridgemont High
　Gremlins
　Night Shift
QUATRO, SUZI
　Annie Get Your Gun
　Times Square
QUAYLE, ANNA
　Chitty, Chitty, Bang, Bang
　Stop the World - I Want to Get
　　Off!!
QUAYLE, ANTHONY
　Oh, Rosalinda!
QUEEN
　Flash Gordon
　FM
　Iron Eagle
　Kind of Magic
QUEEN'S HALL LIGHT
　ORCHESTRA
　Music for Films
QUEENSLAND SYMPHONY
　Franz Waxman
QUEENSRYCHE
　Adventures of Ford Fairlane
QUESADA, CHRIS
　Savage Wild
QUESTEL, MAE
　Bajour
　Funny Girl
QUESTION MARK AND THE
　MYSTERIANS
　More American Graffiti
QUICK, DIANA
　Billy
　Brideshead Revisited
QUICKSILVER MESSENGER
　SERVICE
　Revolution
QUIGLEY, MYRA
　Second Shepherd's Play
QUIJANO, JOE
　Fiddler on the Roof
QUILLEY, DENIS
　Boys from Syracuse
　Cat and the Fiddle
　Grab Me a Gondola
　High Spirits
　Show Boat
QUIN, RICHARD
　Hollywood Party
QUINN, AIDAN
　Handmaid's Tale
QUINN, AILEEN
　Annie
QUINN, ANTHONY
　Zorba
QUINN, JAMES
　Do Black Patent Leather Shoes
　　Really Reflect Up?
QUINN, MICHAEL
　Anya
QUINN, PAUL
　Letter to Brezhnev
QUIROZ, SALVADOR
　My Fair Lady
QUITAK, OSCAR
　Pickwick
QUIVAR, FLORENCE
　Porgy and Bess
QUONG, ROSE
　Flower Drum Song
RCA VICTOR SYMPHONY
　ORCHESTRA
　Evening with Lerner and Loewe
　Great Music from the Movies
　Jungle Book
　Mario Lanza Sings Because
　Pure Gold Movies
　Victory at Sea
　Yankee Doodle Dandy
R.E.M.
　Athens, Ga. - Inside / Out
　Bachelor Party
　Dream a Little Dream
　Made In Heaven

REO SPEEDWAGON
　Goonies
RKO STUDIO ORCHESTRA
　Bundle of Joy
RABBITT, EDDIE
　Every Which Way But Loose
　Growing Pains
　Roadie
RABEN, PEER
　Berlins Alexanderplatz
　Lili Marlene
　Music from the Films of Rainer
　　Werner Fassbinder
　Querelle
　Veronika Voss / Lola
RABIN, YITZAK
　It's Time to Pray, America!
RABINOWITZ, HARRY
　Grizzly
　Heat and Dust
　Manhattan Project
　Masters of the Universe
　Nicholas Nickleby
　Song and Dance
RACHEL, ANNIE
　Salvation
RACHINS, ALAN
　Oh! Calcutta!
RADD, RONALD
　Buccaneer
RADIC, DUSAN
　Genghis Khan
　Long Ships
RADNER, GILDA
　Gilda Radner Live
　Saturday Night Live
RADNEY, DON
　Music Man
RADO, JAMES
　Hair
RADY, SIMON
　Emperor Waltz
RAE, CHARLOTTE
　Littlest Revue
　Rodgers and Hart Revisited
　Something for the Boys
　Three Wishes for Jamie
　Threepenny Opera
RAEL, ELSA
　Beauty and the Beast
RAFFERTY, GERRY
　Local Hero
RAFT, GEORGE
　Co-Star
　Golden Age of the Hollywood
　　Musical
RAGE
　For Your Eyes Only
RAGLAND, ROBERT O.
　Grizzly
　Q the Winged Serpent
　Seven Alone
　Ten to Midnight
RAGNI, GEROME
　Dude (the Highway Life)
　Hair
RAGOTZY, JACK
　Co-Star
RAGS, J.P.
　If It's Tuesday, This Must Be
　　Belgium
RAGS AND RICHES
　Breakin' 2 - Electric Boogaloo
RAGTIME
　Teen Wolf Too
RAGTIMERS
　Schoner Gigolo - Armer Gigolo
　　(Just a Gigolo)
RAHEEM
　Lost Angels
RAHN, MURIEL
　Gigi
RAIKEN, LAWRENCE
　Woman of the Year
RAINBIRD, JAMES
　Empire of the Sun
RAINER, LUISE
　Great Ziegfeld
RAINES, CHRISTINA
　Sunshine

RAINEY
Girls Just Want to Have Fun
RAINEY, FORD
J.B.
RAINGER, RALPH
Paris Honeymoon
Waikiki Wedding
RAINGER-PARKER
Big Broadcast of 1936
RAINS, CLAUDE
Evening with William
Shakespeare
Shakespeare In Hollywood
RAITT, BONNIE
Air America
Urban Cowboy
RAITT, JOHN
Annie Get Your Gun
Broadway Highlights
Carousel
Four Television Musicals
Joyful Noise
No Man Can Tame Me
Oklahoma
Pajama Game
Richard Rodgers
Show Boat
They Stopped the Show!
Three Wishes for Jamie
RAKHA, ALLA
Gandhi
RAKOV, THERESA
Zorba
RAKSIN, DAVID
David Raksin Conducts His
Great Film Scores
David Raksin / Music for Films
David Raksin / Music for Films
(Vol. 2)
Duel In the Sun
Film Music
Hollywood: The Post War Years
(1946 - 1949)
Premier Radio Performances
Sylvia
What's the Matter with Helen?
Will Penny
RAKSIN, RUBY
Lollipop Cover
RALEIGH, DON
Exodus
Pal Joey
RALKE, DON
Bourbon Street Beat
C'mon, Let's Live a Little
Oklahoma
Snoopy Come Home
RALL, TOMMY
Cry for Us All
Kiss Me Kate
Milk and Honey
Seven Brides for Seven
Brothers
That's Dancing!
RALPH, SHERYL LEE
Dream Girls
Mighty Quinn
RALSTON, ALFRED
Billy
Oh What a Lovely War
Young Winston (Churchill)
RALSTON, TERI
Company
Little Night Music
RAMAKRISHNAN, T.K.
Gandhi
RAMAL, BILL
Young America Dances to TV's
Greatest Themes
RAMBEAU, MARJORIE
Joan Crawford
RAMIN, JORDAN
Scent of Mystery
RAMIN, SID
Say Darling
Stiletto
Where Do We Go from Here?
RAMIREZ,CARLOS
Kurt Weill In Hollywood
RAMIREZ, COCO
Hello Dolly!

RAMONE, PHIL
Flashdance
White Nights
RAMONES
Get Crazy
National Lampoon's Vacation
Over the Edge
Rock 'N' Roll High School
Times Square
RAMPAL, JEAN-PIERRE
Reds
RAMSEY, GORDON
Carmelina
RAMSEY, HARLAN
Memorable Music from the
Movies
RAMSEY, LOGAN
Elephant Calf
RAMSEY, MARION
Eubie
RANDALL, ANTHONY
Jewel In the Crown
RANDALL, FRANKIE
Run for Your Wife
Wild on the Beach
RANDALL, SHARON
Wonderful O
RANDALL, TONY
Littlest Angel
Odd Couple
Oh Captain!
Power Is You
RANDAZZO, TEDDY
Girl from U.N.C.L.E.
Hey Let's Twist
It's My Turn
Jamboree!
Mister Rock and Roll (Scene 2)
RANDELES, ROBERT
Nobody's Perfect
RANDI, DON
Bloody Mama
Three In the Cellar
Up In the Cellar
RANDLE, BILL
James Dean Story
RANDOLPH, BOOTS
Blue Hawaii
Follow That Dream
Girls! Girls! Girls!
Kid Galahad
Kissin' Cousins
NARM's Golden Decade
Roustabout
This Is Elvis
Tickle Me
RANDOLPH, ELSIE
Sunny
RANDOLPH, JAMES
Ballad for Bimshire
Guys and Dolls
RANDOLPH, MIMI
All In Love
RANIERI, KATYNA
Yellow Rolls-Royce
RANK AND FILE
Sylvester
RAPHAEL, GERRIANNE
Ernest In Love
Seventh Heaven
RAPOSO, JOE
Great Muppet Caper
House of Flowers
Man's a Man
Raggedy Ann and Andy
Sesame Street
Sing Muse!
You're a Good Man, Charlie
Brown
RAPP, MICHAEL
Ulysses - The Greek Suite
RASCALS
Big Chill
Big Chill (More Songs from the
Original Soundtrack)
Legal Eagles
Platoon (And Songs from the
Era)
RASCH, RAY
Nina, the Pinta, and the Santa
Maria

RASKIN, JUDITH
Desert Song
Vagabond King
RASKIN, TOM
Whoop-Up!
RAST, JIM
Virgin
RATHBONE, BASIL
Adventures of Robin Hood
Aladdin
Christmas Carol
Co-Star
Dinosaurus!
Hansel and Gretel
House of Fear
Oliver Twist
Sherlock Holmes
Stingiest Man In Town
RATHBURN, ELDON
Labyrinth
RATHBURN, ROGER
No, No, Nanette
RATKEVICH, PAUL
Boy Meets Boy
RATT
Golden Child
RAUBER, FRANÇOIS
Jacques Brel Is Alive and Well
and Living In Paris
Playtime
RAVEL, MAURICE
10
RAVEN, PAUL
Jesus Christ Superstar
RAVENSCROFT, THURL
Desert Song
Island at the Top of the World
Nina, the Pinta, and the Santa
Maria
Savage Sam
Seven Dreams
Snoopy Come Home
RAVYNS
Fast Times at Ridgemont High
RAWLS, LOU
Cannonball Run
Here Comes Garfield
Soul of Nigger Charley
RAWSON, DENYS
Man of La Mancha
RAY, ALDO
Miss Sadie Thompson
RAY, ANJE
Believers
RAY, GENE ANTHONY
Fame
RAY, JAMES
Dylan
RAY, JOHNNIE
Last Picture Show
There's No Business Like Show
Business
RAY, MARLA
Schnapsie
RAY, ROBIN
Tomfoolery
RAY, SATYAJIT
Shakespeare Wallah
RAYE, DON
Alice In Wonderland
RAYE, CAROL
Bonanza Bound
RAYE, MARTHA
Four Jills In a Jeep
Here Come the Girls
Judy Garland
Jumbo
$1000 a Touchdown
Pufnstuf
Rodgers and Hart In Hollywood
Rhythm on the Range
RAYMOND, GARY
Irma La Douce
She Loves Me
RAYMOND, HELEN
Music Man
RAYMOND, LEW
Around the World In 80 Days
My Fair Lady
Pal Joey

South Pacific
Themes from the Movies
RAYS
School Daze
RAZ, RIVKA
To Live Another Summer, to
Pass Another Winter
RE-FLEX
Breakin'
REA, STEPHEN
High Society
READING, BERTICE
Valmouth
READY FOR THE WORLD
Beverly Hills Cop II
Running Scared
REAGAN, RONALD
Freedom's Finest Hour
REAL LIFE
Once Bitten
Rad
Savage Streets
Teen Wolf Too
REAL TO REEL
Nothing In Common
REALE, MARCELLA
Interrupted Melody
REAMS, LEE ROY
Applause
42nd Street
Lorelei
REARDON, JOHN
Do Re Mi
Flood
Hello Out There
Lady In the Dark
Merry Widow
New Faces of 1956
Old Maid and the Thief
On the Town
Saint of Bleecker Street
Song of Norway
REBELS
Schoner Gigolo - Armer Gigolo
(Just a Gigolo)
RECHT, COBY
Apple
RED CLAY RAMBLERS
Far North
Lie of the Mind
**RED GUARD ACCORDION
BAND**
Last Emperor
RED HOT CHILI PEPPERS
Pretty Woman
RED MOUNTAIN JUG BAND
Strawberry Statement
RED RIDER
Vision Quest
RED 7
Explorers
Manhunter
RED WARRIORS
Tokyo Pop
REDCOFF, KARL
Zenda
REDD, FREDDIE
Connection
REDD, SHARON
Clams on the Half Shell
REDD, VERONICA
Believers
REDDIN, EARL
Brigadoon
REDDING, GENE
Harrad Summer
REDDING, OTIS
Dream a Little Dream
Monterey Pop
Platoon (And Songs from the
Era)
REDDS AND THE BOYS
Good to Go
REDDY, HELEN
All This and World War II
Pete's Dragon
REDFIELD, LIZA
Ernest In Love
REDFIELD, WILLIAM
Hamlet

Stop the World - I Want to Get
Off!!
RHODES, RED
Prison
RHYS-DAVIES, JOHN
Raiders of the Lost Ark
RHYTHM BOYS
Bing Crosby In Hollywood
(1930-1934)
RHYTHMAIRES
Bing's Hollywood
Just for You
Road to Bali
Themes from the Movies
RHYTHMMAKERS
Bing's Hollywood
RIBANOFF, JAYE
Peter Pan
RIBUCA, LINDA
Flower Drum Song
RIBUCA, YVONNE
Flower Drum Song
RICARDEL, JOSEPH
Evening with Jerome Kern
RICE, BOBBY G.
Louisiana Hayride
RICE, JOAN
Robin Hood
RICE, SARAH
Sweeney Todd (The Demon
Barber of Fleet Street)
RICE, TIM
Blondel
Chess
Evita
Jesus Christ Superstar
Joseph and the Amazing
Technicolor Dreamcoat
RICH, BUDDY
Ship Ahoy
RICH, CHARLIE
Benji
Every Which Way But Loose
RICH, DORIS
Medea
Redhead
RICH, IRENE
New Orleans
RICH, JOHN
Christmas to Elvis
RICHARD, CLIFF
Endless Love
His Land
Summer Holiday
Swinger's Paradise
Two a Penny
Wonderful to Be Young
Xanadu
RICHARD, MAE
Tallulah
RICHARD, ZACHARY
Big Easy
RICHARDS, ANGELA
Cole
High Society
Robert and Elizabeth
RICHARDS, BILLIE
Rudolph the Red-Nosed
Reindeer
RICHARDS, CAROLE
Bob Crosby Show
Brigadoon
Call Me Madam
It's Always Fair Weather
Silk Stockings
RICHARDS, DONALD
Finian's Rainbow
Guys and Dolls
Merry Widow
RICHARDS, EMILY
Nicholas Nickleby
RICHARDS, GLEN
Curtain Going Up (Musical
Guide to Play Acting)
RICHARDS, JESS
Love Song
Musical Chairs
RICHARDS, LEONE M.
Jamboree!

RICHARDS, NORMAN
Thousand Miles of Mountains
RICHARDS, PAUL E.
Merry Widow
Tevya and His Daughters
RICHARDSON, CLAUDE
Grass Harp
Lola
RICHARDSON, IAN
Every Good Boy Deserves Favor
My Fair Lady
RICHARDSON, NATASHA
Handmaid's Tale
High Society
RICHARDSON, PETER
Twins
RICHARDSON, RON
Big River (the Adventures of
Huckleberry Finn)
RICHARDSON, SIR RALPH
Christmas Carol
RICHERT, WANDA
42nd Street
RICHIE, LIONEL
Endless Love
Thank God It's Friday
RICHMAN, HARRY
Legends of the Musical Stage
Puttin' on the Ritz
RICHMAN, JONATHAN
Up the Academy
RICHMAN, REBECCA
Bei Mir Bistu Schoen
RICKETTS, DAVID
Echo Park
RICKLES, DON
Bold Ventures
Foster Brooks' Roasts
Hollywood Squares
RIDDLE, NELSON
Adventures of Rin Tin Tin
Batman
Best of Nelson Riddle
Can-Can
Come Blow Your Horn
El Dorado
Girl Most Likely
Great Gatsby
Harlow
Harper Valley P.T.A.
Hey Boy, Hey Girl
How to Succeed In Business
Without Really Trying
Johnny Concho
Li'l Abner
Lolita
Magnavox Presents Frank
Sinatra
Merry Andrew
More Hit TV Themes
On a Clear Day You Can See
Forever
Paint Your Wagon
Paris When It Sizzles
Profiles In Courage
Pure Gold Movies
Rage to Live
Rio Bravo
Robin and the Seven Hoods
Rogues
Route 66 Theme and Other
Great TV Themes
St. Louis Blues
That's Entertainment, Part 2
Tone Poems of Color, Frank
Sinatra Conducts
Untouchables
What a Way to Go!
RIDER, BRICK
She's Called Virginia
RIDGWAY, STAN
Slam Dance
RIESMAN, MICHAEL
Thin Blue Line
RIFF
Lean on Me
Teenage Mutant Ninja Turtles
RIGG, DIANA
Follies
Little Night Music

RIGGS
Heavy Metal
RIGGS, RICHARD
Arnold's Wrecking Co.
RIGHTEOUS BROTHERS
Stardust
Swingin' Summer
RILEY, CHUCK
Story of Tron
RILEY, JAY
Mrs. Patterson
RILEY, JEANNIE C.
Harper Valley P.T.A.
Proudly They Came
RILEY, TEDDY
Do the Right Thing
RIMMER, SHANE
On the Town
RIMSHOTS
Patty
**RIMSKY-KORSAKOV,
NIKOLAI**
Song of Scheherazade
RINA, BOBBY
Jack and the Beanstalk
RINDER, LAURIN
In Search of
RINGHAM, LAURIE
Oliver!
RINGLAND, DALE
They're Playing Our Song
RINKER, AL
Aristocats
RIO, CHUCK
Big Top Pee-Wee
RIORDAN, IRENE
Committee
RIOS, AUGUSTINE
Jamaica
RIP CHORDS
Swingin' Summer
RIPTIDES
Mondo Hollywood
RITCHARD, CYRIL
Aladdin
Alice's Adventures In
Wonderland
Dangerous Christmas of Red
Riding Hood
General Motors' 50th
Anniversary Show
Happiest Girl In the World
La Perichole
Peter Pan
Roar of the Greasepaint - The
Smell of the Crowd
Sugar
RITCHIE, JUNE
Gone with the Wind
Threepenny Opera
RITCHIE, RENA
Gigi
RITCHIE FAMILY
Can't Stop the Music
RITENOUR, LEE
American Flyers
Officer and a Gentleman
Tequila Sunrise
RITNER, GEORGE
Oh Captain!
RITSCHEL, JACK
My Cousin Josefa
RITTER, TEX
Songs from the Western Screen
What Am I Bid?
RITTER, THELMA
New Girl In Town
RITTER, WALT
My Cousin Josefa
RITTMAN, TRUDE
Peter Pan
RITZ BROTHERS
On the Avenue
RIVAS, CARLOS
King and I
RIVERA, CHITA
Bajour
Bring Back Birdie
Broadway Magic

Bye Bye Birdie
Chicago
Mister Wonderful
Rink
Seventh Heaven
Sondheim: A Musical Tribute
Sweet Charity
West Side Story
Zenda
RIVERA, MARTIN
Lovers
RIVIERAS
Good Morning, Vietnam
RIZO, MARCO
Crossover Dreams
ROACH, BERT
Love Me Tonight
ROACH, HAL
Go Johnny Go!
ROACHFORD, ANDREW
Twins
ROACH
Pumping Iron 2 - The Women
That Was Then, This Is Now
ROANE, FRANK
Lost In the Stars
ROBARDS, JASON, JR.
After the Fall
ROBARDS, JASON
Hughie
Night They Raided Minsky's
ROBB, ROBBIE
Bill and Ted's Excellent
Adventure
ROBBINS, CINDY
By the Beautiful Sea
ROBBINS, FRED
Opening Night at the
Wintergarden - Mame
ROBBINS, GALE
Three Little Words
ROBBINS, JANA
Good News
ROBBINS, MARTY
Alamo
Honkytonk Man
ROBBINS, PETER
Boy Named Charlie Brown
ROBBINS, REX
Dime a Dozen
1776
ROBBINS, RICHARD
Bostonians
Heat and Dust
Maurice
Quartet
Room with a View
Slaves of New York
ROBBINS, ROCKIE
Beverly Hills Cop
ROBBINS, SHIRLEY
Brigadoon
ROBERT AND JOHNNY
Christine
ROBERTA, ABBEY
Surfer Girls
ROBERTS, ANTHONY
How Now, Dow Jones
ROBERTS, AUSTIN
Josie and the Pussycats
ROBERTS, BEATRICE
Flash Gordon
ROBERTS, BOB
Tom Jones
ROBERTS, BRUCE
Main Event
ROBERTS, CHAPMAN
Salvation
Your Arm's Too Short to Box
with God
ROBERTS, HOWARD
George M!
Guys and Dolls
Raisin
ROBERTS, JOAN
Oklahoma
Roberta
They Stopped the Show!
ROBERTS, KEITH
Promises, Promises

ROBERTS, LYNN
Ballroom
Jack and the Beanstalk
Thousand Miles of Mountains
ROBERTS, MURIEL
Flower Drum Song
ROBERTS, MYRON
Begatting of the President
ROBERTS, PERNELL
Bonanza - Christmas on the
Ponderosa
Bonanza - Ponderosa Party
Time
Carousel
ROBERTS, PETE
Summer Stock
ROBERTS, RHODA
Hot September
ROBERTS, RUTH
Curtain Going Up (Musical
Guide to Play Acting)
ROBERTS, TONY
Play It Again, Sam
Promises, Promises
Sugar
ROBERTSON, BAXTER
Karate Kid
ROBERTSON, BRIAN
Pirate Movie
ROBERTSON, CLIFF
Girl Most Likely
ROBERTSON, DON
Fun In Acapulco
It Happened at the World's Fair
ROBERTSON, DOUGLAS
My Fur Lady
ROBERTSON, LIZ
Dance a Little Closer
Jerome Kern Goes to
Hollywood
ROBERTSON, PAT
It's Time to Pray, America!
ROBERTSON, ROBBIE
Carny
Color of Money
King of Comedy
Scrooged
ROBESON, PAUL
Othello
Show Boat
Sing for Your Supper
ROBIN, LEO
Anything Goes
Bing's Hollywood
Gang's All Here
Gentlemen Prefer Blondes
Girl In Pink Tights
Hit the Deck
Just for You
Lorelei
Love Me Tonight
Meet Me After the Show
Mr. Cinders
Paris Honeymoon
Ruggles of Red Gap
State Fair
Stooge
Waikiki Wedding
ROBINSON, ALMA
Hair
ROBINSON, BILL
Blackbirds of 1928
Stormy Weather
ROBINSON, BRUCE
Romeo and Juliet
ROBINSON, CARDEW
Camelot
ROBINSON, DEBRA
Seven Brides for Seven
Brothers
ROBINSON, EARL
Lonesome Train
Sandhog
Sing for Your Supper
ROBINSON, EDWARD G.
Shakespeare In Hollywood
ROBINSON, GORDON
Sincerely Yours
ROBINSON, HARRY
Benny Hill - Words and Music
Dracula

ROBINSON, J. PETER
Believers
Return of the Living Dead, Part
II
ROBINSON, LAURA
All Night Strut
ROBINSON, MARTIN P.
Little Shop of Horrors
ROBINSON, MATT
Save the Children
ROBINSON, PHYLLIS
Cry for Us All
ROBINSON, RICHARD
Flood
New Moon
Student Prince
ROBINSON, ROBERT
Amen Corner
**ROBINSON, SMOKEY, AND
THE MIRACLES**
Big Chill
Big Time
Cooley High
Fine Mess
Last Dragon
Nothing But a Man
Platoon (And Songs from the
Era)
T.C.B. (Takin' Care of Business)
ROBINSON, VENUSTRAK
Runaways
ROBINSON, VICKI SUE
Nocturna
ROBINSON, WAYNE
Story of the Gnome-Mobile
**ROBINSON-WAYNE,
BEATRICE**
Four Saints In Three Acts
ROBISON, BARBARA
Jud
ROBSON, FLORA
King's Story
ROCKATS
Where the Boys Are '84
ROCHE, EUGENE
Secret Life of Walter Mitty
ROCHE, SARITA
Postcard from Morocco
ROCKERS ALL-STARS
Rockers
ROCKWELL
Last Dragon
RODD, MARCIA
I Can't Keep Running In Place
Love and Let Love
Your Own Thing
RODEHEAVER, HOMER
Billy Sunday
RODEN, JESS
They Call It an Accident
RODFORD, JIM
Return to Waterloo
RODGERS, ANTON
Pickwick
Scrooge
RODGERS, BOB
Billy Barnes Revue
**RODGERS, DOUGLAS
FLETCHER**
Plain and Fancy
RODGERS, EILEEN
Anything Goes
Fiorello!
Oh Captain!
Tenderloin
RODGERS, ERIC
James Bond - 10th Anniversary
RODGERS, JIMMIE
Co-Star
Gaily, Gaily
Long Hot Summer
RODGERS, MARY
Feathertop
Mad Show
Once Upon a Mattress
Three to Make Music
Working
RODGERS, MICHAEL
Coming to America

RODGERS, NILE
Soup for One
White Nights
RODGERS, PAUL
Karate Kid II
RODGERS, RICHARD
Allegro
American Idea Souvenir Album
American Musical Theater
Androcles and the Lion
Babes In Arms
Ballet Music from MGM
Musicals
Boys from Syracuse
By Jupiter
Carousel
Chee Chee
Cinderella
Connecticut Yankee
Dearest Enemy
Do I Hear a Waltz?
Evening with Beatrice Lillie
Ever Green
Flower Drum Song
Fly with Me
Gentlemen Marry Brunettes
Girl Friend
Higher and Higher
Hollywood Party
I Married an Angel
I Remember Mama
Jumbo
King and I
Life and Times of a She-Devil
Love Me Or Leave Me
Love Me Tonight
Magic of Musical Comedy
Me and Juliet
Melachrino Orchestra Plays
Medleys
Mississippi
Musical Comedy Favorites
No Strings
Odd Couple
Oklahoma
On Your Toes
Oscar Hammerstein II
Memorial Album
Pal Joey
Pipe Dream
Rex
Richard Rodgers
Rodgers and Hammerstein
Deluxe Set
Rodgers and Hart 1927-1942
Rodgers and Hart In Hollywood
Rodgers and Hart Revisited
Sharky's Machine
Slaughter on 10th Avenue
Sound of Music
Sound of Richard Rodgers'
Music
Soundtracks, Voices and
Themes from Great Movies
South Pacific
State Fair
Tea for Two
Together with Music
Too Many Girls
Two By Two
Valiant Years
Very Best of Richard Rodgers
Victory at Sea
With a Song In My Heart
Words and Music
Yankee Doodle Dandy
Young Man with a Horn
RODGERS, WILLIAM
Cleopatra
RODMAN, DAVID
Touch
**RODRIQUEZ, MARIO
ALBERTO**
My Fair Lady
ROECKER, EDWARD
Mademoiselle Modiste
ROEPER, NOLA
My Cousin Josefa
ROEVES, MAURICE
Ulysses
ROGER, ROGER
Folies Begere

ROGERS, ANNE
Boy Friend
She Loves Me
Zenda
ROGERS, DAVID
Flowers for Algernon
ROGERS, EARL
Camelot
Trouble In Tahiti
ROGERS, GINGER
Alice In Wonderland
Barkleys of Broadway
Choice Cuts
Cinderella
50 Years of Film
Flying Down to Rio
Fred Astaire and Ginger Rogers
Gay Divorcee
Ginger Rogers
Hooray for Hollywood
Kitty Foyle
Miss Ginger Rogers
That's Dancing!
Twenty Million Sweethearts
**ROGERS, GLENN,
ORCHESTRA**
Cabaret
ROGERS, JEAN
Flash Gordon
ROGERS, KENNY
Fools
Growing Pains
Kenny Rogers and the First
Edition Rollin'
Urban Cowboy
ROGERS, MARY
Ali Baba and the 40 Thieves
ROGERS, NOEL
Sweet Bye and Bye
ROGERS, ROY
Age of Television
Best of Broadway / Best of
Hollywood
Mackintosh and T.J.
Rustler's Rhapsody
Smokey and the Bandit II
Wyatt Earp, Cheyenne and
Other TV Favorites
ROGERS, SHORTY
Fools
Man with the Golden Arm
St. Louis Blues
Tarzan the Ape Man
Wild One
Zoot Suit
ROGERS, SUZANNE
Follies
ROGERS, WILLE
Gospel at Colonus
ROGERS, WILL
Show Biz (From Vaude to Video)
ROGIER, FRANK
Medium
Roberta
ROJAS, CRISTINA
My Fair Lady
ROLAND, GILBERT
French Line
ROLAND, NORMAN
Candide
ROLAND, STEVE
I Had a Ball
110 In the Shade
ROLIN, JUDI
Alice Through the Looking
Glass
ROLL, EDDIE
By the Beautiful Sea
Terms of Endearment
West Side Story
ROLLE, ESTHER
Don't Play Us Cheap
ROLLING STONES
Jumpin' Jack Flash
ROLLINS, JACK
Frosty the Snowman
ROLLINS, SONNY
Alfie
ROLPH, MARTI
Good News

ROMAN, BOB
Tom Jones
ROMAN, PAUL REID
Fly Blackbird
Godspell
ROMAN HOLLIDAY
Teachers
ROMANGUERA, JOAQUIN
Sweeney Todd (The Demon
Barber of Fleet Street)
ROMANIS, GEORGE
Eight on the Lam
ROMANN, MIMI
Among Friends - Waa-Mu Show
of 1960
ROMANN, SUSAN
Promenade
ROMANO, RONALD
Haunted
ROMANO, TONY
Frances Langford Presents
ROMBERG, SIGMUND
Deep In My Heart
Desert Song
Girl In Pink Tights
Maytime
Merry Widow
New Moon
Student Prince
ROME, HAROLD J.
Call Me Mister
Destry Rides Again
Fanny
Gone with the Wind
I Can Get It for You Wholesale
Kissing Bandit
Memorable Moments In
Musical Comedy
Pins and Needles
Wish You Were Here
Zulu and the Zayda
ROME, RICHARD
Mame
ROME, SYDNE
Schoner Gigolo - Armer Gigolo
(Just a Gigolo)
ROME PHILHARMONIC
Re-Animator
ROME SOUND STAGE
ORCHESTRA
Cleopatra
ROME SYMPHONY
ORCHESTRA
Ben-Hur
Golden Coach
Trip to Italy
V.I.P.S
ROMEO'S DAUGHTER
Nightmare on Elm Street 5 -
The Dream Child
ROMERO, CESAR
American Spirit
Co-Star
That Night In Rio
ROMOFF, COLIN
Fade Out Fade In
Kwamina
ROMOFF, WOOD
She Loves Me
RONETTES
Dirty Dancing
Quadrophenia
RONNELL, ANN
Kurt Weill In Hollywood
RONSARD
Don Quichotte
RONSTADT, LINDA
American Tail
FM
Hail Hail Rock 'N' Roll
Irving Berlin: 100th
Anniversary Collection
Pirates of Penzance
Urban Cowboy
ROOFTOP
Crossover Dreams
ROOK, WILLIE
Survival of St. Joan
ROONEY, MICKEY
Babes In Arms

Care Bears Movie
Cut! Out-Takes from
Hollywood's Greatest
Musicals
Fox and the Hound
Girl Crazy
How to Stuff a Wild Bikini
Journey Back to Oz
Judy Garland
Magic of Lassie
Merton of the Movies
Mister Broadway
Pete's Dragon
Pinocchio
Rodgers and Hart In Hollywood
Santa Claus Is Comin' to Town
Sugar Babies
That's Entertainment
Thousands Cheer
Words and Music
ROONEY, PAT
Guys and Dolls
ROOSEVELT, FRANKLIN D.
John F. Kennedy
Quick and the Dead - The Story
of the Atom Bomb
Years to Remember
ROQUEMORE, LARRY
Anyone Can Whistle
ROREM, NED
Miss Julie
ROSA, ROBBY
Salsa
ROSAMOND, J.
Porgy and Bess
ROSATO, MARY LOU
Cradle Will Rock
ROSE, ARTHUR
Me and My Girl
ROSE, BILLY
Funny Lady
ROSE, CLIFFORD
Marat (De) Sade
ROSE, DAVID
All-Star Salute, the Very Best of
Gershwin
Americanization of Emily
Another Evening with Fred
Astaire
Astaire Time
Best of the Great Motion
Picture Themes, Volume 5
Bonanza
Box-Office Blockbusters
Butterfield 8
Cimarron
Cleopatra
David Rose and His Orchestra
Play the Music of George
Gershwin
David Rose Among the Stars
Double Impact
Evening with Fred Astaire
Everything I Have Is Yours
Forbidden Planet
Frances Langford Presents
Gigi
Girls...And More Girls
Great Books, Great Movies,
Great Songs
Jamaica
Judy at the Palace
Man from U.N.C.L.E.
Motion Picture Themes
Music from Motion Pictures
Night and Day
of Human Bondage (And Other
Great Themes)
Quick Before It Melts
Rich, Young and Pretty
Theme from Exodus (And Other
Great Themes)
Themes from Box-Office
Blockbusters
Three Evenings with Fred
Astaire
Whoop-Up!
Winged Victory
Wonderful World of the
Brothers Grimm
ROSE, EMMETT
Best of Burlesque

ROSE, GAYLE
Jetsons: The Movie
ROSE, GEORGE
Canterbury Tales
Coco
Dance a Little Closer
Hamlet
My Fair Lady
Mystery of Edwin Drood
Pirates of Penzance
Walking Happy
ROSE, JANE
Car Wash
ROSE, MARGOT
I'm Getting My Act Together
and Taking It on the Road
ROSE, MICHAEL
Mighty Quinn
ROSE, PATRICK
Bistro Car
Jubalay
ROSE, RALPH
Oliver Twist
ROSE, REVA
You're a Good Man, Charlie
Brown
ROSE MARIE
Hollywood Squares
Top Banana
ROSE ROYCE
Car Wash
ROSELLI, JIMMY
Buona Sera, Mrs. Campbell
ROSEN, ROBERT
Shenandoah
ROSENBERG, IRENE
Onward Victoria
ROSENBLATT, BARBARA
Hollywood Party
ROSENFELD, MOISHE
Golden Land
ROSENMAN, LEONARD
Barry Lyndon
Beneath the Planet of the Apes
Bound for Glory
Chapman Report
Cobweb
Dick Powell Presents (Music
from the Original Soundtrack
of Four Star Productions)
James Dean Story
Lord of the Rings
Man Called Horse
9-30-55
Star Trek IV: The Voyage Home
Tribute to James Dean
Twilight Zone
ROSENSTOCK, MILTON
Bells Are Ringing
Bring Back Birdie
Can-Can
Funny Girl
Gentlemen Prefer Blondes
Girl Crazy
Gypsy
High Button Shoes
Hot September
Jimmy
King and I
Lorelei
Make a Wish
One Night Stand
Prettybelle
So Long 174th Street
Stop the World - I Want to Get
Off!!
Subways Are for Sleeping
Sugar Babies
This Is the Army
Two's Company
ROSENTHAL, LAURENCE
Anastasia - The Mystery of
Anna
Becket
Brass Target
Clash of the Titans
Comedians
Dylan
Hotel Paridiso
Island of Dr. Moreau
Man of La Mancha
Meetings with Remarkable Men

Music from the Galaxies
Music Man
Rashomon
Return of a Man Called Horse
ROSIE AND THE ORIGINALS
Hometown U.S.A.
ROSKO
You Are What You Eat
ROSS, ADRIAN
Lilac Time (Blossom Time)
Merry Widow
ROSS, ANNIE
Real Ambassadors
ROSS, BILL
Danny Elfman: Music for a
Darkened Theatre
ROSS, DEBBIE
Double Deckers
ROSS, DIANA
Cooley High
Diana!
Endless Love
Evening with Diana Ross
Funny Girl
It's My Turn
Lady Sings the Blues
Land Before Time
Looking for Mr. Goodbar
Mahogany
On Broadway
T.C.B. (Takin' Care of Business)
Thank God It's Friday
Wiz
ROSS, ELIZA
All About Life
ROSS, HARRY
Do Re Mi
ROSS, HOWARD
Carmelina
Philemon
ROSS, HUGH
Golden Apple
ROSS, JAMES
Different Times
ROSS, JAMIE
Oh Coward!
Woman of the Year
ROSS, JERRY
Damn Yankees
Pajama Game
ROSS, JOE
Crystal Heart
She Loves Me
ROSS, JUSTIN
Chorus Line
ROSS, KATHERINE
Fools
ROSS, LANNY
All Star Color TV Revue
My Fair Lady
Pure Gold Movies
ROSS, LYNN
First Impressions
ROSS, MARILYN
Flahooley
ROSS, MARION
Carousel
ROSS, NORMAN
Progress In Sound
ROSS, PHIL
Zorro
ROSS, SHIRLEY
Bob Hope In Hollywood
Rodgers and Hart 1927-1942
ROSS, TED
Wiz
ROSSBACH, HANS
Gypsy Moths
I Love You Alice B. Toklas
Sundowners
ROSSELLINI, RENZO
Trip to Italy
ROSSI, MARIO
Alexander Nevsky
ROSSI, STEVE
Last of the Secret Agents
ROSSINI, GIOACCHINO
Clockwork Orange
Legend of the Lone Ranger
Melba

ROSSITER, LEONARD
Hooray for Daisy!
ROSWAENGE, HELGE
Threepenny Opera
ROTA, NINO
Amarcord Nino Rota
Boccaccio '70
Clowns
Death on the Nile
8½
Fellini Satyricon
Fellini's Roma
Godfather
Godfather Part II
Godfather, Parts I and II
Great Original Soundtracks and
Movie Themes
Hurricane
Juliet of the Spirits
La Dolce Vita
Leopard
Much Ado About Nothing
Music from the Films of
Federico Fellini
Rocco and His Brothers
Romeo and Juliet
Taming of the Shrew
War and Peace
Waterloo
ROTH, ALLEN
All Star Color TV Revue
ROTH, DAVID LEE
Down and Out In Beverly Hills
ROTH, LILLIAN
I Can Get It for You Wholesale
I'll Cry Tomorrow
70 Girls, 70
ROTH, SIGMUND
Rise and Fall of the City of
Mahogany
ROTHLEIN, ARLENE
In Circles
Peace
ROTHENBERGER,
ANNELIESE
Oh, Rosalinda!
ROTONDO, GUY
To Broadway with Love
ROUGH TRADE
Cruising
ROUND, THOMAS
Lilac Time (Blossom Time)
Merry Widow
Song of Norway
ROUNDS, DAN
Boy Meets Boy
ROUNDTREE, RICHARD
Man from Shaft
ROUNSEVILLE, ROBERT
Candide
Carousel
Man of La Mancha
Merry Widow
Mikado
Student Prince
Tales of Hoffmann
ROURKE, M.E.
Jerome Kern Goes to
Hollywood
ROUSE, ERVIN T.
Smokey and the Bandit
ROUTERS
Surf Party
ROUTLEDGE, PATRICIA
Cowardly Custard
Darling of the Day
Little Mary Sunshine
ROVIN, ROBERT
Mixed Doubles / Below the Belt
ROWAN, DAN
Rowan and Martin's Laugh-In
ROWE, VERN
Pennies from Heaven
ROWLANDS, BRUCE
Mahoney's Last Stand
Man from Snowy River
Phar Lap
Return to Snowy River
ROWLES, JIMMY
College Confidential

ROWLES, POLLY
No Strings
ROXETTE
Pretty Woman
ROXY MUSIC
Miami Vice II
Times Square
ROXY THEATER ORCESTRA
My Fair Lady
ROY, HERVE
Emmanuelle
ROY, SHEILA
Coach with the Six Insides
ROY, WILLIAM
Dressed to the Nines
Four Below Strikes Back
Pieces of Eight
ROYAL COURT OF CHINA
Lost Angels
ROYAL FARNSWORTH
SYMPHONY ORCHESTRA
Around the World In 80 Days
ROYAL LIVERPOOL
SYMPHONY
Last Rebel
ROYAL OPERA HOUSE
ORCHESTRA
Murder on the Orient Express
Peter Rabbit and Tales of
Beatrix Potter
ROYAL PHILHARMONIC
Broadway Extravaganza
Carousel
Concert John Barry
Death of a Salesman
Digital Trip Down Broadway
Francis Lai Performs His Great
Film Music
Greystoke - The Legend of
Tarzan, Lord of the Apes
Inn of the Sixth Happiness
Jarre By Jarre
Mad Max - Beyond
Thunderdome
Miklos Rozsa Conducts His
Great Film Music
Mountbatten: The Last Viceroy
Quo Vadis?
Screen Themes
Shooting Party
Splash
Time After Time
To Kill a Mockingbird
Top Secret
Torn Curtain
200 Motels
ROYAL SCOTTS DRAGOON
GUARDS
Invasion of the Body Snatchers
ROYALE SINGERS AND
ORCHESTRA
Can-Can
Me and Juliet
My Fair Lady
Show Boat
ROYALTY
Earth Girls Are Easy
ROZHDESTVENSKY,
GENNADL
2001: A Space Odyssey
ROZSA, MIKLOS
Ben-Hur
Ben-Hur, Vol. II
Best of the Great Motion
Picture Themes, Vol. 5
Beyond the Sound Barrier, Vol.
2
Bible
Blood on the Sun
Brute Force
Classic Miklos Rozsa Film
Themes
Crisis
El Cid
Eye of the Needle
Fedora
Film Music of Miklos Rozsa
Golden Voyage of Sinbad
Hollywood: The Post War Years
(1946 - 1949)
Ivanhoe

Julius Caesar
Jungle Book
King of Kings
Knights of the Round Table
Last Embrace
Lost Weekend
Love Themes from Motion
Pictures
Lust for Life
Madame Bovary
Miklos Rozsa
Miklos Rozsa Conducts His
Great Film Music
Miklos Rozsa Conducts His
Great Themes
Miklos Rozsa - Music for Films
Music for Films
Music from Great
Shakespearean Films
Music from Hollywood
Power
Premier Radio Performances
Providence
Quo Vadis?
Red House
Rhapsody Under the Stars
Richard Boone Reads the Story
of Jesus for Children
Rozsa Conducts Rozsa
Rozsa: Suites for the Films
Sodom and Gomorrah
Song of Scheherazade
Spectacular World of Classic
Film Scores
Spellbound
Strange Love of Martha Ivers
Thief of Bagdad
Theme Music from Great
Motion Picture Scores
Time After Time
Time to Love and a Time to Die
V.I.P.S
Wide-Screen Spectaculars
Young Bess
RUBACH, EDWARD
Salad Days
RUBENS, CHRISTINE
Let My People Come
RUBENSTEIN, DEIDRE
Boy Friend
RUBENSTEIN, JOHN
Jeremiah Johnson
RUBIN, ARTHUR
Follies
Here's Love
Juno
Kean
Most Happy Fella
Producers
RUBIN, RON
Can Heironymus Merkin Ever
Forget Mercy Humppe (And
Find True Happiness)
RUBIN, STAN
Dixieland Goes Broadway
RUBINI, MICHAEL
Band of the Hand
Hunger
Manhunter
RUBINOOS
Revenge of the Nerds
RUBINSTEIN, ARTHUR
Blue Thunder
Goodtime Charley
War Games
RUBINSTEIN, DONALD A.
Martin
Tales from the Dark Side (the
Movie)
RUBINSTEIN, JOHN
Pippin
RUBY, HARRY
Evening with Beatrice Lillie
Gentlemen Marry Brunettes
Three Little Words
Ziegfeld Follies of 1919
RUDEL, JULIUS
Silverlake
RUDENSKI, SHMUEL
Fiddler on the Roof
RUDLEY, MARION
Cradle Will Rock

RUE, ROBERT
Candide
Juno
RUFF, GARFEEL
Hitter
RUFFELLE, FRANCES
Les Miserables
RUFFIN, GARY
Survival of St. Joan
RUFFIN, HANK
Survival of St. Joan
RUFUS
Breakin'
Night Shift
RUGGIERO, GABRIELLE
Saint of Bleecker Street
RUGGLES, CHARLES
Anything Goes
Love Me Tonight
RUGOLO, PETE
Gigi
Impact
Jack the Ripper
Music for a Private Eye
Richard Diamond
Sweet Ride
Thriller
Time Remembered
TV's Top Themes
RUHL, EDDIE
King and I
RUHL, PAT
Dressed to the Nines
RUICK, BARBARA
Carousel
Cinderella
Oh Kay!
Oscar Hammerstein II
Memorial Album
RUIZ, RANDY
Runaways
RULE, CHARLES
Goodtime Charley
RULE, JANICE
Happiest Girl In the World
RUN - D.M.C.
Ghostbusters II
Krush Groove
RUNDGREN, TODD
Rock 'N' Roll High School
Undercover
RUOFF, DEE
Best of Broadway 1973
RUPERT, GENE
Evening with Richard Nixon
Time for Singing
RUPERT, MICHAEL
Festival
Happy Time
March of the Falsettos
Sweet Charity
Three Guys Naked from the
Waist Down
RUPP, FRANZ
Lady from Philadelphia
RUS, MARJAN
Merry Widow
RUSH, MERRILEE
Bob and Carol and Ted and
Alice
RUSHTON, WILLIAM
John F. Kennedy
RUSK, DEAN
ABC Scope
RUSK, JAMES
Among Friends - Waa-Mu Show
of 1960
RUSSELL, ANNA
Anna Russell's Little Show (All
By Myself)
RUSSELL, BETTY
Harvey Girls
RUSSELL, BOBBY
Grasshopper
RUSSELL, BRENDA
Soul Man
RUSSELL, BRYAN
Bye Bye Birdie
So Dear to My Heart

RUSSELL, CONNIE
Playgirls
RUSSELL, CRAIG
Outrageous
RUSSELL, DAVID
Shenandoah
RUSSELL, JACK
Night In Venice
RUSSELL, JANE
Double Dynamite
French Line
Gentlemen Marry Brunettes
Gentlemen Prefer Blondes
Girls...And More Girls
RUSSELL, JESSICA
Carmen Jones
RUSSELL, KARL
Blacula
RUSSELL, KURT
Adventures of Jamie
McPheeters
Fox and the Hound
Now You See Him, Now You
Don't
RUSSELL, LEON
Joe Cocker: Mad Dogs and
Englishmen
RUSSELL, LILLIAN
They Stopped the Show!
RUSSELL, NIPSEY
Wiz
RUSSELL, PEE WEE
Jazz Dance
RUSSELL, REBECCA
Heart of Dixie
RUSSELL, ROSALIND
American Spirit
Gypsy
Shakespeare In Hollywood
They Stopped the Show!
Wonderful Town
RUSSELL, THERESA
Insignificance
RUSSELL, TONY
Tell Me Lies
RUSSO, CLAUDIA
Solomon King
RUSSO, COS
Shame / Lighthorsemen
RUSSOM, LEON
Oh! Calcutta!
RUSTICHELLI, CARLO
Bebo's Girl
Birds, the Bees and the Italians
Divorce Italian Style
Original Soundtracks and Music
Seduced and Abandoned
RUTH, GEORGE HERMAN
"BABE"
Not So Long Ago
Years to Remember
RUTH, LEWIS, BAND
Threepenny Opera
RUTHERFORD, MARGARET
Wacky World of Mother Goose
RUTHERFORD, MIKE
Against All Odds
RUTLES
All You Need Is Cash
RUTS
Times Square
RVARK, JOHN
My Fair Lady
RYAN, IRENE
Beverly Hillbillies
Pippin
RYAN, MARK
Evita
RYAN, ROBERT
Flush Left, Stagger Right
Inheritance
King of Kings
Mr. President
RYDELL, BOBBY
Bye Bye Birdie
RYDELL, CHARLES
Ben Bagley's Ira Gershwin
Revisited
Painted Smiles of Cole Porter
Rodgers and Hart Revisited

Secret Life of Walter Mitty
RYDER, RICHARD
Piano Bar
RYE, JOHN
Funny Thing Happened on the
Way to the Forum
RYUN, JIM
It's Time to Pray, America!
S.S.Q.
Return of the Living Dead
SABAN, HAIM
Secrets of the Sword
SABAR, JEAN PIERRE
Madame Claude
SABELLA, ERNIE
Lion King
SABIN, DAVID
Now Is the Time for All Good
Men
Preppies
Threepenny Opera
SABLON, JEAN
L'Etoile Du Nord
SABU
Jungle Book
SACHS, ANDREW
Fawlty Towers - Second Sitting
SADD, SUE, AND THE NEXT
Roadie
SADLER, SSGT. BARRY
More American Graffiti
NARM's Golden Decade
SADLER'S WELLS OPERA
COMPANY
Angel's Springtime World of
Light Opera
SAFAN, CRAIG
Lady Beware
Last Starfighter
Nightmare on Elm Street 4 -
The Dream Master
Stand and Deliver
Thief
Warning Sign
SA-FIRE
She-Devil
SAFKA, MELANIE
All the Right Noises
R.P.M.
Swedish Fly Girls
SAGA
Johnny Be Good
SAGER, CAROLE BAYER
Champ
It's My Turn
Night Shift
They're Playing Our Song
SAHL, MORT
Dean Martin Testimonial Dinner
SAHM, DOUG
More American Graffiti
SAIDENBERG, DANIEL
Grandma Moses Suite
SAIDENBERG, THEODORE
Grass Harp
My Fair Lady
On a Clear Day You Can See
Forever
SAINT, EVA MARIE
Our Town
SAINT JAMES, SUSAN
Outlaw Blues
ST. LOUIS CAROL
ASSOCIATION
Christmas Sing with Bing
SAINT-SAENS, CAMILLE
Days of Heaven
SAINTE-MARIE, BUFFY
Officer and a Gentleman
Performance
Revolution
Strawberry Statement
SAINTON, PHILIP
Moby Dick
SAKAMOTO, RYUICHI
Black Rain
Handmaid's Tale
Last Emperor
Merry Christmas Mr. Lawrence

SAKI, YAMA
Flower Drum Song
SAKINAH
Cotton Comes to Harlem
SALAMA, GAMAL
Story of Tutankhamen
SALAS, PETER
Earthquake
SALERNO, MARY JO
Snow White and the Seven
Dwarfs
SALES, SOUPY
Soupy Sales Show
SALGADO, EFRAIN
Brother from Another Planet
SALIVA SISTERS
Evening with Richard Nixon
SALLEE, JEANETTE
Stephen Foster Story
SALLERT, ULLA
Ben Franklin In Paris
SALLIS, PETER
Baker Street
Cabaret
SALONGA, LEA
Miss Saigon
SALSBURY, BAKER
Great American Fourth of July
Parade
SALT, WALDO
Sandhog
SALT LAKE CITY
TABERNACLE CHOIR
Christmas Sing with Bing
SALT-N-PEPA
Colors
SALTARELLO CHOIR
Thief of Bagdad
SALTER, HANS J.
Classic Horror Music of Hans J.
Salter
Evening with Boris Karloff and
His Friends
Fantasy Film World of Hans J.
Salter
Far Horizons - The Western
Film Scores of Hans J. Salter
Film Music of Hans J. Salter
Ghost of Frankenstein
Hitler
Horror Rhapsody
Maya
Scarlet Street
Themes from Classic Science
Fiction, Fantasy and Horror
Films
Themes from Horror Movies
War Lord
Wichita Town
SALVATION COMPANY
Earl of Ruston
SAM THE SHAM AND THE
PHARAOHS
Full Metal Jacket
When the Boys Meet the Girls
SAMBORO, RICHIE
Adventures of Ford Fairlane
SAMMES, MICHAEL
Aristocats
Brigadoon
Cat and the Fiddle
Doctor Dolittle
Fiddler on the Roof
Great Waltz
Half a Sixpence
Kismet
Man of La Mancha
My Fair Lady
Paper Tiger
Prudence and the Pill
Redhead
Swinger's Paradise
Wonderful to Be Young
Words and Music
SAMOSSUD, JACQUES
Kurt Weill In Hollywood
SAMPLE, JOE
Sharky's Machine
SAMUDIO, SAM
Border

SAN FRANCISCO
IMPROVISATIONAL
GROUP
Wide Wide World of War
SAN FRANCISCO MIME
TROUPE
Steel Town
SAN JUAN, OLGA
Kurt Weill In Hollywood
Paint Your Wagon
SANBORN, DAVID
King of Comedy
Lethal Weapon
Lethal Weapon 2
Tequila Sunrise
SANCHEZ, JAMIE
Karl Marx
SAND, PAUL
From the Second City
Mad Show
Paul Sills' Story Theater (of
Magical Folk-Rock Fables)
SANDALS
Endless Summer
Last of the Ski Bums
SANDAUER, HENRY
Destination Moon
Israel Now
SANDBERG, TRICIA
We'd Rather Switch
SANDEEN, DARRELL
Young Abe Lincoln
SANDERS, FELICIA
Baker Street
SANDERS, GEORGE
Batman
Call Me Madam
Conversation Piece
Frances Langford Presents
In Search of the Castaways
SANDERS, JEAN
Johnny Johnson
SANDERS, WAYNE
Hello Dolly!
SANDERSON, JULIE
Memorable Moments In
Musical Comedy
SANDISON, GORDON
Nightingale
SANDLOFF, PETER
Threepenny Opera
SANDORD, WILLIAM
Pretty Boy Floyd
SANDPIPERS
Beyond the Valley of the Dolls
Sterile Cuckoo
Westward Ho, the Wagons
SANDRICH, MARK, JR.
Ben Franklin In Paris
SANDS, BOB
Hear! Hear!
Kiss Me Kate
SANDS, DIANA
Honeybaby
Raisin In the Sun
SANDS, EVIE
John and Mary
SANDS, GENE
Flower Drum Song
SANDS, JODIE
Jamboree!
SANDS, PETER
Athenian Touch
SANDS, ROBERT
Desert Song
Evening with Johnny Mercer
SANDS, TOMMY
Babes In Toyland
In Search of the Castaways
Parent Trap
Sing Boy Sing
Summer Magic
SANFORD, CHARLES
Adventures of Marco Polo
Lady In the Dark
Little Me
SANI, AMRU
New Faces of 1956

SANKEY, TOM
Golden Screw
SANNES, LLOYD
Magic Show
SANTA CECILIA ACADEMY
Dog of Flanders
SANTA CECILIA ORCHESTRA
L'Etoile Du Nord
Leviathan
Unforgiven
SANTA ESMERALDA
Thank God It's Friday
SANTAMARIA, MONGO
April Fools
SANTANA, CARLOS
La Bamba
Woodstock
SANTELL, MARIE
Peace
SANTIAGO AND HIS SILVER STRINGS
Broadway Show Stoppers
SANTIAGO, AUGUSTINA
13 Daughters
SANZ, NIKKI
Earthquake
SAPPINGTON, MARGO
Oh! Calcutta!
Promises, Promises
SAPPIR, JERRY
Zorba
SARANDON, CHRIS
Liberty
SARANDON, SUSAN
Rocky Horror Picture Show
SARAYA
Shocker
SARDE, PHILIPPE
Bear
Choix Des Armes (Choice of Arms)
Coup De Torchon (Clean Slate)
Four Original Soundtrack Recordings By Philippe Sarde
Ghost Story
L'Etoile Du Nord
Manhattan Project
Pirates
Quest for Fire
Sunday In the Country
Tess
SARGENT, JOSEPH
Pied Piper of Hamelin
SARGENT, SIR MALCOLM
Beggar's Opera
Heifetz on Television
Midsummer Night's Dream
Mikado
SARIDIS, ANGELO
Zorba
SARNE, MICHAEL
Joanna
Seaside Swingers
SARNO, JANET
Dylan
Survival of St. Joan
SARNOFF, DOROTHY
King and I
SARO, TOMAS
My Fair Lady
SAROYAN, WILLIAM
Hello Out There
SATO, ISAO
Pacific Overtures
SATO, MASARU
Yojimbo
SATO, REIKO
Flower Drum Song
SATTON, LON
Revenge of the Pink Panther
SATURDAY REVUE
Wild Wheels
SAUERBAUM, HEINZ
Rise and Fall of the City of Mahogany
SAULTER, JOE
I Love My Wife

SAUNDERS, ANDREA
Billy Noname
SAUNDERS, GERTRUDE
Shuffle Along
SAUNDERS, JACK
Around the World In 80 Days
Scent of Mystery
SAUNDERS, MERL
Heavy Traffic
SAUNDERS, RICHARD
Camelot
SAUNDERS, TERRY
Joseph and the Amazing Technicolor Dreamcoat
King and I
SAUSSY, TUPPER
Mary Poppins
SAUTER, EDDIE
Mickey One
SAVAGE, ARCHIE
Kiss Me Kate
SAVAGE, JOHN
Hair
SAVAGE, MARGARET
Fiddler on the Roof
SAVAGE, TOM
Musical Chairs
SAVIDENT, JOHN
Card
SAVINA, CARLO
Amarcord Nino Rota
Ben-Hur
Bible
Black Orchid
Breath of Scandal
Clowns
Fellini's Roma
For the First Time
Garden of the Finzi-Continis
Godfather
Great Original Soundtracks and Movie Themes
It Started In Naples
Juliet of the Spirits
L'Etoile Du Nord
Music from the Films of Federico Fellini
Sondheim
Stavisky
Tess
SAVINO, DOMENICO
Most Happy Fella
My Fair Lady
SAVOY PLAYERS
Gilbert and Sullivan
SAVOYARDS
Mikado
SAWTELL, PAUL
Big Circus
Dog of Flanders
Kronos
Music of Republic
SAWYER, CAROL
Fiddler on the Roof
SAWYER, MIKE
Cindy
SAX, SYDNEY
Wild Rovers
SAXON, DON
Street Scene
SAXON, LUTHER
Carmen Jones
SAXON, RECE
Hansel and Gretel
SAY, JACK
Most Happy Fella
SAYERS, LEO
All This and World War II
Inside Moves
SCAGGS, BOZ
FM
Inside Moves
Looking for Mr. Goodbar
Two of a Kind
Urban Cowboy
SCALA, DELIA
My Fair Lady
SCALES, PRUNELLA
Fawlty Towers - Second Sitting

SCANDAL
Easy Money
SCANLON, MEG
Irene
SCANTLIN, RAY
Joseph McCarthy Is Alive and Well and Living In Dade County
SCANTTIN
A-5,6,7,8
SCARBURY, JOEY
River Rat
SCARDINO, DON
Angel
Homer
I'm Getting My Act Together and Taking It on the Road
King of Hearts
SCARLETT, JIMMY
Body Slam
Garbage Pail Kids
SCARLETT AND BLACK
Hiding Out
SCHAAL, RICHARD
Paul Sills' Story Theater (of Magical Folk-Rock Fables)
SCHAEFER, HAL & LEE
Finian's Rainbow and Brigadoon Remembered
SCHAEFER, JERRY
Ben Franklin In Paris
SCHAEFFER, SANDRA
Promenade
SCHAFER, KERMIT
Burlesque Show
SCHAFER, MILTON
Bravo Giovanni!
Drat! the Cat!
SCHAFER, NATALIE
Four Television Musicals
SCHAFFER, LARRY
Mission: Impossible
SCHARF, WALTER
Bundle of Joy
Cinderfella
Dangerous Christmas of Red Riding Hood
French Line
Funny Girl
Geisha Boy
Harold Lloyd's World of Laughter
If It's Tuesday, This Must Be Belgium
Journey Back to Oz
Living It Up
Man from U.N.C.L.E.
Wilderness Trail
Willy Wonka and the Chocolate Factory
SCHECTMAN, SAUL
Carnival
Hello Dolly!
SCHEERER, BOB
Boy Friend
Top Banana
SCHEFF, JERRY
Easy Come, Easy Go
Elvis In Concert
Elvis: Aloha from Hawaii Via Satellite
That's the Way It Is
This Is Elvis
SCHEFRIN, ADAM
Tea Dance
SCHEIMER, ERIKA
Secrets of the Sword
SCHELL, MAXIMILIAN
Black Hole (the Story of the Black Hole)
Judgment at Nuremberg
SCHERMAN, THOMAS
Cinderella
Our Town
Three to Make Music
SCHERTZINGER, VICTOR
Bing's Hollywood
Fleet's In
Love Me Tonight
SCHICKELE, PETER
Oh! Calcutta!

Silent Running
SCHIFRIN, LALO
Amityville Horror
Between Broadway and Hollywood
Boulevard Nights
Brotherhood (And Other Themes)
Bullitt
Che!
Cincinnati Kid
Competition
Cool Hand Luke
Eagle Has Landed
Enter the Dragon
Film Music
Fourth Protocol
Fox
Gone with the Wave
James Bond
Kelly's Heroes
Liquidator
Man from U.N.C.L.E.
Mannix
Medical Center
Mission: Impossible
Murderer's Row
Nunzio
Once a Thief
Osterman Weekend
Rise and Fall of the Third Reich
Rollercoaster
Sol Madrid
Sting II
Sudden Impact
Twilight of Honor
Voyage of the Damned
Way...Way Out
SCHIMMEL, JOHN
Pump Boys and Dinettes
SCHIPPERS, THOMAS
Amahl and the Night Visitors
Medium
Saint of Bleecker Street
SCHISGAL, MURRAY
Luv
SCHLAMME, MARTHA
Kurt Weill Cabaret
Threepenny Opera
SCHLATTER, CHARLIE
Heartbreak Hotel
SCHLEE, ROBERT
Doctor Selavy's Magic Theater
Threepenny Opera
SCHLOSS, ZANDER
Straight to Hell
SCHMIDT, HARVEY
Bad Company
Celebration
Colette
Fantasticks
I Do! I Do!
110 In the Shade
Philemon
Shoestring Revue '57
Two Film Scores for Solo Piano
SCHMIDT, JOSEPH
My Song Goes Round the World
SCHMIDT, JULES
Cradle Will Rock
SCHMIT, TIMOTHY B.
Fast Times at Ridgemont High
Secret Admirer
SCHNEIDER, CHARLES
Your Own Thing
SCHNEIDER, ELMER "MOE"
Pete Kelly's Blues
SCHNEIDER, JOHN
Dukes of Hazzard
SCHNEIDER, WILLIAM
Nervous Set
SCHOEN, VIC
Bing's Hollywood
Court Jester
Knock on Wood
Manhattan Tower
Mr. Music
Music from Shubert Alley
Red Sky at Morning
SCHOENFELD, MAE
Kosher Widow

810

811

813

SILWELL, RICHARD
Stephen Foster Story
SIM, ALASTAIR
Ruling Class
SIMA, OSKA
Oh, Rosalinda!
SIMEONE, HARRY
Broadway's Best Shows, 1963
Broadway's Big Hits
SIMIEN, TERRANCE, AND
THE MALLET PLAYBOYS
Big Easy
SIMIONATO, GIULIETTA
Met Stars on Broadway
SIMMONDS, STANLEY
Jimmy
Li'l Abner
Mack and Mabel
Maggie Flynn
SIMMONS, BONNIE
Cats
SIMMONS, JEAN
Guys and Dolls
Hamlet
Little Night Music
SIMMONS, JEFFREY
Naked Angels
SIMMONS, JIMMY
Eleven Against the Ice
SIMMONS, MAUDE
Finian's Rainbow
SIMMS, LU ANN
Arthur Godfrey
How to Stuff a Wild Bikini
SIMON, AVI
Fly with Me
SIMON, CARLY
James Bond 13 Original
Themes
Karate Kid II
Nothing In Common
Odd Couple
Soup for One
Spy Who Loved Me
Taking Off
Working Girl
SIMON, HERB
Godspell
SIMON, JOE
Cleopatra Jones
SIMON, JOHN
Last Summer
You Are What You Eat
SIMON, LOWRELL
Three the Hard Way
SIMON, NEIL
Opening Night at the Palace -
Sweet Charity
Opening Night at the
Wintergarden - Mame
SIMON, PAUL
Graduate
More American Graffiti
One Trick Pony
Saturday Night Live
Two a Penny
SIMON AND GARFUNKEL
More American Graffiti
SIMONDS, DOUGLAS
Double Deckers
SIMONE, NINA
Nina Simone Sings Porgy
SIMONETTI, CLAUDIO
Creepers
SIMONS, TED
Go Fly a Kite
New Faces of 1968
SIMPLE MINDS
Breakfast Club
SIMPSON, BILLY
Little Prince
SIMPSON, BLAND
Diamond Studs
SIMPSON, TONY
Pickwick
SIMS, ZOOT
Silent Partner
SINATRA, FRANK
Anchors Aweigh
Anything Goes / Panama Hattie

Can-Can
Cut! Out-Takes from
Hollywood's Greatest
Musicals
Dean Martin Testimonial Dinner
Dick Tracy In BB
Double Dynamite
50 Years of Film
Finian's Rainbow
Frank Sinatra Sings George
Gershwin
Guys and Dolls
High Society
Higher and Higher
It Happened In Brooklyn
Judy Garland
Kiss Me Kate
Kissing Bandit
Magnavox Presents Frank
Sinatra
Movin' with Nancy
On the Town
Our Town
Pal Joey
Robin and the Seven Hoods
Ship Ahoy
South Pacific
Take Me Out to the Ball Game
That's Entertainment
Tone Poems of Color, Frank
Sinatra Conducts
Victors
Young at Heart
SINATRA, FRANK, JR.
Once Upon a Tour
SINATRA, NANCY
Full Metal Jacket
James Bond 13 Original
Themes
Movin' with Nancy
Speedway
You Only Live Twice
SINATRA, RAY
Because You're Mine
Mario Lanza Sings Because
Memorable Moments In
Musical Comedy
That Midnight Kiss
Toast of New Orleans
SINCLAIR, MONICA
Tales of Hoffmann
SINDEN, DONALD
Island at the Top of the World
SINER, GUY
Biograph Girl
SINFONIA OF LONDON
Batman
Boy Who Could Fly
Danny Elfman: Music for a
Darkened Theatre
Exodus
Gone with the Wind
Robocop
Snowman
Vertigo
Young Sherlock Holmes
SINGER, LORI
Fame
SINGING STRINGS
Salute to Bogie: Humphrey
Bogart
SINGLETON, MARGIE
All American
SINGLETON, SUE
Bye Bye Birdie
SINGLETON, ZUTTY
Stormy Weather
SIOUXSIE & BANSHEES
Out of Bounds
SIR DOUGLAS QUINTET
Officer and a Gentleman
SIR JULIAN
La Strada
SIRAVO, GEORGE
Richard Rodgers
SIREN
My Stepmother Is an Alien
SIRETTA, DAN
Coco
SIROLA, JOSEPH
Golden Rainbow

SISSLE, NOBLE
Shuffle Along
SISTER CAROL
Something Wild
SISTER SLEDGE
Action Jackson
Coming to America
Playing for Keeps
Soup for One
SISTERS
Pirate Movie
SITWELL, DAME EDITH
Facade
SIVUCA
Joy
SKAFISH
Urgh - A Music War
SKEGGS, BUSTER
Pal Joey
SKELTON, GEOFFREY
Marat (De) Sade
SKELTON, RED
Cut! Out-Takes from
Hollywood's Greatest
Musicals
Lovely to Look At
Proudly They Came
Ship Ahoy
Thousands Cheer
Three Little Words
Ziegfeld Follies of 1946
SKERRITT, TOM
M*A*S*H
SKIDOOS
Thoroughly Modern Millie
SKILES, STEVE
Now Is the Time for All Good
Men
SKINNER, CORNELIA OTIS
Paris '90
SKINNER, EDNA
Mister Ed
SKINNER, FRANK
Back Street
Evening with Boris Karloff and
His Friends
Imitation of Life
Interlude
Madame X
Magnificent Obsession
Man of a Thousand Faces
Shenandoah
Snow Queen
Written on the Wind
SKINNER, KEITH
Romeo and Juliet
SKINNER, TOM
It's Time to Pray, America!
SKINNY PUPPY
Bad Influence
SKIPWORTH AND TURNER
Pumping Iron 2 - The Women
SKULNIK, MENASHA
Zulu and the Zayda
SKYLAR, SUNNY
Gems from Gershwin
SKYLARKS
Beau James
White Christmas
SKYLINERS
Daddy Long Legs
Hometown U.S.A.
SKYY
Action Jackson
SLADE
Follow That Girl
Hooray for Daisy
SLADE, JULIAN
Salad Days
Wildest Dreams
SLANE, ROD
Revenge
SLANEY, IVOR
King's Story
South Pacific
SLATER, B.J.
1776
SLATER, JOHN
My Fair Lady

SLATKIN, LEONARD
Exorcist
Red Sky at Morning
SLATON, DON
Best Foot Forward
SLAVE RAIDER
License to Drive
SLAVIN, MILLIE
To Broadway with Love
SLAYER
Less Than Zero
River's Edge
SLAZER, JON
Revenge
SLEDGE, EDDIE
Kiss Me Kate
SLEDGE, PERCY
Big Chill (More Songs from the
Original Soundtrack)
More American Graffiti
Platoon (And Songs from the
Era)
SLEEP, WAYNE
Cats
SLEZAK, WALTER
Emil and the Detectives
Fanny
SLICK, DANIEL
Down In the Valley
SLICK, GRACE
Kent State
SLICKERS
Harder They Come
SLOANE, EVERETT
Citizen Kane
High Tor
Medea
SLOOPYS
Doctor Goldfoot and the Girl
Bombs
SLY AND ROBBIE
Good to Go
SLY & FAMILY STONE
Woodstock
SMALL, MARYA
Grease
SMALL, MICHAEL
Ballyhoo
Bright Lights, Big City
Klute
Sporting Club
SMALL, NEVA
Golden Land
Henry, Sweet Henry
SMALLENS, ALEXANDER
Babes In Toyland
Porgy and Bess
SMALLS, CHARLIE
Wiz
SMART, BOB
State Fair
SMARTT, MICHAEL
Nefertiti
SMEATON, BRUCE
Iceman
SMILEY, MICK
Ghostbusters
SMITH, ALEXIS
Follies
Hollywood Canteen
Platinum
Sondheim: A Musical Tribute
SMITH, ANDREW
Porgy and Bess
SMITH, BESSIE
Angel Heart
Lucky Lady
SMITH, BOB
It's Howdy Doody Time
World (Original Cast Starring
Howdy Doody)
SMITH, CHARLES
Light of Day
Three Little Girls In Blue
SMITH, CLIVE
Liquid Sky
SMITH, DEREK
Hannah and Her Sisters

814

SMITH, ELLEN
Wild Rovers
SMITH, GLORIA
By the Beautiful Sea
SMITH, GREGG
Blue Monday
Rise and Fall of the Third Reich
SMITH, GWEN
Billy Jack
SMITH, HAL
Happy Prince
SMITH, HOWARD K.
ABC Scope
SMITH, HOWLETT
Me and Bessie
SMITH, IAN
Hot Rock
SMITH, JABBO
One Mo' Time
SMITH, JACK
An Hour with Irving Berlin
On Moonlight Bay
SMITH, JENNY
Sophie
SMITH, JIMMY
Dance to the Music of Irving
Berlin
Get Yourself a College Girl
SMITH, JOHNNY
Flower Drum Song
SMITH, KATE
America Sings
Proudly They Came
Show Biz (From Vaude to Video)
SMITH, KELLY
Hey Boy, Hey Girl
Kiss Me Kate
South Pacific
SMITH, KENNETH
Down In the Valley
SMITH, LORING
Gay Life
Hello Dolly!
Texas Li'l Darlin'
SMITH, LORRAINE
Gypsy
SMITH, LUCILLE
Music Man
SMITH, MAGGIE
Much Ado About Nothing
New Faces of 1956
Oh What a Lovely War
Share My Lettuce
SMITH, MICHAEL GLENN
Celebration
Philemon
SMITH, MIKE (Dave Clark Five)
Having a Wild Weekend
SMITH, MIKE
Evita
SMITH, MILDRED
Beggar's Holiday
SMITH, MURIEL
Carmen Jones
Crowning Experience
South Pacific
SMITH, NORWOOD
Night In Venice
SMITH, O.C.
Shaft's Big Score
SMITH, OSBORNE
Irma La Douce
SMITH, PATTI
Sixteen Candles
Times Square
SMITH, PAUL J.
Cinderella
Living Desert
Nikki, Wild Dog of the North
Perri
Pinocchio
Pollyanna
Popeye
Secrets of Life
Snow White and the Seven
Dwarfs
Uncle Remus
Vanishing Prairie

Walt Disney's True Life
Adventures
Westward Ho, the Wagons
SMITH, PAUL
Carnival
Let No Man Write My Epitaph
Music Man
SMITH, PREACHER
Rock Baby Rock It
SMITH, PRESTON
Cobra
Cocktail
SMITH, REX
Pirates of Penzance
SMITH, ROBERT B.
Sweethearts
SMITH, RUFUS
Annie Get Your Gun
Paint Your Wagon
SMITH, RUSSELL
Honky-Tonk Freeway
SMITH, SALLY
Aspects of Love
Roar of the Greasepaint - The
Smell of the Crowd
SMITH, SAMMY
How Now, Dow Jones
How to Succeed In Business
Without Really Trying
Wish You Were Here
SMITH, SCOTT
Among Friends - Waa-Mu Show
of 1960
SMITH, SHEILA
Hans Brinker
Sugar
Taking My Turn
SMITH, STEPHEN DOYLE
Happening
SMITH, TED
Hiding Place
Time to Run
SMITH, TRUMAN
Kean
SMITH, TUCKER
Anyone Can Whistle
West Side Story
SMITH, WILLIE "THE LION"
Jazz Dance
SMITHEREENS
Burglar
Dangerously Close
I Was a Teenage Zombie
Under the Boardwalk
SMITHS
Pretty In Pink
SMOTHERMAN, MICHAEL
Always
SMOTHERS, TOM
Goin' Back to Indiana
SMOTHERS BROTHERS
Magic Moments from the
Tonight Show
Smothers Brothers Hour
Smothers Brothers Show - Tour
De Farce of American History
SMYRL, DAVID LANGSTON
Working
SMYTH, PATTY
Caddyshack II
SNAKES
Heart of Dixie
SNEED, GARY
Lovers
Mixed Doubles / Below the Belt
SNOW, HANK
Last Picture Show
Movin' On
SNOW, HARRY
Carousel
King and I
Once Upon a Mattress
SNOW, MARK
Jake Speed
Skateboard
SNOW, NORMAN
Cradle Will Rock
SNOW, PHOEBE
Rude Awakening

SNOWDEN, ERIC
Christmas Carol
SNYDER, CINDY
Ulysses - The Greek Suite
SNYDER, E.
Time to Sing
SOBOLOFF, ARNOLD
Anyone Can Whistle
Cyrano
Sweet Charity
SOEUR SOURIRE
Singing Nun
SOFAER, ABRAHAM
Quo Vadis?
SOKOLOFF, ALAN
Pins and Needles
SOKOLOFF, ALEXANDER
Christy
SOKOLOSKY, BRANDON
Papa Was a Preacher
SOLES, PAUL
Rudolph the Red-Nosed
Reindeer
SOLES, R.J.
Rock 'N' Roll High School
SOLLEY, MARVIN
Hark!
One Way Ticket to Broadway
SOLLY, BILLY
Boy Meets Boy
Great American Backstage
Musical
SOLOFF, LEW
Insignificance
SOLOMON, HOWIE
Arnold's Wrecking Co.
SOLTIS, LAURA
Jerry's Girls
SOLTZER, DAVID
Among Friends - Waa-Mu Show
of 1960
SOMERS, VIRGINIA
Plain and Fancy
SOMERSET ORCHESTRA
South Pacific
SOMERVILLE, PHYLLIS
Over Here!
SOMETHING HAPPENS
Courier
SOMMER, BERT
Hot Parts
SOMMER, HANS
Ballet Music from MGM
Musicals
Everything I Have Is Yours
Lili
SOMMER, KATHY
Romance / Romance
SOMMERS, JOANIE
Lively Set
Mouse on the Mayflower
On the Flip Side
SONDHEIM, STEPHEN
American Musical Theater
Anyone Can Whistle
Candide
Company
Do I Hear a Waltz?
Follies
Funny Thing Happened on the
Way to the Forum
Gypsy
Into the Woods
Little Night Music
Mad Show
Marry Me a Little
Merrily We Roll Along
Pacific Overtures
Reds
Side By Side By Sondheim
Sondheim
Sondheim: A Musical Tribute
Stavisky
Stephen Sondheim Evening
Sunday In the Park with George
Sweeney Todd (The Demon
Barber of Fleet Street)
West Side Story
SONG SPINNERS
Tom Sawyer

SONIC YOUTH
Lovedolls Superstar
Pump Up the Volume
SONNY AND CHER
Buster
Good Times
Wild on the Beach
SONS OF THE PIONEERS
Johnny Appleseed
Rio Grande
Themes of TV's Greatest
Westerns
Wyatt Earp, Cheyenne and
Other TV Favorites
SOO, JACK
Flower Drum Song
SOPER, GAY
Betjemania
Billy
Canterbury Tales
I and Albert
SORENSON, ARTHUR
Five After Eight
SORVINO, PAUL
Baker's Wife
Carmelina
SOSNIK, HARRY
Ethel Merman
Judy at the Palace
Let's Face It
Memorable Moments In
Musical Comedy
Mexican Hayride
Roberta
SOTHERN, ANN
Cut! Out-Takes from
Hollywood's Greatest
Musicals
Ladies of Burlesque
Lady In the Dark
Nancy Goes to Rio
Rodgers and Hart In Hollywood
Words and Music
SOUL ASYLUM
Lost Angels
SOUL CHILDREN
Wattstax (the Living Word)
SOUL II
Black Rain
SOUL, WALTER, SINGERS
South Pacific
SOULE, OLAN
Happy Prince
SOULES, DALE
Magic Show
SOUND STAGE CALLIOPE BAND
Carnival
SOUND STAGE ORCHESTRA
Flower Drum Song
SOUNDGARDEN
Lost Angels
Pump Up the Volume
SOUNDS OF HARLEY
Hard Ride
SOUNDS OF SUNSHINE
Heroes
SOUNDS SPECTACULAR
Great New Motion Picture
Themes
SOURCE
Bullet for a Pretty Boy
SOUSA, JOHN PHILIP
Stars and Stripes Forever
SOUSTER, TIM
Hitch-Hikers Guide to the
Galaxy
SOUTH, HARRY
Miss Ginger Rogers
SOUTH, JOE
Cometogether
SOUTHER, J.D.
About Last Night
Always
Permanent Record
Urban Cowboy
SOUTHERN PACIFIC
Pink Cadillac
Police Academy IV - Citizens on
Patrol

SOUTHERN, JERI
Fire Down Below
SOUTHGATE, WILLIAM
Utu
SOUTHSIDE JOHNNY
Karate Kid II
Tuff Turf
SPACEK, SISSY
Coal Miner's Daughter
SPAGNOLO, GIANNA
Moses the Lawgiver
SPALL, TIMOTHY
Gothic
SPANG, LAURETTE
Battlestar Galactica
SPANGLER, DAVID
Nefertiti
SPANIELS
American Hot Wax
SPANO, VINCENT
Black Stallion Returns
SPARACINO, SPUTZY, AND DELILAH
Day of the Dead
SPARKLERS
On Moonlight Bay
SPARKS, RANDY
Advance to the Rear
Angel Unchained
Hang Your Hat on the Wind
Singing Nun
SPARKS
Fright Night
Get Crazy
Rad
SPEAR, BERNARD
Little Me
Man of La Mancha
Music Man
SPEAR, DAVID
Fear No Evil
Festival
SPEARMAN, RAWN
House of Flowers
SPEARS, ERIC
Chaplin Revue
SPECIALS
Dance Craze
SPECT, DONALD
Kingsmill Suite
SPECTOR, RONNIE
Just One of the Guys
SPECTRE GENERAL
Transformers - The Movie
SPECTRUM
Bliss of Mrs. Blossom
SPEERS, JAN
Leave It to Jane
SPEKTOR, MIRA
Housewives' Cantata
SPENCE, JOHNNY
Elizabeth Taylor In London
Marry Me, Marry Me
SPENCE, JUDSON
Wonder Years
SPENCE, SAM
Music from National Football League Films
SPENCER, BOB
Sing Muse!
SPENCER, CHRISTINE
Ballad for Bimshire
Zulu and the Zayda
SPENCER, HERB
Island In the Sky
SPENCER, KENNETH
Show Boat
SPIELMAN, FRED
Stingiest Man In Town
Tom Thumb
SPIER, WILLIAM
Sorry, Wrong Number
SPINETTI, VICTOR
Taming of the Shrew
SPINNERS
Car Wash
Inside Moves
Jo Jo Dancer, Your Life Is Calling

Spaceballs
Twins
SPIRO, BERNIE
Christy
SPLASH
Speed Zone
SPOLIANSKY, MISCHA
Music for Films
Saint Joan
SPRIGGS, ELIZABETH
Every Good Boy Deserves Favor
SPRINGER, PHILIP
Tell Me That You Love Me, Junie Moon
SPRINGFIELD, DUSTY
Buster
Casino Royale
Corrupt Ones
Growing Pains
Paris Was Made for Lovers
Peking Medallion
Stunt Man
Sweet Ride
SPRINGFIELD, RICK
Hard to Hold
Iron Eagle II
Private School
SPRINGSTEEN, BRUCE
Ruthless People
SPUNKADELIC
Teenage Mutant Ninja Turtles
SQUALLS
Athens, Ga. - Inside / Out
SQUEEZE
Brimstone and Treacle
SQUIER, BILLY
Fast Times at Ridgemont High
Metropolis
St. Elmo's Fire
ST. DARR, DEBORAH
Candide
ST. JOHN, DICK AND SANDY
Truth of Truths
ST. JOHN, HELEN
Flashdance
Superman III
ST. JOHN, JILL
Four Television Musicals
ST. JOHN, HOWARD
Gift of the Magi
Li'l Abner
ST. LOUIS, LOUIS
Grease
ST. PAUL'S BOYS CHOIR
Leonard Bernstein and the New York Philharmonic on Christmas Day
ST. REGIS
Karate Kid
STABILE, DICK
Artists and Models
Pardners
Stooge
STACK, LENNY
C.C. and Company
STACY, JESS
Great Gatsby
STADLEN, LEWIS J.
Candide
Minnie's Boys
STAFFORD, JIM
Any Which Way You Can
STAFFORD, JO
Guys and Dolls
Kiss Me Kate
Last Picture Show
Oh Captain!
South Pacific
STAFFORD, JOSEPH
Peter Pan
STAFFORD, RONALD
Magic Show
STAFFORD, TERRY
Born Losers
Doctor Goldfoot and the Girl Bombs
Wild Wheels
STAHNS, STEVEN
Sunnyside

STAHUBER, ADOLF
Odessa File
STAIGER, LIBI
By the Beautiful Sea
Most Happy Fella
Sophie
STAINTON, CHRIS
Joe Cocker: Mad Dogs and Englishmen
STALLION
Night of the Comet
STALLONE, FRANK
Over the Top
Paradise Alley
Rambo: First Blood - Part II
Rocky III
Staying Alive
STALLONE, SYLVESTER
Paradise Alley
Rhinestone
STAMFORD, JOHN
Girl In Pink Tights
STANDELLS
Get Yourself a College Girl
Riot on Sunset Strip
STANDLEY, JOHNNY
Beg, Borrow Or Steal
STANDWELLS
Showcase Album, 1967
STANFORD AGENCY
Side By Side 75
STANFORD, DOC
Johnny Concho
STANG, ARNOLD
Alakazam the Great
Top Cat
Wonderful World of the Brothers Grimm
STANLEY, GORDON
Joseph and the Amazing Technicolor Dreamcoat
STANLEY, HAL
Pied Piper of Hamelin
STANLEY, HELEN
Cinderella
STANLEY, IVOR
South Pacific
STANLEY, PAT
Fiorello!
Goldilocks
STANLEY, RALPH
Sing Muse!
STANLEY, ROBERT
This Is the Army
STANLOCH
A-5,6,7,8
STANNARD, PETER
Lola Montez
STANTON, MICHAEL
Another 48 Hours
STANTON, OLIVE
Cradle Will Rock
STANTON, PATRICIA SMITH
Bathrooms Are Coming
STANWAY, BRONWEN
Nunsense
STANWYCK, BARBARA
Hollywood Canteen
Ladies of Burlesque
STAPLE SINGERS
Landlord
Last Waltz
Let's Do It Again
Soul to Soul
Wattstax (the Living Word)
STAPLES, MAVIS
Piece of the Action
Wildcats
STAPLETON, CYRIL
Big Hits from Broadway
Gigi
King and I
STAPLETON, JEAN
All In the Family
All In the Family - 2nd Album
Bells Are Ringing
Damn Yankees
Funny Girl
Juno

STAPLETON, MAUREEN
Airport
Bye Bye Birdie
Rose Tattoo
STAPLEY, DIANE
Bistro Car
Jubalay
STARGARD
Sgt. Pepper's Lonely Hearts Club Band
STARK, FREDERICK
Grand Canyon Suite
STARK, SALLY
Dames at Sea
STARKIE, MARTIN
Canterbury Tales
STAROBIN, MICHAEL
In Trousers
Mystery of Edwin Drood
STARR, BRENDA K.
License to Drive
She's Out of Control
STARR, EDWIN
Hell Up In Harlem
STARR, PAT
Anne of Green Gables
STARR, RANDY
Clambake
Double Trouble
Frankie and Johnny
Paradise, Hawaiian Style
Roustabout
Spinout
STARR, RINGO
Give My Regards to Broad Street
Last Waltz
Magic Christian
Tommy
STARS OF FAITH
Black Nativity
STARS OF HEAVEN
Planes, Trains, and Automobiles
STARS ON 45
Bad Guys
STARSHIP
Cocktail
Youngblood
STASERA, MEGLIO
Pink Panther
STATLER, RUDOLPH
Funny Girl
My Fair Lady
Songs from Hello, Dolly! and Funny Girl
STATLER BROTHERS
Smokey and the Bandit II
STATON, MERRILL
Broadway Chorus Call
David Merrick Presents Hits from His Broadway Hits
Here's Love
Show Boat
Sounds Broadway! Sounds Hollywood! Sounds Great!
Student Prince
STATUS QUO
All This and World War II
STEARNS, MICHAEL
Chronos
STEBER, ELEANOR
New Moon
Vanessa
STECK, GENE
Oliver!
STECKO, JOSEPH
Leave It to Jane
Secret Life of Walter Mitty
STEEL PULSE
Do the Right Thing
Urgh - A Music War
STEEL, BRIAN
Captain Jinks of the Horse Marines
STEEL, JOHN
Ziegfeld Follies of 1919
STEELE, ERIC
Porgy and Bess

STEELE, JEUETTA
Gospel at Colonus
STEELE, PATTI
Music Man
STEELE, SUZANNE
La Vie Parisienne
STEELE, TOMMY
Cinderella
Finian's Rainbow
Half a Sixpence
Hans Andersen
Happiest Millionaire
Official Grammy Awards
Archive Collection
Singin' In the Rain
STEELE, WES
Tarot
STEELY DAN
Air America
FM
Mask
STEER, GEOFF
Seven Brides for Seven
Brothers
STEFFE, EDWIN
Anya
Four Television Musicals
Most Happy Fella
STEIGER, J.
Solomon King
STEIGER, ROD
Court Martial of Billy Mitchell
Longest Day
Oklahoma
Pawnbroker
Showcase Album, 1967
W.C. Fields and Me
STEIMANN, MAX
Chaliapin As Boris
STEIN, GERTRUDE
Four Saints in Three Acts
Gertrude Stein's First Reader
In Circles
Mother of All of Us
STEIN, HERMAN
Themes from Classic Science
Fiction, Fantasy and Horror
Films
Themes from Horror Movies
STEIN, JULIAN
Anything Goes
Fantasticks
Half Past Wednesday
Saga of the Dingbat
STEIN, RONALD
Getting Straight
Man Called Dagger
Of Love and Desire
Psych-Out
STEINBERG, BEN
Peter Pan
STEINBERG, DIANNE
Sgt. Pepper's Lonely Hearts
Club Band
STEINBERG, WILLIAM
My Fair Lady
STEINER, FRED
City Backgrounds
Down to the Sea In Ships
Fantasy - Space
Impact
King Kong
Star Trek
Twilight Zone
STEINER, JOHN
Marat (De) Sade
STEINER, MAX
Adventures of Don Juan
Aisle Seat
Band of Angels
Beyond the Forest
Big Sleep
Bird of Paradise
Caine Mutiny
Captain Blood: Classic Film
Scores for Errol Flynn
Casablanca: Classic Film
Scores for Humphrey Bogart
Classic Film Scores for Bette
Davis
Come Next Spring

Death of a Scoundrel
50 Years of Film
Gay Divorcee
Gone with the Wind
Great Music from the Movies
Helen of Troy
John Paul Jones
King Kong
Love Themes from Motion
Pictures
Marjorie Morningstar
Max Steiner - Four Classic Film
Scores
Max Steiner - Great Love
Themes from Motion
Pictures
Max Steiner: Memories
Max Steiner: Music for
Westerns
Max Steiner Revisited
Max Steiner - The Magic of
Max Steiner: The RKO Years
(1932-1935)
Max Steiner: The Warner Years
Mildred Pierce (And Other
Melodramatic Ladies)
Music By Max Steiner
Music for Westerns
Music from Hollywood
Now, Voyager: The Classic Film
Scores of Max Steiner
Parrish
Rome Adventure
Searchers
Since You Went Away
Spectacular World of Classic
Film Scores
Star Is Born
Steiner Touch
Theme Music from Great
Motion Picture Scores
This Is Cinerama
STEINMAN, JIM
Footloose
STEIRLING, RANDY
Naked Angels
STELL, JOHN
One Mo' Time
STELLARI, GIAN
Great Songs from Italian Films
STEPHENS, GARN
Grease
Mrs. Brown, You've Got a
Lovely Daughter
STEPHENS, MADGE
Camelot
STEPHENS, ROBERT
Much Ado About Nothing
Romeo and Juliet
STEPHENSON, VAN
Secret Admirer
Wild Life
STEPLIGHT, RANDALL
Carmen Jones
STEPPENWOLF
Candy
Easy Rider
Legal Eagles
Mask
Satisfaction
STERLING, PHILLIP
Evening with Richard Nixon
STERN, DICK
Man Named Brown
STERN, EMIL
Marry Me, Marry Me
STERN, ERIC
Legs Diamond
STERN, ISAAC
Midsummer Night's Sex
Comedy
STERNBACH, JERRY
A-5,6,7,8
STERNBERG, ANN
Gertrude Stein's First Reader
STERNER, STEVE
Beauty and the Beast
Lovers
STERNHAGEN, FRANCES
Angel
STETSASONIC
Lean on Me

STEVEN, TONY
Sondheim: A Musical Tribute
STEVENS, CARL
Hit Motion Picture Themes
STEVENS, CAT
Stardust
STEVENS, CONNIE
Cole Porter In Paris
Hawaiian Eye
Littlest Angel
Palm Springs Weekend
Rowan and Martin's Laugh-In
STEVENS, CRAIG
Here's Love
STEVENS, DODIE
Alakazam the Great
STEVENS, FRAN
How Now, Dow Jones
STEVENS, JOEL
Second Shepherd's Play
STEVENS, KAY
Playgirls
STEVENS, LEITH
Christmas Carol
Destination Moon
Dick Powell Presents (Music
from the Original Soundtrack
of Four Star Productions)
Doctor Strangelove (And Other
Great Movie Themes)
Exploring the Unknown
Five Pennies
Gene Krupa Story
Hell to Eternity
Interns
James Dean Story
New Kind of Love
Private Hell 36
War of the Worlds
Wild One
STEVENS, LESLIE
La Cage Aux Folles
STEVENS, MARTI
High Spirits
Oh Kay!
STEVENS, MIKE
Cycle Savages
STEVENS, MORTON
Hawaii Five-O
Man from U.N.C.L.E.
Mister Wonderful
Porgy and Bess
Slapstick of Another Kind
STEVENS, NAPUA
13 Daughters
STEVENS, PAULINE
Porgy and Bess
STEVENS, RAY
Cannonball Run
STEVENS, RISË
Carnegie Hall
Chocolate Soldier
Journey Back to Oz
King and I
Lady In the Dark
Little Women
Met Stars on Broadway
Porgy and Bess
Show Boat
STEVENS, ROBERT T.
Point of Order
STEVENS, SALLY
Fox
Hammersmith Is Out
Secret of N.I.M.H.
Washington Behind Closed
Doors
STEVENS, SHADOE
Airplane!
STEVENS, TRUDY
White Christmas
STEVENSON, ADLAI
Three Billion Millionaires
STEVENSON, BOB
On the Brighter Side
STEVENSON, SCOTT
Good News
STEWARD, RON
Believers

**STEWART-WILLIAMS AND
COMPANY**
Porgy and Bess
STEWART, CAROL
Three Little Girls In Blue
STEWART, CHARLOTTE
Eraserhead
STEWART, DANNY
From Here to Eternity
STEWART, DONALD
Gentlemen Prefer Blondes
STEWART, DOUG
Saturday's Warrior
Threads of Glory
STEWART, IAN
Mahoney's Last Stand
STEWART, JAMES
Born to Dance
Man Who Shot Liberty Valence
Proudly They Came
Shenandoah
That's Entertainment
Two Rode Together
STEWART, JERMAINE
Perfect
She-Devil
STEWART, JOHN
Crystal Heart
Hot September
Smokey and the Bandit III
STEWART, JOHNNY
High Button Shoes
STEWART, LARRY
Paper Moon
STEWART, LEON
Festival
STEWART, MARTHA
Landlord
STEWART, MELVIN
Simply Heavenly
STEWART, MICHAEL
Barnum
European Holiday
Gigi
I Love My Wife
Mardi Gras
Oklahoma
Themes from Hollywood
**STEWART, MIKE, AND THE
STABLE HANDS**
Mister Ed - Straight from the
Heart
STEWART, NICODEMUS
Uncle Remus
STEWART, PATRICK
Every Good Boy Deserves Favor
STEWART, PAULA
Wildcat
STEWART, PRINCESS
Black Nativity
STEWART, REX
Redhead
STEWART, ROBB
Chrysanthemum
STEWART, ROD
All This and World War II
Innerspace
Night Shift
Tommy
STEWART, SANDY
Go Johnny Go!
Mr. President
Unsinkable Molly Brown
White Nights
STEWART, SCOTT
Sugar Babies
STEWART, STEVE
In Search of
STEWART, THOMAS
Johnny Johnson
STICKNEY, DOROTHY
Cinderella
STICKNEY, MARTHA
Among Friends - Waa-Mu Show
of 1960
STIERS, DAVID OGDEN
Magic Show

817

STILLER, JERRY
Sex Life of Primate (And Other Bits of Gossip)
STILLMAN, AL
Julie and Carol at Carnegie Hall
STILLROCK
Magic Garden of Stanley Sweetheart
STING
Brimstone and Treacle
Party Party
STIRLING, PETER LEE
Goodbye Gemini
STITES, JULANE
Promises, Promises
STITT, DON
Do Black Patent Leather Shoes Really Reflect Up?
STOCK, NIGEL
Goodbye Mr. Chips
STOCKHOLM RADIO ORCHESTRA
European Holiday
STOCKHOLM STRING ORCHESTRA
Best of Victor Herbert
STOCKWELL, HARRY
Snow White and the Seven Dwarfs
STOKER, GORDON
Christmas to Elvis
STOKES, BARRY
Betjemania
STOKES, ED
Casablanca
Don Ameche
STOKES, LEONARD
Annie Get Your Gun
H.M.S. Pinafore
Oklahoma
STOKES, SIMON
Outlaw Riders
STOKMAN, ABRAHAM
Kurt Weill Cabaret
STOKOWSKI, LEOPOLD
Fantasia
Plow That Broke the Plains
River
STOLL, GEORGE
Anything Goes
Athena
Bing's Hollywood
Cabin In the Sky
For the First Time
Girl Crazy
Hit the Deck
I Love Melvin
In the Good Old Summertime
Judy at the Palace
Jumbo
Kissing Bandit
Meet Me In St. Louis
Mississippi
Nancy Goes to Rio
Rose Marie
Two Weeks with Love
Wizard of Oz
STOLLER, MIKE
Elvis (NBC-TV Special)
Fun In Acapulco
Girls! Girls! Girls!
Jailhouse Rock
King Creole
Loving You
Roustabout
Tickle Me
STOLOFF, MORRIS
Al Jolson Story Soundtrack: Outtakes and Alternate Takes
Cowboy
Doctor Strangelove (And Other Great Movie Themes)
Eddy Duchin Story
Fanny
Finian's Rainbow
Girl Crazy
Guys and Dolls
Jeanne Eagles
Jolson Sings Again
Kiss Me Kate

Miss Sadie Thompson
Naked City
Pal Joey
Picnic
Reprise Repertory Theater
Rita Hayworth
Salome
Song Without End
Soundtracks, Voices and Themes from Great Movies
South Pacific
Sunny Side of the Street
Three for the Show
STOLZ, ROBERT
Merry Widow
White Horse Inn
STONE, CHRISTOPHER L.
Prison
STONE, ELLY
Jacques Brel Is Alive and Well and Living In Paris
O Marry Me
STONE, EZRA
This Is the Army
STONE, JON
Sesame Street
STONE, KIRBY, FOUR
My Fairfax Lady
Parade of Show Stoppers
STONE, LEONARD
Redhead
STONE, LEW
Oklahoma
STONE, MARK
Cindy
STONE, OLIVER
Midnight Express
STONE, PADDY
Joyce Grenfell Requests the Pleasure
STONE, SID
Sugar Babies
STONE, SLY
Burglar
Soul Man
STONE, T.J.
Deep Throat Part II
STONE, WILSON
Take It from Here
STONEBAUER, SAM
Different Times
STONEHAM, HARRY, TRIO
Evening with Peter Sellers
STONEHILL, RANDY
Time to Run
STOPPARD, TOM
Every Good Boy Deserves Favor
STORCH, LARRY
Littlest Revue
STORDAHL, AXEL
Bing's Hollywood
By the Light of the Silvery Moon
Frank Sinatra Sings George Gershwin
Road to Bali
Tea for Two
Young at Heart
STORM, WAYNE
Last of the American Hoboes
STORRS, DAVID
Invaders from Mars
STORY, TIM
Ichabod (the Legend of Sleepy Hollow)
STORYBOOK
Psych-Out
STOSKA, POLYNA
Street Scene
STOTHART, HERBERT
Film Music of Herbert Stothart
Great Ziegfeld
Naughty Marietta
Rogue Song
Rose Marie
Unfinished Dance
Wizard of Oz
Ziegfeld Girl
STOTT, WALLY
Great American Show Tunes

STOUFFVILLE GRIT
B.S. I Love You
STOUT, JEAN
Young Girls of Rochefort
STRACHAN, MICHAELA
Seven Brides for Seven Brothers
STRADIVARI STRINGS
Exodus
Merry Widow
Music from the Films
Show Boat
STRAIGHT, WILLARD
Athenian Touch
STRAIGIS, ROY
Devil In Miss Jones
STRAM, HENRY
Cradle Will Rock
STRANEY, PAUL
Zorba
STRANGE THINGS
John and Mary
STRANGE, BILLY
Bunny O'Hare
De Sade
Movin' with Nancy
STRANGLERS
Permanent Record
STRATHAM, KEITH
Share My Lettuce
STRATTA, ETTORE
Music from the Galaxies
STRATTON, CHESTER
Connecticut Yankee
STRAUS, OSCAR
Chocolate Soldier
Love Me Tonight
STRAUSS, EDWARD
Anything Goes
Me Nobody Knows
STRAUSS, JOHANN
Die Fledermaus
Great Waltz
Night In Venice
Oh, Rosalinda!
2001: A Space Odyssey
STRAUSS, RICHARD
2001: A Space Odyssey
STRAVINSKY, IGOR
Flood
STRAW, JACK
Pajama Game
STRAWBERRY ALARM CLOCK
Beyond the Valley of the Dolls
Psych-Out
STRAY CATS
Sixteen Candles
STREEP, MERYL
Silkwood
Velveteen Rabbit
STREET, DANNY
Lassiter
STREET, DAVID
State Fair
STREISAND, BARBRA
Barbra Streisand...And Other Musical Instruments
Broadway Babies
Broadway Magic
Broadway Musicals
Color Me Barbra
Eyes of Laura Mars
50 Years of Film
Filmusic Scene
Funny Girl
Funny Lady
Harold Sings Arlen
Happening In Central Park
Hello Dolly!
I Can Get It for You Wholesale
Judy Garland
Magic of Musical Comedy
Main Event
My Name Is Barbra
Nuts
On a Clear Day You Can See Forever
Owl and the Pussycat
Parade of Show Stoppers
Pins and Needles

Star Is Born
Way We Were
Yentl
STRICK, LINDA
Assault of the Killer Bimbos
STRICKLER, JERRY
Mr. President
STRIKE, LIZA
Friends
STRINE, HELEN
Regina
STRITCH, ELAINE
Ben Bagley's Oscar Hammerstein Revisited
Broadway Magic
Company
Follies
Goldilocks
Make Mine Manhattan
On Your Toes
Pal Joey
Rodgers and Hart Revisited
Sail Away
Song and Dance
STRODE, WOODY
Black Stallion Returns
STROKA, JERRY
Godspell
STRONG, BARRETT
Cooley High
Flamingo Kid
STRONG, MICHAEL
After the Fall
STRONG, STEVE
Bathrooms Are Coming
STROUD, DON
Angel Unchained
STROUD, GREGORY
Sally
STROUSE, CHARLES
All American
Annie
Applause
Bonnie and Clyde
Bring Back Birdie
Bye Bye Birdie
Dance a Little Closer
Flowers for Algernon
Golden Boy
I and Albert
It's a Bird, It's a Plane, It's Superman
Mayor
Night They Raided Minsky's
Nightingale
Shoestring Revue '57
Shoestring Revues
STROUT, DICK
Now You See Him, Now You Don't
STRUMMER, JOE
Permanent Record
Straight to Hell
Walker
Wired
STRUNK, JUD
Last of the Ski Bums
STUART, ALICE
Fritz the Cat
STUART, CHAD
Three In the Attic
STUART, EDDIE
James Dean Story
STUART, GLORIA
Hooray for Hollywood
STUART, ISOBEL
Ambassador
STUART, JAY
All About Life
STUARTI, ENZO
Music and Lyrics By Cole Porter
Night In Venice
STUBBLEFIELD AND HALL
Best of the Best
STUBBS, LEVI
Little Shop of Horrors
STUBBS, UNA
Cowardly Custard

STUDIO LONDON
ORCHESTRA
James Bond
STUDIO 78
FM
Thank God It's Friday
STUNNERS
Jetsons: The Movie
STUTTGART SCHOLA
CANTORUM
2001: A Space Odyssey
STYLE COUNCIL
Absolute Beginners
Vision Quest
STYLER, ALAN
Mikado
STYNE, JULE
Anchors Aweigh
Bells Are Ringing
Dangerous Christmas of Red
Riding Hood
Darling of the Day
Do Re Mi
Fade Out Fade In
Funny Girl
Gentlemen Prefer Blondes
Gypsy
Hallelujah, Baby!
Hazel Flagg
High Button Shoes
It Happened In Brooklyn
Living It Up
Look to the Lilies
Lorelei
Meet Me After the Show
One Night Stand
Peter Pan
Prettybelle
Ruggles of Red Gap
Say Darling
Starlift
Subways Are for Sleeping
Sugar
Two on the Aisle
What a Way to Go!
Words and Music
STYNER, JERRY
Beach Blanket Bingo
Bikini Beach
Cycle Savages
Devil's Eight
Doctor Goldfoot and the Girl
Bombs
Golden Breed
How to Stuff a Wild Bikini
Killers Three
Pajama Party
Savage Seven
Sidehackers
Thunder Alley
STYX
Roadie
SU, CONG
Last Emperor
SUAREZ, MIGUEL
My Fair Lady
SUBRAMANIAN, L.
Salaam Bombay!
SUDWESTFUNK
ORCHESTRA
2001: A Space Odyssey
SUE ANN
Beverly Hills Cop II
SUES, ALAN
Rowan and Martin's Laugh-In
SUFFIN, JORDAN
Shenandoah
SUGAR GLAZE
Best of Burlesque
SUGIHARA, WILLIAM
Fly Blackbird
SUICIDAL TENDENCIES
Repo Man
SUKMAN, HARRY
Around the World, Under the
Sea
Eddy Duchin Story
For Whom the Bell Tolls
If He Hollers, Let Him Go
Singing Nun
Song Without End

SULLET, KEN
Stan Freberg Shows
SULLIVAN, ARTHUR
Evening with W.S. Gilbert
Mikado
Pirates of Penzance
SULLIVAN, BARRY
Caine Mutiny Court Martial
SULLIVAN, BRIAN
Street Scene
SULLIVAN, ED
Age of Television
SULLIVAN, ED, ALL STAR
CAST
Annie Get Your Gun
Brigadoon
Carousel
Finian's Rainbow
King and I
Kiss Me Kate
My Fair Lady
Oklahoma
Pal Joey
Porgy and Bess
Roberta
Show Boat
South Pacific
SULLIVAN, ERIN
Boy Named Charlie Brown
SULLIVAN, FRANK
Man In the Moon
SULLIVAN, JO
Chocolate Soldier
Most Happy Fella
Threepenny Opera
SULLIVAN, LEE
Brigadoon
SULLIVAN, PETER
Pirate Movie
SUMAC, YMA
Flahooley
SUMMER SAXOPHONES
Born Losers
SUMMER, DONNA
Deep
Fast Times at Ridgemont High
Flashdance
Looking for Mr. Goodbar
Thank God It's Friday
SUMMER, HENRY LEE
Iron Eagle II
Twins
SUMMERHAYS, JANE
Sugar Babies
SUMMERS, ANDY
Band of the Hand
2010
Wild Life
SUMMERS, BOB
Purple People Eater
Teenage Rebellion
SUMMERS, DAVID
Faggot
SUMMERS, ELAINE
In Circles
SUMMERS, LYDIA
Consul
SUMMERS, MICHELLE
Dearest Enemy
SUMNER, J.D.
Elvis In Concert
Elvis: Aloha from Hawaii Via
Satellite
SUNDGAARD, ARNOLD
Down In the Valley
Kittiwake Island
Promised Land
Young Abe Lincoln
SUNDSTROM, ANDY
Quiet Days In Clichy
SUNSET SINGERS
Thoroughly Modern Millie
SUNSET STRINGS
Film Music Italian Style
SUNSHINE GENERATION
Hair
SUPREE, BURTON
Pomegranada

SUPREMES
Girl Groups: The Story of a
Sound
Jumpin' Jack Flash
More American Graffiti
SURF M.C.'S
Under the Boardwalk
SURFERS
Blue Hawaii
Hit Motion Picture Themes
SURVIVOR
Karate Kid
Rocky III
Rocky IV
SUTHERLAND, CLAUDETTE
How to Succeed In Business
Without Really Trying
SUTHERLAND, DONALD
*M*A*S*H*
SUTHERLAND, KEN
Papa Was a Preacher
SUTTON, JUNE
By the Light of the Silvery Moon
SUTTON, SHANE
Jetsons: The Movie
SUTTON, VERN
Postcard from Morocco
SUZUKI, PAT
Broadway Magic
Flower Drum Song
Official Grammy Awards
Archive Collection
SWADOS, ELIZABETH
Doonesbury
Rap Master Ronnie
Runaways
SWALES, ROBERT
High Society
SWAN SILVERTONES
Big Easy
SWANKY MODES
Tapeheads
SWANN, DONALD
At the Drop of a Hat
At the Drop of Another Hat
SWANN, ROBERT
Gone with the Wind
SWANSON, BEE
Christy
SWANSON, GLORIA
Ben Bagley's Oscar
Hammerstein Revisited
Boulevard
Stars of the Silver Screen,
1929-1930
SWAYZE, PATRICK
Dirty Dancing
SWEET INSPIRATIONS
Elvis In Concert
Elvis: Aloha from Hawaii Via
Satellite
Idolmaker
That's the Way It Is
SWEET OBSESSION
Iron Eagle II
SWEET PEACE
Jesus Christ Superstar
SWEET SUE AND HER
SOCIETY SYNCOPATERS
Some Like It Hot
SWEET, JAN
Albert Peckingpaw's Revenge
SWEET, RACHEL
Hairspray
SWEETEN, CLAUDE
Tale of Two Cities
SWEETLAND, LEE
California
New Moon
Student Prince
SWEETLAND, SALLY
Ice Follies
Mikado
Sky's the Limit
SWEIER, VICTOR
Aristocats
SWENSON, INGA
Androcles and the Lion
Baker Street
New Faces of 1956

110 In the Shade
SWENSON, LINDA
Karl Marx
SWENSON, SUSAN
Joyful Noise
SWENSON, SWEN
Little Me
Wildcat
SWIFT, ALLEN
Thousand Miles of Mountains
SWIFT, KAY
Paris '90
SWINBURNE, NORA
Quo Vadis?
SWINFORD, SUSAN
Wedding In Paris
SWINGERS
Swingin' Summer
SWINGERS
Star Struck
SYDNEY, BASIL
Hamlet
Three Worlds of Gulliver
Treasure Island
SYERS, HSU
Pacific Overtures
SYERS, MARK
Evita
SYLVANUS
Angels Die Hard
SYLVESTER
Sylvester
SYLVIA
One Mo' Time
SYLVIAN, DAVID
Merry Christmas, Mr. Lawrence
SYMINGTON, JIM
Body In the Seine
SYMPHONY OF THE AIR
River
SYMS, SYLVIA
Whoop-Up!
SYNERGY
Jupiter Menace
SYREETA
Fast Break
Loving Couples
Night the Lights Went Out In
Georgia
SYSTEM
Beverly Hills Cop
Coming to America
Fatal Beauty
SZARABAJKA, KEITH
Doonesbury
SZELL, GEORGE
Midsummer Night's Sex
Comedy
T-CONNECTION
Bad Boys
TKA
Lean on Me
Modern Girls
T.S.O.L.
Dangerously Close
Suburbia
Return of the Living Dead
Undercover
TABBERT, WILLIAM
Babes In Arms /Jumbo
Evening with Jerome Kern
Fanny
South Pacific
TABORI, GEORGE
Brecht on Brecht
TAJ MAHAL
April Fools
Brothers
Sounder
TAKA, MIIKO
Sayonara
TAKE 6
Do the Right Thing
Growing Pains
Shag
TAKEI, GEORGE
Fly Blackbird
TAKEMITSU, TORU
Ran

TALBOT, IRVING
Greatest Show on Earth
One-Eyed Jacks
TALBOT, NITA
Bundle of Joy
Ladies of Burlesque
TALBOT, SHARON
Housewives' Cantata
TALIAFERRO, MABEL
Bloomer Girl
TALK TALK
Night Shift
TALKING HEADS
King of Comedy
Stop Making Sense
Times Square
TALL BOYS
Return of the Living Dead
TALMADGE, JIM
Best of Broadway 1973
TALMADGE, LAUREL
Best of Broadway 1973
TALVA, GALINA
Call Me Madam
TAMAGNI, ROBERT
Time Changes
TAMBLYN, RUSS
Hit the Deck
Seven Brides for Seven
  Brothers
Tom Thumb
West Side Story
Wonderful World of the
  Brothers Grimm
TAMMY AND THE TULIPS
American Hot Wax
TAMPONI, FRANCO
Bluebeard
TANDY, JESSICA
Glass Menagerie
TANGERINE DREAM
Firestarter
Flashpoint
Legend
Near Dark
Risky Business
Shy People
Sorcerer
Thief
Three O'Clock High
Wavelength
TANNER, STELLA
On the Town
TANNER, TONY
Oliver!
Stop the World - I Want to Get
  Off!!
TARALLO, BARRY
Joseph and the Amazing
  Technicolor Dreamcoat
Summer Dog
TARLOW, FLORENCE
Inner City
Promenade
TARRAGO, RENATA
Deadfall
TARRY TOWN TRIO
How the West Was Won
TARVER, BEN
Man with a Load of Mischief
TASK, MAGGIE
Prettybelle
TASTE OF HONEY
Hitter
TATE, BABY
Blues
TATE, DAVID
Hitch-Hikers Guide to the
  Galaxy
TATE, GRADY
Hot Rock
Silent Partner
TATE, STEPHEN
Jesus Christ Superstar
TATI, JACQUES
My Uncle
Playtime
TATUM, ART
All-Star Salute, the Very Best of
  Gershwin

TATUM, MARIANNE
Barnum
TAUBE, SVEN-BERTIL
I and Albert
TAUBIN, AMY
Doctor Selavy's Magic Theater
TAUPIN, BERNIE
Friends
TAVARES
Saturday Night Fever
TAVERNER, DEREK
Maid of the Mountains
TAXXI
Secret of My Success
Weird Science
TAYLOR, ANDY
American Anthem
Miami Vice II
Tequila Sunrise
TAYLOR, BILLY
Kwamina
Lyrics By Lerner
TAYLOR, BOBBY
Far Out Man
TAYLOR, CHRIS
Breakin'
TAYLOR, CLARICE
Wiz
TAYLOR, DELORES
Trial of Billy Jack
TAYLOR, ELIZABETH
Elizabeth Taylor In London
50 Years of Film
James Dean Story
Little Night Music
Taming of the Shrew
West Side Story
Who's Afraid of Virginia Woolf?
TAYLOR, HOLLAND
Colette
TAYLOR, IRVING
Pied Piper of Hamelin
TAYLOR, JAMES
FM
Ghostbusters II
TAYLOR, JOHNNIE
Wattstax (the Living Word)
TAYLOR, JOHN
Charlie Girl
9½ Weeks
TAYLOR, LAURETTE
Peg O' My Heart
TAYLOR, LES
America, Why I Love Her
TAYLOR, LINDA
Stormy Monday
TAYLOR, MIKE
Sunshine
TAYLOR, NEILSON
Annie Get Your Gun
TAYLOR, RENEE
Bunch
Producers
TAYLOR, ROBERT
Quo Vadis?
TAYLOR, ROBIN
Festival
TAYLOR, RON
Little Shop of Horrors
TAYLOR, TERRY
Creepers
TCHAIKOVSKY, PYOTR
  ILYICH
Loves of Isadora
Nutcracker
Romeo and Juliet
Sleeping Beauty
TCHERINA, LUDMILLA
Oh, Rosalinda!
TE KANAWA, KIRI
Citizen Kane: The Classic Film
  Scores of Bernard Herrmann
Kiri Sings Gershwin
My Fair Lady
Room with a View
South Pacific
TEAGUE, ANTHONY
How to Succeed In Business
  Without Really Trying

TEAGUE, SCOOTER
110 In the Shade
TEBALDI, RENATA
Met Stars on Broadway
TEBOW, ROBERT
Pennies from Heaven
TECH AND EFFX
School Daze
TEDDY AND DARRELL
Mondo Hollywood
TEDESCHI, GIANRICO
My Fair Lady
TEDESCO, TOM
Elvis (NBC-TV Special)
Smokey and the Bandit II
TEELEY, TOM
Night In Heaven
TEEN DREAM
Lean on Me
TEEN QUEENS
Hometown U.S.A.
TEETER, LARA
On Your Toes
TEIG, DAVID
John F. Kennedy
TEIJELO, GERALD M.
On a Clear Day You Can See
  Forever
TELSON, BOB
Bagdad Cafe
TEMPERTON, ROD
Running Scared
TEMPLE, DOT
Oh Boy!
TEMPLE, RENNY
Tuscaloosa's Calling Me (But
  I'm Not Going)
TEMPLE, SHIRLEY
Bambi
Complete Shirley Temple Song
  Book
Dumbo
Littlest Rebel
Shirley Temple's Hits
TEMPO, NINO
Idolmaker
TEMPTATIONS
Air America
Big Chill
Born on the Fourth of July
Coupe De Ville
Fine Mess
Last Dragon
Loving Couples
On Broadway
Save the Children
T.C.B. (Takin' Care of Business)
Where the Buffalo Roam
TEN CC
Moment By Moment
Sunburn
TEN YEARS AFTER
Woodstock
TENNANT, VICTORIA
Winds of War
TEPPER, ROBERT
Rocky IV
TEPPER, SID
Blue Hawaii
Clambake
Double Trouble
Follow That Dream
Frankie and Johnny
Fun In Acapulco
G.I. Blues
Girl Happy
Girls! Girls! Girls!
Harum Scarum
It Happened at the World's Fair
Jamboree!
King Creole
Kissin' Cousins
Loving You
Paradise, Hawaiian Style
Roustabout
Speedway
Spinout
TERRELL, SMOKYE
Selma
TERRI, SALLI
Kismet

Wonderful O
TERRIS, NORMA
Show Boat
TERRY, CLARK
Hot Rock
Silent Partner
TERRY, HELEN
Electric Dreams
Quicksilver
TERRY, SONNY
Book of Numbers
Finian's Rainbow
TERRY-THOMAS
Robin Hood
Those Magnificent Men In Their
  Flying Machines
Three Billion Millionaires
Tom Thumb
Wonderful World of the
  Brothers Grimm
TESTA, MARY
In Trousers
TETLEY, WALTER
Rocky the Flying Squirrel and
  His Friends
TEXAS OPERA COMPANY
Any Which Way You Can
TEXAS PLAYBOYS
Places in the Heart
TEXTOR, SYLVIA
Themes from Great Films
Themes from Hollywood
THACKER, BERNARD
Porgy and Bess
THACKER, CLIVE
O Lucky Man
THACKER, RUSS
Do Black Patent Leather Shoes
  Really Reflect Up?
Grass Harp
Your Own Thing
THATCHER, HEATHER
Christmas Carol
Primrose
Sally
THE "N"
Earth Girls Are Easy
THEM
Good Morning, Vietnam
THEOBALD, TERENCE
Pieces of Eight
THEODORAKIS, MIKIS
Day the Fish Came Out
Film Music from France
Hostage
Original Soundtracks and Music
Phaedra
Serpico
State of Seige
Z
Zorba the Greek
THEODORE, DONNA
Shenandoah
THEODORE, LAURA
Beehive
THEVENY, GRACE
You Never Know
THEYARD, HARRY
Man of La Mancha
THIGPEN, HELEN
Girl Crazy
THIGPEN, LYNNE
Godspell
THINKMAN
Better Off Dead
Blacula
THIRD LANGUAGE
Assault of the Killer Bimbos
THIRD WORLD
Rockers
THIRTEENTH COMMITTEE
Wild Wheels
THIRTEENTH POWER
Wild In the Streets
THIRTY-EIGHT SPECIAL
Teachers
THOMAS, B.J.
Butch Cassidy and the
  Sundance Kid
Growing Pains

TOLAN, MICHAEL
Death of a Salesman
Showcase Album, 1967
TOLKIEN, CHRISTOPHER
Silmarillion
TOM TOM CLUB
Married to the Mob
TOM, LAUREN
Doonesbury
TOMACK, SID
Beg, Borrow Or Steal
TOMASSON, VERNA
Prince and the Pauper
TOMKINS, DON
Wildcat
TOMLIN, LILY
Appearing Nightly
Hollywood Squares
Mixed Doubles / Below the Belt
Saturday Night Live
TOMLIN, PINKY
Paper Moon
TOMLINSON, DAVID
Bedknobs and Broomsticks
Mary Poppins
TOMMY TUTONE
Last American Virgin
TOMPALL AND GLASER BROTHERS
Tick . . . Tick . . . Tick
TONE, FRANCHOT
Strange Interlude
TONE, RICHARD
Parade
TONE LOC
Adventures of Ford Fairlane
TONE NORUM
Summer School
TONIO K
Summer School
TONYS
Border Radio
TOO NICE
I'm Gonna Git You Sucka
TOOTS
Bad Influence
TOPOL
Fiddler on the Roof
Winds of War
TOPPER, BURT
Teenage Rebellion
TOPPERS
Themes from the Movies
TORA TORA
Bill and Ted's Excellent Adventure
TORCH, SIDNEY
Music for Films
TORCH SONG
Texas Chainsaw Massacre Part 2
TORIGI, RICHARD
Camelot
King and I
My Fair Lady
Oklahoma
Show Boat
TORK, PETER
Head
Stardust
TORME, MEL
Artie Shaw Plays Cole Porter
Boy Meets Boy
Higher and Higher
Man Called Adam
Porgy and Bess
Rodgers and Hart In Hollywood
TORO, YOMO
Crossover Dreams
TOROK, MITCHELL
Norwood
TORONTO
Where the Boys Are '84
TORRES, ANDY
Billy Noname
TOSCANINI, ARTURO
Romeo and Juliet
TOSH, PETER
Rockers

TOTO
Dune
TOUCH
Rocky IV
TOUCH LTD.
Young and the Restless
TOUCHE AND DUM DUM
Reluctant Dragon
TOUCHSTONE
Tarot
TOUPS, WAYNE
Steel Magnolias
TOURS, FRANK
Irene
TOWBIN, BERYL
Family Affair
TOWERS, CONSTANCE
Anya
King and I
Show Boat
TOWNES, CAROL LYNN
Breakin'
Breakin' 2 - Electric Boogaloo
TOWNSEND, JOHN
Night of the Comet
TOWNSEND, K.C.
No No Nanette
TOWNSHEND, PETE
Kids Are Alright
Mahoney's Last Stand
McVicar
Playing for Keeps
Quadrophenia
Tommy
TOWSKI, LILLY
Fiddler on the Roof
TOYE, JACQUE
What's a Nice Country Like the U.S. Doing In a State Like This?
TOYE, WENDY
Oklahoma
TOZZI, GIORGIO
Desert Song
Great Waltz
Rose Marie
South Pacific
Student Prince
Vanessa
TRACEY, ANDREW
Wait a Minim!
TRACY, ARTHUR
Pennies from Heaven
TRACY, DORIS
Mama I Want to Sing
TRACY, SPENCER
Judgment at Nuremberg
TRAFFIC
Here We Go Round the Mulberry Bush
TRAMA, JOHNNY
Top Banana
TRAMMPS
Saturday Night Fever
TRAN, MYHANN
Oliver and Company
TRANSVISION VAMP
Cookie
New York Stories
TRAPP FAMILY SINGERS
Sound of Music
TRASHMEN
Full Metal Jacket
TRAUBEL, HELEN
Cut! Out-Takes from Hollywood's Greatest Musicals
Deep In My Heart
Mikado
Pipe Dream
TRAVALINI, TONY
It's My Turn
TRAVERS, VINCENT
Seventeen
TRAVIS, DEBRA
Riot on Sunset Strip
TRAVIS, FRANCIS
2001: A Space Odyssey

TRAVIS, RANDY
Pink Cadillac
Rustler's Rhapsody
TRAVIS, TONY
Time Remembered
TRAVOLTA, JOHN
Broadway Magic
Grease
Over Here!
TREACHER, ARTHUR
Anything Goes
Mary Poppins
TREIBER, ELEONOR
Half a Sixpence
TREIGLE, NORMAN
Carousel
TREKMAN, EMMA
Walking Happy
TRENK-TREBITSCH, WILLY
Threepenny Opera
TRENNER, DONN
Shirley MacLaine Live at the Palace
TRENT, BRUCE
Cinderella
Girl Friend
No, No, Nanette
West Side Story
TRENT, DANIEL
Joseph McCarthy Is Alive and Well and Living In Dade County
TRENT, JACKIE
Card
TRENT, SYBIL
Cinderella
What Do You Want to Be When You Grow Up?
TRESMAND, IVY
Hit the Deck
TREVES, FREDERICK
Christmas Carol
TRIBUSH, NANCY
Oh! Calcutta!
TRIKONIS, GUS
Bajour
TRIOLA, ANNE
Roberta
TRIPP, PAUL
Bremen Town Musicians
Christmas That Almost Wasn't
Flood
Hans Christian Andersen
Sleeping Beauty
Snow White and Rose Red
TRIPP, PETER
Big Bad Wolf
TRISTAN, DOROTHY
California Dreaming
TRONTO, RUDY
Boys from Syracuse
Irma La Douce
Secret Life of Walter Mitty
TROOBNICK, EUGENE
From the Second City
TROOST, ERNEST
Dead Heat
TROTTER, JOHN SCOTT
Bing's Hollywood
Blue Skies
Boy Named Charlie Brown
Going My Way
Holiday Inn
Just for You
Paris Honeymoon
Road to Singapore
Show Boat
Star Maker
TROUBLE FUNK
Good to Go
TROUNCE, MIKE
Jesus Christ Superstar
TROUP, BOBBY
Frances Langford Presents
That Darn Cat
TROUT, ROBERT
Quick and the Dead - The Story of the Atom Bomb
TROVAIOLI, ARMANDO
Boccaccio '70

Ciao, Rudy
How Funny Can Sex Be?
Rugantino
Seven Golden Men
Treasure of San Gennaro
Yesterday, Today and Tomorrow
TROXELL, BARBARA
Mikado
TROXELL, TOM
Hard Job Being God
TROY, LOUISE
High Spirits
Tovarich
Walking Happy
TRUDEAU, GARY
Doonesbury
Rap Master Ronnie
TRUE BELIEVERS
Blue City
TRUE BRETHREN
Paul Sills' Story Theater (of Magical Folk-Rock Fables)
TRUEBLOOD, PAUL
Band Wagon
Four Below Strikes Back
TRUEX, PHILIP
This Is the Army
TRUFFAUT, FRANÇOIS
Confidentially Yours
TRUMAN, HARRY S
Age of Television
Not So Long Ago
Quick and the Dead - The Story of the Atom Bomb
Years to Remember
TRUST
Heavy Metal
TRUTH
Miracle Goes On
TRZCINSKI, EDMUND
Cyrano De Bergerac
TSCHUDIN, MIKE
No Hard Feelings
TSUKERMAN, SLAVA
Liquid Sky
TUBBS, HUBERT
Blind Date
TUBES
Heavenly Bodies
Xanadu
TUBIN, STEVE
Tea Dance
TUCKER, BOBBY
Wiz
TUCKER, FORREST
American Spirit
TUCKER, JAN
Greenwillow
TUCKER, RICHARD
Die Fledermaus
Man of La Mancha
TUCKER, SOPHIE
Irving Berlin Tribute
Legends of the Musical Stage
Lost Films: Trailers from the First Years of Sound
Paper Moon
Show Biz (From Vaude to Video)
Show Boat
Stars of the Silver Screen, 1929-1930
TUCKER, TANYA
Hard Country
Night the Lights Went Out In Georgia
Smokey and the Bandit II
TUCKER, TERRY
Clockwork Orange
TUCKER, WAYNE
Cradle Will Rock
TUCKS, FRED
Selma
TUDOR, RAY
Leave It to Jane
TUFF INC.
Rappin'
TUFO, RICHARD
Three the Hard Way

823

VAN CLEAVE, NATHAN
City Backgrounds
Twilight Zone
VAN CLIBURN
Death In Venice
Song of Norway
VAN DAMME, ART
All American
VAN DOORN, TRUDI
Tom Brown's School Days
VAN DORP, GLORIA
Arabian Nights
VAN DYKE, DICK
Age of Television
Bye Bye Birdie
Chitty, Chitty, Bang, Bang
Magic of Musical Comedy
Mary Poppins
Merriest Songs
Official Grammy Awards
Archive Collection
VAN DYKE, JERRY
Palm Springs Weekend
VAN DYKE, LEROY
All American
What Am I Bid?
VAN DYKE, MARCIA
Tree Grows In Brooklyn
VAN EPS, GEORGE
Pete Kelly's Blues
VAN FLEET, JO
Cinderella
James Dean Story
VAN GROVE, ISAAC
Desert Song
Merry Widow
VAN HALEN
Over the Edge
Spaceballs
VAN HALEN, EDWARD
Wild Life
VAN HEK, LIN
Terminator
VAN HEUSEN, JAMES
Anything Goes
Bing's Hollywood
Carnival In Flanders
Come Blow Your Horn
Emperor Waltz
Going My Way
High Time
Jack and the Beanstalk
Les Poupees De Paris
Let's Make Love
Only Love
Our Town
Pardners
Paris Holiday
Pleasure Seekers
Pufnstuf
Road to Bali
Road to Hong Kong
Robin and the Seven Hoods
Say One for Me
Skyscraper
Some Came Running
This Earth Is Mine
Thoroughly Modern Millie
Walking Happy
Words and Music
World of Suzie Wong
VAN HEUSEN, JOHN
Journey Back to Oz
VAN NUTTER, RIK
Thunderball
VAN PATTEN, DICK
Sanford and Son
What Do You Want to Be When
You Grow Up?
VAN PATTEN, JOYCE
Spoon River Anthology
VAN PATTEN, VINCENT
Survival Run
VAN PEEBLES, MARIO
Rappin'
VAN PEEBLES, MELVIN
Ain't Supposed to Die a Natural
Death
Don't Play Us Cheap
Sweet Sweetback's Baadasssss
Song

Watermelon Man
VAN SCOTT, GLORY
Billy Noname
Fly Blackbird
**VAN VALKENBURGH,
DEBORAH**
King of the Mountain
VAN WAY, NOLAN
Oh Captain!
VANCE, KENNY
Heart of Dixie
Warriors
VANCE, PAUL
Dino
VANCE THE PIG
Big Top Pee-Wee
VANCOUVER SYMPHONY
Platoon (And Songs from the
Era)
VANDALS
Suburbia
VANDER PYL, JEAN
Flintstones
VANDIS, TITOS
Illya Darling
On a Clear Day You Can See
Forever
VANDROSS, LUTHER
Bustin' Loose
Goonies
Made In Heaven
Ruthless People
VANELLI, ROSS
Speed Zone
VANGELIS
Blade Runner
Chariots of Fire
Cosmos (Music of)
VANITY
Action Jackson
Last Dragon
National Lampoon's Vacation
VANLEER, JAY
Don't Play Us Cheap
VANONI, ORNELLA
Rugantino
VARDI
Great Movie Hits of the Thirties
Sound of Hollywood Strings
VARNEY, AMELIA
Cindy
VARRONE, GENE
Bravo Giovanni!
Drat! the Cat!
Goldilocks
Grand Tour
Little Night Music
Subways Are for Sleeping
VARS, HENRY
Ski Crazy
VARTAN, SYLVIE
He's My Girl
VASCONCELOS, NANA
Bad Influence
VASQUEZ, RAY
Music Man
VASSELLI, JUDITH
Rogue Song
VASSY, KIM
Rhinestone
VATICAN CHOIR
Christmas Sing with Bing
VAUGHAN, DAVID
Boy Friend
In Circles
Joan
Peace
Pomegranada
VAUGHAN, FRANKIE
Let's Make Love
VAUGHAN, KENNY
House Party
VAUGHAN, SARAH
Cactus Flower
Murder Inc.
Sharky's Machine
South Pacific
VAUGHAN, STEVIE RAY
Back to the Beach

VAUGHN, BEN
I Was a Teenage Zombie
VAZQUEZ, JAVIER
Crossover Dreams
VEE, BOBBY
C'mon, Let's Live a Little
Stardust
VEGA, SUZANNE
Pretty In Pink
VEGA, TATA
Howard the Duck
Wildcats
VEITCH, LAUREL
Boy Friend
VEJAR, RUDY
Kismet
VELEZ, LUPE
Stars of the Silver Screen,
1929-1930
VELIE, JAY
Call Me Madam
70 Girls, 70
VELONA, TONY
Clown and the Kids
VELVELETTES
Girl Groups: The Story of a
Sound
VENET, NICK
Out of Sight
Skatedater
VENNERI, DARWIN
Darwin's Theories
VENORA, DIANE
Bird
VENORA, LEE
Carousel
Kean
King and I
Kismet
Show Boat
VENTURA, NINO
Merry Widow
VENTURA, RAY
Love Is My Profession
VENTURES
Trini Lopez Show
Wired
VENUTA, BENAY
Annie Get Your Gun
Carousel
Hazel Flagg
VERA, BILLY
Blind Date
Haunted
Iron Eagle II
VERA-ELLEN
Connecticut Yankee
Rodgers and Hart In Hollywood
Three Little Girls In Blue
Three Little Words
Two Weeks with Love
VERDI, GIUSEPPE
Carnegie Hall
VERDON, GWEN
Broadway Magic
Can-Can
Chicago
Damn Yankees
New Girl In Town
Opening Night at the Palace -
Sweet Charity
Redhead
Sweet Charity
VEREA, LISETTE
Merry Widow
VEREEN, BEN
All That Jazz
Funny Lady
Grind
Jesus Christ Superstar
Pippin
License to Kill
VERNO, JERRY
Gypsy
Water Gipsies
VERNON, JACKIE
Frosty the Snowman
VERNON, RICHARD
Hitch-Hikers Guide to the
Galaxy

VERSON, EDWARD
I Can Get It for You Wholesale
VESTOFF, VIRGINIA
Baker Street
Crystal Heart
Love and Let Love
Man with a Load of Mischief
Robber Bridegroom
1776
VICHI, GERRY
Woman of the Year
VICKERS, JIM
Bye Bye Birdie
VICKERS, LARRY
Shirley MacLaine Live at the
Palace
VIDAL, MARIA
Body Rock
Once Bitten
VIDNOVIC, MARTIN
Baby
King and I
Olympus on My Mind
VIENNA BOYS CHOIR
Mouse on the Mayflower
**VIENNA PHILHARMONIC
ORCHESTRA**
Apocalypse Now
**VIENNA SYMPHONY
ORCHESTRA**
Cleopatra
River
Scandalous Life of Frankie and
Johnny
**VIENNA THEATER-KONZERT
ORCHESTRA**
Merry Widow
**VIENNA TONKUNSTLER
SYMPHONY ORHESTRA**
South Pacific
VIGIL
Nightmare on Elm Street 4 -
The Dream Master
VILLA, CARLOS
Great Waltz
VILLAGE ALLSTARS
Nina Simone Sings Porgy
**VILLAGE OF NEUILLY
CHILDREN'S CHOIR**
Christmas Sing with Bing
VILLAGE PEOPLE
Can't Stop the Music
Schoner Gigolo - Armer Gigolo
(Just a Gigolo)
VILLARD, MICHEL
Music from the Films of Charlie
Chaplin
VILLI, OLGA
Ciao, Rudy
VILLO-LOBOS, HEITOR
Forest of the Amazon
**VINCENT, GENE, AND HIS
BLUE CAPS**
Girl Can't Help It!
Hot Rod Gang
VINCENT, JAN-MICHAEL
Winds of War
VINCENT, ROMO
Whoop-Up!
VINCENT, STAN
Looking for Love
VINCENT, VINNIE
Nightmare on Elm Street 4 -
The Dream Master
VINCENT, WARREN
Annie Get Your Gun
Around the World In 80 Days
Can-Can
Gigi
VINES, MARGARET
Macbeth
VINNEGAN, L.
Li'l Abner
My Fair Lady
VINOVICH, STEPHEN
Grand Tour
VINTON, BOBBY
More American Graffiti

VIOLENT FEMMES
I Was a Teenage Zombie
VIPERS
River's Edge
VISCOUNTS
Christine
VISITORS
Wild Angels
VITAL SIGNS
*Bill and Ted's Excellent
Adventure*
VITI, GERALDINE
Golden Apple
VIVALDI, ANTONIO
Golden Coach
Kramer Vs. Kramer
VIVANCO, MOISES
Flahooley
VIVIAN, ANN
Saga of the Dingbat
VIVINO, DONNA
Les Miserables
VLAD, ROMAN
Picasso
Romeo and Juliet
VOET, DOUG
Order Is Love
VOGUES
Good Morning, Vietnam
VOICES ELEVEN
How the West Was Won
VOICES, INC.
Believers
VOICES OF CHRISTMAS
Christmas Sing with Bing
VOICES OF EAST HARLEM
Soul to Soul
**VOICES OF THE ACCADEMIA
MONTEVERDIANA**
Lion In Winter
VOKETAITIS, ARNOLD
Carry Nation
VOLLAIRE, GEORGE
Lady Be Good
VON BRAUN, DR. WERNER
Conquest of Space
VON KARAJAN, HERBERT
Shining
2001: A Space Odyssey
VON PINELLI, ALDO
Uncle Tom's Cabin
VON RITZ, MADELYNN
Cruising
VON STADE, FREDERIKA
Show Boat
Sound of Music
VONDRA, MIMI
Saga of the Dingbat
VOODOOIST CORPORATION
Married to the Mob
VOORHEES, DONALD
Mikado
VOORMAN, KLAUS
Popeye
VORSE, HEATON
Reds
VOSBURGH, DAVID
Doll's Life
1776
VOSKOVEC, GEORGE
Hamlet
VOSS, STEPHANIE
Four Musketeers
Lock Up Your Daughters
VOUTSINAS, ANDREAS
Producers
VUL, POPOL
Nosferatu
VYE, MURVYN
Carousel
WACKER, ROBERT
*Seven Brides for Seven
Brothers*
WADDELL, LINDEN
Stages
WADDINGTON, PATRICK
Kean

WADE, ADAM
Brother on the Run
WADE, WARREN
Anthing Goes
WADSWORTH, DEREK
Hair
WAGNER, CHUCK
Into the Woods
WAGNER, GERRARD
*Joseph McCarthy Is Alive and
Well and Living In Dade
County*
WAGNER, JEANINE
New Moon
WAGNER, RICHARD
Excalibur
Lisztomania
Ludwig
Magic Fire
WAGNER, ROBERT
Say One for Me
WAGNER, ROGER
Desert Song
New Moon
Story of Christmas
Student Prince
WAGONER, PORTER
Honkytonk Man
WAILER, BUNNY
Rockers
WAIN, RICH
Together Again
WAITE, JOHN
About Last Night
Days of Thunder
Vision Quest
WAITRESSES
I Was a Teenage Zombie
WAITS, TOM
Frank's Wild Year
One from the Heart
Paradise Alley
Sea of Love
WAKEFIELD, ANN
Boy Friend
WAKELING, DAVE
She's Having a Baby
WAKELY, JIMMY
James Dean Story
WAKEMAN, RICK
Burning
Crimes of Passion
*Journey to the Center of the
Earth*
Lisztomania
*White Rock - Innsbruck Winter
Games*
WALBROOK, ANTON
Call Me Madam
Oh, Rosalinda!
Wedding In Paris
WALCHA, HELMUT
Slaughterhouse-Five
WALCOTT, COLIN
Raga
WALDEN, GRANT
Best Foot Forward
WALDEN, NARADA MICHAEL
Bright Lights, Big City
Innerspace
WALDEN, STANLEY
Oh! Calcutta!
**WALDEN STREET RHYTHM
SECTION**
*Doonesbury's Jimmy
Thudpucker*
WALDMAN, FREDERICK
Hello Out There
WALDMAN, ROBERT
Robber Bridegroom
WALDRON, MAL
Cool World
Sweet Love, Bitter
WALKEN, GLENN
Best Foot Forward
WALKEN, RONALD
Best Foot Forward
WALKER, BARBARA
Five After Eight

WALKER, BETTY
*Who's Harry Kellerman and
Why Is He Saying Those
Terrible Things About Me?*
WALKER, BILL
Kimberley Jim
Wildcat
WALKER, CHRIS
Follies
Tomfoolery
WALKER, CINDY
Oil Town, U.S.A.
WALKER, JIMMY
Vanishing Point
WALKER, JOE LOUIS
Feds
WALKER, JOSEPH
Believers
WALKER, JUNIOR
*Jo Jo Dancer, Your Life Is
Calling*
WALKER, NANCY
*Cut! Out-Takes from
Hollywood's Greatest
Musicals*
Do Re Mi
Gershwin Rarities
Girl Crazy
Look Ma I'm Dancin'!
Lute Song
My Square Laddie
*Nancy Walker the Broadway
Bombshell Sings Show
Stoppers*
On the Town
Sondheim: A Musical Tribute
WALKER, ROBERT
Kurt Weill In Hollywood
WALKER, SHIRLEY
Batman
Black Rain
Children of a Lesser God
*Danny Elfman: Music for a
Darkened Theatre*
Darkman
Night Breed
WALKER, TIPPY
Four Television Musicals
WALL, MAX
Pajama Game
WALL OF VOODOO
Urgh - A Music War
Weird Science
WALLACE, ART
*Now Is the Time for All Good
Men*
WALLACE, BENNIE
Blaze
Bull Durham
WALLACE, GEORGE
Jennie
New Girl In Town
Pipe Dream
WALLACE, IAN
Aladdin
Kismet
Tom Thumb
WALLACE, JEAN
Maracaibo
WALLACE, MELVIN
Porgy and Bess
WALLACE, OLIVER
Alice In Wonderland
*Darby O'Gill and the Little
People*
Dumbo
Lady and the Tramp
Mickey and the Beanstalk
Old Yeller
Peter Pan
Samoa
WALLACE, PAUL
Gypsy
WALLACH, ELI
Gift of the Magi
Luv
WALLENSTEIN, ALFRED
Oklahoma
WALLER, FATS
Ain't Misbehavin'
Stormy Weather

WALLER, GORDON
*Joseph and the Amazing
Technicolor Dreamcoat*
WALLEY, DEBORAH
Summer Magic
WALLICHS, GLENN
Dean Martin Testimonial Dinner
WALLIN, BENGT ARNE
Dear John
WALLIS, BILL
*Hitch-Hikers Guide to the
Galaxy*
WALLIS, SHANI
Call Me Madam
Can-Can
Oliver!
Time for Singing
WALSH, BOB
Young Warriors
WALSH, GENE
Something for the Boys
WALSH, JOE
FM
Fast Times at Ridgemont High
Great Outdoors
Urban Cowboy
Warriors
WALSH, KEN
Sweet Charity
WALSH, MARY JANE
Let's Face It
Too Many Girls
WALSH, VALERIE
Come Spy with Me
Gentlemen Prefer Blondes
Gypsy
Pieces of Eight
WALSTON, RAY
Damn Yankees
Mary Poppins
Music from Shubert Alley
Popeye
South Pacific
WALTER, CY
Oh Kay!
Porgy and Bess
WALTER, EUGENE
Romeo and Juliet
WALTER, JESSICA
Kiss Me Kate
WALTERS, ELIZABETH
Bill and Coo
WALTERS, INGRAM
God's House
WALTERS, JULIE
Threepenny Opera
WALTERS, TEDDY
Artie Shaw Plays Cole Porter
WALTON, ADAM
Tom Brown's School Days
WALTON, BOB
Preppies
WALTON, FRED
Cat and the Fiddle
WALTON, JIM
Follies
Merrily We Roll Along
WALTON, SIR WILLIAM
Battle of Britain
Digital Space
Hamlet
Henry V
*Music from Great
Shakespearean Films*
*Music from Shakespearean
Films*
Music from the Films
Richard III
*Walton Conducts His Great Film
Music*
WAND, BETTY
Gigi
West Side Story
WANG CHUNG
Breakfast Club
Innerspace
To Live and Die In L.A.
WANN, JIM
Diamond Studs
Pump Boys and Dinettes

WANNBERG, KEN
Blame It on Rio
Losin' it
Philadelphia Experiment
WAR
Fatal Beauty
Youngblood
WARD, BURT
Batman
WARD, CLARA
Time to Sing
WARD, JACKIE
Hey There, It's Yogi Bear
Washington Behind Closed Doors
WARD, KEN
Ka-Boom!
WARD, NANCEE
Best of Burlesque
WARDEN, JACK
Body Beautiful
Who's Harry Kellerman and Why Is He Saying Those Terrible Things About Me?
WARFIELD, CHRIS
Cradle Will Rock
WARFIELD, JOEL
Go Fly a Kite
O Say Can You See!
WARFIELD, WILLIAM
Magnificent Moments from MGM Movies
Porgy and Bess
Show Boat
WARING, DEREK
Cowardly Custard
WARING, FRED
Broadway '55
Broadway Cavalcade
Hear! Hear!
Miss Liberty
Music Man
Proudly They Came
Richard Rodgers
South Pacific
WARNER, DAVID
King's Story
WARNER, FRED
Sweet Charity
WARNER, GENEVIEVE
Student Prince
WARNER, JACK L.
Opening Night at the Winter Garden - Mame
WARNER, JOHN
Salad Days
WARNER, NEIL
Man of La Mancha
WARNER, STEVEN
Little Prince
WARNER BROTHERS ORCHESTRA
Parrish
Sincerely Yours
Top TV Themes '64
WARNES, JENNIFER
All the Right Moves
Blind Date
Dirty Dancing
Officer and a Gentleman
Ragtime
Twilight Zone - The Movie
WARNICK, CLAY
Adventures of Marco Polo
Donnybrook!
WARNING, DENNIS
Baby
WARREN, BETTY
Buccaneer
WARREN, FRAN
Mister Imperium
WARREN, JEFF
Call Me Madam
Can-Can
Wedding In Paris
WARREN, HAL
Among Friends - Waa-Mu Show of 1960
WARREN, HARRY
Affair to Remember

Artists and Models
Belle of New York
Bing's Hollywood
Cinderella
Death on the Nile
42nd Street
Gang's All Here
Golden Age of the Hollywood Musical
Harvey Girls
Hooray for Hollywood
Just for You
Orchestra Wives
Pagan Love Song
Shinbone Alley
Summer Stock
Sun Valley Serenade
Tea for Two
That Night In Rio
Three Little Girls In Blue
Yolanda and the Thief / You'll Never Get Rich
Ziegfeld Follies of 1946
WARREN, JEFF
Brigadoon
WARREN, JENNIFER LEIGH
Little Shop of Horrors
WARREN, JIMMY
Oklahoma
WARREN, JULIE
Connecticut Yankee
Winged Victory
WARREN, KENNETH J.
Canterbury Tales
WARREN, LESLEY ANN
Cinderella
Drat! the Cat!
Happiest Millionaire
One and Only, Genuine, Original Family Band
110 In the Shade
Victor / Victoria
WARREN, MARK
From Hell to Texas
WARREN, ROD
All About Life
WARREN, VINCENT
Crystal Heart
WARRENN, DALE
Wattstax (the Living Word)
WARRICK, RUTH
Citizen Kane
Irene
One Too Many (Hit Songs From)
WARWICK, DIONNE
Love Machine
Slaves
Valley of the Dolls
What's New Pussycat?
Woman In Red
WARWICK, NORMAN
Pickwick
WAS (NOT WAS)
Wonder Years
WASHBURN, JACK
Mr. President
WASHINGTON, DINAH
Tempest
WASHINGTON, LAMONT
Hair
WASHINGTON, NED
Fire Down Below
Impact
Love Themes from Motion Pictures
Miss Sadie Thompson
Naked City
Pinocchio
Search for Paradise
WASNER, FATHER FRANK
Sound of Music
WASSERMAN, ROB
Rain Man
WATANABE, GEDDE
Pacific Overtures
WATANABE, LESLIE
Pacific Overtures
WATERBURY, LAURA
Onward Victoria
WATERMAN, DENIS
Music Man

Oliver!
WATERS, ETHEL
At Home Abroad
At Home with Ethel Waters
Blackbirds of 1928
Cabin In the Sky
Heart Is a Rebel
Hollywood Canteen
That's Entertainment, Part 2
WATERS, JAN
Do Re Mi
High Spirits
WATERS, JANET
Gigi
WATERS, JOHN
They're Playing Our Song
WATERS, MUDDY
Jo Jo Dancer, Your Life Is Calling
Last Waltz
Risky Business
WATERS, ROGER
Body
Obscured By Clouds
WATKIN, LAWRENCE EDWARD
Darby O'Gill and the Little People
Robin Hood
WATKINS, COOKIE
Beehive
WATKINS, MILES
Dark Star
WATSON, BETTY JANE
Oklahoma
WATSON, BRYAN
Joseph and the Amazing Technicolor Dreamcoat
WATSON, DAVID
Great Waltz
WATSON, DOC
Banjoman
Places In the Heart
WATSON, DOUGLASS
Over Here!
WATSON, GENE
Any Which Way You Can
WATSON, JOHNNY "GUITAR"
Thing-Fish
WATSON, LAURENCE
Shuffle Along
WATSON, MERLE
Banjoman
WATSON, RICHARD
Mikado
WATSON, ROGER
Joseph and the Amazing Technicolor Dreamcoat
WATSON, SUSAN
Ben Franklin In Paris
Bye Bye Birdie
Carousel
Celebration
Joyful Noise
No, No, Nanette
Very Warm for May
WATSON SISTERS
Fritz the Cat
WATTERS, HAL
Berlin to Broadway with Kurt Weill
Two
WATTERS, MARLYS
Show Boat
WATTINE, HERVE
Hair
WATTIS, RICHARD
Come Spy with Me
WATTS, CHARLES
James Dean Story
WATTS, ELIZABETH
Destry Rides Again
WATTS, SAL
Solomon King
WAX
Burglar
WAXMAN, FRANZ
Captain Blood: Classic Film Scores for Errol Flynn

Casablanca: Classic Film Scores for Humphrey Bogart
Classic Film Scores for Bette Davis
Crime In the Streets
Digital Premiere Recordings from the Films of Alfred Hitchcock
Down to the Sea In Ships
Enchanted Cottage
Evening with Boris Karloff and His Friends
50 Years of Film
Film Music
Flash Gordon
Hemingway's Adventures of a Young Man
Humoresque
Love Themes from Motion Pictures
Music from Hitchcock Films
Music from Hollywood
Mutiny on the Bounty
My Geisha
Nun's Story
Original Soundtracks and Music
Paradine Case
Peyton Place
Sayonara
Silver Chalice
Spectacular World of Classic Film Scores
Spirit of St. Louis
Sunset Boulevard: The Classic Film Scores of Franz Waxman
Taras Bulba
Twilight Zone
WAXMAN, JEFF
Doonesbury
Downriver
WAYBILL, FEE
Dream a Little Dream
Nobody's Perfect
Running Scared
St. Elmo's Fire
WAYLAND, NEWTON
Berlin to Broadway with Kurt Weill
WAYNE, ALVIS
Teen-Age Cruisers
WAYNE, CYNTHIA
Penney Proud
WAYNE, DAVID
Archy and Mehitabel / Echoes of Archy
Finian's Rainbow
Four Television Musicals
Glass Menagerie
Happy Time
Huckleberry Finn
Ruggles of Red Gap
Say Darling
Show Boat
WAYNE, FREDD
Texas Li'l Darlin'
WAYNE, JEFF
War of the Worlds
WAYNE, JOHN
Alamo
America, Why I Love Her
Island In the Sky
Longest Day
Man Who Shot Liberty Valence
Rio Bravo
Sons of Katie Elder
WAYNE, PAULA
Best Foot Forward
Golden Boy
WAYNE, ROGER
One, Two, Three
Original Motion Picture Hit Themes
WAYNE, SID
Clambake
Double Trouble
Follow That Dream
Frankie and Johnny
Fun In Acapulco
G.I. Blues
Girl Happy
It Happened at the World's Fair
King Creole
Roustabout

WHEATLEY, DAVID
  Speed Zone
WHEATLEY, JOANNE
  Miss Liberty
WHEATRIDGE, CECIL
  Oklahoma
WHEEL
  Magic Garden of Stanley
    Sweetheart
WHEEL, PATRICIA
  Cyrano De Bergerac
WHEELER, BERT
  Ship Ahoy
  Three Wishes for Jamie
WHEELER, BILLY EDD
  Young Billy Young
WHEELER, HAROLD
  Ain't Supposed to Die a Natural
    Death
  Don't Play Us Cheap
  Promises, Promises
  Sunnyside
  Two Gentlemen of Verona
WHEELER, JOHN
  Sgt. Pepper's Lonely Hearts
    Club Band
  Sweet Charity
WHEELER, KIMBALL
  Red Mill
WHISKEYHILL SINGERS
  How the West Was Won
WHITAKER, DAVID
  Dracula
  Hammerhead
  Run Wild, Run Free
  Sword and the Sorcerer
WHITAKER, FOREST
  Bird
WHITAKER, JOHNNIE
  Littlest Angel
  Sigmund and the Sea Monsters
  Tom Sawyer
WHITE, BARRY
  Catch My Soul
  Together Brothers
WHITE, GARY
  Santa Claus Is Comin' to Town
WHITE, JANE
  Nefertiti
  Once Upon a Mattress
WHITE, JESSE
  Linus the Lionhearted
  Stan Freberg Shows
WHITE, LILLY
  Best of Burlesque
WHITE, LORD JOHN
  Courier
WHITE, MAURICE
  Armed and Dangerous
WHITE, PETER
  Boys in the Band
WHITE, RAY
  Thing-Fish
WHITE, ROBERT
  Showcase Album, 1967
WHITE, ROGER
  Lady in the Dark
  Oh Kay!
WHITE, SAMMY
  Show Boat
WHITE, SHEILA
  Biograph Girl
  Dames at Sea
  Oliver!
WHITE, TERRI
  Barnum
WHITE, TONY JOE
  Catch My Soul
WHITE, WILLARD
  Porgy and Bess
WHITE BOYS
  Blue Iguana
WHITE LIGHTNIN'
  Zachariah
WHITE SISTER
  Fright Night
WHITEHEAD, PAXTON
  Beyond the Fringe '64

WHITELAW, REID
  Nocturna
WHITEMAN, PAUL
  Bing Crosby In Hollywood
    (1930-1934)
  Paper Moon
  Thanks a Million
WHITFIELD, ALICE
  Jacques Brel Is Alive and Well
    and Living In Paris
WHITFIELD, JUNE
  Love from Judy
WHITFIELD, NORMAN
  Car Wash
WHITING, JACK
  Anything Goes
  Golden Apple
  Hazel Flagg
  Of Thee I Sing
  On Your Toes
WHITING, LEN
  Love for Love
WHITING, LEONARD
  Romeo and Juliet
WHITING, MARGARET
  Ben Bagley's Ira Gershwin
    Revisited
  Evening with Johnny Mercer
  Taking My Turn
WHITING, NEVIL
  Ambassador
WHITING, RICHARD
  Anything Goes
  Hollywood Hotel
  Love Me Tonight
  Stooge
WHITING, ROBIN
  Anything Goes
WHITLOCK, TOM
  Top Gun
WHITMAN, JERRY
  Electric Company TV Show
    (Songs From)
  Movie Movie
  Promises, Promises
  Showcase Album, 1967
  Teen-Age Cruisers
  Time to Run
WHITMAN, SLIM
  Jamboree!
WHITMORE, JAMES
  Give 'Em Hell Harry!
  Kiss Me Kate
  Oklahoma
  Will Rogers' U.S.A.
WHITMORE, PATRICIA
  Fiddler on the Roof
  Hair
  Hollywood Party
WHITSUN-JONES, PAUL
  Fiddler on the Roof
  Oliver!
WHITTEMORE AND LOWE
  Best of the Great Motion
    Picture Themes, Volume 5
WHITTINGHILL, DICK
  Spoon River Anthology
WHITTINGTON, DICK
  Rowan and Martin's Laugh-In
WHITWORTH, PAT
  Gigi
WHO
  Kids Are Alright
  Quadrophenia
  Tommy
  Woodstock
WHODINI
  Jewel of the Nile
WHYTE, RONNY
  All About Life
WIATA, INIA
  Most Happy Fella
WIBLER, P.
  Wild In the Streets
WICKWIRE, NANCY
  Under Milk Wood
WIDDOES, JAMES
  Is There Life After High School?
WIDDOES, KATHLEEN
  Showcase Album, 1967

WIEDLIN, JANE
  Pretty Woman
WIEGERT, RENE
  Boys from Syracuse
  Cats
  Different Times
  Evita
  Oh Coward!
WIGGINS, GERALD
  Around the World In 80 Days
WIGGINS, TUDI
  My Side of the Mountain
WILBUR, RICHARD
  Candide
WILCOX, CAROL
  Captain Jinks of the Horse
    Marines
WILCOX, DAVID
  Great Outdoors
WILCOX, MARTHA
  We'd Rather Switch
WILCOX, MARTIN
  Joseph and the Amazing
    Technicolor Dreamcoat
WILCOX, RALPH
  Ain't Supposed to Die a Natural
    Death
WILCOX, TOYAH
  Urgh - A Music War
WILD, JACK
  Oliver!
  Pufnstuf
WILD BILL BAND OF
  STRINGS
  Where the Buffalo Roam
WILD MEN OF WONGA
  Weird Science
WILD TCHOUPITOULAS
  Big Easy
WILDE, COLETTE
  Christmas Carol
WILDE, DAVID
  Lisztomania
WILDE, EUGENE
  Playing for Keeps
WILDE, KIM
  Fletch
  Running Scared
  Secret Admirer
  Weird Science
WILDE, MARTY
  Bye Bye Birdie
  Half a Sixpence
WILDER, ALEC
  Alice's Adventures In
    Wonderland
  Clues to a Life
  Hansel and Gretel
  Kittiwake Island
  Peter Pan
  Pinocchio
  Sand Castle
  Tone Poems of Color, Frank
    Sinatra Conducts
WILDER, GENE
  Little Prince
  Producers
  Stir Crazy
  Willy Wonka and the Chocolate
    Factory
  World's Greatest Lover
  Young Frankenstein
WILDER, JO
  She Loves Me
  Threepenny Opera
WILDER, MARC
  Zenda
WILEY, LEE
  Show Boat
WILEY, MICHELLE
  Unmarried Woman
WILKERSON, ARNOLD
  Don't Bother Me, I Can't Cope
  Hair
WILKERSON, DAVID
  It's Time to Pray, America!
WILKERSON, LAURNEA
  Sing
WILKES, PAT
  Body In the Seine

WILKIE, EARLE
  New Moon
  Student Prince
WILKIN, JOHN BUCK
  American Dreamer
WILKINS
  Salsa
WILKINS, ERNIE
  Jamboree!
WILKINS, GEORGE
  Wacky World of Mother Goose
WILKINSON, C.T.
  Evita
WILKINSON, COLM
  Les Miserables
WILKINSON, GEOFFREY
  Treasure Island
WILKINSON, JOHN
  Elvis In Concert
  Elvis: Aloha from Hawaii Via
    Satellite
  That's the Way It Is
  This Is Elvis
WILKINSON, MARC
  Enigma
  Love for Love
  Rosencrantz and Guildenstern
    Are Dead
WILKOF, LEE
  Little Shop of Horrors
WILL POWERS
  Pumping Iron 2 - The Women
WILL TO POWER
  Speed Zone
WILLENS, DORIS
  Piano Bar
WILLIAMS, ALYSON
  Less Than Zero
WILLIAMS, ANDY
  Andy Williams Show
  Broadway Musicals
  55 Days at Peking
  Filmusic Scene
  Life and Times of Judge Roy
    Bean
  More American Graffiti
  Music from Shubert Alley
  Songs from My Fair Lady and
    Other Hits
WILLIAMS, ANN
  Applause
WILLIAMS, ANTONY
  Gypsy
WILLIAMS, ARTHUR
  In Circles
WILLIAMS, BARBARA
  Different Times
  Evening with Alan Jay Lerner
WILLIAMS, BEN
  New Moon
  Under Milk Wood
WILLIAMS, BERT
  Ziegfeld Follies of 1919
WILLIAMS, BILLY
  Inside U.S.A.
WILLIAMS, BILLY DEE
  Empire Strikes Back
WILLIAMS, BONNIE LOU
  South Pacific
WILLIAMS, CAMILLA
  Porgy and Bess
WILLIAMS, CARA
  Ladies of Burlesque
  Playgirls
WILLIAMS, CARLTON
  Selma
WILLIAMS, CHARLES
  Apartment
  Music for Films
WILLIAMS, CHRIS
  Selma
WILLIAMS, CINDY
  First Nudie Musical
WILLIAMS, DAVE
  Creative Freakout
WILLIAMS, DEBBIE
  Ice Follies
WILLIAMS, DENIECE
  Footloose

WILLIAMS, DICK
Ain't Supposed to Die a Natural Death
WILLIAMS, DON
Smokey and the Bandit II
WILLIAMS, DUKE
Simply Heavenly
WILLIAMS, EARLY
Tom Sawyer
WILLIAMS, ELEANOR
On Your Toes
WILLIAMS, ESTHER
Girls...And More Girls
Golden Age of Movie Musicals
Pagan Love Song
Take Me Out to the Ball Game
25 Years of Recorded Sound
WILLIAMS, GEORGE
Daddy Long Legs
WILLIAMS, GRANT
Ballad of Baby Doe
WILLIAMS, GUY
Zorro
WILLIAMS, HAL
Sanford and Son
WILLIAMS, HANK, JR.
Kelly's Heroes
Pink Cadillac
Pressure Is On
Roadie
Time to Sing
Your Cheatin' Heart
WILLIAMS, HANK, SR.
Blaze
Last Picture Show
Your Cheatin' Heart
WILLIAMS, HARCOURT
Hamlet
WILLIAMS, JACK
On Your Toes
WILLIAMS, JACK ERIC
Sweeney Todd (The Demon Barber of Fleet Street)
WILLIAMS, JOE
City Heat
Jamboree!
Lion King
Sharky's Machine
Sing
Torch Song Trilogy
WILLIAMS, JOHN
Accidental Tourist
Aisle Seat
Always
Beyond the Sound Barrier, Vol. 2
Big Hits from Columbia Pictures
Born on the Fourth of July
By Request: The Best of John Williams and the Boston Pops
Checkmate
Cinderella Liberty
Close Encounters of the Third Kind
Diamond Head
Digital Premiere Recordings from the Films of Alfred Hitchcock
Digital Space
Dracula
E.T. - The Extra-Terrestrial
Earthquake
Eiger Sanction
Empire of the Sun
Empire Strikes Back
Fiddler on the Roof
Film Music
Fitzwilly
Fury
Goodbye Mr. Chips
Heidi
How to Steal a Million
In Hollywood
Indiana Jones and the Last Crusade
Indiana Jones and the Temple of Doom
Jane Eyre
Jaws
Jaws 2

John Williams Orchestra Plays Sounds from Screen Spectaculars
John Williams' Symphonic Suites
Lost Angels
M-Squad
Missouri Breaks
Monsignor
Music from Hitchcock Films
Music from the Galaxies
My Fair Lady
1941
Not with My Wife, You Don't
Official Music of the XXIIIrd Olympiad, Los Angeles 1984
Penelope
Raiders of the Lost Ark
Reivers
Return of the Jedi
River
Space Organ
Spacecamp
Spectacular World of Classic Film Scores
Star Wars
Star Wars - Return of the Jedi
Star Wars / Close Encounters of the Third Kind
Star Wars Trilogy
Stevie
Superman - The Movie
Superman III
Thomas and the King
Tom Sawyer
Towering Inferno
Valley of the Dolls
Witches of Eastwick
WILLIAMS, JOHNNY
Penelope
WILLIAMS, JOSEPH
Goonies
Return of the Jedi
WILLIAMS, KENNETH
Cinderella
One Over the Eight
Pieces of Eight
Share My Lettuce
WILLIAMS, LARRY
Christine
Running Scared
WILLIAMS, LAURA
Lion King
WILLIAMS, LENNY
Penitentiary III
WILLIAMS, LLOYD
National Lampoon's Animal House
WILLIAMS, MARION
Black Nativity
Showcase Album, 1967
WILLIAMS, MAURICE, AND THE ZODIACS
American Hot Wax
Dirty Dancing
WILLIAMS, MAYNARD
Joseph and the Amazing Technicolor Dreamcoat
WILLIAMS, PAT
Harrad Summer
How Sweet It Is
Just Between Friends
King Kong
WILLIAMS, PATRICK
Blade Runner
Casey's Shadow
Gulliver
How to Beat the High Cost of Living
It's My Turn
Marvin and Tige
One and Only
WILLIAMS, PAUL
Agatha
Bugsy Malone
Muppet Movie
One on One (the Story of a Winner)
Phantom of the Paradise
Secret of N.I.M.H.
Star Is Born

WILLIAMS, RALPH VAUGHAN
Digital Space
She Loves Me
WILLIAMS, RITA
Angel's Springtime World of Light Opera
Fiddler on the Roof
Lilac Time (Blossom Time)
Love from Judy
Redhead
White Horse Inn
WILLIAMS, ROBIN
Popeye
WILLIAMS, ROGER
More Than a Miracle
Somewhere In Time
WILLIAMS, RON
Five After Eight
WILLIAMS, RUPERT
Selma
WILLIAMS, RUSS, ORCHESTRA
Camelot
WILLIAMS, SAMMY
Stages
WILLIAMS, SYBIL
Under Milk Wood
WILLIAMS, TREAT
Hair
WILLIAMS, VALERIE
Ka-Boom!
WILLIAMS, VAUGHN
Digital Space
Music for Films
WILLIAMS, VESTA
Soul Man
WILLIAMS, WENDY O.
Reform School Girls
WILLIAMS BROTHERS
Going My Way
WILLIAMS SINGERS
Oliver!
On the Town
Show Boat
Song of Norway
WILLIAMSON, FRED
*M*A*S*H*
WILLIAMSON, LAMBERT
Countess from Hong Kong
Romeo and Juliet
WILLIAMSON, MALCOLM
Watership Down
WILLIAMSON, NICOL
Excalibur
Rex
WILLIAMSON, STU
Mission: Impossible
WILLIS, ANDREA
Lost Horizon
WILLIS, IKE
Thing-Fish
Under the Boardwalk
WILLIS, SALLY
El Grande De Coca Cola
WILLISON, WALTER
Front Street Gaieties
Two By Two
WILLOUGHBY, LEVEEN
What's a Nice Country Like the U.S. Doing In a State Like This?
WILLOWS
Hometown U.S.A.
WILLS, CHILL
James Dean Story
WILLS, GLORIA
Allegro
WILLSON, MEREDITH
American Musical Theater
Here's Love
Music Man
Unsinkable Molly Brown
WILLSON, RINI
Music Man
WILMER, DOUGLAS
Christmas Carol

WILSON, ALFRED
Joseph McCarthy Is Alive and Well and Living In Dade County
WILSON, ALLAN
Fly II
Hellbound: Hellraiser II - Time to Play
WILSON, ANN
Golden Child
Tequila Sunrise
WILSON, BRIAN
Almost Summer
Police Academy IV - Citizens on Patrol
She's Out of Control
WILSON, CANDY
Threads of Glory
WILSON, CARRIE
Promenade
WILSON, DEMOND
Sanford and Son
WILSON, DOOLEY
Bloomer Girl
Casablanca
50 Years of Film
Higher and Higher
They Stopped the Show!
WILSON, EARL, JR.
Let My People Come
WILSON, EILEEN
Call Me Madam
Kurt Weill In Hollywood
Rodgers and Hart In Hollywood
WILSON, ELIZABETH
Threepenny Opera
WILSON, FLIP
Flip Wilson Show
WILSON, FRANK
Lola Montez
Wild, Wild Winter
WILSON, JACKIE
American Hot Wax
Go Johnny Go!
WILSON, JACQUES
Creative Freakout
WILSON, JANE
Down In the Valley
Miss Liberty
New Moon
Student Prince
WILSON, JULIE
Beggar's Holiday
Jimmy
Kiss Me Kate
Legs Diamond
Playgirls
This Could Be the Night
WILSON, KELLY
Gypsy
WILSON, MARIE
Ken Murray's Blackouts
WILSON, MARY LOUISE
Bunch
Dime a Dozen
Dressed to the Nines
Flora the Red Menace
WILSON, MICHAEL
Red Mill
WILSON, MICHELLE
Trial of Billy Jack
WILSON, NANCY
Romantic Favorites from Stage and Screen
Save the Children
Showstoppers
WILSON, PATRICIA
Fiorello!
WILSON, RANDAL
Duel
WILSON, RICHARD
What's the Meaning of This?
WILSON, ROBIN
Henry, Sweet Henry
WILSON, RON
Lively Set
WILSON, ROSS
Twentieth Century Oz
WILSON, S.J.
Double Impact

WILSON, SANDY
Aladdin
Boy Friend
Buccaneer
Call It Love
Divorce Me, Darling!
Valmouth
WILSON, STANLEY
Lost Man
M-Squad
Mating Urge
Shotgun Slade
Wagon Train
WILSON, TEDDY
Benny Goodman Story
Gypsy
WINANS
Lean on Me
WINCHELL, PAUL
Goldilocks
WINCHELL, WALTER
Beau James
Irving Berlin Tribute
WINDE, BEATRICE
Ain't Supposed to Die a Natural
Death
WINDING, KAI
Baker Street
WINDOWS
Run, Angel, Run
WINDSOR, BARBARA
Boy Friend
Come Spy with Me
Half a Sixpence
WINDSOR, JOHN
Festival
WINDSOR, NANCY
Happiest Girl In the World
WINFIELD, PAUL
Huckleberry Finn
WING-DAVEY, MARK
Hitch-Hikers Guide to the
Galaxy
WINGER
Karate Kid III
WINKLE, WILLIE
Music Man
WINKLER, EDITH
Merry Widow
WINN, JERRY
Bambi
Young and the Restless
WINNINGER, CHARLES
Show Boat
Ziegfeld Girl
WINOGRAD, ARTHUR
Trouble In Tahiti
WINSLOW, MICHAEL
Police Academy IV - Citizens on
Patrol
WINSLOWE, PAULA
Count of Monte Cristo
WINSON, SUZI
Nunsense
WINSTON, GEORGE
Country
Velveteen Rabbit
WINSTON, HATTIE
Billy Noname
Electric Company TV Show
Me Nobody Knows
WINSTON, MORTON
Cabin In the Sky
WINTER, EDGAR
Air America
WINTER, EDWARD
Promises, Promises
WINTER, LOIS
Camelot
Gigi
Mardi Gras
Music Man
My Fair Lady
Oklahoma
WINTERHALTER, HUGO
Aaron Slick from Punkin Crick
Broadway Classics
Bundle of Joy
General Motors' 50th
Anniversary Show

Gershwin Holiday
Great Music Themes of
Television
Peter Pan
Two Tickets to Broadway
WINTERS, DAVID
Half Past Wednesday
WINTERS, JONATHAN
Alakazam the Great
American Spirit
European Holiday
Little Prince
Progress In Sound
WINTERS, LAWRENCE
Call Me Mister
Devil and Daniel Webster
Porgy and Bess
WINTERS, RENEE
Annie Get Your Gun
Best Foot Forward
WINTERS, ROLAND
Little Women
WINTERS, SHELLEY
Ladies of Burlesque
Minnie's Boys
Pete's Dragon
WINTERTON, DEE
Order Is Love
WINTHROP, FAITH
Gigi
WINTOUR, DAVE
Hair
WINWOOD, STEVE
Here We Go Round the
Mulberry Bush
They Call It an Accident
Tommy
WISDOM, NORMAN
Androcles and the Lion
Jingle Jangle
Night They Raided Minsky's
Walking Happy
Where's Charley?
WISE, FRED
Blue Hawaii
Frankie and Johnny
Fun In Acapulco
G.I. Blues
It Happened at the World's Fair
Kid Galahad
King Creole
Kissin' Cousins
Paradise, Hawaiian Style
Roustabout
Spinout
Tickle Me
WISE, JIM
Dames at Sea
WISE, SCOTT
Jerome Robbins' Broadway
WISNER, JIMMY
Scrambled Feet
WISSLER, RUDY
Al Jolson Story Soundtrack:
Outtakes and Alternate
Takes
WITHERS, IVA
Carousel
WITHERS, BILL
Looking for Mr. Goodbar
Man and Boy
WITT, EVALON
Flowers In the Attic
WITT, PAUL FRANCIS
Flowers In the Attic
Nightmare on Elm Street 2 -
Freddy's Revenge
Power
WITTER, WILLIAM C.
Barnum
WODEHOUSE, P.G.
Jerome Kern Goes to
Hollywood
Leave It to Jane
Oh Boy!
Show Boat
Three Musketeers
WOLCOTT, CHARLES
Saludos Amigos (Music from
South of the Border)
Uncle Remus

WOLCOTT, DEREK
O Babylon
WOLDIN, JUDD
Light Fantastic
Painted Smiles of Cole Porter
Raisin
WOLF, TOMMY
Nervous Set
WOLFE, BETTY
Broadway Magic
My Fair Lady
WOLFE, KARIN
Best Foot Forward
Gigi
WOLFE, LESLIE-ANNE
Musical Chairs
WOLFF, BEVERLY
Carry Nation
Trouble In Tahiti
WOLFGANG, CARL
Atlantis In Hi-Fi Iforbidden
Island)
WOLFINGTON, IGGIE
Cinderella
Music Man
Thousand Miles of Mountains
Tom Jones
WOLFMAN JACK
More American Graffiti
WOLFSON, MARTIN
Baker Street
Threepenny Opera
WOLPE, LENNY
Mayor
Onward Victoria
WOLVIN, ROY
My Fur Lady
WOMACK, BOBBY
Across 110th Street
WONDER, STEVIE
Copley High
Jungle Fever
Last Dragon
Nothing But a Man
Speed Zone
Woman In Red
WONG, BARBARA JEAN
Christmas Carol
WONG, PATRICIA
Flower Drum Song
WONG, PAUL
81 Proof
WOOD, CHARLES
Kiss Me Kate
WOOD, CYRUS
Maytime
WOOD, DEEDEE
Li'l Abner
WOOD, DENNIS
Joseph McCarthy Is Alive and
Well and Living In Dade
County
WOOD, G.
Kittiwake Island
WOOD, GLORIA, CHORUS
Carousel
WOOD, HELEN
Seventeen
WOOD, JIMMIE
Echo Park
WOOD, LAUREN
Pretty Woman
WOOD, LINDA
Spoon River Anthology
WOOD, MARY LAURA
Bye Bye Birdie
WOOD, NATALIE
Gypsy
Penelope
WOOD, PEGGY
Cat and the Fiddle
WOOD, PETER
They Call It an Accident
WOOD, RAYMOND
Boy Meets Boy
WOOD, RON
Last Waltz
Mahoney's Last Stand
Wild Life

WOOD, ROY
All This and World War II
WOOD, TERRY
Nobody's Perfect
WOODARD, CHARLAINE
Ain't Misbehavin'
WOODMAN, TOM
I Remember Mama
WOODRUFF, CAROLE
Saga of the Dingbat
WOODS, AUBREY
Flowers for Algernon
Four Musketeers
I and Albert
WOODS, BARBARA
My Fair Lady
WOODS, CAROL
Grind
WOODS, ILENE
Cinderella
WOODS, LEECY R.
Earl of Ruston
WOODS, LOUISE
Shuffle Along
WOODS, MICHELE-DENISE
Cradle Will Rock
WOODS, PHIL
Show Boat
WOODS, REN
Brother from Another Planet
WOODS, RICHARD
Second Shepherd's Play
WOODSON, WILLIAM
Feeling Good with Annie
Happy Prince
Who Framed Roger Rabbit?
WOODTHORPE, PETER
Darling of the Day
WOODVINE, JOHN
Nicholas Nickleby
WOODWARD, CHARLES
Up with People!
WOODWARD, EDWARD
Breaker Morant
High Spirits
WOODWARD, JOANNE
Ladies of Burlesque
**WOODWARD, PEGGY
TAYLOR**
Le Mans
WOODWARD, WALT
Care Bears Movie
WOOLEY, SHEB
Hootenanny Hoot
WOOLFOLK, WILLIAM
Porgy and Bess
WOOLLARD, ROBERT
Three Musketeers
WOPAT, TOM
Dukes of Hazzard
WORDEN, MARVIN
Hello Out There
WORDSWORTH, RICHARD
Lock Up Your Daughters
WORKING WEEK
Absolute Beginners
WORKMAN, MIRIAM
Trouble In Tahiti
WORLEY, JO ANNE
Mad Show
Rowan and Martin's Laugh-In
WORLOCK, FREDERIC
Count of Monte Cristo
Zenda
WORSTER, HOWETT
New Moon
WORTH, BILLIE
Call Me Madam
WORTH, COLEY
70 Girls, 70
WORTH, IRENE
Cocktail Party
WORTH, JOY
Gigi
WORTH, MARA
How Now, Dow Jones
WORTH, PENNY
Annie

Irene
WRAY, BILL
Private School
WREFORD, EDGAR
Christmas Carol
WREN ORCHESTRA
Gandhi
WREN, JENNY
Edward and Mrs. Simpson
WRIGHT, ANDREA
Ka-Boom!
WRIGHT, BEN
Into the Woods
WRIGHT, BETTY
True Love
WRIGHT, DORSEY
Hair
WRIGHT, EUGENE
Around the World In 80 Days
WRIGHT, GARY
Cobra
Fire and Ice
WRIGHT, GERALDINE
Happy As a Sandbag
WRIGHT, GRAHAM
My Fur Lady
WRIGHT, GREG
Loving Couples
WRIGHT, HELENA-JOYCE
Jerry's Girls
WRIGHT, IRA
Flower Drum Song
King and I
WRIGHT, JOHNNY
Full Metal Jacket
WRIGHT, MARGARET
Joan
Peace
Pomegranada
WRIGHT, MARTHA
Censored
Firefly
H.M.S. Pinafore
Mikado
Musical Comedy and Operetta
  Favorites, Vol 2
WRIGHT, RALPH
Perri
WRIGHT, ROBERT
Anya
Great Waltz
Kean
Kismet
Merry Widow
Song of Norway
Stingiest Man In Town
WRIGHT, RON
Van Nuys Blvd.
WRIGHT, SAMUEL E.
Over Here!
WRIGHT BROTHERS
Thank God It's Friday
WRIGHTSON, EARL
Blossom Time
Connecticut Yankee
Desert Song
H.M.S. Pinafore
Kiss Me Kate
Mikado
Naughty Marietta
New Moon
Night with Jerome Kern
Night with Rudolf Friml
Red Mill
Student Prince
Sweethearts
Vagabond King
WRUBEL, ALLIE
Hooray for Hollywood
Uncle Remus
WYATT, JERRY
Too Many Girls
WYLAM, WILLIAM
Houdini, Man of Magic
WYLE, GEORGE
Robin Hood
WYLER, GRETCHEN
Silk Stockings
WYLIE, BETTY JANE
Beowulf

WYMAN, BILL
Creepers
Green Ice
WYMAN, JANE
Bing's Hollywood
Hans Christian Andersen
Hollywood Canteen
Just for You
Ladies of Burlesque
Pollyanna
WYMARK, PATRICK
Finest Hours
King's Story
WYMORE, PATRICE
Starlift
**WYNCOTE ORCHESTRA AND
CHORUS**
Carpetbaggers
WYNER, YEHUDI
Benito Cereno
WYNETTE, TAMMY
Five Easy Pieces
Hooper
*Night the Lights Went Out In
  Georgia*
Run, Angel, Run
WYNN, ED
Babes In Toyland
Daydreamer
Magnificent Rogue
Mary Poppins
Merriest Songs
WYNN, KEENAN
Annie Get Your Gun
Finian's Rainbow
Kiss Me Kate
Santa Claus Is Comin' to Town
WYNN, MAY
Caine Mutiny
WYNN, NAN
Bing's Hollywood
Rita Hayworth
WYNTER, MARK
Charlie Girl
Phil the Fluter
WYNTERS, GAIL
American Game
X
Decline of Western Civilization
XTC
She's Having a Baby
Times Square
Urgh - A Music War
XXL
Jetson: The Movie
YA YA
Revenge of the Nerds
YACONELLI, FRANK
Four Television Musicals
YADIN, YOSSI
Fiddler on the Roof
YAGER, JOHN
Dark Star
YAGHJIAN, KURT
Amahl and the Night Visitors
Duel
Jesus Christ Superstar
YAMA, CONRAD
Flower Drum Song
Pacific Overtures
YAMASHITA, STOMU
Man from the East
Tempest
YANA
Cinderella
YANCY, EMILY
Hello Dolly!
YANKOVIC, WEIRD AL
Transformers - The Movie
YARBROUGH, GLENN
Hobbit
YARBROUGH AND PEOPLES
Penitentiary III
YARDBIRDS
Blow-Up
YARED, GABRIEL
Betty Blue
Invitation Au Voyage
YARNELL, BRUCE
Annie Get Your Gun

Camelot
Happiest Girl In the World
Moon In the Gutter
YARROW, PETER
You Are What You Eat
YATES, MARTIN
*Seven Brides for Seven
  Brothers*
YATOVE, JAN
Girl In the Bikini
Playtime
YEATS, WILLIAM BUTLER
Five One Act Plays
YELLO
Adventures of Ford Fairlane
Mighty Quinn
She-Devil
YELLOWJACKETS
Star Trek IV: The Voyage Home
YESTON, MAURG
Nine
YOERGLER, HAL
Bugaloos
YOHN, ERICA
Lenny
YORK, DON
Clams on the Half Shell
YORK, JEFF
Savage Sam
YORK, MICHAEL
England Made Me
Much Ado About Nothing
Romeo and Juliet
Taming of the Shrew
YORK, SUSANNAH
Man for All Seasons
YOSHIDA, FUSAKO
Pacific Overtures
YOUMANS, VINCENT
Hit the Deck
Musical Comedy Favorites
No, No, Nanette
*Salute to Vincent Youmans:
  Four Great Hits from Hit
  Shows*
YOUMANS, WILLIAM
*Big River (the Adventures of
  Huckleberry Finn)*
YOUNG, ALAN
Aaron Slick from Punkin Crick
Mister Ed
Tom Thumb
YOUNG, ALEXANDER
Oh, Rosalinda!
YOUNG, ANGUS
Who Made Who
YOUNG, BOB
ABC Scope
YOUNG, CHARLES
Mame
White Horse Inn
YOUNG, CHIP
Elvis
YOUNG, CHRIS
Bat-21
Flowers In the Attic
Fly II
*Hellbound: Hellraiser II - Time
  to Play*
Hellraiser
*Nightmare on Elm Street 2 -
  Freddy's Revenge*
Power
Pranks
YOUNG, CY
Divorce Me, Darling!
Four Below Strikes Back
Rodgers and Hart Revisited
Subways Are for Sleeping
YOUNG, DONA JEAN
On the Flip Side
YOUNG, DORIS
Devil and Daniel Webster
YOUNG, DOUG
Quick Draw McGraw
YOUNG, EVE
Roberta
YOUNG, FARON
What Am I Bid?

YOUNG, JESSE COLIN
1969
YOUNG, JOHN
*Monty Python and the Holy
  Grail*
YOUNG, K.
*Mrs. Brown, You've Got a
  Lovely Daughter*
YOUNG, LES
Pal Joey
YOUNG, LESTER
Sound of Jazz
YOUNG, LORETTA
Les Poupees De Paris
Littlest Angel
YOUNG, MARGARET
My Fair Lady
Oklahoma
YOUNG, MARY ANGELA
That Other Woman's Child
YOUNG, NEIL
Journey Through the Past
Last Waltz
Strawberry Statement
Where the Buffalo Roam
Woodstock
YOUNG, PAUL
Ruthless People
YOUNG, PHYLLIS
Ladies Don't Spit and Holler
YOUNG, PEGGY
Selma
YOUNG, RALPH
Whoop-Up!
YOUNG, RETTA
Patty
YOUNG, RIDA JOHNSON
Mademoiselle Modiste
Maytime
Naughty Marietta
YOUNG, ROLAND
New Moon
YOUNG, RONALD
Boy Friend
Different Times
YOUNG, THOMAS
Duel
Woman Called Moses
YOUNG, VICTOR
Around the World In 80 Days
Bing's Hollywood
Brave One
*Casablanca: Classic Film
  Scores for Humphrey Bogart*
Christmas Carol
Cinema Rhapsodies
Count of Monte Cristo
Emperor Waltz
For Whom the Bell Tolls
Going My Way
Golden Earrings
Greatest Show on Earth
Hans Christian Andersen
Happy Prince
Ichabod and Mr. Toad
Johnny Guitar
Judy at the Palace
Knock on Wood
Kurt Weill In Hollywood
Lady and the Tramp
Littlest Angel
*Love Themes from Motion
  Pictures*
*Memorable Moments In
  Musical Comedy*
Mr. Music
Moby Dick
Music of Victor Young
New Moon
Paper Moon
Pinocchio
Quiet Man
Rio Grande
Run of the Arrow
Sands of Iwo Jima
Seven Hills of Rome
Seventh Heaven
She Loves the Movies
Show Boat
Snow Goose
Somebody Loves Me
Student Prince

Varèse Sarabande Records:
Overview and Soundtrack Discography

By Dr. Robert L. Smith

Between 1977 and 1989, Varèse Sarabande, a small independent Los Angeles-based record company, produced many of the most collectible soundtrack albums of vinyl's last era. Their output was unusual, risky, and prolific, at times flooding the soundtrack bins. They made reissues of many of the rarest soundtracks of the '50s and '60s – in short, a soundtrack collector's dream. Also, the first record releases of many of today's most active and prominent film composers came out on this eclectic label.

Varèse (var-ez) Sarabande Records, with its characteristic label design (an inkblot), was formed in 1977 by a merger between Varèse International Records and Sarabande Records. Varèse, named for composer Edgar Varèse, was headed by Chris Kuchler. Sarabande (a dance) was headed by Tom Null. After the merger, Null became vice-president of Varèse Sarabande.

The company first concentrated on releasing rare classical titles reissued from the long lost catalogs of Remington, Urania, and Decca. Fortunately, the Decca vaults also contained many of the best soundtrack recordings of the 1950s – *Samson and Delilah / Quiet Man*, *A Time to Love and a Time to Die*, *The Young Lions* and *Boy on a Dolphin* – to cite just a few. Titles like these became Varèse Sarabande's initial soundtrack releases, and they were an instant hit with collectors.

The consistent best sellers, however, were not the classic soundtrack reissues but new titles from the horror and fantasy genres. Efforts were then concentrated in these genres in early 1979 when Scot Holton joined the company. Holton had extensive experience in the so-called "fantastic" genres and would play a vital role at Varèse Sarabande. As a result of *Star Wars* and the science fiction explosion of the mid-to-late 1970s, Varèse capitalized on that market with almost perfect timing.

Early horror titles included Pino Donaggio's *Tourist Trap*, Goblin's *Dawn of the Dead*, Brian May's *Patrick* and Fred Myrow's *Phantasm*. These non-mainstream releases again hit a nerve with collectors.

Throughout the 1980s, the label grew and became well-established. Their output consisted of reissues from the Colpix, Decca, and Warner Bros. catalogs, an occasional classical title (though founded as a classical label, these recordings would eventually play only a small role at V.S.) and, most importantly, exclusive releases for current films.

Varèse Sarabande introduced little-known composers to the soundtrack world, predominantly James Horner who would become one of the most prominent film composers of the '80s and '90s. Others with significant early releases on Varèse include Basil Poledouris, Danny Elfman, David Newman, Thomas Newman, Howard Shore, Alan Silvestri, and Christopher Young. Varèse was instrumental in augmenting the careers of this new wave of film composers.

Industry giants, such as Jerry Goldsmith, Maurice Jarre, and Elmer Bernstein, also had scores released on Varèse Sarabande, significant because without Varèse many important '80s scores by established composers would not have been released.

Use fees and limited market potential have severely restricted the output of soundtrack recordings. Re-use fees are amounts paid to the Musicians Union in the United States when a soundtrack is issued. The music is essentially "re-used" a second time for the production of a record (the first "use" being the film's actual background soundtrack). The music is sold in 15 minute blocks, each of which can cost several thousand dollars. The actual amount depends on the number of musicians in the orchestra.

Varèse Sarabande either worked around the re-use fee or confronted it directly. Since the re-use does not apply to scores recorded outside the US, several European film recordings were released by the label. Re-use also did not apply to reissues, such as the vintage Decca soundtrack recordings. Those fees had been paid at the time of the original record release.

Varèse Sarabande Records utilized several numbering schemes, including an "STV 81000" series, "VS5200" series, and a "704.000" series. The numbering schemes are key to better understanding their soundtrack releases, as well as to why some are more collectible than others.

As with any record label, some titles are more common than others. In the main STV 81000 series, the scarcest titles are *The Red Pony* (Copland), *The Ewok Adventure* (Peter Bernstein), *Marie Ward* (Elmer Bernstein), *Lionheart, Vol. II* (Goldsmith), *In a Shallow Grave* (Sheffer) and *The Serpent and the Rainbow* (Fiedel).

Not widely distributed, *Marie Ward* – an original Elmer Bernstein score from a German film – was extremely difficult to find at the time of its release. Likewise with *Lionheart, Vol. II*, a significant Jerry Goldsmith release.

The Serpent and the Rainbow was the last issue of the STV 81000 series. *Sky Bandits* provides an excellent example of the splashy and brilliant cover art which so frequently adorned albums in this series.

Curiously, one of the 81000 series was destined to be a soundtrack collectible. *The Flamingo Kid* (STV 81232) was simultaneously released by two record labels in 1984, one of those being Varèse Sarabande. Due to licensing and legal problems, this situation has occurred on a few occasions in the soundtrack business. Although a compilation album, the Varèse issue was extremely limited in distribution and is much rarer than the other commercial Motown release. It is unquestionably one of the toughest Varèse Sarabande issues to find.

Regarding the 704.000 series, this is a group of new digital recordings and were made distinct by a unique numbering series. The last few issues in this series, from 1988-'89, are very scarce. They include *Eight Men Out, D.O.A., Betrayed* and *Poltergeist III*, the latter rumored to have been withdrawn.

The most confusing series is the VS 5200 line. When Varèse Sarabande began releasing compact discs as an almost exclusive format in the late 1980s, another numbering scheme was developed for the vinyl releases to match the CD numbers. In this series, the numbering is erratic and some are even skipped. During this time (1988-'89), not all Varèse CDs had a vinyl counterpart. The VS 5200 series represents the last of Varèse Sarabande's vinyl output. Many of these titles are from high profile movies and are not scarce. In contrast, however, few people were buying new vinyl releases at that time and thus many of these titles may be rare on vinyl. The last Varèse Sarabande vinyl issue was *Pet Sematary* (VS 5227), from the spring of 1989.

Under the Varèse Sarabande umbrella were several other labels including Citadel, Chalfont, and Starlog Records.

Citadel was established in 1976 by film music historian Tony Thomas for the purpose of issuing scores by Golden Age composers, such as Max Steiner, Miklos Rozsa, Hans Salter, and others. Varèse Sarabande acquired Citadel in 1980 and reissued several titles. As a result, one might find two Citadel issues for a given film (e.g. *Blue Max, Patch of Blue*). Two separate numbering schemes also exist. Many Citadel albums were extremely limited upon release and are scarce and valuable today. Adding to the confusion is that some are limited or promotional titles, not licensed for public sale.

Some very desirable Citadel titles are *The Midas Run* (Bernstein), *The Cassandra Crossing* (Goldsmith), *The Film Music of Alex North* (actually an aborted 1950s RCA Victor companion album to *North of Hollywood*) and *A Walk With Love and Death* (Delerue).

The Chalfont label was primarily used for digital audiophile re-recordings of both a classical and soundtrack nature. There are only two important film score recordings on Chalfont: Charles Gerhardt's *Kings Row* (a landmark release) and *The Empire Strikes Back*, both by the National Philharmonic Orchestra.

Starlog Records (in conjunction with *Starlog* magazine) had only three releases: Ferde Grofé's *Rocketship X-M, Fantastic Film Music of Albert Glasser, Vol. 1* and Bernard Herrmann's *It's Alive II*.

Varèse Sarabande continues to be an industry leader in soundtrack recordings to this day, though their output has been exclusively on compact disc and cassette since 1989. Recently, the company, behind Catalog A&R and Licensing Vice President Cary E. Mansfield, has branched out into vintage pop, rock, and jazz reissues from the 1950s and '60s and thus their output of soundtracks is somewhat less than that of the vinyl era. (For a current catalog, write: Varèse Sarabande Records, 11846 Ventura Blvd. Suite 130, Studio City, CA 91604. Please do not attempt to order older product from them – none is available.)

In the 12 years from 1977 to 1989, Varèse Sarabande Records released between three and four hundred significant soundtrack and film music recordings. As soundtrack collectibles, these recordings are quite desirable for their high quality vinyl pressings (many audiophile in nature), excellent production technique, and cover art. These releases account for most of the collectible vinyl soundtrack recordings of the period. They are all likely to increase substantially in value.

The following catalog lists all known Varèse Sarabande soundtrack and related vinyl records. All issues have been verified to exist. Classical selections not of interest to soundtrack collectors have been omitted.

Varèse Sarabande

VC 81028	First Nudie Musical	Bruce Kimmel
VC 81053	Lust for Life	Miklos Rozsa
VC 81070	Master of the World	Les Baxter
VC 81071	36 Hours	Dmitri Tiomkin
STV 81072	Silent Running	Peter Schikele
VC 81073	Samson and Delilah / Quiet Man	Victor Young
VC 81074	Written on the Wind / Four Girls in Town	Alex North
VC 81075	A Time to Love and A Time to Die	Miklos Rozsa
VC 81076	This Earth is Mine	Hugo Friedhofer
STV 81077	Themes from Classic Science Fiction, etc.	Various
VC 81078	Goliath and the Barbarians	Les Baxter
VC 81081	Jonathan Livingston Seagull	Lee Holdridge
VC 81082	Brass Target	Laurence Rosenthal
VC 81083	Stages (original cast)	Bruce Kimmel
VC 81084	Village of Eight Grave Stones	Yasushi Akutagawa
VC 81102	Tourist Trap	Pino Donaggio
VC 81103	Dunwich Horror	Les Baxter
VC 81104	Rozsa: Suites for the Films	Miklos Roasa
VC 81105	Phantasm	Fred Myrow / Malcolm Seagrave
VC 81106	Dawn of the Dead	Goblin

VC 81107	Patrick	Brian May
STV 81108	Fedora	Miklos Rozsa
STV 81109	A Little Romance	Georges Delerue
STV 81115	Young Lions	Hugo Friedhofer
STV 81116	Island in the Sky / Song of Bernadette	Hugo Friedhofer
STV 81117	Golden Earrings / Blood and Sand	Young / Gomez
STV 81118	Magnificent Obsession	Frank Skinner
STV 81119	Boy on a Dolphin	Hugo Friedhofer
STV 81120	One Step Beyond	Harry Lubin
STV 81121	Man of A Thousand Faces	Frank Skinner
STV 81122	It Started in Naples	Alessandro Cicognini
STV 81124	Rio Grande	Victor Young
STV 81125	Anastasia	Alfred Newman
STV 81126	Piranha	Pino Donaggio
VC 81127	Martin	Donald Rubinstein
STV 81128	Knights of the Round Table	Miklos Rozsa
STV 81129	Meetings with Remarkable Men	Rosenthal / Hartmann
STV 81130	Destination Moon	Leith Stevens
STV 81131	Bloodline	Ennio Morricone
STV 81132	Almost Perfect Affair	Georges Delerue
STV 81133	Eye of the Needle	Miklos Rozsa
STV 81134	Escape from NY	John Carpenter
STV 81135	Seventh Voyage of Sinbad	Bernard Herrmann
STV 81136	Devil At 4 O'clock	George Duning
STV 81137	Prince of the City	Paul Chihara
STV 81138	1001 Arabian Nights	George Duning
STV 81139	Home Movies	Pino Donaggio
STV 81140	Day Time Ended	Richard Band
STV 81141	True Confessions	Georges Delerue
STV 81142	Seven Samurai	Hayazaka
STV 81143	Maniac	Jay Chattaway
STV 81144	Mad Max	Brian May
STV 81145	Wild Bunch	Jerry Fielding
STV 81146	John Paul Jones	Max Steiner
STV 81147	Island	Ennio Morricone
STV 81148	Dressed to Kill	Pino Donaggio
STV 81149	Enola Gay	Maurice Jarre
STV 81150	The Howling	Pino Donaggio
STV 81151	Night of the Living Dead	Various
STV 81152	Halloween II	John Carpenter / Alan Howarth
STV 81153	Formula	Bill Conti
STV 81154	Swamp Thing	Harry Manfredini
STV 81155	Road Warrior	Brian May
STV 81156	Andy Warhol's Dracula	Claudio Gizi
STV 81157	Andy Warhol's Frankenstein	Claudio Gizi
STV 81158	Sword and the Sorcerer	David Whitaker
STV 81159	Twelve Chairs	John Morris
STV 81160	Creepshow	John Harrison

STV 81162	BuMing	Rick Wakeman
STV 81163	Slapstick of Another Kind	Michel Legrand
STV 81164	Eating Raoul	Arlon Ober
STV 81165	Friendly Persuasion	Dmitri Tiomkin
STV 81166	Last Embrace	Miklos Rozsa
STV 81167	Man from Snowy River	Bruce Rowland
STV 81168	Camelot	Lerner / Loewe
STV 81169	Secret of Nimh	Jerry Goldsmith
STV 81170	Forbidden Zone	Danny Elfman
STV 81171	Twilight Zone, Vol. 1	Various
STV 81172	10 to Midnight	Robert Ragland
STV 81173	Videodrome	Howard Shore
STV 81174	Beastmaster	Lee Holdridge
STV 81175	Night of the Shooting Stars	Nicola Piovani
STV 81176	Halloween	John Carpenter
STV 81178	Twilight Zone, Vol. 2	Various
STV 81179	Magic Fire	Erich Wolfgang Korngold
STV 81180	Winds of War	Bob Cobert
STV 81181	Liquid Sky	Slava Tsukerman / Others
STV 81182	Year of Living Dangerously	Maurice Jarre
STV 81184	Hunger	Rubini / Yeager
STV 81185	Twilight Zone, Vol. 3	Various
STV 81186	Young Warriors	Rob Walsh
STV 81187	Hercules	Pino Donaggio
STV 81189	Invitation Au Voyage	Gabriel Yared
STV 81190	Leopard	Nino Rota
STV 81191	Fog	John Carpenter
STV 81192	Twilight Zone, Vol. 4	Various
STV 81193	Minor Miracle	Rick Patterson
STV 81194	Heat and Dust	Richard Robbins
STV 81195	Revenge of the Ninja	Rob Walsh
STV 81197	Brainstorm	James Horner
STV 81198	Osterman Weekend	Lalo Schifrin
STV 81199	Evil Dead	Joe Lo Duca
STV 81202	Blind Date	Myers / Kongos
STV 81203	Children of the Corn	Jonathan Elias
STV 81204	Making the Grade	Basil Poledouris
STV 81205	Twilight Zone, Vol. 5	Various
STV 81206	Gorky Park	James Horner
STV 81207	Wavelength	Tangerine Dream
STV 81208	Lassiter	Ken Thorne
STV 81209	Mutant	Richard Band
STV 81210	Blame it on Rio	Wannberg / Spiegel
STV 81211	Sahara	Ennio Morricone
STV 81212	The Republic Years (Roy Rogers)	Various
STV 81217	Berlin Alexanderplatz	Peer Raben
STV 81219	Top Secret	Maurice Jarre
STV 81220	Cousteau / Amazon	John Scott

STV 81221	Careful He Might Hear You	Ray Cook
STV 81222	Fourth Man	Loek Dikker
STV 81224	Swann in Love / Katharina Blum	Hans Werner Henze
STV 81225	Sheena	Richard Hartley
STV 81226	Until September	John Barry
STV 81227	Sunday in the Country / The Pirate	Philippe Sarde
STV 81228	Bolero	Peter Bernstein
STV 81229	Places in the Heart	Doc Watson
STV 81230	Phar Lap	Bruce Rowlands
STV 81231	Supergirl	Jerry Goldsmith
STV 81232	Flamingo Kid	Various
STV 81233	Starman	Jack Nitzsche
STV 81234	Runaway	Jerry Goldsmith
STV 81235	Shooting Party	John Scott
STV 81236	Nightmare on Elm Street	Charles Bernstein
STV 81237	Witness	Maurice Jarre
STV 81239	Certain Fury	Payne / Kunkel
STV 81240	Aviator	Dominic Frontiere
STV 81241	Cat's Eye	Alan Silvestri
STV 81242	Company of Wolves	George Fenton
STV 81243	Gods Must Be Crazy	John Boshoff
STV 81244	Emerald Forest	Junior Homrich
STV 81245	Christopher Columbus	Riz Ortolani
STV 81246	Rambo II	Jerry Goldsmith
STV 81247	Wetherby	Nicholas Bicat
STV 81248	Red Sonja	Ennio Morricone
STV 81249	Lifeforce	Henry Mancini
STV 81250	Music of Republic	Various
STV 81251	Dance with a Stranger	Richard Hartley
STV 81252	Jagged Edge	John Barry
STV 81253	Black Cauldron	Elmer Bernstein
STV 81254	The Bride	Maurice Jarre
STV 81255	Edith's Diary	Jurgen Knieper
STV 81256	Flesh and Blood	Basil Poledouris
STV 81257	Agnes of God	Georges Delerue
STV 81258	Love Songs	Michel Legrand
STV 81259	Red Pony	Aaron Copland
STV 81260	Return to Eden	Brian May
STV 81261	Re-Animator	Richard Band
STV 81262	Zone Troopers and Alchemist	Richard Band
STV 81263	Invasion USA	Jay Chattaway
STV 81264	Silver Bullet	Jay Chattaway
STV 81265	Marie: A True Story	Francis Lai
STV 81266	Year of the Dragon	David Mansfield
STV 81267	Transylvania 6-5000	Lee Holdridge
STV 81268	Marie Ward	Elmer Bernstein
STV 81269	Subway	Eric Serra
STV 81270	Spies Like Us	Elmer Bernstein

STV 81271	Enemy Mine	Maurice Jarre
STV 81272	Final Conflict	Jerry Goldsmith
STV 81273	Mountbatten: The Last Viceroy	John Scott
STV 81274	Clan of the Cave Bear	Alan Silvestri
STV 81275	Nightmare on Elm Street II	Christopher Young
STV 81276	F/X	Bill Conti
STV 81277	Fellini's Ginger and Fred	Nicola Piovani
STV 81278	April Fool's Day	Charles Bernstein-86
STV 81279	Crawlspace	Pino Donaggio
STV 81281	Ewok Adventure	Peter Bernstein
STV 81282	Manhattan Project	Philippe Sarde
STV 81283	Aliens	James Horner
STV 81284	Apology	Maurice Jarre
STV 81285	Jake Speed	Mark Snow
STV 81286	Raw Deal	Cinemascore
STV 81287	Pirates!	Philippe Sarde
STV 81288	Vamp	Jonathan Elias
STV 81289	Fly	Howard Shore
STV 81290	Where the River Runs Black	James Horner
STV 81291	Deadly Friend	Charles Bernstein
STV 81292	Blue Velvet	Angelo Badalamenti
STV 81293	Tai-Pan	Maurice Jarre
STV 81294	Link	Jerry Goldsmith
STV 81295	Peggy Sue Got Married	John Barry
STV 81296	Crocodile Dundee	Peter Best
STV 81297	Sky Bandits	Alfi Kabiljo
STV 81298	Crimes of the Heart	Georges Delerue
STV 81299	Boy Who Could Fly	Bruce Broughton
STV 81300	52 Pick Up	Gary Chang
STV 81301	Let's Get Harry	Brad Fiedel
STV 81303	Firewalker	Gary Chang
STV 81304	Lionheart. Vol. I	Jerry Goldsmith
STV 81305	Down Twisted	Berlin Game
STV 81306	84 Charing Cross Road	George Fenton
STV 81307	Bedroom Window	Gleeson / Shrieve
STV 81308	Kindred	David Newman
STV 81309	From the Hip	Paul Zaza
STV 81310	Death Before Dishonor	Brian May
STV 81311	Lionheart, Vol. II	Jerry Goldsmith
STV 81312	Amazing Grace and Chuck	Elmer Bernstein
STV 81313	Evil Dead 2	Joe Lo Duca
STV 81314	Nightmare on Elm Street III	Angelo Badalamenti
STV 81315	Whistle Blower	John Scott
STV 81317	Good Morning Babylon	Nicola Piovani
STV 81318	Raising Arizona / Blood Simple	Carter Burwell
STV 81319	Three for the Road	Barry Goldberg
STV 81320	Desperately Seeking Susan	Thomas Newman
STV 81322	My Demon Lover	David Newman

STV 81324	House / House II	Harry Manfredini
STV 81327	Julia and Julia	Maurice Jarre
STV 81328	Believers (1987)	J. Peter Robinson
STV 81329	Hope and Glory	Peter Martin
STV 81330	Robocop	Basil Poledouris
STV 81333	Masters of the Universe	Bill Conti
STV 81334	No Way Out	Maurice Jarre
STV 81335	Russkies	James Newton Howard
STV 81336	Nowhere to Hide	Brad Fiedel
STV 81338	Housekeeping	Michael Gibbs
STV 81339	Three O'Clock High	Tangerine Dream
STV 81340	Prince of Darkness	John Carpenter
STV 81341	The Dead	Alex North
STV 81343	Man on Fire	John Scott
STV 81344	Nightflyers	Doug Timm
STV 81345	Near Dark	Tangerine Dream
STV 81346	Tough Guys Don't Dance	Angelo Badalamenti
STV 81347	Whales of August	Alan Price
STV 81348	Surrender	Michael Colombier
STV 81349	The Hidden	Michael Convertino
STV 81350	Weeds	Angelo Badalamenti
STV 81352	No Man's Land	Basil Poledouris
STV 81353	Anna	Greg Hawkes
STV 81354	Five Corners	James Newton Howard
STV 81355	Sister, Sister	Richard Einhorn
STV 81356	Running Man	Harold Faltermeyer
STV 81357	Shy People	Tangerine Dream
STV 81358	Flowers in the Attic	Christopher Young
STV 81359	In A Shallow Grave	Jonathan Sheffer
STV 81360	Noble House	Paul Chihara
STV 81361	Prison	Richard Band
STV 81362	Serpent and the Rainbow	Brad Fiedel
VS 5201	Crossing Delancey	Paul Chihara
VS 5202	BAT-21	Christopher Young
VS 5203	Nightmare on Elm Street IV	Craig Safan
VS 5204	Madame Sousatzka	Gerald Gouriet
VS 5205	Halloween IV	John Carpenter
VS 5208	Screen Themes	Various
VS 5209	Wisdom	Danny Elfman
VS 5210	Criminal Law	Jerry Goldsmith
VS 5211	Cocoon: The Return	James Horner
VS 5215	Talk Radio / Wall Street	Stewart Copeland
VS 5216	Farewell to the King	Basil Poledouris
VS 5219	Three Fugitives	David McHugh
VS 5220	Fly II	Christopher Young
VS 5223	Heathers	David Newman
VS 5226	Leviathan	Jerry Goldsmith
VS 5227	Pet Sematary	Elliot Goldenthal

SV 95001	North By Northwest	Bernard Herrmann
SV 95002	First Men in the Moon	Laurie Johnson
ASV 95003	Avengers	Laurie Johnson
704.180	Adventures of Robin Hood	Erich Wolfgang Korngold
704.210	Star Wars Trilogy	John Williams
704.250	Music from Hitchcock Films	Various
704.260	Miklos Rozsa	Miklos Rozsa
704.270	Star Trek, Vol. 1	Various
704.280	John Wayne, Vol. 1	Elmer Bernstein
704.290	Splash, Beastmaster, etc. (Holdridge compilation)	Lee Holdridge
704.300	Star Trek, Vol. II	Various
704.310	North and South / Right Stuff	Bill Conti
704.320	Bride of Frankenstein	Franz Waxman
704.340	Ghost and Mrs. Muir	Bernard Herrmann
704.350	John Wayne, Vol. 2	Various
704.370	Pee-Wee's Big Adventure	Danny Elfman
704.380	Sea Hawk	Erich Wolfgang Korngold
704.390	Suspect	Michael Kamen
704.400	Wall Street / Salvador	Copeland / Delerue
704.420	Zelly and Me	Pino Donaggio
704.430	Au Revoir Les Enfants	Franz Schubert
704.450	Off Limits	James Newton Howard
704.470	White Mischief	George Fenton
704.510	Return to Snowy River	Bruce Rowlands
704.520	Two Moon Junction	Jonathan Elias
704.530	Lady in White	Frank Laloggia
704.540	Dominick and Eugene	Trevor Jones
704.560	Bad Dreams	Jay Ferguson
704.570	Dead Heat	Ernest Troost
704.590	Stand and Deliver	Craig Safan
704.600	Eight Men Out	Mason Daring
704.610	DOA	Chaz Jankel
704.620	Poltergeist III	Joe Renzetti
704.700	Betrayed	Bill Conti
VCDM 1000.20	Digital Space	Various

Citadel

CT 7005	Songs by Korngold and Steiner	Korngold / Steiner
CT 7006	Bell, Book, and Candle	George Duning
CT 7007	Blue Max	Jerry Goldsmith
CT 7008	Patch of Blue	Jerry Goldsmith
CT 7009	Captain Horatio Hornblower	Robert Farnon
CT 7010	Lydia (Film Music for Piano)	Stein / Korngold / Rozsa
CT 7011	Freud	Jerry Goldsmith
CT 7012	Horror Rhapsody	Hans Salter
CT 7013	Cry of the Banshee	Les Baxter
CT 7014	South Seas Adventure	Alex North

CT 7015	Captain from Castile and others	Alfred Newman
CT 7016	Touch of Evil	Henry Mancini
CT 7018	Three Worlds of Gulliver	Bernard Herrmann
CT 7019	Come Next Spring / Last Command	Max Steiner
CT 7020	Day after Halloween	Brian May
CT 7021	Eternal Sea / Make Haste to Live	Elmer Bernstein
CT 7022	Dark Star	John Carpenter
CT 7023	Inseminoid	John Scott
CT 7024	Lone Wolf McQuade	Francesco Di Masi
CT 7026	Johnny Guitar	Victor Young
CT 7027	Sands of Iwo Jima / Sun Shines Bright	Victor Young
CT 7028	Walk on the Wild Side	Elmer Bernstein
CT 7029	To Kill A Mockingbird	Elmer Bernstein
CT 7030	Miss Bette Davis Sings!	Various
CT 7031	Pranks	Christopher Young
CT 7034	Barabbas	Mario Nascimbene
CT 6003	Hollywood Maestro - Alfred Newman	Alfred Newman
CT 6008	Blue Max	Jerry Goldsmith
CT 6015	Touch of Evil / Night Visitor	Henry Mancini
CT 6016	Midas Run	Elmer Bernstein
CT 6019	Freud	Jerry Goldsmith
CT 6020	Cassandra Crossing	Jerry Goldsmith
CT 6022	Wichita Town	Hans Salter
CT 6023	Film Music by Alex North	Alex North
CT 6024	Victor Young	Victor Young
CT 6025	A Walk With Love and Death	Georges Delerue
CT 6028	Patch of Blue	Jerry Goldsmith
CT 6031	Blood on the Sun	Miklos Rozsa
CTD 8100	Liberty	William Goldstein

Chalfont

| SDG 305 | Kings Row | Erich Wolfgang Korngold |
| SDG 313 | Empire Strikes Back | John Williams |

Starlog

SR 1000	Rocketship X-M	Ferde Grofé
SR 1001	Fantastic Film Music of Albert Glasser, Vol. 1	Albert Glasser
SR 1002	It's Alive II	Bernard Herrmann

BUYERS & SELLERS DIRECTORY

The pages in every Official Price Guide Buyers-Sellers Directory are packed with personal and business ads, certain to appeal to anyone with an interest in music collecting – whether you're buying or selling.

The Buyers-Sellers Directory is an excellent and inexpensive way to locate those elusive discs you've been seeking for your collection. For over 22 years, the results of advertising in the Osborne books have proven to be tremendous. We are especially proud of our high rate of repeat advertisers, one that far surpasses industry standards.

Look the ads over carefully. You might just find the dealer or contact you've been wanting to assist you in building your collection. When responding, be sure to say you saw their ad in this publication.

You can advertise in the next *Official Price Guide to Movie/TV Soundtracks & Original Cast Albums* or any of the other books in our series. Simply contact our office and ask for complete details.

Osborne Enterprises
Box 255
Port Townsend WA 98368
Phone: (360) 385-1200 — Fax: (360) 385-6572
www.olympus.net/personal/jpo — e-mail: jpo@olympus.net

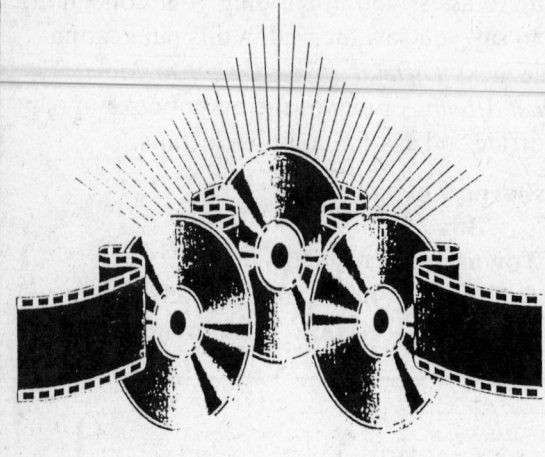

847

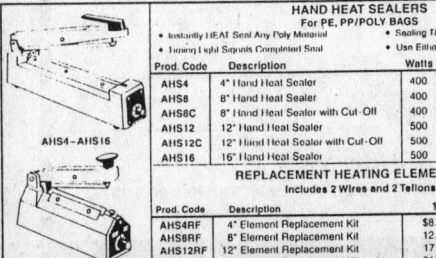

853

858

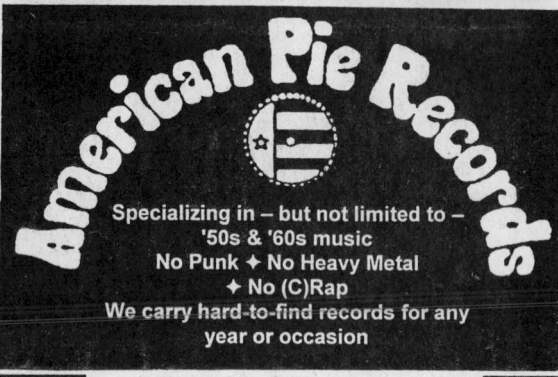

Contents

SECTION III: TRANSFORMATION

SECTION IV: INTERPRETATION

List of Maps, Tables, and Color Plates

MAPS AND TABLES

COLOR PLATES

Following p. 130:

George Catlin, Catlin Painting the Portrait of Máh-to-tóh-pa—Mandan
Karl Bodmer, Péhriska-Rúhpa, Hidatsa Man
Charles Deas, A Group of Sioux
John Mix Stanley, Last of their Race

Following p. 370:

George Caleb Bingham, The Jolly Flatboatmen in Port
Emanuel Leutze, Westward the Course of Empire Takes Its Way *(mural study)*
Thomas Moran, The Grand Cañon of the Yellowstone
An unidentified Oglala Lakota artist, Warrior's Shirt

Following p. 514:

David Hockney, Rocky Mountains and Tired Indians
Arthur Amiotte, Prince Albert, 1989
Carmen Lomas Garza, Cakewalk
Wayne Thiebaud, Corner Apartments *(study)*

Following p. 754:

Frederic Remington, Ghosts of the Past
Georgia O'Keeffe, From the Faraway Nearby
Fritz Scholder, Super Indian No. 2
Skeet McAuley, Navajo Window Washer, Monument Valley Tribal Park, Arizona

To our children—Catherine Carol Milner,
Charles Clyde Milner, Adam Sandweiss Horowitz,
and Sarah Sandweiss Horowitz—
who have inherited our love of the West, and to
Bob Horowitz, who shared this long trail.

Preface

This book is both a harvest and a celebration. It is a harvest of revitalized scholarly interest in the American West that began in the 1950s and continues to grow. It is also a celebration of the renewed recognition of the significance of the West in American history—a recognition that has increased through the efforts of numerous scholars. Some of those scholars have written chapters for this volume, and many others have made vital intellectual contributions that influenced what was written.

Books are often created with idealistic intentions. This volume is no exception. It is meant to serve as a reference work for readers who desire interpretation of large topics instead of exhaustive details about all topics. Important case studies and lively vignettes are incorporated into the individual chapters to illustrate significant points of interest. The editors have encouraged the creation of chapters meant to engage an attentive reader much as a masterful speaker tries to engage a listening audience. A good speaker does not exhaust his listener with particulars, and the good writing exhibited in this volume has a similar purpose. Every chapter in this volume could be a book in its own right, but our authors have generously attuned their efforts to readers who wish to be well informed, but not overwhelmed.

The illustrations for this book serve a similar idealistic purpose. They are a distinct contribution to each chapter's contents, often presenting information not incorporated into the text. The idea was to avoid constantly repeating visually what has been presented in writing.

Through the eighteen chapters of its first three sections, our volume flows forward chronologically. We begin in the era before the West's native peoples encounter Europeans and conclude with the challenges in the late twentieth century for the region's established residents and recent immigrants. The book's final section of five chapters explores the ways in which the West has been interpreted, not only in historical studies but also in literature and art, as well as in popular culture and international comparison. These different interpretations continue to influence how much of the world understands the West, at times regardless of the region's history.

◆ ◆ ◆

The formal planning for *The Oxford History of the American West* began in the spring of 1988. Clyde Milner and Carol O'Connor outlined the organization for the book and invited the twenty-five contributing authors. Marni Sandweiss planned the book's visual contents including the maps. She wrote all the captions and coordinated all illustrations with the authors as well as helped to edit several chapters.

For each of the three editors, it was a happy opportunity to work together. We received our Ph.D.'s from the same institution, Yale University, and two of us, Clyde Milner and Marni Sandweiss, had the same dissertation director, Howard R. Lamar. In addition, Carol O'Connor and Clyde Milner are husband and wife as well as professors in the same department at Utah State University. A colleague several years earlier had jokingly insisted that a married couple so fortunately situated owed the profession at least one joint book. Perhaps this volume will fulfill that informal obligation.

The editors' most generous thanks go first to each of our contributors. These authors shared our vision of the book and made the most essential intellectual contribution. It is always humbling when such talented people will go the extra mile to complete such a large project. Thanks too should go to many people whose names do not appear as authors but who helped us greatly. At an early stage of development, William H. Goetzmann and Howard R. Lamar gave very useful advice. Peter Nabokov, Patricia Nelson Limerick, and Paul Andrew Hutton contributed ideas for three chapters that kept the book moving forward.

Colleagues, students, and friends have also given us support. At Utah State University, Clyde Milner and Carol O'Connor wish to thank the staff of the *Western Historical Quarterly* and of the Department of History. Barbara L. Stewart, Carolyn Fullmer, Ona Siporin, and Jane A. Reilly aided efforts to produce readable texts, multiple documents, and timely communications. R. Edward Glatfelter, head of the history department, supported mailing costs and telephone budget and thoughtfully avoided asking when this huge project would finally end. He also endorsed the utilization of Milner's and O'Connor's year-long sabbaticals in 1990–91 to work on this book. C. Blythe Ahlstrom, the university's assistant provost, provided aid during and after this on-campus sabbatical leave.

Utah State University has its own history of nurturing the study of the American West. The creation of this book arose in this special place where a group of talented colleagues have been very supportive. David R. Lewis, Barre Toelken, Steve Siporin, F. Ross Peterson, Thomas J. Lyon, and Anne M. Butler—the latter three authors of chapters—are all making major contributions to the understanding of the West. Until he took early retirement in 1989 and moved to far southern Utah, a good friend and mentor, Charles S. Peterson, would have been part of this group. Appropriately, the three editors also wish to thank D. Teddy Diggs, who received her master's degree in history at Utah State after working two years as a graduate editorial assistant at the *Western Historical Quarterly*. Teddy Diggs is now a successful free-lance editor in Little Rock, Arkansas. She applied her keen editorial eye to the text of this volume and helped ensure the quality of its final production.

At Amherst College, whose location in the Pioneer Valley of western Massachusetts bespeaks the existence of America's old frontiers, Marni Sandweiss thanks her colleagues in the American Studies Department and the Mead Art Museum for their good fellowship and support throughout this project. Jerry Smolin provided useful assistance with picture research, and Lois Mono helped coordinate a seemingly end-less string of letters, photocopies, phone calls, and faxes. Particular thanks, however, go to Elizabeth Burke, who helped track down picture sources and patiently orga-nized and managed all of the paperwork involved in securing illustrations from more than 150 sources around the world. The many librarians, curators, and archivists who responded to these queries deserve our gratitude.

At the Cartographic Laboratory at the University of Wisconsin-Madison, our thanks go to Onno Brouwer and his staff, particularly Daniel J. Maher, who pro-duced the maps included in this book.

Finally, the three editors wish to thank individuals at Oxford University Press in New York City. Linda Halvorson Morse extended the original invitation to Clyde Milner, in 1988, to begin the planning of this work. She has remained our editor since that time. We thank not only Linda for her support but also Liza Ewell, and most especially, John Drexel and Liz Sonneborn, the development editors at Oxford who worked closely with us to ensure the book's completion.

We dedicate *The Oxford History of the American West* to our children—Catherine Carol Milner, Charles Clyde Milner, Adam Sandweiss Horowitz, and Sarah Sandweiss Horowitz—and to Marni Sandweiss's husband, Bob Horowitz. Our own westering adventures have been immeasurably enriched by their love and companionship.

Introduction

America Only More So

Often a dream, sometimes a metaphor, the American West is a place that millions of people can visualize. Certain landscapes of mountain and desert are instantly recognizable. So are certain residents, if they ride horses and wear broad hats or feathered headbands. In these nearly universal images, the West seems grandly conceived and easily explained. It is the West that serves as popular myth and national symbol.

The American West of historical interpretation is much more complex. The people of the West are not readily stereotyped. Lakotas, Navajos, and other Native Americans retain distinct cultural identities, as do a cornucopia of immigrants whose cultural heritages may be traced to Europe, Africa, or Asia but who sometimes arrived from farther north via Canada, from farther west via the Pacific Islands, or from farther south via Mexico and Latin America.

Like its residents, the location of the American West has changed over time. One generation's West became another generation's Midwest or Upper South. Such was the case for Andrew Jackson, who served as president of the United States from 1829 to 1837. In the late 1780s, after two years of studying law in Salisbury, North Carolina, while still in his early twenties, Jackson moved first to Martinsville in North Carolina and then to Jonesboro across the Appalachian Mountains in what would become the state of Tennessee. By the fall of 1788, he had arrived in the log-cabin village of Nashville, where he made his home and established his political career. Throughout his adult life, Jackson called himself a "westerner," and his avid supporters reveled in "Old Hickory's" regional identity.

By the late decades of the twentieth century, a western president could no longer hale from Tennessee, and his western identity needed to relate to cowboys of the open range rather than pioneers of the backwoods. Ronald Reagan fit both the image and the location. He owned a ranch, rode a horse, and wore cowboy boots. Reagan grew up in Illinois, but he found personal and political success in California. In his career as an actor, he spent four years on screen in western clothes as the announcer for the television series *Death Valley Days*. He became governor of California, which made him an important political figure. California had not been part of the United States during Jackson's lifetime, but even before Reagan's presidency (1981–89), it had the largest population of all the states, not only in the West but also in the nation.

Historical study recognizes the significance of change over time. One story of change explains how the West of the nation's political map once included Tennessee but not California and then at a later time included California but not Tennessee. This story of change emphasizes the nation's expansion westward. But there is another way to tell the historical story of the West. This story forms around the idea of place—a West firmly located beyond the Mississippi River. In this trans-Mississippi West, various historical factors, including the expansion of the United States, have shaped the story.

This volume will view the American West primarily as a distinct place whose historical interpretation follows no one master narrative and no single factor of plot. Instead many narratives, themes, and ideas, like the many peoples of the region, are brought together. In other words, the large and complex story of the West stretches across a shared historical terrain. It is a terrain containing many discrete locations, separate voices, and diverse ideas. For example, the West's story has many beginnings—first in the different origin tales of the region's native peoples and then in the tales of exploration created by the new peoples from Europe. The West's geographic boundaries are also variable. The *eastern* boundary takes form beyond the Mississippi River where the aridity of the Great Plains is clearly established, such as along the ninety-eighth meridian, which roughly coincides with the isohyetal line of less than twenty inches annual rainfall. The *western* boundary extends beyond the coast of the Pacific Ocean to the Aleutian Islands of Alaska and to the chain of islands, atolls, and reefs that make up the state of Hawai`i.

Alaska and Hawai`i represent a greater West that connects to the history of the United States in both the nineteenth and twentieth centuries. Their inclusion also recognizes the grand geographic diversity of the American West. Just as the West has no fixed set of external boundaries, it has no fixed geographic or cultural unity. Crosscut with various subregions, disparate states, and distinct peoples, the West demonstrates an intentional oxymoron, what the historian Richard Etulain has called a "fragmented unity."

In this complex and puzzling place, in this "fragmented unity" that is the West, the clearest boundaries may be those delineated by the people within the region. The historian Martin Ridge has stated: "There is a location on the plains of the West where, for some undetermined reason, people think of themselves as being westerners. . . . There is a psychological fault line that separates regions. As these people see it, they are not from the South but from the Southwest; not from the Middle West but from the West." Travelers sense this same fault line. Somewhere beyond the Mississippi, the horizon is more distant, the land more open, and the sky much larger. Well before they reach the Rocky Mountains, they know they have reached the West.

Archaeologists and historians know that crossing the plains was not the only way to reach the West. The first major migrations by native peoples came from the north, whereas the first major incursion by Europeans came from the south. These Spanish expeditions arrived in the homelands of well-established settlers. Did either group know that they were *in* the West? Of course not.

The American West is an idea that became a place. This transformation did not occur quickly. The idea developed from distinctly European origins into an American nationalistic conception. The western edge of several European empires, especially the British, moved into the hinterlands of North America. The United States inherited this westward edginess and made it the main directional thrust of its own empire. Once across the Mississippi, these American lands did not fill up with a steady progression of settlers. Overlanders and gold seekers pushed ahead to Oregon and California. The mountains, plains, and deserts would be filled in later, if at all. Throughout the nineteenth century, the United States laid claim to more and more of its West, culminating in 1898 with the annexation of Hawai`i. All of this occurred because a nation established mainly by African and European peoples created a region that replaced a world—a homeland once defined exclusively by native peoples.

Throughout the twentieth century, the West became a very American place with an increasingly diverse population. To expand on a statement about California, attributed to the writer Wallace Stegner, the West is America *only more so*. In this light, the culmination of America's history occurs in the West in the last half of the twentieth century. Writing the history of the West becomes, therefore, a vital aspect of understanding the history of the United States. Such a perspective is hardly new, but it should be carefully considered. The important distinction is whether the West is created and shaped primarily by the forces of American history both from within the region and from without, or whether the history of the West is what shaped the history of the United States. The latter proposition, in somewhat different formulation, has generated an astoundingly long-lived scholarly debate.

For several intellectual generations, a dispute has raged over the concept of the "frontier" as articulated by Frederick Jackson Turner in his 1893 essay "The Significance of the Frontier in American History." Turner first presented his famous frontier thesis on an especially warm July evening in 1893, when as a young, thirty-two-year-old historian from the University of Wisconsin, he gave the final talk at the last session on the second day of the World's Congress of Historians and Historical Students organized as part of the Columbian Exposition in Chicago. His audience did not respond with any enthusiasm, but four other speakers had preceded him. So it was a long meeting after a very hot day, yet Turner's essay would not be forgotten.

Turner's published version of his talk began with a quotation from the 1890 bulletin of the superintendent of the census. "Up to and including 1880 the country had a frontier of settlement, but at present the unsettled area has been so broken into by isolated bodies of settlement that there can hardly be said to be a frontier line." The census bureau defined the frontier as the outer margin of non-Indian settlement with a density of two persons per square mile. Turner made more of the frontier than just a line of population scarcity. He told his readers: "Up to our own day American history has been in a large degree the history of the colonization of the

Great West. The existence of an area of free land, its continuous recession, and the advance of American settlement westward, explain American development." Turner went on to claim that the frontier also explained American democracy and American character. The challenges of the wild land forged the values of the American citizen. If nothing else, Turner's thesis expressed a vital moment in the conception of the nation's history.

More than a century after its presentation, Turner's frontier and its scholarly significance have undergone extensive revision—at times to praise his ideas and at other times, such as in recent years, to bury them. Even his advocates are aware that Turner's words occasionally exhibit the ethnocentric perspective of a bygone era. Early in his essay, he refers to the frontier as "the meeting point between savagery and civilization." Of course, anthropology and ethnohistory now recognize the complexity of native life that seems more "civilized" in many locations than the behavior of the invading nonnative peoples. Other critics remain frustrated by the vague use of the term *frontier* itself. In this case, Turner candidly admitted, "The term is an elastic one, and for our purpose does not need sharp definition."

Turner ended his essay on a grandly apprehensive note by asserting, "The frontier has gone, and with its going has closed the first period of American history." He did not apply his "elastic" term into the next century, although others have done so. This volume does not ignore the concepts of Frederick Jackson Turner or his intellectual legacy, but its assembled authors make their own case for the significance of the history of the American West in all centuries under examination. It is a significance not based on one thesis but built on the authors' own thoughts and the work of numerous other scholars. It also is an attempt to free the history of the American West from what could be termed "the Mount Rushmore dilemma."

The four gigantic presidential heads carved into the granite of a prominent mountain in the Black Hills of South Dakota represent American nationalism in its most artificially monumental form. George Washington's nose alone is longer than the entire head, from the chin upward, of the Great Sphinx at Giza. Three of the four historical figures seem out of context for such a distinctly western setting: Washington, Thomas Jefferson, and Abraham Lincoln never visited the area. Theodore Roosevelt spent three years, from 1884 to 1886, ranching in the Badlands of the Dakota Territory. But Roosevelt was not chosen because of his sojourn in the West. According to Lincoln Borglum, the son of Gutzon Borglum, who designed the monument, then-president Calvin Coolidge made the decisive argument. Coolidge admired Roosevelt on the questionable assessment that he was a president who had protected the rights of working men.

In 1923 and 1924, Doane Robinson, the state historian of South Dakota, conceived the idea of a monument that depicted the great heroes of western history such as Lewis and Clark, John C. Frémont, and Red Cloud. Borglum accepted the challenge to find the appropriate mountain, but as his son reported, "He had become convinced that the proposed theme—heroes of western history—was too regionally circumscribed, too insignificant nationally." In effect, Borglum had decided that the West did not have historical figures grand enough to match its own mountains. Both Robinson and Borglum thought of heroic men and considered no representation of women. The elimination of Red Cloud only increased the irony that surrounds this monument, since his people, the Oglala Lakota Sioux, consider the Black Hills to be sacred land.

The dilemma of the Mount Rushmore monument is that it presents a visual argument for the *in*significance of western history, whereas the dilemma of Frederick Jackson Turner's frontier thesis is that it presents a scholarly argument for too much significance. No one monument and no single theory can either eradicate or explain the history of the American West. Instead, during what is now at least four decades of revitalized study, a set of significant themes has emerged. Four are worthy of some consideration here; others will become evident to the readers of this volume.

The Non-Vanishing Native Americans. The persistence of native peoples today would startle visitors from the nineteenth century. Even the best "friends" of the Indians assumed that Native Americans would die out, culturally if not physically. Native population reached its nadir in the 1890s at approximately 250,000. In the same decade, the non-Indian population of the United States grew to over 75 million. These original residents had not lived exclusively in what the United States considered its West. But governmental efforts in the first half of the nineteenth century attempted to relocate all Indians to lands beyond the Mississippi. The removal policy did not eliminate eastern Indians, but it did concentrate even more native peoples in the West, especially in the Indian Territory, which eventually became the state of Oklahoma.

A hundred years after its nadir, federally recognized Native American population is approaching 2 million. These native peoples exist in greater numbers and have greater landholdings in the American West than in any other region of the nation. Native peoples, their cultures and histories, have not been eradicated. They are living proof of the centuries of human history connected to what is now the American West.

The Impact of the Federal Government. In a region supposedly characterized by personal freedom and rugged individualism, the federal government has played an astonishingly large role. In political terms, the federal government created the territories and states of the trans-Mississippi, and it has not left them alone. From the explorations of Meriwether Lewis and William Clark in 1804–6 to the atmospheric testing of nuclear bombs in southern Nevada from 1951 to 1958, projects funded by Congress and administered by federal agencies have affected life in the West. Federal land grants underwrote the establishment of four transcontinental railroads after the Civil War, and military spending transformed the West's economy during and after World War II.

The federal government remains the greatest single landholder in the West. National parks and national forests are only two examples. In 1944, the federal government controlled 99 percent of the land in Alaska and 87 percent of the land in Nevada. Currently, the average for all twelve states from the Rocky Mountains westward, excluding Hawai`i, is over 50 percent. Not surprisingly, water, forest, and land-management programs continue to shape the West through the sometimes heavy-handed implementation of national policy.

The Exploitation of a Golden Land. The West's majestically scenic landscape has inspired not only artists but also entrepreneurs. Many of the latter sought wealth, not only on the western land but also beneath it in the mining of gold and silver and then of copper, coal, and uranium. Only a few made their fortunes. Many more toiled for little gain and often greater loss. Oil, especially in Texas, Oklahoma, and California, developed a similar story of boom and bust. Even wheat farming in the Red River valley of North Dakota had a bonanza era in the late 1870s and early 1880s.

For regional, national, and global markets, the economic development of the West has exploited a cornucopia of resources from timber in the Northwest to hydroelectric power on the Colorado River. Yet, in a term coined in the 1960s by Arizona's Stewart Udall, the "myth of super-abundance" has obscured a troubled and fragile natural environment. Water is an especially problematic resource in a predominantly arid West. The large-scale environmental cost of economic development began in the nineteenth century but became a major public issue only in the final decades of the twentieth century.

The Global Population of an International Borderland. The grand American story of mobility and immigration culminates in the American West. To some excited observers, it seemed nearly the entire world rushed toward California after 1848 to pan for gold. The influx of diverse peoples has continued to the present day, especially along the Pacific coast and in Hawai`i. The American West began as an international borderland between native peoples, the Spanish, Russians, French, and British. Today the international borderlands are even more significant with connections directly to Canada in the north, Mexico to the south, and numerous Asian nations via the Pacific. Immigrant groups who first arrived on America's east coast have representative populations in the West, as do peoples from Latin America, Asia, Australia, and the Pacific Islands. Just as the West's economy since the nineteenth century has increasingly connected to world markets, its population has increased its connections to the world's peoples.

◆ ◆ ◆

Ultimately, the case for the significance of the history of the American West moves beyond the national context to the world's stage. The world knows the American West through mass media images and occasional tourist visits. It also knows the

West in the nationalistic rhetoric of journalists and politicians. The West has been oversold and oversimplified as a vast vista of mountain, plain, and desert occupied by heroic, often male, archetypes noted for their violent actions. Through these misrepresentations, the world's peoples, and even the people of the United States, have little knowledge of the history of this distinctively American region. The authors in this volume have undertaken the important task of replacing easy assumptions about the West with thoughtful analysis of the West's past. In so doing, we desire to supplant widespread distortions with informed insight. This objective is perhaps the first, best purpose for any historical writing. We leave it to our readers to judge whether we have obtained our goal.

CLYDE A. MILNER II

Logan, Utah

Heritage

One West of the popular imagination is a place of spacious landscapes and few people. It is beyond the fringe of settlement on the frontier of national, and even international, expansion. It is natural wilderness, defined as a place where people are not, more often than as a place where people are. This imagined West ignores the well-established presence of native peoples and the diverse groups of nonnatives who have arrived in the region. It neglects the human heritages that have shaped the West both from within and from without. New peoples from across the Atlantic contributed to the mixture of cultures on the continent. Well before these developments, native cultures met and mixed in the West.

The European and African newcomers to North America did not settle an empty land. Some travelers, traders, and explorers may have observed a great wilderness with few native inhabitants, but what they did not understand was how the arrival of new peoples had created the depopulation that made a "wilderness" possible in many places. Over a dozen infectious diseases, led by smallpox, measles, and typhus—diseases common, or endemic, to one-half of the world in Eurasia and Africa—devastated the native peoples of the other half. The death rates from the "virgin soil epidemics," which spread among peoples with no resistance to these illnesses, are appalling. More than one of these killers could strike at the same time, driving the death rate up to as high as 90 percent.

As many as fifty million may have died in the decades after first contact. Not surprisingly, the most devastated were areas of dense population such as the Aztec and Inca empires of present-day Mexico and Peru and the Mississippi Valley of what is now the United States. After initial outbreaks, diseases often spread ahead of contact with Europeans and Africans. In areas of sparse settlement, or where the inhabitants had migratory patterns for subsistence, the onslaught might be delayed. For example, along the upper Missouri River of North America's Great Plains, major epidemics of smallpox were still occurring in the late 1830s.

The impact of disease after 1500 in the Western Hemisphere produced the greatest demographic disaster in human history. It also has produced many troubling questions. The first concerns the number of native peoples who inhabited this half of the planet before diseases took their toll. Historical demographers and other interested scholars keep revising their estimates. The geographer William Denevan compiled all the scholarly recalculations produced between 1976 and 1992 for native population. He estimated there were fifty-four million people in North and South America, with slightly less than four million north of present-day Mexico. But Denevan warned that his range of error was approximately 20 percent.

A second troubling question concerns the lack of comparable Native American diseases that could kill Europeans and Africans. Native residents migrated over a land

The Mandan chief Mató-Tópe's drawing of his slaying of a Cheyenne chief suggests the complexities of cultural exchange in the West. Its subject conveys the long history of intertribal tensions on the plains, whereas the detailed and carefully modeled drawing reveals the influence of the white artists Karl Bodmer and George Catlin on traditional plains art. A friend of both painters, Mató-Tópe died a bitter man, cursing the European-American people who had introduced the smallpox that proved fatal to him and many of his people.

Mató-Tópe (ca. 1800–1837). Mató-Tópe Battling and Killing a Cheyenne Chief with a Hatchet. Watercolor and pencil on paper, 1834. Gift of the Enron Art Foundation. Joslyn Art Museum, Omaha, Nebraska.

bridge from Asia thousands of years ahead of the newcomers from across the Atlantic. In this earlier passage to what was then a truly New World, the diseases of Asia may not have survived, or they may not have even existed in the migrant populations. The most deadly of the diseases that arrived after 1500 were eruptive fevers that evolved from microbes that initially may have infected various species of domestic animals and pets. For example, the microbe that produces rinderpest in cattle is closely related to the measles virus. Humans and domestic cattle have lived in proximity for eight thousand years, during which time the rinderpest virus, which does not affect humans, may have evolved into the measles virus, which does not affect cattle. Native Americans did not have domestic cattle. In fact, the only domestic animal found throughout the hemisphere was the dog.

Ironically, the domestic animals of Europe, especially horses, cattle, pigs, and sheep, flourished in the Western Hemisphere and greatly affected native societies. For example, the horse after 1500 would produce a cultural revolution for native peoples, especially on the Great Plains.

The eventual domination of Europeans in their New World differs from other stories of European expansion. After all, European empires tried to control much of Africa, India, and China, but today it is not peoples of European heritage that are the dominant population in these parts of the world. If diseases had not done their deadly work, what population today would dominate in North and South America? Indeed, would these two continents even carry such names?

And what of the heritage of the American West? Could the Spanish empire have pushed so far north? Could the Russian-American Company have established itself in Alaska and along the Pacific coast? Would only a few French traders, British explorers, and Christian missionaries have found their way across the plains and even out to the Hawaiian Islands? Would there have been sufficient room for non-Native Americans east of the Mississippi River to create a United States of America and then to acquire a western region for that nation?

Such questions are merely conjecture. They do not alter certain historical realities. Native Americans are still the first "westerners"—the original inhabitants of the region. Despite the impact of diseases and the arrival of nonnatives, many native cultures retain a vital existence. Perhaps one of the best-established groups is the Pueblo peoples of the modern-day Southwest. These villagers first dealt with the Spanish in 1540. From an estimated population of sixty thousand in the mid-1550s, the Pueblos shrank in number to a little over nine thousand residents by 1790. But they did not die out, and their population eventually increased to nearly fifty-three thousand in 1990. To the present day, the Pueblo peoples retain their cultural identity, religious traditions, and historical memories, particularly of their successful revolt against the Spanish in 1680.

Native peoples made their home on the land that became the American West, and they have not left it. Europeans began arriving in these homelands nearly five centuries ago. Many more immigrants are still arriving, and not just from Europe. The West has become a region of mixed heritages that originated both from within the region and from outside. It is a place defined initially by the histories of native peoples and by the arrival of newcomers—first from the nations of Europe and then from a new nation to the east.

— Clyde A. Milner II

CHRONOLOGY

28,000 B.C.	Clear signs of human settlement in what would become North America.
A.D. 1,000	Two oldest Pueblo communities of Acoma and Hopi in existence. Polynesians well established on Hawaiian Islands.
1200–1400	Navajos arrive in the Southwest.
1492	Christopher Columbus's landfall in the Bahamas inaugurates centuries of cross-cultural exchange.
1540–42	Francisco Vásquez de Coronado leads Spanish expedition from Arizona to Kansas.
1565	The Spanish found St. Augustine, Florida.
1580	Over five hundred European vessels fish for cod off coast of Newfoundland.
1598	Juan de Oñate establishes towns for Spain in northern New Mexico.
1607	The English plant a permanent settlement in Jamestown, Virginia.
1608	The French found Quebec.
1614	The Dutch establish Fort Nassau on the Hudson River.
1616–19	"Virgin soil epidemic" decimates native peoples in coastal New England.
1620	English Pilgrims settle at Plymouth, formerly Patuxet.
1620s	Tobacco boom in Virginia; fur trade flourishes.
1630–42	"Great Migration" from England to New England.
1664	The English take over New Netherland.
1680	The Pueblo Revolt expels the Spanish from New Mexico.
1682	La Salle reaches the mouth of the Mississippi.
1692–96	Diego de Vargas reconquers the Pueblos.
1707	Lakota pictographs show these native peoples trading for horses.
1718	The French establish New Orleans.
1741	Vitus Bering and Aleksei Chirikov explore the coast of Alaska for Russia.
1763	Treaty of Paris ends French and Indian War and cedes French Canada and lands east of the Mississippi to Great Britain. Spain holds former French lands to the west.
1778	Captain James Cook visits the Hawaiian Islands.
1781	Representatives of New Spain found El Pueblo de Nuestra Señora la Reina de los Angeles in Alta California.
1783	Treaty of Paris ends the American Revolution and extends U.S. borders to the Mississippi.
1785	Ordinance passed by Congress establishes standard survey grid for the United States.
1786	The viceroy of New Spain announces a new Indian policy.
1787	Northwest Ordinance establishes procedures by which U.S. territories can become states.
1791	Defeat of Arthur St. Clair's troops by forces led by Little Turtle on Wabash River.
1799	Aleksandr Baronov establishes a fort in southeastern Alaska near present-day Sitka.
1802–3	France regains Louisiana from Spain and then sells it to the United States.
1811	Tenskwatawa's village on Tippecanoe Creek falls to Indiana militia under William Henry Harrison.
1812–14	War with Great Britain allows the United States to fight Indians opposed to Anglo-American domination of the trans-Appalachian region.
1821	Mexico secures its independence from Spain.

Chapter One

Native Peoples and
Native Histories

PETER IVERSON

Perhaps thirty thousand years ago, the first settlers arrived in the land that would come to be known as North America. These pioneers did not travel by ship, nor did they claim territory for any monarch, but they did discover America. Migrating on foot across a land bridge that spanned the narrow Bering Strait during the Ice Age, they gradually made their way throughout the continent and down into South America, all the way to the tip of present-day Argentina. They sought not empires to swell national treasuries but new hunting grounds to feed growing populations. Of course, it took generations for these first explorers to become well established in specific locations. By A.D. 1000, or even before then, some groups occupied the territory they still claim today. Others continued to migrate, to create new homes and new customs for themselves. Even after the first Europeans made it to American shores, obviously uncertain of where they were or what the land might hold, many of the people they labeled "Indians" remained in motion.

Both for relative newcomers and for more established Indian settlers in any region, the process of building communities and traditions was essentially the same. Around winter fires or on the hunt, while working in the fields or participating in religious rites, the younger members of each group learned from the older members. Their elders taught them about the creatures who shared the earth and sky with them and about the origins of their people. Through this instruction, they understood from an early age that their people belonged to the land they occupied. Creation stories often contained accounts of migration, but these stories also reassured people that the place where they lived was meant to be their home.

One such legend has been told for at least ten centuries by the people of Acoma Pueblo in present-day western New Mexico. That community traced its beginnings to Sipapu, a mythical place beneath the ground. In the legend, a spirit named Tsichtinako met up with two sisters, Iatiku and Nautsiti, who lived in the underworld. The spirit taught them to speak and prepared them to leave the darkness for the strong light of the world above ground. When they were ready, Tsichtinako gave the sisters baskets filled with seeds and with images of the animals who were to live in their new home. The sisters planted four kinds of pine trees underground according to the spirit's guidance. One of the pine trees grew faster than the others and pierced a small hole in the earth above, causing the image of the Badger to come alive.

The middle figure at the top of this painting by a young Acoma artist is Iatiku, a central figure in the Acoma Pueblo creation myth. Framed by mothers of the first-born girls, she is surrounded by symbols of the natural world and fetishes specific to Acoma culture.

Wolf Robe (Kiwa, also known as William Henry, 1905–77). Fire Society Altar. *Watercolor on paper, 1928. Smithsonian Institution, National Anthropological Archives (#45014-C), Washington, D.C.*

At the request of the sisters, Badger climbed the pine tree and enlarged the hole, then returned to the underworld. The sisters rewarded him with a happy life in a place that would be neither too hot nor too cold. Next, Locust came to life and the sisters asked him to smooth the edges of the hole with plaster. Before returning from his task, however, Locust ignored the sisters' prohibition and ventured out into the light. On his return, he lied about his transgression, and the sisters punished him. They condemned him to a short life, although they allowed him to be born again each year.

Iatiku and Nautsiti came into the world above ground through the hole prepared by Badger and Locust. When they arrived, they sprinkled plant pollen and sacred cornmeal from their baskets in prayer to the Sun. Each chose a name for the clan of her descendants, Iatiku settling on Sun and Nautsiti on Corn. The sisters then set about creating the mountains, plains, mesas, and canyons that characterize the Acoma homeland. From these, they gained a sense of the four directions. Next, they grew plants from the seeds in their baskets and animals from the images, in the process learning how they belonged to the land and all that lived upon it. Evil entered the world when one of the images came to life as a Snake. Snake tempted Nautsiti to become pregnant by the rain that fell from a rainbow. From then on, the sisters became increasingly unhappy with each other; eventually they chose to go their separate ways. After the sisters split up, signs of discord multiplied among the birds and animals: Magpie, for instance, ate the intestines of a deer that had been killed by a puma; as a result, Magpie forgot how to hunt and was reduced to scavenging.

Nautsiti left the region, but Iatiku remained behind and in time bore many children. Each child's name became the name of a different Acoma clan. Iatiku also brought to life the spirits of the different seasons as well as the katcinas, the spirits who became so prominent in the beliefs and rituals of generations to come. The katcinas would help Iatiku's descendants to be brave, to learn how to lead good lives, and to grow corn. In homage, the Acomas would imitate the katcinas in dances and ceremonies. After creating the katcinas, Iatiku decided the time had come for the people to build their homes. She told them how to construct their homes and how to design the village they would inhabit. Following Iatiku's instructions, the people built a sacred room, a kiva, in their village. The kiva symbolized Sipapu, the mythical place from which Iatiku had entered the aboveground world. For worshipers inside, its ceiling represented the Milky Way and its walls symbolized the sky. The kiva reminded the people of their origins, of their links with the earth and the sky.

Thus, the legend recounts the origins of Acoma Pueblo. Visitors to the pueblo, built high atop a mesa in a magnificent valley, can still appreciate why the Acomas believe the place to be the center of the world.

The American Indian West

By 1500, the first inhabitants of the American West had created many such centers of the world. Still more would emerge in the years leading up to the early nineteenth century as different peoples continued to migrate, to settle in new homes, and to endow important places—prominent mountains or hidden lakes—with sacred significance. Although European intruders would misunderstand the Native American peoples as a single, monolithic population, many different cultures—varying in size, ambition, and economy—inhabited North America.

In the salubrious environment of the northwestern Pacific Coast, for example, a relatively dense population of related peoples thrived. Small groups occupied compact niches where the abundant land and sea supplied everything they needed. They had no need to conduct extended hunting or gathering forays, but they enjoyed a lively trade with groups from the interior. Through that trade, they acquired items useful for ceremonial purposes and in turn provided the interior peoples with abalone shells and other items unavailable in the less bountiful mountains, valleys, and deserts.

By contrast, fewer tribal groups lived where resources proved scarce and hard to find, for people in these regions had to traverse a wide terrain in order to survive. The passage of the seasons dictated annual cycles of hunting and gathering; the people came to appreciate and even respect the plants and animals with which they shared the earth. In areas burdened with uncertain weather, hunger remained a perennial possibility, but even under challenging circumstances, many communities attempted to farm. Depending on the amount of rainfall, soil conditions, and the length of the growing season, some farmers could coax significant yields from fields of maize, squash, and beans. But they knew their success depended on more than their own diligence, so they performed rituals to call forth the rain.

Although the diversity of the many native communities of the American West makes it difficult to generalize about them, they did share certain fundamental features that set them apart from Europeans. Perhaps most notable was their dedication to community. In general, each person stayed in his or her community of origin from birth to death, never leaving it for the next village, the next tribe, or the next hemisphere. Such permanent affiliation daily reminded individuals of their obligations, values, and loyalties. Individual expression, achievement, and recognition no doubt had a place within indigenous cultures, but people never forgot their role within their group. In a world without horses or rifles to assist in the hunt or win the war, success absolutely depended on cooperation.

This rejection of individualism shaped native attitudes toward the land. Individuals did not own parcels of real estate, so status and power had nothing to do with the acquisition of acreage, as it did in Europe. Nor did groups as a whole own land, although this does not indicate an absence of territoriality. Each people claimed the right to use the land in a given area; communal priorities dictated how the resources there were employed. If their population increased or if drought or a reduction of available resources forced them to move, Indians would attempt to expand their hunting and gathering domain through war with their neighbors. Skirmish or war could often be avoided, but both before and after the Europeans arrived, Indians occasionally fought over land.

Despite this tendency to territorial disputes, Indians did not, as historians too frequently have written, have "ancient" or "traditional" enemies. Each group surely had its allies and enemies, but such relationships were neither permanent nor necessarily long-lived. Alliances changed and animosities withered or flared, both before and after European contact. Probably far more frequently than they fought with each other, different peoples learned from each other. As they moved about, Indian bands transported old ways of doing things to new places and at the same time picked up improved methods of building houses, growing crops, hunting animals, or weaving rugs. Their flexibility carried over into the postcontact period, when many groups incorporated European technology into their culture. Absorbing new influences—whatever their source—did not signal the decay or diminution of any culture. On the contrary, these additions kept cultures viable and eventually seemed as much a part of their traditions as older ways did. The people created stories to explain such augmentations: we have always had horses; the holy people gave us sheep; the Black Hills have been sacred ground from time immemorial.

But even before the introduction of European technology, the American Indian West was a place of progress and innovation. The challenges faced by the people living there—the altitude, the wind, and the aridity—highlight the economic and cultural success enjoyed by many native societies. The resourcefulness of Plains buffalo hunts, the sophistication of Northwest Coast art, and the complexity of Navajo philosophy all point to the vitality of the aboriginal peoples of North America. Imagine what the Yavapais knew about plants, what the Inuit learned about whale hunting, or what the Pueblo peoples observed in the heavens. Consider the rich symbolism of tribal stories or the vibrant imagery of native songs. Far from primitive, the first Americans had a great knowledge of the world, a wisdom that benefited those Europeans open to it.

Likewise, the Europeans possessed knowledge and goods that the Indians wanted. But problems arose between these potentially equal peoples when the Europeans tried to impose undesired new ways on the Indians or tried to achieve their own goals at the expense of those who had first settled in the American West. Because this economic, religious, and social friction did not disappear with time, echoes of confusion and misunderstanding reverberate in the West even today. At the heart of the contemporary conflicts stand the centuries-old issues of land, language, law, sovereignty, and identity. Any insight into the history of the American West must therefore start with an examination of the nature of native societies in the first centuries after Columbus sailed and of the effect the European arrival had on those communities.

The Southwest

To the casual observer, Acoma and the other Pueblo communities of the American Southwest before the European incursion may appear to have been changeless worlds, where one generation after another repeated the familiar patterns of life and where innovation and imagination were devalued. Indeed, the Pueblo peoples cultivated continuity and respect for tradition, but their ancient stories establish that they were not frozen in a quaint ethnographic tableau. These cultures maintained continuity through change. By adaptation, experimentation, and trial and error, they discovered what worked and what did not.

The history of the different Pueblo communities of present-day Arizona and New Mexico centers on change. Acoma and Hopi are probably the two oldest surviving communities, both dating back at least a thousand years; some scholars contend that the Hopi area has been occupied for several thousand years. In the centuries before the Spaniards arrived, the village populations at Acoma and Hopi swelled from immigration.

The Anasazi peoples, who had occupied such fabled sites as Mesa Verde and Chaco Canyon, dispersed, perhaps because of drought, soil depletion, or disease; this brought new residents to old villages and led to the formation of new settlements. Some of the people from Mesa Verde drifted down to Acoma while others ventured to the Rio Grande valley. At the same time, people from the Marsh Pass and Kayenta areas to the north migrated to Hopi.

By the early 1500s, these Pueblo peoples had learned a great deal from numerous contacts with other Indian groups through raiding, war, immigration, and most often, trade. Items and ideas from hundreds or even thousands of miles away arrived with the transient traders and foreign immigrants, some of whom were permitted to reside in the Pueblo villages. The arrival of newcomers probably prompted a renaissance in Hopi pottery technique at the beginning of the 1300s, which transformed the distinctive black-on-white designs to black-on-orange. At Acoma, meanwhile, migrants from the Cebollita area altered not only the local pottery but also housing construction: villagers abandoned adobe in favor of horizontal, wet-laid masonry.

Even though the Pueblo peoples had previously encountered strangers and some-times learned to accept the changes they brought, the arrival of the Spaniards inaugurated a new era. The initial stages of Spanish-Indian contact churned with misinterpretations and violence. In 1539, for instance, the Zuni people met and killed Esteban, a North African who eight years earlier had trekked from the Gulf of Mexico to present-day Mexico City with the party of Alvar Núñez Cabeza de Vaca. Esteban arrived at Zuni as an advance scout for an expedition headed by the Franciscan padre Marcos de Niza. This group had been dispatched to investigate persistent rumors of wealthy cities in the shadowy reaches of northern New Spain. Shrouded in mystery, Esteban's untimely demise is said to have been the response of his initially hospitable Zuni hosts to Esteban's inappropriate requests and violations of proper behavior.

A frightened Marcos de Niza quickly fled to the south. Uncertain why Esteban had been killed, he reported to his superiors that he did not know whether the Zunis had any wealth. His report may have been ambiguous, but it inspired the historic expedition of Francisco Vásquez de Coronado in search for El Dorado, the "city of gold." From 1540 to 1542, Coronado's large expeditionary force lumbered around the Southwest, even stumbling as far east and north as present-day Kansas. Kansas did not look like El Dorado to the weary travelers, who in 1542 retraced their steps south and west past the Zuni village of Hawikuh, which they had fought and brought under their control in July 1540.

Coronado not only explored the Southwest but also sought to conquer the people who lived there. He occasionally prevailed, yet both New Spain and the native inhabitants of the Southwest paid a terrible price for his efforts. At the end of the century, the colonizer Juan de Oñate encountered fierce resistance at Acoma. The Indians there had no doubt heard about the fate of other Pueblo Indians along the Rio Grande, whose villages had been plundered or whose occupants had been burned at the stake by Coronado's men. Told again and again during the decades before Oñate's arrival, the stories of horror were seared into the Indians' consciousness. They did everything possible to repel Oñate, who nevertheless suppressed the Indians.

Despite Oñate's cruelty, the Acomas in time accepted the missionary Juan Ramirez, who from 1629 to 1649 brought fruit trees and livestock to the mesa. He lived in a way that inspired the people; they even helped him build an imposing, thick-walled church. But his successor, Lucas Maldonado, had the misfortune of being stationed on the mesa during the great revolt of 1680. Some of the people seized him as the embodiment of Spanish colonialism and hurled him off the mesa to his death on the rocks below. He died for the sins of his Spanish ancestors. The Spaniards did not abandon their northern outpost at Acoma in the aftermath of the revolt. Instead, in 1692 they returned under the resolute Diego de Vargas. Recognizing the risks of violence, Vargas tried to rein in his men. But he was no pacifist, and after one flare-up of resistance in the summer of 1696, he shot five Acoma captives and destroyed the Acoma cornfields.

By the turn of the eighteenth century, however, an uneasy peace appeared to prevail. Indians and Spaniards seemed to recognize that both were there to stay and that neither could be totally subjugated. Although this realization did not force the Franciscans to take a vow of perpetual pluralism, they naturally hoped to avoid a recurrence of the revolt that had killed their predecessors a generation before. As a result, they were unlikely to raid the kivas in the future. Similarly, especially in the Rio Grande area, where the Spanish population was more concentrated, the Pueblo peoples often became Catholics. They practiced their new religion while continuing to participate in traditional ceremonies that fulfilled native needs. Outside the realm of religion, the Indians found some Spanish ways useful and even pleasing. They already farmed, but the Spaniards introduced new things to grow, such as peaches, apples, and wheat. The sheep, cattle, goats, and horses brought from Europe offered food, clothing, and transportation to the Pueblo peoples; in time they could not imagine that they had ever lived without these animals.

Nonetheless, resistance to Spanish influence did not disappear. In the final two decades of the seventeenth century, various fragmented Pueblo communities reestablished themselves to avoid either absorption or control by the Spaniards. One band of refugees, from the Rio Grande valley near present-day Albuquerque, traveled hundreds of miles to the Hopi mesas to seek shelter. They established the Tewa-speaking community of Hano on First Mesa and maintained a separate community in the years to come. Other Pueblo Indian communities were absorbed into the expanding clan structure of the Navajos, and yet another group initially sought shelter at Acoma. In the very last years of the 1600s, this last group founded a new pueblo of their own, the relatively recent subdivision of Laguna.

But it was the Hopis, the westernmost Pueblo people and the most removed from contact with the Spaniards, who most staunchly rejected European influence. In 1700 they destroyed Awatovi, the one Hopi village that had tried to adopt Christianity. Six years later, they attacked the nearest Pueblo village of Zuni to protest the return of Christian influence there. The Spaniards repeatedly sent military emissaries out to chastise the Hopis for their obstinacy, but the Hopis repelled the unwanted delegations in 1701, twice in 1707, and again in 1717. Likewise, Franciscan and, later, Jesuit priests came away chagrined on several different occasions. Father Silvestre Vélez de Escalante made an unsuccessful overture in 1775, Father Francisco Garces in 1776, and Governor Juan Bautista de Anza in 1780. The case of the Hopis illustrates a general truth about the nature of intercultural contact: more frequent encounters with outsiders do not necessarily erode community identity. Indeed, the Hopis gained greater community cohesion over the years; the arrival of the Spaniards heightened Hopi identity rather than diminished it.

California

The Spaniards extended their campaign of economic, political, and social colonization beyond the contemporary borders of Arizona and New Mexico. Because of the general Spanish interest in the resources of the Pacific coast, California received considerable attention. In California, where the extraordinary topographical diversity had produced a corresponding diversity in its first peoples, the Spaniards encountered a great range of smaller native communities.

Here too, as in Acoma, native children learned about the world around them through stories told by their elders. According to the Modocs, volcanic Mount Shasta was once the home of a spirit who kept a fire in his lodge for himself and his family; the smoke from the fire came out of the hole in the top. They also believed grizzly bears were their ancestors and so should not be harmed. The Maidus, meanwhile, said the Sacramento River had been created when a hole had been poked in a mountainside, allowing the waters of a great flood to surge into the valley below.

Within the different environmental zones of California, Indian communities had a range of economic and cultural activities. Especially along the coast, ample land and water resources permitted localized economies and worldviews. Young people assumed they would live their entire lives within the boundaries of an area that would seem small to postindustrial Americans but that did not feel confining to the first Californians. Indeed, Spanish accounts testify to the richness of that world. In addition, the Indians knew how to manipulate or alter the land for their own benefit. In grassland, woodland, and chaparral regions, they employed regulated, seasonal burning to control brush, stimulate the growth of crops, and improve conditions for hunting.

Human activity within the world of the first Californians was carefully regulated by ritual. Hunters, the Indians believed, did not succeed solely by virtue of their own stealth and cunning but in proportion to their respect for their prey. Just as rituals were meant to bring rain in the Southwest, in California they brought deer to the hunter. A Pomo deer hunter, for example, applied to his body the pleasing smell of angelica and peppertree leaves, thereby showing his respect for his prey and its feelings and emotions.

As their rituals show, the natives of California believed that arrogance and insensitivity toward nature led to disaster. That disaster often took the form of drought, making many areas inhospitable to humans. Some Indians, most notably the Paiutes of the Owens Valley, diverted water for agricultural purposes, but most groups had little need for this technology. Instead, they simply chose to live wherever water was more plentiful. There they could take advantage of the easy life made possibly by an adequate water supply. They did not feel compelled to make the land more fruitful, for they did not seek to dominate nature. Proper living and respectful attitudes preserved this harmonious way of life by ensuring that the rains came. If drought came instead, the people revised their rituals or moved away. Not so the Spaniards, the Mexicans, or the

Americans, who sought to conquer nature by manipulating the water supply to create artificial environments.

These concerns, however, did not vanish. Indeed, they became magnified over time. For example, in 1925, a Wintu named Kate Luchie contrasted the actions and beliefs of whites and Indians. Whites, she said, had never cared for the land or its creatures. Disregarding the pleas of the rocks and the ground, they plowed up the earth, pulled up the trees, and killed the animals. "They blast rocks and scatter them on the earth," she wrote. "The white people dig long deep tunnels. They make roads. They dig as much as they wish. They don't care how much the earth cries out. How can the spirit of the earth like the white man?" Someday, she predicted, the water would come down from the north in retribution for all the white man had done, and all humanity would drown. When all the Indians died, the world would end. Her warnings echoed the centuries-old teachings of California's Indians.

When the Spaniards appeared on the scene, they imported other stories and other dictates. The Franciscan Junípero Serra and his compatriots established mission stations along the coast and set about informing the Indians that they had not been worshiping properly, for according to the Spaniards, humans were superior to animals. White historians until recently portrayed Serra as a kindly man who gently instructed his native charges on the error of their ways. But in the late twentieth century, the prospect of sainthood for Father Serra brought a different, though equally long-held, image to the fore. Indian history called Serra little more than a slaveholder who made prisoners rather than converts of native Californians.

Whether Serra was a saint or a scorpion, there can be little doubt that the Spanish presence adversely affected many Indian communities in California. European diseases reduced the native population by perhaps half. Indians who lived within mission walls suffered severe restrictions on their freedom and, over time, lost their culture. But Spanish domination did not extend to all the peoples of California. Those, such as the Yahis, who lived farther in the interior—in the foothills of the northern Sierra Nevada—were more than a hundred miles from the nearest mission at San Francisco and escaped the worst ravages of the period.

Moreover, some Indians resisted Spanish subjugation. For example, members of the Ipai-Tipai villages attacked Mission San Diego de Alcalá on 4 November 1775, killing Padre Luís Jayme and two other Spaniards. Thousands of southern California Indians rebelled in 1824, destroying Mission Santa Ynez, taking over Mission La Purísima Concepción, and fighting white soldiers called in to protect Mission Santa Barbara. The Spaniards quelled these and other rebellions, but Indian resistance continued. Indians often tried to run away from the missions, and other forms of more passive resistance no doubt also took place.

In the far northern part of California, the Yurok village of Tsurai on Trinidad Bay affords an instructive and well-documented glimpse of native encounters with different Europeans. After initial observation of the bay by the Portuguese sailor Sebastian Rodriguez Cermeno in 1595, the Yuroks apparently had little contact with European vessels until the arrival in 1775 of the Spanish captains Don Bruno de Hezeta and Don Juan Francisco de la Bodega y Quadra. The Spanish entrance into Trinidad Bay convinced whites and Indians alike that a new day had come to northern California.

Bodega y Quadra's journal noted: "The commandant took possession of those lands with all the dignity and solemnity that the accommodations of the port afforded. Mass was celebrated, a sermon was preached and many volleys of cannon and guns were fired as an act of thanks to the creator." He observed that the Indians "were terrified by these noises," believing "that those volleys could demolish the nearby mountains." The Spaniards clearly saw the area as a land of great promise for farming and ranching and noted the "well-ordered" hunting, fishing, and gathering economy of the natives. Perceived again and again as timid and docile, the local people did not appear to threaten European or American ambitions and prerogatives.

Late in the eighteenth century, the British captain George Vancouver stopped in Trinidad Bay a few months before another Spanish ship anchored there. At that point, starting in the early 1800s, sea otters in the bay began to attract various trading ships. The Yuroks grew increasingly enmeshed in the global economy and its conflicts; in an 1806 clash, whites from a ship called the *O'Cain* killed a Yurok. Owned by Americans, the *O'Cain* fulfilled a Russian contract, carried Aleut hunters, and landed in territory still claimed by Spain. The *O'Cain* incident heralded the beginning of the end of Indian autonomy in northern California.

The Pacific Northwest Coast

Stretching fifteen hundred miles from southern Oregon to the Gulf of Alaska and spanning no more than one hundred or two hundred miles east to west, the Pacific Northwest Coast is a long narrow strip that housed native peoples in a world between

A member of a Russian exploring party that arrived in San Francisco in 1816, Ludovik Choris became one of the few Europeans to depict Indian life in Spanish California. Here, in front of Mission San Francisco de Asís, members of an unidentified tribe dance under a towering cross, suggesting the accommodation of cultures that marked Spanish-Indian relations during the early 19th century.

Ludovik Choris (1795–1828). Danse des Californiens. Watercolor over pencil on paper, 1816. Courtesy, The Bancroft Library, University of California, Berkeley.

mountains and ocean. Water defined the region, in the tides and waves of the sea, in the flow of the rivers and creeks, and in the frequent showers of falling rain. The skies ranged from light to dark gray, but the indigenous residents probably did not complain too much. Not only was it the only world they knew, but in it they found abundant resources and prosperity. Along nearly the entire coastline, Sitka spruce and western hemlock flourished, together with yellow cedar in the north and Port Orford cedar in the south. The natives usually selected cedar for their world-renowned woodworking, but they used a variety of woods for different implements, weapons, and ceremonial objects.

Chinook, coho, sockeye, pink, and chum salmon ran in seemingly inexhaustible numbers from fresh water to the ocean and back again to fresh water. Halibut, herring, and other saltwater fish, as well as various sea mammals, supplemented the local diet. On a seasonal cycle, the people hunted bears, beavers, and other land animals. Far more frequently than Indians in many other parts of North America, they could anticipate a surplus during the brief, leaner winter months. The region's rich resources also allowed the people to spend time nurturing a highly creative artistic culture, whose accomplishments included stylized woodworking and splendid twined basketry.

The Cascade Mountains split present-day Oregon and Washington into two regions: to the east, the land is dry, and resources are less plentiful. But some indigenous peoples say this has not always been so. A long time ago, according to Quinault legend, Ocean sent his sons and daughters, Clouds and Rain, to the dry country in answer to the pleas of its residents. Fearing the return of drought, the eastern people refused to allow Clouds and Rain to leave after their visit. A distraught Ocean beseeched the spirits to punish the people. In response, the spirits built a barrier of dirt between the eastern people and the abundant west. This partition became the Cascades; the hole from which the dirt was taken filled with water to form the Puget Sound. From that time on, the eastern peoples struggled to survive in an arid land with few resources.

West of the Cascades, though, many different communities formed along the bountiful coast, including Eyaks, Tlingits, Haidas, Tsimshians, Bellacoolas, Kwakiutls, Nootkas, Makahs, Quileutes, and Tillamooks. No single culture can be said to represent all these communities, but many of the people shared certain characteristics. Like other peoples throughout the area, the Tlingits told stories about mischievous Raven, whose exploits, travels, and travails amused and instructed listeners. Tlingit myths and texts also describe many other beings important to the people, including the orca, otter, porcupine, wolverine, beaver, halibut, clam, salmon, frog, sea lion, and bear. In these tales, the lives of animals and fish intermingled with those of humans. A woman married a frog, a man entertained the bears, a salmon chief talked to a fisherman, a devilfish married a woman and impregnated her. From childhood, Tlingits learned that other beings had feelings and impulses and that all beings were capable of good and evil.

The Tlingits' seasonal pattern of hunting and fishing brought them into contact with many different creatures of the land and sea. Because of their beliefs, Tlingit hunting and fishing assumed the character of a holy quest, in which participants carefully prepared to enact their sacred duty. Boys learned early that the proper response to success on the hunt was not arrogance but gratitude. To heighten their chances of snaring their quarry, hunters wore charms made by shamans, the Tlingit religious leaders. The charms reflected not only the artistic ability of the shaman but also his or her relationship with the spirits.

Armed with religious rituals and proper behaviors, as well as the appropriate implements and a detailed knowledge of animal and fish behavior, the Tlingit people ably harvested the resources of the region. Hunting sea lions, bears, or other imposing prey required sophisticated physical and spiritual knowledge on the part of hunters. The Tlingit people also learned the effectiveness of strategy and cooperation between fellow hunters while tracking and felling large animals. Based on aboriginal spears, bows and arrows, harpoons, and traps, their hunting techniques changed little with the introduction of European technology. They might have added a metal tip to a weapon or fashioned a tool more quickly, but their basic approach and essential equipment remained largely the same.

Although the Tlingits valued self-sufficiency, they enhanced their lives through trade. Neighboring peoples, including the Eyaks, Haidas, Tsimshians, and various Athapaskan-speaking groups, traded with them for items of utility and decoration. Tlingit communities especially sought the furs that interior tribes could provide in return for coastal products such as seal oil. Heavily reliant on canoes, they knew how to make good ones, but the Haidas appeared to make still better ones. A large Haida canoe, impressive not only in its size but in its capacity and overall beauty, was a prized acquisition.

Sometimes the exchange of material items was involuntary because in the Tlingit world, relationships rested not only on goodwill but also on power. Within a community, one clan might be strong enough to dictate trading terms to other clans. It might demand a blanket of surpassing beauty or even a human being to be used as a slave. The social stratification that arose as a result of the prosperity of the Northwest Coast peoples included slavery and turned people into a highly valued commodity. Spread out along a strategic part of the coast, the Tlingits were particularly well situated to profit from the unfortunate tradition of human bondage.

When Europeans intruded into the Tlingit world of the eighteenth century, they sailed into a complex social, economic, and cultural environment. Spanish, British, French, Russian, and American exploring parties disembarked during the next two centuries, complicating an already confusing scene. The first whites to make contact with the Tlingits, the Russians, were the most firmly established European presence in the region by the late 1700s. When Tlingits recount the arrival of the first Russians, they recall how they thought perhaps the famed Raven had paid them another visit:

> At one point one morning
> a person went outside.
> Then there was a white object that could be seen
>   way out on the sea
> bouncing on the waves
> and rocked by the waves.
> At one point it was coming closer to the people.
> "What's that?"
> "What's that, what's that?"

"It's something different!"
"It's something different!"
"It's something different!"
"Is it Raven?"
"Maybe that's what it is."
"I think that's what it is—
Raven who created the world.
He said he would come back again."

The story tells how the people heard strange sounds coming from the object:

Actually it was the sailors climbing around the mast.

Finally, two brave young men paddled out in their canoe to examine the huge boat of the white men. When the crew brought them into the ship's cabin, they saw odd and confusing things:

. . . they saw—
they saw themselves.
Actually it was a huge mirror inside there,
a huge mirror . . .

And in the ship's galley:

There they were given food.
Worms were cooked for them,
worms.
They stared at it.
White sand also.

After they hesitantly tasted the rice and sugar, they were given alcohol to sample:

They began to feel very strange . . .
to feel happiness settling through their bodies.

They then returned to tell the people all the remarkable things they had experienced, and their tale has been retold among the Tlingits ever since.

The European newcomers had just as much difficulty understanding the peoples they encountered, but their early accounts leave little doubt that certain elements of Tlingit material culture impressed them. The French visitor Jean Francois La Perouse, for one, remarked on the unique skill of Tlingit basket and hat makers. Illustrations by Tomás de Suría, a gifted artist who accompanied the Spanish explorer Alejandro Malaspina, support this view. One shows an intricate ceremonial hat woven of spruce root and perhaps worn by a leader of a Tlingit village.

The Chilkat blanket represented the peak of Tlingit creativity. Emblazoned with a stylized crest figure, it featured long strands of wool dangling below the design. Crests belonged to the different clans and portrayed the animals and places significant to those clans. Thus, Chilkat blankets not only demonstrated the artistic genius of their creators but also preserved the meaning of traditional symbols and associations. A Chilkat

Es un Principe Don *tari y cs n*

V/principe

Jefe del Puerto de Mulgrabe nombrado Ankáuu

In November 1788, the Spanish crown authorized Alejandro Malaspina to lead an exploring expedition to the northern Pacific. When the artists assigned to the survey became ill, Tomás du Suría, an engraver at the Mexican mint, replaced them. His pictures of the residents of Port Mulgrave documented the material culture of an exotic people unlike any the Spanish had previously encountered and became part of the report that Malaspina sent to Madrid.

Tomás du Suría (1761–?). Portrait of the Head Man, Port Mulgrave. Ink on paper, 1791. Beinecke Rare Book and Manuscript Library, Yale University, New Haven, Connecticut.

Framed by the spectacular house screen and carved house posts of the Whale House is a broad selection of Tlingit objects including a well-worn Chilkat dance apron, spruce-root hats, and a mask. The large woven basket on the left, known as the "Mother-Basket," was a prized possession of the Gaanaxteidi clan and was used to serve food on ceremonial occasions.

Lloyd Winter (1866–1945) and Percy Pond (ca. 1872–1943). Interior of the Whale House, Klukwan. *Photograph, 1895. Winter and Pond Collection (#PCA 87-13), Alaska State Library, Juneau.*

blanket attested to the power of a clan's religious and political leaders and strengthened the bonds of kinship within the clan, linking the generations that passed the prestigious possession among themselves.

Suría's work also indicates that by the late eighteenth century, Tlingit warriors were very well equipped. Clad in a kind of armor fashioned from wood, sinew twine, and leather, they also wore helmets of wood, copper, and shell. Through trade with the English, some Tlingit soldiers acquired copper knives to attach to their lances. European-made knives and hatchets made their way into battle and the hunt, and even muskets became part of the Tlingit arsenal. So armed, Northwest Coast peoples such as the Tlingits could not be easily controlled by outside forces.

And the Tlingits needed their weapons, for tension as well as friendship characterized early relations between whites and Indians. Three years after Aleksandr Baranov founded a fort near present-day Sitka in 1799, Tlingits raided it and took it over. In 1804, the Russians evicted the Tlingits and erected another fort, New Archangel, which soon served as the hub of Russian America. But despite such clashes, the Russian arrival was not as disruptive to Tlingit culture as it might have been. Missionaries of the Russian Orthodox church criticized traditional Tlingit religious practices and worked to convert the people to a new faith, but they were less determined to transform the Tlingit way of life. Most of them recognized that the people worked hard, spoke an advanced language, and created fine things from wood and other natural elements. The Russian missionaries understood that the Tlingits had come to terms with their environment; the people could not be faulted as hunters or as fishermen. Unlike the American missionaries, the Russians did not hope to make the Tlingits into farmers. Perhaps in part because the Northwest Coast resembled their own home, the Russians could appreciate more of Tlingit culture on its own terms.

The Russians did, however, seek to tap into the existing trading patterns along the coast. Eventually, especially after the British-chartered Hudson's Bay Company arrived on the scene, trading relationships between whites and Indians may have made the Tlingits dependent on Europeans and Americans for certain goods that they could not produce. But from the end of the eighteenth century through the first half of the nineteenth, the trade network that linked the Tlingit people to the rest of the world did not erode their tribal economy or culture. Instead, it often revitalized or expanded some elements within that economy and culture.

For instance, the Tlingits had a fully developed woodworking technique before they started trading with whites. As they acquired iron and then steel tools from the foreigners, they carved and sawed with greater speed, efficiency, and perhaps, imagination. Metal tools allowed them to refine the elaborate carving they applied to various objects, including the house posts known as "totem poles" to the whites. Enhanced by the introduction of new tools, the remarkable evolution of Tlingit art and craft was revealed in such achievements as the interior of the Whale House of the Raven in Klukwan, Alaska, constructed early in the nineteenth century. Approximately fifty feet wide and slightly longer, it boasted a central rain or raven screen and wonderfully detailed house posts. The house posts reflected the aesthetic preference of the people for emphasized eyes, eyebrows, noses, and mouths. As elsewhere in Tlingit art, Whale House artisans used curved shapes defined by black paint and filled in with red. The results were bold and striking.

The Tlingits had many neighbors who also benefited from trade with the whites. To the south, for example, the Haidas prospered as shrewd traders who sometimes declined to trade with one ship in the expectation of making a better deal with another. Similarly, the Bellacoolas played the British and the Americans off each other for many years. All along the Northwest Coast, the indigenous peoples gained much from contact with whites until about the middle of the nineteenth century. American missionaries and other intruders forced some cultural changes on many peoples, but they did not manage to destroy them for a long time.

Alongside the missionaries, the destructive force of smallpox, tuberculosis, malaria, and other diseases hit various Indian groups in epidemics that ran their course in a year or two. Native populations in the region noticeably declined during the nineteenth century, in many instances to half their original size. But even those peoples hit hardest by sickness displayed a consistent resilience that prevented the immediate collapse of their cultures. In Northwest Coast tribal populations, which were large enough to withstand the sudden loss of elders who passed along traditions, disease was less devastating than in other parts of the Americas, where smaller groups could not easily spring back. Demographers debate the precise extent and nature of population decline in the Northwest, but its peoples' survival cannot negate the horrors of the epidemics or their tragic consequences. Those cultures showed a strength and cohesion that permitted them to carry on under unprecedented pressure. Disease killed many native people, but it did not always kill their cultures.

Both in spite of and because of its implications for the Indians, the incursion of whites into the Northwest was an important historical event. Considerably to the south of Tlingit territory, near the mouth of the great river that the whites would name the Columbia, the local residents encountered a famous American exploring party. Meriwether Lewis, William Clark, and their team met the Chinookan peoples of the Oregon coast early in the nineteenth century. Obviously ethnocentric, their observations of native groups reflected white attitudes of the time. Nearly two hundred years after this expedition, the much-maligned Chinooks are still coming into focus.

That the coastal peoples of Oregon were not portrayed favorably by Lewis and Clark is not very surprising. The entourage may have been overjoyed at the sight of the Pacific Ocean, but they were less than thrilled with other dimensions of their stay at Fort Clatsop during the winter of 1805–6. Depressed by the eternally damp weather, they battled exhaustion after their long trek from St. Louis and tried to survive on dwindling supplies. They treated the local people badly, complaining about Indian thievery while rationalizing their own theft of an Indian canoe.

Nonetheless, Lewis and Clark recorded many plodding but valuable ethnographic details of Chinookan life. Unimpressed by the Indians' physical appearance, they yet admired the hats that kept them dry. "They are nearly waterproof, light and I am convinced, are much more durable than either chip or straw," wrote Lewis. Demonstrating the most sincere form of appreciation for Indian craftsmanship, Lewis and Clark bought the hats. When they did, they no doubt discovered the Chinooks' exasperating insistence on getting a good deal. Eons of native trade, as well as contact with non-Indian traders, had taught the people the fine art of bargaining.

Lewis and Clark never formally recorded the frustrations of trading with the Indians of the region, but their disdain for their temporary neighbors was obvious. Like previous white visitors, they found fault with the local people for making a home in a place the explorers found thoroughly unappealing. Fort Clatsop could never be home to Lewis and Clark. At best a stopover on a long and uncertain journey, it had in their view nothing to recommend it to the permanent settler. The Indians, meanwhile, marveled that the white men could not appreciate the environment that had for generations provided them with a comfortable home.

The Plains

In the northern plains, the arrival of Lewis and Clark marked the start of a new era. Only a few months into their westward sojourn, the American explorers had a tense encounter with Black Buffalo and his band of Brulés, a branch of the Dakotas—the Lakotas, or Western Teton Sioux. As representatives of separate and sovereign nations, the two parties tried to impress each other and establish themselves as forces to be reckoned with. Although their posturing probably made everyone apprehensive, they avoided bloodshed that autumn of 1804. The incident would eventually lead to violence, however, for Lewis and Clark's expedition journals labeled the Sioux the vilest miscreants of the savage race. Unless the U.S. government acted firmly and swiftly to uproot them from

George Catlin was deeply impressed by the Mandan villages he visited on the upper Missouri in 1832. Trying to capture the "thrilling panorama" that lay before him, he included in his painting of Mandan earth lodges a drum-like shrine in the center of the open area, a medicine lodge, the distant scaffolds of a Mandan cemetery, and many small scenes of daily life. Catlin's romanticized records of tribal life acquired greater historical value after a smallpox epidemic ravaged the upper Missouri tribes in 1837.

George Catlin (1796–1872). Bird's-eye View of the Mandan Village, 1,800 Miles above St. Louis. *Oil on canvas, 1837–39. National Museum of American Art, Washington, D.C./Art Resource, New York, New York.*

the Missouri River country, the explorers asserted, the fledgling nation would never be able to wrest control of the northern plains from the Indians. Unfortunately, there are no comparable written Brulé journals to offer a record of the 1804 encounter from the natives' perspective. No streams of invective inked in defiant Lakota give a balancing account of the event. But by the early nineteenth century, there could be no doubt that there were not one but two expanding powers on the northern plains.

During the autumn and winter of 1804–5, Lewis and Clark came across the Hidatsas, Arikaras, and Mandans, whose way of life contrasted with that of the increasingly nomadic and broadly territorial Lakotas. These village peoples of the upper Missouri River country demonstrated a remarkable ability not merely to survive but to prosper in country that would ruin the less knowledgeable. For well over a thousand years, Indians had farmed in the plains region, successfully confronting the icy winters and searing summers. People identified specifically as Mandan may be traced back perhaps nine hundred years.

The Mandans and other northern plains farmers prospered because they knew the land and saw the earth itself as a living thing. Following time-honored ways, they never forgot how to plant and harvest, hunt and preserve. As a result, despite their harsh environment, they rarely knew famine. The world they lived in demanded that they make full use of whatever they found, caught, or grew. They used more than seventy wild plants for food, ritual, and healing; they mined flint beds along the rivers for arrow- and spearpoints, scrapers, and knives. In this spare and unsparing world, children grew up knowing that their mothers, fathers, aunts, uncles, grandmothers, and grandfathers knew things that they did not.

Northern plains villagers reached maturity wanting to succeed within the natural and social boundaries of the world prescribed for them. In the early twentieth century, an old Hidatsa woman described these boundaries when she remembered the earth lodge of her childhood in the 1840s. She considered it to be alive, with "the door for a mouth" and four living posts, ten to twelve feet long, to support the roof. Inside, space was methodically allocated: the fireplace, of course, marked the center, with beds, a food-storage platform, a cache pit, a place to store sacred bundles, a place for honored guests to sit, and other specific spots lining the walls. As this orderliness suggests, northern plains villagers learned to do things in certain ways. As children, they entered and moved about their lodges in a counterclockwise fashion, sat down only when told they could do so, and ate the food provided whether or not it tasted good and whether or not they were hungry.

Most often the food tasted good, for it was gathered and prepared according to long tradition. Staple crops, such as maize and squash, were cooked in a variety of ways or dried and stored from one year to the next. Bison meat could be preserved and consumed over an extended period of time. As they farmed or hunted, the people observed ceremonial dictates to enhance their chances of success. Not to do so would be to risk hunger or starvation, but few on the northern plains would dare tempt fate in this way. To people steeped in cultural tradition and social discipline, such inattention to ritual would have seemed absurd and unacceptable.

For so long threatened only by the possibility of raids by peoples less blessed and productive than they, the villagers of the northern plains faced a more insidious danger when whites arrived. Their strength, derived from a large population based in permanent settlements, contributed to their vulnerability because they could not easily avoid the new diseases brought by the whites. Nor could they quickly abandon a way of life so proven and satisfying to take advantage of the newly arrived horse, which made a valuable contribution to other communities.

The smallpox epidemic of the late 1830s, well-known to historians because it wiped out perhaps half the region's indigenous population, represented a final blow rather than an initial onslaught. In 1795, one observer recorded that the Arikaras were devastated by a smallpox outbreak that obliterated thirty of their thirty-two villages and killed thirty-five hundred of their four thousand warriors. Fourteen years earlier, the Mandans and the Hidatsas had suffered similar catastrophes. By the time Lewis and Clark arrived, the Hidatsa population stood at about twenty-seven hundred, perhaps half the total before the importation of European disease.

The horrible experience of the sedentary farmers of the northern plains made their way of life far less attractive to migrating tribes than it once had been. Near the end of the eighteenth century, the various branches of the Lakotas and the Cheyennes had paused along their westward migration from the eastern woodlands to sample life in this seemingly secure world. For a few years, they shifted their focus away from migratory hunting and toward farming and village life. But once they acquired horses and witnessed the terrifying consequences of smallpox, the Lakotas and the Cheyennes scattered with the winds.

The horse came surprisingly late to these prototypical inhabitants of the plains. Not until the last decades of the 1700s and the first years of the 1800s did they accumulate sufficient numbers of horses to begin the transformation of their cultures. But in time, the horse changed them by giving them greater mobility. It increased the territory they could try to control and expanded their capacity to hunt bison and carry out raids. Thus, the village peoples of the upper Missouri River and other more narrowly circumscribed populations, such as the Omahas, which remained settled longer and adapted to horses later, lost their dominant status on the plains.

The popular image of the Lakota and Cheyenne plains peoples, of mounted warriors in feathered headdresses, reflects only the later stages of their evolution. Not only had they lived most of their history without the horse, but they also arrived in the region fairly late. Migration, adaptation, and culture building characterized their way of life from the time they left their original home in the woodlands to the East. Each group has its own story about the reason for that long migration from the upper Midwest. The Ojibwas, for example, say they forced the Sioux, their word for "enemy," out of Minnesota, but the Lakota people do not subscribe to this story. Instead, they speak of their imagination and initiative in following the bison and tell how they sought out opportunities for trade and expansion, which could be realized only in the West.

The Cheyennes, meanwhile, traditionally divide their history into four periods. According to their legends, they originally lived in the Northeast between the Great Lakes and Hudson Bay. An epidemic forced them southward during the second era, known as the time of the dogs. Part-wolf dogs traveled with them until the third age dawned, that of the time of the buffalo. With the buffalo as the key to tribal prosperity, they enjoyed a phase of plenty. Then, when they followed the buffalo onto the plains, they entered the fourth period, the time of the horse. The number four is sacred to the people, so their history gave special significance to this time.

Although the early experience of the Cheyennes is clouded with uncertainty, recent studies have turned up evidence of a migration similar to that recounted by the elders. Originally hunters and gatherers of wild rice, the Cheyennes also farmed and probably did know wolves in the Mississippi River country. Before 1700, they moved west to southwestern Minnesota and settled along the Minnesota River. For almost a century, they lingered in the prairie at the edge of the plains. Then the westward retreat of the buffalo, combined with the growing number of horses in their herds, drew the Cheyennes to the interior plains.

As they claimed a new homeland, the Cheyennes redefined the heart of their culture. They designated a great mountain in the western Dakotas as the most sacred place in their universe and named it Noaha-vose, "The Hill Where the People Are Taught." This solitary promontory resembled a bear to the Lakotas and came to be known to Anglo Americans as Bear Butte. In the Cheyenne belief system, "Nothing lives long except the rocks," as the historian John Stands in Timber put it. Accordingly, the Cheyennes looked to enduring Noaha-vose as the source of power—the power to heal and renew them in the years to come.

They expressed their beliefs in the story of Sweet Medicine and his Woman, who came to a cave in this sacred mountain. Ma-heo-o, the Creator, met Sweet Medicine there and gave him four arrows with special powers. To learn how to care properly for them, Sweet Medicine remained at Noaha-vose for four years. While receiving instruction from Ma-heo-o, he saw Neve-stanevoo-o, the Four Sacred Persons who bless the people from their homes at the Four Directions of the universe. Other holy beings who occupied the Cheyenne universe, such as Sun, Moon, and Thunder, revealed themselves to Sweet Medicine as well, along with the Ahtonoone-etaneo-o, the Underground People. When Sweet Medicine finally left Noaha-vose, his Woman carried Maahotse, the Sacred Arrows, down to be bestowed on the Cheyennes. These four arrows symbolized Ma-heo-o's love for and commitment to the people. Two of them granted the Cheyennes power over the buffalo, and two gave them power over human enemies. Ever since Sweet Medicine's sojourn, the Cheyennes have linked their collective well-being to these forces and entities.

According to Cheyenne legend, Sweet Medicine lived among them for many years before he died. During that time he taught them how to live properly by following the principles he had learned at Noaha-vose. In the uncertain and trying world of the plains, the people were always concerned with simple survival. As they made the transition to a less agricultural way of life, they faced the persistent possibility of not merely hunger but starvation. The vast, open plains country offered little protection, not only from the wind, the snow, and the sun but also from rival groups such as the Pawnees. The arrows bestowed by Ma-heo-o and the ideas communicated through Sweet Medicine reassured the people that they would endure in the face of adversity.

The Cheyennes say that Sweet Medicine warned them to hold fast to their values, for strange people would someday come into their country. They would recognize the newcomers by their light-colored skin and short hair. Speaking a harsh and incomprehensible language, the strangers would pose an unprecedented threat to the Cheyenne way of life. After they came, the buffalo would disappear, and in its place would appear another hoofed animal with a long tail, whose meat they would learn to eat. First, though, they would learn to ride a round-hoofed animal, which would allow them to travel quickly on the hunt or from one camp to another.

As with other indigenous Americans, the arrival of white people did not spell immediate doom for the Cheyennes. They probably encountered the first light-skinned strangers in the early 1700s. Spanish traders and French trappers and traders made their way into Cheyenne territory well before Anglo Americans such as Lewis and Clark traversed the country. Accustomed to trading with other Indians, the Cheyennes began to exchange commodities with non-Indians. Over time, through trade and raid, they acquired horses, guns, and metal implements that eventually had a significant impact on their lives.

New technology changed the way Cheyennes did things more than it altered their values and priorities. They had decided to follow the buffalo herds long before they obtained horses; horses merely allowed them to hunt the buffalo more effectively. Long before they obtained guns, they had fought their enemies; guns simply made them more lethal warriors. Likewise, they had made arrow tips of stone or bone since time immemorial; the introduction of metal only enabled them to make better points. Thus, the items they gained through trade or other means promised to make life better. The Cheyennes also avoided the worst of the epidemics of the late eighteenth and early nineteenth centuries because they were so widely scattered across the land. (Cholera may have been more of a killer than smallpox during this period.) By the second decade of the 1800s, most Cheyennes looked to the future with some measure of confidence.

The Cheyennes could afford to feel confident, because their economic and social order seemed to function well in a world that included a few whites. But they did feel some concern about blending their old values with new technology. The increasing use of horses threatened to make individuals more independent, less likely to participate in traditional, cooperative social and economic endeavors. Similarly, rifles might allow people to hunt by themselves, without working with their peers as in the old days. Given the opportunity to acquire various material possessions, families could hoard rather than share their wealth. And a more nomadic way of life, some worried, was likely to compromise the physical well-being of the elders. The new age clearly posed these and other challenges to the collective well-being of the Cheyennes.

Still, they managed to sustain the behavioral ideals that had always informed the patterns of their life. In times of peace and in times of war, the urge toward individual achievement or action was tempered by the need for group cohesion. Young men wanted to be known for their daring deeds, so they tried to count coup on their enemy in the heat of battle, to stay and fight when retreat might have been tempting, to steal horses even when the odds of a successful getaway seemed slim. Those particularly skilled in wartime exploits or on the hunt had every right to feel proud. Yet individuals did not and could not live apart from the community. Warriors had to move with the group when it moved and fight alongside others if an enemy suddenly attacked the village. In countless ways, individual life was inextricably bound up with the people's common fate. As a result, men generally adhered to the social expectations placed on them from birth. They measured their worth not by what they took or hoarded from others but by what they shared. Reciprocity permeated Cheyenne life, influencing the distribution of food, clothing, housing, and horses.

Among the Cheyennes, altruism and generosity counted for more than ambition, and these admirable traits were fostered by a reward system. Individuals who aspired to lead in the Council of Forty-Four, the organization that oversaw tribal life in times of peace, had to live by certain values and behave in a certain way. Those charged with religious duties also had to live in the proper way. To earn the honor and responsibility of leading a religious ritual, for example, a Cheyenne had to be judged a good person. Otherwise, the ritual was unlikely to achieve the desired results.

For those who made mistakes or committed undesirable or outlawed acts, the Cheyennes developed an elaborate system of law and order that emphasized rehabilitation rather than extended punishment of the individual. Obviously, the Cheyennes had no jails; other than a degree of social isolation within the camp or temporary exile, an individual could not be effectively ostracized. In the rare case of a murder within the community, the perpetrator was apprehended immediately to prevent a spiral of revenge and retribution. The Cheyennes also believed that a murderer left undiscovered in the group would smell bad to the buffalo, and the buffalo would stay away from the hunters. This example graphically illustrates how the individual's fate intertwined both with that of the community and with the workings of the natural world.

During the first half of the nineteenth century, the Cheyennes preserved their traditions while absorbing white influences. At this stage, buffalo were still fairly abundant on the plains, but already the people who hunted them had to keep moving into the interior plains and venturing farther south to find their prey. Like a number of Plains Indian groups, the Cheyennes continued to migrate. A portion of the tribe moved south of the North Platte River in Wyoming and Nebraska, down into eastern Colorado and western Kansas, and toward the Arkansas River. Indian trading networks expanded in the process and began to mesh with those of the Anglo Americans. The growing white economic presence led to the construction in 1833 of Bent's Fort, a landmark on the plains in southern Colorado. Soon afterward, the stresses of migration, tribal politics, economic changes, and war led to the division of the people into the northern and southern Cheyennes.

Other groups who made major migrations included the Kiowas and the Comanches. Formerly peoples of the North, they were linked to the traditions of the Shoshonean Great Basin area by language and economics. By the late eighteenth century, though, the Kiowas and the Comanches both made their way from Wyoming down to the southern plains and established new homelands between the Arkansas and Red rivers. They also abandoned their traditional enmity with each other in favor of greater intertribal harmony. In oral accounts, both groups preserved tribal memories of their move, in stages, to the southern plains. According to Ko-sahn, a Kiowa woman:

> There are times when I think that I am the oldest woman on earth. You know, the Kiowas came into the world through a hollow log. In my mind's eye I have seen them emerge, one by one, from the mouth of the log. I have seen them so clearly, how they were dressed, how delighted they were to see the world around them, I must have been there. And I must have taken part in that old migration of the Kiowas from the Yellowstone to the Southern Plains, for I have seen antelope bounding in the tall grass near the Big Horn River and I have seen the ghost forests in the Black Hills. Once I saw the red cliffs of Palo Duro Canyon. I was with those who were camped in the Wichita Mountains when the stars fell.

The last event, the Leonid meteor shower, occurred early on the morning of 13 November 1833, by which time the Kiowas had established themselves on the southern plains.

Even as the Kiowas and the Comanches migrated out of the Great Basin region to the southern plains, other peoples remained in the Basin. This area, which encompasses present-day eastern Oregon, southern Idaho, western Wyoming, western Colorado, the California-Nevada border territory, and all of Utah and Nevada, was home to a culture dominated by branches of the Shoshone, Bannock, Ute, and Paiute nations. In part because it was among the last areas to be penetrated by Europeans, it remains the least-known portion of the American West.

By the time of the American Revolution, Spanish officials had a nebulous concept of the northern reaches of New Spain. In the same month that Thomas Jefferson signed his name to the Declaration of Independence, two Spanish missionaries set out on an expedition at once remarkable and unrecognized. They were the Mexican-born

Francisco Atanasio Dominguez and the Spanish native Silvestre Vélez de Escalante. Their small party found much to note along an elliptical route that started and ended in Santa Fe, New Mexico. Escalante's journal described peoples who forged a living from apparently meager territory that yet offered adequate resources to those who knew how to exploit the land.

Encountering peoples and places that did not always match their expectations, the bearded travelers at one point came on men with beards so long "they looked like Capuchin or Bethlemite fathers." The priests lamented the fate "of those miserable little lambs of Christ who had strayed only for lack of the Light," but they were impressed by the natives' willingness to help them search for a missing member of their group. The expedition's artist, mapmaker, and astronomer, Don Bernardo de Miera y Pacheco, provided images of the bearded Indians, clothed in nearly knee-length shirts, wearing moccasins, and clutching animal-skin quivers, a net, and a rabbit.

These Indians, the western Utes, hunted by driving rabbits into fences of soapweed, sagebrush, or hemp cords. They netted sage grouse the same way and hunted deer and elk with particular effectiveness in the drifts of winter snow. Wearing deerskins as a disguise, the hunters crept up as close as they could to surprise their prey. In the streams and lakes of their home country, the people used spears, arrows, weirs, nets, and traps to catch fish. Seeds, fruits, nuts, and berries added variety to the Ute diet, with piñons (pine nuts) being a favorite staple. When necessary, they ate rattlesnakes, lizards, cicadas, crickets, and ants. Europeans frowned on such foods, but the Utes were a practical people in an environment that demanded pragmatism. They either ate what the land provided or went hungry.

The Utes had little in common with the Acomas, the Tlingits, or the Hidatsas. Nevertheless, in the years leading up to the period of white contact, various Indian peoples all over the West sought to build cultures and homes, often in new territory. As they made their way onto new lands, they redefined their view of the world around them. They mixed old ideas and ways with new ones, hoping to forge alliances both with other peoples and with the environment itself. In time, the horse and the gun combined with migration to produce greater competition for natural resources, which led to conflict as well as coexistence among Indians. War broke out whenever groups struggled over territory and the right to establish an economic base.

When white people began to appear in growing numbers at the end of this period, Indians saw them not only as enemies or competitors but also as potential allies or pawns. Small communities threatened by more powerful tribes sometimes perceived whites as a useful means toward survival. Certainly, the first whites who struggled onto the plains or into the Great Basin gave the indigenous groups little reason to worry. But the ultimate effect of the white incursion remained to be seen.

The Navajos

A final example of migration and adaptation in the Southwest produced the largest Indian nation of the modern American period: the Diné, known as the Navajos. Their humble beginnings, centuries before, hardly foreshadowed their eventual rise. Linguistic analysis links the Navajos to the large family of Athapaskan-speaking peoples, now

In this image representing one of the central stories of Navajo cosmology, four figures surround the place of Emergence, where, according to myth, the Navajo people migrated into this world. The figures represent the sectors of the sky and the sacred mountains that mark the cardinal points of the Navajo world. Rivers flowing from these mountains nourish the food-producing plants that grow from the Emergence ladder. Though sand paintings were widely used in Navajo ceremonials, these ephemeral images were rarely recorded until the 20th century.

Louie Ewing (1908–83). Emergence Sand Painting. *Serigraph, 1949 (after a sand painting recorded by Mrs. John Wetherell). From Mary C. Wheelwright,* Emergence Myth *(1949).*

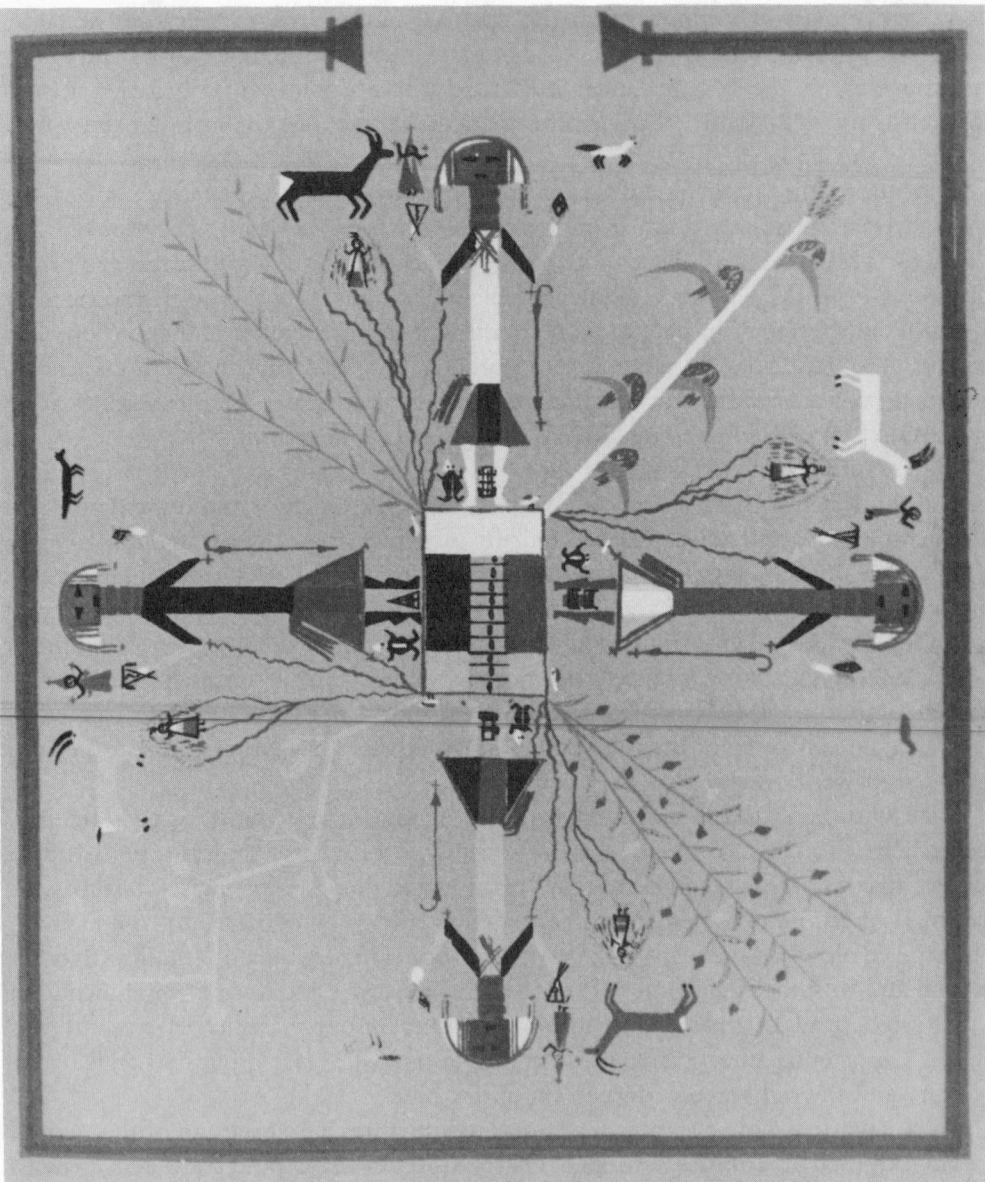

scattered over a wide portion of northern North America. The Navajos and the Apaches are the only Indian communities of the Southwest to speak a language of this classification. But their speech clearly ties them to peoples in Alaska and western Canada, such as the Eyaks, Haidas, and Kutchins. The languages as spoken today are not identical, but even to the relatively untutored ear the cadences and accents sound quite similar.

The Navajos are also tied to the North by the stories they tell. When the anthropologist Franz Boas studied Indian societies a century ago, he discovered striking parallels between some of the tales told by Athapaskan-speaking peoples now separated from one another by thousands of miles. More than coincidence, the commonality was another important piece of evidence that the Navajos had lived in the North before making their way to the American Southwest. Why and how—and even when—the Navajos decided to make this extended trek remain uncertain. It is unlikely that they moved as one group; it is even more unlikely that they moved directly from the far North to the Southwest. What seems more probable is that theirs was a gradual, halting migration by stages, which took them through the Rocky Mountains into northern New Mexico. When they arrived, the Navajos may have contributed to the general reshuffling of southwestern populations in the thirteenth and fourteenth centuries. Internally, the Navajos underwent their own adjustment. More hunters than gatherers, and decidedly not farmers, they slowly came to terms with their new environment.

Like the Cheyennes, the Navajos in time redefined themselves. Children learned that their people had always lived in the Southwest, that they belonged in the place called Diné Bikéyah, or the Navajo country. The Indians marked the boundaries of this territory by four sacred mountains: the San Francisco Peaks (Dook'o'oosliííd) were the sacred mountains to the West, Mount Taylor (Tsoodzil) was the sacred mountain to the South, Blanca Peak (Sis Naajiní) was the sacred mountain to the North, and Hesperus Peak (Dibé Nitsaa) was the sacred mountain to the East. Adorned, respectively, in abalone, turquoise, white shell, and jet, these mountains were not the only places with sacred significance to the Navajos. In their stories, they designated as holy the part of Diné Bikéyah called Dinétah ("among the people"), where they believed they originated. Archaeological evidence corroborates Navajo legend, identifying the region as the first the people occupied when they entered the Southwest.

The Navajos' story of their beginnings is one of emergence, of long migration from one world to the present world. According to the tale, the central figures of Navajo mythology lived in Dinétah. First Man, First Woman, and the children of Changing Woman occupied Huerfano Mountain; Changing Woman resided at Gobernador Knob. The adventures of the children of Changing Woman, Monster Slayer, and Child Born for Water gave meaning to other natural features of Navajo territory. For example, the story refers to the lava flow near present-day Grants, New Mexico, as the dried blood of the creature felled by Monster Slayer. Throughout the tale, other beings, such as animals and insects, appear as an integral part of life itself.

Indeed, the similarities between the Navajo origin story and the origin stories told by the different Pueblo communities are so striking that it seems the Navajos reworked a version of another story to create their own. Such adaptation would be very much in keeping with Navajo character, for the great strength of the Navajos, the key component of their expansion and prosperity, was their ability to learn from others and to incorporate new ways of life into their culture. In time, acquisitions such as the content of stories, the crafting of silver, or the raising of sheep became part of traditional Navajo life.

Essentially a hunting people at first, they became a people who not only hunted but also farmed. In the two or three centuries before the Spaniards came, the Navajos probably learned a great deal from their more established neighbors, the Pueblo Indians, about how to exploit the southwestern environment. The Navajos, of course, do not tell the story that way. Rather, they tell of early Navajos who learned how to grow corn or how to weave from the holy people. Spider Woman, according to their legends, instructed them in the art of weaving. In some respects, it does not matter who taught the Navajos their skills. What matters is that before the Spaniards arrived in the area, the Navajos had thoroughly adapted to their new home, which lay in country remote from the main regions of Spanish incursion.

The Navajos developed an elaborate system of ceremonies designed to promote harmony within themselves and within the larger universe. Hunting remained far more important than agriculture in the different chantways, evidence that the Navajos did not discard all their old beliefs when they migrated. But at the same time, the cornfield became a primary image in the Navajo cosmos. Corn pollen and the corn plant are central to the Navajo ceremonial world.

Nearly a century and a half elapsed between the first Spanish foray into the Southwest and the revolt of 1680. During this period, the Navajos learned about the Spaniards' religion, language, and culture and gradually determined the usefulness of these things. Few Navajos saw any point in converting to Catholicism, but some Navajo names do show up in the baptismal records kept by the missions of New Mexico. Nor did Spanish replace the Navajo language, although many Indians saw the value of learning a few key words for the purpose of communication and trade. Horses, sheep, cattle, and goats, however, were another matter entirely.

Because they had adopted a more sedentary life-style and had claimed a large, relatively uncontested country, the Navajos were ideally situated to incorporate Spanish livestock into their economy. In addition to the meat that all the animals could provide, the horse also promised a new dimension in transportation, and the sheep offered wool, the ideal material for weaving. Once again, new additions to the culture became gifts from the gods, who had always possessed them and only now had seen fit to bestow them on the people.

The Navajos said that horses had originally belonged to the Sun, who kept four of the animals corralled separately to the North, South, East, and West. The coats of the horses showed different colors, one for each of the four directions. When Turquoise Boy journeyed to see the horses, he saw a white shell horse to the East, a turquoise horse to the South, a yellow abalone-shell horse to the West, and a spotted horse to the North. Different Navajo accounts give different versions of how the people acquired the horses, but they all recount the joy with which the Navajos accepted these wonderful animals. One account praises the horse of the South:

> The turquoise horse prances with me.
> From where we start the turquoise horse is seen.
> The lightning flashes from the turquoise horse.
> The turquoise horse is terrifying.
> He stands on the upper circle of the rainbow.
> The sunbeam is in his mouth for a bridle.
> He circles around all the people of the earth
> With their goods.
> Today he is on my side
> And I shall win with him.

As demonstrated by the successful introduction of the horse, contact between the aboriginal Navajo community and the invading Europeans did not lead instantly to decline. To be sure, some dimensions of the Spanish presence—the capture of Navajos for the regional slave trade, for example—were clearly destructive. But just as certainly, the Navajos could not have reached the cultural pinnacle they now occupy were it not for the Spanish influence. Acquisition of Spanish livestock provided them the necessary means to complete their transformation into a people not only with a rich past but also with a viable future.

Even the revolt of 1680 benefited the Navajos by increasing their numbers. In the generation following the rebellion against Spanish oppression, thousands of Pueblo peoples fled their home villages. Some of them established new communities, but others joined existing groups such as the Navajos. In turn, their children became Navajos, and the number of Navajo clans expanded. The Jemez Pueblo people, for instance, migrated to Navajo country and established the Coyote Pass Clan (Ma´ii Deeshgiizhnii), while other immigrants founded the Mescalero Apache Clan (Naashgalí Dine´é) and the Mexican Clan (Naakaii Dine´é). These new arrivals had an immediate demographic impact on the Navajos, swelling the tribal ranks in the wake of the revolt. But they also enhanced Navajo culture by contributing to the art of weaving, the skill of farming, and the technology of animal husbandry. Almost overnight, the Navajos found themselves on the brink of a century of unprecedented expansion, cultural development, and prosperity.

During the seventeenth and early eighteenth centuries, the Spaniards could not contain the growth of the Navajo people or curtail their independence. Meanwhile, through trade and war, the Navajos greatly increased their wealth. True to their time-honored traditions, the Navajos conducted warfare and raiding only after performing the appropriate ceremonies. These rituals—as well as the prospect of proving their valor and acquiring riches—inspired Navajo warriors to perform daring exploits in combat and on raids. For protection and courage, they called on the power of animals and imagined that they assumed the form of these animals. They chanted:

> I am a big black bear.
> My moccasins are black obsidian.
> My leggings are black obsidian.
> My shirt is black obsidian.
> I am girded with a gray arrowsnake.
> Black snakes project from my head.
> With zigzag lightning projecting from the ends of my
>   feet I step . . .
> Black obsidian and zigzag lightning stream out from me
>   in four ways.
> When they strike the earth, bad things do not like it.
> It causes the missiles to spread out.
> Long life, something frightful I am.
> Now I am.

The Navajos must sometimes have seemed frightful to other native peoples of the Southwest. Sometimes friendly and sometimes hostile to their neighbors, the Navajos absorbed other peoples, trading with them, raiding them, and learning from them. Like

In the early 20th century, many artists presented a timeless image of a romanticized Indian world that obscured the many changes that had transformed native life since European contact. Although images of Navajo sheepherders and Lakota chiefs on horseback might seem to reflect unchanging cultural patterns, they in fact underscore the theme of adaptation in Native American life by emphasizing the cultural transformations initiated by the introduction of the sheep and horse.

Laura Gilpin (1891–1979). Shepherds of the Desert. *Gelatin silver print, 1934. © 1981, Laura Gilpin Collection, Amon Carter Museum, Fort Worth, Texas.*

Edward S. Curtis (1868–1952). The Prairie Chief (Pine Ridge Agency, South Dakota). *Photogravure, 1907. From Curtis,* The North American Indian, *supplement to vol. 3. Courtesy Special Collections, Amherst College Library, Amherst, Massachusetts.*

the Lakotas of the northern plains, they were an expanding power as the American era dawned.

At the end of the second decade of the nineteenth century, the American era was about to begin in the West. In 1821, Mexico claimed its independence from Spain, only to lose a large part of its territory in the revolt in Texas and the war with the United States. In the meantime, the first wave of Anglo-American explorers, missionaries, trappers, traders, adventurers, miners, farmers, and urban entrepreneurs began to arrive in the region. No one could predict that the stream of settlers would soon turn into a flood.

Indeed, the previous experience of indigenous peoples with various Europeans in the West bore little hint of the onslaught that lay ahead. Despite the massive toll exacted by disease, Spanish imperialism, Catholic mission work, and all the other upheavals caused by contact, the many surviving Indian communities had reason to be cautiously optimistic about the future. The Spaniards, the British, the Russians, and the first Anglo Americans had many designs on them and their lands, but the native peoples had not been displaced. Their tenacity thus far suggested that they would not disappear quickly in the decades to come. Thus, although the history of the native peoples of the American West is one of migration, adaptation, and change, it is also one of settlement, persistence, and continuity. The presence of Indians in the West obviously altered the course of Anglo-American history, just as the arrival of outsiders changed the direction of Indian history.

Too often in histories of the American West and of the United States as a whole, Indians greet boats filled with whites, fight and lose to the invaders, and in the end totter on the verge of assimilation and extinction. They are always on the defensive. But from the early sixteenth century to the early nineteenth century, native peoples experienced gain as well as loss, and expansion as well as contraction. Like the history of Anglo Americans, theirs is a tale of discovery and new beginnings.

The great ceremony of the Navajos, the Blessingway, includes a song about finding yucca and corn. The words say just as much about the Indians of the West, people who belonged to the land:

> When I found it I became fabrics of all kinds.
> When I found it I became jewels of all kinds.
> When I found it I became game of all kinds.
> When I found it I became plants of all kinds.
> When I found it I became corn of all kinds.
> When I found it I became horses of all kinds.
> Now I am long life, now happiness as now I found it.
> Before me it is blessed, behind me it is blessed,
> Below me it is blessed, above me it is blessed,
> Around me it is blessed, my speech is blessed,
> All my surroundings are blessed as I found it, I found it.

Bibliographic Note

Any attempt to synthesize the experiences of the many native peoples of the West depends heavily on the work of others. The following list of sources suggests works especially important in the field and in the writing of this essay. Readers should consult the extensive bibliographies of the Smithsonian Institution's *Handbook of North American Indians* series for a comprehensive collection of work. In addition, the D'Arcy McNickle Center for the History of the American Indian at the Newberry Library in Chicago has also sponsored a series of critical bibliographies that will prove helpful to those seeking additional sources.

The origin story of Acoma Pueblo is told in Matthew W. Stirling, *Origin Myth of Acoma and Other Records*, Bureau of American Ethnology Bulletin No. 135 (Washington, D.C., 1942). The classic overview of relations between and among the Indians, Spaniards, Mexicans, and Anglo Americans is Edward H. Spicer, *Cycles of Conquest: The Impact of Spain, Mexico, and the United States on the Indians of the Southwest, 1533–1960* (Tucson, 1962). Many authoritative articles on Indian communities and on relations between Indians and non-Indians may be found in the volumes published by the Smithsonian Institution. See in particular the *Handbook of North American Indian* series: *California* (volume 8, 1978), *Southwest* (volume 9, 1979), *Southwest* (volume 10, 1983), *Great Basin* (volume 11, 1986), and *Northwest Coast* (volume 7, 1990). Peter Nabokov and Robert Easton, *Native American Architecture* (New York, 1989), is a richly illustrated study, telling us much about buildings but also about their cultural context.

Traditional stories from California, the Pacific Northwest, and Canada may be found in Katharine Berry Judson, *Myths and Legends of California and the Old Southwest* (Chicago, 1912), Ella E. Clark, *Indian Legends of the Pacific Northwest* (Berkeley, 1963), and Ella E. Clark, *Indian Legends of Canada* (Toronto, 1960). Robert F. Heizer and John E. Milles, *The Four Ages of Tsurai: A Documentary History of the Indian Village on Trinidad Bay* (Berkeley, 1952), provides details of the different encounters between the Yuroks and the Europeans and Anglo Americans. Norris Hundley offers an authoritative examination of choices made about water in *The Great Thirst: Californians and Water, 1770s–1990s* (Berkeley, 1992).

Erna Gunther, *Indian Life on the Northwest Coast of North America, as Seen by the Early Explorers and Fur Traders during the Last Decades of the Eighteenth Century* (Chicago, 1972), is a thorough, well-illustrated overview, including a chapter on the Tlingits. The Tlingit oral historical narratives quoted in the essay are from Nora Marks Dauenhauer and Richard Dauenhauer, eds., *Haa Shuká, Our Ancestors: Tlingit Oral Narratives* (Seattle, 1987). The standard collection of Tlingit stories was recorded by John R. Swanton in *Tlingit Myths and Texts*, Bureau of American Ethnology Bulletin No. 39 (Washington, D.C., 1909). Sergei Kan provides a perceptive introduction to his translation of the Russian Orthodox priest Anatolii Kamenskii's *Tlingit Indians of Alaska* (Fairbanks, 1985).

Richard White's "The Winning of the West: The Expansion of the Western Sioux in the 18th and 19th Centuries," *Journal of American History* 65 (September 1978), is a stunning explanation of Lakota ascendancy. James P. Ronda, *Lewis and Clark among the Indians* (Lincoln, 1984), is a masterful study of the explorers' relations with both Plains and Northwest Coast Indian peoples. Carolyn Gilman and Mary Jane Schneider, eds., *The Way to Independence: Memories of a Hidatsa Indian Family, 1840–1920* (St. Paul, 1987), takes full advantage of the pioneering work of Gilbert Wilson and adds new essays about upper Missouri River native life by W. Raymond Wood, Gerard Baker, Jeffrey R. Hanson, and Alan R. Woolworth.

Peter John Powell's magnificent studies of the Northern Cheyennes are essential readings; see his *Sweet Medicine: The Continuing Role of the Sacred Arrows, the Sun Dance, and the Sacred Buffalo Hat in Northern Cheyenne History* (Norman, 1969) and *People of the Sacred Mountain: A History of the Northern Cheyenne Chiefs and Warrior Societies, 1830–1879, with an Epilogue, 1969–1974* (New York, 1981). E. Adamson Hoebel, *The Cheyennes: Indians of the Great Plains*, 2d ed. (New York, 1978), is a good introduction. George Bird Grinnell, *The Cheyenne Indians: Their History and Ways of Life* (1923; reprint, New Haven, 1973), presents a thorough examination of Cheyenne society. Margot Liberty and John Stands in Timber, *Cheyenne Memories* (New Haven, 1967), is the account by a respected tribal elder. The Kiowa writer N. Scott Momaday includes Ko-sahn in his splendid essay "The Man Made of Words," in Geary Hobson, ed., *The Remembered Earth: An Anthology of Contemporary Native American Literature* (1979; reprint, Albuquerque, 1981), and writes of the Kiowas' great migration to the southern plains in *The Way to Rainy Mountain* (Albuquerque, 1969). Herbert E. Bolton, *Pageant in the Wilderness: The Story of the Escalante Expedition to the Interior Basin, 1776* (Salt Lake City, 1950), is the standard translation and explication of the Escalante diary. Gloria Griffen Cline, *Exploring the Great Basin* (Norman, 1963), outlines the paths taken by various entrants into the region. Omer C. Stewart has written widely about the different peoples of the area; one of his introductory essays is "Ute Indians: Before and After White Contact," *Utah Historical Quarterly* 34, no. 1 (1966): 38–61. Joseph Jorgensen, *The Sun Dance Religion: Power for the Powerless* (Chicago, 1972), is an important study that brings Ute history into the modern era.

Aileen O'Bryan, *The Diné: Origin Myths of the Navaho Indians*, Bureau of American Ethnology Bulletin No. 163 (Washington, D.C., 1956), and Pliny E. Goddard, *Navajo Texts*, Anthropological Papers of the American Museum of Natural History, vol. 34 (New York, 1934), are important sources. LaVerne Harrell Clark, *They Sang for Horses: The Impact of the Horse on Navajo and Apache Folklore* (Tucson, 1966), also employs material from O'Bryan and Goddard that is quoted in this essay.

Sam Bingham and Janet Bingham, eds., *Between Sacred Mountains: Navajo Stories and Lessons from the Land* (Tucson, 1984), is a wonderful collection of material gathered by people at Rock Point School on the Navajo Nation. James F. Downs, *The Navajo* (New York, 1972), and Peter Iverson, *The Navajos* (New York, 1990), present overviews of Navajo history, society, and culture. Ruth Underhill, *The Navajos* (Norman, 1956), and Clyde Kluckhohn and Dorothea Leighton, *The Navaho* (Cambridge, Mass., 1946), remain helpful. The quotation from the Navajo Blessingway ceremonial is from the translations of Father Bernard Haile in Leland C. Wyman, ed., *Blessingway* (Tucson, 1970).

A sweeping survey of western Indians at the time of the Columbus landing may be found in Peter Iverson, "Taking Care of Earth and Sky," in Alvin M. Josephy, Jr., ed., *America in 1492: The World of the Indian Peoples before the Arrival of Columbus* (New York, 1992). Edward Spicer and his students and associates have contributed greatly to our understanding of Indian continuity and change. See, for example, a book of essays in Spicer's honor edited by George Pierre Castile and Gilbert Kushner, *Persistent Peoples: Cultural Enclaves in Perspective* (Tucson, 1981), as well as Edward Spicer and Raymond H. Thompson, eds., *Plural Society in the Southwest* (New York, 1972). Anya Peterson Royce, *Ethnic Identity: Strategies of Diversity* (Bloomington, 1982), is a persuasive study of the symbols employed by groups in their efforts to maintain flexible, working identities.

Peter Nabokov was originally assigned this chapter and was unable to complete it because of events in the Middle East that led to the war in Kuwait and Iraq. His ideas about the structure of the chapter certainly influenced my approach, and I would like to express my thanks to him.

Chapter Two

The Spanish-Mexican Rim

DAVID J. WEBER

I n 1826 a Pueblo Indian appealed to New Mexico officials to stop non-Indians from acquiring land belonging to his community. As alcalde, or mayor, Rafael Aguilar claimed to represent the "principal citizens of the Pueblo of Pecos," a once-powerful town that lay astride a key pass between the Rio Grande valley and the western edge of the high plains. Writing in phonetic Spanish, Aguilar reminded authorities that Pueblo Indians enjoyed the rights of citizens, that the law guaranteed their ownership of four square leagues of land around their pueblo, and that non-Indians had no right to acquire Pueblo lands. Aguilar's petition was one of several formal complaints lodged in the 1820s by natives of Pecos to protect their farms and pastures. In legal terms, the petitions paid off. In 1829 the New Mexico legislature ordered non-Indians to vacate Pecos Pueblo lands.

Like other Pueblo Indians, the *pecoseños*, or residents of Pecos, for whom Aguilar spoke, had remained a culturally distinctive people. Nonetheless, as personified by Aguilar, over two centuries of exposure to Hispanic neighbors and missionaries had profoundly altered Pueblo culture. Like many Pueblo leaders, Alcalde Aguilar held a Hispanic office, understood how and when to appeal to Hispanic law, communicated with Hispanics in their language, and identified himself with a Spanish surname and a Christian given name. [*Please see "A Note about Language" on p. 75.*]

Moreover, Hispanic influence went beyond law, language, politics, and religion into the economic life of Pueblo communities such as Pecos. On farmlands, such as those Aguilar sought to protect, Pueblos raised crops they had not known before the Spaniards arrived in the sixteenth century. In addition to the corn, beans, squash, and cotton they had cultivated for centuries, Pueblos grew tomatoes, chiles, and new varieties of corn and squash brought by Spaniards from central Mexico, as well as exotic coriander, wine grapes, cantaloupe, watermelon, wheat, and other imports from the Old World. Pueblos also tended apricot, apple, cherry, peach, pear, and plum orchards and raised sheep, goats, cattle, horses, mules, donkeys, oxen, and flocks of chickens—all previously unknown to them.

By adopting these foreign crops and stock, Pueblos, like many other Indians, enriched their economy and diet. Changes introduced by Spaniards, however, also had deleterious effects. For over a century before Aguilar wrote his petition, the number of *pecoseños* had declined steadily. Spanish-introduced diseases had taken a toll, and so had raids by Apaches and Comanches. Those raids had apparently intensified as Old World crops and livestock made the Pueblos more productive and thus more tempting as targets for raiders well equipped to strike astride Spanish-introduced horses.

Among the earliest surviving Indian images depicting contact with Spaniards, is this pictograph of Spanish horsemen drawn high on a canyon wall in Canyon del Muerto, Arizona. The riders with long capes, broad-brimmed hats, and flintlock guns may represent the soldiers of Lt. Antonio Narbona who led a raid against the Navajos in 1805.

Attributed to Dibé Yázhí Nééz (Tall Lamb). Spanish Horsemen. Pictograph, ca. 1805. Canyon del Muerto, Arizona. Photograph by Helga Teiwes. Arizona State Museum (#28883), University of Arizona, Tucson.

Spanish Exploration, 1519–1660

Whether from emigration or premature death, the population of Pecos fell from about 1,000 in 1700 to fewer than 150 by the end of the century. By the 1830s, it hardly mattered that Aguilar had won a legal victory against Hispanic encroachment, for there were too few *pecoseños* to prevent unscrupulous Hispanics from killing the Pueblos' stock, poisoning their water holes, and otherwise making their lives intolerable. In the late 1830s, the last residents of Pecos, numbering fewer than 20, abandoned the town and moved across the Rio Grande to Jémez Pueblo, which became their permanent home.

In general, the story of Pecos Pueblo exemplifies the Hispanic impact on the Pueblo world, but many of the details of the story are unique to Pecos. Even among Indians as seemingly similar as the Pueblos of New Mexico, Hispanic influence varied with time, place, and circumstance. Some Pueblo communities became extinct much earlier than Pecos, but others, strengthened by their adaptations to the Hispanic world, have survived to the present day. Whatever the rate or quality, the changes that Spaniards engendered in indigenous communities were remarkably pervasive. Directly or indirectly, Spanish influence extended beyond the Pueblo world across the southern rim of what is now the American West, from California to the Mississippi and northward to Oregon and Washington, the Great Basin, the Central Rockies, and the upper Missouri.

Between 1821 and 1846–47, when Americans seized the West in the war with

Mexico, much of this area had constituted the far northern frontier of independent Mexico. Before 1821, Spain had claimed the western half of the continent as the northern reaches of the viceroyalty of New Spain. Never numerous but highly influential, Spaniards had invaded and explored much of the West in the first half of the sixteenth century and had begun to settle on its southern rim before 1600. For the next two and a half centuries, Hispanics remained and expanded their presence in the region. In the process, they transformed the indigenous landscapes and peoples of what is today the American Southwest.

The story of the Hispanic transformation of southwestern North America has been poorly understood. For Hispanics themselves, the vast region lay "at the ends of the earth . . . remote beyond compare," as one conquistador wrote in 1692. In 1800, a Spanish mining engineer reported to the king that in central Mexico, "the people speak with as much ignorance about the regions immediately to the north as they might about Constantinople." Many Indians also forgot much about the changes that occurred when Hispanics invaded their lands. Over time, for example, as the historian Elizabeth John has noted, the origin of some of the new crops introduced by Spaniards to the Pueblos "faded from memory . . . [and] came to be accepted as 'Indian food,' eaten in the kivas and named in rituals and prayers." Anglo Americans, who began to push into the region toward the mid-nineteenth century, displayed little curiosity about the Hispanics who had preceded them. Blinded by anti-Spanish and anti-Mexican biases, many of the earliest Anglo Americans preferred to imagine the trans-Mississippi West as a virgin land and readily overlooked the region's long Hispanic past.

First Encounters

The transformation of the continent's Spanish-Mexican rim began in the first half of the 1500s, when Iberians introduced Native Americans to the predatory ways of Europeans. The Spaniards who invaded, explored, conquered, and settled much of the Western Hemisphere in the wake of Columbus's discovery arrived with several beliefs that suited them well for these tasks. Their society glorified and rewarded the warrior, whose skills had been hardened in the crucible of a seven-century struggle to drive Muslims out of Iberia—a task completed in 1492. This protracted war had nourished Iberians' zeal and intolerance and bolstered their self-confidence. Like other Christians, Spaniards understood that their god had given them "dominion" over all creatures on the earth, including the newly discovered infidels. Indeed, Spain's onward-moving Christian soldiers crossed the sea with the conviction that the New World belonged to them, since the Spanish pope, Alexander VI, had given it to the Crown of Castile in the famous papal donations of 1493 (the next year, Spain inadvertently granted the eastern edge of South America to Portugal, in the Treaty of Tordesillas).

Spaniards also arrived in the New World with a variety of practical advantages that enabled them to turn their fantasy of superiority into a reality. Peculiar weaponry, including steel swords and explosives, and animals strange to the New World, especially horses and greyhounds, gave Spaniards tactical and psychological advantages that helped them defeat overwhelming numbers of Indians on their native ground. Certain pathogens, foreign to the Western Hemisphere before the 1500s, traveled on Spanish ships and became the microscopic allies of the conquistadores by killing vast numbers of Native Americans, who, unlike Spaniards, lacked immunities. Then too Spaniards arrived as representatives of an emerging state society, with institutions designed to enforce social order—armies, police, and bureaucracies adept at manipulating written symbols. Still fragmented into rival kingdoms, Spain had not yet coalesced as a single nation, but in North America, Iberians found tribal societies far less unified than their own. Like other Europeans in America, Spaniards used Indian disunity to their advantage.

The Spanish reconnaissance of what would become the American West began along the Gulf of Mexico in the same year that Hernán Cortés discovered the Aztec empire. In 1519, in search of a sea lane to Asia, Alonso Alvarez de Pineda set out from Jamaica for the western coast of Florida, where Juan Ponce de León had preceded him, then continued westward to discover the northern shores of the Gulf of Mexico, including the Texas coast. Although Pineda's voyage contributed substantially to Spanish geographical knowledge, it had no direct effect on North American natives, since he did not land on North American shores.

The first Spaniards to set foot in what would become the American West arrived unintentionally, fleeing from a disastrous attempt by Pánfilo de Narváez to conquer and colonize Florida. A storm drove the refugees' makeshift craft onto the Texas coast at or near Galveston Island in the autumn of 1528 as they sailed from Florida toward sanctuary in Mexico. Four men reached Mexico to tell the tale: Alvar Núñez Cabeza de Vaca and three companions, including a black Moorish slave named Esteban. After six years of living among Indians on the Gulf coast, the four had crossed Texas and much of northern Mexico before uniting with fellow Spaniards.

Cabeza de Vaca's lost party contributed little to cartographical knowledge, but his return sparked more purposeful exploration. Despite his apparent reluctance to exaggerate what he saw, or perhaps because of that reluctance, Cabeza de Vaca's reports seemed to substantiate earlier rumors of a wealthy civilization to the north of Mexico and kindled the ambitions of powerful men. Cabeza de Vaca did nothing to dispel these rumors when he hurried to Spain to request a patent to settle Florida. He arrived too late. Hernando de Soto, fresh from enriching himself in the conquest and plunder of Peru, had received royal permission in 1537 to explore and colonize Florida, which then included all of southeastern North America. Two years later, De Soto landed in Florida with a large, costly expedition of nine vessels carrying over six hundred men and assorted livestock.

Meanwhile in Mexico, a private fleet belonging to Cortés had begun to explore Pacific waters to the northwest, and the viceroy of New Spain, Antonio de Mendoza, had laid his own plan to stave off these rivals. In the autumn of 1538, Mendoza put a peripatetic Franciscan, Marcos de Niza, in charge of a reconnaissance of the lands to the north of Mexico, reckoning that a small expedition led by a priest would draw little attention. Within a year Fray Marcos returned to Mexico City, stirring up waves of sensational rumors. He claimed to have seen, but not have entered, a city "bigger than the city of Mexico." The natives, the friar had learned, called this place Cíbola, perhaps from an Opata word meaning Zuni (Spaniards later applied the word *cíbolo* to the curious "cattle" they found on the Great Plains—the buffalo). Fray Marcos described Cíbola as just one of seven cities in a country that appeared to be "the greatest and best of the discoveries"—an extravagant recommendation from a man who knew firsthand the wealth of Mexico and Peru.

On the strength of Fray Marcos's reports, Viceroy Mendoza authorized one of the most elaborate and significant of Spain's reconnaissances of the interior of North America—one to rival De Soto's expedition to Florida. Mendoza, who entertained the idea of leaving the comforts of Mexico City to lead the expedition himself, finally entrusted it to a protégé, thirty-year-old Francisco Vázquez de Coronado. The party included three hundred Spanish adventurers (at least three of them women), six Franciscans, more than one thousand Indian "allies," and some fifteen hundred horses and pack animals. In search of precious metals and great cities, Coronado made his way into the heart of today's Southwest in 1540, establishing a base among Pueblo farmers on the Rio Grande who could supply food, clothing, and shelter. From there, Coronado's band explored parts of Arizona, New Mexico, Texas, Oklahoma, and Kansas. Meanwhile, De Soto had landed at Tampa Bay in 1539 and cut a sanguinary path across eight of the present southern U.S. states. In 1541, after De Soto had crossed the Mississippi into Arkansas and Coronado had marched into Kansas, only some three hundred miles separated the two expeditionary forces.

Neither Coronado nor De Soto succeeded in finding another Mexico or another Peru. In the spring of 1542, Coronado and his entourage retraced their route to Mexico. De Soto's party, far from the vessels that had brought them to Florida, found it more difficult to leave North America. After De Soto took sick and died in the spring of 1542, the remnants of his group tried to make their way back to Mexico by land. Somewhere in eastern Texas they grew disheartened and turned back to the Mississippi. There they built small boats and sailed for Mexico, reaching safety in the autumn of 1543.

Meanwhile, in June 1542, before the results of the Coronado or De Soto expeditions were known, another venture sponsored by Viceroy Mendoza set out for the Pacific coast of North America. Led by Juan Rodríguez Cabrillo, three small ships sailed from the Pacific port of Navidad in 1542 and beat their way up the western coast of Baja California. In 1539, Cortés had sent Francisco de Ulloa to explore that same coast, and Ulloa had made it three-quarters of the way up the peninsula. Beyond that point, Cabrillo's expedition entered waters that no European had seen before. Along the rocky shores of what is today southern California, Cabrillo staked out claims for his sovereign, Carlos I, and mapped the principal harbors—including the ports of San Diego, San Pedro, and Santa Barbara. Cabrillo died while the expedition waited out the winter on Santa Catalina Island, but the next spring his chief pilot, Bartolomé Ferrer, pushed the expedition north to the Rogue River, beyond the present California-Oregon boundary, before turning back.

By 1543, then, the reports of the De Soto, Coronado, and Cabrillo-Ferrer expeditions had opened new horizons to the north of Mexico for Europeans. As a result, the contours of the western half of the continent began to appear on European maps, and Carlos I indulged himself in the common European conceit that discovery gave a claim to lands actually held by a variety of native peoples.

In North America itself, the earliest Spanish expeditions set powerful forces into motion, altering native populations and institutions. European infectious diseases, particularly smallpox and measles, accompanied or preceded Spain's earliest explorers.

If this presidial soldier followed special regulations issued in 1772, he carried 123 pounds of accoutrements in addition to food and water. His weighty equipment included a heavy, knee-length sleeveless coat made of seven layers of buckskin. Designed to deflect Indian arrows, the coat alone weighed 18 pounds. These Spanish soldiers were ambulatory arsenals, able to defend themselves but too burdened down to effectively pursue Indian raiders.

Raymundus à Murillo. Presidial Soldier. Watercolor on paper, 18th century. Archivo General de Indias (Uniformes 71), Seville, Spain.

Deadly to natives, who had no previous exposure and, therefore, no immunities, these diseases took a heavy toll in certain times and places. Cabeza de Vaca reported that shortly after he and his companions arrived ill on an island off the coast of Texas, "half the natives died from a disease of the bowels and blamed us." Neither extant documents nor present archaeological evidence permits informed appraisals of the extent of decline in native populations during the early sixteenth century in what is now the West. Judging from the better-documented demographic collapses that occurred elsewhere in the hemisphere, however, it seems likely that some native communities suffered heavy losses. Wherever those occurred, societal transformations followed. With diminished populations, for example, some native groups must have found themselves suddenly weak in comparison with their neighbors and, in extreme cases, forced to abandon their communities. In the most complex societies, greatly reduced populations would not support specialized functions, undoubtedly causing some simplification.

Along with deadly microbes, the earliest Spanish expeditions also left a legacy of ill-will. Coronado's men, for example, although vastly outnumbered, had taken advantage of firearms and hard steel to seize by force what they could not gain by persuasion. Pueblo Indians who refused to cooperate learned the cost of resistance. Word of Spanish atrocities spread quickly and far. At San Diego in September 1542, Cabrillo met surprising hostility from Ipai Indians who, he learned, were alarmed because "men like us were traveling about, bearded, clothed and armed . . . killing many native Indians, and . . . for this reason they were afraid."

The violent aggression of the earliest Spanish explorers affected Spanish-Indian relations for generations thereafter. Indeed, late in the nineteenth century, Pueblos at Zuni, whose towns Coronado had seized by force, reportedly still remembered that the first Spaniards had worn "coats of iron, and warbonnets of metal, and carried for weapons short canes that spit fire and made thunder." They recalled, "These black, curl-bearded people drove our ancients about like slave creatures."

Spanish exploration and the mutual discovery that it engendered did not end, of course, in 1543. Exploration, and its intentional and unintentional consequences, continued as long as Spain and Mexico held the region. For several decades after 1543, however, Spanish exploration of western North America halted. The new vistas to the north had revealed few tangible attractions—no rich civilizations and no strait through the continent to carry Spanish mariners toward the riches of Asia. For the time being, Spain's American colonies developed around the mineral- and labor-rich realms of the vanquished Incas and the Aztecs, leaving western North America beyond the periphery of the Spanish empire.

Settlers, Friars, and Pueblos in Seventeenth-Century New Mexico

Late in the sixteenth century, as memories of previous exploration dimmed and fresh rumors of another Mexico to the north rekindled their interest, Spaniards returned to New Mexico. This time they stayed. New Mexico became the first permanent European colony in what is today the American West and the second enduring European settlement in what is now the United States (preceded only by St. Augustine, founded by Spain in Florida in 1565).

New Mexico's colonizer, Juan de Oñate, led a small contingent north from Mexico in 1598. Some of his 130 soldier-settlers traveled with their wives, children, and servants, bringing the expedition's number to over 500. All were Spanish subjects, but few were born of Spanish parents. Most of the Spaniards who settled in northern New Spain over the next two centuries were mixed-bloods (mestizos and mulattoes), and some were Mexican Indians and blacks. After pausing at what later became El Paso, where Oñate proclaimed Spanish dominion over the new land and its inhabitants, "from the leaves of the trees in the forests to the stones and sands of the river," the party moved up the Rio Grande, and across the great dry stretch that would come to be called the Jornada del Muerto, into the heartland of the Pueblo Indians. North of present-day Santa Fe, Oñate made his headquarters at the Tewa-speaking pueblo of *ohke*. He declared the pueblo a Spanish town, renamed it for San Juan, and forced the king's new vassals out of their apartments. He kept the natives close at hand, however, to provide labor, food, and clothing.

The Pueblos probably acceded to Oñate's demands to avoid the deaths and damage that Coronado, as well as more recent expeditions by Antonio de Espejo and Gaspar Castaño de Sosa, had inflicted on the Indians when they failed to offer hospitality to Spaniards. Oñate reinforced the lesson. Before his colony was a year old, Pueblos at Acoma resisted Spanish requisitions of food and clothing and killed eleven Spanish soldiers in a single surprise attack. Oñate retaliated swiftly and audaciously, sending a small force against the almost impregnable mesa-top pueblo, where Acomans enjoyed the numerical as well as logistical advantage. Oñate's men succeeded brilliantly. They destroyed Acoma, killing some five hundred men and three hundred women and children and taking perhaps eighty men and five hundred women and children captive. Tried and found guilty of murder, the adult Acoman prisoners received a punishment calculated to make them living reminders of the cost of resistance. Oñate sentenced all captives between the ages of twelve and twenty-five to twenty years of personal servitude, and he condemned males older than twenty-five to have one foot severed. The mutilations, a common punishment for miscreants in Renaissance Europe, were carried out in public.

Like Coronado, De Soto, and other leaders of legitimate Spanish expeditions, Oñate had entered North America as a private contractor, under an arrangement with the Crown that permitted him to settle New Mexico at his own expense. He planned to realize a handsome return from his investment by building a transcontinental empire that would include rich mines, abundant Indian labor, a strait through North America, and seaports on both oceans. Like many of his contemporaries, however, Oñate had underestimated the distance across the continent, and his luck was no better than Coronado's.

Exploring west to the Gulf of California and northeast to the edges of Kansas, Oñate found no wealthy Indians or mines, much less a transcontinental strait. The colonists and the king quickly grew disillusioned and prepared to abandon New Mexico, but Franciscans had baptized so many Pueblo Indians that the project received a royal reprieve. Rather than move the baptized Pueblos south, or see them revert to paganism, Felipe III permitted Franciscans to stay.

For much of the seventeenth century, New Mexico endured largely as a missionary outpost. Isolated over eight hundred miles beyond the edges of Mexico's mining frontier, it attracted few immigrants. The number of Spaniards in New Mexico in the 1600s probably never exceeded three thousand. This scanty population could support only one formal municipality, Santa Fe, established in about 1610 by Oñate's successor, Pedro de Peralta, at an altitude of seven thousand feet amidst piñon and juniper at the foot of the Sangre de Cristo Mountains. No military garrison or presidio existed in New Mexico in the 1600s, but the king expected his vassals to serve as soldiers as well as settlers—particularly those who had received a specified number of natives in trust, or in *encomienda*. Rewarded by Oñate and his successors according to their rank and services to the Crown, *encomenderos*, or holders of *encomiendas*, enjoyed the privilege of receiving tribute from one or more pueblos or fractions of pueblos.

Many of New Mexico's pioneers lived outside of the province's single urban center in clusters of fortified farmhouses or ranches too small to call towns. To be close to the province's single source of revenue, the labor of Pueblo Indians, the Hispanic population scattered up and down the Rio Grande, from Taos Pueblo to below Albuquerque (founded in 1706). Farther south along the Rio Grande, where Oñate had first entered New Mexico, a mission was built in 1659 at present-day Ciudad Juárez, across the river from today's El Paso, Texas, but no civilian community developed there until the 1680s.

In contrast to the slow growth of the civilian population, the number of missions in New Mexico expanded rapidly. By 1629, according to the enthusiastic count of Fray Alonso de Benavides, Franciscans had already overseen the construction of fifty churches and residences for priests in New Mexico. Central to Spain's enterprises in America, missions had become the dominant institution on the frontiers of the Spanish empire by the seventeenth century. Comprehensive Orders for New Discoveries, promulgated by Felipe II in 1573, had made missionaries the Crown's primary agents for exploration and pacification. "Preaching the holy gospel," Felipe II had noted, "is the principal

La V.ᴹ.ᵉ Maria de Iesus de Agreda, Predicando á los Chichimecos del Nuebo-mexico. Antᵗ.ᵒ de Castro f.

The work of mission building in New Mexico advanced in the 1620s, Franciscans said, due to the appearance of a Spanish mystic and nun, María de Jesús de Agreda, who journeyed miraculously to America and persuaded Indians to seek out missionaries. Although the nun later repudiated the story, it served as an inspiration to Franciscans in Texas and California in the 18th century.

Unidentified artist. María de Jesús de Agreda Preaching to Chichimecos of New Mexico. *Woodblock print, 1730. From the first printing of a letter that Fray Alonso de Benavides wrote from Madrid in 1631 to his fellow Franciscans in New Mexico,* Tanto que se sacó de una carta . . . *(Mexico, 1730).*

purpose for which we order new discoveries and settlements to be made." The regulations also prohibited the entry of unlicensed parties into new lands and prohibited the use of the word *conquest* to describe future "pacifications." Those habits proved impossible to break, for there remained an inherent tension between the Crown's imperative to save souls and its interest in exploiting new lands and peoples.

If the age of military conquest had ended, spiritual and cultural conquest had not. Through interpreters, Oñate had spelled out the new Spanish agenda when he ordered Pueblos to accept Spanish rule in 1598. Submission, Oñate said, would bring peace, justice, protection from enemies, and the benefits of new crops, livestock, and trade. Obedience to the Catholic church would bring even greater rewards: "an eternal life of great bliss" instead of "cruel and everlasting torment."

Missionaries embarked on a program to eradicate Pueblo religion and replace it with Catholicism. Using techniques they had honed over time in other areas, Franciscans, many of them skillful and zealous, persuaded Pueblos to build churches and to receive baptisms and religious instruction. In some cases, the friars probably succeeded in bringing about complete conversions; in most cases, it appears, Pueblos simply adopted those features of Catholicism that they found congenial while maintaining their traditional spiritual beliefs.

Many Spanish priests, like their English counterparts, could not imagine that a people could become Christians unless they lived like Europeans. Thus, in the ideal mission, Franciscans sought to reshape the natives' temporal lives by teaching them to dress, eat, and live like town-dwelling Spaniards. Depending on climate, soils, and local needs, Franciscans in New Mexico taught native converts the Spanish trades: to husband such European domestic animals as horses, cattle, sheep, goats, pigs, and chickens; to cultivate European crops, from watermelon to wheat; to raise European fruit trees, from peaches to plums; to use such iron tools as wheels, saws, chisels, planes, nails, and spikes; and to practice those arts and crafts that Spaniards regarded as essential for the civilization they knew. The Franciscan program for the cultural transformation of these tribal societies enjoyed the financial support of a large state apparatus, presided over by the Spanish Crown, which saw missions as a practical and pious way to advance the frontier and to increase the number of Hispanicized subjects without having to export more Spaniards.

Franciscans accomplished some of their purposes through persuasion, gifts, and the promise of spiritual rewards, but they also resorted to force and the threat of force (for Pueblos, for example, memories of Spanish atrocities at Acoma and elsewhere must have lingered). Schooled in a time and place where the good of the community prevailed over the rights of the individual, Franciscans justified the use of force as beneficial to the common good. Thus, once natives consented to receive baptism, Franciscans commonly relied on military force to prevent converts from slipping back into apostasy—a danger to the common weal as well as to the individual soul. Soldiers aided Franciscans in compelling baptized Indians to live in mission communities as Spanish law required, hunted down neophytes who fled, and administered corporal punishment to natives who continued religious practices that Spanish priests found loathsome. From the Spaniards' viewpoint (but certainly not the Indians'), whipping seemed a particularly appropriate punishment in an era when the lash was applied to Spanish miscreants, from schoolchildren to soldiers, and when Franciscans whipped themselves in atonement for their sins. As they had done since the earliest stages of the conquest of America, the Franciscans smashed, burned, or confiscated objects sacred to the natives—what one friar in New Mexico described as "idols, offerings, masks, and other things of the kind which the Indians were accustomed to use in their heathenism."

Believing they had something to gain by accepting the new religion and the material benefits that accompanied it, or too much to lose by resisting it, Pueblos initially cooperated. Like other native societies that had not been vitiated by war or disease, Pueblos adopted from the outsiders what they perceived as both useful for and compatible with their essential values and institutions. Ideally, they sought to add the new without discarding the old, or to replace elements in their culture with parallel elements from the new—as they had done long before the arrival of Europeans. In the religious sphere, for example, many Pueblos simply added Jesus, Mary, and Christian saints to their rich pantheons and welcomed the Franciscans into their communities as additional shamans. However selective neophytes might have been in adopting aspects of Christianity and Spanish culture, their decision to accept missionaries began to transform their cultures—often in ways that neither they nor the missionaries intended. By cultivating certain European crops and raising European domestic animals, for example, natives often enriched their diet, lengthened the growing season, deemphasized hunting in favor of agriculture, and made it possible for their villages to support denser populations. Their prosperity, on the other hand, also made them more attractive targets for raids by nomadic Indians and forced them to devote more resources to defense.

For the Pueblos, the bright future that Franciscans offered at the outset of the courtship lost its luster as the terms of exchange shifted. Along with gifts and access to trade goods came demands for labor and resources. For individual Indians, those demands increased as the size of their communities, their land base, and their productivity declined. Obedience to the Franciscans and their god had not stopped the spread of diseases strange to the natives. From 1598 to 1680, the Pueblo population fell by at least half, to some seventeen thousand.

Violent eruptions, which Spaniards characterized as rebellions but which Indians probably saw as armed struggles for freedom, broke out in New Mexico on a number of occasions. Spaniards suppressed them, sometimes brutally. In 1680, at a time of unusual stress precipitated by drought and starvation and aggravated by Apache raids and Spanish religious persecution, Pueblos revolted with near unanimity. In their carefully planned offensive, the Pueblos caught the Spaniards off guard. Reports of a plot had reached the Spaniards, but they could not have guessed the magnitude of this unprecedented campaign, which involved over two dozen independent towns spread out over several hundred miles and separated by at least six different languages and numerous dialects, many of them mutually unintelligible. Within two weeks, Pueblos had cleansed New Mexico of Spaniards. The natives had killed over four hundred of the province's twenty-five hundred foreigners (nearly all in the initial days of the rebellion), destroyed or sacked every Spanish building, desecrated churches and sacred objects, killed twenty-one of the province's thirty-three missionaries, and laid waste to the Spaniards' fields. The survivors and some Pueblos who remained loyal to them fled south to El Paso. There could be no mistaking the deep animosity that natives, men as well as women, held toward their former oppressors. "The heathen," wrote one Spanish officer in New Mexico, "have conceived a mortal hatred for our holy faith and enmity for the Spanish nation."

Some Pueblo leaders urged an end to all things Spanish as well as Christian and counseled against speaking Castilian or planting crops introduced by the Europeans. This nativistic resurgence succeeded only partially in reversing the cultural transformation that Spaniards had set in motion. Some reminders of Spanish rule, such as forms and motifs in pottery, seem to have disappeared, but Pueblos continued to raise Spanish-introduced livestock and to make woolen textiles. Just as they had selectively adapted certain aspects of Hispanic culture, so too did they selectively reject them.

Pueblos had carried out one of the most successful Indian rebellions against Spanish colonizers anywhere in the hemisphere, but only briefly did they enjoy freedom from

Christian strictures and obligations of labor and tribute. In 1692, Diego de Vargas began a slow and shrewd reconquest of the Pueblos—a task he completed after smashing another bloody Pueblo rebellion in 1696.

Exhausted from war, their property and population diminished, Pueblos did not launch another major offensive while under Spanish rule. To the contrary, threatened by Apaches and other common enemies, Pueblos became loosely allied with Spaniards and fought with them to defend the province. Spaniards, in turn, feared another rebellion and did not offer as much provocation. After the 1696 revolt, pragmatic

Franciscans displayed less zeal in attempting to stamp out Pueblo religious practices, and colonists and officials eased (but did not end) their demands on Pueblo laborers.

This cycle of initial acceptance, growing tension, rebellion or attempted rebellion, and mutual accommodation—the native-Spaniard relationship that manifested itself in seventeenth-century New Mexico—reoccurred in the eighteenth century as Spanish missionaries attempted conversions among other sedentary peoples in far northern New Spain, from the Caddos of East Texas to the Pimas of southern Arizona and to the coastal tribes of Alta California.

Defensive Expansion: Texas and Louisiana

Throughout most of the seventeenth century, New Mexico stood alone on the northern fringes of New Spain, the only permanent Spanish settlement in what is now the western United States. Only temporarily had Franciscans extended the province westward into what is today Arizona, to the land of the Hopis in the high, arid northeast corner of the state. But Hopis had expelled the Franciscans in the 1680 revolt and maintained their independence until the end of the Spanish era. Not until 1700 did Jesuits, building a chain of missions along the Pacific slope of New Spain, cross the future U.S.-Mexico border and establish an ongoing Hispanic presence in present-day southern Arizona. In the parched, cactus-covered desert of southern Arizona, which Spaniards called the land of the Upper Pimas, or Pimería Alta, Jesuits altered the lives of Pima farmers much as Franciscans had effected changes in the Pueblo world. After Spain expelled the Jesuits from all of its territories in 1767, Franciscans carried on their work in Pimería Alta. Meanwhile, Spanish Arizona had attracted few colonists. A modest influx of miners and ranchers began in the 1730s but ended with the bloody Pima rebellion of 1751—a widespread nativistic reaction to Spanish intrusion. As a part of Sonora rather than a separate province, Hispanic Arizona remained confined largely to the Santa Cruz Valley between the present-day border and Tucson. Its non-Indian population seldom exceeded one thousand because it had little to offer would-be colonists and, for much of the century, because it held no strategic importance to attract the attention of government officials.

By the late seventeenth century, defense rather than conversion had become Spain's foremost concern in western North America—notwithstanding the Crown's frequent assertions to the contrary. Indeed, with the exception of the Jesuit advance into Pimería Alta, geopolitics more than religious considerations lay behind all Spanish expansion into North America from the 1690s on. Even the decision of Carlos II to support Diego de Vargas's reconquest of the Pueblos was based in large part on the strategic value of the province in the face of perceived threats to northern New Spain by Frenchmen and Indians.

Beginning in the late 1600s, a growing French presence in the Gulf of Mexico and in the upper reaches of the Mississippi Valley ended Spanish hegemony on the western half of the continent and weakened Spain's ability to control Indians. French traders broke the Spanish monopoly by offering an alternative source of European trade goods and a market for furs while making no demands that Indians change their culture or religion. Moreover, French trade goods, lower priced and better made than Spanish merchandise, included arms and ammunition. In contrast, based on the belief that firearms made natives more effective adversaries, Spanish law had prohibited furnishing guns to Indians. Its enforcement would leave Spaniards at a disadvantage.

Even before French traders appeared on the eastern horizon, New Mexico was under siege by Apaches and other tribes whose cultures had been transformed by Spanish-introduced horses. (Spain had tried, but failed, to keep Indians from acquiring horses.) Mounted and highly mobile, nomadic and seminomadic tribes from the plains raided New Mexico settlements, including those of the Hispanicized Pueblos, and threatened the mining regions of northern New Spain. In the early eighteenth century, southward-moving Comanches, some armed as well as mounted, pushed Apaches farther south and west. As Comanches took possession of the high plains, they alternately raided and traded in New Mexico and Texas.

Initially, Spanish policymakers faced the growing French and Indian threats in Texas, where they relied on an antiquated solution to a new problem. Galvanized by La Salle's bold effort to plant a colony on the Texas coast in 1685, and disturbed by the penetration of the lower Mississippi Valley by Canadian-based French traders, Spain sent a small detachment of soldiers and Franciscans into Texas in 1690. Spanish officials hoped to continue the tradition of advancing and defending frontiers with peaceable and inexpensive missions. Thus, they bypassed the strategic Gulf coast, with its intractable hunting and gathering tribes, and targeted Caddo agriculturalists, the most sophisticated peoples in Texas, as having the greatest potential to become Christians and allies. In the rolling piney woodlands of the "Kingdom of Tejas" in what is now East Texas, at a site some six hundred miles from the Rio Grande over a difficult land route and inaccessible by sea, Father Damián Massanet founded two missions among the Tejas, or Hasinai Indians—the westernmost Caddo confederacy. Spain, however, failed to impose an ecclesiastical and cultural solution to a defensive and commercial problem. Decimated by European diseases, aggrieved by Christian arrogance, and uncompensated by trade goods, the Hasinai forced the defenseless and hopelessly isolated Spanish missionaries to leave three years later, in 1693.

Thereafter, as the French threat to Texas and the Gulf coast seemed to subside, so did the interest of an overextended and bankrupt Spain. In 1716, however, the specter of widening commercial influence from French Louisiana (which had grown slowly from shaky beginnings at Biloxi Bay in 1699 and Mobile Bay in 1702) led Spain again to try to settle Texas. This time the Crown succeeded. Returning to the Kingdom of Tejas, a small party of about seventy-five—soldiers, Franciscans, and colonists, including women—built four small wooden churches and a presidio in the summer of 1716. While that work proceeded, the expedition's leader, Captain Domingo Ramón, continued east, beyond the Hasinai lands, to Natchitoches, the westernmost French trading post in Louisiana. Evoking the papal donation of 1493, Spain officially denied that France had a legal right to be in Louisiana, but Captain Ramón tacitly acknowledged Natchitoches as the western limit of the French colony, and he took measures to check its growth. Just to the west of Natchitoches, he founded two more missions in nearby Caddo communities: San Miguel de los Adaes and Dolores de los Ais.

Undermanned and remote from the nearest Spanish settlements and sources of supplies, the fledgling colony represented little more than a symbol of Spain's interest in maintaining Texas. The weakness of Spain's position became painfully evident when war broke out between France and Spain in 1719. Seven Frenchmen invaded Texas from Louisiana and managed to panic the colonists, soldiers, and missionaries into abandoning the Caddo country. They fled to San Antonio, a civil, military, and ecclesiastical complex founded the year before as a way station on the trail between the Rio Grande and the East Texas missions.

The French "invasion" shocked Spanish officials into reinforcing Texas. In 1721 the wealthy marqués de San Miguel de Aguayo recaptured eastern Texas with the most imposing force Spain would send into the province—some five hundred men, four thousand horses, and assorted other livestock. Aguayo bolstered the presidios at San Antonio and East Texas and built two more. One rose at the very site of La Salle's failed enterprise on Matagorda Bay and another at Los Adaes, just twelve miles from Natchitoches. The post at Los Adaes, where Aguayo left a one-hundred-man garrison and six cannon, became the capital of Texas, a position that it held while the French flag flew over Louisiana.

If Texas succeeded in checking further French expansion, it was largely because of the corresponding weakness of Louisiana. Texas itself stagnated. Under Spain, it failed to develop significantly beyond the points reinforced by the marqués de Aguayo. The mission system, effective in promoting the expansion of earlier Hispanic frontiers, failed across much of Texas. The Hasinai, who recalled prior experience with Christians, declined to receive baptism. "They have formed the belief," one Franciscan wrote, "that the [holy] water kills them." Thanks to French traders, the Hasinai, together with mounted nomadic or seminomadic tribes such as Comanches and Apaches, had better options; they could not be induced to embrace the restricted lives of neophytes in Spanish missions. Only along the San Antonio River did missionaries have modest success at recruiting. San Antonio de Valero and the four other stone-walled missions that developed nearby between 1720 and 1731 provided refuge for small bands of linguistically diverse hunters and gatherers, who found themselves squeezed between Hispanics moving northward into Coahuila and Tamaulipas and Apaches moving southward. At their peak in mid-century, the five San Antonio missions were home to about a thousand neophytes, many of them Coahuiltecan-speaking peoples. A few other missions along the coastal plain attracted modest numbers, but none achieved the potential that the dense native population of Texas seemed to offer.

Texas also failed to attract a significant number of immigrants. In part, it lacked a large pool of tractable Indian laborers, and it suffered, as did all of Spain's frontier provinces, from remote markets and from restrictive economic policies that stifled commerce. In normal times, Spanish mercantilism limited legal trade to a few key ports in the New World that were to be supplied only by Spanish goods carried on Spanish vessels. None of the natural harbors along the Texas coast were among these ports. Fearful of encouraging smuggling, Spain kept the Texas coast closed to shipping until the end of the colonial period, despite occasional entreaties from Texas officials. These commercial restrictions jacked up transportation costs for exports and imports while stifling consumption and production across the northern frontier.

Notwithstanding the relative lack of economic opportunity, Texas attracted some immigrants because the Spanish government, eager for bodies to man the barricades against French expansion, offered incentives. Giving free passage, land, and the title of hidalgo, officials managed to sell Texas to a small number of poor farmers from Tenerife in the economically depressed and overpopulated Canary Islands. Fifteen families (fifty-five persons) arrived in San Antonio in 1731 after a year-long journey by way of Havana, Veracruz, and Saltillo. Together with the colonists who had come to Texas with earlier expeditions, the Canary Islanders brought the Hispanic population of the province to perhaps 500. By 1763, Hispanics in Texas—not counting Hispanicized mission Indians—numbered 1,850, the sparsest Hispanic population of any province in New Spain. Nonetheless, members of the small but resourceful *tejano* community managed to develop a ranching economy adapted to the harsh conditions of life on the frontier. They also found ways to circumvent trade restrictions by trading illegally with Frenchmen in Louisiana.

Spanish Texas endured primarily as a buffer colony, controlled largely by Indians and sparsely populated by Hispanics. When it no longer served imperial purposes, Spain nearly abandoned the province. After Spain acquired Louisiana from France in 1762, it withdrew its missionaries, soldiers, and settlers from East Texas by royal order and relocated them at San Antonio, which, together with nearby La Bahía, was too heavily populated to shut down. Nonetheless, *tejanos* soon drifted back to the edge of Louisiana, where they founded Nacogdoches in 1779. The new town, a center for contraband, rivaled San Antonio through the end of the colonial period.

Just as Spain expanded into Texas in response to a foreign threat, so it acquired western Louisiana for purely defensive reasons. Louisiana promised to become a financial liability for Spain, as it had been for France, but Spain needed it. An immense province, western Louisiana stretched from the mouth of the Mississippi into the Illinois country, with a vague and seemingly limitless boundary to the west. If Louisiana fell into English hands, Spain would face its most powerful imperial rival on the doorstep of New Spain. On the other hand, if Spain occupied Louisiana, it could hold England at arm's length. As one of the king's advisers argued, the Mississippi River would form a "recognizable barrier, a good distance from the population centers of New Mexico." After weighing costs and benefits, Carlos III reluctantly accepted the expensive gift of Louisiana from his French cousin Louis XV in a secret treaty signed in 1762.

After a dilatory and stormy beginning, Spain asserted its sovereignty over Louisiana's French population. The Crown built fortifications and encouraged immigration, as it had in Texas, but it did not attempt the large-scale conversion of French-influenced Indians. Compared with residents of Texas or New Mexico, Louisianians enjoyed economic prosperity under Spain, perhaps because Spanish officials adopted France's more liberal trading policies, opened Louisiana to direct trade with Spanish ports, and welcomed non-Spanish immigrants. On the other hand, even without these policy changes, a growing contraband trade with neighboring Anglo Americans had invigorated Louisiana's economy. Nonetheless, although Louisiana's colonists prospered more under Spain than they had under France, the province remained a net liability for the Spanish Crown.

Spain held title to Louisiana for nearly four decades but failed to Hispanicize it, much less profit from it. Numerically, Frenchmen simply overwhelmed Spaniards. Through incentives, Spanish officials managed to lure Canary Islanders to Louisiana, as they had to Texas. Beginning in the late 1770s, some two thousand Canary Islanders reached Louisiana, along with a trickle of immigrants from other parts of Spain. A hundred or so colonists from Málaga, for example, founded New Iberia in 1779. The number of Spanish immigrants, however, never exceeded the fifty-seven hundred Frenchmen who lived in Louisiana in 1766, when the first Spanish governor arrived to take possession of the province. Moreover, the number of Frenchmen increased dramatically under the Spanish regime as French residents of lands to the east of the Mississippi fled British rule. In addition, Acadian refugees from Nova Scotia swelled the French population of Louisiana by perhaps three thousand.

By 1800, Spaniards in Louisiana were outnumbered not only by Frenchmen but also by Anglo Americans. Eager to regain the Floridas, which it had lost to Britain in 1763, Spain had joined the Americans in 1779 in their rebellion against England and had driven British forces out of the lower Mississippi, Mobile, and Pensacola. The United States, however, with a burgeoning population and manifest designs on the trans-Mississippi West, proved more dangerous than Britain. As early as the 1780s, Spanish officials began to regard Americans as analogous to the "barbarians" who had swept into the Roman empire centuries before. To halt Anglo Americans who swarmed into Louisiana illegally, Spain permitted some to settle legitimately. The idea—that the settlers would become loyal Spanish subjects—soon seemed ill conceived. Unable to limit the number of westward-moving Americans or to ensure their loyalty, a weakened Spain yielded to pressure from Napoleon Bonaparte to return Louisiana to France. Spain still regarded Louisiana as the key to the defense of northern New Spain but would henceforth depend on France to hold the line against the Americans. Thus, the lengthy Franco-Spanish negotiations, finally completed in 1802, proceeded in secret for fear that the United States would invade Louisiana to prevent the transfer. The invasion never came. Breaking his agreement with Spain, Napoleon sold Louisiana to the United States the following year.

When Louisiana passed into the hands of the Americans in 1803, demographics and longevity had combined to ensure that French culture still predominated. Many descendants of old Spanish families stayed in American Louisiana, but in the popular imagination they became culturally indistinct from the more numerous Frenchmen, and their era was nearly forgotten. New Orleans was rebuilt in Spanish style after fires obliterated the French-built city in 1788 and 1794, but the Spanish-built heart of New Orleans remains known today as the French Quarter.

War and Peace

Even though Spain failed to stop the flow of Anglo Americans into Louisiana in the late eighteenth century, it did succeed in coming to terms with Apaches, Comanches, and other Indian nomadic tribes who had long plundered northern New Spain. With their lands threatened by the continuing expansion of the Spanish frontier and with their liberty at risk from slaving parties and missionaries, some Indian raiders had powerful motives besides loot. They fought Spaniards bitterly and successfully, initially meeting little effective resistance.

In the seventeenth century, Spain had no presidios west of the Mississippi, but the destruction of New Mexico in 1680, the Indian rebellions that rippled across northern Mexico, and the growing threat from foreigners had led Spain to increase its professional military forces on the northern fringes of its empire. Friars with crosses and small military escorts no longer filled the bill. In New Mexico, authorities constructed a presidio at El Paso del Norte in 1681, after survivors of the Pueblo Revolt had taken refuge there. As Diego de Vargas reasserted Spanish control over the Pueblo country in 1693, he began construction of a presidio in Santa Fe, authorized by the viceroy. In 1716, when Spaniards returned to Texas to counter French influence, they built presidios to protect every population center—a total of five by mid-century. In Pimería Alta, too, where threat from Apaches grew, Spain constructed a number of presidios, with Tubac (1752), Tucson (1776), and Terrenate (1776) all to the north of the present border.

As the burden of defense in these provinces shifted to presidial troops paid by the king, economic power increasingly resided with the military and its access to the government payroll. Slowly, the military supplanted the missions as the dominant institution on the Spanish rim in the eighteenth century, and soldiers and their families became the mainstay of many communities. Despite its strong presence, however, the military failed to end the chronic insecurity that characterized the lives of Hispanic frontiersmen. Underfunded and headed by an officer staff riddled with corruption, the frontier fortifications were a model of inefficiency for much of the century. Presidial soldiers—cheated of their pay by their officers, vastly outnumbered by their adversaries, and ill equipped and badly trained for either conventional or guerrilla warfare—soon became demoralized, seldom winning a victory. Nonetheless, the presidios themselves enjoyed a reputation as secure places of refuge from hostile Indians. That, however, had less to do with the effectiveness of the soldiery or the strength of the structures than Indians' reluctance to incur losses by laying siege to a fortification.

In the late eighteenth century, Spain ended this dreary chapter in its relations with hostile tribes by making two fundamental changes: it reorganized the administrative structure of the frontier provinces, and it took a fresh approach to its treatment of Indian adversaries. The administrative restructuring aimed to make the presidial soldiers more efficient, to coordinate military campaigns, and to foster immigration and economic development. These activities, the Crown recognized, required closer supervision than a distant viceroy could give. In 1776, four years after restructuring the military command, Carlos III granted semiautonomous status to the northern region of New Spain, long known as the interior provinces. This new administrative entity, the Comandancia General de las Provincias Internas, included much of the present-day northern tier of Mexican states—then known as the provinces of Baja California, Sonora, Sinaloa, Nueva Vizcaya, and Coahuila—together with today's American Southwest, from California through Texas (Louisiana fell within the general jurisdiction of the viceroy of New Spain but came under the immediate supervision of Havana and was never regarded as one of the interior provinces of New Spain). At the head of the Comandancia General was a military officer with the title of *comandante general*, or commander in chief, who had authority over governors of individual provinces and individual military posts, thus enabling Spain to construct a comprehensive military strategy and execute interprovincial campaigns.

In various permutations, the Comandancia General remained in place for the rest of the colonial era and achieved some successes. The first commander in chief, for example, Teodoro de Croix (1776–83), found imaginative ways to increase the flexibility and effectiveness of the frontier military against guerrilla forces. Croix, like most frontier commanders, hoped to win peace through force of arms, but success came only when Spain imitated its French and English competitors, put diplomacy ahead of warfare, and took Indian interests into account.

The individual most responsible for this shift, Bernardo de Gálvez, had experience with war on the Apache frontier and peace in Louisiana. In 1769, as a well-connected twenty-two-year-old officer assigned to Chihuahua, Gálvez had acquired a respectful understanding of Apaches—along with serious wounds from a lance and arrow. In 1776, as a youthful governor of Louisiana, Gálvez observed firsthand how the French and English used trade rather than war to maintain harmonious relations with natives. He noted that French and English traders, by making Indians dependent on them for "sundry conveniences," including guns and ammunition, had caused Indians to forget the use of the bow and arrow and to rely entirely on Europeans for powder to hunt and to defend themselves.

Other Spanish officers had made similar observations, but as the nephew and protégé of José de Gálvez, the powerful and dynamic minister of the Indies in charge of American policy, Bernardo de Gálvez had a unique opportunity to influence Spanish policy. In 1778 Bernardo de Gálvez urged his uncle to adopt the French-English model for the northern frontier of New Spain. Although he had no illusions that trade would rapidly alter Indian cultures, he thought the approach better than a costly, ineffective, and unwinnable war. Through trade, he argued, "the King would keep [Indians] very contented for ten years with what he now spends in one year in making war upon them."

Bernardo de Gálvez's cost-cutting recommendation met a ready reception in Madrid as Spain prepared to enter the war against England on the side of the thirteen rebellious colonies. In 1779, José de Gálvez instructed the commander in chief of the interior provinces, Teodoro de Croix, to halt plans for a large-scale offensive and to seek alliances based on trade and gifts, including firearms. Prompted by the fiscal stringencies of wartime, Gálvez's instructions of 1779 seemed temporary. Instead, they became the foundation of an enduring Indian policy when, seven years later, José de Gálvez indulged his penchant for nepotism by appointing his nephew viceroy of New Spain. As viceroy, Bernardo de Gálvez prepared a detailed exposition, his well-known *Instructions of 1786*, which reconciled conflicting practices with a three-pronged approach. First, he urged the maintenance of military pressure on Indians, to the point of exterminating Apaches if necessary. Second, he endorsed the building of alliances, such as those that Spaniards had long enjoyed with Pueblos and other tribes. "The vanquishment of the heathen," he coldly noted, "consists in obliging them to destroy one another." Third, he argued for the extensive use of trade and gifts to make Indians who sought peace dependent on Spaniards.

In his explanation of how to increase Indian dependency on Spaniards, a policy that he termed "peace by deceit," Bernardo de Gálvez surpassed his uncle in imagination and cynicism. He urged that Indians be furnished with firearms and ammunition, but he specified that guns be made of poorly tempered metal with long barrels that would make them awkward to use and easy to break. Natives, then, would depend on Spaniards for repairs or replacements. As to ammunition, Gálvez believed that Indians should be given an abundance of it. The more they used powder and shot, the less they would use arrows. Soon, they would "begin to lose their skill in handling the bow," which Gálvez correctly understood to be a more effective weapon than the firearm. In short, Gálvez planned to use tried-and-true English and French practices to destroy the basis of native culture as the first step toward turning nomadic Indians into Spaniards. By this means, the military might succeed in bringing about the cultural transformations that missionaries had failed to achieve through less violent and less cynical means.

With various modifications and embellishments, the *Instructions of 1786* governed Spanish-Indian relations on the northern frontier for the remainder of the colonial period. Spain, strapped for funds and arms for its own army, lacked sufficient resources to buy a peace entirely, and there is no evidence that Spanish agents provided significant amounts of alcohol to Indians. But Gálvez's *Instructions* did establish clear rules under which some of Spain's ablest officers could play a new game that included gifts, access to trade fairs, cooperation against mutual enemies, and more equitable and consistent treatment than Indian belligerents had received in the past. Those Indians who had resisted Spanish domination and military pressure had, in effect, forced Spanish leaders to make these concessions.

Thus, conciliation and negotiation, previously subordinate to force, became the cornerstone of a new Spanish policy in the interior provinces. Coupled with military pressure, this policy achieved remarkable results—even before Bernardo de Gálvez reformulated it in 1786. One of the most notable successes occurred in New Mexico under the leadership of Juan Bautista de Anza, a third-generation presidial officer whose father had been killed by Apaches on the Sonora frontier. As governor of New Mexico from 1778 to 1787, Anza won an enduring peace with western Comanches, who had been the scourge of the province since mid-century. Once he had secured peace with Comanches, Anza went on to lay the foundations for an alliance with Navajos, who were soon persuaded to turn on their former allies, the Gileño Apaches. In the face of such evident shifts in the balance of power, Gileños began to sue for peace and its attendant benefits. Similar successes occurred all across the northern frontier, and in many locales Apaches settled down to lives as farmers and ranchers. Near some presidios, at what Spaniards called "peace establishments," soldiers began to distribute goods and instruct Indians in the ways of Spaniards.

This turning point in Spanish-Indian relations occurred during the administration of the experienced and exceptionally able Jacobo de Ugarte, who served as commander in chief of the interior provinces from 1786 to 1790. Ugarte benefited from the groundwork that his predecessors had laid, and he continued to provide the overall coordination to prevent hostile Indians from playing off one Spanish province against the other. Peace, of course, was never absolute. Raids and occasional acts of violence continued on all sides, but minor infractions by individuals were overlooked by Spanish and Indian leaders alike. Both Spanish and Indian leaders had come to believe, as Bernardo de Gálvez hoped they would, that "a bad peace . . . would be more fruitful than the gains of a successful war."

In the interior provinces, the understandings that Spaniards had with Comanches, Apaches, Navajos, and other tribes lasted until the 1810s. Then, when rebellion in Mexico diverted resources away from the frontier, making it difficult to continue to buy friendships or offer a steady supply of trade goods, the peace establishments began to collapse and alliances weakened. On the Texas frontier in particular, the chaotic intermural quarrels between Spanish royalists and Spanish insurgents, both of whom solicited the aid of Indians, made Spaniards undependable and unpredictable allies.

To California

The reorganization of the interior provinces and the forging of a successful Indian policy during the long reign of Carlos III (1759–88) was accompanied by Spanish expansion to the Pacific coast—Spain's last defensive thrust into the western half of the continent. In 1769, the same year that Spanish troops took forcible possession of Louisiana, sea and land expeditions pushed into the northwest of New Spain to occupy the bays of San Diego and Monterey. Had they known of it, they would also have raised the cross on the magnificent Bay of San Francisco, but it had remained concealed from Spanish mariners behind the narrow, fog-shrouded Golden Gate. After a land party discovered the bay later in 1769, Spain built a presidio and mission at the tip of the San Francisco peninsula in 1776.

As in Texas and Louisiana, Spain's motives for expanding into Alta California were purely preemptive. Missionaries and mariners had long urged the Crown to occupy the Pacific coast of North America, all of which Spaniards termed "California," but not until Spain perceived the area as threatened by foreigners did it commit resources for such an enterprise.

The architect of Spanish expansion to the Pacific was José de Gálvez, who served as a nearly omnipotent royal inspector in New Spain from 1765 to 1770, before becoming minister of the Indies. Gálvez regarded both England and Russia as threats to Spanish claims. Beginning with Francis Drake in 1579, English mariners had entered California waters from the south; if England's well-publicized search for the Northwest Passage succeeded, Gálvez feared that English vessels would soon enter the Pacific from the north. At the same time, he predicted that Englishmen would continue westward from Canada and the Mississippi, finding their way to California along great rivers. "There is no doubt," Gálvez wrote in 1768, "we have the English very close to our towns of New Mexico and not very far from the west coast of this continent." The threat from Russian fur traders seemed still more immediate. In 1759 a book by a Spanish Franciscan, José Torrubia, had appeared in Italy with the alarming title *Muscovites in California*.

On his own initiative, the energetic and ambitious Gálvez began to lay the foundations for Spanish expansion to the northwest of New Spain. In 1768, when reports of large numbers of Russians settling the California coast prompted Madrid to order him to secure Monterey Bay, Gálvez was prepared to move swiftly. Strapped for resources and volunteers, he relied heavily on Franciscans, led by Fray Junípero Serra, and soldiers, commanded by Captain Gaspar de Portolá.

Missions had fallen from vogue among the Enlightened ministers of Carlos III, who had expelled the Jesuits from Spain and its colonies in 1767, and Gálvez himself believed them antiquated. Nonetheless, they flourished in Alta California even as they were being secularized in Texas, New Mexico, and Arizona—that is, the missions converted into parishes with parish-supported secular priests and their communal property divided among the remaining Indians. Using the mixture of rewards and punishments that had

worked among the Pueblos, Pimas, and Coahuiltecans, Franciscans supervised the construction of twenty-one missions between San Diego and Sonoma, the last completed in 1823. At the height of their occupancy in the early 1820s, the California missions housed some twenty-one thousand Indians—on the average, five times as many per mission as in the San Antonio missions at their zenith. As elsewhere, Franciscans along the densely populated coast met resistance of various types, including rebellion and flight, but the linguistically diverse natives, organized into tiny units and without benefit of horses, guns, or French or British allies, proved more tractable than Apaches or Comanches. Bernardo de Gálvez had hoped in vain in 1786 that the "innocence" and "tranquility" of the California tribes might by maintained and that they might be denied "the use and handling of the horse."

Despite the populous missions and salubrious climate, Alta California attracted few colonists. The government offered material rewards to encourage immigration and sent some convicts and orphan girls as colonists, but the area remained too distant from population centers and markets to attract willing immigrants. In effect, Alta California was an island through most of the colonial period, dependent solely on occasional ships from New Spain to bring additional colonists and supplies and to provide access to markets. Baja California had provided soldiers, missionaries, and livestock for the initial settlement of Alta California in 1769, but the impoverished peninsula had spent itself. In 1774, California's isolation diminished when Juan Bautista de Anza blazed a trail from Pimería Alta to California via the critical Yuma crossing of the Colorado River. The Quechans at Yuma revolted in 1781, however, destroying two nearby missions and closing Alta California's only land connection to Mexico, which Spain never reopened. As much through natural increase as through colonization, then, the Hispanic population reached about three thousand by 1821—five hundred more persons of European descent than lived in Texas that same year and three times the number who lived in Arizona. New Mexico, the least populated of today's border states, had by far the largest population of Hispanics in 1821—some thirty thousand.

California's Hispanic population was thinly dispersed, clustered in well-watered valleys along a five-hundred-mile stretch of dry coast. The province had only three self-governing municipalities under Spain: Los Angeles (1781), San José (1777), and Branciforte (today's Santa Cruz, 1797). Civilian communities also developed near some of the missions, such as San Luis Obispo and San Juan Capistrano, and around the province's four ill-equipped presidios: San Diego, Santa Bárbara, Monterey, and San Francisco. Appropriate to the Enlightenment, Spanish scientists reconnoitered Pacific waters far into present-day Alaska, but Spain never took effective control of the coast beyond San Francisco. In 1790, Spain's short-lived attempt to occupy Nootka Sound on Vancouver Island, off the coast of present British Columbia, ruptured relations with England. A much-weakened Spain surrendered its exclusive claims to the Pacific Northwest rather than go to war with England. In 1812, while Spain was preoccupied with rebellions in its American colonies, Russian fur traders, whom Gálvez had feared, established Fort Ross on Bodega Bay, to the north of San Francisco.

Impacts and Adaptations

Small in numbers, the Hispanics who moved into California in the late eighteenth century made a powerful impact on the land and its native peoples—as they had wherever they settled along the Spanish rim. Largely because of European diseases, the native population of California fell from an estimated 300,000 in 1769 to 150,000 in 1821. Some Indian survivors fled into the interior, but those who remained along the coast found their traditional cultures eviscerated. Unlike the Pueblos, whose permanent, cohesive towns had provided a measure of refuge against forced culture change, many of California's hunting and gathering peoples had been lured into institutions whose routines, regulations, economic and social activities, and housing and sleeping arrangements differed radically from those they had known before. With the breakup of the missions in the 1820s and 1830s, most of these Indians became marginalized outsiders without a firm footing in either Hispanic or Indian culture.

As Indian populations declined in California, as elsewhere along the Spanish rim, European domestic animals proliferated. The temperate climate along the California coast and the grasslands of South Texas proved especially congenial for cattle and horses, which multiplied with few natural predators. The introduction of European quadrupeds, like the addition of any new species of flora or fauna, had a ripple effect throughout the ecosystem. Voracious, sharp-hooved grazing animals, for example, destroyed protective ground cover and compacted soils; on hillsides or gently sloping land, their well-worn trails deepened into gullies that carried rainwater off too swiftly. In the Spanish era, overgrazing and "gullying" did not turn vast areas of grassland into desert (that process did not become apparent until the late nineteenth century, hastened perhaps by a change in climate), but by the eighteenth century the effects of overgrazing began to be felt in Hispanic and Indian communities alike.

The new pastoral economy also altered the types of plant life that characterized the region because cattle, horses, and sheep (which thrived in New Mexico) exterminated native species of grasses and left a void that more aggressive European species rushed to fill. Wherever they went, Old World grazing animals effectively transported the seeds of Old World grasses—including those, such as Kentucky bluegrass, that we have come to think of as 100-percent American. For centuries, European grasses had adapted to close cropping and bare or compacted soil and had developed seeds specially equipped to travel with grazing animals. In California alone during the Spanish era, Mediterranean forage plants and weeds—bromegrasses, common foxtail, curled dock, Italian ryegrass, red-stemmed filaree, sow thistle, wild oats, and other plants—moved well beyond areas of Spanish settlement into northern California and the interior valleys of the San Joaquín and Sacramento rivers. As in much of the Southwest, the transformation of grasslands in California from native to alien species was not completed until late in the nineteenth century, but the process was well under way before the American era in California and along the Spanish rim.

Just as Spaniards made a powerful impact on the land and the natives from California to Texas, so did the land and the natives have a powerful impact on Spaniards. For example, Spaniards adapted most readily to the same temperate zones where European Spanish domestic animals flourished—along the California coast, in the high country of northern New Mexico where altitude mimics latitude, and on the well-watered, fertile, and salubrious prairies inland from the Texas coast. In contrast, much of the desert remained alien to many European species and, therefore, to Spaniards as well. Across the region, microenvironments also shaped, but did not determine, Hispanic life and institutions. In the mountainous villages of northern New Mexico, scant farmland and the need to share water put a premium on cooperation and intensified Iberian communitarian traditions, including communal ownership of land. Below Santa Fe, where the widening Rio Grande floodplain offered more farm- and rangeland, large, privately held estates became common.

Human geography also transformed the lives and institutions of Hispanics in the far North, whose societies never became mirror images of their metropolis but rather resembled other Hispanic frontiers, such as those in Chile or Argentina. For example, no place on the Spanish rim offered the large, docile, and sophisticated Indian labor force that supported the elegant institutions (universities, seminaries, libraries, and guilds) and complex hierarchical society of central New Spain. To be sure, the frontier societies had at their apex a small aristocracy whose status derived from family, racial purity (real or imagined), land, livestock, and governmental or ecclesiastical positions. At the broad base of the frontier societies one could, of course, also find exploited Indian labor, including Indian servants and slaves (who were seldom called "slaves," since enslaving Indians was prohibited). Across much of the Spanish rim, however, the demands of frontier life forced a high percentage of Hispanics, even those with a few unpaid servants, to work their own land and tend their own livestock—at times simultaneously defending themselves from hostile nomadic tribes. Such circumstances may have shaped the character of Hispanic frontier peoples, making them more

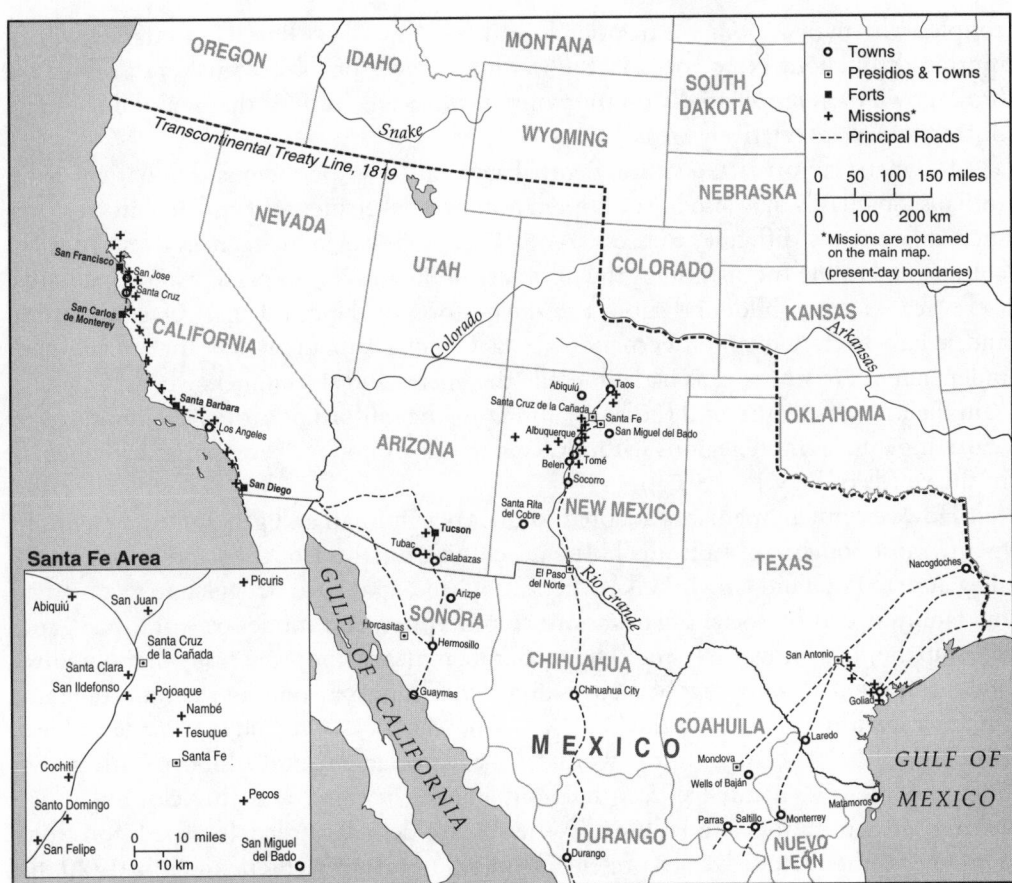

The Spanish-Mexican Rim, 1821

independent, self-reliant, and hardy, as contemporaries such as Alexander von Humboldt and Miguel Ramos Arizpe believed. More concretely, Indian raiders distorted Spain's institutions and society on the frontier, discouraging immigration, initiating the preeminence of the military in the eighteenth century, and making a disproportionate percentage of widows in places like San Antonio, where fighting was most intense.

In contrast to the English colonies, where Indian influence on the formation of Anglo-American cultures appears to have been slight and limited to initial contact, the Spanish colonies experienced ongoing and profound contact with Indians. In many parts of the frontier, the fate of Spaniards remained intertwined with that of their Indian neighbors, on whom they initially depended for subsistence and from whom they learned to adapt to the new land. From Pueblo women, for example, Spanish women learned to plaster adobe, which became women's work among Hispanics as it was among Pueblos. Some Spaniards acquired competence in Indian languages, consulted with Indian physicians, and used Indian drugs, including peyote on occasion. *Atole*, chocolate, pinole, *posole*, tortillas, and other Indian foods became integral to the diet of Spanish frontier folk.

At its deepest level, Spanish-Indian contact included the ongoing amalgamation of races as Spaniards, mestizos, blacks, and mulattoes came north from Mexico and coupled with natives along the frontier, in and out of wedlock. Racial boundaries, which blurred throughout New Spain in the waning decades of the colonial era, seemed to break down even more rapidly on the frontier, where institutions that maintained such distinctions were relatively weak.

In what California Governor Pedro Fages called a "pernicious familiarity" with Indians, Spaniards may also have adopted nonmaterial elements of Indian cultures, but such influence is difficult to assess. As early as 1631, a Franciscan in New Mexico complained to the Inquisition of the difficulty of life in New Mexico, where Spaniards were "reared from childhood subject to the customs of these Indians." Over a century and a half later, Governor Fernando de la Concha lamented that the unruly and independent New Mexicans had adopted "the liberty and slovenliness which they see . . . in their neighbors the wild Indians." Similarly, the californios earned a reputation for scattering into "remote regions without King to rule or Pope to excommunicate them," in the words of Fray José Señán.

However much Spaniards adapted to their new human and geographical environment, most sought to replicate Hispanic culture on the frontiers and to maintain allegiance to Pope and Crown. Like other Europeans, Spaniards struggled to reconstruct the family structure, social organization, communities, and modes of work, play, and worship they had known at home. The greater their means, the more easily they obtained and maintained the trappings of their civilization. The possessions, for example, of Juana Luján, a wealthy widow who died at her ranch near Santa Cruz de la Cañada in New Mexico in 1762, included, in the words of the historian Richard Ahlborn, "silver and porcelain utensils, painted chests, religious images, jewelry, and fine clothing from central Mexico, Europe, and China." When Pedro de Villasur led an expedition from Santa Fe to the Platte River in present Nebraska in search of Frenchmen in 1720, he traveled with silver dishes, cups, and spoons, a silver candlestick, an inkwell, writing paper, quills, and a saltcellar.

Spaniards, who possessed the technological, economic, and political strength of a large state society, succeeded so well in rebuilding their familiar world on the frontiers that members of tribal societies, such as Rafael Aguilar, the alcalde of Pecos Pueblo, probably borrowed more from Spaniards than Spaniards did from them. Ultimately, however, the extent of cultural borrowings depended on so many contingent circumstances, including time, place, and class, that no composite picture can be drawn for the entire Spanish rim. *Californios* differed from *arizonenses*, who, in turn, differed from *nuevo mexicanos* and they from *tejanos*. To cite graphic examples, the carved wooden saints, or *santos*, associated with late colonial New Mexico and valued today by aficionados of folk art, had no counterpart elsewhere along the Spanish-Mexican rim, and the red-tile roofs common to the missions of California toward the end of the colonial era did not exist in New Mexico.

Independent Mexico and American Manifest Destiny

In the first two decades of the nineteenth century, Spain's New World empire crumbled. In 1821, when New Spain followed other former Spanish colonies in declaring its independence, the provinces from California to Texas quietly endorsed the new order. Mexico and the United States agreed to an international boundary that put much of what

Hispanic art in New Mexico found its most creative expression in the form of naive but powerfully evocative wooden carvings of saints, or santos, and paintings of saints on pine boards, known as retablos. The earliest Anglo-American visitors to New Mexico denigrated these objects as "miserable pictures of the saints," but modern-day santeros are now regarded as heirs to one of the few indigenous artistic traditions in the United States.

Miguel Herrera (active 1880s). Our Lady of Sorrows. Gesso, natural pigments on wood, ca. 1880s. Photograph by Blair Clark. Charles D. Carroll Bequest to the Museum of New Mexico, Museum of International Folk Art, Museum of New Mexico, Santa Fe.

is now the American West, including all of Nevada, Utah, and parts of Colorado, Kansas, and Wyoming, as well as the four border states of California, Arizona, New Mexico, and Texas, under the jurisdiction of independent Mexico. But the region remained part of Mexico only briefly. Texas rebelled successfully in 1836; a decade later, in 1846, American troops invaded New Mexico, southern Arizona, and California.

In this quarter century from 1821 to 1846, Anglo Americans and other foreigners moved into the region for the first time in significant numbers as Mexico nullified Spanish restrictions against foreign residents and foreign commerce. The newcomers entered a frontier zone whose landscape and peoples often seemed to them exotic, even though it had been deeply transformed by Europeans. Moreover, foreign visitors found themselves in a region undergoing an immediate turmoil of rapid structural transformations imposed from the outside. In its first decades, independent Mexico made fundamental changes in the nation's political, economic, military, and ecclesiastical institutions. Those changes, intended to modernize the nation, came about so rapidly and imperfectly that they promoted profound discontent along the frontier.

After a brief flirtation with monarchy, Mexico attempted to convert itself into a republic, with its Constitution of 1824 modeled in part after that of the United States. But to lawmakers in Mexico City, it seemed clear that the northern frontier's sparse and relatively unschooled population could not afford to operate the institutions of state government. The compromises that ensued left the frontier populace with inadequate government and with little hope for political reform. The entire region from California to Texas lacked political autonomy at the provincial level and adequate representation or influence at the national level. The situation worsened when Mexico's political institutions collapsed in the early 1830s. The following years of chronic instability disaffected many frontiersmen and contributed to separatist movements that culminated in Texas in 1836 and that had undercurrents in California and in New Mexico from the mid-1830s through the mid-1840s. "Hopes and promises are only what [New Mexico] has received . . . from its mother country," one disenchanted New Mexican, Manuel Chávez, wrote in 1844.

At the same time that Mexico's weakening political institutions began to lose legitimacy in the eyes of some frontier oligarchs, the authority of its ecclesiastical institutions diminished. The mission system ended, and the last Franciscans departed. Like the political changes on the frontier, the demise of the missions came about in part because of efforts to modernize Mexico. The liberal view that missions represented antiquated institutions had been articulated by Spanish thinkers in the late eighteenth century and prevailed in Mexico in the 1820s and early 1830s. Among other things, liberals asserted that missions oppressed Indians by holding them forcibly and denying them the full equality accorded other Mexican citizens. However noble the philosophy, the dismantling of the missions produced a spiritual crisis on the frontier, where the secular church failed to replace the departing Franciscans, who had ministered to Indian and non-Indian alike. Many priests preferred more comfortably familiar parishes in the nation's heartland.

Meanwhile, Mexico's military position on the frontier never fully recovered from the tumultuous decade of civil war that preceded Mexico's final declaration of independence in 1821. The frontier military declined in relation to the strength of Apaches, Comanches, and other nomadic tribes partly because of the reluctance of the Mexican army's highly politicized officer corps to fight Indians in the remote North. Greater awards awaited officers whose units stood poised near Mexico City when governments tottered and fell—as they frequently did. Then too, money for gifts for Indian allies appears to have diminished in the Mexican era. As a result, the frontier presidios never reached the level of effectiveness that they enjoyed before the Mexican wars for independence, and the burden of frontier defense fell on the frontiersmen, who organized themselves into ill-equipped militia. As military effectiveness declined, the firepower of Indian adversaries increased, due largely to American gunrunners. By the

1830s, American merchants had broken into the Indian trade as far west as Arizona, and some of them traded weapons for loot that Indians stole from Mexicans.

In this and other ways, Americans who entered the borderlands became participants in the region's transformation. When independent Mexico sought to invigorate its economy by opening its borders to foreigners and foreign trade, it succeeded notably on its northern frontier. From the nearby United States in particular came manufactured goods, capital, access to markets, and colonists. The tempo of economic life increased, as Mexico hoped it would, but Hispanic frontiersmen from California to Texas grew dependent on outsiders, especially Americans, for manufactured goods, and Americans came to dominate commerce and local industry even before the United States acquired the region between 1845 and 1848.

In the first half of the nineteenth century, westering Americans represented a society that had rapidly outstripped fledgling Mexico in economic productivity and population growth. While the American economy expanded remarkably between the so-called panics of 1819 and 1837, the once robust economy of Mexico withered as a result of the dislocations that accompanied the wars of independence. After independence, Mexico's gross national product fell to less than half of its 1805 peak and would not surpass that figure again until the 1870s. A similar disparity occurred in population growth. In 1820, the population of the United States had reached 9.6 million, more than doubling since 1790; by 1840, it had nearly doubled again, to over 17 million. Meanwhile, the number of Mexicans had fallen by about 10 percent during the turbulent 1810s, to 6.1 million, and remained relatively static for several decades.

Like the encounter between the Spanish state and the North American tribal societies of the sixteenth century, then, this latest contest for control of the Spanish-Mexican rim was lopsided. The new winners enjoyed not only demographic and economic advantages but also a mercantile ethos and a certitude in what they believed to be the superiority of their race, religion, and political institutions. Those conceits lay behind the Americans' sense of their own manifest destiny and served them well as rationalizations for conquering and transforming northern Mexico, much as Spaniards' ethnocentric values had facilitated their domination of indigenous Americans several centuries earlier. But if the contest between the United States and Mexico was lopsided, the transformation that followed the American invasion of 1846 was not entirely one-sided. Just as Hispanic frontiersmen altered and enriched their culture by borrowing from vanquished Indians, so did Anglo Americans embrace aspects of the culture of the defeated Hispanics, whose influences can still be seen today in the Southwest, especially in architecture, diet, language, literature, laws, and ranching and farming techniques.

Constructing and Reconstructing the Hispanic Past

The American transformation of the Spanish-Mexican rim extended to the rewriting of its past. Initially, Anglo Americans dismissed the long Spanish-Mexican tenure in the region as a time of despotism, religious intolerance, and economic stagnation and Hispanics themselves as indolent, vicious, and superstitious (characteristics that Span-iards had often applied to Indians). Painting the Hispanic past in dark hues enabled Anglo Americans to draw a sharp contrast with the enlightened institutions that they imagined they had imposed on the region. Hispanophobic interpretations of the

Carleton E. Watkins systematically photographed all of the California missions in 1880–81, and marketed his large-scale views to buyers who valued the ruined buildings as nostalgic relics of the Spanish West. The renewed late 19th-century interest in the Spanish past was closely linked to efforts to stimulate the California tourist industry.

Carleton E. Watkins (1829–1916). Mission, San Juan Capistrano. Albumen silver print, 1880–81. Department of Special Collections, University Research Library, University of California, Los Angeles.

Spanish-Mexican era never died, but in the late nineteenth century a rosier view emerged. In the 1880s, as demographic changes reduced the influence of Mexicans and Mexican Americans in the region, Anglo Americans could afford to indulge in nostalgia about the Hispanic traditions they had nearly obliterated. A sanitized and quaint rendition of the Hispanic past provided a pleasant sense of place for rootless newcomers and added an aura of exoticism and romance that lured tourists and their dollars. Artifacts from the Hispanic past came to be treasured, architecture and building materials (including the once-despised adobe) emulated, and crumbling missions restored. As Charles Lummis, southern California's most energetic Hispanophile, crassly put it, "The old missions are worth more money . . . than our oil, our oranges, or even our climate."

Historians simultaneously shaped and reflected this new appreciation of America's Hispanic past—an appreciation that prevailed through much of the twentieth century and has continued to the present day in some circles. Most vigorous were those historians associated with Herbert Eugene Bolton and the so-called Borderlands school, many of whom sought to enlarge Americans' understanding of the nation's multicultural origins. To correct the Hispanophobic distortions of the past, they emphasized the heroic achievements of individual Spaniards and the positive contributions of Hispanic institutions and culture. In so doing, many lost sight of the cultural and racial blending that made the societies of northern New Spain essentially Mexican. Anglo Americans had fallen under the spell of what Carey McWilliams, in a pioneering 1949 history of Mexican Americans, called "a fantasy heritage." The fantasy, which McWilliams described as "an absurd dichotomy between things Spanish and things Mexican," enabled Anglo Americans to glorify the region's "Spanish" heritage while ignoring or discriminating against living Mexicans. So too did it allow older Mexican Americans to disassociate themselves from recent immigrants from Mexico by imagining themselves of pure Spanish ancestry. The fantasy implicitly denied Mexicans and Indians their historic roots in the region.

Although a small number of scholars decried the "fantasy heritage," their objections were largely ignored until the late 1960s. Then, the coincidental rise of the Chicano movement and a growing interest in the prosaic questions of social history gave impetus to a fuller and less poetic rendering of the past. Younger scholars, who tended to sympathize with the exploited rather than the exploiters, examined themes that resonated with the problems of contemporary Mexicans in America as well as the concerns of social historians: workers, migration, women, class, race, miscegenation, acculturation, urban life, crime, punishment, social control, family, faith, and the fortitude and adaptability of common folk who endure in times of stressful change.

Hispanophobic and hispanophilic interpretations of the past continue to have strong adherents, but the more inclusive history of today seems likely to prevail until future historians feel the need once again to reimagine the past in order to make it more useful for their generation. At present, we understand the Spanish-Mexican rim as a place where Hispanic men and women, most of them mestizos, contended for power and resources with Indians, with European rivals, and with one another. As both the exploiters and the exploited, they transformed the human and natural geography of southwestern North America and in the process were themselves transformed. Similar transformations continue in this place, which we now know as the American Southwest.

Bibliographic Note

A Note about Language. Spaniard and *Hispanic* have political overtones in certain contexts. In this essay, I usually use those words to designate peoples in the past who identified themselves as culturally more Spanish than Indian, whatever their racial background. Because ethnicity is decidedly contextual and ethnic labels are constructed in opposition to some other group, meanings change with time and place. In the sixteenth century, for example, Iberians would normally have defined themselves by region or city—that is, as Castilians, Aragonese, or *sevillanos* rather than as Spaniards or Hispanics. In the New World, however, the word *Spaniard* acquired currency and took on racial connotations, signifying a person born of Spanish parents as opposed to an Indian or a mestizo. I am not using *Spaniard* in that restricted sense.

Like *Spaniard* or *Hispanic*, the terms *Native American* and *Indian* are ideologically charged and conceal the obvious political and cultural diversity of many specific peoples. I use these words largely to distinguish Native Americans in the aggregate from non-Indians.

In this essay, *North America* refers to the continent above present-day Mexico. Although the northern rim of Spain's empire extended across the continent to Florida, I have treated only the western half of the continent.

Much of this essay draws heavily from my own work *The Spanish Frontier in North America* (New Haven, 1992), which contains citations to many of the quotes as well as guidance to more specialized literature on which I have depended.

Readers in search of a short, well-illustrated overview of the Spanish era and its aftermath will enjoy *The Spanish West* (New York, 1976), by the staff at Time-Life Books. Peter Gerhard, *The North Frontier of New Spain* (Princeton, 1982), is the best reference work. For the Mexican era from California to Texas, see David J. Weber, *The Mexican Frontier, 1821–1846: The American Southwest under Mexico* (Albuquerque, 1982). An overview that examines the Spanish impact on native peoples is the anthropologist Edward H. Spicer's *Cycles of Conquest: The Impact of Spain, Mexico, and the United States on the Indians of the Southwest, 1533–1960* (Tucson, 1962). Spicer focused on northwestern New Spain and the Pueblo world; for insight into the indigenous worlds in northeastern New Spain, from the Rio Grande to Louisiana, see the detailed narrative by the ethnohistorian Elizabeth A. H. John, *Storms Brewed in Other Men's Worlds: The Confrontation of Indians, Spanish, and French in the Southwest, 1540–1795* (College Station, Tex., 1975).

The best surveys of sixteenth-century Spanish exploration are in David B. Quinn, *North America from Earliest Discovery to First Settlements: The Norse Voyages to 1612* (New York, 1977), and Carl Ortwin Sauer, *Sixteenth Century North America: The Land and the People as Seen by the Europeans* (Berkeley, 1971). Biographies of individual explorers include Harry Kelsey, *Juan Rodríguez Cabrillo* (San Marino, Calif., 1986), and Herbert Eugene Bolton's classic *Coronado: Knight of Pueblos and Plains* (Albuquerque, 1949). See too Stewart L. Udall, *To the Inland Empire: Coronado and Our Spanish Legacy* (Garden City, N.Y., 1987), with its handsome photographs and unabashed advocacy.

If one could read only a few books on Hispanic New Mexico, several recent titles should be among them: Marc Simmons, *The Last Conquistador: Juan de Oñate and the Settling of the Far Southwest* (Norman, 1991); John L. Kessell, *Kiva, Cross, and Crown: The Pecos Indians and New Mexico, 1540–1840* (Washington, D.C., 1979); and Ramón A. Gutiérrez, *When Jesus Came, the Corn Mothers Went Away: Marriage, Sexuality, and Power in New Mexico, 1500–1846* (Stanford, 1991).

For Arizona too, the lively narratives of John L. Kessell stand out: *Mission of Sorrows: Jesuit Guevavi and the Pimas, 1691–1767* (Tucson, 1970) and *Friars, Soldiers, and Reformers: Hispanic Arizona and the Sonora Mission Frontier, 1767–1856* (Tucson, 1976). Hispanic families are the focus of the anthropologist James E. Officer's *Hispanic Arizona, 1536–1856* (Tucson, 1987).

The authoritative works of Robert S. Weddle provide fine reading on Texas: *Spanish Sea: The Gulf of Mexico in North American Discovery, 1500–1685* (College Station, Tex., 1985); *Wilderness Manhunt: The Spanish Search for La Salle* (Austin, 1973); *San Juan Bautista: Gateway to Spanish Texas* (Austin, 1968); and *The San Sabá Mission: Spanish Pivot in Texas* (Austin, 1964). Jack Jackson, *Los Mesteños: Spanish Ranching in Texas, 1721–1821* (College Station, Tex., 1986), looks at the province's most important economic activity and its participants. Donald E. Chipman, *Spanish Texas, 1519–1821* (Austin, 1992), is the best overview.

There is no recent single-volume overview of Spanish Louisiana in English, but among the books that shed light on important aspects of life in the colony are John Preston Moore, *Revolt in Louisiana: The Spanish Occupation, 1766–1770* (Baton Rouge, 1976), Jack D. L. Holmes, *Gayoso: The Life of a Spanish Governor in the Mississippi Valley, 1789–1799* (Baton Rouge, 1965), and Gilbert C. Din, *The Canary Islanders of Louisiana* (Baton Rouge, 1988).

Spanish expansion to California and the Pacific Northwest is treated in magisterial fashion in Warren L. Cook, *Flood Tide of Empire: Spain and the Pacific Northwest, 1543–1819* (New Haven, 1973). Iris H. W. Engstrand, *Spanish Scientists in the New World: The Eighteenth-Century Expeditions* (Seattle, 1981), explores one little-known aspect of that expansion. The California missions received a hardheaded look in Robert Archibald, *Economic Aspects of the California Missions* (Washington, D.C., 1978). For the secular world, C. Alan Hutchinson, *Frontier Settlement in Mexican California: The Híjar-Padrés Colony and Its Origins, 1769–1835* (New Haven, 1969), is rich in insight and detail.

The best overview of Spanish military policy and practice is Max L. Moorhead, *The Presidio: Bastion of the Spanish Borderlands* (Norman, 1975). The analogous volume on frontier society is Oakah L. Jones, Jr., *Los Paisanos: Spanish Settlers on the Northern Frontier of New Spain* (Norman, 1979). Michael C. Meyer, *Water in the Hispanic Southwest: A Social and Legal History, 1550–1850* (Tucson, 1984), explores one aspect of the reciprocal relationship between man and environment. Thomas D. Hall, *Social Change in the Southwest, 1350–1880* (Lawrence, 1989), is an unusual effort, by a sociologist, to place southwestern history in a theoretical framework.

Carey McWilliams, *North from Mexico: The Spanish-Speaking People of the United States* (Philadelphia, 1949), is a sprightly, perceptive, and influential commentary on the past by a passionate social reformer. John R. Chávez, *The Lost Land: The Chicano Image of the Southwest* (Albuquerque, 1984), reveals a new historical sensibility in the making.

The above recommendations are to secondary books. Numerous essays and articles, many of them essential to understanding the field, have appeared in scholarly journals over the years. Some are gathered together in David J. Weber, ed., *New Spain's Far Northern Frontier: Essays on Spain in the American West, 1540–1821* (Albuquerque, 1979). Still other important articles have been written specifically for a single volume, such as those that appear in David Hurst Thomas, ed., *Columbian Consequences*, 3 vols. (Washington, D.C., 1989–91).

For those inclined to the pleasure of reading original narratives and documents, an astonishing number have been published in English translation, from the classic work translated and edited by Cyclone Covey, *Cabeza de Vaca's Adventures in the Unknown Interior of America* (New York, 1961), to the recently discovered correspondence translated and edited by John L. Kessell, *Remote Beyond Compare: Letters of Don Diego de Vargas to His Family from New Spain and New Mexico, 1675–1706* (Albuquerque, 1989).

For valuable critiques of this article I am indebted to many generous colleagues: the historians Susan Deeds, Northern Arizona University, Ramón A. Gutiérrez, University of California at San Diego, Elizabeth A. H. John, of Austin, Oakah L. Jones, Jr., Purdue University, John L. Kessell, University of New Mexico, and Clyde Milner, Utah State University, as well as the anthropologists Bernard Fontana, University of Arizona, and David Hurst Thomas, Museum of Natural History in New York. Of the splendid support that I receive from my own university and the Robert and Nancy Dedman Chair in History, none is more valuable than the research assistance of the efficient and affable Jane Lenz Elder. As always, my most reliable critic, Carol Bryant Weber, Esq., went through the manuscript line by line, wringing clarity out of obscurity.

Chapter Three

Empires of Trade, Hinterlands of Settlement

JAY GITLIN

Antoine Le Page du Pratz left the French port of La Rochelle in May 1718 and arrived in America—at the entrance to Mobile Bay—on 25 August. Le Page was an educated man, a professional architect with training in mathematics and engineering. He had fought for Louis XIV in the War of the Spanish Succession. He came to Louisiana as a *concessionaire*, a man of means with a grant from John Law's Company of the West, ready to invest his energy, capital, and skills in this New World.

Several days after his arrival Le Page purchased a female Indian slave, "in order to have a person who could dress our victuals." Le Page and the young woman could not speak each other's language, but they could communicate by signs. Le Page decided to establish his settlement on Bayou St. John, half a league from New Orleans, the new capital of the colony. At the time, New Orleans was—in Le Page's words—"only marked out by a hut, covered with palmetto leaves." After choosing his land and having that choice confirmed by the resident company agent, Le Page built a hut of his own, then made a fire. Then the following incident occurred:

> It was almost night, when my slave perceived, within two yards of the fire, a young alligator, five feet long, which beheld the fire without moving. I was in the garden hard by, when she made me repeated signs to come to her, I ran with speed, and upon my arrival she shewed me the crocodile, without speaking to me; the little time that I examined it, I could see, its eyes were so fixed on the fire, that all our motions could not take them off. I ran to my cabin to look for my gun, as I am a pretty good marksman: but what was my surprize, when I came out, and saw the girl with a great stick in her hand attacking the monster! Seeing me arrive, she began to smile, and said many things, which I did not comprehend. But she made me understand, by signs, that there was no occasion for a gun to kill such a beast; for the stick she shewed me was sufficient for the purpose.

The anecdote related by Le Page raises the expectation of a dramatic confrontation between an American "monster" and a European hero, a "pretty good marksman" at that. But the drama is undercut by surprise and, finally, an ironic smile: Le Page discovers that the native girl and her stick were "sufficient for the purpose." Stephen Greenblatt, in his book on European exploration of the New World, *Marvelous Possessions*, describes

The earliest European eyewitness picture of America, this image of French explorers and Timucua Indians in Florida suggests the willful optimism of Europeans' first New World visions but masks the surprise and disappointment that often greeted settlers. The artist depicts a bountiful land of obedient and worshipful natives, but the French colony he visited was, in fact, near collapse due to the Frenchmen's inability to supply their own food or cooperate with local Indians.

Jacques Le Moyne de Morgues (1533–88). René de Laudonnière and Chief Athore. *Gouache and metallic pigments on vellum with traces of black chalk outlines; date depicted, 27 June 1564. Bequest of James Hazen Hyde, Miriam and Ira D. Wallach Division of Art, Prints and Photographs, The New York Public Library, Astor, Lenox and Tilden Foundations, New York, New York.*

the anecdote as the "principal register of the unexpected." As such, it is the perfect form for conveying the experience of discontinuity, the sense of surprise and dislocation that belongs in our histories but is too often missing. A textbook might state that John Lederer, a German physician, led three early expeditions to explore the western lands of Virginia in 1669 and 1670. Would it add that the sight of the Blue Ridge Mountains literally stopped him in his tracks, turning him back emotionally to the more familiar coastal landscape? In just such a moment, Le Page could only stop and marvel at the actions of his Indian slave. Like these early colonists and natives, we should expect the unexpected when studying these early frontiers—not because alligators were lurking behind every stump but rather because ordinary people doing ordinary tasks were caught in the act, as it were, by the strange transposition effected by the European colonization of America.

Of course, natives and colonists soon regained their composure and attempted to make sense of their experiences. Naturally, they relied on their respective cultures to inform their interpretations and guide their responses. On a personal level, the narrative of colonization, this frontier history is truly a dialogue between the familiar and the unfamiliar. The use of languages illustrates this point. Indian people learned how to speak European languages—not just Spanish, English, and French but also Dutch, Portuguese, and German—and colonists, in turn, learned a daunting array of Indian languages. In colonial Louisiana, many Europeans, Indians, and Africans spoke Mobilian, a trade language based on several Western Muskhogean languages. *Nanta shnu bana shnu chumpa*—"you want it, you buy it"—was a phrase recognized by all. Trade jargons and lingua francas sprang up all over North America, two of the more famous being the Chinook jargon in the Pacific Northwest and the Delaware jargon used in New Netherland and New Sweden. Even late in the colonial period, an Englishman in New Jersey would understand *How's't netap* as a greeting to a friend, and a Connecticut colonist might say a word of thanks—*taubut ne*—to a Pequot neighbor.

This is also a story of—in the words of the historian Fernand Braudel—"dietary frontiers." Colonies were places where people learned to eat "other people's bread." Europeans and Africans in Louisiana learned to use bear oil for cooking and, when it hardened, for spreading over bread as a substitute for butter. A trade in food commodities developed, one that even used Indian standards of packaging and measurement in the case of "deers [deer heads] of oil" and "mococks of maple sugar." Europeans learned to eat various corn-based native dishes such as sagamité and supawn. Delaware Indians learned to raise chickens—which they named *tipas* after a Swedish word used to call domestic fowl. The Pequots came to appreciate *beesh* (peas) and *boige* (porridge). They also came to despise *beksees* (pigs), for these European animals destroyed cornfields, oyster banks, and clamming sites.

Not all such exchanges were beneficial. Europeans learned to smoke tobacco, and Indians learned to drink brandy. And exchanges were often predicated on values rooted in different worldviews, different economies, different environments. The contrast might prove amusing. Europeans obtained land—or, at least, thought they had—for mere "trinkets." The Montagnais of Canada noted, "The English have no sense; they give us twenty knives like this for one Beaver skin." Ultimately, the values or prices set

From a modern perspective, early native and European depictions of one another seem rife with ambiguity. A French pipe featuring an Indian woman sitting on a chamber pot hints at a world of complex social interactions and cultural jokes.

French (near Kaskaskia, Illinois). Clay Pipe. Clay, 18th century. Erwin Peithman Collection, Illinois Historic Preservation Agency, Springfield.

on North American resources or products by Europeans in the New World reflected European needs in the Old World, and the commercialization of the American landscape disrupted Indian economies. Conflicts were often accompanied by complaints of Indian duplicity and European greed.

The sad truth is that mediation and mutuality were, in the long run, overshadowed by misunderstanding and conflict. America became a contested terrain, and five hundred years after Columbus first arrived, the very history of American colonization has become the object of some struggle. From a European perspective, Columbus made a great discovery. From a Native-American perspective, he began an invasion. Historians struggling to eliminate bias from their work describe the arrival of Columbus as an encounter. Although such neutral terms have their uses, there is no disguising the fact that the arrival of Europeans and their plants, animals, and germs generated a demographic catastrophe for Native Americans. The narrative of colonization is, indeed, a story with tragic dimensions, but it is also a story of adventure and empowerment. The fact that history itself has become a contested terrain simply shows that the story set in motion five hundred years ago is an ongoing one.

Models of Colonization and Appropriation

When Columbus reached the Bahamas on 12 October 1492, a new era of surprising discoveries began; yet this landfall was hardly an accident, a mere chance encounter. The

Columbian voyages represented the summation of past European experiences as much as they generated a field of new ones. The merchants of Genoa and Venice had been expanding the commercial interests of Europe in the eastern Mediterranean for centuries. They controlled the bulk trades, importing grain from Constantinople and the cities of Egypt and Syria and exporting oil, wine, and cheese. The most lucrative ventures were the trades in luxury goods: silks from China or Cathay and Persia; linen and cotton cloths such as damasks and calicoes, whose names reveal their place of manufacture. The spice trade was the most important of all, and in the later Middle Ages, "spices" included not only condiments for food but also perfumes, dyes, and cosmetics. This trade functioned within a complex and far-flung network of merchants, cities, caravans, and shipping routes. In cities such as Alexandria and Aleppo, the Italians lived in protected merchant colonies or Latin quarters, called *fondaci*. Throughout the Levant and the Maghrib, merchants learned the lessons of cross-cultural trade. They learned how to convert currencies, how to conduct negotiations that were both diplomatic and commercial, and above all, how to extract profits while residing in a foreign land. These lessons were fundamental to the evolution of colonial culture. The fur trade in North America, especially as it was pursued by the French, resembled a net of mercantile enclaves cast over a vast, animal-rich environment. At its height, this American enterprise became—in the historian Philip Curtin's words—"a series of European trade diasporas meeting a series of native American trade diasporas at convenient sites on major waterways." The merchants at New Orleans, St. Louis, New Amsterdam, and a number of other colonial entrepôts kept one foot in their host society and one in their cultural home. It was their business to be a part of the larger world—to keep abreast of the conditions of trade and to regulate the flow of commodities they were sending and receiving. Their connections were their source of identity and prosperity.

The Mediterranean provided another model of colonial expansion, one that reached its fullest expression in lands lapped by the waters of the Atlantic. In the islands of the eastern Atlantic Ocean, colonization "avec des gros bagages"—that is, colonies based on the importation of settlers, animals, and plants—developed. The cross-fertilization of Mediterranean and Atlantic worlds had been sparked by the Arago-Catalan conquests in the Balearic Islands and the expansion of Aragon and Castile into Andalusia, Valencia, and Murcia. The island of Majorca, in particular, became a center of maritime information, ideas, and technology. This Catalan colony took the lead in what the historian Felipe Fernández-Armesto has dubbed the late medieval "space-race" into the Atlantic.

European mariners explored a new zone of navigation defined by the Atlantic wind system. The prevailing westerlies in the north, the northeasterly trade winds that produce the clockwise-moving ocean currents in the North Atlantic: here was the basis for the linking of distant coasts.

The Canary Islands off the northwestern African coast and the Madeiras and Azores to the north served as stepping-stones—way stations on the routes connecting the New World and the Old; they also became laboratories for colonial experimentation. The patterns of ecological displacement, the destruction and transfer of biota, began to take shape here. These islands also witnessed the creation of plantation societies that would eventually link Africa, Europe, and new American lands.

Sugarcane arrived in Madeira by the 1450s, after experiments with honeybees and wheat and after the destruction of the island's forests by fire, pigs, and cattle. By the end of the century Madeira had become the world's leading producer of a commodity destined to become a reliable source of wealth in the New World. In addition, an ecological epilogue to this story of Madeira would be replayed elsewhere: wood, needed as fuel for the boilers in the sugarhouse, became a scarce commodity on these once-forested islands. Regulations were issued—but too late.

The Canaries had a similar experience with sugar, but it was delayed: the Canaries had an indigenous population. The Guanches were described as being olive-colored, tall, and—when necessary—fierce. They were isolated from the mainland, lacking any nautical traditions, and were therefore subject to the ravages of virgin-soil epidemics. Although the Guanche population may have been as high as one hundred thousand, the people were divided, spoke different dialects, and were never able to unite against their invaders. The invaders, of course, exploited divisions among the natives and were aided in this task by missionaries. The Guanches barely survived the fifteenth century. As one sixteenth-century diplomat noted about European expansion, "Religion supplies the pretext . . . gold the motive."

Sugar plantations—which combined agricultural and industrial processes—required large numbers of unfree laborers. With the explosion of sugar production in the Madeiras and islands off the African coast, the traditional sources of slave labor proved insufficient. The Portuguese, searching for African gold, which they found, also found new supplies of African slaves at places much closer to the islands generating the demand. The Senegambia region soon became the focal point of African-European—and ultimately—American exchange. Senegambia not only became the center of the slave trade but also witnessed the transfer of crops: yams (possibly from the Wolof word *nyami*, "to eat"), millet, bananas, okra, and rice were carried to the Americas; peanuts, papayas, manioc, and maize came to Africa. Colonization required the uprooting of plants and people, and in the pursuit of profits, American enterprises would consume large numbers of African slaves. It was to be a tragic connection, and the linkage of color with slavery would fix European perceptions of Africans for centuries. In his second voyage to the New World, Columbus brought sugarcane from the Canary Islands to Hispaniola. African slaves soon followed.

It is worth noting that this lengthy prehistory of American colonization is not merely about precedents and patterns that shaped that colonization; it is about the consistent importance of the larger European and global context. The importance of that context goes beyond the early settlements in Virginia or Louisiana. It continues to Alaska and Hawai`i. This larger perspective sheds light on social and economic links, even on personal connections. How can we explain, for example, the presence in late-eighteenth-century Natchez on the Mississippi River of merchants such as Domenico Tevezola, a native of Genoa with a French-Creole wife and an English-speaking African slavewoman, and of Francisco Bazo, a native of Palma in Majorca? The ubiquity of such Mediterranean businessmen seems somehow less surprising when we consider the long-standing "western" interests of Majorcans and Genoese. The father of Manuel Lisa, the famous Missouri River trader and adventurer, was born in the old Catalan frontier province of Murcia. An important merchant in St. Louis, Bartolomeo Bertolla, was a partner with

Pierre Chouteau, Jr., and imported glass beads for the fur trade from his brother Alessandro in Venice. The Fort Berthold Indian Reservation in North Dakota preserves the memory of this Venetian connection. Where, indeed, does the American West begin?

In terms of exploration, efforts in North America proceeded by fits and starts throughout the sixteenth century. Members of the international community of mariners and scholars such as Giovanni Verrazzano and John Cabot Montecalunya established claims for patrons in France and England. In the process, the national and religious rivalries and conflicts of Europe were exported to the Americas. Europeans mapped the outlines of a new continent, but their searches for a Northwest Passage and for rumored places of great wealth such as Quivira, Saguenay, and Cíbola accomplished little more than the alienation of native hosts, on whom they depended for survival.

The English, who would eventually dominate North America, were just beginning to think about the process of living and thriving away from home. The idea of subduing Ireland by means of plantations—by seizing native lands, converting them into an English system of land tenure, and distributing them to English settlers—would have a formative influence on English colonies in America. English perceptions of the natives of Ireland would also have an impact on their stereotypes of Native Americans. The "Wild Irish" were seen as uncivilized; that is, they lacked proper towns, spoke a different language, were pastoral and therefore were not sedentary agriculturalists, had long hair, and wore rough clothes made of animal skins. English activities in Ireland and America were connected and roughly contemporary. The first English attempts to colonize Virginia in the 1580s were dismal failures. Promoters underestimated the effort necessary to feed the colonists. Unless the natives fed them, the Europeans starved.

It was the Dutch—together with the spectacular rise of Amsterdam after 1576—who created the preconditions for the subsequent development of North America. Improvements in shipbuilding and marine insurance contributed to Dutch supremacy as the shippers of choice. The use of printed bills of exchange and the formation of the Bank of Amsterdam in 1609 helped make Amsterdam the central money market of Europe until the nineteenth century. Although an old inclination for domination by warfare and the control of land lingered, the English looked at the Dutch, a people once on the periphery and now grown rich through trade, and began to change their tune. The English now started to look for "merchantable commodities" that they might ship, store, and trade in an emerging world-system of markets. The English had their first success at Chesapeake Bay with the cultivation of tobacco, and this success owed a direct debt to pioneer Dutch planters in Guiana. The Dutch presence in the Caribbean, due in part to their search for an alternative source of salt for the herring trade, kept the Spanish on the defensive and allowed the French and the English to gain a foothold in the Americas.

Until the advent of tobacco, only the Newfoundland codfishery made a trip to North America worthwhile. By 1580 there were over five hundred ships from La Rochelle and Bordeaux, from the ports of Normandy and Brittany, from Portugal and England, in the waters around Newfoundland. Fish was an essential part of the European diet, and the North American fishery became a major European industry, employing as many as fifteen thousand men. It fact, the fishery was the only significant European enterprise in North America during the entire sixteenth century, and it was located on the periphery of the continent. The discovery of America and the appropriation of its resources were part of the global expansion of European activities. Within that context, America—with the important exception of the silver mines of Peru and central Mexico—had proven to be a sideshow compared with the theater of the Orient. Other than one defense post in Spanish Florida, no permanent European settlement existed in North America. The French and the English had shown no ability to survive, let alone flourish, in an unfamiliar environment. Certainly the natives had little to do with this; on the whole, they had shown themselves to be gracious hosts. Although the Europeans had explored much of the Americas, in most cases they had—in Braudel's words—"left no more trace behind than a ship does in the sea." (The pathogens the Europeans brought, however, had a tremendous impact.) Only the fishermen in the North Atlantic had any continuous interaction with the North American environment, and they were a transient group living on or near their ships. On the land of North America, the Europeans were like fish out of water.

From Tsenacomoco to Virginia

In 1606 James I acquiesced to the wishes of several groups of merchant adventurers and committed the crown to the colonization of North America by creating the "King's Council of Virginia." This royal council was to oversee the efforts of the Virginia Company—in reality, two private companies centered in Plymouth and in London. The two companies divided the North American coast between them, with a curious overlap in the region between present-day New York and Washington, D.C., and each sent would-be colonists to their respective turfs in 1607. The Plymouth Company's colony along the Sagadahoc (Kennebec) River in present-day Maine lasted only one miserable and contentious winter. The London Company's colonists at Jamestown in the Chesapeake Bay region may well have wished that they too had returned home. Indeed, Sir Thomas Dale, appointed governor of the colony in 1611, reported "a generall desire in the best sort to returne for England." (In our inclination to put a positive spin on the efforts of the pioneers, we often ignore the pleas and complaints of those who regretted their actions. Two centuries after Dale's remarks, Margaret Dwight, a young Connecticut woman on her way to Ohio, wrote: "We have concluded the reason so few are willing to return from the Western country, is not that the country is so good, but because the journey is so bad.")

Ignorance of Virginia's climate prompted optimistic directives from the home company to plant oranges, lemons, sugarcane, and olive trees, and gentlemen colonists starved while frantically pursuing gold. The Europeans were still strangers in a strange land. Clearly, all European colonists came to America with preconceived notions of the situations in which they hoped to find themselves. Their projections and the realities they found were often a bad match. Throughout the history of America, the gap between speculation and occupation has produced comic and tragic episodes, from Jamestown to "swampy acres" subdivisions in twentieth-century Florida. Moreover, the search for viable situations—which usually translated into a search for marketable commodities—was

Eager to encourage further English settlement in Virginia, John White depicted the native communities as clean, prosperous towns where—the Indians' strange customs notwithstanding—fertile soil and a long growing season ensured the well-being of would-be colonists. His optimism proved unfounded. Following his first trip to Virginia in 1585, White returned in 1587 for a brief stint as governor of the Roanoke colony. When he came back to Virginia again in 1590, he found no trace of the European settlement.

Theodore De Bry after John White. The Town of Secota. Engraving, 1590. From Thomas Hariot, A Brief and True Report of the New Found Land of Virginia (1590). Courtesy Virginia State Library and Archives, Richmond.

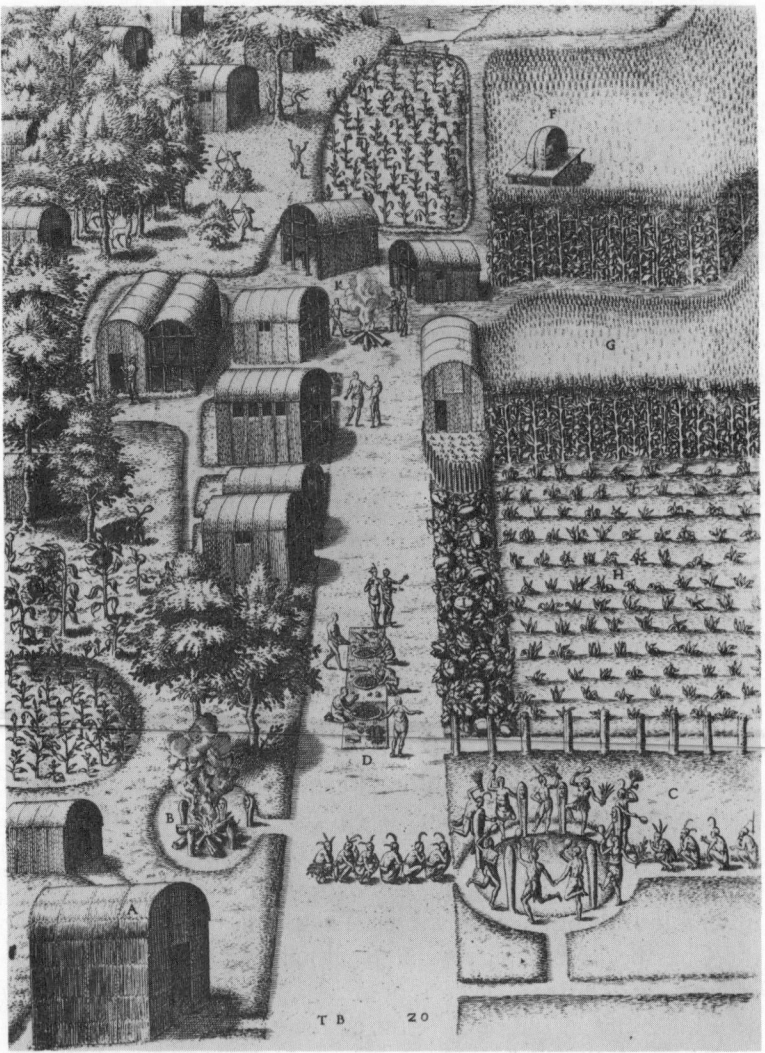

often impeded by a predilection for conquest. Commerce and conquest would remain connected throughout the history of European expansion on this continent, but the former would increasingly shape the latter over time.

As Europeans attempted to secure—in the words of the geographer D. W. Meinig—a "point of attachment," many variables influenced their efforts. There was, of course, the land: its shape, soils, climate, plants, and animals. The site of Jamestown was chosen because of its anchorage, its view downstream, and its potential as a fortress situated on the neck of a peninsula. Unfortunately, it was a low and marshy place with an inadequate water supply. Typhoid fever, dysentery, and malaria plagued the colonists and gave the colony a reputation as a sickly place. Most natives wisely lived upstream and inland.

The historian Timothy Breen has described the European immigrants who first arrived in America as "charter groups." More so than later immigrants, the first colonists had an enormous impact on the "rules of the game": the labor systems, the patterns of behavior and transmission of European customs, the reaction to and treatment of native peoples, even the incorporation of later immigrants. Similarly, the situations that emerged in the first permanent colonies of New France, New England, Virginia, and New Netherland might be described as "charter" frontiers that had a seminal influence on later developments in America. Although every frontier situation was unique, these early colonial frontiers involved the creation of conditions that, to some degree, determined the nature of European expansion westward into the interior of North America. The first frontier settlements served as models for the creation of additional Euro-American settlements. We will focus first on two fundamentally rural frontiers, Virginia and New England.

All European colonists in America entered an occupied land. Estimates of the number of Algonquian-speaking natives living in coastal Virginia in 1607 range from fourteen thousand to twenty thousand. Both in Virginia and in New England, it took roughly forty to fifty years for the European population to approximate the indigenous population. In short, the Europeans built their new homes in the midst of Indian country. The first English adventurers in Virginia hoped that they, like the Spanish, might encounter stratified Indian societies that they could live among and exploit as an imperial elite. Failing that, they might live on plantations like their counterparts in Ireland and reap the rewards of other people's labor. But the natives of Virginia—Tsenacomoco, as they knew it—had no wish to labor for Englishmen, men they perceived to be pale and prone to disease, ugly (too hairy), and needy. (It was logical for the natives to assume that the English had come to their land to acquire maize, trees, and women.) The English, on the other hand, soon recognized that the Indian villages of Virginia lacked gold or spices, indeed lacked any commodity worth stealing. Unlike the Indian groups who lived on the upper Potomac, Susquehanna, and Delaware rivers, these natives did not even have a tradition of preserving or processing valuable beaver pelts.

The Indians of the region were primarily agriculturalists. Men cleared the land around a village by the slash-and-burn method. Women planted the crops, weeded the fields, and gathered nuts and berries. The primary crops were maize, beans, squash, and tobacco. Men went fishing. Seasonal hunting trips were often a communal affair. This economy was fairly common throughout the eastern coast. One historian has described the coastal Algonquians as "sedentary commuters" or "seasonal nomads." In 1607, many of the villages or tribes were part of a state, a chiefdom led by a paramount chief *(mamanatowick)* named Powhatan, or Wahunsonacock. Powhatan's state was surrounded by hostile Siouan and Iroquoian peoples west of the fall line. The newly arrived English represented either a potential ally or another threat. Two years of posturing and bullying on both sides decided the matter: they were a threat. More than three decades of hostilities followed, including three Anglo-Powhatan wars. In the end, Tsenacomoco was devastated. Virginia had replaced it.

A quarter century of conflict drove home many lessons. As early as 1609, the Virginia Company changed its opinion about the Powhatans and wrote, "If you make friendship with any of these [Indian] nations, as you must doe, choose to doe it with those that are farthest from you and enemies unto those amonge whom you dwell, for you shall have least occasion to have differences with them." Few English colonists were ever able to find "common ground" with their Indian neighbors. (Powhatan's daughter, Poca-hontas, did marry a colonist and even visited England, where she died in 1617.) Too many factors stood in the way of peaceful coexistence: conflicting ways of managing the land and its resources; the lack of institutions for regulating cross-cultural conflict; the simple absence of anything that might promote cooperation, such as extensive intermar-riage and mutually profitable trade relations. The English in Virginia had no use for the natives, and so the natives had to go. Even if the Indian communities they encountered had been able to supply valuable commodities, it is doubtful that the English would have been comfortable living as tolerated foreigners under an alien jurisdiction. Their traditions had prepared them to live as conquerors, not as intercultural brokers like the Genoese and Jewish merchants of Asia Minor. The English were only beginning their education in multiculturalism. As soon as the second Anglo-Powhatan war ended, the English constructed a six-mile palisade on the Virginia peninsula passing through Middle Plantation (Williamsburg). This tangible boundary served two purposes: it kept cattle in and Indians out. After a third war broke out in 1644, the English position became quite clear. A treaty of submission signed in 1646 forced the new Indian leader to become a vassal of the English king. The natives agreed to leave the Virginia peninsula from the fall line to the coast. Any Indian found in the area could be shot on sight, unless he was a messenger wearing a special striped coat. The defeated and marginalized "tributary" Indian communities were positioned on the edge of European settlement by colonial authorities to serve as a barrier to the aggressions of larger, independent tribes. It was now the Indians who found themselves strangers in their native land.

Emerging during these war years were several story lines that would be repeated again and again in the drama of European westward expansion. Before the second Anglo-Powhatan war of 1622, native spiritual leaders may have begun to preach purification as a prelude to resistance and rebellion. A spiritual vision—a prophecy of an Indian millennium—may have served to unite communities experiencing conflict not only from without but also from within as European goods, habits, and values upset an established social consensus. The English, for their part, began to realize the distance between the cultural hearth and the fires at home. The Virginia Company's attempts to promote interethnic harmony were not well received by colonists embroiled in total war and race hatred. It would not be the last "east-west" division over Indian policy.

Other problems separated the company back in England and its colonists in Virginia. The company, throughout its brief history, had a vision of orderly, self-sustaining Virginia settlements with company tenants producing valuable commodities on company land until their term of service expired. The reality did not even come close. The only commodity to emerge in the colony was tobacco, the one crop the company discouraged the planters from raising. The first shipment of Virginia tobacco was sent to England in 1617. The market price was an incredibly high three shillings a pound. Tobacco plants were soon being raised on every available plot of land. Far from being self-sufficient, the colonists relied on maize taken from Indian villages during hostilities or purchased from Indian allies. Tobacco exports, on the other hand, rose from sixty thousand pounds in 1619 to a half million pounds in 1628. Although prices fell drastically by 1630, production spiraled upward for the rest of the century.

The historian Edmund Morgan has described the Virginia of the 1620s as a "boom" colony. High prices for tobacco meant fast profits. Land and labor were the necessary ingredients. Although tobacco cultivation did not require an inordinate amount of either, the work was hard, and more hands meant greater profits. Our notions of the independent, hardy pioneer are certainly not sustained by the history of the tobacco colonies. Most men and women were either masters or servants. And few Englishmen came to America prepared for the backbreaking work of converting forests to fields. One observer in Bermuda noted, "[Settlers] do sigh to see how many trees they have to fell, and how their hands are blistered." Not surprisingly, Europeans were quick to seize cleared Indian lands, a fact pointed out by Indians outraged by squatters in their cornfields. Land was abundant and cheap in Virginia. Labor was harder to come by, and a labor market quickly developed—one controlled by an entrepreneurial elite. A coercive labor system was predictable, given the high demand and the long terms of service agreed to by those colonists who could not afford to pay their own way. Masters simply bought and sold men and women for the time remaining on the contracts. Some planters apparently used servants as stakes for gambling.

Life was indeed cheap in Virginia. Some seventy-two hundred settlers came to Virginia between 1607 and 1624. Around twelve hundred were still alive in the latter year. The vast majority died of diseases—usually in "seasoning" time, the dreaded Virginia summer. One colonist estimated that only one out of every six immigrants survived the year. Greed and the uncertainty of survival, combined with the absence in Virginia of English laws and courts designed to protect servants, contributed to a system many laborers found intolerable. By the time Virginia became a royal colony in 1625, it was clear that the vision of the now-defunct Virginia Company had not been realized. Like mid-nineteenth-century California during the gold rush, mid-seventeenth-century Virginia was a transient place. Planter and servant alike crowded passing ships and turned them into floating saloons. Men outnumbered women by three to one. The majority of the colonists were under thirty years old. Demographic and economic factors shaped a place that lacked a sense of permanence or order. Few substantial houses were built. Observers noted that Jamestown was a shabby little village. It was obvious that those who survived hoped to prosper and return to England.

Conditions in Virginia gradually improved. The European demand for tobacco continued to rise, and despite lower prices—tobacco was being grown in Europe in substantial quantities by the 1650s—the annual income of the colony rose from less than ten thousand pounds sterling in 1630 to over seventy thousand by 1670. Immigration increased after the 1630s. The vast majority of new arrivals were still servants, but families with resources responded to perceived opportunities in the colony. By 1660, Virginia and Maryland combined had over thirty-five thousand colonists. By the end of the century, the southern colonies—now including the Carolinas—were home to over one hundred thousand settlers.

Although Virginia was no longer a "boom" colony by the 1660s, Governor William Berkeley reported that the elite of Virginia were still "looking back on England" in hopes of retiring there on the profits made from tobacco. Virginia had become a somewhat sleepy, provincial place on the periphery of the English metropolis. Indeed, after the 1660s, many competitors of the Chesapeake region stopped producing tobacco, in part because of the superior product grown in Virginia and because soil exhaustion threatened a limited supply of land. Planters on islands such as Barbados, Jamaica, Martinique, and Guadeloupe switched from tobacco to crops such as sugar or indigo, which required greater investments in labor and equipment but were far more valuable. Tobacco planters were the poor relations among the producers of cash crops.

Virginia planters, on the other hand, began to diversify. Some planters became farmers and abandoned tobacco for wheat. Most stayed with the leaf but combined that crop with grain production, livestock, and orchards. Unlike planters in the West Indies, those in Virginia could not afford the luxury of becoming absentee proprietors. On the contrary, the ideal in Virginia became the independent gentleman living in an autonomous, self-enclosed world. When African slaves replaced white servants toward the end of the seventeenth century, the picture was complete. A successful plantation appeared to be a world easily controlled. "Economic privatism" had been from the beginning, in the words of Breen, the "colony's central value," and the landscape reflected this. "An extreme form of individualism, a value system suited to soldiers and adventurers," had been transformed into "a set of regional virtues, a love of independence, an insistence upon personal liberty, a cult of manhood, and an uncompromising loyalty to family." Indeed, in a landscape that valued distance from one's neighbors and enjoyed only sporadic contact with the wider world, who else could be trusted? Historians have also suggested that persistently high mortality rates led parents to encourage independence in their offspring. As the Virginia countryside achieved a settled, English appearance, the illusion of English country life tended to obscure the colony's ultimate dependence on global markets. Planters in the eighteenth century, dependent on Scottish factors in Virginia and commission agents back in Great Britain, forgot—to their peril—that connections based on debt and credit could not be expressed simply in personal terms. When the fluctuations of world trade rudely reminded Virginians in the 1760s that they lived on the edge of the metropolis, Thomas Jefferson captured the bitterness of the moment. Virginians, after all, were "a species of property annexed to certain mercantile houses in London."

New England, with Reservations

An eminent historian of colonial America recently wrote, "It would be difficult to imagine how any two fragments [the Chesapeake colonies and New England] from the same metropolitan culture could have been any more different." There are many reasons for this difference, including the native worlds encountered, the economic and environmental conditions, the process of migration, and the regional origins of the immigrants. The earliest English efforts in New England were of little consequence. A small group of dissenting Separatists attempted to settle the Magdalen Islands in the Gulf of St. Lawrence. In the words of the English historian K. R. Andrews, they "dissented from each other and everyone else." The project came to naught. After several expeditions and the failed colony at Sagadahoc, the *Mayflower*, carrying 101 passengers, landed at Plymouth Rock in 1620. The situation they encountered in this region was quite different from that faced by the first Virginia immigrants.

Southern New England—defined roughly as encompassing the present-day states of Connecticut, Massachusetts, and Rhode Island—had a native population before 1616 of between 70,000 and 140,000 people. The people in this region spoke a variety of dialects and languages belonging to the Eastern Algonquian group. The languages were similar, and it is said that neighbors speaking different languages were able to comprehend each other. Tribes—if we may call them that—consisted of allied villages with kinship ties and a system of episodic political, economic, and military relations. Sachems and sagamores exercised leadership based on consensus. Europeans, used to less egalitarian arrangements, tended to magnify the importance of native leaders. Three "nations" inhabited the coast from southern Maine to Cape Cod, from north to south: the Pawtuckets, the Massachusetts, and the Pokanokets or Wampanoags. The Narragansetts lived in Rhode Island, and the Pequot-Mohegan people occupied eastern Connecticut. A variety of smaller groups lived in central Connecticut and Massachusetts. (In fact, various Native-American communities are still in the region today, some of them as federally recognized tribes.)

Two important events occurred in the years immediately preceding the founding of Plymouth. First, French traders along the Massachusetts coast and Dutch traders along the Long Island Sound and up the Hudson and Connecticut rivers initiated a commerce in furs that undoubtedly resonated with existing native exchange networks. The fur trade had begun and, with it, the competition among European nations for spheres of influence in the region. Establishing jurisdiction in this area would not be a simple matter of Indian versus European. A complex series of alliances and struggles encompassing various Indian and European groups would ultimately establish the boundaries we know today.

The second event, probably related to the first, was a virgin-soil epidemic (possibly chicken pox or smallpox) that killed from 75 percent to 90 percent of the people in the coastal villages of the Pawtuckets, Massachusetts, and Wampanoags from 1616 to 1619. The tragedy that devastated the coast had many implications. Tribes that were not hit, such as the Narragansetts and the Pequots, assumed a new-found dominance in the region. Survivors from decimated villages formed new composite villages. Spiritual confidence was undermined. Traditional political and social relationships were disrupted, and even the wisdom and technical knowledge of the people—held in common and transmitted orally by elders—was, to some degree, dissipated by the enormous loss of life. Into this situation sailed the Pilgrims in November 1620, looking for the site of Patuxet (Plymouth), an Indian village they knew to be depopulated.

Although half the colonists died that first winter, the colony survived, thanks in large measure to Squanto—a native of Patuxet who had been kidnapped and brought to England during the time of the great epidemic and had returned before the *Mayflower* arrived. According to William Bradford, governor of the colony, Squanto "directed them how to set their corne, wher to take fish, and to procure other comodities, and was also their pilott to bring them to unknowne places for their profitt, and never left them till he dyed." For the Pilgrims, Squanto was a godsend. For Squanto, the Pilgrims were probably a source of power in a world turned upside down. The local Pokanokets and their sachem, Massasoit, also welcomed an alliance with the English as a bulwark against their traditional enemies, the Narragansetts.

After several seasons, the Pilgrims were producing a surplus of corn, or maize. (Some settlers had already switched to the cultivation of English grains.) The surplus was exchanged for furs from Abenaki villages farther north along the coast. This profitable relationship was overshadowed by the fur trade of the Dutch, who had discovered the value of wampum or wampumpeag—called *sewan* by the Dutch—in 1622 and had established a monopoly with those tribes who controlled its production. Fathoms of wampum were produced from the white and the purple shells of whelks and quahogs by Indians living on the shorelines of the Long Island Sound. The demand for this commodity altered relationships between tribes and facilitated the commerce in furs with inland tribes. In fact, wampum was used as currency by Europeans in New England and New York, and the number of beads in a fathom fluctuated with exchange rates in Europe. (Wampum remained legal tender in specie-starved New England until 1661 and was used as change in the more remote areas of the region into the eighteenth century.) Wampum producers, agriculturalists, and hunters were thus linked with Europe in a market economy. The Dutch and the Pilgrims worked out an arrangement that designated respective trading zones, and throughout the 1620s the colonists at Plymouth discouraged, even threatened, other Englishmen who attempted to settle around Massachusetts Bay. In so doing, they unwittingly prepared the way for a powerful new enterprise forming in England.

In 1629 the Massachusetts Bay Company, with the support of patrons such as Robert Rich (the second earl of Warwick), William Fiennes (Lord Saye and Sele), and Nathaniel Rich, received a royal charter. Although originally designed as a typical joint-stock company, the venture was quickly transformed by influential Puritans such as John Winthrop, a lawyer from Suffolk and first governor of the colony, who divided the commercial and governmental aspects of the company between trustees and colonists. A unique settlement was about to begin.

English Massachusetts was populated quickly and carefully. Over twenty thousand people arrived during the "great migration" from 1630 to 1642. In a generation, the English population doubled, so that by 1660, New England contained approximately twice as many Europeans as the Chesapeake region. And by 1660, most New Englanders were native-born; an Anglo-American colony had developed. After a rather short "starving" time, the English in Massachusetts had become self-sustaining. Birthrates were high and infant mortality was low. The first generation of colonists lived on average to the age of seventy—quite a contrast to life expectancy in Virginia. Although immigration to New England diminished significantly after 1642, in 1700 the descendants of these first New England settlers constituted 40 percent of the colonial population of North America.

Simple population figures do not tell the whole story. This Puritan migration was a family affair, a chain migration of neighbors and relatives. Over 70 percent of the first colonists of Massachusetts came as part of a family group, and the ratio of men to women was a remarkably low 1.5 to 1. The "great migration" was also a middle-class movement, the majority being farmers, artisans, and merchants with some resources at their disposal—almost 75 percent of the adults coming over paid their way. Literacy among the adult males of Massachusetts was twice as high as in old England. Harvard College was founded in 1636, and laws requiring towns to establish schools were passed in the 1640s.

What does all this mean? In part, it means that the transfer of English culture to New England was unusually successful. (This transfer, of course, was influenced by the Puritans' social and religious ideology.) Social relations were not disrupted by the move. Patterns of deference to traditional secular and clerical leaders were brought to the New World; indeed, many leaders themselves made the trip to New England. The environment initially offered no serious challenge to the transfer of English grains such as wheat, oats, rye, and barley. More important, perhaps, the environment was not hospitable to the production of "boom" crops such as sugar. English farms, not tobacco plantations, were carved out of New England soil. Land systems in individual New England townships mirrored the local customs of the English birthplaces of the colonists. Many settlers came from East Anglia (Suffolk, Norfolk, Essex, and Hertfordshire), a region of small towns, enclosed farmsteads, and an active market in land. The historian David Grayson Allen has shown that people in Massachusetts towns such as Ipswich and Watertown simply and effectively reestablished the patterns of their former regions. Origins were of great importance throughout the colonization of North America. Local allegiances and habits were more deeply felt than national ones. The merchants of Creole St. Louis, for example, came primarily from the French provinces of Aunis and Saintonge, and their patterns of family formation and distribution of wealth reflect their place of origin.

Luckily for the Puritans, the land they first settled on lacked powerful native communities. By 1633 some three thousand English settlers had gathered in communities around Massachusetts Bay. By contrast, there were only several hundred natives, and local Indian leaders almost immediately acknowledged the protection offered by the newcomers. (There were, of course, many natives living elsewhere in the region. Thirty thousand resided around Narragansett Bay.) The leaders of the colony, with a natural ethnocentric bias reinforced by a somewhat arrogant sense of mission, quickly extended their jurisdiction over the natives. The policies adopted by Massachusetts were to have a powerful impact on cross-cultural relations in North America. The leaders of the colony attempted both to assimilate and to segregate the small native communities nearby; that is, Massachusetts established reservations.

At first the magistrates were content to restrict the comings and goings of Indian neighbors. In the 1640s a committee led by the Roxbury minister John Eliot formulated a plan for "praying towns," settlements of native converts. Natick was the first, established in 1651, with thirteen others following in the next quarter century. The goal was to bring the good news of Christianity to Native Americans, and that goal was best achieved by weaning native people from their traditional habits. After all, old actions supported old ways of thinking. Besides, many Indian habits were offensive to English sensibilities. To "reduce them to civility," Eliot supervised the Natick Indians in the construction of English-style houses. Commuting to the woods could not be reconciled with the fixed habits of churchgoers. In addition, English leaders wanted to know where the Indians were at all times, both to allay fears of attack and to have it, in the words of one colonial English soldier, "more in our power to Distress them [the Indians]." (Wigwams were retained by many Indians, however, since they were warmer in the winter and cooler in the summer.) Numerous Indian offenses were listed, among them long hair, naked breasts, and gambling. The dangers of multiculturalism were suggested in a Connecticut law of 1672, which prohibited any English person from "playing with any Indian" or laying "any wager with, or for, any Indian." Clearly, Englishmen must have been doing exactly that.

Puritan leaders were quite anxious about the possibility of Englishmen "going native." Great care was taken to maintain adequate cultural distance. Early immigrants built English-style wigwams covered with Indian mats as temporary shelters—clearing fields and planting crops being the top priority. This practice was soon prohibited. Tobacco was also banished from the colony, and lobsters and clams—staples of the Indian diet—were not looked on with great favor by the English, at least not at first. The colonists retained their own ways, preferring "pease porridge"—which developed into the well-known New England baked beans—and brown bread. Indeed, the brown bread of the Puritans might serve as a symbol of cultural interaction on this frontier. Made from a mixture of wheat flour and Indian cornmeal—when a wheat rust forced a greater reliance on rye flour, the mix was known as "rye 'n' injun"—the bread was English in conception and function but borrowed from Indian culture.

In the end, the local native communities of Massachusetts were situated in small enclaves surrounded by English people, grasses, and animals. Indeed, all Native American groups in southern New England suffered the same fate after two devastating wars in the seventeenth century—what the Puritans called the Pequot War of 1637–38 and the even bloodier King Philip's War in 1675–76. Tribal communities, already weakened by death and disease, were further undermined by religious cleavages. Native leaders who served as intermediaries in land transactions and the execution of English justice lost face with their fellow villagers. By the eighteenth century, tribesmen were looking around for support in their struggles against hereditary sachems, some of whom had been corrupted by English speculators or had simply become alcoholics. One Narragansett leader, King Tom Ninigret, was educated in England and spent sixty thousand pounds on a palace designed by an English architect and built in Rhode Island. His debts mortgaged the tribal estate and provoked a declaration of independence by his tribesmen—a decade before the Narragansetts' English neighbors declared their independence from King George. The signs of cultural breakdown were all around by the eighteenth century: migration, alcoholism, pauperization. Yet, many New England natives remained, adapted, and survived. They built fences, sold wood, made baskets, worked as domestic servants, even doctored English neighbors with herbal medicines. Native and European spiritual values were combined by "new light" Indian preachers who responded to the Great Awakening of the 1740s and the new emphasis on the spoken word. On a more limited scale, they continued to use a variety of habitats to produce and gather food. But the land had changed. Hogs had ruined clam banks. Wild turkeys were disappearing. Deer hunting was first regulated in Massachusetts in 1694 (Virginia in 1699). Overhunting, competition from domestic livestock, and the

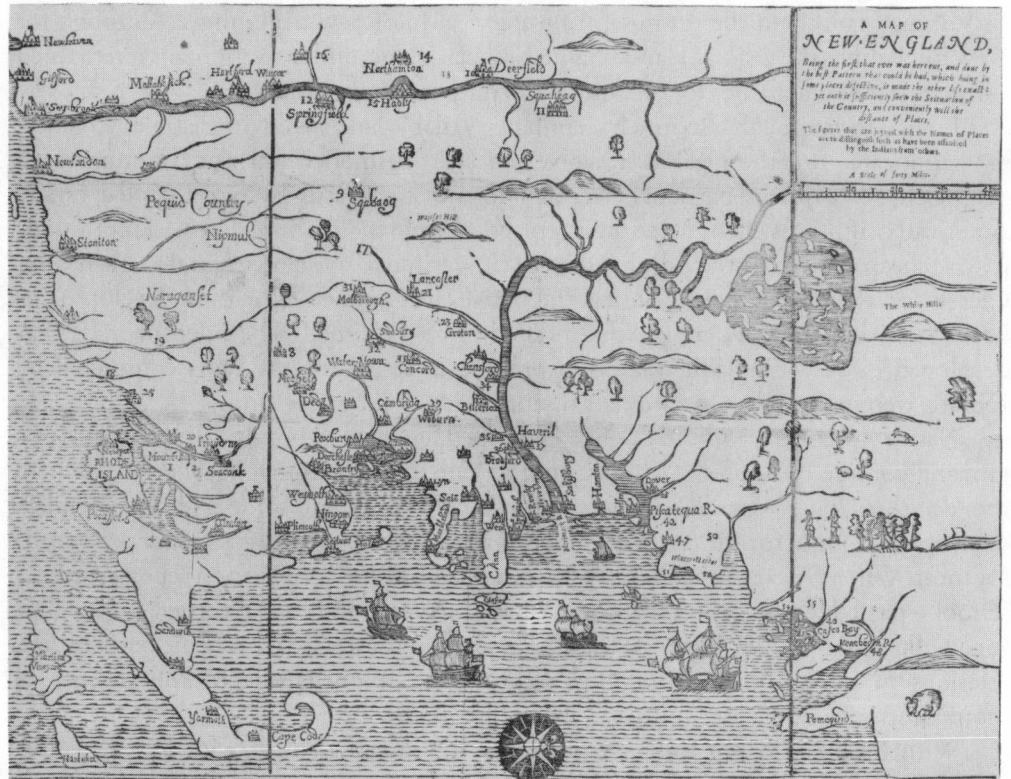

This map, widely recognized as the first printed in the present United States, appeared in a narrative of New England Indian wars written by William Hubbard and published in Boston in 1677. With the direction of west appearing at the top and Cape Cod at the lower left, the map effectively illustrates how English settlers quickly took control of strategic riverfront and harbor sites, pushing Indian communities inland.

John Foster (1648–81). A Map of New England. Woodcut, 1677. Courtesy of the John Carter Brown Library at Brown University, Providence, Rhode Island.

disappearance of areas of open forests with attractive grasses for deer and other herbivores—grasses created by careful Indian burning—caused the decline in animal populations.

In the first sixty years of the seventeenth century, around a quarter of a million people left Britain. Perhaps seventy-five thousand of them moved to North America; most of the rest went to Ireland and the Caribbean. Seen in this larger context, North America was hardly a strong magnet for immigrants. Nevertheless, settlements had been secured; indeed, the English in North America were no longer fish out of water. They had moved beyond their first palisades and were running all over the countryside. In many ways, by the 1670s the links with old England were becoming weaker on the farms and plantations of Virginia and Massachusetts. In New England, writers were already glorifying the achievements of the first Puritan immigrants. New England was a new homeland, one with a history. Boston merchants were developing their own carrying trade, and the colony schools were producing a homegrown elite. Observers were less certain about the achievements of Virginia. Critics, from Captain John Smith to Thomas Jefferson, were not proud of Virginia's past and preferred instead to dwell on Virginia's future. The rather thin social and political life of seventeenth-century Virginia had an improvised flavor.

The two colonies had similarities. Both had fewer institutions, fewer social classifications, and fewer rules than old England. But America had land, and land assumed a central, defining power in both regions. In New England, land was essential because it conferred the ability to define community without interference from ungodly quarters.

In Virginia, land held the promise of future wealth, of new beginnings. Although for New Englanders the vision of land retained a social frame, and for Virginians it remained essentially individualistic, for all colonists land promised mastery.

It is fair to assume that so much seemingly available land was an irresistible attraction for Europeans. But the ideal as it evolved in North America was not common to all people; the British, in particular, seemed to measure status by one's landed estate. American conditions encouraged an imported cultural inclination. The basic commodity was cheap enough. It was only a matter of converting native land to rural English land. Clearly, on these settlement frontiers the natives were mere obstacles to development, part of the "howling wilderness" that needed to be reclaimed. The brief fur trade that developed in New England was but a prelude to settlement as debts contracted by Indians were eventually—as animals disappeared—paid off in land.

Native Americans and the English developed few, if any, bonds. Intermarriage was rare and commerce limited. (This was not as true in the Carolina backcountry, where the deerskin trade assumed major importance.) Although some New Englanders developed a conqueror's interest in Indian survival, race hatred was probably the norm for most. When Eleazar Wheelock—a Yale-trained missionary and founder of an Indian school—passed his collection plate at a church in Windsor, it was returned empty "but for a bullet and flint." As James Axtell, one of the foremost scholars of European-Indian relations in the colonial period, has written, the colonists viewed the Indians as "sometime adversaries and full-time contraries."

With no links to the Indians and rather infrequent contact with Europe, most colonists settled down to a simple rural life. Seen from a European perspective, these colonies were sleepy provinces—in historians' terms, the periphery. For colonists born in America, their towns and farms were the center of the universe. Those with the money to do so tried their best to be fashionable in a European manner. Some traveled to old England and were reluctant to return to America. Increase Mather, the famous Puritan minister, was one who longed for London life. He envied his son Samuel, who had moved to the metropolis where he could "furnish himself with variety of books." For those with a cosmopolitan inclination, the problem with English America in the seventeenth century was not only its distance from Europe but also its lack of urban amenities and social distinctions. Ann Eaton, wife of the governor of New Haven, was anxious to return to England. Lady Deborah Moody, a friend of the Winthrops and a proper Puritan, left Massachusetts in part for religious reasons but also because she found the social atmosphere stifling. She chose to move to New Netherland.

Handelstijd: Dutch New Netherland

The golden age of the Dutch Republic coincided with the first wave of colonizing efforts that swept over North America in the seventeenth century. Viewing the commercial opportunities of the entire world, many Dutch merchants concluded that North America had limited possibilities; nevertheless, a few—such as Arnout Vogels and Lambert van Tweenhuysen—sent ships to the region referred to by 1614 as New Netherland. When Dutch sea captains and traders explored the Noordt Rivier (Hudson River), they looked over the country with Dutch eyes. They searched for places to trade and people to trade with, for routes into the interior and ways to connect. As the historian

Donna Merwick has reminded us, the Dutch were true townsmen who valued communication and "purposeful movement." In Holland, the countryside was dependent on the city; the city was a world in motion encompassing the activities that brought virtue and prosperity. Heroes and leaders came from a *burgerlijk* society and represented its values. They were not landed aristocrats. Jeremias van Rensselaer, sensing the need to know more about the English, who might take over New Netherland, wrote home and asked for a map of England. Dissatisfied with the first one he received, he wrote, "Send me another map . . . but the country must be set off better by cities, for . . . the other map was no good, there were no cities shown on it."

The Dutch came to North America to possess the commerce of the country. Occupying the land was, at best, a secondary consideration. The value of agricultural land had to be compared with the value of other commodities. A good yacht, a consignment of beaver pelts, or a prime location in Manhattan might be worth considerably more. New Netherland did not remain Dutch for long: only until 1664 with a brief Dutch interlude in 1673–74. Nevertheless, Dutch culture in New York had considerable staying power. The Dutch created what would become the dominant city in North America and modeled and named it after Amsterdam. Even distant Beverwijck (Albany), named for the commodity that justified its existence, had its *stadhuis* (town hall) and prominent *handelaars* (merchants). Connections mattered most to the inhabitants of a frontier trading post. Traders literally knew their world. Many Beverwijck burghers had property in New Amsterdam and business associates in old Amsterdam. Distances were deceiving: rivers were meant to be navigated, and people, their letters, and business accounts traveled back and forth. The pioneers of New Netherland, in short, were pioneer agents of trade poised to create markets in the wilderness.

This was, perhaps, a more exciting prospect than the conversion of Indian acres into European farms. How far and in which directions might a trading area extend? Which lines of trade would prove profitable? Which goods would satisfy native customers, and what might these customers produce that would sell in Amsterdam? Indeed, native North America had cultivated acres and boundaries before Europeans, but there were no stores, no merchants. Here was an opportunity: a power to shape, in a sense, virgin territory. Rural colonies, of course, had their entrepôt cities; tidewater Virginia was exceptional. Hartford, New Haven, Boston—these pioneer market towns gathered—in the words of the geographer James E. Vance, Jr.—the "periodic threads of trade" from their hinterlands into a ball of sufficient magnitude to allow for transatlantic exchange. In New Netherland and New France, where the fur trade greased the flow of transatlantic commerce, frontier entrepôts such as Detroit, Michilimackinac, St. Louis, and Beverwijck sprang up in Indian country. Moreover, these places and the larger cities they were connected to—Nouvelle Orleans, Montreal, and Nieuw Amsterdam—dominated the life of the colonies in which they were situated. Historians who have studied these places have been surprised to find merchants on the edge of the "wilderness" in regular contact with European correspondents, enjoying an unexpected array of urban amenities. If life on this frontier was fundamentally urban, even from the beginning, what difference did this make?

It made a difference in cross-cultural relations. Trading posts required profitable links with host communities. The Mahicans gave the Dutch permission to establish Fort

Nassau on the Hudson in 1614, opposite a Mahican village. There the chief trader became fluent in Mahican—an Algonquian language—and enjoyed good relations with his customers. When the Dutch abandoned Fort Nassau and established Fort Orange near present-day Albany in 1624, the Mahicans moved their village nearby on the opposite shore. Generally speaking, the Dutch got along with their Indian trading partners. (They were less diplomatic with natives who could not supply furs.) Unlike French traders, most Dutch traders did not make a regular practice of visiting, residing in, or marrying into Indian villages. They did, however, eagerly desire the natives to come to Fort Orange or Beverwijck. During the trading season—*handelstijd*—from 1 May to 1 November, hundreds of Indian people arrived. Sheds and temporary houses were erected outside the palisades of the town. Some Indian families even stayed at burghers' homes.

Trade required communication. The Unami- and Munsee-speaking Delaware people who traded with the Dutch on the South (Delaware) River and around New Amsterdam developed a trade jargon. The Munsee-speakers also borrowed Dutch words for *appel, knoop* (button), *komkommer* (cucumber), *melk, pannekoek* (pancake), *suiker* (sugar), and many other items. The Jersey Dutch, in turn, used the words *spanspak* and *tahaeim* (Munsee for cantaloupe and strawberries). These examples give us some idea of the nature of the cultural exchange occurring. (The Delawares also borrowed a Dutch slang word for penis, which suggests another kind of exchange.) Although the two peoples lived apart and maintained some distance, physical and social, between one another, good business demanded a certain degree of mutuality. The Indians themselves probably put it best in the following complaint, made several decades after the English takeover of the colony: "When the Dutch held this country long ago, we lay in their Houses; but the English have always made us lie without Doors."

It should be understood that good relations were helped immeasurably by the simple fact that trading posts and incipient cities held small numbers of Europeans and kept them in an enclosed space away from native lands. Indeed, many shareholders in the Dutch West India Company (the Westindische Compagnie, or WIC), the national joint-stock company responsible for administering the colony, wished to keep the trading-post regime as uncomplicated as possible. Unfortunately for the advocates of a pure trading-post regime, the French and the English protested against the presence of Dutch traders in the region. Therefore, in 1624, the WIC settled thirty Walloon (French-speaking) families at four locations on the Delaware and Connecticut rivers, at newly built Fort Orange and on Governor's Island in New York harbor. In short, the new colonists were sent to stake out Dutch claims in North America and thus to substantiate the limits of the proposed colony.

Settlement increased slowly at first, but friction between Indians and the Dutch grew with a series of incidents at Staten Island and Pavonia in 1640 and 1641. When Director General Willem Kieft led a massacre of over eighty Indians outside Communipauw in Pavonia in 1643, a full-scale war ensued. Kieft's policy was not supported by all the colonists: influential men such as the trader David de Vries, who negotiated a temporary peace in 1643, and Dominie Everardus Bogardus, New Amsterdam's Dutch Reformed minister, were vocal in their opposition. Officials back in the United Provinces were also displeased with Kieft and—after a combined Dutch-English force destroyed Indian villages at Hempstead, Fort Neck (Massapequa), and Pound Ridge—replaced him with Peter Stuyvesant in 1647. Stuyvesant was generally more conciliatory, but conflicts occurred again in 1655—the so-called Peach War—and in 1659 and 1663. Many of these struggles hinged on incidents typical of agricultural resource competition: the stealing of a peach or the appropriation of an Esopus Indian field. Indian villagers eventually responded by moving away and establishing refugee camps with neighbors farther inland.

The fur trade also played a role in these conflicts. Kieft had attempted to extort wampum from Indian coastal villages in 1639, but the Mahicans were more successful in extracting tribute from their Indian neighbors. The Wiechquaeskecks massacred by Kieft in 1643 were, in fact, seeking refuge from Mahican attacks. The Mahicans dominated the coastal villages and the supply of wampum and joined the attack on the Indians of western Long Island in 1655. The Mohawks, reacting to a depletion of animals in their own territory and encouraged by the Dutch, attacked northern tribes allied with the French in the 1640s and 1650s in an effort to control the flow of furs. (They also sought captives to be adopted into Iroquois villages to replace members lost through violence and disease.) From 1662 to 1675, the Mohawks, the Mahicans, and their respective Indian allies fought a series of battles for supremacy in the region. The competition between these regional rivals spread to distant areas as the search for furs and allies reached the lands of the Cherokees and the Creeks to the south and the Miamis and the Ottawas in the Great Lakes region. In short, a complex set of conditions involving trade, refugee movements, and Indian and European diplomatic and military attempts to control native decisions over a wide area had evolved by the late seventeenth century. If game depletion, alcoholism, the breakdown of traditional Indian society, and the continuing arrival of European settlers ultimately stacked the deck against many Native American communities and resulted in dependency and enclavement, it still must be said that the story was played out in large measure through Indian agency.

What can be concluded, then, about Dutch-Indian relations? Despite a great degree of cross-cultural contact and exchange, Dutch occupancy of the land resulted in the destruction or removal of Indian villages. Away from the areas of Dutch farms, Indian people retained a measure of autonomy and were necessary to Dutch interests. Many voices in the colony spoke in favor of good relations. At least after Kieft's administration, negotiations were generally favored over confrontations. Efforts to convert the natives were minimal. Measures aimed at preserving the peace were enacted. A law of 1640 ordered colonists to keep their livestock from straying into unfenced Indian fields. The best that can be said is that the Dutch had Indian allies and, therefore, endeavored to live with them.

It was clear to the Dutch by the 1640s that the trade diaspora models in Asia Minor and the Far East were not applicable to North America. A small foreign merchant community living within a host city was not possible: there were no native cities, and food surpluses were hard to extract from native villages. Therefore, the Dutch created new cities. Beverwijck came into existence in almost classic Old World fashion. The patroon of Rensselaerwyck, who owned the land around Fort Orange, had been granting trading privileges and lots to artisans who wished to live near the fort in hopes of grabbing a piece of the fur trade. Director General Stuyvesant, determined to protect the WIC's

Framed by two Indians exchanging furs, New Amsterdam appears in this Dutch print as an urban community dependent on commerce with the hinterlands, its prosperity intertwined with that of the Native Americans.

Engraved by Aldert Meijer. Nieu Amsterdam at. New York. *Colored engraving; date depicted, 1673; date issued, ca. 1700. I. N. Phelps Stokes Collection, Miriam and Ira D. Wallach Division of Art, Prints and Photographs, The New York Public Library, Astor, Lenox and Tilden Foundations, New York, New York.*

prerogatives, restated its claims to all land within a nineteen-hundred-foot radius of the fort in 1652 and declared Beverwijck to be a chartered town (*dorp*). The following year, New Amsterdam was finally granted municipal status. A city government was immediately installed, consisting of two burgomasters, a *schout* (sheriff), and five *schepens* (aldermen). The *vroedschap* (municipal council) exercised the city's privileges, which included collecting an excise tax on beer and wine and regulating bakeries, slaughterhouses, ferries, and other important urban institutions. The city also confirmed property titles within its jurisdiction. (Even Stuyvesant had to go to the city magistrates to perfect a title to land that he had granted to himself in the name of the WIC.) In all they did, the magistrates of Beverwijck and New Amsterdam followed the customs and practices of old Amsterdam back in the fatherland, or *patria*, as they called it.

The cities of New Netherland also came to resemble their counterparts in the *patria* visually and physically. Space was limited at first, and prime commercial property was at a premium. Even the initial house lots were small. In Beverwijck, they ranged from one-half to one-twentieth of an acre. Garden lots were smaller. By comparison, lots in New England market towns were rarely smaller than one acre. And in New Netherland, lots were quickly subdivided. Narrow frontage and close neighbors quickly became the norm. Merwick has calculated that house density in Beverwijck was remarkably similar to that of small towns in the Netherlands—an average of five houses to the acre—almost from the beginning, and "deeds frequently carried clauses covering damage resulting from a neighbor's downspout." Joint ownership of city property was not uncommon, and renting was a feature of New Amsterdam life early in its history. Dwellings made of wood were gradually replaced by ones made of brick and stone with stepped gables facing the street. Rather late into the colonial period, New York City still had a Dutch appearance, with tall buildings made of special red-and-yellow brick covered with red-and-black tile. One feature marked Beverwijck as different from the Dutch Old World and the English New World: an area to the west of town remained forested so that traders might "walk in the woods" with Indian customers.

Pioneer Dutch urbanites bought property outside of town; but when they did, it was often dispersed fragments of real estate—an investment, not a source of status. Status and power, on the contrary, derived from city rights—*burgerrecht*. Even in the English period, New Yorkers paid a fee for the *burgerrecht*, which brought the privilege of doing business. (In 1675, a shopkeeper paid six beavers, and an artisan paid two.) Business was the lifeblood of New Netherland's towns. Interdependency, not self-sufficiency, was the rule. Everyone specialized in at least one trade, and many inhabitants had more than one source of income. In Beverwijck, a tailor was also a half-owner of a bakery. A cordwainer also served as a notary. Capital was meant to be invested, and investments were spread around in any number of ventures. The Dutch practice of partible inheritance reflected a commitment to a dynamic economy that put resources into as many hands as possible. The hands included those of women, since Dutch sons and daughters received equal shares from the estates of their fathers and mothers. Spouses combined their property in a community of goods, which was divided in half at the death of either one. The custom of *boedelhouderschap* continued the community of goods after the death of a spouse and protected the widow's right to manage the estate. Not surprisingly, many women in New Netherland were experienced in business affairs. Many inns were kept by women, and many other women were merchants. Women also engaged in the fur trade, and one was thought to be the best interpreter in the colony.

New Netherland's commerce increased along with its population in the 1650s. With the collapse of the WIC's colony in Brazil in 1654, the passage of the first English Navigation Act in 1651—which was aimed at reducing the Dutch share of the carrying trade—and the Anglo-Dutch war of 1652–54, Dutch merchants and officials took a new and rather anxious interest in New Netherland. Propaganda and incentives produced the desired effect: a substantial migration of young families to the colony. Although the estimates are rough, the colony's population may have grown from twenty-five hundred in 1645 to around nine thousand in 1664. The population, never homogeneous, grew increasingly heterogeneous. People of Dutch ethnicity constituted less than half of the colony's population in 1664, with nearly 20 percent of the total being German, another 15 percent English, and substantial Scandinavian, French, Belgian, and African minorities. (The African minority, both free and slave, was itself ethnically diverse and came to represent a sizable segment of the population later in the colonial period.) As early as 1643, an observer in New Amsterdam noted eighteen different languages being spoken. Except for the Indians and the Africans, the colony's ethnic diversity was reminiscent of old Amsterdam. Indeed, when a group of Jewish refugees from New Holland in Brazil arrived in New Amsterdam in 1654, Stuyvesant—a confirmed anti-Semite—and the orthodox *predikanten* (ordained preachers) of the colony protested. The directors of the WIC told Stuyvesant to mind his own business and hold his tongue lest he offend the Jewish shareholders in the company. They repeated that advice some years later when Stuyvesant was involved in persecuting Quakers.

Living in or near a frontier city was different from being situated on and defined by the land. Living in New Netherland meant being connected to Europe by the Atlantic, not separated by it. Even the Dutch farmers of Brooklyn and Jersey came to the city often. On Tuesday and Saturday, the market days, the country people came to town, reenacting the customs of the Netherlands. As in the *patria*, waterways connected the countryside and the city. Traveling and communicating were crucial because the city held the keys to this culture, and in Merwick's words, the "*lantsman* who simply farmed . . . remained a person without status." But in this New World, partaking of the city meant something more, especially in New Amsterdam/New York where diversity meant that no one cultural tradition could be taken for granted. For those who lived farther away, traveling to Brooklyn or Manhattan meant renewing one's sense of identity—tasting the food of home, visiting the old church. The city was a reference point, a crucible of ethnicity. Braudel has remarked that cities served as "social amplifiers of markets." In the New World, they also amplified cultural traditions, providing the critical demographic mass necessary to reproduce social identities and form consumer communities for the products of the home country. For a colonial people who valued their sense of being connected, the city was a truly central place.

The Dutch wanted to see each other; they likened themselves to bees in a hive. English visitors always remarked on the crowded feel of places like New Amsterdam or French Detroit. The existence of "free" land clearly cannot explain everything about our American history. How the resources of the country were exploited—indeed, which resources were exploited—explains a great deal, but the cultural values Europeans cherished led them to live on the land in ways that must have seemed marvelously inappropriate to their Indian neighbors.

The irony of New Netherland seems to be that its colonists desired direct connections to both Indian country and Europe. Perhaps the irony derives from hindsight influenced by the Anglo-American perspective. In the rural settlements of the English colonies, Indians came to be regarded as alien, inhuman "others." The settlers' fear of declension, the fear that European standards of civility were disappearing among themselves, reinforced fears about the natives. In New Netherland, communication with Europe and with Indian communities assuaged anxiety over the savage within and without. In New England, captivity narratives described horrible scenes of frontier women being abducted by the "savages" and carried into the wilderness. This was the stuff of English nightmares. In New Netherland, women traders visited Indians at their villages and sold them goods for a profit.

Comptoirs: French Traders and Their Partners

The French, like the Dutch, were in North America to trade—although they did not know it at first. When Jacques Cartier crossed the Atlantic in 1534, his orders from the French crown were to search for gold and other precious metals and for a route to China (a search mockingly memorialized in Montreal, where the embarkation point above Sault-Saint-Louis is known as Lachine). Cartier discovered the Gulf of St. Lawrence, and then a group of Micmac (Mi'kmaq) Indians discovered Cartier and suggested that the

French forget China and trade for furs. The Micmacs showed great patience, waiting out several attempts by the French to frighten them off with weapons. The Micmacs returned the following day and persuaded the French to take their skins in exchange for knives, "other Iron wares, and a red hat to give unto their Captaine." The fur trade, of course, became a central, organizing factor in the life of the colony. For the remainder of the sixteenth century, seasonal cod-fishing expeditions and fur-trading fairs at Tadoussac, at the mouth of the Saguenay River, grew in importance without the benefit of permanent European establishments. Samuel de Champlain, who emerged as the first leader of New France in the first decade of the seventeenth century, finally established a habitation at Quebec in 1608. He also secured an alliance with the Hurons and through this alliance secured the Hurons' Iroquois enemies. Champlain began a policy of sending young traders to Indian villages to learn native languages and customs. The first such *hivernant*, or "winterer," was Étienne Brulé, who lived with the Hurons. According to the report of one missionary, he was familiar with too many Huron women, so his hosts killed him and ate him. W. J. Eccles—in one of the classic lines of Canadian history—observed, "He was the first Frenchman, but by no means the last, to be completely assimilated by the Indians."

Canada, like New Netherland, remained little more than a fortified warehouse, a *comptoir* in Indian country, for decades. Cardinal Richelieu formed a joint-stock company, the Compagnie des Cent-Associés, in 1627 in an attempt to build up the colony. The company got off to an inauspicious start when its ships, loaded with colonists and provisions, were captured by English privateers in 1628. The following year Champlain surrendered Quebec to an Anglo-Scottish expedition. A treaty restored French claims, and Champlain began to rebuild in 1633. The population of the colony remained low. As late as 1650, New France contained only 675 permanent settlers, one-quarter of the population of New Netherland and far less than the colonial population of New England.

Two factors complicated the task of establishing trading-post empires in North America: competition from rival European claimants and the lack of native cities and merchants. (Native Americans did, however, trade through fairly elaborate networks, traveling well-worn paths to distant communities.) In both New Netherland and New France, colonial officials recognized the need to establish and defend imperial boundaries—usually with the aid of native allies—and to encourage the growth of a European agricultural sector, though rural settlements in these colonies remained of secondary importance to the main business of trade. In the cities, *marchands* and *négociants* (the larger merchants who handled exports and imports) and the smaller *traiteurs* and *voyageurs* (the traders who handled cross-cultural exchange) made their homes. In Canada and Louisiana, as in New Netherland, cities—or villages in the process of becoming entrepôts—held the keys to development, the symbols of status, and the institutions that maintained cultural traditions. And so, the Dutch re-created Amsterdam on the Hudson, and the French left a trail of cities in North America, from Montreal to Detroit, New Orleans to St. Louis, St. Paul to Kansas City.

The fur trade provided the foundation. If the conversion of Indian land into European farms and plantations underwrote colonial development in Anglo-America, the production of furs and skins by Indian men and women and the consequent rise of native purchasing power underwrote the building of French-Canadian and Creole cities. The beaver was the main object of European affections. The soft, barbed underfur of the pelt was used in the manufacture of felt hats. *Castor gras* (greasy beaver)—a fur that had been worn for several seasons—was more valuable than *castor sec* (dry beaver) because the long guard hairs had been worn off. Markets also existed for moose hides and deerskins, worked into leather for a variety of manufactures. Finally, there were the peltries, or *pelleterie* (skins worn as furs), such as marten, raccoon, otter, and black fox.

Indian labor produced the majority of these furs. Men did the hunting and trapping; women processed the furs and hides through a variety of tasks such as scraping, stretching, rubbing, and curing. For many of the tribal peoples involved, such techniques were part of their cultural repertoire. Some groups had to learn: the Miamis, when the French first encountered them, were in the habit of roasting beavers—burning off the fur—and eating the animals. Women of the Crow tribe of Montana, on the other hand, were esteemed for their processing skills. Indian producers became Indian consumers. Axtell has described the infiltration of European goods into native societies in the seventeenth and eighteenth centuries as the "first consumer revolution." Indeed, metal tools soon became essential items. Iron axes, awls, chisels, knives, fishhooks, and kettles were more durable than their native equivalents and reduced the amount of labor required for many daily tasks. Red-and-blue woolen duffels and strouds, calico shirts, brandy and rum—these items were always in demand. Native Americans could be shrewd bargainers, playing off competing traders and demanding "good measure" and the extension of credit. They also had an eye for quality and fashion. Small paper packets of vermilion—used for body and face paint—came from distant China. Fashion-conscious Indian men counted European mirrors among their prized possessions. Glass beads desired during one trading season could easily be passé during the next.

Baron de Lahontan observed in 1690, "The trade in goods usually brings in a 700 per cent profit for the Indians get skinned" (*écorche les Sauvages*). The markup on trade goods was high, but the profits were not. The Canadian historian Louise Dechêne has calculated normal margins for traders and merchants to be around 10 to 15 percent. The trade involved many middlemen and many burdensome expenses, among them the distribution of gifts to Indian clients. The trade was not simply conducted or expressed in European terms. Indian customers usually articulated exchange in the language of reciprocity, of mutual gift-giving. For Indian villages, the arrival of European traders meant much more than commerce: it meant the establishment and maintenance of social and political relations. Of all the European groups involved in the trade, the French entered most deeply into native worlds.

At first, the French—like the Dutch—waited for native groups to come to them. Montagnais, Nipissing, and Huron canoes brought furs to Quebec in the 1630s, but Iroquois enemies to the south—eager to obtain furs to trade with the Dutch—began attacking parties of Frenchmen and their native partners. Thus began a pattern of warfare and destruction that would last until 1701 and encompass a vast area from the St. Lawrence to the Great Lakes. Iroquois actions forced French reactions. In 1634 a post was built at Trois-Rivières at the mouth of the St.-Maurice River to protect one transportation route to the north. The village quickly became an important training center and jumping-off point for the trade. The French experience began to diverge from that of the Dutch: French traders were leaving home and traveling to Indian communities. Another crucial distinction between the Dutch and the French colonies was the presence in the latter of active missionaries, eager to confront Indian societies and convert them to the true faith.

The paths to Indian country were followed not only by traders but also by clerics and soldiers. (This was true in seventeenth-century Canada and equally true in the nineteenth-century United States, when missionaries and soldiers followed fur traders from St. Louis up the Missouri River.) Recollet friars arrived first, reaching Quebec in 1615, but they had little success in Canada. Their standards of European civility and Franciscan models of reduction—based on experiences with sedentary Mexican natives—were of no use in this northern country. The Jesuits arrived in Canada in 1625 and, at first, pursued a similar plan based on the economic and social Frenchification of the natives. Failures at the reserve at Sillery, founded in 1637 several miles from Quebec, and at a *séminaire*, or boarding school, for Indian children north of the city forced the Jesuits to reconsider. By 1640, the Jesuits were ready to travel with Indian bands and take up residence in distant native villages. Depending on one's perspective, the Jesuits might be congratulated for their insights into native cultures and brave attempts to translate between worlds or condemned for their insidious efforts to undermine traditional gender roles, patterns of authority, and cultural inventories. One thing is definite: their knowledge of Indian customs and languages and their annual *Relations*, which publicized their work and the needs of the colony, were a great resource for the colonists. Nevertheless, not every Jesuit enterprise brought success. From 1647 to 1649, the Iroquois attacked the Hurons and destroyed not only their villages but also the Jesuit missions.

Ste. Marie, the largest of the missions, went up in flames in 1649. The Iroquois, searching for beaver, hunting grounds, captives to replenish their villages, and prisoners to torture, targeted the Hurons because they were the main trading partners of the French. The Iroquois then attacked several allied groups, the Eries, the Neutrals, and the Petuns, and pursued the refugees to the *pays d'en haut* (Great Lakes basin), where they attacked a number of Algonquian-speaking groups such as the Miamis, the Mascoutens, and the Ottawas. In short, for twenty years—from 1647 to 1667—the Iroquois blazed a path of destruction and created a new landscape of refugee communities in a vast area from Ontario to Illinois. The chaos disrupted the fur trade. French farms along the St. Lawrence also came under attack. An Iroquois chief claimed that the French "were not able to goe over a door to pisse."

At this critical point in the history of New France, Louis XIV and his minister, Jean-Baptiste Colbert, decided that the colonies were worth keeping and undertook an ambitious series of reforms to strengthen them. The crown's first act was to take the colony out of the hands of the Compagnie des Cent-Associés. By 1674, New France had become a royal colony. Colbert established a new form of government, designated the Coutume de Paris as the exclusive body of law in the colony, and reorganized the seigneurial system—the plan of settlement.

The seigneurial regime had the appearance of a feudal system, but in fact the seigneur's privileges were limited, and his relationship to his settlers, or *censitaires*, was contractual. In essence, the seigneur was a developer sanctioned by and responsible to the state. It was a system that guaranteed the construction of mills and provided for a minimum level of support for all newcomers. Land was granted to all in exchange for the payment of a nominal annual tax—the *cens*—and rents. A settler could sell his land, but a tax—the *lods et ventes*—had to be paid by the purchaser. The seigneur could also be replaced by the intendant if he neglected his duties. In short, it was a system that encouraged orderly development and discouraged speculation. Speculation was unlikely anyway. Land was cheap and markets were inaccessible. (Canadian ports were closed for over half the year.) Although grain surpluses were produced by Canadian farmers, West Indian markets were dominated by the English colonies. Colonial merchants had no interest in investing in land. Profits accrued from imports.

Rural Canada then was a self-sufficient, isolated world. The landscape assumed a familiar pattern: long, narrow rectangular lots fronting the river, grouped into areas, or *côtes*, that shared physiographic traits. Farmhouses situated along the river brought habitants closer together. This pattern of settlement facilitated the building and upkeep of roads and made ploughing easier—decreasing the number of times a team had to be turned around. Social life centered on the parish church. By the end of the French regime, farms stretched along the north and south banks of the St. Lawrence, giving the appearance of a continuous village. The forest remained intact behind the seigneuries.

That the *côtes* filled in at all was due in large measure to Colbert's policies. From 1665 to 1673, the crown sent approximately one thousand young women, the *filles de roi*, to Canada to help compensate for the pronounced gender imbalance—that is, to provide wives for the colonists and produce children. These young women were, for the most part, orphans and other girls without resources. The king provided dowries. In addition, grants and other incentives were provided for parents of ten children or more. The strategy seemed to work: the colony had a very high birthrate. Recent research has shown that immigration, though never comparable to the flow of people to British North America, was higher than previously thought. There were perhaps as many as sixty-seven thousand men and women emigrants to Canada during the French regime. Many, however, returned to France, giving a net migration calculated at roughly twenty thousand.

Of all those that came over, the soldiers of the Carignan-Salières regiment had the most immediate impact. This force of twelve hundred men arrived in 1665, built three forts on the Richelieu River—the route of Mohawk war parties—and took the war to Iroquois country. Although the French had limited success in battle, they burned enough cornfields to force the Iroquois—who were already fighting the Susquehannocks and the Mahicans on other fronts—to press for peace in 1667. Peace led to a new expansion of trade in the west. Although a flood of beaver depressed prices, the profits were still considerable, and engagés and unemployed soldiers headed for new fur frontiers in the *pays d'en haut*. A new governor, Louis de Buade de Frontenac, pursued an expansionist policy that ran counter to Colbert's plan to concentrate men and resources in the St. Lawrence region. Frontenac had a fort built—named after himself—on the eastern end of Lake Ontario in 1673. That same year Louis Jolliet and Father Jacques Marquette journeyed down the Mississippi. Supported by Frontenac, René-Robert Cavelier, Sieur de La Salle, explored the Illinois and Mississippi rivers and established a chain of posts. By 1680 there were reportedly eight hundred illegal traders, or *coureurs de bois*, in the western Indian lands. The trading fairs of Montreal (founded in 1642) declined and disappeared. Exchange now took place in Indian country.

The Iroquois, freed by 1677 of their other battles, responded to what they saw as an attempt to rob them of furs and hunting grounds. Other natives, however, forged tentative alliances with the French. In 1683 the French sent troops to fortify trading posts in the Great Lakes basin, thus beginning a succession of commandants who pursued private interests while—hopefully—following orders. Attacks in Illinois country in the 1680s gave way to attacks in Iroquoia in the 1690s. By 1701, Iroquoia was decimated. The fur trade at Albany had suffered during the war; convoys had continued to reach Montreal. The Grand Settlement of 1701 established a general peace. An illicit trade, known in New York as the Canada trade, developed between Albany and Montreal, with the Mohawks at Caughnawaga acting as intermediaries. (In the 1730s two Canadian sisters named Desaunier were directing smuggling activities.)

Despite a glut of furs, a severe drop in prices, and a temporary decision in 1696 to abandon the western country, the French were there to stay. The crown, faced with the threat of an English expedition from the Carolinas, ordered Pierre Lemoyne d'Iberville to establish a colony at the mouth of the Mississippi in 1698. (The ministers reasoned that Louisiana would check the expansion of the English colonies and also provide a strategic position from which to attack or defend Spanish possessions, depending on the outcome of the impending war over the Spanish succession.) Detroit, founded in 1701 by Antoine de la Mothe Cadillac, and Michilimackinac, located on the passage between Lakes Huron and Michigan, became the centers of the *pays d'en haut*. Canadian merchants opposed the establishment of Detroit because it was too close to the Iroquois and Albany and of Louisiana because a new port on the Gulf of Mexico would loosen their control over the trade and the traders who were in their debt. Imperial policymakers won the day, and their plans were carried out by a new generation of Canadian-born soldiers and entrepreneurs, many of them members of the Lemoyne clan, ready to realize profits and policy at the same time.

New France, entering its golden age in the first three decades of the eighteenth century, now had two distinct socioeconomic worlds: one was rural, self-sufficient, and rather static; the other was urban and dynamic. Canada came to be more and more a strictly European colony. In Louisiana, the Illinois country, and the Great Lakes basin, French cities and villages developed alongside Indian villages. On this frontier, described by one historian as "one cabin with two fires," Europeans and natives lived side by side. There were violent struggles between the French and certain tribes such as the Fox and the Natchez; indeed, there were problems, large and small. Nevertheless, as the historian Richard White has noted, "Their knowledge of each other's customs and their ability to live together . . . had no equivalent among the British." Here, natives and Europeans found that their different goals were complementary. The French posed no demographic threat. Although French villages in the Illinois country developed agricultural surpluses and although Louisiana, including Illinois, had a colonial—African and European—population of some ten thousand by 1750, the landscape of Indian life had not been seriously altered. The fur trade depended on the integrity of that landscape. (Of course, there came a point when game animal populations were depleted. Once that point was reached, cross-cultural relationships often deteriorated.) Exchange also depended on a variety of bridges such as language and marriage.

In the first few decades of the eighteenth century, French-Indian marriages in Illinois predominated. Intermarriage and clan adoption were ways of going beyond bridges; they formed the basis of a true middle ground. People of mixed ancestry—métis—became an important part of this shared world. Some, like Jean-Baptiste Richardville, of Indiana, assumed positions of authority within Indian society. He became the principal chief of the Miamis in 1814 and was said to be one of the richest men in Indiana at the time of his death in 1841. Others, like Antoine Leclaire, the founder of Davenport, Iowa, and the son of a Canadian trader and a Potawatomi woman, opted for status in the non-Indian world. Ultimately, when this frontier had passed into history, many métis people came to regard themselves as a distinct people. In eighteenth-century Illinois, however, intermarriage was simply one expression of peaceful coexistence.

Another intriguing expression of cultural negotiation can be found in some of the deeds from colonial Illinois. One such deed between a Frenchman and a French husband-and-wife couple advises the purchaser that the deed is valid *unless* the Indians decide to take back the land in question. Such caveats would not be found in a deed from New England, where Englishmen simply assumed that English sovereignty was final and complete. In early Illinois, the French made no such assumptions.

So Louisiana and the Illinois country—which became part of Louisiana in 1717—represented, perhaps, the logical outcome of a trading-post frontier in native North America. In a region without cities, the French established New Orleans in 1718 and St. Louis in 1764. Though they conceived the cities, French colonists relied to an extraordinary extent and for an unusually long period of time on Indian communities for food supplies. Some Indian communities relocated to the suburban districts to serve such a function. Even in the nineteenth century, Indian vendors continued to bring wild turkeys, venison, filé powder, and other products to the markets of New Orleans, Natchez, and St. Louis. African, Indian, and French cooks all contributed to the development of such regional delights as jambalaya and gumbo. Louisiana would later become famous for another unique regional contribution to our national heritage, jazz. It has been suggested that the term *jazz* derives from the French word *jaser*, "to chatter." How appropriate that this polyphonic musical form would be born on a frontier so full of cultural conversations.

Adjustment

The four different frontiers each represented an extension of European languages, laws, people, plants, and animals. Each one represented, in addition, a unique way of mediating between the Old World and the New. European permanence in Virginia and New England required the transformation of the land and the social reorganization of its management. The Dutch and the French, primarily concerned with the acquisition of commodities produced by native peoples, built urban bases. In areas shared by French and Indian peoples, a mixed culture began to develop. All colonies depended on capital

Pierre Chouteau, Jr., and Jean Baptiste Richardville grew up in a world of cross-cultural exchange and conversation. Though both became wealthy businessmen, they chose different cultural paths. Chouteau thrived in the American world and passed along his social prestige to his descendents, who occupied positions of status in St. Louis. Richardville, the son of a French-Canadian man and a Miami Indian woman, abandoned white dress and stopped speaking French or English in his later years. His Miami world in Indiana was shattered by the policies and practices of the United States and its citizens.

Unidentified artist. Pierre Chouteau, Jr. *(1789–1865). Oil on canvas, ca. 1820s. Art Collection (#POR-C-106A), Missouri Historical Society, St. Louis.*

James Otto Lewis (1799–1858). Jean Baptiste Richardville *(ca. 1761–1841). Lithograph, ca. 1835. Marion Public Library, Indiana.*

investments—living away from home was an expensive proposition. Economic activities certainly played a major role in shaping new societies, but there were other factors. The New England landscape reflected a social and religious agenda born in England and nurtured on American soil. The crowded, narrow streets of New Amsterdam recapitulated old Amsterdam without any reference to the available space of seventeenth-century Manhattan. In Virginia, the seeds of independence were planted in American soil by a status-conscious would-be landed gentry. The Creole and Indian world of the Mississippi Valley was forged in the crucible of North American geopolitics.

Ultimately, international rivalries produced a transoceanic war—the Seven Years War—fought on two continents. In 1763, the British emerged victorious on each front, and the French nation lost its North American empire. But the French people did not leave, nor did their native allies. Frenchmen and -women continued to occupy key settlements from Mobile to Detroit, from Quebec to Montreal. Only the imperial maps had changed significantly. While British land speculators projected their visions onto

Founded as a commercial center on the edge of a frontier, St. Louis exemplified the French form of community-building in the New World. Its strategic location near the confluence of the Mississippi and Missouri rivers made it an ideal base from which merchants could operate as middlemen between the Indian communities to the west and the burgeoning American populations to the east. The trade and transportation links established during the French period later helped the city become a leading American transportation and industrial center in the late 19th century.

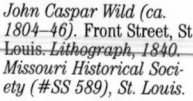

John Caspar Wild (ca. 1804–46). Front Street, St. Louis. Lithograph, 1840. Missouri Historical Society (#SS 589), St. Louis.

surveyors' grids, Creole merchants and their Indian partners continued to travel up and down rivers and continued to live in those supposedly empty spaces.

The process of adjusting frontiers, of remaking the maps, created some wonderful ironies. When George Rogers Clark recaptured Vincennes in 1779 during the American Revolution, his troops included Illinois Frenchmen. The "British" army that surrendered to the Americans was composed of French militiamen from Detroit. Some of the French held commissions from both armies. French settlers at Vincennes became quite adept at taking oaths of allegiance. This masquerade in present-day Indiana led to the extension of Virginia's jurisdiction and eventually to the inclusion of this frontier within the boundaries of the United States. Across the Mississippi River in Spanish St. Louis, French-Creole traders such as Auguste Chouteau—whose portrait suggests a self-styled western Napoleon—and their native partners continued about their business, even after the transfer of sovereignty in 1804, which necessitated a new oath of allegiance. Pierre Chouteau, Jr., Auguste's nephew, created a fur-trade empire in the trans-Mississippi West from 1813 to 1865. Chouteau's fur company realized a centuries-old French colonial dream. Company steamboats plied western waters; the Chouteau name was emblazoned on flagpoles and stamped on Indian medals. Government officials, tourists, artists—all who traveled in the vast regions united by company trading posts—relied on Chouteau's good offices and the company's hospitality. At the same time, Chouteau and his firm looked toward the settlement frontier advancing from the east. With connections to tribesmen in Indian country and to federal officials and politicians in Washington, the company—in a perfect position to assist in the process of extinguishing Indian title—pioneered the use of government funds to pay tribal debts in land-cession treaties. Lobbyists pressured Congress to pass appropriations favorable to the company. When emigrants on the Oregon Trail needed military protection, Chouteau sold Fort

Laramie to the government. Money from all these sources was reinvested in railroad stocks, steamboat lines, and iron mines. Several frontiers intersected in St. Louis. Chouteau, in many ways an old-fashioned, French-speaking *négociant* presiding over a family firm, understood this confluence and profited during this critical period of adjustment. He died a very wealthy man, and with his death—in 1865—the roar of national expansion drowned out the faint echoes of passing colonial frontiers.

Bibliographic Note

Many innovative studies of the colonial era have appeared in the last two decades. Jack P. Greene and J. R. Pole, eds., *Colonial British America: Essays in the New History of the Early Modern Era* (Baltimore, 1984), contains thematic essays by the leading historians in the field. T. H. Breen's contribution, "Creative Adaptations: Peoples and Cultures," elaborates on the notion of "charter groups" and the cultural "conversations" that generated new societies in North America. Three broad reinterpretations of colonial British America have appeared in the last decade. David Hackett Fischer, *Albion's Seed: Four British Folkways in America* (New York, 1989), and Bernard Bailyn, *The Peopling of British North America: An Introduction* (New York, 1986), both emphasize the process of transplantation, but there the resemblance ends. Jack P. Greene's *Pursuits of Happiness: The Social Development of Early Modern British Colonies and the Formation of American Culture* (Chapel Hill, 1988) offers the concept of "social development" as a key to understanding the interaction between metropolitan "inheritance" and American "experience." D. W. Meinig's *The Shaping of America: A Geographical Perspective on 500 Years of History*, vol. 1, *Atlantic America, 1492–1800* (New Haven, 1986), casts a wider spatial and temporal net in an effort to conceptualize the interactions between "three Old Worlds": Europe, America, and Africa.

Histories of Europe and the forces that led to and encompassed the colonization of America abound. Fernand Braudel's magisterial *Civilization and Capitalism, 15th-18th Century*, published in English translation in three volumes—*The Structures of Everyday Life*, *The Wheels of Commerce*, and *The Perspective of the World* (New York, 1982–84)—is comprehensive yet full of insightful analysis and rich detail. Immanuel Wallerstein, *The Modern World-System*, 3 vols. (New York, 1974–89), focuses more strictly on the history of European and global economies and the relationship between core-states and peripheries. The early patterns of European expansion are discussed in Charles Verlinden, *The Beginnings of Modern Colonization*, trans. Yvonne Freccero (Ithaca, N.Y., 1970), and Felipe Fernández-Armesto, *Before Columbus: Exploration and Colonisation from the Mediterranean to the Atlantic, 1229–1492* (Basingstoke, Hampshire, 1987). J. H. Parry, *The Age of Reconnaissance* (Cleveland, 1963), remains a lucid overview of European exploration and conquest, with a concise discussion of the means and preconditions of discovery. Carlo M. Cipolla, *Guns, Sails, and Empires: Technological Innovation and the Early Phases of European Expansion, 1400–1700* (New York, 1965), examines in greater depth the impact of developing technologies.

The Columbian quincentenary witnessed a flood of books on the Genoese mariner, the age of discovery, and the consequences of the encounters between Europeans and Native Americans. Alfred W. Crosby, Jr., *The Columbian Exchange: Biological and Cultural Consequences of 1492* (Westport, Conn., 1972), pioneered the study of "species shifting." His *Ecological Imperialism: The Biological Expansion of Europe, 900–1900* (Cambridge, Eng., 1986) contains an examination of what he terms "Neo-Europes." Crosby's work inspired a Smithsonian exhibit and companion volume to mark the Columbian anniversary: Herman J. Viola and Carolyn Margolis, eds., *Seeds of Change: A Quincentennial Commemoration* (Washington, D.C., 1991). Stephen Greenblatt's *Marvelous Possessions: The Wonder of the New World* (Chicago, 1991) is an elegant and sophisticated reading of the encounter. Those wishing to explore the sometimes depressing, often surprising, and always fascinating history of native-colonial interaction should begin with any of James Axtell's collections of essays: *The European and the Indian: Essays in the Ethnohistory of*

Colonial North America (New York, 1981); *The Invasion Within: The Contest of Cultures in Colonial North America* (New York, 1985); *After Columbus: Essays in the Ethnohistory of Colonial North America* (New York, 1988); and *Beyond 1492: Encounters in Colonial North America* (New York, 1992).

David B. Quinn, *North America from Earliest Discovery to First Settlements: The Norse Voyages to 1612* (New York, 1977), provides a comprehensive and clear overview of European exploration and settlement in this early period. Ralph Davis, *The Rise of the Atlantic Economies* (Ithaca, N.Y., 1973), and K. G. Davies, *The North Atlantic World in the Seventeenth Century* (Minneapolis, 1974), remain useful surveys of imperial systems. Two volumes by Philip D. Curtin—*Cross-Cultural Trade in World History* (Cambridge, Eng., 1984) and *The Rise and Fall of the Plantation Complex: Essays in Atlantic History* (Cambridge, Eng., 1990)—are invaluable for their global perspective and thematic focus. Kenneth R. Andrews, *Trade, Plunder, and Settlement: Maritime Enterprise and the Genesis of the British Empire, 1480–1630* (Cambridge, Eng., 1984), provides an urbane inquiry into a variety of topics pertaining to English expansion.

As for the literature on specific colonial frontiers, Edmund S. Morgan's *American Slavery American Freedom: The Ordeal of Colonial Virginia* (New York, 1975) remains the best single examination of North America's first boom-time frontier. Essays by E. Randolph Turner and Frederick J. Fausz in William W. Fitzhugh, ed., *Cultures in Contact: The Impact of European Contacts on Native American Cultural Institutions, A.D. 1000–1800* (Washington, D.C., 1985), and Helen C. Rountree, *The Powhatan Indians of Virginia: Their Traditional Culture* (Norman, 1989), round out the narrative of Indian-English relations on that frontier. T. H. Breen, *Tobacco Culture: The Mentality of the Great Tidewater Planters on the Eve of Revolution* (Princeton, 1985), is a revealing study of the colony's values and habits. Some of Breen's seminal essays on Virginia and New England are collected in *Puritans and Adventurers: Change and Persistence in Early America* (New York, 1980). The theme of continuity and the persistence of local traditions in New England is pursued in depth by David Grayson Allen, *In English Ways: The Movement of Societies and the Transferal of English Local Law and Custom to Massachusetts Bay in the Seventeenth Century* (Chapel Hill, 1981). David Cressy, *Coming Over: Migration and Communication between England and New England in the Seventeenth Century* (Cambridge, Eng., 1987), is a brilliant and lively account of the move itself and provides many insights into the self-selection process. Francis Jenning's *The Invasion of America: Indians, Colonialism, and the Cant of Conquest* (Chapel Hill, 1975) provides a thoroughly revised narrative of New England's settlement, taking into account the natives of the region and their treatment at the hands of the English. Neal Salisbury, *Manitou and Providence: Indians, Europeans, and the Making of New England, 1500–1643* (New York, 1982), provides an in-depth ethnohistorical account of the region's formative years. William Cronon's *Changes in the Land: Indians, Colonists, and the Ecology of New England* (New York, 1983) offers a brilliant and original assessment of the conflicting ways natives and colonists managed natural resources and the ecological transformation effected by the English invasion.

Donna Merwick's *Possessing Albany, 1630–1710: The Dutch and English Experiences* (Cambridge, Eng., 1990) captures the distinctiveness of the Dutch approach to the New World. It should be supplemented with Oliver A. Rink, *Holland on the Hudson: An Economic and Social History of Dutch New York* (Ithaca, N.Y., 1986). Joyce D. Goodfriend, *Before the Melting Pot: Society and Culture in Colonial New York City, 1664–1730* (Princeton, 1992), a valuable study of ethnicity and community, sheds much light on Dutch culture in colonial America. Allen W. Trelease, *Indian Affairs in Colonial New York: The Seventeenth Century* (Ithaca, N.Y., 1960), remains the standard treatment but should be used in conjunction with Daniel K. Richter, *The Ordeal of the Longhouse: The Peoples of the Iroquois League in the Era of European Colonization* (Chapel Hill, 1992). Thomas Elliot Norton, *The Fur Trade in Colonial New York, 1686–1776* (Madison, 1974), traces the activities of Dutch and British Albanians in a later period.

Historians of New France, appropriately enough, have been among the leaders in the effort to write narratives that include native peoples as significant actors. In addition to the work of

James Axtell, Cornelius J. Jaenen's *Friend and Foe: Aspects of French-Amerindian Cultural Contact in the Sixteenth and Seventeenth Centuries* (New York, 1976) explores the effects of a variety of cross-cultural relationships. Bruce G. Trigger, *Natives and Newcomers: Canada's "Heroic Age" Reconsidered* (Kingston, 1985), revises the early period of the colony's history, and Olive P. Dickason, *Canada's First Nations: A History of Founding Peoples from Earliest Times* (Norman, 1992), provides an Indian-centered narrative of Canadian history. The standard surveys are W. J. Eccles: *The Canadian Frontier, 1534–1760*, rev. ed. (Albuquerque, 1983) and *France in America* (New York, 1972). Louise Dechêne, *Habitants and Merchants in Seventeenth Century Montreal*, English ed. (Montreal, 1992), originally appeared in 1974 and has achieved the status of a classic over the years. Richard White, *The Middle Ground: Indians, Empires, and Republics in the Great Lakes Region, 1650–1815* (Cambridge, Eng., 1991), explores the French and Indian world of the *pays d'en haut* with the creativity and mastery of a novelist. Daniel H. Usner, Jr., *Indians, Settlers, and Slaves in a Frontier Exchange Economy: The Lower Mississippi Valley before 1783* (Chapel Hill, 1992), rescues Louisiana from historiographical oblivion and reveals a fascinating and colorful story. William E. Foley and C. David Rice, *The First Chouteaus: River Barons of Early St. Louis* (Urbana, 1983), examines the first generation of a remarkable Creole dynasty. Jacqueline Peterson and Jennifer S. H. Brown, eds., *The New Peoples: Being and Becoming Métis in North America* (Lincoln, 1985), provides an essential introduction to the subject. Carolyn Gilman, *Where Two Worlds Meet: The Great Lakes Fur Trade* (St. Paul, Minn., 1982), is perhaps the best short overview of the fur trade and is beautifully illustrated. Finally, R. Cole Harris, ed., *Historical Atlas of Canada*, vol. 1, *From the Beginning to 1800* (Toronto, 1987), a visual feast of charts and maps, is a textbook in and of itself.

A sauvage avec ses anciennes Armes, arc et Fleche —

G Sauuages dansant le calumet, auec le chichicoüa a la main

B, sauvage piqué, auec ses Armes Nouuelles

Chapter Four

American Frontier

ELLIOTT WEST

I is any word in the American idiom more evocative and elusive than *frontier*? Few persons can agree on what the frontier was, yet few will deny that it existed and that before its passing it somehow helped shape the nation.

Trans-Appalachian America is a case in point. The frontier certainly left its stamp on this region of more than half a million square miles between the Appalachian plateaus and the Mississippi River. Through the region's standard histories walk figures—from Daniel Boone and the "men of western waters" to Tecumseh and William Henry Harrison—who became, even in their own lifetimes, icons of the "pioneer experience." That vague phrase, and particular images of this American frontier, are bound up as well with popular perceptions of the American people and their emerging character.

Just what the frontier was, however, remains something of a puzzle. It refers in some way to the emigration from the East of thousands of hunters, trappers, traders, farmers, merchants, soldiers, and other assorted floaters. This intrusion into the lands beyond the Appalachians was under way by 1763, and by 1820 its work there was largely done.

That much is clear enough. But the particulars of the frontier's meaning—its definition and its results—are slippery. It is helpful to think of the frontier as both a condition and a historical force. This frontier had certain traits that set it apart from the rest of the continent during these years. Those traits in turn shaped the land and people of trans-Appalachia, leaving marks that ever since have helped define that country as one of the nation's distinctive regions. Besides a condition and force, the frontier was also an anticipation. After 1820, as the wave of emigration rolled beyond trans-Appalachia, most of these traits would reappear in the lands between the Mississippi and the Pacific. Then the Far West, in its turn, would feel the frontier's shaping power.

Of the frontier's defining characteristics, five were paramount. First was its human diversity. Between the Appalachians and the Mississippi was a wider range of cultures than east of the mountains—more than thirty widely varied Indian groups as well as French, English, and Spanish communities, all of them joined by an influx of westering emigrants of many different cultural traditions. That, in turn, contributed to the second characteristic—an intricate set of power relationships. Native peoples exercised a high degree of autonomy. Doing so, they dealt with other centers of power, older nations in Europe and a new one on the Atlantic coast. The strength of these nations, although much greater than that of particular Indian groups, was exercised from afar. Like an expanding circle of light, that power was often felt rather dimly in trans-Appalachia, so whites and Indians were frequently on something close to an equal footing. The resulting play of authorities was arguably more complex than anywhere else in the Western world.

The trans-Appalachian frontier was a dynamic place of cultural exchange between Indians and Europeans. As this watercolor sketch by a French officer in Louisiana suggests, Native Americans quickly adapted European technology for their own purposes.

Behind this interplay of power was the frontier's third defining trait—a diversity of appealing resources. These were certainly not unused; Indians had flourished on the land's bounty for at least ten millennia. But newer arrivals wanted to use the land in new ways. And besides, the region's potential—its economic meaning—was changing rapidly with the stirrings of industry and the rise of a capitalist, market-oriented economic system on both sides of the Atlantic. Value, like beauty and perversion, depends on who does the looking, so the country's promise expanded with the changing economic perspectives of Indians and whites alike. This evolving economic meaning was basic to the fourth element of the frontier—its symbolic significance, most of all for the people of the youthful United States. To them, the country not only offered opportunities to individuals but also ensured a true independence and survival of the nation's distinctive virtues. The frontier became inseparable from the Republic's sense of itself.

All four elements combined to make the fifth. This American frontier was a region of extraordinarily dynamic changes, transformations that were arguably of greater depth and scope than anywhere else in the Atlantic community. The frontier was a competitive arena of a few dozen powers whose varying strengths were ebbing and surging. It was a place of rich cultural exchanges among a changing mix of different, evolving peoples. Here a new nation tested and modified its emerging institutions. The land itself, and perceptions of it, changed dramatically. So did what people wore, how they fought, and why and how they hunted deer and sought salvation.

This American frontier was only the latest of many to enter trans-Appalachia. Indian peoples had been moving into this country in successive waves for at least ten thousand years. In 1763, more than one hundred thousand Native Americans occupied the region. They included more than two dozen groups, varying in population from a few hundred to twenty thousand. In contrast to the common image of Indians rooted for eons to their home sod, most of these peoples had been in movement for generations—some migrating from the East under pressure of European expansion, some being displaced by newcomers, and others expanding their range against weaker competitors. Their cultural, religious, and artistic lives were varied, rich, and complex. Certainly this frontier was not what its most famous scholar, Frederick Jackson Turner, once called it—"the line between civilization and savagery." It was, rather, a zone of exchange and conflict among many civilizations.

Indian peoples had felt the presence of Europeans for more than two centuries before 1763. The *entrada* in the 1540s of the Spanish conquistador Hernando de Soto was the first European intrusion into the interior of the Gulf Coast. Afterward, the Spanish concentrated their attention on the Atlantic side of the Florida peninsula and only in 1698 did they establish an outpost at Pensacola to counter French influence. By then English traders among the Cherokees and Creeks were causing grave concern among both the Spanish and the French. The English also had established themselves as patrons of the powerful Iroquois of western New York, and by the 1740s their traders were among the Indians of the Ohio Valley.

The French, however, were the dominant European force in trans-Appalachia. After establishing a base at Quebec on the St. Lawrence River in 1608, the French, eager to expand their lucrative fur trade, began one of the most remarkable campaigns of exploration of the modern era. By the mid-1630s, they were west of Lake Michigan, and

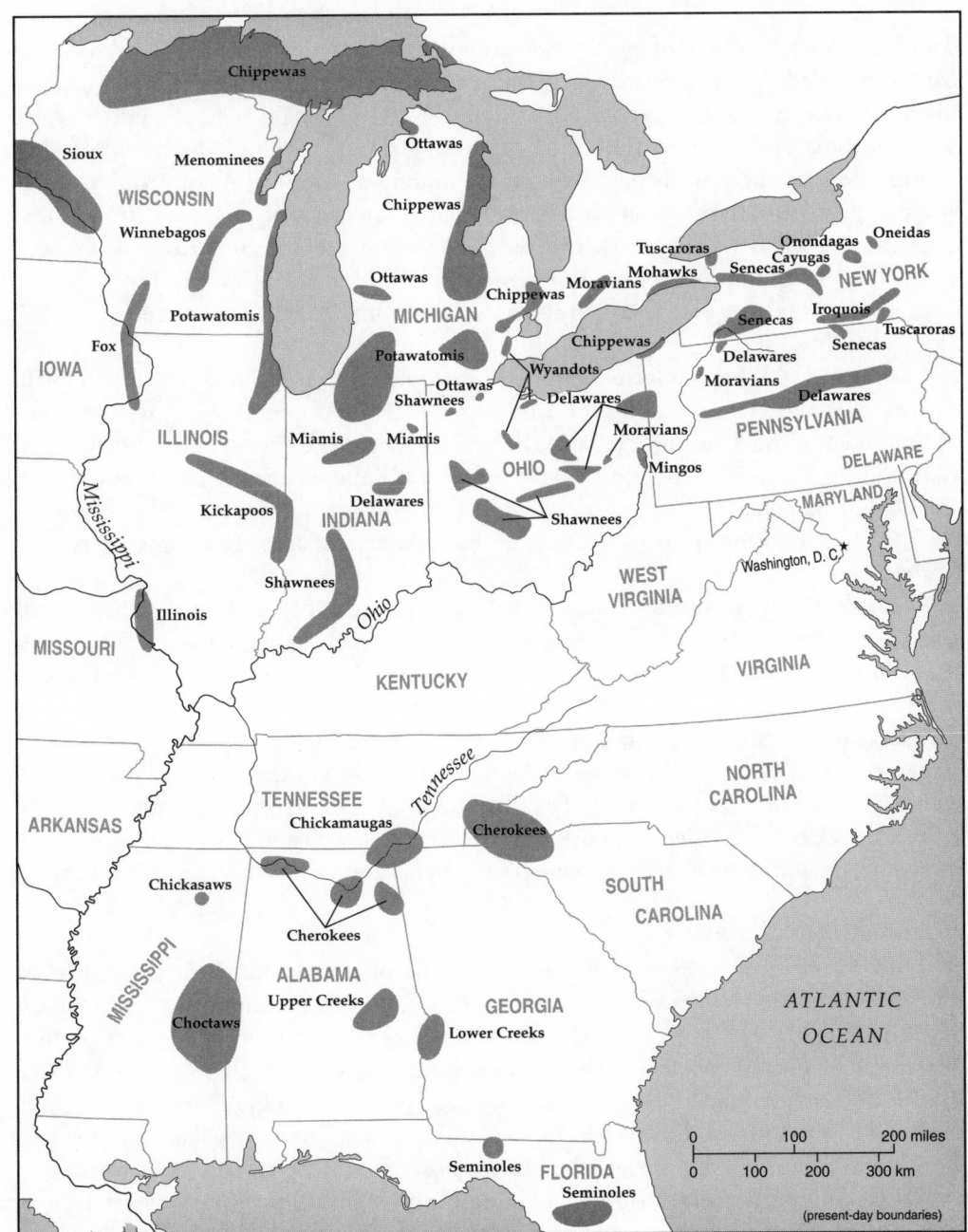

Trans-Appalachian Indian Settlement, 1760–94

by the 1670s, they were in the lower Ohio Valley. Soon they explored and founded posts down the Mississippi and along the Gulf coast. When Sieur de Bienville founded New Orleans in 1718, French traders were probing up the Missouri River and southwest toward the upper Rio Grande. Based on La Salle's voyage down the Mississippi to its mouth in 1682, the French claimed the land stretching from the Appalachian crest westward to the continental divide of the Rocky Mountains. Their presence was concentrated in a string of posts and settlements from the Great Lakes down the Mississippi Valley and eastward along the coast. But their influence radiated outward from that axis. By 1750 they had outposts in northern Alabama and the upper Ohio Valley, on the upper Missouri, and on the southern Great Plains. Their hold on this country depended on an intricate diplomacy among a score of Indian peoples. They lavished gifts and attention on natives even at the far edges of this orbit. In 1724, a delegation of Otos was escorted from their homes on the Missouri River to France, where they hunted in the Bois de Boulogne and basked in admiring gazes at the court of Louis XV. The travelers returned to report that women of the French court smelled like alligators.

Then, in 1763, France surrendered it all. In that year, the diplomatic map of North America was redrawn, at least from Europe's perspective. After nearly seventy-five years of hot and cold wars among England, France, and Spain, England emerged the clear victor. From France, Britain received eastern Canada and all French claims east of the Mississippi; Spain ceded Florida to England. With little use now for its holdings beyond the Mississippi, France transferred the enormous western half of Louisiana to its ally, Spain.

This shuffling marked the start of the frontier era considered here. The next fifty-seven years can be divided into three periods, each with its own theme. The years between 1763 and 1783 saw the first European settlers from east of the mountains and the combat and realignment of powers that came with the American Revolution. During the next three decades, as the nation born of that revolution exerted its authority over trans-Appalachia, the swelling tide of emigration brought rapid change to the land and its peoples. In the final stage, from 1812 to 1820, the United States tightened its grip on the region. But even then, as in the first two periods, the changing frontier conditions in turn changed the new arrivals, their government, and their various institutions.

A Muddling of Powers

In 1763, England suddenly found itself the master of eastern North America. Just as quickly, it began to learn how success bred difficulties. Most Indians of the Ohio Valley and Great Lakes had long been the allies of France. Understandably wary of this expansion of English power, the natives were infuriated when British commanders drastically reduced the annual gifts that were a staple of the Indians' economy. In the spring of 1763, Indians throughout the region launched ferocious assaults against the British and captured every installation except Forts Detroit, Pitt, and Niagara.

This war, traditionally attributed to the ambitions of the Ottawa leader Pontiac, was in fact a wide-ranging attempt to establish a native position of power at a time of uncertainty and change, and although the British retook their posts by 1765, the natives' point was made. In later calculations, the English would weigh Indian perceptions and demands more heavily. In the fall of 1763, as the war raged, London issued orders meant to stabilize conditions in the West to avoid giving Indians further cause for discontent. The Proclamation of 1763 recalled all settlers from west of the Appalachian crest, forbade emigration there until further notice, and authorized trade with Indians only by licensed government agents.

The success of the proclamation, or rather the lack of success, illustrated an important element in understanding the changes coming to this region. The frontier was not a place beyond the reach of authority. Rather, it was an area where many competing authorities were imperfectly exercised. Each of the three centers of settlement that appeared during the dozen years after 1763 took advantage of this situation.

The first, at the headwaters of the Ohio, already existed at the time of the proclamation. After 1758, when English and colonial forces captured France's Fort Duquesne, traders and settlers quickly moved into the area. Renamed Fort Pitt, the garrison offered protection and a market, and by 1760, an officer reported, the country was "over run by a Number of vagabonds, who under pretense of hunting, were making settlements." The second group of settlements, in eastern Tennessee, was fed by discontent in western North Carolina, where predominantly Scotch-Irish farmers complained of corruption, insensitive local officials, too many taxes, and not enough representation. After the one-battle "War of the Regulation" in 1771, many regulators crossed the mountains to join James Robertson, Arthur and John Campbell, and other early settlers, believing this country was part of Virginia. When they discovered their error, they set up a semi-independent government, the Watauga Association.

The third region, Kentucky, was doubly appealing. Besides being known as a beautiful and fertile land teeming with game, it had no permanent Indian settlements, although Shawnees, Miamis, and Cherokees ventured there often to hunt and fight. The prime movers behind Kentucky's earliest white settlement were eastern speculators, well connected and well-to-do. Since the 1740s, various groups had maneuvered to grab the region through vast but ill-defined grants and land bounties originally given to officers of the French and Indian War. By 1775, agents of several Virginia interests were surveying the area, but the most aggressive group was the Transylvania Company of Judge Richard Henderson, a North Carolinian. At Sycamore Shoals on the Tennessee River, Henderson "purchased" from Cherokee leaders about twenty million acres in central Kentucky, then he sent Daniel Boone and thirty companions to cut an emigrant road to the Kentucky River. Soon Henderson and several families were settled around the new outpost of Boonesborough.

In these first beachheads could be seen the most common patterns of settlement, both in trans-Appalachia and farther west: an uneasy partnership between settlers and an outpost of government power, a spontaneous movement of independent pioneers, and a speculative grab by wealthy interests who brought settlers with them. And in each case, the frontier's endemic confusion of interests and authorities helped open the way. Nowhere was this shown more clearly than in Kentucky. The land "Carolina Dick" Henderson hoped to colonize was claimed by Virginia and closed by the Proclamation of 1763. His right to title through Indian purchase was based on a highly dubious legal opinion, and in any case, the Cherokee signatories were giving away land that was not theirs in the first place. Henderson, the Fort Pitt "vagabonds," and the Tennessee regulators all used government claims and the military presence if their needs demanded; they all ignored prohibitions when it suited them. On this frontier, as on later ones, overlapping authorities, geographical ignorance, and ill enforcement of laws brought opportunities as well as problems.

All this was happening during the final stages of the crisis of empire. The history of the frontier and that of the American Revolution are intimately bound together, although the relationship is a bit problematical. Earlier historians, influenced by the ideas of Frederick Jackson Turner, considered the frontier the cradle of democratic ideals that ultimately fostered the discontent causing the breach between the colonies and England. This line of reasoning is far too simplistic, yet some connection between the empire's troubles and conditions on its outer rim is undeniable. For one thing, a concern with defense of the West led Parliament to pass the Stamp Act and other money-raising measures, which in turn brought the first serious colonial protests.

The frontier had a deeper, if vaguer, influence on the imperial crisis. By the middle of the century, many rural Americans had come to associate personal independence with possession of enough land to support a family—a hundred acres was generally considered a minimum. The French immigrant J. Hector St. John de Crèvecoeur wrote that as he stood on his own land, he was elated by "the bright idea of property, of exclusive right, of independence." A lack of land for family freeholds, by contrast, was linked to social corruption and eventual economic and political tyranny. By 1775, as the eastern population grew and farms were divided over and over to provide for maturing children, landholdings were shrinking alarmingly. But to the west (as long as one ignored the native inhabitants) was land to ensure a free and healthy society, especially after the victory over France in 1763. "Now behold!" wrote Nathaniel Ames, of Dedham, Massachusetts. "The farmer may have . . . land enough for himself and all his sons." To the people of his Virginia parish, the Reverend John Brown reported, the country across the mountains was like "a new Paradise." Even those who would never venture west still could see the region as the stuff of independence. It followed that any attempt to stem the emigration was a threat to a free society.

But slowing frontier expansion was just what many British officials advised. Not only would westward emigration bring war with the Indians and increase the imperial debt; the growing colonies would also draw away from England many thousands of tenants and badly needed laborers. Some opposed expansion for the very reasons that American farmers wanted it. To the earl of Hillsborough, secretary of state for the colonies, an expanding society of freeholders threatened "a just subordination to and dependence upon this kingdom." The home government consequently imposed first the Proclamation of 1763, then its modification, the line of 1768, which was to hold settlement east of the Allegheny River and in far eastern Kentucky. To dampen the speculative frenzy after 1770, London in 1773 forbade any new grants to speculators. The Quebec Act, passed the next year, closed land north of the Ohio River to all but the most limited settlement and trade.

The frontier, then, was certainly not a prime cause of the Revolution, but it was a provocation. The West was an occasion for conflict between the home government and particular economic interests, some of them quite powerful. For a far larger group of Americans, the western country was a symbol of possibilities and a hedge against baleful social tendencies. From the Republic's birth, many associated the nation's continuing independence, its unique virtues, even its very identity, with the frontier.

The phrase "War of Independence," when applied to the region beyond the

Appalachians, is both misleading and ironic. In one sense it was not an internal struggle within the British Empire but an imperial rivalry among four nations—three older ones and one just emerging—for control of the continent. In another sense the phrase is accurate, although not in the way it is usually used. American Indians were trying, once again, to salvage a measure of independence and control over their lands, and as usual that meant maneuvering among the various newcomers, lining up with the particular Euro-Americans who seemed at the moment to be the least threatening.

The fighting in the West was an extension of a conflict that had been gathering force for several years as the population around Fort Pitt grew and surveyors ventured into Kentucky. Rising tensions led to Lord Dunmore's War in 1774, after which Shawnees and Delawares allowed white settlement in Kentucky, at least for the time being. To the south, Creeks struck out in 1773 against the advancing Georgia frontier. It was hardly surprising, then, that virtually all Indian groups aligned with Great Britain against the colonists. Nonetheless, British leaders first pleaded with the natives to stay out of the fray, realizing that these people, acting out of their own motives, were thus ultimately uncontrollable. In fact, distant British and colonial commanders found their white frontier "allies" as unpredictable as the Indians, and partly for the same reasons. The changing patchwork of western Whig and Tory support depended on a complex of reasons, including speculation on which side would control land and trade after the fighting. Indians and settlers fought for their own goals, so leaders on both sides hoped to avoid relying on them.

Making matters even less predictable were the other two imperial rivals, Spain and France. Both opposed England, but neither looked favorably on colonial expansion. By 1781, the governor of Spanish Louisiana, Bernardo de Gálvez, having taken Natchez, Mobile, and Pensacola, hoped to control the coastal region as far north as the Cumberland River. French aid to the revolutionary cause was indispensable, and former French citizens sometimes gave direct aid to revolutionary forces in the West. But the French recognized no American claims west of the mountains. Few would have been surprised if the French tried to reassert themselves among their old Indian allies of the Great Lakes and Upper Mississippi.

The war in the West was fought in three theaters. Conflict began south of Kentucky when Cherokee leaders, against the pleas of the British agent John Stuart, struck white pioneer settlements along the Watauga and Nolichucky rivers in the summer of 1776. After a counterattack by white settlers destroyed Indian villages and corn supplies, Cherokees surrendered most of the Tennessee River valley. In the northern theater—upstate and far western New York and northwestern Pennsylvania—loyalists and Iroquois warriors battered colonials with hundreds of raids overseen by the British colonel John Butler and the brilliant Mohawk strategist Joseph Brant. Revolutionary Generals John Sullivan and John Clinton led a brutal retaliatory campaign into the Mohawk Valley, razing forty towns and burning 160,000 bushels of corn and other foodstuffs. By the end of the war, the region was devastated.

Between the northern and southern theaters lay the battleground of Kentucky and western Pennsylvania. Beginning in 1777, Shawnees, Delawares, and their Indian allies struck with such ferocity that "the year of three sevens" became synonymous with loss

and bloodshed in white folklore of the region. Scores, perhaps hundreds, of settlers died over the next five years. Twice Boonesborough was besieged. In 1778, George Rogers Clark with 175 men descended the Ohio and with help from French in the area took the three major British outposts in the Illinois country—Kaskaskia, Cahokia, and Vincennes. At the last of these, he captured the British western commander, Major Henry Hamilton. His audacious campaign, a tonic to colonials, eased the pressure on the upper Ohio. But within a year Clark had withdrawn, and Shawnees and Delawares lashed out with new energy. Colonials in turn swept north of the Ohio, destroying villages and food. These exchanges—bloody, destructive, but ultimately inconclusive—pushed the level of bitterness on both sides progressively higher.

The most striking result of this bloody conflict was the lack of a result. Little territory changed hands, and although white population west of the mountains had grown, Native American and British forces were, if anything, on the ascendant at the end of the war; one of their greatest victories, an ambush at Blue Licks, came in August 1782, nearly a year after the surrender of Cornwallis at Yorktown. So, on the face of it, the terms of the Treaty of Paris (1783) seem astonishing. Great Britain granted the new nation both its independence and an extraordinary western domain stretching in the north to the St. Lawrence and the Great Lakes, in the west to the Mississippi, and in the south to the thirty-first parallel. It was a great gulp of land. The addition of this territory, unwon and mostly unoccupied by colonials, was greater, as a percentage of territory actually controlled, than the expansion of the Louisiana Purchase.

British actions—military stalemate, then apparent generosity—seem a paradox but are easily resolved, for Great Britain in fact was acting out of self-interest. In the short term, London was giving up nothing. Given the new nation's pitiful military and limping economy, British soldiers, agents, and traders could stay in the region indefinitely, counseling the Indians and profiting from the fur trade. England was also guaranteeing its former colonies a host of troubles. The western country was filled with native peoples hostile to white settlement. And Spain, having reestablished itself in the lower Mississippi Valley, now claimed a band of land, roughly the southern half of modern-day Alabama and Mississippi, that the British supposedly were giving away. But what if the republican experiment survived? In the long term, an American nation with western resources and room to expand would depend less on French support and protection. By isolating the Americans from England's two prime rivals, Spain and France, Great Britain was playing a game—that of balance of power—at which it had no peers.

England's bet-hedging strategy was a fitting coda for this first era of the trans-Appalachian frontier. As it showed, this and later frontiers were unusually subject to the swings in diplomatic fortune among distant powers. Great nations were drawn to the country's resources, but their grip on the land was tenuous. In barely twenty years, three nations had passed title of the region among themselves—four if Spain's bid for the south is counted. This, with the changing allegiances among the many Indian groups and these competing nations, made for kaleidoscopic patterns of power and an extraordinary instability.

A Long Reach Westward

During the second period, from 1783 to 1812, one of these powers, the emergent United States, asserted its political control over the country beyond the mountains. Saying this, however, conceals as much as it describes. Behind this apparent grasp, which did not come unresisted, were changes of dazzling complexity. The government itself and its institutions were modified in the process of taking control. Westering emigrants adapted to demands and opportunities of the new country even as they brought their own changes. The many peoples already in trans-Appalachia influenced and were influenced by the newcomers, and all felt the effects of powerful outside economic forces.

Looking westward, the government of the nascent United States first had to unsnarl the conflicting claims of several colonies to country beyond the mountains. By 1786, Virginia, Connecticut, and Massachusetts had surrendered to the national government all claims north of the Ohio River and west of Pennsylvania. This Northwest Territory, or Old Northwest, was the first land over which the central government had exclusive jurisdiction. There, consequently, the frontier first shaped and expanded the government's power.

The national legislature now passed the two most important laws in the history of westward expansion. The Ordinance of 1785 ordered the Northwest Territory surveyed into sections (one mile square, or 640 acres), which were to be grouped into townships (six miles square, or thirty-six sections). Surveyed land was to be auctioned—part in sections, part in townships—in several eastern cities; the minimum price would be a dollar an acre. Next the Ordinance of 1787, or Northwest Ordinance, set out a plan of government for the territory that legislators assumed (incorrectly) would soon be sold and settled. The region would eventually be organized into three to five territories, which would mature into states by a metamorphosis of three stages. In the first, a new territory would be ruled by a governor, his secretary, and three judges, all appointed by the national government. Once five thousand free males had arrived, a legislature would be elected, though the governor could veto its actions. Finally, when sixty thousand settlers were counted, the territory could petition for statehood and, when admitted, enjoy the same rights and powers as its counterparts in the Republic. To establish a social and political order, the ordinance extended English common law into the Northwest Territory, guaranteed freedom of religion and other civil rights, forbade slavery, and set aside one section in each township to support public schools.

Although modified slightly over the decades, both laws were eventually extended to most of the Republic, first to the gulf coastal frontier and then to lands beyond the Mississippi. The ordinances determined the political form the growing nation would take. In principle, the first central government could have created a colonial system, with the original thirteen states as the parent country and the western settlements as perpetual children, but the Northwest Ordinance provided that the expanding nation would be one of sovereign states with equal rights. The three-stage evolution specified by the 1787 ordinance set the framework for the early political life in thirty-one of the thirty-five states west of the Appalachians.

The Ordinance of 1785 had a heritage at least as enduring as that of the Northwest Ordinance. In 1786, government surveyors laid out a baseline westward from the precise point where the Ohio River left the State of Pennsylvania. From there, they laid off the first townships and sections, then built more onto those, range after range, throughout the Old Northwest and eventually in virtually all the region southward to the Gulf of Mexico and westward to the Pacific. That first square inch of the first surveyor's stake was a kind of polestar of national development, the anchored point of reckoning for more than a billion acres. Nowhere else in the world would an area of such size be laid out in a uniform land system.

The survey's rigid predictability was meant to avoid the hopeless tangle of claims and boundaries found in the early land system of Kentucky and Tennessee. But there was far more to the ordinance than that. Adapted from the survey system used in southern New England, this vision of a gargantuan national grid also expressed that passion for reason and symmetry typical of the enlightenment mentality of the founding fathers, particularly Thomas Jefferson. And behind this dream of reason were assumptions of breathtaking audacity.

The system, first, presumed its own growth. With each range serving as the base for the next, the grid was an infinitely reproducible pattern, the perfect machine for national expansion. But the assumptions went deeper, to the very nature of the expanding society. "The art of civilization is the act of drawing lines," Oliver Wendell Holmes wrote later. He might have been referring to this ordinance, for the way the land was plotted profoundly influenced how new settlers thought of it, treated it, and lived on it. The system allowed a simple exchange of parcels of land. Squares, after all, are easily divided and combined: here was the ideal geometry for wheeling and dealing. This encouraged impulses already abroad in the new nation—a restless mobility, a search for profit through transforming a place and moving on, a tendency to see land as a commodity. The arrangement virtually dictated particular styles of farming, most obviously the devotion of one rectangle of soil to one crop, the next to another, with each plowed into straight lines among straight fences beside straight roads.

The Ordinances of 1785 and 1787 were in some ways terribly flawed. In one sense, the grid system was an illusion, one that presumed to impose a sameness on a magnificently diverse landscape. Surveyors would plot out the same legal checkerboard on mountains, canyons, prairies, pine barrens, gullies, deltas, plains, hummocks, and bogs. The rigidly linear brand of agriculture dictated by the survey was woefully unsuited to some regions, including much of the Far West. The result would contribute to later environmental calamities. The ordinances were also at odds with themselves. The provisions for representative government, education, and civil liberties spoke to the farmers of modest means who were close to Jefferson's heart. The land was surveyed not into huge tracts but into parcels that could be easily subdivided; this too seemed to presume a society of yeoman freeholders. Yet other terms clearly favored wealthy speculators. At auctions, to be held not on the frontier fringe but in eastern cities, the smallest unit offered was a section, far more than a family could use, and its minimum price of $640 was several times the annual income of a typical rural household. Besides simply trying to raise money quickly, politicians were recognizing those two groups—monied interests and common squatters and farmers—whose energies had first pushed the frontier over the Appalachians. Playing to both sets of interests, this first western policy was bound to be disharmonious.

In an even more obvious conflict, the government set down a plan of settlement for land that was already occupied. To be sure, the tens of thousands of Indians in the Northwest Territory were not ignored by the government. Its promise to the natives was unambiguous: "The utmost good faith shall always be observed towards the Indians; their lands and property shall never be taken from them without their consent; and, in their property, rights, and liberty, they shall never be invaded or disturbed, unless in just and lawful wars authorized by Congress; but laws founded in justice and humanity, shall from time to time be made for preventing wrongs being done to them, and for preserving peace and friendship with them." But what was the context of this pledge? These words composed the third article of the Northwest Ordinance. We shall protect the Indians and their ancestral lands, the government promised, and we shall lay out the means, step by step, for that land to be sliced up, sold, cleared by the ax and broken to the plow, then layered over by English common law, parliamentary republicanism, and traditions carried by white families and the common school. A policy that could make such promises, all within the same pair of documents, had moved beyond contradiction to schizophrenia.

Not surprisingly, these muddled intentions led to policies that were often at war with themselves, as seen when the new government began to dispose of its land. During the mid-1780s, speculators once more scrambled to control enormous tracts of western lands. They were eagerly received by state and national governments starved for income and groaning under huge debts. In 1787, the national government sold five million acres in southern Ohio to the Ohio Company of Associates, which in turn sold three and a half million acres to the Scioto Company, a group with several members of Congress among its principals. The terms—including discounts for swampland and payment by inflated certificates of indebtedness—came to barely nine cents an acre. Virginia interests purchased veterans' land warrants, which they used to claim great stretches of Kentucky. By 1792, New York had dispensed more than five million of its western acres at prices that averaged under twenty cents an acre. Surely the most outrageous transaction, and probably the most infamous land steal in the nation's history, came in 1795, when a thoroughly bribed Georgia legislature sold more than thirty-five million acres reaching to the Mississippi for half a million dollars, or just over a penny per acre. Georgia soon repudiated the "Yazoo fraud," which the acid-tongued Virginian John Randolph later called a "many-headed dog of Hell," but the U.S. Supreme Court eventually upheld the contract.

These land deals inevitably raised the ire of settlers, a constituency that, if not as powerful as wealthy speculators, was certainly more numerous. Some emigrants, to be sure, were settling land in hopes of selling for a profit when the country filled up; "squatters" and "speculators" sometimes differed only in degree of ambition. That said, the settlers' hostility toward speculators was both genuine and justified. The frenzied dealing naturally drove up the price of land. Many speculators, furthermore, simply held on to their grants, waiting for their value to rise, and thereby closed millions of acres to settlement. Some, like William Blount, the future territorial governor of Tennessee, engaged in outrageous chicaneries. The investors' complex dance—the trades within trades, the dubious transactions, and the outright frauds—muddled titles for generations to come.

Soon after the end of the war, Kentuckians were petitioning Congress, saying they would never be "Slaves to those Engrossers of land" who lived "at ease in the internal parts of Virginia." Some threatened to head down the Mississippi to take up land among the Spanish. Others asked to settle north of the Ohio. Those courses obviously would complicate the government's already troubled diplomacy. Some politicians nonetheless sympathized with families chafing to move into Ohio. When families went there on their own, a congressman later asked his fellows, would Congress "then raise a force to drive them off"? The answer was yes. In fact, troops were patrolling the northern bank of the Ohio as early as 1785, confiscating arms, expelling squatters, and burning their houses.

Pulled between conflicting interests, the government revised the system of land sales. A new law in 1796 opened land offices in Pittsburgh and Cincinnati, thus appealing to settlers, but then raised the minimum price at auction from one to two dollars an acre. With the Harrison Land Act of 1800, however, Congress dramatically shifted its favors. Henceforth settlers could buy land in parcels as small as 320 acres, a size more practical for the typical family. More important, land now was sold on credit; after a down payment of a fourth of the price, purchasers had four years to pay the rest.

The government's pirouette—first nodding one way, then bowing another—suggested the varied economic interests that fueled westward growth. The performance also anticipated the shifting, often contradictory policies that would become familiar as the frontier pushed farther west.

As it tried to appease its constituents, the new government also faced a collection of powerful adversaries across the Appalachians, not only a few dozen Indian groups but also two of the world's great colonial powers, England and Spain. All were determined to push back, or at least retard, the Republic's expanding frontier settlements.

Despite the deep hostility at the end of the revolutionary war, fighting among whites and Indians receded after 1783. Both sides were ready for a rest, and some Indians argued for an accommodation and a search for a middle ground. But the Treaties of Fort Stanwix (with the Iroquois in 1784), Fort McIntosh (with the Wyandots, Delawares, Ottowas, and Chippewas in 1785), and Fort Finney (with the Shawnees in 1786) proved ineffectual. The Indians received nothing for ostensibly surrendering part of western New York and western Pennsylvania and most of what is today Ohio, the fallacious reasoning being that as losers in the recent war, they were merely turning over its spoils. Besides, many Indian groups who lived or hunted in the surrendered regions were not even present at the negotiations. Meanwhile thousands of emigrants were descending the Ohio, and squatters were crossing the river to build on its northern shore. Several towns sprouted along the river in the Ohio country, most of them connected to land speculation schemes; by 1790 Marietta, the first, had been followed by Cincinnati, Steubenville, Gallipolis, Waterford, and a few others.

The uneasy peace was rapidly unraveling by 1786. English agents, still operating in posts they had promised to cede to the new nation, now provided substantial nonmilitary support to natives in the region and worked to fashion a confederation of the more than thirty Indian groups in the Ohio Valley and Great Lakes region. For several years Indians acted with a remarkable degree of unity in their dealings with the new American government, and at one point English officials suggested the formation of an Indian state in the Northwest. Buoyed by encouragement from London, native leaders were increasingly impatient with government policies. Led by the Miami chief Little Turtle, some were soon lashing out at farmsteads in northern Kentucky. "Scarcely a week has passed without some person being murdered," wrote a militia leader. These attacks were followed by retaliatory raids into the Illinois country and against the Shawnees, who so far had been mostly peaceful. By 1789, when the American government tried to pay for the surrender of the upper Ohio in the Treaty of Fort Harmar, events had raised the Indians' alarm past reconciliation. Arthur St. Clair, appointed governor of the Northwest Territory in 1788, summed up the situation with wry understatement. The natives found white intentions so clear and dreadful that there was "little probability of . . .

General Anthony Wayne led his troops in a charge against Indian opponents in the Battle of Fallen Timbers, 1794. After fighting just 40 minutes, Wayne reversed a string of recent American military defeats and gained concessions to vast areas of land north of the Ohio River, land that soon opened to white American settlement.

Frederick Kemmelmeyer (active 1788–1803). General Wayne Obtains a Complete Victory over the Miami Indians. Oil on canvas, ca. 1794. Courtesy, Winterthur Museum, Winterthur, Delaware.

cordiality." He added, "The idea of being ultimately obliged to abandon their country rankles in their minds."

Faced with the consequences of these ineffectual, conflicted policies, President George Washington authorized in 1790 a punitive expedition against "certain banditti of Indians from the northwest side of the Ohio." But after General Josiah Harmar's command razed a few towns and destroyed corn crops, a contingent of his troops was ambushed and badly mauled by Little Turtle's warriors. Washington then ordered Governor St. Clair himself, a revolutionary veteran who had served at Valley Forge, into Ohio. In November 1791, Little Turtle, leading a coalition of several groups, sprang a second trap, this time on St. Clair's poorly trained, ill-disciplined soldiers and their accompanying families, camp followers, and rum sellers. Caught at dawn in an open area against the Wabash River, the expedition was raked for hours by gunfire and attacked by Indians "so thick we could do nothing with them," a combatant wrote later. Of the 1,400 troopers, 630 were killed. Also lost were twelve hundred muskets and eight cannons (including two taken from Cornwallis at Yorktown). In some ways, it remains the worst defeat in the nation's military history.

After Indian leaders turned aside renewed efforts at another settlement, this one on far more favorable terms, Washington reached once again for a military solution. This time General Anthony Wayne, a seasoned commander, led a well-prepared expedition methodically northward toward Fort Miamis, recently built by the English on U.S. soil near the western end of Lake Erie. Four miles from there, on 20 August 1794, Wayne soundly defeated a force of about eight hundred Indians of the confederation on a storm-littered field called Fallen Timbers.

Paradoxically, this combination of dismal failures and a single success made a point that an initial victory would not have. The Republic's armies might often be guilty of tactical blundering and carelessness, but behind this pitiful floundering were, compared with what the Indians could muster, massive resources and, more important, the willingness to commit them in a war of attrition. Driving the point deeper was another realization by the Indians. At Fallen Timbers, the confused and panicked warriors had bolted toward Fort Miamis, calling for sanctuary as they approached its walls. But the fort's commander, unwilling to risk a crisis with the United States, had barred the gates. The Indians were devastated, and for good reason. Only a power like Britain had resources to match those of the United States. The natives, however, could never depend on such help, because Britain's stance toward the Indians was only one of dozens of factors in that nation's complex, ever-changing foreign policy. The barred gates of Fort Miamis showed the natives that their fate was ultimately subject to the veer and sway of European interests.

And those interests were changing rapidly indeed. In 1783, both England and Spain had given high priority to opposing the expansion of the frontier. The former wished to keep the profits flowing from the region's fur trade; more than half the pelts processed at the great market of Montreal came from the forests of the new nation. Spain feared American expansion would ultimately threaten Spanish Florida and Louisiana. Although neither nation gave outright military aid to its Indian allies, both provided moral support and gifts and encouraged natives to form a united front against Anglo-American expansion. In bald violation of treaty terms, English agents remained in six posts and several Indian towns around the Great Lakes and Ohio Valley. The Spanish funneled up to fifty thousand dollars in goods annually to the Creeks and in 1793 built an Indian post, aptly named Fort Confederation, on the Tombigbee River. Spain took further advantage of its control of the lower Mississippi, heavily taxing foreign commerce and periodically banning American traffic from the river that was the pioneers' only practical avenue for exporting goods. At the same time the Spanish—hoping, like the Romans, to assimilate the barbarians—offered full access to the river and generous land grants to westerners who would emigrate to Spanish territory in present-day Missouri.

For a while the English and Spanish had reasons for confidence. While the coalition of northern Indians stung the pioneer settlements and their militia forces, the southern groups held firm against further cessions. Discontented westerners seemed to flirt with the Spanish; at one point the district around Nashville was named Miro after the governor of lower Louisiana. Yet in 1795 both England and Spain conceded virtually everything the United States wanted. In Jay's Treaty, Britain agreed to remove all agents and soldiers from U.S. soil in exchange for concessions on certain maritime issues. Spain's capitulation was even more complete. The treaty of San Lorenzo (or Pinckney's Treaty) set the boundary with Florida at the thirty-first parallel, as provided in the Treaty of Paris, and guaranteed U.S. citizens the use both of the Mississippi and of New Orleans as a site to unload and reship their goods.

Why? England's and Spain's acquiescence, like the story of the Treaty of Paris, demonstrated how distant developments could have profound effects on the American frontier. Events between 1789 and 1795—the French Revolution, the onset of continental wars, and the surprising successes of the French—forced European governments to reevaluate their diplomatic postures. England, now almost wholly without allies, had to anticipate a lengthy conflict with France; Spain prudently looked toward an alliance with the French and, with that, war with England. Neither nation could afford the possibility, however remote, of serious troubles with the United States, and Spain in particular feared that England and the United States might unite to seize Florida and its Caribbean holdings. England and Spain both saw the sense of settling squabbles in a part of the world that was now on the periphery of their main concerns. Once more, an unsettled Europe had worked to the new nation's advantage.

But behind England's and Spain's abandonment of the Indians, and behind the Indians' retreat, was a more fundamental force. The population of the United States stood at more than four million, or nearly fifty times that of the Indians and Europeans to the west. Most citizens of the Republic would never see beyond the Appalachians, but as their sense of nationhood took vague shape, many of them thought of the western country as vital to the Republic's security and future possibilities. A "wall of public opinion" supported white U.S. settlement across the mountains, as a Spanish official put it. The new government, whatever its contradictions and clumsy use of power, would ultimately respond to that popular notion, as well as to the economic concerns of powerful interests.

More immediately, the number who *were* moving westward, though only a tiny portion of the larger society, far outweighed their opponents. The annual white emigration to just one part of the frontier, western New York and Pennsylvania, was at least ten times the number of warriors who fought at Fallen Timbers. During 1788, the average number of people floating on flatboats down the Ohio *each month* was greater than the entire population of the Shawnees; the total for the year nearly equaled the population of the largest southern group, the Cherokees.

Emigration to the frontier was a great weight leaning westward. Standing against that weight was a collection of interests of varying strengths and in unstable combination. They had in common a determination to hold the frontier where it was. But that coalition was vulnerable to events, whether a defeat in the field or upheavals on another continent. The westward-leaning weight, by contrast, continued to build despite military embarrassments, economic sanctions, and diplomatic opposition. Eventually the opposing coalition was bound to crack, and when it did, the force of population would fill any openings and wedge them wider.

Politicians later waxed eloquent on how a superior society, blessed by God and made strong by republican virtue, inevitably triumphed over lesser peoples in its westward march. But if this triumph was inevitable, numbers were the most obvious explanation. On this frontier, as on later ones, demography was destiny.

Land Pikes and Cotton Gins, Libraries and Taxes

The growing wave of settlers from the East, more than military engagements and diplomatic maneuvering, explains how the United States secured control of trans-Appalachia. This emigration in part told of the public's increasing infatuation with the

HERITAGE:

Encounters in the West

◆

No other aspect of the West's complex cultural heritage fascinated European and American artists during the mid-nineteenth century as much as the region's many Indian cultures. Though each artist ventured west with his own interests in mind, most depicted native peoples with a mixture of anthropological curiosity, romantic awe, and a firm conviction that Indian cultures would disappear with an increased American presence in the region.

Fearful that the western Indian cultures he observed in the 1830s would soon disappear, George Catlin placed himself squarely in the forefront of the effort to preserve a record of Indian life with his prodigious output of paintings, prints, and books documenting Native American cultures.

George Catlin (1796–1872). Catlin Painting the Portrait of Máh-to-tóh-pa—Mandan. *Oil on composition board, 1857–69. Paul Mellon Collection. National Gallery of Art, Washington, D.C.*

Karl Bodmer's detailed and lucid watercolors of Indian life on the upper Missouri reflect the widespread international interest in the West's native peoples. A Swiss-born artist who studied in Paris, Bodmer came to America in the employ of the Prussian prince Maximilian zu Wied, an ardent explorer and amateur naturalist. Many of his paintings, such as this portrait of a distinguished Minnetaree leader, were later engraved for an international audience. Bodmer combined ethnographic detail with a romantic admiration for native life.

Karl Bodmer (1809–93). Péhriska-Rúhpa, Hidatsa Man. *Watercolor on paper, 1833. Gift of the Enron Art Foundation. Joslyn Art Museum, Omaha, Nebraska.*

St. Louis–based artist Charles Deas was praised for his attention to frontier subjects and the "essentially American" themes that would attract interest from a European audience. Perhaps his most successful painting, this small narrative picture depicts a group of Sioux Indians as they pause in flight from intertribal warfare. The detailed renderings of material objects suggest the artist's general familiarity with Sioux life, though the scene is clearly one he never observed.

Charles Deas (1818–67). A Group of Sioux. Oil on canvas, 1845. Amon Carter Museum, Fort Worth, Texas.

The tragic but inevitable demise of Native American cultures became an increasingly popular theme in American art of the second half of the 19th century. In this allegorical painting, John Mix Stanley depicted representative figures from both eastern and western tribes at the westernmost edge of the continent as the sun—and by implication their cultures—disappeared over the horizon.

John Mix Stanley (1814–72). Last of Their Race. *Oil on canvas, 1857. Buffalo Bill Historical Center, Cody, Wyoming.*

Daniel Boone's efforts
to settle Kentucky
were first outlined by
John Filson in 1784.
The artist George
Caleb Bingham ap-
pealed to popular
mid-19th-century
thinking about Boone
by depicting the fron-
tier hero as a latter-
day Moses, leading
his people through
darkness into the
promised land.

George Caleb Bingham
(1811–79). Daniel Boone
Escorting Settlers through
the Cumberland Gap. *Oil
on canvas, 1851–52. Gift
of Nathaniel Phillips, Boston, 1890. Washington
University Gallery of Art,
St. Louis, Missouri.*

West. When Benjamin Franklin disembarked in France to seek aid during the American Revolution, he wore the fur cap that Europeans associated with backcountry pioneers. With characteristic insight, Franklin caught an essential truth—that on that continent and his own, the emerging nation's identity was inextricably bound to the imagined possibilities of its hinterland. Prominent frontier figures were already suffering the fate of many to come, transmogrified from flesh and bone into mythic creatures. In John Filson's *The Discovery, Settlement, and Present State of Kentucke* (1784), Daniel Boone's wilderness ordeals change him from a mere hunter into a kind of Moses who embodies a people reborn by their occupation of the new land. His passage and theirs is as much spiritual as physical. This vision, expressed in songs and fireside stories and jokes, set more and more Americans in motion. From Connecticut, an observer wrote of social gatherings where young people "marched to rude melodies which taught them to dream that toward the setting sun lay an earthly paradise with gates open to welcome them. From hill and valley the processions hurried away."

Emigrants moved across the mountains in broad, parallel streams—northeast to northwest, southeast to southwest—so that the Ohio Valley was dominated by settlers from New England, New York, and Pennsylvania, while Kentucky, Tennessee, and the Gulf frontier filled with Virginians, Carolinians, and Georgians. This settlement, however, was never an unbroken, steadily advancing line. Settlers spilled from western Pennsylvania and the Carolinas into the next closest regions—Kentucky, Tennessee, and southern Ohio. But others moved up the Tombigbee into south-central Alabama, down the Tennessee to its great bend, and into the Mississippi delta around Natchez, forming islands of Anglo-American population hundreds of miles from the closest settlement to the east.

By the turn of the century this emigrant society was supporting itself with a surprisingly diverse economic system. The majority of newcomers were farmers, mostly of the "backwoods" sort who would become, in the popular mind at least, the essential frontier common folk. Their lifeways, evolved in the woodlands east of the mountains, were well tested in this new setting.

They first faced the overwhelming fact of trees. "O the woods! the interminable woods!" wrote a visitor to Kentucky in the 1830s. Farmers opened a few acres in this thick forest by girdling or felling the largest trees. Trunks and brush then were burned to clear ground for planting and to enrich the soil with ash. Among the green stumps, families planted corn, which produced four times the food value of wheat with a tenth of the seed. Farmers often intercropped, usually with beans and squash, with the vines of the former climbing the corn stalks and the latter spreading over the soil to choke out weeds. Pioneers grated green corn to make pudding they flavored with berries and grasshoppers; they ate the culms, the soft inner lining of the stalks, like asparagus; they ground some kernels into meal for bread and unleavened johnnycake and boiled and pounded others for hominy; they washed it all down with whiskey distilled from fermented seed. In their gardens they grew potatoes, pumpkins, peas, gourds, and tobacco, and from the surrounding woods they gathered pecans, walnuts, papaws, sassafras, and medicinal herbs and roots. Backwoodsmen fished the streams and preyed on deer, bears, raccoons, squirrels, and opossums. A family kept some chickens, a dog or two, and perhaps a cow for milk, but most valuable were pigs, which roamed the forest on their own, flourishing on roots and acorns. Lean and rangy (some called them "land pikes"), a woodland porker was a walking, grunting smorgasbord. Besides hams, chops, and bacon, families ate the ribs, intestines, lungs, and brains. They made head meat into pies. These essential animals became folkloric figures; it was said they could jump through fences by turning sideways in midair and swim heroically through floods to roost safely in trees. For shelter a family usually began with a lean-to, then turned to the simple, utilitarian log house that visitors found emblematic of the backwoods frontier, then expanded that into a dogtrot (or saddlebag) house, with two rooms separated by a covered breezeway. Around the farmstead they built a sapling or split-rail fence in either the straight "post-and-rider" or, more likely, the zigzag "snake" or "worm" style.

The earliest arrivals practiced extensive and subsistence farming. They exploited the land vigorously for a maximum yield, then moved on to begin anew after a few years when that yield began to decline. And they were almost wholly self-supporting, concentrating on diverse production of things immediately usable. A surplus meant not gain but wasted effort. If the family could not eat it, wear it, drink it, or smoke it, what was the point? A second agrarian wave, overlapping the first, hoped to stay longer on the land. They too began by planting corn among the stumps of felled trees, but soon they began plowing, first around the stumps but eventually in fields cleared of the rotting remains. (Their familiar labors became political metaphors—"log rolling" for cooperation and "plowing the green stump" for avoiding a stubborn problem.) A signal of this intensive agriculture was the appearance of wheat in cleared fields whose potential was conserved by rotating crops and fertilizing with manures. These farmers looked outward, hoping to sell their products at local and distant markets. In one sense this trade was nothing new. As early as 1746, the French on the Wabash and Illinois rivers had sent flour to New Orleans, and by the late 1770s, farmers of western Pennsylvania marketed wheat as far away as the West Indies. By 1811 this trade had grown many times over. Cargoes floating past Louisville included about two hundred thousand barrels of flour, eighty thousand bushels of corn, sixteen thousand barrels of whiskey, twenty-two thousand barrels of pork, and a million pounds of bacon.

On the southern frontier, the most important commercial crop by far was cotton. The gulf coastal plain between Georgia and eastern Texas, with its long, humid summers and its bottomlands of rich, black soil, was the largest region on earth in which short-staple cotton could be grown. After the invention in 1793 of the cotton gin—with its mechanical combs easily removing seeds previously taken out laboriously by hand—cotton suddenly could be produced cheaply and sold dear. A gin was operating in Natchez only two years after Eli Whitney had built his first model. During the following twenty years, production expanded substantially around Natchez, along the lower Tombigbee River, and near the "great bend" of the Tennessee River. In one way, Natchez was at the forefront of the cotton culture; between 1805 and 1810, a local landholder experimented with a newly imported type of cotton, "Mexican upland," to develop the primary strand that would be used throughout the inland South. This cultivation brought its distinctive labor system. Slavery was well entrenched in the Mississippi delta by 1800, and by 1810, slaves were working extensive fields in the Tennessee Valley and the northern Mississippi Territory.

This frontier—and these frontiersmen—were unlike any others that had come across the Appalachians. Dedicated to commercial farming, these settlers were establishing a system of large-scale staple agriculture at the outset, with no preliminaries or transition. Many were planters of means who brought capital, equipment, and slaves. They lived with huge investments and onerous debts and succeeded or failed by shifts among complex markets and by the distant decisions of investors.

Their appearance, in turn, taught something about the dynamics of expansion. Trans-Appalachia by now was part of an expanding capitalist economy emanating from Europe and commercial centers of the Atlantic Coast. The value of this land depended on its potential, and that potential, in a world of growing markets and technological wizardry, expanded or shrank with events hundreds or thousands of miles away—in this case, when Whitney made a prototype of a cotton gin in the guest room of a Georgia plantation house. Land is, in a sense, what people see in it, and so this country, before a single tree was cut or an acre plowed, had become another place, one instantly desirable to squatters and wealthy eastern landholders alike. In the history of westward expansion, there would be no better example of how the accidents of an international economy could profoundly affect the far fringe of the frontier.

Another commercial enterprise—cattle raising—also flourished in the Old Southwest. By the early eighteenth century, Spanish colonials were raising cattle in substantial numbers on the sea islands off the Alabama coast, and after 1750, visitors reported many thousands of grazing animals on the prairies northwest of New Orleans, along the

The popular mythology of the lone frontiersman long obscured the actual importance of families in frontier settlement. After the Civil War, as an eastern interest in domestic culture spread westward, popular prints such as this one reimagined families as central to the frontier experience.

After Frances Flora Palmer (1812–76). Published by Currier & Ives. The Pioneer's Home: On the Western Frontier. Lithograph, 1867. The Harry T. Peters Collection (#57.300.23), Museum of the City of New York.

Mississippi in the Natchez district, and in the valleys of the Perdido, Tombigbee, and Chickasawhay rivers to the east and north of Mobile. By the War of 1812, more land was devoted to cattle raising than to any other economic activity. Cattle were driven by herders on horseback to New Orleans, Mobile, and other ports, then shipped to the West Indies and to cities along the Atlantic coast. Profits were good. Even as the cotton economy boomed, delta planters would "yearly mark thousands of calves, and send them to the prairie to feed," a visitor wrote. As the historians John Guice and Thomas Clark have suggested, many estates in the Old Southwest could have been more accurately called ranches rather than plantations.

In frontier towns, yet another economic pattern could be found. Despite the popular image of trailblazing pioneer farmers opening new regions to settlement, towns typically preceded the agricultural frontier. Their economic patterns varied according to geography and historical circumstances. Some turned to manufacturing goods that could not be profitably imported over the primitive roads across the Appalachians. For this, Pittsburgh's location was ideal. Whatever was made in the town could be floated down the country's grandest distribution system, then marketed from towns along the Ohio and Mississippi rivers. By 1815, with a flourishing iron and glass industry, Pittsburgh was the region's largest urban center. Lexington turned locally grown hemp into cloth and rope worth half a million dollars a year by 1809. Cincinnati and Louisville sold Pittsburgh-made iron goods, light manufactures from the East, and sugar, cotton, and molasses carried from the lower Mississippi Valley by keelboat to the rapidly filling Ohio and Kentucky countryside. These towns also sent downriver the harvests from the developing farms, foodstuffs produced with farm implements made in the shops of local artisans. St. Louis and Natchez did much the same, and they profited as well by exporting the frontier's furs and cotton. New Orleans, at the opposite end of the water highway from Pittsburgh, reshipped goods from upriver to the outside world, sent local cotton both upstream and off to England, and supplied the gulf coastal frontier with imported necessaries.

For all their differences, all these towns exploited the frontier's dynamic changes—its vigorous migration and its evolving rural economy. They had a vibrance that visitors found exciting, if not always appealing. Walking the streets of St. Louis, one would see trappers, merchants, and slaves, planters and their families, boatmen and Indians, loafers and thieves. By 1815, Cincinnati residents could choose among the shops of thirty merchants. Below the bluffs of Natchez was the town's shadowy brother, Natchez-under-the-Hill, where rivermen and traders mixed with murderers, prostitutes, and mountebanks in gambling houses and whiskey holes as repulsive and dangerous as in any eastern city. The respectable town above supported several physicians, artisans in two dozen trades, and perhaps the ultimate sign of a maturing economy: eight lawyers.

These economic changes were part of a wave of influences washing westward over the mountains. The new patterns in turn mingled with ones already there, making this American frontier, like those to follow, a cultural swapping-ground as well as a land of conflict and conquest.

White pioneers carried a mix of traditions. Those that served their needs survived and spread so successfully that they were often seen, incorrectly, as unique creations of the frontier. Just whose traditions were most influential, however, is a matter of dispute. Grady McWhiney and Forrest McDonald have vigorously argued that Celtic lifeways took root and flourished, particularly on the southern frontier and in the Old Northwest closest to the Ohio River. These influences, they have written, explain the most distinctive differences that emerged between the developing South and the North, which drew its traditions from England's southeastern lowlands. Others have stressed the contributions to pioneer life of the Germans who settled in western Pennsylvania. More recently, Terry Jordan and Matti Kaups have written that another group—the Finns who emigrated from the wooded eastern part of their homeland to Pennsylvania's Delaware Valley in the mid-1600s—brought methods of farming, hunting, housing, and herding that others took westward into the vast central woodlands of trans-Appalachia.

Besides these broad influences stretching back across the Atlantic, much of the dominant national culture was being transplanted. "Higher" culture was most apparent in cities, which sat along the best lines of communication with the East and which had the money and population to support cultural institutions. Subscription libraries were established early, and the private book trade could be substantial; a shipment of thirty-five hundred books was auctioned in Natchez in 1808. Even communities of modest size boasted newspapers that offered news and, as the *Missouri Gazette* (St. Louis) advertised in 1808, "Belles Lettres [and] historical and Poetical extracts." Churches appeared early and in surprising numbers. Methodists in Pittsburgh established eight congregations during the decade after 1796, and Cincinnati residents could choose among six denominations by 1815. Protestants, especially Methodists, Presbyterians, and Baptists, dominated cities of the Ohio Valley, while Catholic churches were sprinkled along the Mississippi Valley, with its French and Spanish heritage. Private schools typically were operating within a few years of the founding of a town. Nor was higher education wholly ignored. Lexington's Transylvania Seminary, founded in 1785, had evolved by 1799 into a university that soon had schools of liberal arts, law, and medicine.

Outside the towns, most settlers had only a casual acquaintance with the written word; "all were illiterate," one frontiersman recalled, "but in various degrees." But even this man's parents brought a small library that included the Bible, Benjamin Franklin's *Autobiography*, and John Bunyan's *Pilgrim's Progress*. Subscription, or "field," schools appeared quite early in many areas, although their terms and attendance were erratic and their quality decidedly mixed. Home schooling was probably at least as effective, especially north of the Ohio in country dominated by pioneers from New England.

In town and countryside, immigrants also brought the attitudes, values, and traditions that constituted the new nation's varied "folk culture." In this, the role of the family was paramount. A common popular impression portrays the archetypal frontiersman as a lone woodsman who savored his isolation. This image could not be more wrong. The need for labor and protection, not to mention companionship, made a family deeply desirable. Families, in fact, were more common on the frontier than in the East. Bachelors and widowers were rarely single for long. Women living on their own were almost unheard of; a recent study found only twenty among a sample of fifty thousand persons on the trans-Appalachian frontier between 1800 and 1840. In the entire region, one demographer estimates, only about two-fifths of 1 percent of the population lived alone and planned to stay that way. Like everywhere else in the nation, the frontier was dominated by nuclear families, but these often clustered near their kin, forming communities of geographically dispersed but closely related households. Families were like cells encoded with instructions for the cultural outlines of the societies into which they would grow. Through them were carried religious and ethical beliefs, standards of behavior, concepts of the proper nature of community and the respective roles of women and men, humor, songs, superstitions, games, and much more.

Local governments also nurtured transplanted ways of life. The first county courts protected and extended the new economic system, recording land titles and imposing harsh penalties for crimes against property; a Tennessee horse thief was pilloried, whipped, and branded and had both his ears cut off. Courts conscripted labor to build public roads that would encourage emigration, the growth of market economies, and cultural connections to the world beyond. An evolving tax system fed this implanting of institutions. In the earliest stage of development, taxes were levied on the raw stuff of settlement—free men, slaves, horses, and cattle. As the labor of men and beasts gave monetary value to the land, taxes came from real estate and licenses for some commerce, taverns especially. This income in turn paid for the expanding government services of a society tightening its grip on the land—judges and courts, care of orphans and paupers, bounties for wolves. Weightier civil and criminal matters were heard in courts of common pleas, quarter-session courts, and the territorial supreme courts, but most people encountered the court system, if at all, through a justice of the peace. This official heard some criminal cases but mostly domestic squalls and squabbles between neighbors. Sessions, which were usually a good show, became social as well as legal occasions. A justice's style was informal and his solutions based more on custom than anything else. Through these courts were transplanted both law and those folk traditions and social mores summed up as "common sense."

In their outward appearances, these agents of authority had the frontier's raw look. Records tell of courts interrupted by nearby tavern noise and by pigs rooting under the floor. But from the lowest level to the highest, territorial governments were both bearers of traditions and powerful reinforcers of the economic and social institutions taking root in the country.

A Swapping Ground of Cultures

Yet this intruding culture did not overwhelm and replace all existing culture—far from it. The pioneers' folk and more formal culture was itself evolving, changed through adaptation to this new setting and shaped by the extraordinary mix of other peoples in the region.

By now this was an old story. For two centuries, Indians and Euro-Americans had been changing one another. Certainly nothing remotely like a pristine native culture had existed for generations. At French, English, and Spanish military and trading outposts and in Indian villages, visitors saw an amalgamation of customs and startling juxtapositions. An Englishman wrote one evening of a gala ball at a Shawnee settlement on the Maumee River, with white and Indian dancers sporting fur caps and ostrich feathers. Soon afterward he told of a warrior proudly displaying a Kentuckian's withered heart, "like a piece of dried venison."

Plumed dancers and body parts: the combination of cross-fertilization and conflict continued after the American Revolution. Nowhere was the phenomenon more apparent than in the region's evolving language, starting with new names on the map. All but two colonies on the Atlantic coast had names drawn from the Old World. But once beyond the mountains, the white invaders, having taken the land from the Indians, then named virtually all their new states after the natives they continued to fight. Many other words, following various paths, entered the American idiom from the frontier. Some came directly from European rivals—*alligator* and *dollar* from the Spanish and *coulee* from the French. Many came from Indians: *pecan* and *caucus,* for instance. Others arrived indirectly. *Bayou* was borrowed from the French, who had taken it from the Choctaw *bayuk.* Old words took on new meanings. Because the hide of an adult male deer brought one Spanish dollar, a dollar was called a *buck. Corn,* which in England meant any grain, applied in America only to Indian maize by the revolutionary era. Then west of the mountains, where corn was the family's mainstay, the word was joined to others to form, by one count, 151 new words and phrases.

The newer arrivals absorbed many influences from the older Euro-American settlements, particularly from French communities in the Illinois country and from the Spanish farther south. Euro-Americans of all backgrounds in turn borrowed heavily from the Native American cultures. Backwoods farmers had learned about girdling and intercropping from Indians on both sides of the Appalachians. Other techniques, like burning trees and brush to increase fertility, were native practices that confirmed and reinforced similar methods brought by settlers; most foods gathered and grown, as well as the family's medicinal plants, were adopted from Indian customs. At least in how they supported themselves—hunting and gathering, cutting and burning—early farmers and Indians were more similar than not.

Hundreds of Anglo-Americans—the "white Indians"—opted to live in native societies. To replenish populations devastated by warfare and disease, Indians captured and adopted white women and children. When later given the chance to leave, many of these refused, and if children were forcibly returned, Benjamin Franklin wrote a friend, they soon fled to the woods, "from whence there is no reclaiming them." Some "white Indians" rose to leadership among their adopted cultures. A Pennsylvanian, seized during a raid at the age of four, grew up to become Old White Chief, a prominent Iroquois. Others moved back and forth between cultures. Simon Girty was captured by Delawares at fourteen, and though he returned to white society a few years later, he spent the rest of his life along the cultural borderland. His raids against Kentucky settlements made him probably the most hated figure of the revolutionary frontier era. Later, while dabbling in land speculation, he advised Wyandot, Mingo, and Delaware leaders and helped command Indian warriors in their crushing defeat of Arthur St. Clair in 1791. In 1818, besotted and crippled by rheumatism, he died in Canada, having lived a life as ambivalent and conflicted as the frontier heritage itself.

The Indians in turn found much to borrow from the white newcomers. For generations they had been exchanging animal pelts for European goods. This fur trade sent a wave of European influence over the region—then on, well beyond the Mississippi—far in advance of the farming frontier. In the 1790s, as the first white towns were appearing on the banks of the Ohio, Indians on the upper Missouri River were trading with British and French agents for a variety of goods, including corduroy trousers and peppermint. Trade goods offered obvious advantages. A metal awl or fishhook was more durable than one made of bone. Factory-made blankets were lightweight and easily maintained. For women who heated water by throwing hot rocks into baskets of tightly woven fibers, an iron pot hung above a fire was a wonder. Apart from trade, colonial governments, particularly the French, gave huge amounts of gifts to keep various groups within their alliance. The result was an often dramatic change on the surface of Indian life—in weapons, in utensils, in playthings. As whites adopted some Indian garments, natives wore linsey-woolsey shirts and painted themselves with imported vermilion. From Europeans, the Indians also acquired horses. That, in turn, brought changes in warfare, hunting, and other areas of economic life. By the early eighteenth century, southern Indians on horseback were tending cattle—another animal immigrant—and Seminoles had become acknowledged masters at breeding and raising horses.

In so much of how they passed their days, Indians and whites were moving toward one another, creating what the historian Richard White has called "the middle ground" in which the various lifeways wove together into rich, complex patterns. Did these peoples approach each other at a deeper level? There are hints. Take, for instance, bear stories. Bears—large, graceful, powerful—walked prominently among Indian legends. Typically they embodied both the threat and the bounty of the natural world. They were asked ritually to give themselves to the hunters' spears, then were thanked afterward,

Bears figured prominently as creatures of semi-divine power in the folklore of both Indian and European-American inhabitants of the trans-Appalachian and Far West. Whether in an illustration for Davy Crockett's epic tales or in an Assiniboin Indian's sketch of a European hunter, the animals appeared in 19th-century illustrations as worthy antagonists for their human pursuers.

Unidentified artist. Perilous Adventure with a Black Bear. *Wood engraving, 1838. From* Davy Crockett's Almanack, of Wild Sports in the West, Life in the Backwoods. . . . *(Vol. 1, No 4), 1838, reproduced in Franklin J. Meine, ed.,* The Crockett Almanacks: Nashville Series, *1835–38 (1955).*

Unidentified Assiniboine artist. Man Shooting a Bear *(detail). Ink on paper, 1853. Reproduced from* Bureau of American Ethnology Forty-Sixth Annual Report, *1928–29 (1930).*

with the understanding that the animals sometimes would take people in their turn. Looking on these animals as semidivine, Indians also recognized a close affinity to bears, which were, after all, the woodland creatures most closely resembling humans. Natives told of women marrying bears and of children wandering into caves and slipping easily into bear families. The line between hunter and prey, like that between man and his natural setting, was ultimately indistinguishable. Backwoods settlers too concocted tales of all-powerful bears of mysterious properties; living in the Indians' world, these people embraced stories that spoke of the same view of life. The classic distillation of these tales was Thomas Bangs Thorpe's "The Big Bear of Arkansas" (1841), in which a seasoned hunter and rip-roarer tells of stalking a giant, elusive animal, first with anger, but then with identification ("I loved him like a brother"), and finally with awe. In the end, pushing ever deeper into the forest, he confronts the bear, which looms "like a black mist." He shoots it, and it dies. But, he concludes, the death came not truly from him, for this was "a creation bear . . . an *unhuntable bear*, [which] *died when his time come*."

So for all its bloody conflict, the frontier was also a place of accommodation and exchange, a zone of mutual influence among one of North America's richest mixes of peoples. Still, that "middle ground" was unstable and shifting. Behind those complex changes was a dynamic that worked again and again in favor of the new arrivals and against native cultures.

Initially, for instance, the Indians' interest in trade goods and gifts was conservative in intent; they wanted pots, blankets, spearpoints, and fishnets because those goods would allow them to live, more efficiently and with less effort, by a way of life that had served them well for generations. But inevitably, traditional skills fell into relative disuse, and natives came to rely on items that only Europeans could provide. Indians also felt a spiraling desire for some of the trade goods, especially alcohol. They then began hunting by a new, self-destructive strategy. To meet an escalating need for goods available only from white traders, Indians killed more and more of the very animals they would require to satisfy that need. Populations of game animals plummeted. The effect was felt first in the Ohio Valley; as early as the 1780s, an observer in Ohio estimated that a Delaware hunter typically killed between 50 and 150 deer each autumn. By 1800, areas as far west as Wisconsin and upper Michigan were severely depleted of white-tailed deer, elk, bear, and bison.

White settlers contributed even more to these ecological changes. Thousands of backwoods families stripped the trees from tens of thousands of acres. Others pulled up the stumps and pushed clearings outward into ever-larger cattle pastures and fields for cotton and commercial food crops. All remade the natural setting, disrupting game habitats and destroying the bounty of wild plants. Cotton cultivation often exhausted the fields. Lowlands became bogs that hosted thick clouds of mosquitoes; topsoil from higher ground washed into streams, killing fish and leaving the fields above scarred and brushy.

Thus Indians entered into a pernicious sequence. Trade initially made their lives easier, but time left them increasingly needful of white goods; yet season by season, Indians controlled less of the land and fewer of the animals essential to acquiring those goods and to supporting an independent existence. At the end of this progression—from advantage to reliance to dependence—the balance of power had shifted from native peoples to the whites. Native Americans saw where this process was taking them, and they responded. The result was another level of complexity in the story of cultural exchange. Whites and Indians developed some behaviors that a casual observer would find quite alike. But beneath the surface similarities, the cultural messages were dramatically different.

Nowhere was this more clearly shown than in two of the Indians' and pioneers' most notable activities—drinking and worshiping. Visitors often noted that alcoholic consumption on the frontier far outpaced that in the East. "When I was in Virginia, it was too much whiskey," a traveler noted. "In Tennessee it is too, too much whiskey!" The habit was especially pronounced among the South's Celtic frontier families, but accounts from all trans-Appalachia told of both sexes, and often children, downing draughts of whiskey and cider at all meals and social occasions. When a congregation drained two barrels of whiskey before ten o'clock one Sunday morning, a visitor wrote, "We could hear them firing, hooping and hollowing like Indians." The comparison was apt. By most accounts the natives too drank quickly, passionately, and in prodigious amounts, with spectacular and appalling results. Witnesses told of brawls and murders, of mass rapes, and of men rubbing burning logs on their heads.

Behind these common alcoholic enthusiasms, however, were different causes. White immigrants drank to relieve the tensions growing from the initial isolation and the heavy labors of pioneering. As for the Indians, there may have been some biological basis for their habits, but their drinking seems mainly a response to—and a cause of—their deteriorating position. In alcohol they found brief escape from dispossession and cultural disruption. Rampant drunkenness worsened problems of disease and sped the unraveling of social structures, which in turn gave Indians more reason to drink. It was a brutal cycle helped along by traders, who understood that the demand for alcohol, unlike that for awls or blankets, increased with the product's use. So frontier drunkenness among whites and natives told of different tensions. One habit expressed the trials of conquest, the other the despair and dependence of the conquered.

Backwoods settlers developed a distinctive style of religion as well. Sermons stressed a stark duality of good and evil and the sudden grace of salvation, when a God with strength beyond man's imagining would banish sin from a soul and, at the End Time, from a world rotten with corruption. This simple theology inspired an astounding emotionalism that found its fullest expression at camp meetings. As a sermon built, listeners would wail and weep and occasionally fall unconscious. Some got "the jerks," powerful convulsions that sent hats and bonnets flying. The evangelist Peter Cartwright claimed that five hundred persons were twitching crazily at one of his sermons. However else this religious style might be explained, it at least reflected lives of unrelenting stress and the dichotomous perspective from a cabin surrounded by a host of dangers.

During the same years new religions arose among the Indians. For all their differences, these religions shared certain traits. In fact, they seem to have been part of a far larger phenomenon, what Vittorio Lanternari called "religions of the oppressed," that appeared among native peoples in settings as varied as central Africa, Micronesia, and Latin America. These movements, typically led by a messiah figure, borrowed some Christian concepts from European conquerors; these concepts were then amended to fit natives' perspectives and needs. Besides stressing self-discipline and a rigorous moral code, cults typically demanded that members preserve precolonial skills and ways of life. Most found one Christian teaching particularly appealing: the Day of Judgment. If followers were firm in their faith and kept to the old ways, messiahs promised, a vengeful God would destroy or banish the colonial masters and restore His people to a golden age. Thus many movements became religions of liberation and cultural regeneration.

At least two such movements arose among Indians during the period studied here. The first, which helped inspire the Indian war of 1763, was led by a shadowy Delaware holy man named Neolin, who apparently demanded retention of traditional lifeways and promised divine protection in a crusade against the white invasion. The second movement, much better known, was associated with the most famous native leader of this era—Tecumseh, a Shawnee of diplomatic and oratorical brilliance who attempted to fashion a confederation of tribes north and south of the Ohio against further expansion of white settlement. But at least as important as Tecumseh was his brother. Known during his first thirty years as Lalawethika, this brother was a lazy blowhard; his name translated as "Noisemaker" or "The Rattle." One-eyed, alcoholic, and a poor hunter with no taste for fighting, he was utterly undistinguished until the spring of 1805, when he fell into a trance (or coma) and emerged from it to say that he had died and had been reborn to teach a new religion entrusted to him by the Master of Life. Its basic tenets were the unity of all Indians, preservation of traditional customs and means of living, rejection of virtually all Euro-American ways and technology, abstinence from alcohol, and monogamous marriages with only Indians. He insisted on a revival of some older rituals and the adoption of some new ones strikingly similar to the Catholic confession and rosary. If natives would follow His teachings, the Master of Life had promised, He would restore harmony to the world and "overturn the land." The prophet told his followers, "All the white people will be covered, and you alone shall inhabit the land." Now a divine messenger, Lalawethika called himself Tenskwatawa, or "The Open Door," from Christ's words, "I am the open door."

Indian and backwoods religions had much in common. All found comfort in Christian precepts and ceremonies; all embraced a chiliastic worldview in which the faithful triumphed through the intervention of a fearsome God. Behind the similarities was a fundamental difference, however. Backwoodsmen and Indians all were wrestling for control in a changing world, but whereas settlers were crying out for protection as those changes were accomplished, "The Open Door" desperately preached to reverse those same transformations. His was a theology of the last chance.

Flood Tide

During the third period of this American frontier, from 1812 to 1820, Tenskwatawa's deepest fears were confirmed. The United States solidified its military and political domination as the tide of white migration grew still greater and the market economy took tighter hold in towns, cotton country, and wheatlands. Ecological changes further eroded Indian independence.

The War of 1812 was a triumph for the expansionist forces in trans-Appalachia. This culminating conflict in fact had begun several months before the declaration of war. The movement for Indian resistance led by Tecumseh and Tenskwatawa, also called "The

Prophet," had gathered support after 1806. Incensed by the surrender of land through a series of treaties negotiated by Indiana's territorial governor, William Henry Harrison, Tecumseh devised a complex and precarious strategy. He would use the appeal of his brother's mystical, apocalyptic vision to fashion a practical policy for the here and now. The Shawnee leader knew the odds against successful military resistance. His main weapon instead would be an inclusive agreement among all Indian groups against any further surrender of land. War might be necessary, but it had to be avoided at all costs until this common front was achieved. Tecumseh traveled through the Ohio Valley, the Great Lakes country, and the Old Southwest, urging conversion to the new religion and an alliance against the expanding white frontier. Younger warriors in particular responded to the movement, and the brothers' village of Prophetstown, on Tippecanoe Creek in western Indiana, grew to a few thousand persons by 1811.

But this reach toward Indian independence failed, partly from one rash action and partly from the frontier's snarl of power relationships and the vagaries of distant diplomacy. Many Indian leaders resisted a new order that would, after all, undercut their authority. Then, while Tecumseh was traveling among the southern tribes, Harrison led a militia force to Prophetstown. When Tenskwatawa broke his brother's cardinal instruction and ordered his followers to attack, Harrison's troops drove the Indians from the village. That day—7 November 1811—was perhaps the darkest for Indian interests in the history of the region. Tenskwatawa's powers, and so his religion, were discredited, and the premature fighting crippled Tecumseh's campaign for a Native American front. With the coming of the War of 1812, Tecumseh had little choice but to link Indian interests once more to the ultimately unreliable British forces. His followers fought in at least 150 engagements, but at the end of the conflict, the United States retained control of the entire region. The Indians' greatest disaster came in October 1813, when Tecumseh, protecting British troops withdrawing into Canada, was killed at the Battle of the Thames.

The most militarily formidable group in the South, the Creeks, was divided into two increasingly hostile factions, the Upper and the Lower Creeks. The former, adamantly opposed to any accommodation with white invaders, not surprisingly were also more receptive to overtures from Tecumseh and Tenskwatawa. Many young warriors, calling themselves Red Sticks, converted to the new gospel. As tension grew during the summer of 1813, Lower Creeks and whites from the Tombigbee settlements took refuge in Fort Mims, a stockade on the Alabama River. But this proved to be not a sanctuary but a slaughter pen. On 30 August, more than seven hundred Red Sticks stormed the fort and killed more than five hundred persons. Seven months later a retaliatory force, commanded by Andrew Jackson, trapped the main body of Upper Creeks in their village of Tohopeka, wrapped on three sides by the Horseshoe Bend of the Tallapoosa River. In a withering cross fire, more than eight hundred died, their retreat cut off by Jackson's Cherokee allies.

In barely five months, Indians hoping to resist white expansion saw their shrewdest leader die and their most effective military force annihilated. In the Treaty of Fort Jackson, the Creeks (both Upper and Lower) surrendered an enormous L-shaped parcel of more than twenty-two million acres that included part of western Georgia and much of present-day Alabama. After signing treaties with the demoralized Indians of the Northwest, the United States moved to build a series of military posts among them. And in the final and most famous battle of the war, Jackson's rout of the British at New Orleans assured western farmers and merchants control of their most vital artery, the Mississippi.

So ended the last hopes of Native Americans and other nations to block the absolute control of trans-Appalachia by the United States. Small wonder, then, that these events lifted to political eminence the men most associated with those episodes. Out of the western campaigns came two presidents, Jackson and Harrison, and a vice president, Richard Johnson, of Kentucky, who after claiming to have slain the greatest Indian of the era, ran for office with the following slogan: "Rumpsey Dumpsey,/Rumpsey Dumpsey,/Colonel Johnson killed Tecumsey."

After 1815, the forces of change that had emerged during the previous thirty years gathered an extraordinary momentum. The stream of white migration became a flood. Between 1810 and 1820, Tennessee grew by more than 160,000 persons; Ohio's population more than doubled, from 230,760 to 581,434. But the most impressive growth was in the next tier of territories, those combining accessibility with the best chances of good land. Indiana's population grew by 600 percent, Alabama's by 1,420 percent. Several factors inspired this "Great Migration." The war that ended resistance from Indians and Europeans also publicized the country's promise. Soldiers once more were paid with public land. The value of that land increased as national and international markets for its products grew. With Atlantic trade lanes reopened, the price of cotton doubled within several months of the last fighting.

The territories' passage to statehood was quickly accomplished. Between 1816 and 1819, a state was admitted each year (Indiana, Mississippi, Illinois, and Alabama). Except when four Far Western states joined the union in 1889, the union of states would never again expand at such a pace. The particulars of the new constitutions suggested regional differences and the continuing pull and tug among economic and social groups. Indiana's constitution reflected the interests of middling farmers on the rise; it prohibited slavery and allowed universal manhood suffrage, popular election of governors, and annual election of the lower house. Mississippi's gave the vote to virtually all white men, but like Kentucky's, it also firmly established black slavery and leaned toward larger landowners. The economic patterns north and south of the Ohio became even more deeply entrenched: north of the river were diversified farms and small market towns; to the south was a mixture of large-scale cotton plantations in the blacklands, smaller subsistence farms in the piney uplands, and commercial cattle and pig farming in both.

Throughout trans-Appalachia, residents engaged in one economic activity—land speculation—with a common, frenzied enthusiasm. Eastern investors bought up military bounties for a pittance in hopes of future profits. An unconfirmed report told of a half section in Indiana purchased for $17.50 and sold for $5,000. As usual, squatters complained that their land was being sold from under them after they had held it against foreign and native competitors, but just as usual, settlers of modest means were playing the speculative game on a smaller scale. By the thousands they bought land on credit, pouring all resources into the down payment on the bet that rising values would allow

them to sell off part to make installments or to dump it all for a handy profit. Sales at an Alabama land office increased from under fifteen hundred acres in 1814 to more than two hundred thousand in 1817. In just three years after 1816, indebtedness to the government for public lands increased nearly 600 percent. Rarely in the history of westward expansion would so many buy so much with so little.

Land sales were directly linked to another government encouragement—migration. As Congress admitted each state, it reserved about 3 percent of the net income from the sale of public lands to construct public roads. The first such project was authorized in 1806. The Cumberland Road, which ran between Cumberland, Maryland, and Wheeling, Virginia, was meant to ease the way across the Appalachian barrier to the upper Ohio Valley. Well before its completion, thousands of farm and freight wagons and throngs of people, cattle, dogs, and pigs filled it each year on their way west. Before the War of 1812, Congress had also paid to build the Federal Road from Milledgeville, Georgia, to St. Stephens on the Tombigbee River, and after the conflict it authorized another overland route, popularly called Jackson's Military Road, connecting New Orleans with Nashville and the upper South generally. As with the Ordinances of 1785 and 1787, the demands of the frontier allowed the national government to expand its powers and to project its shaping force into the future of the growing Republic.

These thoroughfares of migration and commerce sealed even more tightly the fate of native peoples and thus deepened the government's well-worn dilemma: how could the United States treat the Indians justly while taking their lands? Especially among the

Set in a mountainous New Hampshire setting, Thomas Cole's painting evokes one of the central tensions of frontier settlement as it was reenacted across the trans-Appalachian West. The sunlit cabin, bountiful garden, and warm domestic scene suggest the idyllic possibilities of frontier life. Nonetheless, the raw tree stumps and fallen logs serve as the artist's warnings about the transformation of the land.

Thomas Cole (1801–48). The Hunter's Return. Oil on canvas, 1845. Courtesy Amon Carter Museum, Fort Worth, Texas.

populous southern tribes, Washington now shifted its emphasis to a strategy of "education." Government-sponsored agents, most of them men of the cloth, would tutor natives, not only in Christian principles but also in the skills and virtues of agriculture—Euro-American style, of course—which would promote orderly communities and a veneration of private property. "We want to make citizens out of them," wrote Thomas L. McKenney, an architect of this policy, "and they must first be anchored to the soil." The various peoples would also be encouraged to abandon native languages for English, "the lever by which they are to elevate themselves into intellectual and moral distinction," and to adopt white concepts of family and white styles of housing, dress, and general propriety. This was thought to be a merciful policy—McKenney called it a "cup of consolation"—that would ensure natives eternal glory and a happy assimilation into the society now pressing hard upon them. Raised up in the ways of the virtuous Republic, Indians would be freed from both outside threats and their own resentments. And the government's dilemma would dissolve.

This optimistic program in one sense reflected certain Enlightenment influences embraced by its early advocate, Jefferson. But in a larger sense this policy was only a newer variation of an assimilative dream as old as the first colonies. And it was as wrongheaded as what had been tried at Jamestown. Indians *were* absorbing white culture (just as whites were absorbing Indian culture), but many of the lessons had little to do with the missionaries' goals. At work was a dynamic of infinite complexity, one that was far beyond the government's understanding and even farther beyond its control. The current policy was bound for frustration, and some already were advocating a final option. In 1817 the government set aside a portion of present-day Arkansas where Cherokees might relocate. Beyond the Mississippi, advocates of removal argued, native peoples would find sanctuary and enough time for a full and final adoption into the national family.

By 1820 the frontier had left its mark on trans-Appalachia. As a historical condition, it had moved on. Its defining traits now prevailed in the country beyond the Mississippi. There the pace of exchange among the many peoples was accelerating. Guns, hawk bells, horses, pelts, blankets, and cloth moved back and forth through a trading network stretching from southern Canada and the upper Missouri to Santa Fe. The scramble of powers had shifted westward. The Adams-Onís Treaty of 1819 rounded out the southeastern boundaries of the United States and projected the nation's imperial energies beyond the great river, where the U.S. government would contest with entrenched European rivals and another few dozen Indian groups. The arm of government was reaching farther west. As Missouri petitioned for statehood, surveyors continued laying out their checkerboard, edging now toward the eastern fringe of the Great Plains, even as Major Stephen Long was mapping part of the region farther west in the latest of several government-sponsored expeditions. The public embraced ever more fondly the idea of the opening West. In 1823 James Fenimore Cooper published *The Pioneers*. Its protagonist, Leatherstocking, would stalk through four other novels before drifting west to die on the plains. A wilderness regenerate, doomed to solitary freedom, brother to and slayer of Indians, Cooper's hero personified a people wedded to the frontier idea in all its obsessiveness, naïveté, hope, and contradictions.

Millions would move west vicariously with Leatherstocking. Of the thousands who went in person, many came from trans-Appalachia. And so the patterns and conflicts of that earlier frontier were begat again. The first serious foray of fur traders up the Missouri River was organized by William Morrison and the Canadian-born Pierre Menard, both Kaskaskia merchants, and Manuel Lisa, a Spaniard from the lower Mississippi Valley. The trapper and scout Christopher "Kit" Carson had moved as a child with his Scotch-Irish parents to Missouri from a Kentucky backwoods farm in 1812. Members of the first party of farmers to cross the plains to California were virtually all from the Ohio Valley and upper South. Guiding them part of the way was John Park, a half-Iroquois hunter.

Among those looking westward was Moses Austin, a Connecticut Yankee who had taken up lead mining in Missouri. In 1820 he won from Spanish authorities the permission to establish a colony of his countrymen in central Texas. A shrewd observer of forces around him, Austin had watched and wondered at the crowds of emigrants he had seen pushing across the Appalachians twenty-five years earlier. "Ask these Pilgrims what they expect when they git to Kentuckey the Answer is Land. have you any. No, but I expect I can git it. have you any thing to pay for land, No. did you Ever see the Country. No but Every Body says its good land . . . here is hundreds Traveling hundreds of Miles, they Know not for what Nor Whither, except its to Kentuckey."

The traits of that crowd—not so much optimism as a driven, unappeasable restlessness—had only gathered strength since then. More "Pilgrims" than ever were pressing westward, but now their promised land was not Kentucky but Texas and other places almost as improbable. As one American frontier closed, another opened.

Bibliographic Note

Anyone curious about the trans-Appalachian frontier can turn first to several excellent surveys. Besides Malcolm J. Rohrbough's *The Trans-Appalachian Frontier: People, Societies, and Institutions, 1775–1850* (New York, 1978), which remains the best and most comprehensive, the reader should consult Reginald Horsman, *The Frontier in the Formative Years, 1783–1815* (New York, 1970), Jack M. Sosin, *The Revolutionary Frontier, 1763–1783* (New York, 1967), Thomas D. Clark and John D. W. Guice, *Frontiers in Conflict: The Old Southwest, 1795–1830* (Albuquerque, 1989), and Francis S. Philbrick, *The Rise of the West, 1754–1830* (New York, 1965). Beverly W. Bond, Jr.'s *The Civilization of the Old Northwest: A Study of Political, Social, and Economic Development, 1788–1812* (New York, 1934), although thin on interpretation, remains a fine starting point for a study of the Ohio Valley frontier. To put this story in context, works on the background of imperial competition are helpful: W. J. Eccles, *The Canadian Frontier, 1534–1760* (New York, 1969); John A. Caruso, *The Mississippi Valley Frontier: The Age of French Exploration* (Indianapolis, 1966); and Jack M. Sosin, *Whitehall and the Wilderness: The Middle West in British Colonial Policy, 1760–1775* (Lincoln, 1961). For a taste of the many approaches to the study of Native Americans and their societies, see Harold E. Driver, *Indians of North America*, 2d ed. (Chicago, 1969), Charles Hudson, *The Southeastern Indians* (Knoxville, 1976), R. Douglas Hurt, *Indian Agriculture in America: Prehistory to the Present* (Lawrence, 1987), and Helen Hornbeck Tanner's superb *Atlas of Great Lakes Indian History* (Norman, 1987), useful for its text as well as its maps and illustrations. There are, as well, anthropological and historical studies of all major native groups of the region.

Solon Buck and Elizabeth H. Buck, *The Planting of Civilization in Western Pennsylvania* (Pittsburgh, 1939), still is an essential introduction to expansion into the upper Ohio; for expansion into Tennessee and Kentucky, one should begin with Thomas P. Abernethy, *From Frontier to Plantation in Tennessee* (Chapel Hill, 1932), William S. Lester, *The Transylvania Company* (Spencer, 1935), John Mack Faragher, *Daniel Boone: The Life and Legend of an American Pioneer* (New York, 1992), and Charles A. Talbert, *Benjamin Logan: Kentucky Frontiersman* (Lexington, 1962). On popular attitudes toward the frontier's possibilities and the revolutionary crisis, I found the research of Alan Taylor, soon to appear in print, especially helpful. As for the war itself, Jack Sosin's *The Revolutionary Frontier* can be supplemented by Thomas P. Abernethy's *Western Lands and the American Revolution* (New York, 1937), which stresses the role of speculation and economic interests.

Two recent studies provide fascinating, but conflicting, ethnic analyses of the roots of frontier society: Grady McWhiney, *Cracker Culture: Celtic Ways in the Old South* (Tuscaloosa, 1988), and Terry G. Jordan and Matti Kaups, *The American Backwoods Frontier: An Ethnic and Ecological Interpretation* (Baltimore, 1989). James E. Davis has given this society a close demographic look in *Frontier America, 1800–1840: A Comparative Demographic Analysis of the Settlement Process* (Glendale, Calif., 1977); to put his conclusions into a larger context, see Walter T. K. Nugent, *Structures of American Social History* (Bloomington, 1981). Richard Wade, *The Urban Frontier: The Rise of Western Cities* (Cambridge, Mass., 1959), remains the best source on the topic. Much can be learned about daily life in the countryside in Charles W. Towne and Edward N. Wentworth, *Pigs: From Cave to Cornbelt* (Norman, 1950), Jared van Wagenen, Jr., *The Golden Age of Homespun* (New York, 1953), and Nicholas P. Hardeman, *Shucks, Shocks, and Hominy Blocks: Corn as a Way of Life in Pioneer America* (Baton Rouge, 1981). Louis B. Wright's brief and highly readable *Culture on the Moving Frontier* (Bloomington, 1955) is a must as an introduction to early cultural development. A classic older study of economic development, Percy W. Bidwell and John I. Falconer's *History of Agriculture in the Northern United States, 1620–1860* (Washington, D.C., 1925), is still full of helpful information, although it should be read with more recent works, such as David C. Klingaman and Richard K. Vedder, eds., *Essays on the Economy of the Old Northwest* (Athens, 1987). On the popular image of the frontier and its complex relationship to Americans' perception of themselves, two classics—Henry Nash Smith, *Virgin Land: The American West as Symbol and Myth* (Cambridge, Mass., 1950), and Arthur K. Moore, *The Frontier Mind: A Cultural Analysis of the Kentucky Frontiersman* (Lexington, 1957)—now have a third companion, Richard Slotkin's *Regeneration through Violence: The Mythology of the American Frontier, 1600–1860* (Middletown, Conn., 1973).

John Barnhart's *Valley of Democracy: The Frontier versus the Plantation in the Ohio Valley, 1775–1818* (Bloomington, 1958) still offers much of value on politics and government, although it should be supplemented by more recent works. Among the best of these is Andrew R. L. Cayton, *The Frontier Republic: Ideology and Politics in the Ohio Country, 1780–1825* (Kent, 1986). Two of the most useful among the many works on land policy are Roy M. Robbins, *Our Landed Heritage* (Princeton, 1942), and Vernon Carstensen, ed., *The Public Lands* (Madison, 1963); Malcolm J. Rohrbough's *The Land Office Business: The Settlement and Administration of American Public Lands, 1789–1837* (New York, 1968) remains the essential book on the distribution of the public domain. Standard studies of the era's diplomacy include Arthur P. Whitaker, *The Spanish-American Frontier, 1783–1795* (Boston, 1927), Jerald A. Coombs, *The Jay Treaty: Political Battleground of the Founding Fathers* (Berkeley, 1970), E. Wilson Lyon, *Louisiana in French Diplomacy, 1759–1804* (Norman, 1934), and two works, both now revised, by Samuel F. Bemis: *Jay's Treaty: A Study in Commerce and Diplomacy*, rev. ed. (New Haven, 1962), and *Pinckney's Treaty: America's Advantage from Europe's Distress, 1783–1800*, rev. ed. (New Haven, 1960).

Indian-white relations and warfare have inspired a voluminous literature. Readers should begin with Richard White's splendid recent study, which blends environmental, cultural, and diplomatic history: *The Middle Ground: Indians, Empires, and Republics in the Great Lakes Region, 1650–1815* (Cambridge, Eng., 1991). Wiley Sword's *President Washington's Indian War: The Struggle for the Old Northwest, 1790–1795* (Norman, 1985) and Reginald Horsman's *Expansion and American Indian Policy, 1783–1812* (East Lansing, Mich., 1967) should be read with earlier standards, such as Randolph C. Downes's *Council Fires on the Upper Ohio* (Pittsburgh, 1940). On government policy and relations with Native Americans, every reader should begin with Francis Paul Prucha's magisterial *The Great Father: The United States Government and the American Indians* (Lincoln, 1984). The best introductions to Tecumseh, Tenskwatawa, and the movement they inspired are both by R. David Edmunds: *Tecumseh and the Quest for Indian Leadership* (Boston, 1984) and *The Shawnee Prophet* (Lincoln, 1983). Vittorio Lanternari's *The Religions of the Oppressed: A Study of Modern Messianic Cults*, trans. Lisa Sergio (New York, 1963), can help the reader understand Indians' new religions in a far larger context, whereas another study is full of insights into dynamics behind the natives' drinking habits: Craig MacAndrew and Robert B. Edgerton, *Drunken Comportment: A Social Explanation* (Chicago, 1969). The complex questions of white perceptions of Indians and how these images were translated into public policy are the subjects of Roy Harvey Pearce, *Savagism and Civilization: A Study of the Indian and the American Mind* (Baltimore, 1953), and Bernard W. Sheehan, *Seeds of Extinction: Jeffersonian Philanthropy and the American Indian* (New York, 1973).

Finally, readers who want to taste the flavor of the times can turn to two fine reprint series. Arno Press has republished early histories and commentaries of the region in the "Mid-American Frontier" series, and University Microfilm's "March of America Facsimile Series" includes reprints of contemporary descriptions and travel accounts.

SECTION II
Expansion

In the course of the nineteenth century, the trans-Mississippi region became the *American West*. Nationalism in all its diverse manifestations enfolded the vast lands and distinct places. The governing of the West and the peopling of the region now acquired a clearly American imprint. The growth of the West in economic and demographic terms not only demonstrated the close connection of this region to the growth of the American nation but also indicated the growing interconnection of the West and the United States to the rest of the world.

The domination of the West by the United States, its incorporation into an American empire, implies a form of political, and even military, control that obscures an important story. Total subjugation of both lands and peoples did not occur. No monolithic power took control of the West. Instead a web of interconnected relationships bound new and old residents of the West to each other, even when they saw each other as enemies. The full story is not one of great victories and clear successes. It is a story of economic boom and financial bust, of natural resources exploited for distant markets, and of agricultural expansion established with great human cost. It is a story marred by violence but shaped by important human institutions—governments appointed and elected, churches traditional and new, communities temporary and sustained, and families separated and united. The actors are not of one generation, one color, or one gender, and the story would not end with the closing of the century.

The complex interconnections of the West's many peoples and institutions can be recognized in some individual lives. Such is the case of the Native American woman whose name was most probably Sacagawea ("Bird Woman" in Hidatsa). In the fall of 1800 at age twelve or thirteen, this Lemhi Shoshoni girl had been captured by the Hidatsas; she was later sold to a French-Canadian fur trader, Toussaint Charbonneau. When the American explorers Meriwether Lewis and William Clark met Charbonneau at Fort Mandan on the Missouri River in present-day North Dakota, Sacagawea, the youngest of the three Indian women with whom he lived, was pregnant with the trader's child. Charbonneau became an interpreter for the Lewis and Clark expedition and took Sacagawea on the epic trek to the Pacific coast and back.

What role did she play in the journey? Lewis dismissed her participation. He reported, "If she has enough to eat and a few trinkets I believe she would be perfectly content anywhere." Clark felt differently. He wrote to Toussaint Charbonneau, "Your woman . . . diserved [*sic*] a greater reward for her attention and services." But what were these services? No direct accounts from Charbonneau or Sacagawea exist, but many legends have been created. The most persistent has Sacagawea guiding the expedition through dangerous lands, thus ensuring the party's survival. A careful reading of the daily accounts left by Lewis and Clark show that only twice did Sacagawea help guide the

The feelings of nationalism inspired by the American victory in the Mexican War created renewed interest in narrative paintings that supported the myth of America's "manifest destiny" as a nation stretching across the continent.

William Tylee Ranney (1813–57). Boone's First View of Kentucky. Oil on canvas, 1849. Courtesy of The Anschutz Collection, Denver, Colorado.

expedition. More often she aided communication with other native groups, especially with her knowledge of the Shoshoni language. Yet her most important role, as the historian James P. Ronda has explained, may well have been as a woman and a mother. Sacagawea gave birth to her son Jean Baptiste Charbonneau early in the journey on 11 February 1805. The presence of a young mother and her baby may have reassured many of the native peoples—women and men—who met the expedition. Clark, with his infamous grammar and spelling, observed: "The Wife of Shabono our interpreter We find reconsiles all the Indians, as to our friendly intentions. A woman with a party of men is a token of peace."

Other women, not as legendary, made their own journeys that interwove with stories set in the West. An African-American woman named Biddy may have started her travel west by oxcart from Georgia. She arrived in southern California in 1852 as a slave, the property of Robert Smith, a Mormon convert from Mississippi. Smith had taken Biddy and another slave woman, Hannah, to Utah in 1851 before migrating with other Mormons to San Bernardino. By 1855, Smith wanted to take Biddy, Hannah, and their twelve children and grandchildren to Texas, but Biddy and Hannah managed to take Smith to court. The judge in Los Angeles granted the mothers and the children their freedom, making special note of Robert Smith's desire to relocate four of the children, born in the free state of California, to the slave state of Texas.

Biddy took the full name of Biddy Mason and settled in Los Angeles, where she worked as a confinement nurse for $2.50 a week. She also did domestic work but soon purchased her own home and eventually bought two city lots. Thus began a successful series of investments in real estate that made Biddy Mason a wealthy woman. She used her house on South Spring Street to aid needy travelers, and she used her money to support education for African-American children. Biddy Mason, like Sacagawea, was a woman and mother who could ensure safety and a form of security for others.

Not all women's lives in the West would have such positive results. Sacagawea was able to facilitate peaceful interactions, but many other Native American women died in brutal attacks, such as the Cheyenne mothers shot down with their children by the Third Colorado Volunteers in 1864 at Sand Creek. And Biddy Mason may have found financial success in the West, but many African-American women found themselves in western prisons, well out of proportion to their numbers in the general population. As the historian Anne Butler discovered, from the 1860s to the early twentieth century, African-American women composed the majority of women in western state penitentiaries. Some were accused of extremely petty crimes, such as stealing a nightgown.

The many lives of the West's many peoples are an indication of the different ways that the history of the American West may be told. Some of these ways may appear familiar at first, examining topics such as the policies of the national government or the pitfalls of economic development. But surprises can emerge—the government was more intrusive and the economy more global than previously recognized. Other perspectives will seem fresh—the creation of animals of enterprise or the multigenerational migrations of families. All perspectives are part of a larger story that improves as much by rethinking as by retelling. It is a story that will expand to include more peoples and more ideas the more often it is told.

— Clyde A. Milner II

CHRONOLOGY

1804–6	Meriwether Lewis and William Clark explore the Louisiana Purchase.
1808	John Jacob Astor founds the American Fur Company.
1821	William Becknell opens the Santa Fe Trail.
1825	William Ashley organizes rendezvous for fur trappers at Henry's Fork on the Green River.
1829	Depletion of sandalwood in Hawaiian Islands and sea otters in southeastern Alaska.
1834	Protestants open mission in Oregon's Willamette Valley.
1836	Texas Revolution results in independence from Mexico.
1837	Epidemic diseases devastate many Plains Indian tribes.
1841	General Preemption Law acknowledges squatters' right to land.
1845	The United States annexes Texas.
1846	Treaty with Britain secures half of Oregon for the United States.
1847	Latter-day Saints (Mormons) arrive in Utah.
1848	Treaty of Guadalupe Hidalgo, ending the Mexican-American War, adds 1.2 million square miles of territory to the United States.
1848	James Marshall discovers gold at Sutter's Mill, California.
1850	Entry of California into the Union forces the most complex legislative compromise in U.S. history.
1857	One-sixth of U.S. Army dispatched to quell presumed rebellion by Latter-day Saints in Utah.
1858	John Butterfield opens overland stage route.
1859	Mining rushes occur in Nevada and Colorado.
1862	Congress passes the Homestead Act, granting 160 acres of public land to settlers after five years of residence.
1864	The Navajos are forced to take the Long Walk to Bosque Redondo. Cheyennes are massacred at Sand Creek in Colorado.
1867	35,000 Texas cattle are driven up the Chisholm trail to Abilene, Kansas. The United States purchases Alaska from Russia.
1869	Completion of the first transcontinental railroad. Wyoming Territory extends the vote to women.
1876	Battle of the Little Bighorn marks short-lived victory for Lakotas.
1877	African-American settlers, "Exodusters," establish Nicodemus in northwest Kansas.
1878	Lincoln County War in New Mexico produces legendary outlaw, Billy the Kid.
1880s	Drought and harsh winters devastate cattle herds throughout the West.
1881	Gunfight near the O.K. Corral in Tombstone, Arizona, results in three deaths.
1882	Huge deposits of copper found at Anaconda mine in Butte, Montana.
1883	North American bison hunted to near-extinction.
1885	Massacre of fifty-one Chinese by miners at Rock Springs, Wyoming.
1886	Division of Forestry formally recognized within Department of Agriculture.
1887	General Allotment Act, or Dawes Act, initiates break-up of reservation lands.
1890	U.S. Census announces that the frontier has closed. Lakota Ghost Dancers shot down at Wounded Knee, South Dakota.
1893	Great Northern Railroad reaches Seattle.
1896	William Jennings Bryan of Nebraska runs for president on both the Democratic and Populist tickets.
1898	Spain cedes Pacific possessions to the United States with treaty ending the Spanish-American War. The United States annexes Hawai`i.

1069. GRAND CAÑON OF THE COLORADO.

W. H. JACKSON & CO. DENVER

Chapter Five

National Initiatives

CLYDE A. MILNER II

W ho owned the Louisiana Territory? Meriwether Lewis and Carlos Dehault Delassus could not agree on an answer. Delassus, a Spanish official, thought that he still administered lands controlled by the French. Rumors of the sale of Louisiana had reached St. Louis in August 1803, but no formal instructions had been sent to Delassus, lieutenant governor of the territory. On 8 December 1803, Captain Lewis had crossed the Mississippi River to meet with Delassus. Lewis knew that the United States had purchased Louisiana from Napoleon's government, but he carried no official documents concerning the sale. So after presenting his credentials, Lewis informed Delassus that he planned to lead an expedition funded by the government of the United States. Perhaps the captain paraphrased the instructions that President Thomas Jefferson had sent to Lewis, his twenty-nine-year-old former secretary, in June. "The object of your mission is to explore the Missouri river, & such principal stream of it, as, by it's [*sic*] course and communication with the waters of the Pacific ocean, whether the Columbia, Oregan [*sic*], Colorado or any other river may offer the most direct & practicable water communication across this continent for the purposes of commerce."

Delassus insisted that the American party not proceed up the Missouri until he received notification of Louisiana's sale. Lewis willingly complied. He crossed back to the east side of the Mississippi and established his winter camp on easily recognized American soil. In January 1804, the residents of St. Louis officially learned that all of the Louisiana country had been purchased by the United States. In March, a formal transfer ceremony occurred in the town. In May, William Clark, who shared command of the expedition with Lewis, led the party across the Mississippi. As many as forty-six men may have begun the ascent of the Missouri. Aside from the two commanding officers, twenty-seven young, unmarried recruits served as permanent members of the "Corps of Discovery." Two nonmilitary personnel also accompanied the corps—York, an African-American slave whom Clark had inherited from his father, and George Drouillard, half French-Canadian and half Shawnee, who worked as a hunter and interpreter for twenty-five dollars a month. Over the journey of twenty-eight months and eight thousand miles, only one member of the corps lost his life. Sergeant Charles Floyd died from what may have been a ruptured appendix. York, Drouillard, Lewis, Clark, and even Lewis's black Newfoundland dog, Seaman, survived the entire transcontinental trek.

A photographer who documented the Rocky Mountain West from 1870 to 1878 as a member of Ferdinand V. Hayden's ambitious geological and geographical survey, William Henry Jackson later created images that romanticized this period as a heroic age of exploration. These two men poised confidently at the edge of a cliff evoke the sense of self-assurance that characterized 19th-century settlement of the western half of the nation.

William Henry Jackson (1843–1942). Grand Canyon of the Colorado. Albumen silver print, ca. 1892, 21 x 17 1/16 in. Collection of the J. Paul Getty Museum, Malibu, California.

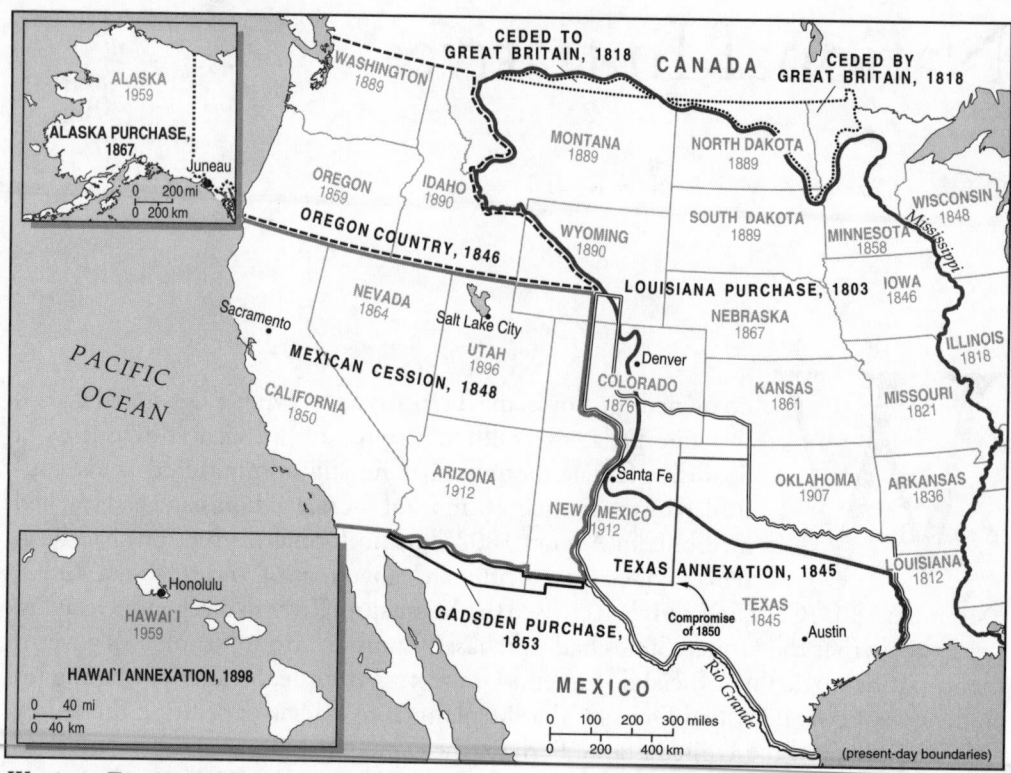

Western Territorial Expansion, 1803–1959

Three centuries earlier, an expedition of three ships under the command of Christopher Columbus had launched an era of European exploration and expansion. On 14 May 1804, an era of American exploration and expansion began when a keelboat and two pirogues carried the Corps of Discovery up the Missouri. Under instructions from the nation's president and with congressional funding, the federal employees of the Lewis and Clark Expedition initiated the incorporation of the trans-Mississippi West into the United States.

During the century that followed, the federal government continued the scientific exploration of land beyond the Mississippi. Yet, federal action did not end with these expeditions. The government not only explored these lands but also claimed new ones. Through purchase, treaty, annexation, and war, the federal government added extensive territory beyond the vague boundaries of the original Louisiana Purchase. The most prominent additions came from what had been Mexican territory with the annexation of Texas in 1845, the cession after the Mexican-American War in 1848, and the Gadsden Purchase in 1853. Britain gave up Oregon, Russia sold Alaska, and numerous Native American tribes lost lands to the growing United States.

More than a century of national expansion culminated on 14 February 1912, St. Valentine's Day, when President William Howard Taft signed the proclamation that made Arizona the forty-eighth state of the United States. Nearly five weeks earlier, his signature had admitted New Mexico to the Union. In less than eleven decades, new states had been formed out of the Louisiana Purchase and the vast lands that bordered it. The two newest additions completed the political incorporation of the contiguous trans-Mississippi West into the United States. Like the acquisition of lands, this process of political incorporation resulted from actions of the federal government and its agents.

Acquisition was simply a claim to western lands that were already occupied by an incredible variety of native peoples, a distinct population of Hispanic settlers, and a diverse representation of fur trappers. Political incorporation meant embracing people as well as lands. Often it involved helping people move to, and settle on, the land. In other words, the federal government promoted the increased occupation of the West as well as its acquisition. Occupation then produced political incorporation. The federal government aided this occupation of the West directly and indirectly. For example, it used the treaty process to reduce the lands held by American Indians and thus to increase the lands that non-Indians might settle. It published the reports of scientific exploration that indicated routes for immigration and lands for cultivation. It protected overland migration and helped supply immigrant parties. It stimulated economic development, especially by building roads, subsidizing stage and wagon lines, and constructing railroads. It also imposed the social, political, and legal models established east of the Mississippi. The U.S. Army supported most of these federal actions, whereas the U.S. Congress prolonged the political apprenticeship of much of the West before granting statehood. As expansion led to acquisition and as occupation led to incorporation, the initiatives of the federal government greatly shaped the history of the American West from 1803 to 1912—and beyond.

Search for a Usable West

The Louisiana Purchase and its aftermath form a long prelude to the more vigorous era of western expansion that began in the 1840s. By the end of that decade, the American presence in the trans-Mississippi had been transformed. Until the 1840s, federal activity in the region extended little beyond a list of scientific, military, and diplomatic initiatives that suited political and economic interests *east* of the Mississippi.

Consider Thomas Jefferson's reasons for sending the Lewis and Clark Expedition across the continent. His explanation to Congress in January 1803 had stressed support of the fur trade through improvement of relations with the Indians along the Missouri River. Jefferson believed that a small party of as few as a dozen men might "explore the whole line [of the Missouri] even to the Western ocean." He noted that improvement of commerce through conferences with the Indians fell within the constitutional powers of Congress. The national assembly accepted the president's plan and appropriated twenty-five hundred dollars for the project. By June, Meriwether Lewis had spent nearly all the initial appropriation, before receiving detailed instructions from the president and before the president had learned of the purchase of Louisiana.

The instructions, dated 20 June, came first. In his letter, Jefferson underscored the purposes that he had presented to Congress and then requested detailed scientific observations of the peoples, weather, rivers, terrain, climate, and natural resources in the lands traversed. On 4 July 1803, a day already reserved for recognition of the signing of the Declaration of Independence, the *National Intelligencer* reported news of the Louisiana Purchase. Jefferson had received notification only the day before, two months after the event. Great news indeed, but how great was the territory acquired? French officials did not know. On 1 October 1800, the French and Spanish had signed the secret Treaty of San Ildefonso, returning Louisiana to France. In the description of the ceded territory, Louisiana contained "the same extent . . . that it had when France possessed it, and such as it should be after the treaties subsequently entered into between Spain and other States." The agreement for the American purchase in 1803 contained the same ambiguous language. In fact, the French had reacquired and then sold Louisiana without establishing political control over all the territory. This explains why in St. Louis, a Spanish official, Delassus, served as lieutenant governor.

Thomas Jefferson knew that his country had acquired a vast territory with most of the new land lying beyond the Mississippi. Some critics considered it a useless wilderness, and no one knew if it contained lands suitable for the yeoman farmers that Jefferson idealized. The president could only guess at the boundaries to the north, west, and south. These would not begin to be clearly defined until 1818, when a convention with Great Britain set the northern boundary along the 49th parallel to the Rocky Mountains and established joint occupation of the Oregon country. The Transcontinental Treaty of 1819 between Spain and the United States, also known as the Adams-Onís Treaty, set the western and southwestern boundaries. Jefferson recognized that the Louisiana Purchase did not stretch to the Pacific Ocean. Yet, he understood that in 1792, an American merchant captain, Robert Gray, had first discovered the mouth of the Columbia River on Oregon's west coast. Gray gave the United States some claim to the Oregon country, so the president instructed Lewis and Clark to cross the entire continent to the Pacific. Jefferson dreamed of an easy portage from the headwaters of a far western river, such as the Columbia, back to the headwaters of the Missouri. Perhaps furs could be collected on the Pacific coast and transported back across the continent instead of across the Pacific or around South America. Of course, others had dreamed of a Northwest Passage that would not only cross the continent but also establish a base on the Pacific coast for trade with Asia, especially China. In 1803, the prospects of profits from both the fur trade and the China trade had captured the attention of commercial interests in Britain, Canada, and the United States. Two great rivals, the British-owned Hudson's Bay Company and the Canadian-controlled North West Company, already had designs on the Oregon country.

On their return in 1806, Lewis and Clark reported to the president. They had not found a Northwest Passage—an easy portage from the Columbia to the headwaters of the Missouri. The Rocky Mountains presented too formidable a barrier. Nor had they found agricultural lands within the Louisiana Territory. But they had collected an immense trove of information about the native peoples, diverse geography, and abundant resources of the trans-Mississippi West. Only a portion of their observations appeared in print. Nicholas Biddle, of Philadelphia, consulted their daily journals to write a narrative of the trip. After modest alterations by Paul Allen, it was published in 1814, along with a map produced by William Clark. Dr. Benjamin Smith Barton had agreed to produce a scientific report, but he died before fulfilling the task. Some materials in his care disappeared, including nearly all the collected plants and animals, the recorded vocabularies of Indian languages, and the astronomical observations.

Without a published scientific report, Jefferson felt that only half of the expedition's story had been told.

Although the trip did not benefit science, agriculture, or commerce in the manner that Jefferson had idealistically envisioned, some people did profit from the Lewis and Clark Expedition. For example, Manuel Lisa, one of the expedition suppliers in St. Louis, established trade with Indian tribes along the upper Missouri River and, by 1807, had built a post at the mouth of the Bighorn River in present-day Montana. In 1809, William Clark, now a brigadier general in the militia and the principal Indian agent for the Louisiana Territory, joined with Lisa, Pierre Menard, and two members of the Chouteau family to create the Missouri Fur Company, based in St. Louis. John Jacob Astor, the squat, German-born, New York merchant, had even grander commercial dreams. He envisioned a series of trading posts that would follow the route of Lewis and Clark all the way to the Pacific. He also desired some sort of relationship with the government. With friendly encouragement from Thomas Jefferson but no formal federal support, Astor forged ahead and founded the American Fur Company in 1808; with Canadian partners, he created the Pacific Fur Company in 1810. Astor launched this latter enterprise by sending both an overland party and a maritime expedition to the mouth of the Columbia where, in March 1811, the overlanders founded Astoria. After the outbreak of the War of 1812, a British warship attempted to take Astoria, but it arrived too late. The North West Company, an enterprise established in Canada under British dominion, had bought the trading post in October 1813 for the bargain price of fifty-eight thousand dollars. This sale under duress, if not quite under the gun, hastened the demise of the Pacific Fur Company, but neither event prevented Astor from becoming one of the wealthiest men in the United States. He continued to profit from the fur trade until 1834, when he wisely left the business, anticipating the decline in the international demand for beaver pelts.

Both before and after this downturn in the market, fur trappers and government explorers used each other's knowledge. For example, fur companies sent their trappers to the upper Arkansas River because of information gathered in 1806–7 by Lieutenant Zebulon Pike's expedition across the Southwest. More typically, fur trappers explored the Far West on their own. Jedediah Smith in the 1820s and Joseph R. Walker in the 1830s undertook astounding journeys. Both men crossed the arid Great Basin and forged through the Sierra Nevada. Smith demonstrated a feasible route through the Rockies at Wyoming's South Pass, which became the main passage for overland travel to Oregon. In the 1840s, Walker helped guide two of John Charles Frémont's expeditions for the U.S. Army Corps of Topographical Engineers. Kit Carson, another famous mountain man, aided three of Frémont's parties, exploring the central Rockies, the Great Basin, Oregon, and California.

Frémont's scientific explorations under military auspices followed the precedent set by the Lewis and Clark Expedition. Throughout the nineteenth century, the federal government supported such explorations with the expectation of commercial, diplomatic, or political benefits. These scientific expeditions produced vital information about the American West, but like the Lewis and Clark Expedition, they did not produce all the benefits expected by the government. Nonetheless, each expedition set out with

Between 1840 and 1863 more than 700 prints of western scenes—virtually all based on eyewitness observation—appeared in government reports documenting exploration of the West. Particularly influential were the Pacific Railroad Survey reports (1855–61), which flooded the market with more than 6.6 million copies of western views. These scenic landscapes, along with carefully drawn scientific illustrations, fueled popular interest in westward expansion.

After W.P. Blake. Mammoth Tree "Beauty of the Forest." *Lithograph, 1856. From* Reports of Explorations and Surveys to Ascertain the Most Practicable and Economical Route for a Railroad from the Mississippi River to the Pacific Ocean, Vol. 5 (Explorations in California), *1856.*

MAMMOTH TREE "BEAUTY OF THE FOREST"

After Heinrich Balduin Mollhausen (1825–1905). Canadian River Near Camp 38 *(Oklahoma). Lithograph, 1856. From* Reports of Explorations and Surveys to Ascertain the Most Practicable and Economical Route for a Railroad from the Mississippi River to the Pacific Ocean, Vol. 3 (Thirty-fifth Parallel Survey), *1856.*

CANADIAN RIVER NEAR CAMP 38.

a plan—a "program"—that outlined the government's intentions about what should be found. The historian William H. Goetzmann has argued that such cultural preconditions distinguish "exploration" from "discovery." The latter may be unexpected and serendipitous, but the former demonstrates cultural values and existing knowledge.

Between 1840 and 1860, the federal government placed great value in what could be learned from scientific explorations. During these two decades, Congress supported such scientific endeavors, as a percentage of the national budget, far more extensively than at any other time in the nation's history, in some years appropriating one-third of total federal expenditures. Most of this money financed what has been called the "great reconnaissance" of the trans-Mississippi. Congress not only paid for these explorations in the West but also published sixty reports—many in multiple volumes, complete with lithographs produced by artists who accompanied the scientists. Typically the U.S. Army Corps of Topographical Engineers carried out these western expeditions. Frémont served in this elite unit, established in 1838 as a separate organization from the army's larger Corps of Engineers. The contributions of the topographical engineers reached their zenith in 1853–55 with the transcontinental railroad surveys. The reports from these surveys appeared in a magnificent set of twelve lavishly illustrated volumes. With extensive maps, detailed geology, elaborate ethnography, and exhaustive ecology, this virtual encyclopedia of the West cost the government over a million dollars to publish—twice the cost of the surveys themselves.

The railroad surveys demonstrate how rapidly the nation had changed by the 1850s. A half-century earlier, such transcontinental routes could not have been predicted. At the time of the Lewis and Clark Expedition, a major question had been left unanswered. Beyond exploration and commerce, what plans did the federal government have for its newest West? Jefferson believed that territorial expansion might not bring national expansion. Ideally, republics should remain compact and homogeneous. In August 1803, he told Senator John Breckinridge that settlement west of the Mississippi would lead to the creation of a second republic—a friendly neighbor sharing a common language and political tradition. "The future inhabitants of the Atlantic and Mississippi states will be our sons."

Later presidents did not share this vision. James Monroe wanted everything east of the Rocky Mountains to join the Union, whereas John Quincy Adams advocated a continental nation stretching from the Atlantic to the Pacific. In his later years, Jefferson too lost his fear of national bigness. In 1817, he talked of the "enlargement of territory" leading to an enduring republic, if that nation was founded "not on conquest, but [on] principles of compact & equality."

As the nation expanded westward, these Jeffersonian ideals did not prevail. Military conquests, unfair treaties, and political inequities sustained government initiatives beyond the Mississippi. For example, in the first major effort to encourage settlement, the government forced the resettlement of American Indians in the trans-Mississippi by removing them from lands east of the Mississippi. As early as 1808, some Cherokees had agreed to go west to hunt and then to settle. After the War of 1812, the Monroe administration became more committed to the idea of exchanging Indian title, and thus changing Indian residency, to lands beyond the Mississippi. Proponents of Indian removal, from Thomas Jefferson to Andrew Jackson, justified this policy as a benefit to

Native Americans. In 1829, President Jackson explained: "[This] just and humane policy . . . recommended them [the Indians] to quit their possessions on this side of the Mississippi, and go to a country to the west where there is every probability that they will always be free from the mercenary influence of White men, and undisturbed by the local authority of the states: Under such circumstances the General Government can exercise a parental control over their interests and possibly perpetuate their race."

The policy of removal clearly benefited agricultural expansion east of the Mississippi, especially after the War of 1812 with the establishment of a cotton kingdom in the Deep South. America's presidents, beginning with George Washington, had advocated European-style agriculture and conversion to Protestant Christianity as the path to social and spiritual salvation for the Indians. Removal forced Indians to emigrate to lands not coveted by American farmers, especially cotton planters. Under the protection of the federal government and under the direction of Christian missionaries, these native peoples, though not recognized as citizens of the United States, might somehow secure "civilization" through cultural assimilation. Removal treaties targeted not only the largest southern tribes—the Choctaws, Chickasaws, Creeks, Cherokees, and Seminoles—but also smaller northern tribes such as the Potawatomis, Shawnees, Ottawas, and Sauks and Foxes. In terms of the American West, the removal policy demonstrated an early variation of what the historian Alfred Runte has called the "worthless land" thesis. The same logic that relegated eastern Indians to "worthless" western lands would later be used to justify the creation of such diverse entities as national parks, nuclear bomb test sites, toxic waste dumps, and numerous Indian reservations.

West of the fertile Mississippi Valley, government explorations led by Lieutenant Zebulon Pike in 1806–7 and Major Stephen H. Long in 1820 had produced vivid descriptions of the Great Plains as a vast arid area. The map that accompanied the publication of Long's report in 1823 labeled most of present-day Kansas, Nebraska, and eastern Colorado as "The Great American Desert." Such information indicated that Indians removed beyond the Mississippi would live, at best, on the far western fringe of usable agricultural lands within the Louisiana Purchase, primarily in the eastern portions of present-day Kansas and Oklahoma.

The government continued its removal efforts into the 1850s. Not all Indians were forced across the Mississippi. After the roundup of thirteen thousand Cherokees by the military, at least two thousand died in late 1838 along the infamous "Trail of Tears" on their way to present-day eastern Oklahoma. Perhaps a thousand Cherokees avoided the military by hiding in the mountains of western North Carolina. Some Choctaws stayed behind in the state of Mississippi. The Senecas of upstate New York swapped the lands reserved for them in the West for a portion of their old homeland. In the Black Hawk War of 1832, belligerent Sauks and Foxes failed to retain their lands in Illinois and Iowa. On the other hand, some Seminoles fought a successful guerrilla war and stayed in the Everglades of Florida. Other natives managed to keep some lands in Michigan and Wisconsin. Nonetheless, most eastern Indians were removed, with the result that American Indian history after the 1840s is overwhelmingly, though not exclusively, set in the West.

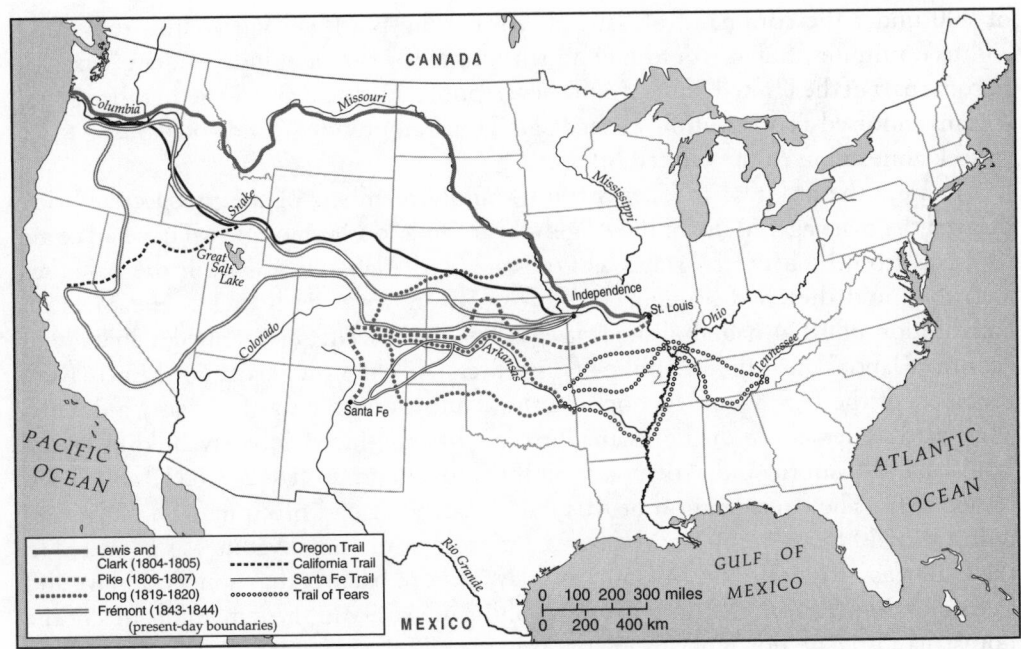

Exploration and Migration Routes, 1804–60

Although Indians in the West did not remain "free from the mercenary influence of White men" as President Jackson had promised, a flood of white settlers did not immediately follow the high tide of Indian removal in the 1830s. In fact, the bulk of the Louisiana Purchase, not just the area of present-day Oklahoma, could still be viewed as "Indian Territory" until after the Civil War. National initiatives leapfrogged beyond the borders of this first trans-Mississippi West—to Texas, the Oregon country, California, and the Great Basin. The Great Plains and the Rocky Mountains were places to pass through or go around. With no settlers in these areas, political incorporation—first with territorial governments and then with state constitutions—had to wait. American citizens were gone to Texas, bound for Oregon, or rushing to California.

Manifest Destiny

Anglo Texans made bad Mexicans. The independence of Mexico, established in 1821, did not produce a loyal citizenry in the frontier province of Texas. Anglo-American settlers had first migrated to Texas in large numbers in the 1820s under the careful direction of an *empresario* from Missouri, Stephen F. Austin. By 1836, open rebellion had created an independent Republic of Texas. Military victory did not come easily. At Goliad, not far from the Gulf of Mexico, one Texas garrison surrendered, only to see Mexican firing squads execute 342 soldiers as pirates on 27 March 1836. Earlier that month, on 6 March 1836, a superior Mexican force commanded by General Antonio López de Santa Anna had stormed the Alamo in San Antonio and killed every one of the Texas and American defenders, more than 180. The victorious Mexicans lost over 600 soldiers in the battle. Then on 21 April, Santa Anna suffered a crushing defeat—730 captured, 630 killed, and 208 wounded—after a surprise attack at siesta time by an army of 900 under the command of Sam Houston. The Battle of San Jacinto took only eighteen minutes, but it would take much longer for the now independent Texas to become part of the United States. In the new republic's first election in September 1836, Texans endorsed a constitution, elected Sam Houston president, and voted 3,277 to 91 to seek annexation to the United States.

Despite the ardor of the Texas suitor, family members of the prospective bride delayed the marriage. Many of the Anglo Texans had southern origins. They had come to Texas from such nearby states as Louisiana and Alabama and from the Arkansas Territory, and they had brought African-American slaves with them. The Mexican constitution of 1824 had abolished slavery, but the Texans maintained a charade of "contract labor" until the Republic of Texas reestablished the institution. Antislavery members of the U.S. Congress opposed the acquisition of Texas for nearly a decade. Westward settlement in the Louisiana Purchase had produced only slaveholding states: Louisiana, Missouri, and Arkansas, joining the Union in 1812, 1821, and 1836 respectively. The consideration of Missouri's statehood had precipitated a dangerous political crisis. In the resulting Missouri Compromise of 1820, Maine was admitted to the Union as a free state and Missouri as a slave state to balance the number of slave and free states. In addition, the compromise prohibited slavery in the remaining area of the Louisiana Purchase north of 36°30'—approximately the extended southern boundary of the new state of Missouri. Texas was not part of the Louisiana Purchase, and in any event, like Arkansas, it was south of the line of compromise. Nonetheless, elaborate political maneuverings, culminating with an extraordinary joint resolution by a lame-duck Congress at the behest of a lamer president, were required before Texas was annexed. Less than a year after this arranged marriage, Texas became a state, on 29 December 1845. Almost exactly one year later, on 28 December 1846, Iowa entered the Union as the first free state carved out of the Louisiana Purchase.

Like Texas, Oregon had not been part of the Louisiana Purchase. In a series of agreements beginning in 1818, the United States and Great Britain recognized their joint occupation of this far northwestern territory. During the decade that Congress by turns debated or ignored the annexation of Texas, Americans began to settle in the Oregon country, especially the fertile Willamette Valley. In 1834, Methodist missionaries from New England, led by Jason Lee, joined some of the first arrivals.

The short trip in the 1820s from the United States to the Austin colony in eastern Texas had few of the physical and psychological challenges produced by the overland trip to Oregon. The American immigrants who declared that they were "gone to Texas" did not have to go far, compared with the journey for Oregon's pioneers. At the time of independence in 1836, the population of the new Texas republic was approaching 40,000. When Texas entered the Union, this figure had soared to 142,000. By 1845, perhaps 6,000 Americans had settled in Oregon. Many were recent arrivals—900 in 1843, known as the "Great Migration." The next year 1,200 immigrants arrived, predominately from Missouri and Illinois. Traveling by covered wagon, on horseback, or, very often, by foot, these overlanders followed the Oregon Trail. Usually starting in Independence, Missouri, they crossed the plains along the North Platte River, rested at Fort Laramie, traveled through the Rockies via South Pass, stopped at Fort Bridger, and headed to Fort Hall on the Snake River. The immigrants survived more barren and mountainous terrain before reaching The Dalles for the hazardous descent of the Columbia River to the Willamette Valley. The journey stretched for two thousand miles and lasted 150 to 180 days.

The success of this overland migration supported the American claim to Oregon. Some political figures wanted all of the territory up to the northern boundary with Russian Alaska. In the 1844 presidential campaign, the Democratic candidate, James K. Polk, of Tennessee, took this position. He also advocated the annexation of Texas. His

DEATH OF LIEUT COL HENRY CLAY JR.
OF THE SECOND REGIMENT KENTUCKY VOLUNTEERS
at the Battle of Buena Vista F'y 23rd 1847.

Although the Mexican War became the first important event in American history to be documented by the new medium of photography, the American public preferred the dramatic fiction of contemporary prints that glorified the war in the name of "manifest destiny."

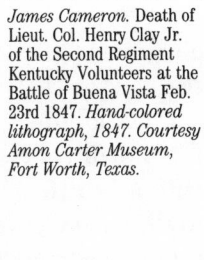

James Cameron. Death of Lieut. Col. Henry Clay Jr. of the Second Regiment Kentucky Volunteers at the Battle of Buena Vista Feb. 23rd 1847. *Hand-colored lithograph, 1847. Courtesy Amon Carter Museum, Fort Worth, Texas.*

Unidentified photographer. General Wool and Staff, Calle Real to South. *Daguerreotype, 1847. Beinecke Rare Book and Manuscript Library, Yale University, New Haven, Connecticut.*

major opponent, Henry Clay, of Kentucky, obfuscated. Polk won a narrow victory. The outgoing president, John Tyler, of Virginia, pushed through the joint resolution for annexation of Texas. After taking office, Polk addressed the "Oregon Question."

The new president articulated one of the major themes of his era—national expansion. His party, the Democrats, especially those in the Mississippi Valley, supported this ideal. In the debate over Texas annexation, an important phrase had appeared: "manifest destiny." John L. O'Sullivan, the editor of the widely circulated *Democratic Review*, placed these two words into print in July 1845. He argued that foreign interference in the acquisition of Texas was attempting to check "the fulfillment of our manifest destiny to overspread the continent alloted [*sic*] by Providence for the free development of our yearly multiplying millions."

In 1751, Benjamin Franklin had talked about a similar demographic destiny for Americans to fill up new western lands. The earlier continental consciousness of presidents like Jefferson, Monroe, and Adams also recognized a form of expansion. But what appeared in the 1840s had a more aggressive tone and nationalistic zeal. The reference to divine purpose and the claim of national superiority underlay an at times idealistic rhetoric that stressed the benefit to all humanity of America's growth. American Indians, who had been subjected to the paternalistic attitude and ethnocentric idealism of the removal policy, were already familiar with such self-serving assumptions.

The government's acquisition of Indian lands in the East closely paralleled the acquisition of western lands under manifest destiny. For its own purposes, the government used various combinations of negotiations, military actions, and treaties. In the case of the Indian removal policy, these aggressive efforts resembled a form of "domestic" foreign policy. In fact, the Supreme Court had created a special legal status for Indian tribes. Chief Justice John Marshall used the phrase "domestic dependent nations" in 1831 when he ruled that the Cherokees were not a foreign nation in relation to the federal government. Instead, the tribes came under the exclusive "protection" of the federal government, as demonstrated by numerous treaties. Marshall claimed that Indian nations occupied "a territory to which we assert a title independent of their will." In the mid-1840s, the administration of James K. Polk assumed that the British and the Mexican rights of possession to certain lands had also ceased. Manifest destiny dictated the removal of old land titles.

The dispute over British claims to the Oregon country ended without war. When James K. Polk said he wanted all of Oregon, he coveted a vast area that stretched from the northern boundary of Alta California to the southern border of Russian Alaska. This latter boundary inspired the political slogan "54°40' or Fight." But diplomatic officials already had begun to discuss the division of Oregon along the 49th parallel. Polk kept his belligerent tone in public statements that cheered expansionist Democrats. Behind the scene, compromise proceeded. Neither British nor American officials wished to push this issue to war. The British protected the fur-trade interests of the Hudson Bay Company by retaining the northern half of Oregon. The southern half had been nearly trapped out, and the company intended to move its major trading post to Vancouver Island. In Britain, the Anti-Corn Law League effectively agitated for peace as part of its campaign for free trade in food. Support for peace grew in the United States, since the government preferred to fight one war at a time and Congress had already declared war with Mexico before the proposed Oregon treaty reached Washington. Ratification quickly followed, on 18 June 1846.

Polk agreed to half of Oregon because the United States hoped to acquire all of northern Mexico. The possibility of open conflict had loomed since the formal annexation of Texas. Within a week after this joint resolution by Congress, the Mexican minister vehemently protested and left Washington. Mexico had refused to recognize the independence of Texas or the claim, made by the new republic, that its international boundary was the Rio Grande. The Nueces River had been Mexico's southern boundary for Texas. Roughly 150 miles separated these two rivers, but President Polk wanted more than this stretch of sandy soil. On his first day in office, he told one of his cabinet members that a prime objective of his administration would be the acquisition of California. He also wanted to settle the numerous claims of American citizens for financial losses in Mexico. Beginning in the 1820s, civil unrest and political turmoil had led to the loss of property by American owners. President Andrew Jackson had demanded repayment, but nothing happened until 1840, when the Mexican government accepted the ruling of a five-member international arbitration commission that awarded American claimants $2,026,000 to be paid in five annual installments. Mexico made three payments and then announced its inability to pay more.

The dispute over land and money led to war. The issue of the Texas boundary provided the flash point. In May 1845, President Polk directed military and naval forces to prepare for actions against Mexico. A few weeks later, American troops under General Zachary Taylor arrived in Corpus Christi, Texas, at the mouth of the Nueces. In November, the president sent a special envoy, John Slidell, to Mexico City. He instructed Slidell to purchase California, assume all claims against Mexico, and settle the boundary along the Rio Grande. Public hatred of the United States had grown so intense that President José de Herrera did not dare receive the U.S. envoy. Despite this anti-American gesture, Herrera's government fell in a bloodless revolution in late December. Slidell informed Polk, "Be assured that nothing is to be done with these people until they shall have been chastised."

The president received Slidell's message on 12 January 1846; the next day he ordered General Taylor to dispatch troops into the area north of the Rio Grande. This action provoked a Mexican response. On 25 April 1846, soldiers under the command of General Mariano Arista crossed the Rio Grande and attacked an American patrol, killing or wounding sixteen men. Truth became the seventeenth casualty when Polk proclaimed to Congress in his war message on 11 May, "Mexico . . . has invaded our territory and shed American blood upon the American soil."

American armies invaded Mexico across its northern frontier, south from the Rio Grande, and eventually inland from its eastern coast. This last campaign occurred in 1847, when General Winfield Scott marched his army through mountainous terrain from Veracruz to Mexico City. The fall of the capital helped Nicholas Trist, Polk's special commissioner, complete the negotiation of a final treaty. In exchange for a payment of $15,000,000, Mexico ceded the vast northern provinces of California and New Mexico to the United States and recognized the Rio Grande as the international border. The United States assumed the claims of $3,250,000 against Mexico by American citizens. Polk, the Democratic president, reluctantly supported the Treaty of

Guadalupe Hidalgo and forwarded it to the Senate. He had started to distrust Trist when the commissioner had become friendly with General Scott, a well-known Whig who, Polk reasoned, might emerge as a potent rival to the Democrats.

Some senators argued that the United States should ignore the treaty and claim all of Mexico by right of conquest. Other senators disagreed. John C. Calhoun, of South Carolina, a noted advocate of states rights and slavery, wanted only the sparsely settled northern lands. Using his best racial logic, he reasoned that Indians had not been incorporated into the Union but had "been left as independent people amongst us, or been driven into the forests." Calhoun warned: "To incorporate Mexico, would be the very first instance of . . . incorporating an Indian race; for more than half of the Mexicans are Indians, and the other is composed chiefly of mixed tribes. I protest against such a union as that! Ours . . . is the Government of a white race."

The Senate ratified the Treaty of Guadalupe Hidalgo by a vote of 38 to 14. Calhoun's rhetoric in defense of the treaty expressed the realpolitik of federal relations with American Indians and Hispanic Americans in the nineteenth century. The federal government willingly acquired new land, but it did not willingly embrace the people inhabiting that land. The remainder of Mexico had too many racially unattractive people to make the land attractive. As for the people within the Mexican cession to the United States, they were left on the margins of American society. A clear sense of racial hierarchy, based on the assumption of white cultural superiority, often led to legal, political, and social exclusion for racial minorities. Even rights guaranteed in a federal treaty could be reversed or ignored. Such was the case with the promised recognition of the title to land in the area ceded to the United States. Over time, the Californios and Hispanos of what had been northern Mexico lost most of their property. By the 1890s, often under the pretense of "clearing" the title to land that predated the Treaty of Guadalupe Hidalgo, Anglo-American lawyers and settlers controlled 80 percent of the original Spanish land grants in New Mexico. Like many American Indians, Hispanic Americans learned that the government of a white race paid little attention to the promises made to peoples of other cultures.

By force of arms, the United States acquired its second trans-Mississippi West in less than half a century. The Mexican-American War fulfilled President Polk's desires for expansion to the Pacific. Combined with the settlement of the Oregon Question in 1846, the Treaty of Guadalupe Hidalgo in 1848 provided the United States with an ample coastline in the Far West. It also increased the nation's internal empire by adding 1.2 million square miles, out of which would be carved the states of California, New Mexico, and Arizona and much of Nevada, Utah, and Colorado. With the fruits of war, the nation had grown by 66 percent.

The Mexican-American War changed the map of the United States, but it did not address the critical issues facing the nation. The apparent fulfillment of manifest destiny in continental terms amplified the need to reexamine the national agenda. Should slavery be permitted to grow westward with the nation, as it had after the Louisiana Purchase? How could a country that stretched from the Atlantic to the Pacific be kept unified? If the modest pace of migration to the West Coast had continued throughout the 1840s and 1850s, the importance of the West in national politics might also have

THE INDEPENDENT GOLD HUNTER ON HIS WAY TO CALIFORNIA.
I NEITHER BORROW NOR LEND

The discovery of gold in California in 1848 drew more than a quarter million immigrants to the area within five years, establishing a powerful American presence in a region only recently won from Mexico.

Unidentified artist. The Independent Gold Hunter on His Way to California. *Lithograph, ca. 1850. Courtesy Amon Carter Museum, Fort Worth, Texas.*

remained modest. But one event brought dramatic changes. News of the discovery of gold in northern California in January 1848 set off a rush of people, tying the fate of America's Far West to the fate of the nation.

The Nation's Region

More than 100,000 people streamed to California in 1849. This flood grew to over 250,000 by the end of 1852. They came from around the globe—from Peru and Chile, from Australia and China, from the British Isles and continental Europe, from the

Hawaiian Islands, Mexico, and Oregon, and from the Mississippi Valley and the eastern United States. Excluding Indians, California's population had been no more than 14,000 at the beginning of 1848. By the fall of 1849, enough people had arrived for a convention at Monterey to draw up a state constitution. This document prohibited slavery because the majority of miners did not want the unfair competition of slave labor in the diggings. The nation's Congress and new president now had to respond to the addition of a free state to the Union.

Since 1846, every northern state legislature, with the exception of Iowa, had endorsed a proviso originally authored by David Wilmot, a Democratic congressman from Pennsylvania. Wilmot advocated the prohibition of slavery in all territories acquired from Mexico. The Senate had blocked the enactment of the Wilmot Proviso into federal law, and President Zachary Taylor believed he could avoid further sectional discord if New Mexico and California immediately applied for statehood and avoided territorial status altogether.

By August 1850, Congress had fashioned an elaborate compromise that ignored New Mexico's application and balanced the interests of North and South. Most significant, a federal Fugitive Slave Law offset Southern opposition to California's admission as a free state. Yet the Compromise of 1850 merely delayed the larger crisis of civil war. During the 1850s, most slave states of the South became convinced that they could no longer stay in the Union. The South feared the subjugation of its political rights and the abolition of its peculiar institution of slavery by a Northern majority in control of the national government.

The South's anxiety expressed a widely held belief about the nature of freedom and government. Before America's Civil War, the concept of freedom often meant freedom from government. Eleven slave states took this position to its extreme and tried to free themselves from the Union as an exercise in radical states rights. The North's victory asserted the power of the federal government to ensure the nation's political unity. In addition, legislation passed during the Civil War demonstrated the government's support of the supposedly "free" enterprises of railroad development and agricultural homesteading. These economic initiatives continued after the war as federal troops and constitutional amendments attempted to politically reincorporate the former rebel states. The West, on the other hand, had come directly under federal power even before the Civil War, in ways that the South did not experience until after the war. Freedom from government did not apply so readily in the nation's newest region. In the West, the national government, aided at times by the U.S. Army, took direct action.

Immigrants appreciated the federal presence in the West. John D. Unruh, Jr., the preeminent historian of the trails to Oregon and California, observed, "Most pre-Civil War overlanders found the U.S. government, through its armed forces, military installations, Indian agents, explorers, surveyors, road builders, physicians, and mail carriers, to be an impressively potent and helpful force." For example, in 1843–44, the second of Frémont's three expeditions for the U.S. Army Corps of Topographical Engineers produced much helpful information about the route to Oregon, including a detailed map drawn by Charles Pruess. The U.S. Senate ordered the publication of ten thousand copies of Frémont's report, which contained the map. In 1846, Pruess produced a second, more elaborate map of the Oregon Trail, which became an oft-used reference.

Overlanders insisted on protection during their travels, as well as information about the route. The federal government provided military support. In fact, soldiers easily outnumbered other groups of federal employees in the West. At times during the 1850s, 90 percent of the U.S. Army was stationed at the seventy-nine posts throughout the trans-Mississippi. In 1860, on the eve of the Civil War, the total reached 7,090 enlisted men and officers. Initially, in the 1840s, the army had relied on expeditions to assert its presence in the West. Along the main immigrant route in 1845, Colonel Stephen W. Kearny took a military force of three hundred to South Pass via the fur-trading post at Fort Laramie. His dragoons wanted to impress the Plains Indians with the might of the United States and prevent any attacks against the overlanders. The next year, Congress approved legislation to establish fixed military posts along the Oregon Trail. By 1850, three had been established: Fort Kearny, on the south bank of the Platte; Fort Laramie, purchased by the government; and what became Fort Dalles, on the Columbia River. The freighting of goods, the rotation of troops, and the communication between posts improved the safety and services along the trail. Supply towns, where passing travelers could find necessities and diversions, grew up near each fort.

Government planning in the 1840s had anticipated increased migration to Oregon's Willamette Valley. By the 1850s, gold in the Sierra Nevada had made California the major destination for cross-country travel. National political leaders advocated the construction of a transcontinental railroad that could ship the riches of California to the East and deliver people and goods to the Far West. The state that contained the eastern terminus would gain a gigantic economic windfall. The railroad frenzy amplified divisions between North and South during the intense political maneuverings in Congress. Not one but four transcontinental surveys were authorized under the direction of the army, in order to determine the best route. Undertaken in 1853–54, these four expeditions produced their own gold mines of scientific information about specific cross sections of the West. Nonetheless, since a southerner—Jefferson Davis, of Mississippi—had overseen these surveys as secretary of war, few were surprised in 1855 when a preliminary report endorsed the southernmost route, along the 32nd parallel.

The North did not want the South to profit from the transcontinental railroad. One attempt in 1854 to preempt a southern route was the Kansas-Nebraska Act organizing the Kansas and Nebraska territories. With the federal government established in these areas, construction of the federally supported railroad could begin in Chicago, the largest city of the home state of the architect of the act, Senator Stephen A. Douglas. Ironically, Douglas had marshaled Southern votes for the two new territories by including in this legislation a repeal of the Missouri Compromise line. Although this meant that slavery could expand into areas that had been considered "free soil" since 1820, Douglas confidently assumed that "popular sovereignty," the political action of the citizens in the new territories, would prevent the growth of slavery. The aftermath of the Kansas-Nebraska Act is well known. Emotions ran high, especially in the North, where a new political party coalesced around the anti-Nebraskaites, who soon took another name—Republicans. The Kansas Territory, which bordered on the slave state of Missouri, plunged into violence and turmoil, with fighting between proslavery and antislavery settlers. The decision about the transcontinental railroad remained unresolved until after the outbreak of the Civil War, when all southern routes were readily eliminated.

Yet, Douglas's assumptions about the workings of popular sovereignty in the West were not impractical. In 1854, slavery was not permitted in the territory of Oregon or the state of California. New Mexico, which shared a border with the slave state of Texas, had proposed a state constitution, written in 1850 and ignored by Congress, that also denied the expansion of slavery. In fact, the Compromise of 1850, whose passage Douglas had engineered, organized the territories of New Mexico and Utah without reference to slavery. Applying the principle of popular sovereignty, Congress had empowered the territorial legislatures of New Mexico and Utah to decide on the slavery issue. Neither had established the South's peculiar institution.

Although these territories were allowed popular sovereignty on the slavery issue, the federal government retained considerable power in the West. As a result, in 1857, the Mormons in Utah Territory found themselves at war with the United States. The territory of Utah had not taken the fast road to statehood but remained under federal domination for decades. After the Mormon pioneers arrived in the Great Basin in 1847, their leader, Brigham Young, advocated the creation of the state of Deseret, which stretched to the southern California coast. Congress rejected a petition for Deseret's statehood in 1849 and instead created the territory of Utah in 1850, with greatly reduced boundaries. A paper government for the state of Deseret continued until 1872, but any possibility of political independence for the Mormons ended in 1857 when President James Buchanan dispatched one-sixth of the U.S. Army to Utah to prevent what his friends and advisers considered a potential rebellion.

What focused the fury of the nation against the Latter-day Saints was not simply Mormon ambitions to control more land. In 1852, the church's leadership had publicly announced what some people had suspected for years. As part of their religious practice, many Latter-day Saints engaged in plural marriage—that is, men had two or more wives at the same time. America now had a second peculiar institution or, as the new Republican party viewed it, a twin evil to slavery. Federal territorial appointees complained that a notorious polygamist, Brigham Young, controlled the Utah Territory through his control of the Mormon Church.

As the historian Howard R. Lamar has explained, President Buchanan's decision to send the U.S. Army into Utah contained several political messages. "The Utah crisis could divert the whole nation from its preoccupation with slavery. The sight of the United States reasserting jurisdiction over a region practically claiming independence would also give pause to Southern secessionists and delimit the more extreme demands uttered in the name of states rights." It would also reassure Northern Republicans that "to believe in popular sovereignty was not to condone polygamy."

The soldiers of the so-called Utah War saw very little fighting. In effect, the national government established military occupation in the territory. Camp Floyd, the major installation in Utah, was located forty miles south of Salt Lake City. A garrison that averaged twenty-four hundred soldiers stayed there until 1860. During 1858 and 1859,

Created by Congress in 1867, the Peace Commission sought to persuade Indians to settle on reservations in exchange for government benefits. Its name notwithstanding, the Peace Commission was backed by the federal army, which stood ready to enforce reservation boundaries if peaceable negotiations failed.

Alexander Gardner (1821–82). Peace Commission Treaty Negotiations with the Cheyenne and the Arapaho at Fort Laramie, Wyoming. *Albumen silver print, 10 May 1868. Smithsonian Institution, National Anthropological Archives (#3686), Washington, D.C.*

as a show of force, the army concentrated more troops at Camp Floyd than at any other location in the United States.

War and the White Road

During the 1850s, the federal government tried to control not only the apparently rebellious residents of Utah Territory but also the diverse native peoples of the trans-Mississippi West. The result was a series of wars that lasted into the 1890s. Sometimes warfare flared because of federal actions and sometimes because of federal inactions. During these four decades, not all Indian tribes fought American troops, but all Indians came under the federal government's policy of cultural assimilation.

After negotiated agreements, military pacification, or a combination of the two, most native peoples relocated to reservations, where federal agents attempted to lead them on the "white road." Through education and missionization, the government hoped to transform tribal peoples into independent Christian farmers. Under the federal government, both civilian and military officials implemented Indian policies. Initially, in 1824, Congress organized the Indian Bureau as part of the Department of War. In 1849, the bureau became part of the newly created Department of the Interior. For the next three decades, advocates of military control of Indian affairs argued that the bureau should be returned to the War Department, since soldiers had more experience and exerted firmer discipline in dealing with native tribes. They pointed to the corrupt financial dealings by some agents and the continued belligerence of some natives. Supporters of civilian control pointed to examples of unnecessary military violence and bloodshed. They argued that soldiers were ill prepared to deal with the Christian, humanitarian needs of the Indians on the reservations. Each side had its supporters and detractors in Congress. The Indian Bureau stayed put, but Indian policy remained a combined, if sometimes contentious, effort by both sides. For example, during the presidency of Ulysses S. Grant, Christian denominations administered specific Indian agencies. Meanwhile, the military attempted to settle all Indians on their assigned reservations, where they would be cared for by the Christian agents. General William T. Sherman described the effect on the Indians as a "double process of *peace* within their reservation and war *without*."

The concerted commitment to a reservation policy had begun during James K. Polk's presidency. William Medill, Polk's commissioner of Indian affairs, advocated the establishment of "colonies" for the Indians native to the region beyond the Mississippi. His was not an original idea. Concentrated colonies, or reservations, had been tried in the East before the removal policy attempted to create a "permanent" Indian frontier. The reservation policy became a form of internal removal within the West. It either reduced the homeland of a native people or moved them to a new location—where they also had less land but were to be protected from evil influences and guided along the road to assimilation. Like the justification of removal, the defense of reservations fused humanitarian concern for the Indians' future welfare with a self-serving ethnocentrism. By the 1880s, in near unanimity, government officials, military officers, congressional leaders, and Christian reformers agreed that allowing tribal landholdings and promoting tribal culture should end. They believed that reservations should disappear along with Indian identity.

Reservations were now seen as obsolete in terms of assimilation. This led to the eventual breakup of many reservations after the passage, in 1887, of the General Allotment Act, often called the Dawes Act after the Massachusetts senator who sponsored the bill. The Dawes Act began a process that further reduced the lands claimed by American Indians. Initially, lands not allotted to Indians became "surplus" and could be sold to non-Indians. Eventually, after the lapse of the government's title in trust, many individual Indians sold their allotments. In 1881, the federal government recognized over 155 million acres as Indian lands. By 1900, the figure had shrunk to under 78 million acres. A few tribes, such as the Navajos and Senecas, managed to escape allotment entirely, but for those who did not, until federal law ended the process of allotment in 1934, Indians under the Dawes Act and its successors lost 60 percent of their lands, which included 66 percent of the lands allotted to individual natives.

The Dawes Act helped create more acreage for non-Indian agriculturalists, but it did not guarantee economic prosperity. In the extensively arid portions of the West, such as the Great Plains, farmers recurrently failed. In the 1870s, drought and grasshoppers doomed many efforts. In the 1880s, a major agricultural depression—tied to deflation, debt, overproduction, and world markets—ruined more farmsteads. In each decade, destitute citizens turned to state governments and federal agencies for relief. Yet, these hard times for white farmers never altered the Jeffersonian idealism that produced the Dawes Act. The government's policy continued to assume that the route to salvation for Indians followed the white road to the church, the school, and the farmstead.

Only a few decades earlier, during the 1850s, the federal government had emphasized treaty negotiations to establish reservations in places such as California and Oregon and to ensure safe passage across the Great Plains. In California, three federal commissioners hastily attempted to set aside 11,700 square miles of land in a series of reservations for 139 small tribes and bands. More than 175 other California tribes were ignored, but that did not matter to the gold-hungry Californians who protested giving to Indians any lands that might contain mineral wealth or that could be used for agriculture. The U.S. Senate refused to ratify these treaties. Many members of Congress believed that California's diverse Indians had no title to the land. By March 1852, Congress did approve California's first superintendent of Indian affairs, the well-intentioned Edward F. Beale. He believed that the old mission system could serve as a model to train the Indians in useful labor, under the guidance not of a Catholic priest but of a federal agent aided by U.S. troops.

In May 1854, Congress learned that Beale was nearly $250,000 in arrears in his official accounts. A later investigation exonerated him, but not before he had lost his appointment. The government's search for parcels of land suitable for Indian resettlement limped along, with modest results and no clear establishment of title. The reservations in California were mostly small and scattered rancherias that, individually, gave some shelter to a few Indians. Meanwhile, the impact of the gold rush had destroyed thousands of other Indians. Some California argonauts hunted Indians like wild animals, and all refused to respect Indian land use. Murder, starvation, and disease created a demographic disaster. In 1845, about 150,000 native people lived in California. By 1856, they numbered as few as 25,000.

The Indian situation in Oregon produced its own set of tragedies. President Polk appointed Joseph Lane, a hero of the Mexican-American War and a politician from Indiana, as the first governor of the Oregon Territory in 1848. As was often the case, the governor was responsible for Indian affairs as well. Lane traveled throughout Oregon to observe the Indians. He also noted the natural riches of the new territory and determined that the rush of settlers to western Oregon would doom the Indians to "poverty, want, and crime" if they were not relocated to "a district removed from the settlements." The territorial legislature followed the governor's advice and asked Congress to purchase native lands and remove the Indians. The territory's delegate to Washington, Samuel R. Thurston, proposed that the Indians be placed east of the Cascade Mountains. In 1850, three federal commissioners were appointed to carry out the extinguishment of titles and the removal of several Oregon tribes. The commissioners reported that removal might prove disastrous, since most of the Indians of the Willamette and lower Columbia valleys survived by fishing. Instead of relocation, the commissioners negotiated six treaties that reduced the Indians' lands but reserved a few sections, including some fishing grounds, for native habitation. Congress never ratified these treaties or thirteen more negotiated by the territory's superintendent of Indian affairs, Anson Dart.

Meanwhile, settlement aggressively expanded under the Oregon Donation Land Law of 1850, which ignored Indian title and granted 320 acres to any citizen or prospective citizen who cultivated the land for four years. The arrival of gold seekers in the Rogue River country, south of the Willamette Valley, created more problems. Army regulars and Oregon volunteers quelled hostilities in the summer and fall of 1853. A treaty of cession left the Rogue River Indians with a small temporary reservation. Tensions increased, and a larger war broke out in the area in 1855. Oregon volunteers and U.S. regulars this time forced the Rogue River Indians to surrender. In the summer of 1856, these Indians were removed to a reservation in the Coast Range. From 1853 to 1855, without open warfare, other Oregon tribes capitulated to federal demands and accepted treaties that left them with small reserves of land and the promise of annual government support in the form of material goods, formal education, and agricultural development. Congress ratified all these treaties by 1859.

In California and Oregon, during the 1850s, new arrivals overwhelmed—and in some places annihilated—the native peoples. On the Great Plains, the Indians' fate did not unfold so rapidly. During the first three weeks of September 1851, an estimated ten thousand American Indians gathered for a treaty council near Fort Laramie. The powerful western Dakotas, known as the Teton Sioux or Lakotas, with their Arapaho and Cheyenne allies dominated the conference. But Assiniboins, Shoshones, Arikaras, Hidatsas, Mandans, and Crows also attended. A former fur trader, David D. Mitchell, of St. Louis, led the U.S. delegation under the protection of 270 soldiers.

The Treaty of Fort Laramie did not establish reservations for its Indian signatories. This agreement simply marked boundaries for the different tribes, to promote peace on the Plains and provide safe passage for overland travelers. It also permitted the government to build military forts and construct roads on Indian lands. Beyond the immediate distribution of numerous presents, the government promised to deliver annually for fifty years useful goods, such as domestic animals and agricultural implements, with a total value of fifty thousand dollars per year. The Senate later reduced these annuities to ten years with a possible five-year extension and increased the annual value to seventy thousand dollars.

The Indians accepted the presents, but they did not necessarily recognize the boundaries imposed by the treaty. Blue Earth, of the Brulés, warned, "We claim half of all the country; but we don't care for that, for we can hunt anywhere." Another Lakota, Black Hawk, of the Oglalas, complained: "You have split the country and I don't like it. What we live upon we hunt for, and we hunt from the Platte to the Arkansas, and from here up to the Red But[t]e and the Sweet Water. . . . These lands once belonged to the Kiowas and Crows, but we whipped these nations out of them, and in this we do what the white men do when they want the lands of the Indians."

The Fort Laramie Treaty of 1851 did not end intertribal raiding or warfare. It did not prevent the eventual hostilities between the U.S. Army and the aggressively expanding Teton Sioux. And it may not even have been necessary to protect the overlanders as they crossed the Plains. The historian John Unruh's careful analysis of the California and Oregon trails from 1840 to 1860 showed that of the approximately 250,000 overlanders who took these routes, fewer than 400 were killed. Of these killings, nearly 90 percent occurred west of South Pass. Despite the great fears expressed by travelers during the journey and the fabricated accounts of Indian attacks in contemporary newspapers and later pioneer memoirs, the trip across the Plains was usually peaceful.

Conquest and Survival

Peace did not continue between the U.S. Army and the Teton Sioux. The fate of the Lakotas on the Great Plains and of another Indian society, the Navajos, in the Southwest demonstrated that military conquest could result in political subjugation but not cultural assimilation. The Lakotas and Navajos exemplify the mixed results of the government's Indian policy in the last half of the nineteenth century. These native peoples lost wars with the United States and were placed on reservations, but they retained their cultural identity and their commitment to a tribal homeland.

Warfare began, at times, from seemingly trivial causes. The first significant armed clash between Lakota warriors and U.S. regulars revealed how miscommunication could produce tragic results. During late July 1854, some four thousand Brulés, Oglalas, and their allies had gathered near Fort Laramie for the distribution of the annuities guaranteed by the treaty of 1851. By mid-August, the federal Indian agent had not arrived to supervise the distribution, and tensions had grown between the outnumbered soldiers at the fort and the Indians encamped in the valley of the North Platte. The nearly constant stream of overlanders along the valley only increased the volatility of the situation. Late on the afternoon of 17 August, a weary cow lagged behind a passing train of Mormon immigrants and wandered among some Brulé lodges, where a visiting Miniconjou Sioux killed it. The Mormon owner demanded punishment of the Miniconjou, so on the morning of 19 August, the commander at the fort sent twenty-nine of his seventy-five infantry, two cannon, and one interpreter, under the command of Brevet Second Lieutenant John L. Grattan, to make an arrest. As this force approached the Brulé camp, the interpreter, drunk with more than courage, called out that the army planned to kill all the Sioux and that he would cut out and devour their hearts. The Brulés did not attack, even when Grattan formed a battle line in the center of their camp. The band's leader, Conquering Bear, had offered many horses in payment for the dead bovine and tried to calm both Grattan and the threatened Miniconjou. The interpreter garbled Conquering Bear's words, and Grattan had his men level their guns at the superior Indian force. Whether the Miniconjou or the soldiers fired first is not clear, but after shots were fired, Conquering Bear urged his people not to shoot. A second volley killed the Brulé leader, and the Indians attacked, killing every member of Grattan's command. The Miniconjou survived. The Lakotas emptied the warehouse and distributed the annuities on their own. They did not attack the fort but split into small bands and left the area.

A year later, in August 1855, after the public outcry over the "Grattan Massacre," the army sent General William S. Harney to lead seven hundred troops out of Fort Leavenworth in Kansas. This show of force began with the annihilation of a Brulé village in western Nebraska, where more than a hundred Indian men, women, and children died. During the fall, Harney marched his men through the heart of the Lakotas' hunting grounds, from Fort Laramie northeast to Fort Pierre on the Missouri. In March 1856, a major council convened at this fort, with representatives from all bands of the Lakotas, including the aloof Hunkpapas. This gathering reaffirmed the Fort Laramie Treaty of 1851. The Lakota leaders also agreed to surrender all warriors still wanted by the army for the Grattan incident.

The federal attack on Indian self-determination during the 19th century included the forcible displacement of tribes, the creation of a reservation system, and the more subtle devaluation of Indian cultures and histories.

Removed more than 300 miles in 1864 to Fort Sumner in Bosque Redondo, New Mexico Territory, these Navajos work under the watchful eye of military guards. In 1868, the Diné were permitted to return to a reservation carved from their former homeland.

Unidentified photographer. Displaced Navajos at Fort Sumner. *Photograph, 1866. Courtesy Museum of New Mexico (#1816), Santa Fe.*

The end of the great buffalo herds aided the government's efforts to confine native peoples to reservations. By the late 19th century, many Plains Indians—like the Lakotas shown here—were increasingly dependent on food and other supplies distributed by government agents.

Unidentified photographer. Dispersement of Government Rations. *Photograph, late 19th century. Smithsonian Institution, National Anthropological Archives (#56630), Washington, D.C.*

By the close of the nine-
teenth century, both
government schools
and privately run
training institutes
encouraged cultural
assimilation and dis-
couraged traditional
behavior. In this photo-
graph, Native Ameri-
cans share a history
class with African
Americans at the
Hampton Institute in
Virginia. Next to a bald
eagle, one native poses
in traditional cloth-
ing—not necessarily of
his own people. The les-
son appears to be that
both the Indian and the
bird are exotic subjects
doomed to survive only
in museums.

Frances Benjamin
Johnston (1864–1952).
Class in American History
(plate from an album of
the Hampton Institute).
Platinum print, 1899–1
900, 7½ x 9½ in. Gift of
Lincoln Kirstein, The Muse-
um of Modern Art, New
York.

Despite Harney's apparent success, the balance of power on the plains had not
clearly shifted in favor of the U.S. Army. The outbreak of the Civil War in 1861 incited
military combat from the Mississippi Valley eastward and left much of the West with
few regular army units. More volunteers replaced the regulars. This change in personnel
did not improve Indian affairs, as demonstrated by one infamous event on Sand Creek
in the Colorado Territory. At dawn on 29 November 1864, one thousand of the Third
Colorado Volunteers, under the command of Colonel John M. Chivington, attacked
the camp of some five hundred sleeping Cheyennes. Black Kettle and White Antelope,
the Cheyenne leaders, believed that a peace treaty was in effect and had turned in their
arms at Fort Lyon. The soldiers slaughtered men, women, and children indiscriminately
and mutilated their bodies. At least one hundred and fifty Indians died. The volunteers
returned to Denver to cheering crowds that admired the scalps and severed genitals
displayed like trophies of battle. A joint congressional committee later investigated the
Sand Creek Massacre and condemned Chivington, but he could not be punished, since
he had left the army.

The Cheyennes retaliated by twice attacking Julesburg, Colorado, and by halting
travel across the plains to Denver. The Teton Sioux, close allies of the Cheyennes, were
already agitated by an uprising in 1862 of the starving Santee Sioux bands in Minnesota,
who had not received their treaty annuities. Militia and volunteer troops had defeated
the Santees, who were expelled from Minnesota. Many Santees fled westward into

Lakota country, but thirty-eight captives were hanged at Mankato on 26 December 1862. Events in Minnesota and Colorado enraged many Lakotas, who also condemned the opening in 1863 of a route from Julesburg, Colorado, to the new gold camps in western Montana. The Bozeman Trail cut through the heart of Lakota territory in the Powder River country, and the U.S. Army had established three forts along the trail to protect travelers and freighters. Red Cloud, of the Oglalas, led the Lakotas' resistance and trapped U.S. troops in all three forts. On 21 December 1866, outside one of these forts, eighty men under the command of Lieutenant Colonel William J. Fetterman died in an ambush skillfully planned by a force of Lakotas, Cheyennes, and Arapahos. As a result of the annihilation of Fetterman's command, along with an ineffective military expedition in 1865–66, Congress advocated negotiations to resolve the Powder River War. After elaborate efforts, the government's peace commission produced a treaty at Fort Laramie late in 1868. Red Cloud promised to keep his Oglala followers out of war, and the army agreed to abandon its three forts. Hostilities had ended, and the Lakotas held the upper hand.

By 1868, in the Southwest, the Navajos had fared much worse in their relations with the United States. War with American forces had come during the years that Americans were fighting each other. The largest Civil War battle in the Far West had been fought in New Mexico at Glorieta Pass in late March 1862. At this engagement, John M. Chivington, who would lead the slaughter at Sand Creek in 1864, helped defeat a Confederate army. The Union's victory ended any serious threat of Confederate control in the Southwest. In August 1862, Brigadier General James H. Carleton arrived in New Mexico in command of a column of California volunteers; with the Confederate force already defeated, he turned to fighting the Indians. Carleton wanted to end raids by the Mescalero Apaches and by the Navajos. He directed his old colleague, Colonel Kit Carson of the New Mexico volunteers, to invade first the lands of the Apaches and then those of the Navajos. By the end of March 1863, more than four hundred Apaches had been relocated to the new reservation at Bosque Redondo, next to the new military post of Fort Sumner. Carson next attacked the Navajos, whose population of ten thousand may have been twenty times greater than that of the Mescaleros. General Carleton had one message for the Navajos: "Go to Bosque Redondo, or we will pursue and destroy you. We will not make peace with you on any other terms."

Carson's men destroyed orchards, crops, and livestock. They marched through Canyon de Chelly, the Navajos' great citadel. To avoid starvation, six thousand Navajos surrendered by the spring of 1864. The military then organized the Navajos' Long Walk—three hundred miles southeast to Bosque Redondo. By the end of the year, eight thousand Indians had been relocated there. Those who refused to surrender hid in isolated areas of their homeland or fled west. One Navajo, Curly Tso, recounted that many of the Diné (Najavos) saw Hweeldi (Bosque Redondo) as a place "where they would be put to death eventually."

Carleton saw the new reservation as a place of cultural transformation where the Apaches and Navajos would take up farming and where their children would learn to read and write and acquire the "arts of peace" and the "truths of Christianity." The superintendent of Indian affairs for New Mexico, Michael Steck, had his doubts. He had been the agent for the Mescalero Apaches and he knew that they considered the Navajos to be "inveterate enemies." He also knew that the land at Bosque Redondo could not support such a concentration of people. Carleton's grand experiment failed, destroyed by the forces of nature as much as by the forces of culture. Drought and insects devastated the crops. The government delivered inadequate supplies. Once more the Diné faced starvation.

In 1868, the same congressionally appointed peace commission that negotiated the new treaty at Fort Laramie sent two representatives to Bosque Redondo. On 1 June the representatives, who saw the suffering of the Navajos, signed a treaty that allowed the people to return to a reservation carved out of the Indians' old homeland. The document still advocated programs such as schooling and farming for the Navajos' cultural "advancement," but it recognized the need for the Navajos to begin again on familiar ground.

What unfolded for the Diné after their return home is a remarkable story. They reestablished their pastoral life-style with herds of sheep, goats, and horses, but they did not continue to raid their neighbors. Before removal, the Navajos had been a people divided into extended families, bands, and clans. But the four bitter years at Hweeldi had increased their sense of tribal unity and expanded the Diné's familiarity with Anglo-American culture. The treaty of 1868 gave the Diné clearly defined borders for their homeland. The historian Peter Iverson has observed, "Their political boundaries had been established: the Navajo Nation had begun." It also began to grow. By 1870, the population reached fifteen thousand. By the early twentieth century, the Navajo Nation was double that figure. The reservation grew as well. From 1878 to 1886, five additions to the original 1868 boundaries quadrupled the Navajos' territory. Most significant, the Navajo reservation was never broken up into individual allotments. The Diné had escaped the deleterious results of the Dawes Act and its successors, and the Navajo population and Navajo lands continued to grow throughout the twentieth century.

The Teton Sioux followed a different road into the twentieth century. Their treaty of 1868 had created the Great Sioux Reserve, which stretched from the Missouri River to the western boundary of the Dakota Territory. In addition, the Lakotas could still hunt in the Powder River country. The agreement contained the usual provisions for promoting "advancement," such as the establishment of farms and schools. It also included an article that promised no future cessions of the reservation without approval by three-fourths of the adult male Indians. Later documents ignored this provision and set the stage, in the late twentieth century, for a legal effort to reclaim Lakota lands. This case eventually reached the U.S. Supreme Court, where in 1980 a favorable verdict for the Lakotas resulted in financial offers from the federal government but no reacquisition of territory.

Many bands among the Lakotas, such as Sitting Bull's Hunkpapas, refused to recognize the Fort Laramie Treaty of 1868. Sitting Bull taunted the apparently cooperative Lakotas who accepted annuities at the government agencies located on the Great Sioux Reserve. He said, "You are fools to make yourselves slaves to a piece of fat bacon, some hard-tack, and a little sugar and coffee." When gold was discovered in the Black Hills, miners invaded the area, destroying an already ineffective peace. Instead of removing the miners, President Ulysses S. Grant, in late 1875, ordered the Lakotas to leave their winter camps and come into the agencies. Few complied, and the Great Sioux War of 1876–77 began.

The most famous battle of this war occurred on 25 June 1876 near the valley of the Little Bighorn River. The destruction of George Armstrong Custer's command by a vastly superior force of Lakotas and Northern Cheyennes became national news on 4 July, just as the United States prepared to celebrate the centennial of its Declaration of Independence. The Indians' one dramatic victory sealed their fate for the longer war. On 7 July 1876, General Philip H. Sheridan, in command of the Division of the Missouri, assured his superior, General William T. Sherman, "I will take the campaign fully in hand, and will push it to a successful termination sending every man that can be spared."

In a massive military effort, the U.S. Army defeated the Lakotas. Even before the final victory, the federal government began to reduce the lands of the Great Sioux Reserve. The president appointed a commission that met with Indian leaders at various agencies during the fall of 1876. The commissioners insisted that the Lakotas cede the Black Hills to the United States. The Indians complied, but this acquiescence did not constitute the approval of three-fourths of the adult males as specified by the treaty of 1868. Another round of reductions and divisions began in 1889 and created six reservations: Standing Rock, Cheyenne River, Lower Brulé, Crow Creek, Pine Ridge, and Rosebud. Eventually the six reservations were to be allotted and "surplus" lands acquired by non-Indians. The Great Sioux Reserve had been shattered.

Shattered too was the Lakota way of life. The loss of the Great Sioux War had been followed by the loss of the great buffalo herds. Some Lakotas turned to cattle raising and crop farming, but most became dependent on the government for food rations. By the late 1880s, the situation was desperate. Disease decimated Lakota cattle herds. Crops failed. Measles, influenza, and whopping cough were epidemic. Crops failed again. The government reduced rations, and the Lakotas starved.

The destitute Lakotas took heart in a new religious movement. The Ghost Dance promised the return of the buffalo and the disappearance of the white people. Nervous neighbors and anxious agents feared another war and asked the army to intervene. Once more the military moved on to Lakota lands, and once more tragedy resulted. The slaughter at Wounded Knee on 29 December 1890 killed 146 Indians, including 44 women and 18 children. Much hope died with them.

Like the Navajos' Long Walk, Wounded Knee placed the Lakotas at their historical nadir. In the twentieth century, their population would grow and their cultural identity would be maintained. But with reduced lands and continued impoverishment, the Lakotas became domestic, dependent peoples—often functioning as economic wards of the federal government. The Diné made a more successful adjustment to economic life in the twentieth century, developing arts, crafts, tourism, grazing, and energy resources on their unallotted reservation. But the Diné have not escaped the droughts, diseases, displacements, and internal divisions that continue to plague the twentieth-century Lakotas. And Indian reservations, whether allotted or not, remain internal colonies controlled to a great extent by a federal bureaucracy. This political status began to improve somewhat in the mid-1930s when the government created a New Deal for America's Indians. Allotment ended. Tribal governments and tribal lands gained legal recognition. But federal supervision continued. Only in recent decades has the possibility of self-determination in economic and political terms been openly considered as national policy.

The Prolonged Territorial Era

Self-determination may not yet fully exist on Indian reservations, but it supposedly came to the federal territories of the American West when they were granted statehood. Yet, admission as a state did not wean the former territories from the agencies of the federal government. During the last half of the nineteenth century, a federal bureaucratic system became well established in the western territories through the Department of the Interior's Indian Bureau, its General Land Office, and its Geological Survey (which after the Civil War expanded on the work of the Army Corps of Topographical Engineers). These federal agencies tried to map, assess, distribute, and develop a vast public domain while limiting the Native American use of that domain. By mid-century, east of the Mississippi, the policy of Indian removal and the massive sale of public lands had resulted in a federal bureaucratic presence limited primarily to institutions like the Post Office and the Customs Service, which also existed in the West. With the exception of the Civil War and the military occupation of the South during Reconstruction, the U.S. Army throughout the nineteenth century was largely a western army, manning posts and pursuing native peoples.

Much more than in the East, the federal government directly affected the lives of the residents of the trans-Mississippi through the actions of its bureaucracies as well as its army. These federal institutions became established in the West along with, or sometimes in advance of, settlements in the region. New arrivals in the West relied on the federal government for military protection, gainful employment, title to land, and relief during disasters. The modern federal government of the twentieth century with its expanded power and bureaucratic structure began to take shape in the American West of the nineteenth century. The historian Richard White has concluded: "While the federal government shaped the West, . . . the West itself served as the kindergarten of the American state. In governing and developing the American West, the state itself grew in power and influence."

Initially, political patronage typically determined appointments within these federal agencies that controlled the West. By the 1880s, in response to the efforts of reformers such as Carl Schurz, secretary of the interior from 1877 to 1881, a professional civil service began to emerge. In that same decade, the federal government started to reserve public lands, which eventually became national forests and national parks. Unlike in the East, vast acreage in the public domain did not pass to private ownership but remained public. Thus in the West when statehood came, the federal government controlled land within the states and retained professional bureaucrats to administer these lands. But statehood itself did not come quickly. With the exceptions of Texas and California, the western territories underwent a prolonged period of apprenticeship within the federal system.

Some people profited during the decades of delay before statehood. Within each territory, self-serving elites acquired much wealth and power as part of a process that the historian Howard Lamar has labeled "the politics of development." During the same era, the impoverishment of Native Americans demonstrated what might be called "the politics of underdevelopment." The loss of reservation lands and natural resources was the result of an assimilationist policy that failed, whereas the economic growth of the West and the admission of new western states might be considered an assimilationist policy that succeeded.

Not surprisingly, the Civil War influenced the commitment to firmer federal control over the western territories. The Lincoln administration extended the territorial system over the remaining unorganized lands beyond the Mississippi. The Republican-dominated Congress also wanted to keep the West in the Union, so in 1861 it organized the Dakota, Colorado, and Nevada territories. Arizona and Idaho followed in 1863, and by 1870, Wyoming and Montana had also become federal territories. Within the contiguous trans-Mississippi, only the Indian Territory remained an exception. But its special status as a reserve for native peoples did not survive once political incorporation into the Union began with the establishment of the Oklahoma Territory in 1890.

Congress readily created territories, but it reluctantly created states. Before the logjam broke in the late 1880s, only four western states had entered the Union—two during the Civil War, Kansas in 1861 and Nevada in 1864, and two after the war, Nebraska in 1867 and Colorado in 1876. Six territories finally gained statehood in 1889 and 1890: North Dakota, South Dakota, Montana, Washington, Idaho, and Wyoming. Four more states had to await admission because of issues delaying congressional approval. In Utah, the Mormon leadership officially abandoned polygamy in 1890; statehood followed in 1896. Oklahoma was next in 1907, after fusion with the remainder of the Indian Territory. Admission came for New Mexico and Arizona in 1912, after Congress reconsidered its attempt to join these territories. In New Mexico, hostile attitudes toward the Hispanic culture and citizenry had prolonged the territorial era for sixty-two years.

The years of New Mexico's territorial status, 1850–1912, are nearly congruent with a period that one scholar has labeled "The Second United States Empire." According to Jack Eblen, the First Empire lasted from 1787 to 1848, or from the passage of the Northwest Ordinance to the admission of Wisconsin. During these sixty years, the United States incorporated all the states through the first tier west of the Mississippi, with the exception of Minnesota. The Second Empire incorporated states across the continent before giving way to a Third Empire, which more firmly established American interests in the islands of the Caribbean and Pacific as well as northward in Alaska.

In terms of territorial policy, the First Empire began with an assumption of federal control over the organization of new lands under the model established by the Northwest Ordinance. Over time, the expansion of voting rights to nearly all adult white males resulted in greater political participation for a new territory's residents, especially in the election of a legislature. By 1836, these democratic ideals reached their culmination in the Wisconsin Organic Act, which replaced the Northwest Ordinance as the model for organizing new federal territories. Of course, federalism itself came under fire during the decades before the Civil War. The democratic rights of territorial residents became part of the debate over states rights and popular sovereignty. For those promoting states rights, the states and not the federal government held title to the territories. It followed, therefore, that if an institution such as slavery was permitted in some states, it could not be excluded from any territory. For the advocates of popular sovereignty, the people of the territory, and not the states or the federal government, should decide issues such as the establishment of slavery.

At least in terms of the slavery question, this debate ended after the Union victory in the Civil War. Federal power again became the guiding force in organizing the territories of the Second Empire, and some controls over popular sovereignty appeared. For example, by 1869, Congress had limited territorial legislatures to a biennial meeting of no more than sixty days. All territorial elections had to be reported to Congress, which reserved the right to resolve disputed elections, especially if they involved the selection of a territorial delegate.

The delegate represented his territory in Washington, but federal appointees represented the national government in the territory. More accurately, these appointees often represented particular political interests and specific factions within the national political parties. Some appointees were crooks. Others were hacks. The most prominent ones were the territorial governors, secretaries, and judges. Nominated by the president, they were confirmed by the Senate. Beyond these appointments, political patronage often determined who held other positions of federal employment in the territories, from surveyor generals, land registrars, and postmasters to U.S. marshals, customs agents, and Indian agents.

Within each western territory, stories of corrupt federal officials abound. Consider the case of Victor Smith, U.S. collector of customs for Puget Sound from 1861 to 1863. An appointee of the new Lincoln administration, Smith, a former newspaper reporter from Cincinnati, was a political crony of a fellow Ohioan, Secretary of the Treasury Salmon P. Chase. Soon after arriving in Port Townsend, Washington Territory's port of entry, Smith began to conspire to move the customshouse to a new townsite, Port Angeles, some forty-five miles to the west. Smith owned twenty-five acres at the Port Angeles site. Since loss of the customshouse would destroy Port Townsend's economy, Smith lied about his intentions while bombarding the secretary of the treasury with letters detailing the attractions of Port Angeles. Smith even returned to Washington, D.C., to help Chase steer through Congress the legal transfer of the port of entry. Meanwhile, the acting customs agent, Lieutenant James H. Merryman, had already written to Chase about Smith's fraudulent use of federal funds. At least $4,354.98 was missing.

Chase did nothing, and Smith returned to Port Townsend aboard the federal revenue cutter *Shubrick*. With the transfer enacted, Smith had come for the customshouse records. The town residents protested, but Smith threatened to have the *Shubrick* shell the customshouse. The ship's commander said he would have to follow Smith's orders. An angry mob of sailors and townspeople backed down in the face of this gunboat diplomacy. The records, along with the customs safe, were delivered to the *Shubrick*. One federal appointee had made off with the town's most important economic asset.

Victor Smith may stand as an example of the corrupt official who tried to profit from the territorial system. Civil service reform only started to take hold in the 1880s and never produced a territorial service for the Second Empire comparable to the colonial service of Great Britain's overseas empire. With patronage in control, men like Victor Smith sought federal jobs in order to rake off some of the funds intended for the

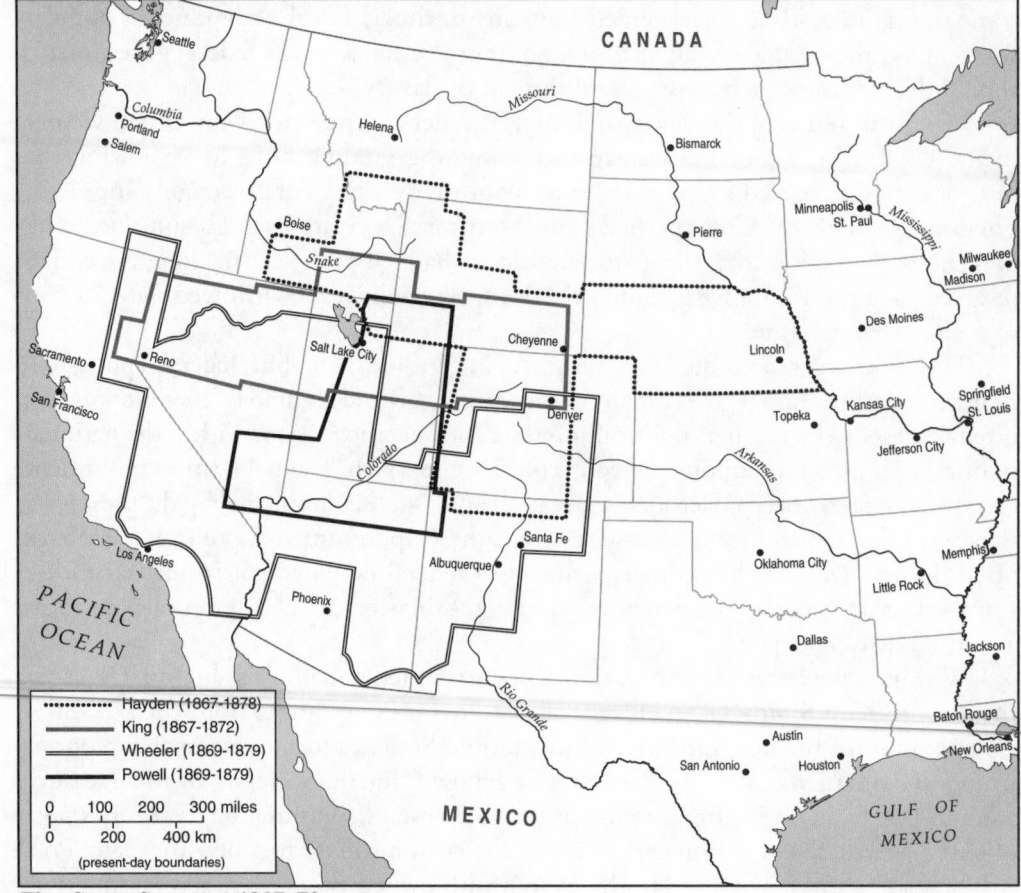

After the Civil War, the federal government renewed its interest in the western territories. Four major survey teams, each accompanied by artists and photographers, scientifically charted the interior West. Led by Clarence King, Ferdinand Hayden, John Wesley Powell, and George Wheeler, these teams produced extensive reports with illustrations that underscored the dramatic features and economic possibilities of the western landscape.

The Great Surveys, 1867–79

territories. They then participated in land investments, railroad schemes, and other business speculations—efforts not always so unwelcomed as the relocation of a customshouse.

Lamar's "politics of development" demonstrated that territorial governments functioned for the benefit of an oligarchy of federal appointees and business leaders. Simply put, the main business of territorial government was business. Mine owners, railroad developers, merchants, cattlemen, and bankers as well as lawyers, judges, and governors played an often profitable role in the politics of development. This fusion of business and government spurred economic development, as did the large federal subsidies to the territories. Along with the salaries of federal appointees and budgets to operate the territorial legislatures, federal funds maintained military posts, land offices, postal routes, and Indian agencies. Federal money also fed Indians on the reservations and built improvements within the territories, such as roads, forts, capitols, and prisons. Because of these expenditures, the federal government became the biggest business in some areas of the territorial West.

But what of the federal appointees who were themselves another form of federal investment in the West? They represented a system of patronage that did not necessarily

The wondrous images of Yellowstone created by artists with Ferdinand Hayden's survey helped persuade Congress to set the area aside as the country's first national park in 1872. For those unable to see the original photographs or watercolors, engraved reproductions in Hayden's annual reports made views of Yellowstone's marvels widely available.

Bisbing, after Thomas Moran and William Henry Jackson. Yellowstone Geysers. *Wood engraving, 1873. From F.V. Hayden,* Sixth Annual Report of the United States Geological Survey on the Territories *(1873).*

Like other survey photographers, Timothy O'Sullivan often included a human figure in his landscapes to give a sense of scale to his dramatic vistas.

Timothy O'Sullivan (1840–82). Shoshone Falls, Looking over Half of the Falls *(for the King Survey, along the Snake River in Idaho). Albumen silver print, 1868. International Museum of Photography at George Eastman House, Rochester, New York.*

produce corrupt or inept officials. Consider, for example, the collective qualifications of all territorial judges. Six hundred and eight individuals received appointments to the territorial courts between 1789 and 1959. Of this number, a majority (57.9 percent) were appointed between 1829 and 1897, from the presidential administration of Andrew Jackson through that of Grover Cleveland. These dates correspond to the years of greatest expansion for the territorial system. The judges of this era typically came from privileged, middle-class families. Well over half of them had attended or graduated from college, which placed their participation in higher education above that of members of the House of Representatives. Less than one-third of these judges had experience in any other court at any other level, a significantly lower rate of judicial service than may be found in other federal courts of the same decades. Sixty percent of the territorial judges had won election to a public office before their appointment, a level of political activism that paralleled that of Supreme Court justices and other federal judges. In other words, territorial and all other federal judges regularly established their affiliation with a political party by running for office. For some, this effort paid off with partisan appointments to the bench.

Territorial judges were well-educated but inexperienced appointees, with active political affiliations. In addition, they were outsiders, and they stayed only briefly on the bench. Between 1829 and 1896, three-quarters of the judges were not originally residents of the territories in which they served. Three-quarters also served less than four years on the territorial bench. The average time of service was 3.2 years, whereas the judges of the other lower federal courts averaged 12.4 years. Rapid turnover was endemic in the western territories. Of the 424 territorial governors, secretaries, and judges appointed between 1861 and 1890, 288 served for less than the four years of their original commission. In the case of territorial judges, most either resigned or were not reappointed. Only about 10 percent were removed from office. Party politics had created a revolving door of territorial appointments. The legal historian Kermit L. Hall notes, "Incumbents on the territorial bench after 1850 must have sensed that, if they did not resign, an incoming administration of the opposition party was likely to replace them."

The constant turnover in territorial appointees may have increased the citizenry's desire for statehood. Taking more government into their own hands could bring some stability, but first statehood needed to be established. And statehood did not come quickly. The case of Montana is typical. Political leaders in Montana, like those in other territories, saw statehood as a certification of successful growth in both economic and political terms. In the push for statehood, the politics of development had been successful enough to produce the politics of home rule. Advocates of statehood recognized that Montana would gain the right to elect its own governor, choose its own judges, and establish its own full representation to Congress. Large grants from federal lands could be used to support education, and a state government had the power to tax local corporations as well as the landholdings of railroads. Knowing the benefits of statehood, the 1883 territorial legislature called for the election of a state constitutional convention. In mid-January of 1884, the forty-one elected delegates gathered in Helena.

Like their election, the convention was generally a nonpartisan affair. Nonetheless, mining and cattle interests had effective representatives, led by the elected president of the convention, William A. Clark, of Butte, one of the wealthiest mining magnates in the United States. In twenty-eight days, the convention produced a document, which borrowed heavily from the constitutions of other states. In November, Montanans gave it their overwhelming approval by a vote of 15,506 to 4,266. They then awaited a positive response from Congress. It took four years.

The national election of 1884 produced a balance between the Democrats and the Republicans. The party of the Democratic president, Grover Cleveland, controlled the House of Representatives, but the opposition Republicans controlled the Senate. Each party blocked the admission of any state that might aid the other party. Since Montana and New Mexico were seen as potentially Democratic states, the Republican Senate stopped their admission. Likewise the Democratic House blocked the admission of Republican Washington Territory as well as a plan to divide Dakota Territory into two states and thus double the gain in Republican votes in Congress.

The election of 1888 gave Republicans control of both houses of Congress as well as the White House. Awaiting the inauguration of Benjamin Harrison, the lame-duck Democrats allowed the passage of an Omnibus Bill that enabled North and South Dakota, Washington, and Montana to proceed to statehood. Grover Cleveland signed the legislation before leaving office. New Mexico was not admitted, but Montana could now join the Union because Republican leaders had become convinced that immigration into the territory would soon produce a Republican majority in the new state. To add to the Republican forces in Congress, Idaho and Wyoming gained admission in 1890.

Fitting the American Mold

A Republican torrent had ended the logjam of admission for six western states. Such forceful partisanship also channeled the admission of the contiguous West's remaining four states. But it did not speed the process. For Utah, Oklahoma, New Mexico, and Arizona, delays continued until each territory had assured congressional leaders that it fit the American mold.

In the case of Utah, an agenda set during the era of Civil War and Reconstruction prevailed. In 1856, the newborn Republican party had denounced the "twin barbarisms" of slavery and polygamy. The Civil War dispatched one barbarism, but Republican Reconstruction ended when the South returned to domination by the Democratic party and the white race. Although Republicans lost their grip on the postwar South, they did not give up the fight against polygamy in the West. They saw Utah as a bastion for one party, the Democrats, under the domination of one church, the Latter-day Saints. Senator George Franklin Edmunds, of Vermont, took the initiative in attempting to reconstruct the Utah Territory. Edmunds had come to the Senate in 1865 as a radical Republican. He served as chair of the Senate Judiciary Committee from 1872 to 1891, with only a brief interruption from 1879 to 1881 under a Democratic majority. In the 1870s he supported legislation to dismantle the Ku Klux Klan and to guarantee civil rights in the South. These efforts had little success. In the 1880s, he pushed to end polygamy and to dismantle the Mormon church. These initiatives had more success.

The Edmunds Act of 1882 established fines and terms of imprisonment for men found guilty of formal polygamy or of informal cohabitation. Belief in plural marriage could exclude citizens from jury duty, public office, and voting. Children born after 1883 of polygamous marriages were declared illegitimate. A federal "Utah Commission" of five men registered voters and oversaw territorial elections. The work of this commission and of the federal courts had some impact, but it did end not polygamy. So by 1887, Senator Edmunds had established more radical powers for the federal government. The so-called Edmunds-Tucker Act of that year gave U.S. marshals wide latitude in arresting offenders. It empowered the Utah Commission to administer a qualifying oath for voters. It also dissolved the incorporated Church of Latter-day Saints and placed church assets in the hands of a non-Mormon receiver.

These antipolygamy laws sent hundreds of Mormon men either to jail or into hiding. The laws so disrupted the work of the Mormon church that after the death of the church president, John Taylor, in 1887, it took two years to go through the ritual of choosing the next president. After prayer and revelation, the new church leader, Wilford Woodruff, instructed his followers to abandon polygamy and to recognize the separation of church and state in the governance of Utah. Woodruff's manifesto in 1890 opened the way to statehood, which nonetheless required six more years of effort by Utahns.

Another Republican principle—homesteading—affected the Indian Territory. The Lincoln administration had produced the Homestead Act of 1862. In legislation such as the Timber Culture Act of 1873 and the Desert Land Act of 1877, Congress expanded the acreage that one settler might claim. By 1887, the homesteading ideal had been applied to Indian lands through the Dawes Act. The goal of Americanizing native peoples through small-scale farming resulted in the Americanization of "surplus" Indian lands by non-Indian farmers. In 1889, Congress authorized the opening of two million acres of "Unassigned Lands" in the middle of the Indian Territory. To claim farmsteads and townsites, fifty thousand people gathered on 22 April to participate in the first of the wild and dramatic "runs." A few months later, these lands formed the basis for the new Oklahoma Territory.

A federal commission chaired by the former governor of Michigan, David H. Jerome, aided the growth of the Oklahoma Territory. Under the principles of the Dawes Act, the Jerome Commission managed to create more surplus lands through the allotment of reservations in the western sections of the Indian Territory. Henry L. Dawes came out of retirement to head another commission that attempted to allot the remaining lands of the Indian Territory. Leaders of the Cherokees, Choctaws, Creeks, Seminoles, and Chickasaws resisted these efforts, but eventually, between 1898 and 1907, over 100,000 Indians from these five tribes were assigned lands. Surprisingly, very few acres became directly available for non-Indian settlement.

The five tribes of the Indian Territory tried to form a separate state that could not be absorbed into Oklahoma. A convention at Muskogee in the spring of 1905 produced a constitution for the proposed state of Sequoyah. Unfortunately, the chairman of the Senate Committee on Territories, Senator Albert J. Beveridge, of Indiana, had become favorably impressed with the "American" settlement of the territory of Oklahoma. The Indian Territory had a population equal to the state of Maine. It contained numerous railroads and incorporated towns. It also had more fertile land and better economic resources than the Oklahoma Territory. Beveridge, who had visited Oklahoma Territory briefly in 1902, believed that the Indian Territory should be joined to the "American" territory of Oklahoma to form one new state. His fellow Republican, President Theodore Roosevelt, agreed and recommended joint statehood in his annual message to Congress in December 1905. On 16 November 1907, the forty-sixth state officially entered the Union.

President Roosevelt and Senator Beveridge so liked "jointure" in the case of Oklahoma that they advocated a similar union for the Arizona and New Mexico territories. Both men belonged to the generation of Republicans influenced more by the Spanish-American War than by the Civil War. Another one of Beveridge's brief visits had been to one of America's newest possessions, the Philippines, which he considered a backward outpost of the former Spanish Empire. His contempt for the Spanish cultural heritage apparently extended to America's own Southwest. A quick tour of that region in 1902 convinced him that neither Arizona nor, most especially, New Mexico was advanced enough for statehood. Nonetheless, Beveridge decided that one vast state might shift the cultural balance toward the more American, but still backward, Arizona. A critic in Congress noted that Beveridge had decided "that one rotten egg is bad, but two rotten ones would make a fine omelet."

Given a chance to vote on "jointure," Arizona and New Mexico hatched different results. The referendum failed in Arizona, whereas it passed in New Mexico with the aid of political gamesmanship and much fraud. President Roosevelt eventually gave up on the proposition and announced in his last annual message to Congress in 1908 that each territory should gain statehood. Beveridge tried to persuade the new Republican president, William Howard Taft, to block admission for partisan reasons—Arizona might become Democratic, and New Mexico supported the wrong Republican faction. By 1910, the opinionated Indiana senator had reluctantly accepted the admission of both states. In 1912, Taft's signature ended this saga.

The admission of New Mexico and Arizona completed the formal political incorporation of the lands that formed the Second United States Empire. But, as some of the final disputes over statehood indicated, a far more complex process of cultural incorporation had not been completed. If anything, the admission of Utah, Oklahoma, Arizona, and New Mexico demonstrated that the American mold would have to be modified to incorporate distinctive peoples within the nation's expanded boundaries.

For decades, members of Congress had viewed the expansion of the nation as a grandly heroic adventure. Indeed, they could daily walk by a dramatic representation of national expansion—a painting that measured twenty by thirty feet on one wall of the U.S. Capitol. Congress commissioned this work in 1860 from Emanuel Leutze, the same artist who had produced the famous portrait *Washington Crossing the Delaware* (1851). In a vividly heroic tableau, Leutze filled a spectacular mountain passage with overlanders emigrating in wagons, mountain men traveling on horseback, women holding babies, men swinging axes, and even a freed slave leading a mule. Inspired by a line in a poem by the eighteenth-century Anglo-Irish philosopher George Berkeley, Leutze titled his work *Westward the Course of Empire Takes Its Way* (see color essay following p. 370). Only one figure, who waves his hat from atop a central pinnacle and resembles John Charles Frémont, hints at any role for the federal government in this great rush through the mountains. U.S. troops, Indian agents, and territorial officials are not part of the picture; neither are the native peoples and Hispanic residents of the Far West. Congressmen, in their own capitol building, could comfortably imagine that national expansion had been the manifest destiny of the American people and not the creation of the nation's government.

Although this image kept the government's cart behind the people's horse, it produced too simple of a picture. At times, the government proceeded westward more like a horseless carriage as it acquired, explored, and administered new lands. Into this vast territory, not only American emigrants but also federal agents and federal policies westward took their way. The initiatives of the nation's government sustained the country's growth, but these actions also enlarged the complexity of the nation's destiny. Thomas Jefferson's ideal of a compact and homogeneous republic could in no way stretch across the expanse of continent that, from east to west, measured itself as one nation. Nor could that nation grow westward in splendid isolation. The resources of the American West brought the country more fully into a global economy. Expansion also opened new doors for immigration from east and west, north and south. Ultimately, the incorporation of the American West multiplied the internal diversity of the United States and increased the nation's interconnections with the rest of the world. Globally the course of empire now would flow.

Bibliographic Note

For many of the topics, events, and individuals presented in this chapter, the best single-volume reference is Howard R. Lamar, ed., *The Reader's Encyclopedia of the American West* (New York, 1977). A revised second edition is in preparation for HarperCollins Publishers. Several books have surveyed the history of the American West with extensive attention to the actions of the federal government. Richard White's *"It's Your Misfortune and None of My Own": A New History of the American West* (Norman, Okla., 1991) presents a most insightful reinterpretation of how the federal government shaped the American West. Patricia Nelson Limerick's *The Legacy of Conquest: The Unbroken Past of the American West* (New York, 1987) gives witty, provocative commentary on some federal efforts. Frederick Merk's *History of the Westward Movement* (New York, 1978) is filled with useful information, whereas Ray Allen Billington and Martin Ridge's *Westward Expansion: A History of the American Frontier*, 5th ed. (New York, 1982) remains a thematically focused, grandly conceived narrative.

The best examination of Thomas Jefferson's interest in the trans-Mississippi West may be found in Donald Jackson, *Thomas Jefferson and the Stony Mountains: Exploring the West from Monticello* (Urbana, Ill., 1981). David Lavender's *The Way to the Western Sea: Lewis and Clark across the Continent* (New York, 1988) is a well-wrought narrative. Under the editorship of Gary E. Moulton, a superb multivolume edition of *The Journals of the Lewis and Clark Expedition* is being published by the University of Nebraska Press. James P. Ronda has considered the expedition in *Lewis and Clark among the Indians* (Lincoln, Neb., 1984) as well as *Astoria and Empire* (Lincoln, Neb., 1990). Three works by William H. Goetzmann have brilliantly explained the significance of American exploration: *Army Exploration in the American West, 1803–1863* (New Haven, 1959); *Exploration and Empire: The Explorer and the Scientist in the Winning of the American West* (New York, 1966), which received the Pulitzer Prize in history for 1967; and *New Lands, New Men: America and the Second Great Age of Discovery* (New York, 1986).

A reassessment of "manifest destiny" awaits a new generation of scholars. A preliminary step is Thomas R. Hietala, *Manifest Design: Anxious Aggrandizement in Late Jacksonian America*

(Ithaca, N.Y., 1985). Frederick Merk's *Manifest Destiny and Mission in American History: A Reinterpretation* (New York, 1963) is the standard work, whereas Reginald Horsman's *Race and Manifest Destiny* (Cambridge, Mass., 1981) is forcefully argued. The grand narrative of Texas is *Lone Star: A History of Texas and the Texans*, by T. R. Fehrenbach (New York, 1968). David Pletcher has considered annexation in *The Diplomacy of Annexation: Texas, Oregon, and the Mexican War* (Columbia, Missouri, 1973). The best military history of the Mexican-American War is John S. D. Eisenhower, *So Far from God: The U.S. War with Mexico, 1846–1848* (New York, 1989).

Before his untimely death in 1976, John D. Unruh, Jr., completed his monumental study of the Oregon and California trails, *The Plains Across: The Overland Emigrants and the Trans-Mississippi West, 1840–1860* (Urbana, Ill., 1979). Among its many insights, this work revised earlier scholarly assumptions about interactions between Indians and emigrants and about the role played by agents of the U.S. government. An effective overview of the political turmoil before the Civil War is provided by David Potter, *The Impending Crisis, 1848–1861* (New York, 1976). This book ignores the "Utah War" of 1857, however. A sound monograph that considers this event is Norman F. Furniss, *The Mormon Conflict, 1850–1859* (New Haven, 1960).

All the writings of Francis Paul Prucha on government Indian policy are models of masterful scholarship. Especially impressive is Prucha's *The Great Father: The United States Government and the American Indians*, 2 vols. (Lincoln, Neb., 1984). Albert Hurtado, *Indian Survival on the California Frontier* (New Haven, 1988), reveals the adaptations made by native peoples before and after the gold rush. The cultural complexities of treaty-making are considered by Raymond J. DeMallie in his essay "Touching the Pen: Plains Indian Treaty Councils in Ethnohistorical Perspective," published in Frederick C. Luebke, ed., *Ethnicity on the Great* Plains (Lincoln, Neb., 1980). Three books by Robert M. Utley are well written and informative: *Frontier Regulars: The United States Army and the Indian, 1866–1891* (New York, 1973); *The Indian Frontier of the American West, 1846–1890* (Albuquerque, N.M, 1984); and *The Last Days of the Sioux Nation* (New Haven, 1963).

Paul Andrew Hutton's *Phil Sheridan and His Army* (Lincoln, Neb., 1985) is an excellent study of the army in the West after the Civil War. The story of the Navajos' removal is told in Gerald Thompson, *The Army and the Navajo: The Bosque Redondo Reservation Experiment, 1863–1868* (Tucson, Ariz., 1976). The later history of the Navajos is presented in Peter Iverson's *The Navajo Nation* (Westport, Conn., 1981). Alfred Runte espoused his "worthless land" thesis in his book *National Parks: The American Experience* (Lincoln, Neb., 1979).

Earl S. Pomeroy, *The Territories and the United States, 1861–1890: Studies in Colonial Administration* (Philadelphia, 1947), and Jack Ericson Eblen, *The First and Second United States Empires: Governors and Territorial Government, 1784–1912* (Pittsburgh, 1968), provide solid overviews of the federal government's administration of the western territories. For the larger story of developments in the West during the territorial era, the work of Howard R. Lamar is unsurpassed. His *Dakota Territory, 1861–1889: A Study of Frontier Politics* (New Haven, 1956) and its marvelous successor *The Far Southwest, 1846–1912: A Territorial History* (New Haven, 1966) are models of definitive scholarship and graceful writing.

Before establishing his fame as a novelist, Ivan Doig wrote about Victor Smith's escapades in "Puget Sound's War within a War," *American West* 8 (May 1971): 22–27. Kermit Hall analyzed the qualifications of territorial judges in his article "Hacks and Derelicts Revisited: American Territorial Judiciary, 1789–1959," *Western Historical Quarterly* 12 (July 1981): 273–89. John Guice has carefully examined territorial courts in *The Rocky Mountain Bench: The Territorial Supreme Courts of Colorado, Montana, and Wyoming, 1861–1890* (New Haven, 1972). Full scholarly histories exist for individual states throughout the West. Two of the best are Michael P. Malone and Richard B. Roeder, *Montana: A History of Two Centuries* (Seattle, 1976), and Arrell Morgan Gibson, *Oklahoma: A History of Five Centuries* (Norman, Okla., 1965).

Chapter Six

Entering the Global Economy

K E I T H   L.   B R Y A N T ,   J R.

James W. Marshall walked along the American River inspecting John A. Sutter's millrace on a cold January morning in 1848. As he tried to determine the water pressure needed to turn the wheel of Sutter's sawmill, Marshall's eyes detected the glint of metal in the stream, yellow metal, and he collected samples. The nuggets he found that morning produced the California gold rush. Some fifty-three years later, Captain Anthony F. Lucas pushed more drill stem into a salt dome at Spindletop, Texas, near Port Arthur. A rumbling noise, a sharp vibration, and the Lucas gusher blew in on 10 January 1901, oil shooting two hundred feet in the air for nine days. Within four years, twelve hundred nearby wells produced over thirty million barrels of petroleum. Between the discovery of gold in California and the coming of "black gold" in Texas, the economy of the trans-Mississippi West was transformed from subsistence agriculture and herding into a modernized and urbanized capitalistic economy integrated into a worldwide structure.

White settlers pressed inexorably westward from the early seventeenth century, but the conclusion of the Mexican War found only a few U.S. citizens occupying the coastal towns on the Pacific while the "Great American Desert" remained largely unoccupied. From the Mississippi River westward to the eastern reaches of the Colorado, Columbia, and American rivers, vast tracts of land beckoned a people whose pioneering spirit permeated the society. The settlement and urbanization processes moved forward vigorously, but the trans-Mississippi West would not be occupied along formal, geographical lines. The slowly moving "frontiers" of the Old Northwest and the Southeast were not replicated in the West.

Endless land, abundant natural resources, scarce labor and capital, a spirit of entrepreneurship, and social and political institutions favorable to economic growth combined to produce a western society undergoing changes that mirrored those occurring around the globe. The favorable movement of the prices of key staples and heavy infusions of capital from the East and abroad stimulated the economy, as did the growing presence of a relatively well educated and technologically sophisticated middle class. Westerners shifted easily and quickly from a rural to an urban environment within a highly mobile society. There was no refuge from change in the region, which imitated the nation and the world as it formed a capitalistic, industrial economy within half a century. Altered consumer demands in the East and in western Europe, the international mobility of both capital and labor, and the global flow of technological information combined to shape the economy of the West.

Painted to illustrate a popular travel guide, John Gast's picture presents a capsule history of western economic development as seen through the rosy guise of manifest destiny. Following a group of Indians come the symbols of American know-how: a wagon train, a horse-drawn stage, and the three lines of the transcontinental railroad. Over them floats a woman wearing the "Star of Empire" and carrying a schoolbook as a symbol of enlightenment and a telegraph line "to flash intelligence throughout the land."

John Gast (active 1870s). American Progress. Oil on canvas, 1872. Gene Autry Western Heritage Museum, Los Angeles, California.

Students of the nineteenth-century West have been overly concerned with a nonexistent uniqueness. Elements of the "mining frontier" in California, Colorado, and Montana could be found in South Africa and Latin America. The impact of the railroad was as significant in India as in Kansas and Texas. A legal structure based on capitalism shaped the American West as well as New Zealand and Australia. Indigenous peoples were subjugated, exploited, and exterminated on all these global frontiers. Some scholars of western American history also fail to differentiate between economic growth and economic development. Dependence on the exportation of raw materials or agricultural products may expand an economy to substantial levels, but that very success may limit diversification and the creation of an infrastructure to sustain industrial and commercial development. This has been the recurring nightmare of colonial and Third World economies. This was not the pattern in the American West before 1900, however, as external investment and internal capital formation produced a diversified regional economy.

Europeans occupied "free land" in North and South America, Asia, Africa, and the South Pacific throughout the nineteenth century. A treasure trove of minerals spurred that process. The movement of peoples into the trans-Mississippi West introduced both material progress and concepts of liberty even as it destroyed those non-European indigenous cultures that resisted. Technologically superior Europeans simply overwhelmed less-sophisticated societies. Transportation and communication accelerated this expansion as peoples of low skill levels were pushed aside. These "frontiers" quickly joined a world-capitalistic core market centered in western Europe. Maturation beyond self-sufficiency brought rising levels of participation in the world economic order to peripheral areas like the American West. As the French historian Fernand Braudel has shown, capitalism is an identifying theme for studying the modern world, for it provides structure and organization for examining relationships within a society. Capitalism emerged as the prevailing force in world history by the nineteenth century and as an all-pervasive aspect of American life, especially in the West.

The trans-Mississippi West formed a segment of several networks of productive processes and commodity chains. The various participants in these networks became interdependent as they sought to maximize capital accumulation. The creation of this world-capitalistic economy was not constant but occurred in wavelike spurts of expansion and contraction. Periods of stagnation led to class struggles, and weaker and less-efficient producers were often eliminated. Western Americans, and many of those who have written their history, saw these boom-and-bust cycles as regionally unique rather than as a reflection of a global economy that had no regard for political boundaries. World trade tied the peripheral economy of the American West to an international market system; then, as the economy of the West matured, it became a part of the core. Transportation, technology, military superiority, and medical science allowed for the inexorable expansion of capitalism, for as the economist Joseph Schumpeter has argued, "Stationary capitalism is impossible."

The economy of the trans-Mississippi West initially shared characteristics with other areas undergoing transformation in the nineteenth century. Like the occupying populations of South Africa, Australia, and portions of Latin America, the settlers of the West were young, largely male, transient, and violent. The absence of women and young children and a low birthrate reflected a restless, transitory society. Demographic characteristics soon changed, however, as the West became urbanized and the population came to reflect national norms. Industrialization produced towns and cities, in some of the most difficult conditions imaginable, in the mountains of Colorado or on the plains of eastern Montana, as westerners sought the amenities of urban life. Schools, churches, and opera houses quickly followed the railroad station, bank, and general mercantile store. If there was a unique element in the American West, it was the speed of this transformation. Mineral rushes produced long lines of wagons headed westward, followed by shining iron rails and singing telegraph wires. Freight lines and steamboats radiated from regional centers as trade routes stimulated traffic in lumber and foodstuffs. Chinese and Irish, Cornishmen and Italians, Australians and African Americans joined thousands of newcomers from the East determined to strike it rich. James Marshall's walk along the American River set in motion a process whereby throngs of settlers sought the "main chance" in the American West.

Mining, Magnates, and Miners

The mineral rushes of the nineteenth century stimulated settlement, forced the early formation of laws and government, created a demand for transportation, and lured labor and capital westward. Waves of pioneers swept into California, Nevada, Idaho, Montana, and the Dakota Territory seeking gold and silver. Ironically, many of these prospectors, miners, investors, and their auxiliaries moved not from east to west but from California eastward into the hinterland.

The forty-niners of the Golden State who flocked to Sutter's Mill found nuggets, "color," or "dust" in the rivers and streams. Placer mining—washing the dirt from the stream in a pan, leaving the heavy grains of gold in the bottom—required little labor, capital, or skill. If the pay dirt proved of sufficient quantity, a wooden box, or cradle, could be used to wash larger amounts of sand and dirt as the box was rocked to and fro. Wooden cleats in the bottom of the box held the gold as the water and earth washed away. A group of men might build a sluice, a series of long wooden boxes fitted with riffle bars across the bottom. They diverted water from the creeks through the sluice, and the flowing water carried away the dirt and sand dumped into the sluice by the miners. Nuggets and dust remained trapped in the riffle bars. Muscle and sweat produced wealth for a few and created a true cornucopia of publicity to lure thousands to the West.

The days of gold placer mining proved short-lived, however. As prospectors moved into the interior, into the Sierra Nevada and the Great Basin, gold and silver were found, but the minerals were locked in quartz lodes, or veins, buried deep in the earth. To reach this treasure, miners had to sink shafts, install timber linings, and use pumps to remove water seeping into these subterranean labyrinths. Capital for mills to crush the quartz and for vessels of mercury to dissolve the gold came not from the prospector but from investors in San Francisco, Philadelphia, and London. Mills, tunnels, machinery, and transportation brought the mining corporation to the strike, along with an army of laborers.

Sutter's Mill in 1848; Virginia City, Nevada, and Cherry Creek, Colorado, in the 1850s; Montana and Wyoming in the 1860s; and the Black Hills of South Dakota in the 1870s saw rushes of prospectors, followed by ramshackle towns filled with lawyers and gamblers, merchants and prostitutes, assayers and drifters. More lasting on the landscape were mineheads, smelters, mills, and tailings heaps, the debris produced by washing and concentrating. These rough, crude communities contributed to a national output of eighty-one million ounces of gold by 1852 and six and a half million ounces of silver by 1863. Virtually all of this treasure came from the Far West. The gold production alone transformed the role of the United States in world trade and led to rising foreign investments in the West. Even more important, the export of gold paid for the importation of steel for the railways and for machines for factories, mills, and mines. The trade surplus generated by western mining encouraged the expansion of credit and brought the United States into the mainstream of the world economy.

The mining rushes began with an initial discovery by a prospector followed by the communication of the news to miners elsewhere, who soon arrived looking for a bonanza. Within a short time, capital requirements brought in corporate investors even as the community moved from tar-paper shacks to wooden stores, stone churches, and brick opera houses. The rapid transformation of the area brought social chaos, physical change, and cultural amenities amid vigilante law, violence among the laborers, and often catastrophe in the tunnels.

All participants, whether a prospector engaging in placer mining along a creek or a mining firm having millions in capital to invest, needed the protection of the rule of law. The absence of legal precedents led westerners to borrow some of the finer points of Spanish and English mining laws as they formulated a body of statutes to protect their interests. Groups of miners elected officers at mass meetings and drafted rules based as much on common sense as common law. "Reasonable" amounts of land could be claimed if clearly marked and filed with a local recorder. The elected officers often settled disputes and allocated water rights. Workable codes, democratically formed, created an idealistic framework that originated in California and was exported to the mining camps of the interior. These spontaneous codes were subsequently incorporated into territorial, state, and federal mining laws. But the miners also conducted lynchings and vigilante actions and displayed disregard for the claims of the Native Americans and Hispanics who preceded them in the area. The mining rushes produced a demand not only for mining law but also for land offices, town marshals, and local governments. These requirements, in turn, led to premature territorial governments and eventual statehood. The mining booms initiated and hastened the arrival of government in the West.

The early Spanish settlers of the Southwest and California, unlike those who first entered Mexico and South America, did not concern themselves exclusively with the acquisition of mineral wealth, but they were not ignorant of its presence. The Catholic fathers of the California missions saw the discovery of gold not as a help in Christianizing the Indians but as a hindrance. Secular elements among the Spanish and then the Mexican settlers did not share that view and initiated modest mining operations in California and elsewhere. The Californios had productive mines long before the Americans arrived, and they taught the new settlers how to crush gold-bearing rocks and to remove the metal. Whereas some miners, known as the "Old Georgians," would come to California from previous diggings in Georgia and North Carolina and would bring their knowledge and skills with them, the Yankees also learned much from the Mexican settlers about the mining of gold.

The early days of placer mining in California were short-lived. Once the ore was mined from rivers and streams, expensive technology was required to obtain the additional gold ore embedded in quartz or buried deep in the earth. An image of easily obtained wealth drew thousands of gold seekers west, but independent miners such as these soon found the richest lodes to be controlled by heavily capitalized corporations.

Unidentified photographer. [Goldminers]. Daguerreotype, half plate, ca. 1850. Courtesy Amon Carter Museum, Fort Worth, Texas.

By mid-March 1848, news of Marshall's discovery at Sutter's Mill reached San Francisco, and within sixty days that small port town seemed deserted as men rushed to sites along the American River and then to other streams that flowed westward from the Sierra Nevada. President James K. Polk formally announced the discovery in his presidential address to Congress that December, and his confirmation of the rumors of vast mineral wealth initiated the rush of the forty-niners. Dozens of boats sailed from East Coast ports, headed around South America and then north through the Pacific to California. Even more intrepid were those would-be miners who took riverboats to Missouri and set out across the Great Plains for the West. In May 1849, some twelve thousand wagons crossed the Missouri River while other wagon trains departed from Fort Smith and Santa Fe. Shipwrecks in the straits of Tierra del Fuego and disease and death along the trails failed to slow the rush to El Dorado. In Dry Diggings, Hell's Delight, and Hangtown, the former shopkeepers, farmers, herders, and sailors panned, sluiced, clawed, and fought to find the illusive nuggets. They sometimes leased sites from the local Indians, but usually the prospectors simply staked claims. When Marshall found his first bits of yellow metal, California had few more than 14,000 U.S. citizens, but by 1852, there were over 250,000 people residing in the area. Immigrants from Asia, Chile, Hawaii, Great Britain, Continental Europe, and Mexico joined the Yankees in their quest.

The mining pattern that emerged in California would be replicated across the American West and in British Columbia. Along rivers and streams, the forces of erosion exposed veins of gold bearing ores and washed the nuggets or dust into the waterway. The first arrivals found easy pickings in their large metal pans and sluice boxes. A prospector might find as much as eight thousand dollars in gold in a day, but the initial discoveries played out quickly. Soon the miners braved the cold waters of upstream sites and resorted to sluices and then to mixing crushed rock with mercury to amalgamate the gold. But even as the output at the sites declined, the cost of food, equipment, and transportation rose; the merchants and freighters soon reaped much of the great bonanza.

Within three years, with dwindling yields from surface mining, corporations entered the diggings to pursue veins hidden beneath the gravel and rock of the land near the streams. Mills to crush the ore and machinery to erode vast quantities of dirt and sand displaced the individual prospectors and miners. Hydraulic mining, the use of water pressure to blast away rock and soil, devastated streambeds and created mountains of rubble. Hydraulic mining required large-scale reservoirs and elaborate flumes and ditches that delivered huge volumes of water at high pressure. Investors in such operations found laborers among the disillusioned forty-niners, who could earn more per day in the mines than with their pans.

Lonely prospectors moved along the Feather River, striking gold there, on the Stanislaus, and in the valley of the Shasta. Each new "rush" created more exaggerated publicity of finds in gulches and ravines, of instant fortunes and riches for all. The ten million dollars in gold produced in 1849 grew each year as miners spread out across the Mother Lode country, but by the end of the next decade, these laborers faced unemployment as technology and capital reduced the need for workers even as output increased. The small-scale miner disappeared, to be replaced by the daily-wage earner.

The gold rush in California created wealth for the few and labor for the many. When the output of gold reached eighty million dollars in 1852, the economy of the region had been transformed. Demands for goods and services made San Francisco a city with merchants, bankers, shipowners, freighting firms, and manufacturers competing for a share of the wealth. Clipper ships sailing round the Horn could not deliver enough clothes, shovels, nails, mercury, and other necessities. The urbanization of northern California initiated a pattern to be found across the West as mining rushes created demands for specialized products. Around the Bay, crowded docks piled high with goods alternated with small foundries and machine shops. Skilled ironworkers could earn far more there than along the streams of the Sierra Nevada or deep in the mine tunnels. The California gold rush set in motion the economic maturation of the West.

Interestingly, the geographical expansion of the mining boom came as a result of digging not by prospectors but by Mormons in the Nevada country. Probably in 1848, but definitely by the following year, members of that religious faith discovered a vein of gold-laden quartz in the Washoe Mountains, a range of hills extending east from the Sierra Nevada into the Great Basin. The Mormons soon lost faith in the area as the amount of dust they found proved negligible. Although the Mormons who made the strike lingered only briefly, miners in California soon heard the news and moved eastward, hoping to find another bonanza. Luck eluded them in "Gold Canyon" until June 1859, when Peter O'Riley and Patrick McLaughlin found the Ophir silver vein. When Henry T. P. Comstock ventured along shortly thereafter and claimed a share of their prize based on his alleged ownership of the spring they were using, the partners acquiesced. The lazy, shiftless Comstock soon had his name attached to this great bonanza, the Comstock Lode. The ore samples sent to California to be assayed contained three-fourths pure silver and one-fourth gold and were worth $3,876 per ton; the Ophir mine was the richest in history.

News of this fabulous strike spread quickly, and investors from California flocked to the Washoe country to purchase claims. Believing that the vein would play out shortly, just as others had, the original owners sold the mine. Judge James Walsh, of Nevada City, and George Hearst, of San Francisco, arrived early, purchased wisely, and prospered greatly.

In the largely treeless and waterless Washoe, the boomtown of Virginia City emerged, and thousands flocked to the forlorn site. Because the gold and silver were embedded in quartz, only crushing machinery could unlock the treasures. Prospectors owned claims, not capital, and sold or leased to others, but only a few of the three thousand sites proved profitable. The major mines—the Ophir, Central, Mexican, and the Gould and Curry—required drilling, blasting, and removal of the ore to steam-powered stamp mills. The tunnels flooded in the spring, and cave-ins marked the paths of the miners. Only heavy timbering allowed the intrepid laborers access to a vein that grew to a width of nearly two hundred feet. Cornishmen with their knowledge from the tin mines, Welshmen with their smelting experience, and Germans with their metallurgy background contributed skills and technology to this mining venture. As the population of Virginia City rose to fifteen thousand, an infrastructure developed to support the mining operations. Freighting, lumbering, and the mercantile trade became almost as profitable as owning a small claim. Yet the greatest days lay ahead, for in 1873 the Consolidated Virginia combine excavated a hole 1,167 feet into the earth and found the "Big Bonanza," a vein fifty-four feet wide filled with gold and silver. A fortune of two hundred million dollars created the "Kings of the Comstock."

Above C Street in Virginia City, the ornate homes of the merchants and bankers looked down on the gaudy, vulgar town, which had swelled to twenty thousand people by the mid-1870s. While the Irishmen, Cornishmen, Germans, Mexicans, and a polyglot of miners labored in the tunnels far below, town matrons sat on their porches eating ice cream and drinking champagne. They toasted their friends and financial allies, such as Hearst, whose capital had made their families a part of the Comstock's elite.

George Hearst had gone to California from Missouri, where he had experience with lead mines. Arriving in 1850, he tried placer and quartz mining but soon engaged in the buying and selling of claims. When news of the strike in Nevada came, he raced to the area to purchase a share of the mighty Ophir mine. Selling all his California holdings, and borrowing money, Hearst put everything into the Ophir. The "Old Californians" like Hearst knew how to register claims, form syndicates, organize stamp mills, and perhaps as important, create a legal mining district. The first thirty-eight tons of ore were packed across the mountains to San Francisco for smelting, but the high quality of the silver from that sample led to the construction of a complete mining operation in Virginia City. Flooding of the mines led to the installation of steam-powered pumps and extensive timbering; it took vast amounts of capital to produce an extraordinary profit. Hearst and his associates retreated to San Francisco, erected mansions, extended their fortunes, and prospered long after Virginia City became a virtual ghost town in the 1890s.

Almost simultaneously with the rise of Nevada as a monumental source of silver and gold, Colorado beckoned both Old Californians and Old Georgians to the foothills of the Rockies. Rumors of gold brought a handful of prospectors, led by Captain John Beck and W. Green Russell, to the headwaters of the Arkansas River in the spring of 1858. Veterans of the California goldfields, they panned along the frontal range of the Rockies. A member of the party hit pay dirt on Cherry Creek near present-day Denver. When residents of "the states" received the news, another rush of epic proportions began. Pilgrims and greenhorns struck out for Pikes Peak and Cherry Creek based on early reports that one need not travel all the way to Nevada or California to strike it rich. Nearly one hundred thousand people headed for Colorado, undaunted by six or seven hundred miles of travel across the semiarid plains of Kansas and Nebraska. Tall tales and the aftermath of the national depression of 1857 sent hundreds to Auraria and Denver City, the twin towns that sprang up along Cherry Creek. Every frontier outpost from Iowa to Arkansas dispatched wagon trains westward to Colorado. "Pikes Peak or Bust" painted on the canvas of their wagons revealed their destination and their determination.

The prospectors found little to warrant their optimism, and half were gone by the next summer. Some of those who remained were rewarded, however, when John H. Gregory hit more pay dirt on Clear Creek. Over five thousand miners swarmed into Central City, the boomtown that developed around Gregory's claim. Although the riches did not rival those of the Comstock Lode, the findings along Gregory Gulch sent hundreds of prospectors into the valleys south and west of Central City. More gold, silver, and lead were found, but Colorado yielded only twenty-five million dollars in gold in the decade after 1858. The greenhorns fled, but the veterans of Georgia, California, and Australia persevered. They had the knowledge and experience required to make the finds, whereas others had the technological skills and capital to develop the strikes.

As the true placers of Colorado played out, it became evident that only shaft mining offered hope for large-scale profits. Pyritic gold ores would not amalgamate with mercury, and thus new processes were required. Undercapitalized, the Colorado mines lacked efficient means to remove the gold, and the boom fell on hard times in the 1860s, but the introduction of smelting soon revived the mines. Smelting converted ores to a fluid state through heat and the use of chemicals, allowing the separation of the various metals. The mining promoters utilized the skills of German-trained metallurgists as well as a large amount of costly equipment.

The failure of early smelting efforts did not deter attempts to build a technologically sophisticated smelter in the mountains. An improved performance led to the removal of the smelter to Denver in 1878, where access to coal and coke made available by the newly arrived railroad allowed for both expansion and greater efficiency. Ores from throughout the Rockies soon came to several smelters in Denver, where foundries and machine shops turned out equipment and parts for the processors and for the mines. An industrial base brought prosperity to the "Mile High City."

The elite of Denver included men who owned mines or shares in mines, but the families who occupied the Cherry Creek Gothic mansions more often obtained wealth based on transportation, banking, smelting, real estate, or food processing. Merchants and bankers such as Jerome B. Chaffee and David H. Moffat used contacts in the East or Great Britain to create such enterprises. Luther Kountze, from Ohio, formed the Colorado National Bank; Amos Steck, also a Buckeye, succeeded in real estate speculation and, along with Kountze, inaugurated horse-drawn street railway service in Denver. Interior towns in the Rockies could only aspire to emulate Denver's growth and prosperity.

Some mining camps failed quickly, but others, such as Leadville and Durango, succeeded in becoming regional centers for mining and transportation. Leadville grew from a village of log huts in the late 1870s into a city of over fourteen thousand by 1880 with schools, churches, a waterworks, and several rail routes to Denver. Hard-rock miners, over one-third foreign born, brought ores containing silver, lead, copper, and zinc to the railway cars. Horace A. W. Tabor, a storekeeper, mayor, and mineowner, made enough money to divorce his wife, marry the famous "Baby Doe," and get himself elected lieutenant governor and later U.S. senator. Tabor went through his riches with dispatch, but his Leadville operations demonstrated the significance of technology and base metals to the mining economy. Gold and silver produced great wealth over short periods, but scientists and technicians showed how to make money from base metals too. Capital came to Leadville to dig new mines and erect smelters for permanent operations. The future of the western economy rested on its ability to attract investors for the long haul and to generate and reinvest its own capital.

Although only a few of the Old Californians traveled east to Colorado, thousands more headed north and west in the 1860s to British Columbia, Washington, Idaho, and Oregon in their quest for the Big Bonanza. A hearty band of prospectors pushed into British Columbia after gold had been found in 1855 near Fort Calville, an old Hudson's Bay Company outpost on the upper Columbia River. The find played out quickly, but some daring souls entered the Fraser River country farther north and discovered a new El Dorado two years later. Thousands of Californians entered British Columbia, only to be disappointed by the paucity of placer sites. While a few continued their quest northward along the Fraser, others moved south into Idaho and the Snake River valley. Elias Davidson Pierce tried his luck in British Columbia, then headed south to the Nez Percé Indian reservation in northern Idaho. He formed a trading partnership in the area, married a Nez Percé woman, and using that position, began to prospect on Indian lands. In 1860 he found gold on the Clearwater River, and despite the protests of the tribe, a rush of prospectors followed. The miners fanned out along the Clearwater and the Salmon rivers and to the south and began to stake claims in the rich placers of the Boise Basin in 1862. That summer a few of them abandoned their Idaho sites to join contemporaries in Oregon, where placers had been found on the John Day and Powder rivers. Because these placers were scattered and small in size, large-scale operations like the Comstock failed to materialize in the Inland Empire. The coming of the "Younder siders" from California did create a demand for farmers and more permanent residents, who initiated the process to organize a territorial government. By the mid-1860s, both Idaho and Montana had achieved territorial status.

As tens of thousands of miners arrived at Portland, Oregon, on their way eastward to the goldfields, that community expanded its role as a mercantile and shipping center. Merchants outfitted the prospectors, and local firms supplied horses, mules, and boats for those headed east. Within the Inland Empire, communities such as Walla Walla

Primary Western Mining Sites, 1848–1900

flourished as more strikes were made. By 1863, Idaho City claimed six thousand residents, who flocked to its saloons, gambling parlors, and bordellos as well as to the stores, theaters, churches, and the hospital. Farmers received $5.00 for a chicken and sold butter for $1.20 a pound as Inland Empire agriculturalists tried to meet the needs of the miners. The Idaho mining communities filled with unskilled laborers, largely American born, but the merchants and skilled workers tended to be foreign-born veterans of other mining regions. The communities were ethnically diverse, and in the absence of widespread property ownership and large numbers of families, their populations often fell drastically, with some simply disappearing.

It would be hard to exaggerate the rootlessness of the miners and those who followed them. Prospectors who reached Idaho and Oregon had hardly wet their pans before news of strikes in Montana sent them headlong to the east. James and Granville Stuart found gold in the headwaters of the Missouri River on Gold Creek in 1862. Their sluice boxes produced modest dust, and the word spread even to Colorado. "Fifty-niners" from Pikes Peak roamed northward, finding a pocket of gold on a tributary of the Jefferson River.

The great Montana gold rush began the next year, with miners coming from the west along the military road from Walla Walla and others coming up the Missouri River from the east in steamboats. Gold on Alder Gulch produced Virginia City, a roaring camp of four thousand people, eight billiard halls, five gambling establishments, and many saloons and bawdy houses. The thirty million dollars in dust and nuggets found in the gulch almost doubled the riches extracted at Last Chance Gulch near Helena, but that town would outlast Virginia City. Helena lay astride the trail between Fort Benton, Bannock, and Virginia City, and the influx of merchants, bankers, and farmers gave it stability. Further, the presence of gold-bearing quartz required crushing operations leading to permanent facilities and large capital investment. Helena also benefited from strikes in Montana and Idaho in the 1870s and 1880s. As late as 1883, a rush in the Coeur d'Alene mountains of northern Idaho saw thousands of miners enter this remote region, only to depart in a few years as the gold played out. That gold rush did lead to discoveries of silver, lead, and zinc and the establishment of permanent operations for the extraction and smelting of base and precious metals in northern Idaho.

Some of the Coeur d'Alene miners, veterans of the Black Hills rush of a decade earlier, carried the scars of that bitter struggle. By the 1870s, clear evidence existed of the presence of gold in the Black Hills of South Dakota. Part of the Sioux Indian lands, the Black Hills fostered rumors and then reality as Indians came to Fort Laramie with nuggets and dust. The army sought to prevent a full-scale invasion of the Sioux reservation, but an expedition into the Black Hills, led by General George Armstrong Custer and intended to lay the rumors to rest, only confirmed what prospectors suspected: gold in extractable quantities existed throughout the area. By the spring of 1875, thousands of miners had gathered at Sioux City, Iowa, and other points around the Black Hills, and the army's thin line of troops could not deter them. Groups of miners penetrated the Black Hills, only to be removed by the soldiers. Escorted off the reservation, the prospectors reentered at other points. When the Sioux refused to relinquish their claims to the land, exasperated federal agents opened the Black Hills to the miners at their own risk. Over fifteen thousand prospectors swarmed in, and by the following April, Deadwood was home to seven thousand people. A wide-open, lawless, frontier town, Deadwood symbolized the last of the famous camps. After the placers and sluices removed the "easy" dust and nuggets, large-scale mining entered the Black Hills, and trained engineers and laborers again replaced the prospectors. The days of thousands of people racing from one place to another, having little or no hard information and enduring hunger, danger, and frequently death, had almost disappeared.

Sometimes the romantic legends of the camps reflected reality, and luck, as when the formerly penniless Irish immigrant Marcus Daly persuaded George Hearst, James Ben Ali Haggin, and Lloyd Tevis, San Francisco investors, to develop a silver mine near Butte, Montana. Armed with their mining venture capital, Daly began operations, only to discover in 1882 that the Anaconda mine had little silver but contained one of the largest copper deposits ever discovered. "The Richest Hill on Earth" would make millionaires of Daly and William A. Clark and add to the fortunes of Hearst and the others. The partners invested nearly four million dollars before producing a profit; soon nearly two thousand people occupied the company town of Anaconda. The largely immigrant laborers, guided by professional engineers and managed by Daly, extracted the copper ore, smelted it, and sent tons of refined copper east to voracious markets. Access to rail transport allowed Anaconda to develop a vast, high-grade copper deposit thousands of feet deep at the beginning of the age of electricity. In 1883, the United States became the world's leading producer of copper, with Montana being a major source of the metal. Anaconda Copper, like other mining giants in the West, depended on technology and science to increase output and reduce costs. A major factor in the rise of industrialization, copper from Montana contributed to the expansion of electrification in the United States and in western Europe.

The "Copper Kings" of Montana engaged in bitter disputes and lengthy litigation to establish control over not only copper output in Montana but also the state's economy and political structure. The copper magnates purchased their primary rival at Butte, consolidated operations, and increased profits. Output from Montana rose from 5,000 tons in 1882 to 176,000 tons in 1916. Anaconda invested huge sums in electrical generating plants, mining equipment, and smelting facilities and joined an international cartel in an effort to corner the copper market. Ultimately Anaconda came to be controlled by eastern investors linked to Standard Oil Company and the powerful National City Bank of New York City. Copper operations in Montana, and later Arizona, symbolized the shift to a highly concentrated and technologically sophisticated metals industry.

The extraction of gold and silver, as well as copper, lead, and other base metals, employed thousands of men across much of the trans-Mississippi West. For decades, mining represented the largest nonagricultural source of jobs in the region. As hard-rock mining supplanted placer operations, more miners became laborers paid by the day or week to work in gangs underground, where "human machines" with strong arms and backs harvested ore for the stamping mills. Life in the tunnels was hard, dangerous, and monotonous, characteristics that led to a highly mobile work force. Itinerants, or floating workers, became the norm as they moved from the silver mines of Nevada to the South Dakota goldfields and then to the copper ranges of Arizona. Some miners broke out of the mold and labored in the smelters or joined railroad construction crews, but many would return to the shafts and pits, only to move on again in a few months. Young, single, and mobile, living in company-owned boardinghouses or tar-paper shacks, many miners failed to settle down, form families, or develop roots. Nevertheless, the sense of adventure and the opportunity for employment attracted workers from around the globe to the mines of the West.

A key characteristic of the labor force was its ethnic and racial diversity. Mining corporations hired gangs of Chinese laborers from headmen, not to work in the shafts but to dump cars, remove surface rubble, cook food, and wash laundry. White miners refused to work with the Chinese in the tunnels, and management feared that the Chinese, unlike other groups, would quit if not paid on time. Nevertheless, the Chinese appeared in large numbers not only in California but also in Idaho, Nevada, and even Colorado. Many Chinese immigrants turned to placer mining, taking over claims abandoned by whites as unprofitable. Chinese and Hispanic miners often accepted the least-skilled and the lowest-paying jobs, the ones that white men did not want.

Working deep in the sweltering shafts of Virginia City's gold and silver mines, Timothy O'Sullivan used magnesium flares to make the first underground photographs of western mining. This image of collapsed timbers suggests the ever-present danger of the work, while the scale of the pick and boot suggest how cramped and claustrophic the shafts could be.

Timothy O'Sullivan (1840–82). Cave-in, Gould & Curry Mine, Virginia City, Nevada. *Albumen silver print, winter 1867–68. Courtesy Amon Carter Museum, Fort Worth, Texas.*

The highest levels of discrimination against the Chinese and the Hispanic workers often came from some of the immigrants who brought a sense of racial superiority and prejudice with them from Europe. Job competition simply exacerbated the racial views of those from Cornwall, Ireland, Wales, Germany, and eastern Europe. An ethnic pecking order developed in some of the mines as a result; the Cornishmen, Welshmen, Irishmen, and Americans labored in the shafts while the southern and eastern Europeans loaded and pushed the cars. Yet all who worked in the mines saw a glimpse of hell.

The tunnels reeked of blasting powder, unclean bodies, rotten timber, and human waste, since there were no toilets. The deeper the shaft, the higher was the temperature and the greater the danger of collapse or flooding. Electricity brought improved light as well as bare copper wires, huge clouds of dust from power tools, and elevators that could become death traps. Mineowners in the West, not unlike those who controlled mines in the East, the United Kingdom, and continental Europe, moved slowly, if at all, to install safety devices and open-air vents and to improve timbering. As the historian Rodman Paul has noted, the absence of concern for the welfare of workers could be found throughout capitalistic economies in the nineteenth century.

The extraordinarily threatening conditions of work within the mining industry led to the first labor action, or strike, in the Comstock Lode in 1864. The Miners' Protective Association sought higher wages, shorter hours, and better working conditions—"bread and butter unionism"—that created a sense of brotherhood among the miners. The union used monthly dues to help the injured or the families of those killed in the mines. It wanted independent hospitals, free from company control, and built union halls as alternatives to the saloons and brothels. The demands of the association, its charter and ideals, spread among the mobile work force. In 1892, miners struck at Coeur d'Alene, Idaho, demanding recognition for their union, and when state and federal troops arrived to break the strike, seven miners died for their cause. The following year the center of union activity shifted to Butte, Montana, where the Western Federation of Miners (WFM) made that city the "Gibraltar of Unionism." The WFM unified local labor organizations in an effort to stop intervention by the military in disputes. Within a decade, the WFM had over fifty thousand members across the region and would serve as a starting point for the more militant Industrial Workers of the World (IWW). The mining corporations and their managers inspired the rise of trade unionism by refusing even to discuss basic issues with their employees and by importing "scabs," calling for the national guard, and seeking injunctions to terminate strikes.

Labor-management relations varied widely from one mining center to another. Some miners joined militant anticapitalist unions, but in other camps, labor remained virtually docile. The WFM elected members to public office in the Comstock, and the miners at Silver City, Idaho, won settlements for better wages and safer working conditions under the leadership of the future militant William "Big Bill" Haywood. But in some Idaho and Colorado camps, class warfare raged. Driven to desperation by the companies, laborers retaliated with dynamite and rifles. Although few California mines unionized, the IWW would later create a virtual commune at Goldfield, Nevada. Even in Butte, the unionists were split between socialists and "bread and butter" Democrats courted by the mineowners Clark and Daly, who wanted their votes. Life for workers in the mining camps of the West differed little from that of miners in the industrial towns of Pennsylvania, the English midlands, and the Ruhr Valley. When corporate mining broke down the relationship between prospectors and townspeople, a polarized labor and management resulted. When absentee ownership collided with demands for the end of paternalism and for an improved standard of living, miners in the West unionized or responded with violence. Mining created wealth, generated significant labor problems, and laid the basis for an expanding economy, especially for a transportation network.

Freighting on the Prairies, Steamboating on Western Waters

Strikes, violence, and militant unionism could not have been further from the minds of the forty-niners headed to the California goldfield as they stood on the docks in New

York, Philadelphia, and Boston, begging ship captains to take their money. The discovery of gold created an enormous demand for transportation and placed a heavy burden on existing shipping facilities between the coasts. Before the War with Mexico, vessels from the United States plied the coast of California. The ships, largely from New England, carried coffee, sugar, metal implements, cloth, shoes, and spices around Cape Horn and into the Pacific. In California, ship captains traded for cattle hides and tallow. Californians greeted each white-sailed clipper with a fiesta, rowing small boats out into the harbor to initiate trading. Voyages of a year to eighteen months could generate profits of 300 percent, unless the straits at Cape Horn swallowed up the vessel.

Shipping companies and their captains knew the routes, and the risks, and after 1848 entered the newly found business to California with a vengeance. The U.S. government initiated mail subsidies to California in 1847, and the United States Steamship Company opened a new route to San Francisco with an overland crossing of the Isthmus of Panama. Cornelius (Commodore) Vanderbilt joined the fray with steamship lines in the Caribbean and the Pacific linked by a land route across Nicaragua. Would-be prospectors and the mail contracts produced demands for faster, and safer, transportation to California. The circuitous routes took thirty days or longer, and the ship lines charged twelve to eighty cents per ounce for letters. A railroad across Panama did open in 1855, reducing the time and dangers of the long voyages. Yet these steps still did not address the issue of cost, with passenger fares from New York to San Francisco averaging over five hundred dollars. Furtive efforts at a mail route through Mexico at the Isthmus of Tehuantepec made clear to Congress that land routes across the Great American Desert were an absolute necessity. An overland route had to be established as freight and passenger traffic to California soared.

Even as demands for an overland route grew louder, shipping firms established a triangular trade across the Pacific. After unloading passengers and cargo in California, ship captains had nothing to haul back to the East Coast. They thus loaded masts, spars, and lumber, which they carried to China and Japan. There they acquired tea, spices, rice, and Chinese goods and set sail for Cape Horn and ultimately New York, London, or Boston. As early as the 1850s, California had entered a global capitalistic economy. Trade with Asia heightened demands for an overland route to the West Coast.

Visionary publicists, political orators, and the promoters of Kansas City, Memphis, St. Joseph, Omaha, and Fort Smith lobbied for the creation of a national road to California, to begin in their town or congressional district, of course. Seventy-five thousand Californians signed a petition in 1856 demanding that Congress establish an overland mail route to the Far West. Clearly, existing services were inadequate. The Brigham Young Express and Carrying Company operated monthly from Independence, Missouri, to Salt Lake City, where a connection reached San Francisco. A military express line extended from Independence to Santa Fe, in the New Mexico Territory, and a monthly mail service linked San Antonio to San Diego. These operations were neither dependable nor inexpensive. As pressure mounted, Congress removed responsibility for road construction from the U.S. Army Topographical Engineers to civilian contractors and authorized improved wagon routes from Nebraska to California over South Pass, from El Paso to Fort Yuma, and from Albuquerque to Needles, California. The Department of the Interior assumed responsibility for the new road work, which was carried out largely by the mail contractors. Using packtrains to carry the mail or handing letters to a freight-wagon driver at St. Joseph offered no guarantee of safety or speed; service had to be improved. The federal commitment to improved transportation in the West accelerated rapidly in the 1850s.

After Congress appropriated an annual subsidy for mail service from the Mississippi River to San Francisco, the leading express firms in the East formed the Overland Mail in a united effort to meet the required delivery schedule of twenty-five days to California. In the midst of a sectional dispute over the expansion of slavery, Congress approved routes from both the North and the South, a compromise beneficial largely to westerners.

The postmaster general, a Tennessean, awarded the mail contract to John Butterfield and William G. Fargo, of New York, experienced express operators. A founder of the American Express Company, Butterfield proposed a route from a rail connection in Missouri, south and west through Fort Smith and El Paso, to Yuma and San Francisco. When howls of protests from the North greeted this decision, the postmaster general defended the southern route as "all weather." Butterfield spent a year building stations along the trail, training drivers, purchasing mules and horses and coaches, and finding agents to operate the stations. He soon had invested more than one million dollars. Service began when a heavy-wheeled stagecoach, its body swaying on leather braces, raced to the West Coast in twenty-four days, arriving on 10 October 1858. The eastbound coach to St. Louis took three fewer days. President James Buchanan telegraphed Butterfield, "It is a glorious triumph for civilization and the Union."

The Overland Mail Company linked the East to the West for three years, offering service twice each month. At the stations, passengers received meals of fried beef or pork, beans, and bread while the agent changed the four horses or six mules for the next leg of the twenty-eight-hundred-mile journey. Blizzards, hostile Indians, and the hellish ride did not deter passengers, who paid two hundred dollars for the adventure. Government subsidies, the mail contract, and passenger fares led to profits for Butterfield and his partners. The postmaster general found the service so reliable that he issued additional contracts for routes from Kansas City to Stockton, California, and from San Antonio to San Diego.

Butterfield, Fargo, and Henry Wells dominated American Express, a powerful firm in the East and Midwest, and now they had a link to California. But even before the opening of the Overland Mail, the Golden State offered prospects as well, and they had challenged the leading firm there, Adams and Company. The enterprise they formed, Wells, Fargo and Company, dramatically reduced rates, driving Adams and Company into bankruptcy in 1855. Wells, Fargo and Company dominated internal transportation in California, with lines from San Francisco to the gold camps of the Sierra Nevada and north toward Oregon. In addition, Wells, Fargo and Company entered the banking business, an increasingly profitable enterprise. The coming of the Civil War in 1861, however, shifted the mail service to the more central California Trail route.

The war led to the consolidation of western operations as the government demanded more frequent and faster service to California. The Overland Mail Company, dominated by Wells and Fargo, established a virtual monopoly in the coaching and freighting business west of the Mississippi River after the failure of two of the greatest names in overland transportation: Russell, Majors, and Waddell; and Ben Holladay.

The acquisition of the Mexican Cession in 1848 meant that the U.S. Army had to establish forts and garrisons throughout the region to protect settlers and traders. The discovery of gold filled the trails with prospectors, and the central routes soon saw caravans of canvas-topped Conestoga wagons heading to California and to the Oregon country. The needs of the military reached mammoth proportions as troop contingents increased in size to protect the trains. Flour, sugar, salt, feed grains, livestock, and military equipment had to be delivered safely and quickly. The Bureau of Indian Affairs guaranteed food, cloth, and other commodities to its wards on the reservations, and the bureau too required considerable transportation. Government alone would have generated vast freighting operations, but the discovery of gold in California, Nevada, and Colorado only exacerbated demand. The response to this need came from large freighting firms, heavily subsidized but with access to substantial capital.

Professional freighters accepted cargoes from the steamboats or railroads at Independence, St. Joseph, Kansas City, Atchison, Omaha, or Nebraska City. These border towns received goods from St. Louis or later Chicago, consigned to the Far West. An experienced trader, Alexander Majors, entered the tough, competitive freight business using oxen rather than mules. The oxen could forage on the plains, he argued, but mules could not, and six yoke of oxen could pull a wagon loaded with six thousand pounds of freight. In 1855 he formed a partnership with William H. Russell and W. B. Waddell, and within three years the firm of Russell, Majors, and Waddell operated thirty-five hundred wagons and employed four thousand men. Armed with a two-year contract to supply the military garrisons in the Southwest, the firm monopolized trade in the region. Extraordinary profits from freight tariffs and subsidies allowed the firm to expand and then to enter stagecoaching, which led to its downfall.

Russell tried to persuade his partners to operate a stage line over the central route, but they refused to join this scheme without a federal subsidy. Russell forged ahead, opening the route to Denver and then on to Salt Lake City, where his line made a connection to California. The operation failed, without a subsidy, and fearing that Russell's collapse would bring down their firm, his partners rescued him. They took over the stage line as part of Russell, Majors, and Waddell, a tragic error.

Faced with a desperate situation, Majors and Waddell followed Russell into yet another ill-conceived scheme, the Pony Express. Hoping to win a federal mail contract for their central route and to prove its superiority, the partners sought to create a means to carry the mail far more rapidly than the Butterfield route. Relays of young riders could move the mail to California in ten days, they reasoned, and they set about establishing 190 stations at ten-mile intervals from St. Joseph to San Francisco. They spread five hundred fine horses along the route, and on 3 April 1860, riders left each terminal at full gallop. Soon eighty riders were in the saddle every day, forty in each direction, tossing the mail pouch to each other at the end of a seventy-mile leg of the journey. The Pony Express was efficient, tightly organized, and very romantic, but hardly profitable, lasting only two years. The Pacific Telegraph Company and the Overland Telegraph Company set the first pole for a transcontinental line in July 1861, and on 24 October, telegraphers tapped out the initial message. Technology killed the Pony Express and helped drive Russell, Majors, and Waddell into bankruptcy.

For several years the firm had received infusions of capital from Ben Holladay, and in 1862 he foreclosed, taking over the leading freight line in the West. Although the Overland Mail Company had won the subsidy for the central mail route, Holladay, the coarse frontiersman, put together a huge freight and coach operation out of the ruins of Russell, Majors, and Waddell. Holladay possessed cunning and managerial skills and recognized the needs of the mining centers far off the main trails. He extended coach lines into Idaho, Montana, and Colorado, becoming the "Napoleon of the West." His five thousand miles of stage routes and twenty thousand wagons produced good profits as he ruled the firm in an absolute manner. The early settlers, miners, and the army depended on his system, but the rates, based on distance and weight, kept costs high and precluded substantial expansion of the regional economy. Holladay purchased surplus army wagons and animals after 1865, moved them west, and extended his freight services. Always shrewd in his business affairs, Holladay saw the effects of the expansion of the railroads and in 1866 sold out to Wells, Fargo, and Company, which had already acquired Butterfield's western interests. The coming of the railways soon relegated the coaches and the freight wagons to secondary routes, but even after 1900 some of these operations continued in remote areas in the region.

Although Wells and Fargo and other investors brought capital for freighting and coaching lines from the East, much of the investment in these transportation services initially came from the Missouri Valley. Families, longtime business associates, and independent draymen formed partnerships to enter the risky and yet often profitable activity. Independent operators, such as Madame Canutson, a female freighter in the 1880s, vied with the larger companies for mercantile traffic when they could not win subsidies or army contracts. From their terminals along the Missouri River, the freighters kept the lifelines open not only to California and Oregon but also to the merchants of Santa Fe, Tucson, and Virginia City as well as to military outposts from Canada to Mexico. This land transportation system often competed with the more efficient steamboats that penetrated western rivers and bays.

Steamboats brought goods to the freight company docks along the Missouri River, carried cargoes up the Columbia River to the Inland Empire, plied Puget Sound with timber and passengers, and transported miners across San Francisco Bay and along its tributaries. In 1859 the Chouteau family of St. Louis constructed a shallow-draft vessel, the *Chippewa*, and steamed up the Missouri almost to Fort Benton, Montana. The discovery of gold in Montana brought seventy boats in 1867, carrying freight for the miners and military goods for the army outposts. As rail lines reached the Missouri River's eastern bank, the point of departure shifted from St. Louis to Omaha and then to Sioux City. Boats on the upper Missouri successfully competed with overland freighting firms.

In California, rankled that the oceangoing ships at their docks were owned by New Yorkers, San Franciscans determined that transportation on the Bay would be locally controlled. Initially a small fleet of sloops and schooners plied the Bay and moved upriver to Sacramento, but the introduction of steamboats revolutionized shipping. The owners of the steamboats formed a monopoly in 1854, the California Steam Navigation Company, a joint-stock firm capitalized at $2,000,000. Since individual steamboats had been owned in shares by builders, merchants, captains, and investors, the new company had a wide-ranging list of stockholders. The firm owned nearly every major vessel linking San Francisco to the interior and over the next two decades earned good profits, paying more than 100-percent dividends on par value stock by 1860. Cash dividends of $225,000 in 1870 enhanced the pocketbooks of the owners and generated capital to be reinvested in mines, factories, railroads, and banks. The Bay steamboats remained a locally owned enterprise and a source of investment capital.

Similarly, the Columbia River served as a water highway into the Inland Empire. The Hudson's Bay Company had initiated river traffic with a fleet of barges transporting furs to Fort Vancouver, and steamboating came to the region in 1850 when the *Columbia* began to ply the Willamette River from Astoria to Oregon City. Transit of the Columbia would not prove so simple, given the rapids at the Cascades and at The Dalles. The solution was the construction of portage tramways around the rapids, with steamers positioned on either side. The *Jennie Clark*, a stern-wheeler, showed that a shallow-draft vessel could navigate the boiling waters of the lower Columbia. Such boats moved upriver from Portland to the Cascades, where freight would be transshipped around the rapids to an awaiting vessel, which moved on to The Dalles. Another portage, more unloading and reloading, and yet a third ship carried the cargo and passengers to a point nearly thirty miles from Walla Walla for transshipment first to wagons and later to a local railway. In 1862, John Ainsworth, Jacob Kamm, and Simeon Reed joined with R. R. Thompson to form the Oregon Steam Navigation Company. Combining their vessels, these men created a virtual monopoly on the river. They replaced the portage roads with steam railroads and added more efficient vessels. At the height of the Idaho mineral rush, the firm earned over $780,000 amid loud complaints by shippers and passengers about high rates. The alternatives, freight wagons and coaches, proved even more expensive. The answer to shipper complaints would come not through state intervention for lower rates but from the railroads, for soon iron rails extended not only up the gorge of the Columbia but also across the plains of Kansas and over the Sierra Nevada. The day of the railroader was at hand.

Railways and Railroaders

"Manifest destiny," economic ambitions, nationalism produced by the Mexican War, a romantic infatuation with "a passage to India," and the lure of the China trade captured the imaginations of many Americans in the 1840s. The New York merchant and China trader Asa Whitney proposed to Congress in 1845 that the federal government grant a strip of land sixty miles wide, from Lake Superior to the Oregon country, to a firm willing to construct a railway to the Pacific Ocean. When Congress failed to respond, Whitney organized a propaganda campaign, and for the next decade he lobbied for an "iron path" to capture the trade of the Far East and to fulfill the national destiny. Residents of California and the leaders of Chicago, St. Louis, and Duluth supported his pleas and bombarded Washington with petitions. Whitney's pleadings were echoed by ambitious politicians such as William Gilpin, who told an audience in Independence,

Documenting the con-
struction of the Union
Pacific tracks, An-
drew Joseph Russell
paused in Granite
Canyon, Wyoming, to
photograph a train
loaded with covered
wagons. Few images
so eloquently suggest
the ways in which
technology, in par-
ticular the railroad,
transformed life in
the American West.

Andrew Joseph Russell
(1830–1902). Train on
Embankment, Granite
Cañon. Albumen silver
print, 1868–70. Beinecke
Rare Book and Manu-
script Library, Yale Uni-
versity, New Haven,
Connecticut.

Missouri, in 1849, that the East was holding the West in bondage by its failure to support
a railroad to the Pacific. Although Whitney and Gilpin might be dismissed as dreamers,
Senator Thomas Hart Benton, of Missouri, could not be so categorized, and he carried
the message to the corridors of power in Washington: the federal government must
authorize a transcontinental railroad. The propaganda and the oratory received greater
attention as California gold flowed into the banks of New York, Philadelphia, and
Boston; finally Congress responded.

From the beginning of the nation, the federal, state, and local governments aided
transportation developments. Funds were directed to the construction of post roads,
canals, and coastal waterways. The Erie Canal and the National Road reminded the
public of the role of government in creating a transportation system. Federal agencies
provided surveys, mail subsidies, and road engineering while state and local governments offered subsidies and land for rights-of-way. The result was the rise of a substantial
transportation system in much of the East and Midwest by the 1850s. Water transportation along the coasts carried products brought to the ports by the railroads and canal
boats. In the interior, roads and canals supplemented an expanding rail network. The
shift from a north-south commercial market based on the Ohio and Mississippi rivers
to an east-west trade using the new trunk rail lines only heightened tensions generated
by the issues of slavery and slavery expansion in the 1850s.

Members of Congress largely agreed that a transcontinental railroad had to be built,
but where would the eastern terminus lie? Senator Stephen A. Douglas contended that

only Chicago would do, whereas Jefferson Davis argued for Memphis or perhaps New Orleans. Acting in its time-honored fashion, Congress asked for a study of all feasible routes, thereby postponing a decision. In 1853 the army initiated the surveys leading to a thirteen-volume report two years later. Four routes were possible: Lake Superior to Portland; the Overland Trail to San Francisco through South Pass; the Red River westward to southern California; and southern Texas to San Diego via El Paso and Yuma. Thus the thorny political issue remained with alternative surveys originating in both the northern and the southern states. Although Douglas triumphed in obtaining territorial status for Kansas and Nebraska to enhance the chances of the central route, he offered a compromise: to build three transcontinentals—one from the North, one from the South, and his own favorite. The staggering sums required to finance three such schemes deterred even the most vocal proponents. It became obvious to all that this gigantic enterprise required loans, land grants, and financial guarantees of enormous magnitude.

The secession of the Confederacy in the spring of 1861, and a Republican party pledge to link the East to the West, gained passage of the Pacific Railroad Act. The catalyst for this action, Theodore D. Judah, had overwhelmed senators and representatives with charts, graphs, engineering drawings, energy, and determination. An engineer by training, Judah left San Francisco and arrived in Washington in the spring of 1861; he was an emissary of Leland Stanford, Mark Hopkins, Collis P. Huntington, and Charles Crocker, San Francisco and Sacramento merchants and bankers. They proposed to construct the Central Pacific Railroad from San Francisco across California to the Sierra Nevada, enter Nevada, and strike eastward to meet a line beginning on the Missouri River. The audacity of the promoters of the Central Pacific Railroad, the persuasiveness of Judah, and the need for transportation to the West in time of war won the day. Congress approved the proposal and incorporated the Union Pacific Railroad to build the link between the Missouri River and the Central Pacific. Lines from Sioux City, Leavenworth, Kansas City, Omaha, and St. Joseph would converge near the one-hundredth meridian before heading to the West, thus ending the furor over the location of the eastern terminus.

The act provided for seemingly substantial subsidization for the project. The railroads would receive a four-hundred-foot right-of-way, ten alternate sections of land for each mile of track, and first-mortgage loans of sixteen thousand dollars per mile in flat country, thirty-two thousand dollars in foothills, and forty-eight thousand dollars in the mountains. Yet even these inducements failed to generate private capital sufficient to initiate work on the Union Pacific. Congress responded in 1864 by doubling the land grant, reducing the government loan to second-mortgage status, and increasing the number of shares of one-hundred-dollar par value stock tenfold, to one million. Thus the scheme began with federal underpinnings in line with land grants to some canals and railroad projects in the East.

Westerners, meanwhile, enthusiastically watched the penetration of the Missouri River valley by the railroads. The Hannibal and St. Joseph reached its western terminus in 1859, and the Missouri Pacific Railroad linked St. Louis to Kansas City in 1865. In Iowa, railroad fever rose to epidemic proportions. The Chicago and North Western reached the Mississippi River in 1855 and pushed on across Iowa to Council Bluffs on the Missouri a dozen years later. The Chicago, Rock Island and Pacific threw the first span across the Mississippi and gained access to Council Bluffs in 1869. With substantial capital from New England, the Chicago, Burlington and Quincy connected its namesake cities and marched westward to Fort Kearney, Nebraska, by 1873. The race to join Chicago with the incipient Union Pacific saw the Illinois Central construct a western branch from Dubuque to Sioux City by 1870. The Union Pacific would have no shortage of connections to the East; what it initially lacked was a massive infusion of capital and material.

Engineers and surveyors plotted a line westward from Omaha across the plains of Nebraska even as company managers competed with military demands for iron rails, locomotives, rolling stock, and labor as the Civil War intensified. When the war ended, track extended only forty miles, but the termination of hostilities brought an influx of rails and equipment as well as gangs of Irish tracklayers. Materials came upriver until 1867, when the Chicago and North Western arrived in Council Bluffs across the Missouri River from Omaha. While the surveyors faced Indian raids and the challenges of the weather, loneliness, and thirst and sought the easiest grades for the roadbed and supplies of water for the locomotives, construction materials piled up in the yards at Omaha. From Boston and New York came urgent telegrams from company executives pleading for more track to be laid, for each new segment of line meant bonds sold and land acquired.

Chief Engineer Grenville Dodge depended on John Stephen (Jack) Casement and his brother Dan to get the track laid, and they, in turn, depended on Irish laborers, many of whom were veterans of the war recruited by the Casements in the East. A brigadier general when the war ended, Jack Casement knew how to mobilize troops, and he used that experience and years of work in railroad construction in New York and Ohio to organize the Union Pacific. He took the "Casement Army" into the field while brother Dan served as quartermaster general in Omaha. Crews of ex-soldiers followed the surveyors, grading the earthen roadbed in one-hundred-mile segments and building wooden bridges. Casement's tracklayers followed, pulling rails from flatcars pushed by a locomotive as crews placed ties on the roadbed. They laid four lengths of rail per minute and in the first six months pushed the end of the track 250 miles. The object was not to construct the best or most efficient route but to move quickly, at the least expense. The trackage was not ballasted with rock, the bridges were often flimsy, and the ties were generally untreated and frequently of poor quality. In 1866 and 1867 the toiling crews drove the shining iron over 500 miles, reaching Cheyenne, Wyoming, in November.

The incredible expense staggered even the most optimistic of the Union Pacific's leaders, and government loans failed to approach even minimal construction costs. Dr. Thomas C. Durant, Oliver and Oakes Ames, and their friends who controlled the line turned to a construction company to raise the necessary funds. The Credit Mobilier, secretly owned by the Union Pacific's leaders, received contracts far in excess of costs to construct the railroad. The Credit Mobilier's profits attracted investors, who ultimately earned over $20,000,000 while creating a railway whose capitalization of $110,000,000 was nearly double its value. "Watered stock," internal corruption, bribes to members of

Congress and the executive branch, and managerial clashes did not deter the Casement Army or the surveyors as crews reached Utah and looked westward. Indeed, the survey teams passed their counterparts from the Central Pacific as both firms sought to lay as much track as possible in order to obtain land and sell mortgage bonds.

The "Big Four" of the Central Pacific—Crocker, Hopkins, Huntington, and Stanford—had gotten their project off to an earlier start after securing a loan of $1,659,000 from the State of California and untruthfully convincing President Abraham Lincoln that the Sierra Nevada began almost at Sacramento, so that the federal subsidy was forty-eight thousand dollars per mile, not sixteen thousand dollars. Using their mercantile contacts in the East, they ordered equipment and rails sent around Cape Horn to San Francisco and upriver to Sacramento. Lumberjacks cut trees in the foothills for ties and trestles, and hundreds of Chinese laborers threw up embankments and graded the right-of-way. Tracklaying began in 1863, but the Central Pacific extended only 115 miles four years later as the construction gangs entered the mountains. Not even Judah anticipated the deprivations and hardships to be faced by Central Pacific employees in breaching the mountains. Seven thousand, then ten thousand, pig-tailed Chinese "coolies" struggled against the rocks, snow, and terrible winds of the Sierra Nevada. Landslides tore away work that had taken weeks or months. Blizzards buried the roadbed and many of the workers, forcing the company to build huge snowsheds to protect the line. Chinese workers swung in baskets suspended by ropes, drilling holes for dynamite in the face of sheer rock walls. They collapsed from heat and humidity deep in tunnels driven through solid granite. Hundreds died, and still they came, recruited in China, brought to California, and taken by rail to the end of the track. They persevered. In the summer of 1867 the Central Pacific crossed the crest of the Sierra Nevada, and the laborers moved swiftly downgrade toward the deserts of Nevada. As Casement's Irish gangs drove westward, the Central Pacific's Chinese raced them to a connection.

As the grading crews passed each other in northern Utah, Congress intervened and ordered the rails joined at Promontory. On 10 May 1869, workers and officials observed the placement of the last tie, laurelwood bound in silver, and the driving of the last spike, fittingly made of gold. They groaned as Stanford missed with the swing of the sledge, but the spike pierced the laurel, and the locomotives moved forward, pilots touching. A telegrapher tapped out, "It is done." The nation, so recently torn by bloody civil war, stood united, east and west.

The construction of the transcontinental railway made millionaires of a few, and some, such as Huntington, reinvested those profits in the region, further stimulating economic growth. Huntington rose from poverty in Connecticut, where he was born, leaving school at fourteen, becoming a traveling salesman, and joining several partners in a hardware store in rural New York. Gold fever took him to California in 1849. Buying and selling commodities in Panama en route gave him five thousand dollars in capital when he arrived in San Francisco. Dry goods, not mining, proved to be his game, and a partnership with Hopkins led to a highly successful hardware business. When the Big Four formed the Central Pacific in 1861, Huntington traveled to Washington to represent the firm in the halls of Congress. Huntington lobbied hard, misrepresenting

Andrew Joseph Russell's photograph of the joining of the transcontinental rail routes at Promontory, Utah, on 10 May 1869 celebrated the triumph of American labor and technology over the vast, often inhospitable, stretches of the western landscape. Excluded from the celebratory image, however, were the Chinese laborers who did the back-breaking work of building the Central Pacific's tracks through the Sierra Nevadas. Joseph Becker, a staff artist for *Leslie's Illustrated Weekly Newspaper,* traveled west aboard the first cross-Rockies Pullman train in 1869 and sketched Chinese workers during a six-week stay in California. Here, as Chinese laborers shake their fists at a train emerging from a snowshed, it is unclear whether they cheer their accomplishments or jeer at the system that subjected them to such difficult labor.

Andrew Joseph Russell (1830–1902). Dodge and Montague Shake [Golden Spike Ceremony]. *Albumen silver print, 1869. The Bettmann Archive, New York, New York.*

Joseph Hubert Becker (1841–1910). Snow Sheds on the Central Pacific Railroad in the Sierra Nevada Mountains, May 1869. *Oil on canvas, ca. 1869. From the collection of the Gilcrease Museum, Tulsa, Oklahoma.*

the length of the railroad and the terrain it occupied, generally following the "ethics" of the day. After the roads were joined at Promontory, he determined to create a rail and steamship empire in California and the West.

Huntington had already purchased independent short-line railroads in California, and he formed the Southern Pacific Railroad as his primary vehicle for expansion. He moved to make the Southern Pacific the major segment of the railroad that Congress had authorized from southern California to Texas. He pushed rails south from San Francisco to Los Angeles and then eastward into Arizona. Clashing with Thomas A. Scott, of the rival Texas and Pacific Railroad, Huntington crushed Scott and drove the Southern Pacific eastward to Yuma, Tucson, El Paso, and on to San Antonio. Even as he reached Texas, Huntington built north from San Francisco, creating a line to Portland. By 1890 his empire stretched from Oregon to Louisiana; railroads, timber, land corporations, ferries, and coastal shipping entered his grasp.

But like others in the West who accumulated vast wealth, Huntington also transferred capital to large-scale investments in the East. As early as 1869, Huntington led a syndicate that seized control of the Chesapeake and Ohio Railroad and rebuilt and expanded that line from tidewater at Newport News, Virginia, into the coalfields of West Virginia. Huntington promoted Newport News as a major port for the export of coal, and he formed a dry dock and shipyard company, making the port one of the largest on the East Coast. Millions of dollars earned in the West migrated eastward to finance railways, terminals, and shipyards. The flow of capital in nineteenth-century America was indeed two ways.

Capital from Boston financed Huntington's major rival in the Southwest, the Atchison, Topeka and Santa Fe Railroad. Founded in Kansas in 1859 by the promoter Cyrus K. Holliday, the company began as an effort to link Atchison, and then Kansas City, to Santa Fe. Financed by Boston investors, construction proceeded to Newton and then Dodge City, where trail herds from Texas created substantial traffic. The company encouraged the migration of farmers to Kansas, and after Russian immigrants introduced hard winter wheat, that commodity generated vast traffic. The Bostonians secured William Barstow Strong as the railway's president in 1877, and under his leadership the firm pushed a line north from Pueblo, Colorado, to Denver, then south toward Santa Fe. Strong and his stockholders abandoned the idea of Santa Fe as the end of the track and, together with the St. Louis and San Francisco Railroad, gained control of the Atlantic and Pacific Railroad, authorized by Congress to construct a line to California. Strong first built to Deming, New Mexico, where a connection with the Southern Pacific formed a through route to Los Angeles. Determined to control its own destiny, the Santa Fe then built a line across Arizona into southern California, reaching Los Angeles over its own tracks by 1887. The Santa Fe acquired more than thirteen million acres of land in Arizona and New Mexico through the Atlantic and Pacific's land grant, but like other carriers, it received the bulk of its capital from private investors, not land sales. Strong extended the company's lines to Chicago and built south from Kansas to connect with the Gulf, Colorado and Santa Fe Railway, giving the firm access to Fort Worth, Dallas, Houston, and Galveston. Acquisition of the Colorado Midland and the St. Louis and San Francisco, combined with headlong expansion, led to bankruptcy in 1893. Reorganization in 1895 created a new entity that proved highly profitable, becoming a major railway in the Southwest. The Bostonians lost control of the carrier to investors from New York and abroad, but both groups sought developmental rather than opportunistic results.

The early literature on capital investment in western railroads emphasized the voracious greed of "robber barons" who fleeced "widows and orphans," constructed poorly built lines across huge federal land grants financed by watered stock, and overcharged farmers and small merchants. Such a simplistic analysis ignored the facts that only a very small percentage of track was laid over land grants, that purchases of railway securities involved great risks for any investor, and that lines across barren prairies did not generate sufficient revenue for years. Arthur M. Johnson and Barry E. Supple have shown that investors had mixed motives. "Developmental" investors committed capital to the railways with the expectation of long-run economic returns as the region matured. Other investors purchased securities for the purposes of manipulation, or for "opportunistic" profits. Whereas the Credit Mobilier clearly represented the latter, the Bostonians who invested in the Santa Fe and the Chicago, Burlington and Quincy saw vast prairies filled with wheat farms; they hoped for the success of Denver's smelters, and they sent their sons and nephews to Los Angeles to purchase real estate, open banks, and construct office buildings and hotels. It has recently been argued that even Jay Gould saw his western investments as developmental in nature.

In a revisionist biography of Gould, Maury Klein contends that after Gould gained control of the Union Pacific, the Missouri, Kansas and Texas (Katy), the Wabash, and the Missouri Pacific railways, he rebuilt and revitalized the properties, sought economic expansion along their routes, and operated the carriers for long-term return rather than for the manipulation of securities. Born on a farm in Delaware County, New York, in 1836, Gould overcame a frail, sickly childhood and entered the business world in 1852. Possessing a quick mind, perseverance, an indomitable will, self-control, and a strong practical bent, he turned his talents first to tanneries and then to Wall Street. Mastering the intricacies of the financial world, he gained a seat on the board of the Erie Railroad, allying himself with Daniel Drew and James Fisk against Cornelius Vanderbilt. The famous "Erie War" won for Gould the sobriquet "The Mephistopheles of Wall Street," yet he tried to make the Erie a trunk-line carrier between New York and Chicago, Klein argues.

Similarly, when Gould gained control of the Union Pacific after the Credit Mobilier scandal and near bankruptcy in 1873, he revitalized the demoralized firm. Within two years the railroad was paying dividends as Gould revamped internal management, formulated lower rates, and labored to create new industries along its routes. Acquiring an encyclopedic knowledge of the Union Pacific, Gould petitioned the federal government to settle a substantial body of issues relating to its charter, the land grant, and the status of the second-mortgage bonds. All the while he developed the company's properties, opened coal mines, and encouraged agricultural settlements. The Union Pacific built branches into Utah and Colorado, planned lines to Idaho and Montana, and purchased the Kansas Pacific running from Denver to Kansas City. By 1878, Gould transferred his ambitions from the Union Pacific to the Wabash Railroad, the Denver and Rio Grande, and more important, the Missouri Pacific and the Missouri, Kansas and Texas. The latter two companies gave Gould a system extending from St. Louis and

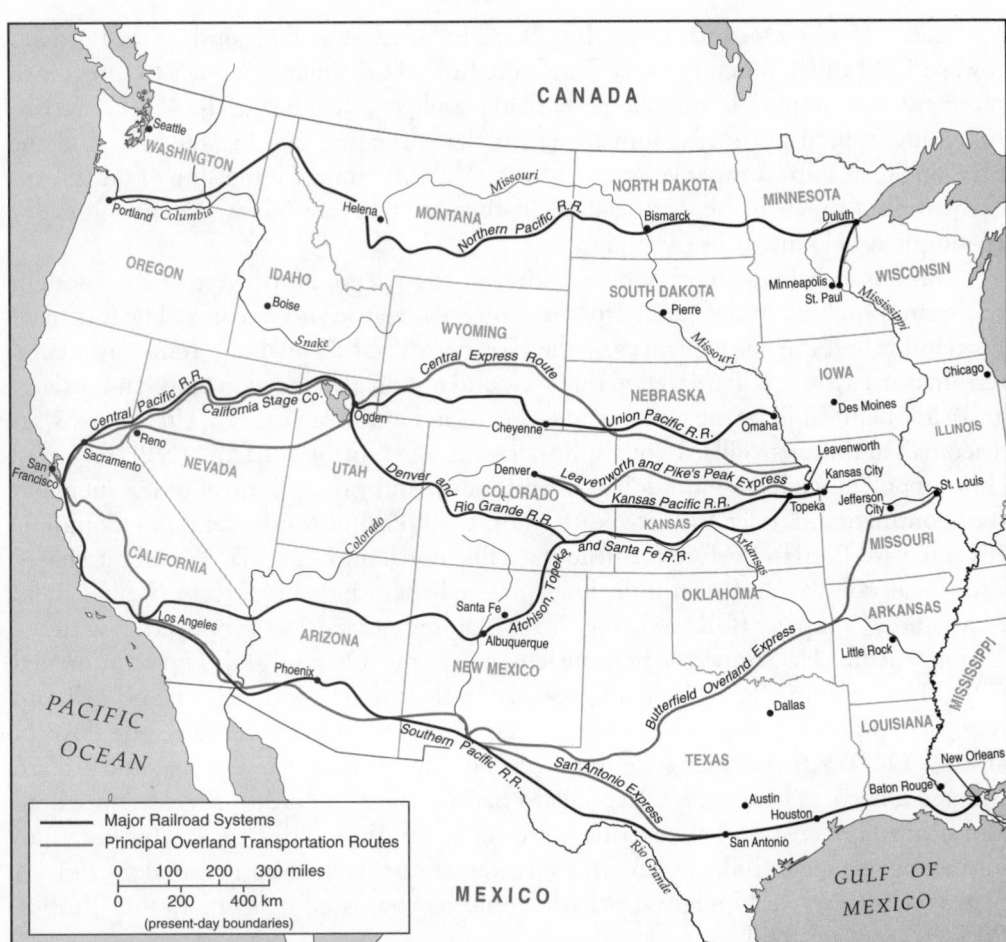

Principal Overland Transporation Routes

Kansas City south and west into Texas and Colorado. The acquisition of additional carriers took the Gould lines to Houston, San Antonio, and Galveston. Klein contends that Gould followed the same pattern with these firms: he purchased new equipment, rebuilt trackage, and modernized the carriers while encouraging economic development along their routes. Through battles with Huntington, the Santa Fe, and the federal government, Gould fought to build or acquire new routes in the West and the Southwest. Though attacked by the press as a scoundrel and seen by the public and later generations of historians as a rapacious manipulator, Gould used his railroad empire to enhance the economic development of large areas of the West.

Even as Gould created his rail system in the Southwest, a young German immigrant, Henry Villard, put together a transportation network in the Pacific Northwest. Born in Bavaria in 1835 as Ferdinand Heinrich Gustav Hilgard, Villard immigrated to the United States in 1853, changed his name, and settled in Belleville, Illinois. Learning English, Villard read law, edited a newspaper, and toured Colorado in the late 1850s and 1860s. Suffering from poor health, he returned to Germany in 1871, where he became involved in financial matters with a group of investors in the Oregon and California

Railroad (O&C). This line, formed by Ben Holladay, extended south from Portland toward California. When the O&C defaulted in 1873, Villard traveled to Oregon to represent the German bondholders. Holladay failed to reorganize the O&C successfully, and Villard persuaded him to return that property, another railroad, and the Oregon Steamship Company to the creditors. Villard assumed leadership of these firms and invested much of his own capital in them, for he saw many opportunities for economic development in the region.

Seeking to enhance Portland's position in the Pacific Northwest, Villard sought transportation links to defeat the city's major rivals, Seattle and Tacoma. The leaders of Portland feared the consequences of the Northern Pacific's goal of a transcontinental terminal at Tacoma. Villard shared that view and sought a connection between Portland and a line being built by the Union Pacific north and west from Ogden, Utah. To thwart Tacoma's ambitions, Villard bought heavily into the Northern Pacific (NP), formed a "blind pool" of eight million dollars with friends, and gained control of the incipient transcontinental. Under Villard's leadership, the NP built south along the Columbia River toward Portland before constructing a line north into Tacoma. Villard purchased additional railways and steamship lines, merged them into his Oregon Railway and Navigation Company (OR&N), and drove that line eastward to a connection with the Union Pacific. He formed a holding company, the Oregon and Transcontinental (O&T), as an umbrella for his enterprises. Alas, the empire dissolved. The NP fell into receivership because of the costs of construction and the paucity of traffic; the OR&N and the O&T lost control of the line from Portland south to California; and Villard suffered a nervous breakdown. Yet Villard had succeeded in creating a substantial rail and steamship network that contributed to the rise of three cities, the establishment of lumbering as a major industry, and the opening of vast tracts to agricultural pursuits. A person of honesty and integrity, Villard would be compared by some to the "Empire Builder," James J. Hill.

While the Northern Pacific struggled from the 1860s to the 1890s to build across its land grant from Lake Superior to Tacoma, falling into bankruptcy twice, Hill constructed the Great Northern Railway (GN) from St. Paul, Minnesota, to Seattle without benefit of a federal land grant and, in the process, created a prosperous region of farms, ranches, mines, lumber camps, and small-scale manufacturing. A Canadian born in 1838, Hill migrated to St. Paul in the 1850s. In that raw, ugly town he saw economic opportunities in many fields, especially transportation. He formed a partnership to put steamboats on the Red River to Winnipeg and organized a firm to bring anthracite coal to St. Paul. When the St. Paul and Pacific railway project to link Minneapolis with Winnipeg floundered, Hill persuaded Canadian and English investors to finance its acquisition. A Minnesota state land grant represented a significant asset for the line, which reorganized as the St. Paul, Minneapolis and Manitoba and resumed construction under Hill's direction. Supported by investors at home and abroad, Hill devoted the next decade to the expansion of the railway.

Hill proposed first to gain access to the Canadian prairie provinces with a through route to Winnipeg, but this was a temporary goal. Only a direct line to the Pacific Coast would keep his carrier independent and profitable. Further, he needed to secure service to Chicago and the Great Lakes from the Twin Cities. Hill and his allies invested in a

subsidiary of the Chicago, Burlington and Quincy that was building a line to St. Paul from Chicago, and they constructed trackage to Superior, Wisconsin, where a line of steamships reached eastward to Buffalo, New York. With these connections secured, Hill drove the Pacific extension of his line, called the Great Northern, across the Dakota prairies toward the Rocky Mountains. His engineer, John Stevens, found Marias Pass through the Rockies and Stevens Pass across the Cascades. As the line crept westward, Hill brought farmers to the Dakotas, urged the settlers to diversify their production, and ordered his surveyors to note the presence of resources along the route. By the time the GN reached Seattle in 1893, Hill had initiated schemes for irrigated farming and for plant breeding along the line.

Hill insisted that the GN be constructed to high standards with quality rail, easy curves, and the lowest-possible grades. Management purchased excellent equipment for the railway and operated at a high level of efficiency. Although the GN reached Seattle as the depression of 1893 began, the railway prospered and, under Hill's tutelage, continued to expand. He visualized a united railway system from the Twin Cities to the Pacific Northwest and twice tried to acquire the Northern Pacific. Failing in those efforts, he did succeed in a scheme for joint control of the Chicago, Burlington and Quincy with archrival Northern Pacific. Hill established an excellent relationship with shippers along the GN, touring the line constantly and speaking to local audiences on economic diversity and the need to develop resources. Hill won the title "Empire Builder," and yet he would often be linked to the nefarious robber barons by those in

With the completion of the transcontinental rail lines, West Coast ports grew in importance as links in an expanded trade network between the western hinterlands and the vast markets of South America, Europe, and the Far East.

Carleton E. Watkins (1829–1916). Pacific Coast Steamship Company Building and Wharf, San Diego. Albumen silver print, 1880. Courtesy of the California State Library, Sacramento.

the West who felt that government should strenuously regulate, or even own, the nation's railways.

Ironically, even as the Farmers' Alliances, the People's Party, and William Jennings Bryan demanded socialization of the nation's railways, competition between the carriers drove rates lower and lower. The efforts by the railroads to form traffic associations and pools to maintain rates were rarely successful and became illegal in 1887. On the Great Northern, for example, the average rate to haul a ton of freight one mile fell from 2.88 cents in 1881 to only 0.77 cents in 1907. Long-distance rates all but collapsed for short periods, a leading cause of the bankruptcies of many lines in the 1890s. Rates charged related not to the distance freight was hauled but rather to the value of the service provided. Most of the costs of carrying the freight were fixed, regardless of how far the cargo was carried. As a result, rates were higher for manufactured products than for heavy, bulk raw materials. The idea that transportation costs should be based on what the traffic would bear did not find favor in Tacoma, Tucson, or Telluride. With Congressman John H. Reagan of Texas leading the way, the federal government initiated efforts to hold down the cost of transporting all commodities, whether the shipment was Washington timber sent to the Dakotas or California oranges dispatched to Chicago. What the critics had overlooked were the major contributions of the railroads to the economic development of the West.

By 1900, the trans-Mississippi West possessed not only an intricate rail network linking the region to all areas of the United States, Mexico, and Canada but also ocean steamship lines operating from Galveston, San Francisco, Los Angeles, Portland, Seattle, and other ports, giving the region access to the trade of Latin America, Europe, and Asia. The railways brought agricultural commodities, base metals, lumber, and manufactured goods to the harbors and returned with industrial products and foodstuffs not indigenous to the region. Along the rail system, farms sprang up like winter wheat in a Kansas spring. The carriers extended loans to farmers and provided them with seeds and free transportation in times of economic distress. Huge "bonanza" wheat farms spread across the Dakotas while irrigated vegetable farms and orchards appeared in New Mexico, Texas, and California. With the resulting agricultural bounty came flour mills, fertilizer plants, meat packers, canneries, dairies, and other food processors in the towns and cities.

Indeed, the urbanization of the West reflected the coming of the railways, with cities as diverse as Dallas, Los Angeles, Tacoma, Spokane, and Denver largely owing their existence, and their growth, to the presence of railways tapping their hinterlands. The detractors of the railroads decried their "capricious" rate making, corrupt financial activities, and political involvement, but the iron and later steel rails gave the region the transportation base necessary to form a viable segment of the world economy.

Loggers, Merchants, Bankers, and Wildcatters

The railways helped to create a vital ingredient in the West's economic growth and in its position in global trade—lumbering. In the region, only the Pacific Northwest, northern California, eastern Texas, and a few mountainous areas of the Rockies received rainfall sufficient to produce trees of a size necessary for efficient timber harvesting. From colonial times into the mid-nineteenth century, the export of logs, masts, spars,

0322. Bachelor Bolt Cutters at Home in Their Little Shake Cabin

and cut lumber helped sustain international trade. The timber industry devastated the hardwood stands of New England and moved westward into the white pine forests of Michigan and Wisconsin in the 1850s and 1860s. Removal of the trees closest to water and rail transportation led these firms to eye the timber of the Pacific Northwest. Lumbering began there with the arrival of the first Europeans; the Russians cut timber at their fur stations along the coast, and the Spanish missions in California produced some wood exports. As has been seen, Californians exported timber to Asia in the late 1840s and 1850s. Only the absence of transportation into the interior prevented large-scale lumbering, and as long as wood remained the universal American building material, a vast potential market existed.

The demand for lumber and timber generated by the mining industry and urbanization led to the opening of forestry operations in the West. New England lumbermen discovered that shipping logs from Maine around Cape Horn made no sense when huge stands of timber reached almost to the coast of the Oregon country; in the 1850s they established sawmills around Puget Sound. Loggers from New England led a lonely, isolated existence at the Sound, cutting timber for the mines of California. Operations expanded slowly into the interior as the firms used waterways to float logs

Surrounded by the tools of their trade, these Washington lumberjacks typify the young, single men who worked as independent logging operators before the turn of the century, when large corporations began to dominate the industry.

Darius Kinsey (1869–1945). Bachelor Bolt Cutters at Home in Their Little Shake Cabin. *Modern print from original glass-plate negative, 1897. D. Kinsey Collection, #10322 (0322), Whatcom Museum of History and Art, Bellingham, Washington.*

to the Sound and the sawmills. An infusion of capital led to the construction of short logging railroads around Puget Sound and in Oregon's Willamette River valley. Later the invention of the steam donkey allowed the harvest of larger trees that could be pulled to a stream or to the rails. In the Oregon country, as in California, loggers simply stripped timber from the public domain and moved on to richer sites.

The forests of the Northwest held Douglas fir, red cedar, and other trees that produced bountiful yields of cut lumber that was transformed into houses, stores, fences, flumes, and even planked streets. The entrepreneurs from Maine, Michigan, and Wisconsin recognized the potential, brought in equipment and veteran employees, and initiated a giant transplanted industry.

The firm of Pope and Talbot provides a case study of the rise of lumbering in the region. In 1850, two lumbermen from East Machias, Maine, Frederick Pope and William Talbot, sent a cargo of lumber from Maine to San Francisco to test the California market. With the successful sale of that shipment, they decided to establish a sawmill at Port Gamble on Puget Sound in 1852 and began a substantial operation. As the business grew, they relocated the company headquarters to San Francisco and built docks, workshops, and living quarters for their loggers at Port Gamble. The timber cut by their employees entered the domestic California market and was exported to Hawaii, South America, and Asia. Their success attracted investors willing to risk even greater capital to build redwood empires.

By the 1880s, firms from New England, the Great Lakes, and San Francisco began to secure title to large blocks of timberland. These contiguous acreages had the capacity to produce vast quantities of lumber. The firms recruited "homeless, womanless" lumberjacks from New England, Michigan, and Wisconsin and initiated operations. The extension of the Oregon and California Railroad to Redding, California, opened the pine and redwood forests of that state to timber operators. The completion of the Northern Pacific meant that lumber from the Northwest could be shipped to the plains states to compete with the Chicago lumber market. Indeed, the harvests of timber reached such proportions that as early as the 1880s, cries for conservation could be heard. Congress gave the president the power to establish forest reserves in 1891, in response to the growing threat to western timberlands.

Conservationists indeed blanched when James J. Hill told an audience in Everett, Washington, in 1892, "Lumber, gentlemen, is your greatest resource today." Hill meant what he said and encouraged Frederick Weyerhaeuser to develop the fir and hemlock forests of the western Cascades. Weyerhaeuser followed a model established by a group of Great Lakes lumbermen who purchased eighty thousand acres of the Northern Pacific's land grant to form the St. Paul and Tacoma Lumber Company on Puget Sound. In the midst of frenzied speculation in timber holdings, Weyerhaeuser purchased nine hundred thousand acres of prime fir lands from the railroad in 1900. The days of the lumber giants began at the outset of the twentieth century.

The coming of a handful of major firms to the industry brought some order to what had been a chaotic business of many small operators, but the situation for the loggers and lumberjacks did not improve. Like those who worked in mining and railroading, the men who came to the timberlands tended to be young, single, and immigrants. There were relatively few Asians or African Americans, but large numbers of Scandinavians could be found in the lumber camps. The work proved hard and dangerous in the forests and in the mills. Companies dammed streams to form small lakes and, after filling the streambeds with logs, blew up the dams, using the cascading floodwaters to move the logs to a nearby river. Men died or lost limbs maneuvering the logs on the water. Crosscut saws ripped into fir trees and into the hands and legs of the loggers. Lumberjacks fell from trees when chains gave way, and they were crushed by trees that fell "the wrong way." Operatives in the sawmills labored over the huge, unprotected blades of circular saws and breathed air filled with sawdust six days a week, twelve to fourteen hours each day. Only a few of the men were considered skilled craftsmen—those who produced shingles, for example—and replacements were easy to find. The rate of industrial accidents in lumbering exceeded that of most other businesses in the West. Nevertheless, lumbering became a substantial contributor to the economy and international trade of the West.

The mill villages, the mining camps, the railroad towns, and even San Francisco all relied on another western business: the mercantile stores with their supplies and services. From early in the nineteenth century, the mercantile traders provided the region with tools, clothes, farm implements, sugar, coffee, and other necessities. The ubiquitous country store served the rural South and Midwest and was replicated across the West as well. Along the Mississippi and Missouri rivers, steamboat companies often established warehouses and retail stores, a pattern repeated by some of the freighting firms west of the Missouri. Local merchants formed partnerships with the boat companies and the freighters, often doubling as their agents and bankers. Western entrepreneurs moved quickly from mercantile interests to transportation, banking, and real estate, as well as town promotion, as their communities matured into towns and cities.

In many communities the merchants and bankers formed the town's elite, both financially and socially. Some were sons or nephews of eastern bankers and merchants and were sent west to open branches or to supervise local investments. An unusually large number were German immigrants, and some were German Jews. Those with European connections often had lines of credit with continental banking houses. While the merchants enjoyed access to capital and social status, the miners, farmers, ranchers, and professional people in their communities frequently resented them because of their privileges. The merchants often controlled transportation facilities, and customers blamed high prices on alleged collusion rather than on the great distances goods had to be carried to their communities. Merchants bought cheap and sold dear, but they were indispensable for economic growth.

Not all merchants were Anglos from the East Coast. In New Mexico and Arizona, Hispanics frequently dominated freighting and the mercantile trade, some families having been engaged in such activities for decades. The Hispanic merchants in New Mexico used their stores as collecting points for wool from local herds, trading that commodity for freight goods brought over the Santa Fe Trail. Some formed partnerships with Yankee traders and served as agents for firms in St. Louis or Independence. They entered the import-export trade and were bankers as well as commission agents. Felipe Chávez, for example, was born in 1835, south of Albuquerque. His grandfather served as the first governor of New Mexico under Mexican rule, and the family had excellent social and economic connections. Chávez attended St. Louis University to study liberal arts and business practices, and he returned to New Mexico to join his father's trading

With the coming of the railroad in 1868, the Mormon leader Brigham Young abandoned his emphasis on economic isolation and the local manufacture of goods. Acknowledging the inevitability of imported products, he instituted a program of church cooperatives in every settlement to keep retail businesses in Mormon hands. Built in 1878, this Lehi store operated as a typical cooperative with stockholders limited to no more than a $200 share in the business.

George Edward Anderson (1860–1928). Peoples Co-operative Mercantile Institution, Lehi, Utah. Modern print from original glass-plate negative, ca. 1885. Harold B. Lee Library, Brigham Young University, Provo, Utah.

company. He opened the Chávez General Merchandise Store in Belen in about 1860, and using his own wagons to transport his trade goods, Chávez flourished. He became interested in the New York Stock Exchange and purchased securities as well as New York real estate. Eventually he purchased a seat on the exchange for his son José, who moved to the East to manage the family investments. A stockholder in the Santa Fe Railway, Chávez worked diligently to have his town located on a low-gradient freight line that the carrier was building across New Mexico. His success mirrored that of Esteban Ochoa in Tucson and other Hispanic business leaders in the Southwest.

Paralleling this story were the careers of many German and Polish Jews who came to the West as merchants, traders, bankers, and incipient manufacturers. Michael Goldwater failed in several ventures in Sonora but established a successful store in Phoenix, where the Goldwater family became prominent members of the community. Aaron Meier tried his luck in the California goldfields before moving to Portland, where he created the Meier and Frank's store in 1857. From a small plant in San Francisco, Levi Strauss provided heavy cotton work clothes to the miners, and I. W. Hellman formed the Farmers and Merchants Bank in Los Angeles. Anti-Semitism could be found in the West, as elsewhere, but that did not deter Jewish families from seizing economic opportunities in the cities and towns.

Merchants have largely been ignored by scholars, as have capitalists of the second echelon whose careers were not as colorful as those of the robber barons. Critics of Montana politics and Anaconda Copper focus their ire on Daly and Clark while failing to see the contributions of men such as Simon Pepin. Neither as prominent nor as controversial as the Copper Kings, Pepin came to Montana after living in Maine and working his way westward first as a riverboat deckhand and then on a freighting outfit to the Utah Territory. A Canadian by birth, Pepin entered the freighting business in Montana by 1864, still a young man in his mid-twenties. As a wagon boss, he gained a favorable reputation and was seen as a "comer." He used his savings to buy a cattle herd, which he sold to the army and the Indian agencies, and then with several partners started a cattle ranch. When the Great Northern Railway built its track through Pepin's ranch, he established a townsite on his property, and Hill agreed to locate a division point in the community. Pepin founded Havre, built a store, hotel, and houses there, and donated land for parks and churches. A banker and developer, Pepin acquired real estate in several Montana communities before his death in 1914.

Transportation allowed towns and cities to grow, and entrepreneurs saw economic opportunities in merchandising, real estate, banking, and construction. Money could be made in transshipping goods, in accepting consignments of equipment, and in developing urban properties. The Mormons of Salt Lake City set examples as they developed freighting firms, trading posts, and stores in Utah and beyond. Brigham Young recognized the impact of the coming of the railroad and entered into construction contracts with the Union Pacific. Mormons built railways north and south out of Salt Lake City and expanded their wholesale houses and small-scale industries. Church leaders planned economic investments and stood united against "Gentile" merchants and bankers. Their concerted efforts succeeded as Salt Lake City grew from 8,236 people in 1860 to over 20,000 two decades later. Salt Lake City, like San Francisco, Portland, and Houston, grew as a result of access to capital and the creation of banking houses with connections in the East and abroad.

Miners, farmers, merchants, builders, promoters, realtors, and westerners generally wanted and needed banks and bankers. Despite the historic image of the banker and the banking system vilified by the press and the populace, in most communities in the region the banks and those who led them were held in considerable regard. Westerners desired sound banks and bankers who could win their respect. Those who formed these institutions usually did so using their own capital and that of a group of partners. Few turned to the East for capital, but they did establish close connections with eastern banks that served as clearinghouses and as sources of currency. The bankers in western communities knew their customers by name, sent their children to school with the town children, and belonged to the same civic organizations and the same churches as their customers. There was little of the venom found in Populist rhetoric directed at local bankers; rather, the ire was directed toward the "monied interests" in the East.

Banking in the West developed largely after the National Banking Act of 1863 and the Internal Revenue Act of 1864, so that western state and territorial governments never had the opportunity to charter their own note-issuing banks or to create a system of "wildcat" banks. It was no longer possible to form banking institutions solely to generate credit by issuing paper money. As a result, most banks in the West were chartered by the states to provide only basic financial services. The regional banking system expanded at an extraordinary pace. The Miners Bank opened in California in 1848, and when Seattle had only four hundred people and a steamer arrived only once a week, it had a bank. The West needed currency more than it needed credit, at least initially. No longer could the regional economy be based on bartering trade goods; an infusion of currency was necessary. This problem had existed from the days of the fur traders and had to be resolved if the economy was to grow and modernize.

In the mining camps the use of gold, gold dust, or raw silver represented a temporary form of currency, but transfer of this currency proved dangerous. As a consequence, gold brokerages, stagecoach lines, and merchants began to accept deposits of the metals and issue certificates in receipt. These certificates of deposit could be exchanged, and thus the firms or individuals issuing them became de facto bankers. One Denver firm even minted coins and put them into circulation, but the arrival of Luther Kountze from Omaha and the establishment of his bank eased the local currency problem. A similar crisis occurred in San Francisco: gold flowed in from the mines, but there was little or no currency to exchange for the dust and bullion. Merchants needed to pay cash for goods ordered in the East, and as a result, banks appeared in rapid order.

The most significant banking house in San Francisco, the Bank of California, opened in 1864 with two million dollars in capital secured by its founders, William Chapman Ralston and D. O. Mills. Born in Ohio in 1826, Ralston worked on the Ohio and Mississippi rivers before going to Panama as a merchant, banker, and shipping agent. By 1854, Ralston moved to San Francisco and joined friends from his steamboat days to form a small bank. In the absence of incorporation laws, such banks were usually partnerships, and their reputations reflected those of the partners. Ralston quickly became a civic leader and served as a director or officer of mining and transportation companies. Although he persuaded Mills to serve as titular head of the Bank of California, Ralston led the firm, and through friendships, opportunism, and sheer energy he took over and consolidated the mines of the Comstock. He built a woolen mill, a winery, and a sugar refinery and invested in a dry dock, an insurance company, and steamships. The coming of the transcontinental railway undermined some of his enterprises, and following the national depression of 1873, Ralston's investments shrank in value, as did the collateral for loans extended by his bank. His empire collapsed in 1875, and Ralston turned over all his personal assets to satisfy his debts to the bank. A lonely swim in the Bay led to an apparent suicide. The economic growth of San Francisco and much of northern California depended on the entrepreneurship of men such as Ralston.

Firms like the Bank of California established branches or corresponding banks in Virginia City and in other mining camps in the West. Whereas the Mormons of Utah issued script to meet their need for currency, bankers in the villages and towns in the region depended on the growing banks of Seattle, Denver, and San Francisco or issued their own notes. Merchants with safes often became the town bankers, and in the absence of state or territorially chartered banks, trust in the banker was the only hope for the depositor. The absence of regulation produced a free-wheeling economy, but by the 1890s, demands for banking restrictions led to new laws in the region. Failures, such as Ralston's, forced legislatures to act to provide minimum protection for banking customers. The states required that both incorporated bankers and private bankers meet certain operating standards.

The depressions of 1873 and 1893, combined with demands from the mining companies and midwestern and southern farmers for the expansion of the nation's currency supply, placed western bankers in a dilemma. While the mining firms and their workers, as well as many other customers, cried out for "free silver," the banking community nationally opposed any movement away from the gold standard. The collapse of small-town banks in farming areas led to louder cries for currency inflation and lower interest rates. From the 1870s into the twentieth century, bankers in the West became more than suppliers of currency; certainly by the late 1880s, they were the primary sources of credit as the regional economy matured. Demand for credit came from many sectors of the economy, but particularly from manufacturing.

The construction of large, elaborate bank buildings in the major cities and the larger towns indicated economic maturation and the development of a commercial and industrial base beyond the extraction of minerals and the harvesting of forests. Although only San Francisco could be described as a city in 1860, by 1900 Houston, Dallas, Denver, Seattle, Portland, Los Angeles, and other urban areas boasted large populations and complex economies. Mining created demands for a wide range of products, from chemicals to candles and even ice, and small firms emerged to supply such items. Denver and San Francisco met some of the demands of miners for consumer goods by opening breweries and small garment plants. More significant, foundries and machine shops began to manufacture equipment for the mines, and over thirteen hundred men labored in such facilities in San Francisco by 1870. Denver and San Francisco attracted the greatest concentration of manufacturing facilities, but other cities also acquired a wide range of industries. Portland, for example, milled flour, produced pig iron, and developed woolen mills. Yet the coming of the railroad hurt these high-cost, high-wage factories; goods from the East or Europe sold for much less in many instances. Some cities that had previously suffered from a lack of labor found large numbers of unemployed men and women filling the streets. Only in the 1880s would the effort to industrialize vigorously advance as wage and transportation differentials achieved some balance and as western urban markets created greater demand. The economy of the region remained urban-centered in 1900, just as it had been since the arrival of the first European settlers; the towns and cities were the vanguards of the settlement process.

At the turn of the century, some western cities stood poised to take advantage of yet another regional resource, petroleum. After the successful development of the oil fields of northwestern Pennsylvania in the 1860s, wildcatting spread to West Virginia, Ohio, and Illinois. Although John D. Rockefeller's Standard Oil Company secured over 90 percent of the crude oil production of the major fields, other firms sought oil across the nation. Commercial production began in Kansas and the Indian Territory in the 1890s, and a large field was discovered south of Dallas near Corsicana, Texas, in 1894. Geologists, speculators, and drillers brought oil booms to the West, but California appeared to be the most promising area before 1900.

As early as the 1860s, oil seepages in California suggested the possibilities of commercial development. But the crude oil of California proved to be of low gravity and to contain excessive carbon, limiting its use as the basis for kerosene, the most important petroleum derivative. It could be used as boiler fuel, however, and was adopted by some industries. In 1892, E. L. Doheny found the enormous Los Angeles field, and other discoveries were made in Coalinga and the Kern River areas. These fields produced boiler fuel for railroad locomotives, steamships, and even Arizona copper smelters. California crude oil could compete with imported coal as a source of heat, and refineries, pipelines, and storage tanks soon dotted the landscape. Capital for the creation of the oil firms came largely from local investors, many of whom, like Doheny, had backgrounds in mining. As the California production grew, Standard Oil Company entered the field by purchasing the independent Pacific Coast Oil Company, soon renamed Standard Oil of California. By 1900 California ranked fifth among the states in petroleum production, and the West contributed 9 percent of the nation's output.

The development of petroleum spread slowly across the West before the discovery at Spindletop in 1901. Fields in Kansas and the Oklahoma Territory yielded good results, as did areas of Wyoming. These widespread discoveries led to the creation of independent oil firms in the region and to a substantial decline in Standard Oil's monopolistic position in crude production after 1900. The oil companies, railroads, and university scientists and geology departments cooperated to expend output, discover new fields, and streamline the refinery processes. By the time the Supreme Court ordered Standard Oil Company of New Jersey to divest itself of major subsidiaries in 1911, the West had replaced the old fields of the Northeast and Midwest as the nation's major source of petroleum. The capital created by regional oil firms contributed to the rise of many cities and towns and was frequently reinvested in other western businesses.

The End of the Beginning

In the last two decades of the nineteenth century, the West grew in population at a rate greater than the rest of the nation even as the rate for the United States as a whole exceeded that of all other industrialized countries. After 1890 the population of the region became more urbanized, and by the turn of the century almost 40 percent of westerners lived in an urban society. The sex ratio moved closer to the national norm as urbanization accelerated. The region retained its large percentage of foreign born while the number of African Americans increased slowly. Economic opportunity attracted this burgeoning populace as the discovery of gold in Alaska in 1896 and then at Tonopah, Nevada, four years later helped to sustain the boom in mining precious metals.

Westerners tended to be boastful, yet there was more than a grain of truth in their claims of economic success. A severe price had been paid in the misuse of natural resources and in the treatment of workers, but the West had functioned within a rising capitalistic system. Westerners were also optimistic, and many believed that although there were areas of poverty and although conservation measures had to be adopted, prosperity and the regulation of business would eradicate these problems in the twentieth century. They would be disappointed.

The economy of the West in the nineteenth century did not develop along the lines of Frederick Jackson Turner's rolling frontier. Rather, it grew in spasms over a widespread terrain and often from west to east. The people of the West adopted and used the system of laws and government they brought with them, but they also borrowed from other societies and cultures. In making use of the natural resources of the region, they incorporated the ideas and experiences of peoples from several other continents. The economy they forged in the West included features common not only to the rest of the United States but also to the world capitalistic economy. Westerners could not lay claim to uniqueness in the creation of a complex regional economy, but they could persuasively argue that few other areas of the world had witnessed such remarkable growth in such a brief span of time.

Bibliographic Note

In the absence of a general survey of the economic history of the trans-Mississippi West, readers should initially turn to the relevant chapters of several histories of the region. Ray Allen Billington and Martin Ridge, *Westward Expansion: A History of the American Frontier*, 5th ed. (New York, 1982), Robert V. Hine, *The American West: An Interpretive History*, 2d ed. (Boston, 1984), and Rodman W. Paul, *The Far West and the Great Plains in Transition, 1859-1900* (New York, 1988), are helpful and suggestive. To place the economic development of the West in a global perspective, William H. McNeill's *The Great Frontier: Freedom and Hierarchy in Modern Times* (Princeton, 1983) is indispensable. Although the jargon can be almost overwhelming, Leften Stavrianos, *Global Rift: The Third World Comes of Age* (New York, 1981), Theodore H. Von Laue, *The World Revolution of Westernization: The Twentieth Century in Global Perspective* (New York, 1987), and Imanuel Wallerstein, *The Politics of the World-Economy: The States, the Movements, and the Civilizations* (Cambridge, Eng., 1984), are critical to placing the economic history of the West in a broader framework. The largely discredited "plundered province" thesis first espoused by Bernard DeVoto in "The West: A Plundered Province," *Harper's Magazine* 149 (August 1934): 355–64, is examined most recently by William G. Robbins in "The 'Plundered Province' Thesis and the Recent Historiography of the American West," *Pacific Historical Review* 55 (November 1986): 577–98. Regional studies are also helpful, such as Carlos A. Schwantes, *The Pacific Northwest: An Interpretive History* (Lincoln, 1989), and Earl Pomeroy, *The Pacific Slope* (New York, 1965).

The mining industry in the West has attracted the interest of many scholars, but the reader should start with Rodman W. Paul's *Mining Frontiers of the Far West, 1848–1880* (New York, 1963), and William Greever's *Bonanza West: The Story of the Western Mining Rushes, 1848–1900* (Norman, 1963). Also important are two works by Clark C. Spence, *British Investments and the American Mining Frontier, 1860–1901* (Ithaca, N.Y., 1958), and *Mining Engineers and the American West: The Lace-Boot Brigade, 1849–1933* (New Haven, 1970), and Richard H. Peterson's *The Bonanza Kings: The Social Origins and Business Behavior of Western Mining Entrepreneurs, 1870–1900* (Lincoln, 1977). For the question of mining law, see Gordon Morris Bakken's *The Development of Law on the Rocky Mountain Frontier: Civil Law and Society, 1850–1912* (Westport, 1983). Lewis Atherton addresses the role of the mining entrepreneur in "The Mining Promoter in the Trans-Mississippi West," *Western Historical Quarterly* 1 (January 1970): 35–50. For mining in California, the best survey is Rodman W. Paul's *California Gold: The Beginning of Mining in the Far West* (Cambridge, Mass., 1947). See also Rudolph M. Lapp, *Blacks in Gold Rush California* (New Haven, 1977). A splendid case study of mining in Nevada can be found in *Treasure Hill: A Portrait of a Mining Camp* (Tucson, 1963) by W. Turrentine Jackson. The emergence of mining in Colorado is traced in Joseph E. King, *A Mine to Make a Mine: Financing the Colorado Mining Industry, 1859–1902* (College Station, Tex., 1977), and Duane A. Smith, *Rocky Mountain Mining Camps: The Urban Frontier* (Bloomington, 1967). Aspects of mining in Washington and Idaho are addressed by John W. Fahey in *The Ballyhoo Bonanza: Charles Sweeny and the Idaho Mines* (Seattle, 1971). For Montana, see Michael P. Malone, *Battle for Butte: Mining and Politics on the Northern Frontier, 1864–1906* (Seattle, 1981). Gold mining in South Dakota is described by Watson Parker in two works: *Deadwood: The Golden Years* (Lincoln, 1981) and *Gold in the Black Hills* (Norman, 1966).

The "new" labor history has produced excellent studies of miners in the West. The lives of these laborers are portrayed by Ronald C. Brown, *Hard-Rock Miners: The Intermountain West, 1860–1920* (College Station, Tex., 1979), Richard E. Lingenfelter, *The Hardrock Miners: A History of the Mining Labor Movement in the American West, 1863–1893* (Berkeley, 1974), Mark

Wyman, *Hard Rock Epic: Western Miners and the Industrial Revolution, 1860–1910* (Berkeley, 1979), and Ping Chiu, *Chinese Labor in California, 1850–1880: An Economic Study* (Madison, 1963).

Prerailroad land transportation in the West is surveyed by Oscar O. Winther in *The Transportation Frontier: Trans-Mississippi West, 1865–1920* (New York, 1964). Studies of various aspects of freighting and stagecoach operations can be found in Raymond W. Settle and Mary L. Settle, *War Drums and Wagon Wheels: The Story of Russell, Majors and Waddell* (Lincoln, 1966), W. Turrentine Jackson, *Wagon Roads West* (New Haven, 1965), Henry Pickering Walker, *The Wagonmasters: High Plains Freighting from the Earliest Days of the Santa Fe Trail to 1880* (Norman, 1966), and Oscar O. Winther, *The Old Oregon Country* (Bloomington, 1950).

No modern survey of railroad expansion into the West has replaced Robert Reigel's *The Story of the Western Railroads* (New York, 1926). Robert W. Fogel, an economist, challenges the significance of the railroads in the modernization process in *The Union Pacific Railroad: A Case in Premature Enterprise* (Baltimore, 1960). Arthur M. Johnson and Barry E. Supple provide insight into the motives of investors in western railroads in *Boston Capitalists and Western Railroads* (Cambridge, Mass., 1967).

Corporate biographies for the period include Maury Klein, *Union Pacific*, vol. 1, *The Birth of a Railroad, 1862–1893* (Garden City, N.Y., 1987), Keith L. Bryant, Jr., *History of the Atchison, Topeka and Santa Fe Railway* (New York, 1974), Ralph W. Hidy et al., *The Great Northern Railway: A History* (Boston, 1988), Richard C. Overton, *Burlington Route: A History of the Burlington Lines* (New York, 1965), Robert G. Athearn, *Rebel of the Rockies: A History of the Denver and Rio Grande Western Railroad* (New Haven, 1962), and John Hoyt Williams, *A Great and Shining Road: The Epic Story of the Transcontinental Railroad* (New York, 1988).

Important biographies of railroad leaders include Maury Klein, *The Life and Legend of Jay Gould* (Baltimore, 1986), Albro Martin, *James J. Hill and the Opening of the Northwest* (New York, 1976), and James B. Hedges, *Henry Villard and the Railways of the Northwest* (New York, 1930). A fine case study of the railway workers is James H. Ducker's *Men of the Steel Rails: Workers on the Atchison, Topeka and Santa Fe Railroad, 1869–1900* (Lincoln, 1983).

Steamboat operations on the Missouri and Columbia rivers as well as in San Francisco Bay and Puget Sound have been well documented. Some of the best studies are Louis C. Hunter, *Steamboats on the Western Rivers: An Economic and Technological History* (Cambridge, Mass., 1949), Jerry MacMullen, *Paddle Wheel Days in California* (Palo Alto, Calif., 1944), William E. Lass, *A History of Steamboating on the Upper Missouri River* (Lincoln, 1962), and Randall V. Mills, *Stern-Wheelers up the Columbia: A Century of Steamboating in the Oregon Country* (Palo Alto, Calif., 1947). Coastal shipping has received far less scholarly interest, but *The Panama Route, 1848–1869* (Berkeley, 1943), by John H. Kemble, is helpful.

The lumber industry and its laborers have been studied by Thomas R. Cox, *Mills and Markets: A History of the Pacific Coast Lumber Industry to 1900* (Seattle, 1974), William H. Hutchinson, *California Heritage: A History of Northern California Lumbering* (Santa Cruz, 1974), William G. Robbins, *American Forestry: A History of National, State, and Private Cooperation* (Lincoln, 1985), Robert S. Maxwell and Robert D. Baker, *Sawdust Empire: The Texas Lumber Industry, 1830–1940* (College Station, Tex., 1983); Ralph Hidy, Frank E. Hill, and Allan Nevins, *Timber and Men: The Weyerhaeuser Story* (New York, 1963), Edwin Truman Coman, Jr., and Helen M. Gibbs, *Time, Tide, and Timber: A Century of Pope and Talbot* (Palo Alto, Calif., 1949), Andrew Mason Prouty, *More Deadly Than War: Pacific Coast Logging, 1827–1981* (New York, 1985), and Daniel A. Cornford, *Workers and Dissent in the Redwood Empire* (Philadelphia, 1987).

One of the important aspects of the western economy is the mercantile trade, but it is also one of the most neglected fields. Only in a few articles and monographs can the role of the merchant be delineated. See, for examples, the following: Lewis Atherton, "The Santa Fe Trader as Mercantile Capitalist," *Missouri Historical Review* 77 (October 1982): 1–12; Richard Griswold del Castillo, "Tucsonenses and Angelenos: A Socio-Economic Study of Two Mexican

American Barrios, 1860–1880," *Journal of the West* 18 (July 1979): 58–66; Peter R. Decker, *Fortunes and Failures: White-Collar Mobility in Nineteenth-Century San Francisco* (Cambridge, Mass., 1978); Floyd S. Fierman, *Guts and Ruts: The Jewish Pioneer on the Trail in the American Southwest* (New York, 1985); and William J. Parish, *The Charles Ilfeld Company: A Study of the Rise and Decline of Mercantile Capitalism in New Mexico* (Cambridge, Mass., 1961).

Bankers fueled the economic engine of the western economy, and a study by Lynne Pierson Doti and Larry Schweikart, *Banking in the American West: From the Gold Rush to Deregulation* (Norman, 1991), surveys the role of banking in the region. A history of Houston's Texas Commerce Bank, by Walter L. Buenger and Joseph A. Pratt, *But Also Good Business: Texas Commerce Banks and the Financing of Houston and Texas, 1886–1986* (College Station, Tex., 1986), is informative, as are Larry Schweikart, *A History of Banking in Arizona* (Tucson, 1982), and L. Milton Woods, *Sometimes the Books Froze: Wyoming's Economy and Its Banks* (Boulder, 1985).

Also neglected by scholars is the story of manufacturing in the West before 1900. Leonard J. Arrington's works on Utah—*Beet Sugar in the West: A History of the Utah-Idaho Sugar Company, 1891–1966* (Seattle, 1966), *David Eccles: Pioneer Western Industrialist* (Logan, 1975), and *Great Basin Kingdom: An Economic History of the Latter-day Saints, 1830–1900* (Cambridge, Mass., 1958)—and H. Lee Scamehorn's *Pioneer Steelmaker in the West: The Colorado Fuel and Iron Company, 1872–1903* (Boulder, 1976) need to be emulated.

The early days of petroleum in the West are related in the following works: Ralph Andreano, "The Structure of the California Petroleum Industry, 1895–1911," *Pacific Historical Review* 39 (May 1970): 171–92; Henrietta M. Larson and Kenneth Wiggins Porter, *History of Humble Oil and Refining Company* (New York, 1959); and Gerald T. White, *Formative Years in the Far West: A History of Standard Oil Company of California and Predecessors through 1919* (New York, 1962).

Chapter Seven

Animals and Enterprise

RICHARD WHITE

I f a roof had been built over the southern plains in the early 1870s, the American zoologist William Hornaday wrote, it would have been "one vast charnel-house." During the fall of 1873 the corpses, stinking and rotting in the sun, lay in a line for forty miles along the north bank of the Arkansas River. William Blackmore, an English traveler, counted sixty-seven bodies in a space not covering four acres. The bodies were those of bison. They died in such numbers and so close together because if a hunter got properly downwind, if a bluff partially concealed him, and if his luck held, he might shoot, reload, and shoot, again and again and again, without the animals stampeding.

In 1872 George Reighard had left Dodge City for the Texas Panhandle with "a buffalo-hunting outfit." He killed, or so he remembered, an average of one hundred bison a day. He killed the bison for the "hide and the money it would bring." Asked, years later, whether he felt pity for the animals as day after day he dropped his hundred, he replied no, he did not. "It was a business with me. I had my money invested in that outfit . . . I killed all that I could."

Money and pity, these are the words that mark a great divide in the history of the American West. Reighard stood at a point where animals were only dollars on a hoof; those who later asked him about pity regarded animals as being worthy of concern within a human moral universe. But for all their differences, those who saw animals as commodities and those who saw them as objects of sentiment stood on the same side of a cultural divide. On the other side was a world in which animals were persons and pity was the sentiment that animals felt toward humans. This earlier West appears to us now at once recognizable and utterly strange. Remembering it, we may feel like Dorothy remembering Oz. Because once, when animals were persons, the West was a biological republic.

It was Indian peoples who had made animals other-than-human persons with whom relationships were social and religious instead of purely instrumental. Indians, like all other humans, certainly sought to order and control the natural world, but the order they constructed was a social order, and control partially came through what amounted to religious negotiation. Indian religions made hunting holy and gave human-animal relations a depth and complexity largely lacking among Europeans. In hunting, some persons died so that others might live. Ceremonies preceded the kill. Animals consented to die; they, or more powerful beings—holy people, keepers of game, or other super-naturals—pitied the hunter and instructed him in the rules and rituals necessary to kill

For many Native Americans, animals formed the bridge by which humans tapped supernatural powers. Working at Fort Union in 1832, Pennsylvania-born artist George Catlin painted this Blackfoot medicine man cloaked in the skin of a grizzly bear, whose strength gave power to the healing ceremonies.

George Catlin (1796–1872). Medicine Man Performing His Mysteries Over a Dying Man. Oil on canvas, 1832. National Museum of American Art, Washington, D.C./Art Resource, New York, New York.

them. Indians killed game as much by prayer, pleading, and reverence as by the arrow or spear. They recognized the obvious wariness of game and the reluctance of animals to die, but they explained it in terms of previous ritual abuse by humans or even supernaturals. The difficulty of obtaining the consent of animals only made strict observance of hunting rituals all the more necessary.

Europeans brought to the West a far more instrumental view of animals, and they brought new animal species that had evolved as instruments of human purposes. Europeans regarded their domesticated animals as sentient tools, and on the basis of utility, they classified them as superior to the native wild fauna. They recognized that their horses, sheep, goats, cattle, burros, and smaller stock gave them an advantage over Indians, for the native North American biota (the continent's native animal and plant life) lacked suitable candidates for domestication. Western Indians had domesticated only the dog and, in the Southwest, the turkey.

Europeans and Indians both linked the success of human endeavors to the biological success of at least some animals, but it was Europeans who made the measure of success commercial and who, like Reighard, could see their own commercial success as tied to the virtual destruction of entire species. Animal persons yielded to animals of enterprise, which gleaned the energy of western ecosystems (the interacting species and the nonbiological environments of the West) to produce hides, meat, and wool that found markets all over the world. Animals ceased to be creatures of a limited set of adjoining ecosystems and became instead, as the historian Alfred Crosby has noted, movable creatures of the biosphere (the entire planetary system that sustains life). By the close of the nineteenth century, human masters took tribute from subject animals and determined their fate. Animals not subject to humans had become, in effect, enemies.

The transition did not come easily or smoothly, and the animals of enterprise themselves, in a sense, rebelled. Without domesticated animals, Europeans would have neither survived nor conquered, but their animals often proved fickle allies. Indian peoples too enlisted the aid of horses, sheep, and cattle. And some domestic stock, disregarding both Indians and Europeans, went wild, turning against their masters' purposes. All of this greatly complicated the history and the mental and physical landscape of the West.

The horse, more than any other animal, exemplified the unpredictability that domesticated livestock introduced into the West. Horses became tools of Indian resistance as well as of European conquest. Horses became persons who entered the visions and dreams of Plains Indians. Among native peoples, the horse greatly increased the efficiency of nomadic hunters and the mobility of raiders. Along with the exotic diseases brought by Europeans, horses shifted the balance of power away from settled horticulturalists—both Indian and Hispanic—and toward nomadic hunters. The horse helped create the flourishing nomadic culture of the Great Plains.

Indians spread horses rapidly and widely across North America. West of the Rockies, they transported the animal to the Snake River valley by 1700 and the Columbia Plateau by 1730. East of the Rockies, the horse reached the central Great Plains by the 1720s and western Canada by the 1730s. Its distribution among Indians of the Pacific Coast was spottier, but by the 1770s the Yokuts of the central valley in modern-day California had adopted horses, and in the Pacific Northwest, Yakimas introduced horses among villagers living in the small prairies on the western foothills of the Cascades. Indians used horses for transport, war, hunting, and more rarely, food. For most groups, a life without horses became unimaginable.

Cattle and sheep did not spread so far or so fast. The Papagos moved from hunting semiwild cattle to herding them; refugee Indians from the East brought livestock with them; and in the early nineteenth century, some groups on the Columbia Plateau became cattle raisers. Before the reservation period, however, most western Indians remained raiders, not ranchers. They plundered Spanish, Mexican, and later American herds. The Apaches, in particular, regarded Spanish and later Mexican herds as virtual supply depots to be tapped at will.

Only the Pueblos and Navajos quickly adopted sheep and cattle. The Pueblos began raising sheep, horses, and cattle in the seventeenth century. The Navajos started as did conventional Apache raiders, preying on the Spanish and the Pueblos. But they quickly became livestock raisers, looking after their sheep, in the words of one Spaniard, "with the greatest care and diligence for their increase." At the end of the eighteenth century the Spanish regarded Navajo herds as "innumerable," and the Navajos found themselves targets of Spanish and Ute raids. As sheep and goats became critical to Navajo subsistence, these animals, like horses, bridged the gap between wild animal persons and domestic animal tools. Navajos regarded sheep and goats as metaphorical mothers and fathers because they sustained life. They were thus loved and identified with the family even as they were killed and regarded as wealth.

It was through raiding, which marked the movement of animals from European to Indian control and back again, that some animals escaped human control entirely. Feral horses and cattle appeared on the margins of human settlements. Not all species of introduced livestock could seize the opportunity to go wild. Domestication had given sheep, even the *churros*—the tough sheep of the southwestern borderlands—too great an inventiveness in finding ways to die. Although hardy and able to withstand drought, sheep could not live without shepherds. By themselves, they could not find water or feed. They died from poisonous weeds, and they could not resist even the most inept predators.

Cattle and horses did go feral, but their populations remained localized, growing as it were from seed animals that Indians and white migrants planted. The mustangs of Texas and other wild horses of the West developed from strays left by raids and from animals abandoned as lame. Wild horses were most numerous in Texas, but there were also significant wild horse populations along the Snake and Columbia rivers and in the San Joaquin Valley of California. There were relatively few wild horses on the northern plains or in the Rocky Mountains before 1800. They did not appear in Nevada, their present-day stronghold, until the transcontinental migrations of the 1840s. At their nineteenth-century peak, only an estimated two million horses grazed between the Rio Grande and the Arkansas River, with perhaps another million in the rest of the West. True wild cattle, as distinct from unbranded stock, had an even more confined range and fewer numbers. Into the nineteenth century, feral Criollo cattle from mission herds remained largely limited to East Texas and the lands around the Arizona missions. After several generations in the wild, they could not be redomesticated. They could only be hunted.

The introduction of new species and their spread created sweeping and significant changes, but these changes still lay on the other side of the great nineteenth-century divide. Western animals had not yet become animals of enterprise. Animals of enterprise are commodities; their value is exchange rather than use. For both Navajos and *nuevo mexicanos*, for example, the *churro* remained primarily a subsistence animal. A full-grown *churro* dressed out to only seventeen pounds of meat, less than a modern lamb, and yielded only about a pound of wool. Such small yields were commercially unacceptable, but they were not liabilities when fresh meat had to be consumed quickly to avoid spoiling. Similarly, *churro* wool (actually closer to hair) was meager but ideally suited to hand spinning.

In a world where social relationships took precedence over economic relationships, commerce took a backseat to other forms of exchange, and such exchanges dominated the transfer of livestock. Indians stole livestock from their enemies, but they gave livestock freely as gifts to friends or relatives. Trade lay in the originally limited region between these extremes; it was a way to seek advantage among those who were not friends but also not clearly enemies. Commerce was thus a form of sublimated theft, and as such, it often shaded easily into outright theft. Plains Indians traded horses at the Mandan and other Missouri River villages, but given the opportunity, traders would quickly turn into raiders. The subtleties of an exchange where the goal was to accumulate wealth at the expense of others and to profit by others' need, but where outright theft was forbidden, were lost on many Indians. And livestock, by its very nature, invited theft. Large domesticated grazers were a plunderer's dream, for unlike all other forms of property, these would gallop off with an insistent thief. Raided by Indians, the Spanish and later the Mexicans raided in turn.

Livestock raiding and its companion, slave raiding, became deeply entrenched in the Southwest and on the Great Plains. The Spanish and later the Mexicans raided and traded for Navajo, Apache, and Pawnee slaves; the Navajos and Apaches took Spaniards and later Mexicans as slaves in turn. In Texas the herds of the missions on the Rio Grande and farther north around La Bahia and San Antonio de Béxar provided inviting targets; first the Apaches, then northern villagers ("los norteños"), and finally the Comanches preyed on these herds. Ute, Apache, Comanche, and Navajo raiders struck deep into the heart of New Mexico, repeatedly devastating sheep herds; in the 1760s the Comanches virtually stripped New Mexico of horses. By the 1840s, Yokut and Miwok horse raiders from the interior had crippled many Mexican ranchos in California, aided by the Indians living on the ranchos.

Under such conditions, cattle, horses, and sheep only slowly emerged as animals of enterprise. The first step in this direction came when they began to serve as capital among both Indians and Hispanics. In eighteenth- and nineteenth-century New Mexico, sheep raising took place on the *partido* system. Sheep essentially became capital lent at interest. The owner (banker) of the sheep turned over a certain number of ewes (capital) to the *partidario* (borrower), who agreed to make set annual payments of wool and lambs, usually 20 percent of the original head count (interest). Eventually, the contracts specified responsibility in case of losses to disease, lightning, and Indian raids. If the *partidario* could realize a return greater than the interest that he paid the owner, he

By the late 19th century, the animal skulls holy to Plains Indian tribes had become for American military troops mere monuments to slaughter.

Karl Bodmer (1809–93). Assiniboin Medicine Sign. *Watercolor on paper, 1833. Gift of the Enron Art Foundation, Joslyn Art Museum, Omaha, Nebraska.*

William Henry Jackson (1843–1942). A Collection of Buffalo, Elk, Deer, Mountain-Sheep, and Wolf Skulls and Bones Near Fort Saunders. *Photograph, 1870. United States Geological Survey (Jackson, W.H. 348), Denver, Colorado.*

profited and could establish his own flock. If he failed, he sank into debt and lost his collateral—land, if he had any, or if not, his own labor. *Partidarios* hoped the arrangement would lead to wealth and freedom, but it often led to poverty and peonage, a form of debt slavery. Sheep owners, on the other hand, succeeded in transferring part of the risks to the *partidarios*, solved their own labor problems in a cash-short economy, and freed themselves from active management of the herds.

Partidario arrangements involved little buying and selling of animals, but livestock gradually became commodities used to acquire other commodities. Comanche and Apache raiders turned easily stolen livestock into more difficult to steal European manufactures by trading what they had stolen. In the nineteenth century, the Yokuts and Miwoks traded stolen California horses to American mountain men and New Mexican adventurers, who drove the horses east to New Mexico and Missouri.

Until the late eighteenth and early nineteenth century, commerce per se remained more an incidental outcome of livestock raising in New Mexico, Texas, and California than a rationale. Indeed, in eighteenth-century New Mexico the governors, fearful of losing breeding stock, placed substantial restrictions on trade in sheep, ordering that only wethers (neutered rams) be sold in the mining towns of Nueva Vizcaya and occasionally forbidding the export of any live animals. Textiles woven from the wool of *churros* remained more important than the direct sale of sheep.

Only in the late eighteenth century did reforms in the Spanish empire and relative peace with the Indians create a commercial boom in sheep raising. By then the *partido* system had concentrated the wealth in the hands of relatively few interrelated families. Large sheep owners became *comerciantes*, rancher-merchants who developed a trade with Chihuahua, Nueva Vizcaya's leading commercial and mining center. By the 1790s, sheep drives had become an annual event as New Mexicans sent roughly twenty-five thousand head of sheep south each year in large caravans guarded by soldiers against the Apaches. Both farmers and *partidarios* were in debt to the *comerciantes*, and the *comerciantes*, in turn, were usually in debt to the merchants of Chihuahua. Only a few *comerciantes* escaped this chain of debt and became *ricos*—the richest tier of New Mexican landowners and merchants. Clemente Gutierréz, born in Aragon and married well in New Mexico, used the *partido* system and the Chihuahua trade to make himself the most powerful of the New Mexican *ricos*. Sheep delivered wealth and power into his hands; he and the other *ricos* dominated New Mexico's economy and politics.

This commerce in sheep, however, remained at the mercy of war and theft. It collapsed in the years of turmoil that led to Mexico's independence. After the revolution, exports resumed, and by 1835, New Mexico was sending eighty thousand sheep south. New Mexican sheep, marketed in Durango, found their way deep into the interior of Mexico, until the Mexican War and the American conquest of New Mexico finally aborted this trade.

The California gold rush redirected New Mexican sheep away from Old Mexico and to the new markets provided by the California mines. Even after the early boom prices in the mines declined, sheep drives continued. In 1858 one hundred thousand New Mexican sheep went west into California. Only the growth of California flocks, to nearly three million head by 1870, closed the California market.

In Texas, the early development of commercial livestock raising was far slower and less successful. Between the 1750s and 1810, ranchos developed in three distinct areas of Texas: between the Rio Grande and the Nueces River (then part of Coahuila and Nuevo Santander), on the San Antonio River, and finally, on the Louisiana border near Nacogdoches. It was on these ranches and on the missions that many of the practices of later western cattle raising evolved. The first Texas cowboys were Indians. When not restricted by raiders, these vaqueros conducted annual roundups to gather and brand free-ranging cattle of the mission herds.

But Texas cattle never quite became full-fledged animals of enterprise during the Spanish era. Indian raids often kept missionaries and ranchers from conducting roundups to brand their cattle. Ownership of these unbranded cattle remained in constant dispute, and they became an irresistible temptation to meat hunters (*carneadores*), soldiers, and, later, soap makers, all of whom slaughtered the unbranded cattle with incredible waste. What was commerce and what was theft remained a matter of considerable disagreement. To make matters worse, legal markets remained limited largely to sales to the king's presidios in Texas and to the south. Burdensome regulations made the transport of cattle to markets in Coahuila and Louisiana difficult and often illegal. This taint of smuggling, plus the endless disputes over the ownership of the unbranded animals, continued to give ranching an aura of criminality. As the slaughter of unbranded stock reduced the once abundant herds, the rancheros turned to gathering and exporting the wild mustangs that also abounded on the range. By 1796, mustangs had supplanted cattle as the province's chief export, until the bloody struggles in the province before the Mexican Revolution stymied the growth of all commerce.

In terms of cattle raising, *californios* succeeded where *tejanos* failed. California missionaries had the good fortune of having a ready market appear virtually at their doors in the form of American and British trading vessels, which arrived to collect hides and tallow—the rendered fat used for candles. Neophytes—the baptized Indians of the missions—and vaqueros working for private ranchos slaughtered the cattle, left the meat to rot, and took away the hides and tallow. After the Mexican government secularized the California missions between 1836 and 1842, much of the mission property intended for the Indian neophytes ended up in the hands of rancheros. The mission herds that had once numbered 150,000 head of horses, sheep, and cattle dwindled to 50,000. The remainder had been slaughtered and sold. The rancheros no longer had to share the trade with the missions.

Fur Trade

By the time New Mexican sheep and California cattle succeeded in becoming full-fledged animals of enterprise, a select group of wild animals had also fallen victim to commodification. To be sure, a small trade in products of the hunt had long existed out of Taos and Pecos. Some hides and buffalo robes traded there continued south, finding an ultimate market in Mexico. Much farther north, at the Mandan villages and Wichita villages, Plains Indians had also bartered deerskins, antelope hides, buffalo robes, and dried meat for corn, beans, and other produce. By and large, these remained local exchanges that disposed of small surpluses gained during normal subsistence activities.

It was not production for the market per se. The large-scale commodification of wild animals emerged only in the late eighteenth century. Even then it affected few species—buffalo, beaver, and sea otters. For these species, however, the results were so dramatic that within a relatively few years, each faced extinction.

In the commodification and killing of wild animals for their furs, two different cyclical patterns met. One was natural. The turning of the seasons made beaver fur and bison wool grow thick in the winter. As long as consumers desired beaver for felt to make hats and bison for wool to make robes, the seasons shaped the hunt. The other pattern was economic and far less regular. On the world markets of emergent capitalism, prices fluctuated, and this cycle too shaped the fate of the animals selected for enterprise. Yet even as human beings conformed to the patterns that nature and the market imposed, they also struggled against them. Producers found new technologies that allowed hatmakers to use lower grades of beaver, and tanners found uses for summer-killed buffalo. The large companies that came to dominate the fur trade unsuccessfully sought monopolies that would allow them to avoid, as much as possible, the cycles of the market.

No animal suffered as rapid a subjection to the market and as rapid a destruction as the sea otter. Sea otters congregated in rafts or schools of up to one hundred animals along the northern Pacific rim from Hokkaido to Baja California. Russian fur traders, lacking the skill to take the animals themselves, virtually enslaved Aleut and Kodiak Indians to hunt the otter during the spring and early summer. They shipped the fur to China, where mandarins prized it for hats and as a trim on their garments. The British somewhat accidentally opened their own direct trade with China in 1778 when British sailors of Captain James Cook's voyage of discovery purchased fifteen hundred otter skins from Indians at Nootka Sound on Vancouver Island. The sailors intended to use the pelts for clothing on their northern voyage, but in China they discovered that, as one sailor said, "skins which did not cost the purchaser six-pence sterling sold . . . for 100 dollars."

The promise of fortunes to be made in the sea otter trade brought English merchantmen sailing to the coast in Cook's wake. The Englishmen, the Russians pushing south from Sitka, and the even more numerous Americans who traded with the Indians for skins from the Pacific Northwest south to California brought the animal to the brink of extinction. As guns replaced bows and arrows in the hunt, otters became increasingly vulnerable. The number of sea otters traded in Canton began dropping early in the nineteenth century. The otter population was badly diminished by the 1820s; by the 1850s, the sea otters had nearly vanished.

It took time for the mainland fur trade to duplicate this pattern of overhunting and near extinction. The western fur trade in beaver and buffalo was an extension of a much older trade that had begun in the East and that had depended on Indians to procure the furs. The French pushed this trade west of the Missouri during the eighteenth century. The dependence of the traders on free Indian labor initially acted to slow the destruction of furbearers, since the Indians of the prairies and plains gave primacy to subsistence hunting over fur trapping. Indeed, many mounted Indians disdained beaver trapping and would engage only in buffalo hunting.

The reluctance of Indians to become wholehearted partners in the slaughter that the traders contemplated had as much to do with the Indians' ideas of a proper economy as

with their ethical beliefs about animals. For Indians, the proper ritual treatment of animals remained essential; as long as hunters killed animals in an appropriate manner, ritually honored the animals, and took game only to fulfill their own legitimate needs, Indians believed animals would return. Because most Indians regarded killing for exchange as a legitimate activity, religion did not offer a significant ideological obstacle to the trade. Indians often interpreted diminishing game in terms of improper treatment rather than overhunting. Thus when the buffalo finally disappeared from the plains, the Sioux did not view their demise as permanent nor the cause as biological. The buffalo had, they believed, gone underground because whites had killed the animals with disrespect. The buffalo would return when Indians could ensure that the animals would receive proper ritual treatment.

Indians could thus, in good conscience, hunt animals even as those animals grew less and less numerous. Yet most Indians did not kill as many animals as they could have because their wants remained limited. The demand for goods and wealth is cultural, and wealth among western Indians took quite specific terms. Horses or medicine bundles were forms of wealth sought by members of many Indian groups. Both the Northwest Coast Indians and the Navajos equated wealth and status, but maintaining status involved the redistribution of accumulated wealth. Most Indians, however, sought only limited amounts of white trade goods. Having met their immediate and limited necessities, they often refused to engage in further hunting. And when they did face shortages, "begging" (asking aid of friends or kinspeople with more than enough to share) or stealing (seizing goods from enemies) seemed to them just as appropriate as engaging in further hunting.

This common Indian refusal to accept European premises of a proper economy led white traders to complain constantly of the capriciousness of Indian hunters, the "laziness" of Indians, and the difficulty in collecting debts. The huge paper profits the trade generated often dwindled beneath the heavy overhead of gifts and the losses to accident and theft. Traders compensated by resorting to alcohol to stimulate greater demand and thus more hunting. Traders themselves dealt in stolen furs, and they favored those Indians who did seek to accumulate wealth, for whatever reason.

The trade thus brought economic and social changes in Indian societies, and these changes increased the impact of Indian hunters on game populations. Among the Blackfeet, a complex brew of material, social, and ideological factors increased their involvement in the British (but not the American) fur trade. In the nineteenth century, Blackfeet chiefs, already distinguished by their wealth in horses, became notable for the number of their wives. A man with many horses could use them to acquire wives or female slaves taken in raids. Because of the gendered labor system of the plains, multiple wives were necessary to process the buffalo hides into robes. A woman could, on average, process eighteen to twenty robes in a winter, and the more wives a man possessed, the more finished robes he accumulated, since a single mounted hunter could kill more buffalo than a single woman could process. Indeed, buffalo hides were useful to a man only if he had wives to process them. Robes, in turn, became critical for chieftainship, for robes obtained the trade goods that chiefs increasingly needed for the gift giving that demonstrated their generosity and maintained their following.

It was women rather than men who made the production of buffalo robes a virtual Indian monopoly before the Civil War. White men could slaughter buffalo, but they could not process robes. By 1840, commercial production had reached about ninety thousand robes a year on the northern plains, and trade robes represented about 25 percent of the total buffalo kill of the plains. The work of Indian women also allowed Indians on the Canadian plains to control the production of pemmican—the mixture of buffalo meat, fat, and berries that formed a basic foodstuff for trappers in the beaver trade.

The production of pemmican linked the work of women to the trade in beaver pelts, but by the early nineteenth century, the work of western Indians, both men and women, was becoming less and less critical to the trade. With western Indian hunters unwilling to supply sufficient furs, white and eastern Indian hunters and trappers replaced them. Operating from fixed posts, American fur-trading companies on the Missouri River had begun to dispatch parties of white men to trap beaver. On the Pacific coast, the Hudson's Bay Company, which had incorporated the earlier North West Company, also used white and Iroquois trappers organized in fur brigades to supplement the Indian trade. A major innovation in the trapping came in the mid-1820s when William Ashley, driven off the Missouri by Arikara attacks and unable to persuade Indians in the central plains to trap on the scale he desired, persuaded his white trappers to stay permanently in the mountains. Ashley sent a supply train to annual rendezvous, where trappers and Indians exchanged furs for supplies and engaged in an extended bacchanal. Because processing a beaver pelt demanded far less skill and labor than processing a buffalo hide, even white trappers who lacked Indian wives or lovers could ready their own catch for shipment. This eliminated the production bottleneck that limited the trade in buffalo robes.

The Rocky Mountain trappers who gathered at the annual rendezvous fell into three broad categories: *engagés*, men supplied and salaried by a fur-trading company; skin trappers, the sharecroppers of the fur trade who operated on credit advanced by a company; and finally free trappers, the small entrepreneurs of the trade who sold their furs to the highest bidder. For all of them, trapping was hard and extraordinarily dangerous work. Trappers may have had the common entrepreneurial ambitions of Jacksonian America, but few other Jacksonians so regularly risked their lives as well as their capital. The lucky ones lived, but they often ended up, in the words of Nathaniel Wyeth, who organized an unsuccessful fur company, "mere slaves to catch beavers for others." The real profits went to the large companies that organized production or brought goods west. These companies would maintain the so-called Rocky Mountain Trapping System, in one form or another, until 1840.

The southern Rockies spawned a final variant on the trade. This was the domain of free trappers who operated, usually illegally, out of Santa Fe and Taos. Kit Carson and other Anglo-American, Franco-American, and Mexican trappers methodically moved through the southern Rockies, stripping the streams of beaver and shipping their furs east along the Santa Fe Trail. After depleting the southern Rockies of beaver, they found themselves unable to compete with the more efficient rendezvous system of the central Rockies.

Between 1820 and 1840, these branches of the trade battled each other, and their contest destroyed the beaver over much of the West. At the height of the beaver trade in 1832, the Missouri and Rocky Mountain systems deployed perhaps one thousand trappers, the Hudson's Bay Company provided another six hundred, and a smaller number of free trappers worked out of Taos. Two large companies came to dominate the fray: the American Fur Company and the Hudson's Bay Company. Each combated its competition as ruthlessly as it slaughtered beaver. The Hudson's Bay Company created a fur desert along the Snake River to stop the progress of American trappers into its stronghold, the Oregon country. The American Fur Company sent its parties to tail those of its competition in the northern and central Rockies. Each side rushed to trap out the streams. Only the Blackfeet country, where the Indians maintained their long-standing animosity to American trappers, retained significant beaver populations.

Sea otters and opium, in an odd way, saved the surviving beaver from slaughter. Sea otter pelts and opium allowed American and European merchants to acquire Chinese silk without expending valuable silver, and by 1833, silk hats had begun to replace beaver hats on fashionable heads in both the United States and Europe. The demand for beaver dropped, prices fell, and the beaver trade went into a precipitous decline. By 1840, it had largely ended. Although substantial, the destruction brought by the mountain men was limited in an important sense: they had destroyed only animals and not habitat. Given a respite, beaver populations staged a recovery in the 1840s and 1850s, only to decline again later in the century from part-time trapping by miners and other western workers and from habitat destruction.

The buffalo, or more properly the North American bison, was the last furbearer to suffer near extinction, and its fate is at once the most instructive and the most mysterious. It is instructive because the buffalo died as an industrial animal rather than as an animal of fashion, like the beaver or otter. The discovery that buffalo hides could be turned into a cheap leather suitable for making machine belts, together with the expansion of the railroad network across the West after the Civil War, sealed the bison's fate. No longer did hunters have to hunt bison in the late fall or winter when robes were full; no longer did Indian women have to painstakingly process hides; and no longer did traders have

to rely on river transport or wagons to move robes to market. Both the seasonal and the Indian bottlenecks on production vanished. Now white hunters could kill buffalo at any season and transport the hides to market on the railroads.

Against Indian resistance, professional buffalo hunters moved onto the southern plains in the early 1870s. The southern hunt peaked between 1872 and 1874. In all, the hide hunters took an estimated 4,374,000 buffalo during these years. To this has to be added the Indian kill of approximately 1,215,000 on the southern plains during this same period, as well as the smaller number of bison killed by settlers and sportsmen. In the 1870s, Congress passed a bill protecting the bison, but President Ulysses Grant vetoed it.

The efficiency of the killing was coupled with a staggeringly inefficient use of the carcass. Virtually all the meat rotted. Some hunters initially did not even know how to skin the animals properly, and they thus wasted the hides. Other hunters killed more bison than they could skin. Contemporary sources estimated that at the peak of the hunt in 1872, three to five buffalo were killed for each hide that reached market. By 1875, the southern herd had largely ceased to exist.

The destruction of the smaller northern herd came later. In 1876 the Northern Pacific Railway reached Bismarck, North Dakota, and began pushing its tracks west into the buffalo country. That same year, the American army began the campaigns that broke Sioux control of the northern plains. In 1880 the assault on the northern herd began in earnest. By 1882, there were an estimated five thousand white hunters and skinners at work on the northern plains; by the end of 1883, the herd had vanished. The slaughter was so thorough and so quick that not even the hunters could believe what they had done. In the fall of 1883, many outfitted themselves as usual. But there was nothing to hunt except piles of bones bleaching in the sun and wind.

The causes and mechanisms of the final slaughter are thus obvious and instructive.

What is mysterious about the fate of the buffalo is that a precipitous drop in bison numbers appears to have occurred in the decades *before* this slaughter, and neither the number killed by Indians nor the early fur trade can account for it. Only quite recently have historians begun to unravel this mystery. Bison numbers on the plains probably peaked at about twenty-five million, well under older estimates. And it now appears that bison were in trouble by the 1840s not so much from overhunting, although this was increasingly a factor, as from a combination of drought, habitat destruction, competition from exotic species, and introduced diseases. During droughts, such as the one that struck the southern Great Plains in 1849, bison had to compete with Indian horse herds and wild mustangs for food and water in critical riverine habitats. At the same time, livestock taken by Indian raiders and cattle driven across the plains by white migrants introduced tuberculosis and brucellosis to the buffalo herds. The expansion of trails through the plains and the settlement of whites along the edges of the region drove the bison from the peripheral habitat on which they had depended as refuges from drought and hunting. The result was a buffalo population already unable to maintain its numbers when the white hunters struck.

The wholesale slaughter of the buffalo eventually abated from a lack of targets, but killing continued for a while on a retail basis with hunters, like the young Theodore Roosevelt, who rushed off to get a trophy before it was too late. Others, however, sought to save the pitiful remnants of the species. Some ranchers started private herds; William Hornaday, of the New York Zoo, organized the Bison Society; and George Bird Grinnell, the editor of *Forest and Stream*, worked to protect the small group of bison in Yellowstone from poachers. The buffalo moved from being a commodity to a symbol of the American West, gracing American coins and exhibited in Wild West shows. Such symbolic status became the last refuge from extinction open to some species whose uniqueness, size, and power allowed Americans to endow them with a special national meaning.

Animals and Energy

The slaughter of the buffalo opened the West for an expansion of the domesticated grazers that would more efficiently provide food, clothing, and energy for humans. Twentieth-century Americans readily think of animals as food, but they forget that for millennia, animals were also energy. Whale oil and tallow provided light. Animals moved people and freight. Before the coming of the railroads, animal-drawn freight wagons hauled the commerce of the prairies, plains, and mountains. Even after the building of the transcontinental railroads, stagecoaches and freight wagons served those areas away from the tracks. Until displaced by the automobile, horses and buggies provided local transportation. Animals pulled the plows that broke the prairies and much of the plains. Oxen dragged logs from the woods; the limits of animal power determined how far from navigable streams early loggers in the Pacific Northwest could go.

In providing energy, the preeminent animals in western enterprises were oxen and mules rather than horses. East of the Mississippi, where improved forage, water, and shelter were readily available, the big, grain-fed Conestoga horses provided the traction for freight wagons. Under the harsher conditions of the West, mules, an infertile cross between a donkey and a horse, stood up better to the rigors of freighting. Although, as the saying went, "without pride of ancestry or hope of progeny," they had the longest working life (eighteen years) of any draft animal, were plagued by few diseases, resisted saddle and harness sores, and could, freighters claimed, do as much work as a horse on one-third the food. There were few mules in Missouri when William Becknell loaded three farm wagons with trade goods, hitched them to horses, and opened the Santa Fe Trail in 1821. But thanks to the Santa Fe trade, mules became a major export of the Mexican borderlands to the American borderlands.

Oxen were slower than mules and more liable to disease, but they had other offsetting advantages. They were much cheaper than other draft animals, and so was their harness equipment. Indians were less likely to steal them, and unlike mules and horses, oxen could live and work on grass alone. The oxen that initially pulled western wagons before the Civil War were not the massive draft animals of the Northeast; they were Texas or Cherokee range cattle. In 1860, what appears to be a partial census counted an estimated 65,950 oxen, valued at $35 each, pulling freight across the high plains; only 7,574 mules, at $125 each, were in harness.

Oxen powered the western freighting industry, but horses and mules supplied the power for western stagecoaches. Transporting freight and people demanded tremendous numbers of animals. Ben Holladay, who in the 1860s briefly reigned as the "Stagecoach King" of the West, supposedly employed 15,000 men on his stage and freight lines and owned 20,000 wagons and 150,000 draft animals. In such operations, freight counted for more than passengers. The Stagecoach King and his competitors relied on federal mail contracts for their essential revenue and tended to regard passengers as so much paying ballast for the coaches. Except in California, passengers did not initially ride in the familiar horse-pulled Concord coaches of western movies. Between 1850 and 1864, a stagecoach trip from Missouri to Santa Fe meant a ride on mule-pulled, watertight wagons that could be dismantled and turned into scows on swollen streams. And since stage stations on this route were often few and far between, passengers and mail shared the wagons with fodder for the mule. Even with the Concord coach, a western stage ticket bought, in the words of a Denver passenger, "fifteen inches of seat, with a fat man on one side, a poor widow on the other, a baby in your lap, a bandbox over your head, and three or four more persons immediately in front, leaning against your knees." Nightfall meant sleeping on "the sand floor of a one-story sod or abobe hut, without a chance to wash, with miserable food, [and] uncongenial companionship." It was a jolting, pounding trip of crying children, swearing drivers, angry passengers, abominable whiskey, and brackish water. Dust was everywhere. Holladay was an ideal man to run such a crude and primitive enterprise. According to the railroad promoter Henry Villard, he was a "genuine specimen" of the successful pioneers of western enterprise: "illiterate, coarse, pretentious, boastful, false, and cunning."

Mules, oxen, and horses had pulled him into great wealth, but Holladay recognized that in long-distance transportation, the days of animal power were numbered. After 1866 he withdrew from freighting and stagecoaching and invested his money in coastal shipping and steamboats on the rivers of the West Coast and, finally, in railroads. Animals, as Holladay realized, were fleeing before steam, and this new source of power, divorced from living ligament and muscle, drove draft animals into more and more

remote sections of the West. In these corners of the West, their capacities continued to mark the limits of enterprise. As long as animal power hauled ore, for example, transportation was expensive and only high-grade ore was worth processing. Low-grade ore or less valuable minerals like copper had to await the railroads. As long as bull teams hauled logs, logging could not penetrate much farther than a mile or two from tidewater or navigable rivers and remain profitable.

Long after steam displaced animals from long-distance transportation, draft animals continued to provide power in the fields. They were in a sense the largest of barnyard stock: animals that lived in close association with humans. There was a surprisingly obvious gendering of the work involved with such domestic animals. Those that produced milk or eggs for consumption or local sale were the domain of women; those animals that produced power, meat, wool, or hides were the domain of men. This changed only when chickens or dairy cattle became fully commercialized. At that point, they too became the domain of men.

The hold of draft animals on American farms proved quite tenacious. Because of their rapid gait, horses were the traction animals of choice over most of the West, but the mule's tolerance for heat gave it the advantage in Oklahoma and Texas. Oxen were less common, although farmers used large oxteams to break raw prairie, particularly wet prairie, until the late 1860s. By the late nineteenth century, steam power had replaced animal power on a large scale only in threshing. Even after the invention of the tractor, many farmers kept their horses and mules because they were far superior for cultivating row crops. Not until 1920 did mechanical power drive most draft animals from the field. By the 1930s, the horse and mule population of the United States had dropped ten million from its peak. As horses and mules vanished, so too did the patchwork of irregularly shaped fields, with their hedgerows and windbreaks that were suited to horse-drawn plows but not to tractors. Thirty million acres of hay, barley, and oats, previously needed to feed traction animals, now became available for the production of other crops. Profits from such crops were necessary, for with the dependence on machinery, the farmers' need for capital rose.

Industrialism, with its creation of new sources of power and products, narrowed the spectrum of animals of enterprise to those that were good to eat or those with skin or wool that was good to wear. Americans were increasingly urban dwellers: 40.3 percent of the people in the Northeast and 20.8 percent in the Midwest lived in cities or towns by 1870, and this growing urban population wanted meat, hides, and hair in quantities greater than ever before. Above all, they wanted beef.

Eastern Tables and Western Beef

Why late-nineteenth-century Americans wanted such vast quantities of beef is not immediately obvious; Americans have not always chosen beef over other meats. If late-nineteenth-century consumers had wanted chicken or pork, or had decided not to eat meat at all, the history of the West would have been considerably different. Before the Civil War, urbanites ate preserved pork, but even then it appears that their desires were turning to fresh beef. Pork may have been on their tables, but beef was on their minds. It was the food that managed to denote both high status and down-to-earth American-ism. The managers of William Henry Harrison's 1840 campaign for the presidency captured the potent symbolism of beef when they coupled Harrison's Indian fighting and log cabin with his diet of "raw beef and salt" to create defining symbols of a rude but democratic American. His opponent, Martin Van Buren, with his weakness for French food and his supposed aristocratic tendencies, seemed effete and elitist by comparison.

Plentiful grass for cattle in the West and eastern consumers hungry for beef were necessary but not sufficient conditions for a prosperous western cattle industry. Range-fed cattle from the grasslands initially provided tough and stringy beef that captured only the bottom end of the growing beef trade: the cheaper cuts of meat in American cities and cured beef for the trade with England. Middle-class Americans, desiring fatter, tenderer meat, bought corn-fed midwestern beef.

Texas Longhorns provided the first inroads into eastern markets. Butchers derided the Longhorn as "eight pounds of hamburger on 800 pounds of bone and horn," but the Longhorns had assets more apparent on the western plains than on the eastern table. Texas Longhorns were a distinct breed of cattle and not merely the description of the horns of a steer. The Spanish cattle of Texas, the Criollos, had long horns, but they were not the Texas Longhorns. True Texas Longhorns did not appear until the early nineteenth century. A backcountry cattle industry had long existed in the American South, and American migrants brought some of these cattle with them into Texas. Criollos thus interbred with American cattle, some descended from a special English breed—the English Longhorns. The crossing of Criollos and Anglo-American stock, like so much of the history of western animals of enterprise, resulted from violent acts. In the wake of the Texas Revolution, raiders from both sides of the border drove off cattle and thus mixed Mexican and Anglo-American animals. Between 1836 and 1865, fertile, long-lived, pugnacious, multicolored cattle with long legs, long tails, long bodies, and long horns (a trait derived from both parent stocks) developed. These cattle were resistant to the tick-carried Texas fever, and they thrived on grass without supplemental feeding.

As southern migrants into Texas abandoned their earlier custom of penning cattle and adopted the Mexican practice of allowing cattle to roam free, the mixing of breeds (including wild Criollos) increased. When the Civil War eliminated both the markets for cattle and many of the men who raised cattle, untended Longhorns bred promiscuously with other range cattle. By the end of the Civil War, Longhorns formed the majority of the roughly five million cattle in Texas. Most of these cattle were unbranded and thus free for the taking. Unlike the feral Criollos, they were manageable, and so they would not remain mere wild cows, the prey of human hunters.

The very biology that gave Texas Longhorns their advantage, however, seemed doomed to limit their commercial prospects. In the arithmetic of enterprise, cattle were only commodities, but cattle continued to demonstrate that they were animals—complicated living things. Texas cattle, for example, carried Texas fever. Although Longhorns had an immunity to Texas fever, when driven out of Texas, the cattle carried the ticks that transmitted the disease. The ticks dropped off and found new hosts, and the new hosts died. Northern farmers did not know how the disease was communicated; they knew only that when Texas cattle came in contact with their domestic stock, their animals died. Northern cattle sometimes sickened simply after crossing a trail used by Texas cattle. The Texans, who never saw their livestock die of the disease, denied that it existed or, at least, that it came from Texas cattle, but they had to face the reality of northern attempts to ban their cattle.

Ticks, as much as markets, determined the initial course of the plains cattle industry. When Texas cattle raisers tried to drive herds north after the Civil War (as they had before the war), Missouri and Kansas farmers violently resisted their passage, shutting off direct access to northern markets. Texas cattle had to stay west of the line of agricultural settlement; thus, except for a small trade to New Orleans, the initial postwar markets for Texas cattle were the mines, military posts, and Indian reservations of the West.

Providing beef to hungry miners in the Rockies had arisen almost as a side effect of transcontinental travel. A percentage of the oxen hauling migrants to Oregon and California and pulling freight wagons within the West inevitably wore out and went lame. J. W. Iliff, who as a failed miner in the 1859 gold rush to Pikes Peak was a sort of human equivalent to these failed oxen, realized that their misfortune might cancel out his own. Iliff established a little store near what is now Cheyenne, Wyoming; in addition to cash sales, he began bartering with passing migrants for lame, footsore, and emaciated cattle and oxen.

Like other early cattlemen in Colorado, Wyoming, and Montana who began roughly similar operations, Iliff discovered that cattle could overwinter with little care on the plains. To easterners, the bunchgrasses of late summer looked scanty and sorry when compared with the big bluestem of the prairies or a bluegrass pasture of the East, but the bunchgrass plains were a storehouse of surprises. Nature annually turned bunchgrasses into hay on the stem. Unlike big bluestem or introduced grasses, bunchgrass retained much of the original plant protein in the dry leaves. And this natural hay remained accessible. Despite cold winters, the light dry snows of the region usually did not crust, thus allowing cattle to push their way down to the grass. On the south-facing slopes, cattle did not have to dig at all, since the winter sun soon melted the snow. In short, it appeared that in the West, animals did not require winter feeding. Footsore cattle, bunchgrass, and hungry miners combined to make Iliff the first of the cattle kings of Colorado and Wyoming.

Iliff's kingdom eventually expanded to thirty-five thousand head; he had cattle in Colorado ranging from Julesburg to Greeley. Whatever the regenerative properties of bunchgrass, however, it could not make oxen reproduce. Iliff built his herds from cattle driven north from Texas. In 1866 Iliff bought cows and bulls that two peripatetic Texans, Charles Goodnight and Oliver Loving, had brought into the Arkansas Valley.

Goodnight, although born in Illinois, was raised in Texas, and he was one of many restless, ambitious Texas cattlemen seeking an outlet for the Longhorns. In 1866 he trailed a cattle herd west from the Cross Timbers to Fort Sumner, New Mexico, where the military needed beef for themselves and for the Navajos and Apaches confined at Bosque Redondo. Goodnight later established a ranch, neither his first nor his last, forty miles south of the fort. By 1870, the federal distribution of cattle to reservation Indians, whose livelihood the Americans had destroyed, required fifty to sixty thousand head a year.

When Iliff began collecting footsore oxen, the mines west of the Rockies had already supported a fledgling cattle industry for a decade. The California gold rush provided the *californio* ranchers with markets virtually at their doorsteps, and cattle once valued for their tallow and hides became beef animals. The *californios* sold cattle to the very miners who had banished them from the goldfields, and they sold cattle in prodigious numbers. Thinking the boom permanent, they spent freely and mortgaged their land at usurious rates to pay the taxes on it and to hire lawyers to defend their ranchos from Anglo squatters. But by 1861, the boom was over. Then came floods, followed by the worst drought southern Californians had endured. Between 1862 and 1864, roughly three million cattle starved to death on the range. Disease administered the coup de grace to the cattle and the ranchos; by 1869, only thirteen thousand cattle remained in southern California. Sheep had replaced them. The ranchos passed into Anglo hands.

By driving down prices, cattle from the Pacific Northwest played their part in destroying the California cattle industry. Some of the Oregon steers that went south to the mines were, in a sense, returning home. They were descendants of California cattle imported by the Puget Sound Agriculture Company, a Hudson's Bay Company subsidiary that had earlier sought to produce tallow, beef, and hides to replace dwindling fur returns as a company export. But most of the cattle for the mines were domestic stock from the eastern United States, stock that in the 1840s had accompanied American migrants west along the Oregon and California trails. More docile, better milkers, and carrying more flesh than the California cattle, they became the preferred stock in Oregon and Washington.

In the 1850s and 1860s, Oregon cattle added much of the interior grass and sagebrush lands of the Great Basin to the bovine empire. They finished their conquest of the region by the 1870s. In Nevada they met herds from the central valley of California fleeing first the drought and then the conversion of interior cattle ranges into wheat fields and orchards. Only Utah resisted the open-range system of Oregon and

California. The Mormons had adapted to the arid Great Basin by creating a unique village-based stock-raising system that combined hay production on irrigated fields, the winter feeding typical of midwestern livestock systems, and summer drives to mountain pastures.

Feeding miners, soldiers, and Indians maintained a small western cattle industry, but as long as Texas fever kept Longhorns from eastern markets, a beef bonanza on the scale envisioned by promoters remained a mirage. At the end of the Civil War, cattle were a glut on the market in Texas, selling for three to four dollars a head, with a fat beeve bringing only five to six dollars. In New York, a three-year-old steer (admittedly of better quality than a Longhorn) brought eighty dollars; in Illinois, a steer brought forty dollars; and even in relatively nearby Kansas, the steer cost thirty-eight dollars.

A tick held all these profits hostage, and they might have remained hostage if the tick could have endured cold. But it could not; a hard freeze killed it. Drovers discovered that when cattle were held on a northern range until after a hard frost, the cattle could be safely shipped. And cattle that spent a year or more fattening on the central and northern plains before shipping were free of fever. Cattlemen did not as yet know how, but the isolation and hard winters of the plains were freeing the profits held hostage by Texas fever.

Joseph G. McCoy claimed credit for being the first to realize the financial possibilities that the convergence of Texas fever, Texas cattle, and the railroads presented, but McCoy was as lucky as shrewd. He was only one among several entrepreneurs who sought out likely spots along the Kansas Pacific and solicited Texas cattle. McCoy helped found Abilene, the first of the cattle towns that enterprise, railroads, and ticks created. Jesse Chisholm, a Texas cattleman of Cherokee ancestry, pushed a trail north from Texas across the Indian Territory to Abilene. During the summer of 1867, an estimated thirty-five thousand Texas cattle came up the Chisholm Trail.

These first drives were not profitable, but McCoy persisted and advertised for more cattle. Over the next twenty years, two million cattle would come up the Chisholm trail and its successors. Traveling ten to fifteen miles a day in herds numbering two to three thousand head, the cattle wore troughs as deep as shallow canals, which remained visible for years. The alliance of ticks and Texas cattle forced a steady westward march of cow towns and the trails that fed them, for once farmers surrounded a town, they banned Texas cattle, from fear of Texas fever. And so the trails led first to Abilene, then later to Ellsworth, Dodge City, and Hays.

McCoy and other cattle-town entrepreneurs solved the problem of moving Longhorns east, but they had not made the Longhorns any more palatable. Northern tastes demanded marbled beef, and Longhorns did not fatten easily when fed grains or, later, cottonseed by midwestern farmers. To get better-quality beef, cattlemen began to interbreed the Longhorns with improved stock from the East. This hybrid stock more easily put on weight on the farm feedlots of Iowa and Illinois. By the late 1870s and early 1880s, midwestern farmers were selling improved cattle in the West and rebuying the steers they produced as feeders. To service these cows, western ranchers began importing purebred Hereford and Shorthorn bulls. Longhorns gradually disappeared as feedlot buyers demanded cattle that could turn a minimum amount of corn into a maximum amount of beef in the minimum amount of time.

ABILENE IN 1867—CELEBRATING THE SHIPMENT OF THE FIRST TRAIN-LOAD OF CATTLE.

Quality was one obstacle the western cattle industry faced; price was another. For beef to be cheap, it needed to be mass-produced, and this could not happen until it could be preserved. Packers had been working on refrigerating beef since the 1860s, but technical problems stymied them until Gustavus Swift created a fleet of refrigerator railroad cars; by 1882 he was successfully marketing refrigerated Chicago beef in New York. Refrigeration allowed shippers to avoid paying freight on the inedible portions of cattle. It cost half as much to ship a dressed carcass as a live animal, and centralized, industrial slaughter allowed a fuller use of by-products. By the 1880s, refrigerated beef undersold fresh beef in the East. The price of prime cuts dropped 40 percent between 1883 and 1889. Because the production of refrigerated beef demanded industrial slaughterhouses, a fleet of refrigerator cars, and a coordinated marketing network, capital costs were high. A few Chicago packinghouses—Swift, Armour, Morris, and Hammond—quickly created an oligopoly that forced smaller regional packers out of business. By the early twentieth century, they, along with Cudahy and Company, produced 82 percent of the beef in the United States. Other meat-packing centers—Kansas City, Omaha, and later Fort Worth—arose as outposts in the dominion of the "Meat Trust."

Americans came to think that they were living in the "Golden Age of American Beef." With cookbooks and magazines dismissing pork as difficult to digest, unwholesome, and unhealthy, fat beef became a health food. The urban Northeast became a world of beef and potatoes; the older hog and hominy diet retreated south. For Anglo Americans, Irish Americans, and German Americans in particular, beef reigned as the symbol of the good life, and the good life became attainable at least at the dinner table. According to the German sociologist Werner Sombart, it was on the "reefs of roast beef and apple pie" that the dreams of American socialists were dashed. And the newer immigrants from eastern and southern Europe soon adopted this preference for beef.

American per capita beef consumption reached a peak in the early twentieth century, only to dip after World War I, before rising to what would be all-time highs after World War II and then falling again.

Making the West Comfortable for Cattle

In the promotion of western stock raising, ideologues were in a sense as significant as the packinghouse magnates. The ideologues were a varied lot: a general of the U.S. Army, James S. Brisbin; a German aristocrat who came as a tourist and stayed as a speculator, Walter Baron Von Richthofen; a surgeon for the Union Pacific, Dr. Hiram Latham; a publicity man for the Union Pacific Railroad, Robert Strahorn; and the entrepreneur and townsite promoter Joseph McCoy, of Illinois, who generously credited himself with creating the cattle industry. It was they who worked for and proclaimed the rise of the cattle kingdom. It was they who urged and celebrated the transformation of the plains, deserts, and mountains from a biological republic to a biological monarchy where humans reigned, where uselessness among lesser living things was a crime punishable by death, and where enterprise was the reigning virtue.

The importance of these boosters was not the example they set; rather, it was the new order they perceived. McCoy soon left the western cattle business; Latham's ranch investments failed; and Richthofen's major livestock experience seems to have been operating a dairy barn for consumptives who rested on second-story porches while sipping fresh milk brought up from purebred cows on the floor below. What the boosters, for all their individual limits, realized was that stock raising was not a romantic retreat from industrial America; stock raising was part of its foundation and its base. Hiram Latham, in particular, conceived of the enterprise in grand, nationalistic terms. He was intent on harnessing useful animals to their rightful task of helping create an industrial power. Industry, in return, provided the railroads, refrigeration, modern packing plants, and urban populations that made beef production practical.

In his 1871 pamphlet *Trans-Missouri Stock Raising*, Latham presented a series of what he regarded as largely self-evident propositions. To maintain a large population of laborers who would sell their products in the competitive markets of the world, the United States must furnish them with cheap food and clothing. The cheaper the food and clothing, the cheaper every article they would produce, and "therefore, in proportion to the abundance and cheapness of our food and clothing, will be our success as a manufacturing nation." This food must include meat, for a solely vegetable diet brought degeneration "to the condition of the Macaroni Eaters of Italy." Cheap meat and cheap wool for clothing demanded cheap lands, but since land prices in the East were rising, the future of stock production was in the West, where there lay "a billion acres . . . boundless, endless, gateless, and all of it furnishing winter grazing."

Cattle and sheep were so many machines to turn grass into meat, hide, or wool, all of which could be readily turned into dollars. Latham's ambitions for sheep and cattle knew no bounds. In a speech to the Colorado Stockgrowers Association in 1873, he said stock raising should not cease until "every acre of grass in Colorado is eaten annually." Latham and the other boomers mastered the arithmetic of optimism. There is, Richthofen assured his readers, "not the slightest uncertainty in cattle raising." In the Spanish proverb that Latham loved to quote, "Whatever the foot of the sheep touches turned to gold." Ideologues and stock raisers alike conceived of sheep and cattle as biological dollars that could mate and produce little dollars with the same regularity with which interest compounded. In their books are tables of investment and yield that have cattle endlessly procreating and cows, heifers, and steers relentlessly transforming themselves into money. At the end of six years, Richthofen estimated a profit of 156 percent on the original investment. Experienced cattlemen, he said, thought it too low.

There was no possibility too remote for this arithmetic of enterprise. For example, a limitless demand for cheese would supposedly push dairy cows into the grasslands. To provide the market, Latham happily imagined the Chinese and Japanese to be cheese eaters—allocating them fifty thousand tons annually—and spiraled the resulting figures into wonderful castles of profits. The Platte River valley alone could support twelve hundred cheese factories and five hundred thousand milk cows and would yield $33,295,000 in profit. As for the scope of such enterprises, Joseph Nimmo, in his *Report in Regard to the Range and Ranch Cattle Business*, prepared for Congress, estimated that in 1885, 44 percent of the United States, exclusive of Alaska, was devoted to grazing. All of it was in the West.

This fascination with the free, apparently limitless grass of the West relegated the old pioneering eastern animal of enterprise—the pig—to the western barnyard, for grass formed only a minor part of a hog's diet. Pigs had accompanied and sustained Anglo-American farmers in the wooded, humid lands of the East, but in the West they prospered only on the prairie margins where farmers grew corn and in rare places such as the western parts of Washington Territory or eastern Texas. Most of the West was inhospitable to the pig. Pigs do not like direct sun and heat; they need access to shade and water. They do not like extreme cold. Pigs became mere animal tourists in the West. They clustered on the edges of Solomon Butcher's famous photographs of Great Plains farms, pampered and peripheral. Unless human beings made them comfortable, pigs wished they had never come west.

The tendency of American universities to name their athletic teams after animals nicely reveals the boundaries between the kingdoms of the cow and the hog. The athletic teams of the University of Arkansas are the Razorbacks. Razorbacks are feral pigs that once abounded in the woods of Arkansas, and University of Arkansas athletes presumably share the better qualities of wild hogs. One state over, to the West, you encounter the Longhorns of the University of Texas. Although eastern Texas proved hospitable to pigs, western Texas welcomed only cattle, and Texas football players today derive inspiration from their identification with neutered cattle.

As pigs lost their pioneering role in the West, they regained it in another sense in the East, for it was on their bodies that entrepreneurs perfected the mechanisms of industrial slaughter. The industrial slaughter of pigs paved the way for the industrial slaughter of cattle. Chicago emerged from the Civil War as the major meat-packing center of the nation. The massive new Union Stock Yards, underwritten by the railroads in 1865, became the central distributing point from which butchers elsewhere bought live cattle. In the 1870s, before refrigeration, most cattle sold in Chicago were still shipped east for butchering, but Chicago was "Hog Butcher to the World." Hogs retained two major advantages over cattle. They more efficiently turned corn into meat, and hogs—whether as bacon, ham, salt pork, or lard—took to preservation better than

beef in the days before refrigeration. Although there was some market for dried and salted beef, most cattle were slaughtered near the point of consumption and sold quickly as fresh beef; pigs could be killed far away and held for sale.

Meat packers transformed slaughterhouses into year-round factories that turned hogs into meat and an increasingly formidable line of by-products. Chicago packing-houses learned to escape the seasonal constraints nature had previously imposed on their enterprise. Using ice, they began, on a small scale, to extend the packing season from the cold-weather months into the spring and summer. The slaughter of hogs increased fivefold between 1872 and 1877. In killing pigs, the packers created a centralized infrastructure that could be expanded to killing and marketing cattle once the packers had perfected a way to preserve the meat.

The western expansion of the railroad network, industrialized slaughter, and the development of refrigeration all allowed western cattle to penetrate more and more deeply into eastern markets. And once cattle found their markets, they became creatures of those markets. When the economy boomed, as it did in the early 1870s and again in the early 1880s, the cattle industry prospered and cattle expanded their numbers and range. When the economy slumped, as it did in the mid-1870s and late 1880s, the cattle industry contracted. The booms of the early 1870s and early 1880s differed, however. The first involved stocking the plains; the second involved stocking butcher shops once cattle became the leading animal of industrial capitalism. During both booms, and in the years that followed, Americans seemed to have no higher ambition than making the awesome western landscape comfortable for cows.

Stocking the Great Plains and the Southwest absorbed most of the cattle produced in Texas. An estimated two-thirds of the cattle driven north out of Texas in the 1870s and early 1880s were yearlings and two-year-olds. Such cattle were too young to market. They, along with a smaller number of cows and calves, were sent to stock the northern grasslands. A second, subsidiary drive, usually numbering 20–25 percent of the northern drive, took cattle into New Mexico and Arizona. The Sioux on the northern plains and the Apaches in the Southwest opposed this expansion, but financial markets proved more deadly than Lakota and Athapaskan warriors.

The optimism of Texas cattle raisers—made tangible in the 600,000 head of cattle they drove north in 1871, the largest total for any year—foundered when one-half the cattle driven north remained unsold. Placed on already overstocked ranges near the cattle towns, many of the cattle died in the harsh winter of 1871–72. The industry was barely recovering from this disaster when the Panic of 1873 cut off the drovers' access to credit. When the banks refused to extend loans, the herders had to ship their young and thin cattle to market, further depressing prices and driving many to ruin. Markets remained depressed, and by 1875 only about 150,000 cattle were going up the trails from Texas. West of the Rockies, the mining boom ended, and the cattle of the Oregon country lost three-quarters and more of their value. This combination of bad weather and bad markets signaled the end of the first boom on the open range.

Although cattle prices remained low until 1881, the industry began to recover in the late 1870s. In 1876 over 300,000 cattle came up the trail from Texas, twice the total of the previous year. For the rest of the decade, the number fluctuated between 200,000 and 250,000 head annually. In the Far West, cattle from southeastern Oregon and southwestern Nevada headed to Winnemucca, Nevada, on the Central Pacific Railroad for shipment to San Francisco. Stocking the central and northern plains quickened with cattle from Oregon joining the herds coming up from Texas.

Oregon and Texas cattle moved onto the plains by their own power; they left the plains in cattle cars provided by the expanding railroads. In 1880–81, Denver became a major sales center with the creation of the Denver stockyards. Farther north, Cheyenne, Wyoming, the headquarters of the Wyoming Stock Growers Association, became one of the capitals of the cattle kingdom. Ogallala, Nebraska, at "the end of the Texas Trail," joined the Kansas cattle towns as a shipping center, as did Miles City, Montana, which went from serving the military sent to subdue the Sioux to serving the cattle raisers who succeeded the buffalo hunters. The eastern demand for western beef grew great enough by the mid-1880s to reach across the Rockies. Ontario, Oregon, replaced Winnemucca as the shipping point in the Great Basin as Chicago superseded San Francisco as the destination of Oregon and Nevada cattle.

In this second cattle boom, large railroad corporations shipped the cattle, and the beef trust slaughtered them. Ranching corporations in the West sought to match this corporate dominance of shipping and slaughtering stride for stride. By the 1880s, western cattle had become creatures of the world capitalist market; the greed of investors became as essential to the propagation of cattle as grass on the western plains. Western banks, particularly those in Denver and Kansas City, had financed much of the early cattle industry at rates of interest ranging from 10 percent to 25 percent, but now eastern and European investors, who commanded much more abundant and cheaper capital, took over the industry.

Cattle corporations were organized in Boston and New York; a large number arose in Great Britain, particularly in Scotland. John Clay, a Scotsman who transplanted to the West, marveled at "this love of money making, enterprise you might call it," that pulled first Scottish investors and then English investors into cattle raising. American investors took money made from mining, railroads, and merchandising and invested it in cattle. In Dundee, Scotland, profits from the jute trade financed western cattle corporations. The thrifty Scot, as Clay remarked, was also the speculative Scot, and this financial schizophrenia found full play in the grasslands. Having gambled on cattle, the Scots tried to enforce precise managerial and accounting techniques in cattle companies that neither knew how many cattle they possessed nor owned most of the land their cattle grazed. The imaginary arithmetic of the cattle business reached new heights in the book count that applied presumed fertility rates to estimates of existing herds and passed off the results as actual cattle. Skeptics in the British financial press complained that purchasing shares of such operations was only playing "poker on joint stock principles." And the players in this particular game—American promoters such as "Uncle Rufus" Hatch, a New York speculator—were not above dealing off the bottom of the deck.

Between 1882 and 1886, as many capitalists as cowboys seemed to be chasing cattle in the West. Much of the total British cattle investment of forty-five million dollars entered the West during these years, and eastern investors outspent the British. Wyoming boasted nearly 100 new cattle companies, New Mexico over 100 (with, however, less funds behind them), Montana 66, and Colorado 176. Some of these corporations grew to gargantuan proportions because the larger the operation, the cheaper it was to raise cattle. Expenses did not increase as a ratio of the size of the herd. In southeastern Oregon, for example, it took three cowboys to care for a herd of one thousand head, but eight thousand head demanded only twelve cowboys.

The holdings of the new cattle companies rivaled European principalities in size. The XIT ranch in Texas arose from the offer in 1879 by a syndicate of Chicago investors to build the Texas state capitol in exchange for the three million acres the legislature intended to sell to pay for the building. The XIT (an abbreviation for "Ten in Texas," referring to ten counties) was unusual not because it was so large but because it owned its land. Other large companies did not hold title. The greatest of them, the Prairie Cattle Company, straddled New Mexico, Texas, and Colorado and contained three divisions, each named after the major river that watered it. Its Arkansas Division in Colorado contained thirty-five hundred square miles; its Cimarron Division in New Mexico had over four thousand square miles. By comparison, its Canadian Division in Texas was relatively tiny: it held only four hundred square miles.

Operations of this size, like other corporations in the West, tried to leave little to chance. They sought a rationalized industry. They wanted to take living animals—cattle—and make the lives of these cattle, from birth to slaughterhouse, as predictable as possible. The companies wanted to control everything about the cattle: their genes, what they should eat and when, how much it should cost to get them to market, and the price they should bring. The cattle corporations wanted to keep labor costs low, and they wanted a dependable, malleable work force.

Cheap labor was one of the appeals of cattle raising, but the corporations wanted to make it even cheaper and far more malleable. The companies' peak labor needs came at roundup and during cattle drives; during the rest of the year, "line riding" cowboys traveled the high ground between watersheds, drifting cattle back toward the ranges claimed by their respective owners. For their labor, these cowboys received only from twenty-five to forty dollars a month plus room and board, and the room was usually as simple as a dugout or a board shack. When cowboys struck for higher wages in the Texas Panhandle in 1883, the Panhandle Cattleman's Association ruthlessly broke their strike. Corporations did not seek romantic heroes for employees; they wanted men who worked cheaply, did as told, and did not get drunk and shoot each other or the cattle. Into the 1880s, the majority of these cowboys were white, with a considerable minority of African Americans working in Texas and Oklahoma, but gradually cattle companies in southern and western Texas began to replace Anglo cowboys with *tejanos* and Mexicans, who drew only one-half to two-thirds the pay of Anglos. Elsewhere, companies began to forbid their cowboys to gamble, drink, or carry six-shooters. R. G. Head, of the Prairie Cattle Company, issued a lengthy circular to his cowboys, reminding them of their moral responsibilities. They took his remonstrances well. Like good company men, the cowboys gave him a silver service when he lost his position as manager.

Cattle raising was becoming an increasingly specialized business by the 1880s. The arithmetic of enterprise, so deceptive in many respects, had accurately revealed that a division of effort best served the industry. A greater percentage of calves survived in Texas than in the cattle country to the north, but young steers fattened more quickly on the northern ranges. The Texas cattleman George B. Loving claimed in 1880 that a Texas steer removed to Nebraska at one or two years old would weigh 1,100 to 1,300 pounds at four years. That same steer, left in Texas, would weigh only 850 to 950 pounds at the same age. Thus, although Texas continued to produce cattle that went directly to market and northern cattle raisers continued to breed their own stock, a rough specialization between southern breeding grounds and northern fattening grounds developed. Many northern cattle raisers annually imported Texas yearlings to fatten on their grasslands.

As specialization increased, a Texas calf (or for that matter a Wyoming calf) was likely to know several owners before its head met a hammer in a Chicago slaughterhouse. Born in Texas and fattened for several years on the northern plains, it might then be shipped to the Flint Hills of eastern Kansas. There it would feed for several months on the lush bluestem grasslands before those grasses began to decline in protein in early July. Now two to three hundred pounds fatter than when it began to gorge on bluestem, the steer would either go directly to slaughter or be sold to a midwestern farmer for further fattening on corn before being killed. By 1883, the Swan Cattle Company had established its own fattening pens near Omaha, where it prepared cattle for the early spring market.

To broker the buying and selling of cattle and the procuring of the grazing land and capital that cattle required, a host of commission merchants acted as middlemen in the business. Most firms were located in Chicago. John Clay was a Wyoming cattleman, but he located his commission firm in Chicago, as did his successful competitor Joseph Rosenbaum.

Cattlemen cultivated an aura of individualism, but the big companies sought oligopoly and a safe market. They organized themselves into powerful local and state associations, which by the 1880s flourished all over the West. The associations held cooperative roundups in the spring to gather and brand newborn calves; they helped establish registry of brands; they hired stock detectives to track down cattle thieves. All attained political influence, but none so great as the Wyoming Stock Growers Association, which faced no major economic rivals within the territory. It represented a concentration of private wealth flaunted in the famous Cheyenne Club, where an eastern visitor reported watching a member simultaneously play tennis and carry on a chess game at the side of the court while periodically refreshing himself with bourbon.

The cattle raisers had trouble extending this regional influence into the national arena. A national organization of cattlemen did not appear until 1883, and it almost immediately split over measures to be taken against the cattle diseases pleuropneumonia and the still prevalent Texas fever. Pleuropneumonia had led to a British embargo of American cattle imports, and northern cattlemen backed an Animal Industry Bill for federal inspection. Southern plains cattlemen, who feared bans on the movement of southern cattle, were already at odds with northern plains cattlemen in the old dispute over Texas fever. As northern cattle raisers turned to improved eastern stock, many came to fear the continued importation of Texas cattle because of both Texas fever and competition for the diminishing grass. In 1885, cattle raisers and farmers in Kansas and Colorado succeeded in getting their legislatures to pass laws that virtually prohibited the driving of Texas cattle into those states. Texans responded with demands that Congress create a national cattle trail so that their herds could move north.

Settling these disputes provided an occasion for the expansion of federal power. Congress established a Bureau of Animal Husbandry but refused to establish a national cattle trail. The Supreme Court ruled that the laws of Kansas and Colorado represented an unconstitutional restraint of commerce by the states, and the federal Bureau of Animal Husbandry took over quarantine inspection and regulation. By the late 1880s, the days of the long drive and the open range were numbered. When Texas yearlings went north, they increasingly went by rail.

Cattle raisers also resorted to soliciting federal intervention to settle disputes with the packers and railroads. Cattle raisers resented the control they believed Chicago packinghouses exerted over prices and the rates the railroads charged. But here they faced powerful enemies, and their victories were minimal. In the 1890s, the Interstate Commerce Commission did secure somewhat lower railroad rates, but cattle raisers failed to get effective federal aid against the packers.

The public domain represented the greatest failure of the cattle corporations to turn regional economic power into national political power. The "free grass" of the public domain that had created the cattle kingdom also presented the greatest danger to the corporations. For if the grass was free to the first cattle raiser to come across it, it was also free to the second, third, and fourth. And not even the wonderful arithmetic of the cattle business could feed an indefinite number of cattle on the same blades of grass. The first or second cattle raisers in an area saw themselves as hardy pioneers and men of enterprise; they saw the third and fourth cattle raisers in an area as "range pirates" stealing "their" grass. To deny competitors access to the ranges already claimed by members, the associations denied range pirates the right to participate in the roundups and refused their herds the protection of stock detectives.

With infinite ingenuity, cattle raisers sought ways to keep grass on public lands for themselves while denying it to competitors. There were legal ways to do this in some

areas, but staying within the law was usually expensive or impractical. In Texas, cattle companies could and did lease state lands. Elsewhere they could purchase railroad lands or school lands. But a company that paid for land was obviously at a disadvantage when competing with a company that got its land for free. And so cattle raisers perfected the technique of obtaining large amounts of grazing land with few purchases. They turned aridity to their advantage by securing water rights and then enforcing extralegal customary rights by which those controlling a stream possessed range rights on its watershed. Controlling the lands bordering a stream thus meant the exclusive use of a much larger area of rangeland lying around the stream. This system of range rights originated in Texas and flourished into the 1880s. In 1882, for example, the Matador cattle company of Texas claimed a range of over a million and half acres on the basis of one hundred thousand acres of waterfront held in fee simple.

When purchasing land or enforcing extralegal rights proved impossible, the cattle corporations resorted to fraud. On occasion, cattle raisers could buy out legitimate homesteaders on riparian lands, but more often they resorted to "dummying" land along the streams. They used their cowboys as "dummy" homesteaders to file fraudulent claims on the land; the cowboys then transferred the land to the cattle raisers. Similarly, cattle raisers filed false claims under the Timber and Stone Act, the Desert Land Act, and the Timber Culture Act.

But barbed wire proved to be the cattle raisers' best friend. In the early 1880s, cattle raisers eagerly used the new technology to defend "their" grass. Before the invention of barbed wire, cattle raisers had bitterly opposed fencing laws designed to confine cattle, but inexpensive barbed wire changed their minds. In the early 1880s they fenced vast acreages of the public domain, even public roads, to keep out competitors, to cut labor costs by preventing their cattle from drifting, and to ensure that their improved bulls did not waste valuable semen on neighbors' cattle. When smaller cattle raisers violently objected, the result was fence-cutting wars such as the one that erupted in Texas in the mid-1880s.

To protect their claims to the public domain, the cattle companies launched a battle for the leasing of federal lands. In doing so, they challenged deep-seated beliefs that agriculture was the proper ultimate use of all land. They also faced popular resentment, for it angered much of the public that foreign corporations could control public lands and exclude American settlers. President Grover Cleveland refused to allow leasing, and in 1885 he issued an executive order for the removal of fences on public land. He evicted herds of cattle trespassing on land in the Indian Territory, and Congress in 1887 passed laws banning foreign land purchases in the territories.

Congress and the White House were the decisive theaters of the battle over land, but a much nastier and often bloody conflict was waged in the West itself. In defense of customary rights, which were sometimes enshrined in state or territorial law, cattle raisers sought to drive competitors—whether sheep raisers, small stock owners (often ex-cowboys), or farmers—from the public domain. The associations redefined legitimate enterprise so that what had once been regarded as the natural progress of enterprise was now seen as theft.

In the early Texas cattle industry, enterprise alone could turn a cowboy into a cattleman. A cowboy who assisted at branding received a portion of the cattle in return. Cowboys too could, with little trouble, take up mavericks (motherless calves), whose ownership could not be determined, and thus become cattlemen. Indeed the gendered terms of *cowboy* and *cattleman* themselves seemed to embody a natural progression that both connected men (but not women) to the raising of large meat animals and correlated the progression from caring for animals to owning them with the growth from boyhood to manhood.

As cattle grew more valuable and range scarcer, large stock raisers sought to stop the mavericking that cowboys had come to regard as their rightful route to independence. Mavericking became an object of dispute in part because mavericks could be created as well as found, and the bigger operations sought to end a practice that at once drained their own herds and created competitors on the public domain. In Colorado, Wyoming, and elsewhere, mavericks were declared the possession of the stock associations and were annually auctioned off. Mavericking—a way to begin a career of enterprise—became rustling—a way to begin a career of crime. Small stockmen did not always agree with this redefinition of enterprise, particularly when the men who claimed higher virtue were themselves appropriating millions of acres of public land while protesting the actions of those who appropriated a few stray cattle. Such differences of opinion lay behind the Johnson County War of 1892, when members of the Wyoming Stock Growers Association hired gunmen to clear out small ranchers whom they accused of rustling.

The Johnson County War was the act of desperate men, for the days of the large cattle corporations were already numbered. They had engineered their own demise. As cattle prices rose in the early 1880s, cattle raisers had crammed animals onto the ranges. Roughly twenty million cattle grazed the American West by 1884, and although both federal studies and some stock raisers denied it, there were fears that there was no longer either enough grass to feed the cattle or enough consumers with the money to buy the beef. When the country once more became mired in depression, cattle, as commodities, went into decline. In 1885 the price for young steers fell dramatically. Too young for prime beef, and with no ranges open to them, they were a glut on the market.

Cattle could not feel their decline in exchange value, but as living things that experienced hunger, cold, and pain, they could feel the consequences of the human greed that had pushed vast numbers of them onto grasslands that could no longer feed them in climates where bad winters could bring enormous suffering. In the 1880s, drought and bad winters combined to inflict damage on western cattle, sickening those who saw it. The winter of 1880–81 brought devastating losses to the herds of the Columbia Basin, reaching 50 percent or more in some counties. Blizzards and bitter cold on the southern plains in the winter of 1884–85 forced hungry cattle to drift before the storms. But the animals' instinctual reaction came up against the new barbed-wire fences, where the cattle piled up and died. Hungry cows aborted their calves. The ones that gave birth were too weak to feed their offspring, and both cow and calf died. The calf crop plummeted. These bad winters moved like serial killers across the West. In 1886–87, a bitter winter followed a hot, dry summer on the northern plains. White arctic owls, for the first time in nearly a generation, appeared in Montana; the chinooks, the warm winds off the Pacific, never arrived, and the result was, as John Clay remembered, "simple murder." Cattle died as they had on the southern plains. Because the cattle companies operated on book counts, no one could be sure how many cattle died, since no one was quite sure how many there had been to begin with. Many companies took the opportunity to claim huge losses and thus remove the discrepancy between their book counts and their actual herds. Probably about 15 percent of the herds died, many more in the hardest-hit areas. Most of the survivors were weak, emaciated, and disfigured from the cold. To meet their loans, cattle raisers rushed many of these steers onto a declining market, pushing prices down farther. In Chicago, cattle worth $9.35 a hundred weight in 1882 brought $1 in 1887. In the Great Basin, 1889–90 was the terrible winter.

The suffering of livestock in these winters affected even hardened cattlemen; they could not, it turned out, fully commodify their animals. Confronted with carcasses of dead cattle and with living animals so weakened that they could not move from the mudholes that mired them, Granville Stuart found what had been a fascinating business suddenly distasteful. "I wanted no more of it. I never wanted to own again an animal that I could not feed and shelter." A concern for the humane treatment of animals destined for slaughter had begun to infringe on the concerns of enterprise well before Stuart's revulsion. The American Humane Society had obtained legislation governing the shipment of cattle as early as 1873, and their disputes with cattle raisers continued for the remainder of the century. Stuart's reaction only revealed the ambivalence of the cattlemen themselves.

Falling markets and the losses of these terrible winters hurt the industry in general, but some companies did better than others. Those companies that, in the derisive words of an English journal, were mere "hunters of wild cattle," although they styled themselves "graziers on a princely scale," did not survive. Better-run companies, such as the Matador of Texas, rode out the bad times, for they had managed to bureaucratize and centralize the business. They endured losses in the 1880s and in the early 1890s, but they bought land, upgraded their stock, leased and purchased northern grazing lands for fattening, and raised hay. Their cowboys became company men who were as likely to dig irrigation ditches, put up fences, or cut hay as ride herd.

But even for the better-run cattle companies, the remainder of the century was more respite than reprieve. There would be another speculative boom, and another bitter collapse after the depression of the early 1890s, but the direction of stock raising had changed. The need to winter feed improved stock changed cattle raising into ranching and reduced its scale. The future lay with small operations of two hundred head or less. These cattle were still seasonally run on the public lands, but they relied on alfalfa and sorghum for the majority of their winter feed. Ranchers also marketed animals more quickly. Because young steers put on weight more rapidly than older cattle, ranchers realized the greatest return on investment by selling steers as soon as their ability to turn feed to fat began to slacken. Eventually, with selective breeding, they could market a steer after only two years. A relatively small herd of improved cattle with a rapid turnover of animals could yield more beef and more profit than the larger herds of the old free-range systems.

As the twentieth century progressed, these reduced operations came to depend on federal permits to run cattle, first in the new national forests and then, after the Taylor Grazing Act of the 1930s, on the remainder of the public domain. Ranchers depended on water from federal projects to fill their irrigation ditches. They raised improved breeds—mainly Herefords—and sent them for fattening to farmers in the corn belt. Corporate control did not vanish; it just became less obvious to outsiders. By the late 1890s, the packinghouses had largely taken over the financing of the cattle industry. The big packinghouses loaned money to commission agents, who loaned it to farmers seeking to buy feeders from the western range. The agents held a mortgage on both the corn and the steer. Long before the steer ever reached Chicago, Kansas City, or Fort Worth, the packers controlled it.

In the late nineteenth and early twentieth centuries, sheep invaded the shrinking domain of cattle. Some of the early boosters had been undifferentiated enthusiasts of grazing animals, and in Montana and elsewhere there were men who ran both sheep and cattle and their range. But on the whole, sheep raisers and cattle raisers competed. Cattle raisers and homesteaders, who resented the presence of tramp sheepmen whose herds consumed grass they wanted for their own cattle and horses, complained that cattle hated the smell of sheep and would not prosper where sheep had grazed. Sharpening this competition was the status of the sheep as an ethnic animal. The owners of sheep were often either immigrants or nonwhites; shepherds were usually Scotsmen, Basques, or Mexican Americans. The Mormons too were often sheep owners; not only were a high proportion of Mormons immigrants, but in the nineteenth-century West, all Mormons were regarded as un-American. To many Anglo-American cattlemen and cowboys, sheep were inferior animals herded by inferior men. The constant care that sheep demanded, the hostility they often created, and their pervasive smell and sound made sheep raising a life utterly without romance.

Yet cattle raisers could not stop the rising tide of sheep. Cattlemen constantly threatened violence; they occasionally slaughtered sheep or burned the haystacks of farmers who sold hay to shepherds; they more rarely killed shepherds. But the numbers of sheep inexorably increased. In New Mexico, the old heartland of sheep, sheep raisers crossbred the *churros* with Merinos, raising the wool yield to four or five pounds, as they found a profitable market for wool in the East. The number of sheep in New Mexico rose to nearly five million in the late 1880s, and their ownership grew even more concentrated. On the upper Rio Grande, Frank Bond and Edward Sargent acquired grazing rights on so much public and private land that many formerly independent *nuevo mexicano* sheep ranchers could not find grazing land and had to sign on as *partidarios* with Bond or Sargent. In Arizona, sheep spilling over from California joined Navajo sheep and Mormon sheep from southern Utah. In northern Arizona, sheep outnumbered cattle ten to one as early as the late 1870s. On the Columbia Plateau, sheep outnumbered cattle four to one in 1890, and by 1900 the more than one million sheep outnumbered cattle eight to one. These sheep were Spanish Merinos and French Rambouillets.

Although cattle raisers did not realize it, their own cattle formed a fifth column paving the way for sheep. As cattle overstocked the ranges and overgrazed the bunchgrasses, they opened up the land to invasion by exotic forbs (that is, nongrasslike herbs). Cattle did not thrive on this weedy growth, but sheep did; in addition, sheep could crop short grasses left behind by cattle. The growth of weedy forbs peaked early, but sheep raisers compensated by adopting a pattern of transhumance, a system of grazing in which herds grazed lowlands in winter and spring when the mountains were covered with snow and then moved into the mountains in the summer as the snow retreated. In the mountains, the sheep, or hoofed locusts as John Muir called them, devastated the mountain pastures.

In the 1880s, sheep raising outside of New Mexico offered poor people the shot at enterprise that the larger cattle companies sought to deny small cattle raisers. In the Columbia Plateau, poor immigrants could work herds on shares, taking minimal pay plus a claim on part of the lamb crop. Sheep required a much smaller initial investment than cattle, and since they matured more quickly, provided quicker returns. They could survive on lands that cattle could not, and they could go much longer without water, thus opening range closed to cattle. The very docility that made them so tempting to predators meant that a single herder and a pair of dogs could control a band of fifteen hundred to three thousand sheep. Their wool was a commodity that could be stored indefinitely, was protected by tariff from foreign competition, and could be harvested annually with little harm to the animal.

But sheep also exacerbated the problems of the open range. Tramp sheep raisers competed with each other, and the only way to keep outfits off a range was, as an observer remarked, "to strip it utterly naked," a practice known as "sheeping off" the range. With the expansion of farming into both the high plains and the Columbia Plateau, and the decision of railroads to ban grazing on their land grants without leases, sheep raisers found their winter ranges constricted; with the creation of national forests, the government began to regulate their use of summer ranges as well. Like cattle raisers before them, sheep raisers found they could not control the open range. Those operations that survived had to turn to leasing lands from the railroads, obtaining grazing permits in the national forests, and purchasing other land to produce hay for winter feed. The capital demands for sheep raising necessarily increased; only those who could meet them would remain in business. And sheep too, as animals of enterprise, were creatures of the market. The Panic of 1893 and the depression that followed sent wool and mutton prices plummeting to their lowest levels since the Civil War.

When sheep battled cattle for the land, the fight was between two industrial animals—animals whose very bodies, whose genetic makeup, humans had altered through selective breeding to fit their needs and whose every part humans processed into a product. Reshaped, these animals, in turn, reshaped the land. The results of their relentless overgrazing differed from place to place, but everywhere they opened up the land to invasion by other exotic species, everywhere they changed the composition of plant communities, and virtually everywhere they brought increased erosion. The changes varied with the local environments that the animals grazed and with the use or suppression of fire. On the Great Plains, the exotic Russian thistle—the tumbling tumbleweed of the cowboy songs—became such a familiar mark of overgrazing that people came to think of it as a native. In the California mountains, light burning and overgrazing by sheep restricted forest regeneration. In the Southwest, overgrazing by cattle and the banishment of fire led to the expansion of juniper and piñon into what had been grasslands. In the Great Basin, overgrazing eliminated native bunchgrasses, stripping the landscape to stark sage-dominated communities whose missing understory provided a vacuum into which exotics like cheatgrass could expand. In the Sangre de Cristos of New Mexico, native grasses such as Thurber fescue and alpine timothy became mere remnants amid the invading bluegrass and forbs such as yarrow and fleabane.

Industrial Animals and Animals of Leisure

The introduction of large herds of cattle and sheep also threatened wild animals, which now became either competitors with or predators on the domestic livestock. Americans, it is true, regarded game animals as useful in the sense that they provided food, but only temporarily useful. These animals were a resource meant to be used up and replaced by domestic stock. Elk, deer, mountain sheep, and any animal that might make a meal fell before the rifle, the victims of a remarkable slaughter.

The slaughter extended beyond animals that pleased the human palate. The western devotion to making the land as comfortable as possible for cattle and sheep led to a relentless campaign against animals that might make a meal of domestic stock. Stockmen shot wolves on sight, but since wolves prudently learned to avoid the sight of stockmen, ranchers and cowboys resorted to putting strychnine in animal carcasses. In a campaign that continues in some parts of the West to this day, bears, mountain lions, wolves, coyotes, wildcats, and lynxes were poisoned, trapped, and shot. Eventually grizzly bears disappeared over most of the contiguous American West, mountain lions over much of it, and wolves over all of it.

Other animals died not because they ate domestic animals but because they ate grass that domestic animals might eat. In Colorado, between 1 August 1885, and January 1886, the Bartholf brothers killed 1,080 antelope that made the mistake of grazing on "their" range. Ranchers also killed elk, which they claimed made their cattle wild. This kind of slaughter continues today on the ranges of Arizona. The carnage extended even to ground squirrels, pocket gophers, jackrabbits, skunks, hawks, and, above all, prairie dogs. Employing the kind of arithmetic that ranchers, U.S. Biological Survey employees, and later agricultural scientists and Forest Service personnel found irresistible in rearranging the western landscape, Frank Benton calculated that the elimination of one huge prairie dog town in Wyoming could alone provide a home and meals for 180,000 more cattle. Wyoming was shortgrass country, but in tallgrass environments, at least, overgrazing by cattle promoted the expansion of the very prairie dogs that cattlemen tried to eradicate. When grazing was restricted, the prairie dog towns shrank. Neither enterprise nor slaughter always yielded the desired results.

Finally, animals died as an unintentional result of livestock raising. Pronghorn antelopes, for example, could easily move through conventional barbed-wire fences, but close-woven sheep fences confined them. They died cornered in blizzards or confined to forage-depleted ranges.

If the citizens of the newly industrialized Republic had retained a strictly instrumental attitude toward animals, species after species would have yielded to the animals of enterprise. But industrialism created not only an intense pride in what human ingenuity had produced but also an increasing nostalgia and fear over what disappeared with that triumph. The loss was cultural. If game animals vanished, Americans could easily replace their meat, but could they, some began to ask, replace the masculine virtue cultivated by killing game?

Sportsmen, as distinct from hunters, began to argue that a particular kind of virtue—hardiness, bravery, self-reliance—impossible to cultivate in an urban, industrial environment was the true product of the hunt. This attitude arose among an eastern elite, who themselves tended to ape the English, but it diffused downward from elite groups like the Boone and Crockett Club to other hunters. Because such killing sought virtue rather than profit, sportsmen had to engage in a "fair chase" and abide by the "sportsman's code." Sportsmen disdained market or subsistence hunters as mere pothunters, and they struggled to institute and enforce state game laws and bag limits. By the early twentieth century, they had clearly won their battle to protect game populations. By dying so that American males could maintain their virility and virtue, game animals achieved a symbolic utility and a protected status.

Relatively few animals, east or west, qualified as game, but other animals benefited from the rise of middle-class nature appreciation. Nature appreciation usually operated within the same middle- and upper-class milieu as sport hunting but on the opposite side of the gender division. Nature appreciation was thought to be appropriate for women and children, who came to treasure the common experiences of wood and field that urbanization and industrialism made rare. Coupled with nature appreciation was the rise of "animal psychology," which sentimentalized and anthropomorphized wild animals. Animals became lovable—"our friends in fur and feathers," as nature stories put it. During the early 1890s, Ernest Thompson Seton and Charles G. D. Roberts developed the animal story into a special genre for which there was a huge popular appetite. Although nature lovers and hunters arose from common roots and appealed to the same classes, there was a latent conflict between the two groups. Both wanted to save Bambi, but the sportsmen wanted to shoot Bambi when he grew up.

Although a product of industrial society, sport hunting and nature appreciation in one sense opposed that society's instrumentalist tendencies; in another sense, however, they opened up a new basis for the commodification of wild animals. Displaced by

Fellow creatures of leisure, a bear and a tourist meet in Yellowstone National Park, where elk, bear, and buffalo populations reflect deliberate wildlife management policies.

Ellen Todd. Yellowstone Bear and Tourist. *Gelatin silver print, ca. 1935. The Denver Public Library, Western History Department, Denver, Colorado.*

animals of enterprise, wild animals became animals of leisure. And it turned out that deer and other game animals could yield revenues as people consumed them while at play. There were the obvious revenues that the state obtained through license fees, but also the revenues that hunters (and sport hunting became a mass sport in the twentieth century) produced in buying supplies and equipment, in travel, and in obtaining food and lodging. Hunters were armed tourists; keeping them happy meant keeping game populations high enough that they had a likely chance of killing something. All of this gave game animals a commercial value, so that even those skeptical about the cultivation of virtue could see convincing financial reasons for maintaining their populations and introducing new and exotic things for people to shoot at. Hunters, and those who profited from hunters, became the main political and economic supporters of wildlife preservation programs, programs whose results became more apparent as the twentieth century wore on.

Some domestic animals too became animals of leisure. The dog and cat had long ago become leisured, and in the twentieth century the horse, for all practical purposes, joined them. These species were almost wholly consumers, creatures that absorbed wealth and did not produce it. Horses, because of their size and the expense of maintaining them, became a special symbol of status, and in the West, part of that status, and part of their perceived value, came from their connection to the Old West of cowboys, Indians, and overland emigrants. The horse's status as an animal of leisure was far more exalted than that of wild game, since horses were usually neither killed nor consumed.

Only predators and rodents initially resisted classification as either lovable or leisured animals. Before Mickey Mouse, rodents failed to be lovable animals, but despite mass poisoning campaigns by the U.S. Biological Survey, they survived. Large predators were not so lucky. Sport hunters disliked predators because they killed game. Ranchers disliked them because they killed domestic stock. Nature lovers disliked them because they killed cute animals. They were, in the early nature-appreciation literature, cruel and murderous. At the turn of the century, even the Audubon Society recommended the killing of hawks, owls, and foxes. In 1915 the federal government took over the war on predators. The U.S. Biological Survey eliminated the last breeding wolf packs in the Dakotas, Wyoming, Colorado, New Mexico, and Arizona by the 1920s. The ecological effect was to make humans the only predator on some large-game species.

These changes in attitude occurred nationally, but they had particular consequences in the West, which contained the largest amount of remaining animal habitat and the largest reservoirs of remaining wild species. Yellowstone National Park represented perhaps the most extreme version of these consequences. It does not appear that Yellowstone was particularly rich in wild animals before white settlement, but the combination of habitat destruction and overhunting outside the park made it an unintentional haven for game. As the twentieth century wore on, elk, bears, and buffalo began to overshadow the geysers and waterfalls as tourist attractions. Government hunters eliminated wolves within the park, and a ban on hunting eliminated human predation. Elk, in particular, increased and thrived even though the park could not provide the whole herd with a winter range. Although presented as a salvaged remnant of aboriginal America, the park by the late twentieth century came more to resemble a petting zoo with a highway running through it. In Yellowstone the commodification of wild animals was everywhere apparent, and a closer look revealed the damage that elk and bison could do by overgrazing a habitat artificially shaped by park boundaries.

Animals of enterprise and animals of leisure were the two sides of the coin of industrialization in the West of the late nineteenth and early twentieth centuries. There was no escape from a logic of commodification that eventually even commandeered the memories of an older West. Animals became symbols of the lost West, symbols of a freedom and wildness that could, advertisers promised, be acquired if one bought an automobile that was also a Mustang, or a Bronco, or an Eagle. Even manitous—the other-than-human persons, often in the form of animals, that Indians conceived of as giving them the qualities they otherwise lacked—could be commodified and mass-produced. Motorized manitous could deliver other-than-human aid without the necessity of the fasting and self-mutilation required to appeal to the older manitous. These new manitous, of course, were not persons; they were only machines. They evoked the old to expand the new. They, as much as the giant feedlots, genetically engineered cattle, or Yellowstone, represented the logical culmination of the triumph of animals of enterprise in the West.

Dances with Wolves, a movie that reached theaters as the twentieth century entered its last decade, reflected even in its title the symbolic burden that animals had come to bear when Americans thought about the West. The first environmentalist Western, the film reversed all of the verities of enterprise. In the film, white soldiers and pioneers were "bestial" in an older sense: they were filthy and greedy, befouling themselves and everything they touched. Their enterprise was mere slaughter and destruction. Animals, especially horses and of course a wolf, were noble and "human": loyal and self-sacrificing. These were animals from the pages of Ernest Thompson Seton—the great sentimentalist of nature and outdoor life. In its depiction and condemnation of the slaughter of bison and its portrayal of a human-animal relationship that went beyond utilitarianism, the film seemed to reject the commodification of animals that had so marked the history of enterprise in the American West. And yet, the film itself was a commodity; the audience paid for the sentiments, and the animals were highly trained. Regarded this way, the film was also what it condemned: yet another stage in the evolution of animals of enterprise in the West.

Bibliographic Note

An interested reader can re-create most of the sources for this article from the bibliographies of recent publications, so I will mention these recent works as well as those sources that readers might not normally consult.

For a wider perspective on these issues, see Alfred W. Crosby *Ecological Imperialism: The Biological Expansion of Europe, 900–1900* (Cambridge, Eng., 1986). For the organization of the livestock industry, see Mary Yeager, *Competition and Regulation: The Development of Oligopoly in the Meat Packing Industry* (Greenwich, Conn., 1981), J'Nell L. Pate, *Livestock Legacy: The Fort Worth Stockyards, 1887–1987* (College Station, 1988), Gene M. Gressley, *Bankers and Cattlemen* (New York, 1966), Margaret Walsh, *The Rise of the Midwestern Meat Packing Industry* (Lexington, 1982), and Sigfried Giedion, *Mechanization Takes Command: A Contribution to Anonymous History* (New York, 1948), for a start. For American dietary habits, see Harvey A. Levenstein, *Revolution at the Table: The Transformation of the American Diet* (New York, 1988).

Works on the plains cattle industry are too numerous and uneven to cite here, but along with the older, classic works, Don Worcester's *The Texas Longhorn: Relic of the Past, Asset for the Future* (College Station, 1987), is recent and worthy of note. Maurice Frink et al., *When Grass Was King: Contributions to the Western Range Cattle Industry Study* (Boulder, 1956), Charles L. Wood, *The Kansas Beef Industry* (Lawrence, 1980), J. Orin Oliphant, *On the Cattle Ranges of the Oregon Country* (Seattle, 1968), W. M. Pearce, *The Matador Land and Cattle Company* (Norman, 1964), Harmon Ross Mothershead, *The Swan Land and Cattle Company, Ltd.* (Norman, 1971), James A. Young and B. Abbott Sparks, *Cattle in the Cold Desert* (Logan, Utah, 1985), and John T. Schlebecker, *Cattle Raising on the Plains, 1900–1961* (Lincoln, 1963), provide regional or corporate studies. The chapter on meat in William Cronon, *Nature's Metropolis: Chicago and the Great West* (New York, 1991), is essential reading.

For sheep and culture in the Southwest, see William deBuys, *Enchantment and Exploitation: The Life and Hard Times of a New Mexico Mountain Range* (Albuquerque, 1985), and John O. Baxter, *Las Carneradas: Sheep Trade in New Mexico, 1700–1860* (Albuquerque, 1987). For the Northwest, see Alexander Campbell McGregor, *Counting Sheep: From Open Range to Agribusiness on the Columbia Plateau* (Seattle, 1982)

For animal power, see Henry P. Walker, *The Wagonmasters: High Plains Freighting from the Earliest Days of the Santa Fe Trail to 1880* (Norman, 1966), Morris F. Taylor, *First Mail West: Stagecoach Lines on the Santa Fe Trail* (Albuquerque, 1971), and Oscar Winther, *The Transportation Frontier: Trans-Mississippi West, 1865–1890* (New York, 1964), as well as W. Turrentine Jackson, *Wells Fargo in Colorado Territory* (Denver, 1982), and Jackson's other works on the Wells Fargo Company.

For the fur trade, see David Wishart, *The Fur Trade of the American West, 1807–1840: A Geographical Synthesis* (Lincoln, 1979). For buffalo, the classic study is still Frank G. Roe, *The North American Buffalo: A Critical Study of the Species in Its Wild State*, 2d ed. (Toronto, 1970), but Dan Flores's recent "Bison Ecology and Bison Diplomacy: The Southern Plains from 1825 to 1850," *Journal of American History* 78 (September 1991), is an extremely important new study. For changing attitudes toward animals, see Thomas R. Dunlap, *Saving America's Wildlife* (Princeton, 1988), and Roderick Nash, *The Rights of Nature: A History of Environmental Ethics* (Madison, 1989).

Chapter Eight

An Agricultural Empire

ALLAN G. BOGUE

From the early nineteenth century through the first decades of the twentieth, settlers created farms in the American trans-Mississippi West. Each life story in this process was unique, but similar elements might be found in all of them. Collectively, these biographies compose the history of American agriculture and settlement west of the Mississippi. The settlers directed torrents of grain and mountains of meat, hides, wool, and cotton to the markets of the older states and of the world and by their example drew millions of hopeful compatriots and immigrants into the American West to share in the adventure of planting European-American settlements.

Among these hopefuls was Joseph Fish's Yankee grandfather, who pushed across the Vermont boundary line, without realizing it, and settled in lower Canada. A generation later, Joseph's mother converted to the religion of the Latter-day Saints (Mormons), and the family moved with other church members to Will County, Illinois, where her husband, Horace Fish, also accepted the faith. In the fall of 1840, when young Joseph was a few months old, the Fish family moved to Nauvoo. During the persecution of the Saints and the ensuing exodus across Iowa, the family lost most of its possessions. In 1850, after three years in Council Point, the family continued to Deseret. Horace Fish prospered at Circleville on a twenty-five-acre holding, but in 1852 he moved to Parowan to join in the development of the southwestern Utah Territory. The family set out in a heavy snowstorm, but twelve-year old Joseph cared not; he was wearing his first pair of new boots.

The forted village of Parowan, where Joseph Fish lived until 1878, lay on Center Creek upstream from Little Salt Lake. Since his father was both miller and tanner, much of the agricultural labor fell to young Joseph. The Fishes had a holding in the community's common field, and there they planted potatoes and grain, with several neighbors typically exchanging work in the cultivation and seeding of their plots. To prepare the community field, the settlers pulled clumps of sagebrush with oxen and chains and used wooden plows reinforced with iron from the rims of wagon wheels. Irrigation was essential; ditching, as well as fencing, had to be done, and water needed to be diverted from the ditches to the crops. Joseph learned to cradle two acres of wheat or oats in a day during harvest. Sometimes he helped guard the community herd or helped drive livestock to new range. In winter, Fish often cut timber for the village homestead or for making pine tar.

The Parowan settlers feared hostile Indians and rustlers; the community militia drilled frequently, and males were armed. Joseph helped build roads and hunted wolves

Though engaged in a common sort of labor, every western farm family had its own story to tell. Like his neighbors, Ether Blanchard relied on family assistance at harvesttime. But Blanchard, who was also a poet, insisted on harvesting the grain on his 13-acre Utah farm with an outmoded cradle scythe.

George Edward Anderson (1860–1928). Ether Blanchard Farm, Maple-ton, Utah. *Gelatin silver print*, 1902. Harold B. Lee Library, Brigham Young University, Provo, Utah.

or waterfowl. However busy they were, residents found time for the religious observances typical of Mormon settlements, for sessions of lay school, and for theatrical entertainment—in which Joseph joined—as well as for frequent games of shinny or horseshoes. This was Parowan during the 1850s and early 1860s.

Farther west, the enumerators of the federal census in California in 1850 recorded several hundred rancheros. Among them was Don Carlos Antonio Carrillo, a prominent resident of Santa Barbara and owner of the Rancho Sespe. Born in 1783, the son of a Spanish Army captain, Carrillo enlisted as a private at fourteen and left the service as a sergeant while still relatively young. Thereafter, he served in the California assembly, as well as representing his region in the National Congress of Mexico. His political fortunes climaxed with his appointment as governor of California, an honor that was contested by a rival who pressed his cause in Mexico City and in California. In 1838, California residents on both sides of the dispute engaged in a short period of comic-opera warfare. When the Mexican government recognized Carrillo's rival, Don Carlos accepted the decision philosophically and returned to the life of a "pobre ranchero," regretting only that his political career had been expensive.

In 1829, Carrillo petitioned the California authorities for six leagues (twenty-four thousand acres) of land along the Sespe, a tributary of the Santa Clara. At the time, Carrillo owned five hundred head of cattle and two hundred horses and mules. Carrillo established his ranch on the Sespe, but he did not perform the ceremonial crossing of his boundaries until 1842, when, according to the rancho's historian, he "pulled up grass, scattered handfuls of earth, broke off branches of trees, and performed other acts and demonstrations of possession." By 1845, he was running approximately three thousand cattle, droves of horses and mules, and flocks of sheep. A two-story adobe house served as headquarters for the rancho, which included two vineyards and two cultivated fields. In these days of the hide and tallow trade with the United States, Carrillo's herds provided a comfortable life marked by visiting, lavish hospitality, fiestas, and rodeos featuring brilliant horsemanship.

The historian of Rancho Sespe pictured Carrillo and his sons leading the leisurely annual expedition of family and servants to the ranch, all astride spirited Arabian horses, saddles and bridles sparkling with silver. The men were clad in "short breeches extending to the knee, ornamented with gold or silver lace at the bottom . . . soft deer skin [leggings] well tanned, richly colored and stamped with beautiful devices . . . tied at the knee with a silk cord . . . with heavy gold or silver tassels . . . long vests, with filigree buttons of gold or silver . . . [jackets] of dark blue cloth . . . long serape or poncho made in Mexico . . . [vicuña] hats imported from Mexico and Peru." Behind rode the women and children in *carretas*, great squeaking oxcarts. At the ranch was the commotion of the annual rodeo: the sounds of bawling calves and pounding hooves mixed with the shouts of vaqueros and with the thick dust that accompanied roundup. The calves were branded and perhaps a herd selected for slaughter.

Hard work was balanced by leisure; the Carrillo men hunted grizzly bears, attended bullfights, and enjoyed the fiesta. Initially, Carrillo benefited under American rule; goldfield markets raised the value of his herds to unimagined levels. In 1852, at age sixty-nine, the old soldier died. The United States Land Commission approved the Carrillos' title to Rancho Sespe in April 1853, and in September, the administrator of the estate auctioned the land. Three brothers named Moore, cattle buyers from Ohio, purchased the rancho for $18,500, about seventy cents per acre.

In Iowa, we find a different story. "Our land is beautiful, though there are few trees . . . . We have good spring water near by. Best of all, the land is good meadowland and easily plowed and cultivated." So wrote Gro Svendsen from Emmet County, northern Iowa, in November 1863. This young woman had accompanied her husband, Ole, from Norway the previous year. After time with friends and relatives in eastern Iowa, the couple established their "new home" in the prairie country drained by the upper Des Moines River. Gro died in 1878 after the birth of her tenth child. The daughter of a respected teacher in Hallingdal, Gro had recorded the details of her life in letters to her parents and siblings in the old country.

Ole Svendsen had hoped to homestead his land and erroneously believed that he must be naturalized to do so. Drafted in 1864, he served in the South with General William Sherman, returning unscathed. Home again, Ole purchased a timber lot to provide boards, rails, and firewood; he tilled more acreage, harvested good crops of wheat, and saw his livestock increase. Meanwhile, Gro made and sold butter. Aided occasionally by work and money from Ole's relatives, the Svendsens never knew abject poverty. But the 1870s were hard years—agricultural prices were low, grasshoppers damaged crops, and the resolution of real estate titles in the area left the Svendsens indebted to a railroad.

The school system was rudimentary in Emmet County; Gro taught her children in both Norwegian and English. She read assiduously, and on summer evenings she liked to sit in the yard and play the alpenhorn. She and Ole were active in the local Lutheran congregation. As the years passed, Gro corresponded less frequently, but her longing for her family remained strong. The Svendsens sent family portraits to Norway and affectionately scanned the pictures of their relatives. However, the recurrent strain of childbearing, her duty as scribe for less-educated neighbors, and constant work wore Gro down. In her thirties, Gro examined a photo of herself and believed she saw an old woman.

The experiences of the Fish, Carrillo, and Svendsen families illustrate the diversity of agricultural settlement in the West. Other examples of the varied backgrounds of western farmers abound: peoples of the southwestern pueblos, residents of the plazas of Hispanic New Mexico, Swedish settlers in Minnesota and Washington, Willamette Valley pioneers, participants in the Oklahoma land runs, and reclamation homesteaders waiting for that first rush of water in "the ditch." In each new environment, settlers were challenged to create productive farms, to modify old ways, to make do with inadequate resources, and to reconstruct the relationships and boundaries of the community.

Of course, European Americans were not the first to utilize the agricultural potential of the North American continent. Earlier migrants, the Indians, had adopted farming practices long before the era of European expansion. Natives of the northeastern woodlands were raising corn, beans, and squash when the Puritans arrived, and centuries earlier, Hohokam Indians had tended irrigation canals where Arizonans today practice a more elaborate water husbandry. Apache Indians channeled water to their crops in New Mexico during the eighteenth century. Although some Indian groups depended on hunting, the natives had identified a range of seeds, nuts, roots, tubers, bulbs, leaves, and

Charles M. Russell
(1864–1926). Trails
Plowed Under. Pen-and-
ink on paper, ca. 1926.
From Trails Plowed Under
by Charles M. Russell.
Copyright 1927 by
Doubleday, a division of
Bantam Doubleday Dell
Publishing Group, Inc.
Used by permission of
Doubleday, a division of
Bantam Doubleday Dell
Publishing Group, Inc.

barks to use for food, fiber, and medicine. They sometimes fostered particular flora by planting seeds or otherwise manipulating the environment. As American settlements expanded, the frontiersmen planted Indian corn, potatoes, squash, and beans side by side with the wheat, oats, barley, and peas of Europe.

Among the European Americans who went West, most dreamed of fertile fields and the bounty that cultivation provided. But there is a no-man's-land between farming and pastoralism in American history. Was the young Hamlin Garland, tending herd on the Iowa prairies in the 1870s, a cowboy or a farm boy? Garland herded cattle on grasslands, but he also knew that he, his pony, and the cattle were an integral part of a nearby farm enterprise. Garland's cowboy days illustrate the tendency of frontier agriculturists to use the free range adjacent to settlements. Access to market was difficult for the pioneer farmer, and livestock provided an ideal crop; cattle, sheep, and hogs could be driven to market by their owners or sold to traveling drovers.

For a time in the plains country of the trans-Mississippi West, the cattle and sheepherders ranged far ahead of the pioneer farmers, and the scale of their operations exceeded such activity east of the Mississippi. Even here, however, the herders built on the foundations of other livestock frontiers—northern, southern, and Hispanic—and found markets for feeder animals and supplies of young range stock or breeding animals in the western farm regions. The agricultural settlers of the trans-Mississippi West failed to oust the graziers from all of their domain, but they followed them doggedly. One of

Charles M. Russell's most poignant sketches shows a cow pony sniffing curiously at the edge of plowed land, its grizzled rider dejectedly contemplating the constricted horizons of his future.

Who Were the Settlers?

For over three centuries, Americans expanded the geographic limits of farming. Many of the new farms were maintained by succeeding generations of the settlers' families, but children and grandchildren also established their own farms, and immigrants joined the native-born. There were about 450,000 European-American farmers by 1800. Fifty years later, the number was almost 1.5 million, and by 1910, it was 6.4 million. By the mid-1930s, the total of farm operators had peaked, well short of 7 million.

Of those 1.5 million American farmers in 1850, only 119,000 were located beyond the Mississippi, most of them in the states along the river from Iowa to the Gulf. Sixteen thousand of them farmed in Texas and in the New Mexico Territory. The census takers reported fewer than 1,000 farmers in Utah and California and 1,200 in Oregon. This distribution foretold the future. Farmers moved west in the hundreds of thousands after 1850, but most trans-Mississippi farmers tilled their fields in the two tiers of states adjacent to the river. Thus, in 1890, the 201,903 farms in Iowa more than doubled the total in Washington, Oregon, and California combined. Moreover, the number of farms in the older states west of the great river continued to grow. The 16,552 farms added in Iowa during the 1880s exceeded the combined total in Montana, Wyoming, and Idaho in 1890 and almost equaled the number in Colorado. Although true pioneering had vanished in the Hawkeye State, farm makers continued to develop unimproved lands, draining wetlands and subdividing older units.

The best-known historian of the West, Frederick Jackson Turner, loved maps. In those the federal census cartographers were drawing during the late nineteenth century depicting American population growth, he found the basic patterns of the westward movement across the Mississippi. From various staging points in the central Mississippi Valley, settlers fanned out to form an area of contiguous settlement that reached the western border of Missouri by 1850 and then advanced into the plains country in a great ellipse, its northern perimeter anchored in Wisconsin and Minnesota, its southern in Texas, with the Indian lands that were to be Oklahoma breaking the pattern until the end of the century. The overleaping movement of pioneer farmers, Mormons, and gold seekers to Oregon, California, and the promised land of the Latter-day Saints during the 1840s and thereafter provided the cartographers with a different configuration—one of vertical bands in the great valleys of the Pacific rim and of strips and islands in the basin, plateau, and mountain country. Here the maps show the tendency for population to move not only westward but also north or south, or even west to east, as farmers followed the miners but were more rigorously confined to river valleys and irrigable areas.

Even on the central plains, settlement did not always surge simply westward. Local settlement jutted out along transportation routes and sometimes proceeded from north to south or vice versa or filled upland gaps between previously settled valleys. The outer margins of the farming frontier reflected the pulsations of the general economy and the alternation of years of little or of generous rainfall. In good times, the agricultural

Based on data from federal census reports, these population-density maps graphically document the westward movement of the American people. In 1890, the superintendent of the census noted, "Up to and including 1880 the country had a frontier of settlement, but at present the unsettled area has been so broken into by isolated bodies of settlement that there can hardly be said to be a frontier line." This observation, vividly supported by the 1890 map, helped inspire the historian Frederick Jackson Turner's famous remarks about the disappearance of the American frontier.

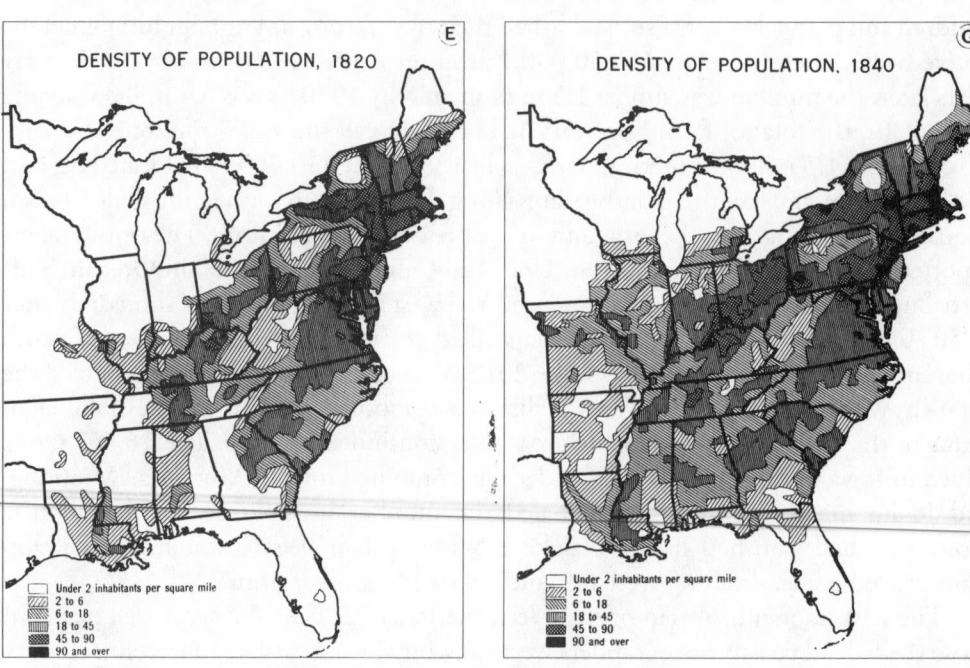

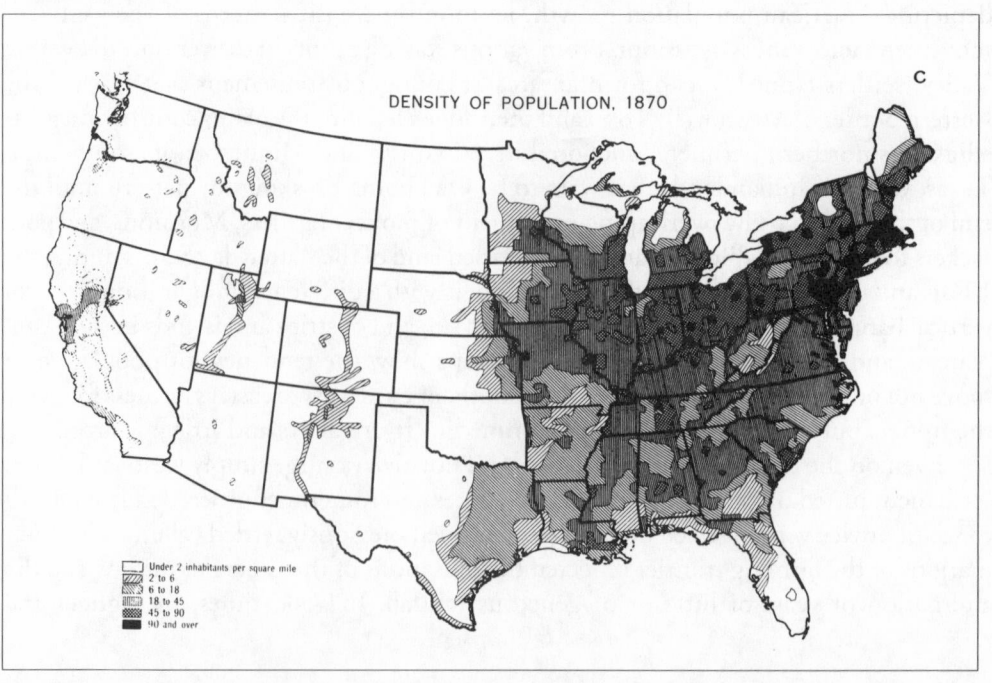

Maps reproduced from Charles O. Paullin, Atlas of the Historical Geography of the United States *(1932).*

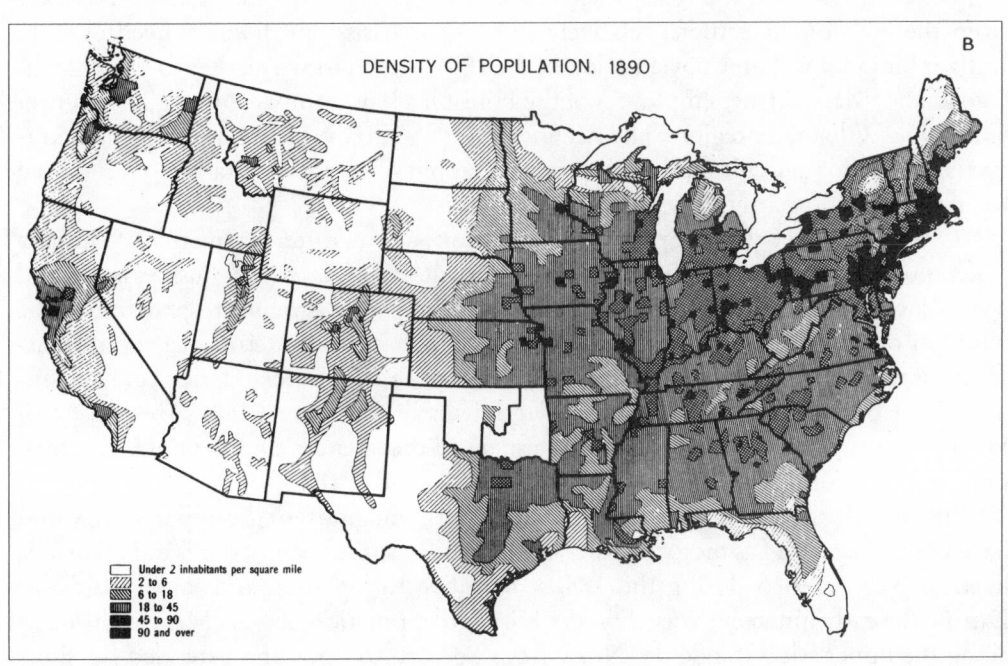

DENSITY OF POPULATION, 1890

B

Under 2 inhabitants per square mile
2 to 6
6 to 18
18 to 45
45 to 90
90 and over

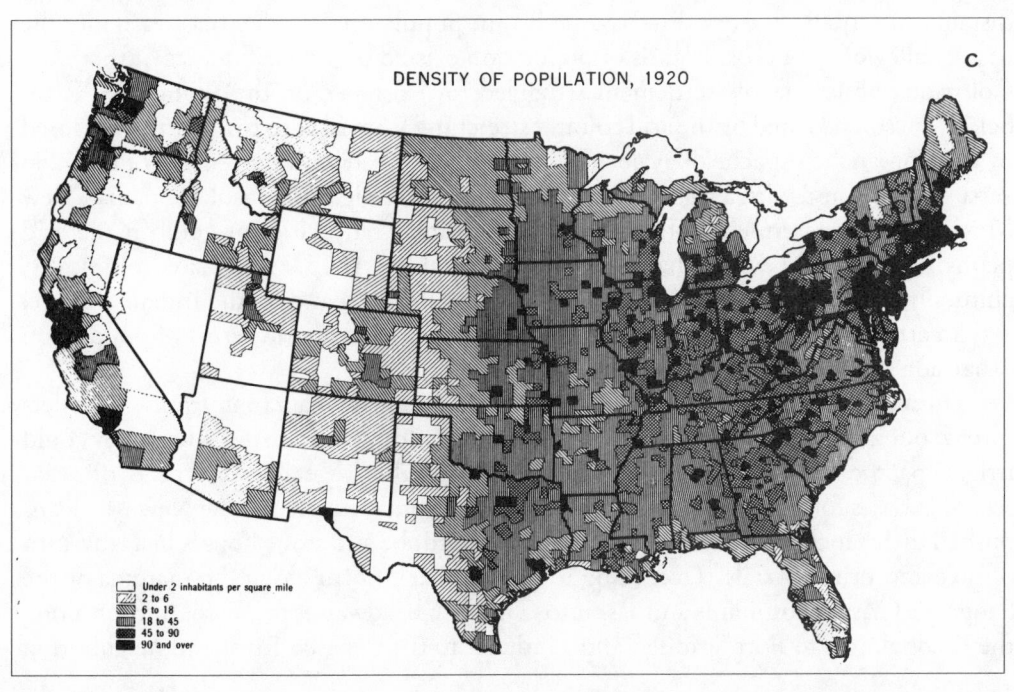

DENSITY OF POPULATION, 1920

C

Under 2 inhabitants per square mile
2 to 6
6 to 18
18 to 45
45 to 90
90 and over

frontier expanded; it remained stationary, or retreated—as in eastern Colorado and western Kansas—during the depression and drought years of the late nineteenth century. In part, such contraction involved the departures of those who failed, those whose will, health, or resources proved inadequate—"in God we trusted, in Kansas we busted" read the wry doggerel. But even in years of prosperity, the population was mobile as new settlers came and residents left.

For the most part, the treaty makers and the soldiers swept the Native Americans from the path of the settlers; relatively few trans-Mississippi pioneers lived close to Indians for long. When the overlanders of the 1840s began to arrive, they found French-Canadian settlers, former employees of the Hudson's Bay Company, living in the lower Columbia-Willamette region. The American settlers drew on this outpost of habitant-métis culture for agricultural knowledge and supplies, but the fur trade left a minimal legacy of agricultural settlement.

Our inheritance from Spanish colonization was a different matter. Within a generation in American California, the argonauts and American businessmen and agriculturists overran a culture of rancho and petty irrigation agriculture, penetrating the world of the thirteen thousand Californios by purchase and intermarriage and transforming it by an expansion of large- and small-scale commercial agriculture on undeveloped Spanish or Mexican grants and federal and state lands. The legacy of Hispanic institutions and landholdings influenced the later development of California, but we cannot distinguish a Hispanic frontier there after 1848.

In New Mexico the situation was different. Although most of the population would have been categorized as mestizo rather than Spanish, some seventy thousand Hispanos lived in New Mexico during the 1840s, near five to ten thousand Pueblo Indians. During the early nineteenth century, the Hispano population of New Mexico clustered along the upper Rio Grande del Norte from Socorro to Taos and extended for short distances up tributary rivers. From Santa Fe, the population branched eastward into the upper valley of the Pecos. Islands of population existed on two tributaries of the Little Colorado, while a feeble settlement struggled for existence on the Santa Cruz River below Tucson. Isolated by the arid country stretching from El Paso to Socorro, pressured by the Comanche, Apache, Navajo, and Ute Indians, riven with the tension of Hispano versus Pueblo, and with a population unschooled and religiously insular, Spanish New Mexico has been termed "a forlorn gateway to imaginary cities of gold on the arid plains." One author wrote that New Mexico in about 1815, "stalemated physically, culturally, and economically by the conditions of the land and by the Indian menace, was an arrested frontier society." It was not, however, arrested in terms of population expansion after 1820.

During the years 1820–70, the Hispanos had their own agrarian frontier. Settlers filtered out from the old communities, developing holdings on streams where they could irrigate patches of grain, corn, beans, peppers, and other vegetables or in canyons that served as bases for grazing flocks. To the east of the old settlements, the New Mexicans pushed their ranchos, or plazas, "crude clusters of adobe and stone houses in a labyrinth of pole and brush corrals" (according to one scholar), north along the margins of the Sangre de Cristo Mountains and east into Canadian headwaters to Tascosa, south along the Pecos almost to Fort Sumner, and southeast to the Penasco River and neighboring streams. To the west, the Hispano pioneers penetrated the San Luis Valley, pushed along various of the Rio Grande's tributaries beyond previous boundaries of settlement, and washed into the headwaters of the San Juan and Little Colorado rivers. When American rule began, this frontier expansion was under way, reflecting population growth and the vitalization of the New Mexican economy that occurred after trade relationships developed with the lower Missouri River valley. After the Mexican War, the American army's efforts to curb the southwestern tribes encouraged the spread of Hispano settlement. By the early 1870s, Spanish-speaking settlers were confronting Texas cattlemen and Mormon farmers. As the Hispanos struggled to hold their lands against these aggressive competitors and to contend with small-scale irrigation agriculture, this frontier thrust lost both its distinctive character and its vitality.

When the American colonists began their great republican experiment, the union was one of cultures as well as one of economic and political institutions. The northeastern states formed a reservoir of Yankees, children both of the sea and the field, who were energetic and commercially oriented and who nurtured a Puritan sense of mission. The people of the middle states were of Dutch and British origins, leavened during the eighteenth century with German and Scotch-Irish settlers who moved into the interior of Pennsylvania and followed the Great Valley into the backcountry of Maryland, Virginia, and the Carolinas. A few representatives of other cultural groups were scattered within this matrix of population. Of the white population of the United States in 1790, some 60 percent were English in origin, and the Scots, Irish, and Germans by birth or descent each made up 5 to 10 percent. Those of Dutch, French, Swedish, or Spanish origins totaled 3 percent or less. From the 1630s onward, on the basis of importation and natural increase, there was a growing African-American population, held, for the most part, in slavery. That institution survived into the late colonial period in the northern colonies and residually into the early national period of some northern states, but it thrived in the southern colonies. The census takers of 1790 estimated that within a U.S. population of 3,929,000 were 697,624 slaves and 59,557 free blacks.

After 1790, a stream of migrants from the northeastern and Middle States flowed westward, occupying western New York and even parts of southern Canada; from these places they moved into the upper areas of the Old Northwest. Simultaneously, settlers from the Virginia and Carolina backcountries flooded into Kentucky and Tennessee and the southern regions of Ohio, Indiana, and Illinois. In turn, the southern border states and the Old Northwest were sources of migrants for the trans-Mississippi Middle West. While some of the population in the southern backcountry moved north and west through the Appalachian chain, another current of southerners trekked along the Gulf, creating a pool of potential settlers for Louisiana, Arkansas, and Texas.

Modest during the first thirty years of the American Republic, immigration quickened in the 1830s, when more than half a million new residents arrived. By the 1850s, the number had risen to almost three million, and five and one-quarter million entered the country during the 1880s. Initially, most of the immigrants in this period were Irish, but by the 1850s, Germans were arriving in comparable numbers. Many newcomers came from the United Kingdom, Scandinavia, and Canada, and almost every European state or province was represented. One historian of American immigration argued that the newcomers shunned the frontier—they were "fillers in." Many did establish themselves in towns or cities or in older farming communities, but immigrants also shared in the agricultural settlement of the trans-Mississippi West. Foreign-born Kansans never totaled more than 13 percent of the population in the period of most rapid settlement in the state, 1860–90, and the proportion in Texas was smaller. But Nebraskans of foreign extraction made up more than 20 percent of the state's residents between 1860 and 1880, dropping to 19 percent in 1890. At that time, 32 percent of Dakotans had been born under other flags. A magnet for gold seekers, California counted 39 percent of its residents as foreign-born in 1860, with approximately 30 percent remaining in that category thirty years later. These facts of population composition and growth are basic to understanding agricultural settlement in the trans-Mississippi West because there, the agrarian culture bearers of the older American North and South mingled with settlers of different heritage, and together they faced new challenges of adaptation.

According to one of the songs of the Mormon handcart migration, "Some may push and some may pull." So it was when individuals considered moving into or within western America. Inability to find farms close to parents or relatives, inhospitable social or religious environments, nagging loads of debt, the conviction that one's locality was ague-ridden or otherwise unhealthy, and clouded land titles—these were factors that pushed people westward. On the other hand, settlers were lured by opportunities for cheap land, tales of rising land values and fantastic crop yields, the urging of relatives in the new country, and newspaper stories or letters singing the praises of a frontier region.

Some westward migrants believed themselves to be agents of destiny. Southern frontiersmen flocking to Mexico and, later, independent Texas considered themselves apostles of republican institutions and were eager to expand their domain. Others who pioneered the overland trail to Oregon or Hispanic California fused the ideology of imperial republicanism with an ambition to prosper in a rich new country. Marching into the Great Salt Lake basin in the wake of Brigham Young and his pioneers, the Latter-day Saints sought not only a religious utopia but also economic security. John Brown and his sons waged war on the slave power in Kansas but staked out land claims there as well.

Some migrants impulsively decided to emigrate; others deliberated at length, push and pull commingled in their minds. Sometimes the embittered bachelor, the bereaved widower, or the independent young woman resolved, in solitary contemplation, to leave his or her home; but usually the decision was a product of family, community, or congregational interaction. Many wives went unwillingly, dreading the disruption of family, the dangers of the trail, and the primitive conditions of pioneering. Others welcomed the adventure and shared their spouses' hopes for success in the West. "A setting hen never gains any feathers," one wife pertly responded when importuned by family members to let her husband proceed her.

The rural householders who left midwestern communities during the nineteenth century were younger than the community mean, possessed less property than those who stayed, and had smaller families. In mid-nineteenth-century Appanoose County, Iowa, for example, the mean total wealth of persisting householders, age thirty to thirty-nine in 1860, was $2,348, whereas those of the same age group who left the county during the next decade possessed assets averaging only $1,401. Such differences were not always present and often were not great. Although family heads in every adult age group migrated, the typical nonpersisters were in their thirties and were not impoverished. Indeed, some members of the initial migration to Oregon and California possessed means beyond the average of the communities from which they came.

For most westering Americans, the decision to emigrate involved the vision of a verdant farm and a thriving family. Land was the lure. Settlers learned of the agricultural possibilities of the West in myriad ways. Land speculators advertised their western holdings with handbills, pamphlets, and newspaper stories. In the early nineteenth century, the American travel account was a popular literary form, and many publications described parts of the American frontier. Although few literary travelers penetrated the land beyond the Mississippi during the first half of the nineteenth century, more of them did so as transportation expanded into the western grasslands and mountain regions. Eastern newspapers featured letters from the West, sometimes from former residents happily reestablished on the new frontiers and on other occasions from eastern newspapermen exploring the region. Early in the nineteenth century, guidebooks became available, describing the natural resources and surface features of western regions and providing digests of the federal land laws and state laws of interest to prospective emigrants, as well as depicting appropriate routes and transportation agencies. Josiah T. Marshall's *Farmer's and Emigrant's Hand-Book: Being a Full and Complete Guide for the Farmer and the Emigrant*, of 1845, was almost five hundred pages long, with chapters on the "Naturalization and Preemption Laws" and a "Miscellany—Containing a vast variety of Recipes, Hints, Tables, Facts, etc. etc., to aid the Emigrant, whether male or female . . . in daily life."

Westerners were keenly aware of the importance of attracting settlers. If others joined them, western economies would thrive; emigrants would be not only comrades in state building but also consumers and producers. Western lawmakers, officials, and community leaders subscribed to the gospel of development. Minnesota established a State Board of Immigration in 1855, and other western states followed suit. Such agencies hired representatives who distributed pamphlets and other materials, trumpeting the abundance of cheap farmlands. By 1864, Kansas was sending emissaries abroad, and after 1872, the thick *Biennial Reports* of the Kansas Board of Agriculture informed readers about crop production and the availability of farmland. In 1887, the governor of the Wyoming Territory promised wonderful futures to "practical, every-day farmers, who will put their hands to the plow and not look back."

The federal government granted public lands to the new western states for the support of education, for the erection of public buildings, and after 1820, for the improvement of transportation. If revenue was to be derived from their sale, the lands must be advertised. By the 1840s, railroads had begun obtaining land grants from the states, and with the advent of the Illinois Central project in 1850, the great era of federal land-grant railroad advertising dawned. Companies like the Union Pacific and the Northern Pacific energetically advertised their imperial domains. Railroad land departments organized excursions for newspapermen and land lookers, sent agents abroad, and printed handbills and pamphlets describing their fertile lands and favorable terms of purchase. The Burlington and Missouri River Railroad Company advertised "millions of acres of Iowa and Nebraska Lands" for sale—on ten years time, at 6 percent interest,

Railroad companies energetically promoted settlement along their western routes, luring prospective homesteaders with pictures of bountiful fields, prosperous farmers, and easy rewards. Enthusiastic (if self-interested) boosters of western settlement into the 20th century, they simply altered their images to keep up with changing times.

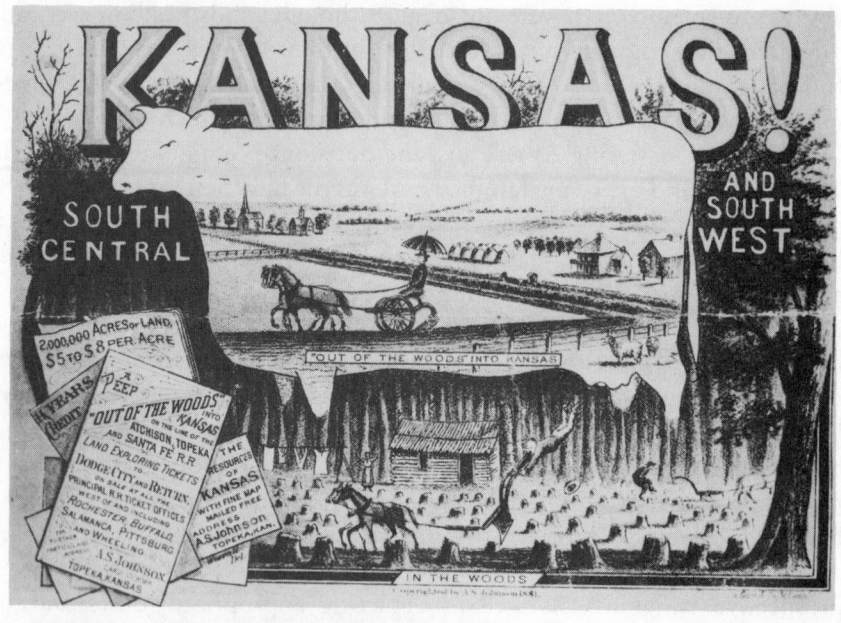

A. S. Johnson, publisher. Kansas! Chromolithograph, 1881. Kansas State Historical Society, Topeka.

Isn't It Time You Owned a Farm? Poster, 1911. South Dakota State Historical Society, Pierre.

payments of principal to begin after two years, and with the cost of a land excursion ticket to be deducted from the first payment if the purchase was made within thirty days. While the settler sought his new farm, his family might wait in "free rooms" in Burlington, Iowa, or Lincoln, Nebraska.

Western community leaders were also active. Local lawyers and real estate men persuaded easterners with capital to invest in western land, mortgages, and tax certificates and to entrust the supervision of such investments to them. In the process, they sang the praises of the country. On the postbellum frontiers, realtors thrived first as claim locators, guiding land seekers to lands that were available under federal laws. Some attempted to attract settlers from the older regions.

The community of black settlers at Nicodemus, Kansas, owed its existence to such activity. "All Colored People that want to GO TO KANSAS, on September 5th, 1877, Can do so for $5.00." So read the handbills that announced the formation of the colony (membership, one dollar) in Lexington, Kentucky, during the summer of 1877. Among those who paid their dollar was the freedman Thomas Johnson. He was part of a group of three hundred who reached the townsite of Nicodemus in Graham County, Kansas, in mid-September, only to find a settlement of bankside dugouts. Arriving later, the wife of an African-American minister saw "various smokes coming out of the ground." "The scenery," she wrote, "was not at all inviting, and I began to cry." A white Kansan from Indiana, W. R. Hill, provided the initial impetus for the establishment of this community of blacks in the valley of the South Fork of the Solomon River, 240 miles west of Topeka. Hill was a townsite promoter and claim locator, and of the five dollars mentioned in the handbill, two dollars was paid to him for his services in locating the colony families on claims, two dollars covered the filing fee at the land office, and one dollar went into the colony treasury.

Western urban centers harboring pretensions (and most did) organized chambers of commerce or boards of trade whose advertising and reports were designed to attract emigrants. By the last third of the nineteenth century, community leaders viewed "booming" editors, such as Marsh Murdock, of the *Wichita Eagle*, as prizes beyond price. In the spirit of the game, the *Kirwin* (Kansas) *Chief* printed Lucy Larcom's "A Call to Kansas" in 1876: "Yeoman strong; hither throng!/ Nature's honest men,/ We will make the wilderness/ Bud and bloom again."

"Boom" went "bust" when the feverish settlement activity of the 1880s in the plains country collapsed amid dust, low prices, and foreclosures. But as western frontier communities prospered in the early twentieth century, community leaders once more sang of opportunity, only now they were "boosters." Their intent was the same.

Although the journalistic scribbling and advertising had an impact, personal contact with western family members or neighbors who returned for visits often provided the incentive to go West. And letters from those in the West were passed from hand to hand within families. Ephraim G. Fairchild, a resident of Jones County, Iowa, in 1857 wrote to a relative, "I think that I can plough and harrow out hear without being nocked and jerked about with the stones as I allways have been in Jersey . . . if Father and Mother and the rest of the family was out here . . . they would make a living easier than they can in Jersey." So worked the process of chain migration. In Scandinavia such letters were

"America Letters" and were read by family networks. The same process occurred in church congregations, spreading migration fever.

Colonies of former neighbors developed in the West, by specific plan or by the accretion of family members, former neighbors, or acquaintances from the same eastern locality or foreign country. Of the organized colonies, none was more exotic than Bethlehem Yehuda, a corporate colony based on socialistic principles established during the early 1880s by idealistic young unmarried Ukranian Jews near Mount Vernon, South Dakota. But as the writer Irving Howe noted, "The leap from a Ukranian *shtetl* to . . . South Dakota—the cultural leap, the economic leap—was simply too great." Bethlehem Yehuda failed.

The last generation of American social historians has shown that nineteenth-century Americans were highly mobile. The federal census takers of one enumeration found less than half of the same pioneer farm households recorded by their predecessors a decade earlier. In the interim, settlers had come and gone. Given that there were fifty-five live births per one thousand of population in the United States in 1820—a figure that stood at thirty in 1910 (as compared with eighteen in 1970)—we might have expected such results. Once fully settled, the rural communities of the nineteenth century produced more children than could be accommodated without drastic subdivision of farms. Barring local urban or industrial opportunities, individuals had to leave, and some went West. That region did not draw equally from the older states and foreign countries; among American migrant residents in western regions, a predominance of settlers came from the nearer states. This held true even in the transcontinental migration to Oregon, where Missourians were most common in the early days. Settlers from more than a few hundred miles away became more common on the plains during the late nineteenth century, when the emigrant's boxcar provided an attractive alternative to the covered wagon.

Although many western farmers moved several times during the course of their lives, the early generations west of the Mississippi blended stability with movement. Most rural communities developed a core of longtime resident farmers; other settlers came and went, and some maturing children sought opportunity elsewhere. Thirty or forty years after the settlement of western rural communities, farmers bearing the surnames of original settlers could still be found, whereas their siblings were farming on new frontiers. In other cases, particularly among some foreign-born settlers, sons and sons-in-law acquired the adjacent lands of aging farmers and established family enclaves within the community.

Acquiring Land

In early June 1873, Henry Ise and his bride, Rosie, reached Henry's homestead and dirt-roofed log cabin in Osborne County, Kansas. Frank and Sam, their team of horses, had pulled the canvas-covered wagon, loaded with supplies, and the husband and wife had alternated between sitting on the wagon seat and driving their small herd of cattle. That day, the sun shone, prairie flowers bloomed in profusion, meadowlarks filled the air with birdsong, and Rosie wore calico and a pink sunbonnet. Although threatened by a flood in Dry Creek at the corner of Henry's claim, the couple arrived at the farmstead safely. The cabin measured eighteen by fifteen feet and was flanked by a straw-roofed stable, a chicken house of sod, a well with wheel and buckets, and a small fenced corral. Within the cabin were a bed, a tiny stove, boxes for chairs, and a nail-box washstand positioned on a floor of cottonwood boards. Nearby patches of sturdy corn, wheat, and oats promised good things to come. Spartan though this was, other homesteader wives found less-developed claims awaiting them.

When the pioneer farmers pushed across the Mississippi during the early nineteenth century, they understood the major features of the federal land-disposal system. Federal surveyors had preceded them, or were soon to follow, leaving a grid of baselines and prime meridians in which were set ranges of townships six miles square, subdivided by survey crews into thirty-six mile-square sections, each further divisible into smaller units. Within the framework of the federal survey, the settlers sought land to their liking. Initially, they used the land auction with its minimum price of $1.25 per acre (after 1820) and the right of purchase by private entry of offered, but unsold, land. Due in part to the political power of the pioneers, Congress liberalized the system, passing preemption, donation, and homestead laws, as well as implementing environmental adaptations like the timber culture laws and the Desert Land Act of the 1870s. But the settlers also found many fertile western lands available only by purchase from railroad companies or western territories or states, as well as from the reviled land speculators.

Congress approved thousands of laws relating to the nation's public domain, but the Homestead Act (1862) symbolized the process of western settlement. Thomas Jefferson wrote, "Those who labor in the earth are the chosen people of God, if ever he had a chosen people . . . whose breasts He has made His peculiar deposit for substantial and genuine virtue." Jefferson hoped that the lands of the United States would be used to foster the development of this class of citizens. The Homestead Act seemingly epitomized such thought. In reality, Congress established a system of land disposal that also served the interests of capitalists and developers. For this reason, as well as the feeling that the law did not meet western needs, historians have sometimes belittled the importance of the Homestead Act and the amendments that increased the size of the grant from 160 to 640 acres and shortened the period of compulsory residence. The facts of farm making between 1860 and 1920 contradict this belittlement. During those years, the number of farms in the United States increased by some 4.4 million. At the same time, 1.4 million homesteaders or their heirs received final patents, equivalent to 32 percent of the increase in farm numbers. So, the Homestead Act probably accounted for a substantial proportion of the new farms opened during this country's greatest period of agricultural expansion. Also, many pioneers filed claims under the law and relinquished them for a sum proffered by other settlers or commuted them to cash purchases. Sometimes commutation reflected poverty and distress; on other occasions the relinquisher or the commuter expected a quick profit. Still, for seventy years the Homestead Act gave legions of Americans inexpensive access to the land market and farm ownership.

Acquiring a farm was not always easy, and over time, it became more difficult. When Congress passed the Homestead Act in 1862, the farm frontier of the prairies and plains still included much of Minnesota, some of northwestern Iowa, most of Nebraska, and two-thirds of Kansas. For over a generation, 160 acres had been an ample unit through much of the unsettled portion of these states and in California, Oregon, and the Washington Territory. But settlers moving into the high plains and the dry plateau and basin country beyond the cordillera found 160 unirrigated acres inadequate to support a family.

The busiest homesteading areas of the nineteenth century were Kansas, Nebraska, and the Dakotas, where more than 430,000 settlers had filed homestead claims by the end of 1895. The most spectacular burst of settlement occurred in the "Great Dakota Land Boom" between 1881 and 1885, when 67,000 settlers took up homesteads in the territory. Between 1896 and 1920, homesteaders were most common in Montana, North Dakota, Colorado, South Dakota, Oklahoma, and New Mexico, each attracting at least 125,000 land entrants. Almost 200,000 settlers poured into James J. Hill's high plains railroad empire in Montana, the flood peaking in the years 1906–10. Of these states, only the Dakotas had seen comparable activity during the nineteenth century. Homesteading also increased after 1900 in the plateau and basin states as settlers moved into the cold desert of southern Oregon and into interior Washington, California to the east of the Sierras, and Arizona. Despite its size and the fact that homesteading began there in 1863, only 114,000 settlers filed homestead claims in California. Nowhere was Jefferson's dream so obscured as in that state.

Gro Svendsen's husband, Ole, was in error when he believed that he had to be naturalized in order to homestead land; he needed only to have declared his intention of becoming a citizen. In this respect, the Homestead Act was a generous one. Its application to the American Indians was ironic; few of them could utilize its provisions. But there were exceptions. During the summer of 1862, warfare blazed in the Minnesota-Dakota borderlands, where starving Santee Sioux rebelled against the exactions of traders and a corrupt Indian service. After a bloody uprising, thirty-eight Indians were adjudged guilty of rape or murder and were hanged. Others went to prison, and the tribe was moved into the Dakota Territory. In 1869, some twenty-five families from the tribe trailed into an unsettled area along the Big Sioux River in South Dakota, determined to live like white farmers. Others joined them; thus emerged the Flandreau Sioux colony, whose members asked to enter individual holdings under the Homestead Act. Friendly government officials and missionaries helped them do so, although the Flandreaus were required at first to surrender their claims on the tribal assets.

Steven Arrow, Big Eagle, David Faribault, their fellows, and their families slowly developed a settlement of log cabins. Initially, they hired oxen from white neighbors, tilled with spades and hoes, and supplemented their husbandry with hunting and trapping. A Sioux Falls merchant reported that they "gave more indications of civilization and industry and 'a show of living like white people than the same number of Norwegian families located a few miles below.'" Like other pioneer farmers, the Flandreau homesteaders faced killing frosts, grasshoppers, and a general shortage of livestock, equipment, and tools; in addition, the Indians confronted defections, factionalism, burdensome taxes, the threat of alcoholism, and the temptation to sell out to white men. But an Indian agent of the early 1880s wrote, " [They] pay their taxes promptly, their word can be relied upon, and they make good neighbors." Few American Indians, however, were able to use the Homestead Act, although an amendment to the statute of the early 1870s was intended to make it generally possible.

The above only outlines the ways in which westering farmers acquired virgin land.

The options of any individual might be limited, but the federal system was varied when viewed in broader perspective. Although the rectangular units within the basic survey grid did not always allow an effective or conserving use of land, settlers found the federal survey easy to understand and, therefore, less a source of boundary disagreements with neighbors than were the haphazard metes-and-bounds surveys found in some older states. Still there were problems. During the early period, when purchase at federal land auction or by private entry prevailed, squatters pushed onto the public domain before land surveyors had completed their tasks. Although such incursions were criticized in Congress and were contrary to law, squatters complained about rapacious speculators who thronged to the ensuing land sales and threatened to bid on claims that the settlers had improved. Among the frontier settlers there were also rascals ready to jump claims. To protect each other's holdings, squatters formed claim clubs or associations. They either ousted claim jumpers or forced them to purchase the claim in question. Club members attended land sales en masse, carrying sturdy walking sticks and threatening unwary capitalists. The squatters' clubs also allowed early settlers to engross land beyond their farming needs and to force latecomers to buy squatters' titles.

With the passage of the general preemption law in 1841, settlers no longer needed to fear speculators. But often thereafter, when land titles were uncertain, claim clubs appeared. In the upper valley of the Des Moines River during the 1850s and 1860s, the assignees of a river-improvement grant found their titles challenged by both a land-grant railroad and settlers hoping to acquire title through the preemption or homestead laws. A settlers' association denounced the other claimants. When the courts ruled on the title to these Des Moines River lands, the squatters learned, to their dismay, that they had to buy their lands from the river lands assignees or the railroad. During the 1850s, settlers poured into eastern Kansas before the federal land surveys, and free state and proslavery settlers used claim clubs to reinforce their positions. Settlers' associations on former Indian reserves and railroad lands in Kansas battled for preemptive rights into the 1870s, and such organizations were common in Nebraska and present in Colorado.

In California, conflict over land titles was complex and confusing. Although farmers were responsible for the first trickle of American overland immigration into California, the gold strikes brought migrants hoping for quick riches. Meanwhile, Congress grappled with the slavery issues attendant on the Mexican Cession and neglected California's land problems. The United States did not establish a California land office until 1853, and the first federal land sales did not occur until 1858. Settling the status of the lands that the Spanish or the Mexican government had granted to individuals was difficult. There were some eight hundred such grants, embracing eleven million acres, and the United States had pledged protection of the property rights of the grantees. Typically, the grants lay in attractive agricultural areas, and in many cases, their boundaries were vague.

The U.S. Congress established a claims commission in 1851 to determine the validity of the Mexican titles. The commission was generous in approving claims, even some of dubious validity; but evaluation proceeded slowly and was further complicated by federal court rulings. In the meantime, squatters settled on undeveloped parts of the grants—some in ignorance of the pending Mexican title, others either believing that the claims were fraudulent or hoping to win preemptive rights to their holdings. California officials complicated the situation by failing to identify state swamplands clearly and by claiming tracts that settlers were already trying to homestead or preempt. The locations of the state agricultural college lands further constricted the acreage available to settlers wishing to use the federal land laws. The allocation of railroad grant lands in areas already occupied by pioneers exacerbated the situation. The Californios were ill prepared to cope with the aggressive, Anglo-American businessmen, legal costs, and tax burdens associated with U.S. sovereignty. Anglos with capital acquired title to all or portions of many of the Mexican grants while others accumulated large holdings of state or railroad lands or of federal lands subject to private entry. Such individuals often refused to acknowledge that squatters had any rights, and the courts became mired in land litigation. In self-defense, the settlers formed claim associations, retained lawyers, and threatened violence against law officers seeking to evict them. Near San Jose in 1861, more than five hundred settlers confronted a posse seeking to evict squatters from the Chabolla grant. Some California farmers were still living on lands with clouded titles in the 1870s.

The New Mexican story of land disposal is even more depressing. Here were hundreds of Hispanic grants, most lying in the corridor of settlement along the Rio Grande and its tributaries but some extending into latter-day Colorado and Arizona. Under these titles a few rich families claimed ownership of large domains, and the Hispano masses held some form of title to modest acreages, with rights to share adjacent range with their neighbors. In New Mexico, grantees submitted their claims to the territorial surveyor general for approval. His rulings, however, could be challenged in the courts, and individuals with resources could beseech the U.S. Congress to confirm titles. Predatory Anglo lawyers and businessmen purchased claims, obtained shares in grants in payment for legal services, and tried to expand the boundaries of their holdings. Exemplified in Stephen B. Elkins and Thomas B. Catron of the "Santa Fe Ring," the Anglo wheeler-dealers found rich pickings, despite charges of corruption. Meanwhile, stockmen used dummy entrymen to obtain control of great stretches of New Mexico range. When Grover Cleveland's advisers considered the administration of public lands, they found widespread belief that "swindling cattle kings, surrounded by a gang of swindling herders, all of whom are in collusion with swindling surveyors, have swallowed our Western acres as a gourmand swallows oysters." New Mexico was the cesspool of the public land system.

With their range rights disregarded and the parent grants within which they lived frequently discredited, Hispano smallholders often hesitated to submit evidence of title and so lost their lands, surviving as hired laborers or renters. Anglo ranchers and settlers manipulated the federal homesteading system more successfully than did the Hispanos. When Congress finally established the Court of Private Land Claims in 1891, the Hispanic land base had already been subjected to four decades of plundering. The court confirmed title to only 2 million of the 37.5 million acres in claims presented.

Spanish Americans did not always suffer the assaults on their land base passively. After fence-building Texas cattlemen invaded the Las Vegas community grant, Hispanic residents, enshrouded in white, responded with night raids. Directed by Juan José

Herrera, "Las Gorras Blancas" (The White Caps) cut fences and burned Texan improvements. The movement was the seedbed of New Mexican populism, and although unsuccessful, this protest contributed to the incorporation of the Las Vegas grant and its continuing occupation by longtime residents.

Federal land disposal in Utah also had unique features. Most farmers here practiced irrigation and lived in villages from which they tended neighboring fields or livestock. In federal eyes, however, the Mormons were, initially, squatters. Not until 1869 did American officials open a land office in the Utah Territory. Meanwhile, church officers supervised settlement and land distribution. With the federal system in place, the Saints moved rapidly to ensure possession of the lands they had occupied, utilizing the Preemption Act, the Homestead Act, the Timber Culture Act, and the Desert Land Act. Many Mormon holdings were less than 160 acres in size, and although the practice was technically illegal, church officers often acquired the acreages allowable under the acts and apportioned them to the settlers occupying them. Wives in polygamous relationships sometimes entered homesteads as family heads and transferred title to their spouses, and villagers evaded the residency requirements of the Homestead Act by periodically camping on their claims. Thus did social realities overcome the technicalities of federal land statutes.

In much of the trans-Mississippi West today, roads, crops, and field boundaries delineate for airborne travelers the checkerboard squares of the federal surveys. Land records in hundreds of county courthouses still show evidence of large holdings amassed in the settlement period, as well as the tendency of ethnic groups to keep and to extend family holdings. In general, the government patent was only one transfer of title on any piece of rural property; there might be many more thereafter. Indeed, in some areas, a quarter-section homestead might be sold several times by relinquishment before the patentee occupied it. Many frontier settlers never acquired land from the government, obtaining their farms from original owners or the latter's assignees. Some of this churning represented the failure of settlers to become independent owners, but in other cases, it tells us that pioneers believed better opportunities lay elsewhere.

Some came to the frontier without means to acquire land. They found landholders willing to rent land to them, and hence, tenancy settled on the frontier along with the freehold farmer. Tenancy also developed because aging pioneers or widows used it in transferring farms to the next generation. For some young farmers, tenant status was a step in their progress toward debt-free farm ownership. But tenancy also indicated that not everyone could enjoy full fellowship in the smallholder's republic lauded by Thomas Jefferson. When the federal enumerators of 1880 counted farm tenants for the first time, they discovered that 24 percent of Iowa farmers were tenants, as were 16 percent of Kansas farmers; in California the rate was also 16 percent. Twenty years later the numbers had risen to 35, 35, and 23 percent.

Mechanization

When American farmers moved into the trans-Mississippi West in the early nineteenth century, their implements were much the same as those used by colonial farmers. Two-wheeled carts or crude wagons, mold-board plows of wood with an iron point and—perhaps—share, drags of heavy planks or tree trunks, harrows of wooden spikes set in triangular plank frames, double-shovel plows for row crops, harnesses, ox yokes, and fittings—these were the major items, along with smaller tools such as scythes, sickles, forks (often of wood), shovels, and coopered pails. The husbandman of the early nineteenth century broadcast his seed from a bag slung over his shoulders; he cut the ripened crop with a sickle or a scythe while others raked it into sheaves and bound them with knotted grain stalks. Eventually, the farmer flailed the grain, taken from barn mow or stack, and winnowed it on a canvas. The settler planted Indian corn with a hoe or, if the crop was sod corn on new breaking, sometimes used an ax. Gathering techniques varied by region; but however it was gathered, ripened corn was stored in cribs while the stalks and leaves provided fodder.

As settlement spread into the prairie states, mechanization accelerated. By about 1820, Jethro Wood had developed the prototype of the walking plow, with all of its earth-turning parts made of iron. Though Wood's plow was an improvement, the dense, matted prairie grass and forb roots defied conventional plows and, once turned, revealed soils that clogged iron-mold boards. Prairie blacksmiths developed massive beamed plows to break the sod, and during the 1830s and 1840s, John Deere and William Oliver led in manufacturing plows with mold boards of steel or polished chilled iron to which these soils did not adhere.

The agricultural inventors worked wonders in reducing work hours for the harvest of wheat and other small grains, hitherto cut with scythe or cradle and bound into sheaves by hand. Cyrus H. McCormick and other machinist-inventors mechanized and melded several processes. For the scythe's short cutting blade, they substituted a long cutting bar with serrated edges set within a framework of metal guide teeth, or fingers, attached to the front of a platform on wheels and pulled by draft animals. In forward motion, gearing motivated by a drive wheel at one end of this platform caused the cutting bar to whicker-snicker within its frame and cut the stalks of grain a few inches above the ground as an elevated reel and guide teeth steered them to the blade. A worker with a rake followed McCormick's contraption of the 1830s, periodically clearing the table of cut grain; but soon this worker was replaced by automatic devices.

The Marsh harvester of the 1870s revolutionized the sheafing and binding process by introducing moving canvases that elevated the cut grain over the drive wheel and dropped it on a shelf for sheaf binders standing on a step attached to the machine. These workers vanished with the introduction of an automatic twine knotter. The resulting grain binder was found in many harvest fields of the trans-Mississippi West by the 1890s. Such binders reduced field labor still more when manufacturers attached sheaf carriers that accumulated the bound bundles. When the driver judged that there were enough to make a stook of grain, he tripped the device.

The final process of separating the grain from the straw had long since left the flail or tramping-floor stage. By the 1840s, crude grain separators that flailed the grain and blew away the chaff and straw with internal fans were in use. Initially, horse treadmills and circular horsepowers drove such machines, but by the 1880s, Pitts or Case threshing machines were trundling down western roads behind steam engines, followed in turn by a horse-drawn water wagon to keep the engine puffing. In the Far West, imaginative rural inventors consolidated the stages of grain harvest; by the 1870s, huge, cumbersome combines drawn by twenty or thirty horses were rattling through the grainfields in the central valley of California, leaving a trail of filled grain sacks behind them. At the turn of the century, combines were conquering the hilly wheat fields of interior Washington. The binder-driver of the plains country encouraged his three or four horses with imprecations and a long whip; the driver of the combine's multiple hitch hung a pail of rocks under his elevated seat and threw them at lazy members of his huge team.

Meanwhile, mechanization proceeded in other areas of husbandry. Practical, if not always reliable, horse-drawn broadcast seeders, grain drills, mowing machines, rakes, and hay loaders had appeared by the 1850s. Plows and cultivators were enlarged and made available as riding machines, and rollers and other tilling machinery also appeared in larger sizes that were stronger and more efficient. The Indian corn crop seems, at first glance, to have benefited less from mechanization than the small grain harvest. Although mechanical planters and twin-row riding cultivators entered the cornfield in the 1860s, handpicking into a horse- or mule-drawn wagon was the general practice until the 1920s. In John Herbert Quick's *The Hawkeye* (1923), Fremont McConkey described the process during the late 1870s:

> Forget the sky, the clouds, the blood drawn by rosebrier or the sharp tips of the kernels of the "hackberry" ears; forget everything but the economy of movement, the making of every second count. Make sure that you do not fail to tear the ear from the stalk and throw it into the wagon by a single movement of the muscles; see to it that

when the right hand returns from the throw, the body has moved forward if necessary to another proper position, and that the left hand has seized another ear and holds it ready for the husking peg; and do not fail to remember that if you husk your hundred bushels in a day, the steady "clump, clump, clump'" against the throw-board must continue hour after hour, even while the trained horses are making the turn at the end of the field.

The settlement era was past when mechanical corn pickers became common in the Middle West during the 1920s.

Mechanization was not the only factor contributing to the efficiency of agricultural production west of the Mississippi during the nineteenth century. The fertility of western soils, improvement of hand skills in tasks such as corn picking, and the tendency of farmers to specialize also enhanced production. But the decline, for example, in the number of work hours expended per hundred bushels in the production of wheat between 1840 and 1900—from 233 to 108 hours—and in the production of corn—from 276 to 135—reflected the use of more sophisticated machinery. By the latter date also, steam, the electric generator, and gasoline engines had begun supplying the energy hitherto provided by Buck and Bright, Fan and Pomp, and Sam and Jenny—the oxen, horse, and mule teams that powered animal-drawn farm machinery.

Climatic Adaptation

The pioneer farmer of the Genesee Valley chopped his farm from a mixed deciduous forest, extending the ramparts of stump and rail by a few acres each year. His son or nephew in central Illinois came to understand the fertility of the tallgrass prairies but preferred a farmstead amid the trees along streams or in the prairie groves, where he found timber for firewood, rails, and lumber. If he moved into the prairie interiors, he might buy a woodlot beside a stream. A generation or two later, settlers on the central or high plains drove their teams as far as forty miles to cut wood. But by this time the railroads were aiding farm making by transporting lumber, milled from logs originating in the pineries of the Great Lakes states—raw material for grassland houses, barns, and fences.

Other western pioneers experienced drastic revisions of their childhood experiences. In the Great Basin of the Mormons, mountainsides to the east were forested, mountain crests glistened white for much of the year, and springtime streams ran full with snowmelt. But the Saints discovered that their accustomed crops of the Mississippi Valley needed supplemental moisture or would fail in all but the most unusual years. Those pioneers who pressed into the coastal regions of upper Washington experienced annual precipitation of seventy inches or more—what the Kansas farmer might expect in several years. In the Central Valley of California, the situation seemed even stranger. One historian imagined the newcomer's first reactions: "The absence of summer rains seemed to prove that the valley was unfit for agricultural purposes. How could crops be raised where there was only a wet and a dry season? How could one farm where the grass turned green in the winter and died in the summer?"

For the farmer who left the Mississippi Valley, a transformation from forest man to grassland man was necessary. The Texan Walter P. Webb dramatized this story: "The whole technique of pioneering and the ways of living which had become habitual with the people and had proved so effective as to become standardized broke down completely when carried from the Eastern Woodland region into the Great Plains." Webb argued that only after waiting from 1825 to 1860 for industrial America to develop such inventions as the six-shooter, barbed wire, and the windmill did pioneer farmers establish themselves beyond the ninety-eighth meridian in the plains country.

No demography demonstrates Webb's claim. The westward march did not stall at the central grassland until the army was equipped with six-shooters and a new technology of settlement adopted. During the 1850s, settlement was incomplete in the states adjacent to the Mississippi. In that decade, preparations for opening the lands beyond the Missouri began—midwestern Indian tribes were moved, formal relations with the Plains Indians were initiated, and territorial governments were established west of Iowa and Missouri. Still, in part, Webb spoke the truth. The pioneer farmers adapted to subhumid environments as they moved westward. Forest man, however, first accepted the challenge of becoming Webb's "new man" on the bluestem prairies of the "prairie triangle," that lazy V of grassland, striped with wooded watercourses, that flares from its apex on the Wabash prairies through northern and central Illinois to include much of southern Wisconsin, more of Minnesota and Missouri, and all of Iowa before merging into the plains proper.

The problem of aridity was manifest in various ways, including home construction. The dominant feature of any new farmstead was the house. The first dwelling of the pioneer was typically the log cabin, which settlers in the grasslands preferred. During the first months of settlement, however, some families lived in lean-tos, or even canvas-topped carts or wagon boxes. Once families could build, cultural influences became apparent, such as the differences between the Yankee and the southern tides of settlement. The well-built, southern-style log cabin had a breezeway through the center. Henry Ise took his bride, Rosie, to a simpler structure near the ninety-ninth meridian. But the dwellings that Rosie saw in the last stages of the journey were mostly dugouts, scooped from the sides of draws or creeks, with front walls of sod, though there were some frame or stone buildings. Elsewhere on the plains, the genuine sod house was common, with walls and usually the roof constructed from rectangles of tough, matted sod.

If many settlers used soddies, few lived in them for long. As the Ises prospered and the family grew, they added a wing to their cabin and built a new house of local stone. More commonly, as railroad lines laced the postbellum West, settlers obtained scantlings, planks, and boards to build claim shanties or the second house that denoted improved circumstances. The new houses were "sawed" rather than "sod" dwellings, one historian notes. When Elinore Plaisted's mother, Em, took her children to the Dakota wheat country late in the century, her husband proudly drove them to a two-story, wooden, framed house where a few years earlier there had been only waving grass. Less-affluent folk lived in wooden shacks, sometimes with an additional coating of tar paper nailed to the board walls, slight shelter against blizzards. Within, the farm wife might stoke her stove with buffalo chips, twisted hay, or stalks of sunflowers or other woody plants if creek-bed wood or coal was unavailable.

On washdays, Em Plaisted carried water from a nearby slough to fill her tubs, but few farms could continue without a good well. Under much of the trans-Mississippi West lay aquifers, but the depth of the water table varied. Sometimes the well-digging

The idealized agrarian image of Currier & Ives' "western farmer's home" reflected eastern sensibilities, not western reality. In the trans-Mississippi West, settlers such as this young Nebraska mother or these African-American homesteaders often started out in simple temporary structures. But dugout homes and claim shanties were not easily incorporated into the popular images that romanticized life on the western farmers' frontier.

Currier & Ives, publishers. The Western Farmers Home. *Chromolithograph, 1871. The Harry T. Peters Collection (#56.300.1448), Museum of the City of New York.*

Unidentified photographer. Our Home (near McCook, Nebraska). *Photograph, 1890. Nebraska State Historical Society, Lincoln.*

A. P. Swearingen (?–1931). Homestead of a Family near Guthrie, Oklahoma Territory. *Photograph, ca. 1889. Western History Collections, University of Oklahoma Library, Norman.*

settler might reach water in less than thirty feet; other times he labored with pick and shovel to greater depths, running the risk that the windlass rope might break or that he might be overcome by well gas.

Loessial in origin and fortified with humus, grassland soils were highly productive if adequate moisture was available. But since the rainfall diminished in amount and increased in variability meridian by meridian, settlers obtained lower average yields per acre as they moved farther west and were compelled to cultivate larger units. The uncertainties of plains country weather also dictated that work be done when conditions were favorable. Larger and stronger farm machinery, illustrated by two and three bottom plows and wider harrows, provided a partial solution to this problem. The trend culminated in the big hitches in which several sturdy teams were combined to pull massive arrays of tillage machinery and in the introduction of the tractor on the high plains wheat frontier of the early twentieth century.

In their eagerness to produce, pioneer farmers managed to raise a half crop of corn on fresh breaking by hacking holes for the seed in the turned sod. During the 1880s, settlers in the Dakotas found that flax grew well as a first-year crop. Beyond the line of the Missouri, however, was a belt of territory where corn thrived during the moist years but where wheat was more dependable in dry periods. When the spellbinding Populist orator Mary Elizabeth Lease exhorted farmers of this region to "grow less corn and raise more hell," she was at least half right on the basis of agronomic principles. During the 1870s and early 1880s, farmers in "The Golden Belt" of central Kansas learned that the hard, red winter wheat that Mennonite settlers had brought from the Russian plains was their most dependable cash crop. Improved milling techniques expanded the market for this grain, which came to dominate a winter wheat region on the central plains. To the north, farmers discovered that spring wheat was more satisfactory. During the dry years of the late nineteenth century, farmers on the high plains found that in their area, sorghums provided a drought-resistant crop.

There were other illustrations of climatic adaptation in the mechanization process. To some Kansas and Nebraska farmers, the droughts of the late nineteenth century revealed the beneficial effects of using lister drills, which allowed the planting of wheat in trenches that ran at right angles to the direction of the prevailing winds. Many plains country farmers adopted the grain header, which cut the small grains just below the seed heads and elevated them into an accompanying wagon for transport to a threshing machine. Thus, they took advantage of the fact that the moisture content of the harvested grain was low and did not need to dry in the shock.

As native timber was consumed, pioneer farmers sought alternatives to rail fences. Herd laws, restricting the stock owner's right to allow his animals to roam at will, were only a partial solution. The prickly Osage orange tree (bois d'arc) provided a popular substitute for fences. If planted thickly and pruned properly, it made a formidable hedge. During the 1850s and 1860s, farmers planted miles of hedge throughout the Middle West but later adopted the more effective barbed wire that northern Illinois inventors had developed. Along with less-punitive wire-mesh fences, barbed wire solved the grassland farmer's fencing problem, but in a way that required an outlay of cash rather than labor.

Real estate agents, officers of land-grant railroads, state officials, and immigration agents assured the farmers who moved into the plains country during the 1870s and 1880s that "rain followed the plow." During some years of those decades this appeared to be true. But the late 1880s and the early 1890s revealed the cruel variability of the grassland climate. Hardy Webster Campbell's gospel of dryland farming sustained the thronging homesteaders after 1900. Publicized by the railroads during the first decade of the twentieth century, the Campbell system dictated that fields be fallowed while moisture accumulated in packed undersoil, topped with a dust mulch. Dubbed "scientific farming," at the urging of railroad executives, dry farming was not complete nonsense. Properly managed, fallowing conserved moisture, but Campbell's system could not withstand a succession of dry years. After 1900, settlers attempted to build a dry-farming empire on the northern high plains served by the Great Northern and the Northern Pacific railroads. From 1917 onward, they suffered recurrent droughts, and many failed, bitterly repeating the aphorism "Dry farming works best in wet years."

Yet, some western farmers grew wheat successfully in areas of low rainfall, unaided by either irrigation or the charlatan rainmakers who preyed on gullible husbandmen during the 1890s. During California's transition from ranching to a varied commercial agriculture, both operators with large mechanized operations and small-scale farmers grew bumper wheat crops on a dryland basis in the Central Valley. After 1900, the farmers of central Washington successfully grew wheat in a region where rainfall was less than twelve inches per year. The timing of the precipitation explains such successes. Although the mountain ranges of the West drained eastward-moving cloud masses and created tributary areas of low rainfall, they also accumulated magnificent snowpacks that created rushing rivers in the spring and early summer. Irrigation, thought visionaries, might create a western oasis. Looking across the heat-shimmering reaches of their kingdom, the Mormons had little choice; if the faithful were to be gathered and to survive, man needed to assist the heavens. In 1847, Mormon farmers in the Salt Lake Valley diverted water to their crops from City Creek. Although some initially tried to harvest crops without irrigation, the Saints built their first highline canal in 1850.

In Deseret, community structure was also church structure, simplifying the mobilization of community effort essential to building an irrigation system. Church officers supervised the construction of the stream diversions and canals and apportioned water quotas. The Saints were, however, human. One pioneer Mormon lurked in the dark near the ditch that provided water for his acres, rock in hand, poised to repulse any neighbor from down the valley who might try to drop the headgate before watering was completed. For a generation and more, Utahns advised residents in other water-scarce regions of the West. There was much to learn about laying out canal systems, constructing impoundments and gates, caring for particular crops, and distributing water evenly. But Utah's irrigation system was a relatively simple one with few elaborate reservoirs or lengthy canals.

In the pursuit of precious minerals, the miners of western regions used water in great quantities. Their activities encouraged the development of agriculture, as onetime farmers realized that eggs at fifty cents apiece and meat and flour at equivalent prices were as rewarding as flakes of gold. With the water rules of the miners in mind, western irrigationists overturned centuries of European and eastern precedent, enunciating a doctrine of prior appropriation in place of riparian rights. The first user was entitled to the amount taken prior to the arrival of others, rather than sharing a right in common with adjacent users and being obligated to return diverted water to streams. During the 1870s, the lawmakers of Colorado and other western states wrote prior appropriation into constitutional and statutory law, although elements of riparian rights lingered, particularly in California.

John Wesley Powell, the intrepid runner of the Colorado canyons and director of the U.S. Geological Survey, was the first government scientist to understand fully the climatic challenges of the West. At the close of the 1870s, he suggested that federal land-disposal laws be revamped—the irrigation farmer needed less than a quarter section to make a good living, whereas the stockman needed more. In the summer of 1889, he told the North Dakota Constitutional Convention, "One year with another, you need a little more [rainfall] than you get." After western developers and politicians drove Powell from the Geological Survey because of his conservative approach to irrigation issues, he continued to perfect his ideas for the development of the West's irrigable lands under a system of self-governing hydrographic basins. As for promoters who dreamed of irrigation as a quick fix, he wrote: "Terpsichorean, sacrificial, and fiducial agencies fail to change the desert into the garden, or transform the flood-storm into a refreshing shower. Years of drought and famine come and years of flood and famine come, and the climate is not changed with dance, libation or prayer." Still, western community builders were convinced that reclamation could help them build populous states. In response, the federal government passed the Carey Act of 1894, providing for the transfer of lands to western states for irrigation purposes. The law was ineffectual.

For the first time in 1890, the federal census takers noted irrigation farmers. They found 54,136 in sixteen western states and territories, one-quarter of them in California. Despite such figures and the success of private developments like the Greeley Colony in Colorado, private or state efforts to develop irrigation were marred by the failures of optimistic entrepreneurs and by land speculators who monopolized reservoir sites or irrigable land. Obviously, argued westerners, the federal government should play a larger role. When Congress passed the National Reclamation Act of 1902, creating the Bureau of Reclamation, the western settler had a new option—homesteading on reclamation developments, as in Arizona's Salt River Project or the Truckee-Carson district of Nevada. In reclamation districts, settlers paid water-user fees that were expected to return the project costs to a revolving reclamation fund from which other developments might be funded. Even federal homestead land was never free, given the farm-making costs involved. Land was certainly not free in the early reclamation projects. By 1923, there were 34,276 farms on twenty-eight western reclamation districts, and in only one district had the settlers met all of their payments.

Commercialization

We can look to the American past and imagine the subsistence farmer, a sturdy fellow living on an isolated farm from which he and his family satisfied all their needs. This individual never existed. But the colonial farmer resembled him more than did the agriculturist of 1850, and the colonial frontier farmers were much more subsistence-oriented than were the farmers of the older settlements adjacent to the markets of colonial ports. In contrast to the self-sufficient husbandman, we can also visualize the commercial farmer, who concentrated on producing the crops that had the greatest market value and who purchased all other necessities.

By the early nineteenth century, American farmers had moved significantly toward the commercial end of the continuum between subsistence and commercial farmers. But even where capitalism had most influenced agricultural production—on the slave plantation—field crops were grown, gardens were tended, and some clothing was made at home. Before the 1820s, in the West, homespun was still common, buckskin was not unknown, and farmers cultivated numerous crops and raised various animals and fowl. Beginning in the 1820s, the transportation system of the United States was revolutionized, expanding the markets for farm produce and making a broad range of manufactured articles generally available. Although nineteenth-century depressions left a residue of failed or financially embarrassed farmers in the less-established communities of the West, agriculturists in general seized market opportunities provided by the expanding economy. In 1863, California's most eminent authority on agriculture reported, "The farmers generally are anxious to make as much money as possible, and as soon as possible." When the railroad vitalized the economy of the hitherto isolated Cache Valley community in Utah, a settler reported, "The jingle of coins was stimulating." Through the last forty years of the nineteenth century, farmers in many western townships or counties supported the purchase of railroad bonds by their local governments in order to amplify that stimulating jingle.

Some historians believe that the early nineteenth century was an era of small-scale farms tilled by hardy republicans who lived a life of community marked by trading of labor and by barter until a subversive capitalism dragged them unwillingly into the marketplace. Trading butter and eggs and other farm products for store goods and bartering labor, goods, and services within the agricultural community *was* common during the early nineteenth century and continued into the twentieth century; but accounting was usually done in monetary units. Whether it was wheat, as on many frontiers, or oats in the Walla Walla Valley, or flax in the Dakotas, the pioneers sought a cash crop that produced a maximum return; they were perennially short of capital and forced to invest much labor in farm improvements from which benefits were derived only in the long run. The United States was born capitalist, and the attendant values did not change, though transformations in transportation, industry, and marketing substantially altered the pioneering process during the nineteenth century. And as farmers learned the peculiarities of their areas and the most remunerative combinations of crops, livestock, capital, and labor—sometimes involving practices that observers called wasteful or exploitive—agricultural regions and subregions emerged.

American institutions encouraged the frontier farmer to think in terms of dollars and cents. The Founding Fathers had established a federal land system that assumed the existence of a market economy. When squatters poured into the Black Hawk Purchase of eastern Iowa during the 1830s, they established claim clubs and purchased and sold claims. They understood also that they must pay the federal government for their claims in money. At the federal land auctions in Iowa, eastern capitalists or their agents made loans to them at 50 percent or more interest. Thus, commerce in land, down payments, and interest charges made even squatters on the Iowa prairie think in terms of markets and cash crops. Once settlers had title to their lands, there were taxes to pay, and western counties did not take payment in kind, although road levies were typically worked off. Before the railroads, some firstcomers were far in advance of organized markets. A few served military posts or Indian agencies. Others satisfied their needs for cash, for iron products, for salt, and for "luxuries" like coffee or cane sugar by selling surplus products to new settlers, by selling livestock to traveling drovers, or by transporting wagonloads of wheat or oats to distant market points.

What did it cost to establish a farm during the nineteenth century? The economist Clarence Danhof estimated the costs of developing a 40-acre farm on the midwestern frontier during the 1850s as "$50-$400 for land, $60–800 for breaking the sod or clearing woodland, $112–320 or more for fencing, $100 for implements, $150–200 for livestock, $40-$80 for the first year's seed, and $25-$450 for housing." On the average, Danhof believed, the midwestern farmer of this era needed about $1,000. Labor shortages during the Civil War stimulated the mechanization process. In 1862, a farm editor published a list of equipment appropriate to a 150-acre holding; the value of the items amounted to $968.

Farmers seldom outfitted themselves completely at one time; some brought secondhand machinery, and others shared the cost of reapers or other more expensive machines with relatives or neighbors. The owners of custom breaking plows did a thriving business, and commercial threshers were a feature of rural life until the 1940s. But the average value of machinery on farms in Johnson County, Iowa, was four times greater in 1890 in constant dollars than it had been in 1860, and in the Ise family's Osborne County, Kansas, the average investment in machinery per farm increased two and one-half times between 1870 and 1890. Some settlers, however, did not initially own draft animals and hoped to work off the claim and thus accumulate farming equipment and stock. Others deferred investment in land by becoming tenants. As mechanization proceeded, the agents of implement manufacturers sold machinery on short-term credit, taking the farmer's note with a chattel mortgage as security.

Throughout the period of our study, the family farmer typified the rural community of the West. This does not mean that all western farmers had equal resources or status. Older farmers had had more time to accumulate property than had younger farmers. Luck, inheritance, business skills, education, good or ill health, and the number of family members all might be reflected in an individual's property holdings, as were the land-disposal systems, land-use patterns, and regional economic development in general. The most common size of farm in Iowa in 1860 was fifty to one hundred acres; in Kansas at that census date the typical holding was twenty to fifty acres; and in California the most common farm was one hundred to five hundred acres. In that year, the census reported seventy-six Iowa farmers who had holdings of five hundred or more acres, with eight such farmers listed in Kansas and eight hundred in California.

Californians developed an agriculture characterized by both small irrigated holdings under intensive cultivation and huge ranches and grain farms, but they were not alone in developing spectacular farm operations. During the 1870s, investors in the Northern Pacific Railroad Company exchanged company bonds on favorable terms for acreage in

In the Guthrie, Oklahoma, land rush of 1889, as in most other federal land sales, those who profited most were often not the actual settlers but the entrepreneurs—like these lawyers—who serviced the settlers' needs.

C. P. Rich. Guthrie, Oklahoma Territory, April 22, 1889, Open Air Law Offices. Photograph, 1889. Western History Collections, University of Oklahoma Library, Norman.

the railroad's land grant in the Red River Valley of the north, and they developed bonanza grain farms on these holdings. Oliver Dalyrymple managed a seven-thousand-acre wheat operation there in 1877. He used "eighty horses, twenty-six breaking plows, forty cross plows, twenty-one seeders, sixty harrows," and harvesting equipment in proportion. But over time the owners of the bonanza farms found it worthwhile to sell out to small farmers.

When settlers first crossed the Mississippi, men of capital had long been investing in raw western lands, expecting to earn large returns as the country developed. By the mid-nineteenth century, well-informed capitalists knew that investments in western mortgages and tax titles were also remunerative. Western lawyers, bankers, and real estate men eagerly served as western agents of such investors. As the tide of settlement flowed into the West after the Civil War, a less visible stream of capital accompanied it. Increasingly in the western county-seat towns and supply centers, loan agents, sometimes also lawyers or real estate men, offered funds to settlers who wished to preempt land, take advantage of the commutation clause of the Homestead Act, or buy supplies, equipment, or livestock. Mortgage agents recruited savings from eastern banks and insurance companies as well as from professionals and small businessmen who were eager to double or triple the 5 or 6 percent paid by eastern savings institutions. Successful western loan men incorporated their businesses, set up branch offices in New York or abroad, offered "guaranteed" mortgages for sale, and began to sell debentures against mortgage paper. Such companies helped finance the "Great Dakota Land Boom" of the 1880s and the flow of farmers into other western states and territories during the same period.

Entrapped in the collapse of the boom, many western settlers failed to meet their mortgage interest or capital payments and abandoned their land. Caught between penniless borrowers and importunate lenders, the mortgage companies foreclosed. But the corporations could not resell the land, and most of them failed also. There had been earlier "wring-outs" in new settlement areas, but none so devastating as that of the late nineteenth century. Populist orators castigated mortgage men, along with railroad companies and land monopolists, for being responsible for the misery of the western farmer during the early 1890s. When Congress passed the Federal Farm Loan Act of 1916, memories of those years of discontent inspired advocates.

On every western agricultural frontier, the commercial production of farmers stimulated the development of an urban superstructure. The villages, towns, and cities of the West provided skills, services, capital, machinery, markets—or gateways to markets—and a good deal of political leadership for rural America. In return, the food, feed, and fiber surpluses of the farmers and their needs for manufactured goods, equipment, and supplies invigorated western trade centers. Above the local level, an urban hierarchy of subregional, regional, and national entrepôts and manufacturing centers developed, sustained by the movement and processing of agricultural products and the needs of hinterlands for manufactured goods, supplies, and services.

Glance at a listing of American millionaires compiled in 1892. In Moline, Illinois, Charles H. Deere controlled the fortune amassed by his father in the plow business. Nearby in Quincy, Edward Wells prospered by packing midwestern hogs; in Chicago, three members of the Armour family became rich in the same business. Thomas Lynch was a millionaire distiller, and Cyrus H. McCormick made millions from the sale of patented mowers and reapers. In Minneapolis-St. Paul, one finds the Pillsburys, enriched by western wheat. Frederick Weyerhaeuser provided thousands of western farmers with milled lumber, and James J. Hill's railroads served the farmers of the northern plains and Pacific Northwest. In St. Louis, D. R. Frances attributed his wealth to dealing in grain options, and Adolphus Busch used western grains to brew "fine beer." In San Francisco, L. L. Baker prospered in the agricultural machinery business, and the millionaire Henry Pierce was a grain dealer. These men exemplify urban individuals or firms that accumulated vast assets during the agricultural settlement of the trans-Mississippi West. Other businessmen derived part of their substantial wealth from rural land speculation. William Jennings Bryan echoed the belief of millions of rural westerners when, at the convention of the Democratic party in 1896, he thundered, "The great cities rest upon our broad and fertile prairies. Burn down your cities and leave our farms, and your cities will spring up again as if by magic; but destroy our farms and the grass will grow in the streets of every city in the country."

Cultural Adaptation

Did cultural groups adapt similarly to the economic challenges of agriculture while they created a vast social mosaic in the West? Did the eagerness of some of these groups to develop commercial agriculture assist their adjustments to western conditions, or did cultural predispositions sometimes obscure economic opportunities? We have seen that two powerful American subcultures were involved—northeastern Yankee and upland southern. Studying early-nineteenth-century regional cultures in Indiana in areas that would soon be sending populations westward, Richard L. Power contrasted hay-gathering, orchard-planting, dairy-oriented, energetic Yankee farmers with corn-growing and hog-raising southern upland or Hoosier agriculturists, who lacked the sense that leisure was sinful. The one ate white bread and chicken "fixens"; the other subsisted on corn bread and "common doins." One used Virginia rail fences; the other preferred posts and straight boards. Yankee and Hoosier farmers even laid out their farmsteads differently. To the cultural options that settlers from such backgrounds brought across the Mississippi, the foreign born added the preferences and practices that they had known. In facing problems, people first consider accustomed solutions—so it was in the trans-Mississippi West.

Cultural proclivity, however, was modified by western realities. Swedish settlers from Upper Dalarna might prefer to make barley their major small-grain crop in Isanti County, Minnesota, as at home in Sweden. But when the local market and natural environment suggested that wheat and oats were more profitable, the immigrants accepted the cue. Had they followed their cultural inclinations, Russian Germans in eastern Nebraska might have concentrated on the small grains of the Russian plains, but a major part of their acreage was soon in Indian corn. The agricultural patterns of ethnic groups did sometimes appear to differ from those of nearby American-born pioneers. These differences tended to disappear in the first generation of settlement. Still, some preferences in farm management continued into the second generation. And sometimes, practices that had been dysfunctional during settlement reappeared. German-Russian settlers in eastern Nebraska were once more growing their homeland crops, flax and rye, during the early 1890s, illustrating cultural rebound. Another adaptation pattern involved the transfer of crops or farming practices from the homeland without any perceptible break in continuity, such as when Mennonites continued to emphasize the wheat crop in the central grasslands.

The manuscript censuses of the late nineteenth century frequently show that ethnic groups differed from colonial-stock Americans in their choice of combinations of crops and livestock. But differences in age of farm operators, in the degree of farm development, in access to capital, in the soils that the groups farmed, in the availability of labor, in the distances to markets, and perhaps in other factors must be considered in such comparisons, and historians have not always done so. Nor did members of particular national ethnic groups invariably behave in the same way. That cultural background might serve as either cue or brake in the immigrant's adaptation to American practice, we cannot doubt. We are tempted to conclude that ethnic differences were less noticeable in making a living than were contrasts in household economy, food preference, work routine, language, religion, neighboring, and family values. Some members of ethnic groups were more strongly committed to passing their farms to the next generation and establishing family members in proximity than were those of Yankee or southern upland descent. Historians have particularly related such behavior to the German settler, but none of the numerous Ise children stayed on the lands painfully accumulated by Henry and Rosie, both impeccably German in origin.

Sometimes the immigrant farmers brought much more to their new country than labor and the will to succeed. The Mennonites' contribution of hard winter wheat is the best known of such legacies. The alfalfa seed that Wendelin Grimm brought from Bavaria was crucial to the later development of American agriculture. Agoston Haraszthy's importations of European vine cuttings made Sonoma County, California, the center of the West Coast wine industry. Thus, immigrant settlers broadened the options open to American farmers, although sometimes their contributions were controversial. When hundreds of industrious Chinese truck gardeners purchased or leased small holdings in California during the 1850s, supplying countrymen, miners, and urban dwellers with vegetables, neighbors criticized their use of night soil in fertilization and urine in pest control as dangerous to the public health and offensive to the nostrils.

Family Ventures

Critics maintain that historians of agricultural settlement have accentuated production to the neglect of cultural values and have emphasized the role of the male head of the farm household while ignoring the farm wife. Such criticism is justified, although the earlier emphases are understandable—if settlers failed to make a living, all else failed as well. But the farm frontier was a family frontier, even though sex ratios were sometimes skewed by the presence of large numbers of bachelors and men improving claims before they brought out families. On the other hand, the censuses of the nineteenth century show that farm households headed by women were present in some numbers, and it is estimated that women represented 10 to 15 percent of the homesteaders in some states during the early twentieth century.

After losing her husband in a railroad accident, Elinore Pruitt moved with her small daughter to Denver, where Elinore worked as a domestic. Hoping to become a homesteader, she advertised her availability as a housekeeper in a region where government land was available. Thus, in 1909, she moved to the ranch of Clyde Stewart near Burnt River in southwestern Wyoming. Soon Stewart proposed marriage, and Elinore accepted.

Elinore Pruitt Stewart filed her homestead claim on land adjacent to her husband's holding, allowing them to build her log cabin as an extension of the Stewart home. Meanwhile, she milked cows, tended poultry and pigs, gardened, cooked, put up preserves, and made clothes for herself and her daughter. She had other children, and she wrote, in 1912, that she wanted "a great many things" that she lacked, but she was neither discontented nor forgetful of her many blessings:

> I have my home among the blue mountains, my healthy, well-formed children, my clean, honest husband, my kind gentle milk cows, my garden which I make myself. I have loads and loads of flowers which I tend. There are lots of chickens, turkeys, and pigs which are my own special care. I have some slow old gentle horses and an old wagon. I can load up the kiddies and go where I please any time. I have the best, kindest neighbors.

With real pleasure, Elinore Stewart proved that she knew how to operate the hay mower.

Frontier wives and mothers did what most wives and mothers were doing elsewhere in America; they tried to provide "proper" homes and give their children a good upbringing. When Anne E. Bingham, a seminary-trained former schoolteacher, journeyed west with her husband in 1869 to a Kansas farm, a woman's suffrage worker in Leavenworth asked for her views on women and the vote. She responded that "voting had better be left to the men, for a woman's place was in the home." Many farm wives of the time would probably have agreed. Still, sixteen of the seventeen states in which women already had the vote before passage of the Nineteenth Amendment were western states. If most of the leaders in winning woman's suffrage were urbanites, rural women had swelled their battalions.

Farms on the frontier were family enterprises. The wife cleaned, cooked, prepared meals, washed dishes and clothes, and mended. At threshing or hog-slaughtering time she fed the extra men. She preserved food—from wild plums to headcheese. During the early nineteenth century, small flocks of sheep were usual, and carding, spinning, and the knitting of socks, mittens, and other apparel were common female tasks. Some women owned looms. Home manufactures were waning by the 1850s, but at this time the treadle sewing machine became available, and many farm women found it indispensable. Although mechanization rapidly changed the character of external farm work after 1850, America's industrialization did less for the farm wife than for her husband. True, the cookstove replaced the fireplace, and the sewing machine was a boon, but the washing machine of the late nineteenth century was a crude device, and few frontier women had running water or an indoor toilet.

The farm woman's work did not stop when she crossed the threshold of her house. Almost certainly, she worked in the garden, she sometimes cared for the barnyard fowl, and she often milked and churned the cream into butter. The dribble of money or store credit from sales of eggs and butter sometimes made the difference between success and failure in the new settlements. Women helped with the binding and shocking of grain in prebinder days and often drove the team or "built the load" at haying time or grain harvest.

In matters of domestic economy there were probably differences depending not only on the material and cultural circumstances but also on the personal inclinations of the women. Some pioneering women found the landscape hostile and the outdoor tasks wearing; others enjoyed the companionship involved in such labor and thrilled to the sights, sounds, and smells of the new land. On large, prosperous farms, the farm wife might be supplied with hired help and never feel the need to venture beyond the household perimeters in her work. Within some cultural groups, outdoor work was an accustomed part of the woman's heritage. On the other hand, Anne Bingham wrote: "My work . . . would have been much harder if I had not had the very best kind of a good husband. Before he went to work morning and noon he saw to it that there was wood and water in the house. I never did any milking and never took care of the poultry, and seldom did the churning. Many women I knew did all these things besides their own housework."

To merely contrast the roles of husband and wife is to oversimplify the social contours of farm life. A demographic analysis of the frontier areas during the years 1800–1840 showed that children constituted at least half of the household in 72 percent of northern frontier households and 83 percent on the southern frontiers. Having "suffered reverses," the Indiana carpenter William Dorsey established a preemption

The farm frontier was a family frontier, where women and children performed essential labor. In addition to producing most of the foods and household goods consumed within the home, women might assist with the care of animals and the planting and harvesting of crops while children performed domestic chores. Their labor would help generate much-needed cash, since the added income brought in from the sale of eggs and dairy products could be critical to a small farm's success.

Unidentified photographer. Farm Women at Work. *Photograph, date unknown. The Denver Public Library, Western History Department, Denver, Colorado.*

Solomon Butcher (1856–1927). Nebraska Lassie (Custer County, Nebraska). *Photograph, date unknown. Solomon D. Butcher Collection, Nebraska State Historical Society, Lincoln.*

claim on the Little Nemaha River in Nebraska in 1857. So lively was the cabin, wrote his diarist daughter Mollie, and so recurrent the demands for hospitality from visitors and the older daughters' beaus that Mother Dorsey often "took the babies and fled to her retreat in the woods . . . to gain her equilibrium." The frontier farm family is best understood when viewed in the context of family interaction and changing family goals as well as from the standpoint of gender polarities.

The full history of American farm labor is unwritten. We know that there were kin and neighborhood work rings, that farmers sometimes hired help at harvest and threshing time, and that there were full-time laborers on large holdings. We also believe that the farmer and his family provided most of the labor on frontier farms. Western children joined the work force at an early age. Seven- or eight-year-old boys could herd livestock, drop corn into waiting hills, and pick potato bugs from infested vines. Increasingly thereafter they shared in farm tasks in the field and at the farmstead. In larger families, boys might hire out to neighbors, with the wages sometimes destined for family coffers. Within the house, the farm wife might move from the position of domestic worker to manager, over daughters who minded younger siblings, learned to cook and sew at an early age, and worked outdoors when needed. On the Little Nemaha it was Mollie, or her sixteen-year-old sister, who milked the cow, rather than their mother, and Mollie also considered herself the chief cook.

One of Rosie's sons wrote a sensitive account, *Sod and Stubble*, of the Ise family homestead and family life on the plains frontier. He depicts the dangers faced by the pioneers: family privations, tragedies, comedy, and victory; the first-born who died and the crippled child among the healthy ones. He writes of the church picnics, the celebration when the mortgage was paid off, the relationships of neighboring and community, the road routing that sparked local conflict, the cultural heterogeneity (leavened with one Democrat), the disdain for "little Dutchies," and the movers and the stayers. In time, the railroad came, and rural-urban differences sharpened. Meanwhile, the Ises developed their farm through times of good returns and periods of drought, grasshoppers, or low prices, slowly accumulating equipment and additional land. Rosie was the dominant force in the Ise family, but the history of the Ise farm is a family story.

Pioneers in the trans-Mississippi West found the first years to be the most difficult. There were exceptions; some came to the new land with ample resources, strapping sons, hired help, strong teams, implements and machines, and the funds with which to buy sufficient land and supplies to bridge the gap before tilled fields began to produce. But for most, the scarcities, hardships, and dangers of pioneering weighed heavily. Drought, grasshoppers, prairie fires, hailstorms, the wheat-attacking Hessian fly, and even jackrabbits on the high-desert homesteads of the twentieth century could turn a year of hope into one of disillusion, or famine. And there were other dangers: poisonous snakes, rabid animals, wandering Longhorns that could tumble through a dugout's sod roof, runaway teams, well-digging accidents, and the errant ax or pitchfork. Medical practice was rudimentary. "Out here," wrote Mrs. Stewart, "we have to dope ourselves." Malaria was common on the nineteenth-century frontier and tetanus always a threat. Other diseases, later rendered minor by vaccine or antibiotic, shattered frontier farm families.

We can make too much of the isolation faced by members of the farm family. The native born were children of an open-country, rural culture and were unused to living in each other's pockets. Remembering a more densely settled countryside, the foreign born sometimes found the absence of close neighbors or the wind of the high plains distressing, even psychologically unsettling. But most pioneer families soon had neighbors, sometimes more than they would have preferred, and among these neighbors almost invariably were relatives, former neighbors, or members of the same religious persuasion. Farm wives visited, quilted, and were active in church activities. Still, Anne Bingham wrote in retrospect of their farm near Junction City, Kansas: "In all the years spent there we never could see a neighbor's light in the evening. I did wish so much we could, to relieve the aloneness."

In the last stage of their epic trek to Oregon in 1843, the Applegate families lost young Warren and Edward in the turbulent waters of the Columbia. In contrast to such tragedy, Herbert Quick's memorable character "Cow" Vandemark wrote: "The prairies took me, an ignorant, orphaned canal hand, and made me something much better. . . . The best prayer I can utter now is that it may do as well with my children and grandchildren." On the other hand, the year 1888 was one of drought in Kansas, and in the fall, the wagons of the "defeated legion" began to roll eastward past the Ise homestead, "grizzled, dejected, and surly men; sick, tired and hopeless women," along with children often unaware of the family tragedy of which they were a part. Given shelter overnight, some left lice, bedbugs, and pools of tobacco juice behind; others tried to steal chickens or pigs. The Ises, therefore, reluctantly agreed when the Hutson family asked for shelter for the sick woman traveling with them. The Hutsons proved, however, to be cultivated people. The sick traveler had lost her husband in an Indian raid in Decatur County, where Hutson had, in two years, lost all of his money. The family was returning to Iowa to begin again. Farmers who enjoyed success comparable to that of "Cow" Vandemark are well represented in the county histories and old settlers' accounts, but such publications seldom tell the stories of victims like Warren Applegate and the Hutsons. Was the settler's story a tale of ruthless and uncaring conquest over man and nature? Sometimes it was that, but more frequently it was a chronicle of hope, new homes, adaptation, family success, and sometimes, tragedy or failure.

Bibliographic Note

Those wishing to carry their reading or research beyond suggestions here should consult the articles, reviews, and indexes in *Agricultural History*, edited at the Agricultural History Center, University of California/Davis, and published by the University of California Press, Berkeley. During the 1960s and 1970s, the center also published a series of helpful regional bibliographies. Critiques of the recent literature dealing with frontier agriculture are provided by Gilbert C. Fite, "The American West of Farmers and Stockmen," in Michael P. Malone, ed., *Historians and the American West* (Lincoln, 1983), 209–33, and James W. Whitaker, "Agriculture and Livestock Production," in Roger L. Nichols, ed., *American Frontier and Western Issues: A Historiographical Review* (New York, 1986), 51–67. Unfortunately, space limitations require that this note focus on the monographic literature without specific mention of relevant articles in the periodical literature.

During the last generation, a number of scholars have written histories of American agriculture that treat the frontier experience from a variety of viewpoints: John T. Schlebecker, *Whereby We Thrive: A History of American Farming, 1607–1972* (Ames, 1975); John L. Shover, *First Majority, Last Minority: The Transforming of Rural Life in America* (DeKalb, Ill., 1976); Willard W. Cochrane (an agricultural economist), *The Development of American Agriculture: A Historical Analysis* (Minneapolis, 1979); and Walter Ebeling (an entomologist), *The Fruited Plain: The Story of American Agriculture* (Berkeley, 1979). Nor should one ignore William Parker's brilliant essay "Agriculture" in Lance E. Davis et al., *American Economic Growth: An Economist's History of the United States* (New York, 1972), 369–417. Several more narrowly focused surveys of agricultural development or settlement are useful: Fred A. Shannon, *The Farmer's Last Frontier: Agriculture, 1860–1897* (New York, 1945); Paul W. Gates, *The Farmer's Age: Agriculture, 1815–1860* (New York, 1960); and Gilbert C. Fite, *The Farmers' Frontier, 1865–1900* (New York, 1966). More broadly conceived and recently published is Rodman W.

Paul, *The Far West and the Great Plains in Transition, 1859–1900* (New York, 1988), which contains relevant chapters.

A number of regional or subregional studies deal with agricultural settlement in the trans-Mississippi West or special aspects of the subject, although the coverage as a whole is incomplete. Despite its age, conceptual weaknesses, and substantive thinness, Walter P. Webb's *The Great Plains* (Boston, 1931) cannot be ignored by anyone who wishes to comprehend the history of the plains country. Basic to understanding the development of agriculture on the prairies, though by no means comprehensive, is Allan G. Bogue, *From Prairie to Corn Belt: Farming on the Illinois and Iowa Prairies in the Nineteenth Century* (Chicago, 1963). The unique developments in the Red River Valley of the North are covered in Stanley N. Murray, *The Valley Comes of Age: A History of Agriculture in the Valley of the Red River of the North, 1812–1920* (Fargo, 1967), and Herman M. Drache, *The Day of the Bonanza: A History of Bonanza Farming in the Red River Valley of the North* (Fargo, 1964). Robert Ostergren, *A Community Transplanted: The Trans-Atlantic Experience of a Swedish Immigrant Settlement in the Upper Middle West, 1835–1915* (Madison, 1988), is an excellent illustration of current approaches to the settlement experience of immigrant groups. Richard L. Power, *Planting Corn Belt Culture: The Impress of the Upland Southerner and Yankee in the Old Northwest* (Indianapolis, 1953), however, is still a classic introduction to American agricultural subcultures.

One of the most talented of western historians, James C. Malin, made the central grasslands his special interest; of his many contributions, *Winter Wheat in the Golden Belt of Kansas: A Study in Adaption to Subhumid Geographical Environment* (Lawrence, 1944) and *The Grassland of North America: Prolegomena to Its History, with Addenda and Postscript* (1947; reprint, Gloucester, Mass., 1967) are central to the concerns of this chapter. Richard G. Bremer develops some of Malin's methods still further in *Agricultural Change in an Urban Age: The Loup Country of Nebraska, 1910–1970* (Lincoln, 1976). Two fine collections from the Center for Great Plains Studies include various relevant papers: Brian W. Blouet and Frederick C. Luebke, eds., *The Great Plains: Environment and Culture* (Lincoln, 1979), and Frederick C. Luebke, ed., *Ethnicity on the Great Plains* (Lincoln, 1980). Mary W. M. Hargreaves, *Dry Farming in the Northern Great Plains, 1900–1925* (Cambridge, Mass., 1957), ably describes the development of that system of agriculture. Terry G. Jordan, *German Seed in Texan Soil: Immigrant Farmers in Nineteenth-Century Texas* (Austin, 1966), and Richard G. Lowe and Randolph B. Campbell, *Planters and Plain Folk: Agriculture in Antebellum Texas* (Dallas, 1987), provide a good introduction to the Texas end of the plains country spectrum.

Several monographs have been basic to our understanding of Mormon settlement: Leonard Arrington, *Great Basin Kingdom: An Economic History of the Latter-Day Saints, 1830–1900* (Cambridge, Mass., 1958); Lowry Nelson, *The Mormon Village: A Pattern and Technique of Land Settlement* (Salt Lake City, 1952); and Nels Anderson, *Desert Saints: The Mormon Frontier in Utah*, 2d ed. (Chicago, 1966).

Turning to the Pacific Northwest, Donald W. Meinig, *The Columbia Plain: A Historical Geography, 1805–1910* (Seattle, 1968), is extremely useful, as is William A. Bowen. *The Willamette Valley: Migration and Settlement on the Oregon Frontier* (Seattle, 1978). Several recent monographs skillfully develop important themes: James R. Gibson, *Farming the Frontier: The Agricultural Opening of the Oregon Country, 1786–1846* (Seattle, 1985); John Fahey, *The Inland Empire: Unfolding Years, 1879–1929* (Seattle, 1986); and Barbara Allen, *Homesteading the High Desert* (Salt Lake City, 1987). Alexander C. McGregor, *Counting Sheep: From Open Range to Agribusiness on the Columbia Plateau* (Seattle, 1982), describes the transition from pastoralism to wheat raising in interior Washington.

Despite California's later position as one of the nation's major agricultural producers, the agricultural history of the state still has many gaps. Various articles in James H. Shideler, ed., *Agriculture in the Development of the Far West: A Symposium* (Berkeley, 1975), are very helpful. See also Rodman W. Paul, "The Beginnings of Agriculture in California: Innovation *vs.* Continuity," *California Historical Quarterly* 52 (Spring 1973): 16–27. Paul W. Gates, ed.,

California Ranchos and Farms, 1846–1862, Including the Letters of John Quincy Adams Warren ... (Madison, 1967), provides the contemporary observations of an agricultural authority. Since irrigated agriculture is such a large part of the California story, Donald J. Pisani, *From the Family Farm to Agribusiness: The Irrigation Crusade in California and the West, 1850–1931* (Berkeley, 1984), is invaluable.

Donald W. Meinig, *Southwest: Three Peoples in Geographical Change, 1600–1970* (New York, 1971), is a fine, if brief, introduction to the settlement history of the Southwest. Henry C. Dethloff and Irvin M. May, Jr., eds., *Southwestern Agriculture: Pre-Columbian to Modern* (College Station, Tex., 1982), contains some useful articles. Water has been the key to the location of cropland agriculture in the Southwest, and Michael C. Meyer, *Water in the Hispanic Southwest: A Social and Legal History, 1550–1850* (Tucson, 1984), contains much of interest.

Much of the monographic literature cited thus far touches on several of the major themes of this chapter. Something should be said of more specialized treatments. Oscar Handlin et al., *Harvard Guide to American History* (Cambridge, Mass., 1954), 152–61, lists many of the best books of travel and description. Two surveys of regional booming activity are David M. Emmons, *Garden in the Grasslands: Boomer Literature of the Central Great Plains* (Lincoln, 1971), and Jan Blodgett, *Land of Bright Promise: Advertising the Texas Panhandle and South Plains, 1870–1917* (Austin, 1988). Paul W. Gates has dominated scholarly study of the disposal of federal lands. He summarized much of his work in *History of Public Land Law Development* (Washington, D.C., 1968). Two of his many articles are particularly relevant: "The Homestead Act: Free Land Policy in Operation, 1862–1935," in Howard W. Ottoson, ed., *Land Use Policy and Problems in the United States* (Lincoln, 1963), 28–46, and "California's Embattled Settlers," *California Historical Society Quarterly* 41 (June 1962): 99–130. John Opie, *The Law of the Land: Two Hundred Years of American Farmland Policy* (Lincoln, 1987), sets the settlement period into chronological perspective.

Almost ignored until 1960, the role of women in western settlement has attracted many scholars during the last generation. Any sampling should include Sandra L. Myres, *Westering Women and the Frontier Experience, 1800–1915* (Albuquerque, 1982), Glenda Riley, *The Female Frontier: A Comparative View of Women on the Prairie and the Plains* (Lawrence, 1988), and Sarah Deutsch, *No Separate Refuge: Culture, Class, and Gender on an Anglo-Hispanic Frontier in the American Southwest, 1880–1940* (New York, 1987). So far, the family in general has been of less interest to scholars than women, but note Elliott West, *Growing Up with the Country: Childhood on the Far-Western Frontier* (Albuquerque, 1989). James E. Davis analyzes the demographic structure of the early-nineteenth-century frontier population in *Frontier America, 1800–1840: A Comparative Demographic Analysis of the Frontier Process* (Glendale, Calif., 1977), but later frontiers still need attention. Also still seeking additional historians are the subjects of frontier agricultural credit and finance and frontier labor, although Allan G. Bogue, *Money at Interest: The Farm Mortgage on the Middle Border* (Ithaca, 1955), David Schob, *Hired Hands and Plowboys: Farm Labor in the Midwest, 1815–1860* (Urbana, 1975), and Thomas D. Isern, *Bull Threshers and Bindlestiffs: Harvesting and Threshing on the North American Plains* (Lawrence, 1990), have demonstrated the promise in these fields.

Chapter Nine

A Saga of Families

KATHLEEN NEILS CONZEN

A family story lies at the heart of American western history. Through the oft-told tales of western conquest and resistance, settlement and development, wind subtle, insistent themes of family, kinship, and community. Consider, for example, one extraordinarily evocative scene from *My Darling Clementine*, John Ford's classic 1946 western film starring Henry Fonda as Wyatt Earp. Silhouetted against the bright southwestern sky rises the skeletal frame of a church tower, a cross at its peak, a joyous bell pealing from its topmost rafters. A lowering mesa broods in the background, nature dwarfing the raw town at its base. In the foreground, two American flags whip bravely in the brisk wind. Men, women, and children, all dressed in their Sunday best, crowd onto the plank floor of the unfinished meetinghouse. And in their midst, knees awkwardly lifted in cautious celebration of the new church, dances the town's tough, gunfighting, poker-playing marshal, tamed by the genteel Bostonian whom he holds gingerly in his arms.

Ford's haunting imagery encapsulates one of the primal themes in the history and mythology of the nineteenth-century American West. Time and again, in memoirs and novels, folk songs and films, political speeches and academic histories, Americans have insisted that the story of western settlement is a story of the conquest of nature and the taming of human nature in the name of the family and of the community that families together form. In this familiar saga, the trajectory from savagery to civilization both defines and legitimates the westward expansion of the American people, and the essence of American civilization lies in its institutions of family and community life. The western drama may seem to be a violent, masculine one, its main protagonists almost exclusively male. Mountain men and miners, cowboys and speculators, native warriors and the U.S. Cavalry, all crowd onto center stage. But sooner or later even the most relentlessly masculine conquest narrative yields to the developmental logic of domestication, and the spotlight shifts to those other archetypal figures who have been waiting in the wings—families trekking westward in covered wagons, wives working alongside husbands to erect a log cabin, warriors setting their hands to the plow, children trudging to a one-room schoolhouse, a community building a church. In popular perception and scholarly interpretation alike, the final integration of the western saga into the nation's ongoing history always seems to turn on those pregnant moments when family and community finally take root, just as Ford's turbulent film pivots on the gentle scene at the church dance.

The fictionalized Tombstone marshal Wyatt Earp danced across an unfinished meetinghouse floor in My Darling Clementine *(1946) with a schoolteacher from Boston, signaling the real and metaphoric centrality of women and the family in the building of western communities. When Earp left town at the conclusion of John Ford's classic film, Clementine remained to preside over the community's transformed domestic order.*

Film still from My Darling Clementine *(1946), directed by John Ford. Courtesy of the Academy of Motion Picture Arts and Sciences, Beverly Hills, California.*

Thus when Ford's boomtown marshal, the fictionalized Wyatt Earp, symbolically embraces the communal and familial values represented by the newly formed Tombstone congregation and by Clementine, the lady from Boston, his feud with the vicious Clantons becomes a crusade for civilization and his success at the O.K. Corral a bittersweet victory that brings to an end the only way of life in which he, with his shooter's skills, could flourish. Ford establishes the essential savagery of both nature and man at the opening of the film with stark camera shots of a pair of menacing gunmen who observe cattle and cowboys in a parched desert setting. But at the end of the film it is a woman, Clementine, the town's new schoolteacher, standing by a tamed, fenced-in landscape, who takes the observer's role as the shooters depart.

The three Earps, seeking to avenge their murdered youngest brother, initially encounter a darkly lit Tombstone of saloons, dance halls, and poker games, a world where Shakespearean tragedians can only degenerate into farce. "Wide-awake, wide-open town, Tombstone! You can get anything you want there." Its denizens are rowdy miners and cowboys, gamblers and whores, its boss a consumptive, alcoholic physician who has turned his back on the civilization of the East. Clementine, his former fiancée, proves unable to reclaim Doc Holliday for Boston and all it stands for. But she begins the taming of Wyatt Earp, and as he primps for her in the local barbershop, Ford lets us glimpse for the first time a different, brighter Tombstone. Beyond the dark of the hotel porch the street floods with sunshine. Wagons and buggies purposefully stream past, families greet one another on the sidewalk, and serving girls in their best hats bustle out of the hotel. "If I wasn't in the territory," Virgil Earp observes, "I'd swear we were back home on a Sunday morning." But the Sabbath has indeed come to the territory. "You know," says Morgan Earp, "there's probably a lot of nice people around here. We just ain't met 'em." Then Wyatt accepts Clementine's ladylike challenge to escort her to church; he slowly leaves the shadows to step with her out into the Sabbath sun. Thus when the Earps subsequently destroy the Clantons at the O.K. Corral, they not only have avenged their brother; they have also, as Wyatt promised, left behind a country where young kids like him "will be able to grow up and live safe," where law and culture are free from ridicule, where the schoolteacher literally replaces the gunslinger. Female sexuality yields to feminine sensibility, and the madam shows herself to be a sensitive nurse. Even Doc Holliday, although too corrupted to be allowed to survive into the new era, is redeemed in death by his belated decision to join Wyatt's crusade.

At the heart of the western saga, Ford would appear to be telling us, lies the civilizing process. The Wild West is an individualistic, solipsistic male world untrammeled by law, morality, higher culture, or feminine domesticity. Its women are deceiving whores and half-breeds, fully deserving the symbolic cleansing in the horse trough that Wyatt administers to Chihuahua, Doc's paramour. Domesticity is as doomed as young James Earp and his plans to marry his sweetheart. "Mac, you ever been in love?" Wyatt asks one of Doc's employees. "No," he replies, "I been a bartender all me life." Women, the family, and the bonds of community can thrive, it seems, only when the West has been tamed. They are the motive that invests the history of western violence with virtue, just as their ultimate triumph signals the end of the uniquely western experience and the final integration of the frontier into the ongoing history of the settled, civilized nation. And in the process they are themselves changed, strengthened, made more robust. A formerly dependent woman like Clementine can now stand alone and shape a role for herself in constructing the new community; the community, like the deacon's womenfolk, can reject the artificial conventions of the East for the wholesome naturalness of western life. Family and community, fresh and reinvigorated, are the rewards that lie at the end of the trail, the ends but not the means of western conquest.

Or are they? Ford's story on one level is indeed the familiar parable of family, community, and the civilizing process that has provided so much of western legend and history with its standard plot. But on another level it charts what can be understood only as a far more complex transformation from one regime of family and community to another. The Clantons, after all, are in Ford's telling also a family of a kind, a dynasty of four brothers held together by their father's will and whip, and the Earps are yet another set of apparently motherless sons, bound in duty and affection to the family economy headed by their Pa back in California. Powerful motives of family honor and vengeance fuel the actions of both clans. Not even Doc Holliday has fully shaken off the claims of family and community. Rather, he is a renegade who prolongs his exile to avoid bringing shame to those who claim him as their own, and in his resistance to the new regime that Clementine represents he even contemplates making his liaison with Chihuahua a permanent one.

Nor is Ford's raucous Tombstone without its own communal structures. It has a mayor and a marshal and the forms of law; when Wyatt Earp marches to the O.K. Corral, he does so with an arrest warrant in his pocket and with the blessings of both the mayor and the deacon of the new church. Untamed Tombstone can constitute itself a moral community in quest of common goals, whether simple entertainment or support for a wounded singer. And it is linked to the wider national community by everything from accounts in the Lordsburg bank to newfangled barber chairs imported from Kansas City. It may not share the moral code of the domesticated, cultured East, but it has its own communal morality nonetheless, a masculine morality that proscribes equally stealing cattle, playing eight-handed poker games, cheating on one's lover, and drawing on a man who is not carrying a gun. Ford's ambivalence about the passing of this order may not be as palpable here as in a later film like *The Man Who Shot Liberty Valance* (1962), with its overt acknowledgment of the falsity of the myths upon which the civilizing process rested. But when Wyatt Earp rides away from Tombstone and its new teacher, it is not just Clementine who is "lost and gone forever" to him. In remaining true to the dictates of one kind of family and community, he has midwifed another, different familial, communal order in which a man like himself can find no place. It is not so much that family and community triumph as that one kind of family order replaces another.

Ford's story, of course, bears only a tenuous relationship to historical reality. It is rather difficult to turn the actual saga of the Earps, the Clantons, Doc Holliday, and the O.K. Corral into a comparable drama of domestication, no matter how ambiguous. The historical Earps were hardly the virtuous retired lawmen and cowboys of Ford's fable. The best recent accounts make it clear that the Earps, though probably not the stage robbers and horse thieves of the revisionist counterlegend, were definitely gamblers, bartenders, brothel keepers, and small-time speculators, as well as sometime lawmen and farmers. The famous shoot-out—not at, but near, the O.K. Corral—had less to do with family vengeance than with tensions arising from economic and political rivalry. And rather than nobly sacrificing his life, Doc Holliday—a Georgian, not a Bostonian—probably initiated the slaughter by drawing first, and lived to trade on his notoriety. Tombstone indeed had a young, single schoolteacher, twenty-four-year-old Lucy McFarland who lived with her sister and her lawyer brother-in-law, but she was from West Virginia, not Boston, and it was not she but the undoubtedly less virtuous Josephine Sarah Marcus, an "artiste" raised in a prosperous German Jewish mercantile family of San Francisco, who attracted Wyatt Earp's wandering eye.

Nevertheless, like their filmic counterfeits, the real Earps inhabited a West defined by distinctive bonds of family and community. They were the offspring of an agrarian Kentucky clan who migrated westward as a family in chainwise fashion, first to Illinois and Iowa, then to Missouri, Kansas, and California, as the various brothers peeled off on a series of continually intersecting trajectories that carried them singly or together through mining camps, railheads, and cow towns from Montana to Kansas and Texas before reuniting them all in 1880 in the new Arizona boomtown of Tombstone. They were, in fact, all married men. Each arrived in Tombstone with his wife, common-law or otherwise, firmly in tow, though Wyatt would replace his partner with Josie during his Tombstone stay. Their women labored for them and moved with them. The Earp brothers were on occasion founding members of church congregations and candidates for public office. They supported and leaned on one another in their efforts for economic advancement, and outside the O.K. Corral they joined to affirm their reputations against not one but two pairs of brothers—McLaurys as well as Clantons—who like them were striving to make it family-fashion in the West. The Clantons, like the Earps, were members of a southern clan seeking to reproduce a familiar pastoral lifestyle in the new territory. The McLaurys, by contrast, were young New York–born, Iowa-raised entrepreneurs who cut loose from their parents to find the fortune that would enable them to found new families of their own. Doc Holliday's initial move west can be seen as a similar attempt by the professional son of well-to-do urban, middle-class parents to establish a home for himself in a healthier climate. The real Tombstone, like its movie version, was overwhelmingly a community of unattached miners leavened by a sprinkling of families like these, to be found mainly within the town's small entrepreneurial class. But the surrounding countryside was punctuated with smaller, family-centered communities—one of them Mormon, several Mexican—that testified to the area's older, deeper domestic roots. And although the only Native American in Ford's film was the drunkard whose literal removal signaled the beginning of Wyatt Earp's crusade to civilize Tombstone, the constant threat of Apache attack was a disturbing reminder to the historical Tombstone of yet another familial tradition in the region.

Thinking about the Family in the American West

In fact as in film, it would seem, the American West was not a domestic tabula rasa. As Ford intuitively sensed, there is indeed a family story at the core of America's western history, but it is something other and more complicated than our familiar fable of domestication and civilization. Many different kinds of family arrangements were to be found in nineteenth-century America's successive Wests, before, during, and after their incorporation into the American nation. Kinship ties could extend across great distances, and family logic could influence even seemingly unattached men and women. Families performed a range of different functions, for their members and for the broader society, that varied with time and place, culture and class. The family in any society is necessarily a cultural and legal construct that invests the basic biological relationship of parents and children with social meaning. Societies determine for themselves what defines a family, who constitutes its members and what their responsibilities are to one another, how far the family identity extends through marriage and consanguinity and across generations, on what basis a family is to be formed, and what societal functions it is meant to fulfill. Tombstone in 1880, no less than Texas in 1820 or Iowa in 1850, was a family frontier in the most literal sense: an arena in which culturally variant constructs of the family, carried by individuals pursuing varying family strategies, met, intermingled, and clashed. These frontier family dynamics played a crucial role in shaping the new societies that emerged, and in turn the struggle to define these new societies helped define the range of regional family models that would survive, the directions in which they would evolve, and their broader influence on American family construction.

Though scholars long neglected the contours and implications of this family frontier, to nineteenth-century Americans the link between western lands and the family was a self-evident though complicated one. "It is in the very philosophy of things, in a country like ours, whose free institutions awaken and bear up the spirit of aspiration from a humble hut, as well as the lofty palace, that the poor man, surrounded by his wife and his children, and animated by a holy love of those endeared objects, with a pure conscience and a resolved purpose, relying upon his own unassisted arm, should go forth to the wilds of the far West to improve his fortunes, and confirm his personal independence," enthused one senator in 1841. To provide for their children, families moved west. In moving west, they escaped the corrupting influences that nineteenth-century American thought attributed to urban life, thereby preserving for the nation its body of independent, freedom-loving householders and, not coincidentally, preserving the West for the nation. As an 1846 observer noted, "All we had to do was to let our women and children go [to the Oregon region] and, without assistance from any one, they would take possession of the country."

Thus easy access by settlers to public land was defended in terms of both its benefits to families and their benefits to the nation. "I know the character of the pioneer," insisted a territorial delegate to Congress in 1852, "and of the men who even now are on their way to the West, and I speak understandingly when I say that it is in such homes as this bill, if adopted, will create, which will forever remain the nurseries of that love of freedom by which alone our present happy form of government can be perpetuated." But by the same token the West could endanger the American family, should it lure away too many of its children or should the family in the West become too isolated from uplifting moral influences, too exposed to the risks of excessive speculative gain. The nation needed strong families; strong families required the independence that western lands could give them; family settlement was the best and cheapest insurance that the West would be tied firmly to the national culture; but familiar models of the family might also prove vulnerable in the West.

Nowhere was the complex circular interplay of family and western opportunity in nineteenth-century American thought better explained than by that acute analyst of Jacksonian America, Alexis de Tocqueville. Without a law of primogeniture, Tocqueville insisted, American families had developed few strong attachments to place or patrimonial land. The resources of the West preserved the promise of economic progress and equality for each new generation on which the belief in American democracy rested, while encouraging the family to reshape itself in democracy's mold. Patriarchy waned, relations of dominance between father and son, and brother and brother, yielded to companionable cooperation, and women, in Tocqueville's reading, achieved and accepted an equal though separate status. Such democratic families raised children appropriately prepared to leave home to make their fortunes; at the same time, these families became a central reason for the stability of American democracy. Order and community in a society lacking strong central authority depended not only on the intersecting self-interests of its self-governing citizens but also on shared mores inculcated by religion and cultivated within the family. But this meant that if the West was the source of the American family's strength, it could also become the nation's weakness, should the bonds of family become too distended in the course of settlement. High levels of speculative profit in the West, Tocqueville feared, too often attracted westwardly mobile men unhampered by kith and kin and thus undisciplined by morality or public opinion. Western opportunity shaped the domesticity on which American democracy depended, but opportunity also placed the family in peril.

American artists in the middle decades of the nineteenth century similarly constructed for their viewers a domestic West, a West peopled by families, a nurturing West for the homes that would cradle the nation's future. The archetypal images were the Madonna-like women whom a stalwart Daniel Boone leads through the Cumberland Gap in George Caleb Bingham's 1851 painting, the three-generational family alongside its covered wagon that listens to a rugged trapper in William Ranney's 1853 *Advice on the Prairie*, and most especially the log cabin domesticity depicted in Thomas Cole's 1845 *The Hunter's Return* (see p. 145). Cole's cozy vine-trellised cabin nestles beneath sublime mountain scenery. A broom and a washtub flank its door, laundry dries beside neat rows of cabbages in the garden, one dog sniffs at the dinner meat airing on a bench and another playfully nuzzles a small child, while smoke drifts invitingly from the cabin's stone chimney and two women eagerly hail their menfolk returning laden from the hunt. No matter that these were in good part images explicitly crafted to celebrate and encourage American expansionism. They worked because they spoke to mid-century Americans' perception of the West as a family resource, the same perception that buttressed antebellum demands for a liberalized homestead law and fueled the attack on slavery in the territories as a threat to family settlement. When the West was portrayed as violent and dangerous, as it often was in paintings of Indian attack, abduction, and rape, it was the threat to the domesticity of the settlers' West that was particularly emphasized, the threat to the purity of its women and the sanctity of its homes. But even the ostensibly untrammeled West of the Native Americans and the fur trappers who

In William Ranney's painting, the men of the family listen intently to an old trapper's tales and absorb the historical lore of the plains, while the Madonna-like mother and child engage the viewer more directly and affirm the family strategies that motivated western settlement.

William Tylee Ranney (1813–57). Advice on the Prairie. *Oil on canvas, 1853. Courtesy Buffalo Bill Historical Center, Cody, Wyoming.*

lived among them was often domesticated by the artists of the 1820s, 1830s, and 1840s, who produced a compelling iconography of Indian daily life and trapper-Indian family unions.

But by the eve of the Civil War, a more somber reassessment was beginning to inform the log cabins that Jasper Cropsey and Sanford Robinson Gifford depicted as inappropriate and unlovely intrusions in the natural landscape, and soon a different kind of artist's West began to take center stage. Families still moved west, their journey now hastened by the railroad, in the popular lithographs of Currier and Ives, but increasingly in western art the domestic middle landscape faded before, on the one hand, a masculine West of soldiers, Indian warriors, and cowboys—Frederic Remington, Charles Schreyvogel, and Charles Russell country—and, on the other, the tourist's delight of unpeopled vistas and valleys, as cultivated by Albert Bierstadt and Thomas Moran. The semiarid lands and boom-and-bust mining camps and cow towns of the post–Civil War West were chancy environments in which to seek family security. The new suburbs of the burgeoning cities back East seemed to offer a safer domestic haven, and in art as in literature a wilder West now shaped the public perception.

It is no accident that it was in the context of this dominant new masculinized and nature-bound western vision that Frederick Jackson Turner in 1893 fashioned his lyric argument for the significance of the West in the nation's development. For the earlier generation of Tocqueville, mores—culture—had taken precedence over environment, and the centrality of the western family seemed self-evident. But by Turner's time, many American reformers had come to doubt the ability of the family to withstand the pressures of the new urban environment. What role, then, could such a feeble institution hope to play in the face of the even greater savagery of the wild? It is little wonder that

"What we want in California," this popular print of mid-century implied, was the civilizing influence of eastern families whose domestic culture would replace the less desirable influence of the single male miners or native California Indians they would inevitably displace.

Britton & Rey, lithographers (active 1852–58). What We Want in California. *Lithograph, ca. 1855. Courtesy, The Bancroft Library, University of California, Berkeley.*

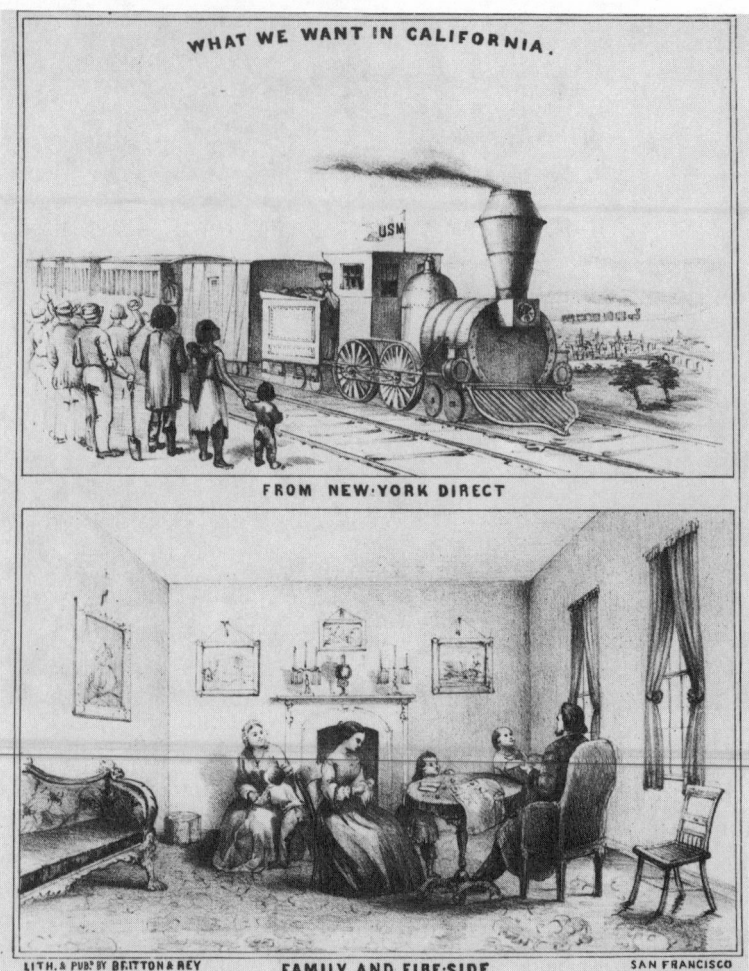

consideration of the family was overwhelmed in Turner's analysis by his emphasis on the competitive individualism of the frontier and that his stage theory of frontier settlement could readily be taken to imply that families culminated rather than coordinated the process. It was left to others, most notably Arthur W. Calhoun in his pioneering 1917 history of the American family, to work out the more specific implications of Turnerian thinking for the relationship between the family and the West. Calhoun noted that the pioneer's necessary focus on "home building and home protection" meant that "the psychology of domesticity was supreme," that a strong "clan-spirit" often developed, and that "the family was the one substantial social institution" on the frontier. But he did not explore the structuring role played by the family in the West, a role that these insights implied. Instead, he focused on the effects of the West on the family, and here his Turnerianism emerged most clearly. The most important formative influence on the American family in the decades after the Revolution, he insisted, was "pioneering and the frontier." Frontier dispersion, hardship, and democracy combined to foster early marriage, high fecundity, easy divorce, the emancipation of children, improved status for women, and insensitivity to the claims of lineage. The frontier, in short, encouraged a fundamental transformation from a regime of "familism" to the "parentalism" that he saw dominating his own era.

By the time that historians began to develop a systematic interest in family history in the 1960s, however, Turnerian approaches were so thoroughly discredited that the question of a specific western or frontier influence on the American family was barely raised. Family historians uncovered a rich and finely textured account of the fundamental transformation of American family patterns and ideology in the course of industrialization, urbanization, national centralization, political change, and ethnic and racial pluralism but made little effort to incorporate geographical expansion and western regional development into their central interpretation. Only as western historians belatedly began to explore the role of women—and children—in the West did family-related issues again receive much scholarly attention. We can now draw on a diverse and growing body of research to sketch, in broad outlines, answers to the four basic questions that structure this essay. How did family auspices influence the processes of migration, settlement, resistance, and integration that peopled the West? What were the resulting variations in western family patterns? Can we identify a distinctive western influence on the development of the American family? And how did the particular values of nineteenth-century American family life shape western regional development?

Family and community were not a simple culmination of western conquest. Nor did new kinds of conditions create a new breed of family or community in the American West. As European and African Americans in the course of the nineteenth century pushed westward over the Appalachians, through the great valley of the Mississippi, across the plains and the Rockies and the deserts to the Pacific and back into the intermountain plateaus and parks, and as Asians moved eastward and Mexicans north, they all carried with them familiar and diverse assumptions about domestic life and firmly established patterns of domestic structures, functions, and relationships. They encountered similarly deep-seated domestic patterns among the Native Americans and French, Spanish, and mixed-descent colonists already inhabiting the land. Bonds of family and community fundamentally shaped the processes of both conquest and resistance, and those processes in turn molded the domestic landscapes that westerners would inhabit by the end of the century. There would be not one form of the western family, one kind of western community, but many. Changing American family and community norms, selective migration, local resource variation, differential incorporation of indigenous peoples, and locally varying degrees of economic integration with the national order all combined to construct a complex and continually evolving domestic landscape in the American West that affected every aspect of western life and influenced evolving conceptions of the American family. Family threads were woven deeply into the fabric of western development from the outset, and western history cannot fully be understood without tracing the patterns they formed. The O.K. Corral showdown was "strictly a family affair," insisted John Ford's Wyatt Earp. The same, we shall see, might almost be said of the West itself.

The Family Logics of Western Settlement

When young Millard Fillmore moved west to Buffalo in 1822, he was both following and breaking a family tradition: following, because he was repeating a pattern set by his father and his grandfather before him; breaking, because whereas they had sought new land on the frontier, it was the new opportunity of a western city that drew the young lawyer who later would become the nation's thirteenth president. Westward migration was certainly an established family habit. In 1765 Millard's grandfather, after seeing his two older brothers move to new settlement areas in Nova Scotia and northwestern Connecticut respectively, set out for frontier Vermont, leaving his youngest brother behind to farm the family land in Norwich, Connecticut. As his sons came of age, they repeated their father's pattern. The two youngest remained behind to take over the Vermont homestead while the oldest moved with his young family to Oneida County, New York, and then on to the Buffalo area as his children approached adulthood.

Then the second and third sons—the second was Millard's father—in their turn joined forces to purchase wild land in Cayuga County, New York. But luck turned against them. Their title proved defective, and they were forced to lease poor land elsewhere in the county. Disgusted with farming under such circumstances, Millard's father, as Millard later recalled, became "anxious that his sons should follow some other occupation" and schemed to apprentice them to such standard rural trades as carding and cloth finishing, carpentry, and masonry. But he soon realized that his talented oldest son could set his sights still higher. Born with the century, in a primitive log cabin, Millard came of age as the pace of local life was quickening in upstate New York. Lending libraries and academies were bringing the culture of a wider world into the backwoods, and Millard arduously scraped together a sort of education for himself in the time he could steal from farmwork, apprenticeship, and winter schoolteaching. So Fillmore senior finally approached his landlord, a wealthy judge, to beg—success-fully—that he give young Millard a chance to read law. When Millard was ready to move on a couple years later, it was Buffalo, portal to the vast western wilderness about to be opened by the Erie Canal, that inevitably attracted—and amply rewarded—his ambitions. Two of his younger brothers would attempt to follow the same path (both died young), and two of his Buffalo-area cousins became local ministers. But the rest of this generation of Fillmores continued to trod the accustomed family paths. One of the Buffalo cousins stayed behind on his father's land while the remaining cousin, and Millard's three other brothers and their families, followed the Great Lakes westward to the new frontier farmlands of northern Indiana, Michigan, and later Minnesota.

Few families produce a future president, distinguished or otherwise. But in other respects the Fillmores typified a fundamental family process that peopled much of the American West. Westward migration for them, as for so many rural American families, was a generationally recurring event, as expected and regular a stage in the normal life course as marriage or retirement. It formed a central element in the family's strategy for providing livelihoods for the coming generation; family considerations governed the timing and composition of migration, and extended family groups sought common destinations. Individualistic loners were probably more common in western legend than in life. No matter how tenuous family ties might seem when a young scapegrace like Millard's cousin Henry Glezen Fillmore drifted into the free and easy life of the Indian trader on Minnesota's northern frontier in the late 1840s, it was no accident that brothers and cousins soon followed in his wake. And when he subsequently married, it

As the three genera-
tions depicted in this
1854 field sketch of
western immigrants
suggest, extended fam-
ilies often moved to-
gether, preserving a
labor force that might
be essential in devel-
oping a new home.

W. C. Weisel (active 1854).
Camp of the Covered
Wagon Train. *Watercolor
on paper, 28 December
1854. M. and M. Karolik
Collection. Courtesy, Mu-
seum of Fine Arts, Boston,
Massachusetts.*

was to a young woman with a similarly extensive local family connection of her own. The story of the family in the West necessarily begins with its varied influences on the peopling of the region itself.

It often seemed to nineteenth-century Americans that there was something inexplicable, even irrational, about the pace and intensity of westward migration. They referred to it in terms suggestive of irresistible natural phenomena. They spoke of "Oregon fever" breaking out, of migrants "swarming" like a hive of bees, of stampedes and epidemics, waves and floods. For the *Cleveland Herald* in 1839, migration was a "tide" that in "the past season [had] been setting toward the west stronger than ever." Americans seemed a breed of restless wanderers, ever seeking elbow room or speculative profits over the next horizon. What but irrational, individualistic ambition or the equivalent of a force of nature could pull so many away from well-tended domestic hearths and the ample opportunities to be found in the more developed sectors of the nation's economy?

Scholars have tended to seek more rational explanations in "push factors" peculiar to a particular time and place—the worn-out fields of New England that by the 1830s could no longer compete with the productivity of new western lands, for example, or the fevers, floods, and low crop prices with which Missourians had to contend in the 1840s—or in uprooting personal crises like bankruptcy or family tragedy. Or they have stressed the "pull" of western opportunity for a striving, entrepreneurial nation—the special "one time only" profits that could accrue to those who reaped the first crops from virgin soil, to those who pastured the first cattle on prairie grasses, trapped the first beaver, mined the first ores. But there were always crises somewhere, and migration was not the only possible response; western opportunity always beckoned, but only some Americans responded. Underlying the complex interactions of specific push and pull factors that help account for the peopling of any given frontier was a family regime that made westward migration for countless American families like the Fillmores—and the Earps—a viable, sometimes even an inevitable, option.

The family, Brazil's noted anthropologist Gilberto Freyre asserted several decades ago, was, for his country, "the great colonizing factor." The same can be said for the United States. The successive Wests that were integrated into the American nation in the course of the nineteenth century were shaped from the outset by the needs and strategies of American families. A number of different and changing family cultures coexisted in the older settled areas of the United States—and in Europe, China, and Mexico—during the nineteenth century. Their varying assumptions about family function, size, and relationships fundamentally influenced who chose to migrate to new frontier areas, when, and with what goals. The varying family patterns of the native peoples already resident in these areas were similarly influential in shaping their ability to resist, adapt, or succumb to the newcomers. Equally significant was the ideological colonization of the West by a powerful new familial ideal that, once embedded in institutions and law, proved able to play an independent role in the shaping of western life.

It was the family cultures of the westward-migrating European-American populations that would be the dominant vectors of change in the new region. Historians have identified the nineteenth century as a time of fundamental transformation in American family life, when a family regime suitable for life in a traditional agrarian society yielded to a new kind of family better adapted to the new industrial order. Various labels have been proposed to capture this transformation—from the "traditional" to the "modern," from the "patriarchal" to the "companionate," from the "instrumental" to the "affective," from the "household" to the "domestic" family—with many recognizing in the nineteenth-century "Victorian" family a style distinctive both from what came before and from the regime that would become dominant in the twentieth century. Whatever the terminology, a new set of assumptions about family life came to be widely shared among nineteenth-century Americans: that the ideal family rested on an affectionate union of a man and a woman who provided one another with love, companionship, and comfort and who carefully and lovingly nurtured their children to be well-developed individuals and productive members of society. Each parent had a separate, distinctive sphere within this family ideal: the man was to be its head, its public representative, its wage earner, and its ultimate source of authority; the woman, its heart and its conscience, kept the home, trained the children, and deferred to the husband while providing gentle moral counsel. No longer a basic unit of production, this new family ideal offered its members a private, sentimental retreat from the rigors of the new, vigorously competitive, capitalist economy. This new style began appearing in prescriptive popular literature discussing family life by the 1810s, and within a generation it overwhelmed the previous emphasis on large, patriarchally governed and productive families with well-defined public roles.

But too much emphasis on the ideal family model defined by the ideology of the times ignores the actual variety of family styles within the nineteenth-century American family regime, and a periodization based on the replacement of one family ideal by another obscures the extent to which older family styles continued to coexist with newer.

If we abandon familiar efforts to classify family styles on the basis of the emotive character of familial relationships or the source of power within the family and turn instead to the economic basis of family organization, we can identify at a very general level four distinctive, coexisting nineteenth-century American family styles that shaped the westward migration process. We can term these the patrimonial, the proletarian, the entrepreneurial, and the slave family styles. Each style had its own distinctive logic of migration.

To understand those logics, we have to recall in very general terms how these styles evolved. American families of all stripes were heirs to what has been termed the western European family system. Any traditional people, dependent on relatively unproductive agriculture, limited craft production, and inefficient trade, necessarily faces the classic Malthusian dilemma of balancing resources and population. With population multiplying over successive generations, land and hence food will run short, resulting, if nature is left to run its course, in famine, disease, and war until the population is again reduced to a level that can be supported by available resources. Of course, nature does not have to be left to run its course, and in traditional western Europe, the most important regulator proved to be the cultural assumption that procreation should occur only within marriage and that marriage should occur only when the new couple were capable of supporting their own household. This meant that the proportions of the population who married, the age at marriage, and consequently the number of children produced by the marriage even in the absense of effective contraception could vary greatly with time, place, and class, depending on the productivity of the local economy and a particular family's place within it. When times were hard, marriages were postponed, birthrates declined, and family size grew smaller. High death rates, particularly among children, also kept family size in bounds. The average western European age at marriage, consequently, tended to be relatively high. The average family was never large, nor were extended multigenerational families residing in the same household very common.

Central to the survival of such a traditional family was the patrimony on which it depended—the land or craft from which it earned its living and which it transmitted from generation to generation. The family passed through a recurrent cycle, from when a young couple married and took over its patrimony, to the maximum earning years when children worked alongside their parents to amass the resources needed for their start in life, to the point when the parents retired to make way for the next generation. In some European regions, the patrimony was divided among all children; in others it remained with one heir while the rest had to find other niches in society. But whatever the specific strategy, the basic principle remained: it was through the family that the individual gained access to a livelihood, and families thus depended on maintaining the patrimony from generation to generation to ensure the livings of their members. Because families were the fundamental units of local society, performing most of its basic functions of reproduction, production, education, welfare, and even governance, they had a fundamentally public character, and local society—formally through the agencies of government and religion, informally through gossip and social sanctions on behavior—paid close attention to the regulation of life within individual families. Wider kinship networks were also important assets. In an age when few institutions existed to guarantee the behavior of strangers, shared blood was one of the best ways of securing trust, and kinship ties could be invoked to ensure everything from emergency assistance to business partnerships, making marriage as much an alliance of two kin networks and two patrimonies as of two people.

Family limitation through delayed marriage was not, of course, the only way that resources and population could be kept in balance. Over the long term, improved productivity released gradually increasing proportions of the western European population from agriculture, paving the way for the quickening of manufacture and trade that would usher in the industrial revolution of the nineteenth century. In the process, two other family styles took shape. One was the proletarian family. Wage earners, urban or rural, lacking either rights in land or a trade that could be passed down to their children, had little reason to think of their families in cross-generational, patrimonial terms. For them, the family economy could be only a pooling of wages for mutual survival. There was little reason to postpone marriage, husband and wife shared the necessity of labor, and additional children were more often regarded in terms of the wages that they would earn rather than the drain on scarce resources that they might represent. Near the other end of the economic spectrum emerged what might best be termed the entrepreneurial family, a family style focused less on the preservation and transmission of the patrimony than on enterprising investment in the constantly changing opportunity offered by the emerging capitalist order. For those with the means to sustain it, the family ceased being the main unit of production. The husband followed his work out of the home into the male world of business, leaving his wife behind to cultivate domesticity, rear their children in the entrepreneurial virtues, and through her tasteful consumption, affirm the gentility of the striving family—in sum, the family ideal that would be propagated as the desired national norm in nineteenth-century America. These families remained enmeshed in the web of kinship and continued to enshrine the ideal of patriarchal authority, but the productive unit of husband, wife, and children—the core of the patrimonial family—was gone, and the number of children declined. Success in the new economy favored those endowed with familial gifts of education and capital but unhampered by constraining obligations to people or place; for such men on the make, the new domestic ideology served as a substitute tether to society's need for the support of women and children.

Accompanying these changes was yet another resolution to the Malthusian dilemma: migration. Even in traditional Europe, those who could not find a niche in rural society often sought opportunity in a nearby town or moved to new lands on the margins of European cultivation. From the early seventeenth century onward, they could also move to America. Their emigration was necessarily influenced by the family economies of which they were a part and which shaped their hopes for life in America. Thus the historian Bernard Bailyn has documented the presence of two very distinct migration streams in the heavy emigration from Britain to America in the mid-eighteenth century. One stream he terms "provincial," made up of mature families with growing children who moved from the agricultural areas of northern England and Scotland with the hope of reestablishing what we have called a patrimonial agrarian family economy on American land. The other "metropolitan" stream consisted mainly of young men, and some young women, who moved as individuals from England's largest cities to seek laboring or entrepreneurial employment in the more urbanized areas of America in particular.

By the time of national independence, some version of the patrimonial family ordered life for the vast majority of Americans who lived in the new nation's rural areas—some 95 percent, according to the 1790 census—and for many in the few but growing cities. The rigorous logic of the proletarian family was, however, also spreading in the cities, and the entrepreneurial family style was beginning to flex its metaphorical wings. Equally in evidence was a fourth generalized family style, formed under conditions of slavery and hence dominant among the roughly 20 percent of the 1790 population who were of African descent. The slave family, as historians have described it in its mature form in the decades before the Civil War, generally centered on a stable two-parent household wherever possible. But parents had little control over either their own work or the fates of their children, and families were constantly at risk of disruption through sale and forced migration. Their situation encouraged general status equality between the sexes and embedded each nuclear family deeply in a broad local net of kin and community that could be called on for the support that the nuclear family was never able to ensure.

The vast expanses of land lying to the west, by European standards lightly used and often lightly defended, almost inevitably played a particularly prominent role in the American family calculus of survival and intergenerational succession. Why delay marriage, why limit children, why divide a patrimony, why cling to the old family hearth, when the limitless resources of the West seemed there for the taking? "To better their condition in an unknown land our forefathers left all that was dear in earthly objects," President Andrew Jackson declared in 1830. "Our children by thousands yearly leave the land of their birth to seek new homes in distant regions. Does Humanity weep at these painful separations from everything, animate and inanimate, with which the young heart has become entwined? Far from it. It is rather a source of joy that our country affords scope where our young population may range unconstrained in body or in mind, developing the power and faculties of man in their highest perfection." Future historians would note that the expenses of establishing a western home could be substantial, precluding this option for many, but European-American families would prove surprisingly capable of marshaling the resources needed for migration when it fit within the logic of their long-term strategies. And because that logic varied with family style, so too did the influence of family on the timing, composition, and goals of migration and hence also on the character of the new communities created in the West.

Two Families Move West

There may be no better way to illustrate this point than to take a closer look at two representative American families as they moved across the continent from 1700 to 1900. The Fillmores can serve as our New England example, whereas the Maxeys, who arrived in Virginia at about the same time as the first Fillmore set foot in New England, provide a southern counterpart, necessary because both slavery and kinship systems created distinctive regional differences. These two families were chosen almost at random from

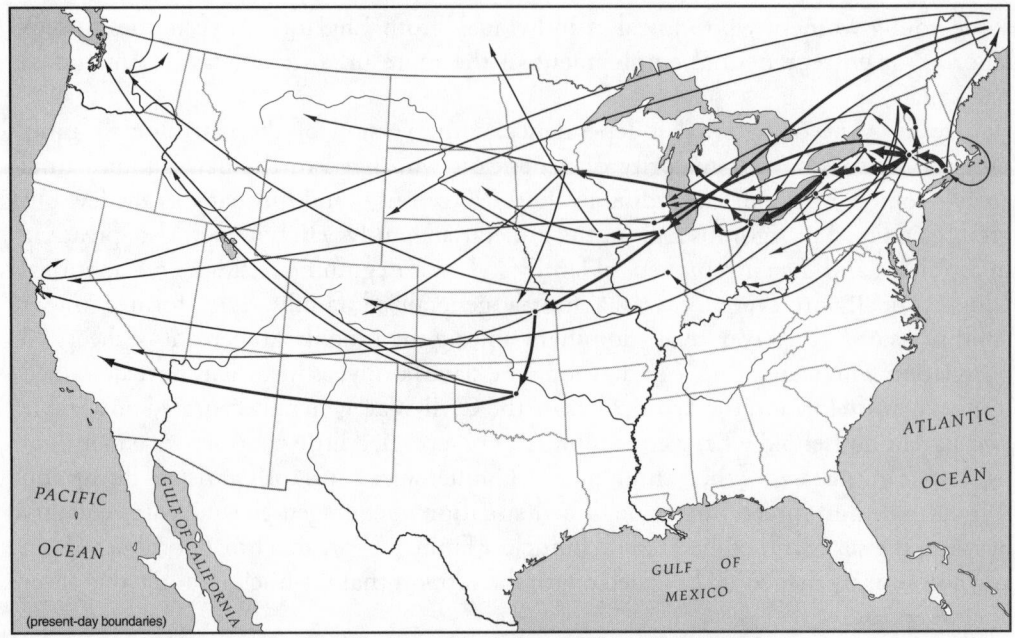

Generalized Fillmore Family Western Migration Paths, 1700-1900

among the plethora of families for whom well-researched genealogies have been published in recent decades. Despite gaps inevitable in even the best-researched record, the basic information about places and dates of birth, marriage, death, landownership, occupation, and the like compiled in Charles L. Fillmore's and Edythe Maxey Clark's authoritative family genealogies yields a surprisingly rich and consistent account of family migration strategies when set within the broader context provided by family and settlement history. Though the Maxey family, unlike the Fillmores, never produced a president, it did number among its members both the wife of Abraham Lincoln's law partner and a Confederate general who later became a Texas senator. More important for present purposes, however, is the very anonymity of most of the more than 1,400 Maxeys and 650 Fillmores whose eight generations of westward migration illuminate the strategies that they shared with countless other European-American families of the time. Like most genealogies, these accounts permit us to follow only the male lines through extended generational sequences, but the daughters of each successive generation are included. It is also important to note that our generalized analysis necessarily skips over many intermediate family moves, side paths, and backtrackings in the interests of interpretive economy.

Either Fillmores or Maxeys participated in virtually every stage of the European-American penetration of the successive Wests of the nineteenth century. Most of the Maxeys, like the Earps and the Clantons in Tombstone, formed part of that vast procession of upland southerners who trailed Daniel Boone across the upper South and lower Midwest to Missouri and points west, while other lines of Maxeys moved, like Doc Holliday's family, through the plantation lands of the lower South and Texas. By

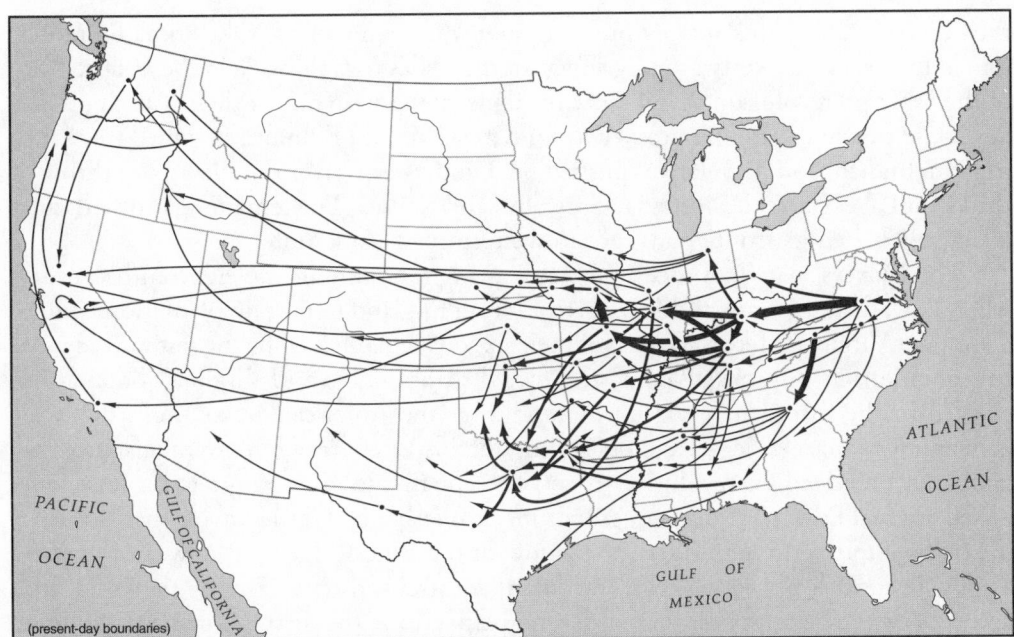

Generalized Maxey Family Western Migration Paths, 1700–1900

contrast, the Fillmores were, like the McLaurys, part of the Yankee diaspora that fanned out to northern New England and upstate New York before and after the Revolution and then pushed westward to the Great Lakes and—barring the occasional southern diversion—California and the Pacific Northwest. Many members of each family would stop and take root at each stage along the westering march, and at each stage urban opportunity soon began to exert a counterpull, but as long as new frontier resources beckoned, there was a Fillmore or a Maxey to answer the call.

The first American Fillmore, John, was a mariner who married in New Hampshire in 1701 and established his family in Beverly, Massachusetts. After his early death at sea, his wife remarried and moved with the children to Norwich, Connecticut. John's younger son remained on the family's Norwich land, but the older son, John junior, began his career as a seaman like his father. John junior's children seemingly shared his broader horizons, and began the family's march westward when service in the 1755-63 war with France exposed them to the opportunity that lay beyond New England's northern and western borders. This time too, it was one of the youngest of the five brothers who remained behind to cultivate his father's Norwich farm, though some of his offspring would subsequently join their uncles and cousins in Vermont or New York and move on westward with them. The oldest of the five brothers settled in New Brunswick, where his progeny participated generation by generation in the slow opening of Canada's Maritime frontier. One line of these Canadian Fillmores, however, followed the logging frontier westward into Ontario and Michigan while another moved to the farmlands of northern Illinois and then on to Iowa, South Dakota, and Manitoba, on the one hand, and to Kansas, Oklahoma, Colorado, and the Pacific Northwest, on the other—a family trek that culminated only when some of the Oklahoma Fillmores joined that last great westward pilgrimage of the Okies to California in the 1930s. Two of the other prerevolutionary Fillmore brothers, along with one of their sisters and her family, settled in the Bennington, Vermont, area. Millard Fillmore stemmed from this migrant branch, and his relatives pushed the family westward from New York through the Great Lakes states to Montana, Colorado, and Kansas. The remaining brother's line effectively halted its frontier advance in western New York State.

The Maxeys' parallel procession westward began early in the eighteenth century when Edward and Susannah Maxey arrived from England to take up plantation land in Tidewater Virginia. Here the oldest of their six sons remained while the rest moved west to plantations in Virginia's Piedmont. Once the frontier beyond Virginia's boundaries opened in the turbulent years during and after the American Revolution, the next generation of Maxeys began to cross the mountains, encouraged in several instances by land grants received for revolutionary service. The first to leave Virginia was Jesse, one of the original Edward's youngest grandsons. His father had settled twenty years earlier in southwestern Virginia under the shadow of the Blue Ridge, and now, in the early 1770s, Jesse with his young wife and infant son trekked down the Great Valley and across Virginia's southwestern border to help create the first permanent colonial settlement in Tennessee. When, during the Revolution, settlers pushed farther west to the Cumberland Valley, forming a local government for themselves at the site of Nashville, Jesse was again among their number. Surviving a severe wound at the hands of the region's native defenders, the "old Indian fighter" and revolutionary veteran lived to see his family well established as slaveholding planters on the rich tobacco and cotton lands of the Cumberland that he had fought to conquer.

It was the Georgia wilderness farther to the south that attracted Jesse's younger brother Walter soon after the Revolution. Choosing to move within his wife's kin group rather than follow his brother, the revolutionary veteran was able to exploit Georgia's generous land lotteries to embed his growing family firmly among the plantation aristocracy of that new cotton frontier. About the same time, other Maxey cousins established a third family foothold across the mountains when they joined the great postrevolutionary Virginia migration that flowed into the Kentucky Bluegrass and then spilled over into the Barrens of southern Kentucky. And in 1804, the son of yet another of Jesse's cousins chose yet another frontier, this one lying to the north, in the Virginia Military District of Ohio. It was probably no accident that Horatio Maxey moved his large family into free territory. Horatio's father, converting to Methodism in the religious revival of the revolutionary years, had emancipated his slaves in 1788, and although three of his sons remained slaveholders, Horatio and his younger brother Bennett, along with a nephew and a niece, sought nonslaveholding lives for their families on the Ohio frontier.

No sooner did one Maxey clan secure a foothold somewhere in the West than they could expect to be joined by siblings, nephews, nieces, cousins, and second cousins. Since most Maxey lines retained some representatives in Virginia, news of settlement opportunities passed quickly along the family grapevine. Kentucky proved particularly enticing. By about 1800, children or grandchildren of all of Edward and Susannah's sons had gravitated to one or the other of the Maxey settlement areas there. For many,

"ALLITO FARM" PROPERTY OF U.S. NYE.
16 MILES NORTHWEST OF WILLOWS COLUSA CO. CAL.

however, Kentucky proved more a staging area than a stopping place, as did Tennessee. By 1815, the first of the Kentucky Maxeys were following their second cousins north to free soil—in this case, Indiana. A couple years later, Jesse's oldest son, like his uncle a Methodist convert, emancipated his slaves and moved his large family from Tennessee to southern Illinois. Within a year or two, one of the Ohio Maxeys was also exploring Illinois opportunity, and soon numerous other Kentucky Maxeys followed, part of the great surge of migration from the upper South into free territory in the decades after 1820. Their children and grandchildren pressed forward with the free frontier to Iowa, Kansas, Nebraska, and the Pacific Northwest or rejoined Maxey cousins farther south. Other Kentucky Maxeys, retaining their commitment to the "peculiar institution," trekked to Missouri as early as 1819; a few of their offspring took the Overland Trail to California and Oregon while others flowed south to Arkansas, Texas, and Oklahoma. The speculative plantation frontier of the antebellum period lured Georgia and Tennessee Maxeys westward to Alabama, Mississippi, Arkansas, and Texas while a later, wilder Texas offered numerous Maxeys a refuge from the war-torn South. And finally, like the Fillmores, Maxeys of all stripes in the 1890s dreamt the frontier dream one last time in the Indian lands of Oklahoma.

A closer look at these migration histories suggests, first of all, the dominant role of patrimonial logic in so many of the Maxey and Fillmore moves. They migrated as family groups, and they migrated for land. The farm that Millard Fillmore's grandfather pioneered in Vermont, for example, could provide a living for only the two youngest of his five sons, one of whom never married; the other three could hope to replicate their

In the many county atlases and histories published from the 1860s to the 1880s, Americans could find idealized images celebrating the virtues of domestic life in the rural West. The owner of this California farm conveyed his own happy prosperity with images of his prize animals, contented children, and farm and domestic laborers and signaled his social connections by including an image of visitors stopping to call at his neat frame house.

Unidentified artist. "Allito Farm": Property of U.S. Nye. *Lithograph, ca. 1880. From Will S. Green,* Colusa County, California *(1880; reprinted 1950, Sacramento Lithograph Company).*

father's success only by moving to a new frontier. By moving after they had married and when their children were still young, they could expand cultivation as their family's needs and labor resources increased and with luck—the luck that eluded Millard's father and uncle—jointly earn farms for both generations. Moving together, or in chainwise fashion, permitted siblings to draw on one another for aid. Fillmore daughters and their husbands and children were an integral part of these sibling chains; a move west for Fillmore women seldom meant leaving all members of their parental family behind.

Indeed, the older generation itself often traveled west with their children and grandchildren, so that their wisdom and labor could aid the family in establishing its new farm and so that their children could assist them in their old age. Thus one of Millard's uncles first moved his young family from Vermont to Oneida County, New York, in 1790 and then, twenty-one years later when his oldest children were approaching marriageable age, transplanted the whole family again to new land in the western part of the state. This land proved able to support one son and his family; two other sons became ministers, and the fourth moved on to Michigan, where he was soon joined by the families of the three sons of his farmer brother, assorted other in-laws, and at least five cousins, siblings of the future president, some of whom then extended the chain to Minnesota.

It was family auspices like these that established the diverging lines of agrarian Fillmores on one frontier after another in the century and a half after 1750. The move from upstate New York to southern Ohio around 1818, the two moves from Vermont to different parts of Illinois in the 1830s, the extended series of frontier moves within the Maritimes, and most particularly the lengthy migration chain that led from New Brunswick in the 1840s all the way to California during the Great Depression—all exhibited the same patrimonial logic as the migrations within Millard's line. The Fillmores who followed the logging frontier from New Brunswick to Ontario to western Michigan in the 1840s and 1850s were engaged in a similarly structured cross-generational family project. Virtually all of these migrants grew up in large families of seven, eleven, or even fourteen children, and virtually all would raise similarly large families on the next frontier.

The Maxeys replicated these basic patrimonial patterns, though not without some distinctive southern accents. For one thing, the generous size of southern land grants gave many early Maxeys, both in Virginia and across the mountains, access to a level of wealth unmatched by most Fillmores, affording parents and some of their offspring the luxury of remaining behind in settled territory while other siblings, able to substitute slave or hired labor for the family labor they lacked, migrated on their own. Thus, for example, many of the initial Maxey moves from Virginia were made by young married couples rather than by older established families, as was common among the Fillmores.

Such moves were facilitated by a second distinctive southern feature of Maxey family strategy: the comparative complexity of the kinship system on which they could draw. Pairs of siblings married other pairs of siblings, and cousins often married cousins; kin relationships constructed in one generation were reaffirmed by new marriages in the next. Migrating Maxeys did not have to rely only on their immediate family for support; they could move within their far-flung networks of kin. Thus, although Edward Maxey remained behind in Virginia when most of his siblings and numerous other kin headed west in the decades after the Revolution, the options for his maturing children in the 1830s and early 1840s were not confined to the weary lands of the Piedmont. Two of his sons joined first cousins in Mississippi, one sought out second cousins in Illinois, and three linked up with third cousins in Missouri; indeed, Patrick, the youngest of the brothers, married one of those Missouri Maxeys and moved on with his in-laws to new land on Missouri's western border.

"I think any of you would be much better satisfied in this country," wrote Walter Maxey from Alabama to his "Dear Brothers and Sisters" in Illinois in 1820. "I think that I can make five dollars here easier than I or you can make one in your country. Trade is so much better. . . . There is a good deal of land in our country to enter and it would not be a hard matter to move from your country here. . . . I would assist any of the connection if they see proper to move to this country. . . . [Brother John] yet lives [in a nearby Alabama county]. He is building a mill but very probable the next time you hear from him he will be living here and they all appear willing." Although Walter's hopes were doomed to double disappointment—not only did the Illinois kin remain in Illinois but John and his family soon left to join them—both his sentiments and his practical offer of assistance demonstrate the kinds of family solder that fused the Maxey migration chains. Thus the same interrelated communities of Maxeys, Bondurants, Fords, and others who moved together from Virginia to Kentucky in the 1780s were to be found in southern Illinois or in Missouri a generation later.

Slavery gave antebellum Maxey migrations a third distinctive twist. There was one kind of Maxey move that almost invariably involved the more mature, often three-generation patrimonial family, even when other kin were already waiting at the destination: the move from slave to free territory. Perhaps so fundamental a transformation in the character of the family itself demanded the emotional support of its most intimate unit. More prosaically, slaves formed part of the patrimony, and any decision to strip the family of that patrimony depended on familial consensus. And once bereft of slave labor, migrating Maxeys were forced to rely on themselves to carve out their new homes on the new frontier and undoubtedly, like the Fillmores, timed their migrations to take maximum advantage of the labor of a maturing family. That certainly became the pattern for subsequent westward migrations among the northern Maxeys, in contrast to many among their southern kin. For example, William Maxey, the son of Jesse, the Tennessee pioneer, after converting to Methodism in his late forties, freed his slaves, sold his cotton mill, and moved his maturing family to Illinois in 1818. Here his eleven children prospered, but many among his numerous grandchildren repeated the family pattern after the Civil War, moving with growing or grown children and grandchildren to new farmlands in western Missouri, Iowa, Arkansas, Kansas, Texas, Oklahoma, Colorado, Idaho, or Washington. Simeon's experience is perhaps representative of this generation. Using borrowed money to purchase forty acres of government land in Illinois in 1853, he set out an orchard and began taking prizes for his fruit at agricultural fairs, his success interrupted only by Civil War service in his brother's company. But with five teenage children to establish by the late 1870s, the arguments for re-investing family resources on new land in the West must have seemed compelling, and he set out on an exploring trip west. He chose the flat Kittitas Valley in the center of the Washington Territory, where the approaching railroad and a series of bad winters that had devastated the cattle herds were forecasting the end of the open range. Here his family began homesteading in 1882, here they established the first of Washington's famed commercial apple orchards, and here they were soon joined by other relatives, friends, and former wartime comrades.

Finally, the incredibly speculative character of the southern market in western lands in the decades before the Civil War encouraged among some Maxey lines one other distinctively southern pattern: frequent joint mobility shared by parents and their married children as the clan moved restlessly from one frontier to the next, using their joint labor less, perhaps, to construct a stable home than to marshal the capital to grubstake a speculative bonanza on the next frontier. Among the less successful players in this game was Simeon's great-uncle Walter, the Alabama correspondent noted earlier. Among the most successful was Walter's cousin William, born in Virginia in 1783, who moved with his parents, siblings, and mother's kin in a complex, intertwining dance that took family members through the land lotteries of Georgia and the federal and Indian land booms of Alabama and Mississippi, prospering as planters and slaveholders seemingly innoculated against the Methodist conscience that plagued others of their kin. The dance culminated for William in 1840, when he sold his large eastern Mississippi plantation, cotton gin, and thirty slaves to his brother in a complicated transaction for twenty-six thousand dollars. Transferring his family and his business to Texas, he carved out, with his children, rich cotton plantations from the tangled lands of the Big Thicket and inspired other relatives to join them on the Texas trail.

But northern or southern, all of these Maxeys exemplified, just as did the Fillmores, the predominant pattern of migration that peopled so much of the American West: the patrimonial migration of kin-linked groups of large rural families, farmfolk or artisans, seeking to preserve a customary family economy by endowing the next generation with the bounty of newly opened public lands. They could, of course, have made other choices, as did Fillmores and Maxeys who remained behind when their kinfolk moved west. If a pioneering venture succeeded, a migrant's children could reasonably expect to live out their lives in the new settlement, but some, at least, of the grandchildren of all but the most prosperous settlers would clearly face the renewed necessity of western migration if they were to maintain both living standards and the customary patrimonial strategy. But pioneering, it seems, was a habit or skill that had to be passed on from parents to children, an option that seldom seemed feasible or desirable unless there was immediate contact with previous migrant generations or relatives already in the West. And as former frontier areas were drawn into the modernizing national economy, more attractive resolutions of the old rural dilemma of balancing population and resources was resolved with attractive options closer to hand. Nearby cities offered market incentives to improve the productivity of local farming. They diffused new ideas about family life and gender roles into their developing hinterlands, encouraging smaller families that placed fewer pressures on available land, and urban opportunity itself proved a potent lure to farmers' children.

Thus the younger of the first John Fillmore's two sons and his male descendants would remain in the Norwich, Connecticut, area as farmers and skilled workmen for five generations. Family sizes soon dropped to fewer than four children, and out-migration, when it finally began, was to the growing cities of the region rather than to the West. The same generational pattern of fertility reduction and subsequent urban migration often in family groups appeared among the other branch of Connecticut Fillmores and among the Fillmores who were subsequently to remain behind in Vermont, New York, Michigan, Indiana, Illinois, and Iowa. Some Fillmores, to be sure, found their way from Vermont and upstate New York to San Francisco and California in the boom years of the 1880s, several generations after their westering kin had departed, but this was new-style city-to-city relocation rather than a late revival of long-forgotten habits of pioneering. The federal patronage that relocated one Nantucket-born Fillmore to a position in the San Francisco Mint in 1863, and one of the Cincinnati branch to an Indian agent's appointment in Oklahoma a generation later, created variants of the same pattern.

Indeed, by the middle of the nineteenth century, when the maturing of any new frontier was becoming a matter of years rather than decades, the logic of patrimonial family migration seemed to be fading even for the most migratory of the Fillmore lines. The march westward halted; the urban drift began. Where westering continued, it now generally took a different pattern. Young people exposed to urban influences might still choose to move west, and families—brothers and sisters, in particular—might still move together or in chains, but they were more apt to move before marriage, and it was urban rather than agrarian opportunity that they seemed to seek on the frontier. Millard provides one early Fillmore example of this alternate strategy. Then there was his cousin's son who grew up on a farm near Buffalo, trained as a physician, and located in a Minnesota frontier town in the 1850s, and whose son, in turn, established his own practice in Kansas in the early 1880s; or the two sons of the Lake Champlain resort hotel owner, one of whom moved to Buffalo and then to newly bustling Zanesville, Ohio, in the 1830s and the other to Milwaukee a decade later; or even the farmer's son from Fillmore Corners near Syracuse who found his urban frontier in the late 1850s in the new coal and iron boomtown of Scranton in the Pennsylvania mountains. Their aspirations were entrepreneurial rather than patrimonial, and the small families that they would establish in the West were testimony to the decidedness of their break with the past.

Northern Maxeys exhibited similar changes in strategy. Various stay-at-home Maxey lines in Missouri, Ohio, Indiana, and central Illinois all responded to new local opportunity with both reduced family size and urban migration. The Illinois land that Joel Maxey chose when he left Kentucky in 1827, for example, happened to be located near the future state capital of Springfield. The agrarian frontier, to be sure, lured one son, Nelson, west in 1847 to join a Kentucky cousin who had settled along the Arkansas River fourteen years earlier. Soon marrying one of the cousin's daughters, he managed to resist the California gold that lured so many along the trail west from Fort Smith and instead turned south to Texas, to the booming cotton lands of the Brazos, where as a deputy sheriff he met a gunfighter's death attempting to make an arrest in the tempestuous years after the Civil War. But remaining at home in Illinois brought both prosperity and a brush with history to his less adventurous brothers, one as an entrepreneurial farmer, the other as a Springfield politician and father-in-law of

Abraham Lincoln's law partner and biographer. One grandson would briefly try his hand at Nebraska farming, and another would die in California in 1866, but most remained in the new middle-class mold that the family had fashioned for itself as Illinois emerged from the frontier.

Southern Maxeys, by contrast, tended to persist much longer in the patrimonial mode. Fewer Maxey lines halted their westward march quite so decisively as did many of the Fillmores. Both the slower southern pace of antebellum modernization and the disruptions and destruction of the Civil War and its aftermath held out fewer incentives to southern Maxeys to abandon familiar family strategies. Families remained large, and well-cultivated kinship connections ensured that westering habits seldom died out completely in any Maxey line. Where they did, the predictable consequence of thinning patrimonial resources was a species of rural proletarianization that underlined just what was at stake in continued family access to ever newer Wests. For southwestern Virginia Maxeys reduced to coal-mine or stone-quarry labor by the late nineteenth century, for example, the West might still offer hope, but for protelarianized families like these it was now the workman's hope of jobs at quarries in Nebraska or at new coal mines in Arkansas or northern New Mexico, where one Maxey died in a mine accident in 1913.

Well-to-do planting families could prove receptive to new kinds of domestic and educational aspirations, and the occasional Maxey planter's son was able to realize an entrepreneurial family style in a nearby town one, for example, became a leading Nashville manufacturer of tin and sheet iron and the city's mayor in the early 1840s, whereas another, after trying an Illinois law practice and the California goldfields, settled down to storekeeping, law, and politics back home in Kentucky. But more often, the limits of the local economy ensured that entrepreneurially inclined southern Maxeys, like their more patrimonial kin, chose to relocate to the frontier as they came of age, drawing on the family network to assist them in their search for urban opportunity in the West. Perhaps the clearest examples occurred in the family of William Maxey, one of those revolutionary veterans who settled in Kentucky in the 1780s. One of his older sons early moved his young family to the Boons Lick area of Missouri and then late in life removed with them farther west in the classic patrimonial pattern; several of William's other children settled into prosperous local farming back in Kentucky. But two of his sons took up the law, one went into local politics, and another became a cabinetmaker, and the next generation continued the family march into the professions and other urban occupations. Not even advantageous marriages into other planter families could secure this family's economic aspirations in Kentucky's Pennyrile, however, and by the late 1840s one young lawyer was on his way to relatives in the Arkansas Valley, and his brother, a former teacher, was in the California goldfields. But it would be Texas where the family's entrepreneurial energies would particularly focus. Samuel Bell Maxey knew the area from service in the Mexican War and from glowing reports by earlier migrating in-laws. So in the summer of 1857, he and his father—William's youngest son—sold their joint Kentucky law practice and, with their households, set out by wagon through Arkansas and Oklahoma to the new boomtown of Paris in the Blacklands of northern Texas. Here Samuel Bell prospered in a legal and political career that brought him to a Confederate generalship and the U.S. Senate. An uncle soon arrived, then an aunt's family left their Tennessee plantation to buy two thousand acres nearby; they were quickly followed by other young cousins—a lawyer, a doctor, a merchant—in an entrepreneurial migration that continued to dispatch young Maxeys westward along the kinship chain to Texas and Oklahoma for more than three decades after the Civil War. When James, a Civil War veteran three years out of law school, left Tennessee for Texas, a law partnership with his father's second cousin, General Maxey, was waiting; his distant Tennessee cousin Napoleon drew on kin in Illinois, where he read law, attended the old University of Chicago, and after a decade of Illinois practice moved with his family to Muskogee to become one of the first two lawyers admitted to the new Oklahoma bar.

Among the Fillmores it was the New Brunswickers, confined like many of the southern Maxeys to a slowly developing periphery of the new economic order, who most resembled them in their resistance to newer family strategies. The two families' migration streams would finally meet as the Canadian line projected the Fillmore patrimonial tradition of large farm families and westering habits through America's final farm frontiers—Kansas, Oklahoma, Idaho—to its sad end in the Dust Bowl trek to California. After three generations of internal colonization in the Maritimes, restlessness—probably induced by family involvement in the logging boom—seemed to strike several of the area's large Fillmore clans after the late 1830s, first sending one group of families to Ontario and later Michigan, then another to northern Illinois and, after the Civil War, points west. Perhaps their northern isolation had left them less prepared to take advantage of newer kinds of opportunity than were their distant cousins reared within the increasingly entrepreneurial communities of the Yankee diaspora. Indeed, at the very time that the first Fillmore moved west from the Maritimes, one of his brothers blazed the trail south to the milltowns of Massachusetts, a trail that many among the increasingly proletarianized subsequent generations would be forced to follow.

Finally, one other pattern of westward migration also becomes more visible in the historical record of both families by the middle of the nineteenth century: the feckless drift or adventuresome quest of the young man who seemingly cuts loose from the family and lights out for the territory, on his own or with others of his kind. The frontier had always tempted the young in this fashion, though such rebels and free spirits are the most difficult for the genealogist to track. Jesse Maxey must have been such a one in his prerevolutionary youth, as surely was Elisha Maxey who, orphaned early, found his way in his early twenties from Tennessee to Stephen B. Austin's young Texas colony on the Brazos. But now there were added inducements. For one thing, the constant series of mineral discoveries that began in 1849 proved a powerful solvent of family bonds, extracting young men from their families' patrimonial strategies and seemingly rewarding most those least hampered by the inflexibility of immediate family responsibility. Gold could be integrated as a resource into the family economy, to be sure, whether by using a grubstake from the goldfields to re-endow the patrimony back East or by establishing a new family line in the West. Two young Maritimers from separate Fillmore branches returned home from California prosperous enough to establish substantial patrimonial families of their own; entrepreneurial Maxeys from Illinois (two), Kentucky, and Tennessee established urban families on similar gold rush foundations.

Another drifted back from California to family farming in Missouri, and yet another made the transition from miner to prosperous commercial farmer and family man in California's Santa Clara County. But others, like the California-bound Maxey, recently widowed, who left his young children with various relatives back in Indiana and was never heard from again, or like the Fillmore father and son of New Brunswick stock who disappeared into the goldfields of the Black Hills in the 1870s, document the disruptive potential of the lure of western wealth.

Other factors also conspired to weaken or supplement family direction of westward migration in the latter decades of the century. Civil War service diverted northerners as well as southerners from planned life paths, and postwar offers of soldiers' homesteads beckoned veterans west to the chancy fortunes of the semiarid plains. The ever more rapid pace of settlement and development compromised the ability of many families to adapt old patrimonial strategies to new circumstances at the same time that the expansion of railroads and natural resource extraction created western wage-earning opportunities largely independent of the agricultural sector to which family pioneering had proven so well-adapted. Even the farming frontier found it easier to dispense with a family work force in this new capitalist era of machinery, hired labor, and speculative homesteading for future sale, as the phenomenon of the single female homesteader attests.

Thus when John Jefferson Maxey left Missouri for the West Coast in 1862 after the death of his father, family planning undoubtedly guided his initial steps. He probably traveled with his sister's family and in Oregon found a home with relatives who had emigrated a couple years earlier. But a political quarrel with his uncle forced him out to earn a living on his own as a farm laborer and miner, drifting down to California and marrying along the way. Quarrels with their stepfather probably launched two of his second cousins, ages twenty-one and twelve, on a similar odyssey from Missouri to the wage earners' frontier in the Pacific Northwest a couple decades later. Yet family still had a way of reasserting its claims. Recall Millard Fillmore's black-sheep cousin, Henry Glezen, who lived a scandalous life in the Minnesota Indian trade but nevertheless drew siblings and cousins to settle nearby once the area opened for white settlement. Or consider Henry's sons, reared by their divorced mother in near poverty on the Minnesota frontier. One ran away early, later surfacing in Montana, but the other, after drifting across the plains from Minnesota to Texas to Colorado and working here as a railcar checker, there as a mule driver or miner, finally married, entered the real estate business, sent for his mother, and put down roots in Kansas City to found the still thriving Unity School of Christianity and to pioneer in radio evangelism. Even the young Illinois Fillmore who rode with the U.S. Cavalry in the Indian wars of the 1870s later settled down to raise a family in the Washington Territory.

For eight generations the frontier was an integral part of Maxey and Fillmore family strategy. Maxeys and Fillmores were loggers in Michigan and fur traders in Minnesota, ranchers in Texas, New Mexico, and Colorado, miners in Arkansas and California, fruit growers in Washington, planters throughout the South, doctors and lawyers in boom-towns across half the nation, and farmers everywhere. Their histories, and those of countless other westering old-stock American families, illustrate the complex ways in which family logic influenced who moved west, with whom, at which stages in their life cycles, where they chose to settle, and what kinds of communities they formed, as well as how the opportunity they encountered in the West shaped subsequent family choices.

Patrimonial strategies undoubtedly peopled most agrarian frontiers, demanding successive generational migrations of young, growing families moving within chains of neighbors and kin in the hope of maintaining the linkage between land that could support the family and the large family that alone could provide labor to work the land. Their dominant form of movement was what might best be termed *colonization*, the uprooting and transplantation of significant segments of a family line, often in conjunction with a larger group of relatives and kin, from an older agrarian region to a newly opened one—the functional equivalent of Bailyn's "provincial" trans-Atlantic migration stream. *Colony*, it might be noted, was a term employed by nineteenth-century frontier folk to describe both highly organized settlement ventures and clustered family settlements. Formal colonization schemes were a feature of virtually every newly developing western region throughout the century, whether organized by land or transportation companies, by religious groups, or by voluntary organizations. But even they relied on colonizing families for their main recruits.

Consider the patrimonial logic of colonization. A farm family with growing children could sell its farm, developed with their common labor, perhaps to an older child who would remain behind, perhaps to a stranger. The family could then invest the profits and its own joint labor—its greatest resource—in cheaper western land, providing farms for the remaining children as they came of age. The migration might occur all at once, or different family members might migrate in stages, some staying behind to earn money and others going ahead to prepare the way. It often made sense for the older as well as the younger generation to head west. Parental wisdom and labor were a critical part of the human capital that the family economy could muster; the parental presence helped keep the children within the cooperative circle of the family, and the children embodied the parents' best hope for a secure retirement. Friends and neighbors often migrated together, turning the wider community into a portable resource that could be carried along rather than left behind and creating chains of linked communities stretching across the nation.

In theory such colonizing families and friends could continue together westward in stages generation after generation. An infant might make her first move with her parents and grandparents when she was still in her mother's arms; as a young bride she might move again with her husband, child, parents, and siblings and move one final time when herself a grandparent. "I had been reared to a belief and faith in the pleasure of a frequent change of country," one southern autobiographer recalled. A move could fail, of course, and all hope of perpetuating the patrimony vanish. Individual children might drift away on their own. The family might be fortunate enough to acquire land enough for more than one generation, permitting members to break the cycle of colonization. Or—and this occurred increasingly over the course of the nineteenth century, as we have seen—the character of local opportunity could change, tempting families to abandon the logic of patrimonial conservation and venture into the world of enterprising individualism. Parents with sufficient resources might decide to remain in place to enjoy the fruits of a developed society; children might take their inheritance in the form of an education preparing them for entrepreneurial or professional life or in the form of capital or credit that would enable them to relocate—on the frontier as readily as in the more developed parts of the country—without the necessity of relying on the pooled labor of the family or the support of a colony. And the West itself changed. By the 1830s, the quickened pace of western development was multiplying urban opportunities for those of an entrepreneurial bent. In the South, frontiersmen with capital could substitute slave for family labor, and everywhere it became increasingly easy for an individual with funds but no family to hire the labor and buy the machinery necessary to establish a farm or a business outside the context of formal family colonization.

The smaller families that broke free of patrimonial logic to take entrepreneurial advantage of the new modernizing economy thus had less dependence on the frontier, but its burgeoning cities and resource speculation could still beckon both young folk leaving home to establish new families of their own and more mature families relocating for a better life. And for those trapped in the hard logic of the proletarian family, the West increasingly in the course of the nineteenth century meant jobs, particularly transient jobs for single migrants whose remitted wages could support family members left behind or free young people from the burden of family demands, even if at the price of long years isolated from the world of the family itself.

The Diversity of Domestic Landscapes in the West

For all their regional and temporal variation, these family strategies for western settlement still rested upon a basic domestic consensus derived from the western European tradition. But as young Volley Maxey, for one, tragically discovered on a summer day in 1872, there were other familial traditions, other family logics, that also played major roles in shaping the nineteenth-century West. Born and raised in a small kin-linked settlement on the northwestern Texas frontier, the six-year-old was playing with his toddler sister and a couple of other children around the woodpile where his widowed Indiana-born grandfather was chopping wood when suddenly his playmates' mother urgently called them back to the cabin. She had seen a raiding party of Comanches, who for generations had supported the family bands in which they lived through raiding and trade in horses, cattle, and captives. Her warning came too late. Volley's grandfather and his two playmates were killed, his baby brother died in his mother's arms, and he and his sister were abducted by the raiding party. When his sister tired and began to cry, she was soon killed. Volley, known to his captors as "Topish," lived three years with them, until the final stages of Comanche resistance to reservation confinement. Horseback, the chief of one of the Quahada bands, traded him and several other young captives to the Quaker agent at the Fort Sill reservation in return for captured Comanche women whom the army was holding. Volley's reintegration into white society was not easy: he had forgotten all his English; he ran from the soldiers when he first saw them; he was rude and, by his family's lights, uncivilized. As an adult he drifted beyond the family's ken.

Maxeys and Fillmores were seldom forced to experience quite so immediately the clash between their family strategies and other family traditions they encountered in the West. Theirs was, after all, the dominant pattern in the region's evolving domestic landscape. Their family system, as Congress had early recognized, ensured the motive and the demographic means to maintain a continual frontier flow, and along with their herds and their household effects, they carried westward their domestic ideology and the power of the American state, which they used to shape the new institutions and law that their family regime required. Family practices different from their own were often central to the critiques they leveled against other groups: to their perceptions of Indians as savage, Chinese as depraved, Mexicans as loose and lazy. Thus family life was irrevocably transformed for the Native Americans who encountered Maxey or Fillmore Indian fighters in Tennessee or Texas or Wyoming and for the African Americans whom Maxeys took west as slaves or sold before their own departure. But it was similarly if more subtly influenced also by the Fillmore Indian agent who sought to impose federally dictated family policy in Oklahoma and by the Maxey judge who coped with the Mormon family system in Utah. In Minnesota Henry G. Fillmore lived and worked within an Ojibwa-French mixed-blood community that soon acquired a German cast; his son made his first money in a Colorado community similarly shaped both by mixed-bloods and by expansionist Hispanic settlers from farther south. Maxey and Fillmore forty-niners undoubtedly confronted Chinese in the California mines. A Fillmore in Cincinnati married a German pioneer's daughter; a San Francisco kinsman took an Irish wife.

Such alternative family traditions were inevitably forced to adapt as they confronted the economic changes and institutional pressures set in motion by the main currents of American westward penetration. But they also proved surprisingly successful in using family as a defensive instrument to ward off some of the consequences of unwanted change and to preserve enclaved cultures, particularly in cases where their family strategies rested on an agrarian patrimonialism strongly defended by religion or geographical isolation.

Thus the rural Hispanic families of northern New Mexico after the American takeover in 1846 drew strength from the communal economies of the extended family plazas that constituted the basic units in their settlement system. They could evade many of the consequences of American governmental and ecclesiastical pressures by retreating into the networks of kin that defined their daily world, effectively converting local justice of the peace courts, communal land rights and community water-control associations, and religious sodalities into alternative forms of local ordering, and hiving off new colonies northward into Colorado as population grew or land was lost to Yankee claimants. For old elites throughout the former Mexican territories, intermarriage with incoming Yankees proved an important tactic in maintaining status and at least partially assimilating the newcomers to accustomed ways. Over the longer term there were real limits to the autonomy of the family. Anglo inheritance laws, Anglo control of land claim courts, and Anglo access to the expanding sectors of the national economy, for example, steadily subverted Hispanic landownership throughout the Southwest, dissolving the vital link between the family and its patrimony. The proletarian niche that increasing numbers of native Tejanos and immigrant Mexicans occupied in later-nineteenth-century Texas involved such family adjustments as more households headed by single persons, more children in the work force, and smaller household size. Nevertheless, even when, at the end of the century, the land of the New Mexico and

Inspired by an encounter with a wagon train of German immigrants moving west through Nebraska, Albert Bierstadt's painting becomes an allegory for the future of the West. As the pioneers move onward, the Indians fade into the sunset.

Albert Bierstadt (1830–1902). Emigrants Crossing the Plains. Oil on canvas, 1867. National Cowboy Hall of Fame and Western Heritage Center, Oklahoma City, Oklahoma.

Colorado plazas was proving inadequate for many a family's support, creative family strategies of seasonal male labor migration channeled the adaptation and helped preserve the distinctive core of community culture.

Mormons migrating from the East similarly constructed a distinctive and enduring society for themselves in frontier Utah resting on the family practices that lay at the core of their religious belief. The Mormon family system was in many ways a logical extension of the patrimonial American family in which it was rooted, and if patrimonial logic yielded to religious fervor in fueling the initial exodus to Utah, it probably played a coequal role in supporting subsequent Mormon colonization throughout the intermountain West. It was doctrine and not economic logic, however, that saw in marriage and childbirth the divine plan for hastening the millennium and in polygamy a path to heavenly exaltation. Life in the Mormon West, accordingly, was fundamentally shaped by early and almost universal marriage, often undertaken without a secure economic base, by very high fertility, and by the practice of plural marriage, which by one recent estimate framed about a third of the men's lives, two-thirds of the women's, and half of the children's. By 1890 this self-confident society could no longer resist federal pressure against polygamy, but its religiously sanctioned patriarchal familism, marshaling family and community resources for both agriculture and trade, remained at the core of its expanding settlement region.

The commitment of various European immigrant groups to their own versions of patrimonial logic planted yet other sets of enduring family cultures in the West. It was long a cliché of western history that immigrants, in contrast to native-born Americans, lacked the skills and resources needed for frontier settlement and that if they entered farming, they did so as "fillers-in" on settled land vacated by the westward-moving native-born. Apparently, as the case of the Irish canal-diggers seemed to suggest, only as proletarian migrants in work gangs of single men could immigrants readily make their way to the West. Certainly the mining towns, lumber camps, and cities of the West always drew more than their share of foreign-born families as well as single workers. But most nonsouthern agrarian frontiers settled after the onset of mass immigration in the 1830s likewise attracted disproportionate numbers of immigrants, either directly from Europe or from older-settled areas to the east. In 1850, for example, when 9.7 percent of the American population was foreign-born, newly settled Wisconsin with 36 percent of its population born abroad was the most heavily immigrant state in the nation; forty years later, almost 43 percent of recently settled North Dakota's population was foreign-born.

The immigrant pioneers came mainly from Germany, Scandinavia, the Netherlands, Britain, the old German colonies in Russia, and even parts of Ireland and Slavic central Europe, products of a predominantly peasant emigration rooted in the old dilemma of growing families and limited land. They were confronted with the same local options as their American counterparts—entrepreneurial transformation for some, proletarianization for most—and when improved trans-Atlantic communication and transportation brought the new lands of the American West within reach, many made the same conservative choice: to move in order to preserve the family system, rather than to change the family in order to stay. The artist Albert Bierstadt encountered a "very picturesque" train of such immigrant families lumbering westward across Nebraska in 1863. "They had," his companion noted, "a large herd of cattle, and fifty wagons, mostly drawn by oxen. . . . The people themselves represented the better class of Prussian or North German peasantry. A number of strapping teamsters, in gay costumes, appeared like Westphalians. . . . All the women and children had some positive color about them, if it only amounted to a knot of ribbons, or the glimpse of a petticoat. . . . Several old women, of less than the usual anile hideousness of the German Bauerinn, were trudging along the road with the teamsters, in short blue petticoats and everlasting shoes. . . . In the wagons all manner of domestic bliss was going on . . . . Many mothers were on front seats, nursing their babies in the innocent unconsciousness of Eve . . . . Every wagon was a gem of an interior such as no Fleming ever put on canvas, and every group a *genre* piece." There is no little irony in the recognition that Bierstadt's luminous archetypal painting of American wagons moving west probably owes much to this immigrant encounter.

The same familial tradition that motivated their emigration lent such immigrant pioneers their greatest strength. With more restricted access to information than the American-born, they tended to migrate within even tighter chains of neighbors and kin, forming clustered communities whose self-segregation within the social walls of linguistic, religious, and cultural difference, buttressed by their control of local schools and government, encouraged the perpetuation of patrimonial values long after they had waned within other western family traditions. As Yankee families like the Fillmores brought their westward march to a halt, immigrants took up the slack, and by 1880, when the foreign-born comprised just over 14 percent of all farmers nationwide, their proportions among the farmers in the predominantly northern-settled states of the post-1840 frontier ranged from 65.5 percent in Minnesota, 60.5 percent in Wisconsin, and 58.4 percent in Dakota to 26 percent in Washington. Even in southern-settled and relatively immigrant-poor states like Kansas, Colorado, and Oregon, they significantly exceeded the national average. Immigrants substituted family labor for the capital they lacked, they transplanted familiar peasant inheritance customs to help bind the next generation to the farm, they used the power of religion to ward off the blandishments of outside opportunity, and when land grew scarce, they exported daughter colonies to the next frontier.

Among those who may have been on the Oregon wagon train that Bierstadt encountered, for example, or one like it, was Franz Nibler, one of Henry G. Fillmore's Minnesota neighbors, a "good solid Backwoods man" of Bavarian birth recently discharged for illness from the Union army. Four years later he returned to lead seventeen families of his German Catholic neighbors and kin in a twenty-six-wagon train from Minnesota across the northern trail to Oregon. His companions were, by and large, married couples in their thirties and forties with six to eight growing children each—Bavarians, Eifelers, Alsatians, and Westphalians who had migrated a decade earlier to the new lands of Minnesota from older German frontiers in Ohio, Michigan, Missouri, and Wisconsin. The extended Schultheis family, for one, had emigrated from Bavaria to Missouri as early as 1836, from whence they trekked in a large family caravan of ox-drawn wagons to Minnesota in 1854. Once in Oregon's Willamette Valley, they became fillers-in for a time, establishing on land abandoned by early American settlers the nucleus of an enduring German Catholic settlement sheltered, like its Minnesota progenitor, beneath the towers of its Benedictine abbey. But when the undulating hills of eastern Washington's Palouse opened to settlement in the mid-1870s, younger members of the Schultheis family headed east to found yet another expansive German Catholic community on yet another frontier.

Family processes like these stretched archipelagos of ethnically defined European settlement islands across successive nineteenth-century Wests. Their family cultures varied from one another in detail and inevitably changed with time. Thus Norwegian families learned that they had to rely more on the labor of the nuclear family than they ever had in Europe; more of their children married, at younger ages, and fertility increased. Women's domestic duties thereby increased as well, while new kinds of farming altered the gendered division of labor in field and barn, and gradually, with time and increasing prosperity, old habits of prenuptial conception disappeared, and bourgeois fertility reduction began. Sharing a familiar patrimonial familism, posing no fundamental challenge to American domestic ideologies, European immigrants like these were able to carve out distinctive and enduring western domestic landscapes.

The pressures of prejudice helped deny other western family cultures the luxury of such relatively autonomous evolution, however, and weakened their ability to directly mediate the settlement process. For the Chinese, for example, it was the absence of family that defined their situation. They left their families behind when they responded to the lure of California gold, seeking as entrepreneurs or laborers the stake that would enable them to maintain or advance family interests back home. In this they differed little from their Yankee counterparts in the mining West or from later labor migrants like the Italians, who would show even less tendency to remain in America than the Chinese. The small numbers of Chinese women who arrived on America's western shore tended to come as prostitutes, perhaps after being sold to relieve their family of the burden of a female mouth or to help finance the advance of more favored members. No more than 5 percent of the region's Chinese population before 1880 was female. Wives remained behind to serve the interests of the family at home, and single men who wished to marry usually had to recross the ocean to do so. The price of these long-distance family strategies was an American life lived in single-sex households and community institutions geared to the needs of single men. Kinship ties, however, forged familiar chains of migration and settlement, and the gradual establishment of local families—by 1880 a third or more of the women in most communities were now wives, though often considerably younger than their husbands, reflecting their relative scarcity—suggested that some of the Chinese were finding motive and means to remain. But from the beginning, they encountered virulent racism that culminated in 1882 in a series of federal exclusion acts effectively curtailing their ability not only to form families in America but even to return from visits to families back in China. It would be well into the twentieth century before a real second generation and a supportive family culture could emerge.

There was even less room for family autonomy among African Americans brought west as slaves before the Civil War. Recent studies suggest that migrant slaves were more youthful than the slave population as a whole, with as many as half still in their teens, but perhaps more evenly divided between males and females than westward-moving whites. "I do not wish families and only desire to purchase those who are YOUNG and likely," advertised a Missouri dealer in 1856. Regardless of whether slaves were sent west by traders or migrated with their owners, such westering almost by definition meant family disruption. Although some masters may have sought to keep slave families together, most apparently did not or could not. Both debt and death could force slave sales; when a master's estate was divided among the heirs, so too were the slaves, and when some family members moved west, so too might their share of the family slaves. Many slaves were hired out on the frontier, as elsewhere, and many frontiersmen owned or rented only a slave or two. Most slaves thus did their pioneering with few of the even minimal supports of family that they may have enjoyed farther east; westering required of them the arduous construction of new domestic ties.

Free blacks, however, shared many of the patrimonial values of white society and were able to participate to a limited extent in the agrarian settlement process. Thus in 1855, two decades after North Carolina–born Walden Stewart and his family settled in Illinois, he pulled up stakes once again at the age of sixty and moved with them north to the Wisconsin frontier, undoubtedly seeking not only more land for his growing family but also freedom from the increasing restrictions that Illinois was placing on people of color. Here they were soon joined by at least ten other black families, a number of them also from North Carolina, and here they prospered and remained, sharing school, church, and ultimately intermarriage with their immigrant neighbors. Similar patrimonial aspirations among relatively self-sufficient African-American farm families from the border South drew increasing numbers to colonies on the Kansas frontier after the Civil War, culminating in the 1879 "Kansas Fever" that for a brief period also spread to the more desperately poor of the lower South. The numbers of westering black families were always small, however, in comparison with those who remained within the South or later moved north. These families had fewer resources of their own than their

INDIAN SUGAR CAMP

Seth Eastman's paintings of Indian life focus particularly on domestic genre scenes. Based on observations made during his tour of duty as an officer at Fort Snelling (Minneapolis) in the mid-1840s, this watercolor sketch of a Winnebago sugar camp suggests the important role played by women in domestic labor and production.

Seth Eastman (1808–75). Indian Sugar Camp. Watercolor on paper, ca. 1850. James J. Hill Reference Library, St. Paul, Minnesota.

white counterparts and drew little institutional support from local society in the West; black homesteaders in the Nicodemus, Kansas, area, for example, were unable to find a local surveyor willing to survey their claims. Their communities, where they survived, could seldom prosper. The substantial African-American presence in the later-nineteenth-century West undoubtedly owed far more to labor-seeking migrants drifting from or with other members of their essentially proletarian families and living in households like the one in Tombstone in 1880 shared by a thirty-year-old South Carolina laborer, his young California-born wife, and eight other African-American men in their thirties and forties—blacksmiths, waiters, porters, laborers, cooks—all, like so many others in Tombstone at the time, without families of their own. The family trajectories of pioneers like these remain largely unstudied.

It was undoubtedly Native Americans, however, who felt the most concerted pressure on their family systems. It is difficult to generalize about the variety of family systems that Native Americans evolved before white penetration into the West. Several points are clear, however. First, few bore much relationship to the patrimonial logic rooted in family rights to privately owned land from which the European-American family system derived. Second, as Volley Maxey learned only too well, systems of kinship, marriage, and adoption, often more expansive, complex, and flexible than those of most European Americans, functioned as effective demographic and economic adaptive mechanisms to the uncertainties of low-technology lives. Third, common practices like polyandry, serial marriage, and women's physical labor, whatever their logic within Indian family systems, struck nineteenth-century European Americans not only as alien but immoral, and inevitably provoked repression. And fourth, like their European-derived counterparts, these family systems were in a constant process of change and adaptation.

Although research has addressed the specific historical contours of such familial transformation, it has tended to focus much more on how various Indian family systems changed or resisted change than on how the family variably influenced adaptation. Often the first consequences of white contact for many Indian peoples, experienced at long distance, were new techniques of hunting and transportation made possible by the horse, or higher standards of living through trade, and family systems were frequently reshaped to take advantage of them. The woodland Winnebagos of eighteenth-century Wisconsin, for example, broke their large agrarian community into small and mobile family bands, the better to hunt for the furs desired by their white trading partners. Polygynous familes organized around groups of co-wives emerged among the early-nineteenth-century Cheyennes as they abandoned agriculture and moved out onto the plains to hunt and trade, an adaptation both to the surplus of females that warfare created and to the need for more women to process the increased products of the hunt. The status of women changed with their exclusion from the hunt, and extrafamilial male sodalities took on a greater societal role. As Cherokees on the trans-Appalachian frontier adapted to closer contact with white settlers and markets in the period before federal removal policies, many exchanged their communalism, clans, and extended family life for agriculture and nuclear families while others, reflecting the same sort of logic that propelled white families to invade their lands, migrated westward across the Mississippi in an effort to preserve the old familial order. Indians in California who survived the initial American onslaught, with its particularly severe attacks on women through rape, prostitution, and disease, frequently had to take what refuge they could in proletarian strategies that left them working for Americans in nonfamily settings with little chance for family life or biological and cultural reproduction.

Native American family systems faced intensified pressures with coerced concentration on Indian reservations in the latter half of the century and again with the subsequent breakup of many reservations into individual land allotments toward the end of the century. For one thing, both federal policy and missionary persuasion aimed at forcing Native Americans into the nineteenth-century American mold of male-supported nuclear agrarian families and female domesticity, using both formal means like schools, supervision by matrons and agents, and Courts of Indian Offenses and even more effective tactics like excluding women from public discussion, channeling annuity payments only through heads of household, designing housing for nuclear families, providing men with wage labor on the agency, and implementing family-based allotment itself. Under such demands, for example, the extended, kin-linked Comanche bands broke up into more numerous, smaller residential clusters often composed of lineally extended family households, and the salience of family and kin increased over that of larger tribal groupings; the gender balance of power within the families and kin groups of the Teton Sioux shifted further in the male direction. The very ability of the family to reproduce itself was endangered when nutrition was compromised, as it so often was, through federal agents' efforts to force behavioral change by withholding

rations or banning traditional medicine or through the sheer incompetence and corruption that plagued the reservation system. But federal policy also worked against intended familial consequences. Thus individual land allotment, in theory designed to anchor Indians irrevocably in the logic of the nuclear family, more often in practice proved a means of stripping their land from them altogether, lending new rationality to still vital traditions of extended family communal living and kin support as a strategy for shared survival. And increasing reliance on cash income from land leases or welfare payments that, thanks to American inheritance laws and domestic ideology, passed equally—or in the case of welfare, primarily to women—could mean that family balance shifted away from the male head.

Indeed, despite severe constraints, Native American family systems, like other western family traditions, were able to influence as well as be influenced by the currents of change, though we know much less than we should about the implications of differing family cultures for Indian negotiations of life in the modernizing West. Thus customs of fictive kinship, adoption, and marriage alliance proved potent means of integrating early traders into Indian society on essentially Indian terms. Through Indian wives, European Americans acquired both access to Indian trade and processors of the pelts and skins for which they traded. Their mixed-race families mediated relations between their two peoples in many areas of the West for generations, with family strategies that sometimes promoted the native relatives' gradual adaptation to newer ways but equally often depended on their ruthless exploitation; in contrast to the case in Canada, however, American circumstances and racial mores ultimately prevented them from consolidating an enduring peoplehood of their own.

But interracial alliances were not the only way that Native Americans could use the family to structure adaptation. Many Winnebagos, for example, converted their small family bands into successful instruments for resistance to removal, repeatedly slipping away from successive reservations in Iowa, Minnesota, and Nebraska to old camps in the forests of Wisconsin, until the government in the 1870s was finally forced to acknowledge their right to claim Wisconsin homesteads of their own. Hopis conserved traditional, sedentary family forms in their densely settled high pueblos at the price of disease, high mortality, and ultimately labor migration and fertility reduction; their more flexible Navajo neighbors adopted pastoralism, then home manufacture and wage labor, maintaining high fertility and high population growth and, like their Hispanic and Mormon neighbors, supporting territorial expansion in the process. Band allegiances often structured settlement location and later allotment choices on Plains Indian reservations, and among the Crows, for example, the clan system provided valuable continuity in marriage regulation despite the unfamiliar reservation setting. Many Indians clearly found their flexible systems of marriage commitment a more rational response to the uncertain vagaries of modernizing life than the lifetime commitment that white society tried to impose and was indeed already in the process of abandoning for itself. Reservation life in effect lent Native American family cultures some of the protective isolation that other enduring western family traditions had also managed to find, but such protection was purchased at a daunting price.

Family Life in the West

There was, then, no single style of family life in the West. America's successive nineteenth-century Wests were shared by a variety of indigenous and colonizing family cultures. Nor could the meanings, functions, and roles that these cultures assigned to the family and to individuals by virtue of their family membership ever be assumed. In the West, as elsewhere, the contours of family culture were constantly evolving through the negotiation, contestation, and unconscious accommodation of family members, in their work sharing, at social gatherings, in bedrooms, even—as in the case of the Fillmores of St. Cloud, Minnesota—on the kitchen floor and in the courtroom.

Mary and Henry Fillmore must have entered their marriage in the early winter of 1853 with conflicting and confused sets of assumptions and aspirations. Mary Georgiana Stone was just sixteen, newly arrived on Minnesota's logging frontier with her family and other relatives from Wisconsin and before that Maine and the Maritimes. Perhaps part of the attraction of Henry Glezen Fillmore, the twenty-five-year-old trader whom she married at a little millsite on the Mississippi, was the éclat of his kinship with the nation's recently retired president. She clearly aspired to much of the life-style promised by the new domestic ideology of the middle class. She had taken dancing lessons in Wisconsin. She enjoyed fine clothes, furniture, and entertaining and was resentful when her husband's business reverses forced her to do heavy housework. Producing a son almost exactly nine months after her marriage, she soon induced her husband to conduct their sexual intercourse so as "not to beget her with child," though "through a mistake on her part of the effect of free and full sexual cohabitation immediately after her menstrual course" she bore a second son three years later. Not only did she seek to restrict her fertility but, Henry would later charge, she gossiped about her methods with her female friends. She was also, it seemed, careless enough in her general demeanor to lend credence to charges of adultery with the housepainter who lived two doors away.

If Mary Georgiana was not fully adept in the practice of the new domesticity, Henry was even less so. His family expectations seemed more old-fashioned; he wanted purity and probity of his wife, of course, but he also wanted more children and more work and expressed his objections to her life-style in a decidedly ungenteel fashion derived more, perhaps, from the rough world of the Indian trade than his patrimonial parents' home. Not only did he beat and curse her often, but once (he admitted) or twice (she charged) he even attempted to rape her on the kitchen floor in front of her children and his young female cousin, declaring, she said, "that he . . . had no other desire to gratify by such intercourse than the desire to abuse . . . and disgrace [her] in the eyes of his . . . family, and bring her . . . to scorn, and loathing." She was, he charged, "a damned whore" who had committed adultery, admitted to being raped by that dancing master in Wisconsin, and bragged that another man had fathered her second child. She resisted him, she said, because he had "a loathsome venereal disease," and once she found out (from her female support network, perhaps?) how such a disease was contracted, she left him in the autumn of 1860 and sought out the judge. After her divorce, Mary succeeded in raising at least one son in the entrepreneurial values to which she aspired and through him achieved a secure old age in the middle-class world of Kansas City. Henry became a horse doctor and lived out his life bereft of family in the male world of St. Cloud boarding houses.

The confusion of family models and practice within the Fillmore household mirrored the mosaic within their broader community. One young neighbor reveled in her companionate marriage, doting over her children, contributing sentimental prose and verse extolling frontier domesticity to a Philadelphia ladies' magazine, and cherishing the sensuously loving letters she received from her attorney husband when he was away. Another was a tough divorced feminist who edited an abolitionist newspaper. Still another was a former schoolteacher who worked with her pioneer husband to carve out a frontier farm for the family and a gracious, busy domestic sphere for herself and who reared their three sons to professional and business occupations. Yet just a few miles down the road were wooden-shoed German immigrant women in thatched-roof log cabins, carefully bargaining with time-honored peasant logic about dowries and family bonds of maintenance for aged parents, and mixed-blood women negotiating the exchange of one partner for another.

The varieties of family cultures to be found in the nineteenth-century West were all subject to the currents of economic and ideological change that were transforming the nation itself. They were influenced also in regionally distinctive fashion by the opportunities and constraints of the western environment, by the self-selection inherent in their migration or local persistence, and by the mutual need to coexist. The result was both regional variation and temporal change. The older agrarian Wests of the first half of the century were the locus classicus of the patrimonial family, with relatively little extractive industry to attract a permanent nonfamily work force, fairly even sex ratios from an early date, and few remaining indigenous families. In the South, slavery created the main variant family style; in the North, prosperity encouraged rapid acceptance of new entrepreneurial family styles for those who chose to remain. Frontiers incorporated after mid-century offered more varied opportunities to attract more varying kinds of families. There were greater numbers of entrepreneurial and proletarian familes to be attracted; new family ideals had filtered even into farming families, and new machinery and labor availability permitted farming without large families; more immigrants were arriving; and indigenous peoples had nowhere left to go. The result was a more variegated domestic landscape in the later Wests, more enclaves of variant family types, and more rapid shifts when, as we saw in Tombstone, one kind of economy replaced another and brought with it a new mix of family styles. Differing family economies were as often symbiotic as competing, as in the case of the farm families who clustered around the edges of mining, ranching, and logging regions to provide them with food and seasonal labor or the entrepreneurial and proletarian families of the towns that serviced the countryside. Yet their cultural incompatibilities were often real and have become the stuff of western legend.

Nineteenth-century observers were indeed more astute than early-twentieth-century commentators: families easternized the region more than they were westernized by it. Men, women, and children brought westward with them habits and aspirations nurtured in the East; like the women who struggled to preserve accustomed domestic ideals in their wagons on the Oregon trail, the settlers used these aspirations to filter and focus their adjustment to the west. Family life changed as people moved west, but it probably would have changed for them had they stayed home. The western women who complained most about loneliness, about being torn from relatives and kin, one suspects, were women who were migrating precisely because their husbands had already broken free of patrimonial ties. For so many others, migration in extended processions of kith and kin was a way of avoiding precisely what, like one Iowa pioneer, so many feared from the changes of the modernizing world: "a drifted family . . . a broken, distorted chain."

Perhaps what was most distinctive about family life in the West, then, was the new lease on life that the region offered a patrimonial logic that was rapidly becoming obsolescent in more settled areas. Fertility ratios were consistently higher on new frontiers than elsewhere, less perhaps because opportunity there encouraged families to have more children, as scholars have often argued, than because families enmeshed in strategies that rested on large numbers of children knew they had to seek the frontier. The West in this sense proved not so much the source of all that was new in American family life as a haven for much that was old, and it was the demographic inexorability of those old forms as much as the speculative entrepreneurship of the new that drove Americans westward. But the region also shared the nation's public aspirations for the new ideals of the middle-class companionate family, however much difficulty westerners like the Fillmores might have had in putting them into practice, and by the end of the century the accelerating pace of economic and cultural transformation was rapidly marginalizing other family styles.

Thus there is a final irony to be wrung from the John Ford saga of western domestication with which this chapter began. In the film, as in the real world of the late-nineteenth-century West, what was really conquered and banished was not so much savagery and anomic individualism as it was the domestic tradition of the extended, patrimonial families whose energies had engulfed and reshaped frontier after frontier in the American mold. It was, after all, Wyatt Earp who drove off into the sunset to rejoin his patrimonial kin group, while entrepreneurial Clementine—single, cultured, now career-oriented, and far from her family of origin—remained to inherit the new community of strangers that foreshadowed the social organization of the twentieth-century West. It was "My Darling Clementine" who claimed both the movie's ending and its title.

Bibliographic Note

At the core of this essay lies an analysis of the thousands of pieces of family information contained in two fine published genealogies: Charles L. Fillmore, *So Soon Forgotten: Three Thousand Fillmores* (Halifax, Nova Scotia, 1984), and Edythe Maxey Clark, *The Maxeys of Virginia: A Genealogical History of the Descendants of Edward and Susannah Maxey* (Baltimore, 1980). The story was supplemented through further research in manuscript census schedules, local histories, and for the Fillmores, "Mary Georgiana Fillmore vs. Henry G. Fillmore," St. Cloud District Court, Civil Case File No. 44, Minnesota Historical Society, and Henry G. Fillmore's obituary, *St. Cloud Journal-Press*, November 15, 1899.

Family history in general is a relatively new field of academic study. Charles Tilly, "Family History, Social History, and Social Change," *Journal of Family History* 12 (1987): 319–30, and Tamara K. Hareven, "The History of the Family and the Complexity of Social Change," *American Historical Review* 96 (1991): 95–124, provide orientation. In "Family Strategy: A Dialogue," *Historical Methods* 20 (1987): 113–25, Leslie Page Moch et al. debate a central concept for this essay. Accessible introductions to the history of western European family systems are Martine Segalen, *Historical Anthropology of the Family*, trans. J. C. Whitehouse and Sarah Matthews (Cambridge, Eng., 1986), David Levine, *Reproducing Families: The Political Economy of English Population History* (Cambridge, Eng., 1987), and James Casey, *The History of the Family* (Oxford, Eng., 1989). Important for conceptualizing nineteenth-century change is Leonore Davidoff and Catherine Hall, *Family Fortunes: Men and Women of the English Middle Class, 1780–1850* (Chicago, 1987).

American family historiography begins with Arthur W. Calhoun, *A Social History of the American Family from Colonial Times to the Present*, 2 vols. (Cleveland, 1917). For its evolution, consult Susan M. Juster and Maris A. Vinovskis, "Changing Perspectives on the American Family in the Past," *Annual Reviews in Sociology* 13 (1987): 193–216. Modern surveys include Carl Degler, *At Odds: Women and the Family in America from the Revolution to the Present* (New York, 1980), Stephanie Coontz, *The Social Origins of Private Life: A History of American Families, 1600–1900* (New York, 1988), and Steven Mintz and Susan Kellogg, *Domestic Revolutions: A Social History of American Family Life* (New York, 1988). John Demos, "Images of the Family, Then and Now," *Past, Present, and Personal: The Family and the Life Course in American History* (New York, 1986), offers an important periodization.

A pathbreaking approach to the family in the American West can be found in Elliott West, *Growing Up with the Country: Childhood on the Far-Western Frontier* (Albuquerque, 1989). James E. Davis, *Frontier America, 1800–1840: A Comparative Demographic Analysis of the Settlement Process* (Glendale, Calif., 1977), explores frontier demography. For the fertility issue, see Richard A. Easterlin, "Population Change and Farm Settlement in the Northern United States," *Journal of Economic History* 36 (1976): 45–75, and Daniel Scott Smith, "'Early' Fertility Decline in America: A Problem in Family History," *Journal of Family History* 12 (1987): 73–84. The history of western women is much better developed than western family history per se; see Susan Armitage, "Women and Men in Western History: A Stereoptical Vision," *Western Historical Quarterly* 16 (1985): 381–95. Overviews include the following: Julie Roy Jeffrey, *Frontier Women: The Trans-Mississippi West, 1840–1880* (New York, 1979); Sandra L. Myres, *Westering Women and the Frontier Experience, 1800–1915* (Albuquerque, 1982); Glenda Riley, *The Female Frontier: A Comparative View of Women on the Prairie and the Plains* (Lawrence, 1988); and Lillian Schlissel, Vicki L. Ruiz, and Janice Monk, eds., *Western Women: Their Land, Their Lives* (Albuquerque, 1988).

Classic narratives of westward migration include Lois Kimball Mathews, *The Expansion of New England: The Spread of New England Settlement and Institutions to the Mississippi River,*

1620–1865 (Boston, 1909), and Stewart Holbrook, *Yankee Exodus* (New York, 1950). For modern approaches, see John D. Unruh, Jr., *The Plains Across: The Overland Emigrants and the Trans-Mississippi West, 1840–60* (Urbana, Ill., 1979), and John C. Hudson, "North American Origins of Middlewestern Frontier Populations," *Annals of the Association of American Geographers* 78 (1988): 395–413. William A. Bowen, *The Willamette Valley: Migration and Settlement on the Oregon Frontier* (Seattle, 1978), analyzes family selectivity and settlement, whereas John M. Faragher, *Women and Men on the Overland Trail* (New Haven, 1979) is a pioneering interpretation of gendered responses to migration; see also Lillian Schlissel, *Women's Diaries of the Westward Journey* (New York, 1982). James N. Gregory, *American Exodus: The Dust Bowl Migration and Okie Culture in California* (New York, 1989), charts the culmination of the family's westward march.

But social historians have tended to pay more attention than western historians to family migration strategies: Gordon Darroch, "Migrants in the Nineteenth Century: Fugitives or Families in Motion?" *Journal of Family History* 6 (1981): 257–77; Allan Kulikoff, *The Agrarian Origins of American Capitalism* (Charlottesville, 1992); Richard L. Bushman, "Family Security in the Transition from Farm to City, 1750–1850," *Journal of Family History* 6 (1981): 238–56; and John Solomon Otto, "The Migration of the Southern Plain Folk: An Interdisciplinary Synthesis," *Journal of Southern History* 51 (1985): 183–200. Studies using genealogies include the following: John W. Adams and Alice Bee Kasakoff, "Migration and the Family in Colonial New England: The View from Genealogies," *Journal of Family History* 9 (1984): 24–42; Russell M. Reid, "Church Membership, Consanguineous Marriage, and Migration in a Scotch-Irish Frontier Population," *Journal of Family History* 13 (1988): 397–414; and Randy W. Widdis, "Generations, Mobility and Persistence: A View From Genealogies," *Histoire Sociale/Social History* 25 (1992): 125–50. Important for methodological and interpretive comparison are Bruce S. Elliott, *Irish Migrants in the Canadas: A New Approach* (Kingston, Ontario, 1988), and Alida C. Metcalf, *Family and Frontier in Colonial Brazil: Santana de Parnaiba, 1580–1822* (Berkeley, 1992).

Gerald McFarland, *A Scattered People: An American Family Moves West* (New York, 1985), offers an evocative case study of generational migration; John Mack Faragher, *Sugar Creek: Life on the Illinois Prairie* (New Haven, 1986), remains the most satisfying explication of family life in a frontier community. Christopher Clark, *The Roots of Rural Capitalism: Western Massachusetts, 1780–1860* (Ithaca, N.Y., 1990), and Hal S. Barron, *Those Who Stayed Behind: Rural Society in Nineteenth-Century New England* (New York, 1984), examine family change within older rural regions. Even when not explicitly family-focused, western social histories suggest how varying family styles interacted in different local contexts: Peter K. Simpson, *The Community of Cattlemen: A Social History of the Cattle Industry in Southeastern Oregon, 1869–1912* (Moscow, Id., 1987); Kathleen Underwood, *Town Building on the Colorado Frontier* (Albuquerque, 1987); Ralph Mann, *After the Gold Rush: Society in Grass Valley and Nevada City, California, 1849–1870* (Stanford, Calif., 1982); and Paula M. Nelson, *After the West Was Won: Homesteaders and Town-Builders in Western South Dakota, 1900–1917* (Iowa City, 1986).

Allan Kulikoff, cited above, provides a valuable introduction to slave migration. Data have been drawn from Peter D. McClelland and Richard J. Zeckhauser, *Demographic Dimensions of the New Republic: American Interregional Migration, Vital Statistics, and Manumissions, 1800–1860* (Cambridge, Eng., 1982), and James William McGettigan, Jr., "Boone County Slaves: Sales, Estate Divisions and Families, 1820–1865," *Missouri Historical Review* 70 (1978): 271–95. Zachary Cooper tells the story of *Black Settlers in Rural Wisconsin* (Madison, 1977), and William Cohen, *At Freedom's Edge: Black Mobility and the Southern White Quest for Racial Control, 1861–1915* (Baton Rouge, 1991), furnishes a starting place for understanding postbellum black family migration.

Larry M. Logue, *A Sermon in the Desert: Belief and Behavior in Early St. George, Utah* (Urbana, 1988), probes Mormon family patterns in a community context, as do essays in Jessie L. Embry and Howard A. Christy, eds., *Community Development in the American West: Past and Present Nineteenth and Twentieth Century Frontiers* (Provo, Utah, 1985). See also Lee L. Bean, Geraldine

P. Mineau, and Douglas L. Anderton, *Fertility Change on the American Frontier: Adaptation and Innovation* (Berkeley, 1990).

An interpretive review of research on immigrant family patterns is sketched in Kathleen Neils Conzen, "Immigrants in Nineteenth-Century Agricultural History," in Lou Ferleger, ed., *Agriculture and National Development: Views on the Nineteenth Century* (Ames, Iowa, 1990). The Nibler and Schultheis story rests on records consulted for a larger study introduced in Kathleen Neils Conzen, "Peasant Pioneers: Generational Succession among German Farmers in Frontier Minnesota," in Steven Hahn and Jonathan Prude, eds., *The Countryside in the Age of Capitalist Transformation* (Chapel Hill, 1985), 259–92; their journey west can be followed in C. S. Kingston, "The Northern Overland Route in 1867: Journal of Henry Lueg," *Pacific Northwest Quarterly* 41 (1950): 234–53. The German wagon train that artist Albert Bierstadt saw is described in Fitz Hugh Ludlow, *The Heart of the Continent* (New York, 1870). For the Norwegian case, see Jon Gjerde, *From Peasants to Farmers: The Migration from Balestrand, Norway, to the Upper Middle West* (Cambridge, Eng., 1985); other examples include Robert C. Ostergren, *A Community Transplanted: The Trans-Atlantic Experience of a Swedish Immigrant Settlement in the Upper Middle West, 1835–1915* (Madison, 1988), and Rob Kroes, *The Persistence of Ethnicity: Dutch Calvinist Pioneers in Amsterdam, Montana* (Urbana, 1992).

For the Chinese family experience, consult Sucheng Chan's *This Bitter-sweet Soil: The Chinese in California Agriculture, 1860–1910* (Berkeley, 1986) and her "European and Asian Immigration into the United States in Comparative Perspective, 1820s to 1920s," in Virginia Yans-McLaughlin, ed., *Immigration Reconsidered: History, Sociology, and Politics* (New York, 1990), 37–75; see also Lucie Cheng Hirata, "Chinese Immigrant Women in Nineteenth-Century California," in Carol Ruth Berkin and Mary Beth Norton, eds., *Women of America: A History* (Boston, 1979), 223–44. Frances Leon Swadesh, *Los Primeros Pobladores: Hispanic Americans of the Ute Frontier* (Notre Dame, 1974), David Montejano, *Anglos and Mexicans in the Making of Texas, 1836–1986* (Austin, 1987), Arnoldo De Leon and Kenneth L. Stewart, *Tejanos and the Numbers Game: A Socio-Historical Interpretation from the Federal Censuses, 1850–1900* (Albuquerque, 1989), and Sarah Deutsch, *No Separate Refuge: Culture, Class, and Gender on an Anglo-Hispanic Frontier in the American Southwest, 1880–1940* (New York, 1987), provide similar access to Hispanic family processes in the West.

The complexities of Native American family history can be approached through S. Ryan Johansson, "The Demographic History of the Native Peoples of North America: A Selective Bibliography," *Yearbook of Physical Anthropology* 25 (1982): 133–52, and Nancy Shoemaker, "Native American Families," in Joseph M. Hawes and Elizabeth I. Nybakken, eds., *American Families: A Research Guide and Historical Handbook* (New York, 1991). Significant articles are collected in Patricia Albers and Beatrice Medicine, *The Hidden Half: Studies of Plains Indian Women* (Lanham, Md., 1983), and volume 15 of *American Indian Quarterly* (1991). Useful case studies include the following: John H. Moore, *The Cheyenne Nation: A Social and Demographic History* (Lincoln, 1987); Nancy Oestrich Lurie, "The Winnebago Indians: A Study in Cultural Change" (Ph.D. diss., Northwestern University, 1952); William G. McLaughlin and Walter H. Conser, Jr., "The Cherokee Transition: A Statistical Analysis of the Federal Cherokee Census of 1835," *Journal of American History* 64 (1977): 678–703; Albert L. Hurtado, *Indian Survival on the California Frontier* (New Haven, 1988); Morris W. Foster, *Being Comanche: A Social History of an American Indian Community* (Tucson, 1991); and S. Ryan Johansson and S. H. Preston, "Tribal Demography: The Hopi and Navaho Populations as Seen through Manuscripts from the 1900 U.S. Census," *Social Science History* 3 (1978): 1–33. For the development of mixed-race families, see Jacqueline Peterson, "Many Roads to Red River: Métis Genesis in the Great Lakes Region, 1680–1815," in Jacqueline Peterson and Jennifer S. H. Brown, eds., *The New Peoples: Being and Becoming Métis in North America* (Lincoln, 1985), 37–71, and Gary Clayton Anderson, *Kinsmen of Another Kind: Dakota-White Relations in the Upper Mississippi Valley, 1650–1862* (Lincoln, 1984).

Finally, those interested in Wyatt Earp can find the film's script in Robert Lyons, ed., *My Darling Clementine: John Ford, Director* (New Brunswick, N.J., 1984). The best recent interpretation is Paula Mitchell Marks, *And Die in the West: The Story of the O.K. Corral Gunfight* (New York, 1989), supplemented for present purposes with older accounts as well as manuscript censuses, county histories, and other local sources; see also Patricia Jahns, *The Frontier World of Doc Holliday: Faro Dealer from Dallas to Deadwood* (1957; reprint, Lincoln, 1979). For the family in western art, consult Dawn Glanz, *How the West Was Drawn: American Art and the Settling of the Frontier* (Ann Arbor, 1982) and Ron Tyler et al., *American Frontier Life: Early Western Painting and Prints* (Fort Worth, 1987). Worry about a "drifted family" can be found in Alfred B. McCown, *Down on the Ridge: Reminiscences of the Old Days in Coalport and Down on the Ridge; Marion County, Iowa* (Des Moines, 1909), 124.

Chapter Ten

Religion and Spirituality

FERENC M. SZASZ AND
MARGARET CONNELL SZASZ

In the spring and summer of 1788, a number of eastern cities staged celebrations in honor of the new Constitution of the United States. The most impressive of these "federal processions" occurred in Philadelphia, where, on 4 July 1788, a crowd of about seventeen thousand watched five hundred people file past in a mammoth parade. According to the eyewitness Francis Hopkinson, the marchers grouped themselves by guild or profession, and eighty-fifth in line (after the lawyers but before the doctors) strolled "the clergy of the different Christian denominations, with the rabbi of the Jews, walking arm in arm." This public display of "charity and brotherly love" by Philadelphia's clergy proved a first, not only for America but probably for the entire world. It pointed to the fact that religion in the new federal Republic would play a vastly different role from anything that had gone before.

The clerics' optimism drew heavily from the political theory of James Madison, the American Enlightenment figure who thought most deeply about church-state relations. Acknowledging that a person's faith could never be determined by reason alone, Madison placed religious belief as the foremost of all natural rights. Since the state existed to protect these rights, it should never unnecessarily interfere with the realm of faith. The Philadelphia Convention of 1787 incorporated Madison's ideas into the Constitution; in 1791, these ideas formed the heart of the First Amendment. Unlike those nations with established churches, which included most of Europe, the United States would never develop any official church. Except for nineteenth-century denominational schools and missions among American Indians, no American church could rely on state support. Rather, each denomination *voluntarily* had to convince others that its position was the correct one. Almost every religious group accepted these boundaries. Each faith would set forth its position as best it could; "the people" would then choose their own religion.

The eminent twentieth-century theologian Paul Tillich once observed, "Religion is the substance of culture and culture the form of religion." Certainly this proved true for the trans-Mississippi West. The religious history of the West is all-embracing. It cannot be limited simply to kivas or churches, ceremonies or sermons, medicine men or clerics. Rather, western religion permeated the realms of politics, culture, and society. Perhaps the key to understanding religion in the West was the land. The vastness of this immense territory, with its many ecological subregions, provided a multitude of homes for native belief systems, as well as for the diverse faiths brought by European, African, and Asian immigrants. In the Great Plains, Rockies, Southwest, Plateau, Great Basin, and Pacific

A region marked by both religious pluralism and tolerance, the West is home to a wide variety of faiths, including the folk Catholicism that flourishes in the Hispanic communities of northern New Mexico.

Eliot Porter (1901–90). Church. Placita de Taos, New Mexico. Gelatin silver print, 1940. Copyright Amon Carter Museum. Eliot Porter Collection, Amon Carter Museum, Fort Worth, Texas.

Coast regions, a variety of religious subcultures flourished. With a few notable exceptions, tolerance and openness characterized the world of western faiths. In the generations encompassed by our story, the West initiated a pattern of religious pluralism in American society—often without a culture-shaping mainstream—that anticipated many developments of the late twentieth century.

We begin with the 1840s, a pivotal decade for both the religious and the political fortunes of the nation. By this time, the main outlines of American religious history had been generally sketched out. The Roman Catholic church had become the nation's largest single denomination, a position it would sustain to the present day. With growth fueled largely by immigration, the church wrestled with multiethnic congregations and a "foreign" image for over a century. The same stream of immigration brought over 250,000 German Jews, who soon scattered across the land. These Jews played vital entrepreneurial roles in the West, and some, such as the clothier Levi Strauss, rapidly rose to the realm of legend. In 1844, when the Latter-day Saints prophet Joseph Smith, Jr., died at the hands of an Illinois mob, the Saints numbered only about 14,000. The pundits of the day predicted their imminent collapse, but their subsequent move to the Great Basin region of Utah and Idaho gave the church new life. The mainline Protestant churches (Methodists, Baptists, Congregationalists, Presbyterians, Episcopalians, Lutherans) congratulated themselves that they had saved the trans-Appalachian region from "barbarism" through their "benevolent empire" of Bible, tract, Sunday school, and education societies. All were looking for new fields to conquer.

Simultaneously, in an era dominated by ideas of "manifest destiny," many Americans pushed across the Mississippi to claim Indian lands in Oregon country or Mexican California. Integral to this mass emigration, the Christian clergy joined the exodus in a race both to convert the Indians and retain the emigrating church members. During the antebellum era, the mainline Protestant denominations wielded the most influence in national affairs. Together, these groups composed what has been termed a "voluntary" religious establishment. While they disputed among themselves over theology and church polity, they agreed on essentials: Christianity had broken into "denominations," each of which had a distinct mission; Protestantism and democratic republicanism were forever intertwined; America had become God's "New Israel"; and the churches felt compelled to carry their mission to both whites and Indians *west* of the Mississippi.

The religious diversity that the European Americans brought west met an equal diversity among the indigenous faiths of the Native Americans. When the historian Robert F. Berkhofer, Jr., spoke of the "multiplicity of [the Indians'] specific histories," he referred primarily to their means of warfare, hunting, fishing, and social organization. But the Native Americans' varied ceremonial life and relationship to the supernatural shared a similar "multiplicity." Thus, in the nineteenth-century West, heterogeneous European-American religions interacted with equally heterogeneous native religions. The resulting blends, as seen in the Pueblo-Roman Catholic, Sioux-Episcopal, and Pima-Presbyterian amalgamations, proved unique in the history of American faith.

Long before the voyages of Columbus, American Indians had engaged in "religious borrowing and synthesis." Thus, when they began to graft European Christianity onto their own faiths, this was, as the anthropologist Robert Brightman has noted, "simply one more instance of a traditional receptivity to religious innovation." A major part of the history of native religion in the West is the story of its interaction with this imported Christianity.

From the 1760s, native groups of southern California had encountered the highly motivated Franciscans, who forced them into mission enclaves stretching from San Diego to San Francisco. The Franciscans retained their hold over thousands of native Californians until the Mexican government secularized the missions in the 1830s. In other regions of the Southwest, including present-day southern Arizona and parts of Texas, natives had also been influenced by Catholicism through missions founded in the late seventeenth and early eighteenth centuries. In the late 1500s, along the Rio Grande valley in what is now New Mexico, Tanoan and Keresan speakers, as well as the Zuni, had come under the control of these Hispanic Catholics, who occupied the region for eight decades—an era dominated by bitter church-state rivalry—before the natives drove them out in 1680. Don Diego de Vargas's *reconquista* of 1692 acknowledged native rights and marked the beginning of a rich blending of native ceremonies and worldview with those of Hispanic Catholicism, a blending that continues into the present. East of the Llano Estacado, crossed by Coronado in the 1540s, former Southeast Woodland tribes—Cherokees, Creeks, Choctaws, Chickasaws, and Seminoles—were settling in. Even before the era of removal forced their emigration, most of these groups had met Protestant missionaries. In general, the Christian messages were well received, especially by the Cherokees, whose leadership, epitomized by the mixed-blood John Ross, welcomed change and the incorporation of European ways. Christianity and traditional values blended among these Indians, historically known as the "Five Civilized Tribes," during their early decades in the Indian Territory.

Elsewhere in the West, however, native religions had remained beyond the thrust of Christian missionaries. In the Northwest Coast and Columbia River Plateau regions, Salishan, Sahaptian, Chinookian, and other linguistic groups had begun extensive cultural borrowing with the opening of the sea otter trade in the late eighteenth century, the startling visit of Lewis and Clark, and the intense international rivalry for beaver. Bargaining for iron pots, metal fishhooks, weapons, or the much desired blue beads had changed their cultures. They had incorporated the epithets of the Boston men into the Chinook trade jargon, and they had sharpened their shrewd trading skills in the vast exchange network that stretched east via the Nez Percés. Moreover, they had been weakened by European disease. But with the exception of a band of Catholic Iroquois, who settled among the Salishan-speaking Flatheads around 1820, and the quasi-religious influence of the Hudson's Bay Company, this cultural borrowing had generally excluded Christianity. Not until the 1830s and 1840s, with the arrival of Oblate and Jesuit priests, plus missionaries from various Protestant denominations, did the North-west Coast and Plateau people begin to address the many messages of Christianity. In the central Rockies, much of the Great Plains, and the western Great Basin, these missionaries arrived even later.

The Intertwining of Politics and Religion

In the mid-1840s, the Utes, Paiutes, and other natives living in the eastern Great Basin met one of the most unusual religious groups in nineteenth-century America. In no other area of the West were politics and religion more closely intertwined, for this region is forever linked with the saga of the Church of Jesus Christ of Latter-day Saints (the Mormons). Western Protestant-Catholic and Christian-Jewish tensions generally remained confined to harsh words and editorials. Only Mormon-Gentile (i.e., non-Mormon) relations crossed the line into mob violence. For many mid-nineteenth-century contemporaries, the Latter-day Saints pushed beyond the limits of America's famed religious toleration.

The story of the angel who led an upstate New York farm boy, Joseph Smith, Jr., to the buried golden plates on Hill Cumorah is well-known. Seated behind a curtain, Smith translated these plates to form *The Book of Mormon*, first printed in 1830. Read literally, *The Book of Mormon* tells the story of ancient Near Eastern peoples who migrated to the Americas: the Jaredites, the Nephites, and the Lamanites (the latter designated as ancestors of the American Indians). The account culminates with the visit of Jesus Christ, shortly after His resurrection, to the Nephites. Read metaphorically, the book depicts the success of those civilizations that follow the Commandments of the Lord and the collapse of those that become filled with pride and arrogance. In either case, *The Book of Mormon* was America's first indigenous holy scripture.

The Mormons invoked controversy wherever they settled. Their new scripture, Smith's 130 special revelations from the Lord—especially those concerning polygamy (an open secret, fueled by rumor, from the late 1830s until officially proclaimed in 1852), Mormon "bloc voting," and their alleged violation of the church-state separation—all played on Gentile fears. The culmination came on 29 January 1844, when Joseph Smith, Jr., announced that he was a candidate for the presidency of the United States.

Consequently, what the novelist William Dean Howells once termed "the foolish mob which helps to establish each new religion" proved a major factor in early Mormon history. Many church leaders, including Smith, were either tarred and feathered or thrown in jail on trumped-up charges. Their northern origins made them especially suspect in slaveholding Missouri, where proslavery settlers and politicians persecuted them mercilessly. As a Mormon hymn writer put it: "Missouri/Like a whirlwind in its fury,/And without a judge or jury,/Drove the Saints and spilled their blood."

When the Saints established the Mississippi town of Nauvoo, Illinois—a well-run prototype for the later Mormon communities in the Great Basin—local outrage could no longer be contained. On 27 June 1844, an angry mob stormed the jail at Carthage, Illinois, to martyr both Joseph Smith, Jr., and his brother Hyrum.

Virtually all observers expected the Saints to collapse with the death of the prophet. Indeed, several schisms weakened them considerably. Sidney Rigdon led a fragment to Pittsburgh, Pennsylvania; James J. Strang headed a larger remnant that thrived in a communal setting on Beaver Island in Lake Michigan, until his assassination; and Joseph Smith III, the prophet's son by his first wife, Emma Hale Smith, rejected polygamy to lead a group that became the Reorganized Church of Jesus Christ of Latter Day Saints, with headquarters in Independence, Missouri. That the entire body of Saints did not similarly fracture may be credited to the skills of the newly appointed prophet, Brigham Young, and his decision to move to the West.

Painted by a Mormon artist, this idealized portrait of the prophet Brigham Young places Mormon family values squarely within the realm of Victorian virtues. Surrounded by traditional symbols that belie the actual western environment, the Youngs appear as prosperous members of Utah society.

William Warner Major (1804–54). Brigham Young's Family. *Oil on canvas, ca. 1847–53. The Church of Jesus Christ of Latter-day Saints, Salt Lake City, Utah.*

The historian Jan Shipps has argued that the great trek from Missouri and Illinois to Utah formed the central event in Mormon history. The journey to the Great Basin carried the Saints not simply to the promised land of Deseret but also "backward" into a primordial sacred time. From this journey, Shipps has suggested, the Mormons emerged as a distinctly new religious faith, as different from Christianity as Christianity was from Judaism.

Both Mormon social practices and theology proved unique. The Saints rejected the Christian trinity and downplayed the concept of original sin. Their communalism, polygamy, and authoritarian church polity formed a sharp contrast to the romantic individualism that dominated contemporary American Protestantism. Believing that God "was once as we are now," the Mormons taught that most devout male Saints would eventually hold similar dominion over future worlds of their own. Their maxim phrased it thus: "As God is at present Man may become." Essentially universalists, the Saints maintained that all of humanity would achieve salvation but that Mormon believers would reach a higher degree of glory. The King James translation of Scripture, *The Book of Mormon* (written in the King James idiom), and Smith's subsequent revelations were accorded equal divine status. The head of the church was assigned the mantle of contemporary prophet.

The evolving Mormon folk religion transcended even the official pronouncements from church leaders. The Saints celebrated special holidays: Joseph Smith's birthday,

Brigham Young's birthday, the birthday of the church; the day of arrival in the Salt Lake Valley (still observed in Utah on 24 July as Pioneer Day). They wove heroic legends of the "Great Trek" west and the suffering of the later emigrants, some of whom pushed handcarts over twelve hundred miles to their new home. They commemorated the sego lily, whose roots the early pioneers ate to avoid starvation, and seagulls, which arrived to devour a plague of crickets that threatened to consume the Saints' first wheat crop. They danced and sang with vigor. When their hymns spoke of "Israel" or the "Camp of Israel," they claimed these concepts for themselves, and thus the term *Gentiles* took on new meaning in the Mountain West. Like the ancient Hebrews, the Saints forged a separate concept of "peoplehood" that persists up to the present day.

The federal government, however, viewed the rise of a semi-independent kingdom in the Great Basin with considerable suspicion. In the mid-1850s, Congress accused Brigham Young of complicity in the harassment of Utah's federal officials. Spurred on by exaggerated coverage by the eastern press, President James Buchanan ordered federal troops to Utah in 1857 to bring the Saints into line.

The Saints viewed the arrival of the federal army as reminiscent of their persecution in Missouri and Illinois. The Mormon leaders seriously considered relocating to Central America or elsewhere. Eventually cooler heads prevailed, and the "Mormon War" ended without direct confrontation. But the tension caused by the war did lead to bloodshed. In August 1857, a wagon train of Missouri and Arkansas settlers crossed southern Utah, where they were attacked by a band of Mormons and their Indian allies. This raid, in which 130 people died, ranks as one of the worst examples of religious violence in American history. The Mountain Meadows Massacre, as it is known, assumed a symbolic role in defining Mormon-Gentile relations.

Politics and religion were equally intertwined in the story of religious expansion into the Pacific Northwest. In 1833, four Flathead and Nez Percé Indians journeyed to St. Louis to inquire about Christian missionaries. This seemingly inconsequential request would help to determine the course of the history of the Northwest. It opened the door for missionaries and migrants and thus became the basis for America's claim to the Oregon Country.

The native appeal for "white religion" probably implied a desire for increased knowledge of a general, all-defusing cultural power. In 1833 and 1837, other groups of Salishan and Sahaptian natives traveled the same path to St. Louis. The retelling of the story created one of the most famous legends of nineteenth-century western religious history. Catholic journals broadcast the Indian journey as a call for "Black Robes" who said "Great Prayers" (the Mass). Protestants declared that the Indians had requested the "white man's book of heaven." Within a few years, both Catholic and Protestant missionaries had begun the arduous trek to the Columbia River Plateau and the Northwest Coast.

In June 1840, the Jesuit Pierre Jean De Smet made the journey from St. Louis to the Flatheads and Pend d'Oreilles. The next year he returned with two more Jesuits, Nicholas Point and Gregory Mengarini, thus inaugurating what a later Jesuit termed "the grandest missionary work of the nineteenth century in its religious, social, economical and political aspect."

De Smet and his fellow Jesuits hoped to encourage the Indians to abandon their nomadic life and adopt a settled agrarian existence. In September 1841, De Smet began St. Mary's Mission in the Bitter Root Valley of Montana. The next year he helped create the Coeur d'Alene Mission of the Sacred Heart on the St. Joe River. The St. Ignatius mission to the Flatheads, St. Paul's to the San Poils, and St. Michael's to the Spokans soon followed.

Generally speaking, the Jesuits looked to their own history, especially their "holy experiment" in the Central Highlands of South America, as a model for this endeavor. During the seventeenth and eighteenth centuries, the Jesuits had established a string of over thirty settlements (called *reducciones*, from the Spanish *reducir*, "to bring together") in the region that is now largely Paraguay. Centered around a market square and a plaza, these communities consisted of several thousand Indians managed by only a handful of clerics. The Jesuits taught the Natives European forms of agriculture, music, architecture, and religion during an experiment that lasted over a century.

Although De Smet's dream of establishing "a new Paraguay," never occurred, these Northwest missions did serve many functions similar to those of their earlier counterparts. St. Ignatius provided a hospital, sawmill, flour mill, and printing press. All missions boasted schools that taught theology, English, and other skills. Rumor had it that every Jesuit mission contained at least one resident genius. Father Anthony Ravalli certainly qualified. During his career at St. Mary's he served as doctor, architect, sculptor, linguist, and expert manager. De Smet himself also proved a skilled negotiator. His peacekeeping efforts on the northern plains saved hundreds of lives, and many regional native leaders held him in esteem.

De Smet also drew on the romantic appeal of the American West to encourage numerous European novices and priests to follow his footsteps. Over the course of the century, perhaps two hundred Jesuits crossed the ocean to serve missions in the northern Rockies and Plateau regions. In spite of this effort, however, the string of Jesuit missions never fulfilled their founders' hopes. The harsh climate of the region proved unsuitable for extensive agriculture, and the Indians preferred their traditional hunting, fishing, and gathering cycle to a settled mission life. (To follow the tribe, for example, Sacred Heart Mission moved three times in thirty-six years.)

Some of these Jesuit missions remain modest tourist attractions today, such as St. Ignatius in Montana or the Cataldo Mission (Sacred Heart) in Idaho. As an entity, however, these missions are not well-known outside the region, and they pale when compared with their internationally known California counterparts. The life of De Smet is respected, but it has never engendered the romance that surrounds California's mission founder, the Franciscan Junípero Serra.

The Methodists were the first Protestant denomination to respond to the Indian journey to St. Louis. In 1834, Rev. Jason Lee, his nephew Rev. Daniel Lee, and three lay associates traveled to the Northwest Coast, settling in the Willamette Valley. Within a few years the Presbyterians sent out Revs. Elkanah Walker and Cushing Eells and their wives, Dr. Marcus and Narcissa Whitman, and Rev. Henry and Eliza Spalding. Narcissa and Eliza were the first European-American women to cross the Rockies into the Columbia River Plateau. Unlike Jason Lee, these missionaries were drawn to the Plateau tribes: Walker and Eells to the Spokans at Tshimakain; the Spaldings to the Nez Percés at Lapwai; and the Whitmans to the Walla Wallas and Cayuses at Waiilatpu. Like the

Jesuits, the Whitmans built a gristmill, sawmill, blacksmith shop, and school; their mission also served as an "emigrant house" for Oregon Trail travelers.

In 1842, when the American Board of Commissioners for Foreign Missions determined to close these missions to the Plateau tribes, an equally determined Whitman traveled east in a dangerous mid-winter trek to argue their case. Like the Nez Percé-Flathead trip to St. Louis, Whitman's dramatic journey to the East has also ballooned into legend. Those who argue that Whitman "saved Oregon" through his travels neglect the fact that by the 1840s, midwesterners with "Oregon fever" were already beginning the migration that led to the resolution of the Oregon boundary issue. The Whitmans' contribution to the American cause may have come later. When Congress learned of the November 1847 native uprising against the Waiilatpu Mission and of the deaths of Marcus, Narcissa, and others, it responded by creating a government for the Oregon Territory, the first official American government established west of the Rockies.

As Protestant and Catholic missionaries competed among the tribes living in the Northwest Coast, Plateau, and northern Rockies, they carried out in microcosm the most persistent American religious theme of the century: Protestant-Catholic hostility. This theme echoed and reechoed throughout the West, where it affected both native and immigrant. The Protestant and Catholic "ladders" developed in the Northwest Coast and the Plateau reflected this antagonism. Borrowing from the Salishan concept of a *sahale* stick ("wood from above"), the French-Canadian father François Norbert Blanchet created a large (six-feet-by-two-feet) paper chart with a time line portraying the life of Christ and basic Christian principles. One version of the "Catholic ladder" depicted Martin Luther as branching off on a road that led to hell. By contrast, Spalding's "Protestant ladder" for the Nez Percés peopled the road to hell with worldly popes and immoral priests.

It is far easier to count missions, sawmills, gristmills, printing presses, and even Christian "ladders" than it is to evaluate the results of the missions among the Indians of the Northwest Coast, Plateau, and northern Rockies. A number of Nez Percés became Presbyterians, and in 1890 a writer pointed out that approximately seven thousand out of ten thousand Montana Indians were Catholics. But counting converts, a popular pastime among nineteenth-century missionary groups, proved as inaccurate as the conclusion, made by some late-twentieth-century historians, that the missions were a general failure. From church buildings to native clergy, the results of both Catholic and Protestant missionary endeavors of the nineteenth century are much in evidence today. Their legacies remain as diverse as the cultures of the native peoples themselves.

Many European immigrants to the Pacific Northwest, like the natives, responded to the missionaries with indifference. By the late twentieth century, this area was widely acknowledged as "the least churched region" of the nation. The nineteenth-century boasts "the Sabbath shall never cross the Missouri" and "no Sunday west of St. Louis" proved prescient. They pointed to the fact that the eastern religious institutions would have difficulty establishing themselves in the wide-open society of the trans-Mississippi West.

Nowhere was the secular image of the new West more pronounced than in California. In 1849, the cry of "Gold, Gold, from the American River" drew thousands

Missionary work in the rural West presented particular challenges to those serving widely scattered populations.

Unidentified photographer. John Jasper Methvin, a Methodist Missionary among Kiowa and Comanche Girls. *Photograph, ca. 1894. Western History Collections, University of Oklahoma Library, Norman.*

Unidentified photographer. Fording River on a Congregational Missionary Tour *(Wyoming). Photograph, date unknown. American Heritage Center, University of Wyoming, Laramie.*

around the Horn, across Panama, or over the trail to San Francisco. The chief goal of forty-niners was seldom that of the spirit. "The Americans," complained a visiting Catholic priest, "think only of dollars, talk only of dollars, seek nothing but dollars."

Nevertheless, a group of clerical forty-niners did their best to stem the tide. By one estimate, four denominations had established about fifty small churches throughout the early "Mother Lode" country. A Unitarian pulpit orator, Thomas Starr King, tried to replicate Boston's values in San Francisco during the 1850s and early 1860s while the Congregationalist Timothy Dwight Hunt attempted to "make California the Massachusetts of the Pacific."

Such was not to be. The historian Kevin Starr has noted that the tumultuous nature of California life could never be confined within traditional religious norms, be they New England parish, Virginia plantation, or Mexican village. California manifested a religious "openness" from its earliest days.

California life also muted all the traditional religious antagonisms. The fact that the territory's first American governor, Peter H. Burnett, was a Catholic convert played absolutely no role in his political career. As a Catholic archbishop noted in 1864, his church "did not face the prejudice which is encountered elsewhere." A generation later, California's small Seventh-Day Adventist community led a successful fight to repeal the state's Sunday regulations. In the cities, the African Methodist Episcopal and African Methodist Episcopal Zion churches provided strong voices for racial equality. John Muir's "religion of nature," a transcendental appreciation for the magnificence of Creation (with little or no role for a redeemer), also drew a number of followers. Worship services by Asian faiths generally went unmolested. In religion, as in so many other areas, California became "the great exception."

Politics and religion were equally intertwined in the American Southwest. In Texas, the nineteenth century was a postmission era. The Franciscan missions, especially those among the Caddo, established in the early 1700s in part to counteract French movement in the lower Mississippi Valley, were defunct, and in the 1840s only a handful of priests still served the Texas Catholic community. After the independence movement established freedom of religion, Jean Marie Odin, the first bishop of Galveston, oversaw the rejuvenation of Texas Catholicism. In addition to the Mexicans, his diocese consisted largely of European immigrants. For example, a band of German Catholics settled the hill country during the mid-1840s, and the Polish Franciscan Leopold Moczygemba led a group of Silesian Poles to Panna Maria in 1856. By the 1850s, however, American immigration had thrust the Baptists, Methodists, and Disciples of Christ into dominance. These evangelical groups have played a major role in Texas religious history to the present day.

The political-religious connection was even more sensitive in the lands taken from Mexico in 1848. All of the Hispanos of the American Southwest were titular Catholics, but everywhere the faithful had long suffered from want of clerical attention. In southern Texas, Arizona, California, and especially New Mexico, the Hispanic settlers had responded to the dearth of priests by creating their own version of folk Catholicism.

This included an intense respect for local patron saints, many of whom were credited with frequent miracles, and a strong Mariolatry, represented by devotion to the Virgin of Guadalupe. The Hispanic communities of the borderlands celebrated a steady round of religious holidays: 17 January, the feast of San Antonio, a day for the blessing of the animals; 24 June, San Juan's Day, which became associated with the first fruits and vegetables of the season; the feast of Corpus Christi, celebrated in the seventh week after Easter; the solemn 1 November, All Saints' Day, and 2 November, All Souls' Day. December was the climax month of celebration, with *Los Pastores*, a Spanish medieval miracle play, plus a reenactment of the nine days that Mary and Joseph wandered in search of shelter in Bethlehem before the birth of Jesus. The historian Arnoldo De Leon has argued that the faith of the Rio Grande borderlands expressed "an attitude consonant more with life experience than theology."

Folk Catholicism permeated the territory of New Mexico. The healing skills of *curanderas*, the lay brotherhood of Penitentes, and the folk carvings of *Santos, bultos*, and *retablos* reflected a deeply held cultural faith. From the early nineteenth century forward, the little chapel at Chimayo, New Mexico, known as "The Lourdes of the Southwest," has drawn those seeking healing. This pervasive New Mexico folk Catholicism proved remarkably tolerant of the influx of Anglo Protestants.

The same basic toleration may be seen in the story of western Judaism. From the 1850s, Jews composed perhaps 10 percent of San Francisco's merchant community. Relying on a credit network that included family members and coreligionists, Jewish families provided vital economic services, both in rural areas, such as New Mexico, and urban centers, such as San Francisco, Portland, Los Angeles, Denver, and Seattle.

Contemporary visitors marveled at how well the western Jews had succeeded. In the Los Angeles 1876 centennial celebration, a young Jewish woman portrayed the "Spirit of Liberty" while a rabbi helped preside over the festivities. In San Francisco's first *Elite Directory* (1870–79), Jews composed over one-fifth of the city's "elite." The historians Harriet Rochlin and Fred Rochlin have counted over thirty nineteenth-century western Jewish mayors, plus countless sheriffs, police chiefs, and other elected officials. Although one can find traces of anti-Semitism, it played a much smaller role in western life than in the contemporary South or Northeast. The historian Eldon Ernst has concluded that California's failure to produce a "religious mainstream" allowed all faiths to flourish on a roughly equal basis. The same could be said for many other subregions in the trans-Mississippi West.

Eastern Churches Move West

In the decades after the Civil War, the American churches moved into the Far West with increasing enthusiasm. Clerics from all denominations followed the recently completed railroad lines in hopes of securing a "first strike" among the mobile frontier settlers. The railroad corporations and various booster organizations aided the church-building frenzy by gladly giving away free lots to virtually every denomination that asked. In their eyes, the presence of church buildings connoted "stability."

Although stability may have been the ultimate goal, both clerics and parishioners remained highly mobile for over half a century. The fluid environment of the early western towns created a unique situation: a brief period of genuine interdenominational cooperation. Initially, frontier clerics sought out not only members of their own denomination but all "interested parties." Thus, the first churches frequently contained people from several different denominations. In these early years, virtually all the Sunday schools on the Great Plains were "union" (multidenominational). Music proved especially ecumenical. The Episcopal choir at Bland, New Mexico, for example, consisted of two Episcopalians, one Catholic, one Mormon, one Presbyterian, and one Congregationalist. A Jew joined the first Episcopal choir in Helena, Montana, and Gentiles sang in the Los Angeles Congregation B'nai B'rith for several years. Westward-migrating Jews occasionally attended Unitarian services, and several Jewish merchants donated to local Catholic and Protestant churches and schools. This "ecumenicism of necessity" diminished when each group gathered enough members to form a church or synagogue of its own. Such cooperation, however short-lived, was seldom duplicated in the annals of American religious life.

The frontier clergy have rarely been given credit for their accomplishments. In addition to building churches and supplying the ordinances of their denominations, they provided the basic institutional infrastructure for the western states and territories. The local and state governments lacked funds, and the federal government was primarily interested in railroad and military affairs. Consequently, the clergy and churches took the lead in providing hospitals, orphanages, old-age homes, and schools.

Every denomination viewed health care as part of its mission. These efforts ranged from the modest "Industrial School and Hygienic Home for Friendless Persons," founded by the Kansas Mennonites in 1890, to the substantial network of Catholic and Episcopal hospitals that graced most major western cities. Catholic bishops spent a great deal of time coaxing women's religious orders west to staff these enterprises. In the last quarter of the nineteenth century, as many as fifteen orders of nuns were active on the northern plains. In addition to founding over twenty schools, the Presentation Sisters established three hospitals in South Dakota, plus one in Montana. The Grey Nuns of Montreal played a similar role in the Pacific Northwest, as did the Sisters of St. Joseph of Carondelet and the Sisters of Loretto in the Southwest. When the Sisters of the Holy Cross walked down the streets of Salt Lake City, curious crowds of Mormon children followed their every move.

The churches and clergy also played a prominent part in establishing and/or teaching in the public school systems. Records from the constitutional conventions of the various western states show that the fiercest arguments frequently revolved around the issue of state funding for parochial schools. Some areas, such as San Francisco, initially divided public funds between private and state-run schools, but this arrangement seldom endured. Protestant clergy frequently taught in the early school systems. The Freethinkers of Cottage Grove, Oregon, even asked the Cumberland Presbyterian minister Will Magee to establish a school. A religious school, these atheists reluctantly admitted, was better than none at all.

Since the fledgling public schools could not accommodate all of the children, many western denominations established parallel educational systems on the primary, secondary, and university levels. San Francisco's first Catholic church served for both worship and education. Many Protestant ministers, or their wives, also taught. The Presbyterians and Congregationalists established elaborate parochial school systems in both Utah and New Mexico. Everywhere, "church" and "school" overlapped.

EXPANSION:
Building an American Nation

◆

In the mid-nineteenth century, as the West acquired a decidedly American imprint, the region became the focus of a particularly nationalistic school of painting that celebrated the region and its recent American settlers as an expression of the country's democratic values and boundless possibilities. Not surprisingly, such art was generally created by those for whom western history seemed a triumph of American culture. Although art by Native Americans conveyed a different story, the incorporation of European-American motifs into traditional art forms also signaled the joined future of the West's different peoples.

Widely praised as a western artist whose paintings captured a distinctively western type of character, the Missouri artist George Caleb Bingham helped bring regional subjects into the mainstream of American art.

George Caleb Bingham (1811–79). The Jolly Flatboatmen in Port. *Oil on canvas, 1857. Museum Purchase, the Saint Louis Art Museum, Missouri.*

This study for a 20-by-30-foot mural in the U.S. Capitol presented familiar icons of westward migration in a triumphant narrative of American expansionism. Painted at the time of the Civil War, the picture reaffirmed the importance of the West as a place of optimism, opportunity, and national unity.

Emanuel Leutze (1816–68). Westward the Course of Empire Takes Its Way *(mural study). Oil on canvas, 1861. National Museum of American Art, Washington, D.C./Art Resource, New York.*

Purchased by Congress in 1872 and put on public view in the
Capitol, Thomas Moran's massive painting of Yellowstone
(7 x 12 feet) became the first American landscape by an American artist to be purchased by the federal government. Acquired
just three months after Yellowstone was designated a national
park, the painting epitomized popular interest in the park as a
romantic wonderland.

Thomas Moran (1837–1926). The Grand Cañon of the Yellowstone. *Oil on canvas, 1872. Lent by U.S. Department of the Interior, Office of the Secretary, National Museum of American Art, Washington, D.C./Art Resource, New York.*

After the 1870s, when many Plains peoples were confined to reservations, new motifs in tribal art emerged to reflect the changed relationship between Native Americans and the federal government. In this Lakota shirt a beaded hand, the traditional symbol of a warrior, is combined with the symbol of another sort of power, the flag of the United States.

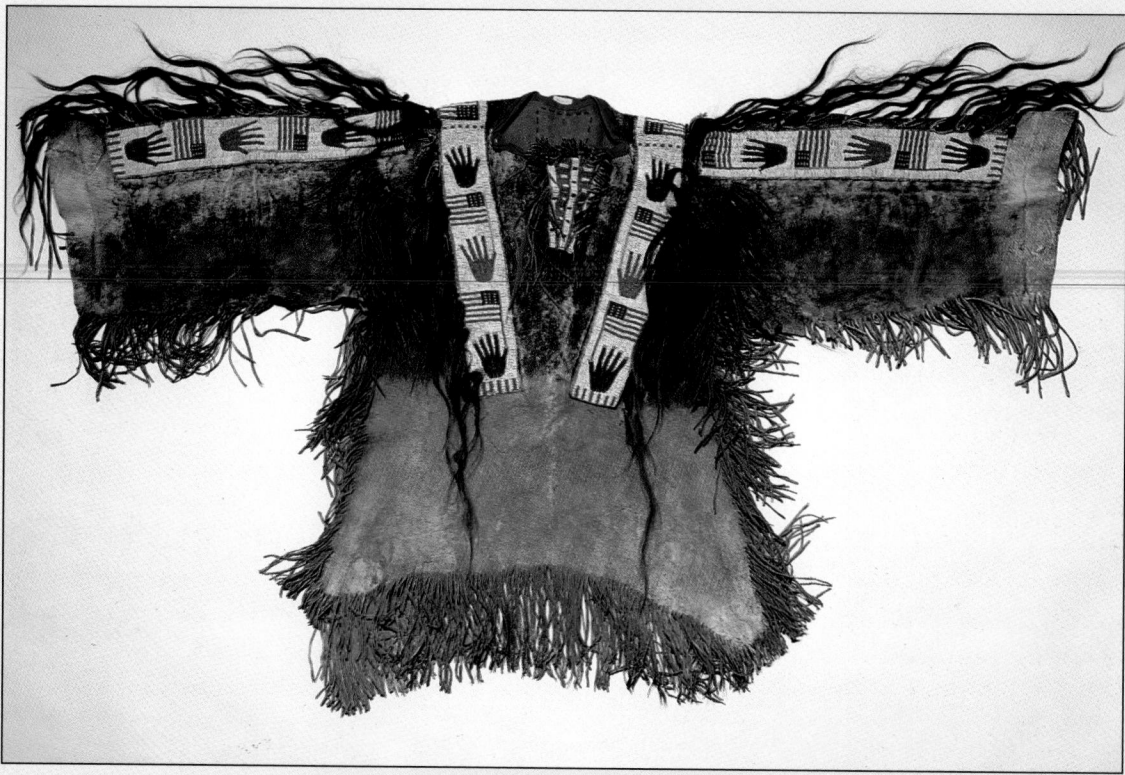

Unidentified artist (Oglala Lakota). Warrior's Shirt. *Native-tanned hide, hair, glass and metal beads, sinew, and blue-green and yellow pigment, ca. 1890. Bern Historical Museum, Ethnography Department, Bern, Switzerland.*

The various denominations devoted much attention to founding colleges. Well into the twentieth century, most western higher education maintained strong denominational links. The oldest institution of higher learning in California is Santa Clara College (now University). St. Ignatius, which later became the University of San Francisco, and St. Mary's, founded by the Christian Brothers, soon followed. Northern Baptists established McMinnville College (Oregon), the Lutherans organized Pacific Lutheran University (Washington), and the Presbyterians founded Occidental College (California), just to name a few. The Methodists established Willamette University (Oregon) and the University of Southern California, whose athletic teams were proudly known as the "Methodists" until 1912, when they became the "Trojans."

The race to found church-related colleges can largely be traced to interdenominational rivalry, but many churches overextended themselves in the effort. Lack of money, interest, and denominational commitment ensured that many of the schools would not survive. Virtually all western states are dotted with "ghost colleges." In California, about fifty church colleges collapsed, and Washington and Oregon lost about fifteen each. The Great Plains are littered with similar ghosts, bearing long-forgotten names such as Mallalico College (Nebraska) or Redfield College (South Dakota). Too many western towns wanted a college, complained a writer in 1891, but it was "immaterial with them whether the institution be a college proper or a normal school or a business college or a school for the feeble minded." By the 1890s, the college-founding boom had largely collapsed.

The clergy from the various denominations also played central roles in the establishment of most western state universities. New England Congregationalists were instrumental in founding the University of California, the University of Colorado, and the entire educational system of South Dakota. Presbyterians helped establish the University of Kansas and the University of Tulsa. The Episcopal St. Margaret's Girls School eventually grew into Boise State University. It was a rare university that did not boast a cleric on the board of trustees. Initially, the University of California had several. The churches saw their educational mission as an integral part of the settlement of the West.

Like the rest of the nation, the West also exhibited its share of free thought: Bohemian and German rationalists in Nebraska and Texas; the prolific, acid pen of William Cowper Brann's *Iconoclast* from Waco, Texas; the Liberal League in Kansas; and the Oregon State Secular Union in the Pacific Northwest. Great Plains freethinkers actually formed a town (Liberal, Kansas), and their Pacific Coast counterparts established a short-lived "Liberal University" in Silverton, Oregon. Despite its often vigorous rhetoric, western anticlericalism had little lasting significance.

The western churches frequently provided the focal point of a community's social life. Revivals and camp meetings, especially on the southern plains, offered an opportunity for isolated ranchers to gather for song and fellowship. Whereas the organizers of these gatherings usually measured "success" by the number of converts, the people were more pragmatic. "However great may have been the need for salvation," one plains woman recalled, "the need for recreation was given preference." In addition, these gatherings helped "democratize" the faith of western Protestantism. Drawing on the persistent tradition of the Great Awakenings, the western evangelists proclaimed a

The oldest cathedral west of the Mississippi, this building (constructed 1831–34) served as an urban monument to the importance of Catholicism in St. Louis, where believers of French and, later, Irish, German, and Italian descent played a major role in local affairs. The completion of an impressive new cathedral in 1914 reconfirmed the central role that the Roman Catholic church played in the religious life of the American West.

After George Morton and Joseph Laveille, lithograph by Leon Pomarede. Front View of the Cathedral of St. Louis. Lithograph, 1835. Missouri Historical Society Photograph and Print Collection (#PB 984), St. Louis.

simple message: mankind was a sinner, but God had redeemed the race through the gift of his only son, Jesus Christ. Humanity was saved through grace, not works, and people had only to open their hearts to the Savior. The truth of this story lay in the Scriptures, easily understood by all. Thus, a simple, democratic, Arminian biblicism formed the heart of western Protestantism. Theology was left to the theologians. The evangelical folk culture of the southern plains still bears the mark of this tradition.

All through the West, churchwomen utilized their denominations for a variety of activities. Excluded from the franchise in all states except Wyoming and Utah, many nineteenth-century women contributed to the social order through church work rather than through politics. Since the local churches were constantly short of money, churchwomen spent considerable energy in fund-raising. Naturally, these gatherings focused on the entire community. An 1882 Catholic church fair in Cheyenne lasted six days and featured dancing. Episcopal churches in Laramie, Cheyenne, and El Paso all sponsored formal dances, as did the Mormon church, but most mainline Protestants considered dancing beyond the pale. Instead, they staged raffles, "beauty contests" (twenty-five cents a vote), box lunches, and bake sales. African-American churches usually sponsored an Emancipation Day supper, with such luxuries as oysters, pound cake, and sweet potato pie. For almost forty years, the Episcopal Charity Ball opened Denver's fall social season, with funds going to St. Luke's Hospital.

Finally, the churches served yet another role on the Gilded Age western frontier: they functioned as training schools for political democracy. The numerous church gatherings introduced citizens to basic democratic principles: the conduct of public meetings via accepted rules of order, the need to speak persuasively to the issue at hand, and (usually) the realization that the majority rules. The discussions also reinforced the virtue of listening, freedom of expression, respect for others' views, and the necessity for compromise. Thus the countless church and political meetings of the era overlapped and reinforced each other.

The clerical accomplishments, however, have never penetrated the popular myth of the American West. Whereas virtually everyone recognizes the names of Billy the Kid, Sitting Bull, Annie Oakley, and Wyatt Earp, only specialists recall Rev. Sheldon Jackson, Father Ravalli, or Rabbi William Friedman. Unlike figures who have been mythologized, the western clergy suffer from the restrictions of denominationalism. Because they can be identified only by denomination, they cannot be "universalized." Thus, their particularity has excluded them from the mythological West and diminished their stature in the public mind.

The pioneer phase of western European-American religious history ended with the first years of the twentieth century. In general, it had been a "brick and mortar" era for most denominations. Religious leaders built schools, hospitals, orphanages, and local churches as fast as their finances would allow. They left an impressive architectural legacy. Denver's Trinity Methodist Church still anchors the city's downtown; when Portland's Beth Israel was built, it reflected the eclectic architecture characteristic of most Reform temples of the era. Virtually every visitor to Salt Lake City acknowledged the Mormon Temple as the most impressive building in the intermountain West. Perhaps the crowning glory came with the new Catholic Cathedral in St. Louis, "the gateway to the West." Completed in 1914, it was an architectural statement of the role that Catholicism had played in shaping the religious life of the American West.

The vastness of the American West also provided space for numerous experiments in communal living. After the Civil War, thousands of immigrants sought alternative living arrangements. The majority of these drew from a shared religious (and often ethnic) framework, and the West provided the setting. The Aurora Colony near Portland (1855–83) reflected the German pietistic roots of its mother organization, Bethel, in Missouri. During the economic crisis of the late nineteenth century, both the Salvation Army and Jewish benevolent societies experimented with religious agriculture communities in the Dakotas and Colorado. In 1867, William Davies, an ex-Mormon, achieved local notoriety when he formed the Kingdom of Heaven colony in Walla Walla and announced that his son was Christ reincarnated (the "Walla Walla Jesus"). The Land of Shalam, in southern New Mexico, was based on a spirit-delivered, second American scripture, the *Oahspe Bible*. Less well-known than *The Book of Mormon*, the *Oahspe Bible* combined convoluted verbiage with practical advice; the community lasted from 1884 to 1901.

California and the Puget Sound area provided homes for more successful utopian colonies. Alturia, Llano del Rio, and Icaria Sporanza were founded in California. Perhaps the most colorful was the Point Loma Theosophical Colony, presided over by Katherine Tingley ("The Purple Mother") with magisterial splendor. The Puget Sound region had fewer strictly "religious" communities, but it was the location of at least five

"Brotherhood of Man" socialist utopias, including Equality, Burley, and Home. Kevin Starr has suggested that for many easterners, the state of California itself seemed to be "utopia" writ small.

The numerous German and Russian-German communal settlements on the Great Plains proved the most successful of all. Descendants of the Reformation Anabaptists, these German peasants moved into Russia in the late eighteenth century. A century later, when the czar introduced a policy of forced Russification, he ordered the Hutterites and Mennonites to move or join the Russian mainstream. All of the Hutterites and over a third of the Mennonites chose to migrate, and a significant number found their way to the American Great Plains.

Both groups initially settled in communal arrangements. In 1874, a group of Mennonite Brethren organized Gnadenau (Meadow of Grace) in Marion, Kansas, a classic model of a communal village. But within three years, the leaders discovered that banding together was less necessary in America than in Russia. Although some branches of Mennonites retained the communal emphasis, the majority became individual farmers.

The Hutterites, however, did not meld into the American mainstream. They have retained their communal style of life up to the present day. Arriving from the Ukraine in the mid-1870s, they settled in the northern plains. Hutterite theology, especially the concept of *Gelassenheit*, demanded that the individual self be subordinated to the will of God. The goal of Hutterite education was to replace the individual will with a group will, bending the emotions (rather than the intellect) through indoctrination. Pacifist, communal, and deeply suspicious of the prevailing *weltgeist*, the Hutterites were also progressive farmers. Unlike their Old Order Amish "relations" (who usually failed when they ventured from the East onto the Great Plains), the Hutterites bought the latest farm machinery and welcomed technical improvements. Their centralization and capital-heavy organization, however, soon brought them into conflict with their South Dakota immigrant neighbors, who termed them "a nepotic corporation." Eventually, South Dakota passed laws restricting Hutterite land purchases, and the anti-Communist agitation of the 1950s drove several colonies into Canada.

In addition to the Russian-Germans, the Great Plains provided a home for numerous other religious-ethnic groups. German Lutherans, Danish Lutherans, Volga German Catholics, and the Bohemians who figure so prominently in Willa Cather's novels all settled on the northern plains. The villages founded by these immigrants often had an obvious ethnoreligious composition. As late as 1926, for example, the only non-Bohemian in Prague, Nebraska, was the depot agent.

Duplicating their ancestral homes in Europe, these immigrants reestablished the church at the heart of their communities. Immigrants who landed in the nation's larger cities could create a variety of institutions for mutual support: foreign-language presses, restaurants, mutual benefit societies, and bakeries. On the plains, however, the ethnic church, the easiest institution to create, had to assume all of these roles. Even those who had been indifferent churchgoers in Europe (such as most males) often became active after they crossed the Atlantic. The plains priest or pastor was always a community leader. The ethnic church played a crucial role in life on the Great Plains: it held the community together.

Native Revitalization Movements and the Challenge of Ethnic Diversity

In the 1870s, a group of Paiutes at Walker River, Nevada, who were becoming anxious about whites moving onto their lands began to focus on a ceremonial dance under the leadership of a prophet known as Wodziwob. The prophet told his people that if they danced, they could communicate with the spirits of their ancestors; he forecast that the world would soon end, the whites would be swept aside, and the Paiutes' ancestors would return to join them on a renewed land. As word of Wodziwob's message spread west to the Monos and Yokuts of northern California and east to the Shoshones, Bannocks, and Utes, word also spread of another prophet, whose dance was performed by the native people of the Columbia River Plateau. This news fueled Wodziwob's movement: the 1870 Ghost Dance. The network that had linked so many native groups in pre-Columbian America continued to hold into the late nineteenth century, binding Indians of the Columbia River Plateau to their counterparts in the Great Basin. A decade later, the tie would reach across the Rockies to encompass the Plains tribes.

The ceremonial cycle of the Sahaptian and Salishan people of the Plateau had long included a Prophet Dance. When native dancers (*Washani*) performed this ceremony, they were acting on their belief in world destruction and renewal, a concept deeply rooted in both Plateau and Northwest Coast cultures. However, after mid-century, this ceremony had incorporated Christian influences, such as observation of a Sabbath. From this time forward, Plateau native groups experienced intensive white pressures, all of which led to anxieties similar to those of the Walker River Paiutes.

In the nineteenth century, a number of Plateau prophets rose to meet these crises. The most important of these leaders was a Wanapum (*river people*) named Smohalla, whose band lived along the Columbia River between Priest Rapids and the mouth of the Snake River. A traditionalist, Smohalla appealed to the conservative groups among the Plateau tribes. During the 1870s, at the height of his influence, he may have had as many as two thousand followers, including Palouses, Nez Percés, Bannocks, and Northern Paiutes. Like his predecessors, Smohalla merged some Christian elements, such as the use of bells, into the ceremonies, but he discouraged his young men from farming, claiming that those who farmed did not have time to dream. He cautioned his followers "to adhere strictly to native dress and custom," and he refused to allow the Wanapum to move from their lands to the Yakima Indian Nation reservation. A dreamer himself, Smohalla's religion became known as the Washani faith or the Pom Pom (Dreamer) religion.

West of the Cascades another native revitalization movement began to grow in the early 1880s. Founded by John Slocum, a Squaxin of lower Puget Sound, the Indian Shakers, so-called because of the nervous twitching that accompanied their prayers and songs, combined shamanistic performances with Catholic ritual and Presbyterian doctrine. Possibly motivated by Smohalla, Slocum's group did not retain the antiwhite sentiment of the Dreamers, but it spread throughout native groups in Washington, Oregon, British Columbia, and northern California.

The widespread religious borrowing of Coast, Plateau, and Great Basin that characterized these native revitalization movements found its way through the Rockies and onto the plains in the late 1880s when Wovoka, the son of an apostle of Wodziwob, revived the 1870 Ghost Dance religion. Because of the catastrophic impact of Wovoka's teaching, his reputation has endured. His message, however, was part of a continuum. Like his predecessors, Wovoka preached that a cataclysmic event would banish the whites and return the ancestors of native people, an event that would be hastened by Indians dancing the Ghost Dance, treating each other as brothers and sisters, and following the old ways. The difference between Wovoka and his predecessors lay in the timing and the circumstances. Smohalla's Washani faith spread in an era of intense anxiety for perhaps two thousand Plateau followers, and it influenced Joseph's band of Nez Percés as well as Northern Paiute Dreamers, who joined the Bannocks in the Bannock-Paiute War of 1878. By contrast, Wovoka's Ghost Dance faith spoke to perhaps twenty thousand Plains Indian followers, whose world was shattering all about them. In the two decades between the Battle of the Little Bighorn and the rise of the Ghost Dance, the Lakotas saw their lives reduced from proud Plains warriors to starving, disease-stricken reservation dwellers. At the same time, their relation to the supernatural had come under attack when the Great Father in Washington had issued new rules prohibiting the old ceremonial dances, including the Sun Dance, and forbidding any interference of the medicine men with schooling or Christianizing. With the news of Wovoka's promised millennium, forecast for the spring of 1891, as well as both the Lakota despair and the Great Father's incredible bungling, conditions were in place for the Seventh Cavalry's massacre of a large number of Lakotas on Wounded Knee Creek in December 1890.

Although this event destroyed the momentum of the Ghost Dance, it also led indirectly to the rise of another pan-Indian revitalization movement that had already captured converts across the southern plains. Peyote, a small spineless cactus with hallucinogenic qualities that was used as a sacred medicine in ancient Mexico, was introduced in the late 1870s and 1880s by border groups, especially the Lipan Apaches, to southern Plains tribes confined to the Indian territory. Like the Ghost Dance, the use of peyote spread rapidly through, in part, European-American devices: the federal boarding school, which inadvertently spurred the growth of pan-Indianism and provided a lingua franca for students in its enforced English-language rule; and the railroads, which eased travel for Indians and aided in transporting hundreds of peyote buttons from the lower Rio Grande to the Indian Territory and the northern plains.

Peyote offered a very different solution from that of the prophet movements. Whereas the Ghost Dance had anticipated a millennium and a renewal, the peyote religion taught the individual Indian how to deal with problems of life here and now. Consequently, it had a wide appeal that ranged from returned boarding school students to Indians with no formal schooling. In the Indian Territory, young, schooled Indians, who found in it a version of Indian Christianity, often became its leaders. As it spread north, some peyotists adopted Big Moon or Cross Fire ceremonies, which were introduced in the Caddo-Oto rituals and included strong Christian elements. Others established the Half-Moon ceremony, adapted from the Kiowas and Comanches and known at the time as the "Quanah Parker Way." This ceremony emphasized the Great Spirit and Mother Earth and included the use of tobacco. As the anthropologist Omer C. Stewart has pointed out, despite these differences, both forms opposed the use of alcohol, and both retained "the ancient persistent belief in the supernatural power of the peyote plant."

By the 1920s, the movement had swept into the Great Lakes and Midwest, as well as Canada. Some tribes accepted it quickly; some rejected it completely; and some were bitterly divided over it. At the same time, peyotists encountered vehement hostility and legal action by many non-Indians, including European-American churches, the Bureau of Indian Affairs (BIA), and the U.S. Congress. The feud over peyote in the early twentieth century is a story in itself. In 1918, after a narrow victory over a congressional bill designed to make peyote illegal, a group of Oklahoma peyotists incorporated the Native American Church to bring their belief system under the First Amendment to the Constitution. However, their action did not resolve all legal problems for the peyote religion.

As Native Americans struggled with the numerous challenges to their faiths, settlers from Europe and elsewhere were meeting other religious difficulties. Within the Judeo-Christian groups, the Catholic hierarchy faced a dilemma unique among the churches: a multiethnic membership. Although the Mass was conducted in Latin, the European immigrants naturally sought a priest who spoke their language. Every bishop wrestled with this question. In Texas, Bishop Odin labored for over two decades to provide ethnic priests for his Belgian, Irish, German, Polish, Swiss, Czech, Alsatian, and Mexican-American enclaves. When the bishop of St. Paul finally sent a Bohemian priest to Tabor, Nebraska, in 1877, the Bohemian congregation openly rejoiced. In urban areas such as Denver, bishops confronted potential "secession" as French congregations refused to be "ruled" by Irish priests, or vice versa.

From the bishops' point of view, the Hispanic Catholics formed perhaps the most perplexing of all the ethnic groups. Recent European immigrants generally shared the same assumptions about the faith. But generations of isolation and poverty had forced

Hispanic Catholics to evolve their own religious folk culture. The first bishops of California, Joseph Alemany and Thaddeus Amat, confronted this dilemma. Amat attacked the Mexican practice of selling burial shrouds and actually suspended some Mexican Franciscans for what he termed "fomenting superstition."

This clash between European-American Catholicism and Hispanic folk Catholicism was highlighted in the territory of New Mexico, where the key player in the drama was Archbishop Jean-Baptiste Lamy. The novelist Willa Cather has immortalized Lamy's efforts to bring Hispanic Catholicism into the Catholic mainstream. But her romanticized portrait of "Bishop Latour" in *Death Comes for the Archbishop* (1927) glosses over Lamy's scorn for Hispanic folk art (which he considered primitive), as well as his attempt to replace it with French imagery. Lamy also had negligible appreciation for the strength of the Penitente lay order (which he tried to suppress) or for the healing shrine at Chimayo. Overall, it is a marvel that the Catholic church survived without ethnic schism.

From their stronghold in the Great Basin, the Mormons confronted a different set of challenges, most related to continuing Gentile hostility. A generation after the Republican Platform of 1856 referred to the "twin relics of barbarism" (slavery and polygamy), Congress finally decided to move against the Saints' "peculiar institution." In 1882, Congress passed the Edmunds Act and five years later the Edmunds-Tucker Act, which forced many Mormon polygamous leaders into jail or exile. In 1890, the Saints agreed to give up the practice of polygamy, a decision that led directly to Utah statehood in 1896. But the "Mormon Question," as it was called, remained a steady theme in federal, denominational, and neighboring state politics until World War II.

Hoping to wean Mormon youth from the faith, several denominations, especially the Presbyterians and Congregationalists, opened a vast network of parochial schools in Utah during the latter decades of the nineteenth century. "To educate the children and youth is to emancipate them," wrote a Congregational woman missionary in 1876. "They can be drawn into the school when the church would fail to reach them." These hopes were never realized. The Protestant parochial schools, located in the heart of Mormon country, provided needed social services, but they garnered relatively few converts. From 1870 to 1930, the Gentile population of Utah grew only in the same proportion as Gentile immigration. Nonetheless, these parochial schools did introduce national holidays and, consequently, helped "Americanize" the Saints' young people. In these decades, the Mormons were a people in transition. The maturing of state politics, the end of polygamy, and the influence of Protestant schooling all helped the Saints move closer to the American mainstream.

The Ferment at the Turn of the Century

In 1871, the Philadelphia Presbyterian Herrick Johnson preached a sermon, "The American City: What Shall We Do with It?" Johnson's plea was the opening shot of a national "education and evangelism" campaign that grew rapidly over the next half century. During these years most of the mainline American churches focused on the problems of urban life: immigration, poverty, urbanization, social services, and political corruption. Their response became known as the "social gospel."

Every western region witnessed a social gospel program. Ministers erected "institutional churches" that provided numerous social services and remained open seven days a week. Episcopal priests led city mission work in Omaha, a meat-packing city whose 1919 population was over half immigrant. Turn-of-the-century clergy voiced their opinions on a wide variety of social issues. In the Southwest, a number of churches teamed with physicians to establish hospitals or sanitoria for people with tuberculosis. These institutional combinations of medicine and faith were widely praised at the time. Such actions for the public welfare formed the "left wing" of the social gospel movement.

But even conservative clergymen, the "right wing," devoted time to reform programs during the fin de siècle years. A Seattle Presbyterian evangelist, Mark A. Matthews, spent over a decade denouncing corrupt mayors, police chiefs, and bootleggers. In nearby Tacoma, Mrs. Birgitte Funnemark and her daughter Christine established a nondenominational Evangelical Seamen's Rest as an alternative to the fleshpots of the region. From 1897 to 1903, they simultaneously ministered to sailors and tried to clean up the worst aspects—including shanghaiing—of Tacoma life. In rural Oklahoma, the Anti-Saloon League billed itself as "the church in action." In all western cities, the Salvation Army and the Volunteers of America reached out to an impoverished segment of society that eluded most other religious groups.

During this period, many western clerics revealed a social concern that extended far beyond their own denominations. They campaigned for clean government and civic responsibility. In Denver, for example, the Catholic priest William O'Ryan led the movement to coordinate the city charities (both Catholic and non-Catholic) into an umbrella Charity Organization, which eventually grew into the Community Chest. The Portland First Congregational Church relief fund eventually became the City Relief Fund. The entire city had become the "parish" for these social gospel clerics.

A second distinct regional manifestation of social gospel concerns was Chinese mission work. The nation's clergy had expressed interest in the West Coast Chinese beginning in the 1850s, when there were perhaps twenty-five thousand Chinese living in California. The clergy argued that the presence of so many Chinese in California was obviously part of God's grand design for Asia. They hoped to convert the Chinese miners, who would return and spread the Christian message throughout China. From the clerics' point of view, the conversion of the Far East lay in the offing. These events never materialized, but their absence did not diminish church support for a wide range of Chinese missions.

Another dimension of the social gospel was the work of eastern Christian reformers who led the fight for the assimilation of western Native Americans. Throughout the late nineteenth century these reformers, who included many ministers and lay church members, had the ear of the Great Father. Their efforts only increased after the demise of President Ulysses Grant's Peace Policy, which had sought to establish church influence over federal Indian programs by assigning specific denominations to each Indian reservation. Christian reformers soon tasted victory with the passage of the disastrous Dawes Act, or General Allotment Act, of 1887, which began to break up the reservations and attempted to end tribal ownership of lands. Two years later the Christian reformers gained a sympathetic commissioner of Indian affairs in Thomas

Jefferson Morgan, a former Baptist minister and educator, who strengthened the 1883 regulations enforcing Indian assimilation. Working directly with the BIA and Congress, the Christian reformers exerted control on Indian religions throughout this era. However, Native Americans demonstrated their resilience. They practiced their ceremonies in secret, and they embraced revitalization movements that brought hope to the despairing.

During this same era, the Southwest began to rediscover its Roman Catholic mission heritage, largely through the efforts of a former Massachusetts Yankee, Charles Fletcher Lummis. The Protestant Lummis spent a lifetime trying to convince California's recently arrived midwestern Protestants that Spanish missions and iconography should become central to their new self-image. He likened the Franciscan missions of California to the Puritan churches of Massachusetts, arguing that one need not be Roman Catholic to appreciate their symbolic power. "The old missions," he wrote in 1918, "are worth more money, are a greater asset to Southern California than our oil, our oranges, or even our climate." Simultaneously, the Catholic bishop of Tucson began to restore nearby Mission San Xavier del Bac, an effort that prevented San Xavier from joining the nearby presidio at Tubac and mission at Tumacácori as crumbling adobe ruins.

Thus, the Southwest began to forge a romantic, mildly nondenominational saga of Catholic missions and missionaries. The fledgling tourist industry soon discovered that "mission tours" were highly profitable. At the center of this revival stood Father Junipero Serra, an eighteenth-century figure whose reputation continued to grow: the state of California eventually placed his statue in the rotunda of the Capitol in Washington, D.C., and the Catholic church inaugurated his canonization process. During the late 1980s, however, several California Native American groups vigorously opposed Serra's proposed canonization on the grounds that the Franciscan missions had enslaved their ancestors. In reply, Catholic defenders argued that Serra should be judged as a man of his times. This controversy, still under way, shows how difficult it is for any religious figure to achieve transdenominational acclaim.

The fin de siècle years also witnessed a bewildering variety of new religious currents. The highly publicized World's Parliament of Religions of 1893 in Chicago focused the nation's attention on the wide range of new faiths, such as the Baha'i movement, Theosophy, the Vendanta Society, and Christian Science. Two of these movements forged deep roots in the American West: New Thought and Pentecostalism.

New Thought, a complex system of metaphysics, maintains that one may control both the physical and the mental circumstances of life by consciously cultivating a "positive" attitude toward one's surroundings. An offshoot of Mary Baker Eddy's Christian Science, New Thought teachers stressed that one should listen to the "voice of the indwelling Presence which is our source of Inspiration, Power, Health and Prosperity." New Thought advocates also insisted that practical results flowed from holding these views: "health" and "success." Both proved capable of endless variations.

The three foremost New Thought organizations—Divine Science, Unity, and Religious Science—were all based in the West. In the late 1880s, the three Brooks sisters of Pueblo, Colorado, began Divine Science in Denver. Nona L. Brooks served as pastor of the church for thirty-one years and shepherded it into the forefront of Denver's faiths.

The Unity movement of Kansas City proved even more successful. Founded by Myrtle and Charles Fillmore, the Unity School of Practical Christianity is now recognized as the most successful of the New Thought groups. California proved especially congenial to metaphysical thinking, and by 1907 boasted more New Thought centers than any other state. The leading California group was Ernest Holmes's United Church of Religious Science, headquartered in Los Angeles. Holmes's *Science of Mind* textbook (1926) has become a minor classic in the field, and his faith gained fame as "the religion of the Hollywood stars." Holmes maintained that the realization that individuals could consciously direct and control "the law of creative force" for their own purposes was "the greatest discovery of all time."

The flexibility of western faiths and the flexibility of New Thought proved a good match. The movement's significance lay less with its actual membership—never large by any count—than with its endless stream of "positive thinking" publications and its eventual incorporation into mainline Protestantism, Catholicism, and Judaism. By the 1990s perhaps the foremost western proponent was Rev. Robert Schuller. With his striking Crystal Cathedral located in Garden Grove, California, his popular television series, and a myriad of best-selling books, Schuller shepherded New Thought from its roots in the West to a prominent role in contemporary American culture.

Few people connect New Thought with the Pentecostal-Holiness movement, but the two have a good deal in common. Emerging simultaneously, they offered spiritual healing to many Americans who, for various reasons, were affected by the professionalization of medicine. Although both these movements fragmented into numerous small groups, their impact reached well beyond their numbers.

The turn-of-the-century Pentecostal movement had tangled roots in both the West and the South and in two interrelated beliefs. One belief emphasized "Christian perfection" or "entire sanctification," a second grace that cleansed the believer from the tendency to sin. The second belief derived from events in the book of Acts and emphasized "speaking in tongues," or glossolalia.

Although historians of Pentecostalism have uncovered scattered references to glossolalia during the nineteenth century, they agree that the 1906 Azusa Street (Los Angeles) revival began modern Pentecostalism. Led in part by William J. Seymour, a one-eyed black minister from the South, the rise of Pentecostalism is a little-known black contribution to white religious life. In the early days, most Pentecostal churches were integrated, but by the 1920s they had separated into primarily white or black congregations.

From Azusa Street, the Pentecostal "full Gospel" revival spread up and down the West Coast and into the rural areas of Oklahoma, Texas, and Missouri. There the Pentecostals also created yet another religiosocial subculture. Their world emphasized spiritual healing, religious ecstasy, glossolalia, and general renewal. The faith demanded a strict personal morality (no cards, jewelry, cosmetics, or bodily ornamentation and minimal amusements). Their musical imagery, which would later influence early rock and roll (for example, the song "Great Balls of Fire"), called for a high degree of participation and emotional release. For many, the profession of the ministry proved a popular road to success. The democracy of the message was obvious. As one minister

With personal dynamism and extravagant staging borrowed from Hollywood, the evangelist Aimee Semple McPherson used her Four Square Gospel Church as a pulpit from which to build a national following for her Pentecostal faith.

H. Harold Fisher. Temple Angelus, Graduation Exercises. *Gelatin silver print, 1930. Department of Special Collections, University Research Library, University of California, Los Angeles.*

stated: "We did not honor men for their advantage, in means or education, but rather for their God-given gifts." In this sense, the Pentecostals reached out to the religious needs of the common people. Not surprisingly, they manifested great strength in old Populist or socialist areas of the West.

The most effective publicist of the Pentecostal movement was Aimee Semple McPherson. Reared in a Salvation Army family, Aimee arrived in Los Angeles in 1918 to establish the Four Square Gospel Church, revealed to her in a vision. A strikingly beautiful woman, she utilized the Hollywood atmosphere to turn her worship services into media productions. "Sister Aimee" also established a religious radio station (KFSG, Kall Four Square Gospel) to spread her message. From the mid-1920s to the mid-1930s, she appeared on the front page of the *Los Angeles Times* approximately three times a week.

McPherson's most notorious escapade occurred in 1926 when she disappeared, probably for a brief romantic tryst with her radio station operator. On her return, however, she claimed to have been kidnapped by two outlaws, "Jake" and "Mexicali Rose." The endless publicity from this event dramatically increased the size of her Sunday audiences and gave her a nationwide reputation.

Beneath the hype and extravagance, McPherson emerged as America's first "superstar" media evangelist. She provided a national platform for the Pentecostal message, one that it would not regain until the 1970s and 1980s. By that time, the charismatic dimension of Pentecostalism had spread into Roman Catholicism, the Episcopal church, and a number of Native American communities and among many televangelists. By the 1990s, Pentecostalism was growing most rapidly in Latin America and Africa.

The Twentieth Century: Pluralism Expands

A revival of religious conservatism occurred in the decades between the two World Wars. The rapid growth of the Ku Klux Klan, which claimed a tenuous link with right-wing Protestantism, provided the most extreme example of this religiosocial backlash. Another form of repression came in the attacks on Native American faiths. During the 1920s, the fundamentalist-modernist controversy split the mainline Protestant churches into two warring camps. All of these national movements affected the trans-Mississippi West.

The Klan proved exceptionally strong in several western states, especially Colorado, Texas, and Oregon. Their anti-immigrant and anti-Catholic message drove some Catholics out of Oregon and Colorado and soured Protestant-Catholic relations in El Paso for a decade. In Oregon, militant nativists introduced legislation in 1922 that would have required all children to attend public school, ostensibly for reasons of "Americanism." The real goal was to destroy the Catholic parochial school system. Catholic resistance found ready allies from the Lutherans, Seventh-Day Adventists, and the American Jewish community, as well as several liberal Episcopal and Presbyterian clergymen. In 1925, the law was overturned by the Supreme Court.

Religious suppression also found its way into the long-festering question of the First Amendment and Indian religious liberties. Through the 1920s and 1930s, Indian religious freedom was a major issue for Native Americans. In the 1920s, the debate pitted Commissioner of Indian Affairs Charles H. Burke against the reformer John Collier. In 1921, Burke issued a circular that reinforced the directive of 1883, prohibiting ceremonial dances and "celebrations" that included actions deemed improper and even harmful. As the historian Francis Paul Prucha has pointed out, this attack infuriated Collier and inspired his "campaign in support of religious liberty for Indians." The ensuing national debate climaxed in 1926 when Collier and his followers defeated a congressional bill that would have legalized Burke's position.

But the fight was not over. In the 1930s, when President Franklin Delano Roosevelt appointed Collier as commissioner of Indian affairs, Collier viewed Indian religious freedom as a cornerstone of his blueprint on Indian policy. Like Burke, he issued a directive. The 1934 circular, entitled "Indian Religious Freedom and Indian Culture," declared that Indians be granted "the fullest constitutional liberty, in all matters affecting religion, conscience, and culture," and that "no interference with Indian religious life or ceremonial expression will hereafter be tolerated." Reversing the centuries-old approach, Collier declared, "The cultural liberty of Indians is in all respects to be considered equal to that of any non-Indian group." At BIA schools, Collier prohibited compulsory attendance at religious services and permitted students to return home for ceremonies. Christian reformers and Christianized Indians saw Collier's circular as a step backward. Some tribes opposed the concept of religious freedom as a matter of principle: it would violate tribal sovereignty by interfering in internal tribal affairs. If the majority of a tribe, such as the Lakotas, opposed the Native American Church, for example, the tribe did not want Washington ordering it to legalize peyote. The issue of religious freedom for Indians was not resolved in the 1930s, but Collier's stand did begin to bring Indian religions under the constitutional guarantees granted to other citizens.

The fundamentalist-modernist controversy, which so disrupted the nation's Protestant churches, also had a strong western component. Two transplanted Pennsylvanians, Lyman and Milton Stewart, used the profits from their Los Angeles–based Union Oil Company to support a series of conservative evangelical causes from the 1890s forward. During the Progressive Era, Lyman Stewart began to attack theological liberals, especially Presbyterian Thomas F. Day, who was eventually dismissed from the San Francisco Theological Seminary in 1912 for teaching Higher Criticism. In 1907, Stewart helped found what would become the Bible Institute of Los Angeles. He also financed the publication of William E. Blackstone's millennial tract *Jesus Is Coming*, which became the most widespread premillennial piece of literature in the world. Finally, Stewart funded the publication of *The Fundamentals* (1912–16), a series of conservative pamphlets that are usually acknowledged as the opening shots of the fundamentalist-modernist controversy. The Stewart brothers helped inaugurate what became the most disruptive twentieth-century controversy among American Protestants. Over the years, the nation's Protestant churches began to divide along theological lines (liberal-conservative) rather than denominational ones. The sociologists Robert Wuthnow and James Davison Hunter have argued that this ever-widening liberal-conservative split lies at the heart of the post–World War II "restructuring of American religion."

After World War II, with the flood of people moving to the Coast and Sunbelt and the meteoric rise of electronic media, western religious culture moved into the mainstream. The evangelist Billy Graham personified this movement. A Wheaton College (Illinois) graduate, William Franklin Graham toured the revival circuits from 1943 to 1948 as merely one of many conservative evangelicals. In late 1949, when the evangelist was in Los Angeles, the publisher William Randolph Hearst allegedly told his editors to "puff Graham." The unexpected publicity brought the young revivalist and his message to the attention of the nation, propelling him into a position of prominence. Graham eventually became the foremost American cleric of the twentieth century. Although Graham could never be called a "western" figure, his national prominence began among the rootless citizens of Los Angeles. Graham's sudden rise personified the religious revival of the 1950s, which sent Americans back to their churches and synagogues in record numbers.

The religiosity of the Eisenhower years furthered the "mainstreaming" of the country's Catholics and Jews. In 1955, the sociologist Will Herberg published *Protestant-Catholic-Jew*, in which he argued that the great historic faiths formed three equally valid routes to becoming "American." Religious life in the West, however, anticipated Herberg's conclusions. By the 1950s, the western Catholic universities of Santa Clara, St. Mary's, St. Martin's, Seattle University, Gonzaga, and the University of San Francisco had long-established strong regional reputations, in both academics and athletics. The Catholic parochial school systems of San Francisco and Denver educated

perhaps one-third of the cities' children. Since the early 1900s, Santa Fe had relied on the romance of Hispanic folk Catholicism (*luminarias, faralitos,* the burning of Zozobra) to entice eastern tourists to its hotels and shops. The California "mission tours" struck the same chord. The "ghetto mentality" that had forced eastern Catholicism to remain on the cultural defensive for over a century was never re-created in the trans-Mississippi West.

The same proved true for western Judaism. The saga of the Jewish forty-niners and the famed success of the great Gilded Age merchandisers, such as I. and J. Magnin, Meyer and Frank, and the Goldwaters, had long been an integral part of the legend of the West. With the larger-than-life stories of twentieth-century film magnates Adolph Zukor, Jesse Lasky, Samuel Goldwyn, Carl Laemmle, Louis B. Mayer, and the Warner Brothers—"the ethnic Horatio Algers who built Hollywood," as one historian phrased it—the legend evolved into myth itself.

The Jewish communities on the urban West Coast had long been intimately involved in the growth of their cities. In 1880, Los Angeles Jews dominated the mercantile world in such fields as dry goods, clothing, and book selling. By any classification, they were middle class. For years, the San Francisco Jews worked closely with the dominant Republican party, contributing politicians who ranged from the infamous city boss Abe Ruef to long-term U.S. Congressman Julius Kahn. From 1930

Important contributors to the economic and political growth of West Coast cities, Jews in San Francisco, Los Angeles, and Portland composed solidly middle-class communities by the late 19th century.

Unidentified photographer. Children's Party at Temple Beth Israel. *Photograph, 1898. Oregon Historical Society (#OrHi 25946), Portland.*

to 1960, San Francisco's major boards and commissions were about 30 percent Jewish, with certain positions traditionally reserved as "Jewish seats." The same tale, with variations, applied to Portland, Seattle, and Denver. Idaho, Utah, New Mexico, and Oregon voters all elected Jewish governors, long before New York or Illinois, with their much larger Jewish populations. In 1913, when San Francisco's mayor, Jim Rolph, extended to Rosh Hashanah and Yom Kippur the same public recognition that attended Good Friday, he was the first big-city mayor to do so. By World War II, impressive temples dotted Los Angeles, Portland, San Francisco, Seattle, Boise, El Paso, Albuquerque, Denver, Phoenix, and numerous other western cities. Thus, the saga of western religious life anticipated Herberg's ideas by at least two generations.

Although it took yet another generation, the "Americanization" process eventually expanded to include the Latter-day Saints. After the Vietnam War and the disruptions of the 1960s and early 1970s that challenged traditional values, the Saints' insistence on conventional morality and family virtues appeared more and more "mainstream." The spread of Mormonism beyond Utah, the opening of the priesthood to African Americans, plus the Saints' success in the business world confirmed this impression. In the early 1980s, the Mormon hierarchy added the phrase "another testimony to the Gospel of Jesus Christ" to the front of *The Book of Mormon.* A decade later, the church quietly dropped the denunciation of non-Mormon clergy from secret temple rituals. Both were indications of the mainstreaming under way. Mormon missionaries continue to stress that their church is the only way to salvation, but if one judges Mormons by life-style and values, rather than theology, the modern Latter-day Saints might well be on their way to becoming simply another American "denomination."

The historian Sydney E. Ahlstrom has argued that the 1960s formed the most tumultuous single decade in American religious history. The Vatican II reforms liberated American Catholicism on many levels but also undermined the church's historic unity of purpose. From the mid-1960s forward, prominent lay and clerical figures publicly disagreed with the official church position on a variety of issues, including abortion, birth control, clerical celibacy, and nuclear disarmament. As the historian Garry Wills has noted, just as Catholicism was accepted in American life, it proceeded to commit hara-kiri.

The mainline Protestants fared no better. From 1960 to 1990, they lost an alarming number of members. In the tumult of the late twentieth century, these aging, liberal denominations often found it difficult to establish a meaningful theology or to retain the loyalty of their youth.

Although they found their influence waning, the mainline churches continued to provide leadership in many western communities. In the urban West, the Catholic parochial schools have proven surprisingly successful in educating children from underprivileged backgrounds. Other mainline churches have inaugurated a variety of modern social gospel programs that are reminiscent of the late nineteenth century: day-care centers, meals for the homeless, hospices, and homes for senior citizens. In polyglot Los Angeles, a downtown Methodist church advertises services in Korean, Vietnamese, Cambodian, and English. These creative adaptations illustrate the continued vitality of the mainstream groups.

From the 1960s, it again became fashionable to search for spiritual values. The quest reached its apogee on the West Coast, especially in California. For a century, California's tolerant, open atmosphere had encouraged a smorgasbord of religious organizations, but the cultural ferment dramatically broadened the offerings. Mainline Protestantism, Catholicism, and Judaism; conservative evangelicalism; a variety of "Jesus People"; saffron-robed Hare Krishnas seeking "Krishna consciousness"; L. Ron Hubbard's Scientology, with its promise to adherents that they could be psychologically "clear"; Rev. Sun Myung Moon's Unification Church, with its emphasis on a "new family"; Black Muslims, with their militant, separatist racial call; the storefront churches, with a bewildering panorama of theological and social messages—all were available in an afternoon's walk in San Francisco, San Diego, or Los Angeles.

In the 1980s, the "unchurched" Pacific Northwest became home for a variety of extreme movements: sexual enlightenment on the Big Muddy Ranch in eastern Oregon, led by the Rajneesh (until he fled to India after pleading guilty to two federal felonies); the Church Universal and Triumphant near Livingston, Montana, whose armed followers went underground to avert the predicted end of the world; and a militant, racist group of Aryan Christians based at Hayden Lake, Idaho. Similar extreme millennial views were expressed by the Branch Davidians of Waco, Texas, whose violent encounter with federal agents ended in the deaths of most members of the group in April 1993.

Amid the bewildering cacophony of voices during the late twentieth century, three larger, nationwide themes emerged: the resurgence of conservative evangelical Christianity, bolstered by its use of television; the popularization of New Age ideas; and the increased visibility of Native American religious concerns. All had strong western components.

Before the 1960s, conservative evangelicals had been somewhat peripheral to the religious mainstream. But the collapse of traditional values in the 1960s called them forth in considerable numbers, bearing their old message of strict biblicism and a call for individual repentance and conversion. Demos Shakarian, a successful California dairy farmer, had created the Full Gospel Businessmen's Fellowship in 1951; its Pentecostal message soon found considerable support within the middle-class business community. The popular Fuller Theological Seminary in Pasadena, which carefully hewed to a moderate biblicism, graduated hundreds of conservative pastors and church workers. Many of these groups began to flex their political muscle.

The conservatives' aggressive use of electronic media, especially television, fueled their growth. Pioneers in the use of radio ministry, in the 1950s and 1960s fundamentalists moved to television, bringing a combined message of folksy, old-fashioned preaching, elaborate staging, and effective fund-raising. Although television audiences are national ones, the westerners Oral Roberts (Tulsa) and Robert Schuller (Garden Grove, California) commanded some of the largest followings.

The New Age movement also attracted growing attention during the 1970s and 1980s. A combination of Eastern mysticism and eclectic folklore, New Age religion celebrates the private individual; it offers the opportunity to "create your own reality." A significant number of New Agers were drawn to Arizona, California, and Washington. The popular West Coast writer J. Z. Knight claimed that she had received messages from a mystic being, "Ramtha," in a fashion similar to the nineteenth-century Theosophist Helena Blavatsky's *Isis Unveiled*. The actress Shirley MacLaine's books, plus various celebrations of "harmonic convergences" at the Black Hills of South Dakota, the San Juan Islands of Washington State, and elsewhere, have given the movement wide publicity. Crystal shops and elixirs, with claims of energy and healing powers, have brought these ideas home to millions. Most modern bookstores have a "New Age" (formerly "Occult") section, and as usual, southern California serves as a welcome home for these questers. By 1990, however, Native American groups began to protest that the New Age movement had stolen traditional native teachings and were using them for financial gain.

Native American belief systems have remained resilient in recent decades, but theirs remains an untold story. Both revitalization movements and traditional ceremonies have retained followers. In the Coast and Plateau regions, Shaker churches and Washat Longhouses are a strong presence in native communities. Throughout Indian country, the Native American Church is ubiquitous. In the trans-Mississippi West, there may be as many as two hundred thousand peyotists. Omer C. Stewart has argued, "Except for the Indian powwow, [peyote] is the most pan-Indian institution in America." In addition, traditional systems of belief persist and continue to provide a focus of ethnic identity. Among the Navajos, many faiths compete. But in times of crisis, Navajos who are Mormons or members of the new Protestant groups may seek help from the traditional ways, incorporating healing ceremonials, such as the Blessing Way. Faced with an increasingly complex world, Navajos view their ancient Diné religion as one symbol of Navajo nationalism.

Above all, however, native belief systems continue to be affected by Christianity. The result is a syncretic blend of faiths: traditional, revitalization, and Christian. When a friend of the anthropologist John C. Ewers paid his last respects to an elderly Blackfeet, the friend noted, "There were lighted candles at his head, a Methodist Bible in his hands, and his weather-worn old medicine bundle at his feet." As the anthropologists Ray J. DeMallie and Douglas R. Parks have written of the Lakotas: "Many of the leaders of traditional ceremonies belong to the Roman Catholic or Episcopal churches. They see no conflict between traditional beliefs and ceremonies and those of Christianity."

Before Vatican II and the upheavals of the 1960s and 1970s, mainstream Christianity had been uncomfortable about accepting the validity of native faiths. Growing religious liberalism, however, combined with increased concern over the deteriorating environment, has brought renewed interest in Native American beliefs. As the Lakota author Vine Deloria, Jr., has concluded, "Many people are seeking answers in American Indian religions, which must involve some form of reconciliation with the American Indian and his lands." Since most of the federal reservations and the largest Indian populations are in the West, this has special meaning for the region.

On Thanksgiving 1987, a group of prominent church leaders in Seattle (Catholic, Lutheran, American Baptist, Disciples, Presbyterian, Methodist, and United Church of Christ) issued an astounding declaration: "a formal apology on behalf of our churches for their longstanding participation in the destruction of traditional Native American spiritual practices." In addition, these liberal churches (no conservative evangelical group participated) pledged to support the 1978 American Indian Religious Freedom Act by helping the native peoples protect their sacred sites. This federal law carried Collier's directive of the 1930s one step further by granting to the American Indians, Eskimos, Aleuts, and Native Hawaiians the right "to believe, express, and exercise traditional religions . . . including access to sites, use and possession of sacred objects and freedom to worship through ceremonials and traditional rites." Other actions included the 1973 return of Blue Lake to Taos Pueblo, the 1975 return of Mount Adams to the Yakimas, and the 1988 halting of the proposed development of Madrona Point on Washington's Orcas Island (sacred to the Lummis). All these events acknowledged the validity of native faiths. As "The Bishops' Apology" concluded, "May God of Abraham and Sarah, and the Spirit who lives in both the Cedar and Salmon People, be honored and celebrated."

What makes the story of western religions distinctive? This is not easy to answer. Clearly, the West never duplicated the theological or literary thrust of New England Puritanism; nor did it produce the umbrella of evangelism that often united the diverse peoples of the American South. Instead, western religion was molded by both the historical moment of settlement and the vast spaces of the western landscape.

The West manifested a bewildering number of faiths: the Native American belief systems; the Hispanic Catholics of the Borderlands; the Latter-day Saints of the Great Basin; German and East European Jews; the faiths of Asia; the Franciscans of California; the Jesuits of the Rocky Mountains; the Russian-German Hutterites and Mennonites, the Greek Orthodox, and other ethnic churches; the Pentecostals of Oklahoma and environs; the Missouri Synod Lutherans of the Middle Border; the evangelical subculture of Texas and the southern Great Plains; and the ubiquitous Congregationalists, Episcopalians, Presbyterians, Disciples of Christ, Methodists, Lutherans, and Baptists. In many areas, these faiths were set apart by both the configurations of the land and the timing of settlement, leading to the creation of religious folk cultures that retain their vitality today.

Thus, the religious history of the American West has flowed in a myriad of parallel currents. Although specific churches may have shaped subregional cultures, no denomination has ever achieved hegemony over the entire West. The West has not produced a "western religious establishment," voluntary or otherwise. In the future, this pluralism, accompanied by the absence of any "culture-shaping" denominational mainstream, will likely characterize religious life across the nation. The pattern of faith established in the American West, therefore, has clearly pointed the way.

Bibliographic Note

The most extensive overview of American religious history is Sydney E. Ahlstrom, *A Religious History of the American People* (New Haven, 1972), although he does not focus specifically on the West. Several recent studies have tried to fill this gap: Ferenc M. Szasz, ed., *Religion in the West* (Manhattan, Kans., 1984); Carl Guarneri and David Alvarez, eds., *Religion and Society in the American West: Historical Essays* (Lanham, Md., 1987); Jay P. Dolan, ed., *The American Catholic Parish: A History from 1850 to the Present*, vol. 2 (New York, 1987); and Ferenc M. Szasz, *The Protestant Clergy in the Great Plains and Mountain West, 1865–1915* (Albuquerque, 1988).

For the Native Americans, see Henry Warner Bowden, *American Indians and Christian Missions: Studies in Cultural Conflict* (Chicago, 1981), and Robert F. Berkhofer, Jr., *Salvation and the Savage: An Analysis of Protestant Missions and American Indian Response, 1787–1862* (1965; reprint, New York, 1972), as introductory overviews. A solid case study is Clyde A. Milner II, *With Good Intentions: Quaker Work among the Pawnees, Otos, and Omahas in the 1870s* (Lincoln, 1982). The late-nineteenth-century reform movement's impact on religion is treated in Francis Paul Prucha, *American Indian Policy in Crisis: Christian Reformers and the Indians, 1865–1900* (Norman, 1976). The revitalization movements are dealt with in a number of works. Recent studies include Robert H. Ruby and John A. Brown, *Dreamer-Prophets of the Columbia River Plateau: Smohalla and Skolaskin* (Norman, 1989). Also consult Click Relander, *Drummers and Dreamers* (Seattle, 1986). On the Ghost Dance, see the classic account by James Mooney, *The Ghost-Dance Religion and the Sioux Outbreak of 1890* (1892–93; reprint, Chicago, 1965). On peyote, consult Omer C. Stewart's works, especially *Peyote Religion: A History* (Norman, 1987). Studies that develop the concept of syncretism include Raymond J. DeMallie and Douglas R. Parks, eds., *Sioux Indian Religion: Tradition and Innovation* (Norman, 1987), Alfonso Ortiz, *The Tewa World: Space, Time, Being, and Becoming in a Pueblo Society* (Chicago, 1969), and David Aberle, "The Future of Navajo Religion," in David M. Brugge and Charlotte J. Frisbie, eds., *Navajo Religion and Culture: Selected Views* (Santa Fe, 1982), 219-31. An American Indian point of view is found in Vine Deloria, Jr., *God Is Red* (New York, 1973). For recent historiography, see Robert Brightman, "Toward a History of Indian Religion: Religious Changes in Native Societies," in Colin G. Calloway, ed., *New Directions in American Indian History* (Norman, 1988), 223–49.

The most comprehensive studies of the missionary thrust into the Pacific Northwest remain Clifford M. Drury, *Marcus and Narcissa Whitman and the Opening of Old Oregon* (Glendale, Calif., 1973), Wilfred P. Schoenberg, *A History of the Catholic Church in the Pacific Northwest, 1743–1983* (Washington, D.C., 1987), and Robert Ignatius Burns, *The Jesuits and the Indian*

Wars of the Northwest (New Haven, 1966). See also Francis Paul Prucha's provocative article "Two Roads to Conversion," *Pacific Northwest Quarterly* 79 (October 1988): 30–37.

Kevin Starr, *Americans and the California Dream, 1850–1915* (New York, 1973), has a good deal on "the great exception," as do Eldon Ernst, "Religion from a Pacific Coast Perspective," in Guarneri and Alvarez, eds., *Religion and Society in the American West*, Robert V. Hine, *California's Utopian Colonies* (1953; reprint, New York, 1966), and Sandra Sizer Frankiel, *California's Spiritual Frontiers: Religious Alternatives to Anglo-Protestantism, 1850–1910* (Berkeley, 1988). Arnoldo De Leon, *The Tejano Community, 1836–1900* (Albuquerque, 1982), Paul Horgan, *Lamy of Santa Fe: His Life and Times* (New York, 1975), and Mark T. Banker, *Presbyterian Missions and Cultural Interaction in the Far Southwest, 1850–1950* (Urbana, 1993), explore religion in the Borderlands region.

The *Western States Jewish Historical Quarterly* provides a mine of information, but one should also consult Max Vorspan and Lloyd P. Gartner, *History of the Jews of Los Angeles* (San Marino, Calif., 1970), Moses Rischin, ed., *The Jews of the American West: The Metropolitan Years* (Berkeley, 1979), and Harriet Rochlin and Fred Rochlin, *Pioneer Jews: A New Life in the Far West* (Boston, 1984).

The literature on the Latter-day Saints is enormous. One should probably start with the overview by Leonard J. Arrington and Davis Bitton, *The Mormon Experience: A History of the Latter-Day Saints* (New York, 1979). The most provocative interpretation of the Saints remains Jan Shipps, *Mormonism: The Story of a New Religious Tradition* (Urbana, 1985). See also Leonard J. Arrington, *Brigham Young: American Moses* (New York, 1985), and Thomas G. Alexander, *Mormonism in Transition: A History of the Latter-Day Saints, 1890–1930* (Urbana, 1986).

Martin E. Marty has begun a four-volume study of religion in the United States under the title *Modern American Religion*. The sociologists Robert Bellah (et al.), *Habits of the Heart: Individualism and Commitment in American Life* (New York, 1985), Robert Wuthnow, *The Restructuring of American Religion: Society and Faith since World War II* (Princeton, 1988), and James Davison Hunter, *Culture Wars: The Struggle to Define America* (New York, 1991), provide the best overviews of post–World War II religious life.

Chapter Eleven

Violence

RICHARD MAXWELL BROWN

T he focus of this essay is the West from the middle of the nineteenth century to 1920—a period in which the violence of the region was not only heavy but destined to become an enduring aspect of the national mythology. First is a discussion of the values that impelled westerners of the time to be violent. Next is an extended treatment of what I have termed the Western Civil War of Incorporation, the key to so much violence from 1850 to 1920. The essay concludes with brief comments on western violence in recent decades, treats the images of western violence so deeply graven in the national consciousness, and closes by addressing two vital questions: Just how violent was the West? Is the West mainly responsible for the American heritage of pervasive violence?

Values

A cluster of beliefs mentally programmed westerners to commit violence: the doctrine of no duty to retreat; the imperative of personal self-redress; the homestead ethic; the ethic of individual enterprise; the Code of the West; and the ideology of vigilantism.

The *doctrine of no duty to retreat* emerged when the West, along with the rest of America, made a transition from the English common law of homicide and self-defense, in which flight or retreat was legally required in combat situations, to the frontier-western-American concept of no duty to retreat. Crucial to the English common law of homicide was the notion of escape: in a personal dispute that threatened to become violent, one must flee from the scene. Should it be impossible to get away, however, the common law required that one retreat as far as possible—"to the wall" at one's back—before violently resisting an antagonist in an act of lawful self-defense.

Following the westward movement of white American settlers beyond the Appalachians, the highest court in state after state canceled the English duty to retreat in favor of the American right to stand one's ground. In 1876 the top Ohio court held that a "true man" was "not obligated to fly" from an assailant. The following year the Indiana Supreme Court got to the heart of the matter: "The tendency of the American mind seems to be very strongly against the enforcement of any rule which requires a person to flee when assailed." An old folk song expressed the popular attitude:

Wake up, wake up darlin' Corrie
And go and get my gun
I ain't no hand for trouble
But I'll die before I'll run

No western gun battle over unbranded cattle or range rights claimed as many lives as Frederic Remington's painting suggests. But the picture, based on a story by Owen Wister, captures the spirit of the no-duty-to-retreat gunplay that characterized violence in the 19th-century West.

Frederic Remington (1861–1909). What an Unbranded Cow Has Cost. *Oil on canvas, 1895. Gift of Thomas M. Evans, B.A. 1931, Yale University Art Gallery, New Haven, Connecticut.*

The climax of the American renunciation of the duty to retreat came with the U.S. Supreme Court's 1921 decision in the case of *Brown v. United States*. The 7–2 majority opinion endorsing no duty to retreat was written by the noted civil libertarian Oliver Wendell Holmes, whose brisk language was a withering dismissal of the duty to retreat. The Supreme Court's decision reversed a federal-court murder conviction of a self-defending Texan who stood his ground and shot to death a knife-wielding assailant. In private correspondence about the case, Holmes noted that in its common and statute law, Texas was the strongest of all states in favor of the doctrine of no duty to retreat. In Texas, Holmes wrote approvingly, "a man is not born to run away."

Throughout the West, the *imperative of personal self-redress* of grievances was strong. In American frontier history Andrew Jackson, who was reared on the South Carolina frontier and established himself in frontier Tennessee, recounted how his mother's 1781 deathbed admonition to him as a youth of fourteen had been never "to tell a lie, nor take what is not yours, nor sue . . . for slander" but to "settle them cases for yourself"—advice by which the future president, who had killed an opponent in a duel, lived. In the West itself the gunfighting Texas-born New Mexico rancher Oliver M. Lee invoked the ethic of personal self-redress to justify the killings in his embattled career. "I never in my life willingly hurt man, woman, or child—unless they hurt me first. Then I made them pay."

Another powerful inspiration for violent behavior by westerners was, time and again, the *homestead ethic*, whose morality went back to the colonial Anglo-American frontier. This grass-roots doctrine had three key beliefs: the right to have and to hold a family-size farm, the homestead; the right to enjoy a homestead unencumbered by a ruinous economic burden such as an onerous mortgage or oppressive taxes; and the right peacefully to occupy the homestead without fear of violence (such as that by Indians or outlaws) to person or property.

Stretching to the highest realm of the American and western economy was a contrasting value: the large-property owner's *ethic of individual enterprise* in a market economy. The individual-enterprise ethic was strongly supported by the greatest capitalists of the West, including such legendary self-made men as the "Big Four" entrepreneurs who built the railroad empire of the Central and Southern Pacific lines and the "cattle kings" such as Captain Richard King of Texas and William C. Irvine of Wyoming. It was not just the big-name industrialists and agrarian magnates who subscribed so ardently to the entrepreneurial ethic but also countless others in small businesses and the professions. Throughout the West, these aggressive men-on-the-make were ever ready to use violence in allegiance to the individual-enterprise ethic and in defense of their landed and industrial property.

As the nineteenth century wore on, the civilians of the West, brandishing revolvers and rifles in the ordinary course of daily affairs, became one of the most heavily armed populations in the world. The uniquely armed and conflicted society of the West—a "legacy of conquest" in the historian Patricia Nelson Limerick's apt phrase—produced notions of western honor culminating in the *Code of the West*. Central to the Code of the West were the doctrine of no duty to retreat, the imperative of personal self-redress, and an ultrahigh value on courage, which often became, in the phrase of one historian, "reckless bravado"—a bravado that, however, was praised for its courage and not derided for its recklessness.

An Englishman who traveled across the West from California to Texas in the 1870s–1880s observed firsthand the Code of the West among his quick-to-shoot cowboy mates on a long 1880s Texas cattle drive. For readers of the British *Cornhill Magazine*, this anonymous Englishman enumerated the elements of what he termed the "somewhat primitive code of honour" of the cowboys: honesty, courage, sensitive pride, stoic indifference to pain, and, above all, a violent vengefulness against insult. With the cowboy, it was "frequently not a word and a blow but a word and a bullet," for the Code of the West was upheld by ready resort to the six-gun. Allegiance to the Code of the West produced a gunfight that claimed a life on this cattle drive. The urban West shared in the code, as the writer Rudyard Kipling found when, at about the same time, he visited the "civilized city" of Portland, Oregon. To his deep distaste Kipling observed that the jury and Portlanders at large viewed a murder case from the perspective of the western code, emphasizing the proper conditions under which a gunfight might legitimately occur and the fairness of such combat. That such prescriptions were often violated was testimony to the view that they were needed.

Nineteenth-century America was obsessed by masculine honor—North, South, East, and West. The Code of the West was a variant of the national emphasis on honor, a variant that was responsive to the particular conditions of western society in which the actuality or threat of gunplay was pervasive. Basic to the Code of the West was what President Dwight D. Eisenhower, in a nationally televised address of 1953, stressed as the essence of that code and as the code of Abilene, Kansas (Eisenhower's hometown), and its frontier marshal James Butler ("Wild Bill") Hickok: "Meet anyone face to face with whom you disagree" and "if you met him face to face and took the same risk as he did, you could get away with almost anything [killing included], as long as the bullet was in front."

Whereas western gunfighting brought the Code of the West into focus, one of the most common institutions of western violence—vigilantism—had its own set of beliefs. The *ideology of vigilantism* was regularized in the vigilante bylaws, constitutions, and oaths to which westerners frequently subscribed. Motivated by the objective of supporting the values of life and property under conditions of frontier and western disorder, vigilante bands took the law into their own hands for the paradoxical purpose of law enforcement—law as they saw it, in its substantive form of justice rather than its procedurally legal sense. Since vigilantes were almost invariably led by the elite, well-to-do members of early western communities, the ideology of vigilantism reflected the need to justify taking the law into one's own hands (in effect, committing a revolution against the State) on the part of those who were ordinarily the most zealous upholders of the legal system of law and order.

At the core of the ideology of vigilantism were three elements: self-preservation, the right of revolution, and popular sovereignty. To vigilantes, self-preservation was "the first law of nature," and thus vigilantism was necessary to preserve the community against outlaw activity. By the same token, although vigilante action was a blow against legal authority, it was justified by the right of revolution, which, in analogy to the intolerable conditions that inspired revolution against the British in 1776, justified vigilante bands, which, likewise, were seen as being like "revolutionary tribunals." By the related doctrine of popular sovereignty, vigilantes as well as Americans at large saw the people as being above the law—a law viewed as ineffective against frontier crime. To its adherents, vigilantism was but a case of the people exercising their sovereign power, in the interest of self-preservation, against the disorderly. Crucial, also, to the ideology of vigilantism was its economic rationale: vigilantism was not only often far more certain and fair than the regular system of law and order but also much cheaper. A Denver newspaper reported the popular view that an 1879 vigilante hanging in nearby Golden was not only "well merited but a positive gain to the county, saving it at least five or six thousand dollars."

Behavior

With well over two hundred vigilante movements west of the Mississippi, few states escaped the severe affliction of vigilantism. From the earliest days of the Anglo settlers, Texas was the most active vigilante state. California, with the giant San Francisco vigilante movement of 1856 (whose six to eight thousand members made it the largest in American history) and with many other movements in the gold rush era, was a prototypical state for western vigilantism. In no state, however, was the ethos of vigilantism more deeply embedded than in Montana, where the state capitol memorializes frontier vigilantes.

Prominent western senators (Leland Stanford, California; Wilbur Fisk Sanders, Montana; William J. McConnell, Idaho) and governors (Stanford, California; John E. Osborne and Fennimore Chatterton, Wyoming; Miguel A. Otero and George Curry, New Mexico) had been vigilantes, as had such members of the economic aristocracy as the capitalists Stanford and William Tell Coleman of California and the cattle king Granville Stuart of Montana. Especially in Texas and occasionally elsewhere, vigilantes terrorized entire communities and, once in a while, as Walter Van Tilburg Clark suggested in his classic antivigilante novel *The Ox-Bow Incident* (1940), punished the innocent. Yet, the offense of vigilantes was far less in violating the spirit of the law than its letter. Violations of the letter of the law, although serious, were widely acclaimed by the people and even by notables of the bench and bar.

The local campaigns of vigilantes were often aspects of a crucial pattern of violence pervading the West from the 1850s to 1920. At its core was the conservative, consolidating authority of capital—the force that was, in the scholar Alan Trachtenberg's conception, "incorporating" America during the late nineteenth century. In the West this process of incorporation was well under way by 1870 and lasted to 1920. Yet, opposing factions and individuals fought the incorporating trend politically and, often, violently.

The polarizing antagonism resulting from the trend of incorporation produced a civil war in the West—one fought in many places and on many fronts in almost all of the western territories and states from the 1850s into the 1910s. In its broadest terms, the "Western Civil War of Incorporation" pitted insurgent or resistant Indians against the political pressure and military force that concentrated them in reservations throughout the West. The Western Civil War of Incorporation also impinged economically and culturally on the traditional lifeways and livelihoods of the Hispanos of the Southwest, who fought back, for example, in northern New Mexico with the Gorras Blancas ("White Caps") and in southern Texas with the *bandidos*. The expansive western farm

Though gunfighters dominate popular imagery of western violence, the perpetrators of violence came from many walks of life. Numerous politicians and business leaders—including the California senator, governor, and railroad magnate Leland Stanford and the Montana cattleman Granville Stuart—participated in the vigilante violence that enforced the interests of conservative businesses in the late-19th-century West.

Walery studio. Leland Stanford, Wife, and Son. *Albumen silver print, ca. 1881. Stanford University Archives, Stanford, California.*

E. H. Train (1831–99). Granville Stuart. *Photograph and pen and ink on paper, 1877. Montana Historical Society, Helena.*

and range country was incessantly rocked by land wars and brigandage while the propertied class curbed the disorder of chaotic boomtowns. In the mines, mills, and logging camps on the wageworkers' frontier of the West, employees resisted corporate industrialists with strikes that frequently ended in violence. An alliance of capital and government fought back with paramilitary efforts to control the far-flung workplaces of the West.

In the forefront of the Western Civil War of Incorporation were the gunfighters of the region. The best known were the two or three hundred glorified gunfighters whose fame and exploits became a part of the legend of the West—gunslingers such as Wild Bill Hickok, Jesse James, John Wesley Hardin, Billy the Kid, and Wyatt Earp. Much more obscure were the thousands of grass-roots gunfighters whose exploits became little or not at all known beyond their own localities. Although generally not as effective as the glorified gunfighters, the grass-roots gunfighters could be deadly. One of them—Walter J. Crow of California—individually exceeded the single-gunfight killings of Hickok, James, Hardin, Billy the Kid, Earp, or any of the other glorified gunfighters. In the range country and boomtowns of the pastoral and mining West, gunmen were the shock troops in the Western Civil War of Incorporation. On one side of this intraregional war were the conservative incorporation gunfighters, whose ranks included glorified gunfighters like Hickok of Kansas, Earp of Kansas and Arizona, and Frank Canton of Wyoming and Oklahoma and grass-roots gunfighters like Crow of California. The incorporation gunfighters were often northern in background and members of the Republican party. Frequently southern or Texan in their roots and Democratic in politics were the dissident resister gunfighters, some of whom, like Jesse James and Billy the Kid, were mythologized as popular heroes—as "social bandits."

Conceptualized by the British historian E. J. Hobsbawm, a social bandit is, in American terms, a notable lawbreaker widely supported, paradoxically, by the law-abiding members of society. In the West the crimes of social bandits were often approved because they expressed the discontents and grievances of those who would never dare commit such crimes on their own. The historian Richard White has traced the grass-roots admiration for social bandits in the tradition of Jesse James, whose bravery and daring was applauded as being that of "strong men who could protect and revenge themselves." Skilled gunhandlers, these social bandits often robbed banks and railroads whose steep charges were deeply resented by peaceable western farmers, ranchers, and townspeople in the post-1865 period when economic conditions caused severe hardship for those of small means. These western social bandits not only were outlaws but also were resister gunfighters in the Western Civil War of Incorporation.

African-American gunhandlers, who fought effectively on both sides of the Western Civil War of Incorporation, were fairly numerous. Among the black resisters was Isom Dart (an alias of Ned Huddleston) of the Brown's Park outlaw faction of Colorado and Wyoming. On the other side of the regional civil war was tall, tough Jim Kelly, a star gunslinger for the magnate I. P. (Print) Olive, whose embattled "gun outfit" of cowboys stormed across ranges in both Texas and Nebraska.

The Western Civil War of Incorporation coincided with a trend from 1865 to 1900 in which wealthy and powerful individuals, companies, and corporations sought either to force settlers off the land or to overcharge them for their occupancy. In effect, this was a land-enclosing movement, which in the West engendered instability and discontent comparable to that caused by the land-enclosure movements in England from the Middle Ages to the eighteenth century. Especially aggressive in the West were the big ranchers, whose gunfighting cowboys tried to exclude small ranchers and homesteading farmers from the ranges. Crucial, also, to the land-enclosing trend were some top railroads of the West, which, through congressional land grants, tied up huge acreages and set the price of land sales to settlers.

It was just such a land grant, to the Southern Pacific Railroad, that bred the Mussel Slough conflict in California. In the agriculturally rich Mussel Slough country thirty miles south of Fresno in California's Central Valley, the homestead ethic of the settlers clashed with the capitalistic entrepreneurial ethic of the "Big Four" owners of the Southern Pacific—Collis P. Huntington, Leland Stanford, Charles Crocker, and Mark Hopkins. In dispute between the settlers and the railroad were thousands of acres for which the pioneers and the railroad had conflicting land claims. The legal dispute over the land's ownership entered the federal circuit court, where in 1879 Judge Lorenzo Sawyer, a friend of Stanford and Crocker, decided in the railroad's favor. The settlers responded with night-riding vigilantism to intimidate local supporters of the railroad and, in a no-duty-to-retreat mood, prepared to defend their richly productive small farms with firearms.

The crisis exploded into the deadliest civilian gunfight in far western history on 11 May 1880, when settlers resisted eviction from their homes. With a final toll of seven deaths, the Mussel Slough shootout far exceeded the three dead of the legendary Earp battle near the O.K. Corral in Tombstone, Arizona, the following year but was entirely the work of grass-roots gunfighters—five pioneers versus two railroad supporters. The five settlers (resister gunfighters) were all killed by the two incorporation gunfighters on the Southern Pacific side, both of whom also died. In killing the five settlers, however, one of the incorporation gunslingers, Walter J. Crow, took more lives than were ever claimed on a single occasion by any of the glorified gunfighters such as Earp, Billy the Kid, or Hardin.

Public opinion in the nation and in California was strongly on the side of the settlers. The conclusion was drawn that a huge American and western corporation, the Southern Pacific, headed by a few millionaires, would not content itself with depriving industrious farmers and family men of their homes but would have them shot down in cold blood. In London, Karl Marx followed the California conflict; after the five farmers died, he wrote to an American correspondent that nowhere else in the world was class conflict— "the upheaval most shamelessly caused" by capitalist oppression—taking place "with such speed" as in California. The Mussel Slough affair and its mordant gunfight burned into the consciousness of late-nineteenth-century Americans. One of the five novels based on the Mussel Slough was Frank Norris's powerful American classic *The Octopus* (1901); its title—long applied to the Southern Pacific in California—was, in effect, a hostile metaphor for the incorporating forces of the American West.

Defeated in both their courtroom and their gunfighting battles with the Southern Pacific, the Mussel Slough dissident farmers, losers in this phase of the Western Civil War of Incorporation, had no choice but to leave their farms or pay the railroad. Most left. The resulting resentment affected an entire generation in California's Central Valley, far more than the hundreds of farmers who had been in direct conflict with the railroad. An outcome of this feeling was the popular admiration for a famous team of robbers, the social bandits Chris Evans and John Sontag, who repeatedly struck Southern Pacific trains from 1889 to 1892. The antirailroad lawbreaking of Evans and Sontag, both glorified and resister gunfighters, was a surrogate for the seething resentment toward the Southern Pacific by peaceful, law-abiding Californians. Evans and Sontag fought in two spectacular shootouts with law officers and railroad detectives, the last of which in 1893 killed Sontag and ended their criminal careers.

Indirectly related to the Mussel Slough conflict was the sensational 1889 killing of David S. Terry of California—an event in which the gunfighter tradition of the West dramatically merged with the Western Civil War of Incorporation. A potent force in the anticorporation wing of the state's Democratic party, Terry had been a strong supporter of the Mussel Slough settlers against the Southern Pacific. Meanwhile, a personal and legal dispute festered between Terry and Justice Stephen J. Field of the U.S. Supreme Court. As the leading member of the Supreme Court in the late nineteenth century and in his concurrent role as a federal circuit judge on the Pacific Coast, Field, a Californian, had spearheaded court decisions favoring the Southern Pacific and other corporations. His judicial associate and protégé, the federal circuit judge Lorenzo Sawyer, had dispossessed the Mussel Slough settlers. As the head of a powerful clique of economically conservative West Coast federal judges that included Sawyer, Field was a pillar of the establishment cause in the Western Civil War of Incorporation and, as such, a political and ideological as well as personal and legal opponent of Terry.

To protect Field from the threats of the violence-prone Terry, who had killed one man in a duel, David Neagle—a tough gunhandling lawman from Tombstone in the era of Wyatt Earp—was hired to serve as Field's bodyguard in the Golden State. When Terry slapped Field in a California railroad depot on 14 August 1889, Neagle immediately shot Terry dead in what quickly became a western and national cause célèbre. The outcome of a legal process reaching the Supreme Court (Field abstaining) found Neagle to be without fault in the killing. Unconvinced were anti-Field partisans, who saw the killing as premeditated murder in the interest of an economic and judicial order that favored incorporating millionaire industrialists.

The range-cattle industry was a major theater of war in the Western Civil War of Incorporation, and it had both urban and rural battlegrounds. In urban terms the conflict was fought in the raw towns of the Great Plains that sprang up where cattle trails met the railroad shipping points to the midwestern packinghouses. In famed boomtowns like Abilene and Dodge City, the incorporating faction of urban merchants wanted to curb the disorder and violence of the Texas cowboys who whooped into town wild for pleasure after months out on the townless trails north of Texas. To intimidate and, if need be, to arrest or even kill cowboys, the mercantile clique used its dominance of boomtown governments to employ skilled gunfighters like Wild Bill Hickok and Wyatt Earp to keep the Texans in line.

The boomtown phase of the Western Civil War of Incorporation had strong political and cultural overtones. Thus, the typical cowboy who roared into the likes of Abilene and Dodge City was a Texan, a southerner in outlook, an ex- or pro-Confederate, and a Democrat. On the other side were the merchants or entrepreneurs like Joseph G. McCoy of Abilene, a northerner who arranged for Wild Bill Hickok to keep order in Abilene. Hickok had established his gunfighting credentials as early as 1861 and became nationally known for his 1865 slaying of Dave Tutt in Springfield, Missouri, in the prototypical western showdown. Hickok, a northerner who fought for the Union in the Civil War and was reared in an Illinois abolitionist family, was a strong Republican in politics. In Abilene in 1871, Wild Bill intimidated violence-prone Texas cowboys and climaxed the season with a face-to-face killing of Phil Coe, a skilled Texas gunfighter and gambler. Incorporation gunfighters and lawmen like Hickok and the Earp brothers were in the van of the movement that safely incorporated Abilene, Ellsworth, Hays, Newton, Wichita, Dodge City, and other boomtowns into a social and economic system dominated by enterprising capital.

In the immense rural range country, the pattern in the Western Civil War of Incorporation pitted the cattle kings against small ranchers, cowboys, farmers, and rustling horse and cattle thieves who resisted the land-monopolizing thrust of the big cattlemen. In Montana, the reign of Granville Stuart and other cattle grandees (including a young Theodore Roosevelt, whose home ranch was across the territorial line in present North Dakota) was challenged by horse thieves in alliance with a motley faction of wolf hunters and ruffians whose outlaw haunts were in the wild Missouri Breaks river country of Montana. The horse-theft operations stretched from the Montana-Canada borderland down into Wyoming. Fed up with these outlaw inroads, "Stuart's Stranglers," as the vigilantes were called, embarked on a devastating campaign that burned the bandit cabins along the wooded shores of the Missouri and killed the inhabitants. Stuart, later to be idolized as "Mr. Montana" (the state's most revered pioneer), deputed a strong force of cowboys, who swept through eastern Montana and on into North Dakota, where those marked for death on a hit list, provided by Stuart, were killed. Theodore Roosevelt knew well the cattle-king leaders of Stuart's vigilante campaign, strongly approved of it until his dying day, and always regretted that Stuart and the others, fearing that the loquacious Roosevelt would talk too much, had kept him out of the triumphant campaign that, with over a hundred fatalities to its credit, was the deadliest of all western and American vigilante movements.

By the time Stuart's Stranglers disbanded in 1884, the Montana-Dakota range country was conquered territory in the Western Civil War of Incorporation. This was far from true across Montana's southern border, where in the late 1880s and early 1890s a Wyoming coalition of small ranchers, homesteading farmers, and cowboy outlaws resisted the growing aggressiveness of a powerful faction of big cattle ranchers. At the core of this faction, eastern and British aristocrats presided over their investments in the cattle country, lording it over the cowboys who toiled for them. Many of the latter struck back at the arrogant employers by rustling from them on the sly in order to break free and establish competing small spreads. By 1892, as the grandees of the Wyoming Stock Growers' Association saw it, wide areas of central and northern Wyoming were held by those who harassed and stole from them. With convictions of accused cattle thieves hard to come by from juries of local folk who were hostile to the cattle kings, the latter perfected their vigilante plans. Defiant Johnson County was marked for the strongest dose of lynch-law medicine.

Political divisions in Wyoming reflected the rising range conflict. The cattlemen tended to be Republican and, indeed, had strong support in 1892 from Wyoming's Republican governor, from its Republican party state chairman (Willis Van Devanter, who as a conservative U.S. Supreme Court member in the 1930s was a staunch opponent of Franklin D. Roosevelt's New Deal), from its two Republican U.S. senators, and as it turned out, from the Republican occupant of the White House, Benjamin Harrison. Tilting against the cattle kings in Wyoming were the insurgent Democrats and Populists. Undoubtedly inspired by the success of Granville Stuart's flawless vigilante campaign only eight years before, the Wyoming big-cattlemen vigilantes (who called themselves "Regulators" in the tradition of the first American vigilante movement, the frontier South Carolina Regulators of 1767–69) replicated Stuart's operation. Like Stuart in Montana, they compiled a victim list (seventy in Wyoming) and prepared a lightning thrust by rail and horse into the enemy country.

The cattle magnate Frank Wolcott headed the Regulators. He enlisted a mercenary band of Texas gunfighters under Frank Canton, a gunfighting ex-sheriff of Johnson County. First by special train and then by horse, this paramilitary force headed for the rustlers' domain. Along the way, however, the overconfident Regulators came to grief. After a notable first success in besieging and killing two resister gunfighters, the rustlers Nate Champion and Nick Ray, Wolcott and company rode on north to Johnson County. South of the county seat of Buffalo, the Regulators were intercepted and pinned down by a giant posse of citizens alerted to the invasion.

Johnson County Cattle Raiders - Prisoners at Ft. D. A. Russell - 1892
A.B.Clark, E.W.Whitcomb, A.D.Adamson, C.S.Ford, W.H.Tabor, G.R.Tucker, A.R.Powell,
J.E.Booke, J.M.Morrison, W.A.Wilson, M.A.McNally, Bob Barlin, W.S.Davis, S.Sutherland,
Alex Lowther, W.J.Clarke, J.A.Garrett, Wm.Armstrong, Buck Garrett, F.H.Laberteaux, J.
Johnson, Alex Hamilton, F.M.Canton, W.C.Irvine, J.N.Tisdale, W.B.Wallace, F.DeBillein, H.Tescé-
maker, W.E.Guthrie, F.G.J.Hesse, Phil DuFran, Wm Little, D.R.Tisdale, J.D.Myners, M.Shonsey,
Joe Elliott, C.A.Campbell, J.Barlings, L.H.Parker, S.S.Tucker, B.Wiley, J.M.Bedford, K.Rickard,
Frank Walcott, B.Schultz, - Names not in order. Copied from Longest Rope by Baber.

Photographed a few weeks after their failed invasion of Johnson County, Wyoming, in April 1892, the self-proclaimed "Regulators," a group of big cattlemen and hired guns, were in temporary defeat. Later set free without a trial, they eventually won their battle with smaller homesteaders and ranchers for domination of the Wyoming range cattle industry.

Charles D. Kirkland (1857–1926). "The Invaders." Johnson County Cattle War (taken at Fort D. A. Russell). Photograph, 1892. American Heritage Center, University of Wyoming, Laramie.

On the brink of annihilation by the Johnson Countians, the Regulators were saved only by the intervention of U.S. cavalry (called out by the Republican chain of influence, which ran from the Wyoming Stock Growers' Association to President Harrison in Washington, D.C.). The cavalry imposed a truce, no bloodshed occurred, Johnson County authorities ran out of money in their legal prosecution of the invaders, and Wolcott, Canton, and all the rest went free. Meanwhile, outraged Wyoming voters avenged the blatant invasion of Johnson County by repudiating the pro-vigilante Republican party in the fall 1892 election. Yet the Johnson County War was only a temporary setback for the big cattlemen of Wyoming in the Western Civil War of Incorporation. From the open violence of a vigilante campaign, the determined cattle barons shifted to the stealth of murderous ambushes by the bounty hunter Tom Horn, who picked off victims until his homicidal career was ended by a legal execution in 1903. The result was a triumph for the big cattlemen. By 1910, possibly even sooner, the range country of Wyoming was a part of the fully incorporated West.

In the Southwest, fence cutting was the major tactic used against the incorporating efforts of the cattle kings. Resistance surged in violence-torn central Texas during the 1880s and 1890s. In county after county, farmers and small ranchers cut the fences of the land-enclosing big cattlemen who were gradually forcing so many of the small operators off the land or on to reduced holdings. The fence-cutting property destruction peaked in 1883–84 and 1897–98 but lost the battle against the broader trend.

In its institutionalization of political violence and assassination from the late 1860s to shortly after 1900, the New Mexico Territory was unequaled in the West. The government in New Mexico lacked the credibility, power, and will to curb the violence of the territory's intricately arrayed, deeply divided elements. In conflict after conflict, the incorporating forces battled against those, like the Gorras Blancas ("White Caps"), who resisted them.

The White Caps were poor Hispanic villagers who struck back—by burning barns, cutting fences, and occasionally using sniper fire—at the aggressive Anglos and *ricos* (rich Hispanos) who used their knowledge of the law and the ways of modern urban society to seize portions of the age-old communal land of the sheepherding villagers. By day these *pobres* ("poor ones") voted Populist and streamed into Knights of Labor lodges, but at night, as White Caps, they destroyed the fences and outbuildings of the *ricos*. White Cap violence was a guerrilla struggle that for a time halted the incorporating trend and through court victories preserved the communal grazing lands. A 1960s throwback to the White Caps of the 1890s was the Alianza movement, formed by Reies Tijerina to reclaim land lost by rural Hispanos to Anglo chicanery, according to Tijerina. Ultimately failing in its objective, Tijerina's crusade came to a climax in 1967 with the violent seizure of the county courthouse in Tierra Amarilla, New Mexico, during which one person died.

In the 1870s, in the northern New Mexico county of Colfax, violence erupted against the incorporating trend. The issue was the Maxwell Land Grant Company, a giant combine of absentee lawyers and capitalists who planned to convert the Maxwell grant in Colfax County into an enormous economic empire. Here the resisters were not Hispanos but Anglo small ranchers, cowboys, and townsmen who used the law as well as the violence of vigilantism and gunfighting to defend their small land claims against the Maxwell magnates. In the Colfax County War, the dissidents rallied around one of the West's most fearsome resister gunfighters, Clay Allison. Anchored by the powerful political support of Republican nabobs in Santa Fe and Washington, D.C., the Maxwell Land Grant Company outlasted the violent resistance of Allison and others and, erecting a land, cattle, and mining empire of nearly two million acres, dominated the county until the 1960s. In central Arizona a lethal vigilante movement on behalf of incorporating big ranching and commercial interests ended the chaotic, bloody Tonto Basin War of the 1880s, which took twenty to thirty lives.

The most enduring range-country episode in the Western Civil War of Incorporation occurred in southern New Mexico and Arizona from the 1880s to 1910. The opposing alignments were similar to those elsewhere, from Texas to Montana and from the Missouri to the Pacific. On the incorporating side was a faction of big cattlemen and Republican capitalists and politicos whose citadels of power were in the growing urban centers of the region. Resisting the incorporators was a typical coalition of small ranchers and cowboy outlaws, whose dissidence was spearheaded by some notable resister gunfighters opposed, in turn, by potent incorporation gunfighters on the other side. Rustling cattle from the large herds of their opponents was a constant tactic of the anti-incorporators, who, in general, tended to be southern or Texan in origin, Democratic in politics, and premodern in their values—emphasizing family and individual loyalty, the no-duty-to-retreat syndrome of personal self-redress, and manly courage. In conflict were not just contrary claims of land and property but two opposed worldviews: one stressing modern, urban, capitalistic values and the settlement of disputes through the legal system (a ground of combat favoring the know-how and sophistication of the incorporators) and the other stressing rural values, kin and friendship loyalties, and the violent settlement of disputes face to face instead of in the courtroom.

Crucial to so much of the trouble that turned southern New Mexico and Arizona into a dark and bloody ground from 1880 to 1910 was the famous Lincoln County War in New Mexico during 1878. The Lincoln County War was a veritable university for gunfighters, with no less than nineteen of them (including Billy the Kid) honing their gunshooting skills in the 1878 conflict. Trouble came from the partnership of Lawrence G. Murphy, James J. Dolan, and John H. Riley, who in the 1870s had, in effect, incorporated Lincoln County into their own economic domain based on the store they operated in the county seat, also named Lincoln. By 1876, when the ambitious young Englishman John Henry Tunstall came into Lincoln County, the small ranchers, farmers, and cowboys were restive under the oppressive domination of town and county by "the House" (the phrase was a reference to the imposing two-story store on Lincoln's single, rambling street—that is, the mercantile house of Murphy, Dolan, and Riley). More than just a store, the House was a corrupt political and economic faction that had much in common with the Tweed Ring of New York City and many other such rings in Gilded Age America and the West. The House in Lincoln County thrived on a complex system of ill-gotten gains. Murphy-Dolan-Riley outlaw hirelings stole cattle from the ranch king, John Chisum, for beef that was sold at inflated prices to the U.S. government's Mescalero Apache Indian Reservation and to Fort Stanton, both located in Lincoln County. In all of this, the House was bolstered by its allies in politics, in the judiciary, and in law enforcement.

Grass-roots discontent with the greed of the House found no practical outlet until the appearance of Tunstall, who forged an alliance with a dissident local lawyer, Alexander McSween, and with the cattle king Chisum, whose cattle losses were illicitly enriching the House. Amply backed by capital from his father's profitable London business, Tunstall (with McSween) soon opened a store in competition with the House. Customers flocked to the new Tunstall-McSween store. No less cynical and selfish than the House, Tunstall hoped to create his own ring and monopolize the mercantile possibilities of the county. Although he hired a band of tough cowboys (including Billy the Kid) to handle his burgeoning ranch (also made possible, like the new store, by munificent loans from his father), Tunstall's English culture led him to accept the ethic of legality and to refrain from violence. The House was not so forbearing. The brutal murder—or assassination—of Tunstall by House hirelings on 18 February 1878 triggered the Lincoln County War. Tunstall's gun-wielding cowboys remained loyal to his memory and to his surviving partner McSween (and his spirited wife, Susan McSween). An all-out range war ebbed and flowed across the county and climaxed in the five-day battle fought along Lincoln's lone street on 15–19 July 1878, resulting in a bitter defeat for the McSween side. After the Tunstall store was set on fire in the battle's conclusion, McSween was shot to death when he fled from the flames while Billy the Kid made one of the most famous of his many escapes.

The Lincoln County War led to the mighty myth of Billy the Kid as a social bandit. Born Henry McCarty in New York City, the lad moved with his widowed mother and his brother through Indiana and Kansas to New Mexico. With his mother remarried to

Sheriff Pat Garrett promoted the mythic stature of his nemesis, Billy the Kid, in 1882 by publishing a popular and widely inaccurate account of the gunfighter's life. Western violence, popular culture, and commerce remain closely linked, with violence still an important theme of much western literature, art, and film.

Pat Garrett (1850–1908). An Authentic Life of Billy the Kid *(Santa Fe, 1882). Western Americana Collection, Beinecke Rare Book and Manuscript Library, Yale University, New Haven, Connecticut.*

a miner, William Antrim, the future Billy the Kid led a normal schoolboy life in Silver City, New Mexico, until 1874, when his mother died and the Antrim family fell apart. The teen-age Billy committed a petty theft, became a fugitive, killed a bully in Arizona, and, back in New Mexico under the alias of William Bonney, became a cowboy working on Tunstall's Lincoln County ranch. The Kid's strong loyalty to Tunstall and the

McSweens drew him into the Lincoln County War; by the end of the battle, he was the top gun on the anti-House side. Not until 1989—more than a century after the Kid's death—did a full, realistic biography of him, by Robert M. Utley, appear. The Kid was neither the hero of myth nor the psychopath of the antimyth but a youth quite typical of the time and place; during his "short and violent life" (Utley's phrase) of twenty-one years, he took not twenty-one lives (one victim for each one of his years, according to the legend) but no more than a far-from-negligible ten. The Kid's career in his last two years collided with the forces of incorporation and became a brief but significant episode in the Western Civil War of Incorporation.

Thrown on his own at the end of the Lincoln County War, Billy the Kid—literate and ambitious—tried and failed to find a niche in law-abiding society. (His nickname was created by newspapers and dime novels in the last year of his life; his friends and enemies in New Mexico spoke of him as "the Kid" but not "Billy the Kid.") John Chisum, the wealthy Tunstall-McSween ally, denied the Kid the combat pay Billy claimed for service in the Lincoln County War—a denial that may have been influenced by Chisum's disapproval of the budding romance between Billy and his niece, Sallie, as well as by the cattle king's famous parsimony. Earlier, the Republican territorial governor of New Mexico, Lew Wallace (a Civil War general and the future author of the best-selling novel *Ben-Hur*), reneged on a deal with the Kid. The governor had promised the Kid a pardon in return for his crucial testimony against two brutal killers. The Kid kept his part of the bargain, but Wallace faithlessly denied him the pardon. With all avenues to a peaceful civilian life closed to him, the Kid became a full-time cowboy outlaw.

Heading a gang of gunfighting veterans of the Lincoln County War, Billy rustled cattle in Lincoln County and the Texas panhandle. This brought down on him the incipient forces of incorporation in Lincoln County, now centered in the mining boomtown of White Oaks and the cattle town of Roswell. A coalition of town businessmen, professional men, and aggressive big cattlemen formed to silence the Kid's deadly guns and end his cattle thefts. But the Kid had resources in this conflict. His sunny nature had earned him a wide circle of Anglo and Hispanic friends throughout southern New Mexico. The rising Roswell entrepreneur Joseph C. Lea and his neighbor, John Chisum, headed the effort to suppress Billy and his gang. The Kid's erstwhile friend Pat Garrett, a tall Texan and former buffalo hunter, was put up for sheriff and elected despite the opposition of the popular Billy, who supported Garrett's rival. Garrett broke up the gang, cornered and arrested the Kid, and saw him tried and sentenced to death for a homicide in the Lincoln County War—the only killer in the war to be tried and convicted. With Wallace's promised pardon definitely withheld, the desperate Kid shot to death two guards and escaped from the Lincoln jail. By now, "Billy the Kid" was a famed figure whose violent career was flaunted in the nation's newspapers and ten-cent paperbacks. Garrett, assisted by the spying of the cattle-range detective John W. Poe, tracked the Kid to one of his favorite haunts: the compound of Pete Maxwell at old Fort Sumner, New Mexico, on the Pecos River. Here, in midnight darkness, Garrett found the Kid and killed him with one shot.

The triumph of Lea, Chisum, Garrett, and Poe over the hapless Billy the Kid ushered in a new incorporated era of dominant town-and-country wealth and large-landed cattle property in southern New Mexico. The new order flourished under the leadership of its rising Republican political boss, attorney, and militia colonel Albert J. Fountain, who enjoyed the crucial support of the large ranchers of the country. Fountain and the big cattlemen had close ties to the lawyer Thomas B. Catron of Santa Fe, the avaricious Republican political boss of New Mexico who came to own or directly control more land than any other American in history. Meanwhile, more and more small ranchers and cowboys from central Texas filtered into the Tularosa basin, which stretched west from the mountain heights of Lincoln County. Ambitious, blessed with incomparable cowboy skills, and proudly bearing the no-duty-to-retreat proclivity to violence of their central Texas backgrounds, these aggressive newcomers saw only one way to survive against the land-enclosing tactics of the established big cattlemen: to steal from the herds and protect themselves with six-guns and rifles. The model and leader of these anti-incorporation Texans was Oliver M. Lee, a natural-born cowman, peerless horseman, and matchless gunfighter. The big cattlemen formed a stockmen's association to fight off the interlopers and employed a most-willing Albert J. Fountain to mount an antirustling militia campaign and legal effort to end the threat of Lee and the Texans to the incorporated state of affairs. Lee formed his own alliance with an ambitious Democratic politico and gunfighting lawyer, the ex-Kentuckian Albert Bacon Fall (who, decades later, with coat turned to the Republican party, became Warren G. Harding's ill-fated secretary of the interior).

Pressed by Fountain's indictment of Lee for cattle theft, Lee, Fall, and the rustling small ranchers seemed to be on the run. That soon changed in 1896 with the disappearance of Fountain and his young son, Henry, as they traveled by buggy from the courtroom in Lincoln back to their home in Mesilla on the Rio Grande. Fountain and his son were never found. It became an open secret to many in the region, and is confirmed by historians, that Lee and two of his cowboys carried out a plot hatched by or, at least, joined in by Fall to waylay Fountain (Fall's personal rival for the political domination of southern New Mexico) and murder him and his son. The bodies were buried in the mountains away from the crime and were never found. Once more, the incorporating faction of cattle kings and powerful Republican politicos led by Thomas B. Catron turned to Pat Garrett, who, again made county sheriff, was given the mission of bringing Lee and his henchmen to justice for killing the Fountains. Garrett eventually arrested Lee, who was brought to trial in 1899. Catron came south from Santa Fe to head the trial team against Lee but turned out to be no match for the histrionics and legal skill of Lee's defense attorney, Albert Bacon Fall. It took only eight minutes for a strongly anti-incorporation, anti-big cattleman, pro-cowboy jury to find Lee not guilty.

The fiasco of Lee's trial was a dramatic but only temporary check of the incorporating trend. The ironic outcome of the Tularosa war was that Fall and Lee soon became incorporators themselves. Deeply conservative in his social and economic views, Fall increasingly felt out of place in a Democratic party dominated by the quasi-populism of William Jennings Bryan. Fall switched to the Republican party and, with his rival Fountain out of the way, succeeded to the leadership of the party in southern New Mexico. In 1912, Fall realized a longtime ambition by being elected to the U.S. Senate from the newly admitted state of New Mexico. Lee's subsequent career was similar to that of his lifelong friend Fall. Lee became one of the largest ranchers in southern New

Mexico, eventually heading the million-acre Circle Cross Ranch (the area's largest) and serving two terms in the New Mexico legislature. In effect, Fall and Lee had used the violence of gunfighting and murder to move from the losing to the victorious side of the Western Civil War of Incorporation. There is no better example of a powerful western and national economic and political career built on violence than that of Albert Bacon Fall—Republican U.S. senator, cabinet member, and power in the high councils of his party as well as heavy speculator in Mexican mining property and baronial New Mexican cattle grandee. Many westerners—and none better than Fall—exemplify the historical sociologist Charles Tilly's maxim that the history of violence is nothing less than the history and organization of power.

By the early 1880s, vast Cochise County in the extreme southeastern region of Arizona was another battleground in the Western Civil War of Incorporation, with conflicts in both the rural range country and the urban streets of the county seat, Tombstone. The opposing forces in Cochise County represented the pervasive pattern of incorporating versus anti-incorporating factions. Headed by the mine owners and managers of booming Tombstone, the incorporating element was mainly Republican in politics, northern in background, urban in culture, and modern in outlook. The opposing faction included urban Democrats of Tombstone but centered on an alliance of small ranchers (many of whom rustled cattle from large ranchers) and cowboy outlaws (including "Curly Bill" Brocius and John Ringo), who were also Democrats as well as mainly Texan or southern in their backgrounds. The cowboy outlaws dominated the backcountry village of Galeyville and periodically rode into Tombstone for boisterous good times that unnerved the Republican elite of Tombstone, which was headed by the mine magnate E. B. Gage and the editor and mayor John P. Clum. Supporting this establishment was the youthful Episcopalian minister Endicott Peabody (later to be the revered schoolmaster and White House chaplain of Franklin D. Roosevelt), who, soon after his missionary period in Tombstone, founded and for decades headed America's most exclusive private school for boys, Groton, in Massachusetts. An exponent of muscular Christianity, Peabody knew and liked Wyatt Earp, for whom he had a lifelong admiration.

Wyatt Earp and his brother Virgil (as well as their younger brothers, Morgan and Warren) were a crucial bloc in the Cochise County conflict. The modernizing Tombstone elite turned to the gunhandling talents of Wyatt and Virgil (and their brothers) in an attempt to end the killings in Tombstone and play down the city's anarchic "man for breakfast" image. In turning to the Earps (and their gunfighting colleague Doc Holliday), the Republican elite hoped to stabilize life in turbulent Tombstone and convince California and eastern investors that the boomtown was a safe field for profitable investment. In contrast to the Earps, the small ranching and rustling families of the Clantons and the McLaurys (along with their cowboy-outlaw allies) were violent protagonists for the unincorporated, premodern, traditional values of the rural cowboy coalition of Cochise County. Strong Republicans of an Illinois-Iowa family of Civil War–era unionists, the Earp brothers were right at home on the side of Tombstone's urban elite, for Wyatt, Virgil, and their brothers were enthusiastic and profitable investors and speculators in Tombstone-area mine and real estate property. Personal clashes with the Clantons and McLaurys brought the Earps (and Holliday) to a violent confrontation with them near Tombstone's O.K. Corral on 26 October 1881. When the Earps fired away at the Clantons and McLaurys in their famous gunfight of that day, they were fighting for their entrepreneurial, Republican, incorporating values as well as their lives. The triumph of the Earps and Holliday (the two McLaury brothers and the one Clanton who faced them were all mortally wounded) was followed by a series of shootings in early 1882. Credited with at least two or three more killings, Wyatt left Cochise County, as did his brothers. They were consoled by their profits in booming Tombstone but saddened by the death of Morgan Earp in a pool-hall ambush. The gunpower of the Earps won a notable victory in the Western Civil War of Incorporation, for their success was to defeat and break up the cowboy-rustler-outlaw faction headed by the Clantons, the McLaurys, Brocius, and Ringo.

Resembling the cowboy-outlaw episode of Arizona was a long-range crime wave in the four-state enclave of Missouri, Kansas, Oklahoma, and Arkansas. An outlaw dynasty flourished in this region from the 1860s to the 1930s—from the time of Jesse James to that of Pretty Boy Floyd. As the historian Paul I. Wellman has shown, Charles Arthur ("Pretty Boy") Floyd (killed in 1934) was "the lineal successor" of William Clarke Quantrill, the Confederate guerrilla leader in Missouri. The fearsome Quantrill was the Civil War mentor of the youthful guerrillas Frank and Jesse James and Cole Younger in the violent arts of riding, raiding, and shooting. Thus began a middle-border outlaw dynasty perpetuated, said Wellman, "by a long and crooked train of unbroken personal connections, and a continuing criminal heritage and tradition handed down from generation to generation." The James-Younger gang (1866–82) began the American outlaw tradition of armed bank robbery at Liberty, Missouri, on 13 February 1866. Although the first train robbery had been by the Reno brothers in Indiana in 1866, it was the James-Younger gang that, again, made this innovative act of American banditry a national tradition. Carrying on this new pattern of gunfight-punctuated bank and train robberies were the 1880s gang of Belle Starr and the 1890s gangs of the Dalton brothers, Bill Doolin, Al Jennings, and Bill Cook. A vital link in the outlaw dynasty was Belle Starr's nephew, Henry Starr, who personally bridged the gap between the nineteenth-century brigands and the likes of the 1920s–1930s gangsters Al Spencer, Frank Nash, and Pretty Boy Floyd. From the James and Younger brothers down to the Dalton and Doolin era, these daring desperadoes fit the pattern of social banditry: men whose audacious exploits won the admiration of rural people wilting under the economic and cultural pressure of a modern, industrializing, corporation-dominated society.

Even as the middle-border outlaw tradition flourished, the Western Civil War of Incorporation was by 1900 making the transition from its main nineteenth-century battle sites in the boomtowns and range country to the early-twentieth-century mining camps, mill towns, metropolises, and commodity-crop fields. The overall issue was the taming of dissident, often radical, labor unionists for toil in a West marked for domination by profit-conscious private investors. The conflict between labor and capital in the Western Civil War of Incorporation predated 1900 but became critical in the new century. The first sustained violence in this industrial phase of the Western Civil War of Incorporation was what the historian George S. McGovern has termed Colorado's "Thirty Years War"—an 1884–1914 conflict amid the state's hard-rock mines and soft-coal fields.

Gunfighting continued, but the variety of violence in the Western Civil War of Incorporation now included the riot and the use of dynamite in connection with strikes and lockouts. High points in the Colorado turbulence occurred in the Rocky Mountain mining camps, where the radical new anti-incorporation Western Federation of Miners (WFM) fought back against repressive mine owners in Leadville (1894), Telluride (1901), and Cripple Creek (1903–4). Bloodiest of all was Cripple Creek, where a typical alignment was the state militia against the mine-and-mill unionists. The WFM was a losing cause in Cripple Creek, even though the professional terrorist Harry Orchard, on behalf of the union, killed thirteen strikebreakers while dynamiting the town's railroad station.

The alliance of industrial corporation and state militia figured in one of the most violent episodes in western history, the Ludlow Massacre of 20 April 1914, which tragically concluded Colorado's "Thirty Years War." This was the climactic event in a long, bitter strike of the United Mine Workers against the Rockefeller-controlled Colorado Fuel & Iron and independent companies in the southern Colorado coalfield stretching northward from Trinidad. Evicted from their company-owned houses, the miners at Ludlow and other coal camps settled into their own tent cities and stayed on strike. Many of the union men were Greek or Hispanic and were subjected to the highly prejudiced harassment of the predominantly Anglo militia, adding an ugly ethnic dimension to the conflict.

At Ludlow on April twentieth occurred the events that shocked America: an all-day gunfight between strikers and militia, the burning of the tent city, and the death by suffocation of thirteen women and children in the "Black Hole of Ludlow"—a declivity beneath a burned-over tent in which the women and children had taken refuge. Enraged by the tragedy, hundreds of miners and their sympathizers roared across the coal-mining counties in a spasm of property destruction that ended only when federal troops were sent in by President Woodrow Wilson to restore order. The U.S. soldiers, unlike the state militia, were impartial in their preservation of peace. The result was a defeat for the union and a costly victory for the Rockefeller family. Young John D. Rockefeller, Jr., never entirely overcame the onus of his disastrous intractability against the union nor, in the eyes of many early-twentieth-century Americans, did the enormous philanthropies of the Rockefeller family fully compensate for the tragedy at Ludlow.

Enmeshed in the Western Civil War of Incorporation was what the labor historian Carlos A. Schwantes terms the "wageworkers' frontier"—the social and industrial context of Colorado's Thirty Years War and other such conflicts. The wageworkers' frontier of the West embodied an explosive combination of the deep tensions of industrialization with the combative frontier psychology of the West. The Pacific Northwest wageworkers' frontier stretched from the mining camps of Idaho and Montana to the coastal logging stands and mill towns of Washington and Oregon. Keynoting the violence was the industrial warfare in the Coeur d'Alene region of the northern Idaho panhandle in the 1890s. The trouble began in 1892 with mineowners and labor unionists trading casualties and temporary victories; soon, to protect mine property from the dynamiting of union forces, state and federal troops intervened and incarcerated hundreds of miners in the infamous "bull pens" of the towns of Wallace and Wardner. Embittered by their defeat in the 1892 struggle, alienated strikers founded the

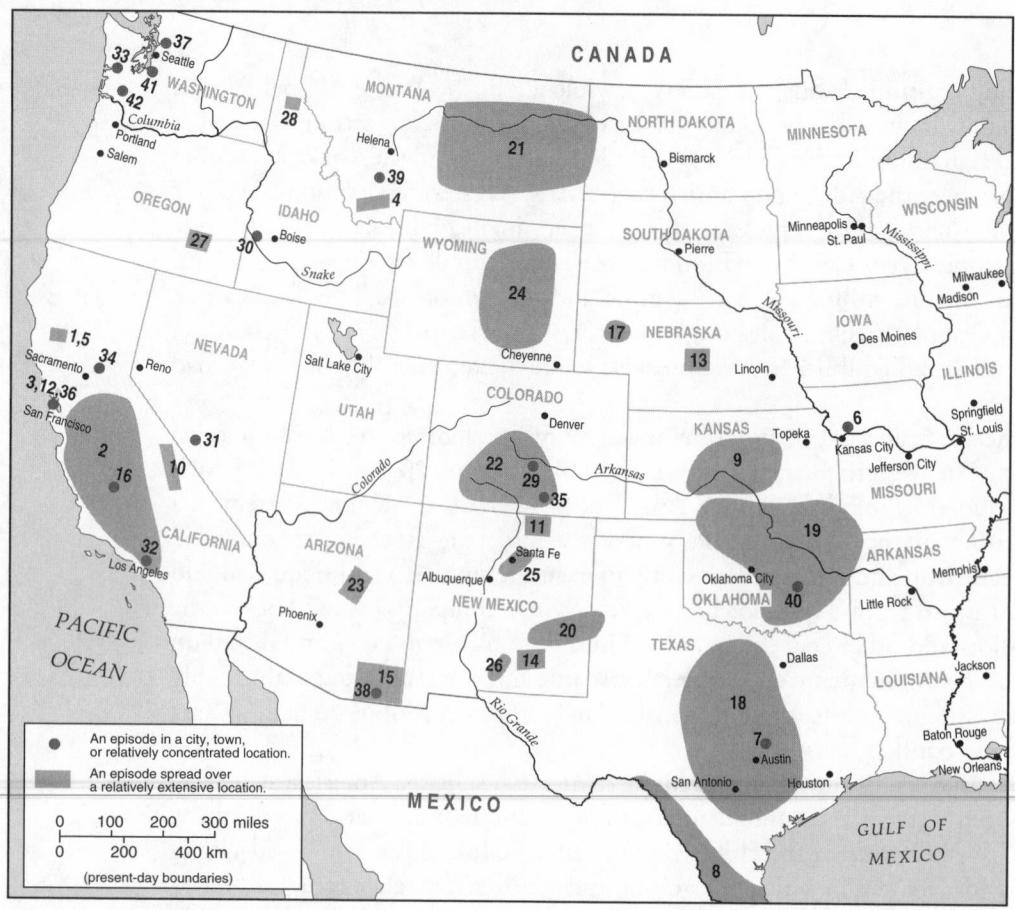

The Western Civil War of Incorporation, 1850s–1919

Below are brief descriptions of the 42 episodes in the Western Civil War of Incorporation, the numbers of which correspond to the numbers on the above map. The following abbreviations are used to designate the outcome of the episodes: **V** = victory for incorporating faction, **D** = defeat for incorporating faction, **A** = ambiguous outcome. (Other abbreviations used: **IWW** = Industrial Workers of the World, **WFM** = Western Federation of Miners, **VIG** = vigilantism was used by incorporating faction.)

1. **First Round Valley War, northwest California, 1850s–1865.** Incorporating white settlers carry on genocidal campaign of dispossession against local Indians. **V**

2. **Mexican outlaws' activity, California, 1850s–60s.** Incorporating California rangers suppress guerrilla-like insurgency of native Mexican outlaws: Joaquin Murrieta, Tiburcio Vasquez, and others. **V**

3. **San Francisco vigilantes, 1856.** Incorporating mercantile elite led by William T. Coleman uses vigilantism against Irish-Catholic working-class element. **VIG V**

4. **Montana vigilantes, 1863–65.** Incorporating faction of vigilantes of Virginia City and Bannack (headed by Wilbur Fisk Sanders, et al.) vs. an outlaw gang led by Henry Plummer. **VIG V**

5. **Second Round Valley War, northwest California, 1865–1905.** Land-enclosing big ranchers vs. small landholders. **V or A**

6. **James-Younger outlaw gang, Missouri, 1866–82.** Bank- and train-robbing outlaws led by social-bandit Jesse James and headquartered in Clay County vs. incorporating industrial, financial, commercial, and state-government forces. **V**

7. **Williamson County War, Texas, 1869–76.** Yegua Notch Cutters outlaw gang vs. Olive family of incorporating big ranchers. (The Olives defeat the outlaws, but their heavy losses force them to move to the more open range country of Nebraska; see #13, below.) **A**

8. ***Bandido* insurgency, south Texas, 1870s–1910s.** Gregorio Cortez, Juan Cortina, and other Hispanic outlaws vs. incorporating force of Texas Rangers. **V**

9. **Kansas cattle towns, 1870s–80s.** Incorporating merchants represented by Wild Bill Hickok and other incorporation-gunfighter law enforcers vs. Texas cowboys in Abilene, Hays, Wichita, Dodge City, and other Kansas cattle towns. **V**

10. **Owens Valley, California, 1870s–80s.** White settlers incorporate local Paiute Indians into labor force. **V**

11. Colfax County War, New Mexico, 1857–76, 1882, 1888. Incorporating large land company (represented by Thomas B. Catron) vs. local settlers (including resister gunfighter Clay Allison) upon whose homes the company impinged. **V**

12. San Francisco, 1877. Incorporating "Pick Handle Brigade" of establishment vigilantes (led again by William T. Coleman) vs. working-class rioters in sympathy with nationwide rail workers strike. **VIG V**

13. Custer County, Nebraska, 1877–79. Incorporating big ranchers led by Olive family from Texas (see #7, above) vs. homesteading small farmers. **D or A**

14. Lincoln County War, southern New Mexico, 1878. Unique conflict between two incorporating factions that nullified each other; the ultimate victor was New Mexico's top incorporator, Thomas B. Catron. **V**

15. Cochise County War, southeast Arizona, 1878–81. Urban, industrial elite of Tombstone (violently spearheaded by the Earp brothers) vs. a coalition of out-county small ranchers and cowboy outlaws. **V**

16. Mussel Slough conflict, California, 1878–82. Incorporating Southern Pacific Railroad headed by Collis P. Huntington, Leland Stanford, and Charles Crocker vs. small-farming settlers in dispute over land. **V**

17. Sand Hills War, northwest Nebraska, 1880s–90s. Incorporating big cattle ranchers vs. homesteaders. **A**

18. Fence-cutting conflict, central Texas, 1880–1900 (including a peak event, the Fence Cutters War, 1883–84, afflicting at least 12 counties). Land-enclosing big ranchers vs. small ranchers and farmers. **V**

19. Outlaws vs. law enforcers; Missouri, Kansas, Oklahoma, and Arkansas; 1880s–1910s. Bill Tilghman, Chris Madsen, Frank Canton, and other law enforcers represent incorporating forces vs. the Belle Star, Dalton brothers, Bill Doolin, and other outlaw gangs that often had popular support as social bandits. **V**

20. Billy the Kid outlaw activity, southeast New Mexico and west Texas, 1880–81. Incorporating big ranchers and business and professional men vs. Billy the Kid's rustling gang. **V**

21. Granville Stuart's Montana vigilante movement of 1884. Incorporating big cattle-rancher vigilantes led by Granville Stuart vs. horse-stealing outlaws. **VIG V**

22. Colorado's Thirty Years' War, 1884–1914. Incorporating mine owners and managers with state-government allies vs. organized labor. (See #29 and #35, below, for two of the major events in the Thirty Years' War.) **V**

23. Tonto Basin War, Arizona, 1886–88. Incoming incorporating commercially-minded large-landholding and ranching elite vs. traditionally-minded early settlers in a war touched off by the Pleasant Valley feud of the Grahams vs. the Tewksburys. **VIG V**

24. Wyoming range conflict, late 1880s–1901. Incorporating elite cattle ranchers and establishment allies vs. small ranchers, homesteaders, and cowboy allies. The latter won a temporary victory in the Johnson County War (1892), but the bounty-hunting kills of incorporation gunfighter Tom Horn (1894–1901) sealed the cattle kings' victory. **VIG V**

25. *Gorras Blancas* (White Caps) conflict, northern New Mexico, 1890s. *Gorras Blancas* spearheading traditional Hispanic pastoral villagers vs. incorporating land-enclosing Anglo and Hispanic elite ranchers and lawyers. **D**

26. Tularosa war, southern New Mexico, 1890s. Incorporating big cattle ranchers and business and professional allies vs. traditionalistic small ranchers and cowboys. **A**

27. Harney County conflict, Oregon, 1890s. Big cattle ranchers vs. homesteaders. **A**

28. Coeur d'Alenes War, northern Idaho, 1890s. Incorporating mine owners supported by state and federal governments and military forces vs. organized labor (including WFM) in the Coeur d'Alenes mining country. **V**

29. Cripple Creek conflict, Colorado, 1894–1904. Incorporating mine owners and managers vs. organized labor, including WFM (part of Colorado's Thirty Years' War; see #22, above). **V**

30. Caldwell, Idaho, assassination of ex-Gov. Frank Steunenberg, 1905, and its aftermath, 1906–07. Anti-incorporating miners' union (WFM) vs. incorporating forces represented by Gov. Steunenberg, who supported the incorporators in the Coeur d'Alenes war (#28, above). An important result is the unsuccessful trial of WFM leaders for the assassination of Steunenberg. **A**

31. Goldfield, Nevada, conflict, 1907. Incorporating mine owners vs. IWW. **V**

32. Los Angeles, 1910. Dynamiting of *Los Angeles Times* building by labor-union conspirators results in significant loss of life, but anti-union backlash results in victory for *Times* publisher Harrison Gray Otis as spearhead of incorporating forces in southern California vs. labor-union movement. **V**

33. Aberdeen, Washington, 1911–17. Incorporating lumber-mill magnates and town allies vs. IWW. **VIG V**

34. Wheatland, California, riot of hop pickers, 1913. Anti-incorporating IWWs and migrant workers vs. owners of Durst hop ranch and law-enforcement allies. **V**

35. Southern Colorado coal-mining conflict, 1913–14. John D. Rockefeller and other incorporating mine-owning forces vs. organized labor. Culminates in miner-families' loss of life in "Ludlow Massacre," 1914 (part of Colorado's Thirty Years' War; see #22, above). **V**

36. San Francisco, bombing of World War I Preparedness Day parade, 1916. Incorporating industrial and business forces vs. organized labor (including its radical fringe). **V**

37. Everett Massacre, Washington, 1916. Conflict between incorporating lumber-mill magnates and allies of vs. organized labor. IWW intervention results in the massacre with labor element's casualties being heaviest. **VIG V**

38. Bisbee, Arizona, conflict, 1917. Incorporating mine interests and town and law-enforcement allies vs. striking miners (including IWW). Vigilantes deport 1,186 strikers and allies. **VIG V**

39. Butte, Montana, lynching of Frank Little, 1917. Little, an anti-World War I activist and IWW organizer, fell afoul of local vigilantes. **VIG V**

40. Green Corn Rebellion, eastern Oklahoma, 1917. Uprising of anti-World War I poor farmers and tenants against incorporating landlords and townspeople.

41. Seattle General Strike, 1919. Incorporating Seattle forces (led by the mayor) defeat the general strike, an event accompanied by turbulence but not violence. **V**

42. Centralia, Washington, massacre and reprisal, 1919. Incorporating town element vs. IWW. **VIG V**

Summary and Analysis of the 42 Episodes: Thirty-four (or about 4 out of 5) of the 42 episodes resulted in clear-cut victory for the incorporators. Yet, the remaining 8 episodes (including 5 with ambiguous outcomes) underscore that, although the overall result of the Western Civil War of Incorporation was victory for the incorporating conservative forces, the resisting elements were strong. In fact, in at least 23 of the 34 episodes, the opposition or threat to the incorporators was significant. (The numbers of these are 2-4, 6-9, 11, 12, 15, 16, 18-20, 22-24, 28, 29, 32, 35, 37, 41.) The era of World War I (in this case, 1916–19) coincided with a final powerful surge of the incorporating trend, resulting in seven episodes (#36-#42). In all but two of these episodes (#37 and #41), the war was a direct factor (#36, #38, #39, #40) or an indirect factor (#42). All seven resulted in clear-cut incorporating victories. Note: The incorporation of Indian tribes through their concentration on reservations and incorporation into local labor forces was widespread in the West. Episodes #1 and #10 are examples of this type of incorporation.

radical, violence-prone Western Federation of Miners (WFM). Striking back in 1899, the WFM attacked the Bunker Hill and Sullivan mine, the leading enterprise of the Coeur d'Alenes, and destroyed its huge, costly concentrator with dynamite. This was too much for Idaho's hitherto prolabor governor Frank Steunenberg, who induced the federal government to send in troops. The latter put the area under martial law and broke the WFM strike by herding six to seven hundred miners into the hated bull pen.

Governor Steunenberg's action and the resulting repression of the WFM in the Coeur d'Alenes led to two dramatic events in the Western Civil War of Incorporation. The first was the organization of the revolutionary, anti-capitalist Industrial Workers of the World (IWW) in Chicago in 1905. The second was the 1905 assassination of Steunenberg by the WFM terrorist Harry Orchard, whose bomb killed Steunenberg (no longer governor) outside his Caldwell, Idaho, home. The aftermath of the crime was not restricted to the life sentence received by Orchard. Charges of conspiracy in the murder of Steunenberg were filed against the charismatic WFM secretary-treasurer, William D. ("Big Bill") Haywood, and two of his associates. The result was one of the greatest show trials in western history, in which the Chicago radical and criminal lawyer Clarence Darrow successfully defended the accused. The acquittal of Haywood and his colleagues was widely viewed by organized labor and its sympathizers as a vindication of the anti-incorporating militant labor movement of the West.

On behalf of the WFM, the charismatic Big Bill Haywood was one of the key founders and leaders of the IWW, whose members were frequently referred to as "Wobblies." Using class struggle as its theme, the IWW spread throughout the West. Some of its strongest support came from the loggers and sawmill workers of the Pacific Northwest. In contrast to its revolutionary rhetoric, the IWW was more often the victim than the initiator of violence, but in the spirit of no duty to retreat, it unhesitatingly fought back in a series of Pacific Northwest confrontations with capital and its supporters. These face-offs were especially acute in western Washington, where the 1916 Everett Massacre killed twelve, mostly Wobblies, and the 1919 Centralia Massacre left five dead, including one Wobbly. In Butte, Montana, in 1917, Frank Little, the IWW organizer and radical opponent of U.S. participation in World War I, died after being swung from a trestle at the end of a vigilante rope. Among many other IWW conflicts in the Western Civil War of Incorporation, Wobbly organizing among hop-field agricultural workers in Wheatland, California, in 1913 led to a strike. The ensuing riot and gunfight between sheriff's deputies and the IWW group produced five deaths, three of them on the anti-IWW side. The Wheatland episode was used by John Steinbeck as the model for the climactic act of violence in his reform novel *The Grapes of Wrath* (1939).

Early in the twentieth century, Los Angeles, in the process of supplanting San Francisco as the metropolis of the Far West, was a bastion of antiunion sentiment. On 1 October 1910, two American Federation of Labor militants, the brothers John J. and James B. McNamara, blew up the *Los Angeles Times* building, killing twenty people. The brothers were angered by the fierce open-shop policy of the *Times'* powerful publisher, Harrison Gray Otis, a prime incorporator of Los Angeles and its sun-drenched environs. Although the loss of life in the destruction of the *Times* building was a traumatic setback for Otis, the backlash of public opinion against labor and its supporters in Los Angeles was, in the long run, a triumph for the *Times* publisher and for the cause of incorporation. Otis was one of the members of the Los Angeles elite whose land speculation in the city's San Fernando Valley area greatly benefited from the early-twentieth-century construction of the Los Angeles Aqueduct, which, by bringing water hundreds of miles from the Owens Valley, gave the city the water supply needed for its booming economic development and vastly increased population. But what helped Los Angeles hurt the Owens Valley, where citizens banded together in 1924 frequently to dynamite the aqueduct in a delayed but fruitless rebellion against incorporation within the imperial outreach of Los Angeles and against the likes of Otis and his successor as *Times* publisher, Harry Chandler.

The conservative forces in the Western Civil War of Incorporation often employed the Pinkerton Detective Agency. The Pinkertons firebombed the family home of Jesse and Frank James and assisted in breaking up the bank- and train-robbing gang. Under the leadership of James McParlan (who earlier had played the key role in the Pinkertons' shattering of the Molly Maguire labor terrorists in the anthracite fields of Pennsylvania), the Denver office of the Pinkerton agency waged an effective but bitterly contested war against the nascent labor unions of the West. Wells Fargo and the Southern Pacific were among the powerful private concerns with their own detective forces.

The public enforcers of the law—local marshals and police, county sheriffs, state agencies such as the Texas Rangers and the Arizona Rangers, U.S. marshals and their deputies—were ambivalent. In numerous cases, these functionaries conducted tough but honorable—even heroic—operations to enforce the law in what was certainly an unruly region. On many other occasions, these law enforcers were willingly co-opted by the conservative side in the Western Civil War of Incorporation—for example, the gunfighting lawmen Wild Bill Hickok and Wyatt Earp and the widespread attack on the IWW. Aside from the involvement of law enforcement in the Western Civil War of Incorporation, local officers had to cope with the rampant disorder of the gunfight-prone West in the late nineteenth century. The bloodiest such confrontation occurred in 1872 in the Indian Territory (present-day eastern Oklahoma). At the community of Going Snake, an internal Cherokee feud and a jurisdictional conflict between a Cherokee court and a U.S. commissioner resulted in a gun battle that killed eleven people, eight of whom were members of a posse led by U.S. deputy marshals. This was the largest massacre in the two-century history of the federal marshal system.

The turbulent 1870s–1880s mining camp of Bodie, California, was typical of the violent pastoral and mining boomtowns where highly homicidal gunfighters were seldom condemned by law or public opinion as long as they observed the Code of the West. Away from these mining camps and prairie towns, however, the rapidly urbanizing West of the late nineteenth century resembled the rest of the United States. According to a study of Alameda County, on the east side of San Francisco Bay, these areas were becoming less violent as the criminal-justice system responded to the mounting public demand for a peaceful civic culture.

Sometimes a part of the Western Civil War of Incorporation and sometimes not were the ethnic, racial, and religious conflicts that all too often yielded massacres and murderous riots. Ethnic animosities were at times related to industrial violence in the West, whereas religious identity was frequently linked to ethnic status. In religion, one key conflict was between Mormons and the Gentiles (non-Mormons) who opposed them. After a violent expulsion from northwestern Missouri, where eighteen died in the Haun's Mill Massacre of 1838, the Mormons created the new metropolis of Nauvoo, Illinois, near which Mormonism's founder, Joseph Smith, was murdered in 1844. Moving again, the Mormons found a new refuge in the West. Established in 1847 under Brigham Young, the Mormon colony in Utah thrived, but trouble rose anew when its practice of polygamy was openly announced. Ensuing tension between the Mormons and the federal government produced a U.S. Army expedition into the Mormon country. Near-hysterical feelings of self-defense swept the Mormons of Utah in 1857 as they prepared to fight for their lives. War was averted, but in late summer a heinous act of violence—the Mountain Meadows Massacre—occurred in southwestern Utah, where, among the frontier Mormon villagers, religious frenzy in the face of the federal threat was highest. The tragic outcome was the slaughter of about one hundred men, women, and older children of a California-bound wagon train of Arkansans by a Mormon-led force of Paiute Indians and local Mormons. Only eighteen of the younger children were spared in what was the largest massacre of white civilians in western history. An order from Brigham Young came too late to save the victims.

The long-term warfare between whites and Indians sometimes passed the line from quasi-military fighting to the massacre of civilians on both the white and the Indian sides. Massacres of Indians by Indians were not unknown, with the last large episode occurring near Camp Grant, Arizona, in 1871 when some one hundred Apaches were killed by a band spearheaded by ninety-four of their traditional Papago enemies who had been incited by Apache-hating Anglos and Hispanos of Tucson. Of massacres of whites by Indians, Marcus and Narcissa Whitman and twelve others were killed by Cayuse at the Whitmans' mission near present Walla Walla, Washington, in 1847. On the Oregon Trail in Idaho were the Ward (1854) and Otter (1860) wagon train massacres, with eighteen and thirty-two lives lost, respectively, to Shoshones. These massacres were exceptions to the rule that Indians far more often aided the overland pioneers than attacked them. One hostile Indian campaign by the Apache band of Josanie (Ulzana) in New Mexico and Arizona killed forty-five civilians in 1885. Much earlier, rebel Indians killed many civilians in the Pueblo revolt of 1680 in New Mexico and in five uprisings by California Indians against Hispanic mission communities in 1775–1824.

Exacting much heavier casualties than Indian massacres of whites were white massacres of Indians: the Bear River Massacre in southeast Idaho in 1863 (90 women and children killed); the Sand Creek Massacre in eastern Colorado in 1864 (about 200 Cheyenne men, women, and children slain); and the Marias River Massacre in northern Montana in 1870 (173 Blackfeet deaths, mostly women and children). Women and children were also killed in the 1868 massacre of 103 Cheyennes on the Washita River in western Oklahoma and the 1890 slaughter of 150 or more Sioux at Wounded Knee, South Dakota. Federal soldiers conducted all of these massacres except for that by the Colorado militia at Sand Creek. Merciless were the genocidal tactics of land-grabbing white men in the fecund Round Valley region of California's northwestern mountains

Buried of the Dead
at the Battle of Wounded Knee S.D.
Copy Righted Jan(31 1891 bythe
North Western Photo Co
Chadron Neb
№ 1

The photographer George Trager recorded the mass burial of 146 Sioux gunned down by the Seventh Cavalry on 29 December 1890 at Wounded Knee, South Dakota. Though the massacre seemed to mark the end of Indian-white warfare, it was part of a continuing pattern of western violence in which federal troops were called on to police internal dissidents.

George Trager (1861–after 1892). Burial of the Dead at the Battle of Wounded Knee, S.D. *Albumen silver print, 1 January 1891. Nebraska State Historical Society, Lincoln.*

in the 1850s and 1860s. Here the population of the Yukis and other Indians fell from over 11,000 to under 1,000.

White fears of Chinese job competition inspired the West's virulent anti-Chinese movement, which was often spearheaded by radical labor reformers. The result was a long chronicle of violence and intimidation: anti-Chinese riots in Los Angeles (eighteen to nineteen Chinese dead in 1871), Seattle, and Tacoma; an 1887 slaughter of ten Chinese miners at Log Cabin Bar, Oregon, on the Snake River; and, two years earlier, a massacre of fifty-one Chinese (with the expulsion of four to five hundred others) at the coal-mining center of Rock Springs, Wyoming.

Violence between Hispanos and Indians early in the years of Spanish colonization in the Southwest was followed by Hispano conflict with the later-arriving Anglos. Violence by Hispanic outlaws and gunfighters against Anglos represented a species of resistance in the Western Civil War of Incorporation but also included the independent factor of ethnicity. This was true of the vigilante lynching of a Mexican woman, Josefa (later often called Juanita), in Downieville, California, in 1851, who had killed a drunken miner who had molested her.

Women, much less involved than men in local murders and assaults, were seldom legally executed, and Josefa was one of only several women lynched in the West. One study shows that black women inmates in the Kansas state prison were disproportionately represented in the female prison population because of racial discrimination. Recent research on physically mistreated wives in the mixed urban and rural society of

Lane County, Oregon, of the 1890s suggests that these women were unusually assertive and that their abusive husbands were economically unsuccessful and psychologically insecure.

From mid-century on, the Hispanic *bandidos* of California and Texas waged an anti-Anglo vendetta. In the Golden State, gunfighting Hispanic outlaws operated in the 1850s–1870s against the Americans who streamed in after the U.S. acquisition of California. Much of this was sheer criminal activity, but the raids and killings by the social bandit Joaquin Murrieta and others also had strong rebellious overtones. Similar animosities operated in a vast zone in southern Texas. Such notable Mexicans as Juan Cortina had the dual identity of border brigand and patriotic Hispanic nationalist. Resembling their outlaw counterparts in California were Gregorio Cortez and other resister gunfighters celebrated by Texas Hispanos in folklore and song as social bandits. Raids back and forth across the Texas-Mexico line found the *bandidos* at war with civilian law officers, Texas Rangers, and, occasionally, U.S. troops. The last such raid was a bold 1915 attack on the Norias unit of the King Ranch north of Brownsville.

Conclusion

By 1920 the Western Civil War of Incorporation was over, with the conservative side emerging strongly victorious. A final surge of seven episodes of the regional civil war had occurred in the 1916–19 era of World War I as the forces of resistance made their last stand. In the overall war, one of the episodes (the White Cap conflict in New Mexico) was a defeat for the incorporators; seven others were ambiguous or unclear in their outcomes. These eight episodes in which the anti-incorporating faction was not clearly vanquished—along with the heavy violence in most of the other episodes—show that resistance to the incorporating trend was dauntless.

Brutality and oppression were plentiful in the Western Civil War of Incorporation but should be viewed in proportion. Mitigating the harsh reality of and coexisting with much of the Western Civil War of Incorporation was a remarkably open, mobile, and expanding society in the West from the 1880s. This enabled a great many of the lower class and middle class not only to avoid the tragic battlegrounds in the regional civil war but to prosper and thrive. Nor should the popularity of the incorporating victory be overlooked and underestimated, for there was a widespread desire—by no means restricted to the elite and the affluent—for the more orderly, structured society that was one result of the Western Civil War of Incorporation. After 1890 a series of social, economic, and political reform movements and advances in popular education for the upwardly mobile softened the impact of the Western Civil War of Incorporation without diminishing the order and stability that was, in part, its legacy.

In the aftermath of the conservative triumph in the Western Civil War of Incorporation, the region, from 1920 to 1960, experienced its least violent times. But the relative calm of that era dissolved into turbulent decades of protest, riot, crime, and assassination. The anti-Hispanic Zoot Suit Riot in Los Angeles in 1943 was a portent of the West's post-1960 period of violence. In its own distinctive way, western violence of the 1960s and after mirrored the postindustrial surge of crime and disorder that afflicted all the technologically advanced democracies of the world, except for Japan. No country was more affected than the United States. Typifying the new turbulence was the unprecedented phenomenon of numerous serial murderers whose relentless violence was exemplified by Ted Bundy's killing of at least nineteen women in Washington, Utah, and Colorado in 1974–75.

Led by the massive Watts riot in Los Angeles, group violence was at its greatest in the black-ghetto uprisings of the 1960s. Watts in 1965 had much earlier precedents in the Texas riots of African-American soldiers in Brownsville in 1906 and Houston in 1917. By the 1980s, ultra-violent drug-dealing gangs of young male African Americans and Hispanos spread through the big cities of the West from their citadels in the ghettos and barrios of Los Angeles. Black gang members spearheaded the Los Angeles riot of 1992, but Hispanos, Asians, and whites were also among the rioters. The riot was a combination of protest, crime, and nihilism, a reflection of late-twentieth-century western racial diversity, and an indication of the growing anomie of western cities.

A throwback to the white-Indian conflict of a century earlier was Wounded Knee II: a fatal 1973 confrontation between Indian militants (two killed) and federal marshals at the site of the 1890 massacre in South Dakota. Most shocking of all was the assassination of President John F. Kennedy in Dallas on 22 November 1963, followed five years later by the scarcely less-unsettling assassination in Los Angeles of Senator Robert F. Kennedy, a younger brother of the president. The western setting of the Kennedy assassinations was an eerie reminder to the historically knowledgeable of a long tradition of assassinations in territorial New Mexico, a tradition that was grounded in the latter's unstable and deeply conflicted society. Aside from the western locations, however, there was nothing uniquely western about the assassinations of the Kennedy brothers.

Many of our images of recent violence in the West come not from the fiction of print or film but from the news seen by millions on television. The presidential motorcade suddenly disrupted by gunfire blasting into the body of John F. Kennedy or the flames searing the horizon of riot-torn Los Angeles are images deeply etched in the national consciousness.

Yet, the most enduring image of western violence is the "walkdown": two holstered westerners, armed with six-guns, pace toward each other down the bleak street of a frontier town, ready to draw and shoot. Climaxed by the inevitable burst of gunfire, the image focuses on one of the men, dying in the dust—dropped by the bullet of the survivor, standing tall in triumph. In this image, the victorious gunfighter is the hero and his fallen foe the villain. In the popular parlance, the hero wears a white hat—the villain a black one.

This image of the western walkdown was fixed in the American mind by its portrayal in the climactic episode of the most influential western novel—*The Virginian* (1902), by Owen Wister. In Wister's book, the heroic Wyoming cowboy, "the Virginian," slays the evil Trampas. So popular was Wister's novel (avidly read by President Theodore Roosevelt, the author's good friend, to whom the book was dedicated) that the walkdown became the central formulaic event in the western fiction of print and film. Yet, as the historian Kent Ladd Steckmesser has suggested, the fictional walkdown in *The Virginian* may have been based on a real walkdown—one at which onlookers by the town square of Springfield, Missouri, saw Wild Bill Hickok gun down his enemy, Dave

The "walkdown," fixed in the popular imagination by the climactic scene of Owen Wister's *The Virginian* (1902), remains a central visual metaphor for western culture. The enduring popularity of the image reflects a public taste for clear-cut moral distinctions between good and evil and an enduring fascination with violence as a means to enforce the rule of law.

Charles M. Russell (1864–1926). The Virginian Looks Down at Trampas. *Drawing reproduced as book illustration in Owen Wister,* The Virginian *(New York: Macmillan Publishing Co., Inc, 18th printing, 1979).*

Film still from The Good, the Bad, and the Ugly *(1968), directed by Sergio Leone. Courtesy of the Academy of Motion Picture Arts and Sciences, Beverly Hills, California.*

Roy Lichtenstein (b. 1923). Fastest Gun. *Magna on canvas, 1963. © Roy Lichtenstein. Courtesy of the artist.*

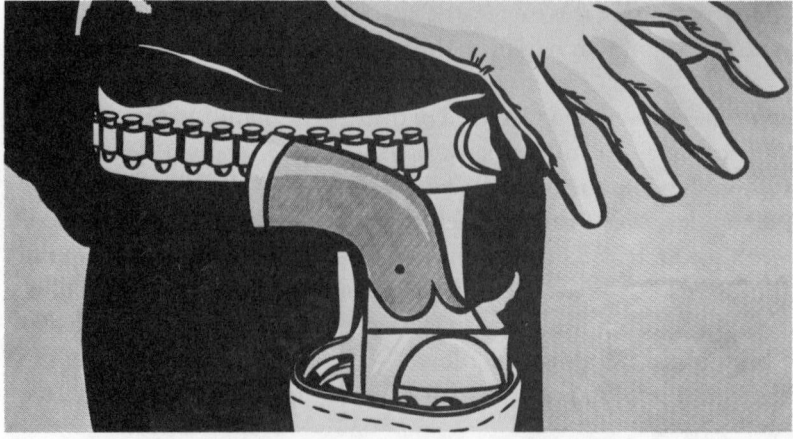

Tutt, in 1865. True to the formula, Hickok was presented as a hero to those who read the account of this prototypical no-duty-to-retreat western gunfight in *Harper's*, the nation's favorite magazine.

Scholars have devoted much attention to popular western fiction, of which *The Virginian* remains the most significant example. Henry Nash Smith traced the origins of the genre to the Leatherstocking novels of James Fenimore Cooper. Smith also emphasized the decline of the popular western into the literarily debased form of the dime novel with its mass readership in the later nineteenth century. Aside from the literary quality of popular western fiction, specialists have focused on the values upheld by it. The scholarly consensus is that popular western fiction, whether in print or film, embodies a deep formula in which the hero, according to John G. Cawelti's study *The Six-Gun Mystique* (1984), mediates between civilization and savagery (or, in the comparable terms of other scholars, between culture and nature, order and chaos). The gunfighting skill of the hero represents the savagery of violence, but his objective of besting evil is in the interest of civilization. In this deep formula the hero is also a transitional figure: one who employs the violence of the frontier West to establish the peaceable society of civilized values that should succeed it. Thus, the hero reflects deeply conservative social values aligned against the threat of anarchy.

Neither Smith nor Cawelti were impressed with the literary quality of formula western fiction, but among recent scholars who take these writings more seriously as literature are Christine Bold, Michael Denning, and Cynthia S. Hamilton. Denning holds that dime-novel authors used the western setting "not only for escapist adventure but to state social conflicts through figures of bank and train robbers," aggrieved cowboys, and range wars. Wister based *The Virginian* on the conflict between the big cattlemen of Wyoming and the rustler element, the conflict that peaked in the Johnson County War. Wister was a firm friend of some of the cattle barons of Wyoming, and *The Virginian* expresses, in literature, their conservative version of the Western Civil War of Incorporation. Wister's villain, Trampas, was modeled on a true bad man—one of the Wyoming rustlers whom Wister himself had met. The heroic Virginian rides with a vigilante band of the kind that took to the field in the Johnson County War.

Since Wister, popular western fiction in both print and film has often reflected the Western Civil War of Incorporation and the emergence of a cognitive split in the mythology of the western hero. The conservative winning side in the Western Civil War of Incorporation bred a socially conservative myth of the hero—for example, the fictional Virginian and the mythic versions of the real-life Wild Bill Hickok and Wyatt Earp. The anti-incorporating side in the regional civil war generated a dissident social-bandit myth in which the heroes were real-life outlaws like Jesse James, Billy the Kid, Joaquin Murrieta, and Gregorio Cortez. Both the conservative mythic hero and the insurgent social-bandit hero have had wide appeal because Americans are deeply ambivalent about established power and dissident protest.

Aside from mass-market formula fiction, many authentic novels of high quality have been based on episodes of western violence: *The Ox-Bow Incident*, by Walter Van Tilburg Clark, the previously mentioned antivigilante novel; *The Lady* (1957), by Conrad Richter, inspired by the tragic deaths of Judge Albert J. Fountain and his son; *A Very Small Remnant* (1963), by Michael Straight, based on the Sand Creek Massacre;

and, with its climax in the slaughter of the Blackfeet on the Marias River, the remarkable *Fools Crow* (1986), by James Welch.

There are two key questions about western violence. First, just how violent was the West? Due to the values of its people, the Western Civil War of Incorporation, and the ubiquity of ethnic, racial, and religious conflict, the West was a turbulent region. This was the result, however, of the particular historical experience of the West. Westerners were not innately more violent than people elsewhere. Leading social, economic, and political blocs freely resorted to violence to advance or defend their interests. Closely connected to key episodes of this western violence were such leading figures and men of power as Leland Stanford, Stephen J. Field, Thomas B. Catron, Albert Bacon Fall, and Granville Stuart. Yet, some qualification is in order.

Many communities and areas of the West were notably violent, but others were not. No region of the West was more violent than central Texas from 1860 to the 1890s, a huge area bounded roughly by Fort Worth, Dallas, Houston, San Antonio, and San Angelo. In this locale of multicultural convergence, Hispanos, German immigrants, and slaveholding southern whites invaded the realm of the native Indians. Violence abounded as a result of the Civil War and its aftermath and also as a result of white-Indian warfare, vigilantism, cattle-range conflict, outlaw activity, community feuds, ethnic and racial tension, agrarian discontent, and political tumult. Gunplay was common, as exemplified by John Wesley Hardin, the West's deadliest gunfighter with over twenty killings arising from his participation in post–Civil War white-black racial strife and in political conflicts and community feuds.

A central Texas culture of violence based on the spirit of no duty to retreat skewed the behavior of the people. As a contemporary wrote, self-defense was "the usual plea of the man-slayer" with "wide latitude" given to its definition. "A look may, if it have . . . sufficient of malice in it, justify resort to the pistol pocket. A touch [to the pocket] frequently justifies instant shooting." Nor was the violence self-contained in the Lone Star State. Central Texas cowboys, cattle kings, and outlaws riding the trails north, northwest, and west took their bent to violence with them, as seen in such gunfighters as Frank Canton in Wyoming and Oliver M. Lee in New Mexico as well as the outlaws John Ringo and Curly Bill Brocius in Arizona. Central Texas expatriates significantly tinctured wide western expanses with the virus of violence.

President Lyndon B. Johnson was born and reared in the heart of the violent region of central Texas. Johnson biographers and Johnson himself have averred the formative influence of his central Texas homeland in shaping his presidential attitudes and values. His relentless determination to defend militarily what he saw as the American national interest in South Vietnam was typical of his central Texas heritage of no-duty-to-retreat violence. As Johnson made his 1965 decision to commit large-scale land forces to the defense of South Vietnam, he invoked the spirit of one of his heroes, a gunfighting Texas Ranger, Captain L. H. McNelly, to admonish the American people that "courage is a man who keeps coming on."

Away from central Texas, disputes over property rights and human rights were endemic in industries like mining, timber, and cattle. Often related to the Western Civil War of Incorporation, such conflicts generated an enormous amount of violence.

Mining, mill, and cattle towns were frequently violent places, but there were also many communities in the West where violence was rare. In 1960, the homicide rate of the West was second to that of the South among the nation's regions. Contrary to this overall sectional pattern, however, two sets of western states had homicide rates in 1960 that were among America's lowest: a Northwest group of Washington, Oregon, Idaho, and Utah; and a Great Plains wedge of Kansas, Nebraska, and the Dakotas. Some basic cultural predispositions were behind the low proclivity to homicide in these states. Both groups of states had strong contingents of core settlers from the Northeast whose regional culture, as the social historian David Hackett Fischer has noted, made them averse to violence.

Governmental structure was a key factor in western violence. Comparative studies of the Canadian and the American West show that miners prone to violence and vigilantism under the loose, permissive rule of the American federal system became peaceable and law-abiding when they migrated to Canada, where the more centralized, stricter government was staunchly intolerant of violence. And yet, as violent as it was, the American West never produced anything like the hundreds of thousands of civilian casualties resulting from the anarchic political violence in the South American nation of Colombia from the 1940s to the 1960s.

Although on a far smaller scale than in Colombia, violence was a principal factor in western U.S. history. This leads to the second question about western violence: has it been mainly responsible for America's unenviable distinction as the most violent nation among its peer group of the technologically advanced democracies of the globe? The answer is no. The turbulent history and values of the West have been a major contributor to our nation's violent heritage but no more so than ethnic, racial, religious, industrial, agrarian, and political conflict or than the crime, lynch-law, and violent examples and legacies of the American Revolution and the Civil War. The West is but one example of the pluralism of American history and society that has yielded both the bane of violence and the blessings of freedom and opportunity. In spite of the incorporating trend of 1850–1920 and the excess of violence, millions of immigrants worldwide have been attracted to the open, democratic society of both America and its western region.

Bibliographic Note

A bibliographical essay is Richard Maxwell Brown, "Historiography of Violence in the American West," in Michael P. Malone, ed., *Historians and the American West* (Lincoln, 1983), 234–69. A comprehensive work on western history that perceptively treats violence is Richard White, *"It's Your Misfortune and None of My Own": A New History of the American West* (Norman, 1991). For my concepts of the Western Civil War of Incorporation and gunfighters, as well as the doctrines of no duty to retreat and the homestead ethic, see Richard Maxwell Brown, *No Duty to Retreat: Violence and Values in American History and Society* (New York, 1991) and "Western Violence: Structure, Values, Myth," *Western Historical Quarterly* 24 (February 1993): 5–20. The general concept of incorporation first appeared in Alan Trachtenberg, *The Incorporation of America: Culture and Society in the Gilded Age* (New York, 1982). The historical context of ethnic and racial violence in the West is compellingly treated in Patricia Nelson Limerick, *The Legacy of Conquest: The Unbroken Past of the American West* (New York, 1987), part 2.

An influential treatment of the frontier myth in relation to American culture and violence is the trilogy by Richard Slotkin, *Regeneration through Violence: The Mythology of the American*

Frontier, 1600–1860 (Middletown, Conn., 1973), *The Fatal Environment: The Myth of the Frontier in the Age of Industrialization, 1800–1890* (New York, 1985), and *Gunfighter Nation: The Myth of the Frontier in Twentieth-Century America* (New York, 1992). The concept of the social bandit in E. J. Hobsbawm, *Social Bandits and Primitive Rebels* (Glencoe, Ill., 1959), is applied by Richard White to "Outlaw Gangs of the Middle Border: American Social Bandits," *Western Historical Quarterly* 12 (October 1981): 387–408. On vigilantism, see Richard Maxwell Brown, *Strain of Violence: Historical Studies of American Violence and Vigilantism* (New York, 1975), Robert M. Senkewicz, *Vigilantes in Gold Rush San Francisco* (Stanford, 1985), and Richard Hogan, *Class and Community in Frontier Colorado* (Lawrence, 1990). Emphasizing the West is W. Eugene Hollon, *Frontier Violence: Another Look* (New York, 1974).

For the Mussel Slough conflict, see Brown, *No Duty to Retreat*, chap. 3. On the Johnson County War, see Helena Huntington Smith, *The War on Powder River* (New York, 1966). The following works address the Lincoln County War and Billy the Kid: Robert M. Utley, *High Noon in Lincoln: Violence on the Western Frontier* (Albuquerque, 1987) and *Billy the Kid: A Short and Violent Life* (Lincoln, 1989); Frederick W. Nolan, *The Lincoln County War: A Documentary History* (Norman, 1992); and Stephen Tatum, *Inventing Billy the Kid: Visions of the Outlaw in America, 1881–1981* (Albuquerque, 1982). C. L. Sonnichsen, *Tularosa: Last of the Frontier West* (New York, 1960), treats the Tularosa war, whereas the Cochise County War and the Earps are dealt with in Brown, *No Duty to Retreat*, chap. 2, and in Paula Mitchell Marks, *And Die in the West: The Story of the O.K. Corral Gunfight* (New York, 1989). For the James-Younger gang and the outlaw tradition initiated by them, see William A. Settle, Jr., *Jesse James Was His Name; or, Fact and Fiction Concerning the Careers of the Notorious James Brothers of Missouri* (Columbia, 1966), Paul I. Wellman, *A Dynasty of Western Outlaws* (1961; reprint, Lincoln, 1986), Glenn Shirley, *West of Hell's Fringe: Crime, Criminals, and the Federal Peace Officer in Oklahoma Territory, 1889–1907* (Norman, 1978), and White, "Outlaw Gangs."

A key article is Carlos A. Schwantes, "The Concept of the Wageworkers' Frontier: A Framework for Future Research," *Western Historical Quarterly* 18 (January 1987): 39–55. The industrial phase of the Western Civil War of Incorporation is reflected in many books dealing with violent episodes from the 1890s to the 1910s. Exemplifying this scholarship are George S. McGovern and Leonard F. Guttridge, *The Great Coalfield War* (Boston, 1972), and Zeese Papanikolas, *Buried Unsung: Louis Tikas and the Ludlow Massacre* (Salt Lake City, 1982), on the Ludlow violence. Norman H. Clark, *Mill Town: A Social History of Everett, Washington, from Its Earliest Beginnings on the Shore of Puget Sound to the Tragic and Infamous Event Known as the Everett Massacre* (Seattle, 1970), strikingly treats the Everett Massacre. John McClelland, Jr., *Wobbly War: The Centralia Story* (Tacoma, Wash., 1987), is the salient work on the Centralia Massacre. Discussing incorporation in California's Owens Valley and its violent legacy is John Walton, *Western Times and Water Wars: State, Culture, and Rebellion in California* (Berkeley, 1992).

Notable works on violent western law enforcement are Frank R. Prassel, *The Western Peace Officer: A Legacy of Law and Order* (Norman, 1972), Larry D. Ball, *The United States Marshals of New Mexico and Arizona Territories, 1846–1912* (Albuquerque, 1978) and *Desert Lawmen: The High Sheriffs of New Mexico and Arizona, 1846–1912* (Albuquerque, 1992), Leon C. Metz, *Pat Garrett: The Story of a Western Lawman* (Norman, 1974), and Robert K. DeArment, *George Scarborough: The Life and Death of a Lawman on the Closing Frontier* (Norman, 1992).

The historiography of western massacres is large. Salient studies include Juanita Brooks, *The Mountain Meadows Massacre* (Norman, 1991), Gary L. Roberts, *Sand Creek: Tragedy and Symbol* (Ann Arbor, 1984), Lynwood Carranco and Estle Beard, *Genocide and Vendetta: The Round Valley Wars of Northern California* (Norman, 1981), and Craig Storti, *Incident at Bitter Creek: The Story of the Rock Springs Chinese Massacre* (Ames, Iowa, 1991). Massacres involving Indians are cited in Robert M. Utley, *The Indian Frontier of the American West, 1846–1890* (Albuquerque, 1984). Hispanic White Caps and *bandidos* are found in Robert J. Rosenbaum, *Mexicano Resistance in the Southwest: "The Sacred Right of Self-Preservation"* (Austin, 1981). David A. Johnson is writing a book on the lynching of Josefa.

Outstanding works are Kent Ladd Steckmesser, *The Western Hero in History and Legend* (Norman, 1965), with chapters on Wild Bill Hickok and Billy the Kid; Joseph G. Rosa, *They Called Him Wild Bill: The Life and Adventures of James Butler Hickok*, 2d ed. rev. (Norman, 1974); Roger D. McGrath, *Gunfighters, Highwaymen, and Vigilantes: Violence on the Frontier* (Berkeley, 1984), on Bodie, California, and Aurora, Nevada; Don Dedera, *A Little War of Our Own: The Pleasant Valley Feud Revisited* (Flagstaff, Ariz., 1988), on the mordant 1880s Tonto Basin War in Arizona; and Gary L. Roberts, *Death Comes for the Chief Justice: The Slough-Rynerson Quarrel and Political Violence in New Mexico* (Niwot, 1990).

Henry Nash Smith, *Virgin Land: The American West as Symbol and Myth* (Cambridge, Mass., 1950), is a classic study. In addition to John G. Cawelti's seminal work *The Six-Gun Mystique*, 2d ed. rev. (Bowling Green, Ohio, 1984), formulaic western fiction is treated in Christine Bold, *Selling the Wild West: Popular Western Fiction, 1860 to 1960* (Bloomington, 1987), Michael Denning, *Mechanic Accents: Dime Novels and Working-Class Culture in America* (London, 1987), Cynthia S. Hamilton, *Western and Hard-Boiled Detective Fiction in America: From High Noon to Midnight* (Iowa City, 1987), and Jane Tompkins, *West of Everything: The Inner Life of Westerns* (New York, 1992).

For the context of late-twentieth-century Los Angeles violence, see Mike Davis, *City of Quartz: Excavating the Future in Los Angeles* (New York, 1992). On central Texas violence, see C. L. Sonnichsen, *I'll Die before I'll Run: The Story of the Great Feuds of Texas* (New York, 1962), and Brown, *Strain of Violence*, chap. 8. For homicide in the West and the peaceful impact of settlers from the Northeast, see Raymond D. Gastil, *Cultural Regions of the United States* (Seattle, 1975), chap. 3, and David Hackett Fischer, *Albion's Seed: Four British Folkways in America* (New York, 1989), 889–93.

SECTION III
Transformation

J ust as scientists map the slant of the West's lands and the flow of its streams, so
historians plot the course of events that have occurred in the region. Both groups
of scholars are looking for watersheds that indicate a significant shift in direction.
For a time, the scholarly world assumed that the year 1890 marked the "continental divide" of western history. The closing of the frontier, as announced by
the director of the U.S. Census Bureau and analyzed by the historian Frederick
Jackson Turner, did not, however, have an immediate impact on settlement patterns or
economic growth. Record numbers of homestead filings lay in the future, as did booms
in copper, lumber, and oil.

Yet the 1890 announcement did represent a psychological turning point, for it led
Americans to question how long the western resources once deemed limitless would
endure. For leaders like Theodore Roosevelt, this awareness had a twofold consequence,
intensifying not only his belief in conservation at home but also his commitment to
imperialism overseas. Not by accident did the United States enter the twentieth century
with a number of new Pacific "possessions": the Hawaiian Islands, American Samoa,
Johnston Island, Wake Island, Guam, and the Philippines.

Some Americans linked the acquisition of these islands to the nation's earlier expansion. "The flag has never paused in its onward march," noted Albert J. Beveridge,
the senator from Indiana. Supporting the McKinley administration's plan to withhold
autonomy from the people of the Philippines, he asked, "If you deny [self-rule] to the
Indian at home, how dare you grant it to the Malay abroad?" Yet even Beveridge
recognized that this analogy could be distorting. The nation's latest acquisitions were not
deemed destination points for Anglo-American settlement, as Indian lands had been,
nor were they (including at first Hawai`i) considered candidates for statehood. Provid-
ing strategic bases as well as raw materials, they would link American manufacturers to
the markets of East Asia.

The nation's new Pacific tilt excited western investors. In 1912 the streetcar magnate
Henry Huntington predicted that the Los Angeles he had helped to develop would
become "the most important city in this country, if not the world." Dismissing the
Atlantic as "the ocean of the past," he glorified the Pacific as "the ocean of the future."
"Europe can supply her own wants," he said. "We shall supply the wants of Asia."

The nation's experiment in colonialism abroad helped parts of the West to outgrow
a quasi-colonial economy at home. Nevertheless, a war in the Pacific transformed the
region even more dramatically than had trade across the Pacific. The two developments
were not unrelated. American economic interests in East Asia and the western Pacific ran
afoul of Japanese ambitions in the area. When Japanese incursions into China and
Southeast Asia led to American economic reprisals, the Japanese attacked Pearl Harbor.

*World War II marked
a decisive moment in
the history of the West.
The money, jobs, and
people that flowed
west with the growth
of defense industries
helped initiate the re-
gion's emergence as a
political and econom-
ic force in postwar
America.*

World War II involved combat on many fronts, but none loomed larger for Americans than the Pacific theater. It was here that the enemy struck without notice, all but crippling the American Pacific fleet and killing thousands of military personnel. Here too, American soldiers retreated from the Philippines. The United States suffered its most stinging reversals of World War II in the Pacific, but the nation responded with decisive action. Able to take the lead in this theater of operations, the United States pushed the Japanese out of the western Pacific and incinerated two home-island cities with atomic bombs. For both the Americans and the Japanese, this was, in the words of the historian John W. Dower, a "war without mercy."

Because the West lay closer than any other part of the nation to this theater of operations, because the region contained vast undeveloped areas ideal for training soldiers and testing bombs, and because westerners lobbied intensively to attract the business of war, the West received a disproportionate amount of U.S. military spending. Moreover, the end of World War II did not mean the end of the spending. Further international crises, including two more wars across the Pacific, helped to complete the West's economic, demographic, and political transformation.

Thus, the year 1941 is a watershed in western history, not only more profound than the artificially derived 1890 closing of the frontier but also more easily demonstrated. The post-1941 new West was a garrison state whose prosperity depended on Americans' willingness to serve as a *posse comitatus* overseas in a not-always cold war. So, in 1965, at a crucial juncture in the U.S. involvement in Vietnam, President Lyndon Johnson explained his response to a Vietcong mortar attack on U.S. Army advisers in Pleiku. "We have kept our gun over the mantel and our shells in the cupboard for a long time now. And what was the result? They are killing our men while they sleep in the night. I can't ask American soldiers out there to continue to fight with one hand tied behind their backs." A popular image of Old West readiness to rebuff Indian raids had become the rationale for initiating a long-term series of air strikes against North Vietnam.

The brutality and ineffectiveness of the Vietnam conflict shook the confidence of many Americans in the legitimacy of their cause. Two decades later, the dissolution of the Soviet Union further confused international issues. The consensus that had created the garrison state eroded, but the West had been forever changed by the decades-long mobilization.

Once a backwater of the nation, the West had grown in wealth and population to become an economic and political powerhouse. Still, its inhabitants were as diverse as ever, its internal discord just as intense. The residents of the region clashed over the development of natural resources, the extension of metropolitan areas, and the retention of the national military presence. They struggled over who belonged in the region, who had the right to name it, and who was allowed to call it home.

The West's history in the twentieth century, no less than in the nineteenth, combines elements sordid and sublime, tragic and triumphant. It is a story both more and less familiar because it has been experienced more than it has been studied. Yet so many dramatic changes have occurred in the twentieth century that this period is an essential part of the region's epic. The fullest understanding of the American West requires a historical appreciation of this watershed era.

— Carol A. O'Connor

CHRONOLOGY

1900	Frederick Weyerhaeuser opens "Sawdust Empire" in the Pacific Northwest.
1901	Major oil find at Spindletop, Texas.
1902	Newlands Reclamation Act establishes federal role in constructing dams and irrigation systems.
1906	Earthquake destroys downtown San Francisco.
1912	New Mexico and Arizona enter the Union. Center of motion picture production shifts from New York to Los Angeles.
1913–14	Strike by the United Mine Workers in Colorado culminates in the Ludlow Massacre.
1916	Congress creates the National Park Service. William Boeing begins building airplanes in Seattle.
1917–18	U.S. entry into World War I stimulates the West's economy but radical labor is suppressed.
1918	The Native American Church is incorporated in Oklahoma.
1922	Colorado River Commission Compact, involving seven states, sets a model for resource planning.
1924	Immigration Restriction Act bars Asians from migrating to the United States and establishes quotas based on "national origins" for groups outside the Western Hemisphere.
1931	Nevada legalizes gambling.
1931–40	Dust Bowl conditions hit the Great Plains.
1934	Great maritime strike ties up ports from San Diego to Seattle. Taylor Grazing Act regularizes stock growers' use of federally owned rangelands.
1939	The Hewlett-Packard electronics firm is founded in a garage in Palo Alto, California.
1941	Japanese attack Pearl Harbor; West becomes staging ground for U.S. operations in the Pacific.
1942	110,000 Japanese Americans are interned in concentration camps.
1943	Servicemen attack Mexican Americans and African Americans in "zoot suit" riots in Los Angeles.
1945	First atomic bomb is tested near Alamogordo, New Mexico. The San Francisco-based Bank of America becomes the world's largest bank.
1947	Congressional hearings on alleged Communist infiltration of the Hollywood film industry.
1955	Disneyland opens in Anaheim, California.
1959	Alaska and Hawai`i become the forty-ninth and fiftieth states.
1960	Del Webb starts selling homes in Sun City, Arizona, an entire community for retirees.
1961–62	The National Aeronautics and Space Administration's Manned Spacecraft Center opens near Houston, Texas.
1964	California passes New York to become the nation's most populous state.
1965	Riots engulf Watts district of Los Angeles. Immigration Act ends the discriminatory aspects of the 1924 law.
1970	Filipino and Hispanic workers win a five-year strike against grape growers.
1973	Members of the American Indian Movement and their Lakota supporters occupy Wounded Knee, South Dakota, for seventy-one days.
1975	Phelps Dodge halts copper production in Bisbee, Arizona. Coal towns like Gillette, Wyoming, profit from the energy boom.
1978	Dan White assassinates San Francisco Mayor George Moscone and Supervisor Harvey Milk.
1986	Immigration Reform and Control Act approved by Congress.
1989	*Exxon Valdez* runs aground in Alaska's Prince William Sound.
1992	Riots convulse metropolitan Los Angeles where members of racial "minorities" make up a majority of the population.

Chapter Twelve

Wage Earners and
Wealth Makers

CARLOS A. SCHWANTES

Thursday morning, 12 July 1917, should have been like any other work-day in Bisbee, Arizona. As dawn backlit the crest of the Mule Mountains surrounding the state's premier mining city, the serpentine streets below should have echoed with the boots of several thousand men coming and going from the mines. The merchants of Brewery Gulch and other downtown streets should have been preparing for another day of brisk sales. It was wartime, and the city worked unceasingly to produce the copper so vital to communications equipment and munitions. Every rifle cartridge contained about half an ounce of the pure red metal. Copper would win the war.

Within the past decade Bisbee had briefly emerged as Arizona's largest city, and even in July 1917 it still ranked with Phoenix and Tucson. Bisbee's nearly twenty thousand residents took pride in the fact that theirs was no insubstantial mining camp. Brick buildings and paved streets, running water and enclosed sewers, and imposing public facilities like the Copper Queen Hotel clearly set Bisbee apart from nearby Tombstone, a once booming but now decaying village of wooden sidewalks and false-front stores typical of the nineteenth-century mining West.

From the mines of Bisbee came fortunes in lead, zinc, manganese, gold, and silver—more gold and silver than from any other place in Arizona—but copper above all else determined the fate of Bisbee. "That depends on the price of copper" was a refrain often heard on the town streets. In Butte, Montana, and Bingham, Utah, and dozens of Bisbee's sister settlements, the red metal equaled prosperity or adversity: a rise in price in Paris or the opening of a new mine in Chile would affect life in remote corners of the American West, and the lingo of mining was the common language of all residents of the copper kingdom regardless of economic or ethnic differences. A slump in the price of copper might close dozens of mines across the West and send hundreds, even thousands, of miners off in search of work in other camps and even to jobs in other major industries, such as logging and agriculture.

Wartime pressures drove the price of copper up dramatically in 1916 and 1917. Miners produced at a hectic pace, working around the clock in successive shifts, soon becoming frustrated by the long hours, together with wages that lagged behind inflation. In Bisbee, approximately three thousand tired miners finally walked off the job on 27 June. The strike remained peaceable, although with each passing day public attention

Staging their own portrait, these Bisbee miners pose with the lunch buckets and candles that helped alleviate the tedium of their work. The light areas on their pants, melted wax from the candles they stuck in the walls to illuminate the mine tunnels, suggest that they have just come off a shift of underground labor.

D. A. Markey. Miners, Bisbee, Arizona. *Photograph, ca. 1895. Bisbee Mining and Historical Museum (#080.73.1), Bisbee, Arizona.*

shifted from the legitimate demands of the mine workers to the radical heresies of the Industrial Workers of the World, widely regarded as the dangerous tool of enemy Germany and the real force behind the unpatriotic work stoppage.

Tension increased until on the morning of 12 July 1917, the streets of Bisbee filled with the sounds of a two-thousand-man *posse comitatus*. Their leader was Sheriff Harry Wheeler, and backing him were the bosses of local copper companies incensed by workers who dared to halt production during a national crisis. Men identified by white armbands raided the homes of known strikers and their sympathizers. Two lines of armed citizens herded twelve hundred "undesirables" aboard the boxcars and cattle cars of a special freight train that sped them east across the deserts of Arizona and New Mexico. Abruptly abandoned along a lonely stretch of track, the prisoners would have died in the July heat had they not received emergency food and water from soldiers stationed nearby to guard the isolated border area from Mexican revolutionaries. In Bisbee, strikebreakers quickly filled the mines, and the community again shouldered its patriotic duty of producing copper to make the world safe for democracy. Next to the roundup of Japanese Americans in World War II, this Bisbee deportation is the greatest mass violation of civil liberties in the twentieth-century West.

Today, most citizens of Bisbee would prefer to forget the infamous episode. Whereas nearby Tombstone attracts busloads of camera-toting tourists by glorifying its violent past, and even occasionally restaging the shootout at the O.K. Corral, Bisbee disdains the shoot-'em-up approach to western history. It retains instead the sober appearance of an industrial center not unlike a steel-mill or cotton-mill town of the East or South. Travelers do come to gaze at a mining landscape dominated by the Lavender Pit, but most Bisbee residents forswear anything that might conjure up images of a raw and immature past.

Still, it is hard to predict what Bisbee's residents will do for a living. Like many of the West's natural-resource-based communities, this one has experienced massive economic dislocation. In 1975, for the first time in nearly a century, the Phelps Dodge Corporation halted its mining operations in Bisbee. In the slump that followed, homes could be purchased for as little as one thousand dollars. By the 1980s, retirees constituted more than 40 percent of the town's eight thousand residents, and a small but visible counterculture accounted for part of the rest. At least residents can be grateful for one thing: Bisbee's mining landscape is not radioactive, as it is in some of the West's uranium mining and processing towns.

The history of business and labor in the West since 1900 is far more than a record of the troubled evolution of natural-resource communities into tourist or retirement meccas (or into ghost towns). Yet at least until World War II, economic life in cities as large as Seattle, Portland, and Denver remained closely linked to the natural-resource hinterlands beyond their doorsteps. This relationship defined the economy of the West in the early twentieth century and continues to do so in many parts of the region today.

The World of Business in the Early Twentieth Century

When the new century dawned, metropolitan centers as large as Seattle, Denver, and El Paso formed urban outposts juxtaposed with vast and lightly populated hinterlands. Many dozens of smaller population islands like Bisbee coalesced around the region's

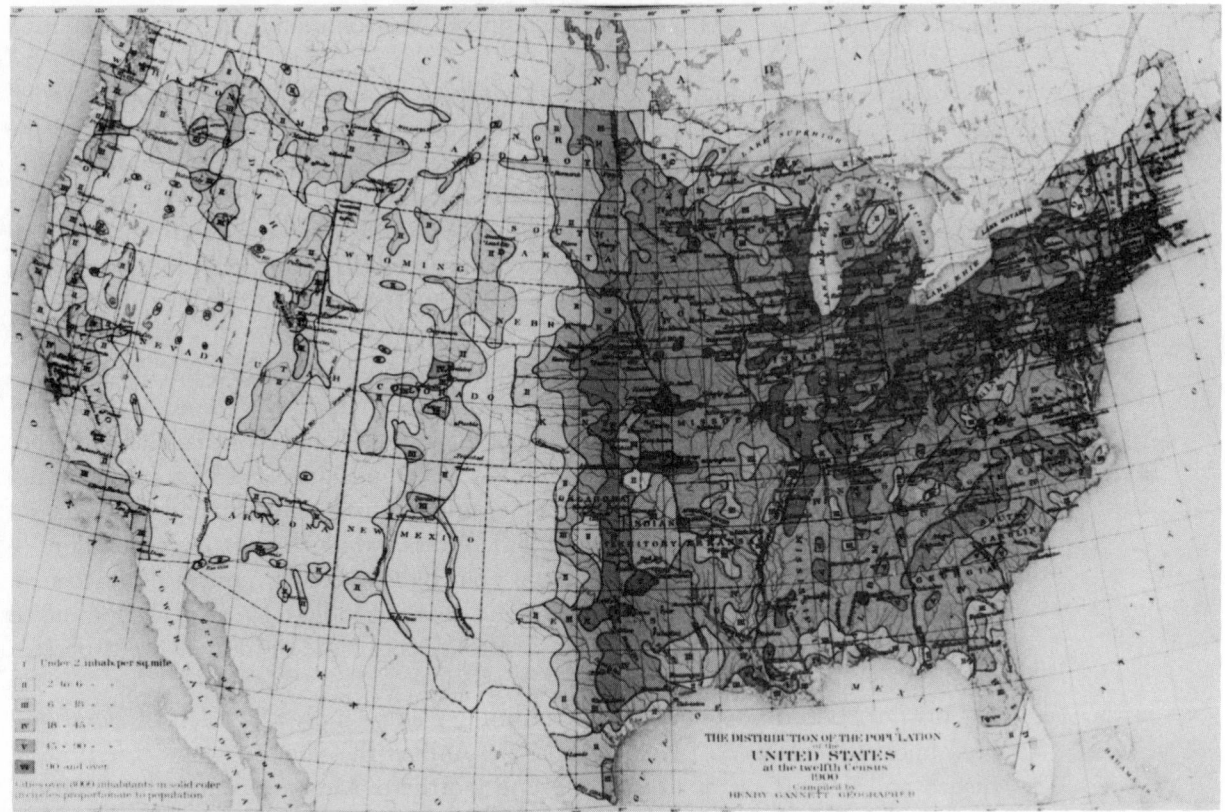

THE DISTRIBUTION OF THE POPULATION
of the
UNITED STATES
at the twelfth Census
1900
Compiled by
HENRY GANNETT, GEOGRAPHER

ubiquitous mineral deposits, some of them isolated at elevations of ten thousand feet or more, where a paralyzing blanket of snow often lasted from October through May, cutting them off from the rest of the world. Separating San Francisco from Salt Lake City, and Los Angeles from Denver, were hundreds of miles of nearly empty deserts, forests, and mountains, and the same imposing physical barriers that isolated so much of the West from itself also separated sizable portions of it from the rest of the United States. Separation took other forms too, notably in California where the coastal area north of San Francisco, with 5 percent of the state's population, received about 40 percent of all surface water, whereas the Los Angeles basin, with 40 percent of the state's population, received about 2 percent of the surface water. Because of the peculiar configuration of resources and settlements, particularly in the arid lands beyond the one hundredth meridian, the work of building a suitable infrastructure of canals and dams, railway lines, highways, and bridges defined the world of business and labor in the early-twentieth-century West. The construction industry necessarily loomed large in the western economy, employing thousands of workers and forming the basis for some of the region's most impressive personal fortunes.

The West's island pattern of settlement was a visual reminder that the regional economy in 1900 was still closely tied to natural resources often found in remote, nearly inaccessible places. This was especially true of the mineral industry. Some 90 percent of the nation's metal reserves were located in the West, and mining in 1900 accounted for 11 percent of the gainful employment in Colorado, 12 percent in Idaho, 13 percent in

The maps drawn from the census of 1900 graphically illustrate the island pattern of settlement that characterized life in the Far West. Population density in the intermountain and Rocky Mountain regions remained tied to the availability of extractable mineral resources or to ample supplies of irrigation water.

Julius Bien & Co., lithographers. Distribution of the Population: 1900. *From the* Twelfth Census of the United States: Statistical Atlas *(1903).*

Montana, and 15 percent in Arizona, as compared with less than 1 percent for the nation as a whole.

By the eve of World War I, the region produced the bulk of the nation's copper, gold, and silver. Gold and silver were glamour metals, but copper, so vital to the expanding electrical and telephone industries after the 1880s, created far more wealth. The West's copper kingdom centered first in Montana, which by the turn of the century had become the nation's leading copper producer, a title it had wrested from Michigan in 1892 and yielded to Arizona in 1910, which has led the country in production since that time. Utah, Nevada, and New Mexico also emerged as significant producers of the red metal.

Copper required enormous sums of money to mine, smelt, refine, and market. Such unprecedented amounts of capital were difficult, if not impossible, to raise in economically undeveloped and lightly settled parts of the United States. For that reason, Bisbee as early as the 1880s became synonymous with Phelps, Dodge and Company, a long-established New York and New England mercantile firm. Rockefeller and Guggenheim money fueled the industry in other parts of the West. In time, three giant corporations—Anaconda in Montana (backed for several years by Rockefeller money), Kennecott in Utah and Alaska (Guggenheim money), and Phelps Dodge in Arizona—dominated production. By 1940 these three eastern-controlled companies accounted for 80 percent of the West's copper output.

It would be a mistake to regard the mining giants simply as soulless corporations. For almost four decades, James Douglas personified the Phelps Dodge enterprise in Bisbee and remote parts of Arizona and northern Mexico. A broadly educated "renaissance man" from Canada, Douglas and various family members developed mine properties on both sides of the international border, arranged for building complex and expensive smelters, and knitted together a railroad system that stretched nearly eight hundred miles across the Southwest. Because of the influence of Douglas, disputes between rival mining companies in Bisbee were settled peaceably, without resort to courts, and the Arizona community was thus spared the "war of the copper kings" that enriched lawyers but wracked Butte's mineral industry. The example of Dr. Douglas's peaceable resolution of disputes was apparently lost on his son, Walter, who played a key role in the Bisbee deportation.

Although copper was synonymous with mining in many parts of the West, the production of precious metals, for which the West had been famous since the California gold rush of 1848, did not disappear. Whereas some production continued as a by-product of copper mining, the Black Hills of South Dakota emerged as a leading gold producer, and Idaho's Coeur d'Alene district did the same in silver production. Far less glamorous than silver or gold or even copper was coal, which could be found in commercial quantities in almost every western state. Coal mining dated back at least to the 1850s and 1860s in Washington. By the 1890s, Colorado alone extracted three million tons of black diamonds a year, ranking it as one of the region's chief producers of coal. Production figures climbed significantly through the first two decades of the twentieth century, but the industry experienced a long-term decline after World War I as the result of an oil glut. Coal rebounded only in the 1970s, when by the end of the decade the West accounted for approximately one-quarter of the nation's output. Much of this was produced by giant machines that stripped seams of coal in the nonunion mines in Wyoming and Montana, unlike in earlier years, when the coal had come from underground, labor-intensive, and often unionized operations.

The first intimation of future trouble for coal can be traced back to January 1901, when a wildcat driller named Captain Anthony Lucas punched through the top of a salt dome near Beaumont, Texas, to tap an enormous underground pool of oil. The black gold gushed out under such pressure that it blew away the drilling apparatus and spewed more than half a million barrels of oil high into the air before it could be controlled six days later. Hundreds of people gathered at Spindletop Field to view the black geyser, the eighth wonder of the world according to its boosters. As thousands more people rushed to form companies and drill wells, the population of Beaumont swelled from nine thousand to fifty thousand in three months. Speculative mania seized all parts of the state. Petroleum was eventually found under more than half the counties of Texas, and it replaced cotton as the primary contributor to the state's economy. Petrochemical production became the state's largest manufacturing industry. From hundreds of small companies, three eventually emerged to dominate the Texas oil industry: Gulf, Texaco, and Humble (now part of Exxon, the modern name for Standard Oil Company of New Jersey). Spindletop and its plume of black gold came to symbolize an entire industry, and oil wealth became synonymous with Texas; but during the first three decades of the twentieth century, California often produced more barrels of oil per year than did Texas.

California oil dated back to pioneer days, but it became a booming industry in the 1890s. New discoveries were made almost every year through the 1920s. A speculative frenzy gripped southern California as production in the state soared from five million barrels in 1900 to fifteen million barrels in 1914, and that was only the beginning. From the San Joaquin Valley to Santa Barbara and Los Angeles, new finds gave rise to a forest of derricks and to the beginnings of industrial giants like Union Oil of California and Standard Oil of California—now Chevron—which was originally only one more part of John D. Rockefeller's giant Standard Oil monopoly. Between 1901 and 1940, California ranked first among American oil-producing states for fourteen years, second for twenty-one years, and third for three years. Oil refining became the state's chief manufacturing industry, and the man-made harbor at San Pedro became one of the nation's chief oil-shipping ports. During the first third of the twentieth century, Oklahoma, Kansas, Colorado, New Mexico, and Montana joined the ranks of major oil producers, but nothing equaled the East Texas boom of 1931, which enabled Texas permanently to dethrone California as the nation's chief oil producer.

If Spindletop in 1901 symbolized a new era for the oil industry, something less dramatic but of similar importance occurred a year earlier to highlight profound changes in the timber industry. As the timber supply of the Great Lakes region dwindled, the extensive forests of the Pacific Northwest emerged from obscurity. Early in 1900, the Minnesota timber baron Frederick Weyerhaeuser and several associates purchased nine hundred thousand acres of the Northern Pacific Railroad land grant—mostly Douglas fir forest in Washington—for six dollars an acre. It was one of the largest private land transfers in American history. Less than fifty years earlier, Weyerhaeuser had been a

young immigrant from Germany beginning his career as a night fireman in a sawmill in Rock Island, Illinois. Eventually his empire totaled more than ninety affiliated companies and dominated timber production in Oregon, Washington, and Idaho.

Weyerhaeuser's show of confidence in the future of timber in the Pacific Northwest precipitated a stampede to buy timberland. Sawmills went up by the hundreds, and Idaho's scenic Lake Coeur d'Alene, for example, resembled an enormous millpond as log booms lined its shores. By 1905 Washington had grabbed the mythical title of the nation's leading timber producer, a position it would maintain for all but one year until Oregon slipped ahead in 1938. The Pacific Northwest became so dependent on the timber industry for its economic well-being that for a time it was aptly labeled the Sawdust Empire. California, however, was never far behind and usually ranked second or third. By 1940, Washington, Oregon, and California together accounted for 40 percent of the nation's lumber production.

Although during the first three decades of the twentieth century the West remained primarily a supplier of raw materials, some processing did take place within the region, usually in or near urban centers. There were smelters, sawmills, food canneries, oil refineries, foundries, and a mixed assortment of manufacturing establishments. Much of the region's manufacturing was devoted either to first-stage processing of raw materials, such as sawing logs into building materials, or to small-scale diversified manufacturing for local markets. The West's only significant steel-manufacturing facility was the Colorado Fuel and Iron Company, which produced enough steel to make Pueblo the Pittsburgh of the West. Value added through manufacturing remained very small in most of the region before World War I.

Unlike manufacturing, service industries loomed larger in the western economy than elsewhere in the U.S. economy in the early twentieth century. Banking, real estate, sales, medicine, and entertainment were all significant. Yet despite the rise of Hollywood after 1915 and even of aircraft manufacturing, which first achieved prominence during World War I, westerners continued for many more years to depend on natural-resource industries and to ride an economic roller-coaster that seemed to deny them any real control over their destiny. Given that the entire West contained a mere 15 percent of the nation's population in 1900, the region could scarcely have avoided becoming enmeshed in what some westerners complained was a colonial relationship, with the richer and much longer established East supposedly plundering the natural resources of the West.

Westerners who subscribed to the "plundered province" thesis most often cited as evidence the domination of eastern capital in Montana, where Anaconda, in addition to its huge copper mines, owned 1.7 million of acres of timberland, municipal waterworks, stores, hotels, and all but one of the seven major daily newspapers of the state. By 1900, Anaconda employed some three-fourths of the wage earners in Montana. A year earlier, Anaconda had come under the control of Rockefeller's Standard Oil and remained so until the copper trust dissolved in 1915. Rockefeller money also dominated the Colorado Fuel and Iron Company in the early 1900s, the Centennial State's largest industrial enterprise. At the opening of the twentieth century, Colorado Fuel and Iron had thirty-eight camps, rolling mills, and steelworks in Colorado, Wyoming, and New Mexico. Its thirteen thousand employees dug coal and iron ore and made coke and steel.

Many factors besides a small population and absentee ownership handicapped the West in any race to compete with manufacturers in the East and elsewhere. These included railroad-rate inequities, usurious interest charges, and tariff protection that favored eastern manufacturers over western consumers. What this "plundered province" complaint often overlooked, however, was that western business interests frequently benefited from an infusion of eastern capital and that some investment money came from the more developed parts of the West itself. For many westerners, nonetheless, the East would remain a convenient scapegoat on which to blame their recurrent economic troubles.

The World of Labor in the Early Twentieth Century

Work life in the early-twentieth-century West was not merely a pale and insignificant reflection of that in the industrial centers of the East and Midwest; instead, several elements gave it a distinctly regional character. As was true for western business generally in the years before World War I, two key concepts explain the most about work life in the West: the island pattern of settlement; and the dependence on natural-resource-based industries infamous for recurrent bouts of cyclical and seasonal unemployment. From the grainfields of the high plains to the oil rigs of Texas and southern California, an army of itinerant laborers supplied the muscle needed to harvest the products of the West's forests, fields, and coastal waters, mine its precious and base metals, drill for its oil, and load its ships. They were indispensable in constructing the West's railroads, dams, irrigation canals, and many other building projects. Before the First World War, the annual wheat harvest of the Pacific Northwest required legions of laborers, and the same was true of California's "factories in the field." In 1910 every hundred miles of railway line required an average of 156 workers for maintenance.

The physical dimensions of the itinerant laborers' domain of toil fluctuated over time. The limits expanded as new agricultural lands and timber and mining camps opened, and the boundaries contracted as natural resources were depleted or, more infrequently, as one of the raw, socially unstable communities survived and matured, as was the case of Bisbee. The domain of the itinerant laborers probably reached its greatest extent in the opening decade of the twentieth century and then diminished after World War I in the face of increased mechanization. Some form of itinerant labor, however, remained a feature of agricultural life in the West's orchards and vegetable, sugar beet, and cotton fields. As one might expect, the still developing West in the early years of the twentieth century had a much higher ratio of laborers to craftsmen and machine-tending operatives than was typical of older, more mature economic regions.

Besides the numerous laborers, the wage-earning work force of the West included printers, plumbers, painters, masons, carpenters, and other skilled workers, who could be found in every major urban center of the West. Forming yet a third group were the operatives, the men and women who ran the machines in sawmills, canneries, and other manufacturing establishments. Although they developed considerable manual dexterity in performing repetitive tasks, most operatives were not highly skilled in the same way that craftsmen were. In some cases the work had been done by craftsmen until machine production opened the way for the less skilled but highly proficient operatives. The craftsmen and operatives of El Paso, Salt Lake City, and any other western community were in many ways not much different from their counterparts in the East and Midwest, although their work lives were shaped to some degree by laborers, who seemed forever on the move throughout the West. Too many itinerant laborers in one locality might, for example, depress wage rates for operatives or tempt employers to hire the outsiders as strikebreakers.

Many operatives were young people, and tending machines was but a step on the road to some other status. Unlike craftsmen or laborers, many operatives were women, who did all types of machine work, from running sewing machines in garment factories to stuffing sausages on production lines in meat-packing plants. In 1939 approximately seventy-five thousand women, mostly Mexican and Mexican-American, worked in California canneries and packinghouses. By the end of World War II, California cannery operatives, 75 percent of them women, constituted one-quarter of the nation's food-processing work force.

Women, however, did not typically hold jobs as laborers. To be sure, women could be found in any mining camp, though not at first in large numbers. A few arrived as wives, others to manage rooming houses and eating places. An unknown number of women worked as prostitutes, especially in the predominantly male world of the laborers. If a mining camp survived to become a town or village, the ratio of males to females tended to normalize as miners married and raised families. In the pre–World War I logging camps, however, which were essentially makeshift work sites in the woods, there were seldom more than a few females. Some loggers, in fact, regarded a woman in camp as bad luck.

Laborers in the pre–World War I era usually worked in all-male gangs and supplied strong arms and backs. They functioned as "human machines" who exchanged physical labor for a daily wage. The work they did was invariably heavy and dirty and often dangerous. Their working hours seemed interminably long, often lasting from five in the morning until eight or later each evening. Some of them remained in a single industry and gained considerable proficiency as miners and loggers, even buying a house and getting married, but in most instances the work was not steady. The average job duration among laborers of the West Coast in 1914 was fifteen to thirty days in lumber camps, sixty days in mining, ten days in construction work, and seven days in harvesting. In extreme cases, an itinerant laborer might remain on the job for as few as three hours before walking off. A common saying in both the timber and the railroad-construction camps was that three crews were connected with any job: "one coming, one going, one on the job."

One scholar who studied their lives labeled them casual workers. Some were indeed casual about work, and some were hoboes and tramps. But many of those found in the ranks of itinerant laborers were at best unwilling conscripts who were ready and able to take steady jobs, if only such work could be found. These itinerant job seekers were in some ways no different from the unemployed of Chicago, New York, or Boston who, on losing one job, might trudge down the street in search of another. Their counterparts in the West, however, were more visible because the loss of a job in one of the region's natural-resource-based island communities often meant having to travel to another island, usually some distance away, to find work, often riding atop or underneath railway freight cars.

Perhaps the single most important reason for widespread itinerancy among western laborers was the cyclical nature of the region's colonial economy. Boom-and-bust cycles heightened workers' sense of dependency and encouraged their mobility. Going hand in hand with cyclical unemployment was the shorter cycle of seasonal unemployment. It became necessary to move around frequently to find work. Depending on the season, a dock worker from Seattle might be found in eastern Washington supplying the muscle needed to sack the annual harvest of wheat. During the course of the year, a metal miner might move from Bisbee to Butte or to the Coeur d'Alene district in Idaho or even to the mines of Alaska before returning to Arizona.

Some of the itinerants were, quite frankly, social misfits, and some were chronic alcoholics. Some were restless by nature and were kept on the move by a frequent surplus of labor in one locality or by reports of high wages being paid somewhere else. The very act of migrating west—which meant at least the temporary loss of the close and stabilizing ties of family, neighborhood, and church—probably contributed to a feeling of rootlessness. And because of the uncertain nature of their employment, some workers found it difficult to forge enduring social relations in new settings.

Because of the seasonal nature of their work, laborers usually spent at least part of the year in one of the West's urban enclaves of employment agencies, cheap hotels and lodging houses, soup kitchens, saloons, and brothels. Every large city had one such district, where laborers congregated and survived between jobs. These urban enclaves, like the logging and construction camps, were predominantly male societies. Seattle, as a result of its close connection with the wageworkers' frontier, in 1900 recorded the highest percentage of male population among American cities of twenty-five thousand or more people (64 percent); Butte, Montana, ranked third (60 percent). It is no accident that both cities featured large and notorious red-light districts.

The laborers of the West came from a variety of racial and national backgrounds. It was common for immigrants of one nationality to gravitate to certain types of work: Scandinavians to logging, for example, and Greeks and Italians to work on railroad construction and maintenance. In California in the early decades of the twentieth century, Japanese could often be found working in fields of sugar beets and berries, Mexicans in the citrus groves and the newly opened cotton fields, and European immigrants in fields of grapes, peas, and artichokes. American whites (sometimes called "tramps") were commonly found harvesting fruit. Few of these were farmhands like those in the East, who enjoyed year-round work and generally boarded with a single family.

There was nothing static about patterns of race and ethnicity in western industry. In 1888 an estimated four-fifths of all Colorado coal miners were English-speaking. That changed after a period of labor strife in 1903–4, when many disillusioned miners left Colorado, and Italians, Austrians, Slavs, Serbs, Poles, Montenegrins, and Greeks filled their places. Many of the first cotton pickers who went west to California and Arizona were whites and blacks from Texas and the South. The composition of cotton-field labor in California changed several times, as Mexican and Filipino laborers came to predominate in the 1920s, followed by families of displaced and desperate whites from Oklahoma, Arkansas, and Texas in the late 1930s. When the defense boom of the early 1940s attracted "Okies" and "Arkies" to urban areas, where they took jobs in shipyards and aircraft factories, Hispanics returned to the fields once more.

Mexicans and Mexican Americans constituted the largest racial or ethnic minority among the workers of the West, although at various times Asians—Chinese, Japanese, and Filipinos—were numerous in certain industries. Compared with the South, the West outside Texas and Oklahoma had relatively few African Americans among its laborers. The proximity of the Mexican border to California's factories in the field, Arizona's copper camps, and Texas's orchards was of crucial importance. The revolution that kept Mexico in turmoil from 1910 to 1920, together with the completion of railway lines north to the border, encouraged thousands of Mexicans to flee to the United States to escape violence and economic uncertainty. Moreover, by taking jobs north of the border, they might triple their wages. In time, the area of Hispanic concentration formed a rough triangle, with its base extending along the Mexican border from San Diego to San Antonio and with its apex located at Denver. Outside California, Texas, and the

Both custom and law enforced the ethnic segregation of western laborers. Italian miners probably gathered in this Bingham Canyon, Utah, boardinghouse by choice, seeking the companionship of their countrymen. But laws could also dictate housing patterns. When this photograph of an all-white Texas housing project was taken in 1942, many Texas communities had three distinct, federally funded housing projects—for whites, blacks, and Mexicans.

Unidentified photographer. Italian Boarding House, Bingham Canyon, Utah. *Photograph, date unknown. Utah State Historical Society, Salt Lake City.*

Unidentified photographer. "No Mexican Children Allowed." *Gelatin silver print, 1942. Library of Congress (#LC-USZ62-89233), Washington, D.C.*

Southwest, Mexican workers remained relatively few until the labor shortages created by World War II gave rise to the Emergency Farm Labor Program (Bracero Program), which dispatched Mexican laborers to work as far north as the fields of Idaho, Oregon, and Washington.

Racial and ethnic prejudice was pervasive. Although some of the harvest workers were fifth-generation Californians or Texans, the Mexicans and Mexican Americans were almost always perceived as cheap and temporary labor. Between 1931 and 1934, in the depths of the Great Depression, an estimated one-third of the Mexican people of the United States were either deported or "repatriated" to Mexico, even though many of them had been born in the United States. In many southwestern mining communities, strict segregation existed between Hispanic and non-Hispanic miners. Other immigrants also were often segregated into distinct ethnic neighborhoods. The copper center of Ely, Nevada, for example, had separate enclaves commonly labeled "Greek Town" and "Jap Town."

In part because of the region's ethnic diversity, labor unions found that organizing in the West was seldom easy, and they never attracted a majority of the region's wageworkers, even in Washington and Colorado, which at various times were among the most highly unionized states in the country. Neither was organized labor's influence uniform throughout the West. Its chief centers of strength were the mining towns of the interior and the Pacific seaports of San Francisco, Tacoma, and Seattle. Labor's power was especially low in Idaho, which had few urban areas and little manufacturing, and in Utah, where the Mormon church vigorously promoted the freedom to work without having to join a labor union, and in New Mexico, where the economy was essentially pastoral. Yet even in Utah, organized labor made some surprising gains, as in 1896 when the state mandated an eight-hour day for workers in mines and smelters—a law the U.S. Supreme Court upheld in the case of *Holden v. Hardy* (1898). Arizona too was friendly to organized workers until the tensions of World War I caused an abrupt about-face.

San Francisco, by far the West's largest city, emerged as perhaps the most highly organized community in the nation in the early twentieth century. Workers in many vital industries were required to join unions. But even in San Francisco, union power fluctuated between periods of strength and weakness. From the depression of the 1890s until the aftermath of World War I, the twenty-five thousand members of the building trades were a dominant force in the economic, political, and social life of San Francisco. Through the Building Trades Council, they helped govern the city, in the process gaining a reputation for corruption. A full-scale effort by local businessmen and the national turn to the right in the 1920s undercut the power of the building trades. The spectacle of San Francisco's "labor barony" frightened businessmen in Los Angeles. As a result, organized labor there confronted some of the country's most outspoken proponents of the open shop, and union weakness was the rule. Leading the battle against organized labor were the powerful Merchants and Manufacturers' Association and Harrison Gray Otis, publisher of the *Los Angeles Times* and a one-time trade unionist turned bitter foe of organized labor.

A distinguishing trait of western organized labor was the popularity of industrial or all-inclusive unions, a natural result of the inordinately large number of laborers employed in the West's natural-resource-based industries. Between 1890 and the First World War, spokesmen for the West's laborers repeatedly asserted that they had little in common with the "labor aristocrats" who belonged to the cautious, craft-conscious American Federation of Labor (AFL) unions and railway brotherhoods. The AFL, in its pursuit of bread-and-butter gains like higher wages and shorter hours, wasted little time trying to organize unskilled laborers and operatives. In the West the AFL's exclusionary philosophy in effect abandoned thousands of workers in natural-resource-based industries to any alternative form of organization that might come along. As a consequence, many were drawn to industrial, inclusive, and even militant forms of labor organization, as well as to populist, anarchist, and socialist associations and political programs.

More than any other labor organization, it was the Western Federation of Miners (WFM) that served as a rallying point for western-oriented industrial unionists in the early twentieth century. Formed in 1893 in the aftermath of a bitter dispute in Idaho's Coeur d'Alene mining district, the WFM functioned as a bridge between the Knights of Labor, an idealistic and inclusive organization popular in parts of the West in the 1880s, and the Industrial Workers of the World (IWW), probably the most famous of all labor organizations in the region. Militant metal miners played a key role in organizing the IWW; events in Colorado supplied the connection between the two unions.

Several notorious examples of industrial violence punctuate the history of work life in the American West, but no state exceeded Colorado in the overall variety, duration, and severity of conflict between labor and management during the thirty years from 1890 to 1920. Nearly one hundred people died during the great coalfield war of 1913–14 with its notorious "massacre" at Ludlow, where in a single day, ten men and a child died in a fierce gun battle between the Colorado militia and striking miners, and two women and eleven children died of suffocation when victorious militiamen finally overran the strikers' tent colony, doused it with kerosene, and set it ablaze. Yet Colorado had been bloodier earlier. Nowhere else in the United States did the level of violence remain so high for so long as in the Colorado labor war of 1903–4, a time of dynamitings, deportations, and shootings. One violent explosion, set by a union sympathizer, ripped through a railroad station near Cripple Creek on the morning of 6 June 1904, killing thirteen nonunion miners.

The WFM, which a year earlier had called 3,500 metal miners of the Cripple Creek area out on a sympathy strike in an effort to support the wage demands of smelter workers, denied responsibility for the 6 June blast. But during the uproar of antiunion hostility that followed, Governor James Peabody imposed military rule on the district. Militia officers questioned 1,569 people and ultimately banished 238 of them. They were marched to Kansas and New Mexico and abandoned, much as would happen later in Bisbee. The WFM did not officially call off the Cripple Creek strike until 1907, although the strike had run its course by the end of 1904. After Cripple Creek, the WFM was for several years but a shadow of its former self. In the camps of Colorado's mineral belt, where in 1902 the WFM could claim a third of its 165 locals and a third of its 27,154 members, the union had virtually disappeared. To get a job, workers were required to hold cards issued by the Mine Owners' Association, and no known union men could get a card. The WFM sullenly licked its wounds, and in Chicago in 1905 it spearheaded the organization of an even more militant and more broadly based union called the Industrial Workers of the World.

Although Wobblies, as members of the IWW became popularly known, did not limit their activities to the West, their union found a more congenial home among the laborers of the West than perhaps anywhere else in the United States. The IWW program seemed especially tailored to meet the needs of those most alienated from the mainstream of society by the brutal working and living conditions frequently encountered in the West's camps and mills. At a time when nationally oriented trade unions concentrated their efforts on skilled white labor, Wobblies emphasized the solidarity of all workers—men and women, whites and blacks (even Asians, who were usually shunned because of their willingness to accept low wages). The IWW kept dues low and ignored political action, which in any case made little sense to workers who seldom remained in one place long enough to qualify to vote. Wobblies refused to sign contracts with employers, whom they regarded as mortal enemies. Confronting some of the roughest working conditions in the United States, the IWW exhibited a strain of militancy that was seemingly a natural by-product of the laborers' struggle for existence.

Wobblies burst into newspaper headlines in 1909 when they launched a spectacular and unorthodox protest called a "free-speech fight," a demonstration designed to call attention to the exploitation of harvest labor in the inland Pacific Northwest. For defying Spokane's ban on street-corner speaking, hundreds of Wobblies were arrested and hauled to jail. Nearly every inbound train brought more Wobblies to Spokane until the city, faced with a lack of jail space, mounting expenses, and bad publicity, declined to pursue the struggle. One of those imprisoned was Elizabeth Gurley Flynn, the "Rebel Girl," who particularly embarrassed city authorities by publishing a description of her sexual harassment in the city jail. The resulting outcry of moral indignation caused the city to provide better treatment for women prisoners. In the end, Spokane released the jailed Wobblies.

Wobblies naturally considered the free-speech fight a success and used the technique wherever they had a grievance to dramatize. But free-speech fights also gave Wobblies a defiant reputation that aroused deep anxieties among westerners and made the union vulnerable to vigilantism and other forms of repressive action. In California in 1910, the IWW had only a thousand members in eleven locals, but the fears they aroused were sufficient to prompt Fresno, San Diego, and several other cities to ban free-speech fights from their streets. This in turn led to confrontation and violence. Free-speech fights eventually spread to Vancouver, British Columbia, and about twenty other western communities before culminating in a bloody "massacre" in the sawmill town of Everett, Washington, in November 1916. In this clash an estimated twelve people, most of them Wobblies, died.

Violence, more than any other characteristic, was attributed to Wobblies, although it must be noted that in the West, violent episodes involving labor antedated Wobblies by more than three decades. The region's sometimes turbulent labor relations owed far more to the special circumstances of its work life than to any single organization or philosophy. Rather than initiate a new and violent era of labor-management relations, the IWW merely elaborated on a strain of militancy, even radicalism, that already existed among western workers. In this way, the Wobblies earned a prominent place in modern western folklore.

Several of the most celebrated episodes of violence in the early-twentieth-century West had nothing to do with Wobblies. These included Colorado's Ludlow troubles as well as the tremendous explosion that leveled the headquarters of the militantly antiunion *Los Angeles Times* in 1910, killing twenty employees. When two union activists, John J. and James B. McNamara, admitted their guilt after first pleading innocent, the whole western labor movement suffered. Widespread public support for organized labor evaporated, and antilabor ordinances passed in several communities. Union labor was stigmatized as a bloody organization.

Another explosion that appeared to have links to organized labor occurred on San Francisco's Market Street on 22 July 1916 during a Preparedness Day parade. The blast killed ten people and wounded forty others. Police arrested Tom Mooney and Warren K. Billings, union activists and labor radicals, but unlike the McNamara brothers, the accused San Francisco murderers maintained their innocence. Labor cried "frame-up." After a long and emotional trial based on the flimsiest of evidence, Mooney was sentenced to death and Billings to life in prison in 1917. The case remained a cause célèbre until Governor Culbert Olson finally resolved it by pardoning Mooney in 1939. The violent episodes of 1916 in San Francisco and Everett foreshadowed the rising tide of antilabor activity in the West during World War I. In time, however, the industrial violence diminished, notably so by the late 1930s, when workers, managers, and government established procedures to settle disputes peaceably. But one thing that did not change in the West were the boom-and-bust cycles that made life unpredictable both for business and for labor.

Living with a Boom-and-Bust Economy

During the years from 1917 to 1941, the West experienced two major cycles of boom and bust, together with the usual vexing seasonal alternations that had long typified the regional economy. The First World War brought unprecedented demands for the resources of the West. Oil producers dramatically stepped up output between 1917 and 1919. A rapidly expanding market for lumber from California, Texas, and the Pacific Northwest brought boom times to the woods. Slogans like "Wheat Will Win the War!" and government officials' lectures to farmers that production of food was their patriotic duty helped push the output of western agriculture to record highs. Farmers planted more acres, often on borrowed money; they expanded recklessly, enjoyed the boom times, and reaped a harvest of troubles when the fighting ceased. But until the bubble burst in 1920, the rural West had never before experienced such prosperity. Manufacturers prospered too during World War I. In the Pacific Northwest, shipbuilding expanded so rapidly that seemingly overnight it ranked second in size to the huge lumber industry. The war stimulated the new aircraft industry centered in Los Angeles, San Diego, and Seattle, where in 1916 a young lumberman named William E. Boeing founded a small company that eventually became a major manufacturer of aircraft.

Jobs were plentiful, both for men and for women, but for labor organizations like the controversial Industrial Workers of the World, the Great War was a disaster. After the United States entered the conflict in April 1917, hostility toward Wobblies

Motion pictures provided both popular western images and a major western industry. Coming of age in the 1920s, the film industry generally prospered during the depression as other businesses faltered and Americans looked to movies as an escape from their economic problems.

Dick Whittington Studio. RKO Pictures. Gelatin silver print, 1929. The Huntington Library, San Marino, California.

increased, since people believed them to be allies of enemy Germany. It was in the context of wartime zealotry that the Bisbee deportation occurred; and the Wobblies likewise suffered harassment in the woods of the Pacific Northwest where federal officials determined to take whatever steps were necessary to harvest spruce, a light, strong wood needed for aircraft construction. The IWW suffered an even more serious blow on 5 September 1917, when agents of the Justice Department, together with state and local officials, systematically raided IWW offices across the country and arrested 160 prominent Wobblies. Wartime prosecution nearly finished the IWW as an effective labor organization.

The war ended on 11 November 1918. Allied victory over Germany and the Central Powers brought Americans joy but not peace of mind. Replacing fear of German imperialism was fear of communism, which some Americans believed had spread from the newly formed Soviet Union to the United States, perhaps even to Seattle, where in February 1919 a general strike by sixty thousand organized workers shut down the city. Although Seattle's four-day "revolution" ended without bloodshed, and radicals did not control the strike (as opponents charged), it cost organized labor popular support and contributed to mounting national hysteria, known as the Red Scare. The culminating act of violence in the immediate postwar years occurred in Centralia, Washington, where on 11 November 1919 at least five lives were lost in a bloody clash between Wobblies and American Legionnaires, the latter group celebrating the first anniversary of the end of the Great War.

The end of war also required some extremely painful economic adjustments. The federal government's precipitous cancellation of war orders threatened the financial well-being of scores of manufacturers and other businesses and cost thousands of jobs. Plummeting commodity prices devastated farmers: from 1919 through 1921, farm prices in the United States fell by 40 percent, and the wartime boom turned into a deep agricultural depression, especially for the farmers and cattlemen of the interior West. One obvious casualty of the 1921 agricultural depression was optimism about the future. Many farmers now faced a period of hardship that lasted until World War II. For most western agrarians, the 1920s were anything but the "prosperity decade" experienced in other parts of the United States.

Whether westerners would remember the 1920s as a time of adversity or prosperity depended to a large extent on where they lived and what they did for a living. Californians would be far more likely than residents of other western states to recall the era positively. Those areas most dependent on timber, mining, and agriculture continued to be buffeted by dizzying cycles of boom and bust, although for a while the region's new commercial enterprises, notably Hollywood and tourism, seemed to offer prosperous alternatives. Tourism was certainly not new to the West in 1920; railroads had lured wealthy tourists west to Colorado, California, and the national parks for decades, but the industry found new prosperity after the automobile made inexpensive family travel possible and heralded the era of the "tin can" tourist.

The rise of Hollywood produced more than an upswing in tourism. After the film industry's beginnings in the Northeast, several moviemakers headed West, lured by a climate suitable for year-round outdoor production on a varied terrain just a short distance from the indoor studios. Some independent filmmakers relocated to the far Southwest and close to the Mexican border as a way to evade Thomas Edison and the "movie trust" with their pesky lawsuits charging nonmembers with infringing on their patents. By 1912 the Los Angeles area had the nation's largest concentration of motion picture companies, with many major studios clustered in the one-time temperance village of Hollywood. Moviemaking came of age during the mid-1920s, when it ranked first among California's thirty-five top industries and grossed far more than the state's fabled gold miners ever did in their heyday. By 1929 the movie industry employed one hundred thousand people; small outfits had grown or merged into industry giants like Metro-Goldwyn-Mayer, created in 1924.

Buoyed by its solid manufacturing base and the rise of new commercial enterprises, California prospered more than any other western state; except for the depression years of the 1930s, it seemed to enjoy a perpetual boom (at least until the 1990s). Even the agricultural depression of the 1920s scarcely fazed the Golden State. Increased irrigation enabled the Central Valley to become the nation's premier fruit and vegetable producer. The decade was also California's foremost era of oil production. The refining of petroleum ranked among the state's largest businesses and for several years after 1925 replaced even food processing as California's number-one manufacturing industry.

Thanks in part to the growing importance of food processing and oil refining, California rose steadily from the nation's twelfth-ranked manufacturing state in 1900 to eighth in 1940.

The population of the Golden State nearly doubled during the decade, reaching 5.7 million people in 1930. Approximately two-thirds of the newcomers settled in the southern part of the state, which experienced another of the spectacular real estate booms that had periodically erupted there since the 1880s. Naturally the state's construction industry thrived during the 1920s, as did seemingly any business related to automobiles. The mild sunny climate that permitted year-round outdoor filming also encouraged year-round driving. By the end of the twenties, California was home to 10 percent of the nation's twenty-three million automobiles and trucks. Los Angeles had the highest automobile registration per capita in the United States. The car culture spawned some of the nation's first shopping centers, supermarkets, and gasoline service stations, in addition to a host of other roadside businesses that catered to motorists.

Some of California's new arrivals during the boom of the 1920s came from Idaho and Montana, which because of continuing economic adversity showed the largest outmigrations of any western states between 1918 and 1933. Neither the stock market crash of 1929 nor the onset of hard times the following year represented an abrupt change from the economic malaise that had plagued the northern Rocky Mountain country since shortly after World War I. When the noted journalist Mark Sullivan visited Idaho in late 1932, he observed that the state was "literally the last community in the United States to feel the depression." He did not mean that as a compliment.

The Great Depression of the 1930s exacted an especially heavy toll in a region still heavily dependent on the production of lumber, minerals, and food for distant markets. The slowdown of manufacturing in the East devastated the natural-resource-based economy of the West. Not surprisingly, during the depression years of the 1930s the West experienced the slowest rate of growth for the entire twentieth century, and some states actually lost population as residents left in search of work elsewhere.

Despite California's enduring image as a land of opportunity, it too suffered along with the rest of the nation during the depression years, although Hollywood seemed to offer a conspicuous exception to the decline. Theater attendance around the nation remained strong, providing the dollars that kept cameras rolling in southern California. Yet even this glamour industry lost $83 million in 1932 and another $40 million in 1933. A worsening oil glut caused by major new discoveries in Texas cost Californians thousands of petrochemical jobs; still more were lost when the state's agricultural revenues plummeted from $750 million a year in 1929 to less than half that amount in 1932. In San Francisco, the unemployment rate shot up to almost 25 percent in 1932 and remained high for several more years. By 1934 there were 1.25 million people on relief in California, almost 20 percent of the state's population. Indigent people concentrated in the area of warm climate in southern California, where they attempted to survive on relief payments of $16.20 a month.

Throughout the West the unemployment crisis elicited a variety of responses. In heavily timbered portions of Idaho, some of the jobless ignited forest fires and then sought work putting them out. Washington apple growers created an enduring symbol

During the depression, overburdened state and local agencies posted warning signs to keep away displaced laborers seeking financial relief.

Unidentified photographer. "No Relief Funds" (eastern Idaho). Gelatin silver print, ca. 1935. Library of Congress (#LC-USF34-65540-D), Washington, D.C.

of the Great Depression when they sold fruit at $1.75 a crate to the unemployed, who then resold the apples, for a nickel apiece, on metropolitan street corners. Hoards of people, reminiscent of the armies of itinerant laborers common in the early part of the century, took to the roads and rails in search of jobs. Their numbers became such a burden in Wyoming that some towns required itinerants to work for room and board in special camps set up for them. The governor of Colorado declared martial law along the southern border and dispatched the National Guard to bar entry to indigent Mexicans, who he feared might take jobs from American citizens. The farce lasted only a few days. California authorities acted similarly after their state was inundated by whole families moving west in a desperate search for work: for several weeks in 1936, Los Angeles officials attempted to erect "bum barricades" on highways leading into the state from the east to turn back the unemployed. Courts ruled the procedure unconstitutional.

A primary response of the federal government to the Great Depression was the New Deal inaugurated in 1933 during the first months of Franklin D. Roosevelt's presidency. Yet even earlier, federal funds had been used to launch the construction of Boulder (now Hoover) Dam and provide loans to start work on the Oakland–San Francisco Bay Bridge. The New Deal dramatically increased the westward flow of federal dollars. Its programs ranged from building roads, dams, sidewalks, courthouses, and other public structures to cutting trails and seeking to eradicate blister rust fungus in Idaho's forests, all activities that created new job opportunities during the dark days of the 1930s. New Deal ameliorative programs pumped more dollars into Rocky

Mountain states per capita than into any others, yet that part of the West still had the highest percentage of unemployed workers in the country in 1940. At that time, 24 percent of New Mexico's work force was unemployed, the highest of any state.

The hard times of the 1930s initially meant continued trouble for organized labor in the West. The unions had endured a series of lean years during the 1920s, when business was clearly in the driver's seat and widespread and continued hostility toward organized labor had forced union members to give up many gains of previous years. The venerable Western Federation of Miners had become the International Union of Mine, Mill, and Smelterworkers in 1916, but like many of its counterparts during the 1920s, it lost important closed-shop agreements. Even in San Francisco, long the bastion of organized labor in the West, the once powerful Building Trades Council gave up ground to the businessmen who brought the open shop to the city. Throughout the West, organized labor in the 1920s showed less strength than at any other time since the 1870s and 1880s.

The 1930s depression brought massive unemployment, but the economic cataclysm also renewed the interest of workers in unions and other forms of collective action. Moribund organizations sprang back to life and made significant gains reminiscent of the opening years of the century. In the Rocky Mountain country, the Mine, Mill Union regained the closed shop in several generally nonviolent strikes. Even Wobblies, thought by many observers to be dead, briefly returned to the woods of northern Idaho and the fields and orchards of Washington's Yakima Valley. Actors like Groucho Marx and Ronald Reagan established a closed shop in Hollywood under the Screen Actors' Guild. Union membership in California tripled between 1933 and 1938, although open-shop sentiment remained strong in the southern part of the state until the rapid industrialization of World War II.

The ranks of organized labor ballooned as a result of federal legislation that encouraged collective bargaining. But the nearly uncontrolled growth of membership worsened friction between advocates of craft unionism and those of industrial unionism, the latter always numerous in the West, even in some AFL unions. When the American Federation of Labor expelled industrial unionists in 1937, dissidents formed the Congress of Industrial Organizations (CIO) the following year. Labor rivalry grew especially bitter on the Pacific Coast, where the aggressive CIO in many ways embodied the fiery militancy of the Industrial Workers of the World. The strength of the CIO lay in the timber and mining industries, in fish canneries, and on the waterfront.

The single most important labor disturbance on the West Coast during the 1930s was the great maritime strike of 1934. It occurred when the International Longshoremen's Association challenged the hated "shape-up" whereby longshoremen arrived on the docks early in the morning and waited for company foremen to select a fortunate few for the day's work, often receiving a kickback from the men chosen. When some 3,500 longshoremen quit work, they were joined by members of various marine unions. Together, they tied up ports from Seattle to San Diego for almost four months. Frightened residents came to believe that the strike was a Communist plot and that the ranks of subversives included the strike leader, Harry Bridges. In San Francisco in July 1934, the dispute erupted into a pitched battle between strikers and police. This in turn led to a three-day general strike that idled 127,000 workers. Shortly after this show of force, the walkout ended; through arbitration, the longshoremen won most of their demands, including an end to the hated shape-up.

Not only strikes but also schism marked this time in labor history. The craft-oriented AFL vigorously warred against the upstart CIO and labor radicalism. Spear-heading the AFL opposition on the West Coast was Dave Beck, a fast-rising star in the Teamsters' Union. Capitalizing on the revolution in motor transport, Beck rapidly moved through Teamster ranks—from organizing laundry drivers in Seattle to being elected national head of the Teamsters' Union in 1952–62. In the mid-1930s Beck was easily the Teamsters' most powerful regional leader and the dominant personality in Northwest labor. For example, in the late 1930s when the forces of Harry Bridges, a labor radical from Australia who headed the Longshoremen's Union of the CIO, attempted to "march inland" from the docks to protect their flanks by organizing warehousemen, Beck countered with club-swinging squads of hired thugs. In time the economy improved, and both the strikes and labor's internecine warfare diminished. Beck even came to be regarded as a respectable citizen of Washington, where he served on numerous state boards and committees (although in the 1960s he served thirty months in prison for income-tax evasion). Bridges remained under a cloud of suspicion despite his repeated denials of being a Communist.

During the same years that Bridges and Beck gained national prominence as labor leaders, two western entrepreneurs gained similar recognition in the fields of banking and construction. Amadeo Peter Giannini and Henry J. Kaiser emerged in the popular mind as visionary leaders of an informal crusade to liberate the region from overdependence on eastern capital and business leadership. Their actions and public pronouncements illustrate how the western complaint of eastern economic colonialism, whether valid or not, might be used to advantage by astute westerners.

Starting in 1904 at the age of thirty-four, with no formal education in banking, Giannini launched his Bank of Italy with modest capital and an equally modest ambition of meeting the financial needs of the common folk of San Francisco. The city's money establishment initially dismissed the upstart as nothing more than a "dago bank" serving the "foreign colony" of the North Beach area. But after the 1906 earthquake, Giannini rapidly expanded and soon became a pioneer in the field of branch banking. In this way he enlarged the Bank of Italy into a giant that by 1930 controlled 40 percent of California's banking capital. Renamed that year as the Bank of America, it grew until in October 1945 its seventy-five-year-old founder proudly announced that the San Francisco–based firm had surpassed New York's Chase National Bank to become the world's largest bank. Throughout his life, Giannini chafed at what he perceived to be the West's subservient status and took inordinate pride whenever western businessmen surpassed their eastern counterparts. During World War II the Bank of America was a leader in financing the West's rapidly expanding industrial base, particularly the California aircraft industry, long dominated by eastern banks.

Another celebrated attempt to declare economic independence from the East was the formation of the Six Companies that built the sixty-story-high Boulder Dam across the Colorado River. Henry J. Kaiser, a highway contractor who would one day control an industrial empire from his Oakland, California, headquarters, regarded the chance to build the massive dam as a key to large-scale industrial development of the West by westerners. He believed that if western contractors combined their talents to build the dam—the world's largest construction venture to that time—they would pick up the lucrative contracts sure to follow. This would end long-standing eastern domination of the construction industry and help shift economic power from the East to the West.

The Six Companies, a consortium mainly of little-known western construction companies, was incorporated in 1931 and won the largest single contract let by the United States to that time (fifty million dollars). The Six Companies successfully completed Boulder Dam four years later, and true to Kaiser's prophecy, individual contractors went on to become multinational giants in their own right. Kaiser himself had a hand in constructing both Bonneville and Grand Coulee dams on the Columbia River and in time became a major player in cement, magnesium, steel, aluminum, and housing. Along the way, an enormous line of credit (forty-five million dollars) from the Bank of America plus money from Uncle Sam helped Kaiser to launch a career in shipbuilding during World War II.

According to Carey McWilliams in *California: The Great Exception*, who sounded a cautionary note, the antiestablishment rhetoric of men like Giannini and Kaiser could be used as a "smokescreen" to conceal certain aspects of California's growing dominance over other western states. California, no less than Wall Street, could become a colonizer of less populous parts of the region. Well before World War II, California had emerged as the colossus of the Far West.

From World War to Cold War

No event in the twentieth century, not even the Great Depression or the New Deal, brought more dramatic economic changes to the West than World War II. In much of the region it touched off an economic boom and significantly altered the traditional reliance on a natural-resource-based economy. On the eve of war, the West was still mainly a producer of raw materials shipped east to be made into finished products. That quickly changed as billions of federal dollars flooded the West to fund construction of a host of new military training facilities and war industries. California alone received 10 percent of all federal spending during the war. Some of those dollars took the form of huge aircraft factories that arose from the pea fields and orange groves of southern California. Here was the West's greatest concentration of aircraft factories, and airplane manufacturing became one of California's chief industries. Lockheed, for example, which built only thirty-seven planes in 1937, produced eighteen thousand between 1941 and 1945. When Uncle Sam poured more than five billion dollars into California for ships, employment in the shipyards of San Francisco Bay expanded from 4,000 to 260,000 jobs. Kaiser put together a shipbuilding empire that stretched from San Francisco Bay to the Columbia River. At the peak of production, his yards launched a new ship every ten hours and earned Kaiser the sobriquet "Sir Launchalot."

Kaiser, who regarded the war as one more chance to promote what he called "higher industrialization," became a major player in the West's new aluminum industry, which began in Vancouver, Washington, in 1940 with the opening of an Alcoa plant. Kaiser eventually built and operated five aluminum plants in the Pacific Northwest. By 1956 his Kaiser Aluminum Company was responsible for 25 percent of the nation's output. Kaiser also wanted to produce steel, but the federal government financed the construction of a big steel plant near Provo, Utah, and leased it instead to a subsidiary of U.S. Steel. Backed by Giannini and his banking muscle, Kaiser persisted and eventually won federal funding for a steel mill at Fontana, California, a site fifty miles east of Los Angeles. When his Fontana plant came on-line, Kaiser boosted the state's output of steel by 70 percent.

Oil production once again boomed in California, Texas, and other parts of the West during World War II. These were also the first prosperous years in two decades for lead and silver in Idaho and for zinc and molybdenum in Colorado. Copper boomed too, bringing newfound prosperity to Arizona, Nevada, Montana, and Utah. The huge open-pit mine in Bingham Canyon alone employed seven thousand of Utah's one hundred thousand workers.

As part of a deliberate effort to decentralize the nation's production of vital war materials, Tucson, Phoenix, Albuquerque, and Denver became sites of new defense-related industries. At the Denver Arms plant, which the federal government built in 1941, Remington Rand and later Henry Kaiser employed as many as twenty thousand workers, about 40 percent of the city's factory personnel, to make armaments such as cartridges, shells, and fuses. Even ships were built in land-locked Denver, such as the USS *Mountain Maid* completed in the spring of 1942. Near Denver, the Rocky Mountain Arsenal and its work force of fifteen thousand made chemical weapons. After the war, Denver's war industries spawned a host of defense-related businesses that included the manufacture of ballistic weapons and space hardware.

During the early years of the war, new production techniques transformed both aircraft and shipbuilding from craft to mass-production industries. This decreased the need for skilled labor and opened the doors to a variety of people who had never before been inside a shipyard or an aircraft factory. Filling thousands of jobs at Lockheed, Douglas, and a number of other aircraft companies were many Okies who had first found employment in California agriculture.

The number of lines in the "help wanted" section of the *Seattle Times* jumped from 28,631 during the first nine months of 1940 to 225,515 during the same period in 1943. Employers paid good wages and competed with one another for workers. Said one Boeing official, "We hired anybody who had a warm body and could walk through the gate." At the peak of wartime aircraft production, Boeing hired fifty-five thousand workers, 46 percent of whom were women. Nearby at the sprawling Puget Sound Naval Shipyard, women formed 21 percent of the thirty thousand workers in 1943. As recently as 1941, the facility had not employed any women outside the offices. During the war, nearly a quarter million blacks, many from rural backwaters of the South, moved to California, where most took jobs in the shipbuilding industries of Los Angeles, Oakland, San Francisco, and Richmond. Thousands more came after the war when California's economy continued to boom.

To deal with the shortage of housing for workers at his Portland and Vancouver shipyards, Kaiser built an entirely new town on the low-lying banks of the Columbia

River just north of Portland. Called Kaiserville and then Vanport, it became one of the largest housing projects in the world. By the end of the war, the instant community of 35,000 people had become the second-largest city in Oregon. The population of Richmond, California, the location of another major Kaiser shipyard, grew from 23,000 to 115,000. San Diego's population doubled. Los Angeles ended the war as America's third-largest city; it also climbed from the seventh-largest manufacturing center before the war to the nation's second largest after Detroit.

Much of the mountain West served as a labor reservoir for booming war industries on the coast. Idaho, except for Camp Farragut and a large naval ordnance plant in Pocatello, contributed mainly its manpower and the traditional products of its mines, forests, and fields to the war effort. The state lost 15,000 residents between 1940 and 1945. Most of them apparently moved to Oregon and Washington, which gained 194,000 and 533,000 new residents respectively. Montanans also headed west to Seattle in record numbers; by late 1943 that state had lost 88,000 people while Seattle gained almost the same number. Pacific Coast shipyards and aircraft factories drew Anglo workers from both Arizona and New Mexico while Hispanics and Indians remained behind to take jobs on railroads, farms, and construction projects.

Organized labor experienced a great influx of new members during the war, but life in the burgeoning union ranks was not harmonious. Industrial workers who were recruited from rural regions and small towns typically regarded unions with apathy or even antagonism and often resented paying any dues. The addition of females and blacks to the industrial work force further disrupted several unions. When blacks in the aircraft and shipbuilding industries applied for union membership, racial antipathy became evident. At Boeing, the union refused to admit blacks and in effect contributed to shaping company policy: Boeing hired only a small number of blacks during the war. Kaiser opposed racial discrimination, but nearly all his employees were members of metal trades unions that had no desire to admit blacks to membership. The Boilermakers' Union, for example, segregated black shipyard workers into auxiliary unions and blocked them from holding skilled jobs. Blacks paid dues but had no voice in union matters, and when the war ended, they found that their classification as temporary members gained them no seniority in the scramble for jobs.

Many westerners feared a return to hard times when World War II ended. In reality, however, the passage from war to peace was surprisingly smooth, especially when compared with the troubled aftermath of World War I. Wartime savings, terminal-leave pay, and unemployment compensation discouraged the kind of desperate search for jobs that had followed the 1918 armistice. Some of the West's war plants closed briefly only to reopen as other industries. Soldiers who had first glimpsed the West in training camps often returned after the war and added to a population boom. For a time, bulldozers ripped out three thousand acres of orange groves a day in Los Angeles County to make way for hundreds of new housing developments. In Arizona, where industrial output fell from eighty-five million dollars in 1945 to fifty-three million dollars a year later, a booming construction industry created many new jobs. An inadequate number of houses built during the Great Depression and war years, coupled with the nation's move to suburbia and an increased rate of family formation, kept the West's forest products industry producing at record levels for several years after the war, although at the cost of further depleting the region's timber supply.

In a real sense, World War II never ended. The infusion of federal dollars into the western economy, which had become so noticeable during the New Deal and World War II years, continued with the cold war. From the 1940s through the 1980s, federal investments in science, defense, reclamation, and highways all combined to further industrialization and urbanization of the West. The rising tide of federal investment in sophisticated military and aerospace technology was especially pronounced in southern California, in the urban Southwest and Texas, and around Puget Sound. "Air power is peace power," declared William Allen, president of Seattle's Boeing Aircraft, which prospered once again from defense orders after a brief postwar slump. Cold war fears kept many of the West's defense plants busy, notably those of the aerospace giants Boeing, Lockheed, and Douglas, all of which manufactured jet aircraft, intercontinental ballistic missiles, and space equipment. In the 1960s, shortly after the National Aeronautics and Space Administration was organized, the new federal agency spent 50 percent of its funds in California.

By 1958, Boeing alone employed seventy-three thousand people and added thousands more to assemble its model 707, the world's first successful jet passenger airplane, as well as to build military equipment. In the process, the state of Washington traded dependence on the forest products industry for dependence on the manufacture of transportation equipment. Defense-based industries also became a major employer in postwar Utah, where as recently as 1941 the economy had been almost entirely dependent on agriculture and mining. The aerospace industry gave Utah's economy a major boost, with the biggest facility being the Thiokol Chemical Company west of Brigham City, which produced the first solid fuel for rockets (and later, as Morton-Thiokol, built booster rockets for the ill-fated space shuttle *Challenger*).

Construction and operation of vast nuclear weapons facilities spurred economic growth in several parts of the West. These facilities ranged from the Hanford Engineer Works in central Washington, where plutonium for atomic bombs was produced, to the Nevada Test Site, where federal authorities conducted 105 atmospheric tests of atomic weapons between 1951 and 1962. Albuquerque boomed as a center of atomic age research. Seventy-five miles north of the city by air was the atomic physics laboratory at Los Alamos, and closer at hand was the Sandia complex that designed bomb cases and components. The number of employees at the Sandia Corporation increased from thirty-eight hundred in 1951 to seventy-eight hundred ten years later, and its payroll became the largest in New Mexico. For a time, Albuquerque proudly billed itself as the nation's "Atomic City." The atomic West also extended into a remote part of Idaho, where federal scientists developed the first atomic reactor to power submarines and trained crewmen for the nation's nuclear navy. They even made plans to use the atom to power airplanes, though the idea was never implemented. By 1990 the Idaho National Engineering Laboratory provided about 5 percent of the state's jobs and employed military and civilian scientists in a variety of research projects involving atomic energy, lasers, and biotechnology. For a time, it seemed as if the cold war would buoy the western economy forever.

The New Economic Equation

Military hardware, aerospace, and electronics, together with tourism, became key elements in the West's new economic equation after World War II. One unlikely pioneer of the high-tech West was Howard Hughes, the playboy son of a Texas oil-bit manufacturer who got his start in the Spindletop boom of 1901. Young Hughes came to Los Angeles in the 1920s and initially used his father's money to distinguish himself as a filmmaker and aviation enthusiast. By the mid-1930s he had established Hughes Aircraft in Burbank, which eventually specialized in electronics. After World War II, Hughes brought thousands of scientists, technicians, and other skilled workers to his southern California facility and cashed in on the first peacetime defense boom in the nation's history. With his holdings in Hughes Aircraft of California and Hughes Tool of Texas, he was probably the wealthiest man in America, although as Hughes grew older and richer he became more eccentric.

William Hewlett and David Packard launched a modest electronics business in a small garage in Palo Alto, California, in 1939. Their first breakthrough product was an audio oscillator. From this seed grew an industry that made both men very rich and transformed the agricultural Santa Clara Valley into the center of high technology now known as Silicon Valley. The name became a byword for California's computer industry, although several similar concentrations of technology emerged in the 1970s and 1980s in Orange County, on Puget Sound, and in cities as diverse as Boise and Phoenix. In Bellevue and Redmond, Washington, the rapid growth of the software giant Microsoft made its chairman, William Henry Gates III, the world's youngest billionaire.

Entrepreneurial westerners also made fortunes from less glamorous endeavors, as John Richard Simplot did from pigs and a small plot of Idaho potatoes. His big boost came when World War II created an enormous demand for dehydrated potatoes, onions, and other food products needed to feed the troops. During the war, Simplot became a supplier of dehydrated food and the world's "biggest potato farmer." The modern J. R. Simplot Company of Boise, a constellation of enterprises that range from food processing and chemical fertilizers to mining and ranching, supplies the McDonald's restaurant business with over half its french fries. In the October 1990 issue, *Forbes* magazine listed Simplot and another of Idaho's homegrown entrepreneurs, the supermarket king Joseph A. Albertson, among the four hundred richest people in America.

During the decades after 1945, several cities of the interior West, including Denver and Phoenix, reached sufficient size to put together much of the financing needed to fuel the postwar boom. The explosive growth of Arizona was financed in part by Walter Bimson and his Valley National Bank, which in their aggressiveness resembled Giannini and the Bank of America. As a result of the economic impact of World War II, Giannini himself bragged, "[The] West has all the money to finance whatever it wants to; we no longer have to go to New York for financing, and we are not at its mercy." Los Angeles and San Francisco banks continued to grow in power with the creation of new giants like Los Angeles–based First Interstate and the expansion of Bank of America through the purchase of Seattle's Seafirst bank. In banking, as in numerous other areas, Los Angeles came to rival San Francisco as a center of economic power on the Pacific Rim, home to a multitude of multinational corporations, banks, and insurance companies. California ranked second only to New York as America's banking and financial power. Long the nation's leading agricultural state, California grew in importance as a manufacturing center, with employment in that sector increasing between 1970 and 1980 at a rate more than five times that of the rest of the country. California, and to a lesser extent other western states, also benefited from the booming trade with Pacific Rim nations, especially Japan. Not without reason would Governor Jerry Brown in the late 1970s refer to his state as "the Pacific Republic of California."

In California, as in several other western states, tourism boomed after the war. When gasoline rationing ended, tourists withdrew money from their bulging savings accounts and swarmed across the "Golden West" in record numbers. The number of visitors to Washington's Mount Rainier in 1946 broke all previous records. National parks had long been recognized as tourist draws, especially so as the region's network of all-weather roads expanded and more Americans acquired the automobiles, money, and leisure time that allowed them to explore all corners of the West. One of the best-known natural attractions was Yellowstone, the nation's oldest national park, which during summer seasons in the mid-1950s lured four times as many people through its gates as lived in the entire state of Wyoming. Glacier National Park attracted more visitors each season than lived in Montana. Interior Secretary Harold Ickes correctly prophesied of Olympic

National Park, which was established in 1938, "In the long run it will mean more for the State of Washington to have a real national park on the Olympic Peninsula than it will be to log this area, either selectively or otherwise."

Another of the West's increasingly popular tourist draws was snow skiing. This industry essentially dates from the mid-1930s when the Union Pacific Railroad opened its posh Sun Valley, Idaho, resort complex, the West's first major ski facility. The demands of World War II temporarily blocked expansion of this promising new form of tourism, and Sun Valley itself was converted into a navy convalescent center. When the conflict ended, just two ski areas in Colorado were operating, with their business confined mainly to weekends. But what Sun Valley began continued after World War II with the development of new winter vacation facilities throughout the West. In Colorado, the pacesetter for winter sports activities, some of the most popular facilities were located in refurbished mining towns like Aspen and Telluride. Still others were in Vail, a new, planned community.

By 1980 tourism had become the largest industry in California. Tourism was actually an old business in the Golden State, but it evolved in a new direction after 1955 when Disneyland opened amid the orange groves of Anaheim. Before that, amusement parks catered mainly to local populations, but Disneyland was a national attraction. It drew four million visitors the first year and in time became one of America's most popular tourist stops. Disneyland also helped to transform the Anaheim–Santa Ana area into a regional rival of downtown Los Angeles. One of Disneyland's popular sections was a fantasy frontier complete with a Mark Twain–era steamboat and a runaway mine train. Outside the park, vestiges of the West's real frontier like Virginia City, both in Montana and in Nevada, discovered how to lure tourists by refurbishing and emphasizing the look of mining boom days, unconsciously, perhaps, borrowing from Disney. In dozens of such communities scattered throughout the West, from Tombstone, Arizona, to Jacksonville, Oregon, look-alike shops sold tourists much the same assortment of trinkets, T-shirts, and taffy.

An unusual form of tourism developed in Nevada, where gambling became a major contributor to the state's economy after World War II. The state had legalized gambling as early as 1931, but old ways of doing business persisted for several more years. Gambling took place in dark, secluded halls where dealers worked in shirtsleeves and wore green eyeshades. Raymond Smith took a different approach at his Harold's Club, which was located on Reno's main street, its glass front revealing brightly lit bars and gaming tables. By the end of the 1930s, Smith's advertisements reading "Harolds Club or Bust" were on billboards scattered across the country and helped launch gambling as a tourist draw.

Until World War II, gambling centered in Reno. Its chief rival, Las Vegas, remained little more than the dusty, railroad division town it had been for the previous forty years. The war, however, changed the character of the town. By 1946 Las Vegas had a population of approximately twenty thousand and was already on its way to becoming the neon-and-chrome oasis it is today. By the 1950 census, it had sixty-five thousand residents, and that was only the beginning of a time of spectacular growth.

The city's first modern casino was the Gold Nugget, which opened in 1946. It was located downtown, but the center of action quickly moved south of Las Vegas to "the

Strip," where a string of new casinos competed with one another in lavishness of decor and Hollywood entertainment. The colorful crime figure Benjamin "Bugsy" Siegel built the Flamingo Hotel, among the first and most lavish casinos on the Strip, with one million dollars of his own money and another six million of borrowed money. When the venture did poorly, Siegel became a victim of a gangland slaying at his home in Los Angeles and drew national attention to the problem of gangster infiltration of Nevada's lucrative new industry. It took a series of unsavory revelations about organized crime before Nevada attempted to clean house. Not until 1955 was any serious effort made to bring the state's gambling industry under government regulation, and nothing substantial happened until the late 1960s. Some problems with organized crime persisted through the 1980s. In any case, gambling accounted for 32 percent of all Nevada jobs in the 1980s, with another 25 percent in related employment.

Overall, the West's new service and high-tech industries enjoyed reasonably good health during the postwar decades, but even they were not immune to the region's old nemesis of boom-and-bust cycles, as the Boeing company demonstrated time and again in western Washington. By the mid-1950s, aircraft manufacturing employed more people in the Evergreen State than logging and lumbering, as compared with less than one-seventh as many before the war. Boeing was by far Washington's largest private employer. Boeing's economic well-being was tied to two markets—civilian aircraft and military weaponry. In 1970, when the company was hard hit by the failure of Congress to fund a supersonic transport plane, employment dropped from a little over one hundred thousand to thirty-eight thousand, and about fifty-five thousand people left the state in search of work. In the Seattle and Everett metropolitan area, unemployment reached 13 percent in 1971, the highest in the United States. The real estate market virtually collapsed, a fact hard to recall twenty years later when the Puget Sound area experienced soaring home prices and a superheated economy. California, like Washington, suffered greatly when recession hit the aerospace industry in the 1970s. Between 1967 and 1972, the number of aerospace jobs in California declined from 616,000 to 450,000. The state's unemployment rate climbed to more than 7 percent, compared with 6 percent for the United States as a whole.

The West's high-tech industries also suffered competitive pressures from Japan, Korea, and Singapore and thus provided no real antidote to boom and bust. For all their glamour, many high-tech industries proved little better than highly sophisticated sweatshops, employing large work forces of unskilled, low-income, nonunion labor. That was only one of the trends that did not bode well for organized workers in the postwar decades. For example, right-to-work laws weakened the power of labor unions in several western states. Arizona passed the first of these in the late 1940s by popular referendum; Nevada, Utah, and Idaho established similar laws during the following decades.

Nationwide, the number of manufacturing workers who belonged to unions fell noticeably in the latter half of the 1980s. The result in Arizona, for instance, was that less than 4 percent of the state's manufacturing workers were unionized. For unskilled workers, the future looked especially grim in the desert Southwest. There the trend toward jobs that required more education and higher levels of skill brought social dislocation to the poorest, least-prepared members of the work force. Still another disconcerting development that began in the 1960s was the rise of *maquiladora* ("twin plant") industrial parks along the Mexican border. Expensive U.S. components were imported duty free into Mexico, where they were assembled in these factories with low-cost Mexican labor and shipped back to the United States, with manufacturers paying duty only for the cost of assembly.

The *maquiladora* system rapidly expanded after devaluation of the Mexican peso; from 620 plants in 1980, the number increased to more than 1,400 by 1988, and the number of jobs the factories provided in Mexico went from 100,000 to 400,000. In Nogales, Arizona, and Mexican Sonora, some fifty companies, including some of the largest in the United States, established twin plants. In 1988 they employed 22,000 people in Mexico and another 1,250 on the Arizona side. Every day one hundred truckloads of *maquila* goods were shipped across the border at Nogales into the United States. This use of low-cost Mexican labor was one way that American automotive and electronics companies sought to meet Japanese competition.

An additional omen of a grim future for western labor was the increasing number of jobs in the tourist industry, which often paid near minimum wages, balanced against a decreasing number of jobs in industries like logging and mining, where the pay was much higher. In an affluent tourist community like Sun Valley, Idaho, which evolved in recent years from a winter sports mecca to a year-round resort, many service workers could not afford the skyrocketing price of local real estate and had to drive to work from homes located as far away as Twin Falls, seventy miles distant. The story was much the same in Jackson Hole, Wyoming, and numerous other upscale resort communities in the West.

Affluence and Anxiety

During the years from 1945 to 1990, it became increasingly clear that there were really two Wests, economically speaking. One was oriented toward sophisticated technology and service industries like tourism, whereas the other was still dependent on the production of natural resources. Timber and mining boomed after World War II and into the 1970s and then, along with agriculture and mining, suffered a collapse that lasted well into the 1980s. The globe seemed awash in natural resources, and this glut hit the West hard. The region suffered its worst economic crisis since the 1930s.

Arizona accounted for 60 percent of the copper produced in the United States until foreign competition flooded the country with copper in the 1970s and caused mines all over the West to close. In Montana, where even the capitol dome is made of copper, the red metal seemed to suffer an especially slow and agonizing death, at least when mirrored in the declining fortunes of the Anaconda Company. The copper giant relinquished control of its several newspapers in 1959; during the next decade Anaconda and its ally Montana Power relaxed their hold on the state legislature. In 1975 Anaconda became a subsidiary of the Atlantic-Richfield Company, but this did not arrest the decline. Five years later, and little more than a century after commercial quantities of copper were first discovered in Montana, the company's closure of its giant smelter at Anaconda cost the jobs of two thousand Montanans. In 1983 the company closed its remaining copper pit in Butte: the great Berkeley pit that Anaconda had opened in 1955 slowly filled with tainted water. Metals mines reopened in Montana in the late 1980s, but when

The western uranium industry, once seen as a boon to Navajo miners and others in the Southwest, is now viewed as an environmental and health disaster responsible for water and soil contamination and widespread illness and death among the miners.

Laura Gilpin (1891–1979). Navajo Uranium Miner (Lukachukai Mountains, Arizona). Gelatin silver print, 1953. Copyright Amon Carter Museum. Laura Gilpin Collection, Amon Carter Museum, Fort Worth, Texas.

production resumed in natural-resource-based industries like mining and timber, facilities were invariably more highly automated, less labor-intensive, and often non-union.

In the early 1980s Nevada was another of the states beset by the worst slump in mining in forty years. Ironically, however, even as copper became an insignificant factor in the state's economy, Nevada experienced a new gold rush, centered in the Battle

Mountain area. Like the low-grade copper deposits of an earlier era, all the new gold mines were open-pit. Microscopic particles of gold could be recovered even from the tailings of earlier mine operations.

Not just metals but also the energy resources of coal, oil, and uranium experienced boom-and-bust cycles in the decades after World War II. For a time in the early 1950s, action centered in uranium deposits on the Colorado Plateau in the Four Corners area. Resembling a new Klondike rush, the search for uranium embodied the American dream of sudden wealth. Any person could stake a uranium claim on public land for $1.00 and, armed with a Geiger counter, might strike it rich. One of the lucky ones was Charles Steen, who made a $150-million uranium find near Moab, Utah, and seemingly overnight transformed the sleepy cattle and ranch center. Moab eagerly embraced the title of "The Uranium Capital of the World." The frenzied hunt was yet another facet of the cold war in the West and the belief that uranium was needed to maintain nuclear weapons superiority over the Soviet Union. Uranium finders thus had a ready customer in the federal government, which was desperate for a domestic source of the yellow metal.

During the uranium boom of the 1950s, Grants, New Mexico, grew from a ranch supply town of five hundred people to become the nation's largest uranium-milling center, with a population of ten thousand. In 1958 the six uranium mills in Grants produced ore worth $115 million. The pace slackened in the early 1950s when the Atomic Energy Commission decreased its uranium purchases, but the yellow metal boomed again in the 1960s and 1970s when the nuclear power industry expanded. The cycle again reversed itself in the early 1980s when the price of uranium plummeted from $43 to $17 a pound amid growing public skepticism about the safety of nuclear power. After the collapse, one thousand men lost their jobs in Wyoming, where Jeffrey City became a uranium ghost town. Of some two thousand uranium workers in Utah in 1960, fewer than four hundred remained employed after the bust. The story was much the same in New Mexico.

Oil, coal, and gas fared better. In the mid-1950s the discovery of oil and gas in the San Juan Basin around Farmington, New Mexico, led to the construction of numerous pipelines, one of which extended sixteen hundred miles to carry natural gas to the Pacific Northwest. In 1949, Montana's oil output for the first time exceeded the value of its copper production, and the city of Billings rode the crest of several successive oil booms. Moving to the forefront of energy development in the late 1970s was the "overthrust belt" in western Colorado and Wyoming. Here California oil giants like Getty, Arco, Champlin, Chevron, and Occidental became new colonizers of the western hinterlands, along with eastern corporations like Exxon. The latter company issued rosy predictions that by the year 2010, production from oil shale in the geologically distinctive overthrust belt would employ 480,000 people in mining, 390,000 in processing plants, and 250,000 in construction during peak years.

Encouraged by rising oil prices and predicted global shortages, Congress in 1980 approved an ambitious goal of producing two million barrels a day from coal and oil shale (synfuel) by 1992. That would mean the construction of thirty to forty mammoth coal and oil shale plants, each costing from one to six million dollars. Residents of Rifle,

Meeker, and other small towns in northwestern Colorado braced for a boom, all the while hoping to avoid becoming another Rock Springs, a Wyoming community that became a byword for social dislocation caused by too rapid development. In the end, the promise of oil from shale proved to be a mirage. By the winter of 1981–82, Occidental Petroleum had closed its operations in the face of economic change, notably the slumping price of conventional oil. Exxon followed by shutting down its Colony Project in May 1982. Once again, the tired refrain of boom and bust led to jobs, good wages, and plenty of overtime followed by massive unemployment and social problems.

In the late 1970s, while energy jobs were plentiful and money abounded, there was an outburst of anger from people who feared another "rape of the West" by "outside" capital, some of which would actually come from places inside the region like Denver and Los Angeles. But by the mid-1980s, oil optimism had run its course, grass grew in the streets of some of the energy boomtowns, and the "sagebrush rebellion" had quieted. *Newsweek* magazine in 1989 evoked the ire of many westerners when it described the northern tier states from Washington to the Dakotas as "America's Outback."

Of all the energy minerals, coal staged the most dramatic and longest-lasting comeback. As late as the 1950s, the western coal industry remained in a declining or, at best, stagnant condition. In 1956 the Northern Pacific Railway liquidated its subsidiary, the Northwestern Improvement Company, which had provided mining jobs at Roslyn, Washington, and Colstrip, Montana. Coal was simply not competitive when the price of oil was three dollars a barrel. But then came a series of sharp price increases for oil, and Colstrip made a remarkable comeback. When the first dedicated coal train left Colstrip for an electric-generating plant in Minnesota in 1969, it marked the dawn of a new era. As in open-pit metal mining, however, the reborn coal industry employed remarkably far fewer people than it had earlier. In Colstrip in 1972, strip-mining methods used only 150 men to produce 5.5 million tons of coal.

In October 1973, the Arab-Israeli War sent the price of oil up to thirteen dollars a barrel and further spurred coal production in Wyoming and Montana. The energy boom of the 1970s and 1980s probably affected no western state more than Wyoming. For a time coal production increased 20 percent annually. The state's Powder River basin, where forty billion tons of subbituminous coal lay buried beneath the soil of Campbell County, became the nation's new energy frontier. During the energy boom, the town of Gillette grew from four thousand people in 1969 to fourteen thousand in 1980. Just to haul the black diamonds to market, railroad construction crews laid 226 miles of new track in the 1970s. A decade later, coal from the Powder River country accounted for 35 percent of the receipts of the Burlington Northern, then the longest railroad in the United States.

Even as the West's coal industry enjoyed its newfound prosperity, the timber industry slumped once again. A variety of economic problems closed sawmills across the Pacific Northwest in the early 1980s. Chief causes of the trouble in timber country were the revival of southern pine forests (which Pacific northwesterners had once cavalierly dismissed as having the quality of weeds), competition from Canadian imports, a housing slump caused by high interest rates, and a shifting market. When the timber industry rebounded, as it did in the late 1980s, innovative technology that included computers and lasers enabled modern sawmills to employ far fewer hands than they had only a decade earlier. These were permanent changes, as they were in the mineral industries, and they clearly illustrated that riding the cycle of boom and bust did not mean that with the return of prosperity would come the return of all the former jobs. In sawmill towns, ranging from Garibaldi on the coast of Oregon to Potlatch in the pine forests of northern Idaho, an era had ended forever. A grassy field replaced the sprawling mill complex in Potlatch, which survived as a bedroom community; Garibaldi's mill became a storage facility for yachts and other pleasure boats. Never again would it be possible to describe the Pacific Northwest as a Sawdust Empire.

A similarly painful and perhaps irony-filled future awaited communities that had once prospered from the cold war. The American economy did not demilitarize after the Allied victory in World War II, so for forty-five years, defense-related spending buoyed the economies of nearly every western state. The apparent end of the cold war in the early 1990s thus forced the West to make some painful adjustments. There was much talk about a "peace dividend" that was supposed to translate not just into the shutdown of redundant military bases but also into massive cutbacks for defense contractors. In mid-1990, for example, the McDonnell Douglas Company trimmed expenses by laying off eight hundred employees at its Mesa, Arizona, and Culver City, California, plants. For the nation's number-one defense contractor, it was the third major set of layoffs since 1989. One study estimated that the closing of the Davis-Monthan air force base in Tucson would cost an estimated ten thousand jobs, produce an exodus of some fifteen thousand people, and cut local spending by about $250 million a year. "Welcome to peace," commented Congressman Jim Kolbe, who represented the Tucson area. "This is going to be a tough road for everybody." Ironically for the Arizona metropolis, when Hughes Aircraft Company moved production of Tomahawk missiles from San Diego to its plant in Tucson in late 1992, it was California that lost twelve hundred defense jobs. For California, which as recently as 1989 had received almost one-fifth of all federal defense contracts, the road to peace would obviously require some very painful adjustments.

Defense contractors talked of using their expertise in military technology for other purposes. Boeing believed that its skill in making satellite-blasting lasers would enable it to design medical equipment for vaporizing cancer cells. Hughes Aircraft, now a subsidiary of General Motors, hoped to transfer its expertise in flight gadgetry to automobiles. In some remote locations, abandoned defense plants and military bases might well have joined ghost towns in symbolizing the West's changing economic fortunes.

In the late twentieth century, the region's natural-resource-based economy left a distinctive signature on the land in the form of abandoned mines, sawmills, and once bustling towns that had withered or disappeared. Many such communities pinned their future hopes on tourism. Some, like Cokedale, Colorado, and Jerome, Arizona, for all practical purposes became living museums of the resource frontier. Cokedale, founded in 1906 by the American Smelting and Refining Company, was placed on the National Historic Register in 1984; but apart from industrial archaeology specialists and Colorado history buffs, not many tourists came to see its huge slag heap or its abandoned coke ovens.

Dependence on natural resources took a toll on the workers of the West, especially in timber and mining, which were two of the most dangerous occupations in the United States. In recent times, legions of agricultural workers have been exposed to a variety of chemicals, which individually or in combination are likely to have a deleterious effect on human health. Probably no group paid a higher price than uranium workers: one especially sinister aspect of the uranium bust of the 1980s was that it not only cost jobs but also left behind radioactive tailings and prospects of a rising toll of lung cancer among workers in the mines and processing plants. Some of the fifteen thousand people once employed as miners believe that uranium companies and the former Atomic Energy Commission conspired to hide the danger of radiation from workers. According to figures supplied by the Centers for Disease Control, 350 of 4,146 uranium miners studied since the early 1950s have died of lung cancer—five times the expected rate. Among the victims were hundreds of Navajos who were sent into the mines without any protective clothing, face masks, or respirators.

Despite the glamour of Nevada gambling and Hollywood films, the computer wizardry of Silicon Valley, and the burgeoning trade of the Pacific Rim, the tragedy of the uranium miners vividly illustrates how the history of business and labor in the twentieth-century West has so often been a tale of relatively short-term prosperity and technological triumphs accompanied by dire long-term consequences. One of the West's growth industries in the years to come will certainly be that of cleaning up the nuclear and chemical messes created during years of cold war prosperity. The West's freewheeling "no-deposit-no-return" post–World War II economy may have left numerous hidden costs.

Bibliographic Note

Individual state histories and historical quarterlies are a rich source of information about business and labor in the twentieth-century West. The *Utah Historical Quarterly*, for example, devoted an entire issue to the state's mining industry (Summer 1963), whereas *Idaho Yesterdays* provided a bibliography of articles on Pacific Northwest labor history (Winter 1985). I make no attempt to provide an exhaustive list of books about even a single topic. The books on western railroads, even for the twentieth century alone, would fill several shelves, and those on the movie industry would occupy many additional shelves. I note only that one of the best summaries of the vast literature on Hollywood is in Kevin Starr's *Inventing the Dream: California through the Progressive Era* (New York, 1985).

What follows is a brief description of books that address aspects of the larger subject. There is, unfortunately, no single book that synthesizes the business and labor history of the twentieth-century West, although two volumes do help to fill the gap: Michael P. Malone and Richard W. Etulain, *The American West: A Twentieth-Century History* (Lincoln, 1989); and Gerald D. Nash, *The American West in the Twentieth Century: A Short History of an Urban Oasis* (1973; reprint, Albuquerque, 1977).

The Bisbee story that was used to introduce this chapter is from Carlos A. Schwantes, ed., *Bisbee: Urban Outpost on the Frontier* (Tucson, 1992). A detailed account of the Bisbee deportation is in James W. Byrkit, *Forging the Copper Collar: Arizona's Labor-Management War of 1901–1921* (Tucson, 1982). Byrkit summarizes his research in James C. Foster, ed., *American Labor in the Southwest: The First One Hundred Years* (Tucson, 1982), a volume that provides an excellent overview of labor in that subregion. In a similar category is Hugh T. Lovin, ed., *Labor in the West* (Manhattan, Kans., 1986). Labor in the Pacific Northwest is the subject of Carlos A. Schwantes, *Radical Heritage: Labor, Socialism, and Reform in Washington and British Columbia, 1885–1917* (Seattle, 1979). David F. Selvin, *A Place in the Sun: A History of California Labor*

(San Francisco, 1981), offers a brief overview of labor developments in a single state. Also useful on California labor and business is Carey McWilliams, *California: The Great Exception* (New York, 1949).

Far more common than state or regional studies of western labor are books on individual strikes, episodes of violence, union organizations, and labor in specific industries. Among the best of these are Robert L. Friedheim, *The Seattle General Strike* (Seattle, 1964), Michael Kazin, *Barons of Labor: The San Francisco Building Trades and Union Power in the Progressive Era* (Urbana, 1987), and Bruce Nelson, *Workers on the Waterfront: Seamen, Longshoremen, and Unionism in the 1930s* (Urbana, 1988), which focuses on Pacific Coast ports.

Labor in the West's mining industry has been an especially popular topic. Among the best studies are the following: Ronald C. Brown, *Hard-Rock Miners: The Intermountain West, 1860–1920* (College Station, Tex., 1979); Howard M. Gitelman, *Legacy of the Ludlow Massacre: A Chapter in American Industrial Relations* (Philadelphia, 1988); George S. McGovern and Leonard F. Guttridge, *The Great Coalfield War* (Boston, 1972), on the troubles at Ludlow, Colorado; George G. Suggs, Jr., *Colorado's War on Militant Unionism: James H. Peabody and the Western Federation of Miners* (Detroit, 1972); James Whiteside, *Regulating Danger: The Struggle for Mine Safety in the Rocky Mountain Coal Industry* (Lincoln, 1990); and Mark Wyman, *Hard-Rock Epic: Western Miners and the Industrial Revolution, 1860–1910* (Berkeley, 1979).

The Industrial Workers of the World has been the subject of numerous studies including Melvyn Dubofsky, *We Shall Be All: A History of the Industrial Workers of the World* (Chicago, 1969), and Robert L. Tyler, *Rebels of the Woods: The I.W.W. in the Pacific Northwest* (Eugene, 1967). A basic research tool is the massive compilation by Dione Miles, *Something in Common: An IWW Bibliography* (Detroit, 1986).

Studies of agricultural and itinerant laborers include Cletus E. Daniel, *Bitter Harvest: A History of California Farmworkers, 1870–1941* (Ithaca, N.Y., 1981), Lawrence J. Jelinek, *Harvest Empire: A History of California Agriculture* (San Francisco, 1979), James N. Gregory, *American Exodus: The Dust Bowl Migration and Okie Culture in California* (New York, 1989), Thomas D. Isern, *Bull Threshers and Bindlestiffs: Harvesting and Threshing on the North American Plains* (Lawrence, 1990), Carey McWilliams, *Factories in the Field: The Story of Migratory Farm Labor in California* (Boston, 1939), Vicki L. Ruiz, *Cannery Women, Cannery Lives: Mexican Women, Unionization, and the California Food Processing Industry, 1930–1950* (Albuquerque, 1987), and Carleton H. Parker, *The Casual Laborer and Other Essays* (1920; reprint, Seattle, 1972), an old but still valuable classic study. On the world of workers, see James B. Allen, *The Company Town in the American West* (Norman, 1966), Norman H. Clark, *Mill Town: A Social History of Everett, Washington, from Its Earliest Beginnings on the Shores of Puget Sound to the Tragic and Infamous Event Known as the Everett Massacre* (Seattle, 1970), and William G. Robbins, *Hard Times in Paradise: Coos Bay, Oregon, 1850–1986* (Seattle, 1988).

Among the general business histories of the West, notably California, are Joel Kotkin and Paul Grabowicz, *California, Inc.* (New York, 1982), and Peter Wiley and Robert Gottlieb, *Empires in the Sun: The Rise of the New American West* (1982; reprint, Tucson, 1985). On transportation, travel, and tourism in the twentieth-century West, see Warren James Belasco, *Americans on the Road: From Autocamp to Motel, 1910–1945* (Cambridge, Mass., 1979), Lawrence R. Borne, *Dude Ranching: A Complete History* (Albuquerque, 1983), Don L. Hofsommer, *The Southern Pacific, 1901–1985* (College Station, Tex., 1986), Ralph W. Hidy, Muriel E. Hidy, and Roy V. Scott, with Don L. Hofsommer, *The Great Northern Railway: A History* (Boston, 1988), Maury Klein, *Union Pacific*, vol. 2, *The Rebirth, 1894–1969* (New York, 1989), Carlos A. Schwantes, *Railroad Signatures across the Pacific Northwest* (Seattle, 1993), and Earl Pomeroy, *In Search of the Golden West: The Tourist in Western America* (New York, 1957).

Studies of important entrepreneurs of the West include Donald L. Barlett and James B. Steele, *Empire: The Life, Legend, and Madness of Howard Hughes* (New York, 1979), Mark S. Foster, *Henry J. Kaiser: Builder in the Modern American West* (Austin, 1989), Marquis James and Bessie R. James, *Biography of a Bank: The Story of Bank of America* (New York, 1954), and Gerald D. Nash, *A. P. Giannini and the Bank of America* (Norman, 1992).

Many of the West's basic business and industrial enterprises have been the subjects of books: Leonard J. Arrington, *Beet Sugar in the West: A History of the Utah-Idaho Sugar Company, 1891–1966* (Seattle, 1966); Ralph W. Hidy, Frank Ernest Hill, and Allan Nevins, *Timber and Men: The Weyerhaeuser Story* (New York, 1963); Harold Mansfield, *Vision: A Saga of the Sky* (New York, 1956), the story of Boeing; Alexander Campbell McGregor, *Counting Sheep: From Open Range to Agribusiness on the Columbia Plateau* (Seattle, 1982); Gerald T. White, *Formative Years in the Far West: A History of Standard Oil Company of California and Its Predecessors through 1919* (New York, 1962); and Carl Coke Rister, *Oil! Titan of the Southwest* (Norman, 1949).

Among the more general industrial studies are Russell R. Elliott, *Nevada's Twentieth-Century Mining Boom: Tonopah, Goldfield, Ely* (Reno, 1966), Robert E. Ficken, *The Forested Land: A History of Lumbering in Western Washington* (Seattle, 1987), A. Dudley Gardner and Verla R. Flores, *Forgotten Frontier: A History of Wyoming Coal Mining* (Boulder, 1989), Andrew Gulliford, *Boomtown Blues: Colorado Oil Shale, 1885–1985* (Niwot, Colo., 1989), and Raye C. Ringholz, *Uranium Frenzy: Boom and Bust on the Colorado Plateau* (New York, 1989).

World War II, which played such a key role in the western economy, is the subject of two books by Gerald D. Nash: *The American West Transformed: The Impact of the Second World War* (Bloomington, 1985) and *World War II and the West: Reshaping the Economy* (Lincoln, 1990). Curiously, no one has yet authored a comparable volume for World War I.

Chapter Thirteen

The Federal Presence

CARL ABBOTT

The federal government pervades the contemporary American West. Federal lands stretch from the fires of Kilauea to the ice cliffs of Glacier Bay, from the nation's highest peak in Alaska to its lowest point in Death Valley. Federal properties range in size and complexity from roadside picnic tables to Hoover Dam. Federal funds protect the ancient homes of the Anasazi on the Colorado Plateau, pay for the scientific research at the Los Alamos National Laboratory, and support the search for nuclear-waste depositories in the sparsely settled hinterlands of Nevada and New Mexico. Westerners are still known to proclaim their independence of the governmental octopus, but they now live in a region whose every corner is linked into networks of federal programs, regulations, spending, and employment.

At the opening of the twentieth century, it *was* possible to think of the federal government as something outside the West. *Honey in the Horn*, the Pulitzer prize-winning novel by H. L. Davis, depicted frontier Oregon in the first years of the twentieth century. Davis's characters move from the foothills of the Cascade Mountains to the Willamette Valley to the Pacific coast and back to the edge of the high desert. They try their hand at sheepherding, hop picking, lumbering, horse trading, and wheat farming. The federal government enters the story as a passive purveyor of cheap homesteads. It figures less in the everyday world of westerners than it does in their fading memories of the Civil War.

When Davis published this work in 1935, a generation after the setting for his story, the federal government had begun to move to the foreground of western life. In the novel's home ground of the Northwest, contractors for the Reclamation Service were at work on the first of the great Columbia River dams. The Agricultural Adjustment Administration was propping up the wheat ranchers of the Palouse and John Day river basins. Federally aided highways had replaced private toll roads. Youthful workers for the Civilian Conservation Corps (CCC) were grading hiking trails through the forests of the Cascades and the Olympics. Regional artists and writers like Davis were beginning to find paying work decorating public buildings and compiling local histories for the Works Progress Administration (WPA).

Forty years later, Edward Abbey published a different sort of best-selling "western." *The Monkey-Wrench Gang* follows an increasingly violent quartet of environmental activists who set out in the 1970s to block the further transformation of the canyonlands of northern Arizona and southern Utah. In Abbey's radical nostalgia, economic development is itself the enemy. The Forest Service, Reclamation Service, Park Service, and Bureau of Land Management, as fronts for the forces of growth, are all part of the problem.

Federal funding helped Las Vegas grow from a town of 5,000 in 1930 to a metropolis of 750,000 in the 1990s. Federal dollars built the dam that generated power for the city's neon lights and constructed the highways that brought in tourists. More federal money poured into the community via the Nevada Test Site and other defense installations. Like many areas of the West, a region of self-proclaimed independence, Las Vegas depends on this outside support.

Unidentified photographer. Las Vegas. Gelatin silver print, 1951. Las Vegas News Bureau Archives, Las Vegas, Nevada.

Even as they fight to reverse the effects of western resource development, however, George Hayduke, Doc Savas, and the other ecoraiders cannot avoid utilizing the same federal investments and institutions that they hate. They drive on U.S. Highways 66 and 89, 160 and 163. They move back and forth from Natural Bridges National Monument to Grand Canyon National Park, from Kaibab National Forest to Glen Canyon National Recreation Area, from the Navajo Indian Reservation to Canyonlands National Park. They sleep in federal campgrounds and cruise on federal reservoirs. They shop in the "neat green government town of Page" near the Glen Canyon Dam. In a story about the vast spaces of the Four Corners in the last quarter of the twentieth century, half the pages would be blank if the federal government were left out.

The difference between the fictionalized Oregon of 1908 and the fictionalized Utah of 1975 captures something of the growing prominence of the national government in the daily life of the West. During the nineteenth century, the federal government was essentially a facilitator of western growth. It explored the region and helped map the terrain. It sold or gave land to individuals or corporations. It confirmed the farm and mining claims of pioneers. It maintained the basis of public order through Indian wars and territorial government until Anglo-American settlers were judged ready to take local affairs into their own hands. In short, it made resources available for private appropriation, investment, and development.

Over the course of the twentieth century, the balance has changed. Uncle Sam is now more active and omnipresent than nineteenth-century pioneers could have imagined. The federal government directly manages the regional resources of grass, timber, oil, and recreational space. It is a primary customer for many of the region's leading businesses and the chief engine behind the area's massive urbanization. Since the Great Depression, it has become an active partner in previously local decisions.

This new federal presence has accumulated in generational layers like the strata of silt laid down along the banks of western rivers such as the Yellowstone or the Platte. The equivalent to periodic floods has been a succession of economic eras of boom and bust and new boom. Each period has involved a new set of federal activities and imperatives. We can follow the expanding federal presence from the era of the federally assisted frontier (1900–1918) through the long regional depression (1919–40), the Pacific war and the rise of the military economy (1940–60), and finally to the era of the West's emergence (1960–90), during which the region increasingly met the world with introductions by Uncle Sam.

A largely inadvertent effect of federal actions has been the transformation of the West from a backwater of the national and world economies of 1900 to a central player at the end of the century, bringing an economic power that westerners only dreamed of in the first generations of American settlement. Policies on resource development, defense, and international relations have moved the southwestern and Pacific states into a prominent position within the contemporary world system. With a series of strong boosts from Uncle Sam, cities such as Seattle, San Francisco, Houston, Dallas, and especially Los Angeles have become contact points and focal points for the world economy in much the same way that Boston, Chicago, and New York grew in the nineteenth century.

Federal actions have also nationalized the West by overriding or eroding regional differences. Almost by definition, federal programs place individual choices, local interests, and regional change within a framework of national requirements and expectations. Federal funds have helped to pave the highways, string the power lines, and build the airports that tie the West to the rest of the nation. At the same time, the organizational state of the twentieth century has had some of its most powerful effects on the "independent" and "individualistic" West that finds itself dependent on farm supports, subsidized water, defense contracts, and mass-transit grants. Although many of the region's public voices hate to admit the obvious, today's West would be far poorer and far more sparsely developed without a century of federal initiatives.

The Federally Sustained Frontier, 1900–18

The first two decades of the twentieth century were the era of the federally sustained frontier. In the nineteenth century, the federal government had created settlement and development opportunities that benefited individual settlers and corporations. After the drought and depression of the 1890s, federal agencies increasingly initiated development on their own. Indeed, visitors to the federal pavilions at the world's fairs that ushered in the new century at Portland in 1905, Seattle in 1909, and San Francisco in 1915 came away with a single impression. What they found on display was a federal government that was taking the lead in the development of western resources through water projects, national parks, and a canal through the Isthmus of Panama. Such activities sustained the development of the American frontier for a full generation after Frederick Jackson Turner had proclaimed its disappearance. At least until 1918, farmers, ranchers, miners, and lumbermen continued to draw on federal help to push into areas previously unsettled or unused by Anglo Americans.

What was perhaps the key legislation in this expansion was authored by Representative Francis Newlands of Nevada. The Newlands Reclamation Act of 1902 established the Reclamation Service as a new agency within the Department of Interior. Led by Frederick Newell, the new bureau took the lead in the construction of irrigation projects throughout the West. In the 1870s and 1880s, many irrigation facilities had been community projects, like the canals that watered the Mormon settlements in Utah or the agricultural colony at Greeley, Colorado. Other projects had been profit-seeking business ventures, like the Highline Canal winding through the suburbs of Denver or the unsuccessful Boise River Project, the setting for the latter chapters of *Angle of Repose* (1971), Wallace Stegner's novelized version of the lives of the writer Mary Hallock Foote and the engineer Arthur Foote.

Under the Newlands Act, profits from public land sales in the sixteen states west of the one hundredth meridian were to be deposited in an "arid land reclamation fund" to pay for major irrigation projects. Users of the water were to repay the U.S. Treasury over ten years, generating a revolving fund for new systems. The Reclamation Service quickly undertook projects beyond the capabilities of profit-oriented corporations. The Roosevelt Dam on the Salt River of Arizona allowed the development of Phoenix. Residents of Reno placed high hopes on tapping the waters of the Truckee River. Orchards blossomed around Delta and Grand Junction in Colorado and Yakima in Washington. Arrowrock Dam on the Boise River, the world's tallest when completed in 1915, finally realized the dream on which Arthur Foote had spent seven years of unrelenting work.

The dam and related projects transformed southern Idaho from desert to farmland as older cities like Boise competed with new towns like Twin Falls for hundreds of thousands of new Idahoans. As Carlos Schwantes has commented, "a whole new Idaho grew out of the sagebrush plains" of the upper Snake River drainage with the irrigation boom of 1900–1917.

The same era of activist government brought the final giveaways of federal lands. Increasingly the federal government acted like a storekeeper trying to move backed-up inventory with price cuts and premiums. The Enlarged Homestead Act of 1909 raised the homestead grant from 160 to 320 acres and reduced the time period before transfer of title from five to three years. The Stock Raising Homestead Act of 1916 raised the grant of rangeland to 640 acres. The General Land Office took on the tone of a railroad immigration department, publishing circulars that listed available homestead acreage in each western county and explained the simple procedures for homestead entry. The result was the extension of settlement into marginal lands. Encouraged by wet years in the 1910s and high food prices caused by war in Europe, farmers pushed into plains lands to plant wheat and sugar beets on acreage better suited to grazing than cultivation. In the first two decades of the twentieth century, eager agriculturalists took up more homestead acreage than in the entire nineteenth century. The "second boom" on the northern plains doubled the mileage of railroads to serve new towns and farmers. North Dakota in 1915, for example, had more towns, railroad mileage, churches, schools, and elected officials per capita than any other state.

The federal government also took the lead in promoting the Anglo-American settlement of Alaska. Interior Secretaries Franklin K. Lane and John Barton Payne published glowing articles on the attractions of Alaska. The failure of private rail companies to penetrate the interior of the territory led Congress to authorize a federal railroad from the Gulf of Alaska to the Yukon River. Woodrow Wilson chose the route from Seward to Fairbanks in 1915; Warren Harding drove the symbolic golden spike in 1923. The Alaska Engineering Commission (AEC) supervised forty-five hundred workers on the federal payroll at the height of construction.

The AEC also found itself in the town-building business, for railroad building required a construction and supply base. In the nineteenth century, towns like Cheyenne on the Union Pacific, Reno on the Central Pacific, and Billings on the Northern Pacific were private promotions. Profit-motivated rail companies or their subsidiaries surveyed the site, sold the lots, and invested in community facilities to encourage settlement. In 1915, in contrast, the AEC planned, built, and managed the new city of Anchorage from 1915 to 1920, anticipating a series of federal construction and science cities in the 1930s and 1940s. Residents resembled those of the earlier generation of private railroad towns, but until the city incorporated in 1920 it was the federally funded AEC that supplied the town manager, graded the streets, laid the water and sewer pipes, constructed the school and the hospital, bought the fire-fighting equipment, and even organized the YMCA to improve the moral tone of four thousand typical frontier townspeople.

The same development impulse also laid the foundations of professional land management by the federal government. The Progressive Era conservation movement, as the historian Samuel Hays has shown, was "an effort on the part of leaders in science,

Unlike the railroad towns of the 19th century, Anchorage was planned and developed by the federal government, which needed a town to supply workers and materials for the construction of a railway through the Alaskan interior. In July 1915, the government auctioned off 655 lots, with strict rules forbidding their development for "immoral" purposes. Just a few months later, Anchorage already resembled a small town, with retail stores, restaurants, and lawyers.

Sydney M. Laurence (1865–1940). Anchorage, 4th Avenue Looking West between G & H Streets, October 8, 1915. *Gelatin silver print,* 1915. Anchorage Museum of History and Art (#B63.16.6), Anchorage, Alaska.

technology, and government to bring about more efficient development of physical resources." As an attempt to sustain and extend the resource development of initial settlement, it was "an aspect of the history of production" whose gospel of efficiency was spread from the top down by dedicated professionals within the Agriculture and Interior departments. The model was the U.S. Forest Service, established under the direction of Gifford Pinchot in 1905 to manage a growing inventory of federal forest reservations that dated to 1891. Theodore Roosevelt entered office in 1901 with 41 million acres in reserves and left in 1909 with 151 million in the rechristened national forests. Pinchot's goal was scientific management to ensure a sustained yield of timber as a lasting contributor to national growth and the stability of local economies. In his view, national forests could protect water supplies for irrigation and western cities, provide cheap grazing for stock raisers, and repay the U.S. Treasury with timber sales.

The National Park Service as both a peer and a rival of the Forest Service was established in 1916 to provide consistent management for an assortment of federally protected parks and monuments. Director Stephen Mather and his chief lieutenant, Horace Albright, were dedicated to preserving the parks for utilization by the public. They constructed tourist facilities, lobbied for paved roads into the parks, granted concessions to private resort operators, and defined the role of the park naturalist as educative entertainment. They hired Robert S. Yard to publicize the parks as tourist destinations with tasteful books on their scenery and attractions. Their work helped to achieve a 900-percent increase in automobile visits from 1919 to 1931. Parks such as Rocky Mountain National Park (established 1915) were originally promoted in terms of local economic development. The rising tide of visitors, however, gave the Park

Service the justification to override local interests in favor of uniform management directives originating in Washington, D.C.

The other federal construction enterprise that spanned the administrations of Roosevelt, William Howard Taft, and Wilson was the Panama Canal, begun in 1905 and opened in 1914 at a cost of $365 million. As with the Alaska Railroad or the Reclamation Service dams, the federal government did what private capital could not. The canal confirmed a Pacific orientation to America's new international power. It improved access to Hawai`i, Guam, American Samoa, and the Philippines, all acquired between 1898 and 1900. It also raised expectations of world trade along the Pacific Coast. Seattle, Portland, and San Francisco all looked forward to what the journalist Wolf von Schierabend called "The Coming Supremacy of the Pacific." The Los Angeles Chamber of Commerce sponsored the book *Los Angeles: A Maritime City* in 1912. Although most Americans thought of Los Angeles as citrus groves and retirees, the author John McGroarty pointed out that the great circle route from Panama to the Far East ran seventy miles from the harbor at San Pedro. West Coast expositions like San Francisco's Panama-Pacific International Exposition and Seattle's Alaska-Yukon-Pacific Exposition were part of the same desire to capitalize on new opportunities served up by the federal treasury by publicizing the attractions of West Coast ports.

The climax of the federally sustained frontier came with World War I. Even more than the new canal, the war linked the West to a warring world with its insatiable appetite for food, lumber, and minerals. As Michael Malone and Richard Etulain have written, "The great wartime boom, with its huge export markets and artificially high prices, climaxed the three-century frontier expansion of American agriculture." The U.S. Food Administration defined markets and guaranteed base prices. Western miners found new profits in industrial metals like zinc, molybdenum, tungsten, and vanadium to make up for depressed silver prices and played-out goldfields. The Emergency Fleet Corporation made Puget Sound and San Francisco Bay into major shipbuilding centers, with thirty thousand workers learning to make steel ships in Seattle's largest yard. By 1919, the federal government had helped to advance American enterprise further than ever before—more deeply into mountain valleys and plateaus, further onto the arid plains, and back from the coastal fringe into the heart of Alaska. It had staked a lasting claim to the Pacific as a field of American enterprise and influence. In the process, western Americans had improved eighty million additional acres of farmland, more than doubling the total in nine states. The western share of national petroleum production had jumped from 29 percent to 68 percent and the share of timber production from 10 percent to 35 percent. Cities like Seattle, Portland, Los Angeles, Denver, Dallas, and San Antonio had doubled and tripled in population. It was the flood tide of the federally assisted frontier.

Regional Planning and the Long Depression, 1919–40

One of the public heroes of America's first crusade in Europe was the westerner Herbert Hoover. Born in Iowa, raised in Oregon, and educated in California, Hoover managed wartime and postwar relief efforts in Europe with American practicality. He was also known in the American West as the director of the wartime Food Administration, which had helped to urge farmers to higher and higher levels of production. As secretary of commerce from 1921 to 1928, he embodied the impulse of progressive efficiency. Given the reputation that he later earned as an advocate of federal inaction during the onset of the Great Depression, it is ironic that, especially before his presidency, Hoover helped to change the federal role in the West from promoter to planner.

The Colorado River Commission Compact of 1922 emerged with Hoover as facilitator; in his role as the congressionally authorized federal representative, he met with delegates of the seven western states along the Colorado River. His goal was to work out compromises in uses and claims on the limited flow of the Colorado River and to provide federal sanction for multistate agreements. Hoover and the delegates met half a dozen times in Washington, in Phoenix, in Denver, and finally for more than two weeks in Santa Fe before hammering out an agreement to divide the river equally between the upper basin states (Wyoming, Colorado, Utah, New Mexico) and the lower basin states (Nevada, Arizona, California). The decisions of 1922 were flawed in detail because of inexact knowledge of the river, but the federally mandated framework for planning the allocation of natural resources stood for the rest of the century.

The Colorado River Compact epitomized the progressive impulse toward "scientific" and efficient development of western resources for the greatest economic return to the nation over time. Hoover filled his very comfortable role as progressive engineer. At the same time, the meetings in Santa Fe anticipated the era of Franklin Roosevelt and Harry Truman, for the compact was a regional planning response to a slowly growing sense that the development of the West could rub up against limits. Over the ensuing quarter century, that growing recognition put a new twist on the idea of efficient use by extending the progressive idea of planning for specific resource types into a broader concern for the comprehensive planning of development by regions.

The federal government in the early 1920s also took part in another effort at regional planning through the creation of a national highway system. Responses to the automobile in the 1910s and early 1920s had followed the western tradition of local community boosterism and private entrepreneurship. Venturesome motorists traveled state to state on a series of privately named highways, bouncing back and forth from paved segments to gravel to graded dirt and even worse. Local groups and governments maintained individual road segments, which national associations grouped into as many as 250 continuous and sometimes logical "routes." Signs were usually a set of color-coded stripes on telegraph poles and fence posts. The best known was the Lincoln Highway, whose red-white-and-blue colors led from Philadelphia to Omaha, Cheyenne, Salt Lake City, Reno, and San Francisco—roughly the route of the first transcontinental railroad west of the Missouri River. The Yellowstone Trail led from Chicago to Seattle. The Old Spanish Trail (red, white, and yellow) started in Jacksonville, Florida, and ended in San Diego. The federal government began to subsidize state highway building with the Federal Aid Highway Act of 1916, but most states allocated their aid funds by logrolling and chance. As one observer noted in the 1910s, "The highways of America are built chiefly of politics, whereas the proper material is crushed rock, or concrete." New legislation in 1921 required states to designate a maximum of 7 percent of their rural roads as primary routes qualifying for federal aid, but planning remained a captive of

Under the aegis of the government's Farm Security Administration, leading photographers traveled the country to document the plight of depression-era America. Pausing in western Oklahoma along Route 66, a popular migration route for displaced farm workers, Dorothea Lange photographed this young Missouri family, hitchhiking their way west in search of work and a better life.

Dorothea Lange (1895–1965). Family on the Road, Oklahoma. *Gelatin silver print, 1938. Gift of Paul S. Taylor, The Dorothea Lange Collection, The Oakland Museum, Oakland, California.*

competitive politics. *Sunset* magazine, for example, reported to its travel-oriented readers that Wyoming had shouldered past Montana as the gateway to Yellowstone Park by using federal dollars to grade and gravel the entrance roads from Casper and Gillette.

The third step toward a planned highway system came when the Bureau of Public Roads within the U.S. Department of Agriculture convened a Joint Board on Interstate Highways. Under the auspices of the Joint Board and its secretary, E. W. James, state and federal highway officials selected and designated "a comprehensive system of through interstate routes" with systematic identification. The outcome amounted to a vast regional planning program. The Joint Board pared a possible 200,000 miles to 75,000 miles of U.S. highways identified by number rather than name. Even-numbered routes supplemented the great trunk railroads—U.S. 10, 30, 40, 90, and the others. Odd-numbered highways paralleled the West's valleys and ranges from north to south—U.S. 99 for the old Pacific Highway, U.S. 89 and 93 through the intermountain West, and U.S. 85 traversing the high plains from Williston, North Dakota, to El Paso, Texas.

The new highway that embedded itself most deeply in American memory through song and television illustrates the shift from local initiative to federally coordinated planning. U.S. 66 originated in the efforts of the Tulsa booster Cyrus Avery. The Joint

Board incorporated pieces of the Ozark Trail into a road that cut diagonally across the national grain, leading from Chicago and St. Louis through the Oklahoma and Texas "dust bowl" region to southern California. Like the other federal highways, it helped to tie the West into a single economic unit. During the 1930s, the fictional Joad family traveled westward on U.S. 66 in *The Grapes of Wrath*. So too did the very real Haggard family follow friends and relatives to California in a 1926 Chevrolet, two years before the birth of their son Merle. A few years later, an even larger migration traveled the same route—war workers, soldiers on assignment, and family members hoping for a few days with departing servicemen in San Diego or Los Angeles.

Whether they left home like the Joads or tried to cling to rural communities, millions of westerners found themselves dependent on the federal government for simple survival during the depression of the 1930s. Through much of the mining and farming country of the Rockies and Great Plains, falling resource prices in the 1920s had already brought individual bankruptcies and bank failures (five hundred in North Dakota alone during the twenties). In Colorado, for example, war-inflated grain and livestock prices fell 60 percent from 1919 to 1921. Unable to expand production to generate more income, small farmers were squeezed between falling receipts and fixed mortgages. The number of tenant farmers who rented rather than owned their land in the state's dry farming areas rose from 23 to 35 percent. Whereas the climatic disasters and market collapse of the 1930s simply deepened existing problems of wheat growers and ranchers, they crippled West Slope orchardists who had protected themselves in the 1920s by cooperative marketing associations. Agricultural statistics for the 1930s told a grim story: population down in all but one plains county; one million acres taken out of cultivation; thirty thousand agricultural jobs lost for Colorado as a whole.

Despite the anti–New Deal posturing of many western politicians, necessity opened the door for a grudging and often limited acceptance of federal aid. Few states had leaders who were prepared to deal with the crisis of the early 1930s. Strict economy in government sat higher on many state agendas than did effective relief. Governors such as Arthur Seligman of New Mexico or Julius Meier and Charles Martin of Oregon believed in the gospel of balanced budgets. By repeatedly striking down new taxes that would have funded state matching money for the Federal Emergency Relief Administration, the Colorado courts forced the termination of needed assistance at the end of 1933. As the historian Robert Athearn has commented: "The West was inclined to bite the hand that fed it. . . . what it amounted to was the unwillingness or inability of the states to reconcile what they conceived to be their rugged individualism, born of the frontier, with the planned society that was implied by the New Deal."

Nevertheless, westerners took what the federal government had to offer, especially after the inauguration of President Franklin Roosevelt and the onset of the New Deal in 1933. New Deal grant and loan programs had a greater relative impact in the West than in any other part of the United States. Figures compiled by the historian Leonard Arrington show that the greater the collapse of a state's level of personal income from 1929 to 1933, the more it received in New Deal assistance from 1933 to 1939. Nevada, with a small population and huge federal construction projects, led the nation with $1,499 received per capita. Next in line were Montana, Wyoming, and Arizona, followed by ten other western states before Minnesota finally broke into the list.

In the rural communities and the city neighborhoods, the New Deal farm support and work relief programs of 1933–35 held crumbling communities together. The longer-lasting federal programs of the later 1930s helped to put the same communities back on their feet. By one estimate, two of every three North Dakotans received federal assistance by 1936 through farm-support programs, business loans, emergency relief, and public works jobs. Just across the state line in Otter Tail County, Minnesota, the people of Fergus Falls, Pelican Rapids, and other small towns found that the new federal agencies kept alive the dream of a normal life, helping one family to hold on to its farm, another to think about college for the children. The CCC enrolled seventy-five hundred workers on Arizona Indian reservations and another five thousand in twenty-nine Indian Conservation Camps in Idaho. The Rural Electrification program, which began in 1935 and continued after the 1940s, raised the number of Idaho farms with power from 30 percent to 54 percent. Beyond direct relief, the federal government helped to reshape the West on paper and on the ground. The New Deal built on the regional initiatives of the 1920s to introduce the idea of systematic planning for regional recovery and future growth. As the historian Richard Lowitt has argued: "Depression, drought, and dust undermined dependence on the marketplace as an arbiter of economic activities. . . . Animating the New Deal in the West was concern for rational planning of resource use. Reports of the National Resources Planning Board, several presidential committees, various regional, state and local boards, all provided guidelines designed to encourage more meaningful regional economic development."

The Taylor Grazing Act of 1934 marked the effective end of the era in which the goal of the federal government was to transfer public lands to private ownership and development. Within two years, the Taylor Act removed 142 million acres of western lands from potential sale and reserved them for grazing under federal control. President Roosevelt reinforced the Taylor Act by officially removing the majority of the public domain from private land claims at the end of 1934. The new Grazing Service of the Department of Interior was to lease grazing rights at reasonable rates while controlling excessive use of the fragile rangelands. The Grazing Service (merged into a new Bureau of Land Management in 1946) has been severely criticized as a captive of local advisory boards that give preferred access and cheap grass to big stock growers at the expense of resource conservation. Nevertheless, the Taylor Act established the principle that virtually the entire remaining public domain should be set aside for federal management rather than sale.

The Soil Conservation Service (expanded from the Soil Erosion Service in 1935) was also part of the new layer of federally mandated regional planning. In the 1910s, the federal government had run a sort of land office fire sale. Twenty years later, H. H. Bennett proposed a regional planning solution to the agricultural crisis of the Great Plains. The Soil Conservation Service tried to work cooperatively with local and state officials, but it set its district boundaries at watersheds rather than county lines. Conservation districts were an experiment in federalism—local government units, established under state laws, implementing a federally defined agenda with the help of federal expertise. The first thirty-seven districts covered nineteen million acres where improved cropping practices, soil retention, and soil restoration became a new credo to replace the soil mining of the frontier generations.

More explicit planning came under the umbrella of an agency known variously as the National Planning Board (1934–35), National Resources Committee (1935–39), and National Resources Planning Board (1939–43). Established in 1934 to advise the Public Works Administration (PWA), the NRPB took on a life of its own. It promoted state planning agencies and established regional planning commissions for the Pacific Northwest, Alaska, Southwest, Intermountain-Great Plains, and Missouri Valley. Planners in Washington, D.C., provided money, manpower, information, and advice for the regional and state agencies. In turn, the regional and state agencies performed first-rate resource inventories and prepared dozens of reports with a focus on natural resources and public works. Reports dealt with individual towns like Sitka, Alaska, with small watersheds like the Upper Gila Basin in Arizona or the Willamette Valley in Oregon, with single states, and with entire multistate regions. The NRPB was perhaps at its strongest in what Lowitt has called the "planned promised land" of the Northwest. Throughout the West, however, it introduced the idea of comprehensive planning for resource conservation and development in areas facing the first stages of a massive economic transition that has now lasted for half a century.

More obvious to most Americans was federal involvement in reshaping the western landscape. The PWA and the WPA built 246 public buildings in the state of Washington, 227 in Montana, and thousands more throughout the West. The PWA and WPA facilities in every state ranged from courthouses to culverts, water-treatment plants to swimming pools, bridges to golf courses. Much of the basis for the postwar boom in tourism was laid in the 1930s as WPA workers built Mount McKinley Lodge in Alaska and Timberline Lodge on Mount Hood and as CCC workers opened trails, leveled campgrounds, and erected rest areas.

The 1930s also brought an engineering marvel for each of the great rivers of the West. Congress had authorized a dam at Black Canyon on the Colorado River in 1928, but the timing of construction made Boulder (now Hoover) Dam a depression-era public works project. The erection of the huge wedge of concrete in the blazing heat that vibrated between the canyon walls captured the national imagination. The current name of the dam is appropriate, for the project represented Hoover's approach to regional growth through carefully planned engineering projects. It gave the Bureau of Reclamation its first large multipurpose project designed for hydroelectric power as well as irrigation. Indirectly, the need to support the dam's thousands of workers and the growing streams of tourists gave birth to the modern city of Las Vegas in place of the small, struggling mining and railroad town of the 1910s and 1920s.

With a span of 3.7 miles, Fort Peck Dam on the Missouri River was the largest earth-fill dam on the continent. The PWA supplied the funds and the Army Corps of Engineers did the building. Drawing on normal construction experience, the Corps built the planned town of Fort Peck City with 280 units for families and 3,200 barracks spaces for single men. In accord with Montana relief regulations, however, three-quarters of the dam builders were married men with dependents, who had to crowd into improvised shelters of barn siding, cardboard, and tenting in instant towns like Wheeler, New Deal, and Delano Heights. The photographer Margaret Bourke-White caught the tone of the towns in a photo essay on "Mr. Roosevelt's New Wild West" for the first issue of *Life* magazine in November 1936. The thousands of "veterans, parched farmers, and plain unemployed parents" who labored on the dam provided "extracurricular work for a shack-town population of barkeepers, quack doctors, hash dispensers, radio mechanics, filling station operators, and light-roving ladies."

Grand Coulee Dam on the Columbia River was the best publicized, from initial PWA funding in 1933 to the generation of the first electricity in 1941. The journalist Richard Neuberger, later to serve in the U.S. Senate from Oregon, proclaimed it "Man's Greatest Structure" and the "Biggest Thing on Earth." New Deal officials were glad to use the awestruck publicity to justify an entire generation of federal activity in the West. In the words of the singer Woody Guthrie, hired to immortalize all the Columbia River dams in 1941, "From the rising of the river to the setting of the sun / the Coulee is the biggest thing that man has ever done." Although its size was what caught the public's attention—550 feet from bedrock to guardrail, with a 15-acre spillway—Grand Coulee would soon prove more important for the electricity it furnished during World War II for Oregon and Washington aluminum plants and for the production of plutonium at Hanford, Washington.

The three pioneer projects introduced a generation of massive western water projects funded with federal taxes. Bonneville, McNary, Chief Joseph, Hungry Horse, and Libby are a few of the dams that tapped the Columbia and its tributaries for irrigation water and electricity. Oahe and Garrison dams on the Missouri, Shasta Dam on the Sacramento River, and Glen Canyon Dam on the Colorado were other key projects. The Colorado-Big Thompson and Fryingpan-Arkansas water diversions took water from the western slope of the Colorado Rockies for the farms and cities of the eastern slope, the former via huge tunnels that pass directly beneath Rocky Mountain National Park.

Big projects required intricate coordination. Congress created the Bonneville Power Administration (BPA) in 1939 to market power from the entire set of Columbia River dams in accord with a rational plan. The BPA's choice was a triangular grid of power lines that marched up and down over the Cascade range to connect Seattle, Spokane, and Portland with essentially equal-price power. Its marketing decision was also a land-use decision, for it favored established centers of economic activity at the expense of new industrial development near the dams. The utilization of Hoover Dam to help implement the Colorado River Compact required coordination of water sales to Imperial Valley and Coachella Valley agribusiness, power sales to private utilities, and both water and power sales to the Los Angeles Water District (the power was used to pump the water west across the desert).

The biggest dam builders offered competing visions and plans for federal development of the West. The Corps of Engineers argued for a water program oriented to flood control and navigation, whereas the Bureau of Reclamation stressed electric power and irrigation. The Soil Conservation Service worked on the sidelines to build small dams for flood prevention and erosion control. Hells Canyon on the Snake River was left undammed in part because a standoff between the Corps of Engineers and the Bureau of Reclamation delayed plans until the 1960s, when a preservationist ethic would begin to alter national policy. On the Missouri River, Colonel Lewis A. Pick of the Corps proposed fifteen hundred miles of levees and six main-stem dams for navigation and flood control, whereas William G. Sloan from the Bureau proposed damming tributaries for hydropower and irrigation. The two men met in Billings in 1944 and hammered out the Pick-Sloan agreement to parcel out development of the Missouri much like European statesmen carving up the map of Africa.

The next logical step of regional river basin development agencies, following the model of the Tennessee Valley Authority, was never taken. Colorado politicians and business leaders shot down the idea of an Arkansas Valley Authority in 1941 as another unwanted intrusion of federal authority that might reduce local control of water resources. A Columbia Valley Authority fared little better. A Missouri Valley Authority, backed by Franklin Roosevelt in 1944, at least carried the New Deal impulse into the 1950s. Advocates like Senator James Murray of Montana hoped to follow wartime prosperity with a coordinated economic transition to prevent postwar depression. Successful opposition came from the power companies, which feared cheap federal electricity, from the railroads, which resented the competition of barge transportation, and from both the Corps and the Bureau of Reclamation, which had already divided up the dam-making job with the Pick-Sloan memorandum. The regional planning idea as a federal initiative reappeared in the 1960s and 1970s with regional commissions to coordinate economic development for the Four Corners (Arizona, Colorado, New Mexico, Utah), the Old West (Montana, Nebraska, Wyoming, the Dakotas), and the Pacific Northwest (Idaho, Oregon, Washington) and with federally mandated River Basin Commissions for the Columbia and Missouri rivers.

The first impression to take away from the 1920s and 1930s is the contrasting styles of project planning and regional planning. The nation's memory of the long depression in the West is one of streams of concrete pouring into wooden forms—the core of a dam, a stretch of federal-aid highway, steps to a new courthouse built by the WPA. Just as important, however, are the hundreds of offices and conference rooms in which federal officials sat down, sometimes with state and local representatives, to plan out a frame-work for future growth. On the dry and desolated plains, the chief actors often reported to U.S. Secretary of Agriculture Henry Wallace, who oversaw such programs as the Agricultural Adjustment Administration, Soil Conservation Service, Farm Security Administration, and Resettlement Administration, which were designed to move the region beyond wasteful practices of agriculture. In the mountain and Pacific states, the final arbiter was most often Interior Secretary Harold Ickes, an old-line believer in the progressive gospel of efficiency whose PWA and other construction programs were designed to redevelop regional resources.

The decision to make the federal government an active planner of western development also left it a permanent partner with western residents. The land retained in permanent federal ownership as national forests, parks and monuments, grazing lands, Indian reservations, and military installations totaled 99 percent of Alaska in 1944 and 87 percent of Nevada. Federal ownership exceeded 50 percent in five other adjacent states in the heartland of western mountains and plateaus—Arizona, Utah, Wyoming, Idaho, and Oregon. Surrounding this federal core were five additional states where federal ownership ranged between 35 and 46 percent. The only significant reductions of federal lands have come in Alaska, where the Native Claims Settlement Act and the National Interest Lands Conservation Act defined the process for transferring 44 million acres to native corporations and 105 million acres to the state by the mid-1990s (leaving 215 million acres in federal ownership). Only in the plains states and Hawai`i was the federal government a relatively minor player, with ownership levels between 1 and 18 percent.

The federal agenda of the 1920s and 1930s hastened the nationalization of American life. Tangible and intangible federal networks—highways, power lines, relief payments, social insurance—helped to incorporate isolated communities into the economic and social mainstream. Ethnic islands that had retained their distinctive cultures through the long decades of Anglo-American conquest found themselves reshaped by contradictory national expectations. The New Deal offered Native Americans and Hispanos a tension between a romantic valuation of preindustrial cultures and a desire to provide upgraded and modernized services. In northern New Mexico, for example, federal officials built roads and improved health care but also tried to "freeze" the styles of folk art and organize production for the tourist trade. The Soil Conservation Service and the Bureau of Indian Affairs forced the Navajos to reduce their herds of sheep and horses in the interest of scientific conservation of the reservation grasslands. At the same time, however, vital infusions of cash and services provided the foundations on which the Navajo people would achieve significant self-determination after 1945.

For westerners who already shared the national values, the regional planning of the 1920s and 1930s was an unambiguous success. Whether residents liked to admit it or not, the federal initiatives saved the West from collapse. There were fewer farmers and miners in 1940 than in 1920, and there were more abandoned towns on the high plains and plateaus. By and large, however, the West in 1940 had new resources in place for an economic takeoff—new electric power, new expertise in large-scale construction, workers with new skills for an industrial economy, and a renewed commitment to the progressive agenda of efficient resource development. "The program of the New Deal," wrote Richard Neuberger in *Our Promised Land* in 1938, "represents the first conscious attempt of government to utilize for all the people the vast, untapped resources of the frontier. Whatever else Mr. Roosevelt may have done to or for our country, that much he has accomplished in the Columbia River basin." Although Neuberger wrote about the Pacific Northwest, his enthusiasm was relevant to a far wider region. "Never again can the natural riches of the hinterlands be left undeveloped as they were in the years before the New Deal."

The West at War, 1940–60

The federal government in 1939 was the leading landlord and largest general contractor in the West. By 1943 and 1944, it was also the dominant employer. In an era when one thousand dollars could buy a very good car, Houston, Fort Worth, Wichita, Seattle, Portland, San Francisco, Los Angeles, and San Diego all received more than one billion dollars in war-supply contracts from 1940 to 1945. The relative impact can be seen in estimates of the proportion of California's personal income derived from the federal government—5 percent in 1930, 10 percent in 1940 after a decade of relief and public works programs, and 45 percent in 1945 after half a decade of a war economy.

Between 1941 and 1964, the United States not only fought its seven-thousand-mile war against Japan but also entered wars against North Korea and China and against North Vietnam. It came to the brink of war at least twice more in the mid-1950s in Indochina and the Formosa Straits. World War II set in motion changes whose impacts

are still being felt half a century later. Taken together, the Pacific war and its Asian follow-ups marked the final transition from the old to the new West and made the federal budget the essential drive wheel of western growth.

The armed forces were no strangers in the West in the nineteenth century, but the region's military establishment had faded in the new century. Indeed, boosters in cities throughout the West labored long and hard during the 1920s and 1930s to secure new military bases to prop up local economies. Cities in the San Francisco Bay area vigorously argued among themselves about the best sites for navy bases but presented a united front in Washington. The San Antonio Chamber of Commerce embraced military aviation as the winning card in that city's rivalry with Dallas and Houston. Kelly Field and Brooks Air Base date to 1916–18 and Randolph Air Base to the 1920s, all to be vigorously defended by San Antonio's congressmen and businessmen. Prewar mobilization in 1940 brought a new wave of booster opportunities. The Dallas Chamber of Commerce and the Citizens Council (representing the city's preeminent movers and shakers) campaigned in Washington to secure a naval reserve aviation base and a North American Aviation Company plant whose payroll would total forty-three thousand by the midpoint of the war. Nearby Fort Worth secured Tarrant Field and a Consolidated Vultee Aircraft (Convair) plant, the latter through the newspaper editor Amon Carter's direct lobbying with Franklin Roosevelt. Similar combinations of local promotion, political influence, and bureaucratic criteria brought Tinker Air Base to Oklahoma City and Hill Air Base and Clearfield Naval Depot to the Salt Lake City–Ogden area.

Anticipating shortages of nonferrous metals, the federal government built a huge plant near Las Vegas to produce magnesium with the help of Hoover Dam electricity and a series of aluminum plants at Spokane, Vancouver, Longview, and other sites in Washington and Oregon served by hydropower from the Bonneville Power Administration.

The Japanese attack on Pearl Harbor and the sustained fighting of 1942 brought the reality of war to American territory. In addition to the attack on Hawai`i and the famous naval battle off Midway Island, Japanese submarines briefly shelled the Oregon and California coasts in 1942, and a large Japanese force invaded the Aleutian Islands in June 1942. The Japanese bombed Dutch Harbor and occupied Attu and Kiska islands until driven off in August 1943. The invasion was preemptive and defensive, for Attu and Kiska were more than one thousand miles closer to the home islands of Japan than to the lower forty-eight states. Nevertheless, the attack helped to trigger a military buildup in Alaska and the assignment of seven regiments from the Corps of Engineers to build the Alaska Highway from Dawson Creek, British Columbia, to Fairbanks. The road was neither necessary nor very useful for the military, but it symbolized the war as a shaper of the western environment.

On 19 February 1942, President Roosevelt issued Executive Order 9066, which authorized the secretary of war to define restricted areas and remove civilian residents. In Alaska, the Japanese attacks and landings caused the military to evacuate native Aleuts from the outlying islands of Alaska. They spent much of the war in substandard conditions in southeastern Alaska and returned to gutted environments. In many ways, their experience mirrored that of more than one hundred thousand Japanese Americans who were removed from California and large parts of Washington, Oregon, and Arizona in the spring of 1942. Those who had not voluntarily moved from the coastal states found themselves in any of ten relocation camps scattered from the mountain West as far east as Arkansas. The political expediency of the removal satisfied a generation of anti-Japanese sentiment kindled into hatred by the war. Most evacuees lost businesses and property. The United States officially recognized its liability with the Japanese Claims Act of 1948 and acknowledged its broader moral responsibility in 1988 when Congress approved redress payments of twenty thousand dollars to the sixty thousand surviving evacuees.

In numbers, of course, voluntary migrants who flocked to war production centers far outnumbered the deportees. The expansion of defense production in 1940–41 and the organization of a huge military enterprise in 1942–43 shifted the national economic balance toward the South Atlantic, Gulf, and Pacific coasts. Small cities like Phoenix and Albuquerque became important urban centers within half a decade. Wartime booms accelerated the long-term development of larger cities like Denver and Salt Lake City. From 1940 to 1943, the states with the highest rates of population growth were California, Oregon, Washington, Nevada, Utah, and Arizona (along with Florida, Virginia, and Maryland). The boom touched every major city in Texas, Oklahoma, the Pacific states, and the Southwest as well as selected production centers in the interior West.

The boom cities of the West suffered a common cycle of problems in which overpriced and insufficient housing forced new workers to locate haphazardly through the metropolitan area and further overburden already overcrowded transit systems. Workers in Seattle's shipyards and Boeing plant scrounged for living space in offices,

Pausing to enjoy their last meal eaten in freedom before their forced evacuation to a relocation camp in the spring of 1942, members of a Japanese-American citizens' league protest their fate with a meal of hot dogs and apple pie, deliberately chosen to reassert their status as American citizens.

Russell Lee (1903–1986). Picnic Lunch for Members of the Japanese-American Citizens' League Just Before Their Evacuation *(San Benito County, California). Gelatin silver print, 1942. Farm Security Administration Collection, Library of Congress (#LC-USF34-TO1-72516D), Washington, D.C.*

tents, and chicken coops. A well-publicized visit by the U.S. House Committee on National Defense Migration in the summer of 1941 found San Diego swamped by ninety thousand defense industry workers and thirty-five thousand military personnel. Operating on their own hurried schedules, federal agencies exacerbated the city's problems by locating defense plants and emergency housing on isolated sites, thus forcing extra service costs and creating painful traffic problems. *Life, Business Week, Fortune,* and the *Saturday Evening Post* all described the crowded schools, overpacked hotels, makeshift trailer parks, and raucous nightlife in the "rip-roaringest coast boom town." San Diego's inadequate and poorly located housing, said one expert, was the "core of every problem and controversy."

After diligently working to secure naval facilities, the cities of the San Francisco Bay area found themselves with more than they had bargained for in 1940 and 1941. The federal government expanded the Mare Island and Hunters Point shipyards, Moffett Field, the Naval Operating Base and new Naval Air Station at Alameda, naval supply depots, and new facilities on Treasure Island. Federal contracts also funded a half-dozen huge private shipyards—General Engineering and Drydock in San Francisco, Western Pipe and Steel in South San Francisco, Bethlehem Shipbuilding in Alameda, Moore Drydock in Oakland, Todd-Kaiser in Richmond, and Marinship in Sausalito. San Francisco itself became a huge dormitory housing war workers, servicemen between assignments, and their dependents. The population of Vallejo and adjoining areas tripled, and workers at Mare Island commuted as far as fifty miles on rationed gasoline. Richmond's job total increased from 15,000 to 130,000. The city imported old elevated railroad cars from New York for a new rail line to Oakland as a way of coping with its transportation problem.

The war also brought entirely new towns. Under the Lanham Act and related programs, the federal government financed one million temporary housing units for wartime use nationwide. Many of the apartments were in the Bay Area at Richmond and the model community of Marin City. Many more—enough for forty thousand residents—were built at the instant "city" of Vanport, Oregon. Rising on the floodplain of the Columbia River, halfway between the Kaiser Corporation shipyards in Portland, Oregon, and Vancouver, Washington, the first of nine thousand apartments in six hundred wooden buildings were ready in December 1942. Painted dull gray to blend into the cold winter rains of the Northwest, the buildings of Vanport included schools, community centers, a day-care program, a post office, cafeterias, a fire district, playgrounds, shops, a 150-bed hospital, and a movie theater that ran three double-bills per week. New "science cities" in the western interior also contributed to the American war effort. Richland, Washington, on a dry benchland along the Columbia River, burgeoned from approximately three hundred people growing peaches and asparagus in 1940 to a community of fifteen thousand technicians supporting the manufacture of plutonium at the Hanford Engineering Works. Los Alamos, New Mexico, on a mesa that faced the sunrise over the valley of the Rio Grande, was built to an equally careful plan. The nuclear physicists and engineers who designed atomic bombs enjoyed gracefully curved streets and public facilities laid out according to the best modern standards of urban design.

The war meant new people as well as planned towns for the Far West. African Americans from Texas, Oklahoma, and the lower Mississippi Valley followed news of labor shortages and high wages to defense production centers. Seattle's black population jumped from four thousand to forty thousand, Portland's from two thousand to fifteen thousand. Within the cities, the newcomers crowded into a few neighborhoods and housing projects carefully set aside in the style of established eastern ghettos. Many found the only affordable housing to be in neighborhoods forcibly vacated by Japanese residents, such as the Western Addition in San Francisco and Little Tokyo east of downtown Los Angeles. Whether in a federal community like Vanport, a housing project like Hunter's Point in San Francisco, or a federally backed subdivision in the East Bay, new housing preserved the distinction between white and black neighborhoods and set a pattern of suburban segregation for the postwar generation.

Tensions also rose between Mexican Americans and Anglo Americans in Los Angeles. During the 1930s, tens of thousands of Mexican Americans had permanently settled in western cities such as Denver when their rural jobs as railroad hands and farm laborers disappeared. New migration in the early 1940s swelled the Mexican community in Los Angeles to an estimated four hundred thousand, prompting discrimination and a steady stream of anti-Mexican articles in the major newspapers. On 3 June 1943, off-duty sailors and soldiers led several thousand Anglos to attack Hispanics on downtown streets and invade Mexican-American neighborhoods. Blacks and Filipinos were incidental targets. The "zoot suit" riots, named for the flamboyant clothes of some young Chicanos, dragged on for a week.

The war was a powerful force for the assimilation of Native Americans. Military service and war production jobs greatly accelerated the process of modernization started by the New Deal. Twenty-five thousand Native Americans served in the armed forces. Another forty thousand moved for off-reservation jobs, utilizing industrial and mechanical skills learned in the Indian CCC and in programs of the National Defense Vocational Training Act. The average cash income of Indian households tripled during the war, and many Native Americans stayed in Los Angeles, Seattle, Phoenix, Denver, and other western cities at the end of the war.

War also opened new opportunities for women, who made up roughly one-quarter of West Coast shipyard workers at the peak of employment, two-fifths of Los Angeles aircraft workers, and nearly one-half of Dallas aircraft workers. The shipyards turned first to women who were already in the labor force in jobs ranging from shop clerk to farm worker. Many of the "housewives" who responded to recruitment campaigns in 1943 and 1944 were women who needed jobs to support their families. As one of the workers recalled of herself and a friend, "We both had to work, we both had children, so we became welders, and if I might say so, damn good ones." The most common shipyard jobs were clerks and general helpers, but the acute shortage of welders opened more than five thousand journeyman positions in the Portland operations. A few women even found positions as electricians and crane operators—far more interesting work than waitressing or sewing in a clothing factory. Aircraft companies, whose labor shortages were compounded by stubborn "whites only" hiring, developed new power tools and production techniques to accommodate the smaller average size of women workers, increasing efficiency for everyone along the production line.

Victory in 1945 forced women out of the factories, but it left the American military extended worldwide. As the "American Century" quickly faded into the realities of the cold war, the United States prepared for the indefinite projection of power in the Pacific and East Asia and for continental defense through nuclear deterrence. The North Korean invasion of South Korea in June 1950 and the Chinese entry into the Korean conflict in December confirmed the American commitment to the dual strategy of advanced and strategic defense. In response, American military planning during the early 1950s created four strategic "layers" that overlapped the western states and territories.

The nation's forward presence in the Far East rested on bases in the Philippines, Central Pacific, Okinawa, Korea, and Japan. The need to anchor this first line of defense in Alaska led to a new surge of federal investment greater than that in either the 1910s or the 1940s. Federal agencies and contractors built the Distant Early Warning Line of radar stations across northern Alaska. They expanded military bases. They upgraded ports, highways, railroads, and airports in the territory's Anchorage-Valdez-Fairbanks core. Alaska's 1950 census counted 1 uniformed member of the armed services for every 4.3 civilians.

Supply depots, training bases, shipyards, and aircraft maintenance bases constituted the second layer in the western military system. Admirals presided over navy commands headquartered at Seattle, San Francisco, San Diego, and Honolulu. Each city lay in a cluster of operating bases, shipyards, and air stations. Army and air force training facilities were especially prominent in Washington, Colorado, Texas, and Oklahoma. The siting of the new Air Force Academy in Colorado Springs to balance the historic

Major Military Installations and Related Institutions, 1992

service academies in Maryland and New York recognized the prominence of the West as a home base.

The strategic strike and defense forces that formed the heart of America's cold war strategy were commanded from the national heartland of the Great Plains. North American air defense was coordinated from a command post sunk deep beneath Cheyenne Mountain at the foot of the Rockies behind Colorado Springs. General Curtis LeMay directed the B-47s and B-52s of the Strategic Air Command from Omaha. By the 1970s, solid-fueled minuteman missiles were targeted for Moscow and Beijing from unobtrusive silos dotting the rolling landscapes of Montana and the Dakotas.

The fourth "layer" of the defense system was strategic weapons production. The Manhattan Project had tested the first atomic bomb at the Trinity site near Alamogordo, New Mexico. After the war, the armed forces experimented with missiles, atomic warheads, and lethal chemicals in the empty reaches of New Mexico, Nevada, and Utah. The Hanford reservation continued to produce plutonium for nuclear weapons, and the Rocky Flats facility north of Denver turned plutonium into triggers for thermonuclear bombs.

Military buildup during the Korean War brought a federally supported uranium boom to the Four Corners region of the Colorado Plateau. In the words of the *National Geographic*, it was "the land of the weekend prospector." Eager amateurs sent fifty-five cents to the Government Printing Office for a how-to pamphlet on uranium mining, stocked up on Geiger counters and USGS maps in Grand Junction, Colorado, and Moab, Utah, and joined Atomic Energy Commission and Geological Survey scientists in the search for bright-yellow carnotite ore. The federal government bought any commercial-grade ore and offered a special finding bonus of thirty-five thousand dollars for each new discovery. Although the prospecting mania died down by mid-decade, radioactive tailings from processing plants in towns like Uravan and Grand Junction, Colorado, and Monticello, Utah, remained serious health hazards for decades.

A city like San Diego showed the results of the peacetime mobilization. By one estimate, the U.S. Navy alone was responsible for adding 215,000 people to the San Diego area in 1957. Weapons makers added tens of thousands more. Most residents seemed to believe that what was good for Convair was good for the country. Cruising the harbor, as the historian Roger Lotchin has pointed out, one would pass a submarine base, a carrier anchorage, dry docks, shipbuilding firms, ammunition bunkers, and barracks ships. "In the bay, ships ply the waters and retired admirals cruise their sailing vessels; overhead, naval helicopters buzz and jets scream; and downtown, sailors throng the streets." The military was a constant presence in social life and civic activities. Scores of community organizations depended on military surplus goods to support their programs. Initiated in 1953, Air Power Day became a local equivalent of the Pasadena rose festival.

The West ended the 1950s deeply dependent on the military budget. Examining defense spending by states for 1952–62, Roger Bolton found a heavy dependence on defense for 25 percent or more of income from out-of-state sources in Washington, California, Hawai`i, Alaska, Utah, and Colorado. He found substantial dependence for 15–24 percent of outside income in Nevada, Arizona, New Mexico, Kansas, Oklahoma, and Texas. A slightly different measurement of defense spending as a stimulus to growth added Montana, South Dakota, and Wyoming to the list of defense-dependent states. Twenty years later there was little change. Six of the ten cities with the largest civilian Department of Defense employment in the 1980s were western. Of the contracts for President Ronald Reagan's Strategic Defense Initiative for 1983–86, 70 percent went to five western states.

The era of the garrison state left cultural as well as economic imprints. Military retirees make up at least 1 percent of the population in Washington, Colorado, Nevada, Arizona, New Mexico, and Hawai`i. They are an inescapable presence in San Diego, San Antonio, and other cities of California and Texas. A retired astronaut would make no sense as a central character in a story set in Buffalo or Detroit but seems perfectly at home in the Houston of Larry McMurtry's *Terms of Endearment* (1975). The West was close to the front lines of our three Pacific wars, serving as a place of embarkation, rest, and reentry. By the 1970s, it was also the new home for three hundred thousand refugees from Indochina. Whether they liked it or not, westerners found that proximity brought them face to face with growing moral dilemmas of American military action. In Herman Wouk's *The Caine Mutiny* (1951), Yosemite National Park is a healing counterpoint to the naval war against Japan. Twenty-three years later, Robert Stone's *Dog Soldiers* offered a compelling analysis of the effects of the Vietnam War on the American character, with the trans-Pacific traffic in drugs as the metaphor for the loss of national innocence. With

Vietnam only a few hours away, the most ordinary streets and ordinary residents of Oakland are pulled into direct confrontation with the moral ambiguities of Saigon. Neither a backwater nor a refuge, the contemporary West in the middle decades of the twentieth century became a central participant in the drama of war and peace.

The West in the World, 1960–90

In 1983, *Time* magazine declared that Los Angeles had become the "new Ellis Island," the destination for immigrants to the United States. A few years later, the Port of Los Angeles renamed itself "Worldport L.A." Security Pacific Bank in 1988 proclaimed that the Los Angeles regional economy was larger than that of Brazil, Australia, or India. As a "focal point of international trade and finance," greater Los Angeles ranked as one of a handful of control points in the world economy. This transformation of a western city into what geographers call a "world city" symbolizes the newest dimension of the federal impact on the West.

In the 1940s and 1950s, emergency mobilization and the entrenchment of the "garrison state" made the American West a staging ground for the projection of national power into world affairs. In the 1960s, a series of federal initiatives reopened American society and economy to the countercurrents of international trade and migration. By the 1970s and 1980s, the West had assumed a new importance in the middle of growing global networks of people, products, and ideas. In substantial part, this regional change was an inadvertent consequence of federal policies devised to handle national needs within world economic and political systems.

The reopening of American borders with the Immigration Reform Act of 1965, for example, responded directly to national economic and humanitarian needs and to the symbolic role of the United States in the world. The removal of Europocentric quotas for immigration, however, opened the door for new migrants from Latin America and Asia, who made the southwestern and Pacific states their primary rather than secondary destinations. Total legal migration to the United States grew from 3.3 million in 1961–70 to 4.5 million for 1971–80 and 6 million for 1981–90. Nearly 5 million of the total for the 1980s were Asians or Latin Americans. Indeed, the migration of the 1980s was large enough to trigger the Immigration Reform and Control Act of 1986, which offered retroactive legalization to many undocumented immigrants while trying to raise new barriers against further illegal immigration.

The liberalization of foreign trade dated to the General Agreement on Tariffs and Trade of 1947, followed by the Trade Expansion Act of 1962. Both measures looked first to the Atlantic economy, but their liberalized trade regulations provided the basis for a shift of foreign commerce to Asian and Pacific partners and ports. Imports and exports totaled 6.8 percent of the gross national product in 1960 and 14.6 percent by 1987, the heaviest orientation of the American economy to overseas trade since 1918. The accompaniment was an unplanned shift of trade to Texas and Pacific ports. By the mid-1980s, western boosters could cite figures that showed U.S. trade across the Pacific to be more valuable than the trans-Atlantic trade.

The West also gained a central role in national policy when the energy industry took center stage in world politics in the 1970s. The crisis of the OPEC embargo and world price increases brought efforts at a national energy independence that depended heavily on the West. Oil leases on federal lands on the North Slope of Alaska triggered a new Alaskan boom. Federal tax credits and subsidies encouraged attempts to extract oil from western Colorado shale deposits. The search for alternatives to fossil fuels looked to western wind and sunlight. Federal funds created the Solar Energy Research Institute in Golden, Colorado, while solar collector fields and windmills blossomed on western bluffs and hillsides. The oil glut of the 1980s resulted in a declining sense of urgency, however, allowing budget-trimming bureaucrats in the Reagan administration to cut off support for most of the experiments. National policy encouraged agricultural exports as a counterbalance to energy imports. Until halted by President Jimmy Carter in reaction to the Russian invasion of Afghanistan, grain sales to the Soviet Union were the most visible sign of a new farm boom, with some painful similarities to the 1910s. Wheat exports increased 2.4 times between 1970 and their peak in 1981. Land prices in the Missouri Valley spiraled upward in the 1970s, only to drop by 40 or 50 percent in the 1980s, with rural bankruptcies and business failures.

If the federal government has remained an ambiguous friend of resource production industries, it supplied the key market for the "fourth wave" industries that led the nation's economic expansion after World War II. Steam engines and the mass production of textiles had led the first wave of worldwide industrial growth from 1790 to 1845. Steel production and railroads had led the second wave from 1845 to 1890. Chemicals, electrical equipment, and automobiles had led a third wave from 1890 until the Great Depression. After the war, the new leaders were the electronics, communication, and aerospace industries. Whereas the first three waves had worked to concentrate industrial power in the manufacturing belt running from Boston to St. Louis, the postwar boom had its most profound impacts on the American West.

It was chiefly in the West, for example, that the aircraft industry of World War I and World War II evolved into the far more extensive aerospace business. By the 1950s, the six cities of Seattle, Los Angeles, San Diego, Dallas, Fort Worth, and Wichita accounted for nearly all of the country's airframe production and assembly. Military contracts sustained Lockheed, General Dynamics, McDonnell-Douglas, Northrop, and scores of related firms. The location of the Manned Spacecraft Center of the National Aeronautics and Space Administration (NASA) on ten thousand acres of donated land brought scores of spinoff businesses to Houston. The national space program also drew on the Jet Propulsion Laboratory in Pasadena, as well as Edwards and Vandenberg air force bases in California.

Federal contracts have been the basic support for the development and utilization of new electronics and information technologies in the newly high-tech cities of the West. Stanford Industrial Park in 1951 was the first planned effort to link the science and engineering faculties of major universities to the design and production of new products. It was the first step in the evolution of Silicon Valley, between San Francisco and San Jose, as a center of the electronics industry. Federal contracts, especially from the Department of Defense, have been a mainstay of Silicon Valley. A broader definition of high-tech, based on a high ratio of research and development to net sales, includes such industries as aircraft, guided missiles and space vehicles, computing machines, communication equipment, electronic components, and drugs. The federal government has been a primary customer for all but the last category. During the 1970s,

Arizona, California, Washington, Kansas, Utah, and Colorado ranked among the top ten states for high-tech jobs as a proportion of total employment.

The promotion of scientific research and applications became another federal industry, especially in the wake of the successful Russian launch of the first *Sputnik* in 1957. The federal subsidy of physical science utilized a combination of federal laboratories, private research-and-development contractors, and universities. One example is Albuquerque, which ranked ninth among all metropolitan areas in its federal research-and-development contracts in 1977. Scientists on the federal payroll have continued to undertake basic research at the Los Alamos National Laboratory. Western Electric operated Sandia National Laboratories under federal contract after 1949. Successful grant applications by faculty at the University of New Mexico made the state a leader in federal research and development in proportion to population. Colorado's pattern has been similar. Martin Marietta Corporation decided in 1956 to build a plant for titan missiles in the Denver suburb of Littleton. Hewlett-Packard, Honeywell, Sundstrand, and Ball Brothers Research were a few of the other high-technology firms attracted by life near the mountains. It was a short step from defense industries and science-oriented corporations to the research division of the University of Colorado and the federal research agencies located in Boulder—the National Bureau of Standards, the National Center for Atmospheric Research, and the National Oceanic and Atmospheric Administration.

The newest era of "big science" continues the western tilt. NASA's controversial manned space station is coordinated from the renamed Johnson Space Center in Houston. Astronomers use the country's biggest telescopes in California and Hawai`i and anticipate new facilities in the mountains above Tucson, Arizona. The end of the cold war has meant an end to plans for an eight-billion-dollar Superconducting Super Collider, slated until 1993 for the Texas prairies south of Dallas. Still, the nuclear weapons laboratories at Los Alamos, New Mexico, and Livermore, California, continue to function, though rapidly diversifying the range of their research.

Big science, it turns out, means big cleanups. The Department of Energy has made the western states the location of choice for disposal of nuclear wastes from military production and private reactors. New Mexico's salt deposits are scheduled to receive contaminated materials from Rocky Flats and other sites. In a multistate contest from which the Energy Department had eliminated all eastern states, Texas and Washington managed to fight off a nuclear waste repository now destined for Yucca Mountain, Nevada. At least nine billion dollars will be required to entomb high-level radioactive materials under the dry basin lands one hundred miles northwest of Las Vegas. At Hanford, Washington, tens of billions of tax dollars will be required for the safe disposal of radioactive liquids that have been sitting for decades in rusting tanks, ponds, and trenches within a few miles of the Columbia River.

In the process of building American scientific capacity, federal initiatives helped to transform western university systems. Research grants and graduate student aid, especially after the passage of the National Defense Education Act (1958), provided vital funding at a time when regional campuses were struggling to cope with the first arrivals from the postwar baby boom. The University of Washington grew from thirteen thousand to thirty thousand students by 1966 with vigorous pursuit of federal grants that equaled direct support from the state general fund. Federal funds had similar effects on university systems in Texas, California, and other western states. The University of California–San Diego was explicitly created to support high-technology research with a hefty gift and strong lobbying from the giant defense contractor General Dynamics. When federal research-and-development funding for universities is compared on a per capita basis, Alaska, Utah, Hawai`i, New Mexico, Washington, California, and Colorado all exceed the national average.

Direct federal funding and federal markets for science-intensive production have helped to make western metro areas some of the best-educated in the country. Sixteen of the metro areas that had five hundred thousand or more residents in 1980 reported that 20 percent or more of their adult population (over twenty-five years old) had completed at least four years of college. Ten of these cities were western: Austin at 28 percent; Denver at 26 percent; San Francisco–Oakland–San Jose at 25 percent; and Seattle–Tacoma, Honolulu, Houston, San Diego, Tucson, Salt Lake City, and Dallas–Fort Worth all at between 20 and 24 percent. The West claimed twenty-eight of the fifty-four metro areas of all sizes with the same high education level—including not only such likely candidates as Colorado Springs and Santa Barbara but also less obvious cities such as Grand Forks, North Dakota; Boise, Idaho; and Midland, Texas.

To gauge the global orientation of the new western metropolis, we can develop a comparative index utilizing data on foreign-born population, foreign trade, foreign banks, foreign investment, importance of foreign markets, and role as international information center. San Francisco–Oakland, the clear leader as an international city in 1960, had yielded first place to Los Angeles by the 1980s. Indeed, Los Angeles is now clearly a "world city" in both its boardrooms and its streets, tied into international flows of people, goods, and data. At one level, it is the New York City of the Pacific Rim. The volume of imports and exports through Los Angeles and Long Beach tripled from 1970 to 1990. Observers such as the *Los Angeles Times* noticed an upturn in foreign investment after 1975. Canadian, Japanese, and other foreign investors have become major speculators in downtown real estate. Several major banks passed into the hands of Japanese and British firms during the 1980s. In turn, the foreign presence has attracted U.S. banks and corporate headquarters.

Los Angeles is very much an immigrant city. Nearly 20 percent of the people in the metropolitan area were foreign-born in 1980, 27 percent in the city of Los Angeles. These new ethnic residents fill the full range of economic roles—low-skill service workers, low-wage garment workers, skilled electronics assemblers, small entrepreneurs in retailing and manufacturing, scientists, and professionals. Specific Asian and Latino enclaves dot Los Angeles and Orange counties. Downtown Los Angeles divides between its English-speaking corporate towers on the west side and its Spanish-speaking theaters and stores east of Broadway. Behind Los Angeles and the Bay Area, San Diego, Honolulu, Seattle, Houston, and Dallas have been pushing forward as second-level centers for international contacts. The landlocked Dallas–Fort Worth "metroplex," for example, has adopted an aggressive global development strategy. The Dallas partnership at the start of the 1990s talked about a future as "a preeminent center of world commerce in the twenty-first century." The adamantly American city of Dallas now cooperates with Fort Worth ("where the West begins") to publish maps showing the metroplex as the navel of the world. In fact, Dallas–Fort Worth has become a second-level center for international banking. Foreign corporations employ thirty-five thousand workers. The city is trying to acquire the critical mass of foreign firms, trade offices, and business agents necessary to rival Mexico City, Chicago, and Los Angeles rather than New Orleans and Houston.

The successful cities of the "New West" have learned how to use federal funds to shape a cityscape appropriate for the information age. Westerners have received far more than their "fair" share of federal dollars for transportation facilities to overcome the added costs and delays of great distances. With a quarter of the national population in the 1970s, the West had received 35 percent of airport construction aid (1946–72) and 42 percent of interstate highway mileage. Only three thousand westerners have to share each mile of interstate within the region, compared with six thousand easterners for each mile in their half of the country.

In contrast to the image of western cities as freeway capitals, many of them showed an initial reluctance to use federal funds that became available for urban revitalization in the later 1940s and the 1950s. Los Angeles and Portland grudgingly accepted public housing as a wartime necessity but backed away from new construction in the 1950s. Tucson rejected federal urban-renewal funds in a noisy political controversy. Politicians and newspaper editors fended off the federal octopus in Phoenix. Fort Worth, Dallas, and Houston declined to hold the local elections required by Texas law. The state of Washington failed even to adopt enabling legislation until 1957, held back, according to Seattle Mayor Gordon Clinton, by the taint of socialism.

Beginning in 1959 in several West Coast cities and in the early 1960s in many of the Rocky Mountain and southern plains cities, new urban-renewal agencies did start up the "federal bulldozer" to clear deteriorated fringes of central business districts. Civic centers, office buildings, and university campuses were the first steps in adapting cities for a global information economy. High-rise cores in Los Angeles, San Francisco, Dallas, Houston, Denver, and Seattle provide the "natural" setting for the information processing and command transactions that dominate the modern world economy. Cities resuscitated failing private bus systems by purchase and expansion with Urban Mass Transit Administration dollars. Downtown streets dedicated to bus service and new rail lines now smooth the commute of the workers who serve the metropolitan decision makers.

Even cities like Phoenix and Houston, whose community ideologies adamantly proclaim the virtues of untrammeled free enterprise, owe much of their growth to federal favor. Federal dollars helped to dredge the Houston Ship Channel that made the city a port and petrochemical center, just as they built Roosevelt Dam outside Phoenix to make the Salt River Valley a major farming center and enable it to support intensive settlement. During World War II, Phoenix acquired three large air bases. Houston ranked sixth in the nation in federal investment in factory facilities, and the federally financed Big Inch and Little Inch pipelines gave Houston a national market for its natural gas. Oil import quotas, depletion allowances, foreign tax credits, and other federal tax subsidies supported the domestic petroleum industry. The expertise of Houston corporations in petroleum research, exploration, production, and refining helped to define and secure American interests in overseas oil fields. Even the unzoned subdivisions of Houston and the sprawling suburbs of Phoenix were built with federally insured or guaranteed mortgages. Like earlier westerners, Houstonians and Phoenicians may have fulminated against the influence of federal bureaucrats, but they were happy to bank the benefits of federal assistance.

The Networked West

The western states and territories entered the twentieth century as a set of isolated resource regions organized around provincial trading centers. Copper miners in southern Arizona, stock raisers in central Wyoming, cotton farmers in Oklahoma, and wheat ranchers in eastern Washington all depended directly on decisions made in New York and Chicago and transmitted through small cities like Tucson, Casper, Tulsa, and Spokane. In a pattern reminiscent of British North America before 1775, most subregions had stronger ties to the East than to each other. In the phrase of the historian Robert Wiebe, the West was an archipelago of "island communities."

Three generations later, the national government's immigration policies, trade policies, resource development policies, infrastructure investments, and defense spending had transformed much of the West. The northern plains and northern Rockies communities found themselves repeating the events of the 1920s, losing old primary industries and scrambling to replace them with the modern resource industry of tourism. The overwhelming majority of westerners, in contrast, lived in the cities of the southwestern and Pacific states—economically diversified communities with the capacity to generate much of their own growth through innovation and import substitution. With Los Angeles–San Diego and San Francisco–Oakland–San Jose as its twin capitals, greater California embraced Arizona, Nevada, Hawai`i, and the northern coastal states within its sphere of trade, finance, and communication. Even in the midst of an energy industry depression, the metropolitan axis of Houston-Dallas-Denver organized a half dozen other states into another economic unit driven by resource production, foreign business connections, high-tech industry, and federal spending.

The political influence of the West rose with its population, making it more and more an initiator of federal policies rather than a recipient. The West added ten U.S. senators after 1900 with the admission of Oklahoma, New Mexico, Arizona, Hawai`i, and Alaska as states. The number of westerners in the House of Representatives rose from 60 in 1900 to 127 in 1980. Theodore Roosevelt in 1901 and Herbert Hoover in 1929 were the first presidents with real western connections. Between 1952 and 1992, genuine or honorary westerners—Eisenhower, Johnson, Nixon, Reagan, and Bush— accounted for thirty-one of forty possible years in the White House.

By the 1980s, western issues had become national issues. Western relations with Japan, OPEC nations, and the newly industrialized countries of East Asia defined much of national economic policy. In the 1990s, conflicting versions of a "sagebrush rebellion" are likely to define long-lasting national choices about the future of the American landscape. The free enterprise rebellion fears that the federal government is preserving and conserving natural resources at the expense of local investment and employment opportunities. The environmental rebels, especially strong in the Pacific states and northern Rockies, fear that the federal government has failed to prevent environmental degradation of lands under its control. Their agenda includes opposition

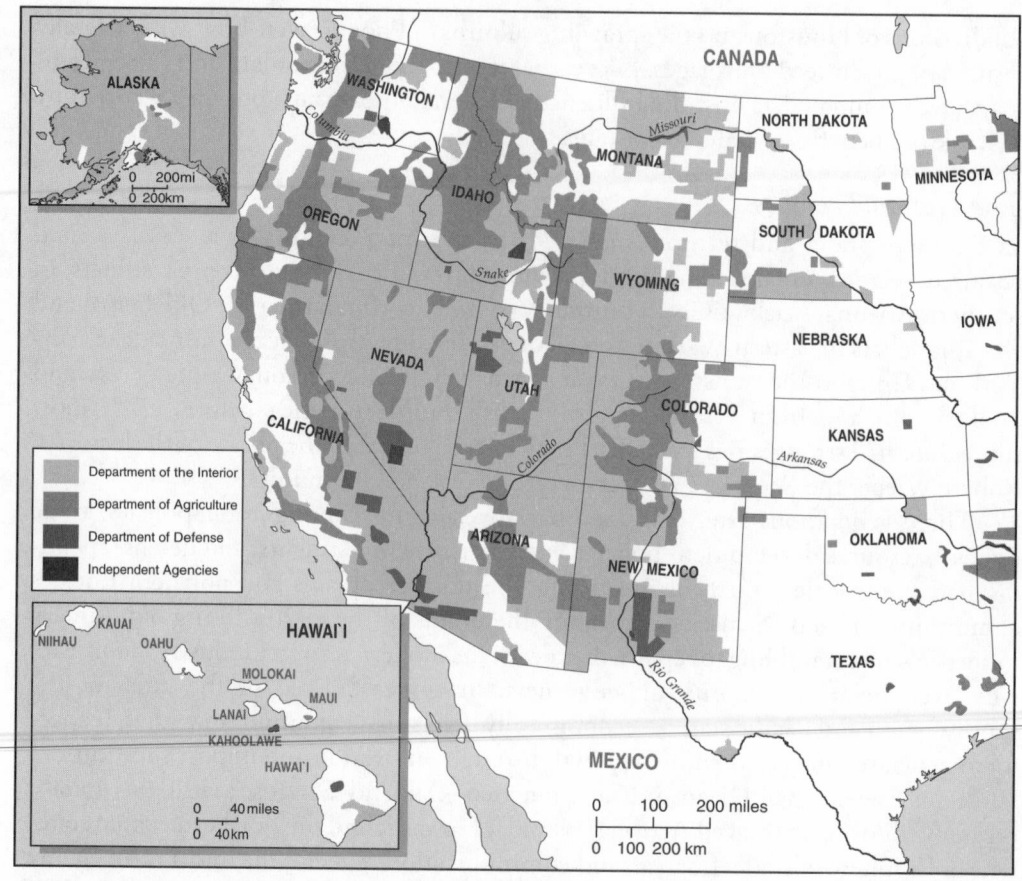

With almost one-half of the total land area of the eleven western-most states in the lower 48—including 86 percent of Nevada—still owned or administered by various federal agencies, the region remains inextricably tied to the federal government.

Legend:
- Department of the Interior
- Department of Agriculture
- Department of Defense
- Independent Agencies

Federal Presence in the Contemporary West

to offshore oil leases and drilling without state regulation and to expansion of military training and testing ranges, concern about the western role as a toxic waste dump, and commitment to the enforcement of endangered species legislation.

At the same time, the West remains inextricably bound to the federal government. From Houston to Honolulu, the region functions within vast networks owned, operated, or defined by the national government. A number of historians and social theorists have argued that a fundamental trend of the last century has been an "organizational revolution" in American life. Individual Americans and their communities have been increasingly caught up in large and extensive organizations—large corporations, big labor, mass communications, and, of course, big government. The effect has been the nationalization of western America, the reduction of differences as subregions and cultures have been incorporated within national systems and found themselves participants in national programs.

In 1893, Frederick Jackson Turner invited his readers to imagine themselves standing at Cumberland Gap to watch the procession of trappers, traders, and pioneer settlers moving inexorably westward. In 1990, we can place ourselves instead to overlook the great gorge of the Columbia River where it cuts to the sea between Mount Adams and Mount Hood. Where Meriwether Lewis and William Clark once forged Turner's path of exploration, Japanese pickups and Korean sedans now weave among the Peterbilts and Winnebagos on Interstate 84. High-voltage lines from the dams at Bonneville and The Dalles cut straight swaths across the timbered ridges to deliver power to Portland and the California intertie. Barges loaded in Idaho pass through federally operated locks in the federal dams, on their way to rendezvous with oceangoing ships that have followed a federally dredged channel upriver from Astoria to Portland. Hikers enjoy trails and campgrounds first cleared by CCC workers and maintained by college students on the temporary federal payroll.

Less visible is the transmission of information and management decisions through the institutional networks of federal land and resource agencies. Fish and Wildlife Service workers watch over research stations and hatcheries on streams that tumble down the steep sides of the gorge. The Corps of Engineers angers local sport fishermen by identifying fishing sites for Native Americans to replace ancestral fishing grounds flooded by the Columbia River dams. Bureau of Land Management and Forest Service managers worry about balancing the demands of stock raisers, timber workers, and tourists. Other Forest Service workers try to administer the Columbia River Gorge National Scenic Area, a 1986 experiment in preserving scenic resources in the midst of continued farming, grazing, and logging.

Apple and pear growers of the Hood River valley work their own land but operate within another set of federal institutions. They draw power through the Hood River Electric Cooperative, which dates from the Rural Electrification Act of the New Deal. They work with representatives of the Soil Conservation Service in the local conservation district. Some of the orchardists are Japanese Americans whose parents were forcibly removed from the county by federal actions in the wartime panic of 1942. All of them worry about the impact of the Immigration Reform and Control Act on the valley's Spanish-heritage labor force.

Indeed, much of the economic life of the Columbia Gorge operates within the international trade rules set by the federal government. Regional lumber mills are squeezed between Japanese demand for raw logs and increased competition from Canada following the free trade agreement of 1989. The trains and barges that pass down the gorge are filled with potatoes for McDonald's outlets in Tokyo, grain for Chinese noodle factories, and bentonite for the oil wells of Indonesia. The fate of returning salmon runs is mired in multinational negotiations over the regulation of Asian fishing fleets.

As much as any private corporation or capitalist, it has been federal programs and federal dollars that have responded to the needs and opportunities of the American West. From the start of the twentieth century, the West has been the vast proving ground for an activist federal government. Thanks to those federal efforts, the West is no longer a region apart. The sparsely settled resource frontiers of 1900 have given way to a new West that lies at the center of national growth and global relations.

Bibliographic Note

The ambiguity in western attitudes toward the federal government is explored in Robert Athearn, *The Mythic West in Twentieth Century America* (Lawrence, 1986), Patricia Nelson

Limerick, *The Legacy of Conquest: The Unbroken Past of the American West* (New York, 1987), and Gene M. Gressley, "Regionalism and the Twentieth Century West," in Jerome O. Steffen, ed., *The American West: New Perspectives, New Dimensions* (Norman, 1979).

Western world's fairs are discussed in Robert Rydell, *All the World's a Fair: Visions of Empire at American International Expositions, 1876–1916* (Chicago, 1984), Burton Benedict, *The Anthropology of World's Fairs: San Francisco's Panama Pacific International Exposition of 1915* (Berkeley, 1983), and Carl Abbott, *The Great Extravaganza: Portland and the Lewis and Clark Exposition* (Portland, 1981).

Federal land policy is summarized in Marion Clawson, *The Federal Lands Revisited* (Baltimore, 1983). The evolution of irrigation policy and the Reclamation Service is treated in Donald Worster, *Rivers of Empire: Water, Aridity, and the Growth of the American West* (New York, 1985). The boom of the early 1900s is most easily approached through state histories and regional studies such as Donald Meinig, *The Great Columbia Plain: A Historical Geography, 1805–1910* (Seattle, 1968). Alaska as a federal frontier is the topic of William H. Wilson, *Railroad in the Clouds: The Alaska Railroad in the Age of Steam, 1914–1945* (Boulder, 1977).

The progressive conservation agenda is delineated in Samuel Hays, *Conservation and the Gospel of Efficiency: The Progressive Conservation Movement, 1890–1920* (Cambridge, Mass., 1959). Also see G. Michael McCarthy, *Hour of Trial: The Conservation Conflict in Colorado and the West, 1891–1907* (Norman, 1977), Elmo Richardson, *The Politics of Conservation: Crusades and Controversies, 1897–1913* (Berkeley, 1962), Harold Steen, *The U.S. Forest Service: A History* (Seattle, 1976), John Ise, *Our National Park Policy: A Critical History* (Baltimore, 1961), and Donald Swain, *Wilderness Defender: Horace M. Albright and Conservation* (Chicago, 1970). The Taylor Act and changing agricultural land policies are treated in John Opie, *The Law of the Land: Two Hundred Years of American Farmland Policy* (Lincoln, 1987).

The starting points for an analysis of the rise of federal planning are Norris Hundley, *Water and the West: The Colorado River Compact and the Politics of Water in the American West* (Berkeley, 1975), Richard Lowitt, *The New Deal and the West* (Bloomington, 1984), and Charles McKinley, *Uncle Sam in the Pacific Northwest: Federal Management of Natural Resources in the Columbia River Valley* (Berkeley, 1952).

A series of pictorial histories traces the evolution of the first federal-aid highway system: George Stewart's classic *U.S. 40* (Boston, 1953); Drake Hokanson, *The Lincoln Highway: Main Street across America* (Iowa City, 1988); Quinta Scott and Susan Croce Kelly, *Route 66: The Highway and Its People* (Norman, 1988). The standard discussion of the adoption of the second federal-aid system in 1956 is Mark Rose, *Interstate: Express Highway Politics, 1941–1956* (Lawrence, 1979).

Primary sources for analyzing the effects of economic depression and the New Deal are the reports of the National Resources Planning Board and its regional and state affiliates, discussed and inventoried in Marion Clawson, *New Deal Planning: The National Resources Planning Board* (Baltimore, 1981). The New Deal at the regional and state levels can be followed in sets of state-level studies published in the *Pacific Historical Review* 38 (August 1969) and in John Braeman, Robert Bremner, and David Brody, eds., *The New Deal: The State and Local Levels* (Columbus, 1975). The comprehensive effects of federal funds are detailed in two articles by Leonard Arrington: "The New Deal in the West: A Preliminary Statistical Inquiry," *Pacific Historical Review* 38 (August 1969): 331–36, and "The Sagebrush Resurrection: New Deal Expenditures in the Western States, 1933–39," *Pacific Historical Review* 52 (February 1983): 1–16.

The great dams are treated in Joseph Stevens, *Hoover Dam: An American Adventure* (Norman, 1988), Murray Morgan, *The Dam* (New York, 1954), Richard Neuberger, *Our Promised Land* (New York, 1938), and Mark Foster, *Henry J. Kaiser: Builder in the Modern American West* (Austin, 1989).

The relations between the New Deal and regional subcultures are discussed in Donald Parman, *The Navajos and the New Deal* (New Haven, 1976), Sarah Deutsch, *No Separate Refuge: Culture, Class, and Gender on an Anglo-Hispanic Frontier in the American Southwest, 1880–1940* (New York, 1987), and Suzanne Forrest, *The Preservation of the Village: New Mexico's Hispanics and the New Deal* (Albuquerque, 1989).

The baseline studies of World War II in the West are by Gerald Nash: *The American West Transformed: The Impact of the Second World War* (Bloomington, 1985) and *World War II and the West: Reshaping the Economy* (Lincoln, 1990).

The military strategy in western city building is discussed in Roger Lotchin, *Fortress California, 1910–1961: From Warfare to Welfare* (New York, 1992), 996–1020. Wartime boom cities are discussed in Carl Abbott, *The New Urban America: Growth and Politics in Sunbelt Cities* (Chapel Hill, 1981), Martin Schiesl, "City Planning and the Federal Government in World War II: The Los Angeles Experience," *California History* 58 (April 1979): 127–43, and Philip Funigiello, *The Challenge to Urban Liberalism: Federal-City Relations during World War II* (Knoxville, 1978). The atomic cities of Richland and Los Alamos can be studied through magazine reports and the postwar hearings of the Joint Congressional Committee on Atomic Energy, as well as in Hal Rothman, *On Rims and Ridges: The Los Alamos Area since 1880* (Lincoln, 1992). Western women as war workers are the topic of Amy Kesselman, *Fleeting Opportunities: Women Shipyard Workers in Portland and Vancouver during World War II and Reconversion* (Albany, 1990).

Aggregate data on the military role in the postwar West are presented in the following: James Clayton, "The Impact of the Cold War on the Economies of California and Utah, 1946–65," *Pacific Historical Review* 36 (November 1967): 449–53; Roger Bolton, *Defense Purchases and Regional Growth* (Washington, D.C., 1966); Rosy Nimroody, *Star Wars: The Economic Fallout* (Cambridge, Mass., 1988); and Ann Markusen and Robin Bloch, "Defensive Cities: Military Spending, High Technology, and Human Settlements," in Manuel Castells, ed., *High Technology, Space, and Society* (Beverly Hills, Calif., 1985). Urban growth in the context of the world energy business is the topic of Joe Feagin, *Free Enterprise City: Houston in Political-Economic Perspective* (New Brunswick, N.J., 1988), and Andrew Gulliford, *Boomtown Blues: Colorado Oil Shale, 1885–1985* (Niwot, Colo., 1989).

The concept of the fourth wave of industrial growth is discussed in Peter Hall and Paschal Preston, *The Carrier Wave: New Information Technology and the Geography of Innovation, 1846–2003* (London, 1988). The aircraft industry is profiled in William G. Cunningham, *The Aircraft Industry: A Study in Industrial Location* (Los Angeles, 1951). Defense spending in southern California is described in Martin Schiesl, "Airplanes to Aerospace: Defense Spending and Economic Growth in the Los Angeles Region," in Roger Lotchin, *The Martial Metropolis: U.S. Cities in War and Peace* (New York, 1984), and David Clark, "Improbable Los Angeles," in Richard Bernard and Bradley Rice, eds., *Sunbelt Cities: Politics and Growth since World War II* (Austin, 1983). The western concentrations of high-tech industries are detailed in Ann Markusen, Peter Hall, and Amy Glasmeier, *High Tech America: The What, How, Where, and Why of the Sunrise Industries* (Boston, 1986).

Data on federal science spending have been summarized by Edward J. Malecki, "High Technology and Local Economic Development," *Journal of the American Planning Association* 50 (Summer 1984): 262–69. The growth of a western science establishment is discussed in Nuel Pharr Davis, *Lawrence and Oppenheimer* (New York, 1968), and Clayton Koppes, *JPL and the American Space Program: A History of the Jet Propulsion Laboratory* (New Haven, 1982).

The emergence of a metropolitan society is discussed in case studies in Bernard and Rice, *Sunbelt Cities*, and in Abbott, *The New Urban America*. An interpretive essay that emphasizes the federally assisted sources of growth is Carl Abbott, "The Metropolitan Region," in Gerald Nash and Richard Etulain, eds., *The Twentieth Century West: Historical Interpretations* (Albuquerque, 1989). The rise of the information-processing city is the focus of Rob Kling, Spencer Olin, and Mark Poster, eds., *Postsuburban California: The Transformation of Orange County since World War II* (Berkeley, 1991), and Allen J. Scott, *Metropolis: From the Division of Labor to Urban Form* (Berkeley, 1988).

Conflicting western expectations about federal resource policy in the past twenty years are described in Thomas J. Gallagher and Anthony F. Gasbarro, "The Battle for Alaska: Planning in America's Last Wilderness," *Journal of the American Planning Association* 55 (Autumn 1989): 433–44, and Samuel Hays, *Beauty, Health, and Permanence: Environmental Politics in the United States, 1955–1985* (New York, 1987).

Chapter Fourteen

Politics and Protests

M I C H A E L   P.   M A L O N E   A N D
F.   R O S S   P E T E R S O N

On an autumn evening along the Pedernales River in the hill country of central Texas, Lyndon Baines Johnson, president of the United States and Texas native, mounted his horse and began riding through his herd of cattle. Dressed in western attire, with ever-present Stetson, the tall Texan rode among the cattle with reckless abandon as Secret Service men in business suits jumped in jeeps and cars in order to stay close to Johnson as he exhibited his riding skills.

Twenty years later, on his ranch near Santa Barbara, California, Ronald Reagan, the transplanted midwesterner, swung into the saddle of his horse and slowly led a small entourage along the hilly trails overlooking one of America's most affluent communities. The planned activity allowed the Secret Service agents to don jeans and boots. The actor-turned-politician became a westerner because of vocation, and his acquired horsemanship came from movie roles, not boyhood necessity.

Different as they were, Lyndon Johnson and Ronald Reagan shared a connection to the American West and celebrated that connection in the course of their presidencies. Moreover, their administrations underscored the western element in American politics in ways that were more than symbolic. The enlargement of federal programs during Johnson's term reflected the West's long experience with the positive impact of government spending, whereas the deregulation and cutbacks initiated by Reagan (with no curtailment of the defense expenditures on which the region was so dependent) grew out of westerners' mounting impatience with federal interference. Though Johnson was the consummate Washington insider, he possessed an individualistic style that marked him as a maverick and strengthened his ties to the people of his home region. Reagan's demeanor was more soothing, but by presenting himself as a political outsider, he too could claim maverick status. That only twelve years separated the end of Johnson's liberal presidential tenure from the beginning of Reagan's conservative one showed how swiftly the West could shift its political direction.

From the 1890s to the 1990s, the West experienced a number of swings from one end of the political spectrum to the other. Yet some concerns remained constant. Primary among these were issues related to the development of natural resources, to the dispersal of federal largesse, and to the expansion of democratic processes. As the West itself changed from a hinterland of the United States to a major population center, the issues that concerned its residents drew increasing national attention.

President Lyndon Johnson used his Texas hill-country ranch to project the image of a quintessentially American leader rooted in the rugged independence associated with the nation's western past.

Bill Hudson. President Lyndon B. Johnson Rounding up a Hereford Yearling on the LBJ Ranch. *Gelatin silver print, 4 November 1964. AP/Wide World Photos, New York.*

Politics in the Era of Closing Frontiers, 1890–1920

During the thirty years from 1890 until the close of World War I, the American West witnessed the last significant land-takings, marking the final closing of the frontier epoch. These were years of economic boom and bust and of consequent social and political turmoil, turmoil that involved the most powerful surges of leftist protest the region has ever seen but that ended with a triumphant rightist reaction. On the Right and especially on the Left, the ideological residues of these formative years lingered long into the future.

In politics, as in other aspects of national life, the tumultuous 1890s formed a watershed decade. Six new states, all of them western, entered the Union in 1889–90: Washington, Montana, North and South Dakota, Idaho, and Wyoming. These entries were heralded at the time as signaling both the governmental maturation of the region and the close of the frontier. In reality, they represented only the breaking of the congressional logjam that had held back western statehood since the entry of Colorado in 1876.

By this time, most of the West had passed beyond the raw, formative stages of territorial politics, beyond the struggles of local economic interests to find their places in the sun and the accompanying clashes between elected legislatures and appointed federal officials. By 1891, only four territories remained in the contiguous United States: Utah, which would gain statehood in 1896, Oklahoma (1907), and Arizona and New Mexico (1912).

As was true throughout the country, politics in the West took shape through the shifting interactions of inherited partisan loyalties and the region's uniqueness. The shadows of post–Civil War politics loomed over the Southwest well into the twentieth century. Thus the Democratic party of the Old South commanded the "borderland" areas—the State of Texas and the Territory of Oklahoma—and even dominated the desert territories of New Mexico and, to a degree, Arizona. Democrats could also contest or even control other states such as Montana, Nevada, or Utah, where Mormondom still shunned the "Grand Old" Republican party, which had deprecated the Mormon religion. Throughout most of the West, though, the Republican party—the party of the North, the Union, and expansion—usually prevailed.

During their territorial years, the western commonwealths had frequently displayed the trait that the historian Kenneth Owens has aptly described as "chaotic factionalism." Inherited party loyalties became confused and convoluted in the new western settings, and rampant factionalism and highly personalized politics were the rule rather than the exception. These characteristics have proven to be abiding. To this day, as the political historian Paul Kleppner has noted, party affiliations have been less stable and the power of personalities and factions stronger in the West than in the older regions to the east. This has made, over the years, for frustrated party organizers and a frequently colorful and hectic political climate.

Each of the western states evolved its own political culture, a product of its peculiar history; and in all of them, the community's distinctive economic and social makeup counted far more than party loyalties in defining behavior. Often, in these years of unblushing governmental manipulation, economic interests unabashedly manhandled the political process. For instance, in the mining states of California, Nevada, Utah,

Colorado, and Montana, millionaires such as William Andrews Clark in Montana or Thomas Kearns in Utah openly "influenced" legislatures in order to be elected to the U.S. Senate. In both Montana and Arizona, years of such abuses finally resulted in thoroughgoing corporate domination. This led some eastern critics to dismiss the more lightly populated western states as "rotten boroughs" and even to question the wisdom of having admitted them to the Union. Other extractive corporations, such as lumber companies, soon exercised similar power in Washington and Oregon.

By far the greatest corporate power lay in the hands of railroads, as Oregon Senator John Mitchell revealed in his famous quote about the owner of the Oregon Central Railroad: "Ben Holladay's politics are my politics and what Ben Holladay wants I want." For years, Nebraska's two major railroads, the Union Pacific and the Burlington, reportedly divided the state's two senate seats between them. In North Dakota, the notorious "machine" headed by "Big Alex" McKenzie acted as a political broker for railroads and other corporations based in Minneapolis and St. Paul. Under the political tutelage of William F. Herrin, the Southern Pacific Railroad exercised such a dominant influence in California that the novelist Frank Norris likened it to an octopus.

It was easy one hundred years ago to assume that the western political order was simply a creature of special interests and a colony of eastern capitalism. The truth was far more complex. Western conservatism, for instance, drew heavily not only on major vested outside interests but also on a wide range of locally based businesses and on the instinctive standpattism of wealthy farmers and ranchers. Similarly, western liberals and radicals also had their natural constituencies. Sizable elements of the region's small middle class and business community chafed at the political ineptitude of the time and at perceived mistreatment by eastern-based railroads and other corporations. Strong regional unions, including four well-organized railroad brotherhoods, were highly active.

However, it was agriculture that set the cadence of western political life in the 1890s, constituting by far the largest social and economic group in most states and territories of the region. Like other westerners, farmers and ranchers varied considerably in their political persuasions. But many of them came from liberal and socialistic backgrounds in Scandinavia and Germany; and many more resented their vulnerability to overcharging by monopolistic railroads, grain storage facilities, stockyards, and other corporations. As events of the 1890s demonstrated, westerners were ready for revolt. The Farmers' Alliance, which claimed four million members nationwide, evolved into the Populist or People's party, the most powerful third-party movement in modern American history. This revolt out of the South and West against eastern domination shook the nation.

Populist parties emerged in Kansas and then in other plains states in the early 1890s. By mid-1892, the Populist movement had grown into a national political party, which held its nominating convention in Omaha. The famous Omaha Platform passed by this gathering signaled the genuine radicalism of the movement. It called for an inflated currency, a subtreasury system of warehouses whereby farmers could secure better credit using stored crops as collateral, the nationalization of railroads and telephone and telegraph lines, a graduated income tax, and the forced forfeiture of "excess" lands granted to railroads. The Populists' political demands for direct election of U.S. senators and for democratic reforms such as the initiative, referendum, and recall substantiated the western theme of bringing power to the people.

In the presidential election of 1892, the Populist candidate James B. Weaver of Iowa did well in the West, carrying Kansas, Colorado, Idaho, and Nevada. Five of Kansas's eight congressional seats went to Populists, who joined the feisty William Peffer, already in the Senate. Populists also gained control of the Kansas State Senate. In Colorado, Populists elected Davis Waite governor and sent a sizable minority, thirty-nine members, to the legislature. These early Populist state governments, like later ones such as that of Governor John Rogers in Washington, faced severe contention because of their unstable alliances with Democrats and the enmity of Republicans. Conversely, in the Farmers' Alliance heartland of Texas, truly dedicated reformers chafed at Populist-style Democrats like Governor James Hogg, politicians who usually preached more reform than they actually achieved.

Populists and their allies in the two established parties gained strength as the hardships of the Panic of 1893 breathed fire into their radical demands. When the Cleveland administration persuaded Congress to repeal the Sherman Silver Purchase Act in November, the resulting closure of mines and smelters wrought havoc throughout the mountain West. As a result, the demand for "free silver," or the resumption of a bimetallic currency, now became the dominant theme of the reformers. It promised both rebirth to the mining industry and a beneficial inflation for debtors. Thus, while the Populists remained agrarian in the plains states and other farming regions, mining and labor interests supported the party in the mountain and Great Basin states.

As the Populist movement gained momentum in the mid-1890s, so too did the arguments of those who reasoned that it could succeed nationally only through "fusion" with an established party. The main force of political marriage was the advocacy of free silver, which appealed to indebted workers as well as farmers. This meant, practically speaking, fusion with the Democrats, as was already common not only in the South but in Nebraska as well. Although there were numerous "Silver Republicans," such as prominent Senators Henry Teller of Colorado and Fred T. Dubois of Idaho, the national Republicans remained overwhelmingly devoted to the gold standard.

During the presidential campaign of 1896, the agrarian crusade crested and then ebbed. The Democratic party, badly divided along regional lines under Grover Cleveland's stumbling direction, nominated the Nebraska congressman and orator William Jennings Bryan after he had carefully campaigned for the post and then captivated the convention with his famous "Cross of Gold" speech decrying conservative, eastern exploitation of the poor, the West, and the South. His nomination rested overwhelmingly on the silver issue; and, to the dismay of many of the more committed reformers, the Populists proceeded to nominate him also, even though this meant that they sacrificed their more substantial reform proposals to silver and its broader appeal. But to have chosen another candidate would have divided the reform-protest forces and ensured the victory of the solid-gold Republican candidate, William McKinley. Nonetheless, McKinley's massive financial support, the comparative narrowness of Bryan's appeal, and the resurgence of prosperity all combined for a GOP victory. McKinley won by an electoral vote margin of 271 to 176 and by a popular vote spread

During his second try for the presidency in 1900, Democrat William Jennings Bryan again crusaded against the eastern exploitation of western workers, linking this opposition to domestic oppression with opposition to President William McKinley's imperialist policy toward the Philippines. For many western farmers, the foreign policy issues remained too abstract, and their votes went to the conservative Republican party.

Neville Williams, publisher. William Jennings Bryan Campaign Poster. Chromolithograph, 1900. Library of Congress (#LC-US262-2144), Washington, D.C.

of almost 600,000, the largest in a generation. In the West and South, however, Bryan and silver nearly swept the field. Only the western states of California, Oregon, and North Dakota went Republican.

Historians have hotly disagreed about the true nature of the Populist party. Writing from a Turnerian vantage, John D. Hicks long ago portrayed the farmer-radicals as genuine frontier democrats who well understood a system that oppressed them and who valiantly tried to change it. The renowned historian Richard Hofstadter, projecting an urban-eastern bias, countered that they were poorly informed cranks and xenophobes who simply lashed out at a system they only vaguely comprehended. Contemporary historians, such as Walter Nugent and O. Gene Clanton, conclude that the Populists were in fact cogent and determined regionalists and reformers.

Clearly, the tumultuous 1890s were a seedtime for the political culture of the modern West. On the one hand, many regional conservatives often demonstrated an exaggerated individualism denoting their frontier origins and also a pronounced belief in unrestrained property rights. They saw little conflict between their dependence on federal largesse on the one hand and their condemnation of federal regulation and ownership on the other. The reformers too were highly individualistic and quite capable of savoring their federal cake even while deploring it. At the heart of their ideology lay the essence of the Populist persuasion: an enmity toward extractive corporations and a government often in league with them, a demand for progressive taxation and effective government regulation, and an encouragement of political participation that included women well before the rest of the country followed suit. For all their rancor, the Populists were true democrats and western regionalists.

Ironically, it was left to another generation of westerners to achieve the political reforms demanded by the Populists. The Progressive movement captured many Populist ideas, revised them, and gave them respectability before a national audience.

In contrast to the 1890s, the early years of the twentieth century were a time of prosperity, calm, and an optimistic belief in the inevitability of progress. Unlike the more narrowly focused and radical phenomenon of the Populist movement, the primary reform thrust of these years took a broader and more orderly approach. Known as "progressivism," an impossibly broad and imprecise term, this new movement was characterized by the urge to curb corporate and political manipulation of the public order by means of expanded democracy, moral regeneration, and increased government regulation of the economy and of society. Progressives drew support from all sectors of society, particularly the rising middle classes; they found effective presidential leadership in Republican Theodore Roosevelt (1901–9) and Democrat Woodrow Wilson (1913–21).

The West responded enthusiastically to progressivism, particularly to the call for tough regulation of railroads and other corporations and to increased participatory democracy. Direct democracy took various forms: the initiative and referendum, which allowed the public to enact and nullify laws when legislatures proved unresponsive; electoral primaries that allowed the voters to nominate party candidates; the direct election of senators by the people; and the establishment of suffrage for women. The progressives' belief that direct democracy would result in moral reform appealed strongly to frontier individualism and to the still smoldering legacy of the Populist party. As the historians Arthur Link and Richard McCormick note, "The most distinctive aspect of western progressivism was its passion for the more democratic, anti-institutional political reforms . . . they were more common there than anywhere else in the nation."

Throughout the country, progressivism energized all levels of government—local, state, and federal—during the years after 1900. In the West, the first wave of reform often came at the municipal level and usually involved the eradication of a corrupt "machine" government, in league with utilities and other businesses contracting with the city, and its replacement with a reform mayor. This is what occurred in Seattle under Reginald Thompson and in Denver, where the reform coalition included the wealthy activist Josephine Roche and two men who went on to national prominence, Judge Ben Lindsey and George Creel. A similar alliance in San Francisco, including the journalist Fremont Older and the millionaire Rudolph Spreckels, scored the region's most spectacular victory by deposing corrupt Mayor Eugene Schmitz and sending the machine boss Abraham Ruef to prison. Of all western cities, however, it was Galveston, Texas, that made the greatest contribution to urban progressivism. After a terrible hurricane and tidal wave ravaged the city in 1900, killing at least six thousand people,

Galveston instituted the businesslike "city commission" form of government, which soon became popular throughout the land.

However, progressives made their greatest mark at the state level of government. Historians have argued at length over whether progressivism derived from the earlier Populist movement or was a new phenomenon that arose primarily in middle-class society. A look at the West offers a commonsense answer. In those states where populism had flourished, progressivism bore a strong agrarian-radical flavor; in those where it had not, the new reformers came more often from urban and middle-class origins.

Two states where populism had a lingering impact were Texas and Kansas. These states passed the first antitrust laws in the nation, and both created strong railroad regulatory commissions. Kansas, under the capable Republican administrations of the reform governors Edward Hoch and Walter Stubbs, and Texas, under the Democrat Thomas Campbell, simply carried forward the efforts begun under Populists in the preceding decade.

The two leading western progressive states were Oregon and California, neither of which had figured largely in the Populist revolt. Both states patterned reforms after the model in Wisconsin. In Oregon, a comparatively middle-class state, a group of clever reformers led by the remarkable William U'Ren and the cagey politico Jonathan Bourne gained sway over the legislature through the Non-Partisan Direct Legislation League. After securing the nation's first general initiative and referendum laws in 1902, the reformers used these weapons to enact the far-reaching "Oregon System," which included the direct primary, the "recall" of unsatisfactory public officials, a corrupt practices act, and a system whereby voters could indicate to legislators their choice for U.S. senator. This constituted a major step toward the constitutional amendment of 1913 allowing popular direct election of senators. A number of basic social reforms followed, such as the defining of maximum workweeks and minimum wages for women and children. By 1912, mass democracy in Oregon had progressed to the point that puzzled voters faced a "bedquilt ballot" nearly a yard long, with 136 candidates and 37 issues to be considered.

In neighboring California, progressivism took a similar middle-class urban profile. Utilizing the new direct-primary law in 1910, the caustic and brilliant Republican Hiram Johnson captured the governorship on a campaign promise "to kick the Southern Pacific Railroad out of politics." Beginning in the 1911 legislature, the Johnson administration enacted a full panoply of progressive laws, including toughened regulation of railroads and utilities and creation of worker's compensation. Both Theodore Roosevelt and Herbert Croly, the main political theorist of progressivism, judged California to be the leading progressive state in the nation.

In national politics, the West stood in the vanguard of progressivism. Theodore Roosevelt carried every western state except Texas in his presidential bid of 1904. In the three-way presidential election of 1912, the reformist Democrat Woodrow Wilson defeated Theodore Roosevelt, who headed an independent Progressive party ticket, and the decidedly unflamboyant Republican William Howard Taft. Taft managed to carry only Utah in the West. In 1916 Wilson, the self-proclaimed reform and peace candidate, carried all but two western states, Oregon and South Dakota. The region produced a number of progressive leaders on the national stage, most of them famed for their

The West led the nation in granting voting rights to women, but the path to full suffrage was not smooth. After winning suffrage in the Washington Territory in 1883, women there were denied the vote in 1887. Not until 1910 did a well-organized campaign result in the restoration of suffrage rights.

A. Curtis. Women in Washington Campaign for Suffrage. *Photograph, 1910. Special Collections Division, University of Washington Libraries (#19943), Seattle.*

individualism and their suspicion of big business. Among them were California's Johnson, the Kansas journalist William Allen White, and Senators George Norris of Nebraska, William Borah of Idaho, and Francis Newlands of Nevada.

The West figured largely in three major facets of national progressivism: woman suffrage, Prohibition, and conservation. Beyond dispute, the region led the nation in the democratic crusade to enfranchise females. Before 1917, the only states that granted women the vote lay in the West. In fact, by the following year—two years before the Nineteenth Amendment made woman suffrage the law of the land—the only western states that had not already done so were New Mexico, Texas, Nebraska, and North Dakota. Naturally, the region also pioneered in females holding political office. Mary Howard of Kanab, Utah, became the first female mayor in the country, Bertha Landes of Seattle the first mayor of a large city, and Jeannette Rankin of Montana the first congresswoman. Miriam "Ma" Ferguson of Texas and Nellie Tayloe Ross of Wyoming became the first governors in 1925. Unlike Ma Ferguson, who fronted for her husband, Jim, Ross really did govern, and govern well.

The sociologist Edward A. Ross voiced the conventional wisdom when he explained, "In the inter-mountain states, where there are at least two suitors for every woman, the sex becomes an upper caste to which nothing will be denied from street-car seats to ballots and public offices." Scarcity was, indeed, a factor, but not the only one. Frontier egalitarianism and individualism affected women as well as men. Promoters often featured the vote to lure women and families westward, and established groups like the Mormons saw the female vote as a counterweight to untrusted immigrant ethnic groups, which tended to be heavily male. Thus, for a variety of reasons—some commendable and others less so—the West truly pioneered a basic political right for America's women.

Again, the conventional wisdom was partly right in linking woman suffrage to the companion progressive effort for the "prohibition" of alcoholic beverages. As the historian Norman Clark has written, "In those states where women could vote on such issues before 1919 (Wyoming, Colorado, Utah, Idaho, Washington, California, Kansas, Oregon, Arizona, Montana, Nevada, New York), all but two—California and New York—adopted by popular vote a state law prohibiting the saloon." In fact, women's organizations did attack the saloon, and various brewers' associations naturally opposed woman suffrage. But it is also true that some suffragists, such as Oregon's realistic Abigail Scott Duniway, viewed Prohibition as a quixotic diversion and a danger to the suffrage campaign.

Nevertheless, the West and South forced national Prohibition on the "wet" cities of the Northeast and upper Midwest. First by "local" or county option and then by statewide vote, one state after another went "dry," often with considerable turmoil, as in closely divided Texas. Among the earliest was Kansas, where Carrie Nation first captured national headlines in 1900 by wading into a Wichita saloon wielding an iron rod and throwing rocks at a painting of "Cleopatra at the Bath." The West soon provided an excellent case study of how an unpopular law cannot be enforced; those westerners who wanted alcohol seldom had trouble getting it.

Of all Progressive Era issues, it was "conservation"—federal protection, regulation, and preservation of natural resources—that most affected the West. On this issue, the region appeared somewhat self-serving and provincial, particularly in its sharp criticism of forest and other land set-asides that threatened to impede development. The Seattle Chamber of Commerce viewed the sequestrations as a "galling insult" to the region. To Colorado Senator Henry Teller, they seemed to create "a system that threatened to reduce western people to a class of servile peons"; to Utah Senator Joseph Rawlins, they were "as gross an outrage as was committed by William the Conqueror." The West strongly supported Interior Secretary Richard Ballinger in 1909–10 when he removed certain lands from the reserves and then came under sharp attack from Gifford Pinchot, head of the Forest Service, for doing so. National progressive sentiment forced Ballinger out of office. Hyperbole aside, such regional reactions were natural enough: westerners were losing their time-honored right of free access to western resources. When eastern conservationists like Pinchot—confident that they were eternally correct—dismissed such western critics as "locals" and "sagebrushers," western anger was understandable, if not endearing. The conflict arising between western property owners and developers on the one hand and conservationists and environmentalists on the other continued as a major political issue throughout the twentieth century.

However, in the area of federally funded reclamation projects, the arid West adamantly supported Roosevelt and his Newlands Act, which created the Bureau of Reclamation. Although numerous water-diversion projects existed throughout the West before massive federal involvement, the progressive engineers were the first to promise water as a consistent resource. From the construction of the Roosevelt Dam in Arizona (1911) to the building of the Jordanelle Dam in Utah (1992), the bureau has played a major part in western politics. Water as a scarce western natural resource became and remains a complicated political issue. Federal and state governments compete with agricultural irrigation districts, municipalities, and recreation interests for a limited resource. From the beginning, the progressive concept of using federal dollars to guarantee water for agrarian users has been viewed as a blessing. Once again the westerner found an internal conflict over progressive programs. On the one hand, most western property owners opposed regulation of the timber and mining industries; yet the same westerners welcomed government programs that created new sources of water.

The progressives left behind a positive, enduring heritage of direct democracy, hope, and reform. However, they also had their limitations, many of which belied their middle- and upper-class origins. For instance, California progressives pushed through a 1913 law prohibiting Japanese from owning land. Western progressives could also have done more to help the region's many workers. Their moderation in this regard left an open field for left-wing radicals during the years before World War I.

Some of the western radicals, like John Reed of Oregon and Bill Haywood of Utah, became Marxists (both are buried in the Kremlin), but most were authentic American leftists who eschewed the Marxian labor theory of value. These individuals came from the ranks of immigrant laborers and small-scale farmers and spoke the language of neopopulism. The most significant group was the Western Federation of Miners (WFM), founded in 1893. This miners' union engaged in a series of violent collisions with exploitive corporations, particularly in Idaho and Colorado. In 1905, members of the WFM led the creation of the Industrial Workers of the World (IWW), America's most famous radical union, which was always strongest in the West.

Overwhelmingly western, the IWW "Wobblies" aimed to meld all workers, regardless of skill, into "one big union." Their class-conscious appeals to exploited farm, forest, and mine workers and their "free speech" campaigns galvanized a harsh conservative reaction. So did their outspokenly anticapitalist leaders, such as Elizabeth Gurley Flynn and Haywood, who spent his final years in the Soviet Union. Joe Hill, a Swedish immigrant, was the poet laureate for the Wobblies, and his songs were sung throughout the West. Hill became a martyr when convicted of a murder-robbery in Utah, where he was executed in 1915.

As in the 1890s, radical support continued to flow heavily from the millions of family farmers who believed "the system" oppressed them. A prime instance was the Nonpartisan League, which exploded into power in North Dakota in 1915 and by the following year counted thirty thousand members there alone. Led by a shrewd ex-farmer named Arthur Townley, the league railed at Twin Cities railroad exploitation of farmers and called for a program of tax reform, state-subsidized insurance, and state-owned banks and grain elevators. As Townley noted, "If you put a lawyer, a banker, and an industrialist in a barrel and roll it down hill, there'll always be a son-of-a-bitch on top." Using nonpartisan tactics, the league gained control of the state GOP and swept the 1918 elections in North Dakota, enacting much of its program in the 1919 legislature. Meanwhile, to the dismay of conservatives and business interests, it swept into other grain states of the Northwest and into Canada.

Drawing sustenance from rural radicals like these, as well as from urban labor, western socialists gained power during the years before World War I. Exemplifying the surge of farm radicalism on the southern plains, Oklahoma was arguably the strongest socialist state in the nation. Although it had only 2 percent of the American population in 1910, it claimed a full 10 percent of national Socialist party membership. And in the elections of 1908 and 1916, it cast the highest vote percentages of all states for the

Socialist party presidential candidate. Socialists won a number of legislative and may-oralty races and in 1911 nearly captured the mayoralty of Los Angeles. A Nevada Socialist party candidate for the U.S. Senate gained over 25 percent of the vote in 1914.

The wide range of political attitudes espoused by westerners, along with their varying ethnic backgrounds, added to the region's confusion over whether to enter World War I. Generally speaking, support for intervention on the side of the Anglo-French "Allies" against the Germans was strongest in the eastern United States, more moderate in the Midwest, and weakest in the West. Seeing the war as an argument among European imperialists, many of the West's labor and agrarian radicals opposed intervention. Obviously, the West's contingents of Germans and Irish resented an English alliance; most Scandinavians, like their homelands, favored neutrality. In 1915 Nebraska's William Jennings Bryan, a friend of the German element at home, resigned as secretary of state rather than support President Wilson's truculent policy toward Germany. Bryan subsequently became a leader of the peace movement. As an example of the power of the hyphenated Americans, the entire three-member North Dakota delegation voted against the war when Congress made its formal declaration in the spring of 1917. On the other hand, representatives from the Southwest, concerned about German meddling in revolutionary Mexico, supported intervention.

Once the nation was at war, an intense atmosphere of patriotic fervor set in. In the West, much of the worst of the repression was aimed at leftist critics. Federally sponsored state "councils of defense" joined state governments and local vigilantes in denouncing anything remotely pro-German or less than "100 percent American." The Colorado progressive George Creel chaired the Committee on Public Information, which produced anti-German material. Governor Will Hobby vetoed the legislative appropriation for the German language department at the University of Texas. An editor in a town nearby opined that, although flogging might be all right for some who declined to volunteer for Red Cross work, others might have to be shot. In Nebraska, regents forced the resignations of two faculty members who were deemed too pro-German. A number of states, including Texas, passed "criminal syndicalism" and "sedition" laws that aimed at stifling dissent. Montana's Sedition Act of 1918 became the model for the federal law passed the same year, which is often considered the most sweeping abrogation of civil liberties in modern American history. Ironically, these attitudes contrasted with the fact that Utah's Simon Bamberger and Idaho's Moses Alexander, both German-born Jews, were elected governors of their states only a few months before U.S. intervention.

Leaders of the Industrial Workers of the World spoke out hotly against the war, but by the end of the war, their organization was a shambles. The public denounced them as "Imperial Wilhelm's Warriors"; and one of their most outspoken leaders, Frank Little, was murdered at Butte, Montana. At Bisbee, Arizona, an army of vigilantes seized hundreds of IWWs and other workers, illegally hauled them out of the city, and stranded them in the New Mexico desert. When the Wobblies called a mass lumber strike in the summer of 1917, the army went into the lumber business; the U.S. Justice Department joined private employers in forming a government union, the Loyal Legion of Loggers and Lumbermen. Federal agents rounded up IWW leaders with mass arrests that autumn, and many received long jail sentences.

Radical farmers faced a similar fate. When motley gatherings of sharecroppers in Oklahoma began protesting the draft by destroying property, in what became known as the "Green Corn Rebellion," they were severely suppressed. At a convention in Walla Walla, Washington, vigilantes ran five hundred members of the Grange movement, a farm-cooperative organization, out of town when they would not disclaim the Nonpartisan League. The league itself came under the severe indictment of superpatriots like ex-president Theodore Roosevelt. Eventually, in 1921, North Dakota Governor Lynn Frazier and Attorney General William Lemke became the first victims of a recall election of state officials in U.S. history as the league, like the IWW, reeled under attacks from the Right.

The national mood of reaction, nastiness, and intolerance, now intensified by fear of the Communist revolution in Russia, carried with full force into the immediate postwar years of 1919–22. In February 1919, a general strike shut down the city of Seattle for four days and deeply alienated public opinion. Miles Poindexter, Washington's formerly progressive senator, turned sharply to the Right and denounced the strikers as "reds." Kansas typified national resentment of militant labor in 1920 when its legislature declared strikes illegal. Severe race riots hit Longview, Texas, in 1919 and Tulsa in 1921; and a pitched battle between veterans and IWWs at Centralia, Washington, in 1919 left at least five dead.

More wary than the nation at large of joining the Wilsonian crusade for war, the West now seemed especially eager to isolate itself from modernity. Idaho actually repealed its 1909 direct primary law in 1919; and its prominent senator William Borah, like Hiram Johnson and other regional progressives, led the effort to defeat America's participation in Wilson's idealistic League of Nations. The U.S. involvement in the Wilsonian crusades of entry into the war, the League of Nations debate, and the oppression of dissenters damaged progressive goals and aspiration. In the West, politicians became more conservative and more concerned with domestic tranquility and foreign isolation. The region's leadership in reform measures was lost to an attitude of internal reclusiveness.

The Era of Transition, 1920–45

Just as the eras of populism and progressivism had given the West a liberal profile during the years before the war, so did the frustrations and xenophobia of postwar reaction turn the region sharply rightward during the early 1920s. However, in a broader perspective, the quarter century following 1920 witnessed a far more significant political transition, to a new and more stable order in which rising federal assertiveness became the major shaping factor. Obviously, the Great Depression and World War II altered the western political framework.

Much of the political negativism of the 1920s derived simply from reaction to postwar frenzy. It also stemmed from the wartime migration into the West of conservative southerners and midwesterners. For example, in the early twenties, Lincoln Steffens concluded that California "today is not a western, it is a middle western state." These newcomers, so different from their predecessors, made southern California dry on Prohibition and generally conservative, in contrast to wet and liberal San Francisco. Southern Californians flocked to radio evangelists like the Methodist minister "Fighting

Bob" Shuler and his sometimes scandalous female counterpart Aimee Semple McPherson. Nevertheless, of all the manifestations of postwar nativism, the most frightening was the reborn Ku Klux Klan (KKK). In contrast to its post–Civil War predecessor, the Klan of the twenties reached far beyond the Old South and not only lashed out at blacks but also violently attacked Catholics, Jews, and other "un-Americans." In one sense, it provided an extension of the immediate postwar superpatriotism.

The Klan's western manifestations mirrored national trends, and the politics of paranoia and hatred lasted until mid-decade. A few specific examples illustrate the Klan's impact on the West. In Texas, Oklahoma, and Kansas, the Klan rocked the established order. William Allen White, the grand old Kansas progressive, took on the KKK in a 1924 gubernatorial race—and lost. The hooded order mushroomed in Oklahoma, leading to the election in 1922 of anti-Klan Governor John Walton. Walton's anti-Klan zeal led to some incredible excesses, culminating in his putting the whole state under martial law. Consequently, the Klan-influenced legislature impeached Walton and removed him from office. Oklahoma's Klan days continued. In 1926, pro-KKK Henry Johnston was elected governor, only to be impeached three years later. Texas too was a cockpit of Klan activity and the homeland of its "Imperial Wizard," Hiram Evans of Dallas. By the early 1920s, the Texas Klan boasted eighty thousand members and a U.S. senator, Earle Mayfield. On the other hand, Miriam Amanda Ferguson's opposition to the KKK contributed to her election as governor in 1924.

The Klan reached into every corner of the Far West. In 1924 it attempted, unsuccessfully, to unseat Montana Senator Thomas Walsh, a devout Catholic. In Colorado, it claimed the election of a senator and a governor, as well as the mayor and chief of police in Denver, before it collapsed in an internal financial scandal in 1925. In the former progressive bastion of Oregon, an overwhelmingly Protestant state, Klansmen helped to elect Harvard-educated Kaspar K. Kubli as Speaker of the House. The state's governor, Walter Pierce, had Klan support, as did the law, enacted by initiative in 1922, that forced all children to attend public schools. The latter measure, intended to destroy Catholic schools, fell before federal district and U.S. Supreme Court rulings in 1924–25. Such were the heights and depths of Klan power before it declined in the mid-1920s, amid the shame of the national leader David Stephenson's disgrace (he was sentenced to life imprisonment for rape and second-degree murder) and the soothing balm of economic prosperity.

The West also mirrored another reality of 1920s politics—the collapse of the Democratic party under Woodrow Wilson's frustrated leadership and the dominance of conservative Republicanism. Every western state except Texas cast its electoral votes for Republican Warren Harding in 1920, all but Texas and Oklahoma voted for Calvin Coolidge in 1924, and then the entire region supported Herbert Hoover in 1928. In addition, numerous western conservative Republicans headed off to Washington, D.C., to participate in the probusiness GOP rule of the era. Utah, for instance, boasted not only of arch-conservative Senator Reed Smoot but also of equally conservative Supreme Court Justice George Sutherland and J. Reuben Clark, the influential undersecretary of state.

Beneath this surface of conservative calm, the old forces of progressivism continued to smolder. Reform governors like Pat Neff in Texas, William Sweet in Colorado, and

Joseph Dixon in Montana got elected in the 1920s, although conservative legislatures usually obstructed their programs. The West led in instituting state pension plans, beginning with Montana and Nevada in 1923, and in the unsuccessful attempt to ban child labor by constitutional amendment. Northwest progressives joined Nebraska's George Norris and pushed for public power. The region suffered from an agriculture depression throughout the decade. In Washington, D.C., angry representatives of the depressed interior West, sometimes dubbed the "Sons of the Wild Jackass" by the eastern press, joined in the "Farm Bloc" to advance the interests of agriculture in the face of solidly probusiness administrations. The McNary-Haugen Bill, which authorized the federal government to purchase and export surpluses, was vetoed twice by Calvin Coolidge.

The problem of the western progressives was that they could neither master a Republican party controlled by conservatives nor stomach a moribund Democratic party controlled by the wet machines of the East. Party irregularity again flared, as in New Mexico, where the maverick reformer Bronson Cutting temporarily switched from the GOP to the Democrats, or in Idaho, which for a time housed the nation's only active Progressive party. The height of irregularity came in the 1924 presidential campaign, which pitted conservative Republican incumbent Calvin Coolidge against John W. Davis—the nominee of a Democratic convention that had deadlocked between the forces of the East and those of the West and South over Prohibition and other issues. When an independent Progressive party ticket of Robert LaFollette of Wisconsin for president and Senator Burton K. Wheeler of Montana for vice president entered the fray, both the weakness of the Democrats and the disorganization of the Progressives became clear. In most states of the West, the Progressives actually outpolled the Democrats. In California, Davis took only 8 percent of the vote. All of this meant that, even in a region sharing only marginally in the vaunted GOP prosperity of the 1920s, the Republicans easily held sway into the 1930s.

By the later 1920s, political turmoil began to abate, and a classic mood of conservatism set in. Although some of the conservative governors of the time were rancorous, like Roland Hartley, the labor-baiting GOP lumberman from Washington, most simply advocated an efficient, low-taxation, and minimal-service government. The political cultures of the western states during the 1920s seemed to be evolving toward acceptance of the new economic stability. Unfortunately, these economic foundations were about to topple, taking with them as they fell the fleeting political calm.

The stock market crash of October 1929 had little initial effect on the West. Agriculture had been depressed throughout the 1920s, and since eastern factories tended to feel the downturn earlier than did the farther-removed sources of raw materials, the West felt the impact somewhat belatedly. However, when the full force of the Great Depression hit in 1930–32, it devastated the western economy. State and local governments, heavily reliant on property taxes, saw their revenue sources dry up with property devaluation. Most westerners demurred at taking on new obligations to help the needy and simply cut back what few services they offered. In effect, they shunted such responsibilities off to an equally hesitant federal government.

Some states did try new approaches to deal with the hard times. In Nebraska, advocates of a unicameral (one-house) legislature had been busy since 1915. Now, with

Drawing on memories of her childhood in a Kingsville, Texas, barrio and the colorful distinctive style of Mexican folk painting, Carmen Lomas Garza creates narrative images that celebrate everyday life in the Chicano communities of southern Texas. Her pictures help create a visual history for a people whose presence was often ignored by earlier artists in the region.

Carmen Lomas Garza (b. 1948). *Cakewalk*. Acrylic on canvas, 1987. © 1987 Carmen Lomas Garza. Photograph by M. Lee Fatheree. Collection of Paula Maciel-Benecke and Norbert Benecke.

Born and raised in the West, Wayne Thiebaud first turned his attention to urban themes when he moved to San Francisco in the early 1970s. One of the few artists of either the 19th or 20th century to find western cities a compelling subject for his work, Thiebaud uses the unique topography of San Francisco as a vehicle for exploring ways to convey space and perspective in his painting. The results are images of a city that appears at once inviting and precarious as it perches at the edge of precipitous hills.

Wayne Thiebaud (b. 1920). Corner Apartments (study). Oil on masonite, 1979. Private Collection.

shrinking budgets, their arguments won favor, and the state adopted this still unique form of government in 1934. The Nevada legislature of 1931 took two controversial steps, both of which turned up new revenue sources while also raising the eyebrows of moralists. The state garnered a larger share of the growing divorce business by lowering the required legal residency period from three months to six weeks; and, in a provocative decision that paid off later, it once again legalized gambling after a twenty-year ban. Warned that legalized gambling might attract organized crime, the sheriff of Reno replied, "Al Capone is welcome in Reno as long as he behaves himself." In reality, most state governments drifted and awaited action from the federal level. The elections of 1930 sent many Democrats into local, state, and congressional office and set the stage for Franklin Roosevelt's 1932 national mandate.

The Roosevelt New Deal program of 1933–39 revolutionized the federal role in the West through a vast array of spending and regulatory innovations. Some of these programs, such as dam construction, the Civilian Conservation Corps, the Taylor Grazing Act, and the Agricultural Adjustment Administration, brought Uncle Sam directly into resource management. Other legislation, such as the omnibus Social Security program and the Federal Emergency Relief Administration, required dollar-matching and other efforts from the states. These latter programs required the states to find new revenue sources from income and sales taxes. In many different ways, therefore, the 1930s became a time of political dynamism at all levels of western government. The voters responded by electing a variety of mavericks as well as effective politicians.

The political upheaval and the rising public demand for drastic action brought a number of eccentrics and publicity seekers into candidacy for office. Kansas's John "Goat Glands" Brinkley, well known for his peculiar cures for infertility, twice ran for governor; and Washington's Vic Meyers, a former orchestra leader who once ran for the mayoralty of Seattle promising stewardesses on streetcars, became lieutenant governor. Oregon's reactionary governor Charles Martin genially advised police to "beat hell out of" labor leaders and called for the chloroforming of demented and elderly folks. Oklahoma's picturesque governor "Alfalfa Bill" Murray gained fame for wearing filthy socks and no shoes, for offering guests tea strained through his handkerchief, and for castigating the rich. The wealthy were also targets of W. Lee "Pappy" O'Daniel, a radio personality who captured the Texas governorship. O'Daniel fronted a band that included the founder of "country swing," Bob Wills. Glen Taylor, a former vaudeville actor and itinerant musician, won one of Idaho's senate seats. For all their haranguing rhetoric, though, politicians like Murray, O'Daniel, and Taylor proved loyal in practice to established economic interests.

Other depression-era radicals were more serious. Governor William Langer of North Dakota issued a general moratorium on hated farm foreclosures, then used the National Guard to halt sheriff's sales on foreclosed land. Langer also issued patently illegal embargoes on wheat and beef, in an attempt to raise prices. After the state supreme court removed him from office following conviction for forcing payments from government employees, he came back to win reelection to the governorship and later to a senate seat. The avowedly socialistic Washington Commonwealth Federation took over the Democratic party of that state for a time in 1936. And in California, the utopian novelist Upton Sinclair captured the Democratic nomination for governor in 1934 on a socialistic EPIC (End Poverty in California) program but lost the election when establishment Democrats opposed him. California, fast becoming a mecca for retirees, also produced the Townsend movement, an impractical scheme featuring monthly pensions for the elderly. Dr. Francis Townsend, a retired doctor, lost his life's savings when his bank failed, and his organization pressured Congress toward Social Security. Townsendism swept the country, but most of its twelve hundred locals were in the West. Sixteen of California's twenty congressmen supported the unsuccessful attempt to write Townsendism into federal law.

Behind all the sound and fury, much of it superficial, worked a profound revolution in federal-state relations throughout the 1930s, a revolution that dramatically affected the West. As James T. Patterson, a student of the New Deal, has commented, the New Deal was primarily a southern-western movement: its heaviest support came from these regions of low per capita income and sparse industry. Roosevelt always carried the Far West, and a significant reason for this stark shift in allegiance from Republicans to Democrats lay in the simple fact that the West benefited inordinately from the new federal dynamism and spending. Near-vacant Nevada ranked first among states in total per capita New Deal spending, at $1,130; Montana ranked second and Wyoming third. The presence of so much federal forest, park, mineral, and public land dictated that numerous reclamation, conservation, and construction projects flourished in the West.

Influential westerners in Washington, D.C., played major roles in forging this new federalism that, through investment and regulation, began the end of the old economic colonialism. Powerful lawmakers like Senators Joseph O'Mahoney of Wyoming, Burton Wheeler of Montana, and Key Pittman of Nevada proved far more able than had their predecessors in channeling new monies to home-state constituents, as they did with the Silver Purchase Act of 1934 and the Agricultural Adjustment Act of 1938. Westerners played key roles among Roosevelt's appointees. Jesse "Jesus" Jones of Houston funneled big investments westward as head of the Reconstruction Finance Corporation; and as governor of the Federal Reserve Board, the Utah banker Marriner Eccles, along with Jones, supported western allies like the California banking titan A. P. Giannini. William O. Douglas, a Washington environmentalist, became an appointee to the Supreme Court.

No western state exercised more federal power, nor better exemplified its results, than did Texas. The Lone Star State had not only Jones at the helm but also Vice President John Nance Garner; Senator Tom Connally, chairman of the Foreign Relations Committee; and a bloc-voting cadre of solidly Democratic congressmen that included no fewer than five house committee chairmen. The master legislator Sam Rayburn rose to become House majority leader in 1937 and then in 1940 became Speaker of the House, a post he held for the next two decades. In 1937 an astute young Texan named Lyndon Johnson won a special House election as a defender of the president and soon became known as FDR's "pet congressman." Allied with the soon-to-be-mammoth construction firm of Brown and Root, he carefully secured funding to complete that company's contract to build the Marshall Ford (later Mansfield) Dam on the Colorado River in Texas. In so doing, he launched the career that would one day make him the region's, and the nation's, most powerful politician.

The inflow of federal dollars and imposition of federal regulation also brought considerable upheaval to the western states. Though welcoming the money, some western elected officials bridled at federal intervention, lusted after and wallowed in the patronage of federal jobs, and railed against federal programs that stipulated the states "match" federal dollars. In Colorado, where a group of Communist-led unemployed actually stormed and occupied the capitol in 1935, anti–New Deal Democratic Governor "Big Ed" Johnson refused to raise matching dollars and openly fought with FDR's relief czar, Harry Hopkins. Other western governors, like Tom Berry in South Dakota and "Cowboy Ben" Ross in Idaho, behaved similarly—taking the money and manipulating the patronage even while yelping about it. When Ross reluctantly forced through a new sales tax to raise the matching funds, the voters turned against him. In the worst cases, as in Langer's North Dakota and Murray's Oklahoma, Hopkins finally took over state relief organizations because of irresponsible governors.

Throughout the United States, the reforming impulse and political popularity of the New Deal Democrats declined sharply in the late 1930s as a gradual economic recovery diminished the sense of urgency. This trend was especially marked in the individualistic West, where traditions of welfare liberalism had been lacking in the first place and where bitter factional struggles broke up Democratic unity in a number of states. Prominent Democratic senators like O'Mahoney of Wyoming and Wheeler of Montana led the effort to defeat the president's ill-fated attempt to "pack" the Supreme Court in 1937. And, typically, FDR failed in his attempt to intervene in the 1938 western primaries to "save" liberals like Congressman Maury Maverick in Texas or Senator James Pope in Idaho.

The rising chorus of protest against New Deal federal activism seemed reminiscent of territorial days. In truth, it smacked of considerable hypocrisy, since these federal investments—particularly those in dams and water systems, in agricultural subsidies, and in Social Security and other federal projects—proved to be enduring and under-wrote a new prosperity and economic stability for the entire region. Even larger federal investments soon followed during World War II; but these investments, primarily in military bases and in huge aviation and shipbuilding industries, would be less contro-versial.

The West was richly rewarded both because of its loyalty to FDR and because of its geography. The arid, underdeveloped West proved perfect for numerous New Deal reclamation, conservation, and agricultural projects. Regardless of whether one's vantage was 1940 or 1945, the political West looked markedly different from that of 1930. Then, Washington had seemed remote, and what little heed one paid to government was usually to sleepy state capitals like Phoenix and Pierre. Now both the state capital and especially the national capital seemed near and vitally important. A new federalism arrived, a new world in which "government" would matter more than the baronial, eastern-based corporations of yesterday.

The bombs that fell on Pearl Harbor in December 1941 brought an abrupt silencing of the political acrimony of the New Deal years. Patriotism and its natural accompani-ment, conservatism, now replaced the fervent reformism of the prior decade. Although many western politicians questioned Roosevelt programs like Lend-Lease and "Cash and Carry," every congressional member except Jeannette Rankin of Montana voted to support the war.

The conclusion of World War II left westerners anxious about continued federal support for the many defense-related projects that had fueled the regional economy. But the cold war ensured an ongoing flow of government money that made the success of regional politicians dependent on their ability to deliver lucrative contracts to their home districts.

Esther Bubley (b. 1921). V-E Day. Mayor Cecil Faris Proclaims V-E Day to Be An Official Holiday in Tomball, Texas. Gelatin silver print, 1945. Standard Oil (New Jersey) Collection, University of Louisville Archives, Louisville, Kentucky.

More to the point, though, the patriotic mood of wartime discouraged political debate. Even such a mass violation of civil rights as the incarceration of more than one hundred thousand Japanese Americans in "relocation centers" throughout the West provoked little protest. A surface harmony prevailed. In California, moderate Republican Earl Warren easily defeated the embattled liberal Democrat Culbert Olson in 1942 for governor. Taking advantage of wartime prosperity and California's unique system of "nonpartisan" cross-filing in both parties, Warren so soothed the electorate that in 1946 he won the nomination of both parties and coasted to a landslide reelection victory. Washington Governor Arthur Langlie successfully employed a similar bipartisan approach. Other state chief executives, like Coke Stephenson in Texas and John Moses in North Dakota, also proved able to cash in on war-born prosperity to stabilize taxes, accrue surpluses, and simultaneously enjoy political peace—the perfect world for most aspiring politicians.

Beneath the calm, however, powerful forces of change were working, driven by massive economic shifts. In Nebraska, venerable Senator George Norris fell to defeat in 1942 at the hands of reactionary Republican Kenneth Wherry, a death knell for the older progressivism. In Oklahoma, the oil magnate Robert Kerr took the governor's chair in 1943, symbolizing the new rich who were grasping political power. As he told the voters, "I'm just like you, only I struck oil." In Nevada, conservative Democratic Senator Pat McCarran routed the brother of his deceased foe, Key Pittman, in his 1944 Senate bid, an intraparty fracas that paved the way for postwar Republican victories. And in the 1944 decision of *Smith v. Allwright*, the U.S. Supreme Court ruled that blacks could no longer be excluded from Texas primary elections, a clear omen that the days of political racial discrimination were numbered.

Amid the rejoicing at the end of war in mid-1945, as westerners nervously looked ahead at what the future might hold, their main fear was that the end of massive wartime military spending might trigger a return to 1930s-style depression. They need not have worried, for quite the opposite happened. The emerging "cold war" soon fueled new rounds of defense spending, much of which flowed westward, particularly to California. Few western military bases were closed, and politicians fought to keep defense dollars moving west. These federal dollars, and many others flowing to such expenditures as reclamation, agriculture subsidies, maintenance of the public lands, and highways, harbors, and airports, would not only underwrite a new regional prosperity but also liberate the West from a dying colonialism. These dollars would, in fact, produce a new regional politics.

Politics of Pork and Protest, 1945–68

The system of federal spending that continued after the war created a new political reality. Because a politician's success depended largely on his ability to deliver federal projects into his home state (few women held national posts in the quarter century after World War II), members of both parties had to work together. But although there were incentives for bipartisan cooperation, there were also reasons for sharp attacks. First from the Right, then from the Left, the politics of the West were rocked by division.

It is easy to see why western politicians rushed to tap the federal coffers. The economic hardships of the past were still sharply remembered; the risks of overdevelopment seemed too remote to be considered. Politicians from both parties joined in and worked together.

This was especially true in matters related to defense. Among the powerful state senatorial teams who combined forces to acquire defense contracts for state-based companies and to expand military facilities within their state were the Democrats Henry Jackson and Warren Magnuson. Known as "the senators from Boeing," they represented Washington for nearly three decades. Representing Texas for a time, in contrast, were such polar opposites as Ralph Yarborough, a Democrat, and John Tower, a Republican. They battled for General Dynamics and for the state's many air bases. Meanwhile, all the legislators from California fought to obtain contracts for Lockheed and McDonnell-Douglas and to secure defense installations, especially along the Pacific coast. Even arch-conservatives like Barry Goldwater of Arizona, contemptuous of federal programs in many other areas, had no qualms pushing for federal dollars for military bases and defense.

The first major questioning of this arrangement occurred in 1961. It came from the out-going president and Kansas-born general who had led the Allied armies to victory in Europe during World War II. In his farewell address to the American people, Dwight D. Eisenhower spoke of "the total influence . . . felt in every city" of "an immense military establishment and a large arms industry." In time, politicians with closer ties to western constituencies would come to question aspects of what "the military-industrial complex"—to use Ike's phrase—was recommending. But in the early 1960s few heeded the former president's warning. Federal expenditures for defense meant unparalleled prosperity for the region.

The defense industry was not the only example of western pork-barrel politics. Federal research contracts for nuclear energy came to Washington, Idaho, and New Mexico. Western geography played a major role in this phase of federal contracts; yet politicians charted the fate of nuclear research based on economic prosperity for their respective states. Simultaneously, internal defense needs were utilized as a reason to create the gigantic interstate highway system. This huge undertaking was especially vital to the West, with its enormous acreage, for it provided up to 95 percent of federal funding for highway construction in the most rural states.

Another area of considerable pork-barrel activity focused on western reclamation projects. Ever since the creation of the Bureau of Reclamation, federally funded multipurpose dams were an accepted way of life in the West. Long before environmentalist organizations fought western projects, almost all politicians sought federal dollars for expansive water projects. The alliance among bureaucrats, politicians, and contractors such as Idaho's Morrison-Knudsen, Nebraska's Peter Kiewit, and the Utah Construction Company produced numerous dams.

Harry Truman originally sought Tennessee Valley Authority–type systems on the Missouri and Columbia rivers. Congress defeated those proposals as it came to rebel against federal government domination and regulation. Instead, numerous dams were constructed on the Missouri, Columbia, Snake, and Colorado river systems. The private power companies, municipalities, and irrigation districts combined with recreation and tourism interests to profit from federally funded projects. With such diverse backing through the 1960s, it is no wonder that western politicians continued to deliver the projects to their states.

While politicians worked together to funnel federal dollars westward, there were times when the political discourse among them attained a high level of vitriol. Initially the sharpest attacks came from the Right. Well before the name of Wisconsin Senator Joseph McCarthy became equated with the phenomenon, western politicians were ferreting out reds and smearing their opponents for being "soft on communism." Under the leadership of Martin Dies of Texas, the House Un-American Activities Committee (HUAC), since its inception in 1938, had been accusing the federal government of harboring radicals. By 1947 HUAC had gained a new member, a young veteran from California who had won his congressional seat through red-baiting tactics and who soon rose to prominence for his role in the Alger Hiss–Whittaker Chambers hearings. Thereafter, Richard Nixon ascended to the Senate in 1950 in part by branding his opponent, Helen Gahagan Douglas, as the "Pink Lady." To placate the McCarthy wing of the party in 1952, Republican kingmakers persuaded Dwight Eisenhower to include Nixon on the national ticket.

Other prominent westerners involved in the virulent anticommunism of the era included Senators Herman Welker ("Little Joe from Idaho"), Kenneth Wherry of Nebraska, and Karl Mundt of South Dakota. Although Republican politicians were most adamant in their charges, anticommunism was bipartisan. Democratic Senator Pat McCarran of Nevada, author of the Internal Security Act, and former Senator D. Worth Clark of Idaho also used McCarthyite techniques.

The search for subversives in the West amounted to the same blend of farce and tragedy as it did throughout the United States. A hunt for Communists among sixty thousand Texas schoolteachers turned up exactly one. In 1948, an investigation by the Washington State Legislature's Canwell Committee forced the dismissal of three University of Washington professors; and at the University of California's Berkeley campus, the Board of Regents fired thirty-two faculty members who refused to take loyalty oaths. After enormous controversy, the state supreme court mandated their reinstatement in 1952.

Perhaps the most celebrated aspect of western McCarthyism occurred when the House Un-American Activities Committee chose to investigate Hollywood's writers, directors, and actors. The California attorney general prepared a list of suspected Communist sympathizers, and the HUAC investigators focused on the "Hollywood Ten." Most of the ten who pleaded the fifth amendment were convicted of contempt of Congress, and all were "blacklisted" by the movie industry. The "fifth amendment" Communists became constant targets of McCarthy and his followers.

Some of the worst excesses of political McCarthyism occurred in the western states during the 1950s. In Idaho, Montana, and Utah, incumbents, usually Democrats, were attacked for being soft on communism. Glen Taylor in Idaho, who ran for vice president as a Progressive in 1948, was victimized by an attack called "The Red Record of Glen Taylor." Elbert Thomas of Utah suffered a media blitz of charges and vicious accusations of Communist sympathy. Some insiders speculated that the suicide of Senator Lester Hunt of Wyoming was precipitated by proposed personal smear tactics. Hunt's death in his Senate office sobered many western politicians. After the famous Army–McCarthy Hearings, the Senate leadership chose Utah's senior Republican senator, Arthur V. Watkins, to chair the special committee that recommended the censure of Senator McCarthy in 1954. Although McCarthy himself faded quickly from public view, the political impact remained for many years.

Indeed, a decade later, the Republicans chose as their presidential candidate a westerner whose intense anticommunism provoked parallels to McCarthy. Barry Goldwater, a department store magnate and senator from the State of Arizona, was hostile to Social Security and the federal role in civil rights. He wanted to abolish the graduated income tax, to sell the Tennessee Valley Authority, and to reduce federal functions at the rate of 10 percent a year. Moreover, he wanted an out-and-out victory over communism and said he was willing to risk war to achieve it.

With Goldwater trumpeting that "extremism in the defense of liberty is no vice," it was easy for the incumbent to present himself as a moderate. After twenty-three years in Congress—first in the House and then in the Senate, including five years as Senate majority leader—Lyndon Baines Johnson had joined the 1960 Democratic ticket as John F. Kennedy's running mate. With their campaign's success, Johnson had discovered that Kennedy and his advisers, eastern-establishment types, looked down on the lowly graduate of Southwest Texas State Teachers College. When Kennedy died on 22 November 1963, in Dallas, the once-disdained vice president became head of state.

Blending the nation's sense of mourning together with his considerable legislative talents, Johnson succeeded in gaining congressional approval for a large number of important measures. By the time he squared off against Goldwater in the 1964 race, the president had to his credit a civil rights bill, a tax cut, and an antipoverty program. Easily defeating Goldwater, he carried every western state except Arizona. Moreover, his party had won large majorities in the House and Senate.

Now president in his own right, Johnson continued to gain enactments of major legislation. In 1965 Congress approved federal aid to education, health care for the elderly, and voting rights for racial minorities. Still, if Johnson had looked to his home region in 1964 and 1965, he might have realized how fragile was the coalition that had elected him.

Two western senators, Wayne Morse of Oregon and Ernest Gruening of Alaska, alone among the members of Congress had voted against the Gulf of Tonkin Resolution in the summer of 1964. This resolution, passed under pretenses the Johnson administration had not bothered to verify, laid the groundwork both for the massive bombing of North Vietnam and for the buildup of U.S. troops in South Vietnam. The nation's actions overseas, as well as the grievances of African Americans at home, were among the issues student protesters wanted to highlight when the Free Speech movement erupted at the University of California at Berkeley in the fall of 1964. From that point through the early 1970s, the West would stand at the forefront of New Left activism.

The early civil rights movement was southern based, but the urban ghetto uprisings of 1964–65, notably the Los Angeles Watts riot of 1965, focused attention on the difficulties of urban discrimination. Thirty-four people died in that prolonged incident, and property worth millions of dollars went up in flames. The militant Black Panthers, created by Huey Newton and Bobby Seale, grew up in the East Bay area during the late 1960s. Claiming to be the godchildren of Malcolm X, the Panthers' violent rhetoric frightened mainstream America. The 1968 Olympic boycott, organized by the San Jose State sociologist Harry Edwards, had western origins. National attention also focused on Angela Davis, then a UCLA philosophy instructor and an announced Communist, when her pro–civil rights and antiwar sentiments, together with her sympathy for black prison inmates, led California Governor Ronald Reagan to attempt to dismiss her.

The more mainstream civil rights political activism centered on Cesar Chavez's National Farm Workers Association. Chavez brought national attention to the plight of Hispanic migrant workers with a series of strikes accompanied by national grape and lettuce boycotts. Chavez's movement spread throughout the Southwest, and although victories were short-lived and opposition was fierce, the national AFL-CIO gave him support.

Native Americans had their own reasons for activism. The 1950s had seen a federal effort to relocate Indians from reservations to cities to improve job opportunities. The national government also attempted to terminate its support of some Native American tribes. This policy of termination created an economic disaster for the targeted tribes such as the Klamaths in Oregon and the Menominees in Wisconsin. Before long termination itself was terminated, but during the unrest of the late sixties and early seventies, both urban and reservation Indians engaged in protests. Russell Means, Dennis Banks, and the American Indian Movement sought "Red Power" or Indian self-determination and economic self-reliance. Native activists seized headlines when they occupied, in protest, Alcatraz Island in 1969 and Wounded Knee in South Dakota in 1973.

The western civil rights movement reached a climax during the primary presidential campaign of Robert Kennedy in 1968. Kennedy campaigned among Chavez's farm workers in Oakland, among African Americans living in Los Angeles, and among the Navajos of the Southwest. His strategy of involvement, concern, care, and support paid

The American Indian Movement attracted national attention to contemporary federal Indian policy with its 71-day occupation of Wounded Knee, South Dakota, in 1973. A negotiated settlement ended the standoff with federal officials, but many of the underlying problems that precipitated the siege on the Pine Ridge Indian Reservation, including poverty and unemployment, remained unresolved.

Unidentified photographer. Armed Escort for Federal Official at Wounded Knee. *Gelatin silver print, 1973. UPI/Bettmann, New York, New York.*

off with a major victory in California's June primary. However, his assassination that night led to despair and frustration among his followers.

In the end, the victor in the presidential election of 1968 proved to be the Californian who two decades earlier had smeared his opponents as "pinkos." Politically, the West had come full circle. Still, the region that helped elect Richard Nixon to the presidency differed from the place it had been before. No longer poor or sparsely settled, the West had entered the national mainstream. Increasingly, it would command respect in major party councils.

State Patterns of Partisan Politics

During the quarter century after 1945, the political culture of each state had been evolving in patterns at once similar yet different, both from each other and from the inherited characteristics of the postfrontier era. Four states of the interior West, North Dakota and Montana in the north and New Mexico and Arizona in the south, provide striking examples of political mainstreaming, of shedding peculiar, postfrontier cultures. The two former states represented the slow-growth political economy of the northern plains, the two latter the fast-changing Southwest.

The unique feature of North Dakota politics after the war was the old Nonpartisan League, still a major force even though postwar voters no longer favored its blend of isolationism and radicalism. In 1956, the minority Democratic party arranged a merger with the league, a move that ended its independence but also made for a genuine two-party rivalry in the state. In neighboring Montana, the corresponding anachronism was the arcane prevalence of the Anaconda Company, which finally sold its heavy-handed chain of newspapers in 1959 but did not collapse until 1983. The state had meanwhile evolved a classic, closely competitive political profile. Liberal forces, drawing on the support of both organized labor and the well-established neo-Populist Farmers' Union, managed to elect progressive congressmen, such as Senator Mike Mansfield, who were lauded for their ability to "deliver" federal pork. Conservative groups, more broadly based and relying on ranchers, large dryland farmers, and extractive corporations, usually dominated state government. Local folks called it "political schizophrenia," but this was simply a dramatic rendering of a trend typical of the interior West.

New Mexico's political culture was especially distinctive, since the Hispanic population not only dominated much of the state but also was assertive. Headed by Democratic Senator Dennis Chavez from the mid-1930s until his death in 1963, the "patron" system of rural Hispanic machines led to many abuses. Nevertheless, the rapid inflow of federal employees and defense workers during and after the war began eroding the power of this fiefdom structure. Although Democratic Senator Clinton Anderson served as the typically western deliverer of largesse, Republicans steadily rose toward parity in state government, exemplified by Edwin Mechem, who served as governor for much of the 1950s and early 1960s.

Of all the western states, Arizona witnessed the most abrupt, revolutionary political upheaval. Traditionally, Arizona embodied the classic southwestern politics: southern-style Democratic dominance, in league with the "3 C's" of copper, cotton, and cattle. Senator Carl Hayden, in Congress from 1912 until 1968, personified this tradition. But the arrival of new corporate giants like Motorola, with hordes of well-paid employees, changed everything after the war. In 1946 a business-agricultural alliance pushed through an antiunion right-to-work law; and with the triumph in 1952 of the conservative Barry Goldwater in a key Senate contest came a clear indication that Republicans were laying claim to the future.

Oklahoma and Texas, the two southern border states of the West, moved from one-party Democratic cultures more slowly. In each state, the ruling Democrats had a lesser liberal wing and a more dominant, oil-allied conservative majority. In Oklahoma the most prestigious of the liberals was the dignified and thoughtful Congressman Carl Albert, who eventually became House Speaker. The dominant conservative, serving first as governor and then as senator, was Robert Kerr, who rose craftily during the 1950s to become one of the strongmen of the Senate. Kerr used his political leverage to advance his Kerr-McGee oil concern and to channel a massive $1.2 billion into making the Arkansas River navigable all the way to Tulsa, one of the greatest pork-barrel forays in American history. By the 1960s, though, business-style Republicans were also winning statewide elections, as did Governors Henry Bellmon and Dewey Bartlett. In other ways, this southern-borderlands state changed only slowly. A large Baptist vote kept the fifty-two-year-old constitutional Prohibition law in effect until 1959.

Texas moved similarly. A vibrant, Populist strain of liberalism lived on here, best articulated by men like Senator Ralph Yarborough and Congressman Maury Maverick. But the Texas "establishment" rested firmly on the foundations of big oil, booming finance and manufacturing, and one-party southern Democracy. Conservative Governor Allan Shivers, whose "Shivercrats" preferred Eisenhower to liberal Democratic leaders like Truman and Adlai Stevenson, represented this class. So too did, in disguised form, Senator Lyndon Johnson, the new Texas strongman. Before his elevation to the Democratic national ticket in 1960, Johnson, along with his venerable mentor House Speaker Sam Rayburn, steered the national Democratic party to smooth cooperation with the Eisenhower administration, meanwhile gathering numerous benefits for Texas and Texas oil.

The silver-haired John Connally, a close associate of Johnson's, governed the state from 1963 to 1969. Connally epitomized the marriage between Texas wealth and the Democratic party, and during his years, new aerospace and other investments transformed the state. But here too, the old order was rapidly changing. By 1958 over one-third of eligible African Americans were registered to vote, and in 1966, federal courts downed the arcane Texas poll-tax law. The genuine power of San Antonio Congressman Henry B. Gonzales symbolized the awakening of Hispanic strength. And GOP Senator John Tower, who garnered the votes of many liberals angry at the Johnson-Connally "machine," signaled both the gradual rise of Republican strength and the aging of one-party Democracy.

Across the dry interior West, a fairly clear pattern emerged during these years of more or less close party competition, with an increasing slant toward conservatism and Republicanism as suburbia grew and the 1970s approached. For instance, in booming Nevada, where the gaming industry increasingly set the pace, the older Democratic organizations led by conservative Senators Key Pittman and Pat McCarran gave way in the 1960s to business Republicans led by Governor Paul Laxalt, even as reports of mafia and teamster influence over state politics raised increasing alarms.

In centrally located Colorado, with its representative mix of urban and rural constituencies, Democrats fretted at the erosion of their blue-collar and Hispanic base in Pueblo and the southeast, and Republicans fattened on the sprawling urban corridor running north and south from Denver. Typically conservative GOP senators like Gordon Allott and Peter Dominick railed at big-spending federal programs, even as Wayne Aspinall, the big-spending Democratic congressman and chairman of the House Interior Committee, worked with them to pour federal investments into Colorado and especially into Denver, America's second-largest center of federal employment.

To the north, thinly populated Wyoming had always been dominated by Republicans and stock growers. With only about twenty-six hundred members, the Wyoming Stock Growers' Association could sometimes lay claim to over half the members of the state senate. As in Colorado, the Democrats saw that their southern power base—along the Union Pacific rail line—was slowly shrinking. Similarly, in neighboring Idaho, Democrats watched the decline of their traditional power bases in the northern Panhandle mining and lumber regions and in the railroad towns, making it increasingly difficult to elect liberals like prominent Senator Frank Church. The booming cities of southern Idaho tended to vote for conservatives like Republican Governor Len Jordan and the exceptionally able Governor Robert Smylie.

In Utah, the political power of the Mormon church was truly awesome: over 90 percent of state officeholders were Latter-day Saints, whereas church members made up only 70 percent of the population; but the power was not as absolute or monolithic as some believed. As in other conservative western states, factional battles between regular Republicans, such as Senator Arthur Watkins, and tempestuous mavericks, such as Governor J. Bracken Lee, who had wooed many conservative Democrats, opened the way for a thoughtful Democrat like Frank Moss to capture a U.S. Senate seat. Farmer-labor Democrats could still win in liberal years or when Republicans became divided.

The strongest Republican heartland in all the West lay in the central Great Plains, where the party had long ago been implanted by homesteading settlers. In South Dakota, Republicans in the early seventies claimed nearly 90 percent of all political contests since statehood. Here, as in Utah, however, a liberal Democrat like the future presidential candidate George McGovern could win by campaigning against the Eisenhower farm policies and later move from the House to the Senate.

Nebraska had a strong Democratic base in Omaha and along the towns of the Union Pacific and Burlington railroads; but as in South Dakota, agriculture set the pace, and set it firmly toward Republicanism and conservatism. For years, the Senate team of Carl Curtis and Roman Hruska ruled as one of the most rightist in America. Nebraska indicated its essential conservatism by maintaining its state government until the mid-1960s with neither a sales nor an income tax. Kansas remained even more of a Republican bastion. Fires of populism and progressivism seem to have banked long ago with the departure of Senator Arthur Capper after the war, and Kansas did not get around to disposing of its antiquated temperance law until as recently as 1986. The only time since the war that the state has voted Democratic for president was in the Johnson landslide of 1964.

Whereas these eastern rim states of the region reflected the Republican conservatism of the adjoining Midwest, the Pacific Coast states were, as earlier, generally more progressive. They seemed more akin to the urban Northeast than to the aridland states that adjoined them. Historically these states, particularly northern California and western Washington, have been oriented toward maritime trade and organized labor, which tilted them leftward. Now, in all three states, sprawling suburbs have recast the political order to the cutting edge of American middle-class rule.

Washington offers a classic example of a state divided politically by geography. The populous Puget Sound area, characterized by burgeoning Seattle, aerospace and maritime industry, and union Democrats, usually outvoted the central and eastern reaches of the state, where Spokane anchored a more conservative political culture. Oregon resembled Washington in its west-east geographic split; but its sociopolitical profile was less industrial-labor and more middle class in nature. Its New England–style politics were typically so Republican yet moderate-progressive that it was sometimes called the "Vermont of the West."

As California evolved into "a nation within a nation," the surface calm of consensual, progressive-Republican governance that Governor Earl Warren had introduced in wartime continued long into the postwar era—through Warren's own nearly three terms, until he was appointed chief justice of the U.S. Supreme Court by Eisenhower, and then under his successor, Goodwyn Knight. By the 1950s, however, the middle road grew bumpy as both liberal Democrats and conservative Republicans moved away from it; and the end of the peculiar cross-filing system in 1959 further undermined the middle. The administration of Edmund "Pat" Brown (1959–67) marked a high-water point for liberal Democracy in California as the legislature enacted most of his reform proposals and a major new water-development plan.

But during the later 1960s, this imperial state spearheaded a major regional and national trend to the Right, with the triumph of arch-conservative actor George Murphy for the Senate in 1964, followed by that of another rightist actor, Ronald Reagan, over Brown for the governorship in 1966. As governor, Reagan won popular support by hacking at budgets, especially for education, and by defying radical students; but in 1967 he was forced to sign into law a record five-billion-dollar budget, with 20 percent of that being tax increases. Still, his show-business style and rightist rhetoric were fast turning him into a national political force.

The West since 1969: A Republican Stronghold?

Ronald Reagan would secure the presidency in 1980, but in 1968 another California Republican, Richard Nixon, squeaked into the White House. With only a fraction of a percentage point separating Nixon's share of the popular vote from that of the Democratic candidate Hubert Humphrey, Republican leaders wondered how they could secure a stronger popular mandate in the future. A book that appeared in 1969, *The Emerging Republican Majority*, provided the answer. The president should ignore the Northeast and Midwest and concentrate instead on winning the South and West. "From space-center Florida across the booming Texas plains to the Los Angeles-San Diego suburban corridor, the nation's fastest-growing areas" were, in the words of the book's author, Kevin P. Phillips, "strongly conservative and Republican."

Phillips's analysis was based on changing demographic patterns. In the West, rural areas were atrophying while urban complexes were quickly rising, particularly in the arc from Houston and Dallas, across the Southwest, to the boom cities of California. The new westerners were neither farmers nor blue-collar workers: they were well-paid middle-class employees, especially of new service, high-technology, and government organizations. They lived in sprawling, sunny suburbs; and if not ideologically rightist, they were inherently middle-of-the-road to conservative, disliking radicals and unions and challenging both with antilabor right-to-work laws. If the two parties had competed relatively evenly in the past, the Republicans were certain to gain the upper hand in the future—especially if the party consciously appealed to this, its natural constituency.

A look at general election trends of the 1970s and 1980s seems to suggest that Phillips was correct: the West tilted to the Right and toward the Republican party. In the Nixon landslide of 1972, the entire West—and nearly the entire country—voted Republican. More tellingly, in the closely fought campaign of 1976, which went to Democrat Jimmy Carter, the only western state to back the winner was Texas. In the two GOP landslides posted by Ronald Reagan in 1980 and 1984, the majority in every western state voted for the Republican presidential ticket. And finally, in the 1988 victory of Texas Republican George Bush, all of the western states except Washington and Oregon voted for the winner.

On closer analysis, however, a more complex reality emerges. The West had, in fact, voted Republican in *every* presidential race between 1952 and 1988 with the exception of the Johnson-Goldwater election. During that thirty-six-year span, the West had voted for the loser only twice, Nixon in 1960 and Gerald Ford in 1976. In other words, the regional voting pattern typically reflected the trend in the nation. Moreover, the Republicans had courted the region with a series of candidates who called the West home (Eisenhower in 1952 and 1956, Goldwater in 1964, Nixon in 1960, 1968, and 1972,

Reagan in 1980 and 1984, and Bush in 1988). Although a number of western Democrats had sought their party's nomination, such as Washington's Henry Jackson in 1972, Idaho's Frank Church in 1976, Arizona's Bruce Babbitt in 1988, and Colorado's Gary Hart in 1984 and 1988, only two western Democrats had succeeded in winning it—Lyndon Johnson in 1964 and George McGovern in 1972. Indeed, even though Bill Clinton was not a westerner, his campaign in 1992 showed that a Democrat who paid attention to the West could crack the Republican stronghold on the region. Clinton won 96 electoral votes from eight western states while Bush garnered 81 electoral votes from eleven states in the region.

Nevertheless, the best evidence that the Republican party's hold on the region was not inexorable came from the discrepancy between the Democrats' poor showing in presidential contests and their success in congressional, state, and local races. The truth was that, in most of the West during the second half of the twentieth century, the two-party system was thriving. Even as presidential candidates like Walter Mondale and Michael Dukakis failed miserably in the region, western Democrats as a whole did well. These Democrats succeeded because they knew how to compete for votes on their own turf. Only in a few locales like western Washington and the San Francisco Bay area could westerners win as unabashed liberals, espousing concern for the poor and needy, equality for minorities, women, and gays, protection of abortion rights, conservation of the environment, and opposition to incursions overseas. Nevertheless, Democrats could get elected in even the most conservative states if they learned to tack their sails, leaning to the Right on some issues like abortion and gays while bearing to the Left on others like the environment.

By making pragmatic choices, two highly skilled Democrats, Calvin Rampton and Scott Matheson, held down the governorship of Utah—arguably the nation's most conservative state—from the mid-1960s until the early 1980s. In Republican Arizona, moderate Democrats like Senator Dennis DeConcini, Governor Bruce Babbitt, and Congressman Morris Udall all demonstrated their popularity. Liberal Senator Alan Cranston, without benefit of any particular charisma, managed to buck the conservative trend in California. And buffeted by farm depression, conservative Nebraskans elected the liberal Democratic Vietnam Medal of Honor winner Robert Kerrey as governor, then senator, and in 1982 enacted the toughest curb on corporate farming in the country.

Yet western politics in the closing decades of the twentieth century were more than a catalogue of winners and losers. The region had to contend with a series of complex issues. On none were the lines more tightly drawn than between those who wanted to protect the West as wilderness and those who wanted to develop it for private business interests.

The modern environmentalist movement, rooted in the conservationism of the Progressive Era, rose to prominence due both to a concern for a deteriorating environment and to the assumption that American affluence could and should afford care for the land and its future. It centered on the West, and on Alaska, the location of most of the public lands.

In the eleven states of the Far West, federal ownership ranged from 29.6 percent in Montana to over 85 percent in Nevada. The managerial agencies that administered huge swaths of federally or publicly owned western land served as custodians of the people's inheritance. The Forest Service, Park Service, and Bureau of Land Management touched every aspect of western life. The governmental policies of fee collection, timber allotment, and development became more and more controversial. The West became the battleground for numerous discussions, debates, forums, and demonstrations. Westerners traditionally sought exploitation and development, but by the 1960s, militant and dedicated environmentalists demanded conservation, preservation, and limited use. Western developers and promoters felt that the federal bureaucrats and environmental allies had thwarted natural economic growth.

A clear beginning occurred in the mid-1950s, with the victory of the Sierra Club and its allies in prohibiting construction of Echo Park Dam in Utah's spectacular canyonlands. More victories followed in the 1960s, such as the creation of Utah's Canyonlands and California's Redwood national parks, even though Governor Ronald Reagan won notoriety for his comment that, having seen one redwood, he had seen them all. A series of major federal environmental enactments called both for effectively using federal lands and for setting aside pristine wilderness areas: the Wilderness Act, Wild and Scenic Rivers Act, National Recreation Area Act, the Federal Lands Policy and Management Act, and the Roadless Area Review and Evaluation Act.

Mainly in the Pacific Coast and Rocky Mountain states, westerners began in the late 1960s to manifest a new ecological concern. Oregon, with its 1971 "bottle bill" and many other measures, became a national leader. Colorado, an especially intense battleground between developers and environmentalists, caused a sensation by voting down the option to host the 1976 Olympic games. Other leaders were California, where a nasty oil spill polluted the Santa Barbara Channel in 1969, and Washington, where Governor John Spellman outraged promoters of the Northern Tier oil pipeline by refusing to allow the siting of its terminal at Port Angeles. In North Dakota, Montana, and Wyoming, ecological "resource councils" formed unlikely alliances in opposition to massive coal strip mining. Throughout the 1980s and into the 1990s, western environmentalists and wilderness advocates seemed steadily to expand their political strength and often to put developers on the defensive. The era of blatant logrolling for economic benefit had ended.

But the developers and users of federal property also mounted their own crusades, epitomized by the "Sagebrush Rebellion." Their main issues were increased regulation and grazing fees on the public land. Beginning in 1979 in Nevada, a state nearly 86 percent federally owned, the sagebrush rebels demanded the cession of federal lands to the states, which would either sell them or otherwise make them more easily accessible to stockmen and other users. Wyoming, which had already defied the federal bureaucrats by refusing to mandate a fifty-five-mile-per-hour speed limit, followed Nevada's lead, as did local politicians in New Mexico, Arizona, and Utah. Senator Orrin Hatch of Utah introduced a bill to transfer 544 million federally owned acres to the states. But other states, like Colorado and Montana, failed to support Hatch's extreme request, and critics like Governors Bruce Babbitt of Arizona and Cecil Andrus of Idaho pointed out the dubious legality, ethics, and benefits of the idea. The fact that most of the land was marginal, could not be sold, and would be expensive to administer forced the states to reconsider. In the end, the rebellion fizzled, even as the Republican presidential

With a straight-talking, straight-shooting reputation won from his career as an actor, Ronald Reagan parlayed his western persona into political capital to become governor of California in 1966. As president from 1981 to 1989, he continued to draw on his western image as a source of popular appeal.

Film still from Tennessee's Partner *(1955), directed by Allan Dwan. Archive Photos, New York, New York.*

candidate Reagan applauded it. Many of its advocates joined only to voice their frustrations, and in that they succeeded while inadvertently stirring up criticism of agencies like the Forest Service and the Bureau of Land Management for their cozy relationships with land users. Controversial environmental issues continue to pervade western politics. Conflict over the endangered spotted owl in Pacific Coast forests became an issue during the 1992 campaign; and coal-fired power plants as well as nuclear waste disposal sites became the subjects of lengthy legal, legislative, and judicial hassles among developers, federal administrators, and conservationists.

The growing complexity, even unpredictability, of western politics was likewise demonstrated in evolving relationships with Washington, D.C. On the one hand, westerners wanted to control the land and their destiny, but on the other, they still wanted federal dollars for special projects. The administration of President Jimmy Carter (1977–81) brought considerable contention between the executive branch and the West. Early in 1977, Carter demonstrated his lack of western political knowledge when he announced his intention to cut funding of eighteen large western water projects with a total price tag of just over five billion dollars. The outrage of western officialdom, from the Right to the Left, demonstrated the extent to which these giant water-reclamation projects had become the lodestone of regional politics, regardless of ideology or partisan ties. Carter beat a retreat, and in the end, all but four of the targeted projects were funded.

Carter once again ran into western frustration when, in 1979–80, he proposed to base the enormous MX (Missile Experimental) program in the deserts of Nevada and Utah. If built, the MX project would have been the greatest public program in history—a system of missile launchers on underground rail carriers covering up to forty-six thousand square miles and costing up to one hundred billion dollars. The outcry from the affected states, and especially from Utah Governor Scott Matheson, showed that even in these prodevelopment areas, which had long accepted nuclear testing, there were new limits to how much "development" was acceptable. In the autumn of 1981, the Reagan administration announced the scrapping of the MX plan and the decision instead to place the missiles in existing silos.

While westerners were beginning to question long-held assumptions, a profound leavening of western politics was occurring during the closing decades of the twentieth century. Women and minorities, hitherto largely excluded from the heart of the political process, now moved to center stage. Sandra Day O'Connor from Arizona became the first female Supreme Court justice when appointed by Ronald Reagan. The only female U.S. senator for years was Republican Nancy Landon Kassebaum of Kansas. The 1992 Senate election dramatically changed that figure as California Democrats Dianne Feinstein and Barbara Boxer, along with Patty Murray of Washington, won seats. Dixie Lee Ray, Kay Orr, Ann Richards, and Barbara Roberts had meanwhile claimed the governorships, respectively, of Washington, Nebraska, Texas, and Oregon. Numerous women succeeded in congressional, mayoralty, and state legislative elections. This trend continues as a proud reminder that western states offered the franchise to women before their eastern counterparts. True to its progressive past, the West bettered the national average in voting for the ill-fated Equal Rights Amendment as only four of its states—Oklahoma, Utah, Arizona, and Nevada—failed to vote for this assurance of political equality for women.

Native and Hispanic Americans were also making their presence known in western politics. Ben Nighthorse Campbell won a Colorado U.S. Senate seat in 1992, and Larry Echohawk became Idaho's attorney general in 1990. Manuel Luhan, a Republican from New Mexico, became the state's governor and then went to Washington as the secretary of interior. Similarly, Democrats Henry Cisneros and Federico Peña served as the mayors of San Antonio and Denver, becoming President Clinton's secretary of housing and urban development and secretary of transportation.

By the 1990s western politics were no longer the exclusive domain of a particular race, class, or gender. Nor could the Republican party claim to hold hegemony. Rocked by a long agricultural depression and by new problems in the once-booming urban states, the loyalties of western voters were clearly up for grabs. Indeed, as major party politicians seemed unable to break the deadlock between business and environmental interests or to wean the West from expensive federal subsidies, the region seemed poised to respond to new voices.

Such an appeal came in 1992 when a Texas billionaire, Ross Perot, mounted a third-party candidacy. As westerners had been doing since territorial days, they again demonstrated their weak party ties and their taste for mavericks. States such as Utah, Idaho, and Kansas gave Perot 29 percent, 28 percent, and 27 percent of their totals respectively. Even in Oregon, Washington, and California, he secured 25 percent, 24 percent, and 21 percent of the vote.

In the aftermath of the 1992 election, the Perot candidacy seemed to contain long-term implications. Whether he himself would again challenge the two-party system or whether another independent candidate would emerge, the West seemed certain to figure in the outcome. With the states from the plains westward accounting for one-third of the Electoral College vote, the West deserved the attention it was getting. Although no candidate could expect to sweep so diverse a region, neither could anyone afford to ignore it.

Bibliographic Note

Although there is no comprehensive, book-length study of politics and government in the modern West, two general histories give considerable attention to the subject: Gerald D. Nash, *The American West in the Twentieth Century: A Short History of an Urban Oasis* (Albuquerque, 1973); and Michael P. Malone and Richard W. Etulain, *The American West: A Twentieth-Century History* (Lincoln, 1989). An important general assessment is Paul Kleppner, "Politics without Parties: The Western States, 1900–1984," in G. D. Nash and R. W. Etulain, eds., *The Twentieth-Century West: Historical Interpretations* (Albuquerque, 1989), 295–338. A bibliographic overview is provided by F. Alan Coombs, "Twentieth-Century Politics," in M. P. Malone, ed., *Historians and the American West* (Lincoln, 1983), 300–322.

State and regional histories are especially helpful. Among those that pay heed to politics and government are Carl Abbott, Stephen J. Leonard, and David McComb, *Colorado: A History of the Centennial State*, rev. ed. (Boulder, 1982), Russell R. Elliott and William D. Rowley, *History of Nevada*, 2d ed. rev. (Lincoln, 1987), T. A. Larson, *History of Wyoming*, 2d ed. rev. (Lincoln, 1978), Michael P. Malone, Richard B. Roeder, and William L. Lang, *Montana: A History of Two Centuries*, rev. ed. (Seattle, 1991), Elwyn B. Robinson, *History of North Dakota* (Lincoln, 1966), Earl Pomeroy, *The Pacific Slope: A History of California, Oregon, Washington, Idaho, Utah, and Nevada* (New York, 1965), and Carlos A. Schwantes, *The Pacific Northwest: An Interpretive History* (Lincoln, 1989).

Also valuable are political studies of states and subregions, such as Robert E. Burton, *Democrats of Oregon: The Pattern of Minority Politics, 1900–1956* (Eugene, 1970), George N. Green, *The Establishment in Texas Politics: The Primitive Years, 1938–1957* (Westport, Conn., 1979), James R. Green, *Grass-Roots Socialism: Radical Movements in the Southwest, 1895–1943* (Baton Rouge, 1978), Jack E. Holmes, *Politics in New Mexico* (Albuquerque, 1967), Roger M. Olien, *From Token to Triumph: The Texas Republicans since 1920* (Dallas, 1982), Jackson K. Putnam, *Modern California Politics, 1917–1980* (San Francisco, 1980), Michael P. Rogin and John L. Shover, *Political Change in California: Critical Elections and Social Movements, 1890–1966* (Westport, Conn., 1970), James R. Scales and Danney Goble, *Oklahoma Politics: A History* (Norman, 1982), and Randy Stapilus, *Paradox Politics: People and Power in Idaho* (Boise, 1988).

Populism is one of the most debated subjects in American history. John D. Hicks's *The Populist Revolt: A History of the Farmers' Alliance and the People's Party* (Minneapolis, 1931) is the classic, appreciative study. The most influential revisionist work is Lawrence Goodwyn's *Democratic Promise: The Populist Moment in America* (New York, 1976). But perhaps the best perspective is offered in Walter T. K. Nugent, *The Tolerant Populists: Kansas Populism and Nativism* (Chicago, 1963), and in O. Gene Clanton, *Populism: The Humane Preference in America, 1890–1900* (Boston, 1991).

There is no general study of western progressivism, but see these state studies: George E. Mowry's classic *The California Progressives* (Berkeley, 1951); Robert W. Cherny, *Populism, Progressivism, and the Transformation of Nebraska Politics, 1885–1915* (Lincoln, 1981); Danney Goble, *Progressive Oklahoma: The Making of a New Kind of State* (Norman, 1980); and Lewis L. Gould, *Progressives and Prohibitionists: Texas Democrats in the Wilson Era* (Austin, 1973).

Prewar radicalism is discussed in Green, *Grass-roots Socialism*, Garin Burbank, *When Farmers Voted Red: The Gospel of Socialism in the Oklahoma Countryside, 1910–1924* (Westport, Conn., 1976), Robert L. Morlan, *Political Prairie Fire: The Nonpartisan League, 1915–1922* (Minneapolis, 1955), and Carlos A. Schwantes, *Radical Heritage: Labor, Socialism, and Reform in Washington and British Columbia, 1885–1917* (Seattle, 1979).

Historians have barely begun to study the West in the 1920s, but see Norman D. Brown, *Hood, Bonnet, and Little Brown Jug: Texas Politics, 1921–1928* (College Station, Tex., 1984), Charles C. Alexander, *The Ku Klux Klan in the Southwest* (Lexington, 1965), and Robert A. Goldberg, *Hooded Empire: The Ku Klux Klan in Colorado* (Urbana, 1981).

Richard Lowitt's pathbreaking *The New Deal and the West* (Bloomington, 1984) does not directly focus on politics, but consult the essays on western states in John Braeman, Robert H. Bremner, and David Brody, eds., *The New Deal*, vol. 2, *The State and Local Levels* (Columbus, 1975), as well as the following state studies: Robert E. Burke, *Olson's New Deal for California* (Berkeley, 1953); Michael P. Malone, *C. Ben Ross and the New Deal in Idaho* (Seattle, 1970); Francis W. Schruben, *Kansas in Turmoil, 1930–1936* (Columbia, 1969); and James F. Wickens, *Colorado in the Great Depression* (New York, 1979).

The political history of the West during World War II remains to be written, but Gerald D. Nash makes a start in *The American West Transformed: The Impact of the Second World War* (Bloomington, 1985). Also valuable is T. A. Larson, *Wyoming's War Years, 1941–1945* (Laramie, 1954).

Historians are only beginning to study the modern, post–World War II West, as Mary Ellen Glass has in *Nevada's Turbulent '50s: Decade of Political and Economic Change* (Reno, 1981). A number of contemporary regional assessments, however, are helpful: Thomas C. Donnelly, ed., *Rocky Mountain Politics* (Albuquerque, 1940); the western chapters in John Gunther, *Inside U.S.A.* (New York, 1947); Neil Morgan, *Westward Tilt: The American West Today* (New York, 1961); Frank H. Jonas, ed., *Western Politics* (Salt Lake City, 1961); and Frank H. Jonas, ed., *Politics in the American West* (Salt Lake City, 1969).

Neal R. Peirce is America's foremost political regionalist. See his *The Pacific States of America: People, Politics, and Power in the Five Pacific Basin States* (New York, 1972), *The Mountain States of America: People, Politics, and Power in the Eight Rocky Mountain States* (New York, 1972), and *The Great Plains States of America: People, Politics, and Power in the Nine Great Plains States* (New York, 1973). For contemporary assessments, consult Neal R. Peirce and Jerry Hagstrom's *The Book of America: Inside 50 States Today* (New York, 1983). Also valuable for contemporary insights are Peter Wiley and Robert Gottlieb, *Empires in the Sun: The Rise of the New American West* (New York, 1982), Richard D. Lamm and Michael McCarthy, *The Angry West: A Vulnerable Land and Its Future* (Boston, 1982), and the regular publications of the *Western Political Quarterly* and the *Almanac of American Politics*.

Finally, although space constraints allow only a brief sampling here, political biographies are also illuminating, for instance: Paolo E. Coletta, *William Jennings Bryan*, 3 vols. (Lincoln, 1964–69); Richard Lowitt's three volumes, *George W. Norris: The Making of a Progressive, 1861–1912* (Syracuse, 1963), *George W. Norris: The Persistence of a Progressive, 1913–1933* (Urbana, 1971), and *George W. Norris: The Triumph of a Progressive, 1933–1944* (Urbana, 1978); Robert A. Caro, *The Years of Lyndon Johnson*, 2 vols. (New York, 1981, 1990); Anne Hodges Morgan, *Robert S. Kerr: The Senate Years* (Norman, 1977); F. Ross Peterson, *Prophet without Honor: Glen H. Taylor and the Fight for American Liberalism* (Lexington, 1974); G. Edward White, *Earl Warren, A Public Life* (New York, 1982); Garry Wills, *Reagan's America: Innocents at Home* (Garden City, N.Y., 1987); and D. B. Hardeman and Donald C. Bacon, *Rayburn: A Biography* (Austin, 1987).

Chapter Fifteen

A Region of Cities

CAROL A. O'CONNOR

On 8 October 1957 the newspapers confirmed what the public suspected. The National League baseball team the Brooklyn Dodgers was moving to Los Angeles. Falling gate receipts at Ebbets Field, which suburban fans found inaccessible, together with the failure of squabbling borough chiefs to agree on a new site for the team, prompted the Dodgers to look elsewhere. Los Angeles, already home to the football Rams, beckoned with an audience of proven sports fans eager for a crack at the national pastime. The advent of nationwide jet passenger service enhanced the city's chances, and bold action on the part of city leaders clinched the deal. Pointing to land formerly slated for "communistic" public housing, they forced out impoverished squatters and offered the Dodgers a site for their stadium at the heart of the metropolitan network of freeways.

The Dodgers's decision, together with the news that the New York Giants were also moving west, endowed Los Angeles and San Francisco with the mantle of major-league status. In the opinion of many Americans, the cities of the West had finally arrived. To some extent such a perception was accurate. With the passing of each year after 1940, the impact of technology and the flow of government dollars furthered the integration of western cities into the national economy and culture. But to the extent that such a perception implied that cities were new to the West, it was wrong. Western history had had a significant urban dimension from the beginnings of nonnative settlement. What was more, in the nineteenth century and especially in the twentieth, western cities contributed to the shape of the American metropolis, helping to determine what modern-day living is all about.

Eastern Models, Western Variations

"Show me a rich country and I'll soon give you a large town." By 1836 this phrase was being cited as a "pioneer proverb," and no wonder. The generation that had witnessed the rise of Cincinnati, Louisville, and Natchez—not to mention the boom then in progress in Chicago—considered the link between frontiers and cities self-evident. With every newly opened region in need of a center for trade, government, and culture, the wise investor could make a fortune. The trick was selecting a viable townsite and then working frantically to promote it.

The trans-Appalachian experience prepared the public for the competitive nature of frontier town building. In other ways, however, the rules of the game changed out West. Who would have anticipated, for example, that so many westerners would inhabit large cities? By 1890, the proportion of residents of the western states who lived in

Enmeshed in the network of freeways that helped define the Los Angeles landscape, Dodger Stadium presented a distinctive alternative to the older ball parks embedded in the densely settled neighborhoods of eastern cities. Its opening in 1962, along with that of San Francisco's Candlestick Park in 1960, signaled a new prominence for western cities in national life.

Unidentified photographer. Dodger Stadium. Gelatin silver print, 1962. Bruce Henstell Collection.

From the start, an impulse toward town building marked American settlement of the West, where nearly every community had urban ambitions. A significant proportion of the region's population has lived in cities since the mid-19th century.

Unidentified photographer. Hogeland, Montana. Photograph, ca. 1930. From the American Geographical Society Collection, University of Wisconsin-Milwaukee Library.

towns of ten thousand or more was larger than that of any other U.S. region except the Northeast.

At first this information startled the statistician Adna Ferrin Weber. But by the time he published *The Growth of Cities in the Nineteenth Century* (1899), Weber had come up with a plausible explanation. In his view, the West owed its urban demographics partly to geography. The forbidding terrain and harsh climate that prevailed in vast sections of the region meant that very few people inhabited much of its acreage, whereas large numbers lived close together in its cities.

The timing of the settlement of the West also contributed to its skewered statistics. As Weber explained, a technological revolution of unparalleled magnitude was occurring—freeing the mass of human beings from the need to produce their own food but not from the need to work in order to purchase the means of subsistence. Most gainful employment now involved the production of goods and services for the purpose of exchange—activities that demanded a concentration of population. Thus, the existing stage of the world economy dictated a West that was relatively urban.

The significance of this shift was not lost on others. In *The Winning of the West* (1896), Theodore Roosevelt contrasted the Kentucky of the 1790s to the Colorado of the 1870s. When Kentucky became a state, not more than 1 percent of its population lived in its largest town and capital city, Lexington; when Colorado joined the Union, fully one-third of its people resided in Denver. "A hundred years ago there was practically no urban population at all in a new country." The future president said, with obvious pride, "Nowadays when new States are formed the urban population tends to grow in them as rapidly as in the old."

But if advances in technology helped to make the West urban, they also made possible a new kind of city. That potential would reach its fullest realization in the Los Angeles of the early-to-mid-twentieth century. Before that time, those involved in shaping western cities seemed to follow an ambivalent course. On the one hand, they wanted their cities to equal those of the East. On the other hand, they wanted their cities to be different and better.

Eastern models had a particularly strong influence on the development of Portland, Oregon. Named in 1844 for the leading city in Maine, it was located on the Willamette River, twenty miles south of the juncture with the Columbia. According to its founders, Portland stood at the head of navigation, as far inland as an oceangoing vessel could travel. The leaders of other would-be harbors disputed that assertion, but by the early 1850s the issue was moot. With a plank road across the western hills to the rich Tualatin Valley and with locally owned steamships running direct to San Francisco, Portland subdued its immediate rivals. Later it succeeded in attracting two transcontinental railroads and fended off, at least for a time, threats from Tacoma and Seattle to its regional supremacy.

Nevertheless, the leading town in the Northwest looked as if it belonged in the Northeast. With its downtown streets sixty feet wide and its blocks two hundred feet on a side, Portland was comparatively compact. Moreover, its architecture resembled that of eastern cities. Indeed, the eastern firm of McKim, Mead and White designed the Portland Public Library as a smaller-scale version of the library it had built for Boston.

Portland's similarity to eastern towns was discernible early. In the 1860s, as the city's population approached seven thousand, a visitor from Massachusetts wrote, "Portland has the air and fact of a prosperous, energetic town with a good deal of eastern leadership and tone to business and society and morals." Forty years later, another easterner affirmed that Portland was living up to its promise. Rather than "a new, crude Western town," Portland, whose population exceeded ninety thousand, was "a fine old city" with the proper "signs of conservatism and solid respectability." Even Portlanders compared their city to those in the East. The editor of an illustrated magazine, the *West Shore*, boasted, "Invoke the spirit of the lamp and transport a resident of some Eastern city and put him down in the streets of Portland, and he would observe little difference between his new surroundings and those he beheld but a moment before in his native city."

According to this type of thinking, what mattered in the Portland of the late nineteenth century were, as indicated by the *West Shore*, "the well-paved and graded streets, the lines of street railway, the mass of telegraph and telephone wires, the numerous electric lights and street lamps, the fire-plugs and water hydrants, the beautiful private residences surrounded by lawns and shade trees suggesting years of careful culture, the long lines of wharves and warehouses on the river front, and the innumerable other features common to every prosperous Eastern city and commercial port." It did not seem to matter that Portland lay within view of three spectacular snow-covered mountains or that an early town father had reserved as green space a long strip of blocks near the heart of the city.

Why was Portland judged so exclusively by eastern standards? As the historian David Hamer has pointed out, the future of urban places in the West depended in large measure on the good opinion of the East and of Europe. After all, thousands of new towns—not just in the United States—were competing for capital and settlers. Most easterners and Europeans judged the West by eastern standards; it was natural that westerners would do so as well.

Yet, even as they adhered to eastern patterns in some ways, the founders of a number of western cities deviated in other, equally telling ways. For example, nineteenth-century Americans must have assumed that God himself, instead of the government land office, prescribed straight streets to cross at right angles, for new townsites followed the gridiron with monotonous devotion. Still, the scale of the grid in the West usually differed from that in the East. Except for towns set in the sides of mountains and narrow gulches (like Virginia City, Nevada, and Deadwood, South Dakota) and in places laid out by the Spanish a century or two before (like San Antonio, Texas, and Santa Fe, New Mexico), western cities tended to have broad streets and large blocks and to spread out in all directions.

Consider the question of street widths. Early in the nineteenth century, the commissioners of the nation's most populous city had established generous standards to accommodate New York's rapid growth. North of 23rd Street, that city was to have 60-foot-wide crosstown streets and 100-foot-wide north-south avenues. Other eastern cities were laid out on smaller dimensions. In Charleston, South Carolina, the broadest streets (those bordering the town square) measured 60 feet across, whereas the standard street width in Cambridge, Massachusetts, was a mere 30 feet.

Out West, however, widths of 80 feet and more were considered the norm. Sacramento, California, platted in 1848, had streets that broad, as did Cheyenne, Wyoming, laid out twenty years later. The standard street in Omaha measured 100 feet across, whereas the city's two major avenues were 20 feet wider. The plan for Topeka, Kansas, called for more variation. Most of the east-west streets were 80 feet wide; most of the north-south streets were 100 feet wide; and the eight major avenues measured an impressive 130 feet from side to side.

In one respect, such broad streets did not make sense. Too expensive for a young municipality to pave, they became, in the words of a European visitor, George Augustus Sala, "a dusty desert" in the summer and "a Slough of Despond" in rain. Yet broad streets tended to typify big plans. The same individual who deplored "the monstrous breadth of the streets" approved of "the resolve characteristic of Americans to make their towns, even in the inception thereof, big things." Coining the phrase "Cities of the Future" to refer to the infant cities of the region, Sala observed, "Every town in the West is laid out on a plan as vast as though it were destined, at no distant date, to contain a million of inhabitants."

From the platting of Houston, Texas, in 1836 to that of Great Falls, Montana, a half century later, western town builders revealed their ambitions time and again. Yet if the nineteenth century had awarded prizes in urban design, one would surely have gone to the Latter-day Saints for Salt Lake City. In founding their Great Basin refuge in the summer of 1847, the Mormons looked to the ideas of their martyred prophet Joseph Smith. His plan for "a City of Zion" had familiar elements. In setting aside land at the center for church structures and land on the outskirts for pastures and farms, it incorporated aspects of the old New England town. Yet Smith's plan also involved some innovations—very broad streets, huge blocks, a required minimum setback for residential structures, and an unusual pattern of changing the direction of the lots on consecutive blocks.

As carried out under the leadership of Smith's successor, Brigham Young, the design

of Salt Lake City followed the prophet's ideas in spirit, though not necessarily in specifics. The streets—132 feet wide with 20-foot sidewalks on each side—were said to be broad enough to allow wagons drawn by teams of oxen to turn around. A quarter of a century later, these same streets easily accommodated mass transit. Nevertheless, their breadth was probably based less on practicality than on a sense of the monumental. This was to be the temple city, the religious capital of the restored true faith. Set beneath majestic mountains on a fertile and well-watered plain, the site suited the city's purpose. Together they called for something special.

The dimensions of Salt Lake City's blocks complemented the breadth of its streets. Measuring 660 feet on a side, each block was divided into eight lots of one and one-quarter acres apiece. Strikingly, this religious group that so emphasized community designed its city in a way that maximized privacy. With one dwelling to a lot, a minimum setback of 20 feet, and, according to a Mormon pioneer, "no houses fronting each other on the opposite side of the street," a family could feel detached from its neighbors. More to the point, in a town that began in the middle of nowhere, an acre and a quarter enabled each family to put in a garden and orchard.

In subsequent years church fathers laid out additional tracts in accordance with the original plan. Modifications, nevertheless, set in. The pattern of alternating frontages, which proved impractical in commercial districts, was gradually jettisoned throughout the city; building lots were subdivided; and new neighborhoods, beginning as early as "The Avenues" section in 1855, were platted on a smaller scale.

Still, Salt Lake City retained many of its original characteristics. One writer, in 1855, dismissed it by saying, "Salt Lake City does not fulfill our ideas of a city, but is rather a gigantic village, or a collection of suburbs." Yet another, in 1886, described it as "one of the most beautiful of all modernly built cities." In the latter's view, what

Barely twenty years old when this photograph was made for a local business directory, Topeka presents a prosperous front with its characteristically wide western streets and dense concentration of commercial establishments.

Leonard and Martin. Kansas Avenue, Topeka, Kansas. Albumen silver print, 1876. Kansas State Historical Society, Topeka.

As urban communities in the late 19th century attempted to incorporate mass-transit systems into existing city grids, western cities, with their wide streets, were well equipped to adapt. The streets of Salt Lake City, once valued because they were wide enough for a team of oxen to turn a wagon around, later provided commodious routes for the city's streetcar system.

Unidentified photographer. Near Main and Second, Salt Lake City. Photograph, date unknown. Utah State Historical Society, Salt Lake City.

Mormons, Gentiles, and visitors alike admired about Salt Lake City had less to do with its impressive buildings and more to do with its site and plan. "There is not yet a single narrow street, not a house wherein the sunlight cannot find its way, nor one whereby a stream does not run, and from which perpetual snow is not visible." From early in its history, Salt Lake's cityscape anticipated the low-density metropolis of the twentieth century. Salt Lake was truly a city—the religious, economic, and political center of a vast territory; but it resembled a suburb—its residents had land around their houses and space in which to move about.

The oldest Anglo-American city in the Rocky Mountain region and visually the most striking, Salt Lake was for a time also the most populous. By 1850 it claimed over 6,000 residents and by 1870 more than 12,000. Thereafter the city acquired railroad connections and a flourishing mining industry, but it did not grow as rapidly as it might have. The continued interference of federal officials in religious matters and of church leaders in economic and political matters contributed to social tensions until the 1890s. By that time Salt Lake City had 45,000 residents; but Denver, Salt Lake's rival to the east, had a population of 105,000, justifying its sobriquet as "Queen City of the Plains and the Rockies."

Founded eleven years after Salt Lake City, the Colorado town could not have been more different. Whereas unified action and utopian vision created the former, the latter grew almost entirely out of the forces of competitive capitalism. From the beginning, its history was chaotic. Within months of the discovery of traces of gold at the mouth of Cherry Creek, three companies had staked out townsites—St. Charles, Auraria, and Highland. Two of the three would not survive. Off scouting for buyers, the founders of St. Charles left too few guards to protect their claim. Soon the members of another company seized the land, replatted it, and named it after the Kansas territorial governor, James W. Denver, who presumably held jurisdiction. Seventeen months later, Denver City absorbed Auraria on the other side of Cherry Creek. Only Highland, which lay across the south fork of the Platte River, maintained its independence.

Despite the aggressiveness of its leaders and a mining bonanza in its hills, Denver's first decade proved shaky. Fire devastated the community in 1863; a disastrous flood followed. The Indian-white tensions that culminated in the massacre of Cheyennes and Arapahos at Sand Creek added to the Denverites' sense of instability. But the town's most fundamental problem resulted from the nature of the clientele it served.

Until 1870 Denver existed to outfit miners headed for the goldfields and to fulfill their needs and desires during slack times and weeks off. During much of the preceding decade, an estimated 100,000 to 150,000 people passed through the town each year. Unattached men for the most part, they brought to the community both money and mayhem. The saloons, gaming parlors, and bordellos they frequented created livelihoods for some Denver residents, but these institutions and the streets outside them were often the scenes of violent crimes.

Some individuals questioned whether such a town was fit to live in. When Lavina Porter arrived in 1860 with her husband and little boy, she found herself "utterly disgusted with Denver." In her view, its society consisted of "the roughest class of all states and nations." She noted, "Drunkenness and rioting . . . existed everywhere." The Porters pressed on to California. Meanwhile, William N. Byers elected to stay. A family man, the founder of the *Rocky Mountain News*, and himself the victim of a kidnapping and attempted murder, Byers agitated for the hiring of a police force and rented to the city, at a discount, a building to use as a jail. Those legal means of crime control were in place by 1862. Before then, local vigilance committees executed a swift if sporadic brand of justice. Wrote Byers in 1867, "That capital punishment had been the salvation of our western communities in their earlier periods, the history of the times proves beyond controversy."

Be that as it may, both the crimes and the retribution exacted for them earned Denver a reputation for violence. One widely read account, William Hepworth Dixon's *New America* (1866), described the town in apocalyptic terms: "As you wander about these hot and dirty streets, you seem to be walking in a city of demons. Every fifth house appears to be a bar, a whisky-shop, a lager-beer saloon; every tenth house appears to be either a brothel or a gaming house; very often both in one. In these horrible dens a man's life is of no more worth than a dog's." Dixon added: "The Vigilance Committee, a secret irresponsible board, . . . has to keep things going by means of the revolver and the rope. . . . Sometimes, when the store-keepers open their doors in Main Street, they find a corpse dangling on a branch."

Denverites responded indignantly to Dixon's portrayal. "You must remember," said one, "Denver only dates from '59; and all beginnings are a little rough." Residents feared that the book had "scared men from coming here." They failed to realize that those who tempted fate would be pleasantly surprised by what they encountered.

For in 1870, Denver entered a new phase of development. The completion of the Denver Pacific and Kansas Pacific railroads secured its position as the leading city on the eastern slope and enabled it to diversify its economy. After a decade in which vast throngs of people had passed through the town with no intention of staying, Denver was about to experience a boom. Its 1870 population of 4,759 people (only 10 more than in 1860) would grow more than seven times over by 1880 and triple again by 1890. At that time, it trailed only San Francisco and Omaha to rank as the West's third-largest city.

No wonder, then, that visitors to Denver were beginning to compare it to older, more established places. An Ohio editor in the late 1870s found "a general absence of frontier ruggedness" and "more of the repose of a settled city than . . . anticipated." A woman from England described it as "a busy place, the *entrepôt* and distributing-point for an immense district, with good shops, some factories, fair hotels, and the usual deformities and refinements of civilization." One easterner, writing in 1881, was especially flattering: "Except that the town is . . . not close knit, it might belong in Ohio, or even in New England. There are shops that would do credit to Broadway, and houses that would fit in our oldest towns."

Yet even while likening Denver to eastern towns, observers recognized a crucial difference. Denver was "not close knit" but was spread out and decentralized. With blocks that varied in size and with sections laid out on different axes, Denver lacked the symmetry of Salt Lake City. Nevertheless, when compared with urban places in the East, Denver, Salt Lake, and many other western cities seemed (like all of Montana) high, wide, and handsome.

Just as the region's geography helped to explain why so many westerners lived in cities, it also played a part in determining why those cities took the form they did. On the plains and between the mountains, the land was flat and, except along the Northwest coast, virtually treeless. Laying out streets with widths of eighty feet and more would have been an arduous task in Portland, Maine, or Portland, Oregon. In much of the West, however, the obstacles to such a scale of development were few.

Technology also affected the form that western cities took. Less than a decade after Denver's first tracts were platted, businessmen laid the groundwork for the first of several horse-drawn railways. By the late 1880s, cable cars were running on thirty-eight miles of city streets, and in 1891 the electric trolley debuted locally. Within two decades, the Denver Traction Company was averaging 240,000 riders a day on the two hundred miles of electrified track that crisscrossed the city.

Some western cities acquired a system of mass transportation earlier in their histories than others. Billings, Montana, for example, was barely one year old when its horsecars started running in 1883. Los Angeles, by way of contrast, had been around for ninety-four years before a street railway opened in 1875. Nevertheless, what mattered was not how old a city was when it acquired public transit but rather how dominant was its core and how much crowding had occurred there. In almost every case, western cities availed themselves of the technology of mass transportation before they entered the most important phases of their growth. As a result, distinct business, governmental, and industrial areas, as well as residential areas distinguished by class, emerged at dispersed locations. A low-density form of development became the norm; the suburbanization of the city had begun.

Thus, the cities of the late-nineteenth-century West proved to be "Cities of the Future" in ways that contemporaries might not have recognized. "It is curious to note," said a British visitor of Denver, "how its future vast proportions seem to exist already in the minds of its projectors. Instead of its new streets and buildings being huddled together as with us in our urban beginnings, they are placed here and there at suitable points, with a confidence that the connecting links will soon be established." What was true of Denver in 1885 was true of cities throughout the western United States. Moreover, the spread-out quality that this observer found so "curious" would increasingly affect cities in other regions and other nations.

The Metropolis on the Bay

San Francisco, the preeminent city of the nineteenth-century West, provided an exception to the regional pattern of low-density urban development. Because it grew early and almost instantaneously, because its raison d'être depended on its docks, and because it stood on a peninsula dotted with steep hills, San Francisco crowded a large population into limited confines. But although its physical growth took a form different from that of other western cities, economically San Francisco proved enormously influential. Writing in 1891, James Lord Bryce compared it to "a New York that has got no Boston on one side of it and no shrewd and orderly rural population on the other to keep it in order." San Francisco, in short, dwarfed the rest of the region.

How did the city come to assert such dominance? Location alone could not explain it, for San Francisco's site was a mixed blessing. On the one hand, the city stood at the entrance to a huge bay offering the best deep-water harbor on the west coast as well as access to the interior by way of the Sacramento and San Joaquin rivers. On the other hand, the location lacked timber, fresh water, and level ground and was wracked by unpredictable winds and fog. Surely some other spot along the bay was better suited to large-scale development.

Still, at the historical moment that mattered, San Francisco, with 800 residents, was the biggest settlement in the area. Moreover, it had recently been rechristened. As part of a ploy by its leaders to monopolize trade on the bay, the former Yerba Buena now bore the name of that famous body of water. Thus, in 1848, when the discovery at Sutter's Mill changed the course of western history, the town of San Francisco, some ninety miles distant, stood poised to profit. It was here that oceangoing clipper ships weighed anchor and unloaded goods and passengers bound for the goldfields. This break in the journey, necessitated by the technology of the day, made San Francisco an instant city. In July 1849 it had 5,000 residents, in 1856 approximately 50,000, in 1870 nearly 150,000, and in 1890 close to 300,000. By this time it ranked eighth in population among the cities in the nation.

As San Francisco grew, its economy broadened; but at first, much like any frontier outpost, it resembled a giant fulcrum. From its hinterland in northern California and Nevada, a chain of merchants collected raw materials—in this case the gold and silver gleaned from the region's streams and mountains—and exchanged them for goods unavailable locally. For a time, these goods included just about everything—from food,

A sprawling, decentralized city that grew rapidly after 1870,
when newly completed rail links assured its commercial prosperity, Denver epitomized the low-density, spread-out form of
most 19th-century western cities. San Francisco, in contrast,
presented a more compact model of urban development that
reflected the city's hilly, water-bound topography and its early
commercial orientation toward a port.

H. Wellge. Perspective
Map of the City of Denver,
Colorado. *Lithograph pub-
lished by the American
Publishing Co., 1889. Ge-
ography and Map Divi-
sion, Library of Congress,
Washington, D.C.*

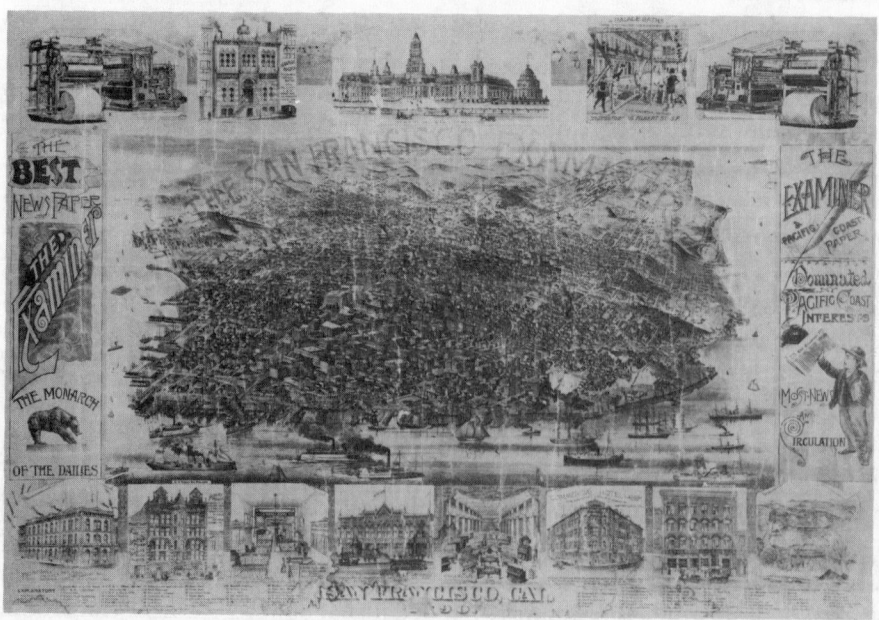

Unidentified artist. San
Francisco, Cal. *Lithograph
published by the* San
Francisco Examiner, *1890.
Arizona Historical
Society, Tucson.*

clothing, and building materials to the equipment needed for mining. Soon, however, some erstwhile miners turned to farming as a surer way to make a living, and by the late 1860s, agricultural products had joined the list of the city's exports.

While agriculture grew in importance in the areas surrounding the city, manufacturing developed within it. By disrupting the flow of finished products from the eastern United States, the Civil War stimulated the demand for local production. By 1870 the city had almost six times more factories and workshops than it had had in 1860 and seven times more people employed in manufacturing. Although it dominated the Far West in both rail and water transport, San Francisco was no longer simply a hinge of commerce. Rather, its workers processed many of the goods—such as foodstuffs, shoes, and clothing—that its merchants distributed. Less than a quarter of a century had passed since the start of the gold rush, yet the number of residents employed in manufacturing exceeded the figure employed in trade and transportation. The economy was on its way to achieving breadth and balance.

San Francisco's rapid rise generated the expectation, especially strong in the 1850s, that those who moved there would prosper. Needless to say, some did. Among those who arrived in the city at mid-century were Mifflin W. Gibbs, an African American from Philadelphia, and August Helbing, a German-Jewish immigrant. While still in their twenties, both established successful business partnerships, Gibbs as a retailer of fine boots and shoes and Helbing as a wholesaler specializing in crockery. But far more common in the ranks of the city's upper and middle classes were native-born whites like Albert Dibblee. The son of a New York merchant and alderman, Dibblee used his commercial and credit connections in the East to become one of the wealthiest commission merchants in the West.

Yet for every male migrant who fulfilled his dreams in San Francisco during the 1850s, many did not. Two year-and-a-half-long booms, two far-longer busts, eight major fires, and a chronic shortage of capital meant that no one could be certain of anything. When S. B. Throckmorton's thriving business failed, he wrote a friend, "I thought . . . that I had at least brought myself to a condition that insured comfort and competency to my family; but I see now I was mistaken." He believed he had made no errors of judgment. "I simply overstaid my tide, and the waters fell and left me aground." In such unstable circumstances, it was not surprising that three-fourths of the men who held jobs in San Francisco in 1852 had left by 1860. That number included the shoe merchant Gibbs, who, denied the right to vote and testify in court, abandoned the city for British Columbia.

In subsequent decades the turnover rate of San Francisco's population began to decline. By 1880 about half the people who had held jobs there ten years earlier remained. With a population more stable than Omaha's but less stable than Boston's, the San Francisco of 1880 suggested a plausible hypothesis. Nineteenth-century Americans moved frequently, but the population of a new town was even more fluid than that of an established center.

While movement in and out of San Francisco in the late 1800s was less intense than at mid-century, movement up and down the social ladder was also less chaotic. As a result of the economic revolution that was occurring internationally, the proportion of higher-status jobs was expanding. In San Francisco specifically, the white-collar share of the work force grew almost 36 percent between 1870 and 1900, whereas at the other end of the scale, the percentage of jobs for unskilled laborers declined 50 percent. This change in the occupational structure, which was as true of Boston as it was of San Francisco, meant that many individuals moved up a notch on the social ladder and that their children rose even higher.

Still, native-born whites had greater opportunities for advancement. The city's many immigrants too often worked at semiskilled or unskilled jobs. This was surprising because San Francisco figured among the nation's most ethnic cities. Between 1850 and 1870, fully half of the population came from abroad. By 1900 that figure had fallen to 36 percent, but another 50 percent consisted of people with one or two immigrant parents.

Within the ranks of the foreign-born, some groups moved ahead more readily than others. The English and the Germans, especially German Jews, rose faster economically than the city's largest immigrant group, the Irish. Held back by a lack of skills and capital, the latter were disproportionately represented on the lower rungs of the social ladder. Nevertheless, Irish immigrants headed the Union Iron Works and the San Francisco Gas Company; others made fortunes in real estate and banking.

Many Irish sought opportunities in politics rather than commerce. In this area they rose early. Led by a second-generation Irish American who learned his politics in New York City, the Irish dominated San Francisco's government in the early 1850s. Inevitably the backlash set in. By mid-decade, David C. Broderick's machine stood accused of "stuffing the ballot-box" and "plunder[ing] the Treasury." Worse, the Irish, as a group, were characterized as "ignorant," "debased," and "dangerous." When a beneficiary of the machine killed an editor who opposed it, the city's elite made new use of a familiar form of frontier justice.

Five years earlier, San Francisco's first Vigilance Committee had hanged four men, whipped another, and banished fourteen. Like similar organizations in Denver, Colorado, and Virginia City, Montana, the committee of 1851 aimed to check a wave of violent crime. The Vigilance Committee of 1856, however, was largely political in nature. Its eight thousand members, drawn almost entirely from the upper and middle classes, focused on corruption more than violence. After executing four men, deporting twenty-five, and causing many others to flee for their lives, the ad hoc committee established an ongoing body that assured elite rule in San Francisco for a decade.

Although the Vigilance Committee targeted the Irish out of proportion to their numbers in the population, they did not disappear from local politics. San Francisco had an Irish-born mayor from 1867 to 1869, a second-generation Irish-American "boss" from 1882 to 1892, and a reforming mayor of wealthy Irish stock from 1897 to 1901. These men—Frank McCoppin, Christopher Buckley, and James D. Phelan—represented a small part of the range of Irish political activity in the city. Additionally the Irish helped to lead San Francisco's labor movement.

The members of another large immigrant group, the Chinese, exercised leadership only in the confines of their district. Inside Chinatown the wealthy merchants of the Chinese Consolidated Benevolent Association, also known as the Six Companies, acted as a quasi-government. Outside this most heavily populated section of the city, the Chinese wandered at their peril.

Chinese immigrants met with hostility in San Francisco almost as soon as they began to arrive in large numbers during the gold rush. The artist of this 1853 book illustration portrayed Chinese cultural traditions and the poor conditions of San Francisco's streets as both deserving of ridicule and derision.

Alonzo Delano (1806–74). San Francisco Scene. *Print, 1853.* From Delano, Pen Knife Sketches; or, Chips of the Old Block *(1853). Rare Book and Manuscript Division, The New York Public Library, Astor, Lenox and Tilden Foundations, New York, New York.*

The Chinese were segregated not only residentially but also occupationally. Elsewhere in the nation, women dominated many of the jobs held by this 90-percent-male group. In 1900 the Chinese (then only 4 percent of the city's population) composed 68 percent of its cigar makers, 52 percent of its laundry workers, 31 percent of its garment and textile workers, and 21 percent of its domestic servants and janitorial workers. Earlier many Chinese had fished, but Italians increasingly dominated this occupation. The Chinese had also peddled foods—usually from baskets carried on poles across their shoulders. Yet this method of hawking products became a misdemeanor in the early 1870s, and before long the city government had found other ways to harass the Chinese population.

The government passed anti-Chinese measures because, unlike European immigrants, Asians were not eligible for naturalization and because the nationality groups that could vote considered the Chinese the source of their troubles. Working-class whites accused them of driving down wages and taking away jobs from other workers. In 1877, a year of high unemployment and numerous strikes, the Irish-born head of the Workingmen's Party, Denis Kearney, tied hatred of the Chinese to hatred of the elite that employed them. Ending his speeches—"The Chinese must go!"—Kearney provoked outbursts of violence by blue-collar whites and more vigilantism from the propertied classes. Although many of its protests were forcibly quelled, the Workingmen's Party enjoyed some short-term successes. As for the Chinese, they began a long-term migration back across the Pacific.

During such times of crisis, the city's compact physical layout may have intensified its social divisions. The protesters of 1877 converged on the sandlots near city hall from their boardinghouses south of Market Street and their rowhouses in the Mission District. After hearing the likes of Kearney speak, they could wander up Nob Hill to agitate outside the mansions of San Francisco's leading industrialists or head over to Chinatown to threaten its residents with arson and violence. Though San Francisco was no longer "the walking city" it had been at mid-century, with rich and poor occupying the same district, it was still a place where a range of class-segregated districts lay within short distances of one another.

Why did San Francisco develop on such a compact pattern? The city did not lack the land: in 1856 it laid claim to the forty-seven square miles that still define its boundaries. And it did not turn its back on mass transit; on the contrary, few other cities in the American West made use of such a wide range of technologies. Horsecars, cable cars, trolleys, commuter trains, and ferries—all operated within or to and from late-nineteenth-century San Francisco. Nevertheless, legal complications resulting from the takeover of Mexican territory delayed the development of parts of the city for a couple of decades. And when that hurdle was cleared, the unusual costs of building mass transit in a hilly terrain—for example, the cost of tunnel construction—further postponed the opening of new districts. Only in 1912, when the city agreed to underwrite the expenses, did streetcar lines start to extend into the southern and westernmost parts of the city.

While the population spread slowly into the outlying districts of San Francisco proper, intensive development occurred along the bay. Those hills that could be leveled were. The resulting fill was then dumped in the water to create more of the flat land that merchants and industrialists desperately needed. As for the hills that could not be leveled, they underwent a transformation in 1873. With the invention of the cable car, the formerly spurned land atop Nob, Russian, and Telegraph hills became highly desirable for residential purposes. The result of this development of inlying locations was surprising: on average, San Franciscans lived closer to their workplaces in the 1870s than they had in the 1850s.

As San Francisco's population continued to grow, the crowding and congestion of its core worsened. By the turn of the century, many of its leading citizens believed that its streets and neighborhoods needed changes. They commissioned Daniel H. Burnham, the best-known American city planner of the day, to draw up a comprehensive urban design. Burnham reported in September 1905. Seven months later a major earthquake and three days of fire destroyed the densely populated core of the city. The opportunity existed to build San Francisco anew.

Yet instead of implementing Burnham's plan, the people of San Francisco reconstructed the city much as it had stood before. Citing the need to act as quickly as possible and at minimal cost, they refused to follow through with the planner's ideas for broader streets and more numerous parks. Yet more than practicality guided their efforts, which were based also on their own and others' affection for the city as it had been. A week after its destruction, Henry Adams, the writer, described San Francisco as "the most interesting city west of the Mississippi" and "more styl[ish] than any town in the east." He added, "I was fond of it and my generation made it."

In rebuilding the San Francisco they remembered, residents honored a city in which heterogeneous groups lived close together. Increasingly, the pattern of urban living that San Francisco represented would become anomalous in the West and in the nation.

The Rise of Los Angeles

During the second decade of the twentieth century, Los Angeles shot ahead of San Francisco to become the West's leading city. Its growth took many observers by surprise.

In their view, San Francisco looked the part of a major city; Los Angeles did not. Indeed, the small downtown, combined with the retail, industrial, and residential sprawl of Los Angeles, drew barbs. "Forty suburbs in search of a city" was one line used to describe it. "There is no there there" (initially coined by the poet Gertrude Stein to describe northern California's Oakland) was another.

Even those whose inquiries were more serious found Los Angeles a puzzle. In 1932 the writer Morris Markey concluded that the types of enterprise touted by the chamber of commerce—such as the branch factories of major industries and the high levels of fruit production—were not "the cause of a city." Rather, they were "the effect rising from an inexplicable accumulation of people." He found it "odd" that "here, alone of all the cities in America, there was no plausible answer to the question, 'Why did a town spring up here and why has it grown so big?'"

Los Angeles baffled men like Markey because it was the prototype of a new kind of city. Recent advances in technology had altered the human relationship to nature. No longer was it necessary for a city to have a natural harbor or its own supply of water. Now a settlement built on arid land in a less than ideal commercial location could become a verdant paradise and the hub of the Pacific. The sunshine, the mountains, and the ocean were what mattered; the rest could be engineered.

Also essential to the rise of Los Angeles was the existence of a class of people more interested in improving their quality of life than in maximizing their financial resources. In this regard the migration to Los Angeles differed from the various rushes for gold. Rather than consisting primarily of single young men eager to make a fortune, the area's residents included retirees and established families who already possessed a comfortable income. Coming largely from the Midwest, these people wished to duplicate, in a more beautiful place and a more benign climate, the small-town atmosphere that they knew.

None of this could have been foreseen in the first sixty-six years of the city's existence. From the time of its founding by the Spanish imperial government in 1781 until the surrender of its Mexican leaders to American forces in 1847, El Pueblo de Nuestra Señora la Reina de los Angeles existed to raise crops and livestock for the forts and missions of the region. Despite the breezes that blew in from the ocean some twenty miles distant, the land was essentially a desert. Only by tapping the waters of the river that flowed from the foothills onto a large plain could the settlers grow something more promising than sagebrush. Still, the pueblo became the center for a thriving cattle trade. On the brink of the American takeover, the population of Los Angeles numbered close to 1,500.

The arrival of the Anglo Americans changed life for the Californios. In 1850, Hispanics composed more than 75 percent of the city's population. Their numbers included rancheros, professionals, merchants, artisans, and skilled and unskilled laborers. By 1880, Hispanics made up less than 20 percent of the city's 11,200 residents. With the rancheros ruined in the 1860s by high property taxes, low cattle prices, and years of drought, Hispanics fell out of the ranks of the major landowners. Still, they maintained a toehold on the professional classes and increased their numbers in skilled laboring positions. Although four-fifths of those employed in 1880 worked as laborers, the same had been true in 1840. What was discouraging was that Mexican Americans were not advancing as quickly as changes in the region's economy might have allowed.

More distressing were the group's encounters with American justice. The state legislature not only restricted such traditional Hispanic entertainments as cockfights, bullfights, and horse races but also subjected unemployed Mexican Americans to fines and imprisonment as vagrants. Even when the laws were not discriminatory, their prosecution could be. Thus, an Anglo found guilty in the 1870s of murdering a Hispanic served only seventy days of a one-year sentence, whereas a Mexican American convicted of disorderly conduct received a ninety-day term. Hispanics (or for that matter Indians) accused of murdering Anglos could count on little mercy from the court. Most of the forty executions held between 1854 and 1870 involved such circumstances, as did the thirty-seven lynchings.

Finding themselves the victims of pervasive prejudice, many Hispanics decided to leave Los Angeles. Some went to Mexico; others stayed in the American Southwest. Meanwhile, new migrants from Mexico and from its former territory kept the Spanish-speaking population of Los Angeles at a few thousand in the late nineteenth century. Though small in numbers and fluid in composition, this segment of the city's population increasingly developed a sense of shared identity. Abetted by several Spanish-language newspapers (none of which had existed before the Anglo-American takeover) as well as by clubs and mutual-aid societies, the Hispanics celebrated their achievements and criticized their persecutors. Distinguishing themselves from the "Anglo-Sajones" or "norte-americanos," they took pride in their membership in "La Raza." As the editor of *El Democrata* noted, theirs was "a glorious race," "embodying the hopes of a race" and "possess[ing] all the secrets of all the mysteries."

As the city's population grew from 102,000 in 1900 to 1,238,000 in 1930, large numbers of blacks and Asians joined the whites and increasing numbers of Hispanics to complicate the racial makeup of the city. In 1930, when racial minorities composed less than 8 percent of the population in Chicago and less than 5 percent in New York, they accounted for more than 14 percent of the population in Los Angeles. At the same time, however, the number of foreign-born whites in the city was comparatively small. Thus, as the historian Robert Fogelson has argued, Los Angeles differed demographically from most eastern and midwestern cities. Whereas native-born Americans and European immigrants divided the latter, in Los Angeles a heavy majority of native-born whites faced a sizable minority of people of color.

The native-born population in the city was remarkable as well. Relatively few Angelenos had begun their lives in California. More came from the Midwest than the Far West; about as many migrated from the South as from the Northeast. These people had made a deliberate decision to move to Los Angeles. Having done so, they considered the city "the choicest part of the earth," and they were resolved, in the words of an early observer, that no one would "have it in his power to point out wherein" their city was wanting. From such basic emotions stemmed the legendary boosterism of the people of Los Angeles.

The city's first generation of promoters made transportation their chief concern. By 1869 the city had a rail link to the coast at Wilmington–San Pedro. In 1876 it acquired ties to northern California and the nation through the Southern Pacific Railroad, and in 1886 the completion of the Santa Fe gave Los Angeles a second cross-country

The image of Los Angeles as a tropical paradise, an image ardently prized and promoted by early civic boosters, continues to influence downtown urban development in the nation's second-largest city.

Douglas Muir (b. 1940). Landscaping at the Sheraton Grande Hotel, Los Angeles, California. *Dye coupler print, 1983. Courtesy of the photographer.*

connection. Only a short time earlier, most forecasters had predicted that San Diego's deep-water harbor would make that city the natural hub of the region. They had not counted on the determination of the citizens of Los Angeles, who taxed themselves to subsidize the railroads, or on the greed of rail officials, who deemed San Diego the greater threat to the value of their San Francisco holdings.

Ironically, then, the inadequacies of the harbor at San Pedro helped Los Angeles secure the Southern Pacific. Yet its citizens did not want their city to remain a tributary of San Francisco. Agreed that the smooth contours of its coastline should not determine the city's destiny, they decided to build an artificial harbor. The project almost collapsed when powerful interests favored Santa Monica as the site, yet the scheme's promoters persevered. In 1896 Congress set aside the first of several multimillion-dollar appropriations for the construction of a major harbor at Wilmington–San Pedro. By 1912 a rock-filled breakwater jutted two miles seaward. By 1932 it extended more than four miles into the ocean and by 1980 more than eight. Meanwhile, the city and private interests devoted comparable amounts of money to dockside improvements. By the mid-1920s, the harbor at Los Angeles was handling more tons of freight than the San Francisco harbor. Despite unpromising beginnings, Los Angeles now boasted the leading port on the west coast of the Americas.

Los Angeles acquired not only an artificial harbor but also an artificial landscape. Neither the royal palm trees that became a symbol of the city nor the citrus groves that bespoke its abundance were native to the region. These, along with the flowers whose January blossoms inspired Pasadena's rose parade, required something the area was short of—water. At first, local residents relied on the Los Angeles River as well as underground aquifers. Then they turned to distant sources. In 1907 Angelenos voted to bring in water from the Owens Valley, 233 miles away. In 1930 they looked to the waters of Mono Lake, another 80 miles to the northeast. By the time World War II broke out, they were tapping the Colorado River, about 250 miles to the east. In the 1970s they began acquiring water from the Feather River near Sacramento, and by the 1990s they had turned their sights to Utah. The sustenance of the city's artificial landscape required the ruin of farming districts elsewhere.

As destructive as these aggressive water policies were to some distant communities, they proved so attractive to neighbors of Los Angeles that many voted to join the city. Between 1915 and 1930, Los Angeles (already swollen by its annexation of Wilmington, San Pedro, and the narrow Shoestring District that connected the harbor to downtown) expanded more than four times over, from 108 to 440 square miles. In terms of area, it was the largest city in the United States in 1930; in terms of population, it was the fifth largest, behind New York, Chicago, Philadelphia, and Detroit.

Yet big as it was, Los Angeles still had a small-town atmosphere. It had this ambiance because that was what the people who were moving there wanted and because the technology existed to make their dream come true. After all, the first great migration to Los Angeles occurred in the late 1880s just as a new form of mass transit was becoming available. In 1887, the very year Julian Sprague built an electric streetcar system for Richmond, Virginia, one was running in Los Angeles. Within three decades, the southern California metropolis had the most extensive system in the world—with nearly four hundred miles of light track in operation in the city and more than eleven hundred miles of track in the area surrounding it.

Here, as in cities across the United States, businessmen financed the building of streetcar lines with the profits they made subdividing adjacent land. But the developers of greater Los Angeles broke from eastern models in one important aspect. Instead of laying out building lots all along the route so that only those at the end of the line enjoyed the beauties of nature, Henry Huntington and others pushed their tracks into the empty countryside—skirting hills, crossing fields, and placing many of their subdivisions in attractive natural settings.

The goal of developers and residents alike was to build a city of single-family, detached houses. They wanted to create what the historian Robert Fishman has called "a suburban metropolis." The squat, spread-out character of Los Angeles was therefore no accident but was the product of a conscious preference on the part of its inhabitants. In 1907 one of them boasted, "Here the tendency is to open and not crowded quarters. . . . Here even the pauper lives in surroundings fit for a king."

Not long after the electric streetcar made possible the spatial expansion of the city, yet another innovation in transportation intensified the process. Angelenos may have enjoyed one of the best light-rail systems in the world, yet they preferred the freedom of movement provided by the automobile. More than the residents of other U.S. cities, they could afford to indulge their preference. There were eight residents per auto in Los Angeles in 1915, four per auto in 1920, two in 1925, and one and one-half in 1930.

If the Los Angeles of the streetcar era seemed decentralized and spread out, it was a model of controlled growth compared with what followed. The automobile opened up for development the land that lay between the streetcars' radial routes. Fields that had formerly produced fruits, grains, or vegetables turned into factories, stores, or block after

By 1888, more than 44 miles of cable and electric railways in Los Angeles facilitated the city's sprawl outward from a small downtown. Despite the concurrent growth of the city and a rapidly expanding mass-transit system, Los Angeles would soon become a metropolis devoted to the automobile.

Unidentified photographer. Second Street Cable Railway, Looking West. Photograph, 1888. Department of Special Collections, University Research Library, University of California, Los Angeles.

block of low-density housing. Moreover, as long as there were streetcars, the city had a hub, a center, where the radial lines converged. Los Angeles, without streetcars, was more free-form and sprawling.

The new shape of the metropolis affected the everyday lives of its inhabitants. As an article in *Westways* magazine in 1937 made clear, Angelenos did not use their automobiles for commuting in the traditional sense of trips to and from the downtown business district. Instead, individual family members set out in a variety of directions, throughout greater Los Angeles, to do a variety of things—to work, learn, shop, and play. By the end of the day, they could easily have covered hundreds of miles of roadway as they crossed each other's paths and those of "countless of thousands of [other people] bent on similar missions." Under such circumstances, the true center of the city was "not in some downtown business district but," to quote Fishman, "in each residential unit." "Each family was its own 'core' in a decentralized city."

Before World War II and the cold war turned Los Angeles into a center for aerospace production and research, at a time when the city's dream makers created the weekend's movies but not the weeknight's television shows, back when the oil rigs of greater Los Angeles produced so much crude it was sold overseas, the city provided a preview of urban living in the future. In the Los Angeles of the 1930s and soon in cities across the United States, the automobile was the vehicle to the kind of life-style people wanted. By allowing individuals to travel on their own schedules and by their own routes, either alone or in company of their own choosing, the automobile provided maximum access to an entire metropolis's opportunities for employment and leisure and minimum exposure to its diverse population groups.

Experimental Cityscapes

Before 1940, western cities were important to the people living in the West. After 1940 they achieved national stature. That stature could be measured by statistics of population

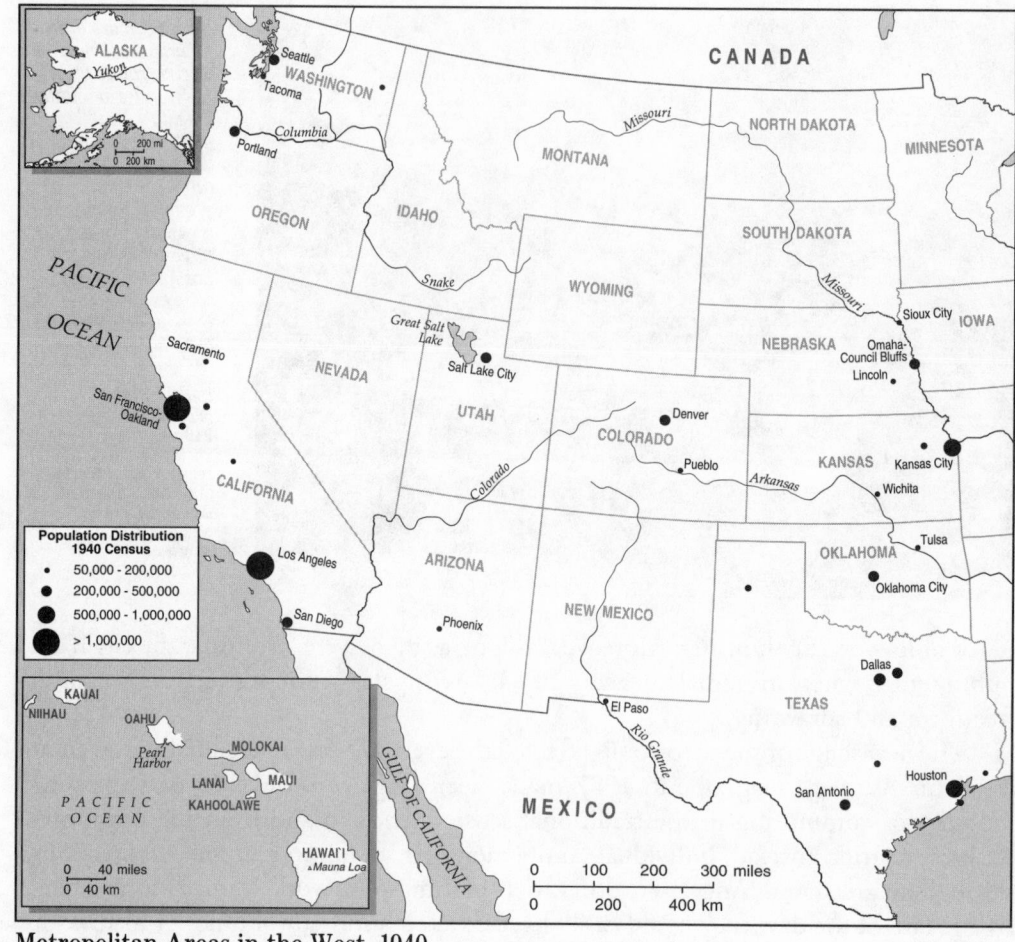

Although the Census Bureau's definition of a metropolitan area remained essentially the same (a core city of at least 50,000 inhabitants plus its contiguous suburbs), the number of metropolitan areas in the West nearly tripled between 1940 and 1990.

Metropolitan Areas in the West, 1940

growth and economic expansion. But it was also indicated by the frequency with which the rest of the nation took up western innovations in urban living and design. Thus the rise of the urban West did not spring entirely from decisions made in congressional cloakrooms or New York City boardrooms. Rather, it resulted from westerners' own success in creating built environments that appealed to their fellow Americans.

In 1900 only San Francisco, of all the cities in the West, ranked among the nation's top ten; in 1940 only Los Angeles could claim that distinction. By 1960 two of the nation's most populous cities stood west of the states that adjoined the Mississippi. By 1990 Los Angeles, Houston, San Diego, Dallas, Phoenix, and San Antonio all ranked among the nation's ten largest cities; of the nation's fifty largest cities, the West accounted for twenty-three.

Western cities grew in population partly because they grew in size. Between 1950 and 1990, San Antonio added 264 square miles to its municipal boundaries, Houston 380, Phoenix 402, and Oklahoma City 557. These cities annexed peripheral areas to prevent the unwieldy crosshatch of governments that typified so many older metropolises. Because they were expanding into newly developed areas whose residents had much

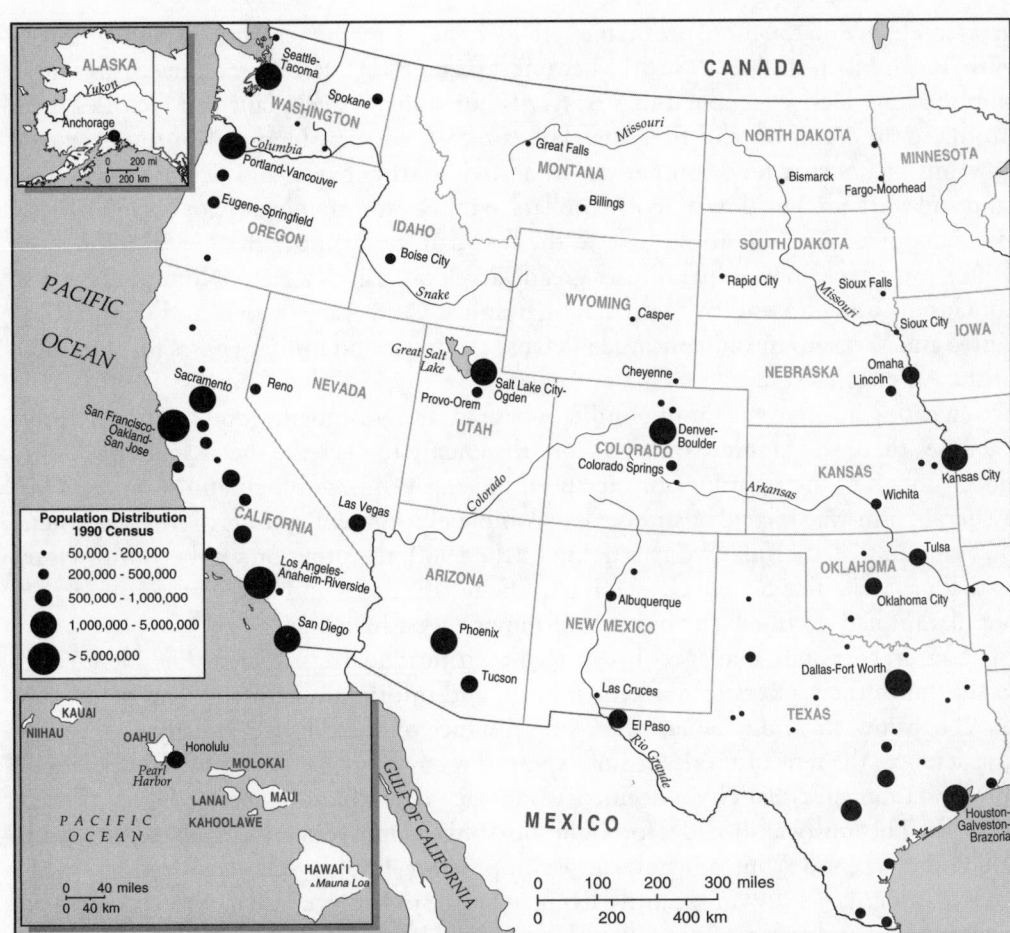

Metropolitan Areas in the West, 1990

in common with those of the city proper, annexation worked in most western cities. The notable exception was San Francisco, which had not added to its territory since the 1850s.

But if San Francisco resembled Boston, Pittsburgh, and St. Louis in the size of its municipal boundaries and in the fact that, for much of the post–World War II era, it was losing population from within those boundaries, the metropolitan area that San Francisco belonged to boomed along with much of the West. Indeed, more significant than the presence of western cities among the nation's top ten was the ranking of the West's metropolitan areas. In 1990 greater Los Angeles, San Francisco–Oakland–San Jose, Dallas–Fort Worth, and greater Houston ranked second, fourth, ninth, and tenth in the nation in population. Economically, as measured by the number of corporate headquarters and the assets of their commercial banks, these four metropolitan areas figured in the nation's top seven.

For each of these metropolitan areas, as for other urban areas in the West, World War II marked a decisive turning point. Federal dollars streamed into the West, changing economies formerly dependent on the light processing of raw materials to greater reliance on the more profitable activity of heavy manufacturing. Long associated with the lumber business, Seattle became a center for aircraft manufacturing and shipbuilding. Denver retained its stockyards but added a steel plant and factories that produced ammunition and firearms. The cotton fields that bloomed in the irrigated environs of Phoenix now competed with airfields, army bases, and defense plants for land and workers. The flow of federal dollars to the West certainly did not begin in 1940 (Phoenix owed its agricultural base to the first dam built under the Newlands Act of 1902), but government expenditures greatly accelerated at that time. Nor did the war's conclusion bring an end to the federal handouts. Cold war tensions and conflicts in Korea and Vietnam meant continued defense contracts and military bases for the cities of the American West.

Locating a defense plant or a military base in the West made good logistical sense. Facilities there were remote enough from the enemy to decrease the risk of attack but close enough to the fighting front to speed the engagement of men and supplies. The owners of non-war-related businesses had completely different matters to consider when they contemplated a move westward, but by the 1960s the situation was becoming clear to them as well. The benefits of staying in the northeastern and midwestern centers of population had declined; the benefits of moving west had risen.

Earlier, corporate managers had placed their headquarters in cities like New York to maximize their access to markets, money, and information. In the days before air travel became safe and reliable, when long-distance phone calls were costly and full of interference, the tens of thousands of experts directly available to businesses operating in Manhattan gave that city a decided advantage. This situation changed after World War II. The postwar decades brought not only improvements in air service and telephone reception but a whole new computer technology that ushered in "The Information Age." Now an executive living in Seattle or Dallas could have access to stock market prices and commodities quotations as quickly as anyone anywhere. Indeed, the non-northeasterner was likely to encounter fewer frustrations like jammed circuits, power outages, and transportation delays.

The question of relocation became pressing to different companies at different times. In the case of Shell Oil, the issue came to the fore in the latter half of the 1960s, when the company's mid-Manhattan offices could no longer accommodate its growing staff. Instead of building anew near Rockefeller Center, where construction costs were astronomical, or in suburban Connecticut, which lacked a large and diversified work force, Shell's board of directors moved its operating headquarters over sixteen hundred miles to Houston, Texas. The move, which involved twenty-two hundred jobs, cost the company twenty-five million dollars. Now ensconced in the state's tallest building, company executives considered the price tag a bargain. In Houston their paychecks went further, since housing and tax costs were lower; meanwhile, their staffs worked longer—a full forty-hour week instead of thirty-five. Additionally, all levels of employees found the journey to work much less of a hassle. Certainly the dollars and cents of the matter were all to Houston's advantage.

Nevertheless, such decisions were not made solely on the basis of economics. Other factors—amenities, they were called—helped to lure Shell Oil to Houston: a fine symphony and opera, respected universities, world-renowned medical facilities, and fashionable shops and stores. Among the latter was the Galleria, on the southwest side of Houston. It included a multistoried, glass-roofed shopping arcade, anchored by a Neiman-Marcus department store and boasting—of all things for the steamy flatlands of Texas—an ice-skating rink in the middle.

The rink represented an exaggerated version of the climate control that was ubiquitous in Houston. Formerly, the city's hot and humid weather had led the British Foreign Service to dub it a hardship post. By 1965, however, Houstonians enjoyed air conditioning not only in their houses, cars, plants, offices, theaters, and shopping malls but also at their sports stadium. "Big-as-all-indoors," the Harris County Sports Dome enabled fans to watch major-league baseball and football in air-cooled comfort. The Astrodome may have helped local residents survive the summer and early fall, but during the other months of the year, Houston, Dallas, Phoenix, and a host of other southwestern cities offered a climate preferable to that of the Northeast or Midwest. Such a consideration took on added value in the latter half of the twentieth century as people lived longer lives and worked a shorter proportion of them.

It was just such an interest in the quality of life that had sparked the growth of Los Angeles in the late 1800s. For decades, citizens of Los Angeles had held on to their vision of creating a new kind of metropolis. "It must not be a second congested London or New York," said John Anson Ford, a Los Angeles County supervisor in 1961, ". . . but a population center with many new characteristics adjusted to the outdoor life of the region, and to the era of greater leisure, greater mobility, and a wider distribution of the skills and culture of modern society." This ideal was seconded by civic leaders elsewhere in the West who accepted the automobile as the primary mode of urban transport and who wanted their cities to "spread widely rather than reach high."

In the very year that Supervisor Ford presented his formula for the future, an associate editor of *Architectural Forum* offered an opposing view. In *The Death and Life of Great American Cities*, Jane Jacobs argued that crowding was part of the essence of cities. The presence of large numbers of people at all times of the day and night made cities economically and intellectually vibrant. It also helped to make them safe. Assaults, rapes, and other major crimes occurred at higher rates, she said, in decentralized cities like Los Angeles than in congested ones like Chicago and New York. Anticipating the looting, arson, and sniper fire that would convulse the Watts district of Los Angeles in 1965, and much of the city in 1992, she called attention to the extent of its racial and economic segregation. In her view the suburbanization of the metropolis meant the addition of yet another barrier to understanding among diverse social groups—namely, physical distance.

In arguing that low-density districts were inherently dangerous, Jacobs relied on limited evidence. True, Los Angeles, along with Dallas and Houston, regularly posted a murder rate that exceeded the big-city average. But a different pattern prevailed in Phoenix, San Antonio, and San Diego. Here the rate of violent offenses (the number of murders, rapes, assaults, and robberies known to the police per one hundred thousand residents) was low; the stunning incidence of crimes against property (such as burglary, larceny, and motor-vehicle theft) drove up the overall crime rate. Moreover, the West boasted at least one large city with an enviable record in both categories. In 1990, of the seventy-four most populous cities in the United States, eleventh-ranked San Jose had the lowest total crime index. Indeed, this sprawling, suburbanized city had less than one-half the rate of property crime and one-third the incidence of violence of its more compact neighbor, San Francisco.

Although Jacobs's book lacked statistical grounding, it certainly had an impact, especially on the field of urban planning. Calling on planners to get people out of their cars and onto the sidewalks, she deserved part of the credit for the revitalization of a number of downtown areas from the 1960s on. Such projects as Pioneer Square in Seattle and Larimer Square in Denver incorporated Jacobs's notion that mixed-use districts were beneficial. Attracting different people for different reasons, such districts allowed cities to be cities. Here, in theory at least, the interactions among a multiplicity of individuals generated an atmosphere that was at once exciting and safe.

Yet influential as Jacobs's ideas proved, Supervisor Ford more nearly captured the trend of the times in his prescription that Los Angeles "must not be a second congested London or New York." By the mid-twentieth century, most Americans equated the good life with owning a single-family home and an automobile. So deeply was this ideal ingrained in the American psyche that the federal government subsidized the sub-urbanization of the nation. By allowing tax deductions for mortgage interest but not for rent, by providing long-term, low-interest house loans, and by financing the construc-tion of an elaborate system of high-speed, limited-access roadways, the federal govern-ment encouraged city dwellers to move miles away from the urban core. When factories, stores, and offices followed, it was clear that other metropolitan areas were coming to resemble greater Los Angeles.

These sprawling metropolises existed not only in the West but also in the East. Analyzing data from more than fifty metropolitan areas in the East and Southwest, Carl Abbott found, in 1990, that the two groups of cities were "not markedly different." The latter *looked* distinctive because their streets were longer and broader and their architecture, with some exceptions, clung to the ground; but in terms of where their residents worked, shopped, and lived, the two had much in common. Both were experiencing the economic and demographic decline of their central business districts (some successful renewal projects notwithstanding) and the rise of peripheral areas in so-called edge cities.

But if the spread-out, multicentered metropolis had become a national phenom-enon, it was nonetheless true that the West had helped to pioneer some of the land uses characteristic of the metropolis. During the immediate postwar decades, as the historian John Findlay has shown, the West developed a new type of workplace, living space, and playground. Built at the outer limits of existing metropolitan areas, these new cultural landscapes stimulated growth in their environs. They also set precedents that would be built upon across the nation and around the world.

Featured in an exhibit at the Brussels World's Fair in 1958 and visited by French President Charles De Gaulle in 1960, the Stanford Industrial Park represented the work environment of the future. Stanford University could have used the several-hundred-acre tract for housing for San Francisco–bound commuters. Instead, it laid out a vast, landscaped expanse, making parcels available to businesses in such fields as computers, aerospace, microwave technology, and pharmaceuticals. With low-slung buildings, a youthful work force, and an informal atmosphere, the Stanford Industrial Park had the look and feel of a college campus. In reality, it was the business center for Santa Clara County, whose agricultural economy was undergoing a rapid transformation. By 1980 the county, better known as Silicon Valley, ranked ninth in the nation for the value of its industrial products. By that time it was hard to remember that the term *industrial park* would once have been thought an oxymoron. By turning a contradiction into a reality, Stanford University created one of the characteristic landscapes of the new American metropolis.

Like *industrial park*, the phrase *active retirement* paired words once viewed as opposites. Adopted by the Del E. Webb Corporation as a slogan for its latest development project, the idea appealed to the emerging market of older Americans who enjoyed good health, a steady income, and no job. In Sun City, Arizona, such people would find what its advertisers termed "a complete community." Indeed, Sun City did have shopping malls, golf courses, recreation centers, and a five-story hospital, but it had no tax-consuming schools (since there were no children) and hardly any minorities. In view of what this walled community had as well as what it lacked, its proximity to Phoenix was important. With the downtown district a mere twelve miles away (and looming ever closer), citizens of Sun City enjoyed access to the amenities of a large city—stores, restaurants, theaters, and museums—without having to confront its realities. In Sun City, retirees discovered a community complete enough that forays to Phoenix could be a matter of choice rather than necessity.

Eventually Sun City drew forty-five thousand residents to its nine thousand acres, and the Stanford Industrial Park employed twenty-six thousand workers on seven hundred acres. By way of contrast, another of the West's new cultural landscapes consisted of a mere seventy acres exclusive of parking, yet it attracted as many as ten million people a year. Without a doubt, Disneyland was the West's single most important contribution to the built environment in the postwar era.

Walt Disney designed Disneyland with certain regional assumptions in mind. Whereas he wanted the amusement park to "be a place for California to be at home, to bring its guests, [and] to demonstrate its faith in the future," he rejected the model of existing parks and especially of Brooklyn's Coney Island. "Dirty grounds," "tawdry rides," "rude patrons," and "hostile employees" were not what he wanted for his brainchild.

In addition, Disney grasped an essential truth. If handled correctly, this venture in outdoor recreation would help to market his films and television shows and vice versa. For this reason Disney hired Hollywood scriptwriters to plan his park; subordinate to them were the engineers, architects, and city planners. Thus emerged in 1955 the world's first theme park. None of the attractions stood on their own. They were all part of an integrated layout that played on the guests' familiarity with Disney characters and stories. Billed as family entertainment, it appealed as much to adults as to children.

Indeed, attendance exceeded all expectations, especially in the park's first fifteen years. To entertain such swarms and keep them coming, Walt Disney Corporation

With Disneyland and the Las Vegas Strip, developers created distinctive new landscapes for the postwar West that capitalized on Americans' increased mobility and expanded leisure time. These new urban sites would become as important to western tourism as the national parks.

Unidentified photographer. Walt Disney Introducing Plans for Disneyland. *Gelatin silver print, 1954. © The Walt Disney Company. The Disney Publishing Group, Burbank, California.*

Unidentified photographer. Floating Craps Game, Sands Hotel. *Gelatin silver print, ca. 1950s. Las Vegas News Bureau Archives, Las Vegas, Nevada.*

doubled the number of attractions, building both above- and underground. The company enlarged the size of the work force five times over and coached employees in how they should look, talk, and act. It also varied the cost structure of attendance. Instead of charging for every ride in addition to general admission, it gradually moved to a single-fee passport. Such permutations helped give the park a positive billing from reviewers. The science fiction writer Ray Bradbury was especially enthusiastic. In his view, Disneyland proved "that the first function of architecture is to make men over, make them wish to go on living, feed them fresh oxygen, grow them tall, delight their eyes, make them kind. . . . Disneyland liberates men to their better selves." A less prominent observer put the matter more succinctly, "[Disneyland]'s as different from the Coney Island type of park as Walt could make it."

All three of these cultural landscapes—the Stanford Industrial Park, Sun City, and Disneyland—showed, according to Findlay, how a carefully planned fragment of the metropolis could lend a sense of order to the postwar sprawl. Yet few development projects were as well thought out as these. A more common feature of the emerging cityscape was the hodgepodge of signs, styles, and services typified by the commercial strip. Here too, the West offered a conspicuous model—the four-mile stretch of Las Vegas Boulevard known simply as the Strip.

The Strip represented the most spectacular part of a remarkable city. Fueled by federal funding, Las Vegas grew from a town of 5,165 in 1930 to a metropolis of 741,000 in 1990. The nation's taxpayers may have subsidized its water, power, highways, airport, and defense jobs, but private investors—at times with ties to the underworld—developed the resorts along the Strip. Beginning in the 1940s with El Rancho, the Last Frontier, the Flamingo, and the Thunderbird, the Strip turned Las Vegas into a major tourist attraction. By the time the Mirage and the Excalibur opened in 1989 and 1990, Las Vegas was welcoming 1.5 million convention-goers a year. In this regard it trailed only New York City, Chicago, Dallas, and Atlanta.

A success with the general public, the Strip was initially panned by critics who presumed to know what a city ought to look like. Nevertheless, in 1972, a trio of professors from the Yale School of Art and Architecture wrote a book extolling it. In *Learning from Las Vegas*, Robert Venturi, Denise Scott Brown, and Steven Izenour contrasted "the deadness . . . of present-day modern architecture" to "the vitality [of the Strip]." In their opinion the former showed the result of "too great a preoccupation with tastefulness and total design." The latter, boasting such resorts as Caesar's Palace and the Sahara, proved, on the other hand, that "people . . . have fun with architecture that reminds them of something else." Mixing allusions to the past and the present, the sacred and the profane, the Strip combined aspects of the appeal of Disneyland, the thrill of gambling, and the glitz of Coney Island. With the neon of its signs set high above the roadway (the sign for the Dunes measured twenty-two stories), the Strip represented "a new landscape of big spaces [and] high speeds." Meant to be traveled by automobile, it offered an architecture for the deconcentrated metropolis.

As much as the West pioneered forms of the late-twentieth-century cultural landscape, it did not monopolize them. Industrial parks, retirement communities, theme parks, and commercial strips soon emerged elsewhere. At times the later examples (such as Florida's Walt Disney World) clearly eclipsed the earlier models. Thus, to some extent, the metropolises of the American East could come to resemble those of the West and even to improve on them.

But in another sense the appeal of western cities did remain distinctive. For, although they could export aspects of their built environment, they could not export their natural environment. Mountains, beaches, oceans, and deserts played a part in the appeal of their settings. After all, where was the eastern metropolis that could rival a Denver, Seattle, or San Diego in offering opportunities for outdoor recreation?

Nevertheless, the lure of western cities rested on an increasingly fragile foundation. As houses grew too expensive to buy and freeways too congested to drive, residents faced a predicament that stemmed from their region's knack for attracting newcomers. Moreover, another characteristic of the region—the westerners' attachment to and dependence on the automobile—was itself fouling the healthfulness and beauty of the places they loved.

By the closing decade of the twentieth century, the day seemed close at hand when western urbanites would live under a near-constant cloud of pollution. On occasion the wind would blow, the air would clear, the landscape would come into view, and people would remember why they lived there. The suburban metropolises of the American West had succeeded too well. The "Cities of the Future" were mired in the present.

Bibliographic Note

From Richard C. Wade's classic study *The Urban Frontier: The Rise of Western Cities, 1790–1830* (Cambridge, Mass., 1959) to William Cronon's prize-winning book *Nature's Metropolis: Chicago and the Great West* (New York, 1991), scholars have stressed the role of cities in transforming rural hinterlands. They have also focused on the impact of new technologies, especially transportation technologies, in reordering the hierarchy among cities and reshaping the space within them.

A comprehensive illustrated account of the settlement of western cities appears in John W. Reps's massive volume *Cities of the American West: A History of Frontier Urban Planning* (Princeton, 1979). David Hamer's *New Towns in the New World: Images and Perceptions of the Nineteenth-Century Urban Frontier* (New York, 1990) adds valuable interpretive insights. His discussion considers locales in Canada, Australia, and New Zealand as well as the United States. Lionel Frost also provides a comparative perspective in *The New Urban Frontier: Urbanisation and City-Building in Australasia and the American West* (Kensington, 1991). Lawrence H. Larsen's *The Urban West at the End of the Frontier* (Lawrence, 1978) examines the twenty-four largest cities in the western United States circa 1880.

For perceptive sketches of San Francisco, Seattle, Portland, Salt Lake City, and Los Angeles, see "The Power of the Metropolis" in Earl Pomeroy, *The Pacific Slope: A History of California, Oregon, Washington, Idaho, Utah, and Nevada* (New York, 1965), 120–64. In *Instant Cities: Urbanization and the Rise of San Francisco and Denver* (New York, 1975), Gunther Barth treats not only the title cities but also the early history of the "City of the Saints." Mary Lou Locke looks at Portland, San Francisco, and Los Angeles to explore a neglected topic in "Out of the Shadows and into the Western Sun: Working Women of the Late Nineteenth-Century Urban Far West," *Journal of Urban History* 16 (February 1990): 175–204. Thomas G. Alexander and James B. Allen, *Mormons and Gentiles: A History of Salt Lake City* (Boulder, 1984), Lyle W. Dorsett, *The Queen City: A History of Denver* (Boulder, 1977), and Eugene P. Moehring, *Resort City in the Sunbelt: Las Vegas, 1930–1970* (Reno, 1989), provide useful information. Thomas J. Noel explores a specific feature of urban life in his highly readable monograph *The City and the Saloon: Denver, 1858–1916* (Lincoln, 1982).

No western city has been more thoroughly studied than San Francisco. Roger W. Lotchin considers the city's beginnings in *San Francisco, 1846–1856: From Hamlet to City* (1974; reprint, Lincoln, 1979). William Issel and Robert W. Cherny pick up the story in *San Francisco, 1865–1932: Politics, Power, and Urban Development* (Berkeley, 1986). Peter R. Decker, *Fortunes and Failures: White-Collar Mobility in Nineteenth-Century San Francisco* (Cambridge, Mass., 1978), Douglas Henry Daniels, *Pioneer Urbanites: A Social and Cultural History of Black San Francisco* (1980; reprint, Berkeley, 1990), and Robert A. Burchell, *The San Francisco Irish, 1848–1880* (Berkeley, 1980), discuss the experiences of specific population groups. William A. Bullough's *The Blind Boss and His City: Christopher Augustine Buckley and Nineteenth-Century San Francisco* (Berkeley, 1979) takes a biographical look at the city's government, whereas Terrence J. McDonald's *The Parameters of Urban Fiscal Policy: Socioeconomic Change and Political Culture in San Francisco, 1860–1906* (Berkeley, 1986) offers a social-scientific analysis. Judd Kahn discusses Burnham's plan for San Francisco in *Imperial San Francisco: Politics and Planning in an American City, 1897–1906* (Lincoln, 1979).

The number of works that focus on Los Angeles is beginning to look impressive as well. At the head of the list is Robert M. Fogelson's pathbreaking study, *The Fragmented Metropolis: Los Angeles, 1850–1930* (1967; reprint, Berkeley, 1993). Two provocative journalistic accounts are Carey McWilliams, *Southern California: An Island on the Land* (1946; reprint, Salt Lake City, 1983), and Mike Davis, *City of Quartz: Excavating the Future in Los Angeles* (London, 1990). The city's early history is examined in Leonard Pitt, *The Decline of the Californios: A Social History of the Spanish-Speaking Californians, 1846–1890* (Berkeley, 1966), and Richard Griswold del Castillo, *The Los Angeles Barrio, 1850–1890: A Social History* (Berkeley, 1979). Los Angeles is one of the cities Mark S. Foster discusses in "The Western Response to Urban Transportation: A Tale of Three Cities, 1900–1945," in Gerald D. Nash, ed., *The Urban West* (Manhattan, Kans., 1979), 31–39. Scott L. Bottles provides an in-depth analysis in *Los Angeles and the Automobile: The Making of the Modern City* (Berkeley, 1987). Robert Fishman's *Bourgeois Utopias: The Rise and Fall of Suburbia* (New York, 1987) contains a perceptive chapter on Los Angeles. Reyner Banham, an architectural historian, and David Brodsly, a city planner, both offer provocative insights in their respective works: *Los Angeles: The Architecture of Four Ecologies* (Middlesex, Eng., 1971) and *L. A. Freeway: An Appreciative Essay* (Berkeley, 1981). Sports fans will not want to miss Neil J. Sullivan's *The Dodgers Move West* (New York, 1987).

A brief introduction to western cities since 1940 can be found in Raymond A. Mohl, "The Transformation of Urban America since the Second World War," in Robert B. Fairbanks and Kathleen Underwood, eds., *Essays on Sunbelt Cities and Recent Urban America* (College Station, Tex., 1990), 8–32. The most comprehensive work on the subject is Carl Abbott's *The Metropolitan Frontier: Cities in the Modern American West* (Tucson, 1993). Abbott's *The New Urban America: Growth and Politics in Sunbelt Cities*, rev. ed. (Chapel Hill, 1987) also remains useful, as does his essay "Southwestern Cityscapes: Approaches to an American Urban Environment," in Fairbanks and Underwood, *Essays on Sunbelt Cities*, 59–86. For more on the Stanford Industrial Park, Sun City, and Disneyland, see John M. Findlay, *Magic Lands: Western Cityscapes and American Culture after 1940* (Berkeley, 1992), a book that is transforming how scholars think about the West and the cities it contains. Findlay analyzes the Las Vegas Strip in *People of Chance: Gambling in American Society from Jamestown to Las Vegas* (New York, 1986). The national context for many of the developments emphasized in this chapter is presented in Kenneth T. Jackson, *Crabgrass Frontier: The Suburbanization of the United States* (New York, 1985), and Joel Garreau, *Edge City: Life on the New Frontier* (New York, 1991).

Readers seeking further sources may consult the following bibliographic essays: Carl Abbott, "The Metropolitan Region: Western Cities in the New Urban Era," in Gerald D. Nash and Richard W. Etulain, eds., *The Twentieth-Century West: Historical Interpretations* (Albuquerque, 1989), 71–98; Lawrence H. Larsen, "Frontier Urbanization," in Roger L. Nichols, ed., *American Frontier and Western Issues: A Historiographical Review* (Westport, Conn., 1986), 69–88; and Bradford Luckingham, "The Urban Dimension of Western History," in Michael P. Malone, ed., *Historians and the American West* (Lincoln, 1983), 323–43.

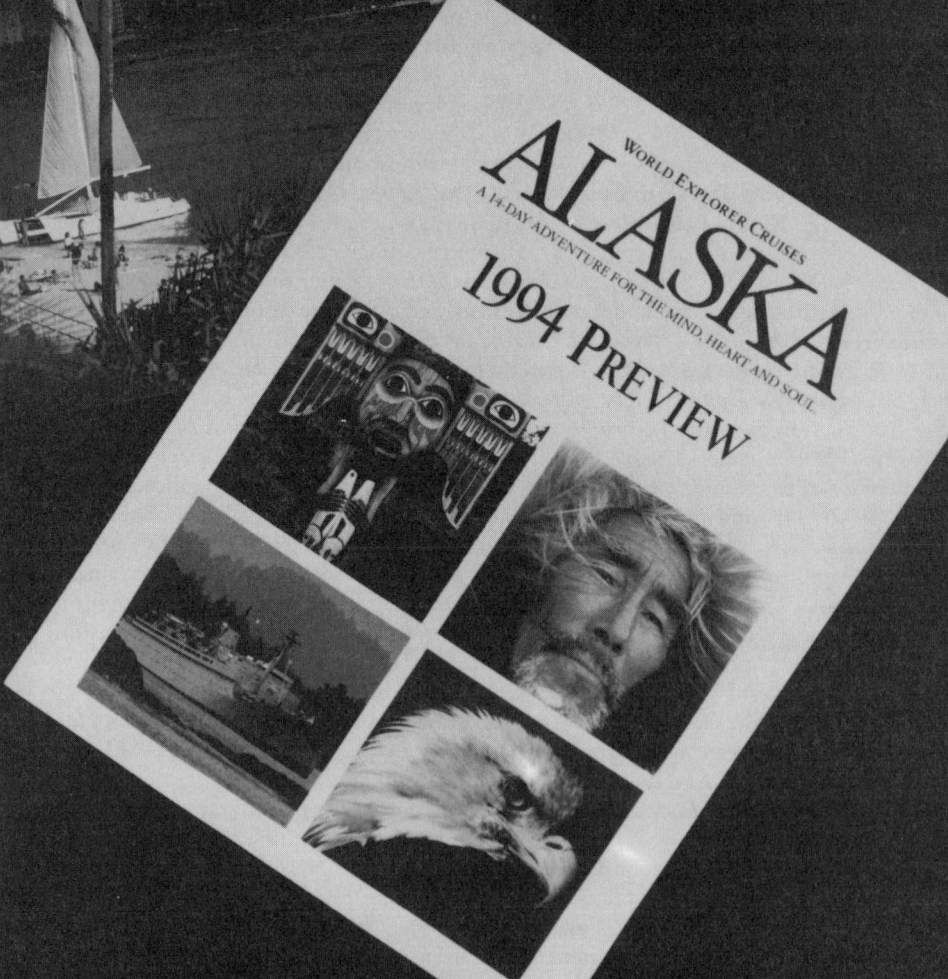

Chapter Sixteen

Alaska and Hawai`i

VICTORIA WYATT

At first blush Hawai`i and Alaska may seem to bear little relation to each other—or to the American West. Americans commonly think of Hawai`i less as part of the American West than as part of the American vacation: an island separated from the stresses of real life by an ocean. Yale University's alumni magazine recently advertised a tour of Alaska under the heading of travel opportunities "abroad"; and according to a common joke, Americans think Alaska is a Pacific island, floating somewhere to the southwest of California, where it basks in warm climes on maps of the nation. Alaska often *is* perceived as a metaphorical island—distanced from the "mainland" by Canada rather than by an ocean, but distanced all the same. To outsiders, Alaska symbolizes a sanitized last frontier, where travelers go to experience spiritual awakening akin to religious conversion. Hawai`i represents a tropical paradise where workaholics can relax and recharge before returning to the stresses of modern American life.

These popular perceptions mask the essential experiences of Alaskans and Hawaiians and their long-standing ties with the contiguous United States. Since Alaska and Hawai`i did not become states until 1959, they seem like new cast members in American history. In fact, many themes central to the development of the American West appeared in Alaska and Hawai`i as early as—and often earlier than—in the contiguous western frontier. These themes include the convergence of indigenous peoples, European newcomers, and non-European immigrants; dispossession of native peoples; economic enterprises based on eastern U.S. or foreign capital; dependence on natural resources for both industry and tourism; and tensions generated by a substantial federal presence in regions far from the center of federal government.

Despite these common themes, Alaska and Hawai`i have tended to remain very much on the periphery in popular concepts of America. World War II was an exception. When both regions were attacked, they suddenly seemed very much a part of America—and certain residents of both felt the impact of the federal government in similar fashion. Thus, examining two World War II experiences seems a fitting way to begin a discussion of Alaska, Hawai`i, and the American West.

Hawai`i and Alaska at War: Two Vignettes

On the morning of Sunday, 7 December 1941, in Honolulu, Hawai`i, Usaburo Katamoto went to the Kokusai Theater to graduate from a first-aid class. A boat builder by trade, he and some of his Japanese friends had been studying first aid to help prepare Hawai`i for war. As they waited for commencement exercises to begin, they heard firing, and a plane came into view. Straining to see it, they finally discerned a Japanese flag painted on its body. Their graduation exercises never took place.

Promoted as exotic sites with dramatic scenery and distinctive indigenous cultures, Alaska and Hawai`i are often viewed as peripheral to the central stories of the western American past. Nonetheless, their histories echo many of the central themes and tensions relating to natural resources, native peoples, and economic development in the contiguous western states.

Tour brochures. *1994. Courtesy Holland America Line and World Explorer Cruises.*

The people who gathered at the Kokusai Theater represented the largest single ethnic group in the islands, for Japanese immigrants and their descendants—including American citizens and aliens—constituted a third of the population of Hawai`i. On that December morning, each Hawaiian resident of Japanese descent instantly became suspect. U.S. Army General Walter Short, supported by President Franklin Delano Roosevelt, called for martial law to help prevent sabotage by Japanese Hawaiians. In an action unprecedented since the U.S. Civil War—when martial law was applied to Southern states that were overtly in rebellion—the Hawaiian people came under U.S. military rule. Although no instances of sabotage were ever found, martial law remained in effect for almost four years.

Fed by the media, rumors spread fast and far. By Monday morning, newspapers and radio stations in Hawai`i and Los Angeles reported that Hawaiian Japanese had blocked access roads to Pearl Harbor during the attack, had cut gigantic arrow shapes in sugarcane fields to point enemy planes toward Pearl Harbor, had poisoned the water supply, and had even shot at American troops. By 8 December, over one hundred local Japanese had been impounded under suspicion of disloyalty. Some were fishermen with radios. Others were suspected solely for their cultural ties and their religious or political leadership positions in local Japanese communities. Twelve Japanese newspapers and three magazines were shut down. Loyalty boards were quickly established on all islands to observe and question thousands of Japanese residents. The expression of Japanese language or culture and the observance of religious holidays were labeled implicitly—and sometimes explicitly—as unpatriotic and suspect.

Almost daily, Katamoto saw friends called in to be interrogated by the FBI. He himself was detailed from his employer to help the U.S. Army Corps of Engineers repair naval ships at Pearl Harbor. His loyalty was not at issue when his boat-building skills were urgently needed. After the urgency slackened and Katamoto returned to his regular job, the FBI abruptly arrested him and dispatched him to an internment camp in Santa Fe, New Mexico. He was suspect, they said, because before the war he sometimes entertained his brother, who was serving in the Japanese navy. Katamoto was held in the camp for almost four years.

Over the course of the war, almost fifteen hundred Japanese Hawaiians were interned. About 37 percent were already U.S. citizens. Some one thousand women and children also left Hawai`i to join the men in the internment camps. Meanwhile, on the West Coast of the mainland, the entire local Japanese population was targeted for internment and relocation. There were some calls for similar actions in Hawai`i, but the Japanese there constituted one-third of the population and a large sector of the skilled labor force. Mass internment was considered essential to national security in West Coast mainland regions, where Japanese represented only 2 percent of the population; ironically, in Hawai`i, where they were the largest demographic ethnic group, selective removal was deemed sufficient.

By June 1942, Usaburo Katamoto from Hawai`i shared the same fate as the 110,000 Japanese residents from the West Coast of the mainland who were being sent to internment camps. Oddly, the Aleut residents of Alaska's Pribilof Islands—two isolated and little-known islands in the Bering Sea—were soon to have much in common with these so-called "enemy aliens." These Aleuts provided the labor for a seal-harvesting

Aleut people from the Aleutian Islands and the Pribilof Islands were forcibly evacuated from their homes during the Second World War and relocated some fifteen hundred miles to camps in southeastern Alaska, where they lived under strict government controls. Only half would return home. Like the Japanese-American internees from mainland western states, they faced a long and difficult process of rebuilding their lives after the war.

Unidentified photographer. Evacuation of Aleut People. *Gelatin silver print, 1942. National Archives, Washington, D.C.*

operation managed by the U.S. Fish and Wildlife Service. In mid-June 1942, a U.S. Navy vessel arrived with an order to evacuate immediately. The unexpected order surprised many. Although the Japanese had attacked the Aleutian Islands the previous week, the tiny Pribilofs lay two hundred miles to the north, had no U.S. military base, and seemed an extremely unlikely target. In fact, military correspondence suggests that the navy wanted to occupy houses on the Pribilofs.

The 290 residents were shipped fifteen hundred miles east to Funter Bay, a small cove sixty miles from Juneau where a few buildings remained from an abandoned cannery and a mine site. The buildings had poor sanitation, no heat, and insufficient floor space for everyone to sleep. The U.S. Fish and Wildlife Service agents in charge protested, and in October 1942 the Pribilof women petitioned the federal government, stating, "This place is no place for a living creature." Their appeals went unheeded, and they spent the winter in these conditions.

The Aleuts at Funter Bay were not under arrest, and their loyalty to the United States was never at question. Yet when Aleut men tried to leave the camp to work in Juneau, the camp superintendent refused to release them. Such control over their movements was not new to Pribilof Islanders. They had first harvested furs for the Russians, who treated them like serfs and demanded work as taxation. When Alaska was transferred to the United States in 1867, the federal government agents stationed at the Pribilofs quickly claimed dictatorial authority. Government agents could deny Aleuts permission to travel off the islands. They selected chiefs, forced labor, controlled wages, threatened banishment to get submission, and—in efforts to increase the population—even engineered marriages.

Thus, when the superintendent at Funter Bay refused to allow men to leave the camp, he was simply assuming authority the government had exercised in the Pribilofs for decades. His motivation for the policy was also the same: to keep the government's Pribilof work force intact. Restricting the movements of free men proved more difficult

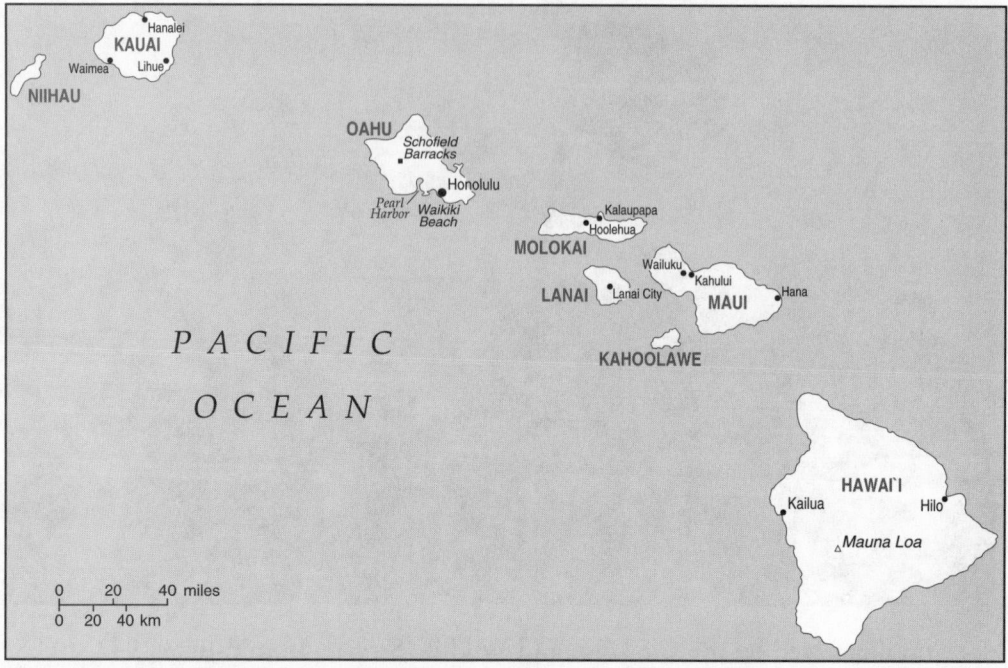

Hawai`i

away from the isolation of the Pribilofs. Other government offices intervened, and some men found work outside the camps.

In May 1944, with the Japanese gone from the Aleutians, the government sent the Pribilof Islanders home. They arrived to find that their houses and other buildings had been vandalized and looted. Personal possessions of value had been stolen, storerooms had been stripped bare, and tools had disappeared. Like the Japanese along the West Coast, the Pribilof Islanders faced a long process of rebuilding and recovery.

Ironically, the evacuation ultimately weakened the federal government's totalitarian control over the Pribilof Aleuts. After the islanders had seen free communities and met native political leaders in Juneau, they resisted the restrictions they had suffered before the war. The unthinkable conditions in Funter Bay had also brought the islanders to the public eye. The government could not reinstate the forced isolation that had made dictatorial policies possible.

Alaska's history, like that of Hawai`i, spotlights paradoxes in the development of the American West. That the government enforced a totalitarian regime in the Pribilofs for three-quarters of a century—that some federal agents sought to maintain this system throughout the disruptions of a world war fought against totalitarianism—is one of those paradoxes. In the Pribilofs, isolation from the rest of the country had made such oppression possible. In Hawai`i, ironically, isolation may actually have prevented the mass deportations suffered by Japanese residents on the mainland's West Coast. Separated from the rest of the United States geographically and no less by popular perception, Alaska and Hawai`i share an island status that fosters historical anomalies. Yet at the same time, as the lives of the Pribilof Aleuts and Katamoto attest, these states are inextricably woven to the rest of the nation. Their histories, like those of colonized islands everywhere, have been informed by continuous dynamics between isolation from the mainland and compelling, unshakable ties to it.

Indigenous Populations and First Contacts with Europeans

Of course, to define Hawai`i and Alaska as "isolated" is to define them in relation to another point of reference, the mainland United States. In fact both Hawai`i and Alaska have long histories of human settlement before U.S. involvement. To the indigenous peoples of both states, being part of a larger government outside the immediate region is a relatively new and culturally artificial phenomenon.

The Hawaiian Islands were formed over hundreds of thousands of years by volcanic eruptions on the ocean floor. Molten rock pushed upward until the tops of some volcanoes rose above sea level. The islands today are composed of volcanoes and their lava flows. The islands stretch over fifteen hundred miles. Their closest neighbors to the north are the Aleutian Islands of Alaska; the North American mainland lies about twenty-one hundred miles away. To the south, their nearest large neighbor is the chain of the Marquesas Islands, two thousand miles distant.

Hawai`i was first settled by Polynesians, who had already developed distinctive cultures on other South Pacific islands. The exact date of their arrival in Hawai`i is not clear. Native Hawaiian legends record that ancestors traveled in double-hulled canoes back and forth between the Society Islands and Hawai`i. These voyages apparently ceased about one thousand years ago, and Hawaiians had no more contact with people from other regions until the arrival of Europeans in 1778. The culture that Hawaiians developed reflects influences of their Polynesian origin, but it also has distinctive qualities born of centuries of isolation.

The first peoples who arrived in Alaska probably crossed from Siberia by land. At various times during the ice ages, the sea levels dropped sufficiently to expose a land mass—known now as Beringia—which lies beneath the Bering Sea today. Some archaeologists believe human beings were living on Beringia forty thousand years ago or even earlier. According to more conservative estimates, the first migration began about fifteen thousand years ago. Whenever they arrived, the first peoples in Alaska were also the first in North America and probably populated both North and South America. Later movements across Beringia followed, separated by thousands of years.

Unlike Hawai`i, Alaska is home to many different indigenous ethnic groups. The Tlingit and Haida peoples of southeastern Alaska have much in common culturally with native peoples of the adjacent Canadian coast. The Déné, or Athapaskan, people of the interior of Alaska share cultural traits with peoples in the Yukon. The Aleut and Eskimo peoples of south-central, southwestern, and Arctic Alaska originate from an entirely different ethnic background from the Tlingit, Haida, and Déné peoples and probably came to North America in a later migration.

The state is composed of 586,000 square miles, stretching 2,400 miles from east to west and 1,420 miles from north to south. It is surrounded on three sides by water and has a coastline of 33,000 miles; thus, many of the Alaskan native cultures adapted to the sea. Long before the arrival of Europeans, native Alaskans developed extensive trading networks along the coastline and rivers.

Because of Alaska's size and the diverse ethnic groups there, native peoples organized

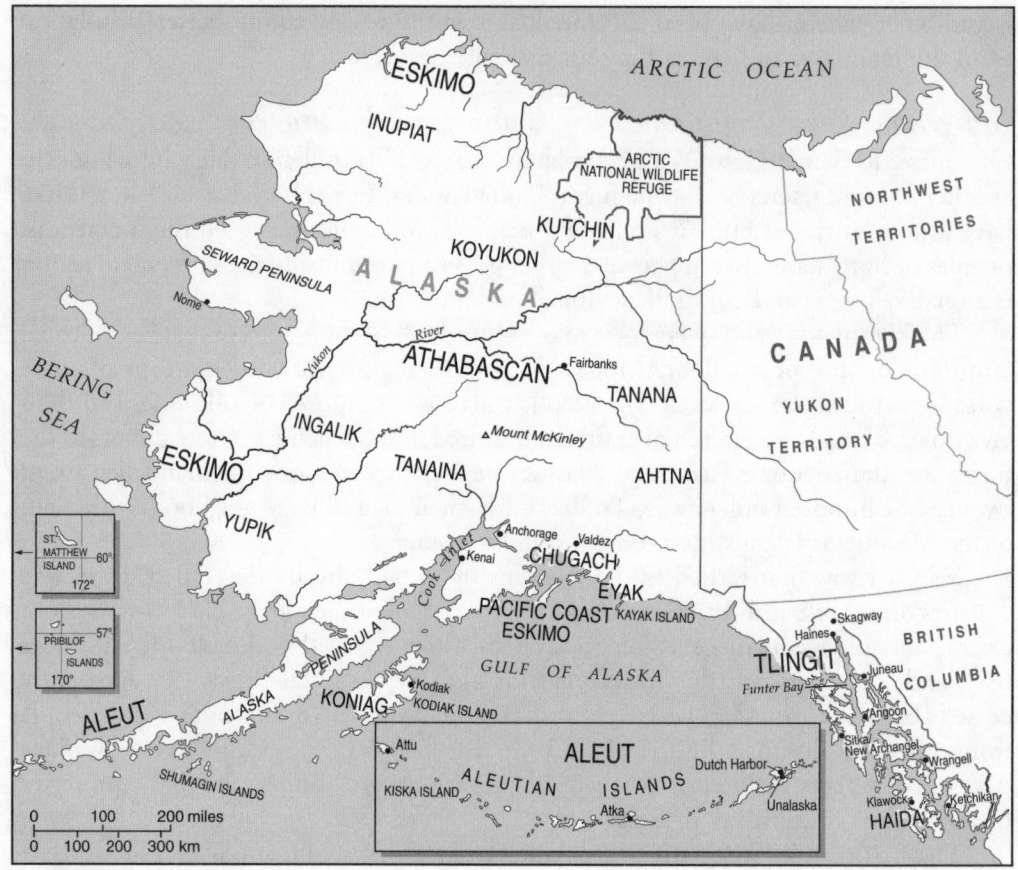

Alaska

themselves locally, usually with different political leaders for each community or village. In contrast, Hawai`i's indigenous social and political system was quite uniform throughout the islands. Social rank was strictly delineated, with many hereditary high chiefs and a complex system of laws and taboos, known as *kapus*. Commoners owed a feudal relationship to chiefs.

The differences between political organization in Alaska and Hawai`i would have an immense impact on native peoples' interactions with Europeans. When British Captain James Cook arrived in Hawai`i in 1778, there were four centers of political power in the islands—four high-ranking chiefs competing for territory and influence. Their battles may have escalated in the decades after Cook's visit as the European traders introduced firearms and explosives. By the turn of the century, one leader, Kamehameha I, controlled all of the islands except Kauai, and Kauai joined his kingdom through diplomatic agreement in 1810. From that time onward, native Hawaiians dealt with foreign nations as one unified monarchy. Europeans and Americans were well accustomed to diplomatic relations with monarchies and could fit Hawai`i easily into their existing political worldviews.

In Alaska, on the other hand, there were many nations of native peoples, each divided into very local political bands. Europeans and Americans had more difficulty recognizing native bands and tribal units as nations. There was no counterpart to Kamehameha—no one monarch whom they could approach and who ruled over all native Alaskans. In the absence of such a monarch, Europeans and Americans often conveniently chose to approach no one, usurping lands and resources without even the pretense of diplomacy between nations.

Eventually, a long history of such injustice led native Alaskans to organize across cultural and geographic boundaries—a monumental task considering the distances and differences involved. In 1966 native leaders throughout the state founded the Alaska Federation of Natives. It became a driving force behind the Alaska Native Claims Settlement Act of 1971, meant to compensate native Alaskans for lands taken without treaty. For decades, however, the colonizers—first Russia and then the United States—simply operated as if there were no native title to land.

Native Hawaiians first saw Europeans in January 1778, when Captain James Cook's expedition sailed past the island of Oahu into Waimea Bay on Kauai. More than two centuries had passed since Hopi and Zuni peoples in the American Southwest had met Francisco Vásquez de Coronado, but native peoples in other parts of the American West would not encounter the expedition of Meriwether Lewis and William Clark for a quarter century more.

In 1778 Cook was on his third major voyage of exploration. He was traveling northward to explore Alaskan waters, seeking a northwest passage. He had learned some of the Tahitian language from his travels in the South Pacific, and he discovered that he could understand portions of the Hawaiian language. The Hawaiians treated him as a high chief; since such chiefs were associated with divinity, Cook may have been considered to have divine origins.

After staying in Hawai`i two weeks, Cook continued his trip. His two ships, the *Discovery* and the *Resolution*, explored parts of what is now the coast of British Columbia, southeastern Alaska, and Prince William Sound and continued on through the Bering Sea to the Arctic Ocean. Cook was certainly not the first European to arrive in Alaska. In 1741 Vitus Bering and Aleksei Chirikov, sailing from Okhotsk, crossed the Bering Sea to explore for Russia. Bering's ship, the *St. Peter*, reached as far east as Kayak Island in the Gulf of Alaska. Sailing back westward, they met and exchanged gifts with some native men in the Shumagin Islands off the Alaskan Peninsula. The parties tried to talk with each other, but without interpreters the obstacles were insurmountable.

Bad weather had diverted Chirikov's ship, the *St. Paul*, early in the voyage. Sailing independently, Chirikov reached as far east as present-day Sitka. He sent men ashore for provisions—none returned. It has often been assumed that they were killed on shore by Tlingit peoples. However, according to Tlingit oral tradition, Chirikov's men voluntarily deserted, and Tlingit peoples welcomed them into their village. There are several documented instances in later years of European seamen who deserted and were sheltered by Northwest Coast native peoples, and the Tlingit account deserves serious consideration.

In any case, after a month of fruitless waiting, Chirikov turned homeward. He traded with Aleut peoples in the Aleutian Chain and reached Kamchatka in October. Bering never returned; he died while his crew wintered on the Commander Islands. Survivors from the *St. Peter* eventually made it back to Kamchatka; like their compatriots on the *St. Paul*, they described the richness of fur-bearing sea mammals they had seen in Alaska.

The Russians already had an active fur trade with China and were eager to exploit the resources in Alaska. They wasted no time, sending a hunting expedition to Bering Island by 1743. In the next two decades Russian hunting expeditions became very active in the Aleutians. The sea otter was the prized fur because, unlike other sea mammals, the sea otter lacks a thick layer of blubber under its skin and must grow a denser fur for warmth. Russian traders wintered in the Aleutian Islands for two or three years, obtaining sea otter pelts from Aleut hunters. They sometimes took Aleuts as hostages to ensure the safety of Russians.

Aleuts and Pacific Coast Eskimos made several unsuccessful attempts to resist the Russian advance. In 1784, the Russian trader Gregorii Shelikhov established a permanent trading settlement on Kodiak Island. By 1799, Russian traders had expanded eastward through south-central Alaska into southeastern Alaska, bringing Aleut hunters with them. Among their establishments in southeastern Alaska was Fort Archangel Saint Michael, built in 1799 near the site of present-day Sitka. In 1802 Tlingit peoples destroyed the fort, but the Russian trader Aleksandr Baranov returned in 1804 with a large military force and reestablished the Russian settlement. This fortified town, called New Archangel, became the Russian capital of Alaska four years later.

Meanwhile, Spain had become concerned about Russia's advancement eastward and sent expeditions up the northwest coastline in 1774 and 1775. Juan Pérez led the first expedition with only one ship; the second was led by Bruno de Hezeta and Juan Francisco de la Bodega y Quadra. The Spaniards traded with coastal native peoples. When James Cook arrived in 1778, he did not know that Spaniards had preceded him to the Northwest Coast, but this soon became evident from the trade goods native peoples showed him.

To prepare for cold weather farther north, Cook and his men obtained sea otter furs from native traders. Later, Cook's crew discovered what Russians had known for three decades: these pelts sold in China for astounding profits. Each pelt was worth a seaman's annual pay. This news spread when Cook's journals were published in Europe in 1784, and very quickly British and American merchants sent trading expeditions to the Northwest Coast. Many reached southeastern Alaska and competed with Russian traders there. Tlingit hunters skillfully used this competition to their best advantage.

Captain Cook did not live to see this sea otter trade. He returned to Hawai`i in November 1778, having failed to find a northwest passage. One night in February 1779, islanders quietly took a British cutter. Cook armed himself the next day and went ashore to invite King Kalaniopuu, the high chief of the island, to his ship. He planned to hold the chief on board until the cutter was returned. However, Cook had not counted on the brashness of his own crew. While he was on shore talking to Kalaniopuu, sailors shot at a canoe and killed a high-ranking chief. News of his death traveled quickly to shore, where fighting broke out. Cook was killed as he retreated into the water. Over the next few days his crew took revenge, burning villages and killing indiscriminately. On 22 February 1779, the *Discovery* and the *Resolution* departed northward toward Alaskan waters, where they again sought a northwest passage.

For the next four decades, Tlingit peoples in southeastern Alaska carried on an active trade in sea otter pelts with Russian, British, and American traders. The Russians conducted their trading in southeastern Alaska from their permanent settlement of New Archangel. They brought Aleut workers from southwestern Alaska to hunt there, ignoring the fact that hunting and fishing areas were traditionally owned by Tlingit families. The British and American traders had no permanent presence in southeastern Alaska and imported no workers; they relied entirely on the Tlingit peoples, and on native peoples in present-day British Columbia, to supply the furs. En route to China, many of the ships stopped in Hawai`i to trade with Hawaiians for provisions. The traders eventually began wintering in Hawai`i, returning to the Northwest Coast for a second summer of trading before heading to China.

The firearms these traders brought to Hawai`i may have helped Kamehameha consolidate the islands under one monarchy. The trading ships also carried European diseases: smallpox, measles, influenza, venereal diseases, and more. Previously unknown in southeastern Alaska or in Hawai`i, these diseases caused devastating epidemics in both places. Social and political stability suffered. High-ranking leaders died, children lost their families, villages were decimated. Survivors faced the rest of their lives with the pain of their tremendous loss and with the ever-present danger of new epidemics.

Hawaiians frequently joined the crews of trading ships and visited other lands, including the Northwest Coast. There are also reports of Northwest Coast native peoples visiting Hawai`i. Artwork and material culture traveled back and forth on the trading ships between the South Pacific and southeastern Alaska. A Tlingit clan in Angoon, Alaska, incorporated a feather collar from the Society Islands into its clan ceremonial regalia. Thus the fur trade led to some exchanges of ideas between indigenous peoples of the two regions. Hawai`i and southeastern Alaska were both far from European and American centers, but they were no longer isolated from each other.

Many British and American seamen left their ships to live in Hawai`i. By 1810, near Honolulu alone, there were several dozen foreigners in residence; by 1819 some two hundred Americans and Europeans lived in the islands. After 1819, Kamehameha and other chiefs allowed foreigners who had skilled trades to own land. These foreigners married Hawaiian women and accumulated estates through gifts from chiefs, for whom they often served as advisers. Hawaiians learned foreign craft skills from them and no longer depended on trading ships for blacksmithing and other craft items. Initially, Europeans and Americans who chose to live in Hawai`i prospered as long as they supported native leaders and joined and contributed to indigenous communities.

The foreigners living in Alaska at this time—the Russians—had a very different relationship with the native peoples. They appropriated land for forts and hunting resources without permission from native leaders. In southwestern Alaska, they forced Aleuts to become serfs who owed labor and tariffs to the Russian tsar. In southeastern Alaska, they established New Archangel through military force and lived behind a barricade. Some Russians married or cohabited with Aleut and Tlingit women, and the progeny of these unions—Creoles—became part of the work force. Otherwise, Russians segregated themselves from native communities. Their presence in Alaska was founded on subjugation and military threat.

Far from behaving as visitors in other peoples' lands, Russians claimed Alaska for their own country. They had no monopoly on ignoring native title, however: Spain and

England claimed the Northwest Coast in similar fashion and almost came to war in the 1790s before Spain backed down. Throughout North America, colonizing nations have tended to claim land first and deal with native title later—if at all. Alaska's history provides no exception.

Nineteenth-Century Commerce

American businessmen and investors became involved in Hawai`i long before they began to develop most parts of the American West. When the first American trading vessel stopped in Hawai`i in 1790, the United States was a new nation, and its "West" was very east. The Northwest Ordinance, providing for governance of lands northwest of the Ohio River, was only three years old. Yet from 1790 onward, Americans were actively involved in commerce in Hawai`i. They quickly became the major actors in the maritime fur trade that linked southeastern Alaska, Hawai`i, and China. About twenty ships from New England stopped in Hawai`i each year to replenish supplies en route to Alaska.

The commercial success of American merchants in Hawai`i was not lost on Russian traders. In 1816 a Russian agent asked a Hawaiian king, Kaumalii, for permission to start Russian trading posts on Kauai and Oahu. Russians felt that here—unlike Alaska—the consent of the local leaders was necessary. Kaumalii granted permission, but Kamehameha I quickly overruled him and forced Russians to leave the following year. Russians did not threaten the dominance of American traders in Hawai`i again.

By 1810 the sea otter population was decreasing on the Northwest Coast, and merchants sought to supplement sea otter pelts with other trade items. American merchants discovered that sandalwood sold well in China, where it was used for wood carving, medicinal and cosmetic oils, and incense. Hawaiian chiefs and New England merchants were both eager to capitalize on the trade. Chiefs sent thousands of commoners deeper and deeper into the mountains to cut sandalwood. Furniture, clothes, carriages, and a myriad of other items flooded from New England to Hawai`i in trade. As the trade escalated, merchants paid chiefs in advance, and chiefs accumulated debts that further increased the pressure to harvest wood. Kamehameha had had the foresight to institute conservation measures early in the trade, but after his death in 1819 these measures broke down. By 1829 the supply of marketable sandalwood was virtually exhausted—leaving many chiefs with large debts from advances on orders they could not fill.

The fate of sandalwood in Hawai`i parallels that of sea otters in southeastern Alaska and the Northwest Coast. The sea otter slaughter was similarly unencumbered by conservation measures, and few sea otter remained in southeastern Alaska by 1829. Realizing the opportunity for immediate profits from sandalwood and sea otter, harvesters and merchants destroyed the very resource on which their commerce depended. Their choice to place short-term gain over long-term sustainable yield is no historical anomaly. The same short-term focus informs the rapid destruction of old-growth forests in Alaska and the Northwest today.

The commercial whaling industry faces similar issues today. Contemporary conservation measures are complicated by the need for international cooperation; and in northern Alaska, subsistence whaling has important cultural implications that must be acknowledged. In 1819, when whaling grounds were discovered off the coast of Japan, the world dealt with no such complexities. Hawai`i quickly became the major supply center for whaling vessels in the Pacific, a great number of which were American ships from New England. They stopped in Hawai`i twice a year to gather provisions and to take oil back to New England. When the sea otter and sandalwood commerce dwindled, whaling was already filling the commercial gap for American maritime businessmen. By 1829 over one hundred whaling ships called in to Hawai`i, and this number grew to four or five hundred a year in the next two decades.

As whaling grounds farther south became depleted, American whaling ships began testing Alaskan waters. In 1835 American ships explored the Gulf of Alaska; by 1852 over two hundred whaling ships were active in the Bering Sea. These whalers traded with coastal Eskimos, hired Eskimo men to work on ship, and commissioned clothing from Eskimo women.

Between 1830 and 1850, the whaling industry generated some six million to ten million dollars' worth of products each year—huge sums in those days. In Hawai`i, mercantile businesses and commercial agriculture grew quickly to meet the needs of the whaling vessels. Americans dominated this commerce, establishing and investing in the enterprises and selling to American fishing fleets. During the sandalwood trade, Hawaiian chiefs had controlled the access to the resource in demand and so had been actively involved in the commerce. They had no analogous role in the commerce that grew from whaling. Americans gained more and more power over the economy in Hawai`i, weakening the power of chiefs.

In Alaska, fur trading remained the focus of commercial activities while affording far more modest profits than whaling. As sea otter populations declined, the Russian-American Company, which enjoyed a monopoly through a Russian government charter, shifted its focus to other sea and land mammals. It also tried to diversify its economic activities in Alaska, without great success. Ice—a plentiful resource in Alaska—could be exported if there was a demand for it in warmer climates. The California gold rush of 1849 created the demand. In southwestern Alaska, the Russian-American Company had their Aleut and Creole workers cut ice; in New Archangel, they paid Tlingit peoples to do so. Up to ten thousand tons of ice were exported annually. Ultimately, though, this industry depended on California demand and declined as the gold rush there subsided. In the 1850s, the company experimented with coal mining, also to serve a California market. However, furs remained the only viable economic product of the Russian-American Company, and fur trading was not a growth industry.

In the first half of the nineteenth century, the economy in Hawai`i flourished and diversified. Hawai`i's isolation actually increased its attractiveness as a wintering and reprovisioning center for ships active in the Pacific, since Hawai`i had no nearby competitors for this commerce. As Americans dominated economic activities there, ties with New England strengthened. By 1845, four hundred Americans were living in Hawai`i—representing two-thirds of the foreign population there.

Politically these Americans were foreigners living in the kingdom of another people. However, unlike the first Europeans and Americans in Hawai`i, their prosperity did not depend on supporting the existing Hawaiian rulers and systems. They did not aspire to assimilate into the local society. Rather, they sought to transplant their own society to Hawai`i. As their economic dominance grew, spurred by investments from New England, they began to resemble colonizers rather than visitors.

In Alaska, the Russian foreigners had been colonizers from the start. From their earliest arrival, they had imposed their rulers and their institutions on local peoples, taxing them in furs for living in their own land. In 1766 Tsarina Catherine the Great declared the native peoples of the Aleutian Islands and the Alaska Peninsula to be Russian subjects. She decreed that they should be treated well, but this was not well enforced. In contrast, tax collecting did become much more systematic after this declaration as the Russian government sent tax collectors along on fur-hunting expeditions. These expeditions competed with one another, often forcing native hunters to work for them.

In 1799 Tsar Paul I granted sole right to trade in Alaska to the Russian-American Company. High-ranking Russian officials were shareholders. Chief Manager Baranov became the director of all Russians in Alaska, a position he held until 1818. Although he married a native woman from Kenai, this did not deter him from abusing Alaskan native peoples. Many of the worst Russian offenses occurred under Baranov's direction. By order of the Russian government, Alaskan natives would not pay taxes, but each year half of the Aleut and Koniag men from age eighteen to age fifty could be forced to hunt furs for the company. These native men could not leave their villages without permission from the company. Baranov also emptied villages of able-bodied men, forcing them to hunt sea otter for the Russians in other regions. These men were unable to hunt for their own families, and women and children starved.

Ironically, Baranov developed a long-distance friendship with Kamehameha, the native ruler of Hawai`i, at the same time that he abused Alaskan native peoples. Baranov and Kamehameha sent gifts and messages to each other through the American fur-trading vessels that visited southeastern Alaska and Hawai`i. Baranov even considered retiring to Hawai`i. He cultivated no such friendship with native leaders in Alaska, viewing them as entirely different from the head of a kingdom.

As colonizers, Russians brought many elements of their own society to Alaska. In Kodiak, the first Russian capital, and later in New Archangel, Russians established a museum, a library, and natural history and scientific collections. The Russian population was never large—in 1839, at its largest, there were only 832 Russians in Alaska, not counting the children of unions between Russian men and native women. However, New Archangel, the Russian-American capital, was a bustling place, with a grand residence for the manager of the Russian-American Company, two churches, a school, barracks, a foundry, a flour mill, a sawmill, a hospital, and a shipyard. Russian officials stationed there enjoyed an active—even gala—social life. In Europe, New Archangel gained a reputation as an oasis of European culture and society.

Missionary Activities

In European and American history, economic and political colonization has been accompanied by social and spiritual colonization. The experiences of indigenous

Alaskans and Hawaiians are no exception. Russians rapidly extended their society's institutions to native populations in Alaska. As early as 1784, Shelikhov and his wife, Natal'ia, founded a school in Kodiak, teaching Russian language and religion to Kodiak children they held as hostages. This school, and others, were soon operated by Russian Orthodox missionaries. Informal missionary activity had started with the earliest Russian fur traders, who began to baptize Aleut hunters. The first recorded baptism took place in 1759, just eighteen years after the Bering-Chirikov voyage. In 1794 ten Russian Orthodox monks went to southwestern Alaska. A Russian Orthodox church was built in Kodiak two years later. Missionaries taught religious, academic, and vocational subjects. When missionaries began complaining to the Russian government about the fur traders' abuse of Alaskan natives, relations between missionaries and fur traders became strained.

After Chief Manager Baranov retired in 1818, the Russian-American Company gave more support to missionaries. Its second charter, issued by the Russian government in 1821, directed the company to maintain "sufficient numbers" of missionaries in Alaska. This charter reflected an upsurge in missionary activity in the Russian Orthodox church, and many Russian missionaries came to Alaska in the 1820s. They began to train native people for positions in the priesthood and especially for service as lay workers. They wanted native lay workers to practice in remote villages where ordained priests were not stationed. They also ran schools for native children, teaching them the Russian language, European academic subjects, and vocational skills.

One of the most influential Russian Orthodox missionaries in Alaska was Ioann Veniaminov, who came to the town of Unalaska in 1824. Missionary work was his first focus, but he also wrote about ethnography and scientific subjects and sent collections back to Russia. He and an Aleut leader, Ivan Pankov, designed an alphabet for Fox Island Aleuts so that they could have a written language—to be used, among other things, for reading religious texts. After ten years in the Aleutians, Veniaminov moved to Sitka, where he worked for another eighteen years. In 1840 he was made a bishop, one of four Russian Orthodox priests in Alaska overseeing churches at Sitka in southeastern Alaska and at Atka, Kodiak, and Unalaska in southwestern Alaska. In addition there were chapels on eight other Aleutian islands.

Russian Orthodox activities continued to expand among native peoples in Alaska. By 1867, when the Russian government withdrew from Alaska, the religion was represented by over thirty Russian Orthodox clergy, with nine churches and thirty-five chapels. Many of the clergy remained active after the Americans occupied Alaska, and they competed with American missionaries for native congregations. In southwestern and southeastern Alaska, Russian Orthodox churches are still vital today.

Religious beliefs are very personal, and few native voices exist from Russian-American times to discuss reasons for native conversions. Some conversions may have been coerced. Certain Russian military personnel were skeptical of native conversions, suspecting that many native converts simply wanted the material benefits that the missionaries bestowed. Nevertheless, a great many native people embraced Christianity through religious conviction. This act did not necessarily imply a rejection of their own spiritual traditions and values. They were accustomed to a range of experiences in

Religious organizations and secular philan-
thropic groups played a significant role in introducing the native peoples of both Alaska and
Hawai`i to the political, cultural, and material
values of mainland American society.

*Vincent Soboleff (ca.
1880–1950). Schoolchil-
dren at Killisnoo [Angoon,
Alaska]. Photograph, ca.
1900. Alaska State Li-
brary (#PCA 1-178),
Juneau.*

*L. E. Edgeworth. Free Kin-
dergarten, Children's Aid
Association. Photograph,
1913. Bishop Museum,
Honolulu, Hawai`i.*

spiritual communication and did not perceive spiritual systems as mutually exclusive
constructs. In Alaska, as elsewhere, many native peoples sought syntheses and relationships between their own beliefs and the colonizers' teachings.

   As Hawai`i became increasingly like a colonized country, native peoples there faced
similar religious issues. Before the first American missionaries arrived in Hawai`i, native
Hawaiians had overtly challenged their own system of *kapus*, the strict laws that governed
dietary restrictions, gender relationships, proper behavior toward chiefs, rituals at births,
marriages, and deaths, and a range of other aspects of daily and ceremonial life. Violating
a *kapu* was sacrilege and warranted severe punishment from human or divine sources.

   However, the presence of foreigners—who operated outside *kapus* and broke them with impunity—severely weakened the *kapu* system. The maritime fur traders disrupted existing social balances by making material goods more widely available, by successfully encouraging Hawaiians to break *kapus*, and by introducing diseases. Kamehameha's political centralization of Hawai`i may also have removed some focus from local chiefs and the deities with whom they were associated. For a complex of reasons, some Hawaiians began to question the contemporary relevance of the *kapu* system and the religious system from which it sprang.

In May 1819, Kamehameha died, and rule passed to his son Liholiho (Kamehameha II) and to one of Kamehameha I's wives, Kaahumanu. Six months later—strongly influenced by Kaahumanu—Liholiho broke a *kapu* in public. Through this action he declared the end of the *kapu* system. To enforce that decision, he ordered the destruction of religious images. Many leaders opposed his action, and one of his cousins, Kukailimoku, challenged him in battle over the issue. Kukailimoku and his wife were killed; the remaining opposition went underground. Traditional religion survived in private, but people no longer practiced it openly.

Meanwhile, Hawaiians had started working on American sailing vessels and at least as early as 1790 were visiting New England. Hawaiian visitors began receiving Christian educations there. One Hawaiian, Obookiah, went to Connecticut in 1809 and trained at a school for missionary teachers run by the American Board of Commissioners for Foreign Missions. The school's leaders sought to extend its influence beyond American shores, and Obookiah's teachers hoped he would return to Hawai`i and preach to his people. In 1818 he died in Connecticut of typhus, but his life and death inspired the American Board to send a Protestant missionary expedition to Hawai`i. The first small group arrived in 1820, followed by reinforcements eight years later. By 1850, 153 missionaries—Presbyterians and Congregationalists—had worked in Hawai`i for the American Board of Foreign Missions.

For a variety of reasons, the American Board felt strongly that missionaries should go as couples. This presented no small hurdle, for between 1819 and 1850, only two of the men accepted by the board for missionary work in Hawai`i were already married. Often a man had to find a wife suitable to the American Board very quickly, since his sailing date had already been scheduled. Women who wanted to be missionaries faced an even tougher predicament: without formal channels to train for missionary work, they often discreetly notified ministers or relatives in theological schools that they would marry aspiring missionaries.

Lucy Goodale's experience was fairly typical. In autumn 1819 she was a twenty-three-year-old schoolteacher in rural Massachusetts when her cousin suggested she marry Asa Thurston—a man she had never met—who was sailing in six weeks to found a mission in Hawai`i. She had dinner with Thurston once and agreed to marry him. They held the ceremony three weeks later and sailed for Hawai`i eleven days after that. For many couples like the Thurstons, moving to Hawai`i meant a total transformation of their personal lives—leaving family and friends, perhaps forever, and taking a stranger as their lifelong spouse.

When missionaries left their country and their families, they did not leave their allegiance to a New England way of life. They came not to assimilate with the Hawaiian people and adopt native customs and values but to transplant American customs and values to Hawai`i. Missionaries' activities went far beyond religious services. They ran schools, administered medicine, and taught Western crafts, farming techniques, and domestic skills. The women, already overburdened with establishing households in settings they considered spartan, sewed European-style dresses for high-ranking Hawaiian women. The missionaries made one concession to their new location—they studied Hawaiian and preached in that language to reach a broad population. But their goal was to make Hawaiians resemble New Englanders, not vice versa.

Missionaries in Hawai`i did face a complication unknown to their counterparts in Alaska: they relied on the permission of the king and the local chiefs to work in the islands. For Protestants—more often than for Catholics—permission was generally granted, provided that the missionaries established missions where the chiefs wanted them.

The missionaries gained congregations quickly, for local populations were eager to explore what the newcomers offered. When Abner and Lucy Wilcox arrived in 1837, just seventeen years after the first mission was established, they noted that the Hawaiians "appeared to be rejoiced to see us." The Wilcoxes reported that 278 Hawaiians had already been accepted as church members and that this was not done lightly—they were made to "stand trial" a long time to ensure that they were truly converted. Chiefs and even commoners gave money and time to build new churches for the missionaries. The Wilcoxes estimated that along a one-hundred-mile stretch of seacoast in the Hilo and Puna districts of the island of Hawai`i, there were already 122 schools with about 4,537 students. Abner Wilcox was impressed with the students' caliber. He stated that their "capacities" equaled those of children in America. He declared, "Give them the advantages of children in our own land and when grown they, I think, will not be a whit inferior." In other words, he felt sure they could learn to live like Americans.

Like missionaries in Alaska, those in Hawai`i faced the challenge of reaching people in remote villages where missionaries were not stationed. They arrived at the same solution: training native teachers to work among their own people. In 1837, Abner Wilcox was delighted to find that native teachers already assisted at the mission in Honolulu and that about one hundred more were training in an adult teachers' school. Missionaries even hoped Hawaiians would provide manpower for missions to native peoples in the Rockies, where the Presbyterian Board of Home Missions was active. The missionaries' enthusiasm was not always matched by solid information about Native Americans: when Wilcox learned that one Hawaiian volunteer had spent three years on the Northwest Coast and could "speak a little of the Indian language," he assumed this meant the man would understand native peoples in the Rocky Mountains.

Missionaries played a strong role in developing American political power in Hawai`i. They quickly gained influential positions within the government and used those positions to lobby for American interests. Two missionaries, Reverend William Richards and Dr. Gerrit P. Judd, became advisers to the king. Missionaries influenced Kamehameha III to replace his feudal government in 1840 with a constitutional monarchy modeled on the monarchies in Europe. This government included an elected House of Commons, a hereditary House of Nobles, and a prime minister. Dr. Judd served as prime minister from 1842 to 1854, during which time he promoted many major changes that shifted power from Hawaiians to whites—who had come to be known as *haoles*.

Despite their eagerness to entrust Hawaiians with church duties, American missionaries in Hawai`i maintained a marked distance from Hawaiian peoples. Their goal was to teach native Hawaiians the American religion and customs, but they did not seek or expect to develop integrated settlements of equals. Although dispersed in missions throughout the islands, the missionaries relied on each other for friendships. They kept their own children away from Hawaiians to protect them from "heathen" influences. They developed their own political and economic base, influencing the king to adopt reforms that benefited *haoles*—and particularly Americans. They often sent their sons to New England to be educated. These sons returned to Hawai`i with their ties to America made all the stronger by firsthand experience. Many of them turned very successfully to politics and commerce. Although born in the islands, they were—like their parents—very much American colonizers.

The Formalization of American Dominance

America's religious colonization of Hawai`i went hand in hand with the growing political and economic dominance of Americans there. This American colonization started considerably earlier in Hawai`i than in some other places in the American West; by the 1840s, when wagon trains started crossing the plains on their way to Oregon, American merchants had been influential settlers in Hawai`i for some fifty years. In Alaska also, Americans—although not permanent settlers—had been active maritime traders for half a century. By the 1840s, inspired by the philosophy of "manifest destiny," American politicians began to consider colonization of Alaska.

From a military viewpoint, American control of North America depended on naval outposts in the North Pacific. Acquiring Alaska from Russia would at once create these strategic bases and eliminate a potential enemy from North America. It would also facilitate U.S. designs on British Columbia. From an economic viewpoint, Alaskan furs were an attractive resource to American companies. Russians already had harvesting systems firmly in place—based on exploitation of native peoples in southwestern Alaska—and American companies could take over the operation without great changes. U.S. exploration expeditions in the 1850s and 1860s revealed vast fur resources that were still untapped. Alaskan settlements would also help develop American markets in Asia.

The American Civil War put a temporary stop to discussions about acquiring Alaska, but these talks quickly resumed after the war. They coincided with a Russian crisis of confidence. The tsar had become concerned that Russia could not defend Alaska if the United States or Britain started a war. In an interesting parallel to events one century later, Russia's foreign affairs closer to home already strained its military budget. The Russian-American Company profits were not great and did not seem to justify the potential costs of overextending the Russian Empire. In spring of 1867, Russia and the United States agreed on a treaty to transfer Alaska to American control. The purchase price was $7.2 million. Those who believed Alaska was one gigantic icebox referred to the purchase as "Seward's folly"—after William Seward, President Abraham Lincoln's secretary of state, who actively promoted the treaty. In fact, the treaty was very popular in the Senate; only two senators voted against it. On 18 October 1867, Alaska officially became part of the United States. By the terms of the treaty, the Russian Orthodox church members owned all Russian churches in Alaska and remained an active presence there. Russians had the option of returning to Russia or becoming U.S. citizens.

Although the transfer of Alaska from Russia to the United States is often called the "Alaska Purchase," Russia did not own Alaska, for the empire had never established agreements with native Alaskans. The United States also moved in without negotiations with native peoples, and the treaty specified that "uncivilized tribes" would be subject to whatever laws the United States adopted toward them. The status of native Alaskans and native rights remained vague for over a century. In some places, such as the Pribilofs, the United States continued Russia's oppressive policies toward native Alaskans.

In 1867 these concerns were far from the minds of Americans, many of whom were eager to explore what Alaska had to offer. Most Americans who came to Alaska immediately after purchase settled in the old Russian capital of New Archangel, renamed Sitka. Some sought adventure and new horizons; others were military and government officials. The army built six posts but quickly eliminated all except the one in Sitka, which also was abandoned in 1877. Civil government was established in 1884, making Alaska officially a U.S. district with a governor appointed by the president.

Many Americans who came to Alaska did not stay long. The economy in Sitka, which boomed right after transfer, soon slowed. Americans there and in the few other settlements dotting the Alaska coast generally relied on fur trading, an industry with declining revenues. More than the Russians, however, Americans explored other industries and rapidly developed fish processing. In 1868 the first American-run fish saltery in Alaska opened in Klawock. Ten years later 2 fish canneries opened in southeastern Alaska; by 1900, 42 salmon canneries in Alaska packed 1.5 million cases annually. The numbers continued to grow, and by 1917 the 118 salmon canneries in Alaska produced half the canned salmon in the world.

Early fishing and canning operations in Alaska were connected to the mainland despite their geographic isolation. Most were operated by absentee companies based in San Francisco, Seattle, and Portland. These companies ensured that the Alaskan fishing operations had an international focus—not only in their markets but also in their labor forces. Then, as now, white Americans tended to be on the upper end of the pay scales, so the companies recruited workers elsewhere. Many native Alaskans moved in the summers to temporary company housing and worked as laborers, increasingly depending on wages as their traditional fishing grounds were appropriated by American industries. Canneries also imported foreign laborers, including workers from China, the Philippines, Japan, and Mexico, who quickly outnumbered native workers. Americans in Alaska did not embrace this ethnic mix, and incidents of violence and racism occurred.

Meanwhile, in Hawai`i, international economic development brought similar demographic shifts. As whale populations decreased and whaling seasons became less consistent, American businessmen in Hawai`i sought a more stable economic product: sugar. American-owned sugar plantations began to gain attention in the 1840s. Initially Hawaiians were hired as laborers, but with the California gold rush in 1848, demands for sugar skyrocketed. Plantation owners formed the Royal Hawaiian Agricultural Society in 1850, to seek cheap labor elsewhere. They brought some 180 Chinese workers over on contract in 1852. Before the end of the century, more than 46,000 Chinese

Brought to Hawai`i in the late 19th century to work in the burgeoning sugar plantations, foreign workers—such as these Japanese men—often remained on the islands when their contracts expired, becoming part of the racially and culturally mixed population that continues to distinguish Hawaiian society.

Unidentified photographer. Japanese Sugar Workers. *Photograph, 1906. Bishop Museum, Honolulu, Hawai`i.*

workers came to sugar plantations in Hawai`i—despite the Chinese Exclusion Act passed by the kingdom in 1886. Also in 1886, Japan agreed to allow Japanese workers to go to Hawai`i, and many came immediately as contract laborers. Between 1852 and 1900, some 15,000 Japanese, 13,000 Portuguese, 1,400 Germans, 600 Scandinavians, and 400 Galicians came to Hawai`i to work in agriculture.

These laborers faced strict contract terms and hard working conditions on the plantations. Most immigrant workers planned to return home to their families after their contracts expired. Some eventually sent for their families and settled in Hawai`i. Contracts in Hawai`i were generally for much longer terms than those in Alaska, where immigrant workers were shipped out at the end of each summer. Thus, contract laborers were more likely to settle permanently in Hawai`i than in Alaska.

Businessmen who focused on agriculture confronted a problem that had not affected whaling: to secure investments, they needed clear title to land, but in Hawai`i, land was traditionally controlled by the king and chiefs. These leaders often allowed foreigners to use land in return for services, but they did not relinquish title. In the 1840s, *haoles* continually pressed for changes in land tenure. With Dr. Judd as prime minister, they had a strong ally in the government, and by 1850 the legislature had abolished the feudal land system. Lands previously owned by the king were divided among the king, the government, and commoners; and aliens were permitted to purchase land. The system was tailor-made for foreign entrepreneurs with capital to invest in land. Influenced by *haoles*, the government was more than willing to sell its land to alien speculators; by 1886, more than two-thirds of the government allocation was owned by *haoles*. Chiefs and commoners were not accustomed to real estate transactions, and many sold their lands to *haoles* at low prices.

A small group of American investors and managers controlled the sugar plantations and dominated Hawai`i's economic development. Some of the investors in sugar plantations were American merchants; many others were American missionaries or their sons. Abner and Lucy Wilcox's son George studied engineering at Yale to prepare for an agricultural career. He devoted his life to the Grove Farm Plantation near Lihue, Kauai, using his engineering skills to introduce innovations in irrigation and agriculture. He also found places for his siblings at the plantation. Like many other missionary families, the Wilcoxes felt that economic power carried obligations; and they made generous donations to public and private charities and established foundations. Their philanthropic contributions were extremely important and testify to their commitment to their adopted land. Thus they returned much of their profit to Hawai`i but on American terms and through American institutions.

With *haoles*—primarily Americans—gaining economic power in Hawai`i, pressures for political reform continued. In 1886, a group of *haoles*, joined by a few part-Hawaiians, formed the Hawaiian League, an alliance designed to remove power from the monarchy. Some members also wanted American annexation of Hawai`i. The Hawaiian League had the support of the Honolulu Rifles, a volunteer militia with more loyalty to the league than to the monarchy. In June 1887, Lorrin A. Thurston, the grandson of the American missionary Asa Thurston, presented a set of league resolutions calling for a new constitution and less involvement by the monarchy in government.

Most Hawaiians supported King Kalakaua and did not want *haoles* to gain more power over the government. Nevertheless, Kalakaua sought to avoid armed confrontation at all costs, and he acceded to the demands. A new cabinet was established, including Lorrin Thurston, who became the primary author of a new constitution. This constitution turned the monarchy into a largely ceremonial institution subordinate to the legislature. Although the king could veto legislation, a two-thirds vote of the legislature would override the veto. Further, the constitution systematically ensured that *haoles* could control the House of Nobles. American and European male aliens could now vote in elections if they swore to support the constitution. Property requirements greatly restricted the number of Hawaiians voting in House of Nobles elections, and Asians were not permitted to vote.

The Constitution of 1887 was an explicit maneuver to make *haoles* the major power in government. However, the *haoles* had more trouble than they anticipated in controlling the legislature, and many wanted further reforms to secure their influence. When King Kalakaua died in 1891, his sister, Queen Liliuokalani, succeeded him. As she made it clear that she would take an active role in government, reformers began to talk increasingly of American annexation.

In January 1893, Liliuokalani announced her intention to revise the constitution and to return powers to the monarchy. Thurston and other reformers decided the time was right for revolution. Gathering arms, the reformers marched on the government building and took control of it, firing only a single shot and injuring one person. Neither policemen nor government loyalists resisted. This may have been because U.S. troops were stationed in Hawai`i, and it was rumored that they would intervene if loyalists resisted. The United States recognized the new provisional government even before the queen capitulated. Perhaps she hoped that the United States would reject the actions of its countrymen. Great Britain had reinstated the monarchy in 1843 when British citizens, acting without authorization, had claimed to cede Hawai`i for Great Britain.

A ceremonial disbanding of Queen Liliuokalani's palace guards marked the usurpation of power by a provisional haole *government in Hawai`i in January 1893. The guards' American-style military dress suggests the extent to which even native Hawaiian institutions had adopted the conventions of mainland culture.*

James J. Williams (1853–1926). Disbanding Royal Household Guards. *Photograph, 18 January 1893. Smithsonian Institution, National Anthropological Archives (#75-11016), Washington, D.C.*

In fact, President Grover Cleveland did feel it was ethically wrong to take the islands, and far from supporting annexation, he asked the Provisional Government to reinstate the monarchy. The Provisional Government refused, Cleveland did not back his request with troops, and the debate over annexation continued for some years. Sugar refiners in the United States opposed annexation, fearing that they would lose their monopoly. In 1896, William McKinley was elected president. Much more than Cleveland, he supported American expansion. When the Spanish-American War broke out, the United States needed a Pacific base. Despite significant opposition, an annexation resolution passed both houses of Congress by 6 July 1898, and the Republic of Hawai`i became a U.S. territory on 12 August 1898.

Hawai`i's annexation was the culmination of a long process in which American residents gathered economic power and political influence. With the help of European aliens, they gradually eroded the monarchy's power. France and England also had interests in Hawai`i, but the early dominance of Americans there left little serious opportunity for them to step in. Although Hawai`i was not technically a U.S. colony, it was certainly colonized by Americans long before it was finally annexed; when it became part of the United States, a substantial and influential group of Americans already controlled the local government.

The opposite was true when Alaska joined the United States. There was no significant American population or American government there in 1867. The United States needed to import a population of colonizers and gradually establish American political institutions. Alaska was organized into a U.S. district, with an Organic Act and an appointed governor, in 1884—a full seventeen years after the United States claimed possession. For the first quarter century after transfer, American populations grew very slowly in Alaska.

American missionaries, however, quickly became active in Alaska. Like their counterparts in Hawai`i, they did much to spread American institutions, and some also gained political power. In 1877 the Reverend Sheldon Jackson, Presbyterian superintendent of the Home Missions of the Territories, brought a lay worker, Amanda McFarland, to establish a mission for native people in Wrangell. The following year, the Presbyterian Board of Home Missions sent the Reverend John Green Brady as a missionary to native people in Sitka, where there was already a Russian Orthodox church. Over several decades, other missionaries from various denominations established missions to work with native Alaskans throughout the district. They also established churches for American immigrants.

Though he never lived for long periods in Alaska, Jackson gained much political influence in shaping the district's religious and political development. Since Alaska government officials were appointed in Washington, D.C., eastern ties were important for political fortunes; Jackson, like some of his counterparts in Hawai`i, had strong eastern ties. Raised in New York State, he was educated at Union College and Princeton Theological Seminary. In 1884, he was appointed general agent for education in Alaska, a position he held until 1908.

As a missionary leader, Jackson took a strong interest in native peoples and focused his attention on native education, health, and welfare. He encouraged various church denominations to open missions in Alaska, partially supporting them with federal funds. He also spent quantities of time in Washington, D.C., lobbying for funds for Alaskan programs. His critics—of which he had quite a few—felt that administering education through missions violated the separation of church and state. They also charged that he put too much effort into native programs and neglected schools for nonnative students. By 1892, the federal government partially supported twenty schools in Alaska, including three for nonnative students in southeastern Alaska and seventeen for native students in church missions scattered throughout the district.

Jackson's friend Brady also gained political influence in Alaska. Although raised in Indiana, Brady had strong eastern ties, for he attended Yale University and Union Theological Seminary. He quickly resigned from his missionary post in Alaska after a policy disagreement with the Presbyterian Board of Home Missions but stayed in Sitka as a merchant. He was appointed a U.S. commissioner in Sitka after the passage of the Organic Act. His proven record of government service—and likely his friendship with the influential Jackson—led to his appointment as governor of Alaska in 1897. He held that office for nine years, coinciding with a period of extremely rapid population growth. As governor, he often served as an advocate for native rights, helping native people lobby for such reforms as native citizenship. Critics felt he was too closely associated with Jackson and Presbyterians in Washington, D.C., whom they felt had excessive influence over Alaskan affairs.

Without doubt, both Jackson and Brady did mix politics and missionary goals. The tremendous influence they both exercised in Alaska's development can be traced in part to their skill in balancing and synthesizing the two. Missionaries in the American West often did not restrict their activities to religion, and neither Alaska nor Hawai`i is an anomaly in this regard. In both places, missionaries strengthened ties between a seemingly "remote" region and seats of power in the eastern United States.

Image and Economics

Since the nineteenth century, many regions of the American West have been strongly affected by popular perceptions. The image of Oregon's Willamette Valley as a promised land urged wagon trains across the Great Plains. The California gold rush attracted new populations spurred by dreams of wealth thought to be attainable—with a little luck—by anyone. In these cases and others, popular image, economic growth, and demographic trends were all integrally connected. Alaska and Hawai`i were no exception. In both places, the American public's perceptions—often greatly exaggerated—have long influenced economic and political developments.

While the year 1898 brought annexation to Hawai`i, changes in Alaska were more sudden and equally far-reaching. This year marked the height of the Klondike gold rush. Thousands of Americans, suffering from economic depression, rushed to Alaska on steamships to start the overland journey to the Klondike. Although their final destination was in Canada, they supported the development of supply towns such as Skagway in southeastern Alaska. Gold was discovered on the Seward Peninsula in 1897, and frustrated Klondike prospectors turned to Alaska. By the summer of 1900, twenty thousand people were camped in the new city of Nome.

In the decade from 1897 to 1907, over fifty new gold-mining camps operated in various parts of Alaska. Most became ghost towns, but some, such as Nome and Fairbanks, survived. Although only a small percentage of prospectors actually became rich, a significant number of American prospectors and suppliers made Alaska their permanent home. Mining corporations quickly replaced independent prospectors, bringing new technologies and company towns. In 1897 Congress authorized railroad building, and many railroad lines sprang up in the opening years of the twentieth century to serve Alaskan mines and ports. Between 1915 and 1923 the Alaska Railroad was built, and in the process Anchorage was founded—now by far the largest city in Alaska.

Alaska's population surge followed similar trends in other parts of the Northwest, which the Klondike gold rush bolstered. Between 1880 and 1900, Seattle exploded from a town of 3,533 to a city of 80,671 residents. Many of the people who came to Alaska had stayed for a time in Seattle, experiencing Washington's rapid growth and seeing the territory gain statehood in 1889. Few American immigrants to Alaska were satisfied with its political status as a district. Seeking more self-government and more representation in the federal government, Alaskans faced the issue of whether to become a territory—the usual next step—or leap to immediate statehood. Proponents of territorial status felt they needed to expand their transportation and communication infrastructure before becoming a state; they feared statehood would eliminate some federal funding. Advocates of immediate statehood, such as Governor Brady, thought that greater home rule and equality with other states in Congress would offset those problems. Pointing to the experiences of Arizona and New Mexico, still territories after some fifty years, Brady feared that if Alaska became a territory, statehood would be a long way off.

To promote immediate statehood, Alaska needed a larger nonnative population. To recruit newcomers, the state had to shake the image of a frozen northern island. That image appealed to the growing tourist traffic but did little to support a true appreciation of Alaska's needs or potential. Many Alaskans felt that federal policymakers knew little about Alaskan conditions and made decisions based on image instead of facts. Successive

As on earlier American mining frontiers, the discovery of gold transformed the Alaskan landscape. A rough tent community in 1900, Nome was by 1908 an established city serving the outlying mines.

B. B. Dobbs (1868–?). Nome, Alaska. *Photograph, July 1900. Alaska State Library (#PCA 12-157), Juneau.*

B. B. Dobbs (1868–?). Front Street [Nome] from Grandstand, Starting of the Dog Teams, All Alaska Sweepstake Race. *Photograph, 1 April 1908. Alaska State Library (#PCA 12-103), Juneau.*

governors traveled to Washington, D.C., correcting congressional misconceptions and striving to provide more accurate information about Alaska's resources. Sometimes this backfired, and they were accused of wintering in Washington to escape Alaska's frigid climate. One frustrated governor published Sitka's average seasonal temperatures in his annual report to prove that he would have been much more comfortable wintering at home than shivering in Washington, D.C.

Overcoming this "icebox" image was a challenge, especially without modern television, film, and transportation. However, Alaska would attract neither population growth nor outside investment until the world knew more about it. Governor Brady took advantage of the St. Louis Exposition of 1904, staging a lavish Alaska Pavilion with attractions such as the huge cabbages that grew in the Matanuska Valley, where twenty-four-hour sunlight offset the relatively short growing season. Photography also helped spread information about Alaskan resources. Some satirists could not resist targeting Alaskan promoters, and one cartoon shows a map of Alaska with a single (Hawaiian?) palm tree rising from the vicinity of Fairbanks. Predictably, neither population nor investments in infrastructure grew fast enough to support a strong statehood movement in the opening years of the century, and in 1912 Alaska became a territory. It would remain a territory for the next forty-seven years.

Today, however, the results of population growth in other parts of the American West have given reason for pause. It is not uncommon in Alaska to hear the comment that if Alaska's environments and quality of living were properly understood, some parts of the state would have the density and pollution of Los Angeles. This may be an exaggeration, but it points to an important irony: many of the people who currently migrate to Alaska go to escape living conditions farther south, and the more people who make that choice, the less of an escape it will be. Other western states face similar dilemmas, as Seattle's skyrocketing population and urban gridlock testify.

If Alaska's exotic image hindered most forms of growth, it spurred the economy in one way. An active tourist industry developed along Alaska's Inside Passage in the late nineteenth and early twentieth centuries. Enjoying deluxe accommodations, tourists dined and socialized on board as their ship glided through narrow channels past rain forests and glaciers. The steamships called in to port cities such as Wrangell, Sitka, and Juneau, where native women lined the docks to offer baskets and carvings for sale. For many travelers, the apogee of their trip was a walk on a glacier, an adventure that was more difficult then than now—especially for women—considering the dress of the day. The protected nature of steamship travel made it acceptable for women to travel on their own, and several women wrote travel journals publicizing the pleasures of an Alaskan expedition. These journals generally emphasized the comforts of traveling on steamships to Alaska, and some explicitly sought to counter misconceptions about the region.

A nascent tourist industry also developed in Hawai`i, although before air travel, the trip was a long one. The first tourist guidebook to Hawai`i appeared in 1875, and by the time of annexation, tourism was bringing in some five hundred thousand dollars annually. The first hotel on Waikiki beach was completed in 1901. However, services for tourists would grow only in response to demand, and demand was hampered partly by the lack of luxury services. This was less of a dilemma in Alaska, where tourists spent most of their time on steamships. In Hawai`i, it meant that the tourist industry grew relatively slowly, a surprising fact considering Hawai`i's beauty and the economic significance that tourism would later assume.

However, Hawaiians were developing other industries that helped diversify their sugarcane economy. In 1903 the Dole plantation experimented with growing pineapples. Under the leadership of James D. Dole, the Hawaiian Pineapple Company purchased the entire island of Lanai in 1922. By the 1930s, pineapples would be Hawai`i's second most important crop. As their opportunities expanded, plantation owners also faced problems. Increasingly, legislation and public pressure regulated treatment of workers on plantations. Workers were also beginning to express resentment of pay scales that were tied directly to racial background. In 1909, some five thousand

By 1920, when this casual snapshot was taken, hula dancing was being promoted to a growing tourist trade as a stereotypical Hawaiian activity.

Ernest Moses. Hawaiian Children in Backyard. *Photograph, ca. 1920. Bishop Museum, Honolulu, Hawai`i.*

Japanese plantation workers went on strike, protesting that they were paid four or five dollars less per month than Portuguese and Puerto Ricans for the same jobs. Plantation owners hired other workers and broke the strike, but they would face more challenges after World War I as workers unionized.

Meanwhile, industrialists in Alaska also faced labor issues. As the number of mines grew there, the Western Federation of Miners became active in Alaska. In 1905 it organized workers at the Treadwell Mines near Juneau, drawing on racial tensions as justification. The miners held a strike in 1905, and federal troops were called in to ensure the mine was not blown up. The Treadwell company met some, but not all, of the workers' demands, and the miners held another strike the next season. This time, though, the company was more prepared and called in workers to break the strike.

The labor tensions in Alaska and Hawai`i were similar to tensions faced elsewhere. Alaska's image as the "last frontier" and Hawai`i's image as a tropical "paradise" made both seem exotic to outsiders. In fact, the people actually living and working in Alaska and Hawai`i struggled with the same economic issues challenging workers in other parts of the American West, the nation as a whole—and the world. As international politics erupted into World War I, Alaska and Hawai`i were by no means isolated.

War and Statehood

The American West has been affected by international ties throughout its history. From the earliest exploration, it was shaped by national rivalries, and it developed under the strong influence of multinational investments and labor forces. In the twentieth century, increasing globalization and advances in technology kept national defense a priority. This emphasis, and the two world wars, changed all parts of the American West, but none more than Alaska and Hawai`i.

One of the arguments for annexing Hawai`i had been to develop a U.S. naval presence in the Pacific. Work began on Pearl Harbor in 1908, and it officially opened in 1911. The navy also built a wireless station on Oahu that enabled communication with ships in the Pacific. Army bases in existence since the Spanish-American War were bolstered, and a large base, Schofield Barracks, opened in 1908 to help protect Pearl Harbor.

World War I affected Hawai`i immediately and intimately, for Hawaiians feared actual attack. When the war broke out, ships in the Pacific, including several German vessels, rushed to Hawai`i to dock in safety. As tensions grew between Germany and the United States, Hawaiians feared that Germany would explode the vessels to destroy Hawaiian harbors. The United States seized the German ships on 5 April 1917, the day Congress passed a war resolution.

Otherwise, Hawaiians responded to the war much as U.S. residents elsewhere. Some islanders went overseas in the military and in support services; those at home bought liberty bonds and worked in relief agencies. Hawai`i experienced the anti-German sentiments prevalent on the mainland. A vigilance corps was formed, teachers had to take loyalty oaths, German language classes were stopped, and some people lost jobs when they were accused of pro-German feelings. The largest firm in Hawai`i, H. Hackfeld & Company, was controlled by German shareholders at the outset of the war and had been the agent for the German ships in Hawai`i. Rumors linked firm officials with pro-German activities. Under the Trading with the Enemy Act, the U.S. government seized most of the shares and sold them to American businessmen in Hawai`i. H. Hackfeld became American Factors, Limited, and remained in American hands after the war, reinforcing American economic dominance in Hawai`i.

Alaska's economy was suddenly and significantly affected by World War I. The tourist industry sagged, since many Americans believed that extended pleasure travel was frivolous. Federal appropriations for transportation and for communication networks slumped during the war, and the development of the infrastructure slowed. In contrast, the major Alaskan industries—fishing, mining, and timber—were tied to international markets for exported resources, and these markets boomed. New salmon canneries and cod-processing plants opened, commercial clam fishing expanded, and crab fishing was undertaken. The war also elevated prices of minerals, and copper mining prospered.

Neither Alaska nor Hawai`i was attacked in World War I. However, at the time—with men and women going overseas, with the economic implications, and with the fear of sabotage in the harbors of Hawai`i—the impact seemed great. Despite their geographic locations, both regions had long been part of global political and economic dynamics.

Like the rest of the country, Alaska and Hawai`i faced significant adjustments in the postwar period. The sudden wartime increases in world demand for Alaskan products were temporary. Some industries, such as fishing, remained active and viable. Others, such as copper mining, suffered more, and many large mines closed in the 1930s. The timber industry had benefited least from World War I, although World War II would bring a much larger boom.

In Hawai`i, owners of large plantations had long recognized the need to cooperate with each other in order to compete with sugar interests on the mainland. By 1933, five firms—known as the "Big Five"—controlled 96 percent of the sugar crop and were also gaining control of the Hawaiian Pineapple Company's operations. The Big Five controlled large shares in transportation, banking, and merchandising.

Many positions of power in the Big Five and its subsidiaries were held by descendants of nineteenth-century American missionary families. These businessmen controlled the Republican party in Hawai`i, and Republicans dominated the territorial legislature. The Big Five also exerted influence over appointments to political and judicial offices. Initially, their Hawaiian Sugar Planters' Association opposed statehood, which would reduce their influence by allowing voters to elect territorial officials. However, in the 1930s, Congress reduced the amount of sugar that Hawai`i could market and increased the quota marketed by states. The association protested, but federal courts ruled that Congress had the right to discriminate against territories when setting such quotas. Thus, when Hawai`i's nonvoting delegate to Congress, Samuel Wilder King, introduced the first Hawaiian statehood bill in 1935, he had the full support of the Hawaiian Sugar Planters' Association.

Racism complicated the statehood issue. Chinese and Japanese immigrants were leaving the plantations and establishing their own businesses in towns. By 1932, about one hundred thousand Japanese lived off the plantations, and their birthrate was high. Their Hawaiian-born children, known as nisei, were U.S. citizens eligible to vote. Some whites feared that if Hawai`i became a state, a Japanese governor would be elected—a prospect that seemed dangerous because Japan was becoming a Pacific power. These concerns about the loyalty of the Japanese in Hawai`i foreshadowed Katamoto's experience in World War II.

Unlike Hawai`i, Alaska was not yet in a position to lobby seriously for statehood. In 1937, only seven cities had over one thousand residents. With just twenty-five hundred miles of public highway built, no road connected Alaska with the contiguous states. In 1940, the territory's population was about seventy-four thousand, a drop in the bucket considering its vast size.

Japan's growing power also caused concern in Alaska. In 1933, Anthony J. Dimond, Alaska's delegate to Congress, warned that Japan was a threat. He requested that Congress bolster military establishments in Alaska and construct a highway between the territory and the rest of the United States to facilitate defense. Aware of Hawai`i's strategic importance in the Pacific, he argued that Alaska was similarly important and should receive similar fortifications. In 1937 he claimed that Japanese fishermen off the coast of Alaska were actually Japanese military spies. In 1940, Congress authorized $29,108,285 for military bases throughout the territory, but construction progressed slowly.

Despite their geographic isolation, it was clear before World War II that both Alaska and Hawai`i were integrally tied to the rest of the United States. Caucasian Americans—as distinct from indigenous peoples or immigrants—dominated both territories political-ly. Leaders in both places were ambivalent toward the federal government; welcoming federal spending, they also felt threatened by some federal policies and wanted more representation in Congress.

The American public, however, did not yet view the two territories as essential to the United States. In 1938, retired Major General Smedley D. Butler had recommended that in the event of an attack on Alaska, the United States should give up the territory without trying to defend it. In January 1940, a poll of Americans in the contiguous states revealed that only 55 percent of respondents felt Hawai`i should be defended if attacked. Ironically, a full 75 percent felt that the United States should help defend Canada in an attack. Clearly, at the brink of World War II, there were major differences of opinion about the importance of Alaska and Hawai`i to the United States.

The American military response to the Japanese invasion of the Aleutian Islands during the Second World War fostered national interest in the region and enhanced Americans' interest in Alaska as a part of their own country.

Unidentified photographer. Japanese Officers, Aleutian Campaign. *Gelatin silver print, 1942–43. National Archives, Washington, D.C.*

Japanese planes bombed Pearl Harbor on 7 December 1941. Hawai`i remained under martial law for almost four years, and the territory was considered a combat zone until April 1944. Perhaps because formal U.S. involvement in World War II started with the attack on Pearl Harbor, awareness of these events remains high today. However, Alaska was actually invaded during World War II—the first time an enemy military had held American soil since the War of 1812.

Japanese aircraft and ships attacked the Aleutian Islands in June 1942. U.S. aircraft fought them off from Dutch Harbor, but the Japanese occupied the islands of Attu and Kiska. From there, they posed a potential threat to military establishments in the Seattle area. The United States and Canada sent bombing raids to Kiska, gradually moving closer and closer as the United States completed air bases on the Aleutians. Some bombers engaged in dogfights with Japanese aircraft. Between combat and treacherous weather conditions, both sides suffered relatively high losses. On 11 May 1943, U.S. forces—infantry, naval ships, and one aircraft carrier—attacked Attu, finally succeeding in retaking it on 29 May. The Japanese evacuated their troops from Kiska before American and Canadian forces came ashore in August.

The war transformed perceptions of Alaska and Hawai`i as the United States rallied to defend them. Residents of both territories fought overseas in the war, contributed to relief work locally, learned first aid, and coped with shortages and rationing. Americans began to think of Alaska and Hawai`i as part of their country—still "exotic islands," to be sure, but islands their neighbor's son had helped protect and islands they might even visit some day.

This shift encouraged a post–World War II boom in tourism. Technological advances in air travel brought both territories closer to the mainland, and the spectacular Alcan Highway made Alaska accessible by car. By the mid-1960s, the number of tourists visiting Hawai`i each year outnumbered the permanent residents. The same would soon be true of Alaska, where in 1975 tourism was already a fifteen-billion-dollar industry.

World War II also brought major demographic changes to both Alaska and Hawai`i, further decreasing isolation. Civilians followed military personnel from the contiguous states, providing support services during the war while seizing the chance to combine patriotism with adventure and economic opportunities. Alaska's civilian population skyrocketed between 1940 and 1950, growing from 74,000 to 112,000 and thus advancing arguments for statehood.

Statehood movements in both Hawai`i and Alaska gained force after the war. Alaskans and Hawaiians still debated the pros and cons of statehood, but by and large residents wanted equal status with states, and new residents from the contiguous states wanted the same representation they had previously enjoyed. The statehood issues became a part of national politics, with both Democratic and Republican parties adopting promises of statehood into their party platforms. However, Alaska and Hawai`i—like many territories before them—found that politics was not a simple proposition. In the early 1950s, the Eisenhower administration supported statehood for Hawai`i—which tended to vote Republican—but was less enthusiastic about Democratic-leaning Alaska. Conservative congressmen from the southern states raised concerns about both territories.

Opponents to statehood worried that "noncontiguity" would destroy the foundation of America's union. With the cold war highlighting national defense, many Americans feared overextension—and saw Alaska and Hawai`i as precedents that would later lead to statehood for places such as the Philippines, Guam, and Okinawa. In American politics, the names of the Founding Fathers are often invoked, and this issue was no exception. Speaking about Hawai`i, Representative Kenneth M. Regan of Texas proclaimed: "I fear for the future of the country if we start taking in areas far from our own shores that we will have to protect with our money, our guns, and our men, instead of staying here and looking after the heritage we were left by George Washington, who told us to beware of any foreign entanglements. I think he had this outpost in the Pacific Islands in mind at that time."

In the conservative climate of the cold war, racism again played a role. According to the 1950 census, Hawai`i's population of about 500,000 consisted of 183,000 Japanese, 114,000 whites, 87,000 native Hawaiians, 33,000 Chinese, and 88,000 people of other ethnic backgrounds including Filipino, Korean, and Portuguese. Alaska's population of 128,643 included some 33,000 native Alaskans. Some conservative Congressmen were loath to admit states that had such ethnic diversity. Reportedly the question cropping up in discussions of Hawaiian statehood was, "How would you like to have a United States senator called Moto?"

For these and other reasons, Alaska and Hawai`i faced a prolonged fight for statehood; leaders from both territories lobbied vociferously throughout the 1950s. Finally, in 1959, Congress voted to admit Alaska as the forty-ninth state and Hawai`i as the fiftieth state.

Hawai`i's economy boomed after statehood, continuing the postwar trend. As in Alaska, the military establishment was a major source of revenue. The cold war ensured that military installations would remain active. The influx of population after the war, and the increase in tourism, supported a major building and industrial surge. Many residents today—especially native Hawaiians and long-term residents who remember the "old" Hawai`i—watch sadly as more and more of the coastline is paved with tourist parking lots and resort hotels. Many parts of the islands are now off-limits to residents who lack the wealth and time to stay at these resorts. Like many other parts of the American West today, Hawai`i is paying the price of popularity—facing the recognition that continued growth may obscure what attracted people in the first place.

In Alaska as well, the debate between development and wilderness preservation continues, pitting economic developers against conservationists. In December 1980, Congress passed the Alaska National Interest Lands Conservation Act, preserving over one hundred million acres of Alaskan lands. Most were closed to development and resource extraction, but this protection can be altered as the economy and political climate dictate. Further concessions were made to developers before the passage of the act, granting subsidies and benefits to help develop other parts of the state. As a result, regions such as Tongass National Forest in southeastern Alaska have been heavily exploited.

With the drop in oil prices in the 1980s, Alaska faced a sudden recession. Its economy had become very dependent on oil revenues; since then, Alaskans have attempted to diversify the economy. The reliance on oil and resource extraction has recently highlighted environmental concerns as disasters such as oil spills clash with pressures to open up the Arctic National Wildlife Refuge for resource exploration. Tourism has been heralded in Alaska, as in the Pacific Northwest, as a way to gain revenue from wilderness lands without destroying them. As Hawai`i's experience demonstrates, however, tourism can bring problems as well as rewards.

Alaska and Hawai`i may still be widely regarded as places to escape to, but they have long been essential participants in the history of the United States and the American West. In the 1990s, Americans increasingly focused on worldwide relationships as well as on national boundaries. No less than the rest of the country, Alaska and Hawai`i are influenced by global events, markets, and ecosystems. The breakup of the Soviet Union revealed tremendous environmental devastation in Siberia, where nuclear residue had been dumped; Alaskans and other Arctic neighbors fear contamination. Problems such as these require broad international cooperation. Alaska's and Hawai`i's isolation has for some time existed only in the popular mind.

Ethnic Diversity and Civil Rights

Throughout the history of the American West, different ethnic groups have mingled in the western landscape. Long before the arrival of nonnative peoples, various Native American groups came together in commerce and in warfare. The American settlement of the West dispossessed Native Americans, and today many of their grievances remain unresolved by the federal government and the courts. Other ethnic groups also faced discrimination. In the twentieth century, issues of civil rights and economic opportunity came to the forefront throughout the American West.

The years following World War I brought changes in native rights in Alaska. Like Native Americans elsewhere, native Alaskans had gained U.S. citizenship under the Citizenship Act of 1924, and this included the right to vote. Some native people in southeastern Alaska had successfully fought for the right to vote a couple of years earlier, but the act of 1924 made their right explicit. That year, William Paul, a Tlingit attorney, was elected to the territorial House of Representatives. One vote in a forty-member House was not substantial, but Paul's election as early as 1924 made a major statement about the potential power of native voters.

The Alaska Native Brotherhood's newspaper, the *Alaska Fisherman*, which circulated in southeastern Alaska, encouraged native people to vote according to their economic interests. Since many were fishermen struggling to remain independent, voting for their economic interests often meant voting against candidates supported by large fishing corporations and other big businesses. Some native peoples in southeastern Alaska were asked to pass tests at the polls—such as reciting the Preamble to the Constitution—before they were allowed to vote. Like African Americans in the American South, they struggled with discrimination in various forms and fought many battles in the succeeding decades.

In Hawai`i, Japanese-born immigrants who had served in the U.S. military returned to discover that they were still ineligible for American citizenship. However, their Hawaiian-born children were U.S. citizens, as were sons and daughters of immigrants of other nationalities. World War I accentuated the strong "melting-pot" sentiments in the United States, and immigrants were encouraged to forget their old country and concentrate on becoming "American." This message was particularly strong in Hawai`i, with its large immigrant population. Here again, Hawai`i's isolation from the mainland United States ended with geography. Immigrants in Hawai`i faced a pressure to assimilate just as did immigrants in the mainland United States.

In the grand tradition of political slogans then and now, the definition of "Americanism" was left somewhat vague. Promoters of "Americanism" insinuated that the country faced a dire moral threat that could be thwarted only by limiting individual liberties. Such sloganism has since proven to be a fundamental part of American politics. During the cold war, similar tactics were used to promote McCarthyism, and in the 1990s the vague but wholesome "family values" slogan spearheaded an assault on liberties deemed dangerous to America's moral fabric. Likewise, in Hawai`i immediately after World War I, "Americanism" actually meant assimilation—the eradication of cultural ties that differentiated immigrants from white Anglo-Saxon Americans.

Champions of "Americanism" targeted foreign-language schools. They viewed these institutions as obstacles to the assimilation of immigrants—and "unassimilated" immigrants, they argued, posed a dire threat to patriotism and national security. The Aloha Chapter of the Daughters of the American Revolution expressed this perception when it declared that its members were "unequivocally opposed to all practices within the borders of the United States of America subversive to the peace and order of our Nation and the undivided allegiance of our people, and unalterably opposed to all foreign-language schools of whatever nationality." Less subtly still, the chapter emphasized that it took a "firm stand for Americanism in its truest and loftiest form, and for one language—that of our heroic Revolutionary ancestors who gave their fortunes and their lives that the United States might live and prosper, and one flag—'Old Glory'!"

With such statements in the air, people who supported foreign-language schools for immigrant children could easily be labeled as subversives. In 1920, the legislature of Hawai`i passed a law entitled "An Act Relating to Foreign Language Schools and Teachers Thereof." As amended in 1923 and 1925, the act imposed special fees on these schools, controlled their curricula, and regulated selection of teachers and textbooks.

The primary targets were 147 Japanese-run schools, which successfully challenged the law in federal courts. The territory then appealed to the U.S. Supreme Court, which upheld the decision in favor of the Japanese schools on the grounds that the law abridged fundamental individual rights guaranteed by the U.S. Constitution. This particular effort to force assimilation was thwarted, but similar language issues are very much evident in the American West today—notably in California, where the use of the Spanish language in schools has become a volatile issue.

The 1930s saw changes in federal policy toward native peoples throughout the United States, including Alaska. In 1934 Congress passed the Indian Reorganization Act (Wheeler-Howard Act) and in 1936 extended the provisions of the act to Alaska, authorizing the U.S. Department of the Interior to establish reservations for native Alaskans. The reservation lands would not belong to native peoples but would be held "in trust" by the U.S. government.

The act raised fears and controversy among both native and nonnative Alaskans. Nonnative developers feared land would be tied up in reservations. Native peoples were well aware that reservations often meant dependency, with too little land and resources to support the communities. At the same time, they had no other way to protect their lands against the encroachment of the growing white population. By 1946, a total of seven reservations had been established—one of which was later ruled illegal—and three villages had voted down reservations. By 1950, some eighty other villages had requested reservations, but by that time the federal government was again encouraging assimilation of native peoples, and the requests were not granted.

The 1930s also saw another movement to protect native Alaskan lands, this one initiated in Alaska by native peoples. In 1929 at the Alaska Native Brotherhood annual convention in Haines, Tlingit and Haida leaders decided to press the federal government for compensation for lands taken when Alaska was transferred from Russia. Before they could do so, it was necessary for Congress to pass a law to authorize them to sue the U.S. government. This law was passed in 1935, but it was 1959 before a decision was handed down, the courts eventually ruling in favor of the Tlingit and Haida plaintiffs. This lawsuit helped lay the foundation for a statewide struggle for native land settlements, a struggle that culminated in the Alaska Native Claims Settlement Act of 1971.

Meanwhile, World War II had an immense impact on intangible attitudes of and toward ethnic groups who had long suffered discrimination. People from Alaska and Hawai`i who had served in the military returned to civilian life with knowledge of how people lived in other parts of the world. They also had demonstrated that they were willing to give their lives for their country. Those who experienced prejudice while in the service, or who faced it when they returned home, were ready for a change. For some time during the war, servicemen in Alaska were prohibited from speaking with native women—and this prohibition extended to native servicemen, who were not permitted to talk to their own sisters. Many Hawaiians who were targets of oppression also served in the military—Japanese, native Hawaiians, Chinese, Portuguese, Filipinos, and Koreans—and returned to Hawai`i knowing that they still faced a domestic struggle. As one Japanese serviceman, Katsumi Komentani, put it: "We have helped win the war on the battlefront but we have not yet won the war on the homefront. We shall have won only when we attain those things for which our country is dedicated, namely, equality of opportunity and the dignity of man." Just as the Pribilof Islanders had returned home from their internment camp with new political ties and a determination to change their status, so too military personnel from Alaska and Hawai`i returned home with much the same resolve. All over North America, the fight for civil rights and equal opportunity escalated after World War II.

In Alaska and Hawai`i, this struggle continued to involve access to land and natural resources. Alaskan statehood made it necessary to distribute land between the state and the federal government, and this process quickly became even more complicated than anticipated. The statehood act entitled the state of Alaska to control 104 million acres of land. Native Alaskans protested the state government's land selections, and in 1966 U.S. Secretary of the Interior Stewart Udall froze selections in an effort to encourage the fair settlement of native claims. The issue—always urgent in the eyes of native peoples— became urgent in the eyes of developers when oil was discovered on the Alaskan Arctic coast in 1969. To build a pipeline, developers needed access to the land Udall had frozen, and they joined those pressing for a solution. Unlike the earlier Tlingit-Haida settlement of 1959, the issue was decided through passage of congressional legislation rather than through the courts. The Alaska Native Claims Settlement Act of 1971 (ANCSA) established twelve regional corporations in Alaska—with land and funds—and a thirteenth corporation, without land, for native Alaskans living outside Alaska. Village corporations were also established. Alaskans born before December 1971 with at least one-quarter native background became shareholders of these corporations. The settlement has proven extremely complex and problematic, and some provisions are under revision today. ANCSA's corporate alternative to reservations has not become a model for native land settlements in the United States or Canada. Nevertheless, native groups and governments in both countries continue to pursue resolution of native land issues through negotiation and legislation rather than through litigation alone.

In Hawai`i, the focus on land distribution intensified after statehood. Due to the centralized power of the Big Five, control of Hawaiian lands was less than democratic. Thirty percent of the land in Hawai`i was owned by twelve families, and 27 percent belonged to much smaller property owners. Most people of native Hawaiian and Asian descent could not afford to purchase land. Many homeowners, then and now, own structures on land that is only leased.

Issues of land distribution, resource control, environment, and development remain central in both Alaska and Hawai`i and promise to spark controversy for some time. Both places are still mingling important grounds for a number of ethnic groups, and both must continue to address questions of civil rights and discrimination. Both retain sometimes tense relationships with the federal government as they balance local autonomy with federal involvement. Tourism continues to grow, with visitors flocking from North America, Europe, and Asia.

These developments echo similar phenomena in other parts of the American West. Alaska and Hawai`i—and the rest of the American West—have long been influenced by international economies and politics. As the twenty-first century opens, there is a growing recognition that political boundaries are purely artificial as far as issues of human welfare, economic prosperity, and biological and cultural diversity are concerned—that the welfare of all countries is vitally connected and must be played out on a global stage. With this shift in perceptions, the apparent isolation of regions such as Alaska and Hawai`i will be deemphasized in view of their integral ties to the United States and the world. Like other areas of the American West, Alaska and Hawai`i have had much experience confronting local concerns in the context of government from afar. Their history will prove valuable as they approach the global challenges of the twenty-first century.

Bibliographic Note

Several general histories of Hawai`i have contributed to this chapter and are useful sources of additional information: Gavan Daws, *Shoal of Time: A History of the Hawaiian Islands* (New York, 1968); Lawrence H. Fuchs, *Hawaii Pono: A Social History* (New York, 1961); Edward Joesting, *Hawaii: An Uncommon History* (New York, 1972); Noel J. Kent, *Hawaii: Islands under the Influence* (New York, 1983); and a three-volume work by Ralph Kuykendall, *The Hawaiian Kingdom* (Honolulu, 1938–67). John Whitehead's article "Hawai`i: The First and Last Far West?" *Western Historical Quarterly* 23, no. 2 (May 1992): 153–77, persuasively points out that many developments in the history of the American West occurred first in Hawai`i.

Eighteenth-century journals of European visitors to Hawai`i reflect early contact between native Hawaiians and Europeans, albeit through European eyes. The journal of Captain James Cook is perhaps the best known. Sketches that explorers made of native Hawaiians, and records of artworks they collected, can lend some insight into early interactions. Sketches are reproduced in Bernard Smith, *European Vision and the South Pacific*, 2d ed. (New Haven, 1985); Adrienne L. Kaeppler's *Artificial Curiosities: Being an Exposition of Native Manufactures Collected on the Three Pacific Voyages of Captain James Cook, R.N.* . . . (Honolulu, 1978), discusses both explorers' sketches and native artwork collected in the South Pacific during Cook's voyages.

Nineteenth-century writings by missionaries and colonists provide information about colonization and also reflect attitudes of the foreign newcomers. One useful account is that of the American missionary Hiram Bingham, who resided in Hawai`i from 1820 to 1840. He recorded both his own observations and his account of Hawaiian history in *A Residence of Twenty-One Years in the Sandwich Islands* (Rutland, Vt., 1981). Alfons L. Korn, ed., *The Victorian Visitors* (Honolulu, 1958), focuses on the period from 1861 to 1866 and quotes from letters of Sophia Cracroft and Lady Franklin and from the diaries and letters of Queen Emma of Hawai`i. Portions of the journal of Mary Chipman, who accompanied her husband on a whaling voyage to Hawai`i in 1856, are reproduced in Stanton Garner, ed., *The Captain's Best Mate: The Journal of Mary Chipman Lawrence on the Whaler Addison, 1856–1860* (Hanover, N.H., 1966). Readers who prefer biography will be interested in Marjorie Sinclair's *Nahi`ena`ena: Sacred Daughter of Hawaii* (Honolulu, 1976), an account of the life of Kamehameha I's daughter, who was influenced by missionaries and the changes brought by colonization but also remained committed to her heritage.

Quite a few other published works and archival sources also reflect activities of American missionaries in Hawai`i. Patricia Grimshaw's *Paths of Duty: American Missionary Wives in Nineteenth-Century Hawaii* (Honolulu, 1989), is particularly useful; it reflects women's perspectives and offers an excellent and detailed impression of missionaries' daily lives and concerns. The information about Lucy Goodale is drawn from this insightful book, which also has an extensive bibliography of published primary and secondary sources. Barnes Riznik, *Waioli Mission House, Hanalei, Kauai* (Kauai, Hawai`i, 1987), provides a very useful case study of an American Protestant mission founded in 1834 and now open to the public as a historical museum. Bob Krauss, with W. P. Alexander, *Grove Farm Plantation: The Biography of a Hawaiian Sugar Plantation*, 2nd ed. (Palo Alto, Calif., 1965), is a biography of George Wilcox, son of the American Protestant missionaries Abner and Lucy Wilcox. It contains much information about their mission work and also documents how the children of missionaries often became active in business, politics, and philanthropy. The Grove Farm Plantation, still a working plantation, is open to the public; its archives include some journals by Abner and Lucy Wilcox as well as plantation records (including pay scales) and photographs. This chapter drew on research conducted in those archives, and I am grateful to the superintendent, Barnes Riznik, and his staff for their welcome and assistance.

Numerous publications explore the mixing of peoples in Hawai`i and/or focus on one ethnic group. A native Hawaiian author, Samuel Kamakau, recorded information about Hawaiian culture and mythology. D. Barrere has edited two volumes of Kamakau's writings: *Ka Po'e Kahiko: The People of Old* (Honolulu, 1964) and *The Works of the People of Old* (Honolulu, 1976). Linda S. Parker, *Native American Estate: The Struggle over Indian and Hawaiian Lands* (Honolulu, 1989), includes information on American appropriation of native Hawaiian lands. Michi Kodama-Nishimoto, Warren S. Nishimoto, and Cynthia A. Oshiro, eds., *Hanahana: An Oral History Anthology of Hawaii's Working People* (Honolulu, 1984), gives accounts by speakers from several different ethnic groups. The experiences of Usaburo Katamoto are presented in this work. Dorothy Ochiai Hazama and Jane Okamoto Komeiji, *Okage Sama De: The Japanese in Hawai`i, 1885–1985* (Honolulu, 1986), Dennis M. Ogawa, *Kodomo No Tame Ni = For the Sake of the Children: The Japanese American Experience in Hawaii* (Honolulu, 1978), and Alan Takeo Moriyama, *Imingaisha: Japanese Emigration Companies and Hawaii, 1894–1908* (Honolulu, 1985), discuss people of Japanese background in Hawai`i. Gary Y. Okihiro, *Cane Fires* (Philadelphia, 1991), considers the anti-Japanese movement in Hawai`i from 1865 to 1945. Works on Chinese immigrants include Tin-Yuke Char, ed., *The Sandalwood Mountains: Readings and Stories of the Early Chinese in Hawaii* (Honolulu, 1975), and Clarence E. Glick, *Sojourners and Settlers: Chinese Migrants in Hawaii* (Honolulu, 1980). Edward D. Beechert, *Working in Hawaii: A Labor History* (Honolulu, 1985), discusses the contract labor system, the development of a labor movement in Hawai`i, and the conditions under which many immigrants work. Another useful book on labor conditions affecting immigrants is Ronald Takaki's *Pau Hana: Plantation Life and Labor in Hawaii, 1835–1920* (Honolulu, 1983). John F. McDermott, Jr., Wen-Shing Tseng, and Thomas W. Maretzki, eds., *People and Cultures of Hawaii: A Psychocultural Profile* (Honolulu, 1980), discusses contemporary circumstances of various populations in Hawai`i, as does Andrew W. Lind, *Hawaii's People*, 4th ed. (Honolulu, 1980). Works of fiction also illuminate ethnic experiences. I gained insights from Milton Murayama's *All I asking for is my body*, new ed. (Honolulu, 1988), about a young Japanese American growing up on a plantation, and from various stories in Frank Stewart, ed., *Passages to the Dream Shore: Short Stories of Contemporary Hawaii* (Honolulu, 1987).

A particularly helpful general introduction to Alaskan history is Joan M. Antonson and William S. Hanable, *Alaska's Heritage* (Anchorage, 1985). Designed as a textbook, this highly readable work is also an excellent source for adult audiences, and it made many valuable contributions to this chapter. Another engaging survey, with a long bibliographical essay, is Claus-M. Naske and Herman E. Slotnick, *Alaska: A History of the 49th State*, 2d ed. (Norman, 1987).

There are many published primary sources from the periods of maritime exploration, the maritime fur trade, and the Russian occupation of Alaska. Journals of maritime explorers such as Captain James Cook and Captain George Vancouver are available in published form. Excerpts from some of these journals are reproduced in Robert N. De Armond, ed., *Early Visitors to Southeastern Alaska: Nine Accounts* (Anchorage, 1978). Sketches made by early explorers to Alaska and the Northwest Coast are reproduced and insightfully discussed by John Frazier Henry in *Early Maritime Artists of the Pacific Northwest Coast, 1741–1841* (Seattle, 1984).

Many important translations of Russian-American writings have been edited by such scholars as Richard Pierce, Lydia Black and Basil Dmytryshyn, and E.A.P. Crownhart-Vaughan. Too numerous to list comprehensively here, they are excellent sources for readers who want more detailed information about the Russian-American period. Petr Aleksandrovich Tikhmenev's *A History of the Russian-American Company*, originally published in 1861–63, has been translated and edited by Richard A. Pierce and Alton S. Donnelly (Seattle, 1978) and is a vital source of information about Russian-American activities. Excerpts from writings of Russian Orthodox missionaries in Alaska can be found in Michael Oleksa, ed., *Alaskan Missionary Spirituality* (New York, 1987). Secondary sources also illuminate the Russian colonization of Alaska and interactions between Russians and native Alaskans. These include, but are not limited to, articles in a very useful anthology edited by S. Frederick Starr, *Russia's American Colony* (Durham, N.C., 1987).

Many secondary sources focus on Alaska after transfer from Russia to the United States. Ted Hinckley's *The Americanization of Alaska, 1867–1897* (Palo Alto, Calif., 1972) is very helpful, as is his biography *Alaskan John G. Brady: Missionary, Businessman, Judge, and Governor, 1878–1918* (Columbus, Ohio, 1982). Missionary writings and travel accounts from the late nineteenth and early twentieth centuries help reveal native-white relations, albeit from nonnative perspectives. Writings by missionaries include the following: Sheldon Jackson's *Alaska and Missions on the North Pacific Coast* (New York, 1880); Eva McClintock, ed., *Life in Alaska: Letters of Mrs. Eugene S. Willard* (Philadelphia, Pa., 1884); *Hall Young of Alaska, "The Mushing Parson": The Autobiography of S. Hall Young* (New York, 1927); and a work by a Quaker missionary, Charles Replogle, *Among the Indians of Alaska* (London, 1904).

Alfred P. Swineford, the second district governor of Alaska, wrote *Alaska: Its History, Climate, and Natural Resources* (Chicago, 1898). Engaging travel accounts of visitors to Alaska, some of whom traveled as tourists on steamships, include Oskar Teichmann, ed., *A Journey to Alaska in the Year 1868, Being a Diary of the Late Emil Teichmann* (New York, 1963), E. Ruhamah Scidmore, *Journeys in Alaska* (Boston, 1885), Septima M. Collis, *A Woman's Trip to Alaska* (New York, 1890), and Ella Rhoads Higginson, *Alaska: The Great Country* (New York, 1912).

The newspaper *Tundra Times* is a useful source of native voices. Some recent publications reflect native perspectives on contemporary developments such as the Alaska Native Claims Settlement Act. These include Robert D. Arnold et al., *Alaska Native Land Claims* (Anchorage, 1976), Frederick Seagayuk Bigjim and James Ito-Adler, *Letters to Howard: An Interpretation of the Alaska Native Land Claims* (Anchorage, 1974), Lael Morgan, *And the Land Provides: Alaskan Natives in a Year of Transition* (Garden City, N.Y., 1974), and Thomas R. Berger, *Village Journey: The Report of the Alaska Native Review Commission* (New York, 1985). Dorothy Knee Jones's excellent and concise work *A Century of Servitude: Pribilof Aleuts under U.S. Rule* (Washington, D.C., 1980) contributed the information about the Pribilof Aleuts found in this chapter.

Several works focus on political history and Alaska's attempt to define a mutually satisfactory relationship with the federal government. Ernest Gruening's *The State of Alaska* (New York, 1968) discusses these themes as seen through the eyes of a prominent Alaskan politician. Ernest Gruening also wrote a short but detailed work on the Alaskan statehood movement, *The Battle for Alaska Statehood* (College, Alaska, 1967). Another concise and helpful book on the statehood movement is Claus-M. Naske, *An Interpretative History of Alaskan Statehood* (Anchorage, 1973).

The Alaska Geographic Society publishes a well-illustrated, highly readable quarterly, *Alaska Geographic*. Some titles in this series focus on regions of Alaska; others address various cultures; still others discuss historical themes or industries. Readers will find more details about material covered in this chapter in *Alaska's Native People* (Anchorage, 1979) and *The Aleutians* (Anchorage, 1980), both edited by Lael Morgan. Likewise, the *Alaska Journal* and *Alaska History* are excellent sources for additional historical information on Alaska.

Many people assisted me in my research for this chapter, and I wish space permitted me to thank them all individually here. I especially want to express my gratitude to the staff of the Grove Farm Plantation and the Bishop Museum for their generous attention during my research visits; to John Whitehead for helpful bibliographic recommendations; to Donald Worster for advice about research in Hawai`i and for recommending research at the Grove Farm Plantation; and to the University of Victoria for a Faculty Research and Travel Grant that made the research trip to Hawai`i possible. I have greatly appreciated the goodwill and good humor of Clyde Milner, Carol O'Connor, and Marni Sandweiss, with whom it has been a pleasure to work. Finally, I thank Geoff Wyatt and Muriel Wyatt for their valuable editorial assistance.

Chapter Seventeen

Landscapes of Abundance and Scarcity

W I L L I A M   C R O N O N

J ust after midnight on 24 March 1989, the *Exxon Valdez* ran aground on Bligh Reef in Alaska's Prince William Sound. Its captain, his judgment clouded by alcohol, had maneuvered the supertanker out of ordinary shipping lanes in an effort to avoid icebergs floating south from the great Columbia Glacier. Accelerating into a mile-wide gap between the ice and the reef, and apparently forgetting that the ship (itself nearly one-fifth of a mile long) required over half a mile to turn, he had already left the bridge when the tanker shuddered to a halt, its hull ripped open as if by an enormous can-opener. So began the worst oil spill in American history.

Over the next two weeks, eleven million barrels of oil flooded into the sound while crews desperately worked to pump the tanker dry. If they had failed in this task, or if the ship had sunk before they completed their work, an additional forty-two million barrels might have spilled into the sea. As it was, the oil formed an enormous slick on the surface of the frigid waters and began to come ashore on islands and beaches in many parts of Prince William Sound. Ultimately, it would drift hundreds of miles to the southwest, traveling the same distance that separates Cape Cod and Cape Hatteras on the Atlantic seaboard. It would coat over twelve hundred miles of shoreline with a black, evil-smelling slime and kill hundreds of thousands of marine birds and mammals, in addition to countless fish and shellfish.

Responses to the catastrophe often seemed frustratingly incompetent. The contingency plans that oil corporations and government agencies had claimed would handle such an event proved grossly inadequate. What was worse, precious time was wasted in the hours immediately after the ship ran aground—the weather stayed calm and the oil dispersed little for almost three days—as officials worried about the legal and political liabilities they might incur by moving too aggressively and thereby perhaps acknowledging their responsibility for the spill. Those who acted first were the owners of small fishing vessels; they instantly realized that the oil threatened their very livelihoods, but they had none of the special equipment or training needed to handle the challenge. Only after the dimensions of the disaster had become clear and public outcry was beginning to swell nationwide were full-scale relief efforts finally mounted. In the end, over ten thousand workers labored for months to clean beaches, save animals, and wash rocky coastlines with heated seawater. Ironically, some of their efforts probably did more harm

The wreck of the Exxon Valdez on 24 March 1989, which sent 11 million barrels of oil into Prince William Sound, dramatically illustrated the environmental costs of the West's extractive industries and underscored the fragility of the great wilderness landscapes of Alaska.

Nick Didlick. Exxon Clean-up of Valdez Oil Spill. *Color photograph, 1989. Reuters/Bettmann Newsphotos, New York, New York.*

than good by disrupting fragile ecosystems even further. The final cost of the cleanup would be measured in the hundreds of millions of dollars, and Exxon's legal liability would be more than one billion dollars. Many experts believed that coastal and marine ecosystems would need decades to recover.

The *Exxon Valdez* story is dramatic enough in its own right, but it can also stand as a symbol for much broader processes that have characterized the environmental history of the West as a whole. The oil spill in Prince William Sound came just three decades after Alaska entered the union as America's forty-ninth state, and the calamity marked a turning point in Alaskan history. Before statehood, much of Alaska had been terra incognita, a vast expanse of land known mainly to its native inhabitants and only lightly touched by development. Like earlier Wests, its very obscurity tempted those who hoped to make a quick fortune from the untapped wealth of nature. Alaska held out the promise of great natural abundance, whether in the goldfields that brought tens of thousands to the Klondike in the 1890s, in the fisheries that annually produced millions of cases of canned salmon in the early decades of the new century, or in the oil fields that were first discovered near Cook Inlet just as Alaska became a state. During World War II, Anchorage emerged as a classic western boomtown, exploding in population as the federal government poured immense sums of money into its military bases and as would-be entrepreneurs began to speculate about the economic potential of its vast hinterland.

Then came the discovery of petroleum at Prudhoe Bay in 1968, and the entire state boomed in an orgy of real and anticipated oil revenues. Along the way, Alaskan natives negotiated the largest (albeit still problematic) land deal in American history, environmentalists mounted a losing but innovative legal battle against the pipeline that would carry North Slope oil to market, and Americans suddenly awoke to the fact that their northernmost state was rich not just in oil but also in wilderness. And so the development of the young state went hand in hand with its *un*development: in 1979, President Jimmy Carter would set aside well over one hundred million acres of national parks, forests, and wildlife refuges in Alaska to make sure that its natural legacy would not be lost as oil lands were tapped. Only in this context can one see that the *Exxon Valdez* represented more than just an economic or ecological calamity; it also threatened the much less tangible spiritual values that America's "last great wilderness" had come to represent.

In the minds of many Americans, Alaska in the twentieth century moved from being a frontier of nearly unlimited natural abundance and exuberant economic promise to being a region that was both fragile ecologically and vulnerable economically. The same might be said of the West as a whole. America's many "Wests" have all begun as frontiers of real or perceived abundance whose regional identities have eventually been shaped by the experience of emerging scarcity. Alaska's identity flowed as much from the failure of the Klondike as from the initial golden dream, as much from the collapse of the canneries as from the early flood tide of salmon, as much from the wreck of Exxon's supertanker as from the extraordinary boom years that followed the discoveries at Prudhoe Bay. In much the same way, most western communities were born in the promise of plenty but did not come into their own until westerners had tested the limits of that promise to forge a new way of life on the land.

In tracing the environmental history of the western landscape, one must carefully distinguish a number of competing narrative trajectories. The story of frontier migration leads eventually to the story of emerging western regions, each with its particular cultural adaptations to the local environment. It is a long tale of people moving to frontier areas, seizing abundance, encountering scarcity, and remaking the land and themselves in the process. The result is the West as we know it today: not one single region but many smaller regions with distinctive environments and cultures. The Great Plains, Texas, the Rocky Mountains, the Colorado Plateau, the Basin and Range, the Desert Southwest, California, the Pacific Northwest, Alaska, and the Hawaiian Islands: each is a region in its own right, with its own smaller subregions like California's Sierra Nevada, Central Valley, Coast Ranges, and the sprawling urban worlds of the Los Angeles Basin and San Francisco Bay. A full environmental history of the West would have to explore the special cultural and ecological landscapes of all these places.

Set against this narrative are stories about institutional forces that have undermined regional diversity and autonomy over the course of western history. Cities and hinterlands have become linked by common markets and have grown to be more like one another. Energy resources like oil and electricity have enabled westerners to ignore the scarcities of their local environments in order to build communities of apparent abundance even in the midst of former deserts. The managerial hierarchies of the modern corporation have brought their own brands of homogeneity to the West, as have the bureaucracies of federal, state, and local governments. These narratives are all about regional (and national) homogeneity, the ability of people to use their technologies and institutions to remake the lands around them so that deserts and forests, mountains and valleys, eventually come to share common cultural forms.

These different stories are all entangled, of course, as the *Exxon Valdez* itself demonstrates. The setting for its special drama was one of the most beautiful and challenging environments of the modern West, a landscape that requires all who live there to change their habits and assumptions to meet the expectations of the land. The ship cargo was profoundly tied to the resource economy that sustains not just Alaska but also the places for which that oil was originally destined. The owners and managers of the ship, even its troubled captain, perfectly represented the corporate institutions that called the ship into being. The legal context of the oil spill, and the political responses it evoked, embody a long tradition of government involvement with interstate commerce, environmental regulation, and western lands. And its effects on the Alaskan "wilderness" lie at the very heart of recent controversies about the future of the western environment. In the long dialectic between scarcity and abundance that has shaped the landscapes of the American West, the ship on Bligh Reef embodies most major themes of the region's environmental history.

Fearing the End of Abundance

An environmental history of the modern West can begin, predictably enough, with the 1890 census pronouncement that Frederick Jackson Turner made famous in his 1893 essay "The Significance of the Frontier in American History." By declaring that "free land" could no longer be the wellspring from which the nation drew its democratic promise, Turner articulated what many Americans were already beginning to fear. America's frontier era was drawing to a close. Ideologues like Frederic Remington and Theodore Roosevelt joined Turner in worrying that the loss of the frontier would sap the nation's virility, exacerbate its class tensions, and undermine the dominance of its white races. Democracy itself might be threatened as a result.

Such fears eventually proved to be mistaken or groundless, but they rested on an even deeper anxiety that has had more lasting consequences. As the historian David Potter has noted, Turner and his compatriots, in declaring that the frontier was coming to an end, were expressing a more general concern that American abundance was giving way to scarcity. Their fears that good farmland would no longer be so easily available for would-be homesteaders suggested that other resources might also disappear from the American landscape. The forests that put roofs over American heads might vanish. The rivers that brought water to American cities might run dry. The coal mines that fueled American factories and heated American homes might give out. If these things happened, the nation's prosperity would surely erode and, with it, the political and personal freedoms that depended on prosperity for their survival. To escape such a fate, Americans must take serious steps to preserve the natural abundance that from the start had been the foundation of their nation's greatness.

Fears about resource exhaustion became increasingly common during the second half of the nineteenth century. In 1864, George Perkins Marsh published *Man and Nature*, a sprawling survey of the role that forests and other resources had played in the rise and fall of civilization. In it, he argued that Greece, Rome, and other Mediterranean civilizations had grown to greatness on the products of the forest and had collapsed when deforestation led to fuel scarcity, soil erosion, and desertification. In particular, he believed that forests at the heads of large watersheds were critical to maintaining the flow of water in navigable rivers: without their regulating effect on runoff, floods and droughts would become more common. Casting his eye on the heavily lumbered forests of his beloved northern New England, he warned that the United States was following the same path as Rome and would reach the same tragic destination if its citizens did not curb their reckless destruction of the woodlands.

In the decades that followed, Marsh's plea would be echoed by growing numbers of scientists, politicians, and corporate leaders. In 1876, an obscure rider to a congressional appropriations bill called on the Department of Agriculture to survey the nation's timber resources to determine "the probable supply for future wants" and "the means best adapted for their preservation and renewal." The result was Franklin B. Hough's *Report upon Forestry*, published in 1878, which looked to Marsh's book for its inspiration. Following Hough's lead, the 1880 census included a massive volume, authored by Charles Sprague Sargent of Harvard, surveying the forestlands of the United States. Although its statistics were roundly attacked by the lumber press, they confirmed Marsh's warnings that deforestation was occurring in many parts of the United States. Partly in response, Congress in 1886 formally recognized the Division of Forestry in the Department of Agriculture, where the German-born forester Bernhard Eduard Fernow began to conduct systematic investigations of the nation's timber resources.

Concerns about resource exhaustion and environmental degradation were not limited to woodlands. In 1878, John Wesley Powell offered to Congress his prescient *Report on the Lands of the Arid Region of the United States*. In it, he argued that the original land survey and homestead laws were radically inappropriate west of the Mississippi

River and would lead to environmental degradation unless significantly modified. Arid land settlement, Powell said, would require either small irrigated farms or large ranches, neither of which could be successfully conducted in the 160-acre units that the Homestead Act mandated. Taking a lesson from Mormon settlements in Utah, Powell urged Congress to revise existing land laws to make western settlement a more collective and regulated process. His views were supported by a report of the Public Land Commission that same year, but Congress failed to act on either set of recommendations. Powell's report joined Marsh's book as a classic of nineteenth-century conservation thought, but half a century would pass before its viewpoint would be fully embodied in government land policy in the West.

Ironically, one of the most important early responses to fears about deforestation came not in the West but in upstate New York—which would in fact become a model for subsequent conservation efforts in the West. In 1883, the New York legislature forbade any new sales on three-quarters of a million acres of public woodland in the Adirondack Mountains. Two years later, all state lands in the Adirondacks were declared to be a "forest preserve," and in 1894 their protected status was written into the state constitution. Henceforth, New York declared, the Adirondacks should remain "forever wild." In making this decision, the legislature was responding to the appeals of wealthy hunters and tourists who had flocked to the mountains in the years following the Civil War, but it was also responding to Marsh's prophecies. Among the most effective arguments on behalf of the Adirondack forest preserve were Marshian claims that deforestation in the mountains would endanger the water supplies of New York City and the Erie Canal by promoting irregular seasonal runoff and altering regional climate patterns. New York might then go the way of Rome: floods and droughts, it was said, would ravage the state's economy if its citizens failed to look after their timbered watersheds.

Despite New York's pioneering role, concerns about deforestation—about the transformation of wooded abundance into treeless scarcity—would have their greatest effect in the American West. Responding to the same public pressures that had created the Adirondack forest preserve, the U.S. Congress in 1891 passed a new statute revising many of the nation's existing land laws. Section 24 of that act, added almost as an afterthought, authorized the president to withdraw from settlement any tract of public land "wholly or in part covered with timber or undergrowth, whether of commercial value or not, as public reservations." As in the case of the Adirondacks, the apparent intent was to protect the heads of navigable rivers, particularly those that flowed past major urban centers, from the disruptions that Marsh had predicted might follow deforestation. Over the next two years, President Benjamin Harrison responded by setting aside fifteen separate reserves totaling over thirteen million acres, all in the trans-Mississippi West. Several contained precious little woodland but were requested by towns and cities whose residents feared their water supplies were threatened by overgrazing.

The 1891 Forest Reserves Act marked a turning point in federal involvement with the American West. Henceforth, there would be a steady reduction in public lands that were still available for private sale and settlement and a corresponding increase in public lands that were permanently reserved for government use. Moreover, the act laid the foundation for an entirely new federal relationship with the American environment. No one at the time had any way of knowing that Section 24 would have these consequences, and in fact it passed with little debate or public comment. But as the number of forest reserves grew, they posed a new problem for the government. Formerly, the chief task of government bureaucrats relative to the public domain had been to sell off land to yield large cash flows for the U.S. Treasury (which still had no income tax as a source of revenue) and for the rapid development of frontier areas in the American West. Now they faced an altogether different task: to oversee the proper use of land that would never pass into private hands and to make sure that government-owned resources were properly managed for the public good. This transition from public land disposal to public land management marked the real start of federal conservation efforts in the West and would become a dominant theme of the region's environmental history for at least the next half century.

Over the next fifteen years, these implications of the 1891 act became abundantly clear to all Americans. The revolution in federal land policy was spearheaded by an elite cadre of professional bureaucrats that Theodore Roosevelt appointed to key posts in his administration. Among these, the most prominent and influential was Gifford Pinchot. Born into a wealthy New York family, Pinchot had been educated to a life of privilege at elite eastern schools, preparing himself for the unlikely career his father had helped him choose: forestry. In 1896, he served on the National Forest Commission of the National Academy of Sciences, which issued recommendations about how best to manage the new western forest reserves. The result was the Forest Management Act of 1897, which would serve for the next sixty years as the fundamental law governing forest policy in the United States. Partly as a result of his experience with the commission, the next year Pinchot succeeded Fernow as chief of the Department of Agriculture's Division of Forestry, thus gaining the platform from which he would launch one of the most ambitious and successful careers in American conservation history.

The Division of Forestry initially seemed a rather unlikely place from which to direct a revolution. It had only eleven employees when Pinchot took office in 1898 and a budget of just $28,520. Worse, since the new reserves were all located in the Department of Interior, the division was without forests to manage. For these reasons, Pinchot's immediate goal was to expand the size of his operation and ultimately wrest control of the reserves from the Interior Department. Within three years, his budget had increased fivefold and his staff more than fifteenfold. By 1902, 179 people were working for Pinchot, many of them young men serving apprenticeships as part of their forestry education.

This remarkable expansion was the indirect product of a tragedy that changed the course of history: on 6 September 1901, an assassin's bullet killed William McKinley just half a year into his second term of office. His death catapulted Theodore Roosevelt into the presidency. Roosevelt had already revealed his fascination for America's frontier past and feared that the "closing frontier" might endanger the nation's democratic heritage. Now he was in a position to protect what he saw as the frontier legacy by conserving America's natural resources and by preserving the remnants of a vanishing

Theodore Roosevelt and John Muir, both passionate outdoorsmen, represented different approaches to land management. Roosevelt believed in the efficient use of forest lands—for both commerce and recreation—through careful government management. Muir, who at first supported such federal control, later repudiated the government's utilitarian aims and turned his attention to promoting the spiritual value of the wilderness.

Unidentified photographer. John Muir and Theodore Roosevelt, Glacier Point, Yosemite. *Photograph, 1903. Courtesy Research Library, Yosemite National Park, California.*

wilderness landscape where one could recover the "vigorous manhood" that the "rough riders" of an earlier day had enjoyed as their birthright. Pinchot immediately gravitated toward Roosevelt, and the two men found much in common with each other. Pinchot soon emerged as the master conservation strategist of the Roosevelt White House, wielding great influence in Washington despite his unexalted bureaucratic position.

The most striking proof of Pinchot's influence came in 1905, when Roosevelt transferred sixty-three million acres of forest reserves—the great majority of them in the West—from the Interior Department to the Agriculture Department and placed them under Pinchot's control as the head of the renamed U.S. Forest Service. But the more important innovation had less to do with who controlled those acres than with how they were managed. More than any other agency, the Forest Service epitomized Progressive Era conservation. Pinchot and his followers committed themselves to promoting professional management, believing that only those with scientific expertise should decide how best to use forest resources. A hunger for quick profits might tempt corporations and private landowners to cut the forest more rapidly than it could replenish itself. Politicians might be wooed too easily by local constituencies eager for rapid development no matter what its cost. Only a scientific forester—so the argument ran—could know enough and be disinterested enough to look after the long-term interests of people and forests alike.

To produce this new style of government manager, Pinchot relied on the new schools of forestry—all more or less inspired by German traditions—that were appearing at Cornell, Ann Arbor, Biltmore, and Yale (the latter financed by a gift from Pinchot's father). Young men—and they were all young men in the early years—who hoped to become foresters got their training from these schools and then made their way into the Forest Service to be inculcated with the values it represented. Energized by an elite esprit de corps and a vision of disinterested public service, the young foresters fanned out across the western landscape with a goal of managing public forests so that frontier abundance could be saved from scarcity and could last forever.

Like other progressives, Pinchot, Roosevelt, and their followers strongly believed in what the historian Samuel P. Hays has called "the gospel of efficiency." For progressives, the greatest villain was the waste of resources, so that "the people" could not enjoy their fullest use. Pinchot liked to borrow and extend Jeremy Bentham's famous utilitarian principle as the central goal of conservation: "the greatest good for the greatest number for the longest time." To waste resources, to use them inefficiently, was to steal from future generations. The correctness of this principle seemed so self-evident that it was hard for conservationists to see their opponents as anything other than venal and corrupt. Short-sighted landowners, dishonest bureaucrats, domineering monopolies, and craven officeholders all had bad motives for putting their own interests above the public good.

There was, inevitably, a darker side to this vision of scientific management. Despite their democratic rhetoric—their apparent defense of "the people" and "democracy" against "monopoly" and "corruption"—the progressive conservationists were suspicious of many democratic institutions. They tended to look more toward executive authority than toward the legislature to enact their reforms, and they saw the good of "the whole" (by which they often meant well-to-do middle-class easterners like themselves) as being more important than the special concerns of individual constituencies. Perhaps because of this, they were attracted to strong leaders who projected a slightly messianic air—Roosevelt and Pinchot being good examples of the type. Progressives preferred expert knowledge to the messier judgments of public debate. They generally preferred centralized authority and decision-making to local control. Pinchot's Forest Service was notable for the decentralized organization of its district system but ultimately derived its authority from Washington rather than from local communities. In their pursuit of what they saw as democratic ends, the progressives sometimes thought it necessary to circumvent democratic means.

And so it was perhaps inevitable that Roosevelt and Pinchot should come into conflict with people who did not share their vision. Among those who opposed the expanding system of national forests were senators and representatives from the western states, who saw more and more of their local landscape being removed from development and placed under Forest Service control. The conflict came to a head in a famous confrontation in 1907. Congress sought to limit Roosevelt's ability to withdraw western land from settlement by passing an appropriations bill that required the president to have congressional permission before creating any new national forests in Colorado, Idaho, Montana, Oregon, Washington, and Wyoming. The list included the most heavily timbered states in the nation and the ones most hostile to Washington's control; all were in the West. Roosevelt had no choice but to sign the bill, but the night before doing so, he ordered the creation of new national forests on sixteen million acres of western lands. These "midnight forests" enraged western congressmen and perfectly express the mingled idealism and arrogance that typified conservation during the Roosevelt years.

Federal conservation efforts at the turn of the century were by no means confined to forests. As politicians identified new environmental problems, they created new laws and bureaucratic institutions to address those problems. For instance, the first two decades of the twentieth century saw significant efforts to diminish threats to key endangered animal species by expanding government regulation of hunting. In 1900, the Lacey Act banned the interstate transport of mammals and birds that had been killed in violation of state law, thereby lending federal support to state efforts at wildlife protection. Recognizing that the reproductive cycles of many species did not respect state or national boundaries, the federal government declared, in the Migratory Bird Act of 1913, that its own jurisdiction took precedence over state laws relating to migratory game and insectivorous birds. This in turn paved the way for the landmark Migratory Bird Treaty with Canada in 1916, establishing for the first time a durable framework for regulating the critical flyways of North America. Free access to an unrestricted hunt, which had been among the defining experiences of American frontier settlement since at least the days of Daniel Boone, would all but vanish in the years ahead, giving way to far more restricted hunting conducted under the watchful eyes of scientists and managers working in the service of a regulatory state. Conflicts over who should have access to traditional hunting grounds often erupted between local communities and newly professionalized game wardens, with representatives of state and national governments working to redefine and expand the concept of poaching. In the process, Indians and other minority ethnic groups were often forced to retreat from hunting and fishing grounds on which they had long depended, sometimes for generations.

Similar efforts at fish and game regulation occurred elsewhere in the government as well. In 1905, the new Bureau of Biological Survey consolidated earlier federal programs designed to research and regulate the effects of animals on agricultural crops. Starting in 1915, it would lay the foundation for a systematic campaign to destroy predators and other "vermin" species—coyotes, wolves, grizzly bears, mountain lions—to protect livestock and to promote the increase of game species such as deer, elk, and moose, which were highly prized by hunters. The Forest Service would also join these efforts. To oversee animal species in less terrestrial environments, the Office of the U.S. Commissioner of Fish and Fisheries moved in 1903 to the Department of Commerce and Labor and became the Bureau of Fisheries, bringing increasingly coordinated oversight to the nation's fish populations, many of the most important of which spawned in western rivers and grew to adulthood off the west coast. Separate agencies overseeing Alaskan fish and fur seal resources would be transferred to the new bureau over the next half decade.

At the same time, the United States joined Canada, Russia, and Japan in seeking to avert the extinction of Alaskan and Siberian seals, eventually signing the Fur Seal Treaty of 1911, which banned pelagic (open-sea) sealing and also tried to regulate hunting at key seal rookeries like Alaska's Pribilof Islands.

Although efforts such as these did not often succeed in stabilizing animal populations at former levels, they did establish the principle that government had an essential role to play in trying to protect—or, in the case of predators, exterminate—wild animal species. More important from the point of view of western environmental history, these early efforts at federal regulation also furnish a classic example of the early abundance of a natural resource giving way to real scarcity, indeed, nearly to extinction. Attempts to respond to such changes created new regulatory institutions that helped alter not just western regional attitudes toward the environment but national ones as well. Increasingly, natural areas and animal populations would be seen not as landscapes of freedom, not as frontiers of endless natural abundance, but as endangered landscapes of scarcity, so fragile in the face of human destructiveness that only careful management could ensure their survival.

This sense of fragility lay behind the Antiquities Act of 1906, which enabled the president to establish national monuments to protect areas of special archaeological, historical, or scientific importance. Despite its apparent emphasis on antiquities—by which its authors generally meant endangered Indian ruins—the act soon became a tool for Roosevelt and his successors to set aside any area of natural or historical value. Thus, within a few years Roosevelt was able to use the act not only to protect places like Montezuma Castle in Arizona and El Morro in New Mexico—both legitimate "antiquities" —but also Arizona's Grand Canyon and a large section of Washington's Olympic peninsula, whose claims to protection clearly rested on their unusual scenic beauty. Roosevelt had already in 1904 stretched the meaning of the 1891 Forest Reserves Act to set aside the first federal wildlife reservation at Florida's Pelican Island—a wetland nesting area whose chief value had far more to do with birds than with trees. It was soon followed by more than fifty other such bird reservations—most of them not especially forested—from Florida to Alaska. When it came to scenic wonders and nesting grounds, at least, the days of limitless abundance, easy exploitation, and unregulated hunting were apparently at an end.

It is important not to misunderstand Roosevelt's interest in protecting game species and areas of extraordinary natural beauty. The goal of setting aside tens of millions of western acres as national forests, of withdrawing them from sale under the public land laws, was not to protect them as permanent natural areas; rather, it was to prevent their destruction so that they could be managed and harvested in perpetuity as a resource for future generations of Americans. The same was true of game refuges and protected nesting grounds: even though hunting was illegal within their boundaries, their purpose was not to abolish hunting but to ensure its perpetuation by protecting the reproductive cycles of key game species. What Roosevelt saw as the uncontrolled freedom of earlier frontier landscapes might have to be abandoned, but the consequence would be to protect the way of life and cultural values that the frontier had supposedly nurtured in America. The progressive conservationists saw no conflict between intelligent exploitation of natural resources and the long-term survival of those resources. Despite their sometimes apocalyptic rhetoric about what might happen if Americans failed to conserve natural resources, conservationists like Roosevelt and Pinchot were fundamentally optimistic about the ability of their own reform agenda to set the country on a course that would ensure permanent national prosperity.

The Reclamation Dream

Nowhere was this optimism more obvious—or more important to the West—than in water policy. By the time Roosevelt became president, westerners had for more than two decades been working on their own and seeking federal support to promote the construction of dams and irrigation systems on rivers and streams throughout the region. The classic dilemma of the western environment was that much of the terrain received far too little rain or snow to permit successful farming. Annual precipitation of much less than twenty inches was the norm almost everywhere except in the mountains and in the Pacific Northwest; in many areas—including the San Joaquin and the Imperial valleys of California—annual precipitation fell below ten inches. No ordinary crop could survive such conditions, though westerners did show considerable ingenuity in pushing the limits of certain crops, notably wheat, in what came to be called "dryland farming." Worse, when rain did fall or the winter snows melted, the resulting floodwaters too often raced down canyons and arroyos in muddy torrents that left little but destruction in their wake. If only these floods could be stayed in their journey and delivered to an otherwise parched earth, then natural scarcity could give way to artificial abundance.

It would be hard to exaggerate the compelling power of this bountiful vision for most Americans during the late nineteenth and early twentieth centuries. The ability of water to transform the arid West seemed wondrous, an unambiguous blessing that tempted irrigationists into flights of impassioned rhetoric that resorted sooner or later to biblical metaphors. "Irrigation," wrote the indefatigable booster William Ellsworth Smythe, "is a miracle." Just as the Nile had once watered ancient Egypt, just as "a river went out of Eden to water the Garden," so might the dry soils of the West burst into flower if the rivers could be made to share their liquid bounty with the land. Anyone who doubted this fact had only to look at what the Mormons had accomplished in Utah since the 1850s. With only the simplest of tools, their own skill, and a powerful religious hierarchy to aid them, they had captured the waters of the Wasatch Range and had turned the valley of the Great Salt Lake into astonishingly fertile farmland. Powell had appealed to the Mormon example in his *Report on the Lands of the Arid Region*, and other irrigationists did likewise. The Rio Grande Western Railroad even went so far as to produce a bird's-eye map of Mormon Utah, which drew direct parallels between its geography and that of the Holy Land. In this striking if rather distorted piece of cartography, Utah's Jordan River flowed toward the Great Salt Lake to water the Mormon Zion in much the same way that Palestine's Jordan River flowed toward the Dead Sea to water the land of Canaan. The title of the map suggests how powerfully its prophetic vision resonated with the American imagination: water would make of the West a "promised land."

Early federal efforts to help fulfill this vision tended, like most nineteenth-century resource policies, to rely on the public land laws. In 1877, Congress passed the Desert Land Act, which was modeled on an experimental effort two years earlier to promote

With high hopes, but little regard for geography or climate, the Rio Grande Western Railroad promoted Mormon Utah as a fertile Garden of Eden in the Promised Land.

Rio Grande Western Railroad, Publisher. Map Showing the Striking Similarity between Palestine and Salt Lake Valley, Utah. *Print, ca. 1899. From William Ellsworth Smythe,* The Conquest of Arid America *(1899).*

irrigated farming in Lassen County, California. Under the act, which applied to all western states except Colorado, individuals could purchase up to 640 acres of land (one square mile, four times the amount available under the Homestead Act) at a price of $1.25 per acre. They were required to pay only 25¢ per acre at the time they filed and then had three years to "make satisfactory proof of reclamation" before paying the balance of their debt to obtain clear title. Land was to go only to those individuals who genuinely intended to settle and improve their land; it was not intended for speculators whose only goal was to resell it after its price had risen. The act's basic intent was to promote irrigation not by direct federal investment but by making land available at relatively low prices to individuals who promised to make private investments in water technology.

Like most such land laws, the Desert Land Act was loosely drafted and poorly enforced, so that abuses of its original intentions were soon common. Would-be owners poured a few buckets of water onto their land and swore they had irrigated it. Dummy entrymen were used by large investors to amass much more than the intended square mile of land. To control water and land for their cattle, ranchers claimed narrow snake-like strips along the banks of streams or dug irrigation ditches that were promptly abandoned as soon as clear title had been obtained. The Desert Land Act undoubtedly encouraged a modest increase in irrigated acreage in parts of the West, but not on anything like the scale that its promoters had hoped.

More important, the Desert Land Act helped identify two questions that would bedevil western water policy until at least the 1920s. The first had to do with who should benefit from federal efforts to promote irrigation. Should irrigation laws, like the Homestead Act before them, encourage the development of a Jeffersonian landscape dominated by small farmers? Or should they permit farms of whatever size, no matter how large, as long as the owners could successfully irrigate the land? Even in this 1877 act, the twentieth-century tension between family farm and agribusiness was implicit. The second question was a corollary of the first: who should provide the capital that would make irrigation possible? Immediately after the Desert Land Act was passed, early critics (including Powell in his *Report on the Lands of the Arid Region*) were arguing that most irrigation districts could not be successfully organized without capital investments of one million dollars or more. From this perspective, it seemed naive to expect individuals who owned only a single square mile to be able to afford the investments in dams, canals, and other water-handling technologies without which farming would be impossible. Wealthy individuals and large corporations would have to supply the needed capital—in which case the limit of 640 acres would almost surely have to be abandoned—or else the government itself would have to make the basic investment. How to resolve these two questions in actual law and practice would be the major challenge of water policy for the next half century.

Not until Roosevelt became president would the federal government abandon its general policy of avoiding direct investment in western irrigation. In the meantime, water policy was left largely to the states and to private individuals. During the second half of the nineteenth century, western water law at the state level acquired the foundations it retains to this day. Under English common law, the use of water in a river or stream was attached as a right of ownership to the land along its banks. One could do whatever one wanted with that water as long as one did not diminish its flow, alter its course, or degrade its purity. Yet this common-law practice had already begun to change in eastern parts of the United States as the owners of canals and water-powered factories began to build dams that flooded riparian lands and fundamentally altered the flow of rivers. So long as such changes constituted "productive use," the courts were willing to tolerate them even though they violated traditional riparian rights. A new body of "appropriative rights" therefore began to emerge in American law.

The arid West posed an even greater challenge to common-law traditions. In desert areas, it was simply not possible to withdraw water from a river, use it for irrigation or other purposes, and then return it without diminishing its quantity or quality. And so westerners, starting with miners who needed water for sluicing gravel in the California goldfields, began to embrace the doctrine that whoever first put water to productive use acquired a permanent right to it. That right was not absolute, since one would lose it if one did not continue "beneficial use," but the divergence from common-law riparian rights was still very great indeed. During the 1880s, Colorado gave its name to this new water doctrine by laying claim to all surface waters within its boundaries, nullifying riparian rights to their use, and taking upon itself the task of enforcing water rights acquired by prior appropriation. If early settlers used up all the water in a stream that flowed through their lands, then later settlers had no claim whatsoever to water for their own use. And so the principle of prior appropriation came to be known as the Colorado Doctrine, which was quickly adopted by most states in the Rocky Mountain region.

Elsewhere, the triumph of appropriative rights was less complete. In California, the famous *Lux v. Haggin* court decision of 1886 held that riparian rights to water did indeed accompany the government sale of lands along a river unless that river's water was already being used by some other landowner at the time the original sale occurred. Under this "California Doctrine," the balance between appropriative and riparian rights depended on which came first, water use or land sale. Riparian rights tended to be favored by large cattle ranchers, whose use of water was relatively passive, whereas appropriative rights were favored by miners, irrigators, and factory owners, whose water use was more active and interventionist. *Lux v. Haggin*, although not a popular decision with the many Californians who believed that riparian rights favored large landowners, did establish the not unreasonable principle that different users of water had different needs, which might in turn entail different ways of conceiving legal property rights to the resource. This principle was in some ways carried to its logical extreme in yet a third body of water law, the Wyoming Doctrine, in which the Wyoming constitution claimed title to all water within the state's boundaries and retained the power to alter any existing private rights or appropriations that did not serve the public interest. This more collectivist definition of water use became the basis for water law in most of the Great Plains states.

In a region where water was at once extremely scarce and absolutely essential for most development, it is hardly surprising that none of these doctrines prevented persistent conflict—and endless litigation—over who should have the right to use this most precious of resources. And yet however problematic these doctrines might be, they did begin to establish the legal framework that made it possible for westerners to exploit the water on which regional economic growth depended. Scarce water was the key that could unlock the hidden abundance of an arid land. Throughout the West, water law rested on the utilitarian premise that both the unused water and the land through which it flowed would be "wasted" unless people intervened to ensure their "reclamation." This usage of the word *reclamation* was fairly new at the time, having appeared in the English language only in the middle decades of the nineteenth century. In England, John Stuart Mill spoke of "the reclamation of waste lands"; in the United States, lands worthy of reclamation were labeled "waste," or "alkali," or "arid," or "new." Whatever the adjective applied to them, they all existed in a state of nature that prevented their exploitation until human ingenuity could "reclaim" their potential—a potential that people tended to see as "natural" even though it served human desires and cultural values far more than the needs of existing ecosystems. So powerful was this sense of a "wasted" "natural" potential waiting to be "reclaimed"—as if a prior *un*wasted landscape had once been lost, Eden-like, and now needed to be claimed again—that by the 1890s virtually all discussion of irrigation and watershed manipulation occurred under the heading of "reclamation." Congress had a Committee on Irrigation and Reclamation of Arid Lands, and the federal agency that would be given responsibility for promoting irrigation would eventually be known simply as the Bureau of Reclamation.

The creation of that agency could not occur until the federal government was willing to embrace the mission of reclamation in a more direct way. That did not happen until it seemed clear that state and private irrigation efforts had reached an impasse. In 1887, California had implemented the Wright Act, creating new irrigation districts that could take collective control of their water rights wherever two-thirds of the electorate so voted; bond issues could then be underwritten by the tax revenues of the district and used to support investments in irrigation. Although the act helped double irrigated acreage in California by the end of the century, and although such districts would play an increasingly important role in promoting the growth of agribusiness in the early twentieth century (after large landowners gained greater control over the bonding process), their initial successes were relatively modest. The same was true in other parts of the West as well. By the 1890s, roughly seven million acres had been "reclaimed" with irrigation, an amount that seemed low relative to the "wasted" potential. Moreover, a large number of the private irrigation enterprises already under way were hardly prospering; by the start of the new century, the majority would be in or near bankruptcy.

And so westerners began to lobby for greater federal intervention. Starting in 1891, a series of "Irrigation Congresses" organized by William E. Smythe brought together engineers, lawyers, journalists, corporate leaders, government representatives, and others interested in promoting irrigation. Their initial goal was to persuade the federal government to extract from the remaining public domain all irrigable land so that it could be turned over to the states for improvement—a policy known as "cession." Washington was not ready for so dramatic a gesture, but in 1894 the Carey Act made available to each western state a grant of one million acres that could be developed by irrigation companies and then sold to farmers. Although this new act encouraged irrigation in some states—most notably Wyoming and Idaho—it shared with the 1877 act a failure to identify adequate sources of capital to "reclaim" the millions of acres it contemplated developing. Neither private corporations nor the states were willing to risk large sums on such risky investments, and so by the end of the century less than twelve thousand acres had been patented under the Carey Act. The facts that it was passed in the midst of a major economic depression and that states differed widely in their ability and willingness to take advantage of it also help explain its apparent failure.

By the time Roosevelt became president in 1901, the modest progress achieved by state, local, and private efforts to develop western irrigation seemed incommensurate with the grand prophetic vision that the word *reclamation* conjured in the minds of westerners and most other Americans. In his first State of the Union message in 1901, Roosevelt made clear his belief that only the federal government was up to the task at hand. "Great storage works," he said, "are necessary to equalize the flow of streams and to save the floodwaters. Their construction has been conclusively shown to be an undertaking too vast for private effort. Nor can it be best accomplished by the individual States acting alone. . . . It is properly a national function, at least in some of its features." Despite the apparent logic of Roosevelt's argument, one might reasonably speculate that the underlying problem with irrigation projects had more to do with the rate at which investment was occurring than with the intrinsic inability of private capital or state governments to provide funding. As with the transcontinental railroads, federal law may have been trying to accelerate developments whose time had not yet come; as with the railroads, an unsurprising consequence was that such ventures initially proved only marginally viable, heading into bankruptcy at an alarming rate. And so one should be careful not to take at face value Roosevelt's conclusion about the necessity or the proper form of federal intervention. The fact that his prophecy came true may say more about the seductive power of the reclamation dream than about the inevitability of the government's role in realizing it.

Roosevelt's prophecy did indeed prove self-fulfilling. When Representative Francis G. Newlands, of Nevada, proposed legislation dramatically expanding the federal role in western reclamation, he had little trouble moving it through Congress, supported as it was by the president and by the vigorous lobbying efforts of the California lawyer George Maxwell's National Irrigation Association. The resulting Reclamation Act of 1902—more familiarly known as the Newlands Act—clearly ranks with the 1785 Ordinance and the Homestead Act as one of the most important American land laws ever passed. The act created a revolving Reclamation Fund, which would receive revenues from the sales of all public lands in sixteen western states. Money from the fund was to be used for constructing dams and irrigation systems in those states. Individuals who purchased the resulting water were to pay high enough fees to replenish the fund within a specified number of years, thereby making it a perennial source of investment capital for reclamation projects throughout the West. (One should note that even if this fund had been fully repaid on schedule—which it was not—it would still have represented a significant federal subsidy, since water users were not expected to pay any interest on the money they had been loaned. As repayment periods stretched from ten to twenty to forty years, the invisible subsidy implied by these interest-free loans ballooned accordingly.) To make sure that the benefits of government-funded irrigation went to small farmers and not to large speculators or corporate farm operations, the act specified that no single landowner could purchase water to irrigate more than 160 acres of land. The act thus sought to continue a long tradition in American land law, dating back to the Homestead Act and before, of trying to promote agrarian communities of single-family farms as the proper foundation for American democracy.

The responsibility for managing the revolving fund was assigned to the new Reclamation Service (renamed the Bureau of Reclamation in 1923). Appealing to scientific expertise and centralized executive authority to legitimate its work on behalf of "the people," the office paralleled Pinchot's Forest Service as an expression of Progressive Era conservation values. From 1902 to 1914, the new agency was headed by Frederick H. Newell, a leading civil engineer who had worked closely with Newlands in framing the Reclamation Act. Work first began on the Salt River Project in Arizona and the Truckee River Project in Newlands' Nevada district, but by 1906 almost all of the western states had projects under way. Newell assembled a superb team of engineers who designed and built not just dams and reservoirs but also the infrastructure—roads, rail lines, cement factories, construction camps—necessary to erect them. Numerous technical problems arose almost from the outset—destructive floods, leaky geological formations, defective designs, faulty construction—but in general the engineering achievements of the act's first two decades were its most impressive legacy.

Measured in economic terms, though, the government's accomplishments under the Newlands Act were more ambiguous. In part because the Reclamation Service had no formal affiliation with the Department of Agriculture, its engineers were less attentive than they might have been to the soil and drainage conditions that farmers would face in adopting irrigation. Speculators tended to buy up land in the vicinity of new dam projects, selling it to farmers at high enough prices that little was left over to pay back the revolving fund. Settlers often moved into an area long before water was available, but they had to stay on their as yet unproductive land for up to five years if they hoped to acquire title to it. Many were undercapitalized—a classic problem of small farmers under the Homestead Act as well—and thus lacked the tools and equipment to make proper use of their government-supplied water once it arrived.

By 1910, it was already clear that farmers were having difficulty meeting their obligations to the Reclamation Fund, so Congress stepped in with the first of what would eventually be a long series of extensions delaying deadlines for making payments. As time went on, the Bureau of Reclamation more or less ignored the rule against sales of water to farm units larger than 160 acres, and large agribusiness operations came to control an increasing share of irrigated acreage in the West. By the early 1920s, federal reclamation projects had produced not much more than an additional one million acres of irrigated land, though the infrastructure was in place for significant expansion in the future. At the same time, local and private efforts based on the model of the California irrigation district had increased their acreage significantly, so that federal projects accounted for only about one-tenth of the regional whole. Throughout the West, whether constructed with private or federal capital, the irrigated rural landscape was dominated by federal bureaucracies and large landowners, with the government showing a clear tendency to favor large long-term water users over small ones. Contrary to the original promise, the society that emerged in "reclaimed" desert areas was a far cry from the Jeffersonian vision of agrarian democracy and single-family farms.

The Power of a Dam

Ironically, it was the Great Depression of the 1930s and the rising urban-industrial demand for electricity that would help secure federal reclamation efforts in the West. In 1928, Congress authorized the construction of a 726-foot-high dam in Black Canyon on the Colorado River. Once complete, it would be the tallest dam in the world. Unlike earlier projects, in which the generation of hydropower had been an incidental by-product of water impoundment for irrigation and flood control, Boulder Dam—so called because the initially proposed construction site was the one the public remembered—was designed to earn back a significant share of its cost from the sale of electricity. Its generators would be owned and operated by the Southern California

Edison Company, the Los Angeles Metropolitan Water District, and the City of Los Angeles—all of which suggested how much the reclamation agenda was shifting from its original rural focus.

Elwood Mead, then serving as head of the Bureau of Reclamation, promoted the Boulder Canyon Project as an example of multipurpose river-basin development. If the bureau conceived of its mandate in an integrated fashion, he argued, it could facilitate regional economic growth by providing construction jobs for unemployed workers, irrigation for farms, flood control for residents of river valleys, water for urban drinking supplies, and electricity for farms, factories, and cities alike. Perhaps most important, sales of electricity to urban and industrial consumers were a far more promising way to pay off deficits in the Reclamation Fund than trying to extract payments from small farmers who were perennially in arrears. In short, Boulder (later Hoover) Dam was the answer to a reclamationist's prayers. Its success would foster a series of integrated projects—Grand Coulee and associated dams on the Columbia, the Central Valley Project in California, the Colorado-Big Thompson Project in Colorado, and other equally grandiose initiatives—each of which would contribute to the Bureau of Reclamation's growing influence throughout the West. More important still, Boulder Dam and the projects that followed it also signified the increasing role that metropolitan institutions and urban political-economic power would henceforth play in reshaping the western environment.

For the Bureau of Reclamation was by no means the only entity promoting major water projects in the West. By 1900, the growing cities of San Francisco and Los Angeles were seeking guaranteed access to water to ensure their growth well into the new century. Civil engineers and politicians in both cities cast their eyes east toward the Sierra Nevada, where cold mountain peaks captured much of the state's precipitation in their winter snowpack. Los Angeles found its "river out of Eden" in the Owens Valley at the southern end of the mountains; San Francisco located its in the Hetch Hetchy Valley just north of Yosemite. Although the struggle to seize these areas for urban water supplies met with severe political resistance—from farmers and boosters who had hoped to develop the Owens Valley for agriculture and from preservationists and nature lovers who sought to protect Yosemite National Park from invasion—in the end the metropolitan demand for water proved irresistible. The Los Angeles Aqueduct was completed in 1913, carrying water 233 miles from the mountains, and the Hetch Hetchy Aqueduct—155 miles long—was finished two decades later. By then, both systems were producing electricity as well as water in such abundance that neither city could use anything close to the full supply. As a result, both cities were in the curious position of being able to sell water to farms and suburban districts in the desert environs around them, yielding important sources of revenue on which both soon became dependent. No matter whether the original source was local, state, or federal, the capital that had been invested to flood Hetch Hetchy, the Owens Valley, and Boulder Canyon made it possible for Californians to enjoy astonishingly cheap water even in the midst of desert landscapes that had never before known such abundance.

One can see in these massive projects and in the other bureaucratic legacies of Progressive Era conservation the compromises that westerners and other Americans

To supply the water and electric power that would ensure the continued growth of Los Angeles, federal and local authorities initiated massive engineering projects that fundamentally altered the landscape of more distant parts of the West. The first Los Angeles aqueduct, completed in 1913, brought water from the Owens Valley 233 miles away and destroyed the economic future of that rural valley on the eastern side of the Sierra Nevada. The construction of Boulder Dam, completed in 1935, led to the creation of Lake Mead in the middle of the Nevada desert.

James Bledsoe. The Alabama Gates of the First Los Angeles Aqueduct. *Gelatin silver print, ca. 1913. Photograph courtesy of the Los Angeles Department of Water and Power.*

Unidentified photographer. Hoover Dam (once Boulder Dam). *Gelatin silver print, ca. 1960. Las Vegas News Bureau Archives Photograph. Courtesy of the Special Collections, University of Nevada-Reno Library.*

were willing to make in the service of the reclamation dream. Turner had argued that the frontier had been a landscape of freedom, in which Americans had discovered the liberty and independence that characterized them as a nation. As embodied in the Homestead Act and in the land-limitation clause of the Newlands Act, frontier settlement was supposed to be for brave individuals, for yeoman farmers in the Jeffersonian mold, for the "little guy" hoping to seize opportunities unavailable in more settled and constricted lands. So said the myth, and for all its distortions it had exercised great influence over Americans' notions of themselves. But the deeper environmental reality was that the frontier had served first and foremost as a landscape of abundance—as mythical as it was material—and this abundance had made possible the way of life Americans considered essential to their national identity. If some measure of personal freedom had to be sacrificed to protect this more fundamental good, then the price might be worth paying. When Pinchot defended "the greatest good for the greatest number for the longest time," he was arguing for constraints on individual freedom—the freedom of people to enter the public domain to cut timber, graze cattle, plant crops, use water in whatever ways they liked—in order to defend a longer lasting, better managed, more collective abundance. Whether confronting the natural scarcities of the western desert or the artificial scarcities of the cutover forest, the conservationist agenda was to manage these scarcities so as to "reclaim" their usurped abundance.

In one way or another, this imperative to manage scarcity in the service of a reclaimed abundance underpinned most western environmental politics in the first half of the twentieth century. Certainly the water reclamation projects derived their emotional and political force from it. So did the famous Colorado River Compact of 1922, in which the states of the upper and lower Colorado River Basin, feuding over the anticipated consequences of the Boulder Canyon Project and finally turning to the federal government to arbitrate between them, agreed to divide the waters of the river into two halves as a not entirely successful way of preventing California from receiving the lion's share of the division. (The compact relied for its statistics on exaggerated estimates of the river's flow, thereby allowing California—the earliest effective user as a result of Boulder Dam—to appropriate more than its proper share of the actual total.) But the imperative to manage scarcity to protect abundance reached well beyond water. Its fullest embodiment was almost surely in the national forests, with their elite cadre of disinterested, scientifically trained foresters managing a natural resource for the national good. Beyond the forests, it was still possible until 1934 for individual homesteaders to stake their claims as farmers or ranchers on the public domain, but in that year the Taylor Grazing Act finally withdrew this right for most of the remaining public lands. Homesteading continued but fell from thousands of new claims per year to a few hundred. Symbolically, 1934 thus marked the culmination of the long process whereby management and regulation replaced open access (or theoretical open access) to the public domain. For all practical purposes, the era of free land was finally at an end.

Arguably, the greatest environmental disaster of that era was the exception to prove the rule. Starting in 1931, the rains failed on the southern plains, so that farms that normally received eighteen inches per year—the minimum for many crops—received as little as eleven or twelve. Crops died as the parched soil cracked in the sun and temperatures soared above one hundred degrees for weeks at a time. The drought would last for a decade, but what really made this climatic event a disaster was the fact that so many plains farmers had expanded their acreage in response to the boom years of World War I, investing in tractors and other new equipment to work farms that were significantly larger than before. The heavy debts they took on to finance this expansion bore heavily on them during the depressed agricultural conditions of the 1920s, so that by the time the rain failed in the early thirties, vast stretches of the southern plains lay open to the blistering heat and windstorms. With no ground cover to hold down the desiccated soil, dozens of extraordinarily severe dust storms occurred every year throughout the 1930s, giving the region a new name: the Dust Bowl. A single famous storm in May 1934 blew three hundred million tons of dust into the air, some of it traveling all the way to New York and Washington and finally landing on ships far out in the Atlantic Ocean. Thousands of families abandoned their homes, took to the road, and headed to California as "Okies," the refugees from Oklahoma and elsewhere whose ordeals were so movingly described in John Steinbeck's *The Grapes of Wrath* (1939).

In the face of such stark proof that the frontier dream of abundance had given way to scarcity and despair, government officials stepped in to offer expert technical assistance with their new techniques of integrated regional planning. The Forest Service organized the planting of over two hundred million trees to form "shelter belts" that would supposedly discourage soil from blowing. The Soil Conservation Service (a New Deal creation of the Franklin Roosevelt administration) promoted new techniques of contour plowing and dry tillage to discourage erosion and retain soil moisture more effectively. The Civilian Conservation Corps provided labor for these and other initiatives. Most striking, the Resettlement Administration declared that in some of the worst-hit areas, farming was simply not viable: the original frontier settlements had been a mistake. In such areas, abandoned farms were bought by the government to be converted to rangeland and pasture. And yet even this symbol of apparent failure and defeat had an optimistic underpinning. In the eyes of the planners, scarcity had been caused by the ignorant and ill-conceived use of natural resources. If settlement patterns and land-use practices could be rationalized, abundance and prosperity could be restored even to so troubled a landscape as the Dust Bowl. In the end, the return of the rains in the early 1940s—and the increasing use of fossil groundwater from the immense Ogallala Aquifer for irrigation—made the dust storms seem like a passing nightmare that technology and better management could prevent in the future. Few bothered to speculate what might happen when the aquifer itself eventually began to give out.

The multiagency assault on the problems of the southern plains was characteristic of the 1930s and carried the progressive conservation agenda to a new level of complexity. For many Americans, it seemed that economic and ecological problems were reinforcing each other in ways that required the integrated perspectives embodied in the Boulder Canyon Project. The result was a new commitment to regional planning and an effort to link conservation initiatives with government programs promoting unemployment relief, investment in economic infrastructure, and social reform. In the East, the most famous example of this new integrated planning approach was the Tennessee Valley Authority (TVA), whose dams, electrical generators, highways, and agricultural reforms transformed the economic life of an entire region. For a time, the TVA seemed to prove that regional planning could solve virtually all the nation's ills.

The nearest parallel in the West was the Columbia River. There, efforts to develop the watershed in an integrated way had to contend with fierce competition between the Bureau of Reclamation and the Army Corps of Engineers over who should develop prime dam sites. Until the appearance of the bureau, the corps had been the government's chief dam builder, and its members were not at all happy about the bureau's growing prominence in the West. In 1937, the corps succeeded in completing the celebrated Bonneville Dam, but in 1941, the bureau finished the even more celebrated Grand Coulee Dam, which at that time was the largest concrete structure in the world, backing up a lake 150 miles long. In the end, the tensions between the two agencies resulted in the creation of a third entity, the Bonneville Power Administration, charged with selling electricity generated from the new dams.

Despite this interagency rivalry over dam construction, the reclamation projects on the Columbia River brought to the Pacific Northwest environmental and economic changes similar to those in California. The actual construction of the dams provided an infusion of relatively stable, high-paying jobs in an otherwise depressed economy. The new water supplies for irrigation had the usual effect of encouraging larger farms and more intensive forms of agriculture. But the most dramatic effects by now clearly concerned electricity. The Bonneville Power Administration was committed to distributing power to municipalities and public utilities so as to foster the widest possible use at the lowest possible rates. By the 1940s, the region had an immense surplus of electricity selling more cheaply than anywhere else in the nation. As a result, it attracted new industries that had especially heavy demands for power. In particular, aluminum production, one of the most voracious industrial users of electricity, concentrated in the region. With the coming of World War II, the availability of this aluminum enabled Seattle's Boeing Airplane Company to enjoy an unprecedented boom, becoming one of the region's most important employers in the postwar era.

It was cheap electricity that linked the Pacific Northwest to one of the most spectacular examples of government-sponsored interregional integration in the 1940s: the effort to develop the atomic bomb. Cheap electricity from the TVA permitted Oak Ridge, Tennessee, to produce uranium-235 via the extremely power-intensive gaseous diffusion process; cheap electricity from the Columbia River helped Hanford, Washington, become the site for a series of nuclear reactors and machine-shop facilities to manufacture plutonium. Both were tied to a network of other sites, the activities of which—collectively known as the Manhattan Project—had to be intricately coordinated in order to make the bomb a reality. Uranium was initially acquired from sources in the Belgian Congo and from the Eldorado mine on the Great Bear Lake in Canada; uncertainty about these foreign sources would soon fuel a uranium mining boom in the West's Four Corners region in the years immediately following the war. The University of California at Berkeley, already a center for nuclear research under the leadership of the physicist Ernest Lawrence, made major intellectual contributions to the bomb-building effort, while the California Institute of Technology contributed its growing expertise in explosives and jet propulsion. Much of the technical work on the actual bomb was conducted at the government's secret laboratory at Los Alamos in New Mexico. And the first nuclear test would occur in New Mexico at a site called Trinity on the desert sands near Alamogordo (postwar nuclear tests would be conducted at an even more isolated location north of Las Vegas, the Nevada Test Site). The extraordinary effort to produce the bomb centered in the West because of its new abundance of power, its large blocks of government-owned land, its isolation, and—paradoxically—its increasing integration with the rest of the nation. The military projects that came to fruition during the war would remain critical to the western economy at least until the end of the cold war era, establishing a partnership among the federal government, the corporate sector, and many western communities—a partnership that would profoundly shape regional development far into the future.

From one point of view, the dramatic changes that transformed the western landscape in the first half of the twentieth century represented unmitigated progress: new communities had sprung into being, parts of the region seemed prosperous as never before, and the desert had indeed bloomed. And yet all had unexpected social and environmental consequences. Residents of the Owens Valley more or less had to abandon their agrarian dreams once their river was tapped to serve Los Angeles; later, the city's growing demand would decrease water levels upstream at Mono Lake, endangering brine shrimp populations and the waterfowl that depended on them. Irrigated farms eventually began to suffer from the salts that accumulated in their soils, necessitating their abandonment or expensive purification techniques. The immense agricultural operations of the Far West required the use of migrant labor for planting and harvesting, creating an underclass of workers who were exposed to any number of toxic substances as growers increasingly came to depend on pesticides to protect their crops. Mine tailings from the uranium boom of the 1950s became a serious health hazard for residents of the Navajo reservation and other communities in the vicinity. Nuclear wastes dumped at Hanford in the years during and after the war created a long-term radiation hazard at that site. Fallout from the above-ground nuclear explosions at the Nevada Test Site killed livestock and elevated human cancer rates in the region lying downwind. The list could go on and on.

But perhaps the most suggestive example of deleterious environmental change occurred on the Columbia River, where the new dams prevented salmon and other anadromous fish from making their annual spawning runs. Salmon had once traveled hundreds of miles upstream to lay their eggs in freshwater locations, where the young fry, once hatched, could grow to maturity without being threatened by the predators they would face in the open sea. Since the spawning runs sustained a large fishing fleet in the waters of Puget Sound and on the open ocean, various efforts were made to protect them. Engineers added fish ladders to the relatively low Bonneville Dam so that adult salmon could still make their way upstream. Unfortunately, young salmon heading back downstream could not find these ladders and had to make the often lethal journey through the dam's pipes and turbines; moreover, the altered temperatures and still water of the new reservoirs made the fishes' journey in both directions more hazardous. On the upper river, high dams like Grand Coulee could not possibly be traversed even by fish ladders, and so heroic airlifts were attempted to capture fish at the base of the dam when its gates were first closed. Above Grand Coulee, salmon would henceforth disappear altogether, permanently ending the spawning runs for hundreds of miles upriver.

To replace those runs, both the fish and the fishing fleet would henceforth have to rely more and more heavily on the artificial output of the fish hatcheries that Washington, Oregon, and the U.S. Fish and Wildlife Service would operate along the Pacific coast. The bitter irony was that efforts to manage the river toward human ends had necessitated an equally elaborate effort—reorchestrating salmon reproductive cycles over thousands of square miles—to manage fish populations that not long before had sustained themselves without any human intervention at all. The long-term success of this massive ecological experiment remains as yet unclear; recent evidence suggests that the genetic uniformity of hatchery fish populations may eventually threaten their viability.

The Urban Wilderness

The newly integrated western landscape that had come into being by mid-century had been mandated by the state, managed by corporations and federal bureaucracies, consolidated by war, and—perhaps most important—concentrated by cities. A handful of metropolitan centers had become foci for the regional economy and homes for most of the West's inhabitants. Los Angeles had emerged as the largest city in the West and before long would surpass Chicago as the nation's second-largest metropolitan area. Joining it were Houston, Dallas, Kansas City, Denver, Salt Lake City, Phoenix, San Francisco, Seattle, and Anchorage, each pulling in the resources of a broad hinterland region—especially water and energy—to sustain itself. Contrary to the frontier myth, the West had for a long time almost led the nation in the percentage of its population living in urban areas; in 1870, only the Northeast had been more urban than the Far West. By the mid-twentieth century, the rest of the nation had caught up, so that the one-half to two-thirds of western citizens who lived in urban places roughly matched the national average of 59 percent. Moreover, western cities had become tied to markets, transportation networks, and administrative systems that were truly national in scope. Like the rest of the United States and much of the world as well, the West had become a metropolitan region by mid-century, with urban and suburban residents consuming and reworking the resources of immense rural districts as part of a fully integrated economy.

As such, they faced many of the same environmental problems and challenges as urban dwellers elsewhere. By 1950, Los Angeles was widely regarded as the extreme example of a new urban landscape peculiar to western cities that had grown to maturity in the twentieth century. Dependent on the automobile for transport, it had sprawled in all directions as its residents had sought to fulfill the suburban dream of isolating themselves from the ills of an urban downtown. In the process, they created a mul-ticentered city with no true focus, in which residents were forced to make long car trips—for work, for shopping, for school, for recreation, for everything—on freeways that became the arteries of the city. But this in fact was the spatial landscape that was developing on the margins of even much older American cities, a fact that became more apparent as the downtown centers of those cities began having more and more trouble competing with their own suburbs. Remove Manhattan, peel away the northeastern forest, and the basic spatial arrangement of Connecticut and New Jersey is not so different from that of Los Angeles. The California metropolis had pointed a way toward the future, and eastern cities soon followed its lead. The long journey between residence and workplace, the endemic traffic jams, the smog, the highway strips, the fast-food joints, and the shopping centers, in addition to the almost invisible systems that deliver water, gas, and electricity while removing sewage and solid waste—these are found to varying degrees in all American cities, not just in Los Angeles or the West. At the same time, the spread of highway systems, rural electrification, household appliances, tele-phone networks, radio and television broadcasting, and national distribution networks for goods have all enabled Americans from similar socioeconomic classes to enjoy similar life-styles whether they reside in cities, suburbs, or rural districts. One of the most important trends of the twentieth-century West, then, has been its steady convergence with the rest of the nation toward a common material life. In a sense, it is precisely this shared material life that has been the real fulfillment of the reclamation dream.

And yet there remains something distinctive about this newly integrated American West, for in fact the western landscape is *not* like the rest of the country. Its aridity makes the competition for water a far more compelling struggle than in the East and much more of a zero-sum game between different places and users. The heat of its desert summers has led it to join hands with the South in adopting air conditioning as a prerequisite for continuing growth. The scale of things often does seem larger in the West than else-where. The long distances—between far-flung metropolises, between sprawling suburbs, between city and country, between one state and another—impose greater travel times and energy costs on even the simplest journeys, making places seem isolated from each other even when in most other ways they are not. One gets used to big things in the West, whether they be mountains or mines or dams or farms. And the enclaved nature of western settlement makes it easy for places of great poverty—Indian reservations, barrios, depressed farming districts, dying towns—to share the regional landscape with the far more affluent inhabitants of well-to-do suburbs and cities. All these qualities mark the West as a special place.

But perhaps the most distinctive feature of the modern western environment has as much to do with the way people *think* about the regional landscape as the way they *use* it. The West has become the nation's greatest repository of "wilderness," a sacred space that for many Americans embodies both the simple virtues of the frontier past and the sublime wonders of pristine nature. Wilderness marks the paradoxical fulfillment of western urbanization. Whereas earlier generations looked to the West and dreamed of a working rural landscape—a place of farms and mines and lumber camps and small towns—urban Americans over the course of the twentieth century have increasingly preferred to think of it in *non*working terms, as a recreational place for escape or play. A similar shift occurred at the same time in national environmental politics: the earlier conservation movement had concerned itself most of all with questions of production and the efficient use of natural resources, whereas the postwar environmental movement—more urban in its basic outlook—became much more interested in problems of consumption, pollution, and the protection of natural systems. As the nonrural population of both the region and the country has grown, the cultural meaning of the western landscape has shifted to reflect predominantly nonrural values. Although wilderness might seem on the surface to represent the least urban of places, the way of viewing the natural environment that it reflects—as a land with no human inhabitants—has in fact come much more easily to urban people than rural ones. Traditional rural inhabitants of the West have been accustomed to earning their living in one way or another from the land and its creatures, activities that by definition involve mingling the natural and the human in ways that one would not ordinarily call "wild." Many modern westerners, on the other hand, accustomed to earning their living from urban markets, do not obtain food or shelter or basic income by working the land. And so, unsurprisingly, when fleeing the city they have often been drawn to *un*worked land: wilderness.

The West has been a destination for leisure-class travelers since the Civil War and before. At the same time that wealthy New Yorkers were first discovering the pleasures of hunting camps in the Adirondacks, Congress was setting aside Yosemite and Yellowstone as the first nonurban American parks. The initial impulse to create national parks came from several sources: a feeling of inferiority relative to the classical monuments of Europe; a desire to preserve the most "scenic" and "picturesque" elements of the American landscape; and a sense that the nation's "natural wonders" were among its most distinguishing features. In addition, powerful lobbies saw possible benefits for themselves in establishing parks. In the earliest years, the major western railroads sought to promote parks along their routes as a way of encouraging transcontinental passenger traffic. Railroad tourism characteristically involved delivering hundreds of well-to-do travelers to a single passenger depot, where they then traveled by

The roads that traverse the national parks not only bring tourists to these sites but also shape the ways in which visitors experience the landscape. For many, the parks are appreciated only from the well-established scenic viewing spots adjacent to the roads.

Roger Minick (b. 1944). Yosemite National Park, California, from Sightseer Series. Ektacolor print, 1980. © Roger Minick 1980. Courtesy of the photographer.

horse and stage to a large hotel capable of catering to their every need. Park hotels had urban amenities and were at best rustic—not "wild"—in their appurtenances. Given the need for destinations that could attract the well-heeled crowds that such hotels required, it made sense for the railroad companies to spend large sums on advertising and other promotional packages to educate Americans about the wonders of the western landscape. Such familiar places as Yellowstone, Yosemite, the Grand Canyon, and most other western parks were introduced to the public in just this way.

By the early decades of the twentieth century, as automobiles became more common and travelers began to consider them as alternatives to the railroads, new forms of western tourism started to emerge. Westerners, and Californians in particular, were prominent among supporters of the "good roads" movement, encouraging state and federal governments to invest significant sums in rural highway improvement. With the passage of the 1916 Federal Aid Road Act, states were given federal money to build and improve a system of "U.S. highways," many of which were soon being designated as preferred tourist routes. As Americans took to the roads in greater numbers, the national parks were among their favorite destinations. In 1916, Congress created the National Park Service to oversee the growing number of parks and monuments. Under the leadership of its first two superintendents, Stephen T. Mather and Horace M. Albright, the Park

Service constructed roads, built tourist facilities, designed brochures, and did everything possible to promote the success of the parks.

By the 1920s, the Forest Service, fearing that the national parks might overtake the national forests in popular affection, was also beginning to promote recreational opportunities on its lands, designating a growing number of sites as "Primitive Areas," with wilder amenities than the parks typically sought to offer. Both bureaucracies increasingly catered to the auto-based tourist, so that small motor campgrounds started to appear as alternatives to the immense railroad hotels. On the outskirts of the parks and elsewhere, "motels"—motor hotels—and other tourist facilities became more common. By the 1930s, the earliest western ski resorts were appearing as winter destinations for western travelers. Averell Harriman persuaded the Union Pacific Railroad to construct a large ski slope at Sun Valley, Idaho, in 1936 as a way of increasing passenger traffic at a time of year that had not previously attracted much of a tourist market. Aspen, Colorado, acquired its first ski lodge the same year. Throughout the West, tourism helped reorient a growing number of local economies, providing important employment alternatives for locals and outsiders alike. One striking example of a traditional western institution shifting from a rural to urban orientation was the dude ranch; throughout the West, marginal grazing operations increasingly turned to wealthy tourists as their chief source of income. Although such ranches billed themselves as places where urban visitors could get back to the basics and experience rustic living firsthand, what they marketed was less a genuine rural way of life than a carefully crafted fantasy for leisure-class consumers. Whatever value such experiences may have had for those who purchased them—and many testified to the considerable benefits for young and old alike—dude ranching was hardly "traditional" life on the land.

With the postwar era came an explosion in tourist travel throughout the West, fueled in part by baby-boom parents seeking to take their offspring to national parks, ski resorts, and even newer destinations like Disneyland, which opened in Anaheim, California, in 1955. In 1956, the popular demand for recreational travel helped secure passage of the Interstate and Defense Highway Act, which provided 90 percent of the funds for an extraordinary new network of divided highways, the largest public works project in American history. The new interstate highways, largely completed during the 1960s and 1970s, reinforced the existing urban system by linking major metropolitan centers and encouraging further growth at these key transportation nodes. At the same time, they made it easier for urban residents to escape the city for the country. The predictable result can be seen in National Park usage. In 1920, total visits to all national parks had only just reached 1 million. By 1950, this number had risen to 33 million; by 1970, it stood at 172 million. Other tourist destinations experienced comparable increases during the same period. The growth in recreational travel far exceeded national population increase.

Not coincidentally, the growing American love affair with western travel fostered new political pressure for the protection of wilderness lands. The United States had been setting aside parks in the West and elsewhere since Yosemite in 1864 and Yellowstone in 1872 but not specifically as "wilderness." Indeed, the act establishing Yellowstone described it as a "public park or pleasuring ground," suggesting the extent to which recreation was intended as its chief use. Only gradually did Americans begin to speak of the "wildness" of parks as one of their special values. Among those who led the preservationist struggle to protect wildlands, John Muir undoubtedly deserves special mention, since his writings about Yosemite, the Sierra Nevada, and the national parks in general were among the principal nineteenth-century texts convincing Americans—many of them elite inhabitants of eastern cities—of the need to set aside wild areas in the West.

In the first decade of the twentieth century, Muir and the San Francisco–based Sierra Club, which he helped found, conducted a nationwide publicity campaign to prevent the construction of the Hetch Hetchy reservoir in Yosemite National Park. Although Muir and his allies were ultimately defeated and the dam was built, Hetch Hetchy would become a battle cry in all subsequent struggles to protect western wilderness areas. More interesting, it also symbolized the growing contradictions between the material and the moral foundations of western American life. On the one hand, the people who sought to defend Hetch Hetchy were principally well-to-do inhabitants of cities—San Francisco chief among them—who viewed Yosemite National Park as a sacred icon of the western landscape as it had appeared before the coming of urban civilization. On the other hand, the people who sought to dam Hetch Hetchy were trying to defend San Francisco from a repetition of the terrible fires that followed the 1906 earthquake, while simultaneously guaranteeing that residents would continue to have water as their city grew. In the decades to come, many of those who would be most committed to saving western wilderness areas would also be drinkers of Hetch Hetchy water.

By mid-century, public enthusiasm for wildland recreation had grown to the point that the Sierra Club's next major battle against a dam would have a very different outcome. When the Bureau of Reclamation proposed building a dam in Echo Park, located within the borders of Dinosaur National Monument, preservationists mounted a major national campaign to lobby against it. This time, they won. Although part of the appropriations bill that protected Dinosaur National Monument also included funds to build a high dam in Glen Canyon—later lamented by preservationists as "the place no one knew"—it was a serious defeat for the bureau, putting it on notice that a significant portion of the American public no longer viewed dams as an unmitigated good. When plans were unveiled in the 1960s for a major reclamation project within the boundaries of Grand Canyon National Park, public outcry swelled to unprecedented levels and once again prevented the dams from being built. Never before had earlier conservation goals and emerging environmentalist values been more starkly contrasted.

The preservationist movement to protect wild areas had its greatest triumph in 1964, with the passage of the Wilderness Act. Under its terms, large tracts of land (most of them initially located in the national forests) were designated as roadless areas in a national system of wilderness preserves. Motorized traffic was not permitted, and—in the absence of new mineral discoveries—any development that might undermine the wild status was forbidden. The vast majority of these new wilderness areas were west of the Mississippi River, though a new law in 1975 mandated the reestablishment of wilderness—restored "virgin land," as it were—on eastern sites that had once been lumbered or pastured. By 1979, roughly twenty million acres had received wilderness protection, and that same year the size of the system quadrupled with the addition of new wilderness preserves in Alaska. Although the administration of President Ronald Reagan sought to cut back on the wilderness system, the resulting public outcry suggested how clearly the wilderness areas embodied environmental values that many Americans held dear.

And yet wilderness also represents one of the deepest paradoxes of the western environment. Standing in a kind of love-hate counterpoint to the urban West, it is quintessentially an urban cultural space if measured by the majority of people who visit it, defend it, and hold it dear. If one plots periods of peak visitation for western parks and wilderness areas, they coincide perfectly with weekends and major holidays as defined by urban workplaces. By the 1960s, Yosemite had acquired smog (and crime) problems that on a smaller, more symbolic scale paralleled those of Los Angeles. Crowding in most parks and backcountry areas had become so severe by the 1980s that permits and reservations—often made months in advance—were necessary if one wanted to experience the "freedom" of the hills. When a major coal-fired power plant was constructed in the Four Corners region to provide electricity to Los Angeles without compounding its pollution problems, the resulting haze would become a perennial problem at the Grand Canyon. Increasingly, those who sought escape from the city by fleeing to the wilderness found the city harder to leave than they thought, for they carried its baggage with them.

Among the most striking examples of the contradictions of wilderness occurred in the country's oldest national park, Yellowstone. Following a policy laid down in the early 1960s, rangers tried to manage the park as if it were a completely natural system, with as little human intervention as possible. As the critic Alston Chase has argued, not all of the results turned out as intended. Bear populations, which may have been kept artificially high by garbage dumps and intentional human feeding dating from at least the 1930s, plummeted disastrously when "natural"-style management was instituted. Even more striking, a decision to reverse the decades-old practice of preventing forest fires and to allow "natural" ones to burn led in 1988 to the largest and most devastating fires in the park's history. In such cases, it was not at all clear that one could just "let wilderness be" so that nature could "take care of itself." The modification of park ecosystems by intense visitor pressure, by fragmentation of habitats, by loss of native species, and by global environmental change suggested that active intervention would be necessary if wilderness was to survive.

In 1977, the Forest Service published a textbook whose title said it all: *Wilderness Management*. A quarter century before, when lobbying for a national wilderness act was still in its early stages, the notion that one could "manage" wilderness would probably have seemed antithetical to the whole concept. Americans in general, and westerners in particular, had sought to preserve wilderness because it stood for natural beauty and frontier freedom, both of which seemed seriously at risk in the modern world. Men and women who no longer earned their livings on the land, whose homes and workplaces were located in immense metropolitan districts, saw in the western wilderness a much-loved alternative to the complicated lives of quiet desperation that they both cherished and maligned. The irony was that those complicated lives—supported by dams and highways and energy resources that had made the desert bloom and had conjured cities in an arid waste to fulfill the reclamation dream—those same lives were themselves the

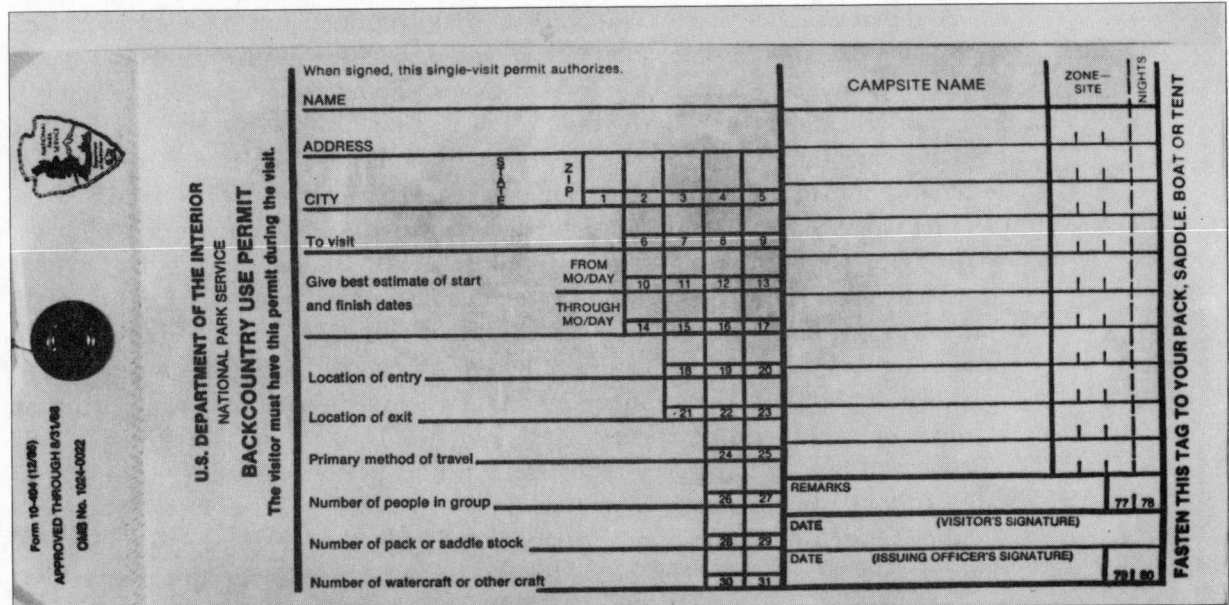

principal challenge to wilderness in the modern world, calling its future into question. Furthermore, the alienated way of thinking about nature embodied in the very concept of wilderness—as a special place where nature could be experienced "pure," isolated from the "artificial" human world that surrounded it—was itself an artifact of American cultural attitudes toward the western frontier. In a very real sense, the wilderness was as much an urban cultural invention as were the dry hillsides of the Owens Valley, the flooded canyons of the Colorado River, or the suburban tracts of Los Angeles.

Furthermore, wilderness was also the ultimate symbol of abundance giving way to scarcity in the modern West. In the nineteenth century, the frontier had stood in the minds of many Americans for the unworked abundance of a savage or prehuman landscape awaiting the touch of human hands to become the site of prosperous farms, mines, factories, and cities. (Indians, of course, were shamelessly ignored or patronized by such thinking.) The progress of the nation was measured by its success in transforming wilderness into fertile countryside. The reclamation dream had extended this vision of frontier plenty even into the drylands of the arid West, making it possible to discover abundance even in the face of seemingly irrefutable scarcity. The growth of modern Los Angeles and other western cities suggests just how triumphant these nineteenth-century dreams eventually proved to be. But in the course of their fulfillment, they also undermined their original promise. The material resources of the West were *not* endless—far from it. The growth of one city could all too easily mean the stagnation of another. The damming of each new canyon left one less source of water and power to be tapped in the future. Perceived abundance gradually gave way to perceived scarcity, and nothing better represented this transition than the well-bounded, carefully managed, fragile western landscapes designated as "wilderness." By the late twentieth century, the wilderness, which had once stood as America's most potent icon of limitless abundance, seemed, in the eyes of many, to be its scarcest resource. Rarely has the reversal of a cultural symbol been more complete.

The "wilderness management" practiced by the U.S. Forest Service and the National Park Service suggests the complexity of contemporary American attitudes toward the land. Once valued for the limitless wildness that seemed to set them beyond the reach of civilization, wilderness lands are now viewed as dwindling resources to be shaped and controlled by human agency.

Backcountry Use Permit, 1993. National Park Service.

And that was why the oil that poured from the ruptured hull of the *Exxon Valdez*, coating the Alaskan coastline with black tar and devastating its marine life, was such a compelling source of outrage even for Americans who had never seen Prince William Sound or visited the far north. By the 1970s, Alaska had come to seem a near-perfect embodiment of America's frontier traditions. Its immense reserves of petroleum had fostered a boom to rival anything one could have found in the nineteenth-century West, creating a smaller, wetter, more northern version of Los Angeles in the city of Anchorage, whose supply lines reached around the world to feed a large urban population that could never have sustained itself with local agricultural resources alone. At the same time, Americans who now cherished "wilderness" as a cultural icon viewed Alaska as the last opportunity to preserve natural areas in their pristine state. Despite its immensity and harshness, the northern environment could thus seem all too small and fragile a remnant of the wonder that had once been North America. In the post-1968 struggles over whether and how to construct the Alaskan pipeline, over whether and how much to protect the Alaskan wilderness, Americans had tried once again to resolve the long-standing tension between abundance and scarcity, between the seductive dream of progress and the sublime icon of wilderness, between American national myth and material life.

Remote as it may have seemed from the day-to-day lives of most Americans, the wrecked Exxon supertanker could not have been more intimately entangled with these central questions of western environmental history. Before running aground, its ultimate destination had been Long Beach, California, where its cargo would have been refined into gasoline to help keep the wheels of Los Angeles turning. The great ship had been sent on its mission by the demands of this and other urban markets and would not have wreaked its havoc without their impetus. The connections were not always easy to trace, but the oily pollution on the shores of Prince William Sound had more than a little in common with the smoggy haze that obscured the waterfalls of Yosemite, the mesas of the Grand Canyon, and the basin of Los Angeles itself. Public outrage may have been directed against the corporations and governmental agencies that failed to prevent the spill, but in a deeper sense its ultimate causes were far too close to home for comfort. In much the same way, public anger in the wake of the spill expressed not just a legitimate outrage about serious ecological damage but an older American resentment about the fading of a pristine dream. Not even Alaska was safe, not even Alaska was far enough away to remain an unsullied landscape of frontier freedom and wilderness escape. Even there, abundance could give way to scarcity, forcing those who had counted on the promise of plenty to confront the consequences of its loss. It was not the first such failed promise in western history, and would surely not be the last.

Bibliographic Note

On the history of the *Exxon Valdez* oil spill, a competent journalistic survey can be found in Art Davidson, *In the Wake of the Exxon Valdez: The Devastating Impact of the Alaska Oil Spill* (San Francisco, 1990); for good photographic coverage, see the special report "Wreck of the Exxon Valdez" in *Audubon* (September 1989).

There is no general environmental history of the West, but Richard White's *"It's Your Misfortune and None of My Own": A New History of the American West* (Norman, 1991) does a better job of surveying environmental issues than any other available western history textbook.

For historiographical essays reviewing relevant literature, see William L. Lang, "Using and Abusing Abundance: The Western Resource Economy and the Environment," in Michael P. Malone, ed., *Historians and the American West* (Lincoln, 1983), 270–99, and John Opie, "The Environment and the Frontier," in Roger L. Nichols, ed., *American Frontier and Western Issues: A Historiographical Review* (Westport, Conn., 1986), 7–25, as well as various essays in Gerald D. Nash and Richard W. Etulain, eds., *The Twentieth-Century West: Historical Interpretations* (Albuquerque, 1989). Although tightly monographic in focus, Richard White's *Land Use, Environment, and Social Change: The Shaping of Island County, Washington* (Seattle, 1980) exemplifies the major themes of western environmental history as well as any available text; useful in much the same way are William deBuys, *Enchantment and Exploitation: The Life and Hard Times of a New Mexico Mountain Range* (Albuquerque, 1985), and Donald Worster, *Dust Bowl: The Southern Plains in the 1930s* (New York, 1979). Also suggestive are the essays in Donald Worster, *Under Western Skies: Nature and History in the American West* (New York, 1992), and my own "Kennecott Journey: The Paths out of Town" in William Cronon, George Miles, and Jay Gitlin, eds., *Under an Open Sky: Rethinking America's Western Past* (New York, 1992).

On the history of American public lands and the laws dealing with them, the standard work remains Paul Wallace Gates, *History of Public Land Law Development* (Washington, D.C., 1968). A more succinct and up-to-date survey can be found in Samuel Trask Dana and Sally K. Fairfax, *Forest and Range Policy: Its Development in the United States*, 2d ed. (New York, 1980). Quite dated but still useful is the anthology edited by Vernon Carstensen, *The Public Lands: Studies in the History of the Public Domain* (Madison, 1962).

Much of the literature on progressive conservation mingles with that on the history of forestry and lumbering in the United States. Overviews of American forest history can be found in Thomas R. Cox, Robert S. Maxwell, Phillip Drennon Thomas, and Joseph J. Malone, *This Well-Wooded Land: Americans and Their Forests from Colonial Times to the Present* (Lincoln, 1985), and Michael Williams's compendious *Americans and Their Forests: A Historical Geography* (Cambridge, Eng., 1989). On the Forest Service and its policies, see Harold K. Steen, *The U.S. Forest Service: A History* (Seattle, 1976), David A. Clary, *Timber and the Forest Service* (Lawrence, 1986), and William G. Robbins, *American Forestry: A History of National, State, and Private Cooperation* (Lincoln, 1985). On the early history of lumbering in the West proper, see Thomas R. Cox, *Mills and Markets: A History of the Pacific Coast Lumber Industry to 1900* (Seattle, 1974).

The classic history of the progressive conservation movement remains Samuel P. Hays, *Conservation and the Gospel of Efficiency: The Progressive Conservation Movement, 1890–1920* (Cambridge, Mass., 1959); for its successor on more recent environmental politics, see Samuel P. Hays, *Beauty, Health, and Permanence: Environmental Politics in the United States, 1955–1985* (Cambridge, Eng., 1987). For an invaluable survey of the predecessors of progressive conservation, see Donald J. Pisani, "Forests and Conservation, 1865–1890," *Journal of American History* 72 (September 1985): 340–59. The best edition of George Perkins Marsh's classic 1864 work is *Man and Nature; or, Physical Geography as Modified by Human Action*, ed. David Lowenthal (Cambridge, Mass., 1965). John Wesley Powell's *Report on the Lands of the Arid Region of the United States* (1878) is available in a reprint edition edited by Wallace Stegner (Cambridge, Mass., 1962).

On wildlife, the best legal history is Michael J. Bean, *The Evolution of National Wildlife Law*, rev. ed. (New York, 1983). General surveys can be found in Thomas R. Dunlap, *Saving America's Wildlife* (Princeton, 1988), and James B. Trefethen, *An American Crusade for Wildlife* (New York, 1975). More monographic works that are quite valuable include John F. Reiger, *American Sportsmen and the Origins of Conservation* (New York, 1975), James A. Tober, *Who Owns the Wildlife? The Political Economy of Conservation in Nineteenth-Century America* (Westport, Conn., 1981), and Theodore Whaley Cart, "The Struggle for Wildlife Protection in the United States, 1870–1900: Attitudes and Events Leading to the Lacey Act" (Ph.D. diss., University of North Carolina at Chapel Hill, 1971). Robin W. Doughty, *Wildlife and Man in Texas: Environmental Change and Conservation* (College Station, Tex., 1983), gives an interesting perspective on wildlife in one important western state. The forthcoming Yale University doctoral dissertations by Jennifer Price and Louis Warren will make important contributions to the history of wildlife in American popular culture and to the history of cross-class and multiethnic local conflicts over new wildlife-management regimes. As for fisheries, the story of western salmon is well traced in Anthony Netboy, *The Columbia River Salmon and Steelhead Trout: Their Fight for Survival* (Seattle, 1980). Finally, on marine resources, Arthur F. McEvoy, *The Fisherman's Problem: Ecology and Law in the California Fisheries, 1850–1980* (Cambridge, Eng., 1986), is in a class by itself as one of the finest environmental histories we have on any western subject.

Western water historiography is immense, and no brief discussion can do it justice. The most important one-volume synthesis of California water history, and the best starting point for anyone seeking a general overview of water in the West, is Norris Hundley, Jr., *The Great Thirst: Californians and Water, 1770s-1990s* (Berkeley, 1992). Broader in coverage and more provocative in argument is Donald Worster, *Rivers of Empire: Water, Aridity, and the Growth of the American West* (New York, 1985); more popularly written and polemical is Marc Reisner, *Cadillac Desert: The American West and Its Disappearing Water* (New York, 1986). For reclamation efforts in the pre–Newlands Act era, the standard work is Donald J. Pisani, *To Reclaim a Divided West: Water, Law, and Public Policy, 1848–1902* (Albuquerque, 1992). On California irrigation, see Donald J. Pisani, *From the Family Farm to Agribusiness: The Irrigation Crusade in California and the West, 1850–1931* (Berkeley, 1984), and Robert Kelley, *Battling the Inland Sea: American Political Culture, Public Policy, and the Sacramento Valley, 1850–1986* (Berkeley, 1989). On the history of individual states and reclamation projects, exemplary monographs include William L. Kahrl, *Water and Power: The Conflict over Los Angeles' Water Supply in the Owens Valley* (Berkeley, 1982), Joseph E. Stevens, *Hoover Dam: An American Adventure* (Norman, 1988), Ira G. Clark, *Water in New Mexico: A History of Its Management and Use* (Albuquerque, 1987), James Sherow, *Watering the Valley: Development along the High Plains Arkansas River, 1870–1950* (Lawrence, 1990), and Daniel Tyler, *The Last Water Hole in the West: The Colorado-Big Thompson Project and the Northern Colorado Water Conservancy District* (Niwot, Colo., 1992). A uniquely valuable reference work is William L. Kahrl, ed., *The California Water Atlas* (Sacramento, Calif., 1979). A superb bibliography and overview of the water literature published before 1980 is Lawrence B. Lee, *Reclaiming the American West: An Historiography and Guide* (Santa Barbara, 1980). Anyone wishing to understand what in this essay I call "the reclamation dream" would do well to read William E. Smythe, *The Conquest of Arid America* (1899), ed. Lawrence B. Lee (Seattle, 1969).

On the role of wilderness in the West and in American culture generally, the classic survey remains Roderick Nash, *Wilderness and the American Mind*, 3d ed. (New Haven, 1982), though one should read its arguments critically; also useful is Craig W. Allin, *The Politics of Wilderness Preservation* (Westport, Conn., 1982). Connections of wilderness to frontier ideology can be explored by reading Henry Nash Smith, *Virgin Land: The American West as Symbol and Myth* (Cambridge, Mass., 1950), G. Edward White, *The Eastern Establishment and the Western Experience: The West of Frederic Remington, Theodore Roosevelt, and Owen Wister* (New Haven, 1968), Richard Slotkin, *The Fatal Environment: The Myth of the Frontier in the Age of Industrialization, 1800–1890* (New York, 1985), and Robert G. Athearn, *The Mythic West in Twentieth-Century America* (Lawrence, 1986). On national park history, the standard history is Alfred Runte, *National Parks: The American Experience*, 2d ed. (Lincoln, 1987). A valuable journalistic survey is Dyan Zaslowsky, *These American Lands: Parks, Wilderness, and the Public Lands* (New York, 1986). The Forest Service textbook mentioned in the text is John C. Hendee, George H. Stankey, and Robert C. Lucas, *Wilderness Management*, Forest Service, U.S.D.A., Miscellaneous Publication No. 1365, (Washington, D.C., 1977). Earl Pomeroy, *In Search of the Golden West: The Tourist in Western America* (New York, 1957), remains one of the best sources on western tourism in the preautomobile era; on auto tourism, see Warren James Belasco, *Americans on the Road: From Autocamp to Motel, 1910–1945* (Cambridge, Mass., 1979), and James J. Flink, *The Automobile Age* (Cambridge, Mass., 1988). Excellent studies of the two best-known western parks are Richard A. Bartlett, *Yellowstone: A Wilderness Besieged* (Tucson, 1985), and Alfred Runte, *Yosemite: The Embattled Wilderness* (Lincoln, 1990). Alston Chase's acute, but not always generous, criticisms of Park Service policies in Yellowstone can be found in his *Playing God in Yellowstone: The Destruction of America's First National Park* (Boston, 1986). On environmentalist battles on behalf of wilderness preservation, see Stephen Fox, *John Muir and His Legacy: The American Conservation Movement* (Boston, 1981), Susan R. Schrepfer, *The Fight to Save the Redwoods: A History of Environmental Reform, 1917–1978* (Madison, 1983), and Michael P. Cohen, *The History of the Sierra Club, 1892–1970* (San Francisco, 1988).

Finally, on the related themes of abundance, scarcity, and a "metropolitan" interpretation of western environmental history, see the following: David M. Potter, *People of Plenty: Economic Abundance and the American Character* (Chicago, 1954); Earl Pomeroy, *The Pacific Slope: A History of California, Oregon, Washington, Idaho, Utah, and Nevada* (New York, 1965); Gerald D. Nash, *The American West in the Twentieth Century: A Short History of an Urban Oasis* (Englewood Cliffs, N.J., 1973); Peter Wiley and Robert Gottlieb, *Empires in the Sun: The Rise of the New American West* (New York, 1982); Carl Abbott, *The New Urban America: Growth and Politics in Sunbelt Cities* (Chapel Hill, 1981); and William Cronon, *Nature's Metropolis: Chicago and the Great West* (New York, 1991).

Chapter Eighteen

Contemporary Peoples/Contested Places

S A R A H   D E U T S C H ,   G E O R G E   J .   S Á N C H E Z ,
A N D   G A R Y   Y .   O K I H I R O

Boyle Heights

Toward the end of the summer of 1924, the *Los Angeles Times Illustrated Magazine* ran a one-page article extolling the virtues of southern California. In "Where Folks Are Folks," the author characterized Los Angeles as "the most American of American cities" because in Los Angeles, in contrast to the East, "the native American" (i.e., the nonimmigrant) was still "in the great majority." Like other important metropolises, Los Angeles had high buildings and high culture. But whereas New York was "overrun with Europeans," its ill-natured crowds "a nightmare to the traveler," Los Angeles was still the archetypical "middle-class American city, a metropolis with small-town ways—American ways." In the mind of this booster, Los Angeles was nothing less than "America regenerated, more eastern than the East," which had "become continental European."

The many promoters of the urban American West in the early twentieth century who extolled the absence of teeming immigrant masses ignored that the industrial and agricultural expansion that generated urban growth had, in fact, attracted large numbers of immigrants. The downtown region of Los Angeles and the areas just south and east of it held heavy concentrations of foreign-born and nonwhite newcomers. Ignored by promoters and largely excluded from the city's ruling elite, the Southside and the Eastside made up the "other" Los Angeles. Boyle Heights, an Eastside community, became the city's most heterogeneous region from the 1920s through the 1950s.

Among the first to settle in Boyle Heights were Mexican workers displaced from the central Plaza area of Los Angeles by rising housing prices and the building of offices during World War I. They shared "the Flats"—a low-lying region next to the river, close to employment by the Southern Pacific Railroad and garment and food-packing factories—with a sizable population of European immigrants, most notably Russian Molokans or "White Russians," a Christian sect that had fled Russia to escape harassment and impressment during the Russo-Japanese War. On the other side of Boyle Heights, a second expanding Mexican community joined a tiny African-American population to form the easternmost neighborhood in the city. Close to the city cemetery, this area—described as "a cheap land area" surrounded "by brick yards, railroad yards,

As this 1939 photograph of a Boyle Heights, Los Angeles elementary school suggests, the West has long been an ethnically diverse region, reflecting a legacy of Native American and Mexican residence and continued migration from Latin America, Asia, Europe, and the eastern United States.

Unidentified photographer. Breed Street School. Gelatin silver print, 1939. Jewish Historical Society of Southern California, Los Angeles.

and manufacturing plants"—was among the least desirable in Boyle Heights. Only housing in the Flats was in poorer condition.

Jewish laborers from the East had also begun to migrate to Boyle Heights during World War I, attracted by the congenial climate and the area's growing needle trades and other industries. They brought a tradition of radical politics and enthusiastic trade unionism. Their militancy made 1920s Boyle Heights home to local chapters of the Workmen's Circle and the hatters, carpenters, and garment workers unions. They also created in Boyle Heights and adjacent City Terrace a bustling, if paler, version of the Yiddish cultural life so typical of Jewish immigrants in New York. According to two historians of Jews in Los Angeles, on Brooklyn Avenue, "Jews bought and sold, Yiddish was freely used, and Saturdays and Jewish holidays were marked by festive appearances and many closed businesses."

Finally, although an enterprising Japanese minister had built a Buddhist temple in Boyle Heights as early as 1904, it was in the 1920s that a large number of Japanese settled there, dotting the central region of Boyle Heights, less concentrated than the Jewish or Mexican communities. Residences, community institutions, and a few businesses lined both sides of First Street. They became an extension of Little Tokyo, the largest center of Japanese life on the West Coast, located directly to the west. Initially the Japanese community consisted primarily of businessmen who preferred "suburban" living in Boyle Heights to the urban congestion of Little Tokyo. But as the 1920s progressed, more working-class Japanese families also ventured across the river, renting apartments and small houses on the Eastside.

The Great Depression pulled these disparate communities closer together. Repatriation campaigns aimed at encouraging Mexican and Filipino immigrants to return to their native countries affected the fringes of Boyle Heights by persuading unemployed Mexicans in the Flats to leave Los Angeles. The Mexicans who remained, largely skilled workers and their families, became steadfast in their commitment to the neighborhood. Some areas of Boyle Heights even grew during the 1930s. Indeed, to depression refugees from other parts of the country, Boyle Heights appeared stable and secure. The Zimmerman family of Cleveland, for example, headed west after losing the family produce business. In Boyle Heights, they could live near other Jewish families and seek employment for adults and older children in local stores and shops. Japanese Americans similarly solidified the ethnic economy they dominated in fruit, produce, and gardening. Dorothy Tomer remembered of her adolescence in Boyle Heights during the 1930s: "Everyone was poor. We pulled together. . . . If you didn't have education and money to back you, you just did anything to make a living."

This situation profoundly affected young people's intergroup perception. Enrolled in the same schools, they valued education as a luxury. Since everyone had to work, it came as no surprise when children dropped out to help the family economy. Jewish and Mexican women, many of them young adults, banded together to form the backbone of the garment and food-packing unions, which grew stronger in the decade.

Local government officials and real estate companies showed some hostility toward this struggling diverse community. For example, in 1939, the Federal Housing Authority gave its lowest possible rating to Boyle Heights precisely because, the agency explained, it was "hopelessly heterogeneous" and its "diverse and subversive racial elements" supposedly made it a bad risk for housing assistance. By 1940 the Jewish population of Boyle Heights totaled about thirty-five thousand, the Mexican population fifteen thousand, and the Japanese population five thousand.

If the depression had pulled the community together, World War II made it clear to most residents that Boyle Heights was not immune to forces out of its control. Roosevelt High School, the only secondary school in Boyle Heights, lost one-third of its population in a matter of months when Japanese-American students were interned. One English teacher encouraged her remaining students to write to interned classmates through round-robin letters kept up until graduation. Internment seemed unjustified to most in Boyle Heights, especially to the youth who had grown accustomed to this mixed environment. Indeed, the experience of living through the forced removal of Japanese-American residents during World War II seemed to leave a distinct impression on non-Japanese in the community, an impression that later translated into efforts on behalf of civil rights for all. The successful race of Edward Roybal, a Roosevelt High School graduate, for the Los Angeles City Council in 1947 was organized by an interracial group out of Boyle Heights.

The end of the war failed to bring normalcy to Boyle Heights; in many ways, peace was as disruptive as war. The severe housing shortage throughout Los Angeles contributed to an instability that left Boyle Heights vulnerable to exploitation under the guise of "development." By 1947, three public housing projects had been built within Boyle Heights by the Los Angeles Housing Authority, an "experiment" that led to the displacement of hundreds of families from the area. Despite the ten thousand residents, money for maintenance and improvement of these facilities evaporated. And between 1943 and 1960, five freeways were built through Boyle Heights, providing pathways for suburban commuters while destroying the cohesiveness of the community and displacing another ten thousand people.

These postwar developments rapidly altered the community's demographics as Boyle Heights became a less desirable place to live. By 1952, the Mexican-American population of Boyle Heights had grown to over forty thousand, forming close to half the population, while the Jewish population had shrunk to fourteen thousand. The Japanese population rested at about sixty-five hundred. For the remaining families, life in Boyle Heights had been transformed. One Jewish family, for example, found it necessary to pay a tough Mexican boy to protect their son through junior high school in the 1950s. Boyle Heights was well on its way to becoming a classic barrio with a population of poorer Chicano residents physically separated by freeways and a river and subject to racial housing restrictions and economic discrimination.

Pearl Harbor

Boyle Heights provided one model of an interethnic community in a contested landscape. World War II wrought others. In 1991, on a clear, bright Hawaiian morning, under the warming sun and with a gentle tropical breeze descending from the Koolau mountains, President George Bush faced the *U.S.S. Arizona* wreckage and memorial at Pearl Harbor. He told the assembled survivors of Japan's attack and the World War II veterans and their families: "No, I have no rancor in my heart. I can still see the faces of my fallen comrades, and I'll bet you can see the faces of your fallen comrades, too. But don't you think they're saying: 'Fifty years have passed. Our country is the undisputed leader of the free world. We are at peace.' Don't you think each one is saying, 'I did not die in vain?'" Although the president posed the question to elicit an affirmative reply, many listeners believed that although America might have won the war, it was being defeated by Japan in the global contest for economic dominance. Like the droplets of oil that still rose to the surface every twenty seconds from the *Arizona*'s tanks, the battle begun on 7 December 1941 continued to be waged on other fronts.

Months before the fiftieth anniversary services that brought President Bush to Pearl Harbor with his message of reconciliation, the Pearl Harbor Survivors Association (PHSA) had lobbied to exclude Japanese representatives from participating in the commemoration. "Would you expect the Jews to invite the Nazis to an event where they were talking about the Holocaust?" asked the national president of the fourteen-thousand-member PHSA. James G. Driscoll, in the *Fort Lauderdale Sun-Sentinel*, editorialized on the government's eventual decision to bar all foreign dignitaries from the fiftieth anniversary proceedings. "The Japanese are not invited to the ceremonies, nor should they be. Their presence would be an affront to those Americans who died there, to those who survived and who will attend and to the families of all."

Thurston Clarke, the author of one of the fifteen books on Pearl Harbor published in America in 1991, explained the legacy of hatred spawned by the Japanese attack. "Since Pearl Harbor was uniquely shocking and humiliating," reasoned Clarke, "it is only logical that American attitudes toward Japan should be uniquely sensitive, and that today's economic disputes should be haunted by Pearl Harbor ghosts. And so Japan's trade policies are likened to a form of 'treachery,' [and] a U.S. senator describes the export of Japanese cars to America as 'an economic Pearl Harbor.'" Japanese purchases of symbolic American properties such as Rockefeller Center, Pebble Beach, and Columbia Pictures, noted Clarke, stimulated among Americans an increased dislike and distrust of the Japanese. Hawai`i, where Japanese yen bought up choice businesses and homes as "minor spoils" of a trade war victory, had become "an economic colony of Japan," charged Clarke, representing "a Japanese victory more enduring than Pearl Harbor." Even the hotel in which the Pearl Harbor and World War II American veterans stayed during the fiftieth anniversary services, observed a *New York Times* reporter, was owned by Japanese. Describing C. A. Murray, a Marine corporal in 1941, who recalled that fateful Sunday, the reporter wrote: "Today he stood on the second floor of the Sheraton-Waikiki Hotel, owned by a Japanese company, and watched Japanese tourists walk by. 'I'm sorry I didn't take Japanese in school,' he said sarcastically, referring to all the signs in Japanese around him. 'I don't have any animosities, but it rubs me the wrong way.'"

Little noticed in the hoopla surrounding Pearl Harbor's fiftieth anniversary was the fact that although Japanese bombs had sparked the conflagration in Asia and the Pacific, America's presence in Hawai`i owed itself to an equally imperialist, expansive thrust during the late nineteenth century. In 1898, the United States had plucked Hawai`i like a ripe pear, the imagery employed by the American minister in Honolulu at the time.

Expansion once again stretched our boundaries and diversified our population. Forty-three years later, the invader became the invaded.

President Bush insisted that Japan had mistaken "our diversity, our nation's diversity, for weakness." He added: "But Pearl Harbor became a rallying cry for men and women from all walks of life, all colors and creeds. And in the end, this unity of purpose made us invincible in war and now makes us secure in peace." Yet Pearl Harbor instead had offered "a golden opportunity," in the words of a leading official of California's Grower-Shipper Vegetable Association in 1942, "to get rid of all Japs, sending them back to Japan either before or after the war is won." Indeed, while smoke still rose from the wreckage that was America's Pacific fleet, Hawai`i's governor proclaimed martial law in the territory, and in Hawai`i and on the mainland, army military police and Federal Bureau of Investigation agents began arresting Japanese aliens and citizens alike. By 19 February 1942, the day President Franklin D. Roosevelt signed Executive Order 9066 authorizing the mass removal and detention of all Japanese Americans along the West Coast, the army and the Justice Department had rounded up several thousand enemy aliens—including Japanese, Germans, and Italians—considered "dangerous" to the nation's security. Before the end of the year, over 110,000 Japanese Americans had been confined to concentration camps in Hawai`i and the American West.

An army leave policy that permitted Japanese-American soldiers to return to the West Coast prompted an "orgy of Jap baiting" in the press during April and May 1943, according to the writer Carey McWilliams. Despite all evidence that Japanese Americans were not the enemy, an editorial appearing in the *Los Angeles Times* on 22 April 1943 argued against the leave policy. "As a race, the Japanese have made for themselves a record for conscienceless treachery unsurpassed in history." Commenting on the leave policy, Lt. Gen. John L. De Witt, head of the Western Defense Command, told the House Naval Affairs subcommittee in San Francisco: "A Jap's a Jap. They are a dangerous element, whether loyal or not. . . . It makes no difference whether he is an American; theoretically he is still a Japanese. . . . You can't change him by giving him a piece of paper." Two California congressmen added, "If you send any Japs back here we're going to bury them." That atmosphere of race hatred and mob violence, wrote McWilliams, "contributed to kindling the fires of racial antagonism in the community."

One of those fires was the "zoot suit" race riot in Los Angeles during the anti-Japanese drive and a police and newspaper campaign against "Mexican crime" in which Mexican and African-American youth were subjected to intimidation and summary arrest. Lt. Edward Duran Ayres of the Los Angeles sheriff's department had testified before a 1942 grand jury that Mexican-American youth were genetically predisposed to criminal behavior. Beginning on 3 June 1943, and lasting for about a week, mobs of white soldiers, sailors, and civilians attacked, beat, kicked, and tore the clothing of Mexican and African Americans in the streets, bars, and streetcars of Los Angeles with apparent impunity. Similar mob violence occurred in Pasadena, Long Beach, and San Diego. During the same summer, race riots also flamed in Philadelphia, Chicago, Evansville, Detroit, Harlem, and Beaumont, Texas.

The war had not produced racial unity. It did, however, provide new employment opportunities for women, Chicanos, African Americans, and Asian Americans. And some of its legacies, notably the GI Bill, which made college education possible for many minorities, boosted the economic and political prospects for these western residents. The war also helped darken the urban West's complexion as California's booming defense industries drew African Americans at the rate of ten thousand a month during the peak wartime migration and as Native Americans too flocked to the urban worksites of the West. At the same time, while U.S.-born Mexicans moved to more lucrative jobs in the cities, the region's factories in the field beckoned braceros from Mexico to plant and harvest the crops. Having repatriated thousands of Mexican nationals back across the border to alleviate relief rolls in the 1930s, including one-third of the Mexican population in Los Angeles County or nearly thirty-five thousand people, by World War II western employers were clamoring for renewed legal immigration from Mexico to provide low-wage labor, particularly in agriculture. The Bracero Program, initiated as a wartime emergency measure, continued until 1964, supplying agricultural employers with a steady labor force whose strict regulation left few options for protest and whose availability could suppress the demand for higher agricultural wages. Even when the Immigration Service launched "Operation Wetback" in the 1950s to return illegal aliens across the border, it often ended up deporting those it had first brought to the United States as braceros. Indeed, potential deportees could be immediately "legalized" if they agreed to work under the contracts provided by the Bracero Program.

Disneyland

Braceros were not the only dream-seeking migrants in the 1950s West. On 17 July 1955, an enterprising Anglo-American transplant to the West welcomed the first visitors to what would become the most recognized site in the region for the rest of the century. As Walt Disney unveiled his uniquely American creation, Disneyland, he also exposed the unbridled optimism in technological progress, industrial expansion, and romantic saga that so marked Anglo-American thinking in the twentieth-century American West. The plaque that was laid that day in Disneyland's Town Square came to symbolize the melding of the western image with that of the nation's future. "To all who come to this happy place: Welcome. Disneyland is your land. Here age relives fond memories of the past . . . and here youth savor the challenge and promise of the future. Disneyland is dedicated to the ideals, the dreams, and the hard facts that have created America . . . with the hope that it will be a source of joy and inspiration to all the world."

Disney's fantasies, as exemplified in Disneyland, were characteristic of an entire migrant generation who made their way to California and other parts of the West in the first half of the twentieth century. Disney had grown up in Marceline, Missouri, a small town northeast of Kansas City, before breaking away from his family and moving west in 1923. Life had not been as idyllic for him as he later depicted on the mythical Main Street of his dream park. Disney's father failed in several business ventures, which perhaps caused the harsh beatings he meted out to his children. The family relied extensively on the income of young Walt and his brother, Roy. For Disney, as for an entire generation of Anglo-American migrants, the move west allowed him to wipe out unpleasant memories and reconstruct his history. That Disney's newfound vision of his past played itself out in a theme park only made his transformation more public than those of others.

Disneyland also represented a frustration with the growing sprawl and diverse population of the urban West and the associated problems of traffic congestion, pollution, overcrowding, and alienation after World War II. Disney saw his park as a leisurely retreat from that civic confusion as well as a platform to show what life in a metropolis could be like if planned correctly. His obsession with eradicating disorder translated into politics as well. A staunch Republican, he was a consistent advocate of combating "internal subversives." As a founder of the Motion Picture Alliance for the Preservation of American Ideals in 1944, Disney argued, "The American motion picture industry is, and will continue to be, held by Americans for the American people, in the interests of America and dedicated to the preservation and continuance of the American scene and the American way of life." This group invited the House Un-American Activities Committee (HUAC) to investigate Hollywood and ferret out supposed Communists who were corrupting the American mind. It was Disney and other conservative southern California businessmen who encouraged Ronald Reagan to abandon acting and turn his attention to politics, particularly after Reagan's role as a star witness identifying Communists to HUAC. Concern with "internal subversives" led Disney to hire only a handful of Jews, Asians, Mexicans, or African Americans at his new park.

Indeed, the vast Disney empire, including movies, television, marketing, and theme parks, began as an attempt by Disney to wrest American entertainment away from the largely Jewish immigrant community that had come to dominate Hollywood by the 1920s. He often equated being Jewish and a movie "mogul" with being a Communist sympathizer, and his vision was to return Hollywood entertainment to "wholesome American ideals." Yet, Adolph Zukor, Louis B. Mayer, and the Warner brothers had all distanced themselves from their immigrant pasts and any affiliation with the Left. Most, like Disney, were staunch Republican party members in the age of Roosevelt. These studio heads willingly fired suspected Communists from their studios to please HUAC in the 1940s and 1950s, even when those fired were talented Jewish writers and directors that they had recruited to Hollywood just a few years before.

A move west had allowed these entrepreneurs, like Disney, to remake themselves into a new elite to take advantage of the economic opportunities in the West, even though they needed to rely on ethnic affiliations and cultural projections brought from the East. While Walt Disney provided Americans with a sanitized version of a simpler midwestern past, the Jewish studio executives were busy appealing to immigrant notions of survival and opportunity. Both Disney and the Jewish movie magnates built institutions that relied on particularistic visions and appealed to a larger, more amorphous public. Ironically, it was their worlds of fantasy and leisure, rather than their own lives, that came to dominate representations of America. Each vision held out the possibility of remaking oneself in the migration to the American West, often by distorting one's own history.

Borders, 1965

Even as Hollywood veered toward film and fantasy, the nation took a different turn. In 1965, Congress enacted sweeping changes in immigration law, altering the racial and ethnic composition of the West and the nation. The new rules emerged in a context of profound national upheaval. Through the 1965 Voting Rights Act, four hundred thousand African Americans registered to vote in the Deep South within three years. The civil rights movement entered a period of transition marked by the full emergence of the Black Power movement, the assassination of Malcolm X, and a profound refocusing on poverty in the wake of the Watts riots, which rocked Los Angeles. Lyndon Johnson launched the Great Society in earnest, introducing the Medicare/Medicaid programs for the elderly and poor as well as creating the Department of Housing and Urban Development. The Free Speech movement had emerged in the fall of 1964 at Berkeley and would eventually spread to other college campuses. At the University of Michigan, the first antiwar teach-in was held to protest the escalation of the Vietnam War and the bombing of North Vietnam.

Amid these transformations, the nation's immigration laws appeared antiquated and racist. The myriad laws that defined who would be welcomed on U.S. shores were products of late-nineteenth- and early-twentieth-century perspectives on race and nationality. The 1924 National Origins Act practically barred legal immigration from Asia while establishing the Border Patrol to manage movement from Mexico and the rest of Latin America. In addition, the act aimed to place severe limitations on immigration from southern and eastern Europe in favor of other parts of that continent, and Europe continued to supply the vast majority of immigrants to the United States well into the 1960s. With victories by the civil rights movement, Third World liberation movements, and a cold war, the U.S. quota system seemed anachronistic at best. As Attorney General Robert Kennedy told Congress in 1964, "Everywhere else in our national life, we have eliminated discrimination based on national origins, yet this system is still the foundation of our immigration law." When the same southern conservatives who fought civil rights legislation fought the new immigration bill in Congress, it was clear that the act would signify a turn away from racial discrimination in immigration.

Recognizing white fears, the bill's proponents argued that it would *not* bring about sweeping changes in the racial makeup of the nation's immigrant patterns. They pointed to the fact that the proposed law did not do away with quotas but rather replaced quotas based on the 1890 national origins of the American population with hemispheric targets and equal allocations among countries. Within the quotas, preferences would be given to professionals, skilled workers, and refugees. Moreover, a special category outside the quota would be set up for immediate family and relatives of U.S. citizens and permanent residents. The *Wall Street Journal* predicted that the family-preference system "insured that the new immigration pattern would not stray radically from the old one." What was impossible to predict, of course, was the massive movement of refugees from southeast Asia and Central America, the deterioration of the Mexican economy, and the rise of illegal immigration.

These developments led to a profound transformation in the racial makeup of the immigrant population of the United States and created new dynamics of race throughout the American West. The national Asian-American population increased fivefold, to five million, in the twenty years following the 1965 Immigration Act while the Latino population increased to fifteen million. Moreover, a new diversity within these groups emerged. Whereas the 1965 Asian-American population had a majority Japanese-

American contingent, two decades later the Chinese and Filipino populations would vie for numerical plurality. Vietnamese, Korean, Asian Indian, Laotian, and Cambodian communities would emerge in areas previously devoid of immigrants from these parts of the world. Although the Latino population remained over half Mexican-origin, new concentrations of Cuban, Salvadoran, Guatemalan, Nicaraguan, Dominican, and Colombian migrants would take their place alongside existing Mexican and Puerto Rican communities. These changes had profound implications for a nation accustomed to thinking of race in black and white terms. The 1990 census, for the first time, recorded that African Americans constituted less than 50 percent of those traditionally considered "minority." With three major umbrella populations (Asian American, African American, and Latino) emerging in the late twentieth century to form almost one-fourth of the U.S. population, in many western localities minorities became the majority.

Nowhere was this transformation more evident than in California. After 1965, one out of every four legal immigrants settled in California, and Los Angeles International Airport replaced Ellis Island as the major port of entry into the nation. In the city of Los Angeles, "minorities" of color by 1990 outnumbered the Anglo "majority," and both the Latino and Asian communities, profoundly augmented by recent immigrants, were larger than the local African-American population. In fact, by 1990, Los Angeles had a larger proportion of foreign-born than New York City, and this proportion was nearly as large as that of New York at the height of European immigration in the early twentieth century.

Probably no other topic so clearly focused the fears of "new" immigration as did language and the "threat" of foreign tongues. California remained in the forefront of the ensuing conflict. In 1971, the U.S. Supreme Court's *Lau vs. Nichols* decision initiated instruction in the native tongue of Chinese-speaking students in San Francisco, mandating bilingual education. And as elsewhere in the United States, new laws resulting from the Supreme Court decision required that bilingual ballots allow non-English-speaking citizens to participate in the electoral process.

Such services produced a backlash from those who considered English to be one facet of the definition of an "American." In 1986, California voters passed Proposition 63, an "English-only Amendment" to the state constitution, designating English as the official language of the state. Though largely symbolic, it spawned a flurry of activity that led to the passage of similar legislation in over half the states in the country. Despite all the calls for increased foreign-language acquisition by the American population in order to compete in the international economy of the Pacific Rim, non-English-speaking immigrants from the Pacific Rim were seen as liabilities. According to the bill's proponents, "Our American heritage is now threatened by language conflicts and ethnic separatism."

Ironically, almost all studies showed that foreign-born adults and children desperately wanted to learn English but that English acquisition was often difficult for older immigrants not in school. State legislators and voters seemed unwilling to provide the services that would allow for successful English language acquisition by the foreign-born. In Los Angeles County in 1986, four hundred thousand adults were on waiting lists to enter the meager number of English-language classes offered by the state's educational system. When State Senator Richard Alatorre introduced a bill to fund more classes the day after Proposition 63 passed, it was roundly defeated by those same legislators most vocal in support of English-only.

The contest over language signified a fundamental ambivalence toward immigration, particularly focused on the West. President Reagan, who emerged from California's multiethnic society, could invoke one perspective when he spoke at the one-hundredth anniversary of the Statue of Liberty. "Call it mysticism if you will, I have always believed there was some divine providence that placed this great land here between the two great oceans, to be found by a special kind of people from every corner of the world, who had a special love for freedom and a special courage that enabled them to leave their own land, leave their friends and their countrymen, and come to this new and strange land to build a new world of peace and freedom and hope." In the same year, former Governor Richard Lamm of Colorado would provoke a different vision of newcomers in his bestseller *The Immigration Time Bomb*. "Today, we Americans must lose the dream of unrestricted immigration and must face the reality behind the dream. We dreamed of America as a country of immigration, and we identified open immigration with freedom. We believed that someone poor, someone downtrodden, someone persecuted—from any other country in the world—could pull up stakes, come to America, and have another chance. . . . It is not a dream we can keep today."

Delano

In 1965, the very year that the immigration law so dramatically changed the racial and ethnic composition of the nation's people, cross-racial alliances in stubborn pursuit of that dream were already emerging in the fields near Delano, California. California's fields were cultivated by a succession of workers, including American Indians, Chinese, Japanese, Koreans, South Asians, Mexicans, Filipinos, and Europeans, who were drawn to the state by opportunities but also by labor recruiters and shippers who plied the Pacific trade. At the locus of production, in the field, these laborers acted as individuals, as women and men, as racial and ethnic groups, and as a class of workers, depending on their individual and collective sensibilities and initiatives and on the conditions under which they labored. At times, racial and ethnic affiliation enabled them to unite for higher wages and better working conditions, but at other times, racial and ethnic affiliation divided them—a condition encouraged by some planters, who employed a mixed labor force, paid differential wages for the same task, and rotated workers in a system of migratory labor.

Racial politics mirrored the racial division of labor. In the late nineteenth century, for example, California's politicians rallied white workers under the banner, "The Chinese Must Go!" And in 1903, when the Japanese-Mexican Labor Association (JMLA) of Oxnard, California, petitioned for a charter from the American Federation of Labor, AFL president Samuel Gompers replied that the agricultural union would be admitted only if it refused membership to Chinese and Japanese. J. M. Lizarras, the Mexican secretary of the JMLA, wrote to Gompers, "We would be false [to the Japanese] and to ourselves and to the cause of Unionism if we . . . accepted privileges for ourselves which are not accorded to them." Workers must unite, he urged, "without regard to their

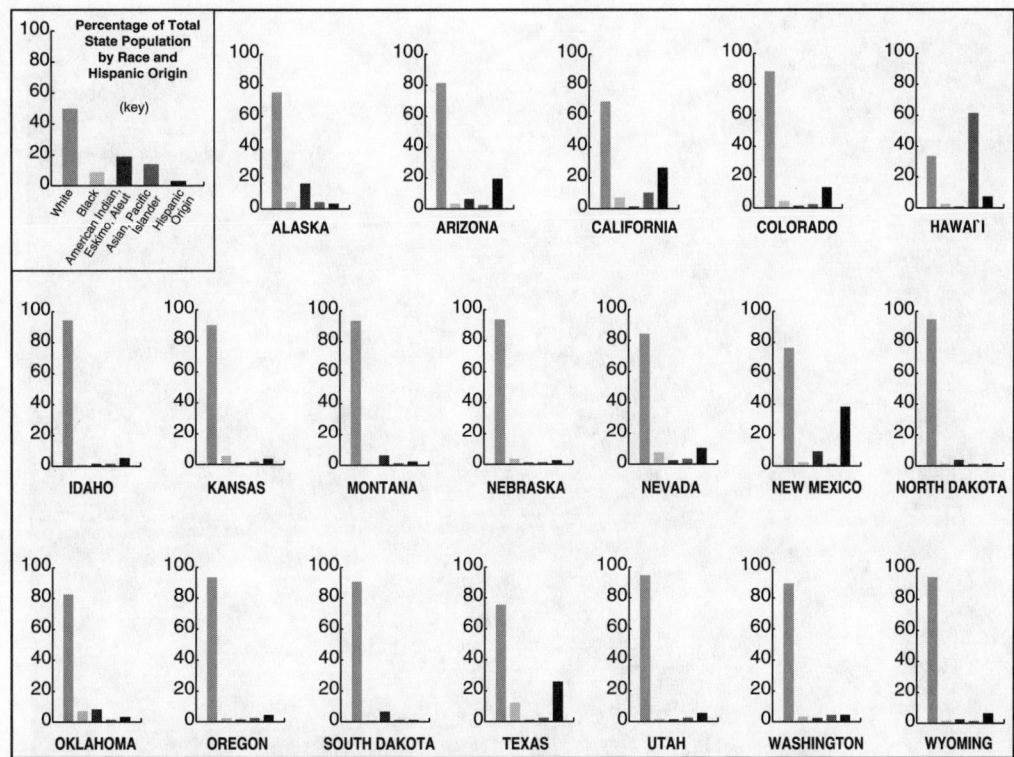

Resident Population by Race and Hispanic Origin, 1990

color or race." The Industrial Workers of the World, in contrast to the AFL, organized farm laborers "without regard to their color or race," including Europeans, Japanese, South Asians, and Puerto Ricans between 1905 and 1917. Asian workers, like whites, acted against their class interest by scabbing on and undercutting fellow Asian laborers. Class and even racial solidarity was clearly imperfect.

But the lessons learned in the fields helped to mold a new generation of leaders, who secured greater equality in the workplace and paved the way for the post–World War II drive for civil rights. When, on the evening of 7 September 1965, Filipino workers sat down in the fields near Delano, California, against the advice of their leaders in the Agricultural Workers Organizing Committee (AWOC), they followed in the footsteps of their early-twentieth-century forebears—Asian, Mexican, and European migratory farm workers who had shown the possibility of organizing and who were, in the words of a Chicago journalist, "the lowliest of workers . . . paid the least and work[ing] the hardest."

The next day, AWOC, with its Filipino organizers Larry Itliong, Ben Gines, and Pete Manuel and its Mexican organizer Dolores Huerta, struck against thirty-three grape growers. Cesar Chavez's National Farm Workers Association (NFWA) joined AWOC eight days later. In walking off his job, a Filipino farm worker in his sixties noted: "For more than thirty years I have been in strikes in the fields. I think we are going to

Emma Tenayuca helped lead a group of Mexican-American pecan shellers concerned about the advent of mechanization in a strike in San Antonio, Texas, in 1938. The workers sought to preserve jobs that paid three dollars for a 54-hour week. The widespread militancy among urban and rural workers in the 1930s laid the foundation for the civil rights and farmworkers' movements in the 1960s.

Unidentified photographer. Emma Tenayuca Leading Workers during the Pecan Shellers' Strike. *Photograph, 1938.* The San Antonio Light *Collection, U. T. The Institute of Texan Cultures, San Antonio, Texas.*

win this one, but whether or not we win, the growers will know they have been in one hell of a fight."

The five-year Delano strike was notable for the gains achieved by farm workers, for Cesar Chavez's rise to national prominence, and for the convergence of issues of labor, civil rights, religion, and education. Philip Vera Cruz, an AWOC member at the time, observed that NFWA was "a mixture of many things," including church and student groups such as the California Migrant Ministry and the Student Non-violent Coordinating Committee, African-American groups such as the Congress of Racial Equality, civil rights workers, and youth volunteers. NFWA, added Vera Cruz, was more than a union bent on raising wages; it was a social movement, "fighting . . . for the rights of people and the dignity of human beings."

Six months into the strike, AWOC and NFWA discussed the need for improved communication and a coordinated effort between the two groups. Both the Teamsters and the AFL-CIO sought to consolidate the strikers under their respective unions. The Teamsters, reported Vera Cruz, told AWOC's Filipinos that NFWA's Mexicans, being more numerous, would soon take their jobs, and both AWOC's and NFWA's members feared that unity would reduce their ethnic autonomy. Yet the groups merged in August 1966 as the United Farm Workers Organizing Committee, despite the misgivings.

The strike became a cause—for a people, for a class, for a nation. Cesar Chavez mused, "We have to find some cross between being a movement and being a union."

As a member of the Senate Farm Labor Subcommittee, Robert F. Kennedy supported the strikers in well-publicized hearings held in Sacramento, Visalia, and Delano in March 1966, joined the picket lines, and with his wife, Ethel, helped to raise funds for the farm workers. When Cesar Chavez ended a twenty-five-day fast on 10 March 1968, Martin Luther King, Jr., telegraphed him: "My colleagues and I commend you for your bravery, salute you for your indefatigable work against poverty and injustice, and pray for your health and continuing service as one of the outstanding men of America. The plight of your people and ours is so grave that we all desperately need the inspiring example and effective leadership you have given."

The strikers' persistence and the grape boycott that affected over one hundred U.S. and Canadian cities led to settlements with the growers in the summer of 1970. The great strike was over, but the farm workers' modern-day battle had just begun. "This is a war," declared the woman warrior Dolores Huerta in 1973, "this is a real war—all of the growers and right-wing elements . . . are trying to crush the farm workers . . . we have to act like it's a real war."

San Francisco City Hall

In the face of new waves of immigration and shifting power relations in the hinterlands, the meaning of the West's vaunted opportunities seemed up for grabs. Other groups who migrated to the region confronted a white population that was feeling increasingly bemused and beleaguered. On 27 November 1978, thirty-two-year old Dan White, a San Francisco native, the son of a San Francisco fireman, a Vietnam veteran, a former member of the city's Board of Supervisors, and a man with an image so clean-cut that an acquaintance told *Time Magazine* that if White " had been a breakfast cereal . . . he would have had to be Wheaties," snuck into San Francisco City Hall and shot Mayor George Moscone and Supervisor Harvey Milk to death.

The *Time Magazine* headline proclaimed it "Another Day of Death." *Newsweek* called it "one more eruption of the San Francisco syndrome, a mindless streak of politically tinged violence that has afflicted the Bay Area with nearly 100 bomb blasts and more than a dozen murder victims in the past ten years." Yet this "day of death" resulted in a gathering of thirty thousand for a torchlight ceremony at city hall, an Oscar-winning documentary on Harvey Milk, a television docudrama, and a stage play. By these vehicles, the public rejected the notion that the shootings had been "mindless" and instead struggled to make sense of the murders. Part of the sense they made was regional. Despite any number of equally lawless incidents across the country, many analysts saw in the incident something peculiarly western.

Moscone's death faded from view as attention centered on the openly gay Milk, the growth of San Francisco's gay population (approximately one-eighth of the city and one-fifth of the city's adults at the time), and the creation of a "gay city" in the Castro, the district that had elected Milk. To these observers, the Castro and the conservative vigilante White echoed images of a West both open and violent.

The story is more complicated, however, than westering gay utopians and lone gun-toters defending "law and order." It also involved San Francisco's shift from a manufacturing to a service city with corporate headquarters and deracinated yuppies. It involved the remnants of blue-collar Irish neighborhoods, an Irish police force, and Irish and Italian political machines. It involved, in short, the postwar, postindustrial transformation of the United States. In this brave new world, "homesteading" was urban, not rural. The gay men flocking to San Francisco in the early 1970s homesteaded in the mixed ethnic blue-collar and increasingly unemployed Castro. Urban or rural, homesteading still recreated the landscape.

Although stories of gay and lesbian life in San Francisco go back as far as the nineteenth century, the Castro as a gay district had two sets of more recent roots, one in World War II and the other in the 1960s. During World War II, the enormous need for men and women in the military had led to a retreat from the military's antigay policies. According to the historian Lillian Faderman, when General Dwight Eisenhower gave Sgt. Johnnie Phelps an order to ferret out the lesbians in her battalion, she replied: "Yessir. If the General pleases I will be happy to do this investigation. . . . But, sir, it would be unfair of me not to tell you, my name is going to head the list . . . . You should also be aware that you're going to have to replace all the file clerks, the section heads, most of the commanders, and the motor pool." Eisenhower responded, "Forget the order." For many gays and lesbians, particularly those from small towns, the war was their first experience meeting sizable numbers of homosexuals. Few of these people wanted to return to the isolation of their former life. They tended to stay in the cities where they had landed on their return to the United States. Moreover, after the war, when the military again adopted repressive measures toward homosexuals, it sent thousands of "undesirable" discharges to the nearest U.S. port. All of these factors helped to produce homosexual enclaves in New York, Boston, Los Angeles, San Francisco, and other cities. Businesses arose to serve a specifically homosexual clientele and, for the first time, could survive.

This was an evolution more urban than western. Indeed, many of the migrants came from a distinctly less open West, from rural Nebraska or Iowa. And yet it was in the West and not in the East that the first gay and lesbian civil rights associations began in the 1950s: the male Mattachine Society, which began in Los Angeles and moved to San Francisco, and the Daughters of Bilitis, which began in San Francisco. Unlike the counterculture simultaneously launched among the beat poets, including the gay Allen Ginsberg, these two societies were relatively conservative. According to the writer Frances Fitzgerald, they aimed primarily to prove the respectability of homosexuals. By 1961, other homosexuals gathered in the city's thirty homosexual bars, and Jose Sarrio, a drag entertainer protesting police harassment, won six thousand votes in his bid for city supervisor.

But this fluorescence was brief. In that same year, 1961, in response to election campaign accusations that he had made San Francisco the national headquarters for sex deviates, the mayor, George Christopher, allegedly launched a police crackdown. Hundreds of men were arrested simply for dancing together or holding hands. Police confiscated copies of Ginsberg's *Howl*. Bars were closed. After 1965, although other gay organizations remained in San Francisco, Mattachine's headquarters moved to New York.

In the late 1960s and early 1970s, Mayor Joseph Alioto ruled San Francisco as an old-time, big-city boss. He relied heavily on ward bosses, who kept his machine running smoothly in the city's Irish and Italian Catholic neighborhoods. But at the end of the decade, the manufacturers and shippers who employed his constituency began to falter. To bolster the city's weakening economy, Alioto lured real estate developers and corporate headquarters to San Francisco. Yet these sectors provided few jobs for blue-collar workers, and Alioto's supporters were leaving town. By the 1970s, only one of San Francisco's eleven voting districts had a blue-collar majority.

While the city's overall population declined in these years, the proportion of people age twenty-five to thirty-four rose by over 25 percent. These young, largely white professionals were lured by San Francisco's new economy. They may have come from blue-collar families, but they were college-educated and did not identify primarily by ethnic heritage. Among them were the gay men who began to gentrify the decaying blue-collar Irish streets of the Castro.

In the 1950s and 1960s gay bars had largely been in the Tenderloin and the decorators' district and, slightly later, in the warehouse district. What made the Castro different was that it was a residential neighborhood. It had shops and homes. It could cultivate a whole gay way of living, twenty-four hours a day. It arose as a result of the changing economy and demographics of San Francisco in the late 1960s and early 1970s.

Highly mobile socially, economically, and geographically, gay or straight, the new city residents were poor fodder for a city machine. The politics of the new West, at least in San Francisco, seemed to call for more accommodation. Richard Hongisto, a civil rights, antiwar activist elected sheriff of San Francisco County in 1971, tried to improve relations between gays and the police. George Moscone, elected mayor in 1977, appointed minorities, women, and gays to city offices. He exemplified the blending of the old and the new. The son of an alcoholic milk-wagon driver (another account has his father as a guard at San Quentin), Moscone had put himself through college and Hastings Law School and then rose through San Francisco's Italian-American political establishment to serve in the state senate. As the majority leader in the state senate, Moscone, along with Assemblyman Willie Brown, who would later serve as speaker of the California state assembly, had helped secure the repeal of state statutes proscribing forms of consensual sex in 1975.

Also elected in 1977 were Harvey Milk and Dan White. Milk was the city's first openly gay man to serve in high public office. Milk and thousands like him had flocked to the cities during the most assertive gay liberation movement to date, which had begun when police raided a New York gay bar, the Stonewall Inn, in 1969. San Francisco had the special attraction of a relatively large and open homosexual community already in place.

But it was not simply that Milk was gay. He was part of San Francisco's yuppie revolution. Born into a middle-class Jewish family on Long Island, Milk had attended teacher's college, served in the navy, taught high school history and math, and worked as a financial analyst for insurance and Wall Street investment companies in New York before coming to San Francisco in 1969 to run a camera store. When Milk first entered politics, in 1973, the Castro was still largely Irish and Catholic. Milk learned how to build coalitions. When, in 1977, a change in election laws meant that city supervisor elections were no longer citywide, Milk was ready for his first success. Because of Milk, gay bars boycotted Coors beer for antilabor practices. With a new haircut and three-piece suits, Milk spoke on issues of education, street cleaning and lighting, and libraries. Labor unions, housewives, teachers, drag queens, gays, and lesbians all supported Milk. Milk had proven to be not only a gay activist but also a good ward boss.

The same year, Dan White was elected from the only district in the city that voted for the Briggs Initiative to drive openly gay teachers out of the classroom. Unlike Milk, White was a native of San Francisco. In high school, he captained the baseball and football teams and was a Golden Gloves boxer. After serving in Vietnam, he worked three and a half years as a policeman before joining the fire department in 1973. While running for office, he was cited for a heroic rescue of a mother and a child from the seventeenth floor of a burning building. White ran as the law-and-order candidate, the hope of a conservative policemen's association. He was the youngest supervisor ever elected in San Francisco.

In June 1978, between 240,000 and 375,000 people turned out for the annual Gay Freedom Day Parade in San Francisco, a city of 700,000 people. Marchers included Gay American Indians, Disabled Gay People and Friends, gay political leaders, the Gay Latino Alliance, a gay Jewish synagogue, a Marilyn Monroe look-alike, Dykes on Bikes, the local Lesbian Association Kazoo Marching Band, and many others. It was, after all, a city with approximately 90 gay bars, 9 gay newspapers, 150 gay organizations, and a gay yellow pages for the clothing stores, stockbrokerages, realtors, churches, and other institutions of the Castro. Estimates of the city's gay population ranged from 75,000 to 150,000.

Were the Milk and Moscone assassinations in late November of the same year the result of a clash over defining the city's landscape? Perhaps, but White was a problematic hero for the old guard. Despite his squeaky-clean image, he had a history of gambling and expensive trips to Reno. On his policeman's salary he had bought first a Jaguar and then a Porsche before taking a leave of absence to hitchhike throughout the United States. After serving for ten months of his term as city supervisor, he had resigned for financial reasons. The potato stand at Fisherman's Wharf he had hoped would support his new wife and infant son and pay for his new house was floundering. White soon changed his mind and asked for his Board of Supervisors job back. In the meantime, it became clear that White's behavior on the board had alienated his fellow supervisors. On a closely balanced board, where narrow victories were common, White was prone to hold grudges and to be a difficult colleague. Moscone decided instead to appoint a symbol of the new accommodating West, Don Horanzy, a real estate loan officer of the federal H.U.D. Horanzy was not an office-seeker but had founded a voluntary "All People's Coalition" in White's lower-middle-class mixed-race and ethnic district. The coalition fought crime and spruced up the neighborhood.

From a radio journalist, White learned he would not be reappointed, and the next day he murdered Moscone and Milk. The trial centered on what became known as the Twinkie Defense—the impact of junk food on depressed people—rather than on city politics, race, and homophobia. When the jury, largely white, working-class Catholics, many of whom lived in White's district, returned a verdict of voluntary manslaughter rather than premeditated murder, five thousand marchers faced down the police at city hall. The police chief, Charles Gain, a Moscone appointee seen as an outsider by the policemen, particularly when he removed the American flag from his office and replaced it with plants, prevented the police from storming the crowd until the crowd began to disperse after three hours. Frustrated police supporters of White tore off their shields to avoid identification and headed for the Castro, where they invaded bars and savagely beat patrons. Sixty-one police and one hundred gay men were hospitalized.

After that violent catharsis, coalition politics reigned in San Francisco. Dianne Feinstein became mayor with 80 percent of the gay vote and appointed a lesbian as police commissioner. But she also removed Police Chief Gain and replaced him with the Irish-Catholic Cornelius Murphy, who had come up through the ranks of the department.

Florence and Normandie

In the mythic West of dime novels and movies, the law enforcers—the marshals and the sheriffs—most often symbolized the heroic, self-denying male who could single-handedly impose order on a chaotic landscape in the best interests of all. The ability of a police force to stand above the fray rather than in it, however, had been laid open to question by the violence in San Francisco, as it had in the race riots of the 1940s. The idea forcefully exploded again in Los Angeles in 1992.

Probably no other event better captured the complexity of the western experience of race than the three days of riots from 29 April to 1 May 1992. On the surface, the Los Angeles unrest was a direct result of the "not guilty" verdicts in the trial of four white police officers for the beating of a black motorist, Rodney King. Yet the reality of racial conflict can never be so easily characterized in the American West, where "race" has always had a multiplicity of meanings. Here, the historical legacy of Native American, Mexican, and Latino populations had confounded the images of race brought by scores of American migrants to the region—white and black. Moreover, Asian immigration, be it Korean, Japanese, Chinese, or Filipino, had consistently been a crucial factor in representations of race in the West, from as far back as the mid-nineteenth century. The meanings of race in the West have barely begun to be explored by eastern commentators—including those who have brought the East with them as migrants. Most Americans still believe that the diversity of the American West is solely of recent origin and can easily be reframed as simply another version of a bipolar racial model: white and "other."

For most who experienced the 1992 disturbances through the media, the most searing image of the Los Angeles riots was taken by a local television helicopter above the corner of Florence and Normandie avenues in South Central Los Angeles on April 30. The image of Reginald Denny, a white truck driver, being pulled from his cab, beaten, and spat on by a group of young African-American males quickly became a counterimage to the inhumane police beating of the black motorist King a year earlier. These two events, both captured on videotape, dominated representations of the rage in Los Angeles, a city haunted by poverty, racism, and police brutality. So powerful, they pushed out other, equally vivid and telling representations, allowing almost all commentators to explain the riot by invoking long-standing notions of racial conflict that speak exclusively of white-black tensions.

A closer look at the victims of violence at the corner of Florence and Normandie reveals not only the complexity of the Los Angeles riots but also the way many academics and social commentators avoided the implications of these events and surrendered to the simplistic notions of race fed to the public by the mass media. Most people outside of Los Angeles were surprised to hear that Denny was not the only person injured on that corner. Mesmerized by video images of a single beating of one white man, people found it difficult to imagine that thirty other individuals were injured at that corner, most pulled from their cars and some requiring extensive hospitalization. Tellingly, almost all the other victims were people of color, including a Mexican couple and their one-year-old child hit with rocks and bottles; a Japanese-American man, stripped, beaten, and kicked after being mistaken for Korean; a Vietnamese manicurist left stunned and bloodied after being robbed; and a Latino family with two five-year-old twin girls, who each suffered shattered glass wounds in the face and upper body. All of these acts of violence occurred before Denny entered the intersection.

Even more complex was the case of Byron Bowers, the adopted son of two African Americans (one of whom was an interracial communications professor), who had only recently learned that he was a product of an interracial union. A mob yelled, "He's white!" Bowers yelled back, "I'm half-black!" His jaw was broken and his car pummeled with crowbars. A twenty-four-year-old Belizian immigrant woman, already suffering a black eye for her efforts, came to the rescue.

The decisions made by young, angry African Americans at that corner as they chose whom to hurt speak volumes on the complexities of racial and ethnic identity in late-twentieth-century America. For some, the decision was not about who was white but about who was not black. For others, it centered on how Latinos and Asians had "invaded the territory" they claimed as their own turf. South Central Los Angeles, in fact, had been demographically transformed since the 1965 immigration law, so that 51 percent of the population was Latino by 1992. According to videotapes, some rioters shouted, "Let the Mexicans go!" But they added, "Show the Koreans who rules!" Whereas the famous 1965 Watts uprising could be read as an African-American community's response to poverty and police brutality, even defining "community" by 1992 became difficult.

Although the violence began as a response to a verdict passed by an almost all-white jury against an almost all-white set of police officers, other people of color were quickly engaged in the deadly discourse. The meaning of racial identities was consistently contested, as at the corner of Florence and Normandie. Over the next three days, the dynamics of racial and class tensions, rage against the police, and antiforeign sentiment came together in violent, unpredictable fashion. The mayhem spread to engulf the city, creating the worst modern race riot in American history. More than fifty people died, residences and businesses suffered about one billion dollars worth of damage, and police made over fourteen thousand arrests. In the first three days of rioting, over four thousand fires were set, and eighteen hundred people were treated for gunshot wounds. The destruction occurred throughout the Los Angeles Basin, and the participants and victims were indeed multiethnic.

Underlying much of the frustration of the riot participants was the collapse of the inner-city economy, the negative flip side of the new "Pacific Rim." Like the transformation of San Francisco's economy, which had set the stage for tensions in the 1970s, Los Angeles had lost 150,000 manufacturing jobs in the previous three years, and each of these jobs was estimated to take another three associated jobs with it. The new jobs

created were disproportionately low-wage and dead-end forms of employment; 40 percent of all jobs created in Los Angeles from 1979 to 1989 paid less than $15,000 a year. Most of these jobs were taken by recent immigrants, leaving African Americans few viable options for secure employment. The average earnings of employed black men fell 24 percent from 1973 to 1989, and unemployment swelled to record levels in the inner city. Middle-income Los Angeles was rapidly disappearing, leaving little opportunity for anyone to move up the economic ladder. This inequality was highly racialized; the median household net worth for Anglos in the city in 1991 was $31,904 but was only $1,353 for non-Anglos.

Clearly, one obvious target of the frustrated residents in the inner city were the Korean merchants in South Central. In 1990, 145,000 Koreans lived in Los Angeles County, a 142 percent increase from ten years earlier and a phenomenal growth from only 9,000 in 1970. Unable to transfer their education and skills to the U.S. labor market, many Korean immigrants had pooled their funds to start small businesses in ethnic communities throughout the city. They had replaced Jews, who had departed after the 1965 Watts riots. They now saw their businesses burn to the ground and suffer widespread looting. These small merchants had filled a vacuum created by the abandonment of the inner city by large retail businesses and by discrimination against African-American entrepreneurs. As Korean immigrants became targets for racial attack, other Asian Americans, particularly American-born Chinese and Japanese, worried that they might be mistaken for Korean and thus distanced themselves from recent immigrants.

Yet much of the damage to Korean businesses occurred in Koreatown itself, where one-third of that community's businesses were located. The residential population of Koreatown was overwhelmingly Latino, and it was this ethnic group that primarily engaged in looting these stores. In fact, 43 percent of those arrested during the riots were Latino; only 34 percent were African American, contradicting the notion that this was simply a black-Korean conflict. At the same time, the Immigration and Naturalization Service took advantage of arrests for curfew violations and deported over two thousand Latino noncitizens.

The situation remained charged in the weeks and months following the riots. Overt citywide battles diminished, but one week in October 1992 witnessed the eruption of racial hostility between black and Latino students in three high schools and one junior high, leading to injuries and arrests. Korean merchants who sought to rebuild their businesses were stymied by community efforts to keep liquor stores and other unwanted enterprises out of inner-city neighborhoods, causing a second financial disaster on top of their burned or looted merchandise. A summer campaign to ensure jobs for African Americans in rebuilding Los Angeles led to confrontations with Latino workers on construction sites. An effort to replace the departing Latino school superintendent with another Latino set Mexican-American organizations squarely against the hiring of a qualified African American. In the wake of the disturbances Rodney King asked, "Can we all get along?" The question seemed directed not toward the city's white population but toward its communities of color.

Zuni Salt Lake

To some of its residents, the contested landscape of the West is hardly new, and the stakes have always been high. The region's various indigenous peoples struggled over the land before European Americans, African Americans, and Asian Americans arrived. Although those disputes continued, in a sense like the battles at the corner of Florence and Normandie avenues, the enormity of the European-American challenge to native rights eventually dwarfed them.

Zuni Salt Lake covers more than eleven hundred acres in western New Mexico. Surrounded by piñon, saltbush, greasewood, and gama grass, the lake lies in a high valley, where only nine inches of rain falls annually. Fresh and salt waters stream and seep into the lake. Long before the advent of Europeans, the Zuni, Hopi, Navajo, and Acoma Pueblo peoples gathered salt there in sacred rituals. In 1540, Coronado called it "the best and whitest" he had ever seen.

In the 1930s, the indigenous peoples still gathered salt at the lake, maintaining the ancient rituals, but they no longer walked their hot, long, and dusty trails and prayed at the shrines along the way. Instead, in pickup trucks, they gratefully headed for the lake along modern roads. Yet, they had not exactly abandoned the old trails. The Hopis still referred to the trails in rituals and prayers. They had once been sacred; they remained sacred.

In 1990, when the Salt River Project, an Arizona Utility Company, developed an 18,612-acre coal mine near Zuni Salt Lake with a forty-mile transportation corridor to a power plant in Arizona, little in this practice had changed. The Hopi's sacred landscape was the geologist's map of resources. One hundred years earlier, the outcome of that conjunction would have been clear. In 1874, after all, the discovery of gold in the Black Hills had ultimately led the U.S. Supreme Court tacitly to condone the violation of a Lakota Sioux–U.S. treaty that had guaranteed that the Lakota alone would possess the,

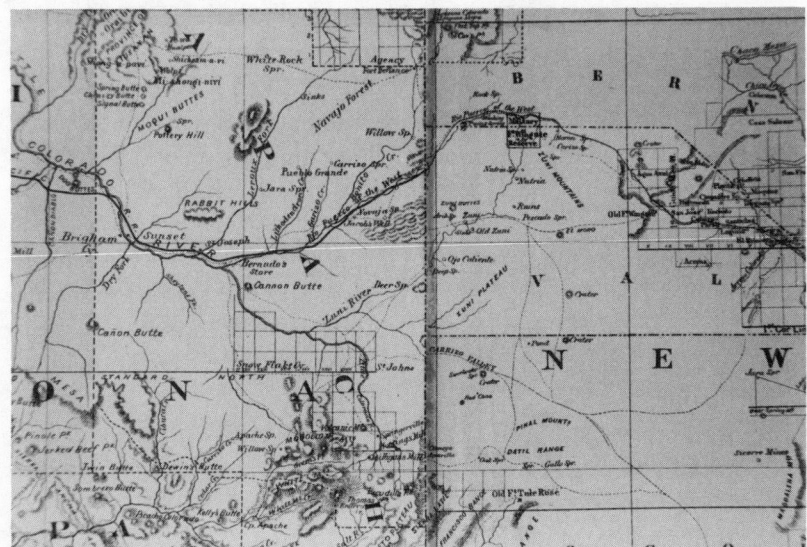

The diverse ways of depicting the physical terrain around Zuni Salt Lake represented in a 19th-century commercial map and a 20th-century Hopi artist's mural, suggest the vast cultural differences to be accommodated in the joint-use venture between European-American and Hopi residents of the Southwest.

S. Augustus Mitchell, publisher. County and Township Map of Arizona and New Mexico *(detail). Lithograph, 1881. Courtesy E. Richard Hart.*

Fred Kabotie (b. 1900). Hopi Salt Pilgrimage. *Mural (located in the Painted Desert Inn, Petrified Forest National Park, Arizona), 1948. Photograph courtesy of the Western Archaeological Center, National Park Service, Tucson, Arizona.*

to them, sacred territory. The settlement offered them money instead. The Lakota rejected the settlement, to no avail. In 1990, Indians owned none of the land involved in the Salt River Project's development. But other factors had changed. As recently as 1965, fewer than a dozen Indians held law degrees; in 1990, between five hundred and six hundred did. This small army of lawyers not only had experienced more success in direct engagements with adversaries but also had become more adept at using laws for their own ends. For example, they had used endangered species legislation to protect sacred lands and traditional uses. In the case of the Salt River Project, they could, if need be, have used historic preservation legislation for the same purposes.

When the research required for the environmental impact statement revealed the concerns of the various tribal groups, however, the Salt River Project pursued the matter cooperatively. Despite the fact that no one alive could remember exactly where the trails were, the Salt River Project asked the tribes to recommend ethnohistorians with whom they felt comfortable working, hired those ethnohistorians, asked each tribe how it would like to proceed, and worked with the subsequent tribal-created research teams to identify the pilgrimage trails and other sites of concern. The composition of the research teams varied with the tribe; some included members of the tribal council, and all included elders.

Such a collaboration was not easy for either side. Each of the thirty-three Hopi clans and each of the ten villages had a private history of its origins, carefully guarded not only from non-Hopis but also from other Hopi clans and villagers. European-American scholars accustomed to academic freedom had to accommodate tribal and individual decisions about confidentiality.

Even beyond notions of history and historical research, this cross-cultural collaboration required extra effort. The degree to which the landscapes of the indigenous peoples and the Salt River Project diverged can be seen in the dramatically different ways each group represented time and space, that is to say, the differences in the maps each produced. The Painted Desert Inn at Petrified Forest National Park displays a mural, *Hopi Salt Pilgrimage*, painted by Fred Kabotie. To European-American eyes, it looks like a nice, geometric picture, with a squiggly line running around the edge of the frame, with some people walking, cooking, bathing, sleeping, and hunting, and with some animals, one rectangle of water, and one plaza. To Hopis, the squiggly line represents the pilgrimage trail, with appropriate symbols as to distance, landmarks such as springs, and behavior appropriate at each site. As early as 1881, a European-American company run by Augustus Mitchell also made a map that included the trail. To European Americans, his map represents "reality." Euro-Americans can "read" this map. Yet it too is full of squiggly lines, dots, grids, and symbols (including writing) that no one sees when walking through the countryside. Each group's map represents a way of thinking about the land, of knowing the land, of possessing the land. The maps are of such different systems that simply superimposing one on the other makes the landscape harder, not easier, to read. In the past, the solution was to erase one map. For Zuni Salt Lake, despite all the difficulties, the two maps would coexist.

The tribal peoples who inhabit this region of the Southwest have had the strength to create an environment in which companies such as the Salt River Project value their contributions in constructing the landscape. But these tribal peoples' power is distinctly limited. They could save their pilgrimage trails. They could not, though they wanted to, prevent the opening of the strip mine.

Since the energy crunch of the early 1970s, increased pressure has been brought to bear on resources within the nation's boundaries. Though the Salt River Project's mine lay outside reservation lands, many of the nation's energy resources do not. With the management of both the nation's resources and the Indian reservations in the same department (Interior), it is not surprising that for years the federal government let leases to develop reservation resources at below market price to non-Indians. In 1976, twenty-five western tribes joined in self-protection to create the Council of Energy Resource Tribes (CERT). These tribes hold approximately half of the U.S. private uranium reserves, 15 percent of all coal in the United States, and 30 percent of all low-sulfur strippable coal in the U.S. West, as well as smaller percentages of oil and natural gas.

Although CERT was able to garner a larger share of the profits from resource extraction for its members, it did not make Indians wealthy. Oil and gas production on CERT reservations earned $169 million in 1980, before energy prices fell, but that still amounted to only $422.50 for each of the four hundred thousand inhabitants. Indeed, the seemingly intractable poverty of reservations despite numerous development and welfare programs mystifies some and exasperates others. At one end of the wide range of explanations lies world systems theory, which argues that expansive, relatively wealthy economies like those of European Americans, in order to sustain their own growth, systematically drain peripheral areas, such as Indian reservations, of resources, thereby not simply neglecting to develop them but rendering them unsustainable. At the other end, theorists blame the lack of entrepreneurial spirit among the communally oriented indigenous peoples. Small business funds, pencil factories, industrial parks, and resorts have all been tried and have failed on these usually remote and often arid lands with little infrastructure. The most successful enterprises seem to involve gambling. For example, bingo cut unemployment among California's Morongo Indians from 64 percent to virtually zero by 1987.

Whatever the cause, on the nation's roughly 270 Indian reservations in 1980, where just over one-half of the 1.4 million Indians lived, unemployment stood at twice the national average and on some reservations hovered near 80 percent. Roughly one-third of rural Native Americans in that year lived below the poverty line, and with this bleak picture, over 40 percent of Indian students entering high school dropped out before finishing. Indians ranked first of all groups in deaths caused by suicide and alcohol consumption. In the cities, Indians fared only slightly better. Just under one-quarter there lived below the poverty line. Most still had close ties to the reservation and planned to retire there. They visited often and left children to grow up in a countryside they hoped was more wholesome than the parts of the cities in which they could afford housing.

In 1984, Indians received a total of $2.6 billion from a wide range of federal agencies; if evenly distributed, the sum amounted to $1,900 per Indian. The Reagan administration and Congress in the 1980s systematically reduced expenditures on Indians, by 18 percent between 1982 and 1984 alone, hurting not only relief recipients but also the almost one-third of employed Native Americans who held government jobs. (Since the 1960s, the percentage of Bureau of Indian Affairs employees who are Native Americans rose steadily, reaching over three-quarters in 1982.) Dwindling resources heightened tensions, even within tribes, about who qualified for these funds, what constituted a Native American, and who should decide.

Despite increasing delegation of responsibilities to tribes, including contracting health and welfare services previously provided directly by the government, the federal government still held the trump cards in both legal and financial resources. It is no accident that one of the most militant Indian rights groups to emerge from the 1960s, the American Indian Movement, continually attacked federally held entities, from Alcatraz in San Francisco Bay to the Bureau of Indian Affairs headquarters in Washington, D.C. In turn, the American Indian Movement became the target of constant federal harassment and infiltration.

As national resources grew scarcer, including water and fish as well as coal, oil, and lumber, conflict sharpened between seemingly remote populations (Hopis and Los Angeles developers, for example) and between intimately contiguous populations (such as Hawaiians and European Americans) who had different notions about the best use of land and water and who still used different maps. Conditions varied tremendously from reservation to reservation, and for most Indians, tribal identities were still far stronger than pantribal ones; yet like many western issues, relations between Native Americans and European Americans became international. The International Indian Treaty Council lobbied the United Nations, and the U.N. Working Group on Indigenous Populations in 1990 rejected any planned triumphal celebration of the quincentenary of Columbus's voyage. As the group stated, "It negates our existence, our systems of government, our cultures, and our pre-columbian and pre-colonial history."

Borders, 1993

Borders, whether Indian reservations or international, whether racial or physical, do not exist in nature. They must be constructed. In the West, those constructions and their human costs have been particularly evident and particularly, perhaps predictably, imperfect.

In April 1993, police in San Diego, California, responded quickly to a report of a kidnapping of a blond preschool boy by a dark-haired Latino at a cafe in a posh neighborhood. Two women dining in the cafe had seen a "suspicious-looking" couple bribing the youngster in Spanish with promises of toys before the man left with the boy in a yellow cab. Police tracked down the taxi and, with guns drawn, entered the house where the two had been dropped off. They feared the kidnapper would quickly take his victim south and disappear into Mexico. Finding the house empty, they began a citywide search before they found the two walking back from a neighborhood park. After several tense moments of interrogation, it became clear that the police had made a terrible mistake. The supposed kidnapper was Guillermo Gómez-Peña, a recipient of one of the coveted MacArthur Fellowships awarded to a few extraordinary individuals each year. He was a world-renowned performance artist whose work highlights life in the hybrid world of the U.S.-Mexico border region. The boy he had been suspected of kidnapping was his own son. At the restaurant, his Anglo ex-wife had transferred the boy to him for an extended weekend visit.

This story contains many themes ever present along the border with Mexico in the late twentieth century. In these borderlands, the terms *alien* and *native* have come to capture the poles of historical and contemporary discussion surrounding social legitimacy in the American West. *Alien* embodies the notion of an outsider to society, an interloper without a claim to an area's resources or history. *Native* paints a picture of one who belongs—an insider, a genuine participant in the society with full legal, historical, almost "natural" rights—one to be counted as part of a particular community. The process by which those once considered native to a region came to be seen as alien and by which those once clearly alien came to be seen as native has been intricately tied to issues of race, colonization, immigration, and law enforcement throughout the century.

A result of the 1846–48 Mexican-American War, the southern border of the United

As much a gate as a barrier, the long border between the United States and Mexico has become a focal point of contemporary debate about the future of U.S. immigration and trade policy.

Douglas Kent Hall (b. 1938). The Border Fence: Tijuana/San Ysidro. *Gelatin silver print.* © Douglas Kent Hall. *Courtesy of the photographer.*

States remains one of the longest continuous borders shared by two nations, spanning a distance of over two thousand miles. In addition, in no other place does such a rich nation share such a long boundary with such a relatively poor country. Though Mexican culture continued to dominate both sides of the border until after the turn of the century, Anglo Americans quickly assumed positions of political and economic power along the border after 1848, and cultural definitions of insider and outsider remained drawn in largely racial terms. In the early twentieth century, the increased migration of Mexicans to work on the railroads, in mines, and in agricultural fields in the Southwest began to concern American public officials. As one worried Labor Department official put it in 1922: "The psychology of the average Mexican alien unskilled worker from Mexico is that when he enters in any manner into the United States that he is only upon a visit to an unknown portion of his own country. . . . To him there is no real or imaginary line." The presence of a strong border culture in which passage had been largely unregulated mitigated against stringent enforcement of immigration regulations already in place by the turn of the century.

In 1917, the U.S. Congress passed an immigration act that placed new restrictions on immigration from Europe, South Asia, and Mexico. Southwestern border officials realized that these new restrictions, which included a literacy test, a medical examination, and a head tax, would lead to increased violations of the law. They were right. For the first time, significant numbers of aliens illegally crossed into the United States to avoid the head tax. The Immigration Service also realized that labor recruiters and southwestern employers cared little how their prospective employees had come to the United States. These conditions led the chief inspector in El Paso to report that supervision of the border was so lax "that practically any alien desirous of entering the

United States and possessed of ordinary intelligence and persistence could readily find the means of so doing without fear of detection." Border officials realized that they were almost completely unable to stem the rising tide of undocumented immigration from Mexico.

Yet, unquestionably, the Border Patrol, established in 1924, was crucial in defining the Mexican as "the other," "the alien," in the region. J. C. Machuca, who worked for the El Paso Department of Immigration in the late 1920s, recalled that some of the early immigration inspectors were members of the Ku Klux Klan, a leading organization in the El Paso region at the time. Those Mexicans who had been long-term border residents could continue to cross in a casual fashion if, and only if, they were granted this special privilege by some Anglo benefactor. Officials would consistently denigrate others who crossed at the bridge, even if their papers were perfectly legal. Eventually, crossing the border became a painful and abrupt event permeated by an atmosphere of racism and control—an event that clearly demarcated one society from another.

Most early immigration officials were, in fact, newcomers to the region. Clifford Alan Perkins, who arrived in El Paso, Texas, in 1908 to begin a fifty-year career as an immigration inspector, remembered his initial impressions. "To a young man from a small Wisconsin farming community with a suspected case of tuberculosis, disappointed in his hopes for a college education and a career in professional baseball, it was a strange and wonderful place. I knew nothing about the people of Mexico, whose history, language and customs were to be so deeply interwoven into the fabric of my life and I was totally unprepared for some of the experiences that were ahead of me, but I was fascinated by what I saw." Perkins must be viewed as a cultural immigrant to the West and, as such, reflects the majority experience of European Americans in the region, much like the European Americans who decided to settle in Hawai`i in the twentieth century. Indeed, the cultural transformation of internal migrants was just as powerful an experience as that of a transnational immigrant, since Perkins arrived in El Paso with little knowledge of the area except a general optimistic portrait of the West.

Still, as a U.S.-born Anglo American, Perkins would become an immigration official within six months of his arrival. He was entrusted with the power, born of the U.S. conquest of the region, to administer the regulations of passage into American society. Because of the state's growing role in the twentieth century, the job of immigration officer came to mark a new cultural dynamic in the region. The administration of national policies made two thousand miles away in Washington, D.C., was handled by a newcomer whose authority was wielded over a population more experienced and at home than he. Though local concerns often encouraged the bending of the immigration laws, the die was cast toward greater restriction of movement. El Paso was defined as a "port-of-entry"—a term developed for seaports where movement implied travel over long distances and few interlocking points of contact between nations. Increasingly, areas hundreds of miles from the nearest ocean—regions defined by common land boundaries—would be asked to serve as politicized points of passage and cultural lines of separation.

By the late twentieth century, the border began to imply a sharp demarcation not only between the United States and Mexico but also between Mexican-origin people

The ongoing tensions over illegal immigration across the Mexico-U.S. border pose a particular problem for U.S. federal agents of Mexican descent, who can find their own identities and loyalties challenged by co-workers as well as immigrants.

Jay Dusard (b. 1937). Agents Larry Dalton, Elvin Harmon, Rogelio Martínez, Domingo Sánchez, and Fabián Casas, U. S. Border Patrol, Rio Grande City, Texas. *Gelatin silver print, 1985. © Jay Dusard 1985. Courtesy of the photographer.*

based on their nativity. In 1993, over 40 percent of all Border Patrol officers were Latino, primarily because of the need for Spanish-speaking personnel. As with the Bureau of Indian Affairs, the position led to tensions about identity. One Mexican-American agent in Texas described those he arrested: "They're not my people. I'm an American. They're here illegally." Having overcome nearly a half-century of questioning whether they were competent to police the border, Latinos found participation in the Border Patrol to be a lucrative, if controversial, avenue for upward mobility in the impoverished border region. Many Latino officials believed that racial bias continued to dominate the Border Patrol. One seventeen-year veteran who filed suit, alleging that he was passed over for promotion because of his Mexican ancestry, also claimed that Latino agents were consistently put under added pressure. He noted: "For Hispanics, there's no in-between. You're either a hard-ass or a bleeding heart."

The new immigration statutes and their administration on the border heightened the significance of the boundary line between Mexico and the United States. Indeed, the modern version of the border implied a rigid line of separation even while the intricate economic relationship between Mexican labor and American capital was perpetuated through labor recruitment agents, government contracts, and specialized exemptions. Here immigration officials, by inspecting new arrivals and border residents and enforcing laws barring illegal entry, made it clear who was alien and who native in this region once part of Mexico. The central role of the immigration inspector was duly noted by an El Paso attorney as early as 1912 when he wrote to Washington, D.C., "His business has brought him in contact with the poor, the ignorant, the friendless and the foreigner, over whom he has practically almost limitless power." This power over the dreams of the individual immigrant became increasingly evident at the border crossing.

To an ever greater extent, that "almost limitless power" has been translated into relationships of violence and intimidation. In December 1992, a U.S. judge in El Paso ruled that the Border Patrol had committed "wholesale violations" of the rights of citizens and noncitizens alike, including unjustified shootings, sexual misconduct, beatings, stealing money from prisoners, drug trafficking, embezzlement, perjury, and indecent exposure. One of the most tragic cases involved the death of twenty-six-year-old Dario Miranda Valenzuela, shot in the back by a U.S. Border Patrol agent, Michael Elmer, near Nogales, Arizona, on 12 June 1992. Rather than calling an ambulance after the shooting, Elmer dragged Miranda's body 175 feet in an attempt to hide the corpse, then threatened his partner if the other agent would not help him cover up the crime. In a landmark trial, Elmer and his colleagues admitted to practices contrary to Border Patrol regulations and to the cover-up, calling the border a "war zone" and the immigrants crossing it "the enemy." The Arizona jury, imbued with a similar notion of the border, refused to convict Elmer even on reduced charges, even for those crimes to which he had readily admitted. Unlike the reaction to the Rodney King trial in Simi Valley, which set off riots in Los Angeles, no one took notice of a verdict that seemed to fulfill the expectations of the power of the native over the alien in the American West.

◆ ◆ ◆

The United States, since its inception, has always looked west and south with the same intensity as, but with more covetousness than, it has looked east. In recent years, relations with Asia and with Mexico and other southern neighbors have increasingly defined the nation's economy, demography, and even culture. These relations are not new, but they are newly powerful, and they are within as well as outside national borders. They have spurred backlashes: Buddhist temple burnings and English as a First Language movements. They have raised the stakes on how the United States, as a nation, defines its western territory and whom it allows to participate in that defining. And these relations have made it crucial that we understand the foundations on which this contested landscape, this multifaceted frontier, of the late twentieth century stands. Most crucial to understand is that the foundation is not a single story but many overlapping stories of invaders who become invaded, of dreams, of histories revised, of identities invented, reinvented, and contested. From that fragmented complexity of individual stories and group experiences emerges a multifaceted history organized around the extremely unequal relations of power that have always marked the region. The West is built as well as riven by that multiplicity.

Bibliographic Note

As more historians turn their attention to the modern West (defined here as post-1930) and its diverse peoples, the field is changing rapidly. Journalistic accounts, such as Carey McWilliams, *Factories in the Field* (Santa Barbara, Calif., 1939) and *North from Mexico* (Philadelphia, 1949),

Peter Wiley and Robert Gottlieb, *Empires in the Sun: The Rise of the New American West* (New York, 1982), and Frances FitzGerald, *Cities on a Hill: A Journey Through Contemporary American Cultures* (New York, 1986), remain crucial but have been supplemented by surveys attempting to incorporate the diversity of the twentieth-century West as a central theme, such as Richard White, *"It's Your Misfortune and None of My Own": A New History of the American West* (Norman, 1991), Patricia Nelson Limerick, *The Legacy of Conquest: The Unbroken Past of the American West* (New York, 1987), and Ronald Takaki, *A Different Mirror: A History of Multicultural America* (Boston, 1993). In addition, surveys of particular ethnic and racial groups in the twentieth-century West include Rodolfo Acuña, *Occupied America: A History of Chicanos*, 3d ed. (New York, 1988), Sucheng Chan, *Asian Americans: An Interpretive History* (Boston, 1991), Ronald Takaki, *Strangers from a Different Shore: A History of Asian Americans* (Boston, 1989), and James S. Olson and Raymond Wilson, *Native Americans in the Twentieth Century* (Provo, 1984). For a brief survey that links gender and racial issues, see Sarah Deutsch, "Landscape of Enclaves: Race Relations in the West, 1865–1990," in William Cronon, George Miles, and Jay Gitlin, eds., *Under an Open Sky: Rethinking America's Western Past* (New York, 1992), 110–31. Peggy Pascoe's pathbreaking work on intermarriage in the West, "Race, Gender, and Intercultural Relations: The Case of Interracial Marriage," *Frontiers* 12 (1991): 5–18, leads a special issue focusing on writing twentieth-century multicultural women's history. This issue also includes Valerie Matsumoto, "Desperately Seeking 'Dierdre': Gender Roles, Multicultural Relations, and Nisei Women Writers of the 1930s," pp. 19–32.

The monographic literature includes regional works on Mexican Americans: David Montejano's award-winning *Anglos and Mexicans in the Making of Texas, 1836–1986* (Austin, 1987), which traces the transformation of race relations and definitions as the result of economic changes; Julia Kirk Blackwelder, *Women of the Depression: Caste and Culture in San Antonio, 1929–1939* (College Station, Tex., 1984), which also includes African-American and Anglo women, and Richard A. García's *Rise of the Mexican American Middle Class: San Antonio, 1929–1941* (College Station, Tex., 1991). On Arizona, see Thomas E. Sheridan, *Los Tucsonenses: The Mexican Community in Tucson, 1854–1941* (Tucson, 1986). On Colorado and New Mexico, see Suzanne Forrest, *The Preservation of the Village: New Mexico's Hispanics and the New Deal* (Albuquerque, 1989), and Sarah Deutsch, *No Separate Refuge: Culture, Class, and Gender on an Anglo-Hispanic Frontier in the American Southwest, 1880–1940* (New York, 1987). On California, see Vicki Ruiz, *Cannery Women, Cannery Lives: Mexican Women, Unionization, and the California Food Processing Industry, 1930–1950* (Albuquerque, 1987), George J. Sánchez, *Becoming Mexican American: Ethnicity, Culture and Identity in Chicano Los Angeles, 1900–1945* (New York, 1993), and Camille Guerin-Gonzales, *Mexican Workers and American Dreams: Immigration, Repatriation, and California Farm Labor, 1900–1939* (New Brunswick, N.J., 1994), which sets Mexican immigrants in the context of the agrarian ideals of American farming and the industrial reality of California agriculture. On the rise of the United Farm Workers in California, see Sam Kushner, *Long Road to Delano: A Century of Farmworkers' Struggle* (New York, 1975), and Margaret Rose, "From the Fields to the Picket Line: Huelga Women and the Boycott, 1965–1975," *Labor History* 31 (Summer 1990): 271–93, and "Traditional and Nontraditional Patterns of Female Activism in the United Farm Workers of America, 1962–1980," *Frontiers* 11 (March 1990): 26–32.

Crossing regional boundaries are Adela de la Torre and Beatríz M. Pesquera, *Building with Our Hands: New Directions in Chicana Studies* (Berkeley, 1993), and Vicki L. Ruiz and Susan Tiano, eds., *Women on the U.S.-Mexico Border: Responses to Change* (Boston, 1987), on women's cross-border experience in *maquilas* and as domestic workers. Border studies are beginning to describe the significant twentieth-century shift toward restriction and control. The best works include Kitty Calavita, *Inside the State: The Bracero Program, Immigration, and the I.N.S.* (New York, 1992), and Raul A. Fernandez, *The United States–Mexico Border: A Politico-Economic Profile* (Notre Dame, Ind., 1977). Leo R. Chavez has written a scholarly analysis of the fate of "illegal aliens" in *Shadowed Lives: Undocumented Immigrants in American Society* (Fort Worth,

1992). First-person accounts include Luis Alberto Urrea, *Across the Wire: Life and Hard Times on the Mexican Border* (New York, 1993), and Marilyn P. Davis, *Mexican Voices/American Dreams: An Oral History of Mexican Immigration to the United States* (New York, 1990). On the dynamics of modern cross-border cultural borrowings, see Rubén Martínez, *The Other Side: Notes from the New L.A., Mexico City, and Beyond* (New York, 1993).

On Asian migrant labor, see Gary Y. Okihiro, *Cane Fires: The Anti-Japanese Movement in Hawaii, 1865–1945*, (Philadelphia, 1991); and Lucie Cheng and Edna Bonacich, eds., *Labor Immigration under Capitalism: Asian Workers in the United States before World War II* (Berkeley, 1984). There are several books that deal with Japanese internment, including Roger Daniels, *Prisoners without Trial: Japanese Americans in World War II* (New York, 1993), and Sandra C. Taylor, *Jewel of the Desert: Japanese American Internment at Topaz* (Berkeley, 1993). On generational change and ethnic identity, see Evelyn Nakano Glenn, *Issei, Nisei, War Bride: Three Generations of Japanese American Women in Domestic Service* (Philadelphia, 1986), Karen Isaksen Leonard, *Making Ethnic Choices: California's Punjabi Mexican Americans* (Philadelphia, 1992), Victor G. Nee and Brett de Bary Nee, *Longtime Californ': A Documentary Study of an American Chinatown* (New York, 1973), Judy Yung, *Chinese Women of America: A Pictorial History* (Seattle, 1986), and Richard Chalfen, *Turning Leaves: The Photograph Collections of Two Japanese American Families* (Albuquerque, 1991), on self-definitions of ethnicity. For the more recent period, see Asian Women United of California, ed., *Making Waves: An Anthology of Writings by and about Asian American Women* (Boston, 1989), Mary Paik Lee, *Quiet Odyssey: A Pioneer Korean Woman in America* (Seattle, 1990), and Craig Scharlin and Lilia V. Villanueva, *Philip Ver Cruz: A Personal History of Filipino Immigrants and the Farmworkers Movement* (Los Angeles, 1992). On Hawai`i see Elizabeth Buck, *Paradise Remade: The Politics of Culture and History in Hawai`i* (Philadelphia, 1993) for a stimulating account of power and culture, and Haunani-Kay Trask, *From a Native Daughter: Colonialism and Sovereignty in Hawai`i* (Monroe, Maine, 1993), for a trenchant case for Hawaiian sovereignty.

For Native Americans in the twentieth century, Kenneth R. Philp, *John Collier's Crusade for Indian Reform, 1920–1954* (Tucson, 1977), presents a policy-centered version of the impact of the New Deal. Very few authors center their work on Native American women's history in this period; Patricia Albers and Beatrice Medicine, eds., *The Hidden Half: Studies of Plains Indian Women* (Washington, D.C., 1983), is a fascinating and useful account. There is, on the other hand, a small industry in books on land claims. A useful introduction is Imre Sutton, et al., eds., *Irredeemable America: The Indians' Estate and Land Claims* (Albuquerque, 1985). For studies more centered on tribal governance and economic development, see Peter Iverson, *The Navajo Nation* (Westport, Conn., 1981), Kenneth R. Philp, ed., *Indian Self-Rule: First-Hand Accounts of Indian-White Relations from Roosevelt to Reagan* (Salt Lake City, 1986), Stephen Cornell, *The Return of the Native: American Indian Political Resurgence* (New York, 1988), and Larry Burt, "Western Tribes and Balance Sheets: Business Development Programs in the 1960s and 1970s," *Western Historical Quarterly* 23 (November 1992): 475–95. Also useful are Alvin M. Josephy, Jr., *Now That the Buffalo's Gone: A Study of Today's American Indians* (New York, 1982), and Peter Iverson, ed., *The Plains Indians of the Twentieth Century* (Norman, 1985). On the Columbian quincentenary, see Margaret Connell Szasz, "American Indians and Outsiders: A Crucial Dialogue of the Columbian Quincentenary," *Montana, The Magazine of Western History* 42 (Autumn 1992): 53–62. On the Zuni Salt Lake, T. J. Ferguson and Richard Hart, both of the Institute of the NorthAmerican West, and Judy Bruncon, of the Salt River Project, all presented research papers that dealt partly with this topic at the 1992 Western History Association Conference in New Haven.

Material is particularly thin for the nonurban twentieth-century African-American experience: see Era Bell Thompson, *American Daughter* (1946; reprint, St. Paul, 1986), on homesteading. Material on urban blacks includes Blackwelder, *Women of the Depression*, and Shirley Ann Moore, "Getting There, Being There: African-American Migration to Richmond, California, 1910–1945," in Joe William Trotter, Jr., ed., *The Great Migration in Historical Perspective: New*

Dimensions of Race, Class, and Gender (Bloomington, 1991), and the last chapter of Douglas Henry Daniels, *Pioneer Urbanites: A Social and Cultural History of Black San Francisco* (Berkeley, 1980).

On Rodney King and the 1992 riots, see Mike Davis, *City of Quartz: Excavating the Future in Los Angeles* (London, 1990), for a Marxist foreshadowing, and David Rieff, *Los Angeles: Capital of the Third World* (New York, 1991), for the recent upsurge in ethnic diversity. Raphael J. Sonenshein, *Politics in Black and White: Race and Power in Los Angeles* (Princeton, 1993), traces the politics of race in the city, and the *Los Angeles Times* staff, *Understanding the Riots: Los Angeles before and after the Rodney King Case* (Los Angeles, 1992), provides a centrist coverage. A more leftist approach is taken by a variety of journalists in *Inside the L.A. Riots: What Really Happened—and Why It Will Happen Again* (Los Angeles, 1992). For more scholarly analyses, see Haki R. Madhubuti, ed., *Why L.A. Happened: Implications of the '92 Los Angeles Rebellion* (Chicago, 1993), and Robert Gooding-Williams, ed., *Reading Rodney King, Reading Urban Uprising* (New York, 1993).

Sarah Deutsch would like to acknowledge the delightfully good nature of her coauthors and the life-saving energy and creativity of her research assistant, Melissa Walker. George J. Sánchez thanks his two coauthors for their congeniality and commitment to collaboration and especially Sarah Deutsch for her persistent yet gentle prodding to get the job done well.

SECTION IV
Interpretation

Just west of downtown Cody, Wyoming, on the well-traveled tourist route to Yellowstone National Park, lies Trail Town, a collection of old wooden buildings moved from remote sites in the Rocky Mountain West and reconstructed as the imagined Main Street of a frontier town. Strung along raised sidewalks in a kind of convivial proximity to one another are homes and schools, shops and workplaces, most transported from considerably more spacious plots. At the end of the single broad dirt street is a small graveyard, surrounded by a Victorian wrought-iron fence, which contains the remains of John "Liver-eating" Johnson (1824–1900), the mountain man and trapper renamed and made famous by Robert Redford in the film *Jeremiah Johnson* (1973). Like most trappers, Johnson was a solitary fellow, but in his lifetime he earned wide renown for his reputed vendetta against the Crow Indians who, in May 1847, allegedly killed and scalped his pregnant Flathead wife. As an early biographer wrote: "For many years thereafter he killed and scalped Crow Indians. Then he ate their livers, raw. He ate them not for hunger's sake but upon principle."

The rugged country stretching from Cody to Yellowstone would have been familiar to Johnson, but he did not die there. After spending his final days in the Veterans Hospital in Los Angeles, he was buried in a military cemetery not too far from present-day Beverly Hills. In 1974, a group of Lancaster, California, schoolchildren, as part of a history project, petitioned the Veterans Administration to have Johnson's body removed and reburied in the mountain West. The schoolchildren raised some money, an airline donated its services, and Trail Town, a private commercial enterprise, paid to reinter Johnson's body and erect the new marker that stands over his grave. More than two thousand people attended the reburial services.

The story of Johnson's ultimate fate presents many ironies, not the least of which is that this self-reliant, violent, and not altogether admirable man should end up being rescued by schoolchildren and corporate largess and transformed into a tourist attraction in a town named for Buffalo Bill Cody, the great western showman Johnson reportedly despised. But this story also serves as an instructive metaphor for the way the West is popularly imagined in American culture: as a place with a particular story line and fixed set of heroes that stubbornly persist despite considerable evidence to the contrary.

Western history has long been a kind of participation sport—as seen in the current popularity of mountain man rendezvous, Louis L'Amour novels, pay-as-you-go cattle drives, Ralph Lauren's ranch clothes, or the Buffalo Bill Historical Center down the road from Trail Town, which draws up to three thousand visitors on a busy summer day. The schoolchildren who initiated the relocation of Johnson's grave were behaving like millions of other Americans of diverse backgrounds who feel empowered to claim western history as a story with particular relevance to their own lives. This is the great strength of a popular western history that celebrates the exploits of mountain men like

The West of myth and memory has long proved an alluring theme for artists, writers, and other interpreters of regional culture who have found their subject matter in an imagined past.

Unidentified photographer. Charles Schreyvogel Painting on the Roof of His Apartment Building in Hoboken, New Jersey. Photograph, 1903. National Cowboy Hall of Fame and Western Heritage Center, Oklahoma City, Oklahoma.

Liver-eating Johnson or extravagant self-proclaimed heroes like Buffalo Bill and constructs a vast region of imagined places like Trail Town, locked forever in a particular stage of community development. It serves as a widely appealing national myth. But the very popularity and accessibility of this myth suggest the problem with this sort of history. As the writer Wallace Stegner succinctly put it, "The western culture and western character with which it is easiest to identify exist largely in the West of make-believe, where they can be kept simple."

The very word *western*, an adjective that has come to serve as a noun, carries popular connotations that suggest the simplicity and limitations of the popular western history celebrated in films and novels, paintings and prints, theme parks and local summer pageants. The word suggests a particular time, place, and cast of characters—a sparsely populated part of the West during the mid-to-late nineteenth century, inhabited by cowboys and Indians, mountain men and cavalry troops, most of whom adhere to a particular moral code of honor. It excludes more people and places in the West than it includes.

Life often imitates art. One of the reasons that the old western myths remain so compelling is that they continue to shape contemporary behavior, as they have ever since Buffalo Bill began dressing up, old cowhands started reading western novels, and tobacco companies began using pictures of ranchers to sell cigarettes. "This is the West, sir," said a small-town newspaper editor in John Ford's classic film *The Man Who Shot Liberty Valance* (1962). "When the legend becomes fact, print the legend." Thus Ford, who understood the popular appeal of the West as well as anyone, ironically acknowledged the power of myth to acquire the trappings of truth and reshape not only the past but the present as well. The popular legend of the West should properly be discounted as good history, but it should not be disregarded as a good story that continues to have a direct impact on American behavior and national beliefs.

Frederick Jackson Turner delivered his seminal 1893 address "The Significance of the Frontier in American History" to an academic gathering in Chicago just a few blocks from a production of Cody's Wild West show. As the historian Ann Fabian argues, "The scholarly pursuit of the western past was joined immediately by an impish popular double." One might make a comparable argument about serious painting in the West, or serious writing. A good history of western creative endeavors must be broad enough to embrace the serious while acknowledging the popular; it must be loose enough to include Georgia O'Keeffe and Robinson Jeffers as well as the modern-day Charlie Russells and cowboy poets.

In the little modern cemetery in Trail Town and through the persona of Robert Redford, Liver-eating Johnson has engaged the imagination of an international audience of tourists and filmgoers who would otherwise remain ignorant of his reputed deeds in the Rockies. Johnson's story thus suggests one final lesson about the history of the American West. Its vitality lies in its continual discovery and reinvention by the artists and writers, historians and schoolchildren, tourists and citizens who come to it with fresh questions. When the West is reimagined from an international perspective, from a contemporary viewpoint, from the perspective of the vast variety of peoples who call it home, it becomes a place even grander than the place of myth—bigger in space and time and infinitely more interesting.

— Martha A. Sandweiss

CHRONOLOGY

1810	Zebulon Pike's record of his expedition to the Southwest sparks public interest.
1814	Extensively edited, the journals of Lewis and Clark appear in published form.
1823	Novelist James Fenimore Cooper introduces the frontier hero Natty Bumppo.
1830s	Painters George Catlin, Karl Bodmer, and Alfred Jacob Miller journey to the interior of the American West.
1849	Francis Parkman taps the mood of "manifest destiny" in his work *The Oregon Trail*.
1859	Painter Albert Bierstadt travels through the Rockies.
1869	Edward Judson, also known as Ned Buntline, discovers William F. Cody in Nebraska.
1871	Photographer William Henry Jackson and painter Thomas Moran accompany the government survey of the Yellowstone country.
1872	Mark Twain recalls his western years in *Roughing It*.
1874–90	Thirty-nine volumes of historical works appear under the byline of Hubert Howe Bancroft.
1887	Reuben Gold Thwaites begins his career at the Wisconsin Historical Society.
1889–1909	Frederic Remington creates more than twenty-seven hundred paintings and drawings and twenty-four editions of bronze sculptures.
1893	Frederick Jackson Turner delivers his address "The Significance of the Frontier in American History."
	Former cowboy Charles M. Russell takes up art full-time.
1894	Naturalist John Muir writes *The Mountains of California*.
1902	Long a subject of dime novels, the cowboy receives artistic treatment in Owen Wister's *The Virginian*.
1903	Arguably the first Western, *The Great Train Robbery* is filmed in New Jersey.
1914	Twenty-five thousand attend the dedication of the new five-story Kansas State Historical Society.
1917	Herbert Eugene Bolton calls attention to Hispanic contributions in "The Mission as a Frontier Institution in the Spanish-American Colonies."
1925	*The Professor's House*, by novelist Willa Cather, addresses postfrontier themes.
1929	Painter Georgia O'Keeffe begins painting in New Mexico.
1931	Walter Prescott Webb publishes *The Great Plains*.
1936	Dorothea Lange's stop at a pea-pickers' camp results in the searing depression photograph "Migrant Mother."
1939	John Ford and John Wayne team up to make *Stagecoach*.
1940	"Gene Autry's Melody Ranch" premieres on radio.
1950	*Westward the Tide*, the first of Louis L'Amour's ninety novels, is published.
1959	Seven of the top-ten television shows in the United States are Westerns.
1962	John Steinbeck receives the Nobel Prize for Literature.
1965	*The Pacific Slope* by Earl Pomeroy presents the twentieth century as integral to western history.
1968	The publication of N. Scott Momaday's *House Made of Dawn* signals a renaissance in Native American writing.
1969	Merle Haggard records "Okie from Muskogee."
1971	Inspired by the life of Mary Hallock Foote, Wallace Stegner writes *Angle of Repose*.
1987	Patricia Nelson Limerick interprets the western past in *The Legacy of Conquest*.
1989	Larry McMurtry's novel *Lonesome Dove* (1985) is re-created as a television mini-series.
1990s	The films *Dances with Wolves* (1990) and *Unforgiven* (1992) gain acclaim, reinterpreting themes of earlier Westerns.
1991	*The West as America* exhibit at the National Museum of American Art stirs controversy.

Chapter Nineteen

The Visual West

BRIAN W. DIPPIE

O n 25 June 1876, Lieutenant Colonel, Brevet Major General, George Armstrong Custer and 209 men with the Seventh U.S. Cavalry died in a battle against Lakota and Cheyenne Indians on the Little Bighorn River in south-central Montana. There were no white survivors of what has gone down in American history as "Custer's Last Stand." The battle did in fact happen, but Custer's Last Stand is a cultural myth created mostly by painters, poets, dramatists, and novelists who found in the news of military disaster out West a heroic lesson. Defeat was victory. It affirmed the pioneering American spirit, the willingness to pay any price for progress, including the sacrifice of self. Today, we reject the presumption of racial and cultural superiority on which the heroic myth of Custer's Last Stand rested. We wonder, with Henry Wadsworth Longfellow, "Whose was the right and the wrong?" We doubt the imperatives of "manifest destiny" and sympathize with the dispossessed, but we do not doubt Custer's Last Stand. Instead, we read its lesson differently. It now seems a cautionary tale about the price of personal ambition and national greed. But we can still visualize Custer's Last Stand, and that is a tribute to the enduring influence of artists who, through the power of imagination, fashioned a reality all their own. Their achievement is what western American art is all about.

Western art commonly refers to representational paintings, drawings, and sculptures showing men (and it is essentially an art by and about men) and animals in unspoiled natural settings. The men are mostly Indians and whites—trappers, miners, plainsmen, soldiers, cowboys—and the viewpoint is exclusively white. The content evokes a historical period, the nineteenth century, but it is historical art of a special kind. Certain storied events like Custer's Last Stand have become standard subjects, but the history in western art is usually generalized. Mountain men frolic at rendezvous, settlers guide their covered wagons westward, Indians and cavalry clash in battle, cowboys tend cattle on the unfenced plains and shoot it out in clapboard towns that squat in the open land suspended between wilderness and civilization. Such images are timeless rather than historical, except in the sense that they constitute a kind of tribal history for white Americans. They seem typical of a time and place because artists, by repeating them, have implanted them in the public's mind. Successive images affirm one another, verifying the truth of the scenes portrayed. Collectively, the artists have created a version of the West, a romantic West that vanished long ago, never to be forgotten. Western art sees to that.

The embattled white heroes of Frederic Remington's painting reiterate one of the central themes and favorite myths of western art—the conquest of the land and its native peoples by Anglo-American frontiersmen.

Frederic Remington (1861–1909). The Last Stand. Oil on canvas, 1890. Woolaroc Museum, Bartlesville, Oklahoma.

Invention, repetition, and refinement define the western art tradition, as Custer's Last Stand can demonstrate. On 19 July 1876, the *New York Daily Graphic* featured a dramatic, full-page illustration by William de la Montagne Cary (1840–1922), *The Battle on the Little Big Horn River—The Death Struggle of General Custer*. It showed Custer and his troopers bravely resisting an overwhelming, savage foe. Though outnumbered and doomed, each soldier still struggles to get off a parting shot as the Indians, armed with rifles and bows and arrows and war clubs, and some wielding scalping knives, close in for the kill. The situation is hopeless, but there, in the midst of chaos, stands Custer, tall and calm, a peculiar light falling on him through the heavy clouds and dust, illuminating his moment of imperishable glory. Saber drawn back, blazing away with a pistol, he scrambles over a fallen horse to get at the enemy and defy death itself. Civilization, never more glorious than in defeat, was never more certain of ultimate victory. That was the message Cary's illustration conveyed. Drawing on his personal experiences among the Missouri River tribes and on his acquaintance with Custer—the credentials that established his authority—Cary had distilled the news, gossip, and rumors then flooding the nation's newspapers into a single compelling image. William Cary had just invented Custer's Last Stand.

Could the battle have been depicted in any other way? In fact, it was. The *Illustrated Police News* a week earlier devoted its cover to a drawing of two Indians rushing at Custer as he reels from a mortal wound. It showed his death, but not why his death mattered. The same was true of the cover of the *New York Illustrated Weekly* that August, which featured a buckskin-clad Custer leading his men in a charge over the corpse of the only Indian in view. What kind of "last stand" was this?

Cary's seminal version of Custer's end might have been lost in a welter of competing images in 1876, denying the battle its distinctive visual form and gutting it of mythic appeal. But that autumn, only months after Custer's death, a full-length biography was rushed into print, Frederick Whittaker's *Complete Life of Gen. George A. Custer*, and among its illustrations was *Custer's Last Fight*. The work of another experienced military artist with western credentials, Alfred R. Waud's (1828–91), painting pared the battle down to essentials and triumphantly reaffirmed Cary's heroic conception. A tight pyramid of soldiers, with Custer at the exact center, parts a surging sea of Indians. It speaks of sacrifice and courage, grace under pressure, good form in dying, and the moral superiority of civilization. Thereafter, artists who essayed the Custer theme—and hundreds have—did their homework in Whittaker and studied in the school of Waud.

That Custer's Last Stand was a cultural creation becomes evident when we consider that a battle renowned for having no survivors actually had hundreds of survivors—the Indian victors. And they viewed things differently. Instead of defiant last stands and military stoicism in the face of death, they remembered panicked soldiers fleeing in disarray, voices crying out and dissolving into sobs, weapons dropped in wild-eyed terror by men desperately seeking a way out. They talked about whiskey or madness to account for the sudden collapse of resistance. And they praised a few who fought hard that day. Custer's Last Stand did not exist for the Indians until time and the persistent demand of white questioners for stories about the heroic death struggle of the chief with yellow hair taught them how they were supposed to respond.

The early depictions of Custer's death, quickly rushed into print after the fateful battle at the Little Bighorn on 25 June 1876, show the rapid evolution of the myth of Custer's Last Stand. Alfred Waud's image, published in the fall of 1876, established Custer as a quintessentially American hero fiercely fighting to defend his nation from an alien threat. The triangular composition of the image, highlighting Custer's own actions, would often be repeated by artists seeking to find, in this moment of white defeat, a redemptive moral for the American people.

Unidentified artist. The Indian War—Death of General George A. Custer, at the Battle of the Little Big Horn River, Montana Territory, June 25. *Engraving, 1876. From the* Illustrated Police News, *13 July 1876.*

William de la Montagne Cary (1840–1922). The Battle on the Little Big Horn River—The Death Struggle of General Custer. *Engraving, 1876. From the* New York Daily Graphic, *19 July 1876. Library of Congress (#LC-US262-60706), Washington, D.C.*

After Alfred R. Waud (1828–91). Custer's Last Fight. *Engraving, 1876. From Frederick Whittaker,* A Complete Life of General George A. Custer *(1876). Brian W. Dippie Collection.*

Commissioned by the
artist Frederic
Remington to create
an account of the
Custer battle, the
Lakota artist Kicking
Bear produced an im-
age that gave a cen-
tral role to the battle's
Indian protagonists.
But his work was in-
fluenced by earlier
white renditions as
well as memory. Ly-
ing just outside the
main group of Indi-
ans, Custer is recog-
nizable by the
buckskins and long
hair made familiar
through other artists'
pictures of the scene.

Kicking Bear (1848–?).
Battle of Little Big Horn.
Muslin painting, 1890–
1900. Courtesy of the
Southwest Museum
(#N 37788), Los Angeles,
California.

An unforgettable event in the tribal history of white Americans barely registered in the tribal histories of the Sioux victors. It did, however, take its place among the exploits of individual Indians who recorded their deeds that day on hides and muslin and sheets of paper. Few of these pictographic accounts, a traditional form of Plains Indian art devoted to battles and hunts, give much comfort to heroic myth. Some, showing overviews of the battle, define defensive positions and support the idea of a final stand. Most portray uniformed soldiers, anonymous in their alikeness, being chased and killed by distinctively costumed Indians. They show an indistinguishable jumble of white corpses and honor fallen warriors identified individually. Custer was conspicuous by his absence in early pictographic accounts, but native artists, under white influence, began including a Custer figure, firing his pistols or lying among the dead. And so a white cultural myth became an Indian myth as well, a process worth tracing.

Frederic S. Remington (1861–1909), the most influential western illustrator in the late nineteenth century, was obsessed with military subjects from the time of his boyhood in upstate New York. His father, a cavalry officer in the Civil War, was his hero, and he filled school notebooks and readers with sketches of soldiers from armies everywhere. He doted on fancy-dress uniforms, the stiff martial bearing, and scenes of combat and carnage. Naturally the sensation created by Custer's defeat in 1876 was irresistible for Remington, an impressionable fourteen-year-old about to enter the Highland Military Academy in Worcester, Massachusetts. That fall, presumably, relying directly on Waud, Cadet Remington drew and colored his own version of Custer's Last Fight. Waud's heroic triangle of soldiers, with Custer at its center, planted itself in the mind of the artist most responsible, in turn, for planting a heroic image of the Indian-fighting army in the public's mind. In 1890 Remington painted a full-scale oil, *The Last Stand*. By then, besides enhanced skill, he brought to the subject a personal acquaintance with the West. After visiting Montana in 1881, he had owned a sheep ranch in Kansas and had patrolled with the U.S. cavalry in Apache country. During the winter of 1890–91 he was on assignment in South Dakota as artist-correspondent covering the Ghost Dance War, though he managed to be absent on 29 December when the Seventh Cavalry took belated revenge on the Lakotas at Wounded Knee. The battle was a last stand for the Indians—more than 150 died—but Remington's painting, reproduced in *Harper's Weekly* twelve days later, remained faithful to myth. Here was Waud's pyramid of troopers, white civilization at bay, still bravely facing the savage foe. The accompanying text wondered, "How many scenes of which this is typical have been enacted on this continent, who can say?" Through repetition, the atypical had become the typical. Custer's Last Stand, a startling exception to the rule of white victory and Indian defeat, by 1890 represented the routine self-sacrifice of countless white Americans in the winning of the West.

Just days after *Harper's Weekly* published Remington's painting, Kicking Bear (1848–19?), a leading Lakota Ghost Dance apostle, formally surrendered to U.S. troops, ending the last major Indian war in American history. Facing exile, Kicking Bear and other Lakota leaders instead chose the option of accompanying Buffalo Bill Cody's Wild West show on a European tour. Their punishment, presumably, was being routed by Cody at each performance. Show business did not reconcile Kicking Bear to the white man's ways—as late as 1902 he was still preaching Ghost Dance gospel on the Fort Peck Reservation in Montana. But he had partly assimilated the white man's view of Custer's Last Stand. In about 1897 Remington commissioned him to paint a pictographic account of the Custer battle, and over the winter he produced a work that rivaled some of the grander nineteenth-century conceptions. Its center was reserved for Indian leaders, including Kicking Bear himself, framed by scenes of battle and dead soldiers. Most prominent among the soldiers, just outside the main grouping of Indians, was the long-haired Custer, sprawled in his buckskins. In Kicking Bear's painting, Custer was not the center of attention, but he was instantly recognizable, looking pretty much as Waud and then Remington had shown him. Artistic contrivance was triumphant—Custer's Last Stand had become a myth for all Americans.

Once established, Last Stand imagery has proven immensely adaptable. Western movies repeatedly borrowed Waud's heroic triangle of soldiers: *The Scarlet West* (1925), *The Plainsman* (1937), and *They Died With Their Boots On* (1941) to honor and praise; *Sitting Bull* (1954) and *Little Big Man* (1970) to vilify and mock. Imagery capable of any refinement, any interpretation, naturally invites parody, and Custer's Last Stand has attracted its share.

Edgar S. Paxson's solemn and gargantuan battle piece *Custer's Last Stand* (1899) derived its impact from sheer size (six feet by nine feet) and its astonishing detail. Paxson (1852–1919) arrived in Montana in 1877 and based his subsequent career on the fact that he was Montana's pioneer painter. His long residency was thought to lend authenticity to his work, in keeping with a cherished tenet of western art: personal experience is everything, validating even the entirely imaginary. In approaching the Custer theme, Paxson augmented what he "knew" with research, since another tenet of western art holds that truth depends on getting the details right, however preposterous the basic conception. Paxson corresponded with officers present at the Little Bighorn, interviewed Indian participants, visited the battlefield, and then, over a five-year period, painted a picture that is almost zanily implausible, so crammed with men, horses, and paraphernalia that, spacious as the canvas is, it feels cramped.

Parodists have paid Paxson tribute. Fritz Scholder (1937–), a Minnesotan of part-native descent and an inspiration for a whole generation of Indian artists, made a reputation in the 1960s and 1970s by pointedly reworking white images of the Indian, exposing their inherent values and reinvigorating them in the process. Playing off stereotypes from photographs and paintings—vanishing Indians, tourist Indians, drunken Indians—he uses brilliant color, simplification, and distortion to jolt the eye into reexamining the familiar and unquestioned. His painting *The Last Stand*, only slightly smaller in size than Paxson's oil, focuses attention on the figure of Custer by reducing the busy details of the Paxson original and unifying the composition through a simplified color scheme. Custer, rendered in buckskin yellow with hair to match, is a golden cloud floating over a turbulent purple sea—and is a ham actor hogging the spotlight. Peter Saul's *Custer's Last Stand* (1972–73), in contrast, is a twisted jumble of figures in cartoon colors, but it too found its inspiration in Paxson's painting. Saul, born fifty years after the Custer battle, was intrigued by Paxson's clutter. Even if his picture parodies Paxson's theme, it pays tribute to a hallmark of western art: surface detail supporting the appearance of truth. The Custer's Last Stand parodies make an additional point crucial to understanding western art. Over time, it has become an art about itself, repeating certain themes and images until they have become enshrined in the collective memory. Western art constitutes its own reality.

First Impressions

Western art as we know it began soon after the United States acquired the Louisiana Territory from France. No artists accompanied Meriwether Lewis and William Clark on their epic exploring trip (1804–6). But while they were still in the field, eastern artists were already portraying Indian visitors from west of the Mississippi River. Later, between 1822 and 1842, through the Office of Indian Affairs, the federal government commissioned nearly 150 portraits, most the work of Charles King Bird (1785–1862). Reproduced to illustrate *A History of the Indian Tribes of North America*, issued in parts between 1837 and 1844, the portraits were among the most familiar likenesses of Native Americans available before the Civil War. But they were studio productions, painted in the comforts of the nation's capital.

The first artists to actually visit the West and make field studies of Indian life accompanied the third of the government-sponsored explorations in the Louisiana Territory. In 1819, Samuel Seymour (active ca. 1797–1822) was appointed painter to Major Stephen H. Long's expedition up the Missouri to the Yellowstone River, and Titian Ramsay Peale (1799–1885), from a prominent Philadelphia family of artists, was hired as assistant naturalist with responsibility for natural history illustration. Aborted by financial constraints, Long's expedition instead traced the Platte River west to within sight of the Rocky Mountains before turning south. Seymour accompanied one party down the Arkansas River, Peale the other down the Canadian (the group was supposed to be on the Red). Disappointed in its original objectives, the Long expedition repaid its frustrations by declaring the region traversed "almost wholly unfit for cultivation, and

of course uninhabitable by a people depending on agriculture for their subsistence"—the Great American Desert. The two artists produced nearly three hundred sketches. Though only a small selection illustrated the official reports, Seymour and Peale had pioneered several themes that would dominate western art. They showed the Rocky Mountains, Plains Indians, and buffalo hunts and set a precedent for artists' participation in the government exploring expeditions that fanned out across the West in the middle of the nineteenth century. John Mix Stanley (1814–72), James W. Abert (1820–71), Richard H. Kern (1821–53), Edward M. Kern (1823–63), Gustavus Sohon (1825–1903), H. Balduin Möllhausen (1825–1905), and Arthur Schott (1813–75) would contribute to the fund of information about the flora, fauna, topography, and native peoples of America's expanding hinterland, firmly establishing the documentary tradition that nourishes western art to this day.

Naturally, the documentarians had their own preconceptions. The historian William H. Goetzmann has argued that explorers are always culturally programmed; the same applies to the artists who accompanied them. The plates by Stanley and Schott illustrating southwestern subjects in Major William H. Emory's official reports of 1848 and 1857 resemble those illustrating the eighteenth-century voyages of Captains James Cook and George Vancouver. All were intended to record faithfully what was seen in order to satisfy the demand for factual information about faraway places and the peoples who inhabited them. The work of the expeditionary artists was a kind of visual naming. It brought to public consciousness what was there but previously unknown, transforming it in the process of showing it. Such is the nature of two-dimensional representation: art creates a separate reality reflecting the artist's cultural values. American exploration artists, Goetzmann notes, shifted from the exotic and pastoral to the sublime and picturesque, keeping apace with the spirit of different ages of discovery. The pastoral mode was appropriate to the earliest phase of exploration, when the West seemed a remote wonderland full of possibilities; the sublime reinvigorated interest in exploration, an activity that had become predictable by the middle of the nineteenth century.

In 1832, when the Missouri River was still redolent of mystery for most Americans, George Catlin (1796–1872) staked his claim as one of the century's great visionaries. The West was a phantom, he said, "travelling on its tireless wing": "it flies before us as we travel, and our way is continually gilded, before us, as we approach the setting sun." Catlin was after an idea, not a place, and in 1832 he headed upriver on the first steamboat to ascend the Missouri to Fort Union near the mouth of the Yellowstone, bound to see unspoiled Indians and paint them "in all their grace and beauty." The eighteen-hundred-mile journey introduced him to the Blackfoot, Crow, and Lakota Indians and all the river tribes, notably the ill-fated Mandans. Catlin subsequently toured the southern plains, the upper Mississippi, and the Great Lakes region. In 1836 he visited the red pipestone quarry on the Coteau du Prairie, concluding his travels in Indian country. His ambition was to win fame and fortune through his enterprise by preserving a pictorial record, "Catlin's Indian Gallery," of all the uncivilized tribes within the borders of the United States. It was an ambition in keeping with an expansionist age.

Catlin's supreme achievement was the gallery itself. Consisting of particulars, all factual he claimed, it was in conception and realization a great act of the imagination, an artistic equivalent of exploration itself. The individual portraits and camp scenes in his gallery—some five hundred paintings—were unified by the sense of purpose that first sent him West to paint Indians. Something vast was happening in America. The new, as ever, was displacing the old; wilderness was yielding to an expanding white population, savagery to civilization. The process was already nearly two centuries old when Catlin was born, but in his lifetime the pace of change had dramatically accelerated. The Old Northwest had appeared on the map of American ambition in the early 1800s and then was engulfed in a wave of speculation, settlement, and statehood. Where Indians had hunted not twenty years before, cities thrived. Only by venturing west could one see "real" Indians—Indians still relatively independent of the white man, still practicing their own rites and garbed in their own costumes, unspoiled by civilization's vices. Catlin was not the most technically accomplished artist to paint Indian portraits, nor was he the first. He was capable of pandering to popular prejudices, and self-interest was never far beneath the surface of his humanitarian professions. He was more often a showman trying to pry coins from a crowd than the serious student of Indian life he had aspired to be. But George Catlin was a magnificent dreamer. Where others saw miniatures, he saw the larger picture, and he created his gallery to mirror it. His generation, he was convinced, was witness to the last act in a great human drama. A race, America's native race, was being extinguished by another, yet his countrymen were mostly oblivious to the fact. His mission was to preserve a visual record of the western tribes before civilization came calling and ruined them forever. In a few years what he saw and painted would be seen no more. Indeed, Catlin counted on this. An artist-entrepreneur, he proposed to invest time and money in the creation of his Indian Gallery and then to retire on the proceeds when his countrymen awakened to the fact that the great drama was already over and that no other record of it survived. It was the power of Catlin's imagination, his ability to harness raw data to a commanding

vision of their meaning, that makes his work collectively the original masterpiece of western art.

Others might disparage Catlin's paintings, pointing to flaws in observation and execution, but his example influenced even his detractors. Two artists followed on his heels in the 1830s, Karl Bodmer (1809–93) and Alfred Jacob Miller (1810–74). Unlike Catlin, they accompanied private patrons, Bodmer traveling with a German prince who toured up the Missouri to the Yellowstone in 1833–34 and Miller with a Scottish nobleman bound for the site of the 1837 fur trade rendezvous on the Green River. With the luxury of time for close observation, Bodmer, a polished draftsman, produced a series of meticulously detailed images of western Indian life, though his portraits, clinical and exact, lacked the human qualities Catlin was able to impart. Miller, who painted some wonderfully evocative watercolors—and several comparatively stilted oils—of mountain men and Indians, thought Catlin a humbug, though literalism was not his forte either. Rather, he created a spacious natural paradise in which time was suspended while his children of nature, white and Indian alike, frolicked to their hearts' content, oblivious to the progress that would outmode them both.

Bodmer and Miller paralleled Catlin on the extremes of scientific observation and romantic indulgence. Artists who painted Indians thereafter usually joined Catlin

Based on his own eye-witness observations, Alfred Jacob Miller's large (69 x 99 inches) painting of the grand entry of the Snake Indians at the annual fur trade rendezvous of 1837 conveyed the exuberant romanticism of the artist's vision. Sir William Drummond Stewart, Miller's patron, acquired the picture for his Scottish castle as a nostalgic memento of his western adventures.

Alfred Jacob Miller (1810–74). Cavalcade. Oil on canvas, 1839. State Museum of History, Oklahoma Historical Society, Oklahoma City.

somewhere in between. Paul Kane (1810–71), Charles Deas (1818–67), Seth Eastman (1808–75), and Stanley each aspired to form an Indian gallery to rival Catlin's and receive some of the recognition and more of the compensation he had been seeking from governments and learned bodies at home and abroad since 1838. Kane, a Canadian, succeeded beyond any of the others. The patronage of the Hudson's Bay Company permitted him wide latitude to roam in the company's vast western empire in the 1840s, and after his return from a tour that had taken him to Forts Victoria and Vancouver on the West Coast, he received a substantial commission for one hundred oil paintings of native life, which constituted an Indian gallery of sorts. Deas was a St. Louis–based painter known in the 1850s for his scenes of frontier trappers. But his plan never got off the ground, since his mental health failed him shortly after he conceived the scheme of painting a gallery of his own. Eastman, an army officer whose postings in the West from the 1820s through the 1850s introduced him to a variety of tribes, came no nearer to realizing his ambition of forming an Indian gallery than serving as the illustrator of Henry R. Schoolcraft's multivolume government-sponsored work *Historical and Statistical Information Respecting the History, Condition, and Prospects of the Indian Tribes of the United States* (1851–57) and as the painter of nine Indian scenes in oil commissioned for the House Indian Affairs Committee room in Washington (1867–70). Stanley was another matter. Western tours, including two as draftsman on official explorations in 1846 and 1853, exposed him to tribes in the Indian Territory, the Southwest, and the

Oregon Territory and along the upper Missouri River, a range that exceeded even Catlin's. Stanley, unlike Deas and Eastman, actually completed and in 1850 began exhibiting a collection of 154 oil paintings of Indians. They were hung at the Smithsonian Institution in 1865, awaiting congressional action on purchase, when fire destroyed the collection, along with Charles Bird King's Indian portraits. Only five of Stanley's paintings were saved, leaving Catlin's gallery unrivaled as a pictorial record of the North American Indian.

Romantic Realism

Because the subject matter of western art is distinctive—Indians, mountain men, cowboys, and the like—there is a tendency to consider the art sui generis. But the obvious links between the work of the American expeditionary artists and their European counterparts alert us to other artistic parallels. Catlin, for example, originally aspired to be a history painter, and the poses in his Indian portraits reflect a conscious classicism. "The native grace—simplicity, and dignity of these natural people," he wrote of the Indians, "so much resemble the ancient marbles, that one is irresistibly led to believe that the Grecian Sculptors had similar models to study from and their costumes and weapons . . . the Toga—the Tunique & Manteau—the Bow—the shield & the Lance, so precisely similar to those of ancient times, convince us that a second (and *last*) strictly classic era is passing from the world."

Catlin's fusion of classicism and romanticism points to a European art movement in the nineteenth century that shared striking parallels with western American art. Orientalism offered colorful Bedouins on horses and camels in lieu of Indians, "these Arabs of the Prairie" as one army officer called them, and harem girls instead of languorous Indian maidens lolling in buckskin dresses, swinging half nude from branches, or performing their toilets by the river. European and American "odalisques" satisfied a taste for the exotic and forbidden. The dry, clear atmosphere, piercing light, and immense expanses of plains and desert linked outdoor scenes, but most of all, western and Orientalist art were linked by the painters' common treatment of their subjects, a supercharged realism steeped in romanticism. Orientalism went out of vogue after the 1860s, though examples lingered into the next century. By then, an emphasis on American exceptionalism (the core of Frederick Jackson Turner's frontier thesis) stressed the Americanness of western art, obscuring the Orientalist connection. But before the Civil War, critics often recognized European parallels. Viewing Miller's painting *Cavalcade*, showing a party of Snake Indians arriving at the rendezvous, a journalist in 1839 wrote: "This is a work which would not discredit Horace Vernet himself, if he had painted it; and by the novelty of the subject and the skilful execution; its evident truth to nature, and the mastery of its difficulties; we fully agree with the uniform opinion expressed by the artists and amateurs who daily congregate around it, that it will attract great attention abroad, and make a favorable impression there of the progress of American art."

Vernet (1789–1863) was one of the most admired French academicians of his day. When Miller visited him at his studio in Rome in 1833 Vernet was working on a battle piece and had yet to discover Arabia. Subsequently, he made Orientalist subjects part of his repertoire, directly influencing some of the American artists who trained abroad. Carl Wimar (1828–62), a St. Louis painter who studied at Düsseldorf, Germany, in the 1850s and later twice journeyed up the Missouri to see for himself the Indians and buffalo and strange rock formations that had so impressed Catlin and Bodmer, translated Vernet's *Arabs Travelling in the Desert* (1843) into an Indian subject, *The Lost Trail* (ca. 1856), while he was still a student in Germany. Years later, Charles M. Russell (1864–1926), born in St. Louis two years after Wimar died, painted a homage also titled *The Lost Trail* (ca. 1915). The trail from Arabia to the American West was rarely so direct. Had Wimar lived longer or been better known in his time, he might today be recognized as a major transitional figure in western art. He went on to paint buffalo herds on the move, buffalo hunts, and panoramic vistas set along the Missouri in the twilight of the Indians' independence; he also painted bloody skirmishes between Indians and whites—a running battle with the cavalry, a war party fleeing with captured horses, an attack on a wagon train, the stout defense of the besieged emigrants—anticipating themes that would preoccupy the next generation of western artists.

Whereas Wimar bridged generations *and* art traditions, the parallels between Orientalist and western art are usually more suggestive than exact. For example, Vernet's first desert scene, *The Lion Hunt* (1836), belonged to the venerable tradition of hunting pictures. It depicted a frenzied melee of horses, lions, men, and a camel and presaged a group of related works on that quintessentially American theme, the buffalo hunt. Eastman in 1848, Miller perhaps two years later, and Stanley in 1853 painted buffalo hunts showing the herd racing away in the left background while the central action in the foreground to the right of center is dominated by an Indian preparing to spear a buffalo that, in the Eastman and Stanley versions, is goring a fallen horse and rider. These buffalo hunts echo Vernet's picture, which showed a spearman, a downed horse and rider, and in lieu of the buffalo, a pouncing lion. In the 1890s Remington and Russell both painted buffalo hunts in which a wounded buffalo vents its fury on a fallen rider while his companions struggle to bring it down. So a lion hunt translated into a buffalo hunt and one buffalo hunt into another, creating through conscious repetition enduring images of the American West long before Custer died on the Little Bighorn and artists invented his glorious Last Stand.

The subjective realism of the painter was challenged in the 1840s by a new technology with apparently unlimited potential for visual documentation. In the very decade that America's "manifest destiny" realized its continental ambitions, photography appeared to offer an objective means of illustrating the Far West. There were drawbacks. The technology was in its infancy, photographic apparatuses were cumbersome, materials were fragile, and the process was time-consuming. Nevertheless, beginning in 1842, artists like Stanley, Wimar, and Albert Bierstadt (1830–1902) made photographs, presumably as aides-mémoire for paintings, since no examples survive. The formal use of photography as part of the record-keeping on surveys, an idea floated during John C. Frémont's Rocky Mountain, Great Basin, and California explorations in the early 1840s, was accomplished on an expedition commanded by Lieutenant Lorenzo Sitgreaves in the Indian Territory in 1850. But three years later Stanley, as expeditionary draftsman with the Pacific Railroad Survey, Northern Route, was still

Though western art, almost by definition, deals with distinctively western themes, its treatment of these subjects is often informed by other artistic traditions. The composition of the French painter E. J. H. Vernet's *Lion Hunt,* for example, presaged a group of paintings on the buffalo hunt, a favorite subject for western artists at midcentury.

E.J.H. Vernet (1789– 1863). Chasse au Lion (The Lion Hunt). Oil on canvas, 1836. Reproduced by permission of the Trustees of the Wallace Collection, London, England.

John Mix Stanley (1814–72). The Buffalo Hunt. Oil on canvas, 1853. Photograph courtesy of The Gerald Peters Gallery, Santa Fe, New Mexico.

using photography to service his art, not to augment the permanent visual record. "I have just returned from a trip of twelve days among the Black Foot Indians," he wrote from Fort Benton on the Missouri. "I have made many interesting sketches of their customs—and daguerretypes [*sic*] of their chiefs—Thus far my trip has been very successful in subjects." But none of his photographs exists today. We do have a small but significant batch of daguerreotypes made during the Mexican War, however, anticipating the role that field photography would play in the Civil War and its role in documenting western expansion after the war.

Photography was first used in a systematic way on government-sponsored surveys of the West in the period 1866–79. Its advantage over art was still thought to be its unblinking factuality, its absolute fidelity to things as they are. It promised to eliminate even the hint of contrivance. Ferdinand V. Hayden, geologist-in-charge of the U.S. Geological and Geographical Survey of the Territories, 1869–78, praised the camera's "uncompromising lens"—an opinion that held sway even after the photographers themselves had asserted artistic aspirations. Preeminent among the western photographers were Carleton E. Watkins (1829–1916), with his almost three-dimensional views of Yosemite; Timothy H. O'Sullivan (1840–82), with his often haunting images, notable for their geological precision and raking light, of the barren lands of the Southwest; and William Henry Jackson (1843–1942), with his compelling pictures of the wonders of what became the nation's first national park, Yellowstone. Each accompanied official expeditions, enjoying freedom from the constraints that commercial considerations imposed on photographers who made their living taking portraits, group pictures, and town views and recording the local attractions, including natives, that would appeal to travelers passing through. Jackson, for example, located in Omaha in 1867 and with a brother operated a successful studio. He did the outdoor work, photographing nearby Indians and scenes along the newly completed Union Pacific Railroad, before he was taken on by Hayden in 1870, beginning an eight-year association that took him all over the West, from the badlands of Wyoming to the cliff dwellings of Arizona and New Mexico. Among expeditionary photographers, Jackson was on the prosaic end of the scale when it came to the aesthetic possibilities of the medium. In his vast body of work, he concentrated on the subject rather than its presentation or its philosophical implications. But he had a natural flair for composition, a talent that was enhanced through contact in 1871 with a gifted landscape painter praised by Hayden as an exquisite colorist, Thomas Moran.

Moran (1837–1926), English-born but American-raised, was highly trained in other aspects of his art as well. Even though he espoused close outdoor study and natural representation, he devoutly admired the English painter J.M.W. Turner. "Literally speaking, his landscapes are false," Moran wrote, "but they contain his impressions of Nature." This was a fundamental distinction, raising again the issue of the artist's subjective input into his art, his *impression* of reality. The Moran-Jackson relationship began on Hayden's 1871 survey of the Yellowstone, and the two proved kindred spirits in their commitment to western landscape as a distinctively American theme. Indeed, Jackson's photograph of Moran at Mammoth Hot Springs calls to mind Asher B. Durand's celebrated 1849 painting *Kindred Spirits*, showing the poet William Cullen Bryant and the painter Thomas Cole viewing the Catskill scenery. Here, photographer and painter contemplate western scenery, one directly, one through the camera's viewfinder. Even as Jackson became more self-conscious about the art in his photography, about selecting vantage points and framing his subjects, he also increasingly manipulated his images through retouching and extensive overpainting. Photography, it turned out, was not nature replicated. Like painting, it was one person's impression of reality.

Moran was not the only western landscape artist to discover his calling on an official

Accompanying Ferdinand V. Hayden's government-sponsored expedition to Yellowstone during the summer of 1871, the photographer William Henry Jackson and the painter Thomas Moran produced compelling views of the region's dramatic scenery that proved useful in enlisting eastern support for the movement to make Yellowstone the first national park.

William Henry Jackson (1843–1942). Thomas Moran at Mammoth Hot Springs, Yellowstone. Albumen silver print, 1871. National Park Service, Yellowstone National Park, California.

expedition. Bierstadt, born in Germany two years before Catlin ascended the Missouri, grew up in America but returned to Germany in the 1850s to polish his craft at Düsseldorf and to hone an ambition, equal to Catlin's, to achieve fame and fortune from his art. His often huge, theatrical paintings of western scenery were long out of favor by the end of his life, victims of changing tastes in art. But in the 1860s Bierstadt was at the pinnacle of popular renown. With a letter of introduction from the secretary of war, he had accompanied an 1859 expedition that was plotting a wagon road through the Rockies, and thus he found his life's work. Moran was always something of a topographical draftsman, despite his enthusiasm for Turner, and his Yellowstone watercolors, brilliant as jewels in their colors and craftsmanship, provided a visual catalog of the major geological wonders. But for Bierstadt, nature was the starting point, not an end in itself, and rearrangement was the artist's role. He gave Americans a western Eden just a little grander than reality. Miniature bear, deer, and Indians cavorted in the foreground while behind them, glimmer-glass lakes, shafts of light, and silver threads of plunging water carried the eye up peaks that soared to extravagant, cloud-piercing heights. He made unspoiled western nature his equivalent of Catlin's unspoiled western natives, staking out a domain (*his* Rockies, *his* Sierra Nevada) separate from that of Frederic Edwin Church, a much-admired contemporary who claimed the rest of the hemisphere.

The West belonged to Bierstadt. A friendly reviewer in 1868 joked that he had "copyrighted nearly all the principal mountains." The next year that noted art critic

George Armstrong Custer praised nature's wonderful ability to imitate the painters. "We are now in the Wichita Mountains . . . a high level plateau, with streams of clear water, and surrounded by a distant belt of forest trees," Custer wrote. "Tom [his brother] and I sat on our horses as the view spread before us, worthy the brush of a Church, a Bierstadt, the structure of the mountains reminding one of paintings of the Yosemite Valley, in the blending of colors—sombre purple, deep blue, to rich crimson tinged with gold." Shortly before departing on his final campaign, Custer lunched in Bierstadt's New York studio; subsequently, Bierstadt contributed fifty dollars to a monument fund for the fallen hero, resisting the temptation to add his version of Custer's Last Stand to the body of American historical art.

Bierstadt did, however, paint the alpha and the omega of the Indian's decline: the landing of Columbus and the last of the buffalo. His most effective statement on progress and change was an allegorical painting whose didacticism was muted by his bravura in handling landscape and light, *Emigrants Crossing the Plains* (1867; see p. 344). A passing caravan of pioneers dissolves into the setting sun; almost invisible behind the wagon train is a tipi village, bearing silent witness to civilization's inexorable advance. Back in 1819, Peale had painted a sunset on the Missouri; the West had then seemed all possibility. But by 1867, history had overtaken the future, and the setting sun, a beacon for the white pioneers, had become instead a symbol of the end of the native way of life. The years after the Civil War marked the final phase in the conquest of Indian America as the government's "Peace Policy," with its humanitarian rationale resting on military force, proved lethally effective. The Piegan, Modoc, Comanche, Kiowa, Lakota, Cheyenne, Nez Percé, Ute, and Apache Indians all felt the brunt of "conquest by kindness" after 1869. Catlin, living abroad in self-imposed exile, fretted over the "spectral picture . . . of well fed soldiers entering the wigwams of these starving and unsuspecting people, with sabres in hand splitting down the heads and mangling the bodies of women and children, crying and imploring for mercy." Now all could see what he had long ago predicted, "the reality of *Extermination* . . . the going down of the sun (and its last glimmering rays) of the North American Indians."

Remington, Russell, and Their Legacy

Born in the decade in which Bierstadt reached the heights of popular acclaim, both Frederic Remington and Charles M. Russell grew up entranced by stories and pictures of Indian-white conflict. Remington took the military side; Russell, while thrilling to the daring antics of dime-novel frontiersmen and real-life counterparts such as Buffalo Bill Cody, shied away from uniforms and favored the Indians. Both early showed their inclinations, which they faithfully followed through careers that spanned the closing of the frontier and the nostalgia of the twentieth century. Remington championed the winning of the West, whereas Russell lamented all that was lost. Each fashioned a distinctive body of work around his commanding theme. They were opposites in every way but one: both were certain they had witnessed the end of something profound. "I knew the wild riders and the vacant land were about to vanish forever, and the more I considered the subject the bigger the Forever loomed," Remington wrote in 1905. Russell said simply, "The West is dead! You may lose a sweetheart, but you won't forget her." It was this conscious awareness of the end of things that impressed their work so indelibly on future generations. Today, Remington and Russell still define western art.

There was never much doubt about Remington—the twig was bent early, and he was still painting and modeling military subjects the last year of his life. Indeed, his natural inclination was as a military, not a western, artist. He became the painter of the Indian-fighting army because Indian wars were all there was. When a foreign war did come along, he champed at the bit to take it in and eagerly awaited a "big murdering" in Cuba in 1898 so that he could be there to see it all. He was there, but it was too late by then. Real war proved messy and horrible, not splendid and glorious, and Remington was too old to be playing soldier. Anyway, time and circumstances had made him primarily a western artist, and the public held him to his task. As a prolific illustrator in the 1880s and 1890s he had relished "men with the bark on"—soldiers, certainly, and mountain men, cowboys, and their ilk. The Indian was for him the necessary foe— brutal, unfathomable, dangerous. Remington had neither empathy nor insight to offer: his was the Indian seen down a rifle barrel.

The Wyoming journalist Bill Nye set the terms for this brand of "western realism." "A dead Indian is a pleasing picture," he observed in 1881. "The picture of a wild free Indian chasing the buffalo may suit some, but I like still life in art. I like the picture of a broad-shouldered, well-formed brave as he lies with his nerveless hand across a large hole in the pit of his stomach." Artists had often depicted Indian atrocities. Paintings of the capture and murder of white women, a venerable tradition in American art, served as visual arguments for retaliation. Massacre scenes—not battles but furious slaughters by monsters in paint and feathers—were a nineteenth-century staple. Illustrations of both subjects filled popular histories of the Indian wars and even school readers. Portrayals of Custer's Last Stand were in the second tradition, and so was Remington. What distinguished his work was its concentration not on Indian savagery but on white heroism in opposing it. Other illustrators portrayed the Indian-fighting army after the Civil War, including Theodore R. Davis (1840–94) and Rufus F. Zogbaum (1849–1925). But Remington saw an epic playing itself out, the winning of the West, and his theme transcended the particulars. He prided himself on a knowledge derived from personal experience. But his imagination was his real strength. He conjured up convincing scenes of cavalry charges and close-quarter combat because he believed in them, and he made others believers too. In his time he was praised not for *creating* much of the imagery still fundamental to western art but for reporting, accurately and unimaginatively, what was. Remington knew better. He did not go to West Point himself, he once explained, because it "might have spoiled it all—it might have paralyzed the sentiment of the thing." And it was the sentiment that counted; facts were simply stepping-stones to larger truths.

Shortly after his return from Cuba, in the fall of 1900, Remington made a dispiriting trip to Colorado and New Mexico. "Shall never come west again," he wrote his wife. "It is all brick buildings—derby hats and blue overhauls—it spoils my early illusions—and they are my capital." Indeed, Remington's priorities changed in the twentieth century. He wanted to be a great artist, not merely an acclaimed illustrator. He wanted to make paintings freed from the demands of the literal. The Old West was mostly an idea, after all, and in increasingly impressionistic oils he gave free rein to his imagination. Color and light, not subject matter, were now his obsessions. Moonlight was a particular challenge, and Remington turned to nocturnes in which dark shadows cloaked a West become mundane, restoring its mystery and allure. Action was often minimized; a hush fell over figures poised expectantly, immobile, as though after three raucous centuries of westering, "of smoke and dust and sweat," only stillness remained. Remington even discovered a late-life regard for the old-time Indian, conquered more by hunger than fair combat and, in retrospect, possessed of a certain "nobility of purpose." But for all his artistic experimentation, Remington never deserted his theme. To the end he painted thundering cavalry charges and believed absolutely in the Anglo-Saxon mastery they represented. And he still defended his original turf against trespassers—artists like the Hoboken, New Jersey, painter Charles Schreyvogel (1861–1912), who in 1900 won a coveted prize from the National Academy of Design for a cavalry picture, *Wounded Bunkie,* and thereafter competed against Remington for popular favor as the painter-historian of the Indian-fighting army.

In truth, Schreyvogel was better equipped to carry on the old, heroic tradition. His West was derived from Buffalo Bill's Wild West show. It was all whooping Indians, dashing cavalry, and plunging horses, pure melodrama untroubled by subtlety or fact. Nevertheless, when Remington decided to expose the pretender, he chose factual accuracy as his grounds. The opportunity came in 1903 when Schreyvogel unveiled *Custer's Demand,* a quiet set piece for once showing a specific historical event—Custer again, though this time parleying with Kiowas on the southern plains seven years before his Last Stand. Remington could not find enough bad to say about it, but he tried, sparking a lively newspaper controversy full of irony as an artist who had disavowed documentary concerns grappled with another who had never embraced them over the issue of "historical correctness." It was a revealing note on which to introduce western art to the twentieth century.

Charles Russell represented an alternative tradition. His work was consistently commemorative, his heart in the past, not the present. He never changed. He fell in love with the wide-open spaces and rough-hewn ways of Montana as a sixteen-year-old in 1880, and he was still in love when he died in Great Falls forty-six years later, though it was the old Montana that commanded his loyalty. Russell came by his title as "the cowboy artist" honestly. He wrangled horses on the roundup most springs and falls from 1882 to 1892, sketching, modeling, and painting on the side. A close observer of what passed before him, he stored up the impressions of roping, riding, and Indian life that became his artistic stock-in-trade. In 1887 his small watercolor *Waiting for a Chinook* caught the public's fancy. It was a plain-spoken document showing a starving cow surrounded by wolves during the terrible winter of 1886–87, yet it had symbolic resonance. That winter marked the beginning of the end for the open-range cattle industry and the cowboy life Russell cherished. By 1890 the outline of a buffalo skull was part of his signature, expressing what he could not yet verbalize: the passing of a distinctive way of life. Soon roving Indians and cowboys, stagecoach drivers and bullwhackers, professional hunters and the rest would be fading memories. Documentation *was* commemoration, so rapidly was change transforming the land. Remington's work speaks to the heroism called forth by the winning of the West, whereas Russell's speaks only to the certainty, and pain, of loss.

Russell took up his art full time in 1893 and settled down for good a few years later when he married Nancy Cooper. She proved a shrewd, tough-minded businesswoman, adept at managing her husband and his career. Success was her goal, and together they achieved it, spectacularly. Russell advanced rapidly in technical sophistication in the twentieth century, but he never advanced an inch in his views. "I often think of you and the good old times we had," he wrote a cowboy friend soon after his marriage, and the years only intensified his nostalgia. "My me[m]ory often takes me back to the range, and camps we knew so well," he wrote another cowboy friend in 1917. "Theres not maney of the old bunch left . . . thirty seven years Iv lived in Mantana, but Im among strangers now." And just months before he died, calling himself a has-been horse wrangler, he mused that he would trade all the canned music in the world "to here the bells of a saddel band like most men of my age my harte lives back on trails that have been plowed under." Art for Russell was the shortest path back to yesterday.

Beginning with a good eye for detail and a wonderful grasp of human and animal anatomy, Russell had a rare knack for portraying action but little knowledge of how to compose a painting. His work through the 1890s was uneven as he learned his craft. At his peak, between 1905 and 1920, everything came together in glowing canvases that integrated figures and landscape to tell stories in paint that still speak of a magic time and place. Personal experience was important to his art. But some of Russell's favorite themes predated his arrival in Montana—Lewis and Clark, intertribal battles, mountain men, even buffalo hunts. His West was a compound of memory, imagination, and research.

Entranced by the romance of the Old West, Charles M. Russell painted a world that existed mainly in memory and imagination. His heroic men of the open range were figures of the past, relics of the days before barbed wire and changing business practices altered the cattle industry that Russell cherished.

Charles M. Russell (1864–1926). Men of the Open Range. Oil on canvas, 1923. Mackay Collection, Montana Historical Society, Helena.

He made it more real than reality. And he never forgot the glue that held it all together, a romanticism that spurned the mundane for the picturesque. "Sinch your saddle on romance," he advised a western writer. "Hes a high headed hoss with plenty of blemishes but keep him moovin and theres fiew that can call the leg he limps on and most folks like prancers." In the last years of his life, nostalgia, not the West, was Russell's real subject. His power—and his enduring legacy to western art—was the ability to make his yearning universal.

Remington and Russell are commonly lumped together as the progenitors of a "Wild West school" of art. But others anticipated them in some respects, and both drew on the older generation of western artists for information and inspiration—notably Catlin, Bodmer, and in Russell's case, Wimar. Still, the pair's influence does constitute a school of sorts. Remington offered advice to artists as diverse as Maynard Dixon (1875–1946), best known for his desert landscapes, and Carl Rungius (1869–1959), a gifted wildlife painter, and his influence was pervasive. It would be safe to say that no western artist after 1890 was entirely unaffected by Remington's example. Certainly Edwin W. Deming (1860–1942), W.H.D. Koerner (1878–1938), Philip R. Goodwin (1882–1935), Frank Tenney Johnson (1874–1939), Schreyvogel, and Russell himself owed Remington a debt. Russell actually had a protégé, the painter Joe De Yong (1894–1975), who from 1914 on sometimes worked beside him in his log cabin studio in Great Falls. And he encouraged a range of cowboy artists who found in him their model, including Will James (1892–1942), E. W. Gollings (1878–1932), and the sculptor Charles A. Beil (1894–1976). Edward Borein (1872–1945), Russell's California counterpart as a cowboy artist, was a close friend, and Russell's influence touched several of the outdoor illustrators of his day, including John N. Marchand (1875–1921), W. Herbert Dunton (1878–1936), and Goodwin (whose technical skills and palette, in turn, influenced Russell's own). The Great Falls painter Olaf C. Seltzer (1877–1957) was a direct imitator, indeed almost a Russell clone. Through calendar reproductions and cheap color prints, Russell's example was broadcast everywhere. Even William R. Leigh (1866–1955), a European-trained and highly polished craftsman given to a Schreyvogel kind of Wild West, named Russell as an inspiration, and members of the Cowboy Artists of America to this day are still proudly in his tradition.

Ageless Cowboys and Sunset Indians

The twin legacies of Remington and Russell have long since passed into the popular culture. John Ford's cavalry western movies relied on Remington for everything from camera angles and color to costume and action bits, and the director Howard Hawks recalled trying to capture Remington's light in a night scene set outside a saloon. The phenomenally successful Marlboro Man advertising campaign, begun in 1954 and still going strong, has played effectively on the notion of the rugged, self-reliant cowboy hero riding free under the "Big Sky" and not about to take advice from Washington bureaucrats like the surgeon general. Imagery and attitude alike are straight out of Remington and Russell. They set the terms for the Old West in the twentieth century. But although the two can be linked as progenitors of a Wild West school, it is equally important to understand their differences. If subject matter connects them, it also distinguishes them from one another. A Montana newspaper in 1902 drew the conventional distinction: "Russell is the acknowledged superior in handling subjects on the ranges and in the cattle country, while Remington's cavalrymen and scouts are the best types of his western work."

The cowboy became a major presence in the American imagination only in the last few decades of the nineteenth century. Artists like James Walker (1819–89) had painted the dashing Mexican vaqueros of California and Texas, but the earliest representations of Anglo cowboys appeared in the popular press shortly after the Civil War, the work of such illustrators as Waud, of later Custer fame. As the mountain man departed the scene, a new individualistic western hero was in order. Plainsmen-scouts in buckskin costumes kept the trappings of the mountain man before the public, but the cowboy was more current. His appeal, like that of the mountain man, stemmed from his free-roaming, transient occupation. One day the beaver would be trapped out, the range would be fenced in, and both mountain men and cowboys, their purpose gone, would be rendered obsolete, mourned as part of the nation's vanished youth. Indeed, their actual youthfulness, their profligate ways—the big blowout at rendezvous or end-of-the-trail cowtowns—and their devil-may-care disregard for convention gave them poignant stature. They would not be here tomorrow. As alternatives to sober-sided earnestness, acquisitiveness, and workaday reality in an ever more urbanized America, cowboys passed through life scornful of money, danger, and the serious business of growing up.

The cowboy story has been characterized as a male escapist fantasy, and the western myth that exalts the cowboy remains overwhelmingly a male myth. Women are plugged into set roles (sunbonneted pioneer mothers, golden-hearted prostitutes, the occasional female outlaw), but their presence is minimal and correspondingly minimal in western art. Again, this reaches to the crux of the matter: western art is about cultural assumptions, not historical realities. It evokes cleaner air and purer water—the greener grass on the other side of the fence or over the next hill. The combination of fiction, showmanship, and art that planted the cowboy's image in the public's mind came at a time when nostalgia was already cloaking the West in the romance of faded youth and better yesterdays. The cowboy promised men they need never grow old; they could be boys forever, leaving behind the cares and duties of ordinary folk and riding off into a "land without end, a space across which Noah and Adam might have come straight from Genesis," as Owen Wister put it in *The Virginian* (1902). In western fiction, the cowboy's work rarely intrudes on the action; indeed, as the Texas writer J. Frank Dobie observed, cowboy stories are notable for the absence of cows. Artists were more faithful to the cowboy's working life. Russell, for one, drew on his rangeland experience to record the technical aspects of cowboying, though his themes were mostly action-oriented: bucking broncos and perilous moments when "ropes go wrong," horses fall, and steers turn hostile and dangerous. The message was mythic.

Besides the cowboy, a more venerable figure took center stage at the turn of the century. The cowboy conjured up a past that need never die; the Indian, decked out in feathers and fairly reeking of pathos, stood for all that was already lost. Before landing in New Mexico in 1918, the influential modernist painter Marsden Hartley (1877–1943)

Echoing contemporary politicians and policy-makers, early 20th-century Anglo artists often depicted Indians as doomed members of a once noble race.

James Earle Fraser (1876–1953). The End of the Trail. Bronze, 1918. Clara Peck Purchase Fund, Buffalo Bill Historical Center, Cody, Wyoming.

confessed that he "wanted to be an Indian, . . . go to the west, and face the sun forever." Neoprimitivism played its part in the reemergence of the "Vanishing American," but nostalgia was the star. "If the cogs of time would slip back seventy winters," Russell wrote in 1920, "thaird be another white Injun among the Black feet Hunting hump backed cows." The cowboy artist loved dressing up in wig and blanket and playing Indian, and he filled his paintings with proud warriors riding across the open plains. It was not that he took no interest in the Indian in the present, but as he remarked, he had "always studied the wild man from his picture side," and his picture side was yesterday. The sculptor James Earle Fraser (1876–1953) achieved lasting renown for his allegorical model *The End of the Trail*, which he worked up on epic scale in 1915. It showed a bowed warrior on a drooping pony, and Fraser dreamed of having it cast in bronze to occupy a promontory above San Francisco Bay. There, horse and rider "would stand forever looking out on the waste of waters—with nought save the precipice and the ocean before them . . . , in very truth, 'The End of the Trail.'" But Fraser's most widely circulated work, the buffalo–Indian head nickel first minted in 1913, told of other trails that had ended as well. The Old West was gone, and the Indian, as its most compelling symbol, now also stood for a vanished America.

Determined to be the George Catlin for a new century, the Seattle-based photographer Edward S. Curtis (1868–1952) in 1900 began creating a comprehensive pictorial history of the western tribes. His enterprise, like Catlin's, would be a calculated fusion of science and romanticism dedicated to a simple proposition: the Indians and their cultures were vanishing. The Indian had long put the putative objectivity of photography to the test. After the Civil War, field photographers had recorded Indian camp life, while studio photographers following in the footsteps of King had made individual and group portraits of Indian delegates visiting in Washington, D.C. Jackson combined both approaches in photographing the Pawnees and Omahas before joining the Hayden survey; subsequently, his ethnological bent found expression in views of the Shoshone, Bannock, Ute, and Pueblo Indians. Other expeditionary photographers were active too, and in 1877 Jackson compiled a descriptive catalog of the government's collection of Indian photographs, over a thousand in number. Hayden, impressed by its size and comprehensiveness (twenty-five tribes were represented), echoed the claims Catlin had made for his Indian Gallery forty years before and declared the government collection unique, irreplaceable, and of inestimable scientific value. The "Vanishing American" still validated the urgent need to preserve a visual record of the native tribes; inevitably, the assumptions it embodied also shaped the record that was being preserved.

Curtis, for example, inaugurated the first volume (published in 1907) in his twenty-volume series *The North American Indian* with a symbolic view of a party of Navajos riding off into the desert haze, toward dark shadows where the light glimmering along the top of a distant bluff provided the only ray of hope for their future. Curtis titled the photograph *The Vanishing Race*. "The thought which this picture is meant to convey is that the Indians as a race, already shorn of their tribal strength and stripped of their primitive dress, are passing into the darkness of an unknown future," he explained. "Feeling that the picture expresses so much of the thought that has inspired the entire work, the author has chosen it as the first of the series." Curtis's pictorial record of the tribes was faithful to this premise. He was not simply out to show Indians; like Russell, whom he later met, he was out to show the romantic and picturesque side of Indian life. Many western towns had a resident photographer in the 1870s, and amateur camera bugs proliferated by the end of the century. They were responsible for some of the frankest, least artfully contrived pictures of Indian reservations, where life, changed as it was, went on. But photographs documenting acculturation never had the emotional appeal of those that suspended time or even rolled it back. To this day, the public prefers pictures of Indians not as they are but as Curtis showed them—colorful, noble, and doomed.

No wonder modern native artists have focused so often on what Scholder has called "Indian kitsch." By defining Indian existence, white stereotypes have defined Indians out of existence. Thus the influence of Scholder's ironic mode: it makes the white images do the work of cultural criticism. Fraser's *End of the Trail* can be turned against itself, for example, exposing the whole self-serving tradition of the "Vanishing American." And Custer's Last Stand is a natural to get at the mythology of the winning of the West.

If the disappearance of native cultures was a subject for European-American artists of an earlier date, the continued vitality of native cultures is an important theme for many contemporary Native American artists. Ironically addressing the cultural stereotypes established by mainstream western art and popular history, the Lakota artist Randy Lee White evokes the imagery of Custer's Last Stand to comment on a fight over gasoline supplies.

Randy Lee White (b. 1951). Custer Revised. Mixed media, 1980. Gift of Manfred Baumgartner, 1984. Collection of the Museum of Fine Arts, Museum of New Mexico, Santa Fe.

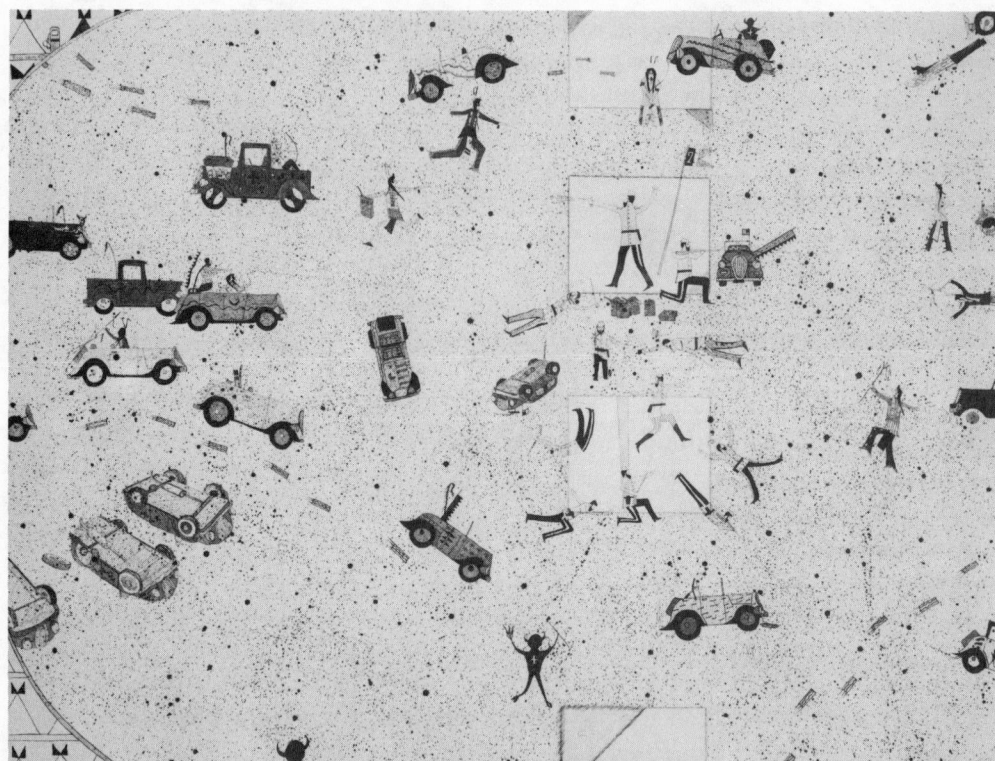

"Custer Wore an Arrow Shirt," a popular Red Power slogan goes; another more bitingly asserts, "Custer Died for Your Sins." These suggest the range of possibilities Custer opens for the native artist. Scholder offered a sly treatment in his amusingly titled painting *Indian, Dog, and Friend* (1973), based on a photograph of Custer at ease with an Indian scout and a hunting dog. His most celebrated student, T. C. Cannon (1946–78), mocked the heroic Custer image in portraits whose titles were also humorous but angrier: *Zero Hero, Ugh*, and *Custer, "Go Gettum."* Randy Lee White (b. 1951), a Lakota, wittily combined Custer's Last Stand and traditional pictographic form to comment on postreservation developments in *Custer Revised* (1980). It shows old-time warriors battling white salesmen, in soldiers' uniforms, who are defending their supply of gasoline, needed to fuel the automobiles that the white men have duped the Lakotas into buying and that, now useless, litter the battlefield. One warrior makes off with his trophy—not a scalp or a rifle but a gasoline can—while a "soldier," still desperately defending his culture's values (here, a fuel hoard), fires a parting shot. Native artists range freely in their choice of subjects. But their work is most clearly part of western art when it overtly comments on white preoccupations and stereotypes, taking visual revenge on the often oppressive mythology that the art sustains.

Outsiders

Cowboys and Indians dominate western art because they express so well its commanding theme of evanescence. This implies, accurately, that the artistic record of the American West is highly selective. Western art omits much in order to emphasize a little, establishing that little, through repetition, as the whole. Fundamentally, it has been a frontier art, and like frontiering, it is about a process, not a result. The West, as the novelist A. B. Guthrie, Jr., noted, "is an adventure of the spirit. . . . more than journey's end, it is the journey itself that enchants us." Repudiating the frontier as a useful historical construct today will change neither its importance for an earlier generation nor the fact that it is now entrenched in western art. As a new generation of historians challenges the inherited story of westering, reevaluation of western art is thus unavoidable, and desirable. An essentially white male escapist fantasy cannot survive unexamined (and perhaps undiscredited) into the twenty-first century. Critics who never did like western art have now found just cause for dismissing it: it is both sexist and racist. Still, the art may prove refractory material for revisionism. Its landscapes remain appealing and its action pieces exciting, and it is encrusted with layers of cultural meaning. Because it is so ideologically charged, it is an exclusionist art. It eliminates alternate visions and even much of the subject matter that a western art should logically embrace.

Urbanization is part of the story of civilization's advance into the wilderness. But a major painter like George Caleb Bingham (1811–79) of St. Louis seems most western not when he is showing political life in Missouri—politicians are still with us—but when he is showing rivermen and trappers, who are not. Western communities were well represented among the popular nineteenth-century bird's-eye views of American towns and cities. The urban intrusion on western nature is evident in prints showing tree stumps pockmarking the hills outside the town. Often, tiny foreground figures serve as aids to perspective and as commentaries on white progress: strolling ladies with parasols and gentlemen in top hats, farmers in their fields, cowboys with their herds, prospectors with their picks, hunters with their faithful dogs, fishermen in their boats, even an artist at his easel. Once in a while an Indian creeps onto the fringe of things. A print made in about 1850 showed an Indian man gazing at Sutter's Mill and Coloma, mute testimony to the devastating impact the gold rush had on California's native population. In an 1849 lithograph of Oregon City, four Indians stand with spears in hand looking across the river at a settlement from which they are both literally and figuratively barred. A view of Omaha, Nebraska, published in 1868 made a similar point. In the foreground, a small forest shelters a lake and a miniature canoe and Indians continuing their traditional pursuits, oblivious to the burgeoning, well-ordered city just beyond the treeline. Sometimes tipis would be sprinkled over the prairies outside the town limits to contrast old and new, past and present.

Despite the occasional concession to such allegorical motifs, western town views were not really concerned with the frontier past. Instead, neat rows of buildings and grids of streets welcomed the future. By the 1980s nearly 83 percent of those living in the West resided in metropolitan areas—the highest percentage in the nation. But this urban reality remains outside the western art tradition. In the nineteenth century, illustrators working for the eastern periodicals might show gambling halls and hurdy-gurdy houses, ignoring the substantial private residences and public buildings that were prominently featured whenever local pride set the artistic agenda. But in western art, towns exist primarily as settings for gunfights and cowboy high jinks. They might be saloon-centered urban oases, but they were never home. *That* was on the range.

Similarly, the farmer is outside western art. Harvey Dunn (1884–1952) gave his

homesteaders, female and male, the monumental stature usually reserved for mountain men, cowboys, and cavalrymen. But western art is attuned to high plains and desert romance, not prairie realism. The farmer may be close to nature, but the land he possesses possesses him, rooting him in the earth and denying him the mythic resonance that comes with moving on. Russell, speaking for the cowboy artist tradition, scoffed at those who thought Dunn a western artist. He could not paint a horse, Russell insisted, and that alone disqualified him. Besides, the farmer was the cowboy's dreary opposite: he represented the triumph of the mundane. "When the nester turned this country grass side down the west we loved died," Russell wrote in 1919. "She was a beautifull girl that had many lovers but to day thair are only a fiew left to morn her the farmer plowed her under . . . the man betwene the plow handls was never a romance maker and when he comes history is dead." Russell's bias is still enshrined in western painting and western fiction. The farmer stands accused of obliterating the picture-and-story part of history—and in western art that is the part that matters.

Beginning in 1898, artists found pictures and stories aplenty in New Mexico. The layering of cultures in the Southwest made for a unique depth in time and for a vibrant present where native, Hispanic, and Anglo intermingled in a setting whose beauty, the writer Mary Austin observed, "takes the breath like pain." Here, in the art colonies that flourished in Taos and Santa Fe, an alternative vision found expression. It showed peoples accommodating, changing, enduring. Western art is predicated on a violent rupture between past and present. It is about transience and loss, whereas southwestern art is about continuity and survival. Explaining his decision to go north and paint for a while on the Crow reservation in Montana, Joseph Henry Sharp (1859–1953), a founding member of the Taos Society of Artists (1915), observed, "I went north because I realized that Taos would last longer." Although the "Vanishing American" lingered in the works of Sharp, Bert G. Phillips (1868–1956), and E. Irving Couse (1866–1936),

Depicting farmers as heroic subjects, the painter Harvey Dunn calls attention both to an important aspect of western development and to the biases of a western art tradition more concerned with mountain men and cowboys than the more numerous homesteaders.

Harvey T. Dunn (1884–1952). The Prairie Is My Garden. Oil on canvas, ca. 1940. South Dakota Art Museum Collection, Brookings.

the defining southwestern motif was permanence. "Of the Southwest of romance and story the vast, inscrutable mountains, the desolate open spaces remain," a journalist wrote in 1919. "The cowboy still herds his cattle on the mesa, and rides gallantly into a settlement to pass a weekend; hard-eyed prospectors seek hidden gold and silver among the mountains; grizzled frontiersmen trap animals for their fur; in short, . . . it is still the storied Southwest, sans hostile Indians." Grand as nature was, it made room for people. Life was on a human scale; it had texture and an ambling pace. Painters like Ernest L. Blumenschein (1874–1960), Oscar E. Berninghaus (1874–1952), Victor Higgins (1884–1949), and Walter Ufer (1876–1936) created languorous set pieces that caught and held the public's imagination into the 1930s. Indians, horses, and wide-open spaces do not necessarily western art make, however. The pastoral vision associated with Taos and Santa Fe stands outside the western art mainstream, promising something still there, awaiting discovery, whereas western art is about a time and a place that have no existence outside the artist's imagination—"The West That Has Passed," as Russell called it.

Western art also excludes women both as practitioners and subjects. Exceptions can be found (Mary Hallock Foote [1847–1938], an author and illustrator with wide experience in the western mining country, is often mentioned), but the rule stands with one great qualifier: Georgia O'Keeffe (1887–1986), the only woman included in most representative collections of western art and the only western artist represented in most collections of modernist American art. Her story has been retold so often that her life and personality are part of common lore. She is today a legendary figure on a level with Russell himself. He was the cowboy whose untutored genius, according to tradition, shaped western art at the end of the nineteenth century; she was the visionary genius who almost single-handedly dragged western art into the twentieth. Friends with Will Rogers, William S. Hart, and a posse of silent film stars, Russell was a deep-dyed traditionalist. Soul mate and wife of the experimental New York photographer Alfred Stieglitz, with whom she shared a stormy relationship at once suffocating and liberating,

Victor Higgins (1884–1949). Pueblo of Taos. *Oil on canvas, before 1927. Photograph by James O. Milmoe. Courtesy of The Anschutz Collection, Denver, Colorado.*

O'Keeffe was an instinctive modernist. Born the year Russell painted his miniature storytelling masterpiece *Waiting for a Chinook*, she visited Taos in 1929, three years after his death. She had located her heartland, her Montana—"for me it is the only place"—and after a protracted tug-of-war between New York and New Mexico, she moved to the West for good in 1949. Legendary ghosts like Billy the Kid had enticed her when she first journeyed west in 1912 to teach in Amarillo, Texas, but it was the land—with its fantastic formations, brilliant hues, and compelling emptiness—that caught and finally held her. In her work the human presence would be left implicit in adobe structures and crosses seemingly as old and durable as the hills.

O'Keeffe has been called a "visionary realist," to differentiate her from the run-of-the-mill realists who populate western art. But Russell, as noted, was a romantic realist himself. Modernists like O'Keeffe are said to evoke rather than describe, to interpret rather than document. Their art, unlike that of the representationalists, is about personal response, not the thing being responded to. However, this generalization risks creating a false dichotomy between western modernists and western traditionalists by implying that modernist works are acts of the imagination whereas traditionalist works are mere factual transcriptions. We might better regard Russell and O'Keeffe not as artistic opposites but as artists who created separate realities true to their times and places, and to themselves. Russell made a buffalo skull his personal insignia because it was visual shorthand for the Old West; O'Keeffe painted skulls and bones as one end of the desert

spectrum, with wildflowers at the other. Fiercely independent in her views, she made her isolation part of her art. Many came to Taos, and most left, just as many streamed through Russell's log cabin studio in Great Falls and his summer cabin on Lake McDonald in Glacier Park, eager to see what he saw but not to stay. Physically and emotionally, he identified with the scenes of his youth, as O'Keeffe would with the scenes of her maturity, and each evolved a distinctive way of expressing this attachment. The world now sees New Mexico through O'Keeffe's eyes, as it long has Montana through Russell's. Calendar reproductions widely broadcast his work during his lifetime, turning his paintings into western icons; he still merits at least one calendar each year. Similarly, O'Keeffe calendars are a growth industry today. As a hero of modernism and women's art, she is in danger of becoming a pinup girl for the 1990s and her strikingly original images the latest western clichés. Scholder has already offered a variation on her magisterial *Ranchos Church, Taos* (1930), and another native artist, David Bradley (b. 1954), has portrayed her as a southwestern "Whistler's Mother." Nevertheless, it is fitting that the painter who ushered western art into the twentieth century should also see it out. Nothing finally makes O'Keeffe a better exemplar of the western tradition than the very visionary realism that supposedly sets her apart.

Given all that western art excludes, it seems fitting to conclude with its own exclusion from American art. Western art did not start out as a regional expression, but it has certainly ended up as one. In the nineteenth century, it expressed an expanding, bombastic nation; today, it is a vital and accepted tradition only in the West. American art surveys may give it a passing nod in a separate chapter, serving merely to emphasize its isolation. Critics routinely ignore it, though some, aroused by a controversial exhibition at the Smithsonian Institution's National Museum of American Art in 1991,

"The West as America," now deplore on ideological grounds what they previously dismissed on artistic ones. The indifference to the actual art—be it traditional or modern, white or native—has led to an enclave existence for western art. Only two museums east of the Mississippi River (and none on the East Coast) house representative collections, though individual works are scattered throughout public collections. The Smithsonian's museums own most of Catlin's works, and the Frederic Remington Art Museum in Ogdensburg, New York, the artist's boyhood home, holds a substantial collection of his work. Otherwise, western art must be seen in the West—in Montana and Wyoming, California and Nebraska, Colorado and Oklahoma, and Texas most of all.

Remington, with a foot planted on both sides of the Mississippi, represents the uneasy current status of western art. In his noisy approval of the "winning of the West," he championed a cause now disapproved with a stridency equal to his own. If revisionism holds, much western art will come to seem as outdated as the triumphalist values it espouses, and images that once seemed timeless will appear increasingly (and embarrassingly) time-bound. But western art is about more than progress and conquest and "manifest destiny." It is also about open spaces and yearning and opportunity and hope. Big Rock Candy Mountains exist in the heart, not the head, and the West is still what Catlin called it a century and a half ago, a "phantom, travelling on its tireless wing." Revisionist history, with its stern lessons about the western past, may yet run that phantom to the ground. Meanwhile, western art continues to appeal to rainbow-chasers everywhere.

Bibliographic Note

Among the surveys of western art notable for scholarship and interpretation are the following: Robert Taft, *Artists and Illustrators of the Old West, 1850–1900* (New York, 1953); John C. Ewers, *Artists of the Old West* (Garden City, N.Y., 1965), which incorporates material from the seminal articles he published on individual artists in the Smithsonian's *Miscellaneous Collections* and *Annual Reports*, extending a tradition that reaches back to the 1920s and the pioneering scholarship of David I. Bushnell, Jr.; Frank Getlein, *The Lure of the Great West* (Waukesha, Wis., 1973); Peter Hassrick, *The Way West: Art of Frontier America* (New York, 1977); Dawn Glanz, *How the West Was Drawn: American Art and the Settling of the Frontier* (Ann Arbor, 1982); William H. Goetzmann and William N. Goetzmann, *The West of the Imagination* (New York, 1986), which draws on ideas first advanced in William H. Goetzmann's *Exploration and Empire: The Explorer and the Scientist in the Winning of the American West* (New York, 1966) and widely broadcast in a companion television series "The West of the Imagination," available on videocassette from Films for the Humanities, Princeton, N.J.; and Jules Prown et al., *Discovered Lands, Invented Pasts: Transforming Visions of the American West* (New Haven, 1992). The latter was produced in conjunction with an exhibition organized by the Thomas Gilcrease Institute in Tulsa, Oklahoma, and the Yale University Art Gallery. Many of the most useful—and sometimes controversial—works on western art have appeared as catalogs accompanying exhibitions. Some provide interpretive approaches (Chris Bruce et al., *Myth of the West* [Seattle, 1990], and William H. Truettner, ed., *The West as America: Reinterpreting Images of the Frontier, 1820–1920* [Washington, D.C., 1991]). Others focus on a group of artists (Charles C. Eldredge, Julie Schimmel, and William H. Truettner, *Art in New Mexico, 1900–1945: Paths to Taos and Santa Fe* [New York, 1986], and Ron Tyler et al., *American Frontier Life: Early Western Painting and Prints* [New York, 1987]) or photographers (Weston J. Naef et al., *Era of Exploration: The Rise of Landscape Photography in the American West, 1860–1885* [Buffalo, N.Y., 1975], and

Martha A. Sandweiss, ed., *Photography in Nineteenth-Century America* [Fort Worth, 1991]).
Most explore the work of an individual. Recent examples include Michael Edward Shapiro et al.,
George Caleb Bingham (St. Louis, 1990), William Wallo and John Pickard, *T. C. Cannon,
Native American: A New View of the West* (Oklahoma City, 1990), Rick Stewart, Joseph D.
Ketner II, and Angela L. Miller, *Carl Wimar: Chronicler of the Missouri River Frontier* (Fort
Worth, 1991), and Nancy K. Anderson and Linda S. Ferber, *Albert Bierstadt: Art and Enterprise*
(New York, 1990). All of the major and most of the minor western artists and photographers have
been the subject of at least one illustrated biography, many of them sponsored by museums like
the Amon Carter in Fort Worth and the Buffalo Bill Historical Center in Cody, Wyoming.
Recently, as the book on Bierstadt indicates, interest in the issue of patronage and western art
has been growing. See, for example, Richard H. Saunders, *Collecting the West: The C. R. Smith
Collection of Western American Art* (Austin, 1988), and Brian W. Dippie, *Catlin and His
Contemporaries: The Politics of Patronage* (Lincoln, 1990). There is also more interest in modern
western art, fueled by the extraordinary popularity of Georgia O'Keeffe. See Patricia Janis Broder,
The American West: The Modern Vision (Boston, 1984), and for O'Keeffe, besides the many
elaborate volumes showcasing her art, see Roxana Robinson's biography *Georgia O'Keeffe: A Life*
(New York, 1989). A helpful compendium of biographical information on the entire range of
western artists is Peggy Samuels and Harold Samuels, *The Illustrated Biographical Encyclopedia
of Artists of the American West* (Garden City, N.Y., 1976). Native art has a huge literature of its
own; a recent sampler is Edwin L. Wade, ed., *The Arts of the North American Indian: Native
Traditions in Evolution* (New York, 1986). *American Indian Art Magazine* is useful for keeping
abreast with activity in its field, whereas *Persimmon Hill* and *Southwest Art* are well-illustrated
journals devoted to western art, past and present.

BEADLE'S Half-Dime POCKET Library

Copyrighted, 1884, by Beadle and Adams. Entered at the Post Office at New York, N. Y., as Second Class Mail Matter. Feb. 20, 1884.

Vol. I. $2.50 a Year. Published Weekly by Beadle and Adams, No. 98 WILLIAM ST., NEW YORK. Price, Five Cents. No. 6.

THE PRAIRIE PILOT; or, THE PHANTOM SPY.

BY BUFFALO BILL.

EXAMINING THE CREVICES IN THE WALL OF ROCK, PRAIRIE PILOT FOUND ONE THAT LOOKED INTO THE ADJOINING CAVERN.

Chapter Twenty

The Literary West

THOMAS J. LYON

apping the western literary range might seem to be a simple job: draw a line down the Mississippi River, and everything west of that is "western." But start talking with critics of western literature, and soon the good feeling of geographical neatness dwindles. Questions arise. Are the elegant detective novels of Ross Macdonald and Raymond Chandler, set mostly in Santa Barbara and Los Angeles, properly western? (Some critics rule out cities—perhaps on the idea that they are not open, western space.) When Henry Miller of Brooklyn and Paris, the author of *Tropic of Cancer*, moved to Big Sur in 1944, did he become a western writer? (Do we go by an author's geographical residence, or is the determinant something more complicated?)

Some students of the West, Walter Prescott Webb and Wallace Stegner among them, have refined the map by describing areas of low rainfall as diagnostically western. Aridity means space: the space between trees and shrubs, struggling to survive in marginal conditions, and also the space between human settlements, ground that is difficult to exploit or settle, thus remaining mostly wild and open. Relatively few people, living in small settlements within an extensive wilderness, comes close to defining the classic western situation.

But a literary map also needs to account for time and change. We need a theory elastic enough to acknowledge, for example, that although megalopolitan Los Angeles of the 1990s may not offer classic westernness to a writer, it nevertheless has been shaped by a definitively western process. It was a sleepy pueblo two centuries ago, became a cattle town in the nineteenth century, then began reaching out and appropriating water, and grew and grew, developing industry, and the end is not yet. The Los Angeles process is, in essence, the "westward movement," the expansion of European-American civilization at the expense of both traditional societies and natural ecology. Such a history is at heart dialectical, a history of conflict, and as Frederick Jackson Turner pointed out back in 1893, the point of interaction between the old (the wildland itself, or Indian culture, originally) and the new (explorers, mountain men, and pioneers, at first) is the frontier. In the traditional understanding, the frontier began at the East Coast and moved westward until closure was declared by the U.S. Bureau of the Census in 1890.

If frontier action defines writing as western, the western map expands considerably. Many critics, indeed, see James Fenimore Cooper's "Leatherstocking Tales," four of which take place in eighteenth-century New York State, as thematically western. Far enough back in time, even Virginia may be a kind of West—Leslie Fiedler once described John Smith's Pocahontas story as an early version of a prominent western

Late 19th-century dime novels depicted the West as a place of adventure and heroic masculine virtues. Although much regional writing is more self-critical, the success of the formulaic westerns is still reflected in an enduring strain of popular western literature.

William F. Cody (1846–1917). The Prairie Pilot; or, The Phantom Spy. From The House of Beadle and Adams and Its Dime and Nickel Novels; The Story of a Vanished Literature, Volume 1, by Albert Johannsen. Copyright © 1950 by the University of Oklahoma Press, Norman.

myth, called by Fiedler "Love in the Woods." But the problems with an exclusively dialectical approach that is not tied in some fashion to geography should be obvious. *Where* the action takes place also counts. It can be argued that the frontier is as old as post-Renaissance European expansion and is worldwide to boot; but on the ground of the American West in the nineteenth century, the drama of invasion achieved its best-known statement. The natives were more resistant than in some of Europe's other frontiers, the landscape was more sublime, and the advancing Anglo-Americans had had several generations of pioneering in which to build an identity as tough practitioners of expansion. What came out of this mix literarily was a durable pattern of romance and myth and a set of images that permeate the broader national culture.

The literature that uses the "frontier" set of myths and values unconsciously—that is, in effect, expansionist by faith, though perhaps tinged from time to time with a certain helpless regret, for example over the plight of the Indians or the loss of the wilderness—such literature has been enormously popular. It may answer some deep American needs, as John G. Cawelti has argued, creating formulas of resolution for the contradictions inherent in a history of violence and aggrandizement. But there is another western literature, one that should be called "postfrontier," whose stance toward the frontier and the frontier ethos is conscious, reflective, and analytic. In general, this writing is not characterized by expansionist sentiments or romance but by a regardful perspective on the environment, a sympathetic view toward Indians, and a realistic bent in historical and social descriptions. A complex self-consciousness stands behind this more mature regional literature. The western literary-critical divide, indeed, is between two literatures: popular and, if the term be allowed, serious. Unfortunately for the sake of neatness, the two kinds of western writing may blend, for example in Jack Schaefer's *Shane* (1949), where the popular myths are stated with such artistry and economy that the novel has been taken very seriously indeed. But in most cases the qualitative differences between frontier and postfrontier mentalities are easy enough to see and make for a reasonably reliable critical gauge.

Early Travel Accounts

The earliest significant writings produced in the West were the journals of the Lewis and Clark expedition, with those kept by Meriwether Lewis making the most substantial claim to literary standing. Lewis frequently went off by himself during the journey, looked over the land with what appears to have been a historical eye or at least a sense of the momentousness of the expedition, and often entered personal reflections in his record. Thus he seemed to have been writing, at times, more than just a log, and several of his more essayistic entries verge on literary territory. He responded to the utter wildness of the land with writing that, as clearly as any other American document, evokes an Edenic feeling. On 25 April 1805, for example, almost three weeks into what would prove to be the least-inhabited section of the continent that the expedition would see (the area of the upper Missouri River, in present-day North Dakota and Montana), Lewis wrote: "the whole face of the country was covered with herds of Buffaloe, Elk & Antelopes; deer are also abundant, but keep themselves more concealed in the woodland. the buffaloe Elk and Antelope are so gentle that we pass near them while feeding, without appearing to excite any alarm among them; and when we attract their attention, they frequently approach us more nearly to discover what we are, and in some instances pursue us a considerable distance apparently with that view."

Lewis's account, beyond its considerable inherent interest, has provided a benchmark against which the subsequent history of the West may be measured literarily, as for example in Archibald MacLeish's bitterly satiric poem "Empire Builders," published in 1933. MacLeish denounced the "Makers Making America," who "fattened their bonds at her breasts till the thin blood ran from them," by using the literary technique of juxtaposing vignettes of capitalist exploitation with images of the purity and abundance that Lewis and Clark had seen. That original vision remains potent to Americans, who in the earliest moments of their consciousness as a people were imprinted, as it were, by newness and pristine nature.

Subsequent nineteenth-century travelers such as the naturalist Thomas Nuttall and the writers Washington Irving and Francis Parkman recorded some of the same awed perception of the wild that had vivified Lewis's journals, but inevitably, with the passage of time, a certain fading of the blossom becomes apparent. By the era of Mark Twain, as early as 1872 and *Roughing It*, it had even become possible to satirize romantic expectations of wilderness and savagery and to cast oneself, as author-persona, in the role of an easterner constantly being disillusioned by the true ordinariness of the West. Nevertheless, there had been genuine beauty and immense, intact wilderness in the Old West, and these realities had fitted remarkably well with the romantic temper of the early nineteenth century. The West was born, literarily, as romantic territory.

Nuttall, one of the most comprehensive of scientists in the "virtuoso" period of American natural history, made three trips into the West, in 1811, 1819, and 1834, but only his *Journal of Travels into the Arkansa Territory, during the Year 1819* (1821) survives. On this adventure, the British-born student recorded his delight in the flowers of the open prairie—a landscape he described as a "magnificent garden"—made satiric comments on many of the settlers he encountered at the fringes of civilization, and dramatized himself as a rapt, dedicated lover of nature. These ingredients signal a consciously put-together literary effort—rather a well-finished one in comparison with Meriwether Lewis's. The innocent note of discovery, the sense of an Adam-like figure walking out into a pristine and beautiful world, comes through strongly in Nuttall's descriptions.

Washington Irving, recently returned from Europe, traveled for some weeks in 1832 in what is now Oklahoma and thought the "glancing rays of the sun," shining through the leaves of a grove of ancient trees along the Arkansas River, were like "the effect of sunshine among the stained windows and clustering columns of a Gothic cathedral." He went on, "Indeed there is a grandeur and solemnity in our spacious forests of the West, that awaken in me the same feeling I have experienced in those vast and venerable piles, and the sound of the wind sweeping through them, supplies occasionally the deep breathings of the organ." In passages like this, not only in the record of his own tour but also in his subsequent western histories *Astoria* (1836) and *The Adventures of Captain Bonneville, U.S.A.* (1837), Irving helped solidify the romantic image of the West. When he described the mountain men as leading a "wild, Robin Hood kind of

Mocking the naïve dreams of Americans who sought quick and easy wealth in the West, Mark Twain challenged the region's romantic image in his travel classic Roughing It *(1872).*

Roswell Morse Shurtleff (1838–1915). The Miner's Dream. *Engraving, 1872. Illustration from Mark Twain,* Roughing It *(Hartford, Conn., 1872).*

life," or a group of Osage Indians as having "fine Roman countenances" and looking in general "like so many noble bronze figures," he was, somewhat ironically, helping to codify the untamed West under the rubric of a received aesthetic convention.

Francis Parkman too was an inheritor of an eastern, hence ultimately European, sensibility. One of his main reasons for traveling westward in 1846 was to see primitive Indians, and this tourist's motive fitted well with his predominantly visual or painter's-eye aesthetic. Some Kanzas Indians, encountered in western Missouri, "made a very striking and picturesque feature in the forested landscape," as Parkman wrote in *The Oregon Trail* (1849), and a little farther west, in Kansas, "the alternation of rich green prairies and groves that stood in clusters, or lined the banks of the numerous little streams, had all the softened and polished beauty of a region that has been for centuries under the hand of man." Similarly conventional vignettes dominate the account throughout, with Parkman's predilection for describing his subject in terms of the visual aesthetic reaching a strange kind of apotheosis in a buffalo-shooting incident near the end of the tour. Coming upon a large group of bison bulls lolling on a dusty patch of ground, he watched them for some time. He described their scruffy appearance and their seemingly pointless rolling in the deep dust at length and then suddenly concluded his account. "'You are too ugly to live,' thought I; and aiming at the ugliest, I shot three of them in succession. The rest were not at all discomposed at this; they kept on bellowing, butting, and rolling on the ground as before." Despite the distance from his subject demonstrated in this passage and perhaps as well in his overall tendency to framed views, Parkman as a historian was aware of the passing of the wild West and appeared to feel the loss personally. "Great changes are at hand in that region," he wrote. "Within a few years the traveller may pass in tolerable security through [the Indians'] country. Its danger and its charm will have disappeared altogether." In prefaces to later editions of *The Oregon Trail* in 1872 and 1892, in tones unmistakably tragic, Parkman treated the West as only a memory, a "withered" and "subdued" region.

It is easy to criticize the hyperbole inherent in the picturesque art of an Irving or a Parkman, but it is also undeniable that the West, at one time, truly was ecologically intact—that is, to European and eastern-seaboard eyes, it was wild. The journals of Warren Ferris and Osborne Russell, two mountain men of the 1820s and 1830s, describe enough solitude, rugged scenery, clear air, and high adventure to justify as romantic an attitude as might be wished. Ferris's rendering of Cache Valley, Utah, written in July 1830 and found in *Life in the Rocky Mountains* (1842), is apropos: "In this country, the nights are cold at any season, and the climate perhaps more healthy than that of any other part of the globe. The atmosphere is delightful, and so pure and clear, that a person of good sight has been known to distinguish an Indian from a white man, at a distance of more than a mile, and herds of buffalo may be recognized by the aid of a good glass, at even fifteen to eighteen miles."

Likewise, Osborne Russell, who kept a diary for nine years of Rocky Mountain adventure, recorded pristine vistas and, on many occasions, a paradise-like abundance of wildlife. His *Journal of a Trapper* (1914) also evinces his own appreciation for wilderness—he often climbed mountains just to see specific, beautiful views. He wrote of the Lamar River valley of Yellowstone, "I almost wished I could spend the remainder of my days in a place like this." The records of Ferris and Russell, along with those of other mountain-man diarists such as James Clyman and Jedediah Smith, amply attest to the West's base of authentic wildness.

But the glory did not last long. Signally, Parkman's first retrospective preface was published in 1872, the same year as *Roughing It*, Mark Twain's classic. Twain showed himself confronting real Goshute Indians (as opposed to Cooperian noble savages, perhaps), being duped into buying a "Mexican plug," and naïvely, ill-preparedly, rushing off to the latest mining strike, among other instructive episodes. *Roughing It* was an early sign that the romantic western mythos would not, henceforth, reign unchallenged.

The Romance of the Frontier

Over the last five decades of the nineteenth century, the overpowering realities of American industrial and population expansion removed most of the West's wildness. But so potent had been the original impression, and so needful of the myths of open land, freedom, individuality, and progress were the denizens of the new, urban-industrial America, that a resolutely frontier-minded body of popular literature began to flourish as early as 1860 and continued to hold sway in the mass imagination for many decades, in spite of—or perhaps because of—the actualities of history.

With the appearance of mass-market "dime novels" in the 1860s, the popular Western began to develop as a distinctive genre. These early paperbacks sold amazingly well almost from the start—one scholar has noted that after just four years in the publishing business, the House of Beadle and Adams had five million of its little books in circulation. Very soon, the dime-novel Western showed certain consistent, indeed programmatic, elements: a hero who represented a synthesis of civilization and wildness; an affirmative finding with regard to progress; an emphasis on action; and a setting of epical import—usually vast, wild, open spaces. Emphasis was laid on the utter self-reliance and individuality of the hero, whose natural nobility led him to do the right thing unerringly. By his actions in the plot, the typical hero supported civilization, dramatizing a faith in progress (this despite any and all contemporary evidence of corruption, uncertainty of economic opportunity, unfairness in distribution of wealth, or environmental degradation), thus lending overall unreality to the developing formula. As the scholar Daryl Jones has noted, "The dime novel operated at the level of fantasy, where conflicts irresolvable in the real world could find swift and clear-cut solutions." When the writer Edward Judson, known as "Ned Buntline," discovered William F. Cody in Nebraska in 1869 and later that year glamorized him as "Buffalo Bill, the King of the Border Men," a story published serially in the *New York Weekly*, the western dime novel had found its most theatrical and perhaps most influential icon. Prentiss Ingraham, Buffalo Bill's press agent, followed Buntline with no less than 121 "Buffalo Bill" novels, nine of them written in 1892 alone. The flood of titles, in synergy with the enormous popularity of Buffalo Bill's own "Wild West Show," helped to solidify the West as a pageant-like realm of adventure in the popular understanding and the Western itself as a formulaic or "automatized" text serving as a key to that never-never land. The characterization of the hero as a knight on horseback, the reliable, moralistic resolution of plot, the extraordinary emphasis on action, and the repetitive and sentimental description of landscape all combined by the end of the nineteenth century to create a dominant literary identity for the West. The rather astonishing proliferation of titles, all representing variations on a few central themes, helped to identify the Western as subliterary, with the result that modern criticism's interest in the genre has been mainly sociological or psycho-historical.

The cowboy, who had arrived on the dime-novel scene in the 1870s, achieved finished and potent description in Owen Wister's 1902 book *The Virginian*. This novel, which went through sixteen printings in its first year and remains in print today, drew all the elements of the mythic West together into an artistic whole, which in turn became definitive for the Westerns of the new century. Its author had had a profoundly rejuvenative experience in Wyoming in 1885, after suffering from nervous exhaustion in his home city of Philadelphia. He had seen beautiful country, had renewed himself through physical exercise, and had been awed by the casual, rugged cowboys on the ranch where he stayed. Over the following several summers, on western excursions, Wister apparently developed a moral geography in which the East represented a certain

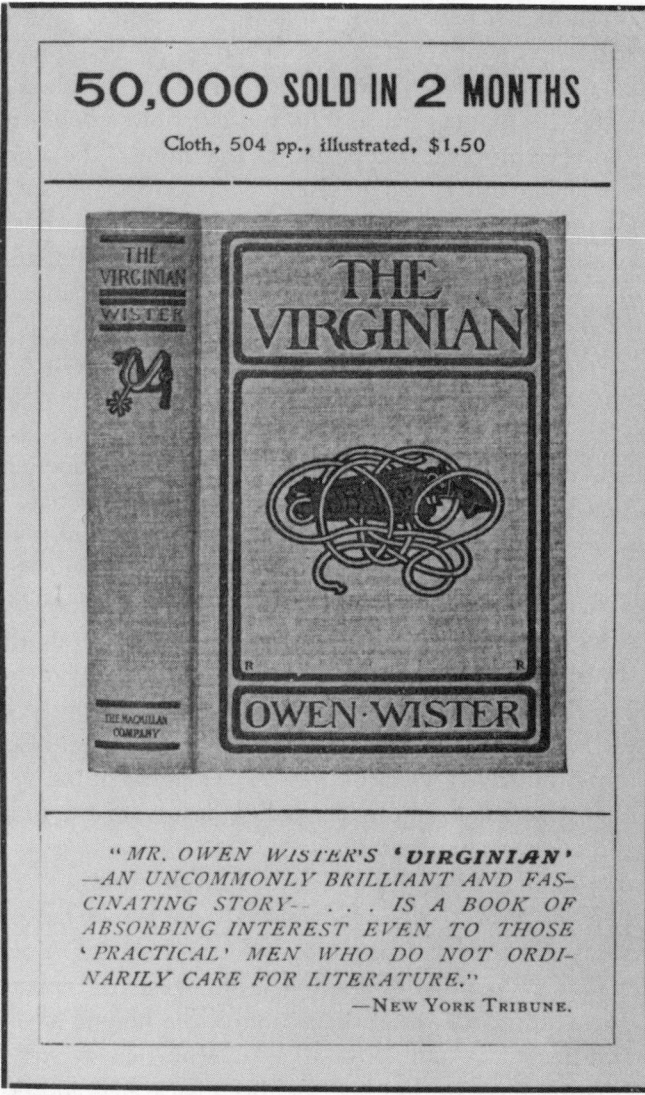

50,000 SOLD IN 2 MONTHS

Cloth, 504 pp., illustrated, $1.50

THE VIRGINIAN

WISTER

THE VIRGINIAN

THE MACMILLAN COMPANY

R · R

OWEN · WISTER

"*MR. OWEN WISTER'S 'VIRGINIAN'—AN UNCOMMONLY BRILLIANT AND FASCINATING STORY-- . . . IS A BOOK OF ABSORBING INTEREST EVEN TO THOSE 'PRACTICAL' MEN WHO DO NOT ORDINARILY CARE FOR LITERATURE.*"
—New York Tribune.

An enormous success, appealing to both easterners and westerners, Owen Wister's The Virginian *sold 50,000 copies in just two months. Dedicated to Theodore Roosevelt, the book helped define the character of the romantic, manly cowboy hero who would come to dominate 20th-century Westerns.*

Publisher's Advertising Brochure for *The Virginian* (New York: Macmillan Publishing Company, 1902). Owen Wister Papers, Manuscript Division, Library of Congress, Washington, D.C.

effete and propriety-regarding mentality—and also intellectual refinement—whereas the West embodied health and decisive individualism. He himself seemed to yearn toward the perceived freedom of the West but at the same time enjoyed his eastern position as a member of the elite professional class, a lawyer who had been graduated from Harvard and who numbered among his many influential friends no less a personage than Theodore Roosevelt. This personal duality can be said to mirror the elements of the historical American dialectic of wilderness and civilization, and when Wister found an artistically satisfactory synthesis of it in the character of the Virginian, his formulation proved immediately and durably agreeable to the American public.

The Virginian, whose mythic status is well symbolized by his having no given name in the novel, is nominally a cowboy but is seldom pictured doing cowboy work. The main emphasis of the book is on his sheer attractiveness as "a horseman of the plains" (the novel's subtitle) and on the testing of his already-beautiful character. He is depicted from the narrator's eastern-tourist perspective—that is, from a suitably hero-making "camera angle"—in the book's opening paragraph: "Then for the first time I noticed a man who sat on the high gate of the corral, looking on. For he now climbed down with the undulations of a tiger, smooth and easy, as if his muscles flowed beneath his skin." The Virginian, for it is he, then proceeds to rope a horse that none of the other cowboys have been able to capture. "The others had all visibly whirled the rope, some of them even shoulder high. I did not see his arm lift or move. He appeared to hold the rope down low, by his leg. But like a sudden snake I saw the noose go out its length and fall true; and the thing was done." The narrator continues to regard the Virginian with wonder and awe and quite early in the novel records his impression that the hero is something more than an uncouth worker: "Here in flesh and blood was a truth which I had long believed in words, but never met before. The creature we call a *gentleman* lies deep in the hearts of thousands that are born without chance to master the outward graces of the type." This intimation of East-West synthesis is borne out in the subsequent plot, as the Virginian courts and wins a young, cultured schoolteacher who has come to Wyoming from Vermont; during the courtship he demonstrates a remarkable ability to read and understand European literature, always bringing to his criticism his innate and practical good sense. Tests of his character come when he has to deal with his former best friend's descent into cattle rustling and with the villainous opposition of yet another rustler, Trampas. The Virginian resolves both of these problems with acts of violence that are presented as absolutely righteous and indeed as marks of the hero's integrity. In the end, he marries the schoolteacher and is last seen as a holder of important coal-bearing lands, a man "with a strong grip on many various enterprises." The hero of the West is seen, in the end, to be a hero of America, bringing his vitality, beauty, and natural morality to bear in the universal movement of progress.

The western romance has had scores if not hundreds of practitioners after Wister, but in general these popular writers' attitudes toward their heroes have resembled Wister's with conspicuous consistency. Zane Grey, whose *Riders of the Purple Sage* (1912) rivals *The Virginian* for popularity among classic Westerns, apparently held social-Darwinist ideas that fitted well with a depiction of the hero as strong, manly, capable of violence when necessary, and above all successful. Like Wister, Grey had grown up in well-off circumstances in the East, had been frustrated and bored in his career there, and had been made an enthusiast of the West by a restorative trip, his to the Grand Canyon in 1907. In his fiction set in the West, the region itself—specifically, spacious and dramatic wilderness country—played a redemptive role. Gary Topping, one of Grey's most astute critics, wrote, "The basic Zane Grey plot is a drama in which a jaded, disillusioned, and perhaps physically frail or ill member of eastern society comes west to find a complete reorientation of values." In *Riders of the Purple Sage*, the person whom the wilderness makes new and strong is Bern Venters, who had journeyed originally from Ohio to southern Utah but had not yet developed independence. When he leaves his protectress's comfortable ranch and, by necessity, spends several weeks being tested by the rugged wilderness of the canyon country, he toughens. He "had gone away a boy—he had returned a man." Throughout *Riders*, Grey pays intense attention to the landscape, charging it with immense emotional and spiritual power. The wilderness is a kind of hovering presence behind all the novel's action. Whatever may be occurring, Grey does not fail to describe the lay of the land, the specific slant and color of the sunlight, and the look of the trees or sagebrush in the area. The descriptions in the aggregate build not a setting but a wild force, a wilderness that somehow encourages the finest qualities in heroic people. *Riders* presents a cowboy-gunman hero of unerring skills, a narrative larded with many chase scenes, and a casually dichotomous moral code by which violence is readily justified—all of these familiar elements of the western romance—but perhaps its most striking characteristic is its hymn to the land. In this, his second Western, Zane Grey struck one of the major western chords, one that also reverberates far back into American intellectual and literary history.

The western themes developed in the dime novels and then brought to fuller expression and more artistic shape by Wister and Grey continued with little fundamental change in both novels and short fiction well into the late twentieth century. Street and Smith's pulp magazine *Western Story* was perhaps the principal descendant of the dime novels when they died out in the 1920s, and in the words of a leading historian of the Western, Richard Etulain, *Western Story* "did much to stylize the new popular genre." Its editors "demanded stories with predictable plots and stereotyped characters." Other "pulp" magazines devoted to the genre arose and flourished; the popular "slicks" such as the *Saturday Evening Post* and *Collier's* also featured western fiction; and writers like Zane Grey and Max Brand continued to produce western novels in abundance. As the decades passed and the public's interest in Westerns did not abate, modifications to the Western were made by Ernest Haycox, some of whose heroes actually learned and developed (rather than simply appearing and remaining as perfected creatures), and by such writers as Eugene Manlove Rhodes and Luke Short, who along with Haycox introduced greater realism of historical and social detail into their western stories. In the post–World War II era, the most popular of western writers to highlight factual detail has, unquestionably, been Louis L'Amour. L'Amour was a self-taught scholar of western history who, in more than eighty novels beginning with *Westward the Tide* in 1950, inserted numberless mini-lectures on fine points of western events, lore, and equipment and who also, in the latter part of his career, transcended the antiquarian emphasis to concentrate on a broad-gauge sense of historical movements. His ecological valuation of nature, seen first in *Hondo* (1953), together with his sensitivity to Native Americans and Hispanic Americans, marks L'Amour as a maker of modern Westerns.

If the Western indeed sanctifies the outcome of American history by a ritual drama in which "civilization and savagery" are fruitfully blended (in the person of the hero and the issue of the plot) and in which violence is vindicated, one could hardly ask for a better epitome than the immensely popular *Shane* (1949), by Jack Schaefer. *Shane* begins, "He rode into our valley in the summer of '89"—a typically well-cut sentence that raises the hero to mythic, pronominal status, sets him in western, epic space (where else can a lone rider be seen "several miles away," as is revealed two sentences later?), and identifies the significant time of the action to come—the last year before the closing of the frontier. The mysterious horseman rides on into the valley, pauses at a fork in the road, then chooses the way that leads toward a row of homesteaders' new places rather than the road to a cattle baron's "big spread." He casts his lot with Joe Starrett, one of the farmers, and joins in the humble work of establishing a farm in a new land. He puts away his gun and his serge trousers, linen shirt, and silk neckerchief and appears to be starting a new life.

But there is trouble in the valley. Fletcher the cattleman, unwilling to lose what he regards as his own free range, has his cowboys harass the homesteaders. Eventually, when Fletcher goes so far as to hire a gunman, Shane faces a stirring moral choice. The valley is far from the machinery of established law and order (we are still in the frontier era, though just barely so), and a man in Shane's position—a man with the skills and tools of violence now desperately needed by the community—can count on no one and nothing but his own resources. Following his inward, natural goodness, he chooses to support the settlers and rides into confrontation with Fletcher and his hired gun. In a stylized scene that seems engineered to highlight Shane's essential morality, he kills those who would drive off the farmers and then rides, wounded, into exile, never to be seen again. He has made the valley safe for progress.

Shane presents the ritual western movement, and the mythically important role of the hero, in perhaps the clearest, most elegant version yet. Schaefer's choice of young Bob Starrett as narrator, "a kid then, barely topping the backboard of father's old chuck-wagon," makes the worshipful description of Shane only appropriate and allows a convincing, homey view of the pioneer family. The narrative as a whole unrolls with the simplicity and inevitability of myth. Despite its being such a definitive statement, however, *Shane* was by no means the final Western. By 1980, after three decades of output, Louis L'Amour's books alone had sold one hundred million copies. Furthermore, contemporary mutations to the form, including not only a minority version of the genre but also parodies, inversions of the standard plot, and even X-rated scenes, have since the time of *Shane* given a new vitality to the "horse opera." In many ways, the Western in the late twentieth century has become *un*predictable, but it is still doggedly alive. A century after the much-cited closing of the frontier, only a brave critic indeed would predict the demise of the Western anytime soon.

Closer Views of the Western Landscape

The frontier mind leans naturally toward romance and favors conventions that are, fundamentally, simplifications of experience. At the "frontier" level of literature, ecologically complex settings are enjoyed, to be sure, but are not investigated closely and are rendered predominantly as scenery; complex moral and psychological situations become straightforward dualities that can be resolved neatly, by characters who in turn are seen as unitary and functional to the all-important movement of the plot, rather than as humanly many-sided. The transition to a postfrontier outlook—and with it to a more mature and subtle literature—involves an opening of perception as a whole, so that a relation-seeing and complex view of existence replaces a simplistic or romantically abstract attention.

Slowing down and then looking closely at one's surroundings (as opposed to being on the move, with eyes on the horizon) are crucial stages in the transition. Simply to observe a place closely is to express the opposite of the tenor of "manifest destiny." In the West, the first writer to make a close study of the land and with that study develop a postfrontier philosophy was John Muir. This well-known figure, famous for environmental effectiveness, offers in his own intellectual history something like a textbook example of the opening and flowering of the relational-complex (that is, ecological) mode of consciousness. Born in Scotland in 1838 and brought to Wisconsin in 1849,

Muir as a youth experienced many of the stern and perhaps mind-narrowing realities of American pioneering. His father ruled the Muir household with rigid, Calvinistic ideas, and the whole family participated in the hard labor of converting wilderness into farmland. Muir grew up within the frontier-minded, American mainstream. But at the University of Wisconsin he encountered two liberating streams of thought—transcendentalism and science—and within a few more years, after working and botanizing in Canada, the Midwest, and the southeastern United States, he was recording in his journal a break with his father's creed. By the time of his first summer in the Sierra Nevada in 1869, Muir's journal shows that he had become a wilderness transcendentalist who took immense delight in nature and who believed that all the creation, including the grasses, rocks, and snowflakes, was a spiritually alive manifestation of a loving, universal God. That "baptismal" summer, to use Muir's term, was the foundation of his life as a postfrontier thinker. But it was in the succeeding years, the early 1870s, that Muir really *studied* the Sierra and melded scientifically precise knowledge with his own experience of an enlarged view, finally to synthesize a totalistic vision of human life and nature.

The impetus for his closer look was a desire to disprove the standard interpretation of the formation of Yosemite Valley. The theory was that in a massive and rather sudden subsidence, in "the wreck of matter and the crush of the worlds," as the California state geologist put it, the valley floor had sunk thousands of feet. Muir responded to this theory with two elements from his own background: first, his limited knowledge of the glaciation hypothesis, gained at the University of Wisconsin, and second, his deeply felt experience of the harmony of the natural world. The slow and stately flow of glaciers, as an agent of mountain sculpture, appealed much more to Muir's sense of things than did geologic cataclysm. But to prove his intuition, he had to go into the Sierra and find evidence—"learn the alphabet" of the range, as he put it. Now began the long, ascetic, solo expeditions into the mountains for which Muir became famous; and now too, many of his journal entries deepened past immediate ecstasy, becoming complex meditations on the nature of evolution, the paradoxical relationship between individual entities and the wholeness of nature, and the progress of the mind itself to ecological awareness. He became a philosopher of the wild. His ruling metaphor, drawn quite naturally from his observations of glaciers, was *flow*. This is a concept that gives precedence not to static entities but to process; it led Muir to an emphasis on cycles and ultimately to a holistic view of nature.

> There are no harsh, hard dividing lines in nature. Glaciers blend with the snow and the snow blends with the thin invisible breath of the sky.
>
> When I look on a glacier, I see the immeasurable sunbeams pouring faithfully on the outspread oceans, and the streaming, uprising vapors entering cool mountain basins and taking their places in the divinely beautiful six-rayed daisies of snow that go sifting, glinting to their appointed places on the sky-piercing mountains, joining ray to ray, forming glaciers amid the boom and thunder of avalanches, and at last flowing serenely back to the sea.

His study of the California mountains also impelled Muir to be a writer. His findings on the glacial history of the Sierra (which have been supported by modern research) were

Combining two distinct approaches to the western landscape, John Muir drew like a scientist but wrote like a poet. His sketches of the Sierra Nevada documented the effects of glaciation, but his texts stressed the transcendental beauty of his subject. He wrote that Starr King, the rounded mountain shown here at the top right, "was one of the first to emerge from the glacial sea, and ere its newborn brightness was marred by storms, dispersed light like a crystal island over the snowy expanse in which it stood alone."

John Muir (1838–1914). Starr King Group of Domes, Sierras. Pen and ink sketches, 1874. From William Colby, John Muir's Studies in the Sierra (1960).

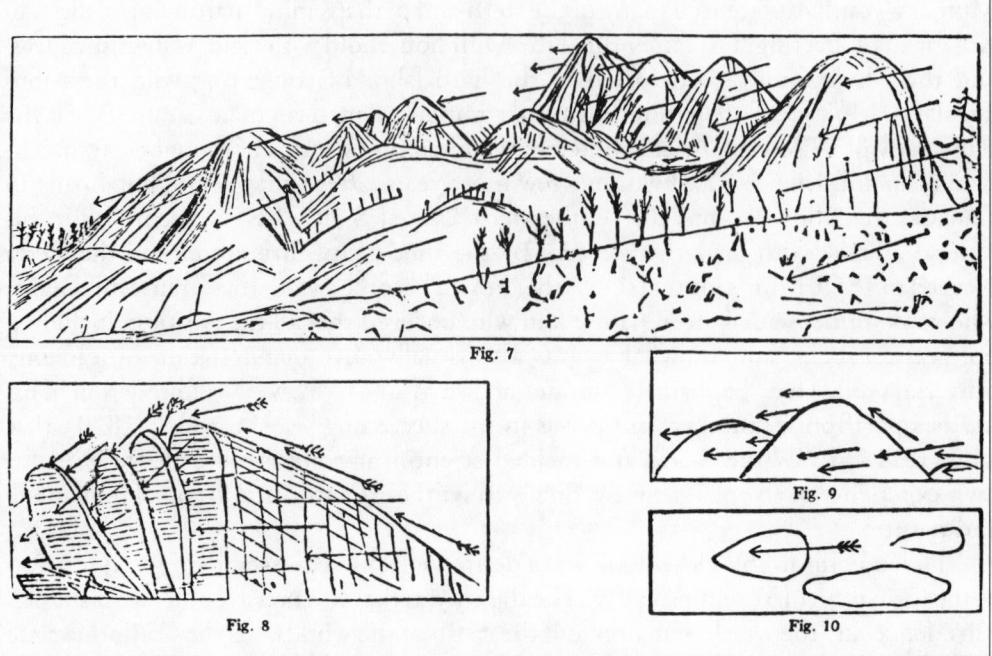

Fig. 7

Fig. 8

Fig. 9

Fig. 10

published in seven articles in the *Overland Monthly* in 1874–75 and helped to establish him as an authority on natural history. Over the following decades until his death in 1914, Muir elaborated on his studies and experiences of nature in a series of influential magazine articles and books, including *The Mountains of California* (1894), *Our National Parks* (1901), and *The Yosemite* (1912). By narrating his own revelatory experiences in the wild, exhorting his readers to recapture a similar range of experience, and thundering against short-sighted exploiters of nature, Muir helped to legitimatize a nonconsumptive, conservation-minded, postfrontier view of the West. His articles on Yosemite had almost immediate practical issue in the legislation establishing Yosemite National Park in 1890. Among other contributions to the "conservation" dimension of the Progressive Era, he influenced Theodore Roosevelt on forest and park policy and stood as a godfather to such important legislation as the Lacey Antiquities Act of 1906 and the enabling act for the National Park Service in 1916.

John Charles Van Dyke had nothing like Muir's impact on American history, but his minutely detailed aesthetic examinations of western landscapes, together with his forthright questioning of certain frontier-era assumptions, mark him as a writer of the mature phase in western literature. A librarian and art historian associated with Rutgers College in New Jersey, and already the author of influential texts on art appreciation, Van Dyke embarked on a remarkable California desert expedition in 1898, knowing little of the terrain he was about to enter and accompanied only by a horse and a small dog. Despite both chronic and acute health problems, he survived the several-month trek and in succeeding years made similar, impressive journeys in other western deserts and wild places. His precise itinerary, however, is always difficult to ascertain, because Van Dyke, of all wilderness travelers, tells the least about himself and his trips. In books like *The Desert* (1901), *The Mountain* (1916), and *The Grand Canyon of the Colorado*

(1920), he concentrates totally on the scene before him, on its line, form, color, and changing image as the sun proceeds through its great arc overhead. As the scholar Peter Wild has pointed out, there are no route descriptions, no extensively described ordeals, and rather surprisingly no other people mentioned in *The Desert*; one might add that there is vanishingly little of the author himself. What this traveler was seeking, apparently, was pure perception, for that is what his books deliver. "He saw his task as one of refining personal experience into an almost disembodied esthetic," Wild has written, and this aim has instructive, postfrontier literary dimensions. Van Dyke wanted nothing tangible from the desert—or the mountains, or the Grand Canyon later. These places were not "resources" to him. A second sign of his having transcended the frontier mentality is that in so casually effacing the intrepid-trekker aspect, Van Dyke demonstrated primary regard for the land itself. Muir apparently went through a similar annulment of the heroic self in his first summer in the Sierra, writing in his journal, "These blessed mountains are so compactly filled with God's beauty, no petty personal hope or experience has room to be." Past a certain crucial, inward divide, the focus turns outward, and both Muir and Van Dyke dramatize the liberation of energy inherent in this particular transcendence and the very close and precise seeing that seems to be concomitant. "In a few weeks we are studying bushes, bowlders, stones, sand-drifts," Van Dyke writes in *The Desert*, "—things we never thought of looking at in any other country." Years later, in *The Grand Canyon of the Colorado*, he restated the needed emancipation: "And we, if we would understand the Canyon, must largely eliminate the human element of it. It is insignificant."

The Desert was the first extended literary appreciation of the American arid lands. It described the desert as "the simplest in form and the finest in color" and "by all odds the most beautiful" of landscapes and addressed its finely detailed, indeed exhaustive, descriptions to a higher and finer sensibility than one that would simply *use* deserts. "The deserts should never be reclaimed. They are the breathing-spaces of the west and should be preserved forever," Van Dyke wrote, making here an attempt at the practical by promoting the benefits of dry and warm air. In the main, however, his moral point of view on the land appears to be founded in the experience of pure seeing. The unrivaled depth and precision of detail in Van Dyke's descriptions, and the seemingly tireless recall of fine points of light and shading—literary characteristics that might signal excess to the modern reader—may in truth be this writer's most revealing signposts to himself and where he had been. Without being overtly self-concerned, he was dramatizing what a freed mind might see.

Mary Austin's work, like that of Muir and Van Dyke, demonstrates the instructiveness of nature and landscape studies in any tracing of the transition to postfrontier western literature. She made the same fundamental move in consciousness whereby nature becomes the primary fact. "Not the law, but the land sets the limit" was the third sentence in her first book, and she reinforced this prescription later in that text with such ecologically minded declarations as "The manner of the country makes the usage of the life there, and the land will not be lived in except in its own fashion." Indeed, the whole of *The Land of Little Rain* (1903) is, as the title suggests, knit tightly around the accepted and basic reality of dryness. As an organizing principle for a book about southeastern California, aridity may seem obvious enough, but Austin's particular genius was to see, and record in process, the innumerable tiny adjustments of plants and animals that, taken together, make up arid biological communities. Her mind was alive to the relational aspect of existence, to detail, and to the patterns that connect. Thus her first book was an ecological text as much in its way of seeing as in its presentation of scientific fact.

Austin's responsiveness to the living and communal quality of nature may have had its origin in a powerful childhood experience. As a six-year-old in Illinois, she experienced a level of perception and consciousness that quite transcended the ordinary mind, and this, she wrote, became "the one abiding reality" of her life.

> It was a summer morning, and the child I was had walked down through the orchard and come out on the brow of a sloping hill where there were grass and a wind blowing and one tall tree reaching into infinite immensities of blueness. Quite suddenly after a moment of quietness there, earth and sky and windblown grass and the child in the midst of them came alive together with a pulsing light of consciousness. There was a wild foxglove at the child's feet and a bee dozing about it, and to this day [1931] I can recall the swift inclusive awareness of each for the whole.

Austin considered the level of being thus revealed to be her true or inner self, "I-Mary," whereas the social or historical identity—less intense, more guarded and conventional—she called "Mary-by-herself." It seems clear that over the years, her ability to recall the peculiar vividness of I-Mary's perception resulted in both the ecological sensitivity and emotional power of her best writing. Her challenge as an author was to create realistic and accessible literary vehicles for her transcendent sense, and she served a long and apparently difficult novitiate to this vocation. Newly married in 1891, and having moved to California only three years previously, Austin was taken by her husband to the remote Owens Valley, east of the Sierra Nevada. Here, while Stafford Austin examined the possibilities of water development, Mary Austin tried to "learn the secret of the mesa life" by taking the exact opposite of the frontiersman's path. She wrote down precise notes on what was around her: creosote bushes, dry lakes, deep echoing canyons, flocks of quail at a water hole. She apprenticed herself to the local Indians and claimed later that she "learned how to write" only after learning how the Indians managed to express a balance between their individual existences and the oneness of nature. The Indians, in their art and in the perceived maturity of their personalities, were a model to the young writer, showing her that a fruitful cooperation might be made between I-Mary and Mary-by-herself. Thus, where John Muir had taken small notice of Native Americans, and John Van Dyke perhaps even less, Mary Austin raised them to the level of tutelary spirits. "Psychologically the state called primitive," she wrote in 1923, "is one of deeply imbricated complexity."

After the publication of her first book, Austin was able to move out into the broader literary world, first to the writers' and artists' colony at Carmel, later to New York, and then to a good deal of travel in Europe. She left the West behind, but apparently, after several years of success among the literati, living in urban situations, she began to long for the missing dimension. "But this life of literary antics which I am leading isn't my real life, and this shell of hardness is only a shell—so far," she once wrote to a friend in

Arizona. In 1923, she made a long motor tour of New Mexico and Arizona, a journey that became (as perhaps she had planned) a return to sources. Once again, she noted the look of piñon-juniper woodland, the dry, exhilarating air, and the long, inspiring vistas of the sort of terrain in which she had learned her craft. In the book that came out of this trip, she spoke conclusively, as if final truths had come to her. She called *The Land of Journeys' Ending* (1924) "a book of prophecy;" its final prediction, among many somewhat oracular statements, is that the western environment itself, operating "subtly below all other types of adjustive experience," is working to create a new, land-harmonious culture. This will be "the *next* great and fructifying world culture." Rarely has the West been celebrated so decisively, but for Austin, a fructifying culture would not be based on exploiting resources or heightening the standard of living. She believed quite the opposite: that adjustment to ecological reality, and attention to the momentous potential in any experience of nature, constituted the true human hope.

Mature-phase Fiction of the West

Generally speaking, the maturation of western fiction is marked by increasing subtlety and complexity of characterization and a diminishment in the weight of plot and ideology. In short, to use the terms of Nathaniel Hawthorne and the critic Richard Chase, the romance gives way to the novel. In the modern western novel, ideas are presented, to be sure, but in less obvious fashion than in a romance. Ideas and themes emerge as the result of the interactions of more or less realistic characters, and thus the ideas have more sides to them, more dimension, and more loose ends. Where issues of justice, retribution, and violence, for example, are handled swiftly and rightfully through the simple goodness of a romance hero like the Virginian, in a mature-phase novel such as Walter Van Tilburg Clark's *The Ox-Bow Incident* (1940), these issues become intensely problematic. Human frailties, the arrogance of power, and the weight of peer pressure all help drive the action. In this novel, a terrible wrong is done, and there are no heroes of the old style. But it is not the lack of a happy ending that makes this book a novel; it is the writer's close attention to humanity.

In addition, postfrontier western fiction writers tend toward an analytic and critical view of American expansion into the West. They do not stand unconsciously inside the history of progress but ask what were, and are, the costs of its march. The West in modern hands, beginning approximately with Hamlin Garland's *Main-Travelled Roads* (1891), is for example not a promised land for upwardly mobile yeomen—the ungiving realities of capitalism need to be reckoned with. These realities, as in Garland's story "Under the Lion's Paw," can and do break good people down. Native Americans, for another example of the greater historical realism of postfrontier fiction, tend not to play stereotyped roles and are not simpleminded; cowboys are working men rather than knights; and the western landscape, though still very much able to arouse a transcendental response, tends to be treated in a less impressionistic and sentimental fashion. All of these improvements in realism are incorporated, in fiction, in the vehicle and test of characterization.

Some of the first moves away from the romantic image of the West were made in the decade immediately following the Civil War, when the growing city of San Francisco became established as a literary center. San Francisco's prominence came about largely through the writings of Bret Harte, Mark Twain, and others of a literary circle that would give birth to the "local color" movement in American fiction. Local color, in turn, became an important precursor to the development of realism as the dominant literary mode later in the century. In the middle 1860s, both Harte and Twain wrote numerous satirical pieces for San Francisco newspapers, emphasizing local peculiarities with great glee. Harte later published a number of rather sentimental, parable-like short stories of California life such as "The Luck of Roaring Camp" and "Tennessee's Partner," but he also edited the important San Francisco literary magazine *Overland Monthly* in its formative years from 1868 through 1871. *Overland* set its sights high, aiming to be the West's *Atlantic*, and published a number of quality essays and astute book reviews over the years, an accomplishment that moved California local color writing from sophomoric satire to more serious and interpretive levels. Twain, for his part, owed much to the sharp eye and ear he developed in his California (and Nevada) days as a journalist; his debunking style of realism and occasional taste for the grotesque, which in his later career were brought to bear on large philosophical issues, may be seen in embryonic form in the early story "The Celebrated Jumping Frog of Calaveras County," a reworking of a California tale he published in 1865.

Though not generally regarded as a western writer, Stephen Crane may be credited with an early and important contribution to the modernizing of western materials. "The Bride Comes to Yellow Sky" (1897), perhaps the most frequently anthologized of Crane's several western stories, exhibits a precisely realistic view of the West and draws on the old, romantic images strictly for comic and ironic effects. In the story, a drunken would-be gunfighter, wanting to "shoot up a town," instead is brought to a state of impotent irrelevance by the mere fact that the town marshal has become a married man. The chief figures, gunfighter and marshal, are of course stock characters of romance, but Crane penetrates the stereotypes to reveal two vulnerable human beings caught in historical transition. His awareness of western myths and the conventions of romance *as* myths and conventions allows him ironic insights, but the ironic view is not so pervasive as to hinder him from portraying authentic courage. The success of Crane's western stories may stem, in part, from the author's insight into his own mixed, ambiguous response to the West—attracted to the mythology and subvertingly conscious of the attraction.

Frank Norris and Jack London, with major publications spanning the period from 1899 to 1916, also made early advances in the scope, realism, and psychological depth of western fiction. Both flirted with high-definition romance at times in their careers—and London's success at swashbuckling adventure has had the ironic effect of obscuring his genuine penetration in several novels and stories—but both conceived of themselves as serious writers, and both attempted broad-gauge views of humanity and of important social issues. Norris, whose background was in the urban, upper middle class (Chicago, San Francisco), was the first western writer to use a city—in his case, San Francisco—as the setting in the action of a serious novel, *McTeague* (1899). This in itself was a major breakthrough. In *The Octopus* (1901), his best-known novel, Norris is concerned with what seems to be a morally dichotomous situation, in which honorable ranchers confront the "octopus" of railroad-based capitalism; but he does not portray the capitalist Cedarquist, or the frustrated mystic Vanamee, or the poet Presley, or the self-absorbed rancher Annixter (who is transformed by love) as one-dimensional characters. They are all quite convincing. Norris died tragically young, in the midst of ambitious novelistic plans; but in the work he did complete he helped move western fiction into the new area of urban life, and he demonstrated a sophisticated handling of powerful, sentiment-arousing materials.

Jack London's contribution to western fiction has probably been underrecognized. Books such as *The Call of the Wild* (1903) and *White Fang* (1906), together with his own celebrity as an adventurer, helped give him an image as a pop-litterateur, but in truth what drove London's fiction as much as animal zest and dramatic event was the author's lifelong intellectual curiosity. From his early days of borrowing armloads of books from the Oakland Free Public Library to his declaredly mind-opening reading of C. G. Jung in the last year of his life, London was a passionate student. Growing up poor, a working boy from the age of nine, he treated ideas as keys to a clarified, liberated realm. Thus developed his active interest in socialism, and his enlightened criticism of egoism and social-Darwinist success, seen for example in *The Sea-Wolf* (1904) and *The Iron Heel* (1907); thus his study of scientific farming, which bore fruit literally at his Beauty Ranch in California and literarily in *The Valley of the Moon* (1913); and thus, finally, his excited discovery and almost immediately successful literary use of Jungian psychology, seen for example in the late story "The Water Baby."

London himself exhibited many of the traditional, romantic western qualities, and he certainly gave expression to the romance of the frontier in several of his stories of the North. But he was not afraid to look within himself analytically. His outlook seems to have included elements of both rational skepticism and mystical confidence; in his most interesting fiction, these dimensions balance and inform each other. For example, two of the novels based on his Sonoma County farming experience—*The Valley of the Moon* (1913) and *The Little Lady of the Big House* (1916)—show London's intellectually critical understanding of the pastoral (read western, frontier-minded, romantic-escapist) urge and, just as firmly, his understanding of the danger of too much science, too much rational ordering of life. Saxon and Billy Roberts of *The Valley of the Moon*, who have escaped the urban distress of Oakland, find that they will need scientific knowledge and technique to make their newfound rural Eden a true success; and Dick Forrest, a hugely prosperous scientific farmer in *The Little Lady*, becomes so efficient that with ironic unconsciousness he destroys life and love all around him. Taken together, these novels demonstrate London's capacity for self-study—it should be noted that he himself began his Beauty Ranch in a mood of retreat from the modern, urban scene—and his artistically balanced handling in fiction of one of the strongest, most central of western themes, the escape to paradise.

A similar artistic equilibrium, giving equal voice both to the western-agrarian urge and to a sober recognition of its incompleteness as a philosophy for a whole life, distinguishes Willa Cather's breakthrough novel *O Pioneers!* (1913). In this novel, a strong woman of the second generation of Nebraska pioneers, Alexandra Bergson, sets her face toward success and achieves it, creating a productive farm on high ground that

Willa Cather's trip to Mesa Verde in 1915 inspired her book The Professor's House *(1925). Like many of her contemporaries, she found in the Southwest powerful reminders of America's rich historical legacy. The ruins of Mesa Verde, her hero proclaimed, "belonged to this country, to the state and to all the people."*

Unidentified photographer. Willa Cather at Cliff Palace. *Photograph, 1915. Private collection.*

had seemed to her father's generation only a mysterious, wild land with a mind of its own. In a profoundly transcendental scene early in the novel, as she and her younger brother drive a horse-drawn wagon into the country of her choice, Alexandra opens her heart to the land, wordlessly declaring complete allegiance.

> When the road began to climb the first long swells of the Divide, Alexandra hummed an old Swedish hymn, and Emil wondered why his sister looked so happy. Her face was so radiant that he felt shy about asking her. For the first time, perhaps, since that land emerged from the waters of geologic ages, a human face was set toward it with love and yearning. It seemed beautiful to her, rich and strong and glorious. Her eyes drank in the breadth of it, until her tears blinded her. Then the Genius of the Divide, the great, free spirit which breathes across it, must have bent lower than it ever bent to a human will before. The history of every country begins in the heart of a man or a woman.

Alexandra is depicted as a founder, and the secret of her success is precisely the pure, uncomplicated love she has for the country. In the great pastoral-romantic tradition, she has merged herself with nature. But as the novel develops, it becomes apparent that life in its entirety cannot be solved as neatly as some of the agricultural problems of early settlement. Alexandra raises her younger brother to enjoy advantages she herself never had, including education and travel, and she entertains a simplistic, accommodating regard for him. This is in keeping with her own directness and essential simplicity. "Her mind was slow, truthful, steadfast. She had not the least spark of cleverness." In a crucial chapter Cather described Alexandra's rather poignant repression of her own sexuality—a habit and characteristic that may have been necessary in her hard life as a builder but that keep her from an important recognition about Emil. Emil is in love with the young wife of a neighboring farmer, but Alexandra's chaste mind does not realize this. "That she [the young wife, Marie] was beautiful, impulsive, barely two years older than Emil, these facts had had no weight with Alexandra." In fact, she had innocently "omitted no opportunity of throwing Marie and Emil together." In a climactic scene, the jealous husband kills the lovers, shocking the pastoral community. What is left for the remaining characters is a rueful, tempered existence. The novel's greatness derives in large part from Cather's sympathetic but discerning dramatization of the minds and personalities of her chief characters. She did not write an essay on the limitations of the agrarian way, or the sacrifices involved in pioneering, but set some real-seeming people, products of a time and place, to interacting.

Cather herself took many years to come to terms with the Nebraska landscape of her later childhood and youth, so that with enough distance from it, but still remembering the power of the land, she could describe the place and its people with the complexity and insight of refined art. Born in Virginia in 1873, she had been brought to the prairie at age nine and apparently experienced great difficulty adjusting. After her college years in Lincoln at the University of Nebraska, she moved eastward, mainly working in journalism, and by 1909 had become managing editor of *McClure's*, one of the leading magazines of the time. In general outline, her career to this point shared in the "revolt from the village" of many nineteenth-century intellectuals; but a trip to the Southwest in 1912 appears to have renewed her sensitivity to wild country and to have reawakened her interest in the pioneer generations. Reflecting on the cliff dwellings of ancient Indians seems to have strengthened Cather's concern with the moral dimensions of living in any certain landscape—indeed with the moral and spiritual dimensions of establishing and maintaining civilizations in general. This moral approach to life and culture is the territory of her mature fiction, in large part, and certainly of her most broadly social western works: *O Pioneers!* (1913), *My Antonia* (1918), *The Professor's House* (1925), and *Death Comes for the Archbishop* (1927).

The Professor's House amply represents Cather's cultural and historical vision—in particular, her acute judgments on modern-day materialism—and also her poetic sense of the redemptive, creative contact with nature that may give an individual, and perhaps even a culture, a basis for right living. The house of the title is an older, undistinguished dwelling in which the professor, Godfrey St. Peter, has lived for many years, writing a prize-winning history of the Spanish explorations and conquests in North America and also helping to raise his and his wife's two daughters, now grown and married. In the first and longest of the novel's three sections, we learn that St. Peter does not want to leave the old house, though with his prize money a new one has been built; that his wife and daughters exhibit varying degrees of consumerist superficiality; that he once had a student, Tom Outland, who was killed in World War I and who has come to represent to St. Peter a fine, upright standard and mentality that his present circumstances seem distressingly to lack; and finally, that he himself, pulled between the remembered world of quality and earnestness on the one hand and the contemporary scene of greed, envy, and trivia on the other, is approaching a spiritual crisis.

When Mrs. St. Peter goes to Europe for a summer, the professor settles back into his study in the old house, planning to edit a diary that Outland had kept while exploring ancient cliff dwellings in New Mexico. Here the novel becomes, in the second section, "Tom Outland's Story"—and also becomes one of the most elemental and stirring evocations of place in all of western literature. Tom had been working as a cowboy and had discovered one day "a little city of stone, asleep," high up on Blue Mesa. During the course of his and his partner's amateur archaeology, and after a falling-out between the two, which begins a period of rich, renewing solitude on the mountain for Tom, it becomes apparent that Blue Mesa is a spiritually cogent place. It is, Cather wrote, "a world above the world." When Father Duchene, a country priest, tells Tom and his partner, Roddy, that "there is evidence on every hand that they [the ancient cliff dwellers] lived for something more than food and shelter," Cather's moral-geographical diagram becomes more sharply apparent. Blue Mesa is a benchmark by which the terrible fall into modern materialism can be decisively measured.

But the novel's treatment of this perhaps familiar, transcendental, and western theme is not programmatic. The piñon-scented air that Tom breathes is not abstractly presented, nor is the slanting sunlight at evening, nor the grasshoppers leaping against the door of the cowboys' line cabin. The landscape is felt and seen, never generalized. And as the "dig" progresses, we learn that the cliff city had its own human imperfections: the partners discover a probable murder victim and take to calling her "Mother Eve"—a good hint of Cather's knowing and complex view of humanity. Furthermore, at the modern end of the diagram, St. Peter himself, though profoundly affected by Tom and thus by Blue Mesa, is not above certain self-pleasuring foibles: he keeps an artificial little garden (quite different from the wild, infinity-suggesting Blue Mesa), enjoys dressing and eating well, and seems withal to be happy enough in his social position as an intellectual and a professor.

In the final section of *The Professor's House*, "The Professor," the novel's two worlds come to a climactic encounter within St. Peter. He is depicted, early in "The Professor," as regaining a certain primary, organic relationship with the earth. "He found he could lie on his sand-spit by the lake for hours and watch the seven motionless pines drink up the sun." "He was only interested in earth and woods and water." He has contacted the "Kansas boy," as the novel calls it, analogous to the western dimension of life that Outland and Blue Mesa represent; but he cannot see what this has to do with his present existence—after all, his wife will soon be returning, and there will be the new house to move into once and for all—and he sinks into a seemingly indifferent, stalled state. "He supposed he did his work; he heard no complaints from his assistants, and the students seemed interested." In the latter pages of the novel, thus, the modern relevance of Blue Mesa—that is, the West, the wild—comes into question. In St. Peter's new experience of nature, a great recovery is hinted at. Yet his spiritual recuperation, when it begins only tentatively to occur after a climactic, near-death incident, is rendered in strictly guarded prose. The novel's concluding sentence rises only to, "He thought he knew where he was, and that he could face with fortitude the *Berengaria* [his returning wife's ship] and the future."

Such restraint is perhaps the essence of Cather's modern and realistic outlook. Her style too, in its rigorous spareness, shows a highly conscious approach. Her refusal to sentimentalize or make too much of her wilderness and pioneering subjects, nevertheless granting them an undeniable, generative energy and moral reference, marks her work as mature western fiction. *The Professor's House* may indeed be, as John J. Murphy has written, "the keystone novel of her career." It is also, in both its sophisticated psychology and its carefully sculpted writing, a type-specimen of a regional literature that had come of age.

After Cather, the line of significant western fiction is continued by a remarkably productive—and in one important respect, closely related—group of writers born between 1890 and 1912: Harvey Fergusson (b. 1890); Vardis Fisher (b. 1895); A. B. Guthrie, Jr. (b. 1901); John Steinbeck (b. 1902); Frank Waters (b. 1902); Wallace Stegner (b. 1909); Walter Van Tilburg Clark (b. 1909); and Frederick Manfred (b. 1912). Among them they have covered nearly all of the thematic range of the West. But for all their immense variety when viewed in the aggregate, each has, in his most representative and consequential work, tried to cut through the peculiarly resistant western mythology and seek, in Stegner's words, "a usable continuity between past and present." These writers have attempted an illusionless point of view and a description of a historical West that plausibly connects with the mixed and real present.

To take just one example, Frank Waters presents a most interesting study on the theme of revision and realism. Although he has been at pains in several books to show western history from the Indians' point of view, and thus his work overturns many "majority" images and beliefs, and although he highly regards detail and fact, placing him again in the realists' camp, nevertheless in the larger dimensions of his worldview there are concepts most realists would regard as mystical, and perhaps mythical. He leans strongly toward an "Indian" sense that humans and nature make one nondual system and that the landscape, seen by the Lockeian eyes of Western civilization as so much matter, is in truth spiritually alive. His psychology is firmly Jungian. These elements of Waters's philosophy are brought to bear in his fiction, with the result that it tends to have prominent ideological content. One early critic, in fact, accused Waters of following a "regional imperative" of landscape-mysticism, to the detriment of novelistic quality. Critics of western fiction confront in Waters's work a radical and pointed example of the postfrontier outlook. The reader of a Frank Waters novel is asked to think beyond the dualistic world, beyond the "white man's" inheritance, psychologically. This requires, among other changes, a revised concept of self and personality—less heroic, less firmly defined and bordered—and in turn, perhaps, a different criterion for characterization. *Shane*'s opening words, "He rode into our valley," with their emphatic statement of individual action, are perhaps accepted without thought because they are part of our traditional frame of reference. Waters's attitude toward character is more relational and "ecological": of his character Martiniano in *The Man Who Killed the Deer* (1942), a person undergoing an emergence into a nonwhite philosophy of life, Waters wrote, "So little by little the richness and the wonder and the mystery of life stole in upon him." The entire process of life is seen differently by Waters: its large and beautiful impersonality is doing the acting, not Martiniano.

The strength of Waters's ideas and assumptions—clearly visible in just this one microcosmic example—may tend in some of his work to cast a fable- or parable-like aura. This is probably so in *People of the Valley* (1941) and *The Man Who Killed the Deer*. But he has also written novels distinguished by an exact and concrete particularization. *The Yogi of Cockroach Court* (1948), an unusual story in that it focuses on the process of meditation and the quest for enlightenment, grounds its subject in the gritty details of life among the underclass of a Mexican border town; in the end, Waters brings off a thoroughly realistic synthesis of these two realms. In one of his best novels, *The Woman at Otowi Crossing* (1966), the course of a woman's spiritual illumination is similarly, and even more successfully, set within an experienceable environment. Readers following Helen Chalmers's inward development understand and feel its progress because they are allowed to perceive her outward world in convincing itemization. The sound of the leaves of the cottonwood trees by her little house, the frosty air of a fall morning, the look of a heron standing on a sandbar of the Rio Grande—all come to the reader as intimate perceptions. In this novel, the northern New Mexico setting is more than setting; its details work in concert with a profound inner response, part and parcel of the character's growth toward a whole and enlightened view of the world. Waters's subtle depiction here gives a new dimension to the concept of realism.

It should be noted that several of the first generation of postfrontier interpreters of the West have written long autobiographical novels, suggesting again a commitment to analytic understanding. Manfred's trilogy *The Primitive* (1949), *The Brother* (1950), and *The Giant* (1951), Frank Waters's *The Wild Earth's Nobility* (1935), *Below Grass Roots* (1937), and *The Dust within the Rock* (1940), subsequently reshaped into *Pike's Peak* (1971), and Vardis Fisher's tetralogy *In Tragic Life* (1932), *Passions Spin the Plot* (1934), *We Are Betrayed* (1935), and *No Villain Need Be* (1936), which became *Orphans in Gethsemane* (1960), are the most extensive treatments, but Wallace Stegner's *The Big Rock Candy Mountain* (1943) and Walter Van Tilburg Clark's *The City of Trembling Leaves* (1945) also deserve recognition for their ardent quest for truth.

In the succeeding generations of western novelists, one does not see quite the intensity of preoccupation with overcoming myth and establishing a true West. It is as if the revolution has been secured, and now a writer is simply free—as any writer normally should be—to write about anything he or she pleases. The almost casual eclecticism of recent and contemporary western novelists may be taken as a sign of a freed literary territory. Among the many successors to the trailbreakers, the Texan Larry McMurtry (b. 1936) may be mentioned for his artistically successful uses of traditional western materials. With seeming ease, he has dealt with the pressure of the Texas mythological inheritance—which is something like the western legacy writ large. Prolific and immensely popular, he has proved difficult to assess or even categorize: his work includes novels honoring the land and the older-generation stewards of it (*Horseman, Pass By* [1961] and *Leaving Cheyenne* [1963]), novels satirizing small-town life and novels describing urban, existential displacement and ennui (*The Last Picture*

Show [1966], *Moving On* [1970], *Cadillac Jack* [1982], and *Texasville* [1987]), and recently, largely realistic novels making use of such hoary western subjects as the trail drive (*Lonesome Dove* [1985]) and Billy the Kid (*Anything for Billy* [1988]). He has left and come back to Texas, in life and also figuratively in critical essays on the state's literary heritage, and his own pronouncements on the thinness of traditional Texas subjects may have complicated the job of assessment. *Lonesome Dove* and *Anything for Billy* came after McMurtry had called for Texas writers "to turn from the antique myths of the rural past and to seek plots and characters and literary inspiration in modern Texas's urban, industrial present." It is clear that McMurtry will not be bound by either the frontier myth or a reactive, antifrontier myth; he appears to have broken through that particular controversy and to have assumed an absolute freedom of subject matter.

Poetry in the West

Western poetry, as a genre, has not been so strongly marked by the specifically regional reappraisal of history that characterizes the West's mature-phase fiction. Poetry in general, as is often noted, tends toward universal themes rather than regionally identifiable ones. Nevertheless, a distinctive western poetic temper does exist and can be seen in the critical retrospect of western poets—their broad-gauge critique of expansionist culture's way in the world—in their willingness to describe transcendental experience of nature, and finally, in their strong allegiance to place.

These defining elements may be seen in the work of the first major poets of the West, John G. Neihardt (1881–1973) and Robinson Jeffers (1887–1962). There had been a great deal of sentimental or genteel western poetry before Neihardt and Jeffers, with occasional pre-flashes of the regional temper: passages in the work of Joaquin Miller, Charles Warren Stoddard, and Edwin Markham still command attention and indeed almost sum up the western achievement before Neihardt and Jeffers. But Neihardt, closely associated with Nebraska and in fact that state's first poet laureate (1921), determined to write epic-scale verse on western themes and did so with critical success; and Jeffers created in his work a California coast that is both a seeable region and a philosophical standpoint from which humanity may be viewed to profound effect.

Neihardt's early verse was mostly lyrical and served as an apprenticeship to his greater ambition. "He believed," his biographer Lucile F. Aly has written, "that at thirty a poet should renounce subjective poetry for work that expressed a wider view of the world." The lyrics allow us to see, however, Neihardt's intensely mystical experience of life, his receptivity to the "Otherness" that fueled all of his poetry. *A Bundle of Myrrh* (1907), *The Stranger at the Gate* (1912), and *The Poet's Town* (1908–12), collected in *Lyric and Dramatic Poems of John G. Neihardt* (1965), express Neihardt's energetic and mystic sense of identity. In "April Theology," he declared,

> O, I know in my heart, in the sun-quickened, blossom-
> ing soul of me,
> This something called self is a part, but the world is the
> whole of me!

His epic-style retellings of western history—*The Song of Hugh Glass* (1915), *The Song of Three Friends* (1919), *The Song of the Indian Wars* (1925), *The Song of the Messiah*

(1935), and finally *The Song of Jed Smith* (1941), all collected in *A Cycle of the West* in 1949—are infused with a broad view of humanity in the cosmos, raising nineteenth-century western materials to classic and universal levels. Neihardt combined extensive historical research (including interviews with old-timers and Indians) with his own sense of nature and destiny, to form a grand-scale vision of the West. From his depiction of the Ashley-Henry expedition of 1822 to the terrible death of the Ghost Dance movement at Wounded Knee in 1890, Neihardt's characters rise to heroic stature by demonstrating such profoundly important, eminently human qualities as physical courage, forgiveness, endurance, and spiritual vision. They are Hugh Glass the mountain man and Wovoka the Paiute Ghost Dance dreamer, but they are also, in Neihardt's presentation, mankind on the earth, in splendid adventure and in deep travail. Neihardt's estimates of his people are evenhanded, compassionate, Shakespearean.

Robinson Jeffers self-published his first work in 1912 (*Flagons and Apples*), was critically praised for *Californians* in 1916, and broke through to his mature style with *Tamar* in 1924. It is interesting to note, in connection with Jeffers's emergence, that Frank Norris's character Presley, in *The Octopus*, had dreamed of becoming the poet of the West—"where the tumultuous life ran like fire from dawn to dark, and from dark to dawn again, primitive, brutal, honest, and without fear." Norris's implicit estimate, that there indeed had been no such West Coast poet yet, seems perfectly just. It fell to Jeffers, after World War I, to write in a way that was "primitive, brutal, honest, and without fear," although in reference to the term *primitive* it must be said that Jeffers was far beyond that state in both his knowledge of classical and modern history and his mastery of poetic form. His view of humanity's course on the earth was sharply critical. In "Original Sin," writing of the very early "man-brained and man-handed ground-ape," he declared his own detached position from our species, "As for me, I would rather / Be a worm in a wild apple than a son of man." A similar stance is seen in the famous "Hurt Hawks," where Jeffers stated he would "sooner, except the penalties, kill a man than a hawk." Several poems depend for their perspective, both visually and figuratively, on the poet's taking a position above and outside the usual concerns and the self-fascination, and indeed the whole history, of humankind. Jeffers referred to his personal philosophy as "Inhumanism," and despite the negative cast of the term itself, he regarded his view as positive, a "falling in love outward," a transpersonal recognition of the beauty and order of the world, a philosophy that revealed humanity in true perspective. Jeffers's may be the most thoroughly revisionist of historical views, for he attempts to consider mankind as a whole, on an evolutionary scale of time, as simply one naturalistic element among many.

The second great dimension of western poetry, transcendental experience of nature, seems to have been a bearing-point in Jeffers's own life. His wife reported that during the building of his stone house, when the poet daily handled rough, heavy, granite boulders, "there came to him a kind of awakening such as adolescents and religious converts are said to experience." The poem "Oh, Lovely Rock" records an instance when Jeffers felt as though he "were seeing through / the flame-lit surface into the real and bodily / And living rock." His character suggestively named "The Inhumanist," in "The Double Axe," cries out to the wilderness around him, "two or three times in my life / my walls have fallen—beyond love—no room for / love— / I have been you." But unlike

Neihardt, Jeffers drew from such experience no positive interpretations about the human potential. His historical vision of mankind remained mordant. What was positive in him emerged in memorable, lyric descriptions of the California coast, either detached from humanity or seen in ironic juxtaposition to our species' foibles. The latter technique provided Jeffers some of his most dramatic effects, for example in "Apology for Bad Dreams," in which the poet stands on a high hill watching the sun set over the ocean, "the fountain / And furnace of incredible light flowing up from the sunk sun," and then sets against this natural glory what he sees below him: in a "little clearing a woman / Is punishing a horse." Jeffers goes on to describe the punishment in some detail and makes the moral implication of his scene-drawing quite clear at the end of the stanza: "What said the prophet? 'I create good: and I create evil: I am the Lord.'"

There are interesting general similarities between Jeffers's work and that of Gary Snyder (b. 1930), who is perhaps—with William Stafford—most significant among contemporary western poets. Both Jeffers and Snyder take human nature and all of human history for their province and view these things naturalistically, that is, from a point outside the usual human self-advertisement, and both write bell-clear descriptions of wild nature, deriving from profound contemplation. But Snyder, who has made a forty-year study and practice of Buddhism, has projected in some of his poetry a calmer detachment than has Jeffers. Jeffers *recommended* dispassion, but his poetic tone is as often tormented as serene. Working from a Buddhistic understanding of entity-hood—that "things" are not as definite and hard-bordered as the dualistic mind perceives them to be but are, in the Buddhist term, "empty"—Snyder at times seems free of the grip of history; he can for example write of Washington, D.C., that "the center, / The center of power is nothing!" In the same vein, he has argued in prose essays that since human nature is not an entity, it is not locked into a course or a destiny, as Jeffers had held. Humanity is free to draw on the past and chart a better future: "whatever is or ever was in any other culture can be reconstructed from the unconscious, through meditation."

But Snyder's work overall is not naïvely or blandly optimistic. His ability to criticize is shown clearly in such poems as "Mother Earth: Her Whales," a scorching indictment of the modern nation-state and its casual destruction of nature, or "Front Lines," which depicts his home territory in the Sierra Nevada as a war zone where logging companies, real estate brokers, and military jets overhead reveal the "cancer" of our time. Though his view of the human potential is Buddhistic and unfettered, allowing at times a near-transcendental confidence (see "Magpie's Song" in *Turtle Island* [1974], for example), his view of the human performance is unblinkingly realistic.

Snyder's strong attachment to his California home ground, and his proposal of "re-inhabitation," or living within ecological parameters and creating a sustainable society, are unmistakable signs of a postfrontier mentality. The poems and essays in *Turtle Island* and *Axe Handles* (1983) record a settled sense of place and stewardship that is the antithesis of the mobile, horizon-scanning frontier mind.

Neihardt, Jeffers, and Snyder show the western poetic temper quite clearly but do not of course cover the whole of the region's range of verse. Among other poets of the first rank, Thomas Hornsby Ferril (1896–1988) of Colorado, with dispassionate assessments of western history in *High Passage* (1926) and *Westering* (1934), made a significant contribution toward the demythifying of the West. Theodore Roethke (1908–63), who arrived in Washington State in 1947 and at the University of Washington became mentor to an entire generation of poets, wrote beautifully of the self in nature, giving to this transcendental theme a psychologically realistic inwardness. Richard Hugo (1923–82) performed an important, Roethke-like tutorship to dozens of poets at the University of Montana, from 1964 until his death. In its own right, his verse expresses an elegiac sense of the West that seems particularly appropriate to the tone and reality of the mid and later twentieth century. William Stafford (b. 1914), whose main poetic loci are Kansas and Oregon, has written some of the most penetrating meditations on humanity and nature, and on the inner life, that have been produced in the West. In *West of Your City* (1960), *Traveling through the Dark* (1962), *Allegiances* (1970), and *A Glass Face in the Rain* (1982), to name only a few of his many books, Stafford very quietly listens to the wilderness as if he could learn something from it, takes a wryly subversive view of all institutions, and proposes in between the lines an ethical revolution in which humankind might take a more modest position in nature. All of this is quintessentially western, in the postfrontier sense.

Native American Literature in the West

Perhaps no more thoroughly revisionist standpoint could be achieved, vis-à-vis the popular image of the West, than to credit the Native American literature of the region with real worth and standing. For the speakers and writers in the two to three hundred tribal communities in the West, before invasion, there was no "great American dialectic" of civilization and savagery at all, no "frontier"—their songs and stories were those of a people entirely at home. Their historical frame of reference was different from that of the European Americans, obviously—and after invasion it became something like the obverse of the whites'—but more important, their metaphysical reference was radically different. The oral literatures of all the different tribes, as various and highly elaborated as they became in widely differing living situations over thousands of years in the region, were marked at the deepest level by a shared worldview. This was a profoundly religious sense of existence as unified. The four major themes in Native American oral literature, as outlined by the modern scholars Larry Evers and Paul Pavich, are the sense of the sacred, the sense of the beautiful, the particular importance of place, and the centrality of community; all of these interweave in a coherent, holistic perception of the world. The "Great Spirit," variously and often inaccurately defined by European Americans, was the unifying reality behind Native American literature and has recently been described by two Native American scholars, Thomas E. Sanders and Walter W. Peek: "Wah'kon-tah is the sum total of all things, the collective totality that always was—without beginning, without end. Neither a force nor a spirit, it is the inexplicable sharing-togetherness that makes all things, animate and inanimate, of equal value, equal importance, and equal consequence because they are all Wah'kon-tah simultaneously, their forms collectively creating the form of Wah'kon-tah which is, obviously, incapable of being anthropomorphized."

Songs and narratives coming forth from such a view will project a different life, and a different concept of human personality, than the atomization and "individualism" that have been the condition and perhaps the pride of the European-American and "frontier" mind. In the native oral tradition, Evers and Pavich wrote, "The individual is constantly reminded that he is part of the whole, not any more important than any creature around him."

The formal structures of traditional songs and stories were highly organized and stylized, indicating long and cherished literary history. It is clear from this alone that literature was integral and important to native culture; the pervasiveness of songs specific to significant occasions, such as the following, a Papago "Death Song," is further evidence that native people were deeply literary, as they were religious:

> In the great night my heart will go out.
> Toward me the darkness comes rattling.
> In the great night my heart will go out.

After the white invasion of the West, from late in the nineteenth century until well into the twentieth, several Native Americans wrote or dictated autobiographies, acutely describing the tremendous and terrible changes they had seen, analyzing Indian-White relations, and in many cases proposing ways by which a fairer accommodation might be made between the cultures. Sarah Winnemucca (ca. 1844–91), an intelligent and forthright Paiute woman, was one of the first in the West to write a book in this genre; her *Life among the Paiutes: Their Wrongs and Claims* (1883) is, among its other qualities, distinguished by a perceptive awareness of her (white) readership. She engagingly

Combining a familiarity with traditional Native American stories and storytelling techniques with a literary style that borrows freely from other modern practices, Leslie Marmon Silko and other contemporary Indian writers have brought Native American fiction to a broad new audience of readers.

Robyn Stoutenburg (b. 1958). Leslie Marmon Silko. *Photograph, 1991.* © *1993 Robyn Stoutenburg/Swanstock, Tucson, Arizona.*

explains her own life and role as an intermediary, dismisses various criticisms of her tribe with documentary logic, and narrates signal events in recent tribal history with a vivid dramatic sense. Her literary success is a testimony to a remarkable adaptability, all the more impressive when we consider, as H. David Brumble III has noted, that "as a young child she had lived with a stone-age, hunter-gatherer people," a people whose first contact with whites occurred in about 1848. Winnemucca's book, like those of the Omaha scholar Francis LaFlesche (*The Middle Five: Indian Boys at School* [1900]) and the Santee Sioux physician Charles Eastman (*Indian Boyhood* [1902] and *From the Deep Woods to Civilization* [1916]), readily and artistically makes use of one of the tools of the conqueror to demonstrate an earned standing in the modern world and to record continuity with the old. This autobiographical tradition has continued to the present and in its way is as varied and dramatic as the nominally more artistic genres of fiction and poetry. For just two further examples of the several hundred on record, *Black Elk Speaks* (1932) and *Lame Deer: Seeker of Visions* (1972) have been widely praised as artistically realized literature; both books have also played a major role in interpreting Native American spiritual thought to a modern, comparatively much more secular world.

The first novel published by a Native American was John Rollin Ridge's *The Life and Adventures of Joaquin Murieta, the Celebrated California Bandit* (1854), a book written in a heightened, romantic style yet unmistakably criticizing the race prejudice of the Anglo gold miners against whom the brave, sensitive Joaquin seeks revenge. But fiction did not, apparently, seem as congenial a mode as autobiography in the urgent and mostly calamitous situation of Native Americans, for it was not until well into the twentieth century that novels began to appear regularly. The first novel published by a native woman was *Co-ge-we-a* (1927), written by Mourning Dove (Cristal McLeod Galler, 1888–1936), an Okanogan. *Co-ge-we-a* takes as its territory the painful dilemmas of the mixed-blood, thereby personally and incisively commenting on the conflicting value systems of the two cultures and the unreasoning prejudice against both Indians and people of mixed lineage. Another important early working of the essentially tragic cross-cultural theme was *The Surrounded* (1936), by D'Arcy McNickle (1904–77), son of a Cree mother who had been adopted into the Salish Kootenai tribe and an Irish father. This novel is both naturalistic and autobiographical, depicting the profound cultural and psychological discontinuities within a mixed-blood protagonist. Like McNickle, young Archilde is sent away from the reservation and his mother to be educated at a "white" boarding school. The dichotomization of Archilde's life, expressed in several symbolic ways in the novel's settings, plot, and characters as well as directly in Archilde's own mind, allows McNickle to comment on the disastrous lack of communication between cultures and on the repressive power of the dominant society. Measured by its plot alone, *The Surrounded* is pessimistic, but it contains a resolute affirmation of the Native American perspective. In its naturalistic recognition of a conflict that will not diminish soon, and its persevering sense of the honor and rightness of the old ways, this novel foreshadows much of the succeeding Indian fiction.

The 1960s and 1970s, a time of turmoil and reassessment in many areas of American life, saw a rebirth of interest in things Indian (perhaps, as some have said, this was a recurrence of a cyclical phenomenon) and at the same time a remarkable creative outpouring—a true renaissance—in Native American writing. In the West, N. Scott Momaday (b. 1934), Leslie Marmon Silko (b. 1948), and James Welch (b. 1940) are widely regarded as important contributors to the new abundance and quality of Indian literature, with Momaday's novel *House Made of Dawn* (1968) usually regarded as bringer of the fire. That book, "the first non-linear, non-chronological, ritual novel written by an American Indian," as the scholar Paula Gunn Allen has said, alone demonstrates enough artistic sophistication, insight into culture and character, and psychologically evocative setting to call into question the stereotype of the "simple" Indian. In broad terms, the novel deals with the conflict of cultures that history itself has established as the "matter" of recent native narrative; but other layers of meaning, reaching back to connect with the traditional world, are also present and lend depth and universality to the story. For example, as Larry Evers has pointed out, the novel's movement from discord to harmony is common in old-time oral narratives, and furthermore this plot is often framed, as is *House Made of Dawn*, on the necessary process of reconnecting with the land. Abel, the protagonist, is alienated from place and culture simultaneously; it is the wholeness of the two with which he must align himself in the proper, ritual fashion.

Leslie Silko's highly regarded novel *Ceremony* (1977), like *House Made of Dawn*, centers on healing. Both novels open and close with ritually appropriate verbal frames, showing in this old way the tellers' awareness that story has a serious, communal, and moral function—a real standing; and both utilize narrative techniques drawn from Anglo and Native American traditions. Momaday and Silko seem to be clearly conscious of the dual literary legacies they work with and appear free to use at any time whatever methods or allusions may be appropriate. This technical free ranging itself suggests a comprehensive outlook; but the authors' ultimate philosophical standpoint, within the coherent, native way, gives their technical virtuosity a grounding and makes their work something more substantial than mere eclectic experimentation. Silko's protagonist Tayo, in *Ceremony*, has been deserted by his mother and traumatized in World War II and exhibits serious psychological problems; concurrently, the Laguna reservation suffers from severe drought. As the novel progresses, it becomes clear that health is not achieved in isolation: Silko's weaving of human personality and land, making a human ecology, reminds a reader that "health" and "whole" are indeed cognate terms. Speaking of comprehensiveness, it may be noteworthy that Betonie, the mixed-blood Navajo who as medicine man works for Tayo's healing, numbers among his tools old St. Louis, Seattle, New York, and Oakland phone books.

James Welch's fiction (*Winter in the Blood* [1974], *The Death of Jim Loney* [1979], and *Fools Crow* [1986]) has inspired a remarkable range of critical interpretation, with much attention given to the author's possible attitude toward his subject matter. The first two novels have seemed unremittingly bleak to many readers; the scholar Peter Wild has written, "*Winter in the Blood* appears to be a 'day-in-the-life-of' novel dogging the sadsack existence of yet another drunken, alienated Native American as he shuffles between his mother's little cow enterprise and the bar-studded towns surrounding the reservation." But as Wild usefully points out, such is only the surface of the book. Through remarkably sharp and memorable images (Welch is a poet as well as a novelist), odd bits of conversation, flashbacks whose significance only slowly begins to emerge, absurdist humor, and surreal dreams, the novel shows that the protagonist is slowly gaining some perspective on himself. The wisest character in the book, Yellow Calf, judges the world to be "cockeyed," and thus—assuming Welch agrees with Yellow Calf—one would expect that any changes for the better will be presented guardedly and will be difficult to see, just as they are in the real world. In the sophistication of his characterization, Welch demonstrates a quality of vision now widely seen in Native American writers: they work from a bicultural and conflicted base, true to history, but they go on to provide insights applicable to the human condition, anytime and probably anywhere.

Recent Indian poetry shows this same combination of a base in the ancient coherence plus a modern freedom of tone, form, and reference. The old world, it must be understood, is not always—or even often—explicitly described, but it is inescapably a generative reference point. The irony, humor, and the tragic sense too, often noted in modern Native American verse, all owe their existence to the brute fact of the two worlds. But there is often a more subtle knitting going on. In the traditional way, song and poetry were methods of naming and praising the wholeness of the world; perhaps in the modern world as well, the poet is attempting to make sense of things, to transcend fragmentation and offer a large enough view, and a view with heart, so that even this anguished, mechanical, and hurried world, so far from *all* human tradition, might be comprehended. Again, the distinctive native flavor derives in large part from the assumption of a communal and moral function for literature—modern Indian poetry shows comparatively little of the poet's obsessive concentration on the self that has trivialized so much American verse in recent years.

This long-term, characteristic depth of intention, and the modern freedom, may be exemplified by showing two Native American poems in juxtaposition. The first is a traditional chant of the Yokuts, the second a recent poem by the New Mexico writer Geary Hobson. Between them, these poems suggest much of what is distinctive and vital in Native American writing, whatever the age or genre.

> My words are tied in one
> with the great mountains,
> with the great rocks,
> with the great trees.
> in one with my body
> and my heart...
> And you, day,
> and you, night!
> All of you see me
> one with the world.

BUFFALO POEM # 1
　　　(or)
ON HEARING THAT A SMALL HERD OF BUFFALO
HAS "BROKEN LOOSE" AND IS "RUNNING WILD"
AT THE ALBUQUERQUE AIRPORT—SEPTEMBER 26, 1975
　　　—roam on, brothers . . .

Other Current Trends

Contemporary literary history is notoriously hard to sort out, but one generalization about recent and current western writing can quite safely be made: something like a creative explosion has been going on for the past twenty or so years, bringing the literary West surely into the modern time. Fiction and poetry by Native Americans, with enough good material for at least three major anthologies between 1975 and 1988 alone, new work by Japanese Americans, Chinese Americans, Filipino Americans, Mexican Americans, African Americans, and Armenian Americans, and a significant increase in the number of books by women writers in the West—all of this "minority" production indicates not a random flurry of activity but a general and positive release from old western stereotypes. Western writers work now as if on liberated terrain. A clear example of the new plasticity of response is furnished by the novels of Tony Hillerman of New Mexico (*The Blessing Way* [1970] and *A Thief of Time* [1988], among many others). In these remarkably original novels, close attention to Navajo thought is blended with clever detective-fiction plotting. Ivan Doig's play of an acute, present-day consciousness over historical materials (*Winter Brothers* [1980]) also demonstrates the contemporary western sophistication. Rediscoveries of ignored or forgotten writers such as Elinore Pruitt Stewart (*Letters of a Woman Homesteader* [1914]) and other western women (noted and honored in such anthologies as Joanna Stratton's *Pioneer Women: Voices from the Kansas Frontier* [1981] and Lillian Schlissel's *Women's Diaries of the Westward Journey* [1982]) are another important aspect of the new West. The proliferation of independent or "small" presses and the continued quality publishing by such established academic outlets as the University of Nebraska Press, the University of Oklahoma Press, the University of New Mexico Press, and the University of Arizona Press—all of whom have made it their business to publish western writers—are further evidence of ground firmly won for serious literature. Each year since the founding of *Western American Literature* in 1966, the number of review and bibliography pages in the journal has grown, reflecting both the increase in western titles and the acceptance of western writing as a field for scholarship. In the public and university-extension sector, conferences of scholars and writers, workshops, and short courses on western literature have all become common and regular features of the western literary landscape over the past twenty years, where as recently as the 1950s and early 1960s, the rare gathering of serious western writers had a trailbreaking, if not maverick, aura. The common note in all this activity is that the West has come into its own, literarily, and is no longer in thrall to the frontier mentality or the romantic western myths.

This release may be seen in certain formal experiments of recent years, such as the widely different minimalist and "magical-realist" schools of fiction, both of which have western adherents, and in jugglings and reversals of old western formulas such as Edward Abbey's *The Brave Cowboy* (1956) and E. L. Doctorow's *Welcome to Hard Times* (1975). But the new West most plainly shows its substance in what the writing says, thematically. Perhaps expectably, there is no clearer exposition of the modern reassessment than in nonfiction, and this is true in particular of writing dealing with nature. In the nature essay, the distinction between frontier mind and postfrontier mind is, as we have seen in the earlier time of John Muir and Mary Austin, fundamental, and the history of the West as an exploited region puts a sharp point on the inner, philosophical divide. Edward Abbey (*Desert Solitaire* [1968], *The Journey Home: Some Words in Defense of the American West* [1977], *Abbey's Road* [1979], and *Down the River* [1982]) is perhaps the most significant and influential of the writers who have engaged the philosophical issues of the nature essay and at the same time taken a new, hard look at the western environment. Although he denied the label of naturalist or nature writer, Abbey (1927–89) certainly examines the relationship of humanity and nature, and civilization and wilderness, with sharp insight. His attack on exploitation is as plain-spoken as one might wish, and such essays as "The Second Rape of the West" describe in precise detail, naming names, the current abusers of what has been called the "plundered province." In addition, his writing is made complex and often blackly humorous—very modern—by an ironic slant on history and humanity, which makes his essays quite different in tone from the usually genteel nature-essay tradition. In Abbey's complex and highly personal work, the nature essay becomes current indeed, though at root this author's allegiances are firmly in the established line.

Other important western essayists who have emphasized a postfrontier awareness include Wallace Stegner (*The Sound of Mountain Water* [1969]), Barry Lopez (b. 1945, *Of Wolves and Men* [1978]) and *Crossing Open Ground* [1988]), Ann Zwinger (b. 1925, *Run, River, Run* [1975]), and William Kittredge (b. 1932, *Owning It All* [1987] and *Hole in the Sky* [1992]). These writers describe—and demonstrate—the deep changes in consciousness and attitude that are required of inhabitants, as opposed to invaders, exploiters, or sentimentalists. In assessing history and speculating on what might be a proper, sustainable basis for human presence in the West, they look first to the details of particular places and the restraints of ecological setting. This shift in priority represents a major change of bearing, toward realism and accountability, and is fundamental to the new western literary outlook.

As a whole, western literature's distinctiveness is that it codifies this transition in full detail. It grew up on the frontier, where myths arise; it has, in its later development, indicated a new pattern: ecological adjustment, cultural refinement, and inward growth. When we consider that the presently dominant world culture—founded on mobility, power, and presumably infinite economic growth—is decidedly frontier-minded in the old sense, the maturation of western American literature assumes a significance far greater than heretofore granted.

Bibliographic Note

Obviously, the preceding offers only an outline. Anyone interested in fuller detail should consult Thomas J. Lyon et al., eds., *A Literary History of the American West* (Fort Worth, 1987), a volume of essays by seventy-one scholars. *LHAW* covers many of the writers mentioned above, but despite its size (1353 pages), the book is far from exhaustive, and an interested reader will find him- or herself piecing together bibliographies and likely scholarly trails from a number of sources. One should probably look first to "The West," in Clarence Gohdes and Sanford E. Marovitz, eds., *Bibliographical Guide to the Study of the Literature of the U.S.A.*, 5th ed. (Durham, N.C., 1984), and to Richard W. Etulain's *A Bibliographical Guide to the Study of Western American Literature* (Lincoln, 1982). In addition, the chapter bibliographies in Fred Erisman and Richard W. Etulain, eds., *Fifty Western Writers: A Bio-bibliographical Sourcebook* (Westport, Conn., 1982), offer good leads. The "Western Writers Series" of pamphlets, published at Boise State University under the editorship of Wayne Chatterton and James H. Maguire, is an excellent guide to a large number of western writers—at this writing, more than one hundred. The annual bibliography of critical books and articles in *Western American Literature*, published each February, and the listings under "Literature and the Arts," found in the "Recent Articles" section of each issue of the *Western Historical Quarterly*, will help keep a student of western literature up to date.

Provocative broad-gauge interpretations include Lucy Lockwood Hazard, *The Frontier in American Literature* (New York, 1927), Henry Nash Smith, *Virgin Land: The American West as Symbol and Myth* (Cambridge, Mass., 1950), Leslie Fielder, *The Return of the Vanishing American* (New York, 1968), and William Everson, *Archetype West* (Berkeley, 1976). For single essays characterizing the nature and history of western literature, it would be hard to surpass Wallace Stegner's "History, Myth, and the Western Writer," in *The Sound of Mountain Water* (1969; reprint, Lincoln, 1985), or Fred Erisman's amazingly comprehensive "The Changing Face of Western Literary Regionalism," in Gerald D. Nash and Richard W. Etulain, eds., *The Twentieth-Century West: Historical Interpretations* (Albuquerque, 1989).

Good anthologies—that is, collections put together with an eye to instructively typical material, and introduced knowledgeably—include J. Golden Taylor, ed., *Great Western Short Stories* (Palo Alto, Calif., 1967), J. Golden Taylor, ed., *The Literature of the American West* (Boston, 1969), Philip Durham and Everett L. Jones, eds., *The Western Story: Fact, Fiction, and Myth* (New York, 1975), Clinton F. Larson and William Stafford, eds., *Modern Poetry of Western America* (Provo, Utah, 1975), James D. Houston, ed., *West Coast Fiction* (New York, 1979), Max Apple, ed., *Southwest Fiction* (New York, 1981), Russell Martin and Marc Barasch, eds., *Writers of the Purple Sage: An Anthology of Recent Western Writing* (New York, 1984), Alexander Blackburn, Craig Lesley, and Jill Landem, eds., *The Interior Country: Stories of the Modern West* (Athens, Ohio, 1987), and William Kittredge and Annick Smith, eds., *The Last Best Place: A Montana Anthology* (Helena, 1988). These collections range across wide regions and times and do not limit themselves to either the popular or the serious-literary level. Perhaps the most comprehensive effort of all is James C. Work's *Prose and Poetry of the American West* (Lincoln,

1990), which with its more than seven hundred pages and its fifty-four authors (representing the time period 1540–1989), as well as the editor's astute historical introduction, is likely to set the textbook standard for years to come.

Notable collections of critical essays include Gerald W. Haslam, ed., *Western Writing* (Albuquerque, 1974), Merrill Lewis and L. L. Lee, eds., *The Westering Experience in American Literature* (Bellingham, Wash., 1977), Richard W. Etulain, ed., *The American Literary West* (Manhattan, Kans., 1980), the aforementioned Erisman and Etulain, *Fifty Western Writers*, and Judy Nolte Lensink, ed., *Old Southwest/New Southwest: Essays on a Region and Its Literature* (Tucson, 1987).

Turning now to more specialized genre and author studies, and framing the list on the preceding essay, I have found the following scholarly examinations to be useful. For ecological and historical definitions of the West applicable to literary criticism, Walter Prescott Webb's *The Great Plains* (1931; reprint, Lincoln, 1981) and *The Great Frontier* (1952; reprint, Austin, 1964), and Wallace Stegner's pithy lectures in *Where the Bluebird Sings to the Lemonade Springs: Living and Writing in the West* (New York, 1992) are invaluable. On the frontier and the "great American dialectic" of civilization and savagery, three landmark studies are Leo Marx, *The Machine in the Garden: Technology and the Pastoral Idea in America* (New York, 1964), Richard Slotkin, *Regeneration through Violence: The Mythology of the American Frontier, 1600–1860* (Middletown, Conn., 1973), and Frederick Turner, *Beyond Geography: The Western Spirit against the Wilderness* (New York, 1980). The latter two studies are strongly revisionist in character.

The early mass-market fiction of the West is covered by Daryl Jones in *The Dime Novel Western* (Bowling Green, Ohio, 1978), and the story of the popular formula is brought forward in two good collections of essays: Richard W. Etulain and Michael T. Marsden, eds., *The Popular Western* (Bowling Green, Ohio, 1974), and James K. Folsom, ed., *The Western: A Collection of Critical Essays* (Englewood Cliffs, N.J., 1979). Probably the most influential interpretation of the formula Western is John G. Cawelti's *The Six-Gun Mystique* (Bowling Green, Ohio, 1970), and students of the field will also want to consult Cawelti's *Adventure, Mystery, and Romance: Formula Studies as Art and Popular Culture* (Chicago, 1977). On Owen Wister, two good sources are G. Edward White, *The Eastern Establishment and the Western Experience: The West of Frederic Remington, Theodore Roosevelt, and Owen Wister* (New Haven, 1968), and Richard W. Etulain, *Owen Wister* (Boise, Idaho, 1973). Zane Grey has been taken seriously and studied to edifying effect by Ann Ronald, *Zane Grey* (Boise, Idaho, 1975), and Gary Topping, "Zane Grey," in Erisman and Etulain, *Fifty Western Writers*. Louis L'Amour is also covered well and fairly in *Fifty Western Writers*, in an essay by Michael T. Marsden. Readers interested in what might be made of Jack Schaefer's *Shane* should consult James C. Work, ed., *Shane: The Critical Edition* (Lincoln, 1984).

John Muir has recently come in for a good deal of instructive study, and useful sources in the wider vein include Michael P. Cohen, *The Pathless Way: John Muir and American Wilderness* (Madison, 1984), and Frederick Turner, *Rediscovering America: John Muir in His Time and Ours* (New York, 1985). Two recent biographies of Mary Austin—Augusta Fink's *I-Mary* (Tucson, 1983) and Esther L. Stineman's *Mary Austin: Song of a Maverick* (New Haven, 1989)—show that Austin, though few of her books remain in print, still has something to say to the modern age. John C. Van Dyke has dropped out of the common view and the literary canon even further than Austin, but Peter Wild's *John C. Van Dyke: The Desert* (Boise, Idaho, 1988) may help spark a rehabilitation.

On the novel in the West, it is useful to consult Richard Chase's distinction between romance and novel in *The American Novel and Its Tradition* (Garden City, N.Y., 1952). The foremost regionally specific studies of the genre have been James K. Folsom, *The American Western Novel* (New Haven, Conn., 1966), and John R. Milton, *The Novel of the American West* (Lincoln, 1980). Roy W. Meyer's *The Middle Western Farm Novel in the Twentieth Century* (Lincoln, 1965) is also valuable, and more widely applicable than its title might suggest. On San Francisco's early days, see Franklin Walker, *San Francisco's Literary Frontier* (New York, 1939). For a cogent analysis of Stephen Crane's West, see Frank Bergon, *Stephen Crane's Artistry* (New York, 1975). Warren French's *Frank Norris* (New York, 1962) will guide readers to further sources in the rich secondary material on this writer. Perhaps the most comprehensive scholar on Jack London is Earle Labor; his *Jack London* (New York, 1974) is a reliable "backgrounder," and his "Jack London's Agrarian Vision," *Western American Literature* 11 (Summer 1976): 83–101, is an excellent example of what might be termed the higher London criticism. Scholarship on Willa Cather represents something of an industry—as befits perhaps the most important novelist of the West—but a student who consults John J. Murphy's *Critical Essays on Willa Cather* (Boston, 1984), David Stouck's *Willa Cather's Imagination* (Lincoln, 1975), and Susan J. Rosowski's *The Voyage Perilous: Willa Cather's Romanticism* (Lincoln, 1986) would engage the most influential and recent Cather criticism. An in-depth study of one text, John J. Murphy's *My Antonia: The Road Home* (Boston, 1989), shows with remarkable critical insight the levels of complexity and layers of reference Cather wove into her work.

On Frank Waters, the series *Studies in Frank Waters*, edited by Charles L. Adams (University of Nevada, Las Vegas), is valuable and current. Terence Tanner's *Frank Waters: A Bibliography with Relevant Selections from his Correspondence* (Glenwood, Ill., 1983) is indispensable. On Larry McMurtry, the collection *Taking Stock: A Larry McMurtry Casebook*, edited by Clay Reynolds (Dallas, 1989), offers many interesting lines of thought. Lucile F. Aly's *John G. Neihardt: A Critical Biography* (Amsterdam, 1959), has established the main lines of interpretation on this important but often overlooked poet. Robinson Jeffers's life and work are surveyed perceptively by Frederic I. Carpenter, *Robinson Jeffers* (New York, 1962); interested scholars will want to delve into Robert J. Brophy's *Robinson Jeffers: Myth, Ritual, and Symbol in His Narrative Poems* (Cleveland, Ohio, 1973) and will keep up to date with the *Robinson Jeffers Newsletter*, edited by Brophy at California State University, Long Beach. Stanford University Press is currently bringing out *The Collected Poetry of Robinson Jeffers* under the editorship of Tim Hunt; two of the four projected volumes have been published (1987, 1989); further criticism and perhaps revaluation seem likely to follow this major western publication. Gary Snyder has been surveyed in Bob Steuding, *Gary Snyder* (Boston, 1976), spiritedly described by Kenneth White, *The Tribal Dharma* (Dyfed, Wales, 1975), and subjected to a variety of approaches in Patrick D. Murphy, ed., *Critical Essays on Gary Snyder* (Boston, 1990); students of this important poet will also want to read Scott McLean, ed., *The Real Work: Interviews and Talks, 1964–1979* (New York, 1980). William Stafford's *Writing the Australian Crawl: Views on the Writer's Vocation*, in the important "Poets on Poetry" series (Ann Arbor, 1978), should be referred to for explication of the poet's motives and values.

Among recent works on Native-American literature, Karl Kroeber, *Traditional Literatures of the American Indian: Texts and Interpretations* (Lincoln, 1981), Alan R. Velie, *Four American Indian Literary Masters: N. Scott Momaday, James Welch, Leslie Marmon Silko, and Gerald Vizenor* (Norman, 1982), Paula Gunn Allen, ed., *Studies in American Indian Literature* (New York, 1983), Brian Swann, ed., *Smoothing the Ground: Essays on Native American Oral Literature* (Berkeley, 1983), Andrew Wiget, *Native American Literature* (Boston, 1985), H. David Brumble, *American Indian Autobiography* (Berkeley, 1988), and Arnold Krupat, *The Voice in the Margin: Native American Literature and the Canon* (Berkeley, 1989), are regarded highly. Two anthologies with useful introductory notes are Thomas E. Sanders and Walter W. Peek, eds., *Literature of the American Indian*, abr. ed. (Beverly Hills, Calif., 1976), and Geary Hobson, ed., *The Remembered Earth: An Anthology of Contemporary Native American Literature* (Albuquerque, 1981). Duane Niatum, ed., *Harper's Anthology of 20th Century Native American Poetry* (San Francisco, 1988), and Simon Ortiz, ed., *Earth Power Coming: Short Fiction in Native American Literature* (Tsaile, Ariz., 1983), should also be consulted. Scholars interested in N. Scott Momaday will want to study his sometimes revealing remarks in Charles L. Woodard's *Ancestral Voice: Conversations with N. Scott Momaday* (Lincoln, 1989). Leslie Silko's work is introduced in Per Seyersted, *Leslie Marmon Silko* (Boise, Idaho, 1980), and James Welch's in Peter Wild, *James Welch* (Boise, Idaho, 1983).

A good critical source on Edward Abbey is James Hepworth and Gregory McNamee, eds., *Resist Much, Obey Little* (Salt Lake City, 1985); readers should also study Ann Ronald's thoughtful critique in *The New West of Edward Abbey* (Albuquerque, 1982).

Chapter Twenty-one

Speaking for the Past

CHARLES S. PETERSON

If historians speak for the past, who speaks for historians? Certainly historians seem endlessly willing to talk about themselves, but on occasion journalists and others too have paid attention. In 1989 and 1990, newspapers and magazines took note of disputes over what became known as the "new western history." National attention may have begun with an article in the *Washington Post* of 10 October 1989 under the wildly western headline: "Shootout in Academia over the History of U.S. West, New Generation Confronts Frontier Tradition." Not to be outdone by its East Coast rival, the *New York Times* published two pieces on this academic showdown in December 1989 and March 1990. In May, *U.S. News and World Report* had a cover announcing "The Old West: The New View of Frontier Life," and in October 1990, the cover of the *New Republic* sourly announced "Westward Ho Hum: What the New Historians Have Done to the Old West."

These reports from the academic front covered the most recent infighting but did not always explain how long the war of words had been under way. For decades an uneasy balance existed between the voices of popular impulse and those of academic professionalism. Without worrying about its subtleties, this constant shifting between general interest and scholarly discipline energized those who spoke for western history even as the very idea of the West changed. Now taken as the trans-Mississippi area, the West looks back beyond the hundred years of its immediate past to historiographic times far more distant and to geographies far wider than its present vastness. Not only has western history had to cope with successive Wests, but it has also had to respond to ongoing change about the meanings and uses of history.

All in all, the converging influences of personality, time, place, and thought make for a field of great appeal. With an ear turned to the seismic stirrings of popular taste, with an almost pathological need to be accepted professionally, and with subfields of growing complexity, western history is at once charming and productive. It has not yet lost its willingness to tell a good story nor abandoned an easy camaraderie, but western historians of widely varied backgrounds are putting together an impressive body of scholarly and popular literature and sustaining the institutional superstructure necessary to develop the story of one of the world's grand adventures.

As in so much else that deals with western history, getting a handle on all this is simplified by the centrality of the person and career of the frontier historian Frederick Jackson Turner. Born in Portage, Wisconsin, in 1861, Turner was a product of middle America and of a republic midway on its course to the present. Wilderness was still near. Old-timers remembered pioneering and Indian wars. Local pride and aspirations ran

The popular appeal of western history, celebrated in this poster as the progressive development from a simple Indian past to a modern urban present, has both inspired and troubled academic historians. If such popular history has created a broad interest in the West, it has also hampered investigation of alternative stories of the region's past.

Unidentified artist. Pageant of Lincoln. Chromolithograph, 1915. Langdon Collection, John Hay Library, Brown University, Providence, Rhode Island.

strong, and as the historian Ray A. Billington has recognized, the views of Thomas Jefferson and Alexis de Tocqueville were still "a common currency." Yet industrial cities were rising, and Populist protest and regional tensions stirred an uneasy land.

Reflecting the situation's complexity was Turner's own experience. As a student at the University of Wisconsin and at Johns Hopkins, he was introduced to history as a social tool and to the ascendant Teutonic germ theory, which rooted American (eastern) development in European influences. Turner returned to teach at Wisconsin, where he devoted himself to seeing the past of his own region in history's larger context. That process involved him with both the popular and the professional elements of history. By 1890 he was lecturing public-school teachers on "The Significance of History," which he described at two levels. On the one hand, history was common, fundamental, apparent. Wherever there remained "a chipped flint, . . . a pyramid, . . . a poem, . . . a coin," there was "history." On the other hand, history was an "ongoing encounter between past and present," written "anew" by each generation in response to the issues of its time and controlled and enlightened by a growing body of historical methodologies and interpretations.

In 1893 Turner delivered his celebrated paper "The Significance of the Frontier in American History." In it he declared, in striking and poetic terms, the centrality of western influences upon America's development. Written as "a programme" or interpretive tool, and "a protest against eastern neglect . . . of the West, and against" the West's own "antiquarian spirit," as he later informed a friend, this famous essay described the frontier both as a process and as the successive lines of advancing settlement. Sensing that the West exerted "a persistent pervasive influence in American life, which did not get its full attention from historians who thought in terms of" European influences or the slavery issue, nor yet from those who were fascinated with "the epic period of the West," Turner tried "to see it [the West] as a whole," to understand "its institutional, social, economic, and political side," and to apply to its study the analytical methods then developing in the social sciences.

At the deepest root of America's past had been "the existence of an area of free land, its continuous recession, and the advance of . . . settlement westward." Progressively distanced from European and even eastern influences, pioneers became a new race, an exceptional people. In Turner's overstated metaphor, democracy emerged fully formed from the American forest, strengthening liberty everywhere and making it the special attribute of Americans. With accessible land functioning as a safety valve, labor agitation, social discord, and violence were muted. Sectional distinctions were in no small part the product of geographical influences. A vital force since earliest settlement, the frontier had closed by 1890, thus ending, Turner warned, "a great historic movement."

The frontier thesis fell on ready ears. Before the end of 1893, Theodore Roosevelt and a few others praised it as a masterful summation of widely held views. In the years that followed, the public and the historical profession capitulated, suggesting Turner's ideas and spirit were firmly based in the general climate of opinion. Turner was widely sought as a lecturer and wrote often for popular journals. Professional papers, of which he delivered many, and monographic works, which were embarrassingly few, bore his

No historian did more to shape the debate about western history than Frederick Jackson Turner, shown here about 1893, the year he delivered his famous address on the significance of the frontier in American history.

Unidentified photographer. Frederick Jackson Turner. *Photograph, ca. 1893. The Huntington Library, San Marino, California.*

trademarks: sweeping generalizations, effective analysis, methodological soundness, and an optimistic and romantic affinity for America and especially the West.

Discovery and an Evolving Literature

To understand Turner's pivotal role it would be well to survey developments that contributed to western history in the centuries before 1900. Formative voices grew from discovery and conquest. Initiated by Renaissance generations, the first age of discovery extended for two centuries, circumnavigated the globe, and worked the Western Hemisphere into the formal record and popular consciousness of Europe. As a statement of history, it was preoccupied with national expansion and extension of the faith as well as filled with allusions to marvels and mythical expectations. Extraordinary only in its claims to priority was Christopher Columbus's first report, which included maritime data, a funding request, and information about the Indies and King Solomon's fabled treasure islands. Similar was Francis Drake's sixteenth-century account of his world-circling raid on the Spanish Empire. Suppressed in England by Queen Elizabeth, it was elsewhere "in every man's mouth," as a contemporary reported. Its distortions spread to the present as either a celebrated memory or a plague on scholarship depending on whom one asks.

The University of Texas historian William H. Goetzmann has explained that a second age of discovery began with the eighteenth century. Explorers no longer sought marvels but, guided by rationalism, set out to order geographical knowledge in terms of Newton's mechanistic model. The data they collected helped create a world culture of science while the "discovery of . . . peoples, who seemingly stepped out of Eden," fostered romantic history and national awareness. By the late 1800s recognition of evolution's workings had added "a linear, history-oriented time-line" to the literature of discovery.

Under these influences the record of exploration was dramatically enlarged in body and meaning. The product of Old World influences, it became increasingly relevant for the New. The United States was both the child of discovery and an active participant. Trade and seagoing industry gave America a recognizable place in the record of maritime discovery, but its unique domain lay in the historiography of land exploration and in a growing awareness of nature's importance.

The influence that discovering nature's purpose had upon the American record is nowhere more apparent than in the thought and policy of Thomas Jefferson. To Jefferson, man and nature were inseparably linked, integral parts of the benevolent design of nature's God. Closely related was the view that equality and independence were not only inalienable rights but, in the natural order of things, the special destiny of America. As the historian Daniel Boorstin has eloquently pointed out, Jefferson's ideas were future oriented rather than historical. In the natural circumstance of the American continent lay a sublime opportunity for individual development unhampered by the past and for the "fruition of a society built on largely naturalistic foundations." Like the agricultural development on which they depended, prosperity and republican virtues were the product of "the environment itself." It was a vision that not only partook of the Age of Reason's confidence in empirical observation but also was moved by the sentiments of romanticism, including nationalistic ardor and a penchant for optimistic expression, qualities still strong in Turner's teaching a century later.

Jefferson's 1803 purchase of Louisiana opened the last great West and vastly expanded America's stake in the historiography of exploration and conquest. A pattern for the record that evolved was Jefferson's *Notes on the State of Virginia* (1785), an "encyclopedic inventory" of old dominion Virginia (from seashore to the Mississippi). As the environmental historian John Opie has written, Jefferson used language that was both empirical and romantic to describe how "human activity" sprang "naturally from Virginia's topography, climate, plants, and animals" and pointed out its potential for future development. After failing to launch transcontinental exploration attempts before he became president, Jefferson improved on the purchase of Louisiana by dispatching the Lewis and Clark Expedition (1804–6) with instructions to record their discoveries in scientific detail.

The journals Lewis and Clark brought back were notable for their factual quality, yet in the fullest sense they were romantic and national history. They were published by Nicholas Biddle of Philadelphia in 1814 along with a "mountain" of supporting accounts, many of which were highly fictionalized. The report focused the attention of reading America on the West, an influence that continues as we approach the bicentennial of the famed expedition.

Something of its early effect may be seen in the experience of Parley Pratt, later a key figure in the Mormon movement westward. In a surge of romantic intensity, the youthful Pratt resolved during the fall of 1826, only months after Jefferson's death, to spend "the remainder of his days" in the "solitudes of the great West, among the natives of the forest." Taking "Lewis and Clark's tour up the Missouri and down the Columbia" to read, Pratt spent a solitary winter in a "holy retreat" west of Cleveland. The "storms of winter raged . . . the wind shook the forest, the wolf howled . . . and the owl chimed in harshly to complete" a "doleful music." To the end of his days Pratt looked West.

Others too looked West, creating a western record as they looked. Significant were Lewis and Clark's followers, official explorers who continued to write reports filled with useful description. One whose account rivaled theirs in popular appeal, and gave a southwestward tilt to American interest, was Zebulon Pike. Ordered to explore the southern reaches of the new purchase, Pike made an extended foray into northern New Spain in 1806–7. His report was filled with information about the Rio Grande and Chihuahua and sold widely in the United States and in numerous foreign editions. Perhaps its most lasting fame grew from Pike's description of the Great Plains as uninhabitable desert.

The national literature of discovery accumulated quickly. Exploration was given a formal place in the military tradition when the U.S. Topographical Bureau was organized during the War of 1812, followed by the Corps of Topographical Engineers in 1838. Later the Department of the Interior and universities incorporated scientific exploration into their functions. The West became a vast laboratory where scientific disciplines defined their perimeters and created a unique literature of western discovery.

Official discovery reports were more or less constant. Transcending journalism and technical data, many of them achieved status as history. Among the most widely read were John C. Frémont's reports of the 1840s and 1850s. Only slightly less acclaimed were exploration accounts from the Mexican War, the Pacific Railroad Surveys of the mid-1850s, and the Utah War of the late 1850s. Even more significant were reports generated by the Great Surveys in the decades after the Civil War. None of these became more deeply embedded in western historiography than John Wesley Powell's benchmark *Report on the Lands of the Arid Region of the United States* (1878). In it Powell called for the rationalization of natural resource utilization through classification and planned use. He also described the geographical regions of the United States and, improving on Pike, defined the West in terms of aridity.

In the meantime, an important western historiography grew out of economic enterprise and settlement in successive Wests. Among the earliest was John Smith's history of Jamestown, which Jefferson found to be "sensible, and well informed" but in style "barbarous and uncouth." More hopefully, as the historian John Higham noted of the Puritan William Bradford, early chroniclers "set down" straightforward narratives "of shared and remembered experience" that possessed "an effortless grasp of human motivation." Much more recently, local historians have written, in parlances humble, nostalgic, or mythic, of beginnings in homestead districts, mining camps, or railroad towns.

Closely related was what might be called the historical journalism of expeditionary enterprise. Existing from the earliest penetration of Europeans, expeditionary accounts took on added relevance with the growth of a market economy and advances in

Generously illustrated with images drawn by eyewitnesses, 19th-century western expeditionary reports such as John C. Frémont's narratives created visual and literary histories of the West's recent past.

After Charles Preuss (active 1845–53). Outlet of Subterranean River. *Lithograph, ca. 1845. From John Charles Frémont,* A Report of the Exploring Expedition to Oregon and North California in the Years 1843–'44 *(1845).*

publication. The first stirrings of this development may be seen soon after the War of 1812 as the fur trade and western enterprise proliferated. By the Mexican War in 1846, it was well established. Sensitive to sales, expeditionaries trafficked in the tastes of the reading public and became slaves to deadlines and profits, giving less attention to stylistic finish, moralistic overtones, and matters relating to public discourse than had earlier literary figures.

Among the best were Richard Henry Dana, Jr.'s *Two Years Before the Mast* (1840), a vivid account of California's coastal trade, and Josiah Gregg's *Commerce of the Prairies* (1844), a description of the Santa Fe trade. With their sights on the entertainment market, expeditionaries enlarged the use of stereotypes, controversy, and humor and increasingly turned to sensational and mythic topics that were proven sellers. For example, the British explorer Sir Richard Burton focused on Mormon polygamy in *The City of the Saints* (1862); and in Mark Twain's *Roughing It* (1872), stereotype and exaggerated humor—the "jackass rabbit" that ran so fast "we could . . . hear him whiz"—are transformed into social commentary of lasting value by a sensitive mix of realism and impressionism.

In the meantime, developments in New England were having an important bearing on western history. First was the evolution of the historical perspective, a subject later addressed by Turner. As Higham points out, the early Puritan commonwealth regarded history as a "vehicle of self analysis . . . and public discourse," only slightly less important than the sermon. This affinity for history persisted in secularized form throughout the eighteenth and nineteenth centuries among what have been called the patrician historians, typically men of private means and conservative social and political temper.

Toward the end of the patrician period, certain "men of letters" emerged whose romantic interests and artistic achievements threw a sophisticated light on western themes. Romantic historians sought to discover and re-create the spirit of the times about which they wrote to, in effect, bring an age to life on the written page. Heroic figures, elites, representative man, flesh-and-blood characters, creative imagination, drama, narrative force—all were tools of romantic historians' art. In their writing the master key was progress; the ill was evanescent, the good was enduring, the "march of destiny" spiraled upward.

In the strictest sense, romantic historians of the American West were few in number but long-lived and prolific. Among the earliest was Washington Irving, an expatriate New Yorker who returned from Europe in about 1830 to make western tours and the fur trade the object of his attention. Central also to romantic interest in western themes were the New Englanders William Prescott, George Bancroft, and Francis Parkman. Prescott's *History of the Conquest of Mexico* (1844) and *History of the Conquest of Peru* (1847) exploited the Hispanic turn in America's past, finding in it the heroic endeavor, the dramatic action, and the narrative power important in western tastes to this day. Romantic nationalism was epitomized in the works of George Bancroft, who brought poetry and prophecy to the heroic events and towering figures described in his twelve-volume *History of the United States* (1834–75).

No one wrote more fully in the "grand manner" to which romantic historians aspired than Francis Parkman. Tapping into the westward current at the time of the Mexican War, *The Oregon Trail* (1849) is an enduring classic. Back from his western tour, Parkman published *The History of the Conspiracy of Pontiac* in 1851 and the seven volumes of his monumental *France and England in the New World* between 1865 and 1892, immersing "himself most completely in" volumes dealing with the discovery of the West. In *Pioneers of France in the New World* (1865), *The Jesuits in North America in the Seventeenth Century* (1867), and *LaSalle and the Discovery of the Great West* (1869), he betrayed a fascination with beginnings and an appreciation for the influence of wilderness. As the historian William R. Taylor suggests, Parkman more than hinted at the environmental interpretation Turner made famous when he explained that "the hard practical wisdom of the forest" accounted for "the triumphant achievements of Champlain, La Salle, and a half-dozen others." Casting his work in terms of a titanic struggle between England and France on the one hand and against nature on the other, Parkman helped make the inevitability of progress an American article of faith, arguing that French culture was predestined to give way to English and, ultimately, to American influences.

In the mold of romantics adjusting to the industrial age was Hubert Howe Bancroft. Of Puritan stock, Bancroft grew up in Ohio, learned the book trade, and followed the gold rush to California, where he succeeded in the book business and by the mid-1870s had acquired a vast and superb collection of western Americana including Spanish materials. To this he applied the techniques of mass production and distribution and, assisted by scores of reductionists and writers, produced under his own byline the thirty-nine volumes of Bancroft's Works (1874–90), along with several lesser series. Bancroft's books were contested in authorship, florid in style, excessive in detail, and thin on integrating interpretation. But they also defined the West in terms of a "Western Shores" or Pacific regionalism and worked out thematic and proportional relationships that have persisted in western history. In addition they brought the Hispanic tradition squarely into the focus of western American history.

Bancroft was a vital link between romantic history and the eclecticism and exhaustive detail of western regionalism. His books were assembled from widely varying elements including an array of literary and historical conventions. Recognizable are biblical, classical, Puritan, Jeffersonian, Jacksonian, and Darwinian influences. But no tradition stands out more clearly than that of the romantics. This shows up in Bancroft's response to nature, his treatment of nationalism, his identification of all progress with developments on the California shore, his discussion of Hispanic themes, and perhaps most emphatically, in his penchant for uncritical, action-driven, male-dominated, fact-based narrative.

Whether embodied in Hernando Cortés, LaSalle, or the California forty-niner, the hero was the transcendent figure in romantic history. After 1840 the western hero also became the central figure in an immense popular literature as well as the symbol for a political era that could no longer claim direct revolutionary involvement but that still sought to distance itself from Europe. Beginning about 1825, politicians exploited the myth of the man of nature as democratic leader using the public media to popularize and give legitimacy to a long generation of western heroes. Eventually these included Andrew Jackson, Henry Clay, Davy Crockett, William Henry Harrison, Zachary Taylor, and Abraham Lincoln. In the process, these heroes gave official form to the country's western destiny, and for many, the westerner became the quintessential American.

Lincoln and Jackson were the most-admired political heroes, but with his willing contrivance Davy Crockett was the most extravagant and served to make the transition to the western hero as a literary figure. "Born in a cane brake, cradled in a sap trough, and clouted in coon skins," Crockett helped launch a myth in his own *Narrative of the Life of David Crockett of the State of Tennessee* (1834) and reveled in the antic legendry of *The Crockett Almanacks* (1835–38). Most significant, he died at the Alamo, following the Wild West into American memory through unnumbered fictional and film renditions.

Exploiting similar impulses was the Wild West of popular taste. In publication, as in politics, biography sold well. Writers turned again and again to well-known western figures including Kit Carson, George A. Custer, and Buffalo Bill Cody, around whom floods of myth-filled biography issued. Regional variations playing on major themes extended well into the twentieth century. Violent heroes like New Mexico's Billy the Kid and Mormon Orrin Porter Rockwell still asserted their hold, attracting biographers both serious and sensationalist. Even the political hero lived on in biographies like Carl Sandburg's superb *Abraham Lincoln: The Prairie Years* (1926) and Marquis James's Pulitzer prize–winning *The Raven: A Biography of Sam Houston* (1929), both written in the nineteenth century's grand tradition of history as literature.

From the early discovery accounts to the popular hero, an enormous body of history-related writing had come into existence. In a very real way this was the voice of western history in 1893 as Frederick Jackson Turner announced the closing of the frontier. It was, however, a voice so dispersed in space, so various in practical function, and so deeply rooted in nostalgia and popular culture as to be only partially realized as western history. It had almost no existence at all as an academic field of study. But developments were under way that soon made it possible for the voice of scholars to be heard on western history as well.

The University and the Professional Historian

In the late nineteenth century, universities multiplied throughout America. History was added piecemeal to the college curriculum, and eastern institutions appointed historians and established departments, giving history a new institutional focus. Initially, graduate work abroad was a common prerequisite, and the first generation of professors tended to reflect class circumstances that made foreign study possible. Soon, however, developing graduate programs enabled scholars to take their entire training in America. Of modest means, many of the new scholars broke with the conservatism of the patricians, tending instead to progressive or liberal social views. Tutorial relationships between student and mentor and debate between professors allowed for widespread exchange of ideas and made for continuity.

Turner's career may be taken as a metaphor for the changes that all this produced in western history. His youth in the Midwest and his education at Wisconsin and Johns Hopkins were typical. This was true also of the nostalgia that dominated his thought, as it was of his return to teach at Wisconsin. He was the creative thinker who linked West and nation to speak to the "ideals and problems of" his own time. He was also the consummate organization man who tended affairs on campus and made his influence felt in the world of history organizations. At both Wisconsin and Harvard, where he moved in 1910, he attracted hundreds of students, scores of whom became dedicated Turnerians.

Turner's threefold influence as sentimental representative of the West, analytical student of American processes, and consummate academic professional was mirrored in the careers of his students and followers. Many maintained regional loyalties, others broadened American history, and still others found ultimate meaning in the frontier interpretation. Perhaps no student reflected the sweep of Turner's thought, and western history's potential for both breadth and responsiveness, more than Carl L. Becker. The Iowa son of a westering German family, Becker did undergraduate work at Wisconsin and graduate study at Columbia under the "new historian" James Harvey Robinson but

Members of the Daughters of the Republic of Texas pose in front of the Alamo, which their organization restored and continues to maintain. The women exemplify the important role played by citizen historians in preserving western historical sites and archives. Often motivated by patriotism or local interests, such groups ensured the survival of major research archives for academic historians.

Hugo L. Summerville Studios (active 1910s–1920s). Officers of the Daughters of the Republic of Texas. Photograph, 1925. Photography Collection, Harry Ransom Humanities Research Center, The University of Texas at Austin.

returned to Wisconsin for his Ph.D. during Turner's day. Thereafter Becker pursued a remarkable teaching and publications career at Dartmouth, at Kansas, and at Cornell. Early on he wrote a rhapsodic essay on Kansas that was in the most atavistic Turnerian mode and did a dissertation on political parties in prerevolutionary New York that reflected Turner's interest in institutional studies. Becker's barometer-like responses to changes in public issues suggest that he endorsed without reservation Turner's conviction that each age rewrites the past in terms of its own moods and needs. But studies on the Revolution and the Age of Reason show that Becker was well prepared to pass from environmental determinism and frontier activism to the impact of institutions and ideas.

Quite different in personality was Edward Everett Dale. Once called the "rarest humorist" in the Mississippi Valley Historical Association, Dale was born in Texas and raised in western Oklahoma's cattle country, where he cowboyed and taught in rural schools for more than a decade before taking his Ph.D. at Harvard in 1922. Although Dale claimed Turner "opened a new Heaven and a new earth" when he introduced him to "American History," Oklahoma and its people remained the focus of his life, of his teaching career (at the University of Oklahoma), and of his prolific writing. Authentic, affectionate, and good-spirited, Dale was not by nature a critic. Like many western historians, he exhibited a professionalism gentled and humanized by native loyalty.

Also useful in understanding the sliding scale between regional enthusiasms and frontier history as scholarly profession was Frederic Logan Paxson. Not a Turner student but sometimes regarded as the truest disciple of all, Paxson was born and educated in Pennsylvania, where he also received his Ph.D. Following professional openings and personal inclinations, Paxson adopted the frontier process as almost his single interpretive tool. At the University of Colorado (1903–6) he taught the full history offering, gained a few professional contacts, and got into western history with several articles on Colorado. At Michigan (1906–10) he enlarged his professional circle and published *The Last American Frontier* (1910), a pleasing application of the frontier process. Riding its success, he took Turner's place at Wisconsin in 1910, continued to advance in his professional connections, worked with good students, and turned out a succession of well-received books including *History of the American Frontier, 1763–1893* (1924), a prize-winning work widely hailed as the masterful frontier synthesis Turner never wrote. Moving to the University of California in 1932, Paxson maintained his reputation as a Turnerian and headed the history department during its great western history era.

Another disciple who embraced Turner's frontier interpretation but went beyond him in connecting with the people was the University of Iowa political scientist Benjamin F. Shambaugh. An Iowa native, Shambaugh threw himself into the affairs of the Iowa Historical Society, which he initially set out to transform from an antiquarian club to a true research institution. However, after World War I, Shambaugh shifted sharply, promoting what the historian Alan M. Schroeder has rightly termed "a lighter, more impressionistic," from-the-ground-up approach to history. This change of emphasis was apparent in the *Palimpsest*, a "magazine of popular history," and in the annual Iowa Commonwealth Conference where, during the late 1920s, representatives of the general public, the press, and national figures mingled enthusiastically.

State Societies and Citizen Historians

Shambaugh's determination "to look at history from the bottom up" and his wholehearted turn to citizen involvement were major attributes of the era's spirit. Historical societies, archives, and individuals were busy throughout the West collecting the record of regional pasts and making it available through study and publication. Although citizen historians worked closely with the scholarly profession, in many ways they represented a second voice for western history that prolonged the influence of epic or classic western themes and emphasized regional treatment.

An early manifestation of this spirit at the personal level, as we have already seen, was the San Francisco collector-historian Hubert Howe Bancroft. Others, like Hiram Chittenden and Elliott Coues, found time during distinguished government careers to indulge personal interests in writing and editing. A Corps of Engineers officer, Chittenden produced the three-volume *American Fur Trade of the Far West* (1902), which is still regarded as the definitive work on the topic, along with studies of Pierre Jean De Smet and steam navigation on the Missouri. In a flurry of historiographical enterprise, surgeon-naturalist Coues edited widely, including thirteen important volumes on the fur trade and Spanish exploration.

Citizen history also took the form of publicly funded historical societies throughout the West. Many counties and municipalities joined in this distinctively western development, but attention here will be directed to the role of state societies. Launched in the 1850s, the Wisconsin Society developed quickly under the untiring work of Lyman C. Draper, a fabulously successful collector, who combined passions for retrieving the pioneer story with a knack for managing Wisconsin's political network. He also possessed the innovative leadership to guide Wisconsin in becoming the first state to make state history an official function and to fund its operations.

Also an important Draper legacy was his 1887 choice of Reuben Gold Thwaites as his successor; Thwaites proved to be his equal as a collector and promoter and his superior as an editor. In his twenty-six years as secretary Thwaites vastly enlarged the society's popular mission, located its library at the University of Wisconsin, and worked closely with Turner and other academics whose cooperation was symptomatic of the close relationship between citizens' history and the scholarly profession. Perhaps most significant, Thwaites published no fewer than 183 volumes of edited documents, including the 73-volume *Jesuit Relations* and the 31-volume *Early Western Travels*. Not surprisingly some of these were not edited to the exacting standards demanded by academic professionals, and some academics saw them as part of the fault line between professional discipline and the popular taste for quantity, beginnings, and narrative.

In 1914 Thwaites was succeeded at the Wisconsin Society by Milo Quaife. An Iowa native with a University of Chicago Ph.D., Quaife rivaled Thwaites's energy and improved on his editorial standards, but Quaife was uneasy in Madison's political community and with the membership of the Wisconsin Historical Society. After a frustrating decade he left for the Burton Historical Collection in the Detroit Public Library. There he continued to edit manuscripts and reprints, wrote numerous books and articles, and edited the *Mississippi Valley Historical Review*, demonstrating again the intimate connection between popular and professional history in the Midwest. Fostering history readable by the public and scholars alike, Quaife pushed the Midwest as a region but was also drawn to the newer West and stood firm against eastern biases. The promising appointment of Joseph Schafer as Quaife's successor at the Wisconsin Society also left something to be desired. A native son and Turner disciple, Schafer came with a strikingly original vision, the "Wisconsin Domesday" proposal, which called for a multivolume cooperative effort to evaluate the contributions of common people in Wisconsin's development. As the University of Oregon historian Richard Maxwell Brown has commented, the Domesday study was far ahead of its times, and in the 1920s and 1930s it found little support.

If they sometimes enjoyed lesser reputations, other state societies also reflected the varying lines of citizens' history. The Kansas State Historical Society, for example, was chartered as a private organization in 1875. In 1879 it became the state's official agent for history but for years functioned as a sister institution to Kansas's almost rabidly patriotic Grand Army of the Republic (GAR), which, like its counterparts elsewhere, was a pressure group composed of Civil War veterans. Challenged, like other post–Civil War state societies, to redefine the position of state loyalties, the Kansas Society was undeviatingly committed to the grandness of Kansas, frankly promotional, thoroughly interested in beginnings, successful in collecting Kansas newspapers, wild about heroes, artifacts, sites, trails, and Indian wars, and willing to bend the truth for good cause. Catching its spirit precisely was Carl Becker's early essay: "The Kansas spirit is the American spirit double distilled. It is a new grafted product of American individualism, American idealism, American intolerance. Kansas is America in microcosm. . . . Within

Framing Monument Valley's distinctive rock formations through the windows of a viewing tower, the photographer Skeet McAuley ironically comments on a place made familiar through countless western films. If the Monument Valley of popular westerns is locked forever in a particular moment of the 19th century, this is a more dynamic site. Its history reaches into the past of "180 million years old" dinosaur track preserved at the lower left and extends into the present of the young Navajo worker who cleans the windows to clarify our view.

Skeet McAuley (b. 1951). Navajo Window Washer, Monument Valley Tribal Park, Arizona. Type C print, 1984. © 1993 Skeet McAuley/Swanstock, Tucson, Arizona.

Directly addressing the romantic image of Native Americans preserved in earlier paintings and photographs, Fritz Scholder depicts Indian subjects who defiantly and humorously refuse to dress or behave in stereotypical ways.

Fritz Scholder (b. 1937). Super Indian No. 2. Oil on canvas, 1972. Courtesy of Nancy and Richard Bloch.

With bleached bones floating over an arid landscape, Georgia O'Keeffe evoked the vast space and clear light of the south-western desert. Though she worked in a modern style that distinguished her from many of her predecessors, she too celebrated the seductive romance of the West. "From the faraway nearby," it was an exotic but accessible place in which one could find physical beauty and psychological freedom.

Georgia O'Keeffe (1887–1986). From the Faraway Nearby. Oil on canvas, 1937 © 1994 The Georgia O'Keeffe Foundation/Artists Rights Society (ARS), New York. Copyright © 1984/88 By The Metropolitan Museum of Art. The Alfred Stieglitz Collection, 1959, (59.204.2). The Metropolitan Museum of Art, New York.

INTERPRETATION:
A Land of Myth and Memory

◆

The romance of the West has remained a central theme for artists in the twentieth century. For some, the romance survives in the vast landscapes of the contemporary West. For others, it exists only in myth and memory, a subject to be mourned with regret or mocked with gentle irony.

Once lauded as a realist, Frederic Remington turned to increasingly moody evocations of the West toward the end of his life. Using a looser, more impressionistic painting style, he suggested that his ever-popular cowboy subjects were actually "ghosts of the past," historical figures more compelling in myth than reality.

Frederic Remington (1861–1909). Ghosts of the Past. Oil on canvas, ca. 1908. Gift of The Coe Foundation, Buffalo Bill Historical Center, Cody, Wyoming.

its borders Americanism, pure and undefiled, has a new lease of life. It is the mission of this self-selected people to see to it that it does not perish from off the earth. The light on the altar, however neglected elsewhere must ever be replenished in Kansas."

First occupying a single showcase, the Kansas Society collections soon filled two rooms in the state capitol, then exploded to most of the basement as records and memorabilia accumulated, including a vile of Dead Sea water and a baby crocodile. In 1909 as the society threatened to take over an entire wing of the statehouse, the legislature authorized a magnificent five-story building. Dedicated in 1914 before twenty-five thousand cheering partisans, half of whom rolled into Topeka on chartered trains, the Memorial Building was shared with the GAR, which mercifully was a diminishing operation by this time. Several early directors were journalists noted for their Kansas propaganda but innocent of training in historical method. One, like Hubert Howe Bancroft, was said to have published works written largely by his subordinates. But the society flourished, making real contributions. Fulfilling its mandate to create a sense of community among a restless people, it proceeded from history dealing with classic, regionwide western themes to studies increasingly confined to the state itself in recent decades. With far-flung programs, a popular journal, respected directors, and a large membership, the modern society is mindful of the work of involved university professionals including James C. Malin's innovative locally based environmental studies, the history-from-the-bottom-up and for-the-sake-of-history-only of George L. Anderson, and the sound work of Homer E. Socolofsky and others. Well might Becker take comfort that the "light on the altar" is still "replenished."

In New Mexico, social and natural conditions made for a rich cultural texture that came to focus in the state historical society. Beginning with Native Americans and the conquistadores and extending through Zebulon Pike, the Mexican War, Spanish land grants, range wars, reclamation, and Los Alamos, a wide variety of writers and scholars worked what the western writer Wallace Stegner called the "broad borderlands of history." In their diversity they greatly enhanced state history, but they also modified its character, giving voice to points of view that went far beyond the conventions of academic professionals and hewed close to romantic western traditions.

Writers with national stature congregated at Taos in the years around 1900. More fully in the regionalist tradition were promoters such as the troubadour-poet Charles F. Lummis who was bent on bringing the entire Southwest to light. Beginning with Ralph Emerson Twitchell and moving through Harvey Fergusson, Paul Horgan, and, with shifting emphasis, Eleanor Adams, Myra Ellen Jenkins, Marc Simmons, and John Kessel, state historians described New Mexico's past, sometimes voluminously, often gracefully. Working from the record of American conquest and from rich Spanish archives, they came close to making the history of New Mexico and its related regions the quintessential western romance.

Meanwhile anthropologists and archaeologists called for "cooperative effort in all fields of history" and employed science as history's "lengthening arm." Known for their color and energy, they operated from bases in Washington, D.C., reveled in fieldwork at New Mexico's pueblos and prehistoric sites, and boasted worldwide connections. The live-in "Zuni" Frank Hamilton Cushing discomfited historians with his conviction that

Interest in local events and nostalgia for the imagined grandeur of the 19th-century past inspired a tradition of popular historical pageants in western communities that continues to the present.

Noel Photo Studio. West on the Lolo Trail, Lewiston, Idaho. *Photograph, 1936. National Museum of American History, Division of Community Life, Washington, D.C.*

the observable present could be used as historical evidence. Adolph Bandelier was considered an "anthropologist in the minds of historians and [a] historian in the minds of anthropologists," as the University of Arizona anthropologist Bernard Fontana has pointed out. And Edgar Lee Hewett was a globe-roaming, money-finagling, site-digging Museum of New Mexico director of almost heroic stature. Together they did much to establish the field of southwestern archaeology. They also complicated and enlivened the career of the New Mexico Historical Society and multiplied the voices of western history.

Regionalism and the Popular Impulse

Implicit in this essay and particularly relevant to the discussion of state history are questions of regionalism. It is a commonplace that the West itself is a region. No less obvious is the fact that it is composed of lesser regions that themselves divide into subregions. All of them vary with time and overlap according to the uses to which they are put. Turner's thesis takes, of course, a regional approach. As a means of understanding, regionalism is closely related to geography but is equally the product of how people identify with place and how one place affects another. Like nationalism, it rises from what Hans Kohn, a historian of Russian imperialism, called "the immense power of habitude" and, among other things, expresses itself in pride, in a sense of self-worth, and in group cohesiveness.

During much of the twentieth century, regionalism attracted wide attention. By extending and adapting a 1983 statement on "The New Regionalism in America" by Richard Maxwell Brown, we can divide western regionalism into three phases. First was the epic regionalism of the open or undifferentiated West that ended about 1890. Second were the six decades after 1890 during which what may be called sentimental and reform regionalism sought historiographic as well as political and economic redress for eastern domination. And third, after a post–World War II hiatus of perhaps three decades, during which regionalism's differentiations were obscured by an explosion of global, strategic, demographic, cultural, and environmental change, came a time of resurgent regionalism as historians sorted through the fallout.

To understand the early era of undifferentiated regionalism, we should recall that with the exception of California and Texas, all western states were territories before they were states. Before that, they had been Indian country, contested empire, unorganized territory, or simply part of the unknown. Across the entirety of this undifferentiated region moved the epic forces of conquest that inspired Prescott and Parkman and thrilled the denizens of the early historical society in Kansas. Wildness, discovery, westward expansion, the fur trade, transportation, and violent conquest—all predated the organization of states. Treated as history, they reached beyond state bounds to become epic regional themes. Vastly broadening the appeal of place, they brought common interests to all state historians, legitimated local studies for native-bred professional scholars, and made regionalists of them all.

Nostalgia for the epic adventures of the nineteenth century continued to dominate western regionalism during the first decades of the twentieth. Historians perpetuated H. H. Bancroft's romantic narrative style, emulated Thwaites and Quaife in publishing documents and new editions of rare books, and waffled between local promotion and a Turner-like mix of sentiment, radicalism, and analysis. In treating the past, they were also joined by people with a wide range of other interests, as we have seen in New Mexico.

Strong since the 1890s, regionalism's reformist mood intensified after 1918. The shock of war, industrial complexity, and depression transformed the disposition of many from the inward-looking and self-congratulatory doctrines of Turner to biting protest against things local, producing an indictment of rural isolationist America. The attack was especially virulent against the West, against the frontier, and against ideas and values associated with them. The western response sometimes added defensive elements to reformism as support formed behind insurgents and defenders. Illustrative were Van Wyck Brooks's despairing critique of the West in *The Ordeal of Mark Twain* (1920) and the spirited defense of Bernard DeVoto in *Mark Twain's America* (1932).

From as early as 1902, reform regionalism had taken an administrative turn in the rise of conservation and reclamation. Accelerating through the enlarged homestead and national park legislation of the Progressive Era, administrative regionalism came to its full reform expression in the New Deal. Relevant to the West's evolving historiography were the Public Records Survey and the Federal Writers' Project (FWP). Conceived as relief measures as well as a means of bolstering sagging pride, the Records and Writers' projects gave on-the-job historical training to thousands of writers and would-be writers in programs organized in state projects.

The effect on western historiography was dramatic. As Jerre Mangione explained in *The Dream and the Deal* (1972), the radical disposition of some prominent FWP figures brought heavy political fire. But influenced by gentler New Deal reformism, rank and filers of the western relief projects often shared popular views and exerted what was in the main a moderate if indeed not a conservative influence, giving the earlier romantic optimism of western regionalism a new lease on life as the New Deal sought to bolster self-confidence. Short-term outcomes for the West included the project's flagship undertaking, the *State Guide* series, as well as distinguished collecting and records survey programs, the promotion of citizen history, and a high interest among publishers and readers.

A longer-term outcome was the influence on a generation of regional historians whose careers were shaped by the project's populistic outlook and reform spirit. Western academics upon whose lives the FWP left a lasting imprint included George P. Hammond, state supervisor for the New Mexico writers' project, UNM professor of history, and longtime director of the Bancroft Library at the University of California. Supervisor of the Massachusetts state project was Ray A. Billington, later history professor at Northwestern University, author of the prestigious textbook *Westward Expansion* (1949), and research director at the privately endowed Huntington Library of San Marino, California. A professional in the broadest sense, Billington restructured and updated Turner in a brilliant and extended interpretive effort, helped transform the regionally oriented Mississippi Valley Historical Association into the more professional Organization of American Historians, held out for mixing buffs and professionals in the newly organized Western History Association, and maintained close contact with a wide range of citizen historians and publishers.

Suggestive of the FWP's influence beyond history was Harold Merriman, the Montana supervisor and English Department chairman at the University of Montana, who drew Pacific Northwest regionalists around him. In Arizona, the artist-illustrator, yarn-spinning free-lancer Ross Santee brought a contagious cowboy enthusiasm to the project, an enthusiasm that he continued to indulge throughout his long life. Idaho's state supervisor, the curmudgeon novelist Vardis Fisher, infuriated the project's Washington office but delighted westerners when he ignored directives and threats, and evaded efforts at physical restraint, to publish the *Idaho Guide* (January 1937) ahead of the guide for Washington, D.C., as well as those slated for powerful eastern states.

A Utah-related case may be used to illustrate the strengths and limitations of the FWP's influence on regional writing, highlighting the extending ripples cast by the project on the one hand and on the other pointing out that it provided no lasting center of gravity. The key figure was the Utah supervisor Dale Morgan, whose youthful energies surged beyond the immediate objectives of the project to a distinguished personal career in fur trade, western trails and maps, and Utah-Mormon history. Perhaps his best-known book was *Jedediah Smith and the Opening of the West* (1953). Without formal training in history, Morgan eschewed historical theories including Turner's. Facts, which he pursued with dogged determination, were the energizing thrust of his historical form. Yet, as Billington noted, Morgan "could write magnificently," combining "word sense with exactness of expression" and an intuitive grasp of history with impeccable scholarship. He also took the New Deal mandate to promote regional history as a continuing personal mission, placing himself at the center of a group of what may be described as Utah-Mormon reform regionalists.

Squarely in the reform tradition was the Utah-born pundit, editor, and historian Bernard DeVoto. He was known nationally for his shrill editorials in *Harper's*, for his "plundered province" approach to western exploitation, and for the neoromanticism of his great trilogy on the West: *The Year of Decision, 1846* (1943), *Across the Wide Missouri* (1947), and *The Course of Empire* (1952). Back home in Utah, he indulged his penchant for pulling "shirt-tails out and setting them on fire," issued emancipation proclamations

against economic and religious suppression, debated issues of Mormon history with Morgan and others, and helped aspiring Utah writers gain access to publishers. Equally in the reform tradition were several remarkable women, including Joseph Smith's biographer Fawn Brodie, Mountain Meadows Massacre historian Juanita Brooks, and novelist of polygamy Maureen Whipple, who were sustained by the tireless Morgan as they explored previously suppressed topics from personal situations largely beyond the reach of academic professionals. With scholarly credentials in the social sciences were Nels Anderson, Lowry Nelson, and Thomas O'Dea, who addressed Mormon themes from sociological perspectives. In a similar form was the historical geographer Donald Meinig who, in a benchmark article published while he was at the University of Utah, defined the Mormon cultural area as a significant western subregion. With creative writers, Morgan, who had majored in literature, maintained even closer touch, making vital contributions to the careers of William Mulder, Ray B. West, and Wallace Stegner, all of whom did significant histories in the reformist mood including Stegner's *Mormon Country*, a vastly underappreciated 1940s portrait of Utah, and his better-known *Beyond the Hundredth Meridian: John Wesley Powell and the Second Opening of the West* (1954). For Utah free-lancers, Morgan was a font of inspiration, a lexicon of information, and occasionally a ghostwriter. Although it has been little appreciated, this group and others who shared the FWP's regional reformism came close to being the established voice of Utah-Mormon history against which the so-called New Mormon History took its measure after 1965.

Although the Utah reform regionalists did impressive work, the ties that bound them slowly relaxed. The Writers' Project passed from the scene as World War II began. The exceptionalist spirit of regionalism, which they embraced wholeheartedly, seemed increasingly anachronistic in the post–World War II time of global crisis. As free-lance historians, they had no students to applaud them and perpetuate their work. Few enjoyed biographers, although Stegner's *The Uneasy Chair: A Biography of Bernard*

Artists as well as writers received funds from the WPA programs that supported the documentation of regional history. Presented in post offices and other public buildings throughout the West, their paintings and murals generally depicted western history as the story of the triumph of the common man.

Everett C. Thorpe (1907–83). Early and Modern Provo. Oil on canvas (study for mural in the Federal Building, Provo, Utah), 1940. Courtesy of Doris B. Thorpe.

DeVoto (1974) is perhaps the best biography done on a Utahn. Death and other interests took them. DeVoto died in 1955. Little recognized at home, Morgan turned, about the same time, to more broadly regional themes at the Bancroft Library. He died in 1971. Social scientists and literature professors gravitated to other states and to professionally focused careers. Stegner's work assumed an increasingly literary turn, although, with a more regionally redefined western historiography taking form, he received the coveted Western History Prize in 1990. He continued to exert widespread influence on the environmental movement until his death in 1993. As the group aged, the thrust and nature of its work kept pace with the West's diminishing sense of its own exceptionalism. It was a process reenacted with variation throughout the region.

A New Regionalism: Paradoxes of Change, Success, and Identity

With these regional influences in mind we may return to the development of western history as a scholarly profession. In important ways scholarly historians were more subject to changing moods and interests than either the public or the more publicly attentive regionalists. Change among them has been explained by the University of California historian John D. Hicks and elaborated by the University of New Mexico professor Gerald Nash as resting on generational rhythms. Attention to successive generations helps explain the nature of the tensions through which western history was working.

From 1890 to 1920, as we have seen, was the era of the Turnerian synthesis. Encouraged by a responsive public, a small and homogeneous cohort of professional historians (two or three hundred strong at the most) hailed the frontier as "an ineradicable influence" for good. Defining it as the engine that powered the rise of an exceptional people, they lamented the frontier's closing, rejected European antecedents, excluded minorities, and ignored environmental costs. Bred to mounting complexity and disillusioned by the rise of industrial urbanism, world wars (hot and cold), the Communist revolution, the depression, and environmental woes, the generations that followed became increasingly pessimistic, questioned the role of the frontier, or, indeed, saw it as a destructive force. According to Richard Hofstadter's *The Progressive Historians* (1968), the very vagueness, impressionism, and overstatement that had given Turnerian doctrines "their plasticity and hence their broad acceptance" came under heavy attack in the decades after Turner's death in 1932. Also increasingly outmoded were his "assumptions about cultural transmission," his view of the West as "safety valve," and the "crippling isolationist implications" his theory had for foreign policy.

Temporarily checked by the affluence and professional opportunity of the years after 1945, pessimism among historians resurged sharply during and after the Vietnam conflict. Western history professionals, who by then numbered perhaps two thousand, hailed from a wide variety of backgrounds. Western history shifted its center of gravity to the Far West, setting up the Western History Association (1961) as the Mississippi Valley Historical Association became the Organization of American Historians (1965), and traditionalists refined nineteenth-century themes and worked to restructure Turner. In time many came to see the West as defunct, its history as passé, and the people attracted to its standard as second rank.

Even in the era of Turner's greatest ascendance there had been alternate voices.

Some, like Charles Beard and Arthur M. Schlesinger, Sr., respectively economic and urban scholars, foreshadowed a move away from Turner and the West. Among the founders of what the historiographers Rodman Paul and Michael Malone have termed the "classic tradition in western historiography," a few "operated outside the Turnerian nexus."

Among the earliest of these was Herbert Eugene Bolton, who "almost singlehandedly opened up and defined" the Spanish Borderlands as a "separate field of historical study." Born not many miles from Turner in Wisconsin in 1870, Bolton worked his way through college, studied under Turner, took a Ph.D. at the University of Pennsylvania, and by 1901 developed an interest in the northern frontiers of New Spain as a junior professor at the University of Texas. He moved first to Stanford and then to the University of California, his career taking on characteristics that became the hallmarks of his own work and that of his numerous followers. Not only did his interest in the Borderlands break with significant elements of the frontier thesis, but in his personal publications he went far toward doing for the Spanish what Parkman had done for the French (he once called it "Parkmanizing" the Spanish). Bolton also became the recognized father of research in Mexico's Spanish archives. Like Thwaites at the Wisconsin Historical Society, Bolton integrated a great collection of western Americana into scholarly research at the Bancroft Library, which he directed for many years after 1916. Also like Thwaites, he was one of western history's great editors, producing among other works *Anza's California Expeditions*, 5 vols. (1930), *Historical Memoirs of California, by Francisco Palou, O.F.M. . . .*, 4 vols. (1926), and *Kino's Historical Memoir of Pimeria Alta . . .*, 2 vols. (1919). He also inspired many of his students as editors. In his determination to put the record in context, he helped set two generations of western historians at work along the trails and through the historic districts as they undertook to make a coherent picture from fieldwork and the surviving records. His students were legion. He taught undergraduates by the thousands and directed the graduate work of some 300 M.A. students and 105 Ph.D.'s.

Nevertheless, Bolton was not universally acclaimed. A few saw him as little more than an antiquarian. He collected data and told its story, but he often stopped short of analysis and generalization. Responding to his work overall and especially to his 1932 address "The Epic of Greater America," other commentators found an unsound Pan-Americanism. Among others, John Francis Bannon and David J. Langrum have pointed out that defenders argued that he neither "ignored nor deprecated analysis or synthesis" but that like H. H. Bancroft before him, and many of his contemporaries, he "felt it was the job of" his generation "to furnish the facts." In sum, Bolton offered an alternative to Turner, yet he maintained much of the same spirit. More than Turner himself, he prolonged the West's taste for fact-loaded narrative history.

Radically different in style and in how he interacted with the scholarly profession and the public was Walter Prescott Webb. Always something of an outsider and a determined provincial, Webb was raised in a hand-to-mouth frontier existence at the southwestern edge of the Great Plains. After a delayed start he proceeded into history through a succession of windfalls and rebuffs. Throughout his career he remained at the University of Texas, where he indulged cross-disciplinary tastes and an instinct for advocacy and reform. Exposed early to "elements of late nineteenth-century social and cultural theory," Webb saw things in terms of a pronounced geographic determinism. However, he was influenced not by Turner but by Lindley Miller Keasbey, a mentor at the University of Texas, who had drawn from some of the same social science theoreticians. Profoundly aware of his own identity and less grounded in the historical method than most academic historians, Webb intuitively worked toward striking insights. These he supported with data gathered from a range of sources and personal observation. At its best, Webb's writing achieved a "feel of authenticity, a confidence and conviction" that, the historiographer Elliott West has said, reached beyond "thought to experience." He took criticism personally and, rather than bow to it, walked out on his Ph.D. program at the University of Chicago. Perhaps because of this experience he developed a "jaundiced view" of professional historians.

It is not surprising that Webb also broke from the crowd in his writing. Nowhere was this more apparent than in his first and perhaps greatest work, *The Great Plains* (1931). A compelling regional portrait that went beyond Turner in the forthrightness of its environmental determinism, it nevertheless served as a western fortification for Turner, in effect, applying exceptionalist doctrines to the very heartland of the West at a time when their influence was under attack elsewhere. Sharply criticized for *The Great Plains*'s tendency to proceed from intuition to evidence, Webb took refuge in the personal aspects of his approach and angrily refused to revise his book.

Nevertheless, the burden of Webb's message changed sharply over the years. Pausing along the way to celebrate the Texas Ranger and work up a handbook of Texas history, and always maintaining an old-boy touch with Texas, Webb shifted in mood from celebration to protest and finally to strident warning. The patent reform regionalism of *Divided We Stand: The Crisis of a Frontierless Democracy* (1935) lamented the ironies and injustices that made the West and South tributary to the Northeast. *The Great Frontier* (1952) detected the early warning signals of global disaster in the collapse of the "400 year boom" that had shaped the liberal tradition. *Divided We Stand* and *The Great Frontier* assailed distant enemies, but in "The American West: Perpetual Mirage," *Harper's Magazine* (1957), Webb indicted his own kind. Making a master key of aridity, he cried out against the thoughtless exploitation that was sweeping the West, bringing an avalanche of protest upon him.

Each of Webb's non-Texas works ran in important respects against the grain. Each was a statement in reform regionalism, and each was an act of scholarly independence. His later career might be said to reflect a spirit something like the despair of Mark Twain, and there can be no doubt that Webb suffered a loss of innocence. Change, however, brought more of sobriety and responsibility, perhaps even more of prophecy, than of despair. Indeed, it may be said that Webb personified both the strengths and the weaknesses of western history's play-off between the provincial influences of popular taste and the sophistication of professional method. He bored or infuriated many professional historians, but he continued to be heard. Important is the fact that in recognizing a vital interplay between region and globe and in shifting from the environmentalism of exceptionalism to the environmentalism of responsibility, Webb pointed the way for western history to make the transition from the buoyant and confident exceptionalisms of youth to maturity's hard responsibilities.

Serving to perpetuate and to broaden western history at a moment of otherwise narrowing interest was the innovative work of Henry Nash Smith in *Virgin Land: The American West as Symbol and Myth* (1950). Texas-born, and trained in cultural and literary criticism, Smith was overtly influenced by the Harvard Turnerian Frederick Merk's "richly factual" treatment of the "West's importance to any understanding of America" and was covertly disposed to many of Turner's ideas, as well as possessing a Turner-like penchant for bold analysis and overstated rhetoric. Concerned with the "ways that regional and cultural identity are shaped" and put off by what Princeton English Professor Lee Clark Mitchell describes as "the intellectual Balkanization that fractured mainstream scholarship," Smith "melded genres"—history and literature—to force an awareness that history is made as well as experienced. "As much an account of imagery and desire as of actual topographies or real events," history rested "upon what people thought they were doing as much as on what they actually had done." Drawing from cultural sources "'high' and 'low,'" Smith portrayed the West not simply as "a separate region of unique events and idiosyncratic assumptions, but as an essential component of . . . [the] national consciousness." Out of his work came a clearer understanding of how "popular beliefs, common assumptions, and government policies" coalesced in the form of symbols and images to become both self-definition and self-fulfilling prophecy for the western experience.

Virgin Land undertook to illuminate the national experience, yet it focused on the West and pertained primarily to the epic themes of conquest, heroic action, and agrarian development with which the westward movement had been identified. On the one hand, it clearly located the West in the mainstream of American history. On the other, it enlivened western history and offered a method by which it could be incorporated in the intellectual studies that were replacing the earlier emphasis on narrative and event-oriented history. *Virgin Land*, like *The Great Plains* and the Borderland studies, was a clear plus for western history, moving in the direction of relevance and broadened spectrums but perpetuating its earlier impetus.

The decades that followed 1950 were a paradoxical period for western history. In many respects it was a productive time, rich with creative energy and sound in the work accomplished. Yet, it was beset with ambiguity and pessimism, and for years its practitioners drifted without new direction in a sea of growing complexity. By the mid-1980s an awakening in regional interests was afoot among scholars and writers who had more than a little in common with the regionalists of the 1940s. This was apparent across a broad disciplinary spectrum, including novelists, journalists, and social scientists who were sensitive to classic western themes and to continuing Turnerian influences, especially as modified by the myth-and-symbol approach of Henry Nash Smith and his followers.

Nearer the traditional heart of western history was the work of a large number of mid- to late-twentieth-century historians who subjected the "individual topics" that made up the epic story of the nineteenth-century West to detailed and often brilliant examination. Considering this work, the historiographers Rodman Paul and Michael Malone called attention to solid progress in such classic fields as grazing, mining, agriculture, territorial history, Mormon history, comparative frontiers, and urban studies. Going further, others scholars broke with Anglo-American traditionalism to inquire into the role of Native Americans, women, and people of other national

The increasing academic attention paid to the historical experiences of ethnic groups in the West is paralleled in the emergence of new art forms depicting western history from the perspective of different cultural groups.

Barbara Carrasco (b. 1955). L.A. History, A Mexican Perspective. Acrylic on masonite, 1981. Courtesy of the artist.

backgrounds. Those concerned with women amended classic fields and worked new ground but initially did so in the nineteenth-century context. With newly developed quantitative techniques, ethnic groups were also considered, frequently in nineteenth-century settings but, in the case of southeastern Europeans and Hispanics, increasingly as manifestations of the twentieth century. Scattered pockets "of recent western history" were also worked vigorously, "among them Populism and the Progressives, conservation, reclamation," and preservation.

For decades the vitality and diversity of this work did surprisingly little to enhance western history as a field. Indeed to some it seemed only to cast further doubt on Turner's assumptions and to point up the inaccuracy and irrelevancies of the romantic tradition and the frontier model. Looking beyond the use of history as celebration, which had moved so many earlier historians, this detailed examination turned to a variety of new methodological and thematic alliances that modified and in many cases weakened their connections with the West.

Both the extent of this scholarship and the centrifugal forces acting upon it were related to the growing numbers of professional historians in the post–World War II years. With college enrollment stimulated by the GI Bill, baby boomers, and a series of Pacific wars, western universities fairly exploded in size. In the late 1940s and 1950s, history departments grew dramatically as Ph.D.'s pouring from distinguished universities were hired. Senior scholars, many of whom had local ties, launched new graduate programs in western history, and libraries vigorously competed for western materials as university after university sought to produce and market Ph.D.'s.

Just as this production line was put in place, markets collapsed. In the post-Vietnam climate, history enrollments diminished, and student interest shifted abruptly. The ensuing job crunch was catastrophic for overstocked history Ph.D.'s generally but was especially critical for graduates coming from institutions with recently founded western history programs, for whom head-to-head competition with candidates from established institutions added to the dilemma of finding employment even in public history and other fields outside the academy. As curricula broadened and faculties became increasingly national, western history's influence on departmental policy slipped sharply, leading old-timers to lament "The Insignificance of the Frontier" with John Caughey, longtime editor of the *Pacific Historical Review*.

While post–World War II momentum was still high, the Western History Association (WHA) had been organized in 1961 with a membership of some three thousand professors, writers, publishers, book collectors, public historians, archivists, and friends of the West. Under the editorship of Russell Mortensen, formerly director of the Utah Historical Society and director of the University of Utah Press, and Gregory Crampton, a Bolton Ph.D. at Utah, the WHA launched the *American West* in 1964. It was hoped that the lavishly illustrated, hybridized journal would help gather the WHA's variegated membership within a single loop and brand it as a popular movement. In a painful exhibition of centrifugal forces at work, WHA membership diminished, and surviving members lived with growing tension, yet the magazine quickly built a subscription list that increased from thirty thousand in the mid-1960s to more than one hundred thousand in the early 1980s. The *American West* first shook off the University of Utah and ultimately the WHA to become by the mid-1980s a glossy, environmentally sensitive, wide-circulation periodical of western life and tours—with only the thinnest, most commercialized veneer of western history. In 1970 the WHA responded to proposals coming from George Ellsworth and Leonard Arrington of Utah State University to set up the *Western Historical Quarterly*, which soon became a respected scholarly journal but made only an occasional bow in the direction of popular interests and did little to reverse tension and attrition in WHA membership.

Professional loyalists called for various fixes. Two proposals merit attention here. At first hearing, Caughey's "Insignificance of the Frontier" statement had a pessimistic ring indeed, but his "larger proposition" was positive and hopeful. Western history would always be "bobtailed and insufficient," he warned, unable to address the problems of the present, much less the future, unless it broke from its "self-imposed imprisonment in the early and antique West" into the twentieth century. A call for twentieth-century awareness made by the University of California professor John D. Hicks as early as the 1930s and 1940s was picked up and amplified by many, including Hicks's student Gerald Nash of the University of New Mexico. Publishing a useful twentieth-century text in 1974, Nash greatly facilitated course work in the twentieth-century history of the West. Simultaneously, graduate studies focusing on the recent past multiplied as the body of twentieth-century records grew.

Another thoughtful response to western history's malaise came from the University of Oregon historian Earl Pomeroy. California-born Pomeroy, like Caughey and Nash, was a UC Berkeley student during the high tide of the great triumvirate of Paxson, Bolton, and Hicks. Like Caughey and Nash, Pomeroy entertained a keen interest in the twentieth-century West, but Pomeroy went well beyond them, offering a larger critique and proposing shifts that would enable western historians to break out of the "self-imposed" constraints Caughey had described. Teaching at Wisconsin, the University of

North Carolina, and Ohio State during the 1940s, Pomeroy published books of lasting value on territorial government and America's dependencies in the Pacific. Later he moved to the University of Oregon, where in the 1950s and 1960s he issued a succession of important historiographic articles.

With the softer touch of one working from within, Pomeroy directed heavy criticism against western history yet paid homage to its early greats. Turner and H. H. Bancroft "sold," he declared, each after his own fashion, "the one as idea, the other as mass, as shelf space—to a public" ready to buy. As time demonstrated, the frontier idea—Turner's "environmental radicalism," Pomeroy called it—was oversold to generations of western historians. Failing to follow Turner in his "larger qualities: his concern for both analysis and synthesis, his effective English style, and the keenness of his mind," many "apostles" became more "orthodox" in their commitment to the frontier thesis than "the prophet" himself, their outlook becoming increasingly restricted as his orthodoxies became outdated. "By stressing differences rather than similarities, by offering escape rather than solution, by celebrating those aspects of the past that seemed least like the present, or least like other parts of the country," Pomeroy told his colleagues, they had been entrapped by the "dead past" of which Turner himself had repeatedly warned. They had failed, in effect, to let "conditions uppermost in their own time" lead them to write "history anew." Working from the large body of Turner criticism that had accumulated by the 1950s but tying his indictment to a call for constructive change, Pomeroy found particular fault with western history's rejection of what was continuous, similar, and comparable in favor of the discontinuities of space and time implicit in the "closed frontier" idea and in the West's strong regional identification. Also at fault were western history's preference for the romantic and heroic over the analytical, its infatuation with Turner's pastoral succession, its short-shrift treatment of cities, and its tendency to exalt the role of the individual at the expense of the territorial system, the federal government, and institutions generally.

Pomeroy's essays posed a significant challenge, not merely to western historians but to himself as well. Fortunately his subsequent books, especially *The Pacific Slope: A History of California, Oregon, Washington, Idaho, Utah, and Nevada* (1965), validated his right to speak. This work was a model of western history, the kind Pomeroy had been calling for. Stressing the interaction of the old and the new, the importance of social, political, and economic ties, the power of the metropolis, limits and growth, and environmental change, it was a masterwork of analysis and synthesis. Rich with insight and invitation to further work, it fully merited Yale westernist Howard Lamar's 1977 characterization as "easily the most complex and sophisticated history of the American West."

Among other things, *The Pacific Slope* was an expression of historical professionalism. A response to the issues of the twentieth century, it broke sharply with the kind of history that Pomeroy had inveighed against at various times as "atavistic," "antiquarian," or "accumulative rather than interpretive." Clearly he sought "solutions" to the issues of the era, rather than "escape." In many respects it was a rejection of the "multiple interest" formula that lay behind the organization of the WHA—a prime example of western history as a formal and sophisticated part of American history. Yet in dealing with the Pacific Slope, it exhibited an exemplary kind of regional connection.

The New Western History and the Quest for Relevance

In short Pomeroy was beginning to define a new and more interpretive point of view for western history. By the mid-1980s his call for analysis and relevance asserted itself in what was increasingly called the "new western history." "Thundering out of New Haven," as the cowboy fictionalist Larry McMurtry described it, the new western history was indeed deeply influenced by broader forces, including Yale's Howard Lamar and numerous other eastern historians and movements, but it also drew from influences from within western history. In one sense the movement experienced a "jump start" effect, as the large body of sound work in individual subfields of the Old West finally assumed the critical mass and momentum necessary to create a dynamic of its own. But beyond this accumulating body of detailed studies, the new western history was also the work of a number of young professionals, many of whom were moved by a passionate concern for late-twentieth-century issues, to which they applied widely varying interests and methodological approaches. To them, relevance and currency were necessary attributes. Most rejected the vagueness of moving frontiers for the physical West that lay beyond the hundredth meridian yet insisted that the western experience be studied in relation to larger national and global issues, an approach that accommodated discussion of the economic forces, twentieth-century developments, and social and natural influences in which they were interested. As expounded in the work of some, the new western history was sharply revisionist, punctuated with anger, confident in its presentist viewpoints, and quite ready to put down the old. Others saw their break with the past in less radical terms, or as the product of a rather clearly defined evolutionary process, and happily acknowledged the continuing worth of earlier viewpoints.

Not surprisingly it was the involved revisionists who gave the movement its most recognizable form. None played a more important role than Patricia Nelson Limerick, a California native, Yale Ph.D., and University of Colorado professor. Carried to the forefront by her *Legacy of Conquest: The Unbroken Past of the American West* (1987), and a taste for the limelight, the irrepressible Limerick based her argument on a neat turn of the shopworn proposition that the romantic spirit and exceptionalist doctrines of the frontier interpretation virtually precluded any understanding of the West's role in the contemporary world. But with much greater ingenuity she moved on, representing the western experience in terms of conflict's legacy, thus bringing to the surface of western history long-suppressed themes including the roles of gender, race, class, industrialization, urbanism, the environment, global influences, and the federal government. Although she could at times be blunt, or even offhanded, in her denunciation of earlier historians, as in her rejection of Ray Billington's career, Limerick's sense of her personal past, and her recognition that relevance required professionals to search for common grounds with the public, revealed an appreciation for popular tastes in history and a conviction that dialogue between professionals and the public was a necessary aspect of history's development.

Also at the forefront of the new western history was the University of Kansas environmental historian Donald Worster. Born in California of Dust Bowl refugee parents, Worster got his Ph.D. at Yale, taught at Hawaii and Brandeis, partook heavily of the developing spirit of the environmental movement, and wrote persuasively about the international development of the science of ecology, about the Dust Bowl, and about the natural and social problems inherent in harnessing the waters of the West. But more to the point of the new western history, Worster condemned western historians for failing "to see themselves as critical intellectuals" and called for a more "penetrating view" of the past, a view freed from the "unthinking acceptance" of myths and explanations, both official and private, a view that would allow them "to discover a new regional identity and a set of loyalties more inclusive and open to diversity than we have known and more compatible with a planetwide sense of ecological responsibility." Worster's was an enlightened statement and an impassioned, almost desperate, appeal. In it were strong elements of the environmentalist mentality, including certain elitist presumptions, the zeal of a crusader, and finally, what strikes one as a conviction that progress is the product of confrontation and partisan activism rather than of scientific objectivity.

Behind the eloquent leadership of Worster and Limerick, the new western history enlarged its impact. In addition to the passion of Worster's environmentalism and the excitement of Limerick's unbroken past, others made continuing and far-reaching contributions. Multiculturalists brought the West as a field of conflict to the fore. Native American history was addressed with renewed sensitivity and breadth. In biography, writers like the gifted and versatile Robert Utley continued to deal with mythic figures, but biography dealing with Hispanics, women, and twentieth-century figures also fared well in prize competitions and commercial markets. The twentieth century came into its own as a subject of historical curiosity. Understanding of the role of women made great strides, passing quickly from stereotype and celebration to penetrating gender-related analysis. Conflict was recognized as a major western legacy. Problems of power and hierarchy were frankly addressed. Frontier and empire were related as global manifestations. Historiography boomed as western historians sought their intellectual roots. And following the examples of Turner, Webb, Smith, and people like DeVoto, Stegner, and Meinig from related fields, as well as Limerick and Worster, western historians struggled to move away from what the latter termed the "camouflage" of "dull gray prose" into the light of stimulating words.

As a field of writing, western history has taken a more relevant stance. In moving toward this position, it has sometimes lashed out against many of the values and attitudes that underlie popular interests. Yet it has attracted a large if undefined public interest, suggesting that substantial elements of the public impulse have also shifted away from a western history of congratulation, escape, and development to one of cultural and ecological responsibility. After a century in which the voices of popular interest and professional effort have sustained and reworked each other, western history again finds itself the product of widely varying voices in which popular impulse and professional responsibility continue to take new forms. Together they promise well for the future.

Bibliographic Note

Of general works let me mention only two. Ray Allen Billington and Martin Ridge's magisterial *Westward Expansion: A History of the American Frontier*, 5th ed. (New York, 1982), first published in 1949, still eloquently anchors western history in America's frontier experience. Less comprehensive but updated in spirit and pointedly concerned with the trans-Mississippi West is Richard White's readable and thought-provoking *"It's Your Misfortune and None of My Own": A New History of the American West* (Norman, 1991).

Historiographical literature about the West is abundant. Couched primarily in terms of the frontier as a broad force in American history are general bibliographies of long-standing usefulness. Included among them are Frederick Jackson Turner and Frederick Merk, *References on the History of the West* (n.p., 1922), and R.W.G. Vail, ed., *The Voice of the Old Frontier* (Philadelphia, 1949). Working from the point of view of successive frontiers but more current in character is the "selective" bibliography that has been part of each of the five editions of Billington and Ridge's *Westward Expansion*. Impressive individually, Billington's bibliographies are even more useful cumulatively, since each new edition pares down the older listing of monographic literature to bring the current work up-to-date. Also serving to maintain the broader role of the frontier in American history are biographical works about frontier historians. For example, see Marcus Cunliffe and Robin W. Winks, ed., *Pastmasters: Some Essays on American Historians* (New York, 1969), which includes essays on Francis Parkman, Frederick Jackson Turner, and Vernon Louis Parrington, names closely associated with frontier history. Ray A. Billington, comp., *Allan Nevins on History* (New York, 1975), offers Nevins's views on Parkman, Turner, and George Bancroft. Clifford Lord, ed., *Keepers of the Past* (Chapel Hill, 1967), presents excellent biographical sketches dealing with the contributions made to state historical agencies by the western historians Lyman C. Draper, Reuben Gold Thwaites, and Edgar Lee Hewett.

Although the frontier idea remains strong and earlier Wests still attract much interest, recent historiographies tend more to the Far West. A useful beginning tool is Rodman W. Paul and Richard W. Etulain, comps., *The Frontier and the American West* (Arlington Heights, Ill., 1977), whose 2,973 entries, although true to the dualism of its title, give earlier frontiers short shrift in comparison to the West as trans-Mississippi region. In Michael P. Malone, ed., *Historians and the American West* (Lincoln, 1983), the editor's introduction and seventeen chapters authored by specialists tie strongly to today's West, yet in chapters dealing with Native Americans, "manifest destiny," and exploration, it too extends to earlier Wests. With a strong twentieth-century focus, Gerald D. Nash, *Creating the West: Historical Interpretations, 1890–1990* (Albuquerque, 1991), follows chronology to emphasize the West of recent times. Without targeting questions of West as region or as frontier, Roger Nichols, ed., *American Frontier and Western Issues: A Historiographical Review* (Westport, Conn., 1986), tends more to the latter than do other works with which it is contemporary. For a wide-ranging and still useful guide to periodical literature, see Oscar O. Winther, *The Trans-Mississippi West: A Guide to Its Periodical Literature* (Bloomington, 1942), for which supplements were issued in 1961 and 1970. The "Recent Articles" and "A Dissertation List" features of the *Western Historical Quarterly* (Logan, Utah, 1970–) have made running lists available in these two categories.

Biography also provides useful historiographic reading. For those with a taste for brief encounters, the "Dedications" in each issue of *Arizona and the West* (Tucson, 1961–85) offered biographical sketches describing and often celebrating the work of deceased western historians. During its first decade (1970–79) the *Western Historical Quarterly* gave the same approach a little different twist in autobiographical essays in which historians explained their interest in western American history and described their own work. Adding to the biographical approach to western historiography are jointly authored books sketching the lives and contributions of historians. Among the most useful are John R. Wunder, ed., *Historians of the American Frontier: A Bio-Bibliographical Sourcebook* (New York, 1988), in which fifty-seven early-twentieth-century figures are treated with what might be termed sympathetic objectivity. Similar in tone but written in greater depth are the eleven essays in Richard W. Etulain, ed., *Writing Western History: Essays on Major Western Historians* (Albuquerque, 1991). Different in the fact that they make a case for the new western history are the jointly produced essays in Patricia Nelson Limerick, Clyde A. Milner II, and Charles E. Rankin, eds., *Trails: Toward a New Western History* (Lawrence, 1991).

Taken together, these historiographies provide evidence that western history continues to have many different voices, some responding to popular and professional impulses and others gravitating around the question of whether the West is frontier or region.

Chapter Twenty-two

Selling the Popular Myth

ANNE M. BUTLER

Wall Drugstore, once a shabby soda fountain shop tucked deep into the South Dakota Badlands, exudes the rugged ambience of a popular culture that embraces the American West. An out-of-the-way pharmacy on the verge of collapse in 1936, the store rocketed into economic vitality when its shopkeepers, Dorothy and Ted Hustead, tied their advertising to the environmental factor that threatened to destroy them—western aridity.

During the viciously dry summer of 1936, a promotional gimmick—offering travelers a free drink of ice water—struck Dorothy Hustead. In a burst of old-time frontier ingenuity, the Husteads used their surrounding regional drabness to capture the attention and money of passersby. A few quaintly lettered road signs, patterned after the famous Burma Shave advertisements, helped the moribund drugstore change into a merchandising bonanza. Hundreds of people, drawn by the refreshing thought of cold water, stopped for a thirst-quenching drink and stayed to purchase western wares from an ever-growing selection.

The Husteads' operation expanded with each passing year. They enlarged the facilities for their famous ice-water well and added dining rooms, home-baked goods, jewelry counters, outdoor displays, a bookstore, a western clothing shop, a museum, and a chapel. Road-weary motorists stopped for water, or breakfast, or gas, but lingered to wander from room to room, shopping for cheap western knickknacks, a ten-gallon hat, a plaster of paris Indian statue, or cowboy art painted on velvet.

Wall Drugstore is both a geographic and a commercial entry point to the American West. Those who stop now do so less out of thirst and more out of curiosity. The aggressive merchandising of a tourist-trap set in neighborly association with the nearby Dakota Badlands surprises the visitor. Over fifty years, the focus of the store shifted from the critically necessary to the completely superfluous—the mass marketing of the commercial baubles of western tourism. The customers browse through rooms of western gewgaws, souvenirs, they believe, of the "real" West. The success of Wall Drug—based on regional commercialism, national imagination, and mass marketing—mirrors much of the twentieth-century selling of the West.

The Husteads, of course, are not the sole cultivators of this boulevard view of the American West. America's western vision grew from older, deeper roots. From the very earliest expansion, the nation built its epic lore. By the nineteenth century, almost three hundred years of exploration, settlement, and human exchanges had molded a popular

For more than 60 years, Wall Drug has successfully marketed the West as a commercial commodity. On a hot summer day, more than 20,000 visitors stop at the store in Wall, South Dakota, to shop in an indoor mall populated with life-size statues of trappers, cowboys, and dance-hall women and displays of Indian jewelry, boots, and mounted big-game trophies.

Unidentified photographer. Wall Drug Mall. *Gelatin silver print. Courtesy Wall Drug, Wall, South Dakota.*

culture that drew energy from song and story, event and myth, heroes and villains. Fact and fancy swirled and merged as a national population of increasing ethnic and cultural diversity struggled for identity. One nineteenth-century character, Davy Crockett, nicely illustrates this wedding of reality and fable, truth and legend. More than 150 years after his death at the Texas Alamo, Crockett maintains his status as an American folk hero. Crockett does so because his life—in both its real and its imagined events—captured important aspects of "Americanness." His gun-and-ax beginnings as a hunter and pioneer in Tennessee marked him as a tough, self-reliant outdoorsman. Although Crockett sprang from humble stock, his elevation to the U.S. Congress in 1827 underscored his place in the era of the Jacksonian self-made man. His adventuresome, impulsive migration to Texas thrust him across frontier worlds and linked him permanently with the Far West. His 1836 death at the Alamo during the Texas revolution defined him as a champion of Anglo-style democracy and a foe of its oppressors.

In all his exploits, some embroidered by his own words, Crockett seemed always "to stand tall" and to face challenge, hardship, and even death with an admirable stoicism, his basic beliefs unshaken. Crockett, by himself and with his compatriots at the Alamo, personified American notions of what it meant to cherish freedom and oppose tyranny. He carried the heritage of the American Revolution into new territories for white America and established a model of independence and feistiness in manhood. Thus, in his own day and for generations that followed, he reminded Americans that the West, a tangible place where one stood for cherished principles, against all odds, was for and of men.

Whether these virtues accurately captured Crockett's opinions and thoughts remains unimportant. His outward actions supposedly demonstrated his inner convictions. His character conformed to a mythical code by which American men can judge themselves. The historian Paul Andrew Hutton summed up the weight that is placed on Crockett's power as a figure of the American West. "We should focus on the positive forces he symbolized. . . . It is through his spirit of unbridled democracy and bold egalitarianism that this magnificent American is best remembered." Critics of Anglo-Texan chauvinism might not agree with Hutton, but his language outlines Crockett's embodiment of the western myth, especially for men and women from an Anglo-European background.

Crockett continues his hold on the national imagination, perhaps because he represents what some Americans want to believe about the West and about themselves. No historical revelation or scholarly analysis will shake Crockett from his pedestal, for his life provides the irrefutable evidence that the West of the popular imagination embraced an epic that belonged to white American males. His feats are tightly woven into the fabric of values that many Americans think they exhibit and cherish: independence, honesty, fair play, self-reliance, loyalty, courage, justice, love of freedom. These boastful Americans assert that if the stories of the frontier, the legends of a Davy Crockett, did not happen, they should have, for these myths give foundation to a modern sense of identity.

Nonetheless, Crockett, born of an eastern forested world, is but a John the Baptist in the face of modern western popular culture, squarely positioned in the trans-Mississippi West. The Far West, with its soaring mountains, shimmering deserts, and

A Tennessee congressman turned land speculator who met his end at the Alamo in 1836, Davy Crockett helped create the image that made him an enduring symbol of popular western culture. Though he often wore formal dress to fit into polite Washington society, he adopted buckskin leggings, moccasins, and a long rifle when he posed for John Gadsby Chapman in 1834. Walt Disney likewise portrayed him as an independent and resourceful frontiersman in a popular television series of 1954–55, but unlike his historical counterpart, the TV Crockett wore a coonskin cap. The Disney show catapulted Crockett to instant celebrity status and initiated the biggest run on raccoon pelts since the 1920s.

John Gadsby Chapman (1808–89). David Crockett. Oil on canvas, 1834. Harry Ransom Humanities Research Center Art Collection, The University of Texas at Austin.

Unidentified photographer. Fess Parker as Davy Crockett. Gelatin silver print, ca. 1955. © The Walt Disney Company. The Disney Publishing Group, Burbank, California.

windswept prairies, with its raging storms, blizzards, and droughts, with its spaciousness and starkness, reconfigured the national conception of wilderness. This dramatically beautiful region—difficult for newcomers to inhabit—demanded mental adjustments. So different from the lush East—really only a codicil of Europe—the arid West came to "explain" the philosophical and psychological development of America, seemingly the most singular of nations. In the search for standards by which to define national character and temperament, Americans often attributed moral and intellectual dimensions to western physical topography and the hardships it imposed. This magical transformation of wilderness into democratic political conventions and national moral principles enabled the movement into the Far West.

In this national mythology, westerners became larger-than-life figures, and the details of their humanity blurred. Gone were the fine lines of visage, the elements of personality, the shadings of culture. Western characters, shapes and voices with no hint of distinction, assumed all the variation of a string of paper doll cutouts. In a short time, America had simplistically defined its westerners and showed no inclination to relinquish the ensuing stereotypical perceptions of western people. The West meant cowboys and Indians, trappers and traders, miners and pioneers. One by one these characters assumed traits like those assigned to Davy Crockett, until they all marched through western history untarnished.

No Place for a Woman

White males controlled the central roles in America's popular West. They explored and settled a tough environment and battled its equally tough peoples. They handed over to the nation more than vast lands. On these champions, Americans hung their sense of winning and, perhaps even more important, their sense of adventure. Cowboys, miners, trappers, soldiers, outlaws, and even farmers seemed to prove to an adoring public that once life had held no tedium, no sense of entrapment. Rather, each day brought risks and challenges that enlivened the spirit and promoted American democratic principles. Whether a dashing cowboy or a raucous outlaw, these heroes—by their style, verve, and independence—"won" the West. Since historical reality never competed very forcefully against the fanciful images, Americans happily crowned their princely models of Wyatt Earp and Wild Bill Hickok. As the frontier era faded in the face of technology and change, twentieth-century Americans made no secret of their nostalgic longing for this grand era when gold was for the finding, land for the taking, and living for the bold.

Their imagined scenario depended on a regular cast of western characters against whom the hero figures regularly triumphed. An advancing white society drew Native American people into enough wars, economic clashes, and social destruction that a popular wisdom easily dismissed all tribes as inferior. Nonetheless, Native Americans, as supporting players in the western saga, were critically important props to document notions of the cultural superiority of white society. Without human adversaries for defeat, the conquering of the West remained incomplete. Although the barren, waterless land held its own terrors, these could not equal the fears generated by mounted foes from unknown cultural traditions. Only with the suppression of those who truly called the West home could white society rest easy in its new surroundings. Few heroic tales of the

West failed to include an obligatory cast of Indian people, either "noble" or "savage," foils who repeatedly reminded white America about the technological strength and power of its own culture.

Other indigenous populations fared badly too. Hispanic groups played a less central but no more dignified part in the tale of Anglo chauvinism. Cast as "colorful" standbys, Spanish-speaking people assumed rigidly defined roles in the popular vision of western history. Painted in the hues of docile peasants, ferocious bandits, or sensual fandango dancers, Mexican Americans provided the "humorous" proof of Anglo superiority. The internal contours of their world and their cultural responses as a community meant nothing in the construction of national myth.

African Americans also found their experiences distorted in the images of the American West. Indeed, the popular memory virtually expunged African-American life from the written and oral records of the western movement, which emerged solely as a tale of white society. Although many black families looked to the West for opportunity after the Civil War, their homesteading and ranching lives never assumed a place in the popular discourse. The "buffalo soldiers" rode with the U.S. Cavalry, five thousand or more black cowboys herded cattle, and nineteenth-century African-American communities sprang up in Colorado, Kansas, Texas, and Wyoming. Despite a well-documented involvement in the Far West, African Americans rarely saw public recognition given to their ancestors' presence in both the rural and the urban areas of the region.

If African Americans suffered from historical neglect, Asian Americans remained invisible in the popular perception of the West. White America vaguely connected Asian people to the 1860s effort to build railroads, but interest in the dynamics of their lives as a western minority group never materialized. Indeed, Asian workers, vital to the construction of the Central Pacific Railroad, were not visible in the famous photographs, taken by Andrew J. Russell on 10 May 1869, that celebrated the joining of the transcontinental lines at Promontory, Utah. Reduced to degrading caricatures, Asians hardly penetrated historical accounts. Their scantily noted experiences barely yielded enough data for a separate focus in the popular culture. Their lives, culture, and language all remained so rigidly peripheral to the interests of mainstream America that Japanese internment, which totally removed one group of citizens from public view during World War II, demanded no parallel excision of Issei elements from western popular culture.

Distortion and neglect characterized the presentation not only of these ethnic groups but also of western women. In the national imagination, nineteenth-century gender definitions intensified. Basic ideas about pioneer women sprang from a national conviction that frontier wives and mothers relentlessly followed a path dictated by courage, patience, and strength. In the American mind, these women, unquestioning of husbands' decisions, sustained families through any trauma of the pioneer West but contributed little of economic or political import.

This tale gathered moral authority from those who remembered pioneer family members. Kathleen Chapman, looking back on her Cripple Creek childhood, spoke for thousands of pioneer youngsters when she said, "I never knew Mama to be idle." The image of the passive, overworked wife and mother has proven a comfortable, unchallenging formula by which to assess the experiences of western women. However, under the scrutiny of historians, a more subtle picture is emerging. Katherine Harris has argued that among homesteading families in nineteenth-century northern Colorado, women as helpmates enjoyed an increase in family responsibility and economic decision making. Elizabeth Jameson stressed the flexibility and interdependence of work roles between men and women, a circumstance that ultimately transcended the family and affected women's roles in the public sector. Carolyn Stefanco expanded this idea with her assessment of the suffrage movement in Colorado, where women capitalized on their experience in church and social organizations to secure the franchise.

Furthermore, stereotypical versions of women's lives provided the basis for an unyielding attachment to racism, further enmeshing ethnic women in social bias and obscuring their historical past. Native-, Mexican-, African-, and Asian-American women struggled under the weight of gender constraints that have never evaporated. Within the popular language of the West, ethnic women rarely assumed any activist character but remained as shadow figures. Linguistic usage—generated from within the white community in academic texts, dime novels, and film—designated minority women as "dusky," "sensual," "earthy," "promiscuous," "exotic," "criminal," and "filthy." Within popular culture, ethnic women simply represented decorations that helped to reinforce the regional uniqueness of the West.

To some degree, this representation applied to all western women—they filled the background as decor. Simplistic definitions of womanly roles gave credibility to the romantic visions of the West, as understood by men. Although the "good" women of the West—presumably white, married, middle-class pioneers—received a sort of obligatory nod in the western scenario, their status could be truly clarified only if they appeared in contrast to the "bad" women of the West. These, of course, included the prostitutes, dance-hall girls, and female outlaws. Within that framework, the mule skinner Calamity Jane, the bandit Belle Starr, and the sharpshooter Annie Oakley fit perfectly, for each could be dismissed as the quirky exception that affirmed the maleness of western society. The secondary players—women and minorities—got their parts only so that they could add greater glamour to the leading men of the West. By the era of mass audiences for radio and television, central casting needed only a sidekick like Tonto to gallop behind the Lone Ranger, or a dance-hall madam like Miss Kitty at the Long Branch Saloon to adore Marshal Matt Dillon of *Gunsmoke*.

New Arenas

The American West has served as a vast national playground for collective and individual dreams. Davy Crockett, along with other historical and fictional figures, paraded through the national imagination. However, these frontier characters were only one aspect of the modern popular attachment to the American West. The place itself took on great significance. Thus, many tourists, from the United States and throughout the world, felt impelled to travel to this hallowed place, to drink in its meaning, to be restored by its atmosphere. In addition, the purchase of western symbols assured tourists they could return home with regional relics that validated their connection to the "real" America. Through keepsakes, the nationalistic values and virtues of the West could be exported to other parts of the country or of the world. Surrounded by their reminders of the West, these mostly middle-class tourists maintained the belief that purple sage and mounted riders meant Americanism.

But consumers did not need to leave home to see the West. Mass marketing brought images of the region to American households. Transformations in industrial production, especially improvements in the technology of printing, and expansion in communication media catapulted cultural images of an earlier age into the twentieth century. For example, after 1900, the production of western art, already a booming business of the nineteenth century, reached industrial proportions. A host of American illustrators took up pen and brush to depict the life and culture believed to be part of the western experience. These artists did so with a new dedication, for the advent of the twentieth century convinced Americans, once more, that rather than "capture" the West, they must "preserve" it. After all, only seven years earlier, the historian Frederick Jackson Turner, in his famous essay "The Significance of the Frontier in American History," had warned that the pioneer West and its democratic virtues had all but disappeared. The very essence of American social and political democracy appeared to be slipping through the nation's fingers.

Certain illustrators, even as they sought personal income, wanted to preserve within the American spirit this meaning of frontier life. Charles Russell and Frederic Remington, each with a highly successful art career, promoted both the frontier concepts and the artistic style that served as guides for others. Turn-of-the-century changes within the publishing industry provided these illustrators with a regular forum for selling works that resonated with their personal visions of national meaning. No fewer than ten thousand magazines appeared on the American market between 1890 and 1940. Publications such as *Cosmopolitan*, *Ladies' Home Journal*, *Collier's*, *Red Book*, and the *Saturday Evening Post* depended on a dozen or more western illustrators for the art that accompanied the western fiction pieces. Among the most successful, Newell Convers Wyeth, William H. D. Koerner, and Frank Schoonover sketched hundreds of western images for these often romantic short stories.

One of the most notable, William H. D. Koerner, exemplifies the impact of these artists on the American mind. During his career, Koerner turned out more than twenty-four hundred illustrations, approximately six hundred of which depicted western themes. He collaborated with a long list of western authors, illustrating the works of Oliver La Farge, Bernard DeVoto, and Zane Grey. His western images graced more than forty stories that appeared in the *Saturday Evening Post* between 1930 and 1935. Koerner's *Madonna of the Prairie* (1922), an earlier portrait of a pioneer woman, around whose head the arch of her Conestoga wagon seems to form a halo, remains one of the most widely recognized of western renderings. He cared deeply about the values that these authors of western fiction tried to portray, and their written tributes to him over his long life demonstrate the success with which authors felt he captured their philosophy.

Like Koerner, all the illustrators turned out appealing images of frontier people and heightened Americans' positive attitude toward western settlement. These artists presented westerners as individuals of character, refinement, and integrity. Perhaps more important, as the nation moved into a world that turned on mechanization and

Molly Wingate, the heroine of Emerson Hough's novel, The Covered Wagon, *traveled west with a wagon train and found true love when she arrived in Oregon. For this book jacket illustration (which subsequently influenced the film version of the story), William Koerner portrayed her as a beatific Madonna of the prairie and gave her a more contemporary look by depicting her with a fashionable 1920s hairstyle.*

William Henry David Koerner (1878–1938). Madonna of the Prairie. *Oil on canvas, 1922. Buffalo Bill Historical Center, Cody, Wyoming.*

industrial growth, these illustrated western stories kept national frontier concepts at center stage for American readers. The work of the illustrators could be found every week in any American home with magazine subscriptions. In the decades spanning World War I, the 1920s, the Great Depression, and World War II, western images accompanied uplifting frontier tales offered for the magazine-reading public.

Not all illustrators took pleasure in this easy market, and some, chafing under the commercial constraints of deadlines and style, determined to break away from the stereotypical magazine portrayals. One of these, Maynard Dixon, in the early twentieth century disappeared on extensive field trips deep into the Southwest in search of remote desert scenes. Dixon wanted to disassociate himself from "traditional," by which he meant commercial, western art and use his brush to capture the harsh grip of weather and environment. Desert aridity fascinated him, and his portrayals of it contradicted the rosy, watered horizons of a group of his colleagues who had, since the late nineteenth century and under the patronage of various railroads, turned out highly promotional western landscapes.

Inadvertently, Dixon convinced Americans that they had yet to understand the "authentic" West. So, his efforts to retreat from the popularized aspects of western art were not entirely successful. The 1939 decision of the U.S. Department of the Interior to place his murals in the Bureau of Indian Affairs pleased Dixon, but the placement of his work in this generic public building pointed to the hopeless task of separating art, popular image, and commercialization in the national visions of the American West.

While illustrators advertised the West and its inhabitants through art forms of every style, other popular entertainments, some of which originated in the nineteenth century, also added to the West's specialized image. For the American public, nothing brought the West more directly into their lives than the Wild West shows. From among fifty or more traveling shows, the one to popularize the American West most successfully was Buffalo Bill's Wild West and Congress of Rough Riders. More than any other figure, Buffalo Bill Cody, himself a mixture of one part reality and two parts fiction, bridged the nineteenth- and twentieth-century evolution of western popular culture. Almost single-handedly he pushed frontier western notions into the modern scenario and made them accessible to a general audience.

By the time Buffalo Bill got around to opening his "Wild West, Rocky Mountain, and Prairie Exhibition" in 1883, he already enjoyed wide fame as a western personality. A well-known scout for the frontier army, Cody assumed celebrity stature during the 1870s due to the literary vision of Edward Zane Carroll Judson, who used the pen name Ned Buntline. Buntline rode the crest of a new wave of western fiction that gave rise to the wildly popular dime novels.

Buntline's decision to develop a fictional frontier hero from the real-life Buffalo Bill was one of the most fortuitous moments in American marketing of the West. The public responded with such enthusiasm to Buntline's books that it proved to be a short hop for Cody from the published exploits in *Buffalo Bill: The King of the Border Men* to the New York stage as an actor in *The Scouts of the Plains; or, Red Deviltry As It Is.* However, it was the traveling Wild West show that made Buffalo Bill the king of international entertainment and cast him as the living definition of the West.

Cody's posters, plastered around the nation, advertised that each of the two daily shows could accommodate twenty thousand people and promised to present "actual scenes, genuine characters" from the West. These vast crowds loved his part-circus, part-pageant, all-West extravaganza. Audiences not only clamored for so-called historical depictions of frontier events—the attack on the Deadwood stage, the defeat of General George A. Custer at the Little Bighorn—but particularly cheered at those outdoor skills so singularly western. Dazzling rope tricks, dangerous bulldogging, and superior marksmanship belonged to the West, and Buffalo Bill filled his show with performers who excelled at these feats.

Americans flocked to Cody's shows convinced he brought them the true West, for, as he promised, he gathered into his performing ranks "genuine characters"—Native Americans of several tribes. As these men, most in flowing headdress and carrying elegantly feathered coup sticks, rode bareback into the arena on stunning painted horses, who among the enthralled viewers questioned how well these appearances replicated tribal life on the Great Plains? In addition, Cody's ability, in 1885, to produce the most famous Indian of all, Sitting Bull, further underscored the reliability of his West.

The Indians themselves, still reeling from recent political and social events that had uprooted traditional economies, found needed employment with Buffalo Bill. Closed out of political decision making within white America, denied access to industrial

Buffalo Bill Cody's touring show helped fix the American cowboy as a daring and dashing figure in the American imagination.

Unidentified artist. Buffalo Bill's Wild West and Congress of Rough Riders of the World. *Color lithograph, ca. 1896, Courier Lithography Co., Buffalo, New York. Buffalo Bill Historical Center, Cody, Wyoming.*

training, and segregated from educational centers, Native American people accepted one of the few jobs they could easily secure—that of entertainment figures. This depressed economic track continued to haunt Indian endeavors throughout the twentieth century, leaving them with few options. Economic opportunities within the context of white America rarely broadened and typically centered on Native Americans' willingness to "play" at being Indians. America's entrepreneurs, such as Buffalo Bill, happily hired Indians who "stayed" native and, thus, furthered their own stereotyping. The Indians who galloped into Buffalo Bill's arena did much more than add a dash of color; they embodied the reality that the twentieth-century forces of commercial capitalism marginalized native peoples who found themselves in a fixed and ungenerous economic structure.

In addition to presenting Indian peoples as glamorous showstoppers completely divorced from their own environment and outside their economic milieu, Cody brought Americans the perfect frontierswoman in the person of Annie Oakley. Her remarkable skills at marksmanship set her apart from effete eastern women, but her genteel appearance and stylish costumes revealed her to be a "true" woman. In one more western paradox, Annie Oakley, born in the East, a child of Ohio, defined the nature of western women—capable and refined—for the country.

These images of Native Americans and white women slid easily into the national consciousness. Indeed, why should any one have challenged the tone and content of the

Cody show? After all, Cody, a product of the West, knew the internal dynamics of the region, and he went directly to the source to secure his talent. His popularity knew no bounds. It was all right with his audiences if Buffalo Bill, transformed by fiction and fame into an elegant, patrician cowboy, became the national caretaker for western authenticity.

Cody not only commanded the admiration of millions of Americans but also saw his international reputation soar. One bronc rider who stayed with the show from 1900 until 1907 traveled around the world more than three and one-half times on tours that included performances in Outer Mongolia. The Cody cast appeared twice before Queen Victoria of England. In 1913, Prince Albert I of Monaco, who knew the American showman from these stunningly well received European tours, journeyed from his tiny principality to Cody, Wyoming, for the chance to "kill a grizzly or two" under the guidance of Buffalo Bill, the Prince of the Frontier.

The magnetism of the Buffalo Bill show could not draw audiences indefinitely. When the program diluted its strictly western themes, the demand for the Cody Wild West show faded. But by the time that happened, Americans had discovered the rodeo as a western entertainment replacement. Predicated on work skills and frontier amusement formed in the earliest days of cattle raising, the rodeo proved a natural for promoters. The thundering action, the magnificent animals, the death-defying cowboys—all swirling around in a sweaty, dust-filled arena—added up to a certain crowd pleaser. For the price of admission, Americans saw, close up, examples of modern men who reflected western toughness, raw courage, and natural strength, living proof that the pioneer spirit of the West remained intact. Once an informal ranch sport that branched into local and regional competitions for seasonally unemployed cowboys, rodeos hit the national big time in the twentieth century.

By 1910, with the sport spreading rapidly and the participants more full-time contestants than part-time cowboys, the competitors at a Denver fair organized the Bronco Busters' Union and demanded five dollars a day for the wild-horse riders. This early unionizing attempt exemplified the tone of rodeo competitions for the next several decades as gate revenues mounted around the country, but low wages and dangerous conditions remained unchanged for contestants. By 1936, both the Boston Garden and New York's Madison Square Garden hosted rodeos that ran for almost three weeks. In New York, audiences totaled nearly a quarter of a million, far surpassing the usual crowds of one hundred thousand associated with rodeos in Cheyenne, Wyoming. Once again, the "Wild West" had hit the eastern pocketbook.

Unlike several areas of western popularizing, the early rodeos made a place for women, who often competed in the same events as the men performers. As early as 1935, Tad Barnes Lucas, a female trick and bronc rider, commanded an impressive annual salary of twelve thousand dollars. Women bronc riders and trick ropers usually appeared under special individual contracts. However, the enigmatically named Cowboys Turtle Association, a union formed in 1936 to promote fairness for rodeo personnel, opened its membership in 1940 to all cowgirl performers.

Rodeo waned during World War II as many of its youthful stars went off to military service and as western communities restricted large public gatherings because of wartime exigencies. In those locations that permitted rodeos, women took up the slack, as they

Although she never ventured west of her home state of Ohio, except when on tour, Annie Oakley came to personify the spirited frontier woman of popular myth. Performing in Buffalo Bill's Wild West show for 17 years, she delighted audiences abroad and at home with her showmanship and skill as a sharpshooter.

Unidentified artist. Annie Oakley: The Peerless Wing and Rifle Shot. Lithograph, 1901, Enquirer Job Printing Co., Cincinnati, Ohio. Circus World Museum, Baraboo, Wisconsin.

did in other war circumstances. In 1944, on the cover of *Hoofs and Horns,* the premier rodeo publication, mounted cowgirls smiled down on three rather aged cowboys welcoming a wounded veteran home from the war. In the post–World War II years, however, rodeos generally barred women competitors, until only barrel-racing events remained for distaff performance.

As public interest continued to accelerate during the postwar 1940s and 1950s, rodeo officials considered ways to further exploit the growing popularity. In 1959, a National Finals Rodeo Commission, which employed the promotional services of a well-known theatrical agency, brought the first rodeo competition to Dallas, Texas, in an event shown on national television.

Major American corporations savored the commercial opportunities in this decidedly nineteenth-century western event broadcast by a decidedly twentieth-century technology. R. J. Reynolds Tobacco, Levi Strauss Clothing, Wrangler Jeans, Justin Boots, Frontier Airlines, Ford Motor, Coors Beer, Schlitz Brewery, Heublein Whiskey, Nestea Foods, and Hesston Farm Machinery all invested in underwriting various aspects of rodeo competition during the 1970s, 1980s, and 1990s. Although market indicators pointed to climbing profits for sponsors, companies insisted they endorsed rodeos because these events reinforced American family values.

In the midst of cow wrangling and bull goring, that rationale remained blurry, yet huge trophies and giant purses drew an ever-increasing number of contestants, many of whom had never worked as cowhands but had trained at rodeo schools to become professional riders. When the national finals, held each December, took up residence in Las Vegas, Nevada, the transformation of rodeo from local pastime to major sport industry was complete. Set in the tinsel mecca of the United States, the national finals now meant a massive influx of fans, costly seats, high-stakes gambling, rodeo stars, ersatz cowboys, and media hype.

For those ersatz cowboys, the rodeo became one of the latest means by which young Americans found a "way out" from a less attractive life. In 1982, Charles Sampson, an African-American cowboy, ranked as the champion rodeo bull rider in the country, with winnings that totaled over ninety-one thousand dollars. Sampson, however, hardly acquired his expertise on the open range. The eleventh of thirteen children, Sampson grew up in Los Angeles, where he credited the YMCA and the Cub Scouts with fostering his interest in the rodeo. He made a clear decision to become a cowboy and studied to do just that. Although Sampson advanced as a national contender, hundreds of his peers found their competitive outlet in the small all-black rodeos sprinkled throughout the Southwest. In 1983, Sampson sustained a serious injury at a rodeo attended by President Ronald Reagan, another self-constructed media cowboy, and subsequently returned to bull riding in rodeos of the Southwest.

Local rodeos proved a popular sport for Native Americans and Mexican Americans as well as blacks. Within ethnic communities the rodeo served to strengthen the bonds of people who often lived great distances from each other. For example, the rodeo amplified earlier Indian social traditions. Building on the custom of tribal powwows, Indians added rodeos to their established social structure. However, within the context of mass marketing, the Indian rodeos, as well as the Mexican-American ones, have remained outside the commercial mainstream. Although ethnic groups have adopted some aspects of the "western" mode—clothing, jewelry, crafts, rodeos—they lack both internal capital and endorsement from big businesses and thus can point to only modest economic results.

Mexican Americans, however, were more successful in using their touring circuses as a source of ethnic support. Well into the 1950s, Mexican circuses brought regular ethnic entertainment to such southwestern cities as San Antonio and Tucson. The Escalante Circus, the Ortiz Brothers, and the Rivas Brothers—from the late nineteenth century—all enjoyed great popularity among Hispanic people. In the twentieth century, national entertainment agencies hired several of the performers from local Mexican circuses to tour on the vaudeville circuit throughout the United States.

The Mexican circuses continued to perform regularly along the Mexican-American border. Known as the *carpa*, these were intimate family-centered circuses, which brought entertainment to small towns in remote western regions. Although Anglos often enjoyed these performances, they overlooked the content of the Mexican-American comic routines that protested against language and social discrimination. The *carpa*, outside the context of the national imagination, points to the importance of localized entertainment, rich with cultural textures and popular with residents within the West.

Putting on the Hat

As American fans propelled rodeos—local and national—into a new status as western sport, they did so to a changing beat of music. New trends in American music began to waft out of southern communities, both white and black, in the 1920s. In the 1930s, as rodeos began to draw wider national attention, American music shifted again, this time with a regional tilt to the West, especially Texas and Oklahoma. Although music in many forms—folk songs, ballads, hymns—had always been central to the pioneer tradition, the transformation in the 1930s from southern-country to country-western represented just one more of the cultural impacts of the Great Depression. Until the 1940s, however, American taste in music continued to divide along urban-rural lines, and the new country-western style stayed popular with a limited audience. Within the West itself, the truly indigenous music of Native Americans and Mexican Americans never acquired the label of "western" music. Like Indian rodeos and Mexican circuses, each ethnic style of music retained an identity limited to the parameters of its own community.

Putting on a cowboy hat not only added a western element to what had been southern-country music but also increased the national audience. Tex Ritter's career furnishes a solid example of how commercial interests shaped music production. As a personality, this well-educated and savvy Texan solidified the singing cowboy image for easterners. Ritter cultivated his western persona in a folksy manner that belied his sharp business sense. He seemed to personify the down-home plain manner that increasingly appealed to an American population beleaguered by the Great Depression. Buoyed by Ritter's success, more and more musicians, often only as genuinely cowboy as the hats and boots they donned, invaded the national music scene—the Prairie Ramblers, the Monroe Brothers, the Blue Sky Boys, and Bob Wills and his western-swing band, the

REPUBLIC PICTURES *presents*
Gene AUTRY
in
'SPRINGTIME IN THE ROCKIES'
with
SMILEY BURNETTE
Directed by
JOE KANE
Original Screen Play by
GILBERT WRIGHT · BETTY BURBRIDGE
Associate Producer
SOL C. SIEGEL
A REPUBLIC PICTURE
REPUBLIC PICTURES

Texas Playboys. All benefited, at least peripherally, from the jingling spurs and simple melodies of the wildly popular and true westerner Gene Autry. Of equal importance to the western music scene was the easy sound of that unauthentic cowboy Roy Rogers, who began life as Leonard Slye from Duck Run, Ohio. Rogers embodied all the personal virtues Americans imagined of cowboys. Clever handlers put those qualities on display for the nation, and Rogers's career took off, eventually landing him on the cover of *Life* magazine in 1943.

Regardless of where these musicians lived or traveled, when the New York songwriters picked up on the distinctive beat and sound, it was not long until all Americans knew tunes for more than "Tumbling Tumble Weeds." Few noticed that easterners increasingly wrote the popular lyrics, managed the publicity, controlled the record distribution, and owned the radio stations that broadcast the new performers. That commercial day soon came when the public cared not who produced or sang western music. In fact, country music no longer required that the performers even offer the pretense of being western cowboys. In the 1940s, both the Andrews Sisters and Bing Crosby cut highly successful country music hits, such as "Biting My Fingernails" and

Through radio shows, films, and later television, Gene Autry became the quintessential cowboy singer. In 82 films made between 1934 and 1959, in which he usually appeared as a fictionalized version of himself, he established the western musical as a film genre, paving the way for other cowboy stars such as Roy Rogers and Tex Ritter.

"Springtime in the Rockies." *Offset,* © *1937, Allied Printing, Essex County, USA. Poster Collection, Prints and Photographs Division, Library of Congress, Washington, D.C.*

"Pistol Packin' Mama." Country music, born with rural southern roots, had used a few cowboy hats to switch from a "hillbilly" to a western identity, which quickly moved beyond region to a national sound.

From its heyday in the 1940s, commercial cowboy music took a substantial nosedive in the 1950s as competing styles within the genre struggled for commercial dominance. Then came the invasion of rock and roll and the eruption ten years later of a brash young group from England, the Beatles. Interestingly, it did not take rock and roll very long to turn to western themes, but these would veer away from the older cowboy lyrics of the nineteenth and early twentieth centuries. Instead, California as a sun-and-surf paradise emerged from the early music of the Beach Boys, only to be replaced in the mid-1970s by the more disillusioned Golden State vision of the Eagles. As groups proliferated and music escalated as a form of social comment, California and the West remained central to the themes, demonstrating once again the mythic power of western symbolism. No longer the Great Depression melancholy of Jimmie Rodgers's "California Blues," the musical message of the Pacific Coast now agonized over drugs, Haight-Ashbury, and America's failed revolution of the 1960s.

In this immense musical renovation, the guitar twangs of country-western music died away as listeners equated the sound with low-class, southern-white origins. American music, in songs like "If I Had a Hammer" and "Blowing in the Wind," took on more and more of the hues of a social protest—a protest that often placed the blame for America's ills in the heart of the South and in the homes of rural people. Country music, however, had not died. It merely waited for a changed climate of social impulses and a new generation of performers, all of whom would be handled by high-powered promoters. By the mid-1960s, as the nation absorbed the shock waves of political assassination, civil disorders, counterculture protests, and debilitating foreign entanglements, country-western music found its moment to go national, as never before. Although television altered production styles and personal costuming for performers, country music's original format—the radio—remained a powerful vehicle for selling the renovated sounds. No longer the music of the South and the West's rural whites, country music attracted the nation's yuppie commuters and blue-collar workers, who tuned their car and truck radios to those lyrics of heartbreak and loneliness, self-reliance and courage. An economic notch or two above the original country music crowd, these fans heaped their approval on a new generation of recording stars, such as Merle Haggard.

Haggard proved to be the perfect new champion of country music. Born to poor Oklahoma farmers, Haggard made the famous depression-style "Okie trek" to California, where he grew up in Bakersfield. After a troubled life that would one day be a press agent's dream, Haggard began to make a steady living with music. Haggard's 1969 hit "Okie from Muskogee," which celebrated people who did not smoke marijuana or burn a draft card, appealed to an entirely new national constituency of listeners: middle-class white Americans, who distrusted notions of social protest and increasingly endorsed conservative values and national conformity. That trend among Americans gained momentum until in the late 1980s and early 1990s two presidents, Ronald Reagan and George Bush, each attended star-studded performances at the Grand Ole Opry in Nashville, Tennessee, the eastern-based Vatican of country music. The importance of these visits—from presidents who pitched their political rhetoric in varying degrees of reactionary language targeted toward the white electorate of the South and the West —was not lost on the American public. Musical statement and political philosophy came together as never before.

Off to the West

Is it any surprise that many Americans longed to tour the West, to watch real cowboys leap into the saddle, to visit the haunting bluffs at the Little Bighorn, to stand at the north rim of the Grand Canyon, to canoe down the magnificent Snake River, to squint out over barren Death Valley? Is it any less surprising that businesses, in addition to the Santa Fe Railway and Frontier Airlines, eagerly hoped to make such adventures possible? Although western tours had always attracted eastern and European visitors, the tourist industry, born in the late nineteenth century, gathered unprecedented steam in the first third of the twentieth century.

The explosion of tourist interest owed much to that self-proclaimed westerner Theodore Roosevelt. In 1888, Roosevelt, who a few years earlier had retreated to the Dakota Territory after the deaths of his wife and his mother, wrote a series of articles about the West for *Century* magazine. A true celebrity, Roosevelt increased the enthusiasm of the American public for firsthand encounters in the wilderness.

Conveniently, the Roosevelt publicity corresponded to the economic misfortunes of many of his Dakota rancher friends, who had lost almost everything in the disastrous winter of 1886–87. Although their cattle profits plummeted, ranchers still owned enormous spreads of land and delighted at the chance to entertain paying guests, drawn largely from an eastern elite. Out of this series of coincidences evolved a new western feature, the dude ranch.

Here, urban visitors, outfitted in appropriate attire, had a chance to experience all the nuances of western life. They rode the range, hiked through national parks, camped in remote areas, and ate by smoky campfires. None of these activities required much adjustment from the cattlemen and their hands, whose daily tasks often followed this same pattern. The happy difference for ranchers concerned the economic benefits accrued from wealthy easterners who frequently stayed for an entire summer season.

The first influx of tourists guaranteed national publicity for the new concept in western vacationing. Among those who heaped praise on and brought attention to dude ranches were the author Mary Roberts Rinehart, the artist C. M. Russell, and the stage humorist Will Rogers. Through the 1930s, thousands of Americans visited the western dude ranches, adding to their own sense of the West and filling the coffers of western ranchers. At the peak of popularity, over 350 dude ranches sprawled from Arizona to Montana. A far cry from the luxury resorts of the modern West, complete with swimming pools and gourmet dinners, the first dude ranches offered no softening amenities and totally immersed visitors in the physical and spiritual meaning of western living, as defined by the ranchers and their hands. The owners of the dude ranches often required that guests plan for a minimum visit of two weeks, since the ranchers argued that to savor the pace and style of western life required an extended stay. Indeed, the ranchers shifted from innkeepers to interpreters of the West with remarkable ease. Once

By the early 20th century, the West's cowboy-and-Indian heritage had become a focal point for tourism.

In the Southwest, Fred Harvey built on the success of his regionally furnished railroad hotels with "Indian Detour" trips that brought visitors directly to the pueblos.

A. J. Baker. Ladies Row, Dude Ranch Camp in Glacier National Park. *Gelatin silver print, 1917. Montana Historical Society, Helena.*

T. Harmon Parkhurst (1884–1952). Detour Buses at Santa Clara Pueblo. Gelatin silver print, ca. 1935. Courtesy Museum of New Mexico (#3813), Santa Fe.

Founded in 1884 as the West's first dude ranch, the Eaton Ranch in Wolf, Wyoming, introduced its guests to the frontier past with pack trips that combined a spirit of "roughing it" with the amenities of civilization. A camp brochure noted, "The tents of the ladies and the gentlemen are carefully segregated for mutual comfort . . . and a special row of tepees is arranged for married couples."

A. J. Baker. Ladies Row, Dude Ranch Camp in Glacier National Park. *Gelatin silver print, 1917. Montana Historical Society, Helena.*

merely the routines of a day-to-day existence, ranch schedules and daily chores trans-muted into secular rituals for understanding the West.

The popularity of the dude ranches coincided with a growing attention to the spectacular scenery of the national parks. Owners of the dude ranches fanned this interest with highly publicized pack trips, which often led visitors into natural areas that were largely inaccessible except by horseback. As the general public expressed more interest in these remote regions, so did the corporate world. Inside Glacier National Park, the Great Northern Railway, like its southwestern counterpart the Atchison, Topeka, and Santa Fe at the Grand Canyon, built several hotels and oversaw the construction of trails to the interior. As early as 1903, Harry Child, who controlled the concessions in the Upper Geyser Basin of Yellowstone National Park, hired an architect to design a visitors' inn that looked out over Old Faithful. Rugged and rustic, the gigantic inn opened in 1904 to national acclaim that has never diminished. By 1920, almost one million tourists a year visited the national parks.

The national parks proved such a draw that in 1936 the businessman and politician-to-be Averell Harriman selected a wilderness site and used the Union Pacific Railroad to carve a private winter resort from the then-isolated Sun Valley, Idaho. The Union Pacific ran a skiers' special to Sun Valley until well into the 1960s. Everything about the trip and the resort catered to the rich and famous until other modes of transportation opened Sun Valley to greater numbers of less aristocratic visitors.

The commercial development of the interior reaches packaged a new western commodity for the American consumer—the wilderness. During the first four decades of the twentieth century, that wilderness remained largely the domain of the moneyed American. However, after World War II, accessibility to wilderness areas changed significantly. The expansion of the interstate highway system, along with a leap in the number of motel chains and campsites, gave American tourism a solid place in the West. A booming airline industry, the fad for oversized recreational vehicles, and the road appeal offered by snappy motorbikes and more gas-efficient cars put domestic travel within easy reach of most Americans. No longer did tourists need dude ranches as outposts from which to organize western sightseeing. Armed with a few guidebooks and a *Rand McNally Road Atlas*, Americans orchestrated their own getaways to the wilderness.

The nineteenth-century national parks, many of which encompassed magnificent western vistas, now threatened to become tourist merchandise. The goals of the conservationist John Muir, who founded the Sierra Club in 1892, changed in ways he could hardly have imagined. Whereas Muir had hoped to jolt Americans into a responsible wilderness awareness, he never anticipated the high-tech by-products of that heightened concern. With travel options maximized, the number of Americans pouring into the West increased at astonishing rates. In 1973, three million more people visited the national parks than in 1972. In the same year, almost four million people went to the Colorado Rockies for skiing. The economic complexities of environmentalism and wilderness preservation crystallized with stunning rapidity.

The national parks, always more closely wedded to economic interests than Americans wanted to realize, faced an avalanche of challenges. In the first place, local economic considerations had often outweighed aesthetic concerns when lands were set aside for the parks. In addition, nineteenth-century conservationists who wanted to preserve natural beauty understood little about ecosystems and biological integrity. As a result, the government often drew boundaries for national parks haphazardly, even before local logging and grazing companies complained about the borders and demanded further gerrymandering.

When millions of nature seekers added themselves to the equation in the post–World War II era, the full tangle of public land management, political pressure, and environmental issues hit the American West. Each year more and more Americans fled from urban pressures, to stack up at the entrances to Utah's Zion National Park or to inch bumper to bumper along the road in Wyoming's Yellowstone. This massive human intrusion placed at risk the very wilderness the visitors believed they cherished. Into the 1980s and 1990s, problems of litter, sewage disposal, wildlife protection, and public safety multiplied at unprecedented speeds. The embattled National Park Service, an agency of the Department of the Interior since 1916, struggled to cope with the flow of visitors even as it warded off conflicting complaints about its overwatchfulness or inattentiveness. As the twentieth century came to a close, less and less of the West fit the description of true wilderness, but more and more Americans believed they needed a pilgrimage to that special environment. Perhaps twentieth-century America revolved around the industry of urban areas, but those drawn to the scenic West appeared to think that the parks made it possible not only to step back into a wilderness paradise but also to capture a personal vision of America, such as the nation's frontier forebears were thought to have possessed.

Always the Cowboy

Vast numbers of people have experienced the West, through literature, art, entertainment, or tourism. Millions more may not have taken as active an interest in things western, but they, nonetheless, would know the singular icon whose image is emblematic for the region—the cowboy. Instantly and internationally recognizable, the cowboy is now a national symbol for America and not just for its western states. His glamour has drooped from time to time as foreign observers or Americans themselves followed other fads, but the cowboy as a beloved figure has demonstrated extraordinary staying power.

The cowboy figure started his heroic career on foot as that noble buckskin-clad pioneer in the eastern woodlands. However, once in the saddle—through story, song, and reality—he evolved into the cowboy of shirt, chaps, and neckerchief on the open western plains. His stature increased, and he quickly passed any other contenders in national prominence. Mountain men, pioneers, scouts, and gold miners cut their own swath in the evolution of western popular history, but they never won the public adoration heaped on the cowboy.

The American cowboy, most often a youthful bachelor, rode into the hearts of Americans with a laconic but honorable manner. No great thinker, he was guided in life by a few simple principles: he was always willing to right a wrong, to save a damsel in distress, and to defend the underdog. With an ever-constant good disposition, the cowboy did not seek violence, but when confronted, he knew how to respond quickly and thoroughly. He was white America's mounted warrior, the defender of a national code of honor, the champion of the open range. He carried a gun and rode a horse, but he did not always herd cattle.

The cowboy became a multimedia figure. He graced the pages of Owen Wister's *The Virginian* (1902) and the later stories of Louis L'Amour's Sackett family. The cowboy galloped across Charlie Russell's turn-of-the-century paintings and inspired the twentieth-century pieces of the European artist Americo Makk. As the Lone Ranger, he rode with youngsters through the pages of their comic books. As Hopalong Cassidy, he loaned his logo to the school lunch-box and the Hoppy thermos, making the sandwiches more appetizing and the milk more cooling. As the singing cowboy, Gene Autry, he crooned "Back in the Saddle Again" to listeners out in radio-land. With Tom Mix and Roy Rogers, he thundered across the silver screen during cliff-hanging Saturday-morning serials. He kept the watch with Marshal Matt Dillon over Dodge City and the Long Branch Saloon.

Actually, Matt Dillon of *Gunsmoke* fame was just one television westerner from a string of shows that proliferated between 1947 and 1960. The western motif proved a successful formula for the burgeoning new world of television. Writers and directors, working under production time constraints, quickly grasped the plot essentials. The underlying theme, as the film historian John Lenihan has pointed out, always concerned society's preoccupation with the conflicts between "individual freedom and social constraint." In the Western, the hero, in the face of nearly overwhelming odds, acted to secure the betterment of the community. This equation required simply a hero, a person to be saved, and an evil force to be defeated—vicious Indians, corrupt cattle ranchers, or heartless bandits. Audiences, well versed in the stock characters of the Western, comfortable with the cowboy as the protector of social values, and familiar with these plot lines, easily accepted the reduction of large movie sets onto the small screen. By 1959, Westerns captured the ratings as seven of the top-ten favorite shows on national television. Americans liked Matt Dillon and his cowboy friends so much that their televisions stayed tuned for *The Rifleman, Rawhide, Maverick, Wanted—Dead or Alive, Wagon Train, Have Gun, Will Travel, Lawman, Bat Masterson,* and *Bonanza.* Indeed, the early years of television saw an almost unending introduction of new Westerns with each season.

In the 1960s and 1970s, changing viewer demands, as well as a shift in the demographics of audiences, sounded the death knell for the Westerns' exaggerated popularity. Family viewing patterns altered, and competition forced network executives to survey carefully the program interests of the nation. Television concentrated on greater news coverage, as well as musical entertainment and sporting events, in part to satisfy an ever-growing population of teenage viewers. The Western faltered as television entertainment.

Yet, the Western survived to make another resurgence. The introduction of cable television in the early 1980s brought the shoot-outs and cattle stampedes back into American living rooms. Reruns of television shows and movie classics offered an available, cheap commodity for network markets that ballooned almost overnight. The Westerns added to their rejuvenated popularity through an appeal to viewers' nostalgia.

The introduction of the home videotape-player allowed television owners to accumulate a private film library, bringing the Westerns and their aging stars back to the attention of the American public. In this new age, the old "B" Westerns of the 1940s and 1950s lacked the sophistication of programming in the 1990s. However, they returned, much like long-lost friends, reminders of an earlier, simpler time. At least for the expanding population of elderly Americans, they provided an easy, inexpensive way to recapture the entertainment of youth, to delight in old stars made whole once more. There again was a dark-haired Jimmy Stewart, an athletic Burt Lancaster, a boyish Steve McQueen. Actor and viewer—everyone was young once more. In a make-believe world that never entirely died, the cowboy heroes rode across the screen, chasing Indians, saving young women, and winning the West.

Certainly this roller-coaster popularity of the film and television Western accounted for the cowboy careers of dozens of actors. Some fell into their cowboy star status by the accident of casting. Others fervently believed that cowboys personified moral integrity and made major contributions to democracy and American life. From William S. Hart to Kirk Douglas, from Joel McCrea to Michael Landon, from Randolph Scott to Jack Palance, from Hoot Gibson to Gary Cooper to Clint Eastwood—all had the western film to thank for major developments in their cinema success.

Typically, women have fared poorly in Westerns. Their screen roles tended to copy the prevailing social attitudes toward womanhood. Accordingly, film heroines of the 1920s and 1930s smiled and simpered as the "gentle tamers," those who brought "civilization" and order to the West. By the 1940s, with American women generally cast into more active and productive economic endeavors to meet the war needs, Hollywood followed suit with films about strong-minded women, such as the 1941 *Gangs of Sonora*, in which a female newspaper editor in Wyoming took on and defeated a corrupt politician. As quickly as the gender trend of self-reliant, independent women lost vogue within American society, Hollywood also dropped scripts that showed females surviving on their own. Within the western genre, women became an environmental adornment, as typified by Joanne Dru in the 1949 *She Wore a Yellow Ribbon*, which pitted John Wayne against the Apache nation.

Jane Russell's sensuous portrayal in Howard Hughes's 1943 film *The Outlaw* presaged a changed tone and texture in women's roles in the Western. By the 1960s, western films assumed greater and greater sexual explicitness, with rape and torture as common themes. Although one might argue that this trend introduced fundamental realities to the Western, often criticized in an earlier era as too sanitary, a counterpoint suggests that filmmakers simply used women characters as the vehicle through which to exploit western violence and gender aggression in more horrifying terms.

This strategy dominated the portrayal of ethnic women. Native-American women seldom emerged as personalities with identities and perspectives. Historically, Native-American women of film appeared only as background "pack animals" to further document the "savagery" of the men or as victims in scenes of village slaughter by marauding army troops, as for example in the 1970 film *Soldier Blue*. Thus Native-American people continued to play their main role in the Western—that of subjects for cultural or political extermination.

In a further distortion, in those rare scripts that called for an actual woman character, directors typically cast Anglo actresses as Native Americans. Thus, Debra Pagent, Jennifer Jones, and Virginia Mayo, in their Indian and mixed-blood roles, helped implant an inaccurate physical image of Native-American women in the minds of moviegoers. In addition, the consistent refusal of the American film industry to hire appropriate ethnic females further codified the economic structures that unrelentingly kept Indian people from reaping personal or collective profits from western popular culture.

It appears Mexican-American women also had little to applaud from the film industry. Along with Native Americans, Mexican Americans found only stereotyping and cavalier treatment of their culture. Scorned as docile and lazy, their speech patterns and language ridiculed, Mexican Americans forcefully held their place in the West despite abuse that dated to the earliest contacts with Anglo culture. The strength and diversity of the Mexican-American culture rarely gained acknowledgment in an entertainment medium that appeared content to create its own image of an entire community. The film characterizations of Mexican women ranged from the elegant

More than any other medium, film is responsible for the image of the West as a place locked in the 19th century and defined by stark encounters between whites and Indians, law and disorder. Although social and political trends have altered the content of western films, the strong, silent man of action—epitomized by John Wayne—remains the central figure.

Film still from Stagecoach *(1939), directed by John Ford. Courtesy of the Academy of Motion Pictures Arts and Sciences Library, Beverly Hills, California.*

Katy Jurado prostitute in the 1952 *High Noon* to the earthy Mexican prostitutes in the 1969 *The Wild Bunch* to the revolutionary Hispanic prostitute in the 1990 *Old Gringo*. In almost forty years of filmmaking, no appreciable refinement in the presentation of Mexican-American or Native-American women graced the American screen.

Despite these glaring weaknesses and offensive biases, the cowboy film continued to draw large audiences, and the intellectual analysis of the genre appealed to film critics, university professors, and cinema buffs. Social critics and scholars like John Cawelti and John Lenihan found something of the national forces and patterns in each era of cowboy films. In the deceptively simple stories, they saw the conflicts and dilemmas of American society—it contradictions, its goals, its fears, and its hopes for itself. Regardless of these sophisticated, often highly perceptive critiques, ordinary folk idolized screen cowboys for their bedrock devotion to American values and codes of behavior seemingly lost to the modern world. Scrubbed and polished in one era, rougher and dirtier in a more recent time, cowboys of film continued to suggest that within the confines of the rocky, barren West could be found valor, freedom, and, above all, justice.

Within that formula, American movie fans avidly followed the roles of their favorite stars and became conversant with Gary Cooper's angst in *High Noon* (1952), Lee Marvin's humor in *Cat Ballou* (1965), Marlon Brando's viciousness in *Missouri Breaks* (1976), or Kevin Costner's sensitivity in *Dances with Wolves* (1990). Cinema buffs can talk for hours about *A Fistful of Dollars* (1964), *Little Big Man* (1970), or *Shane* (1952). But no one did more to perfect the cowboy figure than John Wayne. Indeed, he so absorbed the flint and fiber of the character that Americans forgot where the actor stopped and the role began. Wayne's screen credentials constituted a catalogue of the film history of the American cowboy. In each—among them *Stagecoach* (1939), *Tall in the Saddle* (1944), *Red River* (1948), *Fort Apache* (1948), *Rio Bravo* (1959), *The Man Who Shot Liberty Valance* (1962), *The Sons of Katie Elder* (1965), *El Dorado* (1967), and *Rio Lobo* (1970)—Wayne offered American viewers a straightforward, easily comprehended performance. Audiences knew what to expect in a John Wayne cowboy film: obvious heroes and villains whose final encounters affirmed that in the West, tough problems had clear-cut, honorable solutions. The Duke, as he was known, helped to cement that philosophy and its cowboy values of decency and honesty, valor and integrity, in living technicolor.

As his list of films grew, Wayne, clearly attuned to the standard he represented, accepted scripts that were apparently more complicated in characterization but that did not undercut cowboy-Wayne virtues. *True Grit* (1969) and *The Cowboys* (1972) made his formula a bit more nuanced and definitely more compelling. Despite his artistic advances, his basic film plots remained uniform and his philosophical solutions unchanged. His cowboy characters typically projected a solid wisdom, convinced that truth and justice would carry the day. As his physical body aged, Wayne's personal values—always very American, very masculine, and painfully simplistic—held constant. Once said to be the most recognized film star in the world, John Wayne personified the cinematic definition of cowboy life.

By the time he made his final appearance in *The Shootist*, a 1976 film about a dying gunfighter in a dying West, Wayne had won over even his critics. A brilliant opening sequence that used clips from a dozen of his earlier films reminded audiences that John Wayne had ridden hard on America's cinematic range for more than forty years; almost half of his nearly two hundred movies had been Westerns. At the end of *The Shootist*, as his character died on the barroom floor, Wayne, himself clearly losing a battle with cancer, seemed to say that the West *had* changed, but not the values he endorsed in those four decades of filmmaking. The American public worshiped this film and its dying cowboy hero, fictional and real. In its aftermath, many wept with the actress Maureen O'Hara, a longtime Wayne friend and costar, when she appeared before a congressional committee to plead that the dying John Wayne be honored with the highly coveted U.S. Medal of Freedom. It seemed fitting, for Wayne himself vigorously held to the conservative, masculine, chauvinistic values that so clearly shaped western films and came to dominate American political thinking in the 1980s. That this amazing career of film achievement had really explained very little about the historical realities of the nineteenth-century West mattered not at all to Wayne's fans, Maureen O'Hara, or the U.S. Congress.

Rather, the ultimate expression of Americans' confidence in John Wayne and the cowboy mentality occurred one year after the Duke's 1979 death, when an elderly ex–film star whose personal identity also seemed carefully woven into the many cowboy roles he played was elected president of the United States. Ronald Reagan stepped out of his job as host for television's *Death Valley Days* and into the White House without any visible transformation, even given an earlier tenure in the California governor's mansion. Though more often seen in a tuxedo than his ranch clothes, Reagan, in many aspects of his presidency, made clear his attachment to the basic western script formula that the "good guys wear white hats."

The Reagan conviction that the West defined the country and democracy revealed itself clearly in the administration's rapid-fire acquisition of numerous works of western art. By 1982, the White House permanent collection boasted forty new pieces—paintings, prints, and sculptures—with western themes. Additionally, almost 130 pieces of art on loan from around the country decorated the halls and offices of the White House. In the official West Wing and Oval Office, Frederic Remington bronzes, Thomas Moran landscapes, and George Catlin Indians surrounded those privy to the inner circle. Upstairs, in their private quarters, Ronald and Nancy Reagan gazed on western landscapes painted by Thomas Moran and Thomas Hill.

The Reagans' choice for artistic decor well matched the general interests of the American public. During this same era, the craze for western design and culture reached new heights throughout the United States. Cowboys themselves, or many who claimed to be, led the charge. For example, the Cowboy Artists Association of America devoted itself to "preserving western tradition." The group, organized in 1966 because members wanted better exposure for their art, held an annual gathering featuring both a trail ride and an auction. By 1981, almost two thousand people flocked to the latter event, which collected approximately $1.46 million for eighty pieces of work.

After cowboy artists established their association, cowboy poets followed suit. By 1985, their organization set Elko, Nevada, as the site of its annual gathering. Within less than a decade of its founding, the cowboy poetry craze had swept the nation. Each year

A shared national
myth about the West
contributes to the on-
going popularity and
success of western mo-
tifs in contemporary
advertising.

Chaps: The New Men's
Cologne by Ralph Lauren.
Advertisement, 1979.
Courtesy of L'Oréal, Cos-
metic and Fragrance Di-
vision of Cosmair, Inc.

attendance at the national meeting expanded, and "cowboys," determined to "preserve our way of life," arrived from all over the country. In an event that quickly assumed commercial overtones, no one seemed ready with a definition of cowboy poetry or of the way of life to be preserved. Did poets or poems make cowboy poetry? Did one have to be a cowboy to write cowboy poetry? Was it necessary only to wear the appropriate attire to become a cowboy poet? Did cowboy poetry have any connection to nineteenth-century values, or did it focus on ranch humor? The answers to these questions remained blurry into the 1990s, but the popularity of and profits for the cowboy poets ballooned. Conferences, symposia, rodeos, and fairs began to invite the better known of these performers, whose subjects and rhymes often remained remarkably mundane and predictable.

Larger marketing schemes continued to sell western culture to the American consumer. In the mid-1970s, first-class eastern department stores sponsored annual trunk shows of silver and turquoise jewelry, complete with a Native American demonstrator. Leather boutiques that sold soft pouches, fringed jackets, and tooled vests dotted the nation's malls. On the clothing scene, the designer Ralph Lauren quickly dominated, setting a national style with his western line of stone-washed denim items, new clothes intended to look old, like the West itself.

By 1983, Lauren altered his western pitch and joined forces with J. P. Stevens, once only a textile company, in the manufacture of a wide assortment of designer products. With the emphasis on decor, advertisements displayed a western background of clay-red ceramic pots, wagon wheels, and giant cactus plants. Customers decorated entire bedrooms—drapes, rugs, bed linens—in color-coordinated matching Southwest patterns. Kitchen decor moved from an eastern country-cupboard style to western rustic ranch.

Lauren, the quintessential self-made man, often spoke about how he "believed in America." He acquired a ranch that encompassed thousands of Colorado acres in 1982, and he appeared, casually attired in plaid shirts and old boots, in his own magazine spreads. Consumers, who had never heard of Frederick Jackson Turner, agreed that Lauren, a child of New York who once considered becoming a history teacher, had rediscovered the meaning of the American West. However, the historian Ann Fabian noted, "Lauren found profits in a reinvented past, and he has been busy retelling in fashions and home decorations a story of white male migration, imperial conquest, and American development."

Between 1978 and 1988, Lauren's advertisements even more blatantly appealed to a distinctly white middle-class clientele that apparently wanted two things—stability and classiness. Sales exploded. Fashion-magazine advertisements sponsored by Lauren and other companies such as Dan Post Boots, Jacques Carcanques Jewelry, and Butterick Patterns framed lean, long-haired young women resting against sun-dappled rocks, old-time saloon fronts, and horse stalls. In various wordings, the advertisements mentioned the "pure America," where clothes in "pretty pioneer styles" had a "sense of adventure" and a "respect for tradition." Among these businesses, the West not only represented the best of the nation's history but also offered solid values, made a fashion statement, and defined style. These photographs captured rustic western images, but by the mid-1980s, slightly Indian-looking models in *Vogue* wore ultra-soft chamois dresses inset with gold panels and edged with gold fringe, frontier-basic in style but upscale in cost with price tags of almost six hundred dollars.

The West had galloped onto Madison Avenue. The country rushed into an era that, perhaps more than any earlier time of western adoration, cared little for the artistic renderings of the individual and only for the image that could be purchased. As a 1982 *Mademoiselle* spread entitled "Colors of the Earth" recommended, fashionable products appeared in "earth shades reminiscent of desert horizons, sun-drenched canyons, and mesas." As the trend mounted, designers who in 1978 had first noted a national demand for authentic "horn"—a nineteenth-century furniture crafted from Texas longhorn steers—profited greatly when prices for individual pieces rose to between five and twenty thousand dollars. Ubiquitous cowboys in Marlboro cigarette advertisements peppered urban billboards and every kind of national publication. Automobile companies set the sleekest new car model, along with an alluring woman, atop a high red-rock butte. Florists recommended a masculine cactus dish-garden for that recently promoted company executive. Architects advocated underground structures for residential and commercial needs, drawing on the frontier sod house for inspiration and design. Appealing to the public for deregulation, a western-based telephone company displayed a rodeo action photo and noted, "Take the bull by the horns or the bull takes you." Amid a clamor of western music, old and new, in 1978, the rusty voice of Willie Nelson rose above all others, urging, "Mommas, Don't Let Your Babies Grow Up to Be Cowboys."

In 1991, Billy Crystal, a stand-up comic from the Catskills, ignored Nelson's advice and tried his hand at cow-punching stardom. In his film *City Slickers*, Crystal teamed with old-time western star Jack Palance to warn young American males that unless they literally plunged back into a nineteenth-century cattle drive and learned "to be men," modern society threatened to emasculate them. In technology and sophistication, the nation had surpassed that nineteenth-century West, but American men needed to cherish the skills, the simplicity, the honesty, and the bravery—the maleness of its day. The grandeur of the scenery, the swelling music, the cowboy plot complete with self-reliance, heroism, and honesty, and the gentle, unchallenging women convinced viewers that two weeks in the West rearranged the values of these overpampered New York executives. *City Slickers* broke records at the box office, and Jack Palance won an Oscar for his role as the tough cowboy who snarled, "We are a dying breed."

In all these ventures, from the nineteenth through the twentieth century, the West meant something special to American consumers. From wilderness tales to splashy television productions, a substantial group of Americans derived national meaning from western expansion, and the experience touched the country's collective spirit. Although the fadlike aspects of western commercialism ebbed from time to time, the affection these Americans harbored for the West never totally died. In general, many Americans displayed remarkable consistency in their willingness to buy into the western myth in almost any form. Clearly, through mass marketing and commercial exploitation, powerful elements in western popular culture escaped the confines of region and embraced the nation. Yet, nagging problems linger about this bonding of national myth with commercial enterprise. Elements—some of them not especially edifying—lurk in the background of this apparent success story.

Essentially, across the span of the nation, many Americans—young and old, men and women—indulged their western fantasies so completely that they tolerated and encouraged misrepresentations of history. As a result, America saddled itself with a popular culture organized around problematic expressions of race, class, and gender. Yet, western popular culture persists in its suggestion that Americans shared a commonality of experience.

Profound contradictions mark the popular culture of the West, but there is no reason to assume that these cultural markers are permanently defined. Smug assumptions that the West is an easy place to understand have been proven wrong before. Revisionist thinking will continue, since the changing configurations of western history beckon to each new generation. Not just white Americans but also the sons and daughters of many cultures will have the opportunity, should they choose, to recast the symbols of the legacy of the West. After all, the images of the West belong to everyone, despite efforts, in both the past and the present, to kidnap them for only a select audience. If anything, the West gave all people a historical arena in which to imagine the opportunity and justice that define America's most positive national values. Although the formula for the popular story of the West often fell short of accuracy, the essentials empower those who demand a reinterpretation of the people and events. Those people, and there are many around the world, feel a sense of kinship with the place and purpose of the West. They can still reclaim its justice, its opportunity, its identity, and its spirit and rework western popular culture into larger, more attractive, more generous patterns. The American West deserves the effort, and who is to say that such a transformation will not happen?

Bibliographic Note

The literature of the popular culture of the American West is as vast and far-reaching as the subject itself. Not all subjects are included in this brief essay.

A number of general studies are useful for acquiring an overview of the broad subject of the West and popular culture: Anne Farrar Hyde, *An American Vision: Far Western Landscape and National Culture, 1820–1920* (New York, 1990), offers a gracefully written assessment of the construction of tourist centers for the American public; Lawrence W. Levine, *Highbrow/Lowbrow: The Emergence of Cultural Hierarchy in America* (Cambridge, Mass., 1988), although not regional in its focus, is valuable for the background it lends; Barbara Novak, *Nature and Culture: American Landscape and Painting, 1825–1875* (New York, 1980), includes fascinating descriptions of the bonding of Americans to the wilderness through developments in art; William Cronon, George Miles, and Jay Gitlin, eds., *Under An Open Sky: Rethinking America's Western Past* (New York, 1992), is a collection of essays that touches on many useful topics, including popular culture and the modern West; Susan Armitage and Elizabeth Jameson, eds., *The Women's West* (Norman, 1987), is a compilation of essays that focuses on many cultural areas for western women; and Richard White's concluding chapter, "The Imagined West," in *"It's Your Misfortune and None of My Own": A New History of the American West* (Norman, 1991), discusses commercialism, the American mind, and the West. For a discussion of heroes in early America, see Michael A. Lofaro and Joe Cummings, *Crockett at Two Hundred: New Perspectives on the Man and the Myth* (Knoxville, 1989), John Mack Faragher, *Daniel Boone: The Life and Legend of an American Pioneer* (New York, 1992), Daryl Jones, *The Dime Novel Western* (Bowling Green, Ohio, 1978), and David M. Emmons, "Social Myth and Social Reality," *Montana: The Magazine of Western History* 39 (Autumn 1989): 2–9.

Much of the interesting and important work on popular culture in the West has appeared in journal articles in publications such as *American West (AW)*, which began in 1963 and is now

American West: Its Land and Its People (*AWLP*), and *Montana: The Magazine of Western History* (*MTMWH*). Both have examined popular culture while still offering the reader solidly researched articles about the American West. Any student of western popular culture would do well to survey these and other journals. Examples of significant articles follow.

For art and the West, see these articles: Keith L. Bryant, "The Atchison, Topeka, and Santa Fe Railway and the Development of the Taos and Santa Fe Art Colonies," *Western Historical Quarterly* 9 (October 1978): 437–53; W. H. Hutchinson, "The Western Legacy of W.H.D. Koerner," *AW* 16 (September/October 1979): 32–44; Peter E. Palmquist, "The Life and Photography of Carleton E. Watkins," *AW* 17 (July/August 1980): 14–29; Clement E. Conger with William G. Allman, "Western Art in the White House," *AWLP* 19 (March/April 1982): 34–41; James K. Ballinger and Susan P. Gordon, "The Popular West," *AWLP* 19 (July/August 1982): 36–45; Ted Schwarz, "The Santa Fe Railway and Early Southwest Artists," *AWLP* 19 (September/October 1982): 32–41; Edith Hamlin, "Maynard Dixon: Painter of the West," *AWLP* 19 (November/December 1982): 50–59; and Richard W. Etulain, "Art and Architecture in the West," *MTMWH* 40 (Autumn 1990): 2–11.

For entertainment and films, see John G. Cawelti, *The Six Gun Mystique* (Bowling Green, Ohio, 1971). John H. Lenihan's *Showdown: Confronting Modern America in the Western Film* (Urbana, 1980), provides the reader with a highly readable, insightful analysis of the Western. Kristine Fredriksson's *American Rodeo: From Buffalo Bill to Big Business* (College Station, Tex., 1985), although not a scholarly analysis, contains a great deal of factual material about American rodeo. See also Richard D. McGhee, *John Wayne: Actor, Artist, Hero* (Jefferson, N.C., 1990), Lonn Taylor and Ingrid Maar, comps., *The American Cowboy* (Washington, D.C., 1983), Richard W. Etulain, comp., *Western Films: A Brief History* (Manhattan, Kans., 1983), and the following journal articles: Paul Andrew Hutton, "Celluloid Lawmen," *AWLP* 21 (May/June 1984): 58–65; Bodie Thoene and Rona Stuck, "Navajo Nation Meets Hollywood," *AWLP* 20 (September/October 1983): 38–44; Stan Steiner, "Real Horses and Mythic Riders," *AWLP* 18 (September/October 1981): 54–59; Paul Andrew Hutton, "Correct in Every Detail: General Custer in Hollywood," *MTMWH* 41 (Winter 1991): 29–57; "The Cowboy's West: A Special Issue," *AW* 14 (November/December 1977); "Darling Beautiful Western Girls: Sweethearts of the Wild West Shows," *AWLP* 22 (July/August 1985): 44–48; and Helene R. Day, "The Prince Who Would Be Mayor," *AWLP* 22 (January/February 1985): 54–58.

For tourism, see Alfred Runte's works: "The National Parks in Idealism and Reality," *MTMWH* 38 (Summer 1988): 75–76; *National Parks: The American Experience* (Lincoln, 1979); and *Yosemite: The Embattled Wilderness* (Lincoln, 1990). See also the following: David Lavender, "The Accessible Wilderness," *AW* 11 (January 1974): 18–27; the entire issue of *AW* 16 (July/August 1979), particularly Richard A. Bartlett, "The Presence of the Past," pp. 16–17, 59, and Lee Silliman, "'As Kind and Generous a Host as Ever Lived': Howard Eaton and the Birth of Western Dude Ranching," pp. 18–31; Peter Skafte, "Rubber Rafting Western Rivers: Yesterday and Today," *AWLP* 21 (March/April 1984): 26–34; and Lawrence R. Borne, "Dude Ranching in the Rockies," *MTMWH* 38 (Summer 1988): 14–27. Borne is also the author of *Welcome to My West: I. H. Larom, Dude Rancher* (Cody, Wyo., 1982) and *Dude Ranching: A Complete History* (Albuquerque, 1983).

For the subject of music, see Bill C. Malone, *Country Music U.S.A.: A Fifty-Year History* (Austin, 1968), the standard work in the field. See also Bill C. Malone and Judith McCulloh, eds., *Stars of Country Music: Uncle Dave Macon to Johnny Rodriguez* (Urbana, 1975), James N. Gregory, *American Exodus: The Dust Bowl Migration and Okie Culture in California* (New York, 1989), and Richard Aquila, "Images of the American West in Rock Music," *Western Historical Quarterly* 11 (October 1980): 415–32.

Other articles include the following: Robert M. Utley, "The Presence of the Past: Promontory Summit," *AW* 17 (March/April 1980): 34–39; Laurie K. Mercier, "Women's Economic Role in Montana Agriculture: 'You Had to Make Every Minute Count,'" *MTMWH* 38 (Autumn 1988): 50–61; Manya Winsted, "On the Trail of the Cowboys Fame and Fortune for CAA," *AW* 18 (March/April 1981): 56–59; William T. Anderson, "Wall Drug: South Dakota's Tourist Emporium," *AWLP* 22 (March/April 1985): 72–76; Thomas W. Pew, Jr., "Summit Powwow at Canyon de Chelly," *AWLP* 21 (November/December 1984): 38–44; Michael Wallis, "New Trails for Old Time Boots, *AW* 18 (January/February 1981): 38–47, 64; James Maurer, "Prairie Dugouts to Underground Dream Houses," *AWLP* 18 (November/ December 1981): 34–41; Alma M. Garcia, "A Mexican American Community's Struggle for Educational Equality," *Journal of Ethnic Studies* 17 (Fall 1989): 133–39; LaVerne Harrell Clark, "The Girls' Puberty Ceremony of the San Carlos Apaches," *Journal of Popular Culture* 10 (Fall 1976): 431–48; Nicolas Kanellos, "A Brief Overview of the Mexican-American Circus in the Southwest," *Journal of Popular Culture* 18 (Fall 1984): 77–84; and Alessandra Stanley, "Presidency by Ralph Lauren," *New Republic*, 12 December 1988.

Chapter Twenty-three

Comparing Wests and Frontiers

WALTER NUGENT

The following pages will employ a wide-angle lens to compare, if only in snapshots, America's Wests with other frontiers, Wests, and regions. There is no doubt that the American West, however defined, was unique. But then, so were the Wests and frontiers of Canada, Australia, South Africa, Brazil, Argentina, and other places. Did they have any-thing in common as Wests and frontiers? Did similar processes take place in all or most of them? Do the processes of change in these other places tell us anything new about the American West? Is it worth looking at them, not only to satisfy our curiosity but also to get other perspectives on ourselves?

The American West itself has not always been where it is now. To the U.S. Census Bureau, the twentieth-century West has meant the thirteen westernmost states, with Montana, Wyoming, Colorado, and New Mexico forming the eastern tier. Unofficial definitions would usually agree, perhaps leaving out Hawai`i or Alaska, perhaps including the western halves of the Great Plains states. As recently as 1910 or 1920, however, the "West" still included Chicago and the Mississippi Valley, as it had for much of the nineteenth century. In the eighteenth century the term referred to any place west of the Appalachians, and in the seventeenth century it included the area west of the Tidewater in the Chesapeake or a few dozen miles from the Atlantic farther north. The West as a region, as it is now known, will stay in the same place because there is no place farther west to go. Historically, however, the western region has been a movable feast.

The places that are no longer Wests are now regarded simply as regions or sec-tions—sizable areas with some sort of distinctiveness. These regions include (among others) New England, the Piedmont, Appalachia, and the Midwest. As transitory Wests, they were once called frontiers—the New England frontier, the southern frontier—and those frontiers-become-regions were themselves complex. A recent history of southern frontiers by John S. Otto, for example, identifies a frontier of occupance (very sparse white settlement), a grazing frontier, an extensive farming frontier, and an intensive farming frontier, as well as "huge frontier enclaves with unique agricultural adaptations." The common element in these southern frontiers is that they were all continuing to progress toward a stable level of rural settlement. Similar distinctions may be made in the history of the Midwest and Great Plains and isolated parts of the present West. Much

Frontier settlement in New Zealand, as in other areas around the world, has been marked by a Europe-an incursion into ar-eas inhabited by indigenous peoples, with the subsequent transformation of the natural landscape and the disruption of indigenous cultural patterns.

Unidentified photogra-pher. Land Clearance at Mangaonoho, Rangitikei. Photograph, early 1900s. Child Collection (#G77631/1), Alexander Turnbull Library, Wellington, New Zealand.

of today's West, however, never became settled in that way. Instead, its history has been marked by frontiers of exploitation and entrepreneurship (mining, stock raising, and lumbering most importantly), and by that definition, it becomes virtually impossible to point to exactly where the frontier in the present West ended, if indeed it has. But whether or not it is still a "frontier," the West is certainly one among several American regions.

In U.S. history, then, what are now regions or sections were once frontiers, and the present West is both. Each place's shift over time from "frontier" to "former frontier" or "postfrontier" has usually been called by American historians the "frontier process"; when this shift has occurred in Latin America it has been called "Third World development." They are different processes but are almost certainly related. Regions presently exist in all of the countries that had, or have, frontiers. Canada, for example, includes the Maritimes, Quebec, Ontario (a nineteenth-century farming frontier that soon became urban and industrial), the prairie provinces, British Columbia, and the North. Argentina has long opposed the city (Buenos Aires) and the pampas. Brazil is a mélange of regions, all once frontiers, among them the Nordeste, Minas Gerais, Rio and São Paulo states, the southernmost "gaucho" state of Rio Grande do Sul, and the still-developing frontiers of the Mato Grosso, Rondônia, and Amazonia in general. Australia divides between coast and "outback"—or, more precisely, between sheep, wheat, and mining frontiers on the one hand and vibrant cities on the other. In all of these countries—all developed by European-stock people since 1492—regions change, beginning as frontiers of settlement or exploitation and becoming settled-rural or urban-industrial, often both.

How then should we define "West"? In American terms it means the present West but also, when speaking historically, those regions that are frontiers no longer. In Canada and Australia the term "West" locates frontiers lying in that direction, but in Argentina, Brazil, and South Africa, "West" is inappropriate. In all of those countries, however, "frontier" seems to cover the place as well as the process by which they evolve into a nonfrontier region. That being so, let us look at several frontier histories, remembering that some of them were also "Wests" at one time or another and that one such region, the western half of the United States, roughly, will remain "the West" for foreseeable time.

"Frontier" was recently defined, waggishly, as a place where white people are scarce—not where they have always been scarce, as in Japan or China, but where they were (or are) scarce but tried not to be. That covers most places outside of Europe where Europeans and their descendants have tried to go. In this sense, Europeans began their expansionism close to the beginning of recorded history. The expansionist efforts of Alexander the Great and the Romans are early cases in point. The Roman Empire was studded with "frontier" army garrisons from Spain to Syria, northern Africa to Britain; and in some cases these were not just outposts but real settlements, such as the "Colonia" on the Rhine that has long since become Köln. Rome increasingly fell back on the device of acculturating the so-called barbarian tribes into Roman ways, rather than populating the empire with Romans themselves. There were simply not enough Romans to go around, and as population pressure from the barbarian tribes intensified, the western empire shrank and finally disappeared in the year 476. A similar process of expansion,

De Insulis nuper in mari Indico repertis

Insula hyspana

Columbus's voyages helped initiate a new era of European expansionism that led to the development of frontier cultures around the world. This first European depiction of Native Americans, published in a 1494 illustrated edition of Columbus's report of his 1492–93 voyage, suggests Europeans' fascination with the inhabitants of the New World but, with the elaborate ship, reasserts the superiority of European culture.

Unidentified artist. Insula hyspana. Woodcut, 1493. From Carolus Verardus, In laudem serenissimi Ferdinandi (Basel, 1494). Beinecke Rare Book and Manuscript Library, Yale University, New Haven, Connecticut.

stabilizing, and retreat took place in the eastern empire, but it continued another thousand years until the Ottoman Turks snuffed it out in 1453.

By then other Europeans showed signs of frontier activity that not only were expansionist but involved colonial settlements. The Norse voyages of the ninth to the eleventh centuries led to colonies in Iceland, Greenland, and present Newfoundland.

The Newfoundland settlement at L'Anse aux Meadows was probably the first colony created in North America. Iceland has had a continuous European-stock history since those voyages. The Norse colony at Greenland lasted over five hundred years until it ended shortly after 1400, probably because of a prolonged cycle of cold weather. The Norse people undoubtedly developed a frontier; they went "where white people were scarce," they were expansionist, and they created colonies of settlement rather than trading posts or army garrisons. Presumably they had contact with the native peoples and carried on economic activity involving the extractable resources of the frontier area (in this case, fishing). These elements—an increasing ethnic presence, expansionism, settlement, and economic extraction—are major parts of a definition of "frontier."

Beginning in the 1490s, European overseas activity expanded dramatically and on a geographic scale far greater than that of Alexander, the Romans, or the Norse people. With the voyages of Christopher Columbus, beginning in 1492, and of Vasco da Gama in 1497 around the Cape of Good Hope to India, followed less than thirty years later by Ferdinand Magellan's expedition around the entire world, the true period of European expansionism—and a whole new set of definitions of "frontier"—took shape. Those voyages introduced the four or five centuries of world history dominated by "the expansion of Europe," the "rise of the West," or in the words of the Texas historian Walter Prescott Webb, "the Great Frontier."

Portuguese and Spanish, then French and English, explorers and colonizers, under governmental blessing and often financial support, headed in several directions away from the traditional centers of European civilization. Even in the early twentieth century, Europeans and their descendants still expanded in economic, social, and cultural ways, but by 1950 they had generally stopped annexing and controlling territory. European empires that developed after 1500 reached their maximum extent by 1914 and have virtually all been dismantled since then, rapidly so after 1945.

In the Americas, the Antipodes, and South Africa, however, settlement accompanied empire building to such an extent that those areas became Neo-Europes. They are what Webb and others have regarded as the frontier lands of modern world history. As capitalism came into being, so did they. As nonanimal power sources—steam, electric, and nuclear—were created, so were they. The characteristics already noted of pre-1500 European frontiers continued into the modern period, but modern technology and economic organization, as well as the global geography involved, so changed the nature of frontier activity as to make it qualitatively different from the ancient cases. The great variety of post-1500 frontiers—colonial or imperial, permanent or temporary, agricultural or extractive, Latin or Anglo-Saxon, centralized or individualistic (and many other sets of opposites)—requires that we push somewhat further in the search for a precise definition of comparable frontiers.

Were Europeans, since Alexander the Great, the only expansionists? By no means entirely. But world history furnishes relatively few cases of expansionism outside of efforts by Europeans. Some of these cases, however, were spectacular. They include the expansion of Islam throughout the Middle East, North Africa, Iberia, and eastward to Indonesia beginning in the seventh century; Muslim expansion into Europe was checked in Spain only in 1492 and was not decisively thwarted until 1683, when the Pole Stefan Batory stopped the Ottomans at the gates of Vienna. From the eighth to the thirteenth centuries, Polynesians peopled the Pacific vastness, including previously uninhabited Hawai`i and New Zealand. The Mongol and Tatar incursions into present Russia and eastern Europe in the thirteenth and fourteenth centuries are another example. The consolidation of central power in China and, in quite recent times, the expansion of Japan into northern Honshu and Hokkaido are others. Nevertheless, Europeans created the lasting settler societies as well as the colonies and outposts that ringed the coasts of Africa and of eastern and southern Asia, at least for some time. In the case of the British Raj in India, Europeans ruled, for nearly two hundred years, one of the largest and most venerable world civilizations.

A distinction may be drawn, however, between Europeans' frontiers and their empires. Frontiers lasted; empires disappeared. The basis of the distinction is the demographic strength of the European incursion in relation to the indigenous people, especially if those people already possessed an advanced culture and technology for their time—and a biological resistance to European diseases. European "expansion" needs to be qualified: was it expansion involving settlement in fairly large numbers relative to the natives, or was it simply expansion in the form of economic outposts or military-naval garrisons? The Raj, despite its size and longevity, was essentially an outpost and garrison.

On smaller scales the British, French, German, Spanish, Portuguese, Belgian, Dutch, and Italian colonies of the nineteenth century in Africa, Asia, and Oceania were also outposts and garrisons. Despite a barrage of propaganda from advocates of colonies, no great masses of Europeans chose to emigrate to them. Instead, during the years of mass emigration from Europe (roughly 1870 to 1914), Italians emigrated to Argentina and Brazil, Spaniards went to Cuba, and Britons populated Canada and (in much smaller numbers) Australia, New Zealand, and South Africa, while just about every European emigrant group entered the United States. In time those thirty-some million European migrants became integrated into the Neo-Europes of North America and the southern temperate zone.

In certain colonial areas, such as Britain's in East Africa, France's in West Africa, and the Netherlands' in Indonesia, plantation settlements arose where a minority European planter elite developed a local resource like coffee or rubber using the local population as a labor force. These efforts were relatively transitory. The elite aside, they did not form frontiers of settlement in the New World or Antipodean sense. On some occasions a frontier of resource exploitation did become a frontier of settlement. This shift occurred in certain areas where an initially thin European presence, interested in exploiting a local resource, expanded demographically or intermarried with the local people so as to become a stable Neo-Europe, if a rather modified one. Cases in point include the fur-trade region of the American and Canadian West, Brazil's Minas Gerais (which began with diamond mining), and various gold rush locales. The distinction between frontiers and empires, as well as that between plantation and small-settler agriculture, was not always thorough or permanent, but it nonetheless helps sort out which places were frontiers and which were not.

"Frontier" thus means frontiers of European settlement in previously non-European areas, with some allowance also for frontiers of resource exploitation. In virtually every instance, the Europeans and their descendants encountered indigenous peoples. After the Europeans established themselves in some numbers (and it did not take many, once European contagious diseases took hold), the native peoples declined in numbers and retreated in space. As is now well known, the victories of Hernando Cortés over the Aztecs and Francisco Pizarro over the Incas in the early sixteenth century were greatly aided by horses and gunpowder, but their real secret weapons were pathogens against which the natives were defenseless.

The Varieties of American Frontier Experience

Within the area that is now the United States, a number of frontiers have existed since the early 1600s when Spanish, French, and British colonization began there. From these frontiers, distinguishable regions have developed such as New England, the Ohio Valley, and the Gulf Plains. The varieties of American frontier experience have been broad, and most of the main types have appeared elsewhere in the world: grain growing, lumbering, livestock raising, gold mining, coal mining, oil drilling, even town building. Each of these involved its own environmental problems, contacts with "Indians," and economic and social organization. All together, they compose the interior history of North America. This history, with its environmental adjustments and exploitation of land and other resources, is still continuing, although some important types of frontiers, most notably the frontier of new agricultural settlement, ended some time ago in North America.

For much of U.S. history the frontier meant a moving zone of contact, a series of places that shifted over time, generally in a western direction but sometimes north or even east, especially after the middle of the nineteenth century. This moving zone of contact, which thereafter became settled-rural and urban areas, expanded very slowly at first and then, almost continuously, accelerated. From the first English settlements shortly after 1600, the western edge of the frontier zone penetrated inland only a few dozen miles by 1700 and involved only about 250,000 people of European and African stock. By 1800 the edge of settlement had crossed the Appalachian chain at all points, had moved westward three to five hundred miles, and had enclosed to the east of it 5.3 million nonindigenous people. By 1870 the western edge of the zone had breached the ninety-eighth meridian at most points, putting the eastern half of the now territorially complete United States behind it, while significant oases of non-Indian populations lived west of the ninety-eighth, in northern California, Mormon Utah, the Denver area, and many smaller places mostly created and sustained by mining, lumbering, stock raising, military forts, and commerce.

By 1920 the area under cultivation had more than doubled since 1870, and the national population surpassed one hundred million. By then more than half of those millions lived in towns and cities. The settled area increased only marginally thereafter. In some places people had already begun retreating from their overly optimistic homesteading of a few years earlier. But urban and suburban development, in the West as elsewhere, continued rapidly. In three hundred years the tentative settlements on the Atlantic seaboard had expanded to encompass the entire continental land mass, and in the process almost everything the European-stock people encountered, including themselves, had changed, for better or worse.

The acceleration was all the more remarkable if one starts the time line with

Columbus. From the 1490s to the early 1600s, hardly any frontiers of any kind existed in the future United States. In that "long sixteenth century," Spain managed to subdue or exterminate the local people and establish firm control over the Caribbean islands, central Mexico, Peru, and related areas, and Portugal did the same along the Brazilian coast. But in the area that later became the United States, sixteenth-century European efforts were unimpressive: the unproductive or downright disastrous expeditions of Hernando de Soto, Francisco Vásquez de Coronado, and a few others (ca. 1539–42), the toy-like Spanish post at St. Augustine (1565), and the abortive English attempt to establish the Roanoke Colony in 1585.

Despite these inglorious episodes, Europeans almost without exception gained the impression that they had a right not only to invade such parts of North America as they wished but also to occupy and make use of these regions as they wished. They considered themselves limited only by their own power, and they showed little regard for any rights, or even for the lives, of the people who had been there since the Ice Age. This idea, seldom modified in the history of Anglo-American expansion except by the conscience-pleasing policy that Indian title could not be extinguished without some kind of treaty, guided action throughout the future of the expansionist process.

As the sixteenth century drew to an end and the seventeenth century began, permanent European settlement in the future area of the United States and Canada started in earnest. Juan de Oñate founded El Paso del Norte in 1598 and planted a line of settlements up the Rio Grande valley to Santa Fe (1609) and beyond; an English stock company put ashore settlers on the northern side of the James River in Virginia in 1607; and France founded Quebec in 1608. These three efforts involved three different modes of settlement, sets of institutions, relations with the home country, and relations with the Indians and the environment; that is, these were three different frontiers. But they had in common the intent to settle at least some Europeans, and they succeeded in that.

The first hundred years of English settlement brought some results: successful footholds in the Chesapeake and New England, and later in the seventeenth century in the Carolinas and along the Delaware River, as well as absorption of short-lived colonization efforts by the Swedes and Dutch. Contact with the Indians was often bloody, as evidenced by the Powhatans' near-extinction of the Jamestown colony in 1622 and, on the other hand, the Puritans' liquidation of the Pequots and other neighbors a few years later. Yet the impact of these rather few Europeans on the vast space of the Atlantic seaboard appeared minimal, even if the English had few doubts about the command in Genesis to use the land as they saw fit. Life was indeed a struggle, and often a short one, but the sense persisted that the struggle could be won and they had a right to win it. Before 1700 or 1720, however, the social and economic organization of the settlements was either peculiar, as in New England, or precarious, as in the Chesapeake. These first hundred years were in a true sense precolonial, because the kind of rural society that so typified American life for the next two hundred years had not yet taken shape. It did so in the early eighteenth century, as a frontier-rural mode that lasted into the twentieth.

Patterns of life in seventeenth-century New England and the Chesapeake have been described elsewhere in far more detail than is possible or necessary here. However, a brief

This image of a model American farm along the St. Lawrence River represents a particularly prosperous example of the kind of rural agricultural settlement that marked the American frontier of the late 18th century. An illustration for the travel account of a Scottish gentleman, the image suggests the kind of cultural borrowing that marked this rural life, with a "Virginia rail fence," "Dutch barn," supply of "Indian corn," and native canoes.

McIntyre, engraver. Plan of an American New Cleared Farm. *Engraving, 1793. From Patrick Campbell,* Travels in the Interior Inhabited Parts of North America *(Edinburgh, 1793). Beinecke Rare Book and Manuscript Library, Yale University, New Haven, Connecticut.*

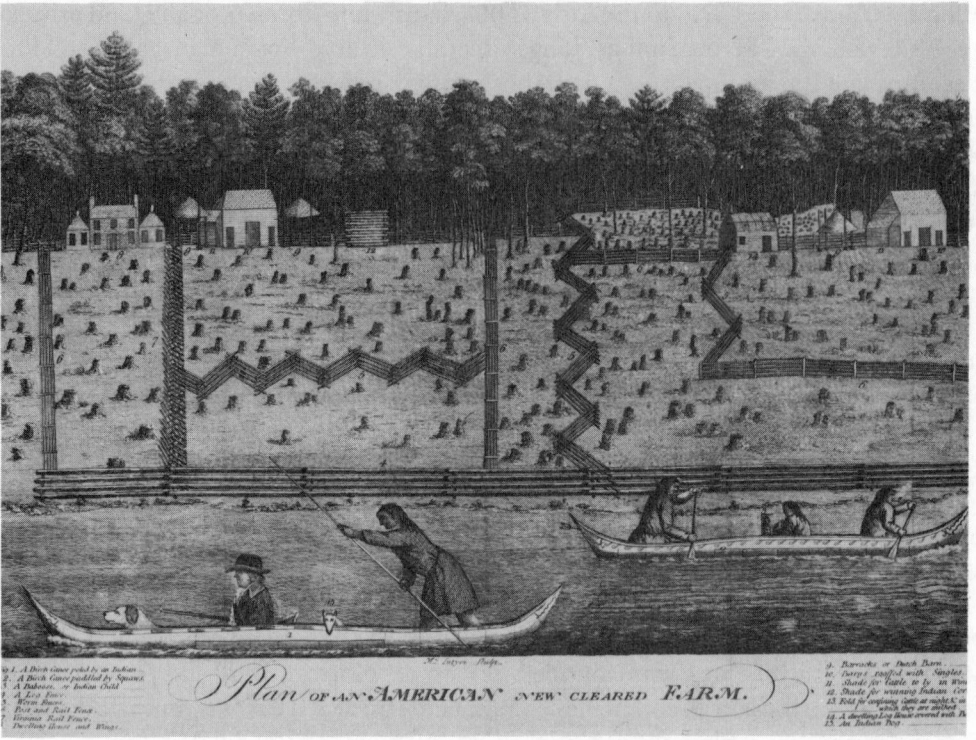

Plan OF AN *AMERICAN* NEW CLEARED *FARM.*

sketch will show how the farm-frontier future developed from these earliest patterns yet differed from them. In the Chesapeake, settlers arrived from England under an indenture of servitude that covered their passage and, after several years of labor, entitled them to land of their own. Individual ownership of land, by smallholders with secure title, became the common practice. Larger plantations also developed and from 1619 began using Africans, whose indenture was permanent; well before the century was over, slave labor was a fixture. Settlement of the Tidewater, much of it by planters raising tobacco for sale in England and shipping directly on oceangoing vessels at their own docks, came early.

But such activity was limited by the line of waterfalls that marked the eastern edge of the Piedmont. Into that backcountry, smallholding settlers rapidly moved. By 1676 they were strong enough to stage Bacon's Rebellion, their uprising to protest taxation and lack of frontier defense. Sometime very late in the seventeenth century, securely by 1720, Chesapeake settlers had finally begun to sustain and enlarge their own population, reproducing themselves more rapidly than they died off, and thus reducing the need for English and African immigrants to keep the settlement going. By the early eighteenth century they had moved well into the Piedmont and down the Great Valley of the Appalachians, subsisting on their own efforts, effective masters of their own small plots of wilderness. By the time of the American Revolution, Virginia was the largest colony in both size and population, home to one of every five Americans.

In New England, meanwhile, a quite different settlement pattern developed out of the Massachusetts Bay Colony, founded at Boston in 1630. This was not the first coastal settlement in New England, but it quickly became dominant. Full membership in the church congregation was identical with full membership in town governance; new settlements combined town and congregation and were created only as the theocratic central authority authorized them. Individuals and families held title to specific pieces of land, but only as granted and permitted by the town-congregation leadership. Private ownership, within the communal structure, typified New England settlement for the next three generations. By the early 1700s, however, the power of the theocracy had seriously eroded. Original family properties could be subdivided no further if the next generation was to earn much of a living from them. Population pressure, the demand for new land, and waning restraints from the theocracy produced a burst of settlements along the rivers leading inland, most notably the Connecticut. The backcountry of New England began to look more and more like the Chesapeake.

From 1720 through the American Revolution, the white English-stock population, reinforced by Rhinelanders and Scotch-Irish in Pennsylvania and western Virginia, pressed into areas new to them and "where whites were scarce." In the North, they cleared the forest and pushed back the Indians in New Hampshire and Vermont. In New York they proceeded up the Hudson and a short distance westward along the Mohawk River until Iroquois resistance stopped them. In Pennsylvania they followed military roads over the mountains to the head of the Ohio River. And in the South they swarmed across the rest of the Piedmont and southwestward to the tip of the Great Valley at Cumberland Gap. By 1776, from New England to South Carolina, they were poised to enter the middle of the continent. When the revolutionary war ended, they immediately did so. Slashing and burning the forest as they went, they produced enough to nourish themselves, and perhaps a little more to sell on a market if they could find one. They lived in large nuclear families and produced children at the biologically maximum rate. In law and politics they neither saw nor respected much human authority, British or colonial, but supported those who upheld their claim to land. They assumed, as always, that they had a right to take and use that land as they saw fit.

In 1783 the United States found itself in possession of not only the thirteen rebellious British colonies but also most of the land east of the Mississippi and south of the Great Lakes that had been French until 1763. Between 1785 and 1790 the new U.S. government established three basic policies regarding its transappalachian areas. First, Indian rights to land could be extinguished only by treaties—a policy never quite broken but greatly bent in governmental and popular practice. Second, western regions from the Appalachians to the Mississippi River would ultimately become states on an equal footing with the original thirteen—thus solving the problem of control that Britain failed to solve between 1763 and 1776 and encouraging western settlement while preserving political unity. Third, the eight states with colonial-era claims to western lands gave them up, allowing these lands to become the public domain of the whole United States; the Land Ordinance of 1785 prescribed how those lands would be surveyed and sold to smallholders. Despite initial major sell-offs to speculator-developers, the government maintained the principle of conveying the land to smallholders, with firm title, as rapidly as it could. By 1848 the area north of the Ohio River became five states, populated mostly by smallholders. The area to the south included a substantial number of large holdings, including new cotton plantations with many slaves in the Old Southwest in the 1820s and 1830s. Even there, however, smallholders (some with a few slaves, many with none) predominated numerically. The acquisition of the Louisiana Territory in 1803, effectively doubling the size of the country, promised to continue these patterns almost indefinitely. As it happened, the deforestation and cultivation of virtually the entire continent was completed by 1920, and the impressment of the native peoples into small reservations was an accomplished fact by 1890.

The uncontested heyday of the frontier-rural mode of life and the agricultural frontier of settlement lasted from the 1780s to the 1840s. In those decades population expanded 35 percent each decade, nearly unaided by migrants from Europe. Almost all of the increase took place on or near farms. The population of the United States doubled itself roughly every twenty-two years, from under three million in 1780 to twenty-three million in 1850. If ever there was a "frontier process," it worked, then, in the interaction of high fertility and abundant available land, with no Malthusian penalties for large families. The young simply left for cultivable areas farther west, depending on the military and the government to force and persuade the Indians to retreat. Crop and livestock technology remained premechanical and appropriate to near-subsistence levels, but forests and wildlife continued to disappear, slowly and inexorably.

The emphasis so far has been on the sameness of frontiers rather than on regional or other differences. This is, however, only a brief sketch, conflating many differences of time and place. One could easily list frontiers as early as the eighteenth century based on different crops or livestock, markets, climate, ownership-tenancy patterns, and the presence or absence of slavery. Here, however, stress has been on the broad similarities affecting people's lives, whether they were northern, southern, or transappalachian, once the frontier-rural mode of life became the American norm early in the eighteenth century.

From a broader perspective, American frontierspeople shared many characteristics, as already indicated. How their frontier-rural mode of life changed over the long run and how it shaded gradually into something quite different need to be pointed out. Their economic activity was initially subsistence agriculture, developing into some involvement with markets in the early nineteenth century. But by about the 1880s, when the American railway network was put in place, they had become participants in—or captives of—regional and even worldwide capitalist markets, placing Polish, Italian, Argentine, and American midwestern wheat farmers in competition with each other.

By that point, although thousands of homesteads were yet to be created on the Great Plains, one may question whether these settlers should be called frontierspeople at all or rather just farmers. Their legal relation to the land had been laid out in the Ordinance of 1785. It established the then-embryonic survey-and-sale system of transferring the public domain from the central government to smallholders, and the system was nurtured into maturity by successive land acts through the Homestead Act in 1862 to the Newlands irrigation law of 1902 and beyond. The survey-and-sale system, to be sure, was diluted by many policies inconsistent with smallholding such as grants to railroads, by inefficient or corrupt administration, and by a failure to adjust to aridity in the western half of the country. Later policies, such as subsidizing irrigation, building massive dams, and leasing rangeland cheaply to stockmen, hastened the West into corporate capitalism.

Nevertheless, the belief that a small farmer or an aspiring one could acquire secure title to a specific tract, and the law's encouragement of that belief, made Americans enviable compared with people on most other settlement frontiers. American demographic behavior was marked for generations by very high fertility, large nuclear families, youthfulness, and a strong propensity to migrate—all connected to the availability of accessible land. The rate of failure among would-be homesteading owner-operators is hard to define and is not definitely known but was probably high. Yet the homesteading urge and ideal remained enormously powerful well into the early twentieth century. By then, rural fertility, though higher than urban, had dropped substantially, family size had decreased, median age had risen (markedly in some settled-rural areas, which had once been frontiers), and migrants were heading for towns and cities rather than unplowed land.

Relations with the Indians continued to be wary and combative. But the U.S. government's successive policies regarding Native Americans—signing treaties (1790s to 1880s) to extinguish Indian title, building military forts in the Mississippi Valley and westward (1820s and later), physically removing eastern Indians to present-day Oklahoma and Kansas (1830s–40s), and finally subduing the Plains and southwestern Indians and confining them to reservations (1840s–90)—made life much easier for land-seeking frontierspeople than it had been in colonial times. Despite the 1787 Northwest Ordinance's pledge to deal with the Indians with "the utmost good faith," results were often brutal. As Alexis de Tocqueville noted in the early 1830s, "It is impossible to destroy men with more respect to the laws of humanity." Frontierspeople's relations with the physical environment continued to include deforestation and unlimited animal kill-offs (of which the destruction of the bison was the most visible but not the sole example; New England whalers did much the same to the great beasts of the oceans). On entering the arid region early in the twentieth century, settlers convinced themselves that "rain follows the plow." Thus they proceeded to disturb the fragile high plains until lack of rainfall forced many of them to retreat, leaving behind dashed hopes and a grievously damaged landscape. The reality of limits began buffeting the myth of limitlessness. In these several ways, the frontier-rural mode gradually changed and finally withered away by 1920, leaving behind a potent mythology that still shapes Americans' perceptions of reality.

In the brief years between the late 1840s and 1865, four events decisively changed American life. Each involved hundreds of thousands, even millions, of people. The first, in the Northeast, was urbanization—the sharp rise in the proportion of town and city dwellers in the population. Then the first massive influx of non-British immigrants began changing the populations of the Northeast, Midwest, and Far West—Irish, Germans, Scandinavians, and on the West Coast, a visible number of Chinese. The third event was the California gold rush of 1849–52, attracting a quarter million fortune-seekers, mostly young men, by land and sea; it was the first of many mining booms. The fourth was the end of slavery and the other outcomes of the Civil War. The frontier-rural way of life continued for several decades, as a moving zone of new settlement shifting ever westward to the Rockies. But because of these changes, in the context of the acquisition of Texas, Oregon, and much of northern Mexico in 1845–48, which brought the United States to the Pacific and provided it with most of its future West, the frontier-rural mode began to have competition from cities and from more blatantly exploitative frontiers.

In 1850 only 15 percent of the U.S. population lived in towns and cities of twenty-five hundred or more people. The proportion had, however, risen almost 5 percent since 1840 and would continue to rise on an average of 5 percent per decade (except for the 1930s) until peaking at about 75 percent urban in 1970. The American people were overwhelmingly (90 to 95 percent) rural until 1840, but thereafter became steadily less so. Moreover, the national figure masked great regional differences; Massachusetts reached an urban majority by 1860, and other northeastern industrial states quickly followed suit. If the end of the settlement frontier may be marked by the date at which a state or section begins exporting more people than it attracts, then New England's frontier days were over no later than the 1820s and New York's and Pennsylvania's by the 1840s. The same may be said for the seaboard South. The South's distinctiveness, however, lay not in urbanization, which made few significant inroads until the early twentieth century, or even in slavery. The region was distinguished by its climate and the fact that one-third of its people were black. The South held over 90 percent of America's black minority as late as 1910. The South would eventually be urbanized, but long after the other regions, especially the West. It is hard to imagine that the expansion of Atlanta, Miami, or any other large southern city after 1945 could have happened without air conditioning. Millions of southern black people, rural dwellers especially, moved to cities in the North, Midwest, and West from 1915 until their net migration flow stabilized in the late 1960s.

Urbanization and the end of slavery thus had enormous consequences. But more needs to be said about the gold rush because it was the first large-scale example of a different kind of frontier, nontraditional in 1850 but visibly outlasting the settlement frontier and in various ways still continuing in the West of the United States. That West—the Far West to some—has consisted of the Rocky Mountain, Great Basin, and Pacific Coast subregions. Within it, after the gold rush, social patterns developed that hardly resemble the 1720–1920 frontier-rural mode, and yet they are frontier patterns, in reality as well as in mythology.

The new type of frontier introduced by gold rush California differed most obviously from the traditional frontier-rural mode in that it was nonagricultural, attempting to exploit what was under the land rather than the surface. Instead of the farm frontier's moving line or zone of settlement, this frontier of resource exploitation became manifest unpredictably almost anywhere and often disappeared just as quickly. In certain cases of rich but technologically challenging mineral deposits, surface mining gave way to hard-rock, deep-shaft, hydraulic, or strip mining. With that, the mining camps became mining towns or cities, thereby losing their frontier character and becoming simply outposts of industrial capitalism.

In its fundamental demographic structure, the frontier of exploitation also differed from the settlement frontier. The 1850 census reported that of the ninety-three thousand people in California, 92 percent were male and 91 percent were in the fifteen-to-forty-four age range. Absent were children, older people, and almost as completely, women. Unattached youths often migrated from opportunity to opportunity. But the young men on mining frontiers were especially footloose and probably as a result were more violent and less careful about resources than people on settlement frontiers, wasteful though they were as well. In any event, mining frontiers and demographically similar ones such as cattle drives, cattle towns, lumber camps, and, in the twentieth century, construction sites, strip mines, oil fields, and other exploitative settlements comprised a kind of frontier essentially different from the traditional frontier-rural mode. If they were that different, do they deserve to be called frontiers at all? Certainly, for two reasons. First, settlement frontiers had their opportunistic and exploitative side too but exploited more slowly. Second, common usage defines cowboys, prospectors, and the like as frontierspeople. And so they were, and are; but they were not part of the frontier-rural tradition.

The frontiers of exploitation, in most cases, lost their bizarre demographic features in the twentieth century but otherwise lasted well beyond the demise of the settlement frontiers. Exploitative frontiers have been especially prominent in the Rocky Mountains, Great Basin, and Pacific subregions, but the type has not been absent from Texas oil fields or the northern Great Plains center-pivot irrigation that has mined irreplaceable water from the Ogallala Aquifer. Because of them, parts of the West lacked settlement frontiers, and frontiers of exploitation existed outside of the West at times. In other words, one can speak of a West without a frontier, a frontier without a West.

The settlement frontier itself met a new challenge after 1860 as it advanced onto the Great Plains. The vast area from the Atlantic Coast to the ninety-eighth meridian had been relatively well watered and was initially timbered or grassy. But settlers entering the arid plains in the late nineteenth and early twentieth centuries encountered decreasing rainfall and groundwater, river systems that were non-navigable and seasonally dry, and land that could not be farmed because it was mountainous or desert. Irrigation began to be touted as a solution from the late 1880s onward, but it never could, and never did, render productive more than a small fraction of the Great Plains and Rocky Mountains.

An early and important exception was Utah. After arriving in this semiarid region in the late 1840s, the Mormons based the survival of their community on irrigation. The Mormons extended irrigation, and themselves, to Idaho's Snake River valley and other areas in the next two generations by means of settlements planned and authorized by the church's central authority. In so doing, they created a town-congregation frontier of settlement paralleled in the American experience only by similarly theocratic New England over two hundred years earlier and at various times by much smaller and shorter-lived communitarian experiments. A complete typology of frontiers should include communitarian theocracies that flourished in inhospitable circumstances because of their ideological cohesion and commitment.

By the late twentieth century, the United States comprised many one-time settlement frontiers that were often losing population although producing more crops and livestock than ever. Farm population declined steadily for fifty years starting in the late 1930s, to about what it was in 1810—except that in 1810 the farm population was 93 percent of the whole and in 1990 only just over 2 percent. Agriculture had become agribusiness, nowhere more aggressively than in California, where massive irrigation networks, government-subsidized, enabled large corporate firms employing migrant workers of a succession of ethnicities to produce for market more crops and livestock than any other state. Ironically, California, the most productive agricultural state in the late twentieth century, scarcely experienced a settlement frontier of the eastern, southern, and midwestern type but included large landholdings since Spanish and Mexican times. Not coincidentally it was also the home of the first major gold rush and two of the most spectacular examples of wealthy urbanization in the world, the Bay Area and the Los Angeles Basin. Urban spread around well-watered Puget Sound and in the irrigated Arizona desert after 1940 was not quite as grand as in California. Together, however, they formed a latter-day frontier of exploitation—capitalist, federally influenced in many ways, multiethnic, and multiracial—in economic and social terms the leading edge of American culture.

Although farm settlement engaged far more Americans over the years than ranching or mining frontiers, the latter produced the legends and much of the cultural definition derived from frontier experience. No farm ballad ever competed with "Home on the Range" or "O My Darling Clementine"; no man with a pitchfork compares as a romantic figure to the forty-niner or even the Marlboro cowboy. American professional football teams call themselves Forty-Niners, Oilers, Broncos, and Cowboys but never Sowers or Reapers or even the more promising Threshers. Macho pursuits, rather than husbandry, seize the national imagination.

Canada's Several Frontiers and Wests

Culturally as well as geographically, Canada is closer to the United States than is any other society. Like the United States, Canada has had several frontiers, some of them closely paralleling the American experience. Canada had an urban frontier, if outposts such as Quebec (1608) and Montreal (1642), dominated by state, church, and commerce, can be called that. It very early had a frontier of exploitation in the fur trade, where *coureurs de bois* roamed from the St. Lawrence Valley westward beyond the upper Great Lakes before there were such places as Canada or the United States. And it had three distinct frontiers of settlement: that of the French *habitants* in New Brunswick and Quebec, beginning in the late seventeenth century; that of Anglophone Ontario in the early and mid-nineteenth century; and that of the prairies and Great Plains from the mid-1880s to 1930.

Canadian historians have long argued whether Canada had a frontier experience anything like that of the United States. It did and did not. The *habitant* and fur-trade frontiers had no counterparts at any time, but Ontario's mid-nineteenth-century farm frontier was very like nearby Ohio's, and Saskatchewan and Alberta were almost of a piece with adjacent North Dakota and Montana around 1910. Canada also, like the United States, had its exploitative frontiers, beginning with the Fraser River gold rush of 1858–67 and proceeding through its cattlemen's frontier of the late nineteenth century, the Yukon gold rush of the late 1890s, and the Alberta oil boom that began in

The generous land policy of the Canadian government drew more than four million settlers to western Canada during the first decade of the 20th century. Many homesteaders were ultimately defeated by the aridity of the lands. Others, like these Alberta ranch hands, became part of a successful cattleman's frontier that strongly resembled older American models.

Unidentified photographer. Canadian Cowboys, Near Thelma, Alberta. Gelatin silver print, ca. 1910. Glenbow Archives, Calgary, Canada.

1909, to the massive mid-century hydroelectric projects in Labrador, Quebec, Ontario, and the Northwest Territories—more a northern than a western frontier.

Canada has always differed from the United States in possessing two "core" cultures, French and English, and this duality affected its frontier and regional history. The European presence in Canada before about 1745 was exclusively French, except for a few English fur traders. French fur traders, missionaries, and soldiers dotted the vast wilderness from Quebec to the Great Lakes and southward to New Orleans and the border of New Spain, scarcely "filling" the region in any real sense. Some French mingled with the Indians in ways that were more benign than English or Spanish contacts. The majority of French, who probably totaled only seventy thousand at the time of the English victory at Quebec in 1759, dwelt in smallholdings hugging the banks of the St. Lawrence, seldom pushing far into a rugged interior. A scattering of towns served the needs of commerce, public administration, and the church. Partly because of their small numbers, but also by design and policy, the French got on well with the Indians, whom they welcomed to *réserves* amid their own riverine settlements, and ventured as guests and traders into the *pays d'en haut*, the backcountry that was the Indians' traditional land.

English fur trading into northern Canada followed the creation of the Hudson's Bay Company in 1670. But English Canada as a settlement frontier did not begin until the middle of the eighteenth century, when several important events occurred in close succession: the founding of Halifax, Nova Scotia, in 1749; the removal of the Acadians to Louisiana in the 1750s; the capture of the French naval base at Louisbourg in 1755; and James Wolfe's defeat of Louis Montcalm at the Quebec citadel in 1759. French authority ceased shortly after that, although the French cultural and economic presence in the fur trade and the Quebec settlements continued to flourish. French Canada, however, never produced an aggressively expanding line of settlement, and after 1759 it remained a self-contained entity. Its population grew not from immigration but from high birthrates in the nineteenth century. But unlike the young Anglo Canadians and Anglo Americans of that time, few young *Québecois* went west to establish frontier farms. Most gravitated instead to Montreal or migrated to New England in search of work. Like many labor-seeking migrants, they often stayed much longer than they had planned.

The American Revolution helped materially to create British Canada. Life became so difficult for American colonials loyal to the Crown that twenty-five thousand of them emigrated to New Brunswick and another six thousand to the upper St. Lawrence and the north shore of Lake Ontario. The latter group in particular built a true frontier of settlement, hacking homesteads out of Crown lands and producing children with amazing frequency. After the War of 1812, migrants from Britain and Ireland swelled the population. By 1850, much of the good farmland in Ontario had been taken up, and the frontier there had virtually closed by 1860.

Certain crucial differences between the Canadian and the American frontier experiences had begun to appear. First, the earliest English-speaking settlers in Ontario explicitly rejected the newly independent United States. They were Loyalists, and for their loyalty the Crown rewarded them with land grants and other compensation. The abortive attempt by Americans to capture Ontario in the War of 1812 reinforced in the Loyalists' children and newly arrived immigrants the idea that Britain was their protector and that they were part of the Empire. Although Canadian nationalism never became as aggressively convinced of its "mission" as the American brand, Canadians continued to believe that their land should be occupied and its borders made secure against further American incursions.

But an intractable problem prevented the extension of Ontario's frontier after 1860. Almost from the beginning, in Upper Canada, settlers had encountered the massive physiographic barrier of the Canadian Shield. With granitic rock lying only a few inches below the topsoil or actually cropping out at the surface and mixing with muskeg and scrub forest, much of Ontario's huge land mass could never be plowed and turned into farms. The Shield extended for hundreds of miles north of an east-west line across southern Ontario, even crossing the St. Lawrence into northern New York at one point; geologically it is eons older than the St. Lawrence and the Great Lakes. The Shield left open to farm settlement only extreme eastern Ontario, the land a few dozen miles north of Lake Ontario, and the southwestern peninsula above Lake Erie and east of Lake Huron and the Detroit and St. Clair rivers.

The Ontario frontier's natural extension was into Michigan and, from there, southwest and west. If the peace treaty of 1783 between Britain and the United States had been based on the actual military situation at the close of the revolutionary war, rather than on politics or diplomacy, then Michigan, Wisconsin, and adjacent areas would have become Canadian. The Shield prevented young Ontarians from continuing the frontier of settlement northwestward, whereas the international boundary meant that they moved out of Canada into Michigan, and beyond to the American Midwest.

The Canadian frontier of settlement was thus interrupted in space—and, as Canadian historians have pointed out, it was also interrupted in time for an entire generation or more, weakening any hold the frontier idea might have had in Canada. Whereas the American frontier experience was continuous from earliest times into the twentieth century, Canada's was fragmented into several nearly discontinuous pieces. The interruptions helped prevent the development of a national mythology of frontier-based exceptionalism, which was so characteristic of the United States.

The southwestward diversion of the settlement flow after 1860, together with the strength of industrial-urban development in New York State and New England, gave Canadian population history a peculiar sieve-like quality in the late nineteenth century. Despite high birthrates and substantial immigration, especially from Britain and Ireland, Canada suffered a net outflow of people for most of the 1870–1900 period. During much of that time, however, the Ottawa government under Prime Minister John A. Macdonald (1867–73, 1878–91) put into effect what he called the National Policy. It secured the area west of the Shield and north of the forty-ninth parallel for Canada, and it promoted there a second frontier of settlement that lasted until 1930. As the historian Carl Solberg noted, Canadians expected a lot from their government, and they got it; the National Policy included protective tariffs, a transcontinental railroad (the Canadian Pacific, or CPR) that bound the West to Ontario and Quebec, and a public land policy aimed directly at peopling the western prairies.

Macdonald's Liberal successor, Wilfrid Laurier (1896–1911), agreed with the basic aims of the National Policy. He and his aggressive interior minister, Clifford Sifton, employed an extensive network of recruiting agents in Europe, a cascade of booster propaganda, and a newfound willingness to admit non-British immigrants such as Ukrainians who were experienced in farming cold, steppe-like regions. As a result, the frontier of settlement in western Canada became a boom country, bringing in over four hundred thousand people *per year* between 1901 and 1911 and transferring sixty-eight million acres from the Dominion lands to settlers and another fifty-two million acres to railroads and other developers.

The law by which the Dominion lands were distributed resembled the American Homestead Act of 1862 but improved on it by requiring only three years' actual residence instead of five and by making available adjoining tracts of CPR land on attractive terms. It unambiguously identified each tract and clearly spelled out how to gain title. Canadian policy, like the American, in the long run worked all too well, enticing thousands of settlers after 1900 into arid and cold regions from which they later had to retreat. These areas included the shortgrass prairie of southern Alberta and Saskatchewan known as Palliser's Triangle, long regarded as too dry to cultivate, and also some settlements well north of Edmonton. Just after the Dominion lands policy ended in 1930, the Canadian geographer W.L.G. Joerg wrote: "The settlement of the Canadian West has exceeded all but the most optimistic estimates. Settlers have invaded Palliser's Triangle; country long designated as grazing country has been homesteaded; the northern forest has been attacked in some areas. Settlers with tractors are as far north as the 58th parallel. . . . All this has not been done, however, without grave human wastage. To the hardships of those pioneers who have succeeded we must add the losses

of those who have failed." In some areas more than half of the attempted homesteads had to be abandoned, even before the economic disaster of the 1930s. As in the United States, a limited acreage east of the Rockies proved amenable to irrigation, sponsored in Canada by railroads and private developers rather than by government. Mormons also irrigated; their successful settlement around Cardston, Alberta (1906), replicated the earlier Mormon frontier in Utah and southern Idaho on a smaller scale.

In the meantime Canada also developed frontiers of exploitation. Canadian historians have often claimed that mining and cattle-raising frontiers were less violent north of the forty-ninth parallel than south of it and that Canada escaped most of the violence associated with American mining camps and cattle towns. They explain this by the presence of the Royal Canadian Mounted Police from 1874 onward, before the arrival of cattlemen, miners, or settlers. The Mounted Police negotiated with the Blackfeet for land and kept order thereafter, fortified by an effective judicial system. Central authority, evidenced also in the National Policy that included the CPR and kept the public lands under Dominion rather than provincial control until 1930, was more constant and continuing than in the United States. Otherwise the Canadian cattlemen's frontier resembled the American. Ranchers resisted farmer encroachment, maintained their presettler alliance with the Mounted Police, and made clearly known their Tory and pro-Empire views. They held the mineral rights on their land, and when oil was discovered early in the twentieth century they became oilmen too. In Canada, sheep ranchers prized individualism but also law and order; the stereotypical hero of the

Canadian West was no Wild Bill Hickok, or Billy the Kid, but was the red-coated man on horseback of the Mounted Police.

The depression of the 1930s forced retrenchment on Canada's several frontiers as it did in the United States. The Dominion Land Policy concluded, according to plan, in 1930, and Ottawa turned over the unoccupied remnants to the provinces. After 1940, agriculture more and more became agribusiness, another latter-day form of resource exploitation.

The Frontiers of Australia, New Zealand, and South Africa

In the nineteenth century, Australia became another frontier of settlement, as well as a series of frontiers of exploitation. Its development differed from that of America and Canada in that the two frontier types were somewhat mixed, since settlement very often involved raising sheep on large grazing tracts rather than crops on small homesteads. Moreover, Australia faced its own physiographic barrier: hills and mountains west of which was no verdant Mississippi Valley but, rather, a prairie that became increasingly arid, soon turning into an uninhabitable desert. Because its arid region is so vast, Australia had no "second chance" at frontier-making, as Canada had after Ontario became filled and then, decades later, when the CPR and settlement on the contiguous American northern Great Plains opened Manitoba, Saskatchewan, and Alberta. Australian settlement remained tied to its eastern and southern coasts. Several writers have attributed the strength of the Labor party in Australian politics to the absence of a frontier of small-farm settlement, which in the United States, at least in theory, siphoned potential workers away from strong labor unions toward farming. Australian egalitarianism, they say, stemmed from Chartism and the importing of undiluted British working-class culture, not from the interaction of Europeans, native peoples, and the environment, as in North America.

Physiography clamped strict limits on Australian frontiers. Although Australia's land mass is almost identical in size to the lower forty-eight American states, its population in the late 1980s was about sixteen million, less than two-thirds of Canada's, and was 85 percent urban. Only 9 percent of the land was considered arable; the lines of twenty-inch and twelve-inch average annual rainfall, about the minimum for raising wheat and livestock, are distressingly close to each other and to the seacoast, limiting farms and stock lands to the coastal fringe from southern Queensland through New South Wales and Victoria into South Australia, together with Tasmania and the extreme southwestern region around Perth. Although some hundreds of thousands of acres west of the mountains proved suitable for the commercial raising of sheep, cattle, and wheat, the great mass of the interior was and is too arid to permit settlement despite optimistic assessments as late as the 1920s. The ancestors of the 50,000 pure-blooded and 150,000 mixed-blood aborigines living in the late 1980s were swept back into the arid interior, displaced by farms and ranchers. They did not resist as the North American Indians did. Australia, as one of its historians noted, has a hinterland but not a heartland. It is a coastal, city-oriented society and has been so throughout its history.

That history began in 1788 when British prisoners were first transported to Botany Bay. The prison-colony period lasted until 1840 in New South Wales and a few years longer in Tasmania. It was followed by several decades of a squatters' frontier, overlaid almost immediately by a gold rush, principally in Victoria, beginning in 1851. "Squatter" applied to anyone, rich or poor, who moved onto Crown land to raise sheep, and by 1850 such people occupied much of the best land. Then came the gold rush, bringing in thousands of young men to a frontier of exploitation much like California's at the same historic moment. After they exhausted the easiest pickings, they formed a large cadre suddenly eager to turn to homesteading. They were blocked, however, by the squatters who had gotten to the land just a few years ahead of them.

Under popular pressure, New South Wales and Victoria passed homestead-type laws in 1861 and with later amendments began a period of "free selection" intended to provide small farmers with land. But squatters bent the laws to their purposes even more effectively than ranchers did in the United States. By the 1880s they owned, freehold, most of whatever land they wanted. The struggle between former squatters with large holdings and the smallholding farmer went on for some years, but from the 1870s through 1900, sheep raising meant large ranches, which were export oriented (especially after refrigerated ships began carrying Australian mutton to England in 1882) and capitalistic. These ranches composed the typically Australian "big man's frontier" so much in contrast to the smallholding frontiers of settlement in Canada and the United States. In Australia, as in the United States and Canada (and for that matter in Scotland and Ireland), something about sheep made people nationalistic. Yet a yearning for unfettered—frontier?—individualism raised the violent highwayman Ned Kelly to the status of a national hero, rather like Jesse James or, less lethally, Black Bart in the American West. Some similar taste raised the jolly swagman of the ballad "Waltzing Matilda" to national legend.

The "small men" gained a foothold only on the fringe, west of the big men in New South Wales and Victoria and well inland in South Australia. Wheat became their export staple. A survey-and-sale system, not unlike that in the United States and Canada though the grid pattern was less rigid, ensured title. The law also allowed a person more than one "selection," permitting him to grow wheat for a few years, move on just before final payment, and select again—thus creating a "hollow frontier," a crop-raising frontier of exploitation. But aridity took a greater toll. Overeager sheepmen and wheat growers alike had to retreat early in the twentieth century from millions of acres that proved to be climatically treacherous, as happened also on the American and Canadian Great Plains. Sheep and wheat have remained Australia's major exports, but the regions of cultivation stabilized not long after 1900, and Australia continued to become more urban than ever.

Although at the national level Australia and the United States had rather different frontier experiences, comparisons at a regional level, such as between northern California and Victoria, have been neatly drawn. Quite unlike the frontier-rural mode of the Midwest, California's frontiers consisted of a gold rush followed by wheat production in large landholdings and eventually production of many staples aided by massive irrigation works. In Victoria too, exploitative gold-seeking preceded rural settlement. Wool production followed, then wheat in the 1880s and 1890s and also irrigation. Though none of these enterprises reached the California scale, the sequence was similar. And each region centered on booming metropolises, San Francisco and Melbourne.

In New Zealand the small settler occupied a much more prominent place than in Australia. The New Zealand smallholder also concentrated on sheep and, like the Australian "big man," was willingly pulled into international markets by refrigerated ships after 1882. A royal governor arrived a week after the first English landing in January 1840, and Crown lands thereafter were distributed in relatively small parcels under strict government control. The many freeholders used near-universal suffrage and an abundance of local-government units to create and preserve, in the words of the historian Donald Denoon, a dictatorship not of the proletariat but of the smallholding sheepman. Large sheep-holdings began to develop on the earlier-settled South Island, but there and later on the North Island the smallholders managed to prevent land monopoly from developing as it did in Australia and, as we will shortly see, in Argentina.

New Zealand's physiography differs greatly from Australia's in being more temperate and mountainous, although the amount of potentially cultivable land is only a fraction of the total. Enough became available to allow settlement to continue through the 1920s. New Zealand's entire "frontier" history thus lasted only eighty or ninety years. It resembled North America's more than Australia's in one major respect: the bloodiness of the conflict between Europeans and the indigenous Maoris, who had reached New Zealand several centuries earlier from Polynesia. The first Maori War, 1843–48, opened the South Island and the second, 1860–70, the North. Treaties relieved the Maoris of most of their best land by 1900. Unprotected by immunities to European diseases, the Maoris declined steeply in number. After 1900 they made something of a comeback, as did Indians in North America after reaching their population nadir in the 1890s. Resources were used ruthlessly, according to a local historian: forests quickly cut for lumber or sheep pasture, gold and coal mined hydraulically, and farming done so extensively as to cause serious erosion—all practices well known in the United States.

South Africa, even more than Australia and New Zealand, is a special case. In the very broadest terms, Australia and New Zealand resembled the United States and Canada in becoming settler societies, with the settlers completely dominating the indigenous population and with settlement ultimately limited by geography more than by other humans. In South Africa the native peoples have continued greatly to outnumber the Europeans. Moreover, South Africa has included two distinct European core groups, which were at times at war with each other, a situation once present in Canada. But the Dutch and English in South Africa together have formed a small minority amid a large African majority. South Africa, therefore, has veered toward the plantation type of European colonization that flourished and then disappeared in Kenya, Zimbabwe, Indonesia, and elsewhere. It would be interesting to measure more precisely why the minority remained in power for so long in South Africa but not in those other places, that is, whether there is a "magic number" or ratio of just enough Europeans to retain control.

The European presence began in 1652 when the Dutch founded their way station to the East Indies at Cape Town; in 1806 the English captured the place to provide a pause on their trips to India. Despite that long history, Europeans were scarce during much of this time, numbering only twenty thousand in 1800 and one million in 1900. Whether Dutch or English, European South Africa for most of its first two hundred years

Aridity has been a major factor shaping settlement patterns in frontier cultures around the world. In Argentina, settlement became most dense in the damp northeastern quadrant of the nation, whereas in Australia, large communities developed only a thin, well-watered, coastal band. In Canada, as in the United States, arid climates east of the Rockies limited frontier settlement and growth.

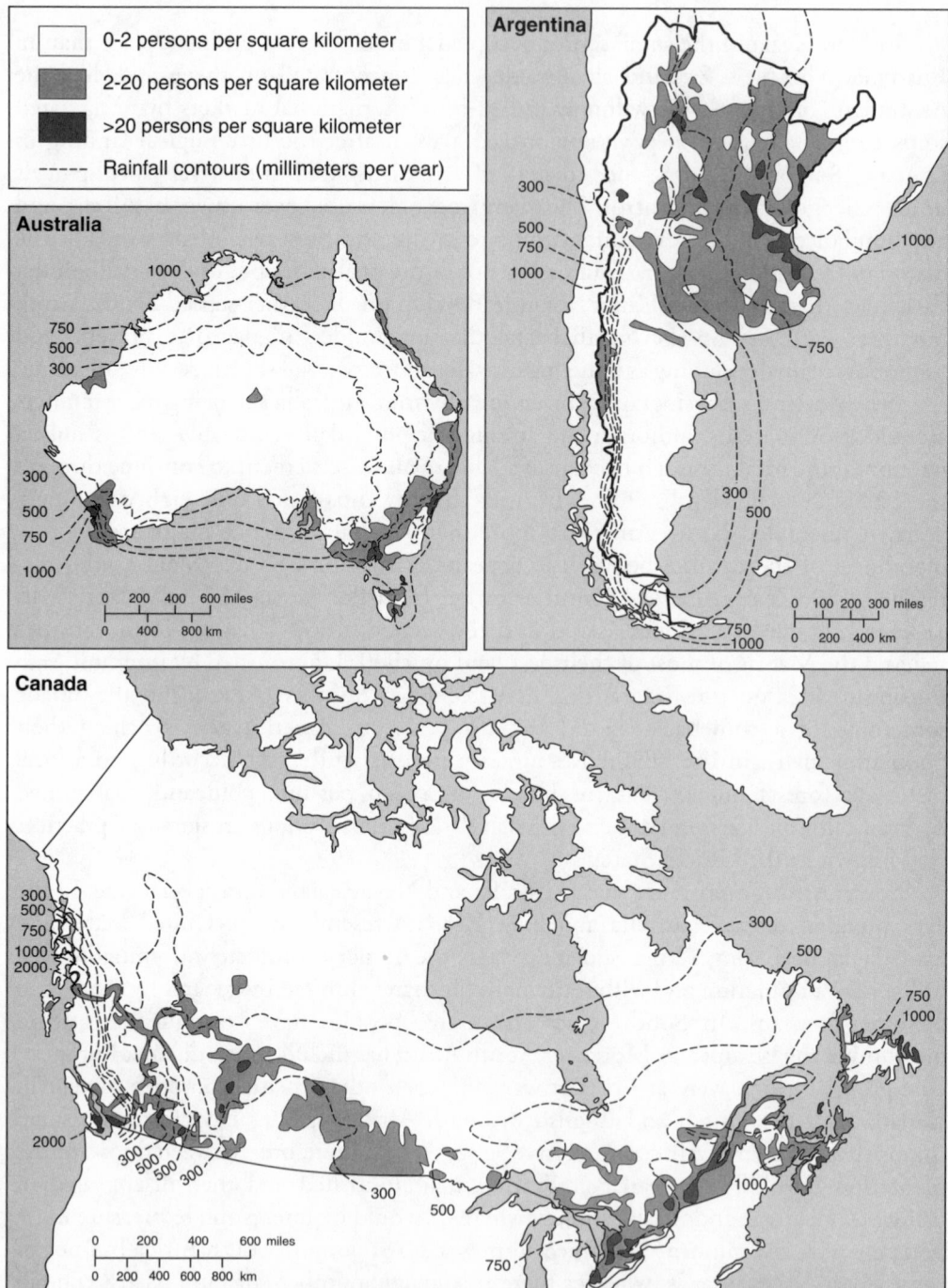

Population Density and Annual Rainfall in Argentina, Australia, and Canada

consisted of "company towns" and a few sheepherders in a riverless, mostly arid land, where they confronted much more numerous native peoples, many of whom in the interior possessed a roughly similar technology.

In their first decades near the Cape, the Dutch pushed back the native Khois and established commercial pastoralism nearby. By the close of the eighteenth century they had occupied further land and had encountered indigenous settled farmers and cattle-herders who more effectively resisted the whites. The Great Trek of 1836–46, involving about fourteen thousand Afrikaners, was only the best-known episode in a continuing push into the interior. (It has been compared, incidentally, to the Mormon migration of the late 1840s. Both were peoples who were united by culture and religion and who sought to create enclaves for themselves well out of reach of hostile neighbors.) The Voortrekkers became an Afrikaner symbol of independence and self-reliance, "frontier" virtues adapted by the Dutch-speaking minority, complete with wagon trains thrusting into the wilderness as happened on the American Overland Trail in the 1840s and 1850s.

Before 1869, however, the "frontier of settlement" by Europeans was pastoral, even to an extent nomadic, marked by continuous searching for new land to replace what they had overgrazed. The Nguni peoples whom the Europeans then encountered raised cattle in much the same way, but their contact with the whites involved them in market relations and increasingly stratified them into wealthy and poor—the latter becoming an increasingly victimized peasantry. The first gold strikes and the beginning of mining for gold and diamonds in 1869 greatly enriched the whites who controlled the mines and access to outside markets. Many Ngunis drifted into low-paid wage labor. European diseases never destroyed the people of southern Africa as they did the Native Americans; Africans possessed many Old World immunities. European force did not immediately triumph either; the Zulus put up a fierce, and for some time successful, resistance to both Dutch and English. But European capitalism succeeded in creating a native economic underclass, who by the twentieth century became a political and legal underclass as well. In its broadest, sketchiest outlines—as just given—South Africa's history involved a thin, moving frontier of pastoralism. Trekking, rather than true settlement, described its pre-1870 history, which was then followed by a frontier of exploitation of gold and diamonds tied to world markets and relying on semimigrant native wageworkers. A land act of 1913 deprived Africans of seven-eighths of the land area, legalizing white farming. Exploitation of grazing land, minerals, and the local people thus characterized the European presence in South Africa, as it did elsewhere, but peculiarly in that the Europeans were so few and the native people remained so numerous.

Other New World Frontiers: Argentina and Brazil

The European frontiers of Latin America began in the first third of the sixteenth century, when Spaniards conquered the Caribbean islands, Mexico, and Peru and Portuguese colonized the coast of Brazil. Much of this activity composed a frontier of exploitation of local resources such as gold and silver, using both native people and imported Africans as a labor force. Missionary activity complemented and at times ameliorated such enslavement. European diseases ravaged the mostly nonimmune indigenous peoples and provided the Spanish and Portuguese with their most effective weapon. But before achieving independence during and after the Napoleonic Wars, Latin America resembled New France in *not* being a major frontier of settlement. Beginning in the late nineteenth century, however, Argentina and Brazil exhibited significant frontier activity comparable to what was then taking place in North America.

Argentina and Australia have been compared by economic historians from those two countries. They "became strikingly alike," in the words of two Australians. "They developed at roughly the same rate, at about the same time, with a similar chemistry of foreign and domestic factors of production, to become competing societies of similar size, wealth and structure." Both battened on British capital investment, developed railroad networks in the late nineteenth century, and became major players in world markets—Australia with sheep and wheat, Argentina with cattle and wheat. Argentina enjoyed the stronger economy from 1890 to 1930, Australia thereafter; but until recently the two economies were seldom far apart. Both countries attracted European migrants—Australia from Britain, Argentina (in larger numbers) from Italy and Spain. Both opened up at much the same time all the frontiers of settlement they would ever have. Buenos Aires as a commercial and administrative center dominated Argentine life just as Sydney and Melbourne did Australian. Argentina, however, included an even larger "big man's frontier" than did Australia.

In other respects, the Argentine frontier paralleled the American and Canadian more closely, such as when the native people were subjugated. Just before the second Riel Rebellion in western Canada (1885), when Americans were conquering the Lakotas in the Montana and Dakota territories (1876–79), General Julio Roca in 1879 destroyed and dispersed the Araucanians and opened the Argentine pampas to white exploitation and settlement. But here the parallels break down, and a key contrast emerges between the Argentine and the North American, and indeed the Australian, frontiers. Because Roca and the government parceled out the pampas to fellow soldiers and friends, ownership became immediately and permanently concentrated in a few hands. Homestead-type laws did pass in 1876 and 1884 but produced only minimal and sporadic results. Land-distribution policy was left to the provinces, in effect meaning the large proprietors, while the central government maintained a laissez-faire stance on land as on other matters.

The Italians who flooded into Argentina mostly became tenant farmers rather than freeholders. Few became citizens. Unlike in North America, no law required homesteaders to be citizens. Thus Argentina's immigrants did not become a political counterforce to the *latifundistas*, demanding roads, schools, agricultural education, or cooperatives. "Argentine agriculture," wrote Carl Solberg, comparing Canada and Argentina, "was built on the systematic exploitation of the nation's tenant farmers rather than on modern production and marketing systems." After World War I the country fell behind Australia, Canada, and the United States in world markets. Climbing the agricultural ladder from migrant worker to sharecropper to tenant to freeholder was not unheard-of in Argentina, but immigrants more often made it to the top through the building trades, the military, the bureaucracy, the professions, and the urban-located occupations that provided services rather than goods. In Santa Fe province, group settlements of family farms, known as "colonies," succeeded well from the 1880s on, yet colonies did not become the national pattern; the *latifundistas* kept control of their ever more valuable real estate. As a Latin American economic historian observed, "The mediocre housing, poor social services, and lamentable infrastructural facilities in most of those melancholy little towns scattered across the pampean zone, were eloquent testimony to the rootlessness of Argentine farming and the weakness of the rural middle class."

Gauchos used their bolas to hunt ostriches—much prized for their feathers—across the pampas of Argentina in the 19th century. The common practice of burning the range to drive the birds out into the open created tension between the gauchos and the big ranchers who lost cattle and grazing lands to the fires.

Emeric Essex Vidal (1791–1861). Balling Ostriches. *Lithograph, 1820. From Vidal,* Picturesque Illustrations of Buenos Ayres and Montevideo *(London, 1820). Courtesy The Edward E. Ayer Collection, The Newberry Library, Chicago, Illinois.*

Argentina lacked a survey-and-sale system of land conveyance, a mortgage and credit market for small farmers, or much rural upward mobility. In fact it lacked a true frontier of settlement aside from the cattle barons and the tenant farmers. It also lacked a gold rush; there was no mining frontier as in North America, Australia, South Africa, or Brazil. National life, despite rapid development of wheat and cattle for world export markets from 1880 to World War I, was dominated rather by its great city, the "Paris of the South," Buenos Aires. In 1914 Argentina compared well in national and personal wealth to almost any country in the world. But after 1945, for lack of true, broadly based development, that was no longer the case.

The gaucho, the mounted cowboy bringing down his animals with his bola, became a stock figure of national definition, although in reality the "conquest of the desert" in 1879 removed the less tameable elements of the gaucho population and changed the rest into ranch hands as dependent for wages on the landowners as Texas cowhands were on ranchers there. The gaucho may have been the hero of ballads, but the *latifundistas* called the shots, both on the pampas and in the governments. It was much the same in Brazil, where the elite of Rio Grande do Sul (the southernmost, most temperate state) like to say they are gauchos, that is, just country boys, whereas that state has disproportionately provided Brazil with its presidents and other leaders.

Brazil, with half the land mass of South America, presents even greater contrasts. Larger in size and theoretically with more available land than the continental United States, its frontier development has been different in almost all important respects from

North America's. In fact, Brazil at the close of the twentieth century was the only large country in the world where the post-1492 frontier process—both of exploitation and of settlement—was still taking place. Brazil's colonial history began with Pedro Alvares Cabral's visit in 1500, a century earlier than the colonial periods of Canada and the United States. But for two centuries or more after Cabral, colonization seldom penetrated deeply inland and was oriented around the larger coastal cities and toward Europe. African slaves began arriving early, providing the labor force for the northeastern sugar economy, a plantation-style frontier of settlement not unlike the cotton plantations of antebellum Alabama and Mississippi. In the early eighteenth century an exploitation frontier emerged some two hundred miles inland from Rio de Janeiro, in the present state of Minas Gerais ("General Mines"), with the discovery of gold, diamonds, and other gems. The Amazon Basin's rubber boom of the early twentieth century formed another plantation-type exploitation frontier.

A real frontier of settlement, however, took very long to appear. The Portuguese Crown made enormous grants of land called *sesmarias* to favored people, and although the grants were seldom developed productively, they precluded mass settlement. The folk figure of the colonial period became the *bandeirante*, the swashbuckling paramilitary leader who roamed, raided, and then returned home. In his classic book comparing Brazilian retardation to North American progress, Vianna Moog claimed that the explanation lay in Brazil's adulation of the romantic but rootless *bandeirante*, whereas in the United States the Jeffersonian yeoman farmer and his family became the ideal and often the reality. Perhaps so. But Moog also pointed out the significance of Brazil's lack of a usable interior waterway system on anything like the scale of the Ohio-Missouri-Mississippi system, as well as its lack of coal, iron, and oil at a time when industrialization required them. From the 1820s through the 1870s, the Imperial Government tried to promote settlement on the land by supporting the establishment of German and Italian colonies in Rio Grande do Sul, Santa Catarina, and Paraná in the south. These colonies included several hundred thousand people by the late nineteenth century, and the Germans in particular continued in unabsorbed enclaves through the twentieth century. But except in the three southern states, the colonists hardly made a dent in Brazil's enormous space.

Change came when Brazil took an early and permanent lead in the world coffee market. Coffee plantations in the state of Rio de Janeiro prospered in the mid-nineteenth century, and then, as soil became increasingly "tired," planters moved west into São Paulo state. Their move was accelerated by the creation of a railroad network from Santos seaport up to São Paulo city in 1867 and then hundreds of miles inland in the next few years. The abolition of slavery in 1888 and the recruitment of tens of thousands of Italians and their families as a replacement labor force caused much of São Paulo and adjoining territory finally to become a settlement frontier.

That frontier, not surprisingly, resembled the Argentine more than the North American ones, except that the immigrants' prospects for improvement were even dimmer. A few thousand did settle in "nuclear colonies," but those lucky immigrants usually brought some capital that enabled them to do so. Much more commonly, the Brazilian settler lived in one or another kind of tenancy arrangement on the land of a *fazendeiro*, a large-holding coffee planter. The government recruited entire Italian families and helped them obtain labor contracts and train tickets out to the plantations, where their living conditions were usually so unenviable that in 1902 the Italian government forbade any further Brazilian recruitment.

Some small freeholding did emerge in São Paulo and the three southernmost states, but the frontier spread only gradually in the early twentieth century, entering the state of Goiás, just north of São Paulo, in the 1930s. The leap into the interior when Brasília was planned in the 1950s and opened in the early 1960s was an event more metaphorical than demographic, more a matter of national pride than of real regional development. Eventually, however, Brasília, together with the later construction of roads into Amazonas, western Mato Grosso, and other remote states and territories, produced a Brazilian frontier of exploitation and of settlement simultaneously. Slash-and-burn agriculture, and the large-scale forest burn-offs that the world began noticing in the 1980s, accompanied the movement of over one million people into Mato Grosso, Pará, Rondônia, and nearby areas in the 1970s. Some of these people obtained plots of land from the government; many others took up unoccupied land as *posseiros*, or squatters (American-style, not Australian). Neither planned colonization nor spontaneous migration led to a contiguous and self-sustaining frontier.

The Indians, who may have numbered five million in 1500, diminished to no more than 150,000 in 1950. They had disappeared from Brazil's coastal regions by the end of the eighteenth century, and with Amazonian development in the late twentieth century their remnant was threatened again. European disease, enslavement, and military raids nearly erased them. Though Indian reserves in remote Amazonia existed, the government agencies in charge—even when sympathetically run, which was not always the case under military rule in the 1970s—were under constant pressure from gold-seekers or other developers, a situation similar to the gold rush in the Dakota Black Hills in 1874–75 that touched off the Custer episode and the ensuing Sioux War. But the Brazilian Indians lacked the ability of the Lakotas to resist.

Despite the massive expansion of São Paulo, Rio de Janeiro, Belo Horizonte, and other cities, the West and Amazonia increased their share of Brazil's population from less than 10 percent in 1940 to about 15 percent in 1980. Very few new settlers lived in official colonies but rather as peasants, squatters, smallholders, and sharecroppers together with the rubber tappers, *mestiços*, and detribalized Indians who were already there. As a whole, however, they were not producing marketable surpluses as on other settlement frontiers. They were precapitalist semisubsistence settlers, more like American frontierspeople of the pre-1870 frontier-rural mode than later market-oriented ones.

An important difference between the continuing Brazilian frontier and the 1720–1920 settlement frontier in the United States was the lack of a survey-and-sale system that securely conveyed land to smallholders. The colonial large holdings were never revoked, despite brave words in the 1850 land law and other laws down through the 1970s. The Program of National Integration of the Medici and Geisel military administrations of the 1970s promised one hundred hectares, six months' start-up pay, cheap credit, a house and implements, and other encouragements to families who would become small farmers in Amazonia. Only seven thousand of the hoped-for one hundred thousand families appeared, and a third of them did not stay long. As an American anthropologist noted, "Laws that protect squatters' rights encourage land invasion and virtually assure access to land for those with the capacity to hire gunmen." In Rondônia in the far west, would-be settlers in the 1970s continued to seek clear title without much success.

In the meantime, in the late 1970s, the government began selling large tracts to private development companies—a practice the U.S. government resorted to in the 1780s when the fledgling survey-and-sale system of the 1785 Ordinance failed to earn revenue and settle the Ohio Valley quickly enough. The differences were that Brazil lacked a land survey and that the quality of land for western Brazilian settlers in the 1980s was much more crucial than for Americans in the 1780s because the Rondônia settlers, to succeed, had to produce surpluses for market very quickly. Capitalist market relations were much more complex in the 1980s, demanding an efficiency in Rondônia and Amazonas that the subsistence American frontierspeople of the late eighteenth century were spared. The Brazilian settlers of the 1970s and 1980s also lacked alternatives; there was almost no further "West" to go to, and city life meant dire poverty.

Treatment of the Indians fluctuated from benevolent paternalism, involving removal and reservations, to harsh repression. Wholesale deforestation topped a list of environmental problems. In a number of ways, the Brazilian frontier story of the twentieth century was a replay, at fast-forward, of most of the mistakes and regrettable features that marked the frontiers of settlement and exploitation of the United States since the eighteenth century.

Frontier, Region, and West Again

These pages have only begun to touch on some of the possibilities of internal and international comparisons in the histories of frontiers, regions, and Wests. Specialists in the history of any of the countries mentioned may rightly object to the sketchiness of the patterns and generalizations given here. However, one may at least see a simple classification scheme distinguishing frontiers of settlement and of exploitation (though concrete cases were often both), plus subtypes such as plantations run by Europeans using slave or wage labor and frontiers directed by central theocratic authority. Certain continuing kinds of interaction, particularly between European-stock people with native people and with the natural environment, seem to appear in all frontier histories, for good or for ill.

The regional uniqueness—and lack of it—in the present West of the United States still deserve clearer definition. The character of that West may help define others and also the ongoing Brazilian situation. Some scholars have looked at the history of frontiers as simply a special case of migration history, sharing the characteristics typical of migrations. Although that is too much of a reduction, it does point up the structural similarity among frontiers in all times and places and invites frontier and western historians to enrich their thinking with the scholarship on international migration. In a very few but very arresting works, theories devised to understand and guide social and economic development in the Third World have been applied to American frontier and western history; modernization, conquest, dependency theory, and center-periphery theory, as well as Antonio Gramsci's idea of hegemony of ruling elites, are cases in point. Insights from cultural anthropology and cultural geography have permitted historians to look with more empathy on native people and with less assurance that the advance of frontiers was beneficial to all concerned.

The term "frontier" will no doubt remain in use and at times be applied in bizarre ways, such as a frontier in space or on Mars—a total misapplication of the term because although exploitation may take place, no true settlement ever can. (If aridity defeated settlement of Australia and the upper Great Plains, it certainly will on Mars.) These would be extreme cases, if they ever happen, of imperial outposts as distinct from real frontiers. Comparisons provide instead the opportunity for interior-directed reflection. They blunt the force either of condemnation or of adulation of frontierspeople, who have had so many varied experiences since 1492; contact among Europeans and natives and the natural environment, inevitable in itself, often turned into exploitation and, it should be said, often into improvement and mutual benefit. These interactions have demonstrated no more and no less than the human condition.

Do comparisons with the histories of frontiers elsewhere help one understand what happened in the United States? No doubt they do, at a minimum to dilute the frontier-derived myth of moral superiority and self-righteous missionizing. Once one starts comparing, one has accepted that American history is not incomparable or unique. On the other hand, does the American story have relevance elsewhere? Surely it would be instructive in Brazil, whose ongoing frontier history has eerily repeated events that have happened elsewhere. Like all histories, comparative frontier histories tell of the good that people have achieved and the ill that they have committed. Thereby these histories indicate what we might expect of ourselves in the future.

Bibliographic Note

Introductions to comparative history in general include the essays by Raymond Grew and others in *Journal of Interdisciplinary History* 16 (Summer 1985) and the essays in C. Vann Woodward, ed., *The Comparative Approach to American History* (New York, 1968). The comparative study of frontiers and regions began with Paul Leroy Beaulieu, *De la Colonisation chez les Peuples Modernes* (Paris, 1874 and later eds.), a work intended to facilitate French imperialism but containing some useful distinctions. Walter Prescott Webb's *The Great Frontier* (Austin, 1952) conceived of Europe as metropolis and the rest of the world as frontier, a conception employed less sympathetically since the 1970s by Immanuel Wallerstein's books on "the modern world-system." Excellent essays on a dozen historical frontiers appear in Walker D. Wyman and Clifton B. Kroeber, eds., *The Frontier in Perspective* (Madison, 1957).

Comparative frontiers in recent times have been discussed from various angles by the following: W. Turrentine Jackson, "A Brief Message for the Young and/or Ambitious: Comparative Frontiers as a Field for Investigation," *Western Historical Quarterly* (hereafter cited as *WHQ*) 9 (January 1978): 5–18; Philip Wayne Powell et al., *Essays on Frontiers in World History*, edited by George Wolfskill and Stanley Palmer (College Station, Tex., 1983); David H. Miller and Jerome O. Steffen, eds., *The Frontier: Comparative Studies* (Norman, 1977); Herbert Heaton, "Other Wests Than Ours," *Journal of Economic History, Supplement VI* (1946): 50–62; Dietrich Gerhard, "The Frontier in Comparative View," *Comparative Studies in Society and History* 1 (1959): 205–29; Walter Nugent, "Frontiers and Empires in the Late Nineteenth Century," *WHQ* 20 (November 1989): 393–408; Donald W. Treadgold, "Russian Expansion in the Light of Turner's Study of the American Frontier," *Agricultural History* 26 (October 1952): 147–52; and William H. McNeill, *The Great Frontier: Freedom and Hierarchy in Modern Times* (Princeton, 1983).

Most of the foregoing range globally, but others have compared two or three Anglophone frontiers: Paul F. Sharp, "Three Frontiers: Some Comparative Studies of Canadian, American, and Australian Settlement," *Pacific Historical Review* 24 (November 1955): 369–77; H. C. Allen, *Bush and Backwoods: A Comparison of the Frontier in Australia and the United States* (East Lansing, Mich., 1959); Robin Winks, *The Myth of the American Frontier: Its Relevance to America, Canada, and Australia* (Leicester, Eng., 1971); and Morris W. Wills, "Sequential Frontiers: The Californian and Victorian Experience, 1850–1900," *WHQ* 9 (October 1978): 483–94. Comparisons that include Latin America are D.C.M. Platt and Guido di Tella, eds., *Argentina, Australia, and Canada: Studies in Comparative Development, 1870–1965* (New York, 1985), Daniel J. Elazar, *Jewish Communities in Frontier Societies: Argentina, Australia, and South Africa* (New York, 1983), and Carl E. Solberg's exemplary *The Prairies and the Pampas: Agrarian Policy in Canada and Argentina, 1880–1930* (Stanford, 1987). An important area of national self-definition and legend is treated in Richard W. Slatta, *Cowboys of the Americas* (New Haven, 1990); urbanism is discussed in David Hamer, *New Towns in the New World: Images and Perceptions of the Nineteenth-Century Urban Frontier* (New York, 1990). For comparisons of Southern Hemisphere societies by their own scholars, see John Fogarty, Ezequiel Gallo, and Hector Dieguez, *Argentina y Australia* (Buenos Aires, Arg., 1979), John Fogarty and Tim Duncan, *Australia and Argentina: On Parallel Paths* (Carlton, Victoria, Austral., 1984), and Donald Denoon, *Settler Capitalism: The Dynamics of Dependent Development in the Southern Hemisphere* (Oxford, Eng., 1983).

Regionalism and frontiers in U.S. history have been discussed copiously. A few of the best treatments include the following: Earl Pomeroy, *The Pacific Slope: A History of California, Oregon, Washington, Idaho, Utah, and Nevada* (New York, 1965); Carlos A. Schwantes, *The Pacific Northwest: An Interpretive History* (Lincoln, 1989); William G. Robbins, Robert J. Frank, and Richard E. Ross, eds., *Regionalism and the Pacific Northwest* (Corvallis, Oreg., 1983), especially Richard M. Brown's essay. See also several articles in the *WHQ*: Donald Worster, "New West, True West: Interpreting the Region's History," 18 (April 1987): 141–56; William Cronon, "Revisiting the Vanishing Frontier: The Legacy of Frederick Jackson Turner," 18 (April 1987): 157–76; Michael P. Malone, "Beyond the Last Frontier: Toward a New Approach to Western American History," 20 (November 1989): 409–27; and William G. Robbins, "Western History: A Dialectic on the Modern Condition," 20 (November 1989): 429–449. Also instructive is John S. Otto, *The Southern Frontiers, 1607–1860: The Agricultural Evolution of the Colonial and Antebellum South* (New York, 1989).

For Europeans' notion that they could do whatever they pleased to new lands and indigenous peoples, see David B. Quinn et al., *Essays on the History of North American Discovery and Exploration*, edited by Stanley H. Palmer and Dennis Reinhartz (College Station, Tex., 1988), and Antonello Gerbi, *Nature in the New World: From Christopher Columbus to Gonzalo Fernandez de Oviedo*, trans. Jeremy Moyle (Pittsburgh, 1985).

Among the many comparative discussions of Canada's frontiers are Michael S. Cross, ed., *The Frontier Thesis and the Canadas: The Debate on the Impact of the Canadian Environment* (Toronto, 1970), A. L. Burt, "If Turner Had Looked at Canada . . . ," in Wyman and Kroeber, *Frontier in Perspective*, and Marcus L. Hansen and John B. Brebner, *The Mingling of the Canadian and American Peoples* (New Haven, 1940). Australia and New Zealand as frontiers are discussed in the following: W.L.G. Joerg, *Pioneer Settlement* (1932; reprint, Freeport, N.Y., 1969); Ronald Lawson, "Toward Demythologizing the `Australian Legend,'" *Journal of Social History* 13 (Summer 1980): 577–87; Peter J. Coleman, "The New Zealand Frontier and the Turner Thesis," *Pacific Historical Review* 27 (August 1958): 221–37; Brian Fitzpatrick, "The Big Man's Frontier and Australian Farming," *Agricultural History* 21 (January 1947): 8–12; J. W. McCarty, "Australia as a Region of Recent Settlement in the Nineteenth Century," *Australian Economic*

History Review 13 (September 1973): 148–67; Donald W. Meinig, "Colonisation of Wheatlands: Some Australian and American Comparisons," *Australian Geographer* 7 (August 1959): 205ff; and Geoffrey Blainey, *The Tyranny of Distance: How Distance Shaped Australia's History* (Melbourne, 1968).

The leading comparative treatment of South Africa is Howard Lamar and Leonard Thompson, eds., *The Frontier in History: North America and Southern Africa Compared* (New Haven, 1981). See also James Gump, "The Subjugation of the Zulus and Sioux: A Comparative Study," *WHQ* 19 (January 1988): 21–36, and W. K. Hancock, "Trek," *Economic History Review* 10, no. 3 (1958): 331–39.

Studded with comparative insights is Alistair Hennessy, *The Frontier in Latin American History* (Albuquerque, 1978). Other important comparative studies include the following: Matt S. Meier, ed., *Latin American Frontiers* (San Diego, 1981); David J. Weber, "Turner, the Boltonians, and the Borderlands," *American Historical Review* 91 (February 1986): 66–81; Carter Goodrich, "Argentina as a New Country," *Comparative Studies in Society and History* 7 (October 1964): 70–88; Sergio Villalobos R., *Relaciones Fronterizas en la Araucania* (Santiago, Chile, 1982); Mark Jefferson, *Peopling the Argentine Pampa* (New York, 1926); Mary Lombardi, "The Frontier in Brazilian History," *Pacific Historical Review* 44 (November 1975): 437–57; C. Vianna Moog, *Bandeirantes and Pioneers* (New York, 1964); Martin T. Katzman, *Cities and Frontiers in Brazil: Regional Dimensions of Economic Development* (Cambridge, Mass., 1977); Frederick C. Luebke, *Germans in the New World: Essays in the History of Immigration* (Urbana, 1990); and Marianne Schmink and Charles H. Wood., eds., *Frontier Expansion in Amazonia* (Gainesville, 1984). The essays by Thomas J. McCormick and Louis A. Pérez, Jr., in *Journal of American History*, June 1990, are a guide to world-systems theory.

Contributors

THE EDITORS

Clyde A. Milner II is Editor of the *Western Historical Quarterly* and Professor of History at Utah State University. He has written on a range of subjects including the work of eastern Quakers among the Plains Indians and the role of memory in creating a western identity. He is the editor of *Major Problems in the History of the American West* and the coeditor with Patricia Nelson Limerick and Charles E. Rankin of *Trails: Toward a New Western History*.

Carol A. O'Connor is Professor of History at Utah State University, where she has taught since 1977. A native of New York, she has authored *A Sort of Utopia: Scarsdale, 1891–1981*, as well as several articles on suburbs and suburbia. She is currently working on a study of middle-sized cities in the West's low-population states.

Martha A. Sandweiss is Director of the Mead Art Museum and Associate Professor of American Studies at Amherst College. A former curator of photographs at the Amon Carter Museum, she has written widely on western photography and art. She is the author of *Laura Gilpin: An Enduring Grace* and the editor of *Photography in Nineteenth-Century America*.

THE AUTHORS

Carl Abbott is Professor of Urban Studies and Planning at Portland State University. He has written extensively on the West in the twentieth century, with particular attention to issues of urban growth, regional development, and land-use planning. His books include *The New Urban America: Growth and Politics in Sunbelt Cities*, *The Metropolitan Frontier: Cities in the Modern American West*, and *Colorado: A History of the Centennial State*.

Allan G. Bogue is Frederick Jackson Turner Professor of History emeritus at the University of Wisconsin-Madison. He has been president of the Organization of American Historians, the Agricultural History Society, the Economic History Association, and the Social Science History Association. He is the author of many books and articles on American western and political history and is currently engaged in a biographical study of Frederick Jackson Turner.

Richard Maxwell Brown is Beekman Professor of Northwest and Pacific History emeritus at the University of Oregon. He was 1991–92 president of the Western History Association and a consultant to the National Commission on the Causes and Prevention of Violence in 1968–69. Among his publications are *Strain of Violence: Historical Studies of American Violence and Vigilantism* and *No Duty to Retreat: Violence and Values in American History and Society*.

Keith L. Bryant, Jr., is Professor of History and Head of the History Department at the University of Akron. His publications related to the economy of the West include *History of the Atchison, Topeka and Santa Fe Railway, Arthur E. Stilwell, Promoter with a Hunch*, and, with Henry C. Dethloff, *A History of American Business*.

Anne M. Butler is Coeditor of the *Western Historical Quarterly* and Professor of History at Utah State University. A specialist in western women's history, she is the author of *Daughters of Joy, Sisters of Misery: Prostitutes in the American West, 1865–1890*. She has also written on subjects as diverse as women in prisons and nuns in the West.

Kathleen Neils Conzen is Professor of History at the University of Chicago. A past president of the Immigration History Society, she is the author of *Immigrant Milwaukee, 1836–1860: Accommodation and Community in a Frontier City* and of numerous articles on definitions of ethnicity and issues of historical methodology. She is completing a study of German immigrant settlement in the Midwest.

William Cronon is Frederick Jackson Turner Professor of History, Geography, and Environmental Studies at the University of Wisconsin-Madison. A MacArthur Fellow, he is the author of *Changes in the Land: Indians, Colonists, and the Ecology of New England* and *Nature's Metropolis: Chicago and the Great West*.

Sarah Deutsch is Associate Professor of History at Clark University, where she teaches courses on social history and gender. She is the author of *No Separate Refuge: Culture, Class, and Gender on an Anglo-Hispanic Frontier in the American Southwest, 1880–1940* and *From Ballots to Breadlines: American Women, 1920–1940*. She is currently working on a study of women in Boston from 1870 to 1950.

Brian W. Dippie is Professor of History at the University of Victoria, British Columbia. A Canadian, he received his Ph.D. in American civilization from the University of Texas at Austin and specializes in the cultural history of the American West. His recent books include *Catlin and His Contemporaries: The Politics of Patronage* and *Charles M. Russell, Word Painter: Letters, 1887–1926*.

Jay Gitlin is a lecturer in American history at Yale University. He is completing a study of the French in the Mississippi Valley in the late eighteenth and early nineteenth centuries. He also performs regularly with the Bales-Gitlin band and is writing a book on the social history of American popular music.

Peter Iverson is Professor of History at Arizona State University. He has written *The Navajo Nation* and *Carlos Montezuma and the Changing World of American Indians* and has edited *The Plains Indians of the Twentieth Century* and with Albert Hurtado, *Major Problems in American Indian History*.

Thomas J. Lyon has taught at Utah State University since 1964, where he edits the journal *Western American Literature*. He edited *This Incomperable Lande: A Book of American Nature Writing* and *On Nature's Terms* and is coeditor, with Terry Tempest Williams, of the Utah Centennial Anthology, forthcoming.

Michael P. Malone is the President of Montana State University and Professor of American History. He is the author of several books, including *C. Ben Ross and the New Deal in Idaho, Battle for Butte: Mining and Politics on the Northern Frontier, 1864-1906*, and, with Richard Etulain, *The American West: A Twentieth-Century History*.

Walter Nugent is Andrew V. Tackes Professor of History at the University of Notre Dame. He has written several books, including *The Tolerant Populists, Money and American Society, 1865–1880, Structures of American Social History*, and *Crossings: The Great Transatlantic Migrations, 1870–1914*, as well as a number of essays on western history, comparative frontiers, and other topics. He is now working on migration and population change in the American West since 1890.

Gary Y. Okihiro is the Director of Cornell University's Asian American Studies Program and Professor of History. He is the author of *Margins and Mainstreams: Asians in American History and Culture* and *Cane Fires: The Anti-Japanese Movement in Hawaii, 1865–1945*.

Charles S. Peterson is Professor of History emeritus at Utah State University and a member of the faculty at Southern Utah University. From 1971 to 1989 he was associated with the *Western Historical Quarterly*, initially as Associate Editor, then as Coeditor, and beginning in 1979 as Editor. He was Director of the Utah Historical Society and Editor of the *Utah Historical Quarterly*. He has written a number of books and more than a score of essays and articles on the subjects of Mormon history, environmental history, and agriculture.

F. Ross Peterson is Director of the Mountain West Center for Regional Studies and Professor of History at Utah State University. The author of *Prophet Without Honor: Glen H. Taylor and the Fight for American Liberalism* and *Idaho: A Bicentennial History*, he is currently working on a biography of Idaho Senator Frank Church.

George J. Sánchez is Associate Professor of History and American Culture at the University of Michigan, Ann Arbor. He has written *Becoming Mexican American: Ethnicity, Culture, and Identity in Chicano Los Angeles, 1900–1945*.

Carlos A. Schwantes is Director of the Institute for Pacific Northwest Studies and Professor of History at the University of Idaho, where he has taught since 1984. He is the author or editor of eleven books, including *The Pacific Northwest: An Interpretive History, In Mountain Shadows: A History of Idaho*, and *Railroad Signatures across the Pacific Northwest*.

Ferenc M. Szasz is Professor of History at the University of New Mexico in Albuquerque. He is the author or editor of over fifty articles and five books, including *The Divided Mind of Protestant America, 1880–1930* and *The Protestant Clergy in the Great Plains and Mountain West, 1865–1915*.

Margaret Connell Szasz is a member of the History Department at the University of New Mexico in Albuquerque. She has written widely in the field of American Indian history, including two books on American Indian education. Her most recent publication is *Between Indian and White Worlds: The Cultural Broker*.

David J. Weber, Dedman Professor of History at Southern Methodist University, is past president of the Western History Association and has been elected to membership in the Mexican Academy of History and the Society of American Historians. His books, many of them prizewinners, include *The Mexican Frontier, 1821–1846* and *The Spanish Frontier in North America*.

Elliott West is Professor of History at the University of Arkansas, Fayetteville. A specialist in the social history of the West and the frontier, he is the author of *Growing Up with the Country: Childhood on the Far-Western Frontier* and *The Saloon on the Rocky Mountain Mining Frontier*.

Richard White is the 1995–1996 president of the Western History Association and is the McClelland Professor of History at the University of Washington. A MacArthur Fellow, his recent books include two prizewinners: *"It's Your Misfortune and None of My Own": A New History of the American West* and *The Middle Ground: Indians, Empires, and Republics in the Great Lakes Region, 1650–1815*.

Victoria Wyatt is Associate Professor in the Department of History in Art at the University of Victoria, British Columbia. Her research focuses on the history and arts of native peoples of Alaska and the Pacific Northwest. She is the author of several articles and two books, *Images from the Inside Passage: An Alaskan Portrait by Winter and Pond* and *Shapes of Their Thoughts: Reflections of Culture Contact in Northwest Coast Indian Art*.

Index

Canada, 818; and cattle raising, 257; and the frontier, 4-5; and history, 746, 749; and manifest destiny, 166; and regionalism, 756; and the trans-Appalachian West, 130; and the trans-Mississippi West, *150*, 151, *151*, 166

Nationalization: of the West, 496-97

Native American Church, 377, 429

Native Americans: absorption of new experiences by, 16; and abundance/scarcity issues, 611, 612, *626*; activism of, 429, 522, *523*; and alcohol, 64, 80, 94, 140, 141, 246, 376, 508-9; alliances/animosities among, 15-16, 35; allotments for, 174, 182, 190; and the American Revolution, 121-22; and animals, *236*, 237-39, *237*, 240, *241*, 244-45; annuities to, 176, 177, 179-80, 182; and the Antiquities Act (1906), 612; in art, 675-94, 695-98; as artists, 678, *678*, 679, *698*; as authors, 732-37; bureaucratic dissension for control of, 173-74; in cities, 487; and classicism, 685; and commercialization of the West, 774-75, 779-81, 783, 792, *793*; common characteristics among, 15-16; community sense of, 15-16; as cowboys, 243; definition of, 75; and the Depression/New Deal, 482; diversity of, 15; as "domestic dependent nations," 166; and economic issues, 487, 661; and the "education policy," 146; European depictions of, *805*; and families, 320-21, 342, 348-51; and farming, 162, 181, 182, 190, 295; and the film industry, 318, 792, *793*; as the "first westerners," 10; and fishing, 497, 611, *626*; and the fur trade, 243-49; and gambling, 661; and gender issues, *348*, 349; and history, 763-64, 768; history of, 697; and homesteading, 290; as hunters, 349, 611; immigrants/migrants fears of, 176; imposition of new ways on, 16; and individualism, 733; and land issues, 143-44, 290, 349, 350, 351; as lawyers, 659; legal status of, 166, 182-83; in literature, 720, 721, 727; in Los Angeles, *638*, *639*; and manifest destiny, 166; and mechanization, 295; and Mexicans, 72-73; and the military, 152, 162, 171, 173-74, *173*,

175, 177, 179-80, 181-82, 248, *523*; in the military, 487; and the mythological West, 9; non-vanishing, 5; and the Northwest Territory, 125-26; as office holders, 531; and political issues, 522, 531; population of, 5, 9; poverty of, 94, 184, 661; as ranchers, 239, 260; relief for, 661; and religion, 141-42, *236*, 237-38, *237*, *241*, 360-61, 364, 383-84, 388-39, 429, 733; romanization of, *40*, 697; sacred lands of the, 658-62, *659*; self-determination for, 522; and settlement patterns, 282, 813; and social change, 246; social stratification among, 23; stereotypes of, 84, 318, 321; and the trans-Appalachian West, 125-26, 138, 143-44, 145-46; and the trans-Mississippi West, 152, 161-62, 166, 171, 173-76, *173*, 175, 177, 179-80, 181-82; treaties with, 143-44; and urbanization, 522; as "Vanishing Americans," *194*, *195*, *344*, 682, 695-98, *696*, 697, 700; and violence, 396, 416; West as home to, 14-16; and white women, 138; and World War II, 454, 486-87; as writers, 673. *See also* Assimilation; British-Indian relations; Disease; European-American and Indian relations; French-Indian relations; Fur trade; Hispanics: Native American relations with; Removal policy; Reservations; *specific tribe*

Native Claims Settlement Act, 481-82

Native revitalization movements, 375-78, 380, 388-89

Natives: and the alien-native problem, 662-66, *663*, *665*; definition of, 662. *See also* Indigenous people; Native Americans

Natural resources, 232, 427, 432-34, *433*, 443, 501, 515. *See also* Abundance/scarcity issues; Conservation; Environmentalism; *specific resource*

Natural rights, 359

Nature: appreciation of, 270-71, 272; conquest of, 316; purpose of, 746; savagery of, 316; writers, 738

Navajo Indians: adaptation of the, 35-41, *40*; allotments to the, 174, 181; and animals, 38, 39, *40*, 239, 240; arrival in Southwest of, 11; in art,

697; assimilation of the, 177, 180-82; ceremonies of the, *36*, 38, 39, 41; clan structure of the, 18; and the Depression/New Deal, 482; enemies of the, 181; and families, 351; as farmers/ranchers, 37, 38, 39, *40*, 181-82, 239, 482; federal relations with the, 482; health of the, 625; as hunters, 37, 38; and land issues, 174; language of the, 35-36; Long Walk of the, 153, 180; and the military, 177; as miners, 465; mythology of the, *36*, 37-38, 41; origins of the, 34-36, *36*; population of the, 39, 180, 181; and the Pueblo Indians, 39; raids by the, 180; and religion, 38, 388-89; removal of the, *178*; and reservations, 180-82; resistance by the, 39; self-determination of the, 482; and settlement patterns, 282; and slavery, 39, 240; Spanish relations with the, 38, 39, *44*, *45*, 64; status among, 245; territory of the, 37; and trade, 39, 245; tribal unity of the, 181; and the uranium industry, *461*, 465

Nebraska: agriculture/farming in, 285, 287, 299, 306, 526, 528; and cattle raising, 260; and the Cold War, 488; cultural adaptation in, 306; Depression in, 514-15; economic issues in, 518; ethnic issues in, 306; immigrants to, 284, 285, 287; land issues in, 289, 290, 291; political issues in, 503, 504, 508, 511, 514-15, 518, 526, 528, 531; and religion, 371, 379; statehood for, 184; as a territory, 215; and violence, 423; and World War I, 511

Neihardt, John G., 729-30, 732

Netherlands. *See* Dutch

Neutral Indians, 105

Nevada: and abundance/scarcity issues, 618-19; agriculture in, 301; animals in, 239; cattle raising in, 254, 260; and the Cold War, 456, 488, 489; copper in, 434; corruption in, 525; and defense issues, *469*, 489; and the Depression/New Deal, 477, 481, 515, 516; economic issues in, 429, 434, 453, 456, 458-59, 461-62, 489, 502-3; ethnic/race issues in, 206; federal-state relations in, 5-6, *468*, *469*, 477, 481, *496*, 530-31; gambling in, 429, 458-59; gender issues in, 531; gold in, 232,